Quizzes for 220
Great Children's Books

Quizzes for 220
Great Children's Books

The Quest Motivational Reading Program

Revised First Edition

POLLY JEANNE WICKSTROM

1996
TEACHER IDEAS PRESS
A Division of
Libraries Unlimited, Inc.
Englewood, Colorado

To my husband, Jim
And to our children
Heather, Adam, and Erica

TEACHER IDEAS PRESS
A Division of Libraries Unlimited, Inc.
P.O. Box 6633
Englewood, CO 80155-6633
1-800-237-6124

Production Editor: Kevin W. Perizzolo
Copy Editor: Tama Serfoss
Layout and Interior Design: Kay Minnis

Library of Congress Cataloging-in-Publication Data

Wickstrom, Polly Jeanne, 1959-
   Quizzes for 220 great children's books : the quest motivational
reading program / Polly Jeanne Wickstrom. -- Rev. 1st ed.
     ix, 307 p. 22x28 cm.
     ISBN 1-56308-383-3
     1. Literature--Study and teaching (Elementary) 2. Children's
stories, English--Examinations, questions, etc. 3. Reading
comprehension--Examinations, questions, etc. 4. Children--Books and
reading. I. Title.
LB1575.W53   1995
372.4'147'076--dc20   95-38594
                                                            CIP

Contents

PART I—TEACHER'S MANUAL *(continued)*

Preface

One Teacher's Story

I have always had an insatiable hunger for books, and when I taught sixth-grade language arts, I wanted to pass the rich tradition of reading on to my students. So I began with the age-old method of asking my students to read books and to provide written and sometimes oral reports on what they had read.

Using this traditional method, however, I ran into some problems. For example, some children seemed capable of producing beautifully written book reports, but incapable of answering a few simple, informal questions about the plot of the book. Other students seemed to dread giving the oral book report or to dread writing the book report—or both—and thus I had the problem of associating something negative with something I wanted to be a very positive experience for my students: that of reading a good book.

After considering these problems, I decided one year that I would try something altogether different. Having selected 20 children's books, I read the books and then wrote short tests for each book. When the tests were prepared, I presented the list of books to my students and asked them to read not one, but several of the books on the list. I explained that no book report and no oral report would be required. Instead, all the students would have to do to receive credit for reading a book would be to take a short and simple objective test over the book. I assured the students that the tests would be easy for anyone who read the books. No trick questions and certainly no studying would be required. Just reading and enjoying the books was the main objective.

The response to this simple system was overwhelming. My students loved not having to write book reports and not having to give oral reports every time they read a book, requirements that I suspected inhibited their reading rather than promoted it, and they loved the simplicity of taking the short test to receive credit for books they read. I noticed that the children seemed to enjoy a feeling of accomplishment that came as a result of having read an entire book on their own, and as success has a way of breeding more success, I observed my students beginning to read more and more books.

In response to my students' enthusiasm, I began to add more quizzes to the program and to develop the program further by assigning point values to books based on their length and complexity. For the following school year, I prepared and launched a full-blown book reading contest with an offering of 50 titles for my students to choose from. The results were staggering. Reading became the "in" thing among sixth graders at the junior high school where I taught, and I had students who read all 50 books in one semester and came to me asking for more. One afternoon I remember in particular, I was in charge of a study hall with over 60 sixth-grade students in a large double room. Supervising study halls was not a favorite task among teachers as the environment too often seemed to lend itself to chaos and disorder. On this particular day, however, the entire room of 60 students was silent and in each set of hands was a book. Behind each book was the face of a child obviously engrossed in a book. It was so quiet in the room, with no sound except the soft rustling of turning pages, you could have heard a pin drop. When another teacher walked in the room to deliver a memo, she stopped in her tracks and stared out over the room with me, sharing my pleasure at this strange and beautiful sight.

As the year went on, the students were reading so fast and asking for more and more titles, that keeping up with the task of writing the quizzes became overwhelming. Thus, the next year, when I left teaching to give birth to my first child, I decided to devote myself to the task of adding many more titles to the program and to seek publication. This is how *Quizzes for 220 Great Children's Books* was born and I pass it on to teachers, library school media specialists, parents, and college professors. May this book be a useful tool for you in accomplishing the worthy goal of launching children into the wonderful world of books.

—Polly Wickstrom

Introduction

A comprehensive reading program not only teaches young people the skill of reading, but also encourages them to develop a lifelong enjoyment of literature. Students build reading skills by reading: the more they read, the better they will read.

For a number of years, teachers have used the book report as the major evaluative component of an individualized reading program. *Quizzes for 220 Great Children's Books* provides an alternative to book reports as a method of determining what, how much, and how well young people read.

In the *Quizzes* program, the student chooses a book from the *Children's Catalog*, reads the book, and then takes a 14-question test about the book. The test is designed both as a comprehension check and to see that the book was finished. After students complete the test successfully, they receive credit or points for their accomplishment. The program is also designed to provide teachers with a method of distributing credit fairly to students based on the length and difficulty of the books they read.

The primary audience of *Quizzes* is students in grades three through eight. However, the program is flexible and can be adapted to almost any grade level. It could be used as part of a program for gifted students in the first or second grades. It could be used by high school teachers, librarians sponsoring summer reading programs, and even by college professors teaching courses in children's literature.

School library media specialists and classroom teachers can use the system to integrate library motivational reading programs with reading skills instruction. *Quizzes* can also provide a means for parents who teach their children at home and encourage children to read widely and carefully.

Not only is the program flexible, it is also expandable. As it stands, the program tests 220 children's books. (If used in conjunction with *More Quizzes for Great Children's Books*, 340 children's books are covered.) That in itself will provide a wide variety of reading materials from which students can choose. The user, however, can easily add an unlimited number of additional books. This option keeps the program from growing stale.

Quizzes takes into consideration the heavy responsibilities of today's teachers and library media specialists by providing several simple methods of tracking what young people read. Perhaps even more importantly, it provides a means for adults to *motivate* children to read and to lay the foundation for a lifelong love of books.

PART
I

Teacher's Manual

Introduction—About the Book Format

The Teacher's Manual

The *Teacher's Manual* describes the program and outlines various methods by which the teacher, library media specialist, or parent can implement the program. The manual also includes a set of black-line masters to be used in record keeping.

The Album of Tests

This volume of *Quizzes* contains a total of 220 tests covering books that have been carefully selected to provide a wide sampling of high-quality children's literature. (*Note: More Quizzes for Great Children's Books* contains an additional 120 tests.)

Each test contains 14 objective questions that test the extent to which students have read and comprehended given books. Most of the questions included on the tests are comprehensive in nature, covering major events that occurred in the book. Some of the questions are literal questions asking the student to recall facts about the characters portrayed in the books. However, the literal questions are *always* questions that should be obvious to any student who actually read that book. For example, a question such as "Did Mrs. Smith have red hair?" would never be asked unless the fact that Mrs. Smith had red hair was part of the story line and was continually repeated throughout the book.

The Answers

A complete set of answers for the 220 tests are in part IV. The user may use binder clips to fasten these pages together while students are using the book to take tests.

The Children's Catalog

The first half of the *Children's Catalog* provides a Subject Index of all the books listed in the program. The second half of the catalog provides brief motivational blurbs about each book. The catalog is designed to help students select books that they will find interesting and books that will be suited to their reading abilities.

The Program Mechanics

Categories of Books

The books have been divided into five categories based on the subject matter, vocabulary, and complexity of plot in each book. Following are the various categories and the appropriate reading levels for participants in the *Quizzes* reading program.

Category	Reading Level
A	Grades 3 and 4
B	Grades 4 and 5
C	Grades 5 and 6
D	Grades 6 and 7
E	Grades 7 and 8

These categories enable the teacher, the library media specialist, or parent to guide students to the category of books best suited to their interests and reading abilities. The categories are meant to serve as general guidelines only. Because of the wide range of preferences and reading abilities within even the same grade level, the user must make the final decision regarding categorical assignments for individual students.

Point Value Assignments

Each book in the program has been assigned a point value based on the length of the book. The point value assignments are as follows:

125 pages or less	5 pts.
126–200 pages	10 pts.
201–275 pages	15 pts.
276–350 pages	20 pts.
351–425 pages	25 pts.
426 pages or more	30 pts.

These point value assignments enable the user to distribute credit fairly to students based on the length of the books they have read.

Note: Because of the large print and very simple vocabulary of some books, these titles have been assigned a low point value regardless of their length in pages.

 # Exploring the Options for Program Use

There are many different contexts in which the *Quizzes* program could be used and many different methods through which it could be implemented. The teacher, library media specialist, or parent may want to use one of the suggestions discussed in this section, or may very well devise a personal system of putting the program to work, so that it will effectively meet local needs.

Using the Program as a Basis for Determining Grades

In a classroom setting, the teacher may want to use the program as a basis for determining part of the students' grades in reading. This could be done by setting up a scale using points. The method for keeping track of the number of points each student has earned over a given period of time will be discussed in the section "Record Keeping."

The first step in setting up a grading scale would be to decide how many average-length books (201–275 pages) the students would need to read over a given period of time to earn an A. Because average-length books are worth 15 points, the teacher would multiply 15 times the number of books to be read. Thus, if the teacher wanted the students to read five average-length books over a period of nine weeks to earn an A, the students would need to earn approximately 75 points.

(*Note:* Average-length books are chosen only for the purpose of setting up a grading scale. Once the grading scale has been established, the student may be invited to read any combination of books to earn points. For example, instead of reading five 15-point books to earn an A, the student could read six 10-point books and three 5-point books. Alternatively, the student could read three 20-point books, one 10-point book, and one 5-point book, etc.)

Teachers can set up their own grading scale by using the following mathematical formula:

X = The number of average-length books students would have to read over a given period of time to earn an A.

$Y = X \times 15$

.90 x Y = Minimum number of points a student would need to earn an A.
.80 x Y = Minimum number of points a student would need to earn a B.
.70 x Y = Minimum number of points a student would need to earn a C.
.60 x Y = Minimum number of points a student would need to earn a D.

Returning to the example of setting a criterion of reading five average-length books to earn an A, the formula used to set up a grading scale would be as follows:

X = 5
Y = (5x15) or 75

By multiplying .90 x 75, the teacher would come up with the minimum number of points a student needs to earn an A. By multiplying .80 x 75, the teacher would come up with the minimum number of points a student needs to earn a B, and so on. Thus, the grading scale for a requirement of five average-length books to earn an A would look like this:

67–75 pts.	A
60–66 pts.	B
52–59 pts.	C
45–51 pts.	D
44 and below	F

A set of model grading scales appears below. Each scale is based on a different number of average-length books that would have to be read by students over a given period of time to earn an A.

Model Grading Scales

2 average-length books per grading period:

27–30	A
24–26	B
21–23	C
18–20	D
17 and below	F

3 average-length books per grading period:

40–45	A
36–39	B
31–35	C
27–30	D
26 and below	F

4 average-length books per grading period:

54–60	A
48–53	B
42–47	C
36–41	D
35 and below	F

5 average-length books per grading period:

67–75	A
60–66	B
52–59	C
45–51	D
44 and below	F

6 average-length books per grading period:

81–90	A
72–80	B
63–71	C
54–62	D
53 and below	F

7 average-length books per grading period:

94–105	A
84–93	B
73–83	C
63–72	D
62 and below	F

8 average-length books per grading period:

108–120	A
96–107	B
84–95	C
72–83	D
71 and below	F

9 average-length books per grading period:

121–135	A
108–120	B
94–107	C
81–93	D
80 and below	F

10 average-length books per grading period:

135–150	A
120–134	B
105–119	C
90–104	D
89 and below	F

An Individualized Grades Approach

If the teacher decides to use the program as a basis for determining grades, those grades should be based on the individual abilities of the students. For example, an advanced reader may be required to accumulate 75 points to earn an A, while a less proficient reader would only be required to earn 50 points. An excellent way to accomplish this individualization would be to use the Student-Teacher Contract. (See the Black-Line Masters section of this manual.)

In setting up Student-Teacher Contracts, the teacher may want to follow some or all of the six steps outlined below:

STEP ONE: Set aside a time during the day to meet with each student for approximately five minutes. Make enough copies of the Student/Teacher Contract so that there is at least one blank contract available for each student.

STEP TWO: During the conferences with the students, be as positive and encouraging as possible. Stress to the students that the information printed on each contract is to remain confidential between the teacher and the student. Try to discourage students from comparing their contracts with those of their classmates.

STEP THREE: Negotiate with the student concerning the number of books that should be read over an agreed upon period of time to earn an A. Once an agreement has been reached, fill in the information on the student's contract.

STEP FOUR: Use the model grading scales or follow the directions given in the previous section to come up with the point scale that will be used to determine that student's grade.

STEP FIVE: Write the scale at the bottom of the student's contract. The contract can then be used at the end of the grading period to determine the student's grade.

STEP SIX: Optionally, the teacher might create a chart similar to the one in figure 1, which shows student progress as a percentage of the goal. The emphasis for all the students is to complete the goal, rather than to compare the number of contracted points.

Using the Program as a Basis for a Reading Contest

The *Quizzes* program lends itself nicely to organizing a book-reading contest within a classroom, a school, a home, or in the case of a very ambitious person, a whole town! The contest could be based on the number of points earned by participants over a period of time. The student earning the most points could be declared the winner, or better yet, the contest could be designed so that every reader is a winner.

One way to track points earned in a reading contest would be to use a large chart. As students earn points by passing tests on books they have read, the teacher or library media specialist fills in the number of points earned by the student on the chart. The chart would look something like figure 2.

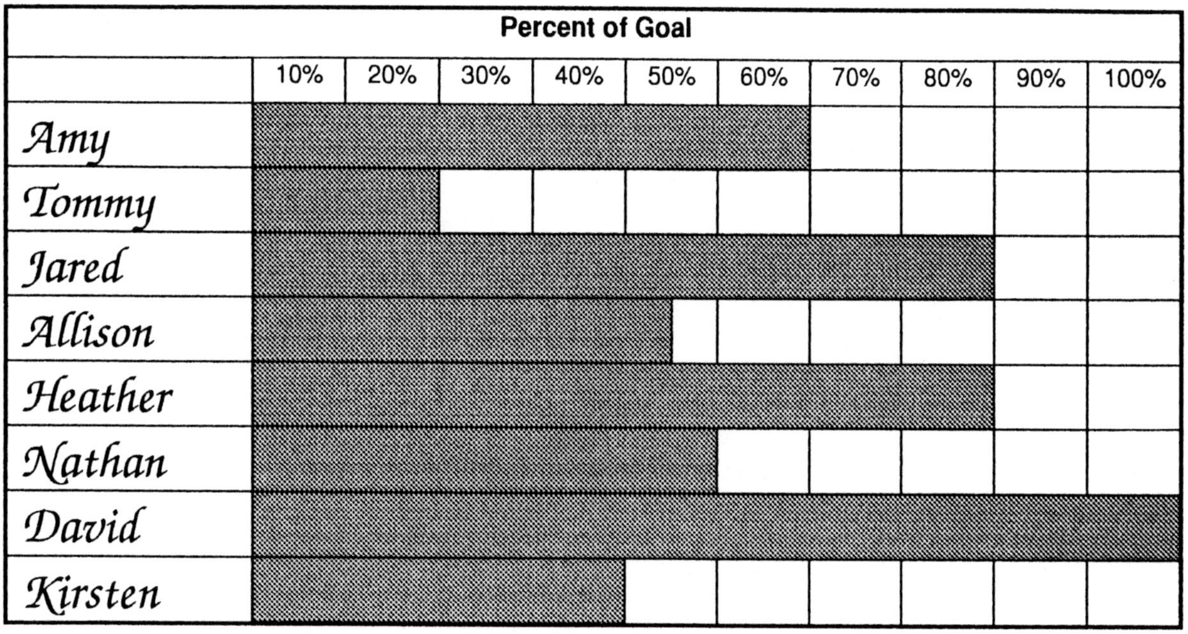

Percent of Goal										
	10%	20%	30%	40%	50%	60%	70%	80%	90%	100%
Amy	████	████	████	████	████	████				
Tommy	████	████								
Jared	████	████	████	████	████	████	████	████		
Allison	████	████	████	████	████					
Heather	████	████	████	████	████	████	████	████		
Nathan	████	████	████	████	████	████				
David	████	████	████	████	████	████	████	████	████	████
Kirsten	████	████	████							

Fig. 1. Chart showing student progress as a percentage of an individual goal.

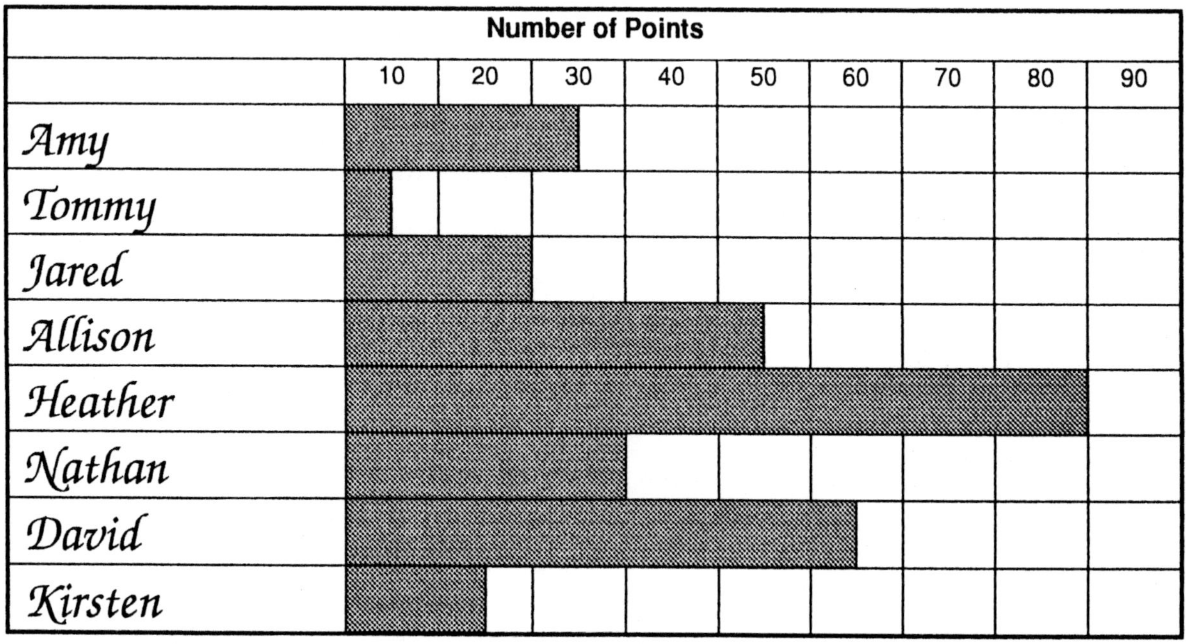

Number of Points									
	10	20	30	40	50	60	70	80	90
Amy	████	████	████						
Tommy	████								
Jared	████	████	████						
Allison	████	████	████	████	████				
Heather	████	████	████	████	████	████	████	████	
Nathan	████	████	████	████					
David	████	████	████	████	████	████			
Kirsten	████	████							

Fig. 2. Chart showing student progress based on earned points.

Regardless of the method (charts or individual record sheets) selected to track progress, the *Quizzes* program can be used in countless ways to implement motivational reading programs for children. For example, at a local library, a program was held in which children ages 9–12 received a ticket every time they read 250 pages. Each ticket earned was signed by the student and then placed in a large box. At the end of the contest, a raffle was held with prizes donated by local businesses. Each child who participated in the contest received a token prize, but additionally, each child had a chance to have his or her ticket drawn in the raffle. The more tickets earned, the more chances the child had of winning extra prizes. The *Quizzes* program could easily be used with ideas similar to this one. Rather than receiving tickets for the number of pages read, children could receive tickets based on the number of points earned.

It should again be emphasized that the ideas suggested in this manual are only a few of the ways in which the *Quizzes* program can be implemented. Other ways in which the program can be used are limited only by the imagination, purposes, or ambitiousness of the user.

Preparing to Implement the Program in a Classroom Setting

As the teacher prepares to incorporate the program into the daily curriculum, there are several things that might enhance the program's effectiveness. While many of the suggestions outlined in this section would be advantageous, they are not crucial to the program's success. The teacher will want to follow some of the suggestions, disregard some of them, and modify others to make them coincide with specific resources, capabilities, and conditions.

Preparing the Classroom

In preparing the classroom, the teacher might do any of the following:

1. Set up an area of the room where students could go to read. One or two beanbag chairs and a small bookcase containing books from the *Quizzes List* (see Black-Line Masters) would make an excellent start for such an area. Later, if resources allow, a few large pillows, posters, a colorful rug, and even a rocking chair could be added to create an inviting place for students to read.

2. Set up a "testing center" where students could sit when taking tests. The testing center could simply be a desk close to the teacher, or it could be a table set up in a corner of the room. Materials that should be kept near the testing center include pencils, blank answer sheets (see Black-Line Masters), and a tray or basket where students could place completed answer sheets.

3. Have as many books from the *Quizzes List* as possible available in the classroom for the students to check out and browse through. Students could be encouraged to bring in old books from the *Quizzes List* that they may have at home, or the books could be purchased inexpensively at used bookstores.

4. Pull books from the school library media center or the public library for use as a temporary room collection.

5. Put up a motivational bulletin board about reading.

6. Display a classroom chart or purchase a set of individual charts (available at most teacher supply stores) to plot students' progress.

Preparing a Time Schedule

One of the nice things about the program is that it provides purposeful activity for the students to engage in when they have completed their other assignments or when the teacher is working with a small group. Students can read silently at any time during the school day, but it would be a good idea for the teacher to set aside a 20-minute period each day entirely devoted to the program.

During this 20-minute period, called the Sustained Silent Reading period, all of the students would read silently. The teacher might also participate in the program and chart personal progress along with the students.

If time permits, the teacher might schedule five minutes before and after the Sustained Silent Reading period to allow students to take tests and to complete the record keeping part of the program. The Sustained Silent Reading period and aspects of scheduling will be discussed in greater detail in the next section.

Preparing the Students

The teacher may want to spend a day or two familiarizing students with the program, outlining expectations for them, getting them excited about reading, answering any questions they might have, and helping them to make book selections. This initial investment of the teacher's time will pay off in the long run by avoiding a barrage of questions and misunderstandings later on.

One way of familiarizing the students with the program and getting them motivated to read books would be to read aloud the introduction to the *Children's Catalog*. The next step would be to allow the students to take turns browsing through the catalog and writing down titles that interest them. Also, if the teacher is planning to assign readings from specific categories of books, this would be a good time to make those assignments.

On the second day, the teacher might take the students to the school library media center so that they could check out books. The teacher might also make copies of the *Quizzes List* for students to take home. Having a copy of the *Quizzes List* at home will allow parents to aid their children in the selection of books.

Once every student had a book from the *Quizzes List*, the teacher would be ready to begin.

Scheduling

To keep the *Quizzes* program running smoothly in a classroom setting, three types of activities—test taking, silent reading, and record keeping—will need to be planned each day. This section suggests scheduling brief periods of time throughout the school day or period to attend to each of these activities separately. However, the program could just as easily be implemented by combining these activities so that they are all accomplished in one 20-minute period.

Test Taking

Each day before the Sustained Silent Reading (SSR) period begins, teachers might wish to set aside a 5–10 minute period for students to take tests. Test taking could be done at the beginning of the SSR period, but if it is taken care of beforehand, the SSR period can be enjoyed without interruptions.

At the beginning of the testing period, students needing to take tests should raise their hands so that the teacher can write their names on the chalkboard. After writing names on the board, the teacher should place this book at the testing center. (*Note:* If desired, the teacher may clip the pages of the *Answers* section together at this time.) Next, the teacher should make a quick check to see that the testing center supplies (pencils and blanks answer sheets) are fresh and that a tray for completed answer sheets is in place.

When the testing center is ready, the child whose name appears first on the list should go to the testing center, find the appropriate test in the book, and complete the test using a blank answer sheet to record his answers. When a student is finished taking a test, he should place his answer sheet in the tray and cross his name off the list on the chalkboard, signifying the next person's turn to use the testing center.

Students who finish taking a test could then spend some time browsing through the *Children's Catalog* and writing down the titles of books that interest them. Some students might be given permission to go to the library media center at this time to review and check out books.

The Sustained Silent Reading Period

The Sustained Silent Reading period is the 20-minute reading period discussed in the last section. During the SSR period, it would be a good idea to have students clear everything off their desks except for the books that they are reading. If a classroom reading area is available, some students might be allowed to take their books to that area. The students should then be asked to read quietly during this time.

Since teachers as well as students need to explore the rich heritage of children's literature, the author recommends that the teacher also use the SSR period to read. The teacher could read books that are not a part of *Quizzes*, adding new books and tests to the program. Over time, the program would grow and become relevant to the particular collection of children's books held in a school or library.

Record Keeping

The teacher will have to complete the record keeping part of the program. Tests need to be graded and the results recorded on the students' individual Data Sheets or the classroom chart. However, this process should take only a minimum amount of time and could be completed during the last five minutes of the SSR period or at some other time during the school day. In fact, students may monitor their own tests and charting depending on each student's ability and responsibility.

Questions and Answers

What should the teacher do if students forget to bring the books that they are reading during SSR time?
These students could be allowed to read one of the books from the *Quizzes List* available in the classroom. By all means, though, the teacher should insist that the students read *something* during SSR time, even if a book from the *Quizzes List* is not available.

What should the teacher do if more than one student at a time wants to browse through the Children's Catalog *after having taken a test?*
It is probably advisable to allow only one student at a time to look through the student catalog, but the other students could be allowed to browse through the books available in the classroom. Also, if such an arrangement is acceptable to the school library media specialist, students could be given a copy of the *Quizzes List* to use in reviewing books at the school library media center.

 # Using the Program for Homeschoolers

The *Quizzes* program is an excellent choice for parents and children involved in homeschooling. Each child may be given a goal for attaining a certain number of points, and progress may be charted. The author recommends that parents adopt any of the ideas and forms listed in this guide for use with individual students.

Books not already a part of the program can be added easily. For example, instead of creating new tests for new titles, the child might read a book, then create a list of four things to discuss with the parent about the book. This list would be used by the parent to ascertain whether the child has read the book and would substitute for the test. The new title and discussion points could be added to the program for use by another child.

Cumulative records like those described in the next section provide a "reading diary" for the student over a period of years. Such a diary can build a source of pride as progress is made in reading more complex and longer books and a wide variety of literature. Parents should remember that the purpose of *Quizzes* is to build reading enjoyment. Reading skill will improve as the number of books read increases. Parents should be careful not to make the *Quizzes* program seem like a negative, work-filled task. Its purpose is positive, fun, and exciting as the personal reading diary grows.

 # Record Keeping

In this section, two different methods that teachers can employ to keep track of students' progress in the *Quizzes* program will be described. The methods differ in the amount of paperwork they require teachers to handle and in the purposes each accomplishes. By reading the brief description of each method, teachers can decide which method will be best suited to their individual needs and preferences.

In addition to these methods, the criteria that students must meet to pass the tests will be discussed. The Data Sheets and the Cumulative Record Sheets will also be mentioned and the purposes for using them will be explored.

Criteria for Passing the Tests

For students to receive credit for a book, they must pass the test on that book. The criteria for passing the tests are set by the teacher, but the author recommends that students be required to answer at least 10 out of 14 questions correctly. These criteria should be easily met by any student who has read a book.

If the student is not able to answer at least 10 out of 14 questions correctly, the teacher should try to discern why the student failed the test. The teacher might set aside a time when the student and teacher can sit down together with the book to discuss it. If the teacher determines that the student actually read the book but the test itself was a problem, then partial or full credit should be given. The emphasis should be placed on reading, not test taking. Teachers should make the entire experience positive— never negative!

It is probably not a good idea to allow students to "study" books repeatedly to pass the tests. Such a practice misses the point of the program.

Record Keeping Plan One

Using Plan One, the teacher uses individual Data Sheets (see Black-Line Masters) to record each student's accumulation of points. In addition to recording point accumulation, the teacher records other information, including the dates on which tests were taken, the number of questions that were answered correctly on each test, and the titles of books read.

One advantage of this method is that it enables the teacher to analyze patterns that may develop in students' progress for the purposes of diagnosis and remediation. For example, a teacher might notice that a student has been taking a test every other day and has been consistently failing the tests. In this case, the teacher might conclude that the student is not reading but probably only skimming the books. The teacher can then encourage that student to devote more time to each book—reading perhaps only a few chapters each day.

On the other hand, a teacher might notice that another student has never attempted to take a test over a book. In this case, the teacher might decide to confer privately with that student to find out what the problem is.

Another advantage of this method is that the Data Sheets provide excellent feedback for parents. By looking at the Data Sheets, parents are able to get a clear picture of the progress their child is making in the program.

Instructions for Record Keeping Plan One

STEP ONE: Make several copies of the Data Sheet and of the Cumulative Record Sheet (see Black-Line Masters). Next, print each student's name on a Data Sheet and on a Cumulative Record Sheet.

Note: If the students participated in the program the preceding year, the teacher would not need to make copies of the Cumulative Record Sheets. Instead, obtain the records from the students' previous teacher.

STEP TWO: Grade any tests that were taken before or during the Sustained Silent Reading period. Write the number of questions the student answered correctly, the point value assignment of the book, and the credit received in the space provided at the bottom of each answer sheet. If the student answered less than 10 out of 14 questions correctly on the test, write a question mark in the blank next to credit received. This will indicate to the student that you wish to meet with him or her to discuss the book before determining the amount of credit that will be given.

STEP THREE: Fill out the Data Sheet for each student who took a test.

STEP FOUR: Fill out the Cumulative Record Sheet for each student who took a test.

STEP FIVE: If the program is being used as a basis for a reading contest, plot each student's additional points on a classroom chart.

STEP SIX: Return the graded answer sheets to the students. If there was a student who failed a test, make arrangements to have a conference with that student and reassure the student that the two of you will discuss the book and the test together and that a joint decision will be made regarding the amount of credit to be received.

Record Keeping Plan Two

Using Record Keeping Plan Two, the teacher will not use the Data Sheets but will only use a classroom chart to record accumulation of points by students. This method has the advantage of requiring very little paperwork on the part of the teacher while still allowing the teacher to use the program to meet the objectives stated in the introduction.

Instructions for Record Keeping Plan Two

STEP ONE: Prepare a classroom chart that will be used to plot each student's point accumulation. The chart should look something like figure 2 (see page 7).

STEP TWO: Make copies of the Cumulative Record Sheet (see Black-Line Masters). Print each student's name on a Cumulative Record Sheet.

Note: If the students participated in the program the preceding year, the teacher would not need to follow this step. Instead, obtain the records from the students' previous teacher.

STEP THREE: Grade any tests that were taken before or during the Sustained Silent Reading period. Write the number of questions the student answered correctly, the point value assignment of the book, and the credit received in the space provided at the bottom of each answer sheet. If the student answered less than 10 out of 14 questions correctly on the test, write a question mark in the blank next to credit received. This will indicate to the student that you wish to meet with him or her to discuss the book before determining the amount of credit that will be given.

STEP FOUR: Shade in the appropriate boxes on the classroom chart for each student who passed a test.

STEP FIVE: Fill out the Cumulative Record Sheet for each student who took a test.

STEP SIX: Return the graded answer sheets to the students. If there was a student who failed a test, make arrangements to have a conference with that student and reassure the student that the two of you will discuss the book and the test together and that a joint decision will be made regarding the amount of credit to be received.

The Data Sheets

The Data Sheets provide detailed information regarding student's progress in the *Quizzes* program. The first three columns of the Data Sheet provide space for the teacher to record the dates on which tests were taken, the number of questions that were answered correctly on each test, and the titles of books read. The fourth column of the Data Sheet provides space to record the number of points the student earned for reading a book along with the point-value assignment of that book. In most cases, the points earned and the point-value assignment will be the same. In the case of a student who failed a test and received partial credit, however, the teacher would note the amount of credit that was given in relation to the amount of credit available for that book.

For example, the book, *It's Like This, Cat*, has a point-value assignment of 10 points. If a decision was made that a student would receive partial credit of eight points for that book, the teacher would write 8/10 in the fourth column of the Data Sheet.

The final column on the Data Sheet allows the teacher to keep track of the total amount of points earned.

A Sample Data Sheet

Figure 3 is a sample Data Sheet illustrating how a teacher would use the form to record information. (*Note:* A blank Data Sheet is provided in the Black-Line Masters.)

By studying the sample Data Sheet, the teacher can see that this student took six tests over a period of approximately six weeks. The student passed four of the tests and received full credit for each of those tests. On the test for *The Secret Garden*, however, the student answered only eight of 14 questions correctly. After a conference with the student, it was decided that partial credit of 15 points instead of the full 20 points would be given.

Data Sheet				
Name: *Janet Carlson*				
Date	**Title of Book**	**Number Correct**	**Points Earned/ Point Value Assignment**	**Total Points**
9/15	*The Tough Winter*	14	10/10	10
9/23	*Ramona Forever*	13	5/5	15
10/4	*Up a Road, Slowly*	12	10/10	25
10/15	*The Secret Garden*	8	15/20	40
10/21	*Little Women*	14	30/30	70
10/30	*The Twenty-One Balloons*	7	?/10	

Fig. 3. Sample Data Sheet.

The final entry on the sample Data Sheet shows that the student took the test for *The Twenty-One Balloons* and answered only 7 out of 14 questions correctly. Thus, the teacher wrote a question mark in the fourth column indicating that a decision had not yet been made regarding the credit to be given for that book.

In the last column, the teacher kept a running total of all the points earned by the student. Each time a student took a test on a book, the credit received for that book was added to the previous total. Keeping a running total in the last column saves the teacher time at the end of the grading period.

Note: Start a new Data Sheet for each grading period. Old sheets can be discarded or saved for parent-teacher conferences.

The Cumulative Record Sheets

The Cumulative Record Sheets are forms the teacher uses to keep a record of books the students have read and been tested on. These sheets provide continuity in the program as students progress from one grade to the next. At the end of each school year, the Cumulative Record Sheets are passed on to the students' next teacher so that the progress each student has already made in the program forms the basis for greater challenges.

One simple method allows the teacher to record information about several different aspects of students' progress in the *Quizzes* program. For each test that is taken, the teacher would record the following:

1. The grade that the child is currently in.

2. In parentheses, the number of questions answered correctly on the test.

3. The number of points earned.

If partial credit was given for a book, the teacher might wish to indicate this by writing an asterisk next to the number representing points earned.

For example, Book #147, *The Call of the Wild*, is a Category C book worth 10 points. If a fifth-grade student answered 13 out of 14 questions correctly on this test, the teacher would write the following in the cell marked 147 in the Category C column of the record sheet:

5 (+13/14) 10

If a fifth-grade student answered 8 out of 14 questions correctly on this same test and partial credit of eight points was earned, the teacher would write:

5 (+8/14) 8*

If a fifth-grade student answered 2 out of 14 questions correctly on this same test and no credit was earned, the teacher would write:

5 (+2/14) 0

Teachers might wish to make progress in each grade even clearer by using a light-colored highlighting marker to highlight all the entries for a given school year. Teachers could agree on a universal color-code system such as third grade = pink, fourth grade = blue, fifth grade = orange, etc., which is appropriate for their school. Writing the color code at the bottom of the record sheet will make the entries easily interpretable.

A Sample Cumulative Record Sheet

Figure 4 is a sample Cumulative Record Sheet illustrating how a teacher might use the form to record information. By studying this form, the teacher can see exactly what type of progress a student made during two years of participation in the program. (*Note:* A blank Cumulative Record Sheet has been provided in the Black-Line Masters section of this manual.)

Cumulative Record Sheet

Quizzes for 220 Great Children's Books—Revised 1st Edition

Student's Name: *Lindsey Moser*

Category A— Grades 3 & 4	Category B— Grades 4 & 5	Category C— Grades 5 & 6	Category D— Grades 6 & 7	Category E— Grades 7 & 8
12—3 (+13/14) 5	16—	10— 4 (+11/14) 10	1—	3—
19—	22—	11—	2—	4—
20—4 (+14/14) 5	23—	13—	6—	5—
21—4 (+13/14) 5	36—	14—	9—	7—
35—	38—	15—	31—	8—
37—3 (+11/14) 5	44—	17—	42—	63—
39—3 (+12/14) 5	69—4 (+13/14) 10	18—	64—	65—
40—	78—4 (+10/14) 10	24—	75—	66—
41—	79—	25—	76—	67—
45—	80—	26—	77—	68—
46—	81—	27—	86—4 (+7/14) 10*	72—
47—	82—	28—	87—	73—
48—	83—	29—	88—	89—
49—	84—	30—4 (+11/14) 10	93—	97—
50—	85—3 (+8/14) 15*	32—4 (+12/14) 10	95—	102—
51—3 (+13/14) 5	90—	33—	96—	103—
52—3 (+14/14) 5	91—	34—	104—	119—
53—	92—4 (+12/14) 10	43—	105—	120—
54—	116—3 (+12/14) 10	71—	106—	121—
55—	118—3 (+10/14) 10	74—	114—	123—
56—	131—	94—	122—	128—
57—	133—	98—	126—	129—
58—	137—	99—	127—	134—
59—	156—	100—	130—	135—
60—	157—	101—	138—	136—
61—	158—	112—4 (+10/14) 15	139—	152—
70—	159—	113—	140—	166—
107—	160—	115—	141—	169—
108—3 (+14/14) 5	174—	117—	142—	170—
109—3 (+13/14) 5	176—	124—4 (+11/14) 10	143—	177—
110—	180—	125—4 (+12/14) 5	144—	181—
111—3 (+12/14) 5	183—	146—	145—	188—
132—	187—	147—	148—	189—
184—	198—	167—	149—	191—
185—	210—	171—	150—	195—
186—	211—	172—	151—4 (+2/14) 0	196—
194—	212—	178—	153—	199—
197—	213—	179—	154—	201—
206—	214—	182—	155—	203—
207—	215—	192—	161—	204—
208—	216—	193—	162—	205—
	217—	202—	163—	219—
		209—	164—	
			165—	
			168—	
			173—	
			175—	
			190—	
			200—	
			218—	
			220—	

Fig. 4. Sample Cumulative Record Sheet.

Looking at figure 4, one would be able to determine that:

- In the third grade, this student read and was tested over a total of 11 books. The student received full credit for 10 of the books and partial credit for one book, Book #85.

- In the fourth grade, this student read and was tested over a total of 13 books. The student received full credit for 11 of the books and partial credit for one book, Book #86. The student answered only 2 out of 14 questions correctly on the test for Book #151 and received no credit for that book.

At the end of the school year, the teacher might use the Cumulative Record Sheets to compile individual summaries of each student's progress in the *Quizzes* program to give to parents. The summaries could contain statements such as the ones provided above, or the summaries could be more detailed, providing the titles and other information about each book the child read that year.

 # Expanding the Program

This book includes tests on 220 books. *More Quizzes for Great Children's Books* includes tests covering an additional 120 books, making tests for a total of 340 books currently available. In addition to tests provided in these volumes, teachers can expand the program even further by adding tests they write themselves. This section will suggest tips for teachers as they write tests and incorporate them into the program.

Writing the Tests

In writing new tests, teachers should attempt to ask questions that cover major events that occurred in the book rather than questions that focus on details. It is also recommended that teachers avoid asking questions that are unrelated to the story line such as, "Who is the author of this book?"

Teachers will find that some books lend themselves to true-false questions while it is easier to write multiple choice questions for other books. Teachers can write the type of questions that best coincide with the book they have read, and they do not need to worry about the ratio of true-false to multiple choice questions in the tests.

After writing the tests, the teacher will want to write corresponding answer keys. One way of storing answer keys for teacher-made tests would be to write them on index cards and then to store them in a card file.

Numbering the Books

For each book on which the teacher writes a test, a book number should be assigned. Any number would work starting from #341, but the author recommends a beginning number of A1, A2, etc. This will allow for the author to add additional volumes of *Quizzes* without interfering with local additions.

Categorizing

When the teacher writes a test for a new book, it will need to be assigned to Category A, B, C, D, or E.

The approximate reading level of each category of books is as follows:

Category	Reading Level
A	Grades 3 and 4
B	Grades 4 and 5
C	Grades 5 and 6
D	Grades 6 and 7
E	Grades 7 and 8

Assigning Point Values

The teacher will also want to assign each new book a point value. The scale for assigning point values is as follows:

125 pages or less	5 pts
126–200 pages	10 pts.
201–275 pages	15 pts.
276–350 pages	20 pts.
351–425 pages	25 pts.
426 pages or more	30 pts.

The Cumulative Record Sheets

The teacher can use the form called Cumulative Record Sheet #2 (see Black-Line Masters) to add the book numbers of the additional tests that have been written. However, because the Cumulative Record Sheets are intended to be passed from teacher to teacher at the end of each school year, all of the teachers using the program in the same school will probably want to devise a system that would enable them to know what numbers their colleagues have assigned to new books. Otherwise a confusing situation could occur.

For example, if Miss Adams, a third-grade teacher, read *Winnie the Pooh* and assigned it a book number of A1, and Mrs. Roberts, a fourth-grade teacher, read *The Wind in the Willows* and also assigned it a book number of A1, the program would begin to lose some of its continuity as far as the Cumulative Records are concerned.

One way of avoiding this situation would be for teachers to meet occasionally and to pool any new tests that they have developed. This way, a universal system of numbering books could be developed, and the program would maintain its continuity. For example, Mrs. Smith could devise tests S1, S2 . . . Mrs. Roberts, R1, R2 . . .

Advertising New Books

As teachers create tests over new books, they will want to let their students know that these new books are available. To do this, teachers may wish to create supplements to add to the *Children's Catalog*.

 # About the Black-Line Masters

This section of the *Teacher's Manual* contains Black-Line Masters which can be copied and used in conjunction with the implementation of the *Quizzes* program.

The Answer Sheet

Students may use the answer sheet to record answers when taking tests.

The Student/Teacher Contract

A form that may be used during student-teacher conferences to set mutually agreed upon reading goals.

The Data Sheet

A form that may be used to record detailed data regarding the reading progress of individual students.

The Cumulative Record Sheet

A form that can be used to record data regarding the reading progress of individual students over several years.

The Cumulative Record Sheet 2

A blank form that can be used to add book numbers when the program is expanded by the user.

The Quizzes List of Great Children's Books

A comprehensive list of the 220 books included in the program arranged alphabetically by author. The teacher might wish to make copies of this list to send home with students at the beginning of the program so that parents can assist their children in the selection of books.

Cumulative Record Sheet

Student's Name:

Category A— Grades 3 & 4	Category B— Grades 4 & 5	Category C— Grades 5 & 6	Category D— Grades 6 & 7	Category E— Grades 7 & 8

The Quizzes List of Great Children's Books

Alcott, Louisa May. *Little Men.*
Alcott, Louisa May. *Little Women.*
Alexander, Lloyd. *The Black Cauldron.*
Alexander, Lloyd. *The Book of Three.*
Alexander, Lloyd. *The Castle of Llyr.*
Alexander, Lloyd. *The Cat Who Wished to Be a Man.*
Alexander, Lloyd. *The High King.*
Alexander, Lloyd. *Taran Wanderer.*
Alexander, Lloyd. *The Wizard in the Tree.*
Armer, Laura Adams. *Waterless Mountain.*
Armstrong, William H. *Sounder.*
Atwater, Richard, and Florence Atwater. *Mr. Popper's Penguins.*
Babbitt, Natalie. *The Eyes of the Amaryllis.*
Babbitt, Natalie. *Goody Hall.*
Babbitt, Natalie. *Knee-Knock Rise.*
Bailey, Carolyn. *Miss Hickory.*
Barnouw, Victor. *Dream of the Blue Heron.*
Blos, Joan W. *A Gathering of Days.*
Blume, Judy. *Otherwise Known as Sheila the Great.*
Blume, Judy. *Superfudge.*
Blume, Judy. *Tales of a Fourth Grade Nothing.*
Brink, Carol Ryrie. *Caddie Woodlawn.*
Burnett, Frances Hodgson. *The Secret Garden.*
Byars, Betsy. *The Cartoonist.*
Byars, Betsy. *The Computer Nut.*
Byars, Betsy. *Cracker Jackson.*
Byars, Betsy. *The Cybil War.*
Byars, Betsy. *Good-bye, Chicken Little.*
Byars, Betsy. *The House of Wings.*
Byars, Betsy. *The Night Swimmers.*
Byars, Betsy. *The Pinballs.*
Byars, Betsy. *The Summer of the Swans.*
Byars, Betsy. *The TV Kid.*
Byars, Betsy. *The Two-Thousand-Pound Goldfish.*
Carlson, Natalie Savage. *A Brother for the Orphelines.*
Carlson, Natalie Savage. *The Empty Schoolhouse.*
Carlson, Natalie Savage. *The Happy Orpheline.*
Carlson, Natalie Savage. *The Letter on the Tree.*
Carlson, Natalie Savage. *The Orphelines in the Enchanted Castle.*
Carlson, Natalie Savage. *A Pet for the Orphelines.*
Carlson, Natalie Savage. *School Bell in the Valley.*
Clark, Ann Nolan. *Santiago.*
Clark, Ann Nolan. *Secret of the Andes.*
Cleary, Beverly. *Dear Mr. Henshaw.*
Cleary, Beverly. *Ellen Tebbits.*
Cleary, Beverly. *Henry and Beezus.*
Cleary, Beverly. *Henry and Ribsy.*
Cleary, Beverly. *Henry and the Clubhouse.*
Cleary, Beverly. *Henry and the Paper Route.*
Cleary, Beverly. *Henry Huggins.*
Cleary, Beverly. *The Mouse and the Motorcycle.*
Cleary, Beverly. *Ralph S. Mouse.*
Cleary, Beverly. *Ramona and Her Father.*
Cleary, Beverly. *Ramona and Her Mother.*
Cleary, Beverly. *Ramona Forever.*
Cleary, Beverly. *Ramona Quimby, Age 8.*
Cleary, Beverly. *Ramona the Brave.*
Cleary, Beverly. *Ramona the Pest.*
Cleary, Beverly. *Ribsy.*
Cleary, Beverly. *Runaway Ralph.*
Cleary, Beverly. *Socks.*
Clemens, Samuel L. (Mark Twain). *The Adventures of Huckleberry Finn.*

Clemens, Samuel L. (Mark Twain). *The Adventures of Tom Sawyer.*
Collier, James Lincoln, and Christopher Collier. *My Brother Sam Is Dead.*
Cooper, James Fenimore. *The Last of the Mohicans.*
Cooper, Susan. *The Dark Is Rising.*
Cooper, Susan. *The Grey King.*
de Trevino, Elizabeth Borton. *I, Juan de Pareja.*
Defoe, Daniel. *Robinson Crusoe.*
DeJong, Meindert. *Hurry Home, Candy.*
DeJong, Meindert. *Puppy Summer.*
DeJong, Meindert. *The Wheel on the School.*
Dickens, Charles. *Oliver Twist.*
Dickens, Charles. *A Tale of Two Cities.*
DuBois, William. *The Twenty-One Balloons.*
Eckert, Allan W. *Incident at Hawk's Hill.*
Edmonds, Walter D. *The Matchlock Gun.*
Edmonds, Walter D. *Two Logs Crossing.*
Enright, Elizabeth. *Thimble Summer.*
Estes, Eleanor. *The Alley.*
Estes, Eleanor. *The Coat-Hanger Christmas Tree.*
Estes, Eleanor. *Ginger Pye.*
Estes, Eleanor. *The Hundred Dresses.*
Estes, Eleanor. *The Lost Umbrella of Kim Chu.*
Estes, Eleanor. *The Middle Moffat.*
Estes, Eleanor. *Rufus M.*
Fitzhugh, Louise. *Harriet the Spy.*
Forbes, Esther. *Johnny Tremain.*
Fox, Paula. *One-Eyed Cat.*
Fox, Paula. *The Slave Dancer.*
Gates, Doris. *Blue Willow.*
Gates, Doris. *The Elderberry Bush.*
Gates, Doris. *A Morgan for Melinda.*
George, Jean Craighead. *A Coyote in Manhattan.*
George, Jean Craighead. *Julie of the Wolves.*
George, Jean Craighead. *My Side of the Mountain.*
George, Jean Craighead. *River Rats, Inc.*
George, Jean Craighead. *Who Really Killed Cock Robin?*
Gipson, Fred. *Old Yeller.*
Gipson, Fred. *Savage Sam.*
Greene, Bette. *Philip Hall Likes Me, I Reckon Maybe.*
Greene, Constance C. *A Girl Called Al.*
Hamilton, Virginia. *M. C. Higgins the Great.*
Hamilton, Virginia. *The Planet of Junior Brown.*
Harris, Rosemary. *The Bright and Morning Star.*
Harris, Rosemary. *The Moon in the Cloud.*
Harris, Rosemary. *The Shadow on the Sun.*
Haywood, Carolyn. *"B" Is for Betsy.*
Haywood, Carolyn. *Back to School with Betsy.*
Haywood, Carolyn. *Betsy and Mr. Kilpatrick.*
Haywood, Carolyn. *Eddie's Happenings.*
Haywood, Carolyn. *Snowbound with Betsy.*
Henry, Marguerite. *Born to Trot.*
Henry, Marguerite. *Brighty of the Grand Canyon.*
Henry, Marguerite. *Justin Morgan Had a Horse.*
Henry, Marguerite. *King of the Wind.*
Henry, Marguerite. *Misty of Chincoteague.*
Henry, Marguerite. *Mustang, Wild Spirit of the West.*
Henry, Marguerite. *Stormy, Misty's Foal.*
Hunt, Irene. *Across Five Aprils.*
Hunt, Irene. *Up a Road Slowly.*
Ish-Kishor, Sulamith. *Our Eddie.*
Kelly, Eric P. *The Trumpeter of Krakow.*
Konigsburg, E. L. *Father's Arcane Daughter.*

Konigsburg, E. L. *From the Mixed-Up Files of Mrs. Basil E. Frankweiler*

Konigsburg, E. L. *Jennifer, Hectate, Macbeth, William McKinley and Me, Elizabeth.*

Krumgold, Joseph. *And Now Miguel.*

Krumgold, Joseph. *Onion John.*

Lasky, Kathryn. *Beyond the Divide.*

Latham, Jean Lee. *Carry On, Mr. Bowditch.*

Lawson, Robert. *Ben and Me.*

Lawson, Robert. *Rabbit Hill.*

Lawson, Robert. *Robbut.*

Lawson, Robert. *The Tough Winter.*

L'Engle, Madeleine. *A Swiftly Tilting Planet.*

L'Engle, Madeleine. *A Wind in the Door.*

L'Engle, Madeleine. *A Wrinkle in Time.*

Lenski, Lois. *Strawberry Girl.*

Lewis, C. S. *The Horse and His Boy.*

Lewis, C. S. *The Last Battle.*

Lewis, C. S. *The Lion, the Witch and the Wardrobe.*

Lewis, C. S. *The Magician's Nephew.*

Lewis, C. S. *Prince Caspian.*

Lewis, C. S. *The Silver Chair.*

Lewis, C. S. *Voyage of the Dawn Treader.*

Lively, Penelope. *Astercote.*

Lively, Penelope. *The Ghost of Thomas Kempe.*

London, Jack. *The Call of the Wild.*

MacLachlan, Patricia. *Sarah, Plain and Tall.*

McKinley, Robin. *Beauty.*

McKinley, Robin. *The Blue Sword.*

McKinley, Robin. *The Hero and the Crown.*

Meigs, Cornelia. *Invincible Louisa.*

Neville, Emily. *It's Like This, Cat.*

North, Sterling. *Rascal.*

North, Sterling. *The Wolfling.*

Norton, Mary. *The Borrowers.*

Norton, Mary. *The Borrowers Afield.*

Norton, Mary. *The Borrowers Afloat.*

Norton, Mary. *The Borrowers Aloft.*

Norton, Mary. *The Borrowers Avenged.*

O'Brien, Robert C. *Mrs. Frisby and the Rats of NIMH.*

O'Dell, Scott. *Island of the Blue Dolphins.*

O'Dell, Scott. *Sarah Bishop.*

O'Dell, Scott. *Sing Down the Moon.*

Paterson, Katherine. *Bridge to Terabithia.*

Paterson, Katherine. *Jacob Have I Loved.*

Pearce, Philippa. *Tom's Midnight Garden.*

Raskin, Ellen. *The Mysterious Disappearance of Leon (I Mean Noel).*

Raskin, Ellen. *The Westing Game.*

Rawlings, Marjorie Kinnan. *The Yearling.*

Robertson, Keith. *Henry Reed, Inc.*

Robertson, Keith. *Henry Reed's Baby-Sitting Service.*

Rodowsky, Colby. *What About Me?*

Sawyer, Ruth. *Roller Skates.*

Sebestyen, Ouida. *Words by Heart.*

Selden, George. *The Cricket in Times Square.*

Seredy, Kate. *The White Stag.*

Shannon, Monica. *Dobry.*

Smith, Doris Buchanan. *The First Hard Times.*

Smith, Doris Buchanan. *Kelly's Creek.*

Smith, Doris Buchanan. *Kick a Stone Home.*

Smith, Doris Buchanan. *Last Was Lloyd.*

Smith, Doris Buchanan. *A Taste of Blackberries.*

Sobol, Donald J. *Encyclopedia Brown-The Case of the Dead Eagles and Other Mysteries.*

Sobol, Donald J. *Encyclopedia Brown Carries On.*

Sobol, Donald J. *Encyclopedia Brown Solves Them All.*

Sorensen, Virginia. *Miracles on Maple Hill.*

Speare, Elizabeth George. *The Bronze Bow.*

Speare, Elizabeth George. *Calico Captive.*

Speare, Elizabeth George. *Sign of the Beaver.*

Speare, Elizabeth George. *The Witch of Blackbird Pond.*

Sperry, Armstrong. *Call It Courage.*

Steig, William. *Abel's Island.*

Steig, William. *The Real Thief.*

Stevenson, Robert Louis. *Kidnapped.*

Stevenson, Robert Louis. *Treasure Island.*

Stolz, Mary. *Cat Walk.*

Stolz, Mary. *The Noonday Friends.*

Stowe, Harriet Beecher. *Uncle Tom's Cabin.*

Taylor, Mildred D. *Roll of Thunder, Hear My Cry.*

Voigt, Cynthia. *Building Blocks.*

Voigt, Cynthia. *Dicey's Song.*

Voigt, Cynthia. *Homecoming.*

Voigt, Cynthia. *A Solitary Blue.*

White, E. B. *Charlotte's Web.*

White, E. B. *Stuart Little.*

White, E. B. *The Trumpet of the Swan.*

Wiggin, Kate Douglas. *Rebecca of Sunnybrook Farm.*

Wilder, Laura Ingalls. *By the Shores of Silver Lake.*

Wilder, Laura Ingalls. *Farmer Boy.*

Wilder, Laura Ingalls. *The First Four Years.*

Wilder, Laura Ingalls. *Little House in the Big Woods.*

Wilder, Laura Ingalls. *Little Town on the Prairie.*

Wilder, Laura Ingalls. *The Long Winter.*

Wilder, Laura Ingalls. *On the Banks of Plum Creek.*

Wilder, Laura Ingalls. *These Happy Golden Years.*

Wojciechowska, Maia. *Shadow of a Bull.*

Wyss, Johann. *The Swiss Family Robinson.*

Yates, Elizabeth. *With Pipe, Paddle, and Song.*

PART II

Album of Tests

1
Little Men
Louisa May Alcott

True or False. Decide whether each statement is true or false. Mark your answer sheet accordingly.

1. Mrs. Bhaer taught Latin and Greek at the Plumfield school.
2. Nan was very ladylike and refused to play outside.
3. Nat knew how to play the violin.
4. Mr. and Mrs. Bhaer did not have any children of their own.
5. Nan was sent away from Plumfield because she was caught smoking cigarettes.
6. Nan fell into a pond and drowned.
7. Demi and Daisy were twins.
8. Demi and Daisy often argued and fought with each other.
9. Demi's father died when Demi was just a baby.
10. Mr. Bhaer wished to leave Plumfield so he could study to become a lawyer.

Multiple Choice. Read each question. Decide which statement best answers the question. Mark your answer sheet accordingly.

11. Why did Dan leave Plumfield?
    A. He was sent away because he kept breaking the rules
    B. His mother was sick and needed him at home
    C. He was going to go to a school that taught advanced mathematics
    D. He was grown and ready to get married
12. Nat was accused of
    A. Cheating on his spelling test
    B. Breaking all the best dishes
    C. Stealing Tommy's money
    D. Hiding Mrs. Bhaer's hen
13. What happened when Nan and Rob were looking for huckleberries?
    A. They got lost
    B. Rob drove a truck
    C. Nan fell out of a tree
    D. They found a lost dog
14. What special gift did Daisy receive at Plumfield?
    A. A magical pony
    B. A little stove that really worked
    C. A baby doll that said "mama" and "papa"
    D. A real baby to feed and care for

2
Little Women
Louisa May Alcott

True or False. Decide whether each statement is true or false. Mark your answer sheet accordingly.

1. Amy was the youngest of the four sisters.
2. Amy liked to draw.
3. Mr. Laurence gave Beth a small piano.
4. Beth had a quick temper that was always getting her into trouble.
5. Laurie's grandfather lived next door to the Marches.
6. Jo liked to write stories.
7. Marmee did not approve of Laurie and would not allow the girls to be near him.
8. Aunt March came to live with the Marches.
9. Jo hated Laurie because Laurie said that he could not love her.
10. Laurie married Amy.

Multiple Choice. Read each question. Decide which statement best answers the question. Mark your answer sheet accordingly.

11. When Jo refused to take Amy to the theater, Amy
    A. Burned Jo's little book
    B. Wrote Jo a letter
    C. Told Laurie that Jo loved him
    D. Broke Jo's best doll

12. What happened when Amy was at school?
    A. A large bear wandered into Amy's classroom and frightened all the students
    B. Amy was punished for bringing a bag of limes to school
    C. The principal announced that the school was going to close because of the war
    D. All of the above

13. When Beth was sick with scarlet fever
    A. Amy was sent to stay with Aunt March
    B. Mr. Laurence took Beth to a hospital
    C. Meg, Jo, and Amy were not allowed to leave the house
    D. Meg and Jo went to find their father in Washington

14. Jo earned some money to send to her sick father by selling
    A. Her favorite pony
    B. Her long hair
    C. Amy's best drawings
    D. Beth's little piano

3
The Black Cauldron
Lloyd Alexander

True or False. Decide whether each statement is true or false. Mark your answer sheet accordingly.

1. Ellidyr and Taran grew up together.
2. Ellidyr tried to capture the Black Cauldron by himself.
3. Orddu, Orwen, and Orgach, the three enchantresses, wanted to turn Taran into a toad.
4. The three enchantresses used their magic to move the Black Cauldron out of the marshes.
5. When Doli entered the Black Gate, he discovered that the Black Cauldron was gone.
6. Ellidyr fell in love with Princess Eilonwy.
7. Ellidyr and Taran were brothers.
8. Gwystyl was a leader of the Sons of Don.
9. Doli had the ability to become invisible.
10. King Morgant rescued Taran from the Huntsmen.

Multiple Choice. Read each question. Decide which statement best answers the question. Mark your answer sheet accordingly.

11. Why did Dallben, the magician, send the armies of men to attack the Dark Gate?
    A. They wanted to capture the Death Lord
    B. They wanted to stop the giant, Gru, before he escaped
    C. They wanted to steal the Black Cauldron
    D. They were trying to rescue the king of the Fair Folk
12. The Black Cauldron was used by the Death Lord to
    A. Create his armies of Cauldron-Born warriors
    B. Make a paste that would protect his Huntsmen from arrows
    C. Make deadly poisons
    D. Make a paste that made his warriors invisible
13. The Huntsmen of Annuvin were difficult to defeat because
    A. They could become invisible at will
    B. If one was slain, the rest would grow stronger
    C. They were immortal
    D. They were three times as strong as ordinary men
14. Taran and his companions found out from the three enchantresses that
    A. They made the Black Cauldron
    B. They stole the Black Cauldron from the Death Lord
    C. The Black Cauldron could only be destroyed by someone dying voluntarily inside it
    D. All of the above

4
The Book of Three
Lloyd Alexander

True or False. Decide whether each statement is true or false. Mark your answer sheet accordingly.

1. When Taran first met Gurgi, he wasn't sure if Gurgi was a man or an animal.
2. Medwyn was a fierce and mighty hunter.
3. The Horned King killed the pig, Hen Wen, and served her to his men for supper.
4. Taran killed the Horned King.
5. Eilonwy fell in love with Prince Gwydion.
6. Achren's castle was destroyed.
7. Taran took Eilonwy back to Caer Dallben.
8. Taran left Caer Dallben because he was chasing the pig, Hen Wen.
9. While in the forest, Taran was attacked by the Horned King.
10. Gwydion and Taran were captured by a dragon from Mount Doom.

Multiple Choice. Read each question. Decide which statement best answers the question. Mark your answer sheet accordingly.

11. In the forest, Taran met Gwydion, who
    A. Was a servant of the Horned King
    B. Was coming to see Hen Wen
    C. Was on a secret mission to kill Coll
    D. Was warning people that the dragons were coming
12. How did Taran escape from Achren's castle?
    A. He was rescued by Gwydion
    B. Eilonwy led him through some secret passages
    C. He stole one of Achren's horses
    D. He climbed down a long rope from his cell's window
13. How did Taran and his companions enter the realm of the Fair Folk?
    A. They followed Hen Wen down a tunnel
    B. They were sucked in by a whirlpool in a lake
    C. King Eiddileg gave them permission to enter
    D. Taran accidentally said the magic word that opened the gate
14. What did Taran find in the realm of the Fair Folk?
    A. Hen Wen
    B. A magic harp
    C. A secret map
    D. A knife that would kill the Cauldron-Born

5

The Castle of Llyr
Lloyd Alexander

True or False. Decide whether each statement is true or false. Mark your answer sheet accordingly.

1. King Rhuddlum wanted Princess Eilonwy to marry Prince Rhun.
2. Princess Eilonwy was excited about becoming a lady.
3. The giant cat, Llyan, loved Fflewddur's harp playing.
4. Princess Eilonwy's bauble would shine with a brilliant light.
5. Magg took Princess Eilonwy to the ruins of Caer Colur.
6. When Taran was questioned by Achren, Achren forced him to tell her the secrets of Eilonwy's bauble.
7. Achren and Magg were both drowned in the flood that destroyed Caer Colur.
8. Prince Rhun was the son of the King of Mona.
9. Magg, the chief steward, was secretly working for Lord Gwydion.
10. Taran and his friends discovered that Glew was trying to turn himself into a giant.
11. After Glew was chased into a cave by the giant cat, Llyan, he grew too big to get out.

Multiple Choice. Read each question. Decide which statement best answers the question. Mark your answer sheet accordingly.

12. Princess Eilonwy was going to the island of Mona because
    A. Dallben wanted her to be safe from the Death Lord
    B. She was going to attend the wedding of the Prince of Don
    C. She was going to be engaged to Math, the High King
    D. Dallben wanted her to be a lady
13. Lord Gwydion was on the island of Mona because
    A. He was looking for his magic sword
    B. He had to kill Prince Rhun
    C. He wanted to protect Princess Eilonwy
    D. He was learning to make shoes
14. After Magg kidnapped Princess Eilonwy, King Rhuddlum asked Taran to swear that he would
    A. Bring Magg back dead or alive
    B. Rescue Princess Eilonwy whatever the cost
    C. Protect and watch Prince Rhun
    D. All of the above

6
The Cat Who Wished to Be a Man
Lloyd Alexander

True or False. Decide whether each statement is true or false. Mark your answer sheet accordingly.

1. Lionel did not tell anyone in Brightford that he was really a cat.
2. Mayor Pursewig was very kind to Lionel.
3. Gillian did not like Mayor Pursewig.
4. Stephanus turned Gillian into a cat.
5. Stephanus was a wizard.
6. Before Lionel went to Brightford, Stephanus gave Lionel a wishbone.
7. Lionel helped Gillian by chasing the rats out of her cellar.
8. At the end of the book, Stephanus tried to turn Lionel back into a cat, but his spell failed.
9. At the end of the book, Mayor Pursewig married Gillian.
10. At the end of the book, the townspeople destroyed the toll gate.

Multiple Choice. Read each question. Decide which statement best answers the question. Mark your answer sheet accordingly.

11. Lionel promised Magister Stephanus that he would
    A. Come home directly
    B. Bring him a present from Brightford
    C. Stay a man for no longer than 24 hours
    D. Earn a lot of money in Brightford
12. How did Lionel get through the toll gate on the way to Brightford?
    A. He used some of the coins Stephanus had given him to pay the toll
    B. He jumped over the toll gate
    C. He used the wishbone to wish himself over the toll gate
    D. He showed the guards at the toll gate a pass
13. When Lionel had a chance to go home, why did he decide to return to Brightford?
    A. He had forgotten to buy a gift for Stephanus
    B. He had not earned enough money to pass through the toll gate
    C. He wanted to help Gillian
    D. He wanted to help the mayor
14. When Lionel and Dr. Tudbelly returned to Brightford
    A. They discovered that the mayor and Gillian were about to be married
    B. They were welcomed by the townspeople with a parade and fireworks
    C. They were locked in a cell
    D. They found out that Gillian had reported them to the police

From *Quizzes for 220 Great Children's Books*, revised 1st ed. © 1996. Teacher Ideas Press. (800) 237-6124.

7
The High King
Lloyd Alexander

True or False. Decide whether each statement is true or false. Mark your answer sheet accordingly.

1. The Cauldron-Born could not be slain.
2. Glew was once a giant.
3. Rhun, King of Mona, was killed trying to rescue King Smoit.
4. Wolves, bears, and hawks all served the Death Lord.
5. Taran found Dyrnwyn, the black sword.
6. Taran decided to go to the Summer Country to marry Eilonwy.
7. Doli was a leader of the Fair Folk.
8. Taran was an Assistant Pig-Keeper.
9. Hen Wen was important because she could tell the future.
10. Hen Wen was a horse.

Multiple Choice. Read each question. Decide which statement best answers the question. Mark your answer sheet accordingly.

11. At the end of the book, Dallben offered Taran the chance to
    A. Become King of Prydain
    B. Go to the Summer Country where he would never die
    C. Become a mighty magician
    D. Marry the beautiful Hen Wen
12. Eilonwy decided to
    A. Go to the Summer Country with her people
    B. Stay and marry King Smoit
    C. Become a great enchantress like her mother and grandmother
    D. Stay and marry Taran
13. Taran found out that his parents were
    A. A lord and lady of the House of Don
    B. Captured by the Cauldron-Born when he was an infant
    C. A prince and princess of the Fair Folk
    D. Unknown by anyone
14. What was unusual about Fflewddur's harp?
    A. It was made of pure silver
    B. It could play by itself
    C. Its strings would break if Fflewddur told a lie
    D. Its music could charm dragons and giants

From *Quizzes for 220 Great Children's Books,* revised 1st ed. © 1996. Teacher Ideas Press. (800) 237-6124.

8
Taran Wanderer
Lloyd Alexander

True or False. Decide whether each statement is true or false. Mark your answer sheet accordingly.

1. Craddoc was Taran's father.
2. The Free Commots were ruled by King Smoit.
3. Hevydd was a farmer who trusted his luck.
4. Dwyvach was a silversmith.
5. Taran and Gurgi protected Commot Isav.
6. At the end of the book, Taran discovered who his parents were.
7. Taran was traveling to find out about his past.
8. Taran started his journey by traveling to see the three enchantresses.
9. Gurgi went with Taran on his journey.
10. Taran found that Doli had been slain by Lord Gast.

Multiple Choice. Read each question. Decide which statement best answers the question. Mark your answer sheet accordingly.

11. Gast and Goryon went to war with each other because
    A. Goryon stole Gast's treasure
    B. Gast stole Goryon's horses
    C. Both Gast and Goryon were in rebellion against King Smoit
    D. A herd of cows was missing

12. Morda, the wizard, was defeated because
    A. Gurgi stole his wand
    B. Morda broke a magic finger bone
    C. The Fair Folk turned his own magic against him
    D. Taran cast a spell over him

13. Craddoc told Taran that
    A. He was a noble lord who had lost his kingdom
    B. He was an exiled prince of the House of Don
    C. He was Taran's father
    D. He was a wizard of greater power than Morda

14. Taran felt great shame because
    A. He wished Craddoc was dead so he could leave
    B. Craddoc was poor, and Taran wished to be rich
    C. He turned in Craddoc to rangers from the House of Don
    D. When enemies attacked, he left Craddoc behind to be captured

From *Quizzes for 220 Great Children's Books*, revised 1st ed. © 1996. Teacher Ideas Press. (800) 237-6124.

9
The Wizard in the Tree
Lloyd Alexander

True or False. Decide whether each statement is true or false. Mark your answer sheet accordingly.

1. Mrs. Parsel was always kind to Mallory.
2. Arbican asked Mallory to bring him some food.
3. Arbican accidentally turned himself into a pig.
4. Scrupnor shot Arbican.
5. Mallory was Arbican's fairy godmother.
6. A maid must kiss Arbican for him to gain back his power.
7. Scrupnor accused Arbican of murdering Squire Sorrel and Mr. Bolt.
8. Mallory rescued Arbican, who was trapped inside a tree.
9. At the end of the book, Mrs. Parsel was to be the new owner of the Holdings.
10. At the end of the book, Mallory went with Arbican to Vale Innis.

Multiple Choice. Read each question. Decide which statement best answers the question. Mark your answer sheet accordingly.

11. Scrupnor insisted that Mr. Parsel
    A. Buy vegetables from Scrupnor and not from Farmer Tench
    B. Give Mallory a whipping
    C. Play chess with him every Saturday night
    D. Divorce Mrs. Parsel

12. Arbican told Mallory that if he did not reach Vale Innis soon, he would
    A. Turn into a star
    B. Die
    C. Lose his fortune
    D. Never see his wife and children again

13. Scrupnor said that he would
    A. Marry Mallory if she would give him her golden trinket
    B. Give the Holdings to Mr. Parsel in return for Mr. Parsel's kindness to him
    C. Give the Holdings to the person who caught Squire Sorrel's murderer
    D. Build Mallory an enchanted castle if Mallory would tell him her dreams

14. Who really murdered Squire Sorrel and Mr. Bolt?
    A. Scrupnor
    B. Mrs. Parsel
    C. The notary
    D. Arbican

10
Waterless Mountain
Laura Adams Armer

True or False. Decide whether each statement is true or false. Mark your answer sheet accordingly.

1. Little Brother brought water back from the Western Sea.
2. Elder Brother killed Crooked Nose.
3. Little Brother spoke Spanish, English, and Navaho.
4. Elder Brother went to jail for killing Crooked Nose.
5. Waterless Mountain did not have any springs on it.
6. A Navaho's real name was announced to the tribe when he was 11 years old.
7. The Soft-footed Chief was a mountain lion.
8. The mask of the Yays was found in an old hogan.
9. Navahos were forbidden to plant crops.
10. Little Brother's daily job was to hunt for rabbits.

Multiple Choice. Read each question. Decide which statement best answers the question. Mark your answer sheet accordingly.

11. Uncle was
    A. A medicine man
    B. A skillful hunter
    C. A mighty warrior
    D. Very old

12. The man called "Grandfather"
    A. Once killed a white man
    B. Was Uncle's father
    C. Ran the trading post
    D. Hated Indians

13. The Navaho believed that the Turquoise Woman lived
    A. In the Western Sea
    B. In Texas
    C. In the Frozen North
    D. By the Lake of Sand

14. The hogan called "Beautiful Under the Cottonwoods" was
    A. The home of the Spider Woman
    B. Where evil spirits dwelt
    C. The place where rainbows grew
    D. Destroyed in a flood

11
Sounder
William H. Armstrong

True or False. Decide whether each statement is true or false. Mark your answer sheet accordingly.

1. The boy's father stole food because his family was hungry.
2. The father went to jail because he had stolen food.
3. Sounder was killed trying to protect the father.
4. The boy took Sounder hunting after his father was arrested.
5. The boy went to look for his father every fall and winter.
6. The boy found his father in a work camp.
7. When the boy's mother was worried or sad, she hummed.
8. While looking for his father, the boy met a teacher who helped him learn to read.
9. The boy lived with the teacher during the winter.
10. The father died while he was hunting with Sounder.

Multiple Choice. Read each question. Decide which statement best answers the question. Mark your answer sheet accordingly.

11. What happened when the boy visited his father in jail?
    A. He was arrested
    B. The jailer was mean to him
    C. His father wouldn't talk to him
    D. He cried and upset his father
12. When Sounder returned, he didn't
    A. Whine
    B. Fetch sticks
    C. Play
    D. Bark
13. What did the mother do after the boy's father was arrested?
    A. She returned what was stolen
    B. She went hunting with Sounder
    C. She begged the police to let the father go free
    D. She visited him in jail nearly every day
14. When the boy's father returned, he was
    A. Blind
    B. Deaf
    C. Rich
    D. Crippled

12

Mr. Popper's Penguins
Richard Atwater and Florence Atwater

True or False. Decide whether each statement is true or false. Mark your answer sheet accordingly.

1. Mr. Popper was a house painter.
2. Every morning for breakfast, Mr. Popper ate a penguin.
3. Mr. Popper took his penguins in a taxi.
4. When the penguins were performing, they liked to interfere with the other acts on the program.
5. One morning, Mrs. Popper turned herself into a penguin.
6. Mr. Popper used a magic wand to turn Mrs. Popper into a penguin.
7. Mrs. Popper learned to play the piano with her gloves on.
8. Mrs. Popper did not know that Mr. Popper was keeping penguins in the house.
9. Mr. Popper kept most of his penguins in his neighbor's barn.
10. Mr. and Mrs. Popper did not have any children.
11. Captain Cook and Greta were Mr. Popper's goldfish.

Multiple Choice. Read each question. Decide which statement best answers the question. Mark your answer sheet accordingly.

12. How did Mr. Popper get Captain Cook?
    A. Mr. Popper bought Captain Cook in a pet store
    B. Mr. Popper found Captain Cook while on vacation in Alaska
    C. Mr. Popper stole Captain Cook from a zoo
    D. None of the above
13. Why did Captain Cook become sick?
    A. He was not getting the right kind of food
    B. He was tired
    C. He was lonely
    D. He was overweight
14. At the end of the book, Mr. Popper decided to
    A. Let Mr. Klein put the penguins in the movies
    B. Let Admiral Drake take the penguins to the North Pole
    C. Sell the penguins to the local zoo
    D. None of the above

13
The Eyes of the Amaryllis
Natalie Babbitt

True or False. Decide whether each statement is true or false. Mark your answer sheet accordingly.

1. Seward told Gran and Jenny that the sign from the sea had to be returned because it was valued.
2. Seward left no footprints and cast no shadow.
3. Jenny's father had hated the sea ever since his father drowned.
4. Gran did not want to return the sign to the sea.
5. Jenny and her grandmother were rescued from the storm by Jenny's father.
6. Jenny found a red amaryllis flower.
7. The husband of the widow, Geneva Reade, was a farmer.
8. The widow, Geneva, searched the shore at high tide every day looking for a sign from the *Amaryllis*.
9. Seward could only be seen by Jenny and her grandmother.
10. The sign that came from the sea was the figurehead of the *Amaryllis*.
11. Seward was the ghost of Nicholas Irving.

Multiple Choice. Read each question. Decide which statement best answers the question. Mark your answer sheet accordingly.

12. When the *Amaryllis* sank
    A. There was no wreckage
    B. Both Geneva and her son, George, were watching
    C. There were no survivors
    D. All of the above

13. Jenny went to stay at her grandmother's house because
    A. Her grandmother had asked her to visit
    B. Her grandmother had broken her ankle and needed help
    C. Her father wanted her to get to know her grandmother better
    D. All of the above

14. What did Nicholas Irving do when the woman he loved rejected him and laughed at his work?
    A. He drowned himself
    B. He killed her
    C. He left Gran's home forever
    D. He hated George for stealing his girlfriend

From *Quizzes for 220 Great Children's Books*, revised 1st ed. © 1996. Teacher Ideas Press. (800) 237-6124.

14
Goody Hall
Natalie Babbitt

True or False. Decide whether each statement is true or false. Mark your answer sheet accordingly.

1. At one time, Hercules Feltwright was an actor.
2. Midas Goody, Mott Snave, and John Constant were all the same person.
3. Willet's father was not really dead.
4. After shopping in the city, Mrs. Goody returned with a carriage full of presents for Willet.
5. Willet never believed that his father was dead.
6. The gypsy gardener tried to kill Hercules.
7. Willet's father was in jail for five years.
8. Mrs. Goody mourned her dead husband for three years.
9. Hercules's mother always believed that Hercules would do great things.
10. At the end of the story, the Goodys gave Goody Hall to the two gypsies.

Multiple Choice. Read each question. Decide which statement best answers the question. Mark your answer sheet accordingly.

11. The blacksmith knew what was happening in Goody Hall because
    A. He worked for Mrs. Goody
    B. His sister worked for Mrs. Goody
    C. He was a relative of Midas Goody
    D. None of the above

12. Hercules Feltwright was going to Goody Hall because
    A. He was related to the gypsy gardener
    B. He was going to be a tutor to Willet Goody
    C. He was a relative of Midas Goody
    D. He was planning to steal the Goody treasure

13. Whenever the thief, Mott Snave, stole something
    A. He would bring it to Midas Goody, who would reward him for it
    B. He would wrap it in wrapping paper and give it to the poor
    C. He would hide it, and John Constant would find it and return it
    D. None of the above

14. When Hercules opened Midas Goody's coffin, he found
    A. The body of Midas Goody
    B. The body of Mott Snave
    C. The statue of Cerberus
    D. Rocks

15
Knee-Knock Rise
Natalie Babbitt

True or False. Decide whether each statement is true or false. Mark your answer sheet accordingly.

1. Ada did not believe in the Megrimum.
2. Ada did believe in the Megrimum.
3. Annabelle was a dog.
4. Annabelle was a cat.
5. Sweetheart broke a clock.
6. Annabelle broke a clock.
7. Egan saw Uncle Ott on Knee-Knock Rise.
8. Uncle Ott told Egan that there was no Megrimum.
9. Egan bought a gift at the fair for Ada.
10. It did not rain the day of the fair.

Multiple Choice. Read each question. Decide which statement best answers the question. Mark your answer sheet accordingly.

11. Who did Annabelle belong to?
    A. Uncle Anson
    B. Ada
    C. Uncle Ott
    D. Aunt Gertrude

12. Who liked to write verses?
    A. Egan
    B. Aunt Gertrude
    C. Uncle Ott
    D. Uncle Anson

13. Who made clocks?
    A. Egan
    B. Aunt Gertrude
    C. Uncle Ott
    D. Uncle Anson

14. Who tapped on the window the night of the storm?
    A. The Megrimum
    B. Uncle Ott
    C. Ada
    D. Sweetheart

16
Miss Hickory
Carolyn Bailey

True or False. Decide whether each statement is true or false. Mark your answer sheet accordingly.

1. Chipmunk took over Miss Hickory's house for the winter.
2. Miss Hickory often worried that Squirrel would try to eat her head.
3. Doe and Fawn lived in a cellar hole.
4. Doe was shot and killed.
5. Fawn was shot and killed.
6. Ground Hog was very friendly and had many friends.
7. The Ladies Aid Society was founded by Miss Hickory.
8. Miss Hickory's friend, Crow, was the leader of Old Crow Week.
9. It was Crow who helped free Bullfrog from the ice.
10. Squirrel ate Miss Hickory's head.

Multiple Choice. Read each question. Decide which statement best answers the question. Mark your answer sheet accordingly.

11. Mr. T. Willard Brown was a
    A. Pig
    B. Cow
    C. Man
    D. Cat
12. Who became like a sister to Fawn?
    A. Miss Hickory
    B. Robin
    C. Wild Heifer
    D. Barn Heifer
13. Bullfrog decided to look for a new home because
    A. He was bored and wanted adventure
    B. He wanted to find a warmer home
    C. He was tired of having stones thrown at him
    D. He wanted to be closer to the other animals
14. What did Bullfrog do with his old "suit"?
    A. He buried it
    B. He swallowed it
    C. He left it where it was
    D. He used it to make oil for his lamp

17
Dream of the Blue Heron
Victor Barnouw

True or False. Decide whether each statement is true or false. Mark your answer sheet accordingly.

1. Wabus's father kidnapped Wabus from his grandparents and sent Wabus to the government school.

2. Wabus's father, White Sky, did not want Wabus to learn to read and write.

3. Wabus's grandfather did not want Wabus to go to the government school.

4. When Wabus arrived at the government school, he was washed and scrubbed, his hair was cut, and he was given new clothes to wear.

5. Wabus was whipped for running away from the government school.

6. Mr. Wickham insisted that every boy go out into the woods at least once a week to fast for his guardian spirit.

7. Wabus never had a dream.

8. Wabus's father was put in jail.

9. Wabus's father, White Sky, accidentally shot Sema.

10. After Sema's funeral, Memengwa went to live at the mill town.

11. After Sema's funeral, Wabus returned to the government school.

Multiple Choice. Read each question. Decide which statement best answers the question. Mark your answer sheet accordingly.

12. Wabus ran away from the government school to
    A. Help his grandparents during the sugaring season
    B. Help his father at the mill
    C. Fast for his guardian spirit
    D. Live on an Indian reservation in Montana

13. Wabus saw Mr. Wickham
    A. Kiss Miss Peterson
    B. Steal money from John Ringboy's wallet
    C. Hide a bag of money in the cellar
    D. All of the above

14. Who, according to Wolf Claw, used bad medicine to make Sema sick?
    A. Wabus
    B. Memengwa
    C. Wabus's father, White Sky
    D. The Runner

18
A Gathering of Days
Joan W. Blos

True or False. Decide whether each statement is true or false. Mark your answer sheet accordingly.

1. Catherine was 21 years old when she began her journal.
2. Matty had dark, curly hair.
3. Catherine's dearest friend was Cassie.
4. Catherine's eyes were blue.
5. Cassie did not have any brothers or sisters.
6. Catherine and her family did not attend church.
7. Catherine was younger than Matty.
8. Teacher Holt never married.
9. Aunt Lucy married Uncle Jack.
10. It was Asa who stole the pies from the Shipman's cellar.
11. The people in the district wanted Teacher Holt to use the newspaper as a text for his students.
12. Daniel became good friends with Asa.
13. Catherine told Mammann about the quilt she had left for the runaway black man.

Multiple Choice. Read the question. Decide which statement best answers the question. Mark your answer sheet accordingly.

14. Asa gave a verse and a ribbon'd lock of hair to
    A. Cassie
    B. Sophy
    C. Catherine
    D. Matty

19
Otherwise Known as Sheila the Great
Judy Blume

True or False. Decide whether each statement is true or false. Mark your answer sheet accordingly.

1. Sheila was afraid of dogs.
2. Libby was Sheila's sister.
3. Libby was older than Sheila.
4. Sheila won first place in the diving contest.
5. Sheila taught Mouse how to do tricks on a yo-yo.
6. Mouse was afraid of Jennifer.
7. Sheila took Jennifer for a long walk every day.
8. When Sheila wrote a camp newspaper, she let other kids form committees to help her.
9. Mrs. Tubman did not have to pay for Sheila's swimming lessons.
10. Mouse was the only girl who came to Sheila's slumber party.
11. At the end of the book, Sheila passed the beginner's swimming test.

Multiple Choice. Read each question. Decide which statement best answers the question. Mark your answer sheet accordingly.

12. What was Bobby Egran's hobby?
    A. Building model airplanes
    B. Collecting stamps
    C. Building radios
    D. Collecting insects
13. Who sat on the toothpaste that was put on the toilet seat?
    A. Libby
    B. Sheila's mother
    C. Sheila's father
    D. Sheila
14. Who was Jennifer?
    A. Sheila's baby sister
    B. The Egrans' dog
    C. The Egrans' cat
    D. Sheila's best friend

20
Superfudge
Judy Blume

True or False. Decide whether each statement is true or false. Mark your answer sheet accordingly.

1. When Peter first heard that his mother was going to have a baby, he was very happy.
2. Fudge and Peter went to the same school.
3. Peter and Alex were in the same sixth-grade class.
4. In this book, Fudge was in the third grade.
5. In this book, Fudge was in kindergarten.
6. Fudge's friend, Daniel, was a fussy eater.
7. Turtle was Peter's dog.
8. Fudge's parents bought Fudge a pet bird.
9. When Jimmy Fargo came to visit, Peter refused to speak to him.
10. Fudge wanted a bike for Christmas.

Multiple Choice. Read each question. Decide which statement best answers the question. Mark your answer sheet accordingly.

11. What did Fudge do to Tootsie?
    A. He covered her with trading stamps
    B. He painted her hair green
    C. He cut off all her hair
    D. None of the above

12. What did Alex and Peter sell to Mrs. Muldour?
    A. Lemonade
    B. Worms
    C. Kittens
    D. Puppies

13. Why was Peter called to the principal's office on the first day of school?
    A. His mother had forgotten to fill out part of his registration card
    B. He had gotten into a fistfight with Alex
    C. They were having trouble with Fudge, and they needed his help
    D. None of the above

14. Fudge kicked Mrs. Hildebrandt because
    A. She wouldn't call him Fudge
    B. She wouldn't let him be the first person in line
    C. She wouldn't let him go to recess
    D. She wouldn't let him play on the jungle gym

21
Tales of a Fourth Grade Nothing
Judy Blume

True or False. Decide whether each statement is true or false. Mark your answer sheet accordingly.

1. Peter's father finally bought Peter a lock for his bedroom door.
2. Peter and Fudge shared the same room.
3. Peter was not home the day of Fudge's birthday party.
4. Peter showed Dribble to the children at Fudge's birthday party.
5. At Fudge's birthday party, Jennie bit Fudge's grandma.
6. At Fudge's birthday party, Jennie went to the bathroom on the floor.
7. Dribble was Peter's hamster.
8. Peter won Dribble at Jimmy Fargo's birthday party.
9. Mrs. Yarby gave Peter a chemistry set.
10. Fudge covered the Yarbys' suitcase with green stamps.

Multiple Choice. Read each question. Decide which statement best answers the question. Mark your answer sheet accordingly.

11. Peter's mother told Peter to stop calling Fudge
    A. Pee-wee
    B. Fang
    C. Farley
    D. Fatso

12. How did Peter's turtle die?
    A. Fudge flushed it down the toilet
    B. Fudge swallowed it
    C. It died of old age
    D. None of the above

13. Which of the following events did NOT take place?
    A. Fudge scribbled on the poster Peter had been making for school
    B. Fudge took some scissors and cut off a lot of his hair
    C. Fudge swallowed Peter's turtle
    D. Fudge tried to eat his shoelaces

14. At the end of the book, what gift did Peter's father bring him?
    A. A new turtle
    B. A new hamster
    C. A dog
    D. A chemistry set

22
Caddie Woodlawn
Carol Ryrie Brink

True or False. Decide whether each statement is true or false. Mark your answer sheet accordingly.

1. Indian John and Caddie were friends.
2. Indian John left his dog with Caddie while he went away to hunt.
3. Tom gave Katie Hyman a valentine.
4. Nero was Indian John's dog.
5. Caddie's father and the circuit rider were enemies.
6. Caddie spent a lot of time playing with Warren and Tom.
7. In the attic, Caddie found some red breeches and clogs that had belonged to her father when he was a little boy.
8. Caddie never showed anyone the scalp belt she was keeping for Indian John.
9. Uncle Edmund gave Caddie a silver dollar.
10. Caddie used her silver dollar to buy a new dress for Clara.
11. Hetty told Mother about the practical jokes being played on Annabelle.

Multiple Choice. Read each question. Decide which statement best answers the question. Mark your answer sheet accordingly.

12. What did Caddie's father do in his spare time?
    A. He built model ships
    B. He mended clocks
    C. He collected stamps
    D. He painted pictures
13. What food did Mrs. Woodlawn serve all winter long?
    A. Beans
    B. Chicken
    C. Squash
    D. Turkey
14. Who was the oldest child in the Woodlawn family?
    A. Hetty
    B. Caddie
    C. Warren
    D. Clara

23
The Secret Garden
Frances Hodgson Burnett

True or False. Decide whether each statement is true or false. Mark your answer sheet accordingly.

1. Colin never learned to walk on his own.
2. The servants did everything that Colin commanded.
3. When Mary first came to Misselthwaite Manor, she was quite overweight.
4. Martha's family was very wealthy.
5. When Mary arrived at Misselthwaite Manor, her uncle was waiting at the door to greet her.
6. Mr. Craven's wife had died of pneumonia.
7. Dickon did not have any brothers or sisters.
8. Martha was Dickon's cousin.
9. Dickon never met Colin.
10. Colin died at the end of the book.
11. Dickon's sister worked at Misselthwaite Manor as a maid.
12. Dickon taught Mary and Colin to do exercises that would strengthen their muscles.
13. Mary and Dickon became good friends.

Multiple Choice. Read the question. Decide which statement best answers the question. Mark your answer sheet accordingly.

14. Who did Mary refer to as a young rajah?
    A. Dickon
    B. Martha
    C. Colin
    D. Ben Weatherstaff

24
The Cartoonist
Betsy Byars

True or False. Decide whether each statement is true or false. Mark your answer sheet accordingly.

1. Alfie's mother did not want Bubba to come home to live.
2. When Alfie heard that his brother, Bubba, was coming home to live, he baked a cake and planned a welcome home party.
3. Alma was not happy when she heard that Bubba would be coming home to live.
4. Alfie's mother liked to watch television.
5. Alfie never showed his mother the cartoons he had drawn.
6. Alfie and Tree got into a fistfight.
7. Alfie's mother was a lawyer.
8. Tree told Alfie that Lizabeth beat him in basketball.
9. Alfie's grandfather lived in the Christian Gentlemen's Nursing Home.
10. Alfie liked to draw his cartoons in the attic.
11. At the end of the book, Bubba and Maureen decided to live with Maureen's parents.

Multiple Choice. Read each question. Decide which statement best answers the question. Mark your answer sheet accordingly.

12. What did Alfie's teacher do when she found out that he had not done his math?
    A. She laughed
    B. She yawned and said that math was boring
    C. She told him that she would like to speak with him after school
    D. She sent him to the principal's office
13. When Alfie told his mother that Bubba had taken Perry Fletcher's car and pushed it down the street into Big Bertha's driveway, she
    A. Was very angry
    B. Laughed
    C. Called Bubba's father
    D. Called the police
14. Alfie's mother used Alma's baby-sitting money to
    A. Buy a birthday present for Alfie
    B. Buy herself a new dress
    C. Buy food for the family
    D. Pay Bubba's fine when he got in trouble

From *Quizzes for 220 Great Children's Books*, revised 1st ed. © 1996. Teacher Ideas Press. (800) 237-6124.

25
The Computer Nut
Betsy Byars

True or False. Decide whether each statement is true or false. Mark your answer sheet accordingly.

1. Willie and Kate were not able to make contact with BB-9 on Willie's Apple computer.
2. Kate introduced BB-9 to her father.
3. Willie did not have any brothers or sisters.
4. Kate's mother had died when Kate was a little girl.
5. Kate's sister was with Kate when she met BB-9.
6. Kate and Willie had to help BB-9 escape a group of angry football fans.
7. Kate's father was a doctor.
8. Kate and Willie met BB-9 at Burger's.
9. BB-9 wanted to make people laugh.
10. Willie Lomax was very skinny.

Multiple Choice. Read each question. Decide which statement best answers the question. Mark your answer sheet accordingly.

11. BB-9 turned out to be
    A. Kate's father
    B. Willie Lomax
    C. Miss Markham
    D. None of the above

12. What kind of party did Kate's sister have?
    A. A slumber party
    B. A popcorn party
    C. A dog party
    D. A baby party

13. Kate promised her sister that
    A. Kate would go on a date with Willie Lomax
    B. Kate would study for her English test
    C. Kate would not contact BB-9 for a week
    D. None of the above

14. Kate got mad at Linda because
    A. Linda would not go with her to meet BB-9
    B. Linda called Mrs. Lomax and told her to tell Willie that Kate called
    C. Linda told everyone at school that Kate believed in UFOs
    D. None of the above

26
Cracker Jackson
Betsy Byars

True or False. Decide whether each statement is true or false. Mark your answer sheet accordingly.

1. Jackson did not have a bicycle of his own.
2. Goat was always getting into trouble.
3. Alma's baby died.
4. Jackson's mother and father were divorced.
5. Jackson told his father about Alma.
6. Alma used to baby-sit for Jackson.
7. Jackson's father was not usually very serious.
8. Jackson's father told him that he should go live with Alma.
9. The palm reader said that Alma would never get married.
10. Alma was collecting Barbie dolls for her little girl.

Multiple Choice. Read each question. Decide which statement best answers the question. Mark your answer sheet accordingly.

11. Who called Jackson "Cracker"?
    A. His mother
    B. Goat
    C. Alma
    D. His father
12. What excuse did Goat find to go to Alma's house?
    A. He pretended to be selling magazines
    B. He pretended that his mother had sent him to borrow a cup of sugar
    C. He pretended to be collecting money for UNICEF
    D. He pretended that he was taking a survey
13. Why didn't Alma show up to talk with Jackson's mother?
    A. Her baby came down with a bad cold
    B. Her husband had beaten her up
    C. She didn't want to tell Jackson's mother about her problem
    D. Her house caught on fire
14. Jackson stole his mother's car so that he could
    A. Visit his father
    B. Go to a party
    C. Go to a football game
    D. None of the above

27
The Cybil War
Betsy Byars

True or False. Decide whether each statement is true or false. Mark your answer sheet accordingly.

1. Tony told a lot of lies.

2. Cybil did not have any brothers or sisters.

3. Simon's father died in a car accident.

4. Simon lived with his grandmother.

5. Cybil invited Simon to come to the pet show and to bring his dog, T-Bone.

6. Harriet Haywood was small and skinny.

7. Simon and Tony had known each other since they were in the first grade.

8. Simon enjoyed his date with Harriet Haywood.

9. Cybil said that Tony was a juvenile.

10. Pap-pap cried a lot.

11. Tony told Simon that Cybil would go to a movie if Simon and Harriet went too.

Multiple Choice. Read each question. Decide which statement best answers the question. Mark your answer sheet accordingly.

12. Tony's dog won the prize for

    A. Best costume

    B. Best tricks

    C. Worst behaved

    D. Smelliest animal

13. What part did Cybil have in the play on nutrition?

    A. A dill pickle

    B. Ms. Indigestion

    C. Mrs. Santa Claus

    D. None of the above

14. When Simon and Tony went to a movie

    A. Simon kissed Harriet Haywood

    B. Simon and Tony got into a fistfight

    C. Cybil fainted

    D. None of the above

28
Good-bye, Chicken Little
Betsy Byars

True or False. Decide whether each statement is true or false. Mark your answer sheet accordingly.

1. Uncle C. C. was 100 years old.
2. Uncle C. C. did not come to the party.
3. Uncle C. C. had killed a lot of people in the Spanish-American War.
4. Jimmie's father was dead.
5. Jimmie's father and mother were divorced.
6. Jimmie and Conrad got into a fight, and Conrad hit Jimmie.
7. Jimmie invited Conrad to come in and enjoy the party.
8. Jimmie and Conrad were together the day Uncle Pete died.
9. Jimmie's mother was not a very good driver.
10. Uncle C. C. lived with Jimmie and his family.

Multiple Choice. Read each question. Decide which statement best answers the question. Mark your answer sheet accordingly.

11. How did Uncle Pete die?

    A. He died in a car accident

    B. He had a heart attack

    C. He died of cancer

    D. None of the above

12. Jimmie was feeling guilty and sad because

    A. He wished he had gone to Uncle Pete's funeral

    B. He wished he had spent more time with Uncle Pete

    C. He wished he had stopped Uncle Pete from walking across the ice

    D. He wished he had learned more about cancer before Uncle Pete died

13. Jimmie's mother

    A. Died at the end of the book

    B. Was deaf

    C. Was in prison

    D. None of the above

14. "Chicken Little" was a name that Jimmie called

    A. Uncle Pete

    B. Conrad

    C. Himself

    D. His father

29
The House of Wings
Betsy Byars

True or False. Decide whether each statement is true or false. Mark your answer sheet accordingly.

1. Sammy's parents did not say good-bye to Sammy when they left him with his grandfather.
2. Sammy's grandfather did not allow animals inside the house.
3. Sammy was not with his grandfather when the crane was captured.
4. Sammy's grandfather had to force-feed the crane.
5. Sammy gave the owl a grasshopper to eat.
6. Sammy's grandfather made Sammy take a bath and go to bed early.
7. Sammy's parents had always been strict with Sammy.
8. Sammy helped his grandfather feed the crane.
9. Sammy's grandfather spent the whole afternoon preparing a hot meal for Sammy.
10. The parrot said "Where's Papa?" and "Good-bye."
11. At the end of the book, Sammy's parents came to get Sammy.

Multiple Choice. Read each question. Decide which statement best answers the question. Mark your answer sheet accordingly.

12. When Sammy's grandfather was a boy
    A. He threw a rock at a bird and killed it
    B. He broke into a hardware store and stole merchandise
    C. He ran away from home
    D. He fell out of a tree and broke his neck

13. Sammy's grandfather discovered that the crane
    A. Was deaf
    B. Was blind
    C. Had a broken neck
    D. Had been bitten by a snake

14. At the end of the book, the crane
    A. Died
    B. Ate a frog by itself
    C. Flew away
    D. Had babies

30
The Night Swimmers
Betsy Byars

True or False. Decide whether each statement is true or false. Mark your answer sheet accordingly.

1. It was Retta's idea to go swimming in the colonel's pool.

2. Roy and Johnny often went swimming in the colonel's pool without Retta.

3. Roy liked to eat peanut butter.

4. Retta did not like Johnny's friend, Arthur.

5. Retta often took Roy over to see the bowlwater plant.

6. Retta was always trying to find free things for the children to do.

7. Retta's mother was dead.

8. Retta's mother and father were divorced.

9. Retta, Arthur, and Johnny were caught stealing from a store.

10. The colonel never found out that the Anderson children had been swimming in his pool.

11. Roy liked to be hugged by Brendelle.

12. Johnny liked to be hugged by Brendelle.

Multiple Choice. Read each question. Decide which statement best answers the question. Mark your answer sheet accordingly.

13. Which of the children nearly drowned in the colonel's pool?

    A. Retta

    B. Johnny

    C. Roy

    D. None of the above

14. Brendelle was

    A. Retta's friend

    B. The father's girlfriend

    C. Retta's stepmother

    D. Retta's aunt

31
The Pinballs
Betsy Byars

True or False. Decide whether each statement is true or false. Mark your answer sheet accordingly.

1. The Benson twins died at the exact same time.

2. Carlie had lived with Mrs. Mason since she was two years old.

3. Harvey was in the hospital on his birthday.

4. Mrs. Mason did not have any children of her own.

5. Mrs. Mason had had other foster children before Thomas J., Harvey, and Carlie.

6. Carlie refused to visit Harvey in the hospital.

7. Harvey liked to make lists.

8. Mr. Mason took Thomas J. to the funerals.

9. Carlie and Thomas J. gave Harvey a puppy for his birthday.

10. Harvey's father gave him a television for his birthday.

Multiple Choice. Read each question. Decide which statement best answers the question. Mark your answer sheet accordingly.

11. The Benson twins were put in the hospital because

    A. They had cancer

    B. They had problems with their hearts

    C. They broke their hips

    D. They were burned in a fire

12. The Benson twins were

    A. A man and a woman

    B. Two women

    C. Two men

    D. A boy and a girl

13. Who had lived with the Benson twins since he or she was a baby?

    A. Carlie

    B. Harvey

    C. Thomas J.

    D. All of the above

14. How did Harvey break his legs?

    A. His father hit him with a baseball bat

    B. His father ran over him with a car

    C. He fell out of a tree

    D. None of the above

32
The Summer of the Swans
Betsy Byars

True or False. Decide whether each statement is true or false. Mark your answer sheet accordingly.

1. Sara's dog, Boysie, was just a puppy.
2. Charlie had a nervous habit of shuffling his feet back and forth on the step.
3. Aunt Willie refused to ride on Frank's motor scooter.
4. Sara tried to dye her orange tennis shoes baby blue.
5. Charlie was proud of his watch.
6. Sara thought that her sister, Wanda, was beautiful.
7. Sara's father came out immediately when he heard that Charlie was missing.
8. Joe Melby stole Charlie's watch.
9. Sara refused Joe Melby's invitation to a party.
10. A search party was gathered to look for Charlie when he was lost.
11. Charlie was found by the police and brought back home.
12. Sara was not close to her father.
13. Sara was younger than her sister, Wanda.
14. Sara's father died at the end of the book.

33
The TV Kid
Betsy Byars

True or False. Decide whether each statement is true or false. Mark your answer sheet accordingly.

1. Lennie earned an A on the science test that the two schoolteachers helped him study for.
2. Lennie and his mother had moved a lot.
3. Lennie did not have any brothers or sisters.
4. The snake bit Lennie on the foot.
5. The snake bit Lennie on the arm.
6. After Lennie was bitten by the snake, he used the telephone in the house on the lake to call for help.
7. Lennie couldn't use the telephone in the house on the lake to call for help because the phone had been disconnected for the winter.
8. After Lennie was bitten by the snake, he used his pocketknife to cut little x's over the fang marks and his bandanna to make a tourniquet.
9. After Lennie was bitten by the snake, he walked three miles to a hospital.
10. Lennie's mother did not come to see Lennie while he was in the hospital.
11. Lennie wrote a report about rattlesnakes.

Multiple Choice. Read each question. Decide which statement best answers the question. Mark your answer sheet accordingly.

12. Lennie's mom
    A. Owned a motel
    B. Was a stewardess
    C. Did not have a job
    D. Was a teacher
13. What was Lennie doing when he was bitten by a snake?
    A. Wading in some muddy water
    B. Sleeping in the bottom of a rowboat
    C. Hiding under the porch of a house
    D. None of the above
14. When Lennie was in the hospital, the policeman
    A. Brought in a friend of his who had been bitten by a snake
    B. Gave Lennie a clock
    C. A and B
    D. None of the above

34
The Two-Thousand-Pound Goldfish
Betsy Byars

True or False. Decide whether each statement is true or false. Mark your answer sheet accordingly.

1. Warren often daydreamed.

2. Warren's mother came to visit him once a month.

3. Warren's grandmother did not have a phone.

4. Warren's mother did not come to his grandmother's funeral.

5. Warren got to talk to his mother on the telephone.

6. When Warren's grandmother was in the hospital, she called for Saffee, Warren's mother.

7. When Warren's grandmother was alive, she spent a lot of time talking about Warren's mother, Saffee.

8. Aunt Pepper refused to talk about Warren's mother.

9. Warren's grandmother caught him looking at old postcards from his mother.

10. When Warren's grandmother died, Aunt Pepper came to live with Warren and Weezie.

11. Weezie planned to become a lawyer.

Multiple Choice. Read each question. Decide which statement best answers the question. Mark your answer sheet accordingly.

12. Warren's mother

   A. Was dead

   B. Was in jail

   C. Had broken the law

   D. Was in a mental institution

13. On the first Monday of each month, at seven o'clock, Warren's mom was supposed to

   A. Meet Aunt Pepper at the grocery store

   B. Call the phone booth in front of the library

   C. Report to her probation officer

   D. Call Warren's grandmother

14. Warren's grandmother kept her money

   A. In the freezer

   B. Under her mattress

   C. In the Bible

   D. In her underwear drawer

35
A Brother for the Orphelines
Natalie Savage Carlson

True or False. Decide whether each statement is true or false. Mark your answer sheet accordingly.

1. Monsieur de Goupil decided to adopt Coucky.

2. Madame Flattot sent Coucky by train to be cared for by her sister in Spain.

3. Josine won some marbles and ball bearings when she played marbles with the boys from the boys' orphanage.

4. Monsieur de Goupil told Madame Flattot that he was going to send Josine to another orphanage.

5. Josine decided to say home with Coucky when Genevieve took the orphelines on a tour of the sewers of Paris.

6. Monsieur de Goupil never found out that Coucky was really a boy.

7. Josine and Coucky had their pictures in the newspaper.

8. Josine found Coucky in a breadbasket.

9. Madame Flattot told Monsieur de Goupil that Coucky could not be moved to the boys' orphanage until Coucky was done making teeth.

10. Josine left the orphanage without permission so that she could take Coucky to the merry-go-round man.

11. The boys from the boys' orphanage told Josine that they were beaten, starved, and worked like donkeys.

12. The boys from the boys' orphanage tried to steal Coucky when Josine wasn't looking.

13. At the end of the book, Coucky's real mother showed up at the orphanage to take Coucky back.

Multiple Choice. Read the question. Decide which statement best answers the question. Mark your answer sheet accordingly.

14. When the merry-go-round man gave the orphelines a free ride
    A. Coucky fell off the merry-go-round
    B. Josine started to feel dizzy and sick to her stomach
    C. Monsieur de Goupil decided to buy the merry-go-round for the orphelines
    D. The horse that Josine was riding galloped off the merry-go-round into the woods

36
The Empty Schoolhouse
Natalie Savage Carlson

True or False. Decide whether each statement is true or false. Mark your answer sheet accordingly.

1. Oralee did not invite Lullah to her birthday party.
2. Lullah got so mad at Oralee that she threw lemonade on her.
3. Mr. Buzzard and Daddy Jobe were good friends.
4. For a while, Lullah was the only student at St. Joseph's School.
5. Emma went with Lullah to see Uncle Vounie.
6. Little Jobe went to school one day with Lullah.
7. Emma did not go to school because she was blind.
8. Father Austin did not want Negro children to attend St. Joseph's School.
9. Lullah was shot in the ankle.
10. Lullah died at the end of the book.

Multiple Choice. Read each question. Decide which statement best answers the question. Mark your answer sheet accordingly.

11. Emma
    A. Worked as a scrub girl at the Magnolia Motel
    B. Quit school in the sixth grade
    C. A and B
    D. None of the above

12. Lullah wanted Uncle Vounie to
    A. Give her a love potion to put in the candy she was going to give to Oralee
    B. Read her palm and tell her what her future would be
    C. Put a spell on Oralee
    D. None of the above

13. What happened when Daddy Jobe took the children to see the sugar mill?
    A. Little Jobe got lost
    B. Some white men beat Daddy Jobe
    C. Little Jobe climbed to the top of the sugar mountain
    D. All of the above

14. Lullah
    A. Did not have any brothers or sisters
    B. Was not old enough to go to school
    C. Would not play with Oralee because Oralee was white
    D. None of the above

37
The Happy Orpheline
Natalie Savage Carlson

True or False. Decide whether each statement is true or false. Mark your answer sheet accordingly.

1. Brigitte prayed every night that she would be adopted.

2. Brigitte did not want to be adopted by Madame Capet.

3. Madame Capet lived in a beautiful palace with golden furniture, velvet curtains, and floors that shone like mirrors.

4. Madame Capet made Brigitte clean up all the dirt in her house, and she didn't give Brigitte anything to eat.

5. Madame Flattot and Genevieve treated the orphelines poorly.

6. When Madame Flattot found out that Brigitte had told a lie, she gave her a spanking.

7. Brigitte and Josine ran away from the orphanage.

8. Brigitte never told anybody that she was an orpheline.

9. Brigitte was queen for the day because she found the bean in her piece of cake.

10. Brigitte let all the wicked dogs in Ste. Germaine loose.

11. Madame Capet took Brigitte back to the orphanage on her bicycle.

12. At the end of the book, Brigitte and Josine were adopted by Madame Capet.

Multiple Choice. Read each question. Decide which statement best answers the question. Mark your answer sheet accordingly.

13. When Brigitte was queen for the day, she commanded that

    A. Monsieur de Goupil come for a visit

    B. Genevieve take the orphelines to the dog cemetery

    C. Madame Flattot let the orphelines stay up all night

    D. Genevieve take them to see Napoleon's tomb

14. Where did Brigitte get a fifty-franc piece?

    A. Madame Flattot gave it to her for her birthday

    B. Madame Capet gave it to her as payment for the cleaning she had done

    C. She stole it from Josine

    D. None of the above

From *Quizzes for 220 Great Children's Books,* revised 1st edition. © 1996. Teacher Ideas Press. (800) 237-6124.

38
The Letter on the Tree
Natalie Savage Carlson

True or False. Decide whether each statement is true or false. Mark your answer sheet accordingly.

1. Bébert did not have any brothers or sisters.

2. Bébert was disappointed when he saw the present that his parents gave him for Christmas.

3. Papa would not allow Bébert to help milk the cows until his sixteenth birthday.

4. Bébert never told his parents about the check he received from Spike Merryfield.

5. Bébert told his parents about the check he received from Spike Merryfield, and they made him send the check back.

6. Charlie spoke both French and English.

7. Charlie spoke English but not French.

8. When Bébert told his parents about Charlie, they called the police.

9. Bébert did not tell his parents about Charlie until after Charlie had left.

10. Bébert's father spoke French but not English.

11. Bébert's parents gave him a toy drum for Christmas.

12. Instead of buying a milking machine, Papa bought Bébert an accordion.

Multiple Choice. Read each question. Decide which statement best answers the question. Mark your answer sheet accordingly.

13. Bébert was a "12-percent boy" because

   A. He could read and write

   B. He did not know how to read

   C. He could speak both French and English

   D. He was smaller than most of the boys in his area

14. Bébert wanted to fix up the cabin so that

   A. Charlie would want to stay there forever

   B. He would have a place to go when he wanted to be alone

   C. He and Pierre could use it as a clubhouse

   D. None of the above

CATEGORY: A
POINT VALUE: 5

39
The Orphelines in the Enchanted Castle
Natalie Savage Carlson

True or False. Decide whether each statement is true or false. Mark your answer sheet accordingly.

1. The girls arrived at the castle before the boys did.

2. The boys had been living in the enchanted castle for 10 years before the girls came to live there.

3. Madame Flattot would not allow the orphelines to have anything to do with the boys until the boys' behavior improved.

4. The boys helped Brigitte and Josine to catch a cuckoo.

5. The boys tricked Brigitte and Josine when they invited the girls on a cuckoo hunt.

6. Because of their naughtiness, the boys were not allowed to go with the orphelines on a tour of the royal palace of Fontainebleau.

7. Madame Flattot liked her old pots and pans better than the new ones.

8. Pierre decided that he would lay the wreath with Brigitte on Bastille Day.

9. One of the boys told Brigitte that Madame and Genevieve only pretended to love the orphelines because they were paid for it.

10. To become full-fledged wolf cubs, the boys had to do a good deed every day.

11. Marcel was too young to become a wolf cub.

12. At the end of the book, Josine and Brigitte were adopted by Monsieur Roger.

Multiple Choice. Read each question. Decide which statement best answers the question. Mark your answer sheet accordingly.

13. One of the boys told Josine that Madame Flattot had

   A. Turned into a hen

   B. Died

   C. Robbed a bank

   D. All of the above

14. As punishment for the trick the boys played on Josine, they

   A. Were kept in the castle for a week

   B. Had to make a public apology to Josine

   C. Were spanked

   D. Were sent to bed without any supper

40
A Pet for the Orphelines
Natalie Savage Carlson

True or False. Decide whether each statement is true or false. Mark your answer sheet accordingly.

1. The orphelines did not go to the charity ball.

2. The boy orphans sang at the charity ball.

3. At the Parc de Bagatelle, Josine found a swan's egg.

4. Madame Flattot's goldfish grew so big that she had to buy a larger tank.

5. Madame Flattot's goldfish went down the bathtub drain.

6. When the plumber came to fix the kitchen sink, he fell down a flight of stairs and broke his leg.

7. When the plumber came to fix the kitchen sink, he brought his crow, Charlot, with him.

8. Monsieur Croquet named his new hybrid cabbage after Madame Flattot.

9. Monsieur Croquet and Madame Flattot decided to get married.

10. Monsieur Croquet brought the orphelines a giraffe and a monkey.

11. Monsieur Croquet brought the orphelines a pony.

12. At the end of the book, the orphelines decided that they did not want a pet after all.

Multiple Choice. Read each question. Decide which statement best answers the question. Mark your answer sheet accordingly.

13. Where did the orphelines find the lost swan?

    A. On the stone steps inside the orphanage courtyard

    B. Under an upside down canoe at the park

    C. Under Josine's bed

    D. None of the above

14. To help the orphelines decide what kind of pet they wanted, Monsieur Croquet suggested that Madame Flattot take the orphelines to

    A. The zoo

    B. A dog show

    C. A cat show

    D. The library

41
School Bell in the Valley
Natalie Savage Carlson

True or False. Decide whether each statement is true or false. Mark your answer sheet accordingly.

1. Uncle Ned and Aunt Ivy insisted that Belle go to school every day.

2. Uncle Ned did not know how to read or write.

3. Annie Love was hit by a train and killed.

4. Uncle Ned lost his job at the railroad.

5. Tom Caigle and his family lived in the blockhouses.

6. Uncle Ned and Aunt Ivy lived in the blockhouses.

7. The blockhouses were where the very richest people lived.

8. Uncle Ned finally agreed to be Lit Caigle's partner in the mule business.

9. The first day that Belle went to school, the other children made fun of her because she couldn't read or write.

10. Annie Love was Aunt Ivy's baby girl.

11. Aunt Ivy helped Tom Caigle's mother by bringing her medicine for her baby.

Multiple Choice. Read each question. Decide which statement best answers the question. Mark your answer sheet accordingly.

12. Mrs. Crissman would not let Belle look after Charlsie any more because

    A. Charlsie told Mrs. Crissman that Belle hit him

    B. Belle stole 10 dollars out of Mrs. Crissman's purse

    C. Mrs. Crissman blamed Belle for Charlsie's accident

    D. Belle took home Charlsie's book

13. Lit Caigle broke his leg when

    A. He fell down a flight of stairs

    B. He was kicked by a mule

    C. He was run over by a carriage

    D. He fell off a horse

14. Who went to find Tom Caigle when he ran away?

    A. His father

    B. Belle

    C. Uncle Ned

    D. Aunt Ivy

42
Santiago
Ann Nolan Clark

True or False. Decide whether each statement is true or false. Mark your answer sheet accordingly.

1. The Old One wanted Santiago to become a burden carrier.
2. The old Indian woman called Santiago "Nightingale" because he could sing so well.
3. Ladinos were Indians who tried to live according to white ways.
4. Jim's father wanted Santiago to go to college in North America with Jim.
5. Santiago's parents wanted him to live in the old ways of his tribe.
6. Jim's parents called Santiago "Little Jim."
7. Santiago decided to work for the government to improve living conditions.
8. Until he was 12, Santiago was raised by Jim's parents.
9. Jim's family ran a banana plantation.
10. Santiago left the Old One's village and went to work on a coffee plantation.
11. After Eduardo was shot by the police, Santiago became a thief.

Multiple Choice. Read each question. Decide which statement best answers the question. Mark your answer sheet accordingly.

12. Santiago was proud because

    A. He could speak Spanish, English, and French
    B. He went to school with North American children
    C. Unlike most Indians, he wore shoes
    D. He was rich enough to buy his own bicycles

13. The Old One took Santiago from Tia Alicia because

    A. Santiago's parents were gone
    B. He was the boy's clansman, and he was responsible for him
    C. He wanted Santiago to be an Indian, not a white man
    D. All of the above

14. Santiago's biggest struggle was

    A. To find a job that would provide for all of his needs
    B. To find out what had happened to Tia Alicia
    C. To discover what his trail in life would be
    D. To gather enough money to visit Jim in North America

CATEGORY: C
POINT VALUE: 15

43
Secret of the Andes
Ann Nolan Clark

True or False. Decide whether each statement is true or false. Mark your answer sheet accordingly.

1. Cusi and Chuto knew of a hidden cave full of the Inca's gold.

2. Cusi learned that his mother had probably been killed in a landslide.

3. Titu, Cusi's father, had tried to keep Cusi from living with Chuto.

4. Amauta came to Hidden Valley to teach Cusi in the way of the Inca.

5. Cusi and Chuto were the only two Incas left alive.

6. Cusi found his family hiding in a ghetto of Cuzco.

7. Cusi and Chuto couldn't leave Hidden Valley.

8. Every morning, Chuto called up the sun.

9. If a llama's load was too heavy, the animal would lie down.

10. On his journey to Cuzco, Cusi was hoping to find a family.

Multiple Choice. Read each question. Decide which statement best answers the question. Mark your answer sheet accordingly.

11. From the mountains around Hidden Valley, Cusi could see

   A. Cuzco

   B. The salt flats

   C. An Indian family

   D. The Ayllu

12. Who lived in Hidden Valley with Chuto and Cusi?

   A. No one

   B. The Inca

   C. The minstrel

   D. Cusi's mother

13. Who led Cusi to the golden sandals?

   A. Chuto

   B. Misti, the llama

   C. Suncca, the shepherd dog

   D. The minstrel

14. The Inca could identify other Incas by

   A. Their language

   B. Their ear plugs of gold

   C. Their coats of llama wool

   D. Their caps of silver

44
Dear Mr. Henshaw
Beverly Cleary

True or False. Decide whether each statement is true or false. Mark your answer sheet accordingly.

1. Leigh's father died when Leigh was very young.

2. Leigh's parents were divorced.

3. Leigh never found out who was stealing the "good stuff" from his lunch.

4. Leigh's mother was unemployed.

5. Leigh lived with his mother.

6. Leigh lived with his father.

7. Leigh's mother was saving money to buy a mobile home.

8. Mr. Henshaw never answered Leigh's letters.

9. Leigh got to eat lunch with a real author.

10. Bandit, Leigh's dog, was run over by a truck and killed.

11. Leigh made a burglar alarm for his lunch box.

12. Leigh wanted to be an author when he grew up.

13. Leigh got to eat lunch with Mr. Henshaw.

Multiple Choice. Read the question. Decide which statement best answers the question. Mark your answer sheet accordingly.

14. Leigh's father was a

   A. Lawyer

   B. Truck driver

   C. Mailman

   D. Teacher

45
Ellen Tebbits
Beverly Cleary

True or False. Decide whether each statement is true or false. Mark your answer sheet accordingly.

1. Ellen and Otis were very good friends.

2. Otis's mother was Ellen's dance teacher.

3. Ellen slapped Austine's face.

4. Austine's mother did not sew as well as Ellen's mother.

5. When Austine's brother saw that Ellen was going to be late for school, he gave Ellen a ride in his bicycle basket.

6. When Austine's brother saw that Ellen was going to be late for school, he laughed at Ellen and splashed muddy water on her.

7. Austine told all the children at school that Ellen wore woolen underwear.

8. Ellen thought that Miss Joyce did not like her because Miss Joyce never asked her to "clap" erasers.

9. Austine helped Ellen when Ellen became tangled up in the Maypole dance.

10. When Ellen went to Austine's house, she and Austine would make brownies.

11. Austine and Ellen finally started talking to each other again when Mrs. Gitler asked them to take the erasers outside and clean them.

Multiple Choice. Read each question. Decide which statement best answers the question. Mark your answer sheet accordingly.

12. To get Miss Joyce to like her, Ellen

    A. Gave Miss Joyce a box of candy

    B. Brought Miss Joyce an apple every day

    C. Brought a beet to school

    D. Offered to help Miss Joyce grade papers

13. Ellen was surprised to find out that

    A. Otis was in the hospital

    B. Austine's grandmother lived with Austine and her family

    C. Otis had untied her sash, not Austine

    D. Otis had stolen her beet, not Austine

14. What happened when Ellen and Austine went horseback riding?

    A. Ellen's horse waded into the stream and would not come out

    B. Ellen fell off her horse and broke her wrist

    C. Austine got scared and would not get on a horse

    D. Austine tried to ride her horse standing up

46
Henry and Beezus
Beverly Cleary

True or False. Decide whether each statement is true or false. Mark your answer sheet accordingly.

1. Scooter had a bicycle.

2. Henry sold all 49 boxes of gum to his classmates.

3. Scooter delivered newspapers.

4. Beezus went with Henry to the auction.

5. Henry had to put new spokes on the bike he bought at the auction.

6. Henry tasted some dog food.

7. The bicycle that Henry bought at the auction was a girl's bike.

8. Ramona did not go to the auction.

9. Scooter wanted Henry to sell Ribsy to the Boy Scouts.

10. A policeman put a ticket under Ribsy's collar because Ribsy was tied to a parking meter.

11. At the end of the book, Henry got a brand new bicycle.

Multiple Choice. Read each question. Decide which statement best answers the question. Mark your answer sheet accordingly.

12. When Ribsy stole the roast from Mr. Grumbie

    A. Mrs. Grumbie called the police

    B. Mr. Grumbie caught Ribsy with a net

    C. A and B

    D. None of the above

13. Where did Henry get 49 boxes of gum?

    A. His dad brought them home from work

    B. He found them

    C. He bought them from a gum factory

    D. None of the above

14. To teach Ribsy not to pick up newspapers, Henry

    A. Squirted him with a water pistol every time he picked up a newspaper

    B. Locked him in the garage every time he picked up a newspaper

    C. Poured a glass of milk on him every time he picked up a newspaper

    D. None of the above

47
Henry and Ribsy
Beverly Cleary

True or False. Decide whether each statement is true or false. Mark your answer sheet accordingly.

1. Henry's mother gave him a haircut.
2. Scooter's mother gave him a haircut.
3. Ribsy was taken to the pound because he bit the garbageman.
4. Henry did not have any brothers or sisters.
5. Mr. Huggins decided not to take Henry salmon fishing.
6. Mr. Huggins decided to take both Henry and Ribsy salmon fishing.
7. Henry's mother decided that she was tired of taking out the garbage.
8. Henry's mother loved to take out the garbage, and she refused to let Henry or Mr. Huggins help her with it.
9. Ramona would not come down from the jungle gym because there was a large snake on the ground.
10. At the end of the book, Ribsy died.
11. At the end of the book, Henry sold Ribsy to Scooter.

Multiple Choice. Read each question. Decide which statement best answers the question. Mark your answer sheet accordingly.

12. Henry's father promised to take him salmon fishing in September if he
    A. Kept Ribsy out of trouble until then
    B. Got all *A*s on his report card
    C. Lost 10 pounds by then
    D. All of the above

13. What did Mrs. Huggins buy at the Colossal Drugstore sale?
    A. Bow ties
    B. White crew socks for Henry
    C. Film for her camera
    D. Electric hair clippers

14. How did Robert's mother and Scooter's mother find out about the sale at Colossal Drugstore?
    A. They read about it in the newspaper
    B. Henry told them about it
    C. They heard about it at the school P.T.A.
    D. Mrs. Huggins called them and told them about it

48
Henry and the Clubhouse
Beverly Cleary

True or False. Decide whether each statement is true or false. Mark your answer sheet accordingly.

1. Henry was the youngest papercarrier in the neighborhood.

2. Mr. Capper did not want Henry to sell subscriptions to the *Journal*.

3. On Halloween, Henry put a mask on Ribsy and took him trick-or-treating.

4. When Henry finally asked the new neighbor if she wanted to buy a *Journal* subscription, she said "yes."

5. When Ramona locked Henry in the clubhouse, he did not get out in time to do his paper route.

6. Mrs. Peabody never found out that Henry's name was not Harry Huggins.

7. Mrs. Peabody wrote a nice letter to the editor of the *Journal* about Henry Huggins.

8. Ramona loved to watch the "Sheriff Bud" program on television.

9. Sheriff Bud never read the letter that Henry wrote him about Ramona.

10. Henry had trouble selling a *Journal* subscription to the new neighbor because when he tried to approach the house, Ranger would chase him away.

11. When Henry forgot about his paper route one Saturday afternoon, his mother started delivering his papers for him.

12. At the end of the book, Henry decided to quit his paper route so that he would have more time to work on the clubhouse.

Multiple Choice. Read each question. Decide which statement best answers the question. Mark your answer sheet accordingly.

13. What did Henry dress up as for Halloween?

    A. An Indian

    B. A cowboy

    C. A ghost

    D. A football player

14. What did Mrs. Morgan give Henry instead of treats on Halloween?

    A. A stuffed owl

    B. A quarter

    C. A dollar bill

    D. A horn for his bicycle

49
Henry and the Paper Route
Beverly Cleary

True or False. Decide whether each statement is true or false. Mark your answer sheet accordingly.

1. Scooter was three years younger than Henry.

2. Henry's class won the paper drive.

3. Scooter's class won the paper drive.

4. In this book, Henry never got a paper route of his own.

5. No one answered Henry's advertisements for the paper drive.

6. Henry's new neighbor was a boy.

7. Henry's new neighbor was a girl.

8. Henry did not have any brothers or sisters.

9. Henry's parents were not mentioned in this book.

10. Mr. Huggins decided to let Henry keep one of the kittens.

Multiple Choice. Read each question. Decide which statement best answers the question. Mark your answer sheet accordingly.

11. How did Henry finally get rid of the kittens that he bought at the rummage sale?

    A. He sold them for one dollar each

    B. He took them to the pet shop and gave them to Mr. Pennycuff

    C. He gave them to Scooter as a birthday present

    D. He took them to the pound

12. Scooter wanted Henry to take his paper route for two weeks because

    A. He had the chicken pox

    B. He wanted to go camping with his dad

    C. His family was going on a vacation to Florida

    D. None of the above

13. Scooter got angry at Henry because

    A. Henry didn't fold his papers correctly

    B. He thought that Henry had stolen his bicycle

    C. Henry wouldn't help him with his paper route

    D. Henry put advertisements for the paper drive in his newspapers

14. What was Murph building?

    A. A go-cart

    B. A tree house

    C. A robot

    D. A pair of stilts

50
Henry Huggins
Beverly Cleary

True or False. Decide whether each statement is true or false. Mark your answer sheet accordingly.

1. Henry bought Scooter a new football with the money he earned collecting night crawlers.
2. Mr. Grumbie paid Henry 25¢ for every night crawler he caught.
3. Mrs. Grumbie sprinkled Doggie-B-Gone on her shrubbery.
4. Ribsy liked the smell of Doggie-B-Gone.
5. When Henry first brought Ribsy home, Ribsy had fleas.
6. Ribsy liked to eat horse meat.
7. Henry bought Ribsy at a pet store for $5.
8. Henry did not receive an allowance from his parents.
9. Henry was the only kid who lived on Klickitat Street.
10. Ribsy won a prize for being the most unusual dog in the dog contest.
11. Ribsy belonged to a different boy before he belonged to Henry.
12. Henry did not want to be in the school play.

Multiple Choice. Read each question. Decide which statement best answers the question. Mark your answer sheet accordingly.

13. Henry was chosen to play the part of the little boy in the Christmas operetta because he was

    A. The shortest boy in the fourth grade
    B. An excellent singer
    C. Very good at sucking his thumb
    D. None of the above

14. When Henry returned his guppies to the pet store, what animal did he get instead?

    A. A bird
    B. A kitten
    C. A catfish
    D. A lizard

From *Quizzes for 220 Great Children's Books*, revised 1st edition. © 1996. Teacher Ideas Press. (800) 237-6124.

51
The Mouse and the Motorcycle
Beverly Cleary

True or False. Decide whether each statement is true or false. Mark your answer sheet accordingly.

1. Ralph promised Keith that he would not ride the motorcycle during the day.

2. Ralph broke the promise he made to Keith.

3. Ralph was sucked into a vacuum cleaner and was stuck inside it for days.

4. When Ralph rode the motorcycle into a pile of sheets and pillowcases, he got tangled up and was dumped into the hamper.

5. Keith never found out that Ralph lost his motorcycle.

6. Keith made a crash helmet for Ralph to wear while riding his motorcycle.

7. Keith's mother loved mice.

8. Ralph was trapped under a drinking glass by a schoolteacher staying at the hotel.

9. Ralph was the only mouse who lived in the hotel.

10. At the end of the book, Ralph decided to live with Keith in Ohio.

11. At the end of the book, Keith told Ralph that he could keep the motorcycle.

Multiple Choice. Read each question. Decide which statement best answers the question. Mark your answer sheet accordingly.

12. Where did Ralph live?

    A. Under the television on the ground floor of the hotel

    B. Inside a mattress

    C. In the knothole in Room 215

    D. In the bridal suite

13. Ralph started the motorcycle by

    A. Making a noise

    B. Putting the key in the ignition

    C. Winding it up

    D. All of the above

14. What did Ralph get for Keith when Keith was sick?

    A. An aspirin

    B. A motorcycle magazine

    C. Some cough medicine

    D. A comic book

52
Ralph S. Mouse
Beverly Cleary

True or False. Decide whether each statement is true or false. Mark your answer sheet accordingly.

1. Ralph never talked to Miss K.

2. Miss K fixed Ralph's motorcycle.

3. Miss K took Ralph home with her.

4. Ralph left the hotel because he didn't want Matt to lose his job.

5. Miss K was terrified of Ralph.

6. Ryan and Brad were in the same class at school.

7. Ryan and Brad could understand Ralph.

8. Ralph never talked to Brad.

9. While living in Ryan's classroom, Ralph liked to sleep in Melissa's boot.

10. Miss K suggested that Ryan and Brad set mousetraps all over the school.

Multiple Choice. Read each question. Decide which statement best answers the question. Mark your answer sheet accordingly.

11. Ryan's mother

    A. Was the principal of Irwin J. Sneed Elementary School

    B. Found Ralph's motorcycle

    C. Worked at the hotel

    D. All of the above

12. The students in Ryan's class

    A. Tried to catch Ralph in a mousetrap

    B. Wrote letters to the editor of the local newspaper

    C. Could all talk to and understand Ralph

    D. Asked Ralph to ride his motorcycle for them

13. How did Ralph's motorcycle get broken?

    A. It was in Ryan's pocket when Brad pushed Ryan

    B. It fell off Ryan's desk

    C. Miss K accidentally sat on it

    D. Ryan broke it on purpose because Ralph refused to run the maze

14. At the end of the book

    A. Brad's father married Ryan's mother

    B. Brad and Ryan became friends

    C. Brad gave Ralph a car

    D. All of the above

53
Ramona and Her Father
Beverly Cleary

True or False. Decide whether each statement is true or false. Mark your answer sheet accordingly.

1. Ramona and Beezus never found out that their father lost his job.
2. Mrs. Quimby did not find out about the burs in Ramona's hair.
3. Picky-picky did not like Puss-puddy.
4. Ramona and Beezus wanted their father to stop smoking.
5. Ramona's mother smoked three packs of cigarettes a day.
6. Beezus was excited about creative writing.
7. Ramona called Mrs. Swink "Pieface."
8. Mr. and Mrs. Quimby did not go to church to watch the Christmas Carol program.
9. Picky-picky ate part of the pumpkin the Quimbys carved for Halloween.
10. Mr. Quimby finally agreed to try to stop smoking.

Multiple Choice. Read each question. Decide which statement best answers the question. Mark your answer sheet accordingly.

11. What surprise did Mr. Quimby bring to Ramona and Beezus on payday?
    A. Hamburgers from Whopperburger
    B. Coloring books and crayons
    C. A bag of gummy bears
    D. A new television set

12. Who used scissors to cut the burs out of Ramona's hair?
    A. Mrs. Quimby
    B. Mr. Quimby
    C. Beezus
    D. Ramona

13. The Quimbys served Puss-puddy to Picky-picky instead of another brand because
    A. Puss-puddy was the cheapest cat food Mrs. Quimby could find
    B. Puss-puddy was recommended by the veterinarian
    C. Mrs. Quimby thought that Puss-puddy had the most vitamins in it
    D. Puss-puddy was the only kind of cat food sold at the market

14. What part did Ramona play in the Christmas Carol program?
    A. A shepherd
    B. Mary
    C. A sheep
    D. None of the above

54
Ramona and Her Mother
Beverly Cleary

True or False. Decide whether each statement is true or false. Mark your answer sheet accordingly.

1. Ramona gave Willa Jean a box of Kleenex.

2. Ramona's mother allowed Ramona to use the sewing machine to sew pants for Ella Funt.

3. Beezus washed her hair a lot.

4. Beezus wanted to use the money she saved to have her hair cut at Robert's School of Hair Design.

5. Beezus did not like the way her hair looked after Lester cut it and sprayed it with hair spray.

6. Willa Jean used scissors to cut the leg off her stuffed bear.

7. Willa Jean used scissors to cut off some of Ramona's hair.

8. Beezus came into the bathroom and saw that Ramona had squeezed out a whole tube of toothpaste.

9. Beezus came into the bathroom and saw that Ramona had dyed her hair orange.

10. Mrs. Kemp had to wash Ramona's clothes because Howie and Ramona had an egg fight.

11. Mrs. Kemp had to wash Ramona's clothes because Ramona came home from school covered with mud.

12. One day, Ramona wore her pajamas to school underneath her clothes.

Multiple Choice. Read each question. Decide which statement best answers the question. Mark your answer sheet accordingly.

13. The Quimbys entertained their neighbors at a New Year's Day brunch to celebrate
    A. Ramona's eighth birthday
    B. Mr. Quimby getting a new set of false teeth
    C. Mr. Quimby finding a job at the Shop-Rite Market
    D. Mrs. Quimby learning to speak French

14. Ramona twitched her nose a lot because
    A. It helped her to think better
    B. She was pretending to be a baby rabbit
    C. She was often nervous
    D. She was allergic to dust

55
Ramona Forever
Beverly Cleary

True or False. Decide whether each statement is true or false. Mark your answer sheet accordingly.

1. Willa Jean sat on the accordion Uncle Hobart gave her.
2. Ramona told Willa Jean to sit on the accordion.
3. Ramona did not like going to the Kemp's house after school.
4. When Picky-picky died, Beezus and Ramona called their mother at work and told her to come home right away.
5. When Picky-picky died, Beezus and Ramona buried him by themselves.
6. Uncle Hobart gave Howie a unicycle.
7. Mr. and Mrs. Quimby decided to let Ramona and Beezus stay home by themselves after school instead of going to the Kemps' house.
8. Uncle Hobart married Aunt Beatrice.
9. When Mrs. Quimby had a baby, Ramona could not visit them in the hospital because she was under 12 years old.
10. Before getting married, Aunt Bea had been a schoolteacher.
11. Howie was the only child allowed to go to Aunt Bea's wedding.
12. Howie was happy when he found out he would be the ring bearer in Aunt Bea's wedding.

Multiple Choice. Read each question. Decide which statement best answers the question. Mark your answer sheet accordingly.

13. Mr. Quimby decided to
    A. Take the teaching job he had been offered in a small town
    B. Take the job he had been offered managing a Shop-Rite market
    C. Stay at home with the children while his wife went to work
    D. Go to Saudi Arabia to look for oil
14. When Ramona first met Uncle Hobart, she
    A. Did not like him because he teased her
    B. Thought that he looked like Santa Claus
    C. Kicked and bit him because he hadn't brought her any presents
    D. Pulled his hair to see if it was a wig or if it was real

From *Quizzes for 220 Great Children's Books*, revised 1st edition. © 1996. Teacher Ideas Press. (800) 237-6124.

56
Ramona Quimby, Age 8
Beverly Cleary

True or False. Decide whether each statement is true or false. Mark your answer sheet accordingly.

1. Ramona's father was going back to college to become an art teacher.

2. Ramona's mother was going back to college to become an art teacher.

3. Howie was Ramona's brother.

4. Ramona enjoyed Sustained Silent Reading at school.

5. Ramona rode the bus to school.

6. When Ramona was sick, her mother stayed home from work to take care of her.

7. Mrs. Whaley was very unhappy with Ramona's book report.

8. When Ramona's family ate dinner at a restaurant, a stranger paid for their meal.

9. Ramona's mother accidentally put a raw egg in Ramona's lunch instead of a hard-boiled one.

10. Ramona's mother accidentally put a golf ball in Ramona's lunch instead of an egg.

11. One night, Mrs. Quimby served tongue for dinner.

Multiple Choice. Read each question. Decide which statement best answers the question. Mark your answer sheet accordingly.

12. What did Ramona call Danny?

    A. Dumbo

    B. Big Mouth

    C. Yard Ape

    D. Super Nuisance

13. On the first day of school, Danny stole Ramona's

    A. Pencil

    B. Lunch box

    C. Eraser

    D. Notebook

14. Who took Ramona home the day she got sick in school?

    A. Her mother

    B. Her father

    C. Beezus

    D. Mrs. Whaley

57
Ramona the Brave
Beverly Cleary

True or False. Decide whether each statement is true or false. Mark your answer sheet accordingly.

1. Ramona was younger than Beezus.
2. Beezus was Ramona's sister.
3. Ramona's teacher, Mrs. Griggs, could never remember Ramona's name.
4. Mr. and Mrs. Quimby decided to take Ramona out of school and teach her at home.
5. The Quimbys were having a new room built onto their house.
6. Mrs. Griggs came to Ramona's house to ask if she could borrow Picky-picky for a couple of days.
7. When Ramona squashed Susan's owl, she had to apologize to Susan in front of the whole class.
8. Beezus liked her teacher, Mr. Cardoza.
9. Ramona liked to color with crayons.
10. Picky-picky was the name of the Quimbys' hamster.
11. Ramona gave Picky-picky to her teacher, Mrs. Griggs.

Multiple Choice. Read each question. Decide which statement best answers the question. Mark your answer sheet accordingly.

12. Ramona squashed Susan's owl because
    A. Susan wouldn't let Ramona use her glue
    B. Susan named her owl Ramona Kitty Cat
    C. Susan didn't invite Ramona to her birthday party
    D. None of the above

13. What game did Ramona and Howie like to play together?
    A. Monopoly
    B. Sorry
    C. Brick Factory
    D. Freeze Tag

14. Why did Ramona need to borrow Mr. Cardoza's stapler?
    A. She needed to staple her papers together
    B. She needed it to make a slipper out of paper towels
    C. She needed it to make a gift for Mrs. Griggs
    D. None of the above

58
Ramona the Pest
Beverly Cleary

True or False. Decide whether each statement is true or false. Mark your answer sheet accordingly.

1. On the first day of school, Ramona's teacher gave her a present.

2. Ramona did not want to wear Howie's old boots to school.

3. Ramona loved to do seat work at school.

4. Each day, Mrs. Quimby stayed with Ramona at school to make sure that she behaved well.

5. On the day of the Halloween parade, Ramona got sick and had to stay in bed.

6. Ramona dressed up as a witch for the Halloween parade.

7. Ramona loved her teacher, Miss Binney.

8. Miss Binney wrote a note to Ramona asking her when she was coming back to school.

9. Ramona rode to school on a horse.

10. Ramona liked to chase Davy around the playground.

11. Ramona liked to pull Susan's curls.

Multiple Choice. Read each question. Decide which statement best answers the question. Mark your answer sheet accordingly.

12. Ramona was sent home from school because

    A. She had the measles

    B. She said that she could not stop pulling Susan's hair

    C. Her mother was sick and needed her at home

    D. She had brought a dog to school

13. Ramona told Henry Huggins, the traffic boy, that

    A. She was going to marry him

    B. His dog, Ribsy, had bitten her

    C. The principal wanted to see him in her office

    D. His pants were ripped in the back

14. Ramona's engagement ring was

    A. A ring that she had gotten out of a gum machine

    B. A rubber band

    C. Made out of Playdoh

    D. A worm

From *Quizzes for 220 Great Children's Books*, revised 1st edition. © 1996. Teacher Ideas Press. (800) 237-6124.

59
Ribsy
Beverly Cleary

True or False. Decide whether each statement is true or false. Mark your answer sheet accordingly.

1. Henry placed an ad in the lost and found section of the newspaper for Ribsy.

2. Mrs. Frawley sold Ribsy to her neighbor.

3. Mrs. Frawley never allowed Ribsy in her house.

4. Henry saw the picture of Ribsy in the newspaper.

5. Henry's parents were with Henry when he finally found Ribsy.

6. Henry Huggins sold Ribsy to Joe Saylor.

7. Ribsy did not know how to shake hands.

8. The Dingley children made Ribsy sleep in a crib.

9. The Dingley children gave Ribsy a bubble bath.

10. Mrs. Frawley called Ribsy "Rags."

11. Henry Huggins finally found Ribsy on a fire escape.

Multiple Choice. Read each question. Decide which statement best answers the question. Mark your answer sheet accordingly.

12. Where was Henry Huggins when Ribsy escaped from the car?

    A. In a shopping center

    B. Camping with his father

    C. At school

    D. None of the above

13. Mr. Woody decided that Ribsy could no longer be the second-grade class mascot after Ribsy

    A. Bit one of the children

    B. Chased a squirrel around the classroom

    C. Barked loudly during a test

    D. Knocked over a can of garbage

14. What was Ribsy doing when he got his picture in the paper?

    A. He was chasing a squirrel around a classroom

    B. He was chasing a football player

    C. He was dressed up in a coat and hat that Mrs. Frawley had bought him

    D. He was swimming in a lake

60
Runaway Ralph
Beverly Cleary

True or False. Decide whether each statement is true or false. Mark your answer sheet accordingly.

1. Garf caught Ralph in his butterfly net.

2. Ralph and Catso were very good friends.

3. Garf found Ralph's motorcycle.

4. Aunt Jill gave Garf a spanking because she was sure that he had stolen Karen's watch.

5. Some of the kids at Happy Acres Camp believed Garf stole Karen's watch.

6. None of the kids at Happy Acres Camp ever believed that Garf had stolen Karen's watch.

7. Catso stole Karen's watch.

8. Garf stole Karen's watch.

9. Ralph stole Karen's watch.

10. Uncle Lester told Ralph that he had to give his brothers, sisters, and cousins rides on his motorcycle.

11. When Ralph ran away from home, he went to Happy Acres Camp.

12. Chum was a cat.

Multiple Choice. Read each question. Decide which statement best answers the question. Mark your answer sheet accordingly.

13. Garf told Aunt Jill that

  A. He wanted other people to stop feeding his mouse

  B. He wanted to be alone sometimes

  C. A and B

  D. None of the above

14. Ralph promised Garf that he would return Karen's watch and clear Garf's name if Garf would

  A. Bring Ralph food every day

  B. Give Ralph a toy ambulance

  C. Give Ralph back his motorcycle

  D. Tell Karen that Ralph wanted to marry her

61
Socks
Beverly Cleary

True or False. Decide whether each statement is true or false. Mark your answer sheet accordingly.

1. George put Socks in the mailbox because he didn't want a bunch of fighting kids to get him.

2. Debbie and George were trying to sell Socks in front of a grocery store.

3. Mr. Bricker bought Socks for $125.

4. Socks liked to be picked up by Tiffy.

5. Charles William cried whenever he saw Uncle Walter's bald head.

6. Socks liked to drink the baby's warm leftover formula.

7. Uncle Walter pointed out that Socks had begun to put on a lot of weight.

8. Socks ate the chocolate pudding Tiffy gave him.

9. When Mrs. Risley came to baby-sit Charles William, she locked Socks in the laundry room.

10. Nana, Mr. Bricker's mother, loved Socks and wanted to take him home with her.

11. Nana did not know how her wig had gotten messed up and pulled apart.

12. Old Taylor and Socks were friends.

13. Charles William called Socks "Ticky."

14. Socks liked to nap on the couch next to Mrs. Bricker.

From *Quizzes for 220 Great Children's Books,* revised 1st edition. © 1996. Teacher Ideas Press. (800) 237-6124.

62
The Adventures of Huckleberry Finn
Samuel L. Clemens (Mark Twain)

True or False. Decide whether each statement is true or false. Mark your answer sheet accordingly.

1. Huck found out that Jim had been sold to a trader from Georgia.

2. Huck pretended to be Tom Sawyer to fool the Phelpses.

3. Tom Sawyer thought up a plan to rescue Jim.

4. Tom Sawyer refused to help Huck rescue Jim.

5. Tom Sawyer told Mrs. Phelps that he was Sid Sawyer.

6. At the end of the book, Miss Watson gave Jim his freedom.

7. The King and the Duke turned Jim in so they could get a reward.

8. The King and the Duke were kind men who helped everyone they met.

9. When Huck Finn escaped from his father's cabin, he made it look like he had been murdered.

10. The Granger Ford family was having a bloody feud with the Sheperdsons.

11. At the end of the book, Huck went back to live with the Widow Douglas.

Multiple Choice. Read each question. Decide which statement best answers the question. Mark your answer sheet accordingly.

12. Huck Finn left the Widow Douglas's house because

    A. He hated the Widow Douglas

    B. He was afraid of the Widow Douglas's slave, Jim

    C. His father made him leave

    D. He hated Miss Watson

13. Jim ran away from the Widow Douglas's place because

    A. He had murdered Huck's father

    B. Miss Watson was going to sell him

    C. He had stolen some money from the Widow Douglas

    D. He thought that a ghost told him to leave

14. When Huck visited a farmhouse dressed as a girl, he learned that

    A. People thought that Jim had killed Huck Finn

    B. Tom Sawyer had run away to Canada

    C. His father had tried to burn down the home of the Widow Douglas

    D. The Widow Douglas had died of a broken heart

63
The Adventures of Tom Sawyer
Samuel L. Clemens (Mark Twain)

True or False. Decide whether each statement is true or false. Mark your answer sheet accordingly.

1. Tom lived with his aunt and two cousins.

2. Huck was the best speller in his school.

3. Becky was Huck's girlfriend.

4. Tom and Becky got lost in a cave.

5. Tom, Joe, and Huck ran away to Jackson's Island to be pirates.

6. After Tom, Joe, and Huck went to Jackson's Island, the townspeople thought that they had drowned.

7. Tom, Huck, and Joe went to their own funeral.

8. Huck warned someone that Injun Joe was after the Widow Douglas.

9. Tom and Huck found Injun Joe's treasure.

10. Injun Joe kidnapped Tom.

11. The townspeople thought that Muff Potter had killed Dr. Robinson.

Multiple Choice. Read each question. Decide which statement best answers the question. Mark your answer sheet accordingly.

12. How did Tom get his aunt's fence whitewashed?

    A. He paid Huck and Jim to do it for him

    B. He held a fence-painting contest

    C. His friends paid Tom to let them whitewash it

    D. Tom's girlfriend had all the girls in town do the job

13. When Huck and Tom were in the graveyard, they saw

    A. Mr. Finn and Hoss Williams burying gold

    B. Muff Potter being buried alive

    C. Injun Joe killing Dr. Robinson

    D. The ghost of Tom's grandmother

14. When Tom saw Becky tear the teacher's book, he

    A. Told the teacher that he had seen Becky do it

    B. Told the teacher that he had seen Alfred do it

    C. Hid the book so that the teacher would not notice the torn page

    D. None of the above

From *Quizzes for 220 Great Children's Books,* revised 1st edition. © 1996. Teacher Ideas Press. (800) 237-6124.

64
My Brother Sam Is Dead
James Lincoln Collier and Christopher Collier

True or False. Decide whether each statement is true or false. Mark your answer sheet accordingly.

1. Most of the people who lived in Redding were Tories.

2. None of the people who lived in Redding were Patriots.

3. Tim's father died on a British prison ship.

4. Sam was shot by his own army for stealing.

5. Tim joined the British army.

6. Tim killed his brother, Sam, to protect his home.

7. Sam and Tim's father was a Tory who ran a tavern.

8. When Sam joined the American army, his father was proud and happy.

9. Sam wanted his father to give him his Brown Bess musket.

10. Tim's father was taken away by cowboys.

Multiple Choice. Read each question. Decide which statement best answers the question. Mark your answer sheet accordingly.

11. Cowboys were

    A. Men who herded cattle

    B. Robbers and cattle thieves

    C. British cattle sellers

    D. Boys who herded cattle

12. At first, the war made life difficult in Redding because

    A. Three major battles were fought in and around the town

    B. Prices kept going up, and money was short

    C. The Black Death killed half of the town

    D. The British burned down the houses and barns in Redding

13. Even though Sam was innocent, General Putnam insisted that Sam be

    A. Kicked out of the army

    B. Locked in prison for five years

    C. Forced to pay a heavy fine

    D. Shot

14. Sam was accused of

    A. Stealing his own cattle

    B. Deserting the army

    C. Selling cattle to the British

    D. Being a coward

65
The Last of the Mohicans
James Fenimore Cooper

True or False. Decide whether each statement is true or false. Mark your answer sheet accordingly.

1. Le Renard Subtil wanted to marry Cora.

2. Cora was in love with Le Renard Subtil.

3. Delaware Indians burned Chingachgook alive.

4. Uncas and Chingachgook both had blue turtles tattooed on their chests.

5. Uncas rescued Cora from Le Renard Subtil.

6. Huron Indians killed Cora.

7. Uncas was killed trying to rescue Cora.

8. When Le Renard came to the fort drunk, Munro had him whipped.

9. When Munro surrendered his fort to General Montcalm, Montcalm's Indians killed the women, the children, the sick, and the wounded.

10. After Munro surrendered, Le Renard Subtil kidnapped Cora and Alice.

11. Hawkeye was able to sneak into the Huron village by wearing a bear skin.

Multiple Choice. Read each question. Decide which statement best answers the question. Mark your answer sheet accordingly.

12. At the beginning of the story, Heyward, Alice, and Cora were
    A. Going to join the girls' father at a British fort
    B. Joined by David, the singer
    C. Guided by an Indian named Le Renard Subtil
    D. All of the above

13. Hawkeye's two friends, Chingachgook and Uncas, were
    A. The last two Indians in their family clan
    B. Scouts for the English army
    C. Spies for the French army
    D. None of the above

14. Hawkeye told Heyward that Le Renard Subtil
    A. Should not be trusted because he was a Huron
    B. Was the best guide in the British army
    C. Was the last living Mohican Indian
    D. Had been educated at Harvard University

66
The Dark Is Rising
Susan Cooper

True or False. Decide whether each statement is true or false. Mark your answer sheet accordingly.

1. Hawkins betrayed Will and Merriman to Maggie Barnes.

2. Hawkins and the Walker were the same person.

3. Only Will's brother, James, knew that Will was an Old One and helped him on his quest.

4. Will's sister, Mary, was persuaded by Maggie Barnes to become a servant of the Dark.

5. The forces of the Dark were at their strongest on the twelfth day of Christmas.

6. Herne and the Yell Hounds were the mightiest servants of the Dark.

7. Farmer Dawson gave Will an iron cross in a circle.

8. Maggie Barnes was a servant of the Dark.

9. The task of the Walker was to give one of the signs to Will.

10. The Dark Rider was able to enter Will's home on Christmas Day because Will's father invited him in.

11. Hawkins was used by Merriman to find the Book of Gramarye.

Multiple Choice. Read each question. Decide which statement best answers the question. Mark your answer sheet accordingly.

12. On his eleventh birthday, Will discovered that

    A. Animals were afraid of him

    B. Radios and televisions didn't work around him

    C. An odd, old man was following him

    D. All of the above

13. The night of his birthday, Will

    A. Traveled back through time

    B. Discovered he was one of the Old Ones

    C. Met the Dark Rider

    D. All of the above

14. Merriman and the Old Lady told Will that his task was to

    A. Slay the Dark Rider

    B. Find the six signs of the Old Ones

    C. Warn the world that the Dark was rising

    D. Find the Walker and bring him to the Old Lady

67
The Grey King
Susan Cooper

True or False. Decide whether each statement is true or false. Mark your answer sheet accordingly.

1. Bran's real father was King Arthur.

2. Bran found out that his mother was the wife of Merlin.

3. The Grey King used Caradog Prichard to try to harm Will and Bran.

4. Will was the only one who could see the milgwn.

5. The Grey King used a Warestone to observe the Old Ones and to transmit his power.

6. Will was the only Old One to see the Grey King.

7. The six sleepers woke because Bran killed the Grey King with a silver sword.

8. Will was sent to Wales because he was sick.

9. A milgwn is an invisible, giant, grey fox.

10. Caradog Prichard killed Cafall because he thought that Cafall killed sheep.

11. John Rowland told Will that Bran's mother was killed by a milgwn when Bran was four years old.

Multiple Choice. Read each question. Decide which statement best answers the question. Mark your answer sheet accordingly.

12. What was unusual about Bran Davies?

    A. His dog appeared blind but could see

    B. He was an albino

    C. He knew that Will was an Old One

    D. All of the above

13. Inside the mountain of Craig yr Aderyn, Will and Bran had to

    A. Pass a test by answering three questions each

    B. Avoid the milgwn

    C. Find the hidden treasure of the Grey King

    D. Find King Arthur's throne

14. What was Will given inside the mountain of Craig yr Aderyn?

    A. A silver sword

    B. A golden harp

    C. A crystal ball

    D. A golden wand

68
Robinson Crusoe
Daniel Defoe

True or False. Decide whether each statement is true or false. Mark your answer sheet accordingly.

1. After many years, Robinson discovered that the cannibals had a village on the other side of the island.

2. Robinson rescued Friday from cannibal tribesmen.

3. Robinson became very sick when he was bitten by a snake.

4. Robinson and Friday rescued Friday's father.

5. Robinson rescued a captain whose crew had committed mutiny.

6. The English captain waited on Robinson's island for the other white men to arrive with Friday's father.

7. Robinson's parents did not want him to go to sea.

8. The first time that Robinson went to sea, he was seasick.

9. Robinson escaped from the Moor by stealing his boat.

10. Robinson had a plantation in the Brazils.

11. One of Robinson's major sources of food was wild goats.

Multiple Choice. Read each question. Decide which statement best answers the question. Mark your answer sheet accordingly.

12. What did Robinson do with Xury, the boy who helped him escape from the Moor?

    A. He took him to Brazil

    B. He let him go off the coast of Africa

    C. He sent him back to the Moor

    D. He sold him as a slave

13. During Robinson's last voyage, a storm came up and

    A. He swam to an island

    B. All of the crew except Robinson drowned

    C. He was killed

    D. A and B

14. After his last voyage, Robinson found that

    A. There were still many useful items left on the ship

    B. The island was filled with dangerous, wild dogs

    C. There was a village of Carib Indians living in the mountains

    D. All of the above

69
Hurry Home, Candy
Meindert DeJong

True or False. Decide whether each statement is true or false. Mark your answer sheet accordingly.

1. At the beginning of the book, the children's mother gave Candy to them as a Christmas present.

2. The children's mother was very concerned about keeping her house clean.

3. The children's mother liked her house to be messy and full of dirt.

4. When the children lost Candy, they were very sad.

5. When the old lady was thrown out of her wagon, Candy guarded her purse until she was found.

6. When the policemen found the old lady who had been thrown out of the wagon, the old lady was already dead.

7. The man at the pound was cruel to Candy and would not give him any food.

8. The bus driver would not allow the captain to get on the bus with Candy.

9. The captain was cruel to Candy.

10. Candy was afraid of brooms.

11. As a reward, the captain gave the children each a new bicycle.

12. At the end of the book, Candy went home with the captain.

Multiple Choice. Read each question. Decide which statement best answers the question. Mark your answer sheet accordingly.

13. Where did Candy get loose and cause quite an uproar?
    A. In the children's ward of a hospital
    B. In the parking lot of a grocery store
    C. On the children's floor of a public library
    D. On the playground of an elementary school

14. What did the captain do with his broom?
    A. He gave it to Candy to use as a toy
    B. He punished Candy with it
    C. He flung it out the window
    D. He sold it to an old woman

From *Quizzes for 220 Great Children's Books*, revised 1st edition. © 1996. Teacher Ideas Press. (800) 237-6124.

70
Puppy Summer
Meindert DeJong

True or False. Decide whether each statement is true or false. Mark your answer sheet accordingly.

1. John and Vestri were visiting their grandparents for the summer.
2. John and Vestri lived with their grandparents all year long.
3. John and Vestri ran away from their grandparents' house to look for gold in the mountains.
4. John hoped to find an arrowhead.
5. John and Vestri bought the three puppies at a pet store.
6. The puppies were named Salt, Pepper, and Sugar.
7. Grandma wanted John and Vestri to sell the puppies.
8. John and Vestri did not like their grandparents.
9. John and Vestri decided to sell the puppies so they could buy bicycles.
10. Grandpa took John and Vestri fishing.
11. When Grandpa was fishing, he caught a little tree that had an Indian ax head in it.
12. When Grandpa was fishing, he got a fishhook caught in his hand.

Multiple Choice. Read each question. Decide which statement best answers the question. Mark your answer sheet accordingly.

13. The punishment for the one found guilty in the Corncrib Court was that he or she had to
    A. Wear the horse's hat
    B. Make supper
    C. Clean out the barn
    D. Do the laundry
14. When Vestri went fishing, she
    A. Fell into the lake
    B. Forgot her fishing pole
    C. Wore gloves
    D. Found a secret cave

71
The Wheel on the School
Meindert DeJong

True or False. Decide whether each statement is true or false. Mark your answer sheet accordingly.

1. Lina was the only girl in her school.
2. The children's fathers put the wagon wheel on the roof of the school during a storm.
3. The teacher and the children put the wagon wheel on the roof of the school.
4. Lina did not have any brothers or sisters.
5. The teacher did not want the wagon wheel on the roof of the school.
6. Janus was at the school the day that the wagon wheel was put on the roof.
7. The teacher said that there would be no school the day that the wagon wheel was put on the roof of the school.
8. Grandmother Sibble III did not want any storks in the town of Shora.
9. To help herself think, Lina stared into her shoe.
10. Lina's father was a fisherman.
11. Grandmother Sibble had a candy tin with pictures of storks on it.

Multiple Choice. Read each question. Decide which statement best answers the question. Mark your answer sheet accordingly.

12. Who found a wagon wheel under a boat?
    A. Jella
    B. Auka
    C. Pier
    D. Lina
13. Who took a wagon wheel from a farmer's shed without permission?
    A. Jella
    B. Auka
    C. Pier
    D. Lina
14. What did Janus have in his yard that he was always guarding from birds and boys?
    A. A swimming pool
    B. A statue
    C. A wagon wheel
    D. A cherry tree

72
Oliver Twist
Charles Dickens

True or False. Decide whether each statement is true or false. Mark your answer sheet accordingly.

1. Fagin trained young people to be pickpockets.
2. Nancy was Bill Sikes's girlfriend.
3. Oliver escaped Fagin's gang but was recaptured by Nancy.
4. Oliver and Artful Dodger became skilled pickpockets.
5. Monks went to Mr. Bumble to find out about Oliver's mother.
6. Mrs. Maylie and Rose took Oliver into their home after their servants shot him.
7. Sikes rescued the Artful Dodger from prison.
8. To protect Oliver, Nancy told Rose all about Monks.
9. Bill Sikes clubbed Nancy to death.
10. Monks turned out to be Oliver's half brother.

Multiple Choice. Read each question. Decide which statement best answers the question. Mark your answer sheet accordingly.

11. When Fagin found out that Nancy had talked to Rose, he
    A. Warned all of his gang to flee London
    B. Took all the gang's money and ran away
    C. Told Sikes to kill Nancy
    D. Locked Nancy in a basement

12. Sikes was
    A. Captured by the police and sent to prison
    B. Killed by his own gang
    C. Captured by Oliver and Rose
    D. Accidentally hung trying to escape the mob

13. Oliver discovered that Rose was
    A. His sister
    B. A member of Fagin's gang
    C. His aunt
    D. Monk's wife

14. At the end of the book
    A. Henry Maylie married Rose
    B. Mr. Brownlow adopted Oliver
    C. Mr. Bumble ended up in his own poorhouse
    D. All of the above

From *Quizzes for 220 Great Children's Books*, revised 1st edition. © 1996. Teacher Ideas Press. (800) 237-6124.

75
Incident at Hawk's Hill
Allan W. Eckert

True or False. Decide whether each statement is true or false. Mark your answer sheet accordingly.

1. Mr. MacDonald refused to let Mr. Burton set traps on his land.

2. Ben liked Mr. Burton very much.

3. Mr. Burton did not check his traps every day.

4. Ben was very small for his age.

5. Badgers do not generally care for their young.

6. Ben began to go out at night to hunt with the badger.

7. When the badger offered her milk to Ben, he refused it.

8. After being rescued, Ben was allowed to keep the badger as a pet and even to sleep with it at night.

9. Memorial services were held for Ben 10 days after his disappearance.

10. A search party of 32 men continued to search for Ben for one month after his disappearance.

11. Ben gained about 20 pounds while he was gone from home.

Multiple Choice. Read each question. Decide which statement best answers the question. Mark your answer sheet accordingly.

12. How many brothers and sisters did Ben have?

    A. One sister and one brother

    B. Two sisters and two brothers

    C. One sister and two brothers

    D. Two sisters and one brother

13. Who found Ben and brought him home?

    A. Lobo

    B. Mr. MacDonald

    C. John

    D. Mr. Burton

14. How long was Ben gone from home?

    A. Three days

    B. Two weeks

    C. Two months

    D. One year

76
The Matchlock Gun
Walter D. Edmonds

True or False. Decide whether each statement is true or false. Mark your answer sheet accordingly.

1. Edward did not have any brothers or sisters.

2. Edward's father died when Edward was very young.

3. Edward's grandmother owned slaves.

4. Edward's grandmother lived with Edward and his family.

5. Edward's mother told him that he was not to touch the matchlock gun, no matter what happened.

6. The matchlock gun was too big for Edward to hold.

7. The Indians were friends with Edward's mother.

8. Edward's mother took him to the Widow Van Alstyne's house until the danger had passed.

9. Edward's mother decided that their own house would be safer than the Widow Van Alstyne's house.

10. The Indians set fire to the barns at the Widow Van Alstyne's house.

11. The Indians threw a tomahawk at Edward's mother.

12. The Indians killed Edward's mother.

13. Edward's mother made a hot supper for the Indians.

14. Edward shot and killed three Indians.

77
Two Logs Crossing
Walter D. Edmonds

True or False. Decide whether each statement is true or false. Mark your answer sheet accordingly.

1. The Haskills were a rich family.
2. John's mother sent him to the judge to beg for money.
3. The judge told John that his father owed him $40.
4. John's mother was pleased when she heard that John had paid back part of the loan.
5. The judge threatened to put John in jail if Mr. Haskill's debts were not quickly repaid.
6. Seth was a French-Canadian fur trapper.
7. Seth taught John how to trap.
8. Seth and John lived in the same cabin and worked the same trap lines.
9. Seth told John to cross rivers by making a bridge of two logs.
10. John lost his entire supply of furs when he fell off a log into a river.
11. John and Seth went trapping together again the next winter.
12. The second winter, John did not lose any furs.
13. John and Seth started a fur trapping business.
14. John found out that the judge never loaned his father any money.

From *Quizzes for 220 Great Children's Books*, revised 1st edition. © 1996. Teacher Ideas Press. (800) 237-6124.

78
Thimble Summer
Elizabeth Enright

True or False. Decide whether each statement is true or false. Mark your answer sheet accordingly.

1. Garnet had two sisters.

2. Garnet had four brothers.

3. Citronella was very thin.

4. Eric was "adopted" by Garnet's family.

5. Garnet wanted to buy an accordion for Mr. Freebody.

6. Timmy won a blue ribbon at the fair.

7. Eric wanted to be a farmer when he grew up.

8. Donald was older than Jay.

9. When Garnet and Citronella were locked in the library, they were not found until the next morning.

10. Garnet went to New Conniston by herself.

11. The day of the fair, Garnet's mother made her wash the dishes before leaving.

12. Garnet and Citronella rode to the fair in Mr. Freebody's truck.

13. Mr. Freebody bought a strawberry ice cream cone for Garnet's pig.

Multiple Choice. Read the question. Decide which statement best answers the question. Mark your answer sheet accordingly.

14. What present was Garnet going to give Eric?

   A. A Wild West book

   B. A black chicken

   C. A bandanna handkerchief

   D. A little aeroplane

79
The Alley
Eleanor Estes

True or False. Decide whether each statement is true or false. Mark your answer sheet accordingly.

1. The burglars broke into Connie's house in the middle of the night.

2. The burglars broke into Connie's house during the day.

3. Nanny was deaf.

4. Nanny often spoke crossly to Billy.

5. Nanny lived in a nursing home.

6. Connie and Billy never found out who the burglars were.

7. Billy and Connie were brother and sister.

8. Connie and Billy liked to play on the swing together.

9. The bullet-head man was one of the burglars.

10. Billy took pictures of the burglars breaking into Bully Vardeer's house.

11. At the end of the book, Connie was sad because Billy went to summer camp.

Multiple Choice. Read each question. Decide which statement best answers the question. Mark your answer sheet accordingly.

12. Connie did not continue to help Billy with his casing because she decided to

   A. Give piano lessons to the children in the Alley

   B. Help her teacher every day after school

   C. Set up a lemonade stand

   D. Teach herself to speak French

13. The bullet-head man asked Connie's mother and Bully Vardeer the same question. What question did he ask them?

   A. "Is there a hospital in the Alley?"

   B. "How many children do you have?"

   C. "Does this dog bite?"

   D. "Are you allergic to dogs?"

14. Connie's mother was sure that

   A. The burglars were people who lived in the Alley

   B. The burglars were dressed in green caps and coats

   C. The policemen had not stolen anything from the houses in the Alley

   D. One of the policemen had taken her diamond ring

80
The Coat-Hanger Christmas Tree
Eleanor Estes

True or False. Decide whether each statement is true or false. Mark your answer sheet accordingly.

1. Ken and Marianna went to the same school.

2. Allie McKaye wanted everybody in school to know that she lived on a barge.

3. Allie brought a gift to school for Marianna.

4. Marianna brought a gift to school for Allie.

5. Marianna told Ken that Allie lived on a barge.

6. Marianna's mother liked to be different from other people.

7. Marianna could see Allie's barge from her bedroom window.

8. Marianna's mother surprised the children by buying them a Christmas tree.

9. Marianna and her family liked to make things.

10. Allie did not know how to run.

11. Allie wished that she had a bureau (chest of drawers).

Multiple Choice. Read each question. Decide which statement best answers the question. Mark your answer sheet accordingly.

12. How would Marianna signal Allie if her mother let them have a Christmas tree?

    A. Blow a whistle three times

    B. Flash her bedroom light on and off

    C. Wink her eye

    D. Wave her flashlight back and forth

13. What did Marianna want for Christmas?

    A. A pair of boots

    B. A pony

    C. A Christmas tree

    D. A bracelet

14. Where did Marianna and Ken put the Christmas trees they brought home?

    A. In the cellar

    B. In Marianna's bedroom

    C. In the garage

    D. In the garden

From *Quizzes for 220 Great Children's Books*, revised 1st edition. © 1996. Teacher Ideas Press. (800) 237-6124.

81
Ginger Pye
Eleanor Estes

True or False. Decide whether each statement is true or false. Mark your answer sheet accordingly.

1. Ginger Pye was a rabbit.
2. Jerry dusted church pews to earn the money to buy Ginger Pye.
3. The Unsavory Character was a woman.
4. The Unsavory Character wore a yellow hat.
5. Mr. Pye was a fish expert.
6. Uncle Bennie was younger than Jerry and Rachel.
7. Jerry Pye had one brother and no sisters.
8. When Jerry grew up, he wanted to be a rock man.
9. Sam Doody was very tall.
10. Mrs. Speedy often said, "You bet!"
11. Ginger was found on Jerry's birthday.

Multiple Choice. Read each question. Decide which statement best answers the question. Mark your answer sheet accordingly.

12. There was a newspaper article written about Ginger Pye because he
    A. Climbed the fire escape into Jerry's classroom
    B. Saved Jerry from drowning in the lake
    C. Killed Mrs. Brown's cat
    D. Caught the man who was trying to break into the grocery store

13. How long was Ginger lost?
    A. A few hours
    B. One day
    C. One week
    D. None of the above

14. Who found Ginger?
    A. Mr. Pye
    B. Uncle Bennie
    C. Dick
    D. Sam Doody

82
The Hundred Dresses
Eleanor Estes

True or False. Decide whether each statement is true or false. Mark your answer sheet accordingly.

1. Maddie and Peggy were sisters.

2. Wanda often spent the night at Peggy's house.

3. Maddie often wished that Peggy would stop making fun of Wanda.

4. Wanda always wore the same pale blue dress to school.

5. Wanda wore a different dress to school each day.

6. Wanda and Peggy were best friends.

7. Maddie sometimes wore Peggy's old dresses.

8. Wanda did not have any brothers or sisters.

9. On their way from Wanda's house, Peggy and Maddie saw old man Svenson.

10. Old man Svenson served cookies and milk to Peggy and Maddie in his living room.

11. Peggy and Maddie wrote a friendly letter to Wanda after she and her family moved away.

Multiple Choice. Read each question. Decide which statement best answers the question. Mark your answer sheet accordingly.

12. Who won the girls' drawing contest?

    A. Peggy

    B. Maddie

    C. Wanda

    D. None of the above

13. What was Wanda's last name?

    A. Brown

    B. Anderson

    C. Smith

    D. Petronski

14. What did Maddie decide that she was never going to do again?

    A. Wear Peggy's old dresses

    B. Stand by and say nothing when someone was being made fun of

    C. Try to be friends with the most popular girl in school

    D. Take the bus to school

83
The Lost Umbrella of Kim Chu
Eleanor Estes

True or False. Decide whether each statement is true or false. Mark your answer sheet accordingly.

1. Kim could not speak Chinese.

2. Kim could not speak English.

3. When Kim came home without the umbrella, her grandmother slapped her.

4. Kim did not have any brothers or sisters.

5. Kim and Mae Lee were friends.

6. Mae Lee did not live in Chinatown.

7. Mrs. Parks, the library teacher, went home with Kim and explained to Kim's grandmother all that had happened.

8. Kim's grandfather had given the umbrella to Kim's father as a birthday present.

9. The umbrella belonged to Kim's father.

10. On the ferry, Kim sat next to a lady who laughed a lot.

11. Kim gave the buffalo nickels she found to the millionaire man.

Multiple Choice. Read each question. Decide which statement best answers the question. Mark your answer sheet accordingly.

12. How did Kim get to the library?

    A. She walked

    B. She rode her bike

    C. Her grandmother drove her there

    D. She took a bus

13. How was the umbrella different from most umbrellas?

    A. The handle could be unscrewed

    B. The handle was made of pure gold

    C. It was invisible

    D. All of the above

14. How did the millionaire man get the umbrella?

    A. He stole it

    B. He found it on the ferry

    C. He bought it from the boy who had stolen it

    D. His wife found it and gave it to him as a gift

From *Quizzes for 220 Great Children's Books,* revised 1st edition. © 1996. Teacher Ideas Press. (800) 237-6124.

84
The Middle Moffat
Eleanor Estes

True or False. Decide whether each statement is true or false. Mark your answer sheet accordingly.

1. Jane's mother did not know how to sew.

2. Jane never got her skates back from Murph.

3. The oldest inhabitant beat Jane at double solitaire.

4. Nancy loved animals.

5. Jane did not give Mr. Buckle a gift on his hundredth birthday.

6. Mr. Buckle called Janey "the mysterious middle Moffat."

7. Jane made her mother an apron for Christmas.

8. Jane had two brothers and one sister.

9. In "The Three Bears," Jane played the part of Goldilocks.

10. When Nancy was angry at Jane, Nancy said, "Jane is a pain."

11. At the end of the book, Jane rode home from the parade in a limousine.

Multiple Choice. Read each question. Decide which statement best answers the question. Mark your answer sheet accordingly.

12. What did Rufus ask Santa to bring him for Christmas?

    A. A live pony

    B. A puppy

    C. A pair of skates

    D. A radio

13. What did Rufus and Joey spend a lot of time doing?

    A. Working on their radio

    B. Looking through their telescope

    C. Building model airplanes

    D. Reading comic books

14. What did Mrs. Price give to the Moffats?

    A. A horse

    B. An organ

    C. A cow

    D. All of the above

85
Rufus M.
Eleanor Estes

True or False. Decide whether each statement is true or false. Mark your answer sheet accordingly.

1. Rufus was allowed to be the backstop for Jane's baseball team, the Fatal Four.
2. Rufus's beans never grew.
3. Rufus found out that the invisible piano player was really just a machine.
4. When Joe and Jane went to visit Miss Myles, Joe talked so much that Jane didn't have a chance to say anything.
5. The eyes in the pipe turned out to be Catherine-the-cat's.
6. Jane and Rufus never found the treasure they buried at the beach.
7. Rufus wanted to learn to be a ventriloquist.
8. Rufus fell into a cellar window at the library.
9. Jane and Rufus sold popcorn to earn money to buy bicycles.
10. Rufus took his cardboard boy to the amusement park.
11. At the end of the book, Sylvie decided that she was never going to get married.

Multiple Choice. Read each question. Decide which statement best answers the question. Mark your answer sheet accordingly.

12. Rufus had to stand in the cloakroom at school because
    A. He said, "Let me out!" when it was quiet in the classroom
    B. He was cheating on a spelling test
    C. His cardboard boy was hitting the other children
    D. He was collecting spiders, frogs, and snakes in his desk

13. After Sylvie's performance of "The Lollipop Princess," the Moffats had to hurry home because
    A. The invisible piano player was coming for dinner
    B. The cardboard boy hadn't had his supper
    C. They were worried that their water pipes might be frozen
    D. They were worried that they had left the stove on

14. The librarian told Rufus that to get a library card, he would have to
    A. Go home to wash his hands
    B. Write his name
    C. Have his mother sign the application
    D. All of the above

86
Harriet the Spy
Louise Fitzhugh

True or False. Decide whether each statement is true or false. Mark your answer sheet accordingly.

1. Mrs. Golly, Ole Golly's mother, was very overweight.
2. Sport wanted to be a ball player when he grew up.
3. Harriet always took a tomato sandwich in her lunch.
4. Harriet did not have any brothers or sisters.
5. Sport's father was a chemist.
6. Janie wanted to be a writer when she grew up.
7. Janie wanted to take dancing lessons.
8. Harriet could not see well without her glasses.
9. Every year in school, Harriet was elected class officer.
10. Harriet and Marion Hawthorne were best friends.
11. Miss Elson chose Harriet to be the editor of the *Sixth Grade Page*.
12. Ole Golly never got married.

Multiple Choice. Read each question. Decide which statement best answers the question. Mark your answer sheet accordingly.

13. Ole Golly left because
    A. Her mother became ill and needed someone to take care of her
    B. Harriet was too much work for her
    C. She was going to get married
    D. She was going to become a nun

14. What part was Harriet to play in the Christmas pageant?
    A. An angel
    B. A soldier
    C. A tree
    D. An onion

87
Johnny Tremain
Esther Forbes

True or False. Decide whether each statement is true or false. Mark your answer sheet accordingly.

1. Cilla was younger than Isannah.

2. Johnny was found guilty of stealing Mr. Lyte's cup.

3. Johnny could not ride a horse because of his burned hand.

4. Rab was a member of the Sons of Liberty.

5. Rab did not believe in carrying a gun.

6. During the Tea Party, Johnny caught Dove shoving tea into his pockets.

7. Johnny hoped that Cilla and Rab would get married.

8. Johnny was Merchant Lyte's grandson.

9. The Laphams were very wealthy.

10. The Lytes were very wealthy.

11. Mrs. Bessie was a Tory.

12. Johnny and Rab never attended a Sons of Liberty meeting.

13. Rab's uncle hoped that Rab would be able to fight in the war.

14. Johnny and Rab were enemies.

88
One-Eyed Cat
Paula Fox

True or False. Decide whether each statement is true or false. Mark your answer sheet accordingly.

1. Ned's mother was confined to a wheelchair.

2. Ned's father was a minister.

3. Ned's father did not want him to have a gun.

4. After shooting the gun, Ned saw someone watching him from the attic window.

5. Immediately after shooting the air rifle, Ned told his parents what he had done.

6. Mrs. Wallis punished Ned for shooting the rifle.

7. The first person Ned told the truth about the cat to was Mr. Scully.

8. Mr. Scully lived in an old mansion across the road from Ned.

9. Mr. Scully hated Ned after he admitted that he had shot the cat.

10. Mr. Scully died in a nursing home.

11. When Mr. Scully and Ned discovered the one-eyed cat, they started feeding it.

Multiple Choice. Read each question. Decide which statement best answers the question. Mark your answer sheet accordingly.

12. Ned helped Mr. Scully because

    A. Mr. Scully was old and needed help

    B. Mr. Scully was Ned's grandfather

    C. Ned's father told him that he had to help Mr. Scully

    D. All of the above

13. When Ned's mother noticed that he seem depressed, Ned

    A. Told his mother that he thought he shot the cat

    B. Cried bitterly for more than an hour

    C. Lied to her

    D. Tried to act as if nothing was wrong

14. When Uncle Hilary offered to take Ned on a trip over Christmas, Ned

    A. Accepted the invitation so he could forget about the cat

    B. Refused the invitation because he felt responsible for the cat

    C. Was happy because he loved Uncle Hilary

    D. Was sad because he would miss his friends

89
The Slave Dancer
Paula Fox

True or False. Decide whether each statement is true or false. Mark your answer sheet accordingly.

1. Jessie was kidnapped and taken aboard a slave ship.

2. Jessie was whipped because he refused to play his fife.

3. The captain killed the mate because he had killed a valuable slave.

4. The slave boy, Rass, led a slave rebellion on the ship.

5. When the captain realized he was about to be boarded by an American patrol ship, he ordered all the slaves thrown overboard.

6. Jessie and Rass were the only two who survived after *The Moonlight* sank.

7. The escaped slave, Daniel, helped Rass escape to the North.

8. Jessie moved to the North to live with Rass and to help other slaves escape.

9. The captain and the mate had living quarters separate from the rest of the crew.

10. When Purvis was wrongly accused of stealing one of the captain's eggs, Ben Stout allowed him to be whipped.

11. One of Jessie's duties on the ship was to empty the slaves' toilet buckets.

Multiple Choice. Read each question. Decide which statement best answers the question. Mark your answer sheet accordingly.

12. After Purvis spent the night tied to the mast

    A. Jessie stole a small boat and escaped from the ship

    B. Jessie and Purvis jumped overboard

    C. Jessie hated Benjamin Stout

    D. The captain locked Purvis in the brig

13. How did the captain of *The Moonlight* plan to avoid being captured by patrol ships?

    A. He had flags and registration papers from various countries

    B. He planned to sail faster than the patrol ships

    C. He sailed only at night when he couldn't be seen

    D. He had many cannons on board to sink the patrol ships

14. When the slaves were first brought on board, they were

    A. Allowed to stay up on deck in the fresh air

    B. Packed down into the hold of the ship

    C. Hidden in the captain's quarters

    D. None of the above

90
Blue Willow
Doris Gates

True or False. Decide whether each statement is true or false. Mark your answer sheet accordingly.

1. Lupé did not have any brothers or sisters.

2. Janey did not have any brothers or sisters.

3. The Larkins did not have a car.

4. Janey had to pay 50¢ to get into the fair.

5. Janey would not accept the eggs that Mr. Anderson offered her.

6. Janey did not like Miss Peterson.

7. When Mrs. Larkin was sick, the doctor insisted that she be taken to the county hospital.

8. Lupé was German.

9. At the fair, Janey used her nickel to buy a package of gum.

10. Miss Peterson brought some bundles for Janey and her family on Christmas Day.

11. Mr. Anderson was the owner of the shack that the Larkins lived in.

Multiple Choice. Read each question. Decide which statement best answers the question. Mark your answer sheet accordingly.

12. When Mrs. Larkin was sick, who went to get the doctor?

    A. Janey

    B. Mr. Larkin

    C. Mrs. Romero

    D. Lupé

13. Which of the following items was NOT bought with Mr. Larkin's prize money?

    A. Tires for the car

    B. A coat for Janey

    C. Dinner at a restaurant

    D. The willow plate

14. What was the name of Mr. Anderson's dog?

    A. Kelly

    B. Courage

    C. Danger

    D. Boxer

91
The Elderberry Bush
Doris Gates

True or False. Decide whether each statement is true or false. Mark your answer sheet accordingly.

1. Julie and Elizabeth were sisters.

2. Father said that he was going to shoot Santa Claus.

3. On the last day of school, Julie and Elizabeth did their recitations barefooted.

4. On the last day of school, Julie and Elizabeth made fun of Ethel Tucker for not wearing shoes.

5. Clara went with Julie and her family on a vacation to the Pacific Ocean.

6. During their two-week vacation at the Pacific Ocean, Julie had the mumps.

7. Julie and Elizabeth were both sick with the mumps at the same time.

8. Mother and Father never found out what Julie had done to Cousin Ruby's paintings.

9. When Uncle Aaron saw what Julie had done to Cousin Ruby's paintings, he laughed.

10. The ladies in Cousin Ruby's paintings did not have faces.

11. Mr. Whipple gave Julie and Elizabeth each a bicycle.

12. Mr. Whipple often said to Julie and Elizabeth, "This is the happiest time of your lives."

Multiple Choice. Read each question. Decide which statement best answers the question. Mark your answer sheet accordingly.

13. What happened the day that Mother and Julie went to town?

    A. It rained

    B. Old Bess ran away

    C. A and B

    D. None of the above

14. How did Mr. Whipple get hurt?

    A. He fell down a flight of stairs

    B. He fell off a ladder

    C. Someone tried to kill him

    D. He tried to kill himself

92
A Morgan for Melinda
Doris Gates

True or False. Decide whether each statement is true or false. Mark your answer sheet accordingly.

1. Melinda's father wanted her to learn to ride a horse.

2. Melinda's brother, Martin, was dead.

3. Melinda's father bought Melinda a horse.

4. Melinda had wanted a horse of her own as long as she could remember.

5. Melinda was happy when Dwight complimented her.

6. Melinda did not like Dwight.

7. Missy was a writer.

8. Missy rode Merry Jo in the Jack Benny.

9. Missy broke her leg the day before she was to ride Merry Jo in the Jack Benny.

10. Missy never met Melinda's father.

11. Melinda told Missy that she really didn't want to learn to ride, but her dad wanted her to learn.

12. Missy gave Melinda a typewriter.

13. At the end of the book, Missy died.

Multiple Choice. Read the question. Decide which statement best answers the question. Mark your answer sheet accordingly.

14. Missy was
    A. A little girl
    B. An old woman
    C. Melinda's teacher
    D. Melinda's sister

93
Coyote in Manhattan
Jean Craighead George

True or False. Decide whether each statement is true or false. Mark your answer sheet accordingly.

1. Tenny did not want to belong to the Street Family.

2. Tenny was the leader of the Street Family.

3. Leon gave Tako to Tenny as a birthday present.

4. Frederick was upset when he learned that his dog had mated with Tako.

5. Tako liked ice cream.

6. Tenny never became part of the Street Family.

7. Tako killed Rancid, Mrs. La Gloria's cat.

8. Tako was not afraid of Tenny.

9. Miss Landry, who fed birds, tried to kill Tako.

10. Poovey was a rabbit.

11. At the end of the book, José told Dr. Lockspur that Tenny had been hiding Tako.

Multiple Choice. Read each question. Decide which statement best answers the question. Mark your answer sheet accordingly.

12. At first, Tenny was not voted into the Street Family because

    A. She was black

    B. She was always getting into trouble with the law

    C. She was too "do-goody" for them

    D. Her father was a policeman

13. Tenny often daydreamed about

    A. Doing good deeds

    B. Marrying José

    C. Becoming a lawyer

    D. Living in a beautiful palace

14. Who lived with Tako in his den during the winter?

    A. Tenny

    B. Poovey

    C. A kitten

    D. Tako's pups

94
Julie of the Wolves
Jean Craighead George

True or False. Decide whether each statement is true or false. Mark your answer sheet accordingly.

1. Jello was the leader of the wolf pack.

2. Daniel was an intelligent young man.

3. The word "gussak" was the Eskimo word for a white person.

4. Julie was glad that she had married Daniel.

5. Naka, Daniel's father, drank too much alcohol.

6. Daniel and his family lived in Anchorage.

7. Julie used strips of caribou skin to make a sled.

8. The wolf pack killed a bear that was going to attack Miyax.

9. Kapu was shot and killed by hunters.

10. Amaroq was shot and killed by hunters.

11. Jello stole Julie's backpack.

Multiple Choice. Read each question. Decide which statement best answers the question. Mark your answer sheet accordingly.

12. The wolves accepted Miyax into the pack after

    A. Miyax saved a puppy

    B. Miyax patted Amaroq's chin

    C. Miyax fed Amaroq

    D. None of the above

13. Miyax got her first food from the wolves

    A. After Jello vomited some of his food for her

    B. When Amaroq brought her a caribou leg

    C. When Kapu led her to a dead caribou

    D. None of the above

14. Which wolf was the "low man on the totem pole"?

    A. Kapu

    B. Nails

    C. Jello

    D. Silver

95
My Side of the Mountain
Jean Craighead George

True or False. Decide whether each statement is true or false. Mark your answer sheet accordingly.

1. Sam did not have any brothers or sisters.
2. Sam was caught stealing food from a local grocery store.
3. The librarian contacted the police when she realized that Sam had run away from home.
4. A lady picking strawberries discovered Sam on the Gribley farm.
5. The lady who had been picking strawberries asked Sam to walk her back into town.
6. Bando was a criminal.
7. The newspapers began to print stories about the wild boy in the woods.
8. Sam was able to train Frightful to hunt for him.
9. Sam's original home was in New York City.
10. When Sam first saw Bando, he thought that Bando was a policeman.
11. Frightful was a skunk.
12. At the end of the book, Sam's family decided to move out to the wilderness, too.

Multiple Choice. Read each question. Decide which statement best answers the question. Mark your answer sheet accordingly.

13. How did Sam know where to find the abandoned Gribley farm?

    A. He read about it in his great-grandfather's diary

    B. The librarian in Delhi helped him to locate it on an old map

    C. A voice from heaven told him where to find it

    D. He met a girl who used to live on the farm

14. In the wilderness, Sam lived in

    A. A hollowed-out tree

    B. A snug cave

    C. The old farmhouse

    D. A lean-to

96
River Rats, Inc.
Jean Craighead George

True or False. Decide whether each statement is true or false. Mark your answer sheet accordingly.

1. Joe and Crowbar wanted lots of people to see them go down the river.

2. Joe and Crowbar were chased by men looking for the urn.

3. As Joe and Crowbar traveled along the river, they met a wild boy.

4. The wild boy ate lizards, snakes, and birds.

5. The wild boy was cared for by some donkeys.

6. Joe named the wild boy "Freddy."

7. Joe taught the wild boy to speak.

8. The boys' raft was destroyed going over Lava Falls.

9. The boys were captured by drug smugglers.

10. Once on shore after their raft was destroyed, Joe and Crowbar weren't sure where they were.

11. When the boys were lost in the desert, Uncle Como helped them find water.

12. At the end of the book, the wild boy went to live with Joe and his family.

Multiple Choice. Read each question. Decide which statement best answers the question. Mark your answer sheet accordingly.

13. On the raft, Joe and Crowbar were carrying

    A. A load of drugs

    B. A funeral urn

    C. Food and supplies for one month

    D. A dead body

14. Joe and Crowbar were supposed to

    A. Take some drugs down the river to Mexico

    B. Drop a funeral urn over Lava Falls

    C. Survive on the river for one month by themselves

    D. Bury a body on the bank of the Colorado River

97
Who Really Killed Cock Robin?
Jean Craighead George

True or False. Decide whether each statement is true or false. Mark your answer sheet accordingly.

1. Detergents were what really killed Cock Robin.

2. Mrs. Robin died.

3. Saddle died.

4. Tony learned all he knew about robins from the mayor.

5. A funeral was held for Cock Robin.

6. Some of Mrs. Robin's eggs never hatched.

7. Saddle was afraid of Tony.

8. Saddle was afraid of Mary Alice.

9. The mayor got all of his information about robins from Mary Alice.

10. Izzy was Tony's brother.

Multiple Choice. Read each question. Decide which statement best answers the question. Mark your answer sheet accordingly.

11. What was wrong with Saddle?

    A. He was blind

    B. He could not fly

    C. He had a broken leg

    D. None of the above

12. Where did Mrs. Robin build her nest?

    A. In the mayor's hat

    B. In Tony's book bag

    C. In Mary Alice's garage

    D. None of the above

13. Mary Alice's father

    A. Owned the Missatonic Mill

    B. Was the mayor

    C. Was dead

    D. Was the editor of the local newspaper

14. The mayor asked Tony to

    A. Perform an autopsy on Cock Robin

    B. Take over the "Cock Robin Hour"

    C. Find out who really killed Cock Robin

    D. All of the above

98
Old Yeller
Fred Gipson

True or False. Decide whether each statement is true or false. Mark your answer sheet accordingly.

1. When Travis was hurt, Lisbeth came to stay with the family.

2. Arliss was afraid of little animals.

3. For awhile, Old Yeller was stealing food from the neighbors.

4. Old Yeller was run over by a truck.

5. Travis's mother said they should burn any animals that died of hydrophobia.

6. Old Yeller fought a mad wolf that attacked Travis's mother and Lisbeth.

7. Travis had to shoot Old Yeller.

8. Travis's father had gone west to fight Indians.

9. Burn Sanderson claimed that Old Yeller belonged to him.

10. When Travis was trapped by wild pigs, Old Yeller attacked the pigs and was badly wounded.

11. Lisbeth brought Travis a puppy.

Multiple Choice. Read each question. Decide which statement best answers the question. Mark your answer sheet accordingly.

12. When Old Yeller first showed up, Travis was

    A. Glad to have another dog around

    B. Happy that Arliss would have another pet

    C. Curious as to who Old Yeller's real owner was

    D. Angry because Old Yeller stole his family's food

13. Travis decided that Old Yeller was a valuable dog when Old Yeller

    A. Found water during a dry spell

    B. Protected Arliss from a bear

    C. Drove off two fighting bulls

    D. Warned the family of an Indian attack

14. Travis and Old Yeller spent many nights in the corn patch to

    A. Keep out coons and skunks

    B. Drive away the crows

    C. Keep the Indians from stealing the corn

    D. All of the above

99
Savage Sam
Fred Gipson

True or False. Decide whether each statement is true or false. Mark your answer sheet accordingly.

1. Little Arliss bit off an Indian's ear.

2. The Comanche protected Little Arliss from the one-eared Apache.

3. The Indians tried not to kill white men during the raid.

4. Travis and the men from the settlement ran into a terrible hailstorm.

5. Gotch Ear killed Savage Sam.

6. Travis's father wanted to give up the chase after Sam lost the trail.

7. The Indians painted Travis and Little Arliss red.

8. Lisbeth's grandfather died of a heart attack while chasing the Indians.

9. Gotch Ear was always trying to impress the other Indians.

10. At the end of the book, Travis killed the Comanche.

Multiple Choice. Read each question. Decide which statement best answers the question. Mark your answer sheet accordingly.

11. What were Travis, Little Arliss, and Lisbeth doing when they were captured by the Indians?

    A. Picking berries

    B. Getting salt from the salt lick

    C. Harvesting corn

    D. Watching Savage Sam fight a bobcat

12. Who first told Travis's father that the Indians were raiding?

    A. Lisbeth's grandfather

    B. Travis's mother

    C. Little Arliss

    D. The mayor

13. The band of Indians who captured Travis, Little Arliss, and Lisbeth were:

    A. Skilled horsemen

    B. Stealing horses from settlers

    C. Able to defeat a group of soldiers

    D. All of the above

14. What happened to Jumper?

    A. He was stolen by the Indians

    B. He got away during the battle

    C. He was eaten by the Indians

    D. Both A and C

100
Philip Hall Likes Me, I Reckon Maybe
Bette Greene

True or False. Decide whether each statement is true or false. Mark your answer sheet accordingly.

1. Philip sent Beth an invitation to his birthday party.
2. Philip liked to play the guitar.
3. Beth was the only child in her family.
4. Philip lived on a turkey farm.
5. Beth was the president of the Pretty Pennies.
6. Friendly was a long-haired dog.
7. Beth was not allergic to short-haired dogs.
8. Beth wanted to be a teacher when she grew up.
9. Beth's family borrowed Mr. Hall's car to drive to the church picnic.
10. Gordon was the president of the Tiger Hunters.
11. Annie loaned her *huaraches* (Mexican slippers) to Beth the day of the church picnic.
12. Annie and Baby Benjamin did not go to the church picnic.
13. The Answer Man never answered Pa's letter about the missing turkeys.
14. Beth won first place in the calf-raising contest.

From *Quizzes for 220 Great Children's Books*, revised 1st edition. © 1996. Teacher Ideas Press. (800) 237-6124.

101
A Girl Called Al
Constance C. Greene

True or False. Decide whether each statement is true or false. Mark your answer sheet accordingly.

1. The principal decided to let Al take shop instead of cooking and sewing.

2. Al's parents were divorced.

3. Al's father took Al out to dinner every Saturday night.

4. Al's mother often left her alone in the apartment.

5. Al's mother did not have a job.

6. Al did not have any brothers or sisters.

7. The narrator's mother invited Al's mother to afternoon tea.

8. Mr. Richards's daughter and grandchildren visited him twice a week.

9. Mr. Richards was homeless.

10. Mr. Richards lived in a mental institution.

11. At the end of the book, Mr. Richards died.

12. At the end of the book, Al's mother died.

Multiple Choice. Read each question. Decide which statement best answers the question. Mark your answer sheet accordingly.

13. Mr. Richards helped Al and the narrator

    A. Study for their history test

    B. Make bookshelves

    C. Find Al's father

    D. Build a tree house

14. Al decided that she would use the money her father gave her to

    A. Help poor people in her city

    B. Buy herself something nice to wear instead of buying food

    C. Buy airplane tickets for Mr. Richards's grandchildren

    D. Help make payments on a house for Mr. Richards

102
M. C. Higgins the Great
Virginia Hamilton

True or False. Decide whether each statement is true or false. Mark your answer sheet accordingly.

1. The Killburns had six fingers instead of five on each hand.

2. M. C. was a lot smaller than Ben.

3. M. C.'s prize for swimming the Ohio River was a car.

4. At the top of M. C.'s pole was a bicycle seat.

5. M. C.'s father's name was Jones.

6. Lurhetta did not know how to swim.

7. M. C. took Lurhetta through the water tunnel.

8. Lurhetta watched M. C. skin a rabbit.

9. Lurhetta owned a car.

10. Lurhetta did not like to travel.

11. Lurhetta came to say good-bye to M. C. before she left.

12. M. C.'s father was a good friend of Mr. Killburn.

Multiple Choice. Read each question. Decide which statement best answers the question. Mark your answer sheet accordingly.

13. What gift did Lurhetta leave for M. C.?

    A. A fishing pole

    B. A knife

    C. A rabbit's foot

    D. A compass

14. What did Ben's grandmother give M. C.?

    A. A rabbit's foot

    B. A snake

    C. A cabbage head

    D. A locket

From *Quizzes for 220 Great Children's Books,* revised 1st edition. © 1996. Teacher Ideas Press. (800) 237-6124.

103
The Planet of Junior Brown
Virginia Hamilton

True or False. Decide whether each statement is true or false. Mark your answer sheet accordingly.

1. The leaders of the planets taught their members to steal to survive.
2. Buddy's parents helped him run his planet.
3. The assistant principal called Junior's mother to tell her that Junior had been skipping class.
4. Junior believed that Miss Peebs's relative was real.
5. Miss Peebs's relative did not really exist.
6. The leader of a planet was called a Tomorrow Billy.
7. When Buddy visited Junior's home, Junior's mother had an asthma attack.
8. Buddy discovered that Junior's piano did not make any noise when it was played.
9. When Buddy and Junior went to see Miss Peebs, she gave Buddy a piano lesson.
10. Whenever something upset Junior's mother, she would have an asthma attack.
11. When Buddy realized that Junior was going insane, he brought Junior to his planet.

Multiple Choice. Read each question. Decide which statement best answers the question. Mark your answer sheet accordingly.

12. What was unusual about Junior's piano lessons?

    A. His teacher fed him a big dinner before every lesson
    B. He had to be wearing white gloves before he was allowed to touch the piano
    C. The lessons were free because he was poor
    D. He was not allowed to touch the piano

13. Miss Peebs told Junior that her relative

    A. Was a famous African pianist
    B. Hated children
    C. Disliked noise and couldn't have any visitors
    D. Was leaving soon to go on a tour of Europe

14. Buddy was part of a system of shelters, called planets, that

    A. Trained underground fighters for the Black Panthers
    B. Were run by the Department of Health, Education, and Welfare
    C. Sheltered poor, homeless boys
    D. Existed only in Junior's mind

104
The Bright and Morning Star
Rosemary Harris

True or False. Decide whether each statement is true or false. Mark your answer sheet accordingly.

1. Ta-Thata did not want to marry Sinuhe.

2. Sinuhe accidentally drank the poison he was supposed to give to the king.

3. No-Hotep was thrown to the crocodiles.

4. Ta-Thata married Tahlevi's son, Henmut.

5. Henmut found a secret passage into the king's tomb.

6. No-Hotep was in love with Thamar.

7. Sinuhe warned the king of No-Hotep's plan.

8. Thamar returned to Kemi because she hoped to find a cure for her son, Sadhi.

9. Ta-Thata was worried that Sinuhe was under the control of No-Hotep.

10. Ta-Thata and Sinuhe were cats that had been dedicated to Ra, the Sun God.

11. Tahlevi and his son helped Hekhti against No-Hotep.

Multiple Choice. Read each question. Decide which statement best answers the question. Mark your answer sheet accordingly.

12. Hekhti helped Sadhi by

    A. Teaching him a sign language

    B. Giving him a magic coin

    C. Teaching him to read and write

    D. Giving him a cane so that he could walk

13. When the king and his family went to visit the royal tomb

    A. They discovered that it had been robbed

    B. The king and queen were locked inside of it

    C. A rock fell from the top and killed Meri-Mekhmet

    D. The priest of Set refused to go inside

14. No-Hotep's plan was to

    A. Become the High Priest of Set

    B. Kill Reuben and become the Prince of Canaan

    C. Steal the temple cats and kill them

    D. Kill the king and the prince and marry Ta-Thata

105
The Moon in the Cloud
Rosemary Harris

True or False. Decide whether each statement is true or false. Mark your answer sheet accordingly.

1. Ham was a kind and generous man.

2. Ham was Noah's uncle.

3. Cefalu fell in love with Meluseth.

4. The ruler of Kemi was a harsh and cruel man.

5. The High Priest of Sekhmet put Reuben in prison.

6. Ham was killed by an elephant.

7. Noah took Reuben and Thamar on the ark.

8. Cefalu talked a lion into going onto the ark.

9. Reuben was worried because Thamar was always stealing money from Ham.

10. Reuben was Thamar's son.

11. Tahlevi was in prison because he had tried to kill the king.

12. Ham promised Reuben that if he brought some animals from Kemi, Thamar could go on the ark.

Multiple Choice. Read each question. Decide which statement best answers the question. Mark your answer sheet accordingly.

13. After Cefalu and Reuben were captured by the men of Kemi, Cefalu

   A. Was turned into a camel

   B. Suddenly had the ability to speak like a man

   C. Became invisible

   D. Was worshipped by the men of Kemi

14. Reuben was given to the ruler of Kemi as a slave because he

   A. Could talk to animals

   B. Was young and handsome

   C. Could play beautiful music

   D. Was as strong as two ordinary men

106
The Shadow on the Sun
Rosemary Harris

True or False. Decide whether each statement is true or false. Mark your answer sheet accordingly.

1. The King of Kemi sent his fleet to capture the Prince of Punt's canoe.

2. M'bu tried to help Reuben rescue Meri-Mekhmet.

3. The Lord God told Reuben to go straight to the prince's village.

4. Reuben killed a giant snake.

5. Kenamut helped Reuben fight M'bu.

6. The King of Kemi married Meri-Mekhmet.

7. The Prince of Punt wanted to sacrifice Meri-Mekhmet to his gods.

8. When the king became deathly ill, Thamar brought Meri-Mekhmet to the palace.

9. Cefalu, the cat, found out what had happened to Meri-Mekhmet.

10. Reuben's enemy, Kenamut, went with Reuben to search for Meri-Mekhmet.

11. When Meri-Mekhmet refused to marry him, the king became stern and cruel.

Multiple Choice. Read each question. Decide which statement best answers the question. Mark your answer sheet accordingly.

12. Why did Reuben and Thamar return to Kemi?

    A. They needed more animals for the ark

    B. Thamar was very sick

    C. Noah wanted them to leave him

    D. The King of Kemi begged them to return

13. Why didn't the King of Kemi want Meri-Mekhmet to know who he was?

    A. He knew that his father had killed Meri-Mekhmet's brother

    B. He was afraid of being killed if he was recognized

    C. He was afraid she would beg him for money

    D. He liked being treated like an ordinary person

14. What problem did the king face when he fell in love with Meri-Mekhmet?

    A. He was already married

    B. He could not marry someone who was not of royal blood

    C. He and Meri-Mekhmet did not believe in the same gods

    D. His nobles feared her power and might revolt if she became queen

107
Back to School with Betsy
Carolyn Haywood

True or False. Decide whether each statement is true or false. Mark your answer sheet accordingly.

1. Mr. Jackson wanted Betsy to teach his dog to read.

2. Mr. Jackson said that he would pay Betsy 5¢ a day if she would check that the workmen locked the doors of his house.

3. Betsy and Ellen were flower girls in Miss Grey's wedding.

4. On the day of Miss Grey's wedding, Betsy had the chicken pox and spent the day at home in bed.

5. As a surprise for Betsy, her father arranged a sleighing party on Christmas Eve.

6. Betsy did not have any brothers or sisters.

7. After Mr. Jackson and Miss Grey were married, they lived next door to Betsy.

8. After Mr. Jackson and Miss Grey were married, Betsy went to live with them.

9. Betsy, Ellen, and Billy bought Miss Grey three goldfish as a wedding gift.

10. Betsy found Thumpy in Mr. Jackson's attic.

11. Thumpy spoiled the dress that Betsy was supposed to wear for Miss Grey's wedding, and Betsy's father had to rush the dress to the cleaners.

12. The janitor accidentally erased the picture that Betsy's class drew on the blackboard.

Multiple Choice. Read each question. Decide which statement best answers the question. Mark your answer sheet accordingly.

13. Betsy found

    A. A robin that couldn't fly

    B. A lost baby

    C. A $5 bill

    D. A diamond ring

14. Betsy's class was surprised to find out that Daisy, the hen

    A. Was really a rooster

    B. Was lost

    C. Could talk

    D. Could write her name

108
"B" Is for Betsy
Carolyn Haywood

True or False. Decide whether each statement is true or false. Mark your answer sheet accordingly.

1. On the first day of school, Betsy found Koala Bear hidden in her schoolbag.

2. On the first day of school, Ellen's dog, Jerry, came into the classroom.

3. Mr. Kilpatrick was the policeman who took the children across the street.

4. Wiggle and Waggle turned into butterflies.

5. When Waggle was lost, the children found him in Mr. Kilpatrick's pocket.

6. When Waggle was lost, the children found him under the wigwam in the sand table.

7. Betsy did not like Ellen.

8. Betsy gave Ellen a set of little dishes for her birthday.

9. Betsy gave Ellen a rabbit for her birthday.

10. Grandma Pretzie was Betsy's teacher.

11. Betsy's mother let her keep the puppy that Mr. Applebee had given her.

12. When Betsy's parents went on a trip, she went to stay with Grandma Pretzie.

Multiple Choice. Read each question. Decide which statement best answers the question. Mark your answer sheet accordingly.

13. How did Betsy usually get to school?

    A. She took a bus

    B. She rode a horse

    C. She walked

    D. She took a taxi

14. While Betsy's mother and father were away on a trip, Betsy

    A. Rode on an elephant in the circus

    B. Went with Grandma Pretzie on a boat ride

    C. Picked some violets that belonged to someone else

    D. Took some money from her father's piggy bank

109
Betsy and Mr. Kilpatrick
Carolyn Haywood

True or False. Decide whether each statement is true or false. Mark your answer sheet accordingly.

1. Most of the children in Betsy's class did not like Mr. Kilpatrick.

2. Betsy's little sister, Star, was too young to go to school.

3. Mr. and Mrs. Kilpatrick did not have any children of their own.

4. Betsy liked Mr. Kilpatrick.

5. The members of the Kilpatrick Club went to meet Mr. Kilpatrick's nieces and nephews at the airport.

6. Mr. Kilpatrick's nieces and nephews did not speak English.

7. Two of Mr. Kilpatrick's nieces came to live with Betsy and her family.

8. Betsy and Star went to Hong Kong to visit Ah Ping.

9. Betsy dressed up as a police officer for the Halloween party.

10. Betsy dressed up as a witch for the Halloween party.

11. The children raised enough money at the Halloween party to take care of Ah Ping for one year.

12. At the end of the book, the children found out that Mrs. Kilpatrick was the new policewoman who would be taking them across the street.

Multiple Choice. Read each question. Decide which statement best answers the question. Mark your answer sheet accordingly.

13. Mr. Kilpatrick's nephews and nieces came to stay with Mr. and Mrs. Kilpatrick because

   A. Their parents had died

   B. Their house had burned down

   C. There wasn't a school for them to go to where they lived

   D. The town they lived in was too cold and was making them sick

14. What did Mr. Kilpatrick call his nieces?

   A. Leprechauns

   B. Colleens

   C. Girlies

   D. Lassies

110
Eddie's Happenings
Carolyn Haywood

True or False. Decide whether each statement is true or false. Mark your answer sheet accordingly.

1. At the beginning of the book, Tookey gave Eddie a calendar that he found in Mrs. Andrew's wastebasket.

2. At the beginning of the book, Tookey gave Eddie a dead frog.

3. Tookey wanted the kids at school to call him "Toothpick."

4. Mrs. Andrews let Eddie bring the dead mouse to school for show-and-tell.

5. Tookey told the kids at school that he had a goat skull.

6. Tookey invited Eddie to his birthday party.

7. Tookey sometimes told stories that weren't true.

8. Eddie's class won the button for having the best George Washington Show.

9. Tookey did not have any brothers or sisters.

10. Tookey and Eddie were in the same class at school.

11. Eddie loaned Boodles a dollar so that he could buy his mother a canary.

12. Mrs. Andrews said that Tookey had an "upside-down" imagination.

Multiple Choice. Read each question. Decide which statement best answers the question. Mark your answer sheet accordingly.

13. How did Eddie get a rocking horse on Christmas Eve?

    A. He bought it with money he had saved

    B. He won it

    C. He found it

    D. His grandfather gave him one

14. What was Eddie going to do with the rocking horse?

    A. Keep it

    B. Sell it

    C. Give it to little Georgie

    D. Give it to Tookey

111
Snowbound with Betsy
Carolyn Haywood

True or False. Decide whether each statement is true or false. Mark your answer sheet accordingly.

1. Susan and Neddie lived next door to Betsy.

2. Betsy did not have any brothers or sisters.

3. Betsy made Christmas presents for Susan and Neddie.

4. The children found Clementine's red feather hat.

5. The hat that the children found belonged to Mr. Kilpatrick.

6. Mrs. Byrd could not call her husband for several days because the telephones were not working.

7. Susan and Neddie would not play with Betsy and Star.

8. Susan made an angel in the snow for Betsy.

9. When the children went to visit Mr. and Mrs. Jackson, they found that the Jacksons could not open the doors of their house and had to climb in and out the windows.

10. The children used orange peels filled with peanut butter to decorate a tree for the birds.

11. Neddie wanted a cocker spaniel for Christmas.

12. The children couldn't use the electric popcorn popper because there was no electricity.

Multiple Choice. Read each question. Decide which statement best answers the question. Mark your answer sheet accordingly.

13. How did Betsy and Billy each get a little Christmas tree of their own?

    A. The men on the truck gave them each one for helping them

    B. They each bought one with the money they earned helping Mr. Kilpatrick

    C. They were the Christmas gifts that each bought for the other

    D. They found them in a garbage can behind the school

14. Betsy put popcorn in the oven because

    A. She wanted to hide it from Star

    B. She wanted it to dry

    C. She wanted to surprise her mother

    D. None of the above

112
Born to Trot
Marguerite Henry

True or False. Decide whether each statement is true or false. Mark your answer sheet accordingly.

1. At the beginning of the book, Dr. Mills examined Gibson and decided that he needed to rest in the hospital.

2. While Gibson was in the hospital, Gibson's father wrote him letters.

3. Gibson's mother was dead.

4. Gibson asked his father to drive Rosalind in the Hambletonian race.

5. Nobody knew who Rosalind's parents or grandparents were.

6. Rosalind won the Hambletonian race.

7. Dr. Mills gave Gibson a book.

8. Gibson's father was a boxer.

9. After releasing Gibson from the hospital, Dr. Mills told him that he was well enough to drive Rosalind in the Hambletonian race.

10. Gibson drove Rosalind in the Hambletonian race.

11. Gibson's father drove Rosalind in the Hambletonian race.

Multiple Choice. Read each question. Decide which statement best answers the question. Mark your answer sheet accordingly.

12. How did Gibson get Rosalind?

    A. He won Rosalind

    B. He bought Rosalind with money he had saved

    C. His father gave Rosalind to him

    D. He found Rosalind wandering in a field near the hospital

13. What happened to Gibson's book?

    A. It was ruined when Gibson accidentally left it out in the rain

    B. Gibson burned it

    C. The book lady picked it up by mistake

    D. Dr. Mills stole it

14. When Dr. Mills realized that Gibson was not improving, he suggested that Gibson's father

    A. Stop writing letters to Gibson

    B. Try to get Gibson interested in boxing

    C. Fill his letters with news about the horses he was training and breeding

    D. Force Gibson to eat five full meals a day

113
Brighty of the Grand Canyon
Marguerite Henry

True or False. Decide whether each statement is true or false. Mark your answer sheet accordingly.

1. Old Timer had always been kind to Brighty.

2. Jake Irons was always kind to Brighty.

3. Uncle Jimmy never found out who murdered Old Timer.

4. Uncle Jimmy was always kind to Brighty.

5. Uncle Jimmy and President Roosevelt were friends.

6. Uncle Jimmy could not get Brighty to walk across the bridge.

7. Jake Irons stole Old Timer's gold watch.

8. Jake Irons murdered Old Timer.

9. President Roosevelt gave Uncle Jimmy a rifle.

10. Brighty died at the end of the book.

Multiple Choice. Read each question. Decide which statement best answers the question. Mark your answer sheet accordingly.

11. What did Old Timer want to do with the money he hoped to earn?

    A. He wanted to buy a house for himself and Brighty

    B. He wanted to buy a rifle for Uncle Jimmy

    C. He wanted to buy his niece, Mimi, a wheelchair

    D. He wanted to buy himself a gold watch

12. How did Uncle Jimmy get Brighty to take some cough medicine?

    A. He put the medicine inside a carrot

    B. He poured it in Brighty's ear when Brighty was sleeping

    C. He tied Brighty up and forced the medicine into his mouth

    D. None of the above

13. President Roosevelt wanted Uncle Jimmy to

    A. Kill Brighty

    B. Be the first man to walk across the new bridge

    C. Capture Brighty and put him in a zoo

    D. Come and live in the White House with him

14. Uncle Jimmy was a(n)

    A. Lion hunter

    B. Schoolteacher

    C. Witch doctor

    D. Animal hater

From *Quizzes for 220 Great Children's Books*, revised 1st edition. © 1996. Teacher Ideas Press. (800) 237-6124.

114
Justin Morgan Had a Horse
Marguerite Henry

True or False. Decide whether each statement is true or false. Mark your answer sheet accordingly.

1. Joel's father bought Little Bub as a gift for Joel.
2. Farmer Beane gave Ebenezer to Justin Morgan to pay off a debt.
3. Justin Morgan asked Joel to "gentle" Little Bub for him.
4. Joel became an apprentice to Mister Chase at Chase's Inn.
5. Joel became an apprentice to Justin Morgan.
6. Mister Chase was not married.
7. Justin Morgan sold Little Bub to Joel for $5.
8. Justin Morgan gave Little Bub to the family who had cared for him during his long illness.
9. Justin Morgan was Joel's father.
10. After Justin Morgan died, his name was given to Little Bub.
11. Joel told the men in the inn that he did not know who Little Bub's father was.
12. Justin Morgan was a farmer.
13. Justin Morgan was a schoolmaster.

Multiple Choice. Read the question. Decide which statement best answers the question. Mark your answer sheet accordingly.

14. The day that Little Bub was to race, Joel brought something in a satchel. When Justin Morgan asked Joel what was in the satchel, Joel would only say, "It's a surprise." What was Joel carrying in the satchel?

    A. Sugar cubes for Little Bub

    B. An apple for Little Bub

    C. A rabbit

    D. A dog

115
King of the Wind
Marguerite Henry

True or False. Decide whether each statement is true or false. Mark your answer sheet accordingly.

1. The constable at Newgate Jail destroyed Sham's pedigree.

2. The constable at Newgate Jail decided not to jail Agba because he thought that Agba was the king's nephew.

3. When Agba was sent to Wicken Fen, he was not allowed to bring Sham with him.

4. When Mister Twickerham came to get Agba from Wicken Fen, Agba told him that Sham was dead.

5. Sham was not allowed to run in the races at Newmarket.

6. One of Sham's sons was awarded the Queen's Plate for winning the race at Newmarket.

7. Sham died before he could see his sons race at Newmarket.

8. Agba was not allowed to attend the races at Newmarket.

9. Agba couldn't talk.

10. Agba was put in jail on the charge of horse theft.

11. When Agba was in jail, he was allowed to keep the cat Grimalkin with him as a companion.

Multiple Choice. Read each question. Decide which statement best answers the question. Mark your answer sheet accordingly.

12. How did Agba feed Sham after Sham's mother died?

    A. An Arab gave him camel's milk, which Agba fed to Sham

    B. Agba milked Signor Achmet's cow and gave the milk to Sham

    C. Each day, Agba went to town and stole a quart of milk from the grocer

    D. None of the above

13. What gift did the sultan send to Louis XV, the boy-king of France?

    A. His daughter

    B. A large treasure chest full of toys and games

    C. The heads of six of Signor Achmet's horse boys

    D. Six of Signor Achmet's best horses

14. Why was Agba sent to Wicken Fen?

    A. He had allowed Sham to fight Hobgoblin, the earl's favorite stallion

    B. He had killed Hobgoblin, the earl's favorite stallion

    C. He had failed to keep Hobgoblin's stall clean

    D. None of the above

116
Misty of Chincoteague
Marguerite Henry

True or False. Decide whether each statement is true or false. Mark your answer sheet accordingly.

1. Paul and Maureen lived with their grandparents.

2. Paul and Maureen lived with their aunt and uncle.

3. Paul's grandfather had to shoot Misty because Misty had a broken leg.

4. Maureen did not know how to ride a horse.

5. Paul brought in Phantom and Misty the day of the roundup.

6. Grandpa did not ride with Paul on the roundup.

7. When Phantom raced against Black Comet, Paul rode her.

8. Phantom won the race on Pony Penning Day.

9. The night of the storm, Paul slept in his grandfather's truck.

10. At the end of the book, Paul gave Phantom her freedom and let her go back to the island of Assateague.

11. At the end of the book, Paul gave Misty her freedom and let her go back to the island of Assateague.

Multiple Choice. Read each question. Decide which statement best answers the question. Mark your answer sheet accordingly.

12. How did Paul and Maureen come to own Phantom and Misty?

    A. Their grandparents bought the horses for them

    B. Their parents sent them enough money to buy the horses

    C. They worked to earn enough money to buy the horses themselves

    D. They won the horses in a raffle on Pony Penning Day

13. Who was the Pied Piper?

    A. A horse

    B. A man

    C. A woman

    D. A cow

14. The man who was going to buy Phantom and Misty backed out because

    A. He heard that Phantom had a broken leg

    B. He tried to ride Misty, and Misty threw him

    C. His barn burned down, and he didn't have a place to keep the horses

    D. His son won the sorrel colt and liked it better than Misty

---

117
Mustang, Wild Spirit of the West
Marguerite Henry

True or False. Decide whether each statement is true or false. Mark your answer sheet accordingly.

1. Annie's little brother died of polio.

2. Annie went to Washington to speak before the judiciary committee about saving the mustangs.

3. Charley, Annie's husband, did not agree that the mustangs should be saved.

4. Charley and Annie wrote letters to schoolchildren telling what was happening to the mustangs and asking them to write letters to their representatives in congress.

5. Annie's bill was never passed.

6. Annie was never able to get any pictures of what was happening to the mustangs.

7. Annie did not go to Washington because Charley needed her at home.

8. To make extra money, Annie and Charley decided to sell their horses.

9. To make extra money, Annie and Charley decided to have a weekend dude ranch for children.

10. Annie's father often called her "Pardner."

11. Large numbers of wild horses were rounded up and slaughtered to make pet food.

12. Large numbers of wild horses were rounded up and slaughtered because it was thought that they were bad luck.

Multiple Choice. Read each question. Decide which statement best answers the question. Mark your answer sheet accordingly.

13. When Annie's father was a baby, he

    A. Was kidnapped by a band of Indians

    B. Was fed the milk of a mustang

    C. Never cried

    D. Was sold to a group of gypsies

14. When Annie's cast was removed, she discovered that

    A. She could not move her arms

    B. She could not walk

    C. The two sides of her face did not match

    D. Her skin had turned yellow

118
Stormy, Misty's Foal
Marguerite Henry

True or False. Decide whether each statement is true or false. Mark your answer sheet accordingly.

1. Many of the wild ponies on Assateague died during the storm.

2. Grandma would not ride in the helicopter.

3. The State Department of Health said that no women or children could return to Chincoteague until all the dead animals had been removed.

4. Maureen became sick with typhoid.

5. Grandpa smuggled Grandma and Maureen back home.

6. Misty gave birth to Stormy before the storm hit.

7. Misty gave birth to Stormy in Grandma's kitchen.

8. Misty gave birth to Stormy at an animal hospital.

9. Paul and Maureen were with Misty when she gave birth to Stormy.

10. Both Paul and Grandpa volunteered to fly back to Chincoteague each day to help clean up the island and repair the causeway.

11. To raise money, Paul and Maureen agreed to allow Misty and Stormy to make appearances at theaters.

Multiple Choice. Read each question. Decide which statement best answers the question. Mark your answer sheet accordingly.

12. When the electricity went out, Paul helped Mr. Terry by
    A. Pumping his bed
    B. Bringing him a supply of candles
    C. Helping him pack his family's food in snow
    D. Chopping wood for his fire

13. Grandpa told Paul that until the tide ebbed, Misty would stay
    A. At the schoolhouse
    B. In Grandma's kitchen
    C. On Assateague Island
    D. In their attic

14. What did the Beebes bring with them to the mainland?
    A. A ham
    B. Grandma's kitchen table
    C. Misty
    D. Stormy

From *Quizzes for 220 Great Children's Books*, revised 1st edition. © 1996. Teacher Ideas Press. (800) 237-6124.

119
Across Five Aprils
Irene Hunt

True or False. Decide whether each statement is true or false. Mark your answer sheet accordingly.

1. Jethro's cousin, Eb, deserted from the Union Army.

2. President Lincoln wrote Jethro a letter.

3. None of Jethro's brothers survived the war.

4. Jethro's mother did not know how to read.

5. Matthew Creighton had a heart attack and died.

6. The Creightons' barn was burned.

7. Jethro served as a drummer boy for the Union Army.

8. Jenny married Shadrach Yale.

9. Shadrach Yale was a local schoolteacher.

10. Jethro's brother Tom was killed at the Battle of Pittsburgh Landing.

Multiple Choice. Read each question. Decide which statement best answers the question. Mark your answer sheet accordingly.

11. When Jethro and his brothers first heard that the Civil War had started, they were

    A. Excited and happy

    B. Sad and depressed

    C. Worried about the future

    D. Fearful that their farm would be burned

12. Several months after the war started, Jethro's brother Bill decided to

    A. Join the Union Army like his brothers had done

    B. Leave home and fight for the South

    C. Go to Canada to avoid the draft

    D. Stay home and help Jethro with the farm

13. Why did Mr. Creighton let his daughter Jenny go to Washington, D.C.?

    A. Shadrach Yale had been wounded and was near death

    B. She wanted to be a nurse

    C. She had been hired as a personal servant to Mrs. Lincoln

    D. He sent her there so that she would be safe

14. Some of Mr. Creighton's neighbors were angry with him because

    A. He predicted that the South would win

    B. He was hiding runaway slaves

    C. He said bad things about President Lincoln

    D. He would not say bad things about his son, Bill

120
Up a Road Slowly
Irene Hunt

True or False. Decide whether each statement is true or false. Mark your answer sheet accordingly.

1. Aunt Cordelia taught school for many years.

2. Aunt Cordelia had never been married.

3. Uncle Haskell wrote and published many books.

4. Uncle Haskell often told lies.

5. Julie was pleased when Jonathon Eltwing told her that she looked just like her Aunt Cordelia.

6. Aunt Cordelia did not want Julie to invite Aggie to her birthday party.

7. Julie did not go to live with her father and Alicia the year before she entered high school as was originally planned.

8. Aunt Cordelia had once been in love with Jonathon Eltwing.

9. Julie had two sisters and no brothers.

10. Brett Kingsman needed help in the subject of geometry.

11. The first time that Julie went to visit Laura, she was envious of Laura's husband, Bill.

Multiple Choice. Read each question. Decide which statement best answers the question. Mark your answer sheet accordingly.

12. Which of the following people did NOT die in this book?

    A. Aunt Cordelia

    B. Aggie

    C. Julie's mother

    D. Uncle Haskell

13. Who was the first person Julie told about her desire to write?

    A. Laura

    B. Uncle Haskell

    C. Aunt Cordelia

    D. Her father

14. Who was the only person besides her husband that Jonathon Eltwing's wife would let touch her?

    A. Julie

    B. Aunt Cordelia

    C. Uncle Haskell

    D. Laura

121
Our Eddie
Sulamith Ish-Kishor

True or False. Decide whether each statement is true or false. Mark your answer sheet accordingly.

1. Eddie wanted to become a Hebrew teacher when he grew up.

2. Eddie wanted to become a medical researcher.

3. Uncle Mark lived in the United States.

4. Uncle Mark and Aunt Sara did not have any children of their own.

5. Mr. Raphel turned down a job that would pay him a higher salary.

6. Mr. Raphel went to the United States because his doctor said that he needed a complete change.

7. Mr. Raphel went to the United States because he hoped to become rich there.

8. Mr. Raphel did not believe in spanking his children.

9. Eddie was fired from one of his jobs because he had stolen some things.

10. Sybil did not attend school in the United States.

11. It was Hal's mother who told him that Eddie had died.

Multiple Choice. Read each question. Decide which statement best answers the question. Mark your answer sheet accordingly.

12. What kind of accident did Eddie have?

     A. He was involved in a car accident

     B. He fell down a flight of stairs

     C. He was hit with a bat during a baseball game

     D. He fell through thin ice when he was skating

13. What did Mr. Raphel do for a living?

     A. He was a dentist

     B. He was a reporter

     C. He was a teacher

     D. He was a truck driver

14. Mr. Raphel came home from work one day because he had been told that one of his children was lost. Which child had been lost?

     A. Lilie

     B. Eddie

     C. Sybil

     D. Thad

122
The Trumpeter of Krakow
Eric P. Kelly

True or False. Decide whether each statement is true or false. Mark your answer sheet accordingly.

1. Tring wanted Nicholas Kreutz to turn brass into gold.

2. Tring was an agent of Peter-of-the-Button-Face.

3. Kreutz stole the Great Tarnov Crystal during Peter's raid.

4. Ivan of Moscow promised to give the Tarnov Crystal to the Tartars if they would attack the Poles in the Ukraine.

5. The king banished Peter and Tring for burning down Krakow.

6. Joseph was in charge of guarding the crystal when his family lived in the Ukraine.

7. The king hid the crystal deep in his vaults to keep it from the Tartars.

8. Andrew Charnetski hid his treasure in a pumpkin.

9. Andrew Charnetski was going to Krakow because he wanted to visit some friends.

10. Nicholas Kreutz, the man who gave the Charnetskis a place to stay, was a cossack agent.

11. Jan Kanty found Andrew Charnetski a job.

Multiple Choice. Read each question. Decide which statement best answers the question. Mark your answer sheet accordingly.

12. What was unusual about the Heynal that was played from the Church of Our Lady Mary?

    A. It was only played on a solid gold trumpet

    B. It had to be played three times a day

    C. A and B

    D. It was never finished by the trumpeter

13. Button-Face Peter's raid on the Charnetski home was

    A. A failure because Joseph heard them coming

    B. Disrupted by Nicholas Kreutz using fire and light

    C. The cause of the fire that swept through Krakow

    D. All of the above

14. Joseph was able to warn Elzbietka of Peter's next attack by

    A. Finishing the Heynal

    B. Ringing a church bell

    C. Sending a message on the collar of his dog

    D. None of the above

123
Father's Arcane Daughter
E. L. Konigsburg

True or False. Decide whether each statement is true or false. Mark your answer sheet accordingly.

1. Winston's family was very wealthy.

2. Winston did not go to school, but was taught at home by a tutor.

3. Heidi had trouble hearing.

4. Bunny thought that Heidi was just as intelligent as Winston.

5. Bunny did not have any children of her own.

6. Sometimes Winston felt jealous of Heidi.

7. When Caroline went shopping for a dress, she took Winston with her.

8. On Saturdays, Winston and Heidi took piano lessons.

9. Shortly after the papers were signed, Caroline moved into an apartment of her own.

10. Heidi had a habit of sucking her thumb.

11. Caroline decided to go back to college to enroll in the agriculture program and learn more about farming.

Multiple Choice. Read each question. Decide which statement best answers the question. Mark your answer sheet accordingly.

12. Bunny Waldheim wanted Heidi to stay with her for a whole day so that she could

    A. Find out about Caroline

    B. Do some testing on Heidi

    C. Talk Heidi into coming to live with her

    D. Teach Heidi how to knit

13. Caroline gave Winston an envelope that contained

    A. A check for $20,000

    B. Evidence that established whether or not she was really Caroline Adkins Carmichael

    C. A copy of Winston's father's will

    D. A picture of Caroline when she was a little girl

14. At the beginning of each chapter, there is a short dialogue between two people. At the end of the book, the reader realizes that this dialogue is between

    A. Heidi and Caroline

    B. Winston and Caroline

    C. Winston and Heidi

    D. Winston and his father

124
From the Mixed-Up Files of Mrs. Basil E. Frankweiler
E. L. Konigsburg

True or False. Decide whether each statement is true or false. Mark your answer sheet accordingly.

1. Claudia decided that while they were at the museum, she and Jamie should try to learn as much about it as they could.
2. Jamie and Claudia took a bath in the fountain of the museum restaurant.
3. Jamie and Claudia found more than $500 in the fountain.
4. Jamie and Claudia called their parents every night during their stay at the museum.
5. There were no night watchmen at the museum.
6. The postman refused to rent a post office box to Jamie and Claudia because they were too young.
7. Claudia was much younger than Jamie.
8. Mrs. Frankweiler had several children of her own.
9. Mrs. Frankweiler was very poor.
10. Jamie and Claudia never told Mrs. Frankweiler the secret of where they had been hiding.
11. Mrs. Frankweiler hid in the museum with Jamie and Claudia and slept in the antique bed.
12. Saxonberg was the children's grandfather.

Multiple Choice. Read each question. Decide which statement best answers the question. Mark your answer sheet accordingly.

13. Why did Claudia take Jamie with her when she ran away from home?
    A. Jamie was old enough to drive a car
    B. Jamie had money and knew how to be careful with it
    C. Jamie had magical powers
    D. None of the above

14. One night, inside of the museum, Jamie and Claudia
    A. Ordered pizza just before midnight
    B. Met some other kids who had been hiding in the museum for months
    C. Used a magic powder to make themselves invisible
    D. None of the above

125
Jennifer, Hectate, Macbeth, William McKinley and Me, Elizabeth
E. L. Konigsburg

True or False. Decide whether each statement is true or false. Mark your answer sheet accordingly.

1. Elizabeth did not have any brothers or sisters.

2. Elizabeth and her family lived in an apartment building.

3. Cynthia dressed up as a pilgrim for Halloween.

4. Most adults liked Cynthia.

5. Jennifer loved to be called "Jenny" instead of Jennifer.

6. Jennifer was shorter than Elizabeth.

7. Elizabeth's parents went to a party on New Year's Eve.

8. Elizabeth was never promoted from an apprentice witch to a journeyman witch.

9. Elizabeth was in the third grade.

10. Elizabeth and Jennifer were in the same class at school.

11. Elizabeth did not go to Cynthia's birthday party.

12. Hilary Ezra was Jennifer's cat.

Multiple Choice. Read each question. Decide which statement best answers the question. Mark your answer sheet accordingly.

13. Elizabeth was chosen to play which part in the Christmas play?

    A. The little puppy

    B. The beautiful princess

    C. A lady-in-waiting

    D. None of the above

14. What was Elizabeth's "forbidden food" at Christmas?

    A. Watermelon

    B. Candy

    C. Eggs

    D. Milk

126
And Now Miguel
Joseph Krumgold

True or False. Decide whether each statement is true or false. Mark your answer sheet accordingly.

1. Miguel did not have any brothers or sisters.

2. Miguel found the lost sheep.

3. Miguel was not able to find the lost sheep.

4. Miguel's father was a criminal.

5. Miguel was given the job of branding the sheep.

6. Miguel did not go to school as he was told to do because he wanted to look for the lost sheep.

7. Miguel liked to be asked to help the men work with the sheep.

8. Miguel fell into a bag of wool that he was sacking.

9. Miguel died at the end of the book.

10. At the end of the book, Miguel went with the men into the mountains of the Sangre de Cristo.

11. At the end of the book, it was decided that Miguel would not go with the men into the mountains of the Sangre de Cristo.

Multiple Choice. Read each question. Decide which statement best answers the question. Mark your answer sheet accordingly.

12. Miguel's wish was to

 A. Go up into the mountains of the Sangre de Cristo

 B. Have a bedroom of his own

 C. Join the army and become a soldier

 D. Have a horse of his own

13. Miguel told Pedro and Faustina that

 A. His parents were building an extra room onto the house

 B. He was dying

 C. He had a plan

 D. His Uncle Deet had asked him to come live with him

14. Miguel's father received a letter telling him that

 A. Miguel's grandfather had died

 B. Miguel's brother had been put in jail

 C. Miguel's brother had to go and be a soldier

 D. Miguel's school had been burned down

127
Onion John
Joseph Krumgold

True or False. Decide whether each statement is true or false. Mark your answer sheet accordingly.

1. Andy's father worked in a hardware store.

2. Andy did not have any brothers or sisters.

3. Onion John's new house took two weeks to build.

4. The Serenity newspaper printed that Andy's father was Onion John's closest friend in town.

5. Onion John suffered a punctured lung when his house collapsed.

6. Onion John never cried in public.

7. Andy did not have any friends his own age.

8. Onion John got most of the things he wore from funerals.

9. Andy's father refused to help build the house on Onion John Day.

10. Andy's father was a member of the Rotary Club.

11. Onion John came back to Serenity for the fish drive.

12. Andy agreed that Onion John should fumigate the town of Serenity to get rid of all the evil spirits.

13. Most of the people who lived in Serenity did not like Onion John.

Multiple Choice. Read the question. Decide which statement best answers the question. Mark your answer sheet accordingly.

14. Andy wanted to run away because

    A. He didn't want to go to General Magneto

    B. Andy's father wouldn't let him be friends with Onion John

    C. He wanted to grow up to be just like Onion John

    D. The kids at school made fun of him because of his friendship with Onion John

128
Beyond the Divide
Kathryn Lasky

True or False. Decide whether each statement is true or false. Mark your answer sheet accordingly.

1. Serena married Mr. Wickham.

2. Serena and Meribah had been friends.

3. Meribah shot and killed Mr. and Mrs. Whiting.

4. Meribah liked to draw.

5. Mr. Billings tried to kill Mr. Wickham when he found out what had happened to Serena.

6. Meribah's father died.

7. Mr. Goodnough never came back to help Meribah as he had promised.

8. Mr. Goodnough's friend stole his boots.

9. Mr. Goodnough's friend never came back to rescue Mr. Goodnough, Meribah, and Will.

10. Meribah's father left his family because he was being shunned by them and by the church.

11. Meribah's father left his family because he was tired of being a farmer.

Multiple Choice. Read each question. Decide which statement best answers the question. Mark your answer sheet accordingly.

12. How did most people in the company feel about what happened to Serena?

    A. They were furious and wanted to kill the men who had done it

    B. They didn't believe that anything had happened to Serena

    C. They all felt sorry for Serena and tried to be especially kind to her

    D. They ignored Serena and felt that she deserved what had happened to her

13. What did Meribah and Mr. Goodnough have in common?

    A. They were both Amish

    B. They both liked to draw

    C. They were both blind

    D. They had both been bitten by a rattlesnake

14. The company abandoned Meribah and her father because

    A. Their wagon was broken

    B. Will was very sick

    C. A and B

    D. None of the above

129
Carry On, Mr. Bowditch
Jean Lee Latham

True or False. Decide whether each statement is true or false. Mark your answer sheet accordingly.

1. Nat was with his wife, Elizabeth, when she died.

2. Nat remarried after his wife died.

3. Nat never remarried after his wife died.

4. Nat attended Harvard College for four years.

5. When Ropes and Hodges sold the chandlery, they released Nat from his indenture.

6. Nat taught himself Latin.

7. Nat learned how to speak French.

8. Nat found so many errors in the tables of Moore's book of navigation that he decided to write his own book.

9. Nat could not find any errors in the tables of Moore's book of navigation.

10. Elizabeth's mother blamed Nat for Elizabeth's death.

11. Polly and Elizabeth had never met.

Multiple Choice. Read each question. Decide which statement best answers the question. Mark your answer sheet accordingly.

12. Mary was worried about marrying David because

    A. David was very poor

    B. David came from a wealthy family

    C. David was a sailor

    D. David was blind

13. How long was Nat indentured?

    A. One year

    B. One month

    C. Two years

    D. Nine years

14. In what cargo did Nat choose to invest $135?

    A. Wine

    B. Boots and shoes

    C. Dresses and skirts

    D. Gold and silver

130
Ben and Me
Robert Lawson

True or False. Decide whether each statement is true or false. Mark your answer sheet accordingly.

1. Amos did not have any brothers or sisters.

2. Amos enjoyed helping Ben with his lightning rod experiments.

3. Ben wore his fur hat wherever he went.

4. Ben never found out about the changes Amos made in *Poor Richard's Almanack*.

5. Amos married Sophia, the beautiful white mouse.

6. Sophia, the beautiful white mouse, was already married.

7. According to this book, the Declaration of Independence was really written by a mouse and copied by Ben Franklin.

8. Red was a timid mouse who did not want anything to do with the war that Amos was planning.

9. Amos lived in Ben Franklin's cap.

10. On Ben's 81st birthday, Amos gave him a new fur hat.

11. Ben went to France because he wanted to raise money for the War of Independence.

Multiple Choice. Read each question. Decide which statement best answers the question. Mark your answer sheet accordingly.

12. In return for Amos's advice, aid, and assistance, Ben agreed to

    A. Deliver food to Amos's family

    B. Allow Amos to live in his fur cap

    C. A and B

    D. None of the above

13. Ben Franklin was interested in

    A. Printing

    B. Electricity

    C. Lightning rods

    D. All of the above

14. How did Amos help Sophia, the beautiful white mouse?

    A. He rescued her children

    B. He brought her some food

    C. He taught her to read

    D. He married her

131
Rabbit Hill
Robert Lawson

True or False. Decide whether each statement is true or false. Mark your answer sheet accordingly.

1. Uncle Analdas did not know how to read.

2. The New Folks had a cat.

3. Little Georgie's parents died when he was very young.

4. The New Folks put a high barbed wire fence all around their garden.

5. The New Folks did not like animals.

6. Little Georgie was hit by a car and killed.

7. The man at the house smoked a pipe.

8. Little Georgie was caught in a trap set out by the New Folks.

9. Uncle Analdas died after eating poisoned vegetables set out by the New Folks.

10. Willie Fieldmouse drowned in a barrel of rainwater.

11. Uncle Analdas was quite elderly.

12. The New Folks set out traps and poison to try and kill the animals.

Multiple Choice. Read each question. Decide which statement best answers the question. Mark your answer sheet accordingly.

13. Who leaped all the way across Deadman's Brook?

    A. Uncle Analdas

    B. Father

    C. Little Georgie

    D. None of the above

14. The man at the house put up a sign that read

    A. "No Trespassing—Private Property"

    B. "Please Drive Carefully—Children at Play"

    C. "Warning—Guard Dog Is Vicious Towards Small Animals"

    D. "Please Drive Carefully on Account of Small Animals"

132
Robbut
Robert Lawson

True or False. Decide whether each statement is true or false. Mark your answer sheet accordingly.

1. At the beginning of the book, Robbut was unhappy because he didn't like his tail.

2. When Robbut saw that the little man was caught in a trap, he laughed and said that he hoped the little man would never get free.

3. When Robbut saw that the little man was caught in a trap, he helped the man get out.

4. The little man agreed to give Robbut a new tail if Robbut would be his servant for the rest of his life.

5. The little man told Robbut that if he did not like his new tail, he could always come back and get a different one.

6. Robbut's father paid the little man $50 to give Robbut a new tail.

7. When Robbut's father saw Robbut's new snake tail, he was very happy and proud of Robbut.

8. When Robbut's father saw Robbut's new snake tail, he was very upset and told Robbut to go away.

9. When Robbut had the tail of a fox, he was chased by a pack of hounds.

10. When Robbut had the tail of a cat, the boy caught him and took him home to keep as a pet.

11. When Robbut had the tail of a cat, the boy threw stones at him.

12. At the end of the book, Robbut's father was shot and killed by a hunter.

13. At the end of the book, Robbut decided that he liked his own tail the best.

Multiple Choice. Read the question. Decide which statement best answers the question. Mark your answer sheet accordingly.

14. Sometimes the little man would hang a sign on his door that said

    A. "Napping—Do Not Disturb"

    B. "Gone Hunting—Be Back Next Month"

    C. "No Trespassing"

    D. "No Rabbits Welcome Here"

133
The Tough Winter
Robert Lawson

True or False. Decide whether each statement is true or false. Mark your answer sheet accordingly.

1. Uncle Analdas warned all the animals that it was going to be a tough winter.

2. Porkey did not see his shadow on Groundhog Day.

3. Willie Fieldmouse came to live with Little Georgie and his family for the winter.

4. The Little Animals on the Hill all liked the Caretaker's dog.

5. Mother was happy when she heard that the Folks at the Big House were going away for the winter.

6. Mother went to live with the Caretaker in the Big House.

7. Many of the Little Animals left the Hill for the winter because there was not enough food.

8. The Folks never returned to the Hill because they liked the Bluegrass Region so much that they decided to live there all year round.

9. Uncle Analdas walked all the way to the Bluegrass Region.

10. Tim McGrath accidentally shot Uncle Analdas.

11. Mr. Muldoon, the cat, tried to eat Willie Fieldmouse.

Multiple Choice. Read each question. Decide which statement best answers the question. Mark your answer sheet accordingly.

12. The Caretaker

    A. Set out food for the Little Animals every night

    B. Tried to shoot Father

    C. Caught Willie Fieldmouse and kept him in a cage

    D. Became very sick and died

13. Father talked a lot about

    A. The Bluegrass Region where he grew up

    B. His grandmother

    C. How hard times were during the war

    D. How well-behaved his brothers and sisters were

14. During the tough winter, there was even less food on the Hill to eat because

    A. There was a tornado

    B. The Caretaker poisoned many of the plants and trees

    C. There was a fire

    D. All of the above

From *Quizzes for 220 Great Children's Books*, revised 1st edition. © 1996. Teacher Ideas Press. (800) 237-6124.

134
A Swiftly Tilting Planet
Madeleine L'Engle

True or False. Decide whether each statement is true or false. Mark your answer sheet accordingly.

1. Gaudior, the unicorn, tried to kill Charles Wallace.

2. After Chuck and Beezie's father died, their mother remarried.

3. Chuck was sent to an institution.

4. Charles Wallace was not able to go within Chuck.

5. The projection was a possible future that the Echthroi wanted to make real.

6. Chuck was Mrs. O'Keefe's brother.

7. On Thanksgiving Day, Meg's father received a call from the president of the United States.

8. At the Thanksgiving dinner, Mrs. O'Keefe called Charles Wallace "Chuck."

9. Pastor Mormain accused Zylle of being a witch.

10. The Echthroi tried to pull Charles Wallace from Gaudior's back.

11. At the end of the book, Gaudior died.

Multiple Choice. Read each question. Decide which statement best answers the question. Mark your answer sheet accordingly.

12. Gaudior told Charles Wallace that he had been called to

    A. Die for the good of his country

    B. Join forces with the Echthroi

    C. Free Madog Branzillo from prison

    D. Find a Might-Have-Been by being sent Within

13. When Gaudior saw that Charles Wallace was badly injured, he decided to

    A. Take Charles Wallace to Gaudior's home

    B. Kill Charles Wallace

    C. Send Charles Wallace back to his own home

    D. Choose another person to accomplish the mission

14. Why did Mrs. O'Keefe call the Murrys in the middle of the night?

    A. She wanted to warn them that Charles Wallace had been captured by the Echthroi

    B. She fell down the stairs and twisted her ankle

    C. She had a letter that she wanted to show them

    D. She thought that she was having a heart attack

135
A Wind in the Door
Madeleine L'Engle

True or False. Decide whether each statement is true or false. Mark your answer sheet accordingly.

1. Charles told Meg that there was a dragon in the garden.

2. Meg was rescued from an Echthros by many little farandolae.

3. The Echthros wanted to keep the farandolae from Deepening.

4. Senex did not want the farandolae to Deepen.

5. Proginoskes Xed himself to save Meg from the Echthros.

6. Proginoskes knew the names of all the stars.

7. Hoping to save Calvin, Mr. Jenkins Xed himself.

8. The creature that Charles Wallace saw was really a cherubim.

9. The Echthroi were evil, destructive spirits.

10. Farandolae lived inside mitochondria.

Multiple Choice. Read each question. Decide which statement best answers the question. Mark your answer sheet accordingly.

11. The teacher, Blajeny, told Meg that

    A. Proginoskes would go to school with Meg

    B. They must try to help Charles Wallace

    C. She must pass three tests

    D. All of the above

12. When Meg got to school, she found that

    A. Charles Wallace had run away

    B. There were three Mr. Jenkinses

    C. The Echthroi were attacking

    D. None of the above

13. If Meg failed in her first test, Proginoskes would have to

    A. Either join the Echthroi or X himself

    B. Leave Earth and never return

    C. Kill Charles Wallace

    D. Become a farandola

14. Louise the Larger was

    A. A snake

    B. A teacher

    C. A and B

    D. None of the above

136
A Wrinkle in Time
Madeleine L'Engle

True or False. Decide whether each statement is true or false. Mark your answer sheet accordingly.

1. Calvin was Meg's oldest brother.

2. Charles Wallace was younger than Meg.

3. Meg did not do well in school.

4. Meg's mother never graduated from high school.

5. Meg's father died when she was very young.

6. Calvin did not have any brothers or sisters.

7. Meg's twin brothers, Sandy and Dennys, did not go to Camazotz.

8. Aunt Beast was kind to Meg.

9. Aunt Beast tried to kill Meg.

10. When the man with the red eyes served the children a turkey dinner, Charles Wallace thought the food was delicious.

11. Mrs. Whatsit said that the danger on Camazotz would be the greatest for Charles Wallace.

12. Meg decided not to return to Camazotz to save Charles Wallace.

Multiple Choice. Read each question. Decide which statement best answers the question. Mark your answer sheet accordingly.

13. What was IT?

    A. An eye

    B. A brain

    C. A heart

    D. A machine

14. What did Meg have that IT did not?

    A. Hate

    B. Pride

    C. Love

    D. Anger

137
Strawberry Girl
Lois Lenski

True or False. Decide whether each statement is true or false. Mark your answer sheet accordingly.

1. Birdie never went to school a day in her life.

2. Birdie and her family were Yankees.

3. Birdie was the only child in the Boyer family.

4. The Slater family was very wealthy.

5. The Boyer family drove more than 100 miles to go to a dentist.

6. Mr. Boyer put barbed wire fence around his land.

7. Mr. Slater cut Mr. Boyer's first barbed wire fence with a pair of pliers.

8. Birdie caught a rabbit and gave it to Shoestring for his pet snake.

9. Mr. Boyer whipped Shoestring for refusing to obey him.

10. When there was a grass fire near the Boyer's house, the Slater family helped the Boyers put it out.

11. Mr. Slater shot all the heads off his wife's chickens.

12. Two of Birdie's sisters were killed in the grass fire.

13. Mrs. Boyer never met Mrs. Slater.

14. Mr. and Mrs. Slater did not have any children of their own.

138
The Horse and His Boy
C. S. Lewis

True or False. Decide whether each statement is true or false. Mark your answer sheet accordingly.

1. Shasta lived with a fisherman in Calormen.

2. Shasta discovered that the fisherman wasn't his real father.

3. Shasta sold Bree to raise money so that he could run away.

4. Bree and Shasta killed a Tarkaan before they fled to Narnia.

5. Aravis and Hwin were talking dogs from Narnia.

6. Aravis, Hwin, Bree, and Shasta were all thrown into jail in the city of Tashbaan.

7. Shasta was mistaken for Corin by the kings and queens of Narnia.

8. Shasta was protected by Aslan when he spent a night at the tombs.

9. Shasta and his friends were chased by Aslan when they traveled to Archenland.

10. At the end of the story, Shasta and Aravis got married.

Multiple Choice. Read each question. Decide which statement best answers the question. Mark your answer sheet accordingly.

11. Why did Prince Rabadash want to raid Narnia?

    A. He wanted to capture Queen Susan and force her to marry him

    B. He was fleeing his evil father

    C. He was a servant of the White Witch

    D. He wanted to kill Aslan and rule the whole world

12. How was King Lune warned about Prince Rabadash's raid?

    A. Bree yelled a warning

    B. Shasta ran ahead and found him

    C. A talking eagle warned him

    D. Aslan told him

13. Aslan told Shasta that

    A. He had been guiding and protecting him

    B. He should fear the great evil of Tash

    C. He must return to Tashbaan to fight the king

    D. He should watch out for giants that wore caps

14. What did Aslan do to Prince Rabadash?

    A. He killed him

    B. He turned him into a donkey

    C. He made him serve Narnia for 12 years

    D. He forgave him and let him go

139
The Last Battle
C. S. Lewis

True or False. Decide whether each statement is true or false. Mark your answer sheet accordingly.

1. Shift, the ape, told Puzzle to wear a lion skin.

2. Shift told the Narnians that Aslan wanted them to work for the Calormenes.

3. Jewel, the unicorn, told the king to believe the ape.

4. King Tirian raced back to Cair Paravel to raise an army against the Calormenes.

5. Roonwith, the centaur, warned the king that it was not time for Aslan to return.

6. Tirian and Jewel surrendered to the Calormenes.

7. The dwarfs were glad to see Tirian and helped him fight the ape.

8. When Tirian called on Aslan to send help, High King Peter appeared.

9. All of the talking dogs went to the aid of the king.

10. When Tirian, Eustace, and Jill rescued the dwarfs, the dwarfs returned to help the king.

11. After Aslan had High King Peter close the stable door, Tirian, Eustace, and Jill met all the heroes and famous citizens of Narnia.

Multiple Choice. Read each question. Decide which statement best answers the question. Mark your answer sheet accordingly.

12. The ape told the animals that

    A. Aslan was never going to come back

    B. Aslan had made Shift the King of Narnia

    C. Aslan was really an ape, not a lion

    D. Aslan and Tash were the same being

13. During the battle in front of the stable

    A. The Calormenes tried to force the Narnians inside the stable

    B. The dwarfs fought both the king and the Calormenes

    C. Some of the Narnians fought against the king

    D. All of the above

14. When Aslan appeared, he

    A. Brought the world of Narnia to an end

    B. Killed all the Calormenes

    C. Brought all the old kings of Narnia with him to fight

    D. All of the above

140
The Lion, the Witch and the Wardrobe
C. S. Lewis

True or False. Decide whether each statement is true or false. Mark your answer sheet accordingly.

1. Edmund had to die because the life of any traitor belonged to the White Witch.

2. King Peter offered to die in place of Edmund.

3. The White Witch and her army killed Aslan.

4. The White Witch escaped Aslan and went to Cair Paravel.

5. The four children all became kings and queens of Narnia.

6. Aslan came to life after being killed by the White Witch.

7. Lucy married the Prince of Cair Paravel.

8. When Edmund entered Narnia, he was met by the White Witch.

9. When Lucy entered Narnia, she discovered that it was always winter there.

10. The creatures of Narnia knew that Aslan was returning because winter began to end.

11. Edmund learned that the White Witch had turned many of the creatures of Narnia into stone.

Multiple Choice. Read each question. Decide which statement best answers the question. Mark your answer sheet accordingly.

12. The adventures of the four children started when

    A. They were exploring an old cave in southern Wales

    B. They were playing hide-and-seek in the professor's house

    C. Their mother and father sent them on vacation in Cornwall

    D. They were visiting an old castle in London

13. Why didn't the other children believe Lucy when she said that she had been to Narnia?

    A. Lucy had a bad habit of telling lies

    B. When they went to the wardrobe, there was nothing there

    C. They thought that she would have been too afraid to have gone into the cave alone

    D. The White Witch put a spell on them

14. When all four children entered Narnia, they discovered that

    A. The faun had been arrested by the White Witch

    B. The winter was ending in Narnia at last

    C. The White Witch was really a fairy princess

    D. They could never return to their own country

141
The Magician's Nephew
C. S. Lewis

True or False. Decide whether each statement is true or false. Mark your answer sheet accordingly.

1. The witch fell in love with Uncle Andrew.

2. Digory and Polly became the first King and Queen of Narnia.

3. The cabby and his wife were turned into stone by the witch.

4. The witch Jadis destroyed her entire world.

5. Digory and Polly entered Narnia by using magic rings.

6. The witch tried to get Digory to eat a magic apple.

7. An apple from Narnia made Digory's mother well.

8. When Polly and Digory first used the magic rings, they found themselves in a forest with pools of water.

9. The first world that Polly and Digory entered had no people, and it was filled with ruins.

10. Uncle Andrew and the witch hated Aslan.

11. Aslan sent Digory on a journey with Fledge, the flying horse, to find a tree with magic fruit.

Multiple Choice. Read each question. Decide which statement best answers the question. Mark your answer sheet accordingly.

12. When Digory hit the bell with the hammer
    A. The Queen Jadis was freed from enchantment
    B. Uncle Andrew magically pulled them back to England
    C. All of the ice and snow melted
    D. Elves appeared and the trees started walking

13. When Uncle Andrew, the witch Jadis, Digory, Polly, the cabby, and his horse first arrived in Narnia
    A. They were greeted by Aslan
    B. They were arrested by two dwarfs
    C. The witch turned everyone else into stone
    D. Aslan was just creating Narnia

14. What did the animals of Narnia do with Uncle Andrew?
    A. They killed him in battle
    B. They banished him to the northern mountains
    C. They put him in a jail cell
    D. They planted him in the ground like a tree

142
Prince Caspian
C. S. Lewis

True or False. Decide whether each statement is true or false. Mark your answer sheet accordingly.

1. The two Telmarine Lords did not want King Miraz to fight Peter.

2. Aslan was forced to kill King Miraz to rescue Peter.

3. The Telmarine army panicked and surrendered when Aslan brought all the trees into the battle.

4. Aslan gave the Telmarines a chance to return to the world from which they had originally come.

5. Aslan told Peter and Susan that they would not return to Narnia again.

6. Miraz, King of Narnia, was Prince Caspian's uncle.

7. Miraz, King of Narnia, was an enemy of all Old Narnians.

8. Miraz, King of Narnia, was the man who killed Prince Caspian's father.

9. The Old Narnians decided to kill Caspian.

10. When Aslan first showed himself to Lucy, the others didn't believe her because they didn't see him.

11. Nikabrik wanted to surrender to King Miraz.

Multiple Choice. Read each question. Decide which statement best answers the question. Mark your answer sheet accordingly.

12. Peter, Edmund, Susan, and Lucy had been away from Narnia for one year when
    A. Aslan came for them while they were at school
    B. They were mysteriously pulled from a train station to an island
    C. The White Witch put a spell on Edmund
    D. None of the above

13. Back in Narnia, the children discovered that
    A. Hundreds of Narnian years had passed
    B. Crowds of fauns were waiting for them
    C. An army of hogs and werewolves was waiting for them
    D. The dwarfs had all left

14. When High King Peter joined Caspian's army, he
    A. Ordered an immediate attack
    B. Waited for Aslan to appear
    C. Challenged King Miraz to a duel
    D. None of the above

143
The Silver Chair
C. S. Lewis

True or False. Decide whether each statement is true or false. Mark your answer sheet accordingly.

1. The prince killed the Queen of Underland.

2. Jill was eaten by the Lady of the Green Kirtle.

3. Instead of returning to Narnia, Eustace and Puddleglum decided to go with Golg to the bottom of the world.

4. The owls went with Jill and Eustace to the House of Harfang.

5. The Queen of Underland had killed the prince's mother.

6. Jill accidentally pushed Eustace over a cliff.

7. Jill accidentally turned Eustace into a Marshwiggle.

8. Jill, Eustace, and Puddleglum discovered that the giants of Harfang were planning to eat them at their Autumn Feast.

9. Eustace, Jill, and Puddleglum found the prince at the House of Harfang.

10. Puddleglum was a gnome.

11. Puddleglum was a Marshwiggle.

Multiple Choice. Read each question. Decide which statement best answers the question. Mark your answer sheet accordingly.

12. Aslan told Jill that she and Eustace must

    A. Kill Puddleglum

    B. Find the lost prince

    C. Find the Queen of Narnia

    D. Destroy the enchanted castle

13. How did Jill get to Narnia?

    A. Aslan blew her there

    B. She walked

    C. Puddleglum carried her there

    D. She accidentally fell into Narnia

14. At the end of the book, Eustace and Jill

    A. Were adopted by Aslan

    B. Became King and Queen of Narnia

    C. Went back to Experiment House

    D. Became King and Queen of Underworld

CATEGORY: D
POINT VALUE: 10

144
Voyage of the **Dawn Treader**
C. S. Lewis

True or False. Decide whether each statement is true or false. Mark your answer sheet accordingly.

1. The three sleepers were in an enchanted sleep because they ate the food at Aslan's table.

2. The old man at Aslan's table told Caspian that to break the sleepers' spell, he had to sail to the end of the world and leave someone there.

3. Aslan, in the form of a bird, guided the *Dawn Treader* away from Dark Island.

4. Eustace became seasick when he first came on board the *Dawn Treader*.

5. The voyagers found an island where everything could be turned into gold.

6. Eustace, Lucy, and Edmund entered Narnia through a picture in Lucy's room.

7. When the children and Prince Caspian reached the Lone Islands, they were captured by slavers.

8. Eustace was a good friend to Lucy and Edmund.

9. Eustace hated being in Narnia.

10. On Dragon Island, Eustace slept on a dragon's hoard and turned into a dragon.

11. Reepicheep was a large talking mouse.

Multiple Choice. Read each question. Decide which statement best answers the question. Mark your answer sheet accordingly.

12. King Caspian was sailing in the *Dawn Treader* to
    A. Find new lands for Narnia
    B. Find the end of the world
    C. Find the seven lords exiled by King Miraz
    D. Sail completely around the world

13. The Island of the Voices was unusual because
    A. Its occupants were all invisible
    B. Its occupants were all talking mice
    C. It was a nesting ground for dragons
    D. No one on the island had ever heard of Aslan

14. The Dark Island was a terrifying place because
    A. It was a nesting ground for dragons
    B. All of its occupants were invisible
    C. It was a land where all dreams came true
    D. No one who went there ever returned

145
Astercote
Penelope Lively

True or False. Decide whether each statement is true or false. Mark your answer sheet accordingly.

1. The people of Charlton Underwood wanted to be isolated.

2. Betsy Tranter died of the Black Death.

3. Goacher showed the "Thing" to Peter and Mair.

4. The ghost of King Arthur was often seen in the wood.

5. Goacher left the wood and hid after the "Thing" was stolen.

6. The people of Charlton Underwood rebuilt Astercote.

7. Luke stole the treasure of Astercote.

8. Goacher had matted hair and old, ragged clothes.

9. Animals did not like Goacher.

10. The "Thing" that Goacher had hidden was a chalice.

11. The "Thing" that Goacher had hidden was King Arthur's crown.

Multiple Choice. Read each question. Decide which statement best answers the question. Mark your answer sheet accordingly.

12. What did the people of Charlton Underwood think would happen if the "Thing" was removed?

    A. The world would end

    B. The Black Death would return

    C. An earthquake would destroy their town

    D. Ghosts would haunt their town

13. After the "Thing" disappeared

    A. Goacher was found murdered

    B. The people of Charlton Underwood started seeing ghosts

    C. The people of Charlton Underwood thought that they had the Black Death

    D. An earthquake hit Charlton Underwood

14. What unusual experience did Mair have in the wood?

    A. She heard bells ringing

    B. She saw Goacher's ghost

    C. She saw King Arthur in Astercote

    D. She found a well that granted wishes

146
The Ghost of Thomas Kempe
Penelope Lively

True or False. Decide whether each statement is true or false. Mark your answer sheet accordingly.

1. James's parents believed in ghosts.

2. James was arrested for throwing a brick through the chemist's window.

3. James told his sister, Helen, about Thomas Kempe.

4. Bert Ellison believed in ghosts.

5. James set Mrs. Verity's house on fire.

6. Thomas Kempe thought that Mrs. Verity was his wife.

7. Thomas Kempe thought that Mrs. Verity was a witch.

8. James wanted Bert Ellison to help him bring Thomas Kempe back to life.

9. James wanted Bert Ellison to help him get rid of Thomas Kempe.

10. James's parents hired Bert Ellison to teach him to ride a horse.

11. At the end of the book, Thomas Kempe asked James to find his resting place and to put his pipe and spectacles there.

Multiple Choice. Read each question. Decide which statement best answers the question. Mark your answer sheet accordingly.

12. What did Arnold and James have in common?

    A. They both went to the same school

    B. They were both related to Mrs. Verity

    C. They had each been blamed for things that Thomas Kempe had done

    D. Neither of them believed in ghosts

13. Thomas Kempe wanted James to tell the archaeologists to

    A. Give half the gold they found to Thomas Kempe

    B. Use their hands to dig instead of their shovels

    C. Dig under Mrs. Verity's house

    D. Let James help them dig

14. Thomas Kempe wrote James a note that said

    A. "I have burned down the witch's house"

    B. "I will not come back to life so please stop bothering me"

    C. "I am going to marry Mrs. Verity on Sunday"

    D. "Buy me the chess set that is on display in Mr. Harvey's store window"

From *Quizzes for 220 Great Children's Books*, revised 1st edition. © 1996. Teacher Ideas Press. (800) 237-6124.

CATEGORY: C
POINT VALUE: 10

147
The Call of the Wild
Jack London

True or False. Decide whether each statement is true or false. Mark your answer sheet accordingly.

1. Buck's owner, the judge, sold Buck to gold miners.

2. Buck learned that a man with a club must be obeyed.

3. Buck killed a wolf to keep it from killing the judge.

4. Buck learned that sled dogs slept under the snow.

5. Spitz, the lead dog, was a good friend to Buck.

6. Buck's first owners were gold miners traveling to Nome.

7. Buck killed Spitz in a fight.

8. After the battle between Spitz and Buck, Buck led the sled team.

9. John Thornton was the only man Buck loved.

10. Thornton won more than $1,000 when Buck pulled a 1,000-pound sled.

Multiple Choice. Read each question. Decide which statement best answers the question. Mark your answer sheet accordingly.

11. Mercedes, Charles, and Hal

    A. Were government mail inspectors

    B. Were private detectives looking for Buck

    C. Didn't know anything about surviving in the North

    D. All of the above

12. Why wasn't Buck killed when Charles and Hal fell through the ice?

    A. He swam to shore

    B. John Thornton had taken him away from Hal before they fell

    C. Mercedes cut him loose so that he didn't drown

    D. None of the above

13. What happened to Thornton and his partners?

    A. They found gold and became the richest men in Dawson

    B. They took over the government mail run

    C. They were killed by Yeehats

    D. They returned Buck to the judge

14. At the end of the story

    A. Buck and Thornton moved to Circle City, Alaska

    B. Mercedes kept Buck as a pet

    C. A miner from Forty Mile Creek adopted him

    D. Buck became the leader of a wolf pack

148
Sarah, Plain and Tall
Patricia MacLachlan

True or False. Decide whether each statement is true or false. Mark your answer sheet accordingly.

1. Caleb did not want Sarah to marry Papa.

2. Anna hoped that Sarah would decide to go back to Maine.

3. Caleb and Anna's mother died when Caleb was a baby.

4. Sarah helped Papa fix the roof.

5. Sarah took Caleb and Anna swimming in the cow pond.

6. Sarah did not sing.

7. Sarah did not like animals.

8. Sarah was unkind to Caleb and Anna.

9. Sarah said that she would marry Papa only if he would send Caleb and Anna away.

10. At the end of the book, Sarah decided to go back to Maine.

11. At the end of the book, Sarah decided to stay.

Multiple Choice. Read each question. Decide which statement best answers the question. Mark your answer sheet accordingly.

12. Why was Caleb worried when Sarah went to town alone?

    A. He thought that she might steal their horses

    B. He thought that she might not come back

    C. He was afraid that someone would try to hurt her

    D. He was worried that she would get lost

13. What did Sarah miss about Maine?

    A. Her brother

    B. The sea

    C. Her aunts

    D. All of the above

14. What did Caleb decide was missing from Sarah's drawings?

    A. The smiles on people's faces

    B. A picture of the house

    C. The colors of the sea

    D. The flowers

149
Beauty
Robin McKinley

True or False. Decide whether each statement is true or false. Mark your answer sheet accordingly.

1. When Beauty went to live with the Beast, she took Greatheart with her.

2. Gervain tried to steal Greatheart from Beauty.

3. The Beast tried to kill Beauty.

4. The first night that Beauty slept in the castle, she discovered that the door to her room was locked.

5. The Beast agreed to let Beauty visit her family for one week.

6. Greatheart was Beauty's horse.

7. Gervain made Beauty promise that she would marry Ferdy.

8. Gervain made Beauty promise to stay out of the forest.

9. Beauty went to live with the Beast to find a husband for her sister, Grace.

10. Beauty went to live with the Beast to save her father's life.

11. At the end of the book, Beauty told the Beast that she wanted to marry him.

Multiple Choice. Read each question. Decide which statement best answers the question. Mark your answer sheet accordingly.

12. What did Beauty ask her father to bring back from the city?

    A. A mirror

    B. A wedding dress

    C. Rose seeds

    D. Some snow

13. What did Beauty's father do that angered the Beast?

    A. He picked an apple from one of the Beast's apple trees

    B. He picked one of the Beast's roses to bring to Beauty

    C. He tried to kidnap Beauty from the Beast's castle

    D. He refused to eat the food that the Beast set before him

14. Why did Beauty beg the Beast to let her visit her family?

    A. She wanted to attend her father's funeral

    B. She wanted to bring them some food so they wouldn't starve

    C. She wanted to tell her sister, Grace, that Robbie was still alive

    D. All of the above

150
The Blue Sword
Robin McKinley

True or False. Decide whether each statement is true or false. Mark your answer sheet accordingly.

1. King Corlath did not listen to Harry when she warned him about the northwest pass.
2. Harry had the gift of kelar.
3. Jack Dedham refused to help Harry.
4. Harry's brother, Jack, was slain in the battle at Ritger's Gap.
5. The filanon, people of the trees, came to help Harry.
6. Harry killed the leader of the Northern army.
7. Corlath married Harry.
8. While Harry was in the town of Istan, she learned that the kingdom of the Hillfolk was free from Homelander control.
9. Corlath captured Harry because his kelar told him to.
10. When Harry drank the Water of Sight, she had a vision and spoke in the Old Tongue.
11. King Corlath gave Harry the sword of Lady Aerin.

Multiple Choice. Read each question. Decide which statement best answers the question. Mark your answer sheet accordingly.

12. Who kept appearing to Harry in dreams and visions?
    A. Lady Aerin, Dragon-Killer
    B. King Tor, the Just
    C. Her mother
    D. Gorthmag, Lord of Thunder

13. King Corlath was seeking aid from the Homelanders because
    A. His people were starving
    B. His kelar told him to
    C. Luthe told him to visit Jack
    D. The Northerners were going to invade his land

14. Luthe told Harry to
    A. Obey Corlath
    B. Trust her horse, her cat, and Lady Aerin
    C. Kill the king of the Northerners
    D. Stay with him and become a wizard

151
The Hero and the Crown
Robin McKinley

True or False. Decide whether each statement is true or false. Mark your answer sheet accordingly.

1. Aerin was always loved and trusted by the people of Damar.
2. Tor was Aerin's best friend.
3. Galanna hated Aerin.
4. Aerin was the most gifted of all the royal family.
5. Only the royal family was allowed to eat the surka plant.
6. Aerin became sick after eating a lot of surka.
7. People kept little dragons as pets in Damar.
8. Aerin befriended the war horse, Talat.
9. When Luthe cured Aerin, Aerin became immortal.
10. Aerin's uncle had Damar's crown.

Multiple Choice. Read each question. Decide which statement best answers the question. Mark your answer sheet accordingly.

11. What did Aerin learn in the Damarian history book?

    A. How to make an ointment that was proof against dragon fire

    B. That some of the great dragons might still exist

    C. Both A and B

    D. None of the above

12. What mistake did the Damarians make after Aerin's battle with Maur?

    A. They buried Aerin alive

    B. They ate some of Maur's flesh

    C. They didn't break Maur's eggs

    D. None of the above

13. Who went with Aerin to find the crown?

    A. Tor

    B. Some wild dogs and mountain cats

    C. A troop of Damarian horsemen

    D. Luthe

14. Why did the people of Damar believe that they could not defeat the Northerners?

    A. Tor had dreams about losing the war

    B. Aerin was gone

    C. The Northerners had dragons to aid them

    D. Maur's head was spreading gloom and despair

152
Invincible Louisa
Cornelia Meigs

True or False. Decide whether each statement is true or false. Mark your answer sheet accordingly.

1. The Alcott family moved many times during Louisa's early life.

2. Louisa's father was a rich and famous artist.

3. Louisa's older sister, Anna, had two sons.

4. Louisa's older sister, Anna, had two daughters.

5. All her life, Louisa kept her hair cut very short.

6. Louisa's youngest sister, May, did not have any children before her death in 1879.

7. Louisa May Alcott died the day before *Little Women* was published.

8. When Louisa nearly drowned in the frog pond, she was saved by her mother.

9. When Louisa nearly drowned in the frog pond, she was saved by a young Negro boy.

10. Mr. Lane tried to persuade Bronson Alcott to give up his family and to live as the Shakers did.

11. After reading the first few chapters of *Little Women*, Mr. Niles was very excited and told Louisa that he was sure the book would be successful.

12. After reading the first few chapters of *Little Women*, Mr. Niles was disappointed, but told Louisa to finish the book even though he doubted its success.

Multiple Choice. Read each question. Decide which statement best answers the question. Mark your answer sheet accordingly.

13. Louisa had to stop working as an army nurse when

    A. She received news that her sister, Elizabeth, had died

    B. She became ill with typhoid

    C. She failed to follow the orders of her commanding officer

    D. She received news that her mother was ill and needed her at home

14. Where did Louisa get the idea to write *Little Women*?

    A. She had always wanted to write a book about her own family

    B. Her mother asked her to write a book called *Little Women*

    C. The book was taken from her childhood diaries

    D. Thomas Niles asked her for "a book for girls"

153
It's Like This, Cat
Emily Neville

True or False. Decide whether each statement is true or false. Mark your answer sheet accordingly.

1. David did not have any brothers or sisters.

2. David's father helped Tom find a job in a flower shop.

3. Mary called her mother by her first name.

4. Kate decided to use the money she inherited to move to a different apartment.

5. Mary's parents were very strict with her.

6. Tom's father didn't seem to care about him.

7. Tom decided to enlist in the army.

8. Tom and Hilda decided to get married.

9. Cat killed one of Ben's salamanders.

10. Mary was afraid of snakes.

Multiple Choice. Read each question. Decide which statement best answers the question. Mark your answer sheet accordingly.

11. Where did David meet Tom Ransom for the first time?

    A. At Coney Island

    B. In a cellar

    C. On the subway

    D. In Connecticut

12. When David visited Kate, she usually served him

    A. Milk and cookies

    B. Cake and ice cream

    C. Tuna fish and Kool-aid

    D. Cottage cheese and iced tea

13. David's father worked as a

    A. Doctor

    B. Insurance salesman

    C. Army recruiter

    D. Lawyer

14. Kate received a telegram saying that

    A. Her father had died

    B. Her mother was very sick

    C. Her brother had died

    C. She had won the lottery

154
Rascal
Sterling North

True or False. Decide whether each statement is true or false. Mark your answer sheet accordingly.

1. Sterling built a canoe in his living room.

2. Sterling's mother loved Rascal and all the other pets.

3. Sterling's father did not allow Rascal in the house.

4. Sterling's father shot Rascal because Rascal had rabies.

5. Sterling's father was very strict with him.

6. Rascal liked to sleep in Sterling's bed.

7. Rascal often ate at the table with Sterling and his father.

8. Reverend Thurman disliked Rascal.

9. Sterling's neighbors insisted that Rascal be kept in a cage because Rascal kept tipping over the garbage cans.

10. Sterling's neighbors insisted that Rascal be kept in a cage because Rascal was eating the sweet corn in their gardens.

11. At the end of the book, Sterling gave Rascal to his brother, Herschel.

Multiple Choice. Read each question. Decide which statement best answers the question. Mark your answer sheet accordingly.

12. Where was Sterling's brother, Herschel?

    A. Studying to be a doctor at the University of Wisconsin

    B. Fighting in World War I

    C. Raising livestock in Janesville

    D. Working as a shoe salesman in Madison

13. What did Edgar Allen Poe, the crow, and Rascal have in common?

    A. They both liked to eat garbage

    B. They were both shot by Sterling's father

    C. They both attacked stray dogs

    D. They both liked bright, shiny objects

14. Poe, the crow, could say

    A. "What fun!"

    B. "Hello, Central"

    C. "What's up, Doc?"

    D. "Polly want a cracker?"

155
The Wolfling
Sterling North

True or False. Decide whether each statement is true or false. Mark your answer sheet accordingly.

1. Mrs. Trent liked to play with Wolf.

2. Mrs. Kumlien died before she could move into her new house.

3. Robbie beat Bub in the Fourth of July horse race.

4. Dan, the hired man, lost his family in the Chicago Fire.

5. Mr. Trent shot and killed Wolf for trying to kill the sheep.

6. Mr. Henderson hired Robbie to take care of his horses.

7. Bub and his father lived on a houseboat.

8. Robbie Trent lived on a farm in Wisconsin.

9. Robbie Trent lived on a houseboat.

10. Mrs. Kumlien was dying of cancer.

11. Mr. Trent did not like Mr. Henderson, who paid low prices for grain and charged too much for machinery.

Multiple Choice. Read each question. Decide which statement best answers the question. Mark your answer sheet accordingly.

12. Thure Kumlien was

    A. A naturalist who owned a small farm

    B. The owner of the sawmill in town

    C. The banker who really owned the Trent farm

    D. The pastor of the Swedish Lutheran Church

13. Robbie said that he would go into the wolves' cave if

    A. He could have all the bounty money from the hides

    B. The men would let the mother and father wolf go free

    C. They would give all the pups to Thure Kumlien

    D. He could have his pick of the litter

14. When Robbie took Wolf to school

    A. Miss Hitchcock tried to shoot him

    B. Wolf bit Inga on the leg

    C. The younger children tried to feed Wolf their lunches

    D. Bub pulled Wolf's ear, and Wolf growled at him

156
The Borrowers
Mary Norton

True or False. Decide whether each statement is true or false. Mark your answer sheet accordingly.

1. Arietty did not have any brothers or sisters.

2. Homily often went into the big house to borrow things.

3. Arietty did not know how to read.

4. Arietty's bedroom was made out of a cigar box.

5. Pod often spoke to Great-Aunt Sophy.

6. Homily would not accept the presents the boy offered.

7. Crampfurl was a Borrower.

8. Arietty often read books aloud to the boy.

9. The boy carried Homily up to the dollhouse in his hand.

10. The Borrowers were much smaller than human beings.

11. Homily never curled her hair.

12. Mrs. Driver and Homily often had tea together.

Multiple Choice. Read each question. Decide which statement best answers the question. Mark your answer sheet accordingly.

13. Who brought the Borrowers some furniture from the dollhouse?

    A. Mrs. Driver

    B. The boy

    C. Crampfurl

    D. Great-Aunt Sophy

14. The boy's real home was in

    A. Africa

    B. China

    C. Asia

    D. India

157
The Borrowers Afield
Mary Norton

True or False. Decide whether each statement is true or false. Mark your answer sheet accordingly.

1. Spiller brought cooked food to Arietty and her family.

2. Spiller saved Arietty's life.

3. Spiller tried to kill Pod and Homily.

4. Homily was always wishing that winter would come soon.

5. Pod told Homily that he wanted to move the family back to the big house where they lived before.

6. Spiller tried to eat Arietty.

7. Spiller wanted to sell Arietty and her family to Mild Eye.

8. Tom Goodenough did not want to hurt the Borrowers.

9. Spiller and Tom Goodenough did not know each other.

10. Old Tom Goodenough showed Arietty's *Diary and Proverb Book* to Kate.

11. Spiller was a Borrower.

Multiple Choice. Read each question. Decide which statement best answers the question. Mark your answer sheet accordingly.

12. Throughout most of the book, Arietty and her family lived

    A. Under the kitchen in the big house

    B. In a stove with Spiller

    C. In an old glove

    D. In a boot

13. When Homily first met Spiller

    A. She told him to go away

    B. Spiller was very dirty

    C. Spiller gave her a cricket

    D. All of the above

14. Homily liked to drink

    A. Wine

    B. Coffee

    C. Tea

    D. Milk

158
The Borrowers Afloat
Mary Norton

True or False. Decide whether each statement is true or false. Mark your answer sheet accordingly.

1. Pod was expected to do all of the borrowing while he, Homily, and Arietty were living with their relatives, the Hendrearys.

2. Aunt Lupy and Uncle Hendreary lived in a boat.

3. Mild Eye tried to catch Pod, Homily, and Arietty.

4. Mild Eye and Arietty were good friends.

5. Mild Eye caught Pod and sold him to the bank manager.

6. Spiller helped Pod, Homily, and Arietty to escape down the cottage drain.

7. Mild Eye brought food to Arietty and her family every night that they were in the teakettle.

8. Young Tom told Arietty that he and his grandfather were leaving.

9. Spiller was a Borrower.

10. The teakettle belonged to Spiller.

11. Mild Eye was a raccoon.

Multiple Choice. Read each question. Decide which statement best answers the question. Mark your answer sheet accordingly.

12. What did Aunt Lupy do for Spiller?

    A. She rescued him from young Tom's grandfather

    B. She taught him to read

    C. She made his clothes for him

    D. She cooked all of his meals

13. What food did Arietty and her family carry through the drain?

    A. A jar of pickles

    B. A cucumber

    C. A tomato

    D. An egg

14. What happened to Homily's skirt?

    A. Arietty used it to make life jackets

    B. Spiller stole it

    C. Mild Eye caught it on his fishhook

    D. Homily sold it to Aunt Lupy

159
The Borrowers Aloft
Mary Norton

True or False. Decide whether each statement is true or false. Mark your answer sheet accordingly.

1. Mrs. Platter did not know that Mr. Platter had kidnapped the Borrowers.

2. Spiller rescued the Borrowers from Mr. Platter.

3. Pod climbed down the outside of Mr. Platter's house and went to get Spiller.

4. Arietty got the idea to build a balloon from the *Illustrated London News*.

5. The balloon carrying the Borrowers crash-landed in Mr. Platter's miniature town.

6. Mr. Platter was planning to make the Borrowers live in a glass house.

7. Homily asked Mr. Platter if she and her family could live in his miniature town.

8. Mr. Pott fixed up a little house with electricity and running water for the Borrowers.

9. Mr. Platter was always spying on Mr. Pott because he wanted his miniature town to be better than Mr. Pott's.

10. Miss Menzies knew about the Borrowers because she had seen and spoken with Arietty.

11. Miss Menzies knew about the Borrowers because she had read about them in a big, black book.

Multiple Choice. Read each question. Decide which statement best answers the question. Mark your answer sheet accordingly.

12. Mr. Platter kidnapped the Borrowers because

    A. He hated tiny people

    B. He wanted to show them on television

    C. He wanted to give them to his wife for her birthday

    D. He wanted to put them in his miniature town

13. Mr. Platter put the Borrowers

    A. In his attic

    B. In a castle in his miniature town

    C. In a coal bin

    D. In his wife's hatbox

14. At the end of the book, the Borrowers decided to

    A. Stay in Mr. Pott's miniature town

    B. Go back and live under the kitchen in the big house

    C. Go live where no people knew about them

    D. Live with Spiller out in the woods

160
The Borrowers Avenged
Mary Norton

True or False. Decide whether each statement is true or false. Mark your answer sheet accordingly.

1. The Platters saw Timmus hiding in the church.

2. Pod, Homily, and Arietty took all of the furniture that Miss Menzies made for them to their new home.

3. Spiller lived with Pod, Homily, and Arietty.

4. The Platters broke into the church one night to capture Timmus.

5. The Platters captured Timmus.

6. Arietty fell in love with Peagreen.

7. Peagreen's family abandoned him when he was a little boy.

8. When the Platters discovered that the Borrowers had escaped from their attic, they looked for them in Abel Pott's little village.

9. Arietty's new home was haunted by three ghosts.

10. Timmus and his parents lived in a teakettle with Spiller.

11. Aunt Lupy's other children had been captured by Mr. Pott.

Multiple Choice. Read each question. Decide which statement best answers the question. Mark your answer sheet accordingly.

12. When Miss Menzies reported the kidnapping of the Borrowers to the local policeman, the policeman
    A. Searched all through the town to find the Borrowers
    B. Notified the local newspapers that the Borrowers existed
    C. Told Miss Menzies that she was crazy and then called a doctor
    D. Acted like he didn't believe Miss Menzies

13. Where was the new home that Spiller found for Pod, Homily, and Arietty?
    A. In the old mill
    B. In a boat
    C. In a teakettle
    D. In the rectory of the village church

14. In their new home, Arietty was surprised to meet
    A. Miss Menzies
    B. A Borrower named Peagreen
    C. A fierce cat
    D. Spiller's parents

161
Mrs. Frisby and the Rats of NIMH
Robert C. O'Brien

True or False. Decide whether each statement is true or false. Mark your answer sheet accordingly.

1. Mrs. Frisby went inside the owl's house.

2. The owl had never heard of Mrs. Frisby's husband.

3. The owl suggested that Mrs. Frisby go to the rats with her problem.

4. Jonathon Frisby and Mr. Ages were with the rats when they escaped from NIMH.

5. Mrs. Frisby was captured by a boy.

6. When Mrs. Frisby went to talk to the rats, she took her son, Martin, with her.

7. Mr. Ages gave Mrs. Frisby some medicine for her sick child.

8. Dragon was a mouse.

9. Dragon was a cat.

10. Jeremy was a crow.

11. At the end of the book, Timothy died.

Multiple Choice. Read each question. Decide which statement best answers the question. Mark your answer sheet accordingly.

12. How did Nicodemus learn to read?

    A. Jonathon Frisby taught him

    B. His mother taught him

    C. He had learned while he was living in the basement of a school

    D. He had learned while he was at NIMH

13. How did the injections that the A-group rats received at NIMH change them?

    A. They would live longer because the aging process seemed to almost stop

    B. They were able to learn more than any rats ever had before

    C. A and B

    D. The injections did not change them at all

14. What was "The Plan"?

    A. To live without having to do any work

    B. To create a pill that would cure all diseases

    C. To live without stealing

    D. To kill Dragon

162
Island of the Blue Dolphins
Scott O'Dell

True or False. Decide whether each statement is true or false. Mark your answer sheet accordingly.

1. Karana's father was killed during a fight with the Aleuts.

2. The laws of Ghalas-at did not allow women to make weapons.

3. Karana jumped off the ship that was taking her people away from Ghalas-at because she saw that her brother, Ramo, had been left behind.

4. Karana made weapons for herself to use against the wild dogs.

5. Karana killed some of the wild dogs on the island.

6. Rontu had been the leader of the wild dogs on the island.

7. Karana had other pets besides Rontu.

8. Karana died on the island of Ghalas-at.

9. Rontu died on the island of Ghalas-at.

10. Karana was never able to capture Rontu's son.

11. When the Aleuts returned to the island of Ghalas-at at the end of the book, Karana became friends with an Aleut girl.

Multiple Choice. Read each question. Decide which statement best answers the question. Mark your answer sheet accordingly.

12. What did the Aleuts do on the island of Ghalas-at?

    A. They brought food to the people on the island

    B. They hunted sea otter

    C. They built a church for the people on the island

    D. They set the island on fire

13. What happened when Karana tried to leave the island of Ghalas-at in a canoe?

    A. The canoe started leaking

    B. A swarm of dolphins swam along beside her

    C. A and B

    D. None of the above

14. When the Aleuts returned to the island of Ghalas-at

    A. Karana became friends with the Aleut chief

    B. Karana became friends with an Aleut girl

    C. Karana decided to return to Russia with the Aleuts

    D. The Aleuts tried to kill Karana

163
Sarah Bishop
Scott O'Dell

True or False. Decide whether each statement is true or false. Mark your answer sheet accordingly.

1. Mr. Morton was a British agent.

2. Some of the people of Ridgeford thought that Sarah was a witch.

3. Sarah joined an Indian tribe.

4. Sarah found and killed the snake that bit her.

5. Sarah was forced to leave Ridgeford because she was accused of spying.

6. Sarah rescued Sam Goshen from a bear trap.

7. Sam Goshen gave Sarah everything she needed to live in the wilderness.

8. Sarah's brother, Chad, died on a British prison ship.

9. Sarah decided to live in a cave.

10. Mr. and Mrs. Longknife helped Sarah survive in her new home.

Multiple Choice. Read each question. Decide which statement best answers the question. Mark your answer sheet accordingly.

11. Why did the Bishops' neighbors dislike Sarah's father?

    A. He was loyal to King George

    B. He supported General Washington

    C. They thought that he was a thief

    D. They thought that he practiced witchcraft

12. Why did Chad and his father have a fight?

    A. Chad wanted to join the king's army

    B. Chad wanted to join the patriots

    C. Chad told the police that his father was a wizard

    D. Chad told the preacher that his father was a wizard

13. What happened to Sarah's father?

    A. He was arrested by British troops and taken to Boston

    B. He died after being tarred and feathered

    C. He was sent to jail for stealing

    D. He moved to France

14. Why did the British arrest Sarah?

    A. They thought that she was trying to kill King George

    B. They were trying to keep her safe

    C. They thought that she was a French spy

    D. They thought that she started a fire near a prison

164
Sing Down the Moon
Scott O'Dell

True or False. Decide whether each statement is true or false. Mark your answer sheet accordingly.

1. Bright Morning's mother did not have any sheep.

2. Bright Morning was a Navajo Indian.

3. Bright Morning was an Apache Indian.

4. One of the Spanish slavers shot and killed Bright Morning's black dog.

5. Bright Morning sold her black dog to Rosita.

6. Bright Morning's parents died when she was very young.

7. Bright Morning married Tall Boy.

8. The white soldiers burned Bright Morning's village.

9. Bright Morning's son died before they reached Canyon de Chelly.

10. Tall Boy finally agreed to return to Canyon de Chelly because he was tired of hearing about sheep.

11. Bright Morning's people called the white soldiers "Long Knives."

Multiple Choice. Read each question. Decide which statement best answers the question. Mark your answer sheet accordingly.

12. Bright Morning's mother would not let her take the sheep to the mesa for a whole year because the first time Bright Morning had that responsibility, she

    A. Let five of the sheep stray

    B. Let the sheep eat a poisonous weed

    C. Left the flock to fend for itself because she was afraid of a storm

    D. None of the above

13. What was Bright Morning doing when she was captured by the Spanish slavers?

    A. Weaving cloth in her tent

    B. Tending sheep on the mesa

    C. Baby-sitting her little sister

    D. Pulling weeds from her garden

14. How was Tall Boy's arm injured?

    A. He was shot by a Spaniard

    B. He fell off his horse

    C. He loaded his gun incorrectly and it backfired on him

    D. He was bitten by a rattlesnake

165
Bridge to Terabithia
Katherine Paterson

True or False. Decide whether each statement is true or false. Mark your answer sheet accordingly.

1. Leslie's family did not have a television.

2. On Easter Sunday, Leslie went to church with Jess and his family.

3. Jess did not have any sisters.

4. Janice Avery told Leslie that her father beat her.

5. Jess did not like Miss Edmunds.

6. Leslie often got in trouble at school.

7. Jess never went back to Terabithia after Leslie died.

8. Leslie's family was very poor.

9. Leslie's parents would not let her keep Prince Terrien.

10. Leslie called her parents by their first names.

11. Leslie did not have any brothers or sisters.

12. Jess gave Leslie a dog for Christmas.

13. Leslie was the fastest runner in the fifth grade.

Multiple Choice. Read the question. Decide which statement best answers the question. Mark your answer sheet accordingly.

14. What did Leslie give Jess for Christmas?

   A. A dog

   B. A baseball bat

   C. A shirt

   D. None of the above

166
Jacob Have I Loved
Katherine Paterson

True or False. Decide whether each statement is true or false. Mark your answer sheet accordingly.

1. Louise thought that the Captain's joke about Wheeze and Cough was funny.

2. Call did not like the Captain.

3. The Captain's house was completely destroyed by the storm.

4. Louise was angry when she discovered that Caroline was using her hand lotion.

5. Caroline and the Captain never met each other.

6. The Captain married Trudy Braxton.

7. Louise's grandmother was always kind to Louise.

8. Caroline was sick when she was an infant.

9. Caroline was a talented singer.

10. Louise never married.

11. Call married Louise.

Multiple Choice. Read each question. Decide which statement best answers the question. Mark your answer sheet accordingly.

12. What did Call and Louise do together to earn money?

    A. They sold lemonade to the fishermen

    B. They ran errands for Louise's grandmother

    C. They caught and sold crab.

    D. They caught bait for the fishermen

13. Where did Louise's grandmother live?

    A. In a nursing home

    B. With Louise and her family

    C. In New York City

    D. None of the above

14. What was finally done with Auntie Braxton's cats?

    A. Call and the Captain drowned them in the river

    B. Caroline and Louise took them home and took care of them

    C. They were drugged and given away to people on the island

    D. They were bought by the owner of a local pet store

167
Tom's Midnight Garden
Philippa Pearce

True or False. Decide whether each statement is true or false. Mark your answer sheet accordingly.

1. Abel, the gardener, could see Tom.

2. Tom often wrote letters to his brother, Peter, about Hatty and the garden.

3. Hatty's aunt could see Tom.

4. Hatty's aunt was always kind to her.

5. Hatty's parents died when she was a little girl.

6. Hatty fell out of the tree house that she and Tom were building.

7. Tom made Hatty promise that when she wasn't using her skates, she would keep them in the secret place under the floorboards.

8. Hatty told Tom that she was a princess.

9. Tom told Hatty that she should carve her name on the trees in the garden.

10. Tom's secret way of signing his name was to make an X.

11. At the end of the book, Tom found out that Mrs. Bartholomew was really Hatty.

Multiple Choice. Read each question. Decide which statement best answers the question. Mark your answer sheet accordingly.

12. Why did Tom stay with his aunt and uncle?

    A. His brother, Peter, had the measles

    B. His parents were going on a business trip

    C. His parents had died

    D. His aunt and uncle were sick and needed his help

13. When did Tom go to play with Hatty in the garden?

    A. During the day when his aunt was out shopping

    B. At night after his aunt and uncle had gone to bed

    C. In the afternoons while his aunt and uncle were napping

    D. During the day while his aunt and uncle were at work

14. Hatty's aunt became very angry when she found out that

    A. Hatty's parents were the king and queen of England

    B. Hatty had been playing with an invisible boy in the garden

    C. Hatty was to blame for the geese getting loose in the yard

    D. Her son, Edgar, had been making fun of Hatty

168
The Mysterious Disappearance of Leon (I Mean Noel)
Ellen Raskin

True or False. Decide whether each statement is true or false. Mark your answer sheet accordingly.

1. Leon disappeared after a boating accident.

2. Mr. Banks managed Mrs. Carillon's money.

3. Augie Kunkel worked for the New York City police.

4. Augie Kunkel made crossword puzzles.

5. Mrs. Carillon fed seals every day because she thought that Leon had turned into a seal.

6. Mrs. Carillon looked for Leon in Chinese restaurants.

7. Mrs. Carillon's favorite racehorse was Christmas Bells, owned by Seymour Hall.

8. Mrs. Carillon was arrested several times for trying to smuggle seals out of local zoos.

9. Leon (or Noel) showed up at Mrs. Carillon's apartment begging for soup.

10. Leon tried to drown himself because Mrs. Carillon told him that she wanted a divorce.

11. Mrs. Carillon and Leon were knocked overboard while Leon was trying to tell Mrs. Carillon something.

12. At the end of the book, Mrs. Carillon discovered that Augie Kunkel was really Leon.

Multiple Choice. Read each question. Decide which statement best answers the question. Mark your answer sheet accordingly.

13. Mrs. Carillon's fortune came from

    A. Gold mines

    B. Gas stations

    C. Feather hats

    D. Soup

14. Mrs. Carillon and Leon Carillon

    A. Were married when both were children

    B. Were separated at an early age

    C. Did not see each other for 14 years

    D. All of the above

169
The Westing Game
Ellen Raskin

True or False. Decide whether each statement is true or false. Mark your answer sheet accordingly.

1. Turtle and Angela were sisters.

2. Chris Theodorakis was confined to a wheelchair.

3. Sydelle Pulaski's partner in the Westing game was Angela Wexler.

4. Sydelle Pulaski's partner in the Westing game was Doug Hoo.

5. Sam Westing's daughter, Violet, died the night before her wedding.

6. Crow murdered Sam Westing.

7. Turtle often kicked people.

8. Angela was engaged to a doctor.

9. The winner of the Westing game was the ghost of Violet Westing.

10. The winner of the Westing game was Turtle Wexler.

Multiple Choice. Read each question. Decide which statement best answers the question. Mark your answer sheet accordingly.

11. What did Turtle do on Halloween?

    A. She went to the cemetery to find Sam Westing's grave

    B. She set off a bomb in the bathroom at school

    C. She went inside the Westing house

    D. She disguised herself as Sam Westing

12. What did Turtle call Flora Baumbach?

    A. Aunt Flora

    B. Mrs. B

    C. Baba

    D. Baumbach

13. What was stolen from Sydelle Pulaski?

    A. Her clues

    B. Her shorthand notebook

    C. Her check for $10,000

    D. Her watch

14. What did Sydelle Pulaski do with her crutches?

    A. She used them as weapons

    B. She painted them

    C. She gave them to Chris Theodorakis

    D. She hung them on her wall

170
The Yearling
Marjorie Kinnan Rawlings

True or False. Decide whether each statement is true or false. Mark your answer sheet accordingly.

1. Baxter's Island was in the middle of the St. John's River.

2. Jody had no brothers or sisters.

3. Penny Baxter was a large man.

4. The Baxters did not have a well.

5. Jody had three dogs and four cats of his own.

6. Fodder-wing had several pets.

7. Old Slewfoot was Fodder-wing's pet cat.

8. Penny was bitten by a rattlesnake.

9. When Flag started eating the corn, Pa told Jody to sell him to the Forresters.

10. When Flag started eating the corn, Pa told Jody to build a fence.

Multiple Choice. Read each question. Decide which statement best answers the question. Mark your answer sheet accordingly.

11. Old Slewfoot was feared because

    A. The only person he obeyed was Fodder-wing

    B. He had rabies

    C. He was a large and dangerous bear

    D. He had killed several small children

12. Jody named his fawn Flag because

    A. That was the name Fodder-wing picked out for him

    B. He found him under an old Confederate flag

    C. His spots looked like stars

    D. He liked to follow parades

13. Why did Pa say that Flag must be killed?

    A. He had rabies

    B. He ate most of the Baxter's crops

    C. They needed him for food

    D. All of the above

14. What finally happened to Flag?

    A. The Baxters had him for supper

    B. Jody shot him

    C. Jody took him into the woods and let him go

    D. Old Slewfoot killed him

171
Henry Reed, Inc.
Keith Robertson

True or False. Decide whether each statement is true or false. Mark your answer sheet accordingly.

1. Mr. Apple said that Agony was his dog.

2. The newspaper printed an article about the firm of Henry Reed, Inc.

3. Henry was not able to sell any of the turtles that he had painted.

4. Mr. and Mrs. Apple often came to Uncle Al's house for dinner.

5. Mr. Glass paid Henry and Midge for the oil they pumped out of the hole they dug.

6. Uncle Al and Mr. Apple had cars that looked exactly alike.

7. Midge and Henry finally caught the white rabbit.

8. Henry never painted Midge's name on the barn.

9. The barn that Henry and Midge used for their research firm belonged to Mr. Apple.

10. On the Fourth of July, Henry accidentally locked Agony in Mr. Apple's car.

Multiple Choice. Read each question. Decide which statement best answers the question. Mark your answer sheet accordingly.

11. Henry said that he would paint Midge's name on the barn if

   A. Midge sold 100 earthworms

   B. Midge contributed two rabbits to the firm

   C. Midge paid Henry $5

   D. All of the above

12. What did Henry paint on the backs of several turtles?

   A. The words "Henry Reed, Inc."

   B. Flowers

   C. Cartoon characters

   D. The names of people who lived in Grover's Corner

13. Midge took a picture of Mr. Apple

   A. Presenting an award to Henry and Midge

   B. Destroying the box trap that Henry had made

   C. Shooting at some deer on his property

   D. Stealing some chickens from Mr. Baine's barn

14. Which of the following statements is true?

   A. Henry had lived in Grover's Corner all his life

   B. Henry's mother had never been to Grover's Corner

   C. Henry would only be in Grover's Corner for the summer

   D. None of the above

172
Henry Reed's Baby-Sitting Service
Keith Robertson

True or False. Decide whether each statement is true or false. Mark your answer sheet accordingly.

1. Midge and Ruth Sebastian were best friends.

2. Midge invited Ruth and Johnny Sebastian to a cookout at her house.

3. Henry Reed's baby-sitting service was advertised on the radio.

4. Henry and Midge never found out who had been making strange noises in the barn to scare the children.

5. Henry and Midge accidentally used horse meat to make hamburgers at the Wittenbergs.

6. Henry had lived in Grover's Corner all his life.

7. Henry had traveled to many different parts of the world.

8. Henry and Midge did not have their driver's licenses yet.

9. Agony was Henry's dog.

10. Agony was Henry's rabbit.

11. The waitress at the dairy bar tripped and spilled the milk shake and soda all over Henry and Herman.

12. At the fair, Midge took a picture of Johnny Sebastian's MG being towed by Henry's tractor.

Multiple Choice. Read each question. Decide which statement best answers the question. Mark your answer sheet accordingly.

13. When Henry was camping with Craig, they heard a noise that sounded like someone screaming for help. What did the noise turn out to be?

    A. A girl who had broken her leg

    B. A mountain lion

    C. Midge trying to scare them

    D. A peacock

14. What was missing when Henry and Herman came back from lunch at the dairy bar?

    A. Their bicycles

    B. The trailer that Herman lived in

    C. All of Herman's pets

    D. All of the above

From *Quizzes for 220 Great Children's Books*, revised 1st edition. © 1996. Teacher Ideas Press. (800) 237-6124.

173
What About Me?
Colby F. Rodowsky

True or False. Decide whether each statement is true or false. Mark your answer sheet accordingly.

1. Dorrie was voted class president for the next school year.

2. Dorrie's mother wanted her to go to Annapolis for June Week with Pat.

3. Dorrie's mother told her that she could not go to Annapolis for June Week with Pat.

4. Guntzie was an artist.

5. Dorrie's mother did not think Dorrie was old enough to baby-sit Fred by herself.

6. Dorrie's parents decided not to move to Maryland.

7. Dorrie wanted to become a lawyer.

8. Dorrie wanted to become an artist.

9. Fred liked the Sears, Roebuck catalog.

10. At the end of the book, Fred went to live with Guntzie.

11. At the end of the book, Fred died.

Multiple Choice. Read each question. Decide which statement best answers the question. Mark your answer sheet accordingly.

12. Dorrie called Fred an idiot when he

    A. Ruined the picture she had been drawing

    B. Refused to play Monopoly with her

    C. Broke the ceramic cat she had made

    D. Ran into her with his bicycle

13. Dorrie became upset when she found out that her parents were planning to

    A. Get a divorce

    B. Put Fred in a home

    C. Hire a full-time baby-sitter for Dorrie and Fred

    D. Move to a small town in Maryland

14. What did Dorrie do to make her father see that she was showing some interest in Fred?

    A. She taught Fred to say his alphabet

    B. She went to work at Fred's school instead of teaching art

    C. She helped Fred make his own ceramic cat

    D. She offered to take Fred with her to the zoo

174
Roller Skates
Ruth Sawyer

True or False. Decide whether each statement is true or false. Mark your answer sheet accordingly.

1. Aunt Emily was happy to hear that Lucinda would be staying with Miss Peters.
2. The Browdowskis were very poor.
3. Trinket died.
4. Uncle Earle called his daughters the "gazelles."
5. One day Lucinda was so bad at school that she was sent home.
6. Tony and Lucinda did not share their picnic lunch with Rags 'n Bottles.
7. Tony's father owned a candy shop.
8. Lucinda was the oldest child in her family.
9. Trinket had many brothers and sisters.
10. Miss Peters was a teacher.
11. Aunt Emily had four daughters.

Multiple Choice. Read each question. Decide which statement best answers the question. Mark your answer sheet accordingly.

12. On what day of the week was Lucinda to go to her Aunt Emily's house?
    A. Monday
    B. Wednesday
    C. Thursday
    D. Saturday

13. What was Uncle Earle's pet name for Lucinda?
    A. Cindy
    B. Snoodie
    C. Lucy
    D. Lindy

14. Who was a great violin player?
    A. Uncle Earle
    B. Trinket's father
    C. Tony's father
    D. Mr. Gilligan

175
Words by Heart
Ouida Sebestyen

True or False. Decide whether each statement is true or false. Mark your answer sheet accordingly.

1. Lena stole some books from Miss Chism.

2. Lena's mother wanted to move to an all-black town.

3. Lena's father hated anyone who mistreated him.

4. Almost everyone in town came to Miss Chism's dinner party.

5. Lena's father was shot by Tater Haney.

6. Lena's father rescued Tater instead of saving himself.

7. Lena's family moved back to Georgia after Lena's father died.

8. Lena's family was the richest family in town.

9. Lena's family was the only black family in town.

10. The Haneys hated Lena's father because Miss Chism gave him Mr. Haney's job.

11. Lena competed in a Bible verse memorization contest.

Multiple Choice. Read each question. Decide which statement best answers the question. Mark your answer sheet accordingly.

12. What happened the night Lena won the contest?

    A. She was given $20

    B. Her little brother was beaten up

    C. Her dog was killed

    D. Her little sister ran away from home

13. Why had Lena's family moved to the West?

    A. They wanted to give the children a better education

    B. They wanted to find gold

    C. Lena's father had killed a man in Florida

    D. Lena's grandmother wanted to see the mountains

14. Why did Winslow stop talking to Lena?

    A. He was mad at her because he lost the contest

    B. He had a crush on someone else

    C. He was afraid of being laughed at

    D. His father told him not to talk with her

176
The Cricket in Times Square
George Selden

True or False. Decide whether each statement is true or false. Mark your answer sheet accordingly.

1. Mario's family was wealthy.

2. Mario did not have any brothers or sisters.

3. Harry Cat was always trying to kill Tucker Mouse.

4. Harry Cat and Tucker Mouse were enemies.

5. The Bellinis did not want other people to hear Chester's beautiful music.

6. Chester liked to eat mulberry leaves.

7. Mama Bellini liked to listen to Chester's music.

8. Mama Bellini sold Chester to Mr. Smedley.

9. Sai Fong supplied Mario with mulberry leaves for Chester.

10. Chester accidentally ate half of a $2 bill.

11. When the animals were having a party in the Bellinis' newsstand, Tucker accidentally set the newsstand on fire.

12. At the end of the book, Chester decided to go back to Connecticut.

Multiple Choice. Read each question. Decide which statement best answers the question. Mark your answer sheet accordingly.

13. How did Chester learn new songs?

    A. Mr. Smedley gave him music lessons

    B. Mario sang songs to Chester that he had learned in school

    C. Chester would listen to songs on the radio and then "play them by ear"

    D. Chester would study the sheet music that Harry Cat brought him

14. Where did Mario get a cricket cage for Chester?

    A. His mother gave him one for his birthday

    B. He made one at school

    C. He bought one from Sai Fong

    D. None of the above

177
The White Stag
Kate Seredy

True or False. Decide whether each statement is true or false. Mark your answer sheet accordingly.

1. Nimrod shot and killed the white stag.

2. When Nimrod died, his two sons became the leaders of the people.

3. When Nimrod died, the people killed his two sons.

4. Hunor and Magyar caught the two Moonmaidens and kept them in a glass jar.

5. Hunor and Magyar each married a Moonmaiden.

6. The Moonmaidens disappeared before Hunor and Magyar could talk with them.

7. Damon, the prophet, was blind.

8. Damon, the prophet, was deaf.

9. Damon, the prophet, could not speak.

10. There were often quarrels between the Magyars and the Huns.

11. When Bendeguz married Alleeta, the enslaved Cimmerians were set free.

12. Bendeguz would not marry Alleeta because she was a Cimmerian.

13. Alleeta gave birth to a son.

14. Alleeta gave birth to a daughter.

178
Dobry
Monica Shannon

True or False. Decide whether each statement is true or false. Mark your answer sheet accordingly.

1. Dobry earned a scholarship to art school.

2. The priest was angry when Dobry made a manger scene out of snow.

3. Dobry's grandfather lost the snow-melting contest.

4. The priest persuaded Dobry's mother to allow Dobry to go to art school.

5. The Bulgarians gave presents to people younger than themselves.

6. The Bulgarians hated and feared the gypsies.

7. Dobry dove through a hole in the ice of a frozen river and brought up a golden crucifix.

8. Dobry's grandfather and mother were gypsies.

9. Dobry's grandfather was famous for his stories.

10. The gypsy bear massaged backs.

Multiple Choice. Read each question. Decide which statement best answers the question. Mark your answer sheet accordingly.

11. To say "no," a Bulgarian would

    A. Wave his finger

    B. Shake his head from side to side

    C. Wrinkle his nose

    D. Nod his head up and down

12. Dobry's father was

    A. A blacksmith

    B. A gypsy

    C. Dead

    D. Living in the United States

13. Bulgarians gave out presents on

    A. Christmas

    B. Christmas Eve

    C. The twelfth day of Christmas

    D. New Year's Day

14. When Dobry's mother found out that he wanted to be an artist, she was

    A. Proud and happy

    B. Upset because she wanted Dobry to become a farmer

    C. Worried that Dobry would get lost in the city

    D. Worried that Dobry would want to live with the gypsies

179
The First Hard Times
Doris Buchanan Smith

True or False. Decide whether each statement is true or false. Mark your answer sheet accordingly.

1. Ancil shared a room with her sister, Zan.

2. Ancil's sisters did not like Harvey.

3. Ancil was happy that her picture was in the newspaper.

4. Lloyd was happy that his picture was in the newspaper.

5. Harvey tried to be nice to Ancil.

6. Harvey had been married and had two children before he married Ancil's mother.

7. Lloyd and Ancil were in the same swimming class.

8. Ancil and Lloyd were friends.

9. Ancil's new stepfather, Harvey, owned the weekly newspaper, the *Hanover Historian*.

10. Ancil's new stepfather, Harvey, was the principal of Ancil's junior high school.

11. Harvey insisted that Ancil take swimming lessons.

Multiple Choice. Read each question. Decide which statement best answers the question. Mark your answer sheet accordingly.

12. Maria wanted Ancil to

    A. Arm wrestle her

    B. Race her

    C. Tell Lloyd that Maria liked him

    D. Come to her slumber party

13. Ancil was upset when Harvey

    A. Forgot to set a place for her at the dinner table

    B. Threw her into the water at the beach

    C. Accidentally threw her homework assignment in the garbage

    D. Would not let her keep the stray puppy she had found

14. Ancil helped Gran

    A. Learn how to skate

    B. Take care of Grandy

    C. Put a jigsaw puzzle together

    D. Make masks of the family

180
Kelly's Creek
Doris Buchanan Smith

True or False. Decide whether each statement is true or false. Mark your answer sheet accordingly.

1. Kelly's father was happy that Kelly had been playing football.

2. Kelly's sister told their parents that Kelly had been talking to a strange man at the creek.

3. Kelly liked to play ball games.

4. Zack liked to play ball games.

5. Kelly and Zack played together every day after school.

6. Kelly was blind.

7. Kelly's parents told him that until he showed some improvement in school, he could not go to the creek.

8. Kelly's mother was angry that Kelly went to the creek when he wasn't supposed to.

9. Kelly's mother asked his teacher to stop sending him to the special class.

10. Kelly's mother asked his teacher to send a note home with him every day.

11. At the end of the book, Kelly died.

Multiple Choice. Read each question. Decide which statement best answers the question. Mark your answer sheet accordingly.

12. Kelly's parents were very proud of him when he learned to

    A. Count to 500

    B. Say the alphabet

    C. Draw a circle and a square

    D. Dress himself

13. Kelly's friend, Phillip, was

    A. Younger than Kelly

    B. An old man

    C. A college student

    D. Blind

14. What did Kelly bring to school to show the other children?

    A. A tooth he had just pulled

    B. A model airplane he built

    C. A puppy

    D. Fiddler crabs

181
Kick a Stone Home
Doris Buchanan Smith

True or False. Decide whether each statement is true or false. Mark your answer sheet accordingly.

1. Miss Dickerson told Sara that she would have to redo her outline.

2. Miss Dickerson told Sara that her outline was the best she had ever seen.

3. Sara and Kay were friends.

4. Sara's parents were divorced.

5. Sara was in love with Sammy.

6. Sara and Sammy were just friends.

7. When Sara grew up, she wanted to be a veterinarian.

8. Sara found out that Kay's parents were divorced.

9. Sara's dog, Tally, was hit by a car.

10. At the end of the school year, Sara wrote Miss Dickerson a note.

Multiple Choice. Read each question. Decide which statement best answers the question. Mark your answer sheet accordingly.

11. Sara hit Johnny Football because

    A. He made fun of her little brother

    B. He called her a name

    C. He said something unkind about Sammy

    D. None of the above

12. At the beginning of the school year, Sara

    A. Transferred out of Miss Dickerson's homeroom

    B. Bumped into Miss Dickerson's car with her bicycle

    C. Invited Miss Dickerson to her house for dinner

    D. Accidentally knocked Miss Dickerson over

13. Why did Sara run out of her Sunday school class?

    A. She realized that she had studied the wrong lesson

    B. She saw Sammy and Kay holding hands

    C. She realized that she had on two different shoes

    D. She realized that her dress was on inside out

14. Sara was shocked when she realized that Dave Kellerman

    A. Was dead

    B. Had broken into their home and robbed them

    C. Was dating her mother

    D. Was a friend of her father's

182
Last Was Lloyd
Doris Buchanan Smith

True or False. Decide whether each statement is true or false. Mark your answer sheet accordingly.

1. Lloyd had a condition called hypoglycemia.
2. Lloyd's mother was on a softball team.
3. Lloyd's mother did not know that he knew how to hit a softball.
4. Ancil was usually the first person chosen to be on a softball team.
5. Lloyd was absent from school a lot.
6. Lloyd walked home from school every day.
7. Lloyd's mother always picked him up from school and drove him home.
8. Ancil never swung at any pitches at softball games.
9. Ancil went to Shafer's birthday party.
10. Lloyd gave Ancil his olive shell.
11. Lloyd gave Ancil a picture of himself.

Multiple Choice. Read each question. Decide which statement best answers the question. Mark your answer sheet accordingly.

12. Kirby told Shafer that he wouldn't go to his birthday party unless Shafer

    A. Paid him $5

    B. Invited Lloyd to the party

    C. Told Lloyd that he was not invited to the party

    D. Did his homework for him every day for a month

13. At Shafer's birthday party, Lloyd

    A. Ate so much food that he got sick

    B. Got into a fistfight with Kirby

    C. Hit a home run

    D. Kissed Ancil

14. Lloyd told Kirby that he wouldn't go to Shafer's birthday party unless Shafer

    A. Begged him to come on his hands and knees

    B. Promised to play softball at the party

    C. Told Ancil that she was not invited to the party

    D. Invited Ancil to the party

183
A Taste of Blackberries
Doris Buchanan Smith

True or False. Decide whether each statement is true or false. Mark your answer sheet accordingly.

1. Jamie thought that his sister, Martha, was a pest, and he was always trying to get rid of her.

2. Mrs. Houser didn't want the children in the neighborhood to play on her grass.

3. Jamie and the narrator were friends.

4. The narrator and Jamie lived in an orphanage.

5. Mrs. Houser asked the narrator if he would ask some of the children to help her get rid of the Japanese beetles on her grapevines.

6. When Jamie was stung by a bee, the narrator ran home and called an ambulance.

7. When Jamie was stung by a bee, the narrator went home and had a popsicle because he thought that Jamie was just trying to get attention.

8. Mrs. Mullins was angry at the narrator when she found out that he had come into her garden without permission.

9. Jamie died after he ate the apple that he had stolen from the farmer's tree.

10. Jamie was allergic to bee stings.

11. The narrator did not go to Jamie's funeral.

12. At the end of the book, the narrator brought a basket of blackberries to Jamie's mother.

Multiple Choice. Read each question. Decide which statement best answers the question. Mark your answer sheet accordingly.

13. What did Jamie, Martha, and the narrator do when they were caught in a thunderstorm?

    A. They stood under a tree

    B. They hitchhiked and were given a ride home

    C. They broke into the school

    D. They ran home as fast as they could

14. Who told the narrator that Jamie was dead?

    A. Martha

    B. Heather

    C. Mrs. Houser

    D. The narrator's mother

184
Encyclopedia Brown – The Case of the Dead Eagles and Other Mysteries
Donald J. Sobol

True or False. Decide whether each statement is true or false. Mark your answer sheet accordingly.

1. In "The Case of the Dead Eagles," Encyclopedia found out that the scoutmaster had poisoned the eagles.

2. In "The Case of the Dead Eagles," Encyclopedia took the eagle eggs home and kept them warm in his winter hat until they hatched.

3. In "The Case of the Parking Meters," Bugs Meany tried to get Encyclopedia and Sally into trouble.

4. In "The Case of the Parking Meters," Bugs Meany told Officer Culp that Sally had been stealing parking meters in the middle of the night.

5. In "The Case of the Hidden Will," Mr. King left one of his sons out of his will.

6. In "The Case of the Old Calendars," Encyclopedia found out that Butch Mulligan had really stolen the calendars from his math teacher.

7. In "The Case of the Old Calendars," Butch Mulligan's math teacher gave him 25 old wall calendars.

8. In "The Case of the Pantry Door," Encyclopedia and Sally were locked into the pantry at Hilda's house by Hilda's cousin.

9. In "The Case of the Pantry Door," Encyclopedia and Sally locked themselves into the pantry and then told Bugs Meany's mother that he had locked them in.

10. In "The Case of the Hypnotism Lesson," Bugs Meany charged Dave a dollar to learn how to hypnotize a lobster.

11. In "The Case of the Mysterious Thief," the thief turned out to be Bugs Meany.

12. In "The Case of Lightfoot Louie," Hoager wanted to enter Lightfoot Louie into the Worm Racers' Club of America.

13. In "The Case of the Broken Window," Mr. Hall wanted Encyclopedia and his father to find out who stole a valuable stamp from his stamp collection.

14. Encyclopedia's father was the principal of the high school.

185
Encyclopedia Brown Carries On
Donald J. Sobol

True or False. Decide whether each statement is true or false. Mark your answer sheet accordingly.

1. During the summer, Encyclopedia refused to solve any cases.

2. During the summer, Encyclopedia solved cases for the children of the neighborhood.

3. Bugs Meany was Encyclopedia's partner in solving cases.

4. In "The Case of the Grape Catcher," Bugs Meany and Edsel tried to get Sally and Encyclopedia into trouble.

5. In "The Case of the Grape Catcher," Sally and Encyclopedia tied Edsel up and threw grapes at him for hours.

6. In "The Case of the Marvelous Egg," Wilford did not really have a square egg.

7. In "The Case of the Marvelous Egg," the children gave all their money to Wilford so they could see his square egg.

8. In "The Case of the Marvelous Egg," Encyclopedia kept the children from giving all their money to Wilford.

9. In "The Case of the Ball of String," Encyclopedia discovered that Cosimo's ball of string was a fake — that it had a basketball in the center.

10. In "The Case of the Giant Mousetrap," the giant mousetrap couldn't be moved off City Hall's front lawn because Salvatore had hidden the key.

11. In "The Case of the Giant Mousetrap," Encyclopedia figured out that Salvatore didn't really own the mousetrap.

12. In "The Case of Bugs Meany, Thinker," Winslow wanted Bugs Meany to let him join the Tigers.

13. In "The Case of the Left-Handers Club," someone tried to break up the meeting by bringing howling dogs into the building where the meeting was being held.

14. In "The Case of the Overfed Pigs," someone was fattening Lucy's pigs so that they would not be able to swim in their act at Submarine World.

186
Encyclopedia Brown Solves Them All
Donald J. Sobol

True or False. Decide whether each statement is true or false. Mark your answer sheet accordingly.

1. Sally and Bugs Meany were good friends.

2. Bugs Meany wanted Sally and Encyclopedia to come to the judo show in the junior high school gym.

3. Sally was Encyclopedia Brown's junior partner in the detective agency.

4. In "The Case of Sir Biscuit-Shooter," Encyclopedia proved that it was not Lionel's Uncle Barney who had robbed and hit Princess Marta.

5. In "The Case of the Frightened Playboy," Mr. Mackey was right in thinking that someone was trying to kill him.

6. In "The Case of the Frightened Playboy," Mr. Mackey thought that someone was trying to kill him because he was the only eyewitness to a gas station burglary.

7. In "The Case of the Wounded Dog," Mr. Harwood told Encyclopedia and his father that he had been shooting at a robber, and he had not tried to shoot the dog.

8. In "The Case of the Wounded Dog," Mr. Harwood told Encyclopedia's father that he believed Encyclopedia had tried to kill the dog.

9. In "The Case of Cupid's Arrow," Encyclopedia was shot in the chest with a very sharp arrow.

10. In "The Case of the Missing Clues," Bugs Meany told Abner that he would give him some fruit for his fruit stand.

11. In "The Case of the Hair Driers," a deaf lady hit Mr. Jorgen in the alley and then robbed him.

12. In "The Case of the Earthenware Pig," Bugs Meany wanted Charlie's teeth collection.

13. Encyclopedia never accepted any money for solving cases for the neighborhood kids.

Multiple Choice. Read the question. Decide which statement best answers the question. Mark your answer sheet accordingly.

14. What had Sally done that no boy under 15 had ever dreamed of doing?

    A. She picked up a rattlesnake with her bare hands

    B. She beat Bugs Meany in a fight

    C. She camped by herself in the woods

    D. She beat Encyclopedia Brown in a fight

187
Miracles on Maple Hill
Virginia Sorensen

True or False. Decide whether each statement is true or false. Mark your answer sheet accordingly.

1. Marly was very angry when her parents decided that they would stay at Maple Hill.

2. When Joe and Marly first came to Maple Hill, Joe would not let Marly go exploring with him.

3. When living at Maple Hill, Joe and Marly went to different schools.

4. Joe became good friends with Harry, the hermit.

5. It was Mother's idea to have Harry, the hermit, spend Christmas at their house.

6. Chrissie said that she hated the sugar season because Mr. Chris worked too hard during that time.

7. Daddy did not get along with Mr. Chris.

8. Mr. Chris died of a heart attack.

9. Joe helped Marly hide the mice so that they would not get caught in the trap.

10. Daddy was much better at Maple Hill.

11. Mother had often visited Maple Hill when she was a little girl.

12. Chrissie was Mr. Chris's mother.

Multiple Choice. Read each question. Decide which statement best answers the question. Mark your answer sheet accordingly.

13. Who was "Annie-Get-Your-Gun"?

    A. The county truant officer

    B. Marly's teacher

    C. The Chris's maid

    D. The county sheriff

14. What did Marly give to Margie for her birthday?

    A. A goat

    B. A jug of maple syrup

    C. A friendship ring

    D. A dozen roses

188
The Bronze Bow
Elizabeth George Speare

True or False. Decide whether each statement is true or false. Mark your answer sheet accordingly.

1. Daniel was a Roman soldier.

2. Daniel's sister, Leah, did not want other people to see her.

3. Samson tried to kill Daniel.

4. When his grandmother died, Daniel decided to stay and take care of his sister, Leah.

5. Rosh did not believe in stealing.

6. Rosh was a Roman soldier.

7. Daniel's sister, Leah, was killed by Roman soldiers.

8. Many people believed that Daniel's sister, Leah, was possessed by a demon.

9. Samson was grateful to Daniel for removing the iron chains from his wrists.

10. Simon asked Daniel to take over his shop.

11. Leah and Thacia became friends.

Multiple Choice. Read each question. Decide which statement best answers the question. Mark your answer sheet accordingly.

12. Why was Daniel living with Rosh on the mountain?

    A. He had run away from Amalek

    B. They were on a camping trip

    C. Rosh kidnapped him from his parents when he was a baby

    D. They were lost

13. When Joel was captured by the Romans, Rosh

    A. Did nothing to help rescue Joel

    B. Sent his men to rescue Joel

    C. Rescued Joel all by himself

    D. Told the Romans to kill Joel

14. How did Samson help Daniel?

    A. He taught Daniel to read

    B. He introduced Daniel to Jesus

    C. He helped Daniel rescue Joel from the Roman soldiers

    D. He taught Daniel how to fight and defend himself during a battle

189
Calico Captive
Elizabeth George Speare

True or False. Decide whether each statement is true or false. Mark your answer sheet accordingly.

1. Susanna and Miriam were sisters.

2. Miriam knew how to sew.

3. The Indians killed Sylvanus because he would not obey them.

4. Sylvanus went with the Indians on a hunting trip.

5. In Montreal, the governor hired James to be his personal bodyguard.

6. Miriam decided to marry Pierre Laroche, the *coureur de bois*.

7. While Miriam was in Montreal, she received a letter from Phineas Whitney.

8. Miriam met Phineas Whitney before she was captured by the Indians.

9. Miriam and Hortense became friends.

10. Miriam and Hortense taught each other words from their own languages.

Multiple Choice. Read each question. Decide which statement best answers the question. Mark your answer sheet accordingly.

11. Madame Du Quesne wanted Miriam to teach her daughter how to

    A. Sew and knit

    B. Ride a horse

    C. Speak and read English

    D. Cook a pot roast and a turkey

12. Madame Du Quesne became angry at Miriam because

    A. Miriam refused to go to Felicité's birthday party

    B. Pierre Laroche paid so much attention to Miriam at the ball

    C. Miriam refused to curtsy when Madame Du Quesne entered the room

    D. Miriam did not know how to sew

13. What did Miriam do with the material the governor's wife gave her?

    A. She made a wedding dress for Hortense

    B. She made a dress for herself

    C. She sold the material to Madame Du Quesne

    D. None of the above

14. Why did the Indians bring Miriam, James, Little Susanna, and Polly to Montreal?

    A. To sell them to the French

    B. To give them their freedom

    C. To kill them

    D. None of the above

190
Sign of the Beaver
Elizabeth George Speare

True or False. Decide whether each statement is true or false. Mark your answer sheet accordingly.

1. Attean's grandfather did not know that Matt was teaching Attean to read.

2. Matt sold the rifle his father had given him to Attean.

3. The rifle that Matt's father had given to him was stolen.

4. Matt read parts of the book *Robinson Crusoe* to Attean.

5. Matt was not with Attean when Attean killed a bear.

6. Matt never met Attean's grandfather.

7. Attean's grandfather invited Matt to go with the Indians on their big hunt.

8. Attean told Matt that after the big hunt, his people would not return to the village.

9. Matt became lost in the woods when he tried to find his way to Attean's village.

10. Matt accidentally shot Attean's dog with his bow and arrow.

11. Matt never met Attean's grandmother.

Multiple Choice. Read each question. Decide which statement best answers the question. Mark your answer sheet accordingly.

12. Who helped Matt free Attean's dog from the trap?

    A. Attean's grandfather

    B. Attean's grandmother

    C. Attean's brother

    D. Attean's sister

13. What did Attean give to Matt before Attean left for the big hunt?

    A. A rifle

    B. His dog

    C. A bear claw

    D. None of the above

14. What did Matt give to Attean at the end of the book?

    A. The book *Robinson Crusoe*

    B. A watch

    C. A Bible

    D. A rifle

191
The Witch of Blackbird Pond
Elizabeth George Speare

True or False. Decide whether each statement is true or false. Mark your answer sheet accordingly.

1. Kit did not know how to swim.

2. Kit's parents died when she was very young.

3. Kit's grandfather was once very wealthy.

4. Kit was born in Barbados.

5. Kit was born in Africa.

6. Kit was afraid of Hannah because she thought that Hannah was a witch.

7. Goodwife Cruff was good friends with Kit.

8. Kit did not go to the corn-husking bee.

9. John Holbrook did not go to the corn-husking bee.

10. Kit was accused of being a witch.

Multiple Choice. Read each question. Decide which statement best answers the question. Mark your answer sheet accordingly.

11. Kit gave a light blue, woolen shawl to

    A. Judith

    B. Mercy

    C. Hannah

    D. Prudence

12. Why had Hannah and her husband been branded and driven out of Massachusetts?

    A. They were Quakers

    B. They were black

    C. They were Catholic

    D. They were Mormons

13. Who put jack-o-lanterns in the windows of William Ashby's house?

    A. Nat Eaton

    B. Kit

    C. John Holbrook

    D. None of the above

14. At the end of the book, who did Kit decide to marry?

    A. Nat Eaton

    B. William Ashby

    C. John Holbrook

    D. None of the above

192
Call It Courage
Armstrong Sperry

True or False. Decide whether each statement is true or false. Mark your answer sheet accordingly.

1. The eaters-of-men captured and killed Mafatu's friend, Uri.

2. Mafatu stole a spearhead from the Sacred Place of the eaters-of-men.

3. Mafatu was wounded by a wild boar on the Forbidden Island.

4. Mafatu made a necklace from the boar's teeth.

5. Mafatu made his own outrigger canoe.

6. The eaters-of-men discovered Mafatu and chased him in their canoes.

7. The king of Polynesia sent war canoes to drive away the eaters-of-men.

8. Mafatu's father was ashamed of him because he was afraid of the sea.

9. Mafatu's only loyal friends were a dog and a bird.

10. Mafatu's mother drowned when he was young.

Multiple Choice. Read each question. Decide which statement best answers the question. Mark your answer sheet accordingly.

11. To prove to himself that he wasn't a coward, Mafatu

    A. Sailed away in an outrigger canoe

    B. Fought a shark with a knife

    C. Killed a wild pig with his spear

    D. Swam across the lagoon at night

12. While Mafatu was at sea, a terrible storm

    A. Sank the canoe

    B. Swept Uri, the dog, overboard

    C. Damaged the canoe, but didn't sink it

    D. Drowned Kivi

13. Mafatu ended up on the island that

    A. Seemed to be empty

    B. Seemed much bigger than his home island

    C. A and B

    D. None of the above

14. Mafatu found that the island was

    A. A breeding ground for walruses

    B. A Sacred Place for the eaters-of-men

    C. The home island of the eaters-of-men

    D. A fortress island for the king of the Polynesians

193
Abel's Island
William Steig

True or False. Decide whether each statement is true or false. Mark your answer sheet accordingly.

1. Abel did not know how to read.

2. Abel stored food in his log for the winter.

3. Abel brought the watch he found back to his log.

4. Abel brought the book he found back to his log.

5. Abel made a statue of the owl.

6. Abel made a statue of Gower, the frog.

7. Abel killed the owl.

8. Believing that Abel was dead, Amanda married another mouse.

9. Abel was happy to see Gower, the frog, leave the island.

10. Abel became good friends with the cat.

11. Abel lost Amanda's scarf when he was swimming across the stream.

Multiple Choice. Read each question. Decide which statement best answers the question. Mark your answer sheet accordingly.

12. What was Abel doing when the storm first hit?

    A. He and his wife were having a picnic in the woods

    B. He was building a log cabin

    C. He and his wife were playing checkers in their living room

    D. He and his wife were at church

13. Abel decided to stop sleeping in the birch tree because

    A. The owl told Abel that the tree belonged to him

    B. The tree was blown over by the wind during a hurricane

    C. One night he fell out of the tree

    D. He discovered that he was allergic to the tree

14. How did Abel finally get off of the island?

    A. Gower, the frog, took him across the stream on his back

    B. He swam across the stream

    C. The owl carried him across the stream

    D. Abel paddled across the stream in a boat he made

194
The Real Thief
William Steig

True or False. Decide whether each statement is true or false. Mark your answer sheet accordingly.

1. King Basil found out who the real thief was and hanged him.

2. The real thief returned all of the stolen treasures.

3. The real thief was happy when he found out that King Basil blamed Gawain for stealing the treasures.

4. Gawain never found out who the real thief was.

5. Gawain found out who the real thief was but did not report him to King Basil.

6. Gawain forgave the real thief for what he had done.

7. King Basil thought that Gawain was guilty because he was the only other person who had a key to the treasure house.

8. The real thief was Derek, the mouse.

9. King Basil was a bear.

10. It was Derek, the mouse, who finally found Gawain.

11. At the end of the book, King Basil appointed Gawain to the office of royal architect.

Multiple Choice. Read each question. Decide which statement best answers the question. Mark your answer sheet accordingly.

12. Why did the real thief steal the treasures?

    A. He stole the treasures because he hated King Basil

    B. He stole the treasures because he wanted to decorate his house

    C. He stole the treasures so that he could sell them to provide food for his family

    D. A and C

13. How did King Basil find out that Gawain was innocent?

    A. More treasures were stolen after Gawain was gone

    B. The real thief came to King Basil and confessed

    C. Gawain passed a lie detector test

    D. None of the above

14. Gawain felt sad because

    A. King Basil had said that he was a disgrace to the kingdom

    B. Gawain admired the king and had agreed to guard his treasures out of love

    C. Even Gawain's friends believed he was guilty

    D. All of the above

From *Quizzes for 220 Great Children's Books*, revised 1st edition. © 1996. Teacher Ideas Press. (800) 237-6124.

195
Kidnapped
Robert Louis Stevenson

True or False. Decide whether each statement is true or false. Mark your answer sheet accordingly.

1. David was related to Ebenezer.

2. Ebenezer was glad to see David.

3. Ebenezer tried to trick David into having a deadly accident.

4. Ebenezer paid Captain Hoseason to kidnap David.

5. Alan Breck Steward helped kidnap David.

6. Alan Breck Steward was a Campbell loyal to the King of England.

7. Alan and David were accused of murdering the Red Fox.

8. Alan shot the Red Fox to help David escape.

9. Alan was in Scotland to collect money for his clan chief.

10. David was angry because Alan lost David's money in a card game.

Multiple Choice. Read each question. Decide which statement best answers the question. Mark your answer sheet accordingly.

11. Why was David accused of murder?

   A. He was talking to the Red Fox when the Red Fox was shot

   B. He was standing next to Alan when Alan shot the Red Fox

   C. He was seen holding a rifle

   D. Captain Hoseason lied to the authorities about him

12. How did Alan and David get out of the Highlands?

   A. Loyal Scots smuggled them over the border

   B. They snuck onto a ship sailing to London

   C. A young girl rowed them across the river

   D. They fought their way over a bridge

13. David got his share of the House of Shaws because

   A. David scared his uncle into giving it to him

   B. Alan threatened to kill him if he didn't

   C. Ebenezer was afraid of Scottish fighters

   D. Alan tricked Ebenezer into admitting that he had David kidnapped

14. At the end of the story

   A. Alan was preparing to return to France

   B. David was planning to go to court to defend James of the Glens

   C. David moved into the House of Shaws

   D. A and B

196
Treasure Island
Robert Louis Stevenson

True or False. Decide whether each statement is true or false. Mark your answer sheet accordingly.

1. Most of the *Hispaniola*'s crew had formerly been pirates with Flint.

2. Jim Hawkins's father had sailed with Long John Silver.

3. Jim Hawkins killed Israel Hands after running the *Hispaniola* aground.

4. Long John Silver told the pirates that he was keeping Jim as a hostage.

5. All the pirates except Long John Silver were killed on Treasure Island.

6. Jim Hawkins, Dr. Livesey, and the squire found that Ben Gunn had Flint's treasure.

7. Long John Silver spent 20 years in prison for his part in the mutiny.

8. The pirate, Ben, told Jim Hawkins to be on the lookout for a man with one leg.

9. Jim found out about the mutiny when he overheard two mutineers talking.

10. Jim found a marooned sailor named Ben Gunn on Treasure Island.

Multiple Choice. Read each question. Decide which statement best answers the question. Mark your answer sheet accordingly.

11. Ben's sea chest contained

    A. A great deal of money

    B. A treasure map

    C. Clothes

    D. All of the above

12. Who helped the squire select the crew of the *Hispaniola*?

    A. Long John Silver

    B. Joe Morgan

    C. Dr. Livesey

    D. All of the above

13. Long John Silver let the captain leave the stockade

    A. Because too many pirates had been killed

    B. Because he felt sorry for the captain and the squire

    C. In exchange for the treasure map and some food

    D. Hoping to follow them to Flint's treasure

14. When the pirates got to the spot where the treasure was buried, they found

    A. The bodies of five men

    B. An empty hole

    C. A treasure chest too heavy to be carried

    D. Both A and C

From *Quizzes for 220 Great Children's Books*, revised 1st edition. © 1996. Teacher Ideas Press. (800) 237-6124.

197
Cat Walk
Mary Stolz

True or False. Decide whether each statement is true or false. Mark your answer sheet accordingly.

1. Jerry, the owner of the gas station, was kind to the black cat with the big white paws.

2. The black cat loved Jerry, the owner of the gas station.

3. After Jerry took the black cat to the veterinarian, he took him to Mr. and Mrs. Jaffee, who owned an animal haven.

4. Mr. and Mrs. Jaffee were cruel to the animals who lived with them.

5. Mr. and Mrs. Jaffee loved animals and took good care of them.

6. Mr. and Mrs. Jaffee named the black cat "Mittens."

7. The black cat left Mr. and Mrs. Jaffee's animal haven because their grandchildren wanted to keep him as a pet.

8. The black cat left Mr. and Mrs. Jaffee's animal haven because he wanted to go back to living in the barn with his mother, his sisters, and his brothers.

9. Jerry's son flung the black cat across a lot and then kicked him.

10. At the end of the book, the black cat was hit by a car and killed.

11. At the end of the book, the black cat went back to the barn to live with his mother, his brothers, and his sisters.

12. At the end of the book, the black cat went back to live with Mr. and Mrs. Jaffee at their animal haven.

Multiple Choice. Read each question. Decide which statement best answers the question. Mark your answer sheet accordingly.

13. What did Missy, the farmer's daughter, do with the black kitten?

    A. She named him Tootsy-Wootsy

    B. She dressed him and pushed him around in her doll carriage

    C. A and B

    D. None of the above

14. What did Jerry, the owner of Jerome's Service Station, do with the black cat?

    A. He gave the cat to his son as a birthday present

    B. He kicked the cat and refused to give it any food

    C. A and B

    D. None of the above

From *Quizzes for 220 Great Children's Books*, revised 1st edition. © 1996. Teacher Ideas Press. (800) 237-6124.

198
The Noonday Friends
Mary Stolz

True or False. Decide whether each statement is true or false. Mark your answer sheet accordingly.

1. Mr. Davis was angry when he found out that Francisco had been hired by Mr. Horney.

2. Mr. Davis lost his job as a shoe salesman.

3. Franny and Marshall often played school together.

4. Mr. Davis helped Francisco get hired as a shoe salesman.

5. Simone and Franny went to the same school.

6. Simone liked to look at beautiful things.

7. On Marshall's birthday, he got to sleep outside in a tent.

8. On Marshall's birthday, he got to stay up all night.

9. Jimmy felt guilty because a man had given him a dollar bill.

10. Jimmy felt guilty because he stole $5 from his father's wallet.

11. Mr. Davis liked to paint.

Multiple Choice. Read each question. Decide which statement best answers the question. Mark your answer sheet accordingly.

12. At 3:00, Marshall always

    A. Left Mrs. Mundy's and waited in the hall for Franny to come home from school

    B. Walked home from school to wait alone until Franny came home

    C. Took his dog for a walk

    D. Took a nap

13. When Marshall and his family went grocery shopping, he

    A. Stole a box of cereal

    B. Got lost

    C. Yelled and screamed for something he wanted

    D. Got into a fistfight with another little boy

14. What did Mrs. Mundy give Marshall on his birthday?

    A. A puppy

    B. A box full of crayons, colored chalk, and paint

    C. A box full of cereal surprises

    D. A pair of shoes

199
Uncle Tom's Cabin
Harriet Beecher Stowe

True or False. Decide whether each statement is true or false. Mark your answer sheet accordingly.

1. Mrs. St. Clare did not sell any of her slaves after her husband died.

2. The Quakers helped Eliza and George escape to the North.

3. George and Eliza were safe once they reached the Northern states.

4. Uncle Tom joined his family back in Kentucky.

5. Mr. Legree let Tom run his plantation for him.

6. Little Eva begged her father to free Uncle Tom.

7. After reaching freedom, George Harris helped many other slaves escape.

8. Eliza and her son crossed the Ohio River by jumping from ice patch to ice patch.

9. When little Eva was dying, she gave everyone a lock of her hair.

10. Mr. Legree believed that slaves should be set free.

Multiple Choice. Read each question. Decide which statement best answers the question. Mark your answer sheet accordingly.

11. Mr. Shelby sold Uncle Tom and Eliza because

   A. They were helping slaves escape to the North

   B. Mrs. Shelby hated Eliza because she was so beautiful

   C. They had been putting on airs and acting like white people

   D. Mr. Shelby needed the money

12. Eliza's husband, George Harris, was sold because

   A. He was too proud and intelligent

   B. His master's wife was in love with him

   C. He was planning to run away, and his master found out about it

   D. His master needed the money

13. Uncle Tom was first sold to Mr. St. Clare to be

   A. The manager of his plantation

   B. The man in charge of the horses

   C. A servant to Mrs. St. Clare

   D. A servant to little Eva St. Clare

14. Uncle Tom was cheerful all the time because

   A. He was a naturally cheerful person

   B. He felt that God was in control of his life

   C. He had a very sheltered and easy life

   D. His masters took good care of him

200
Roll of Thunder, Hear My Cry
Mildred D. Taylor

True or False. Decide whether each statement is true or false. Mark your answer sheet accordingly.

1. Cassie's family lived in town.

2. The black schools used books that the white schools no longer wanted.

3. Both black and white children attended Cassie's school.

4. Cassie's mother worked as a maid.

5. Cassie's mother was fired because she took some food from her boss.

6. Mr. Morrison worked for the Wallaces.

7. Papa bought only from the Wallaces' store.

8. Stacey and Cassie refused to talk with T. J. because he helped get their mother fired.

9. When Cassie accidentally bumped into Lillian Jean, Mr. Simms made her get off the sidewalk and apologize to Lillian Jean.

10. On the way back from shopping in Vicksburg, Papa found a $50 bill.

11. On the way back from shopping in Vicksburg, Papa was attacked by some white men.

Multiple Choice. Read each question. Decide which statement best answers the question. Mark your answer sheet accordingly.

12. Why did Cassie, Stacey, Little Man, and Christopher-John dig a hole in the road?

    A. They were making a crayfish pond

    B. They wanted to hurt the school bus

    C. Little Man thought that there was gold there

    D. None of the above

13. Mr. Granger wanted the Edwards' farm because

    A. He hated the Edwards

    B. He wanted all the land that had once belonged to the Grangers

    C. He needed it to build a sawmill

    D. He knew that an airplane factory could be built there

14. How did Papa stop the night riders from attacking his home?

    A. Papa got Mr. Wallace to stop them

    B. Papa told Mr. Granger that they were coming

    C. Papa killed the leader of the night riders

    D. Papa set fire to his own cotton fields

201
I, Juan de Pareja
Elizabeth Borton de Trevino

True or False. Decide whether each statement is true or false. Mark your answer sheet accordingly.

1. Juan had lived with Master Velazquez ever since he was born.
2. When Master Velazquez found out that Juan had been secretly painting for many years, he wrote a letter that said that Juan was no longer a slave.
3. Juan bought a gold necklace for Paquita when she was a little girl.
4. Juan bought a kitten for Paquita when she was a little girl.
5. Paquita was not allowed to keep the gift that Juan bought her.
6. Juan's wife was not given her freedom from slavery.
7. Master Velazquez became good friends with the king.
8. Master Velazquez painted the king's portrait.
9. Master Velazquez died before his daughter, Paquita, was married.
10. Juan did not believe in prayer.
11. Juan was very devoted to Master Velazquez.
12. Master Velazquez was a talkative person.

Multiple Choice. Read each question. Decide which statement best answers the question. Mark your answer sheet accordingly.

13. Why had Juan been painting in secret for so many years?

    A. In Spain it was unlawful for slaves to paint

    B. Juan thought that his master would be jealous of his paintings

    C. Juan knew that he was not a skillful painter and did it only for his own enjoyment

    D. None of the above

14. Which of the following events did NOT occur in this book?

    A. Master Velazquez died

    B. Paquita died

    C. The king died

    D. Master Velazquez's wife died

202
Building Blocks
Cynthia Voigt

True or False. Decide whether each statement is true or false. Mark your answer sheet accordingly.

1. Brann returned to his own time by sleeping in the block fortress.
2. Suzanne returned to the present with Brann.
3. Uncle Andrew begged Mr. Connell to let Kevin work on his farm.
4. Brann told his father to sell the farm to raise some money.
5. Brann's parents sold their house and moved to Uncle Andrew's farm.
6. Brann's mother decided not to go to law school.
7. Brann's father became a famous doctor.
8. Mr. Connell did not let Kevin go to Uncle Andrew's farm because he wanted Kevin to work at home.
9. When Kevin's family ate breakfast, no one started until Kevin's father arrived.
10. Mr. and Mrs. Connell had Kevin do a lot of work because he was the oldest child.
11. When Brann and Kevin went into the cave, they got lost.

Multiple Choice. Read each question. Decide which statement best answers the question. Mark your answer sheet accordingly.

12. Brann's parents were fighting because
    A. Brann's mother wanted a divorce
    B. Brann's father wanted to move to Vermont
    C. Brann's mother wanted a new car
    D. None of the above

13. What happened to Brann when he fell asleep in the block fortress?
    A. He traveled back in time
    B. He was taken to the planet Voltron
    C. He slept through both lunch and supper
    D. He dreamed that he was a grownup living in Chicago

14. What happened to Suzanne, Brann, and Kevin when they were caught trespassing?
    A. Mr. Connell spanked them with his belt
    B. A guard threw rocks at them
    C. A wild dog bit Suzanne
    D. None of the above

203
Dicey's Song
Cynthia Voigt

True or False. Decide whether each statement is true or false. Mark your answer sheet accordingly.

1. Dicey's grandmother died in this book.

2. Dicey's mother died in this book.

3. Dicey was the oldest of the four children in her family.

4. Dicey worked part-time at the town library.

5. Millie, the store owner, was very intelligent.

6. Maybeth could play the piano.

7. Maybeth had a hard time learning to read.

8. Dicey earned an A in her home economics class.

9. Mina's father was a preacher.

10. Mina disliked Dicey.

11. Dicey's teacher accused her of copying the essay she wrote from a book.

12. Gram went to Sammy's school and took on the second-grade class at marbles.

13. James was blind.

Multiple Choice. Read the question. Decide which statement best answers the question. Mark your answer sheet accordingly.

14. What did a man in a shop give Dicey?

    A. A piano for Maybeth

    B. A box of clothing

    C. A box to put her mother's ashes in

    D. A box of candy to take to her mother

204
Homecoming
Cynthia Voigt

True or False. Decide whether each statement is true or false. Mark your answer sheet accordingly.

1. Sammy was the youngest of the four children.

2. Sammy stole a bag of food from some picnickers.

3. Dicey's grandmother was wealthy.

4. Cousin Eunice wanted to become a nun.

5. Cousin Eunice lived in a huge house next to the ocean.

6. Dicey thought that Maybeth was retarded and should be put in an institution.

7. When Dicey's grandmother found out that the children were living with Cousin Eunice, she wrote and asked if the children could come live with her.

8. James was very intelligent.

9. Cousin Eunice did not allow the children to do any housework.

10. Cousin Eunice liked to keep her house very neat.

11. Cousin Eunice took Maybeth to church with her.

Multiple Choice. Read each question. Decide which statement best answers the question. Mark your answer sheet accordingly.

12. Which of the four children was a slow learner?

    A. Dicey

    B. James

    C. Maybeth

    D. Sammy

13. Sergeant Gordo of the Missing Persons Department told Dicey that they had located her mother. Where had Dicey's mother been found?

    A. In a state hospital in Massachusetts

    B. Working in a small bakery

    C. Living on the streets of New York City

    D. Hiding out in an abandoned farmhouse

14. How did Dicey earn money while she was living in Bridgeport with Cousin Eunice?

    A. She baby-sat for the children who lived next door

    B. She delivered newspapers

    C. She shined shoes

    D. She washed windows

205
A Solitary Blue
Cynthia Voigt

True or False. Decide whether each statement is true or false. Mark your answer sheet accordingly.

1. Melody was very wealthy.

2. Melody felt strongly about women's rights.

3. Jeff thought that Melody was beautiful.

4. When Gambo died, she named Jeff as the heir to her property.

5. When Gambo died, she named Melody as the heir to her property.

6. Dicey never met Jeff's mother.

7. Jeff had to repeat the eighth grade.

8. The second time that Jeff visited Melody, the two of them were able to spend a lot of time together.

9. Jeff's father was a professor at the university.

10. Jeff's father never published any books.

11. Melody told the professor that she wanted custody of Jeff.

12. Jeff visited Melody every summer from the time he was six until he was 15.

Multiple Choice. Read each question. Decide which statement best answers the question. Mark your answer sheet accordingly.

13. What did Jeff call his father?

   A. Dad

   B. Horace

   C. Father

   D. Professor

14. Who gave Jeff his guitar?

   A. Brother Thomas

   B. Melody

   C. The professor

   D. Dicey

206
Charlotte's Web
E. B. White

True or False. Decide whether each statement is true or false. Mark your answer sheet accordingly.

1. Charlotte did not go to the fair with Wilbur.

2. Templeton did not go to the fair with Wilbur.

3. When Wilbur was very small, Fern fed him with a bottle.

4. Avery was older than Fern.

5. After Charlotte started writing things in her web about Wilbur, people came from miles around to look at Wilbur and to read the words in Charlotte's web.

6. Mrs. Zuckerman gave Wilbur a buttermilk bath before taking him to the fair.

7. Wilbur never got to see any of Charlotte's children.

8. Templeton was a rabbit.

9. Templeton was a rat.

10. One of the words that Charlotte wrote in her web was "oops."

11. The last thing that Charlotte wrote in her web was "sorry."

12. Charlotte died at the end of the book.

Multiple Choice. Read each question. Decide which statement best answers the question. Mark your answer sheet accordingly.

13. Mr. Arable was going to kill Wilbur when he was first born because

    A. Wilbur was a large pig, and Mr. Arable wanted to cook him up as sausage

    B. Wilbur was a wild pig, and he was killing all of the other pigs

    C. Wilbur was small and weak, and Mr. Arable thought he'd only cause trouble

    D. None of the above

14. Who found the words for Charlotte to write in her web?

    A. Fern

    B. Templeton

    C. Avery

    D. Mr. Arable

207
Stuart Little
E. B. White

True or False. Decide whether each statement is true or false. Mark your answer sheet accordingly.

1. Stuart's brother, George, was smaller than Stuart.

2. Stuart met a girl who was a little smaller than he was.

3. Stuart and Snowbell, the cat, were good friends.

4. One day, Stuart's mother accidentally locked him in the refrigerator.

5. Snowbell, the cat, ate Margalo.

6. Margalo always slept in the Boston fern on the bookshelf in the living room.

7. Stuart never wore any clothes.

8. Stuart liked to get up very early in the morning.

9. Margalo flew away from Stuart's house because she thought that he did not love her any more.

10. Stuart left his home because he wanted to search for Margalo.

11. At the end of the book, Stuart and Margalo decided to get married.

Multiple Choice. Read each question. Decide which statement best answers the question. Mark your answer sheet accordingly.

12. How did Stuart get a car?

 A. His father gave him one

 B. His friend, the dentist, gave him one

 C. Stuart stole one from a hobby store

 D. Stuart bought one at an auction

13. How did Margalo save Stuart's life?

 A. She rescued him from a garbage dump

 B. She told Mr. and Mrs. Little that Snowbell had trapped him

 C. She saved him from drowning when he fell into the bathtub

 D. None of the above

14. Where was Stuart when his family thought he had gone down the mouse hole?

 A. Hiding underneath his bed

 B. Locked in the refrigerator

 C. Caught in the window shade

 D. Outside taking a walk

208
The Trumpet of the Swan
E. B. White

True or False. Decide whether each statement is true or false. Mark your answer sheet accordingly.

1. Sam kept a diary.

2. Louis kept a diary.

3. Sam's father is never mentioned in this book.

4. Sam did not receive Louis's telegram asking him to come to the Philadelphia Zoo.

5. Louis learned to read and write by going to school with Sam.

6. Louis earned more than enough money to repay the storekeeper for the trumpet and the damages done to the store.

7. Louis asked Sam to take a razor blade and slit the web on his right foot.

8. Louis was born without a voice.

9. Louis needed Sam's help at the Philadelphia Zoo because the Head Man in Charge of Birds had stolen all of Louis's money.

10. Louis needed Sam's help at the Philadelphia Zoo because the Head Man in Charge of Birds wanted to keep Serena captive by clipping the tip of one wing.

11. At the end of the book, Louis's father was shot and killed.

Multiple Choice. Read each question. Decide which statement best answers the question. Mark your answer sheet accordingly.

12. Which of the following items did Louis NOT wear around his neck

    A. A trumpet

    B. A lifesaving medal

    C. A moneybag

    D. A pair of glasses

13. Who gave Louis the trumpet?

    A. Sam

    B. Louis's father

    C. Serena

    D. None of the above

14. Louis wanted to earn money to

    A. Pay for Sam's college education

    B. Impress Serena with how wealthy he was

    C. Buy trumpets for all of his brothers and sisters

    D. None of the above

209
Rebecca of Sunnybrook Farm
Kate Douglas Wiggin

True or False. Decide whether each statement is true or false. Mark your answer sheet accordingly.

1. Rebecca did not have any brothers or sisters.

2. Rebecca's father was dead.

3. Rebecca sold 300 cakes of soap to Mr. Ladd.

4. Emma Jean was Rebecca's roommate at Wareham.

5. Rebecca never graduated from Wareham.

6. Aunt Miranda died and left the brick house to Rebecca.

7. Aunt Miranda was often cross with Rebecca while Rebecca was growing up.

8. Aunt Jane was kinder to Rebecca than Aunt Miranda was.

9. Emma Jean and Rebecca were enemies.

10. Rebecca wanted to sell cakes of soap to earn enough money to buy a special Christmas present for Aunt Miranda.

11. Rebecca wanted to sell cakes of soap to help the Simpson children win a banquet lamp.

Multiple Choice. Read each question. Decide which statement best answers the question. Mark your answer sheet accordingly.

12. What did Rebecca decide to do as self-punishment for ruining her dress?

    A. Cut off her hair

    B. Wear a stone in her shoe

    C. Throw her pink parasol into the well

    D. All of the above

13. Why did Rebecca wear her new pink dress to school without permission?

    A. She wanted Seesaw Simpson to notice her

    B. None of the other girls at school believed that she had a new dress

    C. A and B

    D. None of the above

14. Rebecca first met Mr. Cobb when he

    A. Came to take Aunt Jane on a date

    B. Saved Rebecca from drowning in Aunt Miranda's pool

    C. Brought Rebecca to Riverboro in the stagecoach

    D. Caught Rebecca stealing a handful of candy from his store

210
By the Shores of Silver Lake
Laura Ingalls Wilder

True or False. Decide whether each statement is true or false. Mark your answer sheet accordingly.

1. Jack was very old when he died.

2. Pa sold Jack to Mr. Nelson before he went with Aunt Docia to the railroad camp.

3. Ma and the girls took a bus to meet Pa in the West.

4. Ma and the girls took a train to meet Pa in the West.

5. Big Jerry tried to steal Pa's horses.

6. The Ingalls family did not stay at Silver Lake for the winter.

7. During the winter, Pa taught Laura to play checkers.

8. Pa shot the wolf Laura and Carrie saw when they went out to slide on the ice.

9. On Christmas Day, the Ingalls family drove out to the Boasts' homestead.

10. Ma gave a handkerchief to Mrs. Boast and wristlets to Mr. Boast for Christmas.

11. Ma did not give Christmas presents to Mr. and Mrs. Boast.

12. Laura wanted more than anything else to become a schoolteacher when she grew up.

13. Ma did not want Laura to go to school.

14. Mary died at the end of this book.

211
Farmer Boy
Laura Ingalls Wilder

True or False. Decide whether each statement is true or false. Mark your answer sheet accordingly.

1. Almanzo was six years old when he started school.

2. Almanzo had two sisters and one brother.

3. The boys from the Hardscrabble settlement liked school.

4. Mr. Corse hit the Hardscrabble boys with a paddle.

5. To keep the ice from melting in the summer, it was packed with sawdust.

6. Almanzo's father gave him two calves to train.

7. On the Fourth of July, a frost destroyed some of the Wilders' corn crop.

8. When Almanzo's dad gave him 50¢, Almanzo bought a pig.

9. Almanzo's pumpkin won third place at the fair.

10. Mr. Corse married Elly.

11. Royal and Almanzo took over their father's farm.

Multiple Choice. Read each question. Decide which statement best answers the question. Mark your answer sheet accordingly.

12. Almanzo's father would not let him play with which of the following animals

    A. The calves

    B. The pigs

    C. The horses

    D. The turkeys

13. Royal wanted to be a

    A. Lawyer

    B. Farmer

    C. Storekeeper

    D. Blacksmith

14. What did Almanzo want to buy with his $200?

    A. A wagon

    B. Lumber to build a cabin

    C. A colt

    D. All of the above

212
The First Four Years
Laura Ingalls Wilder

True or False. Decide whether each statement is true or false. Mark your answer sheet accordingly.

1. Laura's first child was a boy who died three days after he was born.

2. After Laura and Almanzo were married, Laura taught two more terms of school.

3. Laura and Almanzo did not owe the bank any money.

4. The sheep that Laura bought were eaten by wolves.

5. Laura named her first child Rose.

6. One day, Indians came to Laura's house while Almanzo was in town.

7. When Laura cooked dinner for the threshers, she forgot to put sugar in the pie.

8. Almanzo bought a pony for Laura so she could learn to ride.

9. Laura became ill with diptheria.

10. Rose became ill with diptheria.

11. Almanzo became ill with diptheria.

12. The day that the fire hit the Wilders' house, they were all in town.

13. Before Laura married Almanzo, she made him promise that he would never give up on being a farmer.

Multiple Choice. Read the question. Decide which statement best answers the question. Mark your answer sheet accordingly.

14. When saying her wedding vows, Laura did not want the minister to use the word

    A. Death

    B. Obey

    C. Cherish

    D. Promise

213
Little House in the Big Woods
Laura Ingalls Wilder

True or False. Decide whether each statement is true or false. Mark your answer sheet accordingly.

1. Laura and Mary stayed home and watched Baby Carrie while Ma and Pa went to the dance at Grandpa's.

2. During the dance, Grandma's stove caught on fire.

3. No children were allowed to go to the dance at Grandma's.

4. On Sundays, Mary and Laura were not supposed to run or shout or be noisy in their play.

5. Pa often told Laura and Mary stories about when he was a boy.

6. None of Laura's relatives came to spend Christmas with her family.

7. Mary was older than Laura.

8. Laura and Mary did not go to school.

9. When Pa went to help Uncle Henry cut his grain, Ma took Laura, Mary, and Carrie to spend the day with Aunt Polly.

10. Cousin Charley did not want to help Pa and Uncle Henry in the field.

11. Laura received a rag doll for Christmas.

12. Laura slapped Mary's face because Mary would not share her candy cane with Laura.

13. Laura's hair was brown.

Multiple Choice. Read the question. Decide which statement best answers the question. Mark your answer sheet accordingly.

14. How was Laura punished for slapping Mary's face?

    A. She had to apologize to Mary

    B. She had to go to bed without any supper

    C. Pa took a strap down from the wall and whipped her

    D. She had to do all of Mary's chores for a week

214
Little Town on the Prairie
Laura Ingalls Wilder

True or False. Decide whether each statement is true or false. Mark your answer sheet accordingly.

1. A mouse cut off some of Pa's hair in the middle of the night.

2. Ma would not allow Laura to work in town as Pa suggested.

3. Laura worked in town as a hired girl in the hotel.

4. Laura worked in town helping Mrs. White with the hand-sewing.

5. Grace went with Pa, Laura, and Carrie to town on the Fourth of July.

6. On the Fourth of July, Pa took Laura, Carrie, and Grace to a restaurant.

7. After Pa shot the blackbirds that had been eating their corn, Ma cooked them for supper.

8. Laura's father was on the school board.

9. Laura, Carrie, and Grace stayed home by themselves for a week while Ma and Pa took Mary to college.

10. Nellie Oleson's father was on the school board.

11. Almanzo Wilder gave his name card to Laura.

12. Laura did not have any name cards of her own.

Multiple Choice. Read each question. Decide which statement best answers the question. Mark your answer sheet accordingly.

13. Which of the following teachers did not like Laura

     A. Miss Wilder

     B. Mr. Owen

     C. Mr. Clewett

     D. None of the above

14. What Christmas gift did Laura accidentally find before Christmas?

     A. A set of hoops

     B. A book of poems

     C. An autograph book

     D. A brown, velvet hat

From *Quizzes for 220 Great Children's Books,* revised 1st edition. © 1996. Teacher Ideas Press. (800) 237-6124.

215
The Long Winter
Laura Ingalls Wilder

True or False. Decide whether each statement is true or false. Mark your answer sheet accordingly.

1. The Ingalls family moved to town for the winter.

2. Pa discovered that Almanzo had been storing his wheat in the wall.

3. The little bird that Pa found in the haystack lived with the Ingalls all through the long winter.

4. The Christmas barrel arrived on Christmas Day.

5. In this book, Pa and Almanzo did not know each other.

6. During the long winter, the trains could not get through.

7. Cap Garland went with Almanzo to buy wheat from Mr. Anderson.

8. Almanzo and his brother, Royal, liked to eat stacks of pancakes.

9. An Indian warned the men in Harthorn's store that it was going to be a hard winter.

10. Mr. Edwards brought a puppy for Laura.

11. Mary didn't go to school with Laura and Carrie because she was blind.

12. Mary was saving money to go to college.

Multiple Choice. Read each question. Decide which statement best answers the question. Mark your answer sheet accordingly.

13. Almanzo

    A. Lived with his brother, Royal

    B. Did not want to sell his seed wheat

    C. A and B

    D. None of the above

14. What did the Ingalls family do when they ran out of coal to burn?

    A. They burned their summer clothes

    B. They went to live with Almanzo for the rest of the winter

    C. They burned sticks of hay

    D. They sold their farm so they could afford to buy coal

216
On the Banks of Plum Creek
Laura Ingalls Wilder

True or False. Decide whether each statement is true or false. Mark your answer sheet accordingly.

1. Laura and Mary went to Nellie Oleson's party.

2. Laura and Mary did not go to Nellie Oleson's party.

3. Nellie Oleson did not come to Laura and Mary's party.

4. Pa had to get a job in the East because grasshoppers ate his wheat crop.

5. When Laura went into water that was too deep, Pa ducked her under the water.

6. When Laura was on her way to the swimming hole by herself, a strange animal stood right in the middle of her path.

7. Laura told Pa that she had disobeyed him, and that she had started to go to the swimming hole alone.

8. While Ma, Pa, and Carrie were in town, the cattle got into the haystacks.

9. Laura and Mary made a button-string to give to Carrie for Christmas.

10. Laura and Mary made a dress to give to Carrie for Christmas.

11. At the end of the book, Laura and her family had to move back into the dugout.

Multiple Choice. Read each question. Decide which statement best answers the question. Mark your answer sheet accordingly.

12. What did Pa want for Christmas?

   A. A new wagon

   B. A cow

   C. Horses

   D. A tractor

13. What very special Christmas gift did Laura receive at church?

   A. A pair of shoes

   B. A fur cape and muff

   C. A slate for school

   D. A puppy

14. How did Laura get back at Nellie Oleson for being so rude?

   A. She did not invite Nellie to her party

   B. She put a snake in Nellie's desk at school

   C. She told Nellie's mother that Nellie had misbehaved in school

   D. None of the above

217
These Happy Golden Years
Laura Ingalls Wilder

True or False. Decide whether each statement is true or false. Mark your answer sheet accordingly.

1. Laura taught in five different schools before she got married.

2. A second-grade teaching certificate was better than a third-grade certificate.

3. The second school that Laura taught in was closer to her home than the first school.

4. Laura was married wearing a black dress.

5. Laura and Almanzo were married in Laura's home.

6. Pa bought Ma a new sewing machine.

7. After teaching her first term of school, Laura discovered that she had fallen behind in her own studies.

8. Laura enjoyed living with Mr. and Mrs. Brewster and Tommy.

9. Mrs. Brewster wanted to move back East.

10. Almanzo never allowed Laura to take the reins of the horses he was trying to tame.

11. Almanzo could not afford to buy Laura an engagement ring.

12. Mary attended Laura and Almanzo's wedding.

Multiple Choice. Read each question. Decide which statement best answers the question. Mark your answer sheet accordingly.

13. What surprise was waiting for Mary when she came home for a visit?

    A. A Bible written in braille

    B. Three new dresses

    C. An organ

    D. A bedroom of her own

14. How many students were there in the first school that Laura taught in?

    A. Two

    B. Four

    C. Eight

    D. Sixteen

218
Shadow of a Bull
Maia Wojciechowska

True or False. Decide whether each statement is true or false. Mark your answer sheet accordingly.

1. Manolo did not look at all like his father.

2. Manolo's father had been a famous bullfighter.

3. Manolo had never practiced before his first real bullfight.

4. Jamie and Juan's father had once worked for Manolo's father as his *banderillero*.

5. Manolo promised that he would invite Juan Garcia to his *tienta*.

6. Manolo's mother did not go with him to his *tienta*.

7. Juan's father did not want him to have anything to do with bullfighting.

8. In this book, Manolo never killed a bull.

9. The six men tried to keep Manolo from becoming a bullfighter.

10. Manolo's mother died when he was two years old.

11. Manolo's father was four years old when he fought his first bull.

Multiple Choice. Read each question. Decide which statement best answers the question. Mark your answer sheet accordingly.

12. How did Manolo's father die?

    A. He was murdered by a man who was jealous of his fame

    B. He was killed by a bull during a bullfight

    C. He died of a heart attack

    D. He died of old age

13. At the end of the book, what did Manolo decide to become?

    A. A carpenter

    B. A lawyer

    C. A doctor

    D. A bullfighter

14. Who did Manolo ask if his father had ever been afraid?

    A. His grandmother

    B. His mother

    C. The six men

    D. All of the above

219
The Swiss Family Robinson
Johann Wyss
(as edited by William Kingston)

True or False. Decide whether each statement is true or false. Mark your answer sheet accordingly.

1. The Robinson family had six children.

2. All of the Robinson children were boys.

3. The winter home at Rockburg was a large cave.

4. The Robinson family spent their first rainy season inside a hollowed-out tree.

5. All the Robinson boys rode zebras.

6. The Robinsons were attacked by cannibals.

7. The Robinsons salvaged equipment and supplies from their stranded ship.

8. Only two members of the ship's crew swam to shore with the Robinsons.

9. The entire Robinson family sailed home on a British ship.

10. When the ship that the Robinson family was on ran aground, it quickly sank.

11. When the Robinsons reached shore, none of the ship's crew could be found.

Multiple Choice. Read each question. Decide which statement best answers the question. Mark your answer sheet accordingly.

12. What did the Robinsons discover about their island?

    A. It was filled with many animals and plants

    B. It was the home of a dangerous tribe of cannibals

    C. It was covered with ancient ruins

    D. All of the above

13. What was unusual about the summer home at Falconhurst?

    A. It was a tent

    B. It was up in a tree

    C. It was in a cave

    D. It was on a small island

14. What happened to Grizzle, the donkey?

    A. He was eaten by cannibals

    B. He was killed by lions

    C. He was swallowed by a boa constrictor

    D. He broke his leg in a ruined city

220
With Pipe, Paddle, and Song
Elizabeth Yates

True or False. Decide whether each statement is true or false. Mark your answer sheet accordingly.

1. Guillaume was part Indian and part French.

2. Monsieur le Comte taught Guillaume to sing.

3. Guillaume's mother was married to Monsieur le Comte.

4. Voyageurs paddled their canoes in total silence.

5. Guillaume was hired to sing to the voyageurs.

6. Everyone in Canada wanted to be a voyageur because it was such an easy job.

7. Voyageurs carried trade goods that would be exchanged for furs.

8. A dream net guarded a sleeper's dreams so that he would only have good dreams.

9. Guillaume didn't stay with Willow Wand because he was homesick for Monsieur le Comte.

10. Guillaume didn't stay with Willow Wand because Willow Wand wasn't in love with him.

11. Guillaume gave Celestine his dream net.

Multiple Choice. Read each question. Decide which statement best answers the question. Mark your answer sheet accordingly.

12. Why was the singer so important?

    A. He helped the men paddle in rhythm

    B. He kept up the men's spirits

    C. A and B

    D. None of the above

13. What happened to Guillaume when his paddle was caught between the rocks?

    A. He fell out of the canoe when he tried to pull it out

    B. He tipped over the canoe when he tried to pull it out

    C. Martin was drowned trying to free it

    D. He lost his pipe and hat

14. How did Guillaume know where to find his voyageurs?

    A. He had a vision while he was sleeping under the dream net

    B. Willow Wand told him where they would be

    C. He found a lob tree with Prosper's initials carved on it

    D. He saw them from the top of a mountain

PART
III

Answers

Answer Key

1
Alcott, Louisa May. *Little Men.*
CATEGORY: D
POINT VALUE: 20

1. F	5. F	9. F	13. A
2. F	6. F	10. F	14. B
3. T	7. T	11. A	
4. F	8. F	12. C	

2
Alcott, Louisa May. *Little Women.*
CATEGORY: D
POINT VALUE: 30

1. T	5. T	9. F	13. A
2. T	6. T	10. T	14. B
3. T	7. F	11. A	
4. F	8. F	12. B	

3
Alexander, Lloyd. *The Black Cauldron.*
CATEGORY: E
POINT VALUE: 15

1. F	5. F	9. T	13. B
2. T	6. F	10. F	14. D
3. T	7. F	11. C	
4. F	8. F	12. A	

4
Alexander, Lloyd. *The Book of Three.*
CATEGORY: E
POINT VALUE: 15

1. T	5. F	9. T	13. B
2. F	6. T	10. F	14. A
3. F	7. T	11. B	
4. F	8. T	12. B	

5
Alexander, Lloyd. *The Castle of Llyr.*
CATEGORY: E
POINT VALUE: 15

1. T	5. T	9. F	13. C
2. F	6. F	10. T	14. C
3. T	7. F	11. T	
4. T	8. T	12. D	

6
Alexander, Lloyd. *The Cat Who Wished to Be a Man.*
CATEGORY: D
POINT VALUE: 5

1. F	5. T	9. F	13. C
2. F	6. T	10. T	14. C
3. T	7. T	11. A	
4. F	8. T	12. B	

7
Alexander, Lloyd. *The High King.*
CATEGORY: E
POINT VALUE: 20

1. T	5. T	9. T	13. D
2. T	6. F	10. F	14. C
3. T	7. T	11. B	
4. F	8. T	12. D	

8
Alexander, Lloyd. *Taran Wanderer.*
CATEGORY: E
POINT VALUE: 15

1. F	5. T	9. T	13. C
2. F	6. F	10. F	14. A
3. F	7. T	11. D	
4. F	8. T	12. B	

9
Alexander, Lloyd. *The Wizard in the Tree.*
CATEGORY: D
POINT VALUE: 5

1. F	5. F	9. F	13. C
2. T	6. F	10. F	14. A
3. T	7. T	11. A	
4. T	8. T	12. B	

10
Armer, Laura Adams. *Waterless Mountain.*
CATEGORY: C
POINT VALUE: 15

1. T	5. T	9. F	13. A
2. F	6. F	10. F	14. D
3. F	7. T	11. A	
4. F	8. F	12. C	

11

Armstrong, William H. *Sounder.*
CATEGORY: C
POINT VALUE: 10

1. T	5. T	9. T	13. A
2. T	6. F	10. T	14. D
3. F	7. T	11. B	
4. F	8. T	12. D	

12

Atwater, Richard, and Florence Atwater.
    Mr. Popper's Penguins.
CATEGORY: A
POINT VALUE: 5

1. T	5. F	9. F	13. C
2. F	6. F	10. F	14. B
3. T	7. T	11. F	
4. T	8. F	12. D	

13

Babbitt, Natalie. *The Eyes of the Amaryllis.*
CATEGORY: C
POINT VALUE: 10

1. T	5. T	9. T	13. B
2. F	6. T	10. T	14. A
3. T	7. F	11. T	
4. T	8. T	12. D	

14

Babbitt, Natalie. *Goody Hall.*
CATEGORY: C
POINT VALUE: 10

1. T	5. T	9. T	13. C
2. T	6. F	10. F	14. C
3. T	7. T	11. B	
4. F	8. F	12. B	

15

Babbitt, Natalie. *Knee-Knock Rise.*
CATEGORY: C
POINT VALUE: 5

1. F	5. T	9. T	13. D
2. T	6. F	10. F	14. B
3. T	7. T	11. C	
4. F	8. T	12. C	

16

Bailey, Carolyn. *Miss Hickory.*
CATEGORY: B
POINT VALUE: 5

1. T	5. F	9. F	13. C
2. T	6. F	10. T	14. B
3. T	7. T	11. D	
4. T	8. T	12. C	

17

Barnouw, Victor. *Dream of the Blue Heron.*
CATEGORY: C
POINT VALUE: 10

1. T	5. T	9. T	13. A
2. F	6. F	10. T	14. C
3. T	7. F	11. T	
4. T	8. T	12. C	

18

Blos, Joan W. *A Gathering of Days.*
CATEGORY: C
POINT VALUE: 10

1. F	5. F	9. F	13. T
2. T	6. F	10. F	14. B
3. T	7. F	11. F	
4. T	8. F	12. T	

19

Blume, Judy. *Otherwise Known as Sheila
    the Great.*
CATEGORY: A
POINT VALUE: 5

1. T	5. F	9. F	13. D
2. T	6. F	10. F	14. B
3. T	7. F	11. T	
4. F	8. F	12. A	

20

Blume, Judy. *Superfudge.*
CATEGORY: A
POINT VALUE: 5

1. F	5. T	9. F	13. C
2. T	6. T	10. T	14. A
3. T	7. T	11. A	
4. F	8. T	12. B	

21
Blume, Judy. *Tales of a Fourth Grade Nothing.*
CATEGORY: A
POINT VALUE: 5

1. T	5. T	9. F	13. D
2. F	6. T	10. T	14. C
3. F	7. F	11. B	
4. T	8. T	12. B	

22
Brink, Carol Ryrie. *Caddie Woodlawn.*
CATEGORY: B
POINT VALUE: 15

1. T	5. F	9. T	13. D
2. T	6. T	10. F	14. D
3. T	7. T	11. T	
4. F	8. F	12. B	

23
Burnett, Frances Hodgson. *The Secret Garden.*
CATEGORY: B
POINT VALUE: 20

1. F	5. F	9. F	13. T
2. T	6. F	10. F	14. C
3. F	7. F	11. T	
4. F	8. F	12. T	

24
Byars, Betsy. *The Cartoonist.*
CATEGORY: C
POINT VALUE: 5

1. F	5. F	9. F	13. B
2. F	6. F	10. T	14. D
3. T	7. F	11. T	
4. T	8. T	12. C	

25
Byars, Betsy. *The Computer Nut.*
CATEGORY: C
POINT VALUE: 10

1. F	5. F	9. T	13. C
2. T	6. T	10. F	14. B
3. F	7. T	11. D	
4. F	8. T	12. C	

26
Byars, Betsy. *Cracker Jackson.*
CATEGORY: C
POINT VALUE: 10

1. F	5. T	9. F	13. B
2. T	6. T	10. T	14. D
3. F	7. T	11. C	
4. T	8. F	12. C	

27
Byars, Betsy. *The Cybil War.*
CATEGORY: C
POINT VALUE: 10

1. T	5. T	9. T	13. B
2. F	6. F	10. T	14. D
3. F	7. T	11. T	
4. F	8. F	12. C	

28
Byars, Betsy. *Good-bye, Chicken Little.*
CATEGORY: C
POINT VALUE: 5

1. F	5. F	9. T	13. D
2. F	6. T	10. F	14. C
3. F	7. T	11. D	
4. T	8. T	12. C	

29
Byars, Betsy. *The House of Wings.*
CATEGORY: C
POINT VALUE: 10

1. T	5. T	9. F	13. B
2. F	6. F	10. T	14. B
3. F	7. F	11. F	
4. T	8. T	12. A	

30
Byars, Betsy. *The Night Swimmers.*
CATEGORY: C
POINT VALUE: 10

1. T	5. F	9. F	13. C
2. F	6. T	10. F	14. B
3. T	7. T	11. T	
4. T	8. F	12. F	

31

Byars, Betsy. *The Pinballs.*
CATEGORY: D
POINT VALUE: 10

1. F	5. T	9. T	13. C
2. F	6. F	10. T	14. B
3. T	7. T	11. C	
4. T	8. T	12. B	

32

Byars, Betsy. *The Summer of the Swans.*
CATEGORY: C
POINT VALUE: 10

1. F	5. T	9. F	13. T
2. T	6. T	10. T	14. F
3. F	7. F	11. F	
4. T	8. F	12. T	

33

Byars, Betsy. *The TV Kid.*
CATEGORY: C
POINT VALUE: 5

1. F	5. F	9. F	13. C
2. T	6. F	10. F	14. C
3. T	7. T	11. T	
4. T	8. T	12. A	

34

Byars, Betsy. *The Two-Thousand-Pound Goldfish.*
CATEGORY: C
POINT VALUE: 10

1. T	5. T	9. T	13. B
2. F	6. T	10. T	14. A
3. T	7. F	11. T	
4. T	8. F	12. C	

35

Carlson, Natalie Savage. *A Brother for the Orphelines.*
CATEGORY: A
POINT VALUE: 5

1. F	5. T	9. T	13. F
2. F	6. F	10. T	14. B
3. T	7. T	11. T	
4. F	8. T	12. F	

36

Carlson, Natalie Savage. *The Empty Schoolhouse.*
CATEGORY: B
POINT VALUE: 5

1. T	5. T	9. T	13. C
2. T	6. T	10. F	14. D
3. F	7. F	11. C	
4. T	8. F	12. A	

37

Carlson, Natalie Savage. *The Happy Orpheline.*
CATEGORY: A
POINT VALUE: 5

1. F	5. F	9. T	13. B
2. T	6. F	10. T	14. D
3. F	7. F	11. T	
4. T	8. F	12. F	

38

Carlson, Natalie Savage. *The Letter on the Tree.*
CATEGORY: B
POINT VALUE: 5

1. F	5. T	9. F	13. C
2. T	6. F	10. T	14. D
3. F	7. T	11. T	
4. F	8. F	12. T	

39

Carlson, Natalie Savage. *The Orphelines in the Enchanted Castle.*
CATEGORY: A
POINT VALUE: 5

1. T	5. T	9. T	13. A
2. F	6. T	10. T	14. B
3. T	7. T	11. T	
4. F	8. T	12. F	

40

Carlson, Natalie Savage. *A Pet for the Orphelines.*
CATEGORY: A
POINT VALUE: 5

1. T	5. T	9. F	13. A
2. T	6. F	10. F	14. C
3. T	7. T	11. F	
4. F	8. T	12. F	

41
Carlson, Natalie Savage. *School Bell in the Valley.*
CATEGORY: B
POINT VALUE: 5

1. F	5. T	9. T	13. B
2. T	6. F	10. T	14. B
3. F	7. F	11. T	
4. T	8. T	12. D	

42
Clark, Ann Nolan. *Santiago.*
CATEGORY: D
POINT VALUE: 15

1. T	5. F	9. T	13. D
2. F	6. T	10. T	14. C
3. T	7. F	11. T	
4. F	8. F	12. C	

43
Clark, Ann Nolan. *Secret of the Andes.*
CATEGORY: C
POINT VALUE: 15

1. T	5. F	9. T	13. B
2. T	6. F	10. T	14. B
3. F	7. F	11. C	
4. T	8. T	12. A	

44
Cleary, Beverly. *Dear Mr. Henshaw.*
CATEGORY: B
POINT VALUE: 10

1. F	5. T	9. T	13. F
2. T	6. F	10. F	14. B
3. T	7. F	11. T	
4. F	8. F	12. T	

45
Cleary, Beverly. *Ellen Tebbits.*
CATEGORY: A
POINT VALUE: 5

1. F	5. T	9. T	13. C
2. T	6. F	10. T	14. A
3. T	7. F	11. T	
4. T	8. T	12. C	

46
Cleary, Beverly. *Henry and Beezus.*
CATEGORY: A
POINT VALUE: 5

1. T	5. T	9. F	13. B
2. F	6. T	10. T	14. A
3. T	7. T	11. T	
4. T	8. F	12. D	

47
Cleary, Beverly. *Henry and Ribsy.*
CATEGORY: A
POINT VALUE: 5

1. T	5. F	9. F	13. D
2. T	6. T	10. F	14. D
3. F	7. T	11. F	
4. T	8. F	12. A	

48
Cleary, Beverly. *Henry and the Clubhouse.*
CATEGORY: A
POINT VALUE: 5

1. T	5. F	9. F	13. A
2. F	6. F	10. T	14. A
3. T	7. T	11. T	
4. T	8. T	12. F	

49
Cleary, Beverly. *Henry and the Paper Route.*
CATEGORY: A
POINT VALUE: 5

1. F	5. F	9. F	13. D
2. T	6. T	10. T	14. C
3. F	7. F	11. B	
4. F	8. T	12. A	

50
Cleary, Beverly. *Henry Huggins.*
CATEGORY: A
POINT VALUE: 5

1. F	5. T	9. F	13. A
2. F	6. T	10. T	14. C
3. T	7. F	11. T	
4. F	8. F	12. T	

51
Cleary, Beverly. *The Mouse and the Motorcycle*.
CATEGORY: A
POINT VALUE: 5

1. T	5. F	9. F	13. A
2. T	6. T	10. F	14. A
3. F	7. F	11. T	
4. T	8. T	12. C	

52
Cleary, Beverly. *Ralph S. Mouse*.
CATEGORY: A
POINT VALUE: 5

1. T	5. F	9. T	13. A
2. F	6. T	10. F	14. D
3. F	7. T	11. C	
4. T	8. F	12. B	

53
Cleary, Beverly. *Ramona and Her Father*.
CATEGORY: A
POINT VALUE: 5

1. F	5. F	9. T	13. A
2. F	6. F	10. T	14. C
3. T	7. T	11. C	
4. T	8. F	12. B	

54
Cleary, Beverly. *Ramona and Her Mother*.
CATEGORY: A
POINT VALUE: 5

1. T	5. T	9. F	13. C
2. T	6. T	10. F	14. B
3. T	7. F	11. F	
4. T	8. T	12. T	

55
Cleary, Beverly. *Ramona Forever*.
CATEGORY: A
POINT VALUE: 5

1. T	5. T	9. T	13. B
2. F	6. T	10. T	14. A
3. T	7. T	11. F	
4. F	8. T	12. F	

56
Cleary, Beverly. *Ramona Quimby, Age 8*.
CATEGORY: A
POINT VALUE: 5

1. T	5. T	9. T	13. C
2. F	6. T	10. F	14. A
3. F	7. F	11. T	
4. T	8. T	12. C	

57
Cleary, Beverly. *Ramona the Brave*.
CATEGORY: A
POINT VALUE: 5

1. T	5. T	9. T	13. C
2. T	6. F	10. F	14. B
3. F	7. T	11. F	
4. F	8. T	12. D	

58
Cleary, Beverly. *Ramona the Pest*.
CATEGORY: A
POINT VALUE: 5

1. F	5. F	9. F	13. A
2. T	6. T	10. T	14. D
3. T	7. T	11. T	
4. F	8. T	12. B	

59
Cleary, Beverly. *Ribsy*.
CATEGORY: A
POINT VALUE: 5

1. T	5. T	9. T	13. B
2. F	6. F	10. T	14. B
3. F	7. F	11. T	
4. T	8. F	12. A	

60
Cleary, Beverly. *Runaway Ralph*.
CATEGORY: A
POINT VALUE: 5

1. T	5. T	9. F	13. C
2. F	6. F	10. T	14. C
3. T	7. T	11. T	
4. F	8. F	12. F	

61
Cleary, Beverly. *Socks.*
CATEGORY: A
POINT VALUE: 5

1. T	5. T	9. F	13. T
2. T	6. T	10. F	14. T
3. F	7. T	11. F	
4. F	8. F	12. F	

62
Clemens, Samuel L. (Mark Twain) *The Adventures of Huckleberry Finn.*
CATEGORY: E
POINT VALUE: 20

1. F	5. T	9. T	13. B
2. T	6. T	10. T	14. A
3. T	7. T	11. F	
4. F	8. F	12. C	

63
Clemens, Samuel L. (Mark Twain) *The Adventures of Tom Sawyer.*
CATEGORY: E
POINT VALUE: 20

1. T	5. T	9. T	13. C
2. F	6. T	10. F	14. D
3. F	7. T	11. T	
4. T	8. T	12. C	

64
Collier, James Lincoln and Christopher Collier. *My Brother Sam Is Dead.*
CATEGORY: D
POINT VALUE: 15

1. T	5. F	9. T	13. D
2. F	6. F	10. T	14. A
3. T	7. T	11. B	
4. T	8. F	12. B	

65
Cooper, James Fenimore. *The Last of the Mohicans.*
CATEGORY: E
POINT VALUE: 30

1. T	5. F	9. T	13. A
2. F	6. T	10. T	14. A
3. F	7. T	11. T	
4. T	8. T	12. D	

66
Cooper, Susan. *The Dark Is Rising.*
CATEGORY: E
POINT VALUE: 15

1. T	5. T	9. T	13. D
2. T	6. F	10. T	14. B
3. F	7. T	11. T	
4. F	8. T	12. D	

67
Cooper, Susan. *The Grey King.*
CATEGORY: E
POINT VALUE: 15

1. T	5. T	9. T	13. A
2. F	6. T	10. T	14. B
3. T	7. F	11. F	
4. F	8. T	12. D	

68
Defoe, Daniel. *Robinson Crusoe.*
CATEGORY: E
POINT VALUE: 25

1. F	5. T	9. T	13. D
2. T	6. F	10. T	14. A
3. F	7. T	11. T	
4. T	8. T	12. D	

69
DeJong, Meindert. *Hurry Home, Candy.*
CATEGORY: B
POINT VALUE: 10

1. F	5. T	9. F	13. A
2. T	6. F	10. T	14. C
3. F	7. F	11. T	
4. T	8. T	12. T	

70
DeJong, Meindert. *Puppy Summer.*
CATEGORY: A
POINT VALUE: 5

1. T	5. F	9. F	13. A
2. F	6. F	10. T	14. C
3. F	7. F	11. T	
4. T	8. F	12. F	

71
DeJong, Meindert. *The Wheel on the School.*
CATEGORY: C
POINT VALUE: 20

1. T	5. F	9. T	13. A
2. T	6. T	10. T	14. D
3. F	7. T	11. T	
4. F	8. F	12. D	

72
Dickens, Charles. *Oliver Twist.*
CATEGORY: E
POINT VALUE: 30

1. T	5. T	9. T	13. C
2. T	6. T	10. T	14. D
3. T	7. F	11. C	
4. F	8. T	12. D	

73
Dickens, Charles. *A Tale of Two Cities.*
CATEGORY: E
POINT VALUE: 25

1. T	5. F	9. T	13. C
2. F	6. F	10. T	14. C
3. T	7. T	11. T	
4. T	8. T	12. C	

74
Du Bois, William. *The Twenty-One Balloons.*
CATEGORY: C
POINT VALUE: 10

1. T	5. F	9. F	13. C
2. F	6. T	10. F	14. A
3. F	7. T	11. F	
4. F	8. F	12. F	

75
Eckert, Allan W. *Incident at Hawk's Hill.*
CATEGORY: D
POINT VALUE: 15

1. F	5. F	9. T	13. C
2. F	6. T	10. F	14. C
3. T	7. T	11. F	
4. T	8. T	12. D	

76
Edmonds, Walter D. *The Matchlock Gun.*
CATEGORY: D
POINT VALUE: 5

1. F	5. F	9. T	13. F
2. F	6. T	10. T	14. T
3. T	7. F	11. T	
4. F	8. F	12. F	

77
Edmonds, Walter D. *Two Logs Crossing.*
CATEGORY: D
POINT VALUE: 5

1. F	5. F	9. T	13. F
2. F	6. F	10. T	14. T
3. T	7. T	11. F	
4. F	8. F	12. T	

78
Enright, Elizabeth. *Thimble Summer.*
CATEGORY: B
POINT VALUE: 10

1. F	5. F	9. F	13. T
2. F	6. T	10. T	14. B
3. F	7. T	11. F	
4. T	8. F	12. T	

79
Estes, Eleanor. *The Alley.*
CATEGORY: B
POINT VALUE: 15

1. F	5. F	9. T	13. C
2. T	6. F	10. T	14. D
3. F	7. F	11. T	
4. T	8. T	12. A	

80
Estes, Eleanor. *The Coat-Hanger Christmas Tree.*
CATEGORY: B
POINT VALUE: 5

1. T	5. T	9. T	13. C
2. F	6. T	10. F	14. D
3. T	7. T	11. T	
4. T	8. F	12. D	

81
Estes, Eleanor. *Ginger Pye.*
CATEGORY: B
POINT VALUE: 15

1. F	5. F	9. T	13. D
2. T	6. T	10. T	14. B
3. F	7. F	11. T	
4. T	8. T	12. A	

82
Estes, Eleanor. *The Hundred Dresses.*
CATEGORY: B
POINT VALUE: 5

1. F	5. F	9. T	13. D
2. F	6. F	10. F	14. B
3. T	7. T	11. T	
4. T	8. F	12. C	

83
Estes, Eleanor. *The Lost Umbrella of Kim Chu.*
CATEGORY: B
POINT VALUE: 5

1. F	5. T	9. T	13. A
2. F	6. T	10. T	14. C
3. T	7. T	11. T	
4. F	8. F	12. A	

84
Estes, Eleanor. *The Middle Moffat.*
CATEGORY: B
POINT VALUE: 15

1. F	5. F	9. F	13. A
2. F	6. T	10. T	14. B
3. T	7. F	11. T	
4. T	8. T	12. A	

85
Estes, Eleanor. *Rufus M.*
CATEGORY: B
POINT VALUE: 20

1. T	5. T	9. F	13. C
2. F	6. T	10. T	14. D
3. T	7. T	11. F	
4. F	8. T	12. A	

86
Fitzhugh, Louise. *Harriet the Spy.*
CATEGORY: D
POINT VALUE: 15

1. T	5. F	9. F	13. C
2. T	6. F	10. F	14. D
3. T	7. F	11. T	
4. T	8. T	12. F	

87
Forbes, Esther. *Johnny Tremain.*
CATEGORY: D
POINT VALUE: 15

1. F	5. F	9. F	13. F
2. F	6. T	10. T	14. F
3. F	7. F	11. F	
4. T	8. F	12. F	

88
Fox, Paula. *One-Eyed Cat.*
CATEGORY: D
POINT VALUE: 15

1. T	5. F	9. F	13. C
2. T	6. F	10. T	14. B
3. T	7. T	11. T	
4. T	8. F	12. A	

89
Fox, Paula. *The Slave Dancer.*
CATEGORY: E
POINT VALUE: 15

1. T	5. F	9. T	13. A
2. T	6. T	10. T	14. B
3. T	7. T	11. T	
4. F	8. F	12. C	

90
Gates, Doris. *Blue Willow.*
CATEGORY: B
POINT VALUE: 10

1. F	5. F	9. T	13. D
2. T	6. F	10. T	14. C
3. F	7. F	11. T	
4. F	8. F	12. A	

91
Gates, Doris. *The Elderberry Bush.*
CATEGORY: B
POINT VALUE: 10

1. T	5. T	9. T	13. C
2. T	6. T	10. T	14. C
3. T	7. F	11. T	
4. F	8. F	12. T	

92
Gates, Doris. *A Morgan for Melinda.*
CATEGORY: B
POINT VALUE: 10

1. T	5. T	9. F	13. T
2. T	6. F	10. F	14. B
3. T	7. T	11. T	
4. F	8. T	12. T	

93
George, Jean Craighead. *Coyote in Manhattan.*
CATEGORY: D
POINT VALUE: 15

1. F	5. T	9. F	13. A
2. F	6. F	10. F	14. C
3. F	7. F	11. F	
4. T	8. T	12. C	

94
George, Jean Craighead. *Julie of the Wolves.*
CATEGORY: C
POINT VALUE: 10

1. F	5. T	9. F	13. A
2. F	6. F	10. T	14. C
3. T	7. T	11. T	
4. F	8. T	12. B	

95
George, Jean Craighead. *My Side of the Mountain.*
CATEGORY: D
POINT VALUE: 10

1. F	5. T	9. T	13. B
2. F	6. F	10. F	14. A
3. F	7. T	11. F	
4. T	8. T	12. T	

96
George, Jean Craighead. *River Rats, Inc.*
CATEGORY: D
POINT VALUE: 10

1. F	5. T	9. F	13. B
2. T	6. F	10. T	14. B
3. T	7. T	11. F	
4. T	8. T	12. F	

97
George, Jean Craighead. *Who Really Killed Cock Robin?*
CATEGORY: E
POINT VALUE: 10

1. F	5. T	9. F	13. A
2. T	6. T	10. T	14. C
3. F	7. T	11. D	
4. F	8. F	12. A	

98
Gipson, Fred. *Old Yeller.*
CATEGORY: C
POINT VALUE: 10

1. T	5. T	9. T	13. B
2. F	6. T	10. T	14. A
3. T	7. T	11. T	
4. F	8. F	12. D	

99
Gipson, Fred. *Savage Sam.*
CATEGORY: C
POINT VALUE: 10

1. T	5. F	9. T	13. D
2. T	6. F	10. F	14. D
3. F	7. T	11. D	
4. T	8. F	12. A	

100
Greene, Bette. *Philip Hall Likes Me, I Reckon Maybe.*
CATEGORY: C
POINT VALUE: 10

1. F	5. T	9. F	13. F
2. T	6. T	10. F	14. T
3. F	7. F	11. T	
4. F	8. F	12. F	

101

Greene, Constance C. *A Girl Called Al.*
CATEGORY: C
POINT VALUE: 10

1. F	5. F	9. F	13. B
2. T	6. T	10. F	14. B
3. F	7. T	11. T	
4. T	8. F	12. F	

102

Hamilton, Virginia. *M. C. Higgins the Great.*
CATEGORY: E
POINT VALUE: 20

1. T	5. T	9. T	13. B
2. F	6. T	10. F	14. C
3. F	7. T	11. F	
4. T	8. F	12. F	

103

Hamilton, Virginia. *The Planet of Junior Brown.*
CATEGORY: E
POINT VALUE: 15

1. F	5. T	9. F	13. C
2. F	6. T	10. T	14. C
3. T	7. T	11. T	
4. T	8. T	12. D	

104

Harris, Rosemary. *The Bright and Morning Star.*
CATEGORY: D
POINT VALUE: 15

1. T	5. T	9. T	13. B
2. T	6. F	10. F	14. D
3. T	7. F	11. T	
4. F	8. T	12. A	

105

Harris, Rosemary. *The Moon in the Cloud.*
CATEGORY: D
POINT VALUE: 10

1. F	5. T	9. F	13. D
2. F	6. T	10. F	14. C
3. T	7. T	11. F	
4. F	8. T	12. T	

106

Harris, Rosemary. *The Shadow on the Sun.*
CATEGORY: D
POINT VALUE: 10

1. F	5. F	9. T	13. D
2. F	6. T	10. T	14. A
3. F	7. F	11. T	
4. T	8. T	12. C	

107

Haywood, Carolyn. *Back to School with Betsy.*
CATEGORY: A
POINT VALUE: 5

1. F	5. T	9. T	13. B
2. T	6. F	10. T	14. A
3. T	7. T	11. T	
4. F	8. F	12. T	

108

Haywood, Carolyn. *"B" Is for Betsy.*
CATEGORY: A
POINT VALUE: 5

1. T	5. F	9. F	13. C
2. T	6. T	10. F	14. C
3. T	7. F	11. T	
4. F	8. T	12. F	

109

Haywood, Carolyn. *Betsy and Mr. Kilpatrick.*
CATEGORY: A
POINT VALUE: 5

1. F	5. T	9. T	13. B
2. F	6. F	10. F	14. B
3. T	7. T	11. T	
4. T	8. F	12. T	

110

Haywood, Carolyn. *Eddie's Happenings.*
CATEGORY: A
POINT VALUE: 5

1. T	5. T	9. F	13. B
2. F	6. T	10. T	14. C
3. F	7. T	11. T	
4. F	8. T	12. T	

111
Haywood, Carolyn. *Snowbound with Betsy.*
CATEGORY: A
POINT VALUE: 5

1. F	5. F	9. F	13. A
2. F	6. T	10. T	14. B
3. T	7. F	11. T	
4. T	8. T	12. T	

112
Henry, Marguerite. *Born to Trot.*
CATEGORY: C
POINT VALUE: 15

1. T	5. F	9. T	13. C
2. T	6. T	10. F	14. C
3. F	7. T	11. T	
4. T	8. F	12. C	

113
Henry, Marguerite. *Brighty of the Grand Canyon.*
CATEGORY: C
POINT VALUE: 15

1. T	5. T	9. T	13. B
2. F	6. F	10. F	14. A
3. F	7. T	11. C	
4. T	8. T	12. A	

114
Henry, Marguerite. *Justin Morgan Had a Horse.*
CATEGORY: D
POINT VALUE: 10

1. F	5. F	9. F	13. T
2. T	6. F	10. T	14. D
3. T	7. F	11. T	
4. T	8. T	12. F	

115
Henry, Marguerite. *King of the Wind.*
CATEGORY: C
POINT VALUE: 15

1. T	5. T	9. T	13. D
2. F	6. T	10. T	14. A
3. F	7. F	11. T	
4. F	8. F	12. A	

116
Henry, Marguerite. *Misty of Chincoteague.*
CATEGORY: B
POINT VALUE: 10

1. T	5. T	9. T	13. A
2. F	6. T	10. T	14. D
3. F	7. T	11. F	
4. F	8. T	12. C	

117
Henry, Marguerite. *Mustang, Wild Spirit of the West.*
CATEGORY: C
POINT VALUE: 15

1. T	5. F	9. T	13. B
2. T	6. F	10. T	14. C
3. F	7. F	11. T	
4. T	8. F	12. F	

118
Henry, Marguerite. *Stormy, Misty's Foal.*
CATEGORY: B
POINT VALUE: 10

1. T	5. T	9. F	13. B
2. F	6. F	10. T	14. A
3. T	7. F	11. T	
4. F	8. T	12. A	

119
Hunt, Irene. *Across Five Aprils.*
CATEGORY: E
POINT VALUE: 15

1. T	5. F	9. T	13. A
2. T	6. T	10. T	14. D
3. F	7. F	11. A	
4. T	8. T	12. B	

120
Hunt, Irene. *Up a Road Slowly.*
CATEGORY: E
POINT VALUE: 10

1. T	5. F	9. F	13. B
2. T	6. F	10. F	14. C
3. F	7. T	11. T	
4. T	8. T	12. A	

121
Ish-Kishor, Sulamith. *Our Eddie.*
CATEGORY: E
POINT VALUE: 10

1. F	5. T	9. T	13. C
2. T	6. T	10. F	14. D
3. T	7. F	11. F	
4. F	8. F	12. B	

122
Kelly, Eric P. *The Trumpeter of Krakow.*
CATEGORY: D
POINT VALUE: 15

1. T	5. F	9. F	13. B
2. F	6. F	10. F	14. A
3. T	7. F	11. T	
4. T	8. T	12. D	

123
Konigsburg, E. L. *Father's Arcane
  Daughter.*
CATEGORY: E
POINT VALUE: 5

1. T	5. F	9. T	13. B
2. F	6. T	10. T	14. C
3. T	7. T	11. F	
4. T	8. T	12. B	

124
Konigsburg, E. L. *From the Mixed-Up
  Files of Mrs. Basil E. Frankweiler.*
CATEGORY: C
POINT VALUE: 10

1. T	5. F	9. F	13. B
2. T	6. F	10. F	14. D
3. F	7. F	11. F	
4. F	8. F	12. T	

125
Konigsburg, E. L. *Jennifer, Hectate,
  Macbeth, William McKinley
  and Me, Elizabeth.*
CATEGORY: C
POINT VALUE: 5

1. T	5. F	9. F	13. A
2. T	6. F	10. F	14. B
3. F	7. T	11. F	
4. T	8. F	12. F	

126
Krumgold, Joseph. *And Now Miguel.*
CATEGORY: D
POINT VALUE: 15

1. F	5. T	9. F	13. C
2. T	6. T	10. T	14. C
3. F	7. T	11. F	
4. F	8. T	12. A	

127
Krumgold, Joseph. *Onion John.*
CATEGORY: D
POINT VALUE: 15

1. T	5. F	9. F	13. F
2. T	6. F	10. T	14. A
3. F	7. F	11. F	
4. T	8. T	12. F	

128
Lasky, Kathryn. *Beyond the Divide.*
CATEGORY: E
POINT VALUE: 15

1. F	5. F	9. T	13. B
2. T	6. T	10. T	14. C
3. F	7. F	11. F	
4. T	8. T	12. D	

129
Latham, Jean Lee. *Carry On, Mr.
  Bowditch.*
CATEGORY: E
POINT VALUE: 15

1. F	5. F	9. F	13. D
2. T	6. T	10. F	14. B
3. F	7. T	11. F	
4. F	8. T	12. C	

130
Lawson, Robert. *Ben and Me.*
CATEGORY: D
POINT VALUE: 5

1. F	5. F	9. T	13. D
2. F	6. T	10. T	14. A
3. T	7. T	11. T	
4. F	8. F	12. C	

131

Lawson, Robert. *Rabbit Hill.*
CATEGORY: B
POINT VALUE: 10

1. T	5. F	9. F	13. C
2. T	6. F	10. F	14. D
3. F	7. T	11. T	
4. F	8. F	12. F	

132

Lawson, Robert. *Robbut.*
CATEGORY: A
POINT VALUE: 5

1. T	5. T	9. T	13. T
2. F	6. F	10. F	14. A
3. T	7. F	11. T	
4. F	8. T	12. F	

133

Lawson, Robert. *The Tough Winter.*
CATEGORY: B
POINT VALUE: 10

1. T	5. F	9. F	13. A
2. F	6. F	10. F	14. C
3. T	7. T	11. F	
4. F	8. F	12. B	

134

L'Engle, Madeleine. *A Swiftly Tilting Planet.*
CATEGORY: E
POINT VALUE: 15

1. F	5. T	9. T	13. A
2. T	6. T	10. T	14. C
3. T	7. T	11. F	
4. F	8. T	12. D	

135

L'Engle, Madeleine. *A Wind in the Door.*
CATEGORY: E
POINT VALUE: 15

1. T	5. T	9. T	13. A
2. T	6. T	10. T	14. C
3. T	7. F	11. D	
4. F	8. T	12. B	

136

L'Engle, Madeleine. *A Wrinkle in Time.*
CATEGORY: E
POINT VALUE: 15

1. F	5. F	9. F	13. B
2. T	6. F	10. F	14. C
3. T	7. T	11. T	
4. F	8. T	12. F	

137

Lenski, Lois. *Strawberry Girl.*
CATEGORY: B
POINT VALUE: 10

1. F	5. F	9. T	13. F
2. F	6. T	10. F	14. F
3. F	7. T	11. T	
4. F	8. F	12. F	

138

Lewis, C. S. *The Horse and His Boy.*
CATEGORY: D
POINT VALUE: 10

1. T	5. F	9. T	13. A
2. T	6. F	10. T	14. B
3. F	7. T	11. A	
4. F	8. T	12. B	

139

Lewis, C. S. *The Last Battle.*
CATEGORY: D
POINT VALUE: 10

1. T	5. T	9. T	13. D
2. T	6. T	10. T	14. A
3. F	7. F	11. T	
4. F	8. F	12. D	

140

Lewis, C. S. *The Lion, the Witch and the Wardrobe.*
CATEGORY: D
POINT VALUE: 10

1. T	5. T	9. T	13. B
2. F	6. T	10. T	14. A
3. T	7. F	11. T	
4. F	8. T	12. C	

141
Lewis, C. S. *The Magician's Nephew.*
CATEGORY: D
POINT VALUE: 10

1. F	5. T	9. T	13. D
2. F	6. T	10. T	14. D
3. F	7. T	11. T	
4. T	8. T	12. A	

142
Lewis, C. S. *Prince Caspian.*
CATEGORY: D
POINT VALUE: 10

1. F	5. T	9. F	13. A
2. F	6. T	10. T	14. C
3. T	7. T	11. F	
4. T	8. T	12. B	

143
Lewis, C. S. *The Silver Chair.*
CATEGORY: D
POINT VALUE: 10

1. T	5. T	9. F	13. A
2. F	6. T	10. F	14. C
3. F	7. F	11. T	
4. F	8. T	12. B	

144
Lewis, C. S. *Voyage of the* Dawn Treader
CATEGORY: D
POINT VALUE: 10

1. F	5. T	9. T	13. A
2. T	6. T	10. T	14. C
3. T	7. T	11. T	
4. T	8. F	12. C	

145
Lively, Penelope. *Astercote.*
CATEGORY: D
POINT VALUE: 10

1. T	5. T	9. F	13. C
2. F	6. F	10. T	14. A
3. T	7. T	11. F	
4. F	8. T	12. B	

146
Lively, Penelope. *The Ghost of Thomas Kempe.*
CATEGORY: C
POINT VALUE: 10

1. F	5. F	9. T	13. A
2. F	6. F	10. F	14. A
3. F	7. T	11. T	
4. T	8. F	12. C	

147
London, Jack. *The Call of the Wild.*
CATEGORY: C
POINT VALUE: 10

1. F	5. F	9. T	13. C
2. T	6. F	10. T	14. D
3. F	7. T	11. C	
4. T	8. T	12. B	

148
MacLachlan, Patricia. *Sarah, Plain and Tall.*
CATEGORY: D
POINT VALUE: 5

1. F	5. T	9. F	13. D
2. F	6. F	10. F	14. C
3. T	7. F	11. T	
4. T	8. F	12. B	

149
McKinley, Robin. *Beauty.*
CATEGORY: D
POINT VALUE: 15

1. T	5. T	9. F	13. B
2. F	6. T	10. T	14. C
3. F	7. F	11. T	
4. T	8. T	12. C	

150
McKinley, Robin. *The Blue Sword.*
CATEGORY: D
POINT VALUE: 15

1. T	5. T	9. T	13. D
2. T	6. F	10. T	14. B
3. F	7. T	11. T	
4. F	8. T	12. A	

151
McKinley, Robin. *The Hero and the Crown.*
CATEGORY: D
POINT VALUE: 15

1. F	5. T	9. T	13. B
2. T	6. T	10. T	14. D
3. T	7. F	11. C	
4. F	8. T	12. D	

152
Meigs, Cornelia. *Invincible Louisa.*
CATEGORY: E
POINT VALUE: 25

1. T	5. F	9. T	13. B
2. F	6. F	10. T	14. D
3. T	7. F	11. F	
4. F	8. F	12. T	

153
Neville, Emily. *It's Like This, Cat.*
CATEGORY: D
POINT VALUE: 10

1. T	5. F	9. T	13. D
2. T	6. T	10. F	14. C
3. T	7. T	11. B	
4. F	8. T	12. D	

154
North, Sterling. *Rascal.*
CATEGORY: D
POINT VALUE: 10

1. T	5. F	9. F	13. D
2. F	6. T	10. T	14. A
3. F	7. T	11. F	
4. F	8. T	12. B	

155
North, Sterling. *The Wolfling.*
CATEGORY: D
POINT VALUE: 15

1. T	5. F	9. F	13. D
2. F	6. F	10. T	14. D
3. F	7. T	11. T	
4. T	8. T	12. A	

156
Norton, Mary. *The Borrowers.*
CATEGORY: B
POINT VALUE: 10

1. T	5. T	9. F	13. B
2. F	6. F	10. T	14. D
3. F	7. F	11. F	
4. T	8. T	12. F	

157
Norton, Mary. *The Borrowers Afield.*
CATEGORY: B
POINT VALUE: 15

1. T	5. F	9. F	13. D
2. T	6. F	10. T	14. C
3. F	7. F	11. T	
4. F	8. T	12. D	

158
Norton, Mary. *The Borrowers Afloat.*
CATEGORY: B
POINT VALUE: 10

1. F	5. F	9. T	13. D
2. F	6. T	10. T	14. C
3. T	7. F	11. F	
4. F	8. T	12. C	

159
Norton, Mary. *The Borrowers Aloft.*
CATEGORY: B
POINT VALUE: 10

1. F	5. F	9. T	13. A
2. F	6. T	10. T	14. C
3. F	7. F	11. F	
4. T	8. T	12. D	

160
Norton, Mary. *The Borrowers Avenged.*
CATEGORY: B
POINT VALUE: 15

1. T	5. F	9. T	13. D
2. T	6. F	10. F	14. B
3. F	7. T	11. F	
4. T	8. T	12. D	

161

O'Brien, Robert C. *Mrs. Frisby and the Rats of NIMH.*
CATEGORY: D
POINT VALUE: 15

1. T	5. T	9. T	13. C
2. F	6. F	10. T	14. C
3. T	7. T	11. F	
4. T	8. F	12. D	

162

O'Dell, Scott. *Island of the Blue Dolphins.*
CATEGORY: D
POINT VALUE: 10

1. T	5. T	9. T	13. C
2. T	6. T	10. F	14. B
3. T	7. T	11. T	
4. T	8. F	12. B	

163

O'Dell, Scott. *Sarah Bishop.*
CATEGORY: D
POINT VALUE: 10

1. F	5. F	9. T	13. B
2. T	6. T	10. T	14. D
3. F	7. F	11. A	
4. F	8. T	12. B	

164

O'Dell, Scott. *Sing Down the Moon.*
CATEGORY: D
POINT VALUE: 10

1. F	5. F	9. F	13. B
2. T	6. F	10. T	14. A
3. F	7. T	11. T	
4. F	8. T	12. C	

165

Paterson, Katherine. *Bridge to Terabithia.*
CATEGORY: D
POINT VALUE: 10

1. T	5. F	9. F	13. T
2. T	6. F	10. T	14. D
3. F	7. F	11. T	
4. T	8. F	12. T	

166

Paterson, Katherine. *Jacob Have I Loved.*
CATEGORY: E
POINT VALUE: 15

1. F	5. F	9. T	13. B
2. F	6. T	10. F	14. C
3. T	7. F	11. F	
4. T	8. T	12. C	

167

Pearce, Philippa. *Tom's Midnight Garden.*
CATEGORY: C
POINT VALUE: 15

1. T	5. T	9. F	13. B
2. T	6. T	10. F	14. C
3. F	7. T	11. T	
4. F	8. T	12. A	

168

Raskin, Ellen. *The Mysterious Disappearance of Leon (I Mean Noel).*
CATEGORY: D
POINT VALUE: 10

1. T	5. F	9. F	13. D
2. T	6. T	10. F	14. D
3. F	7. T	11. T	
4. T	8. F	12. T	

169

Raskin, Ellen. *The Westing Game.*
CATEGORY: E
POINT VALUE: 15

1. T	5. T	9. F	13. B
2. T	6. F	10. T	14. B
3. T	7. T	11. C	
4. F	8. T	12. C	

170

Rawlings, Marjorie Kinnan. *The Yearling.*
CATEGORY: E
POINT VALUE: 30

1. F	5. F	9. F	13. B
2. T	6. T	10. T	14. B
3. F	7. F	11. C	
4. T	8. T	12. A	

171
Robertson, Keith. *Henry Reed, Inc.*
CATEGORY: C
POINT VALUE: 15

1. F	5. T	9. F	13. C
2. T	6. T	10. T	14. C
3. F	7. F	11. B	
4. F	8. F	12. B	

172
Robertson, Keith. *Henry Reed's Baby-Sitting Service.*
CATEGORY: C
POINT VALUE: 15

1. F	5. T	9. T	13. D
2. T	6. F	10. F	14. B
3. T	7. T	11. T	
4. F	8. T	12. T	

173
Rodowsky, Colby F. *What About Me?*
CATEGORY: D
POINT VALUE: 10

1. T	5. F	9. T	13. D
2. F	6. F	10. F	14. B
3. T	7. F	11. T	
4. T	8. T	12. C	

174
Sawyer, Ruth. *Roller Skates.*
CATEGORY: B
POINT VALUE: 10

1. F	5. T	9. F	13. B
2. T	6. F	10. T	14. B
3. T	7. F	11. T	
4. T	8. F	12. D	

175
Sebestyen, Ouida. *Words by Heart.*
CATEGORY: D
POINT VALUE: 10

1. T	5. T	9. T	13. A
2. T	6. T	10. T	14. D
3. F	7. F	11. T	
4. F	8. F	12. C	

176
Selden, George. *The Cricket in Times Square.*
CATEGORY: B
POINT VALUE: 10

1. F	5. F	9. T	13. C
2. T	6. T	10. T	14. C
3. F	7. T	11. T	
4. F	8. F	12. T	

177
Seredy, Kate. *The White Stag.*
CATEGORY: E
POINT VALUE: 10

1. F	5. T	9. F	13. T
2. T	6. F	10. T	14. F
3. F	7. T	11. T	
4. F	8. F	12. F	

178
Shannon, Monica. *Dobry.*
CATEGORY: C
POINT VALUE: 10

1. F	5. T	9. T	13. D
2. F	6. F	10. T	14. B
3. F	7. T	11. D	
4. F	8. F	12. C	

179
Smith, Doris Buchanan. *The First Hard Times.*
CATEGORY: C
POINT VALUE: 10

1. F	5. T	9. T	13. B
2. F	6. T	10. F	14. D
3. F	7. T	11. T	
4. T	8. T	12. B	

180
Smith, Doris Buchanan. *Kelly's Creek.*
CATEGORY: B
POINT VALUE: 5

1. T	5. F	9. F	13. C
2. T	6. F	10. T	14. D
3. F	7. T	11. F	
4. T	8. T	12. C	

181

Smith, Doris Buchanan. *Kick a Stone Home.*
CATEGORY: E
POINT VALUE: 10

1. T	5. F	9. T	13. C
2. F	6. T	10. T	14. B
3. T	7. T	11. D	
4. T	8. T	12. A	

182

Smith, Doris Buchanan. *Last Was Lloyd.*
CATEGORY: C
POINT VALUE: 5

1. F	5. T	9. T	13. C
2. T	6. F	10. T	14. D
3. F	7. T	11. F	
4. F	8. T	12. B	

183

Smith, Doris Buchanan. *A Taste of Blackberries.*
CATEGORY: B
POINT VALUE: 5

1. F	5. T	9. F	13. B
2. T	6. F	10. T	14. D
3. T	7. T	11. F	
4. F	8. F	12. T	

184

Sobol, Donald J. *Encyclopedia Brown— The Case of the Dead Eagles and Other Mysteries.*
CATEGORY: A
POINT VALUE: 5

1. F	5. T	9. F	13. T
2. F	6. F	10. T	14. F
3. T	7. T	11. F	
4. F	8. T	12. T	

185

Sobol, Donald J. *Encyclopedia Brown Carries On.*
CATEGORY: A
POINT VALUE: 5

1. F	5. F	9. F	13. F
2. T	6. T	10. T	14. T
3. F	7. F	11. F	
4. T	8. T	12. F	

186

Sobol, Donald J. *Encyclopedia Brown Solves Them All.*
CATEGORY: A
POINT VALUE: 5

1. F	5. T	9. F	13. F
2. T	6. T	10. F	14. B
3. T	7. T	11. T	
4. T	8. F	12. T	

187

Sorensen, Virginia. *Miracles on Maple Hill.*
CATEGORY: B
POINT VALUE: 10

1. F	5. F	9. F	13. A
2. T	6. T	10. T	14. C
3. T	7. F	11. T	
4. T	8. F	12. F	

188

Speare, Elizabeth George. *The Bronze Bow.*
CATEGORY: E
POINT VALUE: 15

1. F	5. F	9. T	13. A
2. T	6. F	10. T	14. C
3. F	7. F	11. T	
4. T	8. T	12. A	

189

Speare, Elizabeth George. *Calico Captive.*
CATEGORY: E
POINT VALUE: 15

1. T	5. F	9. T	13. A
2. T	6. F	10. T	14. A
3. F	7. T	11. C	
4. T	8. T	12. B	

190

Speare, Elizabeth George. *Sign of the Beaver.*
CATEGORY: D
POINT VALUE: 10

1. F	5. F	9. F	13. B
2. F	6. F	10. F	14. B
3. T	7. T	11. F	
4. T	8. T	12. D	

191
Speare, Elizabeth George. *The Witch of Blackbird Pond.*
CATEGORY: E
POINT VALUE: 15

1. F	5. F	9. F	13. A
2. T	6. F	10. T	14. A
3. T	7. F	11. B	
4. T	8. F	12. A	

192
Sperry, Armstrong. *Call It Courage.*
CATEGORY: C
POINT VALUE: 5

1. F	5. T	9. T	13. C
2. T	6. T	10. T	14. B
3. F	7. F	11. A	
4. T	8. T	12. C	

193
Steig, William. *Abel's Island.*
CATEGORY: C
POINT VALUE: 5

1. F	5. F	9. F	13. C
2. T	6. T	10. F	14. B
3. T	7. F	11. F	
4. F	8. F	12. A	

194
Steig, William. *The Real Thief.*
CATEGORY: A
POINT VALUE: 5

1. F	5. T	9. T	13. A
2. T	6. T	10. T	14. D
3. F	7. T	11. T	
4. F	8. T	12. B	

195
Stevenson, Robert Louis. *Kidnapped.*
CATEGORY: E
POINT VALUE: 20

1. T	5. F	9. T	13. D
2. F	6. F	10. T	14. D
3. T	7. T	11. A	
4. T	8. F	12. C	

196
Stevenson, Robert Louis. *Treasure Island.*
CATEGORY: E
POINT VALUE: 20

1. T	5. F	9. T	13. C
2. F	6. T	10. T	14. B
3. T	7. F	11. D	
4. T	8. T	12. A	

197
Stolz, Mary. *Cat Walk.*
CATEGORY: A
POINT VALUE: 5

1. T	5. T	9. T	13. C
2. T	6. F	10. F	14. D
3. T	7. T	11. F	
4. F	8. F	12. T	

198
Stolz, Mary. *The Noonday Friends.*
CATEGORY: B
POINT VALUE: 10

1. F	5. T	9. T	13. C
2. T	6. T	10. F	14. C
3. T	7. F	11. T	
4. T	8. T	12. A	

199
Stowe, Harriet Beecher. *Uncle Tom's Cabin.*
CATEGORY: E
POINT VALUE: 30

1. F	5. F	9. T	13. D
2. T	6. T	10. F	14. B
3. F	7. F	11. D	
4. F	8. T	12. A	

200
Taylor, Mildred D. *Roll of Thunder, Hear My Cry.*
CATEGORY: D
POINT VALUE: 15

1. F	5. F	9. T	13. B
2. T	6. F	10. F	14. D
3. F	7. F	11. T	
4. F	8. T	12. B	

201
de Trevino, Elizabeth Borton. *I, Juan de Pareja.*
CATEGORY: E
POINT VALUE: 10

1. F	5. F	9. F	13. A
2. T	6. F	10. F	14. C
3. F	7. T	11. T	
4. T	8. T	12. F	

202
Voigt, Cynthia. *Building Blocks.*
CATEGORY: C
POINT VALUE: 10

1. T	5. T	9. T	13. A
2. F	6. F	10. T	14. A
3. F	7. F	11. T	
4. F	8. T	12. D	

203
Voigt, Cynthia. *Dicey's Song.*
CATEGORY: E
POINT VALUE: 10

1. F	5. F	9. T	13. F
2. T	6. T	10. F	14. C
3. T	7. T	11. T	
4. F	8. F	12. T	

204
Voigt, Cynthia. *Homecoming.*
CATEGORY: E
POINT VALUE: 10

1. T	5. F	9. F	13. A
2. T	6. F	10. T	14. D
3. F	7. F	11. T	
4. T	8. T	12. C	

205
Voigt, Cynthia. *A Solitary Blue.*
CATEGORY: E
POINT VALUE: 10

1. F	5. F	9. T	13. D
2. T	6. F	10. F	14. C
3. T	7. T	11. T	
4. T	8. F	12. F	

206
White, E. B. *Charlotte's Web.*
CATEGORY: A
POINT VALUE: 10

1. F	5. T	9. T	13. C
2. F	6. T	10. F	14. B
3. T	7. F	11. F	
4. T	8. F	12. T	

207
White, E. B. *Stuart Little.*
CATEGORY: A
POINT VALUE: 5

1. F	5. F	9. F	13. A
2. T	6. T	10. T	14. C
3. F	7. F	11. F	
4. T	8. T	12. B	

208
White, E. B. *The Trumpet of the Swan.*
CATEGORY: A
POINT VALUE: 10

1. T	5. T	9. F	13. B
2. F	6. T	10. T	14. D
3. F	7. T	11. F	
4. F	8. T	12. D	

209
Wiggin, Kate Douglas. *Rebecca of Sunnybrook Farm.*
CATEGORY: C
POINT VALUE: 20

1. F	5. F	9. F	13. D
2. T	6. T	10. F	14. C
3. T	7. T	11. T	
4. T	8. T	12. C	

210
Wilder, Laura Ingalls. *By the Shores of Silver Lake.*
CATEGORY: B
POINT VALUE: 20

1. T	5. F	9. F	13. F
2. F	6. F	10. T	14. F
3. F	7. T	11. F	
4. T	8. F	12. F	

211
Wilder, Laura Ingalls. *Farmer Boy.*
CATEGORY: B
POINT VALUE: 25

1. F	5. T	9. F	13. C
2. T	6. T	10. F	14. C
3. F	7. T	11. F	
4. F	8. T	12. C	

212
Wilder, Laura Ingalls. *The First Four Years.*
CATEGORY: B
POINT VALUE: 10

1. F	5. T	9. T	13. F
2. F	6. T	10. F	14. B
3. F	7. T	11. T	
4. F	8. T	12. F	

213
Wilder, Laura Ingalls. *Little House in the Big Woods.*
CATEGORY: B
POINT VALUE: 15

1. F	5. T	9. T	13. T
2. F	6. F	10. T	14. C
3. F	7. T	11. T	
4. T	8. T	12. F	

214
Wilder, Laura Ingalls. *Little Town on the Prairie.*
CATEGORY: B
POINT VALUE: 20

1. T	5. F	9. T	13. A
2. F	6. F	10. F	14. B
3. F	7. T	11. T	
4. T	8. T	12. F	

215
Wilder, Laura Ingalls. *The Long Winter.*
CATEGORY: B
POINT VALUE: 20

1. T	5. F	9. T	13. C
2. T	6. T	10. F	14. C
3. F	7. T	11. T	
4. F	8. T	12. T	

216
Wilder, Laura Ingalls. *On the Banks of Plum Creek.*
CATEGORY: B
POINT VALUE: 20

1. T	5. T	9. T	13. B
2. F	6. T	10. F	14. D
3. F	7. T	11. F	
4. T	8. T	12. C	

217
Wilder, Laura Ingalls. *These Happy Golden Years.*
CATEGORY: B
POINT VALUE: 20

1. F	5. F	9. T	13. C
2. T	6. T	10. F	14. B
3. T	7. F	11. F	
4. T	8. F	12. F	

218
Wojciechowska, Maia. *Shadow of a Bull.*
CATEGORY: D
POINT VALUE: 10

1. F	5. T	9. F	13. C
2. T	6. T	10. F	14. A
3. F	7. F	11. F	
4. T	8. T	12. B	

219
Wyss, Johann. *The Swiss Family Robinson.*
CATEGORY: E
POINT VALUE: 25

1. F	5. F	9. F	13. B
2. T	6. F	10. F	14. C
3. T	7. T	11. T	
4. T	8. F	12. A	

220
Yates, Elizabeth. *With Pipe, Paddle, and Song.*
CATEGORY: D
POINT VALUE: 15

1. T	5. T	9. F	13. A
2. T	6. F	10. T	14. C
3. F	7. T	11. T	
4. F	8. T	12. C	

PART
IV

Children's Catalog

Introduction

Welcome to the *Children's Catalog*. Before you select a book, ask your teacher to recommend a category of books (from A—E) for you to read. Within each category, a book's point value depends on the length of the book. Your teacher should give you a goal for the total number of points you should acquire.

When you have read a book, the teacher will give you a short test about the book to see if you understood the story.

In choosing the books you will read during this program try to choose books from all kinds of topical headings. By doing this, you will find out if there are types of books that you enjoy that you might not otherwise have read. It's kind of like going to an ice cream shop that sells 33 flavors of ice cream. You may know that you love dill pickle with pistachio nuts ice cream, but if you always order that flavor, you may never find out that you like fishy fruit better!

So go ahead and read a few mysteries if you like mysteries, but also read a book or two about friendship, horses, or ships. You might be surprised at the types of books you find yourself really enjoying!

The first half of the *Children's Catalog* presents a Subject Index of all the books included in the program. The books for each subject are listed by category (from A—E). The second half of the catalog gives short annotations describing each book. Within each category, the books in the second half of the catalog are listed alphabetically by author.

Using the *Children's Catalog* is easy. Browse through the Subject Index and jot down the titles of several books that interest you. Next to each title, take note of the book's author and category. When your list is complete, turn to the second half of the catalog to read the annotations. If, for example, one of the books you have listed is *Sign of the Beaver* by Elizabeth George Speare, turn to Category D in the second half of the catalog. Then, scanning the list of authors in Category D, look under "S" for Speare, and here you will find the annotation. After reading the annotations for the books on your list, decide which of the books you would like to learn even more about. Next, you might ask your teacher if you may visit the school library to locate and review the books on your list before choosing the next book you would like to read.

The *Children's Catalog* will be a useful tool for you to use in selecting books you are sure to enjoy. On the next page, you will find a complete listing of all the topics included in this program. So start browsing . . . and happy reading!

List of Subjects

Abandonment
Adventure
African Americans
Animals
Animals as Talking Characters
Babies
Baby-Sitting
Biography
Boy–Girl Relationships
Boys Growing Up
Brothers
Brothers and Sisters
Cats
Children Living Alone
Christmas
Computers
Courage
Crime
Death/Dying
Divorce
Dogs
Domestic Violence
Family Life
Family Problems
Fantasy
Farms—Living on a Farm
Fathers
Foster Care
French Revolution
Friendship
Frontier Life and Pioneer Life
Gangs/Street Life
Ghosts
Girls Growing Up
Grandparents
Handicaps
Historical Fiction
Homelessness
Horses
Hospitals—Being in a Hospital
Humor

Islands
Jewish People
Kidnapping
Kindergartners
Make Believe
Mental Illness
Mice/Rats
Mothers
Murder
Mystery
Native Americans
Nature
Neglect
Newbery Medal Books
Orphans/Orphanages
Pets
Poverty/Financial Hardship
Prejudice
Rabbits
Rape
Relatives—Living With Relatives
Rivers
Romance
Runaways
Salem Witch Trials
School
Sea
Ships
Single Parents
Sisters
Slavery
Stepparents
Summer Vacation
Survival
Villages—Living in a Village
Wagon Trains
War
War—Civilian Life During Wartime
Witches/Witchcraft/Sorcery
Wolves

Subject Index

ABANDONMENT—Being Abandoned By One Or By Both Parents

(*See also*: Children Living Alone, Family Problems, Foster Care, Neglect—Being Neglected By One Or By Both Parents, Orphans/Orphanages.)

Category: C

Byars, Betsy. *The House of Wings.*
Byars, Betsy. *The Two-Thousand-Pound Goldfish.*

Category: D

Byars, Betsy. *The Pinballs.*

Category: E

Voigt, Cynthia. *Dicey's Song.*
Voigt, Cynthia. *Homecoming.*
Voigt, Cynthia. *A Solitary Blue.*

ADVENTURE

(*See also*: Fantasy, Frontier Life and Pioneer Life, Islands—Living on an Island, Rivers, Sea, Ships, Survival.)

Category: C

Du Bois, William. *The Twenty-One Balloons.*
London, Jack. *The Call of the Wild.*
Sperry, Armstrong. *Call It Courage.*

Category: D

George, Jean Craighead. *River Rats, Inc.*
Kelly, Eric P. *The Trumpeter of Krakow.*
Yates, Elizabeth. *With Pipe, Paddle, and Song.*

Category: E

Clemens, Samuel L. (Mark Twain). *The Adventures of Huckleberry Finn.*
Clemens, Samuel L. (Mark Twain). *The Adventures of Tom Sawyer.*
Cooper, James Fenimore. *The Last of the Mohicans.*
Defoe, Daniel. *Robinson Crusoe.*
Stevenson, Robert Louis. *Kidnapped.*
Stevenson, Robert Louis. *Treasure Island.*
Wyss, Johann. *The Swiss Family Robinson.*

AFRICAN AMERICANS

(*See also*: Prejudice, Slavery.)

Category: B

Carlson, Natalie Savage. *The Empty Schoolhouse.*

Category: C

Armstrong, William H. *Sounder.*
Greene, Bette. *Philip Hall Likes Me, I Reckon, Maybe.*

Category: D

Sebestyen, Ouida. *Words by Heart.*
Taylor, Mildred D. *Roll of Thunder, Hear My Cry.*

Category: E

Fox, Paula. *The Slave Dancer.*
Hamilton, Virginia. *M. C. Higgins, the Great.*
Hamilton, Virginia. *The Planet of Junior Brown.*
Stowe, Harriet Beecher. *Uncle Tom's Cabin.*

ANIMALS

(*See also*: Animals as Talking Characters, Cats, Dogs, Farms—Living on a Farm, Horses, Mice/Rats, Nature, Pets, Rabbits, Wolves.)

Category: C

Byars, Betsy. *The House of Wings.*
George, Jean Craighead. *Julie of the Wolves.*
Henry, Marguerite. *Brighty of the Grand Canyon.*

Category: D

Eckert, Allan W. *Incident at Hawk's Hill.*
George, Jean Craighead. *Coyote in Manhattan.*
North, Sterling. *Rascal.*
North, Sterling. *The Wolfling.*
O'Dell, Scott. *Island of the Blue Dolphins.*

Category: E

Rawlings, Marjorie Kinnan. *The Yearling.*

ANIMALS AS TALKING CHARACTERS

(*See also*: Animals, Cats, Dogs, Fantasy, Farms—Living on a Farm, Horses, Make Believe, Mice/Rats, Pets, Rabbits, Wolves.)

Category: A

Cleary, Beverly. *The Mouse and the Motorcycle.*
Cleary, Beverly. *Ralph S. Mouse.*
Cleary, Beverly. *Runaway Ralph.*
Lawson, Robert. *Robbut.*
Steig, William. *The Real Thief.*
White, E. B. *Charlotte's Web.*
White, E. B. *Stuart Little.*
White, E. B. *The Trumpet of the Swan.*

Category: B
> Bailey, Carolyn. *Miss Hickory.*
> Lawson, Robert. *Rabbit Hill.*
> Lawson, Robert. *The Tough Winter.*
> Selden, George. *The Cricket in Times Square.*

Category: C
> Steig, William. *Abel's Island.*

Category: D
> Harris, Rosemary. *The Bright and Morning Star.*
> Harris, Rosemary. *The Moon in the Cloud.*
> Harris, Rosemary. *The Shadow on the Sun.*
> Lawson, Robert. *Ben and Me.*
> O'Brien, Robert C. *Mrs. Frisby and the Rats of NIMH.*

BABIES

(*See also*: Baby–Sitting.)

Category: A
> Blume, Judy. *Superfudge.*
> Carlson, Natalie Savage. *A Brother for the Orphelines.*
> Cleary, Beverly. *Socks.*

BABY–SITTING

(*See also*: Babies, Kindergartners.)

Category: C
> Robertson, Keith. *Henry Reed's Baby–Sitting Service.*

BIOGRAPHY

(*See also*: Historical Fiction.)

Category: E
> Meigs, Cornelia. *Invincible Louisa.*

BOY—GIRL RELATIONSHIPS

(*See also*: Boys Growing Up, Friendship, Girls Growing Up, Romance.)

Category: A
> Carlson, Natalie Savage. *The Orphelines in the Enchanted Castle.*
> Cleary, Beverly. *Henry and Beezus*

Category: B
> Burnett, Frances Hodgson. *The Secret Garden.*

Category: C
> Byars, Betsy. *The Computer Nut.*
> Byars, Betsy. *The Cybil War.*
> Greene, Bette. *Philip Hall Likes Me, I Reckon, Maybe.*
> Pearce, Philippa. *Tom's Midnight Garden.*
> Smith, Doris Buchanan. *Last Was Lloyd.*

Category: D
> Alcott, Louisa May. *Little Women.*
> Paterson, Katherine. *Bridge to Terabithia*

Category: E
> Hamilton, Virginia. *M. C. Higgins, the Great.*
> Paterson, Katherine. *Jacob Have I Loved.*
> Smith, Doris Buchanan. *Kick a Stone Home.*

BOYS GROWING UP

(*See also*: Boy–Girl Relationships, Brothers, Brothers and Sisters, Family Life, Family Problems, Friendship, School.)

Category: A
> Blume, Judy. *Superfudge.*
> Blume, Judy. *Tales of a Fourth Grade Nothing.*
> Cleary, Beverly. *Henry and Beezus.*
> Cleary, Beverly. *Henry and Ribsy.*
> Cleary, Beverly. *Henry and the Clubhouse.*
> Cleary, Beverly. *Henry and the Paper Route.*
> Cleary, Beverly. *Henry Huggins.*
> Cleary, Beverly. *Ribsy.*
> Haywood, Carolyn. *Eddie's Happenings.*

Category: B
> Carlson, Natalie Savage. *The Letter on the Tree.*
> Cleary, Beverly. *Dear Mr. Henshaw.*
> Estes, Eleanor. *Rufus M.*
> Smith, Doris Buchanan. *Kelly's Creek.*
> Wilder, Laura Ingalls. *Farmer Boy.*

Category: C
> Armer, Laura Adams. *Waterless Mountain.*
> Babbitt, Natalie, *Knee-Knock Rise.*
> Byars, Betsy. *The Cartoonist.*
> Byars, Betsy. *Good-bye, Chicken Little.*
> Byars, Betsy. *The TV Kid.*
> Byars, Betsy. *The Two–Thousand-Pound Goldfish.*
> Robertson, Keith. *Henry Reed, Inc.*
> Robertson, Keith. *Henry Reed's Baby–Sitting Service.*
> Shannon, Monica. *Dobry.*
> Smith, Doris Buchanan. *Last Was Lloyd.*
> Sperry, Armstrong. *Call It Courage.*
> Voigt, Cynthia. *Building Blocks.*

Category: D
> Alcott, Louisa May. *Little Men.*
> Clark, Ann Nolan. *Santiago.*
> Collier, James Lincoln, and Christopher Collier. *My Brother Sam Is Dead.*
> Edmonds, Walter D. *The Matchlock Gun.*
> Edmonds, Walter D. *Two Logs Crossing.*
> Forbes, Esther. *Johnny Tremain.*
> Fox, Paula. *One–Eyed Cat.*
> George, Jean Craighead. *My Side of the Mountain.*
> George, Jean Craighead. *River Rats, Inc.*

Krumgold, Joseph. *And Now Miguel.*
Krumgold, Joseph. *Onion John.*
Neville, Emily. *It's Like This, Cat.*
Speare, Elizabeth George. *Sign of the
    Beaver.*
Wojciechowska, Maia. *Shadow of a Bull.*
Category: E
Clemens, Samuel L. (Mark Twain). *The
    Adventures of Huckleberry Finn.*
Clemens, Samuel L. (Mark Twain). *The
    Adventures of Tom Sawyer.*
Defoe, Daniel. *Robinson Crusoe.*
Dickens, Charles. *Oliver Twist.*
Hamilton, Virginia. *M. C. Higgins, the
    Great.*
Hamilton, Virginia. *The Planet of Junior
    Brown.*
Ish–Kishor, Sulamith. *Our Eddie.*
Latham, Jean Lee. *Carry On, Mr. Bowditch.*
Rawlings, Marjorie Kinnan. *The Yearling.*
Stevenson, Robert Louis. *Kidnapped.*
Stevenson, Robert Louis. *Treasure Island.*
de Trevino, Elizabeth Borton. *I, Juan de
    Pareja.*
Voigt, Cynthia. *A Solitary Blue.*

BROTHERS

(*See also*: Boys Growing Up, Brothers and
Sisters, Family Life, Sisters.)

Category: A
Blume, Judy. *Superfudge.*
Blume, Judy. *Tales of a Fourth Grade
    Nothing.*
Category: C
Byars, Betsy. *The Cartoonist.*
Category: D
Collier, James Lincoln, and Christopher
    Collier. *My Brother Sam Is Dead.*
Category: E
Hunt, Irene. *Across Five Aprils.*

BROTHERS AND SISTERS

(*See also*: Boys Growing Up, Brothers,
Family Life, Girls Growing Up, Sisters.)

Category: A
DeJong, Meindert. *Puppy Summer.*
Category: B
Henry, Marguerite. *Misty of Chincoteague.*
Henry, Marguerite. *Stormy, Misty's Foal.*
Category: C
Byars, Betsy. *The Night Swimmers.*
Byars, Betsy. *The Summer of the Swans.*
Byars, Betsy. *The Two–Thousand–Pound
    Goldfish.*
Konigsburg, E. L. *From the Mixed–Up
    Files of Mrs. Basil E. Frankweiler.*

Category: D
Paterson, Katherine. *Bridge to Terabithia.*
Rodowsky, Colby F. *What About Me?*
Category: E
Konigsburg, E. L. *Father's Arcane
    Daughter.*
Speare, Elizabeth George. *The Bronze Bow.*
Voigt, Cynthia. *Dicey's Song.*
Voigt, Cynthia. *Homecoming.*

CATS

(*See also*: Animals, Animals as Talking
Characters, Dogs, Farms—Living on a
Farm, Horses, Mice/Rats, Pets, Rabbits,
Wolves.)

Category: A
Cleary, Beverly. *Socks.*
Stolz, Mary. *Cat Walk.*
Category: D
Alexander, Lloyd. *The Cat Who Wished to
    Be a Man.*
Fox, Paula. *One–Eyed Cat.*
Neville, Emily. *It's Like This, Cat.*

CHILDREN LIVING ALONE

(*See also*: Abandonment—Being Abandoned
by One or by Both Parents, Foster Care,
Gangs/Street Life, Neglect—Being
Neglected by One or by Both Parents,
Orphans/Orphanages.)

Category: C
Armer, Laura Adams. *Waterless Mountain.*
George, Jean Craighead. *Julie of the
    Wolves.*
Konigsburg, E. L. *From the Mixed–Up
    Files of Mrs. Basil E. Frankweiler.*
Category: D
George, Jean Craighead. *My Side of the
    Mountain.*
George, Jean Craighead. *River Rats, Inc.*
O'Dell, Scott. *Island of the Blue Dolphins.*
Speare, Elizabeth George. *Sign of the
    Beaver.*
Category: E
Hamilton, Virginia. *The Planet of Junior
    Brown.*
Voigt, Cynthia. *Homecoming.*

CHRISTMAS

(*See also*: Family Life.)

Category: B
Estes, Eleanor. *The Coat–Hanger
    Christmas Tree.*

COMPUTERS

Category: C
    Byars, Betsy. *The Computer Nut.*

COURAGE

Category: A
    Blume, Judy. *Otherwise Known as Sheila the Great.*
Category: C
    Byars, Betsy. *Good-bye, Chicken Little.*
    Sperry, Armstrong. *Call It Courage.*
Category: E
    Speare, Elizabeth George. *The Bronze Bow.*

CRIME

(*See also*: Domestic Violence, Gangs/Street Life, Kidnapping, Murder.)

Category: A
    Steig, William. *The Real Thief.*
Category: C
    Babbitt, Natalie. *Goody Hall.*
Category: E
    Dickens, Charles. *Oliver Twist.*
    Stevenson, Robert Louis. *Treasure Island.*

DEATH/DYING

Category: B
    Burnett, Frances Hodgson. *The Secret Garden.*
    Smith, Doris Buchanan. *A Taste of Blackberries.*
Category: C
    Blos, Joan. W. *A Gathering of Days.*
    Byars, Betsy. *Good-bye, Chicken Little.*
Category: D
    Alcott, Louisa May. *Little Women.*
    Collier, James Lincoln, and Christopher Collier. *My Brother Sam Is Dead.*
    Paterson, Katherine. *Bridge to Terabithia.*
Category: E
    Ish–Kishor, Sulamith. *Our Eddie.*
    Voigt, Cynthia. *Dicey's Song.*

DIVORCE

(*See also*: Family Problems, Single Parents—Living in a Single Parent Home, Stepparents.)

Category: B
    Cleary, Beverly. *Dear Mr. Henshaw.*
Category: C
    Byars, Betsy. *Cracker Jackson.*
    Byars, Betsy. *The Summer of the Swans.*
    Greene, Constance C. *A Girl Called Al.*
Category: E
    Voigt, Cynthia. *A Solitary Blue.*

DOGS

(*See also*: Animals, Animals as Talking Characters, Cats, Farms—Living on a Farm, Horses, Mice/Rats, Pets, Rabbits, Wolves.)

Category: A
    Cleary, Beverly. *Henry and Ribsy.*
    Cleary, Beverly. *Henry Huggins.*
    Cleary, Beverly. *Ribsy.*
    DeJong, Meindert. *Puppy Summer.*
Category: B
    DeJong, Meindert. *Hurry Home, Candy.*
    Estes, Eleanor. *Ginger Pye.*
Category: C
    Armstrong, William H. *Sounder.*
    Gipson, Fred. *Old Yeller.*
    Gipson, Fred. *Savage Sam.*
    London, Jack. *The Call of the Wild.*

DOMESTIC VIOLENCE

(*See also*: Divorce, Family Problems, Neglect—Being Neglected by One or by Both Parents.)

Category: C
    Byars, Betsy. *Cracker Jackson.*

FAMILY LIFE

(*See also*: Boys Growing Up, Brothers, Brothers and Sisters, Family Problems, Fathers, Girls Growing Up, Grandparents, Mothers, Sisters.)

Category: A
    Cleary, Beverly. *Ramona and Her Father.*
    Cleary, Beverly. *Ramona and Her Mother.*
Category: B
    Brink, Carol Ryrie. *Caddie Woodlawn.*
    Enright, Elizabeth. *Thimble Summer.*
    Estes, Eleanor. *The Middle Moffat.*
    Estes, Eleanor. *Rufus M.*
    Gates, Doris. *Blue Willow.*
    Gates, Doris. *The Elderberry Bush.*
    Lenski, Lois. *Strawberry Girl.*
    Wilder, Laura Ingalls. *By the Shores of Silver Lake.*
    Wilder, Laura Ingalls. *Farmer Boy.*
    Wilder, Laura Ingalls. *The First Four Years.*
    Wilder, Laura Ingalls. *Little House in the Big Woods.*
    Wilder, Laura Ingalls. *Little Town on the Prairie.*
    Wilder, Laura Ingalls. *The Long Winter.*
    Wilder, Laura Ingalls. *On the Banks of Plum Creek.*
    Wilder, Laura Ingalls. *These Happy Golden Years.*

Category: C

> Blos, Joan. W. *A Gathering of Days.*
> Wiggin, Kate Douglas. *Rebecca of Sunnybrook Farm.*

Category: D

> Alcott, Louisa May. *Little Men.*
> Alcott, Louisa May. *Little Women.*
> MacLachlan, Patricia. *Sarah, Plain and Tall.*
> Taylor, Mildred D. *Roll of Thunder, Hear My Cry.*

Category: E

> Hamilton, Virginia. *M. C. Higgins, the Great.*
> Hunt, Irene. *Up a Road Slowly.*
> Meigs, Cornelia. *Invincible Louisa.*
> Rawlings, Marjorie Kinnan. *The Yearling.*
> Wyss, Johann. *The Swiss Family Robinson.*

FAMILY PROBLEMS

(*See also*: Divorce, Domestic Violence, Family Life, Neglect—Being Neglected by One or by Both Parents, Poverty, Single Parents—Living in a Single Parent Home, Stepparents.)

Category: B

> Cleary, Beverly. *Dear Mr. Henshaw.*
> Sorensen, Virginia. *Miracles on Maple Hill.*
> Stolz, Mary. *The Noonday Friends.*

Category: C

> Byars, Betsy. *The Cartoonist.*
> Byars, Betsy. *Cracker Jackson.*
> Byars, Betsy. *Good-bye, Chicken Little.*
> Byars, Betsy. *The House of Wings.*
> Byars, Betsy. *The Night Swimmers.*
> Byars, Betsy. *The Summer of the Swans.*
> Byars, Betsy. *The TV Kid.*
> Byars, Betsy. *The Two-Thousand-Pound Goldfish.*
> Shannon, Monica. *Dobry.*
> Smith, Doris Buchanan. *The First Hard Times.*
> Voigt, Cynthia. *Building Blocks.*

Category: D

> Byars, Betsy. *The Pinballs.*
> Collier, James Lincoln, and Christopher Collier. *My Brother Sam Is Dead.*
> Rodowsky, Colby F. *What About Me?*

Category: E

> Hunt, Irene. *Across Five Aprils.*
> Ish-Kishor, Sulamith. *Our Eddie.*
> Paterson, Katherine. *Jacob Have I Loved.*
> Voigt, Cynthia. *Dicey's Song.*
> Voigt, Cynthia. *Homecoming.*
> Voigt, Cynthia. *A Solitary Blue.*

FANTASY

(*See also*: Adventure, Animals as Talking Characters, Make Believe.)

Category: D

> Alexander, Lloyd. *The Cat Who Wished to Be a Man.*
> Alexander, Lloyd. *The Wizard in the Tree.*
> Harris, Rosemary. *The Bright and Morning Star.*
> Harris, Rosemary. *The Moon in the Cloud.*
> Harris, Rosemary. *The Shadow on the Sun.*
> Lewis, C. S. *The Horse and His Boy.*
> Lewis, C. S. *The Last Battle.*
> Lewis, C. S. *The Lion, the Witch and the Wardrobe.*
> Lewis, C. S. *The Magician's Nephew.*
> Lewis, C. S. *Prince Caspian.*
> Lewis, C. S. *The Silver Chair.*
> Lewis, C. S. *Voyage of the* Dawn Treader.
> McKinley, Robin. *Beauty.*
> McKinley, Robin. *The Blue Sword.*
> McKinley, Robin. *The Hero and the Crown.*

Category: E

> Alexander, Lloyd. *The Black Cauldron.*
> Alexander, Lloyd. *The Book of Three.*
> Alexander, Lloyd. *The Castle of Llyr.*
> Alexander, Lloyd. *The High King.*
> Alexander, Lloyd. *Taran Wanderer.*
> Cooper, Susan. *The Dark Is Rising.*
> Cooper, Susan. *The Grey King.*
> L'Engle, Madeleine. *A Swiftly Tilting Planet.*
> L'Engle, Madeleine. *A Wind in the Door.*
> L'Engle, Madeleine. *A Wrinkle in Time.*

FARMS—LIVING ON A FARM

(*See also*: Animals, Cats, Dogs, Horses, Mice/Rats, Nature, Pets, Rabbits, Wolves.)

Category: A

> DeJong, Meindert. *Puppy Summer.*
> White, E. B. *Charlotte's Web.*

Category: B

> Lenski, Lois. *Strawberry Girl.*
> Sorensen, Virginia. *Miracles on Maple Hill.*
> Wilder, Laura Ingalls. *Farmer Boy.*
> Wilder, Laura Ingalls. *The First Four Years.*

Category: C

> Wiggin, Kate Douglas. *Rebecca of Sunnybrook Farm.*

Category: E

> Hunt, Irene. *Across Five Aprils.*
> Rawlings, Marjorie Kinnan. *The Yearling.*

FATHERS

(*See also:* Family Life, Family Problems, Mothers, Stepparents.)

Category: A
Cleary, Beverly. *Ramona and Her Father.*

Category: B
Sorensen, Virginia. *Miracles on Maple Hill.*

Category: C
Barnouw, Victor. *Dream of the Blue Heron.*
Byars, Betsy. *Cracker Jackson.*
Voigt, Cynthia. *Building Blocks.*

Category: D
Neville, Emily. *It's Like This, Cat.*
Krumgold, Joseph. *Onion John.*

Category: E
Ish–Kishor, Sulamith. *Our Eddie.*
Konigsburg, E. L. *Father's Arcane Daughter.*
Lasky, Kathryn. *Beyond the Divide.*

FOSTER CARE

(*See also:* Abandonment—Being Abandoned by One or by Both Parents, Children Living Alone, Neglect—Being Neglected by One or by Both Parents, Orphans/Orphanages.)

Category: D
Byars, Betsy. *The Pinballs.*

FRENCH REVOLUTION

(*See also:* Historical Fiction, War.)

Category: E
Dickens, Charles. *A Tale of Two Cities.*

FRIENDSHIP

(*See also:* Boy—Girl Relationships, Boys Growing Up, Girls Growing Up, School.)

Category: B
Burnett, Frances Hodgson. *The Secret Garden.*
Smith, Doris Buchanan. *A Taste of Blackberries.*
Stolz, Mary. *The Noonday Friends.*

Category: C
Blos, Joan. W. *A Gathering of Days.*
Byars, Betsy. *Cracker Jackson.*
Konigsburg, E. L. *Jennifer, Hectate, Macbeth, William McKinley and Me, Elizabeth.*
Pearce, Philippa. *Tom's Midnight Garden.*

Category: D
Krumgold, Joseph. *Onion John.*
Paterson, Katherine. *Bridge to Terabithia.*
Speare, Elizabeth George. *Sign of the Beaver.*

Category: E
Clemens, Samuel L. (Mark Twain). *The Adventures of Huckleberry Finn.*
Clemens, Samuel L. (Mark Twain). *The Adventures of Tom Sawyer.*
Hamilton, Virginia. *The Planet of Junior Brown.*
Paterson, Katherine. *Jacob Have I Loved.*
Speare, Elizabeth George. *The Bronze Bow.*
de Trevino, Elizabeth Borton. *I, Juan de Pareja.*

FRONTIER LIFE AND PIONEER LIFE

(*See also:* Adventure, Family Life, Historical Fiction.)

Category: B
Brink, Carol Ryrie. *Caddie Woodlawn.*
Wilder, Laura Ingalls. *Little House in the Big Woods.*
Wilder, Laura Ingalls. *The Long Winter.*
Wilder, Laura Ingalls. *On the Banks of Plum Creek.*

Category: C
Gipson, Fred. *Old Yeller.*
Gipson, Fred. *Savage Sam.*
London, Jack. *The Call of the Wild.*

Category: D
Edmonds, Walter D. *The Matchlock Gun.*
Speare, Elizabeth George. *Sign of the Beaver.*
Yates, Elizabeth. *With Pipe, Paddle, and Song.*

Category: E
Cooper, James Fenimore. *The Last of the Mohicans.*
Lasky, Kathryn. *Beyond the Divide.*
Speare, Elizabeth George. *Calico Captive.*

GANGS/STREET LIFE

(*See also:* Children Living Alone, Crime, Homelessness, Runaways.)

Category: E
Dickens, Charles. *Oliver Twist.*

GHOSTS

(*See also:* Mystery, Witches/Witchcraft/ Sorcery.)

Category: C
Babbitt, Natalie. *The Eyes of the Amaryllis.*
Lively, Penelope. *The Ghost of Thomas Kempe.*
Pearce, Philippa. *Tom's Midnight Garden.*

GIRLS GROWING UP

(*See also*: Boy–Girl Relationships, Brothers and Sisters, Family Life, Family Problems, Friendship, School, Sisters.)

Category: A

Blume, Judy. *Otherwise Known as Sheila the Great.*
Carlson, Natalie Savage. *The Happy Orpheline.*
Carlson, Natalie Savage. *The Orphelines in the Enchanted Castle.*
Carlson, Natalie Savage. *A Pet for the Orphelines.*
Cleary, Beverly. *Ellen Tebbits.*
Cleary, Beverly. *Ramona and Her Father.*
Cleary, Beverly. *Ramona and Her Mother.*
Cleary, Beverly. *Ramona Forever.*
Cleary, Beverly. *Ramona Quimby, Age 8.*
Cleary, Beverly. *Ramona the Brave.*
Cleary, Beverly. *Ramona the Pest.*
Haywood, Carolyn. *Back to School with Betsy.*
Haywood, Carolyn. *"B" Is for Betsy.*
Haywood, Carolyn. *Betsy and Mr. Kilpatrick.*
Haywood, Carolyn. *Snowbound with Betsy.*

Category: B

Brink, Carol Ryrie. *Caddie Woodlawn.*
Enright, Elizabeth. *Thimble Summer.*
Estes, Eleanor. *The Alley.*
Estes, Eleanor. *The Hundred Dresses.*
Estes, Eleanor. *The Middle Moffat.*
Gates, Doris. *Blue Willow.*
Gates, Doris. *The Elderberry Bush.*
Gates, Doris. *A Morgan for Melinda.*
Lenski, Lois. *Strawberry Girl.*
Sawyer, Ruth. *Roller Skates.*
Sorensen, Virginia. *Miracles on Maple Hill.*
Stolz, Mary. *The Noonday Friends.*
Wilder, Laura Ingalls. *By the Shores of Silver Lake.*
Wilder, Laura Ingalls. *Little House in the Big Woods.*
Wilder, Laura Ingalls. *Little Town on the Prairie.*
Wilder, Laura Ingalls. *The Long Winter.*
Wilder, Laura Ingalls. *On the Banks of Plum Creek.*
Wilder, Laura Ingalls. *These Happy Golden Years.*

Category: C

Blos, Joan. W. *A Gathering of Days.*
Byars, Betsy. *The Summer of the Swans.*
George, Jean Craighead. *Julie of the Wolves.*
Greene, Bette. *Philip Hall Likes Me, I Reckon, Maybe.*
Greene, Constance C. *A Girl Called Al.*
Konigsburg, E. L. *Jennifer, Hectate, Macbeth, William McKinley and Me, Elizabeth.*
Smith, Doris Buchanan. *The First Hard Times.*
Wiggin, Kate Douglas. *Rebecca of Sunnybrook Farm.*

Category: D

Alcott, Louisa May. *Little Women.*
Fitzhugh, Louise. *Harriet the Spy.*
George, Jean Craighead. *Coyote in Manhattan.*
O'Dell, Scott. *Island of the Blue Dolphins.*
Rodowsky, Colby F. *What About Me?*
Taylor, Mildred D. *Roll of Thunder, Hear My Cry.*

Category: E

Hunt, Irene. *Up a Road Slowly.*
Paterson, Katherine. *Jacob Have I Loved.*
Smith, Doris Buchanan. *Kick a Stone Home.*
Voigt, Cynthia. *Dicey's Song.*
Voigt, Cynthia. *Homecoming.*

GRANDPARENTS

(*See also*: Family Life, Relatives— Living with Relatives.)

Category: B

Estes, Eleanor. *The Lost Umbrella of Kim Chu.*
Henry, Marguerite. *Misty of Chincoteague.*
Henry, Marguerite. *Stormy, Misty's Foal.*

Category: C

Babbitt, Natalie. *The Eyes of the Amaryllis.*
Barnouw, Victor. *Dream of the Blue Heron.*
Byars, Betsy. *The House of Wings.*

Category: E

Paterson, Katherine. *Jacob Have I Loved.*
Voigt, Cynthia. *Dicey's Song.*
Voigt, Cynthia. *Homecoming.*

HANDICAPS

Category: B

Smith, Doris Buchanan. *Kelly's Creek.*

Category: C

Byars, Betsy. *The Summer of the Swans.*

Category: D

Forbes, Esther. *Johnny Tremain.*
Rodowsky, Colby F. *What About Me?*

Category: E

Konigsburg, E. L. *Father's Arcane Daughter.*
Voigt, Cynthia. *Dicey's Song.*
Voigt, Cynthia. *Homecoming.*

HISTORICAL FICTION

(*See also*: Biography, French Revolution, Frontier Life and Pioneer Life, Salem Witch Trials, Wagon Trains, War, War—Civilian Life During Wartime.)

Category: B

Brink, Carol Ryrie. *Caddie Woodlawn.*
Wilder, Laura Ingalls. *By the Shores of Silver Lake.*
Wilder, Laura Ingalls. *Farmer Boy.*
Wilder, Laura Ingalls. *The First Four Years.*
Wilder, Laura Ingalls. *Little House in the Big Woods.*
Wilder, Laura Ingalls. *Little Town on the Prairie.*
Wilder, Laura Ingalls. *The Long Winter.*
Wilder, Laura Ingalls. *On the Banks of Plum Creek.*
Wilder, Laura Ingalls. *These Happy Golden Years.*

Category: C

Blos, Joan. W. *A Gathering of Days.*

Category: D

Collier, James Lincoln, and Christopher Collier. *My Brother Sam Is Dead.*
Forbes, Esther. *Johnny Tremain.*
O'Dell, Scott. *Sarah Bishop.*
O'Dell, Scott. *Sing Down the Moon.*
Yates, Elizabeth. *With Pipe, Paddle, and Song.*

Category: E

Cooper, James Fenimore. *The Last of the Mohicans.*
Dickens, Charles. *A Tale of Two Cities.*
Fox, Paula. *The Slave Dancer.*
Hunt, Irene. *Across Five Aprils.*
Lasky, Kathryn. *Beyond the Divide.*
Latham, Jean Lee. *Carry On, Mr. Bowditch.*
Speare, Elizabeth George. *The Bronze Bow.*
Speare, Elizabeth George. *Calico Captive.*
Speare, Elizabeth George. *The Witch of Blackbird Pond.*
Stowe, Harriet Beecher. *Uncle Tom's Cabin.*

HOMELESSNESS

(*See also*: Children Living Alone, Gangs/Street Life, Poverty.)

Category: D

Krumgold, Joseph. *Onion John.*

Category: E

Voigt, Cynthia. *Homecoming.*

HORSES

(*See also*: Animals, Animals As Talking Characters, Cats, Dogs, Farms—Living on a Farm, Mice/Rats, Pets, Rabbits, Wolves.)

Category: B

Gates, Doris. *A Morgan for Melinda.*
Henry, Marguerite. *Misty of Chincoteague.*
Henry, Marguerite. *Stormy, Misty's Foal.*

Category: C

Henry, Marguerite. *Born to Trot.*
Henry, Marguerite. *King of the Wind.*
Henry, Marguerite. *Mustang—Wild Spirit of the West.*

Category: D

Henry, Marguerite. *Justin Morgan Had a Horse.*

HOSPITALS—BEING IN A HOSPITAL

Category: C

Byars, Betsy. *The TV Kid.*
Henry, Marguerite. *Born to Trot.*
Henry, Marguerite. *Mustang—Wild Spirit of the West.*

Category: D

Byars, Betsy. *The Pinballs.*

HUMOR

Category: A

Atwater, Richard, and Florence Atwater. *Mr. Popper's Penguins.*
Blume, Judy. *Otherwise Known as Sheila the Great.*
Blume, Judy. *Superfudge.*
Blume, Judy. *Tales of a Fourth Grade Nothing.*
Cleary, Beverly. *Ellen Tebbits.*
Cleary, Beverly. *Henry and Beezus.*
Cleary, Beverly. *Henry and Ribsy.*
Cleary, Beverly. *Henry and the Clubhouse.*
Cleary, Beverly. *Henry and the Paper Route.*
Cleary, Beverly. *Henry Huggins.*
Cleary, Beverly. *The Mouse and the Motorcycle.*
Cleary, Beverly. *Ralph S. Mouse.*
Cleary, Beverly. *Ramona and Her Father.*
Cleary, Beverly. *Ramona and Her Mother.*
Cleary, Beverly. *Ramona Forever.*
Cleary, Beverly. *Ramona Quimby, Age 8.*
Cleary, Beverly. *Ramona the Brave.*
Cleary, Beverly. *Ramona the Pest.*
Cleary, Beverly. *Ribsy.*
Cleary, Beverly. *Runaway Ralph.*
Cleary, Beverly. *Socks.*

Category: B

Bailey, Carolyn. *Miss Hickory.*
Estes, Eleanor. *Ginger Pye.*
Estes, Eleanor. *The Middle Moffat.*
Estes, Eleanor. *Rufus M.*

Category: C

>Byars, Betsy. *The Computer Nut.*
>Greene, Constance C. *A Girl Called Al.*
>Konigsburg, E. L. *From the Mixed–Up Files of Mrs. Basil E. Frankweiler.*
>Konigsburg, E. L. *Jennifer, Hectate, Macbeth, William McKinley and Me, Elizabeth.*
>Robertson, Keith. *Henry Reed, Inc.*
>Robertson, Keith. *Henry Reed's Baby–Sitting Service*

Category: D.

>Alexander, Lloyd. *The Cat Who Wished to Be a Man.*
>Alexander, Lloyd. *The Wizard in the Tree.*
>Fitzhugh, Louise. *Harriet the Spy.*
>Lawson, Robert. *Ben and Me.*

ISLANDS—LIVING ON AN ISLAND

(*See also*: Adventure, Nature, Rivers, Sea, Ships.)

Category: B

>Henry, Marguerite. *Misty of Chincoteague.*
>Henry, Marguerite. *Stormy, Misty's Foal.*

Category: C

>Du Bois, William. *The Twenty–One Balloons.*
>Sperry, Armstrong. *Call It Courage.*
>Steig, William. *Abel's Island.*

Category: D

>O'Dell, Scott. *Island of the Blue Dolphins.*

Category: E

>Defoe, Daniel. *Robinson Crusoe.*
>Paterson, Katherine. *Jacob Have I Loved.*
>Stevenson, Robert Louis. *Treasure Island.*
>Wyss, Johann. *The Swiss Family Robinson.*

JEWISH PEOPLE

(*See also*: Prejudice.)

Category: E

>Ish–Kishor, Sulamith. *Our Eddie.*
>Speare, Elizabeth George. *The Bronze Bow.*

KIDNAPPING

(*See also*: Crime, Slavery.)

Category: C

>Gipson, Fred. *Savage Sam.*

Category: D

>O'Dell, Scott. *Sing Down the Moon.*

Category: E

>Cooper, James Fenimore. *The Last of the Mohicans.*
>Fox, Paula. *The Slave Dancer.*
>Speare, Elizabeth George. *Calico Captive.*
>Stevenson, Robert Louis. *Kidnapped.*

KINDERGARTNERS

(*See also*: Baby–Sitting, Humor, School.)

Category: A

>Blume, Judy. *Superfudge.*
>Cleary, Beverly. *Ramona the Pest.*
>Haywood, Carolyn. *"B" Is for Betsy.*

MAKE BELIEVE

(*See also*: Animals as Talking Characters, Humor, Fantasy.)

Category: A

>Atwater, Richard, and Florence Atwater. *Mr. Popper's Penguins.*

Category: B

>Bailey, Carolyn. *Miss Hickory.*
>Norton, Mary. *The Borrowers.*
>Norton, Mary. *The Borrowers Afield.*
>Norton, Mary. *The Borrowers Afloat.*
>Norton, Mary. *The Borrowers Aloft.*
>Norton, Mary. *The Borrowers Avenged.*

MENTAL ILLNESS

(*See also*: Family Problems.)

Category: E

>Hamilton, Virginia. *The Planet of Junior Brown.*
>Ish–Kishor, Sulamith. *Our Eddie.*
>Voigt, Cynthia. *Dicey's Song.*

MICE/RATS

(*See also*: Animals, Animals as Talking Characters, Cats, Dogs, Farms—Living on a Farm, Horses, Pets, Rabbits, Wolves.)

Category: A

>Cleary, Beverly. *The Mouse and the Motorcycle.*
>Cleary, Beverly. *Ralph S. Mouse.*
>Cleary, Beverly. *Runaway Ralph.*
>Steig, William. *The Real Thief.*
>White, E. B. *Stuart Little.*

Category: C

>Steig, William. *Abel's Island.*

Category: D

>Lawson, Robert. *Ben and Me.*
>O'Brien, Robert C. *Mrs. Frisby and the Rats of NIMH.*

MOTHERS

(*See also*: Family Life, Family Problems, Fathers, Stepparents.)

Category: A

>Cleary, Beverly. *Ramona and Her Mother*

Category: B
  Brink, Carol Ryrie. *Caddie Woodlawn.*
  Estes, Eleanor. *The Coat–Hanger Christmas Tree*
Category: C
  Byars, Betsy. *The Cartoonist.*
  Byars, Betsy. *The Two–Thousand–Pound Goldfish.*
  Shannon, Monica. *Dobry.*
Category: E
  Voigt, Cynthia. *A Solitary Blue*

MURDER

(*See also*: Crime, Mystery.)
Category: C
  Barnouw, Victor. *Dream of the Blue Heron.*
Category: E
  Dickens, Charles. *Oliver Twist.*
  Raskin, Ellen. *The Westing Game.*

MYSTERY

(*See also*: Ghosts, Murder.)
Category: A
  Sobol, Donald J. *Encyclopedia Brown—The Case of the Dead Eagles and Other Mysteries.*
  Sobol, Donald J. *Encyclopedia Brown Carries On.*
  Sobol, Donald J. *Encyclopedia Brown Solves Them All.*
  Steig, William. *The Real Thief.*
Category: C
  Babbitt, Natalie. *The Eyes of the Amaryllis.*
  Babbitt, Natalie. *Goody Hall.*
  Babbitt, Natalie. *Knee-Knock Rise.*
  Lively, Penelope. *The Ghost of Thomas Kempe.*
  Pearce, Philippa. *Tom's Midnight Garden.*
Category: D
  Lively, Penelope. *Astercote.*
  Raskin, Ellen. *The Mysterious Disappearance of Leon (I Mean Noel)*
Category: E
  George, Jean Craighead. *Who Really Killed Cock Robin?*
  Raskin, Ellen. *The Westing Game.*

NATIVE AMERICANS

(*See also*: Historical Fiction, Prejudice, Slavery.)
Category: B
  Brink, Carol Ryrie. *Caddie Woodlawn.*
Category: C
  Armer, Laura Adams. *Waterless Mountain.*
  Barnouw, Victor. *Dream of the Blue Heron.*

Clark, Ann Nolan. *Secret of the Andes*
Gipson, Fred. *Savage Sam.*
Category: D
  Clark, Ann Nolan. *Santiago.*
  Edmonds, Walter D. *The Matchlock Gun.*
  O'Dell, Scott. *Island of the Blue Dolphins.*
  O'Dell, Scott. *Sing Down the Moon.*
  Speare, Elizabeth George. *Sign of the Beaver.*
Category: E
  Cooper, James Fenimore. *The Last of the Mohicans.*
  Speare, Elizabeth George. *Calico Captive.*

NATURE

(*See also*: Animals, Farms—Living on a Farm, Islands—Living on an Island, Rivers, Sea.)
Category: B
  Bailey, Carolyn. *Miss Hickory.*
  Burnett, Frances Hodgson. *The Secret Garden.*
Category: D
  George, Jean Craighead. *My Side of the Mountain.*
Category: E
  George, Jean Craighead. *Who Really Killed Cock Robin?*

NEGLECT—BEING NEGLECTED BY ONE OR BY BOTH PARENTS

(*See also*: Abandonment—Being Abandoned by One or by Both Parents, Children Living Alone, Family Problems, Foster Care, Orphans/Orphanages.)
Category: C
  Byars, Betsy. *The Night Swimmers.*
  Byars, Betsy. *The Summer of the Swans.*
  Greene, Constance C. *A Girl Called Al.*
  Voigt, Cynthia. *Building Blocks.*
Category: D
  Byars, Betsy. *The Pinballs.*
  Fitzhugh, Louise. *Harriet the Spy.*
Category: E
  Ish–Kishor, Sulamith. *Our Eddie.*
  Paterson, Katherine. *Jacob Have I Loved.*
  Voigt, Cynthia. *A Solitary Blue.*

NEWBERY MEDAL BOOKS

(Listed with the year, in parentheses, in which the award was given.)
Category: B
  Bailey, Carolyn. *Miss Hickory.* (1947)
  Brink, Carol Ryrie. *Caddie Woodlawn.* (1936)
  Cleary, Beverly. *Dear Mr. Henshaw.* (1984)

Enright, Elizabeth. *Thimble Summer.* (1939)
Estes, Eleanor. *Ginger Pye.* (1952)
Lawson, Robert. *Rabbit Hill.* (1945)
Lenski, Lois. *Strawberry Girl.* (1946)
Sawyer, Ruth. *Roller Skates.* (1937)
Sorensen, Virginia. *Miracles on Maple Hill.* (1957)
Category: C
Armer, Laura Adams. *Waterless Mountain.* (1932)
Armstrong, William H. *Sounder.* (1970)
Blos, Joan. W. *A Gathering of Days.* (1980)
Byars, Betsy. *The Summer of the Swans.* (1971)
Clark, Ann Nolan. *Secret of the Andes.* (1953)
DeJong, Meindert. *The Wheel on the School.* (1955)
Du Bois, William. *The Twenty–One Balloons.* (1948)
George, Jean Craighead. *Julie of the Wolves.* (1973)
Henry, Marguerite. *King of the Wind.* (1949)
Konigsburg, E. L. *From the Mixed–Up Files of Mrs. Basil E. Frankweiler.* (1968)
Shannon, Monica. *Dobry.* (1935)
Sperry, Armstrong. *Call It Courage.* (1941)
Category: D
Edmonds, Walter D. *The Matchlock Gun.* (1942)
Forbes, Esther. *Johnny Tremain.* (1944)
Kelly, Eric P. *The Trumpeter of Krakow.* (1929)
Krumgold, Joseph. *And Now Miguel.* (1954)
Krumgold, Joseph. *Onion John.* (1960)
MacLachlan, Patricia. *Sarah, Plain and Tall.* (1986)
McKinley, Robin. *The Hero and the Crown.* (1985)
Neville, Emily. *It's Like This, Cat.* (1964)
O'Brien, Robert C. *Mrs. Frisby and the Rats of NIMH.* (1972)
O'Dell, Scott. *Island of the Blue Dolphins.* (1961)
Paterson, Katherine. *Bridge to Terabithia.* (1978)
Taylor, Mildred D. *Roll of Thunder, Hear My Cry.* (1977)
Wojciechowska, Maia. *Shadow of a Bull.* (1965)
Category: E
Alexander, Lloyd. *The High King.* (1969)
Cooper, Susan. *The Grey King.* (1976)
Fox, Paula. *The Slave Dancer.* (1974)
Hamilton, Virginia. *M. C. Higgins the Great.* (1975)
Hunt, Irene. *Up a Road Slowly.* (1967)
Latham, Jean Lee. *Carry On, Mr. Bowditch.* (1956)

L'Engle, Madeleine. *A Wrinkle in Time.* (1963)
Meigs, Cornelia. *Invincible Louisa.* (1934)
Paterson, Katherine. *Jacob Have I Loved.* (1981)
Raskin, Ellen. *The Westing Game.* (1979)
Seredy, Kate. *The White Stag.* (1938)
Speare, Elizabeth George. *The Bronze Bow.* (1962)
Speare, Elizabeth George. *The Witch of Blackbird Pond.* (1959)
de Trevino, Elizabeth Borton. *I, Juan de Pareja.* (1966)
Voigt, Cynthia. *Dicey's Song.* (1983)

ORPHANS/ORPHANAGES

(*See also*: Abandonment—Being Abandoned by One or by Both Parents, Children Living Alone, Foster Care, Neglect—Being Neglected by One or by Both Parents.)
Category: A
Carlson, Natalie Savage. *A Brother for the Orphelines.*
Carlson, Natalie Savage. *The Happy Orpheline.*
Carlson, Natalie Savage. *The Orphelines in the Enchanted Castle.*
Carlson, Natalie Savage. *A Pet for the Orphelines.*
Category: D
Alcott, Louisa May. *Little Men.*
Category: E
Dickens, Charles. *Oliver Twist.*

PETS

(*See also*: Animals, Animals as Talking Characters, Cats, Dogs, Farms—Living on a Farm, Horses, Mice/Rats, Rabbits, Wolves.)
Category: A
Atwater, Richard, and Florence Atwater. *Mr. Popper's Penguins.*
Blume, Judy. *Otherwise Known as Sheila the Great.*
Blume, Judy. *Superfudge.*
Blume, Judy. *Tales of a Fourth Grade Nothing.*
Carlson, Natalie Savage. *A Pet for the Orphelines.*
Cleary, Beverly. *Henry and Ribsy.*
Cleary, Beverly. *Henry Huggins.*
Cleary, Beverly. *Ribsy.*
Cleary, Beverly. *Socks.*
DeJong, Meindert. *Puppy Summer.*

Category: B
    DeJong, Meindert. *Hurry Home, Candy*.
    Estes, Eleanor. *Ginger Pye*.
Category: C
    Armstrong, William H. *Sounder*.
    Byars, Betsy. *The House of Wings*.
Category: D
    Fox, Paula. *One–Eyed Cat*.
    George, Jean Craighead. *Coyote in Manhattan*.
    Neville, Emily. *It's Like This, Cat*.
    North, Sterling. *Rascal*.
    North, Sterling. *The Wolfling*.
Category: E
    Rawlings, Marjorie Kinnan. *The Yearling*.

POVERTY/FINANCIAL HARDSHIP

(*See also*: Family Problems, Homelessness, Survival.)

Category: B
    Carlson, Natalie Savage. *The Letter on the Tree*.
    Estes, Eleanor. *The Hundred Dresses*.
    Gates, Doris. *Blue Willow*.
    Stolz, Mary. *The Noonday Friends*.
Category: C
    Byars, Betsy. *The Cartoonist*.
Category: D
    Edmonds, Walter D. *Two Logs Crossing*.
    Krumgold, Joseph. *Onion John*.
Category: E
    Dickens, Charles. *Oliver Twist*.
    Ish–Kishor, Sulamith. *Our Eddie*.

PREJUDICE

(*See also*: African Americans, Handicaps, Jewish People, Native Americans, Slavery.)

Category: B
    Carlson, Natalie Savage. *The Empty Schoolhouse*.
    Estes, Eleanor. *The Hundred Dresses*.
Category: C
    Armstrong, William H. *Sounder*.
    Barnouw, Victor. *Dream of the Blue Heron*.
Category: D
    Sebestyen, Ouida. *Words by Heart*.
    Taylor, Mildred D. *Roll of Thunder, Hear My Cry*.
Category: E
    Clemens, Samuel L. (Mark Twain). *The Adventures of Huckleberry Finn*.
    Fox, Paula. *The Slave Dancer*.
    Lasky, Kathryn. *Beyond the Divide*.
    Stowe, Harriet Beecher. *Uncle Tom's Cabin*.
    de Trevino, Elizabeth Borton. *I, Juan de Pareja*.

RABBITS

(*See also*: Animals, Animals as Talking Characters, Cats, Dogs, Farms—Living on a Farm, Horses, Mice/Rats, Pets, Wolves.)

Category: A
    Lawson, Robert. *Robbut*.
Category: B
    Lawson, Robert. *Rabbit Hill*.
    Lawson, Robert. *The Tough Winter*.

RELATIVES—LIVING WITH RELATIVES

(*See also*: Grandparents.)

Category: B
    Burnett, Frances Hodgson. *The Secret Garden*.
    Henry, Marguerite. *Misty of Chincoteague*.
    Henry, Marguerite. *Stormy, Misty's Foal*.
    Sawyer, Ruth. *Roller Skates*.
Category: C
    Wiggin, Kate Douglas. *Rebecca of Sunnybrook Farm*.
Category: E
    Hunt, Irene. *Up a Road Slowly*.
    Speare, Elizabeth George. *The Witch of Blackbird Pond*.
    Voigt, Cynthia. *Dicey's Song*.
    Voigt, Cynthia. *Homecoming*.

RIVERS

(*See also*: Adventure, Islands—Living on an Island, Nature, Sea, Ships.)

Category: D
    George, Jean Craighead. *River Rats, Inc*.
    Yates, Elizabeth. *With Pipe, Paddle, and Song*.
Category: E
    Clemens, Samuel L. (Mark Twain). *The Adventures of Huckleberry Finn*.

ROMANCE

(*See also*: Boy—Girl Relationships, Friendship.)

Category: B
    Wilder, Laura Ingalls. *The First Four Years*.
    Wilder, Laura Ingalls. *Little Town on the Prairie*.
    Wilder, Laura Ingalls. *These Happy Golden Years*.
Category: C
    Wiggin, Kate Douglas. *Rebecca of Sunnybrook Farm*.
Category: D
    Alcott, Louisa May. *Little Women*.
    McKinley, Robin. *Beauty*.
    O'Dell, Scott. *Sing Down the Moon*.

Category: E
> Hunt, Irene. *Up a Road Slowly.*
> Paterson, Katherine. *Jacob Have I Loved.*
> Speare, Elizabeth George. *Calico Captive.*
> Speare, Elizabeth George. *The Witch of Blackbird Pond.*

RUNAWAYS

(*See also*: Children Living Alone, Gangs/Street Life.)

Category: C
> Konigsburg, E. L. *From the Mixed-Up Files of Mrs. Basil E. Frankweiler.*

Category: D
> George, Jean Craighead. *My Side of the Mountain.*

Category: E
> Clemens, Samuel L. (Mark Twain). *The Adventures of Huckleberry Finn.*

SALEM WITCH TRIALS

(*See also*: Historical Fiction.)

Category: E
> Speare, Elizabeth George. *The Witch of Blackbird Pond.*

SEA

(*See also*: Adventure, Islands—Living on an Island, Nature, Rivers, Ships.)

Category: C
> Babbitt, Natalie. *The Eyes of the Amaryllis.*
> Sperry, Armstrong. *Call It Courage.*

SCHOOL

(*See also*: Boys Growing Up, Girls Growing Up, Friendship, Kindergartners.)

Category: A
> Blume, Judy. *Tales of a Fourth Grade Nothing.*
> Cleary, Beverly. *Ellen Tebbits.*
> Cleary, Beverly. *Ramona Forever.*
> Cleary, Beverly. *Ramona Quimby, Age 8.*
> Cleary, Beverly. *Ramona the Brave.*
> Cleary, Beverly. *Ramona the Pest.*
> Haywood, Carolyn. *Back to School with Betsy.*
> Haywood, Carolyn. *"B" Is for Betsy.*
> Haywood, Carolyn. *Betsy and Mr. Kilpatrick.*
> Haywood, Carolyn. *Eddie's Happenings.*

Category: B
> Carlson, Natalie Savage. *The Empty Schoolhouse.*
> Carlson, Natalie Savage. *School Bell in the Valley.*

> Cleary, Beverly. *Dear Mr. Henshaw.*
> Estes, Eleanor. *The Hundred Dresses.*
> Smith, Doris Buchanan. *Kelly's Creek.*
> Stolz, Mary. *The Noonday Friends.*

Category: C
> Barnouw, Victor. *Dream of the Blue Heron.*
> Blos, Joan. W. *A Gathering of Days.*
> Smith, Doris Buchanan. *Last Was Lloyd.*
> Wiggin, Kate Douglas. *Rebecca of Sunnybrook Farm.*

Category: D
> Fitzhugh, Louise. *Harriet the Spy.*

Category: E
> Hunt, Irene. *Up a Road Slowly.*
> Smith, Doris Buchanan. *Kick a Stone Home.*

SHIPS

(*See also*: Adventure, Islands—Living on an Island, Rivers, Sea.)

Category: E
> Fox, Paula. *The Slave Dancer.*
> Latham, Jean Lee. *Carry On, Mr. Bowditch.*
> Stevenson, Robert Louis. *Treasure Island.*

SINGLE PARENTS—LIVING IN A SINGLE PARENT HOME

(*See also*: Divorce, Family Problems, Stepparents.)

Category: B
> Cleary, Beverly. *Dear Mr. Henshaw.*

Category: C
> Blos, Joan. W. *A Gathering of Days.*
> Byars, Betsy. *The Cartoonist.*
> Byars, Betsy. *Cracker Jackson.*
> Byars, Betsy. *Good-bye, Chicken Little.*
> Byars, Betsy. *The Night Swimmers.*
> Byars, Betsy. *The Summer of the Swans.*
> Byars, Betsy. *The TV Kid.*
> Greene, Constance C. *A Girl Called Al.*
> Smith, Doris Buchanan. *Last Was Lloyd.*

Category: E
> Hamilton, Virginia. *The Planet of Junior Brown.*

SISTERS

(*See also*: Brothers, Brothers and Sisters, Family Life, Girls Growing Up.)

Category: A
> Cleary, Beverly. *Ramona and Her Father.*
> Cleary, Beverly. *Ramona and Her Mother.*
> Cleary, Beverly. *Ramona Forever.*
> Cleary, Beverly. *Ramona Quimby, Age 8.*
> Cleary, Beverly. *Ramona the Brave.*
> Cleary, Beverly. *Ramona the Pest.*

Category: B
> Wilder, Laura Ingalls. *By the Shores of Silver Lake.*
> Wilder, Laura Ingalls. *Little House in the Big Woods.*
> Wilder, Laura Ingalls. *Little Town on the Prairie.*
> Wilder, Laura Ingalls. *The Long Winter.*
> Wilder, Laura Ingalls. *On the Banks of Plum Creek*

Category: C
> Blos, Joan. W. *A Gathering of Days.*
> Byars, Betsy. *The Computer Nut.*

Category: D
> Alcott, Louisa May. *Little Women.*

Category: E
> Paterson, Katherine. *Jacob Have I Loved.*

SLAVERY

(*See also*: African Americans, Native Americans, Prejudice.)

Category: D
> O'Dell, Scott. *Sing Down the Moon.*

Category: E
> Clemens, Samuel L. (Mark Twain). *The Adventures of Huckleberry Finn.*
> Fox, Paula. *The Slave Dancer.*
> Stowe, Harriet Beecher. *Uncle Tom's Cabin.*
> de Trevino, Elizabeth Borton. *I, Juan de Pareja.*

STEPPARENTS

(*See also*: Divorce, Family Problems, Single Parents—Living in a Single Parent Home.)

Category: C
> Blos, Joan. W. *A Gathering of Days.*
> Smith, Doris Buchanan. *The First Hard Times.*

Category: D
> MacLachlan, Patricia. *Sarah, Plain and Tall.*

SUMMER VACATION

(*See also*: Boys Growing Up, Family Life, Girls Growing Up.)

Category: A
> Blume, Judy. *Otherwise Known as Sheila the Great.*
> DeJong, Meindert. *Puppy Summer.*

Category: B
> Enright, Elizabeth. *Thimble Summer.*
> Gates, Doris. *The Elderberry Bush.*

Category: C
> Byars, Betsy. *The Summer of the Swans.*
> Byars, Betsy. *The TV Kid.*
> Robertson, Keith. *Henry Reed, Inc.*

Robertson, Keith. *Henry Reed's Baby-Sitting Service.*

SURVIVAL

(*See also*: Adventure, Animals, Frontier Life and Pioneer Life, Islands—Living on an Island.)

Category: C
> George, Jean Craighead. *Julie of the Wolves.*
> London, Jack. *The Call of the Wild.*

Category: D
> Eckert, Allan W. *Incident at Hawk's Hill.*
> George, Jean Craighead. *My Side of the Mountain.*
> George, Jean Craighead. *River Rats, Inc.*
> O'Dell, Scott. *Island of the Blue Dolphins.*

Category: E
> Lasky, Kathryn. *Beyond the Divide.*
> Wyss, Johann. *The Swiss Family Robinson.*

VILLAGES—LIVING IN A VILLAGE

Category: C
> DeJong, Meindert. *The Wheel on the School.*

Category: D
> Lively, Penelope. *Astercote.*

Category: E
> Clemens, Samuel L. (Mark Twain). *The Adventures of Tom Sawyer.*

WAGON TRAINS

(*See also*: Frontier Life and Pioneer Life, Historical Fiction.)

Category: E
> Lasky, Kathryn. *Beyond the Divide.*

WAR

(*See also*: Historical Fiction, War—Civilian Life During Wartime.)

Category: D
> Collier, James Lincoln, and Christopher Collier. *My Brother Sam Is Dead.*
> Edmonds, Walter D. *The Matchlock Gun.*
> O'Dell, Scott. *Sarah Bishop.*

Category: E
> Cooper, James Fenimore. *The Last of the Mohicans.*

WAR—CIVILIAN LIFE DURING WARTIME

(*See also*: Historical Fiction, War.)

Category: B
> Estes, Eleanor. *The Middle Moffat.*
> Estes, Eleanor. *Rufus M.*

Category: D
  Alcott, Louisa May. *Little Women.*
  Collier, James Lincoln, and Christopher Collier. *My Brother Sam Is Dead.*
  O'Dell, Scott. *Sarah Bishop.*
Category: E
  Hunt, Irene. *Across Five Aprils.*

WITCHES/WITCHCRAFT/SORCERY

  (*See also*: Ghosts, Salem Witch Trials.)
Category: C
  Konigsburg, E. L. *Jennifer, Hectate, Macbeth, William McKinley and Me, Elizabeth.*

WOLVES

  (*See also*: Animals, Animals as Talking Characters, Cats, Dogs, Farms—Living on a Farm, Horses, Mice/Rats, Pets, Rabbits.)
Category: C
  George, Jean Craighead. *Julie of the Wolves.*
  London, Jack. *The Call of the Wild.*
Category: D
  North, Sterling. *The Wolfling.*

Annotations—Category A

Atwater, Richard, and Florence Atwater. 1938. *Mr. Popper's Penguins*. Boston: Little, Brown. Category: A. Point Value: 5. Book #12.
What will Mrs. Popper say when she finds out that Mr. Popper has ordered some penguins to keep in the house as pets?

Blume, Judy. 1972. *Otherwise Known as Sheila the Great*. New York: E. P. Dutton. Category: A. Point Value: 5. Book #19.
"Keep your filthy old dog away from me!" Sheila tries to cover up the real truth, which is that she is terrified of dogs as well as an assortment of other things.

Blume, Judy. 1980. *Superfudge*. New York: E. P. Dutton. Category: A. Point Value: 5. Book #20.
Life with Fudge is one disaster after another, and just when Peter thinks that it can't get any worse, his mother announces that she's going to have another baby!

Blume, Judy. 1972. *Tales of a Fourth Grade Nothing*. New York: E. P. Dutton. Category: A. Point Value: 5. Book #21.
Peter's little brother, Fudge, is a pest! Peter puts up with Fudge most of the time, but then Fudge does something *really* awful.

Carlson, Natalie Savage. 1959. *A Brother for the Orphelines*. New York: Harper & Row, 1959. Category: A. Point Value: 5. Book #35.
The girls are excited when they find out that a baby has been left in a breadbasket at the door of the orphanage. The only problem is that the baby is a *boy*, and this is an orphanage for girls only!

Carlson, Natalie Savage. 1957. *The Happy Orpheline*. New York: Harper & Row. Category: A. Point Value: 5. Book #37.
Brigitte is an orpheline who does not want to be adopted because she loves living at the orphanage with Madame Flattot. When she finds out that Madame Capet is thinking of adopting her, Brigitte does something really wicked to make her change her mind.

Carlson, Natalie Savage. 1964. *The Orphelines in the Enchanted Castle*. New York: Harper & Row. Category: A. Point Value: 5. Book #39.
The orphelines move to a new home, an old castle in the forest of Fontainebleau. The castle is exciting enough, but when the boy orphans arrive to share their home, things really get lively!

Carlson, Natalie Savage. 1962. *A Pet for the Orphelines*. New York: Harper & Row. Category: A. Point Value: 5. Book #40.
Monsieur de Goupil said that the orphelines could have a pet, but when it came time to choose what type of pet to get, the orphelines could not agree.

Cleary, Beverly. 1951. *Ellen Tebbits*. New York: William Morrow. Category: A. Point Value: 5. Book #45.
Ellen and Austine had been best friends until the day that Ellen slapped Austine's face. What can Ellen do to make Austine like her again?

Cleary, Beverly. 1952. *Henry and Beezus*. New York: William Morrow. Category: A. Point Value: 5. Book #46.
Henry is disgusted when his friend, Beezus, picks out a girl's bicycle for him at the auction.

Cleary, Beverly. 1954. *Henry and Ribsy*. New York: William Morrow. Category: A. Point Value: 5. Book #47.
Henry's father makes a deal with him, but the deal involves keeping Ribsy out of trouble until September. Will Henry be able to keep his end of the bargain?

Cleary, Beverly. 1962. *Henry and the Clubhouse*. New York: William Morrow. Category: A. Point Value: 5. Book #48.
Mr. Capper wants Henry to ask his new neighbor if she would like to subscribe to the *Journal*. Henry wants to ask her, but he can't get near her house!

Cleary, Beverly. 1957. *Henry and the Paper Route*. New York: William Morrow. Category: A. Point Value: 5. Book #49.
How can Henry convince Mr. Capper that he is old enough and responsible enough to have a paper route of his own?

Cleary, Beverly. 1983. *Henry Huggins*. New York: William Morrow. Category: A. Point Value: 5. Book #50.
Henry enters Ribsy in a dog contest. Ribsy wins a prize but not for the reasons you might expect!

Cleary, Beverly. 1965. *The Mouse and the Motorcycle*. New York: William Morrow. Category: A. Point Value: 5. Book #51.
Vroom! Ralph, a daring young mouse, becomes friends with a boy who teaches him how to drive a toy motorcycle.

Cleary, Beverly. 1982. *Ralph S. Mouse*. New York: William Morrow. Category: A. Point Value: 5. Book #52.
When Ralph's friend, Ryan, takes him to school, Ralph becomes the object of a class experiment.

Cleary, Beverly. 1977. *Ramona and Her Father*. New York: William Morrow. Category: A. Point Value: 5. Book #53.
When Mr. Quimby loses his job, the family must make some difficult adjustments.

Cleary, Beverly. 1979. *Ramona and Her Mother*. New York: William Morrow. Category: A. Point Value: 5. Book #54.
A box of Kleenex? That's the gift that Ramona gives to little Willa Jean, and what do you think Willa Jean will do with it?

Cleary, Beverly. 1984. *Ramona Forever*. New York: William Morrow. Category: A. Point Value: 5. Book #55.
Ramona is back! A third-grader now, Ramona is just as full of spunk as ever. Read the book and find out about all the changes that are about to take place in the Quimby family.

Cleary, Beverly. 1981. *Ramona Quimby, Age 8*. New York: William Morrow. Category: A. Point Value: 5. Book #56.
The Quimby family must be very careful with their money because Mr. Quimby has decided to return to college.

Cleary, Beverly. 1975. *Ramona the Brave*. New York: William Morrow. Category: A. Point Value: 5. Book #57.
Ramona is sure that her first-grade teacher doesn't like her. Ramona tries to be good, but she just can't seem to stay out of trouble!

Cleary, Beverly. 1968. *Ramona the Pest*. New York: William Morrow. Category: A. Point Value: 5. Book #58.
When Ramona, a kindergartner, refuses to stop pulling her classmate's hair, she is sent home from school until her behavior improves.

Cleary, Beverly. 1964. *Ribsy*. New York: William Morrow. Category: A. Point Value: 5. Book #59.
Henry is brokenhearted when he realizes that Ribsy is lost. He puts an ad in the newspaper, but he doesn't hear anything for months. Will Henry get a new dog?

Cleary, Beverly. 1970. *Runaway Ralph*. New York: William Morrow. Category: A. Point Value: 5. Book #60.
Ralph has had it! His brothers, sisters, and cousins are driving him crazy, so he decides to run away!

Cleary, Beverly. 1973. *Socks*. New York: William Morrow. Category: A. Point Value: 5. Book #61.
Socks is just a kitten when he is sold to Mr. and Mrs. Bricker, a young couple about to have their first baby. What will his life with the Brickers be like?

DeJong, Meindert. 1966. *Puppy Summer*. New York: Harper & Row. Category: A. Point Value: 5. Book #70.
John and Vestri are spending the summer with their grandparents. The summer is off to a fantastic start when their grandparents let them have not just one puppy—but three!

Haywood, Carolyn. 1943, 1980. *Back to School with Betsy*. New York: Harcourt, Brace. Category: A. Point Value: 5. Book #107.
Betsy is excited when she finds out that one of her favorite teachers, Miss Grey, will be moving in to the house next door.

Haywood, Carolyn. 1939. *"B" Is for Betsy*. New York: Harcourt, Brace. Category: A. Point Value: 5. Book #108.

Betsy is unhappy. Tomorrow she will go to school for the very first time, and she is sure that she will not like it. But soon Betsy learns that school is a fun place where she will make a lot of new friends.

Haywood, Carolyn. 1967. *Betsy and Mr. Kilpatrick.* New York: William Morrow. Category: A. Point Value: 5. Book #109.
Betsy is disappointed when she finds out that her friend, Mr. Kilpatrick, won't be taking the children across the street any more.

Haywood, Carolyn. 1970. *Eddie's Happenings.* New York: William Morrow. Category: A. Point Value: 5. Book #110.
Yuk! Eddie and his teacher find a mouse that drowned in a jar of purple paint!

Haywood, Carolyn. 1962. *Snowbound with Betsy.* New York: William Morrow. Category: A. Point Value: 5. Book #111.
One morning when Betsy wakes up, she sees a strange girl sleeping in the extra bed in her room. Who could this girl be?

Lawson, Robert. 1948. *Robbut.* New York: Viking Press. Category: A. Point Value: 5. Book #132.
Robbut is a young rabbit who does not like his tail. He meets a Little Man who gives him a new tail, but then Robbut has more problems than ever!

Sobol, Donald J. 1975. *Encyclopedia Brown—The Case of the Dead Eagles and Other Mysteries.* Nashville, Tenn.: T. Nelson. Category: A. Point Value: 5. Book #184.
Someone is killing eagles on the camp grounds. The mother eagle is still alive, but Encyclopedia must find out who the hunter is before she is shot too.

Sobol, Donald J. 1980. *Encyclopedia Brown Carries On.* New York: Four Winds Press. Category: A. Point Value: 5. Book #185.
Encyclopedia solves 10 more baffling mysteries. See if you can help Encyclopedia figure them out before reading the solutions at the end of the book!

Sobol, Donald J. 1968. *Encyclopedia Brown Solves Them All.* Camden, N.J: T. Nelson. Category: A. Point Value: 5. Book #186.
No mystery is too difficult for Encyclopedia Brown—a boy detective who makes sure that no man, woman, boy, or girl gets away with breaking the law.

Steig, William. 1973. *The Real Thief.* New York: Farrar, Straus & Giroux. Category: A. Point Value: 5. Book #194.
Gawain is accused of stealing the king's treasures. Even his friends believe that he is guilty—but Gawain is innocent!

Stolz, Mary. 1983. *Cat Walk.* New York: Harper & Row. Category: A. Point Value: 5. Book #197.
A kitten runs away from his young owner who likes to dress him up in doll clothes. The poor kitten is treated terribly as he searches for a new home, which he finally finds with an elderly couple who love animals.

White, E. B. 1952. *Charlotte's Web.* New York: Harper & Row. Category: A. Point Value: 10. Book #206.
Wilbur, a young pig, is feeling lonely and depressed. Then he hears a friendly voice coming from the corner of the barn—who could it be?

White, E. B. 1945, 1973. *Stuart Little.* New York: Harper & Row. Category: A. Point Value: 5. Book #207.
Can you imagine what your life would be like if your brother was a mouse? In this book, you will read about a mouse who was born to human parents.

White, E. B. 1970. *The Trumpet of the Swan.* New York: Harper & Row. Category: A. Point Value: 10. Book #208.
Lewis is a young swan who was born without a voice. He falls in love with a lovely swan named Serena, but he is unable to attract her attention.

Annotations—Category B

Bailey, Carolyn. 1946, 1978. *Miss Hickory*. New York: Penguin Books. Category: B. Point Value: 5. Book #16.
Miss Hickory must find a new home, but moving can be dangerous if you are a doll with a hickory nut for a head!

Brink, Carol Ryrie. 1945. *Caddie Woodlawn*. New York: Macmillan. Category: B. Point Value: 15. Book #22.
Caddie Woodlawn has always been allowed to be a tomboy, but now that she is 12, her mother wishes she would start acting more ladylike.

Burnett, Frances Hodgson. 1949. *The Secret Garden*. Philadelphia: J. B. Lippincott. Category: B. Point Value: 20. Book #23.
At night, in her uncle's house, Mary hears the sound of a child crying. When Mary asks the maid about the crying, she is told that it is only her imagination. But later, Mary discovers not only the secret of the crying but a beautiful, secret place as well.

Carlson, Natalie Savage. 1965. *The Empty Schoolhouse*. New York: Harper & Row. Category: B. Point Value: 5. Book #36.
Ten-year-old Lullah was excited when it was announced that black children would be allowed to attend the parochial schools in Louisiana. Her happiness did not last long, however, because things started to happen—terrible things.

Carlson, Natalie Savage. 1964. *The Letter on the Tree*. New York: Harper & Row. Category: B. Point Value: 5. Book #38.
Bébert comes up with a plan for getting the accordion that his father cannot afford to buy him, but it is a plan that Bébert knows is wrong.

Carlson, Natalie Savage. 1963. *School Bell in the Valley*. New York: Harcourt, Brace. Category: B. Point Value: 5. Book #41.
When 10-year-old Belle Mundy goes to school for the first time, the other kids make fun of her because she does not know how to read. Belle is humiliated, and she vows never to go back.

Cleary, Beverly. 1983. *Dear Mr. Henshaw*. New York: William Morrow. Category: B. Point Value: 10. Book #44.
Leigh's parents are divorced, and Leigh is bothered by the fact that his father rarely calls or visits him.

DeJong, Meindert. 1953. *Hurry Home, Candy*. New York: Harper. Category: B. Point Value: 10. Book #69.
Candy, a small dog, is being treated cruelly by his owners. He must escape, but where can he go?

Enright, Elizabeth. 1938. *Thimble Summer*. New York: Holt, Rinehart & Winston. Category: B. Point Value: 10. Book #78.
On a very hot day, Garnet and her brother decide to go for a swim in the river. Near the river, Garnet finds a silver thimble that she is sure will bring her good luck all summer long.

Estes, Eleanor. 1964. *The Alley*. New York: Harcourt, Brace. Category: B. Point Value: 15. Book #79.
The Swinger. That's what the kids in Connie's neighborhood call her. What did Connie do to earn that name?

Estes, Eleanor. 1973. *The Coat-Hanger Christmas Tree*. New York: Atheneum. Category: B. Point Value: 5. Book #80.
No Christmas tree?! Marianna and her brother don't understand why their mother won't let them have a Christmas tree. Perhaps they can get her to change her mind before Christmas.

Estes, Eleanor. 1951, 1990. *Ginger Pye*. San Diego, Calif.: Harcourt Brace Jovanovich. Category: B. Point Value: 15. Book #81.
When Jerry and Rachel find out that their beloved dog, Ginger, is lost, they are broken-hearted. Will they ever be able to find him?

Estes, Eleanor. 1944, 1974. *The Hundred Dresses*. New York: Harcourt Brace Jovanovich. Category: B. Point Value: 5. Book #82.

A hundred dresses all lined up. That's what Wanda says she has in her closet. Does Wanda really have a hundred dresses?

Estes, Eleanor. 1978. *The Lost Umbrella of Kim Chu*. New York: Atheneum. Category: B. Point Value: 5. Book #83.
When Kim comes home without her father's umbrella, her grandmother slaps her. Kim must go out again and find the umbrella, but what could have happened to it?

Estes, Eleanor. 1942. *The Middle Moffat*. New York: Harcourt, Brace. Category: B. Point Value: 15. Book #84.
Not the oldest and not the youngest in her family, Janey is the middle Moffat.

Estes, Eleanor. 1943. *Rufus M*. San Diego, Calif.: Harcourt Brace Jovanovich. Category: B. Point Value: 20. Book #85.
Rufus, the youngest member of the Moffat family, is always up to some kind of interesting activity!

Gates, Doris. 1940. *Blue Willow*. New York: Viking Press. Category: B. Point Value: 10. Book #90.
Janey and her parents never stay in one place for very long. Will Janey's father ever find a steady job so that they can have a home and all of the other things that Janey dreams of?

Gates, Doris. 1967. *The Elderberry Bush*. New York: Viking Press. Category: B. Point Value: 10. Book #91.
Julie and Elizabeth are off with their family for a two-week vacation at the Pacific Ocean, but then something happens to Julie that threatens to spoil her fun.

Gates, Doris. 1980. *A Morgan for Melinda*. New York: Viking Press. Category: B. Point Value: 10. Book #92.
Melinda is terrified of horses, but her father dreams of the day that she will become a skilled rider. Melinda does not want to disappoint her father, but she doesn't know if she can overcome her fears.

Henry, Marguerite. 1947. *Misty of Chincoteague*. Chicago: Rand McNally. Category: B. Point Value: 10. Book #116.
The horses on the island of Assateague are wild, and the Phantom is known as the wildest of them all. On the day of the roundup, though, it is a young boy who captures the Phantom and brings her in.

Henry, Marguerite. 1963. *Stormy, Misty's Foal*. Chicago: Rand McNally. Category: B. Point Value: 10. Book #118.
Paul and Maureen are worried about their horse, who is about to give birth, when they are forced to leave Chincoteague after it has been hit by a terrible storm.

Lawson, Robert. 1944. *Rabbit Hill*. New York: Viking Press. Category: B. Point Value: 10. Book #131.
The animals on Rabbit Hill are worried when they find out that some New Folks are moving into the big house. They become even more worried when they find out that the New Folks have a cat!

Lawson, Robert. 1954. *The Tough Winter*. New York: Viking Press. Category: B. Point Value: 10. Book #133.
Uncle Analdas warns the animals on Rabbit Hill that a long, hard winter is coming, but the animals do not take his warning seriously.

Lenski, Lois. 1945. *Strawberry Girl*. Philadelphia: J. B. Lippincott. Category: B. Point Value: 10. Book #137.
The Boyers and the Slaters are having a feud. Why does Mr. Slater insist on being so unneighborly?

Norton, Mary. 1953. *The Borrowers*. New York: Harcourt, Brace. Category: B. Point Value: 10. Book #156.
Have you ever wondered what happens to those little objects like safety pins, thimbles, and bits of cloth that just seem to disappear? Perhaps you have a family of borrowers living under the floorboards of your house! That's exactly what you'll read about in this book—tiny little people called Borrowers!

Norton, Mary. 1955. *The Borrowers Afield*. New York: Harcourt, Brace. Category: B. Point Value: 15. Book #157.
The Borrowers are back! After Arietty and her family flee the big house where they had lived comfortably for years, they seek shelter in an old boot that Pod finds lying in an open field.

Norton, Mary. 1959. *The Borrowers Afloat*. New York: Harcourt, Brace. Category: B. Point Value: 10. Book #158.
The Borrowers are back again—this time making their home in a teakettle!

Norton, Mary. 1961, 1974. *The Borrowers Aloft*. New York: Harcourt Brace Jovanovich. Category: B. Point Value: 10. Book #159.
The Borrowers have been captured by a man who wants to put them on display. Will the Borrowers be able to escape this awful fate?

Norton, Mary. 1982. *The Borrowers Avenged*. New York: Harcourt Brace Jovanovich. Category: B. Point Value: 15. Book #160.
After escaping from the Platters' attic, Spiller finds a new place for the Borrowers to live.

Sawyer, Ruth. 1936. *Roller Skates*. New York: Viking Press. Category: B. Point Value: 10. Book #174.
When Lucinda's parents go to Europe for a vacation, Lucinda hopes that they will leave her with friendly Miss Peters instead of stern Aunt Emily.

Selden, George. 1960. *The Cricket in Times Square*. New York: Ariel Books. Category: B. Point Value: 10. Book #176.
A cricket who has always lived in the country is shocked to find himself in a busy subway station in New York City.

Smith, Doris Buchanan. 1975. *Kelly's Creek*. New York: Crowell. Category: B. Point Value: 5. Book #180.
Kelly has a learning disability that makes it difficult for him to learn to do even the simplest tasks. The only place he really feels "smart" is at the creek, and now his parents have told him that the creek is off limits.

Smith, Doris Buchanan. 1973. *A Taste of Blackberries*. New York: Crowell. Category: B. Point Value: 5. Book #183.
A young boy is shocked when he finds out that his best friend is dead.

Sorensen, Virginia. 1956. *Miracles on Maple Hill*. New York: Harcourt, Brace. Category: B. Point Value: 10. Book #187.
Marly's father is just not the same since he returned home from the war. It will take a miracle to make Marly's father well again, but 10-year-old Marly believes in miracles.

Stolz, Mary. 1965. *The Noonday Friends*. New York: Harper & Row. Category: B. Point Value: 10. Book #198.
Franny's father is out of work, and the family never seems to have enough money to buy the things they need. In spite of their lack of money, however, the family's love helps hold the family together.

Wilder, Laura Ingalls. 1939. *By the Shores of Silver Lake*. New York: Harper & Brothers. Category B. Point Value: 20. Book #210.
Pa takes a job at a railroad camp in Dakota Territory where he has been told that he can make as much as $50 a month! He sends for his family, and together the Ingalls begin a new chapter of their life.

Wilder, Laura Ingalls. 1933. *Farmer Boy*. New York: Harper & Brothers. Category: B. Point Value: 25. Book #211.
Almanzo lives on a farm in New York with his family. Running a farm is a lot of work, and Almanzo is kept busy with chores from morning till night.

Wilder, Laura Ingalls. 1971. *The First Four Years*. New York: Harper & Row. Category: B. Point Value: 10. Book #212.
Laura and Almanzo get married and spend four happy but difficult years on their small prairie homestead.

Wilder, Laura Ingalls. 1932. *Little House in the Big Woods*. New York: Harper & Brothers. Category: B. Point Value: 15. Book #213.
Laura lives with her family in a log cabin. You will enjoy being a part of Laura's happy family as you read this book!

Wilder, Laura Ingalls. 1941. *Little Town on the Prairie*. New York: Harper & Brothers. Category: B. Point Value: 20. Book #214.
Laura is excited when Almanzo Wilder, the man who will eventually become her husband, gives her his name card.

Wilder, Laura Ingalls. 1940. *The Long Winter*. New York: Harper & Brothers. Category: B. Point Value: 20. Book #215.
Even though Laura and her family had been warned that a hard winter was coming, they weren't prepared for it to be as long and hard as it turned out to be.

Wilder, Laura Ingalls. 1937. *On the Banks of Plum Creek*. New York: Harper & Brothers. Category: B. Point Value: 20. Book #216.
Can you imagine living in a dugout? That's what Laura and her family did until Pa was able to build them a new house.

Wilder, Laura Ingalls. 1943. *These Happy Golden Years*. New York: Harper & Brothers. Category: B. Point Value: 20. Book #217.
Fifteen-year-old Laura accepts a teaching position in a town 12 miles from home. The job is terribly difficult, but she is determined to stick it out.

 # Annotations—Category C

Armer, Laura Adams. 1933, 1993. *Waterless Mountain*. New York: Knopf. Category: C. Point Value: 15. Book #10.
A young Navaho boy makes a long journey by himself to the Western Sea.

Armstrong, William H. 1969. *Sounder*. New York: Harper & Row. Category: C. Point Value: 10. Book #11.
The boy's father was being taken to jail for stealing food, but the boy knew that his father had only done it to feed his family.

Babbitt, Natalie. 1977. *The Eyes of the Amaryllis*. New York: Farrar, Straus & Giroux. Category: C. Point Value: 10. Book #13.
Thirty years after her husband has drowned in the sea, Geneva Reade still waits and watches for her husband to send her a sign.

Babbitt, Natalie. 1971. *Goody Hall*. New York: Farrar, Straus & Giroux. Category: C. Point Value: 10. Book #14.
Mr. Hall has been dead for five years, but his son insists that he is still alive. Can you guess what happens before reading the last page?

Babbitt, Natalie. 1970. *Knee-Knock Rise*. New York: Farrar, Straus & Giroux. Category: C. Point Value: 5. Book #15.
The villagers wake from their sleep and shudder in horror when they hear the sound of the Megrimum's terrible cry. Egan, however, does not believe that the Megrimum exists. He decides to climb the Rise and find out for himself what is causing that terrible noise!

Barnouw, Victor. 1966. *Dream of the Blue Heron*. New York: Delacorte Press. Category: C. Point Value: 10. Book #17.
Wabus's father insists that he go to the government school, but Wabus is an Indian at heart and does not want to learn the white man's ways.

Blos, Joan W. 1979. *A Gathering of Days*. New York: Scribner. Category: C. Point Value: 10. Book #18.
Catherine's mother is dead, and her father is about to remarry. What will her new mother be like? Catherine writes about this difficult time of life in her journal, which she begins in 1830.

Byars, Betsy. 1977. *The Cartoonist*. New York: Harper & Row. Category: C. Point Value: 5. Book #24.
Alfie loves to stay upstairs in his attic room drawing cartoons. His room is the only place he can really call his own, but now his mother says that he will have to give his room to his brother, Bubba.

Byars, Betsy. 1984. *The Computer Nut*. New York: Viking Kestrel. Category: C. Point Value: 10. Book #25.
"BB-9, are you there?" Kate receives a message from an alien who calls himself BB-9 on her computer. Is somebody trying to play a joke on her, or is this the real thing?

Byars, Betsy. 1985. *Cracker Jackson*. New York: Viking Kestrel. Category: C. Point Value: 10. Book #26.
Alma is in trouble! A young boy is sure that his old baby-sitter, Alma, is being beaten by her husband. He wants to help her, but Alma warns him that he must stay away.

Byars, Betsy. 1981. *The Cybil War*. New York: Viking Press. Category: C. Point Value: 10. Book #27.

Simon is in love with Cybil Ackerman, but winning Cybil's love in return is difficult because of his best friend, Tony.

Byars, Betsy. 1979. *Good-bye, Chicken Little.* New York: Harper & Row. Category: C. Point Value: 5. Book #28.
When Jimmie's Uncle Pete falls through some thin ice and is killed, Jimmie feels guilty because he didn't stop his uncle from crossing the frozen river.

Byars, Betsy. 1972. *The House of Wings.* New York: Viking Press. Category: C. Point Value: 10. Book #29.
Sammy cannot believe that his parents left him with his grandfather without even saying good-bye. Will they ever come back to get him?

Byars, Betsy. 1980. *The Night Swimmers.* New York: Delacorte Press. Category: C. Point Value: 10. Book #30.
After one of their neighbors has gone to bed, Retta and her brothers sneak into his pool and take a swim. How long will they be able to do this without getting caught?

Byars, Betsy. 1970. *The Summer of the Swans.* New York: Viking Press. Category: C. Point Value: 10. Book #32.
A 14-year-old girl searches frantically for her mentally retarded brother after he wanders out during the night and becomes lost.

Byars, Betsy. 1976. *The TV Kid.* New York: Viking Press. Category: C. Point Value: 5. Book #33.
A young boy breaks into one of the empty summer houses near the motel where his mother works. Just as he turns the doorknob, he is startled by the sound of a car.

Byars, Betsy. 1982. *The Two-Thousand-Pound Goldfish.* New York: Harper & Row. Category: C. Point Value: 10. Book #34.
Warren hasn't seen or talked with his mother in three years. He begins to suspect that his sister, Weezie, knows where their mother is, but she refuses to answer his questions.

Clark, Ann Nolan. 1952. *Secret of the Andes.* New York: Viking Press. Category: C. Point Value: 15. Book #43.
Hundreds of years after the white men take over, a secret Inca civilization still exists.

DeJong, Meindert. 1954. *The Wheel on the School.* New York: Harper. Category: C. Point Value: 20. Book #71.
The children of Shora want to know why there are no storks living in their village. They have been told that many years ago, Shora was filled with storks that lived on the rooftops. Why had the storks gone away and never returned?

Du Bois, William. 1972. *The Twenty-One Balloons.* New York: Viking Press. Category: C. Point Value: 10. Book #74.
Professor Sherman decides to make a trip in a giant balloon over the Pacific Ocean. He lands on the island of Krakatoa and is amazed at the type of civilization he finds there.

George, Jean Craighead. 1972. *Julie of the Wolves.* New York: Harper & Row. Category: C. Point Value: 10. Book #94.
A young Eskimo girl runs away from home and gets lost on the North Slope of Alaska.

Gipson, Fred. 1956. *Old Yeller.* New York: Harper. Category: C. Point Value: 10. Book #98.
Travis hates the mangy dog that has been hanging around the family farm, but he has a change of heart when the dog does something really heroic!

Gipson, Fred. 1962. *Savage Sam.* New York: Harper & Row. Category: C. Point Value: 10. Book #99.
Travis, Little Arliss, and Lisbeth are captured by a band of raiding Indians. Their only hope of rescue is a dog named Sam. Sam is a skilled tracker, but can one dog save the children from death or slavery?

Greene, Bette. 1974. *Philip Hall Likes Me, I Reckon, Maybe.* New York: Dial Press. Category: C. Point Value: 10. Book #100.
Beth is in love with Philip Hall. Can she get Philip to like her back without having to let him be first in everything?

Greene, Constance C. 1969. *A Girl Called Al.* New York: Viking Press. Category: C. Point Value: 10. Book #101.
Al is having a hard time growing up. Her father never comes to see her, her mother is gone all the time, and she is gaining so much weight that her clothes don't fit her any more.

Henry, Marguerite. 1950. *Born to Trot.* Chicago: Rand McNally. Category: C. Point Value: 15. Book #112.
Gibson wants to prove to his father that he is old enough and strong enough to drive a horse in a race.

Henry, Marguerite. 1953. *Brighty of the Grand Canyon.* New York: Rand McNally. Category: C. Point Value: 15. Book #113.
Old Timer has always taken good care of Brighty, but now Old Timer has been murdered by a wicked man. What will become of Brighty now?

Henry, Marguerite. 1948. *King of the Wind.* Chicago: Rand McNally. Category: C. Point Value: 15. Book #115.
A young horse boy is excited when he finds out that he and his horse have been chosen to make the long journey to France, where they will be presented as a gift to the king.

Henry, Marguerite. 1966. *Mustang—Wild Spirit of the West.* Chicago: Rand McNally. Category: C. Point Value: 15. Book #117.
The mustangs are in danger of becoming extinct! A young woman is determined to save them, but there are others who want to slaughter them and sell them as pet food.

Konigsburg, E. L. 1967. *From the Mixed-Up Files of Mrs. Basil E. Frankweiler.* New York: Atheneum. Category: C. Point Value: 10. Book #124.
Claudia decides to run away from home just long enough to make her parents realize how much they'd miss her. She takes her brother, Jamie, with her, and the two of them hide out in the Metropolitan Museum of Art.

Konigsburg, E. L. 1967. *Jennifer, Hectate, Macbeth, William McKinley and Me, Elizabeth.* New York: Atheneum. Category: C. Point Value: 5. Book #125.
Elizabeth did not have any friends until she met Jennifer. Jennifer, who claimed to be a witch, promised to let Elizabeth be her apprentice.

Lively, Penelope. 1973. *The Ghost of Thomas Kempe.* New York: Dutton. Category: C. Point Value: 10. Book #146.
The ghost of a seventeenth century sorcerer wants young James to be his apprentice. When James does not cooperate, the ghost becomes angry and destructive.

London, Jack. 1912. *The Call of the Wild.* New York: Macmillan. Category: C. Point Value: 10. Book #147.
Buck is kidnapped from his master and forced to be a sled dog in the Yukon.

Pearce, Philippa. 1958. *Tom's Midnight Garden.* Philadelphia: Lippincott. Category: C. Point Value: 15. Book #167.
When the clock strikes midnight, Tom gets out of bed and sneaks out of the apartment. He opens the door to a garden that seems to exist only at this strange hour.

Robertson, Keith. 1958. *Henry Reed, Inc.* New York: Viking Press. Category: C. Point Value: 15. Book #171.
Henry Reed, ambitious as always about finding ways to earn money, starts a research firm in which he becomes involved in all kinds of projects.

Robertson, Keith. 1966. *Henry Reed's Baby-Sitting Service.* New York: Viking Press. Category: C. Point Value: 15. Book #172.
Henry wants to earn money during summer vacation so he decides to start a baby-sitting service. Midge becomes his partner, and the two of them are kept busy all summer long!

Shannon, Monica. 1934. *Dobry.* New York: Viking Press. Category: C. Point Value: 10. Book #178.
More than anything else, Dobry wants to go to art school, but his mother insists that he stay at home to work on the family farm.

Smith, Doris Buchanan. 1983. *The First Hard Times.* New York: Viking Press. Category: C. Point Value: 10. Book #179.
Ancil's new stepfather tries his best to become friends with Ancil, but she resents him because she believes that her real father might still be alive.

Smith, Doris Buchanan. 1981. *Last Was Lloyd.* New York: Viking Press. Category: C. Point Value: 5. Book #182.
Strike three, you're out! No one at school ever wants Lloyd to be on their softball team because Lloyd is known as the "Strikeout King." There is something about Lloyd, though, that the kids at school don't know.

Sperry, Armstrong. 1940. *Call It Courage.* New York: Macmillan. Category: C. Point Value: 5. Book #192.

When you live on a small island, being afraid of the water is considered cowardly. Mafatu is terrified of the water, but he tries to prove his courage by doing what he fears the most.

Steig, William. 1976. *Abel's Island*. New York: Farrar, Straus & Giroux. Category: C. Point Value: 5. Book #193.
Abel is a noble mouse who risks his life to retrieve his wife's scarf that has blown away during a storm.

Voigt, Cynthia. 1984. *Building Blocks*. New York: Atheneum. Category: C. Point Value: 10. Book #202.
When Brann falls asleep in the block fortress, he travels back in time and becomes a visitor in his father's childhood home.

Wiggin, Kate Douglas. 1965. *Rebecca of Sunnybrook Farm*. Racine, Wis.: Whitman Publishing. Category: C. Point Value: 20. Book #209.
Rebecca is sent to live with her two old-maidish aunts, one of whom she finds impossible to please.

 # Annotations—Category D

Alcott, Louisa May. 1965. *Little Men*. Racine, Wis.: Whitman Publishing. Category: D. Point Value: 20. Book #1.
When Aunt March dies and leaves Plumfield to Jo, Jo and Professor Bhaer turn the huge old house into a wonderfully different kind of school for boys. Everyone who enjoyed reading *Little Women* will want to read this delightful sequel.

Alcott, Louisa May. 1965. *Little Women*. Racine, Wis.: Whitman Publishing. Category: D. Point Value: 30. Book #2.
Jo and her sisters are finding out that growing up is not always easy. At times, everything seems dreary and dull for the girls, but when they meet the boy next door, all kinds of interesting things begin to happen.

Alexander, Lloyd. 1973. *The Cat Who Wished to Be a Man*. New York: Dutton. Category: D. Point Value: 5. Book #6.
Lionel is a wizard's cat who wants to be a man. His master finally agrees to turn him into a man, but then Lionel gets into all kinds of trouble!

Alexander, Lloyd. 1975. *The Wizard in the Tree*. New York: Dutton. Category: D. Point Value: 5. Book #9.
Arbican has finally been rescued from a fallen tree where he has been stuck for many years. Will he still have his powers after not having used them for so long?

Byars, Betsy. 1977. *The Pinballs*. New York: Harper & Row. Category: D. Point Value: 10. Book #31.
Harvey got two broken legs when he was run over by his father's new car. He is then sent to live in a foster home where he meets another boy and girl, who also come from difficult family situations.

Clark, Ann Nolan. 1955. *Santiago*. New York: Viking Press. Category: D. Point Value: 15. Book #42.
Santiago had lived all of his life with a rich Spanish woman in the city when suddenly a dusty Indian appeared at the door demanding Santiago to leave with him.

Collier, James Lincoln, and Christopher Collier. 1985. *My Brother Sam Is Dead*. New York: Four Winds Press. Category: D. Point Value: 15. Book #64.
Tim's family is caught in the middle of the Revolutionary War. His father and brother disagree over which side to support.

Eckert, Allan W. 1971. *Incident at Hawk's Hill*. Boston: Little, Brown. Category: D. Point Value: 15. Book #75.
After wandering away and becoming lost on an open prairie, a six-year-old boy is cared for by a badger.

Edmonds, Walter D. 1941. *The Matchlock Gun*. New York: Dodd, Mead. Category: D. Point Value: 5. Book #76.

A courageous young boy helps his mother fight off an Indian attack.

Edmonds, Walter D. 1943. *Two Logs Crossing.* New York: Dodd, Mead. Category: D. Point Value: 5. Book #77.
A young boy must earn $40 to repay a judge.

Fitzhugh, Louise. 1964. *Harriet the Spy.* New York: Harper & Row. Category: D. Point Value: 15. Book #86.
Harriet is a spy! She spies on her friends and neighbors and then writes about them in her notebook. Harriet really has problems, though, when her notebook is found and read by the people she has been spying on!

Forbes, Esther. 1943. *Johnny Tremain.* Boston: Houghton Mifflin. Category: D. Point Value: 15. Book #87.
After a tragic accident, a young boy looks for work but has difficulty finding a job because of his maimed hand.

Fox, Paula. 1984. *One-Eyed Cat.* Scarsdale, N.Y.: Bradbury Press. Category: D. Point Value: 15. Book #88.
Ned fired his air rifle at a dark shadow. His father had told him not to even touch the rifle that he had received as a gift. What will happen if his father finds out that Ned disobeyed him?

George, Jean Craighead. 1968. *Coyote in Manhattan.* New York: Crowell. Category: D. Point Value: 15. Book #93.
A coyote has been let loose in New York City by a young girl who wants to protect him from being captured and killed.

George, Jean Craighead. 1988. *My Side of the Mountain.* New York: Dutton. Category: D. Point Value: 10. Book #95.
A young boy tries to survive on his own in the mountains of Pennsylvania.

George, Jean Craighead. 1979. *River Rats, Inc.* New York: Dutton. Category: D. Point Value: 10. Book #96.
Two boys make their way down the Colorado River on a raft. When their raft capsizes, they become stranded alone in the desert.

Harris, Rosemary. 1970. *The Bright and Morning Star.* New York: Macmillan. Category: D. Point Value: 15. Book #104.
This third book in Rosemary Harris's trilogy tells the story of an evil priest who is plotting to kill the king so that he can marry the king's daughter.

Harris, Rosemary. 1968, 1969. *The Moon in the Cloud.* New York: Macmillan. Category: D. Point Value: 10. Book #105.
Have you heard the story of Noah's Ark? This is a story of what might have happened when God told Noah that there was going to be a huge flood.

Harris, Rosemary. 1970. *The Shadow on the Sun.* New York: Macmillan. Category: D. Point Value: 10. Book #106.
This second book in Rosemary Harris's trilogy tells the story of how Meri-Mekhmet, a beautiful young woman, steals the heart of the king, is captured by the Prince of Punt, and is finally rescued by the king's friend, Reuben.

Henry, Marguerite. 1945. *Justin Morgan Had a Horse.* Chicago: Wilcox & Follett. Category: D. Point Value: 10. Book #114.
This is the story of the sturdy little horse who became the ancestor of the famous American breed of Morgan horses.

Kelly, Eric P. 1928. *The Trumpeter of Krakow.* New York: Macmillan. Category: D. Point Value: 15. Book #122.
Peter-of-the-Button-Face will stop at nothing to steal the Charnetski family's valuable treasure.

Krumgold, Joseph. 1953. *And Now Miguel.* New York: Crowell. Category: D. Point Value: 15. Book #126.
Miguel is a boy who wants to be a man. Why can't his father see that he is old enough to go with the men on their yearly trip into the mountains of the Sangre de Cristo?

Krumgold, Joseph. 1959. *Onion John.* New York: Crowell. Category: D. Point Value: 15. Book #127.
Onion John lives in a house made of piled up stones and four old bathtubs. He wears two long coats, shops at the town dump, and attends every funeral in town. When 12-year-old Andrew and Onion John become

best friends, Andrew's father worries about Onion John's influence on his son.

Lawson, Robert. 1939. *Ben and Me*. Boston: Little, Brown. Category: D. Point Value: 5. Book #130.
Amos is a mouse who lives in Ben Franklin's cap. Amos is sure that Ben could not get along without him, so he strikes up an unusual bargain with Ben.

Lewis, C. S. 1954. *The Horse and His Boy*. New York: Macmillan. Category: D. Point Value: 10. Book #138.
Narnia is about to be invaded! Will Shasta and his friend, Bree, a talking horse, be able to warn King Peter in time?

Lewis, C. S. 1956. *The Last Battle*. New York: Macmillan. Category: D. Point Value: 10. Book #139.
The final battle is fought and lost as Aslan brings Narnia to an end.

Lewis, C. S. 1950. *The Lion, the Witch and the Wardrobe*. New York: Macmillan. Category: D. Point Value: 10. Book #140.
Four children find their way into Narnia, a magical land, where animals talk and many kinds of fairy tale creatures exist. The children meet an evil witch, friendly giants, and a wise, golden lion named Aslan.

Lewis, C. S. 1955. *The Magician's Nephew*. New York: Macmillan. Category: D. Point Value: 10. Book #141.
Narnia is a land full of talking animals. This is the story of how Aslan, the great lion, created this magical land.

Lewis, C. S. 1951. *Prince Caspian*. New York: Macmillan. Category: D. Point Value: 10. Book #142.
Peter, Edmund, Susan, and Lucy have been away from Narnia for one year when they are mysteriously pulled from a train station to a strange island.

Lewis, C. S. 1953. *The Silver Chair*. New York: Macmillan. Category: D. Point Value: 10. Book #143.
Eustace and Jill are sent on a mission by Aslan to find a prince who has been missing for many years.

Lewis, C. S. 1952. *Voyage of the* Dawn Treader. New York: Macmillan. Category: D. Point Value: 10. Book #144.
Lucy's cousin, Eustace, is turned into a green dragon when he steals gold from a dragon's hoard.

Lively, Penelope. 1970, 1971. *Astercote*. New York: Dutton. Category: D. Point Value: 10. Book #145.
The people in a small village begin to think that they are dying from the Black Death, but the fact is that no one has died from the Black Death in more than 600 years. Why do they think that the Black Death is returning now?

MacLachlan, Patricia. 1985. *Sarah, Plain and Tall*. New York: Harper & Row. Category: D. Point Value: 5. Book #148.
Anna's father goes about finding a new wife in a very unusual way after his first wife died during childbirth.

McKinley, Robin. 1978. *Beauty*. New York: Harper & Row. Category: D. Point Value: 15. Book #149.
When Beauty's father picks a rose from the Beast's garden, the Beast is very angry. The Beast says that he will spare the man's life only if he sends his daughter, Beauty, to live with him.

McKinley, Robin. 1982. *The Blue Sword*. New York: Greenwillow Books. Category: D. Point Value: 15. Book #150.
Harry is a young woman who is kidnapped by King Corlath, the ruler of the mysterious Hillfolk.

McKinley, Robin. 1985. *The Hero and the Crown*. New York: Greenwillow Books. Category: D. Point Value: 15. Book #151.
Lady Aerin wins the respect of her countrymen by killing the small dragons that cause her people so much trouble.

Neville, Emily. 1963. *It's Like This, Cat*. New York: Harper & Row. Category: D. Point Value: 10. Book #153.
David's father is about to blow his top! He didn't like the idea of David having a cat in the first place, and now the cat has jumped out of their car window right in the middle of traffic!

North, Sterling. 1984. *Rascal*. New York: Dutton. Category: D. Point Value: 10. Book #154.
Can you imagine having a raccoon for a pet? In this book, you will read about a boy who has many exciting adventures with his pet raccoon named Rascal.

North, Sterling. 1969. *The Wolfling*. New York: Dutton. Category: D. Point Value: 15. Book #155.
A young boy is allowed to raise a baby wolf and keep him as a pet.

O'Brien, Robert C. 1971. *Mrs. Frisby and the Rats of NIMH*. New York: Atheneum. Category: D. Point Value: 15. Book #161.
Mrs. Frisby has a terrible problem. If she does not get help soon, her small son may die. She goes to the owl for advice, but the owl sends her to the rats. Will the rats be able to help her?

O'Dell, Scott. 1960. *Island of the Blue Dolphins*. Boston: Houghton Mifflin. Category: D. Point Value: 10. Book #162.
Karana and her small brother are stranded alone on an island in the Pacific. Alone, that is, except for the vicious wild dogs that roam the island. Will they be able to survive?

O'Dell, Scott. 1980. *Sarah Bishop*. Boston: Houghton Mifflin. Category: D. Point Value: 10. Book #163.
Sarah's father and brother have both been killed in the Revolutionary War. Now Sarah, herself, is being chased by British soldiers who think that she is trying to free American prisoners.

O'Dell, Scott. 1970. *Sing Down the Moon*. Boston: Houghton Mifflin. Category: D. Point Value: 10. Book #164.
Two young Navajo girls are captured by Spaniards and sold as slaves in a strange city far from their home. Tired of waiting to be rescued, they plan an escape.

Paterson, Katherine. 1977. *Bridge to Terabithia*. New York: Crowell. Category: D. Point Value: 10. Book #165.
When Jess first meets Leslie, he avoids her because she is different. The two of them eventually become friends, however, and share a very special and meaningful friendship.

Raskin, Ellen. 1971. *The Mysterious Disappearance of Leon (I Mean Noel)*. New York: Dutton. Category: D. Point Value: 10. Book #168.
Poor Mrs. Carillon! She spends years searching for her husband who has left her only a few clues as to his whereabouts.

Rodowsky, Colby F. 1976. *What About Me?* New York: Watts. Category: D. Point Value: 10. Book #173.
Dorrie is a sophomore in high school who is dealing with the many mixed emotions she has towards her mentally retarded brother.

Sebestyen, Ouida. 1979. *Words by Heart*. Boston: Little, Brown. Category: D. Point Value: 10. Book #175.
Lena's family is the only black family in town. When Lena wins a Scripture memorization contest, some of the townspeople become jealous, and the family is threatened with violence.

Speare, Elizabeth George. 1983. *Sign of the Beaver*. Boston: Houghton Mifflin. Category: D. Point Value: 10. Book #190.
A young boy is left alone for several months in the log cabin that he and his father built, while his father makes a long journey to get the rest of the family.

Taylor, Mildred D. 1976. *Roll of Thunder, Hear My Cry*. New York: Dial Press. Category: D. Point Value: 15. Book #200.
Cassie and her family become the target of hatred and violence when they won't cooperate with those who are trying to take advantage of them.

Wojciechowska, Maia. 1964. *Shadow of a Bull*. New York: Atheneum. Category: D. Point Value: 10. Book #218.
Manolo's father was a famous bullfighter who was killed fighting a bull. Manolo is not so sure he wants anything to do with bullfighting, but he is pressured by the townspeople who knew his father and eagerly await the day Manolo will face his first bull.

Yates, Elizabeth. 1968. *With Pipe, Paddle, and Song*. New York: Dutton. Category: D. Point Value: 15. Book #220.
Splash! One of the men on a canoe full of French voyageurs has gone overboard into fast-moving rapids. Will they be able to rescue him?

Annotations—Category E

Alexander, Lloyd. 1965. *The Black Cauldron.* New York: Holt, Rinehart & Winston. Category: E. Point Value: 15. Book #3.
The Black Cauldron must be destroyed. Gwydion will try to destroy it, but will the magic of the cauldron be too much for him?

Alexander, Lloyd. 1964. *The Book of Three.* New York: Holt, Rinehart & Winston. Category: E. Point Value: 15. Book #4.
Taran wants to be a hero, but he's only an Assistant Pig-Keeper. His country is in danger—perhaps he can save it.

Alexander, Lloyd. 1966. *The Castle of Llyr.* New York: Holt, Rinehart & Winston. Category: E. Point Value: 15. Book #5.
A princess is sent to an island to learn how to be a lady. When she gets there, however, she finds out that an evil enchantress is waiting!

Alexander, Lloyd. 1968. *The High King.* New York: Holt, Rinehart & Winston. Category: E. Point Value: 20. Book #7.
Taran and his friends are fighting a losing battle against Arawn Death Lord, and their country is about to be destroyed.

Alexander, Lloyd. 1967. *Taran Wanderer.* New York: Holt, Rinehart & Winston. Category: E. Point Value: 15. Book #8.
Taran was never told by the wizard who raised him what had happened to his parents, and in this book, he sets out to find them. To be successful in his quest, Taran must survive enchantment, capture, and a host of other evils.

Clemens, Samuel L. (Mark Twain). 1896. *The Adventures of Huckleberry Finn.* New York: Harper & Brothers. Category: E. Point Value: 20. Book #62.
Huck has many exciting adventures with his friend, a runaway slave, while floating down the Mississippi River on a raft.

Clemens, Samuel L. (Mark Twain). 1885. *The Adventures of Tom Sawyer.* Hartford, Conn.: American Publishing Co. Category: E. Point Value: 20. Book #63.
Can you imagine surprising your friends and relatives by showing up at your own funeral? That's exactly what Tom and his friend, Huck, did in this book!

Cooper, James Fenimore. 1899. *The Last of the Mohicans.* New York: Macmillan. Category: E. Point Value: 30. Book #65.
Two girls are kidnapped by a group of Indians.

Cooper, Susan. 1973. *The Dark Is Rising.* New York: Atheneum. Category: E. Point Value: 15. Book #66.
On the night of Will's eleventh birthday, some unusual things happen that make him realize that he is not an ordinary human.

Cooper, Susan. 1975. *The Grey King.* New York: Atheneum. Category: E. Point Value: 15. Book #67.
The Grey King, an evil being, is doing everything in his power to stop two boys from carrying out the mission given them by the Old Ones.

Defoe, Daniel. c.1897. *Robinson Crusoe.* Boston: Lothrop Publishing. Category: E. Point Value: 25. Book #68.
Robinson Crusoe is shipwrecked alone on an island that is visited only by cannibals.

Dickens, Charles. 1839. *Oliver Twist.* Philadelphia: publisher unknown. Category: E. Point Value: 30. Book #72.
Oliver Twist is an orphan raised in a poorhouse. He runs away only to be captured by a gang of thieves who force him to work for them.

Dickens, Charles. 1867. *A Tale of Two Cities.* Boston: publisher unknown. Category: E. Point Value: 25. Book #73.
Charles Darnay is about to have his head chopped off for something he did not do. Will this injustice be stopped in time, or will Charles become another innocent victim of the French Revolution?

Fox, Paula. 1973. *The Slave Dancer.* Scarsdale, N.Y.: Bradbury Press. Category: E. Point Value: 15. Book #89.

A young boy is kidnapped and taken aboard a slave ship where he is forced to play his fife for the slaves held captive on the ship.

George, Jean Craighead. 1971. *Who Really Killed Cock Robin?* New York: Dutton. Category: E. Point Value: 10. Book #97.
When Cock Robin dies, the townspeople are in an uproar. The mayor wants to find out the cause of Cock Robin's death, and a young boy becomes his #1 investigator.

Hamilton, Virginia. 1974. *M. C. Higgins, the Great.* New York: Macmillan. Category: E. Point Value: 20. Book #102.
M. C. Higgins dreams of the day that he and his family will be able to escape the life of poverty that they are now living.

Hamilton, Virginia. 1971. *The Planet of Junior Brown.* New York: Macmillan. Category: E. Point Value: 15. Book #103.
When Junior Brown begins talking to imaginary people, his street-wise friend, Buddy, realizes that Junior needs help.

Hunt, Irene. 1964. *Across Five Aprils.* Chicago: Follett Publishing. Category: E. Point Value: 15. Book #119.
Jethro and his brothers are excited when they hear that the Civil War has begun. Their excitement fades, however, when the family begins to experience hardships brought on by the war.

Hunt, Irene. 1966. *Up a Road Slowly.* Chicago: Follett Publishing. Category: E. Point Value: 10. Book #120.
After her mother's death, Julie is sent to live with her "no nonsense" Aunt Cordelia.

Ish-Kishor, Sulamith. 1969. *Our Eddie.* New York: Pantheon Books. Category: E. Point Value: 10. Book #121.
Eddie's father is hard to understand. He is offered a job that will pay more money, but he refuses to accept it even though his family is in desperate need.

Konigsburg, E. L. 1976. *Father's Arcane Daughter.* New York: Atheneum. Category: E. Point Value: 5. Book #123.
Winston was surprised when he came home from school and met a young woman who claimed to be his father's long-lost daughter.

Lasky, Kathryn. 1983. *Beyond the Divide.* New York: Macmillan. Category: E. Point Value: 15. Book #128.
When Meribah's father is shunned by the members of their church and by their own family, Meribah decides to go with him on a long journey by wagon train to California.

Latham, Jean Lee. 1955. *Carry On, Mr. Bowditch.* Boston: Houghton Mifflin. Category: E. Point Value: 15. Book #129.
This is the story of a young boy who grows up to become a famous mathematician.

L'Engle, Madeleine. 1978. *A Swiftly Tilting Planet.* New York: Farrar, Straus & Giroux. Category: E. Point Value: 15. Book #134.
Charles Wallace is 15 now and his quest is to stop the destruction of the world by a mad dictator named Madog Branzillo.

L'Engle, Madeleine. 1973. *A Wind in the Door.* New York: Farrar, Straus & Giroux. Category: E. Point Value: 15. Book #135.
Charles Wallace is dying! In this companion volume to *A Wrinkle in Time*, Meg, Charles Wallace, and Calvin make another dangerous but exciting journey in which they again fight the forces of evil.

L'Engle, Madeleine. 1962. *A Wrinkle in Time.* New York: Farrar, Straus & Giroux. Category: E. Point Value: 15. Book #136.
Meg, her small brother Charles Wallace, and their friend, Calvin, are taken on a strange journey in which they help save Meg's father and keep IT from taking over the whole world.

Meigs, Cornelia. 1968. *Invincible Louisa.* Boston: Little, Brown. Category: E. Point Value: 25. Book #152.
This is the true story of Louisa May Alcott, a famous author. Anyone who enjoyed reading *Little Women* and *Little Men* will want to read this book as well!

Paterson, Katherine. 1980. *Jacob Have I Loved.* New York: Crowell. Category: E. Point Value: 15. Book #166.
Even though Louise and Caroline are twins, they are very, very different from each other. Louise resents Caroline who is favored and pampered by the people they know—including their own parents.

Raskin, Ellen. 1978. *The Westing Game.* New York: Dutton. Category: E. Point Value: 15. Book #169.
If you like puzzling mysteries, then you've got to read this book! See if you can figure out which one of the many characters is Sam Westing's murderer!

Rawlings, Marjorie Kinnan. 1985. *The Yearling.* New York: Scribner. Category: E. Point Value: 30. Book #170.
Jody's father agrees to let him raise a fawn whose mother was shot for food.

Seredy, Kate. 1937. *The White Stag.* New York: Viking Press. Category: E. Point Value: 10. Book #177.
A white stag and a red eagle lead the people to their promised land.

Smith, Doris Buchanan. 1974. *Kick a Stone Home.* New York: Crowell. Category: E. Point Value: 10. Book #181.
Fifteen-year-old Sara Jane Chambers is having all kinds of problems. Her history teacher doesn't like her, a boy touches her in an improper way, she is asked out on her first date by a boy she's not sure she likes, and the boy she does like doesn't seem to know she's alive.

Speare, Elizabeth George. 1961. *The Bronze Bow.* Boston: Houghton Mifflin. Category: E. Point Value: 15. Book #188.
Daniel is obsessed with his hatred for the Romans and his desire to start a revolution that will free the land from Roman control.

Speare, Elizabeth George. 1957. *Calico Captive.* Boston: Houghton Mifflin. Category: E. Point Value: 15. Book #189.
Miriam and her relatives are kidnapped by a group of Indians who plan to sell them to the French.

Speare, Elizabeth George. 1958. *The Witch of Blackbird Pond.* Boston: Houghton Mifflin. Category: E. Point Value: 15. Book #191.
Having nowhere else to go after her father's death, Kit travels to Massachusetts to live in the house of her harsh Uncle Matthew. Kit is miserable in her uncle's house, but things get even worse when she is accused of being a witch.

Stevenson, Robert Louis. date unknown. *Kidnapped.* Philadelphia: Macrae & Smith. Category: E. Point Value: 20. Book #195.
David's evil Uncle Ebenezer arranges to have David kidnapped so that David will not get his share of the family fortune.

Stevenson, Robert Louis. 1895. *Treasure Island.* Boston: Roberts Brothers. Category: E. Point Value: 20. Book #196.
Jim Hawkins and his friends are sailing on a ship filled with bloodthirsty pirates who will stop at nothing to capture Flint's treasure.

Stowe, Harriet Beecher. 1852. *Uncle Tom's Cabin.* Boston: J. P. Jewett. Category: E. Point Value: 30. Book #199.
Uncle Tom's master is in debt. To pay off his debt, he sells Uncle Tom to a slave trader forcing him to leave his wife and children behind.

de Trevino, Elizabeth Borton. 1965. *I, Juan de Pareja.* New York: Bell Books. Category: E. Point Value: 10. Book #201.
For most of his life, Juan is the personal slave of a great artist. Juan, himself, becomes very interested in art, but he is forced to practice his painting privately because Spanish law prohibits slaves from becoming artists.

Voigt, Cynthia. 1982. *Dicey's Song.* New York: Atheneum. Category: E. Point Value: 10. Book #203.
The story of Dicey and her family continues. Even though the children now have a place to stay, their problems are far from over.

Voigt, Cynthia. 1981. *Homecoming.* New York: Atheneum. Category: E. Point Value: 10. Book #204.
A group of children are abandoned by their mother outside a shopping mall.

Voigt, Cynthia. 1983. *A Solitary Blue.* New York: Atheneum. Category: E. Point Value: 10. Book #205.
Jeff's mother says that she wants to see him. Jeff is sure that she loves him even though she hasn't shown any interest in him for years.

Wyss, Johann. 1898. *The Swiss Family Robinson.* New York: University Publishing. Category: E. Point Value: 25. Book #219.
A Swiss family is stranded on an island filled with every kind of animal imaginable.

Thomas Herzog

Pneumatic Structures

A Handbook of Inflatable Architecture

with contributions by
Gernot Minke and Hans Eggers

New York
Oxford University Press
1976

This edition published 1976 by
Oxford University Press, New York
All rights reserved
including the right of reproduction in whole
or in part in any form
Copyright © 1976 by Verlag Gerd Hatje, Stuttgart
Library of Congress Catalog Card Number: 76—9247
ISBN 0-19-519895-6

Printed in West Germany

Contents

Preface

The first volume of Frei Otto's work *Tensile Structures* appeared in 1962. It contained a long chapter on a field of construction which had hitherto received little attention: pneumatic structures. These are based on a physical principle that is frequently found in nature, both organic and inorganic, and has been applied in the field of technology for centuries.

The initiative given by Otto's detailed description of the present state of development was taken up by many people from the end of the 1960s, especially after the first International Colloquium on Pneumatic Structures which took place in Stuttgart in 1967. In England, the Netherlands, Austria and the western United States especially there were countless experiments within and on the periphery of the pop scene; the motive behind them was less that of scientifically orientated interest than of pleasure in the possibility of personally creating "environments" with a minimum of material expenditure in a short period of time. The pneumatic buildings at Expo '70 in Osaka represented a temporary high point in the history of air structures; the pioneer buildings of earlier exhibitions, such as the Crystal Palace, the Eiffel Tower, the Barcelona Pavilion and the German Pavilion in Montreal found in them successors of equal rank.

In the general application of pneumatic structures, architecture – as has happened so often since the industrial revolution – again lags a good way behind other technical fields. In the field of balloon construction, for example, and, somewhat later, of the construction of airships, there have been fundamental developments with regard to membrane material, its cutting and surface protection since the end of the 18th century. These developments, however, have only recently had any influence on architecture. Significantly – apart from a few exceptions – pneumatic structures were until the last few years seen as pure "engineering structures" and the majority of architects, true to their tradition since the 19th century, ignored the whole subject. But, on the other hand, pneumatic forms offer enormous possibilities in shape and colour with a great new design potential.

For some decades – as a result of the increasing mechanisation of the building process – architecture has been dominated by plane, mostly orthogonal forms with hard, cold, machine-produced surfaces. While nearly all previous attempts to oppose this with a sensuous plastic world have meant a negation of the technical/structural dimension of architecture, building with pneumatic structures offers the possibility of a synthesis. They employ forms that are technically highly developed, using soft, flexible, movable, roundly spanned, "organic" shapes, which can be of great sensous beauty when sensibly used.

For the production of a constant internal climate that differs from the external climate, energy must be supplied to buildings. In the case of large buildings the internal climate is determined primarily by the regulating effect of the outer walls. The energy-based heating need only have a limited additional effect in adjusting temperature. If the mass of the outer walls is reduced, as perhaps in the skeleton structure, the interior climate is dependent primarily on the partial of full air conditioning installations which are then necessary.

In the case of pneumatic structures an additional feature is that the stability and variability of the form is directly related to the supply of energy. The pneumatic principle will therefore doubtless play an important role in the realisation of "kinetic architecture" which is increasingly widely discussed.

This book is a report on the state of development. It begins with a general introduction. This is followed by a detailed documentation of completed and projected structures, in which not only pneumatic structures related to architecture are shown, so that a better overall picture of the subject can be obtained and the forms that are relevant for use in the building field can be better located in the spectrum of what is basically possible. The technical descriptions following the picture section show in detail how pneumatic structures hitherto have been constructed. By summarising the details the various solutions to a special problem can be visualised. The two last chapters are made up by excursuses on structural problems with tables for calculating air supported structures, as well as on pneumatic structures used as form work for shell structures.

In summer 1972 the manuscript was in its first draft and underwent supplements and corrections until early 1974. I obtained the time and opportunity for my work through my position at the Institute of Construction at the University of Stuttgart and by means of a scholarship for a period of study in the German Academy of Villa Massimo in Rome.

I thank Gernot Minke and Giuseppe Morabito for their expert advice, Axel Menges for the editorial work on the text and Ursel Prehn for her laborious work in collecting the material.

Special thanks are also due to Rainer Hascher, Claudia Häfele, Erna Herzog and above all to my wife, Verena Herzog-Loibl, without whose co-operation this book would never have been completed.

Thomas Herzog

1. The phenomenon of pneumatic structures

1.1. Introduction

If a flexible *membrane* which is only capable of supporting tension is stressed by the differential pressure of a gas, normally air, then a pneumatic form (from the Greek "pneuma" breath of air) arises. It is deformed in the direction of the less dense agent until its surface is stable in both position and form.

Each pneumatically stressed membrane is capable of resisting external forces. In making use of this capacity, the stressing medium becomes the *supporting medium* and therefore a structural element. The resulting structure becomes a *pneumatic loadbearing structure*. This can be formed either as a *single* or as a *double loadbearing membrane structure*. The number of membranes between the space to be utilised and the exterior determines whether it is a single or a double membrane structure. Figs. 1 and 2 make the principal difference clear. Figs. 3–6 give further schematic examples, Figs. 3 and 4 representing single membrane structures and Figs. 5 and 6 double membrane structures.

In the case of Figs. 1, 3 and 4 the supporting medium must be air and must have a physiologically harmless density. In the case of Figs. 2, 5 and 6 a different gas or high grade compressed air can also be used. In both cases it is necessary to make the pressure area as airtight as possible. These are termed *closed* pneumatic structures (this includes all pneumatic buildings and parts of buildings so far known). However it is possible for the *membrane* itself – apart from small openings for regulating pressure – to be *closed* or to be only one part in the formation of an externally closed cavity. In the latter case the *membrane* is *open* but the *pneumatic building* is *closed* (Figs. 1–4).

If a pneumatically stressed membrane does not form a closed cavity and is not part of the formation of such a cavity, then it is termed an *open pneumatic structure*. The membrane is purposely formed thus so that it benefits from part of the energy of the applied air pressure (sails, parachutes, kites).

1.2. Design rules for pneumatic structures

As pneumatic structures in nearly all technical applications until now have used membranes which have only slight elasticity, their final form in the non-inflated state must be generated by suitable cutting patterns. For determining this form soap film models with a thickness of 0.1 to $1\,\mu$ have proved useful. They have an outer and inner liquid surface – as opposed to droplets with only an outer liquid surface.

With regard to their surface all shapes produced with soap bubbles can be thought of as "ideal" pneumatic forms since, because of the fluidity of their film, forms always occur in which there are equal membrane stresses at every point on the surface. Within the prescribed boundary conditions the largest possible volumes and the smallest possible surface areas always form. One refers to *minimal surface* areas. Thus an optimisation of form in relation to use of material takes place. The dead weight and the resulting deformation are so small in the case of soap film models with a span of less than 10 cm that they can generally be ignored.

The most important of the design rules for boundary surfaces are described briefly below (detailed explanations in Bibl. 22; Bibl. 119; Bibl. 167). In any case deformations which arise from outside forces are ignored.

If a soap bubble is suspended freely in space, it is not bound by any boundary conditions. It is affected only by the intermolecular cohesive powers of the soap film and the inner relative pressure. The lamella forms a spherical surface as the only finite surface of constant curvature which is free from singularities (Fig. 7). It conforms to the general equation that defines the relationships of any stable fluid surface (Bibl. 167, p.15) and also applies to all soap bubble tests described below:

$$p = \sigma \left(\frac{1}{r_1} + \frac{1}{r_2} \right), \qquad (1)$$

in the specific form of the sphere:

$$p = \frac{2\sigma}{r} = \text{constant, as} \qquad (2)$$

$$r_1 = r_2 \text{ or}$$

$$\sigma = \frac{p \cdot r}{2}, \qquad (2')$$

where:
p = the pressure in the bubble,
σ = the surface tension,
r_1 = the largest radius of curvature of the surface,
r_2 = the smallest radius of curvature of the surface.

Moreover the two radii of curvature in the case of the sphere are equal and therefore describe a surface which is *doubly curved in the same direction* or *synclastic*.

From the interaction shown in equation 2 it follows that, as a result of the different radii of curvature in bubbles of different sizes, the internal pressure in the smaller bubbles must be larger. This is confirmed by the fact that when two soap bubbles are brought into contact with each other the smaller one inflates the larger (Fig. 8; Bibl. 167, p.11).

Cylindrical surfaces also fulfil the equilibrium condition in accordance with equation 1, but cannot be produced as unbounded surfaces and therefore need sealing at both ends. If one uses coils of wire, places a cylindrical lamella between them and closes the structure by means of spherical segments, then according to equation 2 the radius of the sphere is twice as large as the radius of the cylinder (Fig. 9). The surface of the cylinder is regarded as *singly curved*.

If one uses spherical segments to terminate the cylindrical surface and selects the same radius for both cylinder and spherical segments, then at the contact circles the "cylinder generatrices" pass over into the tangents of the spherical segments (Fig. 10).

The membrane tension σ_1 in the spherical skins continues in the same degree in the longitudinal tensions of the cylinder skin. It follows therefore that the transverse or "ring" tensions σ_2 become twice as large as σ_1, which can lead to the collapse of buildings under extreme wind loading. For cylinder ring tensions

$$\sigma = p \cdot r. \qquad (3)$$

If a soap bubble floats on a liquid surface, then it adjoins on that surface a denser medium, into which the tensions of the lamella surface are introduced at the edge (Fig. 11). The higher internal pressure compresses the floor of the bubble down a little. The bubble forms a hemisphere with synclastically curved lamellae and its cross-section forms a circle with the fluid upper surface. By the introduction of further boundary conditions, cross-sections that differ from the circle are formed.

For example, if one uses a three- or four-angled wire frame, then in the area of the angles surfaces are formed which are *doubly curved in opposite directions* or *anticlastic;* they are also called saddle surfaces (Figs. 12, 13).

Also, depending on the size of the bubble, more or less strongly defined anticlastic surfaces are formed at the areas of constriction by means of "restrictive" wire loops (Figs. 14, 15). Numerous forms of pneumatically stressed soap films can be found conforming to the sectional shapes used (Fig. 16).

Several bubbles always have the tendency to pile up together, as the outer skin of an agglomeration of bubbles also tends towards a circular shape, i.e. tends to occupy the smallest possible surface in relation to its volume.

Up to four cohesive bubbles can, if they are the same size and have the same internal pressure, form identical spherical sections in which all internal lamellae are planar.

If the bubbles are of different sizes, then the internal lamellae are arched in the direction of the larger bubble. There is a direct relation for the radius of this arching to the radii of the bubbles concerned:

$$r_3 = r_1 \cdot r_2 (r_1 - r_2). \qquad (4)$$

At one edge only three lamellae and in one point only four edges, or four bubbles, can meet together. The lamellae always meet at an angle of 120°. Four edges always form an angle of 109°28' (Morandi angle).

Fig. 17 gives an illustration of simple bubble combinations. Larger three dimensional agglomerations are called foam. If the bubbles are of equal size, then all inner bubbles have plane contact surfaces and form polyhedrons (Figs. 18, 19). Only the outer lamellae are curved. If the bubbles have different volumes, then the lamella framework inside consists of more or less strongly arched concave and convex single lamellae according to the size of the bubble. This means that all pneumatic structures whose surfaces represent adjacent spherical sections can be constructed. Moreover, by means of additional inner stresses the total size of the structure, which is otherwise limited in its dimensions by the strength of the membrane, can in theory be extended indefinitely (analogous foam).

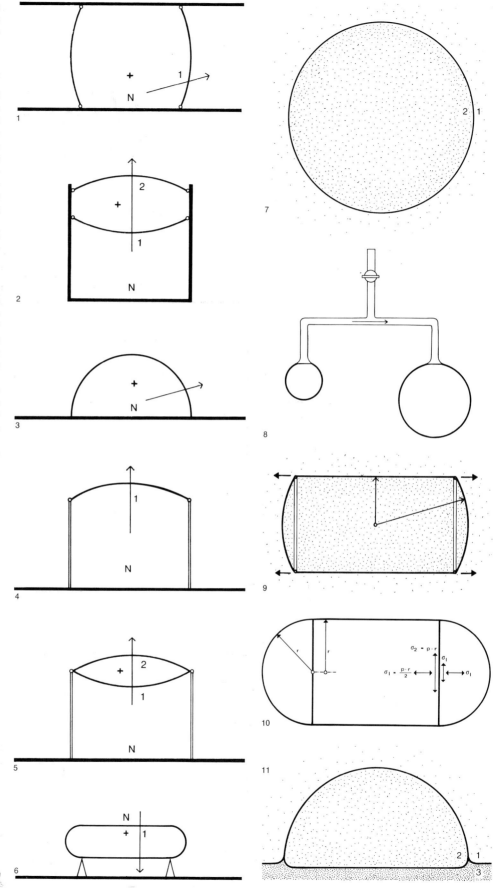

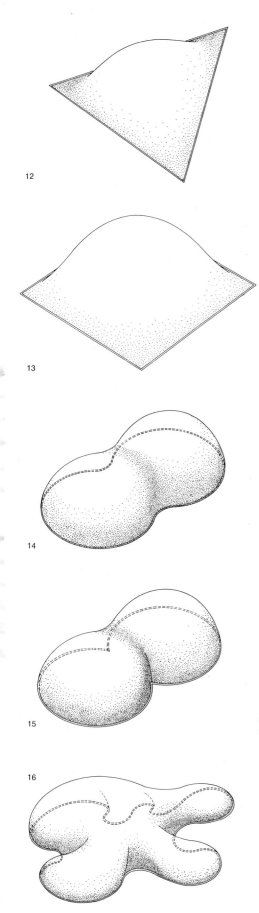

12

13

14

15

16

For the study of pneumatic forms in which the membrane tensions are not the same at every point on the surface and which therefore cannot be represented by soap bubble models, resilient rubber membranes with a thickness of 0.1 to 0.4 mm are particularly suitable when used within their linear area of elasticity.

With the aid of such membranes, for example, it is possible to mould any shape in which spheres, arranged in a straight or curved line, can be inscribed without leaving any excess volume (Figs. 20, 21; Bibl. 119). This can give rise to unilaterally curved, synclastic and anticlastic surface areas.

At places where the radii of curvature are small, zones of lesser stability occur due to a corresponding decrease in the membrane tensions.

If membranes are stressed by means of negative pressure then the imaginary spheres describing the upper surface are found on the outside, for in this case the membrane is stressed by the relative positive pressure of the surrounding atmosphere. However, additional stabilising elements are always necessary, as it is not possible to have a "free" negative pressure structure consisting of only one membrane without boundary conditions (Figs. 24–27). Here too the total of the radii of curvature is always decisive for the evaluation of the surface tension.

Where in the case of soap bubbles wire frameworks have to be used for producing the shape, special boundary conditions are also necessary in the case of pneumatic structures made of non-flexible or slightly flexible materials. The tensions at various points on the membrane are otherwise so different that wrinkles can occur. For example, a structure with the basic shape of a square cushion tends to take on the form of a sphere (Fig. 28). Then there is no tensile stress in the opposite direction to the wrinkle. In order to still produce the tensile stresses necessary to resist the external forces, additional support elements must be introduced (Fig. 29).

In the case of entrances, windows, connection points for fans, etc., there are openings in the membrane which also are subject to specific design laws.

If one places a loop of thread into a plane soap lamella spanned inside a wire ring and pierces the lamella within the loop, the loop forms a circle as a result of the overall equal tensile stresses (Figs. 30, 31).

If one fastens a slack thread in two places on the wire ring and pierces the lamella as shown in Figs. 32 and 33, the thread forms an arc of a circle (Bibl. 167).

This fact should be taken into account in the edge formation of membranes when using tensile stressed cables for the transmission of force.

If in a membrane the tensile stresses prevailing in different directions are not equal (as e.g. in the case of cylindrical forms with hemispherical ends) the shape of the opening should – to avoid wrinkles – be adapted to these forces.

As the membranes of pneumatic structures, apart from special forms, do not form plane surfaces, the curves of openings are correspondingly distorted in three dimensions.

1.3. Morphological classification of pneumatic structures

In the following classification (Table 1) pneumatic structures are described and compared by means of formal characteristic properties. Phenomenological variables other than those used here are certainly possible, but the author has limited himself to categories already in use, as it seemed more sensible to him to create method in the framework of practised terminology than to introduce additional criteria and formulations.

It was stated that pneumatic *structures* could be *open* or *closed*. Equally *membranes* can be *open* or *closed*.

As explained in the chapter on "design rules", the sphere and its sections represent the optimum pneumatic form on account of the equal stress in their surface. If one recognises the sphere as a structure which has the same proportions in three dimensions, then it is natural to classify deviation from this form on the basis of *differing proportions*.

Differentiation should therefore be made between structures with:
— two dimensions of similar size and one larger dimension, e.g. "tubes", "masts", "columns", "towers";
— two dimensions of similar size and one smaller dimension, e.g. "cushions", "lenses", "discuses", "mattresses";
— three dimensions of similar size, e.g. "balloons", "balls", "spheres", "bubbles".

Naturally there are borderline cases between these alternatives. In assessment, therefore, the main directions of extension are compared in their relationship one to another; if a structure is twice as long as it is wide but its height only amounts to a third of its width, then the relationship between width and height is the decisive factor in its classification. The absolute dimensions play no role in this differentiation factor.

The form can be further classified according to the *types of curvature of the outer surface*.

As already shown, it can be:
— singly curved,
— doubly curved in the same direction or synclastic,
— doubly curved in opposite directions or anticlastic.

Plane membrane sections can also occur in pneumatic structures when there are interior skins whose edge is attached to the outer membrane (similar to the inner lamella in the case of equal sized soap bubbles). However, these skins are not stabilised in plane, because there is no difference in pressure. They obtain their tension through the tensile forces acting at the edge.

A further aspect of classification is the establishment of whether an object represents an individual pneumatic structure or comprises several pneumatic structures, and whether these structures are the *same* as each other or *different*.

If the structures are bound together so that they are *not separable* from each other then it is a *combination*. This is the case when adjacent elements possess common membranes so that one element must be destroyed in order to separate

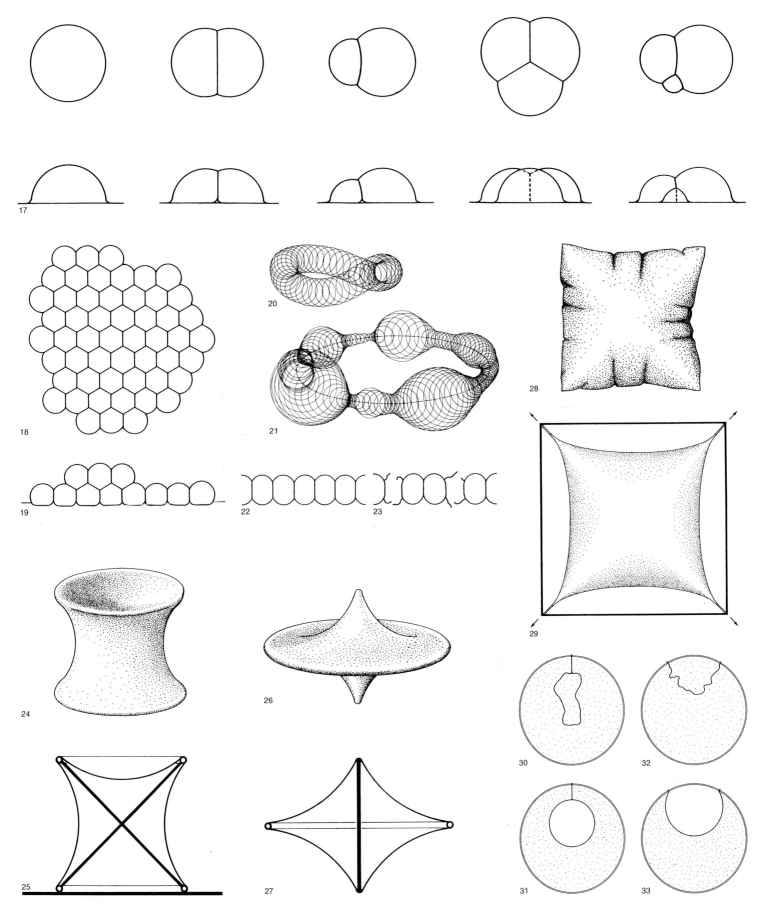

17

18

19

20

21

22   23

24

25

26

27

28

29

30   32

31   33

11

Table 1. Morphological classification of pneumatic objects

feature	alternatives		
type of membrane type of structure 6 alternatives	membrane open structure open	membrane closed structure closed	membrane open structure closed
proportion of structure 7 alternatives	one dominant dimension	two dominant dimensions	three dimensions of similar size
type of curvature 7 alternatives	singly curved	doubly curved in the same direction	double curved in opposite directions
type of connection 7 alternatives	no connection	additions	
		equal structures	unequal structures

possible mixtures of forms			
membrane open and membrane closed, structure closed	membrane open, structure open and structure closed	membrane open and membrane closed, structure open and structure closed	
one dominant dimension and two dominant dimensions	one dominant dimension and three dimensions of similar size	two dominant dimensions and three dimensions of similar size	one dominant dimension and two dominant dimensions and three dimensions of similar size
singly curved and doubly curved in the same direction	singly curved and doubly curved in opposite directions	doubly curved in the same direction and doubly curved in opposite directions	singly curved and doubly curved in the same direction and doubly curved in opposite directions
combinations		additions and combinations	
equal structures	unequal structures	equal structures	unequal structures

the next but one element from the first (Figs. 22, 23).

If, on the other hand, they are *separable* structures, then they can be separated from each other by releasing the connecting mechanism (the same applies to the assembly). The object that is formed by such individual structures represents an *addition* (additive system). (The terms addition and combination are also used as features for connections in the description of support structures.)

The question of the kind of connection between individual structures is important when considering production, erection, dismantling, transport volume, prefabrication and development of structural details, as well as for replacement of damaged parts.

The morphological features for differentiation of pneumatic structures are shown in the first three lines of Table 1. Each horizontal line gives the alternative characteristics and shows which mixtures of forms are possible within one line of alternatives.

The fourth line describes the possible types of connection of individual pneumatic structures to an object. In the first lines the "type of membrane" and "type of structure" are summarised, as they can only occur in the way shown. (The connection of closed membranes to open structures is not possible.)

The principle employed for this representation is in accordance with the morphological box (Bibl. 168). Each alternative of a form variable can be joined to every other alternative of another form variable.

The diagrams of examples should illustrate the actual feature. They are sketches of simple elements which also possess features from every other line of alternatives, but in which the feature by which they are classified is especially marked.

Within this classification there are about 2,000 different possibilities for describing a pneumatic object according to morphological viewpoints. Some of the lines of connection might seem at first to make no sense. However, certainly none of the possible solutions given in the schedule should be excluded, as so far only a small number of these have been realised or projected, and the schedule should also help to find new solutions by means of new forms of alternative connections.

It is not possible to schematise all the single forms possible within the rules of formation. Therefore a criterion such as the geometry of the structure (cylinder, sphere, cone, etc.) must be abandoned at this point, although such a procedure is obvious at first and is found in the bibliography, albeit with clear limitation of the possible spectrum of forms. The fact that geometrically simple structures have previously been preferred in use is consistent with the favourable exploitation of membrane webs with regard to models, the simplified production and calculation process and the possibility of standardisation. However, the standard types represent only a fraction of the possible forms.

2. Pneumatic buildings – structural design alternatives in pneumatically stabilised membrane structures

Gernot Minke

2.1. Introduction

2.1.1. Function and aim of the investigation

Buildings supported by air are among the lightest structures known. With a weight of 1 to 2 kp/m² in relation to the covered ground surface it is possible, for example, to achieve spans of 100 m.

The principle of the membrane stabilised by positive pressure has been used by mankind for thousands of years, but in building technology it was introduced only about 25 years ago, so that the associated problems are still relatively unexplored.

Before one can make a well founded judgement on the possible uses of pneumatically stabilised structures or loadbearing elements, a basic investigation of the structural design alternatives is necessary. For this reason, with the help of the following systematic representation of the different systems and types of pneumatically stabilised membrane structures, a survey is given of the many possible formations of these lightweight structures.

In this survey the different systems are fully discussed; the individual types – which represent the specific characteristics of the system – are partially discussed by example only.

2.1.2. Definition of terms

A loadbearing structure has the function of transferring certain forces within prescribed boundary conditions. It can be allotted to a specific support system and to a specific support form.

The *structural system* is a static system that is neither formalised nor materialised. If additional (secondary) stabilising elements occur in a loadbearing system then it seems logical to divide the system, according to type and formation of the secondary elements, into sub-systems which are called *structural types*. One should refer to a *structural form* when the longitudinal and cross-sectional proportions are known; thus a structural form is a building which is certainly formalised but not materialised. One should refer to a loadbearing *structure* if material and size as well as system and form are given, that is when it is a materialised building. If the loadbearing structure is not yet finally defined or if a specific quantity of structures is referred to, then the term *structural kind* is used henceforth.

If the consideration of pneumatic structures is restricted to their function as a loadbearing structure, then pneumatic structures are *loadbearing structures stabilised by differential pressure*. The differential pressure is necessary for the loadbearing function and consequently the stabilising medium is part of the structure; by this definition sails, hot air balloons and parachutes are not pneumatically *stabilised* but pneumatically *stressed* structures. If one relates the term "pneumatic" to the direct stabilisation, then it can only refer to loadbearing structures made of flexible surface elements – of membranes; loadbearing structures made of curved, stiff surface elements remain shells even when they are pneumatically stressed (high pressure containers) or in addition pneumatically stabilised. Then the specialised term *pneumatically stabilised membrane structure* is used instead of the general term "pneumatic structure".

A membrane structure stabilised in plane does not generally change its form and its loadbearing behaviour significantly if a liquid or granular medium is used to stabilise it instead of a gaseous one. Therefore the term "pneumatic structure" is frequently wrongly used for all three kinds of membrane structure stabilised in plane (Table 1).

The following discussion includes only "buildings" that are accessible, artificially produced structures, fixed to their bases. Furniture, containers and all air controlled structures (air cushioned vehicles, counter-air currents) and structures moved by wind (sails, windmill sails) are not considered.

2.1.3. Criteria of differentiation and alternatives of form

Pneumatically stabilised membrane structures can be sub-divided by a series of different features:
- type of differential pressure,
- degree of differential pressure,
- type of support medium,
- formation of membranes,
- number of membranes,
- dimension of additional stabilising elements,
- formation of additional stabilising elements,
- arrangement of additional stabilising elements,
- type of surface curvature,
- dimension of main directions of expansion,
- magnitude,
- type of usage,
- type of membrane material,
- degree of variability.

For each of the above mentioned features there are different "characteristics". For example two "characteristics" are used to distinguish the type of differential pressure: positive pressure and negative pressure. That is, a distinction is made between positive pressure systems and negative pressure systems.

In Table 2 eleven features (criteria of differentiation) of pneumatically stabilised membranes are shown with two to nine different characteristics in the form of a "morphological box".[1] In contrast to other methods, this method of classification, made famous by Zwicky (Bibl. 168) makes possible a simple and clear representation of very many features and characteristics and is therefore especially suitable as an aid to produce variety. However, it is necessary in the use of this method for the main features of the problem area (here, pneumatically stabilised membrane structures) to be defined in sufficient detail. In Table 2 a feature with its respective characteristics is shown on every line. The combination of every single characteristic from every line gives

[1]Notes see p. 29.

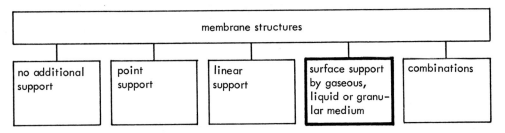

Table 1. Classification of membrane structures.

1,492,992 different alternatives. However, as some of the combinations are mutually exclusive ("incompatible") there are only 250,560 genuine ("compatible") alternatives. In this classification survey the characteristics of the first three features decide the *structural system.* For the classification of the low pressure system it is logical to mention also the combination of point (b) and linear (c) support in the type of secondary support.[2] Thus 16 different structural systems are defined. These are represented in Table 3 and explained in Section 2.2. Within these morphological boxes, however, no combinations of different characteristics of the same feature are shown; these are basically feasible, but would in this case strongly detract from the clarity of the chosen classification scheme. If all possible combinations of characteristics were considered then the number of possible combinations would greatly increase.

The characteristics of features 4 to 6 decide the *structural type,* but it should be noted that this differentiation occurs only in the case of structural systems with additional (secondary) support. The structural types are therefore to be regarded only as their sub-systems. These are explained in greater detail in Section 2.2.4.

The characteristics of features 7 and 8 describe the *structural form,* while the characteristics of features 9 to 11 deal with the loadbearing structure as a materialised building, i.e. they describe the *structural kind.*

With these eleven features and their characteristics 250,560 different kinds of loadbearing structures can be distinguished and described.

The development of classification in the form of the illustrated morphological box may encourage, by means of a systematic procedure, the discovery of new kinds of support structures or the compilation of description schedules or lists of criteria for the description and assessment of different kinds of loadbearing structures.

However suited this form of representation is to clearly illustrating a great number of different kinds of structures, it is not very suitable for plain visualisation of the individual systems and types of pneumatically stabilised membrane structures. For this the matrix seems to be the most suitable form of representation. The following sections give a survey of the possibilities for the structural formation of pneumatically stabilised membrane structure. Here only features 1 to 6 (Table 2), which define the different structural systems and types, are considered. Features 7 and 8, which define the structural form, have already been explained in Section 1.3 in the phenomenological description of pneumatic structures.

Features 9 to 11, which define the kind of loadbearing structure, are not considered in any more detail here.

number	feature	group	characteristics	variety
1	formation of membranes	structural system	a) single b) double	2
2	kind of pressure		a) positive b) negative	4
3	kind of additional support		a) no b) point c) linear	12
4	formation of additional stabilizing elements	structural type	3 b: a) rosette b) ring c) bulged surface 3 c: d) cable e) truss f) arch	28

5	arrangement of additional stabilizing elements		3 b: a) single b) in row c) crossed
			     d) radial e) irregular
			3 c: f) single g) one way h) radial
			     i) tangential k) two-way
			     l) three- (and more) way m) irregular
				148

6	formation of tertiary support		3 b, c: a) no b) tension c) compression d) bending	580
7	dimension of main directions of expansion	structural form	a) one b) two c) three	1 740
8	kind of curvature		a) single b) synclastic c) anticlastic	5 220
9	kind of membrane material	structural kind	a) elastic b) thermoplastic c) non-elastic/ adjustable d) non-elastic/rigid	20 880
10	degree of span		a) up to 20 m b) 20 - 100 m c) more than 100 m	62 640
11	kind of addition		a) no b) one direction c) two directions d) three and more directions	250 560

Table 2. Classification of pneumatically stabilised membrane structures in the form of a "morphological box".

2.2. Low pressure systems

2.2.1. General characteristics

In the surveys of the different systems of pneumatically stabilised membrane structures, two primary systems can be differentiated: low pressure and high pressure systems.

In the case of *low pressure systems* (Table 3) the differential pressure of the media divided by the membrane generally amounts to 10 to 100 mm of water pressure. The membrane is thus stressed by a normal pressure of 10 to 100 kp/m^2. In the case of *high pressure systems* the differential pressure generally amounts to 2,000 to 70,000 mm of water pressure. This means that the membrane is exposed to a differential pressure of 2,000 to 70,000 kp/m^2. The variable static function of these two groups of systems is explained in the description of the high pressure system in Section 2.3.1.

2.2.2. Single membrane systems, double membrane systems

According to the formation of the membrane the low pressure systems can be divided into *single* and *double* membrane structures. In single membrane structures an (accessible) space under positive or negative pressure is formed or closed by one membrane. In double membrane structures, however, the (accessible) space formed or closed by the membrane structure is not under positive or negative pressure. In this case the parts of the membrane surrounding the support medium are always curved in opposite directions to each other. Double membrane structures can, by reason of their appearance, also be called "cushion structures". As some authors also use this term for high pressure tubular structures (see Section 2.3) it will not be used here.

2.2.3. Negative pressure systems, positive pressure systems

The second division of low pressure systems into *negative pressure systems* and *positive pressure systems,* according to the kind of internal pressure, may seem insignificant at first, as in the stabilisation of the structure only the differential pressure of the media divided by the membrane is important. As the diagrams in Table 3 indicate, the kind of pressure differential has, however, a great influence on the structural form and hence also on the structure of the boundary formation, on the static and dynamic loadings of the membrane and on the spatial form.

In positive pressure systems the membrane is always curved outwards (convex), whereas in negative pressure systems the membrane is always curved inwards (concave) – except in the area of secondary support. As a result, in negative pressure systems snow and water pockets can very easily occur in the roof as well as instabilities of form due to aerodynamic loading in wind – disadvantages that are not usually present in positive pressure systems. Moreover negative pressure systems usually require high supports at the edge or in the centre. This means relatively expensive secondary structures. These disadvantages have meant that negative pressure systems have so far hardly been used. However, it must be mentioned here that these systems, in combination with positive pressure systems and high pressure tubular structures, can be very suitable for some purposes.

2.2.4. Systems with additional support

2.2.4.1. Type and application of the principle

The third feature of the low pressure system is the kind of additional, i.e. secondary, stabilisation of the membrane used.

As the types of air supported buildings with large spans which have been realised so far lead one to conclude that the significance of the principle of additional support has not yet been properly comprehended, the characteristics and application of this principle will be investigated in greater detail in this section on structural support systems and in the following sections on the corresponding structural support types.

Additional support within the membrane surface (for example by means of cables) is generally suitable in the case of large spans, in order to decrease the radius of curvature and thereby reduce tension in the membrane. By this means it is possible to use conventional flexible membrane materials, which are simple to manufacture and to work on, even for the largest spans.

The following consideration should serve to clarify this principle (Fig. 1): if one assumes the same air pressure, then in an air supported building with a semicircular cross-section, when the span is doubled, the stress in the membrane doubles. However, as the total height also doubles, the stress from wind forces increases. In order to achieve the same stability as in case A the internal pressure must be increased in case B, which would cause another increase in membrane stress. A further disadvantage in case B is the greater relative volume of the interior in relation to the floor space. Because of this, energy costs for heating and pressurisation increase.

If these two disadvantages are to be avoided then, reducing the height of the envelope, at an identical maximum height of C and A and the same internal pressure, the stress in the membrane in case C is 2.5 times larger than in case A. Thus if one wishes to increase the span without obtaining a greater volume and greater mem-

Table 3. Classification of low pressure systems.

low pressure systems				
I single membrane structures				
	0 no additional support	P additional point support	L additional linear support	P+L additional point and linear support
I n negative pressure	I n 0	I n P	I n L	I n P+L
I p positive pressure	I p 0	I p P	I p L	I p P+L
II double membrane structures (inflated)				
	0 no additional support	P additional point support	L additional linear support	P+L additional point and linear support
II n negative pressure	II n 0	II n P	II n L	II n P+L
II p positive pressure	II p 0	II p P	II p L	II p P+L

17

brane tension, this is only possible by reducing the radii of curvature with the aid of additional stabilising elements, as in case C.

If the reduction of the radii of curvature is achieved by means of channel cables, care must be taken that the tension in a cable is directly proportional to its radius of curvature (Fig. 3, 4, 5). If the cables show the same curvature as the total form of the air supported building, then no reduction of the total tensile stress can be obtained (Figs. 3, 6). Thus in the formation of structures in this system it is important to curve the cables as strongly as possible, which can be achieved through the development of boundary restrictions and through tertiary internal anchorings (Figs. 4, 5). As Fig. 2 shows, any large surfaces can be bridged by such internal anchorings.

In the past it was frequently ignored that for pneumatically stabilised membrane structures, the dynamic load and not the internal pressure is of primary significance for the dimensioning of the membranes, the secondary stabilising elements and the anchorages. The crucial factor with flat structures is the tensile stresses caused by wind suction on the side facing the wind below the vertex (see Section 6.3.3). As it is possible for the stress in the membrane due to wind suction or to instabilities of form (oscillation in wind) to be many times higher than the statics calculation from the normal differential pressure shows, an optimisation of form is necessary in the case of larger spans, above all in respect of the aerodynamic loading. Quite generally it can be said: the flatter the total form, the less is the effect of wind suction and of wind pressure. In the case of very flat structures the occurrence of wind pressure can be almost completely avoided.

If theoretically maximum spans of 2 or 3 kilometres can be achieved with aerodynamically favourable forms, such structures are not practicable without reduction of the radii of curvature with the aid of strongly curved channel cables, as they are much too expensive in terms of material (Fig. 3).

If low membrane tensions, distribution of space and low air volume are determining factors for the choice of system, then in a span of 30 m a reduction in radii of curvature by means of additional stabilising elements can be economical (Figs. 4, 6); for buildings with a short design life and spans less than 10 m this also applies where

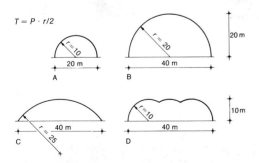

$T = P \cdot r/2$

1. Relationship between tensile stress (T), internal pressure (p) and radius of curvature (r).

membranes are made of thin inexpensive plastic foils (see p. 131).

For additional stabilisation of the membrane two basically different kinds of support can be distinguished: point or linear. The different formations are described in more detail in Sections 2.2.4.2 and 2.2.4.3.

Additional point supports are usually suitable for average and large spans, but the development of support points is generally complicated and expensive in terms of material, so that it is normally more economic to make use of the principle of additional linear support.

With certain boundary formations and with some fields of use it can be practical to combine the principle of point and linear support, i.e. if it is thereby possible to produce sufficient curvature in all areas of the membrane or if, for example, funnel-shaped areas of larger diameter are required in the membrane surface for the drainage of rainwater or snow.

Thus there are four separate characteristics for the feature of additional stabilisation by means of secondary elements. These, together with the two previously mentioned classification features for the group of low pressure systems, define 16 different systems, which are presented in Table 3 in system diagrams and are provided with a mnemo-technically constructed code.

2.2.4.2. Additional point supports

On the principle of point supports

If one attempts to strengthen the curvature of the surface in a balloon made of an elastic rubber membrane by pressing with a pencil point on the membrane, it becomes clear that at the "support point" very high tensions occur in relation to the rest of the membrane, which can very easily lead to the skin splitting. On the other hand, if one expands these individual support points to a circular band or a rounded-off bulged surface, then it is possible, if this expanded support surface is large enough in relation to the whole membrane, for the membrane to show the same tension distribution at every point and thus the danger of the membrane breaking at the support points is no greater than at any other point.

The proof for this, i.e. that with compatible formation of the support elements there is equal tension distribution, can be achieved with the help of soap membranes (Figs. 7–10; Bibl. 120).

The relationship between the size of the point support areas, the extent of deformation and the size of the total membrane can be defined with analogous soap bubble models.

If one introduces a circular support element into a flat membrane from below, then the membrane becomes anticlastically deformed (Fig. 10). A membrane of this kind thus forms a minimum surface with equal stress distribution.

The support ring can, however, only be raised to a certain height before the membrane tears. The larger the ring in relationship to the membrane surface, the higher it can be raised and the larger the possible deformation of the originally flat surface.

On the development of point supports

With point supports three different formations can be defined: "rosette", "ring" and "bulged surface" (Table 4). The term *rosette* is used only when a tensioned element is concerned in which the forces from the membrane are collected into edge cables and from there into tertiary support elements (Figs. 7, 8, 11). It is also possible to use only a single cable, which is then referred to as a "loop". This loop forms a curve of the same curvature in space. As each section of the loop lies in the plane of the membrane immediately adjacent and the membrane tensions are the same at all points, the radii of curvature of the loop – each measured in the tangent plane of the membrane – must also be the same.

The term *ring* is used for a circular element under bending stress as well as tensile or compressive stress (Fig. 10). The bending stress, which usually predominates, results from the angle between membrane plane and ring plane as well as from the support of the ring by tertiary elements.

The term *bulged surface* is used when there is a spherical rounded-off support surface which is mainly under compressive stress. The bulged surface can be a balloon (Fig. 12) which adapts to increasing curvature and directs forces away from the membrane. It can, however, be formed from flexible star-shaped lamellae or clover leaf shaped discs under bending tension or, in special cases, be resolved in individual disc-like surfaces – formations which are already well known from tent construction (Figs. 13, 14).

In the case of ring and rosette supports in pneumatically stabilised membrane structures, the surface within the support element must be closed. This is most easily achieved by means of a low tensioned membrane, which at high points becomes a "dome" (Fig. 11) and at low points a "funnel".

Survey of the different types of loadbearing structure

In Table 4 on the horizontal axis the three basic forms of additional point stabilisation are defined, while on the vertical axis five of their typical arrangements are given. The combination gives 15 different alternatives, which are defined as structural types. As these alternatives are the same for positive and negative pressure systems as well as for single membrane and double membrane systems, 60 different types of pneumatically stabilised membrane structures with additional point support are defined in all.

In this survey the types are given only with their code. Thus the first place gives the number of membranes (I = single membrane, II = double membrane), the second place the kind of internal pressure (p = positive pressure, n = negative pressure), the third place the type of additional support (P = point, L = linear), the fourth place the formation of the additional loadbearing elements (ro = rosette, or loop, ri = ring, bu = bulged surface) and the fifth place the five possible arrangements of the individual supports, as shown in the first column. The first three places of the code thus define the structural system, the following places the structural type.

2

3

4

5

6

2. Greenhouse, study project. Design: Frei Otto and Conrad Roland, 1959.

3. City in the Arctic, project. Design: Atelier Warmbronn (Frei Otto and Ewald Bubner), 1970/71.

4, 5. Study projects. Design; Seminar Pneumatische Konstruktionen, Institut für Umweltplanung, Ulm, under the direction of Gernot Minke, 1971.

6. Multi-purpose hall on the English South Coast, study project. Design: Croucher, Minke and Salt, 1969.

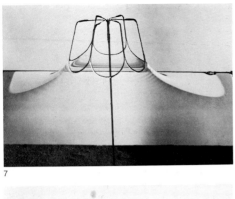
7

8

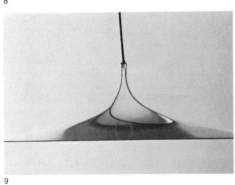
9

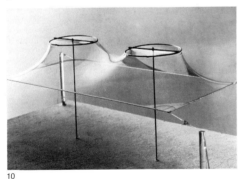
10

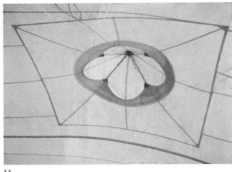
11

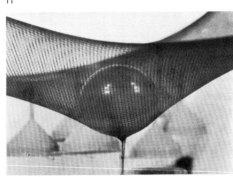
12

13

14

Moreover, if one includes the kind of tertiary support, then 120 different types of structure in this group of systems can be distinguished in all. If one ignores tertiary elements under bending tension which are in general not practicable, then in the case of positive pressure systems internal tertiary supports are under tensile stress, and external ones under compressive stress, while it is the other way round with negative pressure elements. For this reason the symbols "T" for tensile stress and "C" for compressive stress were introduced into the code.

As the *formation* of the tertiary support is in this case more significant for determining the characteristics of the structural type than the *arrangement* of the point secondary supports, the arrangement of the secondary elements is not considered in the diagrammatic representation of the structural types in Table 5. Thus in these diagrams only the 24 basic types of pneumatically stabilised membrane structures with additional point support are shown.

Examples of alternatives of design and usage
As Figs. 15 and 16 show, systems stabilised by negative pressure with point supports seem to differ very little in appearance from non-pneumatically stabilised membrane structures with point supports. However, if one looks at the curvatures of the surface, these systems can be clearly identified: while in the case of pneumatically stabilised membrane structures there is a predominance of curvatures with two sides in the same direction (synclastic) – curvatures with two sides in opposite directions (anticlastic) can only appear in boundary and support areas – in simple membrane structures without pneumatic stabilisation synclastic curvatures never occur, but only anticlastic ones.

The synclastic surfaces, which in the case of negative pressure systems are always curved inwards, can be dangerous because of the formation of water or snow pockets. It is therefore necessary in the formal development of these systems to take care that at every place on the membrane there is sufficient slope for water drainage.

In the case of the multi-purpose hall shown in Fig. 15, the point support was achieved by high pressure balloons. The shape of the hall was determined with a subsequently stiffened rubber membrane deformed by negative pressure; this resulted in an almost uniform tension at all points on the surface. The project shown in Fig. 16 is a double membrane system in which the inner skin forms a part of a spherical surface. For normal wind loadings a negative pressure of only 0.001 excess atmospheric pressure gives sufficient stabilisation in this case.

In the case of additional point stabilisation of positive pressure systems, the development of these secondary support elements requires a considerable amount of structural expenditure. However, structural systems of this kind offer a relatively large variety of forms. In the projects shown in Figs. 17 and 18 the low points are fixed by means of a guyed ring; the membrane continues in funnel-shaped pipes in which rain and snow can be drained away. In the project shown

7–10. Deformation of an originally flat soap membrane by means of individual supports. Investigation by the Entwicklungsstätte für den Leichtbau under the direction of Frei Otto.
11. Roof covering for the swimming pool in Boulevard Carnot, Paris. Design: Robert Taillibert and Frei Otto, 1967. Rosette shaped support of the membrane.

12. Bird cage in Hanover, study project. Design: Thomas Klumpp, 1970. Support of the membrane by a balloon.
13, 14. German Pavilion, Expo '67, Montreal. Design: Frei Otto and Rolf Gutbrod with Hermann Kendel, Hermann Kiess and Larry Medlin. Proposals for the support of the roof membrane.

in Fig. 19 the low points are produced by a "bulged surface", whereby the membrane curvatures are shaped so that rainwater can be drained away outside even in the area of the bulged surface.

2.2.4.3. Additional linear supports

On the type and development of linear supports
Additional linear support in a pneumatically stabilised membrane structure acts exactly like point support in increasing the curvature in the membrane surface and thus reducing the tension in the membrane. However, while it is relatively difficult in the case of a point support to maintain a uniform distribution of stress to the membrane, this is generally easy to achieve with linear support. In the case of additional linear support of the membrane, three different formations can be defined: "cable", "beam" and "arch".

The term *cable* should be applied as a general term for all linear flexible elements which are only under tensile stress. This also includes, for example, chains, threads, wires and cords. The cable appears in positive pressure systems as a "channel cable" and in negative pressure systems as a "ridge cable".

With a relatively small reduction in the radius of curvature it is practicable, instead of a cable, to use a plaited or woven cord of metal, natural fibres or synthetic fibres. In special cases it is even possible to obtain the same effect just by a multiplication of the membrane layers in a sort of banded area. The kind of formation is therefore primarily dependent on the extent of the desired reduction in the radius of curvature (Figs. 4, 5). However, production, transport (packaging) and erection, as well as the possibility for simple connection to tertiary guying elements, can also be decisive factors for the kind of formation of these secondary stabilising elements. An especially interesting formation of a linear support under tensile stress, for which the overall term "cable" was introduced, is the "membrane rib".

By "membrane rib" is understood a flat membrane which, just like a cable, produces an extra linear guying of the pneumatically stressed membrane. Using membrane ribs it is possible for the resultant channels to show only a very small curvature or even to run in a straight line (Figs. 20–27). In order to keep the lowest possible forces in the boundary cables of the membrane ribs, these must be relatively strongly curved. (The tension in the cable is directly proportional to its radius of curvature and the surface tension from the membrane rib.)

Membrane ribs are especially suitable for positive pressure double membrane systems (Figs. 26, 27), particularly as the enclosed volume can be greatly reduced by this.

Table 4. Kind of formation and arrangement of additional point support.

The membrane rib can also simply help to divert forces from the pneumatically stabilised membrane into a cable net lying below it and running parallel to it (Fig. 25). As the example of the American pavilion in Osaka has shown (see pp. 116, 117), a combination of roof membrane and cable net can be created, which is very simple in terms of production and erection and which also offers the advantage that the cable net lies below the roof membrane and is protected from the weather.

The term *beam* was chosen for all linear support elements mainly under bending stress.

The beam is a stiff, primarily straight element, which is only introduced for extra support in exceptional cases. Such an exception can occur where a very small span is concerned or if the beam also takes on further functions at the same time, for example that of track for a crane runway.

The term *arch* is used for all linear support elements mainly under compressive stress.

The arch is a curved stiff element that is predominantly under compressive stress. The use of arches for additional support will only come into question for small and average spans, as they are limited by the dead weight of the element. As a rule the use of the arch will only be practicable for negative pressure systems.

Survey of different types of structure
The differentiation of structural systems into structural types results from the above mentioned *formation* and *arrangement* of the additional support elements. There are seven different kinds of arrangements shown in Table 6.

formation / arrangement	rosette/loop ro	ring ri	bulged surface bu
single 1	I p P ro 1 I n P ro 1 II p P ro 1 II n P ro 1	I p P ri 1 I n P ri 1 II p P ri 1 II n P ri 1	I p P bu 1 I n P bu 1 II p P bu 1 II n P bu 1
row 2	I p P ro 2 I n P ro 2 II p P ro 2 II n P ro 2	I p P ri 2 I n P ri 2 II p P ri 2 II n P ri 2	I p P bu 2 I n P bu 2 II p P bu 2 II n P bu 2
two (and more) way 3	I p P ro 3 I n P ro 3 II p P ro 3 II n P ro 3	I p P ri 3 I n P ri 3 II p P ri 3 II n P ri 3	I p P bu 3 I n P bu 3 II p P bu 3 II n P bu 3
radial 4	I p P ro 4 I n P ro 4 II p P ro 4 II n P ro 4	I p P ri 4 I n P ri 4 II p P ri 4 II n P ri 4	I p P bu 4 I n P bu 4 II p P bu 4 II n P bu 4
irregular 5	I p P ro 5 I n P ro 5 II p P ro 5 II n P ro 5	I p P ri 5 I n P ri 5 II p P ri 5 II n P ri 5	I p P bu 5 I n P bu 5 II p P bu 5 II n P bu 5

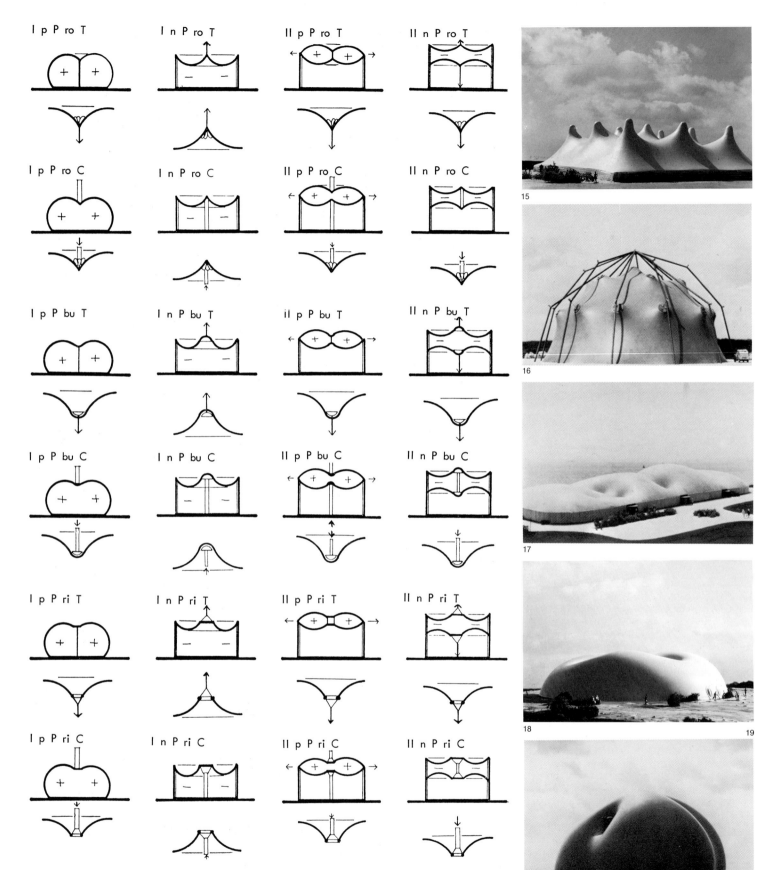

Table 5. Basic types of pneumatically stabilised membrane structures with additional point support.

22

In this survey on the horizontal axis the three basic forms of additional linear support (cable, beam, arch), in this case for single membrane positive pressure systems, are shown; on the vertical axis seven typical arrangements of these supports are given (single, parallel, radial, tangential, two-way, three [and more]-way, irregular). If one disregards the combinations of the three different kinds of support then there are 21 different type definitions in all. As these apply to positive and negative pressure systems as well as to single membrane and double membrane structures, a total of 84 different structural types of pneumatically stabilised membrane structures with additional linear support are defined.

In Table 7 the twelve type groups, for which the seven different possible arrangements are defined, are represented in the form of a mnemo-technical code and in the form of diagrams.

Table 8 shows the 84 defined types of single- and double-membrane structures with linear support.

The division of the 84 types described here systematically should serve as inspiration and/or working aid for analytical and synthetical sub-processes in the design of such structures. In a representation of all 84 types, it becomes clear that one series of types is evidently less practicable or structurally less efficient for application than another. Some types can even be regarded as useless solutions. As, however, an assessment of a structure is not possible without data on size, material and usage, this fact is purposely ignored in this systematic representation.

Examples for possible design and use

It can be recognised from the negative pressure systems shown in Figs. 28 and 29 that with additional linear support significantly different forms occur than with non-pneumatically stabilised membrane structures. The membrane elements of the examples shown would not be stable against wind suction and wind pressure without pneumatic stabilisation, as their corners lie on a plane. The additional linear support can, as is clear from these examples, offer an advantage over point support in that all membrane parts show the same cutting pattern.

Fig. 30 on the other hand shows a project that can be developed in a similar form as a non-pneumatically stabilised membrane structure or as a cable structure. In these two cases the areas round the crown of the arch are only curved very slightly to form a saddle so that normally additional measures against deformation caused by wind must be taken there. However, in the case of negative pressure systems there is generally sufficient curvature and thus also adequate stability against deformation. The surface of these areas is synclastically curved.

In the case of positive pressure systems channels always arise through additional linear support. In the examples shown in Figs. 31 to 37 various possible arrangements are illustrated: parallel (Fig. 31), tangential (Fig. 32) and radially arranged cables (Fig. 33) as well as regular (Figs. 34 and 35) and irregular (Figs. 36 and 37) nets.

15. Multi-purpose hall, study project. Design: Seminar Pneumatische Konstruktionen, Institut für Umweltplanung, Ulm, under the direction of Gernot Minke. Single membrane negative pressure system.

16. Demountable exhibition hall, study project. Design: Seminar Pneumatische Konstruktionen, Institut für Umweltplanung, Ulm, under the direction of Gernot Minke, 1971. Double membrane negative pressure system.

17. Multi-purpose hall on the English South Coast, study project. Design: Croucher, Minke and Salt, 1969. Single membrane positive pressure system.

18. Exhibition hall in Delft, study project. Design: Gernot Minke with students of the Technische Hogeschool Delft, 1971. Single membrane positive pressure system.

19. Exhibition hall, study project. Design: Seminar Pneumatische Konstruktionen, Institut für Umweltplanung, Ulm, under the direction of Gernot Minke, 1971. Single membrane positive pressure system.

20–27. Linear support by means of membrane ribs.

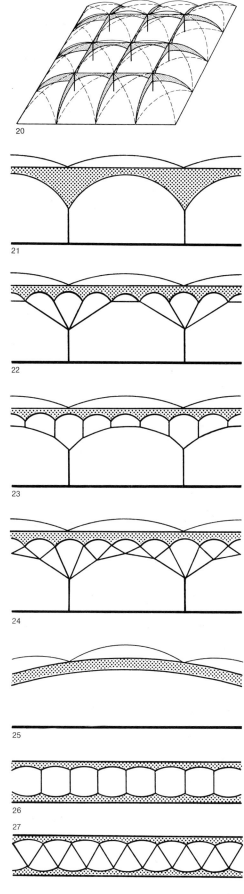

stress / arrangement	tension (cable) ca	bending (truss) tr	compression(arch) ar	combinations
single 1	l p L ca 1	l p L tr 1	l p L ar 1	ca 1 + tr 1 ca 1 + ar 1 tr 1 + ar 1 ca 1 + tr 1 + ar 1
parallel 2	l p L ca 2	l p L tr 2	l p L ar 2	ca 2 + tr 2 ca 2 + ar 2 tr 2 + ar 2 ca 2 + tr 2 + ar 2
radial 3	l p L ca 3	l p L tr 3	l p L ar 3	ca 3 + tr 3 ca 3 + ar 3 tr 3 + ar 3 ca 3 + tr 3 + ar 3
tangential 4	l p L ca 4	l p L tr 4	l p L ar 4	ca 4 + tr 4 ca 4 + ar 4 tr 4 + ar 4 ca 4 + ar 4 + tr 4
two-way 5	l p L ca 5	l p L tr 5	l p L ar 5	ca 5 + tr 5 ca 5 + ar 5 tr 5 + ar 5 ca 5 + tr 5 + ar 5
3-(and more) way 6	l p L ca 6	l p L tr 6	l p L ar 6	ca 6 + tr 6 ca 6 + ar 6 tr 6 + ar 6 ca 6 + tr 6 + ar 6
irregular 7	l p L ca 7	l p L tr 7	l p L ar 7	ca 7 + tr 7 ca 7 + ar 7 tr 7 + ar 7 ca 7 + tr 7 + ar 7

Table 6. Kind of acting force and arrangement of additional linear support.

28. Pendopneu, study project for an exhibition hall. Design: Gernot Minke with students of the Technische Hogeschool Delft, 1971. Single membrane negative pressure system.

29. Hanover fair stall, study project. Design: Gernot Minke with students of the Technische Universität (TU) Hannover, 1970. Double membrane negative pressure system.

30. Sports hall, study project. Design: Seminar Pneumatische Konstruktionen, Institut für Umweltplanung, Ulm, under the direction of Gernot Minke, 1972. Single membrane negative pressure system.

31. Exhibition hall, study project. Design: Gernot Minke with students of the Technische Hogeschool Delft, 1971. Single membrane positive pressure system.

32. Exhibition hall on the English South Coast, study project. Design: Minke, Stevens and Warne, 1969. Single membrane positive pressure system.

33. Roof covering of the Alpamare swimming pool, Bad Tölz. Design: Gernot Minke, 1971. Single membrane positive pressure system.

34. Factory in Delft, study project. Design: Gernot Minke with students of the Technische Hogeschool Delft, 1971. Single membrane positive pressure system.

35. Demountable roof structure for a touring exhibition, study project. Design: Hirst, Kamel and Minke, 1969. Double membrane positive pressure system.

36, 37. Exhibition hall, study project. Design: Seminar Pneumatische Konstruktionen, Institut für Umweltplanung, Ulm, under the direction of Gernot Minke, 1971. Single membrane positive pressure system.

additional support / primary structure	linear support		
	cable ca	truss tr	arch ar
	tension	bending	compression
single membrane — positive pressure	I p ca	I p tr	I p ar
single membrane — negative pressure	I n ca	I n tr	I n ar
double membrane — positive pressure	II p ca	II p tr	II p ar
double membrane — negative pressure	II n ca	II n tr	II n ar

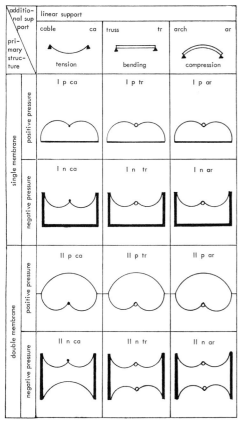

Table 7. Basic types of pneumatically stabilised membrane structures with additional linear support.

28

33

29

34

30

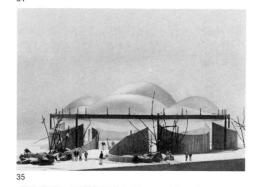

35

31

32   36

37

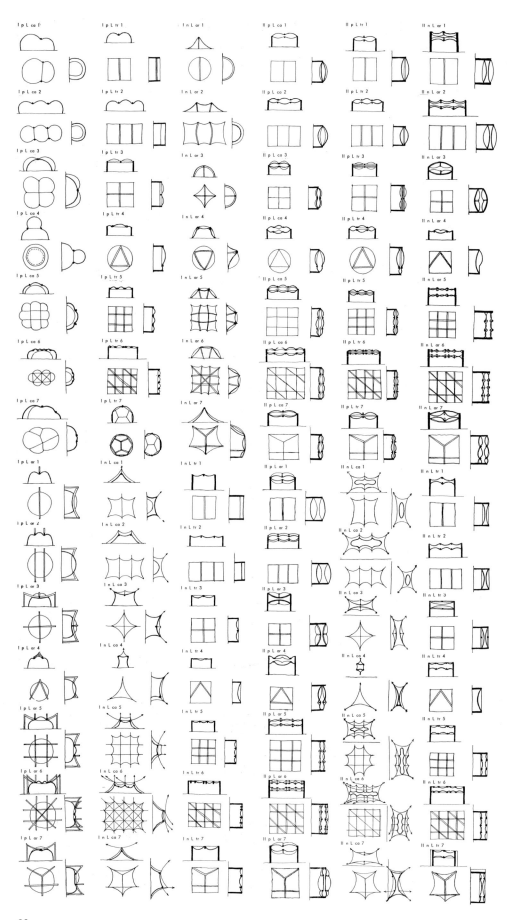

Table 8. The 84 possible types of single- and double-membrane structures with additional linear support.

Table 9. Combinations of negative and positive ▷ pressure systems.

In the case of the project shown in Fig. 32 the central zone was formed by a stronger membrane. As its radius of curvature is three times as large as the radius of curvature of the edge zones, a membrane tension three times as large occurs in the central zone.

Due to the channel cables in the roof of the Alpamare swimming pool in Bad Tölz (Fig. 33) a favourable distribution of internal space could be created and the internal pressure required could be reduced to 0.002 excess atmospheric pressure. Because of the low internal pressure the glass walls needed no additional reinforcement.

2.2.5. Combinations, additions

Although pneumatically stabilised membrane structures have so far mostly been realised as individual structures, a practical economic application for a number of systems seems to be made possible through combination with other pneumatically stabilised systems.

The term *combination* is used if two or more structures of the same or different kinds are directly joined together to form a new structure. If two or more structures are joined together with the help of connection points then this is called an *addition*. In this case each structure is maintained as an autonomous support element.

By means of a logical combination it can be possible to cancel out the disadvantages of individual systems. Thus negative pressure systems show a series of disadvantages (formation of water pockets, aerodynamically unfavourable form), which in certain circumstances can be avoided by combination with positive pressure systems.

The diagrams in Table 9 show examples of the 64 possible simple combinations of the eight negative pressure systems in Table 3; in some cases a vertical as well as a horizontal combination is illustrated.

This representation by means of examples of some of the possible combinations should show how new kinds, forms or types of structures can be found by means of synthesising processes with the help of classification. It should also demonstrate that the spectrum of structural and design possibilities is still by no means fully comprehended and that as yet only a very small number of the alternatives offered to us in the field of loadbearing structures have been realised. Whether the synthetically determined alternatives are practicable for specific uses can only be put to the test when there are constructive requirements related to a specific project.

In the case of additions the formation of the secondary support elements at the edges and the type of connection are generally decisive for the economy of the whole structure. In the possible applications of a system of prefabricated units made of four double membrane standard elements shown in Figs. 38 and 40, the elements are self-supporting by means of an internal compression stressed structure and connected by means of movable connection units so that a secondary support structure can be omitted. In

the test structure shown in Fig. 41 the membrane is stressed by means of flexible, compressed, thermal insulating material.

2.3. High pressure systems

2.3.1. Type and formation

High pressure systems under pneumatically stabilised membrane structures consist of tube-like elements and are therefore termed "tube structures" (in special cases these can also be spherical as Figs. 12 and 44 show). The tube elements show a very strong curvature in one direction, but a very small or no curvature in the other direction, and are able to transfer transverse forces in the direction of low curvature. They can, for example, take on the support function of a beam, an arch, a grid or a lattice shell (Table 10) and thus belong to the group of frame structures. As the membrane of this structure can only take up tensile forces, the compressive forces arising in load application must be compensated for by a corresponding initial stressing of the membrane. The differential pressure required for this generally lies between 2,000 and 70,000 mm of water pressure and this is 100 to 1000 times as large as in low pressure systems. Thus high pressure systems differ from low pressure systems in the differential pressure, the structural function and the type of support action.

The high pressure systems, in comparison with other structures transferring transverse forces, have a relatively low structural efficiency (Bibl. 105, p. 50–53; Bibl. 107) and are thus only used when requirements such as easy erection and dismantling, low weight and low transport volume are decisive factors for the choice of structural system. This is the case, for example, in floating structures for short term use (Fig. 42). A significant property of tube structures is that their form within certain limits can adapt to stresses through external forces. Thus they are particularly suitable as support elements for cable net and membrane structures which are subject to strong changes in form and tension (Figs. 12, 42–44): if the tension in the tensile stressed skin increases then the support surface increases.

2.3.2. Survey of the various structural support systems

As high pressure systems have different structural functions and characteristics from low pressure systems, the differentiating features for low pressure systems given in Table 2 are not applicable here.

In order to distinguish between high pressure systems the following features should be taken into account:

1. The pattern of the elements,
2. The kind of connection of the elements to each other.

In the case of the first feature the three characteristics "straight", "buckled" and "arched"

38

39

40

41

38–40. Buildings for agricultural use, study projects. Design: Gernot Minke with students of the Technische Hogeschool Delft, 1971.

41. Test structure for student working areas. Design and execution: Seminar Leichtbaukonstruktionen, SHfbK Hamburg, under the direction of Gernot Minke, 1973.

high pressure systems			
	S single elements	D discontinuous	C continuous
s straight	Ss	Ds	Cs
b buckled	Sb	Db	Cb
a arched	Sa	Da	Ca

Table 10. Classification of high pressure systems.

42. Information centre Kenniskapsule, Delft. Design and execution: Gernot Minke and Sean Wellesley-Miller with students of the Technische Hogeschool Delft, 1971.
43, 44. Test structures in Delft. Design and execution: Gernot Minke with students of the Technische Hogeschool Delft and Stevin Labor, 1971.

42

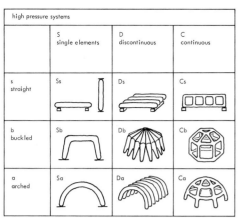

43

44

should be considered; with the second feature the three characteristics are "single elements", "discontinuous" and "continuous".
The nine systems thereby defined are put together in the form of a matrix in Table 10. They are provided with a mnemo-technically derived code and presented as system diagrams.
The terms "straight", "buckled" and "arched" relate to the axis of the element. In the case of system "Ss", with the loadbearing effect of a beam, for example, a small curvature can occur in the longitudinal direction for structural or manufacturing reasons, or the beam can be put together from two truncated cones.
Through addition and combination (see Section 2.2.5) surface structures, which represent a discontinuous or continuous system for transferring forces, can be developed from individual elements.

2.3.3. The different types of loadbearing structures

The nine systems for high pressure structures shown in Table 10 can be divided according to their structural performance into structural types and these can if necessary be divided again according to the type of surface curvature and the arrangement of their elements into structural forms, as is usual in the case of frame structures.
Thus with system "Ss", for example, the "beam" type of structure can be distinguished from the "column" type and with system "Ds" the "plate" type can be distinguished from the "disc" type. In the case of system "Cs" the "Vierendeel truss" and single layer and multi-layer grid types occur; these types of systems can have one, two or three main directions of expansion and thus a one, two or three dimensional loadbearing effect.
The lattice shell system ("Ca") can be split up according to the kind of surface curvature into unilaterally, synclastically or anticlastically curved structural types, or into rotation, translation and ruled surface types, and further, according to the arrangement of elements for example, into net, radial, lamella and geodesic dome types.
The differentiation of kinds of structure can correspond to the classification of low pressure systems stated in Table 2.
As pneumatic high pressure tube structures have the same systems, types and forms of structure as frame structures and as their use is appropriate in only a very few loadbearing buildings, a detailed description of their structural types is not given here.

Notes

[1] The features were limited for reasons of clarity to low pressure systems, because high pressure systems (as is explained in more detail in Section 2.3.1) take on other structural functions and thus have extensively different characteristics.
[2] The suggested classification was tested in relation to its analytical and synthetical function in the comprehension of loadbearing structures so far built, and in the design of loadbearing structures not yet realised, in the following seminars led by the author: T. U. Hanover, January 1970; T. U. Delft, February and September 1971; I. U. P. Ulm, December 1971. The following systematic diagrams came from the reports on these seminars or are based on the studies carried out there (Bibl. 83; Bibl. 84; Bibl. 123).

3. Examples of pneumatic structures from nature and historical technology

3.1. Examples from nature

Some 62% of all animals can fly. A majority of these use as sail surfaces skins which, when they are not pneumatically stressed, lie folded together on the body or hang down limply. These are all open membranes.

The wings of the blue dragonfly *(Aeschna cyanea)* consist of fine membered ribs and between these are spanned membranes which inflate quite weakly under stress (Fig. 1). The strenght of the skin amounts to approximately 3 u and has an equivalent weight of 3.7 g/m². (Bibl. 74, p. 78, 79, 84.)

The flying frog of the Sunda Islands *(Rhacophorus reinwardtii)* has, between his greatly lengthened toes and fingers, skins which give him a controlled fluttering flight (Fig. 2; Bibl. 132, p.154).

Amongst mammals capable of flight the best known are bats (Fig. 3). There are about 500 different types; the largest have a wing span of 90 cm. (Bibl. 132.)

Organic cell structures are not pneumatic forms. If the cell walls consist of solid material then they are self-supporting compartments or shells – similar to those in industrially manufactured foams made of latticed polyurethanes, polystyrenes or glass. If the cell walls consist of flexible membranes, then they are stabilised in their position and form not by gases but by fluids.

Soap bubbles or bubble agglomerations in the sea foam are, however, genuine pneumatic forms with closed membranes.

The law of different internal pressure in liquid bubbles of different sizes can be seen illustrated in the photograph of the broken egg (Fig. 5). One sees how the inner lamellae curve each to the larger bubble.

An interesting experiment was carried out by the (British) Royal Aircraft Establishment in shooting a bullet through a soap bubble (Figs. 6–9). In Fig. 6 the shot flies towards the soap bubble. In Fig. 7 it is in the centre, and in Fig. 8 it comes out again on the opposite side. A fraction of a second later the bubble breaks (Fig. 9), uniformly and symmetrically, a proof of the equal tension in its surface.

A good example of a pneumatic form with a closed membrane is also offered by the natterjack toad *(Bufo calamita)* with its deafening rasping on warm summer nights and its impressive inflatable sack in its throat (Fig. 4).

3.2. Examples from historical technology

The fact that an open, limp membrane surface is stressed under wind loading, thereby changing its form, and that defined forces occur at its edge is one of the early technical experiences of mankind.

The appearance of a sailing ship is very well known, so only one example is shown here (Fig. 10).

The same principle was used in land vehicles by the lesser known sail carts, which were used primarily on flat land – above all in coastal areas. About 4,000 years ago Amenemhet III drove into

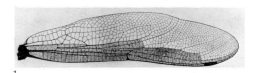

1

2

3

4

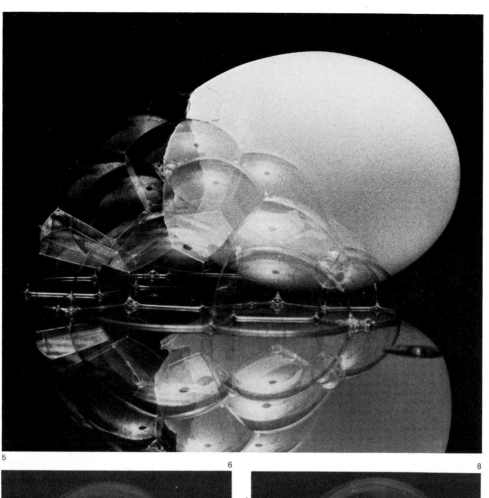

10

11

5

6

8

12

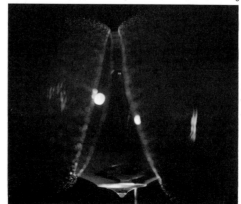

7

9

1. Wing of the blue dragonfly *(Aeschna cyanea).*
2. Flying frog of the Sunda Islands *(Rhacopho-rus reinwardtii).*
3. Bats.
4. Natterjack toad *(Bufo calamita).*
5. Broken egg.
6–9. Different phases of the destruction of a soap bubble damaged by a bullet.
10. Ship of the "invincible Armada", 1588.
11. Vehicle with sails, 1599.
12. "Partenza di Pulcinella per la luna".

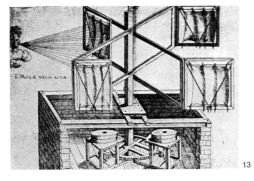

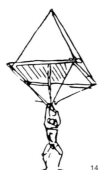

13

14 15

18

19

the desert "with shafts and sails". In China the sail was also known as an aid to the movement of carts. The sail cart built in 1599 by Simon Stevin for Moritz, Prince of Orange, shows clearly in the structure of the cart body the relationship to sailing ships (Fig. 11). The vehicle held 28 men and ran behind a flying sheet at a speed of 7 miles per hour. The same prince is also said to have "gone out for recreation" to the Dutch shores after the Siege of Nieuport (1600) with another vehicle of this kind. (Bibl. 58, p. 1270 ff.)

A "space ship", a mixture of sailing boat and sail cart, is shown in the "partenza di Pulcinella per la luna" (Fig. 12), the curious vision of a moon journey which generously neglects several physical laws.

In 1595 the Italian, Fausto Veranzio, designed a wind wheel with hinged blades for driving two mills (Fig. 13). The surfaces, which serve to catch the wind, consist of membranes supported linearly by cables.

Long before their introduction into air travel, parachutes can be found in drawings and engravings. A sketch by Leonardo da Vinci, originating about 1500, shows a "tent roof made of compressed canvas", whose deformation

through wind has, however, been ignored in the illustration (Fig. 14) – in contrast to the parachute from the machine book by Veranzio, for which the latter proposes a structure related to his millwheel (again with linear cable supports) (Fig. 15).

On a copperplate engraving for the novel Ariane by Desmarets (Paris 1639) the prisoner flees by means of a parachute jump using a sheet. A somewhat complicated apparatus is used in the abduction of Christine by Victorin in an illustration for the novel La Découverte Australe by Restif de la Bretonne (Leipzig 1781). Atop a fantastic flying apparatus a parachute is fixed which is closed in ascent and open in descent (Figs. 16, 17). It is interesting that the illustrator has shown more perception of the form of a pneumatically inflated membrane in the representation of the flight membrane than in that of the parachute, which looks like an umbrella unstressed by air pressure. (Bibl. 58, p. 279–282.)

Sail and box kites are still favourites as toys with children today. The latter were first discovered by. L. Hargrave in 1896.

Sail kites have been known for centuries. Their basic form is an inverted isosceles triangle on top of which is a circle segment or an obtuse

angled triangle. The membrane is made of material, parchment or paper.

In the times of the Dacians, Scythians, Parthians and Persians – the Romans also since Constantine – mobile kites were used as banners. In the early Middle Ages Christian armies carried them; they were also known in India at that time. (Bibl. 23; Bibl. 58, p. 198 ff.)

On the frieze of Trajan's Column in Rome Dacians with their field kites are depicted (Fig. 18). The kites consisted of open metal caps and membrane tubes fixed to them; these were inflated by air to look like bodies of animals. (Bibl. 121.) Sometimes burning torches were put into the mouths of the kites at night. They gave the impression of beasts spewing forth fire and smoke, moving through the air under their own power. Even in the year 1241a "Christian army" is said to have been put to flight by such a banner carried by the Mongols.

Complete animal bodies with clawed feet and stabilising wings on either side were constructed in the 15th century. In an armoury book from Frankfurt on Main dated 1490 there is a dragon kite which is inflated by hot air, moves forwards by means of a rocket in the hind part of the body and is held only by a long string (Fig. 19).

16

17

20. Warm air balloon by the brothers Joseph Michel and Jacques Etienne Montgolfier, 1783.
21. Hydrogen balloon by Jacques Alexandre César Charles, 1783.
22. Balloon with sail by Terzuolo, 1855.
23. Balloon by Giffard, 1852.
24. Airship by August von Parseval, 1906.
25. Stratosphere balloon by Auguste Piccard, 1931.

24

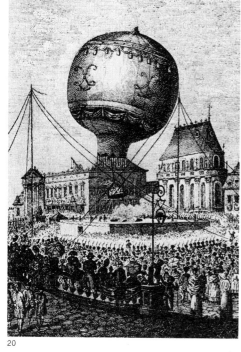

20

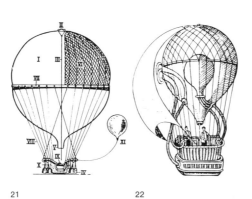

21

22

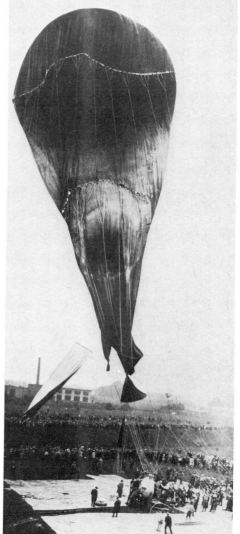

25

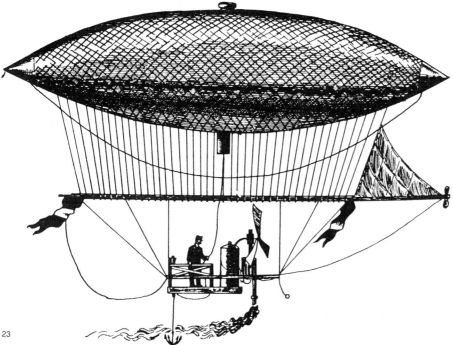

23

119,339

PATENT SPECIFICATION

Application Date, Nov. 20, 1917. No. 17,063/17.

Complete Left, June 20, 1918.

Complete Accepted, Oct. 3, 1918.

PROVISIONAL SPECIFICATION.

An Improved Construction of Tent for Field Hospitals, Depots, and like purposes.

I, FREDERICK WILLIAM LANCHESTER, of 41, Bedford Square, London, W.C. 1, Engineer, do hereby declare the nature of this invention to be as follows:—

The present invention relates to an improved construction of tent for field hospitals, depots, and like purposes.

The present invention has for its object to provide a means of constructing and erecting a tent of large size without the use of poles or supports of any kind. The present invention consists in brief in a construction of tent in which balloon fabric or other material of low air permeability is employed and maintained in the erected state by air pressure and in which ingress and egress is provided for by one or more air locks.

The present invention further consists in a tent maintained in the erected state by air pressure in the provisions for ingress and egress, for rendering pressure tight, and for lighting hereinafter described.

A tent constructed according to the present invention may be conveniently designed either as a segment of a sphere or as a segment of a cylinder.

In one mode of carrying the present invention into effect a rectangular sheet of balloon fabric suitably reinforced by bands, ropes or nets, is pegged to the ground along two of its parallel edges, a flap being left beyond the point of attachment which is turned under. The ends of the said rectangular sheet have stitched to them extensions cut after the manner of a spherical balloon to form quadrant segments of spherical or approximately spherical form. These extensions likewise have a marginal flap which is turned under.

The whole of the above having been securely staked and if necessary loaded by ballast the interior is inflated by moderate air pressure by a centrifugal fan, and the whole so inflated forms a tent of segmental form terminated by dome-like ends. The marginal flap initially turned under in laying out the envelope now forms an air seal in contact with the ground, and where necessary is loaded by sandbags in order to maintain it in close contact and minimise air leakage. One or more doors in the form of an air lock, constructed as hereinafter described, are arranged at suitable points according to the use to which the tent is required to be put. For the purposes of lighting either the fabric employed for the envelope may be made of some translucent material or portions of it may be of translucent material, oiled silk being used for this purpose. Alternatively artificial lighting may be relied upon.

Assuming balloon fabric of fair quality to be employed and the sealing in contact with the earth to be good the supply of air required to maintain inflation against leakage is small in comparison with that required to inflate

[*Price 6d.*]

2 119,339

initially and a comparatively small installation is supplied for permanent running. It is desirable to have a certain moderate amount of leakage in order to provide for adequate ventilation. Disused balloon fabric may therefore be used for constructing tents in accordance with this invention.

The pressure required is of the same order of magnitude as that needed in balloons of the non-rigid type and is considerably less than 1 lb. per square inch. The pressure necessary is related to the velocity of wind and may be increased in bad weather or in order to maintain the envelope against a weight of snow. The peripheral anchorage requires to be calculated and provision made according to the maximum pressure which it is contemplated will be employed. Where the soil provides an insufficient anchorage the latter may require to be assisted by ballast.

The present invention is more particularly applicable to tents of large size, and permits of a very great span being employed. There is no engineering difficulty in constructing a tent for example of 100 feet span and any length required. The technique of construction in such matter as roping, netting, reinforcing, *etc.*, may closely follow similar well known methods at present practised in connection with dirigible balloons.

In constructing an air lock in accordance with the present invention a section is conveniently fitted at one or both of the ends of a tent or elsewhere constructed as hereinbefore described, this construction consisting of quasi temporary structure arranged in the following manner. In a case where the tent is required for purposes not involving the movement in or out of objects of large dimensions such as when used as a field hospital or hutments, each air lock consists of a cabin of suitable size furnished with two sets of doors opening inwards after the manner of an ordinary river or canal lock. The anchorage of the envelope at the point where the lock is fitted is carried on to the structure of the cabin itself which requires to be sufficiently strong to take the stresses. In one modification the cabin is made of "A" form, thus allowing the stresses from the envelope to be carried diagonally direct to the ground parallel to the two sloping rims of the "A." The doors are arranged beneath the bar of the "A" the upper portion being fixed partition. In some cases it is convenient to provide access to the tent by a cutting and ramp the air lock being arranged in the cutting or in a short tunnel in the ground.

Where it is necessary to provide for large objects being taken in or out as for example in employing the tent as an aeroplane hangar, one or both ends of the cylindrical envelope is, or are, filled in with steel or timber structure and the air lock is fitted with sliding doors of the usual pattern adapted to sustain the necessary pressure. The structural ends are preferably anchored securely to reinforcements on the fabric of the envelope, so as to better withstand the pressure to which they are subjected.

Dated this the Twentieth day of November, 1917.

F. W. LANCHESTER.

COMPLETE SPECIFICATION.

An Improved Construction of Tent for Field Hospitals, Depots, and like purposes.

I, FREDERICK WILLIAM LANCHESTER, of 41, Bedford Square, London, W.C. 1, Engineer, do hereby declare the nature of this invention and in what manner the same is to be performed, to be particularly described and ascertained in and by the following statement:—

119,339 3

The present invention relates to an improved construction of tent for field hospitals, depots, and like purposes.

The present invention has for its object to provide a means of constructing and erecting a tent of large size without the use of poles or supports of any kind. The present invention consists in brief in a construction of tent in which balloon fabric or other material of low air permeability is employed and maintained in the erected state by air pressure and in which ingress and egress is provided for by one or more air locks.

The present invention further consists in a tent maintained in the erected state by air pressure in the provisions for ingress and egress, for rendering pressure tight, and for lighting hereinafter described.

A tent constructed according to the present invention may be conveniently designed either as a segment of a sphere or as a segment of a cylinder.

In one mode of carrying the present invention into effect a rectangular sheet of balloon fabric suitably reinforced by bands, ropes or nets, is pegged to the ground along two of its parallel edges, a flap being left beyond the point of attachment which is turned under. The ends of the said rectangular sheet have stitched or laced to them extensions cut after the manner of a spherical balloon to form quadrant segments of spherical or approximately spherical form. These extensions likewise have a marginal flap which is turned under.

The whole of the above having been securely staked and if necessary loaded by ballast the interior is inflated by moderate air pressure by a centrifugal fan, and the whole so inflated forms a tent of segmental form terminated by dome-like ends. The marginal flap initially turned under in laying out the envelope now forms an air seal in contact with the ground, and where necessary is loaded by sandbags in order to maintain it in close contact and minimise air leakage. One or more doors in the form of an air lock, constructed as hereinafter described, are arranged at suitable points according to the use to which the tent is required to be put. For the purposes of lighting either the fabric employed for the envelope may be made of some transparent or translucent material or panels or portions of it may be of transparent or translucent material, oiled silk may be used for this purpose. Alternatively artificial lighting may be relied upon.

Assuming balloon fabric of fair quality to be employed and the sealing in contact with the earth to be good the supply of air required to maintain inflation against leakage is small in comparison with that required to inflate initially and a comparatively small power installation is required for permanent running. It is desirable to have a certain moderate amount of leakage in order to provide for adequate ventilation. Disused balloon fabric may therefore be used for constructing tents in accordance with this invention.

The pressure required is of the same order of magnitude as that needed in balloons of the non-rigid type and is less than $\frac{1}{4}$ lb. per square inch. The pressure necessary is related to the velocity of wind and may be increased in bad weather or in order to maintain the envelope against a weight of snow The anchorage requires to be calculated and provision made according to the maximum pressure which it is contemplated will be employed. Where the soil provides an insufficient anchorage the latter may require to be assisted by ballast.

The present invention is more particularly applicable to tents of large size, and permits of a very great span being employed. There is no engineering difficulty in constructing a tent for example of 100 feet span and any length required. The technique of construction in such matters as roping, netting, reinforcing, *etc.*, may closely follow similar well known methods at present practised in connection with dirigible balloons.

Referring to the accompanying sheets of diagrammatic drawings:—

Fig. 1 is an elevation and Fig. 2 is a plan, of part of a tent constructed in accordance with the present invention.

4 119,339

Fig. 3 is a transverse section showing two air locks in elevation.

Fig. 4 is a side elevation of an air lock in greater detail.

Fig. 5 is an end elevation of same.

Fig. 6 represents an appropriate anchorage.

Fig. 7 is a section showing an alternative anchorage where the maximum angle of slope is small, as for example where it is important that the tent shall cast no shadow.

Figs. 8 illustrates a method of air lock construction giving access to the structure where the general ground level is above the level of the service road.

Fig. 9 is an example of the employment of anchorage given in Fig. 7.

With reference to Figs. 1, 2 and 3 a number of ropes a^1 are secured to appropriate means of anchorage at their extremities; a central ridge rope is provided a^2 terminating in a "banjo" member a^3 from which radial ropes a^4 and a^5 are arranged, similarly connected to a land anchorage, to form the retaining members for the end of the tent or structure. One or more longitudinal rope members a^6 are provided and, at the points where provision is made for an air lock or entrance, diagonal ropes a^7 are provided to reinforce the structure locally and take the place of the transverse ropes that are omitted; as shown more particularly in Figs. 1 and 2, and in Fig. 5.

The air lock Figs. 3, 4 and 5 conveniently takes the form of a van body in which two sets of doors are provided opening inwards, as indicated in the plan view Fig. 2.

The van body is adapted to be utilised as a means of packing the whole outfit when transporting the tent from place to place. The diagonal rope members a^7 adjacent to the air lock or entrance, Fig. 5, form, together with the roof of the air lock aforesaid, the figure of the capital letter A and where it is not desired to make the outfit portable the air lock may comprise structural panels filling in the triangular spaces included between the sides and roof of the air lock Fig. 5 and the adjacent rope members aforesaid.

Beneath the rope network constructed and arranged as hereinbefore described a canvas or fabric envelope is provided of low air permeability, the said envelope being cut and sewn or jointed to fit the rope network just as in the case of a balloon of the non-rigid type. The edges of the envelope do not terminate on the ground line, but allow of a flap extending inwards, as shown more particularly in Figs. 3 and 4, the said flap either being pressed to the ground by internal air pressure or, where necessary, being loaded by sand bags as shown at b^1, Figs. 3 and 4. Where the envelope is cut to permit of the insertion of the air locks or entrances a flap is likewise provided and this may be sealed by a sandbag, as shown at b^2 or by strips and bolts as shown at b^3, or both methods may be utilised and the flap may be additionally nailed, as indicated at b^4. Reinforcement ropes or bands may be provided as at a^9, a^9. The van bodies serving as air locks are arranged with doors, one pair at each end, c^1, c^2, and c^3, c^4, opening in like direction, and apertures may be provided c^5, c^5 fitted with sliding doors, both to equalise the pressure when it is desired to open the doors, acting thus in the manner of the sluice gates of a lock, and to allow of observation if required to ascertain that the lock is not otherwise engaged.

For the purpose of lighting the fabric or canvas employed may be translucent or other means may be provided. For example port holes may be fitted in the canvas in the interspace between the adjacent transverse ropes, at a suitable level for lighting purposes and to allow of observation from the interior of the tent, as shown by way of example at a^8; for this latter purpose the height of the port holes from the ground level requires to be regulated at about five feet. Alternatively, and as is frequently desirable from a military standpoint, the material of the envelope should be opaque and artificial means of lighting exclusively relied upon.

The means of anchorage for the transverse ropes depicted in Fig. 6 comprises wooden planks or baulks d^1, d^2 with an iron tension bar d^3 cottered at d^4 and

119,339 5

with a coupling at link d^5, the said link being connected to its corresponding transverse rope member by a rigging screw or lanyard. The method of constructing the anchorage is to dig a trench of the necessary width and depth, drive the timber in place, and, with the tension bar d^3 in position, fill in and tamp. The vertical component of the load on the tension bar is taken mainly by the filled in and tamped earth, but in part by the driving of the horizontal timber member d^2 under the virgin soil as indicated, the timber member d^2 inserted in an inclined position, being driven down by its butt end while the chamfered end forces its way into the undisturbed soil.

In cases where camouflage is important, as in a military zone, where liable to aerial observation, the tent or structure is made of considerable span and minimum altitude, so that the maximum roof angle is insufficient to cast a shadow. In such cases the transverse tension members or ropes a^1, a^1, a^7 may be held by double, triple or multiple picketing, as indicated in Fig. 7.

In erecting a tent or structure in accordance with the present invention it is desirable to employ a centrifugal fan of considerable delivery capacity, the outlet of the fan being coupled up by a flexible conduit to any convenient point in the envelope and the inflation volume being sufficient to take charge of considerable leakage. While inflated by this means the tent may be entered by passing beneath the sealing flap and sand bags, *etc.*, may be loaded on to the sealing flap at points of leakage in order to make good; also the air locks may be inserted and the sealing round them be made secure. When this is done the permanent air pressure plant, consisting of a comparatively small motor and fan, may be set to work and will be sufficient to maintain the inflation pressure. An appropriate inflation pressure under ordinary weather conditions is about one inch water gauge, but in stormy weather as much as two or three inches water gauge may become necessary.

In place of the definite distribution of transverse and longitudinal ropes herinbefore described the ropework may take the form of a net in which the whole of the members are diagonally knotted or cross fastened in any well known manner.

In the case of a tent of circular form the method hereinbefore described as concerns the ends of the structure may be adhered to, the tent taking the form of two ends with no cylindrical portion as figured on the left of Figs. 1 and 2.

If air locks in the form described are insufficient in size, as in the case of stowage for aeroplanes, special locks may be employed of larger dimensions or the whole end of a building may be occupied by an air lock. In such structures it is necessary, however, that the air lock should be of semi-permanent character and either steel or ferro concrete may be conveniently employed to form end buildings containing the lock adapted to be connected by a cylindrical inflated roof constructed as hereinbefore described.

In other cases and on sites where the conditions indicate the method as suitable, access to the structure may be obtained by a tunnel or "cut and cover" with a ramp leading upward to the floor level and such construction is indicated where the site chosen is adjacent to a sunken road; a diagrammatic example of this is given in Fig. 8.

In order to provide for the excess inflation pressure required when there is a high wind a cowl raised on a stand pipe, or suitably mounted on the top of the tent structure, may be employed, the cowl consisting of a wind catcher pivotally mounted and directed by a weather vane. The wind catcher may consist merely of a right angle bend or hood with the vane so attached that the aperture of the bend is always facing the wind and the said aperture may be flaired or made funnel shaped in order to obtain the maximum effect. This device is similar to the ordinary chimney cowl except that the vane is arranged to act in the diametrically opposite sense.

Having now particularly described and ascertained the nature of my said

6 119,339

invention and in what manner the same is to be performed, I declare that what I claim is:—

1. A tent or roof structure supported by internal air pressure with means of access comprising an air lock.
2. A tent or roof structure in accordance with Claim 1, in which a rope network is picketed or anchored to the ground and contains a canvas or fabric envelope of low air permeability provided with an inwardly turned sealing flap and adapted to be sustained by air pressure supplied by a fan or blower or by a wind cowl, or by both means in combination.
3. A tent or roof structure in accordance with Claims 1 and 2, in which the air locks take the form of van bodies adapted for the stowage of the network envelope and anchorage material for the purpose of transport.
4. A tent or roof structure in accordance with Claims 1 and 2 substantially as and for the purposes hereinbefore described.

Dated this the 19th day of June, 1918.

F. W. LANCHESTER.

Redhill: Printed for His Majesty's Stationery Office, by Love & Malcomson, Ltd.—1918.

26

26. Patent specification *An Unproved Construction of Tent for Field Hospitals, Depots and like purposes* for F. W. Lanchester, 1918.

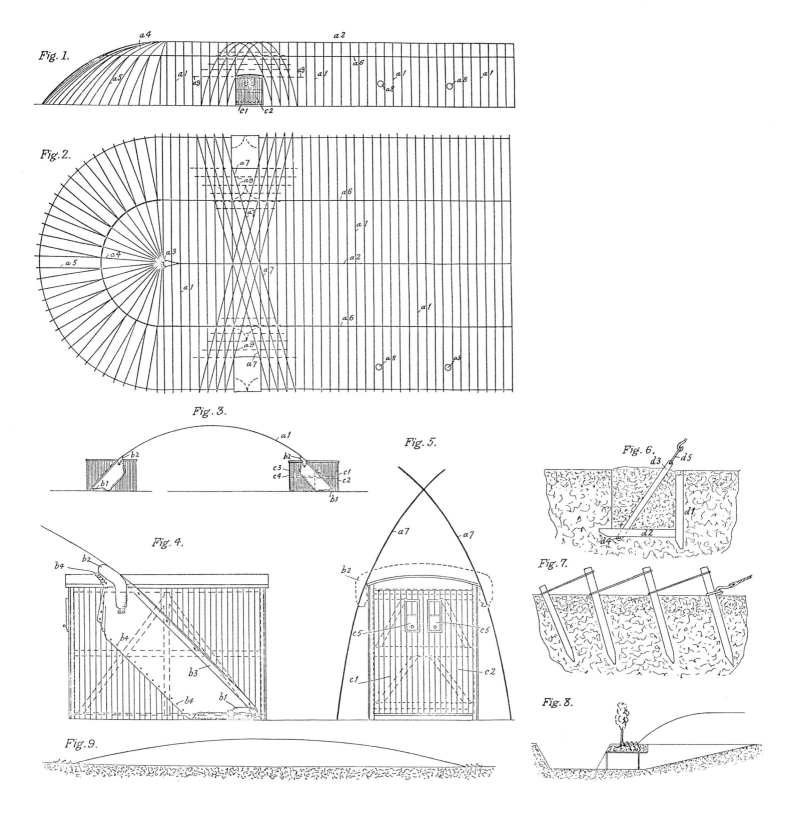

Fig. 1.

Fig. 2.

Fig. 3.

Fig. 5.

Fig. 6.

Fig. 4.

Fig. 7.

Fig. 9.

Fig. 8.

35

Here we are already dealing with closed membranes which can be viewed as forerunners of the later hot air balloons. (Bibl. 58, p. 653, 658.)

In 1826 G. Pocock built in England a vehicle that was pulled by large kites – the sail carts of 1600 had probably been forgotten.

Kites were first used for scientific purposes by Wildon in 1749 for the measurement of atmospheric temperature and in 1752 by Franklin for the proof of thunderstorm electricity. Kites were very important as research apparatus in meteorology. (Bibl. 23; Bibl. 58, p. 651 ff.)

Free and captive balloons are generally regarded as forerunners of present day pneumatic structures. As we have seen, pneumatic forms have existed for very much longer, yet balloons have remained by far the most important prototypes to date.

Historians today are still not agreed on the intellectual authorship of these hollow membrane spheres. To many the warm air balloon made out of a canvas envelope lined with paper by the brothers Joseph Michel and Jacques Etienne Montgolfier still counts as the first structure of its kind (Fig. 20). The balloon went up on 5th June 1783, at first unoccupied, months later with animals, then with a man aboard.

However, the brothers cannot be considered as the discoverers of the balloon. In his Utopian novel *Les Etats et Empires du Soleil* Cyrano de Bergerac (1619–1655) describes a smoke-filled balloon that, with the assistance of a sail, carries a cabin in space. A copperplate engraving of this fantasy appeared in 1657. Round about the same time the Jesuit, L. Laurus, also developed the idea of a warm air balloon. On 8th August 1709 in Lisbon the Brazilian cleric, Bartholomew Lourence de Gusmao, finally ascended 200 feet into the air in a hot air balloon. The following extract is taken from a Russian manuscript: "In the year 1731 in Asen an official of the province of Nerechtes Krjakutnoi made a large ball and blew it up with horrible stinking smoke. To it he fastened a loop and sat himself in it, and the evil spirit raised him higher than the birch trees and then threw him against the bell tower, but he grasped the rope used to ring the bells and thus lived". (Bibl. 58, p. 64 ff.)

Much more significant for the future of balloon travel, however, was the discovery by the French physicist, Jacques Alexandre César Charles, who only some two months after the ascent of the "Montgolfière" sent up the first hydrogen balloon (Fig. 21). In its basic structure it remained the prototype for all gas balloons until the present day. "The envelope took the form of a sphere and was tear resistant and airtight. It was made of silk, which was strengthened inside with the help of liquid rubber. On top there was a gas valve which could be opened from the basket with a release cord. In this way one could release gas and prevent an undesired ascent, just as an undesired descent could be prevented by throwing out ballast in the form of sandbags. The inflation tube remained open. Because air pressure forced the gas into the balloon, the gas could not escape on the ground despite the openings. But in the air the open gas cylinder manifold prevented the balloon bursting, for because of the low air pressure the surplus gas, which then expanded, could escape automatically. Naturally the loss of momentum, which would have led to a crash if near the ground, had to be compensated for by throwing out ballast". (Bibl. 99.)

It is also significant that the "Charlière" basket was already fastened to a cable net that fed the forces of its deadweight uniformly into the balloon membrane.

The stratosphere balloon of Auguste Piccard, which in 1931 starting from Augsburg set a new height record (exactly 16,000 m), was the largest balloon in the world at the time. By means of the gradual expansion of the hydrogen it only obtained its spherical shape at the highest point (Fig. 25).

The efforts following the discovery of the balloon as a means of transport were primarily concerned with propulsion and steering. By using the muscles of man working with air oars, of horses working with air blades, and even of tamed eagles, attempts were made to be independent of the wind.

Again and again projects appeared using sails dependent on the wind (Fig. 22), the means of propulsion.

With the arrival of more suitable means of propulsion, in particular internal combustion engines, balloons were given a longer shape which was aerodynamically better (Fig. 23; Bibl. 23; Bibl. 99).

The Parseval airship (Fig. 24) is regarded as the first really practicable dirigible airship in the world, a successor to the famous Parseval-Sigsfeld kite balloon.

The bodies of later airships, in particular the famous Zeppelins, are not pneumatics. They have metal frames which are covered on the outside by a skin. The gas which produces the uplift is in closed chambers inside.

The idea of also using the pneumatic principle in buildings originates from the English engineer F. W. Lanchester; in 1918 he even obtained a patent on it (Fig. 26). The largest of the pneumatics that he designed in the following period was to have a diameter of 650 m! Regrettably he did not live to see the breakthrough of his idea.

4. Examples of pneumatic structures from the technology of today

The following section gives a survey of pneumatic structures of various kinds as they are designed or produced in the field of technology of today. The term "technology" is used in its original sense – as an antithesis to nature rather than to art.

It has already been stated that not all the pneumatic structures shown in the classification system have yet been realised. In the following details, therefore, only those differentiating features have been chosen for which examples can be found.

These are arranged according to:

type of structure – structure open (So), structure closed (Sc);

type of membrane – membrane open (Mo), membrane closed (Mc);

proportion – one dominant dimension (1 di), two dominant dimensions (2 di), three dimensions of similar size (3 di);

additional support – no additional support (0), additional point support (P), additional linear support (L).

Classification according to usage has purposely been omitted, because usage can change and is frequently interchangeable. It is also the result of temporary interpretation.

1

2

1, 2. Parachutes

Today, more than ever before, parachutes are used as a means of transport. Increasing air traffic and their low transport volume make them irreplaceable for both civil and military purposes. The illustrations show how the weight of the live load is transferred to the membrane by means of a great number of cables. These cables at the same time bring about a reduction of the total membrane curvature and correspondingly a reduction of the membrane stresses.

3. Bat glider
Development and manufacture: Ryan

There are problems involved in the use of a parachute in space travel as it falls almost vertically, cannot execute any controlled flight movements and cannot cover any extensive flight path over the earth in a desired direction. Its advantage, however, is that it can be folded up very compactly.

The bat gliders, which were developed by order of NASA, combine the advantages of the parachute with those of the glider plane; they can be folded up and are also manoeuvrable.
(Bibl. 74, p. 85.)

3

4, 5. Heavy Lift Balloon, Model 530K
Design and manufacture: RAVEN Industries, Inc.

This recently developed balloon is intended for heavyweight transport over impassable terrain. In its lifting characteristics it is similar to the helicopter, but considerably cheaper to produce and maintain. It only has to be grounded in wind speeds of 50 km/h and more. The photograph shows that the balloon on the ground has a strong similarity to a pneumatic structure.

6. Mylar – Sphere
Design and manufacture: RAVEN Industries, Inc.

Such a balloon made of approximately 0.1 mm thick foil can carry scientific apparatus over 50,000 m high into the stratosphere. In August 1960 a pneumatically stressed sphere of this kind, whose surface was covered with a vapour deposit of aluminium, was sent as "Echo 1" into an earth orbit. Further reflector bodies followed it. The diameter of Echo I, which was inflated in outer space, was 30 m, yet its packing diameter in the nose of the rocket was less than 70 cm.

5

4

6

7, 8. Information pavilion at Expo '70, Osaka
Design: Taiyo Kogyo Co., Ltd.
Manufacture: as above, 1970

The pavilions invite comparison with the Berlin SPD pavilion (Fig. 9). The structures are of similar size; they are each anchored to a steel ring in the bottom third of the structure (see p. 155) and their intended usage is also similar. In the case of the SPD pavilion the structure is certainly of the single membrane type, but how should the Japanese example be classified? If one regards it as part of the roof, then it is a double membrane structure. This is a border-line case which makes clear the dependence of these differentiating features on the use.

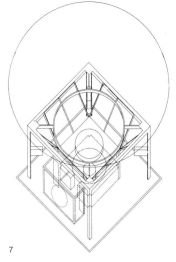

7

8

9

9. SPD publicity pavilion in Berlin
Design: L. Stromeyer & Co. GmbH
Manufacture: as above, 1962

This building is remarkable in that it represents a complete sphere (with a diameter of 12 m), whereas all later spherical single membrane structures consist only of spherical sections. The form relationship with the Field Constable's House in Ledoux is striking.

10, 11. Winter protection for the construction of the TV tower in Dresden
Design: Deutsche Post, project office (H. Rühle, I. Bauer, G. Drechsler, E. Macher)

As in the previous examples a pneumatically stressed envelope is attached to a steel ring with a diameter of 5 m. The retaining ring is connected to the climbing framework of the tower; sealing is effected by a skirt running around the hem. (Bibl. 144, p. 121.)

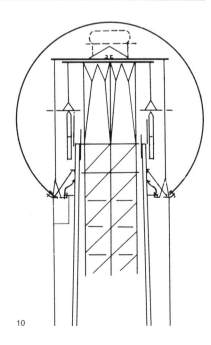

10

11

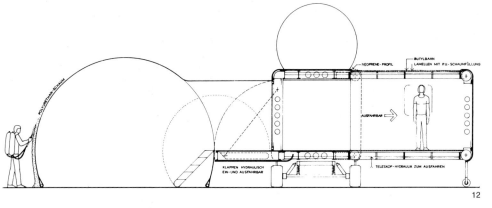

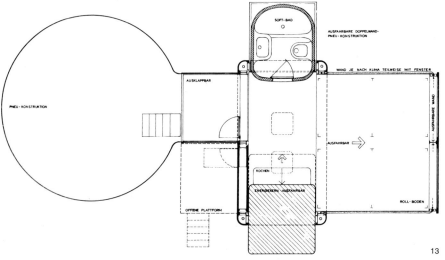

12–14. Mobilhaus
Design: Manfred Schiedhelm, 1970

The idea of this design, which was a contribution to a Japanese competition, is to create a mobile "container" house, having a functional area that can be greatly increased by pneumatic components being extended and attached as additional rooms. These alterations can be made quickly and selection of the different volumes, and of their size, is to be left to the user. However, this is an unrealistic proposition in terms of the current availability of suitable structural materials.

12

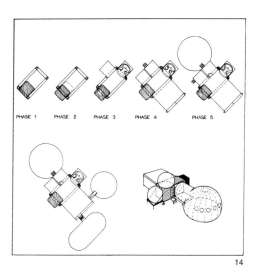

13

14

15

15. Environment Bubble
Design: François Dallegret, 1965

The sketch appeared as an illustration of an article by Reyner Banham, published in 1965, which indicated the role of the technical utility systems in the development of modern architecture. The pneumatic bubble, equipped with a utility element, should enable the user to lead the life of a modern nomad. (Bibl. 7.)

16–18. USA Pavilion for Expo '70, Osaka, initial projects

Design: Davis, Brody, Chermayeff, Geismar, de Harak Ass., 1968

The design team had won the competition for the US Pavilion (Fig. 16) with its first project of a double membrane cube structure made of synclastic panels. Neither the first nor the second (Figs. 17, 18) project was built, because of the cost. (Congress cut the budget from 16 million dollars to 10 million, of which only 4 million remained for the pavilion and all the exhibition items.)

The version finally built (see pp. 116, 117) is far less spectacular but certainly just as suitable for demonstrating the scope of pneumatic structures.
(Bibl. 44, p. 208 ff.)

16

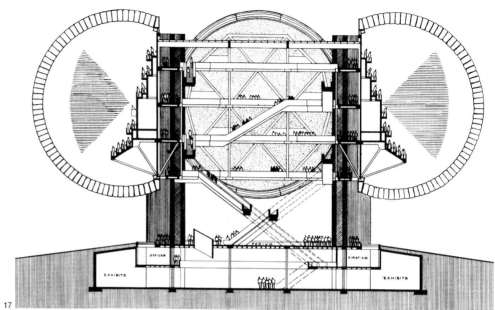

17

18

19

20

19, 20. Water walk
Design and manufacture: Eventstructure
Research Group, 1968

These pneumatic tetrahedrons, which allow
walking on water, consist of 0.5 mm thick transparent or translucent PVC foils. Entrance is by
airtight and watertight zip fasteners.

21

**22, 23. Die Wolke – Das Haus aus der Dose
(The cloud – house out of a can)**
Design: Coop Himmelblau, 1968

The cloud represents a mobile pneumatic unit of
space, equipped with a variable platform which
can be used in various ways. The total unit is to
be transported packed in a giant can.

Without doubt the proposal has a certain technical appeal, but it is better not to question the
relationship of cost to work space, nor the general validity of such a structural system in the
face of the present living and environmental
problems.

22

23

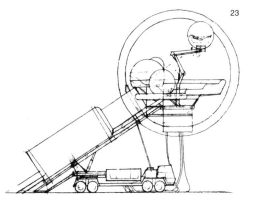

24

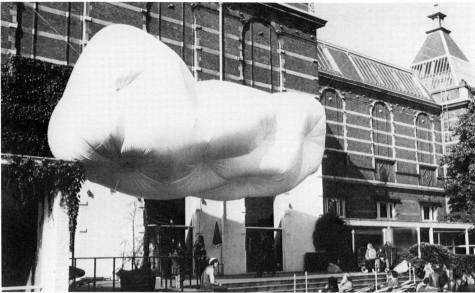

25

24, 25. Cloud, Stedelijk Museum, Amsterdam
Design: Eventstructure Research Group, 1970

The structure presents the rare case of a closed membrane with additional point support. It has no cutting pattern which would anticipate the final shape; thus a large number of wrinkles formed which, however, in this case were not meant to be avoided.

◁ **21. Michelin man**
Design and manufacture: Ballonfabrik — See- und Luftausrüstung GmbH + Co. KG, 1970

This "Pneuman" looks like a predecessor of early space suits. The constrictions were achieved, not by additional stabilising elements, but by the cutting pattern of the material.

26

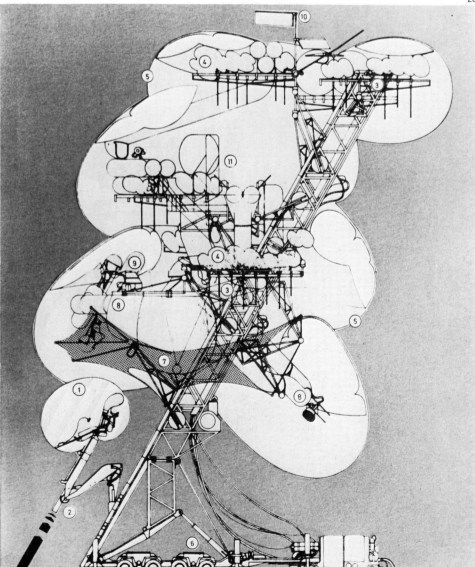

26. Wolke – Gruppendynamischer Wohnorganismus (Cloud – group dynamic living organism)
Design: Coop Himmelblau, 1968

"Cloud" is clearly a favourite name for pneumatic structures. The illustration comes from a research programme for future living forms. However, the design laws for pneumatically stressed membranes have not been fully complied with.

27–29. Ricoh Pavilion, Expo '70, Osaka
Design: Nikken Sekkei, Ltd.
Manufacture: Taisei Construction Co., Ltd., and
Goodyear Aerospace Corp., 1970

A light source of 300 electronically controlled
lamps was installed inside the luminous yellow
balloon. Linear anchoring of cables and membrane ribs gave the balloon its characteristic
shape and reduced the radii of curvature. It had
a pipe connection to a "parent balloon" in the
basement, from where the internal pressure was
kept constant. In storms, or for maintenance
purposes, the balloon was drawn in by means of
winches.

28

27

29

30, 31. High tension test station for Felten & Guilleaume Carlswerk AG, Cologne-Mülheim
Design: Frei Otto
Manufacture: L. Stromeyer & Co. GmbH

The double sphere was achieved by means of a centre cable which forms a deep groove.

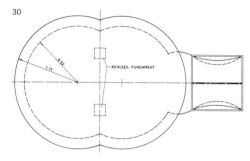
30

31

32–34. Brass Rail Restaurants, New York World Fair, 1963–64
Design: Victor Lundy
Structural calculations: Severud-Elstad-Krueger
Manufacture: Birdair Structures, Inc., 1963

Brass Rail Restaurants are a particularly successful example of the early attempts by Lundy to exhaust the possibilities of form in pneumatic structures.
The elegant lightweight structures were 23 m high and had a diameter of 18 m. The impression of piles of spheres was produced by means of guy ropes fastened to a central steel mast.

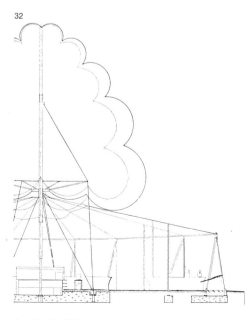
32

33

34

35. Boston Arts Centre Theatre
Design: Carl Koch and Margret Ross
Structural calculations: Paul Weidlinger
Manufacture: Birdair Structures, Inc., 1959

The theatre has 2,000 seats; its diameter is 44 m and the height of the cushion roof in its centre is 7 m. The membrane forces are taken up at the edge by three cables that are anchored to the corners of a polygon made out of steel sections. Thus the edge beams are only loaded for buckling stress (see also p. 157). The internal positive pressure of the cushion is 25 mm of water pressure. Originally it was intended to be used as form work for a concrete shell dome, but it was found that the pneumatic structure functioned very well; it remained completely intact after a bad hurricane in 1960. (Bibl. 119, p. 110.)

35

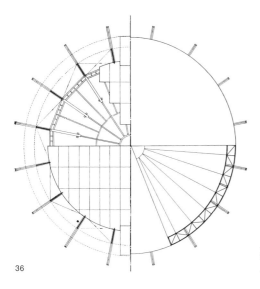

36

36—38. Mobile pavillon for RAI (Radiotelevisione Italiana)
Design: Achille and Pier Giacomo Castiglioni
Manufacture: IPI, 1967

The Italians call this pavilion for travelling exhibitions a "flying saucer" (disco volante). The translucent material of the roof and walls consists of PVC coated polyamide fabric. Only the roof is a pneumatic structure. As can be seen from the section, the radius of curvature of the upper membrane is considerably smaller than that of the lower membrane. Because of its relatively flat shape the roof surface is less strongly stressed by wind pressure than by wind suction, so that the upper membrane, which because of its strong curvature can resist higher loadings, actually is more heavily loaded.

38

37

39

40

39–42. Roof of the Festival Plaza, Expo '70, Osaka

Design: Kenzo Tange
Structural calculations: Y. Tsuboi and M. Kawaguchi
Manufacture: Toray Industries, Inc., 1970

Tange's roof is considered by some people to be magnificent and masterly, by others to be gargantuan.

The steel space framework was set at a height of 30 m over the Festival Plaza; it weighed 5,720,000 kg and measured 108 × 291.6 × 7.60 m on a grid of 10.80 × 10.80 m.

The structure was rectangular in plan, but there was a "break" formed by a circular opening of approximately 58 m diameter, through which emerged the 60 m high "Tower of the Sun". The pneumatically stressed double membrane elements which were used as covering were light, translucent and unaffected by thermal stress in the steel structure (see also p. 157).

The upper membrane consisted of six different layers of polyester film – a weather protective layer (200 u), a heat reflecting layer (200 u), three "loadbearing" layers (250 u each) and an air-sealed coating (50 u). The lower membrane did not have the heat reflecting layer.

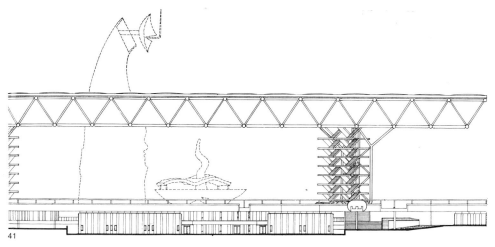

41

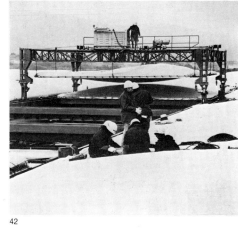

42

A life span of six to seven years was assumed. The elements were flame resistant, and if a fire had occurred under the huge roof the sheeting would have melted to form outlets for the smoke and heat. The internal positive pressure was 50 mm of water pressure in calm weather and 100 mm in storm conditions. The structure had been developed to such maturity that it needed only a few control instruments to maintain the positive pressure.

In Fig. 42 two assembly cars for the air cushions can be seen. They ran in grooves which at the same time served as drainage channels.
(Bibl. 88, p.5ff; Bibl. 148.)

43, 44. Leisure centre with alterable air cushion roof at Rülzheim, near Germersheim
Design: Rudolf Kleine, Georg Kuhn, Klaus Richrath and Albert Schieber
Structural calculations: Wulf Witte
Manufacture: Krupp Universalbau, 1974

The air cushion roof consists of two membranes of which the outer one has the shape of a spherical segment while the inner one curves in the opposite direction with two different radii. The latter is supported by a circular gallery. The diameter of the structure is 36 m. Steel cables inserted in the membranes in the form of arches transmit the uplift forces produced by the internal pressure in the cushion roof into 16 anchorages. Hinged steel plates retain and arrest the cable ends as well as the so-called travelling cables. When the structure is closed both membranes are fixed to the concrete foundation. In summer the anchorages are released from the ground plates and, being raised by the internal pressure, the roof glides 4 m upward. It is then held in position by the travelling cables. In case of high wind load the internal pressure of 30 mm of water pressure is being increased.

Being open on all sides in summer the structure serves as coffee shop for the visitors of the neighbouring swimming pool (see p. 133) and is also used for open air theatre performances. During the cold season when the walls are closed the structure, which can be heated, is to be used for exhibitions, lectures, theatre performances and so on.

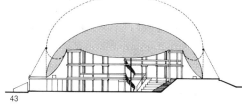

43

44

45, 46, Movil

Design: José Miguel de Prada Poole
Manufacture: Tolder S.A. and students of the Escuela Tecnica Superior de Arquitectura, Madrid

This is a prototype whose potential uses have not yet been thoroughly investigated. The structure becomes mobile by controlling the positive pressure of the cushions, which are independent of one another. It is a solution related to the "Dynamat" (see p. 56) whose further development promises interesting results.

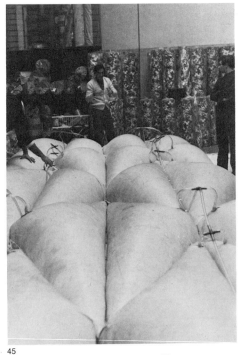

45

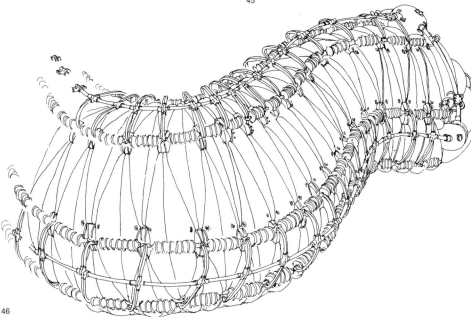

46

47, 48. Discontinuous structure – trial construction for Expoplastica 69

Design: José Miguel de Prada Poole, 1968
Manufacture: Alcudia S.A., 1969

Hexagons made of two layers of plastic foil were attached at their edges and inflated. Fig. 47 shows the model built in 1968, in which each individual cushion is connected to a central fan by means of an external air pipe. The prototype shown at the exhibition was about 5 m high.
The structure is worthy of mention because here the attempt was made to erect a dome from low pressure cushions without a supporting framework.

49. Projection screen at the Deutsche Industrieausstellung 1968, Berlin

Design: Frei Otto and Bernd-Friedrich Romberg
Manufacture: L. Stromeyer & Co., GmbH

This structure became known as the first membrane structure stressed by internal negative pressure.
In contrast to positive pressure structures producing an interior cavity that can be utilised in case of low pressure, membranes stressed by negative pressure need additional auxiliary structures – here a steel frame with tension cables – which keep apart the membrane surfaces as they are drawn inwards.
The scope for negative pressure structures in architecture has received little investigation as yet.

50. Modular inflatable cushion structures

Design: Eventstructure Research Group, 1970

Triangular cushions with a lateral length of 8 m are flexibly connected and can be assembled in various different forms. The apexes are held by a central mast with cables.

47

48

49

51

51–56. Modular Construction system made of self-supporting elements
Design: Gernot Minke, 1972

These polyhedrons also have flexible connections between their lateral surfaces. They consist of flat pneumatic cushions that are self-supporting and can be added to form structural shapes of all kinds.

57–59. Filling elements for grid shells
Design: Gernot Minke with students of the Technische Hogeschool Delft, 1971

The studies were also carried out with double membrane elements in the form of regular polygons. The intention was not to seek new detail solutions but to show some possibilities existing in the connection of light grid shells and pneumatically stabilised cushions. With flat structures such as these an easily visible anticlastic curvature appears at the corners.

54

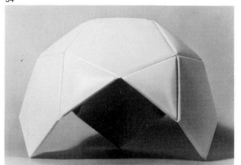

57

52

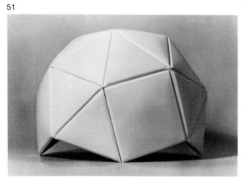

55

58

53

56

59

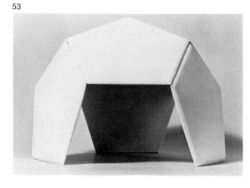

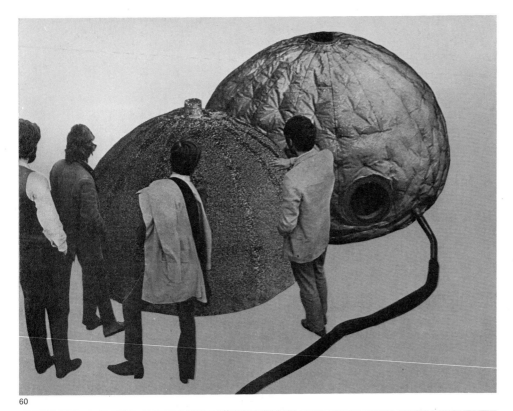

60

61

63

62

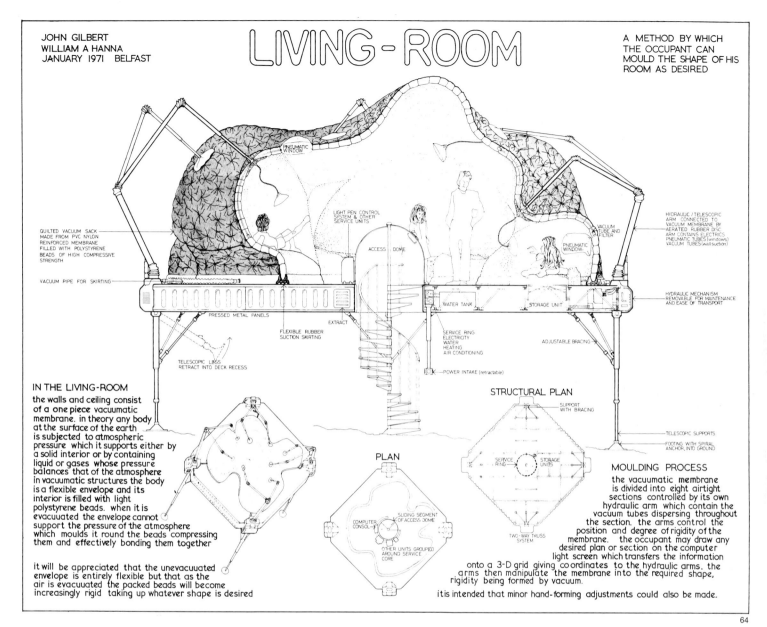

LIVING-ROOM

JOHN GILBERT
WILLIAM A HANNA
JANUARY 1971 BELFAST

A METHOD BY WHICH
THE OCCUPANT CAN
MOULD THE SHAPE OF HIS
ROOM AS DESIRED

PNEUMATIC WINDOW

LIGHT PEN CONTROL
SYSTEM & OTHER
SERVICE UNITS

QUILTED VACUUM SACK
MADE FROM PVC NYLON
REINFORCED MEMBRANE
FILLED WITH POLYSTYRENE
BEADS OF HIGH COMPRESSIVE
STRENGTH

ACCESS DOME

VACUUM
TUBE AND
FILTER

PNEUMATIC
WINDOW

HYDRAULIC / TELESCOPIC
ARM CONNECTED TO
VACUUM MEMBRANE BY
AERATED RUBBER DISC
ARM CONTAINS ELECTRICS
PNEUMATIC TUBES (windows)
VACUUM TUBES (wall suction)

VACUUM PIPE FOR SKIRTING

HYDRAULIC MECHANISM
REMOVABLE FOR MAINTENANCE
AND EASE OF TRANSPORT

PRESSED METAL PANELS

EXTRACT

WATER TANK

STORAGE UNIT

FLEXIBLE RUBBER
SUCTION SKIRTING

SERVICE RING
ELECTRICITY
WATER
HEATING
AIR CONDITIONING

ADJUSTABLE BRACING

TELESCOPIC LEGS
RETRACT INTO DECK RECESS

POWER INTAKE (retractable)

STRUCTURAL PLAN

SUPPORT
WITH BRACING

IN THE LIVING-ROOM

the walls and ceiling consist
of a one piece vacuumatic
membrane. in theory any body
at the surface of the earth
is subjected to atmospheric
pressure which it supports either by
a solid interior or by containing
liquid or gases whose pressure
balances that of the atmosphere
in vacuumatic structures the body
is a flexible envelope and its
interior is filled with light
polystyrene beads. when it is
evacuuated the envelope cannot
support the pressure of the atmosphere
which moulds it round the beads compressing
them and effectively bonding them together

it will be appreciated that the unevacuuated
envelope is entirely flexible but that as the
air is evacuuated the packed beads will become
increasingly rigid taking up whatever shape is desired

PLAN

COMPUTER
CONSOL

SLIDING SEGMENT
OF ACCESS DOME

OTHER UNITS GROUPED
AROUND SERVICE CORE

SERVICE
RING

STORAGE
UNITS

TWO-WAY TRUSS
SYSTEM

TELESCOPIC SUPPORTS

FOOTING WITH SPIRAL
ANCHOR INTO GROUND

MOULDING PROCESS

the vacuumatic membrane
is divided into eight airtight
sections controlled by its own
hydraulic arm which contain the
vacuum tubes dispersing throughout
the section. the arms control the
position and degree of rigidity of the
membrane. the occupant may draw any
desired plan or section on the computer
light screen which transfers the information
onto a 3-D grid giving coordinates to the hydraulic arms. the
arms then manipulate the membrane into the required shape,
rigidity being formed by vacuum.

it is intended that minor hand-forming adjustments could also be made.

64

60—64. Vacuumatics

Design and manufacture: John Gilbert, Marcus Patton, Chris Mullen, and Stanley Black, under the direction of Ivan Petrović, 1970

Vacuumatics have developed as a result of a course on space cell construction at Queen's University, Belfast. The novelty of the technical principle involved, the care taken in its working out and the resulting prospects for its use certainly make this structure one of the most significant since Lanchester's time in the field of pneumatic structures.

The vacuumatics consist of two membrane layers between which is a filling of light granular material. When the air between the membranes has been extracted the external atmospheric pressure forces the membrane against the filling material which in turn is more strongly compressed. In order to maintain a plane structure the membranes are coupled together by local individual connections. The filling material also provides point support to the membrane.

As the negative pressure increases the resulting shell becomes stiffer. Thus the rigidity of such a "negative pressure mattress" can be increased or decreased as required and the form of the structure can thereby be changed.

Vacuumatics are on the fringe of pneumatic structures. The loadbearing capacity is produced only under negative pressure by a compound material with a porous composition (granulate) and reinforced boundary areas (membranes). Without the availability of this negative pressure the structure would consist only of slack membranes with granular filling. Thus the negative pressure is a structural element. The rounding-off of the membrane, which

is characteristic of pneumatic structures, takes place in the micro area, as the section shows.

The significant advantages of "Vacuumatics" over conventional pneumatic structures are the random variability of form produced by a temporary reduction in negative pressure as well as the outstanding properties of thermal insulation inherent in the use of light synthetic globules (e. g. Styropor).

The domes shown in Fig. 60 were investigated to find their loadbearing capacity under snow load and their thermal insulation properties. A further six geometric forms were tested for maximum tension. Nine different membrane materials and six different filling materials were compared with each other in twenty technical properties. The prototypes were constructed out of nylon reinforced PVC membranes with Styropor filling.

65

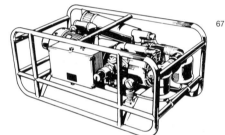

67

68

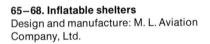

66

69

65–68. Inflatable shelters
Design and manufacture: M. L. Aviation
Company, Ltd.

The series-produced pneumatic sandwich panels, of which an English example is shown, have excellent mechanical properties. The insulation capacity is also very high. The panels manufactured by the M. L. Aviation Company are 12 cm thick and consist of two membrane coatings each of which is built from several layers. The two coatings are held apart by nylon threads positioned very close to each other (further details see p. 145). The panels form segments of polygonal buildings of different sizes and shapes. The buildings are guyed on the outside so that the dome in Fig. 66, for example, can withstand wind velocity of 160 km/h without damage. Technical components such as air conditioning equipment, electrical switchgear and a generator to maintain the internal pressure of the panels (which can also act as a decompressor – Fig. 67) are also supplied with this highly

developed system of construction. Fig. 68 shows a half cylindrical structure with spherical ends (as shown in Fig. 65, but with three central sections) when packed for transportation.

69. Inflatostair – emergency exit for aircraft
Design and manufacture: Goodyear Aerospace Corp.

Inflatable escape slides have long proved their value in aircraft crash landings on land and sea. Gangways, which can also be inflated in seconds, are more comfortable. The wall construction is similar to that of the pneumatic sandwich panels. The example illustrates the complicated individual forms that can be produced when using pneumatic elements. (Bibl. 44, p. 157 ff.)

70–73. Emergency first aid stations
Design and manufacture: Krupp Universalbau

This modular construction unit consists of a tent system, in which a light steel framework is spanned by "air mattresses". Only the covering for the access locks is made out of non-pneumatically stressed membranes. The additional metal support structure was chosen to prevent a collapse in the event of extensive damage to the membrane.

The air space in the "mattresses" provides heat insulation and can also be supplied with cooled air according to external conditions. The tent interior is under a light positive pressure of 10 to 15 mm of water pressure.

70

71

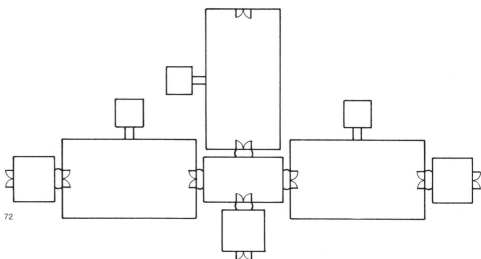

72

73

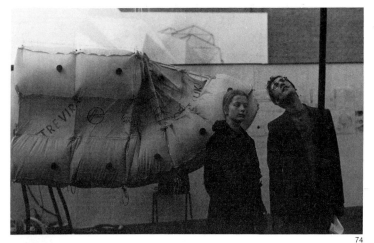

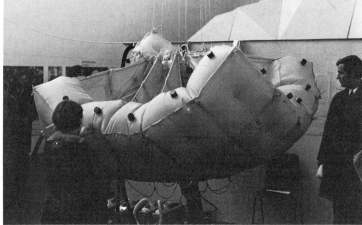

74

75

74–78. Dynamat
Design: Simon Conolly and Mark Fisher, 1971

The elements presented here also originate from the British Isles, as do so many innovations in the field of pneumatic structures. The Dynamat, whose prototype was exhibited at the DEUBAU 1971 in Essen, is one example of a whole series of similar attempts in which the user is given the opportunity of creating an environment for himself and of manipulating its form. The volume of the folded mat is over one hundred times smaller than the envelope when opened out.

The changes in shape are not achieved by mechanical means but by mere alteration of the air pressure in the individual cells, which are separated from each other by airtight divisions. These cells are connected to the central control by 3 mm tubing, and are held vertically by rigid alloy tubes.

By regulating the air input, individual or total movements of the structure are carried out centrally or decentrally.

The mat consists of individual square elements, which can be composed to form surfaces of any size by means of zip fasteners. The stage of development shown cannot, however, be viewed as final since the taking up of transverse forces, for example, has not yet been fully mastered structurally.
(Bibl. 38.)

77

78

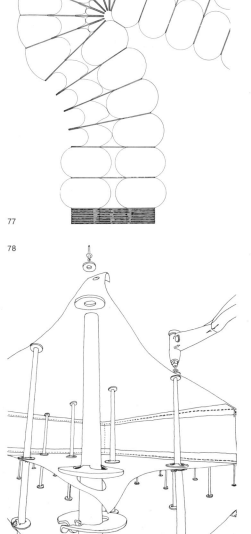

76

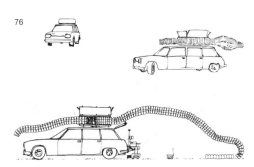

79–81. Air cushion roof over the stage of an open air theatre in Ratingen near Dusseldorf
Design and manufacture: Krupp Universalbau, 1962

The roof is only used during the season and is suspended by cables from a light steel mast. The lower membrane is additionally supported by a band of parallel cables, and the air cushions are connected to each other by tubes.

82–84. "Helium Lifted Canopy" for covering Wembley Stadium, London
Design: Arthur Quarmby
Structural advice: David Powell

The very flat helium cushion is anchored against wind loading by means of guy cables all round the Stadium. Whether the uplift of the gas is sufficient to prevent fluttering of the membrane which spans round the remaining area of the Stadium would still have to be investigated.

85, 86. Pavilion for a travelling exhibition of the U.S. Atomic Energy Commission
Design: Joseph Eldredge
Manufacture: Birdair Structures, Inc., 1964

The lower membrane was supported by cables which ran from the footings to the top of a mast standing in the middle of the building. Thus a strong profile was created from below, which considerably improved the acoustic quality of the room. On its outside the structure obtained the significant shape of a dome with guys at its perimeter between which the membrane forces were taken up by cables.

The travelling exhibition visited Central and South America.

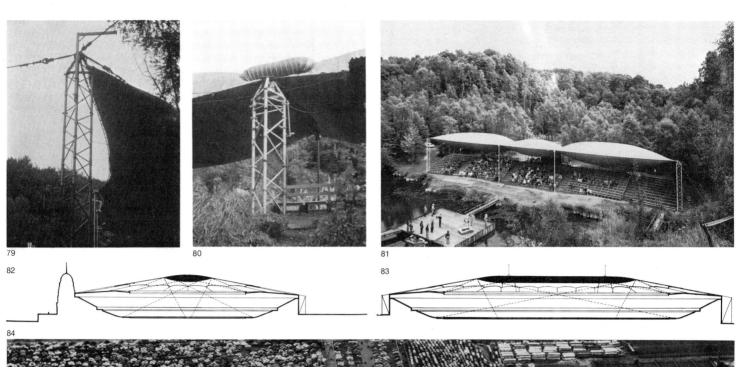

79

80

81

82

83

84

85

86

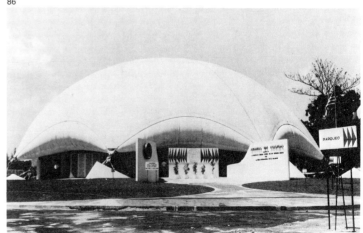

87

88

89

AUFHÄNGESEILE

B

A

A

STÜTZTELLER ZUR HALTERUNG
DER OBEREN HAUT BEI DRUCKAUSFALL

B

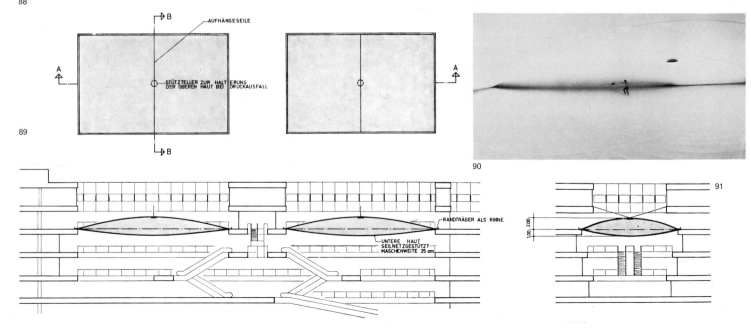

90

91

RANDTRÄGER ALS RINNE

UNTERE HAUT
SEILNETZGESTÜTZT
MASCHENWEITE 25 cm

1.00 | 2.00

87–91. Roof covering for the inner court of Forum Steglitz, Berlin
Design: Bernd-Friedrich Romberg
Manufacture: L. Stromeyer & Co. GmbH, 1970

There were somewhat less than four months available for the planning and execution of these pneumatics. The skeleton structure was already completed, and it permitted only low additional loadings from the added structure. On the narrow sides it was not possible to make a connection to the ceilings. Here IPB 800s are arranged as horizontal supports, able to receive a considerable load due to the low arching of the cushion in that area. As only a very slight sag was permitted in the lower skin of the cushion, additional support nets of 4 mm thick steel cables with a mesh size of 25 cm are stretched beneath it (see p. 156). The upper skin is arched with a rise of 2 m maximum over the top edge of the concrete ceiling. The internal pressure is 10 mm of water pressure. Both the upper skin and the lower net-supported skin are accessible for maintenance and cleaning purposes. Zip fasteners in the upper skins provide this access.

The interior of the cushion cannot be described within conventional categories. With almost shadowless illumination floor and ceiling meet along an equidistant horizon, and the floor yields at every step like a trampoline. This room – an unforeseen and unintended "by-product" of cushion design – seemed to the architect in retrospect to be the most important outcome of the work.

The air supply of the pneumatics is by means of continuous fans. As the low internal pressure is not sufficient for full snow loads and as, on the other hand, snow covering would seriously impede the passage of light, the air input is warmed to +45 °C in winter. The constant air flow produces a sufficiently high surface temperature on the outer skin for any snow falling on it to immediately melt and run off. The gutters are also heated.

In the tops of the cushions there are additional support discs which are carried by cables. When the air flow is interrupted, e.g. for maintenance and cleaning work, they prevent dropping and reverse sagging of the upper skin.

Inside lighting is installed which automatically switches on when daylight ends.

Each cushion weighs about 750 kg and receives 10,000 m³ air per hour. To avoid the formation of condensation inside, the air supply consists of 60% fresh air and 40% recirculated air.
(Bibl. 138.)

92

93

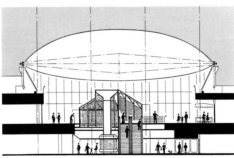

94

92–95. Roof covering of the shopping street in the "City" of Marl
Design: H. Kloss, P. Kolb + Partner – H. Drinhausen, 1970
Manufacture: Krupp Universalbau and Steffens & Nölle, 1974

As roof covering for the 185 m long shopping street, sliding roofs were first taken into consideration. However, the idea was renounced because of the free span being as much as 28 m wide. Steel and glass structures such as the 19th century passages had also to be ruled out – mainly for architectural reasons and on account of their architectural reasons and on account of their low suitability for mining subsidence areas.

The pneumatic structure eventually chosen consists of three not interdependent cushions supported by cables. The two outer cushions are 58.80 m long, the middle one being 67.20 m long, and their width throughout is 29.40 m. A steel framework with bending resistant edge girders and guyed compression struts, which take up the horizontal forces from the membrane cables, serves to stabilize the structure and to maintain its from. The membranes are made of PVC coated polyester fabric; the fibre materials is Diolen superfest produced by Enka Glanzstoff AG.

Each cushion has an inflation unit of its own. Each unit includes two radial fans one of which is enough to maintain the necessary pressurisation of 30 mm of water pressure in the interior of the cushions.
(Bibl. 169.)

95

96, 97. Roof covering for radar and television aerials

Design: William Fischer and Sandy Hook
Manufacturer: Air Cruisers Company

In contrast to the usual radomes made of single membranes, this structure is so rigid that contact between the membrane and the antennae because of wind load is virtually impossible.

The membranes consist of neoprene coated Dacron with an outer Hypalon coating. They are divided up into eight curved sections, anchored to the ground by means of guyed flanges. In some cases tubes for water ballast are also built into the wall. The wall sections are connected to each other by stainless steel clamps through which runs a fastening cable (see p. 148). The dismantling of individual sections allows large items to be transported in or out. The internal positive pressure in each wall is 400 to 1,400 mm of water pressure according to wind loading, and is produced by electric compressors. The walls are separated into individual chambers by internal membrane ribs that give linear support to the external membrane.

The radome has a weight of 770 kg and a diameter of 13 m; the wall thickness is 2 m at the ground and 1.40 m at the top. Erection takes about 3 hours.

A total of about 20 such buildings have been erected throughout the world.

(Bibl. 131, p. 163 ff and p. 236; DBP 1 559 112.)

98–100. Transportable air supported bridge

Design and manufacture: Military Engineering Experimental Establishment (England), 1965

The 350 kg bridge under high pressure can carry a load of 1,000 kg at a span of 5.50 m. The central section as well as the two ramps are divided along their length into separate chambers by internal membrane ribs. In the tension zone there run wires similar to the reinforcement in reinforced concrete. The membrane consists of a three layered neoprene coated fabric.

101–103. Inflatable structures with variable shape and volume

Design: Michel Fourtané, 1969

These are flat structures which are put together from inter-connected chambers. Air is not only the support medium, for when its pressure changes air also causes the structures to change their shape and move in a predetermined manner. (DBP 1 961 523.)

96

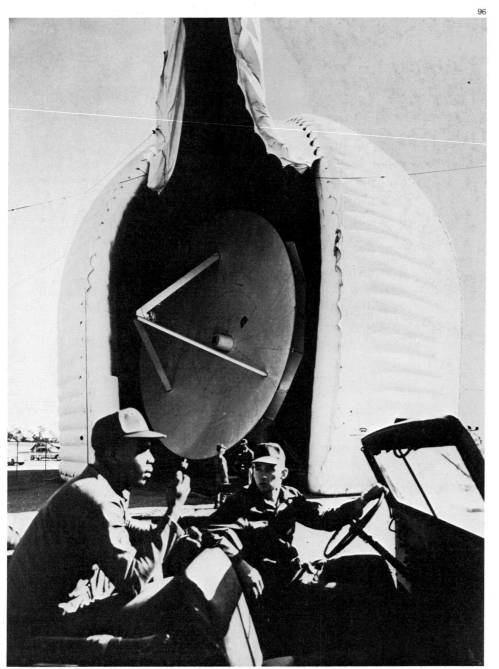

97

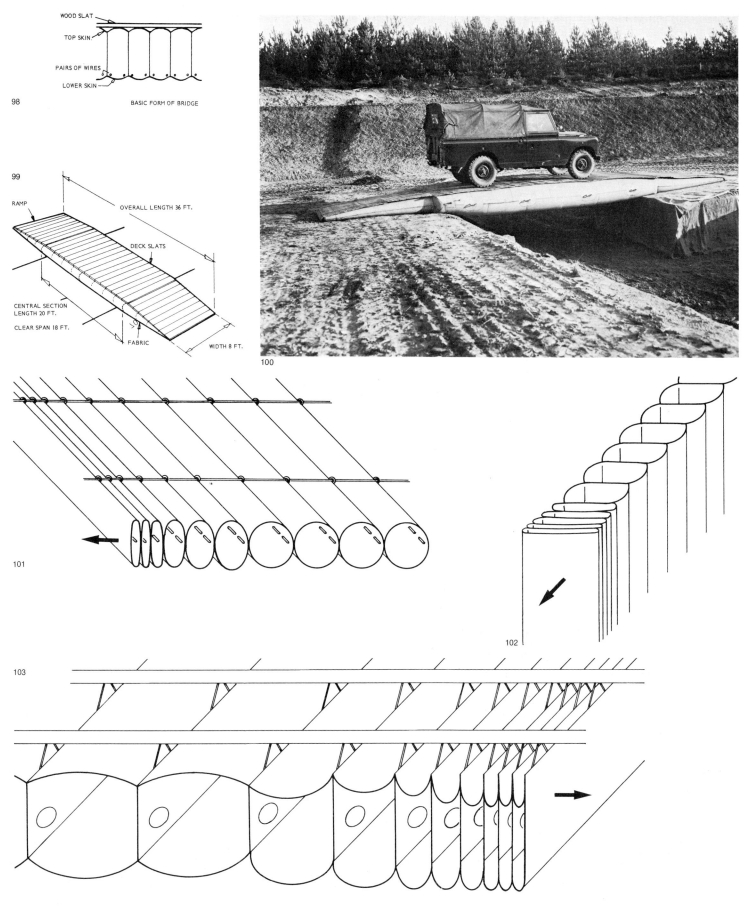

WOOD SLAT

TOP SKIN

PAIRS OF WIRES

LOWER SKIN

98   BASIC FORM OF BRIDGE

99

RAMP

OVERALL LENGTH 36 FT.

DECK SLATS

CENTRAL SECTION
LENGTH 20 FT.

CLEAR SPAN 18 FT.

FABRIC

WIDTH 8 FT.

100

101

102

103

104. Pneumatic environment

Design: Quasar Khan
Manufacture: Kléber Renolit Plastiques, 1968

Khan, a Vietnamese living in Paris, who has become world famous through his blow-up furniture, has created this transparent environment out of PVC foil. The flat form of the room boundaries was produced by internal membrane ribs. The joints are welded.

104

105–108. Roof of the all weather swimming pool at Unterlüss, near Celle

Design: Bernd-Friedrich Romberg, 1968–72
Manufacture: Steffens & Nölle, L. Stromeyer & Co. GmbH, and C. Haushahn, 1972

A traversable envelope made of PVC coated polyester fabric and fixed to three of the steel arches spanning the swimming pool enables the installation to be used as an indoor pool when closed and stabilised with positive pressure of 30 min of water pressure, and as an outdoor pool when open.

The central arch has a span of 26.35 m and a rise at centre span of 13.58 m, while the two outer arches have spans of 20.70 m each and a rise at centre span of 10.75 m. In the longitudinal direction of the hall the arches are stabilised against tilting by means of two guy ropes, anchored to two terminal foundations far outside the hall. Six pulleys run along each arch, between which supporting wires span longitudinally. The envelope in the limp condition is folded up over these wires. On the firmly anchored side the envelope is fastened to a profile on the upper edge of the sloping ramp surface above the roof of the massive cloakroom block; the movable side is bounded by a square pipe. The envelope consists of two layers of polyester fabric with an intermediate air space of 3 cm which is additionally aerated for better insulation and in order to prevent condensation. The two layers are connected to each other at 50 cm centres by means of pointed plastic spacers.

The opening and closing of each takes five minutes only. The roof can be laid completely folded on the sloping ramp over the large block, so that when open only the three arches with the guy cables over the swimming pool can be seen. (Bibl. 154.)

105

106

107

108

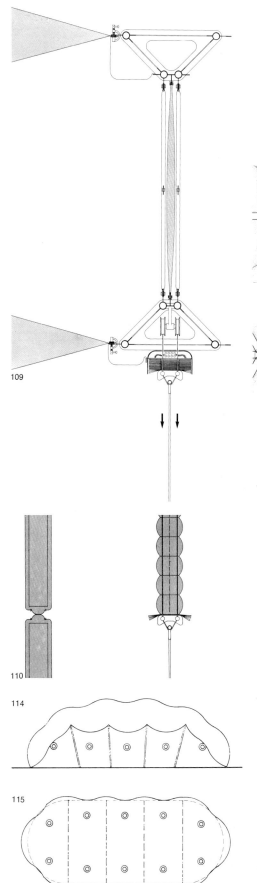

109

110

114

115

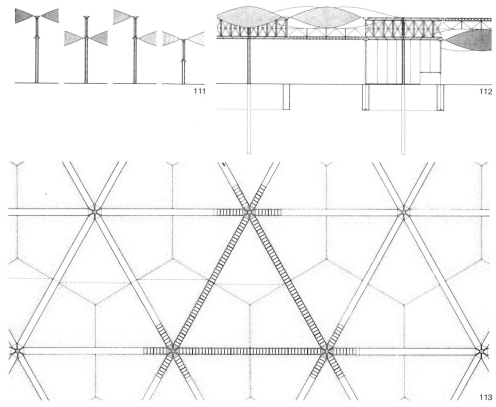

111

112

113

109–113. Alterable fairground halls
Design: Thomas Herzog, 1972

For the solution of the problem of spanning a fairground with an alterable roof a construction has been developed which is based on a 60° grid pattern with 28.8 m lateral sides supporting a steel frame structure with pneumatically stressed membranes as roof and façade elements. In consideration of the purpose to use the site either as an open air fairground or to cover the whole of it with a roof or to use only part of it to put up exhibition pavilions, a principle of construction appeared to be called for which would enable the structural members to change their volumes to an extreme degree. To obtain this objective pneumatic structures have so far proved to be much more suitable than any other principle of lightweight construction.

At all the crossing points of the grid there are vertical shafts inside which steel pillars are sunk in the ground. These steel pillars can be extended up to a maximum length of 11 m by motors which are installed at the two ends of the 4 m high truss girders. If the drive assemblies are being reversed the girders "climb" up the pillars.

The façade elements are drawn up with the girders. They can be arrested at any point by a holding up device. The air not only serves to stabilise the façade parts but also to move them.

114–116. Hall roofs
Design: Ana Sklenar, 1972

The double membrane structure is point supported by means of rings on the outer membrane and linear supported by means of pressure arches on the inner membrane.

116

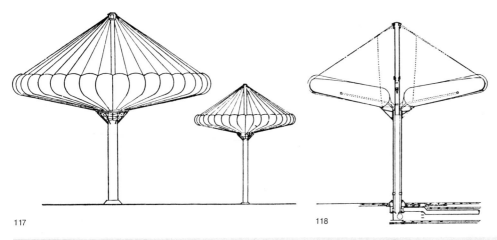

117   118   119

117–122. Mobile roofs at Expo '70, Osaka

Design: Tanero Oki & Ass.
Structural calculations: Shiger Aoki & Ass.
Manufacture: Taiyo Kogyo Co., Ltd., 1970

The mushroom-shaped red and yellow double membrane structure stood in "Expoland", the amusement park of the world exhibition. The diameter of the mushrooms when open varied between 15 and 35 m.

The pneumatically stabilised surfaces were guyed with radial cables to the centre masts, and if the cables were retracted the mushrooms closed.

When open the support pressure was 200 mm of water pressure; when closed it was 400 mm under wind speed loadings of over 15 m/sec. The membrane material was PVA and polyester fabric with PVC coating.

120

121

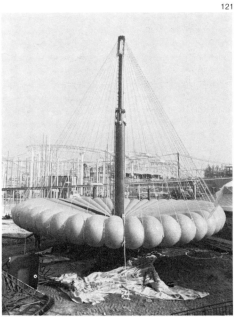

122

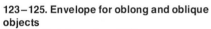

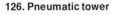

123 · · · 124 · · · 125

123–125. Envelope for oblong and oblique objects
Design: Frei Otto, circa 1960

The model shows a rotational body with harmonic stress distribution in different inclinations.

126. Pneumatic tower
Design and manufacture: RAVEN Industries, Inc.

The cone is some 30 m high. The membrane tensions are decreasing toward the apex, a fact which manifests itself clearly in slight wrinkles at the top.

127. Air supported tower
Design and manufacture: Birdair Structures, Inc., 1959

Here the tensions run more uniformly, but the tower is so slender that it has to be guyed. The height is 24 m.

128. Inflatable mast
Design and manufacture: Ministry of Technology, Research Development Establishment (England)

Here the cross-section is cylindrical right to the top. The height of this quickly erected mast is 30 m and the positive pressure is 1,400 mm of water pressure.

126 · · · 127 · · · 128

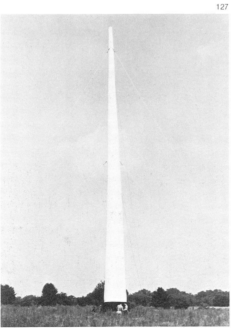

129, 130. Fabridam

Design: N.M. Imbertson and Associates
Manufacture: Firestone Coated Fabrics Company, 1957

The first dams constructed by Firestone were 1.50 m high and 40 m long. Today the height can be over 4 m and the length over 600 m.
The membrane tube made of heavy neoprene coated polyamid fabric is screwed on to a concrete base in the river and is filled with water or air. The overflow height can be raised or lowered simply through pumping or discharging.

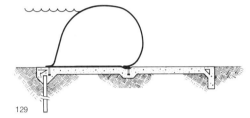

129

130

Within a few minutes the internal support medium can be completely emptied and the membrane will then lie flat on the concrete base; such a quick reaction to tidal waves is not possible with any conventional structure.
If the outside of the membrane is regularly given a new coat of Hypalon, then a life span of about 20 years can be anticipated.
Fabridams cost 75% less to manufacture than conventional dam constructions.
(Bibl. 10.)

131, 132. Dipole antenna

Design and manufacture: RAVEN Industries, Inc.

The membrane of this dipole antenna, which has been developed for use in outer space, is stabilised only by weak positive pressure.

133. Inflatable hoist for lifting persons or goods

Design and manufacture: Ministry of Technology, Research Development Establishment (England), 1970

A cradle made of a pair of rollers and a strap device for carrying goods is fixed to a fire hose. The rollers are closely fixed so that they clamp the hose airtight. If this is inflated from one end, then the rollers and the goods travel to the other end. To raise a man of average weight vertically, a positive pressure of 2,000 mm of water pressure is required (the maximum load capacity is 280,000 mm of water pressure).
The British Central Electricity Authority uses the inflatable hoist for the inspection and maintenance of overhead lines. Small rockets shoot a retaining line over a suitable attachment point. The compressor is carried in the car.
(Bibl. 44, p. 152.)

131

132

133

134

135

136

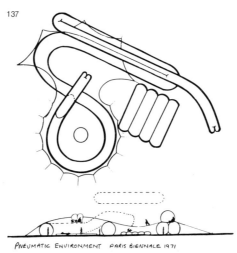

137

PNEUMATIC ENVIRONMENT   PARIS BIENNALE 1971

138

139

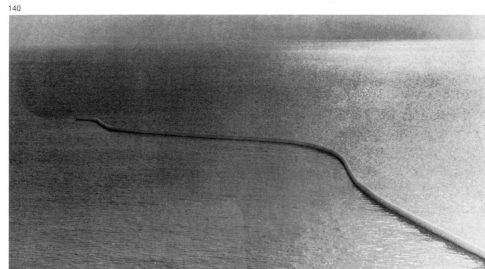

140

139, 140. Wavetube
Design: Graham A. Stevens, 1967

Concerned are ways and means of transporting persons and cargo through long tubes stabilised by air pressure.

In its simplest form the Wavetube is a locked-up tube floating on water, in which a kind of hovercraft is "surfing" shorewards with the waves. To translate this into a system usable over ground and independent of waves, a smaller, open ended tube with air passing through it is laid along the bottom. A hoverpallet serves as vehicle. Its weight creates a partial seal and the pressure build-up creates a wavefront which pushes the pallet forward.

The system is simple and if adequately elaborated can be used in a wide range of conditions and dimensions.
(Bibl. 155.)

141, 142. Passage connecting two buildings in Milan
Design: Studio d'Architettura e Industrial Design, 1968
Manufacture: Plasteco Milano, 1968

This PVC tunnel, which connected the Palazzo Esposizioni with the Padiglione della Produzione Italiana at the 14th Triennale, was 60 m long. Four positive pressure tubes formed the loadbearing part and the walls were single membranes not pneumatically stabilised, which were stressed by a cable running above the tunnel. The window frames were small pneumatically stressed ring tubes.

141

142

134, 135. Bridge over the Maschsee, Hanover
Design and manufacture: Eventstructure Research Group, 1970

This tube bridge was installed during the street art programme in August 1970. It was 250 m long and had a diameter of 4 m. In order to prevent rotation of the structure a small waterfilled hose was installed underneath which acted as ballast as soon as it came out of the water at one side.

The upper part of the tube consisted of 0.4 mm thick PVC sheet, the lower of coated fabric. The bridge was fixed to the floor of the lake at 4 m intervals.

136–138. Pneumatic Environment
Design: Graham A. Stevens, 1971

This arrangement was designed by Stevens on the occasion of the Septième Biennale de Paris. It was intended to demonstrate possible means of expression in form rather than technical functions.

143–149. Inflatable Kindergarten

Design and manufacture: Seminar Pneumatische Konstruktionen, Institut für Umweltplanung, Ulm, under the direction of Gernot Minke, 1972

The 60 m² trial structure consists of 120 m² PVC sheet with a thickness of 0.5 mm and 60 m² PVC coated polyester fabric.

Access is by "lip doors"; the membrane pouches, which open inwards, are pressed together by positive pressure so that they are self-sealing.

The fan has a power input of 0.16 KW. With 15 changes of air per hour it produces a positive pressure of 10 mm of water pressure.

143

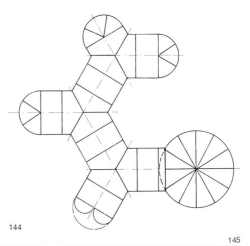

144

145

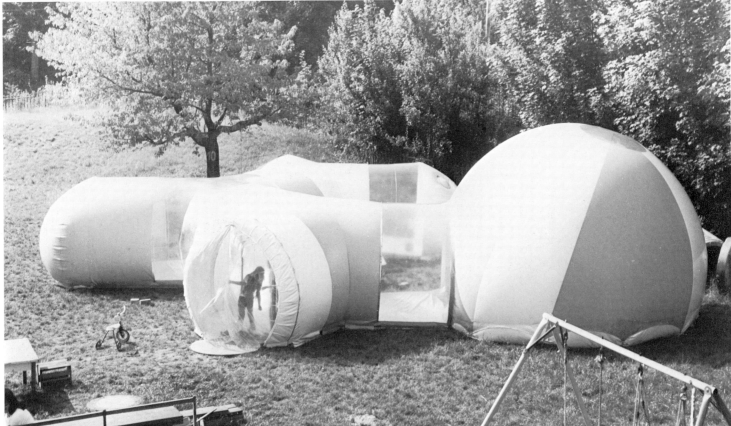

146
147
148

149

150

151

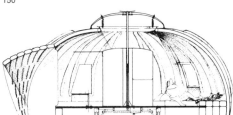

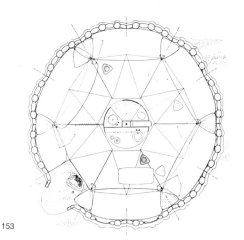

153

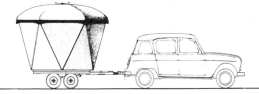

150–152. Pneumatic spiral

Design and manufacture: Tom Colborn, Paddy Acheson, William A. Hanna, and Robin McKelvey under the direction of Graham Hardy, 1968

Because of its cutting pattern the spiral has a tendency to draw together so that the coils are pressed hard on one another. Thus in addition to the normal membrane stresses, there are also torsional and bending stresses, which act like "prestress" on the structure and give it a certain stiffness against lateral forces. It would be even better if the individual lays of the spiral could be prevented, by means of additional connections, from displacing each other.

153, 154. Caravan with variable volume

Design: Jean Louis Lotiron and Pernette Martin-Perriand, 1967

During the journey the volume of the caravan is reduced to the utility unit and takes up a mere 6 m³. On arriving at its base, the small compressor attached to the car motor can inflate the dome in less than half an hour. The dome consists of individual tubes and covers an area of almost 25 m².
The floor of the dome is formed by the folding-down casing of the utility unit; its top part is a pneumatically raised light and ventilation dome. Six pneumatic beds. and six swivelling wardrobes are supplied as furniture.
(Bibl. 50, p. 16.)

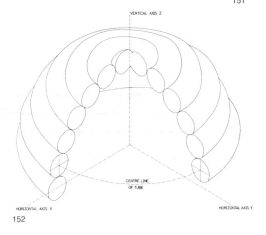

152

157, 158. RFD rescue islands

Design: RFD-GQ, Ltd.
Manufacture: RFD-GQ, Ltd.; Autoflug GmbH

These "floating shelters" are supported by two tube-like pontoons that inflate automatically and with great reliability in seconds. They are carried on ships and aeroplanes.

155

156

155. MUST (Medical Unit, Self-contained, Transportable)

Design and manufacture: Air Cruisers Company

MUST consists of sections of 12 tubes each with a cross-section of 30×50 cm, which when placed one behind the other form barrel-shaped rooms of any length. The air spaces in the tube are separated from each other but are inflated simultaneously. The membranes are made of Dacron fabric with neoprene coating and an outer Hypalon coat. For safety reasons, inside every tube there is a second tube made of nylon with a neoprene coating. The positive pressure is 1,000 mm of water pressure.

A building made of four sections can be erected by eight people in 30 minutes. It is subsequently secured by guys and can thus withstand wind speeds of up to 130 km/h.

About 400 buildings of this kind have been used since 1968 as field hospitals in Vietnam.
(Bibl. 131, p. 161 ff.)

156. Numax house

Design and manufacture: RFD-GQ, Ltd.

The Numax house is mainly used in the military field and as a shelter in disaster areas, where the small volume of the pack and quick erection (some eight minutes) are particularly important features.

The tubular framework supporting a weather proof membrane is called a low pressure structure (1400 mm of water pressure) by the manufacturer and in the technical literature (Bibl. 44, p. 138; Bibl. 131, p. 211). Air expansion bags are attached to the tube structure in order to compensate for the increasing pressure due to heating by solar radiation.

Inflation of the structure is achieved by use of a fan that can be connected to car batteries, or by means of bellows. The valves are at the front ends.

157

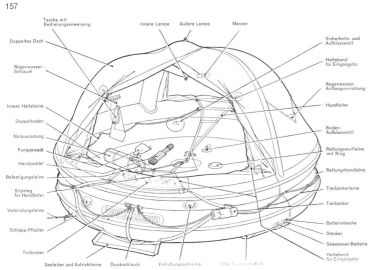

158

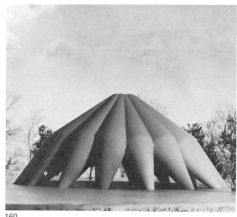

160

159

159, 160. Beach pavilion
Design: Frei Otto, before 1962

The double cones are connected at the points of contact and can therefore be inflated from one point. The compressor is situated under one of the cones.

161

162

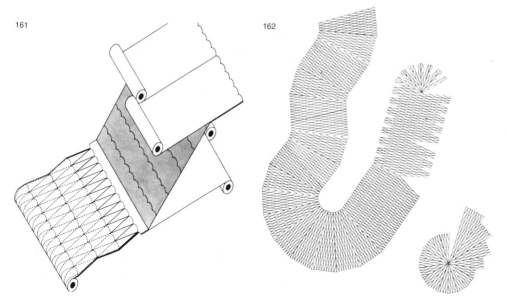

161–171. Construction system for pneumatic shells
Design: Winfried Wurm, 1968

In contrast to the double cones of Frei Otto's beach pavilion, these elements are not buckled on the inside, thus allowing also curved cross-sections of the building to be produced.
The factors to be considered in the manufacture of these structures from two membrane layers are of special interest (Fig. 161). As the seams run through there are no connection problems between the elements of a section. The inner membrane is made up by the coated fabric running from the roll without any cutting pattern or any processing. The outer membrane is folded by the roll into lengths corresponding to half the length of the double cone and sewn as folded into the shape of an arch. Then the inner and outer membranes are matched and sewn together in a straight line.

If high thermal insulation and resistance to snow loads are required, rigidising foam is used instead of pressurised air in the chamber. This foam is a mixture of resin, an expanding agent and a hardening agent that rises up of its own accord and produces an adjustable positive pressure before it hardens after about three minutes. In this construction system the membranes are, in fact, being stressed by a pneumatic process; however, this process serves to create a sandwich-like structure densified towards the upper surface which no longer represents an air supported structure.

The number of breaks in the curve of a structure can be arbitrarily laid down. On it depends the ratio of slenderness of the double cone. There are mathematical formulae that on the one hand represent the form relationships between the number of breaks, the length of the cone and the largest cone diameter, and on the other hand permit the statically correct dimensioning of the structure.

By combining differently constructed individual sections many different plan forms can be produced (Fig. 162).

In collaboration with the DLW Aktiengesellschaft and the Kunststoffbüro München GmbH & Co., a prototype was made with a span of 9.5 m and an average diameter of the cone of 0.8 m. PVC coated polyester fabric with a tensile strength of 300 kp/5 cm was used for the membrane. Polyurethane foam with a density of 60 kg/m³ and a compression strength of 4 kp/cm² served as a foaming agent. The structure corresponded to expectations in terms of manufacture and costs. However, an early structural failure occurred under snow and wind load. A span of only 4.5 m could be achieved with semicylinders and of 9.8 m with domes.

By using thicker foam and firmer membrane material domes with spans of 50 m are supposed to be feasible.

(DBP 1 930 563.)

164

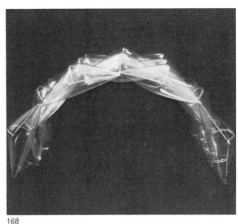
168

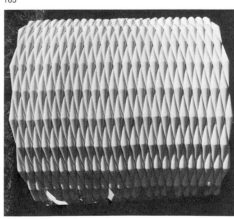
165

169

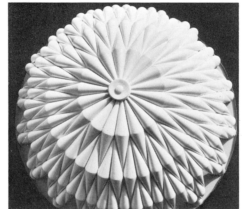
166

167

163

170   171

172–183. Fuji Pavilion, Expo '70, Osaka
Design: Yutaka Murata
Structural calculations: Mamoru Kawaguchi
Manufacture: Taiyo Kogyo Co., Ltd., and Ogawa
Tents Co., Ltd., 1970

This construction, which is the largest multi-membrane structure so far built, has become world famous for its magnificent organic form. It consisted of 16 arched tubes with a diameter of 4 m and a length of 78 m, whose bases defined a circle with a diameter of 50 m. This arrangement caused the two ends of the building apex to jut forward by 7 m. The tubes were held together at 4 m intervals by an encircling horizontal band of 50 cm width. The centre arch was semicircular, the others arched higher and higher as their bases came closer together. The openings of 10 m width at both fronts served as entrances.

The tubes consisted of PVA with a tensile strength of 200 kp/cm and a weight of 3.5 kg/m². The exterior was coated with Hypalon, the interior with PVC. The lower ends were anchored in steel cylinders.

The internal pressure was normally 1000 mm of water pressure and 2500 mm in storm conditions. All tubes were connected to a central turbocompressor by means of a peripheral system of steel pipes. This turbocompressor was very efficient and could react even in a strong wind.

A slowly evolving turntable was installed inside from which a fascinating 20 minute show could be watched. Multi-projectors specially developed for this purpose threw their light on to the white interior of the tubular wall (the tubes were only coloured on the outside). Under the turntable was a pneumatic single membrane structure which sealed off a control room from dust, as well as small double membrane domes housing a bar and toilets.

When the World Exhibition was over the pavilion was destroyed (Fig. 182). In the brief time available for planning it had not been possible, in view of the many basically new technical developments, to make the building completely dismountable.

(Details see pp. 147, 148, 154.)

172

173

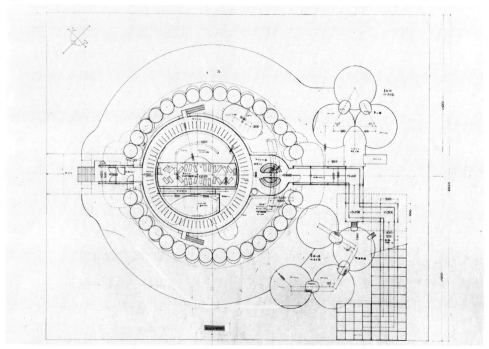

174

175

176

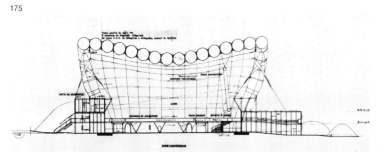

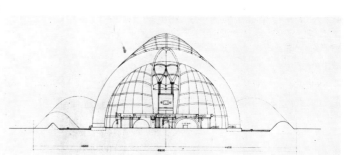

177

178

179

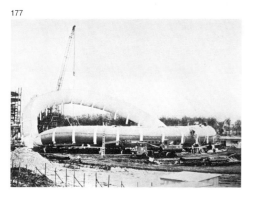

181

183

184–191. Federal German Pavilion for Expo'70, Osaka. Competition design
Design: Wolfgang Rathke and Eike Wiehe, 1968

This structure could certainly have held its own against its Japanese competitors. However, the jury gave preference to another design.

From the architects' explanatory report:

"The proposal includes the integration of building and exhibition, as desired by the competition committee, by means of the many possibilities in the programmed play of structure, space, light and shade. The cloud-like roof formation of PVC balloons can be made of transparent, translucent and coloured material that is changed in appearance by the introduction of light in the programmed play. The possibility of free agglomerations of the cellular roof formations offers every capacity for adaptation to special demands for different exhibitions or operating cycles . . . External and internal wall joints are effected by prismatically connected glass or plastic lamellae which are introduced into the balloon structure of the 'cloud'"."

In order to test the basic theories a model, scale 1:2, was erected out of 100 "pneumatic rods" under the supervision of Professor Polyoni at the Technical University in Berlin. The recorded results formed the basis of the expertise given by him, which states:

"The structure described below uses a new kind of loadbearing system that is produced by the joining together of individual air filled, vertical cylindrical balloons by means of several horizontal belt nets. This loadbearing system, which seen as a whole resembles a plane loadbearing structure in the usual sense, is able to resist bending tension and because of its low deadweight is suitable for covering large spaces with any kind of ground plan".

The structure consists of any number of cylindrical balloons and at least two horizontal belt nets. The balloon should have a diameter of 1.25 m and a height varying between 5 and 15 m. The material used is PVC coated Diolen (Polyester). At the front of each balloon there is an air inlet with a nonreturn valve. The belt nets are also made of Diolen; alternatively other fabrics or wire ropes can be used. The fabric forms a hexagonal net whose nodal points are formed by metal connection elements.

The balloon membranes are put into the prefabricated belt nets in a non-inflated state. All the balloons are connected by air tubes and all receive the required calculated pressure. Thus initial tensile stress is present in the belt net. The balloons press one against the other and take on a hexagonal form, similar to a honeycomb. Thus the two main loadbearing elements of the structure, balloon and belt net, are under tensile stress while in an externally unstressed state. The lower belt layer takes on further tensile forces when used as roof covering, while in the upper belt the tensile forces are reduced. The internal pressure of the balloon remains largely constant throughout. Thus tensile stresses occur in the structure even under load.

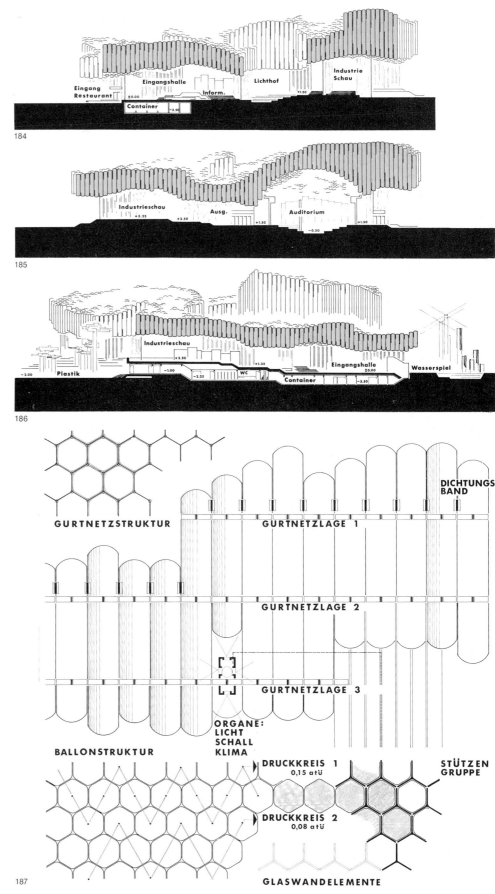

188

189

190

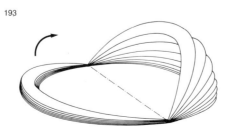

191

192

193

192, 193. Inflatable structures with variable form and volume
Design: Michel Fourtané, 1969

The similarity of these two mobile structures, both termed roofs, to Ramstein's theatre (Figs. 194–197), is striking. Certainly in the next few years buildings will be erected according to these principles.
(DBP 1961 523.)

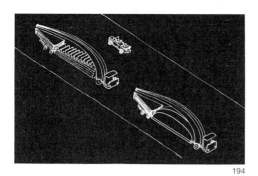

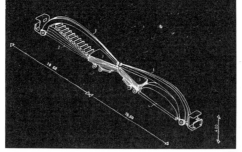

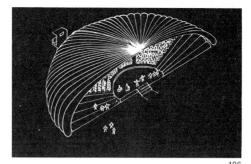

194

195

196

194–197. Travelling theatre
Design: Willi Ramstein, 1961

The significance of this project lies in the fact that as long as 15 years ago the designer recognised the opportunities offered by compressed air as a stabilising medium and as a means to move building components.

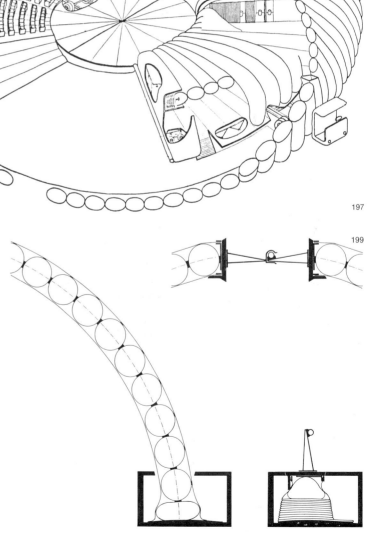

197

198, 199. Mobile roof covering
Design: Robert Laporte, Pierre Malachard des Reyssiers, 1970

This is a kinetic pneumatic structure in which the technical details have been carefully worked out.
The two halves of the building are individually inflatable and form two self-supporting structural units. When deflated each half lies in a box shaped cross-section. The uppermost tube is connected to the lid of the box which is elevated during inflation. On the lid is a stiff element made of transparent material which serves to illuminate the inside of the building and to which is attached an apparatus for connecting the two halves of the building.
(DBP 2 053 702.)

199

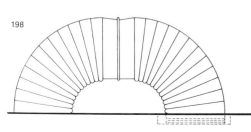

198

age and steel cables as guys against wind loading.

Christo said afterwards that the most important experience he gained from the project was to be made aware of the enormous difference between project and realisation (Bibl. 50, p. 50) – a recognition of great significance for pneumatic forms in general.

The installation shows clearly how linear support of the membrane by cables leads to a change in the radius of curvature.

201, 202. Air cushion roof for the Waldstadion, Frankfurt am Main
Design: Bernd-Friedrich Romberg, 1971

For the World Cup in 1974 FIFA required a great number of covered stands. The Frankfurt stadium, one of the grounds selected, would, according to Romberg's proposal, have a stand roof made of open membrane sections and supporting steel trusses. The architect wrote of his project (Bibl. 139):

"The envelopes forming the surfaces are made of durable, very strong, coated and flame resistant material and are mounted between the steel trusses above and below as well as on the inner and outer edge of the roof. The junction of the envelopes and the T-shaped upper and lower chords of the trusses is achieved by means of clamping bands which, together with the chords, hold the edges of the envelopes. An almost airtight connection is achieved by means of tightly screwing the components. The envelopes thus mounted form a continuous accessible inner space which stretches over the whole stadium. This space is maintained at a specific pressure by means of compressors. These stabilise and support the whole envelope without external prestress having to be applied. The roof structure is transparent, and this is of par-

200. 5600 Cubic Meter Package, 4. documenta, Cassel
Design: Christo
Engineering consultants: Dimiter S. Zagoroff and R. Trostel
Manufacture: Wülfing und Hauck, 1968

On 25th June 1968 a first attempt was made to realise this sensational project. Not until 3rd August – at the fourth attempt – was the plan successful. The total costs (borne by Christo by selling everything he had), including the expensive helium gas for inflation which was imported from the USA, amounted to 60,000 dollars.

The object was 85 m high, had a diameter of approximately 10 m and was made of 2,000 m² of PVC coated polyester fabric with a thickness of 2.5 mm. Ropes served as "string" for the pack-

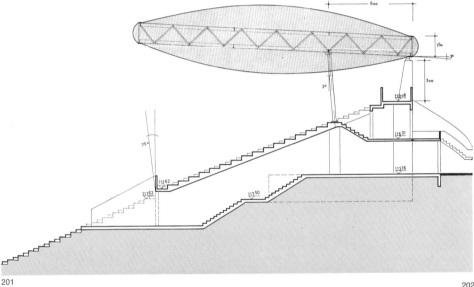

201

202

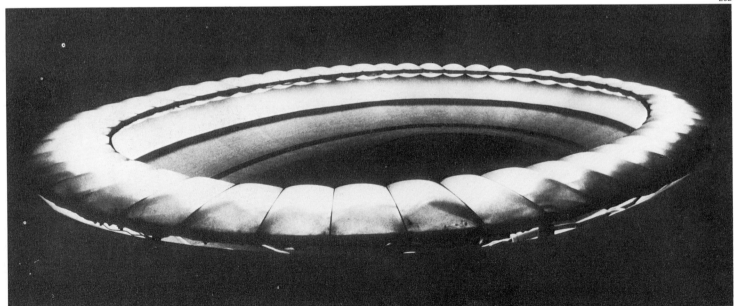

ticular importance for television transmission. Floodlights installed in the protected interior of the roof produce a very good, non-dazzling illumination of the stands. The internal pressure is safeguarded by four compressors. These compressors are adjusted so that for normal operation one of them is sufficient. The internal pressure can be adapted to external weather conditions. A key-operated device raises the internal pressure by increasing the speed of the compressor when there is increased loading on the membrane. This system would also function if there was a leak . . .''

To be precise, this circular tube structure should be classified as a series of open membranes, because the membrane sections between the steel girders are independent of one another. However, because the interruption of the membrane is so insignificant this point is disregarded.

203–205. Diolen Compositum, Hanover Fair 1970

Design: Wolfgang Rathke and Wilfried Lubitz
Manufacture: Conrad Scholtz AG, 1970

Eight pneumatic tubes made of PVC coated Diolen with a length of 10 m and a diameter of 45 cm are held together at each end by two light metal nodes. The two pairs of nodes are connected by a guy rope running in the centre of the horizontal axis. The interior expands when the cable is tightened. By tying the tubes together it is possible to "control" exactly the shape of the space inside.

The space cell was fixed on a cushion base filled with granules. Entry to the inner space was obtained through three smaller cushions.

This modification of the system of a pneumatic cell structure (see pp. 79, 80) proposed by Rathke and Wiehe for Expo '70 was meant to demonstrate the material properties and packaging possibilities of PVC coated Diolen fabric. The sponsor for the study was Enka-Glanzstoff GmbH.

204

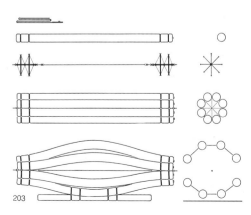

203

205

206

207

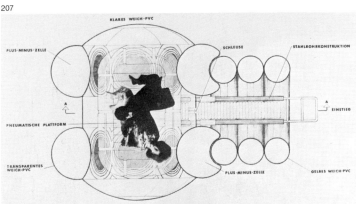

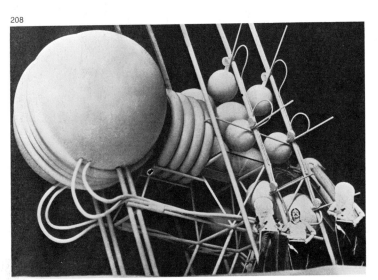

208

209

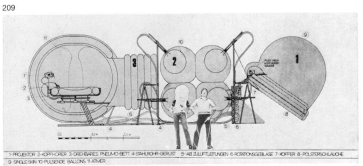

Sc, Mc / 3 di + 2 di + 1 di / 0

206, 207. Gelbes Herz (Yellow heart)
Design and manufacture: Haus-Rucker-Co., 1968

The "heart", made of PVC foil, expands and contracts rhythmically by means of a corresponding control of the air aggregate. As the foil is marked by points, the alteration in the spatial dimension can also easily be seen on the surface.

208, 209. Villa Rosa
Design: Coop Himmelblau, 1969

A pneumatic recreation room which is variable, pulsating and has a swivelling couch, is fixed in a framework of steel tubes. Light, shade and smell can be controlled inside.

210–212. Pneumacosm
Design: Haus-Rucker-Co., 1967

The design is of interest as a translation of the idea of a pneumatic living cell into the dimension of the town. The great number of problems existing there, will, however, hardly be solved this way. "Oasis No. 7", exhibited at documenta 5 in Cassel, was a kind of prototype. Transparent PVC and very strong Trevira were used for the membrane. The diameter was 7 m.

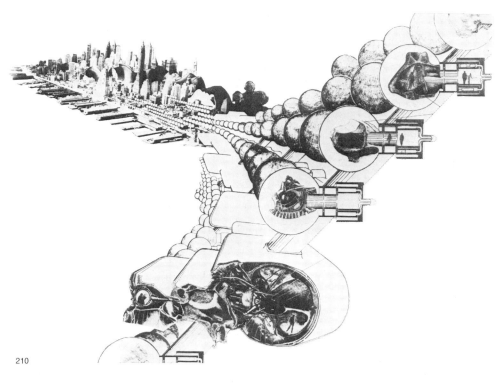

210

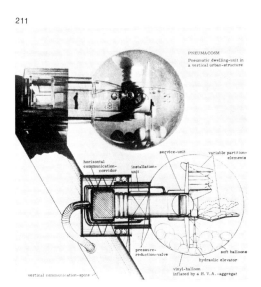

211

212

213–221. Dyodon
Design: Jean Paul Jungmann, 1967

Jungmann seems to have carefully studied the laws of form for pneumatically stabilised structural elements made of closed membranes. However, the expenses required for his design are well beyond the amount firms are at present prepared to spend for trial structures; it was clearly less important for him to find an economical solution by using identical parts, than to design an object which illustrated a great spectrum of pneumatic forms.

A framework of tubes in the form of a polyhedron is infilled by means of rigid and flexible filling elements. The building is stabilised against wind loads by guy ropes in several places.

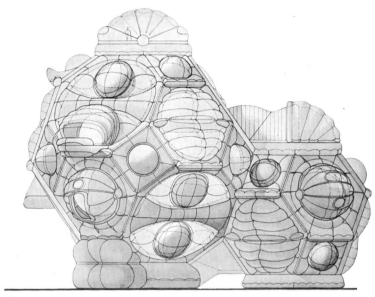

213

214

215

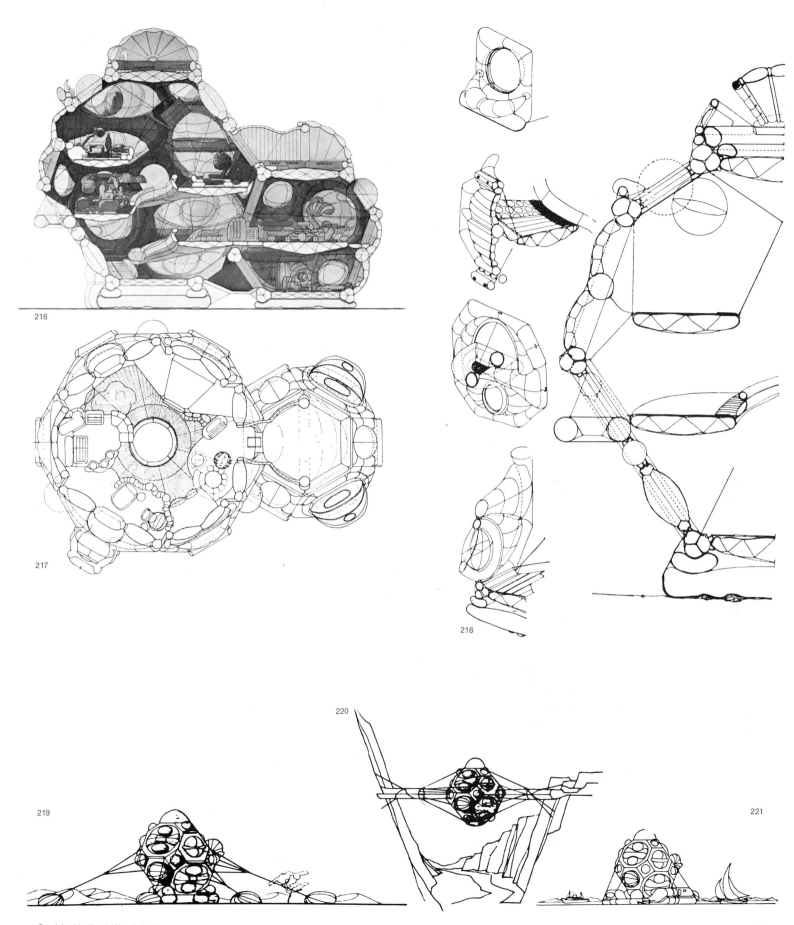

216

217

218

219

220

221

Sc, Mc / 3 di + 2 di + 1 di / L

222

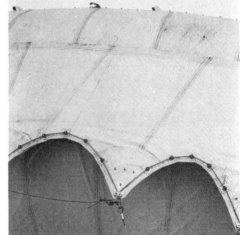

223

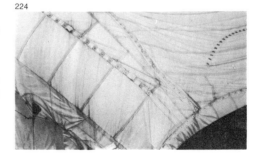

224

222–228. Floating theatre, Expo 70, Osaka
Design: Yutaka Murata
Structural calculations: Mamoru Kawaguchi
Manufacture: Ogawa Tent Co., Ltd., 1970

The upper roof membrane spanned three tubes made of two layers of PVC coated polyester fabric, and the lower membrane was held by five steel cables. The space in between was under a negative pressure of 10 mm of water pressure below atmospheric, which was raised to 20 mm of water pressure below atmospheric in storm conditions in order to prevent membrane flutter. The tubes had a positive pressure of 1,500 mm of water pressure in normal wind conditions and 3,000 mm in storm conditions.
Behind the theatre seats a steel pipe ran in the hem of the membrane, and the two ends of this pipe were fixed to the floor by hinges. The steel arch was held in place by a cable pull which counteracted the negative pressure. When it was released it elevated and made a wide entrance opening for visitors. (Detail see p. 154.)

The building stood in a small artificial lake on a circular steel structure which in turn floated on 48 PVC balloons. An automatic control system adjusted the air pressure and thereby the buoyancy of the individual floating bodies so that the theatre always stayed horizontal, regardless of the changing loading caused by visitors.

229–231. Truckin' University
Design: Ant Farm, 1970

The Truckin' University, which takes all its equipment with it, is formed by quickly inflatable pneumatic structures corresponding to the concept of great mobility.
A circular tube acts as an opening and for air distribution, and the net over it as wind and lightning protection.

Sc, Mc / 2 di + 1 di / L

225

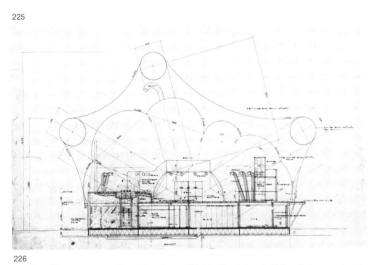

226

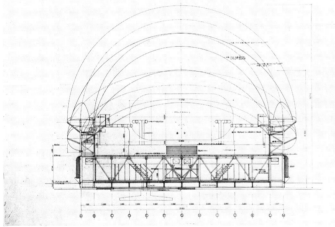

227

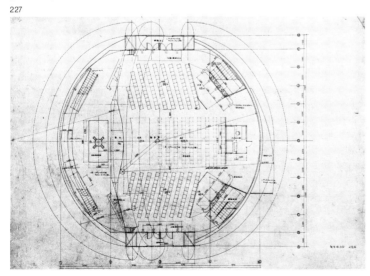

228

229

230

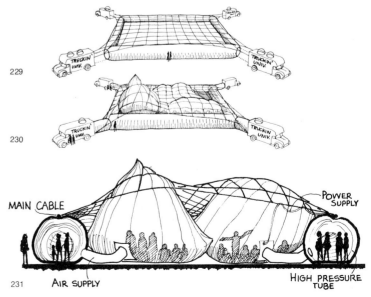

MAIN CABLE

POWER SUPPLY

231   AIR SUPPLY

HIGH PRESSURE TUBE

232-236. Trial structure in Delft

Design and manufacture: Gernot Minke with students of the Technische Hogeschool Delft, 1971

An arch-shaped high pressure tube with a height of 3.70 m, a span of 7.05 m and a diameter of 1.20 m, together with two elastic high pressure globes, supports a saddle-shaped cotton membrane. The tube is made of PVC coated polyester fabric; pressure is 2,000 mm of water pressure.

232

234

233

235

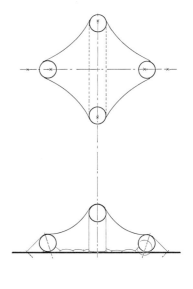

236

237

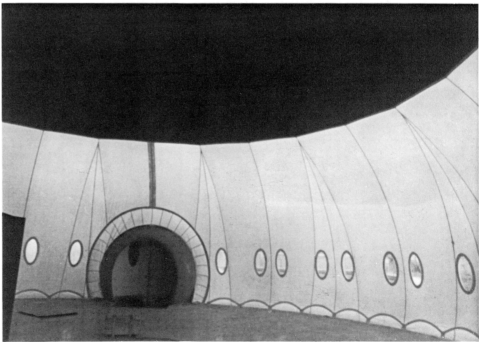

238

237, 238. Dome
Design: José Miguel de Prada Poole
Manufacture: Tolder S.A., 1971

This small hall has had many predecessors throughout the world. However, what makes it worthy of mention is the detail design which is usually completely disregarded in such simple buildings, for example the anchor hem, the window, the door, etc. As the formation of wrinkles shows, however, the cutting pattern for the connection collar to the door was not quite successful.

239

239. Pneumatic paraboloid
Design and manufacture: Arthur Quarmby with students of the Bradford School of Architecture, 1963

The experiment was meant to show where the limit for low pressure systems lies, but it was clear that it was not reached with this trial structure. The "wart" on the top was developed for reasons of production engineering. The individual lengths made of polyethelene foil could be more easily welded together with this special cutting pattern. The structure was anchored by means of a water filled circular tube with a diameter of 38 cm. The dome was 7.5 m high and could be inflated in two minutes.

240   241

240, 241. Pneu-dome
Design and manufacture: Chrysalis, Los Angeles

Not only the pneumatic envelopes of these elegant domes, but also their foundations are made of membrane material. The latter is a water filled circular tube lying on the ground. Its diameter is over 8 m.
The night photograph shows the cutting of the membrane and the slipping doors especially well.

244—247. Radome at the Sternwarte Bochum ▷
Design and manufacture: Krupp Universalbau, 1964

The PVC coated membrane fabric has a thickness of 1.2 mm. The sheets are welded. The total weight of the envelope, which has a diameter of approximately 40 m, is 3,500 kg. The erection of the radome over the already installed antennae was tested by the manufacturer in its individual phases on a model (scale 1:10). At the bottom the radome is encircled by a 4 m high wall. The internal pressure of 40 mm of water pressure is increased in wind to a maximum of 100 mm. The normal supporting pressure can be produced by just one of the four compressors. (Bibl. 8, p. 12 ff.)

242, 243. Radome
Design: Société Industrielle L'Angevinière et
Joué-les-Tours, 1963

This French invention (DBP 1 255 908) is primarily concerned with the method of anchoring the
membrane which is here meant to be connected
to a steel cylinder (see also p. 153).

242
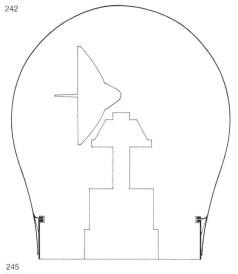

243
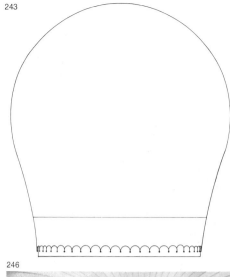

244

245

246

247

249

248

248–251. Pavilion for travelling exhibitions
Design and manufacture: Krupp Universalbau,
1958

As underground anchoring is often not possible
because of destruction to road surfaces, for this
construction a transportable ground and anchorage structure was developed with individual, easily demountable circle sections arranged
round a central steel ring.

250

251

252, 253. Pentadome
Design and manufacture: Birdair Structures, Inc., 1958

The five large domes were exhibition areas for the US Army. The centre dome had a diameter of 49 m, while the diameter of the smaller domes was 33 m. The long cylindrical structure served as a lock unit for large exhibits, e.g. rockets. Twelve compressors in all were installed, producing a positive pressure of 20 mm of water pressure. The building covered an area of 4,650 m² and was in its time the largest air supported building used for military purposes. (Bibl. 119, p. 35.)

253

252

254

— 255

257

258

254. Exhibition hall
Design: Seminar Pneumatische Konstruktionen, Institut für Umweltplanung, Ulm, under the direction of Gernot Minke, 1971

In this example individual supports guyed inwards are expanded to bulged surfaces. The author does not know of any pneumatic structures of this kind that have been put into practice.

255, 256. Studies in form
Design: Frei Otto, circa 1960

Frei Otto's model tests show very clearly the influence exerted on a very elastic rubber membrane by guying with additional linear elements. The pressure inside the membrane is constant. It can be seen that such support of the membrane does not only bring the advantage of reducing the radii of curvature and thereby the membrane tensions (part of the tensile stress is absorbed by the cables) but also considerably affects the total appearance – a point that is of great significance for the design of pneumatic objects.

257, 258. Test structure in Eindhoven, the Netherlands
Design and manufacture: Gernot Minke with students of the Technische Hogeschool Eindhoven, 1972

The test building is the first example of a webbing stabilised air supported structure which is composed of prefabricated standard elements (regular hexagon, regular pentagon, half of a regular hexagon).
The webbing straps which are connected to each other to form a net take up the main forces and transfer them from the skin to the anchorage. In case of rupture the tear cannot extend farther than a strap, since the straps, being connected with the membrane, act as tear stoppers.
The straps consist of stretched polyester fibres. In contrast to to steel cables they can be calculated so as to have about the same expansion as the membrane. This is a special advantage in the event of extreme wind loads. Due to the webbing stabilisation the internal pressure necessary is only 10 mm of water pressure.

256

The focussing effect of the reflected sound waves usually occurring with cylindrical and spherical shapes is avoided by the mode of curvature of the elements.

With this structure a new manufacturing technique was successfully tried: the elements were joined together by stainless steel staples shot by means of a pneumatic tool; the staples had been specially treated so that they automatically bent. Apart from cementing this is the only available technique which allows the jointing of elements in two axes without any limitation in size since the material need not be rolled up in the process. The whole membrane of the structure could thus be prefabricated in one piece.

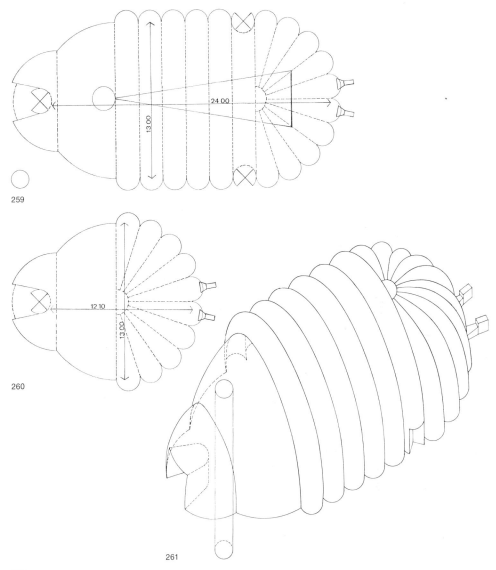

259

260

261

262

259–261. Exhibition building for Hidronor S.A. for the 1st Exhibition of South Argentina, Patagonia and Comahue
Design: Airestructures SRL, 1971

In this project the cable supports have the main function of plastically refining the shape of the structure. The axially symmetrical design of the ground plan and the arrangement of the entrances and compressors illustrate the strong aesthetic desire that is the basis of this project. In some places, however, clear deviations from the planned ideal form would probably occur if the project was carried out.

262. Dome
Design and manufacture: Birdair Structures, Inc.

A clear reduction of the tension in the transverse direction results from the arrangement of radial cables as in this American dome.

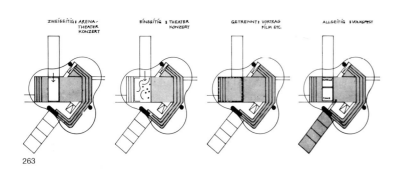

263

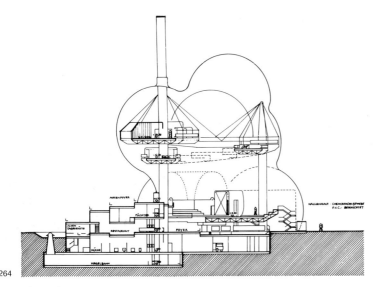

264

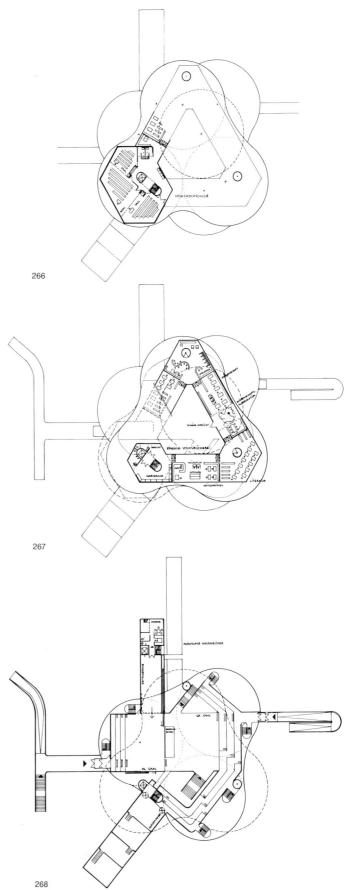

266

267

268

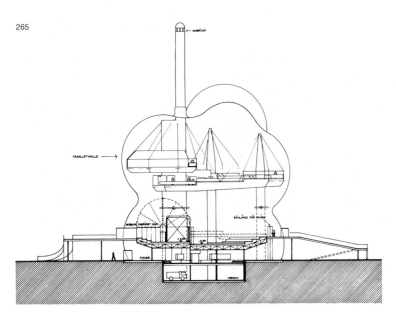

265

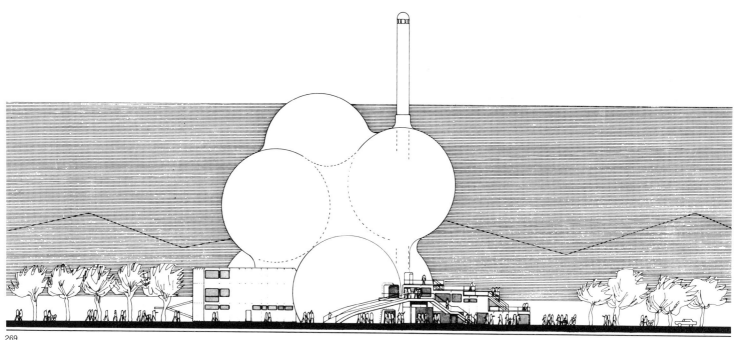

269

270

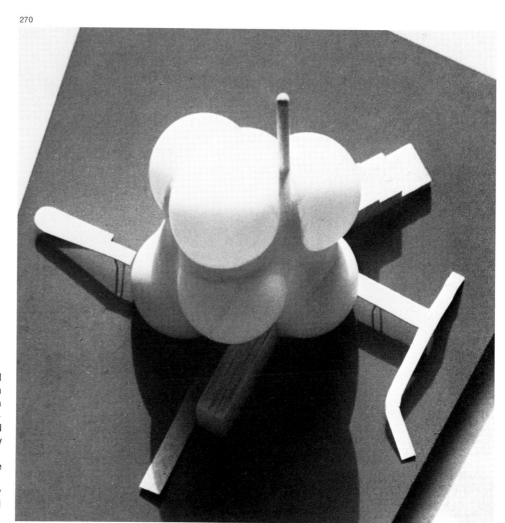

**263–270. Civic centre in Sprendlingen,
near Frankfurt am Main**
Design: Manfred Schiedhelm, 1967

The envelope was to consist of transparent and
opaque sections. As in the German pavilion in
Montreal and the project for the French pavilion
in Osaka (see p. 118) this membrane is independent of the steel platforms inside. Additional
support of the membrane was to be achieved by
means of localised reinforcement of the skin.
However, structural problems would in any case
arise on account of wind loading, and stabilisation of the skin with guy cables would certainly
be necessary in many places, both inside and
outside.

271

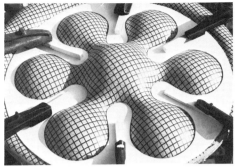

272

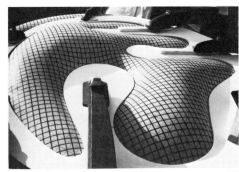

273

271–273. Test model
Design: Frei Otto, before 1962

Otto's model tests show something of the multiplicity of possible design forms for plane structures. Constrictions and undercuts present no problems. As one can see, anticlastic areas occur on the surface.

274

274, 275. Information pavilion in Sonsbeek, Holland
Design: Eventstructure Research Group
Manufacture: Hoogerwerff B. V., 1971

The peculiarity of this structure was its membrane surface. It was coated with synthetic grass which hardly differed from the adjacent lawn and made the building look as though it was a swelling in the park ground.
Also of interest are the entrances, now the subject of a patent application, in which two lip-shaped membranes are pressed against each other by internal positive pressure.

275

276

277

276–279. Swimming pool roofs
Design and manufacture: Birdair Structures, Inc.

The problem of transitions from the membrane to openings, such as doors and windows, is solved here by a particularly interesting method. Arched cables take up the membrane tensions and transfer them to the anchorages. Within these areas different skin sections which are more strongly curved and thus have less tension can be inserted.

278

279

280

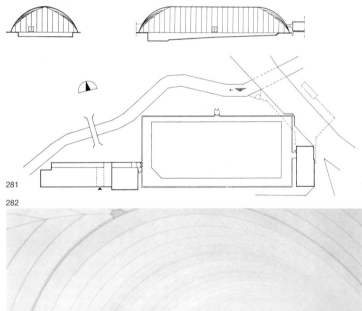

281

282

280–282. Roof covering for a former open air swimming pool in Kaufungen, near Cassel
Design: H. Volmar
Manufacture: Wülfing und Hauck, 1970

The hall is 57.5 m long, 26 m wide and is 10 m high at the highest point; the volume is 12,500 m³. The construction was manufactured in four parts and was assembled and made airtight by using approximately 2,000 aluminium clamping plates and as many stainless steel bolts.

The membrane is translucent and consists of high strength synthetic fabric coated on both sides.

Two electric hot air compressors with controllable fresh and recirculated air operation each have an air output of 36,000 m³/h and a heat output of 450,000 kcal/h. Heating is oilfired. One of the compressors is in reserve. Water heating is by means of a thermal pump. The total apparatus is automatically controlled and during the pool's hours of use gives out an air temperature of +28 °C, a water temperature of +24 °C and a relative air humidity of 40%.
(Bibl. 150.)

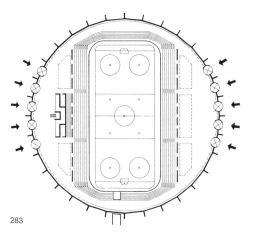

283

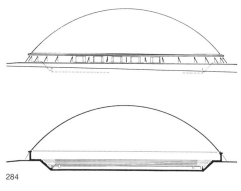

284

285

283–285. Roof of the ice rink palace in Forssa, Finland
Design: Antti O. Bengts
Structural calculations: Timo Suällström
Manufacture: Oy Urheilli-Vaatetus-Ruka, 1971

The hall has a ground area of 4,000 m² and at present is the largest air supported sports hall in the world. The diameter of approximately 71 m and the shallow curvature was possible because of the use of high strength PVC coated synthetic fabric and extensive preliminary investigations on a model hall on which the exact cutting pattern was also determined. As the temperature in the top of the building is always a minimum +12 °C, snow loading can be disregarded in the calculations as the snow melts immediately.
The material was supplied by Enka Glanzstoff GmbH.

286, 287. Cover – roof for Haus Lange, Krefeld
Design: Haus-Rucker-Co.
Manufacture: Wülfing und Hauck, 1971

In the foreword to the catalogue for the exhibition "Cover – Überleben in verschmutzter Umwelt" (Cover – survival in a polluted environment) Haus-Rucker wrote: "Cities are buried under coverings of smog. The dust that is swallowed by the inhabitants of these cities can be measured in lorryloads. The streets have changed into gas chambers, the rivers into viscous poison brews. The sun has become a 40 watt bulb; wandering rubbish dumps eat grass and trees . . .
Despite massive campaigns against environmental pollution the continuity of the process and constant adaptation to the ever worsening conditions prevent an instinctive grasp of the extent of the danger. Death will not come as quickly through the environment as through a H bomb, but it will be just as final.
"Cover" makes a jump in time and shows the

situation that will arise if increasing contamination of the environment continues: life in artificial reservations.
As an example, the Lange house, a one family house in its structural concept, is enveloped in a pneumatic protective covering (air supported structure). A climatic "island" is created which, equipped with the necessary technical apparatus, becomes a self-sufficient life cell. Quartz lamps are suns. Audio-visual sceneries simulate changing weather and landscapes. The illusion becomes a substitute for the real experiences that are lacking. A small synthetic cosmos surrounds the house from which it is impossible to break out.
Noah's ark is launched again.
"Cover" tries to make people conscious of this situation. Consciousness through total simulation of future conditions . . ."
Inside the house further pneumatic "climate zones" were installed to satisfy basic human needs – true objects of horror of future existence.

286

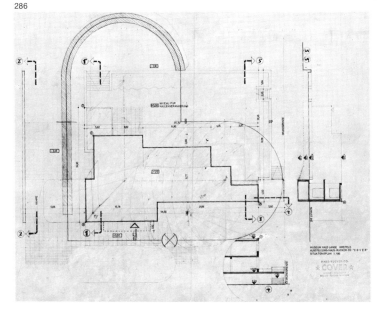

287

288

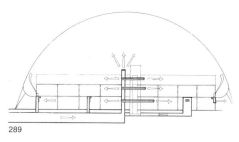

289

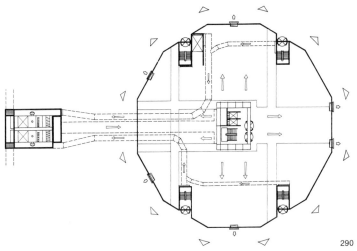

290

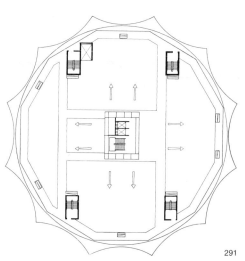

291

292

293

288–291. Air supported pavilion with arcade

Design: Friedrich Krupp GmbH, Zentralinstitut für Forschung und Entwicklung, 1970

The study is part of a research work on pneumatically stabilised membrane structures (Bibl. 91). A spherical segment with a diameter of 65 m is placed on a frustum of a cone cut by 12 parabolic arches. Above the arches the membrane skin is divided into two. The inner part of the skin seals the hall while the outer part conducts the membrane forces into the ground anchors. Through this profiling an arcade is created around the pavilion. On the inside are shop windows, revolving doors and lorry ramps. By dividing the interior into storeys the ground floor can remain pressure-free. Thus expensive lorry and personnel air locks are avoided.

292, 293. Roof covering for the skating rink in Anegasaki, Japan

Design: Japan Engineering Consultant Co.
Manufacture: Taiyo Kogyo Co., Ltd., and Taisei Construction Co., Ltd., 1971

The building has a certain similarity to the preceding project as far as the transfer of membrane forces to the ground and the formation of the membrane apron is concerned. The bottom edge is divided into two parts, one of which serves as an anchorage and the other as a seal. A clear difference in colour turns this structural measure into a distinguishing motif.
The structure covers an area of close to 3,300 m². It has a length of 79 m, a width of 53 m and a height of 16 m.
(For details of the fixing of the membrane to the anchorage see p. 153, Fig. 70.)

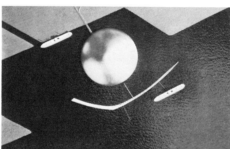

294

295

294, 295. Pneumatically stressed bulk goods container

Design: Frei Otto, before 1962

Conical surfaces, like cylindrical surfaces, are only curved in one direction and therefore offer the advantage of a favourable material cutting pattern. As the longitudinal tensions decrease considerably towards the peak, the difference in the skin tension of the cone must be counteracted by a rounding-off of the tip.
The use of this form suggested by Otto as a bulk goods container has the advantage of optimum use of space. The fuller the container becomes, the less supporting air is required to keep the internal pressure constant.
(Bibl. 119, p. 78 ff.)

296

296. Project for covering Wembley Stadium, London

Design: Arthur Quarmby, 1967
Structural consultant: David Powell

In this alternative proposal to the "Helium Lifted Canopy" (see p. 57) a single membrane structure is to cover the football pitch. The whole stadium would be under positive pressure, which would entail considerable sealing measures in the present buildings.

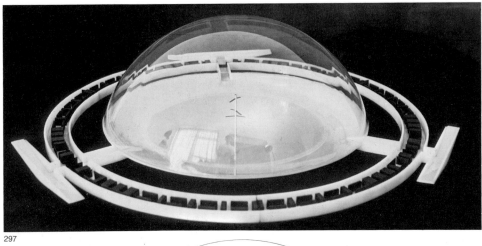

297

300

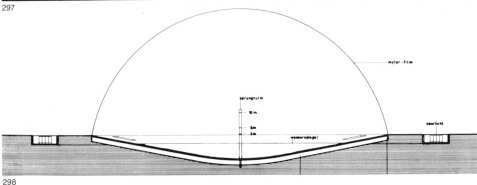

298

299

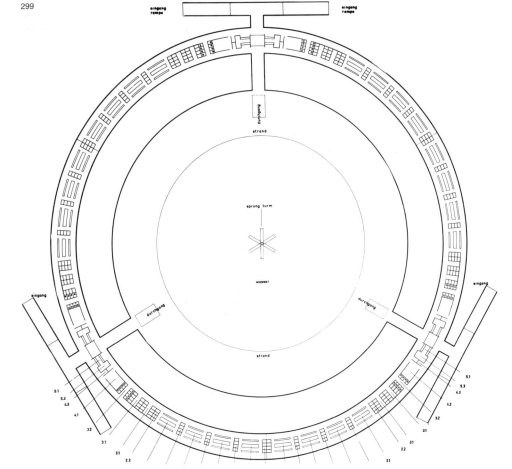

297–300. Indoor swimming pool
Design: Gil Hirt and Willi Ramstein, 1959

The authors wrote at the time about their project, which is fascinating by the clarity of its concept:
"The projection of this object was based on the following ideas:

The passage from land to water should not be by a direct separation (e.g. steps) but by a gentle slope of about 17%. In order to produce this transition from beach to water on all sides, the pool is constructed as a flat spherical segment with a diameter of 100 m. The water surface itself has a diameter of about 76 m and is surrounded by a 12 m wide beach.

Permanent use can be guaranteed by covering the pool. An unhindered entry of light, strong visual connection with the green of the surrounding parkland and an easily produced structure led to a solution in the form of a pneumatic roof covering. The envelope of transparent Mylar film is supported by a light, scarcely noticeable positive pressure.

On the beach, seats can be created for almost 5,000 onlookers. This centre will be used for cultural as well as sporting purposes. For example, theatre, variety, shows, fashion shows, etc. can be performed on floating walkways and stages.

In conjunction with dwelling units the swimming pool can be placed in a spacious park. No superstructure disturbs the landscape and only the light envelope, in which sun and water are reflected, rises into the air".

301

301. Dome for covering part of New York City
Design: Richard Buckminster Fuller, 1962

Fuller's dome for New York City is one of the best known Utopian pneumatic structures in architecture. Even if it were possible to realise such a project – apart from the fact that our knowledge of the climate (heating, cloud formation) created inside is greatly lacking – the attendant city structure is also lacking; it is one without exhaust gases, without dust, without fire, more or less sterilised, with buildings whose exteriors no longer have the function of protection against the weather . . .
This is, therefore, a Utopia whose realisation must begin with the changing of the environment that the dome encloses.

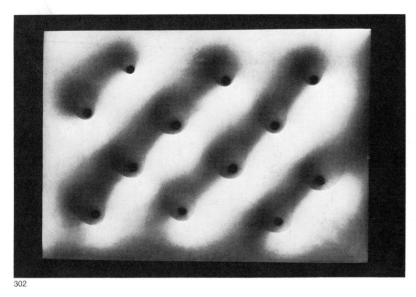

302

303

304

305

302, 303. Form study of a membrane with internal drainage
Design: Frei Otto

The plaster model shows a rectangular membrane with 12 guys.

304, 305. Exhibition pavilion
Design: Gernot Minke with students of the Technische Hogeschool Delft, 1971

The ground plan of the pavilion is circular; the membranes are anchored at three low points inside.

306

306. Multi-purpose structure

Design: Seminar Pneumatische Konstruktionen, Institut für Umweltplanung, Ulm, under the direction of Gernot Minke, 1971

By means of high pressure balloons used as support elements a rather uniform stress distribution is achieved in the membrane which is stabilised by negative pressure.

307–309. Demountable exhibition pavilion

Design: Seminar Pneumatische Konstruktionen, Institut für Umweltplanung, Ulm, under the direction of Gernot Minke, 1971

This pavilion too is a negative pressure structure. By means of circular individual supports the outer membrane is held apart from the inner membrane, which is only fixed at the base.

309

307

308

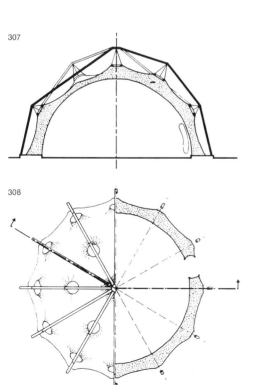

310–312. Form studies
Design: Frei Otto, before 1962

Frei Otto's model tests show the influence of cables and nets on the design. The total radii of curvature are increased by nets; within the mesh the membrane forms surface areas with smaller radii of curvature (Fig. 312).
In the use of cables, care has to be taken that the tensile forces of the membrane on both sides are applied at equal tangential angles if possible.

313. Exhibition pavilion
Design: Gernot Minke with students of the Technische Hogeschool Delft, 1971

The membrane is arched over a circular ground plan. It is additionally supported by means of two cables forming grooves.

314. Cable reinforced pneumatic for exhibition purposes
Design: Friedrich Krupp GmbH, 1973

The exhibition hall is put together from spherical sections in whose seams cables are laid. This formation causes small radii of curvature and correspondingly low membrane forces. Air supply and recirculation take place on both sides of the longitudinal axis of the hall, which is 228 m long, 72 m wide and 25 m high.

310
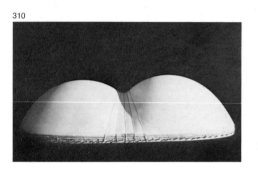

311
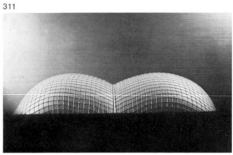

312
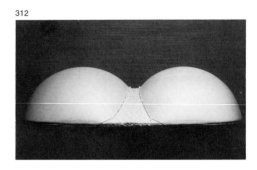

313

314
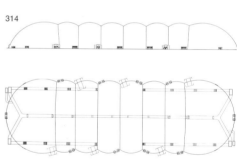

315

315. Multi-purpose hall on the English South Coast
Design: Gernot Minke with Croucher and Salt, 1969

A pneumatically stressed positive pressure membrane reinforced by intersecting cables was to span an area of 2,000 m².
The model demonstrates how, by means of diagonally running cable supports, the appearance of a building can be changed as compared to the previous examples.

316–318. Large span roof for a greenhouse
Design: Frei Otto, before 1962

Support of the membrane is achieved in the interior of the structure by restraining membrane ribs. The cross-section is slightly arched toward the outside to facilitate drainage. Additional ties to the ground reduce the tensions in the cables. (Bibl. 119, p. 104.)

316

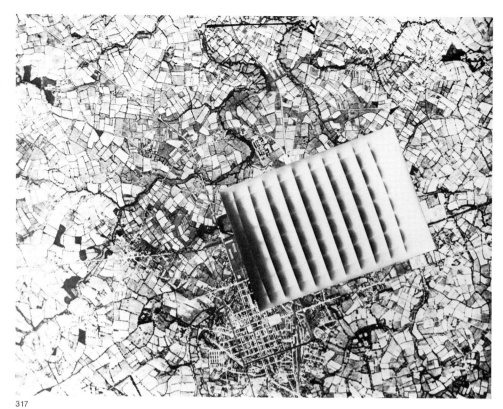

317

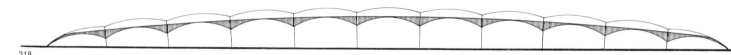

318

319, 320. Plastic foil structure stabilised by positive pressure
Design: Otto Walter Neumark, 1962

The design is based on the idea of covering a cable net, which is anchored at its edges only, with overlapping, laterally fixed foil lengths. The overlapping edges are to be tightly pressed against each other by the internal pressure.
In the (somewhat modified) drawings omitting a uniform scale the possible total dimension and the overlapping covering can be recognised. (DBP 1434 630.)

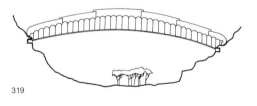

319

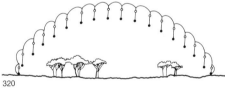

320

321. Structure supported by positive pressure with cable net
Design: Paul Desmarteau

As in Frei Otto's greenhouse the cable tensions here are greatly reduced by means of intermediate guying. (DBP 1219 656.)

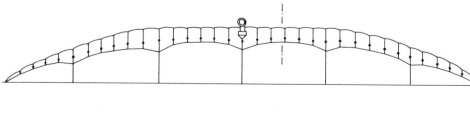

321

322

322–324. Padiglione Abitare, Milan
Design: Studio d'Architettura e Industrial Design
Manufacture: Plasteco Milano, 1969

The cable reinforcements crossing at 90° divided the building into four equal sections. By using a transparent strip in the lower area a spatial relationship was created between interior and exterior. The membrane consisted of high frequency welded PVC lengths 1.2 mm thick.

323

324

325

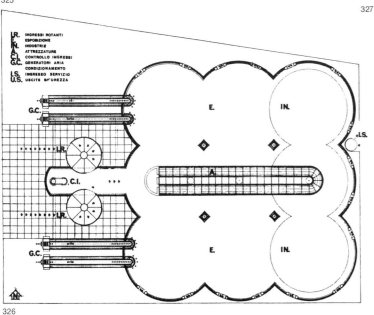

LR. INGRESSI ROTANTI
E. ESPOSIZIONE
IN. INDUSTRIE
A. ATTREZZATURE
C.I. CONTROLLO INGRESSI
G.C. GENERATORI ARIA
CONDIZIONAMENTO
I.S. INGRESSO SERVIZIO
U.S. USCITE SICUREZZA

326

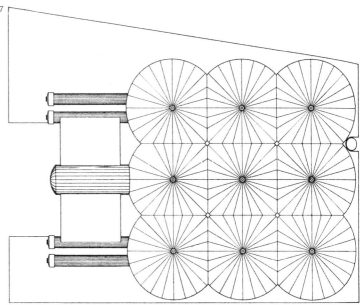

327

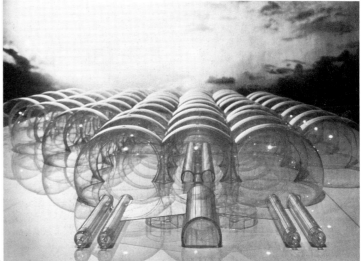

328

325−328. Italian pavilion for Expo '70, Osaka. Competition design

Design: Studio d'Architettura e Industrial Design, 1968

The design represented a further development of the structural system already used by the designers in the Padiglione "Abitare". They proposed a large envelope of dome-shaped membrane sections, which were to be assembled in the manner of modular construction. The 17 m high spherical segments were to be made of 24 lengths of high frequency welded PVC and cover an area of 3,850 m². The internal positive pressure was to be 20 mm of water pressure.

Two months were estimated for the total production of the structure and one week for erection.

329

329–332. Pneumatic roofs for recreation centres

Design: Yutaka Murata, 1972

The projects hardly differ from the two preceding Italian examples. The basic idea aims at offering a modular pneumatic construction system with interchangeable elements. For part of the fixtures and fittings Murata also proposes pneumatic elements which are particularly light, cheap and easily produced.

331

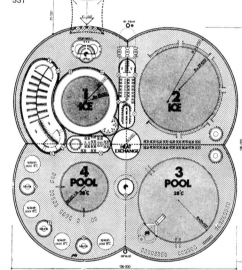

330

332

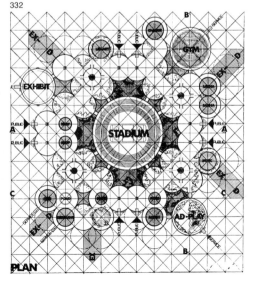

333–335. City in the Arctic

Design: Atelier Warmbronn (Frei Otto and Ewald Bubner), 1970–71
City planning advice: Kenzo Tange & URTEC
Structural advice: Ove Arup & Partners
Material tests: Farbwerke Hoechst AG

The study project commissioned by Farbwerke Hoechst AG provides for a pneumatically stabilised, climate-regulating shell with a diameter of 2,000 m, a height of 240 m and a dome radius of 2,200 m for a city with 15,000 to 45,000 inhabitants.

The transparent membrane is supported by a net of intersecting cables. The researches revealed that a cable net made of polyester fibres is superior to a steel cable net. Because of the low E modulus and the resulting high flexibility of the polyester material, considerable changes in volume (in the region of 200 to 300%) must oc-

cur before the cables fracture or slacken, and deviations of this order of magnitude can be disregarded. The project provides for cables with a diameter of 270 mm at 10 m centres. Under normal load conditions this means a safety factor against breaking of 12. Because of the low loading there is no fear of creep. Anchoring is by means of a ring foundation.

Fig. 334 shows the stages of the construction process for the large shell. Before the cables are laid out on the ground, erection balloons are distributed and anchored. Then the cable bands are attached to each other, lightly prestressed and the membrane is fastened. Finally the foundations are closed, the erection balloons filled and the shell is inflated. The internal pressure varies between 25 and 40 mm of water pressure. The designers predict that in the early eighties the first projects of this kind will be realised. (Bibl. 77.)

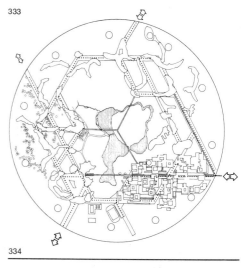
333

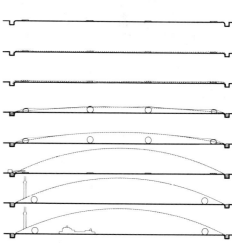
334

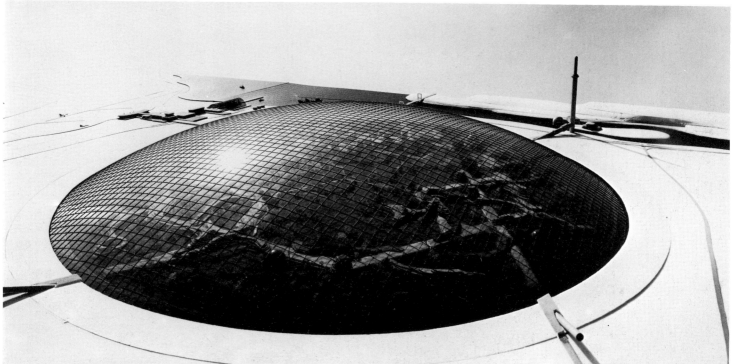
335

337

338

339

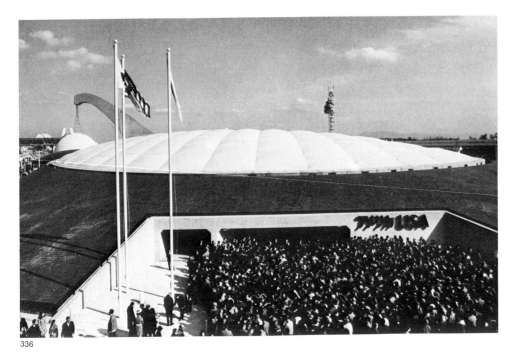

336

336—342. USA Pavilion, Expo '70, Osaka
Design: Davis, Brody, Chermayeff, Geismar, De Harak Ass.
Structural calculation: David H. Geiger
Manufacture: Ohbayashi-Gumi, Ltd., and Taiyo Kogyo Co., Ltd., 1970

The oval covered by the membrane was 142 m long and 83 m wide. The membrane had a rising height of only 6.10 m. The shallow curvature was made possible because the envelope was subtended by a net made of 32 cables, each having a diameter of 48 mm. The weight of the cable net was about 45,000 kg; that of the membrane,

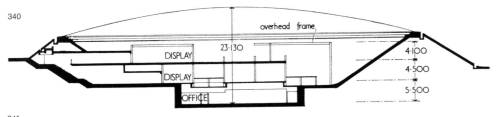

340

DISPLAY

23·130

overhead frame

4·100

DISPLAY

4·500

OFFICE

5·500

341

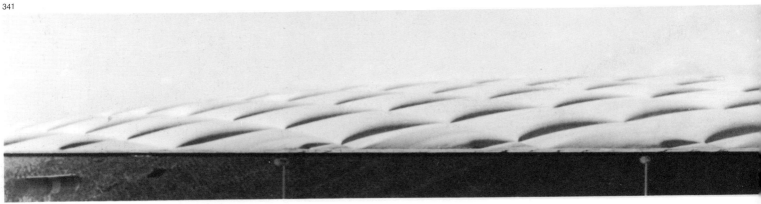

312

which was made of PVC coated high frequency welded glass fibre fabric, was about 15,000 kg. The internal pressure was 27 mm of water pressure, even in a strong wind; under snow loading it was raised to 63 mm of water pressure. (Details see pp. 153, 155.)

The Pavilion was one of the largest buildings at Expo 70. Its effect lay not in its size, however, but in the mixture of understatement and sophisticated design.

As the section shows, the structure was partly sunk into into the site. The excavated soil was piled up as a sloping wall around the periphery. Inside were steel platforms which were used for the display of the exhibits, and as traffic areas for visitors.

The restraint exercised with regard to the outer appearance was interpreted in Japan as a reflection of American political morale in South East Asia. However the great curtailment in the budget seems to have been at least as decisive a factor for the design.

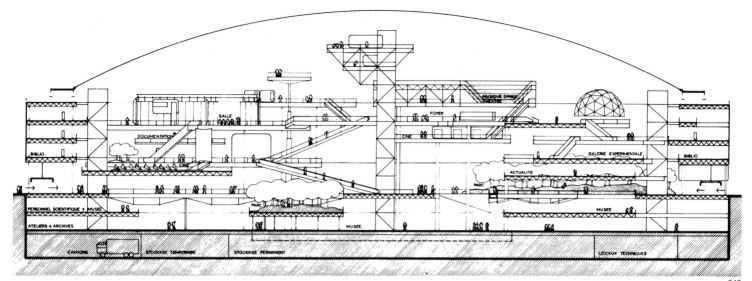

343

343–345. Centre Beaubourg, Paris.
Competition design

Design: Manfred Schiedhelm with Atilla Berker and Myra Wahrhaftig, 1971

The structure, a mixture of building and quarter, is covered by a pneumatic dome which is supported by a steel cable net.

The interior is a large spatial garden with small wooded areas on different levels. Supported by the latest communications techniques, cultural activities of all kinds were to take place here. The areas for library, exhibitions, theatres, museum, etc. are solidly installed yet demountable.

Despite the large total expanse of the structure the scale in its interior corresponds to that of the surrounding built-up area.

344

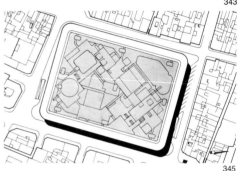

345

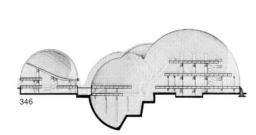

346

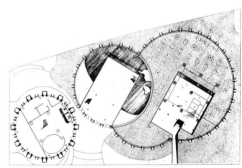

347

346, 347. French Pavilion for Expo '70, Osaka.
Competition design

Design: Jean le Couteur and Denis Sloan, 1967

Concrete shells in the ground were to be supplemented above ground by pneumatic membranes to form complete spheres. Inside multi-storeyed steel platforms were planned, similar to those in the German tent in Montreal. These platforms were not to touch the envelope at any point.

The project was not executed primarily because there was a feeling of uncertainty about the technical problems.

348–350. Investigation into the covering of university buildings with pneumatic structures
Design: Rurik Ekstrom, Charles Tilford and Blair Hamilton (Antioch College, Columbia, Maryland), 1970
Manufacture of prototype: Students of Antioch College, 1972

The investigation resulted in a prototype (Fig. 350) which spans an area of 60×60 m. Technical support for its execution was given by the Goodyear Corporation whose Research Division carried out the relevant experiments. The envelope is made of two PVC sheets with a 36 to 60 cm air gap between them to reduce the build-up of heat; this is also restricted by air conditioning. The two main cables have a diameter of 27 mm; they are each guyed down twice. The diameter of the secondary cables is 7 mm. The entrances are inset into a surrounding embankment.

The building contains art studios and theatre facilities, as well as lecture, seminar and faculty rooms for about 100 students.

In May 1973 the first Conference on Pneumatic Structures in the Educational System took place in which architects, engineers and educationalists from all over the world took part.

348

349

350

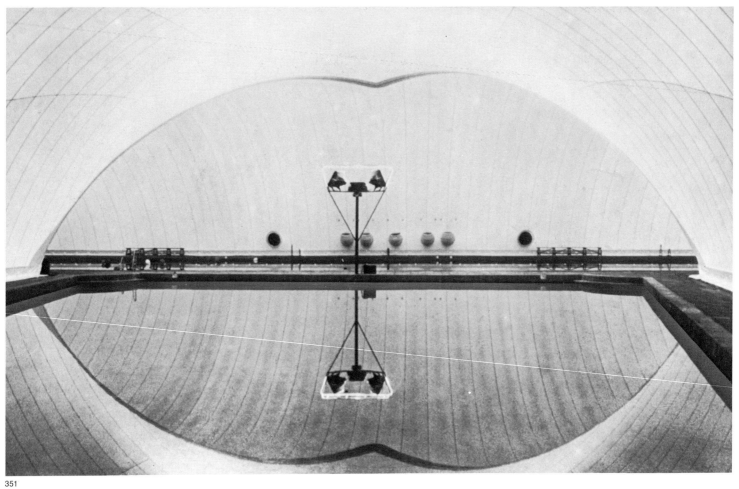

351

352

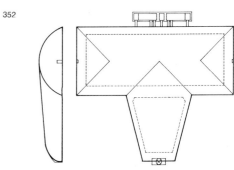

353

354

351, 352. Indoor swimming pool
Design and manufacture: Krupp Universalbau, 1971

As well as the swimming pool a non-swimmers pool with a trapezium-shaped ground plan had to be covered. The problem of manufacture lay in the cutting of the three dimensional elements, a cylinder section and a frustum of a cone.

In order to take up the linear forces which increased from the peak of the hall to its base, the membrane was reinforced along the cutting lines with several layers of the material. All the calculated cutting patterns were tested on a model, scale 1:20, and corrected where necessary. In the arc of the frustum the sheets had to be lapped, as the sloping silhouette made strongly curved cutting patterns necessary. For visual reasons the lapped edges were arranged in continuous lines.
(Bibl. 28.)

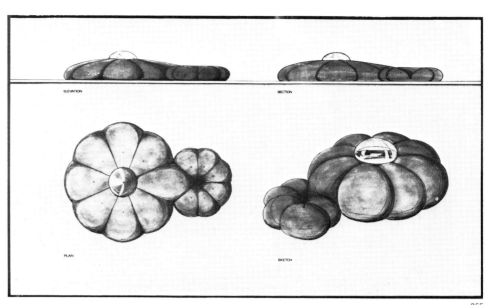

355

353, 354. Roof of the Alpamare wave bath, Bad Tölz
Design: Gernot Minke
Manufacture: L. Stromeyer & Co. GmbH, 1971

The demountable membrane of PVC coated polyester covers a ground area of 1,400 m². On account of the six radially arranged cables restraining the structure a favourable organisation of the interior could be achieved and the volume of air for heating and circulation could be reduced.

Two electric hot air fans with automatically controlled fresh air/recirculated air operation bring a heat output of 400,000 kcal/hour and an air output of 32,000 m³/h. Temperature and humidity are automatically controlled. In the event of power failure a reserve fan will switch on.

The shadow outline of the surrounding trees on the skin acts as a graphic element inside. Thus even when the pool is covered a relationship to nature is created.

355. Project for Brighton Marina
Design: Arthur Quarmby

The two inter-connected roofs were to have diameters of 93 and 150 m. This study illustrates particularly well the design possibilities provided by the arrangement of radial cables.

356. Exhibition hall on the English South Coast
Design: Gernot Minke with Coppin and Galloway, 1969

The membrane, which is to be fixed to a 3 m high surrounding concrete base, is divided by restraining cables into five sections.

357, 358. Cabledome
Design and manufacture: Birdair Structures, Inc., 1971

Spans of over 200 m can be achieved with this structure. The membrane is overspanned by a net made of three bands of cables which intersect each other at the same angle.

The uniform distribution of the net over the surface permits the formation of an almost exact spherical segment — in contrast to the flatter domes with varying curvatures which are restrained by radial cables. The cables do not need to be spliced at the points of intersection but require only positioning clamps; this greatly simplifies manufacture and erection. The fixing of the membrane to the cables is achieved by membrane flanges which are joined in situ over the cables and sewn to a closed loop profile.
(Details see p. 155.)

356

357

358

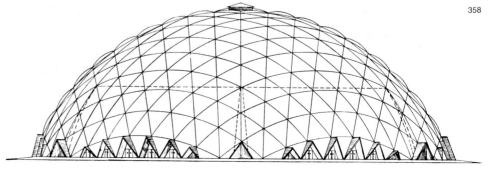

359

360

361

362

366

363

367

359–369. Krupp standard halls
Design and manufacture: Krupp Universalbau

Fig. 359 shows the two most frequently used types of standard hall: one is constructed on a rectangular ground plan; in the other semicircular sections are attached to the narrow side of the rectangle. Figs. 360 and 361 give examples of the range of these two types; the structure built on pure rectangles covers an area of 12,600 m², the other an area of 6,500 m². Figs. 362–365 show various access and connecting structures. Figs. 366–369 give an idea of the erection of a standard hall from transport of the packaged membrane to inflation.

364   365

368   369

370

371

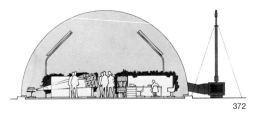

372

370–375. Temporary office building for Computer Technology, Ltd., Hemel Hempstead, England
Design: Foster Associates with Loren Butt
Manufacture: Polydrom, 1970

In the quickly growing computer industry it is often necessary to create new buildings at very short notice. After a number of alternatives had been' investigated, this air supported structure proved to be by far the cheapest solution. Eight weeks elapsed between commissioning and going into operation and erection took only 55 minutes. After some two years use the 60 m long and 12 m wide building that was erected on the asphalt of a car park was dismantled again.

In the event of an emergency a double row of lamp standards would have supported the membrane and kept the escape ways free. The lights were fitted with neon tubes and indirect light sources were projected on to the white membrane which in turn acted as a reflector.
A combined heating and ventilation system with an output of 150 KW produced a maximum input temperature of +50 °C in winter. The ventilation supply was about 10,000 m³/h. The room temperature was found to be quite acceptable in winter, but in summer the air heated up as high as +32 °C. In the case of a longer working life of the building a cooling system would have had to be connected to the ventilators.
(Bibl. 44. p. 192 ff.)

373

374

375

376. Air supported structure for a winter building site in Anzère, Switzerland
Design and manufacture: Sarna-Hallen AG, 1967

In order to be able to work on a hotel site at 1500 m above sea level even in winter, a construction firm commissioned the erection of the illustrated air supported hangar which is 67 m long and 27 m wide. The membrane was manufactured from soft PVC sheeting reinforced with a polyester lattice web. It weighed 3,500 kg and was produced, transported to the site and erected within four weeks.

Two compressors with an output of 10,000 m³/h kept the pressure inside at 10 to 15 mm of water pressure. In strong wind forces the internal pressure was increased to approximately 30 mm of water pressure.
(Bibl. 11.)

377, 378 Krupp exhibition hall, Hanover
Design and manufacture: Krupp Universalbau, 1966

The air supported hall has a length of 106 m, a width of 35 m, a height of 17.5 m and covers an area of 3,300 m². Four cold air compressors provide a frequent change of air during the period of the fair. The air is ducted to the hall in concrete channels lying under the anchorage structure and is dispersed vertically upwards. At each deflection of the air flow, air deflectors keep the unavoidable loss of pressure to a minimum. The

376

378

377

surplus air is carried outside in regulated air-outlet conduits. When the fair is closed only one compressor is operating. This compressor alone produces a pressure that safeguards the hall against high wind loadings. If the internal pressure falls – due to a pane of glass cracking, for example – then a second compressor switches on automatically and off again after replacement of the damaged part. Even hurricane gusts cannot endanger the hall, because the ventilation system reacts by means of wind speed gauges. In the event of a power failure an internal combustion engine starts automatically and takes care of the run-on of one compressor. The heating installations provide fresh air heating and are designed for a temperature differential of about 20 °C. The heating output is 80,000 kcal/h. Heating is by town gas that has a lower calorific value of 4,000 kcal/Nm³. The equipment is connected to the cold air compressors.
(Bibl. 25.)

379

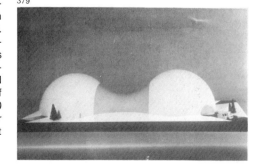

379. Combination of rotation surfaces and hemisphere
Design: Friedrich Krupp GmbH, Zentralinstitut für Forschung und Entwicklung, 1970

The model illustrates that it is also possible to form anticlastic surface areas in cases of large air supported halls with internal positive pressure. The project is ready for execution. Progressive firms are apparently making efforts to supply a greater variety of air supported halls.

380

380–384. Instant City
Design: José Miguel de Prada Poole, 1971

The initiative to build this pneumatic village, which accommodated young participants in the ICSID Congress of 1971, came from some architectural students in Barcelona. José Miguel de Prada Poole, who has already collected a good deal of experience in the field of pneumatic structures, developed a general plan and a "grammar of form" as a guide for manufacture and assembly. The lengths of transparent or coloured PVC were 0.3 mm thick and were fixed to each other by clamps. The ground anchorages were ballast pockets which were made by placing the membrane skirt in a 30×30 cm trench and loading it with the excavated earth.
The "grammar of form" was used very flexibly by the builders. When someone new arrived he built on as he liked — yet everyone kept to the prescribed structural details.
(Bibl. 112.)

381

382

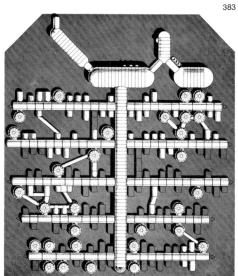

383

EJECUCION DE LAS ZANJAS DE ANCLAJE

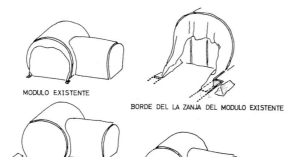

MODULO EXISTENTE

BORDE DEL LA ZANJA DEL MODULO EXISTENTE

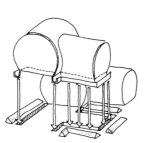

EJECUCION DE LA ZANJA DE 30X30 cms.

COLOCACION DEL BORDE DEL NUEVO MODULO EN LA ZANJA

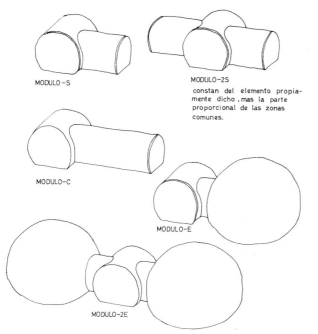

RELLENADO Y APISONADO DE LA ZANJA

AXONOMETRIA DEL CONJUNTO

REPERTORIO GENERAL DE FORMAS NEUMATICAS SIMPLES

MODULO-S

MODULO-2S

constan del elemento propia-
mente dicho, mas la parte
proporcional de las zonas
comunes.

MODULO-C

MODULO-E

MODULO-2E

REPERTORIO GENERAL DE LA GRAMATICA DE USO

Comprende los siguientes elementos:

SIMPLES	DOBLES	MIXTOS
M-S	M-2S	M-SC
M-C	M-2C	M-SE
M-E	M-2E	M-CE

COMPOSICION DE LAS PIEZAS

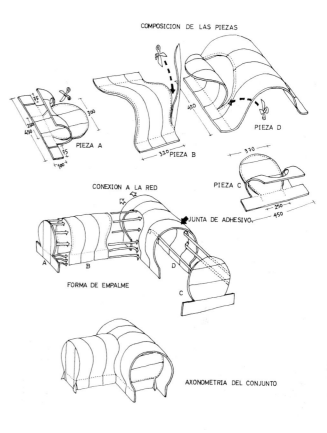

PIEZA A

PIEZA B

PIEZA D

PIEZA C

CONEXION A LA RED

JUNTA DE ADHESIVO

FORMA DE EMPALME

AXONOMETRIA DEL CONJUNTO

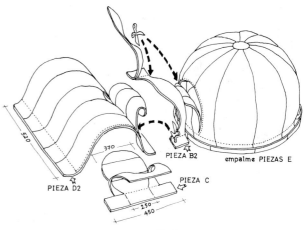

PIEZA D2

PIEZA B2

empalme PIEZAS E

PIEZA C

COMPOSICION DE LAS PIEZAS QUE
FORMAN EL MODULO E (6 PERSONAS)

AXONOMETRIA DEL CONJUNTO

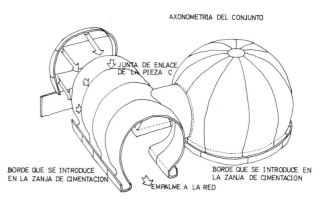

JUNTA DE ENLACE
DE LA PIEZA C

BORDE QUE SE INTRODUCE
EN LA ZANJA DE CIMENTACION

EMPALME A LA RED

BORDE QUE SE INTRODUCE EN
LA ZANJA DE CIMENTACION

Sc, Mo / 2 di + 1 di / 0

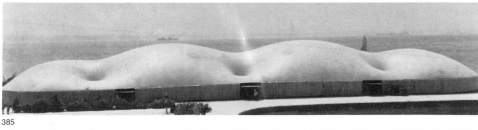

385

386

385, 386. Multi-purpose hall on the English South Coast
Design: Gernot Minke with Croucher and Salt, 1969

As far as the author knows, this is the first time anyone has thought of using additional point support on a structure in which a main direction of extension is dominant. The rubber membrane of the model was guyed first at five and then at eight points. The hall was to have a ground surface of 2,000 m²; the membrane would consist of PVC coated polyester fabric and be fastened to a 3 m high base.

387. Hemispherical combination
Design: Friedrich Krupp GmbH, Zentralinstitut für Forschung und Entwicklung, 1970

The central spherical element is cut so that two quarter circles appear on the outside contour when viewed from above. Such a definition achieves an equal division in the encircling arcade. (Bibl. 91, p. 28.)

388, 389. Roof over an open air swimming pool in Wolfsburg
Design and manufacture: Krupp Universalbau, 1971

The difficulty in this roof lay in the transition area between the rectangular hall and the spherical section covering the diving pool. It was designed with the help of model studies so that the cutting line in the loaded state remains approximately as an arc. The tensile stresses concentrated here are taken up by a steel cable and diverted to the foundations. A "soft" transition would also have been possible, but for various reasons was not chosen.
Air vent valves are put in various places to ensure tolerable temperatures in the event that the structure is not dismantled in summer.
(Bibl. 28.)

387

388

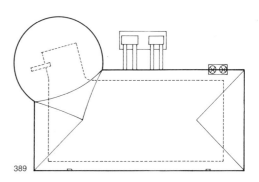

389

390–394. Modern Art Museum, Munich
Design and manufacture: J. B. Sanders & Söhne, 1971

The building is 35 m long and 15 m wide in the centre. From a central hemisphere emerge two half cylinders, at the ends of which are placed quarter spheres in which in turn are cut the entrances. At the transition areas to the half cylinders and to the vehicle lock the membrane forces of the main dome are transferred to the foundations by means of sewn in cables. The formation of wrinkles at the transition areas between the various structural parts shows that the choice of cutting pattern was not completely successful.

390

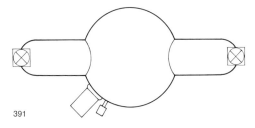

391

392

393

394

395

395. Pavilion of the national Argentinian oil company
Design and manufacture: Airestructuras, 1972

The pavilion acts as a demonstration room for a travelling exhibition. In contrast to the originally intended constriction of the main room by means of a cable, in production the area was designed as a band that is bounded by a cable on both sides. The fan is neatly placed at its foot. As well as the design of the constriction the cutting pattern of the membrane is remarkable. The membrane sections do not converge at the top but at the connection points or access doors. Thus not only is assembling simplified, but the spatial impression is favourably affected in as far as in the spherical sections the zenith has no special emphasis.

396

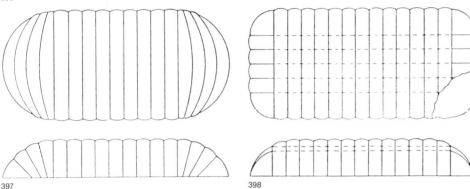

397 398

399

396−398. Cabled fieldhouse
Design and manufacture: Birdair Structures, Inc., 1972

Cables which reduce the curvature of the skin and considerably improve the internal acoustics run at 6 m intervals on the inside of the membrane.
The manufacturer offers two different forms of end section (Fig. 397, 398).

399. Cable reinforced ship cover
Design and manufacture: Birdair Structures, Inc., 1971

The 140 m long by 25 m wide prototype helps to investigate a new process, that of "mothballing" a ship. It is a great advantage to be able, by means of suitable adjustment of the internal climate, to keep the corrosion of the superstructure under considerable control.

400−406. Pneumatically stabilised plastic foil greenhouses
Design and manufacture: H. Brügge, Abt. Zugbeanspruchte Konstruktionen

Normal plastic foil greenhouses are already very cheap. When they are also pneumatically stabilised they can scarcely be beaten for price. A net made of polyamide fibres or coated steel cables was laid over a film of PVC or – as here – polyethelene. More accurate cutting patterns are of no interest in this type of use and for this reason no effort is made to avoid the formation of wrinkles.
The green houses shown in Fig. 400 are each 80 m long and 12 m wide. Figs. 401 to 406 demonstrate the erection.

400

401

403

405

402

404

406

407–410. Conference pavilion, Arnhem, Holland

Design: Eventstructure Research Group
Manufacture: Hoogerwerff B. V., 1971

The Arnhem conference pavilion had two levels that were connected by means of a spiral staircase with a wooden platform. The lower level served as a foyer, the upper as a conference room. The positive pressure amounted to 60 mm of water pressure below, but only 15 mm above, so that the ceiling between the two levels was pressed upwards. It consisted, as did the upper dome, of yellow PVC coated polyester fabric and was held in place at 1 m centres by cables to which sand bags were fastened below. Thus it was point supported so that seats were formed above. Up to thirty people could be seated on this surface under the above mentioned pressure differential. The upper dome, which was fastened all round by a zip fastener, could be detached in fine weather. The outer skin of the foyer consisted of transparent 0.8 mm thick PVC which, because of its great elasticity, was linearly reinforced by polyester bands. As a comparison of the building with the section shows, deformation of the membrane was different from what the designers had presumed.

The building was 9 m high and had a diameter of 18 m. The wooden stage lay 2 m above ground level and had a diameter of 5 m.

407

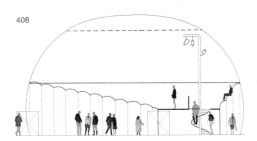
408

409

410

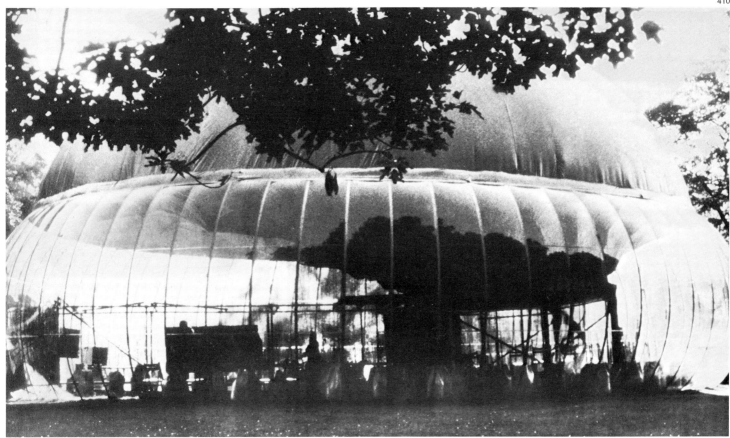

411

412

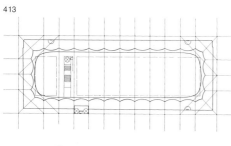

413

411–414. Interchangeable air cushion roof over a swimming pool in Rülzheim, near Germersheim
Design: Kleine und Richrath with Krupp Universalbau
Manufacture: Krupp Universalbau, 1972

This combination of air supported structure and air cushion offers interesting possibilities.
In the simplest form the membrane of a normal air supported hall is designed in two layers and the intermediate space is also under pressure. By using suitable cutting patterns different forms of buildings can be produced, as for instance structures which, with horizontal upper and vertical side cushions, are similar in outline to conventional air supported halls. If in pneumatic buildings of this kind the roof cushion is suspended on masts, the side membranes can be rolled up giving free access to the outside. In the example illustrated here two swimming pools lying one behind the other are covered by such a structure.
(Bibl. 29.)

414

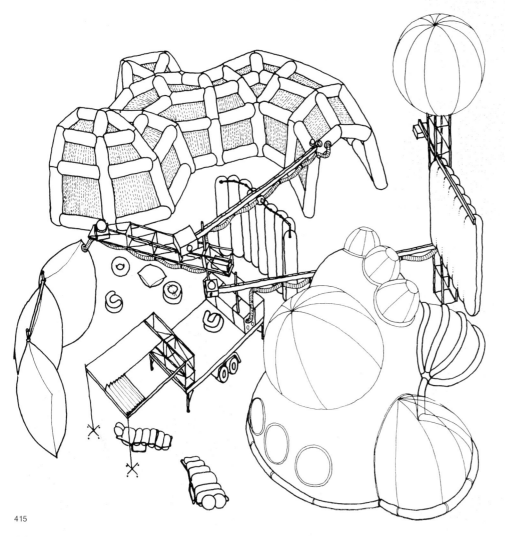

415. Mobile multi-purpose system
Design: Simon Conolly and Mark Fisher, 1970

Pneumatic forms of all kinds are extended from a transport vehicle to form an alterable environment.
(Bibl. 111.)

416—419. Pavilion "Atoms for Peace"
Design: Victor Lundy
Structural calculations: Severud-Elstad-Krueger Ass. and Birdair Structures, Inc.
Manufacture: Birdair Structures, Inc., 1960

The pavilion served as a travelling exhibition for the United States Atomic Energy Commission which was sent throughout Central and South America. It combined a refined technical concept, which has not been bettered in any way since, with an architectural efficiency of the highest rank.

The envelope was formed by two membranes made of vinyl coated polyamide fabric with a 1.20 m air space between which was divided into several compartments. The positive pressure in this air space was 40 mm of water pressure; inside the pavilion, which housed a cinema with 300 seats, workrooms and a test reactor covered by another air supported dome, the pressure was 50 mm of water pressure.

The entrances were rigid frameworks with revolving doors. While the exhibits were moved in and out of the building the entrance canopies,

415

416

417

419

which were linearly supported by internal lamellae, together with these entrance frames and
temporary outer membranes, which were later
dismantled again, functioned as airlocks.

The building was 100 m long, 40 m wide, 18 m
high and covered a surface of some 2,000 m².
The weight of the outer envelope was less than
6,000 kg. Erection lasted 3 to 4 days and was
carried out by 12 men.
(Bibl. 44, p. 41 ff.)

418

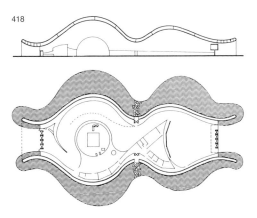

420

421

422

423

Sc, Mo + Mc / 1 di

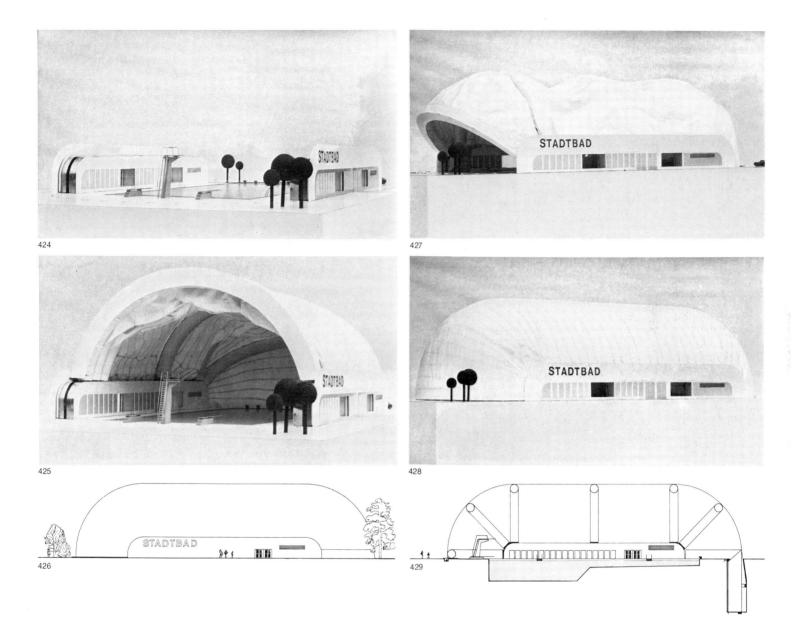

424

427

425

428

426   STADTBAD

429

420, 421. The Bubble
Design and manufacture: Research Development Establishment

The device is used for carrying goods or land vehicles over water, swamps, etc. A tubular closed membrane with a diameter of 60 cm functions as a floating body. Its internal positive pressure is 1,400 mm of water pressure. Attached to it is an open membrane which forms a canopy over the goods to be transported. On the inside of this canopy cables are fixed by means of loops and the goods are fastened to these cables. If the inner space is put under positive pressure the goods are raised up. An air cushion is created on which the vehicle can be moved. Sealing to the ground or water surface is provided by an encircling membrane apron. An outboard motor is used for travelling over water. The cargo is loaded or unloaded while air is let

out on both sides in the central portion of the tube, thus creating a joint which allows the structure to hinge open and shut.

Because of its low transport volume the craft, together with inflation equipment, can be conveyed on a normal vehicle trailer.

Fig. 421 shows the transport of a lorry with a dead weight of 4,250 kg and a cargo of 3,750 kg.

422, 423. The Ark
Design: Research Development Establishment

This is a smaller design of lifting vehicle. It can be stowed away in a trunk and weighs only about 100 kg, while the weight of the transported car amounts to 1,500 kg.

424–429. Alterable air supported hall with air tubes
Design: Krupp Universalbau, 1971

Until now air tubes have seldom been installed as loadbearing structures for large spans. They must have large diameters and high internal pressure to withstand wind forces. However, they are highly suitable as erection aids for light membranes. The illustrations show a 50 m swimming pool with diving tower that can be used with or without the encircling envelope according to the weather conditions. The air tubes support the membrane only when it is being pulled across and tilted; they do not need to be designed for the usual wind loadings as the hall is only opened or closed in calm weather. When closed the hall is operated with internal positive pressure, i.e. as a pure air supported hall. (Bibl. 28.)

5. Pneumatic structures – technical details

5.1. Material properties of the membrane

5.1.1. Survey of materials

Tests have been carried out on all kinds of materials. However, requirements for tensile strength, flexibility and durability heavily restrict the range of suitable materials. A summary is given by the following classification which is divided up into isotropic and anisotropic materials. (Isotropic materials show the same strength and stretch in all directions; anisotropic materials have direction orientated properties.)

5.1.1.1. Isotropic materials

Plastic films
Plastic films are primarily produced from PVC, polyethelene, polyester, polyamide, polypropylene, polyvinylfluoride, polyterephthalate or synthetic rubbers (polisobuthylene, chloroprene).

Fabrics
This covers fabrics made of glass fibres or synthetic fibres which are coated in a PVC, polyester or polyurethane film.

Rubber membranes
Rubber membranes are very flexible. They are particularly useful as test specimens, as a wide range of forms can be constructed from them without a complicated cutting pattern. They are not very suitable for permanent pneumatic membranes of larger dimensions because of their low modulus of elasticity and their low weatherability. They are used particularly in special pneumatic concrete and synthetic forming processes, which make use of their great ability to deform. (Bibl. 119, p. 168.)

Metal foils
Metal foils possess a very high gas diffusion resistance and their tensile strengths range up to 90 kg/mm². However, they have very low breaking loads and can only be used for pneumatic structures when they are fairly ductile. Aluminium foils are mainly used in outer space because of their high reflective properties.
Rocket research in recent years has provided information on the application of chrome-nickel steels for membrane structures. At the moment investigations are being made on how far such materials can be economically applied in architectural situations. The author does not know of any completed projects.
One of the major problems in the use of metal foils is the need to produce very exact cutting patterns.

5.1.1.2. Anisotropic materials

Woven fabrics
Woven fabrics have two main directions of weave initially at right angles, but some angular displacement between threads is possible. They can be made of:

organic fibres, e.g. wool, cotton, hemp or silk,
mineral fibres, e.g. fibre glass,
metal fibres, e.g. thin steel wires, or
synthetic fibres, e.g. polyamides (Perlon, Nylon, Dederon), polyesters (Dacron, Diolen, Grisuten, Terylene, Trevira), polyacrylnitrilene (Dralon, Dolan, Orlon, Redan) or polyvinyl (Rhovyl).
Organic fibres are seldom used today for pneumatic structures. Deterioration processes can be largely prevented by additive materials; however they have a considerably lower durability and a less favourable elasticity after outside exposure than mineral or synthetic fibres.
The lowest elasticity under loading is shown at the moment by the fibre glass fabrics (breaking strengths of 3 to 4%). However, because of the low elasticity their spatial deformability is relatively low despite the angle displacement of the fabric threads and thus their ability to adapt to synclastic or anticlastic surfaces (which frequently occur in pneumatic structures) is also low, so that a very accurate cutting pattern is necessary. It is for this reason too that metal fibres have hardly ever been used in practice despite their great strength.
A great variety of materials is used for coating these fabrics, in particular rubber, bitumen, paraffin, polyester, acrylester, polyacrylic acid (Plexigum), plasticised PVC, polychloropor, (Neoprene, Perbunan), chlorysulfonated polyethelene (Hypalon), alkathene, athylene/propylene-Terpolymerisat (Holstapren), butyl and polyurethane. (Bibl. 15; Bibl. 57, p 3ff; Bibl. 104; Bibl. 119, p 168; Bibl. 123, p 38; Bibl. 144, p 102.) They must be specially applied and provided with additives for ultra violet protection and flame resistance.

Gridded fabrics
Gridded fabrics are coarse weaves made of organic, mineral or synthetic fibres or metallic networks with mesh sizes of 3 to 20 mm. They are often embedded in several layers of synthetic films by means of casting or rolling processes. Gridded fabrics are particularly recommended when maximum light transmission plus high strength is required.

5.1.2. Synthetic films

Synthetic films are especially suited for use in pneumatic structures because of their high gas diffusion resistance and their great flexibility. They also offer advantages in their easy workability (welding and cementing) and their high light transmission.
Like all synthetic materials, however, under constant load they show an increased tendency to stretch so that they only maintain their form over a period of time if relatively low loads of less than 10% of the short term tear resistance are applied.
Furthermore, limits are placed on the use of films on the basis of their relatively low tensile strength of 3 to 20 kg/mm², their low tear-propagation resistance and their low weather resistance. The strength of thin films is affected primarily by ultra violet rays in conjunction with

Collaborators to this chapter: Rainer Hascher, Claudia Häfele and Verena Herzog-Loibl.

water vapour and can be greatly reduced within the first few months after an object was erected. The durability can be considerably increased by the use of absorbent carbon coatings or vaporisation or lamination of metals (above all aluminium) for protection against ultra violet rays – although at the expense of transparency, which is in any case greatly reduced by dirt in the course of time. If high light penetration is required it is often most economical to use the cheapest possible material (to which category most films belong) and not to clean this when it gets dirty but simply to change it.

5.1.3. Coated woven fabrics

5.1.3.1. Interaction of fabric and coating

As already stated, woven fabrics are anisotropic surface forms with two right angled preferential directions whose angles can be displaced. In the weaving process the threads are stretched more strongly in the warp direction (Fig. 1); thus this has a lower elasticity in comparison with the weft. In an extreme case the warp lies flat in the weave. In a fabric with the same form in both directions there is a somewhat lower stretch or higher modulus of elasticity due to the coating in the warp direction.

Other properties of the uncoated fabric, such as tear-propagation resistance and flexibility are also directly affected by the coating. For example, if the coating has a very high adhesive strength, then the long term tearing resistance is reduced.

However, one can state basically that the uncoated fabric is primarily responsible for strength and elasticity. Further important requirements, such as high gas diffusion resistance, flame resistance, resistance to ultra violet rays, insensitivity to mechanical influences and chemicals, must be provided by the coating.

Coatings vary greatly with regard to colour and light penetration.

5.1.3.2. Strength properties

Comparison with other construction materials
A comparison of the strength properties of these materials stressed only by tensile forces with other structural materials is offered by the tension length. It is measured on any constant cross-section and signifies the length at which a vertically hanging thread or rod breaks off by its own weight at the point of suspension. The size and shape of the cross-section are unimportant. The tension length is specific to each material and is expressed in terms of the breaking strength and the specific weight. It signifies the capacity of a material in terms of the possible spans within a structure.

The concept has long been used in the textile industry, because textile threads, which have no clearly measurable cross-section, can be best defined by their performance in material tests by means of weighing and tearing.

A thread or rod breaks when its weight cor-

responds to the breaking load. This is equal to the maximum weight (GMax). As:

$$R = \frac{V\,max}{F} \quad \text{and}$$

$$F = \frac{G\,max}{\sigma} \quad \text{and}$$

$$\gamma = \frac{G\,max}{V\,max} \quad \text{equals}$$

$$R = \frac{\sigma}{\gamma},$$

where:
R = the breaking length in km,
V = the volume of the rod in cm³,
γ = the specific weight in g/cm³,
F = the cross-sectional surface in mm²,
σ = ultimate stress of rupture of the material in kg/mm².

Table 1 shows tension lengths of freely suspended profiles with prismatic cross-sections (Bibl. 137, p. 5). From this it can be seen that, disregarding the duration of load application, temperature and other limiting factors, the best values are achieved by those materials which have low volumetric weight and are able to take up high tensions. Under short term loading natural and synthetic fibres have a greater tension length than high strength steel wires (St 200/220), as they have a considerably lower specific weight. Today tension lengths of over 80 km can be achieved with high strength synthetic fibres as well as with glass fibres; even higher values can be attained by monocristal fibres (e.g. silizium-carbide), so-called whiskers, which have tensile strengths of 2000 kp/mm² and more.

In theory considerably larger spans can be achieved with Perlon wires than with metal wires. Because of the relatively low modulus of elasticity, the flow behaviour under permanent load, the comparatively low fatigue strength and the considerably higher safety factors which are therefore required, Perlon is still inferior to steel in terms of the maximum spans which can actually be achieved.

Using a safety factor of 5 on a typical fabric as used today, the maximum span of a flat dome without additional stabilisation is about 40 m.

Tensile strength and stretch
The actual strength of the cross-section of fabric membrane is not clearly definable; construction and non-homogeneity of the materials used make an exact definition of the tension in kp/cm² impossible.

The tensile strength of woven fabrics is usually given in kp/5 cm. To determine the tension length samples of 50 mm widths (in accordance with DIN 53 354) are torn with a free clamping length of 300 mm and a speed of 300 mm/min. Up until now the strength behaviour of coated fabrics has generally been tested successively in the weft and warp directions.

The actual tensile strength of a woven fabric depends on the number of threads per cm, on the thread denier and on the type of weave.

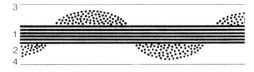

1. Diagrammatic cross-section through a coated fabric in the warp and weft direction. Key: 1 warp, 2 weft, 3 top side, 4 bottom side.

Material	σ (kg/mm²)	γ (g/cm³)	R (km)
lead	1.7	11.4	0.15
aluminium wire	17	2.7	6.5
structural steel St 52	52	7.8	6.7
duraluminium	50	2.8	18
pine wood	10	0.5	20
steel wire	220	7.8	28
silk	–	–	45
cotton	–	–	26–40
perlon wire	57	1.14	50
aluminium oxide whisker	2000	3.3	606
graphite whisker	2,100	1.4	1,500

Table 1. Tension lengths of different materials.

(Denier expressed by "den" is the weight of a 9000 m long thread in grammes. Some time ago the unit of measurement "tex" was also introduced. 1000 den corresponds to approx. 110 tex, or 1100 dtex.)

High pressure structures require woven fabrics with strength values of over 1000 kg/5cm and thicknesses of several millimetres; in low pressure structures, which make considerably lower demands on strength and stretch behaviour, strength factors of 200 to 600 kp/5 cm and thicknesses of 0.7 to 1.2 are usually sufficient.

Table 2 shows the results of uniaxial tensile tests on an uncoated and a PVC coated polyester fabric. The higher elongation in the weft is characteristic of coated polyester fabrics. It can be either smaller or larger depending on the method of production. It depends primarily on the shrinkage allowance during the coating process.

In contrast to these uniaxial tensile tests the biaxial ones offer a better insight into tension/elongation behaviour in practice, where the membranes are nearly always equally tensioned in both directions.

The bursting test, in accordance with DIN 53869, is made to establish the strength and elongation of laminar textiles during bulging due to air or fluid pressure up to bursting point of the ring clamped sample. The bursting pressure is generally given in kp/cm². For example, for a polyester fabric that has a tensile strength of 400 kp/5 cm in both the weft and warp, it amounts to 20 kp/cm². (Bibl. 103.)

Table 3 shows an evaluation of the cross-test described by M. I. Petrowkin (Bibl. 144, p. 103).

For larger mechanical stress so far polyamide fabrics (e.g. Nylon, Perlon, Dederon) have been employed. These elastic, friction resistant fibres are used especially in barrage dam construction. For normal pneumatic structures polyesters are almost exclusively used in Europe today because of their high dimensional stability. Polyester fibres have somewhat lower elongation and strength than polyamides, although the difference, especially in strength, between polyester and polyamides is now small.

Polyester threads can be produced in normal strengths and high strengths. For the manufacture of coated and rubberised fabrics the high strength, low shrink types are used almost exclusively. (Bibl 103).

Tear-propagation resistance and adhesion
Tests to determine the tear-propagation resistance give information regarding the "tear-propagation load" (kp) at which a sample, which is already notched on one edge, tears on. This kind of measurement of tear-propagation resistance, in accordance with DIN 53356, is disputed and attempts are being made to find other methods. On the other hand the present method is easy to carry out.

The adhesion strength expressed in kp/cm specifies the resistance of adhesion of the coating to mechanical separation from the woven fabric generated by tensile forces (not by shear forces). For testing purposes two freshly coated strips of fabric 5 cm wide were laminated under

light pressure; the force which is required to separate the two layers of fabric is given as the adhesive strength in kp/5 cm (DIN 53357). The test procedure is called a "Peeling Test".

In contrast to woven fabrics made of rough fibres, thick woven fabrics made of smooth fibres offer the coating a mechanical anchorage that is inadequate for the usual fields of use.

Without an adhesive agent the adhesive strength of polyester fabric 1000, den 60 T/m, 9.2/9.7 threads/cm, for example amounts to only 4 to 5 kp/5 cm. It is different in the case of open and lattice weaves, where an adhesive agent is not usually necessary, as here a welding of the coatings can take place by means of the formation of small plugs.

In the case of PVC coatings on polyester fabrics, isocyanates in conjunction with polyesters have proved successful as adhesive agents. Increased additions of isocyanate do not further improve adhesion and usually lead to a stiffening of the fabric.

In the case of polyurethane coating on polyester the addition of adhesive agents is unnecessary as the isocyanate itself is present in a very concentrated form.

Today adhesive strengths of up to 25 kp/5 cm can be achieved. However, as a decrease in the tear-propagation resistance occurs simultaneously with an increase in the adhesive strength, 12 kp/5 cm cannot usually be exceeded.

The tear-propagation resistance is also influenced by the fabric form, the type of weave, the formula of the coating paste and the twist of the thread.

In woven fabrics with a denier of 1000 the tear-propagation resistance is usually between 20 and 30 kp. The lowest tear-propagation resistance – here approximately 7 to 8 kp – occurs when each thread tears separately and the threads remain separated from one another.

For low pressure structures woven fabrics are most frequently used at the moment in basket or mat weave. Regardless of the value of the tensile strength, in general one can estimate the tear-propagation resistance at 10 to 15% of the tensile strength. (Bibl. 27; Bibl. 103.)

Relationship between strength behaviour and load duration, temperature and humidity
The long term tensile strength of coated fabrics is considerably lower than the tensile strength which can be determined from a short term test in accordance with DIN 53354.

Tests with PVC coated polyester fabrics showed that under permanent loads of 80% of the tearing strength some samples tore after only hours, many after several days.

The samples resisted continuous loads up to 10,000 hours at 50% of the tearing strength. In a subsequent short term test no reduction in strength worth mentioning could be distinguished. (Bibl. 104.)

Table 4 shows the stretch of the fabric in both thread directions under different loads and the increase in stretch under load continuing for some time. The increase in length stopped when a specific final value for the load in question had been reached.

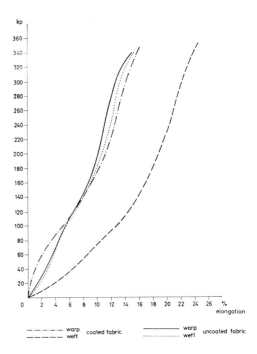

--- --- warp coated fabric   —— warp uncoated fabric
——— weft   .... weft

Table 2. Diagram of a uniaxial tensile test on an uncoated and PVC coated polyester fabric 1000 den, 9/10 threads/cm.

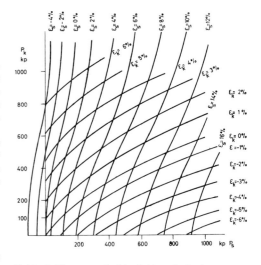

Table 3. Diagram of a biaxial tensile test.

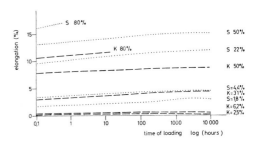

Table 4. Progress of elongation of a PVC coated polyester fabric in warp (k) and weft (s) direction under permanent load (loadings in % of breaking load).

Breaking elongations of 14 to 20% in the weft or warp direction were rarely attained in low pressure structures because of the usual factor of safety of 5 to 6.

Strength and stretch are dependent on temperature. With an increase in temperature, stretch increases and strength decreases. The material reacts conversely when it is cold. In any case one can state that temperatures of –25 °C to +70 °C are normal for coated and rubberised synthetic fabrics and within this range the influence on strength and stretch behaviour is low. (Bibl. 27.)

Even in temperatures of under –30 °C such fabrics are still stable; however flexibility is considerably reduced so that tears could be initiated by a sharp kink.

In Tables 5 to 8 the stretch behaviour in the warp and weft direction is shown for PVC coated polyester fabric under different temperatures (Bibl. 104).

If polyester fabrics are vulcanised, then even after several hours storage in the drying cupboard at +180 °C no loss of strength in the material can be established.

The influence of humidity is also important for the dimensional stability of a woven fabric. The better dimensional stability of polyester fabrics under the influence of temperature and humidity as against polyamide fabrics (in damp conditions polyamides show a tendency to lengthen and have a higher humidity absorption than polyester) is itself a decisive reason why polyester fabrics are used in preference today. (Table 9; Bibl. 27.)

5.1.3.3. The different coatings

PVC coating

Good weather stability, favourable price, easy workability and above all variation in respect of colour and transparency account for the fact that in over 90% of cases in Europe synthetic fabrics are PVC coated.

Usually it is stipulated that a PVC coating should have a thickness of at least 0.2 mm over the crossing points of the threads. For reasons of price and weight it is not in any case economical to greatly exceed this figure.

The support fabric hardly ages when the coating is strongly pigmented (e.g. with carbon).

If transparency or translucence is desired, it is usual to try to make good the lack of colouring by adding ultra violet absorbents (e.g. Tinuvin or Uvinul). (Table 10.)

Single membrane structures are often completely made out of translucent material, whereby in certain conditions additional transparent plastic sheets or acrylic glass windows can be inserted. Although translucent material only has a light transmittance of 5 to 10%, with an external brightness of 1200 lx light values of 120 lx are achieved inside such buildings. This corresponds to the brightness in a conventional office under the same external conditions. (Bibl. 104.)

A light transmittance of over 50% with a strength of approximately 300 kp/5 cm is provided by a special polyester lattice fabric with transparent coating.

Rotting due to mould or bacteria cannot occur in synthetic coatings or in synthetic woven fabrics. A reddish colouring which was observed in the membrane was found after investigation to be due to metabolic products of a fungus type whose nutritive substratum was probably fine dust. Even this could be prevented by special additives in the PVC. (Bibl. 104.)

Even atmospheric elements (water, oxygen, ozone, industrial gases) have hardly any effect on the PVC coating. The coating can if necessary be additionally provided with very thin rolled metal foil or even be damped with aluminium. A final coat of varnish, which for ultra violet protection can be strengthened with the finest aluminium lamellae, mica or quartz granules, prevents plasticiser dispersion and thereby sticking or smearing on the surface and, in the case of coloured coatings, diffusion of coloured pigments. As these varnishes are very smooth, they also reduce the effects of pollution and allow water to drain away more quickly.

Rubberising

In contrast to PVC coatings the durability of synthetic rubbers is considerably affected by industrial gases.

Translucence can also be achieved in rubberised coatings, as in the use of chlorosulfonic polythelene (e.g. Hypalon) and ethylenepropylene rubber; polychloroprene (e.g. Neoprene, Perbunan) is only suitable for dark coatings because of its tendency to yellowing. (Bibl. 103.)

Rubber coatings are practical especially when a greater mechanical tensioning has to be taken into account, e.g. in pneumatic barrage dams.

Table 5, 6. Stretch behaviour of PVC polyester fabric (high strength Trevira) at different temperatures.

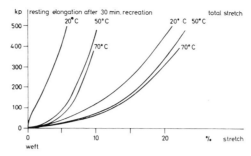

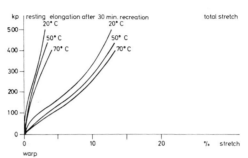

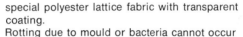

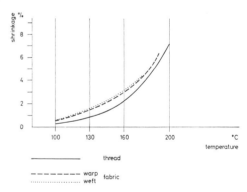

Tables 7, 8. Strength and stretch behaviour of a rubberised polyester fabric (high strength Trevira) at different temperatures.

Table 9. Shrinkage behaviour of a low shrink polyester fabric (high strength Trevira 1000 den).

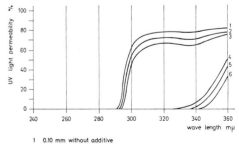

1 0.10 mm without additive
2 0.15 mm without additive
3 0.20 mm without additive
4 0.10 mm with 0,5 tsp Uvinul N 35
5 0.15 mm with 0,5 tsp Uvinul N 35
6 0.20 mm with 0,5 tsp Uvinul N 35

with Titanoxide 2 tsp TiO or 0,5 tsp Tinuvin P no transparency

Table 10. Ultra violet permeability of PVC foils

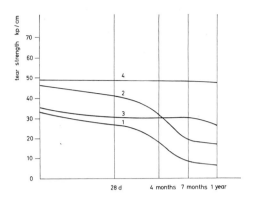

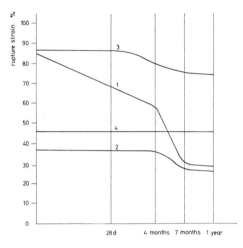

1 transparent material in weft direction
2 transparent material in weft direction
3 dark material in weft direction
4 dark material in weft direction

Table 11, 12. Aging of polyamide rayon fibre fabric DC15 coated with PVC on both sides.

Other coatings

Despite various advantages such as high flexibility, abrasion resistance and resistance to cold, polyurethane coatings have not much been used due to their high price and the fact that in the long run they are being attacked by hydrolytic decomposition (Bibl. 57).

The most weather resistant coating at the present time can be achieved with polytetrafluorethelene (Hostavan, Mylar). However, due to its high price and difficult workability it is only used in special cases.

5.1.4. Safety factors and data on durability

In coated woven fabrics the fatigue strength is considerably less than the tensile strength, the seam strength is usually lower than the material strength and a gradual decomposition through ultra violet rays cannot be completely eliminated. Therefore in low pressure structures today a safety factor of 5 to 6 is generally applied for the tensile strength of high performance woven fabric structures.

In tests to determine the suitability of specific materials more significance is given to the results of external weathering, in so far as this is carried out over a sufficiently long period of time, than to those of artificial weathering. The durability of synthetic materials is particularly affected by ultra violet rays. In the case of uncoated fabrics a higher degree of failure is usually expected in the weft direction, as in the cross-woven areas the weft threads are above the warp threads. (Bibl. 104.)

Tables 11 and 12 show the effect of aging on the strength and stretch behaviour of polyamide fabric DC 15 which is coated with PVC on both sides (Bibl. 144, p. 103); Table 13 gives information on the expected durability of coated high strength polyester fabrics in relation to the coating (coating strength as generally used in practice). (Bibl. 86; Bibl. 104.)

From the economic viewpoint the durability of coated woven fabrics is completely satisfactory, if it is borne in mind that any slight damage can easily be repaired in situ by a piece of replacement material and special adhesive agent and that apart from occasional cleaning to improve the light transmission, no maintenance of the envelope is necessary. (In this connection the caution of the German manufacturers, who at the moment will only furnish guarantee periods of 2 years maximum even for standard air supported halls, is difficult to comprehend.)

5.1.5. Behaviour in fire

Previous evidence of the behaviour of pneumatically stressed membranes has been gained from tests on single membrane structures with internal positive pressure ("air supported halls"). The information gained should not therefore be directly generalised.

Subsequent tests have been carried out by the Institut für Baustoffe and the Institut für Grubensicherheit in Weimar (Bibl. 153). The tests were made on a hemispherical membrane of 25 m diameter made of polyamide fabric with an inflammable PVC coating. During the tests the following weather conditions prevailed:

The air temperature was –6 °C and humidity was 52%; the wind speed on the ground was 1.8 m/sec. and at 14 m height 3.85 m/sec.

1. At a distance of 1 m from the membrane a row of wax torches was installed inside at varying heights. After 12 minutes the first hole appeared in the membrane. It increased in size only slightly due to the fact that the flame was drawn out by the air pressure differential and extinguished. It was deduced from this that the dimensions of burn holes depend only on the size and heat of the furnace.

2. In the centre of the hall 50 litres of benzine was ignited on a surface of 3 sq m. After 2.5 minutes the interior was completely filled with smoke; after less than a further half minute as a result of the increase in pressure caused by the increase in volume, a hole appeared at the top of the membrane through which the smoke was drawn; after 18 minutes the building began to sink in. The greatest heat inside occurred after 5 minutes.

3. At a distance of 1 m from the inside of the membrane a pile of wood with a ground surface of 60 × 60 cm and a height of 1 m was lit over a container with 10 litres of benzine. 3 to 4 m high flames licked at the membrane but did not ignite

Coating	Durability
PVC, transparent, 0.5% UV absorber	3– 8 years
PVC, translucent, 2 to 6% TiO$_2$, 0.5% UV absorber	8–12 years
PVC, opaque, pigmented	10–18 years
chloroprene	8–12 years
chlorosulfonated polyethylene	12–20 years
polyurethane	4– 6 years

Table 13. Durability of coated high strength polyester fabric in relation to the coating.

Country	Material	Weight g/m²	Thickness mm	Tearing resistance kp/5 cm	
				warp	weft
FRG	Hostaphan	53	0.04	45	36
USA	Mylar	16	0.015	8.2	5.5
USA	polyterphthalic acid ester, aluminised	110	0.127	~ 15	~ 11
USA	polyvinyl chloride	285	0.25	36	32
USSR	polyethylene	53	0.065	4.5	4.5

Table 14. Technical data for different foils.

it. After 3.25 minutes heat radiation caused a hole in the membrane; after 4.1 minutes the pile of burning wood was extinguished; after 7 minutes the fan switched off – the building began to sink in. The greatest internal heat arose between the 4th and 5th minute.

4. At a distance of 1 m from the inside of the membrane four piles of wood, each with 5 litres of benzine, and another in the centre of the hall were ignited. After 0.6 minutes the increase in pressure caused a hole at the top of the membrane; after 1.8 minutes heat radiation caused holes in the region of two furnaces; after 2.8 minutes the third hole appeared; after 3.3 minutes the fourth hole appeared; after 10 minutes the fan switched off; although two of the openings made were several square metres in size the hall did not collapse for 25 minutes. The greatest internal heat came after 6 minutes.

Similar combustion tests were undertaken by the Swedish Research Laboratory (Bibl. 131, p. 33 ff.).

The first test was undertaken on an air supported hall made of polyester woven fabric with PVC coating. The wind speed was 5 to 7 m/sec.

At the edge of the hall inside a furnace was installed. After 2.7 minutes a hole appeared in the membrane. The flames penetrated through to the outside without directly touching the membrane. No further damage occurred.

The second test was carried out on a hall made of polyethelene lattice foil with polyamide fibres. The wind speed was 2.2 to 2.7 m/sec.

Here also a small furnace was installed at the edge of the hall. After 5 minutes a large hole appeared and the hall collapsed so severely that the furnace lay in the open air.

In the Krupp work reports the following test was described (Bibl. 28): "In order to test a water spraying apparatus 8 plates with various sprays, toothpastes, tins, etc. were set on fire by means of remote ignition. The hall was a hemisphere of 11 m diameter. The sprinkler was set to switch on at 68 °C and reacted with most success after 57 seconds. The pressure rose from 27 mm water column to over 50 mm water column and the temperature from 10 °C to 22 °C; the oxygen content was almost constant. The rise in pressure caused the nonreturn valve in the draft channel to close automatically".

The results of these tests showed that the combustion danger for air supported halls made of rubberised and coated fabrics was very low, as long as they were not used for storing inflammable goods, and that the same fire protection conditions could be applied as for solid structures. Smoking is permitted. Welding work can also be carried out as long as the usual safety precautions are fulfilled. (Bibl. 28; Bibl. 104; Bibl. 153.)

Safety measures are specific (Bibl. 102; Bibl. 131, p. 34, 68):
– use of flame resistant material;
– adequate escape routes (maximum intervals 30 m);

Table 15. Technical data for different coated fabrics.

Country	Material	Weight g/m²	Thickness mm	Tearing resistance kp/5 cm		Tear propagation resistance kp		Breaking elongation %	
				warp	weft	warp	weft	warp	weft
FRG	PVC coated high-strength Trevira fabric, dtex 1100 f 200, 9.5/9.5 threads/cm, linen weave 1/1	850	0.75	330	310	35	35	14	20
FRG	PVC coated high-strength Trevira fabric, dtex 1100 f 200, 11/12 threads/cm, mat weave 2/2	1,000	0.9	400	400	70	70	15	21
FRG	PVC coated high-strength Trevira fabric, dtex 1100 f 200, 14/15 threads/cm, mat weave 2/2	1,100	1.0	500	500	70	70	15	23
FRG	high-strength Trevira lattice fabric, foil coated on both sides, translucent, dtex 1100, 5/5 threads/cm, linen weave 1/1	420		200	190	56	56	16	16
FRG	PVC coated super-strength Diolen fabric, 12/11.6 threads/cm, mat weave	873		451	362	43	56.3	17.3	21.5
FRG	PVC coated super-strength Diolen lattice fabric, dtex 1100, 17/18 threads/cm	1,250	1.02	550	625	70	62	20	28
CSSR	PVC coated Atmotol 800/TE 516, 7/7 threads/cm	691		226	234			20	28
CSSR	polyurethane coated Chemlon TE 514-TH 370, translucent, 14/13 threads/cm	532		562	479.6			43.2	31
CSSR	butyl rubber coated Chemlon TE 522, 11/10 threads/cm	770		406	326			25.4	39.2
GDR	PVC coated polyamide fabric	760	0.76	375	370				
UK	PVC coated polyester fabric	540	0.51	180	115			52	
France	PVC coated polyester fabric	650		230	200				
France	PVC coated polyester fabric	730		300	270				
France	PVC coated polyester fabric	850		400	360				
Japan	Hypalon coated PVA fabric	980	0.92	770	720	48			
Japan	PVC coated "Vinylon KV 71,000" PVA fabric	1,000	0.95	600	575	45	60	24	24
Japan	PVC coated "Vinylon KV 70,600" PVA fabric	600	0.6	325	300	12	14	25	20
Japan	PVC coated "Tetoron TT 51,000" polyester fabric	600	0.45	375	850	50	50	25	30
Japan	"Vinylon KV 40,629" PVA fabric, Hypalon coated on the outside and PVC coated on the inside, double ply	3,200	3.5	c. 2,000	c. 2,000			37	33
Japan	PVC coated "Cordoglass X-340/864" fibre glass fabric	1,000	1.2	550	500	30	26	4	15
Japan	PVC coated "Tetoron TT 4,000" polyester fabric, double ply	3,700	3.2	c. 630	c. 920	300	350	25	30
Japan	PVC coated "Tetoron TT 55,000" polyester fabric	1,100	0.7	c. 750	c. 750	60	60	25	30
Sweden	type 199 PVC coated nylon fabric	950	0.8	490	410	60	60	16	28
Sweden	type 196 PVC coated nylon fabric	708	0.6	300	260	35	30		
Sweden	PVC coated nylon fabric, dtex 840, 5/5 threads/cm	750	0.8	201	170	56	74	25	30
USA	Hypalon coated dacron fabric, double ply below 45°	2,380	1.78	910	910	180			
USA	silicone rubber coated dacron fabric	540	0.51	270	270	41			
USA	PVC coated nylon fabric	610	0.66	360	305	50			
USSR	rubber coated polyamide fabric No. 24	1,200		270	216			32.9	39.6
USSR	rubber coated polyamide fabric No. 806	1,200		180	130			28	28

– emergency exits in the form of single doors opening to the outside; however, these have the disadvantage that the high loss of pressure which occurs when they are opened hastens the collapse of the building;
– provision of spare fans, to maintain support pressure for as long as possible;
– rigid support structures preventing the membrane from collapsing completely;
– fire extinguishers;
– smoke vents at the top of the building;
– sprinkler equipment.

In Federal Germany it is usually stipulated that the envelope should comply with the combustion chamber test in accordance with DIN 4102. In the FRG guidelines for the construction and operation of air supported halls (Bibl. 136) brought in in 1971 proof of this was also required.
In order to comply with the strict demands of this Standard the coating must be made sufficiently flame resistant. This is achieved by means of flame resistant plasticisers (e.g. alkylarylphosphate) and other additives.

The air supported hall materials produced in Federal Germany are flame resistant materials Class B. 1. It is frequently said that this test is too stringent for coated and rubberised fabrics. Thus for the development of flame resistant materials initial tests are carried out in accordance with DIN 53 906 and DIN 53 907 (determination of the flame resistance of textiles with vertically and horizontally clamped specimens). The decisive criteria for the evaluation of combustion tests are undecomposed surface lengths of the sample, combustion time, afterburn time, after-glow time and flue gas temperature. The least stringent test is that complying with DIN 53 907, where surface decomposition and after-burning are lowest. The combustion chamber process (DIN 4102) compared with the combustion tunnel process developed by the construction materials testing office in Hamburg, has a somewhat lower proportion of undecomposed surface length and is therefore the more stringent test. DIN 53 906 provides the hardest test. Because of longer after-burn times the sample material is often completely destroyed. However a longer after-burn period can also give proof of low combustibility of the material. (Bibl. 57.)

H. L. Malhotra at the International Symposium on Pneumatic Structures in Delft in 1972 reported on a series of fire tests carried out mainly in England and Sweden. The observations made there deviate slightly from the test result described so far (Bibl. 102). It became clear how problematic generalisations of individual test results are and that as regards fire behaviour one is often obliged to deal with prognoses.
It is comforting to know that the number of cases of combustion of single membrane structures is very low (approximately 0.5% in the USA). For all other kinds of pneumatically stabilised membrane structures no evaluated test results were known at the time of writing.
For low pressure double membrane structures it can, however, be stated that destruction will normally take place more quickly because the internal air volume is less than in single membrane structures and because in most cases the loadbearing structure is stressed by bending, torsion or buckling. If the loadbearing structure consists of individual compartments whose air spaces are not connected to each other, then in certain circumstances only parts are destroyed. In this case it is, however, important that the membrane material does not continue burning of its own accord.
In the case of high pressure loadbearing structures damage to the membrane, including fire damage, could cause an immediate collapse.

5.1.6. Summary tables

Tables 14 and 15 show the most important technical values of the most commonly used membrane materials as at Spring 1972 (Bibl. 44, p 94, 98; Bibl. 82; Bibl. 103; Bibl. 104; Bibl. 131, p 168, 169; Bibl. 144, p 104). The indication of a country in which a material is manufactured or used does not preclude the fact that this or a similar material may be manufactured or used in other countries, but means simply that the technical details originate there.

5.2. Development of the membrane envelope

5.2.1. Structural design

In almost all cases single layer membranes are used. In places where concentration of forces occurs (anchorages, connections to other structural parts or triangulations) reinforcement is provided by superimposed flanges, so that the forces are conducted away from the membrane surface (Fig. 2; Bibl. 131, p. 235).
Doubled membranes are structurally necessary over the whole surface when – perhaps because of an above average internal pressure (e.g. in special high pressure structures) or of a lower than average membrane curvature – the forces in the envelope become so large that they can no longer be taken up by a single layer of the membrane material available.
It was not to increase strength, but in order to avoid corrosion through ultra violet rays, that the physicist Dr. Laing developed a three layer membrane with an outer coating of glass fibre fabric, a middle one of aluminium foil and an inner one made of plastic foil to which were attached revolving aluminium lamellae (Bibl. 96, p. 163; see also p. 162).
A multi-layered membrane is also produced by spraying insulating synthetic foam or by sticking soft lamellae on the membrane. Such measures bring about an additional stiffening. If the coating is so stiff that the pneumatically stressed membrane is structurally superfluous, then this can subsequently be removed. Then the building can naturally no longer be referred to as a pneumatic design.
There are two main possible designs for pneumatic envelopes made of two membrane layers separated from one another by a support medium:

1. The space to be utilised receives the same atmospheric pressure as the exterior (Figs. 3, 5).
2. The space to be utilised receives a higher or lower atmospheric pressure than the exterior space (Figs. 4, 6). In the cases illustrated here the support pressure is reduced from layer to layer towards the outside so that the inner membrane is stressed by the support pressure of the utilised space.

In Example 1, the most simple design, the membranes touch only at the ends. Lenslike cross-sections are formed (Fig. 5). If the membrane surface is damaged, the support air escapes and the membranes become slack, although the structural part will not collapse. Only in the event of severe applied forces need subsequent damage be expected. Lower heights with smaller radii of curvature in the membrane are achieved with positive pressure by means of guys (Figs. 7–11) or with negative pressure by means of supports (Fig. 12, 13). A large number of proposals which have not yet been executed can be found in Bibls. 83, 84 and 119. In the case of larger spans it is recommended that the space between the membranes be divided into individual compartments so that if the skin is damaged only single parts of it fail (Figs. 14–16).
The main advantage of a structure such as Example 2 is that in the event of external damage there is still a reserve membrane available (Fig. 17, 18).
A combination of both principles is represented in "pneumatic sandwich plates". Fig. 19 shows an English design in which both layers are joined together by narrow, parallel threads. The internal positive pressure is between 0.2 and 0.8 excess atmospheric pressure. The lamellae are produced in Great Britain as well as the USA and are available in different thicknesses. They are characterised by a high thermal insulation capacity as well as a high resistance to wind loading. Because of their relatively high price they have been used almost exclusively in the military field.

5.2.2. Cutting pattern

The commercial semi-finished material for membranes in the case of foils and coated fabrics is lengths which in Europe are usually supplied in widths of 150 cm, less often 120, 140, 160 or 200 cm. At the sides overlaps of 2 to 4 cm are required, so that an untreated width of 150 cm for simply curved surfaces gives finished widths of 146 to 148 cm according to the type of bonding used.
Overlaps are formed by localised linear reinforcements of the skin, which, depending on the cutting pattern and construction of the seam, can lead to a reduction in the radius of curvature of the skin – similar to that in the use of cables as additional structural elements.
With a doubled skin (See Section 5.2.1) the joints of the membrane lengths in the individual mem-

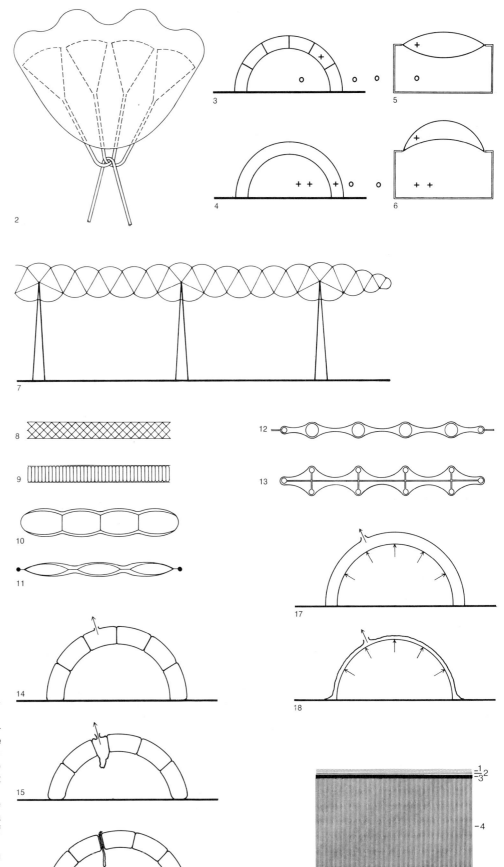

2. Surface diversion of forces for triangulations.

3, 5. Double membrane structures with the same pressure in the space to be utilised and outside.

4, 6. Double membrane structures with different pressures in the space to be utilised and outside.

7–11. Sandwich type positive pressure structures.

12, 13. Sandwich type negative pressure structures.

14–16. In the case of double membrane structures with the same pressure in the space to be utilised and outside, it is recommended that the space between the membranes be divided into individual compartments so that only parts of it fail if the skin is damaged.

17, 18. If the utilised space of double membrane structures is also under positive pressure then a reserve skin is always available in the event of external damage.

19. Pneumatic sandwich plates, M. L. Aviation Co. Ltd. Key: 1 Hypalon, 2 ply, 3 air sealed layer, 4 nylon threads.

brane layers can be staggered so that the stability is practically the same in all directions.

With synclastic and anticlastic surfaces the lengths must be cut in rounded contours according to their form. The less flexible the material and the less the possibility of generous deformation, the smaller the surface elements must be which comprise the total form.

In the case of Fig. 20 the seams increase – in relation to the same surface unit – towards the top of the dome. The reinforcement of the membrane towards the top leads to unequal elongation on the skin and thus to a deviation from the ideal form of the spherical section.

Fig. 21 shows another cutting pattern in which the seams are fairly equally distributed over the whole surface. However, manufacturing costs are higher in this case; furthermore there is a greater danger of failure under aerodynamic stress.

Figs. 22 to 26 show typical cutting patterns for standard halls by different manufacturers.

When geometrically different partial forms are put together, then various membrane tensions occur which can easily lead to wrinkles forming at the transition areas. In order to predetermine such tensions and to adapt the cutting pattern accordingly, exact dimensioning models are necessary.

Cutting pattern drawings of standard halls are today being prepared by programme controlled plotters. Further simplification will be brought by automatic pattern cutters, which are directly linked with computers to avoid the intermediate step "drawing".

5.2.3. Jointing techniques

5.2.3.1. Inseparable joints

The production methods used in envelope manufacture depend primarily on the basic material and sometimes on its coating. The requirements made of the joints are:
– a strength equal to that of the main material;
– as great a flexibility as possible, so that no kinks or break points occur in inflating and deflating the envelope;
– a density which will prevent the escape of air and penetration of surface water;
– a low relief so that there is little susceptibility to meteorological factors.

For the production of inseparable joints the possibilities are as follows:
– sewing,
– cementing,
– vulcanising,
– welding,
– riveting,
– clamping.

Sewing

Suitable forms of seam are the double and multiple sewn simple and double overlaps. There are also various special forms (Fig. 27; Bibl. 144, p. 113).

In the case of natural fibre fabrics the seams seal themselves through swelling of the damp fibres;

in the case of synthetic materials methods of seam sealing must depend on the actual material used.

In the case of coated fabrics wrinkles occasionally occur in the seams; the use of saddle making machines with combined lower, upper and needle carriage as well as thread with contra-rotation and chromium plated round pointed needles is therefore recommended. (Bibl. 57, pp. 6, 8.)

The strength of sewing threads is decreased by ultra violet rays. It is therefore best if the point with the highest loading, the overlap between the upper and lower thread, can lie deep in the material. Effective protection of the seam can be achieved by coating the seam area with a pigmented protective varnish or a pigmented foil. (Bibl. 104.)

The strength of a seam depends largely on the strength of the seam thread and the number of stitches. With too many stitches tears occur in the perforated skin; with too few stitches and weak sewing thread tears occur in the seam.

Cementing

Cementings usually have very high strengths. In peeling tests the cemented area is often stronger than the bond between fabric and coating. In the course of time the adhesive strength of soft PVC cementings falls considerably when affected by higher temperatures – probably due to plasticising diffusion in the cement.

Cementing is fairly complicated and comparatively expensive. Therefore it is only worthwhile for very high grade materials such as butyl rubber, neoprene or Hypalon, for repairs in rather inaccessible places and in the production of complicated forms.

Vulcanising

Vulcanisation can be used for joining together rubber skins or rubberised fabrics.

Welding

From the point of view of the time involved, welding, which can be carried out on all thermoplastic synthetics, is one of the best bonding techniques. In the case of PVC coated fabrics with adequate adhesive strength the bondings are stronger than the basic material. The main requirement is that not more than 60% of the coating should be on one side of the basic fabric. (Bibl. 20, Table 3; Bibl. 44, p. 37.)

There are three different processes: the hot key, the hot air and the high frequency welding process.

In the hot key process the materials to be bonded are fused to the seams by means of a heated key on the surface and bonded under pressure by means of two pressure rollers. Portable hot key welding machines exist which under favourable conditions can reach a working speed of 5 m/min. Welded seams 30 mm wide are now possible; usually however a seam width of 20 mm is adequate. (Bibl. 57, p. 9 ff.)

In the hot air process the membrane material is fused by means of jets of hot air. Here also bonding occurs through pressure of rollers.

In the high frequency welding process a high

frequency field is set up between electrodes which are usually ridge-shaped. This high frequency field heats the parts to be welded to the necessary temperature at the area of bonding. The welded joint is achieved by means of simultaneous pressure of the electrodes on the seam. The process works discontinuously. The seam length depends on the actual length of the electrodes. After each individual welding stage the whole machine moves one electrode length further. The working speed can, according to machine size and width of seam, go up 3 m/min including insertion time. The advantages of high frequency welding are that more than two layers as well as very thick materials can be bonded in one stage.

Riveting

Sealing is achieved using "pop" rivets placed at short intervals, while the inner membrane is pressed against the outer at the point of overlap. The process is little used.

Clamping

In this process metal clamps which look like large wire staples and which are equally deformed when applied, are shot in with air pistols at short intervals. The process is new and was first used on some temporary structures.

5.2.3.2. Separable joints

Separable joints can be necessary:
– in order to be able to insert movable parts within a section of the envelope;
– in order to be able to exchange parts of the envelope for other or new parts;
– in order to be able to separate large envelopes into parts suitable for transport and erection;
– in order to be able to manufacture large individual sections as standard elements and to combine them into buildings according to individual requirements;
– in order to be able to achieve a compound structural effect with individual pneumatic parts;
– in order to be able, in the case of expansion or reduction of the building, to add or remove sections.

With single membrane structures the possibility of changing size can only be planned in a few places for inseparable seams are considerably cheaper than any separation mechanism.

Separable seams, when they lie between zones of different pressure, must be as airtight as possible. If several individual pneumatic designs are joined together and the same pressure applies inside the building as outside, then the bondings only have to satisfy mechanical requirements.

From the point of view of technical practicality the following are available:
– zip fasteners,
– press fasteners,
– lacings,
– peg joints,
– connecting strips,
– different combinations of clamps, springs,

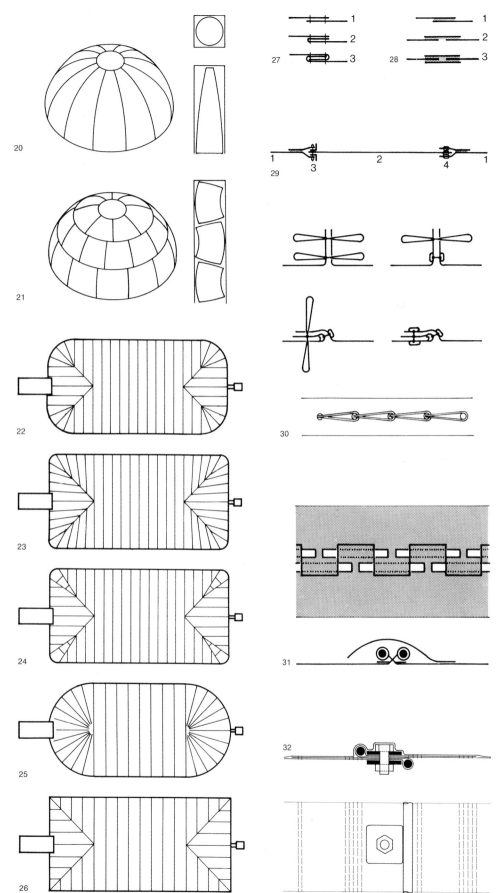

20, 21. Different cutting patterns for a hemisphere.

22–26. Cutting patterns of standard halls.

27. Sewn seams. Key: 1 simple lap joint, 2 simple overlapping seam, 3 double overlapping seam.

28. Welded and glued joints. Key: 1 simple lap joint, 2 connection with single cross-section, 3 connection with double cross-section.

29. Interchangeable window. Key: 1 envelope, 2 window, 3 L profile, screwed, 4 press stud.

30. Simple tent lacing ("Dutch lacing").

31. Peg joint.

32. Separable clamp joint with metal plates. Fuji Pavilion, Expo '70, Osaka.

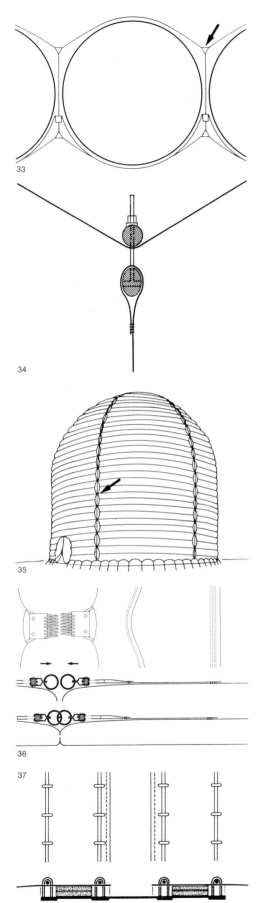

33

34

35

36

37

rings, material loops or membrane belts with inserted cables, link chains, etc.

There are zip fasteners for pneumatic structures in gas and watertight as well as normal specifications. Products with rubber or PVC coated support bonds (according to the envelope material) are also used.

Press fasteners are only used in "shear" tensioned structures (and even then the tension must not be very high). They serve to secure membrane sections to openings (Fig. 29) or to mount membrane flaps on the skin surface.

Simple tent lacings are usually carried out by "Dutch lacing". Hooks run along one side and cable loops along the other. Fig. 30 shows the phases of lacing. This is a type of joint which can be performed in one direction only at each seam.

Peg joints consist of membrane loops linked together and stabilised in position by round pegs which are pushed in sideways. They form a simple and safe joint which can be protected against meteorological factors by an overlapping apron which is welded onto one side during manufacture (Fig. 31).

A clamp joint with metal plates is shown in Fig. 32. In order to distribute the tensile forces of the membrane within the screwed joints and to prevent the skin from slipping through, continuous round profiles (steel or plastic rods, cables or pipes made of steel or plastic) are inserted at the edge of the membrane. The detail shown here is from the Fuji pavilion in Osaka (see pp. 76–78). The seams were covered on the outside by a protective paint.

Figs. 33 and 34 show the jointing of the high pressure tubes of the Fuji pavilion. 50 cm wide girdles were used which encircled the whole building horizontally both inside and out and were guyed against each other. The girdles were jointed outside the guying by the principle of the peg joints.

Figs. 35 and 36 show a further process of jointing closed pneumatic forms. Metal springs are fixed on to flaps and fastened to sewn-in cables. When the steel springs are pushed into one another, the pneumatic forms are pressed together. A cable is pushed through and holds the joint in position. (In accordance with DBP 1559112.)

The separable joint shown on the single membrane structure in Fig. 37 is also formed by a cable being pushed through. Brackets placed on a strip of synthetic material are inserted through the hooks of the membrane sections and four cables are drawn through the upper part of the bracket. Sealing is by means of strips of expanded rubber. (In accordance with DBP 1172025.)

33, 34. Separable joint for high pressure tubes. Fuji Pavilion, Expo '70, Osaka.
35, 36. Separable joint for flat pneumatic forms. DBP 1559112.
37. Separable membrane joint. DBP 1172025.

5.3. The anchorage of pneumatic envelopes to the ground

5.3.1. General

The anchorage has the task of conducting to the foundations the vertical and horizontal forces carried by the membranes. These forces result from the internal positive or negative pressure and the external loading. Figs. 38 to 40 show the dependence of the vertical and horizontal force components, which stress the anchorage, on the tangential angle at the base of the membrane. These are tensile forces.

To take up the vertical forces the deadweight of the anchor can be used or an applied load.

To take up the horizontal forces either the "passive earth pressure" of the directly adjacent ground is used or the friction generated along the anchorage surface.

Most anchorages represent mixtures of different types. Fig. 41 gives a schematic survey (Bibl. 94). The most important types of anchorages are briefly described below. In some diagrams the connection to the membrane is also illustrated for further clarification. Detailed illustrations of tensile anchorages can also be found in the Bibliography 119, p. 279ff. and in the technical literature on foundation engineering and soil mechanics.

5.3.2. Anchorage structures

5.3.2.1. Ballast anchors

In the case of ballast anchors lying on the ground, the size of the permissible tensile force Z is dependent on the deadweight of the anchor as long as it is only vertically tensioned. In the case of transverse tensioning the vertical force components are taken up by a friction force which acts horizontally. Their size is dependent on the roughness of the friction surface and the condition of the subsoil.

Cast-in-situ concrete strip foundations (Fig. 42) are usually only used in large permanent pneumatic structures.

Special precast concrete parts (Figs. 43, 44) can be formed in such a manner that structures with curved (polygonal) as well as those with rectilinear outlines can be anchored. Standard components such as concrete pipes (Fig. 45), road building slabs (Fig. 46), canal shells (Fig. 47) and barrels filled with gravel or sand (Fig. 48) are sunk as appropriate; after the dismantling of the building they can be redirected to their original uses.

Ballast pockets or ballast containers are filled with bulk material or water. Figs. 49 and 50 show the use of sandbags (Bibl. 20; Bibl. 144, p. 110). In Fig. 51 a very primitive form of pocket for small buildings is illustrated, formed by wrapping the lower end of the membrane skin around stones (Bibl. 3). The method shown in Fig. 52, in which a box made of steel plate with brackets welded on is used, is more solid (Bibl. 144, p. 110). In Fig. 53 the use of water tanks is shown (Bibl. 20). Ballast pockets have proved especial-

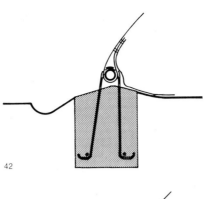

38

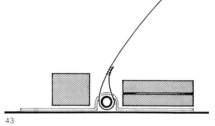

39

40

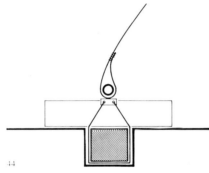
42

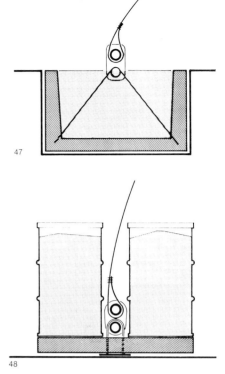
47

43

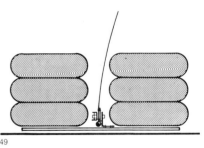
48

38–40. Force components at the membrane edge in relation to the tangential angle at the base of the membrane.

41. Schematic survey of the various types of anchorages.

42. Ballast anchorage – cast-in-situ concrete strip foundation.

43, 44. Ballast anchorage – precast concrete parts.

45. Ballast anchorage – concrete pipes.

46. Ballast anchorage – road building slabs.

47. Ballast anchorage – canal shells.

48. Ballast anchorage – barrels filled with gravel or sand.

49, 50. Ballast anchorage – sandbags.

51. Ballast anchorage – stones around which the lower end of the membrane is wrapped.

44

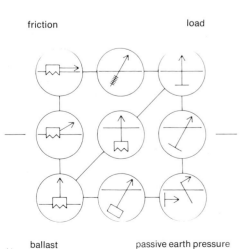

49

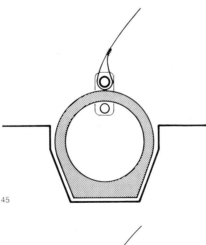
45

50

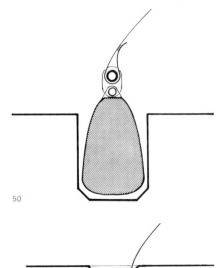

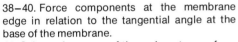

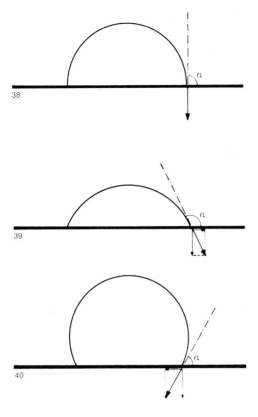

friction

load

ballast

passive earth pressure

46

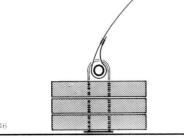

51

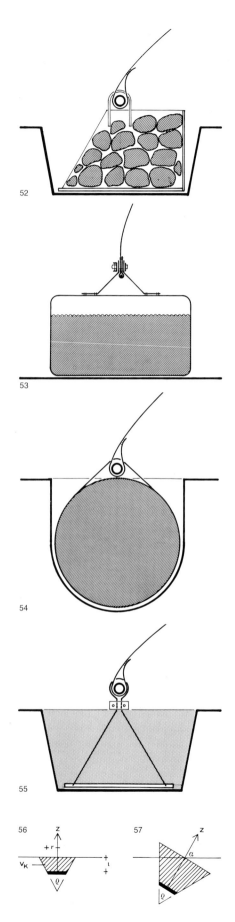

52

53

54

55

56

57

ly good for use in average sized structures with a span of 15 to 20 m.

Circular flexible tube foundations are particularly suitable for small structures. They are filled with water or sand and, like the skin of a pneumatic structure, are made of membranes and to a certain extent are part of the envelope. Fig. 54 shows an embedded water tube (Bibl. 15); yet flexible tubes, which can adapt up to a certain degree of unevennes in the site, are just as suitable for setting on top of the ground.

5.3.2.2. Ground-load anchors

Anchor plates (Fig. 55) are usually made of steel or reinforced concrete. In the case of vertical application of stress the possible tensile force results from the deadweight of the anchor and the weight of the earth frustum above it. If the application of stress is not vertical (as in Fig. 56) but oblique (as in Fig. 57), then as the angle between the direction of stress and the horizontal under constant stress is reduced, the horizontal component becomes larger and the vertical component smaller. For an approximate calculation of the earth resistance one can also take as a basis the weight of the earth frustum and ignore consideration of the skin friction of the frustum or the passive earth pressure, as long as α is not less than $90° - {}^2/_3\,\varrho$. Anchor plates are a simple, often very cheap type of anchorage (Bibl. 144, p. 110). A variation is provided by anchor beams which are dug deep in order to guarantee the necessary load application.

Screw anchors can be tapped or driven in according to profile. The anchor must have sufficient inherent rigidity against the buckling and torsion stress which arises. There are screw an-

chors where the shaft and the boring blade are securely connected and those in which an anchor line is connected to the boring blade. The shaft serves to install the anchor which cannot then be withdrawn. Anchor lengths of 60–300 cm are usual with plate diameters from 10 to 35 cm. Fig. 58 shows various possibilities for the design of the screwing blade. The short boring blade is particularly suitable for permanent anchorages, while those with long threaded screws are more appropriate for short term anchorages.

Screw anchors are capable of alteration in use. The force which is to be conducted into the ground can, in most cases, be transferred into the anchor axis by an adequate thread direction. In very dense soils, which the anchor cannot penetrate, a hole must first be augered; this is later backfilled after the anchor has been installed, e.g. with tamped concrete. In order to compress the earth, stakes can be driven in around the anchorage.

Large anchor screw depths do not necessarily mean greater grip. This is only the case when firmer earth strata lie below.

Because of the possible loosening of the subsoil when screwing down, a safety factor of at least 3 should be incorporated as the basis of the calculation of loadbearing capacity of screw anchors. In an area of ground water in cohesive soils a negative effect of frictional resistance has to be taken into account, and with uniform sandy soils a positive effect through the washing effect of the ground water.

Table 16. Holding power of screw anchors in relation to type of soil, disc size and reach of the screw. According to Lange/Glienke.

Disc diameter (mm)	Reach of screw (m)	Rich clay, dried-up, also containing stones	Well-graduated gravel and sand mixtures; equal-grained gravel with few fine components	Sand and gravel, coarse-grained, close-packed	Loam, firm (easily to hardly kneadable)	Filling-up, unconsolidated, loosely bound; sand, fine-grained
1	2	3	4	5	6	7
100	0.70	615	520	420	320	250
	1.00	950	800	650	500	400
130	0.70	910	780	600	450	380
	1.00	1,400	1,200	950	750	600
	1.50	2,550	2,300	2,100	1,500	1,000
150	0.70	1,100	950	700	600	450
	1.00	1,700	1,450	1,100	880	720
	1.50	3,000	2,800	2,400	1,800	1,200
	2.00	5,500	4,000	3,200	2,500	2,200
200	0.70	1,600	1,450	1,100	900	700
	1.00	2,500	2,200	1,700	1,300	1,100
	1.50	4,500	4,000	3,600	2,700	1,800
	2.00	7,350	6,000	4,800	3,800	3,500
250	0.70	1,500	1,400	1,100	800	700
	1.00	2,300	2,000	1,600	1,200	1,000
	1.50	6,600	5,500	3,300	2,500	1,700
	2.00	7,500	5,800	4,300	3,300	2,500
300	1.00	3,300	2,800	2,200	1,800	1,400
	1.50	5,800	5,200	4,600	3,500	2,300
	2.00	9,000	7,500	5,700	4,300	3,300
350	1.00	4,200	3,600	2,800	2,200	1,800
	1.50	7,500	6,800	6,000	4,500	3,000
	2.00	12,000	10,000	8,000	6,300	5,700

The loadbearing capacity of screw anchors is calculated as follows (Bibl. 94):

$$P_z = \frac{1}{V_s} \cdot q_r \cdot t \cdot d_s \cdot \pi.$$

where

P_z = permissible bearing capacity (kg),
V_s = safety factor (3),
q_r = specific frictional resistance (kg/cm^2),
t = screw length (cm),
d_s = screw diameter (cm).

Screw anchors can be used individually or in combination (Fig. 59). They are cheap and can be moved with simple equipment or machinery. Their possible applications depend very much on the type of soil.

Table 16 shows the holding power calculated by one manufacturer (Lange/Glienke) in relation to type of soil, disc size and reach of the screw.

Driven-in anchors (Fig. 60) have shovel-like blades which are joined together by means of a hinge. They are driven a fair way into the ground and contract further under tension. (Bibl. 144.)

Spreading anchors (Fig. 61), which are driven into the ground like stakes, under tension spread barbs. They can usually be used only once and thus are relatively expensive. (Bibl. 119, p. 302.)

Large spreading anchors, for which a hole has first to be augered in the site, consist of a round anchor plate of a diameter similar to that of the hole, a screwed-in tensile bar and two, three or four "resisting" surfaces, which folded together are set up over the round plate and connected by hinges. Pressure is applied by means of a tube or special tool, which grips the central tensile bar, to the hinge of the anchor plate which is then expanded and pressed into the earth. Finally the hole is backfilled.

Hinged anchors (Fig. 62) consist of a hinged tip, which is rammed into the earth by means of a tube which is subsequently withdrawn, and cables which transfer the tensile forces. A further cable regulates the position of the hinged tip and recovers it.

Injection anchors act as frictional resistance anchors. So-called "needle anchors" are frequently used. These are tubes, often provided with barbs or pins, which are open at the lower end. Using these under a pressure of 30 to 40 excess atmospheric pressure, cement or other hardening agents or agents effecting petrifaction of the earth are pressed in. Thus around the needle anchors a solidified, hardened mass arises, which offers sufficient frictional resistance in its tension loading.

The process is particularly suitable for difficult unconsolidated soils. Sand or gravel strata are especially suitable for the use of injection anchors. The cavities of a gravel structure can easily be injected with cement so that in the area of force entry or compression a solid anchorage is formed. Even when cement grout cannot penetrate into a sandy soil then a spread footing forms as a result of the high pressure and the subsequent local compression of the sand. The size of this footing is to a large extent dependent on the soil conditions, especially on the thick-

52. Ballast anchorage – metal boxes filled with stones.
53. Ballast anchorage – tanks filled with water.
54. Ballast anchorage – flexible tube filled with water.
55. Ground-load anchorage – anchor plates weighted with sand.
56, 57. Operation of a ground-load anchorage consisting of entrenched anchor plates.
58, 59. Screw anchors.
60. Driven-in anchor.
61. Spreading anchor.
62. Hinged anchor.
63. Screw plug with screw socket.
64. Screw plug with glued socket.

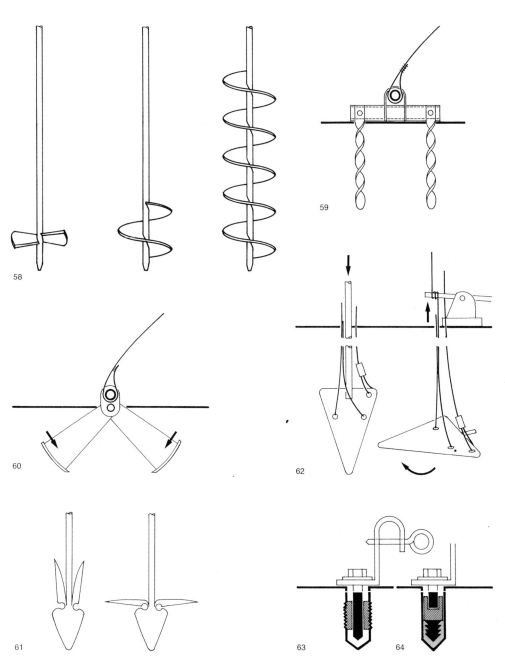

58

59

60

61

62

63   64

ness of the sand stratum. In the case of cohesive soils certain differences have to be considered with regard to the type of soil (distribution of granules) and the water content (consistency). Although cohesive soils cannot take up any compression mass, with the aid of an additional work process, injection anchors can still be produced in clay, loam and glacial marl of a firm to soft consistency and in silt of a firm to stiff consistency. The maximum working load is 25 to 30 Mp per anchor. (Bibl 94.)

Socket anchors are required for fixing on very hard ground such as rock or concrete slabs. Screw sockets with screw plugs (Fig. 63) are used as much as glued sockets (Fig. 64). The connection to the membrane is frequently made by means of shackles (Fig. 63). (Bibl. 20.)

The anchorage chosen in each individual case depends on the condition of the site. When using frictional resistance anchors it is advisable to carry out extraction trials on the intended site. Naturally the applied load is also governed by the distance between the anchors which in the case of individual anchors is usually 60 to 90 cm.

If different tensions occur in the membrane, perhaps because of the geometry of its surface, then the anchorages are correspondingly tensioned. They must be dimensioned according to the strongest tension or be adapted to the different tensions.

5.3.3. Fixing of the membranes to anchorage structures

In order to conduct the membrane forces into the anchorage a hem is made into which a cable, rod or tube is pushed and this transfers the tensile forces of the membrane to the individual anchorages. In order to prevent air escaping an air apron in the form of a membrane flap is attached to the inside. In the case of continuous anchorages the hem of the envelope is clamped by clamps, splints or cover plates. An airtight lower seal is usually automatically guaranteed in this kind of anchorage.

5.3.3.1. Single membrane structures

Securing of point anchorages
In a "one pipe system" the pipe running through the envelope hem is connected to the foundation by means of bolts (Fig. 65; Bibl. 15), hooks (Fig. 66; Bibl 92) or brackets (Fig. 67; Bibl. 54). There are notches in the hem where the anchorages grip.

The so-called "two pipe system" is somewhat more independent of the accuracy of erection of the anchor. As Fig. 68 shows, one pipe runs through the hem of the envelope and a second between the hem and the foundations. (Bibl. 92.) When cables are inserted a "garland line" arises between the individual anchors, which has to be taken into account in the cutting pattern for the envelope. As to the cutting in the case of small foil structures the cable can be assumed to be straight as the foil stretches to correspond with the tension. A simple project is shown in

Fig. 69 (Bibl. 20) and a more expensive one in Fig. 70 (see p. 104, Figs. 292, 293). In the case of Fig. 71 the cable takes on the membrane forces at the periphery of the building and conducts them into the individual anchorages while the cables running across the building to the opposite side serve to reduce the membrane forces on the surface (Bibl. 131, p. 118).

Cables can be sewn in during manufacture. Because of the possibility of simple and quick erection and dismantling, such structures are particularly suitable for "flying buildings".

Figures 72 to 74 show the boundary point of the USA Pavilion at the world exhibition in Osaka (see pp. 116, 117). A cable was sewn into the hem at the edge of the membrane, which was anchored to a huge concrete ring foundation by means of tensile cables.

Securing of continuous anchorages
The envelope hem is usually compressed with clamps against a continuous anchorage profile and a profile sewn into the hem prevents the membrane from slipping out. The disadvantage of greater erection costs contrasts with the advantages of this type of fixing, namely uniform conduction of forces, airtight sealing and good control of the drainage of the skin surface.

In Figs. 75 to 77, connections to profiles consisting of wood, concrete and steel are shown.

In the fixing detail of a radome skin to a steel cylinder shown in Fig. 78 clamps are used to produce the bearing pressure (see p. 93).

The detail shown in Fig. 79 illustrates a combination of continuous and point anchoring: a tube which runs in the hem and bridges the distance between the clamps is connected with individual clamps to the steel profile.

5.3.3.2. Double membrane structures

From the details given so far analogous solutions can be deduced for multi-membrane structures. The provision of an inner membrane apron for sealing is, however, no longer required.

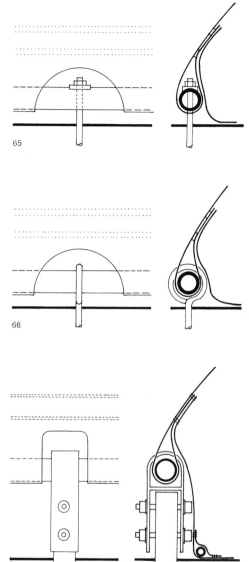

65–67. Fixing of membrane to point anchorage by means of single pipe ("one pipe system").
68. Fixing of the membrane to point anchorage by means of two pipes ("two pipe system").
69–71. Fixing of the membrane to point anchorages by means of boundary cables.
72–74. Fixing of the boundary cable to a concrete ring foundation. USA Pavilion, Expo '70, Osaka.
75. Fixing of the membrane to a continuous wooden anchorage profile.
76. Fixing of the membrane to a continuous concrete anchorage profile by means of a steel clamp.
77. Fixing of the membrane to a continuous steel anchorage profile by means of a steel clamping rail.
78. Fixing of the membrane to a steel cylinder by means of a steel clamping rail pressed on to it by screwed clamps. DBP 1 225 908.

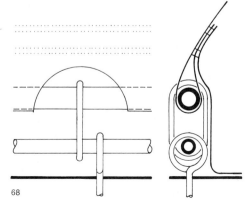

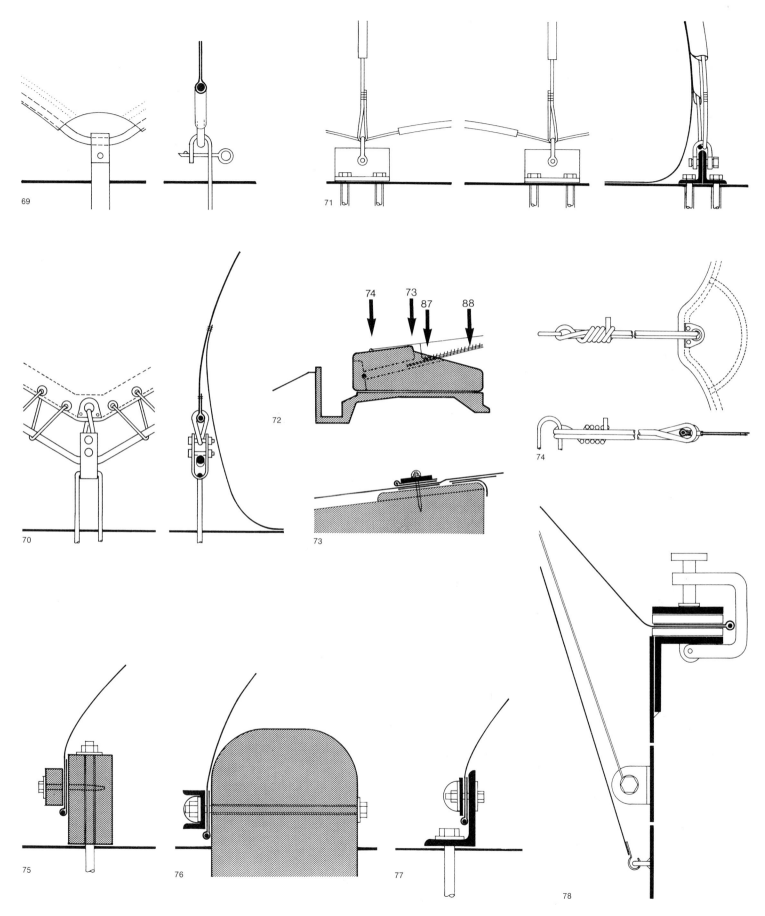

69

70

71

72

73

74

74 73 87 88

75

76

77

78

153

79. Fixing of the membrane to a steel profile by clamps.

80. Boundary formation of a mobile membrane apron. "Floating Theatre", Expo '70, Osaka.

81. Fixing of the membrane of a high pressure structure to the anchorage by means of closely spaced flat steel clamps. Fuji Pavilion, Expo '70, Osaka.

82, 83. Fixing of the membrane to the anchorage structure by means of flaps held by press studs. DBP 1 684 972.

84. Simple fixing of the membrane to a wooden framework.

85. 86. Fixing of the membrane to a steel ring. Information Pavilion, Expo '70, Osaka.

87, 88. Fixing of the membrane to a cable net construction by means of skirts of membrane material. USA Pavilion, Expo '70, Osaka.

89. Fixing of the membrane to a cable net construction by means of clamps.

90. Joining of individual membrane sections by means of sewn-in boundary cables. DBP 1 434 630.

91, 92. Fixing of the membrane to a cable net construction by means of loops; the cables are held together at the points of intersection by means of positioning clamps. Cabledome.

93. Internal drainage: fixing of the membrane to a rainpipe anchored in the ground.

94. Internal drainage: fixing of the membrane to a circular pipe guyed by cables to a concrete foundation.

95. Internal drainage: fixing of the membrane to a rainwater collection vessel.

96. Internal drainage: fixing of the membrane to a special precast component.

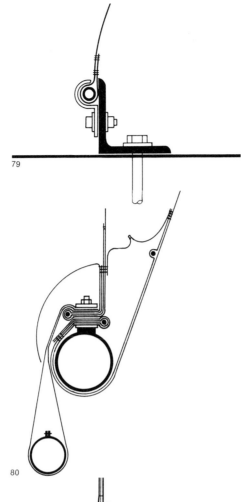

79

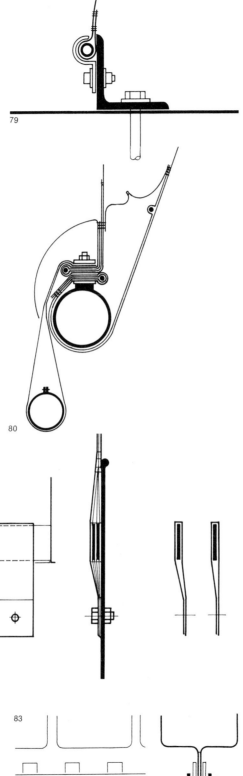

80

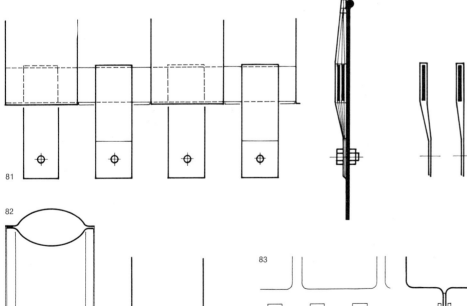

81

82

83

In addition some special forms are illustrated here:

Fig. 80 illustrates the "mobile" anchorage of the "Floating Theatre" at the world exhibition in Osaka (see pp. 88, 89). The two tubes were flexibly fixed at each end. The upper tube followed exactly the curvature of the envelope; the lower was the connection point on the ground. As there was negative pressure between the membranes, the tube arches were raised up so that they released a large opening which acted as an entrance and exit for visitors to the theatre. In order to close the opening, the lower tube and thus the whole envelope was drawn down.

The securing of the membranes of the high pressure tubes on the Fuji Pavilion (see pp. 76–78; see also pp. 147, 148) had to withstand an extremely high loading. Closely positioned flat steel clamps held two flat steel rings which ran through the uniformly divided hem of the envelope (Fig. 81). In this way the membrane was not weakened at any place on the hem.

In the solutions suggested in Figs. 82 and 83 the membranes are held by flaps which are fastened with press studs (DBP 1 684 972). The membrane tensions produced by the internal pressure are not transferred to the fastening. It is affected only by external forces.

5.4. Fixing of pneumatic envelopes to other structures

5.4.1. General

In the same way as they are fastened to ground anchorages, membrane ends are also fastened to other structural components. The main task is always that of conducting the membrane forces into the other structural elements.

5.4.2. Single membrane structures

The fixings to a simple wooden framework (Fig. 84) or to a steel ring (Figs. 85, 86; see also p. 39, Figs. 7, 8) show the relationship to the ground anchorages detailed above: the membrane is compressed on to a guide profile by clamps and also secured under heavy loading by cables or synthetic profiles sewn into the hem (Bibl. 46; Bibl. 119).

The skin of the USA Pavilion in Osaka (see pp. 116, 117; see also p. 153) was subtended by a diamond grid cable network. The membrane forces were conducted into the net by means of narrow vertical fabric skirts attached to the cables (Fig. 87). As the bands of cables lay on two planes because of the intersections (Fig. 88), these fabric skirts had to have different heights. (Bibl. 46.)

A similar construction was carried out in 1972 on two warehouses in France. Here also the membrane was additionally stabilised by subtended cables. Fig. 89 shows how the membrane forces are transferred into the cables by means of two clamps and fabric loops. According to the manufacturer this detail is considerably cheaper than that on the USA Pavilion.

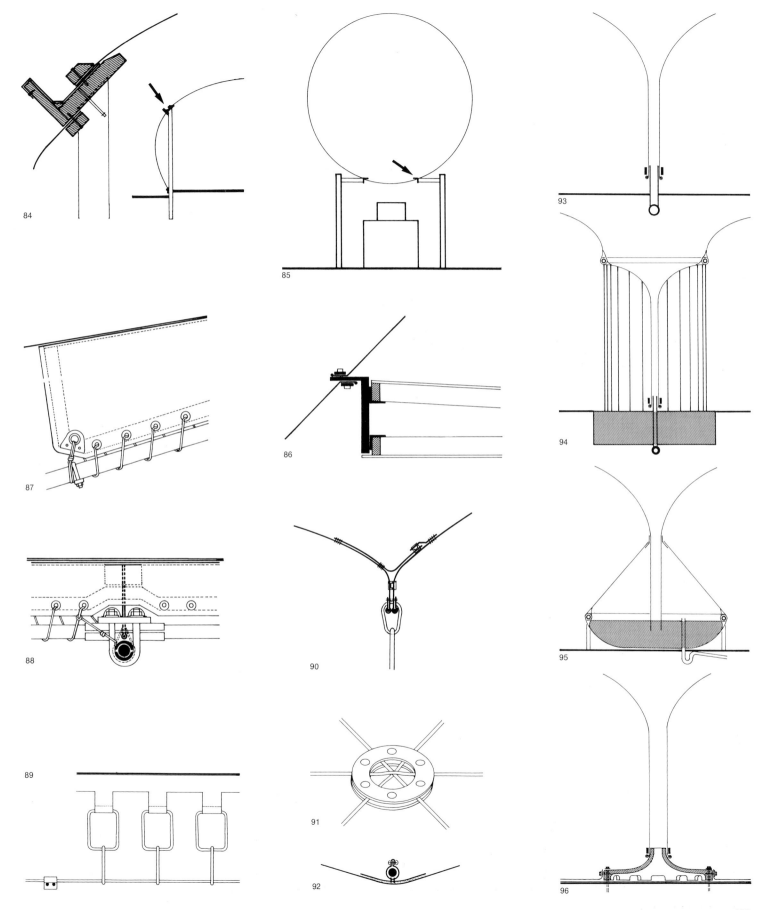

84

85

86

87

88

89

90

91

92

93

94

95

96

97, 98. Simple connections of cushion structures to steel profiles.

99, 100. Connections, sealed with synthetic profiles, of cushion structures to steel profiles. DBP 1 937 998.

101, 102. Fixing of a cushion structure to a flat steel profile. Forum Steglitz, Berlin.

103, 104. Fixing of individual cushions to a tubular frame. Festival Plaza, Expo '70, Osaka.

105. Cable guyed cushion framework.

106. Cushion structure guyed against an arched framework.

107–109. Connection of a cushion structure to a framework of horizontal I profiles. Boston Arts Centre Theatre.

110. Connection of two cushions to a pipe.

111. Rectilinear cable net as support for a cushion structure.

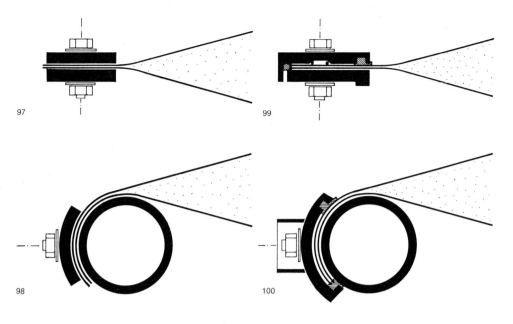

97

99

98

100

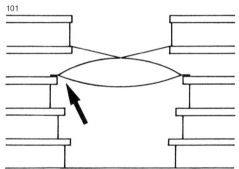

101

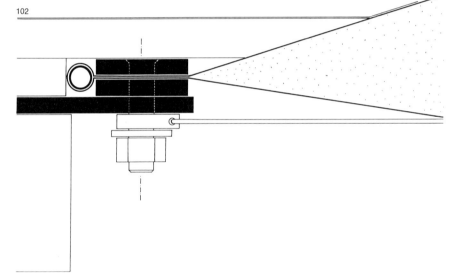

102

Another solution is shown in Fig. 90. Here individual membrane sections are joined together by means of sewn-in boundary cables. The resulting groove is protected against rainwater by a flap which is sewn on to one side and attached to the other by press studs. (DBP 1 434 630.)

For the "Cabledome", a development by Birdair in 1971 (see p. 121), a very simple detail was found for joining the cables to each other. The cables, which are arranged in three sheaves on the outside of the membrane, pass through from base to base and are held in the intersections by positioning clamps (Fig. 91). Loops serve to fasten the membrane to the cables (Fig. 92).

Compared with a reinforcement of the membrane by a cable net lying on the outside a subtended net has clear advantages:

– the connection points between membrane and

cable are not exposed to weather and pollution by the atmosphere;

– the connections do not need to be rainproofed;

– the cables do not chafe on the skin when this moves under the effect of wind;

– erection is simplified as the membrane lies on the cable net instead of being suspended from it.

If the rainwater is drained off inside the building, then there are additional places at which the membrane must be connected to other structural components.

Fig. 93 shows the direct connection to a rainpipe anchored in the ground. In Fig. 94 the membrane forces are taken up by a circular pipe which is guyed by cables to a concrete foundation. Further possibilities are the connection to a water collection vessel with overflow (Fig. 95) or

to a precast component (Fig. 96) which channels the water into a double membrane which forms the floor. (Bibl. 119.)

5.4.3. Double membrane structures

Patented connections to steel profiles in simple solutions such as those illustrated in Figs. 97 and 98 (DBP 1 937 998) have already been used several times.

The central hall of Forum Steglitz in Berlin (see p. 58) is covered by two large air cushions. Fig. 101 shows the position, Fig. 102 the details of the boundary connection. The cable net, which is used for safety reasons, is attached to the bolts that hold the flat steel profiles in place. (Bibl. 138.)

The large air cushions of the Festival Plaza in

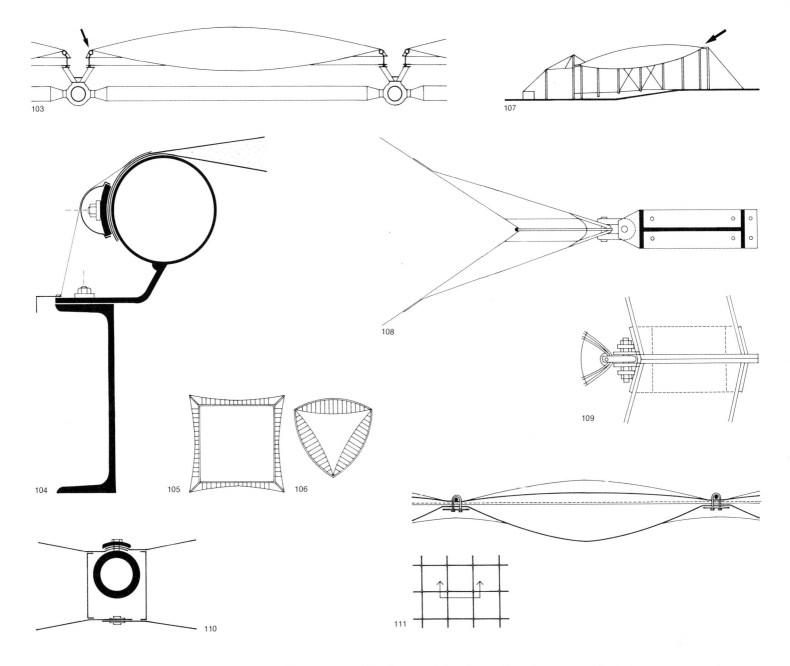

103

107

108

104 105 106

109

110 111

Osaka (see pp. 48, 49) were erected on a tubular framework which in turn sat on a framework made of ⌷ profiles (Figs. 103, 104). Aprons were drawn over the screwed joints to drain off the rainwater.

Where greater sealing is demanded the connections can be further improved by the insertion of flexible profiles (DBP 1937 998) (Figs. 99, 100).

Frameworks for cushion structures can be guyed by cables on the outside, as in Fig. 105, in order to reduce the strong bending moments in the frame profiles. In Fig. 106 the membrane forces are conducted by means of cables into arched frame elements mainly under compression stress. (Bibl. 119.)

In a theatre in Boston (see p. 47) in 1959 the combination of an encircling framework of horizontal I profiles with cables which resisted the membrane forces had already been realised.

(Figs. 107–109.) The framework is polygonal in plan form. Three cables are sewn in to the edges of the cushion and these run together into the corners of the polygon. Thus bending tension in the framework elements as a result of membrane forces is avoided.

Figs. 110 and 111 show combinations of pipes and cable nets with double membranes (Bibl. 119). Neither idea has been executed so far.

5.5. Access constructions

5.5.1. General

Buildings whose utilisation space has a higher or lower pressure than the exterior need special access structures which are as airtight as possible when closed and keep the leakage of air as

low as possible during the passage of persons or materials.

5.5.2. Passage of persons

Alongside the rigid conventional doors which are generally used in building, there are some special constructions for installation in membranes.

Trapdoors, which are situated in cable reinforced round sections of the envelope (Fig. 112), are kept in balance under a central axis of rotation and low internal pressure of the building (Bibl. 119). Under an eccentric axis of rotation the regulation of pressure must be achieved by means of springs or weights. The loss of air is controlled by the period of opening. According to Bibl. 136 trapdoors are only permitted as sup-

112. Trapdoor.
113. Simple membrane apron.
114. Slipping-through door.
115. Lip door.
116. Cushion door.
117. Revolving door for personnel.
118, 119. Air locks.
120, 121. Air locks with revolving doors. DBP 1559208.

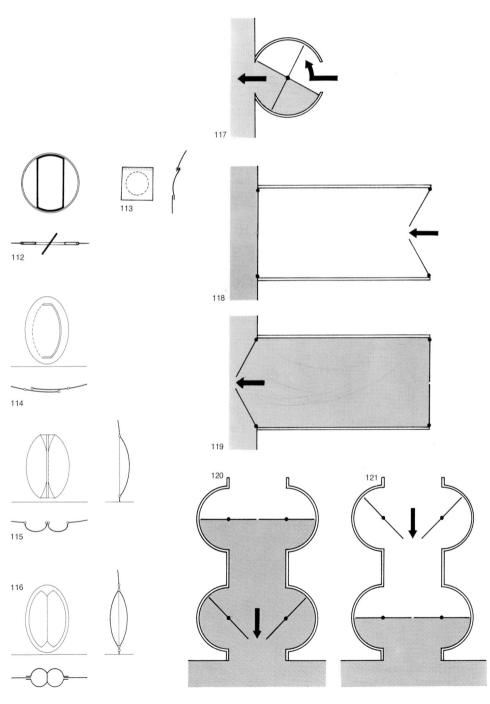

117

113

112

118

114

119

115

120   121

116

plementary doors; simple trapdoors, such as the one illustrated in Fig. 113, are at the most allowed in primitive "bubbles" which do not require authorisation. The same applies to all other access openings not intended as emergency exits.

Slipping-through doors consist of two membranes of which the inner one is pressed against the outer one (Fig. 114). They are difficult to open from both sides and the apex and base are in danger of splitting.

With lip doors two lip-shaped pouches are pressed against one another by the internal pressure (Fig. 115). Lip doors are easy to open from the outside, but less easy from the inside. Here also the apex and base are at risk.

With cushion doors two elongated rolls are pressed against each other by their internal pressure (Fig. 116). Usually no satisfactory sealing is achieved at the base and apex. The positive pressure in the rolls must be separately maintained independent of the pressure inside the building; it must be higher than the pressure inside the building.

Revolving doors (Fig. 117) are always under stable balance. They are the most frequently used type of access and permit constant through traffic in both directions without great losses in pressure.

5.5.3. Passage of material

Because of the high loss of pressure from large openings, single doors can only be used in the case of an automatically controlled short period of opening, or in very large structures.

Air locks (Figs. 118, 119) must have doors at both ends of the air lock which open and close alternately. They are particularly suitable for the transport of bulk goods and the use of vehicles within the building. (Bibl. 144, p. 114.)

A particularly expensive air lock is illustrated in Figs. 120 and 121 in which the doors are positioned in the centre (DBP 1559208). In order to produce the necessary pressure inside the air lock, small supplementary fans can be installed in the wall of the air lock. The side walls of the air lock can consist of stiff material or of a framework with a skin covering.

The connections between the flexible membrane and the stiff access construction are particularly difficult. Abrupt tension differentials always occur in the membrane when no transition elements are provided. Therefore the tension from the membrane must be properly intercepted, i.e. with a sewn-in boundary cable, then a membrane collar (for example) must form the joint from the cable to the access construction.

According to the FRG guidelines (Bibl. 136) every pneumatic structure must have at least two exits situated as far apart from each other as possible, which must be easily and safely accessible and may be no further than 35 m from any point in the building. In addition, near to air locks and revolving doors, outward opening doors leading directly outside can be required.

These access constructions show very clearly

how little aesthetic interests have concentrated up until now on pneumatic structures and how much architects have ignored this field.

In the last decade thousands of pneumatic structures have been produced and yet, from the aesthetic point of view, it will hardly be possible to find among them any satisfactory solutions for those structural elements which are not part of the membrane.

5.6. Stabilisation measures

5.6.1. General

The stabilising pressure of the membrane is an important structural element in a pneumatic structure. Its production and maintenance as well as its constant control require the provision of special technical equipment.

In the case of buildings and building elements the stabilising pressure is usually produced by inflation devices which are arranged on the outside of the structure.

As an additional measure for positive pressure structures, especially those with large spans, it has been repeatedly suggested that the wind pressure be intercepted by large funnels and conducted into the interior of the pneumatic structure. Thus under external wind loading one would also at the same time be able to produce a higher internal pressure. However this is not practical for very flat forms where the surface is stressed only by wind suction. (However the author knows of no instance of this idea being put into practice.)

Further possibilities are seen in the use of gases (helium, coal gas, hydrogen) for multi-membrane structures. Such solutions will, however, always remain special cases, as gases are either too expensive or too explosive.

More realistic is the exploitation of the uplift forces of warm air in buildings with large spans. These are effective both for single membrane structures which are situated in cold climatic zones and for buildings which are heated in winter.

For smaller structures, say up to the size of small camping tents, the use of high pressure gas cylinders for inflation has proved effective. The process is, however, only practicable for hermetically sealed elements. The same applies for bellows and hand pumps.

5.6.2. Mechanical equipment

A distinction is made between axially, radially and tangentially working inflation devices according to the control of the air current.

In the case of *axially* working devices (Fig. 122) the air current flows in the direction of the axis of the device, whereby several devices can be arranged in series. The noise at high speeds is greater than with other devices. The capacity can be increased by the arrangement of propellers rotating in opposite directions. The direction of the air current can be easily reversed by reversing the direction of the propeller.

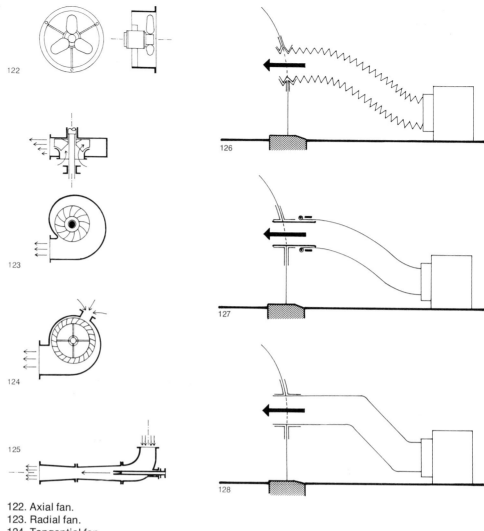

122. Axial fan.
123. Radial fan.
124. Tangential fan.
125. Jet compressor.
126–128. Diagrams of various possible joints between fan and envelope.

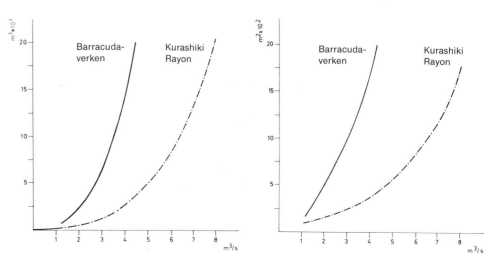

Table 17. Relationship between fan capacity and building volume or ground surface of building in the case of standard air supported halls.

In the case of *radially* working devices (Fig. 123) the air is sucked in sideways, forced outwards centrifugally by the rotation of a cylinder and blown out at right angles to the air intake. Because of air deflection the devices cannot easily be added to each other. High running speeds are necessary to produce the air pressure. The direction of flow cannot be reversed.

In the case of *tangentially* working devices (Fig. 124) a shaft with fins which act as impellers revolves inside a cylinder. The air is sucked in tangentially in the area of the cylinder casing and also blown out tangentially. This device is usually only produced in small sizes. It is used in preference where increased demands for operational quietness are made. They are especially suitable for producing negative pressure. However, the direction of flow is not reversible.

According to the air capacity a distinction is drawn between fans, blowers and compressors.

A *fan* is an apparatus with a low pressure capacity but large cross-sections for the air current. An (axial) propeller fan needs the most power when producing a low air current under high pressure (e.g. at the end of the inflation of a building), a (radial) centrifugal fan needs the most power producing a strong air current under low pressure (e.g. at the beginning of the inflation of a building).

A slightly higher pressure can be produced with *blowers* than with fans. Radial blowers can only be installed under certain conditions because they have only a moderate volumetric capacity. The best energy yield is offered by circulating displacement blowers, in which no internal compression develops. They work with minimal pressure and gradually develop only as much pressure as is required by the counter pressure of the pneumatic structure. Their pressure capacity adapts and is only a little above the actual internal pressure of the structure at any time.

Compressors, as the name suggests, are appliances with high compression and therefore high pressure production. Aerodynamic compressors are expensive high speed machines of which the main disadvantage is the high temperature of the discharged air (over 200 °C); the output is over 3 excess atmospheric pressure.

With positive displacement compressors, which have at their disposal a fixed internal compression ratio and a constant delivery flow, pressures of up to 7 bar can be produced which makes them suitable for use in high pressure structures. In the case of low pressure structures such a high pressure output is not desired because the air expands again after entering the structure; furthermore, the enormous force of the air current can lead to damage to the membrane. If one still wishes to work with compressors on low pressure structures, one can add to the compressors jets, in whose air vent area air from the surroundings is carried forward by negative pressure (Fig. 125). In this way the positive pressure of the main air current is reduced and a larger quantity of air is transported with the same amount of energy.
(Bibl. 163.)

In contrast to the distinction made here, in line with general usage the term "fan" will be used henceforth even when blowers or compressors are being discussed.

5.6.3. Fan specifications and their control mechanisms

Determination of the required fan capacity results from the anticipated quantity of air leakage as well as the characteristics of the fan and the supply channels.

In the case of single membrane structures the need for support air does not increase linearly with increased building volume conditioned by the relatively low proportion of openings. Table 17 shows the relationship between fan capacity and volume of building or building ground surface. (Bibl. 44, p. 100.)

The average current consumption can be estimated according to the following formula (Bibl. 25):

$$\text{KW required} = \frac{\text{covered surface (m}^2)}{200 \text{ to } 250} \cdot$$

Occasional fluctuations in support pressure can become very dangerous in the presence of snow or wind loading. Therefore in the first place the support air in winter should always be warmed (approx. +12 °C is sufficient inside, measured at the apex), so that no snow remains. In the second place it should be possible to adjust the fan capacity to the actual wind pressure. In the case of buildings with almost equal main directions of extension, the internal pressure must be raised when the wind loading increases in order to further stabilise the membrane in position. With flat structures the wind loading acts in the form of suction forces. Here the internal pressure must be reduced by decompression or automatically controlled positive pressure valves, so that the membrane tension is not increased too much.

If the interior of a pneumatic structure is used by living beings, then the fan equipment has the function of air renewal as well as the task of producing support pressure. In small buildings, because of leaks the air supply must be maintained high enough to ensure adequate ventilation. With large halls one calculates 1 to 2 changes of air per hour.

To ensure uniform distribution of the inflowing air current and to reduce the air speed, the provision of "air current distributors" is recommended, perhaps in the form of an air distributing ring system with a great number of small discharge openings (Bibl. 44, p. 104).

In Figs. 126 to 128 different kinds of air supply lines are illustrated. Fig. 126 shows a concertina type tube whose length is variable; Fig. 127 shows a membrane tube, whose connection to the building envelope is reinforced by a piece of pipe. A stiff supply system is shown in Fig. 128; it has the advantage of an exactly controllable air supply but a considerable disadvantage in that it cannot yield to movements in the building without transition members which can lead to tension peaks in the membrane.

For conventional air supported halls the following rules can be compiled for the establishment of stabilisation equipment (Bibl. 44, p. 101; Bibl. 144, p. 114).

1. The fan installations must be suitable for continuous operation and be designed in such a way that they meet even maximum demands. The maximum stabilisation pressure must be quickly and reliably attainable.

2. Two or more fans, where under normal conditions only one would be operated, guarantee that in the event of a mechanical defect another fan can be switched on. Valves prevent loss of air due to non-functioning fans.

3. Care must be taken that no snow can collect in the area of the fan intakes so that the supply of airs is not reduced.

4. The injection pressure should be just above the internal pressure. This will make the best use of the energy supplied.

Further detailed directions can be found in Bibl. 136.

5.7. Transport and erection

How small the transport volume in relation to the final volume and the weight of the pneumatic structure is and of how few individual parts it consists becomes especially evident in the transport and erection procedure; this aspect also makes pneumatic structures particularly suitable for use in remote, e.g. polar, areas and in outer space.

In all structures the erection and dismantling procedure has to be carefully thought out for each individual case, as in this phase the membrane is not stabilised in position and is especially susceptible to damage.

In particular the following properties have a favourable effect on transport and erection (Bibl. 44, p. 121 ff.; Bibl. 144, p. 105 ff.).

1. With the exception of anchoring on site all parts of the structure are normally prefabricated. The anchoring too can be formed from prefabricated parts.

2. The weight of the structure is extremely low. It is essentially defined by the weight of the membrane, which is about 3 kg/m² including localised reinforcements.

3. The proportion of erection costs to total expenditure is only 8 to 25%.

4. The structure can be transferred to other sites and also be used after lengthy storage.

5. The erection and dismantling times are very short. Depending on the size of the building, ground conditions, type of anchorages, size of erection team – usually 5 to 8 men – erection for a standard hall lasts 1 to 4 days, dismantling less than 1 day including packing for transport.

5.8. Structural/physical factors

5.8.1. Humidity control

Almost completely airtight and watertight membranes are logically only used for high pressure structures, while in buildings whose positive or negative pressure zones are occupied by men a certain air and moisture penetration is even desirable (Bibl. 119, p. 168).

If highly impervious synthetic foils are used in single membrane structures, ventilation flaps are indispensable as an aid to greater circulation of air (Bibl. 131, p. 33). By using coated fabrics such flaps can usually be dispensed with if there are at least 4 to 5 changes of air per hour.

Even in pneumatic swimming pool roofs condensation formation can be brought under control to a large extent and even completely eliminated by means of additional measures. Thorough investigations into this were made by a German air supported hall manufacturer and the results are reproduced below (Bibl. 28): If the water temperature is 23 ° to 24 °C then the air temperature should be about 26 °C. This does not only mean that the room temperature is pleasant, but also limits the amount of water evaporating from the surface.

If the fresh air in the inblown air volume is so proportioned that almost total absence of condensation is assured, a temperature difference of at most 30 °C can be bridged with the usual fans so that at an internal temperature of +26 °C the hall membrane remains dry down to an external temperature of −4 °C. If the proportion of fresh air is reduced and the proportion of recirculated air is correspondingly increased, then a temperature difference of 40 °C is attainable, so that an internal temperature of +26 °C can be maintained down to an external temperature of −14 °C. With the reduction of the proportion of fresh air the drying effect, e.g. the absorption capacity for humidity, is reduced; however, the film of condensation on the interior of the membrane is usually insignificant. Moreover, the temperature stratification within the room, i.e. the situation that the warmer air rises to the upper zones, has a favourable effect.

As the heat storage capacity of the water is considerably greater than that of the air, it is more practical to make allowance for a slight cooling of the water during the night than to continually draw off warm air to the outside. Even with a night temperature outside of 0 °C to +5 °C and corresponding air temperatures in the hall of +15 °C to +18 °C, considerable amounts of condensation occur on the inside of the membrane when the pool water is constantly kept at bathing temperature. If the pool is covered at night with a sheet of foil, then the hall membrane will remain completely dry down to an external temperature of some −30 °C and a corresponding internal air temperature of up to +10 °C.

5.8.2. Thermal control

It is clear that such thin and light materials as foils and woven fabrics can only offer extremely low thermal insulation and heat storage. PVC coated polyester weaves have at 4.0 to 4.5 more or less the same calorific value as a normal window pane.

Considerably lower coefficients of heat transmission can be achieved by laminating the membrane with insulating material. Flexible foams made of rubber, polystyrol, PVC and polyurethane are most frequently used and these are either stuck on in sheets or sprayed on direct as a foam. The calorific value attainable here is about 3.0 (Bibl. 123, p. 53). In Southern France air supported halls were used for refrigeration as well as for quicker ripening of fruit and vegetables. The required internal temperatures of +3 °C to 27 °C could be achieved without difficulty by pasting on 80 mm thick sheets of polyurethane foam. (Bibl. 60, p. 8.)

The pasting on of stiff and relatively thick foam sheets results in a shell-like stiffening. With such stiffened halls a very high internal pressure is necessary in order to prevent the changes in form due to aerodynamic loading. If the air supported hall frequently has to be erected and dismantled, this method cannot be used for the sheets can only be pasted on when the structure is already erected and the insulating layer must be removed again before the structure is dismantled.

Another solution is offered by the membrane sandwich construction described on p. 145 which has a calorific value of 2.6.

A further possibility of achieving a higher thermal insulation is the use of multi-layered membranes with enclosed air cushions. An example of this is the American exhibition pavilion "Atoms for peace" by Victor Lundy (pp. 134, 135). However, it should be remembered that with a membrane distance of over 5 cm an increased heat transfer can take place by means of convection in the vertical direction within the individual chambers.

In contrast to conventional buildings whose great thermal inertia demands constant heating, pneumatic structures only need to be heated while in use, so that short term heating systems, such as hot air or radiation systems, are the most suitable.

Propane gas burners are not recommended, as they are dangerous to health and increase the formation of condensation on the inside of the membrane (Bibl. 44, p. 124). In preference to these, heat exchange systems should always be chosen. A very uniform temperature distribution is obtained when the ventilated warmth caused by the loss of air is transmitted through the ventilation ducts or in their immediate proximity. The necessary transmission warmth is expediently supplied by heating elements arranged regularly in the interior of the hall. (Bibl. 144, p. 115.)

The warm air fans most frequently installed are provided with directly lit heat converters run off heating oil. Hot water or steam heating is only occasionally used. Heating by electricity is uneconomical for the most part.

In the cushion structure of Forum Steglitz in Berlin warm air heated up to 45 °C is blown in so that an accumulation of snow, which is not only undesirable on structural grounds but also reduces translucency, is prevented.

The heating of the air inside air supported halls in strong sunlight is only a problem when the hall is low in height. Large halls with a height of 10 to 20 m even in strong sunlight have a temperature in the main hall only a little above that outside, although the membrane temperature at the top of the hall could be +40 °C and more; this is because thermal convection causes the temperature to reduce from top to bottom at the rate of about 1 °C per metre (Bibl. 25).

The higher temperature in the upper area is anyway convenient in so far as it helps in melting snow and ice in winter. Thus in order to achieve the melting temperature of +12 °C laid down in the FRG guidelines, it is sufficient in the case of an external temperature of −10 °C and a 10 m high hall for the air volume at 1 m (height) to be heated up slightly above 0 °C. It is recommended that the proportion of fresh air be kept as low as possible and that the fans run with more recirculated air in order to save thermal energy. (Bibl. 28.)

In the case of small halls, cooling the supplied air in summer is indispensable; tests show that in sunlight even near the floor temperatures of more than 10° above the external temperature can occur.

In the case of halls being less than 5.5 m high, cooling the supplied air is not feasible for economic reasons. However, here also favourable temperature conditions can be achieved by means of a higher rate of change of air, the possibility of ventilation in the crown of the membrane, local lifting of the internal skirt and water spraying apparatus from perforated tubes or pipes. (Bibl. 28; Bibl. 104.)

The colouring and surface treatment of the hall membrane have a decisive influence on the heating of the hall interior by means of sun radiation. White and silver coatings show the highest reflection values and therefore result in the least heating. For this reason PVC coatings are frequently provided with an additional aluminium varnish. In the case of dark membrane surfaces the internal temperatures are 3 °C to 5 °C higher than with light membrane surfaces.

The significance of colour for reflection values can be seen in Table 18 (Bibl. 103); Table 19 shows the transmission and reflection curves of two white PVC coated polyester fabrics (Bibl. 104).

In 1967 N. Laing published a very interesting research work on the problem of the hothouse effect – great heating up of the air strata in the hall interior in sunshine and quick cooling when the sunshine goes and the temperature outside drops.

In his institute, variable transmission wall constructions of thin very light membrane material were developed, which in connection with radiation control systems use the sun for heating up and extra terrestrial space for cooling down. With minimal energy contributions for the servo system these wall elements can give frost temperatures in the Sahara and sub-tropical conditions in Newfoundland.

Some 20 different wall systems have been developed by which the internal climate of buildings can be widely controlled in respect of all classic climatic factors – radiation, air temperature, air humidity, precipitation and air current.

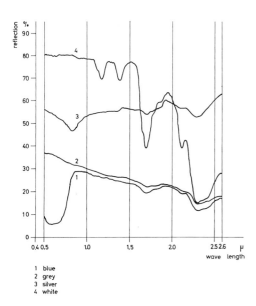

1 blue
2 grey
3 silver
4 white

Table 18. Reflection curve of PVC coated polyester fabrics in various colours.

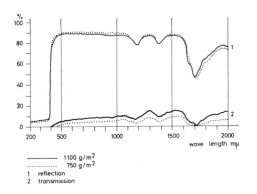

—— 1100 g/m²
········· 750 g/m²
1 reflection
2 transmission

Table 19. Reflection and transmission curves of two white PVC coated polyester fabrics.

Questions of manufacture and structural realisation as well as installation and maintenance expenses have already been extensively clarified.

In the simple wall construction shown in Fig. 129 an example of the operation of these variable transmission wall systems is explained (Bibl. 96).

The outer skin (A) consists of a fibre glass net; this is coated with a foil which has a certain optical quality. On the inside are channels made of very thin transparent film which are tightly filled with gas. Within these channels a partly metallised foil flap (K) is fixed which can be pneumatically moved to positions L and R.

The surfaces marked in black are made reflective on both sides by metal vaporisation. If the foil flap is in the position depicted on the left, then atmospheric radiation and ground reflection enter without hindrance through the wall.

In the position depicted on the right the wall acts like a polished screen that prevents the entry of any radiation.

With such walls coefficients of heat transmission of less than 0.8 Kcalories/m²h°C have been achieved, which corresponds to the thermal insulation of a 30 cm thick cavity brick wall.

Dietz suggests another system for regulating the climate (Bibl. 47):

He believes that one should view the outer membrane as a kind of "solar trap" and provide blackened surfaces at intervals on the inside which can be heated up by sunlight. By means of appropriate fan equipment, air can be conducted past these surfaces which will transmit the heat to a central storage unit. From there it could be recalled for heating or cooling purposes by means of a heat converter.

The main problem lies in the choice of the storage medium, whose energy output must be controllable in small stages corresponding to changing demands. At the moment, appropriate model tests are being carried out at the Massachusetts Institute of Technology.

5.8.3. Acoustics

No completely satisfactory solutions for pneumatic structures have yet been found as regards acoustics. In the case of single shell structures a high weight per unit area and great rigidity are decisive for good sound attenuation, so that sound transmission is hardly affected in single membrane structures with their very light envelope systems in comparison with other materials.

In order to protect exhibition areas in pneumatic structures against noise, attempts were made to provide curtains made of leaded vinyl which, however, at the same time caused a greatly increased reflection of sound waves.

There are also suggestions for shielding pneumatic structures from outside noise by connecting a second sound absorbing skin to the envelope system or incorporating a sound absorbent material.

It is interesting that the sound insulation values of pneumatic structures did not prove to be as bad as had been expected. Detailed investigations into the influence of internal pressure in double and multi-membrane structures as well as investigations into the influence of tension conditions in the membrane have still to be carried out. Also inferences for acoustically improved envelope systems have still to be drawn.

In this connection it is also worth mentioning the phenomenon that the intensity of sound waves from the noise of speaking is hardly reduced at all by a single pneumatically stressed membrane, but the sound waves are transposed so that on the other side no speech but only noises can be heard.

The acoustic behaviour of air supported halls also is generally better than was first expected by the experts. With correctly installed loudspeaker facilities, even lectures can be presented easily in very large halls. However, air supported halls are still unsuitable for musical performances with high acoustic demands.

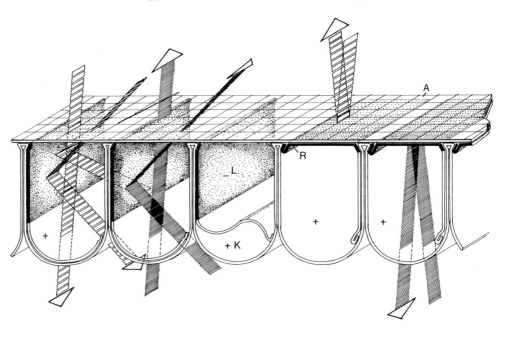

129. Variable transmission wall construction. N. Laing.

In a hall for 2,500 people with a covered surface of 1900 m² there was an average reverberation time of approx. 1.3 seconds over the total frequency range of 100 Hz to 1 Hz, while it should be 1.7 to 2 seconds in rooms of this size. When the internal pressure of the hall is reduced the reverberation time increases by 10% but is still not satisfactory. As a result of the acoustically transparent envelope music does not have an adequate sound volume. It sounds similar to an open air performance. In addition there are flutter echoes, whose fade-out time is sometimes longer than the reverberation time. The vaulted roof cross-section is the main cause of these flutter echoes. They are certainly moderated when the hall is full, but not suppressed. (Bibl. 28.)

Improvements in acoustics can be achieved by means of sound dispersing hanging surface elements, mobile sound absorbing curtains and by the pasting on of absorbent, soft porous materials. (Bibl. 123, p. 49).

6. On the statics and dimensioning of air supported structures

Hans Eggers

6.1. Introduction

For the last ten years air supported structures have been built in an increasing number as industrial, sports, store and exhibition halls. The important stages in their production are:
- design and selection of geometry,
- proof of load safety,
- selection and calculation of cutting pattern,
- manufacture,
- erection.

Only the first four points are dealt with here. Special emphasis is laid on design, calculation and construction methods for relatively small, simple, air supported structures. More detailed investigations and model tests are required for very large or complicated structures.

Even in the choice of membrane form one has to take into account the fact that the envelope can only take up tensile forces. Following on from the soap membrane comparison, in Section 6.2 the design of an unwrinkled membrane over any ground plan is shown. Cylindrical and spherical forms have been especially successful on account of their simple cutting pattern and their trouble-free manufacture. Even for these simple forms the calculation process is relatively complicated when the large deformations of the membrane can no longer be ignored. The numerical effort involved in solving the non-linear equations is usually great. The loading – specifically the wind loading – is often known only in the order of magnitude. Therefore approximation methods, designed for practical use, are only given here which are sufficiently accurate to calculate the membrane forces and the displacements. The diagrams shown in Section 6.6 considerably simplify the calculations of spherical and cylindrical membranes. They are specifically laid down for the design load and proof of load safety given in Bibl. 136. Their practical use is shown in Section 6.7.

At this stage I would especially like to thank Professor Duddeck at whose suggestion this work was originated and who has greatly assisted it. Apart from that I thank all the companies who have helped me both with practical advice and by placing test results at my disposal, as well as Mrs. Lack for her very careful production of the drawings.

6.2. Membrane geometry

6.2.1. Soap film analogy

One of the simplest membrane forms is the soap film (Bibl. 119). It encloses a prescribed volume with the minimum surface area. Characteristic of the form law of the soap film is the identical disappearance of the shear forces:

$$n_{12} \equiv 0. \tag{1}$$

This condition is only fulfilled for any co-ordinate lines when the maximum value

$$\max n_{12} = \frac{1}{2} \sqrt{(n_{11}-n_{22})^2 + 4(n_{12})^2} = 0 \tag{2}$$

also disappears. From equations 1 and 2 it follows that only the hydrostatic membrane force state

$$n = n_{11} = n_{22} \tag{3}$$

can occur in the skin. If one ignores the minimal selfweight, then the membrane force n is constant in the whole skin (tangential equilibrium). The equilibrium, normal to the surface, is determined as follows:

$$b_\alpha^\alpha = \frac{p}{n} = \text{const.} \tag{4}$$

The mean curvature b_α^α ($= 1/R_1 + 1/R_2$ for rectangular co-ordinates) can be given for arbitrary co-ordinates with the help of the tensor calculation. For a given curvature b_α^α depends only on the relationship between internal pressure p and membrane force n. For the Cartesian co-ordinates according to Fig. 1 the equation 4 is converted to

$$\frac{z_{,xx}(1+z_{,y}^2) + z_{,yy}(1+z_{,x}^2) - 2z_{,xy} \cdot z_{,x} \cdot z_{,y}}{(1+z_{,x}^2+z_{,y}^2)^{3/2}} = \frac{p}{n} \tag{5}$$

where a comma denotes the partial derivatives

$$(\ )_{,x} = \frac{\partial(\ )}{\partial x}, \quad (\ )_{,y} = \frac{\partial(\ )}{\partial y}$$

Exact solutions of this partial non-linear differential equation are known only for special cases. Therefore it is solved in general iteratively. Because of the non-linear connection between the geometry and the curvature several equilibrium positions are possible. In the transition to a new state of equilibrium the membrane changes its form suddenly.

The soap film model is very clear and is usually replaced in the experiment by an inflated thin rubber membrane. Envelopes formed in accordance with the soap film analogy are uniformly tensioned by internal pressure and are free of wrinkles. For this loading – usually permanent load – the soap film is the ideal membrane form.

6.2.2. Choice of geometry

In general a pneumatic structure should be free from wrinkles. This condition can only be fulfilled for a "pneumatically formed geometry" in which only tensile forces occur under internal pressure. The membrane will not take compression forces. It changes the geometry through the formation of wrinkles, so that a tensile structure re-occurs. Even under short term wind and snow loadings the membrane should not bulge in order to avoid an uncontrolled increase in external loadings (see Section 6.3). Manufacturing discrepancies, distortions of the cutting pattern, as well as various stiffnesses of the seams and fabric in the weft and warp direction lead to unexpected membrane forces which are not usually taken into account in the calculation. They considerably influence the development of the membrane forces, however, as the measured bearing loads in Bibl. 114 and Bibl. 67 show. In order to include these influences approximately, a wrinkle-free membrane should satisfy the condition.

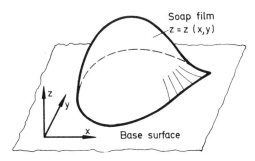

1. Soap film.

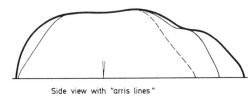

Side view with "arris lines"

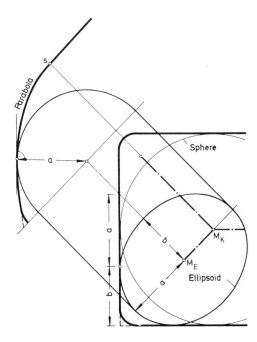

2. Envelope construction by inscribed spheres.

3. Angle construction by inscribed ellipsoids.

The curvature of a membrane must be steady. Even with complex geometries the curvatures must change over from one to another as uniformly as possible. Small jumps in the curvature are compensated for by the elasticity of the material and only rarely lead to the formation of wrinkles. Ridges, flutes and peaks can only be produced by additional forces. Theoretically conical apexes are formed by internal pressure, but are always rounded-off for reasons of stability. However, as $n_{11} = n_{22} = 0$ they do not comply with condition 6.

The geometry of a soap film is usually too complicated for practical application. Furthermore the flat corner areas are often undesirable. The soap film is, however, a very clear membrane form from which the geometry can be changed and simplified.

A very simple rule for the construction of wrinkle-free membranes is given by Frei Otto (Bibl. 119):

"A geometry can be formed pneumatically when spheres with a steadily changing radius can be included, the centre points of which lie on a curve and when at least one parallel of latitude of the generating sphere rests on the whole length of the membrane".

Condition 6 is approximately satisfied for spherical radii $R_{min} \geq 0.2 \cdot R_{max}$. In Fig. 2 the construction of a membrane according to Otto's rule is shown. In this example the centres of the sphere lie on the dotted line in the ground plane. The spheres touch the bearing line in at least two points. In the corner they transform into conical surfaces which are indicated by their generatrices. The base circles of the largest and smallest sphere are shown for comparison when $R_{min} = 0.2 \cdot R_{max}$. Furthermore the form of the membrane can also be affected by shifting the centre point of the sphere from the ground plane. In the vertical plane branchings of the central point lines are also possible.

The straight generatrices in the corner area do not look very attractive even when the tip of the cone is rounded-off by a sphere. A more pleasing form arises when the sphere is replaced by an ellipsoid that is tangential to the base lines and to a parabola in the direction of the angle bisectors (Fig. 3). Experience shows that even this geometry remains unwrinkled. The corner should always be rounded-off, as wrinkles can easily occur here otherwise.

The choice of geometry is difficult when the envelope is constricted by individual cables but there is still no cable net (Fig. 4). Then only the cable length is given, while the form of the cable lines are determined by the equilibrium conditions. In the first approximation the cable lines are estimated and then a membrane geometry is chosen following Otto's rule. Constricted membranes usually undergo much greater deformation than the simple smooth envelopes. Thus small errors are usually balanced out. With larger, more complicated structures the geometry and the membrane forces should always be defined by tests and more accurate calculations.

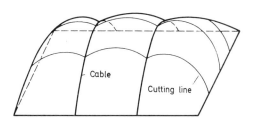

4. Membrane reinforced by cables.

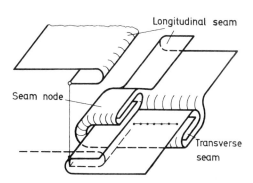

5. T-nodes on a folded seam.

6.2.3. Membrane cutting patterns

The envelope of a pneumatic structure is usually made of coated fabric or synthetic film. The material, which is supplied in a bale, is cut like a suit and either sewn, glued or welded. As simple and economic a cutting pattern as possible is sought for a given geometry. The seam pattern on the skin is chosen according to the following criteria:

– regular and large surfaced patterns are preferred to a 'patched' pattern because the seams in the inflated membrane can be clearly recognized;

– if seam nodes cannot be avoided, then as few seams as possible should converge at one point (in the T-node shown in Fig. 5 ten layers are sewn together and in a crown node sixteen layers);

– for reasons of reduced strength in the seam area, seams in the direction of the greatest main tension are more economical than those running at right angles to it;

– the wastage is generally less in short lengths than in long;

– seams running in the direction of the steepest gradient facilitate the slipping off of snow and the membranes dry more quickly after rain.

Fig. 6 shows some seam patterns for the front joint of a cylindrical membrane. The 'armadillo' pattern is the simplest for production. Exact calculation of the cutting pattern is – apart from specific geometric forms and seam patterns – only possible with an electronic calculator. In Fig. 7 the individual membrane strips are cut out from the surface F through planes E_i. They are approximated by means of very small, flat, triangular elements whose corners lie on the surface of the membrane and on the planes E_i. If the triangles on the broken line K are folded into a

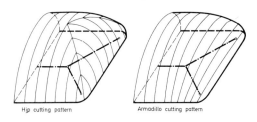

Hip cutting pattern   Armadillo cutting pattern

6. Forms for cutting patterns.

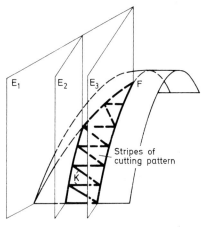

Stripes of cutting pattern

7. Membrane cutting pattern for the hip type.

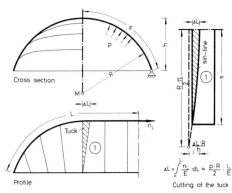

Undistorted   Distorted ($\gamma \approx 0,08$)   Approximated developed from 5 lengths

8. Distortion of the cutting pattern.

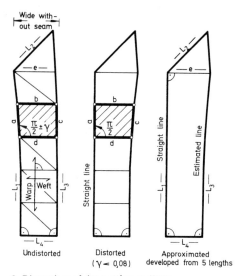

Cross section

Profile

Cutting of the tuck

$$\Delta L = \int_0^L \frac{n_L}{E} \, dL \approx \frac{p \cdot R}{2} \cdot \frac{L}{E}$$

9. Cutting pattern of a strained membrane.

plane, the cutting sector appears. Its form is influenced by the distance and inclination of the planes E_i so that only a low wastage occurs. If one also makes use of the extreme shear flexibility of the material, then more simple cutting patterns are possible. The sections are so distorted without extension of the warp and weft direction, that with equal cutting pattern lengths a straight edge occurs. The permissible shear distortion depends on the material and on the membrane forces. Experience shows that shear strains of 5 to 8% are possible without wrinkles forming.

Approximation methods, as used in tent construction, are suitable for determining the cutting pattern. Commencing with a straight length, the cutting pattern is "developed with the curve template" over the length of the seams and one or two intermediate points (Fig. 8). Small errors are balanced out in the membrane. The use of the approximation method is very simple, although it requires a certain amount of experience.

With larger structures the elongation of the membrane due to the internal pressure (about 1 to 3%) should be taken into account in the cutting pattern. Usually the narrower cutting pattern of individual strips is adequate for adjustment of the membrane elongation (Fig. 9). The distance between the tucks must not be chosen too large because the membrane might be restrained by door and gate constructions in the side of the hall. A tuck width limited to $\Delta l \leqslant 20$ cm is approved.

6.3. Load assumptions

In pneumatic structures very large deformations can occur which affect wind and snow loading through the changed geometry of the envelope. The load is approximately applied to the undeformed membrane and "affixed" there. Conservative loads, such as deadweight and snow, remain true to direction; internal pressure and wind act always normal to the deformed membrane.

6.3.1. Internal pressure

Air supported halls maintain their form by internal pressure. The size of the internal pressure depends on the geometry of the membrane, loading and permissible deformations. Furthermore the membrane must not wrinkle or flutter in the wind stream. Tests have shown that, depending on the geometry, minimum internal pressures of 50 to 100% of the wind pressure are required for this. More detailed instructions on the minimum internal pressure are contained in the Japanese (Bibl. 32) and East German (Bibl. 158) guidelines. In Table 1 they are compared with the test results according to Bibl. 14 and Bibl. 114.

The minimum internal pressures measured for cylindrical membranes have to be increased by about 15% if one also wishes to avoid wrinkles in the end calottes. In shallow-stretched mem-

branes only suction forces occur so that a low internal pressure is adequate for stabilisation.

In West Germany a minimum internal pressure of $p = 30$ kp/m² is prescribed for envelopes with a height of more than 8 m. This value is not sufficient to stabilise high membranes erected over small ground areas. For any geometry the minimum internal pressure can be determined by restriction of the displacements and by a margin of safety against folding in.

The maximum possible internal pressure is the bursting pressure $p_{Br.}$, which depends on the geometry and on the fabric strength. In the fabrics used today it is generally less than the critical internal pressure p_{crit} at which the membrane suddenly expands and changes to another state of equlibrium (Bibl. 119, p. 64). In Bibl. 53 the formula

$$p_{crit.} = 0.296 \cdot D/R_o \tag{7}$$

is given for the critical internal pressure of a spherical rubber membrane. Here R_o is the radius of the undeformed sphere and D the tensile stiffness of the membrane ($D = E \cdot t$, modulus of elasticity E, membrane thickness t). For cylinders the first factor is replaced by the value 0.25. For a coated fabric the equation 7 provides an approximate value.

6.3.2. Deadweight

The specific gravity (γ) of the envelope material lies between 0.8 and 1.6 kp/m² per mm fabric thickness. The fabrics usually used ($t \leqslant 1$ mm, $g \leqslant 1$ kp/m²) are very light, so that the dead-load can be ignored in structural calculations. Because of the low weight a pressure difference of 1 to 2 mm water column is sufficient to maintain the envelope in its shape. Even when there are large openings in the envelope the membrane collapses slowly.

Tests are now being run to foam up insulating materials on the inside of the fabric in order to reduce the loss of heat in winter and overheating in summer. A considerably greater dead load must be taken into account in the structural calculation. In cylindrical air supported halls a larger envelope deadweight can also be approximately disregarded if the working pressure exceeds the internal pressure used as a basis for the structural calculation by the value:

Geometry	p/q Building code (Bibl. 158)	p/q Wind tunnel tests (Bibl. 14, Bibl. 114)
Sphere on a tower	1,0	—
Three-quarter sphere	0,85	1,0
Hemisphere	0,65	0,70 ··· 0,74
Cylinder with spherical callottes	0,65	0,60 ··· 0,62
Cylinder over rectangular base	0,55	0,62 [1]

[1] Semicylinder, for a quarter cylinder p/q ≈ 0,5

Table 1. Minimum internal pressure p: wind back pressure q.

$$\Delta p \approx \left[1.1 - \frac{h}{b} \cdot \left(1 + \frac{g}{2\,p} \right) \right] \cdot g \qquad (8)$$

where $h/b \leqslant 0.6, \quad g/p \leqslant 0.5$

This increase in pressure only balances out the reduction in membrane forces generated by the deadweight. Likewise in the spherical membrane the increase in pressure

$$\Delta p \approx g \qquad (9)$$

where $h/b \leqslant 1.0, \quad g/p \leqslant 0.1, \quad g/q \leqslant 0.1$
(q = wind back pressure)

does not lead to any excess in the membrane forces.

6.3.3. Wind load

For the dimensioning of an air supported structure the load condition "internal pressure and wind" is decisive. The membrane forces arising purely from wind pressure are generally greater than those caused by internal pressure. Because of the low mass and great damping no galloping vibrations occur. An approximation of the wind loading is calculated according to the formula

$$w = c \cdot q \qquad (10)$$

where $q = \varrho/2 \cdot v_e^2$ and $\varrho/2 \approx 1/16$
$[kp \cdot s^2/m^4]$.

Here the normalised form function c describes the distribution of wind pressure over the surface, while the back pressure q as a function of the wind speed v_e defines the size of the compression load.

The back pressure q is dependent through the wind speed on the geographical position and height above the ground. Both influences are contained, for example, in the Japanese guidelines (Bibl. 32) of the back pressure distribution (dimensions in kp, m, s):

$$q = \frac{v_e^2}{16} \sqrt[4]{\frac{h}{10}} \geqslant 30 \ kp/m^2 \qquad (11)$$

Because of the low mass of pneumatic structure for v_e the squall speed, with a duration of effect of a few seconds, is critical. Determining factors of the squall speed and its frequency are published in Bibl. 37 for West Germany. According to this the squall speed of $v_e = 35$ m/s lasting 2 to 10 seconds is exceeded only on 2 days a year, if one disregards particularly exposed positions such as high mountain peaks and immediate coastal areas. Special local conditions, such as the nozzle effect in the vicinity of high buildings for example, are not taken into account in the determining factors. In Table 2 the assumed back pressures for various countries are given for comparison. The form function c for the wind distribution can be determined only by tests. It is dependent on the geometry, the deformation and the wind direction. Reynolds Number and the surface roughness of the generally smooth membranes have little influence on the distribution of pressure. Tests on cylindrical membranes gave a greatly varying pressure distribution with distinct suction peaks. Wind directions inclined towards the cylinder axis lead to particularly large wind loadings in the vicinity of the up-

stream calotte. The greatest measured wind pressure distribution (given in Bibl. 114) for the cylinder with spherical calottes affected by transverse and slanting crosswinds is contrasted in Table 3 with the values given in Bibl. 136.

The influence of the deformations on the pressure distribution is slight for a cylinder. The evolved geometry adapts without wrinkles to the support line for the loading, so that even large deformations alter the aerodynamic conditions very little. In contrast to this a spherical membrane takes up randomly distributed wind pressures without appreciable deformations. Only when compressive stresses arise does the membrane bulge locally (snap through). The bulging in the back pressure area influences the form function considerably (Bibl. 14). In Table 4 the form functions c, measured in accordance with Bibl. 114, for different internal pressure conditions are given and compared with the values for the cylinder given in Bibl. 136. When normal to the wind direction the pressure distribution is almost axially symmetrical.

The gradual approximation of the back pressure usual in West Germany is particularly unfavourable. The high back pressure in the apex area coincides with the large ordinates of the form function. The membrane forces calculated according to Bibl. 136 are therefore too large. In comparing Tables 3 and 4 it should be observed that the test results only apply for a constant back pressure distribution.

The internal pressures prescribed for air supported halls are only necessary for stabilisation on a few stormy days in the year. For the rest of the time lower internal pressures are adequate. If the internal pressure is altered to suit every weather condition, then running costs are lower and the life of the envelope is somewhat extended (lower permanent loading). The internal pressure can be easily controlled by means of a wind gauge, whereby the minimum values can still be dependent on the time of year. In Bibl. 61 air valves are suggested to control the internal pressure. The wind presses open the valves as soon as the back pressure exceeds the internal pressure (Fig. 10). Tests (Bibl. 61) and theoretical investigations (Bibl. 56) show that even relatively small valves are sufficient to raise the internal pressure by some $0.7 \cdot q$. Practical testing for the control of varying internal pressures has still to be carried out.

6.3.4. Snow loading

The snow loading of a membrane is dependent on the geometry, the stability of form and the temperature. According to Bibl. 136 no snow will settle on heated membranes with internal temperatures of more than 12 °C. In unheated air supported structures very large deformations occur under snow loading (Figs. 11, 12), which affect snow deposits because of the changed geometry. The shaking effect of the wind combined with the increased snow drift on pneumatic structures usually leads to one-sided snow deposits. The interrelations have been only partly researched.

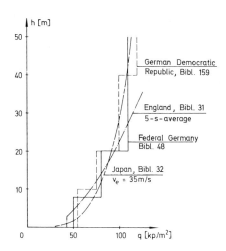

Table 2. Wind back pressures.

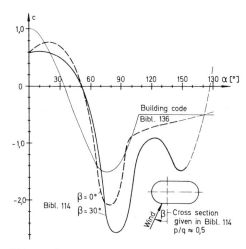

Table 3. Form function c of a semicylinder with quarter sphere, end, test readings (Bibl. 114) – guideline (Bibl. 136).

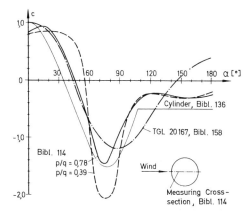

Table 4. Form function c of the hemisphere, test readings (Bibl. 114) – DDR Standard (Bibl. 158).

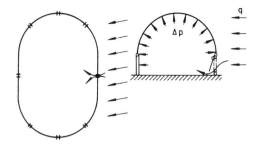

10. Wind valves – see Bibl. 61.

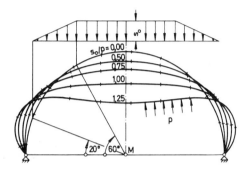

11. Cylinder under full snow loading.

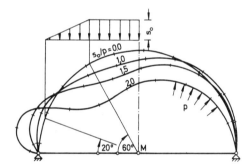

12. Cylinder under one-sided snow loading.

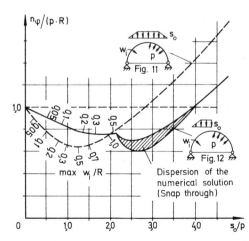

Table 5. Membrane forces of the semicylinder under snow loading.

Snow loading reduces membrane tensions (Table 5) so that splitting of the skin need not be feared. The deformations must be limited according to the use of the structure, so that the envelopes do not "impale themselves" on the installations. Furthermore no pockets of snow should be allowed to arise which could harm the overall stability. As increased snow loading does not increase the risk for the user nor for the structure, the large standard snow loadings (Bibl. 48) based on a 95% probability factor of the annual maximum are not justified. A standard snow load of

$$s_o = 35 \text{ kp/m}^2 \qquad (12)$$

is suggested, as is applied in Bibl. 48 for "buildings for temporary uses". Snow deposits over 10 cm high must be shaken off by varying the internal pressure. Only in regions with great snow falls can the full snow load occur, as here it is often not possible to shake it off. In order to prevent snow pockets arising on cylindrical envelopes and to maintain stability of form, the displacements should not exceed the value

$$\max w \leqslant 0.1 \cdot R. \qquad (13)$$

By comparison in Bibl. 67 $\max w \leqslant 0.03 \ldots$ $0.05 \cdot R$ is suggested for the semicylinder. The minimum internal pressure is defined by the restriction of deformation (13). Spherical membranes bulge inwards locally under snow load (snap through). The minimum internal pressure which prevents bulging is determined by a folding condition in accordance with Section 6.4.1.

6.4. Calculation procedure

6.4.1. Folding conditions

The principal normal forces of a membrane are calculated by the equation

$$n_{\substack{\max \\ \min}} = (J_1 \pm \sqrt{(J_1)^2 - 4 \cdot J_2})/2 \qquad (14)$$

with the invariants

$$J_1 = n_{11} + n_{22}, \quad J_2 = n_{11} \cdot n_{22} - (n_{12})^2. \qquad (15)$$

If the membrane forces in the whole envelope fulfil the condition

$$\min n \geqslant o \qquad (16)$$

it is a pure tensile structure. Equivalent to the "folding condition" (16) is the restriction of the invariants

$$J_1 \wedge J_2 \geqslant 0 \qquad (17)$$

or

$$\min n \geqslant J_2/J_1 \geqslant 0. \qquad (18)$$

The very thin membranes do not absorb any compression forces. In order to avoid folding in, the membrane forces actually present must not violate the folding condition (16). However, the actual membrane forces are not known – only known are the calculated forces which can still be influenced by manufacturing accuracy and load scattering. In order to prevent any wrinkle formation, the calculated tensile forces

in the membrane must not become too small. As a criterion for the folding safety under working load the quotient

$$\nu = \frac{\min n \ (\min p, g, s \vee w)}{\max n \ (\min p, g)} \geqslant 0.2 \qquad (19)$$

is introduced. In equation 19, min n is the smallest membrane force determined for the deformed state with the load combinations (min p, g, s) or (min p, g, w), and min p is the smallest working pressure at which the fans start. Folding safety over $\nu = 0.2$ is not generally required. If one disregards the low deadweight of the membrane, equation 19 for the load condition "internal pressure" is converted into condition 6.
The folding safety defined in Bibl. 136 $\bar{\nu} \approx 1/(1 - \nu)$ assumes the superimposition principle and thus a calculation according to the First Order Theory. The definition fails in the case of membranes which can only take up specific loads in the deformed state.

6.4.2. Basic equations of the membrane theory

The basic equations of the membrane theory can be formulated for any membrane forms in tensor notation (sign conventions see Fig. 13). They are given for the linear case in Bibl. 66 and for membranes with large deformations in Bibl. 69. The partial differential equations can be solved for any geometries only numerically. In the following, therefore, only axially symmetrical membranes are investigated for which exact solutions or sufficiently precise approximations are known.
Cylinder co-ordinates as in Fig. 14 are introduced for the axially symmetrical membrane. They run in the direction of the (orthogonal) main lines of curvature. The geometry of a surface element is uniquely described by the following geometric values (Fig. 14):

lengths $\sqrt{a_{11}} = r$, $\sqrt{a_{22}} = \sqrt{1 + r_{,z}{}^2}$, $\qquad (20)$
area $\sqrt{a} = \sqrt{a_{11} \cdot a_{22}}$,
curvatures $b_1^1 = -1/\sqrt{a}$, $b_2^2 = r^3 \cdot r_{,zz}/a^{3/2}$,
gauss curvature $K = b_1^1 \cdot b_2^2$,
change of lengths $(\sqrt{a_{11}})_{,z} = \Gamma_{12}^1 \sqrt{a_{11}}$,
$$(\sqrt{a_{22}})_{,\varphi} = 0,$$
christoffel symbol $\Gamma_{12}^1 = r_{,z}/r$.

With the specific geometry of the rotational membrane, the physical components of the forces and displacements and the abbreviations,

$$d_1 = \frac{\partial(\ )}{\sqrt{a_{11}} \, \partial\varphi}, \quad d_2 = \frac{\partial(\ )}{\sqrt{a_{22}} \, dz}, \qquad (21)$$
$$\Gamma = \Gamma_{12}^1 / \sqrt{a_{22}}$$

the membrane equations derived in Bibl. 66 are converted into
a) equilibrium

$$\begin{bmatrix} d_1 & 2\ \Gamma + d_2 & o \\ -\Gamma & d_1 & \Gamma + d_2 \\ b_1^1 & o & b_2^2 \end{bmatrix} \cdot \begin{bmatrix} n_{11} \\ n_{12} \\ n_{22} \end{bmatrix} + \begin{bmatrix} p_1 \\ p_2 \\ p_3 \end{bmatrix} = 0, \quad (22)$$

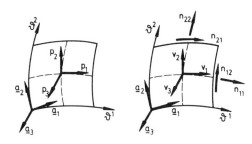

13. Sign convention.

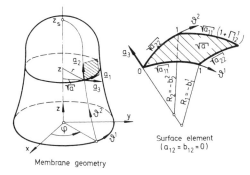

Membrane geometry

14. Rotational membrane.

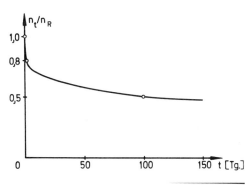

Table 6. Qualitative time-dependent tensile strength for nylon fabrics.

b) strains

$$
\begin{bmatrix} d_1 & \Gamma & -b_1^1 \\ d_2 - \Gamma & d_1 & o \\ o & d_2 & -b_2^2 \end{bmatrix} \cdot \begin{bmatrix} v_1 \\ v_2 \\ v_3 \end{bmatrix} = \begin{bmatrix} \alpha_{11} \\ 2\,\alpha_{12} \\ \alpha_{22} \end{bmatrix} \cdot \quad (23)
$$

The equilibrium conditions (22) are adequate only for calculating the membrane forces when the boundary and transition conditions can also be formulated free of deformation (no cable reinforcements). The displacements then result from the strains and the material laws given in Section 6.4.3. In the case of large deformations the equilibrium conditions depend also on the displacements (Bibl. 69).

For Gauss curvature $K \leqslant 0$ singular solutions ($\alpha_{\alpha\beta} = 0$, $v_i \neq 0$) exist for the strain equations (23). These "stretch-free deformations" do not occur in pneumatic structures with fixed edges. However, the low shear stiffness of coated fabrics (28) can lead to large shear strains ($\alpha_{12} \neq 0$, $\alpha_{11} \wedge \alpha_{22} \approx 0$) and thus to large deformations even with small membrane forces. This effect, which is related to stretch-free deformation, essentially occurs only with very small or negative Gauss curvatures.

Usually the decisive loading for dimensioning of air supported halls – wind loading – is only known in the first approximation. The calculation method may also be equally "rough", as long as it includes the essential loadbearing effects. All the more accurate calculation processes, e.g. the finite element methods, are very expensive numerically. However, they really provide more accurate results only when the wind and snow loading as well as the material laws are known from measurements and tests.

In convex-curved, smooth membranes the deformations remain small as long as folding in is prevented by sufficiently great internal pressure. Alternatively large displacements can occur when
– the load is only transferred by the low shear stiffness of the membrane,
– there are Gauss curvatures $K \leqslant 0$,
– no equilibrium is possible in the undeformed state.

Large deformations have to be taken into account only if stability investigations are required or if the membrane is cable reinforced. Under all other conditions a calculation according to the First Order Theory results in membrane forces being too large. In the deformed state the membrane curves more strongly in the area of heavy load, so that the membrane forces decrease in accordance with the "barrel formula" (Fig. 34). The following rule is valid:
A pneumatic structure calculated by the First Order Theory and dimensioned for the maximum occurring membrane forces is sufficiently safe as long as no instability can occur.

6.4.3. Material laws and dimensioning

The material properties of synthetic films and coated fabrics cover a very wide range. They are not fully described by tensile strength, rupture strains and subsequent tensile strength, even

with the seam strengths determined by short term tests. In particular, aging under ultra violet radiation reduces the material strength. Thus after several years use the tensile strength can decrease by 25%, the subsequent tensile strength by 50% and the water vapour permeability (watertightness) by 65%[1]. Furthermore the long term tensile strength of synthetic materials is relatively low (Table 6). These values show already that dimensioning is problematic using the short term tensile strength as prescribed in Bibl. 136. In order to cover the strength losses caused by aging and permanent loading, large safety factors

$$
v_R \leqslant \frac{n_R}{\max n} \quad (24)
$$

are necessary (max n = largest calculated membrane force).

In Bibl. 136 $v_R = 5$ is laid down for the membrane and $v_R = 3.5$ for the seam. As the creep strength is often not known, they suggest a "safety" which is not available in older air supported structures.

Equation 24 only applies for working conditions. As in the linear theory the membrane force is bounded by

$$
\text{perm. } n = n_R/v_R \geqslant \max n. \quad (25)
$$

The coefficient v_R states nothing about a possible increase in load. In an envelope with large deformations the non-proportional growth of the membrane forces can only be determined by a limit design investigation. For proof of load-bearing safety

$$
\max n \,(v_1 \cdot \max p, \; v_2 \cdot g, \; v_3 \cdot w) \leqslant n_t \quad (26)
$$

the v_i fold loadings are applied to the system. Through the time-dependent tensile strength n_t the durability t of the structure is brought into the dimensioning. The following safety factors are recommended:

internal pressure $\qquad\qquad\qquad v_1 = 1.2;$

deadweight $\qquad\qquad\qquad\qquad v_2 = 1.0;$

wind (Bibl. 143)
– warehouses, agricultural structures $\quad v_3 \geqslant 1.2,$
– public buildings $\qquad\qquad\qquad\quad v_3 \geqslant 1.5,$
– meeting halls $\qquad\qquad\qquad\qquad v_3 \geqslant 1.8,$
– structures with particularly great stability,
e.g. radar protection domes $\qquad v_3 \geqslant 2 \ldots 2.5.$

The coefficient v_1 is relatively small as the greatest internal pressure $v_1 \cdot \max p$ achieved by the fan is generally only a little above the maximum working pressure max p.

[1]All values given here were determined in 5 to 10 year old PVC coated Nylon and Trevira fabrics. They are intended to give no more than a survey over the order of magnitude of the anticipated loss of strength under long term tensioning. For dimensioning reference should be made to the material characteristics given by the manufacturer of the relevant fabric and supported by test certificates.

In the case of small strains and equal safety factors ν for all loadings, according to the model law (Bibl. 114) the dimensioning formulae 24 and 26 are equivalent

$$\nu \cdot n \,(p, g, w) = n \,(\nu \cdot p, \, \nu \cdot g, \, \nu \cdot w). \qquad (27)$$

Apart from stability cases, for large deformations and for $\nu_1 < \nu_3$, dimensioning by the limit design theory is more favourable. In buildings for short term use, e.g. exhibition halls, the increased short term tensile strength leads to an especially economic dimensioning.

The material law of the membrane is required for all deformation calculations. In approximation films act isotropically and coated fabrics rectilinearly anisotropically. The material constants can be determined for films only by uniaxial tensile tests. For coated fabrics extensive tests (in accordance with Bibl. 100) under two-dimensional tensioning are required, in order to include the link between the warp and weft direction as well as the non-linear effects related to the material and the fabric structure. The material laws, determined by tests, are very complex as stated in Bibl. 100.

Characteristic is the very weak coupling between the shear strain and the tensile strains in the thread direction as well as the low shear stiffness

$$S \approx 0.05 \ldots 0.1 \cdot D_k \qquad (28)$$

compared with the tensile stiffness D_k in the warp direction.

For practical use complicated non-linear material laws are less suited. In the operating condition the errors made by their linearisation are relatively small. Inaccuracies in manufacture, distortions in the cutting pattern, increased seam stiffnesses, as well as wrinkles which only pull smooth by higher internal pressure, often change the stress distribution considerably more. These influences, together with the aging of the membrane, are difficult to determine. Tests have to be made on whether or not very simple material laws, such as for example

$$
\begin{bmatrix} \varepsilon_{kk} \\ \varepsilon_{ks} \\ \varepsilon_{ss} \end{bmatrix} =
\begin{bmatrix} \dfrac{1}{D_k} & o & -\dfrac{1}{D_k + D_s} \\[2mm] o & \dfrac{1}{15\,D_k} & o \\[2mm] -\dfrac{1}{D_k + D_s} & o & \dfrac{1}{D_s} \end{bmatrix} \cdot
\begin{bmatrix} n_{kk} \\ n_{ks} \\ n_{ss} \end{bmatrix} \qquad (29)
$$

give sufficiently accurate results. In equation 29 the index k refers to the warp direction and s refers to the weft direction; D is an average secant stiffness taken from the n-ε-diagrams (Table 7). Simple material laws also covering oblique angled fabric directions, creep or plasticising are given in Bibl. 117.

6.4.4. Rotationally symmetric membranes

In convexly-curved membranes (Gauss curvature K ≫ 0) the deformations are small, so that the linear equations 22 and 23 give sufficiently accurate results. If one eliminates n_{11} in equa-

---

tion 22/3, then according to Bibl. 52 the substitution

$$N_{22} = \frac{r^2}{\sqrt{a}} \cdot n_{22}, \quad N_{12} = r^2 \, n_{12} \qquad (30)$$

gives the equations

$$N_{12,z} + r \, r_{,zz} N_{22,\varphi} = -\, r\sqrt{a}\, p_1 - a\, p_{3,\varphi}, \quad (31)$$
$$N_{12,\varphi} + r^2 N_{22,z} = -\, r^3 p_2 + r^3 \, r_{,z} \; p_3.$$

Similarly the elimination of V_3 in equation 23/1 and the substitution

$$V_1 = \frac{v_1}{r}, \quad V_2 = \frac{\sqrt{a}}{r} \, v_2 \qquad (32)$$

leads to the set of equations

$$V_{2,z} + r \, r_{,zz} V_{1,\varphi} = r \, r_{,zz} \, \alpha_{11} + \alpha_{22}, \qquad (33)$$
$$V_{2,\varphi} + r^2 V_{1,z} = \sqrt{a}\, \alpha_{12}.$$

The homogenous equations 33 for the strains have the same form as the equilibrium conditions 31. They are solved by the same scheme. For rotationally symmetrical loadings the derivatives ( )$_{,\varphi}$ disappear so that equations 31 are uncoupled. Integration and resubstitution gives

$$n_{22} = \frac{\sqrt{a}}{r^2} \int_{z_s}^{z} (-r \cdot p_2 + r \cdot r_{,z}\, p_3)\, dz + C_1,$$

$$n_{12} = -\frac{1}{r^2} \int_{z_s}^{z} r \sqrt{a}\, p_1 \, dz + C_2, \qquad (34)$$

$$n_{11} = \sqrt{a}\, p_3 + \frac{r^3 \cdot r_{,zz}}{a}\, n_{22}.$$

For distributed loadings the membrane forces in the zenith remain finite. Equilibrium at the cut-out zenith element provides the integration constants (Fig. 15)

$$C_1 = \sqrt{a} \cdot p_3/2, \quad C_2 = 0. \qquad (35)$$

The given surface loads are dispersed in the directions of the moving trihedral $\mathbf{a}_i$.

Internal pressure p:

$$p_1 = p_2 = 0, \quad p_3 = p, \qquad (36)$$

Deadweight g:

$$p_1 = 0, \quad p_2 = -r \cdot g/\sqrt{a},$$
$$p_3 = -r \cdot r_z \, g/\sqrt{a}. \qquad (37)$$

Snow s_0, referring to the basic area $x - y$:

$$p_1 = 0, \quad p_2 = -r^2 \cdot r_{,z} \cdot s_0/a,$$
$$p_3 = -(r_{,z} \cdot r)^2 \cdot s_0/a. \qquad (38)$$

The membrane forces due to internal pressure are given for some membrane forms in Table 8. The evaluation of equations 34 for ellipsoids is shown in Table 18 for internal pressure and in Table 19 for snow load in accordance with Bibl. 136.

In the case of unsymmetrical loads the membrane forces and loadings are developed in Fourier's series:

$$p_1, N_{12} = \sum_{m=0}^{\infty} \binom{m}{\,} \cdot \sin(m\varphi),$$

$$p_2, p_3, N_{11}, N_{22} = \sum_{m=0}^{\infty} \binom{m}{\,} \cdot \cos(m\varphi). \qquad (39)$$

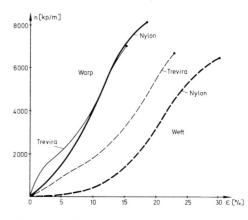

Table 7. n-ε-diagrams for coated fabrics.

15. Equilibrium on the zenith element.

The elimination of the shear force in equations 31 leads to the normal differential equation

$$\overset{m}{N}_{22,zz} + \frac{2\, r_{,z}}{r}\, \overset{m}{N}_{22,z} + \frac{r_{,zz} \cdot m^2}{r}\, \overset{m}{N}_{22} = \overset{m}{F} \qquad (40)$$

where

$$\overset{m}{F} = \frac{\sqrt{a}}{r}\, \overset{m}{m}\, p_1 - \frac{a\, m^2}{r^2}\, \overset{m}{p}_3 + \frac{1}{r^2} \left[r^3 \left(-\overset{m}{p}_2 + r_{,z}\, \overset{m}{p}_3 \right) \right]_{,z}. \qquad (41)$$

The equation leads for the ellipsoid (Bibl. 52)

$$r = \sqrt{R^2 - \alpha \cdot z^2},$$
$$\alpha = R^2/H^2, \qquad (42)$$

(see Table 8) with the substitution

$$\omega = \operatorname{artanh}(\sqrt{\alpha} \cdot z/R) \qquad (43)$$

to a differential equation with constant coefficients

$$\overset{m}{N}_{22,\omega\omega} - m^2 \overset{m}{N}_{22} = \frac{r^4}{R^2\, \alpha}\, \overset{m}{F}. \qquad (44)$$

The solution of the differential equation and the resubstitution give for the wind load

a) m = 0:

$$\overset{0}{n}_{22} = -\frac{\sqrt{a}\, \alpha}{r^2} \int_{z_s}^{z} z \cdot \overset{0}{w}\, dz, \qquad (45)$$

b) m = 1:

$$\overset{1}{n}_{22} = \frac{\sqrt{a}}{r^3} \left[-z \int_{z_s}^{z} r \cdot \overset{1}{w}\, dz + (1 - \alpha) \int_{z_s}^{z} r \cdot z \cdot \overset{1}{w}\, dz \right], \qquad (46)$$

c) m ⩾ 2:

$$\overset{m}{n}_{22} = \frac{\sqrt{a}}{2\, m \sqrt{\alpha}\, R\, r^2} \left[J_1\, e^{-m\omega} + J_2 \cdot e^{m\omega} \right] \qquad (47)$$

where

$$J_1 = \int_{z_s}^{z} \overset{m}{G} \cdot e^{m\omega}\, dz,$$

$$J_2 = \int_{z_u}^{z} \overset{m}{G} \cdot e^{-m\omega}\, dz,$$

$$\overset{m}{G} = (-a\,m^2 - \alpha\, r^2 + 2\,\alpha^2\, z^2)\,\overset{m}{w} - \alpha\, z\, r^2\,\overset{m}{w}_{,z}, \quad (48)$$

$$e^{m\omega} = \left(\frac{R + \sqrt{\alpha}\, z}{R - \sqrt{\alpha}\, z}\right)^{m/2}.$$

The integration constants are determined for $m = 0{,}1$ by the equilibrium conditions $\Sigma V = 0$, $\Sigma M = 0$ in the zenith (Fig. 15). For the higher series elements $m \geq 2$ residual stress conditions exist, which affect only the form of the membrane force distribution. The integration constants are so adapted that the solution also remains finite in the vertices z_s, z_u. The remaining membrane forces follow from

$$\overset{m}{n}_{12} = \left(-\alpha \cdot z \cdot \overset{m}{p}_3 - \left(\frac{r^2}{\sqrt{a}}\,\overset{m}{n}_{22}\right)_{,2}\right)/m \quad (m > 0),$$

$$\overset{m}{n}_{11} = -\frac{\alpha\, R^2}{a}\,\overset{m}{n}_{22} + \sqrt{a} \cdot \overset{m}{w} \quad \text{(all m)}. \quad (49)$$

For the ellipsoid the wind loading given for the cylinder in Bibl. 136 is slightly modified (Fig. 16). The integration of the equations 45 to 47 and the superimposition of the series elements are numerically very expensive. The extreme values of the membrane forces which are decisive for dimensioning and for proof of folding safety are given in Tables 20 and 21 for the ellipsoid under constant wind pressure and in Tables 22 to 24 for the sphere under gradually changing wind pressure ($m \leq 8$). Numerical results for the spherical membrane under wind loading (Bibl. 158) are also given in Bibl. 62.

The membrane forces for the first two Fourier elements can also be determined by the equilibrium at the dome when cut off at height z (Fig. 15). For the wind load the following equations are obtained for any membrane form:

$$\Sigma V = 0: \quad \overset{0}{n}_{22} = -\frac{\sqrt{a_{22}}}{r} \int_{z_s}^{z} \overset{0}{w} \cdot r \cdot r_{,\zeta}\, d\zeta,$$

$$\Sigma H = 0: \quad \overset{1}{n}_{12} = -\frac{2\sqrt{a_{22}}}{r} \int_{z_s}^{z} \overset{1}{w}\, r\, d\zeta, \quad (50)$$

$$\Sigma M = 0: \quad \overset{1}{n}_{22} = -\frac{2\sqrt{a_{22}}}{r^2} \int_{z_s}^{z} \overset{1}{w}\,(r^2\, r_{,\xi} + r(\zeta - z))\, d\zeta$$

where

$$\overset{i}{w} = \frac{1}{2\pi} \int_0^{2\pi} w \cdot \cos(i\varphi)\, d\varphi \quad \text{for } i = 0,1. \quad (51)$$

The ring force results from the equilibrium condition 22/3

$$\overset{i}{n}_{11} = \sqrt{a}\,(\overset{i}{w} + b_2^2 \cdot \overset{i}{n}_{22}) \quad \text{for } i = 0,1. \quad (52)$$

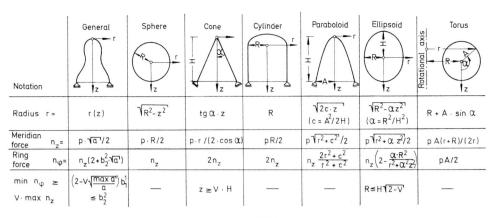

Notation	General	Sphere	Cone	Cylinder	Paraboloid	Ellipsoid	Torus
Radius $r =$	$r(z)$	$\sqrt{R^2 - z^2}$	$tg\,\alpha \cdot z$	R	$\sqrt{2c \cdot z}$ $(c = A^2/2H)$	$\sqrt{R^2 - \alpha z^2}$ $(\alpha = R^2/H^2)$	$R + A \cdot \sin\alpha$
Meridian force $n_z =$	$p \cdot \sqrt{a}/2$	$p \cdot R/2$	$p \cdot r/(2 \cdot \cos\alpha)$	$pR/2$	$p\sqrt{r^2 + c^2}/2$	$p\sqrt{r^2 + \alpha z^2}/2$	$p\,A(r+R)/(2r)$
Ring force $n_\varphi =$	$n_z(2 + b_2^2\sqrt{a})$	n_z	$2n_z$	$2n_z$	$n_z\dfrac{2r^2 + c^2}{r^2 + c^2}$	$n_z\left(2 - \dfrac{\alpha \cdot R^2}{r^2 + \alpha^2 z^2}\right)$	$pA/2$
min $n_\varphi \geq$ / $V \cdot$ max n_z	$\left(2 - V\sqrt{\dfrac{\max a}{a}}\right)b_2^1$ $\leq b_2^2$	—	$z \geq V \cdot H$	—	—	$R \leq H\sqrt{2 - V}$	—

Table 8. Membrane forces under internal pressure p, see Bibl. 85.

6.4.5. Cylindrical membranes

Cylindrical membranes take up in the ring direction only axially symmetrical loading (barrel formula). All unsymmetrical parts of the load are transferred to the stiff end calottes by shear and longitudinal forces. The low shear stiffness of the membranes leads to large deformations without folds arising in the cylinder. With very short cylinders the First Order Theory provides a good approximation for the membrane forces. For longer cylinders the membrane form changes approximately into the support line for the loading. Both idealisations are further investigated here.

6.4.5.1. Undeformed membranes

For the cylinder the curvature b_2^2 and the Christoffel symbol Γ_{12}^1 disappear, so that the equilibrium conditions 22 are uncoupled and can be directly integrated

$$n_{11} = p_3 \cdot R,$$

$$n_{12} = -\int_0^z (p_1 + p_{3,\varphi})\, dz + C_1(\varphi), \quad (53)$$

$$n_{22} = -\int_0^z \left(\frac{n_{12,\varphi}}{R} + p_2\right) dz + C_2(\varphi).$$

For symmetrical loadings in the longitudinal direction the constants $C_1(\varphi)$ disappear. The

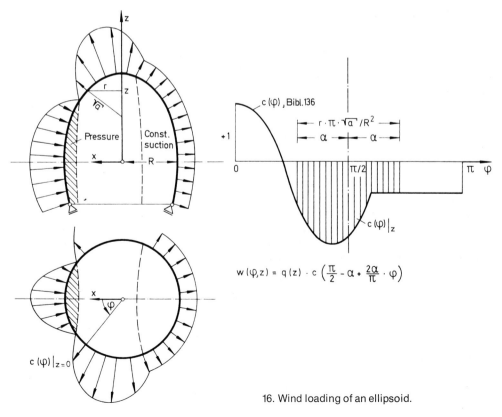

$$w(\varphi, z) = q(z) \cdot c\left(\frac{\pi}{2} - \alpha + \frac{2\alpha}{\pi} \cdot \varphi\right)$$

16. Wind loading of an ellipsoid.

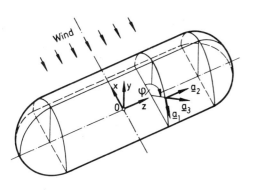

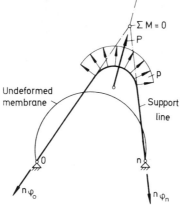

17. Cylinder membrane.

19. Support line – see F. Rudolf (Bibl. 147).

18. Support line.

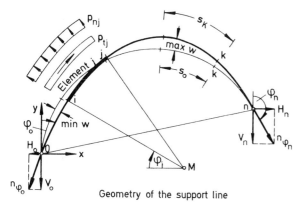

Geometry of the support line

Deformed element

shear forces of the cylinder must be taken up by the end calottes. $C_2(\varphi)$ are the normal forces transferred from the calottes to the cylinder. They are transmitted through the cylinder membrane and are first taken up by the calotte opposite. A detailed calculation of the membrane forces for spherical end calottes is contained in Bibl. 119. Similarly simple formulae for cylinders over rectangular ground areas are not known.

The maximum membrane forces for the dimensioning can be determined without complex calculations. For the load condition internal pressure p and wind w it follows from equation 53/1 that

$$\max n_{11} = (\max w + p) \cdot R. \qquad (54)$$

In the longitudinal direction the membrane force is approximately given by

$$\max n_{22} \approx \max n_{11} - p \cdot R/2. \qquad (55)$$

These membrane forces, which are calculated by the linear theory, are too large. They are in part considerably reduced by the related changes in curvature.

6.4.5.2. Cylinder as a line of pressure

If one disregards the load distribution in the longitudinal direction, the cylinder can deform without tension. Equilibrium is only possible for

the line of pressure of the loading (Fig. 18). The non-linear differential equation of the line of pressure and its numerical solution is shown in Bibl. 142. F. Rudolf's approximation method (Bibl. 147; Fig. 19) is considerably clearer and simpler. In this the membrane, idealised as a cable, is divided into small sections and constantly loaded element by element .

For the known initial values $n_{\varphi i}$, φ_i, x_i, y_i the variables at the end of the element can be calculated in accordance with Fig. 19:

$$n_{\varphi j} = n_{\varphi i} + p_t \cdot s_o,$$
$$x_j = x_i + 2 R_M \cdot \sin(d\varphi) \cdot \sin(\varphi_i + d\varphi),$$
$$y_j = y_i + 2 R_M \cdot \sin(d\varphi) \cdot \cos(\varphi_i + d\varphi),$$
$$\varphi_j = \varphi_i + 2 \cdot d\varphi \qquad (56)$$

where

$$R_M \approx \frac{n_{\varphi i} + n_{\varphi j}}{2 p_n},$$
$$d\varphi = \frac{s_o}{2}\left(\frac{1}{R_M} + \frac{p_n}{D}\right) \qquad (57)$$

Starting from one bearing point all the intermediate membrane points are calculated one after another for the prescribed initial values $n_{\varphi o}$, φ_o.

The initial values are then improved iteratively until the calculated end of the cable and the bearing point coincide. At each iteration cycle deadweight and snow loadings must be re-

divided into the components which are tangential and normal to the element.

Tests (Bibl. 14; Bibl. 114) show that even with relatively short cylinders the line of pressure appears as an approximation. Therefore only the smaller membrane forces of the line of pressure are used for dimensioning. For wind and snow load the largest membrane and bearing forces and the largest displacements can be taken from Tables 13 to 17.

6.4.6. Membranes guyed by cables

The cable guys of a pneumatic structure generally only take up the deflection forces from the kink. Variable tangential displacements are scarcely affected by the very pliable connection of the cable with the membrane (Fig. 26). If one disregards even the minimal deadweight, the cable force is

$$S = \text{constant}. \qquad (58)$$

The curvatures $\varkappa$ (s) and the torsion ϱ (s) clearly define the cable line. Both quantities can be determined by the membrane geometry (compatibility) and the equilibrium conditions.

6.4.6.1. Compatibility

For a given membrane geometry the cable curve **r** (s) is also known (Fig. 20). From the tangential vector of the cable

$$\mathbf{e}_1 = \mathbf{r}_{,s} = \frac{1}{\cos\varphi} \cdot \overset{R}{\mathbf{a}}_3 \times \overset{L}{\mathbf{a}}_3 \qquad (59)$$

the curvature $\varkappa$ and torsion ϱ can be determined by means of the Frenet formula

$$\frac{d}{ds}\begin{bmatrix}\mathbf{e}_1\\\mathbf{e}_2\\\mathbf{e}_3\end{bmatrix} = \begin{bmatrix}0 & \varkappa & 0\\-\varkappa & 0 & \varrho\\0 & -\varrho & 0\end{bmatrix} \cdot \begin{bmatrix}\mathbf{e}_1\\\mathbf{e}_2\\\mathbf{e}_3\end{bmatrix} \qquad (60)$$

6.4.6.2. Equilibrium

The deflection forces of the cable must be taken up by the membrane (Fig. 21). The condition leads to the vector equation

$$\overset{L}{n_u} \cdot \overset{L}{\mathbf{u}} + \overset{R}{n_u} \cdot \overset{R}{\mathbf{u}} = \varkappa \cdot S \cdot \mathbf{e}_2. \qquad (61)$$

In the longitudinal direction of the cable the equilibrium for S = constant is automatically fulfilled; for the normal direction $\mathbf{e}_2$ and binormal direction $\mathbf{e}_3$, the equilibrium conditions

$$\overset{L}{n_u} \cdot \cos\overset{L}{\varphi} + \overset{R}{n_u} \cdot \cos\overset{R}{\varphi} = \varkappa \cdot S,$$
$$\overset{L}{n_u} \cdot \sin\overset{L}{\varphi} - \overset{R}{n_u} \cdot \sin\overset{R}{\varphi} = 0. \qquad (62)$$

are obtained.

The derivation of equation 61 with respect to the arc length s and taking into consideration the Frenet Formula (60) lead to the torsion

$$\varrho = \frac{1}{\varkappa S}\left[\overset{L}{n_{u,s}} \cos\overset{L}{\varphi} - \overset{R}{n_{u,s}} \cos\overset{R}{\varphi}\right]. \qquad (63)$$

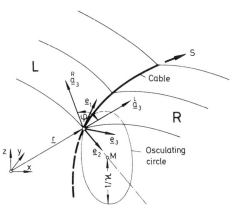

20. Geometry of the cable line.

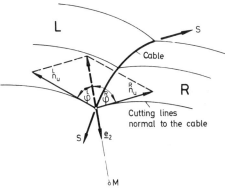

21. Equilibrium on the cable.

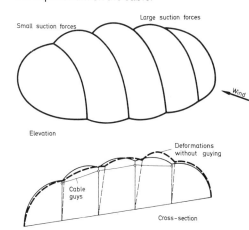

22. Membrane formed with torus zones.

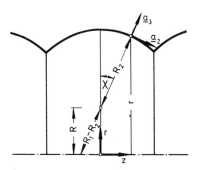

23. Torus geometry.

The actual cable line must fulfil the equilibrium and compatibility conditions. In the undeformed state that is only possible for a definite load condition – usually deadweight and internal pressure – and a geometry selected specifically for it. In all other load conditions large displacements occur, until the cable line which results from the changed geometry can take up the deflection forces from the membrane. Membranes constricted by individual cables must always be calculated by the Second Order Theory. Very large deformations easily lead to "flutter" under wind loading, so that special structural measures for stabilisation are usually necessary.

The membrane formed from torus zones (Fig. 22) fulfils all equilibrium and compatibility conditions in the undeformed state under internal pressure. Unequally distributed wind suction forces in envelopes exposed to cross winds lead to the large deformations illustrated. They are usually prevented by special cable guys.

The membrane forces under internal pressure p are calculated with the geometry quantities (Fig. 23)

$$\sqrt{a_{22}} = 1/\cos\chi, \qquad \sqrt{a} = r/\cos\chi = R_1,$$
$$b_1^1 = -1/R_1, \qquad b_2^2 = -1/R_2 \qquad (64)$$

according to Table 8, Column 1

$$n_{22} = p \cdot r/(2 \cdot \cos\chi), \qquad (65)$$
$$n_{11} = n_{22} \left[2 - \frac{r}{R_2 \cos\chi} \right].$$

In order to get the membrane forces max $n_{11} \geq \nu \cdot$ max n_{22} in the ring direction of the envelope, the folding condition

$$R_2 (1 - \nu) \geq R \qquad (66)$$

must be fulfilled.

6.5. Structural indication

6.5.1. Introduction of forces and cable reinforcements

Loops are sewn on to the membrane for anchorage. Steel pipes or cables are pushed through which take up the membrane forces (Bibl. 36). The anchorage using galvanized metal tubes, which can be pushed into each other with 1 to 2 mm clearance, is particularly simple. At the junction the tubes are telescoped and secured against undesired displacements with a small bolt (Fig. 24).

In the rounded-off corner area first the short pipe bend and then the connecting straight anchorage tubes must be threaded and joined. A special anchorage of the pipe bend is not necessary for radii of $R \leq 1.0$ m as the membrane forces are small. Reinforcement of the anchorage in the connection area of the cables and replacements is made possible without difficulty by telescoping one tube into the other. In dimensioning, according to the limit design theory, the bearing capacity of both tubes is fully exploited (Bibl. 42). Galvanized water pipes are only suitable for anchorage when they achieve the minimum material strength. In Federal Germany this is not laid down in DIN 2 440. Moreover the threaded sleeve joint is a very expensive pipe connection which weakens the cross-section. In substructures made of concrete the clamp anchorage is also usual (Fig. 25).

Larger air supported structures are reinforced by individual support cables. The transition to cable net structures, where the membranes only span the individual fields, is fluid. For protection against weather the cables are drawn in on the inside of the envelope, with which they are connected tension-proof (Fig. 26). The mount-

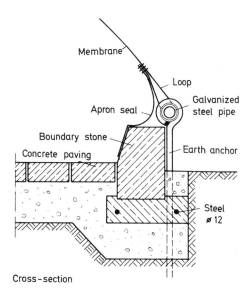

Cross-section

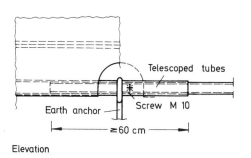

Elevation

24. Loop anchorage with telescope joint.

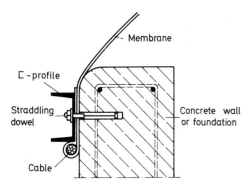

25. Clamp anchorage – see Bibl. 36.

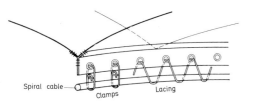

26. Cable/membrane connection.

Type given in Fig. 28	D mm	F_N cm²	G kg/m	S_{Br} Mp [1]	E [2] Mp/cm²
A	8,5	4,31	0,35	6,25	
	9	4,95	0,40	7,18	
	10	6,36	0,52	9,22	
B	11	7,22	0,61	10,45	≈ 1800
	12	8,59	0,72	12,45	
	13	101	0,84	14,65	
	14	117	0,98	16,95	
	16	153	1,28	20,15	
	18	193	1,62	28,05	
	20	239	2,00	34,60	

[1] Tensile strength of the single wire G_{Br} = 14,5 Mp/cm²
[2] after stretching

Table 9. Spiral cables – see Bibl. 59.

Type of anchorage	η
Hook or grommet with clamps	0,80
Hook or grommet (spliced)	0,95
Drawing casing, compression socket	0,90
Sealing attachment	1,00

Table 10. η-values for cable anchorages ($\varnothing \leqslant 20$ mm).

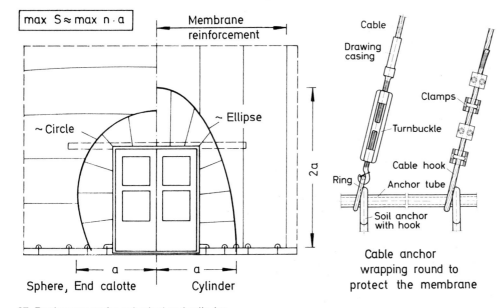

$$\boxed{\max S \approx \max n \cdot a}$$

Membrane reinforcement

~ Circle   ~ Ellipse

2a

Sphere, End calotte | Cylinder

a   a

27. Replacements for spherical and cylinder membranes.
28. Cable forms.

Cable
Drawing casing
Clamps
Turnbuckle
Cable hook
Ring
Anchor tube
Soil anchor with hook

Cable anchor wrapping round to protect the membrane

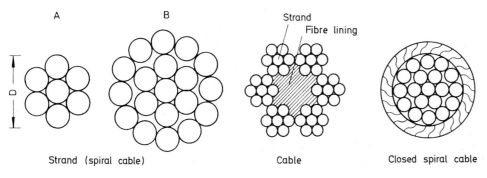

A   B   Strand   Fibre lining

D

Strand (spiral cable)   Cable   Closed spiral cable

ing of the cables in sewn-on loops is very time consuming and only practicable for boundary cables and short gate replacements. When tensions are minimal the cables are also replaced by sewn-on strips of material.

In the case of door and gate replacements boundary cables take up the membrane forces. Thereby additional membrane deformations occur, because parts of the internal pressure will be carried by the gate construction. The geometry of the boundary cable depends only on the membrane forces introduced, whose direction is influenced by the additional deformations. In order to keep deviation from the prescribed membrane form low, the boundary cable for the load condition internal pressure is adapted in approximation to the line of support. Under other load conditions increased membrane forces sometimes occur in the replacement area, as the boundary cable can only take up the forces after large deformations and force rearrangements in the membrane. For cylindrical and spherical membranes the form of the cable line and also an approximation of the largest cable forces are given in Fig. 27.

The support cables usually consist of galvanized steel wires, less frequently of synthetic or organic fibres. The overwhelming choice of steel cables is due to the large E module, the insensibility to environmental influences and the high heat resistance. For pneumatic structures and cable nets spiral strands are mainly used (Fig. 28).

Cables in which several strands are whipped around a fibre centre have a low E module and are more difficult to anchor. They are specially suited to running over a roller. A detailed summary of the different types of strands and cables, their end anchorage and breaking strength is contained in Felten & Guilleaume's catalogue (Bibl. 59). Table 9 is taken from this: from a diameter of 15 mm locked spiral cables are also produced. The cable strength S_{Br} is not the criterion for the dimensioning of the cable, but the, in part, considerably lower strength $V_{Br} = \eta \cdot S_{Br}$ of the end anchorage. The reducing coefficient η is dependent on the type of anchorage and on the cable diameter. With thin cables and a well executed anchorage the η-values given in Table 10 are usually exceeded (Bibl. 13).

6.5.2. Anchorages

Air supported structures can be produced very economically and they have a life of 8 to 15 years. Extensions, alterations or removal to a new site are relatively easy. The membrane anchorage should be just as adaptable and economic. So as not to prejudice later use of the site, the withdrawal or dismantling of the anchorage should not involve any great expense. The membrane forces in pneumatic structures are usually relatively small at 1 to 2 Mp/m. In a direct anchorage of the membrane many anchor points with low strengths are required. They are developed as gravity or earth anchors.

Some gravity anchors are shown in Fig. 29. The anchor forces depend basically on the weight of the anchor only and they disperse very little. For dimensioning of the anchor body two limiting cases have to be investigated (Fig. 30):

a) The horizontal components of the membrane force are taken up by the ground or by an inserted concrete floor. The anchor weight compensates only the vertical component ($N_{Br.} = n_R \cdot$ anchor interval)

$$G \geqslant V_{Br.} \qquad (67)$$

b) The anchor body turns round and begins to glide unfavourably in the direction of the membrane force. The anchor weight must exceed the value

$$G \geqslant \frac{N_{Br.}^2}{V_{Br.} + \varrho \cdot H_{Br.}} \qquad (68)$$

(ϱ = sliding friction between anchor and floor). Thereby large displacements occur, which do not affect the loadbearing behaviour of the membrane. They are only of significance with respect to the structural development of the anchor point and the components.

Tests must be made to determine whether the safety factor $\nu = 1.5$ cannot be reduced in the case of well defined anchorage bodies. The peak values of the membrane forces originate from briefly occurring wind loadings, whose effect is broken down by the mass of the anchor body and by the damping in the ground.

In contrast to gravity anchors, soil anchors are generally easier to place and to remove. Fig. 31 shows a screw anchor and a spread anchor. The screw anchor is especially suitable for lighter soils, while the spread anchor can also be rammed into heavy soils. The lamella of the ground anchor can snap together in highly consistent soils with very great shear strength without a body of earth shearing off. The instability of the lamella is connected with a sudden loss of loadbearing capacity and is prevented by pressing out of the spread anchor foot with concrete.

Under diagonal tension the anchor shaft bends without reducing the bearing capacity significantly. An inclined approach of the anchor or a head plate made of concrete, with which several anchors can be fastened together, prevents the shaft bending.

The loadbearing capacity of the earth anchor depends on the soil physics characteristics – in particular the shear strength – which determine the size of the sheared off earth body. In the area near to the surface drying out, soaking

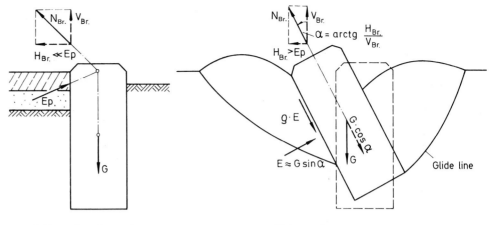

a) Upper boundary value   b) Lower boundary value

30. Limit values of the anchor forces.

or freezing changes the strength properties of the ground. In order to keep the seasonal variations in anchorage capacity as small as possible, the foot of the anchor should lie at least 70 to 100 cm under this zone. Thus one obtains minimum anchor depths of some

$$\min t \approx 1.2 \ldots 1.5 \,(m) \qquad (69)$$

in Federal Germany. In the case of stratified soils the loadbearing capacity of the anchor is dependent mainly on the shear strength of the earth layer directly above the anchor foot. The equation

$$S_{Br.} \approx d \cdot (2.25 \cdot t - 1) \cdot S_o$$

where $1.0 \leqslant t \leqslant 2.0\,[m]$, $0.1 \leqslant d \leqslant 0.35\,[m]$ (70)

gives a cautious indication for the loadbearing capacity of the earth anchor.

Equation 70 only applies for the given anchor depths t and foot diameter d (Fig. 31); the factor S_o can be taken from Table 11. The measured anchor forces disperse over a wide range and in part exceed considerably the values given in equation 70. In the low anchor depths sudden changes in the ground characteristics cannot be excluded. It is therefore suggested that every 5th to 10th anchor in an air supported hall be subjected to a tensile test. In order not to destroy the anchors by the test, only 1.25 times of the working load should be applied.

Larger anchor forces, such as arise in the cable guys of air supported structures and in cable net constructions, are taken up by groups of anchors, reinforced concrete anchor piles or larger gravity anchors. The anchorage costs increase quickly with the size of the force to be anchored, so that large cable forces should be avoided if possible in air supported structures.

6.5.3. Checking of the construction

Air supported halls and their operating installations must be regularly controlled and maintained. A thorough check should be made especially before a large storm gets up. Defects

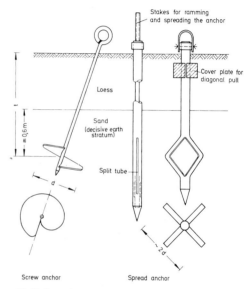

31. Soil anchors.

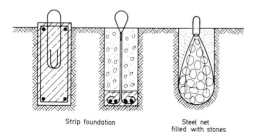

Strip foundation   Steel net filled with stones

29. Gravity anchors.

Type of soil	S_0 [Mp/m²]
Rich, well drained clays, mixed with rubbles and stones	8,9
Well graduated gravel-sand mixture, one grain gravel	7,5
Firmly supported rough grained gravel-sand	6,1
Semi-firm, cohesive soils, loam, marl, loess loam	4,7
Filled in, non-compressed soil	3,7

Table 11. Soil coefficients S_o.

No.	Check	References	Date checked				
1	the envelope, by sector, for tears, holes or overstraining						
2	for excessive air leakage around the base						
3	that the envelope is free of tears at the connections with cables, door constructions or components						
4	every old patch for leaks						
5	the proper distance between the envelope and the components or the storage of material	min a =					
6	the firmness of the anchorage, the adjustments and the rust protection						
7	for changed ground conditions (excavations, foundation-trenches)						
8	the ground anchorage of the components						
9	the door linkages and controls for proper operation (doors should not remain open by mistake)						
10	the proper operation of the pressure gauge or manometer						
11	the proper on-off control of the blowers by internal pressure	min p = max p =					
12	the regular servicing of the blowers						
13	the cleanness of the blower intake, the blower and the flexible connection with the envelope – leaves, paper, snow, etc., must be removed						
14	the presence of the warning and direction plates, the snow rope and the repair kit for small leaks						

Table 12. Check list for maintenance – see Bibl. 36.

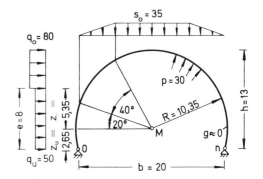

32. Loading scheme. Wind loading – see Bibl. 136.

and deficiencies which are revealed should be repaired immediately. Small tears in the envelope can otherwise quickly tear further and lead to destruction of the whole structure. During a storm the largest permissible internal pressure should be maintained in order to prevent the membrane folding in and the considerably greater wind loadings which follow. A typical check list for maintenance is shown in Table 12, which is taken, somewhat abbreviated, from Bibl. 36.

Alongside this maintenance the operating safety and stability of the air supported structure should be controlled at larger intervals (every 2 years say). Only when the whole structure comes through the next maintenance period with adequate safety will the operating permit be extended. Here a special difficulty of such an inspection becomes clear: a rusted anchor or brittle concrete is easy to recognise, but the residual tensile strength of the aged membrane and seams is not. The owner generally only agrees to sample tests in exceptional cases, as the patches in the membrane stand out very clearly.

A membrane test which satisfies the safety regulations and does not destroy the membrane is offered by "squeezing". In this method of testing, which is taken from pipe construction, the internal pressure on a still day is increased until the membrane force reaches the value

$$\max n \ (p_{test}) \approx 1.1 \cdot \max n \ (p, w). \qquad (71)$$

Factor 1.1 approximately takes in the loss of strength of the membrane in the next maintenance period and the dynamic effect of the wind. The fixed fan installations usually do not attain the test pressure p_{test}. Therefore a specially strong (portable) fan must be connected for the test, which can be borrowed from

the technical inspection authority or from the manufacturer. Only the additional connection nozzles must already be provided on the membrane. Weak points on the membrane are discovered immediately through this "squeezing". Prompt repair avoids greater damage in the next storm.

6.6. Diagrams for membrane calculation

With the following diagrams cylindrical and ellipsoid membranes can be calculated. They are prepared so that the structural quantities necessary for the dimensioning and anchoring of the envelope can easily be read off. The loading corresponds to the data in Bibl. 136. The wind distribution given there for the cylinder is also approximately correct for ellipsoids. The selfweight and the membrane elongations are disregarded. The formulae in Section 6.4 form the basis of the diagrams. Their application is shown in an example in Section 6.7.

In cylinder membranes the deformations must not be ignored. Comparative calculations have shown that only a few parameters considerably influence non-linear behaviour. Those parameters are explicitly contained in the diagrams. The low dispersion of the solution through the unrealised parameters is revealed by the envelope curves of the diagrams. Tables 15 and 16 apply only for constant wind pressure. They may be used in approximation for gradually changing wind pressure.

The membrane deformations of the ellipsoid are very small and can be ignored. Local bulging must be avoided by an adequately large internal pressure. In Tables 19 to 21 only the extreme values of the membrane forces as a function of the z coordinates are shown. The

superposition of the individual load conditions provides the maximum membrane forces for the dimensioning and the minimum for proof of folding safety. Furthermore the extreme values of the membrane are given for the sphere under gradually changing wind pressure.

6.7. Calculation examples

For lack of space the handling of the diagrams given in Section 6.6 is shown here for one load condition only. For a limit load investigation the internal pressure and the back pressure of the wind will be multiplied by the safety factors v_i, given in Section 6.4.3. The membrane forces, calculated for the v_i-times of the loading, must not exceed the long term tensile strength of the envelope. In our example a cylinder membrane with spherical calottes will be determined for the load conditions p, w $\vee$ s. The loading scheme is shown in Fig. 32 (dimensions in kp, m). In cylinders with rectangular base the wind load decreases because of higher turbulences. Therefore the membrane forces are smaller than the values determined here.

In the following calculation all the coefficients taken from the diagrams are set in bold type. The reading scheme is marked on the diagrams for example.

6.7.1. Cylinder membrane

6.7.1.1. Input parameters

$h/b = 13/20 = 0,65$,
$e/h = 8/13 = 0.615 \approx 0.6$ (rounded down),
$p/q_u = 30/50 = 0.6$,
$p/q_o = 30/80 = 0.375$,
$p/S_o = 30/35 = 0.857$.

6.7.1.2. Membrane forces

Snow load reduces the membrane forces so that the load condition wind is critical for dimensioning. From Table 13 is taken the membrane force for constant wind pressure and estimated separately for q_u and q_o:

$n_\varphi(q_u) = \mathbf{0.8} \cdot (30 + 50) \cdot 10.35 = 662 \text{ kp/m}$,

$n_\varphi(q_o) = \mathbf{0.765} \cdot (30 + 80) \cdot 10.35 = 872 \text{ kp/m}$.

For gradual wind distribution the membrane force generally lies between these two critical values. Only in the specific input parameters present here is the membrane force $n_\varphi(q_o)$ slightly exceeded. The final membrane force is calculated in accordance with Table 14:

$n_\varphi(q) = -\mathbf{0.025} \cdot 662 + (1 + \mathbf{0.025}) \cdot 872$

$= 877 \text{ kp/m}$.

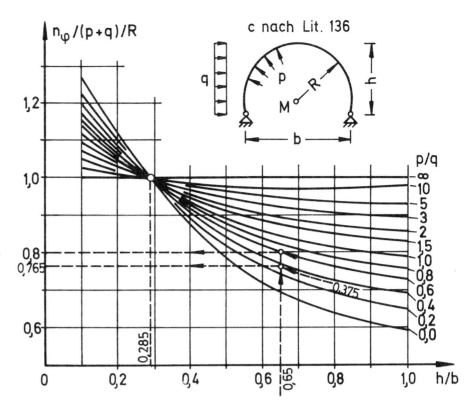

Table 13. Membrane forces of a cylinder under wind loading.

Table 14. Factor λ in gradual wind loading.

$$n_\varphi(q,p) = \lambda \cdot n_\varphi(q_u,p) + (1-\lambda) \cdot n_\varphi(q_0,p)$$

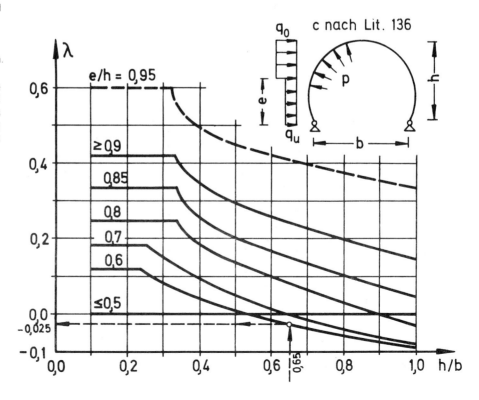

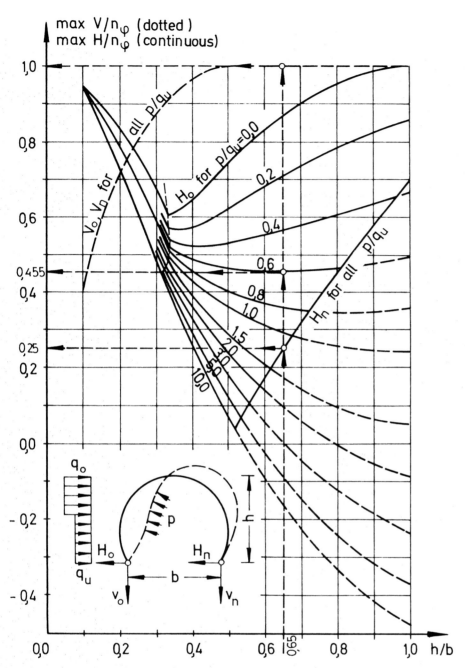

max V/n_φ (dotted)
max H/n_φ (continuous)

V_o, V_n for all p/q_u

H_o for $p/q_u = 0.0$

0.2
0.4
0.6
0.8
1.0
1.5
2.0
3.0
5.0
10.0

H_n for all p/q_u

Table 15. Bearing forces of a cylinder under wind loading.

6.7.1.3. Anchorage forces (load condition wind)

In flat cylinder sections when $h/b \leq 0.5$ the horizontal anchorage forces $H_o \geq H_n$ are always directed outwards. They can change the sign in membranes where $h/b > 0.5$. The anchorage forces are taken from Table 15:

$H_o = \mathbf{0.455} \cdot 877 = 400$ kp/m,
$H_n = \mathbf{0.25} \cdot 877 = 219$ kp/m,
$V = \mathbf{1.0} \cdot 877 = 877$ kp/m.

H_o is directed outwards, H_n inwards.
The maximum forces H and V occur at different bearing points and they are marked off in Table 15 by envelope curves. Therefore

$$n_\varphi(q) \leq \sqrt{H^2 + V^2}$$

is valid.

6.7.1.4. Deformation of non-flexible membranes

a) Load condition wind according to Table 16

max $w \approx \mathbf{0.2} \cdot 10.35 = 2.07$ m.

The deformation caused by wind must generally be proved for membranes where $h/b \geq 0.5$. The greatest displacement occurs in the wind back pressure area.

b) Load condition snow in accordance with Table 17

max $w = \mathbf{0.52} \cdot 10.35 = 5.38$ m.

Only in special cases is snow loading taken into consideration for unheated membranes. The one-sided snow loading leads to lower deformations.

The internal pressure must be significantly raised so that the deformations do not exceed the permissible values max $w \leq 0.1 \cdot R = 1.035$ m as given in equation 13.

6.7.1.5. Internal pressure for max $w = 0.1 \cdot R$

a) Load condition wind in accordance with Table 16
emp. $p \approx \mathbf{1.8} \cdot 50 = 90$ kp/m².

b) Load condition snow in accordance with Table 17
emp. $p = \mathbf{2.5} \cdot 3.5 = 87$ kp/m².

Normally one begins with this proof to establish the operating pressure p.

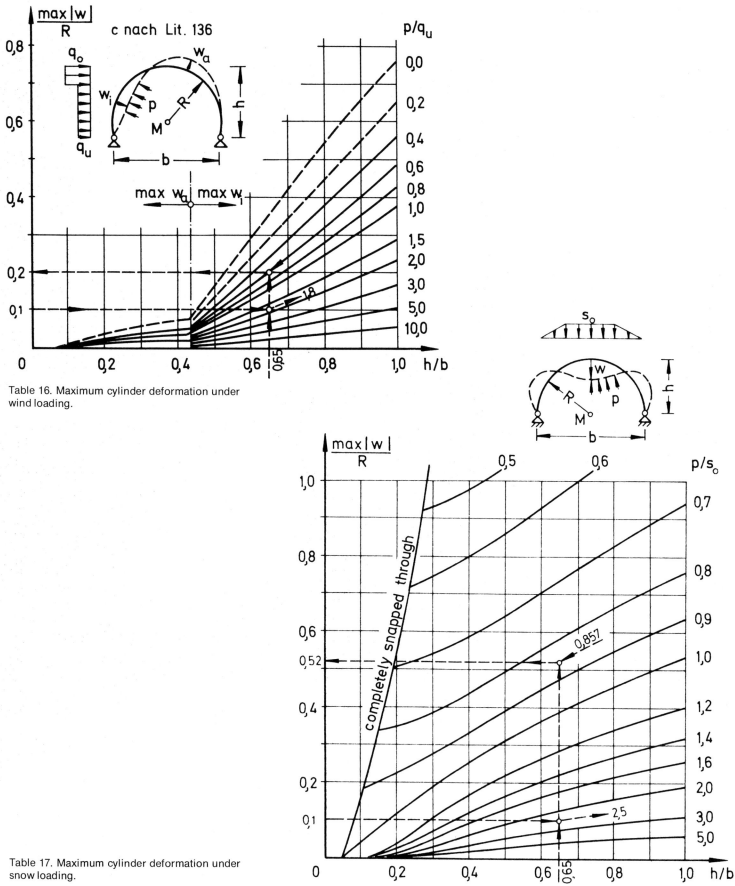

Table 16. Maximum cylinder deformation under wind loading.

Table 17. Maximum cylinder deformation under snow loading.

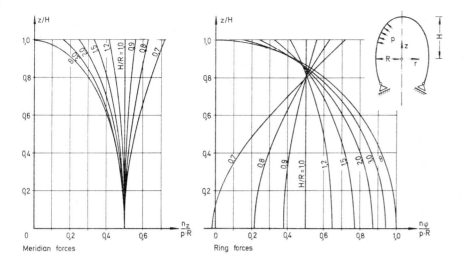

Table 18. Ellipsoid under internal pressure.

Table 19. Ellipsoid under snow loading.

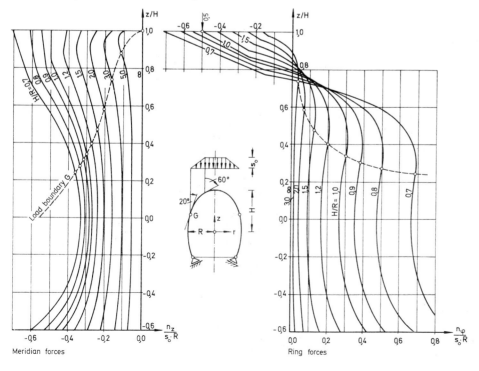

6.7.2. Spherical calottes

The deformations of the double curved end calottes are very small and can be ignored. Thus the superposition principle is maintained. Instead of the deformation restriction of the cylinder membrane folding in must now be avoided by using the necessary margin of safety.

6.7.2.1. Input parameters

$H/R = 1.0$,
$z_u/R = -2.65/10.35 = 0.266 > 0.6$,
$z_O/R = 5.35/10.35 = 0.517$,
$q_u/q_o = 50/80 = 0.625$.

6.7.2.2. Membrane forces

The wind loading is also critical for the dimensioning of spherical membranes. The membrane forces from internal pressure (Table 18) are superimposed with the maximum values from wind (Tables 22, 23):

$$\max n_\varphi = \mathbf{0.5} \cdot 30 \cdot 10.35 + \\ + \mathbf{1.26} \cdot 80 \cdot 10.35 = 1198 \text{ kp/m},$$

$$\max n_z = \mathbf{0.5} \cdot 30 \cdot 10.35 + \\ + \mathbf{1.14} \cdot 80 \cdot 10.35 = 1100 \text{ kp/m}.$$

The membrane forces in the end calottes are 25 to 35% larger than the forces in the cylindrical part (see Section 6.7.3).

The dimensioning forces for a sphere can be very easily determined. For ellipsoids one must plot and superimpose the extreme values of the membrane forces (Tables 18–21) given for the individual load conditions as a function of z. The envelope is dimensioned for the largest membrane forces in the area $z \geq z_u$.

6.7.2.3. Anchorage forces

Approximately the anchorage is dimensioned for the maximum membrane forces n_z:

$$\max H \approx \max n_z \cdot z_u/R = -1100 \cdot 0.266 = \\ = -292 \text{ kp/m},$$

$$\max V \approx \max n_z \cdot b/2/R = \\ = 1100 \cdot 20/2/10.35 = 1060 \text{ kp/m};$$

max H points inwards.

6.7.2.4. Formation of wrinkles

a) Load condition wind in accordance with Table 24:

$$\min n_w = -\mathbf{0.43} \cdot 80 \cdot 10.35 = -368 \text{ kp/m}.$$

The minimum membrane force occurs mostly at the jump point of the wind pressure. It does not occur in this order of magnitude in a steady wind distribution.

b) Load condition snow:

$$\min n_s = -\mathbf{0.5} \cdot 35 \cdot 10.35 = 181 \text{ kp/m}.$$

The prescribed internal pressure produces in the end calottes in accordance with Table 18 only the constant membrane force

$$n_{\phi} = n_z = \mathbf{0.5} \cdot 30 \cdot 10.35 = 158 \text{ kp/m} < |\min n|.$$

In the end calottes wrinkles occur under wind and snow loading. However, it has not yet been taken into account that the cylinder membranes, by reason of the large deformations, hang on at the stiffer spherical heads.

6.7.2.5. Minimum internal pressure for folding safety ν

Wind loading, which produces the greatest compressive membrane forces, is the critical load condition for calculating the minimum internal pressure.
The minimum internal pressure:

$$\min p = \frac{|\min n (w)|}{(1-\nu) R/2} = \frac{386}{0.8 \cdot 10.35/2} =$$

$$= 86 \text{ kp/m}^2.$$

arises from equation 19 for folding safety.
In Bibl. 136 the folding safety $\nu = 1.2$ for spherical membranes is prescribed ($\nu \approx (\bar{\nu} - 1)/\bar{\nu} = 0.17$ in accordance with equation 19). The folding safety $\bar{\nu} = 2.0$ ($\nu \approx 0.5$) given there for cylinders with quarto-spherical heads is unrealistic and should be avoided.

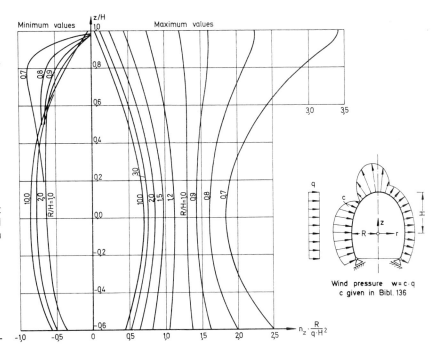

Table 20. Ellipsoid under wind loading, extreme values of the meridian forces.

Table 21. Ellipsoid under wind loading, extreme values of the ring forces.

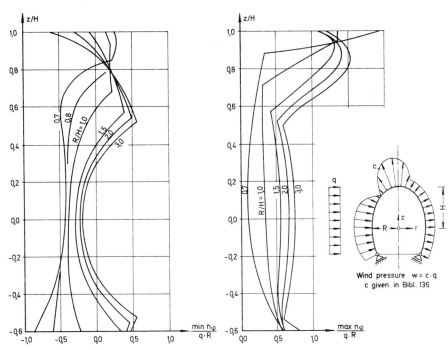

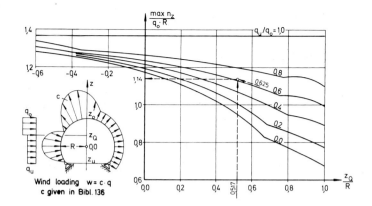

Table 22. Sphere under wind loading, maximum meridian tensile force in the region $-0.6 \leq z/R \leq 1.0$.

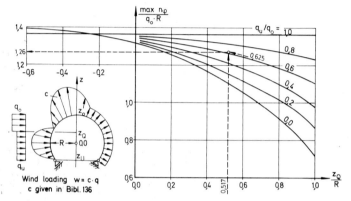

Table 23. Sphere under wind loading, maximum ring tensile force in the region $-0.6 \leq z/R \leq 1.0$.

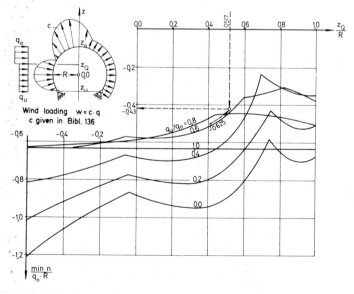

Table 24. Sphere under wind loading, maximum membrane compression force in the region $-0.6 \leq z/R \leq 1.0$.

6.7.3. Discussion of the results

At first glance it is surprising that the maximum membrane forces of the sphere are larger than those of the cylinder. The favourable load-bearing behaviour of the sphere under internal pressure no longer applies for wind loading.

Fig. 33 gives a view of a wind loaded spherical shell. The rings 1, normal to the wind direction, are loaded symmetrically in respect to rotation for the assumed wind distribution c. They bear the wind suction – like the cylinder – mainly in line with the barrel formula. In the wind direction the rings 2 receive pressure and suction so that no large membrane forces can arise which could significantly relieve the load in the transverse direction 1.

In contrast the cylinder adapts better to non-uniform loading. Peaks in the membrane forces such as occur in the sphere are reduced by the deformation of the support line. In the area of higher loading the support line curves more strongly so that only the longitudinal force

$$n_\varphi = \max(p + w) \cdot \min \varrho < \max(p + w) \cdot R$$

arises (Fig. 34).

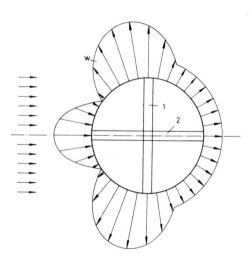

33. View of a wind loaded shell sphere.

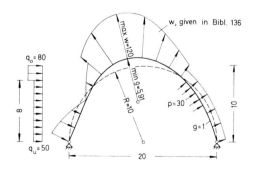

34. Cylinder deformation. Dimensions in kp, m.

182

7. Excursus: Pneumatic structures as form work for shell construction

As long ago as the early forties the American engineer W. Neff constructed a number of buildings by spraying concrete on to rubber balloons. In the process, however, considerable technical problems arose as there was excessive deformation of the form work due to insufficient internal pressure and furthermore it was not possible to maintain a constant internal pressure during fluctuations in temperature. As a result the concrete shells started cracking. (Bibl. 119, p. 163.)

It was about 20 years before the idea, which was not at all far fetched, reached technical maturity with the Domecrete technique by Haim Heifetz (Fig. 1–4; Bibl. 44, p. 149ff.; Bibl. 70; Bibl. 72). Here a 3 or 4.5 or 6 cm thick coat of high grade concrete is applied or sprayed in layers of 15 mm on to high pressure structures the size of a house. The pneumatic form work can be removed within 90 minutes after application of the concrete. In less than a day a dwelling house including a Vermiculite insulating layer, inside and outside plastering (total wall thickness 10 cm), electricity and water supplies, as well as windows and doors, can be completed.

The production costs are 30 to 56% lower, according to the type of usage, than conventionally produced buildings. Expenses for the special equipment are so moderate that they are usually recovered on the first building.

1

2

1–4. Various houses manufactured by the Domecrete technique

3   4

5. Binishell with fan not yet removed.
6. Diagram of the Binishell process.

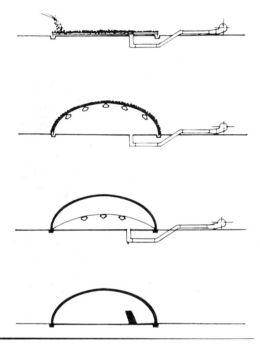

The Bayer Igloo (Figs. 7–10), by Farbenfabriken Bayer AG, was developed as an emergency shelter for use in disaster areas. It is built by spraying polyurethane foam on to a balloon made of PVC film reinforced with fabric. While the pneumatic form work is rotated on a turntable, consisting of a dismountable lightweight steel structure, the spray gun moves up and down on a tripod placed over the form work. The reaction mixture foams up immediately, expands to about 30 times its initial volume and cures after a few seconds. Several layers of spray foam are applied one on top of the other up to a total thickness of 10 cm.

As rigid polyurethane foam also possesses excellent insulating properties, the English firm P. Frankenstein and Sons, Ltd. used this material to develop a shelter for polar regions (Bibl. 44, p. 150). The main difference from the Bayer Igloo is

that the air supported structure serving as form work is not only coated from the outside but also from the inside. After the curing of the foam the membrane is no longer structurally necessary, although it cannot be re-used.

A similar process is offered by the American firm Basic Products Development Company. There the inside is also reinforced with steel.

A method combining the above mentioned processes was been developed by the firm of Garteway Towers. Rigidising polyurethane foam is sprayed from the inside on to a pneumatic form work for reinforcement. In addition a steel reinforcement is laid over the outside and covered with concrete by the Torcret technique.

7–10. Various stages in the manufacture of a Bayer igloo.

In the Binishells (Figs. 5, 6; Bibl. 17; Bibl. 44, p. 147 ff.) developed by Dante Bini and manufactured by Du Pont de Nemours International S.A., the form work consists of a flat, 2 to 3 mm thick rubber or neoprene membrane which, because of its high elasticity, can be inflated to hemispherical shape. The setting time of the concrete of which the shell is made is 12 to 48 hours. Removing the form work is particularly simple as the membrane falls back flat again as soon as the tension is slackened.

The reinforcement consists of coiled springs which can adapt well to the arched shape.

The shells can be heat insulated from the inside or the outside. In addition a second concrete shell can later be applied from the outside. Openings are cut out with a saw.

The buildings achieve high strengths and need no scaffolding or cranes in erection. According to the quotations of various firms the price is about 50% below that of a comparable conventional structure.

The rubber form work used by NOE-Schaltechnik, a West German firm, for the production of in-situ concrete conduits (Figs. 11, 12) is particularly economic in the case of large cross-sections of pipes with high loading, but can also be used to manufacture small conduits such as ventilation shafts, chimneys, etc.

First the base is concreted, the external casing erected and, if necessary, reinforcement applied. Then the rubber form work is laid in and inflated.

The form work can also be used in the building of curved pipe conduits; the smallest possible bending radius amounts to about 20 times the tube diameter.

11

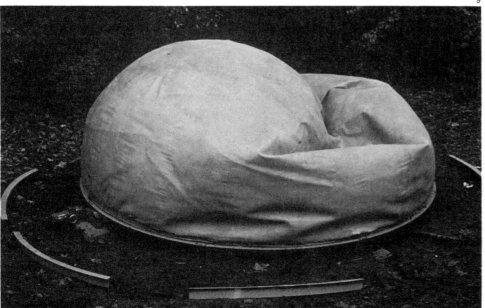

9

10

12

11, 12. Examples of the production of in-situ concrete conduits as developed by the firm of NOE-Schaltechnik.

Appendix

Bibliography

1. David Allison. "A great balloon for peaceful atoms". *The Architectural Forum* (New York), Nov. 1960.

2. Fred Angerer. *Bauen mit tragenden Flächen.* Munich, 1960.

3. Ant Farm. *Inflatocookbook.* Sausalito, California. 1971.

4. *Architectural Design* (London), 1968, 6.

5. Ballonfabrik—See- und Luftausrüstung GmbH + Co. KG, Augsburg. *Ballonhallen.* Company brochure, Nov. 1970.

6. Ballonfabrik—See- und Luftausrüstung GmbH + Co. KG. *BFA auf einen Blick.* Company brochure, 1972.

7. Reyner Banham. "A Home is not a House". *Art in America* (New York), 1965, 4.

8. *Bauen mit Kunststoffen* (Institut für das Bauen mit Kunststoffen e. V., Darmstadt), 1965, 2.

9. *Bauen mit Kunststoffen,* 1965, 4.

10. *Bauen mit Kunststoffen,* 1965, 5.

11. *Bauen mit Kunststoffen,* 1968, 4.

12. *Bauen mit Plasten.* Seminar report. Technische Hochschule Darmstadt, 1971.

13. J. Beck. *Die Befestigung von Drahtseilen mit aufgezogenen Stahlhülsen.* Thesis. Technische Hochschule Stuttgart, 1940.

14. G. Beger and E. Macher. "Results of Wind Tunnel Tests on some Pneumatic Structures". In: *Proceedings of the 1st International Colloquium on Pneumatic Structures.* Technische Hochschule Stuttgart, 1967.

15. Roland Benesch. "Das Bauen mit Membranen und Netzen". *kib Kunststoffe im Bau* (Heidelberg), 7 (1967).

16. Roland Benesch. "Pneumatische Wände". In: *International Symposium on Pneumatic Structures Delft 1972. Proceedings.* Technische Hogeschool Delft, 1972.

17. Dante Bini. "A New Pneumatic Technique for the Construction of Thin Shells". In: *Proceedings of the 1st International Colloquium on Pneumatic Structures.* Technische Hochschule Stuttgart, 1967.

18. Walter W. Bird. "The Development of Pneumatic Structures. Past, Present, Future". In: *Proceedings of the 1st International Colloquium on Pneumatic Structures.* Technische Hochschule Stuttgart, 1967.

19. Walter W. Bird. "Air structures span space in building revolution". *Rubber World,* 1972, 1, and 1972, 2.

20. Birdair Structures, Inc., Buffalo. N.Y. *Airshelters.* Company brochures, 1971.

21. T. Botschuiver and J. Shaw. "Eventstructures". In: *International Symposium on Pneumatic Structures Delft 1972.* Proceedings. Technische Hogeschool Delft, 1972.

22. C. V. Boys. *Soap bubbles, their formation and the forces that mould them.* London, 1960.

23. *Der Große Brockhaus.* 15th ed., Leipzig, 1928—35.

24. H. Brügge. Zugbeanspruchte Konstruktionen, Marienfeld. *Die Brügge-Innendruck-Lager-Halle.* Company brochure, 1970.

25. Rudolf Brylka. "Belüftung und Beheizung von Traglufthallen". *Haus der Technik — Vortragsveröffentlichungen* (Essen), 124 (1967).

26. Rudolf Brylka. "Zur Konstruktion von Traglufthallen". *Bauen + Wohnen* (Munich), 1968, 6.

27. Rudolf Brylka. "Entwicklung und Anwendungsmöglichkeiten von Traglufthallen". *Der Architekt* (Essen), 1968, 10.

28. Rudolf Brylka. "Traglufthallen heute". *Technische Mitteilungen Krupp* (Fried. Krupp GmbH, Essen), vol. 28 (1970), 2.

29. Rudolf Brylka. "Neue Ausführungsbeispiele und Projekte von pneumatischen Konstruktionen". In *International Symposium on Pneumatic Structures Delft 1972. Proceedings.* Technische Hogeschool Delft, 1972.

30. Rudolf Brylka. "Richtlinien für den Bau und Betrieb von Tragluftbauten in der Bundesrepublik Deutschland". In: *International Symposium on Pneumatic Structures Delft 1972. Proceedings.* Technische Hogeschool Delft, 1972.

31. BSI-Code. 1972. (England.)

32. Building Centre of Japan, Pneumatic Structures Committee. *Pneumatic Structure Design Standard and Commentary.*

33. Philip S. Bulson. "The Behavior of some Experimental Inflated Structures". In: *Proceedings of the 1st International Colloquium on Pneumatic Structures.* Technische Hochschule Stuttgart, 1967.

34. Philip S. Bulson. "3 Metre Diameter Air Bags under Severe Local Loads". In: *International Symposium on Pneumatic Structures Delft 1972. Proceedings.* Technische Hogeschool Delft, 1972.

35. Z. Bychawski. "Rheological Large Deformation of Rotational Membranes". In: *International Symposium on Pneumatic Structures Delft 1972. Proceedings.* Technische Hogeschool Delft, 1972.

36. Canvas Products Association International, Air Structures Division. *Minimum Performance Standard for Single-Wall Air-Supported Structures,* March, 1971.

37. W. Caspar. "Maximale Windgeschwindigkeiten in der Bundesrepublik Deutschland". *Die Bautechnik* (Berlin), vol. 47 (1970), p. 335ff.

38. Simon Conolly and Mark Fisher. "Auto-mat". *Architectural Design* (London), 1971, 4.

39. Simon Conolly, Mark Fisher and O. W. Neumark. "Experiments and Observations on the Use of Pressure Tensioned Membrane Systems for Locomotion and Flight". In: *International Symposium on Pneumatic Structures Delft 1972. Proceedings.* Technische Hogeschool Delft, 1972.

40. H. J. Cowan and J. G. Pohl. "A Preliminary Investigation into the Load-Bearing Capacity of Open-Ended Cylindrical Columns, Subjected to Internal Fluid Pressure". In: *Proceedings of the 1st International Colloquium on Pneumatic*

Structures. Technische Hochschule Stuttgart, 1967.

41. Justus Dahinden. *Stadtstrukturen für morgen. Analysen, Thesen, Modelle.* Stuttgart, 1971. English: *Urban Structures for the Future.* London and New York, 1971.

42. Deutscher Ausschuß für Stahlbau. *Richtlinien zur Anwendung des Traglastverfahrens im Stahlbau.* May, 1972.

43. Roger N. Dent. *Pneumatic Structures in Architecture with Special Reference to Arctic and Lunar Application.* Thesis. University of Liverpool, 1968.

44. Roger N. Dent. *Principles of Pneumatic Architecture.* London, 1971.

45. Roger N. Dent. "A Unique Pneumatic Application". In: *International Symposium on Pneumatic Structures Delft 1972. Proceedings.* Technische Hogeschool Delft, 1972.

46. *Detail* (Tokyo), April, 1970.

47. Albert G. H. Dietz. "Solar Energy for Air-Supported Buildings". In: *International Symposium on Pneumatic Structures Delft 1972. Proceedings.* Technische Hogeschool Delft, 1972.

48. *DIN 1055. Lastannahmen für Bauten.* Sheet 4, March 1963 issue, and sheet 5, March 1973 draft.

49. *Domus* (Milan), 455 (Oct., 1967).

50. *Domus* (Milan), 467 (Oct., 1968).

51. Milford W. Donaldson and John B. McNicholas. "First Steps in the Development of a Photoelastic Model Technique for the Study of Pneumatic Structures". In: *International Symposium on Pneumatic Structures Delft 1972. Proceedings.* Technische Hogeschool Delft, 1972.

52. H. Duddeck. "Die Biegeberechnung technischer Rotationsschalen mit Rändern entlang den Breitenkreisen". *Der Bauingenieur* (Berlin), vol. 39 (1964), p. 435 ff.

53. E. Dulácska. "Stability of Rubber Ballons". In: *International Symposium on Pneumatic Structures Delft 1972. Proceedings.* Technische Hogeschool Delft, 1972.

54. Dynamit Nobel AG., Troisdorf. *Traglufthallen aus beschichtetem Trevira-hochfest-Gewebe.* Company brochure, 1970.

55. Dynat Gesellschaft für Verschlußtechnik und Feinmechanik mbH, Hildesheim. Company brochure on gas-, water- and pressure-tight fasteners, 1969.

56. G.-A. Euteneuer. "Druckanstieg im Inneren von Gebäuden bei Windeinfall". *Der Bauingenieur* (Berlin), vol. 45 (1970), p. 214 ff.

57. Farbwerke Hoechst AG, Frankfurt/Main. *Information T 21: Vergleichende Prüfung von beschichteten und gummierten Geweben aus Trevira-hochfest auf Schwerentflammbarkeit bzw. Schwerbrennbarkeit.* (Sept. 1967.)

58. E. M. Feldhaus. *Die Technik der Vorzeit, der geschichtlichen Zeit und der Naturvölker.* Leipzig and Berlin, 1914.

59. Felten & Guilleaume Carlswerk AG. *Drahtseile für alle Verwendungszwecke.* Suppliers survey.

60. *Fertigteilbau + Industrialisiertes Bauen* (Waiblingen), 1970, 3.

61. Vladimir Firt. "Air-Supported Structures with Automatic Adjustment of Inner Overpressure". In: *International Symposium on Pneumatic Structures Delft 1972. Proceedings.* Technische Hogeschool Delft, 1972.

62. W. Förster and K.-H. Schüßler. "Der Membranspannungszustand der windbelasteten Kugelschale". *Der Bauingenieur* (Berlin), vol. 42 (1967), p. 21 ff.

63. Bernard Fournier and Donald P. Greenberg. "A Graphical Analysis Approach for Pneumatic Spherical Membrane Structures". In: *International Symposium on Pneumatic Structures Delft 1972. Proceedings.* Technische Hogeschool Delft, 1972.

64. M Fourtané. "Structures Pneumatiques à Géométrie Variable et Structures Mixtes de Grande Portée: Gonflable – Ferme – Cable". In: *International Symposium on Pneumatic Structures Delft 1972. Proceedings.* Technische Hogeschool Delft, 1972.

65. J. E. Gibson, M. Barnes, M. Smolira and W. W. Frischmann, "A Multi Pneumatic Loading System". In: *International Symposium on Pneumatic Structures Delft 1972. Proceedings.* Technische Hogeschool Delft, 1972.

66. A. E. Green and W. Zerna. *Theroretical Elasticity.* London, 1954.

67. J. Grepl. "Die Belastung der Membranen von Überdruckhallen durch Schnee und durch inneren Überdruck". In: *International Symposium on Pneumatic Structures Delft 1972. Proceedings.* Technische Hogeschool Delft, 1972.

68. Blair L. Hamilton. "Pneumatic Structures, Cybernetics and Ecology". In: *International Symposium on Pneumatic Structures Delft 1972. Proceedings.* Technische Hogeschool Delft, 1972.

69. R. Harbord. "Berechnung von Schalen mit endlichen Verschiebungen – Gemischte finite Elemente". *Bericht des Instituts für Statik der Technischen Universität Braunschweig,* 1972, 7.

70. Gershon Har'El and Haim Heifetz. *Realisation of Inflatable Forms Simplifies Hastens and Reduces Cost of Shell Structures.* Publication no. 169 (July, 1971) of the Israel Institute of Technology, Haifa.

71. Eberhard Haug. "Finite Element Analysis of Pneumatic Structures". In: *International Symposium on Pneumatic Structures Delft 1972. Proceedings.* Technische Hogeschool Delft, 1972.

72. Haim Heifetz. "Development in inflatable forms". *Build International* (Barking), Jan./Feb., 1970.

73. Heinz Herlinger. "Über die Herstellung von Chemiefasern". *Süddeutsche Zeitung* (Munich), June 2, 1971.

74. Heinrich Hertel. *Struktur, Form, Bewegung.* Mainz, 1963.

75. Alfons Holslag and Suzan van Westenbrugge. *Pneumatiese Konstrukties,* Technische Hogeschool Delft, 1972.

76. Zdenek Holub. "Neue Lösungen der Stützschlauchkonstruktionen mit höherer Betriebssicherheit". In: *International Symposium on Pneumatic Structures Delft 1972. Proceedings.* Technische Hogeschool Delft, 1972.

77. *IL 2. City in the Arctic.* Institut für leichte Flächentragwerke, Universität Stuttgart, 1971.

78. H. Isler. "Clear – Transparent Roof for a Court". In: *Proceedings of the 1st International Colloquium on Pneumatic Structures.* Technische Hochschule Stuttgart, 1967.

79. H. Isler. "Pneumatic Shape for Concrete Shells". In: *Proceedings of the 1st International Colloquim on Pneumatic Structures.* Technische Hochschule Stuttgart, 1967.

80. Kazuo Ishii. "On Developing of Curved Surfaces of Pneumatic Structures". In: *International Symposium on Pneumatic Structures Delft 1972. Proceedings.* Technische Hogeschool Delft, 1972.

81. Yoshito Isono. "Abstract of 'Pneumatic Structure Design Standard' in Japan". In: *International Symposium on Pneumatic Structures Delft 1972. Proceedings.* Technische Hogeschool Delft, 1972.

82. Yoshito Isono. "The Development of Pneumatic Structures in Japan". In: *International Symposium on Pneumatic Structures Delft 1972. Proceedings.* Technische Hogeschool Delft, 1972.

83. *iup* (Institut für Umweltplanung, Ulm), 7 (1972).

84. *iup,* 9 (1972).

85. V. V. Jermolov and others. *pnevmaticeskie konstrukcii.* Moscow, 1973.

86. Laurent Kaltenbach and Guy Naizot. "Utilité des Gonflables". *Techniques & Architecture* (Paris), 1969, 5.

87. Laurent Kaltenbach, Louis Paul Unsteller and Michel Maillé. "Une Structure Gonflable de 100 m de Portée Résille de Câbles". In: *International Symposium on Pneumatic Structures Delft 1972. Proceedings.* Technische Hogeschool Delft, 1972.

88. Mamoru Kawaguchi and others. *Engineering Problems of Pneumatic Structures.* Lecture manuscript, 1971.

89. Carl Graf von Klinckowstroem. *Knaur Geschichte der Technik,* Munich and Zurich, 1959.

90. Celal N. Kostem. "Thermal Stresses and Deformations in Pneumatic Cushion Roofs". In: *International Symposium on Pneumatic Structures Delft 1972. Proceedings.* Technische Hogeschool Delft, 1972.

91. Fried. Krupp GmbH, Essen. *Untersuchungsbericht 130/70: Leichte Flächentragwerke, Entwürfe und Ideen zur Struktur und Form.*

92. Krupp Universalbau, Essen. Construction drawing on Standard halls, 1970.

93. Krupp Universalbau, Essen. Price lists nos. 1 and 2 for Krupp air-supported halls, Oct., 1970.

94. H. Kurschat. "Zuganker". In: *Räumliche Tragwerke.* Seminar report. Universität Stuttgart, 1968/69.

95. Wolfgang Längsfeld. "Sonsbeek 71". *Süddeutsche Zeitung* (Munich), July 24/25, 1971.

96. N. Laing. "The Use of Solar and Sky Radiation for Air Conditioning of Pneumatic Structures". In: *Proceedings of the 1st International Colloquium on Pneumatic Structures*. Technische Hochschule Stuttgart, 1967.

97. A. Libai. "Pressurized Cylindrical Membranes with Flexible Supports". In: *International Symposium on Pneumatic Structures Delft 1972. Proceedings.* Technische Hogeschool Delft, 1972.

98. Josef Linecker. "Pneumatische Konstruktion für Hallenbäder". In: *International Symposium on Pneumatic Structures Delft 1972. Proceedings.* Technische Hogeschool Delft, 1972.

99. Wolfgang Lochner. *Weltgeschichte der Luftfahrt,* Würzburg, 1970.

100. M. H. Losch. *Bestimmung der mechanischen Konstanten für einen zweidimensionalen, nichtlinearen, anisotropen elastischen Stoff am Beispiel beschichteter Gewebe.* Thesis. Universität Stuttgart, 1971.

101. Victor A. Lundy. "Architectural and Sculptural Aspects of Pneumatic Structures". In: *Proceedings of the 1st International Colloquium on Pneumatic Structures*. Technische Hochschule Stuttgart, 1967.

102. H. L. Malhotra. "Fire Behavior of Single-Skin Air-Supported Structures". In: *International Symposium on Pneumatic Structures Delft 1972. Proceedings.* Technische Hogeschool Delft, 1972.

103. Herbert Mewes. "Beschichtete und gummierte Gewebe aus Trevira-hochfest". *Chemiefasern* (Frankfurt/Main), 1964, 12 u. 1965, 1.

104. Herbert Mewes. "Beschichtete Gewebe aus hochfesten Polyester-Fäden für Traglufthallen und leichte Flächentragwerke". *kib Kunststoffe im Bau* (Heidelberg), 14 (1969).

105. Gernot Minke. *Zur Effizienz von Tragerken.* Stuttgart and Bern, 1970.

106. Gernot Minke. "Pneumatische Konstruktionen". *Bauen + Wohnen* (Munich), 1971, 11.

107. Gernot Minke. "Die konstruktive Effizienz der pneumatischen Stütze". In: *International Symposium on Pneumatic Structures Delft 1972. Proceedings.* Technische Hogeschool Delft, 1972.

108. Gernot Minke. "Übersicht über die Systeme und Typen der pneumatisch stabilisierten Membrantragwerke". In: *International Symposium on Pneumatic Structures Delft 1972. Proceedings.* Technische Hogeschool Delft 1972.

109. C. J. Moore and B. Rawlings. "Inflated Metal Structures – Some Small and Large Scale Tests". In: *International Symposium on Pneumatic Structures Delft 1972. Proceedings.* Technische Hogeschool Delft, 1972.

110. Erwin Mühlestein. "Blow up". *Werk* (Winterthur), 1970, 5.

111. Erwin Mühlestein. "Air Structures Design". *Bauen + Wohnen* (Munich), 1971, 3.

112. Toal'o Muiré. "Instant City Ibiza". *Architectural Design* (London), 1971, 12.

113. Yoshio Nakahara. "The Mechanical Behavior of Circular Membrane Fabric under Uniform Lateral Pressure". In: *International Symposium on Pneumatic Structures Delft 1972. Proceedings.* Technische Hogeschool Delft, 1972.

114. Hans-Jürgen Niemann. "Zur Windbelastung von Traglufthallen". *Konstruktiver Ingenieurbau Berichte* (Ruhruniversität, Bochum), 13.

115. Hans-Jürgen Niemann. "Wind Tunnel Experiments on Aerolastic Models of Air-Supported Structures: Results and Conclusions". In: *International Symposium on Pneumatic Structures Delft 1972. Proceedings.* Technische Hogeschool Delft, 1972.

116. A. Nölker. "Windkanalversuche an Modellen von Traglufthallen: Versuchstechnik und Modellherstellung". In: *International Symposium on Pneumatic Structures Delft 1972. Proceedings.* Technische Hogeschool Delft, 1972.

117. J. T. Oden and W. K. Kubitzka. "Numerical Analysis of Nonlinear Pneumatic Structures". In: *Proceedings of the 1st International Colloquium on Pneumatic Structures*. Technische Hochschule Stuttgart, 1967.

118. Frei Otto. "Bauen im Weltraum". *Bauwelt* (Berlin), 1963, 17.

119. Frei Otto (ed.). *Zugbeanspruchte Konstruktionen.* Vol. 1. Frankfurt/Main and Berlin, 1962. English: *Tensile Structures.* Vol. 1. Cambridge, Mass., and London, 1967.

120. Frei Otto (ed.). *Zugbeanspruchte Konstruktionen.* Vol. 2. Frankfurt/Main and Berlin, 1965. English: *Tensile Structures.* Vol. 2. Cambridge, Mass., and London, 1969.

121. Erasmo Pistolesi and Salvatore Busuttil. *La Colonna Traiana.* Rome, 1846.

122. *Plasticonstruction* (Munich), 1972, 1.

123. *Pneumatische Konstruktionen.* Seminar report. Technische Universität Hanover, 1970.

124. Jens G. Pohl. "Multi-Storey Pneumatic Buildings as a Challenge to the Plastics Industry". *Australian Building Science and Technology* (Sydney), June, 1967.

125. Jens G. Pohl. "Pneumatic Structures". *Architecture in Australia* (Sydney), July, 1968.

126. Jens G. Pohl. "The Structural Pressurized Flexible Membrane Column". *Architectural Science Review* (Sydney), June, 1970.

127. Jens G. Pohl. "The Reinforcement and Bracing of Multi-Storey Pneumatic Buildings". *Architectural Science Review* (Sydney), March, 1971.

128. Jens G. Pohl and H. Cowan. "Multi-Storey Air-Supported Building Construction". *Build International* (Barking), April, 1972.

129. Jens G. Pohl. "Multi-Storey Fluid-Supported Building Systems". In: *International Symposium on Pneumatic Structures Delft 1972. Proceedings.* Technische Hogeschool Delft, 1972.

130. J. M. Prada and R. Aroca. "Some Properties and Possibilities of Third Generation Pneumatic Structures". In: *International Symposium on Pneumatic Structures Delft 1972. Proceedings.* Technische Hogeschool Delft, 1972.

131. Cedric Price, Frank Newby and others. *Air Structures.* London, 1971.

132. August Pütter. "Die Entwicklung des Tierfluges". In: Bernhard Lepsius and Richard Wasmuth (ed.). *Denkschrift der ersten Internationalen Luftschiffahrt-Ausstellung (ILA) zu Frankfurt am Main 1909.* Vol. 1. Berlin, 1910.

133. Wolfgang Rathke. "Pneumatisches Zellentragwerk". In: *International Symposium on Pneumatic Structures Delft 1972. Proceedings.* Technische Hogeschool Delft, 1972.

134. *Règles NV 65.* (France.)

135. G. F. Reitmeier and Milton B. Punnett. "Design Developments in Large Span Cabled Structures". In: *International Symposium on Pneumatic Structures Delft 1972. Proceedings.* Technische Hogeschool Delft, 1972.

136. "Richtlinien für den Bau und Betrieb von Tragluftbauten". July 1971 version. *Ministerialblatt für das Land Nordrhein-Westfalen,* 1971, p. 1658 ff.

137. Conrad Roland. *Frei Otto – Spannweiten. Ideen und Versuche zum Leichtbau.* Berlin, Frankfurt/Main and Vienna, 1965. English: *Frei Otto – Structures.* London, 1972.

138. Bernd-Friedrich Romberg. "Lichtdecken über dem Forum Steglitz in Berlin". *Bauwelt* (Berlin), 1970, 19.

139. Bernd-Friedrich Romberg, "Aufgeblasen". *db-Deutsche Bauzeitung* (Stuttgart), 1972, 3.

140. Bernd-Friedrich Romberg. "Konstruktion und Anwendungen von Luftkissen". In: *International Symposium on Pneumatic Structures Delft 1972. Proceedings.* Technische Hogeschool Delft, 1972.

141. Bernd-Friedrich Romberg. "Verfahrbare Raumhüllen aus luftgetragenen Häuten". In: *International Symposium on Pneumatic Structures Delft 1972. Proceedings.* Technische Hogeschool Delft, 1972

142. E. W. Ross. "Large Deflections on an Inflated Cylindrical Tent". *Journal of Applied Mechanics* (New York), 1969, p. 845 ff.

143. H. Rühle. "Development of Design and Construction in Pneumatic Structures". In: *Proceedings of the 1st International Colloquium on Pneumatic Structures*. Technische Hochschule Stuttgart, 1967.

144. H. Rühle. *Räumliche Dachtragwerke.* Vol. 2. Cologne, 1970.

145. H. Rühle. "Reale Entwicklungstendenzen pneumatischer Konstruktionen im Bauwesen". In: *International Symposium on Pneumatic Structures Delft 1972. Proceedings.* Technische Hogeschool Delft, 1972.

146. H. Rühle and R. Schulz. "Pneumatische Konstruktionen". *Deutsche Architektur* (East Berlin), 1968, 5.

147. F. Rudolf. "A Contribution to the Design of Air-Supported Structures". In: *Proceedings of the 1st International Colloquium on Pneumatic Structures*. Technische Hochschule Stuttgart, 1967.

148. Seiji Sawada. "Die Kunststoffbauten der Expo '70 verschwinden". *Plasticonstruction* (Munich), 1971, 5.

149. P. R. Smith and Jens G. Pohl. "Pneumatic Construction Applied to Multi-Storey Buildings". *Progressive Architecture* (New York), 1970, 9.

150. *Sport- + Bäderbauten* (Düsseldorf), 1971, 1.

151. Stefan A. Szcelkun. *Shelter, Survival Scrapbook 1,* Brighton and Seattle, 1972.

152. Rudolph Szilard. "Pneumatic Structures for Lunar Bases". In: *Proceedings of the 1st International Colloquium on Pneumatic Structures.* Technische Hochschule Stuttgart, 1967.

153. R. Schulz. "Fire Tests on an Air-Supported Structure". In: *Proceedings of the 1st International Colloquium on Pneumatic Structures.* Technische Hochschule Stuttgart, 1967.

154. Steffens & Nölle GmbH, Berlin. *Das Schwimmbad der Zukunft. Eine neuartige Konstruktion des Allwetterbades. Dargestellt am Beispiel der Gemeinde Unterlüß.* Company brochure, 1972.

155. Graham A. Stevens. "The Development of the Wavetube and Participation as a Working Method". In: *International Symposium on Pneumatic Structures Delft 1972. Proceedings.* Technische Hogeschool Delft, 1972.

156. *Techniques & Architecture* (Paris), 1969, 5.

157. *The Tent. Soft Shell Structures at Expo '70.* Taiyo Kogyo Co., Ltd., Tokyo, 1970.

158. *TGL 10728, Gruppe 20000: Traglufthallen, Technische Normen, Gütevorschriften, Lieferbedingungen.* (G.D.R.)

159. *TGL 20167, Gruppe 700: Lastannahmen für Bauten.* (G.D.R.)

160. I. Torbe. "Deformation of a Plane Surface of an Inflated Fabric Structure due to Localized Normal Load". In: *International Symposium on Pneumatic Structures Delft 1972. Proceedings.* Technische Hogeschool Delft, 1972.

161. F. J. H. Tutt. "The Effect of Concentrated Loads on Load Bearing Inflatable Structures". In: *International Symposium on Pneumatic Structures Delft 1972. Proceedings.* Technische Hogeschool Delft, 1972.

162. F. J. H. Tutt. "Inflatable Jacking Systems". In: *International Symposium on Pneumatic Structures Delft 1972. Proceedings.* Technische Hogeschool Delft, 1972.

163. F. J. H. Tutt. "A Survey of Inflation Requirements and Methods for Inflatable Structures". In: *International Symposium on Pneumatic Structures Delft 1972. Proceedings.* Technische Hogeschool Delft, 1972.

164. Tekal Vishwanath and P. G. Glockner. "Arbitrarily Large Deformations of Flat Circular Membranes under External Loads and Inflation Pressures". In: *International Symposium on Pneumatic Structures Delft 1972. Proceedings.* Technische Hogeschool Delft, 1972.

165. W. Weisz. "Air-Supported Constructions for Hard Winter Conditions". In: *International Symposium on Pneumatic Structures Delft 1972. Proceedings.* Technische Hogeschool Delft, 1972.

166. Sean R. Wellesley-Miller. "Control Aspects of Pneumatic Structures". In: *International Symposium on Pneumatic Structures Delft 1972. Proceedings.* Technische Hogeschool Delft, 1972.

167. K. L. Wolf. *Tropfen, Blasen und Lamellen.* Berlin, Heidelberg and New York, 1968.

168. Fritz Zwicky. *Entdecken, Erfinden, Forschen im Morphologischen Weltbild.* Munich and Zurich, 1966.

Addendum

169. Henning Drinhausen (editor). *Das Dach von Marl.* 1974. Brochure on the air-cushion roof of the shopping centre in midtown Marl. (The brochure can be ordered free of charge from: Enka Glanzstoff Ag, Ressort Technische Gewebe, D 5600 Wuppertal 1.)

170. *IL 9. Pneus in Nature and Technics.* Institut für leichte Flächentragwerke, Universität Stuttgart, 1976.

171. *IL 12. Convertible Pneus.* Institut für leichte Flächentragwerke, Universität Stuttgart, 1976.

172. *IL 15. Air Hall Handbook.* Institut für leichte Flächentragwerke, Universität Stuttgart, 1976.

173. Frei Otto. "Les pneus – le système des structures pneumatiques". *Techniques et Architecture* (Paris), 304 (1975).

174. David Pelham. *The Penguin Book of Kites.* Harmondsworth, 1976.

Addresses of manufacturers

Air Cruisers Company, P.O.B. 180, Belmar, New Jersey 07719, USA

Air-Tech Industries, Inc., 9 Brighton Road, Clifton, New Jersey 07012, USA

Autoflug GmbH, Industriestraße 10, 2081 Egenbüttel, Western Germany

Badische Anilin- & Soda-Fabrik AG, 6700 Ludwigshafen, Western Germany

Ballonfabrik – See- und Luftausrüstung GmbH + Co. KG, Austraße 35, 8900 Augsburg 3, Western Germany

Barracudaverken, P.O.B. 25, 18251 Djursholm 1, Sweden

Bayer AG, 5090 Leverkusen, Western Germany

Birdair Structures, Inc., 2015 Walden Avenue, Buffalo, New York 14225, USA

H. Brügge Zugbeanspruchte Konstruktionen, 4831 Marienfeld, Western Germany

CIDAIR Structures Company, 130th & Indiana Avenue, Chicago, Illinois 60627, USA

E.I. du Pont de Nemours & Company, Fabrics and Finishes Department, Wilmington, Delaware 19898, USA

Dynamit Nobel Aktiengesellschaft, Postfach 1209, 5210 Troisdorf, Western Germany

Dynat Gesellschaft für Verschlußtechnik und Feinmechanik GmbH, Bergmühlenstraße 10, 3200 Hildesheim, Western Germany

Enka Glanzstoff AG, Ressort Technische Gewebe, Postfach 13 01 20, 5600 Wuppertal 1, Western Germany

Farbwerke Hoechst AG, Verkauf Fasern, Postfach 80 03 20, 6230 Frankfurt (Main) 80, Western Germany

Felten & Guilleaume Carlswerk AG, Schanzenstraße 24, 5000 Köln 80, Western Germany

Firestone Coated Fabrics Company, Firestone Drive, Magnolia, Arkansas 71753, USA

Goodyear Aerospace Corporation, 1210 Massillon Road, Akron, Ohio 44315, USA

Hoogerwerff B.V., Wattstraat 1, Alblasserdam, Holland

KIB Konstruktion und Ingenieurbau GmbH, Flexible Konstruktionen, Frohnhauser Straße 95, 4300 Essen 1, Western Germany

Kléber Renolit Plastiques S.A., 67 Avenue de Verdun, 77470 Trilport, France

Otto Kleyer KG, Lübbecker Straße 12a, 4950 Minden, Western Germany

Krupp Universalbau, Abteilung Flexible Konstruktionen, *since April 1st, 1976* → KIB Konstruktion und Ingenieurbau GmbH, Flexible Konstruktionen

Metzeler AG, Westendstraße 131, 8000 München 2, Western Germany

M.L. Aviation Company, Ltd., Maidenhead, Berkshire, England

NOE-Schaltechnik – Georg Meyer-Keller KG, Kuntzestraße 72, 7334 Süssen, Western Germany

Ogawa Tent Co., Ltd., 28 Fukagawa Fuyukicho, Koto-ku, Tokyo, Japan

Plasteco Milano, Via Ugo Foscolo 13, 20030 Senago, Italy

Polydrom, *taken over in the meantime by* → Smireko AB

RAVEN Industries, Inc., P.O.B. 1007, Sioux Falls, South Dakota 57101, USA

RFD-GQ Limited, Godalming, Surrey, England

J. B. Sanders & Söhne, Postfach 140, 4550 Bramsche, Western Germany

Sarna-Hallen AG, 6078 Lungern, Switzerland

Conrad Scholtz AG, Am Stadtrand 55, 2000 Hamburg 70, Western Germany

Smireko AB, P.O.B. 55, 19060 Bålsta, Sweden

Steffens & Nölle GmbH, Gottlieb-Dunkel-Straße 20/21, 1000 Berlin 42, Germany

L. Stromeyer & Co. GmbH, Stromeyersdorf, 7750 Konstanz, Western Germany

Taisei Construction Co., Ltd., 5, 2-chome, Ginza, Chuo-ku, Tokyo, Japan

Taiyo Kogyo Co., Ltd., 22–1, Higashiyama 3-chome, Meguro-ku, Tokyo 153, Japan

Wülfing und Hauck, Ernst-Abbe-Straße 2, 3504 Kaufungen 1, Western Germany

Index

The Freedom~Seekers
Blacks in Early Canada

The
Freedom~
Blacks

Seekers
in Early Canada

Daniel G. Hill

The Book Society of Canada Limited
Agincourt, Canada

Book design by Robert Burgess Garbutt
Cover illustrations by Alan Daniel
Text illustrations by Jock MacRae
Maps by Catherine Farley

Typeset by ART-U Graphics
Printed and bound in Canada by John Deyell Company
1 2 3 4 5 6 7 8 JD 88 87 86 85 84 83 82 81

Canadian Cataloguing in Publication Data
Hill Daniel G.,
    The freedom-seekers

Bibliography: p.
Includes index.

ISBN 0-7725-5283-5   (boards)
ISBN 0-7725-5284-3   (paper)

1. Blacks—Canada—History. I. Title.

FC106.N4H55   971'.00496   C81-094235-6
F1035.N3H55

Acknowledgements

I WISH TO express my thanks to my wife, Donna, who worked tirelessly throughout the preparation in this manuscript; to Lorraine Hubbard and Joan Kaczmarski, my research assistants; to Arnold Bruner, for advice on style; and to Jo File of the Book Society of Canada Limited, for her valued advice, enthusiasm and editorial skills.

Finally, I wish to thank the many families across Ontario who so generously shared with me their scrapbooks, documents, photographs and family stories.

The faith and interest of all who helped made this work possible.

D.G.H.
Don Mills, 1981.

THE AUTHOR AND publishers wish to express their thanks for permission to include material in *The Freedom-Seekers: Blacks in Early Canada* as follows: the Abbott family; Nellie Lightfoot Wells; Amistad Research Centre; Barrie Public Library; The Bettman Archive, Inc.; L.N. Bronson; Ed and Harold Butler and families; H. Campbell; Canadian Baptist Archives; Chatham-Kent Museum; Cincinnati Museum Association; Jim Cooper; Culver Pictures Inc.; Rita Duval Cummings; Board of Trustees, First Baptist Church, Toronto, Ontario; Board of Trustees, First Baptist Church, Windsor, Ontario; W. Allen Fisher; Fort Malden National Historic Museum (Parks Canada); Gary French; Grey County and Owen Sound Museum; Nora Hodgins; Fred Hubbard; Johnson Publishing Company, Inc.; Audrey Miller Laurie; the late Professor Fred Landon; Les Presses de l'Université Laval; Marguerite McLean; Victor Metoyer Jr.; Metropolitan Toronto Library Board; Moorland-Spingarn Research Center of Howard University; National Gallery of Canada; North Buxton (Ontario) Museum; the Nicholson family; Nova Scotia Museum; Ontario Department of Travel and Publicity; Ontario Historical Society; Oro Town Council; Owen Sound Sun Times; Public Archives of Canada; Public Archives of Ontario; Public Archives of Nova Scotia; Raleigh Township Historical Museum; Arlie Robbins; St. Catharines Historical Museum; Morton Scott; Peter Scott; Simcoe County Museum and Archives; Donald G. Simpson; Josie Butler Sloman; City of Toronto Archives; Uncle Tom's Cabin Museum, Dresden, Ontario; Hiram Walker Historical Museum; University of Toronto; University of Western Ontario; Van Nostrand Reinhold Limited; Colonel Charles de Volpi; Robin Winks.

The author and publishers also wish to thank Judy Saunders, Archivist at the Market Gallery of the City of Toronto Archives for her co-operation and assistance.

Contents

The Freedom~Seekers
Blacks in Early Canada

1
Slaves and Slave-Holders

The French Régime

IN THE YEAR 1628 a British ship sailed up the St. Lawrence River to New France. It carried in its cargo a lone Black child from Madagascar. This six-year-old was the property of David Kirke, a famous privateer who, with the blessing of King Charles I, was making raids on the young French colony. The child from Africa was the first known Black resident of Canada.[1] He came as a slave.

In that same year Kirke and his brothers captured the first convoy of settlers and supplies sent out to Canada by the newly formed Company of New France.[2] The following year David Kirke captured Québec City from its founder, Samuel de Champlain. We know little about the life of the small Black slave who witnessed the struggle for control of Canada-to-be, but David Kirke seems not to have been his master for long. Soon after he took Québec, he left the colony in the hands of his brother Lewis. Before he himself returned to England, he sold his little slave for 50 half-crowns to a French clerk, Le Baillif. The clerk sold the child to Champlain's master-builder, Guillaume Couillard,[3] who saw to it that he was taught his catechism.

By the terms of the Treaty of St-Germain-en-Laye, Lewis Kirke handed Québec back to the French in

Mattieu da Costa, though not a permanent resident of Canada, was the first known Black to set foot on Canadian soil. He came with the expedition of Pierre de Gua, sieur de Monts, which founded Port Royal in 1605. It is probable that da Costa had spent some time in Canada even earlier, for he served as interpreter for the French Habitation with the friendly Micmacs of the area.

1632. In that same year Father Paul LeJeune arrived from France to become Superior of the Jesuit Order's Canadian mission. The following year he baptized the young slave lad. The child was given the Christian name 'Olivier' in honour of the Company's head clerk, Olivier Letardif, and Father LeJeune's own surname: at his baptism he became 'Olivier LeJeune'.

About 1638, shortly before Father LeJeune returned to France, Couillard set Olivier free. He died, still a young man, in 1654. The colony's burial register records that he had been a *domestique*.

In 1663 the Company of New France gave up its charter after 35 years of disastrous rule. King Louis XIV then tried to strengthen the colony. He appointed a governor and an intendant to carry out his wishes. The first intendant, Jean Talon, encouraged farming, mining and fishing. By 1688 the population of New France numbered 9000, but the chief citizens still complained of the shortage of servants and workers. They asked the governor, Jacques-René de Brisay, Marquis of Denonville, and the intendant, Jean Bochart de Champigny, for permission to buy Black slaves "... in the Islands at the arrival of the ships from Guinée [Guinea, West Africa]."

Although the law of France forbade slavery, Louis XIV gave it limited approval in Canada. An official letter informed the colonists on May 1, 1689:

> His Majesty finds it good that the inhabitants of Canada import negroes there to take care of their agriculture, but remarks that there is a risk that these negroes, coming from a very different climate, will perish in Canada; the project would then become useless.[4]

After they received the King's permission, the French colonists bought Blacks and 'Panis' [Pawnee Indians]

This engraving shows Québec as it was in 1640 when the young Olivier LeJeune worked in the town as a **domestique.**

and set them to work as household servants and field-hands.

In 1701 the ambitious fur-trader and colonizer Antoine de Lamothe Cadillac travelled west with 100 French soldiers and settlers to establish Fort Ponchartrain beside the Detroit River. Black slaves were among the first inhabitants of this new fur-trade outpost. They did much of the heavy work of the frontier community, "... for many of the peruked and elegant colonists disdained rough work and, what is more, refused to do very much of it."[5] At first, in fact, the new French arrivals had tried to enslave Indians to do their heavy work. When they could not hold these wilderness-wise prisoners-of-war bought from local tribes, they turned to Black slaves. They bought them from Southerners who had moved north with their chattels to settle in the Detroit Territory, from Indians who had captured slaves when they raided Southern plantations, and from slave-merchants in the East.

In 1709 Louis XIV gave full permission for the long-standing practice of slavery in New France: he authorized its colonists to own slaves "... in full proprietorship." There were fewer slave-owners in New France than in the neighbouring English colonies to the south, but the attitude to slaves was similar:

Louis XIV, King of France

Often in inventories slaves were enumerated with the animals. A Negro was a slave everywhere and no one was astonished to find him in bondage.[6]

The British Régime

In 1562 Captain John Hawkins was the first Englishman to bring a cargo of slaves to the New World. Over the next five years he made three trips to Africa to buy slaves. He sold them at a profit in the Spanish American settlements. The first shipload of 20 African slaves to reach British North America was landed at Jamestown, Virginia in 1619.

Almost a century later, in 1713, the French territory of Acadia was ceded to the British by the Treaty of Utrecht. Settlers from New England moved north into the area, which was re-named 'Nova Scotia'. Some

America's first Blacks arrive at Jamestown. They were traded to the colonists for food by the captain of a Dutch ship.

of them may well have brought Black slaves, for slaves helped to build Halifax when it was founded in 1749. Many of these Blacks were skilled tradesmen who were re-sold in the American colonies when they were no longer needed in Halifax. The Boston *Evening Post* of 1751 advertised, for instance:

> Just received from Halifax, and to be sold, 10 strong hearty, negro men, mostly tradesmen, such as caulkers, carpenters, sailmakers and ropemakers.[7]

When the British conquered New France in 1760, the slave system of Québec passed smoothly into the British régime. General Jeffrey Amherst of the conquering British forces assured the Marquis de Vaudreuil, the last governor of New France:

> Negroes and panis [Indians] of both sexes shall remain in their quality of slaves in the possession of the French or Canadians to whom they belong; they shall be at liberty to keep them in the colony or sell them ...[8]

This assurance was included in the Articles of Capitulation signed at Montréal. Perhaps the deposed French governor, a slave-owner, found this comforting.

When General James Wolfe died on the Plains of Abraham, General James Murray, who took over his command, became the first British governor of

Halifax in 1750 was surrounded by a palisade and protected by bastions.

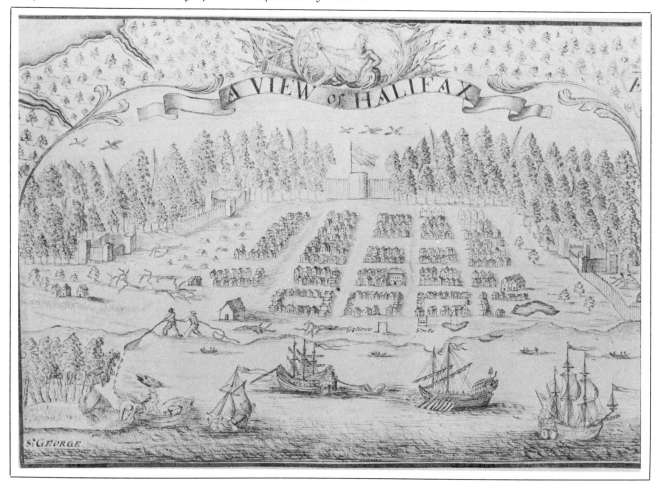

The British régime in Canada began in September, 1760. A modern artist, A.S. Scott, has recreated the scene of the ceremonial transfer of power from the French at Montréal.

Québec. In November, 1763 Murray sent an urgent request for Black slaves to John Watts of New York:

> I must most earnestly entreat your assistance, without servants nothing can be done, had I the inclination to employ soldiers, which is not the case, they would disappoint me, and Canadians will work for nobody but themselves. Black Slaves are certainly the only people to be depended upon, but it is necessary, I imagine, they should be born in one or other of our Northern Colonies, the Winters here will not agree with a Native of the torrid zone, pray therefore if possible procure for me two Stout Young fellows, who have been accustomed to Country Business, and as I wish to see them happy, I am of the opinion there is little felicity without a Communication with the Ladys, you buy for each a clean young wife, who can wash and do the female offices about a farm, I shall begrudge no price, so hope we may, by your goodness succeed.[9]

It was fashionable for His Majesty's officers to own slaves. Lieutenant-Colonel Christie of His Majesty's 60th Regiment[10] owned Bruce:

> ...a Negro Servant, Tall, well made with a high nose and very Black Complexion about 35 years of age ...[11]

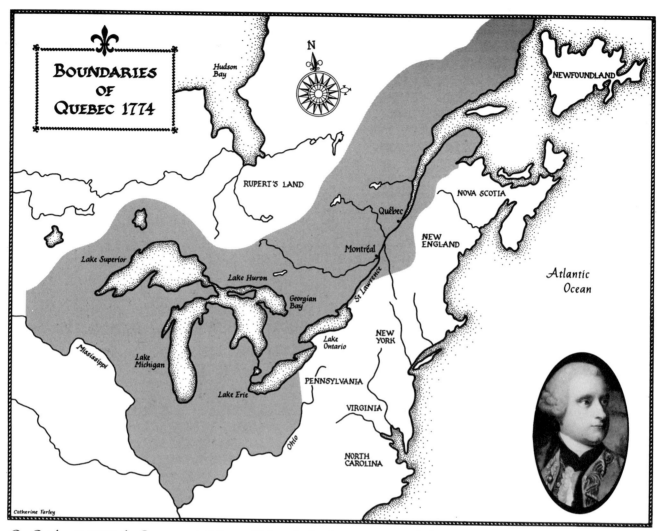

On October 7, 1763 the Government of George III issued a Proclamation setting the boundaries in North America of lands ceded to Britain by the Treaty of Paris. This put an end to the Seven Years War in America. The Proclamation created the new British colonies of Québec (including much of later Ontario), Nova Scotia (including later Prince Edward and Cape Breton Islands) and Newfoundland (including most of Labrador, Anticosti Island and the Magdalen Islands).

When the French surrendered Québec to Brigadier-General Sir James Murray (lower right) in 1774, its territory included much of the present provinces of Ontario and Québec.

Possibly because of the American Revolutionary War, Christie expected to be away from Montréal for some time in the summer of 1777. He gave Bruce written permission to support himself by finding work, but made it plain that the slave was not to go very far or to think that he would be set free even if his master died:

The Bearer—Bruce...being my property, has my Leave and Permission at his own Request to hyer himself to any Master or Mrs. as a Servant or take any other honest and Lawfull Way of Employing himself for his own Sole benefit and advantage providing he do not Embark on Board of any vessell by Sea or to go beyond

Albany in the Province of New York giving due notice to me or my agent at Montreal from time to time Where he is as often as he Changes places ...

This Leave to be only during my absence from this Province or the Good behaviour of Said Negroe, or till the Same is recal'd verbally or by other notice either from me, My Agent heirs Executors or assigns and no longer, and in no Shape to be construed into any freedom or discharge from Claim of Right or Property of Said Negroe aforesaid.

Given under my hand in Montreal this Thirtieth day of June in the Year one thousand seven hundred and seventy-seven.[12]

Many prominent citizens were also slave-holders. The Reverend David Charbrand Delisle of the Church of England in Montréal[13] bought a slave named 'Charles' in 1766. Two years later a wealthy North West Company merchant, James McGill[14], bought

... a Negro woman named Sarah, about the age of 25

The advertisement below appeared in The Royal Gazette And The Nova Scotia Advertiser.

years for the sum of fifty-six pounds lawful money of the Province.[15]

Much of the dealing in slaves was carried on through the newspapers. When Fleury Mesplet founded the *Montreal Gazette* in 1778, he announced in his paper that he would "... give notice to the public at any time of ... slaves deserted from their masters."[16] Trading in slaves was brisk. On April 3, 1790, a Black youth named 'Antoine' went from Oliver Hastings to Chevalier Charles Boucher de la Brière in exchange for 90 *minots*[17] of wheat. George Westphall, a British officer, borrowed 20 louis[18] from Richard Dillon in 1797. He gave as security a female slave named 'Ledy', who served Dillon until Westphall paid off the principal and interest of the loan.

It was not only in Québec that slavery continued to flourish under the British Régime. By the Articles of Capitulation, the British took Detroit from the French in 1760. Ten years earlier a census had counted 33 slaves in Detroit's population of 450. By the early 1770s the town had 1291 white residents and 96 Blacks. By 1778 the 2017 whites living there owned 127 Black slaves.

The Loyalists and Slavery

When 13 American colonies rebelled against the government of Britain's George III in 1775, United Empire Loyalists began to leave the dissident territories and move north. Their goal was to re-establish their families in the Maritimes and in Québec. The British government encouraged the Loyalists. It offered them military commissions, administrative positions, generous grants of land and permission to bring slaves.[19]

It is ironic that soon after the Revolutionary War broke out, the British offered to free any slaves who would join their forces. Both the slaves and their owners responded quickly. Many owners sent their slaves to places far behind the British lines. Some of the colonies passed new laws to banish, sell or execute slaves who were caught escaping. Slave patrols were even stricter than usual. In spite of all these measures, thousands of slaves tried to escape.[20] Some of these managed to make their way to Canada, or were taken there in British ships when the War ended. About 10 per cent of the Loyalists who reached Nova Scotia were Black.

Great Britain recognized the birth of the United States in 1783 and made peace with its former colonies. At that time Québec west of Montréal—the area soon to become Upper Canada, then Canada West and finally Ontario—was a vast wilderness with fringes of white settlement along the Upper St. Lawrence River and the lower Great Lakes. The end of the Revolutionary War left in a hostile and dangerous environment about 100 000 American colonists loyal to Britain. These people included soldiers of American units who had fought on the British side. About 40 000 of these chose to resettle in the British North. Approx-

Upper class colonists and their slaves, loyal to Britain, landed at Shelburne, Nova Scotia, in 1783.

imately 30 000 of these settlers, mostly upper-class colonists from established Eastern communities, packed themselves and the remnants of their fine belongings into sailing ships. They were making for the wilds of Nova Scotia, which included the territory that later became New Brunswick. Among the possessions they took with them were their Black slaves.

Almost 500 Black Loyalists received land grants in Nova Scotia. About half the grants were in Annapolis County; the rest were in the counties of Shelburne, Halifax and Guysborough. Most of the grants were small: some were less than a half-hectare, though grants of 16 to 20 ha were more common. Except for the land in the Annapolis Valley, the soil was poor and

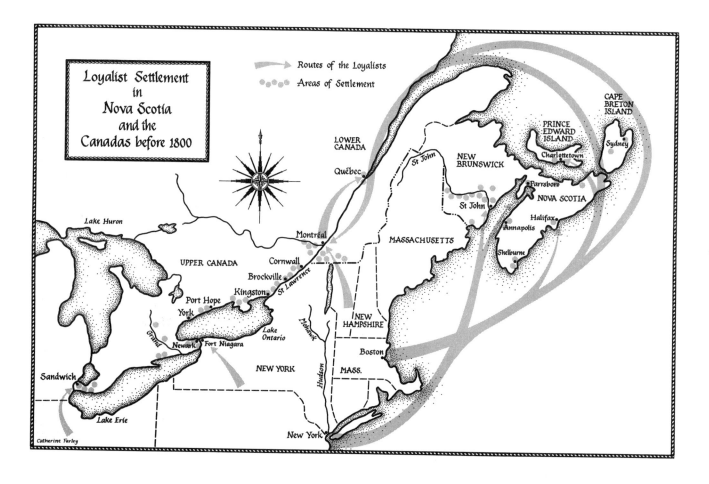

Loyalist Settlement in Nova Scotia and the Canadas before 1800

Routes of the Loyalists
Areas of Settlement

rocky. The settlers faced great hardship, especially in the early years.

About 10 000 Loyalists headed west to Québec. Most of them travelled overland through the dark wilderness. Most of them were veterans of loyal regiments; some were frontier farmers. Wives and children accompanied their husbands. Moving in the same direction were the main bodies of Mohawk and Iroquois Indians who had fought for Britain and had been given huge grants of land. All these groups—and thousands of land-hungry American settlers who followed them—helped to establish the character of English Canada. All of them included owners of Black slaves.

Many of these Blacks were a great help to their owners even before they reached their new homes. Sometimes the journeys by wagon or in open boats took many weary weeks. The slaves of some of the Loyalist refugees had been confiscated along with the rest of their property, but the owners had bought others. Some Loyalists had been left a few of their slaves, and many of these came along of their own accord. Often Blacks rowed the heavy *bateaux* to increase or replace their sailing power. At night these same Blacks often made camp and guarded the exhausted families who slept fitfully around campfires kept alight to ward off the lynx or bear or wolves that might be lurking in the dark forest.

Adiel Sherwood, one of the first settlers near Brockville, wrote in 1868 "... as regards slaves...":

> I only recollect two or three which settled in the district of Johnstown[21]; One in particular, named Caesar Congo, owned by Captain Justus Sherwood, who came with his family in the same brigade of boats that my father and family did, and located miles above Prescott. They were the very first actual settlers. Well I remember Caesar Congo, then a stout, strong young man, and who often took the late Justice Sherwood of Toronto, and myself on his back, to assist us along, while the boats were drawn up the rapids. Caesar was sold to a half-pay officer named Bottom[22]... After twenty years' service, Mr. Bottom gave Caesar his freedom. Caesar then married a free colored woman, and settled in the Town of Brockville where he lived many years and died.[23]

When the Loyalist settlers reached their destinations, their slaves helped to build the first homes and to clear and farm the land. Many of the 285 veterans of Butler's Rangers[24], who settled in Niagara Township, brought Black slaves with them. A Sheriff Ruttan once recalled a family tradition about two Black slaves, "... faithful and hard working fellows," belonging to his uncle. During a famine, the two slaves were sent from Adolphustown in Prince Edward County to Albany, New York to buy

> ... four bushels of Indian corn; a dreadful hazardous journey through the forest, with no road, and the snow very deep. They executed this mission, and returned in safety.[25]

Some Loyalist settlers bought slaves from livestock merchants who brought their wares to Canada. A Colonel Clark of Ernestown in Prince Edward County wrote in his memoirs:

Loyalists camping on their way up the St. Lawrence River in 1784.

C.W. JEFFERYS

Joseph Brant at the Grand River.

> ... drovers used to come in with droves of horses, cattle, sheep and negroes, for the use of the troops, forts, and settlers in Canada, and my father purchased his four negroes, three males and one female, named Sue.[26]

Native people, too, sometimes owned or traded in slaves. The Shawanabe and Potawatomis and other western tribes brought slaves from Ohio and Kentucky and sold them in the north, particularly in the Detroit area. Settlers farther east bought slaves from the Mississaugas. Traders of the Six Nations sold slaves to settlers in the Niagara region. Sarah Ainse, a famous Native trader, owned "one or two" Black slaves. With their help she worked her huge property: she had bought "... from the Chippewas the entire north bank of the Thames from the mouth to the Forks,[27] to a depth of 150 acres."[28]

Another famous Native slave-holder was Thayendinaga, or Joseph Brant. This Mohawk chief, who fought as a British ally in the Indian and Revolutionary Wars, was granted land on both sides of the Grand River. Black slaves whom Brant had captured in war did much of the work in his home *Brant House* at Burlington Beach and in his more modest house at Oshweken near Brantford. Other slaves worked on his land and tended his horses. In all, Brant owned 30 to 40 Blacks. Ironically, he allowed escaped slaves from the United States to settle on his land and to marry among his people.[29]

The hard life of the wilderness did not always teach slave-owners humane ways. Colonel Matthew Elliott served as a British Liaison Officer with the Indians during the American Revolution. He took part in a number of raids in Kentucky and captured Black slaves as loot. In this way he got most of the 60 slaves that he took with him when he moved to Amherstburg in 1784. There, on his government grant of about 800 ha, Elliott installed a lashing-ring for his slaves in a "...bloody whipping tree." In spite of treating his Blacks so harshly, the Colonel prospered from them. Their value was a considerable part of his wealth, and their hard work turned his property into a model of prosperous living. Within a few years Elliott's farm was well known for its productivity and its good buildings.

Wherever the Loyalists brought their slaves, the latter formed the beginnings of Black settlements: at Birchtown, near Shelburne, in Nova Scotia; along the Detroit frontier, at Sandwich and Amherstburg; throughout the Niagara Peninsula; at York (later Toronto) and around Kingston and Prescott. Although most of the Blacks who entered Canada during the Loyalist period came as slaves, hope was beginning to dawn for some of them. In 1787 the young United States passed the first anti-slavery law in North America.[30] This law applied in its Northwest Territory, where government authority was blurred for years. The British had taken the land from the French in 1760. In theory the U.S.A. received it in 1783 by the terms of the Treaty of Versailles. In fact, the British continued to govern in Detroit until 1796, two years after Jay's Treaty was signed. When Upper Canada came into being in 1791, Detroit was treated as part of the new province, and many of the town's residents held office in the government of Upper Canada. This meant that the district was at the same time 'free' American territory and 'slave' British territory. After the Ordinance of 1787 abolished slavery in the American Northwest Territories, British subjects still living there ignored the new law, but some of the slaves living in Upper Canada did not. Several of them swam across the Detroit River to freedom.

2
Opposition to Slavery

John Graves Simcoe

THE VOICES OF leaders opposed to slavery were already being heard when Upper Canada was founded in 1791.[1] In that same year the reformer William Wilberforce first introduced in the British House of Commons a bill to stop the importation of slaves in Britain's colonies. One of his supporters was Lieutenant-Colonel John Graves Simcoe. Simcoe was well known in England as a soldier who had led the Queen's Rangers in the American Revolutionary War and as the Member of Parliament for St. Mawes, Cornwall. He spoke against slavery in the Commons, arguing that Christian teaching opposed it and the British constitution did not allow it.[2] Shortly afterwards Simcoe left England to take up his appointment as the first Lieutenant-Governor of Upper Canada. When he arrived at its capital, Niagara (which he re-named 'Newark'), he pledged himself never to support any law that "... discriminates by dishonest policy between the Natives of Africa, America or Europe."[3]

There were barely 14 000 people living in the pioneer province of Upper Canada when Simcoe arrived. He immediately realized that its ruling class took slavery completely for granted. His earliest advisers included prominent slave-owners. Nine members of the Legislative Council, the appointed upper house, were slave-owners or members of slave-owning families. These members included Alexander Grant, James Baby, Robert Hamilton, Richard Cartwright Jr. and Peter Russell. These five men were also members of Simcoe's Executive, the Cabinet of the time. In the lower house, the elected Legislative Assembly, six of the original 16 members owned slaves.

Early in 1793 Simcoe learned of a brutal incident involving a slave. In an official letter to London he reported

> ... a violent outrage committed by one Fromand [*in fact, Vrooman*] ... residing near Queens Town [*Queenston*] ... on the person of Chloë Cooley a Negro girl in his service, by binding her, and violently and forcibly transporting her across the [*Niagara*] River, and delivering her against her will to certain persons unknown ...[4]

Although few American slaves were branded, none had personal or legal rights that an owner was bound to respect.

Lieutenant-Governor John Graves Simcoe

Chief Justice William Osgoode

Although Peter Russell supported Upper Canada's law to ban the importing of slaves, he continued to own and sell them.

The sale of Chloë Cooley dramatically illustrated a slave's total lack of protection. It stunned and offended Upper Canadians and became a *cause célèbre* for all opponents of slavery. On March 21, 1793 her case was brought before Simcoe's Executive Council in the Navy Hall at Newark. With Simcoe were the colony's first Chief Justice, William Osgoode, and the Receiver General, Peter Russell. Two witnesses testified. One was Peter Martin, a Black slave of Colonel John Butler. The other witness, William Grisley (or Crisley) of Mississauga Point, stated:

> That on Wednesday evening last he was at work at Mr Froemans near Queens Town, who in conversation told him, he was going to sell his Negro Wench to some persons in the States, that in the Evening he saw the said Negro girl, tied with a rope, that afterwards a Boat was brought, and the said Frooman with his brother and one Vanevery, forced the said Negro Girl into it ... and carried the Boat across the River; that the said Negro Girl was then taken and delivered to a man upon the Bank of the River by Froomand, that she screamed violently and made resistance, but was tied in the same manner ... and in that condition delivered to the man.[5]

Grisley said he also saw a Black man on the bank tied in the same way. He claimed he had heard that many other people planned to do the same with their Blacks. The Council was shocked by the tale and passed a resolution: "That it is necessary to take immediate steps to prevent the continuance of such violent breaches of the Public Peace."[6] It directed Attorney General John White to prosecute Vrooman, but White, a lawyer, knew that there was no case since English law regarded slaves as mere property. A slave had no rights that an owner was bound to respect. In law, Vrooman had no more committed a breach of peace than if he had been handing over his heifer to a new owner.

Although nothing came directly of the Council's instruction to prosecute Vrooman, the incident encouraged Simcoe to work for the abolition of slavery in Upper Canada. Chief Justice Osgoode drafted a bill to prohibit the importing of slaves into the colony. On June 19, 1793 Attorney General White introduced this bill in the second session of Upper Canada's first Legislative Assembly. It was passed, as White put it, "... with much opposition but little argument."

Peter Russell, member of Governor Simcoe's Executive Council.

Robert I.D. Gray, Solicitor General of Upper Canada.

The new law was a bitter disappointment to Simcoe, for it was far from the outright ban on slavery that he and Osgoode had wanted. It ruined White's political career and it did not free the slaves. It was compromise legislation, holding out only the promise of their gradual freedom. Even so, it had to be pushed through the Assembly and it was loudly opposed by some of the slave-owning legislators and by many land-owners who insisted that slave labour was necessary in an agricultural economy.

The new act repealed the Imperial Statute of 1790 which had allowed settlers to bring slaves into the province, but confirmed the status of slaves already there, only requiring that their owners feed and clothe them properly. The act did provide, however, that any child born in Upper Canada of a slave mother would become free at the age of 25. Any owner who set a slave free must make sure that he or she would not become a public charge. Finally, no voluntary contract of service could extend for more than nine years.

Simcoe was not the only person disappointed by the new anti-slavery law. David William Smith, a barrister, wrote:

We have made no law to free the slaves. All those who have been brought into the Province, or purchased under any authority legally exercised, are slaves to all intents and purposes, and are secured as property by a certain act of parliament. They are determined, however, to have a bill about slaves, part of which, I think, is well enough, part most iniquitous. I wash my hands of it. A free man who is married to a slave — his heir is declared by this act to be a slave. Fye! Fye! The laws of God and man canot [sic] authorize it.[7]

In 1798, after Simcoe had returned to England and Peter Russell sat in his place, opponents of the anti-slavery law tried to bring back the right to import slaves. A bill "... to authorize and allow persons coming into this Province to settle to bring with them their negro slaves" was introduced in the Legislative Assembly. Its chief opponent was the Solicitor General, Robert I.D. Gray, the Member for Stormont, himself a slave-owner. Gray moved the rejection of the bill, but his motion was defeated by eight votes to four. The measure went to the Legislative Council, where the majority of members were slave-owners. Russell, however, argued against taking an immediate vote. A motion to 'hoist' (postpone) the vote for three months was moved and seconded.[8] The matter was never raised again.

In spite of its limitations, Simcoe's law helped to change public attitudes to slavery. After the turn of the 19th century, most Canadian Blacks were free. For decades they had served their owners as domestics and attendants, and farmed and cleared their land. After 1800 they began to work as tradespeople and labourers needed by the fledgling province. Moreover, Simcoe's action in support of human rights affected thousands of Blacks in the United States. Learning that they would not be enslaved north of the American border, they soon began the trek to freedom and a greater measure of security in Upper Canada.

Slavery in Decline

At the turn of the 18th century, opposition to slavery was growing in Lower Canada as well in Upper Canada. In 1792 a bill to abolish slavery was introduced in the first Legislative Council of Lower Canada. It was defeated. Seven years later Joseph Papineau, father of the reformer Louis-Joseph Papineau, presented a citizens' petition to abolish slavery; after this, several anti-slavery bills were introduced in the Council. While all of them were defeated, a movement toward the abolition of slavery was clearly under way. In 1794 William Osgoode was named Chief Justice of Lower Canada. In 1803 he handed down the historic decision that slavery was inconsistent with British law.[9] While this judgement did not legally abolish slavery, it set free the 300 slaves in Lower Canada.[10] From that point on, citizens who wanted to trade in slaves were left without the protection of the courts. Commerce in slavery in Lower Canada went into decline.

In Upper Canada, too, the decline of slavery was inevitable. The Canadian climate with its short agricultural season ruled out crops such as cotton, which required a cheap, plentiful labour force. Besides, it was expensive to keep slaves fed, clothed and housed through a long unproductive winter. For these reasons slaves did not become a necessary prop for Upper Canada's economy. Abolitionist sentiment rose sharply, and more and more slaves were set free.

When the War of 1812 ended, Sir Peregrine Maitland, then Lieutenant-Governor of Upper Canada, began to offer Black veterans grants of land in what was to become the Township of Oro. This area lay between Kempenfeldt Bay on Lake Simcoe and Penetanguishene Bay on Lake Huron's much larger Georgian Bay. Maitland hoped, too, that runaway slaves from the United States might find sanctuary there. He tried to be discreet, however, in helping Black refugees, for two powerful Americans, Secretary of State Henry Clay and John Quincy Adams, were exerting pressure to have runaway Blacks returned to American soil. Maitland refused, citing the opinion of his Attorney General that any Black who reached Canada was free forever. Maitland's intention of quietly combining "policy and humanity" appears in a confidential letter dated September 24, 1819; it was written by his civil secretary, George Hillier, to Henry Goulbourn, a British official.

Sir Peregrine Maitland, Lieutenant-Governor of Upper Canada, 1818-1828.

Blacks were among the musicians and on-lookers at a dance in Lower Canada about 1807.

... There is another point which I was instructed to mention. Sir Peregrine Maitland has granted land in several instances to Blacks and persons of Color, all in the same settlement, which is on a line parallel to the Road running from Lake Simcoe to Gloucester Bay on Lake Huron, generally known by the name of Penetanguishene Road. Those already settled have proved industrious and steady, and the Lt. Governor proposes to himself considerable advantages from the measure both in view of policy and that of humanity. The reason for not making this the object of an official report will I daresay be obvious to you. An application was made a short time ago by Mr. Quincy Adams to the British Chargé d'Affaires at Washington, to know if American slave owners could follow fugitive slaves into His Majesty's Provinces with a hope of recovering their property. Mr. Antrobus sent to Gr. P. Maitland who forwarded him in reply the opinion of the Attorney General for Upper Canada, which was decidedly negative to the proposition. This however had no reference to the subject I have mentioned, but was brought on by two or three slaves having been traced from the Michigan Territory to some of our most Western Settlements ...[11]

About this time, judges who favoured abolition were handing down more and more court decisions against slave-owners. In fact, so difficult did slave-holding become that very few slaves were likely left in Upper Canada when the British Imperial Act of 1833 abolished slavery throughout the Empire. In that year two young Blacks named 'Hank' and 'Sukey', slaves of a Mrs. O'Reilly of Halton County, claimed their freedom. They were perhaps the last slaves in Upper Canada to be set free.

The number of abolitionist sympathizers grew in Canada in the decades that followed. As more Black refugees entered Canada, these sympathizers formed groups to influence public opinion and to help the freedom-seekers who were making their way north. The Toronto Anti-Slavery Society, for example, was formed on February 26, 1851. George Brown of the *Globe* was one of its founding members. The *Globe* reported:

> The largest and most enthusiastic meeting we have ever seen in Toronto was held in the City Hall last night. His Worship the Mayor in the chair .... The meeting was called to enable the citizens of Toronto to enter their protest against the manifold and unspeakable iniquities of slavery.[12]

A number of resolutions were passed at the first meeting and a platform that proclaimed: "Slavery is an outrage on the laws of humanity [*and its*] continued practice demands the best exertions for its extinction."[13] The Society further declared that it would fight slavery by every lawful means and would help the many "houseless and homeless victims of slavery flying to our soil."[14] It set up a powerful committee to carry on its business. This committee included George Brown[15] and Oliver Mowat, who would later become premier of the province.

Many Blacks were drifting into Toronto, destitute and disoriented from the effect of weeks and months spent in planning and making their escape. The Society was dedicated to caring for the fugitives, finding places for them in schools and jobs, and helping them to get started in their new lives. A Women's Auxiliary was formed, and during its first year raised nearly $1000. With the money, it clothed, fed and housed 300 refugees.

The Society's work did not end at the city's boundaries. Samuel Ringgold Ward was appointed an agent to go across the province lecturing about slavery. Ward's slave parents had escaped with him from Maryland when he was three. He was educated in New York and became a Congregational minister there. He later worked among Black fugitives in Chatham and Toronto and organized branches and auxiliaries of the Anti-Slavery Society throughout Canada West. Commenting on the strong anti-slavery opinion in and near Toronto, Ward declared:

> Toronto is somewhat peculiar in many ways, anti-slavery is more popular there than in any city I know save Syrcuse.... I had good audiences in the towns of Vaughan, Etobicoke, Markham, Pickering and in the village of Newmarket. Anti-slavery feeling is spreading and increasing in all these places. The public mind literally thirsts for the truth, and honest listeners and anxious inquirers will travel many miles, crowd our country chapels and remain for hours eagerly and patiently seeking the light.[16]

John Brown

It was probably because of Canadian sympathy that John Brown arrived in Canada on April 29, 1858. Brown, the ardent white abolitionist from Kansas, was planning to overthrow the American government and, with it, the slave system. He believed that he could do this by training a highly disciplined band of men to wage what is now known as 'guerilla warfare'. From a base in the Appalachian Mountains, his men would make surprise strikes at plantations and immediately enlist in their ranks all the slaves they freed.

Brown chose Chatham in Canada West as the ideal place to develop his military strategy and draw up a constitution for the provisional government he planned to set up. He arranged to meet with sympathizers on Saturday, May 8, 1858 to begin work on the new constitution. Ten days before the meeting, Brown arrived in Chatham with a corps of 13 supporters. His men put up at the Black-owned Villa Mansion Hotel, while Brown was a guest of James Bell, a well known Black poet and writer, who lived at 153 King Street.

For several days before the meeting, Brown drilled his men in Chatham's Tecumseh Park. Because he wanted to conceal his true purpose, he announced that he had come to Chatham to form "a new colored lodge of the Masonic order." His real intention, however, began to appear after he mailed out a form letter to a select group of friends:

Chatham, Canada West
April 29th 1858

Dear Sir

You are earnestly requested to meet quite a number of the friends of freedom at this place on Saturday the Eighth of May and bring with you any others that you know *to be absolutely true men to the cause* and who will have sufficient interest in the matter to meet the *expense* of the journey. There are already so many collected here that it has been decided to make *this* the point for a most *quiet convention.* Had we the means of bearing your travelling expenses we would most gladly do so. Western friends are on the grounds *now* waiting.

Very respectfully your Friends
Charles L. Remond Esqr.   John Brown
                                 M. R. Delany
                                 J. M. Bell[17]

At this first meeting, held in Chatham's British Methodist Episcopal Church, John Brown outlined his plan. He would attack the American arsenal at Harpers Ferry, West Virginia, arm his followers and then march south, smash slavery and set up a provisional government of the U.S.A. At the close of the meeting, the Reverend Toyer and a number of Chatham Blacks, frightened by Brown's revolutionary plans, refused him further use of the church and withdrew their support from the convention. Toyer warned his congregation to have nothing more to do with the project "in case they ended this life before a firing squad." The Presbyterian minister William King of the Elgin Settlement backed Toyer's view, for he, too, feared that Brown's plan would accomplish nothing but the massacre of many Blacks.

There were other Blacks, however, who continued to support Brown. Alfred Whipper, a local teacher, made hurried arrangements to hold the afternoon meeting in the Princess Street School. There Brown began his second address in ringing oratorical style, claiming that he had been appointed by God to carry out his plan. The meeting adopted *The Provisional Constitution and Ordinances for the People of the United States,* and Brown's supporters signed the document.

The next day, on Brown's 59th birthday, he and his supporters attended First Baptist Church. It was there that Brown held his third meeting on Monday, May 10; 35 Blacks and 11 whites were present. They confirmed the proceedings of the second meeting and elected officers to serve in Brown's provisional government. Brown was to be its Commander-in-Chief, Richard Ready its Secretary of State, and John Kagi its Secretary of War. Then the "strangest convention which has probably ever been held"[18] adjourned.

Brown stayed on in Chatham for a short while, awaiting friends from New York. Some of his men found a few days work around Chatham; others left by boat for Cleveland. Brown, learning that proslavery interests were endangering his work in Kansas, soon returned there. He had to change his detailed military plans when he discovered that "a traitor" had leaked news of the Chatham convention to American authorities. His uprising was postponed for over a year and ended in disaster.

Brown received considerable moral support from Chatham Blacks. The Shadd family backed Brown and gave him the use of their offices and printing press. Isaac Holden, captain of the town's Black Fire Brigade, helped Brown, and so did J.M. Bell, who took care of his correspondence and mail. Isaiah Matthew, Edward Nolan and Aaron Highgate, a local teacher, went to Detroit on their way to join Brown's army of liberation, but turned back when they heard that Brown had been captured at Harpers Ferry. It is claimed that Brown had also 'signed up' Blacks from Buxton, Ingersoll, Hamilton[19] and St. Catharines to support his movement.

Only one Canadian Black actually took part in the ill-fated raid on Harpers Ferry. He was Osborne Anderson, who had been elected a congressman in Brown's provisional government. Anderson, who had come to Canada from Delaware with the Shadd family,

John Brown's (left) attack on
the American arsenal at
Harpers Ferry, West Virginia
(above), *has been called 'the
opening battle of the Civil
War'.*

place on October 16, 1859. The attack was one of the major incidents in the long struggle over slavery in the United States. Of the 21 men who fought with Brown that day, 10 were killed, 6 escaped and 5 were later hanged. On October 31 Brown himself was tried for treason, conspiracy with slaves to rebel and first degree murder. The verdict was 'Guilty'. Brown was hanged in Charlestown, West Virginia, on December 2, 1859.

The Harpers Ferry raid made a deep impression on Canadians. The newspapers of Canada West took particular note of Brown's efforts, and some proclaimed him a hero. After his execution funeral bells tolled and memorial services were held in many churches. Brown was seen as a martyr and soon became a symbol of freedom. Two years after he was hanged, Americans were locked in deadly civil war, and Union troops, marching south to fight against slavery that had already cost so much misery and so many lives, sang as they tramped along:

John Brown's body lies a-mouldering in the grave ...
His truth goes marching on.[20]

It was the same issue of freedom that brought about the last great demonstration of anti-slavery sentiment when the great American President Abraham Lincoln was assassinated on April 15, 1865. The shocked citizens of Toronto closed their businesses as a mark of respect during the time of Lincoln's funeral; throngs attended memorial services held in the city's churches; Black citizens held a mass meeting; for 80 days "people of colour" wore black arm-bands or some other symbol of mourning. During that time many Canadians and many Americans must have pondered the question Lincoln put so unforgettably to his own people when he spoke about slavery at Gettysburg: "... whether that nation or any nation so conceived and so dedicated could long endure."[21]

survived the raid and escaped back to Canada. With Mary Ann Shadd he later wrote the booklet *A Voice From Harpers Ferry*. One other Canadian also fought with Brown: Stewart Taylor, a white man from Uxbridge, died of wounds he received in the raid.

John Brown's raid on the American arsenal took

3
The Road to Freedom

The Underground Railroad

I'M ON MY way to Canada
That cold and distant land
The dire effects of slavery
I can no longer stand —
Farewell, old master,
Don't come after me.
I'm on my way to Canada
Where coloured men are free.[1]

Word of Simcoe's anti-slavery legislation spread slowly in the United States. At the end of the 18th century Canada was as remote to the Southern slave as the prospect of freedom. Soon after the War of 1812, however, John Beverley Robinson, Upper Canada's Attorney General, declared that residence in Canada made Blacks free, and that Canadian courts would uphold that freedom. Slaves in the American border states began to hear that in Canada Blacks were free, and that their rights were protected by British law.

It was the slave-owners' account of Canada, however, that Blacks generally heard first:

The Detroit River to Canada is 3000 miles wide … Canada is … a barren country where only black-eyed peas can be grown …[2] Abolitionists are cannibals, they get you darkies up there, fatten you up and then boil you.[3]

But such lurid warnings could not hide the truth for long. There were no bars to communication between 'free' and 'slave' states, and news of free Blacks living in 'the land of promise' was passed on by word of mouth. Slaves sold from northern states to the deep South carried stories of Canada. Slaves from the South sold into Kentucky, Maryland and Missouri learned that they could find their way to freedom by following the North Star beyond the American border. Black men and women who prized freedom more than life were not long in putting their new knowledge to use. Their determination to win liberty for themselves and their children, a growing awareness of Canada's small, free, Black population, and the urgent need of a sanctuary for escaped slaves, gave birth to the Underground Railroad (UGR) movement.

The legendary Underground Railroad, with its mythical 'trains' running through the northern states to terminals in Canada, had no track and no rolling stock. It was 'underground' in the sense that it was a secret operation carried out by courageous people linked only by their hatred of slavery and their willingness to hide, feed and help onward fugitive slaves. But the image of a secret underground railroad was so effective that in the 1800s many people believed that a train ran through a tunnel deep in the earth carrying runaways from the South to freedom in the North. Quakers and Methodists, city people and farmers, freed Blacks and slaves, most of them working out of border and northern states, used railroad terms to confuse the public and deceive slave-holders. 'Conductors' drove carts, carriages or farm wagons loaded with passengers and produce — and with slaves hidden in false compartments. 'Stations' where abolitionists transferred or temporarily hid their 'cargo' were barns, farmhouses, secret passages, cellars, attics and church belfries.

The UGR movement seems to have started among the Quakers of Pennsylvania:

Harriet Tubman, nurse, scout and spy in the Union Army.

... some cases of kidnapping and shooting of fugitives who attempted to escape occurred in Columbia, Pa., in 1804. This incited the people of that town, who were chiefly Friends [Quakers] or their descendants, to throw around the colored people the arm of protection, and even to assist those who were endeavoring to escape from slavery ... This gave origin to that organized system of rendering aid to fugitives which was afterward known as the 'Underground Railroad'.

Thus begun, the service rapidly extended, being greatly favored by the character of the population in southeastern Pennsylvania, which was largely Quaker, with here and there some important settlements of manumitted [freed] slaves. It was on account of the large number of runaways early resorting to Columbia that it became necessary to have an understanding with regard to places of entertainment for them along lines leading to the Eastern states and to Canada, whither most of the fugitives were bound.[4]

The Quakers had many of the qualities necessary for an effective UGR 'employee'. By their quick wit, confident bearing and good humour they often threw slave-hunters off the track of runaways. But the UGR could not have operated without other 'stockholders' as well: sympathizers who provided the money to pay boat-operators and wagon-drivers and to buy food and clothing vital to the secret movement of the 'passengers'. Women were deeply involved in the aboli-

Slaves cultivating rice.

tionist cause. Some were 'conductors'; others were 'station-keepers', who received, fed, clothed and hid new arrivals at transfer points.

The Underground Railroad had to operate informally, without open meetings, reports, letters or officers. Its members communicated by means of passwords, signals and cryptic messages. The arrival of refugees might be announced by a bird call, a special knock or a coded letter:

Dear Sir — By tomorrow evening's mail you will receive two volumes of the "Irrepressible Conflict" bound in black. After perusal, please forward and oblige ...

Or:

Dear Grinnell: Uncle Tom says if the roads are not too bad you can look for those fleeces of wool by tomorrow. Send them on to test the market and price, no back charges...[5]

Some refugees were actually packaged and shipped as freight on real trains and boats. In one dramatic escape, a hotly pursued slave was put into a coffin in Kentucky and shipped to Sandusky, Ohio. The coffin, a crude wooden box, had knot holes for air and shavings as a cushion for the fugitive's head. When the coffin arrived, it was taken to the home of a Sandusky abolitionist and opened. This man looked at the figure in the box and found that "... the eyes were bloodshot, the mouth was foaming and the poor fellow was nearly dead." But he revived quickly and was soon well enough to be sent on his way.

The Underground Railroad developed a complicated system of connecting lines that included many networks and many routes to Canada. Progress on these lines was seldom straightforward. Paths zig-zagged, changed course and even doubled back to throw off pursuing slave-owners and their hired hunters. Stations were generally 25 to 30 kilometres apart.

About the beginning of the 19th century some midwestern states passed laws to limit the rights of 'free' Blacks. Ohio's Black Codes of 1804 and 1807 banished Blacks and "mulattoes" unless they could show a certificate of freedom from the courts. Employers could be fined for hiring a Black who had no certificate. Blacks were not allowed to settle in the state at all unless within 20 days they showed proof that they could support themselves, posted a $500 bond and gave other assurances of good behaviour. Even then they were not allowed to give evidence in court against whites or to serve on juries. Fines for hiding Blacks who were in Ohio illegally were raised from $50 to $100.

The chief effect of these repressive measures was to give impetus to the abolitionist movement. The Quaker Levi Coffin, for example, made his home in Cincinnati a major UGR centre by building secret cellars and other hideaways. Coffin was born in North Carolina in 1796 of a Quaker abolitionist family. He moved to Indiana before he settled in Cincinnati where he worked for the abolitionist cause for over 35 years. Coffin, a key 'stockholder' in the UGR, hid 100 or more refugees in his Cincinnati home every year. As the owner of a store in the city, he was able to persuade other business people to take out 'stock' in the UGR: that is, to give money to support the work of operators, station-keepers and conductors. In time Coffin became known as the 'president' of the Underground Railroad. Once, when he was asked why he held this title, Coffin replied: "It was given to me by slave-hunters, who could not find their fugitive slaves after they got into my hands."[6]

UGR conductors often disguised refugees to throw suspicious onlookers off the track. The Quaker woman's costume with its full-skirted dress and veiled bonnet made an ideal disguise. A refugee who could be identified by light skin was blackened with burnt cork and given a wig. Another might be handed a hoe or scythe and told to walk at a leisurely pace in a certain direction, as if going to work.

John Fairfield, a Virginian, was especially good at developing ruses and disguises to help fugitives. Although he was a Southerner from a slave-holding family, he despised slavery and chose a career as a conductor on the UGR. He toured the South in search of 'passengers', often posing as a slave-trader or an egg-pedlar. In Cincinnati during the 1820s Fairfield solved the problem of safely moving 28 refugees by preparing a mock funeral procession. Closed coaches carried the escaping Blacks at a slow and solemn pace through the streets of the city while unsuspecting

A lake steamer approaches Niagara. Many such steamers carried Black refugees to Underground Railroad terminals in Canada.

slave-hunters looked on. Fairfield considered this success his greatest single UGR achievement.

Another group of fugitives just arrived from the South were hiding in Cincinnati, not daring to show themselves since slave-hunters were watching all the streets leading out of the city. UGR workers decided to organize a bold escape in broad daylight. They collected colourful costumes like those worn by Cincinnati's well-to-do Blacks and dressed the fleeing men like women and the women like men. Then they drove the fugitives quickly through the streets in expensive carriages. The slave-hunters, who were watching closely for a group of tattered, bedraggled runaways, never gave a thought to the group of 'prosperous' Blacks.

By 1820 the UGR had established definite routes into Canada from Kentucky, Indiana, Ohio, New York, Virginia, Maryland, Delaware, Missouri, Michigan and other states. Though more and more 'passengers' travelled these routes, some Blacks made their own escape without the help of the UGR. On August 10, 1823, for instance, the Canadian Steamer *Chief Justice Robinson* picked up a Black man floating on a wooden gate in Lake Ontario. He explained that he had run away from Tennessee to upper New York State. He was frightened when he saw a crowd of white people waiting to board the Lewiston ferry which crossed the

Niagara River to Canada. Too fearful to board the boat, he stole a gate and tried to float across the river to Queenston. The current had carried him well past his goal, for he was 18 km from the mouth of the river. When he learned that he was on a Canadian ship, he dropped to his knees and cried, "Thank you, Lord, for delivering me to Canaan!"

During the 1830s and '40s many UGR terminals were set up in Canada. About 20 of these were located along the Lake Erie shore, the Niagara River and the Detroit frontier, particularly at Amherstburg, Sandwich and Windsor. Fugitives also travelled by land and water to Toronto, Hamilton, St. Catharines, Brantford, Kingston and Prescott. The side-wheel paddle steamers *Bay City, United States, Arrow* and *Mayflower* normally travelled between Sandusky, Ohio and Detroit, but they also stopped at Canadian ports to set Black refugees ashore. So did the *Forest Queen*, the *May Queen* and the *Morning Star,* which travelled between Cleveland and Detroit, and the *Phoebus,* which sailed between Toledo and Detroit.

Many of the Great Lakes ships—the *Arrow* among them—carried runaways without charge. So did boats owned by William Wells Brown, a former slave. Brown had escaped from Missouri in 1840 and, with the help of friends in Cleveland, set himself up in business on the Great Lakes in 1842. Though he usually sailed between Cleveland and Detroit, Brown recorded: "In the year 1842 I conveyed, from the first of May to the first of December, sixty-nine fugitives over Lake Erie to Canada."[7] Small groups of Blacks waited on the Cleveland wharf for Brown's boats, knowing that he would charge them nothing for their passage.

During this period the Reverend Calvin Fairbank was a leading conductor on the UGR. In 1843 he went to Arkansas to rescue William Minnis, a young slave with a light skin and an impressive appearance. Fairbank found that Minnis looked very much like a gentleman who lived near Little Rock. He decided to make use of this resemblance. He fitted Minnis out with a wig, a false beard and moustache, and clothes like those of his model.

Minnis was quickly drilled in the deportment of his assumed rank, and, as the test proved, he sustained himself well in his part. On boarding the boat that was to carry him to freedom he discovered his owner Mr. Brennan, but so effectual was the slave's makeup that the master failed to penetrate the disguise.[8]

Fairbank later spent 17 years in prison for his "slave-abducting" activities before he was given a full pardon. In his autobiography he wrote:

Forty-seven slaves I guided toward the north star, in violation of the slave codes of Virginia and Kentucky. I piloted them through the forests, mostly by night; girls, fair and white, dressed as ladies; men and boys, as gentlemen, or servants; men in women's clothes and women in men's clothes; boys dressed as girls, and girls as boys; on foot or on horseback, in buggies, carriages, common wagons, in and under loads of hay, straw, old furniture, boxes and bags; crossing the Jordan of the slave, swimming or wading chin deep; or in boats, or skiffs; on rafts,

Major routes of the Underground Railroad were travelled by thousands of fugitives like the one (lower right) *first depicted on a notice advertising for the return of a runaway slave.*

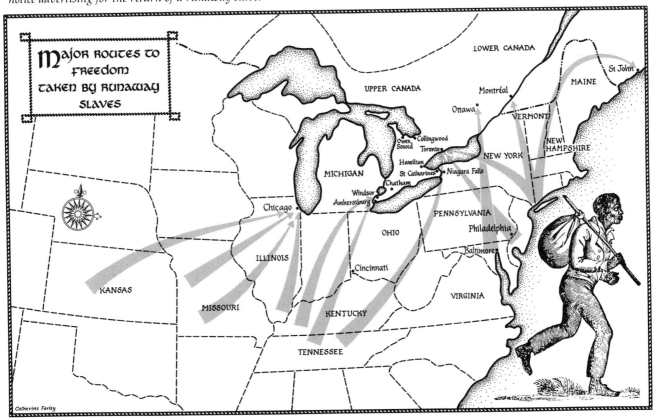

Most slaves lived a life of almost endless drudgery from dawn to dusk. Their two meals a day were often scant and always monotonous, and their quarters were bare, comfortless and cold in winter. Slaves (left) *harvest sugar cane,* (below, left) *dig trenches,* (centre) *harvest grain,* (right) *pole a barge and* (bottom left) *pick cotton. After the passing of the Fugitive Slave Act in 1850, slaves who had escaped to 'free' states in the North lived in fear of slave-catchers* (bottom right).

and often on a pine log. And I never suffered one to be recaptured.[9]

The Fugitive Slave Act passed by the American Congress in 1850 dealt a severe blow to the abolitionist cause. The Act was promoted by Southern congressmen stung by their constituents' complaints that their slaves were escaping to 'free' states. The Act gave slave-owners and their agents the right to track down and arrest fugitives anywhere in the U.S.A.[10] In practice, free Blacks, as well as runaways, were often kidnapped by bounty-hunters and taken off to slavery in the South.

Even before the Fugitive Slave Act was passed, danger dogged the footsteps of runaways and their helpers until that final moment when they reached free soil. The Act was a powerful stimulus to the anti-slave movement, but it multiplied the risks of escape. Many of the UGR conductors were caught and jailed, but abolitionists who remained free worked even harder for their cause, and the UGR carried more Blacks to Canada than ever before. According to the Black historian John Hope Franklin, 100 members of one Black Baptist church in Buffalo fled to Canada when the Act was passed. Nearly all the 114 members of the Baptist Church in Rochester, N.Y. also set out for Canada. Most of the Black waiters in the Pittsburgh Hotel armed themselves with pistols and bowie knives and headed for the Canadian border "... determined to die rather than be captured."

By 1850 Great Lakes steamers carried Blacks from ports in Wisconsin and Illinois to Detroit or Amherstburg, from Rochester to St. Catharines *en route* to Toronto, and from Chicago to Collingwood and Owen Sound, the most northerly of the UGR terminals in Canada West.[11] Scows, sailboats, steamboats—almost any craft that floated—were used by agents of the UGR to deposit their 'cargo' on Canadian shores. The *Toronto Colonist* of June 17, 1852 noted that every boat arriving in the harbour from the U.S.A. seemed to carry fugitives.

In April, 1853 an advertisement in a Detroit newspaper announced the safe arrival in Windsor of a group of refugees and requested help for them:

**Stockholders
of the Underground
R.R. Company
Hold on to Your Stock!!**

The market has an upward tendency. By the express train which arrived this morning at 3 o'clock, fifteen thousand dollars worth of human merchandise, consisting of twenty-nine able-bodied men and women, fresh and sound, from the Carolina and Kentucky plantations, have arrived safe at the depot on the other side, where all our sympathising colonization friends may have an opportunity of expressing their sympathy by bringing forward donations of ploughs, etc., farming utensils, pick axes and hoes, and not old clothes; as these emigrants all can till the soil.

N.B. Stockholders don't forget the meeting to-day at 2 o'clock at the ferry on the Canada side. All persons desiring to take stock in this prosperous company, be sure to be on hand.

Detroit, April 19, 1853   By Order of the
BOARD OF DIRECTORS[12]

In 1854 W.P. Newman, editor of the Black newspaper, the *Provincial Freeman,* wrote:

The accession to our numbers has been great during the winter past, at this, and other points west of us. Nearly all who have joined us have been directly from the south, fugitive slave bill and bloodhounds to the contrary notwithstanding. Those who have reached this point have been mostly from the "Old Dominion" [Virginia] and I assure you that some of them are not only 'the dare-devils of the South' but also the choice sons and daughters of Virginia's best blood.[13]

During one week in the same year 23 fugitives and 43 other Blacks arrived in Windsor by way of the Underground Railroad.

Seymour Finney, who kept a hotel at Detroit's Woodward and Gratiot Avenues, operated a UGR station. Later a second station was set up at Griswold and State Streets. Runaways were taken from these stations to the ferryboat *Gem,* which carried scores of Black refugees from Detroit to Windsor between 1856 and 1865. The *Gem's* captain was Thomas Chilver, an

The steamer Chief Justice Robinson *landing passengers in Toronto Bay in 1852. According to the* Toronto Colonist *of that year, there may well have been fugitives among her passengers.*

ardent abolitionist. His family handed down many stories about his exploits and the fears and hopes of fugitives as they sat "trembling on the boat until they got into Canadian waters."

Transportation by land and by water became more efficient in the 1850s. Expanding rail systems made it possible for UGR workers to send their human cargo by train, but fugitives did not simply board the trains with the rest of the passengers. They usually travelled hidden in the baggage or freight cars or among the livestock. The railroads were generally sympathetic to the abolitionist cause. The Grand Trunk, running from Portland, Maine through northern New Hampshire and Vermont into Canada, regularly charged fugitives half the usual fare and occasionally gave them passes.

One of the directors of the New York Central Railway, Horace White, secretly gave free passes for fugitives. His son, Dr. Andrew White, heard about the matter after his father's death from "an old abolitionist" in Syracuse:

> He said to me that he had often come to my father's house, rattled at the windows, informed my father of the passes he needed for fugitive slaves, received them through the window, and departed, nobody else being the wiser.[14]

Among the most daring of the UGR workers was a Canadian doctor from Belleville. Alexander Ross was an ornithologist as well as a doctor, and he often used his interest in birds as a cover for his UGR activities. Ross' parents had discussed the evils of slavery with him when he was a lad, and when he read Harriet Beecher Stowe's *Uncle Tom's Cabin,* he made a lifetime commitment to the abolitionist cause. In later years Ross said of Stowe's novel:

> It excited the sympathies of every humane person who read it in behalf of the oppressed. To me it was a command; and a settled conviction took possession of my mind that it was my duty to help the oppressed to freedom…[15]

When Ross met refugees and anti-slavery groups in Toronto, he translated his sympathies into action. His Black acquaintances told him about the secret lines of the Underground Railroad and gave him names and addresses of station-keepers in Ohio, Pennsylvania and Michigan. As an ornithologist Ross then travelled through the South, particularly Virginia, Tennessee, South Carolina, Mississippi and Alabama. Unsuspecting plantation-owners let him roam their estates, with no inkling that the flights he hoped to see were not those of birds, but of their slaves.

Ross planned every operation carefully. Each time he visited the South, he arranged through his contacts to meet secretly at night with groups of trustworthy slaves. At every meeting Ross would describe in detail

(Above) *Alexander Milton Ross, M.D.* (Below) *Underground Railroad workers help escaping slaves to disembark at League Island, Philadelphia.*

the best escape route to Canada and the sites of the stations where UGR conductors would help the fugitives. He advised runaways to travel only at night.

At one meeting in Richmond, Virginia, 42 slaves gathered, and nine of them accepted Ross' offer of help to escape. The others, who chose not to make the dangerous attempt, promised to encourage more slaves to escape and to pass along information about the UGR. Ross later recalled of the fugitives: "To each I gave a few dollars in money, a pocket compass, a knife, and as much cold meat and bread as each could carry with ease."[16]

Many times Ross personally conducted slaves over the whole journey from a southern state to Canada. A black woman in Nashville whose husband had already escaped once pleaded with Ross to help her join him in Canada. She had been severely whipped when she had refused to marry another man chosen by her owner. Ross disguised her as his valet and took her on foot and by boat to St. Louis, Chicago and Detroit. There they rested at the home of another conductor while Ross telegraphed friends in London, Chatham and Amherstburg to try to find the woman's husband. One evening, under a pitch-dark sky, Ross and his 'valet' rowed across the Detroit River to Windsor. When she reached Canadian soil ... "She dropped on her knees, and uttered a sincere prayer to the Almighty to protect and bless me for bringing her to Canada."[17]

Ross had learned that the woman's husband was living in London, and he arranged to have her sent there. Husband and wife were happily reunited after a separation of two years. Later they invited Ross to visit them. He recalled: "I dined with them ... at their pretty little home which they had paid for with the proceeds of their industry and thrift."[18]

By the time of the American Civil War, Ross had become so well known for his abolitionist activities that Abraham Lincoln invited him to the White House and asked him to help break a Confederate spy ring based in Montréal. After several months of detective work Ross uncovered the ring, which was led by a Southern woman who used the pseudonym 'Mrs. Williams'. She had been travelling regularly by train from Montréal to Rouses Point, N.Y., near Lake Champlain,

to pass on messages from Confederate agents working in Canada. Ross introduced himself to 'Mrs. Williams' as a 'Canadian friend' and arranged to accompany her to Rouses Point after he had alerted American detectives. 'Mrs. Williams' was arrested when the train crossed the American border. Detectives found 82 dispatches sewn into her petticoats. President Lincoln received Ross again after his success to thank him for his services to the Union.

Ross continued to work for Blacks into the 1870s. After that he turned his attention more to the problems of Native people. He died at Detroit on October 27, 1897.

Another famous UGR conductor was John Mason, a fugitive slave from Kentucky. During the 1850s he continually risked his life by returning there to spirit over 1300 slaves into Ohio. In one 19-month period he personally brought 265 slaves out of Kentucky. Mason's key contact in Ohio was the Reverend W.M. Mitchell, a Black missionary. Many of Mason's 'passengers' were cared for in Mitchell's home and then sent on to Canada. Mason was once captured in Kentucky. He was badly beaten, and both his arms were broken before he was returned to slavery. Months later he was re-sold in New Orleans, where he escaped again. He used his excellent contacts to make his way north to Hamilton, where he settled. He kept in touch with Mitchell, who was later sent to Toronto by the American Baptist Free Mission Society to minister to Black refugees.

Most notable of all 'slave-abductors' was Harriet Tubman, called the 'Black Moses' of her people. She was born a slave about 1820 on a large plantation in Bucktown, Maryland. After her escape about 1849, she made at least 19 trips into the South to guide Blacks to the North. When it became hazardous for runaways to remain there, she made at least 11 more trips to bring more than 300 'charges' to Canada. Most of these rescue forays ended at St. Catharines, at the home of the Reverend Hiram Wilson, the leader of the refugee community there.

Working with free contacts and trusted slaves, Tubman arranged to meet in swamps and forests with small groups of Blacks whom she then piloted through

(Top left) *Slaves met in the woods at night to plot escape.* (Top centre) *William Wells Brown* (Top right) *Ellen Craft escaped from slavery disguised as her master.* (Bottom left) *Henry Box Brown was shipped from slavery to freedom in a packing crate.* (Bottom right) *A Quaker woman's costume often disguised refugees.* (Opposite) *A fugitive in hiding.*

Maryland, Delaware, New Jersey, Pennsylvania and on to Canada. She travelled only at night, and her compass was the north star; on cloudy nights she guided herself by the moss growing on the north side of trees. Her parties used disguises while they travelled through the South and fake passes when they reached Northern states. They took shelter in chimneys, barns, haystacks and potato holes, dugouts used to store produce.

Tubman could neither read nor write, but she was considered a military genius, a master of logistics and strategy. She was a rigid disciplinarian on the march North and would not allow any of her 'passengers' to drop out of the group or turn back. Once when she was leading a group of 25 runaways, they had to spend a day and much of a night hiding in a swamp, without food. When Harriet judged that it was time for them to move on, one of the men decided to go back instead. He was sure that the whole group was going to die, and he preferred to take his chances at the plantation. Tubman wasted no time in argument. She stepped up to the discouraged refugee and aimed a revolver at his head. "Dead men tell no tales," she warned him. "Move or die." He went on with the rest, and in a few days the whole group was safe in Canada.

Tubman made Rochester, N.Y. a key stop-over on her trips. There her fugitives received help from the Black emancipator, Frederick Douglass, before they went on to small towns farther upstate. They were hidden in cellars and cubbyholes in Williamston before they were smuggled to the docks of Puttneyville. Captains of lake boats took them from there to Niagara

Harriet Tubman (left) *with some of her 'passengers'.*

St. Catharines, Canada West, 1850.

Falls, where they crossed over the suspension bridge into Canada. Government officials evidently looked the other way.

St. Catharines, the chief 'terminal' of Tubman's activities in Canada, was her favourite Canadian town. She could count on the willingness of its citizens to help former slaves. Her elderly parents and three brothers were among the refugees she brought there. But the new freedom in the North was tempered by hardships, particularly during one winter when Harriet arrived in St. Catharines with 11 escaped slaves.

> It was a severe winter for runaways. They earned their bread by chopping wood in the snows of a Canadian forest; they were frostbitten, hungry and naked. Harriet kept house for her brother and the ex-slaves boarded with her. She worked for them, begged for them, encouraged them and carried them through the hard winter.[19]

At the height of Tubman's activities, a group of slave-owners put a price of $40 000 on her head. Undaunted, she carried on. Dr. Michael Willis, the principal of Knox College in Toronto and president of the Anti-Slavery Society of Canada raised money for her to make more trips.

Tubman met John Brown when he visited St. Catharines in April, 1858. Brown asked her to be the chief guide to Canada of all Blacks that he expected to free after the Harpers Ferry raid. Harriet assured Brown of her support and promised "... to bring to his side her own personal following of fugitives in Canada West." Brown's defeat at Harpers Ferry and his execution were hard blows for Harriet. For the rest of her life she honoured his memory, claiming to her death that he was one of the great emancipators of her people.

Shortly before the outbreak of the American Civil War Harriet returned to the U.S.A. She joined the Union Army and served as nurse, scout and spy. After she finally retired in Auburn, N.Y., she founded a home for the aged. She died there on March 10, 1913 after a lifetime of courageous service to her people.

There is considerable argument over the exact number of slaves who reached Canada *via* the UGR. Its activists were inclined to inflate the figure, claiming that between 1830 and the mid '50s from 60 000 to 75 000 Blacks made their way into Canada West.[20] On the other hand, doubtful Canadian census figures showed 4669 Black residents in 1851 and 11 223 in 1861. The fact is that no accurate figures can be given for the number of fugitive or free Blacks in the British North American provinces. Many Blacks who set out for Canada died or disappeared along the way. Many who reached Canada decided to 'pass' for white, and many fugitives claimed to be 'free' Blacks because they mistakenly feared that Canadian authorities would return them to their former owners. Many Blacks were simply not enumerated. At a conservative guess, 30 000 fugitives may have reached Canada between 1800 and 1860.

Whatever the actual figures may be, the Underground Railroad was a phenomenal success. By the 1860s Blacks were clustered throughout Canada West, involved in the difficult task of setting up and developing their new communities.

Kidnappers and Slavers' Agents

The heroic work of the Black freedom-seekers and their abolitionist helpers did not go unopposed. As

Great Western Station, London, Canada West, 1858.

early as 1796 attempts were made to force Canadian runaways living in Detroit to return to their owners,[21] and slave-holders continued for years to try to rid Detroit of escaped Canadian slaves. Later there were many attempts to kidnap Black refugees living in Canada and return them to the U.S.A. Slave-catchers and kidnappers roamed the border towns, and Black refugees faced the constant threat of kidnapping by whites and Blacks who meant to force or trick them back into slavery.

Moves and counter-moves followed one another in the contest for the lives of fugitives. The proprietor of the Clifton House at Niagara, for example, co-operated with American kidnappers who were trying to return to slavery Sarah Jane Giddings, a servant in his hotel. A number of young Blacks learned of the plan and removed her to safety. Southern families often visited Niagara Falls, N.Y., bringing some of their slaves with them. Canadian abolitionists sometimes tried to encourage these slaves to cross the river and claim their freedom in Canada, but their owners threatened reprisals against their families back home.

Black refugees could not always trust their security to their own people. There were 'Negro vagabonds' who were prepared to use deceit and force to prey on fugitives for profit. In 1843 a letter to the *Chatham Journal* warned:

> To the Colored People residing in the Province of Canada:
> My Friends and Countrymen.
> ... Some time last month, I was decoyed by one George Wilson, a man of color, to go into the State of Ohio, under pretence of his rendering me a service, but on my arrival at Pettysburg, Ohio, according to my appointment, instead of meeting me with the proferred services gratuitously promised by the deceiver, I was met by the Agent of a Slave-holder, and arrested as a runaway slave; but through the interference of two professional gentlemen of that place, I was set at liberty, on a promise on my part to see them fairly remunerated for their trouble.
> In making this brief statement to my colored friends, I have two objects in view.
> The first is to caution you against the impropriety of placing too much confidence in any person, particularly those of color, who can thus be guilty of such nefarious conduct to his own people, on a mere superficial acquaintance.
> And secondly, as many of you whom I am now addressing, have by permission of a kind Providence been allowed to make your escape from slavery and bondage, and through the wise and liberal policy of the British Government been allowed a place of refuge; I now with confidence appeal to your sympathy and humbly solicit of you such assistance as you in your different circumstances can spare in order to enable me to honorably and honestly redeem my promise to those my benefactors, thereby showing to the world, that though we once were slaves, that now we are free we will be honest.
> Henry Gouins[22]

For the most part, however, Canadians co-operated to prevent the re-enslavement of any of their fellows. In 1840 the *New York Albion* reported:

RIOT AT NIAGARA FALLS, SEPT. 16, 1840

A pleasure party from the southern States having two coloured servants [presumably slaves] entered Canada at Chippewa and proceeded to a resort hotel near the Falls. While the group was at dinner, the hotel was surrounded by a large party [40 or 50] of coloured militia men then in service on the Niagara frontier who desired to 'rescue' the coloured females. Finally, after three hours, the mutinous company withdrew. No charges.[22]

Elijah Leonard, one time mayor of London, Canada West, recounted a more successful incident:

> The year after I was Mayor ...[in] 1858 ... I came very near getting into a scrape by encouraging the keeping of a colored lad in Canada. A recognition of the injustice of slavery was, I suppose, born in me from the first, as it was in all Northerners. It was the only blot on the American people as a nation, and I disliked it the more I heard stories of so many escaped slaves. Canada was then their only safe place of residence. I was at the Great Western Station one noon on the arrival of the train from Suspension Bridge, when I first noticed a dandy sort of a fellow pacing up and down the platform with a bright negro boy[23] at his heels, acting as his body servant, and sending the little innocent to buy his papers and cigars. He was rather communicative, and told in my hearing how much the boy was worth when he got him south. I had heard stories of this illegal traffic going on in

The homestead of the Baby family at Sandwich, Upper Canada.

the North but had never come face to face with it. I knew in a moment this creature had been east and had enticed this boy, perhaps from his home. In turning around I saw on the station Anderson Diddrick, [24] the colored man who carried the Union Jack in front of our firemen when in procession. I told him I was afraid that boy was going into slavery and it was too bad to see him dragged off free British soil to work all his life for some one else, and perhaps be badly treated. The train started, the man whistled to the boy, and off they started for Detroit. This brought tears to Diddrick's eyes. I asked him if he knew anyone in Chatham. "Yes, several." "Would they take this boy away from this man?" "Yes, they would," but he added he had no money to telegraph. I gave him some, and he immediately wired the state of affairs, which was responded to in great shape. When the train stopped at Chatham, sure enough there were nearly a hundred colored men and women with clubs and staves who surrounded and boarded the train and demanded the boy. He was handed over by his greatly surprised master without much ceremony and taken up town. Mr. Kidnapper was very glad to get off with a whole skin from this desperate company. The railway company had these people all summoned for disturbing the peace, and quite a fuss was made about it. I was summoned to attend court in Chatham, but the papers miscarried. I believe, when the magistrate learnt the whole truth, he bound over some of the foremost, and the act of trespass was in a short time forgotten. I have been given to understand the boy lived for many years afterwards near Chatham. [25]

Many Canadians whose families had once owned slaves gradually took on anti-slavery attitudes. In 1830, for instance, Charles Baby, whose parents and grand-parents had been important slave-owners, hired a Black refugee named 'Andrew' as a farm-hand. Andrew's former owner traced him from Kentucky to the Baby household, where he soon appeared. He accused Andrew of stealing a horse and offered Baby $2000 to help him take his runaway back to Michigan. Baby, believing Andrew's word that he was innocent, replied: "We don't barter in human flesh in Canada; your proposition I look upon as an insult, and the sooner you get out of this country, the better for you." [26]

Andrew's former owner returned to Detroit and hired five kidnappers. These men rowed across the Detroit River on a Sunday morning, expecting that the Baby family would be at church. Fortunately Baby had stayed at home that day and was able to call on neighbours to help drive off the attackers.

> This was sufficient proof that there was no safety for him to be with us and the next day Andrew was paid off, a subscription was made up among our friends, and he was advised to go to Toronto by stage.... When Charles [Baby] met him repeatedly for several years after, he was ever grateful for our sorely tried friendship, and remained contented and prosperous in his place of refuge. [27]

There are records of Americans kidnapping former slaves in Toronto in the 1840s. Peter Gallego expressed concern about American slave-owners who were tracking their 'property' into Canada in the hope of getting back the runaways by kidnapping or extradition. A report appeared in the *Toronto Patriot* of July 3, 1840:

> Two persons, Irishmen we believe by birth, but Yankee-fied by habit, were charged on Thursday last, before Aldermen Gurnett and King, with an attempt to kidnap a coloured man whom they asserted to be their slave, and with drawing bowie knives on another person.
>
> The parties after being suitably reprimanded by the sitting Aldermen for the brutal and cowardly practice of carrying bowie knives, and made aware that under Monarchical Institutions and British Laws, there existed no excuse for wearing such weapons, were severally fined Five Pounds, and held to bail for their future good conduct.

Toronto citizens formed vigilance committees to prevent kidnappings and published notices warning all newcomers that slave-owners had their agents in the city. Gallego continued to be active: he wrote to Queen Victoria, arguing that it would be wrong to extradite runaway slaves on criminal charges since they would not be given fair trials or fair sentences in American courts.

Of course, the payment of bounties for returning escaped slaves meant that bounty-hunters continued to operate. Toronto, with its relatively large population, had perhaps more than its share of active searchers. From March 24, 1855 the *Provincial Freeman* printed a warning in each edition:

CAUTION!!

COLORED PEOPLE

OF BOSTON, ONE & ALL,

You are hereby respectfully CAUTIONED and advised, to avoid conversing with the

Watchmen and Police Officers of Boston,

For since the recent ORDER OF THE MAYOR & ALDERMEN, they are empowered to act as

KIDNAPPERS

AND

Slave Catchers,

And they have already been actually employed in KIDNAPPING, CATCHING, AND KEEPING SLAVES. Therefore, if you value your LIBERTY, and the *Welfare of the Fugitives* among you, *Shun* them in every possible manner, as so many *HOUNDS* on the track of the most unfortunate of your race.

Keep a Sharp Look Out for KIDNAPPERS, and have TOP EYE open.

APRIL 24, 1851.

Posters like this warned slaves in the 'free' states of their danger, and many fled to Canada.

CAUTION

From information received from reliable sources, we learn that parties are at present in Toronto endeavouring to induce coloured persons to go to the States in their employ as servants. From the character of the propositions, there is reason to believe "foul play" is intended. Possibly that Constable Pope's designs on the fugitives and others are being carried out.

Individuals have proposed to women to go to Detroit to live in their service, and another party under circumstances of great suspicion to a boy, to go as far south as Philadelphia. We say to our people, listen to no flattering proposals of the sort. You are in Canada, and let no misplaced confidence in this or the other smooth-tongued Yankee, or British subject either, who may be mercenary enough to ensnare you into bondage by collusion with kidnappers in the States, deprive you of your liberty.

Chatham, like other towns which attracted a number of refugee slaves, attracted slavers' agents. In August, 1857 John W. Wells of Lynchburg, Virginia and T.G. James of Bashville, Tennessee arrived in Chatham and put up at the Royal Exchange Hotel. They had come to recover "... a smart colored lad named Joseph Alexander" 20 years of age. Word quickly circulated among the town's Blacks, and a large crowd, including the wanted man himself, assembled in front of the hotel. James told the crowd that Joe was "... a good boy ..." but almost "... too big and saucy." He claimed that he had whipped Joe only once because he had got drunk and let a span of horses run away and smash a fine carriage.

Then Joe Alexander spoke for himself. He told the crowd that James and Wells owned one of the largest slave pens in the South. This pen, behind the St. Charles Hotel in New Orleans, held at least 500 slaves on any ordinary day. At this, the visiting Americans, realizing that the Blacks in the crowd would not let them seize their former slave, turned to Joe and offered him $100 to go with them to Windsor. But this sudden 'change of heart' in no way deceived their intended victim. Appealing to the crowd, Joe said firmly:

> "I am positive from what I know of him [James] that as soon as he got me out he would shoot me dead and then leave me for he would just as soon shoot a man as a black squirrel and a white man as a Black man, and his nephew [Wells] is just like him."
>
> Whereupon the crowd escorted the men to the train and saw them out of Chatham.[28]

Joe Alexander had finally won his freedom.

4
Refugees and Their Havens

Early Arrivals

WHILE MOST BLACKS who made their way into Nova Scotia[1] and 'the Canadas' before the end of the American Civil War came as fugitives and refugees, there were a considerable number of free Black settlers. The first of these arrived in the period of Loyalist settlement just before and just after the American Revolutionary War.

The earliest group of free Blacks to reach Nova Scotia was the 'Company of Negroes' evacuated from Boston with other British troops in 1776. Thousands of slaves had claimed the British offer of freedom to all who would desert to them, and many of these thought that migration to remaining British territory was their only hope of avoiding re-enslavement. By the terms of the Provisional Peace Agreement[2] between Britain and its former American colonies, refugees who had been behind the British lines for 12 months were to be allowed to leave the U.S.A. Many Black refugees and Loyalists were appalled to learn that their former masters disputed their right to safe conduct to continuing British territory. While British and American authorities argued the claims of Black Loyalists and their former owners, the British Brigadier General Samuel Birch began to issue certificates to any Black who could prove that he had been a refugee for the past year. These certificates guaranteed the bearer permission "... to go to Nova Scotia or anywhere else He may think proper."[3] Any Black leavinq New York, the last British outpost held against American forces, might be

Mary Ann Cousby (opposite) *and her husband were among Owen Sound's first Black settlers.*

Black troopers fought on both sides in the American Revolutionary War.

Niagara, Upper Canada, with a view of the American Fort Niagara across the river, about 1790.

haled before a Board set up by Commander-in-Chief Sir Guy Carleton to examine disputes relating to the embarkation of Loyalists and their goods. A "Book of Negroes" was compiled to record the name, age and description of every Black who wished to leave New York, together with all details relating to his or her former status, escape and military record. A ship's captain who carried an unlisted Black was liable to prosecution. The names of 3000 Blacks were listed in "Carleton's Book of Negroes". These went directly to Nova Scotia. In the following year several hundred Black Loyalists who had gone from New York to East Florida migrated to Halifax.

Massachusetts-born Peter Long was a Loyalist who left the southern colonies and settled in New Brunswick. As a gunner on the schooner *Nova Scotia* he fought against the Americans on the St. John River in 1779-80. Deciding that life would be less difficult for Blacks in Upper Canada, he moved his family of ten[4] to 'Muddy York' in 1793. They settled east of the Don River. Long died at Prescott in 1813. He had been proud that his name was on the United Empire Loyalist list,[5] but it was removed without explanation before 1818.[6]

Black Loyalists, like others who were moving into 'the Canadas' in the 1780s and '90s, settled first close to the rivers and lakes of the borderlands. Some Blacks, for example, came to Sandwich in the 1780s when Loyalist fur-traders and merchants from Detroit moved across the river to Upper Canada. Butler's Rangers, a company of commando-style wilderness fighters based at Fort Niagara were disbanded in 1783, when the Fort was handed over to the Americans. Some of the veteran Rangers, Blacks among them, also settled near Sandwich on a 25-km stretch of the Lake Erie shore granted to their Colonel William Caldwell by Native chiefs. Colchester Township's earliest Black landowner was James Robertson, a veteran of the Rangers, who was recorded there in 1787. By 1794 several Blacks owned land in Gosfield Township, including Prince Robertson, another man named 'Prince' and James Fry, also a veteran. James Richardson, too, had applied for 100 ha of Crown land in the township.[7]

During the same two decades the Niagara region attracted most of the settlers in Upper Canada's central area. In 1788 a man named 'Diamond' settled near the Welland River beside a spring in a grove. A free Black and the first non-Native settler in Caistor Township, Diamond fished and hunted, built himself a stone house and cleared some land for crops. By 1792 he held almost 325 ha. At that point, he sold his land and disappeared. Henry Dochstader, the Loyalist who bought it, was the first white settler in the township.

In 1794, 19 free Blacks living in the Niagara area, who had probably been given their freedom as a reward for military service, petitioned Governor Simcoe for a grant of land to establish a Black settlement. They attested that among them were "… many who had been soldiers during the late war between Great Britain and America."[8]

The residents of York (later re-named 'Toronto') included Blacks from the town's earliest days. Its first Black business people were two contractors, Jack Mosee and William Willis, who in 1799 undertook to open a road westward from Yonge Street through 'the Pinery'. Their first attempts failed to satisfy Upper Canada's surveyor, who found the road improperly cleared and too narrow, but in time the job was satis-

factorily finished. In 1799, 15 Blacks were counted in York, without distinction between free and slave. By 1802 there were 18 free Blacks, including six children.

Even before the turn of the 19th century a few free Blacks were moving into the inland areas of Upper Canada. Edward Smith, a former American slave and a United Empire Loyalist, received a land grant in the second concession of Raleigh Township in Kent County. He is said to have been the only Black to own land along the Thames in 1793. Smith had been captured by Cherokee Indians in the Revolutionary War and released at Detroit through the influence of the commandant, Colonel DePeyster, who then hired him as a servant. Five other Blacks were listed as residents of Raleigh Township in '93: James Jackson, Bango Smith, Abram Gray, John Gun and 'Tobias'. There is also mention at about the same time of a Black preacher named 'Steve White' and a 'Darkey' Rhodes. Even earlier, in 1790-91, the first official survey of Chatham Village recorded an unnamed Black living in a cabin on the north side of the Thames River. This

York, the new capital of Upper Canada, in 1803.

might have been a man called 'Croucher' who 'squatted' on the flats north of the Thames River. Croucher, though handicapped—"... the lower portion of his legs, from the knees down, spread out at a 45° angle"[9]—kept pigs which were evidently a source of some distress to his neighbours south of the river.

Chief Areas of Black Settlement

There was no major movement of Blacks into Upper Canada before its first Legislative Assembly abolished slavery there in 1793, but from then on Black immigration began. Simcoe's anti-slavery legislation undoubtedly made many fugitive American slaves decide that Upper Canada's first capital, Newark (later Niagara-on-the-Lake), would be the safest place for them to settle. An army sergeant who, as a child, had lived in Newark's Red Barracks in Navy Hall[10] told of watching a party of 11 escaped slaves arrive at King's Landing Wharf. As word of a safe refuge for runaways began to get abroad, their number grew. American officers who had been stationed near Fort Malden during the War of 1812 carried back stories of a country that welcomed Blacks. For this reason great numbers of escaped slaves began to make their way north to Malden (later Amherstburg).

The first major wave of fugitive slaves arrived in Upper Canada between 1817 and 1822, and the Ferry (later Windsor) and Sandwich Township became the first sanctuaries for many of them. Others settled in small groups wherever the boats set them down. From the 1820s onward, refugees migrated into the townships, villages, and towns of Essex County, including Anderdon, Mersea, Gosfield, Colchester, Maidstone, Rochester, Fort Malden, Harrow, New Canaan and Amherstburg. This last town was the Canadian port most accessible to escaping slaves because the Detroit River was narrowest there. It was even possible to swim across the river at that point, but most fugitives built makeshift rafts or boarded boats, with or without the co-operation of their crews. In winter refugees walked across the ice to the Canadian side. Captain Charles Stuart, a British officer and an ardent abolitionist, reported that roughly 150 Blacks entered the area between 1817 and 1822. Captain Stuart formed a real affection for these Blacks and secured for them a government grant of "... a small tract of land in the rear of the village".[11] An early visitor reported:

> The negro village and the clearances were then but just begun. As it was a very rainy season, the land seemed to be a swamp and the huts very indifferent affairs, but were thought to be palaces by the freemen who inhabited them. Subsequently heavy crops were obtained from their farms.[12]

Bertie Township, often called 'the Quaker Township' in Upper Canada's early years, was a reception centre for some of the first Black refugees. They were given shelter in the white-columned Bertie Hall, which stood on the bank of the Niagara River at Fort Erie. The Hall, which was rumoured to contain secret cellars and passages to hide runaway slaves, had been built by two abolitionist brothers, Brock and Nelson Forsyth. The Lake Erie homestead of Benjamin Schooly, a Quaker who came originally from Hardwick, N.J., was also a place of refuge.[13] It is estimated that by 1830 nearly 600 Blacks were settled along the Detroit River and the Lake Erie shore.

The shore of Lake Ontario also had its share of refugees. There were Blacks in the village of Hamilton during the 1820s and '30s, and at about the same time Black squatters settled on Hamilton Mountain under the protective eye of two of Hamilton's oldest families, the Burkholders and the Greens. In the Burkholder Cemetery, the oldest pioneer cemetery on Hamilton Mountain, are buried a number of former slaves; some of their graves were made as early as 1820.[14]

During the 1830s and '40s the Black population of Upper Canada continued to grow, but at a somewhat slower rate. By 1835 Hamilton's Black population had increased enough to open an African Methodist Episcopal (A.M.E.) church in a small log building on Cathcart Street. This church was probably organized under the direction of J.C. Loguen who had been an A.M.E. lay preacher in the United States.

Toronto in 1834 was the third largest city on the Great Lakes.[15] As it grew, the corresponding boom in industry and business created a keen demand for skilled tradespeople and workers, as well as opportuni-

View of Amherstburg, 1813 *by Margaret Reynolds.*

ties for merchants and other business people. The time was ripe for the city's first wave of Black immigrants.

Word filtered into the U.S.A. that there was work to be had in Toronto. For free Blacks in the northern states, it was a city within easy reach, and for runaways it was far enough from the American border to offer safety from pursuing masters. In time, Toronto became a major haven for runaways, and many of them settled in the old Ward 4, west of the present University Avenue. Although the growing Black community created a new refugee group which settled chiefly in a working-class area, it turned out to be self-supporting and no drain on the public purse. In 1837 James Birney observed that the city's Blacks were

> ... exempt from pauperism, from intemperance and from the grosser forms of vice ... The gentlemen from whom I had this testimony more especially were of the radical party in politics, and as such were opposed by the colored people generally who belong to the Government party. The testimony therefore, is the more valuable.[16]

John Dunn, then Upper Canada's Receiver General, wrote to an American abolitionist: "Negroes ask for

Amherstburg (above) *and London* (below), *Canada West, 1838.*

charity less than any other group, and seem generally prosperous and industrious."[17] This view was affirmed by an old Black named 'Robertson' who "... while complaining that his fellow Negroes would not help him, said that there were plenty of Negroes who were well off, not a few in Toronto."[18] Later Benjamin Drew observed that most Toronto Blacks owned their own homes, and some had valuable property.[19]

Amherstburg remained a centre of Black population during this period. Levi Coffin, the 'president' of the Underground Railroad, visited the town in 1844, considering it the principal Canadian terminal for the UGR. On the same tour he also visited Blacks in London, Dawn, Wilberforce and smaller settlements along the Thames River. There were small Black settlements, too, at Niagara Falls, Drummondville[20] and Niagara-on-the-Lake where at least 14 Black families came as refugees between 1830 and 1840.[21] These families, including the Andersons, the Bannisters, the Birds, Brights, Carrets, Martins and Spriggs, lived on Mary Street.

Lake steamers and small craft often dropped runaways at Fort Erie, and a small village called 'Little Africa' soon grew up on the town's outskirts. By about 1840 there were 80 Blacks living there. Its population grew to 200 before they scattered to other parts of

Ontario about 1880, when a dwindling wood supply and an increasing demand for coal to fuel the railroad trains deprived these people of their chief livelihood.

Other Black families chose to settle farther inland to remove themselves from the threat of kidnappers searching for escaped slaves, and to find cheaper land. By the early 1830s Blacks had begun to settle in London, which had been founded in 1826 at the forks of the Thames River. In 1832 Benjamin Lundy, a Quaker abolitionist who was passing through London, noted that there were about 25 to 30 "colored people" in the town. A Black man carried a flag at the head of an "Orange Tory procession" in London during the summer of 1836. A few Blacks settled in small towns nearby: Strathroy, Woodstock and St. Thomas. Twelve Blacks started their own church in St. Thomas in the 1830s, and Blacks from the town attended a St. George Day rally held by Colonel Thomas Talbot, an early promoter of settlement in the area.

The village of Brant's Ford began with the arrival of a few non-Native traders among the Six Nations Indians of Mohawk Village on the Grand River near Upper Canada's main east-west highway. After the village of Brantford was surveyed in 1830, it attracted not a few settlers. John Boylston, a blacksmith, was the only Black property-owner listed among Brantford's residents in that year. By 1832, however, with the help and encouragement of Captain John Brant, three more Black families had moved into the village and bought lots. These were the families of Adam Akin, a "common labourer", who built a house for his large family on Darling Street, James Anderson, a blacksmith, who lived with his family on Dalhousie Street, and Samuel Wright, a barber, who built a log house on Colborne Street. Another early Black settler in the village was William Taylor,[22] a member of the Bridge Guard commanded by Captain Brown. By 1846 about 15 Black families lived in or near Brantford.

About 1840, Black and white squatters began to move into the wilderness of the Queen's Bush, part of

Brantford, Canada West, about 1840.

the great tract of land in the Huron area that covered almost 800 000 ha and included Waterloo, Wellington, Dufferin, Grey and Bruce Counties. There was no organized settlement program for Blacks in the Bush. They went in as individual families and they managed on their own. In 1844 missionaries reported 108 Black families living in the Bush on lots of less than 40 ha apiece. Most came without money or supplies; sometimes they had only an axe and a few clothes. There were no roads, no markets, no grist mills to grind grain for flour. The settlers existed at first in common shelters, and their first food was simply "... a species of greens gathered in the woods and boiled in salt."[23] But they survived and hewed out of the bush small homes, a mission church and, in time, a school.

The chief area of Black settlement in the Bush was around Conestoga, a little north of the present cities of Waterloo and Guelph. Among the first Black settlers there were an ex-slave William Jackson and his father, who cleared the land and farmed, and Sophia Pooley, once a slave of the Mohawk chief, Joseph Brant. She chose to move into the Bush with other Blacks for she thought that they would care for her in her old age. She seems not to have been disappointed.[24]

John Little, a Black refugee from North Carolina, and his wife, Eliza, had been slaves in Petersburg, Virginia. They escaped to Chicago, where the UGR helped them to get passage on a boat to Detroit; from there they crossed the river to Windsor. Six months later they moved on to the Queen's Bush, where they had heard that settlers could buy land at a reasonable price. Little later described their early experiences:

> We had not a second suit of clothes apiece; we had one bedquilt and one blanket, and eighteen dollars in money. I bought two axes in Hamilton, one for myself, and one for my wife; half a dozen plates, knives and forks, an iron pot, and a Dutch oven: that's all for tools and furniture. For provisions I bought fifty weight of flour, and twenty pounds of pork. Then we marched right into the wilderness, where there were thousands of acres of woods which the chain had never run round since Adam. At night we made a fire, and cut down a tree, and put up some slats like a wigwam. This was in February, when the snow was two feet deep. It was about fourteen years

ago. We made our bed of cedar boughs from a swamp. Thus we travelled three or four days, seeing plenty of deer: wolves, as plenty as sheep are now, were howling about us, and bears were numerous ...

> The settlers were to take as much land as they pleased, when it should be surveyed, at various prices, according to quality. Mine was the highest price, as I had taken of the best land. It was three dollars seventy-cents an acre. I took a hundred acres at first, and then bought in fifty ...

> I raised that year one hundred and ten bushels of spring wheat, and three hundred bushels of potatoes on land which we had cleared ourselves, and cultivated without plough or drag. All was done with the hoe and hand-rake. This I can prove by my nearest neighbors. I got the seed on credit of some Dutchmen[25] in the towns, by promising to work for them in harvest. They put their own price on the seed, and on my labor.[26]

At first Little wished to put as much distance as possible between himself and white people, Americans and Canadians alike, for he claimed that they had harrassed him for years. As time went on, however, the many kindnesses shown to him and his family by white settlers gradually changed his attitude. After he had lived in the Bush for five or six years, he realized: "It was not the white man I should dislike, but the mean spirit which is in some men, whether white or black. I am sensible of that now."[27]

Before the middle of the 19th century small Black communities were firmly rooted in six areas of Canada West: along the Detroit frontier, that is at Windsor, Sandwich, Amherstburg and their environs; in Chatham and its surrounding area, where the all-Black settlements of Dawn and Elgin were established; in what was then the central section of the province, particularly London, the Queen's Bush, Brantford and the Black settlement of Wilberforce (now Lucan); along the Niagara Peninsula at St. Catharines, Niagara Falls, Newark (Niagara-on-the-Lake) and Fort Erie; in the larger urban centres on Lake Ontario, that is, Hamilton and Toronto; at the northern perimeter of Simcoe and Grey Counties, especially in Oro, Collingwood and Owen Sound. Besides these centres of Black population, small clusters of Blacks, as well as individual Black families, were settled throughout Canada West.

When the American Congress passed the Fugitive

A settler's house in the bush. The first crops were often planted among the stumps.

Slave Act of 1850, Canada's second wave of Black refugees began to arrive. As a result Canada West's Black population increased dramatically between 1850 and 1861. Most of the refugees came directly from the South; others, like James Smith of Colchester, had lived for a while in the northern states:

> I stayed upward of three years in the free states, married there a few days before I left in 1850 and came to Canada. I left the United States in consequence of the Fugitive Slave Bill . . .[28]

By the early 1850s Windsor was beginning to emerge as the commercial and industrial centre of the Western District of Canada West. At least 50 Black families lived in the village in 1851, and 50 Blacks were employed by the Great Western Railway, "chopping wood and grading the line". Windsor's refugee centre in the early 1850s was the barracks on the present City Hall square. There newly-arrived Blacks were helped to find housing and jobs. Work was plentiful, for several fugitives stated:

> . . . there is no need of raising money to aid the colored people here, unless a day or two when a fugitive family first comes in. Women get half a dollar for washing and it is difficult to hire them at that.[29]

Windsor's Black community continued to grow as the town prospered and became, too, a major terminal of the UGR. In 1855 Benjamin Drew estimated that of Windsor's 1400 residents, 259 were Black. In 1859 another visitor, the Reverend William Mitchell, estimated that Windsor had 700 to 800 Black residents in a total population of 2500. Most of the Blacks lived on the eastern edge of the town. MacDougall Street was dotted with their homes for over a mile. Blacks also lived on Assumption, Pitt and Goyeau Streets, and seven families had their homes on the Baby farm. By 1867 assessment rolls showed an estimated Black population of well over 600.

Sandwich, not far from Windsor, was also a centre for Blacks. In 1855, according to Benjamin Drew, 22 Black refugee families were living there. By 1861 the assessment rolls of Sandwich East listed 41 heads of

Black families, most of them farmers. The many Black churches, schools, missions and colonization schemes that developed in Windsor and Sandwich through the 1850s and the early '60s reflected the growth of Black population in the area.

In 1853 the Convention of the Amherstburg Regular Missionary Baptist Association set the number of Black settlers there at 600; those in Malden Township numbered 900. By 1859 the number of Blacks in Amherstburg had peaked at 800.

Like Windsor, the town of Chatham prospered in the 1850s and became a bustling commercial centre supporting a variety of industries.[30] As the town grew, its Black population grew with it. The census of 1851 showed a total population of 2070, including 353 Blacks, members of 122 families. Eighty of Chatham's Blacks were Canadian-born, mostly of refugee parents. Blacks from all over the American South came to Chatham through the 1850s. Beyond Prince Street, King Street East was lined with log cabins and small houses, most of them occupied by refugees. Garden plots surrounded most of these cabins, and their owners grew corn, beans, pumpkins, potatoes, squash and other vegetables, as well as flowers to brighten the plain exteriors of their homes. The *New York Herald* of 1854 reported that begging did not exist among the town's Blacks, and only two or three refugees had to be helped from municipal funds. In fact, it informed its readers, in Chatham's largest market-place, the greater number of wagons or carts with vegetables for sale seemed to belong to Blacks.[31] The more prosperous Black families owned two-storey frame homes, usually painted white, and surrounded by well-kept gardens. These homes were the equal of homes of white families of similar means. The poorer Black families had "... one or two bedsteads, with bedding, a chest or two, chairs, tables and cooking utensils and sometimes a looking glass, clock or bureau."[32]

In 1856 the estimated population of Chatham was 4000, including 800 Blacks. The records of the British Methodist Episcopal conference of 1859 stated of Chatham:

> Here the colored people are full one third of the population; they poll one third of the votes at the election; they pay one third of the taxes; own one third of the dwelling houses; in a word, they contribute their full share to the wealth, intelligence, industry and enterprise of the town. Their moral and religious character will compare favourably with their white fellow citizens.[33]

The Black community of Chatham reached its zenith by the opening of the American Civil War; from that time it declined quickly. In 1861 a census showed 1254 Blacks in the city, members of 441 families. By the turn of the 20th century Chatham's Black population was halved, although the city continued to be the largest centre for Blacks in Ontario until well into the 1900s.

The estimated Black population of London in 1848 was 480. Many of these people lived on Thames Street, below the river level, in a Black neighbourhood often called 'Nigger Hollow' in newspaper reports. James Brown, a Scot who wrote a book about his eight years of travel in Canada, recorded:

> Generally speaking, this coloured portion of the population, both in the country parts and in the towns and villages of Canada live apart from white inhabitants. They were usually found to be collected together in the least valuable corners of the towns—their houses and style of living most frequently denoting a scale of civilization greatly inferior to the mass of the population surrounding them; among whom, it can scarcely be doubted, they too bitterly feel themselves to be merely "the hewers of wood and drawers of water".[34]

This report contrasts with information given to Benjamin Drew in 1855 by Black settlers, who generally spoke of good times and prosperity for Blacks in London. A few, however, were critical of some Blacks who went about the town begging for money and clothes, "for other refugees". Most Blacks frowned on this practice for plenty of work was available.

Estimates of London's Black population in the 1850s ranged from 350 to 500. The town was a centre for social, religious and educational activities of Blacks who lived in the surrounding areas. In April, 1853, for instance, a large convention of "colored refugees from slavery" met there, and Blacks travelled great distances to attend.

St. Catharines was a major centre of Black settle-

London, Canada West, 1853.

St. Catharines, Canada West, 1850.

ment in Canada West in this period. A great many Blacks arrived there in the '50s by boat, by train and on foot.[35] Benjamin Drew put the total population of St. Catharines during this decade at 6000, including 800 Blacks. This was somewhat higher than the figures published in the *St. Catharines Constitution* on November 7, 1855, that is, 500 Blacks in a population of 7060. The assessment rolls for that year show that 123 Black families were living in the town, chiefly on North, Geneva, St. Paul, Concession, Queenston, Niagara, Cherry and William Streets. The same area housed 94 Black families in 1857, and the number rose to 117 in 1861.

While most of St. Catharine's Black residents had arrived as fugitives, some ex-slaves were brought there in unusual circumstances:

> ... a few days since, some twelve slaves arrived in this town, honourably manumitted by their late owner, now deceased. These people were not only released from slavery, but also had bequeathed them $1,000 each. They were carefully brought here by one of the executors of the will, and though a slave holder himself, and now holding the wife of one of the manumitted slaves, yet to the letter of the will he has carried out the intention of the deceased owner. This gentleman refuses $600 for the liberty of the wife of one of the released slaves ...[36]

Drew considered St. Catharines a true haven for refugees: "The houses occupied by the colored people are neat and plain without; tidy and comfortable within."[37] Other influential Blacks agreed: Mary Ann Shadd, editor of the *Provincial Freeman*, commented on the snug homes of the "colored people" there and on the enterprise and resourcefulness of the refugees. Harriet Tubman and Frederick Douglass chose St. Catharines as the main reception centre for the runaways they helped to escape.

The Black population of Brantford, unlike that of other refugee settlements of the period, actually dwindled at the beginning of the 1850s. Some families may have moved because of discrimination, while others may simply have decided to go into the Queen's Bush and other areas. At any rate, by 1852 the esti-mated Black population of Brantford and its environs was fewer than 100 persons.

Black settlers in the Queen's Bush fared badly during the 1840s and '50s. In fact, Black settlement there was doomed from the outset, for the Blacks had settled on clergy reserves.[38] They found out later that it would be almost impossible for them to buy their land. In their dismay, they repeatedly petitioned officials for the right to buy their squatters' lots. In 1845, for instance, 10 Blacks sent a petition to "James, Earl of Elgin and Kincardine, Governor-General of British North America". They argued that a proclamation issued in 1840 had offered a free grant of 20 ha of land in the Queen's Bush, with the option to buy another 20, to every "man of colour" who helped to quash the Rebellion of 1836-38. Although no such proclamation has ever been discovered in government records, many settlers had acted on this rumoured offer. The 10 petitioning Blacks claimed that they had undergone nine years of "privation and hard labour" and had cleared, on an average, 16 ha and made "corresponding improvements". Sadly, the Crown Land Agent in Elora informed the petitioners that they had been given false information, that they had no case, and that "their farms and improvements were on the market."

In a similar petition directed to the Earl of Elgin in 1847, Black settlers acknowledged that they had squatted on their land: "We are aware that an apology for our boldness of squatting into the Queen's Bush the way we have done, should be reasonably looked for ..."[39] But they pleaded that they had no means of making a living except as day-labourers, and that if the new plan of requiring cash for the land was put into effect, it would wipe them out, for they had no way of paying. They claimed that they had taken over unsettled land when it had "... no more use than being a rendez-vous of the wolf and bear ..."[40] and asked to be allowed to buy lots of 80 ha on favourable terms.

In 1850, 91 Black settlers made a last attempt to buy their land from the government through a petition presented to Lord Elgin. They claimed to have shown their loyalty "... to our governing Queen Victoria ..." during the 1837 Rebellion and to have cultivated and

William Henson escaped from slavery in Maryland and settled in Grey County in the 1820s.

fenced the land they held and built homes and roads on it. Again they asked for time to pay and pleaded:

> ... [if] driven from our little Homes our distress will be great not knowing what to do many of your petitioners has large families to support and no means of supporting them if your petitioners has to leave these lands ...[41]

Finally the government of Canada West heeded the petitions that settlers already on the land be allowed to pay for it in instalments, but the terms of payment were difficult, and Blacks, generally inexperienced in business, could not deal successfully with hard-driving land agents. Other settlers arriving with cash in hand, eager to buy land already under cultivation, drove most of the squatters out of the Bush. One of these Black squatters, John Francis, described his experience:

> Then came a land agent, to sell and take payments. He put up public notices, that the settlers who had made

Henry Cousby and his wife settled in Sydenham Village.

improvements were to come and pay the first instalment, or the land would be sold from under them. The payment was to be in ten annual instalments of 15s 6d. currency, 5s to the dollar. It was then hard times in Canada, and many could not meet the payment. The agent, as we now know, transcended his powers, for some people, white and colored, still hold their lands, not having made payments. The agent had a percentage for collecting. His course in driving people for money, ruined a great many poor people here in the bush. Fearing that the land would be sold, and they get nothing for their betterments, they sold out for very little and removed to other parts. The agent himself told me he would sell my land unless the instalment was paid. I sacrificed my two cows and a steer, to make the payment that I might hold the land. Others did not do that and yet hold. One man, fearing to lose all he had done, sold out for ten dollars, having cleared eight or ten acres — that property is now estimated at $15,000. Some borrowed money on mortgages, and some paid a heavy per cent. for money to meet that instalment: which was very hard on the poor settlers who had their hands full in trying to live, and clearing land so that they could live. But it was done: and it has kept many back by trying to meet that borrowed money, and others by their moving where they would have to begin again: that is what has scattered the colored people away from here.[42]

The exodus of Black squatters from the Queen's Bush, which began in the 1850s, was complete by the end of the American Civil War. Bishop Nazrey of the BME Church reported in 1865: "I visited Peel Township and found scarcely enough people there to give our minister good support."[43] Those Black settlers who did not return to the United States moved on to Owen Sound or Chatham to seek the security of their thriving Black communities.

Escaped slaves and free Blacks had continued to push north through the 1850s until they reached Grey County and Sydenham Village (later Owen Sound) on Georgian Bay, 63 km west of Collingwood. The first Blacks to make their home there were John Hall and his family. Soon after Hall built his cabin in the growing village, other Black families settled there and established squatters' rights to their land. Among these were the families of Thomas Henry Miller, Henry Cousby, Edward Patterson, Thomas Green, William

Henson and Chauncy Simmons. Henson, who was related to Josiah Henson, had escaped from slavery in Maryland, was pursued through Pennsylvania and New Jersey, and finally reached safety in Grey County. Other Blacks arrived there from the Queen's Bush, particularly from Waterloo County, after they had been evicted from their squatter settlements in Peel and Wellesley Townships. These settlers, with John Hall, formed the nucleus of Owen Sound's original Black community.

The town of Collingwood was founded about 1854 on Nottawasaga Bay, in the northwest corner of Simcoe County. Its small Black community began with the town itself. Collingwood grew quickly with developing commercial and passenger routes along the Great Lakes. During the 1850s when the movement of Black refugees into Canada West was at its height, shipping routes connected Collingwood to Chicago, Milwaukee, Sault Ste. Marie and many other Great Lakes' ports. During this same decade the Northern Railway was built to serve Collingwood and the large American steamers that plied between the town and Chicago.

There are few records to show how Blacks first reached Collingwood, but it is most probable that UGR workers put fugitive slaves aboard steamers headed for Georgian Bay ports. Chicago was a major port of embarkation for UGR refugees. Steamers ran three times a week from there to Owen Sound and Collingwood. Some Blacks, too, in more settled areas of Canada West — Chatham, London, Toronto and Oro — became discouraged or restless and began to look for better opportunities elsewhere. Blacks moved often from one district to another, sometimes in search of friends and relatives, sometimes in search of new experiences. Members of the Bush, Morrison, Munroe and Smith families, for example, moved from Oro to Collingwood in the 1850s and '60s. The assessment rolls of 1858 listed three heads of Black families in the town's west ward: Elizabeth Piecraft, Abraham Sheffield and Joseph Rodney.

By the 1850s there was an established Black community, commonly called 'Little Africa', on Hamilton Mountain. For many years Black families had been squatting in small shacks dotted along the Mountain. Between 1851 and 1853 William Bridge Green, who owned considerable land there, gave small lots to eight heads of Black families: William Nelson, George Washington, Isaac Davis, Washington Scott, Henry Johnson, Lewis Miles Johnson, Edward Johnson and David Nelson. Green and Jacob Thomas Nottle gave land to another Black, William Jaggard. The only condition of the donors was that the new owners must farm their land. The property donated by Green became the heart of 'Little Africa'.[44] There were 208 Blacks living in Hamilton in 1853;[45] by 1856 Blacks numbered 274.

During the 1850s Toronto's Black population swelled to about 1000 out of a total 48 000 residents. Possibly because of its relatively large number of Blacks, the city was chosen as the place for an historic convention in 1851. On September 10 of that year the North American Convention of Colored Freemen met in Toronto's new St. Lawrence Hall. The convention's leaders included H.C. Bibb, Josiah Henson and J.T. Fisher. They and other leaders had earlier discussed holding their meetings in the Windsor area or in some Northern town, but decided that Toronto was the safest place to gather. Hundreds of Blacks converged on the city from Canada, the Northern U.S.A. and England. The Convention resolved to encourage American slaves to come to Canada instead of going to Africa since Canada was the best place from which to direct anti-slavery activity. After discussing the problems of resettlement, particularly in Canada West, the Convention's leaders stated "… that the British government was the most favourable in the civilized world to the people of colour and was thereby entitled to the confidence of the Convention."[46] And into Canada West the refugees continued to come.

Free At Last!

Arrival on Canadian soil often had an electrifying effect on slaves who had reached the end of a dangerous journey and suddenly found themselves free. Captain Chapman, who commanded a ship on Lake Erie, gave the following account of two Blacks he carried from Cleveland to Canada:

St. Lawrence Hall, Toronto, 1868.

While they were on my vessel I felt little interest in them and had no idea that the love of liberty as a part of man's nature was in the least possible degree felt or understood by them. Before entering Buffalo harbor, I ran in near the beach … They said, "Is this Canada?" I said, "Yes, there are no slaves in this country… Then I witnessed a scene I shall never forget. They seemed to be transformed; a new light shone in their eyes, their tongues were loosed, they laughed and cried, prayed and sang praises, fell upon the ground and kissed it, hugged and kissed each other crying, "Bless de Lord! Oh! I'se free before I die."[47]

On the other hand, it is not surprising that the stress of body and mind that many refugees experienced during their escape to Canada tempered their joy in their safe arrival and left them vulnerable to all the difficulties of climate and circumstance that they still had to face. J.W. Loguen, for example, who arrived in Hamilton in 1835, later wrote:

Twenty-one years ago I stood on this spot penniless,

Fugitive slaves arriving at the farm of Levi and Catharine Coffin. Three thousand refugees were sheltered here before they were sent on to Canada.

ragged, lonely, homeless, helpless, hungry and forlorn. Hamilton was a cold wilderness for the fugitive when I came here.[48]

On his trip to Canada in 1844 Levi Coffin, 'president' of the UGR, looked into the conditions in which refugees were living. No doubt his services to hundreds of escaping slaves had opened his eyes to the very great difficulties of adjustment which most refugees heroically overcame. When Coffin returned to Cincinnati to collect food and clothing for the refugees in Canada, he reported:

Many fugitives arrived weary and footsore, with their

clothing in rags, having been torn by briers and bitten by dogs on their way, and when the precious boon of freedom was obtained, they found themselves possessed of little else, in a country unknown to them and a climate much colder than that to which they were accustomed.[49]

But in spite of all the dangers, difficulties and discouragements, the determination to be free nerved thousands of Blacks to risk and endure everything to achieve their goal. Many very old slaves were just as determined to escape to freedom as younger men and women. Philip Younger, for instance, came to Chatham at the age of 77. He had fled slavery in Virginia after working almost his whole life on a plantation. He spoke, perhaps, for many more of his people than he knew when he summed up his life's experience:

Many awful scenes I have seen while moving about. I have had to put chains on men, myself, to go into a chain gang: I have seen men whipped to death, — have seen them die. I have ridden hundreds of miles in Alabama, and have heard the whip going, all along from farm to farm, while they were weighing out cotton … I came here in consequence of the passage of the Fugitive Slave Bill. It was a hardship at first; but I feel better here — more like a man — I know I am — than in the States.[50]

5

Black Colonies and Communities

made the first day of January in the year of our Lord One
Thousand Eight Hundred and Sixtysix in pursuance of the
Act passed in the Thirteenth and Fourteenth years of the
Reign of Her Majesty Queen Victoria Chapter one hundred and
fiftyfive entitled "An Act to incorporate the Elgin Association
for the settlement and moral improvement of the coloured
Population of Canada" **Between The Elgin Association**
of the first part and **Levi Anderson** of the Township of
Raleigh in the County of Kent yeoman of the second part
Witnesseth that the said Elgin Association for and in consideration of the sum of **Three Hundred Dollars**
of lawful money of Canada now paid by the said party of the
second part the receipt whereof is hereby acknowledged the
said Elgin Association doth grant unto the said Levi Anderson his heirs and assigns forever **All and singular**
that certain parcel or tract of land and premises situate
lying and being in the Township of Raleigh in the County of
Kent being Composed of the northwest half of lot number six
in the thirteenth concession containing one hundred acres
more or less **To have and to hold** unto the said Levi
Anderson his heirs and assigns to and for his and their
sole and only use forever Subject nevertheless to the reservations limitations provisoes and conditions expressed in
the original grant thereof from the Crown The said Elgin
Association covenants with the said Levi Anderson that
they have the right to convey the said lands to the said
Levi Anderson notwithstanding any Act of the said
The Elgin Association And that the said Levi Anderson
shall have quiet possession of the said lands free from
incumbrances And that the said Elgin Association will
execute such further assurances of the said lands as
may be requisite and will produce the title deeds and
allow copies to be made of them at the expense of

Birchtown, Nova Scotia

IN THE FINAL days of the Revolutionary War a Loyalist townsite was chosen at Port Roseway, Nova Scotia, to be a model settlement in loyal British North America. The settlement's name was shortly changed to 'Shelburne' in honour of the British Secretary of State. Among the first arrivals there in 1783 was a unit of troops, the Black Pioneers, who helped to lay out and build the new town. On its northwestern fringes they

(Opposite) *First page of a deed for land in the Elgin Settlement.*

also set up a townsite for themselves; in gratitude to General Birch, they named it 'Birchtown'. Though Benjamin Marston, the local deputy-surveyor, tried to obtain fair treatment for the Black Loyalists in the granting of town lots and farmland, the Blacks of Birchtown were given smaller lots than their white neighbours, and those few who were finally given farms found that they were harder to clear and cultivate than those of white colonists. Other Black Loyalists were even less fortunate, for they had to wait up to six years for the land promised them, while they were more than once moved from sites they had improved. Even then, the grants were much smaller

On the outskirts of Shelburne, N.S. (below) *Black Loyalists founded the community of Birchtown.*

than they had been promised. A few small grants were made to Blacks at Brindley Town[1], close to Digby, and at Little Tracadie on the Tracadie River.

The difficulty of supporting themselves in the face of discrimination and of adverse conditions of climate and the economy convinced many of Nova Scotia's Blacks that they would be better off to leave the province. Some went to New Brunswick, some to 'the Canadas', but most took advantage of the British government's offer of transport to Sierra Leone, where a settlement for free Blacks was to be established. Thomas Peters, a former sergeant in the Black Pioneers, encouraged his people to accept the British offer. In 1791 almost 1000 of Nova Scotia's Blacks took ship from Halifax for Africa.

Oro

In 1808 the rolling farmland that lies between Ontario's Lake Simcoe and Georgian Bay was an almost trackless wilderness. In that year Samuel Wilmot, Upper Canada's Deputy Provincial Surveyor, explored from Lake Simcoe's Kempenfeldt Bay to Penetanguishene Bay to assess whether a road could be built between them. Wilmot's assistant was probably Daniel Cokely, a Black who in 1807 had applied to lease land in the area. He was the first Upper Canadian Black to travel as far north as Simcoe County.

In 1811 Wilmot surveyed a road through the area he had explored. At the same time he laid out lots on both sides of the road from Kempenfeldt Bay to a military and naval base at Penetanguishene, about 50 km distant.

After the War of 1812 the governments of Britain and Upper Canada encouraged veterans and other British subjects to settle in the growing province. Officials thought that such settlers would help to protect Upper Canada's 'back door' from a possible American attack *via* Lake Huron and Georgian Bay. Partly to promote Upper Canada's defence and partly because of his sympathy for Blacks, Sir Peregrine Maitland, the province's first Lieutenant-Governor, decided to offer land grants in Simcoe County to Black veterans of the War of 1812. He seems also to have

thought that the area might become a sanctuary for runaway slaves from the United States.

On April 26, 1819, Maitland's Executive Council authorized the settlement of Oro along a road one concession[2] east of Penetanguishene Road. The road planned as frontage for the Black settlement was named 'Wilberforce Street' after the famous British abolitionist:

> It being desirable to open the road to Penetanguishene, which commences in the north side of Kempenfeldt Bay in Lake Simcoe, His Excellency in Council is pleased to order that to such persons qualified to receive grants from the Crown as are able to and willing to perform settlement duty, locations of two hundred acres [80 ha] will be made upon their undertaking to begin their settlement duty within one month after receiving the certificate of location and continuing the same until a dwelling house be erected and ten acres [4 ha] cleared adjacent to the road and one half of the road in front of the location also cleared.[3]

Most white settlers were granted 80 ha, though many received much more land,[4] but Maitland's government, for all his good intent, apparently discriminated against Blacks, for they generally were given only 40 ha. Most of the Blacks who were offered land accepted it, but failed to settle on it, for the site was too remote and the move too difficult for those living in established areas of Upper Canada. Although special provision was made to settle refugees from the U.S.A. along Wilberforce Street, Oro was too inaccessible[5] to be a terminal for runaways arriving by the UGR. Twenty-three Black veterans of militia units, including Captain Runchey's Colored Corps, obtained from the Surveyor General's office tickets of location for grants along Wilberforce Street. But of the 23, only 19 actually settled on their grants, and only eight stayed long enough to gain title by building a house and clearing four hectares.

The Blacks who were granted land on Wilberforce Street were among Simcoe County's first settlers. They included Charles Faulkner of the Canadian Regiment, a unit of the British army; Samuel Edmunds, who had been a private in Captain Runchey's Corps; Solomon Albert of the 104th Regiment; John Long, son of Peter Long of York; John Call[6] who had served

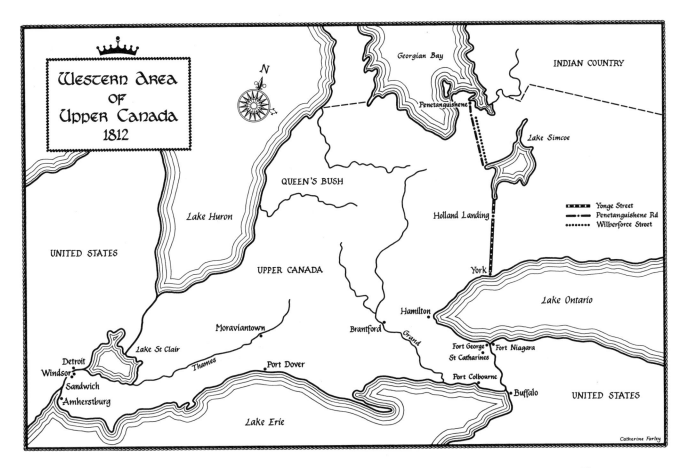

Western Area of Upper Canada 1812

Catherine Farley

with his brothers Richard and Stephen in Runchey's Corps; John Delay, a former sergeant in Runchey's Corps, who moved to Oro after the house he had built in Wilberforce burned down in 1823[7]; George Darkman, who was granted Lot 15[8]; William Davenport, originally from Amherstburg, who settled on Lot 2 with his five children in 1824.

After 1827 Oro's original settlers were joined by Blacks from Ohio[9] and other places. Some Blacks from Wilberforce (later Lucan) in Biddulph Township, unhappy over bickering and financial problems in the Wilberforce settlement, moved north to Oro. They settled there under the supervision of Peter Robinson, the newly appointed provincial Commissioner of Crown Lands. While the government continued to grant Black settlers land on Wilberforce Street until 1829, Robinson began to place new families in other areas. The land-grant system had changed by the time

Robinson was appointed, and tickets of location were no longer required. Land was sold to Blacks at "one shilling per acre [.4 ha]". Between 1828 and 1831 Robinson sold property in Oro Township to about 39 Black families.

In 1831 the provincial District Surveyor, Samuel Leslie Richardson, was instructed to find out whether the first Black settlers on Wilberforce Street were meeting the requirements for their land grants. Richardson's report was gloomy: while 30 new families had joined the original nine, and the settlement now numbered more than 90 people, most of them were poor, and only a few seemed to be prospering. Nineteen Blacks who had been granted land had never settled on it or had soon abandoned it. Of about 2350 ha inspected by Richardson, only 58 had been cleared.

This report had painful consequences for one original Oro settler, George Darkman. In 1819 he had been granted 40 ha on Lot 24, but he was not living on his land when Richardson inspected it, and he had not cleared the required four hectares. For these reasons the elderly man was turned off his land. He made an appeal supported by affidavits and a petition of his neighbours, pointing out that he was 70, in poor health and had lost five toes. His neighbours attested that he had put up a sturdy house, cleared the road and .8 ha and done other work that made his property worth £25. But Peter Robinson rejected the appeal:

> The Location Ticket enclosed expresses in plain terms what he should have done, and his not having complied with the terms subjected him, as well as other persons similarly situated, to the forfeiture of the lot.[10]

Darkman's lot was sold for £25 to a white man, John Gosling,[11] but Darkman was given another chance. He lived on Lot 15, Concession 2, until his death ten years later.[12]

In 1831 the new Lieutenant-Governor, Sir John Colborne, adopted a plan to encourage European immigrants to settle in the Kempenfeldt area. Peter Robinson was to carry out the plan, and Colonel Edward O'Brien, originally of York Township was to administer the Oro settlement. The government began to sell land at "five shillings an acre [.4 ha]" in three townships, including Oro, though some people thought that Colonel O'Brien and his wife were more interested in attracting British immigrants to Oro than in settling Blacks there:

> Instead of settling coloured immigrants, Mrs. O'Brien and her husband were occupied in welcoming white settlers such as the Gardiners, the Lallys, the Campbells, the Goods, the Monks, the Moberleys, the Frasers, and [a] great crowd of Islay immigrants ...[13]

By the 1830s and '40s the village of Edgar was the main centre of Black life in Oro. A farm at the northwest corner of Edgar belonged to a Nelson Morrison, and the farm at the northeast corner to a Black named 'Monro'. Well known family names in this period included Morrison, Bush, Case, Barber, Sumner, Caughly, Hepburn, Johnston, Jennings, Smoots, St. Dennis, Thompson, Turner, Jackson, Banks, Hawkins, Eddy and Johnson. Richardson and other officials mentioned Blacks who were successful farmers. Benjamin Turner, who settled in Oro about 1830, cleared at least five hectares. He gave other land as a burial ground for the Black community and placed it in the charge of James and Mark Bush, trustees for the Black church.

Whenever serious illness or death struck a family of Oro, Blacks gathered from the whole area to help and comfort one another. According to James Smith of Edgar:

> When there was sickness in one of the Negro families, visitors of their own color came from miles around. Mrs. Eddy, the last of the ex-slaves, died this spring. Before her death as many as 20 people were there at one time ... In the early days one old woman, a Mrs. Banks, was exceedingly skilful in the use of herbs; she was the doctor for the settlement.[14]

In 1831 a census recorded 97 Black residents in Oro Township. Two very different figures are on record for 1848, a census figure of 65, and what is probably a more reliable figure of 127. From that point Oro's Black population declined. In 1861, 101 Blacks lived there; in 1871 there were 79; by 1900 there were no Black families in Oro.

It is possible that the poor land allotted to Blacks and their extreme poverty when they arrived kept them from succeeding. To support their families they had to hire themselves out as axe-men, choppers and farmhands to their better-off white neighbours. As horse-drawn machines gradually replaced human labour, and poor Irish immigrants began to compete with their Black neighbours for the available jobs, times became even harder. Blacks who had to pay fees of a shilling per .4 ha to obtain clear title to their land were hard put to it to raise the money. It may even be that the Black settlement of Oro came to grief because of Lieutenant-Governor Colborne's wish to settle white immigrants in the area at a time when land values were rising, for Blacks were strongly tempted to sell their land at a profit to white settlers eager to buy. Quite a few sales took place, and most Blacks drifted to other parts of the province, including Barrie, Collingwood, Owen Sound, Chatham, Buxton and Toronto. A few families held on, intermarried with whites and kept their farms until the early 20th century. Among them were the families Smith, Thompson, Bush, Eddy

James Dixon Thompson was the last known survivor of the original Black settlement at Oro.

and Davenport.[15] The last known survivor of the original Black settlement was James Dixon Thompson,[16] a sheep-shearer and a grandson of David Thompson. James Thompson died in Barrie on December 21, 1949.

Today beside the small frame church and cemetery in Edgar stands a cairn with a plaque bearing the names of Oro's 13 original families. It is all that remains of the Black community of Oro.

The Wilberforce Settlement

Although Ohio abolished slavery in 1802, its legislature was strongly influenced by sympathizers with the slave-holding South, and in 1807 Ohio, like many other states, adopted the notorious Black Code. Before 1829 the Code was leniently administered — even virtually ignored — in Cincinnati, but as that city's Black population rose to 3000, tough enforcement began. Unruly whites, finding excuse and opportunity in the Code, provoked serious race riots in the Black district, which compounded the Blacks' suffering.

Many Blacks now decided that to remain in Cincinnati would be very dangerous. They formed a colonization group headed by James C. Brown, a former slave and a successful mason, who had refused to post the $500 'good behaviour' bond which the Code required. The group decided to send a committee including Israel Lewis, Thomas Cresap and Stephen Dutton to the town of York to ask Sir John Colborne, Upper Canada's Lieutenant-Governor, to help them find a new home. Colborne gave them an encouraging reception and replied to their request:

> Tell the Republicans on your side of the line that we Royalists do not know men by their color. Should you come to us you will be entitled to all the privileges of the rest of His Majesty's subjects.[17]

The committee returned to Cincinnati with a favourable report and began to negotiate with the Canada Company[18] for suitable land. They chose a site where the town of Lucan now stands in Biddulph Township, Middlesex County. The Company agreed to sell the Blacks from Cincinnati about 1600 ha for $6000 due in November, 1830. The city fathers of Cincinnati heard of this arrangement and began to reconsider their strict enforcement of the Black Code. Fearing that they would lose much of the city's cheap labour, they promised to do their best to repeal the oppressive Code. This change of policy greatly reduced the number of Black emigrants: fewer than one-third of the expected 3000 set out, and most of those did not go to the new settlement.

In October, 1829 James Brown arrived in Biddulph Township with only five or six families. A few weeks later 15 families from Boston joined the tiny group. Each family received between 19 and 20 ha to cultivate, but the little settlement could not meet the promised payment. The Canada Company resented the new settlers' failure to pay, and the Company's agent,

Sir John Colborne

decided to return to Cincinnati.[19] Brown's going left a gap in the colony's leadership which was filled by three men: Austin Steward, a businessman from Rochester, Nathaniel Paul, a minister, and the latter's brother, Benjamin Paul. Israel Lewis, a member of the original Cincinnati group, had persuaded Steward to give up his successful butcher and grocery business and settle in Upper Canada. When he arrived in 1820, the settlers quickly recognized his abilities and made him their president. He suggested re-naming the settlement 'Wilberforce' after the British philanthropist and abolitionist, and the group readily agreed. A seven-member board of directors was set up, but the settlement's affairs were really controlled by Steward, the Paul brothers and another newcomer, Peter Butler, a former slave from Maryland.[20]

The settlement badly needed funds and more settlers to expand its labour force. It also needed houses, equipment to build them and farm implements. Steward convinced the settlers that they needed responsible agents to raise money for their project. Unexpected support came from the *Cincinnati Gazette*:

> The blacks who emigrated last summer from this vicinity to Upper Canada have named their colony Wilberforce. They have commenced opening and improving the land obtained by purchase and expect to cultivate small crops this season. But they are still in great need of pecuniary assistance. Israel Lewis, the agent ... has addressed a letter to the clergy in [N.Y.,] Pa. and Ohio, requesting that collection may be made in the churches in aid of this colony on the 4th of July next. Ought not we in Cincinnati to aid those driven out from amongst us, rather than the colony at Liberia?[21]

In the meantime Steward cleared about four hectares for himself and put up a house and barn. Later he found that Israel Lewis had sold him land without a clear title, which the Canada Company still controlled. Although this was a serious hardship to Steward, he managed to remain on the property. He described the harsh life of the settlement:

> The township was one unbroken wilderness ... and of course [the settlers'] lands must be cleared of the heavy timber before crops could be got in, hence, there was a great deal of destitution and suffering before their

a Mr. Jones, vowed that no other Blacks would be sold "a foot of land" in the area. Quakers from Ohio and Indiana, alerted to the settlers' plight, sent an agent, Frederick Stover, who bought 325 ha from the Canada Company and gave them to the Blacks.

American abolitionists who were watching the colonization scheme spread word of it, and the Quaker Benjamin Lundy gave it considerable publicity in his journal, *The Genius of Universal Emancipation*. He described the settlement's fertile soil, the climate, the advantages to Blacks of living under British rule. He also published a map, which was widely distributed, showing different routes to Biddulph Township. As a result emigrants from other Northern cities were attracted there.

Soon after the first group of settlers arrived, Brown's wife became dissatisfied, and the family

harvest could ripen after the land was prepared for the seed ... All was one vast forest of heavy timber, that would compare well with that of Western New York.[22]

Game was plentiful, but hunting could be dangerous, even close to home:

The forest abounded with deer, wolves, bears and other wild animals. Bears were plenty, and very troublesome because so dangerously tame ...

Having a little spare time, I went out with my rifle, in search of deer; but soon came upon a large wolf, which I wounded with the first shot; he, however, sprang aside and was gone. On looking about for him I espied another! — reloading my rifle, I fired, and he fell dead at my feet, while my dog at the same time I heard barking furiously. Having dispatched this second intruder, I saw that my dog had the first one, entangled in the branches of a fallen tree. I searched for my [bullets] and was vexed to find that I had left them at home. In this predicament I cut with my knife a knot from a beech limb, put it in my rifle, and took deadly aim at the enraged wolf. The wooden ball struck him between the eyes and killed him on the spot.[23]

Israel Lewis, as it turned out, had damaged the name of the settlement by soliciting over $700 which he refused to turn over to the settlers. Even after the latter discharged him as their agent, he went on collecting money, claiming falsely that it was for Wilberforce.

After dismissing Lewis, the Wilberforce settlers named the Reverend Nathaniel Paul their land agent and gave him power of attorney "... for the purpose of soliciting aid for the erection of houses for worship, and for the maintenance of schools in the colony."[24]

Paul went off to England on this mission,[25] but although he raised about $8000, he claimed that his expenses for the trip amounted to $7000; in addition he charged the colony $50 a month for the three years he was away, so that the settlement did not benefit at all. Paul even claimed on his return that the settlers still owed him $1600 in fees and expenses.[26]

In spite of all its difficulties, Wilberforce made some progress. When Benjamin Lundy visited it in 1832, he praised its 32 families for their work of clearing about 80 ha, 25 of which were sown in wheat. The settlers had 100 head of cattle, a few horses and pigs, "... a good substantial sawmill ... and two good schools ... dwellings ... as yet constructed of logs — some of them hewed — and a few have well shingled roofs."[27] In that year, however, an early frost killed all the settlers' crops.

The settlers built homes much like those they had left in the southern U.S.A., with fireplaces and outside chimneys built "... of thin sawn timber, placed horizontally, and mixed with clay."[28] The Reverend William Proudfoot, a Presbyterian minister just out from Scotland, thought little of these houses and less of the Blacks who owned them:

Austin Steward

The dwellings of the Negroes seem to be wretched, they are ill constructed, ill built, very small ... The Blacks are indolent and do not seem susceptible of early improvement.[29]

Quakers in Oberlin, Ohio, raised funds for a school at Wilberforce. White students as well as Black attended its classes in an old log house with "notched down corners, elm bark roof and basswood planed floors." Benjamin Paul's son taught the boys, and one of his daughters taught the girls; Austin Steward was in charge of the Sunday School.

By 1832 the Baptist and African Methodist Episcopal churches were active in Wilberforce. The AME had no church building of its own, but its members held meetings led by circuit preachers or by Austin Steward in one another's homes. There were three Baptist lay preachers among the settlers: the Paul brothers and the Reverend Daniel A. Turner. The tiny Baptist congregation built a small log church on the Turner farm, probably late in 1852, and Turner conducted

> ... stirring camp meetings and revivals where the colored people would assemble in large numbers and sing many old Southern songs as well as listen to the discourses of local and travelling clergymen.[30]

In spite of small successes, Wilberforce was in difficulty

Slave quarters on a Southern plantation.

from its beginning. By 1835 it had dwindled to 20 families, and local prejudice had reinforced the Canada Company's decision to sell no more land to Blacks. During the 1830s many immigrant Irish families settled in the district. They successfully petitioned the government to support this policy. Lieutenant-Governor Sir John Colborne informed the Colonial Office of his constituents' fears that

> ... the Wilberforce Settlement would become a place of refuge for fugitive slaves and [they prayed] that people of color might not be encouraged to take up their residence in the province.[31]

Any effort to attract settlers to Wilberforce was finished by 1835, and except for a few families, the residents scattered. Austin Steward left in 1837 to become a full-time minister in the AME Church. Israel Lewis died a pauper in Montréal in 1839. The Reverend Benjamin Paul died at Wilberforce in 1836, and his brother Nathaniel died at Albany, N.Y. in 1839. The settlement's first leader, James Brown, had long been following his trade as a mason in Chatham. The Reverend Turner moved to London and founded that town's Black Baptist church. The Baptist church in Wilberforce managed to keep its doors open until 1856, when it was forced to close.

Wilberforce failed because of poor luck, bad management, the dishonesty of some its leaders and the prejudice of some of its neighbours. All the same, the wide publicity given it by Benjamin Lundy and other abolitionists encouraged American Blacks to keep coming to Canada West. An historical plaque and the subdivision of Wilberforce Heights now honour the memory of the Black families who were the first settlers in Biddulph Township.[32]

Dawn

The idea of the Dawn Settlement took root in the mind of Josiah Henson when he saw the need of his fellow refugees for land of their own and an education that would teach them to farm it efficiently. In Colchester Township, near Amherstburg, Henson founded a temporary settlement for Black refugees.

Josiah Henson

There he came to know Hiram Wilson, a Congregational missionary, teacher and abolitionist from Boston. In 1844 Henson and Wilson began to plan a settlement and school for escaped slaves, but they sorely needed a benefactor. Wilson decided to write to James C. Fuller,[33] a Quaker philanthropist of Skaneateles, N.Y., outline the project and invite him to come to Upper Canada to see for himself the desperate needs of Black refugees. Fuller accepted the invitation and became convinced of the need for a Black colony and a school. He joined Wilson and Henson in planning the Dawn Settlement. He had excellent contacts among the Society of Friends (Quakers) in England and he decided to go and ask for their support for Dawn. He succeeded in raising $1700 to use as he saw fit for the benefit of fugitive slaves in Canada.

A sawmill in West Flamborough Township, Ontario, about 1880.

On his return, Fuller decided to discuss the use of these funds with members of Toronto's Black community. His chief contact there was James C. Brown, the first leader of the Wilberforce settlement. Brown and Fuller called a meeting of Toronto's Black citizens, but it broke up in a row when part of the audience protested that neither Fuller nor Brown was authorized "... to beg and collect money for them." Thinking that their project might win more support in London, Fuller, Henson, Wilson and Brown decided to organize a meeting there. At this second meeting, it was decided to buy land for a settlement, and a board of six trustees was chosen. The three white members of the board were Fuller, the Reverend John Roof of Toronto, and Frederick Stone of Norwich, who was elected chairman. The board's three Black members were George Johnston of Dawn, and Peter B. Smith and Brown of Toronto. Henson, Wilson and a J. Shelby were chosen as a property committee to find a suitable site.

Many Blacks had already settled in Dawn Township when, about 1842, it was chosen to be the site of the new school and settlement. Its Board bought 80 ha at $8.00 each on the bank of the Sydenham River.[34] The school was to be called 'The British American Institute', and it was to offer an elementary education with emphasis on industrial and manual training. Property around the school was to be reserved for families connected with it. The school's curriculum was

> ... designed not to supersede, but greatly to subserve, the interests of common schools, by training up teachers; [it] is to be conducted strictly on the manual labour system. Students over fifteen years of age are to have instruction free of cost, and to be furnished with plain but wholesome diet and lodging, at one dollar per week, to be paid in work, for which they will be allowed five cents per hour. They are to be trained thoroughly upon a full and practical discipline, which aims to cultivate the entire being, and elicit the fairest and fullest possible developments of the physical, intellectual, and moral powers.[35]

Dawn was fortunate to have excellent timber. Since an efficient sawmill was needed to capitalize on this asset, Henson decided to visit lumber towns in New England and New York and study their operations. With the help of Boston friends he and his colleagues raised enough money by 1844 to build both a sawmill and a school; about 1848 a gristmill was added.

The school at Dawn was a log building where Hiram Wilson and Elias Kirkland taught the first classes. In 1844 the Canada Missionary Society sent four more teachers for the school's 60 students, half of whom were adults. Twenty-two of the students were boarders who worked on the land. The sawmill began production in 1845, and black walnut lumber was shipped to England and the United States.[36]

In its very early years the Dawn Institute grew — it had 70 students by 1845 — and seemed to be headed for success, but serious problems soon developed. The sawmill and the school were treated as independent operations and had different supervisors. This led to competition, jealousy and conflict, compounded by mismanagement of funds. Some Blacks in Chatham argued, too, that a segregated institution simply encouraged prejudice. The goal of Blacks, they insisted, should be to integrate with other Canadians. Wilson and Henson protested that the Dawn Institute included Native and white students, as well as white and Black teachers, agents and members of its Board. Nevertheless, criticism of the small settlement mounted.

In 1854 the Reverend William P. Newman came to Dawn to take charge of the sawmill and to be secretary-treasurer of the Institute's executive committee. After examining the financial records, he asked Henson to return from one of his lumber-sales trips to explain deficits in Dawn's accounts. Henson returned, and he and Wilson denied vehemently that they had misappropriated funds. In the end the committee charged with looking into the matter cleared both men of any wrongdoing.[37] Still, financial troubles continued, and by 1849 Dawn's debts had risen to nearly $8000. James C. Fuller had died, and several members of the Board had given notice that they would no longer be responsible for the Institute's debts. Newman moved to Ohio, but his continuing attacks on Dawn in letters to American newspapers and later, as editor of the *Provincial Freeman*, damaged the Institute's name and the morale of its staff.

The final stage of Dawn's ruin began in 1851 when Henson took some of his finest walnut lumber to the Industrial Exhibition in London, England. He hoped to raise money to pay off the settlement's debts, but wherever he went, a most embarrassing document was circulated. It described the failure of Dawn and its managers, including Henson, and forecast its end. A committee of Henson's friends acted quickly to clear his name and to send John Scoble, secretary of the British and Foreign Anti-Slavery Society, to Canada to look into problems at Dawn and set up a new system of management there.

Scoble and Henson had been quite friendly in England, but their friendship waned as soon as Scoble arrived at Dawn and began to take over from its trustees all the deeds and powers of the Institute. These Scoble at once began to use for his own benefit. He cut hundreds of cords of the settlement's wood and shipped them to Detroit, giving no account of payment received. He moved into the best house at Dawn and claimed the best livestock and equipment. He failed to build a promised new school and allowed the property to become badly run down. His manner and behaviour offended Canadian Blacks, and they complained publicly. The Canadian Anti-Slavery Society, J.C. Brown and the editors of the *Provincial Freeman*, Mary Ann Shadd and W.P. Newman, all attacked Scoble and, to a lesser extent, Henson. In 1860 Dawn's few trustees who had not turned their powers over to Scoble began

The Wilberforce Educational Institute, Chatham, in 1922.

a legal action against him. The court battle raged until 1872, when the Institute's affairs were finally handed over to a new board. Four years earlier Scoble, facing a new series of scandals, had decided to leave. The new Board sold the Institute's land and assets and used the $40 000 they brought to set up the Wilberforce Educational Institute[38] in Chatham. For all real purposes Dawn and the Institute were finished.

The Colored Industrial Society

From the early days of slavery in North America, the church was important to Black culture. It is not surprising that it took a part in planning settlements for refugees. In 1845 the African Methodist Episcopal Church founded in Sandwich Township a small mission which in 1851 was re-named 'The Colored Industrial Society'. In effect, the church was promoting a land-colonization plan for members of the AME Church and other Black refugees. The Reverend Israel Campbell and the Reverend John Jackson were the Society's first representatives; its trustees declared:

> We have been appointed a Board of Trustees to establish a settlement of colored people in the township of Sandwich, Canada West, and an institution in which that class of the community may receive a liberal education and thereby improve their present illiterate state and also to promote such religious and orderly conduct among them which will tend to their spiritual as well as their temporal happiness.[39]

From its very beginning the Society was plagued with difficulties, and it carried on for only a very few years. With funds raised in the U.S.A. by a Reverend Willis, it bought over 80 ha on the third concession of the Township of Sandwich and divided the land into four-hectare lots. Soon after a dispute arose in the Society, and Willis, who had proposed the plan and raised the funds, vanished. Three AME trustees, George Williams, Alfred Kelly and Phillys Moton, took over the direction of the settlement.

By 1855 the project had failed. David Cooper of Windsor, one of the early settlers, reported to Benjamin Drew that the original terms of sale were a down payment of $3.00 and another $6.00 payable over the next two years. This was evidently considered no bargain, for only eight families had bought lots, and only 16 ha had been cleared. The buyers had had to hire themselves out as day-labourers to make ends meet, leaving their own land uncleared and unworked. The British Methodist Episcopal Church stepped in and tried to minister to the few families that stayed on, but the settlement itself was dissolved.

The Refugee Home Society

The seed of the Refugee Home Society was sown in 1846 at a Windsor convention organized by Isaac Rice, a white Presbyterian missionary, T. Willis, a Black Methodist preacher, and some philanthropists from Detroit. The convention, concerned that the increasing number of refugees from the U.S.A. was making it harder for Blacks to find jobs in Canada, formed the Sandwich Mission to buy land north of Amherstburg and re-sell lots to refugees on easy terms. By 1851 Willis, purchasing agent for the Mission, had bought 80 ha for re-sale, but the plan did not flourish.

In May, 1851 another meeting, attended largely by supporters of the Sandwich Mission, was held in Detroit. There Henry Bibb, who had just founded the Black newspaper, the *Voice of the Fugitive*, proposed a similar land scheme; it was to be called the 'Refugee Home Society'. Bibb and his wife Mary were chosen to lead the Canadian Branch,[40] along with Josiah Henson and David Hotchkiss, an American Missionary Association (AMA) worker in Amherstburg. The new Society's constitution outlined its plan to buy 20 000 ha in Canada to "... assist the refugees from American slavery to obtain permanent homes, and to promote their social, moral, physical and intellectual elevation."[41]

Half the money from the Society's sale of land was to be used to buy more property, while the other half was to be used for building and supporting schools and churches. About 10 ha apiece were to be sold only to refugees from slavery; the first four of these were to be free, if they were cleared and under cultivation within three years of purchase. Once a refugee had bought a lot, it could not be re-sold for 15 years. The

Society had the right to repossess the land of any settler who failed to meet these requirements.

Fund-raisers across the U.S.A. collected enough money for the Society to buy 680 ha within its first year. The main tract of this land lay about 15 km from the Detroit River, southeast of Windsor, in the Townships of Sandwich and Maidstone.[42] By 1855 half the Society's land had been re-sold and occupied by 150 settlers. In 1858 the Society bought from Horace Hallock, one of its trustees, another 120 ha along the Puce River.

The Society differed from other similar groups in buying land here and there in areas already settled. It fostered isolated groups of Blacks in Maidstone, Puce, Belle River, Spruce River, Pine Creek and Pelet. Some of the settlers managed very well; one reported:

> I commenced here in the bush three years ago and have gone over about eight acres [3 ha] — I think the biggest clearing there is. Those near round me are well satisfied with their homes ...[43]

Thomas Jones, an escaped slave from Kentucky, stated:

> They are poor, some of them, but all able to have enough to eat and wear, and they have comfortable homes, with few exceptions.[44]

In this heyday of the community many crops were grown: wheat, sweet potatoes, apples, cherries, peaches, plums, pears and grapes. Work was plentiful, and a man could earn $1.50 a day as a labourer. A woman's wage for similar work was $1.50 a week, but she could earn 50 cents a day as a laundress.

The teacher of the settlement's school recorded that there were at one time 70 or 80 students attending who had learned to read and write. As well as teaching day classes, she also held a Sabbath School which was well attended by both children and adults. Her students, she reported, were "... very diligent and progressing rapidly."

Even so, the Society's few successes were short-lived, for both settlers and prominent members of Windsor's Black community were dissatisfied with some of its policies. The Society solicited donations to operate relief centres, but it was charged with continuing this practice long after new settlers no longer

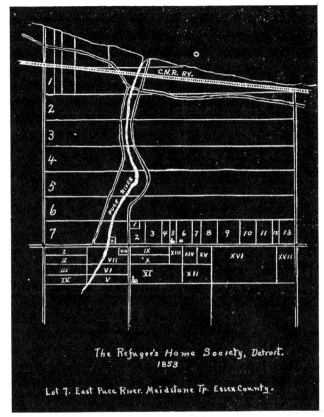

Plan of the Refugee Home Society's holding at Puce River in Essex County, Canada West, 1853.

required support. Outraged refugees and others complained that fund-raising had degenerated into 'begging'.

Mary Ann Shadd and the prominent Samuel R. Ward used the *Provincial Freeman* to voice the criticism of an organized opposition. Ward had earlier supported the Society, but disapproved of its 'begging'. Shadd argued that there was absolutely no need for the Society to exist since its land scheme offered no advantages to fugitives that government offers did not duplicate or exceed. She claimed that many settlers who had bought independently in the area had paid a lower price on better terms than the Society asked.

Charles Foote defended the Society's policy on the ground that the fugitives were unable to handle their own affairs and needed control to prevent their losing their land to speculators. He claimed that the Society's lots were kept to a maximum of 10 ha because money was raised from poor people in New England who thought that a large enough allotment.

In August, 1854 Henry Bibb died. Leadership passed to Foote, who struggled to keep the Society going in spite of opposition. But by 1855 only 40 lots had been settled by 20 families, and disputes continued between the Society and settlers. When the former tried to raise the price of land and introduce stricter regulations, strong opposition forced it to drop its proposals. Later Foote sued some settlers for non-payment, but lost the case.

In the meantime, the Society became more closely linked to the AMA. Foote raised funds from the AMA to build schools at Puce River, Little River and Chatham. By 1861, 60 families had settled on 100 lots, but as the Civil War drew to a close, so did the Refugee Home Society. Some families migrated to Haiti, and some to other parts of Canada West. The AMA finally withdrew its support, and Foote returned to the States, leaving behind the remnants of an experiment that had failed.

The failure of the Society grew in part out of many of its goals. Its land policies were narrow and paternalistic; they excluded many potentially capable settlers and attracted those who expected hand-outs. The Society made no attempt to organize and develop leadership among the settlers, although such a policy might have had a positive and unifying effect. Instead, its paternalism encouraged apathy. Finally, the exposure of corruption among many of its officers and agents badly discredited its reputation. In the end, it only added another discouraging chapter to the tale of segregated Black settlements in Canada.

The Elgin Settlement/The Buxton Mission

The Elgin Settlement, including the Buxton Mission, was the brainchild of a tough-minded, intelligent Presbyterian, the Reverend William King. Born on November 11, 1812 in Ireland, King attended Glasgow University where he was influenced by a group of social reformers and by the work of the famous British abolitionists William Wilberforce, Thomas Clarkson and Sir Thomas Foxwell Buxton.[45]

In 1834 King emigrated with his parents to America, where the family settled on a large Ohio farm. The following year he went south to Jackson, Louisiana, to become Rector of Matthews Academy, a private school for the children of wealthy planters. There he met and married Mary Phares, the daughter of a wealthy planter; they had two children. Although King spoke out publicly against slavery, his wife brought with her four slaves who helped about the Academy and worked as servants in their home. King tired of Louisiana and of teaching and decided to study theology in Edinburgh. His son Theophilus died on the way there in 1844, and his wife and his daughter, Johanna, two years later. In spite of his bereavement, King continued his studies and in 1846 became a minister and missionary of the Presbyterian Church in Scotland, posted to do missionary work in Canada West.

King quickly came to know the province and the Black immigrant groups who were moving into its southern districts. It was while working among the refugees in Essex and Kent Counties that he formed a plan to establish a Black settlement. Family problems intervened. His father-in-law died, leaving him 14 slaves, a legacy and a tangled will. King, greatly embarrassed, had to inform the Toronto Synod that he was a slave-owner. The Synod asked King to resign until he had disposed of his slaves. He agreed, on the understanding that after he had resolved his problems, he could submit his proposal to settle Blacks in Canada West.

By 1848 King had settled the family squabbles over the will. He returned north by steamboat with his 14 slaves, picking up another Black child on his way. At his family's farm in Ohio he told the 15 Blacks that they were now free. If they chose, they could stay on the King farm for the winter and then join him in Canada to live as free persons in his proposed settlement. King's ex-slaves accepted his offer. In the meantime they were to attend school and learn all they could about farming, carpentry and other skills they would need in Canada.

On King's return to Toronto, the Synod greeted

him as an emancipator for piloting 15 slaves out of the South and freeing them in Ohio. He was reinstated as a minister of the Presbyterian Church and quickly took advantage of his new reputation to push his settlement plan. He wanted to establish a refuge for Blacks entering Canada whether they were escaping from Southern slavery or from the hideous Black Codes of some Northern states:

> And to accomplish this I believed it was necessary to provide them with homes where the parents could support themselves by their own industry and their children with the blessings of a Christian education. Three things were necessary for that end: land to place the families upon; a church where they could assemble on Sabbath and hear the gospel; and a day school where the children could receive a good Christian education.[46]

King was convinced that his project could succeed

The Reverend William King

only if Blacks could own land on easy terms and gain enough education to make them independent and masters of the skills of farming. He asked the Synod to help him find a suitable place for the settlement, where he could buy clergy-reserve or crown land at a reasonable price.

Although the Presbyterian Church favoured King's proposal, it moved cautiously. The Synod wanted to control the plan, but it also wanted widespread community support. To this end it set up a committee of 17 members, including Presbyterian ministers and prominent people in both Canada West and Canada East.[47] This powerful committee met with the Governor General of Canada, James Bruce, Earl of Elgin, who pledged that both he and his government would support the plan. Next the committee met with the Commissioner of Crown Lands, James H. Price, who gave them maps of "... fertile, timbered crown land in Essex, Kent and Hamilton Counties ..."

Early in 1849 King and Price set out to look at a clergy-reserve tract of about 3600 ha in Raleigh Township between the small settlements of East Tilbury and Chatham. The land, bounded on the north by the Thames River and on the south by Lake Erie, had distinct advantages: it was only 160 km from London, 65 km from Windsor and Detroit, and it was accessible to those towns by water and by 'the Old Talbot Road'; it was covered with rich stands of oak, hickory, elm and walnut. King recognized the value of the timber as an immediate cash asset and its potential for making pearl ash and potash.

Eager to act quickly, King and his committee drew up a plan.[48] This was approved by the Synod, and all stock required to finance the new settlement was sold in just two months. King was appointed managing director of the new Elgin Association, and an advisory committee from Chatham was chosen under the chairmanship of Archibald McKellar. Meanwhile, opposition led by Edwin Larwill, an English-born Tory, was growing in Chatham. Larwill had come to the town in 1841 and opened a tinsmith's shop on King Street. Since then he had become a Raleigh Township Councillor, a member of the Western District Council, editor of the Chatham *Journal*, a Member of the Legislature and the school commissioner for the district.

Woods near Chatham about 1840.

Larwill was inexorably opposed to Black settlement anywhere near Chatham. Enraged at King's planned community, he organized a campaign of letters, protest meetings, petitions and deputations to halt the project. He argued that Blacks were inferior, that nearby property would be devalued and that many established, respectable settlers would leave the area if Blacks were admitted. Convinced that he had public support, Larwill arranged a public meeting in Chatham to debate the proposed settlement. The sheriff of Kent County authorized the meeting, but warned King that his life was in danger, for Larwill was organizing a vigilante committee backed by most of Chatham's citizens.

The public meeting was held on August 18, 1849 at the Royal Exchange Hotel. Over 300 people gathered, including a group of Blacks whose presence assured King's support and safety. Archibald McKellar was the only local white person to stand on the balcony of the Royal Hotel with King and face the unruly crowd. When King started to speak, he was booed and hissed, but he refused to be intimidated:

> I have come two hundred miles to attend this meeting, and you cannot put me down. Besides, I am from Londonderry and Londonderry never did surrender.[49]

The threatened violence did not break out, but only a few of his audience supported King's defence of his proposed settlement. Larwill's fears of Blacks and his argument that they should settle in "... any other place" but Chatham prevailed.

Soon after the public debate King called a meeting in Chatham's Presbyterian Church to answer arguments against Black settlers. He was the only speaker: no one argued with him, and no questions were asked. The crowd that filled the church remained silent and sullen. After the meeting, as King walked along the dark streets to his hotel, 12 armed Black men quietly formed a guard about him to make sure that he would get there safely.

In October Larwill and his supporters persuaded the Western District Council to send another protest to Parliament. Without the Council's knowledge Larwill added several recommendations of his own: that Blacks should be barred from public schools and public office; that they should pay a poll tax; that the whole question of allowing them to vote should be examined; that they should be required to post bonds if they wished to stay in Canada. Taking this independent action hurt Larwill, for many of his supporters concluded that he was an extremist and gradually withdrew from his campaign.

All the protests and clamour were useless. William King moved into the Elgin Settlement with the first settlers, his 15 former slaves, on November 28, 1849. These people were King's strongest allies in the settlement's early days and they set a continuing example

The Royal Exchange Hotel and King Street West, Chatham, 1860.

to later arrivals of self-discipline, hard work and devotion to the principles on which Elgin was founded. Two distinct groups handled Elgin's administration. The Elgin Association attended to secular business. It was a company, later incorporated by the province, with a constitution and by-laws which its stockholders adopted on June 8, 1850. It had a highly prestigious board of 24 directors who ran Elgin's financial and social affairs, raised capital to buy land, made regulations relating to the property and the building of homes, and looked after the group's legal affairs. The Buxton Mission supported by the Presbyterian Church supervised the community's chapel, schools and Christian work. In order to support these services a Buxton Mission Fund was set up, and a collection for it was taken every year in all Canadian Presbyterian churches. The Elgin Association and the Buxton Mission worked well together throughout the life of the settlement.

When the first settlers arrived, the land had already been surveyed and divided into 20-hectare lots served by seven concession roads. Each family head was to pay approximately $4.50 per hectare in 12 annual instalments in order to receive a deed and clear title to the land. King was determined that Blacks should own their property and pass it down to their heirs or sell it to other Blacks. His first concern was to protect Elgin's settlers and the work they had invested in their holdings. He reasoned also that Blacks who owned their property over a period of years would eventually gain the political power they needed to protect their interests. To bring this about he had a clause written into the deeds so that settlers could not transfer their land to a white person for ten years, and the land could not be rented or sharecropped until it was fully paid for. Elgin's history proved King right, and later he was able to point out that the restrictions had kept the settlers together and given them a measure of voter-strength.

King recalled that the settlers found it quite easy to buy their land:

> When a fugitive came to me who had not a cent, I said to him, "You can go to work, and earn twelve dollars and a half, and pay the first instalment on your land, and have ten years in which to pay the rest." They were all able to pay the first instalment, for the railroads were being built at that time, and they could readily get work. I taught them never to ask for a cent, if they could earn it themselves. You would hardly ever see one of them begging, and we have endeavored to cultivate that principle throughout the whole.[50]

Each settler was required to begin work at once on a log house built to the Association's minimum specifications: the house must measure at least eight by six metres and be four metres high. All houses had to be set back eight metres from the road, with a picket fence in front. King's home lay at the heart of the settlement where Centre Road and Middle Road met. King owned 40 ha and his commodious, low-built, log house was larger than most. He and his second wife, whom he married in 1853, employed four of his former slaves as house-servants. King's somewhat easier circumstances provoked some criticism, but he was so deeply loved and respected that his work was not damaged. In fact, King gave his whole life-savings and property to support and develop the settlement.

The first settlers faced no easy task. In the middle of the winter of 1849-50 they had to build homes, cut down and burn trees, clear brush and open roads. Because the land was level, they had to dig drainage before they could sow a crop. King had gained first-hand knowledge of like problems when his family had homesteaded in Ohio. He and his original 15 settlers taught newcomers all the skills they needed, but handed out no supplies of money, food or clothing. This policy taught the new settlers pride in their own work, self-reliance and the independence needed for success. All the newcomers were encouraged to plant vegetables and flowers as soon as the weather permitted. Since the soil was the most fertile in Kent County and the climate was relatively mild, the settlers soon produced fine vegetables, fruits and crops, including wheat, hemp and tobacco.

The settlers' self-reliance grew more easily because they could earn the annual payments on their land by a few months' work for the railroad close by. King warned them, however, not to depend too much on railroad money, for they would earn more in the long

Plan of the Elgin Settlement.

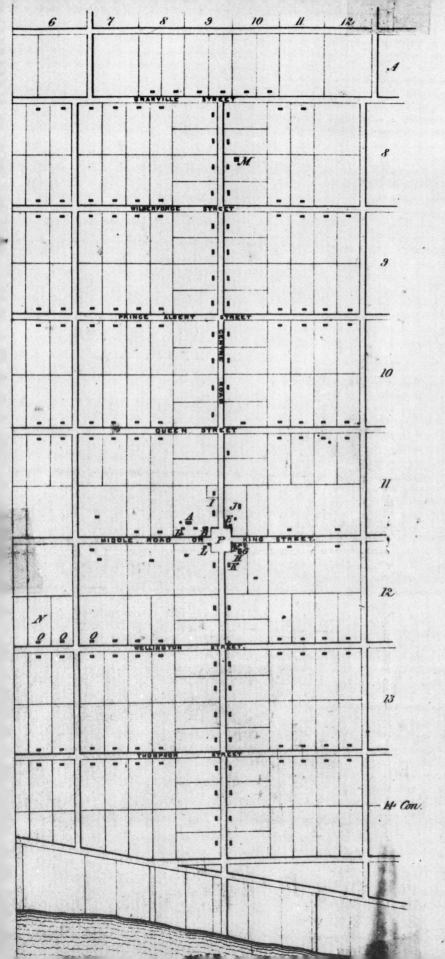

Note.

The Elgin Association was incorporated by Act of Parliament 10th August, 1850, for the social and moral improvement of the Colored Population of Canada.

The settlement is nearly 6 Miles long and 3 Miles wide containing about 200 Families embracing about 1000 Souls.

The land is divided into Farms of 50 acres each, and the Houses built along the Concessions after a model 18 feet by 24 — 12 feet high, and set 33 feet from the Road enclosed in front with a picket fence.

For further information see Annual Report of the Elgin Association.

PLAN
OF THE
ELGIN SETTLEMENT
IN THE
TOWNSHIP OF RALEIGH,
COUNTY OF KENT,
CANADA WEST.

ELGIN SETTLEMENT in the Township of Raleigh, County of Kent, Canada West, founded by the Revd. WILLIAM KING, the Clayton of Mrs Stowe's "DRED." (See Chapter 56

References.

A. Revd W. King's House.	I. Brick Yard.
B. Mission Church.	J. Steam Saw and Grist Mill.
C. Buxton Post Office.	K. Carpenter's Shop.
D. Mission School.	L. Shoe Shop.
E. Store.	M. District School.
F. A two story brick Hotel.	N. Lots of 50 Acres each.
G. Blacksmith Shop.	O. Houses on Lots.
H. Pearlash Factory.	P. Buxton Square.

Isaac Riley, his wife and their four children were Elgin's first settlers. After escaping from slavery in Missouri, they lived in St. Catharines for a few months. There Isaac, who could read, saw a copy of King's prospectus and learned that the Elgin Settlement would have a church and school. He walked 480 km to the district land office at Sandwich and asked for a location ticket for the 40 ha nearest the proposed school. When King returned to Elgin with his 15 free Blacks, the Rileys were waiting in his barn. Isaac soon became a leader in the settlement.

(Right) *A clearing near Chatham in the 1840s.*

run by developing their land. A community spirit grew strong, and morale was high as the settlers went about their work:

> One by one those that escaped slavery came dropping in and we were all as busy as bees, chopping, burning, boiling (black ash), singing and talking. Taking dinner in the bush one day, I remember we were one plate short and I can hear King's cheery voice yet as he shouted, "Bring me a chip, Jacob, I can eat off a chip." Those were days of hardship but they were happy days, and we were frolicsome as kittens.[51]

In 1850 a post office and a church/school building were put up at the centre of the settlement, close to

gave the pupils a classical education. In time Blacks and whites from Ontario and the U.S.A. competed for places in the Buxton school.

The young settlement continued to grow. By 1853 it had attracted 130 families numbering 320 persons; 200 ha had been cleared, and about 68 ha partly cleared; about 160 ha were still being developed. The settlers owned 128 head of cattle, 15 horses, 30 sheep and 250 hogs. The settlement's timber was said to be worth $125 000. But the community still needed a sawmill, a gristmill, a brickyard and a good country store.

Two enterprising ex-slaves who had learned brick-making in the U.S.A. borrowed money from King to open a brickyard. Within a year they had turned out 300 000 bricks, which were in high demand, for there were very few kilns in Essex and Kent Counties. In a few months they had fully repaid King's loan.

Two successful businessmen who sent their children to the Buxton school, W.R. Abbott of Toronto and Henry Thomas of Buffalo, used their considerable influence to promote businesses at Elgin. In a short time they raised $3000 and were able, in March, 1852, to form the Canada Mill and Mercantile Company. Its board of directors was Black, except for William King and George Brown, publisher of the *Globe*. By 1854 the new company was operating two mills and a country store at Elgin. In order to make good use of the abundant timber, King brought a friend from Ohio to teach the settlers how to produce pearl ash and potash, which were in great demand for fertilizer and industrial use in the district.

As businesses quickly developed, the problem of transporting goods to a port on Lake Erie remained. Although Centre Road had been opened through the settlement and pushed 15 km to the lake, heavy rains sometimes made it a totally impassable quagmire. The difficulty was solved by building a railway line with wooden rails from Elgin timber sawn in the settlement's mill. The line was completed within a month, and a team of oxen was bought to draw large loads in heavy wagons which rolled along the greased rails. The sawmill, brickyard, gristmill and pearl-ash factory could now send their products fairly easily to ready markets in Buffalo and Detroit. Barrel-staves were another of the settlement's fast selling products, for

King's home. Since both labour and timber were plentiful, the church/school, which measured eight by ten metres and could seat 200 people, cost only $400; this money King himself gave. A service was held there every Sunday and a prayer-meeting every Thursday evening.

King opened the Mission school in April, 1850 to all children and adults at Elgin and in nearby communities. On opening day 14 Black children and two whites enrolled: Mr. and Mrs. Joshua Shepley, who lived close by, had decided that the Buxton Mission School would be better than the district common school and sent their two children. Several excellently trained young teachers from Knox Presbyterian College in Toronto

King's house in North Buxton.

pickled pork was shipped down the Ohio River in barrels. The settlers got good prices, too, for their crops of wheat, corn, oats, tobacco and timber. Small secondary businesses, including a blacksmith's shop, a cobbler's shop and a carpenter's shop, were set up to serve Elgin's growing needs.

During the 1850s the settlers' homes began to show their prosperity:

> The puncheon floors of the early settlers now gave place to fine, planed oak floors and the primitive mud chimneys of the log cabins were replaced with brick, and some of the log cabins themselves gave place to frame buildings, and one settler named West erected a fine, two-storey brick temperance hotel, the first brick building erected in the settlement.[52]

An American journalist writing a story on Elgin noted:

> In [one] house, besides the ordinary bed and bedding, chairs, tables, etc. we found a rocking chair and a large new sofa — a recent importation from Yankee land. On asking for a glass of water, it was brought in a clean tumbler and upon a plate.[53]

King was a staunch Presbyterian, but understanding that many of the settlers wished to continue in the churches of their slave background, he helped the African Methodist Episcopal and Baptist groups to organize congregations at Elgin. The First Baptist Church of Buxton was founded in 1853 by George Hatton, Alfred West, William H. Jackson and Isaac Washington; by 1856 it had 56 members. Thomas Stringer was the chief organizer of the AMEs, and the spirit of community co-operation was so strong that when the group was ready to build a church, the Presbyterians and Baptists turned out to help. The AMEs, who had started with 30 members, had a congregation of 299 by the 1860s.

The Elgin settlers valued education highly, and it was soon widely acknowledged that the Buxton Mission School was a great deal better than the nearby district (government) schools. By 1854 half Buxton's students were white, and, according to a leading educator in the area, "The black school [was] becoming the fashionable academy of that region." A second school was built about 1855, and a third two years later. The Elgin children often taught their parents who had no time to attend school during the day, but many adults were so eager to learn that they walked through the forest in the dark to evening classes. King wrote:

> All the ones who could not read seemed anxious to learn and applied themselves with diligence, although they found it a hard task to master the elements of the English tongue. But, by diligence and perseverance, they soon began to make progress and by the end of six months quite a number of them could read a little, and by the end of the first year many who did not know the letters when they came to me were able to read slowly large print in the Testament.[54]

In 1857 King reported that over 250 pupils had attended Mission schools. Some students went on to teach in the U.S.A. and Australia, and others in nearby communities. King disagreed with the common notion that all Blacks should be trained to do manual work in a society that would not accept them as professionals, no matter what their education. Experience at Buxton proved him right. To the amazement of some visitors, 10-year-old children could recite the Catechism from memory. Isaac Riley, one of the first Elgin settlers, had a son who could recite in flawless Latin long passages from Vergil's *Aeneid*. By 1856 King had a group of students so well grounded in Greek and Latin that they were ready to enter Knox College in Toronto. This astounding achievement by people so lately slaves brought applications pouring in from Canada and the States, and the Buxton schools could not find places for all the applicants. The Presbyterian Church could no longer wholly finance Buxton Mission's church and schools, and King decided to take his own savings, mortgage his land and travel in England, the U.S.A. [55] and Canada West to find new support for their work.

As Elgin grew and thrived, its settlers gradually overcame the prejudice and opposition of their white neighbours. By the mid-1850s Elgin's people had cleared and cultivated over 480 ha on which they grew a variety of crops to market throughout the southwest of the province. They owned more than 200 head of cattle, 80 oxen, 300 hogs, 52 horses, sheep and other livestock. The industries they had established were thriving and were useful to nearby white communities, as well as to themselves. The final proof of the settlers' independence and good business sense was the Buxton

Savings Bank which accepted for deposit "... sums of ten cents and upwards ..." and which consolidated the settlement's many investments and kept the settlers' money in their own community.

Chatham whites were now ready to acknowledge Elgin's achievements and to celebrate its success with their Black neighbours. On September 14, 1856 nearly 1000 settlers entertained an equal number of Chatham people, most of them white, on the lawn of St. Andrew's Presbyterian Church. The guests sat together in a huge pavilion made from lumber dressed in Elgin's sawmill. Flowers from Elgin's gardens decorated the tables, and rope made at Elgin supported the climbing plants that decorated the outside of the church. Guests and hosts

... dined on venison and wild turkey, both hunted in Buxton's own forests. They also had a choice of beef, mutton and pork from Buxton's own herds and drank milk from Buxton's two hundred milk cows. They ate bread baked from flour ground in Buxton's own gristmill out of wheat raised on the one thousand acres [400 ha] of land cleared and under cultivation only seven years

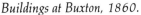

Buildings at Buxton, 1860.

SCHOOL HOUSE   REV. Mr KING'S HOUSE   POST OFFICE   CHURCH

St. Andrew's Presbyterian Church at Buxton. [16]

after the first Negroes arrived. The vegetables came from approximately two hundred front-yard gardens of two hundred homes in Buxton.[56]

Dr. Willis and Dr. Reid of the Presbyterian Synod made after-dinner speeches. Guests from England were introduced. But the greatest applause was for Archie McKellar, the Chatham lawyer who had supported the settlement in the face of almost unanimous local opposition.

Later that same year local Blacks showed that they had come of age politically, as well as economically. Their toughest opponent, Larwill, was now a Member of Parliament, for he had defeated McKellar for the Kent County seat in 1854. As property owners, the Elgin settlers were entitled to vote and they organized effectively for the fall election of 1856. On election day Blacks gathered from all over Kent County; they marched in a body to the Court House and cast their votes. One small triumph they enjoyed was that every Black voter was able to sign his name in the register,

although many white voters could only 'make their mark'. Larwill was trounced, and the settlers' hero Archibald McKellar became Kent County's Member of Parliament. Larwill's defeat ended his political career, and King recorded: "From that time forward all opposition to me and the coloured people ceased."[57]

Elgin had reached its zenith, and its decline was soon to follow, but not before it had produced some distinguished citizens for Canada West and the U.S.A.: Anderson Ruffin Abbott, the first Canadian-born Black doctor; James T. Rapier, an American Congressman who worked for a bill to improve public education in the South and for the Civil Rights Act passed in 1875; Harry Thomas, whose extensive knowledge of herbal medicine was widely used in Kent County; William Parker, a former slave who became a Raleigh Township Councillor; many members of the famous Shadd family, who became doctors, teachers and public servants; Charles Watt, a Justice of the Peace in Raleigh Township; John Richard Travis, who hewed railway ties for the Canadian Southern Railway and made axe-handles sold by merchants in Chatham and the surrounding towns.

The outbreak of the American Civil War brought changes to Elgin. Forty of its men enlisted at once in the First Colored Regiment based in Detroit. Among these was Abraham W. Shadd, who became one of the very few Black commissioned officers in the Union Army. Just before the War began, $6000 had been raised to build another church and more schools in Elgin, but with Lincoln's Emancipation Proclamation and the end of the War, some of the settlement's Black families started the long trek back to the American South. There was no need to enlarge Elgin's facilities. The Buxton schools, which in 15 short years had offered excellent education to more than 700 children and many adults, soon merged with the local common schools. Half of the $6000 building-fund was used to build a Presbyterian church and manse; the other half went for an annuity for William King in his retirement.

Although the tremendous enthusiasm of the 1850s waned, Buxton continued to operate on a reduced scale through the 1860s. Samuel Gridley Howe, commissioned to study the life of Canadian Blacks for the American Freedmen's Bureau, reported in 1864:

Archibald McKellar about 1880.

Buxton is certainly a very interesting place. Sixteen years ago, it was a wilderness ... There are signs of industry and thrift and comfort everywhere; of idleness, of want, nowhere. There is no tavern and no groggery, but there is a chapel and a schoolhouse. Most interesting of all are the inhabitants. Twenty years ago, most of them were slaves who owned nothing, not even their children. Now they own themselves; they own their houses and their farms; and they have their wives and children about them. They are enfranchised citizens of a government which protects their rights. The present condition of all these colonists, as compared with their former one, is remarkable.[58]

King told the Howe Commission that prejudice in the Chatham area began to disappear when the Elgin settlers were able to cast over 200 votes for M.P.s and more for township councillors, and to elect their own school trustees and path-masters. King claimed that Elgin's people were temperate, serious and hardworking. Liquor was not sold in the settlement, and when a tavern was opened just outside its bounds, it closed within a year for lack of customers. Contrary to popular notion, the Black settlers suffered no more from the cold Canadian winters than did whites, and the general health of Elgin's people had been excellent. Their moral standards were high, and there had been almost no crime at Elgin from 1849 to 1864.

Abraham W. Shadd served in the 24th Kent Militia. He joined the Union Army at Detroit in August, 1863. Later he became captain's aide and chief clerk to Major Martin R. Delany of the 104th U.S. Colored Troops.

In 1873 the Board of Directors of the Elgin Association, satisfied that it had fulfilled its purpose, disbanded. The Association left no debts: all land had been properly sold and deeded, and all stockholders paid off.[59] All fees, salaries, and other expenditures, to a total of $24 365.29, had been paid and accounted for. With its final report to the Province of Ontario the Board submitted a notarized statement of these figures.

King was pensioned off, but he continued as the settlement's minister until 1880. He had served Elgin without fee for 25 years and had contributed to its improvement over $15 000 of his own savings. In recognition of his services the Presbyterian Church elected him Moderator for one year. In his final years King moved to Chatham, where hundreds of his friends and former students visited him. He died there of malaria on January 5, 1895 and was buried in Maple Leaf Cemetery.

King successfully established Canada's only self-supporting all-Black community. At a time when most people doubted the natural abilities of slaves or freed

The Reverend William King about 1870.

Casting their first votes.

The children of School Section #13 Raleigh, North Buxton, with their teacher, George Cromwell, about 1910.

persons, Elgin proved that Blacks could develop and progress enormously. Some still argue that Elgin did not prepare Blacks to take a full and equal place in Canadian communities. On the other hand, Anderson R. Abbott wrote in 1894:

> A large number of white settlers now occupy the land, but that makes no difference. The two classes work together on each other's farms, go to the same churches, their children attend the same schools, the teachers are white and coloured, and the pupils fraternize without any friction whatever. The teacher of the North Buxton School, Alfred Shadd, is an Afro-Canadian. He holds a second-class certificate from the normal school, Toronto, and has been a successful teacher for a number of years. One third of his pupils are white. There are three hundred pupils in the schools. The various offices of the municipality, such as councillors, school trustees, path masters, constables and justices of the peace are fairly distributed among both classes. The coloured farmers who now occupy the land are of the best class. Very few of them had any means at first; their only resources were their courage and determination to succeed ... When they appear in the Chatham market side by side with their white neighbors, as vendors, there is nothing to distinguish but their colour.[60]

Whatever else may be said, it is a fact that by educating hundreds of Blacks and by developing among them a group of leaders, Elgin lit a strong beacon of hope during a critical time in the history of a people struggling from slavery to freedom.

6
Justice and Injustice

Blacks and the Law

CRIMINAL AND CIVIL law of the 18th and early 19th centuries exacted penalties that seem dreadfully harsh by the standards of Canadian society today. Where such penalties fell on Blacks, and particularly on Black slaves, it is easy to wonder if racial discrimination was to blame. In fact, there is little evidence that white dependents in like situations could have hoped for more humane treatment from the courts. Yet there are some tragic records of Canada's early Blacks and the law.

In the spring of 1734, for example, Angélique, a Black slave of François Poulin of Montréal, was told that she was to be sold. In her fear and resentment she set fire to her master's house. The house and other nearby property were destroyed, and Angélique was arrested, convicted of arson and sentenced to hang. A rope was tied around her neck, signs bearing the word 'Incendiary' were fastened on her back and chest, and she was driven through the streets in a scavenger's cart. Worse was to come: she was tortured until she confessed her crime before a priest; then her hand was cut off and she was hanged in public.

In 1775 Judge William Dummer Powell, who later became Chief Justice of Upper Canada, sentenced "... a black boy, slave to Mrs. Benton, widow of the Late Commodore of the Lakes ..." to be hanged at Kingston. Because he was only 15 years old and had been brought up in slavery, the Judge recommended a pardon and expressed the hope that he "... would not be the first capital example."

In fact, Joseph Cutten, one of John Askin's many Black slaves, was the first person to die on the gallows in Upper Canada. All his short life Cutten had been bought and sold like a piece of property. On February 18, 1785, when he was about 22 years old, he was sold by Elija Cooper, a Boston farmer and shoemaker, to John Turner of Montréal for a gray horse and £32.10.0

A street in old Montréal.

in Québec currency, worth about $130 in Canadian funds of the day. Little more than a month later Turner sold Cutten for £50 to David Rankin, a Montréal merchant. Somehow, on January 13, 1787, Cutten arrived in Detroit where the firm of William St. Clair and Company, merchants, sold him to Thomas Duggan for £120 in New York currency, payable in Indian corn and flour. Duggan sold Cutten to Askin on March 28, 1791 for "... a farm on the River Tranch[1] of Nine acres [7.4 ha] in front, more or less." Arthur McCormick, a teacher who had come to Detroit from Kingston, became Cutten's half-owner.

On October 18, 1791 Joseph Campeau accused Cutten of stealing rum and furs and brought him before his part-owner, John Askin, who was a Justice of the Peace. Two months after Askin committed Cutten to trial, on December 26, 1791, the Province of Upper Canada was born. The village of L'Assomption (later Sandwich) became the official seat of its Western District, which included Detroit and therefore the unfortunate Joseph Cutten. On May 16, 1792 Askin bought out McCormick's interest in Cutten for £50. The receipt McCormick gave acknowledged "... full consideration for all my right title & interest to a negro man Named Joseph Cotton now in Prison for Felony ... which Negro man should he Suffer Death ... I am not Answerable for."[2]

On September 3, 1792 Cutten was tried and found guilty by Judge Powell, who owned slaves himself. In his summation the Judge told the convicted man:

> This crime is so much more atrocious and alarming to society, as it ... cannot be guarded against without the same precautions which are used against the wild beasts of the forest, who, like you, go prowling about at night for their prey. A member so hurtful to the peace of society, no good Laws will permit to continue in it, and the Court in obedience to the Law has the painful duty imposed upon it of pronouncing its sentence, which is that you be taken from hence to the Gaol from whence you came, and from thence to the place of execution, where you are to be hanged by the neck until you are dead.[3]

The stern sentence was carried out that same month. Joseph Cutten's unhappy life was cut off before he

The Honourable William Dummer Powell, Chief Justice of Upper Canada 1816-1825.

was 30 at the end of a rope. The young province paid the hangman £2.0.0—about $8.00—to perform his duty.

Jack York, another Black convicted by Judge Powell at Sandwich in 1800, took his fate into his own hands. York, convicted of breaking into a house and raping a woman, was sentenced to death, but Judge Powell delayed the execution to learn the pleasure of

Lieutenant-Governor General Peter Hunter. When word came that the sentence must be carried out, York broke out of jail and disappeared.

The death sentence was carried out on the slave Ann Wyley who "... was hanged for stealing six guineas from the firm of Abbott and Finchley and buried face downward."

On March 1, 1811 Secretary Jarvis[4]

John Beverley Robinson, Attorney General of Upper Canada.

... informed the Court that a negro boy and girl, his slaves, had the evening before been committed to prison for having stolen gold and silver out of his desk ... and escaped from their said master.[5]

They had done this with the help of a free Black named 'Coachly' who was also in jail. The Court

... Ordered, — That the said negro boy named Henry, commonly called Prince, be re-committed to prison ... and that the girl do return to her said master, and Coachly be discharged.[6]

In spite of this sorry record, Canadian law soon came to the defence of thousands of Black refugees. Upper Canada's Attorney General, John Beverley Robinson, stated in 1819:

Since freedom of the person [is] the most important civil right protected by the law of England...the negroes [are] entitled to personal freedom through residence in [Canada] and any attempt to infringe their rights [will] be resisted in the courts.[7]

In April, 1826 a law like the Black Code of Ohio was passed in the Detroit Territory. It required every free Black to register with the county clerk and to post a $500 bond to guarantee 'good behaviour'. Any Black who did not comply would be forced to leave the Territory. Sixty-six Blacks living in Detroit registered, but there were probably others who did not, for by this time the pendulum of social approval was swinging against slavery, and the new law was not strictly enforced. Fugitives continued to flee to Detroit and to cross over from there to Canada if their status was too closely questioned.

The American Secretary of State, Henry Clay, who was a slave-owner, resented the readiness of Upper Canada to accept escaped slaves. He declared this policy a growing evil and several times asked Britain to order fugitive slaves returned, but with little success. British courts upheld the principle that "... every man is free who reaches British ground," and always rejected American appeals to extradite refugees. In 1827 England agreed to pay indemnities for American property, including slaves, taken during the War of 1812, but refused to return the slaves themselves. Upper Canadian courts usually took the same stand and treated refugee slaves justly and fairly. The support of the courts raised the morale of the newcomers enormously and assured them that life was far safer for them in Canada than in the U.S.A.

Canadians often rallied to the aid of refugees who were threatened with return to their former masters. In 1837, for example, Solomon Moseby, a fugitive from Kentucky, was accused by his former master of stealing a horse. Moseby was found in Newark and arrested, but hundreds of Blacks attacked the jail and freed him. Two men were killed during the attack, and most of the attackers were arrested and jailed; they were set free later on condition that they join the Militia. Moseby himself fled to Montréal and later to England. The incident was widely reported, and Moseby's name became a household word. A plaque at Niagara-on-the-Lake now marks the spot where the people of Niagara rescued him:

Here stood the Court House and Gaol of the Niagara

The court house and jail at Niagara, Canada West.

District. Erected in 1817, they were considered to be among the finest public buildings in the Province ... In 1837, an escaped American slave, Moseby, threatened with return to his master was forcibly rescued here by local negroes abetted by other residents of Niagara ...

In the same year Paola Brown, a leader of Hamilton's Black community, led a protest against the arrest and imprisonment of Jesse Happy, a refugee from Kentucky who was accused of stealing his master's horse to escape North four years earlier. An American visiting Hamilton recognized Happy and reported him to the town's authorities, who at once had him arrested. Happy denied the charge of theft. He claimed that he had borrowed the horse, ridden it only a short distance north and then sent a message to his master, telling him exactly where he could recover the animal; he had made the rest of the journey to Canada on foot.

Feelings in the district ran high, for many people believed that a charge had been trumped up in order to have Happy returned to his former master. A petition was sent to Lieutenant-Governor Sir Francis Bond Head to ask for Happy's release. Bond Head's Executive Council met and decided that since the case was complex and might affect Upper Canada's relations with the U.S.A., it should be referred to Her Majesty's government in London, England. Sir Francis therefore asked the advice of Lord Glenelg, British Secretary of State for the Colonies; but in October, 1837, before a reply came from England, the Council decided to reject the application for Happy's extradition because of insufficient evidence. Happy was set free on the ground that to send him back to Kentucky would automatically return him to slavery, a condition that British law considered illegal. In February, 1838 the British Secretary of State, speaking for the British Law Office, confirmed the Council's action: Happy had simply made "... an unauthorized use of a Horse, without any Intention of appropriating it."[8] For Happy, who had gained his freedom five months earlier, the decision was no longer crucial, but it set a most important precedent for other fugitives in Canada.

The outcome was different for Nelson Hackett, a Black refugee from Arkansas, where he was accused of theft and rape. When he was discovered in Chatham, he had a fine horse, saddle and watch, which his former master claimed he had stolen. Hackett was arrested, charged and held in the Chatham jail pending trial. After 15 Black soldiers armed with bayonets tried unsuccessfully to free him, he was moved to the jail in Sandwich and later extradited to Arkansas by order of the Lieutenant-Governor and Council of Upper Canada. When Hackett arrived in Arkansas, he was not tried, but promptly handed over to his master. The case drew wide attention in Canada and the U.S.A., for many Canadians believed that false charges had been laid in order to create an example that would frighten other slaves from running away. The matter was later raised in the British House of Commons. The House declared that, although the events were regrettable, the government of Upper Canada had acted within the law.

By the 1850s Canadian law and public opinion generally supported Black refugees. In 1852 a group of Windsor Blacks resolved at a public meeting:

> That we have reason to thank God for the impartial character and administration of the laws of this our adopted country, and for the easy conditions offered us in common with other settlers, to appropriate the soil to our comfort and support.[9]

While there could still be injustices, they were generally opposed. In 1856, for example, Archie Lanton, an escaped slave, was caught in Windsor and accused of stealing two horses from his former master. Two local magistrates, Adolphus Woodbridge Sr. and a man named 'Wilkinson', allowed Lanton to be left in the care of several American slave-catchers. Naturally the latter promptly whisked Lanton across the border into the U.S.A. As a result, the Attorney General dismissed the two magistrates.

Occasionally an incident that brought a Black to the notice of the law was amusing. A Collingwood newspaper of 1857, for instance, reported that a Black citizen had defied the town constable:

> I saw a little western life that morning, for the town constable arrested a big colored man called Wesley Collings; he got him as far as the Montgomery Hotel, but he refused to go further, until he had had a drink. The

Father Thomas Henry Miller, a lay preacher, served the Black communities of Collingwood and Owen Sound.

three other men were beating Anderson to prevent his escape, Anderson stabbed Diggs and fled; he had gone first to Chatham and later settled in Brantford. Anderson was arrested and brought to Toronto to be tried before Chief Justice Robinson and the Court of Queen's Bench. In a packed courtroom with a crowd waiting outside, the Court decided for Anderson's extradition. Only Mr. Justice Richards dissented, arguing that Anderson's master had kept him working without reward for most of his life and then tried to have him killed when he wished to escape; Anderson was justified in making a bid for freedom, even at the cost of life and "... in doing so he exhibited a heroism of which we all might feel proud."

Toronto's Black community was keenly aware of the verdict's injustice. The Toronto Anti-Slavery Society and the *Globe* attacked the Court's judgement and invited the public's support. Thomas D'Arcy McGee, later a Father of Confederation, spoke out on Anderson's behalf. On February 16,1861 Anderson's counsel, Samuel B. Freedman, lodged an appeal before the British court of Common Pleas, where it was found that there was a flaw in the original charge: Anderson, the court ruled, should have been charged with manslaughter since, under British law, a slave could not be accused of a crime if the act was a necessary part of escape. This judgement set Anderson free.

Racism

While Blacks were steadily, if slowly, gaining equality before Canadian courts, they had to wage a harder and less successful battle against the prejudice of some Canadian citizens. The roots of racial prejudice in Upper Canada were older than the province itself: they could be traced to the early acceptance of slavery along the St. Lawrence River and Lower Great Lakes. Although Lieutenant-Governor Simcoe's legislation of 1793 changed the legal status of the 600 or so slaves then in Upper Canada, the legacy of slavery remained. For many years that legacy affected the economic and social position of Blacks. No repressive laws were passed in Upper Canada to 'keep Blacks in their place',

constable pulled out a revolver, and threatened to shoot if he went in. He went in all the same, and he had his drink, and the constable did not shoot. When he got him to the lock up, Daddy Miller [a local Black preacher] lectured him on his duties as a citizen and Collins danced a jig on the platform before they locked him in.[10]

In 1860 a Black man became angry with a fellow refugee who was living in Brantford under the name of 'John Anderson'. The former man reported to the authorities that 'Anderson' was really Jack Benton who had killed Seneca T.P. Diggs, a friend of his Missouri master, seven years before. When Diggs and

for in most districts they were a small and insignificant minority. But they were a visible minority with a traditionally low status, and many Canadians considered them inferior and useful only for menial work. Thus Blacks were an obvious target for discrimination throughout the 19th century.

North of the town of York, about the beginning of that century, Robert Franklin, a free Black, settled on a farm. Franklin had been a slave of Peter Russell, Receiver General of Upper Canada and one of its most powerful men. When Franklin applied to buy land on Yonge Street, he was refused. This refusal may have been one of the first acts of racial discrimination in York Township. In the years that followed, there were others. Settlers who thought Blacks inferior were sometimes tolerantly patronizing, sometimes actively hostile. Mary O'Brien, for example, described her household's relations with the Blacks of Oro in a tone that was good-natured, but unmistakably patronizing.

> Shanty Bay, May 16th, 1832.
> The three black men we employed before have returned raising our black establishment to six. You would suppose we were slave holders when you got upon our place—It is chiefly due to our popularity amongst our sable neighbors or perhaps our absence of prejudice against them that we have been able to do nearly as much in the six weeks that we have been here as the others have done since the winter set in.[11]

Again, of her nearest neighbour, Mary O'Brien wrote:

> On the way [to Capt. Oliver's] we called on our black neighbour, the most cheerful chattering body in the township ... we have sent some [bear meat] as a dainty present to our black neighbour Mrs. Jackson who is delighted ...[12]

The O'Brien home at Shanty Bay.

These remarks are fairly typical of the attitude of many well-intentioned white Canadians of the 19th century, for few treated Black neighbours as equals, even though they may have been civil or even sympathetic to them.

In fact, not all white Canadians showed even such limited good nature. One newly-arrived immigrant, for example, wrote to his sister in England:

> Here by the way, I may mention as illustration of the state of society, that every one is called, it matters not in what position or occupation they stand, as Mr. or Mrs., or this Gentlemen, or that Lady, even the Niggers ...[13]

Even established Canadian families and professional people sometimes showed ignorant prejudices. For example, Dr. T. Mack of Chatham considered Blacks unfit for the harsh Canadian climate:

> The disease they suffer most from is pulmonary — more than general tubercular; and where there is not real tubercular affection of the lungs there are bronchitis and pulmonary affections. I have the idea ... that this climate will completely efface them.[14]

Some Canadians were positively hostile to Blacks. When community leaders were strongly prejudiced, their influence could have serious effects. The notorious Edwin Larwill of Chatham, for example, claimed in a petition opposing the Elgin Settlement:

> The Negro is a distinct species of the Human Family and, in the opinion of your Memoralists is far inferior to that of the European. Let each link in the great Scale of existence have its place. Amalgamation is as disgusting to the Eye, as it is immoral in its tendencies and all good men will discountenance it.[15]

In a later petition against Elgin he warned:

> Would not offices of trust Honor and Emolument, ultimately fall to their Share? Imagine our Legislative Halls Studded and, our principal Departments managed by, these Ebony Men. It would be impossible to keep them out of the Smaller elective offices. Black Councillors, School Trustees, Pathmasters, etc. The Genious [sic] of our Institutions would be destroyed.[16]

Although Larwill failed to block the Elgin Settlement, his strong personality and his ability to attract support may well have contributed a good deal to Chatham's notorious discrimination against Blacks. Indeed, while Larwill was lobbying to stop Elgin's establishment, George Bullock, the influential Warden of the Western District, wrote to the Legislative Assembly on behalf of the District Council:

> In the opinion of your petitioners such a settlement in any part of this District would be highly deleterious to the morals and social conditions of the present and future inhabitants of this District, as well as to the prosperity in every other respect.[17]

In other districts, too, white citizens often opposed Black settlement. For instance, complaints were made against the Wilberforce settlers to a Mr. Prior, land agent for the Canada Company. Prior passed them on to Lieutenant-Governor Sir John Colborne who, in turn, relayed them to the British Colonial Office. According to Prior's informants:

> ... the greater number were people of bad character, idle and dissolute; dissention [sic] soon crept in amongst them, a great many disallowed the authority of these agents, everything fell into confusion and the most respectable with Mr. Paul at their head expressed a strong desire to separate themselves from the rest and obtain land elsewhere ... The general bad conduct of the men of colour was such as to preclude all prospect of realizing the hopes of the commissioners and began to be felt as a serious obstacle to the sale of adjacent lands, unfortunately aiding the prejudice of the white people to settle in their neighbourhood.
>
> The commissioners, therefore, refused to sell them any more land, offered to take back the 800 acres [324 ha] and pay the full value of the improvements thereon on a liberal scale to enable them to follow their inclinations in some new place.[18]

White residents of Amherstburg made a similar charge in 1835, when they petitioned the magistrates of Upper Canada not to remove troops from Fort Malden. If the troops were withdrawn, they claimed, the whites of Amherstburg would be defenceless against "... the very numerous and troublesome Black populations ... who are almost daily violating the laws."[19]

Since most Black refugees were inexperienced in

A settler's house on the Thames River, 1842.

business matters and knew nothing of their rights in Canada, it was often all too easy for them to fall prey to greedy or unscrupulous neighbours. Some Blacks were forced off land they had cleared when they could not meet payments; others were pushed off homesteads by whites who claimed that the Blacks were mere squatters not legally entitled to their holdings. In Colchester Township, for example, one Black farmer told Benjamin Drew:

> The colored people have cleared up two-thirds of what has been cleared in this township. Those who came first, bought lands of individuals and lost them again: but when they began to buy of the government, they began to have good claims on the land.[20]

Again, in the turbulent young town of Brantford, some white settlers were determined to get rid of their Black neighbours and have them sent to the Queen's Bush. A local historian contended:

> The whites were English, Irish and Scotch chiefly, with quite a sprinkling of native Canadians, United Empire Loyalists and Americans. There was also a large inflow of escaped colored slaves from the United States, who fraternized with the Indians, and the village became a very turbulent and disorderly place. A meeting of all the whites was held, and an urgent request unanimously signed, addressed to the Government, requesting that the negroes be sent to the Queen's Bush, and settled upon the land. Good grounds for such action must have

been shown by the white settlers, for a large majority of the escaped slaves were received and settled in different parts of Western Canada. Shortly afterwards the Indians surrendered all their lands at Mohawk, and retired to their present location, and a considerable inflow of whites began to arrive and the village to prosper.[21]

George Sunter, a local Black, tired of claims that Blacks had brought no wealth into Canada, that they were an inferior race "intermediate between man and monkey" and would be better off if they were sent back into slavery in the U.S.A., came to his people's defence. In a letter to the *Brantford Expositor* he protested:

> Not because we are black but because you suppose us weak and ignorant, and because we are friendless and oppressed, *therefore* you meanly give us additional kicks. You deny us the opportunities of improvement, and then reproach us with our degradation. Your horror of amalgamation is a lying pretence; "niggers" may shave you, cook for you, serve your tables, dress your fair ladies, and be the bedfellows even of your "patriarch" brethren of the "States" so long as they will consent to be your slaves ... They would have to be negroes of the baser sort that would not be degraded by amalgamation with the like of you. You reproach us with our poverty; we bring no wealth to the province, forsooth! We bring what is better, a test of your morals, an occasion for the exercise of that *justice*, the meaning of which you have well nigh forgot, and for a reinstatement of those principles of *liberty* which you would betray and banish.[22]

Upper Canadian Blacks received harshest discrimination in the schools. In Hamilton, London, St. Catharines, Sandwich, Windsor and Chatham Black children were excluded from the common (public) schools or made to sit at the back of classrooms. The refugees — hard-working, tax-paying citizens — petitioned against this discrimination, but without success.[23] Most school districts continued the practice of segregated education, often without the support of the law. By 1832, for example, seven Black families were living in the growing village of Chatham, and although pupils of both races were supposed to attend the common school, the villagers' prejudice was so strong that Black parents kept their children at home. Indeed, the villagers tried to banish Israel and Juliana Williams and their

six children on the ground that they were troublesome. In reality, it may have been because the Williams, escaped slaves from Virginia, tried to send their children to school. They did not succeed because the teacher was afraid that to admit them would displease his employers. When Larwill later became School Commissioner in Kent County, he opposed admitting Black children to its common schools or giving them any chance for an education. Although he did not wholly succeed, he helped to set up a segregated school system that lasted for decades in the county.

In the Windsor area, too, local people kept Black children out of the common schools. When Black landowners and farmers in Sandwich, who could well afford to pay their taxes and any school fees, tried to send their children to the common school, they met determined opposition:

> The prejudice against the African race is here very strongly marked. It had not been customary to levy school taxes on the colored people. Some three or four years since, a trustee assessed a school tax on some of the wealthier citizens of that class. They sent their children at once into the public school. As these sat down, the white children near them deserted the benches: and in a day or two, the white children were wholly withdrawn, leaving the school-house to the teacher and his colored pupils. The matter was at last 'compromised': a notice — 'Select School' — was put up on the school-house: the white children were selected *in*, and the black were selected *out*.[24]

One Black settler, Mrs. Henry Brant, explained:

> One thing which makes it bad about getting our children into school here is, we are so near Detroit. The people would feel ashamed to have the Detroit people know that they sent the white into the same school with the colored. I have heard this from a white woman.[25]

Isaac Rice, a Presbyterian missionary working among refugees near Amherstburg confirmed:

> Local trustees would cut their children's heads off and

A school for Black children was held in the upper storey of the Sexton's House of St. Andrew's Presbyterian Church, Niagara.

throw them across the roadside ditch before they would let them go to school with niggers.[26]

But even in the most unpromising situations, Black parents did not give up the struggle for their children's education. When Black pupils were excluded from the common schools, they sometimes hired private teachers; more often abolitionist and Christian groups funded mission schools in areas of heavy Black settlement. The issue remained a sensitive one, and Black organizations and newspapers made bitter attacks from time to time on the common school system. But Black children needed educating, and their parents unwillingly settled for separate schools. The Common Schools Act of 1850 provided for separate common schools for Black children; its wording implied that the provision was made to satisfy the wishes of the Black community:

> ... and upon the application in writing of twelve or more heads of families resident in any city, town, or incorporated village, being coloured people, the council of such township or the board of school trustees of any such city, town, or incorporated village, shall authorize the establishment therein of one or more separate schools for coloured people, and in every case such council or board (as the case may be) shall prescribe the limits of the section or sections of such schools.[27]

This legislation, intended to protect the rights of Black parents and children, had the opposite effect. Although it was supposed to allow Blacks to have separate schools if they wished, it was interpreted by Dr. Egerton Ryerson, Superintendent of Education, to mean that trustees could establish segregated schools against the wishes of Black parents and require Black pupils to attend them. This meant that the prejudice that had closed the schools of Chatham to Black children in 1840 was sanctioned by Ryerson's interpretation of the legislation of 1850.

Later judicial decisions upheld the Common Schools Act of 1850. In 1857 Black parents petitioned the trustees of No. 6 School District of Malden Township to admit their children to the white common school. The trustees had provided separate schools for the children of the district's 48 white families and 23 Black families in 1856-57, but the school for Blacks had been

Dr. Egerton Ryerson

open for only three months, and the parents were naturally dissatisfied. In spite of the circumstances, the trustees were keenly antagonized by the Blacks' petition:

> ... Now [the Blacks] want to drop their school and send to our school. This the white people will not submit to they will take their children from the school and our teacher will not teach black children nor be bound to teach at all if the black children come. We want to keep them separate to themselves. They have numbers and means enough to keep up a school themselves if they would act right.[28]

In January, 1859 Clayborn Harris, a Windsor Black, wrote to the Windsor school board asking that his son be admitted to the common school. He claimed that the rented 'house' provided as the school for Black children was no more than a coop measuring about five by six metres, and was filled to capacity; nearby was a school for white children "… with comforts, not near filled up."[29] Harris hired a London lawyer, William Horton, to fight his case, but lost.

In the case of *Simmons vs Chatham*, heard in 1861, a court confirmed the total exclusion of Black pupils from the town's schools. These children were afterwards assigned to one of Chatham's two segregated schools, no matter how far they had to go to attend.

In spite of such discouragements, Black parents kept working through the 1850s and '60s for better schools for their children. In Hamilton, for instance, schools were officially integrated after Blacks petitioned government authorities in the 1840s. Even so, prejudice persisted, and in 1860 a non-denominational Christian school was built on Concession Street in the heart of Hamilton's 'Little Africa'; most of its pupils were Black, and "… the dark skinned children sat with the white ones conning over their lessons." Former slaves, eager for the education denied them in childhood, attended evening classes there, particularly in the winter. They "… labouriously traced out verses from the Bible in the hope of learning to read the Gospel's message." White Hamilton citizens made no objection to Black children's attending the Mission school, but continued to object to their attending the common schools. Isaac Buchanan, Hamilton's Member of Parliament for Canada West, who was a known supporter of Blacks, commented:

I think we see the effects of slavery here very plainly. The children of the colored people go to the public schools but a great many of the white parents object to it, though their children do not that I know of. I suppose

In a few Canadian schools Black and white children learned their lessons together.

James Hawkins farmed near Windsor.

I shall have to emigrate to the West Indies to educate my children, for, the other day, my two daughters were refused admission into the Female Academy because they are coloured.[31]

Even some churches discriminated against Blacks. As a result some Black groups formed their own congregations. In 1845, for example, the Amherstburg Regular Missionary Baptist Association (ARMBA) established itself after some disputes with white Baptist groups in Michigan and Canada West. This action was resented by the Long Point Baptist Association of Canada West, which resolved that:

> ... an Association lately formed in the Western District composed of African churches is not recognized as being "in fellowship".[32]

Elder Hawkins of the Amherstburg group responded angrily charging that "persons of colour" had been refused membership in some churches affiliated with the Long Point group. He flatly stated:

> We desire no fellowship with anti-christians, if we had, we would have stayed with them and covered up their inequities ... What, in the name of truth, do they baptize Blacks for if they are not Christians — to make a mockery of a divine institution?[33]

His rebuke evidently had some effect, for by 1853 the two groups were friendly.

The wardens of Colchester's Christ Church (Anglican) would not allow Blacks to be buried in the churchyard. In spite of this evidence of prejudice, the Reverend William Troy, minister of nearby Windsor's First Baptist Church, expressed a cautious optimism: "... prejudice is being removed slowly but it is being removed; it is not as strong as it has been. Yet it is very powerful."[34]

During the 1850s London's Black citizens were discouraged from attending some of the town's 10 white churches, and when they did, were often insulted by white members. All the same, Aby Jones, a Black businessman, claimed that Black refugees had little difficulty in becoming members. St. Paul's Anglican Church set an example of integration for other white congregations. The Reverend M.M. Dillon, Superintendent of the Mission, said:

if the question was put to vote, the people would vote against having the negroes remain here.[30]

Blacks were also refused admission to private schools. One of Hamilton's prosperous Black businessmen, distressed about his daughters' plight, wrote:

Our work has been greatly assisted by the kind manner in which the rector, church wardens and congregation of St. Paul's have aided us in breaking down existing prejudices against the coloured people by admitting them into all parts of the church; and opening to them every pew during the afternoon service.[35]

Blacks were also discriminated against on steamboats, stagecoaches and in hotels, and feelings sometimes ran so high that violence broke out. Peter Gallego, while travelling by boat between Toronto and Kingston, was told to keep out of the captain's dining room. When he defiantly entered, the captain attacked him. Gallego knocked the man down and proceeded, undisturbed, to eat his meal. When the ship reached Kingston, the captain charged Gallego with assault. Gallego, in turn, charged the captain with denying him his natural rights. The case went to court, where both men were fined, Gallego £5 and the captain £20.

In 1852 a Black named 'Harris' was stoned by a white person. When the police refused to help him lay a charge, Harris took the matter into his own hands: he returned to his attacker and gave him a beating. In the riot that followed, considerable damage was done to Black homes. Charges were laid, and the court ordered the white rioters to pay for all the repairs.

Some hotels refused to serve Blacks, particularly in towns such as Chatham and St. Catharines, where there was a sizeable Black population. In 1854 Blacks protested that omnibuses belonging to the St. Catharines House and the nearby American Hotel would not carry them. The hotels' owners gave in and accepted Black guests when influential citizens planned a boycott and their Black waiters threatened to quit their jobs.

Blame for discrimination and segregation is often placed on Americans, many of whom came to Canada for summer holidays. At the height of the American Civil War not a few Southern families took refuge in St. Catharines and the Niagara area. These former slave-owners had money and status and they resented the presence of Blacks in local schools and hotels. In order to keep these wealthy clients happy, some hotel-owners refused to admit Blacks. But it is unrealistic to place the major blame for Canadian racism on visiting Americans. A more likely explanation is the rapid growth of Canada's Black population during the 1840s and '50s. As early as 1851 there were at least 35 000 refugees in Canada West, and prejudice was plainest in the areas where most Blacks had settled. Chatham's Blacks, for instance, at one time made up one-third of its residents, and the town was considered both a mecca for refugees and the most prejudiced community in Upper Canada. A disenchanted Black minister, reporting to American government officials studying the conditions of refugees, commented: "There is no place in Canada where the whites are more prejudiced against the colored than in Chatham."[36]

Similarly when Blacks were refused the right to buy town lots in Windsor in 1855, the *Windsor Herald* argued that refugees were fortunate to be living in Canada and should not 'rock the boat' by trying to buy property where they were not wanted:

> If a certain locality is prohibited, let them avoid it, as they will experience no difficulty in finding places for settlement; but if they endeavor to force themselves into positions where they are not wanted, under the idea that the British constitution warrants them in so doing, they may discover in the end that the privileges which they now enjoy will become forfeited ...[37]

In Toronto, farther from the American border, the percentage of Black residents was much smaller. There Blacks met less prejudice since they represented little threat to white residents. Even so, there was some uneasiness. *The Colonist* of June 17, 1852 noted that every boat arriving in Toronto Harbour from the U.S.A. seemed to carry "... several fugitive slaves ... as passengers." Clearly apprehensive about their numbers, *The Colonist* later commented:

> Large numbers of slaves continue to escape into Canada daily from the United States. One of the Detroit papers tells us that on the 15th instant no less than eighteen of them crossed the river into Canada. We fear they are coming rather too fast for the good of the Province. People may talk about the horrors of slavery as much as they choose; but fugitive slaves are by no means a desirable class of immigrants for Canada, especially when they come in great numbers.[38]

The Black community did not accept this attack passively. The *Provincial Freeman* published a militant reply, attacking *The Colonist* for dishonouring the many Blacks who had succeeded in their adopted country. It noted that there were no objections to poor European immigrants who had yet to contribute to the province. But *The Colonist* received support from Colonel Bruce, a Member of the Legislature for Essex County, who introduced a bill to impose a poll tax on every fugitive slave entering Canada West; the bill failed to reach a third reading. Perhaps the best reply to *The Colonist* and Colonel Bruce came from crime statistics for the period. In the mid-1850s Toronto had about 50 000 residents, including 1200 or so Blacks. Chief of Police Samuel Sherwood reported a lower crime rate for Blacks than for whites. In 1856, for example, 5346 persons were arrested by Toronto's police, and of these only 78 were Black.

Such evidence of good citizenship did not impress everyone. Colonel John Prince, a member of the Legislative Council, observed in 1857:

> Of the coloured citizens of Toronto I know little or nothing; no doubt some are respectful enough in their way, and perform the inferior duties belonging to their station tolerably well ... I believe that in this city as in some others of our Province, they are looked upon as necessary evils, and only submitted to because white servants are so scarce. But I now deal with these fellows as a body and I pronounce them to be as such the greatest CURSE ever inflicted upon the two magnificent counties which I have the honour to represent in the legislative council of this Province ... It has been my misfortune and the misfortune of my family to live among these blacks (and they have lived upon us) for twenty-four years.[39]

In reply Toronto Blacks held a mass protest meeting, and Toronto papers contradicted and condemned Colonel Prince's remarks, for while prejudice did exist there, it was not general.

It did nothing to help erase discrimination, however, that during the 1840s and '50s Blacks constantly competed with British immigrants for jobs. One Chatham resident of the '50s spoke for many of his neighbours when he wrote:

> ... the darkies are coming here in droves and work is not that plentiful to accommodate them. I've heard both

> Dawn and Buxton have all they can handle ... And not all are capable and industrious. They go fishing along the river and lie in the sun sleeping, too lazy to hold a fish-pole. "Black-snaking" it is called ...[40]

Even some established Black Canadians confessed uneasiness about the newcomers, for they feared that their position was being endangered and that the goodwill they had slowly gained for their small communities would be damaged by the influx of refugees.

Building Together

Although Canadian Blacks faced bigotry, they also had the continuing help and support of countless white allies and friends. The American Revolutionary War and the War of 1812 created strong anti-American opinion in Upper Canada, and much of this was translated into abolitionist sympathy. Indeed, after Simcoe's legislation of 1793 and the abolition of slavery throughout the British Empire in 1833, many Canadians came to hate the American slave system and began to support anti-slavery societies and the Underground Railroad. A number of Canadian newspapers ran strong editorials denouncing prejudice and racism wherever it occured. George Brown, publisher of the Toronto *Globe*, strongly opposed racism and did much to create a positive climate of opinion for Black refugees. Brown outspokenly backed William King of the Elgin Settlement and consistently used the *Globe* to attack Larwill and others like him. In describing the infamous protest meeting Larwill organized against Elgin, for example, the *Globe* editorial reported:

> Three things struck me as peculiarly deserving of reprobation, viz: the gross partiality displayed by the Chairman, the intemperance of the speakers and the behaviour of the crowd. Among the latter drunkenness abounded and obscene language and shocking oaths were bandied from mouth to mouth.[41]

When Brown became a candidate for Canada West's Parliament, he received a letter bearing 150 signatures, which stated that if he would agree to press for a law to keep Blacks out of the common schools and put a poll tax on Black immigrants, the signatories would

The Honourable George Brown, editor of the Toronto Globe.

ministerial platforms, and government offices. There is no doubt some prejudice here, but those who have it are ashamed to show it. This is at least true of Toronto.[43]

Samuel Ringgold Ward, an editor of the same paper, often commented on the relatively secure economic position of Toronto's refugees, as well as on the absence of serious racial problems in the city. Ward was particularly pleased that there were no Black schools, which were beginning to be opened in other parts of the province, and that churches and other institutions did not discriminate against Blacks. He concluded: "If we are asked how [racial equality] affects them, we answer that a more intelligent, enterprising and independent class of coloured people, we have yet to see."[44]

Even in centres where the Black population was relatively large, there was considerable sympathy and support for the abolitionist cause, and groups were formed to help refugees. One such group in St. Catharines was the Refugee Slaves' Friends Society. It was supported by Elias Adams, the town's mayor, and William H. Merritt, an influential benefactor of local Blacks. In other towns Anglican, Presbyterian, Congregational and Quaker churches formed refugee-aid societies and set up depots to give food and clothing to newly arrived runaways. Some churches also organized schools for children of refugees.

There were supporters, too, of integrated schools. In Hamilton, for instance, Mr. McCullum, principal of the Hamilton High School, urged integrated education:

> I had charge of the Provincial Model School at Toronto for over ten years, and I have had charge of this school over four years, and have had colored children under my charge all that time. They conduct themselves with the strictest propriety, and I have never known an occasion where the white children have had any difficulty with them on account of color. At first, when any new ones came, *I used to go out with them in the playground myself, and play with them specifically,* just to show that I made no distinction whatever; and then the children made none. I found this plan most healthy in its operation.
>
> Little children do not show the slightest repugnance to playing with the colored children, or coming in contact with them. I never knew of a case. But sometimes parents will not let their children sit at the same desk with a

vote for him; otherwise they would support his opponents. Brown's disgusted comment was: "There were 150 men degraded enough to sign such a paper and send it to me."[42]

Largely through the influence of Brown and other citizens of like mind, an atmosphere generally favourable to Blacks developed in Toronto. W.P. Newman writing in the *Provincial Freeman* stated:

> Here there is no difference made in public houses, steamboats, railroad cars, schools, colleges, churches,

Mal Nicholson (**right**), *later a successful contractor in St. Catharines, Ontario, with a friend about 1905.*

colored child. The origin of the difficulty is not being treated like other children. We have no difficulty here. We give the children their seats according to their credit-marks in the preceding month, and I never have had the slightest difficulty The moral conduct of the colored children is just as good as that of the others.[45]

Some clergy and churches actively opposed discrimination. The Reverend Mr. Geddes, an Anglican clergyman who was a staunch friend of Hamilton's Blacks, rebuffed several white parishioners who objected to their daughters' associating with Blacks in the Sunday School, where two Black women, members of the church, taught "... white children of respectable parents." Geddes responded to the complaint:

I am sorry that any persons belonging to the Church of England are so narrow-minded as to suppose their children will be injured because there are a few colored persons in the same school; but of course we cannot change our principle, and the young [white] ladies must leave.[46]

In Toronto Blacks and whites worshipped together in many churches. James G. Birney, a white American visitor to the city in 1837, wrote:

On Sunday I attended, in the morning the "English (Episcopal) Church". I saw here *several colored people sitting promiscuously with the whites.* In the afternoon I went to a Baptist Church, the pastor of which is Mr. Christian, a colored man, a native of Virginia, and formerly a Slave. The Congregation, which was larger than the building could well accommodate, was composed of about an equal number of whites and colored persons. There was no distinction in seats, nor any, the least recognition, so far as I could discern, of a difference made by complexion or any other cause. There is a considerable number of the members of the Church that are whites. I never saw a better looking, or a more orderly Congregation assembled. In their persons they were neat—in their attention to the services decorous and exemplary.[47]

Birney further commented that any Black "... of good health and steady conduct..." could succeed in Toronto and Canada West since the laws were just and were administered without regard to race.

A less encouraging report followed the Reverend John Hurst's attempt to form an integrated Sunday School in Windsor's All Saints Church (Anglican). He later reported:

> A few weeks before Christmas we commenced teaching the children, both colored and white, some Christmas and other hymns, for a special service in the Church. In the afternoon of the Sunday before Christmas this service was held. About 30 members of the colored Sunday school were present, over 200 white children, and many adults. Apparently everything went off well. All read the Psalms, responded, and sang together in a manner that astonished and delighted every one. ... We were all pleased, and thought we had succeeded in bringing white and colored children together. But in this we were greatly deceived, for next Sunday not a colored child appeared; they had taken offence at something, and gave us one more proof that the time has not come when colored and white can be brought together at Windsor. It can be done in Toronto and other towns east of this, but not here.[48]

Though he was disappointed, Hurst did not give up. He spoke for many Canadians who were battling discrimination when he later said: "We cannot do what we would, so we do what we can."

The Black community itself did much to counteract prejudice. As time went on, it met discrimination with more and more effective protest. Hamilton's Black Abolitionist Society, for instance, protested its exclusion from the parade that marked the laying of the cornerstone for the city's Crystal Palace. Their protest was supported by many white residents. The editors of the *Spectator* pointed out that Black Hamiltonians had contributed much to the city's life and done many acts of good citizenship. The next year Blacks were included in the major parade, "... not only in the procession but near its head, before any of the other ethnic societies, in fact, where they marched resplendent in white hats."[49]

In Toronto Wilson Ruffin Abbott and other Blacks finally grew weary of white American actors performing plays and skits that ridiculed Blacks. They also objected to circuses and "freak shows" that featured Black persons. In July 1840, a deputation to the City Council argued that such performances caused Toronto's Blacks "... much heart burning and led occasionally to violence." The group presented a petition signed by almost all the city's Black business people, as well as by George Brown of the *Globe*: there were 15 signatures in all. The Council replied that it had no authority to prevent such performances, but the next month it passed a by-law to license travelling theatrical groups and circuses, although it took no further action. The Black community renewed its deputations and petitions every year until July, 1843, when the mayor, backed by the Council, refused to let a travelling circus perform acts that would hurt the feelings of "the gentlemen of colour." The only complaint was that of one citizen who protested that the mayor had not stopped the Orangemen from parading, which would have "...gratified a more respectable and larger portion of the community."[50]

In all, it seems fair to claim that, while the record of justice for Blacks in Canada is certainly not without flaws, their many successes in the early period of our history would not have been possible without co-operation between whites and Blacks and without the strong principles and courageous action of people who believed in social justice and practised human kindness. It must be added that one can only marvel at the courage of thousands of fugitive slaves who risked their lives to reach a new land where they hoped and struggled for acceptance and achievement. Most of them arrived weary, destitute, illiterate and unskilled, but determined not to accept bondage. That determination was perhaps their greatest success.

7
Blacks and the Armed Forces

Black Loyalist Troopers

ON JANUARY 17, 1871 in Cornwall, Ontario, the death was announced of

> ... a coloured man named John Baker who attained his 105th year ... He came as chattel of the late Col. James Gray in 1792 having seen service in the Revolutionary War. Subsequently he served throughout the War of 1812. He was wounded at the Battle of Lundy's Lane and has drawn a pension for 57 years.[1]

In some ways John Baker's career was unique. He may well have been the last surviving Upper Canadian slave. After he was freed by Robert I.D. Gray, he worked at York (later Toronto) for Chief Justice William Dummer Powell. In 1815 Baker sailed to England, joined the 104th Regiment and fought under the Duke of Wellington at the Battle of Waterloo. "I saw Napolean riding on his fine white horse and jumping ditches,"[2] Baker recalled in later life when he had settled in Cornwall. He tried to enlist again in 1854 for service in the Crimean War, but was rejected. Before his death he saw his adopted country become in turn Upper Canada, Canada West and the Dominion of Canada. He had helped it to survive through its first precarious years and its early growing pains.

Although Baker's astounding record set him apart in some ways, in others his life mirrored that of many Canadian Blacks, slave and free, who took up arms to defend their country. Hundreds of Blacks fought on the British side in the American Revolutionary War and many of them afterwards came into continuing

A Pioneer of the 54th Regiment of Foot, the 'West Norfolk Regiment', 1782.

British territory as Loyalists. The Black Pioneers, a unit of Black troops commanded by white officers, were evacuated from New York with other British troops and helped to establish Loyalist settlements in Nova Scotia. Peter Long, who settled first in Nova Scotia and later in Upper Canada, was for a time a gunner on the schooner *Nova Scotia*. Richard Pierpoint and James Robertson[3] were privates in Butler's Rangers under Colonel John Butler, a slave-owner. Every member of this unit "... considered himself the equal of several Indians in woodcraft or in a fight."[4]

Colonel John Butler

The Maroons

A group of 600 freedom-fighters landed in Halifax on July 22, 1796. They were the Maroons, immigrants from Jamaica who were part of the community of escaped slaves who, from 1655, had guarded their freedom in the mountains of that island and for over a century had fought off all attempts to re-enslave them. Some of them, finally overcome by the superior resources and false assurances of British and Jamaican forces, surrendered in 1796 and were exiled to Nova Scotia aboard three small transport ships, the *Dover*, the *Mary* and the *Ann*. To help them settle in their new home, the Jamaican government supplied a fund of £25 000.

Sir John Wentworth, Governor of Nova Scotia, and Prince Edward, Duke of Kent, Commander-in-Chief of the province's forces, gave a hearty welcome to the Maroons. They were impressed by their record of brave resistance and by their impressive physical appearance. When the Duke of Kent offered them work building new fortifications on Halifax's Citadel Hill, the Maroons accepted his offer and volunteered to work without pay. The Duke, however, ordered that they should be paid at the regular rate of nine pence a day, "… besides provisions, lodging and clothing."

The Maroons quickly finished their assignment of building the 'Maroon Bastion' to reinforce the new province's defences. They also formed a militia unit in

The Maroons in ambush in one of their Jamaica strongholds.

Halifax from the citadel, 1801.

which two of their leaders, Montagne and John, were made colonels, and two others, Bailey and Jarret, were made majors. At first the people of Halifax were delighted with the added protection and prosperity which the Maroons provided, with their combat experience and their soldiers' pay to spend in the community; but before long there was trouble. The independent spirit and the determination to keep to their own ways that had been the life of the Maroons through a century and a half of guerrilla warfare seemed arrogance to the Nova Scotians, and there were several attempts to have the newcomers expelled. The Maroons found the climate of their new land harsh, the food unpalatable, and the dislike of their neighbours difficult to bear. In 1797 they asked to be sent to a warmer climate, but it was not until January, 1800 that the government decided to send them to Sierra Leone. In August of that year 550 Maroons boarded the ship *Asia* for their new homeland which they finally reached in October.

Black Troops in the Michigan Territory

The first governor of the Michigan Territory, William Hull, used runaway Blacks to help defend Detroit against Indian raiders of the Sauk, Kickapoo and Mascouten tribes. In 1805 or '06 Hull gave permission for fugitive Blacks to form a military unit under the command of Peter Denison, a Black. In 1807 George, a 15-year-old slave of John Askin, was sent from Upper Canada to Detroit on an errand. Men, probably belonging to Denison's corps, were drilling in the town square. The lad was offered a weapon and urged to throw off the bonds of slavery and accept the freedom offered by the United States.[5] George considered the offer, but after asking his mother's advice, he returned to his master.[6]

The presence of Canadian Blacks, especially armed ones, in the Michigan Territory disturbed local slave-owners, and a committee headed by Judge Woodward passed a number of resolutions charging Hull with misgovernment, claiming that to arm Blacks was injurious to "proprietors of slaves." Hull was asked to submit to the Legislature copies of military commissions or "... other authorities issued to slaves." In a report on the resolutions, Hull stated that Peter Denison's men often "appeared under arms" and showed good conduct. They were loyal, and the governor considered it legal to arm them since they were living in Michigan Territory as free people. In spite of Hull's practical view, the Black militia unit was demobilized.

The War of 1812

On the Canadian side of the Detroit River, shortly before the War of 1812, the veteran Richard Pierpoint petitioned the government to raise a company of "coloured" troops to help protect the Niagara frontier. Pierpoint had been born in Bondou, Africa. About 1760, when he was 16 years old, he was caught by slave-traders, shipped to America and sold to a British officer. He came to Upper Canada in 1780, one of the 10 Blacks on the U.E.L. list.

The government of Upper Canada granted Pierpoint's petition, and a company of Blacks was formed under the command of a white officer, Robert Runchey Sr. The unit, called 'Captain Runchey's Company of Coloured Men', was made up of Blacks from Niagara, York, St. Davids, St. Catharines and the Bay of Quinte district. It was probably the earliest all-Black company in Canadian military history. Other Blacks, too, were welcomed into Upper Canadian units about this time. Thirteen Blacks joined the 3rd Regiment of York Militia[7], and one, at least, the 10th Regiment[8]; others later joined the Glengarry Light Infantry.[9]

In June, 1812 the bitterness that had smouldered between the British and Americans ever since the Revolutionary War broke into open conflict. Canada became a prime military target since the Americans believed that their new western frontiers would never be safe until they expelled the British from North America. For the Americans it was

> ... a second war of independence; and for Canada a second struggle against American invasion ... far more

important than it was for Britain, and much more dangerous than it was for the United States.[10]

For Canadian Blacks the War of 1812 raised the spectre of being dragged back into American slavery. The Legislature of Upper Canada made stirring appeals for loyalty to the people of the young province, many of whom had strong ties to Britain and bitter memories of the Revolutionary War. The call "... to defend everything they called precious ..."[11] touched free Blacks, who feared and hated the American slave system, and they eagerly joined Upper Canadian fighting units. Black volunteers fought and distinguished themselves at Queenston Heights, Fort George, Niagara Town, Stoney Creek, Lundy's Lane and in other border skirmishes. James Long, probably the eldest son of Peter Long, was captured on November 11, 1812 on board the British ship *Elizabeth* in Lake Ontario. He was imprisoned by the Americans, but found his way back to York in 1813.

Among the Blacks who fought at Queenston Heights were 50 former American slaves who had escaped in the 1790s and taken refuge on the Grand River Reserve, where the famous Mohawk chief, Joseph Brant, gave them homesteads. Aaron Eyres, the son-in-law of Peter Long, was among them. General Roger Hale Scheaffe, who took command at Queenston after General Brock was killed, deployed 380 men of the 41st Regiment and 300 men of the York Militia to reinforce about 200 Canadians. In the afternoon 140 Indians and 50 Blacks led by John Brant, the 18-year-old son of Joseph Brant, arrived on the battle scene:

> The left flank of the British line was of very varied character, consisting of one company of the 41st Regiment, one company of coloured men, and a mixed body of militia and Indians. The men advanced in gallant style, delivered a volley, and then charged, driving in the American right at the point of the bayonet.
>
> Scheaffe opened the battle at about 4:00 by directing Lieutenant McIntyre, with the Light Company of the 41st on the left of his column, supported by a body of

The Battle of Lundy's Lane.
The Battle of Queenston Heights.

Black fugitives waiting on the shore of Maryland's Chesapeake Bay for a British ship to take them to freedom.

militia, Indians and negroes under Captain Runchey, to fall upon the American right. They fired a single volley with considerable execution, and then charged with a tremendous tumult, the white men shouting and the Indians ringing out the fearful war-whoop and hideous yells. The Americans were overpowered by the onslaught and gave way ...[12]

As news spread of the exploits of free Blacks under arms in Canada, slaves in Maryland and Virginia were supporting the British cause. In the spring of 1813 British naval units were ordered to launch attacks along Maryland's Chesapeake Bay to divert American attention from Canada. As the British commanders began these operations, they offered freedom and protection to any Blacks who helped them. Two hundred slaves in Maryland and Virginia joined the British militia, and others volunteered to act as spies, guides, messengers and labourers for the British forces.

Through 1813[13] and '14 Runchey's Corps saw service in the Niagara district, and in May, 1813 took part in a brave attempt to repulse an American landing near Two Mile Creek:

Our troops advanced to charge ... but the tremendous fire from ... fort and shipping rendered it impossible. ... Our brave troops advanced to dispute the ground but ...

found themselves still more exposed. ... A retreat was most unwillingly resorted to.[14]

Soon after, on June 6, the Coloured Corps fought at the Battle of Stoney Creek. In June, 1814 the Corps was at Fort George; on July 8 it was in Fort Mississauga and it remained there as a garrison force when the main body of troops fell back to Twenty Mile Creek. By the War's end the Coloured Company was attached to the Quartermaster General's Department. It had become a labour corps commanded by Captain George Fowler.

The men of the Coloured Company were promised six months' severance pay on their discharge from the militia, but some, at least, may never have received it. A letter of complaint records

... that Sergeant William Thompson (a black) who voluntarily went from the 3rd Regiment York Militia to Niagara in October 1812, with thirteen men of colour, and enlisted in a Company commanded by Capn. Wrenchy [Runchey], and afterwards by Lieut. James Robinson [Robertson] complains, that at the reduction of the 24th March last, they were promised six months pay, as they were considered on the same footing with the incorporated Militia, but since upon application to the said Lieut. Robinson, he can obtain no satisfaction

Fort George, Upper Canada, from the American Fort Niagara.

except, being told that he must go and look for his pay himself.[15]

Some members of Runchey's Corps received land grants. Robert Jupiter[16] was granted a lot in Garafraxa Township, Wellington County; Sgt. W. Thompson, Corp. Humphrey Waters, Corp. Francis Willson, John Call, Daniel Cokely, Sgt. John Delay, Samuel Edwards, formerly of York, and John Jackson received grants in Oro Township; James[17] and John Long applied for grants in Oro, but decided not to settle there.

Richard Pierpoint, who had proposed the first all-Black company, fell on hard times. In July, 1821, when he was an old man, he petitioned the government of Upper Canada to send him back to his native Bondou in Africa to live out his remaining years. Unfortunately no record of a reply to his petition has been found, and Pierpoint's fate is unknown.

The Mackenzie Rebellion

Before the outbreak of the 1837 Rebellion, few of Upper Canada's militia units included Blacks, although they were eager to serve in defense of the Crown. Indeed, William Lyon Mackenzie, writing to the American Anti-Slavery Society on January 30, 1837 reported:

> That nearly all of Upper Canada's Blacks are opposed to every species of reform in the civil institutions of the colony—they are so extravagantly loyal to the Executive that to the utmost of their power they uphold all the abuses of government and support those who profit by them ... I regret that an unfounded fear of a union with the United States on the part of the colored population should have induced them to oppose reform and free institutions in this colony, whenever they have had the power to do so.[18]

As soon as the Mackenzie Rebellion broke out, however, Upper Canada's government was glad to enroll Blacks in the province's forces:

> A week after the Toronto rising it was realized that trouble was imminent on the Niagara frontier. On

December 11th, [1837] the Adjutant General of Militia wrote to Thomas Runchey of Niagara to raise a corps of negroes, and on December 15th James H. Sears had fifty colored men under his command. Still another colored unit was embodied, probably about the same time, under the command of Hugh Eccles of Niagara. The formation of these units was an emergency measure and probably not preceded by the usual routine at military headquarters. Later Orders regularized them.[19]

Captain Sears' company of 50 Blacks

> ... was on duty along the bank of the Niagara opposite Navy Island on the night of December 29th, when the "Caroline" cutting-out party left on its adventurous enterprise.[20]

This American ship was defiantly carrying supplies and men to Navy Island to strengthen the rebels for an all-out attack on Upper Canada when Commander Drew, R.N., caught up with it, set it on fire and put it out of commission. The *Caroline* was swept away by the strong current of the Niagara River and carried over the Falls.

Even before the government enlisted their support, Blacks of several communities formed volunteer units and drilled on their own. In Windsor, for instance, Josiah Henson commanded a company of Black volunteers, which was part of the Essex Militia. When the schooner *Anne*, manned by rebels and their sympathizers, sailed down the Detroit River firing its gun into the town of Sandwich, its fire was immediately returned. The captain lost control of his ship, and it drifted ashore on Elliott's Point. The Essex Militia, including Henson's detachment,

> ... were quickly on the spot and a party waded out to the stranded vessel and took possession of her without opposition. Her crew were made prisoners and the vessel and its contents became a prize of war.[21]

Henson's unit helped to defend Fort Malden from Christmas, 1837 to May, 1838, and another company of 123 Black volunteers, Captain Caldwell's Coloured Corps, was also stationed at Fort Malden for two months during the Rebellion. Benjamin Turner, who settled in Oro about 1830, served as a private in Captain Edward Lally's Company, the 1st Simcoe Militia,

William Lyon Mackenzie (right) led the brief Rebellion of 1837-38. When the rebels were dispersed at Montgomery's Tavern, he fled to Navy Island in American waters, hoping to carry on the rebellion from there. Canadian troops destroyed his ship, the Caroline (left), and put an end to Mackenzie's hopes.

The barracks at old Fort Malden, 1913.

The barracks at Chatham, Upper Canada, 1838.

and James Pleasant Bush, Jeremiah Munroe and George Eddy, all of Oro, joined Captain Alex Laing's Company of Medonte Volunteers.

On December 18, 1837, 18 of Hamilton's Blacks signed a "Loyal statement of people of colour ..." proclaiming that it was "... the duty of every Loyal man at the present crisis to come forward in support of the Government of our Most Gracious Queen."[22] They formed a company under Captain William Allen, Lieutenant Leonard Mead and Sergeant John Tory. The *Hamilton Gazette* later reported:

> On Tuesday about 100 of the 5th Gore Militia arrived here, under the command of Captain Fyfe — they were principally from Esquesing. On the same day from 150 to 200 additional volunteers left town to join Col. McNab on the frontier, amongst whom, we are happy to say, almost every coloured man in town appeared.[23]

Later dispatches attested to the excellent service record of Hamilton's Black company:

> This is to certify that the Colored Company commanded by Captain Allan and attached on the 26th December last to the 5th Gore Militia under my command did their duty while on the Frontier in every respect to my satisfaction, and I do not hesitate for a moment to say that should they again be employed (as they desire to be) they would not disgrace Her Majesty's Service, and I strongly recommend that Captain Allan be allowed to raise a volunteer corps to serve until the 1st day of July next.
>
> Wm. M. Jarvis, Coll.
> 5th Regt. G.M.
>
> . . .
>
> The men under Captain Allan were always ready and willing and they conducted themselves to my entire satisfaction.
>
> Allan N. McNabb[24]

Lieutenant-Governor Sir Francis Bond Head, acknowledging the loyalty of Black Canadians, reported to the Legislature of Upper Canada on March 6, 1838:

> When our colored population were informed that American citizens, sympathising with their sufferings, had taken violent possession of Navy Island, for the double object of liberating them from the domination of British rule and of imparting to them the blessings of republican institutions, based upon the principle that all men are born equal, did our colored brethren hail their approach? No! On the contrary, they hastened as volunteers in wagon loads to the Niagara frontier to beg from me permission ... that they might be allowed to be foremost to defend the glorious institutions of Great Britain.[25]

In May, 1838 the Black companies stationed at Drummondville (later Niagara) and commanded by Runchey and Sears were merged into one corps and moved to Chippawa and Black Creek under the command of Lieutenant-Colonel Ogden Creighton. Before the corps was temporarily disbanded in the summer of that year, it had reached a strength of two captains, three lieutenants, two ensigns, five sergeants, six corporals and 127 privates.

Sir Francis Bond Head

Armed citizens and drilling soldiers on 6th Street, Chatham, 1838 were ready to ward off Mackenzie's rebels or American invaders.

Chatham Blacks, too, formed a voluntary drill company, using arms borrowed from British regular units. Colonel Chichester, commandant for the area, wrote to the Deputy Adjutant General on October 16, 1838:

> I should wish to mention that there are a number of coloured people in the neighborhood, all well disposed, they might be formed into a company, as it is they do assemble for drill and I lend them arms, but there is no authority for it, they do it on their own accord.[26]

Chichester received prompt permission to form a company of Black militiamen, but he faced some problems: it was hard to find white officers willing to command Black troops, and Black volunteers who were poor and had families to consider, objected to enlisting for the mandatory term of six months. But these difficulties were overcome, and two Black companies were formed in November, 1838. Captain William Muttlebury commanded the 1st Coloured Company, and Lieutenant James Perrier commanded the 2nd Coloured Company. The combined strength of the two units was 80 men.

At about the same time the government of Upper Canada learned that the border was again threatened by groups of men who were gathering arms to invade the province. Militia units were quickly activated, and a call went out for volunteers. Black units were reactivated in November, 1838 under the command of Major Richard Webbe, and a notice appeared in the *Niagara Reporter* on the 16th of that month:

TEN DOLLARS BOUNTY!
EIGHTEEN MONTHS SERVICE

BRAVE AND LOYAL COLOURED MEN: Your services are once more required to defend the Liberty you now enjoy.

VOLUNTEERS

(not Slaves) are now called to rally round the British Constitution, which proclaims LIBERTY TO THE WHOLE COLOURED RACE.

Being authorized to raise a Coloured Corps for eighteen months, TEN DOLLARS BOUNTY will be paid on joining at Head Quarters at Niagara, deducting only what will complete each man's Kit to

3 Shirts,	3 pairs Socks,
1 pair Boots,	2 Shoe Brushes,
1 Razor,	1 Strop,
1 Shaving Brush,	1 Comb.

They will also be supplied free of cost with the following articles of clothing—

One Coatee or Jacket,
One pair Half Boots,
One pair cloth Trowsers,
One Cap, one Stock,
One [Great Coat],
One Knapsack,
One Canteen,
One Haversack.

These last named articles to be returned at the expiration of their service.

With the same pay as Her Majesty's Forces, and *Free Rations*—14 days pay in advance, when disbanded at the expiration of their service.

RICHARD P. WEBBE
Major Commanding.
Pavilion, Niagara Falls, Nov. 12th, 1838.
Apply to Captain CLENCH, Niagara.

"GOD SAVE THE QUEEN"

The government had acted none too quickly. On December 4 the rebels captured the unprotected steamer *Champlain* berthed in Detroit. With a force of 200 men they then crossed the river to the Ferry (later Windsor) and captured it. As the attack began, a Black civilian on guard in the area was killed. Two hours after the news got out, 50 Black volunteers had gathered ready to fight. Joined by British regulars, they quickly recaptured the town and restored order. By the spring of 1839 the threat of the Rebellion had passed, and Major Webbe's Colored Corps, which had reached a strength of 155 men, was shortly afterwards disbanded.

Keeping the Peace

In April, 1843 the Coloured Company of Chatham was also disbanded, to the joy of many of the town's white residents. The *Chatham Journal* noted:

> The colored company of the Second Battalion stationed at this place, were paid off on Thursday last, and were all conveyed yesterday by the splendid steamer *Kent* to Sandwich, there to be disbanded. They all left apparently in high spirits, with music and colors flying, cutting up the greatest "nigger shines" imaginable, and followed, if not by many good wishes of our inhabitants, at least with one—that they may never return again. The officers in command, Captain Cameron and Lieutenant Perrier carry with them the kindest feelings [for their gentlemanly conduct and the] discipline and orderly manner in which they have kept these almost unruly sort of people under subjection.[27]

This seems strange thanks for the services the Company had performed. Under the direction of Captain Cameron, for instance, its men had served as Chatham's main fire-fighting force in 1842. In March of that year, when fire destroyed a barbershop and two frame houses, the Company's swift action prevented the blaze from spreading.

Three years earlier, in 1840, another Black corps had been formed under the command of Captain Alexander MacDonald; it was to serve for more than a decade. Its first assignment was to build the Cayuga Road between Drummondville and Simcoe, but road-building and forest-clearing soon gave way to keeping the peace along the construction route of the Welland Canal. The Irish workmen, or 'canallers', divided themselves into opposing forces, according to whether they were Roman Catholics or Protestant Orangemen, and the local police could not control their fighting.

In July, 1840 the most serious incident in the building

of the canal took place at Slabtown, a community of canallers on the outskirts of Merritton (now a district of St. Catharines) that got its name from its shacks made of the slabs that could be bought cheaply from nearby sawmills. The 'battle of Slabtown' started when about 50 Orangemen were holding a celebration at Duffin's Inn. While they were dining, several hundred Catholic canallers surrounded the inn and fired shots into it. The Orangemen inside were armed, and they returned the fire. A fracas started and an urgent call went out for troops to restore order. Twenty-five Black troopers arrived and quelled the disturbance, but two men were killed and seven wounded. The government, the officials of Merritton and most of the public were grateful, but the Irish workers were far from pleased: "... it was the climax of humiliation to be kept within the bounds of law and good order by 'a naygur in a red coat'."[28]

The Negro Volunteer Military Company was formed in Victoria, B.C. about 1860 to protect the British colony. The Hudson's Bay Company lent the volunteers muskets. The unit was disbanded in 1864 when Governor A. Kennedy advised that it had been illegally organized.

The Earl of Elgin, Governor General of Canada.

During a strike, when the canallers had little to keep them occupied, a group of them decided to attack the Black troops stationed at Port Robinson. They marched out in a body to confront the troops who, with loaded guns and fixed bayonets, were drawn up across the road to block the canallers' path. It seemed that a bloody fight was unavoidable, but at the critical moment the canallers' priest, Father MacDonagh, galloped up on his famous black horse. While the canallers loved and admired Father MacDonagh, they had a healthy awe for this fearless and militant man. He rode up between the advancing canallers and the Black troops, jumped off his horse and with his riding crop drew a line across the dirt road. Then he turned on his parishioners and told them that he would put the ban of the Church on any man who dared to put a foot across the line. The canallers paused, and the priest sprang into the saddle and rode into their ranks, striking out with his riding crop at any man he could reach. This distraction took the crowd's attention, and it scattered without making the attack it had intended.

Although there was plenty of conflict during this troublesome decade of strikes and fights, the Black soldiers were well behaved, kept their tempers and did not abuse their power. Groups of ill-wishers often set upon some of the Blacks when they were off duty and unarmed, but they were strong enough to fight off such attacks and put their attackers to flight.

The Governor General, Lord Elgin, spent considerable time in Drummondville in 1849. He also made a tour of inspection of the canal and paid a state visit to Port Robinson. Lord Elgin and his family were escorted on these trips by a guard of honour made up of the Black Corps' finest men. Officials of the town of Thorold later said of the Coloured Corps: "They were a fine set of fellows, very jealous for the honour of their company and exceedingly proud of the trust reposed in them."[29]

When the canal was completed in 1850, the Coloured Corps was no longer needed. It was officially disbanded in 1851. Its members settled throughout the Niagara Peninsula where many of them became active helpers of the Underground Railroad and the refugees it brought into the Niagara area.

8

Blacks and the Churches

The Earliest Years

FROM THEIR EARLIEST dealings with Blacks, white Canadians tried to teach them their religion and convert them to their beliefs, seeming not to find slavery inconsistent with Christianity:

> Nowhere, either under the French or the English régime, did any bishop declare, in his proclamations or in his letters, the slightest opposition to a state of things that the State had legalized in 1709; furthermore, the Church in French Canada accepted slavery as normal and even profited by it.[1]

Roman Catholic clergy offered Blacks the rites of their church: they baptized and married them and recorded the births of their children, for the Roman Church "... favoured the integration of slaves into society." With the permission of a master, a slave could marry another slave or even a free Canadian, and marriages between Indians and French Canadians and Blacks and Canadians were blessed by the priests.

> Sometimes the baptism of a Black or Indian slave took on the colouring of a social event, as in the case of the Negro Pierre-Louis-Scipion, 20 years old, when in 1717 thirteen persons were brought together to sign his baptism certificate. The slave could serve as a godmother or godfather. He could take communion. On his deathbed, he received the reassurances of a priest; there was a funeral which might attract a large gathering of people. He was buried in the same conditions as a free man: we know of an Indian woman, Marie-Athanase, slave of the merchant Charles Hamelin de Michillimakinac, who had

The British Methodist Episcopal Church at Niagara Falls, Ontario, about 1900.

the signal honour of being buried under the church itself, near to her dead mistress.[2]

On the other hand, the Roman Church did not accept Blacks as priests and allowed a person who unknowingly married a slave to have the marriage annulled. By and large, however, the Roman Church had a more moderating influence on slavery in Canada than had the early Protestant churches in the American colonies and states. The latter, for the most part, definitely supported slavery.

Among Canada's Protestant Loyalists, as among the Catholic French, slavery was not generally considered to conflict with strong religious convictions. Indeed, some ministers of the church in Upper Canada actually owned slaves. The Reverend John Stuart of Kingston, the first minister of the Church of England in Upper Canada, recorded in his diary that he had brought his slaves with him from Mohawk Valley where he had been a missionary to the Indians. Commenting on his departure during the American Revolution, he wrote:

> My Negroes being personal property, I take with me, one of which being a young man, and capable of bearing arms, I have to give 100 pounds security to send back a white prisoner in his stead.[3]

During the era of slavery the church was the only social organization that American slave-owners permitted to Blacks. Slaves and oppressed freedmen found in the Christian doctrine of salvation hope of escape from their earthly troubles. While American churches shared this doctrine with Blacks, they excluded them from white congregations. As a result, Blacks began to form their own Christian groups. In 1816 Richard

The Reverend John Stuart and his wife, Jane Okill Stuart.

Christian slaves, rejected by most white congregations (below), formed their own churches. Their services were strictly monitored, however, and slaves could not hold a funeral (opposite) or even mark their fellows' graves without their owners' permission.

Allen established the African Methodist Episcopal (AME) Church in Philadelphia, and other Black churches were formed later.

It is small wonder that these people looked forward to the freedom of the 'promised land' beyond death, for the more important slavery became to the American economy, the more strictly legislation restricted the slaves' earthly life. Eventually the Black Codes and other regulations completely controlled them. In some districts, for example, Blacks were not allowed to gather in groups of more than five, except in church. There they could meet, with their owners' permission, provided that their services were strictly religious and musical. The churches thus became a force for unity among people whom slavery had stripped of their family ties, their culture and their African heritage.

Early in the 19th century, when some religious groups—particularly the Quakers—undertook to combat slavery by the Underground Railroad movement, Blacks began to come into Canada, first in small numbers, later in thousands. Their churches, which had been an important part of their life before they fled from the U.S.A., were quickly transplanted to Canadian soil and carried on their ministry there. The earliest and most important institutions in all Black Upper Canadian communities were the churches.

During Upper Canada's earliest years, its Blacks were too few to organize and support their own congregations, and they were served by predominantly white churches. As early as 1793 the baptisms of many slave children were recorded at St. Mark's Anglican Church, Niagara.[4] An American missionary, Joseph Hickox, served along the Thames River between 1815 and 1819, and his charge included 160 members, four of them Blacks. The Blacks at Oro at first attended religious services along with their white neighbours. Most of the refugees at Niagara-on-the-Lake attended a Baptist church which included some white members. At the Black burial ground, still tended by the city, is an inscription:

> Here stood a Baptist church erected in 1830 through the exertions of a former British soldier, John Oakley, who although white, became pastor of a predominantly Negro population.

Missions and Missionaries

As more and more Black refugees entered Canada, British and American missionary organizations saw in the growing fugitive settlements a great opportunity for their work. These groups encouraged the development of Black congregations by giving funds and sending missionaries. While most Canadian Blacks were Baptists or Methodists, other denominations generously supported missions to refugees. An article in the *Provincial Freeman* of November 10, 1855 commented:

> It is a fact that the colored people of Canada are almost entirely of the Baptist or Methodist persuasion and nearly all the teachers sent among them have been either Presbyterian or Congregationalists. No one need wonder at their failure since *Black* people have conscientious conviction of their duty as well as white ones. We thank our Presbyterian and Congregationalist friends for what they intended to do for us. They meant well! But we must admonish our Baptist and Methodist friends, that they are sadly in fault since they [have] neglected their duty and done but little or nothing for us, when they have been earnestly entreated to do something; nor are our "Free Mission Baptists" friends to be excused, in this case.

A Congregational Church was founded at Oro in 1838 by Ari Raymond, a white abolitionist sent there from Boston to minister to the settlers. In 1841, with a membership of six families, two Black and four white, the congregation built a small church. Raymond also built a tiny mission school where he taught five days a week. The church and school and Raymond's home burned down in 1845, but his Black neighbours willingly took him in and supported him. The Methodist Church was also active in Oro. John Lever, missionary to North Simcoe from 1841 to 1843, Luther Rice, missionary from 1847 to 1849 and James L. Slater, missionary from 1860 to 1862, all of them white clergymen, served Oro's Blacks.

Isaac Rice, a white Presbyterian minister, gave up a comfortable charge in Ohio in 1838 to establish a work among refugees in Amherstburg, where he built a shack on a back street in the town's Black district. His eccentric views and behaviour offended some potential supporters as well as many Blacks, although the inter-denominational Union Missionary Society continued to support his Union Border Mission until about 1849, when the American Missionary Association (AMA) took over its control. But its support lasted only one year, for complaints about Rice forced the AMA to drop the connection. Rice tried to keep his Mission going with the help of the town's First Baptist Church which used his headquarters as their meeting place. Later this congregation, too, withdrew their support, for the Union Border Mission's appeals for charity for the "... poor degenerate fugitives ..." soon earned it the nickname of 'the Begging Society'. Amherstburg's Black residents, who prided themselves on their industry, fiercely resented Rice's making their condition seem worse than it was, for most newcomers were able to find jobs within a week of their arrival.

Besides this, scandalous stories were circulating about the Mission: drunkenness "... and other abominations ..." were said to be going on there. Local Blacks were enraged when, in 1855, while fighting a fire at the Mission, they found a very ill old man living in wretched conditions. Their anger reached fever pitch when they learned that Rice had just received a grant of $725 to help fugitives, but had spent only $10 of the amount for a few bits of clothing. The *Provincial Freeman* attacked Rice and his policies regularly and scathingly. Mary Ann Shadd suggested in one editorial that he was responsible for Amherstburg's segregated schools and churches:

> The testimony of reliable persons here is that years ago before Rice and his co-adjutors came hereabouts, the children were in the same schools and the fathers worshipped at the same altars, but the missions recommended schools, churches and donations for the fugitives and hence the separations, prejudices, distrust, etc.[5]

The Refugee Home Society (RHS), which began its active work in 1851, also looked to the AMA for the religious element of its program. Its constitution required that it provide land and money to support the religious and educational welfare of its settlers. Although Baptist, Presbyterian and Methodist churches had already been established throughout the districts where the Society operated, their work was not directly connected with that of the Society. The AMA, through its churches at Pike Creek, Puce River, Little River and Sandwich, took most of the responsibility for religious and educational work among the Society's settlers.

When the RHS opened a new frame school in the Puce River district in 1852, Henry Bibb and Charles Foote, its chief officers, asked Laura Haviland, a white, Canadian-born Quaker, to teach there. As well as teaching, she undertook to serve the religious needs of the settlers. Since the separation of the Society's settlements made a central meeting place impractical, and since there were settlers of several different denominations to be served, Laura Haviland suggested that a Union Church be formed. She later explained:

> There were in this colony a mixed religious element — Baptist, Methodist, Presbyterian and Free-will Baptist — deeply interested in Sabbath school and class meetings, open to all who wished to enjoy them. An organization was proposed. The proposition came from the Methodist element, but I did not deem it wise to organize from any one denomination, as divergent opinion would create controversy ... Consequently I proposed to organize a Christian Union Church without disturbing the Church relationship of anyone ... after a little discussion and explanation it was adopted.[5]

The new church was a great success, and attendance was high until Haviland left the settlement. Then the Baptists separated to form their own church, and the Union Church was discontinued. Since most of the Black settlers at Puce River were Methodist, their church eventually became known as 'Methodist Episcopal'.

From the mid-1860s the Anglican Church, working through its Colonial Church & School Society (CCSS), served Windsor's Black community. The CCSS was formed to minister to "... the downtrodden and oppressed ..." refugees streaming into the southwestern part of the province. A Coloured Mission Fund was set up, and the Reverend John Hurst[7] who was working among the refugees in Amherstburg, was given a grant to begin a similar work in Windsor. In

1863 he moved to Windsor's All Saints' Church to begin his work for the CCSS. As a matter of practical policy, rather than conviction, Hurst kept his services, Sunday School and mission activities racially separate. He explained:

> Although feeling runs high between colours, the same white person can, by the exercise of prudence, and by quietly labouring away, discharge his duty to both colours without much prejudice from either.[8]

The CCSS recognized the need to encourage and co-operate with existing Black churches in Windsor. Hurst divided the town into wards and, with a small group of teachers, went into its streets to find Black children who needed religious and secular schooling:

> In that way we found several families where the children went to no school, and their ignorance something dreadful, actually heathens.[9]

In spite of Hurst's activity, the CCSS Mission in Windsor gradually declined. Hurst explained in 1870 that most of the people it had served had moved to Toronto or returned to the U.S.A. to join their relatives.

Times of Change

From the 1820s on, the growing numbers of Black refugees entering Canada tended to form their own congregations. At first these were not directly linked with American denominations, but simply served to bring together the few Blacks in various Canadian communities. A small log building called 'Salem Chapel' was built in 1820 on North Street, St. Catharines to serve local Blacks, and it seems to have been the centre of their activities. In Amherstburg a church was formed in 1826 to meet the religious needs of the growing refugee community. Its first pastor was the Reverend George Ferguson. This church was likely the forerunner of the AME Nazrey Church organized by Noah C. Cannon in 1828. In 1839 its congregation was able to erect a church building.

It was not until 1847 that Oro's Blacks decided to form their own congregation and called to serve them

the Reverend Richard S. Sorrick. This fiery former slave and self-trained preacher had escaped from Maryland, where he was imprisoned for holding services and preaching among his fellow slaves. During his brief stay in Oro, Sorrick made himself known as a spell-binder, and it was reported of him: "During the old-time revivals the coloured congregations went fairly crazy under the spell of this man's passionate eloquence."[10]

Sorrick said later of his Oro congregation:

> I went to Oro, where I found some fifty persons settled; many [are] comfortable and doing well, but many suffer a great deal from poverty. I showed them about agriculture, and instructed them as far as my limited learning would go. When I came away, many were poor, but they were not vicious: I never lived among a more teachable people.[11]

The Reverend Richard Sorrick

The African Episcopal Church at Edgar, Canada West.

In 1848 the small Black community of Oro built a wooden church on a half-hectare of Lot 11. Noah Morris, an early Black settler, sold the land to the church for one pound. The congregation chose the name 'African Episcopal Church', perhaps after the AME Church, for some of the Oro Blacks had originally come from Maryland and Virginia and were likely of AME background. Certainly the name of the Oro church did not show any strong denominational preference, for its members often called themselves 'British Methodists', and local whites often attended its services. Since the congregation was too poor to support a full-time minister, it was served by itinerant pastors; one of these was the Reverend William Ban-

yard, who ministered there from 1859 to 1863. Later the Reverend J.H. Harris, an Anglican, was sent to Oro by the New England Missionary Society. Finally one of Oro's own Blacks, Elder Bush, led the congregation's services and helped its other members to keep their church alive. Between the 1830s and '70s Oro's African Episcopal Church served about 40 families, including early settlers from Wilberforce and Blacks who lived in nearby concessions and townships.

Although the records are not clear, at least one and possibly two small churches served the community of 'Little Africa' at Fort Erie. Josiah Henson, founder of the Dawn settlement, is said to have organized services of worship there. The community's first meetings

Members of Toronto's Grant African Methodist Episcopal Church in the 1890s.

were held outside, and then in the homes of the people until a log church was built. Tradition has it that a small Black burial ground called 'Donahower Cemetery' lay for many years across from St. John's Anglican Church, Ridgemount.

Owen Sound's first Black church, 'Little Zion', was a log building on the Sydenham River, where the city's Market Square now lies. This congregation was served by a lay preacher, Father Miller, who was respected by the whole community. One newspaper article commented: "He didn't get much pay for preaching, and did painting and gardening to support his family."[12]

Black Methodist Churches

Since most Blacks who settled in Canada had belonged to Methodist or Baptist groups in the U.S.A., they tended to attach themselves to the denominations familiar to them. The Reverend Nathan Bonga, a Methodist minister, was the first Black clergyman to serve in Amherstburg; he became pastor of the AME Church there.

The AME Church formed a congregation in Toronto in 1833 and built a church on Richmond Street, east of York Street. In 1851 it had 128 members, and the

following year, at the Church's annual conference, it was the third largest of six reporting districts: its Sunday School had six teachers and 50 pupils. The congregation moved to several locations: Elizabeth, Sayer and Elm Streets. It finally settled in its present place on Soho Street.

In 1835 the AME Church formed a congregation in Brantford, though there were "... only a handful of members." By the same year Hamilton's Blacks opened an AME church in a small log building on Cathcart Street. J.C. Loguen, who had been an AME lay preacher in the U.S.A., probably organized its congregation. In 1847 this church called the Reverend Richard Sorrick from Oro to become its pastor. He later had difficulties with its members and was replaced by the Reverend M. Broadwater. In 1856 the AME church moved from Cathcart to Rebecca Street.

The Reverend Richard Sorrick with his wife and son.
(Below) *St. Paul's AME Church stood on Rebecca Street in Hamilton. The Reverend J.W. Crosby* (upper left) *was one of its ministers.*

About 1836 the small Black community of Drummondville (later Niagara Falls) built an AME chapel at the intersection of Murray and Allan Streets.

W.R. Abbott and two other Blacks, acting for the Coloured Wesleyan Methodist (CWM) Church of Toronto, bought property[13] on Richmond Street near York Street in July, 1838 for £125. The congregation, which started out with 40 members, seems to have been founded because of the indignation its members felt at Toronto's white Wesleyans who were in fellowship with pro-slavery churches in the American South. By 1850 the CWM Church of Toronto had over 100 members. In time a decided rift appeared, especially with well-to-do members, who began to consider that Black churches impeded Black integration with the rest of the community. The split in the AME Church in the mid-1850s made itself felt within the CWM group. Some of its better-off members, too, began to argue that Black churches hindered social mingling of Blacks and whites. The congregation continued, however, until 1875, when the death of many members and the emigration of others to the U.S.A. closed their church. In later years W.R. Abbott and other former members joined the Anglican Church of St. George the Martyr on John Street.

By 1840 Brantford was the heart of an AME missionary circuit which included the Queen's Bush and London. This circuit was served by the Reverend James Harper. Methodist circuit-riders also served the St. Catharines area, holding revival meetings wherever they could, sometimes in private homes and sometimes outdoors. In 1846 a Reverend S. Brown, an AME circuit preacher, was assigned to cover the Queen's Bush. In that year 16 ministers from all over Canada West gathered in the Bush for their annual AME conference. In this same period Chatham's third Black church, the Episcopal Methodist, was organized; this brought the total membership of the town's three Black congregations to 217 people.

In Windsor the AME Church was the first organized religious group to minister solely to Blacks. In 1851 the town's AME congregation announced in the *Voice of the Fugitive* that it had bought a lot and solicited donations for building a church. There is no evidence, however, that the building was begun. The congregation was split by a growing movement to part with its

The Very Reverend Walter Hawkins, Bishop of the British Methodist Episcopal Church, earlier served as pastor to its Brantford congregation.

parent American denomination and lost most of its strength. Not until 1889 did an AME congregation start up again; its 18 members met in a new building at the corner of Mercer and Assumption Streets.

It was about the mid-'50s that a division developed within the AME denomination. Some members wished to drop the American connection in order to identify more closely with British ideals and government. This group had a practical reason, as well as an ideological one, for their view: they thought that Blacks newly arrived in Canada, and mostly fugitives, would be more likely to find justice and security if they belonged to a church with a British name, made up of British subjects. At the 1854 AME Canadian Conference the Reverend Benjamin Stewart successfully proposed a motion to form a separate body. This was accomplished at the Annual Conference in Chatham

in September, 1856, where the new British Methodist Episcopal (BME) Church was formed under the direction of the Reverend Willis Nazrey, an AME minister who agreed to become the first bishop of the new denomination. The Chatham BME Church flourished. By 1859 it was located on Princess Street near Wellington in a $6000 brick building which would seat 1000 people. The congregation had more than 300 active adult members and a large Sunday School taught by 14 teachers.

Before he became a bishop, the Reverend Nazrey had worked to found BME churches through Canada West. A BME congregation was formed in St. Catharines, and a frame church built at Geneva and North Streets, with funds raised largely by J.L. Lindsay, Lloyd Peet and Edmund Hoyt. The new church was dedicated on November 4, 1855 by Bishop Payne of Cincinnati, Ohio.

Other BME congregations were formed in the same period in Hamilton, Niagara Falls, Brantford, Windsor

(Left) *Brantford's BME Church about 1900. The congregation was established in 1865.*
(Lower left) *The B.M.E. Church in Guelph about 1890.*
(Lower right) *The BME Church at Fort Erie about 1900.*

and Collingwood. The BME group at Niagara Falls met at first in a chapel on Murray Hill; later its members built a larger church at Grey and Peter Streets. During the 1860s the Reverend William Banyard ministered there to the 42 members. The 50-member congregation at Brantford built a small frame church at Murray and Darling Streets. Owen Sound's Little Zion Church joined the new BME group in 1856, and the Reverend Josephus O'Banion was appointed pastor. By 1864 its congregation numbered 120 people.

In 1863 Windsor's BME congregation built a church at McDougall and Assumption Streets. According to tradition, this church was built at night, when its members had finished their daily work. The women carried water from the Detroit River, with which they helped to mix the mortar, while the men took turns working and holding torches to provide light. The new church's early pastors were the Reverend Messrs. Oliver, Blunt and Washington. By 1865 its congregation numbered 146; its Sunday School had 10 teachers and 84 pupils, and a library of 500 books.

In Collingwood a Mr. Woods held services for many years in the homes of BME members. Only in 1871 had these people gathered the funds to build a church. Its first pastor was the Reverend Robert Johnson of Brontë; he was followed by a number of itinerant pastors. In 1898 the church and parsonage burned down, but were rebuilt a few years later on their original 7th Street site.

Black Baptist Churches

Most of the Black refugees who came to Canada had belonged to Baptist churches, and they remained loyal to their denomination. The first Baptist group began in Toronto in 1826, when 12 slaves who had fled to freedom in Canada met for prayer on the shore of Toronto Bay. Elder Washington Christian[14], a native of Virginia, who came to Toronto in 1825, organized the Black worshippers into a congregation which became First Baptist Church. Christian had been ordained in the Abyssinia Baptist Church of New York in 1822.

Elder Washington Christian

The first building erected by the congregation of Toronto's First Baptist Church (above) stood on March Street, now Lombard Street.
From 1841 to 1905 Toronto's First Baptist Church stood at the corner of Victoria and Queen Streets.

Responding to the call to serve Black refugees in Canada West, he founded Baptist churches in Toronto, St. Catharines and Hamilton. Toward the end of his career, he also served as a pastor in the town of Niagara. The Toronto congregation grew in number until, in 1827, its members leased St. George's Masonic Hall for Sunday meetings. Their faithfulness and enthusiasm attracted some of Toronto's white residents, and they soon organized a congregation of their own:

> A few coloured people sixty years ago by organizing themselves into a Baptist Church, stimulated a few white people that attended their services to start out for themselves; from the latter, the old Bond Street church originated and from that the present Jarvis Street edifice started.[15]

The congregation of Toronto's First Baptist Church continued to grow. From 1834 to 1841 it met in a building on Lombard Street. Late in 1841 the congregation built a frame church on the northeast corner of Victoria and Queen Streets, on a lot donated by the family of Squires McCutcheon. In 1843 Elder Washington Christian, founder of the original congregation, left for a two-year stay in Jamaica. He returned with enough money donated by Baptists there to permit the Toronto group to pay off the mortgage on their church. First Baptist Church, situated today at D'Arcy and Huron Streets, has the distinction of being Toronto's oldest Black institution.

Another Baptist congregation was founded in St. Catharines in 1838 by Elder Christian. The group named its church 'Zion Baptist'. In 1840 the AME Church sent a circuit preacher, Alexander Helmsley, to serve the town's Blacks. The next year the AMEs of St. Catharines built a meeting house on land given them by one of the Black community's chief benefactors, William H. Merritt, a pioneer merchant and businessman of the town, who suggested the idea of building the Welland Canal. Henry Gray, a leader of the Black community, recorded the history of the church building in an open letter published in the *St. Catharines Journal* of March 11, 1841:

To My Colored Brethren
    When I first came into the province of Upper Canada, I settled in St. Catharines, and being a poor man myself,

I learned from my friends, that Mr. Merritt was the poor man's friend. Since that time, I have had no reason to change my opinion of him. To the colored population, he has been very kind and lenient; at least to ten or fifteen people of color, of my acquaintance who have, for a long period of time, held land of his, for which they bargained, but have never been able to pay; but they have not been distressed by him, nor turned off the land; and he has not even demanded from them the interest of the money due on the land.

I with many of my colored brethren, was desirous of having a chapel erected, for the sole use of people of color; but was fearful lest we could not raise money enough to buy the ground necessary to erect it upon; and I consulted with some of my brethren, and we formed a committee to go to Mr. Merritt and enquire, upon what terms he would let us have a lot of land sufficient for building a chapel upon — and much to our surprise, he immediately offered us, free from all charge, a lot of land, provided we would have a chapel built in five years — which we did, and then got our deed. The above land was granted to the Methodist people of color.

Between two and three years ago, a Baptist Society was formed, in this place, and we were desirous of erecting a meeting-house, for the Society's use. This we attempted to do by subscription. As we had to purchase the land, we were desirous of buying it from Mr. Merritt: but not finding any which, from its situation would suit us, we applied to H. Mittleberger, Esq., who offered us a lot, for $300—fifty of which he deducted as his subscription; the remainder to be paid in yearly instalments, of $50 each. A great many put their names on the subscription list, but afterwards refused to pay; and we failed in our endeavors to pay for the land, in consequence. When we went to Mr. Merritt, for the purpose of asking him to put his name on the list, he told us that when we had paid for the land, to come to him again; and he would help us to build the meeting-house. As I said before, we could not pay for the land, and went to Mr. Merritt and stated our failure to him. He told us to meet him at 9 o'clock the next morning, and he would give us a lot. This filled us with surprise and gratitude; for we could not have expected that he would have given us two lots.

In consequence of his generosity to the colored people, they have now one chapel built, in which they can worship God, and another they hope to be able to build soon — and in their prayers they always remember him,

as the poor man's benefactor, and the friend of the despised African.

Henry Gray

St. Catharines, March 6, 1841.

By 1844 Zion Baptist Church had become the reality Henry Gray had hoped for, and its pastor, the Reverend John Anderson, was serving 40 members. In the 1850s its pastor was the famous Black preacher Anthony Burns whose earlier capture in Boston and re-enslavement had caused great disturbance in the U.S.A. The congregation flourished, for as late as 1890 its Sunday School was still serving 80 or more children. In the early 20th century, however, its members reported: "Though few in number, we who love the old landmark will struggle on to preserve it, as a heritage, to pass on to the future generations in this place."[16] In spite of their best efforts, the "old landmark" has disappeared. In 1958 it was torn down to make room for a parking lot.

Amherstburg's First Baptist Church was founded between 1838 and 1841 under the leadership of the Reverend Anthony Binga, although the congregation did not manage to put up a building until 1845. In 1841, however, the members joined with their fellows in Detroit and Windsor to form the Amherstburg Regular Missionary Baptist Association (ARMBA). The group's goals were to promote unity among Black Baptists, to exchange ideas and to meet the religious needs of Blacks that had been neglected by the white churches of the area. An invitation to local Blacks to attend an organizational meeting stated:

> Resolved that we the Second Baptist Church of the City of Detroit believing that the time is Now Come that We ought to form ourselves into an association because We cannot enjoy the Privileges we Wish as Christians with the White Churches in Canada ... and believing that many of our fathers have gone down to the grave not enjoying their just privileges and rights in the Christian churches among the Whites ...[17]

As well as preaching the gospel, ARMBA gave personal and financial help to fugitives. The Association employed three Baptist ministers[18] who travelled through the southwestern districts of Canada West to hold services at missions too small to support their

A Sundary School class of First Baptist Church, Amherstburg, in the 1890s.

own minister. In 1847 Elder Wilks founded the First Regular Baptist Church of Colchester and arranged for it to join ARMBA. By the late 1850s 12 congregations in Canada West and five in Michigan had joined the Association.

Organized religious activity in Sandwich began in 1840 when its First Baptist Church was founded by a few ex-slaves who met at the foot of Huron Road. These people, led by Henry Brown, John Hubbs and Willis Jackson, called themselves 'The Close Communion of Baptists'. ARMBA and the congregation of the Second Baptist Church of Detroit helped the 11 founding members of the new group. It met at first in homes or out of doors. Its pastor in 1842 was a Brother J. Hubbs, a licentiate, who was assisted by itinerant ministers. By 1847 the group had 29 members and was mostly served by Elder G. Jacobs and Deacon H. Brown. In the following year the congregation built a small church. This was no mean accomplishment, for most of its members were farmers and labourers who built their church themselves in their limited spare time:

> After a long day of hard labour the men would spend their evenings hewing out logs to build a place for worship, a small log cabin that served as a church.[19]

As the number of Blacks in Sandwich continued to grow, the congregation needed larger premises. Rather remarkably, the members were able to persuade the government to grant land for a church and a graveyard. A crown patent was given to Henry Brant to permit him to hold just under a half-hectare for church purposes. The congregation undertook to raise funds for their new building, and the women's group shared their work:

> Dinner will be furnished by the Ladies for twenty-five cents per ticket—Refreshments may be had during the day and supper in the evening. The proceeds will be appropriated towards erecting a Baptist Church.[20]

According to the minutes of ARMBA each able-bodied male member was required to make a certain number of bricks for the new church at night. The building, which stood on Lot 22, West Peter Street, was completed in 1851. The Reverend M.J. Lightfoot was chosen to be the new minister. Unfortunately, friction developed among the members two years later, and a splinter group broke away to become 'The Frame Church Brethren'. ARMBA was able later on to reconcile the two groups, and by 1859 they had settled their differences amicably. In 1865 the congregation had 45 members, and in 1940, on its 100th anniversary, the church was still open, although its membership was very small. In that year one of its members wrote:

> Few in number are we, but the church doors are never closed.
>
> We are looking forward to a great meeting, in spirit, on this our one hundredth anniversary.
>
> As I close, it seems that in my vision I can see, again, the church filled with sweet memories of the past, of the pioneer fathers singing the songs of Zion. How firm a foundation!
>
> And on memory's page I can see again "the church by the side of the road."[21]

During the 1840s a few of Chatham's 200 Blacks founded a congregation. In 1843 the Reverend Stephen White led a group of nine Baptists into ARMBA. The Reverend Horace H. Hawkins, son-in-law of the Reverend Benjamin Paul of the Wilberforce Settlement, was ordained in the new Chatham congregation in 1845 and became its pastor in 1852; he also served as an ARMBA missionary throughout the district.

Thirty Blacks founded Chatham's Second Baptist Church in 1846; they called the Reverend Eli Highwarden from serving a Baptist group in Colchester to be their pastor. The newly organized group was eager to build a church, and successfully petitioned in the fall of 1848 for the grant of Lot 10 on the north side of Park Street for this purpose. They stated:

> ... that a very considerable number of the descendants of the natives of Africa have made their escape from the United States and taken up their residence in Chatham, where they are proud to find that the same encouragement for Education is held out alike to all classes without respect to colour: That your petitioners have for a considerable time past had to labour under considerable difficulty for want of a proper House wherein to worship God. That your petitioners are poor but willing and will voluntarily erect a Building if one half acre of land [.2 ha] can be obtained for them.[22]

It seems, too, that a third Baptist congregation, the Union Baptist Church, was founded about this time, possibly as a result of friction among members of the First and Second Baptist Churches. This possibility seems to be upheld by a report from Second Baptist Church read to the Annual Conference of 1854:

> We are thankful to God to meet you in our annual meeting. God has been good ... There has not been as much *union* among us as is desirable. We have had *no* pastor, a part of the year, though we have had preaching regularly.[23]

An account still exists of a baptismal service held by the Union Baptist Church:

> On Sunday afternoon 4th inst. ... 7 persons converts of the ... [Union] Baptist church were emerced [*sic*] in McGregor's Creek, by the Rev. Mr. Campbell. The day was pleasant and afforded an opportunity for a large turnout of the citizens. Some six hundred or more per-

The Reverend S.H. Lynn, founder of the Union Baptist Church in Dresden, Ontario.

sons were in attendance, crowding the banks on either side of the stream, all seeming anxious to witness the performance, and hear the sermon (which last, was concise, but appropriate,) rendering the scene both interesting and solemn.[24]

Whatever the churches' internal troubles may have been, they were evidently concerned with larger issues that affected the lives of Blacks beyond Chatham. In 1854, with 79 members served by the Reverend Stephen White, Second Baptist Church hosted a meeting of the Canadian Anti-Slavery Baptist Association. On December 3, 1855 the *Provincial Freeman* reported an interdenominational meeting in the church to hear a plan by Henry Garrett of London for freeing slaves in the United States. Garrett proposed to raise money from sympathisers in order to buy slaves and set them free, but the meeting rejected his plan because "... it recognized the legality of slavery."

By September, 1856 Chatham's three Black Baptist congregations must have come to terms, for the 1857 minutes of ARMBA refer to harmony among them:

> *Whereas.* There has [sic] been divisions and subdivisions among the colored Baptist denomination in Chatham, which resulted in several distinct and separate church organizations, each retaining and advocating Baptist sentiments in faith and practice. And whereas a proposition having been made — The 1st. Baptist, 2nd. Baptist, and the Union Baptist Churches did on the 18th. day of September 1856, in a meeting called for the purpose, unite themselves in one body in membership and property, namely "The First Colored Baptist Congregation of Chatham, Canada West," with a view to better promote and sustain the public and social worship of God among us, and in this community, and aid the growing interest at home and abroad of the Great Redeemer's Kingdom, separate and distinct from all slaveholding interests, holding no fellowship with Slavery, adopting for our articles of faith and practice, such as are known and recorded in the Baptist religious Literature of America. Done and recorded by order of the 1st colored Baptist congregation of Chatham.[25]

Chatham's First Baptist Church, on King Street between Prince and Princess Streets, served as a meeting place for the town's Black community. Besides providing Sunday services and weekly prayer-meetings, it became the headquarters of anti-slavery campaigns. It hosted meetings called to deal with the problems of Josiah Henson's Dawn Institute. Later it opened its doors to the abolitionist John Brown as he tried to organize Canadian Blacks to support his projected raid at Harpers Ferry.

The Reverend Daniel Turner, Sr., born in Baltimore in 1805, had come to Canada to minister to the Black settlers at Wilberforce. He is credited with founding the Second Baptist Church of London. In 1845 Aby

SUNDAY SERVICES
9 BIBLE SCHOOL
11 A.M. WORSHIP 7 P.M.

LET THE CHILDREN COME TO
ME DO NOT HINDER THEM. FOR
TO SUCH BELONGS THE KINGDOM
OF GOD

THE FIRST
BAPTIST CHURCH.
1858.

Jones bought from W. Welch a property at 260 Horton Street, west of Wellington, and donated it to the congregation. Jones also gave money to help put up a frame building on the site. The 30 or so members of the new church arranged for it to join ARMBA in 1856. Within two years the congregation had more than doubled its membership to 73 persons. Its early officers and deacons included the Jones brothers, George Duncan, John Pope and John Reeves. Daniel Turner died in 1860 and was succeeded by the Reverend B. Miller and Elder Marshall. The emigration of many members to the U.S.A. during the American Civil War reduced the membership to 62 by 1863 and to 37 by '65. In spite of its small numbers and consequent financial difficulties, the church kept its doors open until it sold its property and disbanded in 1929.

Hamilton's Coloured Baptist Church was founded in 1847 through the work of Elder Washington Christian who had started the Baptist movement in Toronto a decade or so earlier. In 1856 Elder A. Brown was pastor of this church on McNab Street between Cannon and Mulberry.

The Baptists were the last of the Black groups to start a work in Windsor. The town's First Baptist Church was founded by the Reverend William Troy who was born on March 27, 1827 in Essex, Virginia, of a free mother and a slave father. Troy made his way from Virginia to Cincinnati, Ohio, where he joined the Zion Baptist Church and was given a basic education by a local Baptist clergyman. He worked for a short time for the Underground Railroad before he moved to Canada in 1854. Troy began as a minister in Amherstburg; while serving there he also commuted to Windsor to organize prayer-meetings in the home of Joseph Faulkner on McDougall Street. In 1856 Troy moved to Windsor to give all his time to organizing a Black congregation there. Its founders were the following men and their wives: Joseph Faulkner, Stephen Holland, Stephen Jones, Samuel Harper, Allen Browning, 'Father' Cole, Samuel Gibbs and Allen Sydney. The new congregation met at first in its members' homes and later in a small frame building on McDougall Street near Albert. In 1856, with 26 members, the group petitioned to join ARMBA. Soon the members needed a larger building. They pooled their resources and sent Troy to England to raise funds. There he made speeches and raised the money needed, including a donation from Queen Victoria who granted him an audience. Troy also found time in England to write a book entitled *Hair Breadth Escapes from Slavery to Freedom*.

The new church building was finally completed in 1862. It was a two-storey brick structure on the east side of McDougall, north of Albert Street. Three years later the congregation reached its peak of 147 members. Its numbers declined after the American Civil War, but its fine brick church remained in use until 1915 when, under the leadership of the Reverend Charles L. Wells, a new church was built at Mercer and Tuscarora Streets. A thriving congregation still meets in this historic church.

The Reverend William Troy (inset) *founded Windsor's First Baptist Church in 1853. Today its congregation meets in a fine brick church* (opposite).

9
Blacks and the Schools

Getting Started

EDUCATION WAS ENORMOUSLY important to the fugitives. As slaves, almost all of them had been kept illiterate, for their owners fully understood that education might lead them to a more urgent quest for freedom. The Black Codes passed in many states prohibited education for slaves, or even exposure to any ideas that might make them restless with their lot. Indeed, to teach a slave to read or write was, in many areas, an offence punishable by a long jail term. For these reasons most adult refugees were untaught, but they were eager to send their children to school so that they might succeed in their new country.

In the 1790s and the early 1800s schools in Upper Canada were few and far between. The better-off settlers living in the Western District taught their own children or hired tutors for them. No district (public) schools were provided for children until 1807, when the District Schools Act was passed. It provided up to £800 to set up government schools in each district. With this assistance, a school was opened at Sandwich; it was managed by a board of trustees appointed by the Governor-in-Council. Unfortunately, it did little to promote general education:

> The school for the Western District was at Sandwich, and was of little benefit to the rural sections. The district schools in general were unpopular, as they were undemocratic in organization and soon became class schools.[1]

The situation improved somewhat after 1816, when

Refugees who could not spare time from their work to go to school were sometimes taught to read by their children at home.

John Strachan, Bishop of Toronto, a staunch conservative and supporter of the privileged upper class, was made responsible for Upper Canada's first 'common school' system.

Upper Canada passed the Common Schools Act. Under this statute $24 000 a year was to be provided to open common (public) schools in the province's 10 districts. The money was to be distributed in proportion to the population and the number of students; any deficits were to be met with fees paid directly by the students' parents. To be eligible for government funding of its school, a community had first to build a schoolhouse, elect three trustees and enrol 20 pupils.

The trustees' duties were to choose textbooks, appoint teachers and prescribe courses; they themselves were responsible to a District Board of Education nominated by the Lieutenant-Governor. The Reverend John Strachan was appointed director of the whole school system.

In 1823 a provincial Board of Education was formed, with Strachan as its president. This Board's duty was to supervise all Upper Canadian schools. Any group of parents with at least 20 school-age children among them could now petition for a common school; local trustees were still empowered to choose the teacher. A government subsidy of £10 per teacher per year made possible some improvement in teachers' salaries, though by no means all that was needed. In the late 1830s many residents of the Western District complained of the poor quality of local education: "[Local teachers are] ill fed, ill clothed, ill paid or not paid at all, always either Scotch or American, and totally unfit for the office they [have] undertaken."[2]

Separate — and Unequal

Added to all the other difficulties of providing schooling for their children that Black parents had to overcome was the fact that, in many communities, Black pupils were not welcome in the common schools. The growing numbers of refugees through the 1830s-'50s increased the problems of the situation. In the Windsor region, for instance, white settlers did not openly oppose the influx of Black fugitives, for the refugees were industrious, and most of them seemed to be providing for themselves and adjusting well to Canadian life. But Black pupils were not wanted in the common schools of Essex County. Although the refugees did not push for immediate entry to these schools, the issue was sensitive, and it simmered and occasionally boiled over in bitter attacks on the common school system by Black organizations and newspapers. Since their children needed education, the refugees were eventually forced to set up Black schools. Ironically, this action caused more division between whites and Blacks and sparked serious quarrels within the Black community. Mary Ann Shadd and Henry Bibb became bitter enemies over these and other matters, and their quarrel left Blacks without a unified voice to speak out against the segregated school system that was spreading through the province.

In 1837 the small Black community of Brantford set up its own school since its children were excluded from the town's common school. The Black school was most successful, and its level of instruction was soon thought to be considerably higher than that of the common school. As a result, so many white parents applied to send their children to the Black school that it looked as if the common school would have to close, and its trustees decided to admit all the town's children, regardless of race. Black parents continued to keep a watchful eye on education, and some years later a teacher who had allowed her pupils to sing "Negro songs" drew the wrath of a Brantford correspondent to the *Provincial Freeman*:

> The national music, as it is styled in the States, may do there; but it is a disgrace to Canadians, and a direct insult to the colored tax payers who help support such schools. It is well understood that such music tends to reconcile Americans to the "institution" of slavery; and its introduction into the public schools in this country cannot have an elevating tendency.[3]

Black children in London and its vicinity had considerable difficulty gaining admission to the town's common school as early as 1840. Benjamin Drew reported:

> Many of the whites object to having their children sit in the same forms with the colored pupils; and some of the lower classes will not send their children to schools where the blacks are admitted.[4]

The London branch of the Bible Society deplored the situation, arguing that London's 200 Blacks paid school taxes and had an "... equal right to participate in the blessings of education." In fact:

> If any Coloured child enters a school, the white children are withdrawn, the teachers are painfully obliged to decline, and the Coloured people, while they acutely feel the anomoly of their painful position, yield to an injustice which they are too weak to redress.[5]

Eventually the Bible Society regretfully recommended

separate schools for Blacks. In 1849 at least one such school was being funded with tax dollars. Miss R.J. Dawsey, a white woman, petitioned London's Town Council in January, 1850 to pay the salary owed her for teaching 40 Black pupils the previous year. Her petition was sent on to the School Board, which settled the debt.

It is heartening that at least one attempt at integrated education had a brief success. In 1840 a Scottish immigrant, James Dougall, arrived in Amherstburg and recognized the need for a

> ... first class school, where the white children including my own, and the colored children, should be admitted on

Going to school.

an equal footing, so as to do away if possible with the growing prejudice existing amongst them.[6]

Dougall sent to Scotland for a relative who was a qualified teacher, and in due time Robert Peden arrived to teach the local children. The school was successful at first, but after six years financial difficulties forced it to close. Still, it had made a mark in the history of Canada West, for it was one of the few schools of that period in which Black children sat side by side with white.

In Hamilton, as in several other parts of the province, the trustees responsible for the common schools refused to admit Black children. Paola Brown and "The Coloured People of Hamilton" officially protested such discrimination to the Governor General, Lord Elgin:

> ... we have tried every lawful and civil means to get our children into the common schools, and as yet have failed in the attempt. ... We are called nigger when we go out in the street and sometimes brick bats is sent after us as we pass in the street.[7]

The Governor General's office asked Hamilton's Board of Police to supply more information. George S. Tiffany, its president, admitted that there was "... a strong prejudice existing among the lower orders of the whites against the Negroes."[8] He expressed the fear that, if Black children were enrolled in Hamilton's schools, white children would be withdrawn. In spite of this, Tiffany took a courageous stand:

> The Board of Police are unanimous in their opinion that whatever may be the state of feeling at present ... it would not be advisable to yield to it, but that the law ought to be enforced without distinction of colour. They think that if a firm stand be taken at first, the prejudice will soon give way.[9]

On the basis of this recommendation, Black children were accepted for a time by Hamilton's common schools.

Hamilton, Canada West, about 1850.

In Chatham an inferior segregated school was opened for Black children about 1840. Years earlier, in 1828, members of the town's Black community had met with Archdeacon Strachan to try to organize a separate school, but they could not subscribe enough money to meet expenses, and no school was provided. Later a few of Chatham's Black families were able to send their children to the Buxton School at the Elgin Settlement, though most families had no choice but to send their children to the local school for Blacks. Sixteen of these families submitted a mildly worded petition to the Solicitor General, John Hillyard Cameron:

> We are all Freeholders in the County, and, as a body we wish to testify our gratitude to the County, which has received us and the Constitution which protects us, by recording our votes in favour of a loyal and good man. That you are such we feel assured; that you will not neglect the educational and other interests of the colored race, we are certain; and again request that you come and receive our votes.[10]

Local school trustees, faced with increasing pressure to improve school facilities, planned to build three more schools. One of these, on King Street, was to be set aside for Black pupils. Their parents, who were deeply discouraged by local prejudice, half-heartedly agreed to the plan, thinking that it would slightly improve their children's chances for an education. Later, however, Henry Bibb, editor of the *Voice of the Fugitive*, harshly criticised the Black parents who had agreed to accept a separate school:

> This request [for a separate school], however, was not made by the intelligent portion of the colored population, but by a lot of ignoramuses who were made tools of, and who knew not what they were doing.[11]

Mission Schools

Some of the churches and mission societies of Canada West were aware of the disadvantages to Black children of their limited opportunities for education. Their members began to found schools and supply teachers for Blacks in some communities. At Dawn, Elgin and London, for example, missions opened private schools for Black children. The Buxton Mission School at Elgin was so successful and became so famous that many white parents in its neighbourhood preferred it to the local common school, which was finally forced to close.

Isaac Rice, the much-criticised founder of the Union Border Mission, made at least one positive contribution to the education of Black children in Canada West. Rice had found it hard to get teaching materials for his school, for most such items had to be imported from the U.S.A. and were subject to high duty. About 1844 he appealed to Governor General Metcalfe for relief from this duty. His action brought attention to the situation, and soon afterward customs officers began to allow school supplies to enter the province without import tax.

In the late 1840s the first school in the Queen's Bush was built with the help of the American Missionary Association. Fidelia Coburn, a wealthy woman from Maine, was its first teacher, and among its first pupils was a sprinkling of white children. One Black settler, at least, was dissatisfied with the school's curriculum. John Francis criticised the teaching given to the children because their teachers did not share the Black parents' abhorrence of slavery and were not stressing the notion of getting ahead and elevating their race. Francis hoped to be able to remedy the situation somewhat himself: "When any children get old enough to read, I intend to instruct them about slavery, and get books to show them what we have been through, and fit them for a good example."[12]

In 1850 the Canada Mission and the Free Baptist Mission opened a school for Black children in Chatham; its teacher was a Miss Huntingdon. At that time the Black common school was taught in a derelict log building on King Street East. Its teacher was James Grant, a Black, who described the town's schools for Black children in a letter to the *Voice of the Fugitive*:

> Two schools, one a Government School, established some twelve years ago, the other Free Mission, started last summer and [is] taught by Miss Huntingdon.
>
> The Government School, here, numbered in 1848, 49 scholars, the first year I took charge of the school. In 1849, 76; in 1850, 91; as follows: Grammar, 7; History and Geography, 9; Writing and Arithmetic, 33; Reading and Spelling, 42; scholars: males, 45; females, 46; average

daily attendance, 45½. This season, the school is free to all children living within the corporation or limits of the town. Attendance in January, 73 scholars, February, 76—to the 31st March, 65. Studies of the same during the quarter, History, Geography, Grammar, Arithmetic, Town's Reader and Test Mat—37; Reading and Spelling—37. Total number of scholars, 86; and might have numbered 100 or over had we a school house sufficiently large to have accommodated all who wished to attend, as it was, we were obligated during the Winter to send some 15 small scholars to my house for instruction by my wife. The Board of Trustees have promised the erection of a school house, large and commodious, this coming Summer. Our Sabbath School numbers from 60 to 100, and sometimes over, according to the state of the roads; it has seven teachers. We need Bibles for the Sabbath School and Bible class, and have many applications for the Bible from the poor and indigent. We need a larger library and a large Sabbath School map, temperance and other tracts for distribution among children and to be read at home to parents during the week. We are also in great need of reading books, slates and some six or seven dozen of Webster's Spelling Book, (the only American Spelling book allowed in Government Schools) for the use of poor scholars. We hope with a little help to be able to continue to keep our schools open to all living without [i.e. outside] the corporation, and that all children may enjoy the benefit of a common school education ...

Yours for the oppressed,
(signed) James E. Grant[13]

In London the Anglican CCSS decided to meet the problem of segregated education head on. In June, 1854 it commissioned the Reverend Martin M. Dillon, then stationed in Dominica, to come and set up a mission and school. Dillon brought with him R.M. Ballantine, a graduate of Mico Training College in Kingston, Jamaica, and two Black student-teachers from Dominica, Sarah and Mary Ann Titré; they became the first Black women to teach integrated classes in the province. The CCSS opened its school to both white and Black pupils in a London barracks on November 20, 1854. On the first day 11 children registered, and by the end of the first week, there were 50 pupils. Dillon proudly claimed: "... it is the first

A Mission School

instance, either in the United States or in this country, in which coloured persons have been introduced as teachers of mixed classes ... It succeeded."[14]

The school soon moved from the barracks to a building that was probably next to St. Paul's Church. On July 12, 1855 Dillon reported that a representative of the Canadian Anti-Slavery Society had visited London's common schools and found only 19 Black pupils in attendance. He was astonished to learn that the Mission School had 75 Black children registered and 64 actually in attendance.

> Next day he returned at play hour and was much pleased to see the freedom with which the white and coloured children played together.[15]

As its enrolment increased, the Mission School hired several more teachers. Its curriculum included Scripture-reading, junior reading, spelling and alphabet, writing on paper, writing on slates, and arithmetic. To the more advanced classes it offered grammar, geography, mental arithmetic, natural history, natural philosophy and needlework. The demand for admission of both white and Black pupils was dramatic: by the end of 1855 the school had 450 pupils and a waiting list of 960 applicants.

In spite of its highly successful beginning, the Mission School had a disastrous winter in 1855-56. The Titré sisters became ill, probably from tuberculosis, and returned to Dominica. Shortly afterwards Dillon, who was under great financial and other pressures, suffered a nervous breakdown. He was relieved of his duties in November, 1856 and returned to England. The end came in 1859, when the Mission School was able to announce that the common schools of London had finally opened their doors to all children, without distinction of race or colour.

The Common Schools Act of 1850

In 1850 Canada West passed provincial legislation which, for the first time, included conditions for the legal establishment of separate public schools for Blacks and whites. Faced with this racist legislation, Black parents responded by setting up private, religiously-oriented schools for their children, while continuing to protest.

In February, 1851, at the request of over 200 Blacks, Paola Brown spoke out against the poor quality of education in Hamilton's common schools:

> It is lamentable that many of our children go to school from four until they are eight or ten and sometimes fifteen years of age, and leave school knowing but a little more about the grammar of their language, than a horse does about handling a musket; and not a few of them are really so ignorant that they are unable to answer a person correctly general questions in Geography, and to hear them read would only be to disgust a man who has a taste for reading ...[16]

Later Benjamin Drew observed that there were 1700 children in Hamilton schools, "... of whom 25 are coloured." Writing of the city's Central School, Drew claimed that of 800 pupils enrolled, only seven were Black. He believed that the number was low because Black parents kept their children out of school to avoid racial animosity.

It was in 1851 that a separate school was opened, under the Common Schools Act, for Amberstburg's Black children. Its first teacher, J. Underwood, was also Black. He was so well liked that after eight months his salary was doubled—to $30.00 a month. The money was not entirely at his personal disposal, however, for Underwood and the teachers who followed him had to rent classrooms and pay for the fuel to heat them out of their salaries.

Underwood was replaced in 1854 by Miss Julia Turner. When Benjamin Drew visited the school in that year, he formed a good impression of her: "She appeared to be one of the working sort, disposed to bear up as well as she could under her many discouragements."[17]

These included "... the frequent absence of pupils" —only 24 were present that day—and the school's limited equipment. It had no blackboard and only two inkwells, which contained a poor grade of ink; the books were in a "... tattered and worn-out condition." Miss Turner finally resigned in December, 1856, after some of her pupils' parents, opposed to a woman teacher, drew up a petition asking for the appointment

of a man. Her replacement, J.B. Williams, did not prove satisfactory and was replaced by Jacob Taylor and a woman assistant, Miss Green. By this time the "coloured school" was held in a house belonging to a Mr. Lewis, at an annual rent of $36.00. Taylor remained as teacher until 1866; two years before he left, the school was moved to a house bought from a Mr. McGuire for $450.00. This house was torn down some years later to be replaced by a school costing $1743.00.

The Blacks of Amherstburg were not satisfied to be restricted to separate schools. Mrs. Levi Foster, for instance, appealed to the District School Board to allow her to send her children to the common school, but was refused. According to the Board, the separate school "... was sufficient for the wants of the colored people."[18]

In Chatham, too, racial segregation continued in the schools. In 1854 Aaron Highgate, a Black, was appointed teacher of the 'coloured school' on Princess Street at a salary of £100 a year. His appointment, effective in September, was conditional until December; it was to be extended if he could then produce a certificate of qualification. This he evidently did, for he taught in Chatham until 1856, when he was replaced by Alfred Whipper. The latter had been teaching in a private school for Blacks that was no more than a room rented from a Mr. Bell for $3.50 a month. In 1858 the municipality had taken over this private school and was running it as a second Black school. In 1860 Whipper was replaced by a white teacher, Peter Nicol. Black parents objected, arguing that their children needed a Black leader, but the Board replied that Nicol, who held a Class A certificate, was the best qualified applicant. While Nicol was teaching there, the Board had an addition built to the overcrowded Princess Street School, but it continued to draw complaints from the Black community. The addition, which cost $299, was a frame structure without a foundation or plumbing. Water was supplied by a pump in the yard and heat by a wood stove. The small-paned windows gave little light. The facilities were probably not much better and not much worse than those of most rural schools of the period. Segregated schools persisted in Chatham until 1890, when public pressure

The 'Old King Street School' of Chatham, Canada West, actually stood on Princess Street. Here John Brown and his supporters held one of their historic meetings.

finally forced its Board of Education to approve truly 'public' schools.

As in other communities, education for Blacks declined in Windsor's common schools after the Act of 1850. Black parents, realizing that their children would be refused admission to the town's common schools, hired Mary Ann Shadd to teach a private school. Shadd opened her classes in the fall of 1851 in Windsor's old and dilapidated barracks. She had been assured that she would have 20 day pupils and an adults' evening class, but she started with 13 day and 11 evening students. Those who could afford to pay sixpence a week toward their teacher's salary were expected to do so; those who could not were admitted free. Soon after classes opened, payments began to fall off, and the school was in danger of closing. Shadd turned to the AMA for support, claiming that a teacher could not live on the salary the parents paid. George Whipple of the AMA arranged for a subsistence grant of $125 a year, which allowed Shadd to continue teaching, but the local Board of Health declared the barracks unfit for human habitation, and some parents kept their children at home because of this. Then an epidemic of cholera struck Windsor in the summer and early fall of 1852. Shadd and some of her pupils fell ill, and the school was closed for a time.

Its attendance picked up again later in the year, and enrolment increased from 20 to 30, with pupils ranging in age from four to 45 years. Meanwhile local Blacks began to raise funds for a small frame schoolhouse, which got under way in October. The fee per pupil was raised to one shilling and sixpence a month for those who could afford to pay; the others were still admitted free. Shadd, who taught 10 different classes, was considered an exceptional teacher and received the praise of the community. Her schedule included:

2 classes in Geography	1 [class in] 3rd Reader
1 class in History	1 [class in] 2nd Reader
1 class in Colburn's arithmetic	1 [class in] Written Arithmetic
2 classes in Grammar	1 [class in] Botany[19]

It was unfortunate that at this point Mary Ann Shadd quarrelled with Henry Bibb, editor of the *Voice of the Fugitive*. Her criticism of some of Bibb's policies and practices provoked his counter-accusation that she had concealed from the Black community the fact of the AMA grant that supported her school. Bibb followed up his accusation in print:

At this we understand, that there was an offence taken by Miss Shadd, where there was none intended by us. We heard her say that she was receiving 'three york shillings, from each of her pupils per month,' which sum was not enough to support her from about 20 children, and after we learned that the above society [AMA] had granted her the sum of $125, we thought that they did well, and we ventured to give publicity to the fact, for the encouragement of our people in Windsor as they were entirely ignorant of it up to that time, so this was good news to them, and as our business is to give the news, and not knowing that she wished this information kept from the parents of the children, we gave publicity to it and for which Miss Shadd has said and written many things which we think will add nothing to her credit as a lady, for there should be no insult taken where there is none intended.[20]

Shadd replied that she had not spoken publicly about the grant because it was not enough to support the school entirely, and she was afraid that parents who learned of it might stop paying fees. The parents' committee to which she was responsible upheld her reasons, but Bibb did not report this. Instead, he attacked her again, claiming that she did not accept white pupils, and he printed no retraction when he

Mary Ann Shadd Cary

There have been large Day, Evening and Sabbath Schools during the winter and up to this time, and I have been requested to continue, but cannot say for how long, even after resuming school duties again should I depend on them alone.

Very respectfully
Yours etc.
Mary A. Shadd[21]

Mary Ann Shadd left Windsor in the spring of 1853, disillusioned by her experiences with Henry Bibb and the AMA. With the collapse of her school, Windsor's Black children had little opportunity for education. In 1854, in fact, the Windsor School Board decided that three new schools were badly needed for the growing Black, Catholic and Protestant communities. Two years later the Catholic and Protestant schools were admitting pupils, but no building was provided for Black pupils until, in the fall of 1858, dilapidated premises were rented for them. In 1862 St. George School was finally built for Blacks on the northeast corner of McDougall and Assumption Streets, and in February, 1863 a committee was chosen to supervise it. By 1864 it had 150 pupils. Schools in Windsor remained segregated until 1888 when, after continual protests, Black children were finally admitted to the city's common schools.

Mary Bibb, the wife of Mary Ann Shadd's enemy, opened a classroom in her home in Sandwich in January, 1851. Within a month the enrolment jumped from 25 to 46 pupils. In February Bibb managed to find a larger room for her pupils, but it was "... ill-ventilated, with uncomfortable seats and a shortage of desks and apparatus."[22] Besides, Mrs. Bibb had to carry firewood quite a distance to heat the schoolroom. In spite of these conditions, the parents of six white children sent them to Bibb's school. Her salary as teacher-caretaker was $10 for a whole eight-month term!

The *Provincial Freeman* of May 26, 1854 claimed in an article by J.W. Loguen that Niagara's school for Black children was inferior, had not been requested by Black parents and would be boycotted:

> The Government school house for colored children, built by American caste and placed in the outskirts of the town by American prejudice, they disdain to occupy.

learned that there had been several white pupils in Shadd's school from the first.

This public quarrel had disastrous effects. The AMA grew increasingly concerned about Shadd's image in the community and finally withdrew its support on the "... trumped-up charge ..." that her religious views were not compatible with its own. In spite of her gifts as a teacher and the success of her school, Shadd decided to leave Windsor. She wrote to George Whipple of the AMA:

> This whole business is really sickening to me. A regular and well executed series of attacks might be resisted by a man of strong physical constitution, but I am not equal to it I confess. ... I must say though, I hope ever to have unrestricted liberty of opinion on all matters of general interest — never to allow interest to become master of principle; and always to act as God requires.

Denied equal school rights by the Government, they scorn the favor which prescribes their equality and dignity. They have braved too much for freedom to consent to the degredation which such a boon implies.[23]

Although some families did carry out this threat, the school soon had 60 pupils ranging in age from five to 25 years. Eagerness to learn obviously outweighed resentment of segregation among some of the refugees. In 1857 the School Board agreed to admit a few Black pupils to the upper grades of 'white' schools, but insisted that the Black children should be seated and taught separately. In 1863-64 Mr. James Brown taught 130 pupils in Niagara's Black school, but by December, 1869 the enrolment had dropped to 34, and the school, taught by Mr. O.F. Wilkins, had been moved to the corner of Catharine and Welland Avenue.

In Amherstburg, too, the legalizing of segregated schools penalized Black children. In 1856 a separate school for the children of the 23 Black families of No. 6 School District of Malden Township was open for only three months. When concerned parents asked that their children be admitted to the 'white' common school, the trustees were very angry. Segregated schooling continued in the district until 1910. After 1870 Black children were, in theory, admitted to King Street Public School, but a separate log building next to the main school was set aside for them.

In St. Catharines the Black community tested the legality of the School Board's policy of segregation in the case of *Hutchison vs. St. Catharines*. Mr. Justice Joseph Curran Morrison of the Court of Queen's Bench heard the case in 1871. The complainant contended that Judge Morrison should deny the Board's right to keep "… any kind or description of schools …" including segregated ones. The Judge found that the Board had opened a separate school in 1846, before the Act of

Canada West's Common Schools Act of 1850 was interpreted in ways that reinforced segregated education.

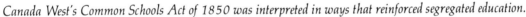

1850 had given it the legal right to do so. But after he stated that the Board's action had been highly irregular, he sidestepped the issue by ruling that there was no room in the common school for the Hutchison children. In this way he tacitly reinforced the fact of segregated schools. As the refugee population dwindled in the 1870s, some of the remaining Black children were admitted to the town's common schools, but it was not until 1883 that a policy of integrated education opened all grade levels to Black pupils there.

In the 1860s a survey of London's seven wards showed that only 50 of the town's 96 Black school-age children were actually in school. Blacks were certainly discouraged from attending, for an American abolitionist, Dr. Samuel Gridley Howe, who visited Canada West in 1862, reported that the principal of London's Union School had told him: "It does not work well to have colored children in school with the whites ..." In that same year a Mr. Webb, one of London's school trustees, proposed a motion to the School Board that included the clause:

> We still recognize the principle that it would be beneficial to all classes of the community (especially to the coloured children) that a distinct and separate class or school be formed for all the coloured children attending the Common schools in the City of London and would recommend the adoption by the Board of such a system as soon as financially practicable.[24]

In December, 1862 the London Board of Education voted one to three in favour of segregated education for Black pupils. An excerpt from the minutes reads:

> In a report presented to the Board by a Committee struck for the purpose of inquiring into the propriety of opening a separate school for coloured children, it was urged that, the indiscriminate attendance, and the mixing together of the white and the coloured children in our schools are productive of evil to both; and if provision were made for a separate education the results would be found beneficial, especially to the coloured portion of the population. The Board in adopting the principle embodied in this Report did not overlook the fact, that in our excellent school system, provision is made for the education of all classes of the community; without respect to colour, creed, nationality or social position, and in dealing with this subject they do not deny to the coloured people any of the rights of fellow-subjects or fellow citizens; neither have they any desire to institute a system of persecution or oppression, but in the performance of their duty, and in the exercise of the powers with which they are invested by the School Act to provide for the coloured people a system of education which will be attended by the best results to them and meet the prejudices which many of the white people entertain to the association and intercourse now existing.[25]

While it is not clearly recorded how far the London Board put into practice its policy of segregated schools, its minutes for July, 1863 show that some action had been taken, for the town was asked for "... the further sum of $500 for providing additional school accommodation for coloured children."[26]

Alfred Jones, a wealthy pharmacist, led the Blacks' opposition to London's segregated schools. Jones told Howe that he had been a slave for 20 years, but that his eight children were born and bred in London, and therefore were British subjects like others. He believed that, if the Board kept up a policy of full segregation, his children would grow up hating their country. Fortunately, segregation was never fully practised in London's schools.

Toronto was unique among the larger communities of Canada West in keeping its schools integrated. There were two chief reasons for this record. In the first place, Toronto was a centre of abolitionist activity, and its anti-slavery sentiment was strong; indeed, the Canadian Anti-Slavery Society was founded there. Secondly, Black immigration took place at a slower rate in Toronto than it did in the southwestern towns and cities of the province, and most of Toronto's residents did not feel threatened by an influx of refugees as some smaller communities did. The influence of George Brown of the *Globe* was also a strong deterrent to any racist policy in the city. Examples of integrated education are many. Emaline Shadd, for instance, won first prize for students at Toronto Normal School in 1855. W.P. Hubbard attended the prestigious Toronto Model School in the 1860s; Anderson Ruffin Abbott graduated from the Toronto School of Medicine in 1857, and A.T. Augusta from Trinity Medical College, Toronto, in 1860. Peter Gallego was a student at Upper Canada College and an early graduate of the Univer-

Anderson Ruffin Abbott

sity of Toronto. The record of Toronto's Black students makes it plain that in practising a policy of integrated education the city reaped a generous reward.

Black Schools in the Maritimes

The first school for Black children in Nova Scotia seems to have been opened in 1784 by a Church of England clergyman, the Reverend John Breynton of St. Paul's Church, Halifax. Later that year a small philanthropic society known as 'The Associates of the Late Dr. Bray' (ALDB), opened a similar school at Digby, with Breynton's encouragement. Within a year ALDB had opened two more schools, one at Birchtown and another at George Brindley Town; a third was opened at Preston in 1788. The policy of ALDB was to provide a few books and a salary of £9 for a teacher if at least 30 pupils were enrolled.[27] The Church of England catechism was part of the curriculum, but children of other denominations could attend, slave as well as free. Teachers were often hard to find and to keep, for any who held "... strange religious tenets..."[28] did not receive their pay! The courses of study were usually limited to reading, writing, simple arithmetic and sewing, and pupils memorized most of the information they were taught. Even so, the schools were useful to the Black community: students became literate, their memories were trained, and a tendency to segregation was slowed because a few white pupils attended. Black teachers gradually replaced white teachers, and women were sometimes hired to teach — at half the salary offered men!

In 1811 Nova Scotia's Assembly passed a School Act which provided school funds for any community that had built a schoolhouse, appointed a teacher and raised £50 towards schooling. While the Act may, in theory, have provided equal help to all communities, no Black community was able to meet its conditions. Again, in 1816, the Assembly authorized its Army Fund to provide two schools for Black children, but neither was actually opened, thought small grants were made to Black schools in Halifax, Bridgetown and Hammond's Plains.

The Society for the Propagation of the Gospel (SPG) opened a school for Black pupils at Preston in 1818 and another at Hammond's Plains in 1820.[29] It also contributed to schools in Tracadie, Yarmouth and Digby.[30]

In 1832 the School Act was amended to allow a grant of up to £70 a year to fund a school in any district that could not afford one unaided; an extra £5 a year was granted for books. In 1836 the Board of School Commissioners was authorized to use some of this money to open schools for Blacks, whether a common school existed or not. The result of these changes in the Act was that Black communities could legally open schools, though they were not actually in a position to do this, and a policy of segregated education was begun.

An African School was opened in Halifax in 1836 after £300 was raised for it by public subscription. Of the town's 300 Black children, 50 attended until the building burned down eight months later. The Reverend John Inglis, Bishop of Nova Scotia, worked hard to raise funds to rebuild the school, and late in 1840 a new and simpler building was erected. The province supported the school until it was struck from the Assembly's annual grants' list in 1844, but funding was resumed after several members of the Assembly visited classes and saw their work in progress. From 1836 to 1854 the teacher was Daniel Gallagher. Although he was handicapped by blindness in one eye, he was a fine teacher; his curriculum included reading, writing, catechism, geography, navigation, palm-weaving and Bible study; his wife taught knitting and other household arts. Gallagher was devoted to his

Halifax, Nova Scotia, 1801.

A young Nova Scotian about 1845.

work, and when he retired, it was discovered that he had paid for the school's furniture, maps and fuel from his own small salary. The school began to decline almost as soon as Gallagher retired, since the ALDB was unable to continue its support after 1861. In that year the school, which had been renamed 'Inglis' Boys School' closed down. The boys' and girls' African Schools reopened in Halifax after the American Civil War; they were funded by the province after 1873.

The progress of Black education in New Brunswick was, if anything, less encouraging. The SPG opened schools for Blacks in St. John, Fredericton and St. Andrews. In Fredericton, too, the townspeople raised £60 and the legislature granted £100 to provide a school for Black children. In general, however, Black schooling in the Maritimes was "… poor, unsystematic, and undependable …"[31] Black teachers did not always have much opportunity for training and were limited by their own experience in poorly equipped schools. The Bishop of Nova Scotia commented sadly in 1856 that white residents of the province "… in general care so little for Blacks, that assistance cannot be obtained."[32]

10
The Work-A-Day World

Settling and Serving

MOST OF UPPER Canada's first Black immigrants entered the colony as slaves. In general, they worked as domestics and labourers, although some were given an elementary education and placed in positions of responsibility. Those owned by French-speaking masters such as Joseph Campeau spoke the language fluently. Mullett, one of Campeau's 10 Black slaves, was his clerk and showed "... integrity and shrewdness in business matters." Hector, who belonged to General John R. Williams, ran the *Oakland Chronicle* newspaper plant, but lost his job when Williams sold the paper. Hector learned of the sale only when Williams had to persuade him to turn over the premises to the new owner.

Pompey, or 'Pomp', one of John Askin's favourite slaves, whom Askin bought about 1775, sailed on the *Mackinac*, one of the Askin schooners. Its skipper, Captain Barthe, was Askin's brother-in-law. He had orders to issue himself and an Indian crew-member a pint of rum each day, and "... Pomp half that amount." Later Askin wrote to Barthe: "We must find a man to go in Pomp's place after this voyage. I cannot do without him."[1] Pomp, whose name appears in many of the Askin letters, took up his duties again at the family warehouse and farm.

The earliest free Black settlers cleared land and farmed it. William Davenport, his wife, Sarah, and his brother Benjamin entered Upper Canada about 1810. After living for a time in Amherstburg, they moved on to Flos Township near Oro. William and Sarah and

Edward Patterson, a lay preacher, drove a stage between Meaford and Owen Sound.

their five children soon settled on Lot 2, Wilberforce Street in Oro. Benjamin stayed in Flos where, in the 1820s, he worked for Alexander Walker, teaming government supplies over the 15-kilometre portage from Kempenfeldt Bay to the Nottawasaga River.

The first permanent settler was a colored man, named Davenport, who for reasons of his own chose to take up a remote lot rather than one of the free grants made to people of his race in Oro. It is a peculiar fact that this man and his brother, who also settled in Flos, were the only successful black pioneers; for while all the other names passed away from the neighbourhood years ago, Davenports of the second generation[2] still hold and work farms in Flos, and are living representatives of the earliest pioneer family in the township ... The first man to bring a horse into the township, or indeed this side of the lake, was Benjamin Davenport, one of the colored brothers.[3]

James Pleasant Bush was one of the more industrious and prosperous Black settlers of Oro. He arrived there with his family on April 25, 1830 from his birthplace of Richmond, Virginia. By 1848 he had cleared and improved 12 hectares and built a house and barn. He received title to his land in 1851.[4]

Henry St. Dennis of Lot 26, Wilberforce Street, was "... tolerably well off." Noah Morris was rated "... very industrious and doing well, 12 acres [5 ha] under crop, slash fence." Jeremiah Munroe, who was Peter Robinson's assistant, was considered a successful farmer.[5] George and Mary Eddy[6] with their large family, worked 10 ha on Lot 12, Concession 4.

New arrivals often used the skills they had learned so painfully as slaves to supplement their meagre incomes while they established themselves on the land. By 1821, for instance, Israel Williams and his family

In this cartoon, first published in England in 1837, a Lower Canadian farmer, his wife and their fieldhands are barring a party of hunters from crossing their cultivated land.

Penetanguishene Bay, 1836.

lived in a log cabin near Chatham on the western stretch of the Thames.[7] Williams owned a slaughter-house nearby and supplied many of the local people with fresh meat. He was "... a smart, active, stout little fellow in good circumstances with several stacks of wheat on his excellent farm."[8]

Along the north shore of Lake Erie, by 1825:

> Black slaves who have run away from their masters in Kentucky arrive in Canada almost weekly and work at raising tobacco; I believe they introduced the practice. One person will attend, and manage the whole process of four acres, planting, hoeing, budding etc., during the summer.[9]

In November, 1826 the *Canadian Spectator* in Montréal printed a letter about the new industry:

> On the 12th August two hogsheads of Leaf Tobacco were shipped at Amherstburg, consigned to you [in Montréal], with a certificate from John Wilson Esq., collector of that port, of their being the growth in this

Slaves cultivating tobacco on a Southern plantation.

province. This tobacco belongs to an industrious, respectable Negro to whom I sold some land and who is one of a number of the same color whom I have advised to settle together and form a village; so far the undertaking is promising and the owner of the two hogsheads informs me that in a very short time he expected that at least sixty hogsheads of the same article would be raised in this small settlement.... I have sold nearly a thousand acres of land in small parcels to a number of these poor fugitives ...[10]

Branching Out

As more and more fugitives began to arrive in Upper Canada, their enterprise showed itself in the variety of work they did. While most Black males worked as labourers, a small number had skilled trades. Others worked in service occupations, and a few opened small businesses or entered the professions.

By 1837 at least 50 Black refugee families had settled in Toronto. Many were from Virginia, where most of the men had been waiters, barbers and cooks. Others had been blacksmiths, carpenters, painters and shoe-makers, who brought with them enough money to start small businesses and buy homes. W.H. Edwards, for instance, kept a successful barbershop on King Street[11] as early as 1839. He advertised that he used "... Vegetable Extract, for Renovating and Beautifying the Hair, cleansing it from all Dandruff, Dust, etc, and giving it a beautiful glossy appearance without the slightest injury to the Hair or Skin."[12] Toronto's first cabman was Thornton Blackburn, a Black, and Richard Gray, another, was one of its early storekeepers.

William Lyon Mackenzie, the outspoken editor and reformer who became Toronto's first mayor, remarked on the business success of one Toronto family during a visit to Philadelphia in 1832:

> They speak of equality in this country [the U.S.A.], but it is in Upper Canada that it can be seen in all its glory. There is a man of colour, a barber and hairdresser in our town of York, named Butler; he is married to a coloured woman and they are respectable, well behaved people in their line; and punctual in their dealings; they have, of course, a black family and (hear it, ye slave-trading, equal rights and independence people) they keep white

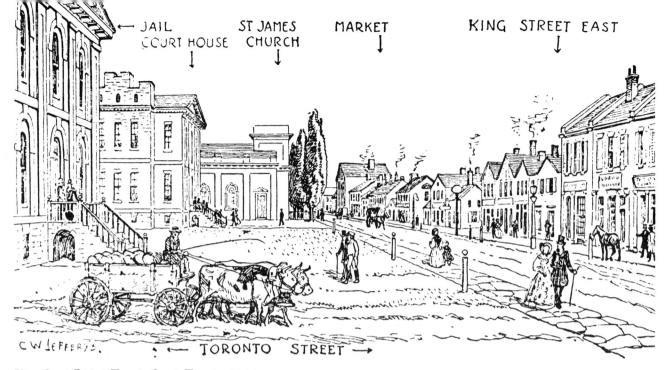

CW JEFFERYS.   ← TORONTO STREET →

King Street East at Toronto Street, Toronto, 1840.

men and women servants from Europe to wait upon them and their black children. This is turning the table on the Southerons, and fairly balancing accounts with the ebony-hearted slave holders.[13]

The earliest wave of Toronto's Black refugees was fairly established by the 1840s. These people provided a new source of unskilled labour and added, as well, to the town's growing trades- and businesspeople. A general pattern of Black socio-economic development appears in a survey of 1841 that listed the following:

Black Occupations — 1840

Cook	6	Carter	3
Baker	2	Dyer	1
Plasterer	3	Hatter	1
Cooper	2	Baptist Minister	2
Inn Keeper	2	Shoemaker	2
Labourer	73	Hair Dresser	3
Tailor	2	Cordwainer[14]	5
Tanner	1	Tobacconist	4
Pauper	1	Grocer	4
Mason	1	Carpenter	13
Seamstress	1	Blacksmith	5
House Painter	3	Widow	10
Barber	4	Retired	
Musician	2	from business	3

Unskilled, 73; Skilled, 60; Businessmen, 13; Others, 13; Total, 159.[15]

The *Toronto City and Home Directory* of 1846-47, published by George Brown of the *Globe*, listed 36 Black labourers, 34 skilled tradespeople[16] and six owners of businesses[17], as well as two ministers, a cabman, a sailor and a teamster. Blacks also owned restaurants: Rescue Inn, Prince Albert Recess, Tontine Coffee House and Epicurean Recess.

During the 1830s and '40s some of Niagara Falls' Blacks worked as waiters in hotels and as tourist guides; others found jobs on boats. The steamship *Chief Justice Robinson*, built in 1842, which travelled between Toronto, Hamilton and Niagara, was recommended for first-class passengers:

> The stewards and waiters are coloured people, clean, neat and active; and you may give sevenpence, half-penny or a quarter-dollar to the man who cleans your boots, or an attentive waiter, if you like; if not you can keep it, as they are well paid.[18]

The *St. Catharines Journal* of November 25, 1847 carried an advertisement for a Thomas P. Casey, "Barber and fashionable Hair Dresser". Casey thanked his many customers and announced:

> … commencing on the 5th of December next, his shop will be closed on Sabbath mornings at half past 10, and to give as many as possible an opportunity of being shaved on Saturday evening he will keep open till 11.

Many of St. Catharines' hotels hired Blacks: the headwaiters at the St. Catharines House and the American Hotel, a Mr. Morris and a Mr. Dyke, were both Black. The Welland House, still in business today, and other hotels in the town were built with the help of Black labour.

Making the Grade

Through the 1850s and '60s Blacks began to work in an even greater variety of ways. Ambitious new arrivals vied for jobs in Canada West, while those who had come a decade or more earlier became more and

Thomas P. Casey and his wife, Mary Ann Casey, owned a successful barber- and hairdressing shop in St. Catharines.

more involved in the professions, business and the trades. Rowsell's *City of Toronto Directory* of 1850-51, limited as it was, listed 69 Black heads of families, including 14 labourers, 27 tradespeople and 7 businesspeople. Levi Lightfoot owned a shoe-repair shop; his two sons later became a dentist and a doctor. Philip Judah owned a tobacco shop as well as a large fruit market on Queen Street near Augusta. The first ice company in Toronto was owned by a Black who cut ice from the mill ponds beyond Bloor Street. This was probably the beginning of the firm of T.F. Cary and R.B. Richards, who owned four ice-houses in the city by 1854. They advertised that their warehouses were "... filled with pure and wholesome spring water ice, from Yorkville ... The ice will be conveyed by wagon daily, to places within six miles of Toronto."[19] Cary also owned several barbershops, including one at 88 King Street West for "... all who wish to be operated upon in the line of either hair cutting, shaving, hair curling or shampooing."[20] In May, 1855 Cary moved his business to Front Street east of Church and opened a bath house which offered "... warm and cold baths at all hours."

T. Smallwood kept a hardware store at 35 Front Street, and his son William later articled with Mr. Justice M.C. Cameron.[21] A.T. Augusta advertised:

Central Medical Hall
A. T. Augusta
Begs to announce to his friends and the public generally that he has opened the store on Yonge St. one door south of Elm Street, with a new and choice selection of

DRUGS, MEDICINES,
Patent Medicines, Perfumery, Dye Stuffs, etc.
and trusts, by strict attention to his business, to merit
a share of their patronage.
Physicians' prescriptions accurately prepared
Leeches applied
Cupping, Bleeding, and Teeth Extracted
The proprietor or a competent assistant,
always in attendance.[22]

(Above) *Captain A.T. Augusta, M.D.*
(Below) *Philip Judah and his wife, Margaret Casey Judah.*

Augusta, a native of Virginia, lived for some years in Philadelphia. Because Blacks were barred from medical schools there, he came to Toronto and enrolled in medicine at Trinity College. He graduated in 1860 and was later appointed physician to Toronto's 'poor house'. He returned to the U.S.A. before the outbreak of the Civil War; there he joined the Union Army and was commissioned a captain in the Medical Corps. He did not return to Toronto.

Augusta's wife, Mrs. M.O. Augusta, was Toronto's only Black business-woman of her time. She owned a "New Fancy Dry Goods and Dressmaking Establishment" on York Street between Richmond and Adelaide, "... where will at all times be found the latest Paris and London patterns".[23]

In 1851 about 170 Black families lived in Hamilton. They included, among 13 businesspeople, two innkeepers, four grocers and four tobacconists. Mrs. Marian Barnes kept an 'eating house' on King Street between James and Hughson; S.O. King had a popular fruit stand at King and Caroline Streets; Charles Patterson owned a fruit market and a barbershop on King Street near McNab. A few years later William T. Cary, son of the ice merchant of Toronto, extended his father's operations to Hamilton, where he opened the East End Pure Ice Company at the foot of Niagara and Ship Streets, beside Hamilton Bay.

A Black cabman of the period told a Hamilton newspaper reporter that he had lived in the town for 17 years and was worth between $12 000 and $15 000. He had worked briefly as a porter in a Hamilton store, but soon gone into 'hacking': by 1854 he owned two carriages and four horses. The town bought the lot on which his house stood for a market, and with the $8000 paid him he expanded his business.

Many of London's Blacks were labourers who lived on Grey Street near the Wellington Street Bridge. They worked as waiters, painters and plasterers; they also cleaned outhouses and cut wood with the railway gangs to fuel the first steam-powered trains that the

Hamilton, Canada West, 1855.

Great Western Railroad began to use in 1853. Others had set up successful businesses: Alfred and Aby Jones, brothers, arrived in London in 1833. Aby was a field-hand, and Alfred had been trained as a miller on a plantation in Madison County, Kentucky. Hearing that " ... coloured men were free in Canada ..." the brothers asked to buy their freedom. When they were refused, they forged 'passes'[24] and escaped to Canada with the help of the Underground Railroad. They were destitute when they reached London, but through hard work they saved enough money to open a co-operative store on Dundas Street between Ridout and Richmond Streets. Alfred also owned one of the town's first apothecary shops, on Ridout Street. A correspondent from the weekly *New York Tribune*, visiting London wrote:

> At London a neat and well-furnished drug store is kept by a black man, who 23 years ago escaped from slavery in Kentucky. At that time he could write a little, sufficient, as he laughingly said, to put his name to a pass. For a long time he had dealt only in herbs and simples, but foreign drugs were gradually added, and we found him hard at work at a little Latin manual, mastering the barbarous Latin in which physicians couch their prescriptions![25]

The two brothers went on to buy even more property, and they held that opportunities such as they had grasped were open to their fellow refugees. In 1853 Alfred said:

> There are colored people employed in this city in almost all the mechanic arts; also in grocery and provision stores etc. Many are succeeding well, are buying houses, speculating in lands, and some are living on the interest of their money.[26]

And Aby concurred:

> I am satisfied, that any colored man coming to Canada, can, in a few years, accumulate property to give himself and family a living ... The future prospects of the colored people of Canada are very favourable. All that is required of them is, to use industry in common with white people.[27]

Another settler, Nelson Moss, who was one of the finest shoemakers in Middlesex County and needed

The Washington family of London, Ontario, about 1880.

an accountant to keep track of his thriving business, stated: "There are a large majority of Blacks who are industrious; a few are wealthy; a good many are well off."[28]

One of the latter was William Hamilton, who owned a popular bakery at the corner of York and Ridout Streets. Another was John Holmes, who had escaped from slavery in Virginia in 1825. He arrived in London in the 1830s and within 20 years owned his own home and eight hectares. Alexander Hamilton entered Canada with just $1.50 in his pocket. He found work in London at once and in time owned three houses and several lots. Hamilton claimed: "The colored people in London are all making a living. There is no beggar among them."[29] He seems to have been right, for in 1853 London's Blacks, not including the prosperous Jones brothers, owned property worth over $13 000.

Prosperity continued through the 1850s. Daniel Taylor became chief engineer of London's largest foundry at Dundas and Adelaide Streets. As a slave, Taylor had been an engineer on the *Eclipse*, an Ohio River steamer. When he escaped to Canada, his owner valued him at $12 000. In the winter of 1865 Taylor was killed in an explosion at the foundry.

Hayden Watters, "... an athletic colored man ..." operated the Washington hand press of the weekly *London Free Press* during the early '50s. Shadd Martin

The Smith family (above) *lived near Dresden, Ontario, about 1875. Smith cooked for 35 years on the boats that travelled the Sydenham River.*
(Below) *Isaac Holden, captain of Chatham's Black fire brigade, Victoria Company No. 3. John Brown held a meeting in the Company's engine house.*

Fire Engine House No. 5

owned a barbershop on King Street during the same period.[30] One of his steady customers was Sir John Carling, the brewery magnate. W.H. Dick kept a boot-and-shoemaker shop on Horton Street between Richmond and Clarence.

Although most of Chatham's Blacks were unskilled labourers in 1851, a few were tradespeople and businesspeople. Among the skilled workers were nine shoemakers, seven carpenters, eight blacksmiths, three bricklayers and six masons. There were also several barbers, tobacconists, cooks, ministers, sailors and farmers. Three years later a *New York Herald* survey recorded Blacks in the following occupations: one gunsmith, four cabinetmakers, some of whom were in business for themselves, six master carpenters, many plasterers, three printers, two watchmakers, two ship's carpenters, two millers, four blacksmiths, one upholsterer, one saddler, six master shoemakers, six grocers and a cigar-maker.

Some of Chatham's Blacks owned prosperous businesses. One of these was James Charity, a shoemaker, who built and rented out a red brick building known as the 'Charity Block' at King and Adelaide Streets. The Block contained four small shops on the ground floor and apartments above. The building housed the *Provincial Freeman* which had been moved from Toronto to Chatham under the ownership of Israel, Isaac and Mary Ann Shadd. Mr. J.M. Jones, gunsmith, kept a downtown store, and George Ramsey, a skilled iron-worker, had a business nearby. Sherwood Butler owned the Villa Mansion Hotel, often used as a conference centre, near the corner of King and William Streets.

Unskilled Blacks in the area found plenty of work on farms, in the mills and cutting, sawing and splitting wood for fuel. Chatham had an all-Black fire brigade, Victoria Company No. 3. This squad, described in a Chatham paper as " ... very efficient ..." had its headquarters in a firehall on King Street East. John Little one of Chatham's Blacks, reported in 1855 that fugitive slaves were "... as thick as blackbirds in a cornfield":

> At every town I meet members of the African race, single or in groups; I see them building and painting houses, working in mills, engaged in every handicraft employment.[31]

A log home in Essex County, about 1900.

In the mid-1850s some of Amherstburg's Blacks left their traditional work of farming to set up small businesses of their own. James Smith, for instance, stated:

> I am doing tolerably well in Canada, and am getting a very comfortable living. I own a lot of land worth about two hundred dollars, and have other property. I keep a grocery and sell to who will buy, without distinction of color.[32]

Other Blacks in the town were provision-store owners, a barber, mechanics and teamsters. The town's best hotel was owned by a Black named 'Hamilton'. Levi Foster, who owned a livery-stable, also kept a tavern for a short while, but one day he attended a public debate at the Sons of Temperance Hall where it was resolved that: "The Slave Holder is better than a tavern keeper." The debate must have stabbed his conscience, for the next day he hung a notice on his closed tavern stating that, since he was a former slave himself, he could not let it be said that he was worse than a slave-holder. He continued in his livery business and built up large holdings of valuable real estate. Eventually he owned several houses and lots along George Street, as well as a 20-ha farm in Anderdon.

Thomas Jones, a Windsor Black who had escaped from slavery in Kentucky, stated that Blacks were getting along well enough in his town: they had all they needed to eat and wear and, with a few exceptions, were living in comfortable homes. Jones himself, when he first came to Windsor, had gone into the bush, chopped wood for a living, built a frame house and started a plastering business. Several years later he claimed to be worth $3000 to $4000.

In nearby Sandwich, where Drew found about 22 Black families living in 1855, the refugees had settled in log cabins and hired themselves out to work. Many considered that they were doing no better and no worse than their white neighbours. Henry Brant, for instance, who had escaped from slavery in Virginia, said that when he settled in Sandwich he received

> ... neither victuals, clothes nor money, —I received only a welcome, that was all I wanted and I was thankful to get it ... I managed to save up what little I got pretty well. I invested in a home, I got me a house and a lot. I own ten acres [4 ha] of bush. Comparing the condition of the colored population here with an equal number of families of white labourers, I think they are about equal in means.[33]

J.F. White, Brant's neighbour, arrived in Canada in 1853 after escaping from slavery. Within two years he had bought 40 ha and was producing grain.

The names of 29 heads of Black families appear on Windsor's assessment rolls in the mid-'50s. Most were labourers, but there were also several preachers, three barbers, two coopers and a drayman. By 1862 there were 97 Black families totalling nearly 500 persons. These included 17 skilled tradespeople: barbers, carpenters, blacksmiths, tailors and masons; there were five grocers and merchants and eight sailors. The others were labourers or in service occupations.

By 1867 Windsor had 20 Black residents who were skilled tradespeople, including nine barbers, three coopers, two blacksmiths, two carpenters, one shoemaker and three masons. There were six businesspeople, six sailors[34], a cabman, a drayman, gardeners, an engineer and three barbers. The Black residential area had grown slightly, and some Blacks were living on Bruce Avenue, Pellisier and Church Streets. Black businesspeople included Benjamin Baylis, who owned a confectionary shop on Goyeau Street, and Thomas Eugene who advertised that he did bricklaying and plastering "... in the best style ... with prices to suit the

Labalinin Harris was a postman in Windsor in 1870.

Refugees sometimes worked as day-labourers on neighbours' farms to support their families while they struggled to clear and cultivate their own land.

times." James L. Dunn[35] & Family opened a paint and varnish store on Goyeau Street in the 1860s and later moved to larger quarters on Ouellette Avenue.

Prosperity was not so easily come by in some other areas of Canada West. Most Oro Blacks of the 1850s and '60s worked as farm hands to eke out a bare existence. Local farmers — Highland Scots, English and Irish pioneers — were glad of Black labour to help clear their land along the Penetanguishene Road and for logging, haying and harvesting. These Black labourers

… were expert with the axe, single-bitted, double-bitted, or the broadaxe, and tall tales were told of their prowess in cutting wood or squaring timbers. They were good hands with the scythe or cradle. One of them, Josiah Smith … had skill in the burning of lime. At that time lime, for local building, was obtained by burning field limestone in small kilns, dug out of hillsides. Joe Smith was employed, for a fee, to say when it was burned enough. On such occasions he came dressed to fit the dignity of his position as an expert, in a long black coat and an old stovepipe hat.[36]

One Oro Black known simply as 'Valentine', became a valued rope-maker for the New Lowell branch of the Jacques and Hay Company. A letter of July 39, 1865 records:

> Mr. Madison ... tells us that Valentine does not use leather as a protection to his hand while spinning and without it, he says, it is impossible to give the rope a hard enough twist, and set it up, as it should and must be done.
>
> You will therefore please request Valentine to commence to use the leather protection for his hands at once. We do not care if he should not spin over 10 lbs. [4.5 kg] a day for the first week or two, he will soon get accustomed to it and in 6 months will be able to spin as much with it as without it, the fact is it must be properly twisted or we will have to give it up altogether, for it is in the twist that the secret is in making strong hair ...[37]

Evidently Valentine followed instructions and rose in the company's esteem, for a letter of May 5, 1869 requests:

> ... We sent you a large quantity of Hog Hair the other day please get Valentine to examine it and let us know if it is all right, the man wants his money at once and we want to know if it is a good article before we pay him.[38]

The first Black known to live in Collingwood was a tavern- and hotel-keeper who, for advertising purposes, called himself 'Collingwood Harris'. He did business at first near the railway station in a log building that the local people called 'Uncle Tom's cabin'. By 1855 Harris' hotel was thriving, and vaudeville acts and other entertainment took place in its dining room. Later Harris bought the Malakoff House, a large frame building at the intersection of Huron, Rodney and Minnesota Streets. He retired to Orillia by 1858, though his sign hung outside the Malakoff House for many years afterwards.

Another well known Collingwood personality was Elizabeth Piecraft. The large red turban she always wore and her stately figure gave her an imposing appearance. She was an excellent cook and strong enough to lift a barrel of flour into a wagon by herself. She was also the first caretaker of Collingwood's Central High School, while her husband, a labourer, was in charge for many years of ringing the town's bell. From 1850 to 1870 he was a popular fiddler and used to play for excursion parties on the *Ploughboy* and *Frances Smith*. "He was also the loudest in his responses in the English Church, at which he was a regular attendant."[39]

Two other Black women were well known in Collingwood. 'Dr.' Susan Libertis was a successful herb-doctor and had a fine home on Sunset Point. Mrs. Bolden owned a hat shop on Hurontario Street.

Most of the town's Blacks worked as whitewashers, lime-burners, bakers, plasterers and labourers. Joseph Rodney was a labourer and lime-burner, David Mason a labourer and David Grant a barber. A Mr. Brackenbury was headwaiter in the Armstrong House, a railway hotel considered the town's leading hostelry, and other Blacks worked as waiters and chefs in hotels and on the boats; there were Black cooks and barbers in the North American Hotel. Abraham Sheffield, a pearl-ash maker came to Collingwood from England "... where after the slaves were released, his family worked for Lord Sheffield, whose name they adopted."[40]

Pleasant Duval, who arrived in Collingwood in 1863 at the age of 30, opened the first barbershop there on Huron Street.[41] He also kept an ice-cream and soft-

The Duval family home at the corner of Sixth and Walnut Streets, Collingwood, Ontario.

drink parlour, while his wife ran a busy dressmaking business in their commodious home on Sixth Street. This home was the social centre for the Blacks of Collingwood, Owen Sound and the whole region, and parties, picnics and other gatherings were held there.

Joseph Cooper, a freedman and veteran of the American Civil War, came to Collingwood in 1866 at the age of 24. He worked as a labourer until he saved enough money to open a cork factory in 1882. His 11 employees delivered their product by horse and wagon through the whole region.[42]

Owen Sound's early Blacks worked as labourers, whitewashers, carpenters, barbers, hostelers and tradespeople. Mary Taylor kept a small eating house and store near the Eighth Street Bridge over the Sydenham River. She was well known for her pies, fruit and oysters. Although she was barely 1.5 metres tall, she was "... of great breadth of form and as strong as a horse." She often sold her wares in the county courthouse, where she dealt most effectively with any young men who teased her: "Mary would grasp them around the waist and carry them despite all struggles out of the building."[43]

The expansion of the railroads in the 1850's to '70s gave work to some Black communities. At Fort Erie, for example, early Black residents often worked at cutting logs to be rafted across the Niagara River for shipment to American centres. In 1860 a railroad line was run from Fort Erie to Niagara-on-the-Lake, through the heart of 'Little Africa' where woodchoppers prepared fuel for the engines. Blacks cut wood for the Canada Southern Railway, built from St. Thomas to Buffalo in 1873, and for the ferries which carried trains across the Niagara River at Fort Erie before the International Railway Bridge was built. When the Northern Railway came through Simcoe County in the '70s, Oro Blacks worked 'farther back in the township' cutting wood for fuel. They delivered the wood to railroad sidings for $1.75 a cord, and their earnings for this heavy work, supplemented by what they produced on their little clearings, "... enabled them just to get by."[44]

(Upper left) *Charles Duval (left) and Fred Bolin in the barbershop established by Charles' father, about 1895.* (Upper right) *Charles and Chestina Duval with their children about 1900.* (Lower left) *A Collingwood family through four generations:* (clockwise from lower right) *Lorna Duval, Mrs. Cane, Rita Duval, Chestina Duval, about 1915.* (Lower right) *The Sheffield brothers were successful businessmen in Collingwood:* (back row, left to right) *Reginald, Bert, Alfred, Richard;* (front row) *Wilfred, Russell, Norman. The photo was taken about 1914.*

11
Black Societies and Celebrations

Cultural and Benevolent Societies

FROM THE 1830s Blacks formed societies to strengthen their culture and to help the needy in their communities. The African Temperance Society of St. Catharines, whose activities were reported in the press during 1835, probably met in the Salem Chapel. The Society had about 40 members, including Henry Gray[1], who had become spokesman for the Black community. The Young Men's Education and Temperance Society[2] in Amherstburg was founded by J. Underwood. In Toronto, Blacks formed the Young Men's Excelsior Literary Association. Windsor's Blacks formed a temperance society led by Robert Ward and Henry Bibb, and Mary Bibb presided over a Mutual Improvement Society organized by "... the Colored Ladies of Windsor." This group met to hear speeches and 'improve their minds'. Blacks also formed a band that played at many local functions:

> The Coloured Gentlemen of the Order of Free & A.M. held a grand Concert in the Town Hall on the 27th Decr. A Band from Windsor (all coloured) was in attendance. A goodly number of the brethren from Windsor and Detroit were invited. On their arrival here they paraded the principal streets, the Band discoursing sweet music.[3]

A rather controversial group headed by William Jones, the Africa Enterprise Society, was criticized on the ground that its purposes were purely selfish and would increase Windsor's prejudice against Blacks.

The *Toronto Directory* of 1859-60 listed a Moral and Mental Improvement Society (African):

> This Society has for its object the improvement of its members by means of essays and debates; it meets every Monday evening in the upper part of No. 120 Elgin Buildings in Yonge Street at 8 o'clock during the summer and 7½ during the winter.

Among the Society's officers were R.P. Thomas, F.G. Simpson, E.G. Bailey, W.H. Taylor, J.W. Cary and G.W. Squirrel.

Established Canadian Blacks formed societies to help refugees who flooded into Canada West in the 1840s and '50s. In Toronto the Liberating Association, formed "... to assist the weary and worn out fugitive that may reach our shore ..." reported in 1856 that Blacks were coming in steadily, "... nine, seven, two ..." at a time. The Society for the Protection of Refugees, the Ladies Coloured Fugitive Association, the Ladies Freedman's Aid Society, the Queen Victoria Benevolent Society led by Mrs. Ellen Abbott, and various church groups helped arriving Blacks. The report of the Toronto Ladies' Association for the Relief of Destitute Colored Fugitives for 1853-'55 stated:

> During the past inclement winter, much suffering was alleviated, and many cases of extreme hardship prevented. Throughout the year, the committee continued to observe the practice of appointing weekly visitors to examine into the truth of every statement made by applicants for aid. In this way between two and three hundred cases have been attended to, each receiving more or less, according to their circumstances.[4]

The total paid out during the year is not mentioned, but subscriptions and donations amounted to a little over £160.

On August 9, 1854 the Provincial Union Association was born. It proposed a broad program for the refugees of Canada West:

Chatham, Canada West, 1854.

This pencil and water-colour sketch made about 1838 was labelled, "The good 'woman of colour' who . . . took in & nursed the poor sick black man. . ." The woman, who lived near Lundy's Lane came to the rescue of a sick neighbour who had been turned out of his lodgings because he could not pay his rent.

> To promote harmony—not based on complexional differences—among her Majesty's subjects.
>
> To encourage and support a press—*The Provincial Freeman* particularly.
>
> To remove the stain of slavery from the face of the earth—and check its progress in America by all legitimate means.
>
> To encourage the rising generation in literary, scientific and mechanical efforts.[5]

Thirty-five Blacks from Toronto, Chatham, Hamilton, Dresden, London and Amherstburg were made officers of the Union. Samuel Ringgold Ward was elected president *in absentia*, but declined the office when the news reached him in England, and W.R. Abbott and T.F. Cary became its leaders. After the *Provincial Freeman* moved to Chatham in August, 1855, it carried little news of the Association's activities, but each issue listed its officers and district representatives and the 14 women on the Ladies' Committee.

The True Band, a benevolent society for men and women, was formed in Malden in 1854 and spread across Canada West. It encouraged refugees to take an interest in one another's welfare, to co-operate in economic ventures, to improve their schools and unite their churches, and to avoid going to law against other Blacks by referring all disputes to a special True Band committee. The group also attacked appeals for charity—"the begging system"—as money-making schemes that wrongly portrayed refugees as destitute and starving. Members agreed that any support for refugees in difficulty should come from the Black community. The Band encouraged Blacks to be politically active and to work for a just Canadian society. In the mid-'50s there were 14 branches in the southwestern part of the province, and their 600 members paid small monthly dues; these brought in enough money to help most destitute fugitives and keep a working balance in the treasury. Of course, not all branches were equally successful, and some members in Chatham and Amherstburg continued to solicit funds in spite of the Band's official rule against "begging".

A Black Freemason's Lodge was active in Chatham, as well as a Benevolent Society led by a Mrs. Charlotte Hunter. A Black band and a glee club performed at meetings of local clubs, which included a debating society, a temperance group and the Victorian Ladies Association.

The Victorian Reform Benevolent Society provided insurance services to the refugees:

> Upon payment of an initiation fee and dues of seven and a half pennies a month, a member could, after one year, begin to collect benefits if sickness prevented him or her from working. The benefits to be paid were five shillings per week for the first three months of sickness, two shillings sixpence per week for a further three months, and if the sickness went beyond one-half year, the directors of the Society would grant a further weekly sum as they thought proper. A further benefit for paid-up members of two or more years' duration was that if a member died it was the duty of the Society to inter him decently in [his church's] burial ground ...[6]

The Society was concerned for the moral, as well as the physical, welfare of its members. It barred "... persons addicted to intoxication, or who have a plurity of living husbands ..."

Members of the BME Church paid a $10 initiation fee into the BME Itinerant Benefits Association to provide for sick or aged BME ministers.

This music group, based in Hamilton, Ontario, about the turn of the 20th century, was noted for its concerts.

The mouth of the Niagara River, about 1825.

Emancipation Day

In August, 1814, soon after the Battle of Lundy's Lane, Blacks met at Niagara to celebrate "... an anniversary of African emancipation ..." with a public dinner on the Battleground at Drummond Hill. Tickets "... for a gentleman and his lady ..." sold for $1.00, and Blacks from St. Catharines and Hamilton joined local residents to give thanks for delivery from slavery.[7] They must have been commemorating Simcoe's anti-slavery legislation of 1793, for the British Act of 1833 was yet to be passed.

The most important social event of the year for Canadian Blacks of the mid-1800s was Emancipation Day, when Whites and Blacks celebrated the Act of 1833 that abolished slavery throughout the British Empire in 1834.[8] The *St. Catharines Standard* of November 12, 1835 described the parade and the service at Salem Chapel, in which young, middle-aged and old took part. The marchers paraded through "...the two principal streets of the village, accompanied with musick, and carrying an appropriate banner, to the African Church." The church was filled, and after the service 60 persons sat down to a dinner prepared by John Thomas. The parade, dinner and celebrations were organized by Charles C. Coburn and James Findley, marshall and assistant-marshall of the day.

In Toronto Blacks celebrated Emancipation Day as early as 1840. Plans for the 1854 celebration were carefully laid several months in advance when Blacks met at First Baptist Church and passed resolutions:

> Resolved, that we celebrate that glorious event which took place in the Year of our Lord 1834, when the British Nation did honour to itself and justice to 800,000 of her coloured subjects in the West Indies;
> Resolved, that we meet in the Second Wesleyan Chapel, Richmond Street at five in the morning to offer up devout Thanksgiving to Almighty God for his past mercies and to engage in fervent prayer for the utter extinction of slavery throughout the United States and other parts of the world where the evil now exists;
> Resolved, that we meet at 9:00 at the Government House, King Street West, form in procession and proceed from thence to Yonge Street Wharf, to meet our friends from Hamilton; thence to St. James Cathedral, King Street East, to listen to a sermon at 11:00 from the Rev. J.H. Gassett after which the procession will proceed through the principal streets of the city to the Government grounds to partake of a Dinner provided by the Committee of Arrangements at two o' clock.[9]

Chatham's Black troops took part in the 1842 celebration of Emancipation Day. About daybreak they fired 21 rounds of ammunition from a cannon on the military grounds. One hundred Black soldiers paraded through the town and afterwards sat down to dinner "... beneath an arbor of boughs sixty feet [18 m] long." The men of the company prepared the feast themselves, and there were generous quantities of beef, ham and fowl. In the evening there was a military ball. Although liquor was plentiful, white guests commented on the exemplary conduct of the men: not a single soldier was drunk. (As a matter of fact, many of the troopers belonged to a temperance society.)

Dr. A.R. Abbott wrote of an Emancipation Day in Toronto in the 1850s:

> On one occasion within my memory they provided a banquet which was held under a pavilion erected on a vacant lot running from Elizabeth Street to Sayre Street opposite Osgoode Hall, which was then a barracks for the 92nd West India Regiment. The procession was headed by the band of the Regiment. The tallest man in this Regiment was a Black man, a drummer, known as Black Charlie. The procession carried a Union Jack and a blue silk banner on which was inscribed in gilt letters "The Abolition Society, Organized 1844." The mayor of the city, Mr. Metcalfe, made a speech ... followed by several other speeches of prominent citizens. These celebrations were carried on yearly amid much enthusiasm, because it gave the refugee colonists an opportunity to express their gratitude and appreciation of the privileges they enjoyed under British rule.[10]

Hamilton's central location made it a key point for Emancipation Day celebrations, and Blacks came 90 km or more to join in the festivities there. They travelled on foot or by wagon or train from St. Catharines, Niagara, Brantford, Ancaster, Toronto and smaller communities to make Hamilton's celebrations the largest and most spectacular of all. For many years the Honourable Isaac Buchanan, M.P.P., gave over his homestead, "Auchman", in Clairmont Park on the Mountain, for the celebration. On August 2, 1859, at about half-past one a stream of people began to climb the mountain. Some rode in cabs; others trudged along gaily on foot. At "Auchman" tables for more than 500 guests, covered with white linen, lay in the shade of big apple trees. When the covers were removed at three o'clock, the guests saw that "... they fairly groaned under the weight of roast beef and fowls and pies and pastry of all kinds."[11] Boxes of oranges and barrels of lemonade were at hand. Although a few dozen whites were present, mainly Buchanan's family and dignitaries, it was a Black people's affair. A group called the 'Sons of Uriah', dressed in black robes, white

trousers and three-cornered cocked hats, paraded around the grounds. One of its members carried a huge axe "... symbolical presumably of the destiny of slave holders." The women wore "... the most effulgent robes, the most splendid silks and satin that can be seen in a day's shopping."[12]

After dinner Buchanan spoke to the crowd on the front lawn. Then there were speeches by Blacks and by M.P.s and a guest from Dawn, the English Mr. Scoble, who recalled the great parliamentary struggle to end slavery in the British Empire in 1833. He reminded the audience that 7 500 000 Blacks were still slaves. The day ended with a soirée, and the press, reporting the event, made much of the fact that the Blacks behaved in model fashion: there was "... not a jar in the whole affair ...", and Buchanan's property was in no way damaged — not a plate had been broken or an apple pulled from a tree, "... even by the boys."

This celebration, though larger than most, was typical of the occasion in Black communities in Canada West, and in Ontario, for the day was celebrated well into the 1870s, even after the Black population had become much smaller. In Amherstburg, for instance, up to 1000 Blacks met in the town park every year on August 1st. Local Blacks would march down to the docks with their bands to welcome friends coming from Detroit and Windsor; then all would return to the park for an afternoon of games, songs and speeches. The Jubilee Singers, a local group of spiritual-singers led by Josephus O'Banyon, probably took a regular part in the program. At night the annual Ball was held in the Town Hall.

Oro's Blacks celebrated Emancipation Day on August 2nd, and an audience came from near and far to see a football (soccer) game between Black players and a local white team.

> The negroes were skilled at hitting the ball with their heads and sending it great distances. Their weak spots were their shins, a fact that their opponents kept in mind.[13]

At Owen Sound, too, the celebrations were held on August 2nd. Blacks usually marched through the town and then sat down to dinner; speeches followed, and "... the day was enjoyed exceedingly." It was common for Owen Sound Blacks to walk all the way to Col-

(Above) *Emancipation Day Parade at Amherstburg, August 1, 1894.*
(Right) *Picnicking at Sunset Point, Collingwood, about 1905.*

lingwood to share in the celebration held on August 1st. Blacks there met in Georgian Bay Park to hear speeches and hold a picnic and a dance in which their white neighbours joined.

While Emancipation Day was a celebration, it was also kept as a day of thanksgiving. In 1855, for instance, the Reverend Martin Dillon of St. Paul's Church, London, recorded: "... between 600 and 700 marched with banners flying and headed by the band from the barracks. I preached from St. John, XIII, 34-36."[14]

The Black Press

The two Black newspapers, the *Voice of the Fugitive* and the *Provincial Freeman*, differed on many issues, but both constantly reminded refugees that they were in a fair and hospitable land where they should be good citizens and take part in the life of their communities. At the same time, they vigorously attacked injustice and racism.

The *Voice of the Fugitive*, owned and edited by Henry Bibb, was the earlier of the two papers. Anti-slavery readers throughout Canada and the U.S.A. considered it literally "... the voice of the fugitive in Canada." Bibb's reports were long and detailed, for he was struggling to gain acceptance for the thousands of Blacks who streamed into Canada after the Fugitive Slave Act was passed in the U.S.A. As well as helping to create a more sympathetic climate for Blacks, Bibb's paper helped new arrivals to adjust by providing an invaluable source of information particularly about the Black communities of Essex County. Many escaped slaves read the paper to locate friends and relatives:

In enumerating the arrivals this week we can count only 17, 10 of whom came together on the express train of the underground railroad. This lot consisted of a mother with her six children, and three men. The next day there came four men, two men arrived and then one came alone. The latter tells us of having had a warm

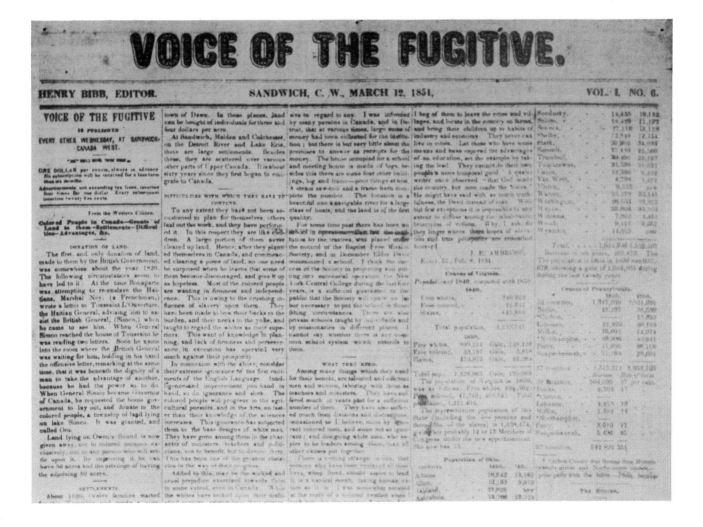

Samuel Ringgold Ward

combat by the way with two slave catchers, in which he found it necessary to throw a handful of sand in the eyes of one of them, and while he was trying to wash it out he broke away from the other and effected his escape.[15]

Before long the *Provincial Freeman,* a more militant paper, was founded in Windsor by Samuel Ringgold Ward. Its first issue appeared on March 25, 1853; a year later the *Freeman* moved to Toronto, and in June, 1855 to Chatham where it was named official printer to the town council; its last issue was published in September, 1857. The *Freeman* contained vivid descriptions of church, business and abolitionist activities, and although it was plagued with difficulties of money and management, it reflected the problems, hopes and thanks of a new refugee group in a strange, but usually friendly land. The motto on its masthead reflected its editorial position: *Self-Reliance is the True Road to Independence.*

In its first issue the *Freeman* stated that its goal was to

> ... represent the 40,000 Negroes, freedmen, fugitives, wealthy and poor, recently arrived in Canada; encourage "the right class" to enter Canada by publishing an account of the country and its advantages; and develop in Canada a society to deny all assertions regarding the Negro's inability to live with others in civilized society.[16]

Basically integrationist in its policy, the *Freeman* fought hard against Black colonization schemes and refugee aid societies that its editors considered dubious:

> Our tour satisfied us abundantly that the coloured people of Canada are progressing more rapidly than our people in the States — that the liberty enjoyed here makes different men of those once crushed and dispirited in the land of chains — that along with the other poor classes who come here and improve themselves in wealth and status, the black people will also arise in some cases very rapidly, but generally slowly, though surely — that the day is not far distant when we shall put to shame the selfish, systematic charity seekers who go to the States, and some of them to the south, to beg partly for fugitives but chiefly for their own pockets — that more money has been begged professedly for Canadian blacks than said blacks ever did, or will ever receive, by a thousand fold — that unless persons going to the States begging for us are the accredited agents of some duly organized

society, with honest, unselfish men at its head, our friends should hold them at arms' length — that what the recently arrived fugitive most needs is not land buying societies, not old clothes, not any substitute for labour, but stimulation to self-development.[17]

The paper's most colourful writer and, later, its first full-time editor, was Mary Ann Shadd, who was well known for her sharp tongue and biting editorials. Shadd is acknowledged the first Black newspaper-woman in North America; she may also have been the first woman publisher of a newspaper in Canada. In her final article as editor she wrote:

> To colored Women we have a word — we have broken the "Editorial Ice" whether willingly or not for your class in America, so go to editing as many of you who are willing and able and as soon as you may, if you think you are ready.[18]

The *Provincial Freeman* urged refugees to educate themselves and enter business, agriculture or the professions. Occasionally it goaded the community. Under a heading "Lectures" it urged:

> One great subject of regret is that the colored citizens of Toronto should so seldom attend lectures, whether the meetings are called by those of their own number, or others. It would be well for them to meet oftener, to look in the face the cause of present discords and former antagonisms, and endeavour to do away with the just imputation of "division, ignorance, disunion, love of menial occupation and the like" that however much we regret it, can be and is brought against them with so much force every day. Why with the abundant opportunities surrounding us — the schools, churches, associations and lectures — need the sad spectacle our people here present be persisted in by them?[19]

While the *Freeman* urged Blacks to use all the opportunities provided by their new country, it also reported many cases of discrimination. In 1854 Blacks met to oppose a plan of the Anglican CCSS to open a normal school for their people in Toronto.[20] On September 20, 1854 in the Wesleyan Church Toronto's Blacks rejected the plan and later published three resolutions about it; the second and third of these read:

> Resolved — That should such schools be opened, and

Provincial Freeman.

DEVOTED TO ANTI-SLAVERY, TEMPERANCE, AND GENERAL LITERATURE.

"Self-Reliance is the True Road to Independence."

VOLUME I. TORONTO, CANADA WEST, SATURDAY, NOVEMBER 18, 1854. NUMBER 35.

PROSPECTUS
OF THE
PROVINCIAL FREEMAN.

The Provincial Freeman will be devoted to Anti-Slavery, Temperance and General Literature. The origin of no particular Political Party, it will open its columns to the views of men of different political opinions, reserving the right, as an independent Journal of tall expressions on all questions of property affecting the people in a political way, and reserving also the right to express emphatic condemnation of all projects having for their object or a great or remote degree, the interests of the principles of the British Constitution, or of British rule in the Provinces.

M. A. SHADD, Publishing Agent.

Business Directory.

CHARLES MARCH.

A. B. JONES,
GROCERIES AND CROCKERYWARE,
LONDON, C. W.

D. FARRAR,

VANKOUGHNET & BROTHER

CHARLES FLETCHER,
BOOKSELLER & STATIONER,
TORONTO.

PUNCTUALITY !!
J. R. BROWN,
Late of Philadelphia

G. HARCOURT'S
CLOTHING STORE,
KING STREET EAST

REMOVAL.
Fashionable Hair Cutting!

F. PARSONS,

Poetry.

Trust in God and Persevere.

Miscellaneous.

The Reformer of Turkey and his Gazette.

Prince Mentschikoff.

What Family Government Is.

The Black Swan—and so Forth.

Agriculture in Japan.

The building on the right was the Chatham headquarters of the Provincial Freeman.

efforts made by the Colonial Church and School Society contrary to our expressed wish and interest, we cannot consistently, and will not, as coloured citizens, give them our support.

Resolved—That we caution our people throughout the province to be careful as to how they give their influence and support to institutions and efforts whether established and made by friend or foe, white or black, that tend to make distinction on account of colour and to destroy the foundation of our liberties.[21]

H.F. Douglass, the last editor of the *Freeman*, believed that those liberties were firmly rooted in the British tradition. On March 28, 1857, during the last months of the paper's life, he urged his readers to become totally British in sympathy. In an article headed "The Duties of Colored Men in Canada," he wrote:

What are the duties of colored men in these provinces, who have been forced here from American despotism and oppression? … We owe everything to the country of our adoption and nothing to that miserable, contemptible despotism and government of the U.S. … Colored men should become as thoroughly British as they can. We are opposed to all separate organizations, whether civil, political or ecclesiastical, that can have no other effect than that of creating a line of demarcation; fostering if not creating a spirit of caste here, such as colored men are compelled to suffer in the U.S. Separated schools and churches are nuisances that should be abated as soon as possible, they are dark and hateful relics of Yankee Negrophobia, contrary to that healthy, social and political equality recognized by the fundamental principles of British common law, and should never be permitted to take root upon British soil.

The Black press tried in vain to re-establish itself in Windsor in the 1860s with the founding of the *True Royalist and Weekly Intelligencer*. The Reverend A.R. Green, a BME preacher, was encouraged by Bishop Nazrey to start the paper. It was to be devoted to "… the cause of Universal Liberty, Emigration, Temperance, Religion, Agriculture, Politics, Science, Literature and General News."[22] The paper lasted barely a year and published very few issues.[23] Its failure may, in fact, have shown that the Black community had learned well the lessons of broader interests and independence that earlier Black editors had urged upon it, for one critic has written:

The *True Royalist* while intended for Negroes, contained little news that was racial, rather discussing dissension within the Church and preaching political conservatism and obedience to the Queen.[24]

Its potential readers had left the narrowness of its editorial policy behind and were marking new horizons as they moved into the latter part of the 19th century.

12
The
Freedom-Seekers

Sophia Pooley

IN THE MID-1850s the American abolitionist and writer, Benjamin Drew, made a trip through Canada West. In the book he later wrote, he recorded his interviews of many refugees who had escaped from the U.S.A. to Canada. "In the settlement of Queen's Bush, now known as the township of Peel..." Drew talked with an elderly woman, Sophia Pooley. She claimed to have been a slave of Joseph Brant, the Mohawk chief, and the first Black woman in Upper Canada. Sophia Pooley's memories of her earliest days in Canada were not perfect. Over the years she had confused the order of some events and may have forgotten or exaggerated some details. But her story, which Drew set down in Sophia's own words, is a rare recollection of a person who lived as a slave in Upper Canada in its earliest days.

> I was born in Fishkill, New York State, twelve miles from North River. My father's name was Oliver Burthen, my mother's Dinah. I am now more than ninety years old. I was stolen from my parents when I was seven years old, and brought to Canada; that was long before the American Revolution. There were hardly any white people in Canada then—nothing here but Indians and wild beasts. Many a deer I have helped catch on the lakes in a canoe; one year we took ninety. I was a woman grown when the first governor of Canada came from England; that was Governor Simcoe.
>
> My parents were slaves in New York State. My master's sons-in-law, Daniel Outwaters and Simon Knox came into the garden where my sister and I were playing among the currant bushes, tied their handkerchiefs over

The Henson family arrives in Canada.

our mouths, carried us to a vessel, put us in the hold, and sailed up the river. I know not how far nor how long—it was dark there all the time. Then we came by land. I remember when we came to Genesee—there were Indian settlements there—Onondagas, Senecas and Oneidas.

I guess I was the first coloured girl brought into Canada. The white men sold us at Niagara to old Indian Brant, the king. I lived with old Brant about twelve or thirteen years as nigh I can tell. Brant lived part of the time at Mohawk, part at Ancaster, part at Preston, then called Lower Block; the Upper Block was at Snyder's Mills. While I lived with old Brant we caught the deer. It was at Dundas at the outlet. We would let the hounds loose, and when we heard them bark we would run for the canoe—Peggy, and Mary, and Katy, Brant's daughters, and I. Brant's sons, Joseph and Jacob, would wait on the shore to kill the deer when we fetched him in. I had a tomahawk, and would hit the deer on the head—then the squaws would take it by the horns and paddle ashore. The boys would bleed and skin the deer and take the meat to the house. Sometimes white people in the neighbourhood, John Chisholm and Bill Chisholm, would come and say it was their hounds, and they must have the meat. But we would not give it up.

Canada was then filling up with white people. And after Brant went to England, and kissed the Queen's hand he was made a colonel. Then there began to be laws in Canada. Brant was only half Indian; his mother was a squaw—I saw her when I came to this country. She was an old body; her hair was quite white. Brant was a good looking man—quite portly. He was as big as Jim Douglass who lived here in the bush, and weighed two hundred pounds [90 kg]. He lived in an Indian village—white men came among them and they intermarried. They had an English schoolmaster, an English preacher, and an English blacksmith. When Brant went

The Village of the Mohawks (above) on the Grand River was sketched by Mrs. Simcoe in 1795. (Left) Joseph Brant's house at Burlington. Black slaves did much of the work here and on Brant's other property.

Joseph Brant in 1797 by William Berczy.

among the English, he wore the English dress — when he was among the Indians, he wore the Indian dress — broadcloth leggings, blanket, moccasins, fur cap. He had his ears slit with a long loop at the edge, and in these he hung long silver ornaments. He wore a silver half-moon on his breast with the king's name on it, and broad silver bracelets on his arms. He never would paint, but his people painted a great deal. Brant was always for making peace among his people; that was the reason of his going about so much. I used to talk Indian better than I could English. I have forgotten some of it — there are none to talk it with now.

Brant's third wife, my mistress, was a barbarous creature. She could talk English, but she would not. She would tell me in Indian to do things, and then hit me with anything that came to hand, because I did not understand her. I have a scar on my head from a wound she gave me with a hatchet; and this long scar over my eye is where she cut me with a knife. The skin dropped over my eye; a white woman bound it up. Brant was very angry when he came home at what she had done, and punished her as if she had been a child. Said he, "You know I adopted her as one of the family and now you are trying to put all the work on her."

I liked the Indians pretty well in their place — some of them were savage, some friendly. I have seen them have the war-dance — in a ring with only a cloth about them, and painted up. They did not look ridiculous — they looked savage — enough to frighten anybody. One would take a bowl and rub the edge with a knotted stick; then they would raise their tomahawks and whoop. Brant had two colored men for slaves; one of them was the father of John Patten, who lives over yonder, the other called himself Simon Ganseville. There was but one other Indian that I knew who owned a slave. I had no care to get my freedom.

At twelve years old I was sold by Brant to an Englishman in Ancaster, for one hundred dollars. His name was Samuel Hatt, and I lived with him seven years. Then the white people said I was free, and put me up to running away. He did not stop me — he said he could not take the law into his own hands. Then I lived in what is now Waterloo. I married Robert Pooley, a black man. He ran away with a white woman, he is dead.

Brant died two years before the second war with the United States. His wife survived him until the year the stars fell. She was a pretty squaw; her father was an English colonel. She hid a crock of gold before she died, and I never heard of its being found. Brant was a Freemason.

I was seven miles from Stoney Creek at the time of the battle — the cannonade made everything shake well.

I am now unable to work, and am entirely dependent on others for subsistence; but I find plenty of people in the bush to help me a good deal.[1]

Josiah Henson

When my feet first touched the Canada shore, I threw myself on the ground, rolled in the sand, seized handfulls of it and kissed them and danced around, till, in the eyes of several who were present, I passed for a madman.[2]

The man who wrote these words was Josiah Henson, the most famous and most controversial slave ever to make his way to freedom in Upper Canada. Many people thought that Henson, one of the founders of the Dawn Settlement, was the model for the character of Uncle Tom in Harriet Beecher Stowe's famous novel, *Uncle Tom's Cabin*[3]. While this is still hotly debated, it is certain that Henson spent many painful, searing years as a slave before he reached Upper Canada.

Josiah Henson was born on a plantation near Port Tobacco in Charles County, Maryland, on June 15, 1789. His mother was a slave of Dr. Josiah MacPherson, a planter. It was MacPherson who named the baby: 'Josiah' after himself and 'Henson' after an ancestor who had fought in the American Revolutionary War. Henson's earliest memory of slavery was brutal and grim. His father had tried to defend his wife against the insults of an overseer. For this he was given 100 lashes, had an ear cut off and was sold deeper south into Alabama. His family never heard from him again.

Not long afterwards Dr. MacPherson died. He left his finances in poor order, and his property had to be sold. Henson's mother looked on "… in an agony of grief as she saw her children sold one by one." Josiah was sold to a stranger named 'Robbs'; his brothers and sisters were sold to other planters, and another, Isaac Riley, bought his mother. She begged Riley to buy Josiah so that she might have at least one of her children with her. Riley agreed, and mother and son were together again.

Josiah's mother was deeply religious, and she brought her son up in the Christian faith. He often stood outside the 'white' church, which he was never allowed to enter, to listen to the preaching. He had heard that God would deliver all His people, "… the rich, the poor, the strong, the weak and even the poor slave in chains."[4] These words confirmed his faith and inspired him to become a preacher himself.

Isaac Riley enjoyed partying, drinking and gambling. One night he got into a fight at a tavern, and Henson, sitting outside, heard the uproar. He came to Riley's aid, helped him out of the tavern into a wagon and drove him home. One of the white men who had been fighting with Riley later waylaid Henson and beat him with a fence-rail until he broke his arm and both shoulder blades. Henson's shoulders did not heal properly, and he could never straighten his arms again.

At a religious service on a neighbouring plantation Henson met a slave named 'Charlotte'; he married her

when he was 21, and they had 12 children of whom eight survived. Because of Henson's hard work and loyalty Riley put him in charge of his farm and the sale of its produce in nearby markets. But Riley got into debt through his poor management and put his plantation up for sale. Before it was sold, he persuaded Henson to travel to his brother Amos' plantation in Kentucky, nearly 1600 km away. Fearful of being sold deeper south, Henson agreed to make the trip. In 1825, with his wife, two children and 28 other slaves, he began the journey, travelling with a one-horse wagon stocked with food. The men walked, and the women and children rode in the wagon. Later Henson sold the horse and wagon and bought a yawl to travel up the Ohio River. When the group reached Cincinnati, the others pleaded with Henson to escape with them into free country. But Henson was loyal to Riley and in April, 1825 delivered the whole group to his brother Amos.[5]

Henson stayed with his new owner for three years. In that time he was promoted from field-hand to manager and unofficial overseer. He was also given privileges including more free time and more freedom to go about. He used his greater privileges to become a Methodist Episcopal preacher and saved the scant fees he was given with the hope of buying his freedom. When he had saved nearly $300, he got a pass[6] from Amos Riley to visit Isaac and arrange the sale. Isaac agreed to free Henson for $450, but knowing that the slave could not read, he drew up papers that named a price of $1000. Henson returned to Kentucky to discover that he had been duped and must remain a slave.

Soon after this Amos Riley asked Henson to go with his son to New Orleans to sell farm produce there. In fact, he had made a deal to sell Henson in Louisiana. Fortunately, while the men were on their way, young Riley fell ill, and they had to return to Kentucky. On their return Henson discovered the plan to sell him. He was furious and decided that he owed the Rileys no further loyalty. He began to plan his escape.

Henson chose a time when he knew that Amos was away. On a moonless night in September, 1830 he and another slave loaded Henson's family into a small boat and crossed the Ohio River. When the party reached the Indiana shore, Henson packed his two youngest children into a knapsack and shouldered it. Two older children walked beside his wife. Travelling by night and hiding by day, they reached Cincinnati within two weeks. Friends helped them on to Sandusky, Ohio, where a sympathetic ship's captain hired Henson to help load his ship for a small wage and free passage for himself and his family to Buffalo. There Henson found a ship to take them to Canada. They reached freedom on October 28, 1830.

For the next three years Henson worked as a farm labourer near Fort Erie and Niagara. The family lived in a small house, bought a horse, a cow and a pig, and enjoyed their new freedom. Josiah's 12-year-old son, Tom, taught him to read, and he began to serve as a local preacher, holding prayer meetings in the home of Benjamin Risely, one of his employers. In these meetings he encouraged his audience to save their money, buy land collectively and farm it.

Slowly the idea of a self-supporting Black colony grew in Henson's mind. In this ideal colony refugees

The Hensons escape by night.

general farming, owning land, and British patriotism. Black refugees often chose to grow only tobacco because they hoped to get a good price for it. In fact, the tobacco market was often glutted and depressed, and farmers who had no other crops to sell suffered severely. Black farmers who rented land and improved it often found that owners would not renew their leases, and others benefitted from their hard work. Henson lectured all through the district about the advantages to Blacks of owning land and growing a variety of crops. He also strongly supported the order and good government that he believed existed in Canada.

Henson led a volunteer company in support of Canada's government in the Mackenzie Rebellion of 1837-'38. In those years, too, he saw part, at least, of his dream of a Black colony beginning to take form. Although the Dawn Settlement never became the ideal community of its founders' dreams, Henson remained loyal to its purpose. He lived on at Dawn in his small frame house, still famous as the 'Uncle Tom' of Stowe's novel. Until his death he lectured through

The Henson home at Dawn Settlement.

This photograph of the legendary Josiah Henson and his wife was probably taken during a visit to England in 1877.

would be self-employed and would have a chance to get a general education. Henson's followers encouraged him to look for a site. He toured the districts near Lake Erie and the Detroit River and, greatly impressed with the quality of the land, hoped to form a colony there. In the meantime he took his followers to Colchester, near Amherstburg, where land had already been cleared. There Henson lectured and preached, often returning to the U.S.A. to help over 100 slaves escape to Canada West.

During Henson's seven years at Colchester he formed three strong convictions: the importance of

Canada and the U.S.A., recounting stories of his meetings with Queen Victoria, the Archbishop of Canterbury, Lord John Russell, then Prime Minister of England, and other famous British abolitionists and Members of Parliament. For Josiah Henson the road from slavery had taken many a turn.[7]

Henson died on May 5, 1883. Later the term 'Uncle Tom' took on a negative meaning for Blacks. They saw Stowe's character as a person too willing to compromise, incapable of militant action on behalf of his people. In view of what Henson tried to do at Dawn, this image is unfortunate. He loved fame and prestige, but he worked with energy and vision to improve life for Upper Canada's Blacks. Although he was a poor administrator, he sincerely tried to bring education and security to the Dawn settlers, and he sincerely practised the patriotism he preached. Henson lived by what he believed. He once summed up his faith and hopes for his people:

> We are a peaceable people and I believe the day is not far distant when we shall take a respectable rank among the subjects of Her Majesty, the excellent and most gracious Queen of England and the Canadas.[8]

Peter Butler and his Family

In 1797 a slave family named 'Bowzer' in Baltimore, Maryland had a son whom they called 'Peter'. As a young man Peter escaped from his master, changed his tell-tale surname to 'Butler' and ran away to sea. He returned to the U.S.A. seven years later[9] and married a Native named 'Salome Squawker'.

About 1829 Peter and Salome Butler moved their young family to Upper Canada. Peter worked for several years as a caulker in Port Stanley, Port Dover and St. Thomas before he learned about the new Wilberforce Settlement. He first visited the colony and later moved his family there. The Butlers settled on Lot 5, north and south of the London-Goderich road.[10] There Peter and Salome farmed, raised seven children and were active in the settlement. Peter became its treasurer in 1836; he also served as its 'doctor', administering herbal medicines to Black and white neighbours.

Butler had an acute business sense and profitted by it. When the Grand Trunk Railway was built across Biddulph Township, John McDonald, Lucan's surveyor, owned a good deal of land along the projected line and wanted the station built on his property. But 'Doc' Butler came to an understanding with the Grand Trunk's surveyor, and the line was run and the station built on Butler's land.

As members of the Wilberforce Settlement moved away, Butler either bought or was given much of their land[11] until his property in Lucan "... extended from about the Central Hotel north past the Public School on both sides of the street."[12] When Butler died in 1872 at the age of 75, his estate, said to be worth over $22 000, was considerable for that time.

Peter Butler II inherited most of his father's property as well as his herbal knowledge. He gathered herbs through the district and kept a large collection of them in his home off Main Street, prescribing remedies for his neighbours as his father had done. He also continued to farm until he died in 1896. He was one of the last of the original Wilberforce settlers, having come to the settlement as "... a babe in his mother's arms."

The Butler homestead in the Wilberforce Settlement.

Mrs. Peter Butler Sr., widow of Peter Butler II, in 1891.

Peter Butler III had been born in Lucan in 1859. Over nearly 50 years he served as Lucan's tough, but fair, county constable and a member of the Ontario Provincial Police (OPP). Butler had amazing energy and was sturdily built. He stood about 1.8 metres tall and weighed about 85 kg. He relied only on a big stick and his sizeable fists to maintain peace and order and occasionally amazed Lucan's residents by walking blithely through the town with a 45-kg bag of sugar under each arm. Although some of the town's British immigrants objected at first to a Black policeman, Butler quickly gained their respect. In 1883 he was made a member of the Middlesex County police and served with them for about 30 years. He joined the OPP in 1913 and remained with the force until he retired in 1936. He carried a gun only when he was taking prisoners to the county jail in London or chasing cattle rustlers. On the latter occasions he also carried an axe to cut brush or the firewood he needed on his overnight searches for rustlers. Although he so seldom carried a gun, Butler was a deadly shot and kept a collection of 38 guns in his home. Most of these he had taken from law-breakers, including the notorious Donnellys.

Butler was known for his kindness and generosity to Lucan prisoners. Every Saturday night he bought a huge bucket of beer for 25¢ and took it to the inmates of the three cells behind the firehall. Often he used his home, rather than the jail, to detain local drunks and other offenders whom he thought should be kept off the streets for a little while.

Butler always helped tramps who came through his property while "... following the rails." He gave each man a meal and a chance to earn a few dollars splitting rails on his farm before he went on his way. Once he learned that a Black 'tramp' he had picked up along the railway was an escaped criminal. After hearing his story, Butler decided not to turn him over to the authorities, but kept him on his farm and let him work for room and board. A grandson recollected: "Grandpa would alway feed them and give them a night's rest and they would catch the train the next day."[14]

Peter Butler III

Butler left his widow, three sons and four daughters, to whom he passed on considerable property.[13]

The three sons, Richard, Frank and Peter III, stayed on in the area and married three McCartney sisters of an immigrant Irish family. One daughter, Elizabeth Hesson, moved to Stratford and opened a successful beauty parlour and wig shop. Along with their farm work, Richard and Frank ran an ice company in the 1880s and '90s, as well as a small contracting business. They built cement silos for local farmers and sidewalks for Lucan's main streets. They grew flax as well, and sometimes worked in Ward's flax mill where the flax was made into linen.

Harriet (Hattie) Butler, wife of Peter Butler III.

Constable Peter Butler, about 1930.

By the time Peter Butler III became a peace officer, about 1880, the family owned about 500 hectares including most of the present town of Lucan. The Butler brothers worked this land with a number of hired hands and 30 horses. The principal farmhouse stood on what is now Princess Street. Butler later sold or gave away a large part of his property, besides leaving a considerable portion to his descendants.

In the early autumn the Butler family held two major events: a threshing party at which dozens of neighbours helped to harvest the crop, and a large picnic to which friends and relatives came from Stratford, London, Listowel and Lebanon.[15] Years later guests recalled:

> Whenever they had a threshing all the community would come in and help, white men would all be there and they'd throw on a big spread for the farmers, you know. It was really a lovely life. None of the kids nowadays remember lives like that ...
>
> [When threshing was finished] ... they joined in an afternoon and evening of eating, dancing and revelry. They'd really whoop it up and then sit down to a good home-cooked meal, prepared in the house and outside, too, over a roaring fire.[16]

About 1900 Butler lost a considerable amount of his property and almost all his savings in a fraudulent scheme for land-development and tourist attractions in British Columbia. The great depression slowed business, but after recovery began, Butler began a salvage enterprise to collect ashes, rags, bones and scrap metal. He and his two sons carted the ashes back to a large cylinder on their farm and covered them with water to leach out the lye. By boiling grease with this liquid the Butlers made soap which they sold in Lucan. The rags, bones and scrap metal they sold in London. Mrs. Butler gathered old railroad spikes, while the men of the family went from farm to farm, bartering pots and pans for scrap metal. The family also collected dead farm animals which farmers paid them to take away. They skinned the animals in the field, disposed of the bodies and sold the hides in London for 75¢ each. In this way they earned about $40 a week, a tidy sum for that time. As an old man, one grandson recalled, Butler "... sat in the yard and told us what to do, and we ran the farm according to his orders."

Constable Butler died in 1943. Local dignitaries from the county and the province, and guests from the U.S.A. attended his funeral. Six OPP officers followed the casket to the family plot at Sauble Hill, the historic resting place of the first Wilberforce settlers. It was a tribute well deserved.

Henry and Mary Bibb

Henry Bibb, son of a white father and a slave mother, was born in Shelby County, Kentucky in May, 1815. From his youth he was fiercely determined to be free, and he ran away from his masters at least six times. Bibb later claimed that he had been "... educated in the school of adversity, whips and chains." His owners were quick to part with such a discontented slave, and Bibb was often sold at prices ranging from $350 to $1200. In 1839 he was sold at auction in New Orleans to a local planter who soon resold him to a Native person. Soon afterward Bibb made his final escape and fled north to Detroit.

During the 1840s Bibb travelled through Michigan, Ohio, New York and Canada West speaking and organizing abolitionist groups. At the end of that decade, despairing of the lot of Blacks in the U.S.A., Bibb moved from Detroit to Windsor, set up a printing business[17] and founded the *Voice of the Fugitive*. Its first issue was published on January 1, 1851. Bibb also founded the Refugee Home Society (RHS) and the local branch of the Canadian Anti-Slavery Society. He reported in his paper the activities of the UGR along the Detroit River, informing his readers of landing places, numbers of Blacks in different districts, job opportunities and new colonization schemes. In June, 1852 he published and distributed *The Anti-Slavery Harp,* a collection of popular anti-slavery songs.[18]

In Sandwich Mary Bibb set up a classroom in her home. In January, 1851 she was teaching 25 pupils; within a month the enrolment jumped to 46. In February she managed to find a larger room for her school, but it was "... ill ventilated, with uncomfortable seats and a shortage of desks and apparatus."[19] Mrs. Bibb was obliged to carry firewood quite a distance to heat the room. In spite of these difficult conditions, six white children attended the school along with the Black pupils. Bibb's salary for that whole eight-month term was $10.00. Mary and Henry also taught a Sunday School. Its 44 pupils received schoolbooks and Bibles from the Bibbs' supporters in Michigan. These two schools offered the area's Black children at least a minimal education during a time when the Sandwich common school was closed to them.

It is sad that Bibb's record was tarnished by evidence of self-interest and fraud in the RHS and by his bitter quarrel with Mary Ann Shadd, who was one of the outstanding women of her time. In a series of articles

Henry Bibb

written for the *Western Evangelist* Shadd attacked the RHS for "begging" and other questionable practices. Her articles provoked strong reaction from prominent abolitionists and anti-slavery groups. They were astounded to learn that the settlers had neither seen nor heard of several hundred dollars donated in response to Bibb's appeals for money to buy axes and hoes. John Martin, one of the settlers, attested:

> The people have been told falsehoods about our freezing and suffering and money has been raised which does no good. It has been reported to us, that thousands of dollars have been raised for our benefit. Of which we have never received the first red cent.[20]

Shadd further charged that, although Bibb denied collecting funds from abolitionists in Indiana to help refugees, his own newspaper[21] had reported that the RHS had received a good deal of money from Indiana for this purpose. At a public meeting held by the RHS on August 25, 1852 it was stated that agents held back an average of 20 to 25 per cent of the funds they collected for fugitives. Later Shadd learned from the Reverend S.H. Baker, chairman of the Society's executive committee, that agents kept for themselves as much as 63 per cent of the funds they collected. Theodore Holly, a junior editor of the *Voice of the Fugitive*, later admitted that Horace Hallock and other members of the RHS, who lived in Detroit, were also involved in the fraud. Another member of the executive committee, George Cary, admitted that he and Bibb still held the deed for the first 80 hectares bought with donations; they had never turned it over to the RHS.

The extent of the fraud explains why Shadd fought so relentlessly against the RHS and Bibb. She insisted that she was not acting from personal interest, but from a sense of duty. Writing to the American Missionary Association in December, 1852, she claimed:

> It is no slander to say that Henry Bibb has hundreds of dollars belonging to fugitives, probably thousands, would be nearer the truth. Henry Bibb is a dishonest man, and as such must be known to the world. To expose him is a duty which though painful, involving as it does loss of confidence, in coloured men, who assume to be leaders of their people, must be performed ... Within the present year and during the time he has been asking for 'donations' etc. to help him out of difficulty, he has built a house, bought a vessel, bought a house and lot on which he lives, leased another, and Mrs. Bibb has purchased a farm, and there are other business operations I can mention beside the paper [*Voice of the Fugitive*], and being in receipt of several hundreds per annum for buildings and lots in Detroit. This is the man who is 'making sacrifices for the fugitives' ... sacrifices are reported—great pecuniary disadvantages—mortgages etc. When at the same time he and she both, buy and build and carry on more extensive operations by land and water, than any colored people within fifty miles on either side of the river.[22]

It is impossible now to discern the motives from which Bibb acted. Certainly he seems to have been a strangely contradictory man. He was hard-working, but aggressive, devoted to the cause of Black freedom, but willing to defraud the very people he worked to help. It is certain that he believed that Black refugees would stay in Canada for only a short time and would return 'home' to the U.S.A. when conditions there improved. This belief may have tempted Bibb and others to provide for their own future at the expense of their fellows.

On October 9, 1853 Bibb's printing office burned down. It was a blow from which he never fully recovered. He continued to put out a one-page sheet packed with interesting news, but he died in August, 1854 still certain that his business had been destroyed by arson. Bibb's energies were lost at the very height of the fugitive slave movement to Canada, but his newspaper had done much by documenting the history of the refugees along the Detroit frontier.

The Shadd Family

One of the earliest families to settle in Raleigh Township was that of Abraham D. Shadd. The family descended from Hans Schadd who was born in Hesse Cassel, Germany about 1725. He went to America in Braddock's army in 1755, was wounded in the Seven Years War and later settled near Westchester, Pennsylvania. His grandson, Abraham D. Shadd, a shoemaker, was born in 1801. He came to Canada with his 13 children in the 1830s and settled near Chatham.

Mary Ann Shadd, Abraham's eldest daughter, early became a well-known activist for Blacks, particularly in the field of education. She once wrote that her only desire

> ... was to get an honest living by teaching persons who have not had opportunities afforded them to learn and at the same time to be privileged to exercise thought and speech as a rational being.[23]

As a young teacher she struggled with every kind of difficulty and discouragement to educate the children who attended her Windsor school. When her criticism of Henry Bibb roused him to attack her through his paper, a supporter wrote in her defense:

> Her presence here is absolutely necessary as a check upon the selfish and ambitious schemes of Mr. Bibb and his wife. I know of no one more competent from her ability and honest straight forwardness to keep things in the right place in the community. She has led a blameless life, although her path has been thorny ... all things considered you could not find a better teacher.[24]

When Shadd left Windsor in the spring of 1853, she joined her brother Isaac in publishing the *Provincial Freeman*. The Shadds promoted the cause of Black refugees in Canada and battled constantly against intemperance, "begging" and Black colonization schemes. They proclaimed the *Freeman* "... the enemy of vice and corruption and a promoter of good morals, devoted to anti-slavery, temperance and general literature."

The *Freeman* had correspondents in London, Windsor, Brantford, Toronto and St. Catharines; it had subscribers throughout Canada West and the U.S.A. Its pages sparkled with newsy items on the life of Blacks in Canada; its editorials urged a relentless war on bigotry and slavery. Mary Ann took a lively personal part in this war:

> One Sunday a slave boy without hat, coat, or shoes who had thus far eluded his pursuers, was overtaken in Chatham and about to be carried off. Mrs. Cary[25] tore the boy from the slave-hunters, ran to the court-house and had the bell rung so violently that the whole town

was soon aroused. Mrs. Cary with her commanding form, piercing eyes, and stirring voice soon had the people as indignant as herself—denouncing in no uncertain terms the outrage perpetrated under the British flag and demanded that these man-hunters be driven from their midst. The result was that the pursuers fled before the infuriated people, happy to get away without bodily harm;...[26]

Mary Ann Shadd finally left Chatham to become a recruiter in the Union Army during the Civil War, then a school principal and at last a lawyer in Washington, D.C. There she died on June 5, 1893.

Isaac Shadd was an avowed militant and a supporter of John Brown. In spite of their outspokenness, he and

(Left to right) *William, Alfred and Charles Shadd, sons of Garrison Shadd, about 1890.*

Mary Ann gained the respect of many of Chatham's residents. A letter in the Chatham *Planet* on March 4, 1858 proclaimed:

> We the undersigned citizens of Chatham and vicinity take pleasure in recommending the Provincial Freeman Newspaper published by Messrs. I.S. Shadd and T.F. Cary and edited by Mr. Shadd and sister (Mrs. Cary) all ardent laborers in the cause of colored people whose elevations and improvements they are seeking to advance.
>
> For three years Mr. Shadd and sister have published the paper independent of the support usually given to papers and Institutions advocating the interests of this class and have unflinchingly held up the standard to incite the colored people to progress, both mentally and morally.
>
> We take, or have patronized the paper and consider it to be a great and efficient means of improving their conditions and prospects and also feel satisfied that wherever it has circulated it has not only been found improving but has reflected credit upon the colored people generally. Consequently, we can in good faith recommend it to the philanthropic everywhere and ask in its behalf their warmest support.
>
> | | |
> |---|---|
> | Charles J.S. Atkin | —Mayor of Chatham |
> | Thomas Crop | —Reeve of Chatham |
> | Richard Monck | —Deputy Reeve Chatham |
> | Francis Martin | —Councillor |
> | | and 5 others |

A brother, Alfred Shadd, taught at the Buxton Mission School, and a younger sister, Emaline Shadd, graduated first in her class at Toronto Normal School in 1855, winning an award of £5.10.0. Emaline taught in Peel and Kent Counties and later at Howard University in Washington, D.C. before she returned to live in Kent County. She died in a train accident in 1895. Another brother, Garrison Shadd[27], became a wealthy farmer in Kent County. It was a family that in many ways contributed much to the development of Canada West.

Wilson Ruffin Abbott

Wilson Ruffin Abbott was born of free parents in Richmond, Virginia in 1801. As a lad he was appren-

ticed to a carpenter, but ran away from home at the age of 15 and went to Alabama, where he worked in a hotel. Later he became a steward on a Mississippi steamboat. He was hurt when a cord of wood fell over on him, and Ellen Toyer, a Black maid who was on the boat, nursed him back to health. The two young people were married and settled down in Mobile, Alabama, where Abbott opened a general provisions store. His wife taught him to read and write, but he needed no one to teach him mathematics. He had been born with a natural ability for figures and could do large sums in his head.

Before long Mobile's city council passed a law

Wilson Ruffin Abbott

requiring all free Blacks to post a bond signed by two white men, guaranteeing their good behaviour, and to wear badges showing that they were under bond. Abbott refused to obey the new regulations. He soon received an anonymous letter warning him of a plot to destroy his store and advising him to leave the city at once. That very day Abbott drew his money out of the bank and put his wife and children on a steamer for New Orleans. He followed them the next day. The warning had been true: Abbott's store was ransacked. Abbott never returned to Mobile, although he tried unsuccessfully to get compensation for his property there.

The Abbotts moved to New York, but finding that Blacks were treated unfairly there as well, decided to settle in Toronto; they arrived there in 1835. Two years later Abbott was one of the city's Blacks who joined Captain Fuller's Company of Volunteers during the Mackenzie Rebellion.

Abbott started up a tobacco shop; when it failed, he began to buy and rent houses, warehouses and offices. By 1875 he owned more than 75 properties in Toronto, Hamilton, Dundas and Owen Sound. He was active in Toronto's Colored Wesleyan Church, the Anti-Slavery Society of Canada and the politics of St. Patrick's Ward, where he lived. Ellen Toyer Abbott founded the Queen Victoria Benevolent Society, which helped hundreds of the refugees who were coming into Toronto.

The Abbotts, who had five daughters and four sons, moved to Elgin for a short time to give their children the advantage of a classical education at the famous Buxton School. They returned to Toronto, where Abbott died in 1876. He was buried on a hillside in Toronto's Necropolis, overlooking the Don Valley.

Anderson Ruffin Abbott

Anderson R. Abbott, a son of Wilson Ruffin Abbott, was born in Toronto in 1837. He became the first Canadian-born Black doctor and served as one of eight Black surgeons in the Union Army during the American Civil War. He himself wrote the following sketch of his life:

(Left) *Anderson Ruffin Abbott, surgeon in the Union Army, about 1863.* (Above) *Mary Ann Casey Abbott, daughter of Thomas P. Casey and wife of Anderson Ruffin Abbott, about 1875.* (Below) *The Abbott home on Dowling Avenue, Toronto, about 1905.*

I was born in the City of Toronto, April 7th in the year 1837 ... I was married on Aug. 9th-1871 to Mary A. Casey daughter of T.P. Casey — a Canadian born in St. Catharines Ont. I received my elementary education in private and public schools afterwards at the Toronto Academy in connection with Knox's College ... A.M. Lafferty, Samuel R. Ward and myself were the only Colored students in attendance — I remained at this school about three years and was very successful in carrying away either prizes or honors in all my classes — I afterwards attended school in Oberlin, Ohio, remained there about three years. On returning home I matriculated in medicine in the University of Toronto and studied medicine for four years under the care of the late Dr. A.T. Augusta M.B. Trinity College, and passed the primary examination for the degree of Bachelor of Medicine at the Toronto University in 1857 also the Medical Board of Upper Canada for a licence to practice in 1861 — I graduated in medicine when I was 23 years of age. In 1863 I was appointed a surgeon in the U.S. Army and ... was placed in charge of [Camp Baker and Freedman's] Hospitals in Washington ... until my resignation April 5th 1866. I ... returned home, was married in 1871 and went into practice in Chatham, Ontario. In Chatham I held the following positions: President of the Wilberforce Educational Institute from 1873 to 1880, Coroner, County of Kent, 1874 ... President of Chatham Literary & Debating Society, President Chatham Medical Society in 1878. In 1881 I removed from Chatham to Dundas. Appointed Doctor for Dundas Mechanics Institute in 1881 ... I removed from Dundas to Oakville in 1889, and in 1890 removed to Toronto — In April of 1890 I was elected a member of Jas. S. Knowlton Post No. 532 Grand Army of the Republic and on Nov. 21st 92 appointed Aide de Camp on the Staff of the Commanding Officers Dept. of N.Y. ... On resigning I was presented with Sword, Sash and Belt by the officers and Comrades of the Post. I was also honored by being presented with a Shepard Plaid Shawl which Mr. Lincoln wore on his way to the 1st inauguration and which formed part of a disguise which it is alleged he wore on that occasion to escape assassination — The shawl was presented to me by Mrs. Lincoln after the assassination of the President.[28]

Abbott was also an active member of the York Pioneers and of the Canadian Institute. In 1894 he became Medical Superintendent of Provident Hospital in Chicago, where he stayed until he retired in Toronto. In his later years he wrote articles for the Chatham

Planet, the Dundas *Banner* and the New York *Age.* He was a leader of Toronto's Black community and attacked discrimination wherever he found it.

James Mink

One of Toronto's wealthiest Blacks in the 1840s was James Mink, owner of the Mansion Inn and Livery on Adelaide Street. Mink was born in Upper Canada, the son of former Canadian slaves who came from New York with the Herkimers, a Loyalist family that settled near Kingston about 1800. James was the eldest of 11 children, "... a fine example physically of a pure Black man; in countenance good humored, open and sensible, stout in figure and inclined to obesity."[29]

Mink's business grew, and he opened stables at 6-7 Terauley Street and on Queen Street. His stagecoaches carried passengers and mail from Toronto to Kingston, where his brother George kept a livery service. For many years Toronto's city council used Mink's livery stables, and minutes of council meetings record many payments to Mink.[30] Mink also brought prisoners from Kingston with four-horse wagons, usually at a cost to the city of £32.10.0. He often appeared before the city council to petition for services and changes to Toronto's cab laws. Even so, he seems to have been in favour with City Hall, for his Mansion House was a polling station in St. James ward for the municipal elections of January, 1847 and '48.

Mink was considered eccentric. He offered $10 000 for a "... respectable white husband ..." for his daughter Minnie. The prize tempted James Andrews, a cabman from Yorkshire, and he married Minnie, took her to the U.S.A. for a 'honeymoon' and promptly sold her into slavery. Months later Mink discovered his daughter's plight and rescued her.

The coming of the Grand Trunk Railway put an end

A coach on the Kingston Road, 1843.

to the expansion of Mink's business. He retired to a mansion in Richmond Hill where he lived quietly.

Martin Delany

Martin Delany, a free Black from West Virginia, received his early education in Pennsylvania and went on to become the first Black to graduate in medicine from Harvard University. Delany came to Canada in February, 1856 and opened an office in Chatham on William Street, east of King. He also joined the Black Masons, wrote editorials for the *Provincial Freeman* and often spoke in public, promoting Black settlement and supporting John Brown at his Chatham convention. When a cholera epidemic broke out in the summer of 1856, Delany suggested to Chatham's authorities a plan to bring the disease under control; to everyone's relief, the plan succeeded.

When Archie McKellar, the long-time friend of Kent County's Blacks, decided to battle the segregationist Edwin Larwill for a seat in Canada West's parliament, Delany organized the Black vote in the Chatham area, while William King promoted McKellar's candidacy at Elgin. On election day 300 Blacks marched in a group from St. Andrew's Church in Buxton to the Court House in Chatham to cast their votes. Each one signed his name in the register, and no doubt this gave them satisfaction, for almost half the white voters could only make their mark. To the joy of the Black voters, McKellar defeated Larwill decisively.

One of Delany's chief interests was finding a homeland in Africa for Canadian and American Blacks who might choose to emigrate there. After John Brown visited Chatham, Delany left for Africa to try to buy from the chiefs of the Niger Valley land for Black immigrants. He bought the land, but the American Civil War broke out and Delany's plan came to nothing.

On his return to Chatham, Delany was named Canada's delegate to the 1860 International Statistical Congress held in London, England, where most of the world's major countries were represented. Delany read a paper that impressed all but the American delegates, who stormed out of the Congress to protest the pres-

Major Martin Delany, M.D.

ence of Canada's Black representative. Both the London *Times* and the Toronto *Globe* criticised the Americans' action.

When the American Civil War began, Delany went to Washington to offer his services as a recruiting officer in the Union Army. His eldest son, Toussaint L. Delany, who had been educated at the Buxton Mission, joined the 54th Massachusetts Volunteers and was promoted to Sergeant-Major. At first Martin Delany was rejected because he was known to have supported John Brown's Chatham convention of 1858, but he would not give up. Somehow he secured a personal interview with President Lincoln who was so deeply impressed with Delany's bearing, intelligence and commitment to the Union cause that he wrote to Secretary of War, Edwin Stanton, recommending that Delany receive a commission.

Delany was made a major, the highest commission conferred on a Black during the Civil War. At the commissioning Stanton said:

> Major Delany, I take great pleasure in handing you this commission of major in the United States Army. You are the first of your race who has been thus honored by the government; therefore much depends on and will be expected of you. But I feel assured it is safe in your hands.
>
> Dr. Delany replied: Honorable secretary, I can assure you, whatever be my failure to meet the expectations concerning me, on one thing you can depend — that this parchment will never be dishonored in my hands.[31]

After receiving his commission, Delany returned to Chatham to raise volunteers for his plan to infiltrate the South and enlist Blacks in the Union cause. He formed the 104th Regiment of Colored Troops and made Abraham Shadd, who had been serving with the 55th Massachusetts, a captain in the new regiment. But by this time the Confederates had surrendered, and Delany was posted to the headquarters of the Bureau of Refugees, Freedmen and Abandoned Lands in Hilton Head, South Carolina. He spent the rest of his life in reading, research and writing. He died in 1885.

Anthony Burns

Zion Baptist Church on St. Catharines' Geneva Street had an eminent minister from 1860 to 1862: the Reverend Anthony Burns. Before he came to Canada, Burns had been the centre of a serious riot and a famous legal battle in Boston. Burns had escaped from his master, Colonel Charles Suttler, in Virginia and fled to Boston in 1854. Suttler traced Burns to Boston and took out a warrant for his arrest. When he found Burns, he asked him sarcastically if Burns remembered the money Suttler used to give him. "Yes," replied Burns, "I do recollect that you used to give me twelve and a half cents at the end of every year I worked for you."[32]

The case came to court and the abolitionist lawyer Richard Henry Dana[33] acted for Burns. News soon spread that in Boston, the cradle of liberty, a Black who had escaped from slavery might soon be enslaved again. Abolitionists denounced the Fugitive Slave Law which required the return to a master of any slave discovered in a 'free' state. Massachusetts newspapers demanded that the Act should not be enforced in New England. A crowd of nearly 2000 gathered for a mass meeting. It stormed the courthouse to try to free Burns, but failed, and one man was killed and several were injured before artillery troops could clear the streets and restore order.

By the time Burns was tried, several days later, the whole American public was interested in his case. The authorities took no chance of another riot: the courthouse was surrounded by chains and guarded by marines and state troopers. Fifty thousand people gathered to hear the verdict. Judge Edward G. Loring upheld the Fugitive Slave Act: he ordered Burns returned to his master in Virginia.

The sentence was decidedly unpopular in Boston. A coffin bearing a sign, 'The Funeral of Liberty', was hung from a building opposite the courthouse. Stores and businesses were draped in black. Back in Virginia, Burns was sold again and sent to North Carolina, but the people of Boston remembered him. Twelfth Baptist Church and its pastor, the Reverend L.A. Grimes, raised funds to buy Burns' freedom. In 1855 a Boston woman sponsored him as a student at Oberlin College, Ohio. There he studied between 1855 and 1857. After that he became pastor of a church in Indianapolis for a short while, but left because of local prejudice against free Blacks. He came to Canada in 1860 to take charge of Zion Baptist Church, St. Catharines. He soon cleared the church of all debt and earned the respect of the community. But his troubles had taken their toll: Burns was not well when he came to St. Catharines; he died within two years, on July 27, 1862. A local newspaper reported:

> On Monday last the mortal remains of the Rev. Anthony Burns, pastor of the colored Baptist Church of this town, were conveyed to their last resting place ... He had been here but a short time. When he came he saw that there was much for him to do and he set himself to do it with all his heart. He was prospering in his work, he was getting the affairs of the church into

Abolitionist feeling ran so high in Boston that, to prevent his rescue, Burns had to be escorted to a ship by troops when he was returned to his master.

good shape ... Mr. Burns' memory will be cherished long by not a few in this town. His gentle, unassuming and yet manly bearing secured him many friends. His removal is felt to be a great loss and his place will not soon be filled.[34]

The Reverend R.A. Ball of the Methodist church commented:

> He was a fine-looking man, tall and broad-shouldered, but with a slight stoop, indicating a weak chest. His colour was light brown. He was a fine speaker and was considered to be well educated. He was unmarried and very popular with both the white people and the people of his own race.[35]

Burns was buried in Victoria Cemetery, St. Catharines. His gravestone reads:

In Memoriam
REV. ANTHONY BURNS
The fugitive slave of the Boston
Riots, 1854
Pastor of Zion Baptist Church,
Born in Virginia, May 31, 1834
Died in the triumph of faith in
St. Catharines,
July 27th, 1862.

Until the year 1951 the signboard hanging outside Zion Baptist Church bore the name 'Anthony Burns'. Tourists still search out the church and the grave of this man who played an important part in the struggle for human equality.

Burr Plato

A remarkable member of the Black community in the Niagara District was Burr Plato who fled Virginia with seven other Blacks in 1856. While a slave, Plato had saved $50 in gold, and this money kept the group of fugitives alive until they reached Fort Erie a month later with only five dollars, a bag of biscuits and a strong desire to work in freedom.

For the next several years Plato worked as a porter and a farm-hand and spent every spare moment learning to read and write. He saved enough money to buy a home on Stanley Street, where he raised a family of 10 children and took a very active part in community and political affairs. He was one of the very few Blacks of the 19th century to win election to municipal office in Canada.

> By thrift and untiring industry he acquired education and a comfortable property and was so respected as an honest and God-fearing citizen that he was on several occasions elected to municipal office by his white neighbours.[36]

Burr Plato died in 1905 and was buried in Drummond Hill Cemetery with other members of Niagara's early Black families.[37]

James Morgan

In an interview reported in the *Elmvale Lance* in 1923, 97-year-old James Morgan said that he was born at Holland Landing in 1831. His father, a 'herb doctor' and a slave on a Virginia plantation had had the good fortune to meet some Quakers who helped him escape to Cincinnati and from there to Canada. Morgan went on:

> Father, wishing to have a piece of land of his own and hearing that land was cheap north of Lake Simcoe, moved up here when I was a very little shaver ... The whole country was solid bush with the exception of our own clearing and the view was no wider than that across the yard where I live now.
>
> What did we have to eat? Whatever we could get. People talk of hard times today. They do not know the meaning of the words. For meat we sometimes had venison from deer killed in the wood by the few who had guns. More frequently we had groundhogs, very nice meat, coons which make an excellent dish, muskrat or porcupines. For bread we thrashed wheat with a flail, threw it in the air from a blanket to get rid of the chaff and then carried it to the Holland Landing to be ground. Flour, shorts and bran were all baked together. We had "mooney tea" and "burr tea" the latter very good made from plants grown in the woods. For vegetables we had cow cabbage and leeks.[38]

The Morgan family, including James' father, who lived to the age of 110, is buried in the New Lowell cemetery.

John Hall

The first Black to settle at Sydenham Village near Owen Sound was the legendary John "Daddy" Hall who arrived about 1843. Hall was born near Amherstburg in 1807 of Black and Native parents. When he was a small child, American slave-hunters raided the Black settlement, seized his mother and all 11 children and sold them to plantation owners in Kentucky.[39] Hall was bought by a Kentuckian named 'Catlett' from whom he eventually escaped. In the

John Hall of Sydenham Village (Owen Sound).

meantime he had married a young slave from a neighbouring plantation. He and his bride decided to make a try for freedom and set off northward, "... keeping to back country trails, sleeping in fields and barns by night and avoiding all towns where citizens were eager to capture runaway slaves for a reward."[40] They reached Canada and settled in Toronto, where Hall claimed that his first, second, third and fourth wives died. His fifth, and last, wife was an Englishwoman from Manchester who had lived next door to him, cared for his children, and moved with him to Rocky Saugeen (now Durham) where they built a cabin. Their later move to Sydenham Village was hard:

> At first they found it impossible to bring all their belongings with them and so for two months, during which Hall was clearing up a place and building a shack, his wife, her baby bound to her back, walked back and forth to her former home to milk their two cows ... She would bring back with her foodstuffs procurable there, but not at Sydenham.[41]

Hall felled trees, cleared the land and built a log cabin in one of Owen Sound's six natural parks.[42] "There were no homes then, just a shanty or two put up for a land agent and surveyor."[43] The Halls reared 10 children[44]—three sons and seven daughters—in Owen Sound. In 1851 John Hall became the town's night watchman, town-crier and bell-ringer. He went about ringing his solid copper bell and announcing auction sales and other events. The town residents called him a 'walking newspaper'. After making his announcements, Hall usually went on to comment on some of them, always closing with the words, "God save our gracious Queen."

Hall served as town-crier for nearly 50 years. He died in 1925 at the presumed age of 118. Stories are still told of him in Owen Sound today:

> Long after he had passed the century mark he got his third set of teeth and though he had been shiny bald for many years he grew new hair and at the time of his death had a luxurious head of snow white curls and a thick beard ... Second sight was another benediction upon his great years. After being nearly blind for a considerable period, "Daddy Hall" was restored to perfect eyesight.[45]

William Hall, V.C.

William Hall was born in Hants County, Nova Scotia in 1827. His father, an escaped slave from Virginia, had reached the province aboard the British ship *Leonard* in 1814. When William was a child, his family moved to Horton Bluff; they lived where the Bluff lighthouse now stands. Hall was only 12 years old when he went to sea. He joined the Royal Navy on February 2, 1852 and served on Nelson's flagship *Victory* at Portsmouth. Later he was posted to *H.M.S. Rodney* and sailed for two years with the Channel Fleet. The Crimean War broke out in 1853, and Hall was decorated for his actions in the Battle of Inkerman and the siege of Sebastopol. After the war Hall was transferred to the frigate *Shannon* stationed at Hong Kong.

When the Indian Mutiny began in the summer of 1857, the *Shannon* was ordered to Calcutta. Hall was one of 410 seamen and marines picked by Captain William Peel to go overland to Bawnpore and Lucknow where Sir John Inglis was desperately holding out against the mutineers. At Lucknow, Hall volun-

William Hall, V.C.

teered to join a gun crew trying to breach the walls of the Shah Nejeef, a temple that the sepoys had fortified. It was virtually a suicidal mission, and when all the other men in the crew had been killed, except Hall and a badly wounded lieutenant, Hall kept sponging, loading and firing their gun until he opened a gap in the wall that allowed the British troops to enter. For his bravery in action Able Seaman William Hall received the Victoria Cross on November 16, 1857. He was the first Canadian sailor and the first Black to win this award.

Hall retired from the navy in 1876 after nearly 23 years of service. He had reached the rank of quartermaster, and it is believed that he was offered a post at Whitehall in London, England, which he declined. He returned to Nova Scotia to live for a time with his two sisters on a farm outside Hansport. When he gave up farming, he moved to Avonpost. He died there on August 25, 1904 and was buried at Lockhartville.[46]

Osborne Perry Anderson

Osborne Anderson

Only one Canadian Black accompanied John Brown on his ill-fated raid. He was Osborne Anderson, whom Brown's provisional government had elected a 'congressman'. Anderson was born in West Fallowfield, Pennsylvania on July 27, 1839. He was well educated, a printer by trade and was living in Chatham when Brown arrived in 1858. Anderson had come to Canada with the family of Absalom Shadd who owned two farms near Chatham. He had brought Anderson from Pennsylvania to help manage and work his farms, but before long Anderson chose to return to printing. He became printer's devil for the *Provincial Freeman*, working for Mary Ann and Isaac Shadd. It may well have been Isaac who influenced Anderson to join Brown's 'army of liberation'.

Responding to Brown's call for volunteers, Anderson went off to train in guerilla warfare at Brown's secret farm in Virginia. He was one of the strike force at Harpers Ferry and one of the few to escape death or capture there. He fled back to Canada with the help of the UGR and there, with

Mary Ann Shadd, wrote a pamphlet about his experiences: *A Voice from Harpers Ferry*. At the outbreak of the American Civil War, Anderson returned to the U.S.A. and became a non-commissioned officer in the Union Army. After the war he retired to Washington, D.C. where he died on December 13, 1872.

Stewart Taylor

Just one other Canadian joined John Brown at Harpers Ferry. He was a white man, Stewart Taylor, who died of wounds received in the raid. Taylor

> ... was born at Uxbridge, some miles north of Toronto, on October 29, 1836, and thus was a few days short of his 23rd birthday when killed at Harpers Ferry.... "His mother, Jane Taylor, married a Mr. Price when Stewart was still a child. He received a fair English education, residing in Canada with his grandfather, David Taylor, till his 17th year, when he started out for the United States, intending to settle in Kansas. However he did not reach Kansas; he became ill in Missouri, then after a jaunt into Arkansas, he located at West Liberty, Iowa, where he found employment in a wagon factory and where, later, he met John Brown and his men ... He had

Stewart Taylor

an inclination to spiritualism and fatalism …'Poor Taylor had told me that he knew he would be shot at the taking of Harpers Ferry, and be one of the first ones, too. He attributed this impression to Spiritualism in which he firmly believed. He was an odd or eccentric person, a day dreamer.'"[47]

He dreamed, it seems, of brotherhood and freedom…

Delos Rogest Davis, K.C.

The most prominent Black of Amherstburg in the late 19th century was probably Delos Rogest Davis. Davis was born in Colchester Township in 1846. He taught school in Colchester North for four years before he was appointed commissioner of affidavits in 1871. Two years later he became a public notary. He studied very hard in the hope of becoming a lawyer, but to be admitted to the Bar, an applicant had to article for a time under a lawyer and then pass the Bar examination. Davis could find no lawyer who would take a Black into his office. Finally, in 1884, he appealed to the Ontario Legislature, asking that the Supreme Court of Judicature admit him to the Bar without articling if

he could pass the exmination and pay the fee. The Legislature granted his appeal. Davis passed the examination, paid the fee and was admitted to the Law Society of Upper Canada on May 19, 1885. The first Black lawyer in Canadian history, Davis went on to achieve for himself and his race another 'first' when he was made King's Counsel in 1910.

Davis' son followed in his father's footsteps and graduated from Osgoode Hall in 1900. The two men established the firm of Davis and Davis, Barristers, on Gore Street in Amherstburg.

Delos Rogest Davis (below) *practised law with his son Frederick Homer Alphonso Davis in Amherstburg.*

Controller W.P. Hubbard, 1906.

Dr. Anderson Ruffin Abbott in his later years.

'Old Cicero' (W.P. Hubbard) in the back yard of his home on Broadview Avenue, Toronto.

William Peyton Hubbard

W.P. Hubbard, son of a Virginian refugee, grew up in the 1840s in a cabin in 'the bush' (now the bustling Bloor Street-Brunswick Avenue district of Toronto). His father, a waiter at the Cataract Hotel in Niagara Falls, sent his son to the Toronto Model School. There he learned the trade of baking, which he enjoyed all his life. There, too, he met his future wife, Julia Luckett.

In his early years Hubbard worked as a livery man in his uncle's business. While driving his cab down the Don Mills Road one day in the 1860s, he saved a passenger from plunging into the Don River. The passenger was George Brown of the *Globe*. Brown hired Hubbard as his driver, befriended him and urged him to go into politics.

Hubbard, a baker for 16 years, invented an oven which he sold through his own company, Hubbard Ovens. In 1874 he and Julia Luckett were married. She had been teaching in Washington, D.C. For the next 20 years, the Hubbards were chiefly busy bringing up their family.

In 1893, at the age of 51, W.P. Hubbard entered civic politics. He was first elected alderman in 1894 in the affluent Ward 4 where he lived; he was re-elected in the next 13 annual elections. In 1897 he topped the polls for the first of many times. Indeed, his gift for oratory earned him the title of 'Cicero of Council'.[48] From 1898 to 1907 he served on the Board of Control, being elected first by his fellow aldermen, then by the citizens at large. From 1904 to 1907 he was vice-chairman of the Board of Control and second in rank to the mayor, for whom he often acted.

Hubbard worked for the 'little man'. When rich laundry owners tried to drive small Chinese laundries out of business by demanding exorbitant municipal licence fees, Hubbard got a gradual increase in fees, which small businesspeople could meet without hardship. In his early years on Council he fought a tough battle to keep Toronto's water supply publicly owned. Later he took up the cause of cheap, publicly-owned electricity. He constantly supported Adam Beck, the founder of Ontario's hydro-electric system. Beck later said that Hubbard was "... always an ally." Hubbard gave most of his time and interest to chair a special 'power committee'. He and others worked for provincial legislation to allow Toronto to generate, develop and lease electricity. Out of this effort came the Toronto Hydro-Electric System. At that period hydro was an unpopular cause with Toronto voters, and the time Hubbard spent promoting it contributed to his defeat in 1908. Ironically, this work was later seen as his greatest gift to the future of his city and his province.

After his defeat, Hubbard moved to Ward 1, east of the Don River; there he built a 14-room house at 660 Broadview Avenue, overlooking the valley. He was back on City Council representing Ward 1 in 1913, but retired at the end of his term because his wife was seriously ill. Before he retired, he was honoured in a gala ceremony in the City Hall chambers, where Adam Beck presented Council with a large oil portrait of Controller Hubbard. The portrait hung for many years in the broad, marble-paved corridors of Toronto's Old City Hall.[49]

Hubbard and his wife were members of St. George's Anglican Church on John Street. He kept a close connection with Toronto's Black community. He was a member of the Home Service Association and the Musical and Literary Society of Toronto. He was also a close friend of Anderson Ruffin Abbott: the Hubbards' son Fred[50] married the Abbotts' daughter Grace, and Abbott spent his last years in W.P. Hubbard's home on Broadview Avenue. Both men were members of the prestigious York Pioneers. Hubbard once wrote to Abbott: "I have always felt that I am a representative of a race hitherto despised, but if given a fair opportunity would be able to command esteem."[51]

Abbott died in 1913. He could not have foreseen the influx of West Indian and American Blacks who were brought to Canada during the First World War by railroad and industrial interests. Hubbard was to witness this development. He lived in retirement to the age of 93 and became known in the press as 'Toronto's Grand Old Man'. He could be counted on to make good copy, and his latter birthdays were covered by the newspapers. When he turned 93 he told a reporter: "Too much leisure makes a man languid. His organs stop functioning as they should and complications develop. It is written that man shall earn his living by the sweat of his brow."[52]

It was Hubbard's last birthday quote. In the spring of 1935 he died. He was buried near the Abbott family plot in the historic Toronto Necropolis. His descendants still live in Toronto.

Notes

1:   **Slaves and Slave-Holders**

1. Matthieu da Costa, a Black, travelled with the expedition of Pierre du Gua, sieur de Monts, to Canada's Atlantic region, 1604-1606. According to some accounts, da Costa was a free man; according to others, he was a servant to de Monts, Governor of Port Royal. Da Costa acted as interpreter between the French and the Micmac Indians of the region, but he did not become a permanent resident of Canada.
2. The Company of New France was also known as the 'Hundred Associates'.
3. Guillaume Couillard, his wife, Guillaumette Hébert, and their children were the only complete family to stay at Québec through the English occupation.
4. Correspondence to Ministre-Secrétaire d'Etat from M. De Dononville and M. De Champyny, August 10, October 31 and November 6, 1688. London: Cross Cultural Centre, University of Western Ontario.
5. "Negroes in Detroit", p. 3. Burton Historical Collection MS, Detroit Public Library.
6. MARCEL TRUDEL: "L'Attitude de l'église catholique vis-à-vis l'esclavage au Canada français", p. 1. Québec: Les Presses de l'Université Laval, 1960.
7. T. WATSON SMITH: *The Slave in Canada.* Collections of the Nova Scotia Historical Society, Vol. X., 1896-98, p. 9. Halifax, 1899, as cited by W.A. Spray in: *The Blacks in New Brunswick,* p. 14. Brunswick Press, 1972.
8. *Montreal Gazette,* March 3, 1962.
9. Murray Papers, PAC, Vol. II, p. 15, as cited by W.R. Riddell, "Notes on Slavery in Canada", *Journal of Negro History,* Vol. V, No. 3. (July, 1920), p. 396.
10. This regiment was also known as the 'Royal American'.
11. Riddell Papers, B-2. Toronto: Public Archives of Ontario.
12. *Ibid.*
13. This is now Christ Church Cathedral of Montréal.
14. James McGill gave a large bequest and his name to Montréal's McGill University.
15. *Montreal Gazette, op. cit.*
16. *Ibid.*
17. One *minot* is about 39 litres.
18. A French gold coin worth about $4.50.
19. The *Act for Encouraging New Settlers in His Majesty's Colonies and Plantations in America,* passed by the British Parliament in 1790, stated that settlers could bring with them any Blacks, household furniture and other personal property "... not to

exceed the value of £50 for each white person in the family and that of 40 shillings [£2] for each Negro."

Some of Canada's most successful, influential, pious and powerful families owned slaves. In the Kingston area, for example, slave-owning families included the Everetts, Herkimers, Fairfields, Richard Cartwright and the future Solicitor General of Upper Canada, Robert I.D. Gray. In 1791 the pioneers of the Niagara district owned about 300 Black slaves, more than in any other part of the territory at that time.

20. Americans claimed that Virginia lost almost 30 000 slaves in 1778; South Carolina 25 000 and Georgia over 12 000 slaves.
21. Now Cornwall, Ontario.
22. Ensign Elyah Bottom whose home was near Maitland, about 10 km above Prescott.
23. WILLIAM CANNIFF: *The History of the Province of Ontario*, p. 575 f. Toronto: A.H. Hovey, 1872.
24. Butler's Rangers was a troop of Loyalist soldiers who served as wilderness fighters (commandos) under Colonel John Butler in the American Civil War. The unit was disbanded in 1784.
25. WILLIAM CANNIFF: *ibid.*
26. *Ibid.*
27. That is, from Lake St. Clair to the site of the present city of Chatham.
28. VICTOR LAURISTON: *Romantic Kent*, p. 26. Chatham: Shepherd Printing Co. Ltd., 1952.
29. Brant's granddaughter, Catherine Morey, who spoke no English, married an escaped Black slave from Maryland, William Henderson. Their children were for many years part of the small Black community of Brantford.
30. The Ordinance of 1787, Article 6, as cited in "Negroes in Detroit", *op. cit.*, p. 6, stated: "There shall be neither slavery nor involuntary servitude in the Said Territory, otherwise than in the punishment of crime, whereof the party shall have been duly convicted."

2: Opposition to Slavery

1. In 1778 the British abolitionist Thomas Clarkson published a book which exposed the African slave trade and became an anti-slavery handbook.

   In 1787 the American Northwest Territories (including Indiana, Illinois, Wisconsin, Iowa and Michigan) became the sixth American jurisdiction to pass anti-slavery legislation. They had been preceded by Vermont, Pennsylvania, Massachusetts, Connecticut and Rhode Island.
2. The eminent jurist, Lord Mansfield, had ruled (in the Somerset case) that a slave could not be made to leave "the free air of Britain" against his will, to be sold and re-enslaved in another country.
3. T.W. SMITH: "The Slave in Canada", *Nova Scotia Historical Society*, X (1900), p. 43.
4. W.R. RIDDELL: "The Slave in Canada", *JNH*, V, No. 3 (July, 1920), p. 55 n.
5. *Ibid.*
6. *Ibid.*

7. "Negroes in Detroit", Burton Historical Collection MS, Detroit Public Library, p. 7.
8. Richard Cartwright made the motion; Robert Hamilton seconded it. Both men were slave-owners.
9. WILLIAM CANNIFF: *The History of the Province of Ontario*, p. 574. Toronto: A.H. Hovey, 1872.
10. W.T. HALLAM: "Slave Days in Canada" (a paper read before the Women's Canadian Historical Society, Toronto, 1919, reprinted in *The Canadian Churchman*, p. 14.
11. PAC. C.O. 42 (Q 326) Vol. 363, p. 117; as cited by Gary E. French: *Men of Colour*, pp. 12-13. Stroud, Ont: Kaste Books, 1978.
12. *The Globe,* March 1, 1851.
13. *Ibid.*
14. *Ibid.*
15. While George Brown used the influence of the *Globe* to support anti-slavery activities, his brother Gordon was considered an even more zealous abolitionist. He is said to have been in no small measure responsible for the *Globe's* continued support of the abolitionist cause when the *Globe* championed the North during the American Civil War and so brought criticism on the paper. After the War, American citizens in Toronto showed their esteem for Gordon Brown's support by presenting him with a gold watch.
16. *The Provincial Freeman,* February 26, 1852.
17. *The Collector,* No. 2 (1960), Stanley Smith Collection, Regional Room, University of Western Ontario.
18. *Ibid.*
19. When John Brown was tried in Charleston, West Virginia, in December, 1859, for his disastrous raid on the armoury at Harpers Ferry, evidence was produced that Hamilton sympathizers had helped to finance his attack. It is also believed that some of the documents and publications carried by Brown and his men had been published in Hamilton.
20. H.H. BROWNELL: "John Brown's Body ..."
21. ABRAHAM LINCOLN: "The Gettysburg Address".

3: The Road to Freedom

1. Various versions of this song were developed from the original "The Free Slave" by George W. Clark, an American abolitionist.
2. WILBUR H. SIEBERT: *The Underground Railroad From Slavery to Freedom*, p. 197. London: Macmillan & Co. Ltd., 1898.
3. ROBERT WEST HOWARD: *Thundergate: The Forts of Niagara*, p. 202. New Jersey: Prentice-Hall, Inc., 1968.
4. WILBUR H. SIEBERT: *op. cit.*, p. 120.
5. *Ibid.*, p. 58.
6. *Ibid.*, p. 111.
7. WILLIAM WELLS BROWN: *Narratives of William W. Brown*, pp. 107 f.; as cited by Wilbur H. Siebert, *op. cit.*, p. 83.
8. REVEREND CALVIN FAIRBANKS: "During Slavery Times", p. 11; as cited by Wilbur H. Siebert: *op. cit.*, p. 160.
9. REVERENT CALVIN FAIRBANKS: *op. cit.*, pp. 104-143; as cited by Wilbur H. Siebert: *op. cit.*, p. 160.
10. Up to that time fugitive slaves had been considered free if they managed to reach a 'free' (non-slave) state.

11. Upper Canada was renamed 'Canada West' in 1841 and kept the name until it became 'Ontario' in 1867.

12. *Border City Star,* April 13, 1929.

13. *The Provincial Freeman,* March 22, 1854.

14. WILBUR H. SIEBERT: *op. cit.,* pp. 80 f.

15. ALEXANDER MILTON ROSS: *Recollections and Experiences of an Abolitionist,* pp. 2 f. Toronto: Rowsell and Hutchison, 1875.

16. *Ibid.,* as cited by Wilbur H. Siebert: *op. cit.,* pp. 181 f.

17. *Ibid.,* p. 20.

18. *Ibid.*

19. SARAH H. BRADFORD: *Scenes in the Life of Harriet Tubman,* p. 77. Auburn: W.J. Moses, Printer, 1869.

20. Benjamin Drew, for example, claimed that 30 000 Blacks were living in Canada West before 1852; Levi Coffin estimated the figure at 40 000.

21. Jay's Treaty of 1794 brought about the evacuation from Detroit of British troops in 1796, but the British residents who remained there were granted immunity from the Ordinance and allowed to keep their slaves. Slavery in Michigan was abolished by the state constitution of 1835. As in Upper Canada, where abolition had become absolute in 1833, the last few instances of slavery would continue to the final possible moment.

22. *Chatham Journal,* December 23, 1843.

23. The lad rescued was St. Louis Powell. He was placed temporarily in the care of the Shadd family. At the turn of the century he was living in Windsor.

24. Anderson Diddrick was employed as a porter by the Great Western Railway. He worked in Toronto, Hamilton, London, Chatham and Windsor.

25. "A Memoir ... The Honorable Elijah Leonard", pp. 1-2. London: Stanley Smith Collection, University of Western Ontario.

26. WILLIAM LEWIS BABY: *Souvenirs of the Past,* p. 138. Windsor, 1896.

27. *Ibid.*

28. *Chatham Planet,* August 5, 1857.

4: Refugees and Their Havens

1. Nova Scotia at first included the territory of New Brunswick. The latter became a separate province in 1784.

2. A Provisional Peace Agreement between Great Britain and the United States of America was signed at Paris on November 30, 1782.

3. Public Archives of Nova Scotia, White Collection, III, doc. 196, 'General Birch Certificate' as cited in James W.St.G. Walker: *The Black Loyalists: The Search for a Promised Land in Nova Scotia and Sierra Leone 1783-1870,* p. 11. New York: Africana Publishing Company and Dalhousie: Dalhousie University Press, 1976.

4. One of Peter Long's daughers, Elizabeth, was married by the Anglican Bishop John Strachan to an Aaron Eyres in 1811.

5. The United Empire Loyalist (UEL) list is the official roster of those British subjects whose allegiance to the Crown caused them to leave the dissident American colonies and settle in the Maritimes or 'the Canadas'.

6. Peter Long's son James tried to have his father's name replaced on the list, but without success.

7. P. MCNIFF: Map of Township of Gosfield, 1794. Windsor: Hiram Walker Historical Museum.

8. "Petitions for Grants of Land", p. 63; as cited by Donald G. Simpson: "Negroes in Ontario from Early Times to 1870" (unpublished Ph.D. thesis, University of Western Ontario, 1970), p. 396. The petition was rejected and the petitioners' dreams deferred until 1819, when the government established the Oro Settlement near Barrie.

9. VICTOR LAURISTON: *Romantic Kent,* p. 26. Chatham: Shepherd Printing Co. Ltd., 1952.

10. The group of buildings which formed Navy Hall was built on the bank of the Niagara River below Fort George to house stores for the Provincial Navy. Governor Simcoe added a Council Chamber where the first Legislative Assembly met. Most of the buildings were burned by the American forces in 1813.

11. JOHN J. BIGSBY, M.D.: *The Shoe and the Canoe,* Vol. I, p. 264. London: Chapman and Hall, 1850.

12. FRED LANDON: "Captain Charles the Abolitionist"; as cited by Donald G. Simpson: *op. cit.,* p. 306.

13. Audrey Miller Laurie Scrapbooks, October 1972 & June 1974 record that one Black family that sheltered there was given permission to take the Schooly name as they began their new life in Canada.

14. Burkholder family records show that two Blacks, William Nelson and Henry Johnston, were gravediggers, and Nelson is referred to as Hamilton's first public gravedigger.

15. Rochester and Buffalo in New York State were larger than Toronto in 1834.

16. Letters of James Gillespie Birney, 1831-1857, I, pp. 395 f. New York, 1938.

17. W.R. RIDDELL: "Interesting Notes on Great Britain and Canada with Respect to the Negro" *JNH* XIII (1928), p. 201.

18. J.G. KOHL: *Travels in Canada,* Vol. II, p. 110. London: George Manwaring, 1860.

19. BENMJAMIN DREW: *The Refugee,* p. 94. Boston: John P. Jewett and Company, 1856.

20. Drummondville later became part of the city of Niagara Falls. The district in which its Black families lived in the 1850s and '60s was called 'Pollytown' after a man named 'Polly' who is said to have helped Blacks settle in the area.

21. The heads of these families applied for Canadian citizenship after they had qualified by living in Canada for at least seven years.

22. In 1840 Taylor petitioned the government for a pension, claiming that while performing sentry duty he had contracted an eye infection that left his right eye sightless and his left eye nearly so. Captain Brown supported his petition, saying of Taylor, "He conducted himself like a loyal and zealous man, and took his turn of duty regularly." Toronto: Broadside Collection, Baldwin Room, Metropolitan Toronto Library Board.

23. DONALD G. SIMPSON: *op. cit.,* p. 383.

24. See Chapter 12 *infra.*

25. This probably refers to one of the German immigrants who moved up from Pennsylvania (Pennsylvania Dutch). There was a very significant German-American migration into the Waterloo-Kitchener-Guelph area, *i.e.* the Bush.

26. BENJAMIN DREW: *op. cit.,* pp. 216-218.

27. *Ibid.*, p. 217.
28. *Ibid.*, p. 353.
29. *Ibid.*, p. 322.
30. Chatham in the mid-1850s had three sawmills, two shingle mills, two potash factories, two sash and blind factories, four flour mills, four brickyards, several iron foundries, distilleries, breweries, wagon factories and many warehouses.
31. *New York Herald*, 1854, as cited by *London Free Press*, June 19, 1971.
32. *Ibid.*
33. *Minutes of the Fourth Annual Conference of the B.M.E. Church,* Chatham, August, 1859, p. 20, as cited by Donald G. Simpson, *op. cit.,* p. 664.
34. ELIZABETH SPICER (ed.): *Description of London and its Environs 1799-1854,* p. 65 f. London: London Public Library.
35. The stories of 23 of these St. Catharines Blacks are contained in Benjamin Drew, *op. cit.*
36. *The St. Catharines Journal*, August 5, 1852.
37. BENJAMIN DREW: *op. cit.,* p. 18.
38. Land set aside by the government of Upper Canada for the use or benefit of the Church of England. The clergy reserves were to be surveyed and put up for sale by 1848.
39. Petition of the Settlers of Queen's Bush to the Earl of Elgin, June 22, 1847. Toronto: Public Archives of Ontario.
40. *Ibid.*
41. Petition of the Settlers of Queen's Bush to the Earl of Elgin, July 4, 1850. Toronto: PAO.
42. BENJAMIN DREW: *op. cit.,* p. 196.
43. *Minutes of the Ninth Annual Conference of the B.M.E. Church* (June, 3, 1865), as cited by Donald G. Simpson: *op. cit.,* p. 815.
44. This area is bordered by the present Concession, Fennell, Upper Sherman and Upper Wentworth Streets. In early times Concession Street was called the 'Old Stone Road'. A Black family named 'Berry' kept a toll gate near the corner of Wentworth and Concession Streets. Other Black families lived along a rough trail known as 'the cow path', which passes well back from the brow of the Mountain between Ancaster and Tapley Town.
45. Hamilton's City Directory for 1853 lists only six Blacks: Francis Anderson, dyer; Mr. Barns, carter; John Bland, barber; John Burns, saloon-keeper; Thomas Butler, shoemaker; Marcus Sargnett, saloon-keeper.
46. *The Provincial Freeman*, September 10, 1851.
47. E.M. PETIT: *Sketches in the History of the Underground Railroad,* as cited by Wilbur H. Siebert: *The Underground Railroad From Slavery to Freedom,* p. 197. London: Macmillan & Co. Ltd., 1898.
48. WILBUR H. SIEBERT: *op. cit.,* p. 198. Loguen experienced a few difficult years as one of the first Black settlers in the wilderness area that was then Hamilton before he moved back to Syracuse in 1841. There he became one of the important UGR conductors ferrying other fugitives to Canada.
49. WILBUR H. SIEBERT: *op. cit.,* pp. 200 f.
50. *Ibid.*, p. 198.

5: Black Colonies and Communities

1. Town lots of .4 ha were granted to 76 Black Pioneers and other Black Loyalists.
2. That is, approximately 2 km.
3. Public Archives of Ontario, Land Book K, p. 92, as cited by Gary French: *Men of Colour,* p. 10. Stroud, Ontario: Kaste Books, 1978.
4. Lots of 80 ha were offered to white settlers until 1828 at least, and some retired officers were granted more than 400 ha.
5. To reach the new settlement refugees would have had to travel north from York by cart or wagon to Holland Landing, about 56 km, then by boat or canoe (later by steamer) about another 50 km to Hawkestone, Hodges Landing or — even farther north — to Orillia along the Lake Simcoe shore; they would then have had to backtrack south on foot to Oro.
6. Call received title to his land in 1831. He died on May 4, 1852, after buying more property in Vespra Township, which he willed to his wife, Ann Call.
7. Delay received title to his property in 1838.
8. The disaster did not break Delay's determination: in 1831 he was living on Lot 11 with about six ha cleared. He received his patent (i.e., clear title) in 1833.
9. Many Blacks left Ohio after the oppressive Black Codes were passed in 1807.
10. W. ALLEN FISHER: *Legend of the Drinking Gourd,* p. 24. Barrie: W.A. & M.W. Fisher, 1973.
11. Gosling later re-sold the property for £103.
12. Darkman's (Dartman) will, leaving the property to his wife Rebecca and two sons still in slavery, was the first to be probated in Simcoe County.
13. W. ALLEN FISHER: *op. cit.,* p. 19.
14. Fred Grant Collection MS, 52, pp. 254-256. Barrie Public Library. Oro Township.
15. Descendants of the Davenports still live in Simcoe County.
16. James Thompson lived in a white frame house on Concession 2, Lot 16, Oro Township.
17. FRED LANDON: "A Pioneer Abolitionist in Upper Canada", Ontario Historical Society, Vol. LII, No. 2 (June, 1960), p. 78.
18. In 1826 this important English firm had bought from the government of Upper Canada for speculation and investment over 400 000 ha in the Huron tract.
19. The Browns, finding themselves no happier in Cincinnati, returned to Canada, settled briefly in Toronto and then moved permanently to Chatham.
20. Peter Butler's descendants remain to this day respected residents of the town of Lucan.
21. AUSTIN STEWARD: *Twenty Years a Slave and Forty a Freeman,* p. 85. New York: 1869.
22. *Ibid.*, p. 180.
23. *Ibid.*, p. 194.
24. *London Free Press*, February 15, 1941, as cited by James K. Lewis: "Religious Life of Fugitive Slaves and Rise of Coloured Baptist Churches 1820-1865 in What is Now Known as Ontario", p. 134. (Unpublished M.A. thesis, McMaster University, 1965.)
25. Upper Canada's Lieutenant-Governor, Sir John Colborne, gave Paul a letter of recommendation which the latter used in his own interest.
26. Paul accomplished one good thing, however, during his three years in England. While he was there, in 1832, he appeared before a Select Committee of the British House of Commons,

which included the Rt. Hon. Sir James Graham, Lord John Russell, Sir Robert Peel, the Marquis of Chandos, Thomas Powell Buxton, and Sir George Murray. The Committee eventually issued a report, based on its hearings, that is a landmark in the history of emancipation in the British Empire.

27. FRED LANDON: "Diary of Benjamin Lundy", *OHS*, XIX (1922), pp. 110-133, as cited by James K. Lewis, *op. cit.*, p. 129.
28. FRED LANDON: "Wilberforce, An Experiment in the Colonization of Freed Negroes in Upper Canada", *Royal Society of Canada*, Section 11 (1937), p. 76.
29. *Ibid.*, p. 77.
30. *London Free Press*, July 8, 1944; as cited by Donald G. Simpson, *op. cit.*, p. 367.
31. FRED LANDON: *op. cit.*, p. 75.
32. The Butlers and a few other Black families continued to live in the area for generations. Two families of Butler descendants still live in Lucan, and local citizens remember other descendants of the Wilberforce Settlement.
33. Fuller "... kept at his own expense a carriage so built as to render it impossible to see who was inside, and several valuable teams of horses, with which he used to transport fugitives through the state of New York and put them over the river at Queenstown." "James Brown on the Dawn Institute." London: Regional Room, University of Western Ontario (January, 1860).
34. Henson later bought another 40 ha for himself next to the communal property.
35. DONALD G. SIMPSON: *op. cit.*, p. 348.
36. Mr. Chickering of the Boston Piano Manufacturing Company bought the first shipment of black walnut from Dawn's sawmill.
37. In 1847 and 1849 Henson was accused again of misappropriating funds. Although he was cleared, there was no doubt that Dawn's finances were badly managed.
38. This school for Black students survived into the 20th century.
39. *Voice of the Fugitive*, January 29, 1851, as cited by Donald G. Simpson: *op. cit.*, p. 599 f.
40. Horace Hallock and E.R. Benham, members of the Michigan Anti-Slavery Society, were chosen to lead the American branch.
41. BENJAMIN DREW: *op. cit.*, p. 324.
42. The settlement stretched from Maidstone 25 km east toward the Puce River region, where a flourishing community of Blacks was already settled.
43. BENJAMIN DREW: *op. cit.*, p. 336.
44. *Ibid.*, p. 327.
45. Eventually King would name the mission at the Elgin Settlement after the anti-slavery spokesman, Buxton.
46. VICTOR ULLMAN: *Look to the North Star*, p. 91 f. Boston: Beacon Press, 1969.
47. Members of this committee were Judge Skeffington Connor, president; Michael Willis, D.D., Principal of Knox College, and Robert Burns, D.D., Moderator of the Presbyterian Assembly, vice-presidents; James Scott Howard, treasurer; Nathan Gatchell, secretary; John Redpath of Montréal, the Reverend John Piraf, Judge R.B. Sullivan, W.E. Thompson, the Reverend James Piper, the Reverend Enoch Wood, James Dougall of Windsor, the Reverend Alexander Gale of Knox Church, Toronto and the Reverend William King.
48. The document they produced was entitled "Prospectus of a scheme for the social and moral improvement of the coloured people of Canada".
49. VICTOR ULLMAN *op. cit.*, p. 115.
50. *Ibid.*
51. *Essex County History*, Vol. 1. Windsor Public Library.
52. VICTOR ULLMAN: *op. cit.*, p. 137.
53. *The Witness*, November 2, 1859.
54. VICTOR ULLMAN: *op. cit.*, p. 151.
55. The Blacks of Pittsburg, Pa. donated a considerable amount of money to the Buxton Schools, as well as a bell weighing almost a quarter-tonne. The donors asked that the bell be rung at sunrise and sunset "to proclaim liberty to the captive". This was done for many years. Eventually the bell was placed in the steeple of St. Andrew's Presbyterian Church in Chatham, where it hangs today.
56. VICTOR ULLMAN: *op. cit.*, p. 142.
57. *Ibid.*, p. 194.
58. SAMUEL GRIDLEY HOWE: *The Refugees from Slavery in Canada West*, pp. 90-91. Boston, 1864.
59. The treasurer reported a cash balance of $198.71, with $200 still due from land sales.
60. VICTOR ULLMAN: *op. cit.*, p. 326.

6: Justice and Injustice

1. Now re-named the 'Thames River' in Ontario.
2. W.R. RIDDELL: "The First Legal Execution for Crime in Upper Canada." *Ontario Historical Society*, XXVII (1931), pp. 514-516.
3. *Ibid.*,
4. William Jarvis, first Secretary General of Upper Canada, held the post from 1792 until his death in 1817. Jarvis was one of the Colony's most prominent slave-owners.
5. HENRY SCADDING: *Toronto of Old*, p. 211 f. Toronto: Oxford University Press, 1966.
6. *Ibid.*
7. JOHN HOPE FRANKLIN: *From Slavery to Freedom*, p. 36 f. New York: Alfred A. Knopf, 1947.
8. J. MACKENZIE LEASK: "Jesse Happy, A Fugitive Slave from Kentucky." *OHS*, LIV, No. 2, (June, 1962), p. 96.
9. *The Globe*, October 26, 1852.
10. JOHN NETTLETON: "Reminiscences 1857-1870." Huron Institute Papers & Records, 11 (1914) 13.
11. Journals of Mary O'Brien, May 16, 1832. Public Archives of Ontario.
12. *Ibid.*, March 10, 1833.
13. *St. Catharines Journal*, September 11, 1856, as cited by D.G. Simpson, "Negroes in Ontario from Early Times to 1870", p. 396. (Unpublished Ph.D. thesis, University of Western Ontario, 1970.)
14. SAMUEL GRIDLEY HOWE: *The Refugees From Slavery in Canada West: A Report to the Freedman's Inquiry Commission*, p. 19. Boston, 1864.
15. VICTOR ULLMAN: *Look To The North Star*, p. 106. Boston: Beacon Press, 1969.

16. WILLIAM PEASE & JANE PEASE: "Opposition to the Founding of the Elgin Settlement," p. 205 f. *Canadian Historical Review*, XXXVIII, No. 3 (September, 1957).

17. *King Papers*, February 19, 1849. Public Archives of Canada.

18. FRED LANDON: "Wilberforce, An Experiment in the Colonization of Freed Negroes in Upper Canada." *Royal Society of Canada*. Section 11 (1937), p. 76.

19. ROBIN WINKS: *The Blacks in Canada*, p. 148. New Haven: Yale University Press with McGill-Queen's University Press, 1971.

20. BENJAMIN DREW: *The Refugee or: The Narratives of Fugitive Slaves in Canada*, p. 371. Boston: J.P. Jewett & Co., 1856.

21. F. DOUGLAS REVILLE: *History of the County of Brant*, p. 97. Brantford: The Hurley Publishing Co. Ltd., 1920.

22. *The Brantford Expositor*, June 10, 1859. Sunter's letter was dated May 15, 1859.

23. Legislative permission for the establishment of racially separate schools continued in Ontario until 1965 when M.P.P. Leonard Braithwaite took the initiative to have it removed.

24. BENJAMIN DREW: *op. cit.*, p. 341 f.

25. *Ibid.*, p. 347.

26. D.G. SIMPSON: *op. cit.*, p. 314.

27. HARRIET CHATTERS: "Negro Education in Kent County up to 1890," p. 36. (Unpublished M.A. thesis, Howard University, 1956.)

28. *Ryerson Papers*. S. Askin to Ryerson, February 26, 1857. Public Archives of Ontario.

29. D.G. SIMPSON: *op. cit.*, p. 642.

30. SAMUEL GRIDLEY HOWE: *op. cit.*, p. 36.

31. REVEREND WILLIAM MITCHELL: *Underground Railroad*, p. 133. London: 1860.

32. Long Point Baptist Association Minutes, 1843.

33. *Pathfinders of Liberty and Truth*, p. 2 f. Amherstburg Regular Missionary Baptist Association, 1940.

34. WILLIAM TROY: *Hair-Breadth Escapes from Slavery to Freedom*, p. 8. Windsor: University of Windsor.

35. Report of the Reverend M.M. Dillon, July 12, 1855.

36. DONALD G. SIMPSON: *op. cit.*, p. 666.

37. *Windsor Herald*, November 3, 1855.

38. *British Colonist* as cited by *The Provincial Freeman*, May 5, 1855.

39. The *Provincial Freeman*, June 20, 1857.

40. GRACE JONES MORGAN: *The Recollections of Edwin Bassett Jones*, p. 24 (1974). For Malden National Historic Museum.

41. Toronto *Globe*, August 25, 1849.

42. SAMUEL GRIDLEY HOWE: *op. cit.* p. 43.

43. *Anti-Slavery Reporter*, April 1, 1858.

44. *Voice of the Fugitive*, October 8, 1851.

45. SAMUEL GRIDLEY HOWE: *op. cit.*, p. 47.

46. *Ibid.*

47. Letters of James Gillespie Birney, 1831-1857, I, p. 395 f. New York, 1938.

48. *Annual Report*, Mission to the Coloured Population of Canada, p. 7 f., as cited by D.G. Simpson, *op. cit.*, p. 637.

49. MICHAEL B. KATZ: *The People of Hamilton, Canada West*, p. 68. Cambridge: Harvard University Press, 1975.

50. Adam Wilson to Robert Baldwin, July 12, 1843, Baldwin Papers. Toronto: Metropolitan Toronto Library Board.

7: Blacks and the Armed Forces

1. R.F. FLEMING: "Negro Slaves with the United Empire Loyalists in Upper Canada." *Ontario Historical Society*, XLV, No. 1 (1953), p. 28. Baker's pension was a shilling a day.

2. *Ibid.*

3. After his service in Butler's Rangers in 1787, Robertson was rewarded with the grant of a lot in the "new settlement" of Detroit.

4. R.M. FULLER: *Windsor Heritage*, p. 91. Windsor: Herald Press Ltd., May, 1972.

5. See Chapter 2, note 1.

6. Simcoe's legislation guaranteed George his freedom in another 10 years, when he reached the age of 25.

7. Before the Battle of Queenston Heights, Sergeant William Thompson and 13 other Black soldiers decided to leave the 3rd Regiment of York Militia and join Runchey's Coloured Corps.

8. Solomon Albert, a gardener from York, later joined Captain Runchey's Coloured Company.

9. An American officer who described the action at Niagara Town and Fort George recalled seeing one dead Black on the battlefield wearing a Glengarry uniform.

10. J.M. CARELESS: *Canada*, p. 131. Toronto: The Macmillan Company of Canada Ltd., 1959.

11. BENJAMIN J. LOSSING: *The Pictorial Field Book of the War of 1812*, pp. 244 f. New York: Harper and Bros. Publishers, 1868.

12. *Ibid.*, pp. 402 f.

13. At some time in 1813 command of the unit passed to Lieutenant James Robertson, formerly attached to the Army Engineer Department.

14. ERNEST GREEN: "Upper Canada's Black Defenders". *Papers and Records of the Ontario Historical Society*, XXVII (1931), p. 369.

15. Lieutenant Colonel W. Cheweth to Lieutenant Colonel Coffin, September 14, 1815. Toronto: Public Archives of Ontario.

16. Jupiter had been a slave of Captain Daniel Servos of Niagara Township.

17. James Long died in Etobicoke in 1852.

18. W.L. Mackenzie to the American Slavery Society, January 30, 1837, as cited in *Papers and Records of the Ontario Historical Society*, XXII (1925), p. 153.

19. ERNEST GREEN: *op. cit.*, p. 371. Tradition tells that Black prisoners were released from jail in Niagara on condition that they join the militia.

20. *Ibid.*, p. 372.

21. *Ibid.*, p. 380.

22. *Loyal Statement of the People of Colour of the Town of Hamilton*, December 18, 1837. Hamilton Public Library.

23. *St. Catharines Journal*, January 4, 1838, as cited by Ernest Green, *op. cit.*, p. 379.

24. Militia Papers, Upper Canadian Military Dispatches 45, as cited by Ernest Green: *op. cit.*, p. 379.

25. ERNEST GREEN: *op. cit.*, p. 372.

26. *Ibid.*, p. 382.

27. *Ibid.*, p. 388.

28. *Ibid.*

29. *Jubilee History of Thorold*, as cited by Ernest Green: *op. cit.*, p. 388.

8: Blacks and the Churches

1. MARCEL TRUDEL: "L'Attitude de l'église catholique vis-à-vis l'esclavage au Canada français", p. 3. Québec: Les Presses Universitaires Laval, 1960.
2. *Ibid.*, p. 10.
3. R.F. FLEMING: "Negro Slaves with the United Empire Loyalists in Upper Canada". *OHS* (Ontario Historical Society), XLV, No. 1 (1953), p. 28. In his will of 1811 the Reverend Stuart bequeathed to "... my beloved wife Jane Stuart my female slave Louise and her children."
4. St. Mark's, founded in 1792 by the missionary, the Reverend Robert Addison, was one of the first churches in the province.
5. *Provincial Freeman*, December 22, 1855.
6. DONALD G. SIMPSON: "Negroes in Ontario from Early Times to 1870", p. 60. London: Unpublished Ph.D. thesis, University of Western Ontario, 1970.
7. Hurst had previously been rector of St. John's Church in Sandwich.
8. DONALD G. SIMPSON: *op. cit.*, p. 633.
9. *Report of Colonial Church & School Society*, 1870.
10. Fred Grant Collection MS, 52: 254-256. Barrie: Barrie Public Library.
11. Benjamin Drew: *The Refugee*, p. 120. Boston: John P. Jewett and Company, 1856.
12. Melba Croft: "Early History of Owen Sound". Owen Sound: *Owen Sound Sun-Times*, 1962.
13. The vendors were John Cawthra and James Leslie. The three buyers were considered the founders of Toronto's Coloured Wesleyan Methodist Church.
14. Christian was a firebrand preacher with a vivid style that drew large crowds. Before a Sunday service in Whitby in 1837, for example, news spread that Elder Christian was to preach at 10:00 a.m., and worshippers gathered hours in advance. Two 'emergency' ministers had to be called on to address the crowds who could not get into the packed church. One member of the congregation reported: "While Christian was preaching, every eye in the house was fixed upon him and while truth fell from his lips it reached many hearts and suffused many eyes with tears." *Haldimand Baptist Association Minutes, 1837*, pp. 5 f., as cited by James K. Lewis: "Religious Life of Fugitive Slaves and Rise of Coloured Baptist Churches 1820-1865 in What Is Now Known as Ontario", p. 32. Hamilton: Unpublished M.A. thesis, McMaster Divinity School, 1965.
15. JOHN ROSS ROBERTSON: *Landmarks of Toronto: A Collection of Historical Sketches of the Old Town of York from 1792-1837 and of Toronto from 1837-1904*, pp. 471 f. Toronto: J.R. Robertson, 1904.
16. *Pathfinders of Liberty and Truth*, (compiled from the Minutes and Historical Essays, written by its Members, 1940), p. 9. Sandwich: First Baptist Church.
17. Amherstburg Baptist Association, MS Minutes (1841), p. 21.
18. Only once in the whole history of ARMBA did it engage a white minister, a Reverend William Pitt, who was pastor of the Amherstburg congregation in 1871.
19. *Pathfinders ...: op. cit.*, p. 91.
20. *Voice of the Fugitive*, July 30, 1851.
21. *Pathfinders ...: op. cit.*, p. 92
22. FRED COYNE HAMIL: *The Valley of the Lower Thames*, pp. 297 f. Toronto: University of Toronto Press, 1951.
23. JAMES K. LEWIS: *op. cit.*, p. 98.
24. *Ibid.*, pp. 99 f.
25. *Ibid.*, p. 103.

9: Blacks and the Schools

1. FREDERICK COYNE HAMIL: *The Valley of the Lower Thames*, p. 215. Toronto: University of Toronto Press, 1951.
2. *Ibid.*, p. 217.
3. *Provincial Freeman*, April 14, 1855.
4. BENJAMIN DREW: *The Refugee*, p. 147. Boston: John P. Jewett and Company, 1856.
5. "W.H. Draper to Tyerson", pp. 355 f. *Ryerson Papers*, April 5, 1847, as cited by Donald G. Simpson: "Negroes in Ontario From Early Times to 1870". London: Unpublished Ph.D. thesis, University of Western Ontario.
6. J. DOUGALL: "The Laying of the Cornerstone of Windsor Central School". (November, 1871). Fort Malden, Ontario.
7. Ryerson Papers, October 19, 1843. Toronto: Ontario Public Archives.
8. *Ibid.*, November 9, 1843.
9. *Ibid.*
10. DONALD G. SIMPSON: *op. cit.*, pp. 331 f.
11. *Voice of the Fugitive*, April 25, 1851.
12. BENJAMIN DREW: *op. cit.*, p. 197.
13. *Voice of the Fugitive*, April 5, 1851.
14. J.I. COOPER: "The Mission to the Fugitive Slaves at London". *Expression*, III, No. 2 (Summer, 1968), p. 28.
15. *Ibid.*, p. 29.
16. PAOLA BROWN: "Address on Slavery" Hamilton, (1851), as cited by Donald G. Simpson: *op. cit.*, pp. 854 f.
17. BENJAMIN DREW: *op. cit.*, p. 348.
18. *Ibid.*, p. 576.
19. Mary Ann Shadd to the American Missionary Association, October 24, 1852. American Missionary Association Archives.
20. *Voice of the Fugitive*, 1852, as cited *ibid.*
21. Mary Ann Shadd to George Whipple, April 24, 1853, as cited *ibid.*
22. DONALD G. SIMPSON: *op. cit.*, p. 596.
23. *Provincial Freeman*, May 24, 1856, as cited by Donald G. Simpson: *op. cit.*, p. 841.
24. London Board of Education Minutes, December 4, 1862.
25. *Ibid.*
26. *Ibid.*, July, 1863.
27. The ALDB agreed to support a school for Black children at Preston, even though only 20 pupils were enrolled.
28. ROBIN W. WINKS: *The Blacks in Canada — A History*, p. 58. McGill-Queen's University Press, Yale University Press, 1971.
29. This school closed in 1834.
30. The SPG also contributed to funding a school in Sackville, after 1833.
31. ROBIN W. WINKS: *op. cit.*, p. 137.
32. *Ibid.*

10: The Work-a-Day World

1. R.M. FULLER: *Windsor Heritage*, p. 53. Windsor: Herald Press Ltd., May 1972. Askin learned to do without Pomp, for a sale recorded in the Michigan Historical Collection shows that a "... certain Negro man Pompey by name ..." went to a new owner for £45, New York currency (about $112.) in the fall of 1794. He was sold again within three months for £50.

2. William Davenport's son Robinson, who moved from Flos to Medonte and Tiny Townships, "... was a Negro of stately appearance who was known to have cut down six acres of grain in one day with a cradle leaving it in a swath. He was also known to have carried a barrel of flour across a concession, the flour enclosed in the barrel making in all two hundred and eighteen pounds." Robert Miller: "Pioneering in Medonte Township", as cited by W. Allen Fisher: *Legend of the Drinking Gourd* p. 17. Barrie: W.A. & M.W. Fisher, 1973.

3. D. MACDONALD: "Township of Flos". Unpublished paper, Simcoe County Museum & Archives, 1881.

4. Bush first settled on Lot 11, Concession 4, and then moved to Lot 12, Concession 5. He had eight children, and members of his family, including his son Mark, owned land in Oro until the late 1930s.

5. Monroe settled on Lot 10, Concession 5.

6. Some of their descendants still lived in Oro in the first part of the 20th century.

7. Between 1817 and 1821 the names of four Blacks appear in the Account Books of John Dolsen of Dover: Tom Surphlet, George Askin, William Booker and Israel Williams.

8. FRED COYNE HAMIL: *The Valley of the Lower Thames*, p. 118. Toronto: University of Toronto Press, 1951.

9. J. PICKERING: *Enquiries of an Immigrant*, p. 142. London: 1831.

10. "Records Illustrating the Condition of Refugees from Slavery in Upper Canada Before 1860". *Journal of Negro History*, XIII, No. 2 (April, 1928), p. 206, as cited by Donald G. Simpson: "Negroes in Ontario from Early Times to 1870", p. 316. (Unpublished Ph.D. thesis, University of Western Ontario, 1970.) Within a very short time this tobacco export trade had increased to 600 hogsheads per year.

11. Edward's business was first located at 102 King Street and later at 77 King Street.

12. *British Colonist*, May 10, 1842.

13. W.L. MACKENZIE: *Sketches of Canada and the United States*, p. 19. London: Effingham Wilson, 1833.

14. That is, a shoemaker.

15. "Number of Coloured Persons Resident in Toronto, July 25, 1840." Metropolitan Toronto Library Board. Another survey was made the following year at the request of Bishop Strachan. It was carried out by Peter Gallego, then a student at Upper Canada College and later a graduate of the University of Toronto and an activist for the defence of Blacks. Gallego's survey found 525 Blacks in Toronto. The majority were labourers, but skilled tradespeople and businesspeople were also listed.

16. These included shoemakers, carpenters, waiters, tailors, barbers and bricklayers.

17. There were three innkeepers and restaurant-owners, one tobacconist and two storekeepers.

18. EDWIN C. GUILLET: *Early Life In Upper Canada*, p. 482. Toronto: University of Toronto Press, 1933.

19. *The Provincial Freeman*, June 3, 1854.

20. *Ibid.*, March 16, 1854.

21. William did not practise law in Toronto; he moved to Mississippi where he died in 1933.

22. *The Provincial Freeman*, April 14, 1855.

23. *Ibid.*, January 11, 1854.

24. Documents showing that slaves were travelling on legitimate business with their owners' permission.

25. *London Free Press*, June 12, 1971.

26. BENJAMIN DREW: *The Refugee or The Narratives of Fugitive Slaves in Canada*, p. 152. Boston: J.P. Jewett & Co., 1856.

27. *Ibid.*, p. 151.

28. *Ibid.*, p. 153.

29. *Ibid.*, p. 178.

30. Martin later left London and became one of the first Blacks to serve in the Union Navy during the Civil War.

31. BENJAMIN DREW: *op. cit.*, p. 176.

32. *Ibid.*, p. 353.

33. *Ibid.*, p. 345.

34. One of these, George Washington, was a deck hand on the Detroit ferry, *Essex*.

35. Dunn was elected an alderman in 1887-88. His brother Robert, his partner in the family business, was an alderman for Windsor's Ward 3 from 1893 to 1903.

36. E.C. DRURY: "The Negro Settlement of Oro". Drury Papers, p. 8. Simcoe County Museum and Archives.

37. Jacques & Hay Collection, July 30, 1865. Simcoe County Museum and Archives.

38. *Ibid.*, May 5, 1869.

39. JOHN NETTLETON: "Reminiscences 1857-1870". *Huron Institute Papers & Records*, II (1914), 41.

40. *The Enterprise Bulletin*, op. cit.

41. The Annual Report of the Collingwood Board of Trade, 1894, p. 77 records:

    Mr. C. Duval's tonsorial establishment on Huron Street nearly opposite the Globe Hotel is the oldest barbershop in town and is managed in a manner which will always bring good business. Mr. Duval and his assistants are always on hand and customers may rely upon finding competent artists to attend to their calls.

42. In 1904 Cooper's sons expanded the family business into a small firm called "Cooper Brothers, Contractors". With its three teams of large horses, cement mixers and other equipment, the firm paved and repaired many of Collingwood's streets. The firm also helped to construct the Old Victoria Public School and a number of the town's factories and buildings. Cooper Brothers closed in the 1930s, when members of the family went into cattle breeding.

43. REVEREND WILLIAM WYE SMITH: "Canadian Reminiscences 1900". XIV, MS, Public Archives of Ontario, p. 194.

44. E.C. DRURY: "The Negro Settlement of Oro". Drury Papers, p. 8, Simcoe County Museum & Archives.

11: Black Societies and Celebrations

1. In 1843 Gray headed a committee of some 20 Blacks to organize the 1843 Emancipation Day celebrations. His name appeared on the city's assessment rolls until 1862, when his

age was given as 78. He lived in a one-storey frame house on Cherry Street.

2. This probably served as a model for the King Street School Literary Society organized during the 1870s. The latter was rather more progressive than the former, for it allowed women to join.

3. Taylor Scrapbook. Fort Malden National Historic Museum.

4. BENJAMIN DREW: *The Refugee*, p. 238. Boston: John P. Jewett and Company, 1856.

5. *The Provincial Freeman*, August 19, 1854.

6. DONALD G. SIMPSON: "Negroes in Ontario from Early Times to 1870", p. 231 ff. (Unpublished Ph.D. thesis, University of Western Ontario, 1971.)

7. After dinner the guests made plans to establish a Methodist Mission in Drummondville (later Niagara Falls).

8. The statute of 1833 abolishing slavery took effect August 1, 1834.

9. *The Provincial Freeman*, June 3, 1854, July 29, 1854. The event was followed by a soirée and fireworks' display to the accompaniment of a cornet band.

10. Abbott Papers. Toronto: Baldwin Room, Metropolitan Toronto Library Board.

11. *Hamilton Spectator*, June 21, 1924.

12. *Ibid.*

13. *The Story of Oro*, p. 31. Oro, 1972.

14. J. I. COOPER: "The Mission to the Fugitive Slaves of London". *Expression*, III, No. 2 (Summer, 1968), p. 29.

15. *Voice of the Fugitive*, December 3, 1851; as cited by *Windsor Daily Star*, January 15, 1938.

16. *The Provincial Freeman*, March 25, 1854.

17. *Ibid.*, January 11, 1854.

18. *Ibid.*, June 30, 1855.

19. *Ibid.*, March 17, 1855.

20. The intention was, presumably, to train Blacks to teach in Africa.

21. *The Provincial Freeman*, March 25, 1854.

22. *The True Royalist & Weekly Intelligencer*, April 29, 1860.

23. Green then left Canada for Washington, D.C.

24. ROBIN WINKS, *The Blacks in Canada*, p. 397. New Haven: Yale University Press, 1971.

12: The Freedom-Seekers

1. BENJAMIN DREW: *The Refugee: or the Narratives of Fugitive Slaves in Canada*, pp. 192-195. Boston: John P. Jewett and Company, 1856.

2. *Press Release*, Ontario Department of Tourism & Information, April 26, 1965, p. 2.

3. Harriet Beecher Stowe wrote *Uncle Tom's Cabin* to expose the horrors of slavery. The novel told dramatically how Uncle Tom and his family tried to escape from a tyrannical overseer, Simon Legree. It vividly described Uncle Tom's daughter, Eliza, making her way across ice floes, pursued by baying hounds and a crazed Legree with his rawhide whip. The book, published serially c. 1851, electrified the American public and caused a stir in Canada and Europe. It sold millions of copies, was translated into 37 languages, and has been credited with inspiring President Abraham Lincoln to end slavery.

4. WILLIAM CHAPPLE, *The Story of Uncle Tom*, 1960, p. 2.

5. Henson later regretted bitterly that he had delivered his fellow slaves into continued bondage.

6. Slaves were not allowed to travel without a 'pass' or permit to show that they were not running away from their masters.

7. Historians continue to argue whether Henson really was the 'Uncle Tom' of *Uncle Tom's Cabin*. Although Harriet Beecher Stowe never definitely stated that he was, she knew Henson and considered him a close friend. In a letter published in the *Windsor Daily Record*, June 18, 1877, she wrote:

   "It is also true that a sketch of his life, published many years ago by the Massachusetts Anti-Slavery Society, furnished me many of the finest conceptions and incidents of Uncle Tom's character ... in particular the scene where he refuses to free himself by the murder of a brutal master. The real history of Josiah Henson in some points goes even beyond that of Uncle Tom in traits of heroic manhood. He once visited me in Andover, and personal intercourse confirmed the high esteem I had for him ..."

   Until Henson was 93, he never directly confirmed or denied that he was 'Uncle Tom'. Only when he was preaching his last sermon in Hamilton's Park Street Baptist Church did he finally claim that distinction.

   Josiah Henson's grave and cabin have become famous tourist attractions at Dresden, Ontario.

8. Research materials, Chatham-Kent Museum.

9. Peter Butler passed down to his children his considerable knowledge of herbal medicine which he claimed to have picked up on his voyages to Africa.

10. Now both sides of Main Street in the heart of Lucan.

11. *London Free Press*, April 22, 1944 recorded that the property originally owned by Ephraim Taylor "... has been in the possession of the Butlers for years."

12. JENNIE RAYCRAFT LEWIS: *The Luck of Lucan* (1967), p. 9.

13. Another Black property owner in Lucan was Green Thurman, an escaped slave from Missouri. Thurman married Anne, a daughter of Peter Butler I. Anne died in 1899 leaving her husband and 10 children. Green, who lived to be nearly 100, died at Lucan in March, 1926.

14. Interview with Harold Butler, March 6, 1977.

15. These annual events continued into the 1930s.

16. Interview with Josie Butler Sloman, April 12, 1977.

17. Bibb took printing contracts from private firms and organizations throughout the county.

18. No known copies of this work have survived.

19. DONALD G. SIMPSON: "Negroes in Ontario from Early Times to 1870," p. 596. Unpublished Ph.D. thesis, University of Western Ontario, 1970.

20. BENJAMIN DREW: *op. cit.*, p. 336.

21. Bibb's paper, *Voice of the Fugitive*, was the official organ of the Refugee Home Society.

22. Mary Ann Shadd to G. Whipple, December 25, 1852. American Missionary Association Archives.

23. Mary Ann Shadd to George Whipple, January 15, 1853. American Missionary Association Archives.

24. Alexander McArthur to George Whipple, December 22, 1852. American Missionary Association Archives.

25. Mary Ann Shadd married T.F. Cary, the Toronto ice merchant, on January 3, 1856. They had two children. Cary died on November 29, 1860.

26. HALLE Q. BROWN: *Homespun Heroines and Other Women of Distinction*, pp. 94 f. Xenia: Aldine Press, 1926.

27. His son, Alfred Shadd, was born in 1870. After Alfred graduated in medicine from the University of Toronto in 1898, he left Ontario to teach school and practise medicine in Kinistino, Saskatchewan. In 1904 he moved to Melfort, Saskatchewan and in 1907 went to Britain for post-graduate medical studies. Shadd was an unsuccessful candidate for the Saskatchewan Legislative Assembly, the first Black in Canada to seek office in a provincial legislature. He died in Saskatchewan in 1915.

28. Abbott Papers, Baldwin Room, Metropolitan Toronto Library Board.

29. *Ibid.*

30. At a meeting on February 20, 1854 seven accounts for the hire of Mink's carriages were presented for payment approval.

31. JOHN FARRELL, "The History of the Negro Community in Chatham, Ontario, 1787-1865". *The Collector*, No. 2 (1960), p. 184. London: Stanley Smith Collection, Regional Room, University of Western Ontario.

32. Audrey Miller Laurie Scrapbooks, July 11, 1959.

33. Author of *Two Years Before the Mast*.

34. *London Free Press*, June 2, 1934.

35. FRED LANDON, "Anthony Burns in Canada," *OHS*, XXII (1925), 165, as cited by James K. Lewis in "Religious Life of Fugitive Slaves and Rise of Coloured Baptist Churches 1820-1865 in What is now Known as Ontario," p. 52. (Unpublished MA thesis, McMaster University, 1965.)

36. ERNEST GREEN: "Some Graves in Lundy's Lane", *Niagara Historical Society*, No. 22, p. 50.

37. Ninety-one other Blacks were buried in this cemetery between 1855 and 1863. These include the Suttons, Littles, Washingtons and Hodges.

38. *Elmvale Lance*, September 13, 1923.

39. This story has never been authenticated. It would be most unusual for a mass kidnapping to have taken place without intervention, even though slavery also existed in Upper Canada at that time.

40. *Owen Sound Sun-Times*, August 24, 1940.

41. *Ibid.*

42. This area was later named 'Harrison Pleasure Grounds' and is now Victoria Park.

43. *Owen Sound Sun-Times*, August 24, 1940.

44. Hall claimed a total of 21 children from his many wives, but not all were with him in Owen Sound.

45. *Owen Sound Sun-Times*, August 24, 1940.

46. The Black branch of the Canadian legion in Halifax is named for Hall. In 1947 the Hansport branch put up a monument to his memory.

47. Stanley Smith Collection: *op. cit.*

48. Marcus Tullius Cicero was a famous orator and politician of the late Roman Republic (1st century B.C.).

49. In 1976, long after it had been taken down, the portrait was rediscovered in good condition. At the time of writing, it hangs in a place of honour in Committee Room No. 1 of Toronto's New City Hall.

50. Hubbard's son Fred, whose house was next door to the family home, served as general manager of the Toronto Street Railway Company. He later became Commissioner and then Chairman of the Toronto Transit Commission.

51. Abbott Papers, *op. cit.*

52. *Evening Telegram*, January 27, 1933.

Bibliography

Abbott Papers: Toronto: Metropolitan Toronto Library, Baldwin Room.

ARMSTRONG, F.H.: "Toronto Directories and the Negro Community in the Late 1840s". *Ontario Historical Society* Vol. LXI, No. 2, 1969.

BÂBY, WILLIAM LEWIS: *Souvenirs of the Past.* Windsor, 1896.

BEARDEN, JIM and BUTLER, LINDA JEAN: *Shadd: The Life and Times of Mary Shadd Cary.* Toronto: N.C. Press Ltd., 1977.

BEATTIE, JESSIE L.: *Black Moses, The Real Uncle Tom.* Toronto: Ryerson Press, 1957.

BERTLEY, LEO W.: *Canada and Its People of African Descent.* Pierrefonds, P.Q., 1977.

BEST, CARRIE M.: *That Lonesome Road, The Autobiography of Carrie M. Best.* New Glasgow: Clarion Publishing Company Ltd., 1977.

BIGSBY, M.D., JOHN J.: *The Shoe and the Canoe,* Vol. 1. London: Chapman and Hall, 1850.

BRADFORD, SARAH H.: *Scenes in the Life of Harriet Tubman.* Auburn: W. J. Moses, Printer, 1879.

BROWN, HALLE Q.: *Homespun Heroines and Other Women of Distinction.* Xenia: Aldine Press, 1926.

BURKHOLDER, MABEL: "Out of the Storied Past". Hamilton Public Library.

CANNIFF, WILLIAM: *The History of the Province of Ontario.* Toronto: A. H. Hovey, 1872.

CARELESS, J.M.: *Canada.* Toronto: The Macmillan Company of Canada Ltd., 1959.

CHATTERS, HARRIET: "Negro Education in Kenty County up to 1890". Unpublished M. A. thesis, Howard University, 1956.

CLAIRMONT, DONALD H. and MAGILL, DENNIS WILLIAM: *Africville, The Life and Death of a Canadian Community.* Toronto: McClelland and Stewart, 1974.

CONNEAU, CAPTAIN THEOPHILUS: *A Slaver's Log Book, or 20 Years' Residence in Africa.* Englewood Cliffs, N.J.: Prentice-Hall, Inc., 1976.

COOPER, J.I.: "The Mission to the Fugitive Slaves at London". *Expression III, No. 2, 1968.*

CRAIG, GERALD M.: *Upper Canada, The Formative Years 1784-1841.* Toronto: McClelland and Stewart Limited, 1963.

DREW, BENJAMIN: *The Refugee: or the Narratives of Fugitive Slaves in Canada.* Boston: John P. Jewett and Company, 1856.

DRURY, E.C.: "The Negro Settlement of Oro". Drury Papers, Simcoe County Museum and Archives.

FARRELL, JOHN: "The History of the Negro Community in Chatham, Ontario, 1787-1865". Unpublished Ph.D. thesis, University of Ottawa, 1955.

FIRTH, E.G.: *The Town of York 1793-1815.* Toronto: University of Toronto Press, 1962.

FISHER, W. ALLEN: *Legend of the Drinking Gourd.* Barrie: W.A. & M.W. Fisher, 1973.

FLEMING, R.F.: "Negro Slaves with the United Empire Loyalists in Upper Canada". *Ontario Historical Society,* XLV, Vol. 45, No. 1, 1953.

FRANKLIN, JOHN HOPE: *From Slavery to Freedom.* New York: Alfred A. Knopf, 1947.

FRAZIER, E. FRANKLIN: *The Negro Family in the United States.* Chicago: Press, 1939.

FRENCH, GARY E.: *Men of Colour.* Stoud, Ontario: Kaste Books, 1978.

FULLER, R.M.: *Windsor Heritage.* Windsor: Herald Press Ltd., 1972.

GRANT, FRED, Collection MS. Barrie Public Library, Barrie, Ontario.

GREAVES, IDA: "The Negro in Canada". *McGill University Economic Studies No. 16, 1930.*

GREEN, ERNEST: "Upper Canada's Black Defenders". *Ontario Historical Society,* XXVII, 1931.

GUILLET, EDWIN C.: *Early Life in Upper Canada.* Toronto: University of Toronto Press, 1933.

HALLAM, W.T.: "Slave Days in Canada". *The Canadian Churchman,* 1919.

HAMIL, FRED COYNE: *The Valley of the Lower Thames 1640 to 1850.* Toronto: University of Toronto Press, 1951.

HENRY, FRANCES: *Forgotten Canadians: The Blacks of Nova Scotia.* Don Mills, Ontario: Longman Canada Limited, 1973.

HENSON, JOSIAH: *The Life of Josiah Henson, Formerly a Slave.* Boston: Arthur D. Phelps, 1849.

HILL, DANIEL G.:"Blacks in Canada: A Forgotten History". *Toronto Star,* February 17, 1979.

———"Black History in Early Toronto".*Multiculturalism,* Vol. II, No. 1. Toronto: Faculty of Education, University of Toronto, 1978.

———*A Brief Pictorial History of Blacks in Nineteenth Century Ontario.* Toronto: Ontario Human Rights Commission, 1972.

———"Negroes in Toronto: A Sociological Study of Minority Group". Unpublished Ph.D. thesis, University of Toronto, 1960.

———*Human Rights in Canada; A Focus on Racism.* Ottawa: Canadian Labour Congress, 1977.

———"Negroes in Toronto 1793-1865". *Ontario Historical Society* LV No. 2, 1963.

———"Toronto's Pioneer Black Politician All But Forgotten". Toronto: *Globe and Mail,* February 14, 1976.

———"Trial and Triumph: Black Progress in Young Toronto". Toronto: *Globe and Mail,* December 11, 1976.

HOWARD, ROBERT WEST: *Thundergate: The Forts of Niagara.* Englewood Cliffs, N.J.: Prentice-Hall, Inc., 1968.

HOWE, SAMUEL GRIDLEY: "The Refugees from Slavery in Canada West: Report to the Freedmen's Inquiry Commission". Boston, 1864.

Identity, The Black Experience in Canada. Toronto: The Ontario Educational Communications Authority in association with Gage Educational Publishing Ltd., 1979.

KATZ, MICHAEL B.: *The People of Hamilton, Canada West.* Cambridge, Mass.: Harvard University Press, 1975.

KILLIAN, CRAWFORD: *Go Do Some Great Thing: The Black Pioneers of British Columbia.* Vancouver: Douglas & McIntyre, 1978.

KOHL, J.G., *Travels in Canada,* Vol. II. London: George Manwaring, 1860.

LANDON, FRED: "A Pioneer Abolitionist in Upper Canada". *Ontario Historical Society,* Vol. LII, No. 2, 1960.

———"Social Conditions Among the Negroes in Upper Canada Before 1865". *Ontario Historical Society,* Vol. XXII, 1925.

———"Wilberforce, An Experiment in the Colonization of Freed Negroes in Upper Canada". *Royal Society of Canada,* Section 11, 1937.

LAURISTON, VICTOR: *Romantic Kent.* Chatham: Shepherd Printing Co. Ltd., 1952.

LEWIS, JAMES K.: "Religious Life of Fugitive Slaves and Rise of Coloured Baptist Churches 1820-1865 in What is Now Known as Ontario". Unpublished M.A. thesis, McMaster University, Hamilton, 1965.

LEWIS, JENNIE RAYCRAFT: *The Luck of Lucan.* Lucan, Ontario, 1967.

LOGUEN, J.W.: *The Rev. J. S. Loguen as A Slave and as A Freeman. A Narrative of Real Life.* Syracuse: J.G.K. Truair & Co., 1859.

LOSSING, BENJAMIN J.: *The Pictorial Field Book of the War of 1812.* New York: Harper and Bros. Publishers, 1868.

MACDONALD, D.: "Township of Flos". Simcoe County Museum & Archives, 1881.

MACKENZIE, WILLIAM LYON to the American Anti-Slavery Society, January 30, 1837. *Ontario Historical Society,* XXII, 1925.

————*Sketches of Canada and the United States.* London: Effingham Wilson, 1833.

MCCURDY, GEORGE F.: *Pictorial on Black History — Nova Scotia.* Halifax: Nova Scotia Human Rights Commission, 1975.

MCKERROW, PETER EVANDER: *A Brief History of Blacks and the Church in Nova Scotia 1783-1895.* (ed: Frank Stanley Boyd Jr.) Dartmouth: Afro-Nova Scotian Enterprises, 1975.

MITCHELL, W.M.: *The Underground Railroad.* London: William Tweedie, 1860.

"Negroes in Detroit". Burton Historical Collection MS, Detroit Public Library.

Pathfinders of Liberty and Truth. Sandwich: Amherstburg Regular Missionary Baptist Association of Ontario, 1940.

PICKERING, J.: *Enquiries of an Immigrant.* London, 1831.

"Race, Religion, and Culture in Ontario School Materials". Toronto: Ontario Ministry of Education, 1980.

REVILLE, F. DOUGLAS: *History of the County of Brant.* Hurley Publishing Company Ltd., 1920.

Riddell Papers, B-2. Toronto: Public Archives of Ontario.

RIDDELL, W.R.: "An Official Record of Slavery in Upper Canada". *Ontario Historical Society,* Vol. XXV, 1929.

————"Interesting Notes on Great Britain and Canada with Respect to the Negro". *Journal of Negro History,* XIII, 1928.

————"Notes on Slavery in Canada". *Journal of Negro History.* Vol. V, No. 3, 1920.

————"Notes on the Slave in Nouvelle France". *Journal of Negro History,* Vol. 7, 1923.

————ROBERTSON, JOHN ROSS: *Landmarks of Toronto: A Collection of Historical Sketches of the Old Town of York from 1792-1837 and of Toronto From 1837-1904.* Toronto: J. R. Robertson, 1904.

ROSS, ALEXANDER MILTON: *Recollections and Experiences of an Abolitionist.* Toronto: Roswell and Hutchison, 1875.

SCADDING, H.: *Toronto of Old.* Toronto: Willing & Williamson, 1878.

SCADDING, H., and DENT, JOHN: *Toronto Past and Present.* Toronto: Alain, Stevenson & Co., 1873.

SIEBERT, WILBUR H.: *The Underground Railroad From Slavery to Freedom.* London: Macmillan & Company, 1898.

SIMPSON, DONALD G.: "Negroes in Ontario from Early Times to 1870". Unpublished Ph.D. thesis, University of Western Ontario, London, 1970.

SMITH, T. WATSON: *The Slave in Canada. Nova Scotia Historical Society,* Vol. X, 1900.

SMITH, REVEREND WILLIAM WYE: "Canadian Reminiscences 1900". XIV, MS, Public Archives of Ontario.

SPICER, ELIZABETH (ed): *Description of London and its Environs 1799-1854.* London Public Library, London, Ontario.

SPRAY, W.A.: *The Blacks in New Brunswick.* Fredericton: Brunswick Press, 1972.

Stanley Smith Collection, Regional Room, University of Western Ontario, London, Ontario.

STEWART, AUSTIN: *Twenty Years a Slave and Forty a Freeman.* New York, 1869.

The Story of Oro. Oro Township, 1972.

STOWE, HARRIET BEECHER: *Uncle Tom's Cabin (or, Life Among the Lowly),* Vol. I & II. Boston: John P. Jewett & Company, 1852.

Taylor Scrapbook, Fort Malden National Historic Museum, Amherstburg, Ontario.

THOMSON, COLIN A.: *Blacks in Deep Snow: Black Pioneers in Canada.* Don Mills, Ontario: J. M. Dent & Sons (Canada) Limited, 1979.

TRUDEL, MARCEL: "L'attitude de l'église catholique vis-à-vis l'esclavage au Canada français". Québec: Les Presses de l'Université Laval, 1960.

TULLOCK, HEADLEY: *Black Canadians: A Long Line of Fighters.* Toronto: NC Press Limited, 1975.

ULLMAN, VICTOR: *Look to the North Star.* Boston: Beacon Press, 1979.

WALKER, JAMES W. ST. G.: *The Black Loyalists: The Search for a Promised Land in Nova Scotia and Sierra Leone 1783-1870.* New York: Africana Publishing Company, and Dalhousie, N.S.: Dalhousie University Press, 1976.

————*A History of Blacks in Canada: A Study Guide.* Ottawa: Ministry of State — Multiculturalism, 1981.

WINKS, ROBIN: *The Blacks in Canada.* Montréal: McGill-Queen's University Press, and New Haven and London: Yale University Press, 1971.

WOODSON, CARTER G.: *The Negro in our History.* Washington, D.C.: The Associated Publishers, Inc., 1928.

Index

Picture Credits

PERMISSION TO REPRODUCE illustrations is gratefully acknowledged as follows. Page numbers on which illustrations appear are listed after each source. Where applicable, reference numbers for individual illustrations follow page numbers in brackets.

Mrs. Robert Aiken 217; Bettmann Archive Inc. 38; Cincinnati Art Museum 60; Culver Pictures Inc. 36 *upper left* (10475); Catherine Farley 8, 10, 29, 65; Enid D'Oyley 156; W. Allen Fisher 133; First Baptist Church, Toronto 138; 139 *lower*; First Baptist Church, Windsor 144; Fort Malden National Historic Museum 172 (LO37519), 215; Grant AME Church, Toronto 134; Daniel G. Hill 36 *upper centre and right*, 67, 87 *right*, 89, 96, 108, 126, 132, 135, 136, 137, 143, 156, 159, 167, 168 *lower*, 170, 171, 175, 176 (*lower right:* courtesy of Collingwood Enterprise Bulletin Ltd.), 181 (courtesy of Van Nostrand Reinhold Ltd.), 184 *lower*, 197, 198, 199, 200, 204, 205, 207; Johnson Publishing Company Inc.: *Ebony* 5, 128 *lower*; Jock MacRae 2, 112, 178, 203; Victor Metoyer Jr. 45, 110; Metropolitan Toronto Library Board 15, 16* *right*, 22, 22-23, 26, 29* *inset*, 30, 31, 34* *lower*, 36 *lower*, 37, 40†, 41†, 42, 44*, 55†, *lower*, 57*, 61*, 69*, 70, 71, 77, 79†, 82, 84*, 86*, 87, 88 *lower*, 90, 91†, 92†, 93†, 94†, 97†, 101†, 103, 104*, 113, 116*, 129, 134*, 139†, 141*, 146, 147, 149, 150†, 152, 157, 160†, 165, 168*, 169†, 173*, 174, 180†, 186*, 190*, 195, 196* *lower*, 206*, 208†, 209, 211, 216; National Gallery of Canada 193 (5777); Nova Scotia Museum 63; Ontario Department of Travel and Publicity 185 (3-L-863), 188, 201; Owen Sound and Grey County Museum 44, 57, 162; *Owen Sound Sun-Times* 212; Parks Canada: Fort Malden National Historic Park 49; Provincial Archives of Nova Scotia, Newspaper Collection 9; Provincial Archives of Nova Scotia, Photographic Collection 213; Provincial Archives of Ontario 14, 17 *right*, 18, 28 (230), 34, 75, 115 *lower* (952.15.11), 155, 171 *lower*, 184 (S12008), 188, 216 (L1267); Public Archives of Canada 4 (C6492, C34183), 5 (C10888), 7 (C11043), 8 (C2834), 11 (C168), 12 (C73449), 13

* Broadside Collection; † John Ross Robertson Collection.

241

(C73421), 16 (C69886), 17 (C69887), 19 (C252), 33 (C69355), 46 (C2035), 47 (C34334), 50 (C11850, C67365), 51 (C17694), 53 (C44633), 55 (C34598), 59 (C4437), 68 (C20764), 78 (C11883), 82-83 (C11811), 97 (C544), 102 (C6303), 107 (C8249), 111 (C69344), 115 (C12093), 117 (C26), 119 (C18172, C5434), 120 (C8876, C11857), 121 (C18789), 122 (C11878), 124 (C22626), 125 (C9790), 128 (C11057, C11058), 148 (C3305), 161 (C9564), 163 (C24589), 180 *right* (C20912), 182 (C31209), 189 (PA84854), 192 (C110101); Raleigh Township Centennial Museum, North Buxton 62, 73, 81, 83, 85, 88; Uncle Tom's Cabin Museum, Dresden 196; University of Western Ontario 24, 72, 213, 215.

DIAGNOSIS AND MANAGEMENT OF ADULT CONGENITAL HEART DISEASE

DIAGNOSIS AND MANAGEMENT OF ADULT CONGENITAL HEART DISEASE

second edition

Michael A. Gatzoulis, MD, PhD, FACC, FESC
Professor of Cardiology, Congenital Heart Disease
Consultant Cardiologist
Adult Congenital Heart Centre and Centre for Pulmonary Hypertension
Royal Brompton Hospital
National Heart and Lung Institute
Imperial College
London, United Kingdom

Gary D. Webb, MD, CM, FACC
Professor of Pediatrics and Internal Medicine
University of Cincinnati
Director, Cincinnati Adolescent and Adult Congenital Heart Center
Cincinnati Children's Hospital
Cincinnati, Ohio

Piers E. F. Daubeney, MA, DM, DCH, MRCP, FRCPCH
Reader in Paediatric Cardiology
National Heart and Lung Institute
Imperial College
Consultant, Paediatric and Fetal Cardiologist
Royal Brompton Hospital
London, United Kingdom

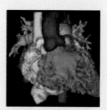
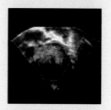

ELSEVIER
SAUNDERS

1600 John F. Kennedy Blvd.
Ste 1800
Philadelphia, PA 19103-2899

DIAGNOSIS AND MANAGEMENT OF ADULT CONGENITAL HEART DISEASE, SECOND EDITION
ISBN: 978-0-7020-3426-8

NOTICES

Knowledge and best practice in this field are constantly changing. As new research and experience broaden
our understanding, changes in research methods, professional practices, or medical treatment may become
necessary.

Practitioners and researchers must always rely on their own experience and knowledge in evaluating and
using any information, methods, compounds, or experiments described herein. In using such information
or methods they should be mindful of their own safety and the safety of others, including parties for whom
they have a professional responsibility.

With respect to any drug or pharmaceutical products identified, readers are advised to check the most
current information provided (i) on procedures featured or (ii) by the manufacturer of each product to be
administered, to verify the recommended dose or formula, the method and duration of administration, and
contraindications. It is the responsibility of practitioners, relying on their own experience and knowledge of
their patients, to make diagnoses, to determine dosages and the best treatment for each individual patient,
and to take all appropriate safety precautions.

To the fullest extent of the law, neither the Publisher nor the authors, contributors, or editors, assume any
liability for any injury and/or damage to persons or property as a matter of products liability, negligence or
otherwise, or from any use or operation of any methods, products, instructions, or ideas contained in the
material herein.

Library of Congress Cataloging-in-Publication Data
Diagnosis and management of adult congenital heart disease / edited by Michael Gatzoulis,
Gary D. Webb, Piers E. F. Daubeney ; foreword by Joseph K. Perloff.—2nd ed.
   p. ; cm.
   Includes bibliographical references and index.
   ISBN 978-0-7020-3426-8 (hardback : alk. paper) 1. Congenital heart disease. I.
Gatzoulis, Michael A. II. Webb, Gary D. III. Daubeney, Piers E. F. IV. Title.
   [DNLM: 1. Heart Defects, Congenital—diagnosis. 2. Adult. 3. Heart Defects, Congenital—
therapy. WG 220]
   RC687.D495 2011
   616.1'2043—dc22
                                                                                    2010031222

Executive Publisher: Natasha Andjelkovic
Senior Developmental Editor: Ann Ruzycka Anderson
Publishing Services Manager: Patricia Tannian
Team Manager: Radhika Pallamparthy
Project Managers: Claire Kramer, Joanna Dhanabalan
Designer: Steven Stave

Printed in the United States of America
Last digit is the print number: 9   8   7   6   5   4   3   2   1

To Julie, Mikey, and William

To Anne, Laura, and Natalie

To Nara, Henry, Beatrice, and Daphne

DAVID ALEXANDER, MBChB, FRCA
Consultant Anaesthetist
Royal Brompton and Harefield National Heart and
    Lung Hospital
London, United Kingdom

ABDULLAH A. ALGHAMDI, MD, MSC, FRCSC
Cardiac Surgery Fellow
Department of Surgery
Division of Cardiac Surgery
University of Toronto
Toronto, Ontario, Canada

RAFAEL ALONSO-GONZALEZ, MD, MSC
Clinical Fellow in Adult Congenital Heart Disease
Royal Brompton Hospital
London, United Kingdom

NASER M. AMMASH, MD
Consultant
Cardiovascular Diseases and Internal Medicine
Associate Professor of Medicine
Mayo Medical School
Mayo Clinic
Rochester, Minnesota

ANNALISA ANGELINI, MD
Associate Professor, Cardiovascular Pathology
Department of Medical-Diagnostic Sciences and
    Special Therapies
University of Padua Medical School
Padua, Italy

RAVI ASSOMULL, MBBChir, MRCP
Research Fellow
Cardiovascular Magnetic Resonance Unit
Cardiologist
Imperial College NHS Trust
London, United Kingdom

SONYA V. BABU-NARAYAN, MBBS, BSc, MRCP
Honorary Clinical Research Fellow
National Heart and Lung Institute
Imperial College London
Adult Congential Heart Disease Fellow
Royal Brompton Hospital
London, United Kingdom

CARL L. BACKER
Professor of Surgery
Northwestern University Feinberg School of Medicine
A. C. Buehler Professor of Cardiovascular-Thoracic Surgery
Division Head, Cardiovascular-Thoracic Surgery
Children's Memorial Hospital
Chicago, Illinois

CRISTINA BASSO, MD, PHD
Associate Professor, Pathology
Department of Medico-Diagnostic Sciences and
    Special Therapies
University of Padua Medical School
Padua, Italy

ELISABETH BÉDARD, MD, FRCPC
Cardiologist
Québec Heart and Lung Institute
Quebec City, Quebec, Canada

D. WOODROW BENSON, MD, PhD
Professor of Pediatrics
Cincinnati Children's Hospital
    Medical Center
Cincinnati, Ohio

LEE BENSON, MD, FRCPC, FACC, FSCAI
Professor of Pediatrics (Cardiology)
Pediatrics
University of Toronto School of Medicine
Director, Cardiac Diagnostic and
    Interventional Unit
Hospital for Sick Children
Toronto, Ontario, Canada

STELLA D. BRILI, MD
Consultant, Adult Congenital
    Heart Disease
First Cardiology Department
University of Athens Hippokration Hospital
Athens, Greece

CRAIG S. BROBERG, MD, FACC
Assistant Professor
Director of Adult Congenital
    Heart Disease
Oregon Health and Sciences University
Portland, Oregon

MORGAN L. BROWN, MD, PhD
Resident, Department of Anesthesiology
    and Pain Medicine
University of Alberta
Edmonton, Alberta, Canada

ALBERT V. G. BRUSCHKE, MD, PhD
Emeritus Professor of Cardiology
Department of Cardiology
Leiden University Medical Center
Leiden, The Netherlands

WERNER BUDTS, MD, PhD
Professor of Medicine
Cardiology
Catholic University of Leuven
Head of Adult Congenital Heart Disease
University of Hospitals and Leuven Clinic
Leuven, Belgium

ALIDA L. P. CAFORIO
Assistant Professor
Cardiological, Thoracic, and Vascular Sciences
University of Padova Medical School
NHS Senior Staff Cardiologist
Azienda Ospedaliera di Padova–
    Policlinico Universitario
Padova, Italy

DENNIS V. COKKINOS, MD
Professor Emeritus
University of Athens
Director Emeritus
Onassis Cardiac Surgery Center
Director Cardiovascular Department
Biomedical Research Foundation
Academy of Athens
Athens, Greece

JACK M. COLMAN, MD, FRCPC
Associate Professor of Medicine (Cardiology)
University of Toronto
Cardiologist
Mount Sinai Hospital
Staff Cardiologist, Congenital Cardiac
    Centre for Adults
Peter Munk Cardiac Centre
Toronto General Hospital
Toronto, Ontario, Canada

**MICHAEL S. CONNELLY, BSc,
MBBS, MRCP**
Clinical Assistant Professor
Department of Cardiac Sciences
Division of Cardiology, Department of Medicine
University of Calgary
Staff Cardiologist
Peter Lougheed Centre
Foothills Medical Centre
Calgary, Alberta, Canada

HEIDI M. CONNOLLY, MD
Consultant, Division of Cardiovascular Diseases
Professor of Medicine, College of Medicine
Mayo Clinic
Rochester, Minnesota

DOMENICO CORRADO, MD, PhD
Professor, Cardiovascular Medicine
Inherited Arrhythmogenic Cardiomyopathy Unit
Department of Cardiac, Thoracic, and
    Vascular Sciences
University of Padova Medical School
Padova, Italy

**GORDON CUMMING, BSc (MeD), MD,
FRCPC, FACC, FAHA**
Board Certified Insurance Medicine
Medical Board
The Great-West Life Assurance Company
Winnipeg, Manitoba, Canada

MICHAEL CUMPER
Chairman
Grown Up Congenital Heart Patients
    Association
London, United Kingdom

**PIERS E. F. DAUBENEY, MA, DM, DCH,
MRCP, FRCPCH**
Reader in Paediatric Cardiology
National Heart and Lung Institute
Imperial College
Consultant, Paediatric and Fetal Cardiologist
Royal Brompton Hospital
London, United Kingdom

BARBARA J. DEAL, MD
Division Head, Cardiology
Children's Memorial Hospital
M. E. Wodika Professor of
    Cardiology Research
Feinberg School of Medicine
Northwestern University
Chicago, Illinois

JOSEPH A. DEARANI, MD
Professor of Surgery
Division of Cardiovascular Surgery
Mayo Clinic
Rochester, Minnesota

GERHARD-PAUL DILLER, MD, PhD
Consultant Cardiologist
Adult Congenital Heart Disease Programme
    and Programme for Pulmonary Arterial
    Hypertension
Royal Brompton Hospital
London, United Kingdom

**KONSTANTINOS DIMOPOULOS, MD, MSc,
PhD, FESC**
Consultant Cardiologist
Adult Congenital Heart Centre and Centre for
    Pulmonary Hypertension
Royal Brompton Hospital and Imperial College
London, United Kingdom

ANNIE DORE, MD, FRCP(c)
Associate Professor of Medicine
University of Montreal
Consultant Cardiologist
Adult Congenital Heart Centre
Montreal Heart Institute
Montreal, Quebec, Canada

JACQUELINE DURBRIDGE, MBBS, FRCA
Consultant Obstetric Anaesthetist
Chelsea and Westminster Hospital
London, United Kingdom

ALEXANDER R. ELLIS, MD, MSc, FAAP, FACC
Pediatric and Adult Congenital Cardiologist
Children's Hospital of the King's Daughters
Assistant Professor
Internal Medicine and Pediatrics
Eastern Virginia Medical School
Norfolk, Virginia

SABINE ERNST, MD
Honorary Senior Lecturer
Imperial College
Consultant Cardiologist
Royal Brompton Hospital
Lead Electrophysiology Research
Royal Brompton Hospital
London, United Kingdom

**SIMON J. FINNEY, MSc, PhD, MBChB,
MRCP, FRCA**
Consultant in Intensive Care
Adult Intensive Care Unit
Royal Brompton Hospital
London, United Kingdom

MICHAEL A. GATZOULIS, MD, PhD, FACC, FESC
Professor of Cardiology, Congenital
  Heart Disease
Consultant Cardiologist
Adult Congenital Heart Centre and Centre for Pulmonary
  Hypertension
Royal Brompton Hospital
National Heart and Lung Institute
Imperial College
London, United Kingdom

SMITHA H. GAWDE, MSc, PhD
Operational Head
Metropolis Healthcare Ltd.
Mumbai, India

MARC GEWILLIG, MD, PhD
Professor
Pediatric and Congenital Cardiology
University of Leuven
Leuven, Belgium

GEORGIOS GIANNAKOULAS, MD, PhD
Clinical Research Fellow
Royal Brompton Hospital
London, United Kingdom

THOMAS P. GRAHAM, JR, MD
Emeritus Professor
Division of Pediatric Cardiology
Vanderbilt University
Nashville, Tennessee

**ANKUR GULATI, BA HONS (CANTAB), MB BChir,
MA, MRCP**
Cardiovascular Magnetic Resonance Research Fellow
Cardiology Specialist Registrar
Royal Brompton Hospital
London, United Kingdom

ASIF HASAN, MB, BS, FRCS
Consultant Cardiothoracic Surgeon
Freeman Hospital
High Heaton
Newcastle upon Tyne
Tyne and Wear, United Kingdom

SIEW YEN HO, PhD, FRCPath
Professor/Consultant
Head of Cardiac Morphology
Royal Brompton and Harefield NHS Trust
London, United Kingdom

ERIC HORLICK, MDCM, FRCPC, FSCAI
Assistant Professor of Medicine
Director, Structural Heart Disease Intervention Service
Peter Munk Cardiac Centre
University Health Network–
  Toronto General Hospital
Toronto, Ontario, Canada

TIM HORNUNG, MB, MRCP
Clinical Senior Lecturer
University of Auckland
Cardiologist
Green Lane Congenital Cardiac Service
Auckland City Hospital
Auckland, New Zealand

HARALD KAEMMERER, MD, VMD
Professor of Medicine
Deutsches Herzzentrum München, Technische Universität München
Klinik für Kinderkardiologie und angeborene Herzfehler
Deutsches Herzzentrum München
München, Germany

JUAN PABLO KASKI, BSc, MBBS, MRCPCH
Specialist Registrar
Royal Brompton Hospital and Great Ormond Street Hospital
London, United Kingdom

PAUL KHAIRY, MD, PhD, FRCPC
Director, Adult Congenital Heart Centre
Montreal Heart Institute
Associate Professor
Department of Medicine
Canada Research Chair, Electrophysiology and Adult Congenital
  Heart Disease
University of Montreal
Montreal, Quebec, Canada
Research Director, Boston Adult Congenital Heart (BACH) Service
Harvard University
Boston, Massachusetts

PHILIP J. KILNER, MD, PhD
Consultant in Cardiovascular Magnetic Resonance
Royal Brompton Hospital and Imperial College
London, United Kingdom

MICHAEL J. LANDZBERG, MD
Assistant Professor of Medicine
Harvard Medical School
Director
Boston Adult Congenital Heart Program (BACH)
Associate Director
Adult Pulmonary Hypertension Program
Associate in Cardiology
Children's Hospital
Boston, Massachusetts

WEI LI, MD, PhD
Royal Brompton and Harefield NHS Trust
London, United Kingdom

EMMANOUIL LIODAKIS, MD
Research Fellow in Adult Congenital Heart Disease
Royal Brompton Hospital
London, United Kingdom

**SIMON T. MACDONALD, BSc(Hons), BMBCh,
DPhil, MRCP**
GUCH Fellow
Grown Up Congenital Heart Disease Unit (GUCH) Office
The Heart Hospital
London, United Kingdom

SHREESHA MAIYA, MBBS, MRCP, DCH
Locum Consultant in Paediatric Cardiology
Royal Brompton and Harefield NHS Foundation Trust
London, United Kingdom

LARRY W. MARKHAM, MD, MS
Assistant Professor
Pediatrics and Medicine
Vanderbilt University
Nashville, Tennessee

CONSTANTINE MAVROUDIS, MD
Chairman, Department of Pediatric and Adult
    Congenital Heart Surgery
Ross Chair in Pediatric and Adult Congenital Heart Surgery
Joint Appointment in Bioethics
Professor of Surgery
Cleveland Clinic
Lerner College of Medicine of Case Western Reserve University
Cleveland, Ohio

DOFF B. MCELHINNEY, MD
Assistant Professor of Pediatrics
Harvard Medical School
Associate in Cardiology
Children's Hospital
Boston, Massachusetts

PETER MCLAUGHLIN, MD, FRCP(C)
Adjunct Clinical Professor of Medicine
University of Toronto
Toronto, Ontario, Canada
Chief of Staff
Peterborough Regional Health Centre
Peterborough, Ontario, Canada

FOLKERT J. MEIJBOOM, MD, PhD, FESC
Department of Cardiology and Pediatrics
University Medical Centre Utrecht
Utrecht, The Netherlands

LISE-ANDRÉE MERCIER
Associate Professor
Department of Medicine
University of Montreal
Cardiologist
Montreal Heart Institute
Montreal, Quebec, Canada

BARBARA J. M. MULDER, MD, PhD
Professor of Cardiology
Academic Medical Center
Amsterdam, The Netherlands

MICHAEL J. MULLEN, MBBS, MD, FRCP
Consultant Cardiologist
The Heart Hospital
University College Hospital London
London, United Kingdom

DANIEL MURPHY, MD
Professor of Pediatrics
Stanford University
Associate Chief, Pediatric Cardiology
Lucile Packard Children's Hospital
Palo Alto, California

NITHA NAQVI, BSc(hons), MBBS(hons), MSC, MRCPCH
Paediatric Cardiology Specialist Registrar
Royal Brompton Hospital
London, United Kingdom

EDWARD D. NICOL, BMedSci, BM, BS, MD, MRCP
Cardiac CT Fellow
Royal Brompton Hospital
London, United Kingdom
Specialist Registrar in Cardiology and General
    (Internal) Medicine
John Radcliffe Hospital
Oxford, United Kingdom

KOICHIRO NIWA, MD, FACC
Director
Department of Adult Congenital Heart Disease and Pediatrics
Chiba Cardiovascular Center
Chiba, Japan

MARK D. NORRIS, MD
Cardiology Fellow
The Heart Institute
Cincinnati Children's Hospital Medical Center
Cincinnati, Ohio

ERWIN OECHSLIN, MD
Associate Professor, University of Toronto
Director, Toronto Congenital Cardiac Centre for Adults
Peter Munk Cardiac Centre
University Health Network
Toronto General Hospital
University of Toronto
Toronto, Ontario, Canada

GEORGE A. PANTELY, MD
Professor of Medicine
Department of Medicine (Cardiovascular Disease)
Oregon Health and Science University
Portland, Oregon

JOSEPH K. PERLOFF, BA, MS, MD
Streisand/American Heart Association
Professor of Medicine and Pediatrics, Emeritus
Founding Director, Ahmanson/UCLA Adult Congenital
    Heart Disease Center
UCLA School of Medicine
Los Angeles, California

JAMES C. PERRY, MD
Director of Electrophysiology and Adult Congenital Heart Programs
Professor of Clinical Pediatrics
University of California San Diego
Rady Children's Hospital
San Diego, California

FRANK A. PIGULA, MD
Associate Professor of Surgery
Harvard Medical School
Associate in Cardiac Surgery
Children's Hospital Boston
Boston, Massachusetts

KALLIOPI PILICHOU, Phd, BSc
Medical Diagnostic Sciences and Special Therapies
University of Padua
Padua, Italy

NANCY C. POIRIER, FRCSC
Associate Professor
University of Montreal
Congenital Cardiac Surgeon
Montreal Heart Institute
Ste-Justine Hospital
Montreal, Quebec, Canada

MATINA PRAPA, MD
PhD student
National Heart and Lung Institute
Imperial College London
Research Fellow
Royal Brompton Hospital
London, United Kingdom

SANJAY K. PRASAD, MD, MRCP
Consultant Cardiologist
Royal Brompton Hospital
London, United Kingdom

JELENA RADOJEVIC, MD
Clinical and Research Fellow
Adult Congenital Heart Centre and Centre
    for Pulmonary Hypertension
Royal Brompton Hospital
Grant Student of the French Society of
    Cardiology
London, United Kingdom

ANDREW N. REDINGTON, MD, FRCP (UK) & (C)
Head, Division of Cardiology
Hospital for Sick Children
Professor of Paediatrics
University of Toronto
BMO Financial Group Chair in Cardiology
Labatt Family Heart Centre
Hospital for Sick Children
Toronto, Ontario, Canada

MICHAEL L. RIGBY, MD, FRCP, FRCPCH
Consultant Cardiologist
Division of Paediatric Cardiology
Royal Brompton Hospital
London, United Kingdom

JOSEP RODÉS-CABAU, MD, FESC
Associate Professor of Medicine
Laval University
Director of the Catheterization and Interventional Laboratories
Quebec Heart and Lung Institute
Quebec City, Quebec, Canada

MICHAEL B. RUBENS, MB, BS, LRCP, MRCS, DMRD, FRCR
Consultant Radiologist
Royal Brompton Hospital
London, United Kingdom

MARKUS SCHWERZMANN, MD
University of Bern
Head, Adult Congenital Heart Disease Program
Swiss Cardiovascular Center
University Hospital Inselspital
Bern, Switzerland

ELLIOT A. SHINEBOURNE,
MD, FRCP, FRCPCH
Honorary Consultant in Congenital Heart Disease
Royal Brompton Hospital
London, United Kingdom

DARRYL F. SHORE, FRCS
Director of the Heart Division
Royal Brompton and Harefield NHS Trust
London, United Kingdom

MICHAEL N. SINGH, MD
Assistant in Cardiology
Children's Hospital Boston
Brigham and Women's Hospital
Instructor
Harvard Medical School
Boston, Massachusetts

MARK SPENCE, BCh, BAO, MB, MD
Honorary Senior Lecturer
Queen's University Belfast
Consultant Cardiologist
Royal Victoria Hospital, Belfast Trust
Belfast, United Kingdom

CHRISTODOULOS STEFANADIS, MD, PhD
Dean of the Medical School
National and Kapodistrian University of Athens
Athens, Greece

JAMES STIRRUP, BSc, MBBS, MedMIPEM, MRCP
Clinical Research Fellow, Cardiac Imaging
Department of Nuclear Medicine
Royal Brompton and Harefield NHS Foundation Trust
London, United Kingdom

KRISTEN LIPSCOMB SUND, MS, PhD
Genetic Counselor
Cincinnati Children's Hospital Medical Center
Cincinnati, Ohio

LORNA SWAN, MB CHB, MD, FRCP
Consultant Cardiologist
Royal Brompton Hospital
London, United Kingdom

SHIGERU TATENO, MD
Department of Adult Congenital Heart Disease and Pediatrics
Chiba Cardiovascular Center
Ichihara, Japan

DYLAN A. TAYLOR, MD, FRCPC, FACC
Clinical Professor of Medicine
University of Alberta
Co-Site Medical Director
University of Alberta Hospital
Stollery Children's Hospital
Mazankowski Alberta Heart Institute
Edmonton, Alberta, Canada

BASIL D. THANOPOULOS, MD, PhD
Associate Professor
Director, Interventional Pediatric Cardiology
Athens Medical Center
Athens, Greece

ERIK THAULOW, MD, PhD, FESC, FACC
Professor
Head Section Congenital Heart Disease
Department of Pediatrics
Rikshospitalet
University Hospital Oslo OUS
Oslo, Norway

GAETANO THIENE, MD, FRCP
Professor
Cardiovascular Pathology
University of Padua Medical School
Padua, Italy

SARA A. THORNE, MBBS, MD
Consultant Cardiologist
Queen Elizabeth Hospital
University of Birmingham
Birmingham, United Kingdom

JAN TILL, MD
Consultant
Paediatric Cardiology
Royal Brompton Hospital
London, United Kingdom

PAVLOS K. TOUTOUZAS, MD, FESC
Department of Cardiology
Hellenic Heart Foundation
University of Athens
Athens, Greece

JOHN K. TRIEDMAN, MD
Associate Professor of Pediatrics
Harvard Medical School
Senior Associate in Cardiology
Children's Hospital Boston
Boston, Massachusetts

PEDRO T. TRINDADE, MD
Consultant Cardiologist
Adult Congenital Heart Disease Clinic
University Hospital Zurich
Zurich, Switzerland

ANSELM UEBING, MD, PhD
Consultant Congenital and Paediatric Cardiologist
Department of Congenital Heart Disease and Paediatric Cardiology
University Hospital of Schleswigs–Holstein, Campus Kiel
Kiel, Germany

HIDEKI UEMURA, MD, FRCS
Consultant Cardiac Surgeon
Royal Brompton Hospital
London, United Kingdom

GLEN S. VAN ARSDELL, MD
Staff Surgeon, Toronto Congenital Cardiac Centre for Adults
Head, Cardiovascular Surgery
Hospital for Sick Children, Toronto
CIT Chair in Cardiovascular Research
Professor of Surgery
University of Toronto
Toronto, Ontario, Canada

HUBERT W. VLIEGEN, MD, PhD, FESC
Associate Professor of Cardiology
Leiden University Medical Center (LUMC)
Leiden, The Netherlands

FIONA WALKER, BM HONS, FRCP, FESC
Clinical Director, GUCH Service
Lead for Maternal Cardiology
National Heart Hospital
University College London Hospitals NHS Trust
London, United Kingdom

NICOLA L. WALKER, MBChB
Honorary Clinical Senior Lecturer
University of Glasgow School of Medicine
Division of Cardiovascular and Medical Sciences
Glasgow Royal Infirmary
Glasgow, United Kingdom

EDWARD P. WALSH, MD
Chief, Electrophysiology Division
Department of Cardiology
Children's Hospital Boston
Professor of Pediatrics
Harvard Medical School
Boston, Massachusetts

CAROLE A. WARNES, MD, FRCP
Professor of Medicine
Mayo Clinic
Consultant in Cardiovascular Diseases
Internal Medicine and Pediatric Cardiology
Mayo Clinic
Rochester, Minnesota

GARY D. WEBB, MD, CM, FACC
Professor of Pediatrics and Internal Medicine
University of Cincinnati
Director, Cincinnati Adolescent and Adult
  Congenital Heart Center
Cincinnati Children's Hospital
Cincinnati, Ohio

STEVEN A. WEBBER, MBChB, MRCP
Professor of Pediatrics
University of Pittsburgh School of Medicine
Chief, Division of Cardiology
Children's Hospital of Pittsburgh of UPMC
Pittsburgh, Pennsylvania

TOM WONG, MBChB, MRCP
Honorary Senior Lecturer
National Heart and Lung Institute
Imperial College London
Director of Catheter Labs
Harefield Hospital
Royal Brompton and Harefield NHS
London, United Kingdom

EDGAR TAY LIK WUI, MBBS, MMed, MRCP
Consultant, Cardiac Department
National University Heart Centre
Clinical Instructor
Yong Loo Lin School of Medicine
Singapore

**STEVEN YENTIS, BSc, MD,
MBBS, MA, FRCA**
Consultant Anaesthetist
Chelsea and Westminster Hospital
Honorary Reader
Imperial College London
London, United Kingdom

JAMES W. L. YIP, MD
Senior Consultant Cardiologist
Department of Medicine
National University of Singapore
Yong Loo
Lin School of Medicine
Singapore

FOREWORD

The Hospital for Sick Children in London was established in 1852 as the first major facility dedicated to treatment of the young, but in reality it was little more than a dim light of hope in the darkness of pediatric medicine.[1] It is altogether fitting that *Diagnosis and Management of Adult Congenital Heart Disease*, a book that originates in large part from another distinguished London hospital, the Royal Brompton, is devoted to a new patient population that represents the success story of pediatric cardiology and pediatric cardiac surgery: adult survival in congenital heart disease.

In the latter part of the 19th century, *Congenital Affections of the Heart* were of "…only a limited clinical interest, as in a large proportion of the cases the anomaly is not compatible with life, and in the others nothing can be done to remedy the defect or even to relieve the symptoms".[2] By contrast, in developed countries in the early 21st century, approximately 85% of infants with congenital heart disease can expect to reach adulthood because the impressive technical resources at our disposal permit remarkably precise anatomic and physiologic diagnoses and astonishing feats of reparative and palliative surgery. Cures, however, are few and far between, so patients remain patients. Postoperative residua and sequelae are the rule rather than the exception, vary widely in severity, and oblige us to assume responsibility for the long-term care of the growing population of adults with congenital heart disease. These patients not only are beneficiaries of surgical advances, but also are beneficiaries of major advances in medical management of both operated and unoperated/inoperable congenital heart disease (see Chapter 1).

The first of eleven sections is devoted to general principles that define the subspecialty: cardiac morphology and nomenclature, genetics, clinical assessment, diagnostic methods, interventional catheterization, operation and reoperation, heart and lung transplantation, and medical management, including noncardiac surgery, electrophysiology, infective endocarditis, pregnancy, exercise, and insurability. Section two includes three types of septal defects. Sections three through five deal sequentially with acyanotic malformations of the left ventricular inflow and outflow tracts and diseases of the aorta, while sections six and seven focus on acyanotic malformations of the right ventricular inflow and outflow tracts. Each of these sections is orderly and comprehensive. Section eight, which is about cyanotic congenital heart disease—both pulmonary hypertensive and nonpulmonary hypertensive—deals with specific malformations and, importantly, with cyanotic congenital heart disease as a multisystem systemic disorder, a topic of special relevance in adults. Section nine deals with the often contentious topic of univentricular heart (double inlet ventricle, univentricular atrioventricular connection) and properly includes atrioventricular valve atresia. Section ten is noteworthy by virtue of focusing on congenital anomalies of the coronary arteries, a topic that tends to be underrepresented in discussions of adult congenital heart disease. Section eleven carries the title, "Other Lesions," and deals chiefly with acquired diseases but includes informative accounts of Marfan syndrome and primary pulmonary hypertension.

Certain malformations necessarily appear in more than one chapter, emphasizing that congenital heart diseases are not static malformations but are anatomically and physiologically dynamic, changing over the course of time, often appreciably.

Diagnosis and Management of Adult Congenital Heart Disease is a comprehensive multisource book that complements rather than duplicates the earlier single-source text whose format is different.[1] The book is a welcome addition to an emerging field, the importance of which is underscored by the appearance of this major work that will appeal to cardiologists whose interest in congenital heart disease ranges from infancy through adulthood. The three co-editors, Michael Gatzoulis, Gary Webb, and Piers Daubeney, are eminently equipped to edit this definitive work.

Joseph K. Perloff

REFERENCES

1. Perloff JK, Child JS. Aboulhosn J: Congenital Heart Disease in Adults. Philadelphia: WB Saunders Co; 2009.
2. Osler W: The Principles and Practice of Medicine. New York: D Appleton & Co; 1894.

Congenital heart disease (CHD), with its worldwide incidence of 0.8%, is one of the most common inborn defects. Advances in pediatric cardiology and cardiac surgery over the past several decades have led to more than 85% of these patients surviving to adulthood. This wonderful medical story has transformed the outcome for CHD and created what is a large and still-growing population of adolescent and adult patients. It was recently appreciated, however, that most early interventions for these patients—surgical or catheter—were reparative and not curative. There is now global consensus that most patients with CHD will require and benefit from lifelong specialized follow-up. Many of them will face the prospect of further surgery; arrhythmia intervention; and, if managed inappropriately, overt heart failure and premature death.

Although provision of care for children with CHD is well in place in most parts of the world, clinical services for the adult with CHD remain scarce or incomplete. Sadly, CHD remains a small part of general cardiology training curricula around the world. Pediatric cardiologists, who excel at cardiac morphology and physiology, are trained to manage children with CHD and may, out of necessity, continue to look after these patients when they outgrow pediatric age. There are clearly other health issues concerning the adult with CHD beyond the scope of pediatric medicine. These issues relate to obstetrics, electrophysiology, coronary disease, high blood pressure, diabetes, and other comorbidities that our patients now routinely face. Adult physicians with a non-CHD background are therefore increasingly involved in the day-to-day management of patients with CHD.

A few years ago, we invested time and effort in our resource textbook addressing this expanding clinical need, written for a wider professional audience. The textbook was about disseminating existing knowledge, and there have been ongoing advances in our understanding of the late sequelae of CHD. The worldwide response and interest in its first edition suggested that the time was right. We return, herewith, with the second edition, which has the same focus but with additional coverage of topics such as computed tomography, critical and perioperative care, obstetric and cardiac anesthesia, and transition of care from pediatrics, thus being inclusive of "new" and related disciplines. Our textbook continues to address the expanding disciplines involved in the care of these patients, medical and nonmedical, although we hope that even the supraspecialized expert in CHD will find some sections of interest and benefit from it. This primary aim shaped the original layout of the textbook, which is characterized by a systematic approach, easy access to information, and an emphasis on management issues. We hope that the reader will appreciate our clinical approach to the challenge and privilege of looking after the patient with CHD.

We are indebted to our wonderful faculty, leading cardiovascular experts from around the world, for donating their precious time, including the additional burden of complying with the unique chapter format to produce excellent chapters and make the second edition of the textbook a reality. We remain grateful to the Elsevier team, in particular to Michael Houston and Anne Lenehan for their enthusiastic support through the first edition of the book and to Natasha Andjelkovic and Ann Ruzycka Anderson, who with their help, patience, and support carried the project through in a timely fashion. Last, but not least, we thank our patients for making this work possible by supporting our endless pursuit through research and education of a better understanding of CHD, its late problems, and the most effective strategies for their treatment.

Michael A. Gatzoulis

Gary D. Webb

Piers E. F. Daubeney

CONTENTS

DIAGNOSIS AND MANAGEMENT OF ADULT CONGENITAL HEART DISEASE

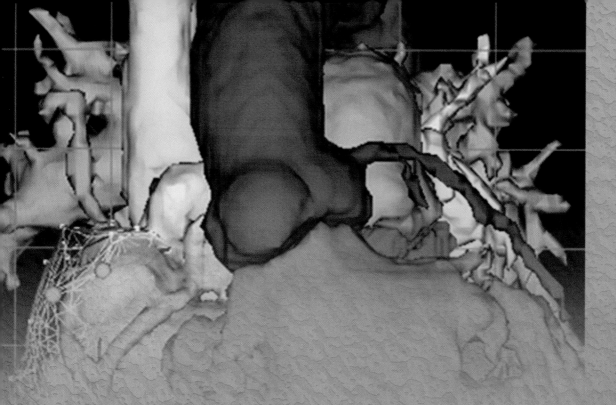

I

General Principles

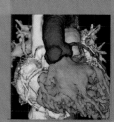

1

Adults with Congenital Heart Disease: A Growing Population

MICHAEL A. GATZOULIS | GARY D. WEBB

Introduction

Congenital heart disease (CHD) is the most common inborn defect, occurring in approximately 0.8% of neonates. Adults with CHD are the beneficiaries of successful pediatric cardiac surgery and pediatric cardiology programs throughout the developed world. Some 50% or more of these individuals would have died before reaching adulthood had it not been for surgical intervention in infancy and childhood. This dramatic success story has resulted in a large and growing population of young adults who require lifelong cardiac and noncardiac services.[1]

It is now well appreciated that most patients with CHD who have had their lives transformed by surgical intervention(s) had reparative, and not curative, surgery. Many of them face the prospect of further operations, arrhythmias, complications, and, especially if managed inappropriately, an increased risk of heart failure and premature death. There are approximately 1 million adults with CHD in the United States.[2] This number will continue to grow as more and more children become adults. With current advances in cardiac surgery and perioperative care and a better understanding of CHD, more than 85% of infants are expected to reach adulthood. A 400% increase in adult outpatient clinic workload was reported in the 1990s in Canada.[3] More recently, data from the Province of Quebec[4] confirmed this exponential growth in numbers and, in addition, demonstrated the increasing complexity of CHD in persons surviving to adulthood (Fig. 1-1). In the United Kingdom the need for follow-up of patients older than the age of 16 years with CHD of moderate to severe complexity has been estimated at 1600 new cases per year.[5] Furthermore, there are patients with structural and/or valvular CHD who present late during adulthood.[6] Most of these patients will also require and benefit from expert care for their adult CHD (ACHD). In general, attendance at a regional ACHD care center is required for:

- The initial assessment of suspected or known CHD
- Follow-up and continuing care of patients with moderate and complex lesions
- Further surgical and nonsurgical intervention
- Risk assessment and support for noncardiac surgery and pregnancy

The majority of patients with ACHD will still require local follow-up for geographic, social, and/or health economic reasons, however. Primary care physicians and general adult cardiologists must, therefore, have some understanding of the health needs and special issues in the general medical management of this relatively new adult patient population. Importantly, community and hospital physicians must recognize promptly when to refer these patients to an expert center. Published management guidelines may be of assistance in this process.[7–9]

A new set of recommendations have been created following the American College Cardiology/American Heart Association[8] and the European Society of Cardiology Working Group on Grown Up Congenital Heart Disease (GUCH)[9] guidelines regarding care delivery systems, improved access to health care, staffing, planning, and training objectives.

Organization of Care

Care of the patient with ACHD should be coordinated by regional or national ACHD centers, fulfilling the following purposes:

- To optimize care for all patients with ACHD and to reduce errors in their care
- To consolidate specialized resources required for the care of patients with ACHD
- To provide sufficient patient numbers to facilitate specialist training for medical and nonmedical personnel and to maintain staff and faculty competence and special skills in the treatment of ACHD
- To facilitate research in this unique population, to work toward the ideal of evidence-based care, and to promote a more complete understanding of the late pathophysiology and determinants of late outcomes in these patients
- To offer educational opportunities and continuous support to primary caregivers, cardiologists, and surgeons so that they may contribute optimally to patient management
- To provide a readily available source of information and expert opinion for patients and doctors
- To help organize support groups for patients
- To provide information to the government and to act as the representative of the specialty

Approximately one regional expert center should be created to serve a population of 5 to 10 million people:

- Adults with moderate and complex CHD (Box 1-1) will require periodic evaluation at a regional ACHD center; they will also benefit from maintaining regular contact with a primary care physician.
- Existing pediatric cardiology programs should identify or help to develop an ACHD center to which transfer of care should be made when patients achieve adult age.
- Similarly, adult cardiology and cardiac surgical centers and community cardiologists should have a referral relationship with a regional ACHD center. Transition clinics should be established (ideally as a joint venture), and timely discussions for risks of pregnancy/family planning and appropriate advice on contraception should be provided.
- All emergency care facilities should have an affiliation with a regional ACHD center.
- Physicians without specific training and expertise in ACHD should manage only adults with moderate and complex CHD in collaboration with colleagues with advanced training and experience in the care of patients, usually based in a regional ACHD center.
- Patients with moderate or complex CHD may require admission or transfer to a regional ACHD center for urgent or acute care.
- Most cardiac catheterization and electrophysiologic procedures for adults with moderate and complex CHD should be performed at the regional ACHD center, where appropriate personnel and equipment are available. If such procedures are planned at the local cardiac center, prior consultation with ACHD cardiology colleagues should be sought.
- Cardiovascular surgical procedures in adults with moderate and complex CHD should generally be performed in a regional ACHD center where there is specific experience in the surgical care of these patients.
- Appropriate links should be made for provision of noncardiac surgery; and the need for developing an integrated team of high-risk obstetricians, anesthetists, and ACHD cardiologists cannot be overstated.

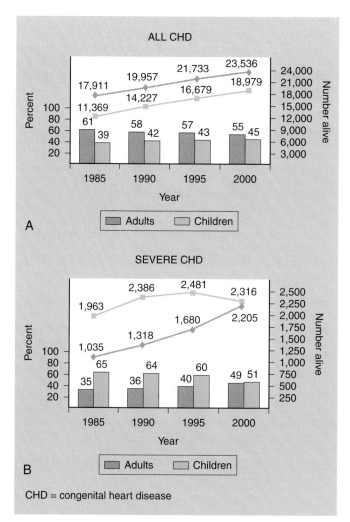

ALL CHD

SEVERE CHD

CHD = congenital heart disease

Figure 1-1 Numbers and proportions of adults and children with all (**A**) and severe (**B**) congenital heart disease in 1985, 1990, 1995, and 2000. (After Marelli AJ, Mackie AS, Ionescu-Ittu R et al. *Congenital heart disease in the general population: changing prevalence and age distribution. Circulation 2007;115:163-172. Copyright, American Heart Association.*)

- Each regional center should participate in a medical and surgical database aimed at defining and improving outcomes in adults with CHD. Appropriate clinical records should be kept in the regional ACHD center and be shared with the primary care provider and with the patient.

Manpower, Training, and Research

The importance of ACHD as a subspecialty of cardiology has been recognized by the Calman U.K. Training Advisory Committee and the 2006 Bethesda Conference. Basic training in adult CHD is now mandatory for adult cardiology trainees. It is also recognized that selected individuals will need to train more comprehensively in the field. The American College of Cardiology Task Force states that a minimum of 2 years of full-time ACHD training is needed to become clinically competent, to contribute academically, and to train others effectively.[9] The small number of available centers that can offer comprehensive training in ACHD at present, coupled with limited resources, remains an obstacle in achieving this goal.[10] Training programs for other key staff (e.g., nurses, obstetricians, imaging staff, technicians, psychologists) in ACHD teams

should also be established. The first set of guidelines for the management of the adult with CHD, commissioned by the Canadian Cardiovascular Society, was recently revised by an international panel of experts[7] and is now available on the Internet (http://www.cachnet.org). These guidelines have been endorsed and have been developed further by North American, European, and other professional bodies. National and international curricula in ACHD are being developed to disseminate existing information on the management of the adult patient with CHD and to stimulate research. A new group of specialized cardiologists in ACHD is required to ensure the delivery of high-quality lifelong care for this patient population, which has benefited so much from early pediatric cardiology and cardiac surgery expertise.[11]

Educational material to guide ACHD patients is being developed. Advice on employability, insurance, pregnancy and contraception, exercise, endocarditis prophylaxis, and noncardiac surgery is being made available. Barriers to multidisciplinary services should be challenged with the objective of making needed expert resources available for all adult patients with CHD who need them.[12]

There is a pressing need for clinical research on potential factors influencing the late outcome of this expanding patient population.[13] Furthermore, the effects of medical, catheter, and surgical intervention need to be assessed prospectively. Clinical and research resources must, therefore, be secured for this large patient population.

Transfer of Care

Structural plans for transition from pediatric to adult care for CHD are being developed. Different models are applied, depending on local circumstances. Individual patient education regarding the diagnosis and specific health behaviors should be part of this process. Comprehensive information including diagnosis, previous surgical and/or catheter interventions, medical therapy, investigations, current outpatient clinic reports, and medication should be kept by the patient and also be sent to the ACHD facility. Advice on contraception for female patients is paramount because sexual activity should be anticipated. The development of a patient electronic health "passport" is to be encouraged and is of particular relevance to patients with complex diagnoses and numerous previous interventions.

There is international consensus that the multiple needs of this population discussed in this and other chapters of this textbook can best be fulfilled through national frameworks with the following objectives:
- To establish a network of regional centers for the adult with CHD
- To foster professional specialist training in ACHD
- To coordinate national or local registries for adults with CHD
- To facilitate research in ACHD

Such a model of care, training, and research for the adult with CHD would be in keeping with the 2001 Bethesda Conference and recent U.K. National Health Service guidelines and has been implemented for some time in Canada. Within this framework, general cardiologists with an interest need to be supported locally in district general hospitals and be facilitated to work with both tertiary and primary care physicians to provide for the adult patient with CHD. Pediatric cardiology expertise must be utilized and transition care programs developed to ensure seamless care for this patient population. Patients need to realize that lifelong follow-up is required for many of them and that they may well require further intervention—medical and/or surgical. Databases shared among pediatric, adult, and nontertiary care centers, and easy access to regional facilities, should be in place to promote this multilevel collaboration. Patient advocacy groups (http://www.achaheart.org and http://www.guch.org.uk) need to continue to develop and participate actively in this dynamic process.

CONCLUSION

Adults with CHD are no longer rare or odd. Many or most need expert lifelong care. The time has come for national ACHD networks, supported by individual departments of health, relevant professional societies, and funding bodies, to care for the beneficiaries of this astonishing success story in the management of CHD.

REFERENCES

1. Perloff JK, Warnes C. Congenital heart diseases in adults: a new cardiovascular specialty. Circulation 2001;84:1881–1890.
2. Warnes CA, Liberthson R, Danielson GK, et al. Task force 1: the changing profile of congenital heart disease in adult life. J Am Coll Cardiol 2001;37:1170–1175.
3. Gatzoulis MA, Hechter S, Siu SC, Webb GD. Outpatient clinics for adults with congenital heart disease: increasing workload and evolving patterns of referral. Heart 1999;81:57–61.
4. Marelli AJ, Mackie AS, Ionescu-Ittu R, et al. Congenital heart disease in the general population: changing prevalence and age distribution. Circulation 2007;115:163–172.
5. Wren C, O'Sullivan JJ. Survival with congenital heart disease and need for follow-up in adult life. Heart 2001;85:438–443.
6. Brickner ME, Hillis LD, Lange RA. Congenital heart disease in adults. N Engl J Med 2000;342:334–342.
7. Silversides CK, Marelli A, Beauchesne L, et al. Canadian Cardiovascular Society 2009 Consensus Conference on the management of adults with congenital heart disease: executive summary. Can J Cardiol 2010;26:143–50.
8. Warnes CA, Williams RG, Bashore TM, et al. ACC/AHA 2008 guidelines for the management of adults with congenital heart disease: a report of the American College of Cardiology/American Heart Association Task Force on Practice Guidelines (Writing Committee to Develop Guidelines on the Management of Adults With Congenital Heart Disease). Developed in Collaboration With the American Society of Echocardiography, Heart Rhythm Society, International Society for Adult Congenital Heart Disease, Society for Cardiovascular Angiography and Interventions, and Society of Thoracic Surgeons. J Am Coll Cardiol 2008;52:e1–e121.
9. Baumgartner H, Bonhoeffer P, De Groot NM, et al. ESC Guidelines for the management of grown-up congenital heart disease (new version 2010): The Task Force on the Management of Grown-up Congenital Heart Disease of the European Society of Cardiology. Eur Heart J 2010 doi:10.1093/eurheartj/ehq249.
10. Report of the British Cardiac Society Working Party. Grown-up congenital heart (GUCH) disease: current needs and provision of service for adolescents and adults with congenital heart disease in the UK. Heart 2002;88(Suppl 1):i1–i14.
11. Karamlou T, Diggs BS, Person T, et al. National practice patterns for management of adult congenital heart disease: operation by pediatric heart surgeons decreases in-hospital death. Circulation 2008;118:2345–2352.
12. Gatzoulis MA. Adult congenital heart disease: education, education, education. Nature Clin Pract Cardiovasc Med 2006;3:2–3.
13. Williams RG, Pearson GD, Barst RJ, et al. Report of the National Heart, Lung, and Blood Institute Working Group on research in adult congenital heart disease. J Am Coll Cardiol 2006;47:701–707.

2

Cardiac Morphology and Nomenclature

SIEW YEN HO

The care of adults with congenital heart malformations has evolved to become a specialty in its own right. The malformations are conceived by the general cardiologist as extremely complex, requiring a sound knowledge of embryologic development for their appreciation. The defects are so varied, and can occur in so many different combinations, that to base their descriptions on embryologic origins is at best speculative and at worst utterly confusing. Fortunately, in recent decades, great strides have been made in enabling these malformations to be more readily recognizable to all practitioners who care for the patient born with a malformed heart. Undoubtedly, the introduction of the system known as "sequential segmental analysis"—hand in hand with developments in angiography and cross-sectional echocardiography—has revolutionized diagnosis.[1-5] The key feature of this approach is akin to the computer buff's WYSIWYG (what you see is what you get) except that in this case it is WYSIWYD (what you see is what you describe). Best of all, it does not require knowledge of the secrets of cardiac embryogenesis!

Cardiac morphology applied to the adult patient with congenital heart disease (CHD) is often not simply a larger version of that in children. Cardiac structures grow and evolve with the patient. Structural changes occur after surgical palliation and correction. Even without intervention in infancy, progression into adulthood can bring with it changes in ventricular mass, calcification or dysplasia of valves, fibrosis of the conduction tissues, and so on. It is, nevertheless, fundamental to diagnose the native defect. The focus of this chapter is on the sequential segmental analysis and the terminology used.

Sequential Segmental Analysis: General Philosophy

To be able to diagnose the simplest communication between the atria to the most complex of malformations, the sequential segmental approach[3-7] (also known as the European approach on account of the promoters of the original concepts) as described here requires that normality be proven rather than being assumed. Thus, the patient with an isolated atrial septal defect in the setting of a normally constructed heart undergoes the same rigorous analysis as the patient with congenitally corrected transposition associated with multiple intracardiac defects.

Any heart can be considered in three segments: the atrial chambers, the ventricular mass, and the great arteries (Fig. 2-1). By examining the arrangement of the component parts of the heart and their interconnections, each case is described in a sequential manner. There are limited possibilities in which the individual chambers or arteries making up the three segments can be arranged. Equally, there are limited ways in which the chambers and arteries can be related to one another. The approach begins by examining the position of the atrial chambers. Thereafter, the atrioventricular junction and the ventriculoarterial junctions are analyzed in terms of connections and relations. Once the segmental anatomy of any heart has been determined, it can then be examined for associated malformations; these need to be listed in full. The examination is completed by describing the cardiac position and relationship to other thoracic structures. The segmental combinations provide the framework to build up the complete picture, because in most cases the associated lesions produce the hemodynamic derangement.

The philosophy of segmental analysis is founded on the morphologic method (Box 2-1). Thus, chambers are recognized according to their morphology rather than their position.[3,6,7] In the normally structured heart, the right-sided atrium is the systemic venous atrium, but this is not always the case in the malformed heart. Indeed, the very essence of some cardiac malformations is that the chambers are not in their anticipated locations. It is also a fact of normal cardiac anatomy that the right-sided heart chambers are not precisely right sided; nor are the left chambers completely left sided (Fig. 2-2).[8] Each chamber has intrinsic features that allow it to be described as "morphologically right" or "morphologically left" irrespective of location or distortion by the malformation.[9,10] Features selected as criteria are those parts that are most universally present even when the hearts are malformed. In this regard, venous connections, for example, are not chosen as arbiters of rightness or leftness of atrial morphology. The atrial appendages are more reliable for identification. In practice, not all criteria for all the chambers can be identified in the living patient with a malformed heart. In some cases there may only be one characteristic feature for a chamber, and in a few cases rightness or leftness can be made only by inference. Nevertheless, once the identities of the chambers are known, the connections of the segments can be established. Although spatial relationships—or relations—between adjacent chambers are relevant, they are secondary to the diagnosis of abnormal chamber connections. After all, the connections, like plumbing, determine the flow through the heart, although patterns of flow are then modified by associated malformations and hemodynamic conditions. The caveat remains that valvular morphology in rare cases (e.g., an imperforate valve) allows for description of connection between chambers, although not in terms of flow until the imperforate valve is rendered patent surgically or by other means.

Morphology of the Cardiac Chambers

ATRIAL CHAMBERS

All hearts possess two atrial chambers—albeit they are sometimes combined into a common chamber because of complete or virtual absence of the atrial septum. Most often, each atrial chamber has an appendage, a venous component, a vestibule, and a shared atrial septum. Because the last three components can be markedly abnormal or lacking, they cannot be used as arbiters of morphologic rightness or leftness. There remains the appendage that distinguishes the morphologically right from the morphologically left atrium. Externally, the right appendage is characteristically triangular with a broad base, whereas the left appendage is small and hook shaped with crenellations (see Figs. 2-2 and 2-3). It has been argued that shape and size are the consequence of hemodynamics and are unreliable as criteria.[11]

Internally, however, the distinguishing features are clear.[12] The terminal crest is a muscular band that separates the pectinate portion—the right appendage—from the rest of the atrium. The sinus node is located in this structure at the superior cavoatrial junction. Because the appendage is so large in the morphologically right atrium, the array of pectinate muscles occupies all the parietal wall and extends to the inferior wall toward the orifice of the coronary sinus (see Fig. 2-3). In contrast, the entrance (os) to the left appendage is narrow, the terminal crest is absent, and the pectinate muscles are limited. The smoother-walled morphologically left atrium, however, has on its epicardial aspect a prominent

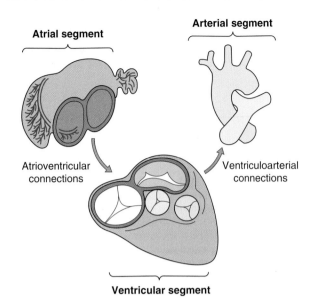

Figure 2-1 The three segments of the heart analyzed sequentially.

BOX 2-1 SEQUENTIAL SEGMENTAL ANALYSIS

- ☐ *Determine arrangement of the atrial chambers (situs)*
- ☐ *Determine ventricular morphology and topology:*
  Analyze atrioventricular junctions:
  Type of atrioventricular connection
  Morphology of atrioventricular valve
- ☐ *Determine morphology of great arteries:*
  Analyze ventriculoarterial junctions:
  Type of ventriculoarterial connection
  Morphology of arterial valves
  Infundibular morphology
  Arterial relationships
- ☐ *Catalog associated malformations*
- ☐ *Determine cardiac position:*
  Position of heart within the chest
  Orientation of cardiac apex

---

venous channel, the coronary sinus, which can aid in its identification (see Figs. 2-2 and 2-3). Where the septum is well developed, the muscular rim around the oval fossa is indicative of the morphologically right atrium, because the flap valve is on the left atrial side.

VENTRICLES

Ventricular morphology is a little more complex than atrial morphology in that some malformations may have only one ventricular chamber or one large ventricle associated with a tiny ventricle.

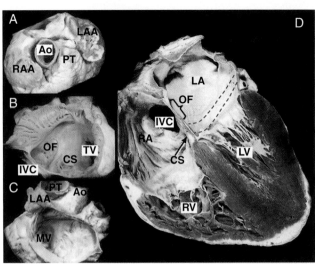

Figure 2-3 **A,** The right and left atrial appendages have distinctively different shapes. **B,** The internal aspect of the right atrium displays the array of pectinate muscles arising from the terminal crest. The oval fossa is surrounded by a muscular rim. **C,** The internal aspect of the left atrium is mainly smooth walled. The entrance (os) to the left appendage is narrow. **D,** This four-chamber section shows the more apical attachment of the septal leaflet of the tricuspid valve relative to the mitral valve. Pectinate muscles occupy the inferior right atrial wall, whereas the left atrial wall is smooth. The *broken blue lines* indicate the course of the coronary sinus passing beneath the inferior aspect of the left atrium. Ao, aorta; CS, coronary sinus; IVC, inferior vena cava; LA, left atrium; LAA, left atrial appendage; LV, left ventricle; MV, mitral valve; OF, oval fossa; PT, pulmonary trunk; RA, right atrium; RAA, right atrial appendage; RV, right ventricle; TV, tricuspid valve.

Normal ventricles are considered as having three component parts ("tripartite"; see Chapter 46): inlet, outlet, and trabecular portions.[13,14] There are no discrete boundaries between the parts, but each component is relatively distinct (Fig. 2-4). The inlet portion contains the inlet (or atrioventricular) valve and its tension apparatus. Thus, it extends from the atrioventricular junction to the papillary muscles. The trabecular part extends beyond the papillary muscles to the ventricular apex. Although the trabeculations are mainly in the apical portion, the inlet part is not completely devoid of trabeculations. The outlet part leading toward the great arteries is in the cephalad portion. It is usually a smooth muscular structure, termed the *infundibulum,* in the morphologically right ventricle. In contrast, the outlet part of the morphologically left ventricle is partly fibrous, owing to the area of aortic-mitral fibrous continuity. The mitral valve is always found in the morphologically left ventricle, and the tricuspid valve is always in the morphologically right ventricle, although these features have no value when the ventricle has no inlet. Similarly, the outlets are not the most reliable markers.

Figure 2-2 These four views of the endocast from a normal heart show the intricate spatial relationships between left (red) and right (blue) heart chambers and the spiral relationships between the aorta and pulmonary trunk. The atrial chambers are posterior and to the right of their respective ventricular chambers. Note the central location of the aortic root. The right atrial appendage has a rough endocardial surface owing to the extensive array of pectinate muscles. The left atrial appendage is hooklike. The left and inferior views show the course of the coronary sinus relative to the left atrium. Ao, aorta; CS, coronary sinus; LA, left atrium; LV, left ventricle; PT, pulmonary trunk; RA, right atrium; RV, right ventricle.

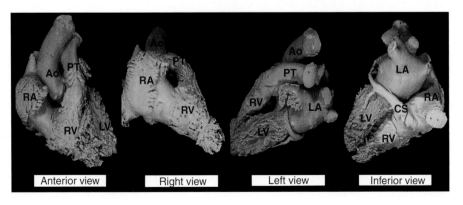

Anterior view | Right view | Left view | Inferior view

Of the three ventricular components, the distinguishing marker is the apical trabecular portion. Whenever there are two ventricular chambers they are nearly always of complementary morphology, one being of morphologically right and the other of morphologically left type. Only one case has been reported of two chambers of right ventricular morphology.[15] Characteristically, the trabeculations are coarse in the morphologically right ventricle and form a fine crisscross pattern in the morphologically left ventricle. Thus, no matter how small or rudimentary, if one or more component parts are lacking, the morphology of a ventricle can be identified.

In addition to right and left morphology there is a third ventricular morphology. This is the rare variety in which the trabeculations are coarser than the right morphology and is described as a solitary and indeterminate ventricle (Fig. 2-5). There is no other chamber in the ventricular mass. More often, the situation is one of a large ventricle associated with a much smaller ventricle that lacks its inlet component (see Fig. 2-5). Because its inlet is missing, the smaller ventricle is described as rudimentary, but it may also lack its outlet component. The third component—the apical portion—is always present. It may be so small as to make identification impossible, but its morphology can be inferred after identifying the larger ventricle. The rudimentary ventricles are usually smaller than constituted ventricles, but not always. Normal ventricles can be hypoplastic, a classic example being the right ventricle in pulmonary atresia with intact ventricular septum (see Fig. 2-5) (see Chapter 46). Size, undoubtedly important in clinical management, is independent of the number of components a ventricle has.

In clinical investigations, the nature of trabeculations may not be readily identifiable. For instance, the fine trabeculations in the hypertrophied morphologically left ventricle can appear thick. Adjuncts for diagnosis must be considered. In this respect, a review of normal ventricular morphology is helpful. The inlet component of the right ventricle is very different from that of the left ventricle. The tricuspid valve has an extensive septal leaflet together with an anterosuperior and a mural (inferior) leaflet. Tethering of the septal leaflet to the septum is a hallmark of the tricuspid valve. At the atrioventricular level, its attachment—or hinge point—is more apically positioned than the point at which the mitral valve abuts the septum (see Fig. 2-3D). This is an important diagnostic feature, recognizable in the four-chamber section. In contrast, the mitral valve has no tendinous cords tethering it to the septum. The normal, deeply wedged, position of the aortic valve between the mitral and tricuspid valves allows direct fibrous continuity between the two left heart valves (see Fig. 2-4). Consequently, the left ventricular outlet lies between the ventricular septum and the anterior (aortic) leaflet of the mitral valve. This passage is detected in cross sections as a cleavage or recess between the septum and the mitral valve. Both the anterior (aortic) and posterior (mural) leaflets of the mitral valve are attached to the two groups of papillary muscles situated in anterolateral and posteromedial positions within the ventricles.

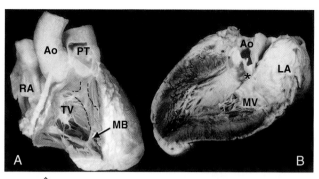
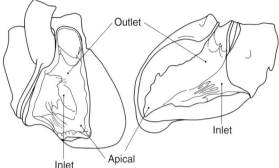

Figure 2-4 **A,** This anterior view of the right ventricle and corresponding diagram show the tripartite configuration of the normal ventricle. The apical portion is filled with coarse trabeculations. The pulmonary valve is separated from the tricuspid valve by the supraventricular crest, which is an infolding of the ventricular wall. The septomarginal trabeculation is marked by the *dotted lines.* **B,** The left ventricle also has three portions, but its outlet portion is sandwiched between the septum and the mitral valve. The apical trabeculations are fine, and the upper part of the septum is smooth. There is fibrous continuity (*asterisk*) between aortic and mitral valves. MB, moderator band. Other abbreviations are as in Figure 2-3.

More accurately, the respective papillary muscles are superiorly and inferomedially situated, as depicted on magnetic resonance imaging.

The normal outlets also have distinctive morphologies. As described earlier, the right ventricular outlet is completely muscular. The conical muscular infundibulum raises the pulmonary valve to occupy the highest position of all the cardiac valves. The infundibulum is not discrete, because it is a continuation of the ventricular wall. In its posterior and medial parts, it continues into the supraventricular crest formed in part by the ventriculoinfundibular fold (see Fig. 2-4). The crest distances the tricuspid valve from the pulmonary valve. Although an outlet septum

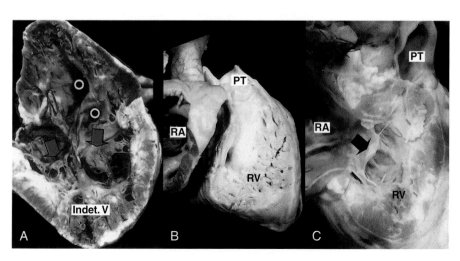

Figure 2-5 **A,** The solitary and indeterminate ventricle (Indet. V) displayed in "clam" fashion to show both right and left atrioventricular valves (*solid arrows*) and both arterial outlets (O). **B,** This heart, with absence of the right atrioventricular connection, shows the rudimentary right ventricle lacking its inlet portion. **C,** This hypoplastic right ventricle in a heart with pulmonary atresia has a muscle-bound apical portion and a small tricuspid valve at its inlet portion (*arrow*). PT, pulmonary trunk; RA, right atrium; RV, right ventricle.

was described previously, close examination shows that this structure is diminutive or lacking in the normal heart but comes into prominence in hearts with malformed outlets, exemplified by the tetralogy of Fallot and the double-outlet right ventricle (see Chapters 43 and 50).[16,17] On the septal aspect, the ventriculoinfundibular fold is clasped between the limbs of another muscular structure characteristic of the right ventricle. This is the septomarginal trabeculation, which is like a Y-shaped strap (see Fig. 2-4). The fusion of its limbs to the fold of musculature forms the supraventricular crest. Further muscular bundles—the septoparietal trabeculations—cross from the crest to the free (parietal) ventricular wall in the outlet portion. The medial papillary muscle of the tricuspid valve inserts into the posterior limb of the septomarginal trabeculation. The body of this trabeculation extends into the trabecular component, where it gives rise to the moderator band that passes across the cavity of the right ventricle to reach the free (parietal) wall. This is no longer the outlet region, but its features are useful diagnostic clues for recognizing a right ventricle. In contrast, the upper part of the septum lining the left ventricular outlet is smooth (see Fig. 2-4). There is no equivalent of the supraventricular crest.

GREAT ARTERIES

The great arteries are recognized by their branching patterns rather than the arterial valves, because the semilunar leaflets are indistinguishable. The coronary arteries arise from the aortic sinuses. As the aorta ascends in a cephalad direction it arches to the left and gives rise to the neck and arm arteries before turning inferiorly to become the descending thoracic aorta. In adults, the pulmonary trunk is recognized as the great artery that bifurcates into the right and left pulmonary arteries. A third vessel, the arterial duct, may be visualized in infancy. In the normal heart the pulmonary trunk passes anterior and to the left of the aortic root. The aorta and pulmonary trunk ascend in a spiral relationship, with the aorta arching over the right pulmonary artery (see Fig. 2-2).

When there are two great arteries it is an easy matter to distinguish the aorta from the pulmonary trunk. The aortic sinuses give origin to the coronary arteries in the vast majority of cases. At the arch the aorta gives branches to the head, neck, and arm. Although some of its branches may be absent in malformations, or its arch may be interrupted, the aorta is the vessel that gives origin to at least one of the coronary arteries and the greater part of the systemic supply to the upper body. The pulmonary trunk rarely gives origin to the coronary artery. It usually bifurcates into the left and right pulmonary arteries (Fig. 2-6). When only one great artery is found this is frequently presumed to be a common arterial trunk (truncus arteriosus) (see Chapter 37). However, care must be taken in making this diagnosis to avoid missing an atretic aorta or atretic pulmonary trunk (see later). A common arterial trunk is defined as one that leaves the ventricular mass via a common arterial valve and supplies the coronary, systemic, and pulmonary arteries directly (see Chapter 37). This needs to be dis-

tinguished from the situation often referred to as "truncus" type IV, in which the solitary trunk does not give rise to any intrapericardial pulmonary arteries (a severe form of tetralogy with pulmonary atresia; see Chapter 44) (see Fig. 2-6). Collateral arteries that usually arise from the descending aorta supply the lungs. A case may be made for such an arterial trunk to be either an aorta or a truncus. For simplicity, this is described as a solitary arterial trunk.

Arrangement of Atrial Chambers

The first step in segmental analysis is determining the atrial arrangement. As discussed earlier, the morphology of the appendage with the extent of the pectinate muscles permits distinction of morphologic rightness or leftness. Even with juxtaposition of the appendages, atrial arrangement can be determined. There are only four ways in which two atrial chambers of either right or left morphology can be combined. The first two variants occur with lateralization of the atrial chambers. The arrangement is described as usual (or situs solitus) when the morphologically right atrium is on the right and the morphologically left atrium is on the left. There is mirror image of the usual arrangement (situs inversus) when the chambers are on the wrong sides (see Fig. 2-7). In the other two variants, the appendages and arrangement of pectinate muscles are isomeric (see Chapter 53).[12] There are bilaterally right or bilaterally left morphologies (Fig. 2-7).

Because direct morphologic criteria are not always accessible by the clinician, indirect ways must be used to determine situs. Bronchial morphology identifiable from the penetrated chest radiograph is a

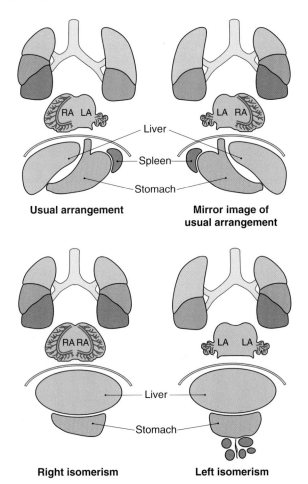

Usual arrangement   **Mirror image of usual arrangement**

Right isomerism   **Left isomerism**

Figure 2-7 These four panels depict the four patterns of atrial arrangement and corresponding arrangement of the lungs, main bronchi, and abdominal organs usually associated with each type. The right main bronchus is short, whereas the left main bronchus is long. LA, left atrium; RA, right atrium.

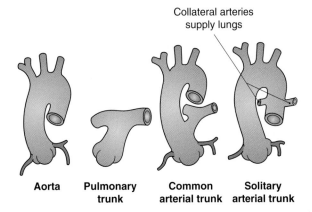

Aorta   Pulmonary trunk   Common arterial trunk   Solitary arterial trunk

Figure 2-6 Four major categories of great arteries. In contrast to the common arterial trunk, the solitary arterial trunk lacks connections with central pulmonary arteries.

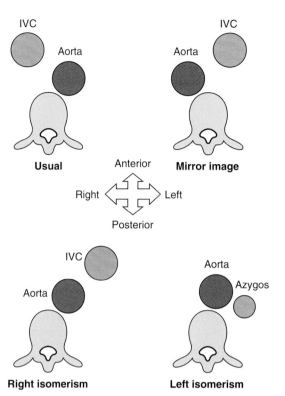

Figure 2-8 The locations of the aorta and the inferior vena cava (IVC) relative to the spine can provide clues to atrial arrangement.

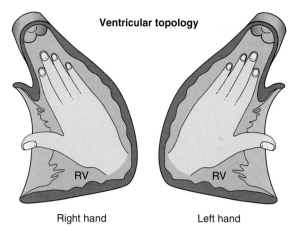

Figure 2-9 Ventricular topology is determined by placing the palm, figuratively speaking, on the septal surface of the morphologically right ventricle (RV) such that the wrist is in the apical portion, the thumb is in the inlet, and the fingers are pointing to the outlet.

good guide, because there is good correlation between atrial and bronchial morphology (see Fig. 2-7). Another method is to study the relative positions of the great vessels just below the diaphragm using imaging techniques such as cross-sectional echocardiography or magnetic resonance imaging. This allows inference to be made of most cases of isomerism (Fig. 2-8). In patients with isomeric situs, the great vessels lie to the same side of the spine. In cases of left isomerism, when the inferior vena cava is interrupted and continued via a posterior hemiazygos vein, as in 78% of postmortem cases,[12] it lies to the same side of the spine as the aorta but posteriorly (see Chapter 53).

In cases with lateralized atrial chambers, the atrial arrangement is harmonious with the remaining thoracoabdominal organs, so that the morphologically right atrium is on the same side as the liver and the morphologically left atrium is on the same side as the stomach and spleen (see Fig. 2-7). The isomeric forms are usually associated with disordered arrangement of the abdominal organs (visceral heterotaxy) (see Chapter 53). Isomeric right arrangement of the appendages is frequently found with asplenia, whereas isomeric left is found with polysplenia (see Fig. 2-7).[18] These associations, however, are not absolute.[6,19,20]

Determination of Ventricular Morphology and Topology

The morphology of the ventricles, the second segment of the heart, was described previously. Briefly, three morphologies are recognized. These are right, left, and indeterminate (see Figs. 2-4 and 2-5). In hearts with two ventricular chambers, however, it is necessary to describe ventricular topology that is the spatial relationship of one ventricle to the other. There are two discrete topologic patterns that are mirror images of each other. Right-hand topology is the normal pattern. Determination of ventricular topology requires, first, identification of the morphologically right ventricle. If the palmar surface of the right hand can be placed, figuratively speaking, on the septal surface so that the wrist is at the apex, the thumb in the inlet, and the fingers toward the outlet, then this is the right-hand pattern (Fig. 2-9). If only the palm of the left hand can be placed on the septal surface of the right ventricle in

the same manner, then left-hand topology is described. This convention allows analysis of the atrioventricular junction in hearts with isomeric arrangement of the atrial appendages (see later). It is also helpful to the surgeon in predicting the course of the ventricular conduction bundles. Ventricular topology in univentricular atrioventricular connections (see later) with dominant left ventricle is inferred from the larger ventricle, because the rudimentary right ventricle lacks at least the inlet portion of the three ventricular components to position the palm properly. Ventricular topology cannot be described for hearts with solitary and indeterminate ventricles.

Analysis of the Atrioventricular Junction

Being the union of atria with the ventricles, the atrioventricular junction varies according to the nature of the adjoining segments. Analysis of the junction involves, first, determining how the atrial chambers are arranged and the morphology (and topology where appropriate) of the chambers within the ventricular mass. Second, the type of atrioventricular junction is described according to how the atria connect to the ventricles. Third, the morphology of the atrioventricular valves guarding the junction is noted.

The arrangement of the atria influences description of the atrioventricular junction according to whether they are lateralized (usual or mirror image of usual) or isomeric. On the other hand, the ventricles exert their influence depending on whether two ventricular chambers, or only one, are in connection with the atrial chambers.

When lateralized atria each connect to a separate ventricle there are only two possibilities. Connections of morphologically appropriate atria to morphologically appropriate ventricles are described as *concordant* (Fig. 2-10). When atria are connected to morphologically inappropriate ventricles, the connections are termed *discordant* (see Fig. 2-10). In contrast, when an isomeric arrangement of the atrial appendages exists, and each atrium connects to its own ventricle, the connections are neither concordant nor discordant. Instead, the connections are described as *ambiguous* (see Fig. 2-10). It is in this setting that identification of ventricular topology is particularly useful. Thus, the three connections—concordant, discordant, and ambiguous—have in common the fact that each atrium is connected to its own ventricle. Self-evidently, these connections can exist only when there are two ventricles, that is, biventricular connections.

There remains a further group of atrioventricular connections. Irrespective of their arrangement, the atria in these hearts connect with only one ventricle, that is, univentricular connections. The distinction from biventricular connections is that even though there are two ventricles in most cases of univentricular connection only one ventricle makes the connection with the atrial mass (Fig. 2-11). Hearts with univentricular atrioventricular connections have been the subject of

Figure 2-10 Biventricular atrioventricular connections are present when each atrium connects to its own ventricle. This diagram depicts the variations possible in the four patterns of atrial arrangement. Ambiguous atrioventricular connections are formed in hearts with isomeric arrangement of the atrial chambers. LA, left atrium; LV, left ventricle; RA, right atrium; RV, right ventricle.

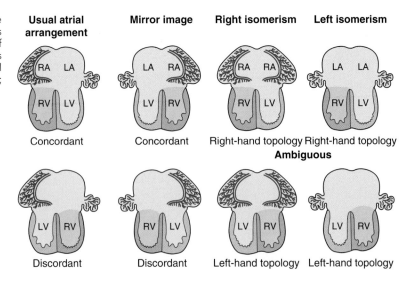

arguments over terminology. Central to the controversy is the issue of the singular nature of the ventricular mass—a single or common ventricle.[21,22] In fact, the majority of hearts with these variants have two ventricles. The ventricles are usually markedly different in size because one of them is not connected to an atrium. Thus, the smaller ventricle lacking its inlet portion is both rudimentary and incomplete. The exemplar pattern is when both atria connect to the same ventricle—a double-inlet connection (Fig. 2-12A) (see Chapter 51). This can be found with any of the four variants of atrial arrangement and when the connecting ventricle is any of the three morphologies (see Fig. 2-11). The atria can be connected to the morphologically left ventricle, in which case the morphologically right ventricle is rudimentary. Similarly, the connection can be to a dominant morphologically right ventricle when the left ventricle is rudimentary. Rarely there is only one ventricle; this is described as a solitary and indeterminate ventricle.

Within the group of univentricular connections the remaining two patterns exist when one of the atria has no connection with the underlying ventricular mass (see Fig. 2-11). These patterns are absence of either the right or the left atrioventricular connections (see Fig. 2-12). Absent connections are the most common causes of atrioventricular valvular atresia (see Chapter 52). The classic examples of tricuspid atresia and mitral atresia have absence of the right or left atrioventricular connection, respectively, instead of the affected valve being imperforate. Although these are convenient shorthand terms, it is speculative to speak of "tricuspid" or "mitral" atresia in these settings when the valve is absent! Either type of absent connection can be found with the other atrium connected to a dominant left, dominant right, or a solitary and indeterminate ventricle. When the connecting ventricle is of left or right morphology, then, as with double inlet, the complementary ventricle is rudimentary and incomplete.

Figure 2-11 The three types of univentricular atrioventricular (AV) connections are double inlet, absent right, and absent left. Variations then exist in atrial arrangement and morphology of the connecting ventricle. LV, left ventricle; RV, right ventricle.

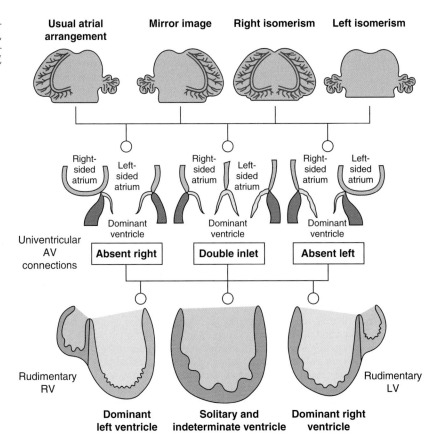

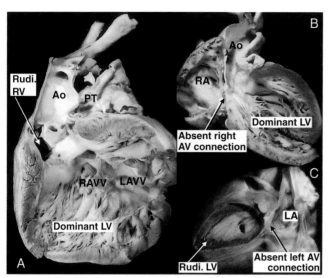

Figure 2-12 **A,** This heart with double inlet shows both right (RAVV) and left (LAVV) atrioventricular valves opening to the same dominant left ventricle (LV). The pulmonary outlet is from the left ventricle, whereas the aorta arises from the rudimentary right ventricle (Rudi. RV). **B,** This heart with absent right atrioventricular (AV) connection shows the blind muscular floor of the right atrium. The left atrium connects to the dominant LV. This section is taken inferior to the rudimentary right ventricle. **C,** This left inferior view of a heart with absent left AV connection shows the rudimentary left ventricle (Rudi. LV) and a small ventricular septal defect, which allows communication with the dominant right ventricle. Ao, aorta; PT, pulmonary trunk.

In the presence of a dominant and a rudimentary ventricle, an aid to diagnosis of ventricular morphology is the relative locations of the ventricles. Rudimentary ventricles of right morphology are situated anterosuperiorly, although they may occupy a more rightward or leftward position in the ventricular mass. In contrast, rudimentary left ventricles are found inferiorly, either leftward or rightward.

The morphology of the atrioventricular valves requires description separately (Table 2-1). Valvular morphology can influence type of atrioventricular connection. Imperforateness of a valve has been alluded to previously. Another situation is straddling and overriding. Straddling valve is the situation in which the valve has its tension apparatus inserted across the ventricular septum to two ventricles. Overriding of the valve, in contrast, describes only the opening of the valvular orifice across the septal crest. When a valve straddles, it most often also overrides; and the same is true the other way round. It is, however, the degree of override that determines the atrioventricular connections present (Fig. 2-13).[23] The valve is assigned to the ventricle

TABLE 2-1	Morphology of Atrioventricular Valves
Atrioventricular Connection	*Morphology of Valve*
Concordant, discordant, ambiguous or double inlet	Two patent valves
	One patent + one imperforate valve (right or left)
	One totally committed + one straddling valve (right or left)
	Two straddling valves
	Common valve (may or may not straddle)
Absent right or left atrioventricular connection	Sole valve, totally committed
	Sole valve, straddling

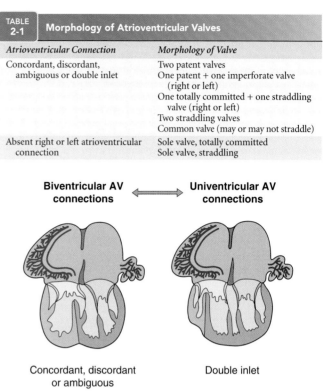

Figure 2-13 The extent of commitment of the valvular orifice determines the atrioventricular (AV) connection. This diagram shows an example of the spectrum between biventricular and univentricular connections depending on the override of the right AV valve.

connected to its greater part. There is then a spectrum between the extremes of one-to-one atrioventricular connections (biventricular) and double-inlet (univentricular) atrioventricular connections.

There is one other pattern that merits special mention. When one atrioventricular connection is absent, the sole valve may be connected exclusively within the dominant ventricle or, rarely, it may straddle and override the ventricular septum. The effect is to produce double outlet from the connecting atrium. The connection is then described as uniatrial and biventricular (Fig. 2-14).[7]

Determination of Morphology of the Great Arteries

As discussed previously, the aorta and pulmonary trunk are distinguished by their branching patterns and origins of the coronary arteries

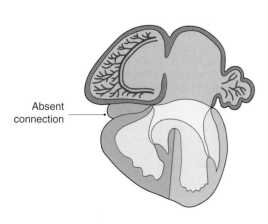

Uniatrial biventricular connection

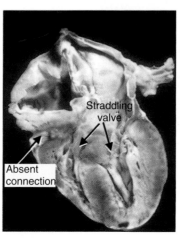

Figure 2-14 An example of uniatrial biventricular connection in a heart with absent right atrioventricular connection. The left atrium opens to both ventricles.

rather than by the arterial valves. These features permit distinction even when the valves are atretic. There are two further variants of great arteries: common arterial trunk and solitary arterial trunk (see Fig. 2-6). When only one great artery is found, however, it must not be assumed to be either of these single-outlet entities. It may be single outlet via an aortic or pulmonary trunk in the presence of an atretic and hypoplastic complementary arterial trunk. A common arterial trunk (also known as *persistent truncus arteriosus*) has a single arterial valve and always gives rise to at least one coronary artery, at least one pulmonary artery, and some of the systemic arteries (see Chapter 37). The pulmonary trunk, or its remnant, and intrapericardial pulmonary arteries are lacking in solitary arterial trunk—also known as truncus type IV or tetralogy with pulmonary atresia and major aortopulmonary collateral arteries (MAPCAs) (see Chapter 44). The lungs are supplied by collateral arteries, which usually arise from the descending aorta.

Analysis of the Ventriculoarterial Junction

To analyze the connections at the ventriculoarterial junction, the precise morphology of both the ventricular and arterial segments must be known. The spatial relationships of the great arteries and the morphology of the ventricular outlets—the infundibular morphology—need to be described separately because they are not determinants of the type of connections. Just as with the atrioventricular junction, concordant and discordant connections are described when each great artery is connected to a ventricle (Fig. 2-15). Thus, "concordant connection" describes connections of the aorta and pulmonary trunk to the appropriate ventricles and "discordant connection" describes the reverse. The combination of usual, or mirror image, atrial arrangement with concordant atrioventricular connections and discordant ventriculoarterial connections gives "complete transposition of the great arteries." This description of so-called *d*-transposition imposes no restrictions on aortic position or developmental implications. Similarly, the segmental combination of usual, or mirror image, atrial arrangement with discordant atrioventricular and ventriculoarterial connections describes "congenitally corrected transposition" (so-called *l*-transposition). The use of the term *transposition* in isolation is meaningless. Double-outlet ventricle exists when one arterial trunk and more than half of the other arterial trunk are connected to the same ventricle, be it of right ventricular, left ventricular, or indeterminate morphology (see Fig. 2-15) (see Chapter 50). Defined in this way, muscular subaortic and subpulmonary outflow tracts (bilateral infundibula) are not essential for diagnosing double-outlet right ventricle. In contrast, a single outlet from the ventricular mass occurs when there is a common or solitary arterial trunk, as defined in the previous section. A single outlet may also be produced by aortic or pulmonary atresia when it is not possible to determine the ventricular origin of the atretic arterial trunk. More usually, atresia is

due to an imperforate valve, in which case the connection can be determined as concordant, discordant, or double outlet.

Description of the morphology of the arterial valves includes stenotic, regurgitant, dysplastic, imperforate, common, or overriding. Overriding valves are assigned to the ventricle supporting more than 50% of their circumference.

The spatial relationship of the aorta relative to the pulmonary trunk is of lesser importance nowadays than in the past era when it was used to predict the ventriculoarterial connections. Two features can be described. One is the orientation of the arterial valves according to anterior/posterior and right/left coordinates. The other is the way the trunks ascend in relation to one another. Usually there is a spiral relationship. Less frequently they ascend in parallel fashion, alerting the investigator to the possible association with intracardiac malformations.

The final feature to note is the morphology of the ventricular outflow tract. The usual arrangement is for the outflow tract of the right ventricle to be a complete muscular infundibulum, whereas there is fibrous continuity between the arterial and atrioventricular valves in the left ventricle. Both outflow tracts can be muscular, as occurs in some cases of double-outlet right ventricle, but this arrangement is not pathognomonic of the lesion (see Chapter 50). Again, although infundibular morphology was used previously to give inference to ventriculoarterial connections, this is no longer necessary with modern noninvasive technologies such as magnetic resonance imaging or echocardiography.[8] Furthermore, direct visualization provides more accurate information of the "plumbing."

Associated Malformations

Sequential segmental analysis cannot be completed without a thorough search for associated lesions. In the majority of cases the chamber combinations will be regular but it is the associated malformation (or malformations) that has the major impact on clinical presentation. Anomalies of venous connections, atrial malformations, lesions of the atrioventricular junction, ventricular septal defects, coronary anomalies, aortic arch obstructions, and so on, must be searched for and recorded.

Location of the Heart

Abnormal position of the heart relative to the thorax is striking. It is usually observed on initial examination but is independent of the chamber combinations. Two features—the cardiac position and apex orientation—need to be described separately. The heart may be mostly in the left chest, approximately midline, or mostly in the right chest. For each of these locations, the cardiac apex may point to the left, to the middle, or to the right. Nominative terms such as *dextrocardia* are nonspecific and may be confusing unless specific description of the direction that the apex of the heart points is also given.

CONCLUSION

The nomenclature for CHD need not be complicated (Table 2-2). The morphologic method overcomes many of the controversies that confer malformed hearts with the undeserved reputation of being anatomically complex. The majority of malformed hearts will have usual chamber connections and relations and will be described segmentally as having usual atrial arrangement, concordant atrioventricular connections, and concordant ventriculoarterial connections. However, in addition, they will have intracardiac defects, such as atrial septal defects (see Chapter 25), atrioventricular septal defects (see Chapter 27), ventricular septal defects (see Chapter 26), or tetralogy of Fallot (see Chapter 43). Some will have associated vascular anomalies such as coarctation (see Chapter 36), vascular slings or rings (see Chapter 38), and so on. Even in these situations, analyzing the heart segmentally is an important checklist that will eliminate any oversight. The segmental approach is particularly helpful in describing hearts with abnormal connections and relationship of chambers, allowing each level of the heart to be analyzed in sequence without having to memorize complex alpha-numeric computations. For example, a heart with a usual atrial

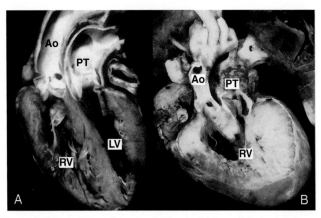

Figure 2-15   A, Discordant ventriculoarterial connections showing an inappropriate great artery emerging from each ventricle. **B,** A heart with both aorta and pulmonary trunk arising from the right ventricle exemplifying double-outlet connections. Ao, aorta; LV, left ventricle; PT, pulmonary trunk; RV, right ventricle.

TABLE 2-2	Examples of How Commonly Occurring Lesions Can Be Described Using the Sequential Segmental Method of Nomenclature
Commonly Used Term	**Sequential Segmental Analysis**
Atrial septal defect	**Usual atrial arrangement, concordant AV, and VA connections** + ASD (oval fossa defect)
Ventricular septal defect	**Usual atrial arrangement, concordant AV, and VA connections** + perimembranous inlet VSD
Atrioventricular septal defect	**Usual atrial arrangement, concordant AV, and VA connections** + atrioventricular septal defect with common valvar orifice
Coarctation	**Usual atrial arrangement, concordant AV, and VA connections** + coarctation
Fallot tetralogy (with anomalous LAD and right aortic arch)	**Usual atrial arrangement, concordant AV, and VA connections** + perimembranous outlet VSD with subpulmonary stenosis (tetralogy of Fallot), overriding aorta, right ventricular hypertrophy, pulmonary valvar stenosis, anomalous origin of LAD from right coronary artery, right aortic arch
Transposition of the great arteries with VSD, aortic stenosis and coarctation	**Usual atrial arrangement, concordant AV, and discordant VA connections** + perimembranous and malalignment VSD, aortic stenosis, coarctation
Congenitally corrected transposition with VSD, PS, and Ebstein malformation	**Usual atrial arrangement, discordant AV, and VA connections** + perimembranous VSD, subpulmonary stenosis, Ebstein malformation
Truncus arteriosus following homograft repair	**Usual atrial arrangement, concordant AV connections, and single-outlet VA connection with common arterial trunk** + muscular outlet VSD, ASD (oval fossa type). Repair with RV to pulmonary artery conduit and patch closure of VSD
Pulmonary atresia with VSD and collaterals	**Usual atrial arrangement, concordant AV connections, and single-outlet VA connection with pulmonary atresia** + perimembranous VSD, systemic to pulmonary collateral arteries
Tricuspid atresia with transposition and coarctation	**Usual atrial arrangement, absent right AV connections, and discordant VA connections** + morphologic left atrium to morphologic left ventricle, VSD, coarctation
Double-outlet right ventricle	**Usual atrial arrangement, concordant AV connections, and double-outlet VA connections from the right ventricle** + VSD, ASD (oval fossa type)
Double-inlet left ventricle with transposition and coarctation	**Usual atrial arrangement, univentricular AV connections to the left ventricle, and discordant VA connection** + double-inlet left ventricle, rudimentary right ventricle in right anterior position, VSD, coarctation
Situs inversus, dextrocardia, double-outlet right ventricle with valvar pulmonary atresia	**Mirror-imaged atrial arrangement, concordant AV connections, and double-outlet VA connections from the right ventricle** + muscular inlet VSD, valvar pulmonary atresia, heart in right chest, apex to right

For each example, segmental analysis of atrial arrangement, AV connections and ventriculoarterial connections are highlighted in bold. Examples of associated lesions are included, illustrating how segmental analysis provides the initial building block on which specific details are added.

ASD, atrial septal defect; AV, atrioventricular; LAD, left anterior descending coronary artery; PS, pulmonary stenosis; RV, right ventricle; VA, ventriculoarterial; VSD, ventricular septal defect.

arrangement, absence of the right atrioventricular connection, and concordant ventriculoarterial connection will mean just that. Further analysis is required to demonstrate that the left atrium is connected to the morphologic left ventricle that gives rise to the aorta, with the rudimentary right ventricle supporting the pulmonary trunk. In other words, this is the more common form of so-called tricuspid atresia but segmental analysis clarifies the "plumbing" (see Table 2-2).

Furthermore, the adult with CHD is likely to have had surgical interventions in childhood. Even so, segmental analysis is applicable in describing the native lesion, with additional surgical repairs or palliations noted (see Table 2-2). The diagnostician should, therefore, be familiar with the various types of palliative and corrective procedure. The availability of noninvasive modalities such as cross-sectional echocardiography, magnetic resonance imaging, and multislice computed tomography provides accurate diagnosis of even the most complicated patterns of chamber combinations and relationships. The best feature of the morphologic method is that it owes nothing to speculations on embryologic maldevelopment!

REFERENCES

1. de la Cruz MV, Berrazueta JR, Arteaga M, et al. Rules for diagnosis of arterioventricular discordances and spatial identification of ventricles: crossed great arteries and transposition of the great arteries. Br Heart J 1976;38:341–354.
2. Van Praagh R. The segmental approach to diagnosis in congenital heart disease. In: Bergsma D, editor. Birth Defects. Original Article Series, vol. VIII. no. 5 The National Foundation—March of Dimes. Baltimore: Williams & Wilkins; 1972. p. 4–23.
3. Shinebourne EA, Macartney FJ, Anderson RH. Sequential chamber localization—logical approach to diagnosis in congenital heart disease. Br Heart J 1976;38:327–340.
4. Tynan MJ, Becker EA, Macartney FJ, et al. Nomenclature and classification of congenital heart disease. Br Heart J 1979;41:544–553.
5. Anderson RH, Becker AE, Freedom RM, et al. Sequential segmental analysis of congenital heart disease. Pediatr Cardiol 1984;5:281–288.
6. Macartney FJ, Zuberbuhler JR, Anderson RH. Morphological considerations pertaining to recognition of atrial isomerism: consequences for sequential chamber localisation. Br Heart J 1980;44:657–667.
7. Anderson RH, Ho SY. Sequential segmental analysis—description and categorization of the millennium. Cardiol Young 1977;7:98–116.
8. Ho SY, McCarthy KP, Josen M, Rigby ML. Anatomic-echocardiographic correlates: an introduction to normal and congenitally malformed hearts. Heart 2001;86(Suppl. 2):ii3–ii11.
9. Lev M. Pathologic diagnosis of positional variations in cardiac chambers in congenital heart disease. Lab Invest 1954;3:71–82.
10. Van Praagh R, David I, Gordon D, et al. Ventricular diagnosis and designation. In: Godman M, editor. Paediatric Cardiology. Vol. 4. Edinburgh: Churchill Livingstone; 1981. p. 153–168.
11. Van Praagh R, Van Praagh S. Atrial isomerism in the heterotaxy syndromes with asplenia, or polysplenia, or normally formed spleen: an erroneous concept. Am J Cardiol 1990;66:1504–1506.
12. Uemura H, Ho SY, Devine WA, Anderson RH. Atrial appendages and venoatrial connections in hearts with visceral heterotaxy. Ann Thorac Surg 1995;60:561–569.
13. Goor DA, Lillehei CW. The anatomy of the heart. In: Congenital Malformations of the Heart. New York: Grune & Stratton; 1975. p. 1–37.
14. Anderson RH, Becker EA, Freedom RM, et al. Problems in the nomenclature of the univentricular heart. Herz 1979;4:97–106.
15. Rinne K, Smith A, Ho SY. A unique case of ventricular isomerism? Cardiol Young 2000;10:42–45.
16. Sutton III JP, Ho SY, Anderson RH. The forgotten interleaflet triangles: a review of the surgical anatomy of the aortic valve. Ann Thorac Surg 1995;59:419–427.
17. Stamm C, Anderson RH, Ho SY. Clinical anatomy of the normal pulmonary root compared with that in isolated pulmonary valvular stenosis. J Am Coll Cardiol 1998;31:1420–1425.
18. Van Mierop LHS, Wiglesworth FW. Isomerism of the cardiac atria in the asplenia syndrome. Lab Invest 1962;11:1303–1315.
19. Anderson C, Devine WA, Anderson RH, et al. Abnormalities of the spleen in relation to congenital malformations of the heart: a survey of necropsy findings in children. Br Heart J 1990;63:122–128.
20. Gerlis LM, Durá-Vilá G, Ho SY. Isomeric arrangement of the left atrial appendages and visceral heterotaxy: two atypical cases. Cardiol Young 2000;10:140–144.
21. Van Praagh R, Ongley PA, Swan HJC. Anatomic types of single or common ventricle in man: morphologic and geometric aspects of sixty necropsied cases. Am J Cardiol 1964;13:367–386.
22. Anderson RH, Becker AE, Tynan M, et al. The univentricular atrioventricular connection: getting to the root of a thorny problem. Am J Cardiol 1984;54:822–828.
23. Milo S, Ho SY, Macartney FJ, et al. Straddling and overriding atrioventricular valves morphology and classification. Am J Cardiol 1979;44:1122–1134.

3

Adults with Congenital Heart Disease: A Genetic Perspective

KRISTEN LIPSCOMB SUND | SMITHA H. GAWDE | D. WOODROW BENSON

As a result of the genetic revolution, the impact of genetics must be considered in the diagnosis, management, and treatment of the patient populations of most specialty clinics. Cardiology is no exception. In fact, it is likely that genetic information will eventually transform the definitions and taxonomy of congenital heart disease (CHD) used in daily practice. Furthermore, as we learn to apply genetics to risk assessment and develop a better understanding of pathogenesis of heart malformations, many of our diagnostic and therapeutic strategies will be impacted. A current challenge is to incorporate such information into the doctor's "little black bag." Because these times are already upon us, an understanding of basic genetics is necessary for "top notch" care in cardiology. The goal of this chapter is to identify and explain key implications of genetic testing for adult congenital heart disease (ACHD). At the conclusion of the chapter, the reader should be familiar with elements of the clinical session that can be used to diagnose a genetic condition, be able to identify resources available to investigate genetic diagnoses and sites for laboratory testing, and be prepared to develop a genetic testing strategy for ACHD.

What Is Congenital Heart Disease?

CHD refers to structural or functional abnormalities that are present at birth even if discovered much later. CHD comprises many forms of cardiovascular disease in the young, including cardiac malformations, cardiomyopathies, vasculopathies, and cardiac arrhythmias.[1-4] Cardiac malformations are an important component of CHD and constitute a major portion of clinically significant birth defects with estimates of 4 to 50/1000 live births. For example, it has been estimated that 4 to 10/1000 liveborn infants have a cardiac malformation, 40% of which are diagnosed in the first year of life. However, bicuspid aortic valve, the most common cardiac malformation, is usually excluded from this estimate. Bicuspid aortic valve is associated with considerable morbidity and mortality in affected individuals and, by itself, occurs in 10 to 20/1000 of the population. When isolated aneurysm of the atrial septum and persistent left superior vena cava, each occurring in 5 to 10/1000 live births,[1] are taken into account the incidence of cardiac malformations approaches 50/1000 live births. The incidence of cardiomyopathy, vasculopathy, and arrhythmias, including channelopathies, is less well characterized, but in light of the just-mentioned considerations an incidence of CHD of 50/1000 live births is a conservative estimate. In this chapter, we will use the term CHD to refer to all forms of pediatric heart disease or cardiovascular disease in the young.

Genetic Evidence for Congenital Heart Disease

There is a long-standing clinical view that most cases of CHD are isolated. Based on studies of recurrence and transmission risks, a hypothesis of multifactorial etiology has reigned for several decades. However, CHD is not purely multifactorial, because cytogenetic abnormalities such as Down syndrome have been identified and other examples of families with multiple affected individuals exhibiting classic mendelian transmission have been reported.[2] In the past decade molecular genetic studies have exploited these observations and provided insight into the genetic basis of CHD.[1-4] These insights have contributed to an impression that the genetic basis of pediatric heart disease has been underestimated. However, inheritance of nonsyndromic CHD is often complex.

From Phenotype to Genotype

On any given day, a cardiologist sees a variety of patients. What findings suggest a genetic etiology? Subtle clues obtained in the clinic can point to a genetic cause. Here we focus on the importance of medical history, family history, and the clinical examination in the investigation of a genetic cause for ACHD.

Detailed assessment of the patient's medical history, and in some cases the pregnancy history, can provide a starting point for classification of genetic disease. Individuals with CHD are likely to have a history of cardiac surgery, previous visits to a cardiologist, and records containing past echocardiographic or electrocardiographic results. In some cases, clinical history will identify the presence of a characteristic trait that would not otherwise be found on clinical examination. One example is the individual who was born with polydactyly but had early surgical removal of extra fingers or toes. This type of information can be crucial for the classification of patients with syndromic versus nonsyndromic phenotypes. A developmental assessment is also part of the medical history. Evaluation of past gross and fine motor skills as well as cognitive development will lead to the recognition of developmental delay, which is more likely to be associated with certain CHD as part of a syndrome. Because this assessment may not have been done since childhood, it is particularly important to explore this aspect of the past medical history with the adult patient.

Family history can distinguish genetic conditions that are not usually inherited (e.g., Down syndrome or trisomy 21) from genetic conditions that exhibit familial clustering (e.g., bicuspid aortic valve). The recognition of familial heart disease has been complicated by three genetic phenomena (Table 3-1) that obscure the familial nature: reduced penetrance, variable expressivity, and genetic heterogeneity. Furthermore, whereas most patients believe family history is important, many are unfamiliar with important clinical details. Too often, in the hustle and bustle of a busy clinic, family history is asked on the initial visit, recorded, and never revisited. This leads to a situation in which family history is an underutilized tool in the recognition of genetic etiology.[5] A precise recording of family history may require revisiting the questions on more than one occasion and obtaining information from more than one family member. In addition, family history, like other elements of the medical history, is dynamic and subject to change with the passage of time.[6] Based on family history and clinical examination, the likelihood for a genetic etiology can be determined. If the condition appears to be inherited, a pedigree, a shorthand way to record family history, may give some indication as to the mode of inheritance. Such patterns of inheritance include autosomal dominant, autosomal recessive, X-linked, and mitochondrial. However, physicians should use caution not to rely entirely on family history because some genetic conditions are not hereditary or do not display a family clustering on a pedigree. Figure 3-1 illustrates the types of simple inheritance and gives examples of genes that cause CHD.

A genetic condition may be identified by recognizing signature cardiac and/or noncardiac findings during the clinical examination. For

TABLE 3-1	Definition of Genetic Phenomena	
Phenomenon	*Attribute*
Genetic heterogeneity	Similar phenotypes, different genetic cause
Variable expressivity	Individuals with same disease gene but different phenotypes
Reduced penetrance	Disease absence in some individuals with disease gene

example, tetralogy of Fallot is a signature cardiac malformation for 22q11 deletion syndrome (del22q11), but a physician evaluating a patient with right ventricular outflow tract malformation may overlook dysmorphic facial features characteristic of del22q11. The presence of syndromic features is strongly supportive of a genetic condition and may be an indication for genetic testing. Even with what appears to be isolated CHD, typical features of the cardiac phenotype may suggest a genetic etiology with known inheritance. For example, electrocardiographic findings of prolonged QT interval or echocardiographic findings of unexplained cardiac hypertrophy would be recognized by most cardiologists as conditions with a strong likelihood of genetic etiology and family clustering.

Online Mendelian Inheritance in Man (OMIM) is a reliable resource that can be used at the bedside as a tool to investigate conditions that may have a genetic etiology. OMIM can be accessed through the website for the National Center for Biotechnology Information (NCBI).[7] Users can enter patient phenotypic information and learn about genetic conditions to help them decide the appropriate testing scheme to pursue.

▣ Clinical Utility of Genetic Testing

If at completion of the personal medical history, family history, and clinical examination a genetic etiology of heart disease is suggested then genetic testing may be considered. A stepwise process for genetic testing identification, counseling, and explanation of results as well as a discussion of the implications follows.

CHOOSING A GENETIC TEST

Decisions about the type of genetic test need careful consideration. If the physician has a strong index of suspicion for a specific genetic or cytogenetic abnormality, then karyotyping, fluorescence in-situ hybridization (FISH), or gene-specific mutation analysis is indicated

based on that suspicion. If the characteristics are not typical for a known condition, karyotyping or comparative genomic hybridization (CGH) may be necessary to identify a rare or novel genetic change. In addition to the *OMIM*, GeneTests, a resource supported by the National Institutes of Health, keeps up-to-date information on genetic condition and clinical/research laboratory testing sites.[8] Figure 3-2 outlines a strategy for choosing an appropriate genetic test.

PREPARING THE PATIENT FOR GENETIC TESTING

Patients who decide to undergo genetic testing should be pre-counseled for the possible test results. A cytogenetic abnormality that has been previously reported or that interrupts or deletes a biologically important gene(s) is likely to be involved with disease pathogenesis. Similarly, a sequence change that occurs in a highly conserved residue, changes the amino acid coding sequence, and segregates with disease in a family is likely to affect gene function (especially during development) and could be expected to be deleterious. Such changes are considered to result in a positive test. Once they are identified there are implications for patient management that extend to family care. If a deleterious change has been identified in a family, and an unaffected family member has a negative result during genetic testing, that person is considered to have a true negative result and does not have that specific genetic risk for heart disease. However, in a family in which no one has had a positive genetic test, a negative test means that the genetic cause has not been determined (it is neither good news nor bad news). That patient and his or her family members are still at risk and should be managed according to their personal or family history. Finally, a variant of unknown significance is a genetic change that may or may not be a risk factor for CHD. This mutation may be a polymorphism, or it may cause disease. More information needs to be gathered before the doctor or patient incorporates this test result into clinical care.

IMPLICATIONS OF GENETIC TEST RESULTS

Once a genetic test result is obtained it can be used to make decisions about management, screening, and prophylaxis. Patients with isolated CHD are at risk for secondary phenotypes that can be caused by their gene mutation. For example, patients with an *NKX2.5* mutation may have undergone successful surgery for a congenital heart defect but they will continue to be at risk for atrioventricular block. They should receive regular electrocardiographic screenings to monitor that risk and encourage early treatment of any abnormal findings. Early detection of

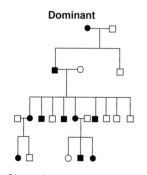

Dominant

- Disease in every generation
- Disease in males and females

- Gene transmission = 50%

- *NKX2.5, TBX5, PTPN11, SCN5A*

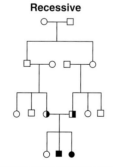

Recessive

- Disease may appear sporadic
- Disease in males and females

- Gene transmission = 25% if both parents are unaffected carriers

- *EVC, EVC2*

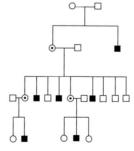

X-linked

- Disease in every generation
- Males are primarily affected with disease Female carriers may show symptoms
- Gene transmission
  - Daughters of affected fathers will be carriers
  - Sons of affected fathers do not have disease
  - Female carriers have 50% chance of passing mutation to next generation—daughters are carriers, sons are affected

- *ZIC3, X-linked cardiomyopathy*

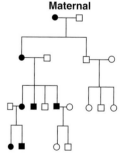

Maternal

- Disease in every generation
- Disease in males and females

- Gene transmission = 100% from mother, 0% from father
- Only passed through females

- *MT-TL1, Rare cardiomyopathies*

Figure 3-1 Illustration of classic mendelian (simple) inheritance patterns. Examples of genes causing CHD associated with each mode of inheritance are shown.

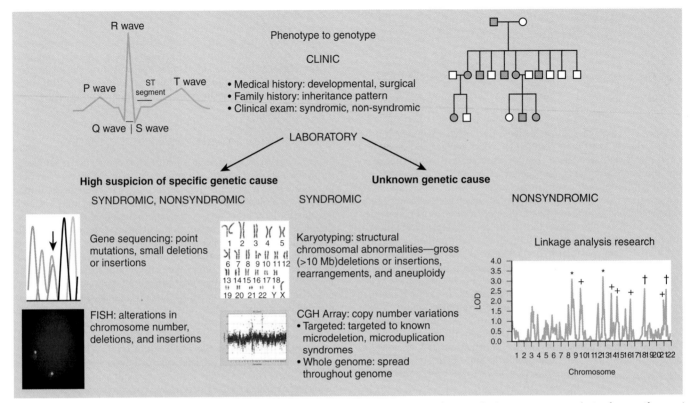

Figure 3-2 Strategy for selection of a genetic test in the cardiology clinic. Test selection may be specific (e.g., mutation analysis of a specific gene) or more general (e.g., karyotyping) if the genetic cause is unknown.

genetic status can improve screening and management; and as we come to understand the underlying pathogenesis, detection will be important for prophylactic treatment, such as the use of an implantable cardiac defibrillator in patients with channelopathies.

IMPLICATIONS FOR FAMILY MEMBERS

Genetic information has health management and psychosocial implications for extended family members, too. Individuals who have not previously had any symptoms or risks for CHD may become candidates for intensified screening owing to the genetic diagnosis of a family member. Family members with a negative clinical history of CHD may think they are not at risk for hereditary heart conditions. Once a genetic cause has been identified, it can be advantageous to rule out individuals who are not at risk for a condition. This can prevent unnecessary, expensive, and sometimes inconvenient screening practices. Information that has implications for family members must be managed cautiously because some family members may not be interested in sharing genetic information, getting genetic testing, or carrying out prophylactic measures that are available to them.

DESCRIBING RECURRENCE RISKS

Recurrence risk is a statistic that estimates the probability that a condition present in one or more family members will recur in another relative in the same or future generations.[5] Improved survival of CHD in recent decades has led to more CHD patients living to reproductive age and to renewed interest in recurrence risks. Ideally, recurrence risk is based on knowledge of the genetic nature of the CHD of interest and the family pedigree. When the disorder is known to have single gene inheritance (e.g., Marfan syndrome), the recurrence risk can be determined from known patterns of inheritance (see Fig. 3-1); this may become complicated when reduced penetrance or variable expressivity are present (see Table 3-1). However, for most forms of CHD, the underlying patterns of inheritance are unknown; in this situation, recurrence risk is based on previous experience. Recurrence risks can be extended to include distant relatives, but adults with CHD are likely

to be primarily concerned with risks to their siblings and their children. One interesting finding of these data is that the risk for transmission appears to be higher when the affected parent is the mother compared with when the father has CHD. The genetic basis of this predilection is unknown, and the phenomenon has not been confirmed based on genetic diagnosis. As more information is published on this topic, clinicians will be able to provide more accurate information to adults with CHD who are concerned about the risks for their family members. Table 3-2 provides recurrence risks for several CHD types.[2,9]

REPRODUCTIVE DECISION-MAKING

Imaging studies (ultrasonography, magnetic resonance imaging, fetal echocardiography), chorionic villus sampling, and amniocentesis are increasingly used for the evaluation of the fetus suspected of having CHD. For example, early, high-resolution ultrasound measurements of nuchal translucency have been used to predict CHD in high-risk families.[10] Chorionic villus sampling and amniocentesis are invasive tests that involve the removal of placental tissue or amniotic fluid for genetic testing in the fetus.[5] Genetic tests can also be used for pre-implantation genetic diagnosis in future pregnancies.[5] This procedure involves external fertilization of embryos, as used for in-vitro fertilization, but adds

TABLE 3-2	Recurrence Risks of Congenital Heart Disease Based on Phenotype
Type of CHD	*Recurrence Risk*
Atrioventricular septal defect	3.0-4.0%
Tetralogy of Fallot	2.5-3.0%
Transposition of the great arteries	1.0-1.8%
Left-sided obstructions	3.0%
Bicuspid aortic valve	8.0%
Hypoplastic left heart	3.8%
Risk of bicuspid aortic valve in HLHS kindred	8.0%
Atrial septal defect	3.0%

HLHS, hypoplastic left heart syndrome.

a genetic screening step prior to re-introduction of the nonaffected embryos to the uterus. Although pre-implantation genetic diagnosis is infrequently used for non–life-threatening conditions or adult-onset disease, its use may be increased as the technology is improved and the cost decreases.[11] Pre-implantation genetic diagnosis has already been used to test for Holt-Oram syndrome[12] and Marfan syndrome.[13]

Current State of Genetic Technology

In the past two decades there have been remarkable advances in the number and type of genetic tests that have become available for patient diagnoses as well as for prenatal and pre-implantation genetic diagnosis. It seems safe to predict that this will continue to change given the pace of advances in technology. For purposes of our discussion, we have grouped clinically available genetic tests into three categories: cytogenetic, molecular cytogenetics, and molecular genetic tests.

CYTOGENETIC INVESTIGATIONS

Standard metaphase karyotype is used to analyze chromosomes with 450 to 550 bands in the case of many chromosomal disorders, especially those with variation in chromosomal number such as trisomy (trisomy 18 or 21), monosomy (45,X or Turner syndrome), and gross chromosomal structural rearrangements such as translocations and large deletions (>10 Mb), duplications, and inversions. However, in some cases a high-resolution banding technique is used to identify subtle chromosomal rearrangements such as microdeletions and cryptic translocations that may go undetected by routine chromosomal analysis. Karyotyping is performed using peripheral blood lymphocytes, cord blood, skin fibroblasts, or bone marrow. In case of prenatal chromosomal diagnosis, cells from amniotic fluid or chorionic villus sampling are used.[5] Cells are cultured, and the chromosomes are arrested at metaphase stage and then used for karyotyping. In an adult patient or unborn fetus, indications for karyotyping include suspicion of an undiagnosed syndrome that might result from recognition of dysmorphic facial features, developmental delay, mental retardation, or other noncardiac anomalies.

MOLECULAR CYTOGENETIC INVESTIGATIONS

FISH is a molecular cytogenetic technique that is used to identify aneuploidies and cryptic chromosomal translocations by localization of specific DNA sequences within interphase chromatin and metaphase chromosomes.[5] This technique uses fluorescent probes that bind to specific sequence on a particular chromosome. Centromeric probes are used to identify aneuploidies, microdeletion probes are used to identify microdeletion syndromes such as CATCH 22q11.2, and telomeric probes are used to identify tiny deletions, duplications, or subtle translocations involving the distal ends of the chromosome (telomeres) because they are difficult to detect by standard or high-resolution karyotype techniques.[14] In addition to these, whole chromosome paint and multicolor FISH probes, which are actually a collection of probes, each of which hybridizes to different sequence along the length of the same chromosome, are also used. Each chromosome is painted with different colors to help in the examination of structural chromosomal abnormalities (e.g., translocations). One of the disadvantages of FISH is that because the probes are locus specific, a pretest decision must be made to determine which probe to use. This requires a high level of suspicion for a specific genetic condition on the part of the clinician. For example, the FISH probes used to identify Williams-Beuren syndrome are very different from those used to diagnose the 22q11 deletion syndrome.

MOLECULAR GENETIC INVESTIGATIONS

Availability of mutation analysis by direct sequencing and CGH or clinical testing is relatively new. Whereas cytogenetic techniques identify large changes in chromosome structure or number, mutation analysis by direct sequencing identifies small changes that occur at the level

of a single nucleotide, and CGH detects loss or gain of allele copy number on a larger scale (up to 10 to 20 Mb). A discussion of these two techniques follows.

DNA mutation analysis is a technique used to identify small changes that cause disease. Ordering DNA mutation analysis requires some knowledge of the gene(s) of interest. Mutation analysis identifies changes in the coding sequence of the gene, including small deletions, insertions, or substitutions of nucleotides that alter the encoded amino acid and consequently protein structure. The most common method used to identify these DNA changes is by direct gene sequencing. Indirect screening methods, such as denaturing high-performance liquid chromatography or single-strand conformation polymorphism, have been used extensively. Additionally, newer, more cost-effective direct sequence analysis methods have become available.[2] Mutation analysis is performed using DNA obtained from peripheral blood lymphocytes, but other tissues, such as skin, liver, muscle, buccal cells, or saliva, may also be used, depending on the availability. Once a sequence variation is identified, it is important to determine whether this variation is disease related. Basic criteria used to establish the disease-causing potential of a nucleotide change are that it (1) is predicted to alter the gene coding sense, a gene splice site, or regulatory region of the encoded protein; (2) segregates with disease in a kindred; (3) is not found in unrelated, unaffected controls; and (4) occurs in an evolutionarily conserved nucleotide. Although each of these criteria should be met by any disease-causing mutation, supporting evidence will come from the demonstration that affected individuals from unrelated families have mutations in the same gene. Another major problem is the interpretation of the biologic importance of mutations. In many instances, little is known about the role of the normal gene product in cardiac development or function; and in some instances, genes were not known to have any role in the heart before mutation identification (e.g., Alagille syndrome). To date, a variety of mutations that cause CHD, including missense and frameshift mutations, have been identified (e.g., *NKX2.5, TBX5, GATA4, JAG1, ZIC3, TFAP2B, TBX1,* and *FOG2.*)[15] Table 3-3 provides a summary of selected genes, their inheritance pattern, and their association with CHD. The extent and heterogeneity of the genes and the mutations identified thus far suggest that they are associated with a variety of pathogenic mechanisms, including loss of expression, inactivation, or loss/gain of function of the mutated products. These genetic findings have provided tools for studies in model systems, which have been informative for cardiac development and the pathogenesis studies of CHD.

CGH offers the additional opportunity to delineate the aberrant chromosomal region with high accuracy. Therefore, an increasing number of genetic laboratories have introduced this technique as a

TABLE 3-3	Mode of Inheritance and Cardiac Phenotype of Selected Congenital Heart Disease Genes	
Gene	*Inheritance*	*Associated with:*
NKX2.5	AD, sporadic	ASD, AVB, VSD, TOF, HCM, TVA
TBX5	AD, sporadic	Holt-Oram syndrome, ASD, AVSD, AVB, TOF
GATA4	AD, sporadic	ASD, VSD, AVSD, PV dysplasia
CRELD1	AD, sporadic	AVSD
ZIC3	X-linked	Heterotaxy, TGA, DORV
SCN5A	AD, sporadic	LQTS, Brugada syndrome, SSS, AVB
JAG1	AD, sporadic	Alagille syndrome, TOF, PS/PPS
FBN1	AD, sporadic	Marfan syndrome, aortic root dilation
PTPN11	AD, sporadic	Noonan syndrome, PS, PV dysplasia, ASD, AVSD, HCM
EVC, EVC2	AR	Ellis-van Creveld syndrome, AVSD

AD, autosomal dominant; AR, autosomal recessive; ASD, atrial septal defect; AVB, atrioventricular block; AVSD, atrioventricular septal defect; DORV, double-outlet right ventricle; HCM, hypertrophic cardiomyopathy; LQTS, long QT syndrome; PPS, peripheral pulmonary stenosis; PS, pulmonary stenosis; PV, pulmonary valve; SSS, sick sinus syndrome; TGA, transposition of the great arteries; TOF, tetralogy of Fallot; TVA, tricuspid valve anomalies; VSD, ventricular septal defect.

diagnostic tool to detect copy number variants. Humans have two copies of each DNA segment (gene), and a copy number variant occurs when a deletion or a duplication results in a respective increase or decrease in that specific segment of DNA. Copy number variants typically involve DNA segments that are smaller than those recognized microscopically (<3 Mb) and larger than those recognized by direct sequencing (>1 kb). This includes so-called large-scale variants (>50 kb) that can be detected using CGH.[16] There are two types of CGH: chromosomal and array based. In chromosomal CGH, differentially labeled test (i.e., patient) and reference (i.e., normal individual) genomic DNAs are co-hybridized to normal metaphase chromosomes and fluorescence ratios along the length of chromosomes provide a cytogenetic representation of the relative DNA copy number variation. The resolution is limited to 10 to 20 Mb. In array CGH, arrays of genomic BAC, P1, cosmid, or cDNA clones are used for hybridization. Fluorescence ratios at arrayed DNA elements provide a locus-by-locus measure of DNA copy number variation and result in increased mapping resolution. Targeted arrays focus on chromosomal regions associated with known microdeletion or microduplication syndromes as well as all subtelomeric regions. Whole-genome arrays permit analysis of deletions or duplications anywhere in the genome without requiring predetermination of a region of interest. As array CGH becomes more commonplace, it is serving an important role in gene discovery for causes of CHD. Studies have found cryptic chromosomal abnormalities in patients with CHD and

additional birth defects, which could not be identified using standard cytogenetic technique.[17] Several studies on copy number variants have resulted in the publication of maps of normal variation in the human genome as well as of disease-specific copy number variants.[18] These may be found in online catalogs such as the DECIPHER database[19] and the Database of Genomic Variants.[20]

DIFFERENCE BETWEEN GENETIC TESTING IN A RESEARCH SETTING AND CLINICAL GENETIC TESTING

The main differences between clinical genetic testing and research testing are the purpose of the test and the recipients of test results. The goals of research testing include identification of unknown genes and interpretation of gene function and pathogenicity to advance our understanding of genetic conditions. The results of testing done as part of a research study are usually not available to patients or their health care providers. Clinical testing, on the other hand, is done to find out about an inherited disorder in an individual patient or family. Patients receive the results of a clinical test and can use them to help them make decisions about medical care or reproductive issues. It is important for people considering genetic testing to know whether the test is available on a clinical or research basis. Clinical and research testing both involve a process of informed consent in which patients learn about the testing procedure, the risks and benefits of the test, and the potential consequences of testing.

REFERENCES

1. Lehnart SE, Ackerman MJ, Benson DW, et al. Inherited arrhythmias: a National Heart, Lung, and Blood Institute and Office of Rare Diseases workshop consensus report about the diagnosis, phenotyping, molecular mechanisms, and therapeutic approaches for primary cardiomyopathies and gene mutations affecting ion channel function. Circulation 2007;116:2325–2345.

2. Pierpont ME, Basson CT, Benson DW, et al. Genetic basis for congenital heart defects: current knowledge: a scientific statement from the American Heart Association Congenital Cardiac Defects Committee, Council on Cardiovascular Disease in the Young: endorsed by the American Academy of Pediatrics. Circulation 2007;115:3015–3038.

3. Hughes SE, McKenna WJ. New insights into the pathology of inherited cardiomyopathy. Heart 2005;91:257–264.

4. Callewaert B, Malfait F, Loeys B, De Paepe A. Ehlers-Danlos syndromes and Marfan syndrome. Best Pract Res Clin Rheumatol 2008;22:165–189.

5. Nussbaum RL, McInnes RR, Willard HF. Genetic counseling and risk assessment. In: Nussbaum RL, McInnes RR, Willard HF, editors. Thompson & Thompson Genetics in Medicine. 6th ed. Philadelphia: WB Saunders; 2004. p. 375–389.

6. Hinton RB. The family history: reemergence of an established tool. Crit Care Nurs Clin North Am 2008;20:149–158.

7. Online Mendelian Inheritance in Man. Available at http://www.ncbi.nlm.nih.gov/sites/entrez?db=OMIM [accessed February 14, 2009].

8. GeneTests. Available at http://www.genetests.org/ [accessed February 14, 2009].

9. Calcagni G, Digilio MC, Sarkozy A, et al. Familial recurrence of congenital heart disease: an overview and review of the literature. Eur J Pediatr 2007;166:111–116.

10. Clur SA, Mathijssen IB, Pajkrt E, et al. Structural heart defects associated with an increased nuchal translucency: 9 years experience in a referral centre. Prenat Diagn 2008;28:347–354.

11. McDermott DA, Basson CT, Hatcher CJ. Genetics of cardiac septation defects and their pre-implantation diagnosis. Methods Mol Med 2006;126:19–42.

12. He J, McDermott DA, Song Y, et al. Preimplantation genetic diagnosis of human congenital heart malformation and Holt-Oram syndrome. Am J Med Genet 2004;126A:93–98.

13. Spits C, De Rycke M, Van Ranst N, et al. Preimplantation genetic diagnosis for cancer predisposition syndromes. Prenat Diagn 2007;27:447–456.

14. Anderlid BM, Schoumans J, Anneren G, et al. Subtelomeric rearrangements detected in patients with idiopathic mental retardation. Am J Med Genet 2002;107:275–284.

15. Hinton RB, Yutzey KE, Benson DW. Congenital heart disease: genetic causes and developmental insights. Prog Pediatr Cardiol 2005;20:101–111.

16. Perry GH, Ben-Dor A, Tsalenko A, et al. The fine-scale and complex architecture of human copy-number variation. Am J Hum Genet 2008;82:685–695.

17. Thienpont B, Mertens L, de Ravel T, et al. Submicroscopic chromosomal imbalances detected by array-CGH are a frequent cause of congenital heart defects in selected patients. Eur Heart J 2007;28:2778–2784.

18. Iafrate AJ, Feuk L, Rivera MN, et al. Detection of large-scale variation in the human genome. Nat Genet 2004;36:949–951.

19. DECIPHER database. Available at https://decipher.sanger.ac.uk/ [accessed February 14, 2009].

20. Database of Genomic Variants. Available at http://projects.tcag.ca/variation/ [accessed February 14, 2009].

4

Clinical Assessment

JOSEPH K. PERLOFF

The main purpose…is to present a brief account of congenital heart disease with special emphasis on those lesions capable of clinical recognition when modern methods are employed (Brown, 1939)[1]

I hope to stimulate clinicians to use the tools at their disposal—the history, physical examination, electrocardiogram and chest x-ray—and to feel that many insights can be gained apart from the laboratory (Perloff, 1970).[2]

Congenital malformations of the heart, by definition, originate in the embryo, then evolve during gestation, and change considerably during the course of extrauterine life.[3] Before World War II, these malformations were regarded as hopeless futilities, a suitable interest for the few women in medicine. Maude Abbott was advised by William Osler to devote herself to the anatomic specimens in the collection at McGill University, and Helen Taussig was advised to occupy herself with the hopeless futilities in the Harriet Lane Children's Clinic at Johns Hopkins University. Congenital heart disease (CHD) in adults was an oxymoron.

Clinical recognition of congenital malformations of the heart has long depended on information from four primary sources—the history, the physical examination, the electrocardiogram (ECG), and the chest radiograph.[1] These sources also now include echocardiography[1,3] (see Chapter 5).

Clinical assessment of CHD is best achieved within the framework of an orderly classification. The classification was proposed by Paul Wood in the 1950s[3] and has now been revised.[7]

In most professions there are certain settings that reveal an inner core. In medicine that core is an encounter between two people—the patient and the doctor during the history and the physical examination. The doctor enters the patient's world. There is a human being behind every disease.

The *medical history* is an interview—a clinical skill not easily mastered. The first necessity is to learn to *listen*. Traditionally, trained psychiatrists serve as models, and an occasional media interviewer can serve the same purpose. Nothing demeans the process as much as the impersonal noninteractive checklists that patients are asked to fill out before an office visit.

The *physical examination* includes the physical appearance, the arterial pulse, the jugular venous pulse, precordial percussion and palpation, and auscultation.[4]

The *chest radiograph* (Wilhelm Conrad Roentgen, 1895) and the *ECG* (Willem Einthoven, 1903) continue to provide gratifying diagnostic insights, even in complex CHD.[3] There is much to be said for learning to read chest radiographs under the tutelage of an expert chest radiologist. And there is much to be said for interpreting ECGs according to the vectorial analysis proposed by Robert P. Grant in the 1950s and by Chou, Helm, and Kaplan in the 1970s.[5]

Echocardiography—two dimensional (2D) echocardiography with color flow imaging and Doppler interrogation—has taken its place almost routinely as a part of the clinical assessment alongside the time-honored ECG and chest radiograph.[3,6]

Maximum information should be extracted from each of the aforementioned sources while relating information from one source to that of another, weaving the information into a harmonious noncontradictory whole. Each step should advance our thinking and narrow the diagnostic possibilities. By the end of the clinical assessment untenable considerations should have been discarded, the possibilities retained for further consideration, and the probabilities brought into sharp focus.

Diagnostic thinking benefits from *anticipation* and *supposition*.[3] After drawing conclusions from the history, for example, it is useful to pause and ask, "If these assumptions are correct, what might I anticipate from the ECG, the radiograph, or the echocardiogram to support or refute my initial conclusions?" Anticipation heightens interest and fosters synthesis of each step with the next. Confirmation comes as a source of satisfaction; error stands out in bold relief.

The face-to-face interview is indispensible in sensing the person behind the patient, in establishing a comfortable relationship between patient and physician, and in determining the reliability of information so derived. With infants and children, the family is the patient. Questions should guide rather than preempt the discourse. Let the patient talk. The doctor should learn to listen.

In outpatient clinics, the patient as a rule lies on an examining table with the physician alongside—standing above the patient, so to speak. Patients often feel that they are being looked down upon, at least in the figurative sense, and are more comfortable when the physician sits at a desk close by looking up to the patient, at least in the literal sense.

Adolescents are neither older children nor younger adults but are *sui generis* and are best seen in adolescent clinics surrounded by their peers. Mature adolescents should be included in the interview and allowed to speak for themselves. Questions should be directed to both patient and parents, with the relative proportion determined by the maturity and receptivity of the adolescent. Immature adolescents manifest undesirable dependency by deferring to their parents. Adolescent girls who are anxious to discuss sexuality may be embarrassed to do so in front of parents or with a male physician. This problem can be resolved by having a female nurse practitioner or a female physician do the clinical assessment.

The History

In adults with CHD the history begins with the family. Has CHD occurred among first-degree relatives? Was there maternal exposure to teratogens or environmental toxins during gestation? Was prenatal care provided by the same obstetrician who attended an in-hospital delivery? Was birth premature or dysmature? How soon after birth was CHD suspected or identified? The maternal parent is likely to be the best source of this important, if not crucial, information. The mother will surely recall whether her neonate remained in hospital after she was discharged and is likely to remember whether the initial suspicion of CHD was a murmur or cyanosis.

Exercise capacity in acyanotic patients can be judged by comparing their ability to walk on level ground with their ability to walk up an incline or up stairs. If squatting is reported, the patient should be asked to demonstrate the position. In judging the presence and degree of symptoms, it is well to remember that patients who describe themselves as asymptomatic before surgery often realize that they are symptomatically improved after surgery.

If an acyanotic neonate were examined in the newborn nursery and pronounced normal by a pediatrician (rather than by a less experienced general physician), and if the same pediatrician heard a prominent murmur a few weeks later at a well-baby examination, it can be suspected that the anatomic but not the physiologic substrate was present at birth. The diagnosis is likely to be a restrictive or moderately restrictive ventricular septal defect that announced itself after the fall in neonatal pulmonary vascular resistance established a left-to-right shunt. Conversely, a murmur that is prominent at birth in an acyanotic neonate implies that the anatomic *and* physiologic substrates responsible for the murmur existed at birth, which would be appropriate for lesions characterized by obstruction to ventricular outflow.

Cyanotic CHD is a multisystem systemic disorder, so the history should include questions that deal with red blood cell mass, hemostasis, bilirubin kinetics, urate clearance, respiration, ventilation, the long bones, the central nervous system, and, in females, gynecologic endocrinology.[8] Symptoms associated with erythrocytosis include headache, faintness, dizziness, light-headedness, slow mentation, impaired alertness, irritability, a petit mal feeling of distance or dissociation, visual disturbances, paresthesias, tinnitus, fatigue, lassitude, lethargy, anorexia, and myalgias and/or muscle weakness.[8] Importantly, a headache per se does not imply symptomatic hyperviscosity because headaches are independently so common. Hemostatic defects are manifested by easy bruising, epistaxis, menorrhagia, excessive bleeding caused by minor injury or minor surgery, and hemorrhage from fragile gums during otherwise innocuous dental procedures.[8] Cholecystitis is caused by hyperbilirubinemia and calcium bilirubinate gallstones. Effort dyspnea may be unrelated to heart failure but instead to symptomatic hyperventilation induced by stimulation of the respiratory center and carotid body in response to the sudden change in blood gas composition and pH caused by an exercise-induced increase in right-to-left shunt.[8] In Eisenmenger syndrome, hemoptysis, which by definition is external, does not reflect the extent of pulmonary hemorrhage, which may be chiefly—and dangerously—intrapulmonary.[8] Abnormal gynecologic endocrinology in an unoperated cyanotic female may be manifested by delayed menarche and, after surgical relief of cyanosis, by dysfunctional bleeding that suggests endometrial carcinoma.[8] Central nervous system abnormalities in adults vary from transient ischemic attacks caused by paradoxical microemboli to seizures caused by a long-since healed brain abscess in childhood.[9] Smoking is always undesirable, but especially in the presence of cyanosis. Airplane travel is chiefly a concern when patients are confronted with rushed last-minute stressful arrivals and annoying delayed departures and is of relatively little concern after the patient is comfortably seated in the aircraft.[8] In-flight dehydration increases the hematocrit, an eventuality that can be avoided by drinking nonalcoholic fluids.

The prevalence of lower-extremity deep vein thrombosis became evident in Londoners who were crowded and relatively immobile in air-raid shelters during World War II. The "economy class syndrome" is analogous among airline travelers as seating becomes more and more cramped and movement more and more restricted. Patients should flex their ankles and knees and stretch their legs as much as possible and walk up and down the aisles at frequent intervals.

A congenital cardiac malformation can be a substrate for infective endocarditis. Questions should focus on routine day-to-day oral hygiene of teeth and gums and on antibiotic prophylaxis before

dental work.[10] Biting and picking of fingernails and fingertips is an autosomal recessive compulsive disorder from which patients cannot desist by being browbeaten. The history should therefore include questions regarding compulsive behavior patterns in first-degree relatives.[11] A psychiatric consultant may recommend an appropriate psychopharmacologic medication.

A history of palpitations can often be clarified by asking the patient to describe the onset and termination of the rapid heart action, the rapidity of the heart rate, and the regularity or irregularity of the rhythm. Physicians can simulate the arrhythmic pattern—rate and regularity or irregularity—by tapping their own chest to assist the patient in identifying the rhythm disturbance.

In mentally impaired patients, the history is necessarily secured through parent or guardian. In Down syndrome, the distinction between symptomatic hypothyroidism and premature Alzheimer disease is resolved by thyroid function tests. A change in established behavior patterns arouses suspicion.

The term *natural history* is an anachronism that has little or no place in modern medical terminology. The *Oxford Dictionary of Natural History* defines *natural* as "a community that would develop if human influences were removed completely and permanently."[12] Julien Hoffman's definition is equally apt: "The natural history of any disease is a description of what happens to people with the disease who do not receive treatment for it."[13] Few or no patients have literally received no treatment. *Natural history* is not synonymous with *unoperated* because survival is modified, often appreciably, by a host of nonsurgical therapeutic interventions that cannot be considered natural. The awkward term *unnatural history* is also not synonymous with *postoperative*. The surgeon should not be cast in the role of perpetrator of the unnatural.

■ The Physical Examination

Physical examination of the heart and circulation includes the physical appearance, the arterial pulse, the jugular venous pulse, precordial percussion and palpation, and auscultation[4] (see earlier). There are few areas of clinical cardiology that physical signs do not illuminate.

PHYSICAL APPEARANCE

Appearance includes gait and gestures, abnormalities of which can result from residual neurologic deficits of a childhood brain abscess. Bitten nails and paronychial infection in a febrile patient with a substrate for infective endocarditis directs attention to staphylococcal bacteremia, whereas poor oral hygiene with carious teeth and infected gums directs attention to *Streptococcus viridans* bacteremia.[10]

Certain physical appearances predict specific types of CHD. Down syndrome (Fig. 4-1) is associated with an atrioventricular septal defect. Coexisting cyanosis predicts a nonrestrictive inlet ventricular septal

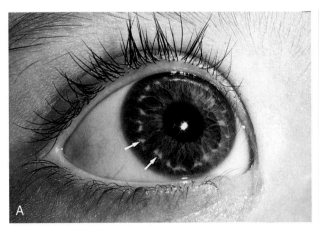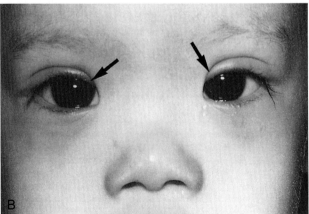

Figure 4-1 **A,** Characteristic Brushfield spots consisting of depigmented foci along the circumference of the iris (*arrows*) in a child with Down syndrome. The sparse eyelashes are also characteristic. **B,** Typical inner epicanthal folds (*arrows*) and depressed nasal bridge in a child with Down syndrome.

defect with pulmonary vascular disease, to which Down syndrome patients are especially and prematurely prone.[3] Williams syndrome is associated with supravalvular aortic stenosis and an increase in the right brachial arterial pulse. The probability of coexisting peripheral pulmonary arterial stenosis demands auscultation at nonprecordial thoracic sites. Differential cyanosis connotes flow of unoxygenated blood from the pulmonary trunk into the aorta distal to the left subclavian artery, a distinctive feature of a nonrestrictive patent ductus arteriosus with pulmonary vascular disease and reversed shunt. Reversed differential cyanosis is a distinctive feature of the Taussig-Bing anomaly in which unoxygenated right ventricular blood flows into the ascending aorta and upper extremities while oxygenated left ventricular blood enters the pulmonary trunk through the subpulmonary ventricular septal defect and flows through a nonrestrictive patent ductus to the lower extremities.[3]

THE ARTERIAL PULSE

With careful practice, the trained finger can become a most sensitive instrument in the examination of the pulse. (James Mackenzie, 1902)[14]

The ancient art of feeling the pulse remains useful in contemporary clinical medicine.[4] The arterial pulse provides information on blood pressure, waveform, diminution, absence, augmentation, structural properties, cardiac rate and rhythm, differential pulsations (right-left, upper-lower extremity), arterial thrills, and murmurs.[4]

When a patient affected by the disease is stripped, the arterial trunks of the head, neck and superior extremities immediately catch the eye by their singular pulsation. From its singular and striking appearance, the name visible pulsation is given to this beating of the arteries. (Dominic Corrigan, 1832)[4]

A visible pulse in the neck should not be mistaken for a kinked carotid artery. The Corrigan pulse is bilateral, but an elongated kinked carotid artery loops back upon itself and is confined to the right side.[4] A *water-hammer pulse,* a term sometimes assigned to the Corrigan pulse, is derived from a Victorian toy that consisted of a glass tube containing mercury in a vacuum. The tube was held between the thumb and the tip of the index finger. As the tube was inverted back and forth, the mercury abruptly fell to the dependent end, imparting a jolt or impact to the thumb or fingertip,[4] analogous to the impact of the Corrigan pulse.

In Williams syndrome, a disproportionate increase in the right brachial arterial pulse is attributed to the exaggerated Coanda effect associated with supravalvular aortic stenosis (Henri Coanda was a Romanian engineer who described the tendency of a moving fluid to attach itself to a surface and flow along that surface).

When coarctation of the aorta obstructs the orifice of the left subclavian artery, the left brachial pulse is diminished or absent while the right brachial artery is hypertensive. A disproportionate increase in the left brachial pulse occurs in coarctation when a retroesophageal right subclavian artery originates distal to the coarctation and courses to the right arm. The tortuous, U-shaped retinal arterioles are unique to coarctation.[3,4]

Arterial murmurs and thrills vary according to patient age. In normal children and young adults, an innocent supraclavicular systolic murmur can be loud enough to generate a thrill that radiates below the clavicles, inviting the mistaken diagnosis of intrathoracic origin. Error is avoided by auscultation above and below the clavicles and by hyperextension of the shoulders, a maneuver that decreases or abolishes the supraclavicular murmur.[4]

THE VEINS—JUGULAR AND PERIPHERAL

In 1902 James Mackenzie established the jugular venous pulse as an integral part of the cardiovascular physical examination,[14] and in the 1950s Paul Wood furthered that interest.[7] The jugular pulse provides information on conduction defects and arrhythmias, waveforms and pressure, and anatomic and physiologic properties.[4] First-degree heart block is identified by an increase in the interval between an a wave and the carotid pulse, which is the mechanical counterpart of the PR interval, as in congenitally corrected transposition of the great arteries; second-degree heart block, which is almost always 2:1 with this malformation, is identified by two a waves for each carotid pulse. In congenital complete heart block, a normal atrial rate is dissociated from a slower ventricular rate that arises from an idioventricular focus. Independent a waves are intermittently punctuated by cannon waves (augmented a waves) that are generated when right atrial contraction fortuitously finds the tricuspid valve closed during right ventricular systole. The slow rate and regular rhythm of sinus bradycardia are distinguished from the bradycardia of complete heart block by the orderly sequence of a and v waves in the former.

In the normal right atrial and jugular venous pulse the a wave is slightly dominant, whereas in the normal left atrial pulse the a and v crests are equal. A nonrestrictive atrial septal defect permits transmission of the left atrial waveform into the right atrium and into the internal jugular vein, so the crests of the jugular venous a and v waves are equal. In tetralogy of Fallot and in Eisenmenger ventricular septal defect, the right atrial pulse and jugular venous pulse are normal because the right ventricle functions normally despite systemic systolic pressure, analogous to a fetal right ventricle that functions normally without an increased force of right atrial contraction.

In Ebstein anomaly, the waveform and height of the jugular pulse are normal despite severe tricuspid regurgitation because of the damping effect of the large right atrium. In severe isolated pulmonary stenosis, jugular a waves are large if not giant because of the increased force of right atrial contraction needed to achieve presystolic distention sufficient to generate suprasystemic systolic pressure in the afterloaded right ventricle (Starling's law). Large a waves in tricuspid atresia coincide with a restrictive interatrial communication; if the atrial septal defect is nonrestrictive, the right atrial waveform is determined by the distensibility characteristics of the left ventricle with which it is in functional continuity. Similarly, but for a different reason, the right atrial waveform after an atrial switch operation for complete transposition of the great arteries is determined by the distensibility characteristics of the left ventricle via the systemic venous baffle. After a Fontan operation, the waveform of the jugular venous pulse necessarily disappears because the right internal jugular vein and superior vena cava reflect nonpulsatile mean pulmonary arterial pressure.

Varicose veins are the most common clinically important vascular abnormality of the lower extremities and are important sources of paradoxical emboli via the right-to-left shunts of cyanotic CHD. Varices are commonly overlooked and often underestimated during routine physical examination because the legs are not exposed when the patient is lying on the examining table. Gravity distends the leg veins, so examination in the standing position is obligatory.[4]

PRECORDIAL PERCUSSION AND PALPATION

Information derived from percussion serves two purposes: (1) determination of visceral *situs* (heart, stomach, and liver) and, much less importantly, (2) approximation of the left and right cardiac borders.[4] Situs inversus with dextrocardia is the mirror image of normal, so gastric tympany is on the right, hepatic dullness is on the left, and cardiac dullness is to the right of the sternum (Fig. 4-2A). All but a small percentage of patients with mirror image dextrocardia have no coexisting CHD, but if the malposition is not identified the pain associated with myocardial ischemia, cholecystitis, and appendicitis will be misleading. In situs solitus with dextrocardia, gastric tympany is on the left and hepatic dullness is on the right but cardiac dullness is to the right of the sternum (see Fig. 4-2B). Predictable patterns of CHD coexist in most, if not all, patients with situs solitus and dextrocardia (see later). In situs inversus with levocardia, gastric tympany is on the right and hepatic dullness on the left (mirror image) but cardiac dullness is to the left of the sternum (see Fig. 4-2C). CHD always coexists, but the type is not predictable.

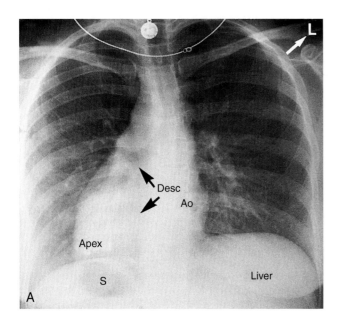

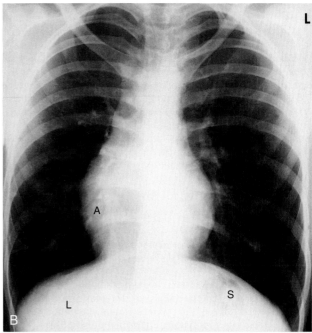

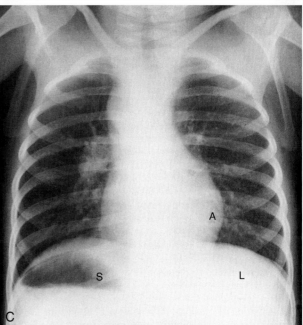

Figure 4-2   Chest radiographs showing the three basic cardiac malpositions in patients without visceral heterotaxy. **A,** Situs inversus with dextrocardia (mirror image). The liver is on the left, the stomach (S) is on the right, and the cardiac apex is on the right. Desc Ao, descending aorta. **B,** *Situs solitus* with dextrocardia. The liver (L) is on the right, the stomach (S) is on the left, and the cardiac apex (A) is on the right. **C,** Situs inversus with levocardia. The liver (L) is on the left, the stomach (S) is on the right, and the cardiac apex (A) is on the left.

Diagnostic conclusions based on palpation assume knowledge of the topographic anatomy of the cardiac and vascular structures that impart movement to the overlying chest wall.[4] At birth, the normal right ventricle generates a gentle unsustained systolic impulse. In tetralogy of Fallot this gentle impulse persists because the right ventricle continues to function as in the fetus, ejecting at but not above systemic resistance. Conversely, an elevated right ventricular pressure in pulmonary valvular stenosis with intact ventricular septum is characterized by a left parasternal impulse that is increased in amplitude and duration and is accompanied by presystolic distention in response to an increased force of right atrial contraction.

AUSCULTATION

Laennec's discovery of the stethoscope advanced physical diagnosis beyond anything previously imagined. The stethoscope is the oldest cardiovascular diagnostic instrument in continuous clinical use, and abnormal auscultatory signs detected with the stethoscope are often

the first suspicion of CHD. A systolic murmur heard at birth because of obstruction to ventricular outflow is in contrast to the delayed onset of the systolic murmur of ventricular septal defect, as pointed out earlier in the section on the art of history taking. Mobile pulmonary valvular stenosis is accompanied by an ejection sound that characteristically varies in intensity with respiration and that introduces an asymmetrical midsystolic murmur at the left base followed by a second sound with a delayed soft second component.

When a normal first heart sound is split at the apex, the initial component is the louder; but when the second component is louder, the cause is likely to be the ejection sound of a mobile bicuspid aortic valve that is functionally normal if there is no accompanying midsystolic murmur. Conversely, an aortic ejection sound preceded by a fourth heart sound and followed by a long symmetrical right basal midsystolic murmur connotes severe bicuspid aortic stenosis (Fig. 4-3), a conclusion supported by a sustained left ventricular impulse with presystolic distention.

Ebstein anomaly of the tricuspid valve generates a widely split first heart sound at the lower left sternal border and a medium-frequency

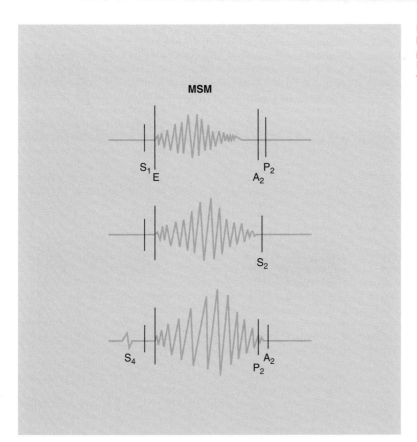

Figure 4-3 Auscultatory signs of mild, moderate, and severe bicuspid aortic stenosis. A$_2$ and P$_2$, aortic and pulmonary components of the second heart sound (S$_2$); E, ejection sound; MSM, symmetric midsystolic murmur; S$_1$, first heart sound; S$_4$, fourth heart sound.

early systolic murmur of low-pressure tricuspid regurgitation. If the anterior tricuspid leaflet is large and mobile, the second component of the split first heart sound is loud, a sign that predicts adequacy for surgical creation of a monocuspid valve.

Time-honored auscultatory features of an atrial septal defect include a short grade 2 to 3 of 6 impure, left basal, midsystolic murmur followed by a wide fixed splitting of the second heart sound. A prominent mid-diastolic medium-frequency flow murmur across the tricuspid valve flow implies a systemic-to-pulmonary flow ratio of at least 2:1. After repair of tetralogy of Fallot, a medium-frequency mid-diastolic murmur in the third left intercostal space represents low-pressure pulmonary regurgitation that is likely to be severe if the right ventricular impulse is easily palpable. A similar mid-diastolic murmur in unoperated tetralogy of Fallot implies congenital absence of the pulmonary valve, especially when accompanied by a prominent midsystolic flow murmur, a combination that creates a distinctive to-and-fro cadence. In unoperated tetralogy of Fallot the length and loudness of the midsystolic murmur vary inversely with the severity of right ventricular outflow obstruction, because the greater the stenosis, the greater the amount of right ventricular blood that is diverted from the pulmonary trunk into the biventricular aorta. Tetralogy of Fallot with pulmonary atresia and a dilated ascending aorta is accompanied by an aortic ejection sound that introduces a soft short midsystolic flow murmur followed by a loud single second heart sound and a high-frequency early diastolic murmur of aortic regurgitation.

Eisenmenger syndrome with a nonrestrictive ventricular septal defect is accompanied by a pulmonary ejection sound that introduces a soft, short midsystolic pulmonary flow murmur followed by a loud single second heart sound and a high-frequency early diastolic Graham Steell murmur.

THE ELECTROCARDIOGRAM

The standard 12-lead scalar ECG, when read systematically and interpreted in clinical context, provides appreciable diagnostic information, even in complex CHD. Attention should focus sequentially on the direction, amplitude, configuration, and duration of P waves; the PR interval; the direction, configuration, amplitude, and duration of the QRS complex; the QT interval; the ST segment; and the direction and configuration of the T waves. In patients with cardiac malpositions the technician recording the ECG requires instructions regarding special lead placements. In complete situs inversus, the reversal of arm leads and recording of mirror-image leads from the right precordium permits the tracing to be read as in situs solitus with levocardia. In situs solitus with dextrocardia, arm leads remain unchanged but right precordial leads should be recorded. In situs inversus with levocardia, arm leads should be reversed whereas standard left precordial leads suffice.

The normal sinus node lies at the junction of a right superior vena cava and a morphologic right atrium. Atrial depolarization generates a P wave that is directed downward and to the left within a narrow range from birth to senescence. P-wave directions that deviate from normal imply that the depolarization focus is not in a normal right sinus node. P waves that are directed downward and to the right are features of atrial situs inversus in which mirror image atrial depolarization originates in a sinus node located at the junction of a left superior vena cava and an inverted morphologic right atrium. In atrial situs inversus with a left atrial ectopic rhythm, an uncommon but distinctive configuration is a dome and dart P wave, with the dome due to early left atrial depolarization and the dart due to sudden delayed depolarization of the right atrium.[3]

When the anatomic junction between a superior vena cava and a morphologic right atrium is deficient or absent as with a superior vena caval sinus venosus atrial septal defect, the sinus node is also deficient or absent. Depolarization then originates in an ectopic focus, so the P-wave direction is necessarily abnormal. In visceral heterotaxy with left isomerism there is no morphologic right atrium to form a junction with a superior vena cava.

Normal P waves have either a single crest or bifid right and left atrial crests separated by no more than 40 ms, because right atrial depolarization is promptly followed by depolarization of the left atrium via Bachmann bundle, a ventral connection between the two atria. When atrial size and wall thickness are normal, the amplitude, configuration, and duration of P waves are normal, conditions that prevail with tetralogy of Fallot and with an Eisenmenger ventricular septal defect, in which the hypertensive right ventricle copes with systemic resistance without the need for an increase in right atrial contractile force. The left atrium in not represented in the P wave in either malformation because in the tetralogy it is underfilled owing to reduced pulmonary blood flow and in Eisenmenger syndrome left atrial volume is curtailed by an elevated pulmonary vascular resistance. In tricuspid atresia, an increase in amplitude of the initial crest of the P wave reflects the response to an increased force of right atrial contraction; the second crest and the prolonged negative P terminal force in lead V_1 reflect volume overload of the left atrium, which receives both the systemic and pulmonary venous returns. Isolated left atrial P-wave abnormalities are reserved for pressure or volume overload confined to the left atrium, such as congenital mitral stenosis, left atrioventricular valve regurgitation of an atrioventricular septal defect, or left-sided Ebstein anomaly in congenitally corrected transposition of the great arteries.

Atrial enlargement is not an ECG diagnosis except in Ebstein anomaly of the tricuspid valve in which the diagnosis of enlargement is based on limb lead P waves and PR interval and on right precordial QRS complexes. The exceptional size of the right atrial compartment of the P wave is responsible for a distinctive, if not diagnostic, ECG combination consisting of an increase in amplitude (right atrial mass), prolongation of the PR interval (an increase in conduction time from sinus node to AV node), and precordial Q waves that extend from lead V_1 to V_3 because those sites correspond topographically to epicardial leads from the enlarged right atrium that extends anatomically as far left as the V_3 position (Fig. 4-4).

Left-axis deviation in CHD is not as simple as the left anterior fascicular block of acquired heart disease. Left-axis deviation is a time-honored feature of an atrioventricular septal defect, but *extreme* left-axis deviation with a mean QRS axis directed toward the right shoulder is evidence of coexisting Down syndrome. In univentricular hearts of left ventricular morphology, the direction of ventricular depolarization tends to be away from the outlet chamber and toward the main ventricular mass. Thus, when the outlet chamber is at the right basal aspect of the heart—the noninverted position—depolarization is to the left and upward (left-axis deviation) or to the left and downward (Fig. 4-5). In the more common form of tricuspid atresia with nontransposed great arteries and a restrictive ventricular septal defect, left-axis devia-

tion is the rule, but that is not the case when the ventricular septal defect is nonrestrictive, which implies coexisting complete transposition of the great arteries. In a cyanotic patient, left-axis deviation of type B pre-excitation is virtually diagnostic of Ebstein anomaly of the tricuspid valve. Left-axis deviation is a feature of double-outlet right ventricle with a subaortic ventricular septal defect. When pulmonary stenosis coexists, the axis is vertical but depolarization remains counterclockwise, so Q waves persist in leads 1 and aVL and serve as ECG markers that distinguish double-outlet right ventricle with pulmonary stenosis from tetralogy of Fallot, which is clinically indistinguishable. Left-axis deviation is a feature of anomalous origin of the left coronary from the pulmonary trunk because regional myocyte replication increases the mass of the posterobasal portion of the hypoperfused but viable immature left ventricle.[3]

An increase in amplitude of R and S waves is a feature of ventricular hypertrophy, but a dramatic increase in limb lead and precordial R and S wave voltages is unique to univentricular hearts of the left ventricular type (see Fig. 4-5). The excessive voltage, together with precordial QRS patterns that are stereotyped, justifies a presumptive diagnosis.

In ostium secundum and sinus venosus atrial septal defects, notching near the apex of R waves in the inferior leads (Fig. 4-6) has been called "crochetage" because of resemblance to the work of a crochet needle. Crochetage is independent of the terminal R wave deformity, but when an rSr' pattern exists with crochetage in all inferior leads, the specificity of the ECG diagnosis of atrial septal defect is virtually certain (see Fig. 4-6). In atrioventricular septal defects, the characteristic notching of S waves in the inferior leads is due to an abrupt change in terminal force direction and is not called crochetage.

An increase in duration of the QRS complex is expected because of prolonged ventricular activation of the bundle-branch blocks. However, prolonged intraventricular activation after right ventriculotomy has a special significance. After intracardiac repair of tetralogy of Fallot a QRS complex duration of 180 ms or more is an independent risk factor for monomorphic ventricular tachycardia and sudden cardiac death, especially if the prolongation occurred over a relatively short time course.[15] The increased QRS complex duration is believed to reflect slow conduction, which is the electrophysiologic substrate that sustains reentry, the mechanism of monomorphic ventricular tachycardia, which is the tachyarrhythmia associated with sudden cardiac death.[16]

Figure 4-4 Electrocardiogram in an adult with Ebstein anomaly of the tricuspid valve. Right atrial enlargement is indicated by tall peaked P waves, PR interval prolongation, and Q waves in leads V_1 to V_3. The QRS complex shows right bundle-branch block.

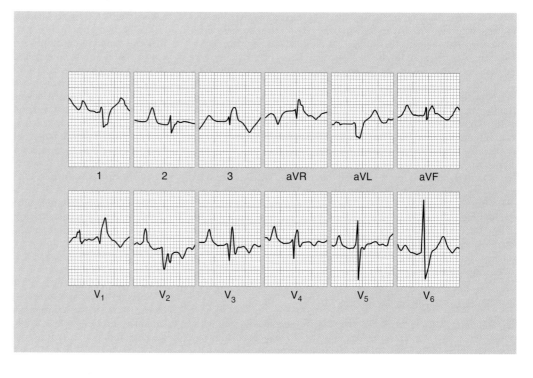

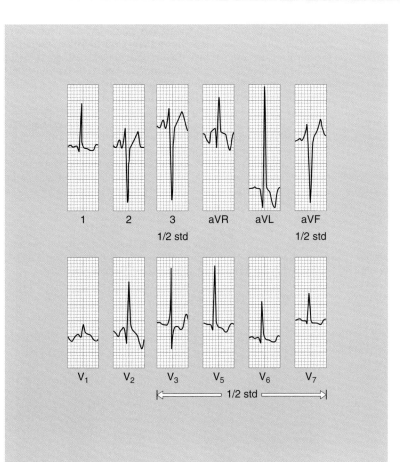

Figure 4-5 Electrocardiogram of a patient with a univentricular heart of left ventricular morphology. There is left-axis deviation. QRS amplitudes are strikingly increased in leads 3, aVL, aVF, and V₃ to V₅. The precordial QRS pattern is stereotyped (one-half standardized).

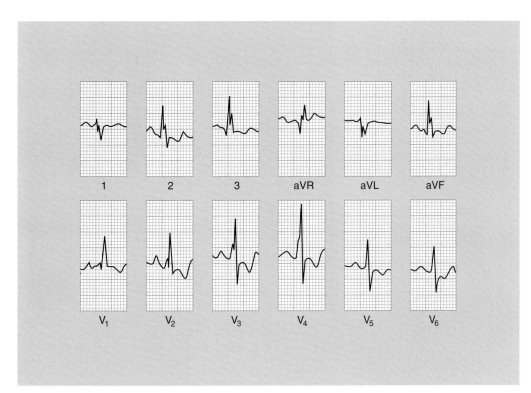

Figure 4-6 Typical electrocardiogram in a patient with an ostium secundum atrial septal defect. There is notching (crochetage) of the R waves in leads 2, 3, and aVF, with an rSr′ in lead V₁.

THE CHEST RADIOGRAPH

For interpretation of chest radiographs, a consistent sequence should be employed to avoid oversight. The sequence includes technique (penetration, rotation, degree of inhalation), age and sex, right-left orientation, positions and malpositions (thoracic, abdominal, and cardiac situs), the bones, the extrapulmonary soft tissue densities, the intrapulmonary soft tissue densities (vascular and nonvascular), the bronchi, the great arteries, the great veins, the atria, and the ventricle or ventricles.

Right-left orientation identified in the posteroanterior chest radiograph sets the stage for assessment of cardiac and visceral positions and malpositions (see Fig. 4-2A). Radiologic recognition of the basic cardiac malpositions and the visceral heterotaxies underscores the value of radiographic interpretation in complex CHD.[3]

A chest radiograph as a rule fortuitously includes the upper abdomen, thus permitting identification of gastric and hepatic situs (see Fig. 4-2). If the stomach bubble cannot be seen, visualization can be achieved by aerophagia—the swallowing of air after deliberate inhalation in adults or from sucking an empty bottle in infants. A transverse liver implies visceral heterotaxy but does not distinguish right from left isomerism. The inferior margin of a transverse liver is horizontal in contrast to the diagonal inferior margin of hepatomegaly in which there are two lobes of unequal size. Bilateral symmetry implied by a transverse liver demands bilateral symmetry of the bronchi. Bilateral morphologic right bronchi establish right isomerism (Fig. 4-7A), and bilateral morphologic left bronchi establish left isomerism (see Fig. 4-7B). Right isomerism predicts the presence of a primitive bilocular heart characterized by common morphologic right atria, a common atrioventricular valve, one ventricular compartment that gives rise to one great artery, and total anomalous pulmonary venous connection.[3] Left isomerism predicts the presence of a less primitive heart characterized by common morphologic left atria, atrioventricular septal defect, two ventricles that give rise to concordant great arteries with obstruction to left ventricular outflow, and inferior vena caval interruption with azygous continuation recognized by a thoracic shadow that can be mistaken for a right descending aorta.[3]

In patients without visceral heterotaxy, three clinically important cardiac malpositions can be recognized on the chest radiograph[3]: (1) situs inversus with dextrocardia, (2) situs solitus with dextrocardia, and (3) situs inversus with levocardia. Situs inversus with dextrocardia (see Fig. 4-2A) is characterized by a stomach bubble on the right, a liver shadow on the left, a right thoracic heart, a morphologic right bronchus with a trilobed lung on the left, and a morphologic left bronchus with a bilobed lung on the right. If the right/left (R-L) label on the radiograph (see Fig. 4-2A, B) is overlooked in a patient with complete situs inversus, the radiograph can be mistakenly read as normal situs. Mirror-image dextrocardia is seldom associated with CHD, but the pain of ischemic heart disease is central or right with radiation to the right shoulder and right arm; the pain of appendicitis is in the left lower quadrant, and the pain of biliary colic is in the left upper quadrant. A coexisting disorder of ciliary mobility is manifested by sinusitis with bronchiectasis (Kartagener syndrome) and male infertility owing to immobility of sperm.[3] Situs solitus with dextrocardia is recognized

by normal positions of the stomach, liver, and bronchi in the presence of a right thoracic heart (see Fig. 4-2B). In this positional anomaly, the normal embryonic straight cardiac tube initially bends to the right (D loop) but then fails to pivot into the left chest. Left-to-right shunts at atrial or ventricular levels usually coexist. When the bulboventricular loop in situs solitus initially bends to the left and then pivots to the right where an L loop "belongs," dextrocardia is once again present and congenitally corrected transposition of the great arteries exists by definition.[3] Situs inversus with levocardia is recognized by mirror-image positions of stomach, liver, and bronchi in the presence of a left thoracic heart (see Fig. 4-2C). A concordant L loop fails to pivot into the right hemithorax, or a discordant D loop pivots into the left side of the chest. CHD invariably coexists, but the types are not predictable.

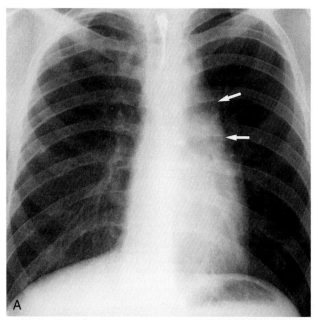

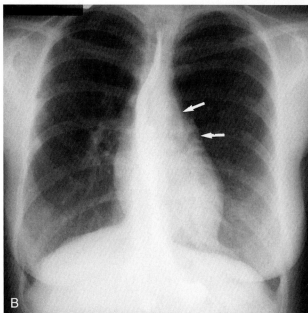

Figure 4-8 **A,** Chest radiograph of a patient with a univentricular heart of left ventricular morphology. The inverted outlet chamber gives rise to the aorta and straightens the left upper cardiac border (*arrows*). **B,** Chest radiograph of a patient with isolated congenitally corrected transposition of the great arteries. The inverted infundibulum gives rise to the aorta and straightens the left upper cardiac border (*arrows*).

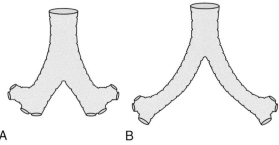

Figure 4-7 **A,** Symmetrical morphologic right bronchi characteristic of right isomerism. **B,** Symmetrical morphologic left bronchi characteristic of left isomerism.

Absence of the 12th rib, a bony abnormality typical of Down syndrome, can be detected in the chest radiograph by counting the ribs. When an absent 12th rib is coupled with extreme left-axis deviation (see earlier), the diagnosis of Down syndrome is virtually conclusive.

Radiologic identification of right and left ventricular chamber(s) can be problematic. Inversion of the outlet chamber with a univentricular heart (Fig. 4-8A) is virtually indistinguishable from congenitally corrected transposition of the great arteries with a biventricular heart (see Fig. 4-8B). The distinction can be made on the ECG (see Fig. 4-5).

CONCLUSION

The increasing array of laboratory methods provides contemporary clinicians with unprecedented diagnostic information, but an intelligent decision on which laboratory method(s) to select requires a new level of knowledge and sophistication.

This chapter was designed to help in this selection process by stimulating clinicians to use the basic tools at their disposal—the history, physical examination, ECG, and chest radiograph.

REFERENCES

1. Brown JW. Preface to Congenital Heart Disease. London: John Bale Medical Publications; 1939.
2. Perloff JK. Preface. In: Clinical Recognition of Congenital Heart Disease. Philadelphia: WB Saunders; 1970.
3. Perloff JK. Clinical Recognition of Congenital Heart Disease. 5th ed. Philadelphia: WB Saunders; 2003.
4. Perloff JK. Physical Examination of the Heart and Circulation. 4th ed. Beijing: Peoples Medical Publishing House USA Ltd; 2009.
5. Chou T, Helm RA, Kaplan S. Clinical Vectorcardiography. New York: Grune & Stratton; 1974.
6. Child JS. Echocardiography in anatomic imaging and hemodynamic evaluation of adults with congenital heart disease. In: Perloff JK, Child JS, Aboulhosn J, editors. Congenital Heart Disease in Adults. 3rd ed. Philadelphia: Saunders/Elsevier; 2009.
7. Wood P. Diseases of the Heart and Circulation. 2nd ed. Philadelphia: JB Lippincott; 1956.
8. Perloff JK. Cyanotic congenital heart disease: a multisystem disorder. In: Perloff JK, Child JS, Aboulhosn J, editors. Congenital Heart Disease in Adults. 3rd ed. Philadelphia: Saunders/Elsevier; 2009.
9. Perloff JK, Saver JL. Neurologic disorders. In: Perloff JK, Child JS, Aboulhosn J, editors. Congenital Heart Disease in Adults. 3rd ed. Philadelphia: Saunders/Elsevier; 2009.
10. Child JS, Pegues DA, Perloff JK. Infective endocarditis. In: Perloff JK, Child JS, Aboulhosn J, editors. Congenital Heart Disease in Adults. 3rd ed. Philadelphia: Saunders/Elsevier; 2009.
11. Guze BH, Moreno EA, Perloff JK. Psychiatric and psychosocial disorders. In: Perloff JK, Child JS, Aboulhosn J, editors. Congenital Heart Disease in Adults. 3rd ed. Philadelphia: Saunders/Elsevier; 2009.
12. Allaby M. The Oxford Dictionary of Natural History. Oxford: Oxford University Press; 1985.
13. Hoffman JIE. Reflections on the past, present and future of pediatric cardiology. Cardiol Young 1994;4:208.
14. Mackenzie J. The Study of the Pulse, Arterial, Venous, and Hepatic, and of the Movements of the Heart. Edinburgh: Young J. Pentland; 1902.
15. Gatzoulis MA, Balaji S, Webber SA. Risk factors for arrhythmia and sudden cardiac death in repaired tetralogy of Fallot. Lancet 2000;356:975–981.
16. Perloff JK, Middlekauf HR, Child JS, et al. Usefulness of post-ventriculotomy signal averaged electrocardiograms in congenital heart disease. Am J Cardiol 2006;98:1646–1651.

5

Echocardiography

EDGAR TAY LIK WUI | JAMES W. L. YIP | WEI LI

Introduction

Echocardiography has been a diagnostic tool in the field of congenital heart disease (CHD) since late 1950.[1] Improved surgical techniques and interventions have enabled patients with complex congenital hearts to survive into adulthood, presenting new clinical challenges. Concurrently, the development of new echocardiographic imaging technologies has allowed us to understand and manage these clinical problems. It is important to appreciate that echocardiography is part of the armamentarium of imaging tools available to the cardiologist and that often a combination of these are necessary for clinical management of patients. The advantages and disadvantages of these tools are presented in Table 5-1.

Using Segmental Analysis to Describe Abnormal Cardiovascular Connections

Segmental analysis was described in Chapter 2. It is important to systematically assess all abnormalities using echocardiography. The subcostal view is used to determine to where the cardiac apex points. This view also allows the assessment of the relationship of the aorta, the inferior vena cava, and the spine to help determine atrial situs. This is followed by assessment of atrioventricular (AV) and ventriculoarterial connections before describing the other associated intracardiac lesions.

Echocardiography in Specific Diagnostic Groups

ATRIAL SEPTAL DEFECT

Atrial septal defect (ASD) is one of the most common defects seen in the adult congenital heart disease (ACHD) clinic.

Type and Location
Secundum Atrial Septal Defect
The majority of ASDs are secundum atrial septal defects. The defect is localized centrally in the intra-atrial septum. There can be multiple defects, and the defect may be fenestrated. This is best viewed in the modified parasternal four-chamber view and the subcostal view (Fig. 5-1).

Primum Atrial Septal Defect
Primum atrial septal defect is less common and forms part of the spectrum of AV septal defect (AVSD) with a common AV junction (Fig. 5-2). The defect is best viewed from the apical four-chamber view. It is often associated with an abnormal left AV valve (trileaflet left-sided AV valve), which is best seen in the parasternal short-axis view.

Sinus Venosus Defect
The sinus venosus defect is positioned outside the limbus of the fossa ovalis, on the right septal surface next to the drainage site of the superior (or inferior) vena cava (superior vena cava 5.3% to 10%; inferior vena cava 2%). The caval veins have a biatrial connection, overriding the septum. Partially anomalous venous return of the right upper pulmonary vein is a common association. This type of defect can be visualized from the modified parasternal view in echogenic adult patients. Transesophageal echocardiography at the mid esophagus with 90-degree caval views is diagnostic.

Coronary Sinus Defect (Unroofed Coronary Sinus)
The coronary sinus defect is located in the wall that separates the coronary sinus from the left atrium. It may be fenestrated or completely absent. An enlarged coronary sinus with a dropout between the left atrium and the coronary sinus is seen. The best imaging view is the four-chamber view with slight posterior angulation.

Size and Hemodynamic Effects
Large left-to-right shunting may result in right-sided heart dilation and raised pulmonary pressure. The following are features of significant shunting:
- Right atrial and ventricular dilation
- Reversed septal motion
- Elevated right ventricular pressure
- Large left-to-right shunt ($\dot{Q}p/\dot{Q}s > 2:1$). This is quantified using the continuity equation (RVOT VTI × RVOT area/LVOT VTI × LVOT area), where RVOT is the right ventricular outflow tract, LVOT is the left ventricular outflow tract, and VTI is the velocity time integral.

Associated Anomalies
Although isolated ASD is common, ASDs can also be associated with many congenital anomalies. The segmental analysis approach should be used to avoid missing important defects.

Interventional Closure
Before starting closure of an ASD, the type, location (only secundum defects are suitable), and its hemodynamic significance is assessed.[2] The size and position of the defect determines the feasibility for closure and the size of the occluder device.

Transesophageal (Fig. 5-3) or intracardiac echocardiographic guidance is used during interventional closure of secundum ASDs. Before device closure, the adequacy of the ASD rims needs to be defined. Three-dimensional (3D) transesophageal echocardiography is increasingly used for this purpose (Fig. 5-4).

After surgical or interventional closure, the following are assessed:
- Presence of residual shunt
- Position of the device relative to other cardiac structures (Fig. 5-5)
- Right and left ventricular size and function
- Presence of pulmonary hypertension
- AV valve function (especially after repair of an ostium primum ASD)

Persistence of right-sided heart dilation is usually the sign of residual left-to-right shunt. Impaired ventricular function (especially of the left ventricle) is common in patients with coexistent coronary artery disease or arrhythmias.

VENTRICULAR SEPTAL DEFECT

The following is a recommended approach for evaluation of a ventricular septal defect (VSD):

Determination of Type of Defect
Perimembranous VSDs (60%) are localized in the membranous part of the septum and are characterized by fibrous continuity between the leaflets of the AV and arterial valve (Fig. 5-6).[3] These defects can have inlet, trabecular, or outlet extensions (Fig. 5-7). Anterior deviation of the outlet part of the septum can cause right ventricular outflow tract obstruction (tetralogy of Fallot). Similarly, posterior deviation can result in left ventricular outflow tract obstruction and can be associated with aortic arch anomalies (coarctation, interrupted aortic arch).

Muscular VSDs (20%) are localized in the muscular septum and can be described as inlet, trabecular, or outlet type, depending on the location of defect. Occasionally, there may be multiple defects.

TABLE 5-1	Advantages and Disadvantages of Imaging Modalities		
Imaging Modality	*Advantages*		*Disadvantages*
Chest radiography	Allows an overview of the heart and adjacent structures (mediastinum, pulmonary vasculature, lungs, and thoracic spine) Inexpensive Highly reproducible		Ionizing radiation (albeit low) Lack of hemodynamic information Inadequate visualization of structures
Transthoracic echocardiography (TTE)	Convenient Portable Real-time acquisition Provides hemodynamic information Modest cost Safe No ionizing radiation		Operator dependent Limited echocardiographic windows and lack of penetration results in suboptimal images
Transesophageal echocardiography (TEE)	Superior imaging for posterior structures		Relatively invasive Limited field of view Limited access to extracardiac structures Doppler alignment to the eccentric jets possibly challenging
Cardiovascular MRI (CMR)	No ionizing radiation Imaging not restricted by body size or poor windows Gold standard for assessment of ventricular volumes Allows hemodynamic assessment and tissue characterization		Expensive and expertise needed Not widely available Not suitable for patients with pacemakers/defibrillators Gadolinium contrast may be contraindicated in patients with significant renal impairment
Multislice computed tomography (MSCT)	Excellent spatial localization and spatial resolution Rapid acquisition time Excellent for visualizing coronary arteries, surgical shunts, collaterals, and stented structures May allow measurement of ventricular size and function with gating		Substantial dose of ionizing radiation Relatively costly Tissue characterization and contrast inferior to CMR Provides less hemodynamic information compared with echocardiography/CMR

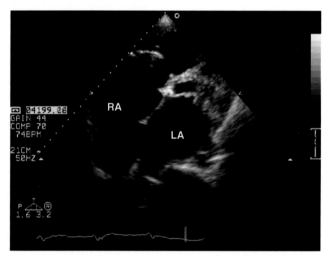

Figure 5-1 Secundum atrial septal defect. The modified apical four-chamber view demonstrates this large secundum defect. LA, left atrium; RA, right atrium.

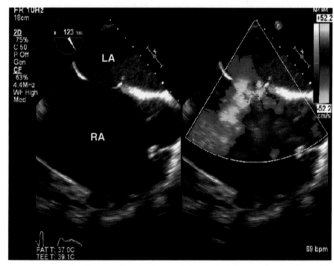

Figure 5-3 Intraprocedural transesophageal echocardiography. The accurate sizing of the defect is performed before closure. LA, left atrium; RA, right atrium.

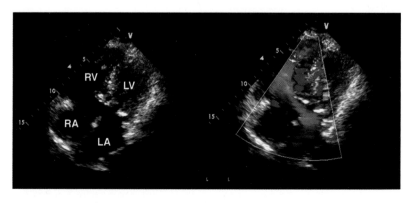

Figure 5-2 Partial atrioventricular septal defect (primum ASD). **Left,** Note the large defect. **Right,** Color flow Doppler image shows that the shunt is predominantly left to right. LA, left atrium; LV, left ventricle; RA, right atrium; RV, right ventricle.

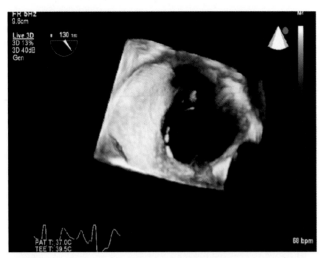

Figure 5-4   3D transesophageal echocardiography. The irregularly shaped defect is better appreciated with this technique.

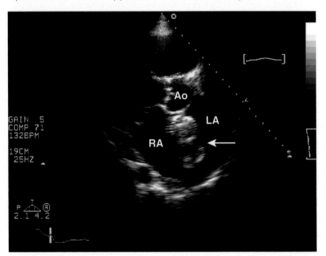

Figure 5-5   Appearance after transcatheter device closure of the ASD. The atrial septal occluder is well seated over the defect (*white arrow*). Ao, aorta; LA, left atrium; RA, right atrium.

Doubly committed VSDs (5%) are localized just below the aortic and pulmonary valve and are characterized by fibrous continuity between the aortic and pulmonary valve.

Defect Size and Hemodynamic Significance

The VSD should be measured in at least two views. The defect can be described as small (<5 mm), moderate (5 to 10 mm), or large (>10 mm).

Figure 5-6   Perimembranous VSD. The color flow Doppler image shows bidirectional shunting. Ao, aorta; LA, left atrium; RA, right atrium; RVOT; right ventricular outflow tract.

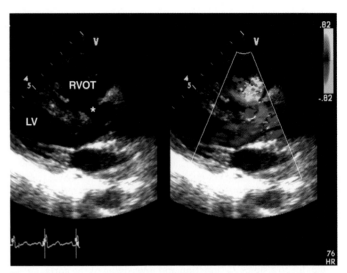

Figure 5-7   Outlet VSD. The *asterisk* marks the defect, which shows predominant left-to-right flow in systole. LV, left ventricle; RVOT, right ventricular outflow tract.

Large left-to-right shunting results in left atrial and ventricular dilation. Left atrial size and volume and left ventricular dimensions should therefore be measured. Functional mitral regurgitation can be associated.

A restrictive VSD has a significant peak instantaneous gradient (>75 mm Hg) and is not associated with left atrial or left ventricular dilation or pulmonary hypertension. A nonrestrictive VSD will have a small peak instantaneous gradient (<25 mm Hg) and have significant left atrial/left ventricular dilation with pulmonary hypertension.

A VSD can be associated with pulmonary arterial hypertension. Right ventricular pressures can be estimated with continuous Doppler interrogation of the gradient across the VSD (Right ventricular systolic pressure = Systolic blood pressure − 4 × (VSD peak velocity^2). Significant pulmonary vascular disease may result in bidirectional or predominantly right-to-left shunting across the VSD (Eisenmenger syndrome).

Qp/Qs greater than 1.5 to 2.0 : 1 quantified with the continuity equation is considered to be hemodynamically significant.

Associated Anomalies

Important associated lesions include prolapse of the aortic cusp with progressive aortic regurgitation and development of a double-chamber right ventricle from hypertrophy of right ventricular muscle bands.

With the exception of muscular defects, most defects are closed surgically if indicated. Some institutions perform catheter closure of perimembranous defects in selected cases. After interventional or surgical closure, the following need to be assessed:

• Residual VSDs
• Subaortic stenosis

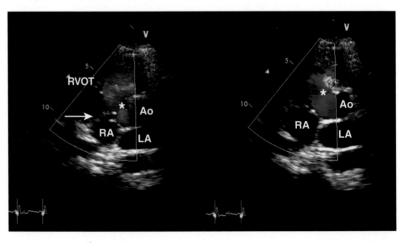

- Subpulmonary stenosis
- Aortic insufficiency
- Left ventricular function

ATRIOVENTRICULAR SEPTAL DEFECT

Most AVSDs seen in adulthood would have been treated surgically in infancy. Unoperated AVSDs with large ventricular components are commonly associated with irreversible pulmonary vascular disease.

Identification of Morphology

There are three main types of morphology:
- A *partial* AVSD is similar to a primum ASD.
- An *intermediate* AVSD is characterized by a primum ASD, a small restrictive VSD, and separate right and left AV valves (which is trileaflet).
- A *complete* AVSD has a primum ASD, a nonrestrictive VSD, and a common AV valve (Fig. 5-8).

There is a lack of offset between the left and right AV valves in the apical four-chamber view.[4] The left ventricular outflow tract is elongated due to a single AV junction and unwedging of the aorta.

The AV valve is made up of five leaflets. AV valve regurgitation can be present. Regurgitation is often seen at the commissure between the bridging leaflets and between the inferior bridging leaflet and the mural leaflet.

Hemodynamic Significance

The atrial and ventricular shunt can result in atrial and ventricular dilation. Pulmonary hypertension is present. The $\dot{Q}p/\dot{Q}s$ should be measured.

Associated Lesions

Associated lesions include secundum ASD, tetralogy of Fallot, transposition complexes, and double orifice of the left AV valve.

Assessment of Repaired Atrioventricular Septal Defect

This assessment includes the following:
- Detection of residual shunts
- Determination of left and right AV valve function. AV valve regurgitation is common, and valvular stenosis may also be present.
- Assessment for left ventricular outflow tract obstruction
- Assessment for the presence of pulmonary arterial hypertension

PATENT DUCTUS ARTERIOSUS

A patent ductus arteriosus (PDA) is not uncommon in adulthood.[5] Significant left-to-right shunting results in left ventricular volume overload and often progresses to pulmonary arterial hypertension and Eisenmenger syndrome in adult patients.

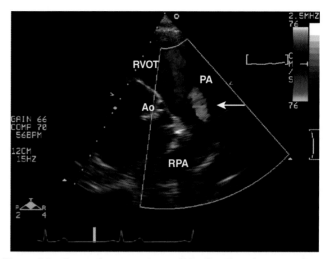

Figure 5-9 Patent ductus arteriosus. Color flow Doppler image shows the left-to-right shunt (*arrow*). Ao, aorta; PA, pulmonary artery; RPA, right pulmonary artery; RVOT, right ventricular outflow tract.

The following should be determined:
- Size and location
- Direction of flow
- Secondary hemodynamic effects: left atrial and ventricular dilation and the presence of pulmonary hypertension
- Associated congenital defects

Size and Location

The duct is commonly located between the descending aorta and the left pulmonary artery (with left-sided aortic arch) (Fig. 5-9). With a right-sided aortic arch the duct can be present between the descending aorta and the right pulmonary artery but more commonly connects the left subclavian artery with the left pulmonary artery. Large ducts with low-velocity bidirectional shunting are difficult to visualize on two-dimensional (2D) echocardiography. Computed tomography (CT) or magnetic resonance imaging (MRI) may be the ideal choice for diagnosis.

Direction of Flow

The shunt size and direction can be assessed by Doppler imaging (Fig. 5-10). With normal pulmonary vascular resistance, flow is left to right and continuous. Flow velocity is high in a restrictive PDA. The peak and mean gradient between the aorta and pulmonary artery can be measured. With increasing pulmonary vascular resistance, flow

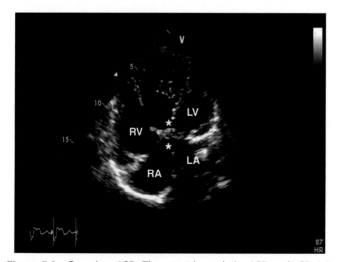

Figure 5-8 Complete ASD. The *asterisks* mark the ASD and VSD. LA, left atrium; LV, left ventricle; RA, right atrium; RV, right ventricle.

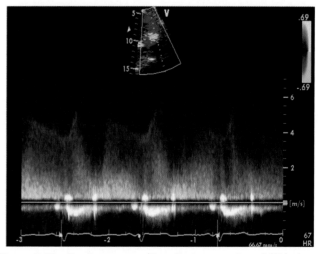

Figure 5-10 Continuous wave Doppler interrogation of PDA shows continuous left-to-right flow of this defect.

becomes bidirectional with right-to-left flow in systole and left-to-right shunting in diastole. With progressive pulmonary vascular disease, the shunt can be exclusively right to left.

Associated Anomalies
Associated anomalies are uncommon in the setting of a PDA presenting in adulthood.

Secondary Hemodynamic Effects
Secondary hemodynamic effects include left atrial and left ventricular dilation, secondary mitral regurgitation, and pulmonary hypertension.

Management
A duct can be closed by surgery or transcatheter techniques using a coil or a duct occluder. After closure, the following should be assessed:
- Device position
- Residual shunt through the duct
- Residual pulmonary hypertension
- Residual left ventricular dilation and mitral regurgitation
- Obstruction of the left pulmonary artery after coil/device placement

AORTIC COARCTATION

The incidence of aortic coarctation varies from 5.3% to 7.5% of all adults with CHD. Patients presenting in adulthood can be divided into those who received prior surgical intervention for coarctation and now have re-coarctation or those presenting for the first time (often with systemic hypertension).

In classic coarctation, the narrowing of the aorta is located distal to the origin of the left subclavian artery at the arterial duct (Fig. 5-11). This narrowing is usually discrete but can be associated with long-segment hypoplasia. Coarctation alone is termed *simple* if it is the only lesion and *complex* if it is associated with other lesions.

Echocardiography can provide the following information:
- Confirmation of the diagnosis of coarctation/re-coarctation
- Location and assessment of severity
- Secondary effects: left ventricular hypertrophy, left ventricular dysfunction, coexistent coronary artery disease
- Associated lesions, especially bicuspid aortic valve, mitral valve disease (parachute mitral valve), and left ventricular outflow tract obstruction
- Assessment of prior interventions (e.g., aneurysms after patch repair)

Diagnosis and Location
The subcostal long-axis view of the abdominal allows screening for coarctation using pulsed wave Doppler imaging. A decreased systolic

flow with diastolic runoff is suggestive of a narrowing on the thoracic aorta. To identify the location of the narrowing, the suprasternal view should be used. The narrowing can often be detected just distal to the left subclavian artery (this window may be limited in adult patients). Color flow Doppler imaging would show flow turbulence.

Hemodynamic Significance
Continuous wave Doppler imaging is used to interrogate the narrowed segment. The modified Bernoulli equation permits measurement of flow velocity across the segment and can be used to estimate the pressure drop across the narrowing (Fig. 5-12). The coarctation is significant if high velocities (>30 mm Hg peak gradient with continuous wave imaging across the descending aorta) with anterograde diastolic flow is seen (diastolic runoff). In severe cases the antegrade systolic flow velocity may be very low. Doppler profile in abdominal aorta (low velocity continuous flow) is helpful in diagnosis.[6]

The following are important caveats:
- PDA or collateral vessels may reduce the gradient across the coarctation.
- The simplified Bernoulli equation is less accurate for long lesions or multiple stenosis.
- Patients with coarctation often have multiple obstructive lesions in series that lead to an increased peak velocity proximal to the coarctation. For this reason the expanded Bernoulli equation should be used if the proximal velocity exceeds 1 m/s: Peak gradient = $4v^2$ max-coarctation − $4v^2$ max-pre-coarctation

Secondary Effects
Left ventricular wall thickness, mass, and systolic and diastolic function should be assessed.

Assessments of Prior Interventions
Aneurysms or re-coarctation can be similarly assessed (Fig. 5-13).[7] In adult patients, MRI is the modality of choice for evaluating suspected aneurysm formation.

RIGHT VENTRICULAR OUTFLOW TRACT OBSTRUCTION

Right ventricular outflow tract obstruction can be classified into valvular and subvalvular stenoses. Valvular stenosis makes up the majority (80%) of cases.[8] The pulmonary valve is best visualized in the parasternal short-axis and parasternal long-axis pulmonary outflow view (leftward and slight superior tilt from the usual parasternal long axis) and apical five-chamber view with further anterior tilt.

Morphology
The valves may be unicuspid, bicuspid, tricuspid, or quadricuspid. The most common type in isolated pulmonary valvular stenosis is the acommissural type. The bicuspid pulmonary valve is less commonly

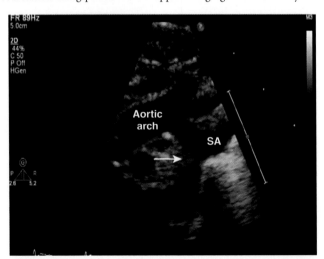

Figure 5-11 Coarctation of the aorta. A discrete narrowing is seen distal to the subclavian artery (SA) (*white arrow*).

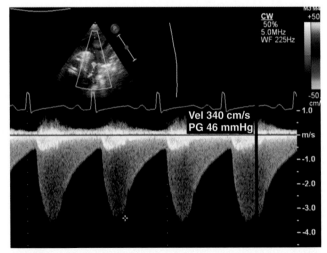

Figure 5-12 Continuous wave Doppler recording through the coarctation of aorta in descending aorta.

seen compared with the aortic valve, and often both cusps are similar in size. The trileaflet valves are often dysplastic. The commissures are not fused, and obstruction is due to the valve thickening and a small annulus (seen in Noonan syndrome). The quadricuspid valve is more frequently seen compared with the aortic site. Only one third of the quadricuspid valves are stenotic.

Degree of Severity
Stenosis is severe if the peak gradient (using continuous wave Doppler imaging) measures more than 80 mm Hg. Right ventricular hypertrophy with restrictive physiology is often seen. Large left-to-right shunts can lead to elevated velocities. Conversely, right ventricular dysfunction, tricuspid regurgitation, right-to-left shunting, or a PDA augmenting pressures distally results in a lower velocity across the stenosis.

Pulmonary Artery Dilation
Post-stenotic dilation often may be present in a patient with valvular stenosis.

Associated Anomalies
Patent foramen ovales (PFOs) or secundum ASDs are frequent.

Subvalvular Stenosis
Subvalvular stenosis includes infundibular stenosis or a double-chamber right ventricle. A double-chamber right ventricle is characterized by muscle bundles dividing the right ventricle into a proximal and distal chamber and is differentiated from infundibular stenosis in that the obstruction is located lower within the body of the right ventricle. A concomitant perimembranous VSD may be identified. This is best seen in the parasternal short-axis view or the apical five-chamber view with anterior tilt.

Infundibular stenosis is located at the lower portion of the pulmonary infundibulum where the infundibulum unites with the trabecular portion of the right ventricle (usually a ring or diaphragm with a central orifice).

LEFT VENTRICULAR OUTFLOW TRACT OBSTRUCTION

The levels of left ventricular outflow tract obstruction can be divided into valvular, subvalvular, or supravalvular.

Valvular Aortic Stenosis
This constitutes 70% of left ventricular outflow tract obstruction. The following are assessed:
- Valve morphology
- Aortic root size
- Annular size
- Severity of obstruction
- Impact on the left ventricle
- Associated abnormalities

Similar to pulmonary stenosis, the valves may be unicuspid, bicuspid, tricuspid, or quadricuspid. In adults, the bicuspid valve is most common (occurring in 1% to 2% of the population) with both leaflets being unequal in size. The larger leaflet may have a bisecting fibrous raphe that does not reach the central edge. In adults, stenosis occurs due to fusion, fibrosis, or calcification of the commissures. Infective endocarditis may accelerate the deterioration of such valves. Quadricuspid valves are more often regurgitant than stenotic valves and usually consist of three normally sized leaflets and one small leaflet.

The short-axis view enables assessment of the number of valves. The bicuspid valve opens like a fishmouth with limitation of leaflet excursion. The inequality of the two valves and its often eccentric closure line make planimetry of the valve area difficult. The parasternal long-axis views show doming of the leaflets and allow measurement of the aortic root.

Aortopathy is common in patients with bicuspid aortic valves. The aortic root has a "water hose" appearance with dilation occurring mainly in the proximal ascending aorta. The dimension of the hinge point, sinuses of Valsalva, and sinotubular junction should also be assessed.

The degree of valve excursion can be assessed by 2D or M-mode color Doppler imaging, which shows turbulence across the valve. Planimetry

on 2D imaging can occasionally be difficult. The highest peak velocity across the valve should be assessed by continuous wave Doppler imaging from multiple windows (e.g., the apical five-chamber view, the apical three-chamber view, and the right parasternal or suprasternal views). The stenosis is severe if the jet velocity is more than 4 m/s, the mean gradient is more than 40 mm Hg, and the valve area is less than 1 cm or less than 0.6 cm/m^2 (indexed).

The left ventricle should also be assessed for left ventricular hypertrophy and diastolic dysfunction, which is often associated with significant stenosis.

Common associated anomalies include PDA, coarctation, and mitral valve stenosis.

Subaortic Stenosis
Subaortic stenosis is a narrowing below the aortic valve (Fig. 5-14). There are two commonly described subtypes: a fibromuscular ridge and a tunnel-type obstruction. Color flow Doppler imaging detects turbulence whereas pulsed wave Doppler imaging helps to localize the origin of acceleration. M-mode and 2D imaging may demonstrate early systolic closure of the aortic valve or fluttering of the aortic valves. Continuous wave Doppler imaging should be used to assess the peak and mean gradients across the lesion. Of importance, the fibromuscular tunnel type is likely to be associated with a small aortic root. This poses more difficulties compared with valvular stenoses with regard to discrepancies in catheter- and Doppler-derived gradients. The maximal

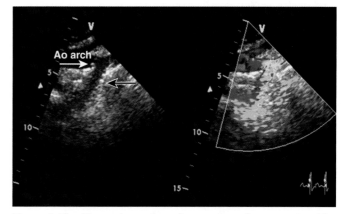

Figure 5-13 Obstruction to flow after stenting of a coarctation. The previous stent is visualized in this suprasternal view (*black arrow*). A small portion of the stent protrudes (*white arrow*) and causes obstruction to flow (*right image*). Ao, aorta.

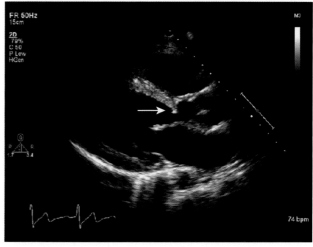

Figure 5-14 Subaortic stenosis. A fibromuscular ridge is seen proximal to the aortic valve (*arrow*).

velocity found in the tunnel may be missed by both Doppler or catheter techniques. Furthermore, the gradients may be further underestimated due to viscous forces along the tunnel.

In the ACHD clinic, subaortic stenosis can also be encountered after AVSD repair, repair of a double-outlet right ventricle (Rastelli procedure), or the arterial switch operation.

Supravalvular Stenosis

Supravalvular stenosis is rare. The stenosis can be membranous, hourglass shaped, or associated with hypoplasia of the ascending aorta (20%). The aortic valve is involved in 30% of cases with valve dysplasia, fibrosis, or thickening, and aortic regurgitation may be present. The coronary arteries can be involved in the narrowing. Associated pulmonary branch stenosis is not uncommon. These changes may be present as part of Williams syndrome.

EBSTEIN ANOMALY

Ebstein anomaly of the tricuspid valve is defined by apical displacement of the septal (more than 0.8 cm/m^2 from the mitral annulus) and posteroinferior leaflets of the tricuspid valve (Fig. 5-15).[9] Typically, the tricuspid valve orifice is rotated superiorly toward the right ventricular outflow tract. The anterosuperior leaflet is often large and redundant (sail-like).

In this condition, the following should be assessed:
- Morphology of the defect
- Presence of tricuspid valve stenosis or regurgitation
- Left ventricular function
- Suitability for surgical repair
- Associated anomalies

The apical four-chamber view allows immediate appreciation of the displacement of the septal leaflet as well as the attachment of the anterosuperior leaflet to the AV groove while the subcostal four-chamber and parasternal long axis with medial angulation views allow assessment of the displacement of the mural leaflet (posteroinferior).

Tricuspid valve regurgitation is often severe. More than one jet may be seen on color flow Doppler imaging if there is fenestration of the tricuspid valve. Qualitatively, the regurgitation is severe if this jet extends to the superior border of the right atrium on color Doppler imaging and if continuous wave Doppler imaging shows a dense spectral signal.

A vena contracta measuring more than 0.7 cm, with a large regurgitant fraction and regurgitant volume of more than 60% and more than 60 mL, respectively, also defines severe tricuspid regurgitation.

In adult patients, color flow Doppler imaging often does not show turbulence owing to the low velocity of the tricuspid regurgitation jet. Also,

continuous wave Doppler imaging would show a reduced peak gradient and even laminar flow of this jet owing to rapid equalization of the right ventricular and right atrial pressures from severe tricuspid regurgitation.

Left ventricular systolic and diastolic dysfunction is commonly seen and relates to late mortality. Intervention on the tricuspid valve appears to have a favorable impact on left ventricular function.[10]

The ability to repair or replace the valve can be assessed echocardiographically. The anterior leaflet should be mobile and of good size. The size of the atrialized portion should also be assessed to decide if plication is necessary. Tethering of the anterior tricuspid leaflet and a large dilated, noncontractile atrialized right ventricle would make repair difficult (Fig. 5-16).

A patent foramen ovale/ASD is common (80%). This should be assessed from the modified four-chamber view at the left sternal edge, the parasternal short-axis view, or the subcostal view. If right atrial pressures are elevated, right-to-left shunting may be seen. Agitated saline contrast may be used to demonstrate this. Other associated conditions include VSD, AVSD, and congenitally corrected transposition of the great arteries (see later).

CONGENITAL ABNORMALITIES OF THE MITRAL VALVE

Parachute Mitral Valve

The parachute mitral valve defect involves the attachment of the chordae tendineae to a single papillary muscle (most commonly the posteromedial papillary muscle).

Double-Orifice Mitral Valve

The double-orifice mitral valve defect is characterized by two separate mitral valve orifices. The first type is associated with AVSD. The second type is caused by reduplication of the mitral valve orifice with two orifices each having their own chordal attachments and papillary muscles.

Isolated Cleft in the Mitral Valve

The isolated cleft in the anterior mitral leaflet not associated with an AVSD (Fig. 5-17). Some studies have suggested that the closer position of the papillary muscles to each other and the larger size of the mural leaflet allow differentiation from AVSD.

Supravalvular Mitral Ring

A supravalvular mitral ring is a shelflike structure found above the mitral valve. It originates from the fibrous annulus.

Continuous wave Doppler interrogation can be used to assess the degree of stenosis. The valve is severe if the mitral valve area (assessed by continuity equation or pressure half time) is less than 1 cm^2, the

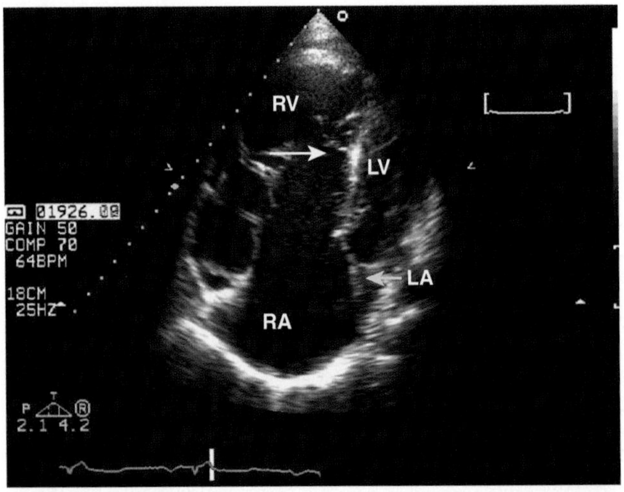

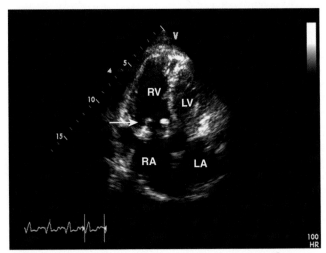

Figure 5-15 Ebstein anomaly. The septal leaflet of the tricuspid valve is markedly displaced apically (*white arrow*). The functional right ventricle is small. The left atrium is compressed by the large right atrium (*yellow arrow*). LA, left atrium; LV, left ventricle; RA, right atrium; RV, right ventricle.

Figure 5-16 Appearance after tricuspid valve replacement and right atrial (RA) plication for Ebstein anomaly. The bioprosthesis is well seated (*white arrow*). LA, left atrium; LV, left ventricle; RV, right ventricle.

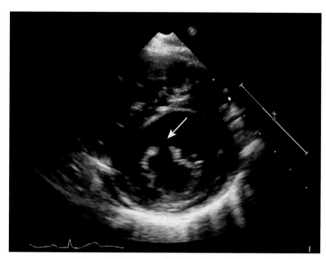

Figure 5-17 Mitral valve cleft (*arrow*).

mean gradient is greater than 10 mm Hg, and the pulmonary artery systolic pressure is more than 50 mm Hg.

COR TRIATRIATUM SINISTER

A fibromuscular membrane divides the left atrium into two separate chambers.[11] The proximal chamber receives the four pulmonary veins. The left atrial appendage is located below the membrane. Occasionally, several orifices in the membrane may be seen. There may be obstruction caused by the membrane, and a mean gradient of more than 10 mm Hg (using continuous wave Doppler imaging) is consistent with severe stenosis. In up to 50% of cases there may be an ASD/PFO. This usually communicates with the distal chamber. Dilated pulmonary veins and associated pulmonary arterial hypertension also suggests significant stenosis. Anomalous pulmonary venous drainage may be present.

TETRALOGY OF FALLOT WITH AND WITHOUT PULMONARY ATRESIA

Tetralogy of Fallot is characterized by anterocephalad deviation of the outlet septum resulting in a subaortic VSD, overriding aorta, infundibular pulmonary stenosis, as well as right ventricular hypertrophy. It is associated with variable degrees of pulmonary valve obstruction and hypoplasia of pulmonary artery branches. Tetralogy of Fallot with pulmonary atresia can be considered an extreme form in which there is no connection between the right ventricle and the pulmonary circulation. The pulmonary perfusion may be duct dependent or be dependent on major aortopulmonary collateral vessels. Most patients presenting in adulthood would have undergone some extent of palliation or primary repair.

Echocardiographic assessment of unrepaired tetralogy of Fallot includes:
- Assessing the size and location of the VSD and the degree of aortic override: perimembranous to outlet (92%), doubly committed (5%), inlet VSD or AVSD (2%). If the aorta overrides the VSD by more than 50%, the term *double-outlet right ventricle* should be used.
- Assessing the level of right ventricular outflow tract obstruction and its severity
- Assessing for pulmonary artery abnormalities, including the absence of central pulmonary arteries, aortopulmonary collateral vessels, or discontinuity between the right and left pulmonary arteries. The size of the pulmonary arteries should also be measured.
- Assessing coronary artery abnormalities (using short-axis views).
- Determining whether the arch is left or right sided and whether there are aortopulmonary collateral vessels
- Assessing associated abnormalities (ASDs, left superior vena cava, additional VSDs, abnormal pulmonary venous return)

Echocardiographic assessment of palliated tetralogy of Fallot requires understanding the type of surgery that was performed and evaluation of the following:
- Residual right ventricular outflow tract obstruction
- Residual VSD
- Right ventricular dilation and right ventricular function
- Peripheral pulmonary arterial stenosis
- Aortic insufficiency
- Left ventricular function

Type of Repair and Its Complications
The most common types of repair include:
- Blalock-Taussig shunt. This shunt is best visualized from the suprasternal views. Color flow Doppler imaging allows detection of turbulence. Continuous wave Doppler imaging shows a peak velocity during early systole that gradually declines before the next systole.
- Waterston shunt. There is communication between the main pulmonary artery and aorta. Distortion of the anatomy of the pulmonary artery may be seen.
- Potts shunt. There is communication between the pulmonary artery and the descending aorta.

Rarer surgeries include interposition grafts between the pulmonary artery and aorta and the Brock procedure (resection of the infundibular stenosis without closure of a VSD).

Pulmonary pressures should be estimated (rarely, pulmonary vascular disease may occur if the shunts were too large).

$$PASP = \text{peak systolic systemic arterial pressure}$$
$$- 4v^2 (\text{peak velocity across the shunt}).$$

Note: It is important to exclude peripheral pulmonary artery stenoses before using this technique.

For late repair, important factors to consider are ventricular function, pulmonary pressures, and pulmonary artery anatomy after shunt surgery. Coronary angiography is still preferable to rule out an anomalous course or coronary artery disease.

Echocardiographic assessment of repaired tetralogy of Fallot includes:
- The degree of pulmonary regurgitation (qualitative assessment)
- Right ventricular dilation and function
- Residual right ventricular outflow tract obstruction
- Residual VSD
- Peripheral pulmonary arterial stenosis
- Aortic dilation and regurgitation
- Left ventricular function

Pulmonary Regurgitation
One of the most common problems after repair of tetralogy of Fallot repair is pulmonary regurgitation (especially after transannular patch), which can result in progressive right ventricular dilation and dysfunction. Replacement of the pulmonary valve can prevent irreversible damage to the right ventricle and arrhythmic complications, but the optimal timing of valve replacement is still being debated.[12] The following are echocardiographic features of severe pulmonary regurgitation:
- Broad laminar retrograde color Doppler imaging diastolic jet seen at or beyond the pulmonary valve (jet width/annulus ratio > 0.7) (Fig. 5-18)
- Dense spectral continuous wave Doppler signal
- Early termination of the pulsed wave spectral Doppler signal (PR index < 0.77) (Fig. 5-19)[13]
- Right ventricular dilation and reversed septal motion implies severity: right ventricular inlet diameter greater than 4 cm and right ventricular outflow greater than 2.7 cm.

Right Ventricular Function
Right ventricular function can be assessed by[14]:
- Visual estimates, two-dimensional fractional area change (FAC), three-dimensional (3D) RV EF. FAC <35% indicates RV systolic dysfunction.
- Calculating the dP/dt (normal = 100 to 250 mm Hg/s)

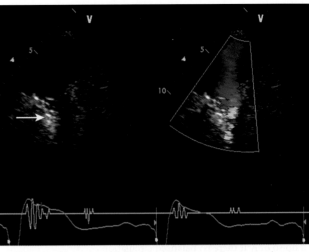

Figure 5-18 Severe pulmonary regurgitation after repair of tetralogy of Fallot. Ao, aorta; PA, pulmonary artery; RVOT, right ventricular outflow tract.

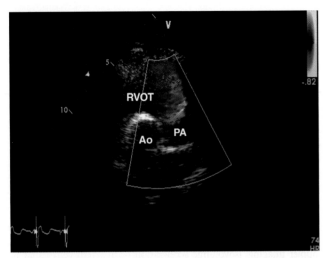

Figure 5-20 Appearance after percutaneous pulmonary valve (*arrow*) replacement. The position of the pulmonary valve can be seen with mildly turbulent flow on this color flow Doppler image.

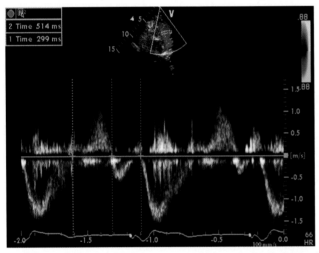

Figure 5-19 Pulsed wave Doppler interrogation at the level of the pulmonary valve. The early termination of the regurgitant flow suggests that the regurgitation is severe, leading to rapid equilibration of pressures between the right ventricle and the pulmonary artery.

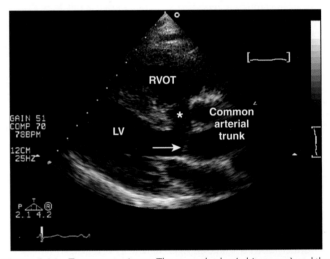

Figure 5-21 Truncus arteriosus. The truncal valve (*white arrow*) and the VSD (*asterisk*) are seen in the parasternal long-axis view in this patient with Eisenmenger syndrome. LV, left ventricle; RVOT, right ventricular outflow tract.

- M-mode of the lateral tricuspid annulus, greater than 1.5 cm = normal ventricular function*
- RV myocardial performance index* (normal = 0.28 ± 0.04)
- Peak systolic tissue Doppler velocity (normal > 11.5 cm/s)
- Isovolumic acceleration (normal = 1.4 ± 0.5 m/s²)[15]
- Strain rate

Restrictive physiology as a feature of diastolic dysfunction has been described in this patient group. Diastolic function can be assessed to look for a restrictive right ventricle. It can be done by assessing the pulsed wave Doppler in the main pulmonary artery. Restrictive physiology is present when there is laminar antegrade diastolic flow in the main pulmonary artery coinciding with atrial systole present throughout the respiratory cycle. Pulsed wave Doppler interrogation of the inferior vena cava flow would show retrograde flow during atrial systole.

Residual Right Ventricular Outflow Obstruction

Residual right ventricular outflow obstruction is classified into mild (peak gradient < 40 mm Hg), moderate (40-70 mm Hg), and severe (>70 mm Hg). Patients with surgical or percutaneous valve

replacement (Fig. 5-20) should also be assessed periodically for stenosis/regurgitation.

Aortopathy

Progressive dilation of the aorta has been detected several years after repair of tetralogy of Fallot. Therefore, the aortic dimension and presence of aortic regurgitation should be closely monitored.

Left Ventricular Dysfunction

Left ventricular dysfunction is increasingly recognized as a marker of increased disease severity.

COMMON ARTERIAL TRUNK (TRUNCUS ARTERIOSUS)

Common arterial trunk is characterized by a single arterial trunk originating from the heart supplying the coronary, pulmonary, and systemic circulation typically associated with a large VSD (Fig. 5-21). The truncal valve has variable anatomy with varying degrees of stenosis and regurgitation. The majority of patients presenting in adulthood would have undergone surgical repair with VSD closure and a right ventricle/pulmonary artery (valved) conduit. Those patients who have not undergone surgery and survived would have developed Eisenmenger syndrome.

---

*Used at the author's institution.

Evaluation of patients who have had surgery for common arterial trunk includes:
- Detecting residual VSDs
- Assessing truncal valve function for stenosis or regurgitation. The truncal valve may be tricuspid, quadricuspid, or bicuspid. Occasionally, the valve may have been replaced with a prosthetic valve.
- Determining neoaorta size
- Assessing the right ventricular conduit for obstruction and/or regurgitation
- Detecting pulmonary branch stenosis
- Assessing ventricular function

TRANSPOSITION OF THE GREAT ARTERIES

Transposition of the great arteries (TGA) is characterized by AV concordance and ventriculoarterial discordance. The incidence is 5% to 10% of all CHD. The majority of adult patients would have had surgical repair in early life. Few patients present in adulthood without repair and do so only if there is "balanced circulation."

The following anatomic features are important for assessment of unrepaired patients:
- VSD in up to 50% of all patients. This can be perimembranous in 33%, a malalignment defect often associated with obstruction of one of the outflow tracts in 30%, a muscular defect in 25%, AV inlet defect (5%), or a doubly committed defect (5%).
- Left ventricular outflow tract obstruction (subpulmonary and pulmonary stenosis) caused by different mechanisms
- Variable coronary artery anatomy. The most common coronary variant is the circumflex originating from the right coronary artery (18%).

Surgery for simple TGA started with the atrial switch procedure (Senning or Mustard operation) and has been subsequently replaced by the arterial switch operation. For TGA with concomitant VSD and left ventricular outflow tract obstruction, the Rastelli operation is performed. This has recently been replaced by the Nikaidoh procedure in selected cases.

Echocardiographic evaluation after the atrial switch procedure (Senning or Mustard) includes addressing the following:
- Assessment of ventricular function (especially the systemic ventricle)
- Assessment for valvular regurgitation
- Establishment of the presence of atrial baffles leak or obstruction
- Assessment of pulmonary artery pressures
- A search for left ventricular outflow tract obstruction
- Residual shunt either at atrial or ventricular level

Systemic Right Ventricular Function and Tricuspid Valve Regurgitation

Systemic right ventricular dysfunction and progressive tricuspid regurgitation are common problems after the atrial switch. Quantification of systemic right ventricular function by echocardiography remains challenging. In most clinical settings, assessment of global right ventricular systolic function is qualitative. Right ventricular long-axis measurements have been used in assessing right ventricular function in this setting. Newer quantitative methods include fractional area change, tissue Doppler imaging, isovolumic acceleration of the right ventricular free wall, and strain calculation in the right ventricular free wall. Recently developed 3D volume measurement has allowed more accurate measurement of right ventricular volumes. Cardiac MRI remains the gold standard for the quantitative evaluation of right ventricular function.

Baffle Obstruction/Leak

The venous pathways must be identified to rule out baffle obstruction or baffle leaks. All venous connections should be assessed. The best view of the atrial baffle is the apical four-chamber view with nonstandard probe angles to display the connection of the superior and inferior venae cavae to the left atrium (Fig. 5-22) and the pulmonary venous connection to the right atrium (Fig. 5-23). The Doppler interrogation with pulsed wave imaging in the superior and inferior venae cavae will demonstrate increased velocities if there are significant stenoses (Fig. 5-24). Peak velocities greater than 1.2 m/s or loss of phasic flow and mean gra-

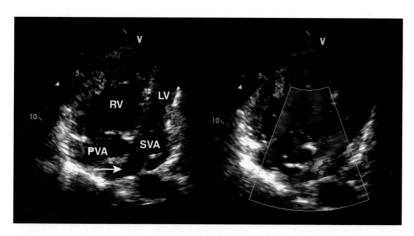

Figure 5-22 Transposition of the great arteries after the Mustard procedure. Demonstration of the connections of the systemic venous circulation (*arrow*). There is laminar flow from the superior vena cava to the systemic venous atrium (SVA) and subsequently to the left ventricle. LV, left ventricle; PVA, pulmonary venous atrium; RV, right ventricle.

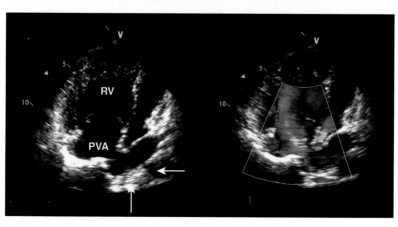

Figure 5-23 Transposition of the great arteries after the Mustard procedure. Demonstration of the connections of the pulmonary venous circulation. Note the position of the pulmonary veins in this view (*white arrows*). There is laminar flow from the pulmonary veins to the pulmonary venous atrium (PVA) and subsequently to the right ventricle (RV).

Figure 5-24 Baffle obstruction at the level of the superior vena cava. Note the elevated velocities on pulsed wave Doppler interrogation. RA, right atrium; RV, right ventricle.

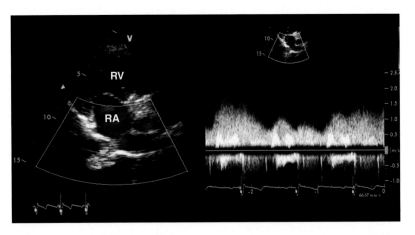

dient greater than 2 to 3 mm Hg also suggest significant obstruction. The Doppler measurements are best made in the apical four-chamber view. Baffle leaks result in an interatrial shunt. This is best appreciated on color flow imaging in the modified apical four-chamber view. In those patients with poor windows, transesophageal echocardiography may be helpful. Contrast echocardiography with injection of agitated saline through a peripheral intravenous cannula can be helpful to detect baffle problems.

Elevated pulmonary artery pressures secondary to pulmonary venous hypertension can be estimated by the modified Bernoulli equation on the mitral regurgitation jet.

Left ventricular outflow tract obstruction in this setting is often due to the bulging septum and anterior movement of the mitral valve. It should be excluded by continuous wave Doppler interrogation.

Echocardiographic Evaluation After Arterial Switch
Echocardiographic imaging involves:
- Assessing for neoaortic root dilation. Is there associated aortic regurgitation?
- Assessing for pulmonary stenosis (best assessed in the parasternal short-axis view) at anastomotic sites
- Assessing the coronary arteries and ventricular size and function

Assessing the Neoaortic Root
Progressive neoaortic root dilation and neoaortic valve regurgitation can occur.

Pulmonary Stenosis
Right ventricular outflow tract obstruction is the most common cause for late reoperation after arterial switch. The obstruction can occur at any level but is most commonly seen at the anastomosis. Because the Lecompte maneuver is performed during this procedure, the pulmonary bifurcation is seen anterior to the aorta (this makes imaging the pulmonary valve challenging). Peak velocities less than or equal to 2 m/s (predicted maximum instantaneous gradient less than or equal to 16 mm Hg) across the distal main pulmonary artery and branch pulmonary arteries are within normal limits after surgery.

Coronary Artery and Ventricular Function
Screening for myocardial ischemia should be performed routinely. Apart from looking for regional wall motion abnormalities, dobutamine stress echocardiography can be used to identify ischemia.

The left ventricular size and function should be measured in every patient after the arterial switch procedure.

Echocardiographic Evaluation After the Rastelli Procedure
In the Rastelli procedure the VSD is closed, creating a tunnel between the left ventricle and the aorta and the right ventricle is connected with a conduit to the pulmonary arteries. Imaging the patients after the Rastelli procedure involves:
- Evaluation of the conduit and branch pulmonary arteries. The conduit is often difficult to visualize on 2D imaging but with continuous wave Doppler imaging the flow velocity can almost always be detected. Hence the pressure gradient can be estimated.

- Evaluation of the left ventricle-to-aortic valve pathway for obstruction and aortic regurgitation. Because of the angulation of the connection, steps must be taken to avoid underestimating the pressure gradient.
- Evaluation of left ventricular function. Left ventricular dysfunction is a potential late complication after the Rastelli operation.
- Exclusion of residual VSDs.

DOUBLE-OUTLET RIGHT VENTRICLE

Double-outlet right ventricle is defined by at least 50% of each great vessel arising from the right ventricle. This includes a wide spectrum of lesions ranging from tetralogy of Fallot type to patients with functionally univentricular hearts. Most patients seen in the ACHD clinic would have had definitive repair or palliative surgery.

Imaging the unoperated patient requires assessment of:
- The relationship of the great vessels and the position of the VSD
- The AV valves
- The variable degrees of outflow tract obstruction with subpulmonary or subaortic obstruction
- Associated lesions such as aortic coarctation or ASD

Interinfundibular Relationship and Position of the VSD
The parasternal short-axis views show the relationship of the pulmonary artery to the aorta. The relationship can be normal, side to side, dextro-malposed where the aorta is anterior and to the right or levo-malposed where the aorta is anterior and to the left.

The VSD is usually large and nonrestrictive. It can be subaortic, subpulmonary, doubly committed, or remote.

The parasternal long-axis view is good in assessing the relationship between the two vessels and VSD. When the VSD is subaortic, the images resemble those of tetralogy of Fallot except that the aortic override is more than 50%.

Assessment of the Atrioventricular Valves
Straddling may be detected. When assessing patients who have had definitive repair, depending on the underlying anatomy, different types of surgical repairs are performed, and the postoperative assessment will depend on the surgery performed. Patients with subaortic VSDs are assessed in a similar fashion to those with postoperative tetralogy of Fallot repair. For more complex lesions, other types of surgery are performed (e.g., arterial switch and VSD closure).

CONGENITALLY CORRECTED TRANSPOSITION OF THE GREAT ARTERIES

There is AV and ventriculoarterial discordance. The left atrium (LA) receives oxygenated blood from the pulmonary veins. The LA connects through the tricuspid valve to the morphologic right ventricle that ejects blood into the aorta (which usually arises leftward). Systemic venous deoxygenated blood enters the right atrium that connects to the morphologic left ventricle through the mitral valve (atrioventricular discordance)

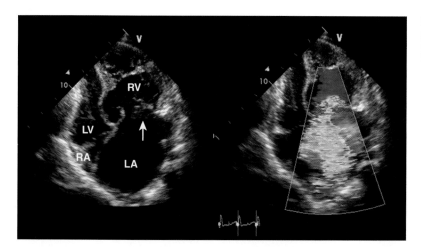

Figure 5-25 Congenitally corrected transposition of the great arteries. The tricuspid valve is dysplastic, and there is associated severe tricuspid regurgitation. LA, left atrium; LV, left ventricle; RA, right atrium; RV, right ventricle.

before delivering blood to the pulmonary arteries. Twenty percent of patients with congenitally corrected TGA have dextrocardia. Associated abnormalities such as pulmonary stenosis or VSDs are common.

The following aspects should be assessed:
- The AV and ventriculoarterial connections
- Ventricular function for both morphologic right and left ventricle
- Presence of valvular regurgitation and quantification of its severity
- Associated anomalies
- Determination if further intervention is required
- Assessment of post-repair patients
- Role of transesophageal echocardiography

Verifying the Diagnosis
In usual situs, the tricuspid valve (more apically displaced AV valve) is on the left (four-chamber view) (Fig. 5-25). Mitral-pulmonary fibrous continuity is demonstrated on the parasternal long-axis view. The ventricles, septum, and great vessels are often vertically oriented and require vertical rotation of transducer in parasternal planes to optimize imaging. The subpulmonary morphologic left ventricle may appear compressed. From the parasternal long axis, the great arteries lie in parallel position and superiorly with vertical orientation. The relationship of the aorta and the pulmonary artery can also be seen from the parasternal short-axis or apical views (Fig. 5-26).

Ventricular Function
Patients with congenitally corrected TGA have the morphologic right ventricle as the systemic ventricle. With time, ventricular dysfunction and heart failure ensues. By the fourth decade, 67% of patients with associated lesions would have developed congestive heart failure. Echocardiography may be able to identify ventricular dysfunction before overt clinical symptoms.

Tricuspid Regurgitation (Systemic Atrioventricular Valve)
Tricuspid valve regurgitation is common. Again, by the fourth decade, 82% of patients would have developed tricuspid regurgitation. Some patients may have associated Ebstein anomaly of the tricuspid valve. Besides tricuspid regurgitation, pulmonary regurgitation and aortic regurgitation should also be noted and assessed.

Associated Anomalies
Anomalies associated with congenitally corrected TGA include:
- VSD (60% to 70%). Perimembranous defects are most common.
- Left ventricular (pulmonary) outflow tract obstruction and pulmonary valvular stenosis (40% to 70%). This is usually subvalvular due to aneurysmal valve tissue, cords, and/or discrete fibrous obstruction.
- Tricuspid valve abnormalities. The pathology is variable (Ebstein anomaly–like, thickened malformed leaflets, straddling valve).
- Mitral valve abnormalities (50%): cleft mitral valve; straddling through the VSD.

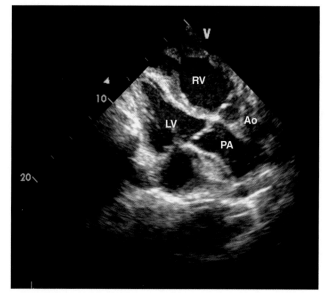

Figure 5-26 Parallel relationship of the great arteries. This view is taken from the apex with anterior tilt. Note the ventriculoarterial discordance. Ao, aorta; LV, left ventricle; PA, pulmonary artery; RV, right ventricle.

- ASD (43%)
- Other associated lesions: aortic stenosis, aortic coarctation, left atrial isomerism, coronary artery variants, complete heart block

Role of Echocardiography in Further Intervention and Assessment After Surgery
Echocardiography can be used to:
- Assess the suitability of repair or replacement of the tricuspid valve
- Evaluate right ventricular function
- Assess the feasibility of biventricular repair or need for pulmonary artery banding
- After pulmonary artery banding, assess left ventricular function, hypertrophy, and tricuspid regurgitation
- After atrial switch and the Rastelli procedure, assess leak or obstruction across the baffles
- Assess for worsening ventricular function and AV valve regurgitation

Role of Transesophageal Echocardiography
Transesophageal echocardiography can be used for:
- Preoperative anatomic assessment
- Intraoperative monitoring of pulmonary artery banding (gradient, left ventricular function)
- Intraoperative assessment of repair

FUNCTIONALLY UNIVENTRICULAR HEART

A functionally single ventricle (left or right morphology) supports systemic circulation. As expected, there can be many anatomic diagnoses. Occasionally, two adequately sized ventricles are present but their anatomy prevents septation (e.g., straddling AV valves or very large VSDs).

Because of its complexity, systematic segmental analysis should be performed. Important aspects include assessing the AV connections and whether there are double-inlet ventricles (DILV, DIRV) (Fig. 5-27), single-inlet ventricles (absent right/left connection), or a common inlet (unbalanced AVSD). Determination of ventricular looping (D or L) and morphology (left/right) is required (multiple imaging planes may be needed). A small superior and rightward subarterial outlet chamber is typically a morphologic right ventricle. An inferoposterior chamber is typically a morphologic left ventricle. The size and location of the accompanying VSD should be determined. This is followed by demonstrating the ventriculoarterial relationship. The AV valve is next assessed for straddling (tricuspid valve is more common) across the VSD as well as stenosis or regurgitation. Restriction at the atrial septum may be important for specific lesions (e.g., absent right/left connection). Finally, ventricular function is assessed and pulmonary hypertension is excluded.

FONTAN CIRCULATION

Fontan circulation is characterized by systemic venous blood being directed to the pulmonary arteries and bypassing the heart. The original Fontan operation (Fig. 5-28) has undergone many modifications. Currently, the total cavopulmonary connection (TCPC) (with the lateral tunnel [Fig. 5-29] or an extracardiac conduit) is commonly performed. A fenestration may be placed between the systemic venous pathway and the atrium to allow a right-to-left shunt that decompresses the systemic venous pathway to maintain adequate cardiac output.

It is important to first establish the exact surgery performed. Echocardiographic assessment includes:
- Assessing the Fontan connection
- Excluding pulmonary venous obstruction
- Assessing for AV valve pathology and ventricular function
- Establishing the presence of collateral vessels and identifying residual communication between systemic and pulmonary circulation

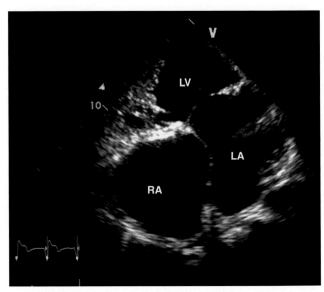

Figure 5-28 Atriopulmonary Fontan procedure. The right atrium is markedly dilated. LA, left atrium; LV, left ventricle; RA, right atrium.

Assessing the Fontan Connections
The steps involved in assessing the Fontan connections include:
- Evaluating the superior cavopulmonary anastomosis and inferior vena cava to pulmonary artery connection to exclude obstruction
- Measuring flow velocities in the superior and inferior venae cavae (usually of low velocity)
- Excluding thrombi. The apical four-chamber view allows visualization of atrial thrombus (Fig. 5-30) especially in the classic atriopulmonary Fontan procedure. Sluggish blood flow with spontaneous echocardiographic contrast is often seen.
- Evaluating the patency and size of the fenestration. The mean gradient across the fenestration using Doppler techniques allows estimation of transpulmonary pressure gradient or pulmonary artery pressure when there is no Fontan pathway obstruction.
- Excluding baffle leaks in the intracardiac type
- Assessing flow to both pulmonary arteries using color Doppler and pulsed Doppler imaging. The typical Doppler spectra using pulsed

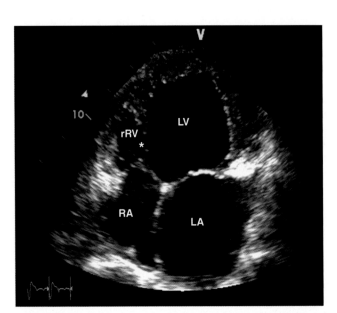

Figure 5-27 Double-inlet left ventricle. Note the presence of a rudimentary right ventricle (rRV) and a nonrestrictive VSD (*asterisk*). LA, left atrium; LV, left ventricle; RA, right atrium.

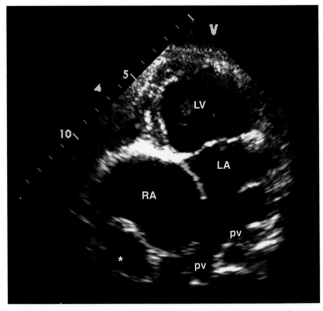

Figure 5-29 Total cavopulmonary connection (*asterisk*). LA, left atrium; LV, left ventricle; pv, pulmonary vein; RA, right atrium.

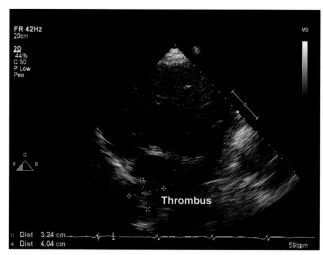

Figure 5-30 Thrombus seen in the markedly dilated right atrium.

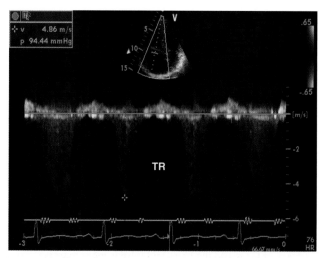

Figure 5-31 Continuous wave Doppler image of the tricuspid regurgitation (TR). This patient had Eisenmenger syndrome from an unrepaired VSD.

wave Doppler imaging shows a biphasic antegrade flow pattern. There is antegrade flow seen from early diastole and peaking at atrial systole; the second period of antegrade flow occurs at ventricular systole. Inspiration increases flow velocity.

- Transesophageal echocardiography may provide better imaging in some cases.

Excluding Pulmonary Venous Obstruction
Pulmonary venous obstruction should be excluded. All four pulmonary veins should therefore be identified after the Fontan operation using 2D, color Doppler, and pulsed wave Doppler techniques. High velocities or loss of phasic variations would suggest obstruction to flow.

Atrioventricular Valve Function
AV valvular stenosis and regurgitation should be evaluated.

Ventricular Function Assessment
Systolic function is assessed qualitatively. The evaluation of diastolic function in the Fontan circulation is extremely difficult owing to abnormal AV valve anatomy and abnormal pulmonary venous flow.

Detection of Aortic-to-Pulmonary Collateral Flow
Eighty percent of patients undergoing Fontan-type operations already have, or subsequently develop, systemic arterial-to-pulmonary arterial collateral vessels as a consequence of preoperative, or continued, hypoxemia. Competitive flow from these aortopulmonary vessels can elevate right-sided pressures, thereby reducing systemic venous flow to the pulmonary arteries. These can be detected from the suprasternal aortic arch views. MRI should be the imaging choice for these patients.

EISENMENGER SYNDROME

Eisenmenger syndrome is characterized by irreversible pulmonary vascular disease due to systemic-to-pulmonary communication (e.g., ASD, nonrestrictive VSD, nonrestrictive PDA, AVSD, aortopulmonary window, surgical systemic-to-pulmonary shunt). An initial left-to-right shunt reverses direction after an increase in pulmonary vascular resistance and arterial pressures.

The following should be assessed:
- Severity of pulmonary hypertension
- Direction of shunting across an intracardiac communication
- Underlying lesion
- Associated lesions
- Biventricular function

Determining the Degree of Pulmonary Hypertension
Right ventricular hypertrophy with flattening and bowing of the interventricular septum in systole ("D" sign) is seen in the parasternal short axis. Systolic flattening occurs with disease progression.

With tricuspid regurgitation and the absence of right ventricular outflow obstruction, the pulmonary artery systolic pressure can be estimated using the modified Bernoulli equation, $4v^2 + RAP$, where v= maximal velocity of the tricuspid regurgitation by continuous wave Doppler (Fig. 5-31) and RAP = right atrial pressure (estimated by the inferior vena cava dimensions and its respiratory variation).

In the absence of a good quality tricuspid regurgitation jet, pulsed wave Doppler imaging of the right ventricular outflow tract using the Mahan equation allows an estimation of mean pulmonary artery pressure[16]:

$$\text{Mean pulmonary artery pressure} = 79 - 0.45(\text{AcT})$$

where AcT = right ventricular outflow acceleration time, which is best obtained by a pulsed wave interrogation across the pulmonary valve from the parasternal short-axis view. This formula is cardiac output and heart rate dependent. Corrections for heart rate are necessary when the heart rate is less than 60 or more than 100 beats per minute.

The end-diastolic pulmonary artery pressure can also be estimated from the end-diastolic pulmonary regurgitation velocity.

Direction of Shunt and Underlying Lesion
The underlying structural defect, coexisting structural abnormalities, and surgical shunts (multiple planes) can be determined. Color flow Doppler imaging helps define the anatomic defect and direction of shunting.

Ventricular Function
With disease progression, right ventricular enlargement and dysfunction occurs (parasternal long and short-axis views, four-chamber view). Impaired left ventricular function conveys a worse prognosis.[17]

Worsening tricuspid regurgitation (increasing afterload, annular dilation, and right ventricular dysfunction) and right atrial enlargement (four-chamber) are the result of disease progression.

Special Topics in Adult Congenital Imaging

ROLE OF ECHOCARDIOGRAPHY IN THE PREGNANT WOMAN WITH CONGENITAL HEART DISEASE

With increasingly successful management of CHD, a large number of patients with complex congenital heart defects are surviving to reproductive age and contemplating pregnancy. Whereas some simple lesions such as repaired ASDs/VSDs pose little problems, more complex lesions may be associated with significant maternal morbidity and mortality and perinatal complications.

TABLE 5-2 Risk Categories of Patients with Preexisting Cardiac Lesions

Class I	Class II	Class II-III	Class III	Class IV
Simple/uncomplicated lesions (operated or not) such as: MVP with mild MR PDA (restrictive or closed) VSD/ASD (restrictive or repaired) Pulmonary stenosis (mild to moderate) Anomalous pulmonary venous drainage (repaired)	Moderate complexity defects or unoperated lesions such as repaired TOF or unoperated large ASD	HOCM Low risk Marfan syndrome Mild left ventricular dysfunction Valvular heart disease (not in class IV)	Prosthetic heart valves Systemic right ventricle Fontan circulation Cyanotic heart disease	Pulmonary arterial hypertension EF < 30% History of peripartum cardiomyopathy with residual left ventricular dysfunction Severe AS/MS Marfan syndrome with aorta > 4 cm

Class I, No detectable increased risk; Class II, slightly increased risk; Class III, significantly increased risk; Class IV, unacceptably high risk.

AS, aortic stenosis; ASD, atrial septal defect; EF, ejection fraction; HOCM, hypertrophic obstructive cardiomyopathy; MR, mitral regurgitation, MS, mitral valve stenosis; MVP, mitral valve prolapse; PDA, patent ductus arteriosus; TOF, tetralogy of Fallot; VSD, ventricular septal defect.

Echocardiography is well suited in the evaluation of such patients because it is noninvasive and safe for the fetus.

Table 5-2 shows the risk categories of the patients with preexisting cardiac lesions.[18] In addition to history and examination, echocardiography provides incremental information for risk stratification. Even where the lesion is mild and hemodynamically nonsignificant, the information is important to reassure patients. In severe lesions, for example in pulmonary arterial hypertension or severe valvular lesions, the discussion should include avoiding pregnancy.

In our center, the echocardiographic examination is usually performed before pregnancy, in early pregnancy as a baseline study, at the end of the second trimester when cardiac stress is at its peak, and 6 months' post partum to assess the impact of pregnancy on the heart. In patients who have complex or high-risk anatomy the frequency of monitoring is increased accordingly (e.g., measuring aortic dimensions in patients with dilated or dilating aortic root in Marfan syndrome or assessing right [and left] ventricular function in those with pulmonary arterial hypertension).

FETAL ECHOCARDIOGRAPHY

In tandem with adult congenital imaging, the field of fetal echocardiography has progressed significantly.

Adult patients with CHD who become pregnant are often advised to undergo fetal screening. Other indications for fetal echocardiography include maternal diabetes, connective tissue diseases, exposure to teratogenic drugs, abnormal nuchal translucency, or suspicion of aneuploidy.

The risk of CHD in an infant born to a parent with CHD is 3% to 7% (slightly higher if the mother has CHD). In fact, the presence of CHD accounts for about 10% of infant deaths.

Technique

A transabdominal approach at 18 to 20 weeks of gestation with five transverse scanning planes is used. These five views allow views similar to that of MRI, namely, abdominal situs, four-chamber, great artery relationship, three-vessel (transverse aortic arch, ductal arch, and superior vena cava), and trachea views. Color and Doppler techniques allow assessment of pulmonary venous flow.

Some cardiac lesions may progress, and serial monitoring may be indicated (e.g., tetralogy of Fallot progressing to pulmonary atresia with VSD).

Other tools include the detection of interatrial restriction or closure of the foramen ovale by observing thickening of the interatrial septum or changes in the pulmonary venous waveform. This is particularly important in patients with simple transposition, hypoplastic left heart syndrome, or critical aortic stenosis because it impacts on subsequent management (e.g., fetal intervention to prevent fetal hydrops). Another useful technique is the monitoring of cerebral blood flow as a surrogate of disease severity in hypoplastic left heart syndrome.

The information obtained helps in counseling of parents, performing fetal intervention, and planning early neonatal cardiac care.

TISSUE DOPPLER IMAGING, STRAIN, AND STRAIN RATE IN CONGENITAL HEART DISEASE

Potential applications for tissue Doppler techniques currently are:
- Assessment of diastolic function
- Isovolumetric acceleration. This may be used to offer a relatively load-independent measurement of cardiac contractility. It has been used in postoperative tetralogy of Fallot and atrial switch patients. Because of its heart rate sensitivity it has been used to study force-frequency relationships in postoperative patients with CHD. Further validation of its use in a clinical setting is required.
- Evaluation of dyssynchrony. This technique has been used in combination with other echocardiographic modalities to identify patients with a failing systemic right ventricle who may benefit from cardiac resynchronization, although its limitation has been stressed by the recent PROSPECT trial.[19]

THREE-DIMENSIONAL ECHOCARDIOGRAPHY IN CONGENITAL HEART DISEASE

3D imaging is useful for anatomic definition and offers superior functional assessment. In CHD, it allows a better appreciation of intracardiac lesions and permits more accurate measurements of cardiac dimensions, volumes, and asynchrony. Full volume data acquisition in a single cardiac cycle and 3D myocardial strain are now being applied. Transesophageal 3D echocardiography also facilitates intraoperative and perioperative assessment.

Functional Assessment
3D echocardiography compares favorably with MRI for measurement of left ventricular volumes, ejection fraction, and mass. It is especially reliable for assessing right ventricular volumes and functional single ventricles using summation of discs.

Assessment of Atrial and Ventricular Septal Defects
Accurate dimensions of the defect and appreciation of the rims around these lesions help in selecting appropriate transcatheter devices to close the defects.

Assessment of Atrioventricular Valve Regurgitation
The entire regurgitant jet is visualized and allows better understanding of the regurgitant mechanism. In addition, orthogonal planes placed through the jet yield the true vena contracta jet area. This information is important for surgeons to decide whether and how the valve can be repaired.

Other clinical situations in which this may be useful include Ebstein anomaly (aids in deciding if the tricuspid valve can be repaired), left ventricular outflow tract obstruction, and double-outlet right ventricle (to define the relations of the great arteries to the ventricle and the position and relation of the VSD).

PHARMACOLOGIC STRESS ECHOCARDIOGRAPHY AND EXERCISE ECHOCARDIOGRAPHY

Pharmacologic stress echocardiography and exercise echocardiography are very sensitive techniques in detecting not only ischemic myocardial dysfunction, which may be more common than we expected, but also dynamic changes in patients with exertional symptoms (e.g., dynamic outflow tract obstruction in patients after a Fontan procedure).[20]

INTRACARDIAC ECHOCARDIOGRAPHY

Intracardiac echocardiography has been used predominantly for guidance of electrophysiologic and percutaneous congenital heart interventions in the catheterization laboratory (most commonly ASD/PFO closure). It allows for the procedure to be done under local anesthesia because it can replace transesophageal echocardiography for imaging (which needs to be done under general anesthesia) and it is cost effective.

CONCLUSION

Echocardiography, with its wide range of modalities, is a great tool in the diagnosis and follow-up of adult patients with CHD. It provides comprehensive assessment of anatomy and physiology and contributes significantly to clinical management many years after surgical or catheter interventional procedures. Despite ongoing challenges with the morphologic right ventricle (in the pulmonary or systemic position) and the so-called single ventricle physiology, echocardiography plays a major role in the assessment of ventricular function. Furthermore, echocardiography is the imaging of choice for detecting asynchrony and, thus, assists decision-making for pacing and other arrhythmia intervention. As developments in both cardiology and the management of CHD continue, so echocardiography will continue to expand its current applications and remain a pivotal tool in managing adult patients with CHD.

REFERENCES

1. Edler I, Lindstrom K. The history of echocardiography. Ultrasound Med Biol 2004;30:1565–1644.
2. Yun CF, Cao QL, Hijazi ZM. Closure of secundum ASD using the Amplatzer Septal Occluder. In: Horst Sievert SQ, Wilson N, Hijazi ZM, editors. Percutaneous intervention for congenital heart disease. London: Informa Healthcare; 2007. p. 265–275.
3. Minette MS, Sahn DJ. Ventricular septal defects. Circulation 2006;114:2190–2197.
4. Li W. Atrioventricular septal defects. In: Li W, Henein M, Gatzoulis MA, editors. Echocardiography in adult congenital heart disease. New York: Springer Verlag; 2007. p. 22–24.
5. Schneider DJ, Moore JW. Patent ductus arteriosus. Circulation 2006;114:1873–1882.
6. Tan JL, Babu-Narayanan SV, Henein MY, et al. Doppler echocardiographic profile and indexes in the evaluation of aortic coarctation in patients before and after stenting. J Am Coll Cardiol 2005;46:1045–1053.
7. Knyshov GV, Sitar LL, Glagola MD, Atamanyuk MY. Aortic aneurysms at the site of the repair of coarctation of the aorta: a review of 48 patients. Ann Thorac Surg 1996;61:935–939.
8. Valdes-Cruz LM, Cayre RO. Anomalies of the right ventricular outflow tract and pulmonary arteries. In: Valdes-Cruz LM, Cayre RO, editors. Echocardiographic diagnosis of congenital heart disease. Philadelphia: Lippincott-Raven; 1999. p. 325–348.
9. Shiina A, Seward JB, Edwards WD, et al. Two-dimensional echocardiographic spectrum of Ebstein's anomaly: detailed anatomic assessment. J Am Coll Cardiol 1984;3:356–370.
10. Brown ML, Dearani JA, Danielson GK, et al. Effect of operation for Ebstein anomaly on left ventricular function. Am J Cardiol 2008;102:1724–1727.
11. Ostman-Smith I, Silverman NH, Oldershaw P, et al. Cor triatriatum sinistrum: diagnostic features on cross sectional echocardiography. Br Heart J 1984;51:211–219.
12. Therrien J, Siu SC, Harris L, et al. Impact of pulmonary valve replacement on arrhythmia propensity late after repair of tetralogy of Fallot. Circulation 2001;103:2489–2494.
13. Li W, Davlouros PA, Kilner PJ, et al. Doppler-echocardiographic assessment of pulmonary regurgitation in adults with repaired tetralogy of Fallot: comparison with cardiovascular magnetic resonance imaging. Am Heart J 2004;147:165–172.
14. Haddad F, Hunt SA, Rosenthal DN, et al. Right ventricular function in cardiovascular disease: I. Anatomy, physiology, aging, and functional assessment of the right ventricle. Circulation 2008;117:1436–1448.
15. Vogel M, Schmidt MR, Kristiansen SB, et al. Validation of myocardial acceleration during isovolumic contraction as a novel noninvasive index of right ventricular contractility: comparison with ventricular pressure-volume relations in an animal model. Circulation 2002;105:1693–1699.
16. Oh JK, Seward JB, Tajik AJ. Pulmonary hypertension. In: Oh JK, SJ, Tajik AJ, editors. The Echo Manual. Boston: Little, Brown; 1994.
17. Salehian O, Schwerzmann M, Rambihar S, et al. Left ventricular dysfunction and mortality in adult patients with Eisenmenger syndrome. Congenit Heart Dis 2007;2:156–164.
18. Thorne S, Nelson-Piercy C, MacGregor A, et al. Pregnancy and contraception in heart disease and pulmonary arterial hypertension. J Fam Plann Reprod Health Care 2006;32:75–81.
19. Chung ES, Leon AR, Tavazzi L, et al. Results of the Predictors of Response to CRT (PROSPECT) trial. Circulation 2008; 117:2608–2616.
20. Li W, Hornung TS, Francis DP, et al. Relation of biventricular function quantified by stress echocardiography to cardiopulmonary exercise capacity in adults with Mustard (atrial switch) procedure for transposition of the great arteries. Circulation 2004;110:1380–1386.

6

Heart Failure, Exercise Intolerance, and Physical Training

KONSTANTINOS DIMOPOULOS | RAFAEL ALONSO-GONZALEZ | ERIK THAULOW | MICHAEL A. GATZOULIS

The patient population with adult congenital heart disease (ACHD) is expanding, posing a significant challenge to medical professionals. Although early surgery has transformed the outcome of these patients, it has not been curative. Exercise intolerance is a major problem for ACHD patients, significantly affecting their quality of life. Physical limitation is common, even in patients with simple lesions, and is most severe in those with Eisenmenger syndrome, single-ventricle physiology, or complex cardiac anatomy. Important systemic complications of the heart failure syndrome are also present, such as renal dysfunction, hyponatremia, and neurohormonal and cytokine activation. Cardiopulmonary exercise testing provides a reliable tool both for assessing the exercise capacity of ACHD patients and for risk stratification and is becoming part of the routine clinical assessment of these patients. Similarities in the pathophysiology of exercise intolerance in acquired heart failure and congenital heart disease (CHD) suggest that established heart failure therapies might be beneficial to ACHD patients with exercise intolerance.

Heart Failure in Adults with Congenital Heart Disease

Heart failure is defined as a syndrome characterized by symptoms of exercise intolerance in the presence of any abnormality in the structure and/or function of the heart. All types of acquired or congenital heart disease, involving the myocardium, pericardium, endocardium, valves, or great vessels, can ultimately lead to the development of heart failure.[1] In ACHD, heart failure is the ultimate expression of the sequelae and complications, which ACHD patients often face even after "successful" repair of their primary defect.

PREVALENCE

Exercise intolerance is the main feature of heart failure. It is common in this population, affecting more than a third of patients in the Euro Heart Survey, a large registry of ACHD patients across Europe. Patients with cyanotic lesions and those with a univentricular circulation tend to be those with the highest prevalence of exercise intolerance, whereas patients with aortic coarctation and Marfan syndrome are the least impaired.[2] Within the cyanotic population, those with significant pulmonary arterial hypertension (Eisenmenger syndrome) tend to be most severely limited.[2,3] Patients with the right ventricle in the systemic position, either as a result of congenitally corrected transposition of the great arteries or after atrial switch operation (Mustard or Senning procedure) for transposition of the great arteries also tend to become severely limited in their exercise capacity, especially after the third decade of life. As many as two thirds of patients with congenitally corrected transposition of the great arteries with significant associated defects and prior open-heart surgery have congestive heart failure by age 45. Patients with univentricular circulation and a Fontan-type operation are also typically limited in their exercise capacity, especially in the presence of ventricular dysfunction, atrioventricular valve regurgitation, or a failing Fontan circulation. In a group of 188 patients with a systemic right ventricle or single ventricle, the frequency of heart failure was high (22% in transposition of the great arteries and atrial switch, 32% in corrected transposition of the great arteries, and 40% in Fontan-palliated patients). However, even patients with "simple" lesions such as closed atrial septal defect often present with reduced exercise capacity, even though often at a later stage (after the third or fourth decade of life).

MECHANISMS OF HEART FAILURE

Identification of the mechanisms responsible for exercise intolerance, both cardiac and extracardiac, is essential in the management of ACHD patients because these can become targets for therapies.

Cardiac Causes of Exercise Intolerance
Ventricular Dysfunction

Cardiac dysfunction is the most obvious cause of exercise intolerance and heart failure in ACHD. A reduction in cardiac output may occur through a reduction in ventricular function (reduced stroke volume) or through inability to increase heart rate to meet demands. Myocardial dysfunction is common in ACHD and can be caused by ventricular overload, myocardial ischemia, and pericardial disease (Fig. 6-1). It can also occur through the effects of medication, permanent pacing, and endothelial and neurohormonal activation.

Hemodynamic overload of one or both ventricles due to obstructive or regurgitant lesions, shunting, or pulmonary or systemic hypertension is common in ACHD. This overload is, by definition in ACHD, of long standing and can lead to severe ventricular dysfunction, as is found in patients with a systemic right ventricle 10 to 30 years after atrial switch repair of d-transposition of the great arteries or after the third decade of life in corrected l-transposition of the great arteries and in patients with Fontan-type circulation. Right ventricular systolic dysfunction is common in patients with significant volume overload, such as those with large atrial septal defects or patients with tetralogy of Fallot and severe pulmonary regurgitation. Ventricular dysfunction can also result from repeated cardiac surgery, anomalous coronary circulation, and abnormal myocardial perfusion, as has been documented in patients after atrial or arterial switch repair for d-transposition of the great arteries. Ventricular-ventricular interaction is not uncommon in ACHD, with right-sided lesions often affecting the left ventricle and vice versa. Significant ventricular interaction is most pronounced in patients with Ebstein anomaly, in whom the left ventricle typically appears small, underfilled, and hypokinetic, almost "compressed" by the dilated right ventricular cavity.

Ventricular dysfunction may also be triggered or exacerbated by arrhythmias, permanent pacing, and medication. ACHD patients have an increased propensity for arrhythmias owing to intrinsic abnormalities of the conduction system, long-standing hemodynamic overload, and scarring from reparative or palliative surgery. Arrhythmias can lead to significant hemodynamic compromise, especially in the presence of myocardial dysfunction, and can become life threatening, especially when fast or ventricular in origin. Even relatively slow supraventricular tachycardias may, however, cause a reduction in cardiac output and exercise capacity through loss of atrioventricular synchrony, especially when of long standing.

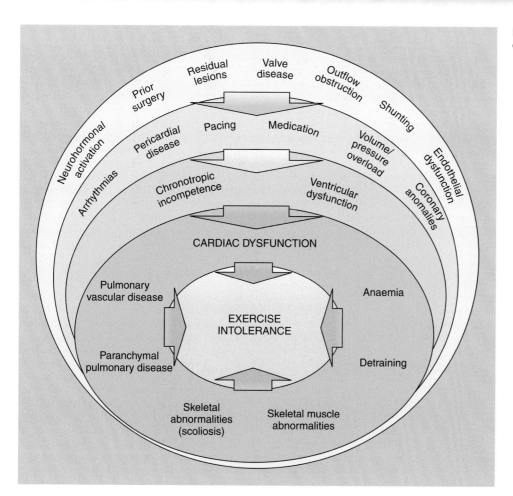

Figure 6-1 Potential mechanisms of exercise intolerance in ACHD.

Diastolic dysfunction is also an important component of ACHD and can affect exercise capacity and ventricular response to overload. A significant number of patients after repair of tetralogy of Fallot present with restrictive right ventricular physiology, which is related to decreased predisposition to right ventricular dilation in the presence of significant pulmonary regurgitation.[4] However, it is associated with low cardiac output and prolonged inotropic and volume support immediately after surgery in this population. In patients with a univentricular heart, the presence of a rudimentary chamber may affect the regional contractility of the dominant ventricle and affect relaxation and diastolic filling. In addition, patients with diastolic dysfunction may also do worse after a Fontan-type procedure. However, evaluation of diastolic properties across the spectrum of cardiac anatomies is difficult because there are no established criteria for this population. Moreover, no data are available on the pharmacologic management of diastolic dysfunction in the ACHD population.

Acquired disease superimposed to the congenitally abnormal heart may also cause deterioration of myocardial dysfunction. Infective endocarditis, systemic hypertension, coronary atherosclerosis, myocarditis, alcohol or other substance abuse (i.e., cocaine), and diabetes mellitus may all trigger or aggravate myocardial dysfunction in ACHD. Infective endocarditis, in particular, is not uncommon in ACHD and can have devastating short- and long-term effects especially in high-risk patients with multiple hemodynamic lesions and/or ventricular dysfunction.

The prevalence of significant coronary artery disease does not appear to be increased in ACHD patients.[5] However, because this population is aging, coronary artery disease should always be suspected when ventricular dysfunction is encountered and traditional cardiovascular risk factors for coronary atherosclerosis should be addressed.

Chronotropic Incompetence

The chronotropic response to exercise is a major contributor to the increase in cardiac output, more so than the increase in myocardial contractility. Chronotropic incompetence may be defined as the inability to increase heart rate appropriate to the degree of effort and metabolic demands. Chronotropic incompetence is common in ACHD, encountered in 62% of ACHD patients in one series, and can be due to intrinsic abnormalities of the conduction system or be iatrogenic.[6] In the ACHD population, chronotropic incompetence is related to the severity of exercise intolerance, plasma natriuretic peptide levels, and peak oxygen uptake. Chronotropic incompetence has also prognostic implications in patients with ischemic heart disease and is a strong predictor of mortality in ACHD patients, especially those with "complex" lesions, Fontan-type surgery, and repaired tetralogy of Fallot.[6]

Medications such as β-adrenergic blockers, calcium antagonists, and antiarrhythmic agents can have significant negative inotropic and chronotropic effects and can affect ventricular performance and exercise capacity.[2] Medication can also unmask latent conduction system disease and lead to sinus node dysfunction, atrioventricular block, or chronotropic incompetence.

Permanent pacing can also affect cardiac output through chronotropic incompetence and ventricular dysfunction. ACHD patients with a permanent pacemaker were, in fact, found to have significantly lower peak heart rate and a trend toward lower peak oxygen consumption ($\dot{V}o_2$) compared with those without.[2] Pacemaker therapy is often required in ACHD for atrioventricular block, which is common in patients with atrioventricular septal defects or corrected transposition of the great arteries and immediately after surgical repair of a ventricular septal defect or muscle bundle resection. Sinus node dysfunction requiring permanent pacing is also common after Fontan operation or atrial switch repair for complete transposition of the great arteries.

Dual-chamber pacemakers are most commonly used to avoid atrioventricular asynchrony, but this is not always possible in patients with complex anatomy. Moreover, despite advances in rate-responsive pacemakers, rate responsiveness at higher levels of exercise in younger patients may be inadequate to produce a sufficient increase in cardiac output. Right ventricular pacing can also cause ventricular asynchrony and in the non-congenital population has been shown to cause long-term left ventricular dysfunction and reduced exercise capacity. The development of sophisticated pacing technologies that encourage more intrinsic conduction, thus minimizing ventricular pacing, holds promise for ACHD patients.

Extracardiac Causes of Exercise Intolerance

Parenchymal and vascular lung diseases are important contributors to exercise intolerance in ACHD. Subnormal forced vital capacity has been reported in patients with Ebstein anomaly, tetralogy of Fallot, corrected transposition of the great arteries, Fontan operation and atrial repair of complete transposition of the great arteries, and even in patients with atrial septal defects. Lung disease affects exercise capacity. The percent FEV_1 has, in fact, been shown to be a powerful predictor of exercise capacity in the ACHD population. Prior surgery with lung scarring, atelectasis, chest deformities, diaphragmatic palsy, pulmonary vascular disease with loss of distensibility of peripheral arteries, and significant cardiomegaly are possible mechanisms for the abnormal pulmonary function observed in ACHD.

Pulmonary Arterial Hypertension and Cyanosis

Patients with Eisenmenger physiology are, by far, the most symptomatic ACHD patients. The vast majority are in New York Heart Association (NYHA) functional class II or more at a median age of 28,[3] suggesting a detrimental effect of cyanosis and pulmonary hypertension. Patients with complex univentricular anatomy are also highly symptomatic, especially in the presence of significant cyanosis.[3]

Both cyanosis and pulmonary hypertension significantly affect exercise capacity and the ventilatory response to exercise. In cyanotic patients who have not undergone repair and who have unrestricted defects, an increase in cardiac output is obtained through shunting, at the expense of further systemic desaturation.[7] At the onset of exercise, oxygen consumption fails to increase, owing to the inability to sufficiently increase pulmonary blood flow. Ventilation increases abruptly and excessively, resulting in alveolar hyperventilation. Although ventilation is increased throughout exercise, ventilatory efficiency is significantly decreased. Pulmonary hypoperfusion, an increase in physiologic dead space through right-to-left shunting, and enhanced ventilatory reflex sensitivity are mechanisms contributing to the ventilatory inefficiency and the failure to meet oxygen requirements in ACHD patients with cyanosis and pulmonary arterial hypertension.

The effect of cyanosis on exercise capacity and ventilation is difficult to distinguish from that of pulmonary hypertension. Significant ventilatory inefficiency has also been described in patients with idiopathic pulmonary hypertension, in the absence of right-to-left shunting. Despite being "inefficient" and likely contributing to the early onset of dyspnea, the exaggerated ventilatory response to exercise in cyanotic ACHD patients appears appropriate from a "chemical" point of view because it succeeds in maintaining near-normal arterial pCO_2 and pH levels in the systemic circulation despite significant right-to-left shunting, at least during mild-to-moderate exertion.[1]

Anemia and Iron Deficiency

In acquired heart failure, anemia relates to exercise capacity and is a predictor of outcome. Anemia results in reduced oxygen-carrying capacity and a premature shift to anaerobic metabolism during exercise and can precipitate heart failure by affecting myocardial function and volume overload. Anemia in ACHD can occur as a complication of chronic anticoagulation, surgery or intervention, hemolysis due to prosthetic valves, intracardiac patches or endocarditis, or hemoptysis in patients with severe pulmonary arterial hypertension. Moreover, anemia can occur due to chronic renal failure or as anemia of chronic disease. Similar to acquired heart failure, anemia is associated with a higher risk of death in noncyanotic ACHD patients.[8]

In cyanotic patients, anemia as conventionally defined is rare. Chronic hypoxia results, normally, in an increase in erythropoietin production and an isolated rise in the red blood cell count (secondary erythrocytosis), which augments the amount of oxygen delivered to the tissues. "Relative anemia," that is, an inadequate rise in hemoglobin levels despite chronic cyanosis can, nevertheless, occur as a result of iron deficiency and can have important detrimental effects on exercise capacity and symptomatic status. No universally accepted algorithm for the calculation of "appropriate" hemoglobin levels exists, and diagnosis of relative anemia is based on serum ferritin and transferrin saturation. Iron supplementation in these patients is associated with an improved exercise capacity and quality of life.[9]

QUANTIFICATION AND FOLLOW-UP OF EXERCISE INTOLERANCE

The first step for assessing exercise intolerance is quantification of its severity. This can be achieved either by subjective (describing patients' perception of their limitation) or objective means. The most commonly used scale for quantifying subjective limitation in ACHD is the NYHA classification (and the almost identical World Health Organization classification for patients with pulmonary hypertension). This scale is preferred because it is familiar to cardiologists who treat ACHD and is simple and easy to apply. When compared with objective measures of exercise capacity, the NYHA classification is able to stratify ACHD patients according to their exercise capacity but overall tends to underestimate their degree of impairment. In fact, many asymptomatic (NYHA class I) ACHD patients have dramatically lower objective exercise capacity compared with normal control subjects, which is similar to that of much older patients with acquired heart failure.[2] It appears, in fact, that ACHD patients tend to be less aware of their exercise limitation, because this has occurred over several decades rather than abruptly as occurs in acquired heart failure. This apparent unawareness of significant exercise limitation in many ACHD patients may impact on the timing and type of therapeutic interventions, possibly supporting a "sooner rather than later" approach. In particular, patients with right-sided lesions, such as patients with severe pulmonary regurgitation after repair of tetralogy of Fallot, tend to remain asymptomatic or very mildly symptomatic for long periods, even in the presence of significant right ventricular dilation and dysfunction. It is, thus, important that objective means of assessment such as cardiopulmonary exercise testing be used for the routine clinical assessment of ACHD patients and aid in the decision-making when considering elective surgery. Moreover, the NYHA classification is not a tool for assessing quality of life and thus not a substitute to a quality of life questionnaire (e.g., CAMPHOR score for patients with pulmonary arterial hypertension).

OBJECTIVE QUANTIFICATION OF EXERCISE CAPACITY

Cardiopulmonary Exercise Testing

The best method for quantifying exercise tolerance in health (athletes) and disease is cardiopulmonary exercise testing. It is a powerful tool for the objective assessment of the cardiovascular, respiratory, and muscular systems and has become part of the routine clinical assessment of ACHD patients. Incremental (ramp) protocols are used to assess functional and prognostic indices such as the peak oxygen consumption, the $\dot{V}E/\dot{V}CO_2$ slope (the slope of the regression line between ventilation ($\dot{V}_E$) and rate of elimination of carbon dioxide [VCO_2]), the anaerobic threshold, and the heart rate and blood pressure response.

Peak VO_2 is the highest value of oxygen uptake recorded during maximal exercise testing and approximates the maximal aerobic power of an individual, that is, the upper limit of oxygen utilization by the body (Fig. 6-2). It is usually expressed in milliliters per kilogram per minute and reflects the functional status of the pulmonary, cardiovascular, and muscular systems. In fact, during steady state, oxygen uptake from the lungs reflects the amount of oxygen consumed by the cells in the periphery. Peak VO_2 is the most reported exercise parameter because it

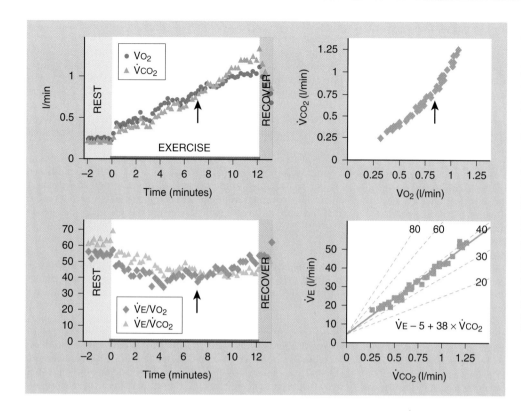

Figure 6-2 Cardiopulmonary exercise test in a 32-year-old patient with transposition of great arteries and an atrial switch repair (Mustard operation). There was mild systemic ventricular dysfunction with mild tricuspid regurgitation and dynamic left ventricular outflow tract obstruction on echocardiography (peak gradient, 55 mm Hg). The patient exercised for 12 minutes on a modified Bruce protocol and achieved a peak Vo_2 of 19 mL/kg/min, which is 64% of predicted for age, sex, and body habitus (mildly impaired). The anaerobic threshold was also mildly reduced (15.1 mL/kg/min). There was an adequate blood pressure and heart rate response and mild desaturation (from 98% to 90% at peak exercise) likely owing to a baffle leak. The VE/Vco_2 slope was mildly increased, possibly reflecting mild pulmonary hypoperfusion owing to the subpulmonary stenosis and the physiologic dead space due to right-to-left shunting. FEV_1 and FVC were within normal limits.

is simple to interpret and carries prognostic power both in acquired heart failure and ACHD.[2] However, peak Vo_2 can be reliably estimated only from maximal exercise tests and is limited by the ability and determination of a patient to exercise to exhaustion. Moreover, it can be prone to technical error/artifacts because it is derived from measurements recorded only during the last minute of exercise (peak).

Cardiopulmonary exercise testing in a large cohort of ACHD patients demonstrated that average peak Vo_2 was depressed in all ACHD groups compared with healthy subjects of similar age and varied according to underlying anatomy (Fig. 6-3).[2] Peak Vo_2 was significantly depressed even in asymptomatic ACHD patients. Patients with Eisenmenger physiology and complex anatomy (univentricular hearts with protected pulmonary circulation) had the lowest average peak Vo_2 values (11.5 and 14.6 mL/kg/min, respectively). Gender, body mass index, cyanosis, pulmonary arterial hypertension, forced expiratory volume, and peak heart rate were independent predictors of peak Vo_2 in this population.

Patients with permanent pacemakers, on β-adrenergic blocker therapy, and those not in sinus rhythm also had lower peak Vo_2. As with acquired heart failure, exercise capacity in ACHD patients was not directly related to resting systemic systolic ventricular function. In ACHD, peak Vo_2 is an independent predictor of the combined endpoint of death or hospitalization at a median follow-up of 304 days, in patients with a peak Vo_2 less than 15.5 mL/kg/min being at a threefold increased risk.[2] Peak Vo_2 is also related to the frequency and duration of hospitalization, even after accounting for NYHA class, age, age at surgery, and gender. Peak circulatory power expressed as peak exercise oxygen uptake multiplied for peak mean arterial blood pressure has also been shown to be a strong predictor of adverse outcome in ACHD.

The anaerobic threshold is the level of Vo_2 beyond which aerobic metabolism is substantially supplemented by anaerobic processes. Above the anaerobic threshold, lactate starts to accumulate and is buffered by plasma bicarbonate, resulting in an increase in CO_2 production

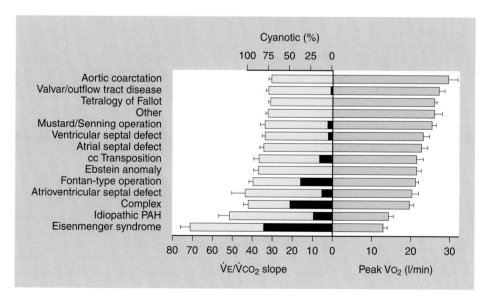

Figure 6-3 Peak Vo_2 (*pink bars*) and VE/Vco_2 slope (*yellow bars*) across the spectrum of ACHD. Groups with a higher prevalence of cyanosis (*black bars*) had the higher values of VE/Vco_2 slope. (*Data from Dimopoulos K, Okonko DO, Diller GP et al. Abnormal ventilatory response to exercise in adults with congenital heart disease relates to cyanosis and predicts survival. Circulation 2006; 113:2796-2802.*)

($\dot{V}CO_2$). Anaerobic threshold can be identified through observation of the $\dot{V}CO_2$ versus $\dot{V}O_2$ relation or by observing the ventilation ($\dot{V}E/\dot{V}O_2$) ratio over time. The anaerobic threshold has obvious pathophysiologic significance because it is the point beyond which aerobic metabolism is unable to sustain energy requirements. It also carries important prognostic information in acquired heart failure and ACHD.[2,10]

The $\dot{V}E/\dot{V}CO_2$ slope is an exercise parameter that is independent of maximal exertion (see Fig. 6-2). It is a simplification of the complex relationship between ventilation and CO_2 production. It is thought to reflect pulmonary perfusion and the degree of physiologic dead space and ventilation/perfusion mismatch, as well as enhanced ventilatory reflex sensitivity.[3] It is easy to calculate, reproducible, and a marker of exercise intolerance strongly related to peak $\dot{V}O_2$. The $\dot{V}E/\dot{V}CO_2$ slope carries important physiologic and prognostic information.

High values of $\dot{V}E/\dot{V}CO_2$ slope compared with normal controls were encountered in all major ACHD groups.[3] Patients with Eisenmenger syndrome were found to have the most disproportionately high $\dot{V}E/\dot{V}CO_2$ slopes (mean 71.2), whereas patients with aortic coarctation had the lowest mean $\dot{V}E/\dot{V}CO_2$ slope (see Fig. 6-3). Cyanosis had a significant impact on the ventilatory response to exercise and was the strongest independent predictor of the $\dot{V}E/\dot{V}CO_2$ slope in this cohort. A linear relation between $\dot{V}E/\dot{V}CO_2$ slope and NYHA functional class was observed, suggesting a link between the ventilatory response to exercise and the occurrence of symptoms. Nevertheless, the $\dot{V}E/\dot{V}CO_2$ slope was, as with peak $\dot{V}O_2$, significantly raised even among asymptomatic patients, further underscoring the importance of objective assessment of exercise capacity in ACHD. When cyanotic ACHD patients were excluded, a $\dot{V}E/\dot{V}CO_2$ slope of 38 or above was an adverse prognostic marker associated with a 10-fold increase in the risk of death within 2 years.[3] The $\dot{V}E/\dot{V}CO_2$ slope can improve after pulmonary valve replacement in patients with tetralogy of Fallot. Those patients who were younger than 17.5 years old at the time of pulmonary valve replacement were more likely to have a normal $\dot{V}E/\dot{V}CO_2$ slope 1 year after surgery.[11]

Other valuable information is also recorded during cardiopulmonary testing, which entails spirometry, electrocardiography, and oxygen saturation and blood pressure measurement. Frequent blood pressure measurement is required in patients with left-sided obstructive lesions. Although physicians are generally reluctant to have small patients with left-sided obstructive lesions exercise, exercise testing in this setting can provide valuable information. Moreover, a fall in systolic blood pressure is best identified in a controlled environment during in-hospital exercise testing. The arm/limb blood pressure measurements are also important, especially in patients with previous Blalock-Taussig shunts and those with aortic coarctation.

6-Minute Walk Test

A simpler means of objectively assessing exercise capacity is the 6-minute walk test. This timed distance exercise test is ideal for significantly impaired patients for whom the distance walked in 6 minutes correlates well to peak $\dot{V}O_2$. Oxygen saturations and perceived exertion through semiquantitative means such as the Borg scale can also be recorded. It is an easy test to perform and reflects the ability to perform ordinary daily activities. It is also more sensitive to changes after intervention compared with peak $\dot{V}O_2$, and is a U.S. Food and Drug Administration (FDA)–approved endpoint for prospective clinical trials in pulmonary hypertension. It should not be used in mildly impaired or asymptomatic patients because there is a "ceiling effect," masking improvement after intervention. An important learning effect has also been described, making direct comparison between the first and subsequent tests difficult.

Systemic Manifestations of the Heart Failure Syndrome in Adult Congenital Heart Disease

The clinical syndrome of heart failure has important systemic manifestations that define the natural history and are the target of modern therapies. Neurohormonal activation, chemoreflex and peripheral ergoreflex activation, as well as organ failure, such as renal and hepatic

dysfunction, are well-described complications of acquired heart failure and affect the outcome of these patients. Neurohormonal and cytokine activation have also been described in ACHD patients, with elevated atrial natriuretic peptide, B-type natriuretic peptide, endothelin-1, renin, aldosterone, and norepinephrine reported across a wide spectrum of congenital lesions and correlating with worsening NYHA class and ventricular function. Neurohormonal activation has also been described in asymptomatic ACHD patients years after surgical repair of even relatively simple lesions and is associated with an increased risk of death.[12]

Endothelial dysfunction is well described in patients with heart failure and has a detrimental effect on myocardial and skeletal muscle function and on exercise tolerance. Evidence of endothelial dysfunction in CHD is available for Fontan operation patients and for cyanotic ACHD patients, owing to impaired release of nitric oxide despite hemoconcentration and increase in shear stress.[13] Patients with Eisenmenger syndrome also exhibit reduced circulating endothelial progenitor cell numbers.[14]

The term *cardiorenal syndrome* is used to define a state of advanced renal dysfunction in heart failure. ACHD patients, even though younger than those with acquired heart failure, have a high prevalence of impaired renal function with moderate or severe dysfunction present in one of five patients.[15] Renal dysfunction in ACHD is likely due to a low cardiac output state with decreased kidney perfusion, activation of sympathetic nervous system leading to arterial vasoconstriction, and activation of the renin-angiotensin-aldosterone system. Cyanotic patients are at highest risk of developing renal dysfunction, suggesting a detrimental effect of chronic hypoxia and, perhaps, hyperviscosity on the kidney. Patients with moderate to severe renal dysfunction were at a threefold increased risk of adverse outcome.

Hypotonic hyponatremia is typical of patients with congestive heart failure, especially those requiring treatment with diuretics, and is a strong prognostic marker in this population and a criterion for transplantation. Hyponatremia has also been found to be common in ACHD patients and is a strong predictor of outcome independent of renal dysfunction and use of diuretics.[16]

Anemia is also common in heart failure patients and has been described in ACHD. Anemia can affect exercise capacity[8] and is also a predictor of outcome in noncyanotic ACHD patients. "Relative" anemia, that is, inadequate increase in hemoglobin concentration (secondary erythrocytosis secondary to chronic hypoxia) is also common in cyanotic ACHD patients and is usually due to iron deficiency.[9] Screening for iron deficiency in these patients is important because it is associated with impaired exercise capacity and quality of life.

Treatment

TREATMENT OF HEMODYNAMIC LESIONS AND CORRECTABLE ABNORMALITIES

Cardiac hemodynamic lesions should be the first target in the effort to improve exercise capacity. Potential therapeutic options include surgical or interventional relief of obstructive lesions, repair of valve abnormalities, and elimination or reduction of shunts.[1,17] Improvement in symptoms has been reported after interventions such as Fontan-type operations, tetralogy of Fallot repair, relief of congenital aortic stenosis, and transcutaneous closure of an atrial septal defect. Other reversible causes of exercise intolerance and ventricular dysfunction, such as ischemic heart disease, anemia, and parenchymal pulmonary disease, should be sought and, when possible, treated.

COUNTERACTING NEUROHORMONAL ACTIVATION

Modern pharmacologic treatment of chronic heart failure is based on counteracting neurohormonal activation with medication such as angiotensin-converting enzyme (ACE) inhibitors, β-adrenergic blockers, and spironolactone, improving not just hemodynamics but also prognosis. Such drugs are increasingly used in ACHD on the basis of similarities in pathophysiology between ACHD and acquired heart failure, despite little evidence of their efficacy in this setting.[18,19] In fact, published trials are mostly single center studies with a sample size significantly smaller compared with similar trials in acquired heart disease. Caution is, however, recommended when extrapolating data from heart failure trials.[20]

TARGETING PULMONARY ARTERIAL HYPERTENSION

Recently, new therapies have become available for patients with pulmonary arterial hypertension, including those with ACHD. Epoprostenol has been shown to improve functional status, systemic saturations, and pulmonary hemodynamics in patients with CHD and pulmonary arterial hypertension.[21] Epoprostenol is, however, limited by the need for continuous intravenous administration and consequent complications such as line infections. Bosentan, an oral dual-receptor endothelin antagonist, improved exercise capacity in patients with Eisenmenger syndrome in several open-label intention-to-treat pilot studies and a randomized placebo-controlled study.[22] The pulmonary vascular resistance index was also decreased in the bosentan arm of the study within 16 weeks of therapy (but not in the placebo), and these results were sustained during open-extension studies. Sildenafil, an oral phosphodiasterase-5 inhibitor, improves functional capacity in patients with pulmonary arterial hypertension, including some with CHD.[23] A small randomized trial of sildenafil in 10 patients with Eisenmenger syndrome found a significant improvement in functional status, exercise capacity, and pulmonary pressures in the Eisenmenger syndrome subgroup. Oral administration of a single dose of sildenafil acutely improved exercise capacity and hemodynamic response to exercise in 27 patients with Fontan circulation. Other large randomized trials using treprostinil, sildenafil, and sitaxsentan have included a minority of patients with ACHD in their population. A minority of ACHD patients were also included in the recently published EARLY study assessing the effect of bosentan on patients with pulmonary arterial hypertension in functional NYHA class II.[24] None of these studies, however, was powered for formal subgroup analysis, leaving doubts on the applicability of their results to the ACHD population. Nevertheless, our group recently reported survival benefits from advance therapies for pulmonary arterial hypertension in a contemporary cohort of adult patients with Eisenmenger physiology (229 patients, mean age 34.5 ± 12.6 years, median follow-up of 4 years) compared with patients from the same cohort managed conventionally.[25] Whether selected patients, in which advanced pulmonary arterial hypertension therapies induce a significant improvement, could safely undergo partial or complete repair of the underlying cardiac defect in a "treat-and-repair" fashion is still a matter of debate.[17]

RESYNCHRONIZATION THERAPY

Ventricular dyssynchrony has been found to affect significantly cardiac function and is a target for therapy in patients with left ventricular dysfunction and intraventricular conduction delay. Although there is mounting evidence that ventricular dyssynchrony is present in patients with CHD,[26] randomized trials of resynchronization in this population are lacking. Implantation of cardiac resynchronization devices in ACHD patients may present significant difficulties owing to the varying intracardiac anatomy and should be performed by appropriately trained operators. The role of resynchronization, like that of implantable cardiac defibrillators, in the setting of ACHD needs to be explored further.

TRANSPLANTATION

The role of transplantation (heart and/or lung) remains relatively limited in ACHD, especially for patients with complex cyanotic disease. The scarcity of donors, the slow deterioration with a mortality rate significantly lower than that of end-stage acquired heart failure, the high prevalence of complications such as renal and hepatic dysfunction in severely symptomatic ACHD patients, and the often complex cardiovascular anatomy result in very few patients actually receiving a transplant.[27] However, transplantation should be considered in highly symptomatic patients who are not amenable to conventional surgery/intervention.

EXERCISE TRAINING

Exercise is defined as movement undertaken by muscles with an increase in energy expenditure above resting metabolism. Leisure activities, labor, sports, and training are all examples of exercise. *Training* can be defined as systematic exercise in which the type of activity, intensity, frequency, and duration all play a role.

Exercise has an effect on the muscular, locomotive, metabolic, and circulatory systems, and its beneficial psychological and physical effects on patients with acquired heart disease are established.[28] However, the recently published HF-ACTION trial, the largest multicenter randomized controlled trial of exercise training in heart failure (n = 2331), failed to demonstrate a benefit on the primary endpoint of mortality or hospitalization.

Isotonic and Isometric Exercise

There are two types of exercise: isotonic (also called dynamic) and isometric (also called static). Isotonic exercise is recognized by rhythmic muscular contractions with changes in muscle length, using a relatively small force. Isometric exercise is recognized by a relatively large force with little or no change in muscle length. Most forms of movement contain both types of exercise, although some are mostly isotonic (jogging, cross-country skiing, and swimming) and others isometric (weightlifting and speed skiing). Isotonic exercise causes a volume overload of the heart and an increase in oxygen consumption, heart rate, stroke volume, cardiac output, and systolic blood pressure. Owing to the decrease in peripheral resistance, the diastolic blood pressure may fall during isotonic exercise. Isometric exercise, which causes mainly pressure overload, induces a sudden increase of blood pressure, whereas the increase in oxygen consumption and cardiac output is limited. The load in isometric exercise may be difficult to control, which makes isometric exercise unsuitable in some young patients with CHD.

Goals of Exercise Training

The goals of exercise programs are general health promotion and improvement in aerobic capacity. Regular isotonic exercise can increase maximal oxygen uptake, stroke volume, cardiac output, and myocardial perfusion through enhanced oxygen extraction, increased capacity of oxidative enzymes, mitochondria, increased amount of myoglobin, and vascularization. Moreover, because ACHD patients (with the exception of cyanotic patients) are at similar risk of coronary atherosclerosis as the normal population,[5] physical fitness is also a means of reducing the risk of coronary disease.

Exercise Training in Adult Congenital Heart Disease

Because the evidence on the risks and benefits of exercise in ACHD is limited, recommendations have rested on individual physician judgment. The 36th Bethesda Conference recommendations for the participation of patients with CHD in sports suggest the use of exercise testing for assessing the impact of exercise on ACHD patients before advising any level of training in the clinical setting.[29] Simple preventive measures such as avoiding excessive dehydration are recommended, especially in patients with cyanotic disease. High-impact sports should be discouraged in patients on anticoagulation therapy or carrying a pacemaker as well as patients with Marfan syndrome. Extreme caution is also recommended in patients who are at high risk of arrhythmia and sudden death, such as those with long QT syndrome, arrhythmogenic right ventricular dysplasia, and hypertrophic obstructive cardiomyopathy. All recommendations should be thoroughly discussed with patients (Box 6-1).

Rather than a therapeutic intervention, exercise training should be approached as a lifestyle change. However, modification of lifestyle is difficult and requires adequate physician and patient education on the benefits of exercise. To establish relationships with adolescents with CHD, a focus on physical activity is often a "key" that can open up a fruitful dialogue and willingness to accept follow-up programs and adjustments to a healthy lifestyle. Individualized recommendations may increase motivation to adopt an active lifestyle. Self-monitoring of physical activity through logs and the use simple devices such as accelerometers may also enhance awareness and motivation.[30] The effort

BOX 6-1 PARTICIPATION IN EXERCISE FOR PATIENTS WITH COMMON ACHD LESIONS

Atrial Septal Defects (ASDs)

The main concerns regarding exercise in patients with ASDs are pulmonary hypertension and the presence of tachyarrhythmias. After surgical or interventional repair, tachycardias and residual myocardial dysfunction are major concerns. Patients with small ASDs with no pulmonary vascular disease or right ventricle dilation as well as those 3 to 6 months after successful repair with no arrhythmias, pulmonary hypertension, or myocardial dysfunction can participate in all competitive sports. Patients with an ASD and mild pulmonary hypertension can participate in low-intensity competitive sports.

Ventricular Septal Defects (VSDs)

Patients with restrictive VSDs and those operated on in early childhood with no pulmonary hypertension and normal ventricular function can participate in all competitive sports. Three to 6 months after repair, asymptomatic patients with no defect or only a small residual defect can participate in all sports when there is no evidence of pulmonary hypertension or ventricular or atrial arrhythmias. Patients with nonrestrictive VSDs and secondary pulmonary arterial hypertension (Eisenmenger complex) are at risk when undertaking strenuous exercise because of risks of precipitating a clinical event.

Patent Ductus Arteriosus (PDA)

Small PDAs with normal left ventricular size are not a contraindication to competitive sports. Larger PDAs with left ventricular enlargement require repair before undertaking competitive sports. After repair of a PDA, asymptomatic patients with no evidence of pulmonary hypertension or left ventricular enlargement can participate in competitive sports. See later for patients who develop Eisenmenger syndrome.

Pulmonary Stenosis

If the peak gradient is less than 40 mm Hg and the right ventricular function is normal, competitive sports can be undertaken with annual review. When the gradient is more than 40 mm Hg, patients can participate in low-intensity competitive sports. However, patients in this category usually are referred for balloon valvuloplasty or operative valvotomy before sports participation. After repair (2 weeks for balloon valvuloplasty or 3 months for surgery), athletes with no/mild residual pulmonary stenosis and no ventricular dysfunction can participate in all competitive sports. If severe pulmonary regurgitation with marked right ventricular dilation is present, less-competitive sports can be undertaken.

Coarctation of the Aorta

Owing to a reduced distensibility of the precoarctation portion of the aorta there is often a marked rise in systolic blood pressure in the proximal part of the aorta during exercise, despite successful repair. Patients with mild coarctation and a resting gradient between upper and lower limb pressure less than or equal to 20 mm Hg, no large collateral vessels, no significant aortic root dilation, and a normal exercise test with peak systolic blood pressure less than 230 mm Hg can participate in all competitive sports. If the systolic arm/leg gradient is more than 20 mm Hg or there is exercise-induced hypertension, low-intensity competitive sports may be undertaken until treated. At least 3 months after repair, sports are allowed if the arm/leg gradient is less than or equal to 20 mm Hg and there is a normal blood pressure response to exercise. However, high-impact sports and those that are high intensity static are to be avoided during the first postoperative year. High-intensity sports should also be avoided in patients with significant aortic dilation, wall thinning, or aneurysm formation.

Aortic Subvalvular, Valvular, and Supravalvular Stenosis

Patients with mild aortic stenosis (operated or nonoperated), normal electrocardiogram, exercise tolerance, and no history of exertional pain, syncope, or arrhythmias can participate in all sports. If aortic stenosis is moderate, athletes can participate in low static/low-to-moderate dynamic, and moderate static/low-to-moderate dynamic competitive sports if they are asymptomatic, there is mild or no left ventricular hypertrophy on echocardiography and no left ventricular strain pattern on the electrocardiogram, and exercise testing is normal with no evidence of ischemia or arrhythmias and normal blood pressure response. Severe aortic stenosis is a contraindication to competitive sports. After repair of left ventricular outflow tract obstruction, annual follow-up and re-evaluation is indicated.

Tetralogy of Fallot

Patients with repaired tetralogy of Fallot and normal right-sided heart pressures, no residual shunting, no significant right ventricular overload, and no arrhythmias can participate in all sports. Age at repair is important in predicting exercise tolerance, because long-standing right ventricular pressure overload often results in reduced compliance and impaired diastolic function. Patients with significant pulmonary regurgitation, residual right ventricular hypertension (≥50% of systemic) or tachyarrhythmias (ventricular of supraventricular) should participate in low-intensity sports.

Transposition of the Great Arteries (TGA)

Patients after atrial switch repair with no or mild right ventricle dilatation, no history of previous arrhythmias or syncope, and a normal exercise test can engage in low and moderate static/low dynamic competitive sports.

There is a growing cohort of patients with previous arterial switch for TGA who are now old enough to participate in competitive sports. Athletes with mild hemodynamic abnormalities or ventricular dysfunction can participate in moderate static/low dynamic competitive sports, provided that their exercise test is normal.

Asymptomatic patients with congenitally corrected TGA without other cardiac abnormalities may be eligible for participation in low-to-moderate intensity competitive sports if there is no systemic ventricular enlargement, no evidence of tachyarrhythmias on electrocardiographic monitoring or exercise testing, and a normal exercise test (including normal maximum oxygen consumption).

Fontan Operation

Patients after a Fontan operation are usually limited in their exercise capacity. Participation in high-intensity competitive sports is not advisable in the presence of ventricular dysfunction or arterial desaturation.

Ebstein Anomaly

Patients with moderate tricuspid regurgitation and no arrhythmia on Holter monitoring can participate in low-intensity competitive sports. Participation in sports is not advisable in patients with severe Ebstein anomaly. After surgical repair, low-intensity competitive sports are permitted if tricuspid regurgitation is mild, cardiac chamber size is not substantially increased, and symptomatic atrial or ventricular tachyarrhythmias are not present on ambulatory electrocardiographic monitoring and exercise testing. In selected cases of excellent hemodynamic result after repair, additional participation on an individual basis may be permitted.

Eisenmenger Syndrome

Patients with Eisenmenger syndrome should avoid moderate- or high-intensity exercise. A fall in systemic vascular resistance and reduced pulmonary venous return may cause significant arterial desaturation, exercise-induced syncope, and death. If more than mild exercise programs are planned, testing of pulmonary hypertensive patients is mandatory to assess blood pressure, heart rhythm, and oxygen saturation response.

---

to bring previously impaired patients to normal activities, such as part-time or full-time employment, is strongly desirable because it can be a powerful means of "re-training" ACHD patients.

It is important to direct patients with CHD into sports at which they can succeed even if cardiac function deteriorates. The social impact of sports is important for their self-esteem. An acceptable effort toler-ance is fundamental for improving social integration and permitting employment and sexual relations, especially in young ACHD patients. Moreover, adequate effort tolerance is fundamental for labor and especially delivery, which requires great isometric effort. Exercise testing in this setting may provide essential information on the hemodynamic responses of individual patients to effort.

REFERENCES

1. Dimopoulos K, Diller GP, Piepoli MF, Gatzoulis MA. Exercise intolerance in adults with congenital heart disease. Cardiol Clin 2006;24:641–660 vii.

2. Diller GP, Dimopoulos K, Okonko D, et al. Exercise intolerance in adult congenital heart disease: comparative severity, correlates, and prognostic implication. Circulation 2005;112:828–835.

3. Dimopoulos K, Okonko DO, Diller GP, et al. Abnormal ventilatory response to exercise in adults with congenital heart disease relates to cyanosis and predicts survival. Circulation 2006;113:2796–2802.

4. Gatzoulis MA, Clark AL, Cullen S, et al. Right ventricular diastolic function 15 to 35 years after repair of tetralogy of Fallot: restrictive physiology predicts superior exercise performance. Circulation 1995;91:1775–1781.

5. Giannakoulas G, Dimopoulos K, Engel R, et al. Burden of coronary artery disease in adults with congenital heart disease and its relation to congenital and traditional heart risk factors. Am J Cardiol 2009;103:1445–1450.

6. Diller GP, Dimopoulos K, Okonko D, et al. Heart rate response during exercise predicts survival in adults with congenital heart disease. J Am Coll Cardiol 2006;48:1250–1256.

7. Diller GP, Dimopoulos K, Kafka H, et al. Model of chronic adaptation: right ventricular function in Eisenmenger syndrome. Eur Heart J 2007;9:H54–H60.

8. Dimopoulos K, Diller GP, Giannakoulas G, et al. Anemia in adults with congenital heart disease relates to adverse outcome. J Am Coll Cardiol 2009;54:2093–2100.

9. Tay ELW, Peset A, Papaphylactou A, et al. Replacement therapy for iron deficiency improves exercise capacity and quality of life in patients with cyanotic congenital heart disease and/or the Eisenmenger syndrome. Int J Cardiol (2010), doi:10.1016/j.ijcard.2010.05.066.

10. Diller GP, Dimopoulos K, Benson LR, Gatzoulis MA. Ventilatory efficiency and heart rate response are the strongest exercise markers of outcome in noncyanotic adults with congenital heart disease. J Am Coll Cardiol 2007;49(9 Suppl. 1):A268.

11. Frigiola A, Tsang V, Bull C, et al. Biventricular response after pulmonary valve replacement for right ventricular outflow tract dysfunction: is age a predictor of outcome? Circulation 2008;118(Suppl. 14):S182–S190.

12. Lammers A, Kaemmerer H, Hollweck R, et al. Impaired cardiac autonomic nervous activity predicts sudden cardiac death in patients with operated and unoperated congenital cardiac disease. J Thorac Cardiovasc Surg 2006;132:647–655.

13. Oechslin E, Kiowski W, Schindler R, et al. Systemic endothelial dysfunction in adults with cyanotic congenital heart disease. Circulation 2005;112:1106–1112.

14. Diller GP, van Eijl S, Okonko DO, et al. Circulating endothelial progenitor cells in patients with Eisenmenger syndrome and idiopathic pulmonary arterial hypertension. Circulation 2008;117:3020–3030.

15. Dimopoulos K, Diller GP, Koltsida E, et al. Prevalence, predictors, and prognostic value of renal dysfunction in adults with congenital heart disease. Circulation 2008;117:2320–2328.

16. Dimopoulos K, Diller GP, Petraco R, et al. Hyponatraemia: a strong predictor of mortality in adults with congenital heart disease. Eur Heart J 2010;31:595–601.

17. Dimopoulos K, Peset A, Gatzoulis MA. Evaluating operability in adults with congenital heart disease and the role of pretreatment with targeted pulmonary arterial hypertension therapy. Int J Cardiol 2008;129:163–171.

18. Dimopoulos K, Diller G, Koltsida E, et al. Prevalence, predictors and prognostic value of renal dysfunction in adults with congenital heart disease. Circulation 2008;117:2320–2328.

19. Dore A, Houde C, Chan KL, et al. Angiotensin receptor blockade and exercise capacity in adults with systemic right ventricles: a multicenter, randomized, placebo-controlled clinical trial. Circulation 2005;112:2411–2416.

20. Warnes CA, Williams RG, Bashore TM, et al. ACC/AHA 2008 Guidelines for the Management of Adults With Congenital Heart Disease. A Report of the American College of Cardiology/American Heart Association Task Force on Practice Guidelines (Writing Committee to Develop Guidelines on the Management of Adults With Congenital Heart Disease). Circulation 2008;118:e714–e833.

21. Rosenzweig EB, Kerstein D, Barst RJ. Long-term prostacyclin for pulmonary hypertension with associated congenital heart defects. Circulation 1999;99:1858–1865.

22. Galie N, Beghetti M, Gatzoulis MA, et al. Bosentan therapy in patients with Eisenmenger syndrome: a multicenter, double-blind, randomized, placebo-controlled study. Circulation 2006;114:48–54.

23. Galie N, Ghofrani HA, Torbicki A, et al. Sildenafil citrate therapy for pulmonary arterial hypertension. N Engl J Med 2005;353:2148–2157.

24. Galie N, Rubin L, Hoeper M, et al. Treatment of patients with mildly symptomatic pulmonary arterial hypertension with bosentan (EARLY study): a double-blind, randomised controlled trial. Lancet 2008;371:2093–2100.

25. Dimopoulos K, Inuzuka R, Goletto S, et al. Improved survival among patients with Eisenmenger syndrome receiving advanced therapy for pulmonary arterial hypertension. Circulation 2010;121:20–25.

26. Uebing A, Gibson DG, Babu-Narayan SV, et al. Right ventricular mechanics and QRS duration in patients with repaired tetralogy of Fallot: implications of infundibular disease. Circulation 2007;116:1532–1539.

27. Dimopoulos K, Giannakoulas G, Wort SJ, Gatzoulis MA. Pulmonary arterial hypertension in adults with congenital heart disease: distinct differences from other causes of pulmonary arterial hypertension and management implications. Curr Opin Cardiol 2008;23:545–554.

28. Piepoli MF, Davos C, Francis DP, Coats AJ. Exercise training meta-analysis of trials in patients with chronic heart failure (ExTraMATCH). BMJ 2004;328:189.

29. Graham TP, Driscoll DJ, Gersony WM, et al. Task Force 2: congenital heart disease. J Am Coll Cardiol 2005;45:1326–1333.

30. Giannakoulas G, Dimopoulos K. Exercise training in congenital heart disease: should we follow the heart failure paradigm? Int J Cardiol 2010;138:109–111.

7

Cardiovascular Magnetic Resonance Imaging

PHILIP J. KILNER

Introduction

Cardiovascular magnetic resonance imaging (CMR) gives unrestricted access to the heart and great vessels noninvasively and without ionizing radiation.[1] It can provide biventricular functional assessment, flow measurement, myocardial viability assessment, angiography, and more. Transthoracic echocardiography remains the first-line approach to imaging the hearts of patients with adult congenital heart disease (ACHD), providing a relatively rapid and comprehensive evaluation of anatomy, function, and hemodynamic indices in most patients. However, the suboptimal penetration of ultrasound is a limitation, especially in adults after cardiovascular surgery. Moreover, echocardiography does not offer CMR's repertoire of tissue contrast options, with or without administration of a contrast agent, and lacks its unrestricted fields of view and volumetric measurements of flow. For these reasons a dedicated CMR service should be regarded as a required facility in a center specializing in the care of patients with ACHD.

CMR is performed with a patient's body located in a strong magnetic field, typically 1.5 Tesla, where the patient will generally have to lie still for a period of 30 minutes or more. Claustrophobia can be problematic in about 5% of patients. Images are acquired by means of a radio signal that passes freely through the body and resonates with the nuclei of hydrogen the body, whose spins are appropriately tuned and re-tuned by magnetic gradients superimposed on the main magnetic field. Images are computed by spectral analysis of re-emitted radio signal, interpreted in relation to the sequence of radio pulses and the magnetic gradients applied. Cardiac gated cardiovascular images are acquired using sequences applied at specific time delays after the R wave of the electrocardiogram, usually through several successive heart cycles, so arrhythmias may degrade image quality.

Safety

Although CMR is noninvasive, nonionizing, and usually safe, the strong magnetic field with its gradient switches can present dangers under certain circumstances (Box 7-1).[2] A patient with a pacemaker should not go near the magnet. Common items of hospital equipment made with steel such as scissors, wheelchairs, or gas cylinders can become lethal missiles if inadvertently taken close to the magnet. However, most metallic devices and clips implanted in the chest are safe, as long as they do not incorporate electrical devices. Ferromagnetic implants cause local artifacts on images, but this does not usually negate the usefulness of the investigation. In recent years it has become apparent that gadolinium chelate contrast agents, which are widely used for CMR angiography or myocardial viability studies, have been linked, albeit rarely and only in patients with renal failure, to the severe complication of nephrogenic systemic fibrosis.[3] In cases in which a contrast agent is indicated, renal function needs to be tested and the potential risks weighed against the benefits of contrast-enhanced rather than noncontrast CMR imaging. Information regarding specific implants and CMR systems is available on the Internet (www.MRIsafety.com).

General Considerations

Where a CMR service is available for investigation and follow-up of patients with ACHD it is soon found to be extremely valuable. Images and measurements obtained complement those from transthoracic and transesophageal echocardiography. They make diagnostic catheterization unnecessary in many cases and expedite subsequent interventional catheterization.[4] However, diagnostic catheterization may still be needed for measurement of pulmonary artery pressure and resistance. Alternatively, multislice computed tomography (MSCT) may be preferable for visualization of coronary arteries and in patients with pacemakers.[5] Combined catheterization and CMR is also feasible. A promising application is for measurements of pulmonary vascular resistance based on simultaneous measurements of pulmonary flow by CMR and pressure by catheter transducer.[6] Work is progressing in the use of CMR for catheter and device guidance, with the potential advantages of three-dimensional (3D) localization, tissue characterization, and the avoidance or reduction of ionizing radiation,[7] although this remains a field for research rather than for mainstream clinical use.[8]

CMR gives unrestricted access to the chest in multiple, freely chosen slices. It is noninvasive, free of ionizing radiation, and usually well tolerated by patients who may need to return for repeated follow-up investigations. It provides clear images of anatomy throughout the chest. Cine imaging depicts movements of myocardium, valves, and flowing blood. 3D magnetic resonance angiography, usually after venous injection of gadolinium, can provide clear views of the pulmonary, systemic, and collateral arterial branches. CMR can answer functional as well as anatomic questions, including the location and severity of stenosis (e.g., aortic coarctation or pulmonary artery stenosis), severity of regurgitation (e.g., pulmonary), the size and function of heart chambers (the right as well as the left ventricle), and measurement of shunt flow.

As an imaging modality, magnetic resonance has unrivaled versatility. The key to this versatility is control of the interaction between radio signals and nuclear spins in the tissues and blood, mainly by means of rapid, carefully designed sequences of applied magnetic gradients. The spins of protons are energized by pulses of radio energy and tuned and re-tuned by magnetic gradient switches. A repertoire of different sequences allows a variety of image appearances or flow measurements to be achieved, usually without administration of a contrast agent (Fig. 7-1).

The versatility of CMR is a great strength but also a potential source of confusion. Different CMR systems, or different individuals using the same system, may use different approaches. Given so much choice, uniformity is not easy to maintain. CMR is also relatively expensive, but the cost of imaging should be weighed against potential costs of inappropriate management, which might entail complicated repeat surgery or more extended hospitalization than necessary. Imaging specialists need not be deterred by anatomic variability found in CHD. The comprehensive anatomic coverage offered by CMR almost always allows useful diagnostic contributions to be made. Although it is recommended that CMR of more complex cases be undertaken by experts in specialist centers, this may not always be possible. If necessary, a relatively comprehensive and technically simple approach is to acquire one or more contiguous stacks of cine images covering the whole heart and mediastinum. Such cine stacks are easy to acquire and review. They reveal functional as well as anatomic information and allow the identification of any jet flow. This approach can be supplemented or replaced by patient-specific protocols as experience and confidence are gained.

Image Display and Analysis

Static films are not adequate for conveying all of the information available in multislice, cine, flow velocity, and 3D angiographic acquisitions. CMR acquisitions need to be replayed and analyzed interactively on a computer using appropriate software. The image display and analysis package should allow ventricular volume and flow measurements. For review of images in the setting of a multidisciplinary clinical meeting, images should be displayed via a computer linked both to the image storage server and to a projector.

BOX 7-1 OBJECTS THAT AFFECT THE SAFETY AND USEFULNESS OF CARDIOVASCULAR MAGNETIC RESONANCE

Unsafe
- Cardiac pacemaker
- Pacing wire (possibly)
- Implants with electric circuits
- Intracranial aneurysm clip
- Steel fragment in a previously injured eye

Safe, But Causing Local Image Artifact
- Prosthetic heart valves
- Stents
- Occlusion devices
- Intrathoracic ligation clips
- Sternal wires
- Implanted spinal rod (Harrington rod)

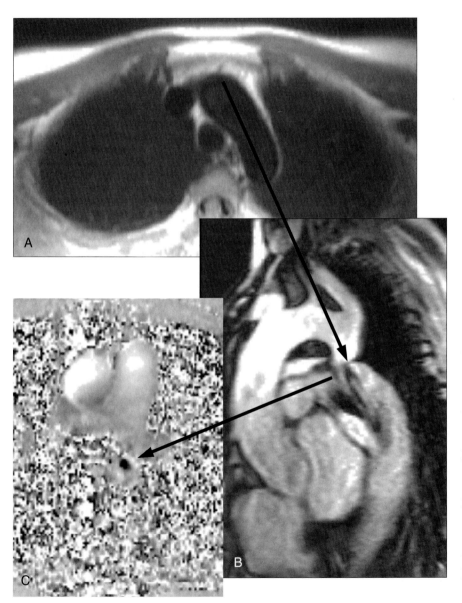

Figure 7-1 Assessment of aortic coarctation by magnetic resonance. **A,** The transaxial dark-blood image is one of a multislice set. This set of images is used to locate an oblique sagittal cine-imaging slice. **B,** The oblique sagittal cine image is aligned with the aortic arch and, more importantly, the region of coarctation. In this case, a systolic jet appears as a bright core outlined by dark lines of signal loss (*arrow*). The jet arises distal to an orifice (not clearly seen) in a discrete membrane that partially occludes the descending aorta. **C,** The phase-contrast velocity map shows a central dark spot (*arrow*) representing the systolic jet through the coarctation orifice. The plane of velocity acquisition transects the descending aorta at the level indicated by the origin of the arrow. Velocities of up to 4 m/s have been encoded through the plane, with black representing flow toward the feet and white representing flow toward the head. A peak velocity of 3.4 m/s was recorded, with slight diastolic prolongation of forward flow.

Techniques

MULTISLICE IMAGING

Transaxial, coronal, and sagittal stacks of multislice images should be acquired in ACHD patients. There are several methods of acquiring these. Bright-blood images using steady-state free precession (SSFP) acquisition have advantages in ACHD patients because they show the pulmonary vessels well and because each slice can be acquired rapidly. Adjacent slices can be acquired in consecutive heartbeats so that 20 or more static slices can usually be acquired in a single breath-hold and then used for accurate alignment of subsequent breath-hold cine acquisitions.

CINE IMAGING

Cine imaging allows visualization of flow and the movements of the heart and vessel walls. Contiguous stacks of transaxial or coronal cine images covering the whole heart and mediastinum are recommended when evaluating patients with ACHD, particularly in more complex cases. Such cine stacks are easy to acquire and review and reveal functional as well as anatomic information, showing the presence of any jet flow. However, because the images are composed of relatively long, thin voxels, the length being the slice thickness (typically 5 to 7 mm), thin structures such as valve leaflets or jet boundaries are seen clearly only where they are orientated perpendicular to the slice. SSFP cine images give good blood-tissue contrast, which is an advantage for imaging and measuring ventricular volumes and mass and for visualizing heart valves. Sequences of this type can outline a coherent jet core clearly, if present, owing to localized loss of signal from the shear layers at the edges of a jet (see Fig. 7-1B), and breath-hold acquisition makes it possible to interrogate a jet area precisely and repeatedly. The approach of "cross-cutting," locating an orthogonal slice though a partially visualized feature such as a valve orifice or jet, is an effective way of "homing in" on a particular jet. An alternative and more comprehensive approach is to acquire an oblique stack of relatively thin (5-mm) cines, without gaps, orientated to reveal all parts of a particular structure or region of interest such as a regurgitant mitral valve.[9]

PHASE VELOCITY MAPPING

If correctly implemented, phase-contrast velocity mapping can provide accurate measurements of velocity and volume flow.[10] However, an understanding of the principles and pitfalls is needed for successful clinical application.[11] Clinical uses include measurements of cardiac output, shunt flow, collateral flow, regurgitant flow,[12] and, where jets are of sufficient size and coherence, jet velocities through stenoses. It is necessary to select a plane, echo time, velocity-encoding direction, and sensitivity appropriate for a particular investigation.

Velocity can be encoded in directions that lie either in or through an image plane. Mapping of velocities through a plane transecting a vessel (velocity encoded in the direction of the slice select gradient) allows measurement of flow volume. The cross-sectional area of the lumen and the mean axially directed velocity within that area are measured for each phase through the heart cycle.[12] From this, a flow curve is plotted, and systolic forward flow and any diastolic reversed flow are computed by integration. Such flow measurements will only be accurate if phase shifts are caused by velocities and not by other factors such as eddy currents, concomitant gradients, motion artifacts, or background noise. Appropriate acquisition sequences must be used. On some systems, either automated correction of phase offset errors, if available, or subsequent correction using corresponding phase maps acquired in a static phantom may be needed to remove errors.[13]

Jet velocity mapping can be useful for assessment of certain stenoses where ultrasonic access is limited, such as in aortic coarctation, ventriculopulmonary conduits, pulmonary artery branch stenoses, and obstructions at atrial and atriopulmonary levels after Mustard, Senning, and Fontan operations. However, the limitations of the technique need to be recognized. The velocities of narrow, eccentric jets through mildly regurgitant tricuspid or pulmonary valves, which may be used in Doppler echocardiography for estimations of right ventricular or pulmonary artery pressure, are unlikely to be measured accurately by CMR.

THREE-DIMENSIONAL ANGIOGRAPHY

To visualize vascular branches and collateral vessels, 3D angiographic acquisitions are used, usually after venous injection of gadolinium chelate. This allows fast acquisition to be combined with good spatial resolution, allowing one or more 3D angiographic datasets to be acquired in a single breath-hold. Magnetic resonance angiography is useful for depiction of branches of the pulmonary artery and aorta, and for assessment of aortic coarctation, re-coarctation, or aortic aneurysm. The presence of metallic stents, sternal wires, or arterial clips can cause localized loss of signal in an angiogram, possibly leading to a false impression of stenosis.

Bright-blood SSFP sequences allow electrocardiographic gated 3D imaging of cardiovascular cavities and structures without the need for a contrast agent. This approach may be more suitable than contrast-enhanced angiography in patients after a Fontan operation because it is not subject to the dilution of contrast from nonopacified caval inflow. It is also used, either in a single breath-hold or using diaphragm navigator respiratory gating, for magnetic resonance coronary angiography. This allows the identification of anomalous coronary origins in most cases, although CT provides superior spatial resolution in shorter acquisition times for noninvasive coronary angiography, but at the cost of exposure to ionizing radiation.

RIGHT AND LEFT VENTRICULAR FUNCTION AND MASS MEASUREMENT

CMR is well suited for volumetric measurements of the right ventricle (RV) as well as the left ventricle (LV).[14–16] The reproducibility of measurements of the LV is excellent.[17] Although published studies have shown good reproducibility,[18,19] measurements of the RV are challenging and not easy to achieve reproducibly in ACHD patients in routine clinical practice. The myocardium of most of the free wall and the apical regions of the RV is highly trabeculated in most individuals. The trabeculations become more apparent when the RV is hypertrophied, but even if clearly visualized they are not easy to outline individually. Furthermore, the base of the RV tends to be more mobile and difficult to delineate than that of the LV. After repair of tetralogy of Fallot, the right ventricular outflow tract (RVOT) can be dilated, is akinetic, and may have no effective pulmonary valve. This can make it hard to decide on distal limits of the outflow tract. Measurements of RV volume and function require meticulous and clearly defined technique. An akinetic or aneurysmal region of the RVOT should be included as part of the RV, up to the (expected) level of the pulmonary valve. In the interests of time and reproducibility, the RV boundary may be traced immediately within the relatively thin compact myocardial layer of the free wall rather than by outlining the multiple trabeculations.[20] However, semiautomated methods that identify blood-myocardial boundaries may become a practicable, even if not directly comparable, alternative.[21] Whichever approach is used, it is crucial that longitudinal comparisons are based on comparable methods of acquisition and analysis. Contour data for volumetric analysis should ideally be stored in a database and remain available for comparison at the time of a subsequent study.

MYOCARDIAL INFARCTION OR FIBROSIS STUDIED BY LATE GADOLINIUM IMAGING

Late gadolinium enhancement inversion recovery imaging is well established for the visualization of previous myocardial infarction and for assessment of myocardial viability.[22] The extent of RV fibrosis identified late after surgery for tetralogy of Fallot or transposition of the great arteries may be relevant to arrhythmic risk stratification.[23,24] However, localized enhancement in the regions of insertion of the RV free wall into the LV is a frequent and nonspecific finding in ACHD and of doubtful clinical significance.

MYOCARDIAL PERFUSION IMAGING

The acquisition and interpretation of first-pass myocardial perfusion images by CMR at rest and during adenosine stress requires training and experience. However, because CMR perfusion imaging does not subject patients to the long-term hazards of ionizing radiation, it is likely to gain a clinical role in the assessment of ischemia in patients with CHD.

Applications of Cardiac Magnetic Resonance Imaging in Specific Diseases

AORTIC COARCTATION, RE-COARCTATION, AND ANEURYSM

The geometry of the aorta is variable in adults with aortic coarctation, especially after different types of repair. Magnetic resonance allows depiction of aneurysms or false aneurysms associated with (repaired) coarctation (Fig. 7-2), depiction of arch anatomy, and measurement of jet velocity (see Fig. 7-1). In this setting, a resting peak velocity of 3 m/s or more is significant, particularly if associated with diastolic prolongation of forward flow (diastolic "tail"), which is a useful indicator of obstructive significance.

With cine imaging and velocity mapping, CMR can generally determine the nature and severity of coarctation[25] and identify dissecting or false aneurysms, if present.[26] Gadolinium enhanced angiography can add information if there is a narrow, tortuous segment or if collateral vessels or an aneurysm need to be visualized. The 3D images provided are valuable for planning catheterization and stenting, if indicated.

Post-stenotic dilation is common, appearing as fusiform dilation beyond a stenosed or previously stenosed region, usually distinguishable by its location and smooth contours from more sinister aneurysmal dilation that may require reoperation or protection with a lined stent. True or false aneurysms may complicate balloon interventions or surgical repairs, particularly those incorporating patches of incompliant fabric such as Dacron (see Fig. 7-2). Leakage of blood through a false aneurysm can lead to hemoptysis. In such cases, para-aortic hematoma is generally well visualized by CMR, appearing bright, usually with diffuse edges, on spin-echo images. Postoperative hematoma is common, however, and sometimes leaves a region of signal adjacent to the aorta, which may only be distinguished from a developing false aneurysm if comparison of images over time is possible. For this reason it is worth acquiring baseline postoperative images in adults who have had recent surgery for coarctation. Repeat surgery for coarctation can be difficult owing to adhesions and weakness of the aortic wall in the previously repaired region. Reoperation carries higher risk than the initial operation, so the relative risks of surgery or catheter intervention need to be weighed against the expected risk of leaving an aneurysm or residual stenosis.

PATENT DUCTUS ARTERIOSUS

Patent ductus arteriosus is identifiable by CMR if sought. Flow through it, usually directed anteriorly into the top of the pulmonary artery close to the pulmonary artery bifurcation, is detectable on cine images or velocity acquisitions. Shunting can be assessed by measuring the pulmonary trunk and aortic flow. Ascending aortic flow will be greater than pulmonary artery flow if duct flow is from the aorta to the pulmonary artery bifurcation.

ATRIAL AND VENTRICULAR SEPTAL DEFECTS

Although atrial and ventricular septal defects are generally assessed satisfactorily by echocardiography, CMR offers unrestricted access in awkward cases and enables measurement of shunt flow from the difference between pulmonary and aortic flow measurements. CMR can also detect associated anomalies, notably the possibility of anomalous pulmonary venous drainage.[27–29]

PULMONARY ARTERIAL HYPERTENSION

CMR allows assessment of RV size and function, the size of the main and branch pulmonary arteries, flow measurement in the aorta or main pulmonary artery for calculation of indexed cardiac output, and identification of anomalies that might contribute to pulmonary hypertension such as patent ductus arteriosus or ventricular septal defect.[30] Contrast-enhanced angiography may be used for the identification of thromboembolic disease or aortopulmonary collateral vessels, although contrast-enhanced CT offers superior resolution in a shorter time, which may matter in patients with limited breath-holding ability.

MARFAN SYNDROME AND OTHER CONNECTIVE TISSUE DISORDERS

CMR studies allow measurement of the aortic root and of any aortic regurgitation. They allow measurements of the entire aorta and its major branches and of ventricular and mitral valve function. Moreover, CMR can detect abnormal aortic elastic properties in affected patients before dilation occurs.[31]

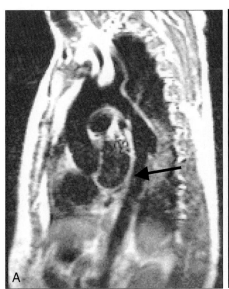

Figure 7-2 Magnetic resonance imaging and angiography of true and false aneurysm formation after Dacron patch repair of aortic coarctation. The patient presented with hemoptysis late after repair. **A,** A spin-echo image shows gray signal (*arrow*), indicating the hematoma of a false aneurysm adjacent to the bulge of a true aneurysm. **B,** Gadolinium-enhanced 3D angiography shows the location and shape of the true aneurysm.

REPAIRED TETRALOGY OF FALLOT

CMR has important contributions to make in the assessment and follow-up of adults with repaired tetralogy of Fallot and related conditions, including those with RV/pulmonary artery conduits.[32] CMR measurements of RV and LV function, pulmonary regurgitation, RVOT obstruction, conduit or pulmonary artery stenoses, and possible residual shunting all contribute to decisions on management, notably the possibility of pulmonary valve replacement for pulmonary regurgitation. The pathophysiology of pulmonary regurgitation differs from that of aortic regurgitation. Free pulmonary regurgitation, with little or no effective valve function, is common after repair of tetralogy of Fallot. It may be tolerated without symptoms for decades and is typically associated with a regurgitant fraction of 35% to 45%.[33] However, RV dysfunction, arrhythmia, and premature death can result. In most centers, surgical pulmonary valve replacement is considered in such patients but when to operate remains controversial, particularly if the patient is asymptomatic and bearing in mind that a homograft replacement may only function effectively for 15 or 20 years.[34,35] Once a conduit is in position, however, progressive stenosis or regurgitation may be treatable by percutaneous placement of a stented valve within the relatively rigid tube of the conduit.[36] Even in the absence of an effective pulmonary valve, the amount of regurgitation depends on factors upstream and downstream. In occasional cases the regurgitant fraction can exceed 50%.[37] This may be attributable to an unusually large and compliant pulmonary trunk and branches, whose recoil in diastole contributes to the regurgitation.[38] Pulmonary artery branch stenosis or elevated peripheral pulmonary resistance, limiting the distal escape of flow, increases the amount of regurgitation.[39] Contrast-enhanced 3D angiography may be used for the visualization of pulmonary artery branch stenosis, and appropriately aligned cines show jet formation and the reduced systolic expansion of pulmonary artery branches distal to a stenosis that is obstructive enough to require relief, either percutaneously or at the time of surgery. Tricuspid regurgitation needs to be identified and assessed, as does any residual ventricular septal defect patch leak and consequent shunting, or global and regional LV function and any aortic root dilation.[40] So, in summary, the evaluation of repaired tetralogy of Fallot requires thorough assessment of the left and right sides of the heart, extending to the branch pulmonary arteries, and each measurement should be interpreted in the context of circulatory factors upstream and downstream.

DOUBLE-CHAMBERED RIGHT VENTRICULAR OR SUBINFUNDIBULAR STENOSIS

Double-chambered right ventricular stenosis is caused by obstructing muscular bands or ridges between the hypertrophied body of the RV and the nonhypertrophied infundibulum. The subinfundibular origin of the RV outflow jet, directed into the nonobstructive infundibulum, is generally visible in routine basal short-axis cines.[41] It is usually associated with a ventricular septal defect into the higher pressure part of the RV and may progress during adulthood. CMR can help to differentiate between a jet through a ventricular septal defect, the subinfundibular stenosis, and possible infundibular or pulmonary valve stenosis, which may be hard to distinguish echocardiographically.

MULTIPLE AORTOPULMONARY COLLATERAL ARTERIES

Contrast-enhanced 3D CMR angiography is valuable for delineation of all sources of pulmonary blood supply before surgical or transcatheter procedures in patients with multiple aortopulmonary collateral arteries associated with severe pulmonary stenosis or atresia.[42] However, CT angiography is likely to depict small vessels more clearly.

EBSTEIN ANOMALY AND TRICUSPID REGURGITATION

In Ebstein anomaly, CMR allows unrestricted imaging of atrial and ventricular dimensions and the location and function of the displaced tricuspid valve. A stack of transaxial cines, supplemented by four-chamber and other oblique cines, is recommended for visualizing the right atrial/

RV anatomy in Ebstein anomaly patients. Transaxial cines may be suitable for volume measurements of the functional part of the RV in these patients, which may be hard to delineate in short-axis slices. In spite of atrialization, higher RV volumes than normal may be found in the presence of severe tricuspid regurgitation. The severity of tricuspid regurgitation can be assessed using through-plane velocity mapping to depict the cross section of the regurgitant stream through a plane transecting the jet immediately on the atrial side of the defect. A tricuspid regurgitation jet cross section, reflecting the regurgitant defect, of 6 × 6 mm or more can be regarded as severe. An atrial septal defect, possibly attributable to atrial distention and gaping of a patent foramen ovale, can be present in about 50% of adult patients with Ebstein anomaly and should be sought with an atrial short-axis cine stack. If present, the resting shunt can be measured by aortic and pulmonary velocity mapping. A long-axis view of the LV aligned with its outflow tract allows visualization of the degree of LV compression by a distended right side of the heart, especially in diastole.

TRANSPOSITION OF THE GREAT ARTERIES TREATED BY ATRIAL SWITCH OPERATION

CMR can assess the atrial pathways and systemic RV function after Mustard or Senning operations (Fig. 7-3).[43] With experience, cines and velocity maps can be aligned with respect to systemic and pulmonary venous atrial pathways.[32] Comprehensive coverage can, however, be achieved using a stack of contiguous transaxial or coronal cines or a 3D SSFP sequence. Because it can be difficult to align a single plane with both superior and inferior caval pathways, cross-cuts may be needed to decide whether pathways are stenosed, and velocity mapping can be performed through a plane transecting a stenotic jet. At atrial level, a peak velocity above 1.5 m/s may be significantly obstructive. Gradual obstruction of one of the two caval paths is generally well tolerated as the azygos vein(s) dilate to divert flow to the other caval pathway. Baffle leaks may not be easy to identify by CMR, the suture line being long and tortuous, but the measurement of pulmonary relative to aortic flow may be useful. As the hypertrophied RV is delivering systemic pressure in these patients it is important to assess its function by cine imaging volume measurements and to assess any tricuspid regurgitation.

TRANSPOSITION OF THE GREAT ARTERIES TREATED BY ARTERIAL SWITCH OPERATION

CMR allows assessment of any RVOT or supravalvar pulmonary artery stenosis, branch pulmonary artery stenosis, the neoaortic valve, and biventricular function.[4] Assessment of the patency of the reimplanted coronary arteries and LV perfusion during pharmacologic stress may be attempted by CMR.[44]

TRANSPOSITION OF THE GREAT ARTERIES TREATED BY RASTELLI OPERATION

CMR allows assessment of possible stenosis or incompetence of the RV-to-pulmonary artery conduit, the LV outflow tract, biventricular function, and possible residual shunt.

FONTAN OPERATIONS FOR FUNCTIONALLY SINGLE VENTRICLE

The Fontan operation aims to eliminate shunting in patients born with only one effective ventricle, routing systemic venous return to pulmonary arteries without passage through an intervening ventricle, so that the one ventricle propels blood to the systemic and then the pulmonary vessels, in series.[45] In this radically altered circulation, pressure is elevated in the systemic veins and it is this residual systemic pressure that maintains flow through the lungs back to the left atrium. Any obstruction of the systemic vein to pulmonary artery flow path easily raises systemic venous pressure to an unsustainable level.[46]

The Fontan operation was originally performed via the right atrium, either through a conduit passing round the aorta or by direct connection of the region of the atrial appendage to the pulmonary arteries. Over the

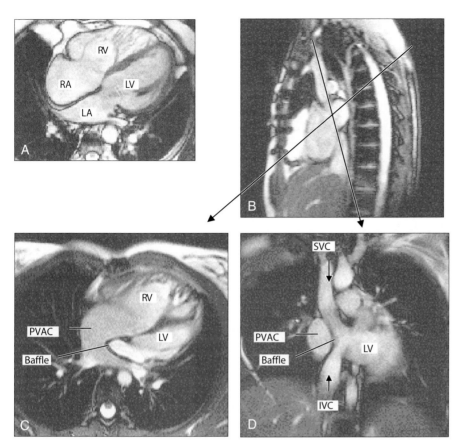

Figure 7-3 Surgically reconstructed atrial anatomy after Mustard operation for transposition of the great arteries (**B-D**) compared with usual anatomy (**A**). **A,** Four-chamber TrueFISP cine image showing usual atrioventricular connections—right atrium (RA) to right ventricle (RV) and left atrium (LA) to left ventricle (LV)—in a patient with repaired tetralogy of Fallot. **B,** Sagittal image through the reconstructed atrial compartments. *Arrows* show the location in **C** of an oblique transaxial slice aligned with the pulmonary venous atrial compartment (PVAC) and in **D** of an oblique coronal image aligned with superior and inferior venae cavae (SVC and IVC), redirected by the baffle to the LV.

past decade or so, total cavopulmonary connection either by intra-atrial tunnel or extracardiac conduit has come to be used. The superior vena cava is connected to the right pulmonary artery from above and from below and flow from the inferior vena cava is channeled by a patch, flap, or conduit up the side of the right atrium to the pulmonary arteries. Right and left pulmonary arteries communicate, and the pulmonary trunk is disconnected from the heart. Whichever variant is used, it is crucial that cavopulmonary flow paths remain unobstructed; and it is important to look for stenosis, typically at a suture line, or for thrombosis in the cavopulmonary flow paths. Comprehensive coverage using a transaxial stack of cines is recommended, followed by appropriately aligned cine imaging and velocity mapping of any jet. A peak velocity of 1 m/s or more is likely to be significant. The peak will coincide with atrial systole after atriopulmonary connection, so use of retrospective electrocardiographic gating can be important. If contrast injection is considered for angiography, the connection of the superior vena cava to the pulmonary arteries and its relation to inferior vena caval flow should be borne in mind. Noncontrast 3D SSFP imaging, or injection of a contrast agent via a leg vein, may be preferable. Evaluation of myocardial fibrosis by late gadolinium enhancement (LGE) may be informative in patients with impaired ventricular function. It is also important to assess contractile function of the ventricle, competence of its inflow valve, and the width of its outflow tract.

COMPLEX CONGENITAL HEART DISEASE

CMR allows clarification of anatomy and function, including anomalous vessels, connections, shunts, and stenoses. Comprehensive cardiac and mediastinal coverage using stacks of contiguous transaxial and coronal cines is recommended. Other sequences such as 3D SSFP can also be useful. Cine images should be aligned with each inflow and outflow valve and with any shunt flow so that connections can be established. They are best described according to sequential segmental analysis.[47] The relative pre-branch lengths of the left- and right-sided bronchi in coronal slices can provide a useful guide to thoracic situs, if in doubt. To distinguish a morphologically right from an LV, useful signs include the presence of a moderator band and additional coarse trabeculations arising from the RV side of the interventricular septum but not from its relatively smooth LV side.

CONCLUSION

CMR gives unrestricted access to structures throughout the chest, including the RV and great arteries, making important contributions to the diagnosis and follow-up of ACHD. A dedicated CMR service should be regarded as a necessary component of a center specializing in the care of patients with ACHD, and adults who were born with relatively complex CHD, including tetralogy of Fallot, should ideally be investigated as well as managed in such a center. Variation of underlying anatomy and surgical procedure among patients means that decisions on selection of planes and sequences may need to be made during acquisition of images. However, a relatively comprehensive and technically simple approach is to acquire one or more contiguous stacks of cine images covering the whole heart and mediastinum. Acquisition and analysis CMR is likely to become more rapid, automated, and comprehensive in the coming years.

REFERENCES

1. Manning WJ, Pennell DJ, editors. Cardiovascular Magnetic Resonance. London: Churchill Livingstone; 2009 (in press).
2. Shellock FG, Spinazzi A. MRI safety update 2008: part 2, screening patients for MRI. Am J Roentgenol 2008;191:1140–1149.
3. Shellock FG, Spinazzi A. MRI safety update 2008: I. MRI contrast agents and nephrogenic systemic fibrosis. AJR Am J Roentgenol 2008;191:1129 1139.
4. Hirsch R, Kilner PJ, Connelly M, et al. Diagnosis in adolescents and adults with congenital heart disease: prospective assessment of the individual and combined roles of magnetic resonance imaging and transesophageal echocardiography. Circulation 1994;90:2937–2951.
5. Nicol ED, Gatzoulis M, Padley SP, Rubens M. Assessment of adult congenital heart disease with multi-detector computed tomography: beyond coronary lumenography. Clin Radiol 2007;62:518–527.
6. Muthurangu V, Taylor A, Andriantsimiavona R, et al. Novel method of quantifying pulmonary vascular resistance by use of simultaneous invasive pressure monitoring and phase-contrast magnetic resonance flow. Circulation 2004;110:826–834.
7. Muthurangu V, Razavi RS. The value of magnetic resonance guided cardiac catheterisation. Heart 2005;91:995–996.
8. Geva T, Marshall AC. Magnetic resonance imaging-guided catheter interventions in congenital heart disease. Circulation 2006;113:1093–1100.
9. Chan KM, Wage R, Symmonds K, et al. Towards comprehensive assessment of mitral regurgitation using cardiovascular magnetic resonance. J Cardiovasc Magn Reson 2008;10:61.
10. Firmin DN, Nayler GL, Kilner PJ, Longmore DB. The application of phase shifts in NMR for flow measurement. Magn Reson Med 1990;14:230–241.
11. Kilner PJ, Gatehouse PD, Firmin DN. Flow measurement by magnetic resonance: a unique asset worth optimising. J Cardiovasc Magn Reson 2007;9:723–728.
12. Rebergen SA, Chin JGJ, Ottenkamp J, et al. Pulmonary regurgitation in the late postoperative follow-up of tetralogy of Fallot—volumetric quantitation by nuclear magnetic resonance velocity mapping. Circulation 1993;88:2257–2266.
13. Chernobelsky A, Shubayev O, Comeau CR, Wolff SD. Baseline correction of phase contrast images improves quantification of blood flow in the great vessels. J Cardiovasc Magn Reson 2007;9:681–685.
14. van den Bosch AE, Robbers-Visser D, Krenning BJ, et al. Comparison of real-time three-dimensional echocardiography to magnetic resonance imaging for assessment of left ventricular mass. Am J Cardiol 2006;97:113–117.
15. Mannaerts HF, Van Der Heide JA, Kamp O, et al. Quantification of left ventricular volumes and ejection fraction using freehand transthoracic three-dimensional echocardiography: comparison with magnetic resonance imaging. J Am Soc Echocardiogr 2003;16:101–109.
16. Grothues F, Smith GC, Moon JC, et al. Comparison of interstudy reproducibility of cardiovascular magnetic resonance with two-dimensional echocardiography in normal subjects and in patients with heart failure or left ventricular hypertrophy. Am J Cardiol 2002;90:29–34.

17. Bellenger NG, Marcus NJ, Rajappan K, et al. Comparison of techniques for the measurement of left ventricular function following cardiac transplantation. J Cardiovasc Magn Reson 2002;4:255–263.
18. Karamitsos T, Hudsmith L, Selvanayagama J, et al. Operator induced variability in left ventricular measurements with cardiovascular magnetic resonance is improved after training. J Cardiovasc Mag Reson 2007;9:777–783.
19. Mooij CF, de Wit CJ, Graham DA, et al. Reproducibility of MRI measurements of right ventricular size and function in patients with normal and dilated ventricles. J Magn Reson Imaging 2008;28:67–73.
20. Winter MM, Bernink FJ, Groenink M, et al. Evaluating the systemic right ventricle by CMR: the importance of consistent and reproducible delineation of the cavity. J Cardiovasc Magn Reson 2008;10:40.
21. Codella NC, Weinsaft JW, Cham MD, et al. Left ventricle: automated segmentation by using myocardial effusion threshold reduction and intravoxel computation at MR imaging. Radiology 2008;248:1004–1012.
22. Wu HD, Kwong RY. Cardiac magnetic resonance imaging in patients with coronary disease. Curr Treat Options Cardiovasc Med 2008;10:83–92.
23. Babu-Narayan SV, Kilner PJ, Li W, et al. Ventricular fibrosis suggested by cardiovascular magnetic resonance in adults with repaired tetralogy of Fallot and its relationship to adverse markers of clinical outcome. Circulation 2006;113:405–413.
24. Babu-Narayan SV, Goktekin O, Moon JC, et al. Late gadolinium enhancement cardiovascular magnetic resonance of the systemic right ventricle in adults with previous atrial redirection surgery for transposition of the great arteries. Circulation 2005;111:2091–2098.
25. Nielsen JC, Powell AJ, Gauvreau K, et al. Magnetic resonance imaging predictors of coarctation severity. Circulation 2005;111:622–628.
26. Therrien J, Thorne S, Wright A, et al. Repaired coarctation: a "cost effective" approach to identify complications in adults. J Am Coll Cardiol 2000;35:997–1002.
27. Wald RM, Powell AJ. Simple congenital heart lesions. J Cardiovasc Magn Reson 2008;8:619–631.
28. Piaw CS, Kiam OT, Rapaee A, et al. Use of non-invasive phase contrast magnetic resonance imaging for estimation of atrial septal defect size and morphology: a comparison with transesophageal echo. Cardiovasc Intervent Radiol 2006;29:230–234.
29. Valente AM, Sena L, Powell AJ, et al. Cardiac magnetic resonance imaging evaluation of sinus venosus defects: comparison to surgical findings. Pediatr Cardiol 2007;28:51–56.
30. Nagendran J, Michelakis E. MRI: one-stop shop for the comprehensive assessment of pulmonary arterial hypertension? Chest 2007;132:2–5.
31. Baumgartner D, Baumgartner C, Matyas G, et al. Diagnostic power of aortic elastic properties in young patients with Marfan syndrome. J Thorac Cardiovasc Surg 2005;129:730–739.
32. Dorfman AL, Geva T. Magnetic resonance imaging evaluation of congenital heart disease: conotruncal anomalies. J Cardiovasc Magn Reson 2006;8:645–659.

33. Samyn MM, Powell AJ, Garg R, et al. Range of ventricular dimensions and function by steady-state free precession cine MRI in repaired tetralogy of Fallot: right ventricular outflow tract patch vs. conduit repair. J Magn Reson Imaging 2007;26:934–940.
34. Henkens IR, van Straten A, Schalij MJ, et al. Predicting outcome of pulmonary valve replacement in adult tetralogy of Fallot patients. Ann Thorac Surg 2007;83:907–911.
35. Frigiola A, Tsang V, Bull C, et al. Biventricular response after pulmonary valve replacement for right ventricular outflow tract dysfunction: is age a predictor of outcome? Circulation 2008;118:S182–S190.
36. Frigiola A, Tsang V, Nordmeyer J, et al. Current approaches to pulmonary regurgitation. Eur J Cardiothorac Surg 2008;34:576–580.
37. Geva T, Sahn DJ, Powell AJ. Magnetic resonance imaging of congenital heart disease in adults. Prog Pediatr Cardiol 2003;17:21–39.
38. Kilner PJ, Balossino R, Dubini G, et al. Pulmonary regurgitation: the effects of varying pulmonary artery compliance, and of increased resistance proximal or distal to the compliance. Int J Cardiol 2009;133:157–166.
39. Chaturvedi RR, Redington AN. Pulmonary regurgitation in congenital heart disease. Heart 2007;93:880–889.
40. Geva T, Sandweiss BM, Gauvreau K, et al. Factors associated with impaired clinical status in long-term survivors of tetralogy of Fallot repair evaluated by magnetic resonance imaging. J Am Coll Cardiol 2004;43:1068–1074.
41. Kilner PJ, Sievers B, Meyer GP, Ho SY. Double-chambered right ventricle or sub-infundibular stenosis assessed by cardiovascular magnetic resonance. J Cardiovasc Magn Reson 2002;4:373–379.
42. Geva T, Greil GF, Marshall AC, et al. Gadolinium-enhanced 3-dimensional magnetic resonance angiography of pulmonary blood supply in patients with complex pulmonary stenosis or atresia: comparison with x-ray angiography. Circulation 2002;106:473–478.
43. Salehian O, Schwerzmann M, Merchant N, et al. Assessment of systemic right ventricular function in patients with transposition of the great arteries using the myocardial performance index: comparison with cardiac magnetic resonance imaging. Circulation 2004;110:3229–3233.
44. Taylor AM, Dymarkowski S, Hamaekers P, et al. MR coronary angiography and late-enhancement myocardial MR in children who underwent arterial switch surgery for transposition of great arteries. Radiology 2005;234:542–547.
45. De Leval MR. The Fontan circulation: what have we learned? What do we expect. Pediatr Cardiol 1998;19:316–320.
46. Rebergen SA, Ottenkamp J, Doornbos J, et al. Postoperative pulmonary flow dynamics after Fontan surgery: assessment with nuclear magnetic resonance velocity mapping. J Am Coll Cardiol 1993;21:123–131.
47. Anderson RH, Becker AE, Freedom RM, et al. Sequential segmental analysis of congenital heart disease. Pediatr Cardiol 1984;5:281–287.

8

Cardiac Computed Tomography

JAMES STIRRUP | EDWARD D. NICOL | MICHAEL B. RUBENS

Introduction

Over the past few decades, advances in pediatric cardiology and cardiac surgery have revolutionized the management of patients with adult congenital heart disease (ACHD). As a result, the majority now survive into adulthood. Although cardiovascular magnetic resonance imaging (CMR) and transthoracic echocardiography (TTE) remain the techniques of choice for the routine assessment and follow-up of patients with ACHD, advances in cardiac computed tomography (CCT) have led to its emergence as both a complementary technique and an alternative to CMR and TTE when these are unavailable or contraindicated. Current CT scanner technology allows cardiac assessment without blurring from cardiac motion and offers superior spatial resolution to both CMR and TTE. CCT images comprise near-isotropic voxels that look identical irrespective of the plane in which they are viewed, allowing rotation of the three-dimensional (3D) dataset in any desired plane even after the completion of acquisition and thus rendering prespecification of imaging planes unnecessary. Although the temporal resolution of CCT remains inferior to both CMR and TTE at present, wider-detector arrays and dual-source radiographic technology offer resolutions of around 75 ms on newer generations of scanners. Exposure to ionizing radiation remains the limiting factor in the widespread application of CCT, a limitation not affecting either CMR or TTE. Most modern CT scanners incorporate dose-reduction algorithms into their cardiac packages and wider-detector arrays (256- and 320-detector scanners), and improved detector sensitivity may lead to dramatic reductions in radiation dose in the future. CCT also lacks the capacity to assess valvular and shunt flow, parameters readily measured by both CMR and TTE. However, CMR and TTE have important limitations. Acquisitions may be time consuming, especially in those with ACHD. Furthermore, CMR is often limited by its availability and claustrophobia may prevent successful acquisition in as many as 1 in 20 patients. Importantly, the ever-increasing prevalence of pacemakers or implantable cardiac defibrillators (ICDs) precludes assessment by CMR, and CCT is an appropriate alternative in these cases. Furthermore, CCT is preferable for the assessment of stents and occlusion devices because images do not suffer from the signal void that these devices create when imaged by CMR. Regardless of the technique selected, all require substantial training and expertise and should be undertaken only by those with the appropriate experience. Reporting of CCT images should follow the standardized segmental approach described elsewhere in this book.

Technical Considerations

CONTRAST PROTOCOLS

Standard retrospectively gated CT coronary angiography (CTA) usually gives clear information about both left ventricular function and coronary lumenography. However, there are few methodologic studies looking at CTA in ACHD. Although most contrast protocols are suitable for all patients, certain considerations should be taken into account when timing administration of a contrast agent for those with ACHD. A manual test bolus tracked to determine the time to peak concentration at the aortic root is recommended owing to the variable transit time and venous hemodynamics of ACHD patients and also allows early identification of other late filling structures. Particular care should be taken in those with presumed or likely pulmonary

arterial hypertension in whom transit times may be especially challenging to calculate despite the use of bolus tracking. In patients who have undergone Fontan repair, imaging may be especially difficult because the contrast bolus may pool and become diluted in the passive right-sided circulation. Additionally, consideration should be given to the limb through which the contrast agent is injected because delivery from either the superior or inferior vena cava may lead to preferential perfusion of one lung. In ACHD, right ventricular function is often of interest; and although reduced pulmonary transit time is likely to be of benefit in right ventricular analysis, it may be detrimental to analysis of the left ventricle. Although it is possible to change the scan timing or CT protocol to optimize right ventricular opacification, this, in turn, limits left ventricular opacification and coronary artery assessment, thus preventing complete cardiac assessment within a single breath-hold. However, using specific intravenous contrast protocols, it is possible to combine CTA with CCT within a single scan protocol to allow comprehensive assessment of the pulmonary and coronary arteries, biventricular function, and valvular anatomy without fundamentally altering the region of interest or the basic scan protocol.[1] Finally, because CCT involves intravenous iodinated contrast, often in excess of 100 mL (e.g., dual- or triple-phase CTA/CCT protocols), the technique is best avoided in those patients with renal dysfunction when alternative techniques are available.

GATING

The improved temporal resolution of current CT scanners (75 to 165 ms) coupled with simultaneous electrocardiographic recording allows image acquisition during multiple phases of the cardiac cycle. This allows selection of the interval of minimum cardiac motion (usually end-diastole) and resolution of structures as small as 0.5 mm. Gating is unnecessary when the predominant clinical question centers on assessment of major extracardiac vascular structures because cardiac motion is less important. Ungated acquisitions are usually used when imaging children because the scans are quicker to perform, easier to process, and involve lower exposure to ionizing radiation. However, rapid cardiac motion prevents adequate assessment of smaller structures such as the coronary vessels in ungated studies. If coronary angiography is required, acquisitions should use either prospective or retrospective electrocardiographic triggering. Prospective acquisitions involve emission of radiation only during a predefined phase of the cardiac cycle, thus reducing radiation dose, and are suitable for patients with a stable heart rhythm in whom the interval of minimum cardiac motion can be predicted reliably. However, because prospective gating provides information on only one phase of the cardiac cycle, functional information cannot be obtained and interpretation of the resultant images is thus limited to anatomy. In retrospective acquisitions, radiation is emitted throughout the cardiac cycle. Gating is useful in patients who do not have a stable heart rate and thus have an unpredictable interval of minimum cardiac motion. Furthermore, acquisition of multiple cardiac phases allows functional assessment of the ventricles and heart valves. Like all imaging techniques, patient selection remains important and the presence of atrial fibrillation or other rhythms with wide beat-to beat variation may lead to significant artifacts within the dataset that, if extreme, may render the scan uninterpretable. In patients with ACHD, retrospective gating is used most often because the incidence of arrhythmia is higher and the functional information provided is helpful.

Cardiac Computed Tomography in Clinical Practice

The major focus of recent CCT research and practice has been non-invasive coronary angiography and, in particular, lumenography for specific conditions such as angina pectoris. With ACHD patients now surviving longer, they are at equal or increased risk of common cardiac conditions that present in adulthood, such as coronary artery disease. Coronary CTA thus retains the same indications as in patients without ACHD.[2] However, the CTA dataset contains substantially more information than that of the coronary arteries alone and a far broader assessment of cardiac anatomy and function is possible from a single acquisition. In essence, any patient who is unable or unwilling to undergo CMR can be assessed by CCT; and although flow data cannot be obtained, most other aspects of a CMR study are available from within the CCT dataset.

CORONARY ARTERY ASSESSMENT

Because of the high incidence of abnormal resting electrocardiograms, stress electrocardiography is often unhelpful for the diagnosis of coronary artery disease in those with ACHD. Abnormal ventricular anatomy also leads to difficulties in the interpretation of myocardial perfusion scans. Many are therefore investigated by invasive coronary angiography, although this may in itself be complicated by the presence of aortic root dilation, variation in the site of the coronary ostia, and unusual coronary anatomy. Furthermore, once these technical issues have been overcome, there is often no evidence of obstructive coronary artery disease. CTA offers excellent negative predictive value for the exclusion of coronary artery disease and is a powerful alternative to invasive coronary angiography in this setting. The use of CTA is especially relevant outside CHD centers where the operator experience required for invasive coronary angiography in ACHD may be limited. Beyond coronary artery disease, CTA is especially helpful in assessing the origin and course of anomalous coronary arteries, which are seen frequently in those with abnormal cardiovascular anatomy (Fig. 8-1A). Aside from common anomalies, such as left coronary artery from right

coronary sinus, CTA may provide the first diagnosis in patients with anomalous left coronary artery from pulmonary artery (ALCAPA) on the rare occasions that this presents in adulthood. CTA is also useful in patients with Kawasaki disease, where the site, size, and number of coronary artery aneurysms can be measured, as can the extent of calcification, thrombus, and contrast enhancement within any aneurysms seen (see Fig. 8-1B). CCT is also a well-established technique for identifying and fully delineating coronary fistulas (see Fig. 8-1C) and cardiac venous anatomy (see Fig. 8-1D). The latter may be of particular importance when planning cardiac resynchronization therapy, a technique that is finding greater use in patients with CHD.[3]

FUNCTIONAL ASSESSMENT OF THE LEFT AND RIGHT VENTRICLES

By reconstructing CCT data at multiple phases of the cardiac cycle (usually every 5% or 10%), it is possible to calculate both end-diastolic and end-systolic volumes of the left and right ventricle and thus stroke volume, cardiac output, and ejection fraction. Ventricular volumes may be calculated either through manual delineation of endocardial and epicardial borders or using a threshold technique that identifies voxels above a certain Hounsfield unit number as contrast rather than tissue (Fig. 8-2A and B). The latter is quicker and probably more accurate, although both depend on adequate opacification of the ventricle to make accurate assessments. CCT agrees well with CMR,[4] TTE,[5] and myocardial perfusion scintigraphic[6] measurements of left ventricular ejection fraction. There is good agreement between CCT and CMR for the calculation of left ventricular volumes, although volumes are significantly greater on CCT than on TTE or perfusion scintigraphy.[7] Right ventricular analysis is more challenging owing to its complex geometry, but calculations of right ventricular function compare well with equilibrium radionuclide ventriculography,[8] and volumes assessed using the threshold technique appear to be accurate when compared with CMR.[1] In addition to volumes, ventricular wall motion, thickening, and thickness can also be derived (see Fig. 8-2C). Measurements of regional wall motion are reasonable when compared with those of perfusion scintigraphy,[6] although the poorer spatial resolution of the

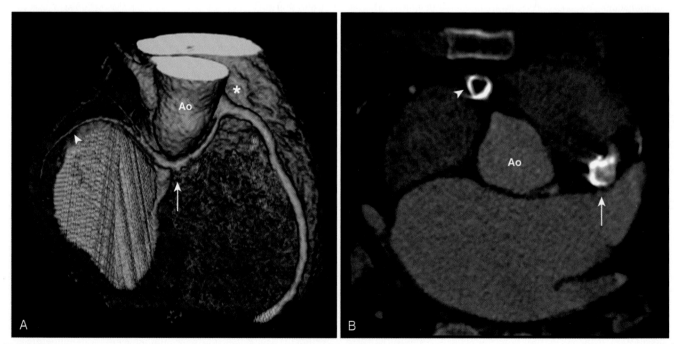

Figure 8-1   Coronary arterial and cardiac venous anomalies. **A,** Anomalous left circumflex artery arising from the right coronary artery (*star*) and following a retroaortic course (*arrow*) to reach to left atrioventricular groove (*arrowhead*). **B,** Calcified coronary artery aneurysms in Kawasaki's disease. The left anterior descending artery aneurysm (*arrow*) is contrast enhanced and is thus patent. The right coronary artery aneurysm (*arrowhead*) shows no contrast enhancement and is thrombosed. Ao, aorta.

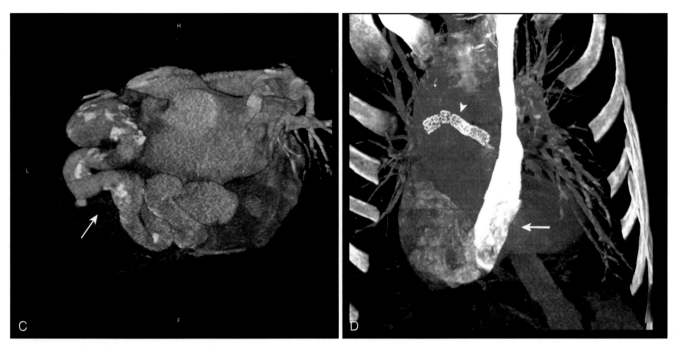

Figure 8-1—cont'd **C,** Coronary cardiac fistula (*arrow*) between the left circumflex artery and coronary sinus. **D,** Persistent left superior vena cava draining into the coronary sinus (*arrow*). This abnormality may be of particular importance when planning electrophysiologic intervention. A stent within the right pulmonary artery is also seen (*arrowhead*).

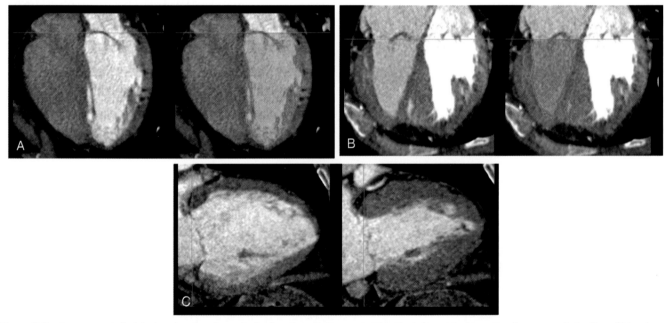

Figure 8-2 Assessment of global and regional ventricular function. **A,** Contrast within the left ventricular cavity allows easy distinction of blood pool from myocardium (*left*) and thus analysis of volumes using a thresholding technique (*right*). In this study, right ventricular contrast is poor and no such assessment can be made. **B,** In pulmonary hypertension there is hold up of contrast in the right sided circulation. In this case, the right ventricular blood pool may be easily distinguished from myocardium, allowing assessment of right ventricular function. **C,** Vertical long-axis view of the left ventricle in end-diastolic (*left*) and end-systolic (*right*) phases. Review of phases in cine format allows assessment of regional ventricular function.

latter may explain why these comparisons are not better. In addition to differences in resolution, the use of β-adrenergic blockade before CCT to control heart rate may lead to discrepancies in functional analysis.[9] Although most studies have evaluated ventricular function in patients without ACHD, available data suggest that CT compares well with CMR for analysis of global and regional left and right ventricular function in those with complex congenital defects.[1]

CARDIAC MORPHOLOGY AND EXTRACARDIAC ASSESSMENT

Although TTE and CMR are widely accepted as the first-line techniques, CCT is often considered because of the ease and rapidity of acquisition. Although axial images are critical for assessment of major vessels, the use of volume-rendered images and the ability to rotate

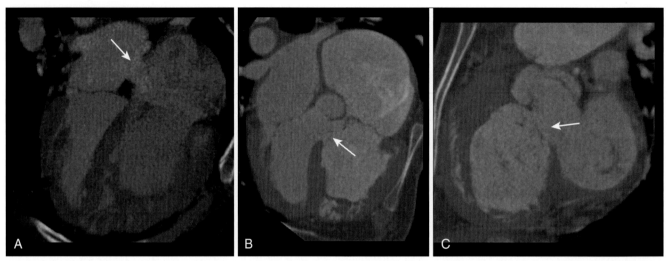

Figure 8-3 Septal defects. **A,** Secundum atrial septal defect (*arrow*). **B,** Ventricular septal defect, also seen in **C** on the short-axis view (*arrow*).

reformatted structures into any plane allows accurate definition of cardiac and vascular anatomy before any planned intervention. The role of CCT in specific conditions is outlined here; fuller descriptions of each condition may be found elsewhere in this book.

Atrial and Ventricular Septal Defects

CCT is able to characterize the location and size of atrial septal defects (ASDs), especially in areas poorly visualized on TTE (Fig. 8-3A). Additionally, biventricular size and function may be assessed, along with any associated anomalies such as anomalous pulmonary venous drainage. CCT may be used as a follow-up investigation after surgical or percutaneous ASD closure, either to evaluate right ventricular function[10] or to assess the state of a septal occlusion device.[11] CCT can also provide detailed anatomic information about size and morphologic features of a patent foramen ovale (PFO).[12] The presence of a short PFO tunnel length and septal aneurysms on CCT correlates well with the presence of a left-to-right shunt on TTE. However, CCT is probably less effective at determining the presence of small defects. Just as for ASDs, TTE remains the technique of choice for the detection of most ventricular and atrioventricular septal defects (VSD/AVSD). The high spatial resolution and 3D capabilities of CCT allow straightforward measurement of VSD size and location when there is diagnostic doubt (see Fig. 8-3B, C).

Patent Ductus Arteriosus

A patent ductus arteriosus (PDA) may be found incidentally on CT acquisitions, particularly during investigation of pulmonary hypertension (Fig. 8-4A). CCT is able to determine the presence and size of a PDA and with 3D reconstruction techniques can provide an accurate roadmap for catheter or surgical closure, where appropriate. Importantly, unlike CMR and TTE, CCT offers the opportunity to quantify calcification within the duct.[13] Those with heavy PDA calcification are at higher surgical risk and are thus referred for transcatheter closure.

Aortopulmonary Window

CCT is able to provide information on the location and size of the aortopulmonary (AP) window (see Fig. 8-4B). This may be useful if planning percutaneous closure because the superior and inferior rims of the defect may be assessed for adequacy to support an occlusion device. Associated lesions such as atrial and ventricular septal defects also may be evaluated from the same acquisition.

Coarctation of the Aorta

CCT allows accurate determination of the location and extent of aortic coarctation and compares well with measurements made by TTE.[14] Although CMR offers information about flow through the coarctation, the aorta in such patients may be tortuous and it can be

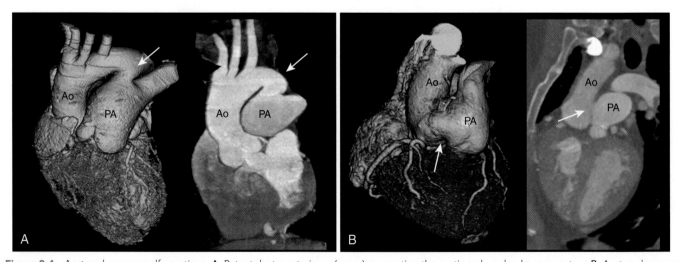

Figure 8-4 Aortopulmonary malformations. **A,** Patent ductus arteriosus (*arrow*) connecting the aortic arch and pulmonary artery. **B,** Aortopulmonary window (*arrow*) connecting the aortic root and pulmonary artery. Ao, aorta; PA pulmonary artery.

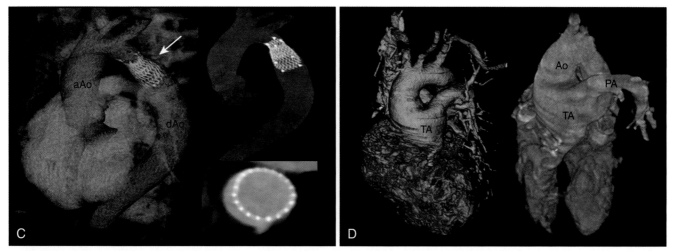

Figure 8-4—cont'd **C,** Stented coarctation of the aorta (*arrow*) at the junction of the transverse arch and descending aorta. Cross-sectional profile of the stent shows it to be widely patent. **D,** Common arterial trunk giving rise to the aorta and pulmonary artery. aAo, ascending aorta; Ao, aorta; dAo, descending aorta; PA, pulmonary artery; TA, truncus arteriosus.

difficult to ensure that the correct imaging planes are selected. The isotropic nature of voxels acquired using CCT allow the selection of any desired imaging plane after acquisition has been completed. In this regard, CCT may be particularly useful in isthmic coarctation.[15] Furthermore, CCT is better than both CMR and TTE at assessing stent position and patency after percutaneous treatment and may thus be a valuable tool in both the diagnosis and follow-up of these patients (see Fig. 8-4C).

Common Arterial Trunk

The value of CCT in patients with truncal abnormalities was suggested more than 25 years ago (see Fig. 8-4D).[16,17] The intravenous use of a contrast agent allows identification of pulmonary artery branches and collateral vessels where present. In those who have undergone surgical repair, CCT is able to accurately assess conduit patency.

Tetralogy of Fallot

Small series have shown good agreement between CCT and TTE for the diagnosis of tetralogy of Fallot.[18] In addition to detailing intracardiac anatomy, CCT allows assessment of the coronary and pulmonary arteries, with information on anomalous courses in the former and stenoses in the latter invaluable when planning operative repair. In those who have undergone surgical repair, shunts and valved conduits may be examined clearly by CCT and patency, size, and potential stenoses can be accurately described (Fig. 8-5). Those with stenotic or regurgitant valved conduits are now often referred for percutaneous pulmonary valve replacement. CCT may be used to assess the conduit and its spatial relationship to other cardiac and noncardiac structure, particularly with regard to the possible path of a coronary artery between the conduit and adjacent epicardium (Fig. 8-6). Deployment and expansion of a stented pulmonary valve within the conduit may potentially lead to compression of an

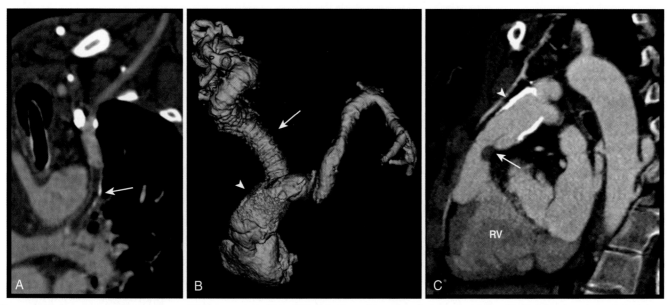

Figure 8-5 Assessment after tetralogy of Fallot repair. **A,** Blalock-Taussig shunt. Thrombus is visible in the distal half of the shunt (*arrow*). **B,** Volume-rendered image of a calcified right ventricular outflow tract homograft (*arrowhead*) and conduit to the right pulmonary artery (*arrow*). **C,** Multiplanar reformatted image of the same patient as in **B** showing the calcified homograft (*arrowhead*) and subpulmonary stenosis (*arrow*). RV, right ventricle.

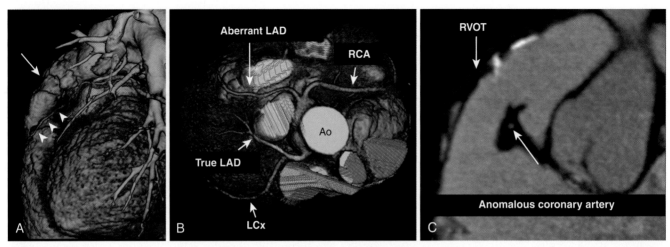

Figure 8-6 Assessment of a patient with previous tetralogy of Fallot repair before percutaneous pulmonary valve replacement. **A,** Right ventricular outflow tract conduit (*arrow*) passing over an aberrant coronary artery (*arrowheads*). **B,** Volume-rendered image with conduit cut away demonstrating dual supply of the left anterior descending artery territory. An aberrant branch arises from the right coronary sinus and passes under the conduit to reach the anterior interventricular groove. **C,** Multiplanar reformatted image demonstrates the space between the conduit and the epicardium through which the aberrant coronary artery passes. Ao, aorta; LAD, left anterior descending artery; LCx, left circumflex artery; RCA, right coronary artery; RVOT, right ventricular outflow tract.

adjacent coronary artery, resulting in myocardial ischemia and, if uncorrected, infarction. Assessment of coronary anatomy by CCT is therefore helpful before the patient undergoes percutaneous pulmonary valve implantation.

Pulmonary Arterial Hypertension Including Eisenmenger Syndrome

CT pulmonary angiography has been the mainstay of diagnostic imaging in pulmonary arterial hypertension for many years, specifically identifying or excluding thromboembolic disease,[19] assessing confluence and size of pulmonary arteries,[20] and identifying pulmonary artery stenoses or aneurysmal dilation of the pulmonary arteries

(Fig. 8-7A). However, the use of CCT in conjunction with standard CTA is useful,[1] particularly for the evaluation of right ventricular hypertrophy and biventricular function and in the differentiation of intrinsic and extrinsic pulmonary arterial pathology. Although flow and pressure measurements are beyond the capabilities of CCT, valve integrity, biventricular function, and the causes underlying pulmonary arterial hypertension may be readily assessed.

Major Aortopulmonary Collateral Arteries

Major aortopulmonary collateral arteries (MAPCAs) develop in conditions such as pulmonary atresia when blood fails to reach the lungs via the pulmonary arteries. The anatomy of these collateral arteries varies widely, and accurate delineation is crucial to clinical management.

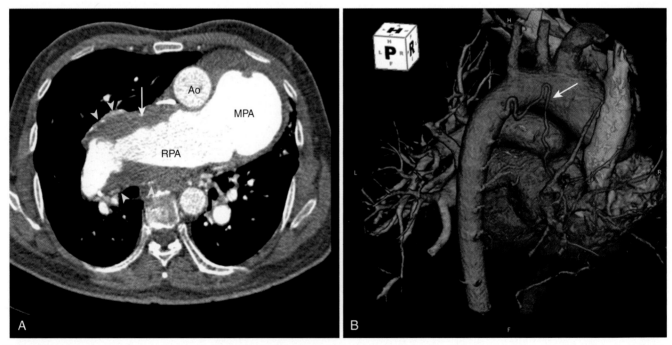

Figure 8-7 Pulmonary artery assessment. **A,** Markedly dilated proximal pulmonary arteries with extensive mural thrombus (*arrow*) and calcification (*arrowheads*) in a patient with severe pulmonary artery hypertension. **B,** Aortopulmonary collateral artery (*arrow*) arising from the proximal descending aorta to supply the right lung. Ao, aorta; MPA, main pulmonary artery; RPA, right pulmonary artery.

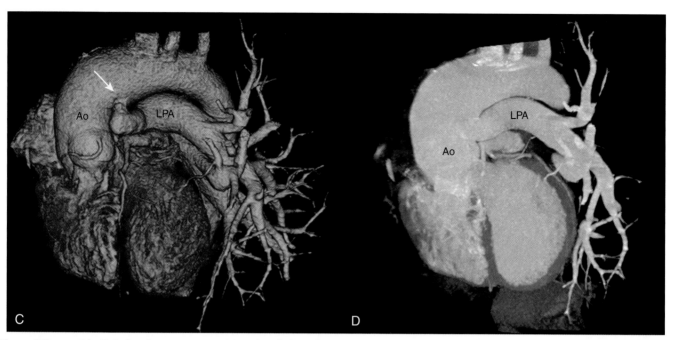

Figure 8-7—cont'd C, Left pulmonary artery arising directly from the aorta (*arrow*). Ao, aorta; LPA, left pulmonary artery; MPA, main pulmonary artery; RPA, right pulmonary artery.

The high spatial resolution and 3D nature of CCT lends itself well to accurate anatomic localization (see Fig. 8-7B, C). CCT compares well with measurements made by invasive coronary angiography[21] and therefore may usefully guide interventional or surgical management.

Transposition of the Great Arteries

In those with congenitally corrected transposition of the great arteries (ccTGA), CCT can be useful in confirming atrioventricular and ventriculoarterial discordance as well as evaluating the state of any anatomic repair and biventricular size and function (Fig. 8-8A). Patients with TGA are usually evaluated after operative repair, and CCT can help to assess the patency of intra-atrial baffles (Mustard and Senning procedures), ventriculoarterial conduits (Rastelli procedure), or the neoaorta and neopulmonary arteries (arterial switch) (see Fig. 8-8B).

In the latter case, the ostia of coronary arteries reimplanted into the neoaorta may be readily assessed by CCT. Precise knowledge of coronary anatomy is required before surgery and CCT may be ideally suited to their noninvasive assessment.

Double-Outlet Right Ventricle

CCT allows assessment of the preoperative double-outlet right ventricle (DORV) and compares favorably with TTE for the characterization of VSD in this setting.[22] Postoperative assessment of ventricular function, conduit patency, and pulmonary branch diameter is also possible when required.

The Functionally Univentricular Heart

True single-ventricle morphology is rare, and obstructions of either systemic or pulmonary outflows with shunting away from the obstructed side,

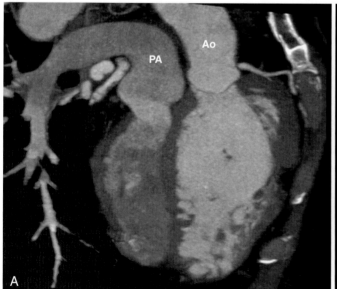

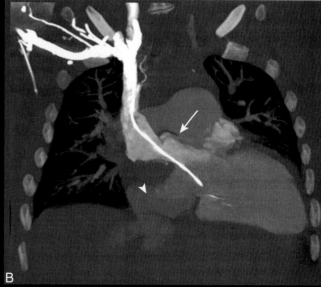

Figure 8-8 A, Congenitally corrected transposition of the great arteries. The aorta (Ao) can be seen to arise from the trabeculated, morphologic right ventricle whereas the pulmonary artery (PA) arises from the morphologic left ventricle. **B,** Mustard repair after transposition of the great arteries. Flow from the superior (*arrow*) and inferior (*arrowhead*) venae cavae is directed to the pulmonary ventricle. Note pacemaker lead traversing the superior vena cava channel, which precludes cardiovascular magnetic resonance imaging.

Continued

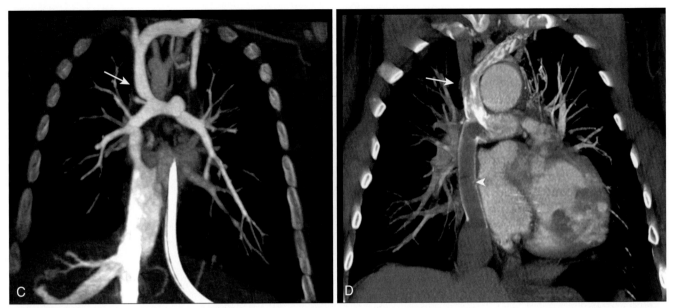

Figure 8-8—cont'd C, Glenn anastomosis. The superior vena cava (*arrow*) is anastomosed to the right pulmonary artery. **D,** Total cavopulmonary connection. There is direct anastomosis of the superior vena cava (*arrow*) with the right pulmonary artery whereas the inferior vena cava is connected using a conduit (*arrowhead*).

usually at the atrial level, are more common. The anatomy of these obstructions and the associated systemic and pulmonary circulations are critical in deciding management. CCT is able to identify virtually all causes of both systemic and pulmonary outflow tract obstructions, listed under separate headings here, in addition to allowing evaluation of ventricular function.

The Fontan Circulation

The Fontan circulation may take many forms and is described elsewhere in this book. In brief, the absence of an adequate-sized subpulmonary ventricle is addressed with a right atrial to pulmonary artery or a venae cavae to pulmonary artery connection (cavopulmonary connection); the patency of this connection in conjunction with low

pulmonary arterial pressure is crucial to maintain pulmonary blood flow. These connections are readily assessed by CCT, which is especially useful at delineating the complex vascular anatomy using 3D reconstruction techniques (see Fig. 8-8C, D). From these data, abnormal vessel dimensions, stenoses and post-stenotic dilation, mural damage (e.g., dissection or calcification), and in-situ thrombosis may all be identified. Right atrial size and pulmonary venous return (and stenoses from external compression) also may be readily assessed.

VALVULAR ASSESSMENT

The anatomy and function of the heart valves may be studied using the standard CCT dataset. However, the major technical limitation of

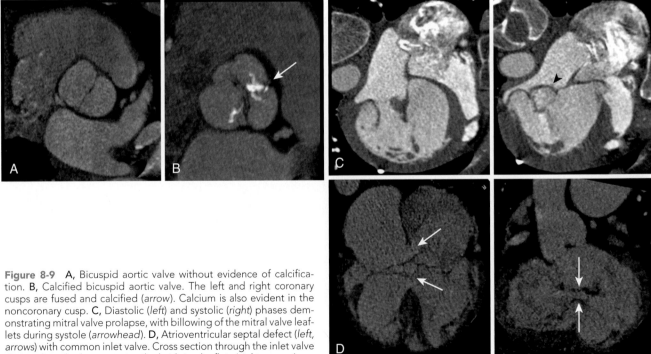

Figure 8-9 **A,** Bicuspid aortic valve without evidence of calcification. **B,** Calcified bicuspid aortic valve. The left and right coronary cusps are fused and calcified (*arrow*). Calcium is also evident in the noncoronary cusp. **C,** Diastolic (*left*) and systolic (*right*) phases demonstrating mitral valve prolapse, with billowing of the mitral valve leaflets during systole (*arrowhead*). **D,** Atrioventricular septal defect (*left, arrows*) with common inlet valve. Cross section through the inlet valve during diastole demonstrates the bridging leaflets (*right, arrows*).

CCT in assessment of congenital heart disease is the inability to assess flow. Any comments on the physiologic effect of an abnormal valve are therefore relatively limited. CCT is well placed to assess valve morphology. It can accurately identify bicuspid aortic valve morphology when compared with transesophageal echocardiography and may even be more accurate than TTE (Fig. 8-9A).[23] Aortic valve calcification may be assessed (see Fig. 8-9B), with moderate to severe calcification correlating well with TTE measurement of stenosis severity.[24] Aortic valve area may be measured using planimetry,[25] although, as for coronary assessment, dense calcifications may lead to underestimation of valve area. The mitral valve leaflets may be assessed for thickening and calcification; the latter may also be seen in the annulus. These features correlate with the presence of mitral stenosis on TTE.[26] Assessment of congenital mitral valve anomalies, such as the parachute-like mitral valve, may also be possible but data are limited to case reports at present. Mitral valve planimetry is also possible and, again, CCT measurements correlate well with TTE.[27] Cardiac gating also allows assessment of valve leaflet mobility and coaptation through the cardiac cycle (see Fig. 8-9C). The size of any regurgitant orifice in the aortic or mitral valves correlates with severity of regurgitation seen on TTE.[28,29] Right-sided valve assessment is often more difficult in the normal heart because of poor contrast density in the right side of the heart. In those with ACHD, such as in those with ASD, VSD, or pulmonary hypertension, assessment is more straightforward, because right ventricular contrast is improved owing to either impaired right ventricular outflow or mixture of contrast agent within the right ventricular blood pool owing to abnormal communication between the left and right sides of the circulation.

Assessment of right atrial and ventricular anatomy allows identification of Ebstein anomaly along with any coexistent ASD, where present. In those with atrioventricular septal defects, a common inlet valve may be seen and bridging leaflets delineated (see Fig. 8-9D). Right ventricular outflow tract obstruction may be demonstrated by CCT, which may be particularly useful in demonstrating the level of stenosis and the presence of calcification. The latter may be important when deciding percutaneous interventions to obstructive right ventricular outflow tract conduit stenoses.

CONCLUSION

CCT allows comprehensive assessment in the majority of patients with ACHD. However, radiation exposure remains an important issue, particularly if multiple examinations are expected over time. Expected advances in CT scanner technology alongside the further refinement of dose reduction techniques are likely to ameliorate this issue. Nonetheless, CMR and TTE are likely to remain the first-line imaging modalities in most circumstances. However, CCT allows an alternative means of assessment for those with either poor access or contraindications to these techniques or the expertise that they require. CCT itself requires considerable expertise when interpreting the complexities of ACHD. Because acquired data can be rotated and postprocessed in any desired imaging plane, CCT is a powerful tool for the assessment of intracardiac and extracardiac morphology and, when used in combination with established investigations such as CTA, offers a far fuller assessment than has been available previously.

REFERENCES

1. Nicol ED, Kafka H, Stirrup J, et al. A single, comprehensive non-invasive cardiovascular assessment in pulmonary arterial hypertension: combined computed tomography pulmonary and coronary angiography. Int J Cardiol 2009;136:278–288.
2. Hendel RC, Patel MR, Kramer CM, et al. ACCF/ACR/SCCT/SCMR/ASNC/NASCI/SCAI/SIR 2006 appropriateness criteria for cardiac computed tomography and cardiac magnetic resonance imaging: a report of the American College of Cardiology Foundation Quality Strategic Directions Committee Appropriateness Criteria Working Group, American College of Radiology, Society of Cardiovascular Computed Tomography, Society for Cardiovascular Magnetic Resonance, American Society of Nuclear Cardiology, North American Society for Cardiac Imaging, Society for Cardiovascular Angiography and Interventions, and Society of Interventional Radiology. J Am Coll Cardiol 2006;48:1475–1497.
3. Cecchin F, Frangini PA, Brown DW, et al. Cardiac resynchronization therapy (and multisite pacing) in pediatrics and congenital heart disease: five years experience in a single institution. J Cardiovasc Electrophysiol 2009;20:58–65.
4. van der Vleuten PA, Willems TP, Götte MJ, et al. Quantification of global left ventricular function: comparison of multidetector computed tomography and magnetic resonance imaging: a meta-analysis and review of the current literature. Acta Radiol 2006;47:1049–1057.
5. Henneman MM, Bax JJ, Schuijf JD, et al. Global and regional left ventricular function: a comparison between gated SPECT, 2D echocardiography and multi-slice computed tomography. Eur J Nucl Med Mol Imaging 2006;33:1452–1460.
6. Nicol ED, Stirrup J, Reyes E, et al. Comparison of 64-slice cardiac computed tomography with myocardial perfusion scintigraphy for assessment of global and regional myocardial function and infarction in patients with low to intermediate likelihood of coronary artery disease. J Nucl Cardiol 2008;15:497–502.
7. Yamamuro M, Tadamura E, Kubo S, et al. Cardiac functional analysis with multi-detector row CT and segmental reconstruction

algorithm: comparison with echocardiography, SPECT, and MR imaging. Radiology 2005;234:381–390.
8. Delhaye D, Remy-Jardin M, Teisseire A, et al. MDCT of right ventricular function: comparison of right ventricular ejection fraction estimation and equilibrium radionuclide ventriculography, part I. AJR Am J Roentgenol 2006;187:1597–1604.
9. Schlosser T, Mohrs OK, Magedanz A, et al. Assessment of left ventricular function and mass in patients undergoing computed tomography (CT) coronary angiography using 64-detector-row CT: comparison to magnetic resonance imaging. Acta Radiol 2007;48:30–35.
10. Berbarie RF, Anwar A, Dockery WD, et al. Measurement of right ventricular volumes before and after atrial septal defect closure using multislice computed tomography. Am J Cardiol 2007;99:1458–1461.
11. Lee T, Tsai IC, Fu YC, et al. MDCT evaluation after closure of atrial septal defect with an Amplatzer septal occluder. AJR Am J Roentgenol 2007;188:W431–W439.
12. Saremi F, Channual S, Raney A, et al. Imaging of patent foramen ovale with 64-section multidetector CT. Radiology 2008;249:483–492.
13. Merkle EM, Gilkeson RC. Remnants of fetal circulation: appearance on MDCT in adults. AJR Am J Roentgenol 2005;185:541–549.
14. Hu XH, Huang GY, Pa M, et al. Multidetector CT angiography and 3D reconstruction in young children with coarctation of the aorta. Pediatr Cardiol 2008;29:726–731.
15. Ou P, Celermajer DS, Calcagni G, et al. Three-dimensional CT scanning: a new diagnostic modality in congenital heart disease. Heart 2007;93:908–913.
16. Baron RL, Gutierrez FR, Sagel SS, et al. CT of anomalies of the mediastinal vessels. AJR Am J Roentgenol 1981;137:571–576.
17. Sondheimer HM, Oliphant M, Schneider B, et al. Computerized axial tomography of the chest for visualization of "absent" pulmonary arteries. Circulation 1982;65:1020–1025.
18. Wang XM, Wu LB, Sun C, et al. Clinical application of 64-slice spiral CT in the diagnosis of the tetralogy of Fallot. Eur J Radiol 2007;64:296–301.

19. Roberts HC, Kauczor HU, Schweden F, Thelen M. Spiral CT of pulmonary hypertension and chronic thromboembolism. J Thorac Imaging 1997;12:118–127.
20. Kuriyama K, Gamsu G, Stern RG, et al. CT-determined pulmonary artery diameters in predicting pulmonary hypertension. Invest Radiol 1984;19:16–22.
21. Greil GF, Schoebinger M, Kuettner A, et al. Imaging of aortopulmonary collateral arteries with high-resolution multidetector CT. Pediatr Radiol 2006;36:502–509.
22. Chen SJ, Lin MT, Liu KL, et al. Usefulness of 3D reconstructed computed tomography imaging for double outlet right ventricle. J Formos Med Assoc 2008;107:371–380.
23. Pouleur AC, le Polain de Waroux JB, Pasquet A, et al. Aortic valve area assessment: multidetector CT compared with cine MR imaging and transthoracic and transesophageal echocardiography. Radiology 2007;244:745–754.
24. Morgan-Hughes GJ, Owens PE, Roobottom CA, Marshall AJ. Three dimensional volume quantification of aortic valve calcification using multislice computed tomography. Heart 2003;89:1191–1194.
25. Abbara S, Pena AJ, Maurovich-Horvat P, et al. Feasibility and optimization of aortic valve planimetry with MDCT. AJR Am J Roentgenol 2007;188:356–360.
26. Willmann JK, Kobza R, Roos JE, et al. ECG-gated multi-detector row CT for assessment of mitral valve disease: initial experience. Eur Radiol 2002;12:2662–2669.
27. Messika-Zeitoun D, Serfaty JM, Laissy JP, et al. Assessment of the mitral valve area in patients with mitral stenosis by multislice computed tomography. J Am Coll Cardiol 2006;48:411–413.
28. Feuchtner GM, Dichtl W, Schachner T, et al. Diagnostic performance of MDCT for detecting aortic valve regurgitation. AJR Am J Roentgenol 2006;186:1676–1681.
29. Alkadhi H, Wildermuth S, Bettex DA, et al. Mitral regurgitation: quantification with 16-detector row CT—initial experience. Radiology 2006;238:454–463.

Cardiac Catheterization in Adult Congenital Heart Disease

ERIC HORLICK | LEE BENSON | PETER MCLAUGHLIN

Introduction

The role of heart catheterization in patient management continues to evolve as anatomic and physiologic imaging with cardiac magnetic resonance imaging (CMR) and computed tomography (CT) improves and as the breadth of interventional catheter techniques dramatically widens. In this chapter this topic has been approached in four ways:

1. Planning the procedure, including consideration of the information required, the potential pitfalls to be anticipated, and the equipment needed for the procedure
2. Execution of the procedure, including the essential points related to the sample run, coronary angiography, chamber angiography, and angiography of selected specific lesions
3. Understanding the role of heart catheterization in the context of recent developments in echocardiography, CMR, and CT
4. Discussing present and evolving interventional procedures as well as the future of heart catheterization.

Planning the Procedure

The quality and usefulness of the diagnostic information provided by a catheterization procedure can be directly related to the quality of the planning and preparation that was undertaken before the catheterization study and the knowledge base and experience of the operator. It is extremely helpful to have discussed a specific case of a patient with complex disease with the referring adult congenital heart disease (ACHD) specialist to understand the specialist's perspective and potential questions that can be resolved at the time of the catheterization.

A detailed review of the patient's clinic chart with specific attention not only to the structural anatomy but also the details of previous surgical repairs is paramount. Review of serial imaging and previous hemodynamic and angiocardiographic evaluations helps to consolidate an understanding of potential problems or issues that require specific attention at the time of catheterization that may not be readily apparent. As an example, the use of an unusual catheter shape or technique to enter a particular anomalous vessel or chamber at a previous catheterization can facilitate the subsequent procedure significantly. Vascular access is another prime example: if a patient is known to have had an occluded right iliac venous system as a child, there is not much hope that it has spontaneously recanalized as an adult, and thus alternative plans can be made that may include interventional reconstitution.

The operator must have a thorough understanding of the anatomy and physiology of congenital cardiac defects, the potential defects associated with the primary defect, the therapeutic options for the defect under investigation, and the information the surgeon/interventionalist will require if the patient is to be referred for treatment.

Before starting it is critical to appreciate the following:

- What information is absolutely essential to establish the diagnosis or plan the treatment
- What information would be useful to obtain but is not critical
- What information is redundant and already available from other imaging studies

When such thought and preparation have been done before the procedure, the catheterization can be performed in an efficient manner, minimizing radiation exposure, procedure duration, and the

volume of contrast media. With the aging of the ACHD population and the accumulation of comorbidities, it is of utmost important to avoid unnecessary renal injury through the pointless administration of large volumes of contrast agent to document anatomy that is already (or better) appreciated through other cross-sectional imaging modalities. If the study is to be an ad-hoc intervention, that is, an intervention decided on after hemodynamic or other information is ascertained, it is mandatory to fully assess the patient clinically and have an unhurried discussion of risks and potential benefits in the clinic setting. An unprepared patient is often disappointed with the procedure duration, conduct, and possible results and is unable to judge whether the risk for a potential benefit is acceptable.

WHAT INFORMATION IS ESSENTIAL?

Not uncommonly, some complex cases will become unintentionally long or, perhaps worse, be completed without obtaining a key piece of information. The most common essential information frequently required for management decisions concerns the pulmonary vasculature: the pulmonary artery pressure and resistance, the reactivity of the pulmonary vasculature, and shunt calculations. If access to the pulmonary artery is difficult, this may mean prolongation of the procedure, but time invested here may be far more valuable than recapturing other data already clear from other diagnostic testing. This is never more true than when surgical shunts or aortopulmonary collaterals contribute flow to the pulmonary circulation. Similarly, the temptation may occur to defer coronary angiography after a difficult procedure in a young adult at low risk for atherosclerosis, thus missing the opportunity to detect a relevant congenital anomaly of the coronary circulation that may directly impact future surgical or interventional decisions.

WHICH CATHETERS TO USE AND THE SEQUENCE OF EVENTS

The prepared operator will go into the cardiac catheterization laboratory with a clear idea of which catheters are likely to be most helpful and the sequence to follow to obtain the required information. For example, it may be useful to begin the right-sided heart catheterization with a steerable catheter such as a Goodale-Lubin catheter to sample for oxygen saturation, probe for atrial septal defects (ASDs) and anomalous venous drainage, and then change to a balloon-tipped catheter to cannulate the pulmonary artery through a difficult right ventricular outflow tract. A modified Judkins right coronary artery catheter with a side hole(s) near the tip is also of great value, with the side hole(s) easing pressure measurements and oximetric sampling in tight spaces.

The operator will be chagrined if he or she realizes that the pulmonary artery has been reached but all the oximetry samples and pressures were forgotten to be obtained on the way up. The operator then faces the choice of compromising the saturation run and pressures after angiograms have been obtained or having to withdraw the catheter, obtain the measurements, and reenter the pulmonary artery, adding to the fluoroscopy and procedure times. It is of critical importance to assure that, as much as possible, the information is obtained in a steady state. A vagal reaction at the beginning of the procedure, which may necessitate atropine, will jeopardize the integrity of the information. Similarly, pain from the access site with catheter manipulation related to an inadequate or improperly administered local anesthetic has a similar effect. This is usually amplified in patients who have had many procedures with dense scar tissue at the site of the puncture. An appropriate amount of sedation for most adults is mandatory. Caution should be exercised to "start low and go slow." The oversedated patient may develop airway obstruction or, independently, hypercarbia/hypoxemia can result in elevated pulmonary pressures, resistances, and arterial hypoxemia. Those with sleep-disordered breathing are most at risk.

To summarize, one should make a checklist at the beginning of the procedure outlining which hemodynamic information must be obtained, which chamber and great vessel angiography must be done, whether the coronary anatomy must be determined, what catheters will be most useful, and the sequence to be followed throughout the procedure. Catheterization is a team event involving nursing, hemodynamic technicians, and possibly a radiology technician; and conducting the procedure in a structured fashion adds value. "Time outs" and checklists in the operating room have been shown to improve safety and efficiency and should be applied to the catheterization laboratory, where increasingly complex work is done. In our laboratory we conduct a diagnostic catheterization in a structured way. We obtain venous pressures and saturations in the same predictable order and obtain all the right- and left-sided hemodynamic information before administering a contrast agent. In this way, it is easy for the team to follow the case and, similarly, if a particular saturation is forgotten, a team member can easily "flag" this for the operator.

What Can Go Wrong

Common problems with cardiac catheterization studies in adult patients with congenital cardiac disease relate to:
- Prolonged catheterization time and contrast administration
- Inadequate, missing, or nondiagnostic information
- Redundant information obtained
- Catheter complications

Many of these problems can be minimized with planning and consultation with the clinician and surgeon involved in the patient's care. Most of these procedures can be expected to take substantially more time to complete than the usual right-sided and left-sided heart procedures in patients with coronary or valvular heart disease, particularly if an unexpected finding arises during the procedure. One way to be sure that the procedures are kept short is to ensure that the invasive test is performed after all relevant noninvasive tests to avoid repeated documentation of known facts.

One is obliged to keep in mind the key questions in the planning of a catheterization procedure:
1. Am I aware of the information that I need to collect to complete the procedure? *Example:* is a descending aortogram required to map an anomalous vessel?
2. How will I gather the essential information required to establish the diagnosis, define the anatomy, define the physiology, define the presence or absence of associated anomalies, and provide the surgeon/interventionalist with the information he or she will require?
3. Should additional noninvasive testing be obtained to better understand the question to be answered?
4. How much contrast will I need for chamber and large-vessel angiography? Has the patient been adequately prehydrated and prepared with N-acetylcysteine? If renal dysfunction is a major issue, how can I reduce the amount of contrast agent required?
5. Are there comorbidities that might add to the risk of a complication and, if so, what are the potential preventive measures? *Examples:* if the patient has acquired heparin-induced thrombocytopenia, has all heparin been removed from flushing solutions? Should general anesthesia be planned for a patient with developmental delay?
6. What sequence of steps should be used to conduct the procedure? *Example:* will I be able to acquire all the hemodynamic measurements before proceeding to angiography?

Although no procedure can ever be entirely free of risk, taking these precautions will lessen the chance of problems occurring.

Equipment for Interventional Cardiac Catheterization

As in adult coronary interventions, a considerable amount of equipment is required to address the varied lesions that present in the catheterization laboratory. Unlike coronary angioplasty and stenting, however, the different types of devices, wires, catheters, and embolization and retrieval equipment can be vast when addressing congenital heart lesions. It is especially challenging in the pediatric laboratory, in which the inventory has to further address varied patient sizes. There are three principles of inventory management: *PLANNING, PLANNING,* and *PLANNING.* There are few things as disappointing to the operator or patient as arriving at a particular point during a procedure when a particular piece of equipment is required to complete the procedure and it is unavailable. It is a definite advantage to care for patients with CHD in a laboratory that is fully equipped for that purpose. A laboratory set up to care for adults is more likely to have to confront these issues as compared with one for pediatric patients. A well-planned procedure will included consideration of the inventory required that should be on hand. As such, there will be some equipment that will need to be discarded because of date of expiration, however; this should be looked on as a "necessary evil."

The equipment needed to cover most interventional cases includes sheaths, guide wires, catheters, guiding catheters, balloons, coils, occlusion devices, stents, covered stents, and retrieval kits.

SHEATHS

A selection of short and long sheaths from 5 to 16 French (Fr) is required. If coarctation stenting is to be offered, a 14-Fr system may be needed (e.g., for covered stent implantation using a balloon-in-balloon delivery system). Whereas in the past we would rarely use a sheath larger than 16 Fr, today 24-Fr sheaths (28-Fr outer diameter) are required for some percutaneous valve procedures; and thus some intermediate short sheaths are useful to stock. There are various Mullins-type sheaths, and they should be purchased with radiopaque tip markers (Fig. 9-1). Additionally, some operators find it helpful to have kink-resistant long sheaths. Such sheaths are advantageous when there is peripheral tortuosity, when large loops in the right atrium are required or the right ventricular outflow tract has an acute angulation, or when delivering devices to the pulmonary arteries.

GUIDE WIRES

A selection of guide wires with sizes from 0.014 to 0.035 inch in lengths from 50 to 260 cm are also needed. They should be super floppy, ordinary, super stiff, and glide wire (e.g., Terumo) varieties. The so-called Amplatz extra stiff and ultra-stiff guide wires (Cook Medical, Bloomington, IN, USA) (0.025 to 0.038 inch) are a mainstay for almost every case and are invaluable for stabilizing balloons across high flow lesions and during stent implantation or valvuloplasty. The Meier Backup wire (Boston Scientific, Natick, MA, USA) has been an invaluable tool for transcatheter pulmonary valve implantation.

Figure 9-1   Left, Photograph of the side-arm bleed-back tap on a Mullins-type long sheath. **Right,** Radiopaque marker tip, which is most useful when initially positioning the sheath and when directing a balloon-stent toward the target lesion.

CATHETERS

A variety of catheters are required: basic configurations such as the Goodale-Lubin, Amplatz, pigtails, cobra, vertebral, and Judkins coronary catheters are essential (Figs. 9-2 and 9-3). We have found it very helpful to stock a series of 4-Fr hydrophilic catheters in lengths of 100 and 120 cm. These catheters will track through almost any tortuous bend to a destination often unreachable by 5- or 6-Fr coronary catheters. They permit pressure monitoring from these locations as well as exchange for stiffer wires to deliver sheaths required for therapy. The Multitrack catheter (NuMed Inc, Cornwall, ON, Canada) allows high-pressure injections without recoil while stabilized by a well-positioned stiff wire and are invaluable, particularly for right ventricular outflow tract/main pulmonary artery injections in the setting of pulmonary insufficiency. As such, they allow angiography and pressure measurements without the need to remove a stable guide wire. They are available with a set of distal marker bands on a 5-Fr catheter for calibration. Some have used guide catheters over a wire for this purpose; however, high-pressure injections via end-hole catheters is discouraged. Long microcatheters with lumens that accept 0.018-inch wire should be

available for coil delivery. Tapered and nontapered catheters, guiding catheters, and balloon wedge (end-hole) and angiographic (side-hole) catheters such as the Berman catheters (Arrow Inc, Reading, PA, USA), are the foundation of any interventional laboratory.

A comprehensive stock of catheters is an asset. Although each operator will choose an appropriate selection and become familiar with their use, sometimes a key piece of equipment is required to complete a maneuver and its absence will result in failure. The more complex the case mix, the greater the variety of catheters that will be needed in the inventory.

MISCELLANEOUS EQUIPMENT

Transseptal needles, using the Mullins transseptal technique, will occasionally be required to enter the left side of the heart or perforate an atretic vascular structure. For the adult, a single length of transseptal needle can be stocked. It is important to be certain the needle fits the long sheath dilators. Additionally, the hub of the dilator should be such that when the needle and hub are engaged, only 2 or 3 mm of the needle is exposed from the tip.

BALLOONS

Although the adult interventional cardiologist is very experienced with a variety of coronary balloons for angioplasty and as a platform for stent delivery, the form and function of the balloons used in interventions in a CHD patient population are very different with regard to size, length, design, material, and limitations. Furthermore, many of the balloons used were not initially produced for intracardiac or pulmonary applications but for peripheral angioplasty. Low-pressure balloons (e.g., Tyshak [I or II], Z-Med [I or II] [NuMed]) are available in a range of sizes, many on 4- to 6-Fr shafts. They are especially advantageous because of their rapid deflation rates, which limit the time an outflow tract is occluded during an inflation cycle. High-pressure balloons also come in a range of sizes and lengths from a number of manufacturers (NuMed [Mullins]; Bard, Murray Hill, NJ, USA [Atlas]). Most balloons can be used as platforms for stent delivery. The NuMed balloon in a balloon (BIB) is very popular for controlled expansion and is especially useful for stent delivery. Despite the enormous selection that is available, one does not need a large number of different makes of balloons; however, a large range of sizes is required (Figs. 9-4 and 9-5).

EMBOLIZATION EQUIPMENT

In patients with congenital heart disorders, standard embolization devices such as coils have in many instances, been supplanted by the application of device implants designed for other locations and indications, such as ductal, atrial, and patent foramen oval (PFO) defect occluders.

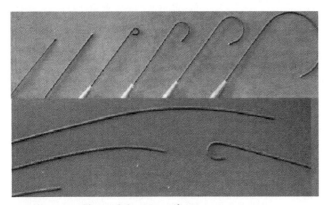
Figure 9-2 Wires of various curves.

Figure 9-3 There is a large variety of catheter curves. The Judkins right coronary, multipurpose, and cobra shapes are very useful. Each operator must determine his or her own preferences for each type of vascular structure that must be traversed.

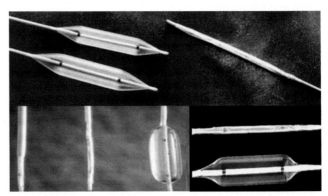
Figure 9-4 Various balloons used for both stent delivery and vessel/valve angioplasty.

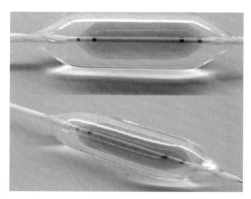

Figure 9-5 The BIB balloon (NuMed, Inc) has an inner balloon, constructed from the same material as the so-called Tyshak II balloon, whereas the outer balloon is constructed from a heavier-gauge material as used in the Z-Med higher pressure balloon. The BIB balloon allows controlled delivery of stents and adjustment of stent position after inflation of the inner balloon. This prevents stent migration, and the balloon design prevents flaring of the stent.

Coils

Historically, the Gianturco free release coil (Cook Inc, Bloomington, IN, USA) has been the primary device for peripheral embolization; however, controlled release coils (where coil release is dependent on an active maneuver from the operator) offer a safer implant especially in higher flow lesions or areas where precise coil implantation is critical. A large variety of sizes, lengths, and shapes are available from various suppliers. Additionally, a selection of guiding and microcatheters should be available (Fig. 9-6). Controlled release coils offer an additional advantage because they can be retrieved and repositioned before release. Some coil formats use an electrolytic detachment, whereas others a mechanical release mechanism. Such coils are atraumatic and result in no damage to the vessel. They offer low radial friction within the delivery catheter lumen for easy placement. For an effective occlusion, a dense mass of coils is needed. As such, they take a longer time to form a thrombus than fibered steel coils.

Atrial and Ventricular Septal Defect Occluder Devices

There are several devices now clinically available for closure of both secundum atrial and ventricular septal defects (primary muscular). The Amplatzer Septal Occluder (AGA Medical Corporation, Plymouth, MN, USA) CardioSEAL, STARflex, BioSTAR (NMT Medical, Inc., Boston, MA, USA), Figulla Occluder (Occlutech AB, Helsingborg, Sweden), and Helex (Gore Medical, Flagstaff, AZ, USA) are just a few of the devices approved for clinical use (Fig. 9-7). What is kept in inventory depends on operator experience and the range and number of defects that are addressed.

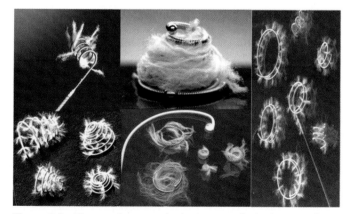

Figure 9-6 The top three panels depict controlled-release implants, and the remaining panels show a few of the many shapes that can be useful in particular locations.

Figure 9-7 Examples of atrial defect implants. **Top,** CardioSEAL (*left*) and Starflex (*right*). **Bottom,** Amplatzer septal occluder (*left*), Cardia (*middle*), and Helex (*right*).

The Amplatzer Septal Occluder has the advantage of being applicable to a wide range of defect diameters but therefore requires a large stock (sizes 4 to 20 mm in 1-mm increments; sizes 22 through 40 mm in 2-mm increments). The most commonly used implant for muscular ventricular septal defects (VSDs) is that designed by AGA Medical Corporation—the Amplatzer Muscular VSD Occluder. It is easy to deliver to the target lesion, is retrievable, and comes in a number of sizes (4 through 18 mm diameter central plug). These devices can also be used for other occlusions (e.g., atrial implants can be used in ventricular defects, in persistently patent arterial ducts, or in fistulas). There is a post–myocardial infarction VSD version of this device that has a waist measuring 10 mm (as opposed to the 7-mm waist on the muscular VSD occluder device) to better conform to the adult septum. It comes in sizes 16 through 24 mm.

ENDOVASCULAR STENTS

There are a number of endovascular stents that are useful in interventional management of the patient with a congenital heart lesion. Operators should be familiar with several types, noting their advantages and limitations. In the adult setting, stocking a range of sizes and lengths can be rationalized, particularly for use in aortic coarctation, baffle stenosis, and in the pulmonary circulation. For coarctation there are a number of choices, including but not limited to Andrastent (Andramed, Reutlingen, Germany), Maxi LD (EV3-Plymouth, MN, USA), XL series (Johnson & Johnson, Warren, NJ, USA), Cheatham-Platinum (CP) Stent (NuMed Inc, Cornwall, ON, Canada), and Wallstent (Boston Scientific, Natick, MA, USA). Covered stents have a role in the primary treatment of coarctation of the aorta. In addition, they have an important role as standby or bail-out. The CP stent is the most commonly used covered stent for congenital lesions. It is made of platinum and iridium, with gold used to strengthen the 0.013-inch thick wire solders. Unlike other implants this stent has rounded leading and trailing edges that reduce the risk of balloon rupture during inflation and of vessel trauma. Its visibility is good, it can be expanded to large diameters (up to 24 mm), and its delivery can be through 12-Fr sheaths with regular balloons and 14-Fr sheaths with the BIB system. Importantly, the implant is compatible with magnetic resonance imaging (MRI), a significant issue when managing an adult patient (Fig. 9-8).

In summary, careful thought in stocking the laboratory with a wide variety of equipment for all types of interventional procedures is required for an effective program. Although considerable variations in the kinds of equipment are required, a rational inventory with a focus on adult applications is easily achievable at a reasonable expense.

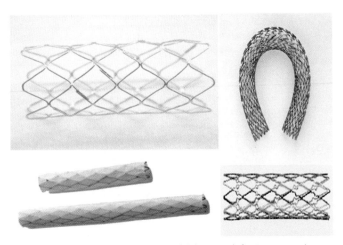

Figure 9-8 Various stents are available. **Top left,** Bare metal stent (NuMed, Inc). **Top right,** Self-expanding Wallstent (Boston Scientific). **Bottom left,** Covered CP stent (NuMed, Inc). **Bottom right,** Genesis balloon expandable stent (Johnson & Johnson).

Flows and Shunts

SAMPLE RUN

In the decision-making process for the patient with a congenital heart lesion, a great deal of significance is placed on oxygen saturation data. As an isolated measurement, the determination of blood oxygen saturation can provide important information about the patient early in the catheterization procedure. Arterial desaturation may reflect a right-to-left shunt or a ventilation/perfusion mismatch. The most common cause of arterial desaturation in the adult catheterization laboratory is hypoventilation owing to sedation. It is of critical importance to identify this issue because a climbing CO_2 in a sedated patient may have a profound impact on pulmonary pressures as well as the oximetric evaluation.

A systemic venous saturation of less than 50% indicates a low cardiac output; a high saturation indicates either a left-to-right shunt or a high-output state. The calculation of cardiac outputs, shunts, and resistances is dependent on an accurate determination of oxygen saturation. However, there are several assumptions in using oxygen as an indicator (see later) and some practical considerations in obtaining oxygen saturation data when potential errors can be introduced. As such, oxygen saturation data are the least sensitive and most prone to error of all the physiologic data obtained in the catheter laboratory.

Assumptions when using oxygen as an indicator include:
1. All measurements are made during "steady-state" blood flow. In other words, there are no changes in blood flow, respiratory rate, heart rate, or level of consciousness.
2. Two or more samples are obtained from at least three sites in rapid succession, which, in the patient with complex congenital heart lesions, can be difficult to achieve. For flow determinations (not discussed here) the assumption is that the samples are taken at the same time that oxygen consumption is measured.

In most adult laboratories the oxygen consumption is estimated based on body surface area and can result in the introduction of significant errors (up to 30%). We often estimate absolute pulmonary blood flow using both the Fick method as well as with thermodilution where appropriate. When the results are disparate, one should consider why that might be and consider favoring one value over another.

MIXED VENOUS SATURATION

There is not a single uniform source for mixed venous blood, because the "mixed" venous blood sample has three variable sources, that is, the inferior vena cava (IVC), the coronary sinus, and the superior vena cava (SVC), with each caval vein having multiple sources of blood with different saturations.

The SVC oxygen saturation may vary by 10%, because it receives blood from the jugular, subclavian, and azygous systems, each with very different saturations and flows (the subclavian and azygos veins have higher saturations than the jugular vein). The IVC also has variable oxygen saturations because the components that make up its flow may vary by 10% to 20%. For example, more saturated blood originates from the renal veins, while less saturated blood comes from gastrocolic and hepatic sources. The "net" mixed sample from the IVC is generally 5% to 10% greater than from the SVC. Coronary sinus blood also contributes to the total pool of mixed systemic return. Despite making up only 5% to 7% of total venous return, the very low saturation in this sample (25% to 45%) can impact the total mixed saturation.

Because there are multiple contributions to the so-called mixed venous sample, there is no practical way to measure each and account for the variations in flow. Not even a sample from the right atrium can completely adjust for streaming. In the absence of a shunt lesion, a sample downstream from the right atrium, such as from the main pulmonary artery, can provide for a thoroughly mixed sample. Also, it has been noted that the SVC blood saturation is very close to that in the main pulmonary artery and can be used as representative of the mixed venous sample unless the patient has a low cardiac output state. Some investigators use a weighted average of SVC and IVC blood (see later) as a calculated mixed venous sample. In the presence of a downstream shunt lesion, several samples, obtained in rapid sequence and found to be near or equal in value, should be used.

Similarly, the mixed pulmonary venous saturation is a combination of all the pulmonary veins, each reflecting different ventilation to perfusion ratios. As such, a pulmonary vein sample may be 50% to 100% disparate from the "true" mixed pulmonary venous sample. In the absence of a right-to-left shunt, a downstream sample is preferable (left ventricle or aorta), rather than using a single pulmonary vein saturation. A pulmonary venous sample may be a critical part of figuring out the cause of arterial desaturation in acquired disease when a right-to-left shunt is questioned through a PFO as a cause.

SAMPLING

When blood is drawn for shunt calculations, the samples should be obtained both proximally and distally to the lesion. Note must be taken of the influence of "streaming" when a saturation gradient may exist. Samples must be drawn in rapid temporal sequence, taking no more than 1 to 2 minutes for the sampling run. Duplicate samples should be obtained when possible and should differ by no more than 1% or 2%. The operator must be aware of potential equipment malfunctions as a source of differing sample values. For example, if blood is splattered on the inside of the saturation reading chamber, an unusually high saturation will be reported until it is cleaned, or if the hemoglobin is very high (>200 g/L) a false reading can be obtained. When a sample is drawn, all flush solution and blood must be cleared from the catheter and the catheter filled with the sample blood by a further withdrawal. If there is a poor connection between the catheter and syringe, or significant negative pressure is applied, then microbubbles can be drawn into the sample, resulting in oxygenation. Samples should not be drawn from the side arm of a bleed-back tap because they contain a chamber where the sample can be contaminated. This also applies to stopcock valves where a small amount of blood remains in the connecting chamber and contaminates the sample.

CLINICAL APPLICATIONS

In patients with CHD in whom a communication between the two sides of the heart or between the aorta and the pulmonary artery allows a shunt to exist, a number of calculations may be made, namely:
- The magnitude of a left-to-right shunt
- The magnitude of a right-to-left shunt
- Effective pulmonary blood flow
- Pulmonary to systemic flow ratio ($\dot{Q}p{:}\dot{Q}s$)

Of these, the only calculation that is of practical value is the pulmonary to systemic flow ratio. This provides a simple and reliable estimate of the extent to which pulmonary blood flow is increased or reduced and provides a useful insight into the severity of the hemodynamic disturbance in most cases. It is also very simple to perform, employing solely the oxygen saturation data from systemic arterial blood, left atrial/pulmonary venous blood, pulmonary artery, and vena caval/right-sided heart samples. The samples need to be acquired in (or be ventilated with) room air or a gas mixture containing no more than a maximum of 30% oxygen. If oxygen-enriched gas is being given (>30% oxygen), the saturation data may not provide accurate information regarding pulmonary blood flow, because a significant amount of oxygen may be present in dissolved form in the pulmonary venous sample (which is not factored into the calculation if saturations alone are used). Under such circumstances, pulmonary flow will tend to be overestimated and the Q̇p:Q̇s ratio will be correspondingly exaggerated.

Pulmonary to Systemic Blood Flow Ratio

This calculation is based on the Fick principle; that is, factors such as oxygen-carrying capacity and oxygen consumption that are used for each individual flow calculation (i.e., pulmonary and systemic flows) cancel out when only the ratio of the two flows is being estimated. This is very convenient because it removes the more difficult and time-consuming parts of the calculation. The resulting equation (after removing the factors that cancel out) is pleasingly simple:

$$\dot{Q}p : \dot{Q}s = (Sat\ Ao - Sat\ MV)/(Sat\ PV - Sat\ PA)$$

where Sat Ao = aortic saturation; Sat MV = mixed venous saturation; Sat PV = pulmonary vein saturation; and Sat PA = pulmonary artery saturation.

Because the aortic and pulmonary artery saturations are routinely measured, the only components that may present any problems are the pulmonary vein and mixed venous saturations (see earlier). If a pulmonary vein has not been entered, an assumed value of 96% may be used (note the potential error). The left atrial saturation can be substituted provided there is no right-to-left shunt at atrial level. Similarly, left ventricular or aortic saturation may be substituted provided there is no right-to-left shunt. For mixed venous saturation the tradition is to use the most distal right-sided heart location if there is no left-to-right shunt. Thus, the pulmonary artery sample should be used if there is no shunt at the atrial or ventricular level.

In practice the SVC saturation is often used, although some prefer to use a value intermediate between that of the SVC and IVC (see earlier). However, it has been demonstrated that the mixed venous saturation more closely approximates that of the SVC rather than the IVC. The following formula is often used:

$$Mixed\ venous\ saturation = (3 \times SVC + IVC)/4$$

Usefulness of the Shunt Ratio in Practice

The Q̇p:Q̇s ratio is very useful, such as in making decisions about surgery for a patient with a ventricular defect. Beyond infancy, a Q̇p:Q̇s greater than 1.8:1 is likely to require intervention whereas one less than 1.5:1 is not. The Q̇p:Q̇s is also helpful in assessing the hemodynamics of many more complex or multiple defects, but it should be recognized that under some circumstances it is of limited practical help. In an atrial defect, if there is evidence of a significant shunt on clinical and noninvasive testing (right ventricular dilation; paradoxical septal motion; cardiomegaly on x-ray; right ventricular hypertrophy on the electrocardiogram [ECG], the shunt ratio should not be used to decide about treatment. This is of critical importance, because atrial shunts depend on ventricular filling characteristics (compliance), which can vary depending on conditions (sympathetic tone, catecholamine concentrations). It is not uncommon for a measured shunt to be small (e.g., <1.5:1) despite other evidence of a significant defect.

◼ Coronary Angiography

In this section all anomalies of the coronary circulation will not be discussed in detail because excellent reviews may be found in the literature.[1,2] Instead the focus is on the more common anomalies faced by the adult congenital angiographer and some possible approaches one may consider. First, it is useful to consider a working classification of the type of coronary anomalies one may see in both structurally normal and abnormal hearts. Freedom and Culham have presented an excellent review of these anomalies and divided the possibilities into four groups as outlined in Box 9-1

For the adult angiographer one of the more common and often frustrating presentations is "the missing coronary artery." A frequent mistake is to assume that the origin of the artery is indeed in its expected position in or just above the midpoint of its facing sinus. The operator may then persist for inordinate lengths of time with the usual Judkins shape catheter, thinking the vessel is there and that further catheter manipulation will identify its origin. If the usual-shape catheter does not quickly identify the origin, one should consider alternatives. Coronary arteries may connect to the aorta immediately adjacent to a commissure, to the ascending aorta well above the sinotubular junction, or to the contralateral facing sinus. In addition, the coronary circulation may have a single main coronary artery, with the right coronary, circumflex, and left anterior descending arteries all arising from the trunk, with the main trunk itself having an anomalous aortic wall or sinus origin. Similarly, it is not uncommon to find an individual artery arising from another coronary artery, for example, the circumflex or left anterior descending artery from the right coronary or the right coronary from the left coronary artery. If one cannot find the left coronary artery with the left Judkins catheter in the left coronary sinus, or if the circumflex or left anterior descending is "missing," the next step is to proceed to the right coronary artery, which will usually identify the missing artery arising from the right coronary trunk. If the right coronary artery is the missing artery, then an aortogram or review of the left ventricular angiogram will often identify the anomalous origin. A nonselective injection in the cusp of interest with a preshaped diagnostic catheter may also be of great value. The operator must then persist or select from a variety of other catheter shapes the best fit for the location in the aortic wall of the origin. Although there are no hard and fast rules, often the Amplatz, and multipurpose catheters will be first choices to reach anomalous origins. When a proximal coronary artery, in particular the circumflex or left anterior descending, has an aberrant course from the anterior facing sinus, it is important to define which of four courses the vessel pursues to reach the left ventricle: retroaortic, interarterial, right ventricular free wall, or infundibular septum. Some criteria are available

---

BOX 9-1   CLASSIFICATION OF CORONARY ARTERY ANOMALIES

I. Anomalies of Origin
 A. Ostial anomalies
 B. Ectopic origin
  1. Anomalous origin from the aortic wall or sinus
  2. Anomalous origin from a coronary artery
  3. Abnormal connection to a pulmonary artery
  4. Origin from a vessel other than the pulmonary artery or aorta
  5. Origin from a ventricular cavity
II. Anomalies of Course
 A. Intramural course
 B. Aberrant course of proximal coronary artery
 C. Myocardial bridge
 D. Epicardial crossing
III. Anomalies of Termination or Connection
 A. Connections to cardiac structures
 B. Connections to extracardiac structures
IV. Anomalies of Coronary Size

From Freedom RM, Culham JAG, Moes CAF. Angiocardiography of congenital heart disease. In: Anomalies of the coronary arteries. New York: Macmillan Publishing Co. 1984:405-421.

and, combined with careful angiography, help to make the correct diagnosis.[3,4] This becomes important if a cardiac surgical procedure is planned. It has become increasingly realized in the era of high-speed gated cardiac CT that our present understanding of how angiographic anatomy relates to pathology may be inadequate. The role of cardiac CT in an experienced center to document the coronary course may become increasingly relevant especially as prospective gating continues to diminish the radiation dose required for these studies.

The other not infrequent finding that will arise for the adult congenital angiographer is one or more coronary arteriovenous fistulas. These may connect from either coronary artery, be quite small or very large, may be single or multiple, and may connect to a chamber, usually right-sided, or to a coronary vein or coronary sinus. Most will be small, exit in a mediastinal vessel, not require any intervention, and will be of passing interest. A small number will be large and associated with symptoms or signs of volume overload and lead to the question of catheter or surgical intervention. In these few cases the angiographer should spend the time and make additional contrast injections in multiple projections to carefully define the exact origin of the fistula, the anatomy of the exit of the fistula, and the location of any coronary arteries arising from the fistulous tract. These will be important in deciding if catheter occlusion is possible or if surgery is necessary and the best interventional or surgical approach to closure.

Chamber Angiography

Accurate anatomic and physiologic diagnosis is the foundation of a successful catheter-based therapeutic procedure. This section includes a discussion of standard angiographic approaches and how they are achieved. Emphasis is placed on the application of these projections as applied to interventional procedures. A detailed description of the physical principles of image formation is beyond the scope of this chapter, and the interested reader is referred to other sources for more detailed information.[5]

ANGIOGRAPHIC PROJECTIONS

In the therapeutic management of the patient with a congenital heart lesion, the spatial orientation and detailed morphology of the heart and great vessels are of critical importance. As the operator enters the laboratory, an understanding of the anatomy should have been synthesized, based on information from other imaging modalities such as chest radiography, echocardiography, CT, and MRI (see earlier). As such, the angiographic projections used in the procedure will be "tailored" to outline the lesion to allow appropriate measurements and guide the intervention.

The heart is oriented obliquely, with the left ventricular apex being leftward, anterior, and inferior, in relation to the base of the heart. The interventricular septum is a complex geometric three-dimensional (3D) structure that takes an "S" curve from apex to base, the so-called sigmoid septum. From caudal to cranial the interventricular septum curves through an arc of 100° to 120°, and the right ventricle appears as an appliqué or overlay on the left ventricle. To address this topology, today's angiographic equipment allows a wide range of projections, incorporating caudocranial or craniocaudal angulations. The up-to-date laboratory consists of independent biplane imaging chains that, with the proper selection of views, minimize overlapping and foreshortening of structures. However, most adult laboratories do not have biplane configurations as is frequently standard in a pediatric laboratory, and these procedures must be performed in a single plane room. As such, a detailed understanding of the anatomy and the goals of the intervention become paramount to a successful procedure.

TERMINOLOGY

Angiographic projections are designated either according to the position of the recording detector (flat panel detector) or the direction of the x-ray beam toward the recording device. In cardiology the convention is usually the former. For example, when the detector is directly above a supine patient, the x-ray beam travels from posterior to anterior and the *angiographic projection* is designated posteroanterior (PA), but based on detector *position*, it is called frontal and the position of the detector by

convention is at 0°. Similarly, when the detector is moved through 90°, to a position beside and to the left of the patient, a lateral projection results. Between 0° and 90° there are a multitude of projections termed *left anterior oblique* (LAO), and when the detector is moved to the right of the patient, a *right anterior oblique* (RAO) projection is achieved. Standard detectors mounted on a C-arm not only allow the above positions, but also the detectors can be rotated around the transverse axis, toward the feet or head, caudally or cranially (Fig. 9-9).

BIPLANE ANGIOGRAPHY

A dedicated interventional catheterization laboratory addressing congenital heart defects ideally requires biplane facilities.[6,7] Biplane angiography has the advantage of limiting contrast exposure and evaluating the cardiac structures in real-time in two projections simultaneously. However, this is at a cost, because these facilities are expensive, and with existing flat panel detectors, extreme simultaneous angulations can be compromised. Standard biplane configurations include RAO/LAO and frontal/lateral projections, with additional cranial or caudal tilt. The possible combinations are endless (Table 9-1; see also Fig. 9-9).

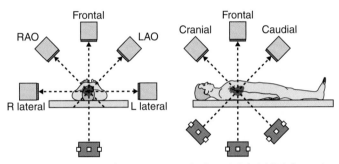

Figure 9-9   Angiographic projections in biplane. L, left; LAO, left anterior oblique; R, right; RAO, right anterior oblique.

TABLE 9-1 Angiographic Projections		
Projection	**Angles**	
Single Plane Projections		
Conventional RAO	40° RAO	
Frontal	0°	
Shallow LAO	1° to 30°	
Straight LAO	31° to 60°	
Steep LAO	61° to 89°	
Left lateral	90° left	
Cranially tilted RAO	30° RAO + 30° cranial	
Cranially tilted frontal (sitting up view)	30° or 45° cranial	
Cranially tilted shallow LAO	25° LAO + 30° cranial	
Cranially tilted mid LAO (long-axis oblique)	60° LAO + 20°-30° cranial	
Cranially tilted steep LAO (hepatoclavicular view)	45° to 70° LAO + 30° cranial	
Caudally tilted frontal	45° caudal	
Biplane combinations	A plane	B plane
Anteroposterior and lateral	0°	Left lateral
Long-axis oblique	30° RAO	*60° LAO + 20° to 30° cranial*
Hepatoclavicular view	45° LAO + 30° cranial	120° LAO + 15° cranial
Specific Lesions		
RVOT-MPA (sitting-up)	*10° LAO + 40° cranial*	Left lateral
Long axial for LPA (biplane)	30° RAO	60° LAO + 30° cranial
LPA long axis (single plane)		60° LAO + 20° cranial
ASD	*30° LAO + 30° cranial*	
PA bifurcation and branches	*30° caudal + 10° RAO*	*20° caudal*

Note: Primary projections are in italics.

ASD, atrial septal defect; LAO, left anterior oblique; LPA, left pulmonary artery; MPA, main pulmonary artery; PA, pulmonary artery; RAO, right anterior oblique; RVOT, right ventricular outflow tract.

Cranial–Left Anterior Oblique Projections

A clear working understanding of cranial-LAO projections is of critical importance in developing a flexible approach to congenital heart defect angiography and intervention. The practice of using "cookbook" projections for each case *may* allow acceptable diagnostic images but will fall short of the detail required to accomplish an interventional procedure. As noted earlier, a comprehensive understanding of the normal and congenitally malformed cardiac anatomy, especially the interventricular septum, allows the operator to adjust the projection to optimally profile the region of interest.

There are a number of "rules of thumb" that allow the operator to judge the steepness or shallowness of an LAO projection:

Of importance is the relationship of the cardiac silhouette to the spine, the ventricular catheter, and the ventricular apex. To optimize the profile of the midpoint of the *membranous ventricular septum* (and thus the majority of perimembranous defects), two thirds of the cardiac silhouette should be to the right of the vertebral bodies (Figs. 9-10 and 9-11). This will result in a cranially tilted left ventriculogram showing the left ventricular septal wall, with the apex (denoted by the ventricular catheter) pointing toward the bottom of the image.

A shallower projection will have more of the cardiac silhouette over toward the left of the spine and profile the inferobasal component of the septum, which is ideal for *inlet-type ventricular defects*. This projection allows for evaluation of atrioventricular valve relationships, inlet extension of perimembranous defects, and posterior muscular defects.

A steeper LAO projection can be used to profile the *outlet extension of a perimembranous defect* and *anterior muscular and apical defects*. As noted in Figure 9-10, the ventricular catheter in the cardiac apex can be used to help guide the projection but only if it enters the chamber through the mitral valve. If catheter entry is through the ventricular defect or retrograde, it tends to be more basal and left lateral.

Modification of the cranial LAO projection will have to be made if there is a discrepancy in chamber sizes, and the septum is rotated, such that a steeper or shallower projection may be required. Also, it is assumed that the patient is lying flat on the examining table, but if the head is turned to the right or there is a pad under the buttocks, it will rotate the thorax such that the LAO projection is steeper and the detector caudal. This has to be compensated for during the setup for the angiogram. The clue in the former case is that more of the heart silhouette is over the spine.

The first step in setting up a cranial-LAO projection is to achieve the correct degree of steepness or shallowness. After that, the degree of cranial tilt has to be confirmed so that the basal-apical septum is elongated. This can be estimated by seeing how much of the hemidiaphragm is superimposed over the cardiac silhouette; the greater the superimposition, the greater the cranial tilt. Additionally, the degree of cranial tilt can be determined by looking at the course of the ventricular catheter, with it appearing to be foreshortened or coming directly at the viewer as the degree of cranial angulation is decreased (Fig. 9-12).

■ Specific Lesions

VENTRICULAR SEPTAL DEFECT

The imaging of specific ventricular defects is beyond the scope of this review but is commented on in detail by various authors.[8] The injections to outline the septum and the margins that circumscribe the defect(s) are best performed in the left ventricle using a power injector (Fig. 9-13). Two orthogonal (right angle) projections will give the best chance of profiling the lesion. Table 9-1 lists single and biplane angulations for the various projections. For the perimembranous defect the midcranial LAO projection, at 50° to 60° LAO, and as much cranial tilt as the equipment and patient position will allow (see Fig. 9-10) should be attempted. Additional projections can include a shallow-LAO with cranial tilt

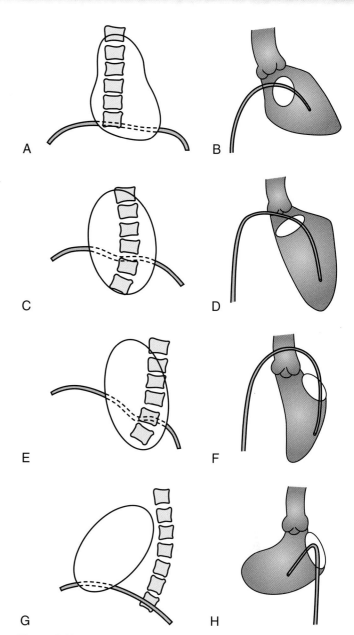

Figure 9-10 Setting up a standard LAO projection. To achieve the LAO projection, attempt to adjust the detector angle such that two thirds of the cardiac silhouette is to the left of the spine (as in **E**). If a catheter is through the mitral valve in the left ventricular apex, it will point to the floor (as in **F**). In this view, the intraventricular septal margin points toward the floor. The so-called four-chamber or hepatoclavicular view is achieved by having one half of the cardiac silhouette over the spine (as in **C**). A catheter across the mitral valve will appear as in **D**. A steep LAO projection will have the cardiac silhouette as in **G**, and a transmitral catheter in the left ventricle will appear as in **H**. **A** and **B** show the frontal projection. *(Modified from Culham JAG. Physical principles of image formation and projections in angiocardiography. In: Freedom RM, Mawson JB, Yoo SJ, Benson LN, eds. Congenital Heart Disease Textbook of Angiocardiography. Armonk, NY: Futura Publishing; 1997:39-93, with permission.)*

(so-called four-chamber or hepatoclavicular view) to outline the basal septum or inlet extension of a perimembranous defect. The RAO view will outline the high anterior and infundibular (outlet) defects.[9]

COARCTATION OF THE AORTA

Biplane angiography should be used to outline the aortic arch lesion (Fig. 9-14). Projections that can be used include LAO/RAO, frontal

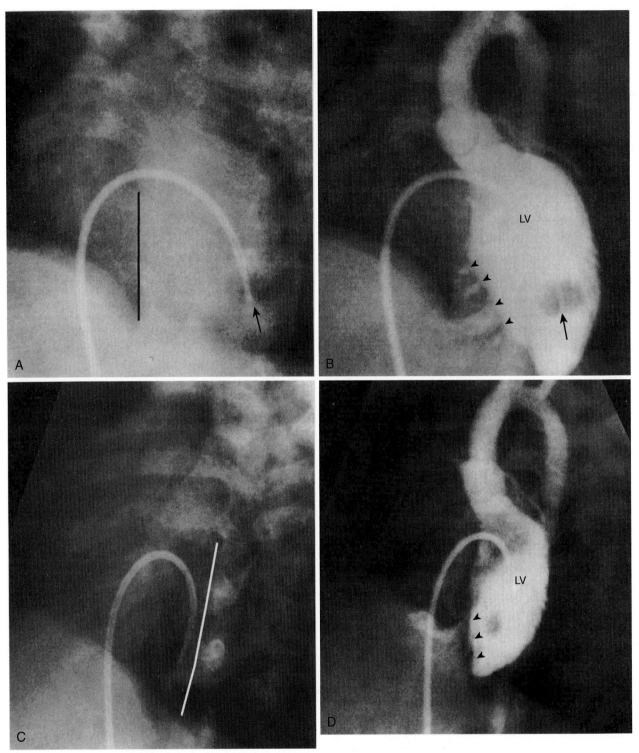

Figure 9-11   Achieving an LAO projection. **A,** For a hepatoclavicular view, one half of the cardiac silhouette is over or just left of the spine, (*line*), with the catheter pointing toward the left of the image. During the injection, the apex and catheter (*arrow*) will point toward the bottom and left of the image. In this example (**B**), the basal (inlet) portion of the septum is intact. Multiple mid-muscular septal defects are not well profiled (*arrowheads*). In **C,** the LAO projection is achieved with the catheter pointing toward the bottom of the frame and the cardiac silhouette well over the spine. During the contrast injection (**D**), the mid-muscular defects are now better profiled. LV, left ventricle. *(Modified from Culham JAG. Physical principles of image formation and projections in angiocardiography. In: Freedom RM, Mawson JB, Yoo SJ, Benson LN, eds. Congenital Heart Disease Textbook of Angiocardiography. Armonk, NY: Futura Publishing; 1997:39-93, with permission.)*

and lateral, or a shallow or steep LAO. Our preference is a 30° LAO and left-lateral, with 10° to 15° caudal tilt to minimize any overlapping structures, such as a ductal bump or diverticulum. Modifications to accommodate a right arch are generally mirror image projections (i.e., 30° RAO and left-lateral). The operator must be cautious to

examine the transverse arch for associated hypoplasia, and this may be foreshortened in the straight left-lateral projection. In such an instance, for a left arch, a left posterior oblique projection may elongate the arch. This is particularly important if an endovascular stent is to be deployed near the head and neck vessels.

AORTIC VALVE ANGIOGRAPHY

In the setting of normally related great arteries with ventriculoarterial concordance, assessment of the diameter of the aortic valve for balloon dilation is best performed using biplane configurations in the long axis and RAO projections (Fig. 9-15; see Table 9-1). Our preference is to obtain the diameter of the aortic valve from a ventriculogram, which profiles the hinge points of the leaflets. Caution must be observed when using an ascending aortogram, because one of the leaflets of the valve may obscure the margins of attachment.

MUSTARD BAFFLE

Over time, patients who have had a Mustard operation may develop obstruction to one or both limbs of the venous baffle. Because atrial arrhythmias are not uncommon in such adult patients, pacing sys-

tems are frequently required for management. To facilitate pacing catheter insertion, enlargement of a stenotic, often asymptomatic, superior baffle is frequently required. The optimum projection to outline superior baffle obstruction for potential stent implantation is a cranially angulated LAO projection (30° LAO and 30° cranial) (Fig. 9-16). This view will elongate the baffle pathway, allowing accurate measurement before stenting. For inferior baffle lesions, a frontal projection will allow adequate localization of the lesion. Leaks along the baffle are more problematic and require modification of the projection. The initial approach should be a frontal projection, with modifications in angulation made thereafter to best profile the lesion for device implantation.

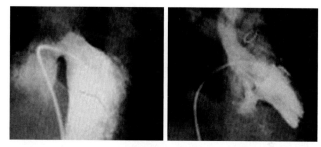

Figure 9-13   **Left,** Long-axis oblique projection of a left ventriculogram, defining a perimembranous ventricular septal defect. **Right,** A mid-muscular defect outlined with a hepatoclavicular left ventricular injection.

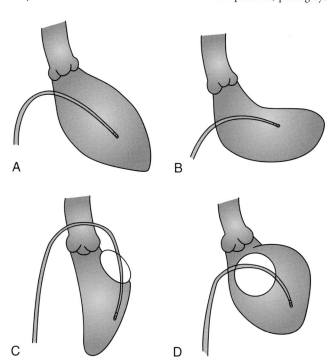

Figure 9-12   Obtaining the cranial tilt. In the standard RAO view (**A**) the left ventricular apex points caudad and to the left. The LAO view (**C**) will open the outflow from apex to base. If there is an upturned apex, as in tetralogy of Fallot the RAO view will appear as shown in **B**. Adding cranial tilt to a mid-LAO projection will not effectively open the apex to base projection, and the appearance will be as looking down the barrel of the ventricles (**D**). *(Modified from Culham JAG. Physical principles of image formation and projections in angiocardiography. In: Freedom RM, Mawson JB, Yoo SJ, Benson LN, eds. Congenital Heart Disease Textbook of Angiocardiography. Armonk, NY: Futura Publishing; 1997:39-93, with permission.)*

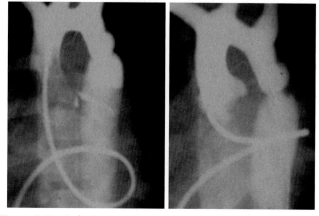

Figure 9-14   **Left,** An ascending aortogram taken with a shallow LAO projection without caudal angulation. The catheter was placed through a transeptal entry to the left side of the heart. **Right,** Although the area of the coarctation can be seen, it is the caudal angulation that identifies the details of the lesion, including a small ductal ampulla.

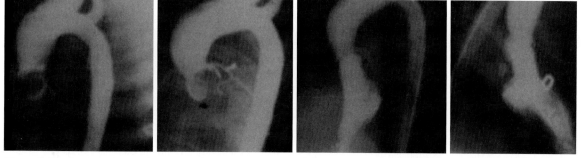

Figure 9-15   Intervention on the aortic valve requires accurate definition of the hinge points of the leaflets. **Left,** LAO views from an ascending aortogram. The margins of the leaflets are not defined due to overlap of the cusps (bicuspid in these examples). **Right,** LAO and RAO views. The left ventriculogram allows easier identification of the leaflet hinge points, where measurements can be made.

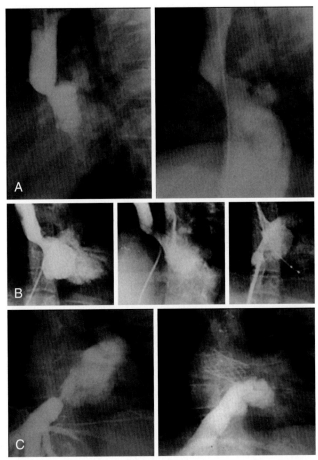

Figure 9-16 As the ACHD population ages, baffle obstruction after a Mustard operation is an increasingly common event. This is particularly important when such patients need transvenous pacing devices. **A,** The presence of a superior baffle obstruction can be identified from the left-lateral projection (*left*). However, only with cranial angulation (cranial-LAO view, *right*) will the full extent of the lesion be detailed. **B,** This is particularly critical when the frontal view (*left*) does not show the full extent of the obstruction and only from the angulated view will the length and diameter of the lesion be outlined (*middle*). A stent is placed, followed by a transvenous pacing system, as shown in a frontal projection (*right*). **C,** For an inferior baffle lesion, the frontal (posteroanterior) projection is optimal, before (*left*) and after (*right*) a stent is placed.

SECUNDUM ATRIAL SEPTAL DEFECT AND FENESTRATED FONTAN OPERATION

Secundum ASDs are best profiled in the 30° LAO projection with 30° cranial tilt (Fig. 9-17). With the injection made in the right upper pulmonary vein, the sinus venosus portion of the septum can be visualized and anomalous pulmonary venous return ruled out. Additionally, any associated septal aneurysm can be outlined. With the application of transesophageal or intracardiac echocardiography there is less reliance on fluoroscopic device positioning. When balloon sizing is performed, this projection will elongate the axis of the balloon for proper measurements. The interventional management of the patient with a fenestrated Fontan operation, whether a lateral tunnel or extracardiac connection, generally requires selective studies of the superior and inferior caval veins and pulmonary circulations, to determine the presence or absence of obstructive or hypoplastic pathways and whether venous collateral vessels have developed. If present, they must be addressed by angioplasty, stenting, or embolization techniques before fenestration closure. Venous collateral vessels after an extracardiac Fontan procedure will generally develop either from the innominate vein or from the right upper hepatic/phrenic vein toward the neo–left atrium, less frequently

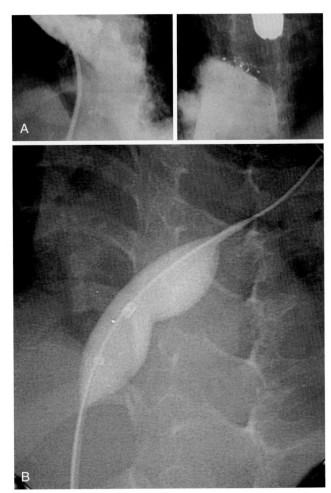

Figure 9-17 **A,** Use of angiography for septal defect definition and device placement in the setting of a secundum atrial septal defect has been supplanted by intracardiac and transesophageal techniques. **B,** However, fluoroscopy is still required for initial device localization, and in many laboratories a short cine-run is done to record the diameter of the static balloon diameter to choose device size. In this case, there is a 30° LAO with 30° cranial tilt to best elongate the balloon to avoid foreshortening.

from the right hepatic veins to the pulmonary veins. The optimum projection to outline these lesions is in the frontal and lateral projections, with selective power injections in the appropriate vessel. The location and dimensions of the fenestration may also be defined in these views, but for ideal profiling some degree of right or left anterior obliquity may be required (Fig. 9-18).

BIDIRECTIONAL CAVOPULMONARY CONNECTION

Second-stage palliation for a number of congenital defects consists of a bidirectional cavopulmonary connection (the bidirectional Glenn anastomosis) (Fig. 9-19). Because the caval to pulmonary artery connection is toward the anterior surface of the right pulmonary artery (rather than on the upper surface), an anteroposterior projection will result in overlapping of the anastomotic site with the pulmonary artery. Therefore, to determine whether the anastomosis is obstructed, a 30° caudal with 10° LAO projection will generally open that region for better definition. Furthermore, this projection will outline the full extent of the right and left pulmonary arteries. The left-lateral projection with or without 10° caudal angulation will profile the anastomosis for its anteroposterior dimension. Contrast injection must be made in the lower portion of the superior caval vein. Examination of venous collaterals can be performed from the anteroposterior and lateral projections in the innominate vein.

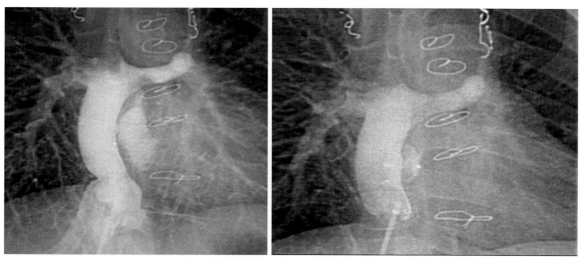

Figure 9-18 Appearance of a fenestrated extracardiac Fontan operation in the frontal projection (*left*), and its appearance after device closure (*right*). Generally, a frontal projection profiles the defect adequately, but at times some angulation is required, where the defect is best profiled in a shallow-RAO view. Also note coils in the left superior caval vein, which developed after the Fontan procedure and required embolization. Occasionally, collateral vessels develop from the hepatic/phrenic vein or innominate vein, the primary view being frontal and left-lateral.

PULMONARY VALVE STENOSIS AND TETRALOGY OF FALLOT

Percutaneous intervention on isolated pulmonary valve stenosis was the procedure that ushered in the present era of catheter-based therapies. Although angiographic definition of the right ventricular outflow tract and valve is not complicated, several features must be kept in mind when approaching angiography for an interventional procedure. In the case of isolated pulmonary valve stenosis and other right ventricular outflow tract lesions, because the outflow tract can take a horizontal curve, a simple anteroposterior projection will foreshorten the structure. Therefore, a 30° cranial with 15° LAO projection will open up the infundibulum and allow visualization of the valve and the main and branch pulmonary arteries. The best definition of the hinge points of the valve, to choose the correct balloon size, is from the left-lateral projection (Fig. 9-20). Occasionally, 10° or 15° caudal angulation of the lateral detector can be used to separate the

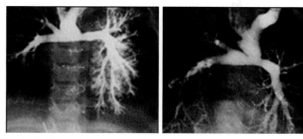

Figure 9-19 **Right,** Because of an offset in the anastomosis between the superior vena cava and right pulmonary artery, the optimal view to see the anastomosis without overlap is a shallow one—with caudal tilt. **Left,** In the frontal projection there is overlap of the anastomosis that obscures a potential lesion, as seen in the angulated view. The combination of an angulated frontal detector and caudal angulation of the lateral tube will allow definition of the anastomosis and the pulmonary artery confluence.

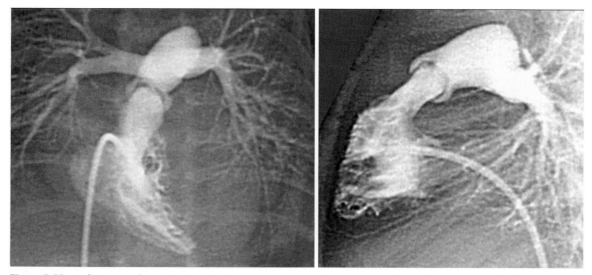

Figure 9-20 **Left,** A case of typical isolated pulmonary valve stenosis in a neonate. The outflow tract is profiled in the cranially angulated frontal projection, with a slight degree of LAO angulation. The right ventriculogram outlines the form of the ventricle, the main pulmonary artery (and ductal bump), as well as the pulmonary artery confluence and branch dimensions. **Right,** The lateral view outlines the valve leaflets (thickened and doming) and allows accurate delineation of the valve structures for balloon diameter determination.

overlap of the branch vessels seen on a straight left-lateral projection. However, this is not recommended, because it will also foreshorten the outflow tract and the valve will appear off plane, giving incorrect valve diameters.

BRANCH PULMONARY ARTERY STENOSIS

Pulmonary artery interventions are common and represent the most difficult angiographic projections to separate out individual vessels for assessment and potential intervention (Figs. 9-21 and 9-22). A cranially tilted frontal projection with a left-lateral or RAO/ LAO projection is frequently the first series of views that can be performed as scout studies to map the proximal and hilar regions of the pulmonary circulation. The injection may be performed in

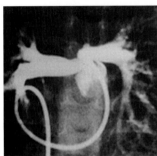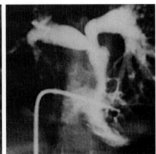

Figure 9-21 Angiography for selective intervention on the branch pulmonary arteries can be most difficult owing to overlapping of structures. No single projection is totally representative and often multiple views are required. A scout film is taken in the main pulmonary artery (*left*) and in the right ventricle (*right*). Both images are taken in the cranial-LAO projection and, in these examples, clearly outline the outflow tracts and branch confluences. In the *left panel* the dilated main pulmonary artery would have obscured the branch pulmonary artery confluence, thus cranial-LAO (*top left*) and caudal left-lateral (see Fig. 9-22) views nicely detail the anatomy for subsequent intervention.

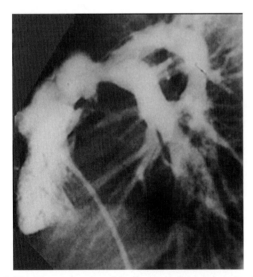

Figure 9-22 This image is taken from a left-lateral projection with caudal tilt. This will separate the proximal right and left pulmonary artery branches and detail the main pulmonary artery. The outflow tract is foreshortened, and this view will mislead the operator when examining the diameter of the valve and the infundibulum. When examining both the infundibulum and the diameter of the valve, a straight left-lateral projection should be performed. In the caudal-lateral projection, the left pulmonary branch will sweep superiorly and toward the upper right corner of the image while the left pulmonary artery will appear more medial and in the center of the image. By using the left-lateral view, stents could be placed in each branch.

either the ventricle or main pulmonary artery. Because there is frequent overlap in viewing the right ventricular outflow tract (see earlier), these standard views can be modified by increasing or decreasing the degree of RAO or LAO and adding caudal or cranial tilt. Selective branch artery injections are best for detailed visualization to plan the intervention. For the right pulmonary artery, a shallow-RAO projection with 10° or 15° cranial tilt will separate the upper and middle lobe branches, while a left-lateral with 15° caudal tilt projection will open up all the anterior vessels. Similarly, to maximize the elongated and posterior leftward directed left pulmonary artery, a 60° LAO with 20° cranial view is very effective, with a caudal tilt on the lateral detector.

THREE-DIMENSIONAL ANGIOGRAPHY

With the introduction of digital image acquisition and flat panel technology, CT images allowing soft tissue visualization can be acquired from the angiographic system. A three-dimensional (3D) CT reconstruction can be produced from the acquisition of two-dimensional (2D) projection images by rotating the C-arm around the patient (Fig. 9-23). The process was initially applied in the electrophysiology laboratory to map the topology of the left atrium but has now been applied for online volume-rendered vessel reconstruction. Its application during interventional procedures during great vessels and pulmonary artery interventions is now being assessed. It appears very promising as an adjunct to the standard imaging techniques.

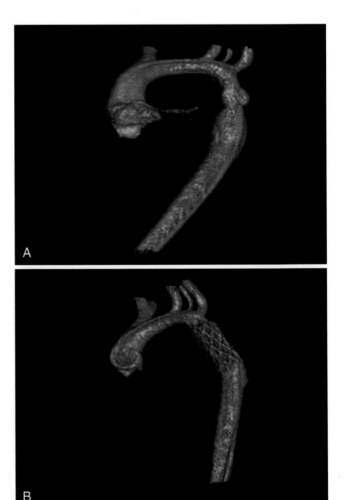

Figure 9-23 Volume-rendered 3D images obtained by rotating the C-arm in this example of coarctation of the aorta, (**A**) before and (**B**) after stent implantation.

Changing Indications for Cardiac Catheterization in ACHD

There has been no greater impact on the care of patients with CHD than new imaging modalities. The heart, once accessible only by the surgeon, angiocardiographer, and pathologist, can now be safely and accurately sliced, rotated, and examined with minimal discomfort to the patient. The development of better imaging has greatly impacted our ability to make decisions and plan percutaneous interventions and surgery. Unfortunately, the clinical appreciation of a patient's anatomy can become quite befuddled as years go by and a patient is cared for by different pediatricians and adult cardiologists or even lost to specialized follow-up. This is never so true as when geographic migrations occur and patients leave the pediatric hospital where they were initially cared for and arrive in a new city without their medical file.

Clinical information about a patient has a hierarchy in terms of its relevance and importance. A tattered 25-year-old surgical report may be the "holy grail" of information. A seasoned surgeon's operative report may carefully describe the native and surgical anatomy in great detail. The report may provide insight into what was repaired, how, and why. A close second in the hierarchy is a good quality CT scan or MR image by an experienced imager. The latest generation of imaging equipment from the major modalities of echocardiography, MRI, and CT permits the appreciation of subtle anatomic details.

More important than the newest technology and costliest equipment is the availability of imaging specialists to conduct the study, expertly interpret it, insightfully report it, and caution us if there are limitations we should know about. Collaboration between the imager and clinical, surgical, and interventional physicians allows the integration of knowledge and facilitates the delivery of excellent patient care. Little is gained from the ability to produce beautiful images that are interpreted in a way that is not meaningful to the clinician. It is as important for the radiologist to know the concerns of the surgeon and interventionalist as is the reverse. Choosing the right modality to answer a particular question or set of questions is key, as is providing the imager with the specific questions to be addressed so that correct protocols are used to obtain the information required.

CARDIAC CATHETERIZATION

What is the role of catheterization? Is it a dinosaur in the face of advanced imaging? Is it barbaric to use catheters to measure pressures and inject dye directly into a cardiac chamber for fleeting seconds when a simple peripheral intravenous injection suffices for detailed cross-sectional imaging?

In counterpoint, catheterization is the only modality that provides the gold standard of pressure measurement in a vessel or chamber. In stark contrast to the complexities of the newest technology, the measurement of intracardiac pressures is simple, reliable, and reproducible. The assessment of the hemodynamic significance of a lesion should never be left to cross-sectional imaging and always be verified by catheter. Some have argued that an aortic valve should never be changed without the patient having had a catheter examination.[10,11] This will be interpreted as an old way of doing things by some, but by others it is a refreshing confirmation of the value of invasive imaging. Some will send patients for operative correction of a defect without catheterization, but they may, on occasion, fall victim to this approach; an anomalous coronary will be missed and transected or ligated or an opportunity to address an unrecognized defect will be missed. It is not uncommon for echocardiographic gradients to be misleading, valve areas to be erroneous, and shunt flows to be misrepresented in the most accredited and experienced echocardiography laboratories. Unfortunately the same can be said for cross-sectional imaging in the same institution. It is important to realize when inconsistencies in data occur. This leads to an inherently difficult problem in management that must be reconciled, in which additional confirmation is required. It may make a significant difference in the decision regarding the need for surgery, intervention, or assessment of risk.

Catheterization is the only method to accurately determine the pulmonary artery pressure and pulmonary vascular resistance. These values are of utmost importance in many patients with CHD. The time-honored practice of oximetry and shunt determination is a confirmatory piece of information, and the weight placed on it is reflected in our present guidelines for intervention in CHD.[12] There are a number of situations in which noninvasive imaging cannot provide the anatomic detail required for decision-making. The recognition that noninvasive imaging may not reliably assess the lumen of a pulmonary artery or collateral vessel after stenting may lead to a further intervention that could improve a patient's quality of life. Coronary angiography provides the only standard used to assess coronary lesions and their suitability for revascularization. The addition of invasive physiologic (coronary flow reserve) and imaging modalities (intravascular ultrasonography) can make the resolution of a clinical question regarding lesion severity a straightforward issue. Diagnostic catheterization is alive and well in CHD.

LOOK AT TODAY'S INTERVENTIONS

Most adult congenital catheterization practices consist of about 70% intracardiac device implantation and about 30% other interventions. The world of device closure for ASDs is divided between ASD and PFO closure.

Atrial Septal Defect Closure

ASDs are present in about 0.317 of every 1000 live births.[13] A variety of devices have been used to close these defects, generally for the indication of right ventricular volume overload. The guidelines for these interventions are drawn from the Canadian and European Grown-Up Congenital Heart Disease (GUCH) recommendations.[12,14] ASD closure is a well-established and safe procedure. It can be performed on an outpatient basis with intracardiac echocardiographic guidance and without the need for anesthesia or transesophageal echocardiography. Such an approach presumes that patients have undergone a detailed transesophageal echocardiography to exclude associated abnormalities including but not limited to anomalous pulmonary venous return, additional secundum defects, fenestrations, and sinus venosus defects as well as the occasional septum primum defect. MRI and CT provide excellent detail with regard to pulmonary venous drainage but are somewhat lacking in specificity and sensitivity when it comes to small fenestrations or other small coexisting ASDs. Transesophageal echocardiography will also exclude left atrial thrombus and confirm the absence of significant valvular heart disease.

The most versatile device for this application is the Amplatzer Septal Occluder (AGA Medical Corporation, Plymouth, MN, USA). It provides the benefit of a self-centering design (an issue with double umbrella devices) and is easy to implant. The residual leak rate after placement is arguably the lowest of any device, and it has the lowest rate of visible thrombus formation of any current device.[15,16] Many series of both short- and medium-term results have been published and have demonstrated excellent results. Patients younger than age 40 generally have a complete return of their dilated right ventricular size to normal over the following 6 months (much of the improvement occurs immediately after the procedure).[17] Many patients older than age 40 have enjoyed the same results. The use of MRI to examine ventricular volumes in adults has been reassuring; in our series the vast majority of adults enjoy the benefits of ventricular normalization. Most adults demonstrate objectively improved cardiopulmonary function after closure, including those who believed they were asymptomatic before the procedure.[18–20] There is a suggestion that patients without arrhythmia before the age of 55 who undergo closure may enjoy a lower risk of subsequently developing an arrhythmia.[21] Although it is a well-established procedure, the long-term safety of ASD device closure remains in question. A number of late device erosions into the pericardium, aorta, or other structures have been reported. The erosion rate is thought to involve about 0.1% of cases.[22,23] Caution has been advised in cases with a deficient superior or aortic rim, with aggressive balloon sizing and device over sizing, as well as with aggressive maneuvers (push-pull) to verify device stability. Some have advocated the abandonment of balloon sizing, but data are lacking to confirm this is a safer approach. What is generally agreed on is that the smallest possible device should be placed in a defect to provide closure and that oversizing should be avoided. Operators who use sizing balloons to decide on device size should use the "stop flow" size and not aim to stretch a defect awaiting a significant waist on the balloon. The prospect of placing a large device (which will result in remodeling and shrinkage of the right side of the heart) into a small person remains a source of concern. Programs that do a lot of these procedures will encounter a severe complication at some point.

Patent Foramen Ovale Closure

Whereas indications for ASD closure are generally accepted, the indications for closure of PFO for the secondary prevention of stroke are not. Although the evidence of benefit is limited, the number of procedures performed and the number of operators performing them continues to grow. Major trials are presently underway (two have completed enrollment) examining whether device therapy is better or worse than medical therapy for secondary stroke prevention. These trials have been slow to recruit patients because many have been treated off label with related devices. The data arguing for closure rest mainly on evidence provided by single centers, with retrospective, non-randomized trials, and with meta-analyses that have taken unfortunate liberties in interpretation and analysis.[24,25] The result is an unclear future for this procedure.

- Which patients will benefit from a percutaneous PFO closure procedure?
- Will it be only those with atrial septal aneurysms or those with multiple prior events?
- Will the complications of PFO closure including arrhythmia, device thrombus formation, recurrent cerebrovascular events, or access complications make this therapy less attractive than medical therapy?
- Will patients with other risk factors for stroke such as diabetes or those with nonsurgical carotid disease benefit from closure as a risk reduction strategy?

Our policy regarding patients referred for PFO closure involves a detailed informed consent in which many of the issues and questions just listed are raised. Patients are rigorously screened with detailed history and physical examination, stroke-neurology consultation, brain MRI and MR angiography, coagulation testing, and rhythm monitoring. We avoid offering therapy to those with nebulous, nonspecific, and questionable symptoms for fear of recurrence of these same symptoms after closure. We offer every appropriate patient entry into a randomized trial to help resolve these issues. We tell each patient that there are no conclusive data to support closure at this time, a position supported by the American Academy of Neurology.[26] The treatment and follow-up of these ASD and PFO patients after device closure is another area of controversy. Most operators will treat with aspirin and clopidogrel for periods varying from 1 to 6 months or longer. The use of bubble studies to follow these patients with transthoracic or transesophageal echocardiography to "confirm closure" is often done as a surrogate marker for "protected"; it is commonly accepted that a minimally positive bubble study likely translates into a reduced risk of paradoxical embolism and is an acceptable result.

Coarctation of the Aorta

Stent placement for coarctation of the aorta is potentially the most hazardous of all interventions performed in the adult congenital catheter laboratory but is generally well tolerated. Patients with either native coarctation or previously treated coarctation may be candidates for therapy. In most patients the intervention will be indicated for a gradient of more than 20 mm Hg across the coarctation site, usually in the setting of proximal hypertension. Covered stents or stent grafts may also be used to treat pseudoaneurysms that have resulted from previous surgery, stenting, or angioplasty. Over the past several years we have modified our approach to this procedure to improve its safety. We routinely obtain access both from the right radial artery and the right femoral artery. This has allowed for simultaneous pressure measurement before and after stenting as well as well as immediate angiography after stent placement to rule out aortic dissection or perforation. Our approach has always been one of direct stenting (primary stenting) in the adult without progressive balloon inflation until dissection is noted and then stenting as advocated by others. Data from several sources suggest that predilation may contribute to complications.[27,28]

We began our experience with the use of the Palmaz-Schatz P5014 stent (Johnson & Johnson Interventional, Warren, NJ, USA), which provided excellent radial strength but relatively poor flexibility, and then moved to the Genesis biliary stent, which provides less radial strength in return for flexibility. In follow-up we have seen the Genesis stents fracture secondary to aortic recoil. Circumferential fractures have also been noted. We have most recently used the CP PTFE-covered stent (NuMed Inc, Hopkinton, NY, USA), which offers protection from aortic perforation and dissection, the most serious complications of this procedure. The other interesting but early observation is that no aneurysms have been observed in early follow-up after the use of covered stents in the literature.[29-31]

We have also addressed the femoral access site as a source of complication by fully anticoagulating these patients and "preclosing" the access site using a suture-mediated closure device (Perclose AT Abbott Vascular Devices, Redwood City, CA, USA). We have found that complete hemostasis is possible with few complications. The large arterial access (up to 14 Fr) required for this procedure remains a source of concern. The introduction of new covered stents for this application is anticipated and will likely become the standard of care.

Patent Ductus Arteriosus

Patent ductus arteriosus (PDA) closure in the adult is usually performed to reduce the risk of endarteritis. Guidelines suggest that all ducts with an audible murmur should be closed. PDA closure has been greatly facilitated using the Amplatzer Duct Occluder (AGA Medical Corporation). This is a well-designed device that has little competition in the adult marketplace. It is a safe and quick procedure that almost uniformly corrects the intended anatomic abnormality.

We, and others, have successfully used this versatile device to close perivalvular leaks around previously implanted mitral or aortic valve prostheses. We have limited these interventions to patients with indications of severe mitral insufficiency associated with heart failure or transfusion-dependent hemolysis who are not surgical or high-risk surgical candidates.

Transcatheter Valve Therapies

Transcatheter valve therapies represent the most exciting evolution of catheter-based therapies since the stent. There have been thousands of aortic valve implants performed with each of the leading systems, namely, the Sapien system (Edwards Life Sciences, Irvine, CA, USA) and the CoreValve Revalving system most recently acquired by Medtronic (Minneapolis, MN, USA). The two systems are remarkably different.

The Edwards system is balloon expandable and consists of a stainless steel stent with sewn bovine pericardial leaflets with a proprietary Thermafix treatment to prevent calcification. The present iteration consists of two different size valves, a 23- and a 26-mm system requiring a 22-and 24-Fr delivery system, respectively. The outer diameters of these systems are 25 and 28 Fr, respectively, and require generously sized iliofemoral systems to be viable from this route. An alternative, for those with inadequately sized iliac arteries, is the transapical route, in which a small left thoracotomy is performed and the apex of the left ventricle is accessed directly while the heart continues to beat. The large sheath is placed through an apical puncture, and the valve is delivered. Both of these approaches utilize rapid ventricular pacing to stabilize the system during balloon expansion and valve deployment. The presence of perivalvular leaks is inevitable, they are usually small and posterior and cause little hemodynamic consequence. The Sapien valve demonstrates excellent hemodynamic performance in many cases superior to comparable surgical tissue valves owing to the increased orifice area made possible by the low profile of the stent scaffolding as compared with the sewing ring of a valve. Structural deterioration has not been observed in medium-term follow-up and the results of the definite randomized U.S. Food and Drug Administration trial comparing the Sapien valve to conventional surgical aortic valve replacement in a very high risk cohort with Society of Thoracic Surgery risk scores of over 10% is nearing the end of the follow-up phase. By mid 2010 a 19-Fr system was available, and a larger 29-mm valve soon followed.

The CoreValve Revalving system consists of a goblet-shaped laser cut nitinol tube 50 mm in length to which a porcine pericardial valve has been sewn. The lower portion of the stent has high radial strength to exert force on the native annulus. The stent is convexoconcave to avoid covering the coronary arteries. The device has gone through several iterations and is presently at 18 Fr; it requires an 18-Fr sheath with an outer diameter of 21 Fr. The implant procedure is slow but deliberate and involves slowly exposing the self-expanding stent within the annulus. This is in stark contrast to the rapid balloon expansion of the Sapien system during rapid ventricular pacing. The CoreValve system is plagued by permanent pacemaker rates in the 30% range, most likely related to leaving the prosthesis too deep in the left ventricular outflow tract, and this number is expected to diminish with improvements to the system and improved training. At present the CoreValve system allows treatment of larger aortic annuli than the Sapien system, more reliable treatment of prosthetic valve stenosis, and a wider population that can be treated transfemorally. For patients with iliac arteries that are too small to accept the 21-Fr diameter required, a left subclavian approach has been performed. The design of the system is likely to change, the delivery system remains at an early stage of development, and there is substantial room for improvement.

Percutaneous mitral valve repair is a far more challenging endeavor than either aortic or pulmonary valve implantation. Whereas implantation of a stent in a tubular structure is a well-practiced technique by interventionalists, the complexity of the mitral valve does not lend itself to an easy solution. The function of the mitral valve requires the integrated function of the annulus, leaflets, chordae, papillary muscles, and ventricle. There are a variety of therapies in various stages of development. The most advanced of these therapies is the Evalve Mitraclip, which was recently acquired by Abbott Vascular (Abbott Laboratories, Abbott Park, IL, USA). The clip is made of titanium and covered with a polyester fabric. It is delivered via the transseptal route and is intended to be steered over the A2-P2 junction, lowered into the ventricle, and then withdrawn to grasp the central scallop of the anterior and posterior mitral valve leaflets, creating a repair similar to the Alfieri stitch. Evalve has completed its trial of the MitraClip versus surgery in selected patients with severe mitral insufficiency. The device has been used for degenerative, ischemic, as well as functional mitral regurgitation.[32] The device is CE marked in Europe and is commercially available.

There are a variety of approaches available for the treatment of functional mitral insufficiency, which results from annular dilation usually related to decreased ventricular function. These approaches include devices that constrict the coronary sinus, direct annular therapies, ventricular reshaping, and atrial therapies that shorten the length between the atrial septum and coronary sinus. At present only one other coronary sinus therapy is CE marked in Europe (Cardiac Dimensions, Kirkland, WA, USA). This is an exciting area of investigation for a target population that is highly symptomatic and that has had mixed results with conventional surgery.

Percutaneous Pulmonary Valve Replacement

The Medtronic Melody valve has been used in more than 1000 patients in the European Union, Canada, and the United States. At present the valve is best suited to implantation in previously placed surgical valved conduits or homografts. There has also been widespread use in patients who have undergone the Ross procedure. The valve consists of a bovine jugular vein sewn inside a CP stent. In general, the hemodynamic performance of the valve has been excellent. Early problems such as the "hammock effect," which is collapse of the middle portion of the valve causing recurrent outflow obstruction, have been overcome. Stent fractures occur but rarely influence hemodynamic performance

and can likely be reduced by prestenting the conduit. Prestenting with bare metal stents has improved scaffolding, reduced recoil, and likely improved hemodynamic outcome. The pursuit of therapies for the native outflow tract in tetralogy of Fallot and other conditions that require right ventricular outflow tract modifications is clearly in sight. There has already been implantation of the Melody valve in a narrowed right ventricular outflow tract after repair of tetralogy of Fallot.[33] There has been early use of a reducing stent in a bench model,[34] animal model,[35] and native outflow tract of a patient with tetralogy. Although the patient with a conduit or previous surgical valve remains an excellent candidate for a percutaneous valve, it is the pursuit of the population with large irregularly shaped outflow tracts that comprise the majority of the population.

The Sapien valve has also been implanted in patients with right ventricle to pulmonary artery conduits.[36] The early results are encouraging in short-term follow-up. The Sapien valve allows for the treatment of patients with conduits too large to anchor a Melody valve, which has a maximum size of 22 mm. The valve is also shorter (14 to 16 mm), which may be helpful in some anatomies. A distinct advantage to the Melody valve is its functionality in size between 16 and 22 mm, whereas the Sapien functions from 21 to 23 mm with the smaller valve and from 24 to 26 mm with the larger valve. Often, with these procedures, the size of the surgical conduit is known but the final size that will be achieved with prestenting is not.

LOOK AT NEW AND EMERGING INTERVENTIONS

A growth of hybrid surgical/interventional procedures that involve sophisticated imaging to examine physiology and anatomy immediately before and after repair is inevitable. Hybrid procedures are gaining popularity in the pediatric world (Fig. 9-24). Until transapical aortic valve replacement became more commonplace these types of procedures were a rarity in the adult. With collaborations established between like-minded surgeons and interventionalists numerous possibilities abound for working together. This may include transapical approaches to the mitral valve (native or prosthetic), approaches to the tricuspid valve on a beating heart of for prosthetic stenosis or regurgitation, or procedures that involve the surgical plication of the main pulmonary artery with subsequent transcatheter valve placement.

Many leading centers have invested in structural heart disease suites that take into account the need for operating room standard ventilation, lighting, anesthesia, and perfusion. The ability to operate in the catheter laboratory as well as the ability to perform cross-sectional imaging with a dedicated CT scanner or with a rotational protocol and a standard C-arm provides a tremendous background on which to grow. The addition of 3D echocardiography, especially in later iterations, will provide unparalleled appreciation of physiology and structure and will be a very helpful tool.

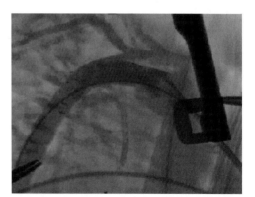

Figure 9-24 Angiogram obtained in the main pulmonary artery outlining the arterial duct after stent implantation. The delivery sheath was placed through an incision in the main pulmonary artery during a hybrid procedure (bilateral pulmonary artery bands and ductal stent) in the catheterization laboratory for management of hypoplastic left heart syndrome.

The teamwork between specialties will no doubt lead to a disruption of our present understanding of our roles in patient care. No longer will a particular silo dictate what a surgeon or interventionalist can and should do as part of practice. Training, experience, and results will dictate who should be doing what and where.

Surgical strategies for repair will take into account interventional advances, and childhood operations will be modified so that an interventional solution to a future reoperation may be possible. An example may be the performance of a modified hemi-Fontan operation to allow for its completion in the catheterization laboratory with a covered stent from the IVC to the pulmonary artery (Fig. 9-25). We may see the implantation of fewer mechanical valves, permitting the percutaneous implantation of tissue valves within failing surgically implanted stented tissue valves, which will serve as a matrix on which to build.

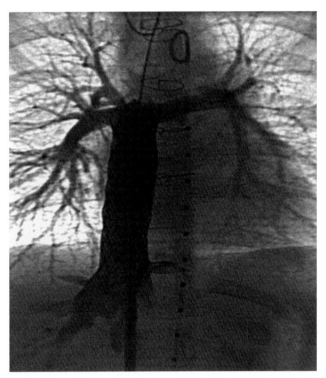

Figure 9-25   Frontal projection of an injection in a covered stent placed percutaneously to complete the Fontan circulation.

Guidance for these new procedures will likely involve 3D imaging modalities and device manipulation and stabilization during the procedures, requiring that new expertise be developed. We live in interesting times, but they are certain to become more interesting as structures as divinely inspired as the mitral valve become the substance of everyday catheterization laboratory repair.

FUTURE ROLE OF DIAGNOSTIC CATHETERIZATION IN THE ADULT PATIENT WITH CONGESTIVE HEART DISEASE

It is probable that what we now know of diagnostic catheterization will change dramatically. A diagnostic catheterization may be expected to be performed in an imaging suite. Who the operator will be remains in question. A structural map may be created with cross-sectional imaging, and then the navigation through tortuous pulmonary arteries, vessel occlusions, or transseptally will be done with a 0.014-inch wire with a pressure transducer and a radiofrequency ablation assembly at its tip. The guidance of this small device may be solely magnetic. A nurse may place a peripheral intravenous line through which such a device is introduced. We may measure oximetry in various chambers using similar wire tip technology without the need for blood sampling. The need for large devices such as balloons and stents will continue to require access to a large or central vein to permit their introduction.

The ACHD patient may no longer wait for different appointments for different imaging modalities but will pass through a series of scanners in the course of an hour. The coronary arteries may be visualized via CT; the stenosed pulmonary artery and the gradient across it assessed by MRI; and this will be followed by the crossing of the stenosis by a magnetically directed wire over which a balloon and stent will be introduced.

Will contrast angiography survive independent of interventional catheterization? It may not, at least not in its present form. Diagnostic catheterization will not disappear; but it will change. It will be less invasive, use less or no contrast enhancement, and may take place with the operator sitting in a control room using navigational equipment. To run an aircraft carrier, one need not turn a crank to drive the propeller.

CONCLUSION

This short introduction to diagnostic and interventional heart catheterization in the adult patient with CHD will allow the reader a point of departure for the invasive assessment and interventional treatment of the most common lesions. However, many cases occur that do not fall into a standard categorization and the operator must be prepared to remember the basic principles outlined in this chapter and use creative approaches to optimally define and treat the lesion. Successful outcomes require patience, perseverance, and the learned experience of others.

REFERENCES

1. Angelini P. Abnormalities of the coronary arteries: normal and anomalous coronary arteries: definitions and classification. Am Heart J 1989;117:418–434.
2. Greenberg MA, Fish BG, Spindola-Franco H. Congenital anomalies of the coronary arteries. Radiol Clin North Am 1989;27:1127–1146.
3. Ishikawa T, Brandt PWT. Anomalous origin of the left main coronary artery from the right anterior aortic sinus: angiographic definition of anomalous course. Am J Cardiol 1985;55:770–776.
4. Serota H, Barth CW, Seuc CA, et al. Rapid identification of the course of anomalous coronary arteries in adults: the "dot and eye" method. Am J Cardiol 1990;65:891–898.
5. Culham JAG. Physical principles of image formation and projections in angiocardiography. In: Freedom RM, Mawson JB, Yoo SJ, Benson LN, editors. Congenital Heart Disease Textbook of Angiocardiography. Armonk, NY: Futura Publishing; 1997. p. 39–93.
6. Beekman 3rd RH, Hellenbrand WE, Lloyd TR, et al. ACCF/AHA/AAP recommendations for training in pediatric cardiology: Task force 3: training guidelines for pediatric cardiac catheterization and interventional cardiology endorsed by the Society for Cardiovascular Angiography and Interventions. J Am Coll Cardiol 2005;46:1388–1390.
7. Qureshi SA, Redington AN, Wren C, et al. Recommendations of the British Paediatric Cardiac Association for therapeutic cardiac catheterisation in congenital cardiac disease. Cardiol Young 2000;10:649–667.
8. Ventricular septal defect. In: Freedom RM, Mawson JB, Yoo SJ, Benson LN, editors. Congenital Heart Disease Textbook of Angiocardiography. Armonk, NY: Futura Publishing; 1997. p. 189–218.
9. Brandt PW. Axially angled angiocardiography. Cardiovasc Intervent Radiol 1984;7:166–169.
10. Griffith MJ, Carey C, Coltart DJ, et al. Inaccuracies of using aortic valve gradients alone to grade severity of aortic stenosis. Br Heart J 1989;62:372–378.
11. Rahimtoola SH. Should patients with asymptomatic mild or moderate aortic stenosis undergoing coronary artery bypass surgery also have valve replacement for their aortic stenosis? Heart 2001;85:337–341.
12. Therrien J, Dore A, Gersony W. Canadian Cardiovascular Society Consensus Conference 2001 update: Recommendations for the Management of Adults with Congenital Heart Disease: I. Can J Cardiol 2001;17:943–1158.
13. Ferencz C, Rubin JD, McCarter RJ, et al. Congenital Heart Disease: Prevalence at Livebirth. The Baltimore-Washington Infant Study. Am J Epidemiol 1985;121:31–36.
14. Deanfield J, Thaulow E, Warnes C, et al. Management of grown up congenital heart disease. The Task Force on the Management of Grown up Congenital Heart Disease of the European Society of Cardiology. Eur Heart J 2003;24:1035–1084.
15. Anzai H, Child J, Natterson B, et al. Incidence of thrombus formation on the CardioSEAL and the Amplatzer interatrial closure devices. Am J Cardiol 2004;93:426–431.
16. Krumsdorf U, Ostermayer S, Billinger K, et al. Incidence and clinical course of thrombus formation on atrial septal defect and patent foramen ovale closure devices in 1,000 consecutive patients. J Am Coll Cardiol 2004;43:302–309.
17. Veldtman GR, Razack V, Siu S, et al. Right ventricular form and function after percutaneous atrial septal defect device closure. J Am Coll Cardiol 2001;37:2108–2113.
18. Giardini A, Donti A, Formigari R, et al. Determinants of cardiopulmonary functional improvement after transcatheter atrial septal defect closure in asymptomatic adults. J Am Coll Cardiol 2004;43:1886–1891.
19. Webb G, Horlick EM. Lessons from cardiopulmonary testing after device closure of secundum atrial septal defects: a tale of two ventricles. J Am Coll Cardiol 2004;43:1892–1893.
20. Brochu MC, Baril JF, Dore A, et al. Improvement in exercise capacity in asymptomatic and mildly symptomatic adults after atrial septal defect percutaneous closure. Circulation 2002;106:1821.
21. Silversides CK, Siu SC, McLaughlin PR. Symptomatic atrial arrhythmias and transcatheter closure of atrial septal defects in adult patients. Heart 2004;90:1194–1198.
22. Amin Z, Hijazi Z, Bass JL. Erosion of Amplatzer septal occluder device after closure of secundum atrial septal defects: review of registry of complications and recommendations to minimize future risk. Catheter Cardiovasc Interv 2004;63:496–502.
23. Divekar A, Gaamangwe T, Shaikh N, et al. Cardiac perforation after device closure of atrial septal defects with the Amplatzer septal occluder. J Am Coll Cardiol 2005;45:1213–1218.

24. Windecker S, Wahl A, Nedeltchev K, et al. Comparison of medical treatment with percutaneous closure of patent foramen ovale in patients with cryptogenic stroke. J Am Coll Cardiol 2004;44:750–758.

25. Landzberg MJ, Khairy P. Indications for the closure of patent foramen ovale. Heart 2004;90:219–224.

26. Messe SR, Silverman IE, Kizer JR, et al. Practice parameter: recurrent stroke with patent foramen ovale and atrial septal aneurysm: report of the Quality Standards Subcommittee of the American Academy of Neurology. Neurology 2004;62: 1042–1050.

27. Qureshi AM, McElhinney DB, Lock JE, et al. Acute and intermediate outcomes, and evaluation of injury to the aortic wall, as based on 15 years experience of implanting stents to treat aortic coarctation. Cardiol Young 2007;17:307–318.

28. Forbes TJ, Moore P, Pedra CA, et al. Intermediate follow-up following intravascular stenting for treatment of coarctation of the aorta. Catheter Cardiovasc Interv 2007;70:569–677.

29. Butera G, Piazza L, Chessa M, et al. Covered stents in patients with complex aortic coarctations. Am Heart J 2007;154:795–800.

30. Tzifa A, Ewert P, Brzezinska-Rajszys G, et al. Covered Cheatham-platinum stents for aortic coarctation: early and intermediate-term results. J Am Coll Cardiol 2006;47:1457–1463.

31. Tanous D, Collins N, Dehghani P, et al. Covered stents in the management of coarctation of the aorta in the adult: initial results and 1-year angiographic and hemodynamic follow-up. Int J Cardiol 2010;140:287–295 Dec 17 [Epub ahead of print].

32. Feldman T, Kar S, Rinaldi M, et al. EVEREST Investigators. Percutaneous mitral repair with the MitraClip system: safety and midterm durability in the initial EVEREST (Endovascular Valve Edge-to-Edge Repair Study) cohort. J Am Coll Cardiol 2009;54:686–694.

33. Momenah TS, El Oakley R, Al Najashi K, et al. Extended application of percutaneous pulmonary valve implantation. J Am Coll Cardiol 2009;53:1859–1863.

34. Vismara R, Laganà K, Migliavacca F, et al. Experimental setup to evaluate the performance of percutaneous pulmonary valved stent in different outflow tract morphologies. Artif Organs 2009;33:46–53.

35. Amahzoune B, Szymansky C, Fabiani JN, Zegdi R. A new endovascular size reducer for large pulmonary outflow tract. Eur J Cardiothorac Surg 2010;37:730–732.

36. Boone RH, Webb JG, Horlick E, et al. Transcatheter pulmonary valve implantation using the Edwards SAPIEN transcatheter heart valve. Catheter Cardiovasc Interv 2010;75:286–294.

10

Late Repair and Reoperations in Adults with Congenital Heart Disease

DARRYL F. SHORE | MATINA PRAPA

Introduction

Advances in cardiology and cardiac surgery have transformed the outlook for patients with congenital heart disease (CHD) so that currently 85% of neonates with CHD survive into adult life. The majority of adults with CHD require lifelong cardiologic surveillance. A number of these patients will require further surgical management related both to the underlying diagnosis and to the techniques employed at the initial reparative surgery. The need for surgical intervention is a constantly fluid situation influenced by length of follow-up, our improved understanding of the late pathophysiology after reparative surgery, and the increasing role of interventional cardiology. Nevertheless, at the present time, surgical needs of the adult patient with CHD pose a rapidly increasing demand on the time of the surgeon who specializes in CHD and carry with them a unique set of complex surgical challenges.

Special Considerations

There are several features in performing reparative surgery in the adult that are either unique or of much greater importance in this population, namely, the systemic effects of chronic cyanosis, ventricular hypertrophy, and abnormalities of ventricular function and the frequency and importance of postoperative arrhythmias (Box 10-1). Cyanosis in adults with CHD undergoing surgery is an independent predictor of early mortality owing to the combined effects of chronic cyanosis on hemostasis and renal and ventricular function.[1] Long-standing cyanosis produces difficulties obtaining postoperative hemostasis. Secondary erythrocytosis and the preceding hyperviscosity are well established in patients with cyanotic CHD and are thought to be major contributors to the coagulation abnormalities often observed in these patients.[2] In addition, chronic cyanosis leads to the development of profuse acquired collateral vessels that are friable and difficult to coagulate. Difficulties in perioperative hemostasis associated with chronic cyanosis may be compounded by extensive suture lines and often long bypass times, leading to decrease in platelet activity and numbers and consumption of coagulation factors with fibrinolysis.

The following measures are employed to assist in postoperative hemostasis:
- Administration of aminocaproic and tranexamic acid
- Meticulous hemostasis during sternotomy and dissection
- Administration of platelets, fresh frozen plasma, and cryoprecipitate guided by laboratory estimation. It is important that these products are available immediately after protamine administration.
- Use of continuous ultrafiltration during cardiopulmonary bypass and modified ultrafiltration after the completion of cardiopulmonary bypass along with a cell saver to raise the hematocrit
- Use of fibrin glue for application to suture lines

Many cyanotic patients have limited cardiac reserve and excessive postoperative blood loss that regardless of whether re-intervention for control of bleeding is needed may lead to hemodynamic instability and may compromise outcome. The importance of meticulous postoperative surgical hemostasis, therefore, cannot be overemphasized for these patients.

Renal dysfunction is a well-recognized complication of long-standing CHD. The prominent feature of cyanotic nephropathy is glomerular damage. Risk factors for postoperative acute renal failure in cyanotic patients are the existence of preoperative glomerulopathy and longer cardiopulmonary bypass time and surgery on complex cardiac lesions, which predisposes to low cardiac output postoperatively.[3] Therefore, renal status in cyanotic patients should influence the planning of surgery; and the maintenance of cardiac output, renal blood flow, and meticulous fluid balance is essential to reduce the risk of postoperative renal failure.

Patients with chronic cyanosis have also an increased propensity to perioperative myocardial injury:
- This propensity to myocardial injury is multifactorial.
- The cyanotic patient is more sensitive to the damaging effects of free oxygen radicals.
- The acquired collateral circulation may involve the coronary arterial tree and result in wash-out of cardioplegia.
- Increased pulmonary venous return may lead to ventricular distention.
- The presence of ventricular hypertrophy also adds to the difficulty of providing adequate myocardial preservation.

These difficulties are overcome by the more frequent administration of cardioplegic solution, venting of the heart to prevent overdistention, and, in some cases, the use of low-flow hypothermic cardiopulmonary bypass.

A common complication of cardiac surgery in adults with CHD is lung reperfusion injury. Cardiopulmonary bypass has been shown to initiate a systemic inflammatory response that can lead to pulmonary dysfunction ranging from subclinical functional changes to acute respiratory distress syndrome. Several potential therapeutic techniques are being applied, such as the use of heparin-coated circuits and continuous hemofiltration. Additional care must be taken when surgery has resulted in an increase in pulmonary blood flow; meticulous fluid balance with maintenance of cardiac output is required in these patients.

Ventricular hypertrophy, together with the attendant difficulties of myocardial preservation during cardiopulmonary bypass and ischemic arrest, predisposes to a postoperative low-output state due to poor ventricular compliance. A relationship between myocardial injury and "restrictive physiology" has been demonstrated in children undergoing repair of tetralogy of Fallot.[4] *Cardiac arrhythmias,* both ventricular and supraventricular, are common in adults with uncorrected cyanotic CHD. Indeed, the occurrence of arrhythmias may be the cause of sudden symptomatic deterioration. In the postoperative period arrhythmias may be responsible for the sudden onset of severe low-output states. Arrhythmias must be immediately evaluated and promptly treated. The surgeon must ensure the presence of functioning atrial and ventricular pacing wires to assist in arrhythmia management.

The management of atrial septal defect, atrioventricular septal defect, ventricular septal defect, pulmonary valve stenosis, coarctation of the aorta, and aortic valve disease are all dealt with in detail elsewhere. The indications for surgery and surgical techniques do not differ significantly from those in the pediatric population, except in the area of arrhythmia management.

The data supporting the view in favor of closing atrial septal defects in the adult population, both for symptomatic relief and for improved prognosis, have now gained universal acceptance.[5] Recently, attention has focused on the importance of postoperative atrial arrhythmias increasing morbidity and mortality after closure and the role of arrhythmia surgery in their prevention. Theodoro and colleagues[6] have demonstrated the efficacy of arrhythmia surgery as an adjunct to surgical repair of Ebstein anomaly and atrial septal defect closure. Although the majority of secundum atrial septal defects are now amenable to transcatheter device closure, surgical closure may be required for a minority of secundum atrial septal defects and presently for all sinus venosus and primum atrial septal defects. Adult patients older than 40 years of age with preoperative atrial flutter or fibrillation should be considered for concomitant arrhythmia intervention at the time of closure of an atrial septal defect.[7] Indeed, the role of arrhythmia surgery as an adjunct to the primary correction of any right-sided lesion in the adult population is a subject for ongoing research and evaluation.

Management of Arrhythmias Associated with Right-Sided Lesions Requiring Surgical Intervention

TYPE OF ARRHYTHMIA

Atrial Fibrillation
Atrial fibrillation almost always originates from the left atrium or the pulmonary vein and should be managed by surgical left atrial ablation at the time of surgical intervention.

Supraventricular Tachycardias Originating Within the Right Atrium
These are mostly reentry tachycardias, which may be atrioventricular reentry tachycardias, atrial reentry tachycardias, or, more rarely, atrioventricular nodal reentry tachycardias. Our current thinking is that these should be treated by mapping and ablation in the catheter laboratory before surgery. The advantage of such an approach is that catheter ablations may abort the need for targeting the arrhythmia at operation, thereby reducing the bypass time and the operative risk. It also reduces the risk of arrhythmia during induction and anesthesia.

Ventricular Tachycardia
When patients present with episodes of documented (or strongly suspected) ventricular tachycardia, they should undergo preoperative mapping and ablation where possible before surgery. Reentry ventricular tachycardia may occur around the right ventricular outflow tract patch, the ventricular septal defect patch, or the scar commonly present in the right ventricular free wall. If at cardiac catheterization the ventricular tachycardia cannot be induced, the site of the ventricular tachycardia can be assessed by pace mapping, following which an ablation line is made from the presumed site of tachycardia to a nonconductable area, for example, the pulmonary valve in the case of an infundibular outflow tract patch or between a right ventricular free wall scar and a right ventricular outflow tract patch. After operation those patients who have poor right and/or left ventricular function, with evidence of extensive ventricular or right ventricular fibrosis

on gadolinium-enhanced cardiac magnetic resonance imaging, and those with a marked prolongation of QRS duration, should receive an implantable cardiac defibrillator. In addition, patients who had inducible ventricular tachycardia without successful ablation also receive an implantable cardiac defibrillator. Patients who have maintained ventricular function, have a narrow QRS complex, and have minimal scarring are clearly a very low risk group. There remains, however, a group in the middle who do not fall into either of the previous categories and for whom the indications for implantation of a cardiac defibrillator remain uncertain at present.

CORONARY ARTERIOGRAPHY

The assessment of any adult with CHD and the need for coronary arteriography before surgery are dictated by the individual features, the sex and age of the patient, the presence of risk factors, the presence of angina or electrocardiographic evidence of ischemia, reduced ventricular function, and history of suspected or confirmed coronary artery disease. There has been a consensus for routine assessment with selective coronary angiography for patients older than 40 years of age referred for CHD surgery.[8]

Coronary arteriography may reveal:
- The presence of atheromatous coronary artery disease
- An anomalous origin of the left anterior descending from the right coronary artery. It is particularly important to be aware of this anomaly in any reoperation involving surgery on the right ventricular outflow tract. Surgical adhesions may prevent identification of this vessel at the time of operation. Iatrogenic damage to the left anterior descending artery during previous surgery may be identified.
- Patients with anomalous origin of the left coronary artery from the pulmonary trunk
- Patients with congenital coronary arteriovenous fistula presenting with a continuous murmur in adulthood

Ultrafast CT angiography is an alternative that is particularly suitable for patients with very large arteries in whom selective coronary cannulation may be challenging or risky.

PRIMARY CORRECTION IN ADULT LIFE

The principal reasons for late correction include the following:
- Late diagnosis; this is particularly true of atrial septal defect and coarctation of the aorta.
- Balanced systemic and pulmonary blood flow in more complex lesions; this can occur either naturally or after palliation.
- When the condition was previously considered inoperable
- When there was no local surgical facility in patients being referred for surgery from overseas

Patients considered for primary correction in adult life can be divided into those with cyanotic and those with noncyanotic heart disease. Those with cyanotic heart disease include patients with a diagnosis of ventricular septal defect and right ventricular outflow tract obstruction, tetralogy of Fallot, and pulmonary atresia with ventricular septal defect. Late repair of patients with univentricular heart circulations is discussed in Chapters 51, 52, and 53.

All patients with cyanotic heart disease and a biventricular heart should be considered for repair. Patients who consider themselves symptom free nearly always have objective evidence of reduced exercise capacity. Deterioration can be due to increasing cyanosis, the development of new arrhythmias, ventricular dysfunction, or the development of aortic regurgitation and coronary artery disease. Patients with pulmonary atresia have the worst prognosis in which survival without surgical repair beyond the fifth decade is exceptional.[9]

Patients with noncyanotic heart disease who are considered for primary repair in adult life include those with a diagnosis of atrial septal defect with pulmonary stenosis, aortic valve disease, and left ventricular outflow tract obstruction, including subvalvular aortic stenosis and coarctation of the aorta.

SELECTION FOR OPERATION

Tetralogy of Fallot

Detailed assessment of the pulmonary vascular tree is essential when considering reparative surgery. Patients with tetralogy of Fallot without pulmonary atresia usually have central pulmonary arteries, although rarely the right or left pulmonary artery may be absent. Either the main or left and right pulmonary artery may be hypoplastic. There may be naturally occurring stenoses or stenoses related to the presence of previously performed shunts. Whenever possible, pulmonary artery pressure should be measured. It is particularly important to exclude the presence of pulmonary vascular disease, which, although uncommon, can occur due to overshunting.

All systemic to pulmonary artery shunts (see Chapter 43) have the potential to cause distortion and narrowing of the pulmonary artery. The Waterston and Pott shunts (now rarely encountered) are those more likely to be associated with pulmonary vascular disease. Their takedown requires the use of cardiopulmonary bypass, and repair of the pulmonary artery is almost always required.

Preoperative investigation should also include an assessment of biventricular function, assessment of the size of the ascending aorta and aortic valve function, presence of multiple ventricular septal defects, presence or absence of major aortopulmonary collateral vessels, and assessment of the coronary artery anatomy.

Pulmonary Atresia and Ventricular Septal Defect

Pulmonary atresia and ventricular septal defect may be associated with central pulmonary arteries and unifocal pulmonary blood supply. In these patients the same considerations discussed in tetralogy of Fallot apply.

The pulmonary blood supply is often multifocal, with segments of one or both lungs supplied by major aortopulmonary collateral arteries. The distribution of the major aortopulmonary collateral arteries must be carefully elucidated together with the pressure within them and the presence or not of peripheral pulmonary artery stenoses. In pulmonary atresia, with multifocal pulmonary blood supply the central, native pulmonary arteries may be present, hypoplastic, or absent.

In patients with pulmonary atresia and multifocal pulmonary blood supply, unifocalization of major aortopulmonary collaterals may be required on one or both sides before, or as part of, surgical repair.[9,10] This is dealt with in more detail in Chapter 44.

Occasionally, when lung segments receive dual blood supply from native pulmonary arteries and major aortopulmonary collaterals, preoperative embolization of the latter should be considered to facilitate operative repair. The remainder of the preoperative assessment mirrors that of tetralogy of Fallot with pulmonary stenosis, although aortic regurgitation and impairment of ventricular function are more likely in patients with pulmonary atresia.

Previous Banding of the Pulmonary Trunk

Occasionally patients are considered for primary repair who originally had left-to-right shunts at ventricular level and had undergone banding of the pulmonary trunk. Pulmonary arterial bands may have been placed in the setting of ventricular arterial concordance or discordance. When considering surgical repair, pulmonary artery anatomy must be defined, particularly the presence or absence of origin stenosis of the right or left pulmonary artery. Furthermore, the pulmonary vascular resistance and the function of the pulmonary valve need to be assessed.

Reoperation

The vast majority of procedures performed on adults with CHD are reoperations. Common reoperations include conduit or pulmonary valve replacement, pulmonary valve insertion for regurgitation after repair of tetralogy of Fallot, redo aortic valve replacement after previous aortic valve surgery or balloon valvuloplasty, and re-coarctation of the aorta. Less common reoperations include Fontan conversion and operations for prosthetic or native atrioventricular valve dysfunction, pathway obstruction after atrial repair for transposition of the great arteries, and endocarditis.

The need for reoperation after reparative surgery is a constantly changing situation. As postoperative follow-up increases, leading to the emergence of new pathologic processes, such as aortic root dilation and aortic valve regurgitation after repair of tetralogy of Fallot,[11,12] and a better understanding of the optimal timing for re-intervention is necessary to prevent irreversible myocardial injury. The surgeon must be fully conversant with the previous operative procedure during the planning phase of reoperation. Wherever possible, he or she should read the previous operative notes to become familiar with any unusual features or complications. The surgeon also should understand the late sequelae related to the operative procedure and the mode of failure of synthetic material(s) and prosthetic valve(s) used in the repair.

A detailed discussion of the indications for reoperation in each diagnostic category is beyond the scope of this chapter and is provided elsewhere. Common to all reoperations is the need for re-sternotomy, which is planned and performed in such a way to eliminate or reduce to a minimum the chances of damage to cardiac structures, great vessels, or extracardiac conduits.

The first requirement is to establish the relationship of these structures to the inner table of the sternum. This is best achieved by magnetic resonance imaging in both the anteroposterior and lateral views. In some cases a clear space can be seen between the inner table of the sternum and the cardiac structures allowing for uncomplicated re-sternotomy. Conversely, there may be either no discernible space or actual distortion or erosion of the inner table, particularly by a dilated right ventricle or extracardiac conduit. Of particular concern is the presence retrosternally of a thin-walled right ventricular aneurysm or dilated ascending aorta. Detailed anatomic information and spatial relationships can be obtained with preoperative magnetic resonance imaging.

In addition to the assessment of the retrosternal space, preoperative assessment for reoperation in the adult follows the patterns for patients undergoing primary correction. Because many of these patients will be undergoing reoperation for right-sided lesions, assessment of the pulmonary vasculature is paramount, particularly in relation to potential pulmonary artery stenosis. The latter, if of long standing, may have a bearing on the durability of replaced valves and conduits. Consideration should be given to balloon dilation and stenting of peripheral pulmonary artery stenosis preoperatively or intraoperatively. Proximal pulmonary artery stenoses are best dealt with surgically at the time of reoperation. If major aortopulmonary collaterals are present, consideration should be given to preoperative embolization. Note should be taken of any aortic regurgitation, because although not necessarily hemodynamically significant, it may have a bearing on the conduct of cardiopulmonary bypass and administration of cardioplegia. In any case, a detailed treatment plan should be created jointly by cardiac surgeons and cardiologists, particularly when presurgical and postsurgical catheter intervention is contemplated.

Conduct of Re-sternotomy

In all cases in which the preoperative investigations suggest risk to right-sided structures, exposure of femoral artery and vein are performed before re-sternotomy, so that in the event of venous hemorrhage, femorofemoral bypass can be established rapidly. This immediately allows blood salvage, control of systemic blood flow, and systemic blood pressure and the lowering of venous pressure, which is usually sufficient to continue retrosternal dissection.

If preoperative assessment suggests a high risk of damage to right-sided structures, then heparinization and femoral-femoral cardiopulmonary bypass should be begun before re-sternotomy. In those cases in which there is a risk of catastrophic hemorrhage, for example, in the presence of an extensive retrosternal right ventricular aneurysm or a markedly dilated ascending aorta closely applied to the sternum, a technique of cardiopulmonary bypass, hypothermia, and a short period of circulatory arrest during re-sternotomy may be employed. When the heart fibrillates during cooling, it may be necessary to massage the heart to prevent distention until cooling is complete. Alternatively, a vent may be inserted through the apex of the ventricle through a small anterior thoracotomy incision.

Replacement of Conduit

Conduits or prosthetic valves used in reconstruction of the right ventricular outflow tract or the establishment of ventricular pulmonary artery continuity will eventually require replacement. Caldarone and colleagues,[13] in a large retrospective study after surgery for CHD, showed a 20-year freedom from valve or valve conduit replacement of 40%. Before conduit replacement the need to evaluate pulmonary and coronary artery anatomy has already been discussed. Tricuspid regurgitation often develops in the setting of conduit stenosis and if more than mild may require tricuspid annuloplasty. Aortic regurgitation associated with dilation of the aortic root can also develop after repair of pulmonary atresia and ventricular septal defect[14] and, more rarely, after repair of tetralogy of Fallot and may be the principal indication for reoperation. Eighty-five percent of conduits require replacement for conduit stenosis with or without regurgitation. Conduit insufficiency in isolation, aneurysm formation, and endocarditis are other indications, albeit uncommon.

Pulmonary Valve Replacement After Repair of Tetralogy of Fallot

As the length of follow-up after repair of tetralogy of Fallot increases, so, too, does the percentage of patients requiring pulmonary valve replacement. The precise indications and timing of pulmonary valve replacement for pulmonary insufficiency and/or residual pulmonary stenosis after repair of tetralogy of Fallot is a subject for ongoing research, and a detailed discussion is outside the scope of this chapter. The presence of symptoms, heart size, arrhythmias, evidence of right ventricular dysfunction, QRS prolongation, tricuspid regurgitation, and impaired exercise capacity may all influence the decision. Interval change in one or more these parameters is an important consideration. Preoperative evaluation follows the principles outlined earlier.

Patients without symptoms who do not meet any of the accepted criteria for surgical intervention must be closely observed. Meijboom and associates[15] reported 11% of their asymptomatic patients with severe pulmonary regurgitation who did not undergo pulmonary valve replacement for the regurgitation per se had an unsatisfactory outcome with prolongation of QRS complex duration, development of arrhythmias, and unsatisfactory resolution of symptoms after later pulmonary valve replacement as a result of this policy. These risks have to be balanced against those of repeated reoperation required as a result of prosthetic valve degeneration from earlier intervention. However, the "preparation" of the right ventricular outflow tract at the time of surgical pulmonary valve replacement for later percutaneous pulmonary valve replacement and the ability to perform percutaneous pulmonary valve replacement into a wider right ventricular outflow tract than is presently possible may tilt the balance in favor of earlier surgical pulmonary valve replacement.

In the absence of a residual atrial or ventricular septal defect and when extensive pulmonary arterial reconstruction or tricuspid valve surgery is not required, the operation can be performed without ischemic arrest of the heart. This also applies to the replacement of right ventricular pulmonary artery conduits and is of particular advantage when right ventricular impairment is present. Severe pulmonary regurgitation occurring in patients operated on in an early surgical era is often associated with the use of large right ventricular outflow tract or transannular patches. It is often possible to excise these large patches and remodel the right ventricular outflow tract and so reduce the size of any akinetic segments. When nonstented valves are used for pulmonary valve replacement, it is important to restore the geometry of the outflow tract at the level of the ventriculoarterial junction to prevent distortion of the geometry of the prosthetic valve and avoid the risk of early prosthetic valve regurgitation. If this cannot be achieved, it is prudent to use a stented prosthesis. In the adult there is little evidence at present to support the use of any particular bioprosthesis in terms of prosthetic valve or patient survival. The guidelines for the management of patients with valvular heart disease by the American College of Cardiology and the American Heart Association state that pulmonary valve replacement is usually performed with a homograft or xenograft with low risk,[16] albeit some studies support that the use of mechanical valve prostheses has promising results.[17] The implantation of a bioprosthesis requires several reoperations with the risk of mortality, whereas the implantation of a metallic prosthesis necessitates anticoagulant therapy with a greater risk of morbidity.

Reoperation After Atrial Switch for Transposition of the Great Arteries

Reoperation is rarely required in the adult population for systemic or pulmonary venous obstruction after atrial switch. In most instances, systemic venous obstruction may now effectively be dealt with by balloon dilation and stenting. Reoperations vary in complexity from simple augmentation of venous pathways to enlargement of the pulmonary venous atrium to complete excision and revision of the intra-atrial baffles, usually where synthetic material was used for the initial repair.

Pathway obstruction after atrial switch may be associated with impairment of right ventricular function. The degree of impairment can be difficult to assess in the setting of pulmonary venous obstruction. Nevertheless, great care must be taken to preserve right ventricular function both by avoiding damage to the right ventricle during re-sternotomy and optimizing myocardial preservation. In our experience, right ventricular dysfunction has not been a cause of low cardiac output after revision of an atrial switch.

Recurrent Coarctation

Re-coarctation occurring in the adult population is rarely a simple problem. Re-coarctation may be associated with hypoplasia of the aortic arch, aneurysmal dilation of the ascending aorta, and coexisting intracardiac pathology, usually in the form of aortic valvular disease. Aneurysm formation at the site of coarctation repair may or may not be associated with re-coarctation. Both true and false aneurysms occur and if not detected on routine follow-up may present at the time of rupture. Cardiovascular magnetic resonance imaging is the diagnostic modality of choice and, therefore, recommended for all patients with previous coarctation repair.

We have reviewed the results of reoperation for re-coarctation in the adult through a left thoracotomy and found the postoperative complications of postoperative bleeding, false aneurysm formation, and residual or recurrent coarctation were all more common, compared with primary repair of coarctation during adulthood.[18]

For this reason in cases of complex re-coarctation (with hypoplasia of the aortic arch, aortic/mitral valve involvement, or ischemic heart disease), we would consider repair through a median sternotomy placing a conduit between the ascending and descending aorta approached through the posterior pericardium. The advantage of this approach is that it deals effectively with associated arch hypoplasia.[19] It avoids the often difficult dissection of the lung and collateral circulation associated with re-thoracotomy. It eliminates the risk of damage to the recurrent laryngeal nerve, which is often intermittently bound to vascular structures by fibrous tissue at the site of re-coarctation. Approach through a re-thoracotomy can still be required for the excision of expanding or ruptured aneurysms associated with re-coarctation or occurring at the site of previous coarctation repair.

Whether for re-coarctation or excision of aneurysm, reoperation must involve careful preservation of perfusion in the descending thoracic aorta. When the collateral circulation is inadequate (often the case of re-coarctation in adults), our preference is to use cardiopulmonary bypass, either atriofemoral or femoral-femoral, to maintain descending thoracic perfusion during the period of aortic cross-clamping. Cardiopulmonary bypass with hypothermia and circulatory arrest may be required in the most complex cases of ruptured aortic aneurysm.

The management of re-coarctation and associated aneurysms is being revolutionized by the application of endovascular stents, and again each case should be discussed jointly between surgeons and cardiologists to determine the most appropriate management strategy.

CONCLUSION

Adults with CHD with or without previous palliative or reparative procedures represent a unique patient population posing constant challenges to the congenital heart surgeon. Additional risk factors exist for these patients—particularly for those with chronic cyanosis—and specialized surgical expertise and specific perioperative measures are required for optimal outcomes. The best model of care for these patients involves a multidisciplinary approach with surgical and cardiologic teams working together. Additional resources for patient care, training, and research are required to provide for this growing patient population.

REFERENCES

1. Dove A, Glancy DL, Stone S, et al. Cardiac surgery for grown-up congenital heart patients: survey of 307 consecutive operations from 1991 to 1994. Am J Cardiol 1977;80:906–913.
2. Tempe DS, Virmani S. Coagulation abnormalities in patients with cyanotic congenital heart disease. J Cardiothorac Vasc Anaesth 2002;16:752–765.
3. Dittrich S, Kurschat K, Dähnert I, et al. Renal function after cardiopulmonary bypass surgery in cyanotic congenital heart disease. Int J Cardiol 2000;73:173–179.
4. Chaturvedi RR, Shore DF, Lincoln C, et al. Acute right ventricular restrictive physiology after repair of tetralogy of Fallot: association with myocardial injury and oxidative stress. Circulation 1999;14:1540–1547.
5. Attie F, Rosas M, Granados N, et al. Surgical treatment for secundum atrial septal defects in patients >40 years old. J Am Coll Cardiol 2001;38:2035–2042.
6. Theodoro DA, Danielson GK, Porter CJ, Warnes CA. Right-sided maze procedure for right atrial arrhythmias in congenital heart disease. Ann Thorac Surg 1998;65:149–154.
7. Gatzoulis MA, Freeman M, Siu SC, et al. Atrial arrhythmia after surgical closure of atrial septal defects in adults. N Engl J Med 1999;340:839–846.
8. Therrien J, et al. Canadian Cardiovascular Society Consensus Conference 2001 update: recommendations for the management of adults with congenital heart disease: I to III. Can J Cardiol 2001;17:940–959, 1029–1050, and 1135–1158.
9. Marelli AJ, Perloff JK, Child JS, Laks H. Pulmonary atresia with ventricular septal defect in adults. Circulation 1994;89:243–251.
10. Iyer KS, Mee RB. Staged repair of pulmonary atresia with ventricular septal defect and major systemic to pulmonary artery collaterals. Ann Thorac Surg 1991;51:65–72.
11. Niwa K, Siu SC, Webb GD, Gatzoulis MA. Progressive aortic root dilatation in adults late after repair of tetralogy of Fallot. Circulation 2002;106:1374–1378.
12. Ischizaka T, Ichikawa H, Sawa Y, et al. Prevalence and optimal management strategy for aortic regurgitation in tetralogy of Fallot. Eur J Cardiothorac Surg 2004;26:1080–1086.
13. Caldarone CA, McCrindle BW, Van Arsdell GS, et al. Independent factors associated with longevity of prosthetic pulmonary valves and valved conduits. J Thorac Cardiovasc Surg 2000;120:1021–1031.
14. Dodds III GA, Warnes CA, Danielson GK. Aortic valve replacement after repair of pulmonary atresia and ventricular septal defect or tetralogy of Fallot. J Thorac Cardiovasc Surg 1977;113:736–741.
15. Meijboom FJ, Roos-Hesselink JW, McGhie JS, et al. Consequences of a selective approach toward pulmonary valve replacement in adult patients with tetralogy of Fallot and pulmonary regurgitation. J Thorac Cardiovasc Surg 2008;135:50–55.
16. Bonow RO, Carabello BA, Chatterjee K, et al. American College of Cardiology/American Heart Association Task Force on Practice Guidelines. 2008 focused update incorporated into the ACC/AHA 2006 guidelines for the management of patients with valvular heart disease: a report of the American College of Cardiology/American Heart Association Task Force on Practice Guidelines (Writing Committee to revise the 1998 guidelines for the management of patients with valvular heart disease). Endorsed by the Society of Cardiovascular Anaesthesiologists, Society for Cardiovascular Angiography and Intervention, and Society of Thoracic Surgeons. J Am Coll Cardiol 2008;52:1–142.
17. Waterbolk TW, Hoendermis ES, den Hamer U, Ebels T. Pulmonary valve replacement with a mechanical prosthesis: promising results of 28 procedures in patients with congenital heart disease. Eur J Cardiothorac Surg 2006;30:28–32.
18. Massey R, Shore DF. Surgery for complex coarctation of the aorta. Int J Cardiol 2004;97:67–73.
19. Connolly HM, Schaff HV, Izhar U, et al. Posterior pericardial ascending-to-descending aortic bypass: an alternative surgical approach for complex coarctation of the aorta. Circulation 2001;104(12 Suppl. 1):1133–1137.

11

Venous Shunts and the Fontan Circulation in Adult Congenital Heart Disease

CONSTANTINE MAVROUDIS | BARBARA J. DEAL | CARL L. BACKER

Introduction

Venous shunts are surgical reconstructions involving an anastomosis between one or both venae cavae to one or both pulmonary arteries. We refer to these venous shunts or anastomoses as connections, which is useful in describing the various types of palliative and corrective operations. In general, these procedures are applied to patients with functionally single ventricles and can be staged during infancy and childhood to achieve eventual separation of the pulmonary and systemic circulations, often referred to as orthoterminal correction.[1] For purposes of definition, we refer to all operations that result in separation of the pulmonary and systemic circulations as corrective, irrespective of the number of functional ventricles (1, 2, or 1½), exercise capacity, quality of life, or expected longevity. As a consequence, venous shunts can be palliative as in the cases of the classic Glenn shunt (Fig. 11-1) and bidirectional Glenn shunt (Fig. 11-2) or corrective as in the case of the Fontan operation (Figs. 11-3 to 11-7).[2–4]

Historical Aspects of Venous Shunts

The right ventricular bypass was first successfully reported by Rodbard and associates in 1949.[5] They anastomosed the right atrium to the pulmonary artery and ligated the main pulmonary artery in dogs.[6] Then in 1950, Italian surgeon Carlo Carlon and colleagues published their canine study of an end-to-end anastomosis between the divided azygos vein and the right pulmonary artery with preatrial ligation of the superior vena cava.[6,7] More than 10 years elapsed before Carlon and colleagues reported their first clinical experience. Although never published, in 1954 at the 40th Annual Clinical Congress of the American College of Surgeons, Harris Schumacker presented the experiments he had been performing in which venae cavae were anastomosed directly with the pulmonary artery.[8] Finally, in 1956, the first description of a successful clinical cavopulmonary shunt was reported by Meshalkin,[9] a Russian surgeon who performed a right-sided cavopulmonary shunt in a young child with tetralogy of Fallot. Also in 1956, Robicsek and associates[10,11] reported on the procedure that they had been performing for 3 years in animals and found that if the azygos vein is uninterrupted while the cavopulmonary anastomosis is done the animals survived and the procedure could be performed with low operative mortality.[12] In 1958, Glenn published his series of superior vena cava to right pulmonary artery shunts, which was largely applied to tetralogy of Fallot patients with excellent palliation.[13] Through a right anterior thoracotomy, the right pulmonary artery was divided and anastomosed to the right side of the superior vena cava, after ligation and division of the azygos vein. The superior vena cava was then ligated at the cavoatrial junction.[14] This operation quickly gained the eponym the *Glenn shunt*. The development of the superior vena cava to main pulmonary artery anastomosis without pulmonary artery division took on the name *bidirectional Glenn shunt*, even though the developers of this shunt were different authors.[15–17] Why certain names and phrases gain universal use despite logical and scientific evidence to the contrary is beyond the scope of this chapter but has been considered with regard to congenital heart nomenclature elsewhere.[18]

The Fontan operation (see Fig. 11-3)[2] and the many modifications, one of which is the Kreutzer procedure (see Fig. 11-4),[3] are characterized by complete separation of the pulmonary and systemic circulations and depend on high systemic venous pressure and low pulmonary artery pressure/resistance to propel nonpulsatile blood flow through the pulmonary circulation. Fontan (1971)[2] and Kreutzer (1973)[3] published their findings within 2 years of each other and proved that systemic venous pressure would be sufficient to propel blood flow through the pulmonary circulation as long as other hemodynamic considerations were optimal. It was Fontan's thought that the right atrium, which is quite thickened in patients with tricuspid atresia, could be made to function as a right ventricle; hence, the necessity for inflow and outflow bioprosthetic valves. Kreutzer's contribution resembles more closely the type of cavopulmonary connections that are used today.

Eventually, the right atrium to pulmonary artery direct connection (both retroaortic and anteroaortic) became standard therapy, as did the Björk modification (see Fig. 11-5),[4] although there were reports of interposition valved conduits between the right atrium and pulmonary artery. These modifications were of limited benefit because the flow across these valved conduits was shown to be nonpulsatile (the valves never closed during the cardiac cycle) and finally the valves calcified with stenosis and perturbed the delicate Fontan circulation, leading to atrial enlargement, arrhythmias, and ascites, among other complications. It was then discovered that many patients with atriopulmonary connections, especially those individuals with anteroaortic connections, were experiencing similar problems. This led to total cavopulmonary lateral tunnel connection,[19,20] which was demonstrated to have superior flow characteristics[21] and theoretically exposed less of the right atrium to the higher venous pressure of the systemic venous Fontan circuit (see Fig. 11-6). The proponents of this strategy reasoned that the newly created low-pressure pulmonary atrium would decrease the progression and incidence of arrhythmias due to atrial stretch. The increased suture load in the right atrium to construct the lateral tunnel was not considered as a future arrhythmogenic part of the procedure. The latest modification of the Fontan operation was the extracardiac connection (see Fig. 11-7), which was introduced by Marcelletti.[22] He and many colleagues[23] showed that an extracardiac tube graft could link the inferior vena cava with the pulmonary artery without the obligatory suture load within the atrium. The consensus among the participating authors was that in addition to the ease of the operation—often requiring no cross-clamp and sometimes being performed without cardiopulmonary bypass—the patient would benefit from a decreased incidence of atrial arrhythmias.

Pathophysiologic Aspects of Venous Shunts

UNIDIRECTIONAL GLENN SHUNT

The early effects of the unidirectional Glenn shunt showed that it was a relatively simple operation, improved oxygen saturation, and provided excellent palliation for many patients.[24] Unfortunately, late deterioration occurred because of decreased effective pulmonary blood flow resulting from systemic venous collateral vessels and pulmonary arteriovenous malformations. Systemic venous collateral vessels developed because of increased venous pressure and

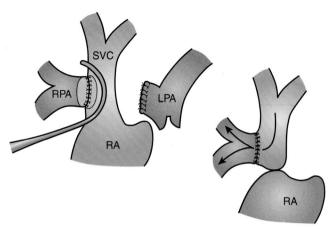

Figure 11-1 The Classic Glenn shunt. End-to-side anastomosis between the right pulmonary artery and superior vena cava after suture ligation of the proximal right pulmonary artery. Also shown is the ligation of the superior vena cava right atrial junction, which completes the operation. LPA, left pulmonary artery; RA, right atrium; RPA, right pulmonary artery; SVC, superior vena cava.

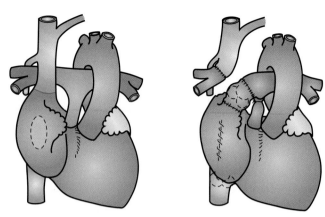

Figure 11-3 The Fontan operation. End-to-side anastomosis of distal end of right pulmonary artery to superior vena cava; end-to-end anastomosis of right atrial appendage to proximal end of right pulmonary artery by means of an aortic valve homograft; closure of atrial septal defect; insertion of a pulmonary valve homograft into inferior vena cava; and ligation of main pulmonary artery. *(Redrawn from Fontan F, Baudet E. Surgical repair of tricuspid atresia. Thorax 1971; 26:240-248.)*

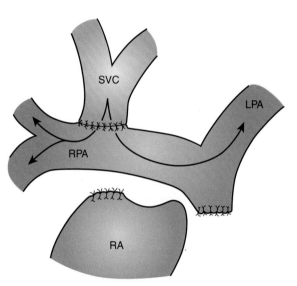

Figure 11-2 Bidirectional Glenn shunt. Superior vena cava anastomosis to the right pulmonary artery with suture ligation of the cardiac end of the superior vena cava. LPA, left pulmonary artery; RA, right atrium. RPA, right pulmonary artery; SVC, superior vena cava.

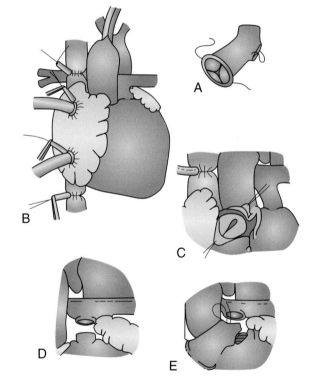

Figure 11-4 Kreutzer surgical technique. **A,** The pulmonary homograft annulus was set on a rigid Teflon ring. The left branch of the pulmonary artery was sutured. **B,** Extracorporeal circulation was started, and the aorta was crossclamped. **C,** Through an incision in the right atrial appendage, the foramen ovale was partially closed. **D,** The pulmonary artery trunk was transected and the proximal pulmonary artery was sutured. **E,** Posterior wall of the end-to-end anastomosis of the right branch of the homograft with the distal pulmonary artery trunk. *(Redrawn from Kreutzer G, Galindez E, Bono H et al. An operation for the correction of tricuspid atresia. J Thorac Cardiovasc Surg 1973; 66:613-621.)*

therefore shunted blood flow away from the pulmonary artery. Pulmonary arteriovenous malformations were initially attributed to lack of pulsatile flow but later found to result from the exclusion of hepatic venous flow from the pulmonary circulation.[24] Nevertheless, the clinical contributions to congenital heart surgery by all the surgeons who worked in this field, both experimentally and clinically, not only proved that the right ventricle could be partially bypassed but also paved the way for Fontan and Baudet's historic operation in 1968 that completely separated the systemic and pulmonary circulations.[25]

BIDIRECTIONAL GLENN SHUNT

The bidirectional Glenn procedure can also lead to systemic venous collateral vessels and pulmonary arteriovenous malformations. As a

result, often this shunt is a short-term, palliative procedure performed in young children (usually < 2 years) who are being prepared for an eventual Fontan procedure. This procedure improves systemic arterial oxygen saturation without increasing pulmonary vascular resistance and is an excellent palliation when systemic venous to pulmonary

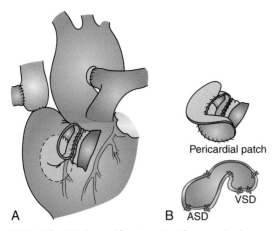

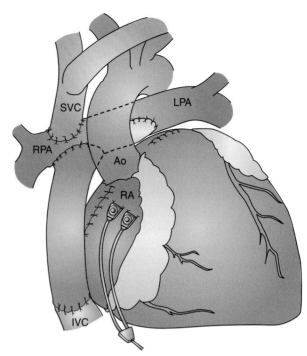

Figure 11-5 The Björk modification. **A,** After patch closure of the ventricular septal defect (VSD) and atrial septal defect (ASD), the posterior wall of the right atrial appendage is sutured to the everted edge of the right ventricular incision. **B,** The *insets* show how the pericardial patch is sutured to the right atrium and the right ventricle to complete the anastomosis. *(Redrawn from Bjork VO, Olin CL, Bjarke BB, Thoren CA. Right atrial-right ventricular anastomosis for correction of tricuspid atresia. J Thorac Cardiovasc Surg 1979; 77:452-458.)*

Figure 11-7 Total cavopulmonary artery extracardiac connection with bipolar epicardial leads on the right atrium. Ao, aorta; IVC, inferior vena cava; LPA, left pulmonary artery; RA, right atrium; RPA, right pulmonary artery; SVC, superior vena cava.

pulmonary artery are not divided owing to small pulmonary arteries to augment pulmonary artery flow in addition to the bidirectional Glenn shunt.

Fontan Circulation Complications

Patients with Fontan operations and Fontan physiology can be hampered by various obstructive, valvular, and associated lesions that can perturb the delicate physiologic balance that allows venous propulsion of blood flow through the pulmonary circulation.

SYSTEMIC VENOUS PATHWAY OBSTRUCTION

Obstructions to the systemic venous pathway can be manifested by stenotic atriopulmonary connections, lateral tunnel stenosis, superior vena cava stenosis, peripheral pulmonary artery stenosis, and right atrial thrombus. The unwanted pathophysiologic consequences of these obstructive lesions lead to decreased pulmonary flow, atriomegaly, atrial arrhythmias, decreased cardiac output, exercise intolerance, ascites, cirrhosis, protein-losing enteropathy, and renal compromise. In particular, atriopulmonary obstructions can be subtle, often showing only 1 to 3 mm Hg hemodynamic stenotic characteristics. More often than not, the obstructive lesions can be better assessed by angiography, which can demonstrate stenotic anastomotic segments. Although these stenotic lesions can occur in any Fontan patient, they are more likely to develop under the following circumstances. They include (1) individuals who had a right atrial to right ventricle or pulmonary artery valved/nonvalved conduit, (2) individuals who had an anteroaortic right atrial to pulmonary artery connection, and (3) individuals who had staged orthoterminal correction resulting in divided pulmonary arteries (Glenn shunt to the right pulmonary artery and right atrioleft pulmonary artery connection).

Their clinical presentation is subtle and insidious. Patients respond to the perturbed pathophysiology by adjusting their activities until the onset of arrhythmias, which can be life threatening. This condition

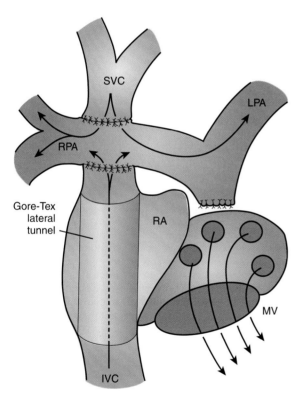

Figure 11-6 Total cavopulmonary artery anastomosis with an intra-atrial Gore-Tex (WL Gore & Associates, Flagstaff, AZ) lateral tunnel directing blood from the inferior vena cava to the inferior portion of the right pulmonary artery. IVC, inferior vena cava; LPA, left pulmonary artery; MV, mitral valve; RA, right atrium; RPA, right pulmonary artery; SVC, superior vena cava.

artery connection must be postponed because of age, weight, or anatomic considerations. It is performed by anastomosing the superior vena cava to the right branch of the pulmonary artery using fine sutures and then dividing the main pulmonary artery. Occasionally, the preexisting systemic to pulmonary artery shunt or the stenotic

establishes the necessity for toxic drug therapy and can lead to ventricular dysfunction resulting from drug therapy and/or arrhythmias. If no intervention is prescribed, the aforementioned cascade of clinical events is ensured.

PULMONARY VENOUS OBSTRUCTION

Pulmonary venous obstruction in Fontan patients usually occurs as a consequence of severe right atrial dilation in the case of right pulmonary vein obstruction (Fig. 11-8) or coronary sinus dilation in the case of left pulmonary vein obstruction (Fig. 11-9). The unwanted consequences of pulmonary vein obstruction are additive to the already established conditions that have led to atrial and coronary sinus dilation in the first instance. These include the induction of increased

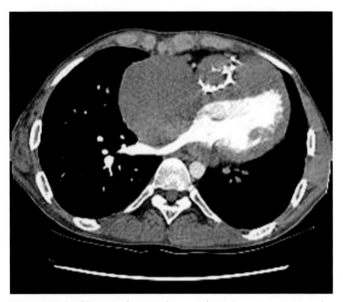

Figure 11-8 CT scan showing large right atrium compressing the course of a right pulmonary vein.

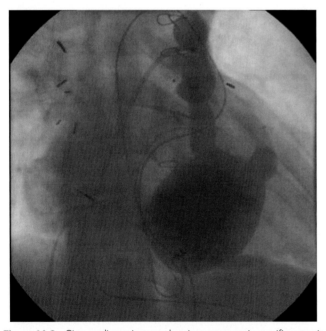

Figure 11-9 Cine cardioangiogram showing coronary sinus orifice atresia after ligation of the left superior vena cava. Lack of venous outflow resulted in a gigantic mass that compressed the left pulmonary veins.

transpulmonary right-sided pressure, decreased systemic oxygen saturation, decreased cardiac output, induction of aortopulmonary collateral arteries (stimulated by cyanosis), and all the consequential cascade of events previously noted. Pulmonary venous obstruction is difficult to assess by echocardiography and is probably better identified qualitatively by computed tomography (CT).

LEFT VENTRICULAR OUTFLOW TRACT OBSTRUCTION

Functionally single-ventricle patients often have associated conditions that can cause left ventricular outflow tract obstruction. Some examples include patients with staged correction of hypoplastic left heart syndrome who develop recurrent coarctation, patients with double-inlet left ventricle and transposition of the great arteries who are subject to a closing bulboventricular foramen (effective subaortic stenosis), and patients with stenotic supra-aortic anastomotic problems from the various forms of Damus-Kaye-Stansel-operations. The unwanted consequences of these conditions relate to increased ventricular afterload, ventricular hypertrophy, decreased compliance, and ventricular hypertension. Decreased ventricular compliance is associated with increased end-diastolic pressure, which has a negative backpressure effect on the Fontan circulation, leading to the cascade of events mentioned previously. In addition to diastolic abnormalities is the ever-present possibility of sudden death when left ventricular outflow tract obstruction exceeds 80 to 100 mm Hg.

VALVULAR ABNORMALITIES

Functionally single-ventricle patients generally have abnormal atrioventricular valves. Even patients with tricuspid atresia have been found to have larger than normal and, in many cases, abnormal mitral valves.[26] The possibility of valve dysfunction, especially in Fontan patients with heterotaxy (common atrioventricular valves) and congenitally corrected transposition (Ebstein anomaly of the systemic tricuspid valve) can be a major therapeutic challenge. The unwanted consequence of valve dysfunction, which is usually regurgitant, is increased Fontan pressure, decreased compliance, atrial and ventricular arrhythmias, decreased ventricular function, and the cascade of events previously noted.

Associated lesions that negatively impact the Fontan circulation include aortic aneurysm, residual atrial and ventricular shunts, right and left ventricular outflow tract obstruction, discontinuous pulmonary arteries, and trapped lung. These lesions can lead to sudden death (aneurysm rupture), pulmonary arteriovenous fistulas, increased cyanosis, and congestive heart failure.

Finally, unrelenting atrial arrhythmias or troubling ventricular arrhythmias negatively effect the Fontan circulation by causing ventricular dysfunction, atrial thrombi, decreased cardiac output, and sudden death. Compounding these problems is the necessary use of cardiolytic antiarrhythmic drugs that can cause further clinical compromise.

◼ Therapeutic Options

The therapeutic options that confront Fontan patients with significant complications are Fontan conversion and cardiac transplantation.

What is meant by Fontan conversion? Our experience is composed of three main parts of the operation. The first is atriopulmonary to total cavopulmonary artery, extracardiac (polytetrafluoroethylene graft) conversion, which involves venous pathway takedown and revision to an extracardiac circuit, right and left pulmonary artery reconnection in those cases where there was an extant Fontan operation consisting of a right Glenn shunt and a right atrium to left pulmonary artery connection, coronary sinus unroofing in those patients who had left pulmonary vein obstruction, and right atrial wall reduction (Fig. 11-10).[27] There are a number of other problematic connections in various diagnostic groups that have required special therapeutic maneuvers and are noted in Figures 11-11 to 11-25.[28,29] The second is

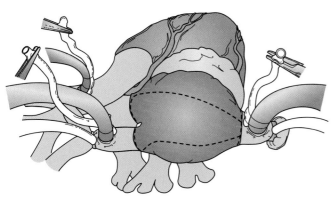

Figure 11-10 Technique of cannulation and right atrial resection. *(Redrawn from Backer CL, Deal BJ, Mavroudis C et al. Conversion of the failed Fontan circulation. Cardiol Young 2006; 16[Suppl 1]:85-91.)*

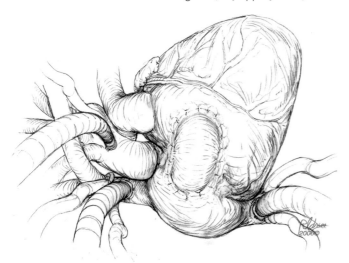

Figure 11-11 Global view of a Björk-Fontan modification showing a right atrial to right ventricular nonvalved connection using a prosthetic graft roof. *(From Mavroudis C, Backer CL, Deal BJ et al. Evolving anatomic and electrophysiologic considerations associated with Fontan conversion. Semin Thorac Cardiovasc Surg Pediatr Card Surg Annu 2007; 10:136-145.)*

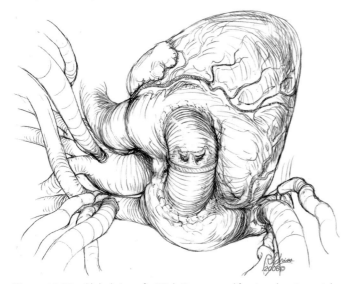

Figure 11-12 Global view of a Björk-Fontan modification showing a right atrial to right ventricular valved connection using a prosthetic graft roof. *(From Mavroudis C, Backer CL, Deal BJ et al. Evolving anatomic and electrophysiologic considerations associated with Fontan conversion. Semin Thorac Cardiovasc Surg Pediatr Card Surg Annu 2007; 10:136-145.)*

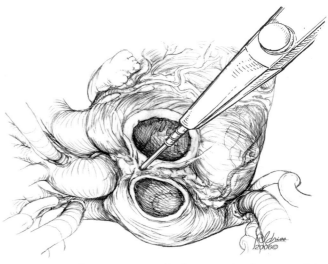

Figure 11-13 Commencement of bulboventricular dissection of the right atrial-right ventricular groove.

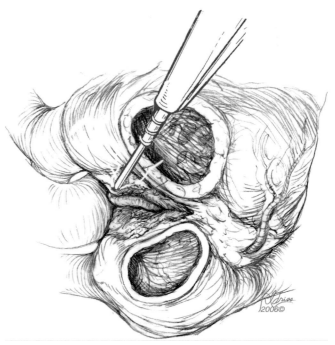

Figure 11-14 Electrocautery dissection at the atrioventricular groove commencing at the base of the aorta with extension to the right ventricular free wall. Care is taken to perform this dissection with a low electrocautery setting to avoid unwanted injury to the right coronary artery. *(From Mavroudis C, Backer CL, Deal BJ et al. Evolving anatomic and electrophysiologic considerations associated with Fontan conversion. Semin Thorac Cardiovasc Surg Pediatr Card Surg Annu 2007; 10:136-145.)*

arrhythmia surgery, by which is meant a right-sided maze procedure for atrial reentry tachycardia (Figs. 11-26 to 11-28),[28] pathway modification for atrioventricular nodal tachycardia (Fig. 11-29),[30] local resection or ablation for focal (automatic) atrial tachycardia (Fig. 11-30),[30] pathway interruption for accessory connections (Fig. 11-31),[30] Cox-maze III procedure for atrial fibrillation/left-sided atrial reentry tachycardia (Fig. 11-32),[27] and various forms of cryoablation/endocardial resection for ventricular tachycardia. All patients receive an antitachycardia, dual-chamber pacemaker with corticosteroid-eluting epicardial leads

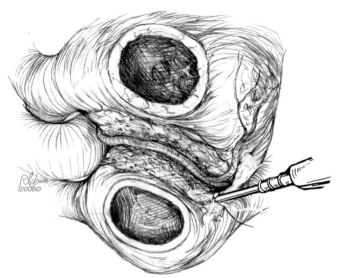

Figure 11-15   Completed electrocautery dissection of the entire atrioventricular groove. The amount of atrium freed during this maneuver allows for a larger atrial reduction and provides unscarred atrial tissue for the atrial pacemaker leads that are placed at the end of the Fontan conversion. *(From Mavroudis C, Backer CL, Deal BJ et al. Evolving anatomic and electrophysiologic considerations associated with Fontan conversion. Semin Thorac Cardiovasc Surg Pediatr Card Surg Annu 2007; 10:136-145.)*

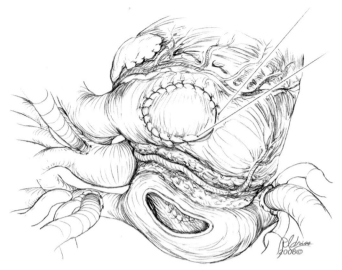

Figure 11-17   Right ventricular polytetrafluoroethylene graft is placed on the right ventricle to ensure right ventricle–pulmonary artery continuity for drainage of thebesian blood flow.

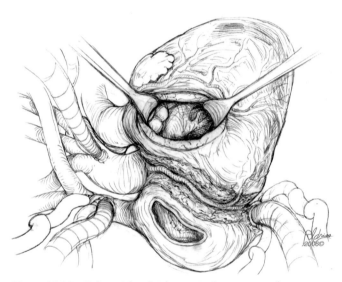

Figure 11-16   Right atrial and right ventricular exposure after atrioventricular groove dissection showing pulmonary valve and the diminutive right ventricle.

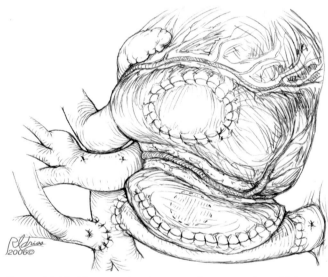

Figure 11-18   The completed extracardiac connections. Right atrial wall reduction and closure is noted by the long atrial suture line. Right ventricular to main pulmonary artery continuity is maintained by a right ventricular patch, thus ensuring outflow of thebesian venous flow and avoidance of right ventricular dilation. *(From Mavroudis C, Backer CL, Deal BJ et al. Evolving anatomic and electrophysiologic considerations associated with Fontan conversion. Semin Thorac Cardiovasc Surg Pediatr Card Surg Annu 2007; 10:136-145.)*

(Fig. 11-33). Some patients have multisite ventricular leads (resynchronization) or automatic ventricular defibrillators. The third is correction of associated lesions, which impact unfavorably on the Fontan circulation and are noted in Table 11-1. Repair of associated lesions almost always involves an extension of the crossclamp time and must be planned appropriately to limit ischemic time, which will optimize the result. The therapeutic alternatives for valve repair are challenging and are complicated by the lack of operative experience, lack of specialized supportive annular rings, especially for complete atrioventricular canal, and the problems of poorly formed valves, as in the cases of Ebstein anomaly of the tricuspid valve. We have used a number of techniques to repair and replace defective valves with inconsistent results (Fig. 11-34).[31,32] Recently, we have had increasing success with the Alfieri valvuloplasty technique and presently would not consider

significant atrioventricular valve insufficiency, per se, as a contraindication for Fontan conversion. Nevertheless, more clinical research and application of specialized rings will be necessary to improve outcomes in these patients.

Results of Fontan Conversion, Arrhythmia Surgery, and Repair of Associated Lesions

The perioperative results for Fontan conversion are shown in Table 11-2. In general, patients benefit significantly from this procedure and, in most cases, have a noteworthy improvement in their exercise tolerance and daily activities. Arrhythmia control is highly

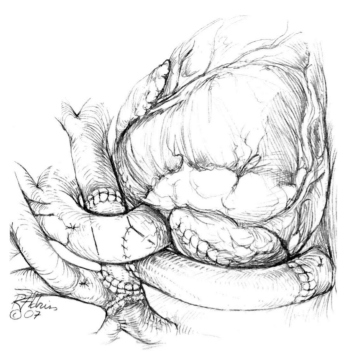

Figure 11-19 Reconstruction of discontinuous pulmonary arteries using polytetrafluoroethylene graft. *(From Mavroudis C, Backer CL, Deal BJ. Late reoperations for Fontan patients: state of the art invited review. Eur J Cardiothorac Surg 2008; 34:1034-1040).*

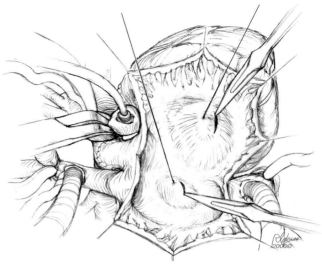

Figure 11-21 Right atrial view of a patient with double-inlet ventricle who had an atriopulmonary Fontan with tricuspid valve isolation and atrial septal defect closure. The isolation patch is sharply removed to uncover the tricuspid valve and the coronary sinus to perform the right-sided maze procedure. *(From Mavroudis C, Backer CL, Deal BJ et al. Evolving anatomic and electrophysiologic considerations associated with Fontan conversion. Semin Thorac Cardiovasc Surg Pediatr Card Surg Annu 2007; 10:136-145.)*

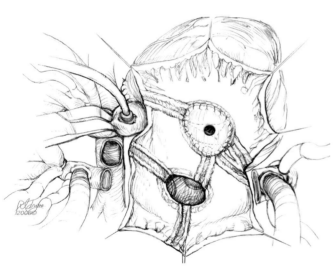

Figure 11-20 Right atrial view of a patient with pulmonary atresia and intact ventricular septum who had a prior atriopulmonary Fontan operation and presents now with arrhythmias and suprasystemic right ventricular pressure. The cryoablation lines are noted for the modified right-sided maze procedure as well as the fenestrated tricuspid valve isolation patch. The idea of the fenestration is to limit the inflow to the right ventricle in diastole, which will decrease the developed pressure of the right ventricle in systole. *(From Mavroudis C, Backer CL, Deal BJ et al. Evolving anatomic and electrophysiologic considerations associated with Fontan conversion. Semin Thorac Cardiovasc Surg Pediatr Card Surg Annu 2007; 10:136-145.)*

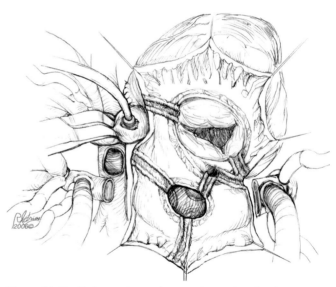

Figure 11-22 Right atrial view showing the results of isolation patch removal and atrial septal defect creation. The cryoablation lesions are shown after proper identification of the tricuspid valve annulus and coronary sinus. The cryoablation lesion from the base of the right atrial appendage to the anterior tricuspid annulus is optional. *(From Mavroudis C, Backer CL, Deal BJ et al. Evolving anatomic and electrophysiologic considerations associated with Fontan conversion. Semin Thorac Cardiovasc Surg Pediatr Card Surg Annu 2007; 10:136-145.)*

successful with an overall recurrence rate of 11.4%. The recurrence rate, however, has been reduced for the most recent cohort of patients to 7.3% (Table 11-3). Kaplan-Meier curves showing freedom from arrhythmia recurrence and freedom from death are noted in Figures 11-35 and 11-36. Interestingly, the freedom from death curve is remarkably constant except for two patients who died of an

anesthetic complication and from injuries sustained in an automobile accident, 2.5 and 11.3 years postoperatively, respectively. The freedom from arrhythmia recurrence curve shows that the atrial fibrillation group had a higher recurrence rate than the atrial reentry tachycardia group. Interestingly, no patient who was treated for atrial fibrillation experienced a recurrence of atrial fibrillation. The recurrences were largely reentry atrial tachycardia in this group, which for the most part were easily treated with β-adrenergic blockade. We also found that risk factors for death or transplantation in our group of patients were protein-losing enteropathy, long

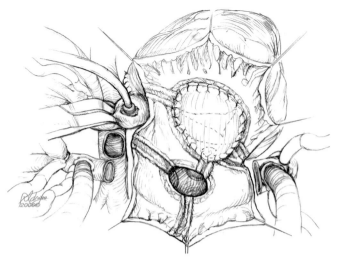

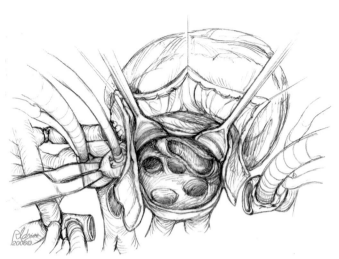

Figure 11-23 Right atrial view of Gore-Tex (WL Gore & Associates, Flagstaff, AZ) tricuspid valve isolation after cryoablation. The suture line for attachment is placed in the valve tissue near the annulus to avoid injury to the atrioventricular node. *(From Mavroudis C, Backer CL, Deal BJ et al. Evolving anatomic and electrophysiologic considerations associated with Fontan conversion. Semin Thorac Cardiovasc Surg Pediatr Card Surg Annu 2007; 10:136-145.)*

Figure 11-25 Left atrial view of the patient described in Figure 11-24. The large coronary sinus was unroofed, thereby establishing proper coronary sinus drainage and relief of the left pulmonary vein stenosis. *(From Mavroudis C, Backer CL, Deal BJ et al. Evolving anatomic and electrophysiologic considerations associated with Fontan conversion. Semin Thorac Cardiovasc Surg Pediatr Card Surg Annu 2007; 10:136-145.)*

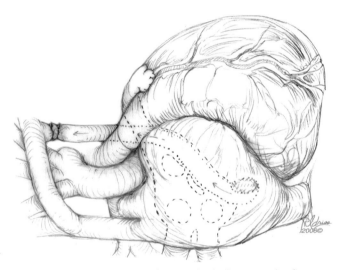

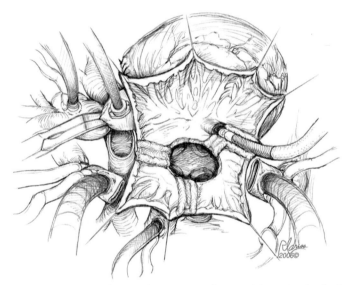

Figure 11-24 Double-inlet left ventricle, bulboventricular foramen, and *l*-transposition of the great arteries with bilateral superior venae cavae. The patient underwent ligation of the left superior vena cava in preparation for an eventual atriopulmonary Fontan procedure without prior knowledge of orifice atresia of the coronary sinus. Lack of ebb flow from the coronary sinus caused sinus dilation and obstruction of the left pulmonary veins as noted. *(From Mavroudis C, Backer CL, Deal BJ et al. Evolving anatomic and electrophysiologic considerations associated with Fontan conversion. Semin Thorac Cardiovasc Surg Pediatr Card Surg Annu 2007; 10:136-145.)*

cardiopulmonary bypass time, atrioventricular valve regurgitation, and right or ambiguous ventricle (Table 11-4).[33] These data have led us to note that there are contraindications for Fontan conversion in patients who (1) have irreversible severe ventricular dysfunction not related to arrhythmias or drug therapy, (2) protein-losing enteropathy in the absence of severe venous pathway obstruction, (3) advanced liver cirrhosis, and (4) severe renal insufficiency. Relative, but unproven, risk factors include (1) significant ascites, (2) severe liver nodularity, (3) renal insufficiency (creatinine > 2.0), and (4) esophageal varices.

Figure 11-26 Atrial view of a patient with tricuspid atresia who had an atriopulmonary Fontan operation after aortic crossclamping and cardioplegic arrest. The inferior and superior venae cavae have been transected, the atrial wall excision has been performed, and the atrial septal patch has been removed. No measures were taken to preserve the sinoatrial node, which is nonfunctional in a significant number of patients. Cryoablation lesions were placed in four areas to complete the modified right-sided maze procedure. The first two cryoablation lesions are standard for all anatomic substrates and are performed by connecting (1) the superior portion of the atrial septal ridge with the incised area of the right atrial appendage and (2) the posterior portion of the atrial septal ridge with the posterior cut edge of the atrial wall, which extends through the crista terminalis. The next part is the isthmus ablation. These lines of block are dependent on the anatomic substrate. In patients with tricuspid atresia, as noted here, the cryoablation lesion is placed to connect (3) the posteroinferior portion of the coronary sinus os with the transected inferior vena cava os. The last session (4) connects the coronary sinus os with the inferior edge of the atrial septal defect. *(From Mavroudis C, Backer CL, Deal BJ et al. Evolving anatomic and electrophysiologic considerations associated with Fontan conversion. Semin Thorac Cardiovasc Surg Pediatr Card Surg Annu 2007; 10:136-145.)*

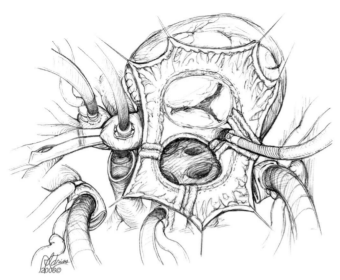

Figure 11-27 The modified right-sided maze procedure in a patient with double-outlet right ventricle and mitral atresia. As noted in Figure 11-26, the two standard cryoablation lesions connecting the rim of the atrial septal defect with (1) the incised area of the right atrial appendage and (2) the posterior cut edge of the atrial wall, respectively, are shown. The isthmus block is accomplished by creating cryoablation lesions (3) to connect the posteroinferior portion of the coronary sinus os with the transected inferior vena cava os and (4) to connect the tricuspid valve annulus with the transected inferior vena cava os. These isthmus block lesions are usually placed across the ridge of the resected atrial compartmentalization patch. An additional lesion (5) connects the coronary sinus os with the inferior edge of the atrial septal defect. *(From Mavroudis C, Backer CL, Deal BJ et al. Evolving anatomic and electrophysiologic considerations associated with Fontan conversion. Semin Thorac Cardiovasc Surg Pediatr Card Surg Annu 2007; 10:136-145.)*

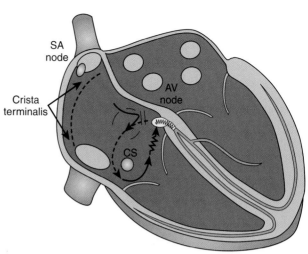

Figure 11-29 Slow-fast or "typical" form of atrioventricular (AV) nodal reentry tachycardia. Atrioventricular conduction encounters a block in the normal fast pathway fibers superior to the compact AV node. The wavefront proceeds toward the atrial isthmus, between the coronary sinus (CS) and tricuspid valve, and encounters slowing through the slow pathway fibers of the AV node. Exiting the isthmus, conduction is now able to reenter the fast pathway fibers, located anteriorly and superiorly, and perpetuate a reentrant circuit; simultaneously, conduction proceeds inferiorly to the ventricles. Of note, conduction to the ventricles is not relevant to the tachycardia circuit. Cryoablation of the inferior isthmus region will interrupt the circuit. SA, sinoatrial. *(Redrawn From Mavroudis C, Deal BJ, Backer CL, Tsao S. Arrhythmia surgery in patients with and without congenital heart disease. Ann Thorac Surg 2008; 86:857-868; discussion 857-868.)*

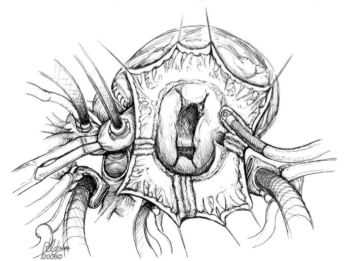

Figure 11-28 The modified right-sided maze procedure on a patient with a single ventricle and unbalanced atrioventricular canal. As noted inFigure 11-26, the two standard cryoablation lesions connecting the rim of the atrial septal defect with (1) the incised area of the right atrial appendage and (2) the posterior cut edge of the atrial wall, respectively, are shown. The isthmus block is accomplished by creating cryoablation lesions (3) to connect the posteroinferior portion of the coronary sinus os with the transected inferior vena cava os and (4) to connect the common atrioventricular valve annulus with the transected inferior vena cava os. These isthmus block lesions are usually placed across the ridge of the resected atrial compartmentalization patch. The lesion connecting the coronary sinus os with the atrial septal defect is not performed because the anatomic ridge is not usually absent. *(From Mavroudis C, Backer CL, Deal BJ et al. Evolving anatomic and electrophysiologic considerations associated with Fontan conversion. Semin Thorac Cardiovasc Surg Pediatr Card Surg Annu 2007; 10:136-145.)*

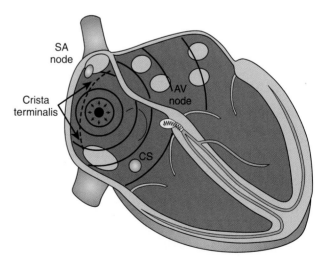

Figure 11-30 Right focal atrial tachycardia. Focal atrial tachycardia is a localized area of impulse initiation that is most commonly automatic in mechanism, firing repeatedly, rapidly, and independent of normal sinus function, which is inhibited. Impulse conduction is spread in a centripetal fashion across the atria, thence to the atrioventricular (AV) node and ventricles. Ablative therapy is aimed at obliteration or isolation of this localized discrete area (hot spot). CS, coronary sinus; SA, sinoatrial. *(Redrawn from Mavroudis C, Deal BJ, Backer CL, Tsao S. Arrhythmia surgery in patients with and without congenital heart disease. Ann Thorac Surg 2008; 86:857-868; discussion 857-868.)*

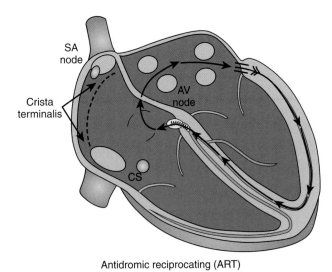

Antidromic reciprocating (ART)

Figure 11-31 Atrioventricular (AV) reciprocating tachycardia. Wolff-Parkinson-White (WPW) syndrome or manifest accessory connection. During sinus rhythm with pre-excitation, conduction from the sinus node to the ventricles proceeds simultaneously over two routes, the atrioventricular node and the accessory connection. The wavefront traversing the accessory connection depolarizes ventricular tissue first, because of intrinsic slowing of conduction at the atrioventricular node. The accessory connection thus pre-excites ventricular depolarization, giving rise to the delta wave. As depicted, there is blocked conduction in the atrioventricular node, with conduction proceeding to the ventricles via the accessory connection (pre-excited). Conduction delay is encountered in ventricular muscle, allowing the wavefront to proceed up the AV node (which has had time to regain conduction) to the atrium. This reentrant circuit is termed *antidromic reciprocating tachycardia*; the playing field includes the atria, accessory connection, ventricles, and the AV node. CS, coronary sinus; SA, sinoatrial. (*Redrawn from Mavroudis C, Deal BJ, Backer CL, Tsao S. Arrhythmia surgery in patients with and without congenital heart disease. Ann Thorac Surg 2008; 86:857-868; discussion 857-868.*)

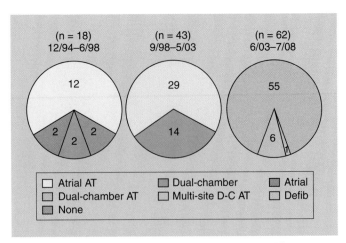

Figure 11-33 Three eras of Fontan conversion using different pacemaker technology.

TABLE 11-1	Children's Memorial Hospital Experience 1994-2007		
Concomitant Surgery	*1994-1996*	*1996-2003*	*2003-2007*
Pulmonary arterioplasty/ interposition	2	13	10
AV valve repair/replacement		10	14
Coronary sinus unroofing, pulmonary vein stenosis, atrial augmentation		4	11
LVOT procedures		1	6
RVOT procedures			5
Thrombectomy		2	3
Residual intracardiac shunt			2
Tricuspid valve patch takedown/ placement			12
Other (decortication, ligation of vessels)			5

AV, atrioventricular; LVOT, left ventricular outflow tract; RVOT, right ventricular outflow tract.

Figure 11-32 The Cox-maze III. Illustrations of opened atrium. Note the superior and inferior caval veins have been transected. Right pulmonary veins have been isolated by an incision. Left pulmonary veins have been isolated by cryoablation. There are lesions from the base of the excised left atrium to the pulmonary vein lesion and from the mitral annulus to the pulmonary venous lesion. The epicardial lesion on the coronary sinus (shown) is created over 2 minutes. (*From Backer CL, Deal BJ, Mavroudis C, Franklin WH, Stewart RD. Conversion of the failed Fontan circulation. Cardiol Young 2006; 16[Suppl 1]:85-91.*)

Alternative therapeutic interventions for severely compromised Fontan patients have included cardiac transplantation. Our experience includes nine patients who had cardiac transplantation for failed Fontan operations either as an elective or emergency procedure. Operative survival was 78% with good long-term survival. Three of four patients with protein-losing enteropathy survived. Because rejection rarely occurred in this group, lower intensity immunosuppression may be warranted. We concluded that heart transplantation is an acceptable surgical alternative for patients with a failing Fontan operation who are not candidates for Fontan conversion. An important corollary is that Fontan conversion does not preclude heart transplantation.

There are, however, a number of patients who present with a failing Fontan operation who have cirrhosis and renal failure (Box 11-1). In some cases, a cardiac transplant can be performed with a subsequent renal transplant if the kidneys do not recover. Others have performed triple-organ transplantation (heart, liver, and kidney) with poor results to date because of uncontrolled bleeding.

CONCLUSION

Fontan conversion with arrhythmia surgery results in excellent outcomes despite increasing complexity among patients. Identified risk factors for death or transplantation include protein-losing enteropathy, moderate-to-severe atrioventricular valve regurgitation, and right or ambiguous ventricle. Although atrioventricular valve regurgitation was

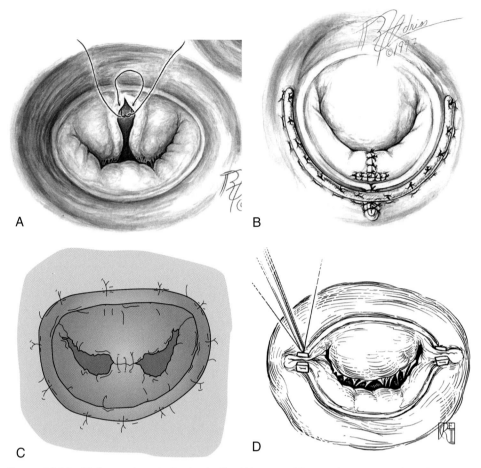

Figure 11-34 Cleft anterior mitral valve leaflet (**A**) repaired by simple, interrupted, and inverted sutures (cleft closure), (**B**) strengthened by a semicircular Gore-Tex (WL Gore & Associates, Flagstaff, AZ) strip (Carpentier annuloplasty), (**C**) Alfieri valvuloplasty, and (**D**) suture annuloplasty. *(From Zias EA, Mavroudis C, Backer CL et al. Surgical repair of the congenitally malformed mitral valve in infants and children. Ann Thorac Surg 1998; 66:1551-1559 and Alfieri O, Maisano F. An effective technique to correct anterior mitral leaflet prolapse. J Card Surg 1999; 14:468-470.)*

TABLE 11-2	Results of Fontan Conversion-Arrhythmia Surgery (n = 123)	
Result	*No. Patients (%) or Duration*	
Reoperation for bleeding	1 (0.8%)	
Sternal infection	3 (2.4%)	
Acute renal failure	8 (6.5%)	
Mean chest tube duration	9.1 ± 4.9 days	
Mean length of stay	13.7 ± 11.9 days	
Early mortality	2 (1.6%)	
Late mortality*	10 (8.0%)	
Heart transplantation	7 (5.7%)	
Improvement in NYHA class	86%	
Recurrent atrial tachycardia	11.4%	

*Three patients after transplant.
NYHA, New York Heart Association.

TABLE 11-3	Fontan Conversion and Arrhythmia Surgery: Children's Memorial Hospital Experience with Arrhythmia Recurrence*		
	No. Patients	*No. Arrhythmias*	*%*
Early period (12/1994-6/1996)†	9	3	33.3
Middle period (12/1996-6/2003)*	55	8‡	14.5
Late period (6/2003-8/2007)*	55	4§	7.3

*Defined as treatment with medication.
†Isthmus ablation technique.
‡5/8 had atrial fibrillation; atrial reentry tachycardia only recurred; 1→Tx; 1→Exp.
§2/4 had atrial fibrillation; atrial reentry tachycardia only recurred; 1→Tx→Exp.

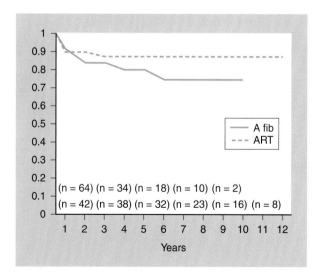

Figure 11-35 Kaplan-Meier curve showing freedom from arrhythmia recurrence in patients who underwent Fontan conversion and arrhythmia surgery.

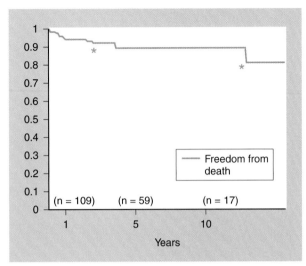

Figure 11-36 Kaplan-Meier curve showing freedom from death of 122 patients who underwent Fontan conversion and arrhythmia surgery: 1994 to 2008. *Asterisks* represent two deaths: one from sedation administration (2.5 years) and one from an automobile accident (11.3 years).

TABLE 11-4	Fontan Conversion with Arrhythmia Surgery: Cox Proportional-Hazards Model for Death or Transplant		
	P Value	*Odds Ratio*	*95% CI*
Protein-losing enteropathy	< .0001	87.1	9.6, 793
Long cardiopulmonary bypass time (>239 minutes)	.0014	15.5	2.9, 83
AVVR (moderate-to-severe)	.0015	11.7	2.6, 53
Right or ambiguous ventricle	.0067	7.7	1.8, 34

AVVR, atrioventricular valve regurgitation; CI, confidence interval.
Adapted with permission from Mavroudis C, Deal BJ, Backer CL et al. J. Maxwell Chamberlain Memorial Paper for congenital heart surgery: 111 Fontan conversions with arrhythmia surgery: surgical lessons and outcomes. Ann Thorac Surg 2007; 84:1457-1465; discussion 1465-1466.

shown to be a risk factor, our recent experience with valve repair has been encouraging. Increasing incidence of atrial fibrillation and left atrial tachycardia parallels increasing complexity of patients. Evolution of pacemaker technology has provided more options for postoperative electrophysiologic management. Fontan conversion does not preclude cardiac transplantation, which will continue to be an important mode of therapy for these patients.

BOX 11-1   FREQUENTLY ASKED QUESTIONS

Question #1
I have a 20-year-old asymptomatic patient who has had an atriopulmonary Fontan operation. He has no arrhythmias, no demonstrated pathway obstructions, no associated lesions, and a large (gigantic) right atrium. What do I recommend for this very bright college student?

Answer
There are reasons for atriomegaly. A careful workup may reveal right pulmonary vein obstruction owing to a large right atrium or left pulmonary vein obstruction due to a large coronary sinus. A Holter monitor may reveal periods of atrial tachycardia, and an exercise study may reveal some objective data to explain the differences between his stated lack of symptoms and the reality of his compromised functional capacity. If all of these tests are negative, we would recommend that this patient be closely followed. Whether the clinician wants to use aspirin or anticoagulant therapy such as crystalline warfarin sodium (Coumadin) is a clinical decision that has no demonstrated clinical basis either for or against its use.

Question #2
I'm treating a 21-year-old Fontan operation patient with mitral atresia and single right ventricle who has had to curtail his activities over the past 6 months. He has severe tricuspid regurgitation and severe ventricular dysfunction. He has controlled atrial arrhythmias (amiodarone), no pathway obstructions, no associated lesions other than tricuspid insufficiency, a large (gigantic) right atrium, and decreased functional status (New York Heart Association class III). What should I recommend for him?

Answer
The clinical situation with this patient is very similar to the era when Mustard/Senning procedure patients were being evaluated for tricuspid insufficiency and ventricular dysfunction. Would tricuspid valve replacement help ventricular function? In the ensuing years clinicians and surgeons found that tricuspid valve replacement rarely helped these patients because the basic condition was ventricular dysfunction, which in turn caused the tricuspid regurgitation. This patient should be considered for cardiac transplantation.

Question #3
I have a moribund 35-year-old patient with a single ventricle, status post Fontan operation whom I have been observing for 30 years. He has severe protein-losing enteropathy and cirrhosis of the liver and has just recently developed anuric kidney failure. Is there anything that we can offer him?

Answer
This unfortunate patient has developed significant complications of the Fontan operation. He is likely to have clotting abnormalities, irreversible kidney failure, and severe ventricular dysfunction. Heroic measures include cardiac transplantation and possible liver and kidney transplantation. His chances for survival are very low owing to the scarcity of organs and a high mortality no matter whether organs are found or not. One would have to consider comfort care with end-of-life protocols. Situations such as these raise ethical questions that, at the forefront, consider the dignity of the individual. Secondary, but not unimportant, issues consider the allocation of precious resources and their application to a moribund patient. These are serious matters that have always been encountered and will require careful and thoughtful consideration by physicians, ethicists, the public, and patients.

REFERENCES

1. Joffs C, Sade RM. Congenital Heart Surgery Nomenclature and Database Project: palliation, correction, or repair? Ann Thorac Surg 2000;69(Suppl. 4):S369–S372.
2. Fontan F, Baudet E. Surgical repair of tricuspid atresia. Thorax 1971;26:240–248.
3. Kreutzer G, Galindez E, Bono H, et al. An operation for the correction of tricuspid atresia. J Thorac Cardiovasc Surg 1973;66:613–621.
4. Bjork VO, Olin CL, Bjarke BB, Thoren CA. Right atrial-right ventricular anastomosis for correction of tricuspid atresia. J Thorac Cardiovasc Surg 1979;77:452–458.
5. Rodbard S, Wagner D. By-passing the right ventricle. Proc Soc Exp Biol Med 1949;71:69.
6. Konstantinov IE, Alexi-Meskishvili VV. Cavo-pulmonary shunt: from the first experiments to clinical practice. Ann Thorac Surg 1999;68:1100–1106.
7. Carlon CA, Mondini PG, De Marchi R. [A new vascular anastomosis for the surgical therapy of various cardiovascular defects.]. G Ital Chir 1950;6:760–774.
8. Schumacker HB. Use of the right auricle as a pump for the pulmonary circuit. Presented at: the 40th Annual Clinical Congress of the American College of Surgeons, Atlantic City, NJ; November 15, 1954.
9. Meshalkin EN. [Anastomosis of the upper vena cava with the pulmonary artery in patients with congenital heart disease with blood flow insufficiency in the lesser circulation.]. Eksp Khirurgiia 1956;1:3–12.
10. Robicsek F, Temesvari A, Kadar RL. A new method for the treatment of congenital heart disease associated with impaired pulmonary circulation; an experimental study. Acta Med Scand 1956;154:151–161.
11. Sanger PW, Robicsek F, Taylor FH. Vena cava–pulmonary artery anastomosis: III. Successful operation in case of complete transposition of great vessels with interatrial septal defect and pulmonary stenosis. J Thorac Cardiovasc Surg 1959;38:166–171.
12. Robicsek F. An epitaph for cavopulmonary anastomosis. Ann Thorac Surg 1982;34:208–220.
13. Glenn WW. Circulatory bypass of the right side of the heart: IV. Shunt between superior vena cava and distal right pulmonary artery; report of clinical application. N Engl J Med 1958;259:117–120.
14. Baum VC. Pediatric cardiac surgery: an historical appreciation. Paediatr Anaesth 2006;16:1213–1225.
15. Dogliotti AM, Actis-Dato A, Venere G, Tarquini A. [The operation of vena cava–pulmonary artery anastomosis in Fallot's tetralogy and in other heart diseases.]. Minerva Cardioangiol 1961;9:577–593.

16. Haller Jr JA, Adkins JC, Worthington M, Rauenhorst J. Experimental studies on permanent bypass of the right heart. Surgery 1966;59:1128–1132.

17. Azzolina G, Eufrate S, Pensa P. Tricuspid atresia: experience in surgical management with a modified cavopulmonary anastomosis. Thorax 1972;27:111–115.

18. Mavroudis C, Jacobs JP. Proceedings of the International Nomenclature and Database Conferences for Pediatric Cardiac Surgery, 1998-1999. Ann Thorac Surg 2000;69(Suppl 4): S1–S372.

19. Puga FJ, Chiavarelli M, Hagler DJ. Modifications of the Fontan operation applicable to patients with left atrioventricular valve atresia or single atrioventricular valve. Circulation 1987;76: III53–III60.

20. Laks H, Ardehali A, Grant PW, et al. Modification of the Fontan procedure: superior vena cava to left pulmonary artery connection and inferior vena cava to right pulmonary artery connection with adjustable atrial septal defect. Circulation 1995;91:2943–2947.

21. de Leval MR, Kilner P, Gewillig M, Bull C. Total cavopulmonary connection: a logical alternative to atriopulmonary connection for complex Fontan operations: experimental studies and early clinical experience. J Thorac Cardiovasc Surg 1988;96:682–695.

22. Marcelletti C, Corno A, Giannico S, Marino B. Inferior vena cava-pulmonary artery extracardiac conduit: a new form of right heart bypass. J Thorac Cardiovasc Surg 1990;100:228–232.

23. Marcelletti CF, Hanley FL, Mavroudis C, et al. Revision of previous Fontan connections to total extracardiac cavopulmonary anastomosis: a multicenter experience. J Thorac Cardiovasc Surg 2000;119:340–346.

24. Freedom RM, Lock J, Bricker JT. Pediatric cardiology and cardiovascular surgery: 1950-2000. Circulation 2000;102(20 Suppl. 4):IV58–IV68.

25. Kopf GS. Tricuspid atresia. In: Mavroudis C, Backer CL, editors. Pediatric Cardiac Surgery. St. Louis: Mosby; 1994, 379–400.

26. Anderson RH, Wilkinson JL, Gerlis LM, et al. Atresia of the right atrioventricular orifice. Br Heart J 1977;39:414–428.

27. Backer CL, Deal BJ, Mavroudis C, et al. Conversion of the failed Fontan circulation. Cardiol Young 2006;16(Suppl. 1):85–91.

28. Mavroudis C, Backer CL, Deal BJ, et al. Evolving anatomic and electrophysiologic considerations associated with Fontan conversion. Semin Thorac Cardiovasc Surg Pediatr Card Surg Annu 2007;10:136–145.

29. Mavroudis C, Backer CL, Deal BJ. Late reoperations for Fontan patients: state of the art invited review. Eur J Cardiothorac Surg 2008;34:1034–1040.

30. Mavroudis C, Deal BJ, Backer CL, Tsao S. Arrhythmia surgery in patients with and without congenital heart disease. Ann Thorac Surg 2008;86:857–868; discussion 857–868.

31. Zias EA, Mavroudis C, Backer CL, et al. Surgical repair of the congenitally malformed mitral valve in infants and children. Ann Thorac Surg 1998;66:1551–1559.

32. Alfieri O, Maisano F. An effective technique to correct anterior mitral leaflet prolapse. J Card Surg 1999;14:468–470.

33. Mavroudis C, Deal BJ, Backer CL, et al. J. Maxwell Chamberlain Memorial Paper for congenital heart surgery: 111 Fontan conversions with arrhythmia surgery: surgical lessons and outcomes. Ann Thorac Surg 2007;84:1457–1465 discussion 1465–1466.

Late Complications Following the Fontan Operation

PAUL KHAIRY | LISE-ANDRÉE MERCIER

Introduction

The univentricular heart encompasses a spectrum of rare and complex congenital cardiac malformations in which a biventricular repair is not possible and, usually, both atria predominantly egress into one functionally single ventricular chamber.[1] Population studies indicate an overall prevalence of approximately 2 per 10,000 live births. Subtypes include hypoplastic right or left ventricles, absence or atretic atrioventricular (AV) valves, common AV valves with only one well-developed ventricle, and heterotaxy syndromes (or cases of isomerism), that is, disorders of lateralization in which the arrangement of abdominal and thoracic viscera differ from normal and mirror-image of normal.

General objectives of initial surgical palliation are to provide unobstructed systemic outflow, unobstructed systemic and pulmonary venous return, and controlled pulmonary blood flow. Most patients will be managed by a staged surgical approach aiming toward a Fontan procedure. A minority will not undergo Fontan palliation because of reasonably balanced systemic and pulmonary circulations or as a result of unfavorable anatomy/hemodynamics. In patients with severe pulmonary obstruction or atresia, initial palliation may consist of aortopulmonary shunts (Fig. 12-1A-D) or a bidirectional cavopulmonary anastomosis (see Fig. 12-1E). In contrast, in patients with unrestrictive pulmonary blood flow, pulmonary artery banding or division may afford initial protection (from developing pulmonary arterial hypertension).

Fontan procedures are typically completed between 18 months and 4 years of age and consist of directing systemic venous return to the pulmonary artery, often without an interposed right ventricle (see Fig. 12-1F-H). Multiple modifications and adaptations have been proposed since its original description in 1971. The classic Fontan operation involved a valved conduit between the right atrium and pulmonary artery. Currently, the majority of adults will have had a modified Fontan procedure, with a direct anastomosis of the right atrium to a divided pulmonary artery (see Fig. 12-1F). De Leval later proposed an end-to-side anastomosis of the superior vena cava to the undivided right pulmonary artery, a composite intra-atrial tunnel using the right atrial posterior wall, and a prosthetic patch to channel the inferior vena cava to the transected superior vena cava (see Fig. 12-1G).[2] Inferior vena caval flow may also be directed to the pulmonary artery by means of an external conduit (see Fig. 12-1H). In addition, Fontan pathways may be "fenestrated" by creating an atrial septal defect (ASD) as an escape valve for elevated Fontan pressures postoperatively.[3] Fenestrations may subsequently be closed percutaneously, conditions permitting.

Patients with univentricular hearts and systemic outflow obstruction, the most severe form being hypoplastic left heart syndrome, constitute the most prevalent subtype. These patients typically undergo a variation of Norwood stages that culminate in a Fontan-type circulation.[4]

Objectives of the *Norwood stage 1* procedure, performed within the first 2 weeks of life, are to provide unobstructed pulmonary venous return, permanent systemic outflow from the right ventricle, and temporary pulmonary blood supply to allow the pulmonary vasculature to develop and mature (see Fig. 12-1I, J).

The *Norwood stage II* procedure, performed before 6 months of age, consists of a bidirectional Glenn shunt or hemi-Fontan connection and closure of the Blalock-Taussig shunt.

At 18 months to 3 years of age, the *stage III* procedure completes the total cavopulmonary Fontan connection by connecting the inferior vena cava to the pulmonary artery.

To understand long-term sequelae in patients after Fontan operations, the Fontan circulation may be viewed as a hemodynamic compromise. In normal biventricular hearts, caval pressures are typically less than 10 mm Hg and mean pulmonary pressures exceed 12 to 15 mm Hg. Fontan physiology imposes systemic venous hypertension with concomitant pulmonary arterial hypotension.[5] Long-term complications, the focus of the current chapter, are numerous, highly prevalent, and increasingly appreciated as the first Fontan recipients approach 4 decades of follow-up. Consequently, lifelong follow-up in centers with expertise in adult congenital heart disease (ACHD) is recommended for all patients.

Clinical Evaluation

Routine follow-up typically involves one to two clinical visits per year. In addition to a thorough clinical history and physical examination, minimum testing includes resting oximetry; 12-lead electrocardiography (ECG); chest radiography; echocardiography with Doppler interrogation; complete blood cell count; biochemical analyses for liver function tests, serum protein, and albumin levels; and occasional Holter monitoring. Additional workup may require transesophageal echocardiography, exercise spiroergometry, cardiac magnetic resonance imaging (CMR), isotopic ventriculography, complete heart catheterization, and electrophysiologic study.

PHYSICAL EXAMINATION

After successful Fontan palliation, the physical examination typically reveals the following:

- A transcutaneous oxygen saturation greater than 94% in patients without fenestrations[6]
- Nonpulsatile mild jugular venous distention
- A single second heart sound that may be loud, depending on the position of the aorta
- No murmur or a soft systolic murmur (e.g., mild AV valve regurgitation)
- Absence of a diastolic murmur

Markedly elevated jugular venous pressures may indicate Fontan obstruction, particularly if associated with hepatomegaly and/or mild cyanosis. Loud systolic murmurs should raise concern for moderate or severe AV valve regurgitation, outflow tract obstruction of the systemic ventricle, or incomplete ligation of the main pulmonary artery, with forward flow. A diastolic murmur may indicate aortic regurgitation or pulmonary regurgitation in patients with particular variants that include pulmonary to aortic connections (e.g., Damus-Kaye-Stansel).

COMMON CAUSES OF HYPOXEMIA

- Progressive deterioration of ventricular function with or without AV valve regurgitation
- Shunting through a baffle leak or residual interatrial communication
- Pulmonary vein compression by a giant right atrium (Fig. 12-2) or aorta[7]

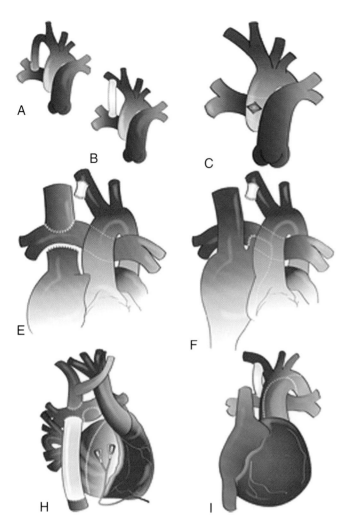

Figure 12-1 Aortopulmonary shunts and variations of Fontan surgery. **A,** The classic Blalock-Taussig shunt. **B,** Modified Blalock-Taussig shunt. **C,** Waterston shunt. **D,** Potts shunt. **E,** Bidirectional Glenn operation. **F,** Modified classic Fontan. **G,** Intracardiac lateral tunnel Fontan. **H,** Extracardiac Fontan. **I,** Norwood stage I procedure. **J,** Sano modification. *(Adapted with permission from Khairy P, Poirier N, Mercier LA. Univentricular heart. Circulation 2007; 115:800-812. Copyright, American Heart Association.)*

- Systemic venous collateralization
  - Present in about 30% of patients with bidirectional cavopulmonary connections
  - Between systemic or hepatic veins and pulmonary veins, left atrium, or coronary sinus
- Pulmonary arteriovenous malformations (Fig. 12-3)
- Particularly in patients with classic Glenn or Kawashima-type operations
- Pulmonary pathology including a restrictive pattern or diaphragmatic paresis
  - Right-to-left interatrial shunting via small thebesian veins

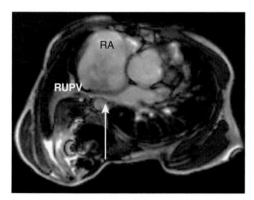

Figure 12-2 Compression of right upper pulmonary vein. Transverse magnetic resonance image of a patient with a modified classic Fontan for tricuspid atresia and severe rotoscoliosis. The *arrow* designates the site where the massively enlarged right atrium (RA) compresses the right upper pulmonary vein (RUPV). *(From Khairy P, Poirier N, Mercier LA. Univentricular heart. Circulation 2007; 115:800-812. Copyright, American Heart Association.)*

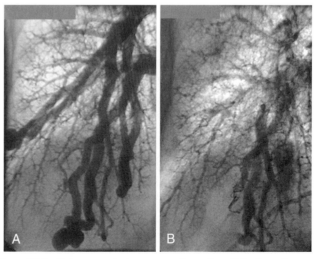

Figure 12-3 Pulmonary arteriovenous malformations. Selective pulmonary angiography of the right lower lobe in a patient with tricuspid atresia and unidirectional Glenn shunt. **A,** Multiple pulmonary arteriovenous malformations are seen. **B,** After transcatheter coil occlusion there is one residual pulmonary arteriovenous malformation. *(From Khairy P, Poirier N, Mercier LA. Univentricular heart. Circulation 2007; 115: 800-812. Copyright, American Heart Association.)*

ELECTROCARDIOGRAPHIC FEATURES

Given the heterogeneity of single ventricles, the ECG appearance is highly variable.[8] It may be particularly helpful in detecting and characterizing rhythm disturbances, particularly atrial tachyarrhythmias. Patients with right atrial isomerism often have two separate sinus nodes, with a P-wave axis that fluctuates with the prevailing pacemaker. In contrast, most hearts with left atrial isomerism do not have a recognizable sinus node, with slow atrial or junctional escape rates. In patients with tricuspid atresia:

- The PR interval is usually normal with tall and broad P waves
- Left-axis deviation is characteristic
- Left ventricular forces are unopposed, as manifested by small r waves and deep S waves over the right precordial leads and tall R waves over the left precordial leads

In the most common subtype of double-inlet left ventricle, that is, with ventriculoarterial discordance, characteristic ECG findings include PR prolongation and possibly higher-degree AV block, absence of Q waves over left precordial leads, and Q waves over right precordial leads and, occasionally, leads II, III, and aVF. In patients with univentricular hearts of right ventricular morphology, including hypoplastic left heart syndrome, typical ECG findings include right ventricular hypertrophy and a superior frontal QRS axis (in over 60%).

RADIOLOGIC FEATURES

The cardiac silhouette may be deviated if the heart is malposed but is usually of normal size if hemodynamics are favorable. The pulmonary vasculature should be normal. Pleural effusions may indicate the need to rule out hemodynamic abnormalities or protein-losing enteropathy.

NONINVASIVE IMAGING

Echocardiography is considered the cornerstone of postoperative assessment. All patients should have periodic echocardiographic and/or CMR by ACHD specialists.[9] Comprehensive echocardiographic examination is outlined in Chapter 5. In general, the underlying diagnosis and morphologic subtype may be fully characterized by a systematic and thorough echocardiographic appraisal that includes apical position; atrial situs; AV relationship; ventriculoarterial alignment; systemic and pulmonary venous anatomy and flow; atrial and ventricular shunts, including bulboventricular foramen, valvular stenosis, and regurgitation; ventricular morphology, size, and function; and aortic and pulmonary artery size and abnormalities, including aortic coarctation. In selected cases, CMR may overcome limitations of echocardiography in demonstrating systemic and pulmonary venous anomalies, aortic arch malformations, and proximal pulmonary artery lesions.

History and Long-Term Sequelae

LONG-TERM SURVIVAL

Long-term survival and modes of death were assessed in a contemporary cohort of 261 patients with Fontan palliation, with right atrium to pulmonary artery connections in 52%, right atrium to right ventricle variants in 10%, lateral tunnels in 38%, and extracardiac conduits in 1%.[10] Over a median follow-up of 12 years, 29% died and 2% underwent cardiac transplantation. Modes of death were as follows: perioperative 68%, sudden cardiac death 9%, thromboembolism 8%, heart failure 7%, sepsis 3%, and other 5%. Importantly, perioperative mortality rates declined steadily over time, from 37% prior to 1982 to less than 2% in 1990 or later.

Actuarial event-free survival at 1, 10, 20, and 25 years was 80.1%, 74.8%, 68.3%, and 53.6%, respectively (Fig. 12-4). In perioperative survivors, freedom from death or cardiac transplantation was comparable among all types of Fontan operations, with survival rates of 96.9%, 89.9%, 82.6%, and 69.6% at 1, 10, 20, and 25 years, respectively. Independent predictors of all-cause mortality or cardiac transplantation were protein-losing enteropathy, hypoplastic left heart syndrome, higher right atrial pressures, and diuretic therapy.

Death from thromboembolism occurred at a median age of 25 years, 9 years after Fontan surgery. Patients in whom thromboemboli were detected clinically and those without antiplatelet or anticoagulant therapy were at increased risk. Heart failure deaths occurred at a mean of 12 years after Fontan surgery, with similar risk factors to total mortality. Sudden deaths occurred at a median age of 20 years, with no identifiable independent predictors. Most were of presumed arrhythmic etiology.

ARRHYTHMIAS

Atrial arrhythmias are a major contributor to late complications and are associated with substantial morbidity. Over 50% of patients experience an atrial tachyarrhythmia by 20 years after Fontan surgery,[11] with a prevalence that continues to increase with follow-up duration. Although initial recurrences may be sporadic, the pattern often progresses toward more frequent and prolonged recurrences.[12] Importantly, patients with Fontan physiology may not tolerate persistent tachyarrhythmias, even with 2:1 conduction. A reduction in ventricular systolic function, increase in AV valve regurgitation, atrial thrombus formation, congestive heart failure, syncope, and rarely, sudden death, may ensue. Acute termination of tachycardia with direct current cardioversion, overdrive pacing, or antiarrhythmic medication is usually warranted after balancing risks of thromboembolic complications (often with transesophageal echocardiography) against delayed cardioversion, with potential worsening of hemodynamic status.

When atrial tachyarrhythmias are detected, underlying hemodynamic causes such as obstruction of the atriopulmonary connection should be sought and anticoagulation pursued. The most common form of tachyarrhythmias are macroreentrant intra-atrial tachycardia circuits, facilitated by fiber orientation patterns, extensive atrial fibrosis, suture lines, and/or anatomic barriers such as the orifice of the inferior or superior vena cava and coronary sinus. Intra-atrial reentry tachycardia is typically confined to the systemic venous atrium in patients with atriopulmonary anastomoses but may involve the pulmonary venous atrium with total cavopulmonary connections. The lateral tunnel modification was developed to improve hemodynamics and limit atrial tachyarrhythmias, with initially promising results. It remains doubtful, however, that a reduction in arrhythmia burden will be maintained long term. By limiting atrial incisions and sutures, extracardiac conduits show promise in reducing the long-term incidence of atrial tachyarrhythmias. Lack of future transvenous access to the right atrium is, however, a major hurdle to long-term therapeutic options in the event of recurrent arrhythmias.

Atrial tachyarrhythmias in Fontan patients are characteristically resistant to antiarrhythmic therapy, although some successes with class IC and class III agents have been observed. With three-dimensional (3D) electroanatomic mapping systems (Fig. 12-5) and irrigated-tip ablation catheters, transcatheter procedures are acutely successful in over 80% of cases in dedicated centers.[13] Although recurrences and development of new arrhythmias remain problematic, in the order of 30% to 50% 6 to 12 months after ablation, quality of life metrics are improved.[14] Difficulties include complex and multiple circuits and inability to create transmural lesions in severely thickened (up to 20 mm) atria. Patients with failing Fontan connections and atrial arrhythmias should be considered for surgical conversion to a lateral tunnel or extracardiac conduit with concomitant arrhythmia surgery.[15]

Bradyarrhythmias, predominantly sinus node dysfunction, have been observed in 13% to 16% of patients with atriopulmonary connections by mid-term follow-up.[16] If the need for a pacemaker arises, Fontan surgery usually precludes direct transvenous access to the ventricle.[1] With classic atriopulmonary connections, transvenous atrial pacing is generally feasible and ventricular pacing via the coronary sinus may be achieved in selected cases. Despite extensive areas of low voltage, acceptable atrial pacing thresholds and adequate P-wave sensing may be attained in most. In patients with total cavopulmonary connections, some variants of intracardiac, but not extracardiac, conduits may likewise permit transvenous access to the atrium and coronary sinus. However, even if transvenous access is possible, opinions differ

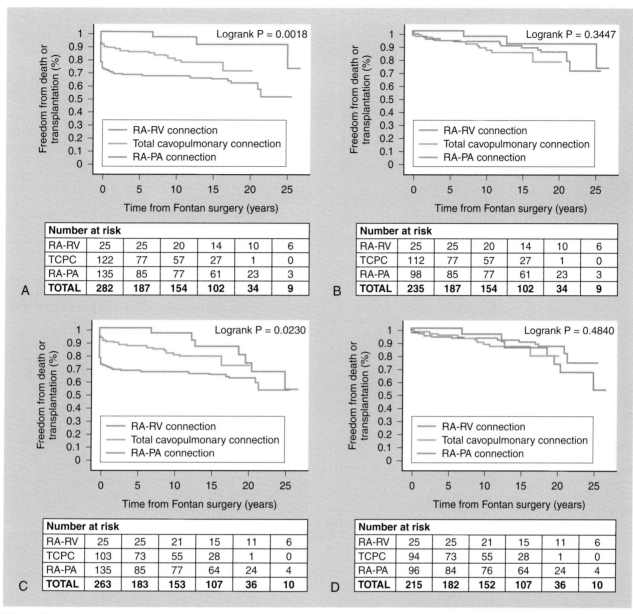

Figure 12-4 Freedom from death or transplantation according to type of Fontan. Two analyses are presented. In **A** and **B**, censoring occurs at the time of Fontan conversion and patient-years are attributed to the Fontan category under observation. In **C** and **D**, patient-years are ascribed to the initial Fontan category without censoring at the time of Fontan conversion. Kaplan-Meier curves in **A** and **C** plot survival free from all-cause mortality or cardiac transplantation in the entire cohort according to type of Fontan surgery. In **B** and **D** freedom from all-cause mortality or cardiac transplantation in perioperative survivors is shown. PA, pulmonary artery; RA, right atrium; RV, right ventricle; TCPC, total cavopulmonary connection. *(Redrawn with permission from Khairy P, Fernandes SM, Mayer JE Jr, et al. Long-term survival, modes of death, and predictors of mortality in patients with Fontan surgery. Circulation 2008;117:85-92. Copyright, American Heart Association.)*

as to whether transvenous or epicardial atrial leads should be favored.[17] Thrombus formation on pacing leads is an important concern, and hemodynamic consequences of pulmonary emboli may be devastating. Whereas some recommend avoidance of transvenous leads in the context of Fontan surgery, proponents generally support long-term antiplatelet or anticoagulation therapy.

When vascular access limitations or thromboembolic risks prohibit transvenous leads for pacemakers or defibrillators, epicardial systems may be required. Creative approaches to defibrillator implantation have included subcutaneous arrays and epicardially or subcutaneously placed leads.[18] However, these approaches are not without complications, including high defibrillation thresholds. In general, placing the defibrillator opposite rather than ipsilaterally to a subcutaneous electrode may result in lower defibrillation thresholds.

HEPATIC DYSFUNCTION

Liver injury is common and has been related to length of follow-up, elevated hepatic venous pressures, low cardiac index, and reduced heart rate.[19] In 34 patients with a median follow-up of 12 years, hepatomegaly was present in 53%, abnormal transaminase levels in 30%, elevated gamma glutamyl transpeptidase levels in 30%, elevated bilirubin levels in 32%, and coagulopathy in 58%.[19] Multiple clotting factor abnormalities include decreased levels of Protein C, Protein S, and antithrombin III. Increased platelet reactivity has also been recognized. Hepatic congestion, sinusoidal fibrosis, and cardiac cirrhosis are common, whereas hepatic adenoma and hepatocellular carcinoma occur less frequently.[20] The presence of a substantial quantity of orcein negative sinusoidal fibrosis suggests a remediable component to liver damage.[21] Dense fibrous bands are predominantly orcein positive and

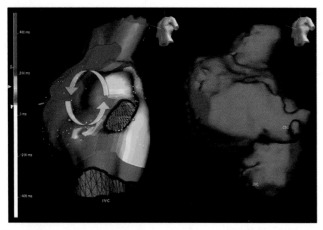

Figure 12-5 Electroanatomic mapping in a right atrium to pulmonary artery Fontan connection. An electroanatomic map (*left*) and imported CMR image (*right*) are shown in a patient with a classic modified Fontan operation and recalcitrant atrial tachyarrhythmias. The gray regions denote areas of dense scar. Local activation times are color-coded, from white to red, orange, yellow, green, light blue, dark blue, and purple. Note the narrow channel of tissue between two dense scars. The arrhythmia circuit propagated counterclockwise around the upper scar and was successfully interrupted by ablating this narrow isthmus. (*From Khairy P. EP challenges in adult congenital heart disease. Heart Rhythm 2008; 5:1464-1472.*)

suggest irreversible damage.[21] The fibrotic process appears mediated by a noninflammatory mechanism. Hemodynamic assessment is required in any patient with ongoing liver dysfunction.

THROMBOEMBOLI

Thrombus formation is a well-recognized source of morbidity, and asymptomatic pulmonary emboli are frequently found. More recently, thromboemboli have been recognized as leading causes of late mortality.[10] In the Fontan mortality study, all patients who died of thromboemboli had atriopulmonary Fontan procedures, except for one patient with a lateral tunnel. Clot was predominantly identified within the right atrium (Fig. 12-6), although a few patients had thromboemboli limited to pulmonary arteries.

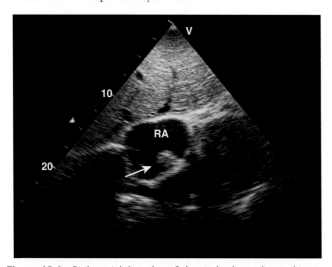

Figure 12-6 Right atrial thrombus. Subcostal echocardiographic view of the right atrium (RA) in a patient with a modified classic Fontan for *d*-transposition of the great arteries, multiple muscular ventricular septal defects, a functional single ventricle, and atrial tachyarrhythmias. The *arrow* indicates a well-delineated thrombus in the dilated right atrium. (*From Khairy P, Poirier N, Mercier LA. Univentricular heart. Circulation 2007; 115:800-812. Copyright, American Heart Association.*)

Anticoagulation is generally indicated in patients with atrial arrhythmias, intra-atrial shunts, atrial or baffle thrombus, prior thromboembolic event, and transvenous pacemaker leads. In the absence of these indications, the role of routine long-term antiplatelet and/or anticoagulation therapy remains poorly defined.

PROTEIN-LOSING ENTEROPATHY

Protein-losing enteropathy is a major complication associated with substantial mortality. Loss of protein via the gastrointestinal tract occurs in approximately 4% of patients with Fontan surgery and is clinically characterized by fatigue, peripheral edema, pleural and pericardial effusions, ascites, and chronic diarrhea. The diagnosis is confirmed by a low serum albumin level and increased fecal α_1-antitrypsin levels. Protein-losing enteropathy is thought to be mediated, in part, by chronically elevated central venous pressures. Other risk factors include longer cardiopulmonary bypass time and morphologic right ventricular anatomy.[22] In patients with generalized edema, the 5-year survival rate is approximately 50%.[23]

Multiple therapeutic approaches have been described with anecdotal successes. These include dietary modifications with high-protein and high medium-chain triglycerides, afterload reducing agents, inotropic agents, heparin, albumin infusions, octreotide, prednisone, creation of an atrial fenestration, Fontan revision or conversion, and cardiac transplantation. Of note, even with cardiac transplantation, protein-losing enteropathy does not always resolve. Because the mean time between Fontan palliation and diagnosis of protein-losing enteropathy is 7 years, most adult survivors will have undergone some form of surgical intervention.

PLASTIC BRONCHITIS

Plastic bronchitis is an uncommon complication in children with Fontan surgery that is even rarer in adults. It is characterized by the production of large pale bronchial casts that obstruct the tracheobronchial tree. These casts may be distinguished from mucus plugs, such as those found in asthma, by their cellular content, dense consistency, and cohesiveness. In patients with Fontan surgery, plastic bronchitis is characterized by an acellular infiltrate with a predominance of fibrin. It is a life-threatening complication that can result in airway obstruction and asphyxiation. Although the pathophysiology remains unclear, it has been associated with high central venous pressures in the setting of a predisposed pulmonary lymphatic system. Treatment successes are limited, with case reports describing favorable response to aerosolized urokinase and tissue plasminogen activator.[24]

EXERCISE TOLERANCE AND QUALITY OF LIFE

Exercise capacity is impaired in adults with Fontan surgery and is characteristically associated with reduced vital capacity, high residual volume-to-total lung capacity ratio, low arterial saturation with hypocapnia, and skeletal muscle dysfunction. A univentricular heart of left ventricular morphology is independently associated with a higher peak oxygen uptake consumption.[25] No pharmacologic agent has yet been shown to improve exercise capacity, including a 10-week course of enalapril.[26] Preliminary data suggest that an exercise program may be safe and beneficial in patients with stable hemodynamics. However, optimal exercise programs remain to be defined and the effects of exercise training on cardiac function, functional capacity, peripheral muscle function, and health-related quality of life require further study.

Despite reductions in exercise tolerance, repeated hospital admissions, and comorbidities, many patients with univentricular hearts and Fontan palliation report a satisfactory quality of life. Younger age is associated with better quality of life. In adults with Fontan physiology, physical functioning, mental health, and general health perception are generally impaired when compared with normal controls. Reoperations, arrhythmias, and thromboembolic events are significantly associated with a poorer quality of life.

PREGNANCY

A univentricular heart with Fontan physiology is not an absolute contraindication to pregnancy. However, risks must be thoughtfully considered (see Chapter 21). In selected candidates with favorable hemodynamics, pregnancy may be successfully undertaken with a relatively low risk of long-term sequelae.[27,28] As in other forms of congenital heart disease,[29] pregnancy is not advisable in women with cyanosis (i.e., oxygen saturation < 90%), NYHA functional class III or IV symptoms, systemic ventricular dysfunction, left-sided heart obstruction, or prior cardiac event or arrhythmias. In patients contemplating pregnancy, a multidisciplinary approach is recommended, including high-risk obstetric care, specialized cardiology assessment and follow-up, and genetic counseling. Careful surveillance may allow prompt recognition of symptoms related to systemic venous congestion, increased AV valve regurgitation, worsening ventricular function, atrial and ventricular arrhythmias, thromboemboli, and paradoxical emboli in the presence of fenestrations or other sources of shunting.[27]

NONCARDIAC PERIOPERATIVE CARE

There is a paucity of data regarding risks and complications related to noncardiac surgery in patients after a Fontan operation. If present, worsening cyanosis should be addressed before surgery. Given the fragile physiology, particular vigilance with close perioperative hemodynamic monitoring is warranted. Pulmonary blood flow is dependent on systemic venous pressures and may be highly sensitive to minor variations in pulmonary vascular resistance, which may be modulated by anesthetics and hypoxemia and postoperative complications such as atelectasis, thromboemboli, and pneumonia. Oxygenation should be optimized and excess volume loading or volume depletion with decreased venous return (e.g., positive-pressure ventilation) avoided. To prevent complications from changes in preload and/or pulmonary vascular resistance, early involvement of experienced anesthesiology and intensive care personnel is advisable.

FONTAN CONVERSION

As patients with atriopulmonary Fontan connections age and their hemodynamic status worsens or complications arise, surgical conversion to total cavopulmonary connections should be considered. This typically involves debulking the right atrium, removing thrombus, excising right atrial scar tissue, performing a modified right atrial maze procedure, adding a left-sided atrial maze procedure in patients with prior documented atrial fibrillation,[15] and epicardial pacemaker implantation. Left-sided maze procedures are not routine, given the longer ischemic time.

Experienced centers report combined perioperative cardiac transplantation and mortality rates of 2% to 15%.[15] Perceived advantages of Fontan conversion to a lateral or extracardiac conduit include improved hemodynamics and a lower incidence of atrial arrhythmias and thrombosis related to atrial distention.[5,15] Importantly, Fontan conversion without arrhythmia surgery affords insufficient protection against atrial tachyarrhythmias.[30]

Case series with short-term follow-up report promising results, with arrhythmia recurrence rates of 13% to 30%.[15] Theoretical advantages of the extracardiac versus intracardiac lateral tunnel include a decreased incidence of sinus node dysfunction and avoidance of suture lines (with arrhythmogenic potential) and thromboembolic risk associated with intracardiac prosthetic material.[5] Comparative studies of the two approaches are required to determine whether extracardiac tunnels are associated with a lower long-term risk of atrial arrhythmias. As previously noted, access to the arrhythmia substrate by means of a trans-baffle puncture may be considerably complicated by an extracardiac conduit.

CONCLUSION

Fontan surgery has been touted as an innovative milestone of historic proportions, and rightfully so, in the evolution of congenital heart disease management. It achieved the seemingly impossible, that is, restoration of a noncyanotic state with complete bypass of the right ventricle. By eliminating surgical and congenital shunts, ventricular volume overload and pulmonary hypertension were avoided. The technique was modified and applied to a wide variety of single-ventricle physiologies. It was later realized, however, that the "perfect" Fontan operation was an elusive goal, because it inherently represents a hemodynamic compromise. Complications are numerous, diverse, and increasingly ubiquitous in aging adult survivors. Common long-term sequelae include severe right atrial dilation, atrial bradyarrhythmias and tachyarrhythmias, thromboemboli, hepatic dysfunction, progressive ventricular dysfunction and AV valve regurgitation, and worsening cyanosis from systemic venous collateralization, pulmonary arteriovenous malformations, and pulmonary vein compression. Quality of life and functional capacity are substantially impaired. Leading causes of late mortality include sudden, thromboembolic, and heart failure–related deaths. The complexity of this patient population and imposing catalog of potential adversities underscore recommendations to concentrate the care of Fontan surgical patients within regional centers supported by multidisciplinary teams dedicated to improving outcomes, education, and research.

REFERENCES

1. Khairy P, Poirier N, Mercier LA. Univentricular heart. Circulation 2007;115:800–812.
2. de Leval MR, Kilner P, Gewillig M, Bull C. Total cavopulmonary connection: a logical alternative to atriopulmonary connection for complex Fontan operations. J Thorac Cardiovasc Surg 1988;96:682–695.
3. Bridges ND, Mayer Jr JE, Lock JE, et al. Effect of baffle fenestration on outcome of the modified Fontan operation. Circulation 1992;86:1762–1769.
4. Norwood WI. Hypoplastic left heart syndrome. Cardiol Clin 1989;7:377–385.
5. de Leval MR. The Fontan circulation: a challenge to William Harvey? Nat Clin Pract Cardiovasc Med 2005;2:202–208.
6. Magee AG, McCrindle BW, Mawson J, et al. Systemic venous collateral development after the bidirectional cavopulmonary anastomosis: prevalence and predictors. J Am Coll Cardiol 1998;32:502–508.
7. O'Donnell CP, Lock JE, Powell AJ, Perry SB. Compression of pulmonary veins between the left atrium and the descending aorta. Am J Cardiol 2003;91:248–251.
8. Khairy P, Marelli AJ. Clinical use of electrocardiography in adults with congenital heart disease. Circulation 2007;116:2734–2746.
9. Warnes CA, Williams RG, Bashore TM, et al. ACC/AHA 2008 Guidelines for the management of adults with congenital heart disease: Executive summary. J Am Coll Cardiol 2008;52:1890–1947.
10. Khairy P, Fernandes SM, Mayer Jr JE, et al. Long-term survival, modes of death, and predictors of mortality in patients with Fontan surgery. Circulation 2008;117:85–92.
11. Weipert J, Noebauer C, Schreiber C, et al. Occurrence and management of atrial arrhythmia after long-term Fontan circulation. J Thorac Cardiovasc Surg 2004;127:457–464.

12. Deal BJ, Mavroudis C, Backer CL. Arrhythmia management in the Fontan patient. Pediatr Cardiol 2007;28:448–456.
13. Triedman JK, DeLucca JM, Alexander ME, et al. Prospective trial of electroanatomically guided, irrigated catheter ablation of atrial tachycardia in patients with congenital heart disease. Heart Rhythm 2005;2:700–705.
14. Triedman JK, Alexander ME, Love BA, et al. Influence of patient factors and ablative technologies on outcomes of radiofrequency ablation of intra-atrial re-entrant tachycardia in patients with congenital heart disease. J Am Coll Cardiol 2002;39:1827–1835.
15. Mavroudis C, Deal BJ, Backer CL. The beneficial effects of total cavopulmonary conversion and arrhythmia surgery for the failed Fontan. Semin Thorac Cardiovasc Surg Pediatr Card Surg Annu 2002;5:12–24.
16. Cohen MI, Wernovsky G, Vetter VL, et al. Sinus node function after a systematically staged Fontan procedure. Circulation 1998;98:II352–II358.
17. Khairy P. EP challenges in adult congenital heart disease. Heart Rhythm 2008;5:1464–1472.
18. Stephenson EA, Batra AS, Knilans TK, et al. A multicenter experience with novel implantable cardioverter defibrillator configurations in the pediatric and congenital heart disease population. J Cardiovasc Electrophysiol 2006;17:41–46.
19. Camposilvan S, Milanesi O, Stellin G, et al. Liver and cardiac function in the long term after Fontan operation. Ann Thorac Surg 2008;86:177–182.
20. Ghaferi AA, Hutchins GM. Progression of liver pathology in patients undergoing the Fontan procedure: chronic passive congestion, cardiac cirrhosis, hepatic adenoma, and hepatocellular carcinoma. J Thorac Cardiovasc Surg 2005;129:1348–1352.

21. Kendall TJ, Stedman B, Hacking N, et al. Hepatic fibrosis and cirrhosis in the Fontan circulation: a detailed morphological study. J Clin Pathol 2008;61:504–508.
22. Powell AJ, Gauvreau K, Jenkins KJ, et al. Perioperative risk factors for development of protein-losing enteropathy following a Fontan procedure. Am J Cardiol 2001;88:1206–1209.
23. Mertens L, Hagler DJ, Sauer U, et al. Protein-losing enteropathy after the Fontan operation: an international multicenter study. PLE study group. J Thorac Cardiovasc Surg 1998;115:1063–1073.
24. Do TB, Chu JM, Berdjis F, Anas NG. Fontan patient with plastic bronchitis treated successfully using aerosolized tissue plasminogen activator: a case report and review of the literature. Pediatr Cardiol 2009;30:352–355.
25. Ohuchi H, Yasuda K, Hasegawa S, et al. Influence of ventricular morphology on aerobic exercise capacity in patients after the Fontan operation. J Am Coll Cardiol 2001;37:1967–1974.
26. Kouatli AA, Garcia JA, Zellers TM, et al. Enalapril does not enhance exercise capacity in patients after Fontan procedure. Circulation 1997;96:1507–1512.
27. Khairy P, Ouyang DW, Fernandes SM, et al. Pregnancy outcomes in women with congenital heart disease. Circulation 2006;113:517–524.
28. Canobbio MM, Mair DD, van der Velde M, Koos BJ. Pregnancy outcomes after the Fontan repair. J Am Coll Cardiol 1996;28:763–767.
29. Siu SC, Sermer M, Colman JM, et al. Prospective multicenter study of pregnancy outcomes in women with heart disease. Circulation 2001;104:515–521.
30. Takahashi K, Fynn-Thompson F, Cecchin F, et al. Clinical outcomes of Fontan conversion surgery with and without associated arrhythmia intervention. Int J Cardiol 2009;137:260–266.

13

Heart and Lung Transplantation in Adult Congenital Heart Disease

STEVEN A. WEBBER | ASIF HASAN | FRANK A. PIGULA

Introduction

Many patients surviving into adulthood with congenital heart disease (CHD) will develop progressive cardiopulmonary dysfunction. Some will develop ventricular failure, some will have pulmonary hypertension, and many will experience progressive cyanosis. Among these patients, some will require cardiac replacement, others will need heart-lung transplantation, and a few may be suitable for lung transplantation with repair of the congenital defect. In many, the risks of transplantation may be prohibitive and continued medical management will be the best option. Risk stratification for this challenging group of patients requires comprehensive evaluation by a multidisciplinary team that includes transplant surgeons as well as cardiologists with special interest and expertise in adult congenital heart disease (ACHD).

Indications

Little is known about the long-term needs for thoracic transplantation in ACHD. The 2008 report of the Registry of the International Society for Heart and Lung Transplantation (ISHLT) shows that only 2% of adult heart transplants are performed for a diagnosis of CHD,[1] although there was a small increase to 3% over the past 3 to 4 years. Similarly, only a tiny proportion of adult lung transplantations are performed for this indication. By contrast, congenital CHD accounted for one third of adult heart-lung transplants reported to the registry between 1982 and 2007.[2] Indeed, CHD remains the most common diagnosis leading to heart-lung transplantation in both children and adults. The number of thoracic transplants performed for the indication of CHD almost certainly underestimates the true need. Many patients are not referred for consideration of transplantation because it is assumed that their disease may be too complex or the risk is too high. Others die while on the waiting list. With almost all forms of CHD now deemed suitable for palliation or repair in infancy and childhood, an ever-increasing population of patients with severe forms of CHD is now reaching adult life. Thus, increasing demand for transplantation in adults with CHD seems inevitable.

Types of Heart Disease Requiring Transplantation

A few patients who have never undergone palliation for their congenital defects survive into adult life. These include patients with simple anatomic defects such as atrial or ventricular septal defect or patent ductus arteriosus who have developed pulmonary vascular disease. Few patients without prior surgery will be suitable for isolated heart transplantation. Another population comprises those patients who were palliated for complex cyanotic heart disease (with reduced pulmonary blood flow) before the modern era of congenital heart surgery. Many of these underwent systemic-to-pulmonary shunts such as Waterston or Potts procedures or a classic Blalock-Taussig shunt. These (relatively) unrestricted shunts provided excellent long-term palliation for many patients but caused chronic ventricular volume overload as well as excessive pulmonary blood flow, resulting in pulmonary hypertension. Many of these patients may therefore be potential heart-lung transplant candidates.

An increasing population of patients being referred for transplant consideration are those palliated with partial (Glenn) or complete (Fontan) atriopulmonary or cavopulmonary anastomoses. It is now recognized that the Fontan procedure is palliative, even though complete separation of the circulations has been achieved.[3] Most patients with Fontan circulation will likely need consideration for heart transplantation at some point in their adult life.

Two final groups of patients form a significant proportion of the adults with CHD referred for consideration of thoracic transplantation. These are patients with tetralogy of Fallot with complex pulmonary atresia and patients with simple transposition of the great vessels who underwent childhood repair with atrial baffling (Mustard or Senning procedure). The former group poses enormous challenges. Most are referred for consideration of heart-lung transplantation with progressive cyanosis. Some have never been palliated, but many have received one or multiple systemic-to-pulmonary shunts often with multiple unifocalization procedures. Patients with right ventricular failure after a Senning or Mustard procedure are also being seen with greater frequency as it becomes apparent that the systemic right ventricle is unlikely to perform well into late adult life. Several years ago it was believed that many of these adults with right ventricular failure could be helped by left ventricular training and subsequent atrial baffle takedown and arterial switch procedure. It is now recognized that the mortality of this approach is very high in the older patient and most of these patients are probably best considered for heart transplantation.

Timing of Transplantation

For patients with ischemic or dilated cardiomyopathy, a number of risk factors for survival have been investigated. Peak oxygen consumption has proved a useful guide for timing of transplantation. In the setting of CHD, no such guidelines exist and each patient's pathophysiology is unique. Life expectancy of less than 2 years can be considered a good indication for listing, given the long waiting times for donor organs in this population. This is not always easy to predict and emphasizes the need for involvement of physicians highly experienced in the management of adults with CHD in the transplant evaluation. Evaluation of quality of life is as important as estimation of survival in determining the timing of transplantation. It must also be remembered that many adults with end-stage CHD may not be suitable for ventricular assist device support as a bridge to transplantation. Therefore, late referral should be avoided.

Pre-transplantation Evaluation

The principles of evaluation of the thoracic organ candidate are covered in detail in standard texts. Specific considerations in the evaluation of the patient with ACHD are summarized in Box 13-1.

ANATOMIC/PHYSIOLOGIC CONSIDERATIONS

Risk assessment and planning of the appropriate operative procedure require comprehensive evaluation of the patient's anatomy and cardiopulmonary physiology. Complete documentation of systemic and pulmonary venous return is required. This must also include knowledge of hepatic venous return. Abnormalities of great vessel relationship should be noted but generally pose few problems for cardiac transplantation. Specific attention must be paid to branch pulmonary arterial anatomy. Stenoses, hypoplasia, distortions, and discontinuity of the pulmonary arteries are commonly present and may determine whether isolated heart transplantation can be achieved. Angiography and magnetic resonance imaging may be required for full evaluation. Assessment of systemic-to-pulmonary arterial shunts and collateral circulation is also critical. Persistence of major collateral vessels will cause an unnecessary left ventricular volume overload that may be poorly tolerated by the freshly ischemic cardiac allograft. Extensive systemic-to-pulmonary collateral circulation also represents an important risk factor for severe perioperative hemorrhage. Chronic secondary erythrocytosis and history of multiple prior thoracic surgical procedures add to the risk of perioperative bleeding. Reports of all prior operative procedures must be directly reviewed. It is not unusual to find important clinical information that directly impacts on surgical planning, such as a history of postoperative mediastinal or pleural infection or even of unilateral pleurodesis that would likely preclude ipsilateral lung transplantation. History of phrenic nerve damage should also be sought. When doubt exists, diaphragmatic motion should be studied with ultrasonography or fluoroscopy. The relationship of conduits or cardiac structures to the posterior aspect of the sternum must also be noted, because inadvertent entry into a cavity must be avoided. Finally, evaluation for the presence of pulmonary arteriovenous malformations must be made in cyanotic patients, especially those with cavopulmonary anastomoses. Those at greatest risk are patients with a prior classic Glenn shunt. When the patient has complex heart disease with incomplete separation of circulations, it may be difficult to determine how much cyanosis is due to this incomplete separation and how much is due to the pulmonary arteriovenous malformation. If the latter is extensive, there will be obligatory cyanosis after isolated heart transplantation. This may be tolerated poorly by the freshly hypoxic-ischemic donor myocardium.

Evaluation of pulmonary vascular resistance (PVR) is as important as the assessment of cardiac anatomy. The adult right ventricular myocardium, when rendered ischemic, may be less tolerant of elevated PVR than the pediatric myocardium. Cardiac transplantation in pediatric candidates has been successfully performed when indexed PVR is as high as 10 IU. This may not be feasible in adults, although little hard data are available in this area. The evaluation of PVR may be very difficult (if not impossible) in the setting of complex heart disease with shunts at pulmonary arterial level and with discontinuous pulmonary arteries. In these complex settings additional clinical information must be incorporated along with hemodynamic data (e.g., intensity of continuous murmurs from systemic-to-pulmonary shunts and systemic oxygen saturations).

MEDICAL EVALUATION

Many adults with end-stage CHD have suffered years of ventricular failure and/or progressive cyanosis. Chronic erythrocytosis may be associated with bleeding diathesis. This may be exacerbated by liver dysfunction in the patient with chronic right-sided heart failure, especially long-term Fontan survivors.[4,5] The latter group may progress to overt cirrhosis[6]; and, on rare occasion, hepatic adenomas and hepatocellular carcinoma may develop.[7] Liver imaging should form part of the pretransplant evaluation of the late Fontan operation survivor, and in selected cases liver biopsy may be indicated. Platelet consumption in the lungs may occur in the patient with advanced pulmonary vascular disease, leading to severe thrombocytopenia in some cases. Long-standing low cardiac output state may also lead to severe renal dysfunction. It may be hard to predict to what extent this will reverse after successful thoracic transplantation. Many patients operated on in earlier eras were exposed to hepatitis B and C viruses from contaminated blood products. When there is evidence of prior infection with these viruses, infectious disease and hepatology consults should be obtained to determine the risk of reactivation of these viruses when immunosuppression is introduced. When there is a history of prior neurologic events (e.g., stroke, cerebral abscess, or seizure disorder), pretransplant evaluation should include brain imaging. Nutritional status should also be carefully evaluated, because cardiac cachexia may be an important determinant of perioperative morbidity and survival. This may be particularly problematic in the patient with protein-losing enteropathy (especially common in the Fontan population). The latter may be associated with hypoalbuminemia, hypogammaglobulinemia, and lymphopenia. This can result in acquired immunodeficiency before transplantation and likely contributes to the high post-transplant infectious mortality in the Fontan patient.

Finally, it should be noted that the high number of pretransplant blood transfusions and the frequent prior usage of homograft material results in significant risk for the development of pretransplant anti–human leukocyte antigen (HLA) antibodies in this population. This increases the risk of hyperacute and accelerated early rejection, as well as the late risk of post-transplant coronary arterial disease (chronic rejection). For this reason, many centers require a negative prospective or "virtual" donor-specific crossmatch before accepting organs for transplantation in adults with CHD who are sensitized against non-self HLA antigens. This may markedly decrease the chances of finding a suitable donor for those patients who are highly sensitized.

▪ Surgical Considerations

Adults requiring cardiopulmonary transplantation for CHD present unique surgical issues.

CHOICE OF PROCEDURE

Whenever possible, isolated heart transplantation is the procedure of choice, since the addition of the lung inevitably impacts negatively on chances of very long-term survival. When complex heart disease (including all cases of "single ventricle" physiology) is associated with severe and irreversible pulmonary hypertension, heart-lung transplantation is the procedure of choice. Selected patients suffering from pulmonary hypertension with simpler forms of heart disease may be offered cardiac repair with lung transplantation. Although it has been our general approach to offer double-lung transplantation to these patients, single-lung transplantation may be offered to select patients, such as those with prior unilateral pleurodesis. When contemplating cardiac repair rather than replacement (mostly for patients with atrial or ventricular septal defect or patent ductus arteriosus), assessment of myocardial function and reserve is critical. Cardiac catheterization, echocardiography, and radionuclide studies should be performed to assess the coronary arteries, valvular function, and myocardial reserve. When cardiac function is deemed unsatisfactory, cardiac replacement becomes necessary.

TECHNICAL CONSIDERATIONS

Cannulation and Cardiopulmonary Bypass
Cannulation strategy assumes great importance in the operative planning for these patients. The presence of right-sided heart failure with history of previous sternotomy should be an indication for peripheral cannulation if sites are available. This is particularly important in the presence of a single, systemic ventricle or previous atrial inversion procedures in which the systemic ventricle is dilated and directly behind the sternum, because even a small amount of intracavitary air may be disastrous.

The conduct of cardiopulmonary bypass needs to be given due consideration in these patients. There is often a considerable amount of collateral flow owing to vascular adhesions or major aortopulmonary collateral arteries that may compromise brain perfusion, and pH stat management is required to protect against cerebral injury.

Cardiac Repair
For patients with atrial septal defect, standard surgical techniques, including superior and inferior caval vein cannulation, are used. With the aorta crossclamped, the defect is repaired using direct or patch closure techniques. Ventricular septal defect repair may be complicated by the sequelae of chronic CHD. Long-standing pressure loading of the right ventricle leads to hypertrophy and fibrosis, rendering exposure of the ventricular septum difficult. In these cases, specialized techniques, such as takedown of the septal leaflet of the tricuspid valve and resection of hypertrophic muscle bundles within the right ventricle, may be required. De Vega annuloplasty may be useful as an adjunctive procedure when there is significant tricuspid regurgitation. The approach to adults suffering from pulmonary vascular disease due to patent ductus arteriosus requires careful planning. Division of the calcified duct should include patch closure from within the pulmonary artery during a brief period of circulatory arrest. Smaller, noncalcified ducts may be clamped, divided, and oversewn during continuous bypass support.[8]

Surgical Considerations for Isolated Cardiac Transplantation
Pulmonary arterial anomalies are frequently encountered in patients with prior systemic-to-pulmonary shunts, pulmonary arterial bands, and cavopulmonary anastomoses. Inadequacy of branch pulmonary artery repair at the time of transplantation can lead to donor right-sided heart failure and/or branch pulmonary artery thrombosis. Repair of caval and shunt insertion sites with donor tissue (aortic, pulmonary, or pericardial) is preferred. When the pulmonary arteries are discontinuous, such as after a classic Glenn shunt, more extensive surgical reconstruction is required. If the lungs are not to be transplanted, the pulmonary arteries with their bifurcation should accompany the heart and bipulmonary anastomosis may be utilized. If the lungs are to be transplanted, a segment of donor aorta serves well as an interposition graft.

Transplantation for failed atrial inversion procedures can pose special problems. There are often calcified baffles and previous stents that once removed can leave a paucity of native tissues for atrial anastomoses. Direct pulmonary venous anastomoses may be performed in these situations. Abnormalities of the position of the great arteries relative to each other (e.g., anterior aorta in transposition of the great vessels) rarely cause problems for cardiac transplantation, although additional lengths of donor great vessels should be procured to facilitate the transplant procedure.

Systemic venous anomalies are probably the single most difficult anatomic variation encountered in young adults requiring heart or heart-lung transplantation. A variety of baffle techniques, directing systemic venous return from left-sided cavae to the right-sided atrium in the new heart have been reported. This allows transplantation in the patient with mirror image arrangement (situs inversus), as well as those with atrial isomerism (heterotaxy syndromes). Because of these anatomic variations, exaggerated lengths of superior vena cava, innominate vein, and donor aorta may be required. In these instances, careful preoperative planning and clear communication with the donor team is essential.

Perioperative Complications
As discussed earlier, long-standing cyanosis leads to the development of highly vascularized mediastinal and pleural structures owing to the development of extensive systemic-to-pulmonary collateral circulation. Chronic erythrocytosis may also be associated with bleeding diathesis, further compounding the risk of life-threatening bleeding. Meticulous attention should be paid to hemostasis of the posterior mediastinum before organ transplantation. Although mortality is similar between patients transplanted via sternotomy versus bilateral thoracosternotomy, the latter technique is preferred for improved access and visualization of the posterior mediastinum in most cases of heart-lung and bilateral lung transplantation. Likewise, avoidance of the posterior mediastinum altogether by performing bibronchial rather than tracheal anastomoses should be considered for heart-lung transplantation. The use of aprotinin (no longer available in many countries) and recombinant activated factor VII (Novo7) may also prove very useful in controlling bleeding in the thoracic transplant recipient.

As with cardiopulmonary transplantation for any indication, primary graft failure may occur. If cardiac repair or other complex reconstructions add significantly to donor ischemic time, then increased risk of graft ischemia-reperfusion injury may be anticipated. Mechanical support may be indicated until independent function of the organ(s) is achieved. However, primary graft failure in this complex setting is likely to be associated with high mortality.

If bleeding is controlled, and early graft function is good, then other early postoperative complications will be similar to those observed in thoracic transplant recipients without CHD. The postoperative intensive care and hospital stays tend to be somewhat longer in those with CHD than among their counterparts with other indications for transplantation. Similarly, intermediate and long-term complications, along with immunosuppressive strategies, are comparable among operative survivors with and without CHD. These topics are therefore not discussed further.

▨ Outcomes

CARDIAC TRANSPLANTATION

There are relatively little data available on outcomes for cardiac transplantation in adults with CHD. Single institutional experiences have produced mixed results and have generally involved very small numbers of patients.[8–11] It is clear that the most challenging group is the late Fontan operation survivor,[12] and perioperative mortality appears to be particular high in this cohort of patients, especially when compared with pediatric candidates carrying the same diagnosis (Fig. 13-1).

Data from the Registry of the ISHLT show that CHD is an important risk factor for death at 1 and 5 years after adult heart transplantation.[1] Most of the excess risk is early and presumably reflects the challenges involved in complex reconstructions and "redo" surgery, compounded by other problems such as coagulopathy, chronic liver disease, and enhanced infection risk (most notably in the Fontan population). Indeed, a diagnosis of CHD is second only to use of short-term circulatory support as a risk factor for death after transplantation. Although

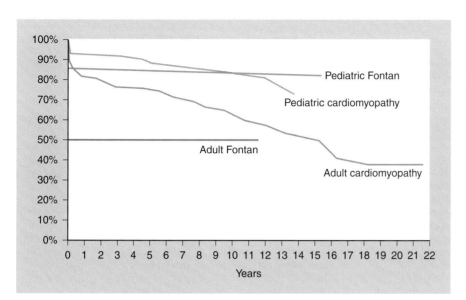

Figure 13-1 Results of transplantation for failed Fontan circulation in children and adults. High perioperative mortality is noted in both groups (compared with cardiomyopathy as indication for transplantation) but is significantly higher in the adult cohort. *(Data from the Cardiothoracic Transplant Department, Freeman Hospital, Newcastle, United Kingdom.)*

perioperative survival for adults with CHD is only approximately 80% in the registry, it is noteworthy that this population (generally younger) carries the best long-term survivals. The recipient half-life for the ACHD population is 13.4 years after transplantation compared with 11 years for those with cardiomyopathy. Conditional survival (half-life for those surviving to 1 year) is 17.1 years for those with ACHD and 13.3 years for those with cardiomyopathy. Of note, the ISHLT registry shows little change in perioperative survival in the most recent cohort (2000–2005) compared with the total registry experience (1982–2005).[1] By contrast, recent data from the U.K. Cardiothoracic Transplant Audit (1985–2008) shows progressive improvements in survival over time for adults with CHD after heart and heart-lung transplantation (Fig. 13-2). In the earliest cohort (1985–1992), 1-year survival was only 54% (95% confidence interval [CI], 43–65). In the most recent period (2001–2008), this had risen to 76% (95% CI, 63–88), although these results still lag significantly behind those for diagnoses other than CHD.

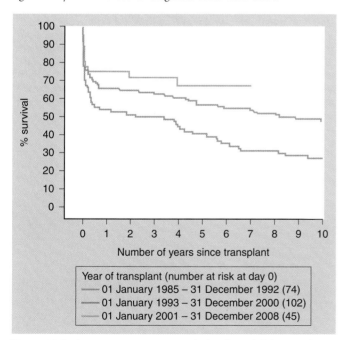

Figure 13-2 Long-term patient survival after first adult heart or heart-lung transplant in the United Kingdom, January 1, 1985, to December 31, 2008, where primary disease at transplant was congenital heart disease. *(Courtesy of U.K. Cardiothoracic Transplant Audit.)*

LUNG AND HEART-LUNG TRANSPLANTATION

The Registry of the ISHLT also reports data on outcomes after heart-lung transplantation for adults with CHD.[2] The registry currently contains data on 869 patients with ACHD who have received heart-lung transplantation. Despite the complexity of the diagnoses in most patients, the recipient half-life for patients with Eisenmenger syndrome is 5.8 years and actually exceeds that for patients with idiopathic pulmonary arterial hypertension who received heart-lung transplant over the same time period. The impact of early mortality is further emphasized by the encouraging recipient conditional half-life (for 1-year survivors) of 10.6 years for adults receiving heart-lung transplantation for a diagnosis of ACHD.

Three large single-center experiences have also reported results of heart-lung and/or lung transplantation for ACHD. The Papworth group from Cambridge, England, analyzed data on 51 consecutive heart-lung transplantations performed for Eisenmenger syndrome and compared the results to 212 heart-lung transplants performed for other indications.[13] Although the authors noted a more complex course in the ACHD group, including greater bleeding and high incidence of return to the operating room, overall survival was identical between the ACHD and non-ACHD groups. Perioperative mortality in the Eisenmenger syndrome group was only 16%. One-, 5- and 10-year survival rates were 73%, 51%, and 28% in the ACHD group and 75%, 48%, and 26% in the non-ACHD group, respectively. Pigula and colleagues examined outcomes for adults with CHD who underwent transplant among a total of 1281 adult cardiopulmonary transplant recipients at the University of Pittsburgh.[8] Both lung and heart-lung transplants performed for ACHD showed comparable outcomes to similar procedures performed for other indications. Other observations from this extensive single-center experience were the comparable results between heart-lung transplantation and lung transplantation with cardiac repair among ACHD patients, along with evidence of significantly improved outcomes for patients who underwent transplant in recent years. Finally, the Hannover group also reported results of heart-lung and lung transplantation for ACHD.[14] Forty-six patients received heart-lung transplants and 5 underwent lung transplantation. Thirty-day mortality was only 11.8%, and 1-year survival was 80%. All three series suggest that heart-lung transplantation or lung transplantation may be performed with acceptable results in the ACHD population in experienced centers.

It is important to recognize that survival without transplantation varies with diagnosis, and patients with Eisenmenger complex have relatively low waiting list mortality.[15] The impact of transplantation on overall survival for patients with pulmonary hypertension and

ACHD has not been clearly determined. Some authorities have even questioned the role of heart-lung transplantation in improving overall survival in this population of patients.

QUALITY OF LIFE

Even less is known about quality of life issues after thoracic transplantation, although interest in this area is increasing.[1,16] The U.K. Cardiothoracic Transplant Audit reported that among patients surviving 1 year from transplantation, 89% of heart and 92% of heart-lung recipients were in New York Heart Association class I. Similar observations are found in the Registry of the ISHLT, although cardiac recipients fair slightly better than lung recipients in this dataset.[1,2] Despite this high level of functional status, it is of interest to note that only a minority of heart or lung recipients are back in the workforce by 5 years after transplantation. The cause for this discrepancy between functional ability and work status requires further investigation. How the ACHD patient fares compared with other thoracic transplant recipients should also be investigated. For further discussion of the topic of transplantation for adults with CHD, the reader is referred to a recent review.[17]

CONCLUSION

Thoracic transplantation in adults with CHD can be summarized as follows:

- ACHD accounts for a tiny minority of heart or lung transplantations but for a third of combined heart-lung transplantations.
- Demand for transplantation in ACHD will increase significantly over the next decade.
- Comprehensive preoperative evaluation and planning are required for successful outcomes.
- Heart transplantation short-term outcomes for ACHD remain inferior to those for other indications.
- Heart-lung and lung transplant outcomes for ACHD are comparable to those for other indications in experienced centers.
- Heart-lung transplant results for ACHD are comparable to those of lung transplantation with cardiac repair. The latter is therefore indicated for simple defects.
- Functional status at 1 year is excellent in most patients, yet only a minority return to work.
- Further quality of life studies are warranted in this population.

REFERENCES

1. Taylor DO, Edwards LB, Aurora P, et al. Registry of the International Society for Heart and Lung Transplantation: twenty-fifth official adult heart transplant report—2008. J Heart Lung Transplant 2008;27:943–956.
2. Christie JD, Edwards LB, Aurora P, et al. Registry of the International Society for Heart and Lung Transplantation: twenty-fifth official adult lung and heart/lung transplantation report—2008. J Heart Lung Transplant 2008;27:957–969.
3. Fontan F, Kirklin JW, Fernandez G, et al. Outcome after a "perfect" Fontan operation. Circulation 1990;81:1520–1536.
4. Camposilvan S, Milanesi O, Stellin G, et al. Liver and cardiac function in the long term Fontan operation. Ann Thorac Surg 2008;86:177–182.
5. Friedrich-Rust M, Koch C, Rentzsch A, et al. Non-invasive assessment of liver fibrosis in patients with Fontan circulation using transient elastography and biochemical fibrosis markers. J Thorac Cardiovasc Surg 2008;135:560–567.
6. Kendall TJ, Stedman B, Hacking N, et al. Hepatic fibrosis and cirrhosis in the Fontan circulation: a detailed morphological study. J Clin Pathol 2008;61:504–508.
7. Ghaferi AA, Hutchins GM. Progression of liver pathology in patients undergoing the Fontan procedure: chronic passive congestion, cardiac cirrhosis, hepatic adenoma, and hepatocellular carcinoma. J Thorac Cardiovasc Surg 2005;129:1348–1352.
8. Pigula FA, Gandhi S, Ristich J, et al. Cardiopulmonary transplantation for congenital heart disease in the adult. J Heart Lung Transplant 2001;20:297–303.
9. Lamour JM, Addonizio LJ, Galantowicz ME, et al. Outcome after orthotopic cardiac transplantation in adults with congenital heart disease. Circulation 1999;100:II200–II205.
10. Coskun O, Coskun T, El-Arousy M, et al. Heart transplantation in adults with congenital heart disease: experience with 15 patients. ASAIO 2007;53:103–106.
11. Izquierdo MT, Almenar L, Martinez-Dolz L, et al. Mortality after heart transplantation in adults with congenital heart disease: a single center experience. Transplant Proc 2007;39:2357–2359.
12. Jayakumar KA, Addonizio LJ, Kichuk-Chrisant MR, et al. Cardiac transplantation after the Fontan or Glenn procedure. J Am Coll Cardiol 2004;44:2065–2072.
13. Stoica SC, McNeil KD, Perreas K, et al. Heart-lung transplantation for Eisenmenger syndrome: early and long-term results. Ann Thorac Surg 2001;72:1887–1891.
14. Goerler H, Simon A, Gohrbandt B, et al. Heart-lung and lung transplantation in grown up congenital heart disease: long-term single center experience. Eur J Cardiothorac Surg 2007;32:926–931.
15. De Meester J, Smits JM, Persijn GG, Haverich A. Lung transplant waiting list: differential outcome of type of end-stage lung disease, one year after registration. J Heart Lung Transplant 1999;18:563–571.
16. Dew MA, Switzer GE, Goycoolea JM, et al. Does transplantation produce quality of life benefits? A quantitative analysis of the literature. Transplantation 1997;64:1261–1273.
17. Hosseinpour A, Cullen S, Tsang VT. Transplantation for adults with congenital heart disease. Eur J Cardiothorac Surg 2006;30:508–514.

14

Noncardiac Surgery in Adult Congenital Heart Disease

MARKUS SCHWERZMANN | JACK M. COLMAN

Introduction

Comprehensive guidelines exist to direct the management of a patient with acquired heart disease before noncardiac surgery.[1] Their principal focus is to reduce the incidence of perioperative myocardial infarction,[2] and they advocate for timely recognition of treatable "active cardiac conditions" that should be addressed prior to elective surgery. Patients with adult congenital heart disease (ACHD) requiring noncardiac surgery are a different patient population from those for whom these guidelines were devised. ACHD patients are usually younger and usually have a lower risk profile for atherosclerotic disease but may be more prone to arrhythmias, to heart failure, and to complications unique to ACHD. It is reasonable to assume, just as in acquired heart disease, that perioperative morbidity and mortality of noncardiac surgery can be reduced in patients with CHD by timely preoperative risk assessment and advance planning.[3] However, published guidelines on perioperative cardiovascular evaluation and care[1] do not address many of the issues unique to the ACHD population and general guidelines for the management of ACHD patients do not cover issues of noncardiac surgery in detail.[4] We propose that this gap among the guidelines may be bridged by using a stepwise strategy for risk assessment similar to that elaborated for acquired heart disease while incorporating issues unique to ACHD patients.

In the preoperative risk assessment of the ACHD patient it is necessary to collect detailed information about the diagnoses, the previous procedures, and the clinical course over many years. Often the patient alone cannot provide complete details regarding the nature of the congenital heart defect or the type of repair because relevant events occurred in infancy or childhood. Parents, too, may have misunderstood, forgotten details, or not transmitted their knowledge to growing children. Nevertheless, details about the era in which cardiac surgery was done, the exact techniques applied, and the types and severity of residua and sequelae may have a significant impact on perioperative management. For example, a patient with repaired tetralogy of Fallot and mild pulmonary regurgitation who has a moderate residual ventricular septal defect with left-to-right shunt may tolerate hypovolemia less well than a similar patient with no residual shunt (see Box 14-2). As another example, after palliative early aorto-pulmonary shunts, the ability to monitor blood pressure in one or both arms may be lost, so alternative strategies must be planned. Few patients will be able to relate their history with the precision required to identify such issues. Surgical treatment in childhood may even have led to the misapprehension of "cure" when, in fact, active issues remain. Frequently, subjective assessment of functional capacity may not correspond to the objective magnitude of cardiac limitation because patients are accustomed to chronic limitation and do not describe it as abnormal.

Preoperative evaluation and noncardiac surgery, especially for patients with ACHD of moderate or great complexity, are best performed at a regional ACHD center where multidisciplinary expertise and understanding of their unique histories and special circumstances may be found. In particular, it is valuable to include on the team an experienced cardiac anesthesiologist who is familiar with the physiology of CHD and how this may be affected by the hemodynamic responses to surgery, the corresponding anesthetic implications, and special issues relating to postoperative pain management. Such an anesthesiologist can rarely be found in a community hospital.

A noncardiac surgeon may not have detailed knowledge of the congenital heart condition with which his or her patient presents. It is in the patient's interest that the ACHD consultant and the cardiac anesthesiologist brief the surgeon regarding the terminology, the anatomy, and the physiology in the patient at hand, emphasizing potential differences in response to surgery in contrast to patients with acquired heart disease.

Assessment of Risk

GENERAL ISSUES

After review of the detailed history, preoperative assessment for ACHD patients should include a physical examination, systemic arterial oximetry, an electrocardiogram (ECG), a full blood cell count, assessment of renal function, and a coagulation screen. Cardiac imaging (echocardiogram, chest radiography, and/or cardiac magnetic resonance imaging) may be necessary depending on the underlying defect, the past medical history, and the length of time since any prior comprehensive assessment.

In patients with major predictors of cardiovascular risk at noncardiac surgery (which includes "active clinical conditions" according to the terminology of the guidelines for acquired heart disease[1]), surgery should be postponed if possible until the patient has been further evaluated and stabilized. These predictors include:
- Decompensated heart failure (New York Heart Association [NYHA] functional class IV or worsening/new-onset heart failure)
- Significant arrhythmias (high-grade atrioventricular block, symptomatic or newly recognized ventricular arrhythmias, symptomatic bradycardia, or supraventricular arrhythmias with ventricular response > 100 beats per minute)
- Severe obstructive valvular disease (symptomatic, or asymptomatic with definite evidence of severe stenosis)
- Unstable coronary syndromes (unstable or severe angina, myocardial infarction within 30 days)

For patients without such major predictors of risk, additional risk stratification should take into account the type of the proposed surgery, the patient's functional capacity, and the presence of other clinical risk factors as defined by the Revised Cardiac Risk Index.[5] A detailed algorithm for risk assessment can be found in the 2007 ACC/AHA guidelines on perioperative cardiovascular evaluation and care for noncardiac surgery.[1] Of note, endoscopic procedures, cataract surgery, breast surgery, and some other ambulatory procedures are considered to be low-risk procedures and, in the absence of major predictors of risk, can be carried out without further risk stratification.

COMORBID CONDITIONS

Comorbid conditions may complicate perioperative cardiac management and increase the anesthetic risk. Added risk may accrue from:
- *Obstructive or restrictive pulmonary disease,* which places the patient at risk of perioperative respiratory complications. The effects of hypoxemia, hypercapnia, and major acid-base disturbances on the pulmonary or systemic circulation can further compromise the cardiovascular system. This may especially hold true for ACHD patients with cyanotic heart disease and severe scoliosis. If significant pulmonary disease is suspected, preoperative lung-function testing including response to bronchodilators should be considered.[6]

- *Diabetes mellitus,* which increases the likelihood of significant coronary artery disease. Insulin therapy is a significant risk factor for perioperative cardiac morbidity. Serum glucose concentration less than 220 mg/dL or less than 12 mMol/L on the first postoperative day may reduce the frequency of postoperative nosocomial infections.[7]
- *Renal dysfunction,* which can complicate perioperative fluid management, especially in a patient with heart failure.
- *Hematologic disorders* such as anemia, erythrocytosis, thrombocytopenia, or thrombocytosis, which can increase the risk of perioperative ischemia and hemostatic problems.

SPECIFIC RISKS IN ADULT CONGENITAL HEART DISEASE

Certain defects, pathophysiologic sequelae, and prior therapies increase the overall risk and should influence the preoperative workup and perioperative management. The following additional markers for increased risk supplement those discussed previously that overlap with acquired heart disease.[4]

High Risk
- Pulmonary hypertension
- Cyanotic CHD
- Severe systemic ventricular dysfunction
- Severe obstructive valvular disease or severe conduit obstruction
- Fontan circulation

Moderate Risk
- Prosthetic valve or conduit
- Systemic-to-pulmonary shunt
- Moderate systemic ventricular dysfunction
- Moderate obstructive valvular disease or moderate conduit obstruction

Perioperative Management

APPROACH

The ACHD cardiologist should distribute a structured plan that clarifies the cardiac anatomy, type of repair, residua and sequelae, and current cardiovascular hemodynamics (Box 14-1). Further preoperative evaluation should be arranged if necessary. The final plan should detail the perioperative risks, anticipated complications, and contingency plans necessary to minimize or deal with them. Recommendations should be made regarding the nature and duration of postoperative monitoring.

BOX 14-1 ASSESSMENT AND MANAGEMENT PLAN THROUGH SURGERY FOR ADULT PATIENTS WITH CONGENITAL HEART DISEASE

1. Define and explain the cardiac anatomy.
   - Underlying congenital defects
   - Type of surgical palliation or repair
   - Residua and sequelae
2. Assess the surgical risk.
   - Global risk factors, including comorbid conditions
   - ACHD-specific risks
3. Suggest additional preoperative testing if necessary.
4. Develop a perioperative management plan.
   - Indication for preoperative interventions
   - Recommendation for infective endocarditis prophylaxis
   - Perioperative medical therapy
   - Potential for perioperative interference with pacemakers and implantable cardiac defibrillators
   - Nature and duration of perioperative and postoperative monitoring
   - Recommendation for prophylaxis of venous thromboembolism
5. Request an ACHD-experienced anesthesiologist.
6. Provide a written summary and plan.

An anesthesiologist knowledgeable in ACHD issues should provide a consultation focusing on the impact of the particular congenital anatomy and physiology on anesthetic technique, perioperative surveillance, and postoperative pain management. Ideally, the documents prepared by the anesthesiologist and congenital cardiologist will complement one another and serve as a reference for less experienced colleagues who may be faced with the patient for the first time in the operating room, in the intensive care unit, or on the ward.

ANTICOAGULATION

The risk of bleeding during surgery has to be weighed against the risk of thromboembolic complications caused by withholding or reducing anticoagulation therapy. The management of chronic anticoagulation has been simplified since a risk-benefit analysis published in 1997 demonstrated convincingly that most patients are well managed by withdrawal of warfarin for 4 or more doses before the procedure (depending on the baseline international normalized ratio [INR]), with resumption of warfarin as soon as safely possible after the procedure.[8] The current guidelines of the American College of Chest Physicians for perioperative management of antithrombotic therapy recommend resuming vitamin K antagonists 12 to 24 hours after surgery if adequate hemostasis has been ensured.[9]

Bridging anticoagulation with heparin should be considered for:
- Patients with mechanical valves at high or moderate risk for arterial thromboembolism
- Patients with rheumatic valvular heart disease and atrial fibrillation
- Patients with atrial fibrillation and a CHADS-2-score[10] of greater than 2
- Patients with a previous thromboembolic event (especially an event within 3 to 12 months before the planned surgery) or with a known thrombophilic condition.

Bridging anticoagulation usually consists of therapeutic-dose low-molecular-weight heparin. In patients receiving a twice-daily therapeutic dose regimen, only the morning dose should be administered the day before surgery. In patients treated with once-daily therapeutic-dose low-molecular-weight heparin, the last dose 24 hours before surgery should be reduced to half the daily dose. In patients who receive bridging anticoagulation with intravenous unfractionated heparin, the infusion should be discontinued at least 4 hours before surgery. Bridging anticoagulation can be resumed 24 hours after surgery, but after major surgery or if a high bleeding risk is perceived it may be wise to delay resumption of heparins for 48 to 72 hours. More aggressive perioperative antithrombotic regimens may be appropriate on an individualized basis.

Patients with a bileaflet mechanical aortic valve without atrial fibrillation who do not have any risk factors for stroke according to the CHADS-2 prediction score[10] are at lower risk for arterial thromboembolism. In such patients, the risk for thromboembolism after interrupting oral anticoagulation is less than 4%/year (and therefore quite low during a few perioperative days without anticoagulation), so in contemplating surgery with high bleeding risk clinicians may avoid bridging anticoagulation altogether.

If vitamin K is used to reverse warfarin anticoagulation preoperatively, temporary blunting of the subsequent response to warfarin should be anticipated; frequency of INR monitoring must be increased until the warfarin dose stabilizes in the expected range based on preoperative history. However, in most patients whose INR is 1.5 to 1.9 on the day before surgery, a dose of 1 mg oral vitamin K is sufficient to ensure a normal or near-normal INR the next day without major blunting of the response to re-anticoagulation.[11]

ANTIPLATELET AGENTS

Aspirin therapy should be interrupted 7 to 10 days before surgery if no antiplatelet effect at the time of surgery is desired. It also takes 7 to 10 days to replace the platelet pool in patients using clopidogrel. Nonsteroidal anti-inflammatory drugs have a reversible effect on platelet function and should be discontinued long enough prior to surgery to ensure no residual antiplatelet effect at the time of surgery. The interval will vary according to the elimination half-life of the drug, from 1 day (e.g., ibuprofen, diclofenac, indomethacin) to 10 days (e.g., piroxicam). Antiplatelet therapy can usually be resumed 24 hours after surgery as long as hemostasis has been assured.

β-ADRENERGIC BLOCKERS

The previously accepted role of β-adrenergic blockers in perioperative care has been challenged by the results of a large trial published in 2008 that did show a benefit of high-dose metoprolol on the risk of myocardial infarction, but at the cost of an increased incidence of stroke and increased overall mortality (POISE—Perioperative Ischemic Evaluation trial).[12] Although it is clear that patients already receiving β blockers before surgery should not discontinue their therapy during the perioperative period, it may not be appropriate to initiate a β blocker preoperatively. Current recommendations restrict the initiation of perioperative β-blocker therapy to patients requiring vascular surgery in whom coronary artery disease or more than 1 clinical risk factor according to the Revised Cardiac Risk Index[5] has been documented.[1]

In most ACHD patients using β blockers chronically, the indication is arrhythmia or heart failure, and the drug should be continued during the perioperative period. In the uncommon ACHD patient believed to require initiation of β-blocker therapy before a surgical procedure, the dose should be gradually increased over several days to weeks, adjusted to heart rate and blood pressure. Long-acting β_1-selective receptor blockers are preferred over short-acting and nonselective β-receptor blockers.[1,2] Initiating full-dose β-blocker therapy the evening before surgery is not encouraged and may have contributed to the negative outcome of the POISE trial.

CYANOTIC HEART DISEASE

In patients with cyanotic heart disease many risk factors for perioperative complications conspire to increase risk. Patients with cyanosis due to a right-to-left shunt may have severe pulmonary vascular disease. They have an increased risk for paradoxical embolism, so air filters should be used for intravenous lines whenever possible and particular attention should be paid to avoid unintentional air injection into an intravenous line.

Reducing the risk of postoperative venous thromboembolism is especially important, because there is the risk of paradoxical systemic arterial embolization in the presence of a shunt, in addition to the possibly exaggerated adverse response to pulmonary embolism in many ACHD patients with already compromised pulmonary circulations or with single ventricle circulations. Preventive anticoagulation may be considered. On the other hand, patients with cyanotic heart disease have abnormalities in platelet function and coagulation pathways, have increased tissue vascularity, and may have aortopulmonary or transpleural collateral vessels, all of which increase the risk of hemorrhage. Serial isovolumic phlebotomy to reduce the hematocrit to less than 0.65 may improve hemostatic function if undertaken shortly before operation (the blood withdrawn at venesection may be reserved for possible autotransfusion). The decision to accept an increased bleeding risk by using preventive anticoagulation therapy to reduce the risk of thromboembolism or vice versa should be made after careful weighing of risks and benefits in the individual patient.

When monitoring hemostatic and hematologic parameters several pitfalls should be kept in mind. Apparent thrombocytopenia can be an artifact of increased red blood cell mass and proportionally reduced plasma volume; absolute platelet count is usually in the low normal range. Standard measures of INR and partial thromboplastin time are subject to error if the hematocrit exceeds 0.55, owing to relative excess citrate in the sampling tube, unless citrate volume is adjusted for the reduced plasma volume in the draw. A so-called normal hemoglobin concentration after surgery may represent a significant anemia in a patient whose hemoglobin is normally much higher but has been reduced by perioperative hemorrhage. Preoperative fasting and/or bowel preparation without adequate fluid replacement may cause hypovolemia and precipitate effects of hyperviscosity in a cyanotic patient with preexisting erythrocytosis.

DOWN SYNDROME

Hypothyroidism occurs in more than 15% of patients with Down syndrome. Signs and symptoms can develop slowly over time and may be difficult to detect.[13] Elective surgery should not be performed in patients with untreated hypothyroidism because hypothermia and electrolyte disturbances are relatively common in this setting.[14] A preoperative anesthetic evaluation is important because of comorbidities such as difficult intubation and sleep apnea syndrome, which may influence the choice of anesthetic technique.

FONTAN CIRCULATION

Many unique issues arise in the management of the single-ventricle circulation of a Fontan patient, some of which vary according to the type of Fontan procedure previously performed. For all Fontan patients, pulmonary blood flow depends directly on the pressure gradient between the systemic veins and left atrium. Furthermore, antegrade flow through the lungs is exquisitely sensitive to changes in pulmonary vascular resistance. Any elevation of pulmonary vascular resistance (as may be provoked by hypoxia, atelectasis, thromboemboli, pneumonia) or of left atrial pressure (as might be caused by ventricular systolic or diastolic dysfunction, mitral regurgitation, loss of sinus rhythm, cannon waves) will decrease pulmonary blood flow and hence cardiac output. Perioperative factors that reduce preload and compromise pulmonary blood flow include hemorrhage, venodilation, inadequate volume replacement, and increased intrathoracic pressure as a result of positive-pressure ventilation. The normal fall in intrathoracic pressure during spontaneous inspiration is an important contributor to pulmonary blood flow in a Fontan operation patient, and therefore spontaneous breathing should be enabled as long as hypercapnia and hypoxemia can be prevented. Abdominal insufflation with carbon dioxide for laparoscopic procedures may be problematic because the consequent increase in intra-abdominal pressure impedes venous return.[15] Atrial arrhythmias are common, are often poorly tolerated, and require prompt antiarrhythmic therapy or cardioversion. In Fontan operation patients with a right atrium/pulmonary artery connection, the right atrium can be grossly dilated and highly compliant, such that continuous central venous pressure measurement will not necessarily reflect acute changes in preload. In selected Fontan operation patients transesophageal echocardiography may be helpful to monitor preload and ventricular contractility in real time.

OBSTRUCTIVE VALVULAR DISEASE

In patients with severe outflow tract stenosis at valvular, subvalvular, or supravalvular levels and noncompliant ventricles, rapid volume infusion may result in an inordinate rise in filling pressure, provoking pulmonary edema or right-sided heart failure. Loss of sinus rhythm and atrial contraction may lead to a fall in cardiac output because of reduced presystolic ventricular filling. Blood flow through a stenotic orifice is relatively fixed, and so profound bradycardia too will lower cardiac output more than otherwise anticipated. Hypovolemia or venodilation will lead to a fall in preload, not easily tolerated by a hypertrophied, pressure-loaded, noncompliant ventricle. To address these risks, relief of severe outflow tract obstruction should be considered before elective surgery, unless the expected risk of the cardiac repair exceeds the risks of adverse effects during noncardiac surgery.

Similar considerations apply to patients with severe inflow tract stenosis. In particular, tachycardia decreases diastolic filling time and is poorly tolerated. Also, in patients with mitral stenosis, pulmonary hypertension can complicate the perioperative course. Obstructive valvular disease can sometimes be associated with an increased bleeding tendency due to a form of acquired von Willebrand syndrome.[16]

PULMONARY HYPERTENSION

Severe pulmonary hypertension due to pulmonary vascular disease imparts a major risk even to minor procedures. The mortality rate for noncardiac surgery in patients with severe pulmonary hypertension is 5% to 10%.[17,18] Among 58 Eisenmenger syndrome patients undergoing noncardiac surgery, there were two deaths, one in a patient undergoing appendectomy in a community hospital.[18] The risk is highest for cyanotic patients with poor functional class, intermediate- or high-risk surgery, and prolonged procedures (duration of anesthesia > 3 hours). Because of the high pulmonary vascular resistance, right ventricular stroke volume and consequently the volume available for left ventricular filling are limited. The ability to increase cardiac output in response to a fall in systemic vascular resistance or increased metabolic demands is restricted. Inadequate preload, systemic hypotension, decreased coronary perfusion, biventricular heart failure, and progressive hypoxemia can engender a vicious downward spiral. If there is intracardiac or pulmonary-to-systemic shunting, as is common in ACHD patients with pulmonary hypertension, a drop in systemic vascular resistance or increase in pulmonary vascular resistance will drive an increase in the right-to-left shunt and so exacerbate hypoxemia. Strategies to minimize the adverse effects of pulmonary hypertension during and after noncardiac surgery include avoiding factors known to increase pulmonary vascular resistance, such as hypothermia, excessive positive-pressure ventilation or positive end-expiratory pressure, acidosis, additional hypoxia, or hypercapnia. In addition, systemic vascular resistance must be maintained or quickly restored and hypovolemia avoided or quickly corrected.

RHYTHM ABNORMALITIES, PACEMAKERS, AND AUTOMATIC IMPLANTABLE CARDIOVERTER-DEFIBRILLATORS

The presence of an arrhythmia should trigger evaluation for an underlying hemodynamic problem, pulmonary disease, drug toxicity, or metabolic or electrolyte disturbance. Arrhythmia suppression is needed only if the arrhythmia is symptomatic and/or hemodynamically significant. There are no current recommendations for prophylactic use of β blockers (including sotalol) or amiodarone in patients at risk for atrial arrhythmias in noncardiac surgery, although these drugs have been shown to be effective after cardiac surgery.[19]

In patients with implanted pacemakers, preoperative device interrogation is advisable to document pacing and sensing thresholds. Electrical current used for electrocautery, intraoperative cardioversion, metabolic derangements, and anesthetic agents may all have an adverse effect on pacing and sensing thresholds. These effects can be minimized by reprogramming the pacer to an asynchronous mode (VOO or DOO) during surgery. A simple but less reliable method to ensure asynchronous pacing is to place a magnet over the device. Of note, a magnet does not change the pacing function of an automatic implantable cardioverter-defibrillator (AICD) but suspends its antitachycardia function. If unipolar cautery is used, the indifferent electrode should be placed in a position where current flow through the pacemaker or AICD is minimized. AICDs should have their tachyarrhythmia detection algorithms turned off during surgery to prevent inappropriate shocks. It is mandatory to continuously monitor the AICD patient whose device has been inactivated. Because electrocautery may interfere with ECG monitoring and complicate the recognition of arrhythmias, continuous pulse monitoring should be used as well to mitigate this problem. After surgery, pacing and sensing thresholds should be rechecked and all devices reprogrammed as necessary.

SYSTEMIC VENTRICULAR DYSFUNCTION

Heart failure (defined as the presence of any of the following: history of congestive heart failure, pulmonary edema, paroxysmal nocturnal dyspnea, an S_3 gallop on auscultation, or pulmonary vascular redistribution on the chest radiograph) is an independent risk factor for poorer outcome in noncardiac surgery.[5] The surgical risk is mediated in part by the severity of ventricular dysfunction and, more importantly, by the degree of current compensation.[20] Hence, delaying surgery to improve signs and symptoms of overt heart failure and to optimize anti-failure therapy is usually justified. The systemic right ventricle and the single ventricle circulation are especially problematic, because intrinsic impairment of ventricular function is frequent in such ventricles, because objective assessment of ventricular performance is not well established or accomplished, and because the approach best suited to treat such a failing ventricle is not well defined.

LESION-SPECIFIC CONSIDERATIONS

Perioperative issues of particular relevance to specific lesions are listed in Box 14-2.

ENDOCARDITIS PROPHYLAXIS

Most patients with CHD have an increased lifetime risk of infective endocarditis. In 2007 the American Heart Association revised its recommendation for antibiotic prophylaxis and no longer recommends prophylaxis for infective endocarditis based solely on an increased risk of acquisition.[21] Rather, infective endocarditis prophylaxis is recommended only for patients with high risk of an adverse outcome of infective endocarditis, including patients with prosthetic valves (biologic or mechanical valves) or prosthetic material used for cardiac valve repair, previous infective endocarditis, unrepaired and palliated cyanotic lesions, in the first 6 months after complete repair of a congenital defect, or when a residual defect exists at the site of a patch or a prosthetic device that interferes with complete endothelialization. In such patients, infective endocarditis prophylaxis is recommended only for dental procedures and procedures on the respiratory tract or infected skin. These revised guidelines have not been unanimously adopted worldwide, and consequently an approach that differs in some details may be recommended by some local or national authorities. Nevertheless, all recent recommendations advise substantially less widespread application of infective endocarditis prophylaxis than had been specified in older guidelines.

ANESTHESIA

Noncardiac surgery in ACHD patients can pose a particular challenge for the responsible anesthesiologist. Insufflation of CO_2 into a body cavity or placing a patient in the lateral, prone, Trendelenburg, or head-up position may have profound effects on ventilation and hemodynamics.[22] The choice of a specific anesthetic technique is best left to the informed anesthesiologist, who should be one with expertise in the management of ACHD patients or one who has consulted with such an expert. The skill of the anesthesiologist in responding to changes in the patient's status is more important that the type of anesthetic agent used. One should not assume that local anesthetic techniques are necessarily "safer" because the risk of inadequate anesthesia may be greater than the risk of the anesthetic agent itself.

INTRAOPERATIVE MONITORING

The extent of intraoperative monitoring will depend on the underlying heart defect and expected degree of physiologic compromise in relation to the surgical procedure planned. Invasive monitoring should be considered for patients with limited hemodynamic reserve in whom a prompt and finely titrated response to changes in systemic or pulmonary blood flow may be necessary. However, problems of vascular access, common in ACHD patients, may limit ability to establish such monitoring. For instance, the presence of a classic Glenn shunt will preclude monitoring of right-sided heart filling pressure via the neck veins. Pulmonary artery catheterization is contentious, because added benefit has not been shown in several studies in unselected patients with acquired heart disease. In addition, in AHCD patients, the catheter is often more dangerous (e.g., in patients with pulmonary hypertension) and more difficult to insert (e.g., traversing an atrial baffle in a Mustard operation patient). In patients with a persistent left superior vena cava, catheters or wires are

BOX 14-2   SOME LESION-SPECIFIC CONSIDERATIONS IN THE PERIOPERATIVE MANAGEMENT OF ADULT CONGENITAL HEART DISEASE

Atrial Septal Defect
- Rule out pulmonary hypertension.
- Hypovolemia is poorly tolerated; a certain circulating volume is needed to maintain the shunt volume in parallel with the systemic blood volume. The response to hypovolemia will be a rise in systemic resistance and a reduction in venous return—a combination that may primarily augment the shunt fraction at the cost of the systemic flow.[15]
- There is an increased risk of paradoxical embolism; leg thrombi entering the right atrium via the inferior vena cava may preferentially stream through the defect into the systemic circulation. Postoperative leg care, early ambulation, and bridging anticoagulation should be considered. Air filters on intravenous lines may prevent unintentional air embolism and should be used even in the absence of known baseline right-to-left shunting.
- Postoperative electrocardiographic monitoring is advised even in patients without a history of arrhythmias, especially in the elderly.
- Central venous pressure is not a reliable measure of right ventricular preload, especially in patients with tricuspid regurgitation or a high shunt volume.

Coarctation of the Aorta
- Assess the aortic valve because aortic stenosis and/or insufficiency in association with bicuspid aortic valve are commonly found.
- Patients with a history of late repair are at increased risk of premature coronary artery disease.
- Blood pressure is usually more accurately measured in the right arm unless there is anomalous origin of the right subclavian artery.
- Lower-limb blood pressure should be assessed in a hypertensive patient because re-coarctation is common.
- Hypertension may be a persistent or developing problem even after effective relief of aortic obstruction.

Complete Transposition of the Great Arteries
- Depending on the type of repair, possible long-term complications should be sought: systemic ventricular dysfunction, residual baffle leaks or baffle stenosis, subpulmonary or supravalvular pulmonary stenosis.
- In patients with a prior arterial switch procedure, myocardial ischemia can be clinically silent. Significant coronary sequelae are found in 5% to 10% of children undergoing routine coronary angiography. Preoperative noninvasive functional tests to detect ischemia may be considered depending on the planned surgery.
- In patients with a prior atrial switch operation, transvenous pacing leads must traverse the superior vena cava baffle to enter the subpulmonary left ventricle. Baffle leaks should be ruled out by transesophageal echocardiography before transvenous pacemaker insertion to reduce the risk of paradoxical embolism, and morphologic assessment of the systemic venous pathway should be carried out to assess for a stenotic systemic venous channel that may impede proper wire positioning and/or increase the chance of systemic venous obstruction by the electrode.

- Central venous pressure measurement is not reliable in a patient with an obstructed superior vena cava baffle.

Congenital Complete Heart Block
- In nonpaced patients with a narrow QRS complex, no history of syncope or near-syncope, and normal exercise capacity there is no need to insert a temporary pacemaker.
- Continuous electrocardiographic monitoring is advised.
- Vagotonic stimuli, especially prevalent in ophthalmic or gastrointestinal surgery, should be minimized and bradyarrhythmias treated promptly with atropine.

Congenitally Corrected Transposition of the Great Arteries
- Assess systemic ventricular function.
- Rule out significant subpulmonary obstruction.
- Even in patients with normal conduction on the standard ECG, continuous rhythm monitoring is advised.
- In patients with an Ebstein anomaly–type malformation of the systemic tricuspid valve, the possibility of pre-excitation should be kept in mind.[24]

Ebstein Anomaly
- Atrial arrhythmias can be a major hazard if the patient has accessory pathways capable of rapid conduction. Continuous ECG monitoring is necessary in patients with delta waves or a history suggestive of pre-excitation.
- In patients with an interatrial communication, the risk of paradoxical embolism should be taken into account.
- Central venous pressure is not a reliable marker of right ventricular preload in patients with a dilated and compliant right atrium.

Tetralogy of Fallot
- Assess potential residua or sequelae of surgical repair such as the presence of a residual ventricular septal defect, pulmonary regurgitation, right ventricular outflow tract obstruction, right ventricular dysfunction, atrial fibrillation, or atrial flutter.
- If pulmonary blood flow is maintained through aortopulmonary connections, systemic hypotension will decrease pulmonary blood flow and exacerbate cyanosis.
- In patients with significant pulmonary regurgitation, pulmonary vascular resistance should be kept low.
- In patients with a more than small residual ventricular septal defect, hypovolemia should be avoided (see earlier discussion on atrial septal defect).
- In patients with severely impaired right ventricular function, hypervolemia and its negative effect on left ventricular function due to ventricular interdependence should be avoided.

Ventricular Septal Defect
- Check for pulmonary hypertension.
- Patients with a more than small shunt are sensitive to hypovolemia (see earlier discussion on atrial septal defect).

best inserted via the right superior vena cava. There is an increased risk of thrombosis if the left superior vena cava is cannulated. Placement of a pulmonary artery catheter via a persistent left superior vena cava is usually not possible and carries a risk of damaging the coronary sinus.

Transcutaneous or Intra-arterial Oxygen Saturation
Pulse oximetry is the single most important monitoring tool in a patient with cyanotic heart disease. It provides a continuous assessment of relative pulmonary and systemic blood flow, and thus instantaneous warning of a deleterious fall in systemic vascular resistance or rise in pulmonary vascular resistance. In a patient with a history of a classic Blalock-Taussig shunt, the ability to reliably measure oxygen saturation in the ipsilateral fingers may be compromised. In such a case, oximetry must be performed at an alternate site.

Intraoperative Transesophageal Echocardiography
Transesophageal echocardiography may be useful for hemodynamic monitoring during noncardiac surgery in patients with complex anatomy

(Fontan circulation, transposition of the great arteries), in whom conventional monitoring may not be sufficient to promptly detect changes in volume status and ventricular function.[15]

End-Tidal Partial Pressure of Carbon Dioxide
End-tidal partial pressure of carbon dioxide ($PETCO_2$) is often used as a surrogate for $PaCO_2$, but in cyanotic patients the $PaCO_2$ is consistently underestimated with this technique. Cyanotic patients also have a blunted ventilatory response to hypoxemia, so controlled ventilation is needed during anesthesia.

Postoperative Management

Close postoperative surveillance is essential. High-risk patients are best managed in an intensive or coronary care unit. Perioperative complications are more likely to occur after than during a procedure. Hemorrhage, infection, fever, thrombosis, embolism, myocardial ischemia, atelectasis, pneumonia, or pulmonary edema may convert a well-tolerated noncardiac surgical operation into a crisis. Early hospital discharge is often not appropriate.

Effective postoperative pain management reduces catecholamine surges, which otherwise promote hypercoagulability, arrhythmias, and elevated blood pressure. ACHD patients who had surgery with inadequate analgesia as infants may have specific centrally mediated pain sensitization and thus increased sensitivity to pain and a greater fear of painful procedures.[23]

In patients with cyanotic heart disease, postoperative postural hypotension is a particular risk because it facilitates right-to-left shunting; position changes should be undertaken gradually to minimize this effect. Supplemental oxygen may be helpful because it may reduce pulmonary vascular resistance even if arterial saturation does not rise significantly. There are detrimental effects, however, such as drying of mucous membranes. Caregivers may need to be reminded of the impossibility of fully correcting oxygen saturation in such patients.

REFERENCES

1. Fleisher LA, Beckman JA, Brown KA, et al. ACC/AHA 2007 Guidelines on Perioperative Cardiovascular Evaluation and Care for Noncardiac Surgery: a report of the American College of Cardiology/American Heart Association Task Force on Practice Guidelines (Writing Committee to Revise the 2002 Guidelines on Perioperative Cardiovascular Evaluation for Noncardiac Surgery) developed in collaboration with the American Society of Echocardiography, American Society of Nuclear Cardiology, Heart Rhythm Society, Society of Cardiovascular Anesthesiologists, Society for Cardiovascular Angiography and Interventions, Society for Vascular Medicine and Biology, and Society for Vascular Surgery. J Am Coll Cardiol 2007;50:e159–e242.
2. Poldermans D, Hoeks SE, Feringa HH. Pre-operative risk assessment and risk reduction before surgery. J Am Coll Cardiol 2008;51:1913–1924.
3. Fleisher LA, Eagle KA. Lowering cardiac risk in noncardiac surgery. N Engl J Med 2001;345:1677–1682.
4. Warnes CA, Williams RG, Bashore TM, et al. ACC/AHA 2008 Guidelines for the Management of Adults With Congenital Heart Disease. A report of the American College of Cardiology/American Heart Association Task Force on Practice Guidelines (Writing Committee to Develop Guidelines on the Management of Adults With Congenital Heart Disease). Circulation 2008;118:e714–e833.
5. Lee TH, Marcantonio ER, Mangione CM, et al. Derivation and prospective validation of a simple index for prediction of cardiac risk of major noncardiac surgery. Circulation 1999;100:1043–1049.
6. Smetana GW, Lawrence VA, Cornell JE. Preoperative pulmonary risk stratification for noncardiothoracic surgery: systematic review for the American College of Physicians. Ann Intern Med 2006;144:581–595.
7. Pomposelli JJ, Baxter 3rd JK, Babineau TJ, et al. Early postoperative glucose control predicts nosocomial infection rate in diabetic patients. JPEN J Parenter Enteral Nutr 1998;22:77–81.
8. Kearon C, Hirsh J. Management of anticoagulation before and after elective surgery. N Engl J Med 1997;336:1506–1511.
9. Douketis JD, Berger PB, Dunn AS, et al. The perioperative management of antithrombotic therapy: American College of Chest Physicians Evidence-Based Clinical Practice Guidelines (8th Edition). Chest 2008;133:S299–S339.
10. Gage BF, Waterman AD, Shannon W, et al. Validation of clinical classification schemes for predicting stroke: results from the National Registry of Atrial Fibrillation. JAMA 2001;285:2864–2870.
11. Woods K, Douketis JD, Kathirgamanathan K, et al. Low-dose oral vitamin K to normalize the international normalized ratio prior to surgery in patients who require temporary interruption of warfarin. J Thromb Thrombolysis 2007;24:93–97.
12. Devereaux PJ, Yang H, Yusuf S, et al. Effects of extended-release metoprolol succinate in patients undergoing non-cardiac surgery (POISE trial): a randomised controlled trial. Lancet 2008; 371:1839–1847.
13. Roizen NJ, Patterson D. Down's syndrome. Lancet 2003;361: 1281–1289.
14. Murkin JM. Anesthesia and hypothyroidism: a review of thyroxine physiology, pharmacology, and anesthetic implications. Anesth Analg 1982;61:371–383.
15. Chassot PG, Bettex DA. Anesthesia and adult congenital heart disease. J Cardiothorac Vasc Anesth 2006;20:414–437.
16. Franchini M, Lippi G. Acquired von Willebrand syndrome: an update. Am J Hematol 2007;82:368–375.
17. Ramakrishna G, Sprung J, Ravi BS, et al. Impact of pulmonary hypertension on the outcomes of noncardiac surgery: predictors of perioperative morbidity and mortality. J Am Coll Cardiol 2005;45:1691–1699.
18. Ammash NM, Connolly HM, Abel MD, Warnes CA. Noncardiac surgery in Eisenmenger syndrome. J Am Coll Cardiol 1999;33:222–227.
19. Crystal E, Connolly SJ, Sleik K, et al. Interventions on prevention of postoperative atrial fibrillation in patients undergoing heart surgery: a meta-analysis. Circulation 2002;106:75–80.
20. Xu-Cai YO, Brotman DJ, Phillips CO, et al. Outcomes of patients with stable heart failure undergoing elective noncardiac surgery. Mayo Clin Proc 2008;83:280–288.
21. Wilson W, Taubert KA, Gewitz M, et al. Prevention of infective endocarditis: guidelines from the American Heart Association: a guideline from the American Heart Association Rheumatic Fever, Endocarditis, and Kawasaki Disease Committee, Council on Cardiovascular Disease in the Young, and the Council on Clinical Cardiology, Council on Cardiovascular Surgery and Anesthesia, and the Quality of Care and Outcomes Research Interdisciplinary Working Group. Circulation 2007;116:1736–1754.
22. Heggie J, Karski J. The anesthesiologist's role in adults with congenital heart disease. Cardiol Clin 2006;24:571–585, vi.
23. Porter FL, Grunau RE, Anand KJ. Long-term effects of pain in infants. J Dev Behav Pediatr 1999;20:253–261.
24. Perloff JK. Congenitally corrected transposition of the great arteries. In: Perloff JK, editor. The Clinical Recognition of Congenital Heart Disease. Philadelphia: WB Saunders; 2003. p. 62–80.

15

Critical Care

SIMON J. FINNEY

Introduction

More than 85% of patients with congenital heart disease (CHD) survive into adulthood.[1] They present to critical care physicians by virtue of their underlying cardiac disease, the need for surgical or cardiologic intervention to replace failing valves and conduits, or with unrelated reasons such as pregnancy or surgery for a noncardiac condition.

The classification adapted from the Canadian Consensus Document[2] provides a useful guideline to the degree of support critical care teams will require from cardiologists specializing in adult congenital heart disease (ACHD), imaging specialists, electrophysiologists, and cardiac surgeons. Thus, patients with mild or surgically repaired lesions such as a bicuspid aortic valve or ligated patent ductus arteriosus often pose few additional problems on the critical care unit aside from considerations of prophylaxis for infective endocarditis or complications following previous surgery. By contrast, patients with complex (e.g., cyanotic disease, univentricular circulation) and moderate disease (e.g., tetralogy of Fallot, Ebstein anomaly) may require considerable resources,[3] some of which may only be present at specialist centers.

In this chapter general considerations are presented for critical care physicians caring for patients with moderate or severe CHD who are being managed through cardiac surgery, cardiologic intervention, or an intercurrent illness. Some clinical problems more common in patients with CHD are outlined in Table 15-1. The consequences of specific anatomic arrangements and pregnancy are considered elsewhere in this book.

Cardiac Anatomy

An appreciation of the patient's cardiac anatomy is paramount. When patients present following cardiac surgery, this will have been well defined preoperatively with a combination of echocardiography, cardiac catheterization, and magnetic resonance imaging. However, the fallibility of these investigations is reflected by the occasional conflicts with observations made during surgery. In the setting of an emergency admission or a patient who has been lost to follow-up, the anatomy may be less well defined. It is important to gather data from the patient, next of kin, and other institutions that have cared for the patient previously. Echocardiography in complex CHD may be difficult and require tertiary expertise. Key questions to attempt to answer are the presence of abnormal shunts, the nature of the systemic and subpulmonary ventricles, and previous palliative or corrective procedures that have been undertaken.

Detailed anatomic knowledge helps physicians predict the effects of interventions such as increasing systemic vascular tone and increasing heart rate. It is often necessary to compromise certain physiologic targets (e.g., the systemic saturations) to achieve other targets (e.g., sufficient cardiac output, systemic pressure). The goal of hemodynamic manipulations is to achieve just enough oxygen delivery to end organs such as the kidney or the brain to prevent damage. This is frequently with parameters different from those in patients without CHD. Because patients with CHD tend to be younger and have less atherosclerotic disease, they often tolerate moderate hypotension better.

Vascular Access

Central venous access is necessary to measure central venous pressures and to administer vasoactive agents. Placement of multiple-lumen catheters is made more difficult by the presence of abnormal venous anatomy (e.g., persistent left-sided superior vena cava) or vessel thrombosis/stenosis due to multiple previous attempts and/or transvenous pacing systems. Real-time ultrasound guidance of line insertion is considered as best practice in these, and perhaps all, patients.

It is also possible to place long catheters across bidirectional Glenn shunts (which connect a right-sided superior vena cava to the right pulmonary artery) into the pulmonary circulation directly. Although this may supply interesting physiologic data if undertaken inadvertently, it is not ideal and such catheters should be withdrawn into the superior vena cava.

Extreme care must be taken when administering medications and fluids to patients with known right-to-left shunts in whom small amounts of air can cross to the systemic circulation and result in neurologic damage. Even in patients with predominant left-to-right shunts there may be transient shunt reversal during the normal cardiac cycle or during coughing.

Invasive arterial access may be difficult in upper limbs on the side of previous Blalock-Taussig shunts.

Infective Endocarditis Prophylaxis

Infections have been reported of shunts, conduits, prosthetic valves, septal defects, surgical cannulation sites, and pacemakers in patients with CHD.[4] Episodes of infective endocarditis are not always anteceded by events that can cause bacteremia such as dental procedures or genitourinary or gastrointestinal instrumentation; indeed, in those that were, antibiotic prophylaxis was not always protective.[4] In the United Kingdom, the National Institute for Clinical Excellence considers that routine antibiotic prophylaxis is not indicated.[5] This advice contrasts to that of the American Heart Association,[6] which considers patients with prosthetic valves, previous infective endocarditis, unrepaired congenital heart defects (including palliative shunts and conduits), repaired defects, or residual defects close to prosthetic materials as having particular risk for a bad outcome after an episode of infective endocarditis. The American Heart Association concludes that the risks of unnecessary antibiotics are outweighed by this risk and therefore recommends the use of antibiotic prophylaxis.

Critically ill patients are at risk of bacteremia due to the presence of central venous catheters. Reported rates of bacteremia from central venous catheters are around 1.4 per 10,000 catheter-days. Meticulous aseptic practice in the insertion, day-to-day care, and timely removal of these lines reduces these infections, a standard that should be afforded to all critically ill patients.[7] There are few data to support the routine change of central lines after a fixed time interval.[8] Nevertheless, many cardiothoracic institutions cognizant of the catastrophic consequences of infective endocarditis have a low threshold for changing central venous catheters. For example, a catheter may be replaced for an otherwise unexplained rise in inflammatory markers despite the absence of local signs of inflammation at the catheter entry site. The use of routine prophylactic antibiotics in patients with invasive lines is unproven and risks complications such as *Clostridium difficile* diarrhea and the development of antibiotic-resistant organisms. Nevertheless, it is practiced by many.

TABLE 15-1	Conditions Associated with Congenital Heart Disease Complicating Critical Illness
System	**Associations**
Respiratory	Congenital pulmonary lesions (e.g., hypoplastic lung)
	Musculoskeletal abnormalities
	Phrenic nerve palsies after cardiac surgery
	Hemoptysis secondary to aortopulmonary collaterals, pulmonary embolism, etc.
Renal	Glomerulosclerosis and renal dysfunction
	Proteinuria
	Hyperuricemia
	Congenital abnormalities of the renal tract
Gastrointestinal	Asplenia
	Congenital abnormalities of the gastrointestinal tract
	Liver dysfunction
	Protein-losing enteropathy (in Fontan circulation)
Endocrine	Thyroid dysfunction
Neurologic	Cerebral abscesses

TABLE 15-2	Techniques of Cardiac Output Measurement
Fick Principle	Oxygen consumption is difficult to measure in the clinical setting. The Fick technique measures transpulmonary flow assuming that there is no intrapulmonary shunting.
Pulmonary Artery Thermodilution	Pulmonary artery catheter is not possible to place if there is no subpulmonary ventricle. This technique measures flow through the subpulmonary ventricle but it is less accurate if there is severe tricuspid regurgitation.
Transpulmonary Dilution	Indicators that can be used are lithium (LIDCO) or thermal (PICCO). They measure through the entire heart presuming minimal intracardiac shunt.
Esophageal Doppler Interrogation	Measures flow in descending aorta and estimates cardiac output based on nomograms of aortic size according to the patient's height and weight. It may not be possible to obtain a Doppler signal if the aorta is right sided. The nomograms may be inaccurate in congenital heart disease.
Fick Partial Rebreathing	Carbon dioxide production is difficult to measure in the clinical setting. Transpulmonary flow is measured assuming there is no intrapulmonary shunting.
Pulse Contour Analysis (Calibrated)	Variable reports about the accuracy of the pulse contour algorithms in patients with congenital heart disease
Pulse Contour Analysis (Uncalibrated)	The accuracy of these devices is low even in normal circulations.
Echocardiography	Provides excellent physiologic and anatomic data at a specific time point but is less useful for real-time titration of therapy

Feeding

Early enteral feeding improves outcome in critically ill patients, whereas inappropriate parenteral nutrition is associated with infections and other complications such as immune dysfunction.[9] Neonates with CHD are prone to necrotizing enterocolitis (NEC) perhaps in part due to reduced splanchnic blood flow in a low cardiac output state coupled with systemic venous hypertension. Therefore, neonates often have enteral feedings introduced slowly because NEC usually does not occur before the beginning of oral feedings. Similarly, some physicians limit enteral feedings in adults with very significant right ventricular dysfunction. There are no specific data to support this practice.

Coagulation Defects and Anticoagulation

Patients with cyanotic heart disease may have an associated thrombocytopenia that may be a result of reduced platelet survival or may be artifactual owing to increased red cell mass and megakaryocytes crossing the right-to-left shunt resulting in larger platelets that are not identified by automated cell counters.[10] Decreased levels of factors V, VII, VIII, and IX and reduced von Willebrand multimers have been reported, although not consistently. These may be manifest as prolonged bleeding, prothrombin, and partial thromboplastin times[11–13] and increased postoperative bleeding. Standard management algorithms should be used that identify and correct specific deficiencies in coagulation and platelet function. The severity of coagulation defect can relate to the degree of secondary erythrocytosis in an individual patient. Preoperative phlebotomy is still practiced in patients with a hematocrit over 65%[14]; there is limited evidence for this practice, however, and care must be taken to not critically compromise oxygen delivery in the preoperative state through hypovolemia or relative anemia.

By contrast, some patients require anticoagulation for mechanical valves and arrhythmias. This is usually undertaken on the critical care unit with infusions of unfractionated heparin. A sudden reduction in the platelet count should alert the physician to the possibility of heparin-induced thrombocytopenia and its thrombotic complications. There are few data to support the use of low-molecular-weight heparins, and warfarin often complicates interventional procedures, which are frequent in the intensive care unit.

Management of Oxygen Delivery

Much consideration is given to maintaining sufficient oxygen delivery to the organs of the body to prevent ischemic organ dysfunction. There is a complex balance between cardiac output, oxygen saturations, hemoglobin levels, the affinity of hemoglobin for oxygen, systemic arterial pressure, and systemic venous pressure. The latter is often overlooked, although systemic venous hypertension in combination with a low cardiac output can be particularly damaging to end organs.

All these parameters are easy to measure apart from cardiac output. In CHD there may be anatomic considerations that limit certain techniques (Table 15-2) and prevent measurement of cardiac output. Cardiac output may be manipulated through fluid therapy, vasoactive drugs, management of pulmonary vascular resistance (PVR), pacing, or mechanical support.

FLUID THERAPY

Fluids can be administered to increase systemic preload to the right side of the heart. Initially, fluid expansion will improve right-sided heart function particularly if it has restrictive physiology, although this will be at the expense of systemic venous hypertension. However, excessive fluid administration may result in ventricular distention and a reduction in cardiac output. Fluids should be titrated to markers of cardiac output (either direct or indirect such as clinical examination, metabolic status, urine output). Patients who have a Fontan-type circulation are particularly dependent on adequate venous filling to ensure transpulmonary blood flow in the absence of a subpulmonary ventricle. There are few data to support the use of a specific colloid or crystalloid solution.

Blood Transfusion

Anemia is common in critically ill patients. Blood is often administered in an attempt to increase oxygen delivery. Moreover, cyanotic patients have increased red cell mass at baseline. This is one part of their adaptation to chronic hypoxemia and is triggered by increased erythropoietin production in the kidney. The increase in red cell numbers is termed correctly as a secondary erythrocytosis, in contrast to a polycythemia, which relates to increases in more than one hematologic lineage. Patients are frequently iron deficient due to consumption by erythropoiesis, inappropriate phlebotomy, gastrointestinal losses, or poor dietary intake.[15]

The hemoglobin threshold that should trigger transfusion is unclear. A large study in critically ill patients demonstrated that targeting hemoglobin concentrations to 7.0 to 9.0 g/dL was as effective and perhaps superior to higher targets.[16] This study excluded patients who had undergone cardiac surgery and most likely patients with cyanotic heart disease because the hemoglobin level had to fall to below 9.0 g/dL within 48 hours of admission to the intensive care unit. Nevertheless, more restrictive targets limit the exposure of the detrimental effects of transfusion that may increase morbidity and even mortality.[17] Transfused red cells are immunosuppressive; have poorer rheologic properties, which reduce microvascular flow; and are deplete in 2,3-diphosphoglycerate, which impairs their oxygen-carrying capacity for some days. Targets should be customized to the patient. Typically, a threshold of 7.0 to 9.0 g/dL is used in currently noncyanotic patients who do not have acute coronary ischemia. Cyanotic patients need higher hemoglobin levels, but the exact levels are hard to estimate. Transfusion is better titrated to markers that suggest oxygen delivery is insufficient (e.g., low venous saturations or poor end organ function) despite optimization of arterial oxygen saturations and cardiac output.

INOTROPES AND VASOCONSTRICTORS

Inotropes are used to increase cardiac contractility in low-output states. Catecholamines such as epinephrine, dobutamine, and dopamine are agonists at β-adrenergic and dopaminergic receptors. Although they may increase the force of contraction by increasing intramyocyte calcium levels, this is often at the expense of an increased heart rate, increased myocardial oxygen consumption, and impaired relaxation of the heart during diastole. Epinephrine per se can induce a hyperlactatemia,[18,19] which may complicate the interpretation of metabolic changes. There are potential advantages to phosphodiesterase inhibitors, such as milrinone and enoximone, and the newer calcium sensitizer levosimendan in patients with significant right ventricular dysfunction.

Milrinone, when compared with dobutamine, causes less tachycardia, more pulmonary and systemic vasodilation, more lusitropy, and has a lesser increase in myocardial consumption.[20] Because the morphologic right ventricle is so susceptible to afterload changes the vasodilating properties are advantageous, even in the setting of needing some vasoconstrictor to maintain systemic pressures.

Levosimendan acts by sensitizing cardiac troponin C for calcium during systole. Because intracellular calcium levels are not elevated there is a lesser increase in myocardial oxygen consumption and better lusitropy. Experimental data suggest it also may be a pulmonary vasodilator.[21,22] This appears to borne out clinically[23,24] and makes it an attractive agent in patients with right ventricular failure and those with pulmonary hypertension. It has been used successfully in pediatric patients with CHD.[25,26]

Norepinephrine is an α-adrenergic agonist that is a systemic and pulmonary vasoconstrictor. It is administered in vasodilated states to restore systemic vascular resistance (SVR) and mean arterial pressure to ensure adequate organ perfusion. Although autoregulation maintains perfusion of organs during hypotension there is a threshold at which this fails, and administration of vasoconstrictors will restore organ perfusion and function such as urine output. Vasodilation is common in critically ill patients owing to sepsis, systemic inflammation postoperatively, and the administration of vasodilating drugs such as milrinone and levosimendan.

Arginine vasopressin (up to 0.04 IU/hr) is an alternative systemic vasoconstrictor to norepinephrine. It acts at vasopressinergic (V1) receptors and may be vasodilating at low doses in the pulmonary circulation through a nitric oxide–dependent mechanism.[27] This may be manifest clinically as a reduction in the PVR/SVR ratio.[28,29] It has been used successfully in severe sepsis and safely in patients with pulmonary hypertension.[30–33] These data provide a rationale for selecting arginine vasopressin above norepinephrine in settings of pulmonary hypertension and systemic vasodilation.

MANAGEMENT OF THE PULMONARY VASCULAR RESISTANCE

Management of the PVR is often the cornerstone to the care of patients with complex CHD. In patients with a failing subpulmonary ventricle,

reduction in the afterload presented by the pulmonary circulation may improve cardiac output; morphologic right ventricles (the usual scenario) are particularly susceptible to fail with acute rises in PVR. The balance between pulmonary and systemic blood flow in patients with unrestricted shunting is influenced by the balance between PVR and SVR. Thus, in high PVR/low SVR settings systemic cardiac output will increase at the expense of decreased pulmonary flow, greater venous admixture, and systemic desaturation. The converse will occur in low PVR/high SVR settings.

Inhaled Nitric Oxide

Inhaled nitric oxide forms a mainstay of acute therapy in many institutions. It increases smooth muscle cyclic guanosine monophosphate, thereby causing arteriolar vasodilation. Since nitric oxide is inhaled and has a short half-life its effects are generally limited to the pulmonary circulation. Administration of inhaled nitric oxide may profoundly drop the PVR. It is important to administer it properly. In general, it is delivered using an injector system that is attached to the mechanical ventilator. Doses used in clinical practice range from 0 to 40 ppm.[34,35] It is clear that ever-increasing doses of nitric oxide do not increase pulmonary vasodilation further and may exacerbate the situation.[34,36] Moreover, data from 20 patients with elevated pulmonary artery pressures due to acute respiratory failure suggest that the dose response to inhaled nitric oxide changes over time[36] and may result in a situation in which a previously efficacious dose is ineffectual. Thus, inhaled nitric oxide therapy should be titrated at least every 48 hours targeting a clear physiologic goal such as cardiac output. Despite concerns about the generation of nitrogen dioxide and methemoglobin, in practice, this seems to be unusual.

Prostacyclin Analogues

Epoprostenol, iloprost, and treprostinil are prostacyclin analogues that differ primarily in their stability and half-lives. All can be administered by continuous infusions, although only epoprostenol is licensed for this in pulmonary hypertension. Although they are pulmonary vasodilators and inhibit platelet aggregation, their use in this form in critically ill patients can be limited by the concomitant systemic vasodilation. By contrast, epoprostenol and iloprost can be nebulized with less systemic effects. The longer half-life of iloprost means that it does not need to be nebulized continuously. All have been associated with rebound pulmonary hypertension on withdrawal.

Phosphodiesterase Inhibitors

Sildenafil is a phosphodiesterase-5 inhibitor that causes vasodilation by increasing intracellular cyclic guanosine monophosphate levels. Because phosphodiesterase-5 is particularly abundant in pulmonary vascular tissues and the corpus cavernosum, the vasodilation is relatively selective to these tissues beds. It has been used with great success in patients with chronic pulmonary hypertension, increasing exercise capacity and improving hemodynamics and symptoms[37] and longevity.[38] Sildenafil may be additive with inhaled nitric oxide,[39] prostacyclin analogues,[40–42] and bosentan.[43]

In general sildenafil is only available as an oral preparation. It has been used acutely in critically ill patients.[44–46] An intravenous form is available on a compassionate basis from the manufacturer and is used at rates of 2 to 16 mg/hr.[47,48] Intravenous sildenafil can be associated with profound systemic vasodilation, particularly when there is concomitant use of inhaled nitric oxide.

Other Factors Influencing Pulmonary Vascular Resistance in Critically Ill Patients

Pulmonary hypertension may be exacerbated by hypercapnia, acidemia, hypoxemia, and pain. With respect to analgesia, fentanyl[49] and thoracic and lumbar epidural analgesia do not affect pulmonary vascular tone.

Mechanical ventilation also increases PVR because elevated airway pressures compress perialveolar capillaries The relationship between positive end-expiratory pressure (PEEP)/lung inflation and PVR is

U-shaped such that low levels of PEEP reduce pulmonary vascular resistance by recruiting collapsed areas of lung, but as PEEP increases further PVR increases.[50] PEEP therefore must be titrated such that PVR is not unduly increased while maintaining lung volumes and preventing hypoxemia. Spontaneous ventilation minimizes airway pressures and is the favored mode of ventilation if possible.

Sedation and neuromuscular blockade is used to facilitate mechanical ventilation on intensive care units. Propofol and midazolam do not increase PVR[51-53] and have been used safely in patients with pulmonary hypertension. Another study in patients undergoing coronary artery surgery demonstrated that PVR was not changed by atracurium, vecuronium, or pancuronium.[54]

Endothelin Receptor Antagonists

Bosentan is a competitive antagonist of both endothelin A and B receptors. It has become an important drug in the treatment of pulmonary hypertension, in which endothelin-1 has been implicated in pulmonary vasoconstriction per se and the proliferation of vascular smooth muscles cells that results in the remodeling of pulmonary arterioles. It increases exercise capacity and hemodynamics and slows disease progression in chronic pulmonary hypertension. It improves exercise capacity and hemodynamics in patients with Eisenmenger syndrome.[55,56] Longevity is improved when bosentan is used as part of a package of pulmonary hypertension management in these patients.[38]

There are few data about the acute use of bosentan or other more selective endothelin antagonists in critically ill patients. Bosentan utility is limited by its availability only as an oral preparation and that it causes an idiosyncratic hepatic transaminitis. It is therefore not recommended in patients who also have Child Pugh class C cirrhosis. It is a known teratogen.

Atrial Fenestration

Occasionally, when pulmonary hypertension is refractory to medical intervention resulting in a low cardiac output state that threatens organ perfusion, an atrial septostomy will allow shunting of desaturated blood to the left side of the heart and an increase in cardiac output, albeit at the expense of systemic desaturation. This intervention can be lifesaving but may fail in the setting of significant left ventricular dysfunction when elevated left atrial pressures will reduce the degree of shunt. Sometimes fenestration will be undertaken at the time of cardiac surgery to allow shunting if pulmonary hypertension occurs. Fenestrations may be closed at a later date, if appropriate, usually by a percutaneous approach.

MECHANICAL SUPPORT

Temporary mechanical support can bridge a patient through the temporary cardiac dysfunction that may occur after cardiac surgery. This temporary dysfunction may be due to relative ischemia while the surgical crossclamp was applied, to myocardial dysfunction associated with postoperative systemic inflammation, or to perioperative elevation of PVR. Intra-aortic balloon counterpulsation lowers the afterload of systemic ventricle and improves coronary blood flow and may be particularly useful in older patients especially if there is concomitant coronary artery disease. Balloon counterpulsation has been undertaken also in the pulmonary artery.[57] Ventricular assist devices are more complex undertakings and may be difficult to place in anatomically abnormal circulations. They are often associated with considerable postoperative bleeding and are reserved for use in centers where technicians are familiar with the range of devices available.

MANAGEMENT OF CARDIAC RHYTHM

Arrhythmias are common postoperatively and in patients with complex lesions. Loss of atrial transport can be associated with a dramatic fall in cardiac output. Atrial arrhythmias tend to be more common owing to the substantial substrate of atrial tissue and often multiple operations and scars. Atrial tachycardias are common particularly in patients with Ebstein anomaly or Fontan circulations. They can be hard to differentiate from sinus tachycardias, but previous electrocardiograms and interrogation of any implanted pacing system may help in this respect.

Management of cardiac arrhythmias follows standard algorithms of replacing electrolytes such as potassium and magnesium, antiarrhythmics, and electrical cardioversion. Amiodarone is often the first drug of choice but can reveal other problems, such as poor sinus node function, atrioventricular/intraventricular conduction delays, and aberrant pathways. A more detailed consideration of arrhythmias is presented elsewhere in the book. Early input from specialist electrophysiologists is highly advisable for rhythm disturbances that do not respond to standard measures.

PACING

Patients who have undergone cardiac surgery generally have an external temporary pacing system attached to epicardial pacing wires on the right atrium and one or both ventricles. Transvenous access to the heart for pacing is not possible in some instances such as following a total cavopulmonary connection. Further difficulties with pacing may occur because previous and extensive surgery often makes electrical capture difficult. In some instances patients will have permanent implanted pacing systems. Optimization of heart rate and atrioventricular delay pacing may lead to rather useful increases in cardiac output. Often echocardiography is used to guide optimization. For example, patients who have restrictive physiology demonstrated on echocardiography (with ventricular filling ending in early diastole) may benefit from an increased heart rate and short atrioventricular interval. Interventricular dyssynchrony may be improved by left ventricular pacing or multisite pacing. Furthermore, biventricular pacing, or pacing with a longer atrioventricular delay may allow the heart's intrinsic pacing pathways to work albeit with a degree of heart block. It is unknown and probably unlikely that conventional criteria for cardiac resynchronization therapy would apply to patients with CHD.

CONCLUSION

Care of complex CHD requires considerable input from critical care physicians, cardiologists, cardiac surgeons, imaging specialists, and electrophysiologists. Indeed observational data of 342 patients admitted to a single center demonstrated that complex disease consumes considerable intensive care resources. Many required three or more vasoactive agents, multiple echocardiograms, inhaled nitric oxide, pacing, renal replacement therapy, and percutaneous tracheostomies over prolonged admissions.[3] Clearly this is easier to provide in larger centers with greater intensive care unit capacity.

REFERENCES

1. Warnes CA, Liberthson R, Danielson GK, et al. Task force 1: the changing profile of congenital heart disease in adult life. J Am Coll Cardiol 2001;37:1170–1175.
2. Connelly MS, Webb GD, Somerville J, et al. Canadian Consensus Conference on Adult Congenital Heart Disease 1996. Can J Cardiol 1998;14:395–452.
3. Price S, Jaggar SI, Jordan S, et al. Adult congenital heart disease: intensive care management and outcome prediction. Intensive Care Med 2007;33:652–659.
4. Li W, Somerville J. Infective endocarditis in the grown-up congenital heart (GUCH) population. Eur Heart J 1998;19:166–173.
5. National Institute for Clinical Excellence. CG64: prophylaxis against infective endocarditis—antimicrobial prophylaxis against infective endocarditis in adults and children undergoing interventional procedures. Available at: http://www.nice.org.uk/nicemedia/pdf/CG64NICEguidance.pdf; 2008 [accessed July 13, 2009].
6. Wilson W, Taubert KA, Gewitz M, et al. Prevention of infective endocarditis: guidelines from the American Heart Association: a guideline from the American Heart Association Rheumatic Fever, Endocarditis, and Kawasaki Disease Committee, Council on Cardiovascular Disease in the Young, and the Council on Clinical Cardiology, Council on Cardiovascular Surgery and Anesthesia, and the Quality of Care and Outcomes Research Interdisciplinary Working Group. Circulation 2007;116:1736–1754.
7. Pronovost P, Needham D, Berenholtz S, et al. An intervention to decrease catheter-related bloodstream infections in the ICU. N Engl J Med 2006;355:2725–2732.
8. Timsit JF. Scheduled replacement of central venous catheters is not necessary. Infect Control Hosp Epidemiol 2000;21:371–374.
9. Marik PE, Zaloga GP. Early enteral nutrition in acutely ill patients: a systematic review. Crit Care Med 2001;29:2264–2270.
10. Lill MC, Perloff JK, Child JS. Pathogenesis of thrombocytopenia in cyanotic congenital heart disease. Am J Cardiol 2006;98:254–258.

11. Ekert H, Gilchrist GS, Stanton R, Hammond D. Hemostasis in cyanotic congenital heart disease. J Pediatr 1970;76:221–230.
12. Perloff JK, Rosove MH, Child JS, Wright GB. Adults with cyanotic congenital heart disease: hematologic management. Ann Intern Med 1988;109:406–413.
13. Broberg CS, Ujita M, Prasad S, et al. Pulmonary arterial thrombosis in Eisenmenger syndrome is associated with biventricular dysfunction and decreased pulmonary flow velocity. J Am Coll Cardiol 2007;50:634–642.
14. Therrien J, Warnes C, Daliento L, et al. Canadian Cardiovascular Society Consensus Conference 2001 update: recommendations for the management of adults with congenital heart disease: III. Can J Cardiol 2001;17:1135–1158.
15. Spence MS, Balaratnam MS, Gatzoulis MA. Clinical update: cyanotic adult congenital heart disease. Lancet 2007;370:1530–1532.
16. Hébert PC, Wells G, Blajchman MA, et al. A multicenter, randomized, controlled clinical trial of transfusion requirements in critical care. Transfusion Requirements in Critical Care Investigators, Canadian Critical Care Trials Group. N Engl J Med 1999;340:409–417.
17. Vincent JL, Baron JF, Reinhart K, et al. Anemia and blood transfusion in critically ill patients. JAMA 2002;288:1499–1507.
18. Heringlake M, Wernerus M, Grünefeld J, et al. The metabolic and renal effects of adrenaline and milrinone in patients with myocardial dysfunction after coronary artery bypass grafting. Crit Care 2007;11:R51.
19. Barcroft H, Cobbold AF. The action of adrenaline on muscle blood flow and blood lactate in man. J Physiol 1956;132:372–378.
20. Grose R, Strain J, Greenberg M, LeJemtel TH. Systemic and coronary effects of intravenous milrinone and dobutamine in congestive heart failure. J Am Coll Cardiol 1986;7:1107–1113.
21. Yokoshiki H, Katsube Y, Sunagawa M, Sperelakis N. Levosimendan, a novel Ca^{2+} sensitizer, activates the glibenclamide-sensitive K$^+$ channel in rat arterial myocytes. Eur J Pharmacol 1997;333:249–259.
22. De Witt BJ, Ibrahim IN, Bayer E, et al. An analysis of responses to levosimendan in the pulmonary vascular bed of the cat. Anesth Analg 2002;94:1427–1433 table of contents.
23. Morelli A, Teboul JL, Maggiore SM, et al. Effects of levosimendan on right ventricular afterload in patients with acute respiratory distress syndrome: a pilot study. Crit Care Med 2006;34:2287–2293.
24. Kerbaul F, Rondelet B, Demester JP, et al. Effects of levosimendan versus dobutamine on pressure load-induced right ventricular failure. Crit Care Med 2006;34:2814–2819.
25. Osthaus WA, Boethig D, Winterhalter M, et al. First experiences with intraoperative Levosimendan in pediatric cardiac surgery. Eur J Pediatr 2009;168:735–740.
26. Egan JR, Clarke AJ, Williams S, et al. Levosimendan for low cardiac output: a pediatric experience. J Intensive Care Med 2006;21:183–187.
27. Eichinger MR, Walker BR. Enhanced pulmonary arterial dilation to arginine vasopressin in chronically hypoxic rats. Am J Physiol 1994;267:H2413–H2419.

28. Jeon Y, Ryu JH, Lim YJ, et al. Comparative hemodynamic effects of vasopressin and norepinephrine after milrinone-induced hypotension in off-pump coronary artery bypass surgical patients. Eur J Cardiothorac Surg 2006;29:952–956.
29. Tayama E, Ueda T, Shojima T, et al. Arginine vasopressin is an ideal drug after cardiac surgery for the management of low systemic vascular resistant hypotension concomitant with pulmonary hypertension. Interact Cardiovasc Thorac Surg 2007;6:715–719.
30. Smith AM, Elliot CM, Kiely DG, Channer KS. The role of vasopressin in cardiorespiratory arrest and pulmonary hypertension. QJM 2006;99:127–133.
31. Vida VL, Mack R, Castaneda AR. The role of vasopressin in treating systemic inflammatory syndrome complicated by right ventricular failure. Cardiol Young 2005;15:88–90.
32. Scheurer MA, Bradley SM, Atz AM. Vasopressin to attenuate pulmonary hypertension and improve systemic blood pressure after correction of obstructed total anomalous pulmonary venous return. J Thorac Cardiovasc Surg 2005;129:464–466.
33. Russell JA, Walley KR, Singer J, et al. Vasopressin versus norepinephrine infusion in patients with septic shock. N Engl J Med 2008;358:877–887.
34. Solina A, Ginsberg SH, Papp D, et al. Dose response to nitric oxide in adult cardiac surgery patients. J Clin Anesth 2001;13:281–286.
35. Solina A, Papp D, Ginsberg S, et al. A comparison of inhaled nitric oxide and milrinone for the treatment of pulmonary hypertension in adult cardiac surgery patients. J Cardiothorac Vasc Anesth 2000;14:12–17.
36. Gerlach H, Keh D, Semmerow A, et al. Dose-response characteristics during long-term inhalation of nitric oxide in patients with severe acute respiratory distress syndrome: a prospective, randomized, controlled study. Am J Respir Crit Care Med 2003;167:1008–1015.
37. Sastry BK, Narasimhan C, Reddy NK, Raju BS. Clinical efficacy of sildenafil in primary pulmonary hypertension: a randomized, placebo-controlled, double-blind, crossover study. J Am Coll Cardiol 2004;43:1149–1153.
38. Dimopoulos K, Inuzuka R, Goletto S, et al. Improved survival among patients with Eisenmenger syndrome receiving advanced therapy for pulmonary arterial hypertension. Circulation 2010;121:20–25.
39. Bigatello LM, Hess D, Dennehy KC, et al. Sildenafil can increase the response to inhaled nitric oxide. Anesthesiology 2000;92:1827–1829.
40. Ghofrani HA, Wiedemann R, Rose F, et al. Combination therapy with oral sildenafil and inhaled iloprost for severe pulmonary hypertension. Ann Intern Med 2002;136:515–522.
41. Ghofrani HA, Rose F, Schermuly RT, et al. Oral sildenafil as long-term adjunct therapy to inhaled iloprost in severe pulmonary arterial hypertension. J Am Coll Cardiol 2003;42:158–164.
42. Stiebellehner L, Petkov V, Vonbank K, et al. Long-term treatment with oral sildenafil in addition to continuous IV epoprostenol in patients with pulmonary arterial hypertension. Chest 2003;123:1293–1295.

43. Gruenig E, Michelakis E, Vachiéry JL, et al. Acute hemodynamic effects of single-dose sildenafil when added to established bosentan therapy in patients with pulmonary arterial hypertension: results of the COMPASS-1 study. J Clin Pharmacol 2009;49:1343–1352.
44. Ng J, Finney SJ, Shulman R, et al. Treatment of pulmonary hypertension in the general adult intensive care unit: a role for oral sildenafil? Br J Anaesth 2005;94:774–777.
45. Ganiere V, Feihl F, Tagan D. Dramatic beneficial effects of sildenafil in recurrent massive pulmonary embolism. Intensive Care Med 2006;32:452–454.
46. Maruszewski M, Zakliczy ski M, Przybylski R, et al. Use of sildenafil in heart transplant recipients with pulmonary hypertension may prevent right heart failure. Transplant Proc 2007;39:2850–2852.
47. Mikhail GW, Prasad SK, Li W, et al. Clinical and haemodynamic effects of sildenafil in pulmonary hypertension: acute and mid-term effects. Eur Heart J 2004;25:431–436.
48. Suntharalingam J, Hughes RJ, Goldsmith K, et al. Acute haemodynamic responses to inhaled nitric oxide and intravenous sildenafil in distal chronic thromboembolic pulmonary hypertension (CTEPH). Vascul Pharmacol 2007;46:449–455.
49. Hickey PR, Hansen DD, Wessel DL, et al. Pulmonary and systemic hemodynamic responses to fentanyl in infants. Anesth Analg 1985;64:483–486.
50. Whittenberger JL, McGregor M, Berglund E, Borst HG. Influence of state of inflation of the lung on pulmonary vascular resistance. J Appl Physiol 1960;15:878–882.
51. Rich GF, Roos CM, Anderson SM, et al. Direct effects of intravenous anesthetics on pulmonary vascular resistance in the isolated rat lung. Anesth Analg 1994;78:961–966.
52. Hammaren E, Hynynen M. Haemodynamic effects of propofol infusion for sedation after coronary artery surgery. Br J Anaesth 1995;75:47–50.
53. Rouby JJ, Andreev A, Léger P, et al. Peripheral vascular effects of thiopental and propofol in humans with artificial hearts. Anesthesiology 1991;75:32–42.
54. Ferres CJ, Carson IW, Lyons SM, et al. Haemodynamic effects of vecuronium, pancuronium and atracurium in patients with coronary artery disease. Br J Anaesth 1987;59:305–311.
55. Galiè N, Beghetti M, Gatzoulis MA, et al. Bosentan therapy in patients with Eisenmenger syndrome: a multicenter, double-blind, randomized, placebo-controlled study. Circulation 2006;114:48–54.
56. Gatzoulis MA, Beghetti M, Galiè N, et al. Longer-term bosentan therapy improves functional capacity in Eisenmenger syndrome: results of the BREATHE-5 open-label extension study. Int J Cardiol 2008;127:27–32.
57. Skillington PD, Couper GS, Peigh PS, et al. Pulmonary artery balloon counterpulsation for intraoperative right ventricular failure. Ann Thorac Surg 1991;51:658–660.

16

Arrhythmias in Adults with Congenital Heart Disease

JOHN K. TRIEDMAN | EDWARD P. WALSH

Introduction

The great successes of congenital heart surgery have created a new class of cardiology patient: the adult with congenital heart disease (CHD). It is estimated that there are more than 1 million patients older than 18 years of age with CHD in the United States, and for the first time ever there are more adults living with congenital heart defects than children with CHD. Cardiac arrhythmias of all varieties (Table 16-1) are prevalent in the adult group, are often complex and difficult to manage, and significantly complicate the long-term care of these patients.

Although the electrophysiology of the cardiomyocyte in CHD patients is generally thought to be similar to that of the normal population, anatomic malformations, the effects of variety of hemodynamic and environmental stressors, and surgical scarring produce a complex arrhythmogenic substrate. The result is a high and increasing frequency of acquired arrhythmias that are rarely seen in normal young adult hearts, including atrial and ventricular reentrant tachycardias, heart block, and sinus node dysfunction. In addition, any arrhythmias prevalent in the normal population may also occur in CHD.

The presence of CHD significantly alters arrhythmia risk, its potential severity, and the safety and feasibility of various therapies.[1] Clinical manifestations of arrhythmia in adult CHD (ACHD) range from clinically occult arrhythmia to sudden death. Incessant arrhythmias may cause progressive hemodynamic deterioration and are associated with thrombosis and embolic events. Symptoms, frequent need for hospitalization, and adverse effects of antiarrhythmic drugs constitute a significant burden on quality of life. Risk assessment for identification of patients appropriately treated with implantable cardiac defibrillators (ICDs) is difficult because ACHD populations are small, are anatomically diverse, and have relatively low rates of sudden death. In this chapter, a review is provided of the identification, evaluation, and management of the more common forms of arrhythmia seen in ACHD.

Bradycardia

SINUS NODE DYSFUNCTION

Gradual loss of sinus rhythm occurs over time after the Mustard and Senning operations and after all varieties of Fontan procedures.[2,3] Patients with heterotaxy syndromes, particularly left atrial isomerism, may also have congenital abnormalities of the sinus node. Loss of sinus rhythm appears to increase risk of mortality and is also highly associated with the occurrence of paroxysmal atrial tachycardias such as intra-atrial reentrant tachycardia, (IART), a form of tachy-brady syndrome.

Direct surgical injury to the sinus node artery and the node itself has been observed and may be the cause of long-term sinus node dysfunction in some patients. However, loss of sinus rhythm is observed to occur in populations of ACHD patients over decades, which implies the action of other ongoing processes most likely related to scarring and chronic hemodynamic abnormality. Abnormalities of atrial electrophysiology identified in postoperative CHD patients include prolonged sinus node recovery times, intra-atrial conduction times, and atrial refractoriness.

ATRIOVENTRICULAR BLOCK

Interventricular conduction abnormalities and particularly right bundle-branch block are common after CHD surgery, but complete and permanent postoperative heart block is relatively rare in recent decades. It is most often seen in small patients undergoing repair of ventricular septal defects of any sort and after left ventricular outflow tract and mitral valve surgeries and is caused either by direct surgical injury to the specialized conduction system or by indirect damage due to inflammatory response. In the era before cardiac pacing systems appropriate for ACHD patients were widely available, postoperative heart block had an extremely high mortality rate, even when an escape rhythm was present.

Complete heart block also occurs spontaneously in patients with certain structural heart defects, especially endocardial cushion defects and congenitally corrected transposition, plausibly related to the aberrant anatomy of the specialized conduction system that renders them vulnerable. Heart block may progress at any stage of life in these patients, irrespective of surgery.

PACEMAKER ISSUES

Pacing is clearly indicated for high-grade heart block in ACHD, most commonly encountered in the postoperative patient. Clinical experience demonstrates the value of atrioventricular (AV) synchrony and favors implantation of dual-chamber pacemakers if size and access permit, but the value of "physiologic" as compared with simpler pacing modalities is not well established in ACHD. Other indications such as sinus node dysfunction with or without concomitant atrial tachycardia are more controversial, and recommendations have largely been based on clinical judgment. In patients with sinus node dysfunction and junctional escape rhythms, severe resting bradycardia, chronotropic incompetence, and/or prolonged pauses, pacing may alleviate symptoms of fatigue, dizziness, or syncope.

Options for cardiac pacing in ACHD patients may be limited owing to congenital and acquired abnormalities of cardiovascular anatomy. The presence of an intracardiac shunt increases the risk of stroke, limiting some patients to epicardial lead placement. Placement of atrial leads by either epicardial or transvenous route may be technically challenging and must avoid inadvertent stimulation of the phrenic nerve. Excellent sensing of atrial electrical activity by pacing systems is crucial to avoid asynchronous atrial pacing, which may provoke atrial tachycardia. The effect of these technical constraints is that pacing systems must not infrequently be adapted on an individual basis to patient-specific lead placement and maintenance issues.

Recently, the utility of cardiac resynchronization effected by multisite pacing has been investigated in ACHD.[4-6] Acute hemodynamic studies and small clinical series suggest the possibility that both left and right ventricular resynchronization may have some clinical value but also highlight the fact that it is exceedingly difficult to construct validated and reproducible measures of ventricular function in this heterogeneous and anatomically complex population (Fig. 16-1).

TABLE 16-1	Relative Risk for Specific Arrhythmias in Common Congenital Heart Defects						
						AV Block	
	Atrial Flutter (IART)	Atrial Fibrillation	WPW	VT/SCD	SA Node Dysfunction	Spontaneous	Iatrogenic
VSD	+			+			+
ASD	+	+					
TOF	++			++			+
AS		+		++			+
D-TGA (M&S)	+++			++	+++		
CAVC	+					+	++
SING V (F)	+++	+		+	+++		
L-TGA	+		++	+		++	+++
Ebstein	++		+++	+			

+++, "high" risk; ++, "moderate" risk; +, "slight" risk

AS, aortic stenosis; ASD, atrial septal defect; AV, atrioventricular; CAVC, common atrioventricular canal defect; D-TGA (M&S), transposition of the great arteries with normal D-looped ventricles, after the Mustard or Senning operation; IART, intra-atrial reentrant tachycardia; L-TGA, "congenitally corrected" transposition of the great arteries with inverted L-looped ventricles; SA, sinoatrial node dysfunction; SCD, sudden cardiac death; SING V (F), single ventricle, after the Fontan operation; TOF, tetralogy of Fallot; VSD, ventricular septal defect; VT, ventricular tachycardia; WPW, Wolff-Parkinson-White syndrome.

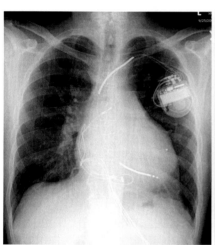 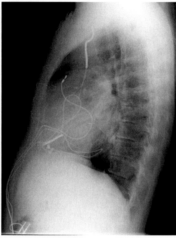

Figure 16-1 Anteroposterior and lateral views of an ACHD patient with congenitally corrected transposition of the great vessels, left-sided tricuspid valve replacement, atrial fibrillation, complete heart block, and nonsustained ventricular tachycardia. This patient has undergone a complex modification of his prior pacing system (initially epicardial but now transvenous) to include placement of a coronary sinus lead for resynchronization as well as an ICD lead in the subpulmonary ventricle.

Atrial Tachycardias

Macroreentrant atrial tachycardias, often denoted as *intra-atrial reentrant tachycardias* (IARTs), are prevalent in many adults with congenital heart defects, including both atypical reentry circuits and more typical forms of atrial flutter noted to occur in the normal heart. These tachycardias tend to have a relatively stable cycle length and P-wave morphology, suggesting that they are organized by a fixed substrate. They are most common among patients who have undergone surgical procedures involving extensive atrial dissection and repair. The importance of surgical injury to the atrium is supported by observations in animal models patterned after Mustard and Fontan surgeries, which reliably cause tachycardias similar to those seen clinically.[7]

Risk factors identified for IART include older age at operation and longer follow-up. About one half of patients with classic right atrial-right ventricular or atriopulmonary Fontan procedures develop IART within 10 years of surgery.[8] Those who undergo the lateral tunnel variant of the procedure with cavopulmonary connection are at lower risk, and this is also expected to be the case for the extracardiac Fontan operation, which is performed using an intercaval tube graft. Patients who have had a Mustard and Senning procedure for transposition of great arteries are at risk of developing sinus node dysfunction and IART, often concurrently. IART is more prevalent than ventricular tachycardia in patients with repaired tetralogy of Fallot and more likely to be associated with symptoms.[9]

Study of late follow-up of patients with a prior surgical history of Fontan, Mustard, or Senning procedures observed mortality including sudden cardiac death at a rate of 1% to 2% per year.[10,11] Although stroke

after cardioversion in ACHD patients seems rare, intravascular and intracardiac thromboses are associated with atrial tachycardias, with a prevalence of intracardiac thrombi in 42% of patients undergoing echocardiography before cardioversion has been reported.[12]

DRUG THERAPY

Although some small studies have suggested otherwise, clinical experience generally suggests that antiarrhythmic drug therapy is unlikely to suppress recurrences of IART. Experimental models of atrial reentry have given us a good understanding of the potential salutary effects of New York Heart Association class IC and class III drugs, and symptomatic arrhythmias can sometimes be suppressed in individual patients using these agents. However, proarrhythmia and adverse effects on ventricular and nodal function may limit their value. Novel antiarrhythmic drugs with pure class III activity have not been widely used in IART and may prove useful.

The frequent occurrence of thrombosis in adult patients with CHD and atrial tachycardia suggests that warfarin or other potent anticoagulant therapy is indicated in most of these patients. AV nodal blocking drugs may also be used but are often difficult to titrate because of the relatively slow cycle length and fixed conduction ratios often seen in IART.

PACEMAKER THERAPY

Atrial antibradycardia pacing alone sometimes results in symptomatic improvement and decreased tachycardia frequency. In patients with sinus node dysfunction, this may also be the result of improved hemodynamics with appropriately timed atrial activation. Automatic antitachycardia pacing has also been of value for some patients. The overall efficacy of the atrial pacing is variable, and there are significant technical difficulties associated with lead placement in these patients. Few endocardial or epicardial sites are generally available and able to generate sensed electrograms of sufficient quality to ensure reliable atrial sensing. Endovascular placement of atrial leads may also increase risk of thrombosis. The potential of other innovative device therapies currently being developed for treatment of atrial fibrillation, such as dual-site pacing and the atrial defibrillator, has not been explored in ACHD.

CATHETER ABLATION

A proposed curative approach to IART has been to create or extend lines of conduction block, using catheter-based and/or surgical techniques. This anatomic approach to therapy involves the design of a lesion or lesions based on an understanding of the relation of macroreentrant circuits to the underlying cardiac anatomy. It can be understood in the same way as catheter and surgical ablation procedures for ventricular tachycardia and the maze procedure for atrial fibrillation.

Acute success rates reported for radiofrequency catheter ablation for IART range from 55% to greater than 90%.[13] Catheter ablation procedures usually target individual macroreentrant circuits, seeking a vulnerable site for application of a radiofrequency lesion. Review of IART ablation experience has shown that, in patients with a right AV valve, the isthmus between that valve and the inferior vena cava commonly supports IART, similar to common atrial flutter.[14] When this isthmus is present, as is the case in patients with Mustard and Senning procedures, tetralogy of Fallot, and other biventricular repairs, techniques developed for atrial flutter may be used to perform and assess the effectiveness of the ablation. Even in these familiar anatomies, however, the observation of multiple IART circuits is common and other anatomic or surgical features relevant to ablation may be difficult to locate fluoroscopically. It may also be difficult to generate the large and confluent lesions sometimes needed to interrupt these circuits. Application of imaging, mapping, and ablation techniques, such as advanced activation mapping technologies and irrigated radiofrequency lesions, is associated with improved acute success rates. Longer-term follow-up after ablation has revealed that arrhythmia symptoms and quality of life are improved in most patients after IART ablation, but recurrences are documented in almost half of the patients.[15] Further advances in our understanding of the arrhythmia substrate and the technology available to visualize and modify it will be necessary to improve this important clinical outcome (Fig. 16-2).

SURGICAL THERAPY

"Old-style" Fontan connection patients—those with a right atrial to right ventricular conduit or an atriopulmonary anastomosis— now frequently undergo revision to cavopulmonary connections or intercaval, extracardiac conduits for hemodynamic reasons. Such surgeries in and of themselves do not appear to prevent arrhythmia recurrence in patients with established atrial arrhythmia. Reports in the past several years of right atrial and biatrial maze procedures based on modifications of the Cox-type maze for atrial fibrillation and performed with surgical and/or cryoablative techniques have shown promising results. Surgical mortality is relatively low, and risk of arrhythmia recurrence appears to be about 15% in the centers performing the largest volume of such surgery.[16] This suggests that maze revision of Fontan procedures can be performed at a reasonable surgical risk and may markedly reduce recurrence of postoperative IART. Additional follow-up studies are needed to ascertain long-term hemodynamic and arrhythmia benefit. There is understandably less enthusiasm for this approach in patients with other forms of heart disease, where arrhythmia control may be the only indication for surgical intervention.

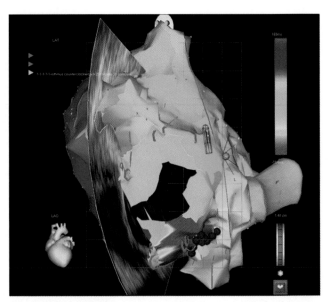

Figure 16-2 Oblique view of the right atrium in a patient with tetralogy of Fallot and atrial flutter visualized and ablated using hybrid electroanatomic catheter mapping and intracardiac ultrasonography. The anatomy of the right atrium, inferior vena cava, and proximal coronary sinus have been recorded by segmentation of multiple echocardiographic acquisitions, with a single echo frame visualized in its relation to the map. The colors applied to the gray endocardial surface represent electrogram activation timings, and blue markers are annotated locations of the tricuspid annulus observed by echocardiography. Red markers clustered in the area of the cavotricuspid isthmus represent ablation lesions.

ATRIAL FIBRILLATION

In a study of cardioversion of patients with ACHD, atrial fibrillation had a prevalence of 25% to 30%.[17] Atrial fibrillation is more frequent in patients with residual left-sided obstructive lesions or unrepaired heart disease. Risk of thromboembolism is thought to be elevated in these patients, and principles of management are drawn from adult guidelines, including anticoagulation and rate control. Cardioversion, prophylactic antiarrhythmic drugs, and atrial pacing are used to prevent the establishment of permanent atrial fibrillation, if possible. In patients with the Fontan procedure, the occurrence of atrial fibrillation may prompt consideration of a Cox-type maze procedure in conjunction with a Fontan conversion.

Accessory Atrioventricular Pathways

Recurrent supraventricular tachycardia caused by an accessory pathway can greatly complicate the management of ACHD. The prevalence of manifest or concealed accessory pathways for most forms of CHD is similar to that in the general population with normal cardiac anatomy, but Ebstein anomaly of the tricuspid valve is a specific and important exception.[18] As many as 20% of Ebstein patients will have Wolff-Parkinson-White syndrome, and in roughly half of these cases multiple accessory pathways are present.[19] The accessory pathway(s) typically occur along the posterior and septal aspect of the tricuspid ring, where the valve leaflets are most displaced, suggesting a developmental link between the valve abnormality and imperfections of electrical insulation along the tricuspid ring. Accessory pathways are also common in patients with congenitally corrected transposition of the great arteries with an ebsteinoid malformation of their left-sided (systemic) tricuspid valve.

Tachycardia events for Ebstein anomaly patients usually begin in childhood, but become especially of concern in adulthood when long-standing atrial dilation can lead to recurrent atrial flutter or atrial

TABLE 17-1	Relative Risk for Specific Arrhythmias in Common Congenital Heart Defects					
Type of ACHD	*IART*		*AP-Mediated Arrhythmia*	*Atrial Fibrillation*	*VT*	*SCD*
Atrial septal defect	+++			+		
Ventricular septal defect				+		
Ebstein anomaly of the tricuspid valve	+ (RA isthmus-dependent flutter)		+++	++		
Tetralogy of Fallot	++			+	+++	+
Transposition of great arteries (post Mustard or Senning)	+++				+	+
Single ventricle (Fontan)	+++			++		
Total cavopulmonary connection	++			+		

Modified from Walsh EP. Interventional electrophysiology in patients with congenital heart disease. Circulation 2007; 115:3224-3234.
ACHD, adult congenital heart disease; AP, accessory pathway; SCD, sudden cardiac death; IART, intra-atrial reentry tachycardia; VT, ventricular tachyarrhythmia.

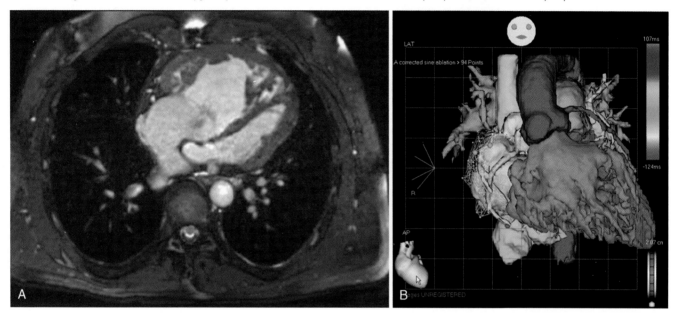

Figure 17-1 **A,** Noncontrast 3D cardiac magnetic resonance imaging of a patient with complex congenital heart disease. **B,** 3D reconstruction using the Polaris software (Biosense Webster) allows understanding of the complex 3D anatomy and potential ways for access.

for the reentry. Whereas simultaneous conduction through the RA inferior isthmus allows demonstration of a "figure of eight" reentry, both "circles" of the eight need to be interrupted to abolish all potential reentrant circuits. Ideally, the "waist" of the eight would represent the simplest ablation target, but catheter stability between the atriotomy scar and the tricuspid annulus can be so challenging that ablation of the RA inferior isthmus and a second line between it and the IVC (e.g., atriotomy) is a reasonable alternative.[11]

TYPICAL ATRIAL ARRHYTHMIAS IN PATIENTS WITH EBSTEIN ANOMALY

Although patients with Ebstein anomaly of the tricuspid valve may present in their early years with accessory pathway–dependent atrioventricular reentrant tachycardia (multiple accessory pathways are very common in this setting), a second type of arrhythmia (i.e., atrial reentry and atrial fibrillation) arises later in life, occasionally after surgical repair or replacement of the tricuspid valve. Many surgeons include intraoperative ablation in their hemodynamic procedure with good results (up to 75% freedom from atrial fibrillation with RA intervention only has been reported).[12]

Typical reentrant circuits for IART in Ebstein anomaly are RA isthmus–dependent reentries, reentry around the atriotomy scar, or reentries caused by conduction gaps in surgically created linear lesions (iatrogenic "gap"-related reentry tachycardia) (Fig. 17-4).

TYPICAL ATRIAL ARRHYTHMIAS IN PATIENTS WITH TETRALOGY OF FALLOT

Although ventricular tachycardias are the most life-threatening arrhythmias in this patient population (see later), RA enlargement can give rise to atrial reentry tachycardia. The latter is often of hemodynamic

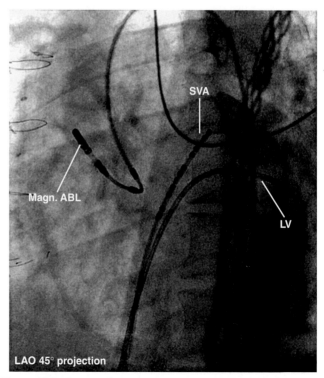

Figure 17-2 Retrograde access using magnetic navigation depicted in left anterior oblique (LAO) 45° projection. LV, diagnostic catheter in left ventricle; SVA, diagnostic catheter (serving as timing reference) in systemic venous atrium.

Figure 17-3 Example of magnetically remote-controlled mapping of the pulmonary venous atrium (PVA) in a patient after Mustard operation. **Top,** Fused CMR 3D reconstruction on the fluoroscopic reference screens in both right anterior oblique (RAO) and left anterior oblique (LAO) projections. **Bottom,** The same situation with the magnetic catheter (magn. ABL) advanced retrogradely via the aorta (Ao) through the right ventricle (RV) into the lateral inferior pulmonary vein of the PVA in a transparent fashion.

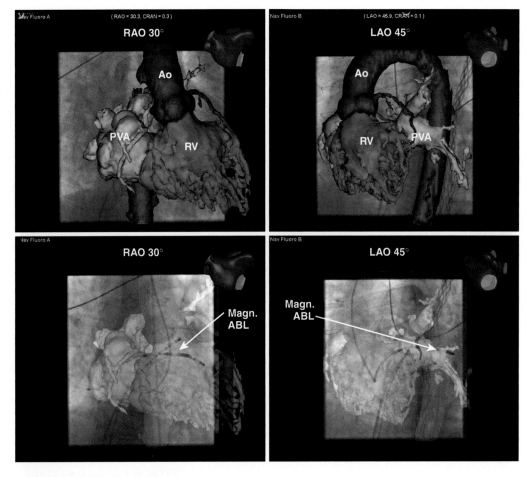

Figure 17-4 Example of catheter ablation of right atrial (RA) isthmus-dependent flutter in a patient with Ebstein anomaly. **A,** 3D reconstruction of the giant RA using the novel mapping system CARTO3 (Biosense Webster) in an anteroposterior projection. The *red line* marks the necessary ablation line connecting the tricuspid annulus (TA) to the inferior vena cava (IVC). **B,** Activation map of the same patient during ongoing tachycardia. The *yellow arrow* illustrates the reentrant circuit around the TA in a counterclockwise fashion. **C,** The effect of radiofrequency current (RFC) delivery along the *red line in A,* which terminates the tachycardia.

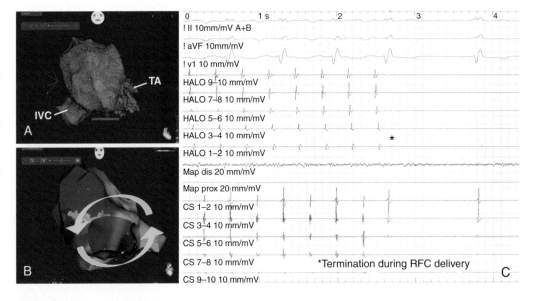

relevance to patients and a significant cause of morbidity.[11] Especially for patients at high risk of SCD (see later) and subsequent need for an implantable cardiac defibrillator (ICD), appropriate sensing and differentiation of rapidly conducted atrial tachycardias are of major clinical relevance as to avoid inappropriate ICD discharges. Because CMR is not an option for patients after ICD implantation, preprocedural 3D imaging is limited to CT, albeit intracardiac 3D echocardiography may have the potential to image the atrial chamber shape and potentially locate the scar(s).[13]

TYPICAL ATRIAL ARRHYTHMIAS IN PATIENTS WITH SURGICALLY CORRECTED TRANSPOSITION OF THE GREAT ARTERIES (MUSTARD OR SENNING)

From the mid 1960s to the mid 1980s patients born with transposition of great arteries (TGA) underwent repair with atrial switch operations using either artificial material (Mustard technique) or heart tissue (Senning technique) to redirect the systemic and pulmonary venous circulation. As a consequence of both operations, the right ventricle carries the workload of the systemic circulation, which may lead to enlargement and subsequent ventricular arrhythmia (see later). Atrial arrhythmias, however, are far more common and arise in as much as 30% of these patients at 20 years after the index operation.[14]

Biatrial reentrant tachycardias around the interatrial baffle are described, but most reentrant circuits are located in the so-called pulmonary venous atrium. Access to the pulmonary venous atrium can be achieved via a retrograde access through the right ventricle or after a transbaffle puncture.[6] Because the reach of conventional mapping catheters renders the mapping and ablation inside the pulmonary venous atrium a significant challenge (irrespective of chosen access), novel technologies such as magnetic navigation play to their full potential in these patients. Our anecdotal recent experience in six patients has shown both safety and efficacy of such advanced technology. Furthermore, there was significant reduction in total fluoroscopy exposure.

TYPICAL INTERATRIAL REENTRANT TACHYCARDIA IN PATIENTS AFTER THE FONTAN PROCEDURE

Patients with univentricular hearts or those whose condition is unsuitable for biventricular repair are often directed toward the Fontan repair. This involves a direct connection between the right atrium and the pulmonary artery. Although a multitude of variations of the original surgical Fontan operation exist, most of them result in a markedly dilated right atrium with a subsequent clear potential for RA-IART.[15] Again, surgical scar areas represent a common source of central barriers that give rise to reentrant circuits, but additional diffuse scaring due to the volume/pressure atrial overload is frequently encountered. The greatest difficulty is an adequate reach of all sites with optimal catheter/tissue contact to allow both correct understanding of the reentrant circuit by 3D mapping techniques and subsequent lesion deployment.

TYPICAL ATRIAL ARRHYTHMIAS IN PATIENTS AFTER TOTAL CAVOPULMONARY CONNECTION

An alternative to the Fontan operation has been a direct connection of the systemic venous return to the pulmonary arteries (the so-called total cavopulmonary connection [TCPC]). This modification has been performed in recent years and has superseded the previous approach of right atrial to pulmonary artery anastomosis. Creation of the "tunnel" is either exclusively by synthetic material or partially by RA myocardium. Unfortunately, IART arises mostly in the "native" atrial chambers (left atrium and remainder of the right atrium) around the surgically deployed scars.[16] Whereas access to the remaining right atrium might be gained through punctures through the TCPC wall, retrograde access is the obvious alternative route. Again, advance techniques such as magnetic navigation with its flexible ablation catheter may allow reaching the extra-tunnel atrial myocardium relatively more easily than with the conventional catheter technique.

Ventricular Arrhythmias

Ventricular arrhythmias, either ventricular tachycardia or fibrillation, are not uncommon in patients with ACHD, particularly so in patients with previous ventriculotomy, patch repair of a ventricle, and dilated or hypertrophic cardiomyopathy. For instance, the incidence of ventricular tachycardia in surgically repaired tetralogy of Fallot is 11.9%.[17] The hemodynamic effects of ventricular arrhythmias are often detrimental and require immediate medical attention.

Reentry is the most common mechanism for ventricular tachycardia in this group of patients, whereas the mechanism of ventricular fibrillation is not yet fully understood. The anisotropic conduction, as a result of nonuniform conduction delay, in areas of functional and fixed conduction block, has been shown to play a pivotal role in the pathogenesis of tachycardia, including ventricular tachyarrhythmias. This is particularly relevant in patients who previously had ventriculotomy and patch repair from surgery in which the incisional scar and patch together with the existing anatomic barriers provide the substrate for

the macroreentry circuit.[18] In addition, fibrodegenerative changes can occur secondary to previous operation(s), pericardial inflammation, and ventricular dilation from chronic pressure and/or volume overload that may also contribute to ventricular tachyarrhythmias.

The onset of clinical ventricular tachyarrhythmia may coincide with or even precede functional decline and cardiac decompensation of congenital heart defects. Therefore, serial cardiac imaging and functional studies to assess the anatomy and the hemodynamics and document any interval change are essential and an integral part of the assessment of a patient with a new-onset ventricular arrhythmia. Intervention to restore the hemodynamics may be necessary; however, the impact of an isolated hemodynamic intervention on the propensity of arrhythmia for the majority of patients is probably limited and, in reality, unpredictable.

Arrhythmia-related SCD is clearly a major risk in the presence of previous history of ventricular arrhythmia. Although randomized control trial data are lacking with respect to the use of an ICD in ACHD patients, it is generally accepted that an ICD should be offered to patients with previous ventricular tachycardia or aborted SCD (for secondary prevention).[19]

Identifying the risk factors for ventricular tachycardia in patients who have had repair of tetralogy of Fallot has been a subject of intense investigations in the past 30 years. The following risk stratifiers of modest predictive value for ventricular tachycardia have been identified[20]:
- Older age at the time of definitive surgery
- History of palliative shunts
- High-grade ventricular ectopy
- Inducible ventricular tachycardia at electrophysiologic study
- Abnormal RV hemodynamics
- QRS complex duration greater than 180 ms

However, how best to employ these clinical variables in guiding the use of ICD as primary prevention of SCD is still unclear. Individualized decisions are currently made for ICD implantation for any given patient based on a balanced view of all these factors, incorporating the patient's personal view.

Ablation of ventricular tachycardia is feasible and in certain pathologic processes, such as tetralogy of Fallot, may convey good symptomatic relief.[18] However, catheter ablation of ventricular tachycardia in this cohort of patients should be considered as primarily an adjunctive therapy to ICD at least until longer-term outcome data of ablative strategies in these patients become available.

Over the past decade many hurdles have been overcome to improve the success in ablating ventricular tachycardia in patients with CHD. The advent of 3D sequential contact and spontaneous noncontact mapping systems has undoubtedly facilitated advanced mapping of ventricular tachycardia, often anchored to the surgically created fixed scar/patch, in patients with surgical repair of congenital cardiac disease. More recently, Zeppenfeld and associates demonstrated the use of such mapping in identifying the substrate of ventricular tachycardia during sinus rhythm in patients who had previous repair of tetralogy of Fallot.[18] In doing so, critical isthmuses bordered by the surgically created scar in the right ventricle and the anatomic barriers were located. The transsection of these isthmuses using radiofrequency ablation catheter abolished ventricular tachycardia with good medium-term clinical outcome. Furthermore, it is well recognized that the ventricular myocardial wall is often hypertrophied from chronic pressure and volume overload and, as a result, the success of catheter ablation may be hampered by the lack of transmurality from endocardial ablation. The availability of cool-tip ablation catheter, which is capable of creating a deeper lesion independent of the variation of regional endocardial blood flow, has significantly improved the prospect of transecting the critical isthmuses in these challenging cases.

Devices in Adult Congenital Heart Disease

CHD presents the pacing physician with a rich and diverse challenge that often requires an innovative approach. Many hearts are uniquely different in structure and function. As in other patients, atrioventricular nodal block and sinus node dysfunction are the usual rhythms that necessitate pacing. Antitachycardia pacing and defibrillators have an important part to play in the prevention of life-threatening rhythms inaccessible to ablation techniques, and most recently resynchronization therapy has been found useful in the management of pump failure in ACHD.

DISEASES REQUIRING PACING

Atrioventricular Nodal Block

Degrees of atrioventricular nodal block are often seen in patients with congenitally corrected transposition of the great arteries or in survivors with left atrial isomerism and atrioventricular septal defect as part of the natural history of these disorders owing to the precarious position of the conduction bundle. Such patients may develop atrioventricular nodal block at any age. Despite the best efforts by cardiothoracic surgeons, surgically created atrioventricular nodal block and sinus node dysfunction cannot always be avoided and still accounts for a proportion of patients requiring pacing, albeit with a decreasing incidence in recent years. Long-term mortality after postoperative complete atrioventricular nodal block has been estimated to be up to 50%; thus there is consensus that patients in this position should undergo pacing. Most units will accept atrioventricular conduction recovery up to 7 days after surgery (some perhaps up to 14 days).

Sinus Node Dysfunction

Sinus node dysfunction is a common occurrence after the Mustard or Senning repair for congenital transposition of the great arteries. It is also common after the Fontan procedure both in the immediate postoperative setting and later. It also occurs in a smaller proportion of patients after sinus venosus ASD repair (in which the defect itself often occupies the area of the sinus node). Pacing the atrium in these patients has been shown to help relieve symptoms of fatigue and poor exercise tolerance and may in itself help prevent atrial tachycardias (bradycardia-tachycardia syndrome). A pacemaker with antitachycardia pacing facilities such as the Enrhythm (Medtronic Inc, Minneapolis, MN, USA) can be very useful in the management of these patients with difficult atrial arrhythmias, although ablation techniques are improving and would now be generally considered the treatment of first choice.

Ventricular Fibrillation and Sudden Cardiac Death

There is a recognized incidence of SCD in many patients with ACHD. It can be expected in approximately 6% of patients with tetralogy of Fallot at long-term follow-up. Sudden death may result from the degeneration of ventricular tachycardia arising from the right ventricle. It is still difficult to accurately predict those at high risk, but in those judged to be in this situation defibrillators are often considered. There is a risk of ventricular fibrillation/SCD in other types of ACHD, but this is less well quantified. After the Mustard procedure SCD may result from ventricular or atrial tachycardia.

The safety and efficacy of ICDs in adult patients with ischemic heart disease or dilated cardiomyopathy has been the subject of large prospective trials, leading to guidelines for primary and secondary prevention. The risk-benefit ratio in a young person with CHD is, however, more difficult to ascertain. The patient will live longer, and additional procedures are to be expected. This is the background on which the consideration of risk of appropriate shock has to be weighed against that of inappropriate shock. Inappropriate shock is more common in this group of patients than older patients with ischemic heart disease owing to inappropriately sensed sinus tachycardia, lead break, or atria tachycardia. The efficacy is often unknown. The recent attempts by industry to downsize leads with the recognized increase in breakage rate in these leads, particularly in young patients who are active and may still be growing, has made only a small contribution to alleviate these fears. Careful programming and follow-up is strongly recommended in young adult patients with CHD with defibrillators after implantation in an effort to minimize complications and inappropriate discharges. The latter can be psychologically very disturbing, particularly so for the younger patient.

IMPLANT CONSIDERATIONS

Transvenous leads still function better in terms of sensing and pacing than epicardial leads and are more robust. In addition, transvenous systems are more popular with patients and physicians, because they can be placed in the catheter laboratory, thus avoiding a sternotomy or thoracotomy. If, however, the chest is open for a surgical procedure, consideration should be given to placing permanent epicardial pacing leads. Epicardial leads are not always possible, especially if the heart has been operated on before. Scar tissue and adhesions may limit access to excitable myocardium or chambers. Similarly, transvenous access to the heart chamber required is not always possible and in some cases carries an unacceptable coagulation risk; therefore, both techniques may be advantageous at times and both should be available in large units caring for ACHD patients. The choice of system may be made after careful consideration of the relative risks.

Transvenous Approach

The usual approach is from the cephalic or subclavian vein. Great care needs to be taken with these veins from early on in the child's life because during a lifetime of pacing requiring repeated instrumentation and chronic lead placement they may become subject to occlusion. When both right and left subclavian or superior caval veins are lost, consideration can be given to the femoral vein. Dual-chamber pacing or defibrillation or biventricular systems can be performed from the femoral vein with implantation of the generator just above the inguinal ligament. Use of the hepatic veins is also an option.

Epicardial Approach

The epicardial approach is usually more invasive unless thoracoscopic facilities are available. Multiple adhesions can limit good lead placement, and poor sensing and high thresholds can be a problem.

RESYNCHRONIZATION THERAPY

Cardiac resynchronization therapy is well established as a treatment of heart failure in adult patients with New York Heart Association classes III and IV with a QRS complex width greater than 120 ms and an ejection fraction less than 35% on optimal medical therapy. In these patients with predominately ischemic heart disease or dilated cardiomyopathy cardiac resynchronization has been shown to decrease symptoms and mortality, especially if combined with defibrillator function. This group of patients will differ from those with ACHD in that they will have a left ventricle in the systemic position and a right ventricle in the subpulmonary position and have left bundle-branch block as a cause of their QRS prolongation. In CHD this accounts for just 9% of patients in heart failure. Furthermore, additional anatomic considerations need to be taken into account (e.g., a systemic right or functionally single ventricle of right or left morphology). Resynchronization has been tried in these hearts, but because of the rich diversity there are not large numbers of any one type of heart defect to which controlled studies can be applied. Several multicenter experiences have been described. It would appear that "biventricular" hearts with a failing systemic ventricle (of left morphology) respond best to conventionally applied resynchronization with a left ventricular lead placed in a tributary of the coronary sinus (Fig. 17-5) on the lateral wall or when placed in a similar position by a surgeon. Such a resynchronization approach should also be seriously considered for patients in whom ventricular function deteriorates after right ventricular pacing. In this latter group evidence is increasing that early placement of a resynchronization lead may prevent ventricular remodeling that leads to dyssynchrony.

The evidence for resynchronization is less clear in other situations. There have been reports of patients with a systemic right ventricle responding well to biventricular pacing. In patients with congenitally corrected transposition this can sometimes be achieved using the coronary sinus. However, this vein is not always well developed in these patients and when difficulty is experienced an early venogram is recommended. In patients who have undergone a Mustard or Senning repair the coronary sinus is not always accessible. The surgeon may baffle the mouth of the coronary sinus to open in the pulmonary venous atrium. The operation note unfortunately may not describe what has been done with this regard because the importance of the coronary sinus was not appreciated in the era most Mustard and Senning procedures were performed. Similarly, some surgeons will patch the entrance of the coronary sinus off from the transvenous operator in closure of atrioventricular septal defects.

There is even less evidence concerning the group of patients with a functionally single ventricle. Multisite pacing has been shown to improve cardiac output perioperatively but fewer long-term patients have been reported.

The other group that merits consideration is the group with a failing right subpulmonary ventricle, such as patients who present years after repair of tetralogy of Fallot (see Fig. 17-5). The right ventricle dilates and the QRS complex reflects broad right bundle-branch block. In the immediate postsurgical period it has been shown that pacing of the outflow tract and therefore shortening the QRS complex width improves cardiac output. To date there are no reports of chronic right ventricular outflow tract pacing in this group. Many units are experimenting with different pacing sites in an effort to preserve ventricular function in the chronically paced adult with CHD.

CONCLUSION

Recent developments have made invasive electrophysiologic studies and subsequent catheter ablation a valuable and effective option for patients with ACHD and atrial or ventricular arrhythmia. Equally, pacing options for ACHD have improved by far, providing a large range of devices and leads. However, especially in patients receiving ICDs, the amount of lead failure and inadequate shocks remains relatively high. Further research in this field and data from electrophysiologic and device registries are clearly warranted.

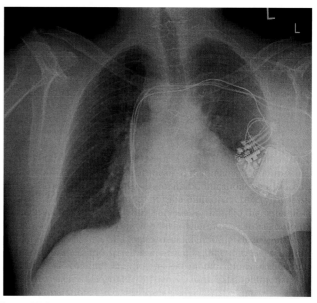

Figure 17-5 CRTD transvenous system in an adult with previous repair of tetralogy of Fallot and biventricular dysfunction. The system was upgraded from ICD in light of ventricular dyssynchrony with good short/mid-term hemodynamic result and improved cardiac output. CRTD, cardiac resynchronization therapy/defibrillator; ICD, implantable cardiac defibrillator. *(Courtesy Dr. Jonathan Clague, Royal Brompton Hospital, London, England.)*

REFERENCES

1. Walsh EP. Interventional electrophysiology in patients with congenital heart disease. Circulation 2007;115:3224–3234.
2. Berul CI, Van Hare GF, Kertesz NJ, et al. Results of a multicenter retrospective implantable cardioverter-defibrillator registry of pediatric and congenital heart disease patients. J Am Coll Cardiol 2008;51:1685–1691.
3. Sorensen TS, Therkildsen SV, Hansen OK, et al. Images in cardiovascular medicine: total cavo-pulmonary connection: a virtual 3-dimensional fly-through. Circulation 2002;105:E176.
4. Ernst S, Chun JK, Koektuerk B, Kuck KH. Magnetic navigation and catheter ablation of right atrial ectopic tachycardia in the presence of a hemi-azygos continuation: a magnetic navigation case using 3D electroanatomical mapping. J Cardiovasc Electrophysiol 2009;20:99–102.
5. McGann CJ, Kholmovski EG, Oakes RS, et al. New magnetic resonance imaging-based method for defining the extent of left atrial wall injury after the ablation of atrial fibrillation. J Am Coll Cardiol 2008;52:1263–1271.
6. El-Said HG, Ing FF, Grifka RG, et al. 18-year experience with transseptal procedures through baffles, conduits, and other intra-atrial patches. Catheter Cardiovasc Interv 2000;50:434–439; discussion 440.
7. Hebe J, Hansen P, Ouyang F, et al. Radiofrequency catheter ablation of tachycardia in patients with congenital heart disease. Pediatr Cardiol 2000;21:557–575.

8. Paul T, Windhagen-Mahnert B, Kriebel T, et al. Atrial reentrant tachycardia after surgery for congenital heart disease: endocardial mapping and radiofrequency catheter ablation using a novel, noncontact mapping system. Circulation 2001;103:2266–2271.
9. Ector J, De Buck S, Adams J, et al. Cardiac three-dimensional magnetic resonance imaging and fluoroscopy merging: a new approach for electroanatomic mapping to assist catheter ablation. Circulation 2005;112:3769–3776.
10. Everett 4th TH, Lee KW, Wilson EE, et al. Safety profiles and lesion size of different radiofrequency ablation technologies: a comparison of large tip, open and closed irrigation catheters. J Cardiovasc Electrophysiol 2009;20:325–335.
11. Nakagawa H, Shah N, Matsudaira K, et al. Characterization of reentrant circuit in macroreentrant right atrial tachycardia after surgical repair of congenital heart disease: isolated channels between scars allow "focal" ablation. Circulation 2001;103:699–709.
12. Khositseth A, Danielson GK, Dearani JA, et al. Supraventricular tachyarrhythmias in Ebstein anomaly: management and outcome. J Thorac Cardiovasc Surg 2004;128:826–833.
13. Peichl P, Kautzner J, Gebauer R. Ablation of atrial tachycardias after correction of complex congenital heart diseases: utility of intracardiac echocardiography. Europace 2009;11:48–53.
14. Gelatt M, Hamilton RM, McCrindle BW, et al. Arrhythmia and mortality after the Mustard procedure: a 30-year single-center experience. J Am Coll Cardiol 1997;29:194–201.

15. Durongpisitkul K, Porter CJ, Cetta F, et al. Predictors of early- and late-onset supraventricular tachyarrhythmias after Fontan operation. Circulation 1998;98:1099–1107.
16. Agnoletti G, Borghi A, Vignati G, Crupi GC. Fontan conversion to total cavopulmonary connection and arrhythmia ablation: clinical and functional results. Heart 2003;89:193–198.
17. Gatzoulis MA, Balaji S, Webber SA, et al. Risk factors for arrhythmia and sudden cardiac death late after repair of tetralogy of Fallot: a multicentre study. Lancet 2000;356:975–981.
18. Zeppenfeld K, Schalij MJ, Bartelings MM, et al. Catheter ablation of ventricular tachycardia after repair of congenital heart disease: electroanatomic identification of the critical right ventricular isthmus. Circulation 2007;116:2241–2252.
19. Khairy P, Harris L, Landzberg MJ, et al. Implantable cardioverter-defibrillators in tetralogy of Fallot. Circulation 2008;117:363–370.
20. Gatzoulis MA, Till JA, Somerville J, Redington AN. Mechanoelectrical interaction in tetralogy of Fallot: QRS prolongation relates to right ventricular size and predicts malignant ventricular arrhythmias and sudden death. Circulation 1995;92:231–237.

Cardiac Resynchronization Therapy in Adult Congenital Heart Disease

JAMES C. PERRY

Electrophysiologists and cardiologists specializing in adult congenital heart disease (ACHD) are just beginning to address the myriad of potential benefits of cardiac resynchronization therapy (CRT) for the adult patient with CHD. Research and large multicenter studies on uses and indications for CRT in adults typically involve a relatively uniform group of patients: the majority have postischemic forms of heart failure, are men in their mid 60s, and tend to have left bundle-branch block (LBBB). In stark contrast, ACHD patients encompass a very wide range of underlying anatomic conditions and physiologies, multiple manifestations of previous palliative surgeries and residual defects, and ill-defined measures of heart failure. They also range in age from 18 years up to some individuals who were early pioneers of congenital heart surgery and are now in their 60s. As a result, there have been no large (and certainly no randomized) studies of the benefits of CRT in adult or pediatric CHD owing to low patient numbers among a range of defects and physiologies.

The development of "guidelines" for the use of CRT has been and will be hampered by these factors. Cardiologists are left with clinical decision-making efforts that attempt to extend the findings in adult ischemic heart failure to these complex ACHD patients. In this chapter the ACHD population is examined based on the presence of heart failure in CHD settings with specific ventricular morphologies and on heart failure etiology and a discussion is presented regarding those groups of patients who are most likely to benefit from CRT interventions.

Cardiac Resynchronization Therapy in Adults Without CHD

An excellent review and meta-analysis of large, adult, multicenter studies of the benefits of CRT came from Bradley and colleagues in 2003.[1] Included were data on 1634 patients from the CONTAK, MUSTIC, MIRACLE, and InSync ICD trials of CRT. The average age of these patients was about 65 years, and most had ischemic heart failure (37% to 69%) and left ventricular (LV) ejection fractions of 30% or less. Additionally, LBBB was present in 54% to 87% of all patients. The authors found that CRT in this population reduced deaths from heart failure by 51% (1.7% with CRT, 3.5% without CRT), reduced hospitalizations by 29%, but had no effect on the incidence of ventricular tachyarrhythmia. None of the patients enrolled in these studies had CHD, and, in fact, CHD patients have been excluded from all published multicenter adult CRT trials as a matter of routine study design.

Recently, there are indications that the actual percentage of time spent with CRT being active (i.e., percentage of time biventricular pacing is occurring) has a direct bearing on the overall measures of success of CRT. In a large study of an adult, non-CHD population composed primarily of postischemic patients in their 70s, those patients who were paced more than 92% of the time had reduced hospitalization, atrial arrhythmia, and mortality compared with those who were paced less than 92% of the time.[2] We do not have such data available for the CHD or ACHD patient. As will be noted later in the chapter, details of CHD anatomy, atrial and ventricular lead location, and programming needs for the atrioventricular (AV) delay will all influence the percent of time an ACHD patient utilizes an implanted CRT system.

First Investigations of Cardiac Resynchronization Therapy in Congenital Heart Disease—Early Postoperative Pediatric Congenital Heart Disease

Credit must be given to the work of Jan Janousek for his work on multisite pacing to resynchronize ventricular activation in pediatric patients after congenital heart surgery who had right bundle-branch block (RBBB).[3] Using temporary wires, an investigational temporary pacing system and extensive hemodynamic monitoring to assess response, he showed mild increases in systolic blood pressure, mean pressure, pulse pressure, and decreases in filling pressures and both ventilator hours and intensive care unit (ICU) days.

Zimmerman and associates then showed the benefits of CRT in young CHD patients using multisite pacing and an examination of echocardiographic indices of function.[4] Interestingly, this early work was done in a mixed group of 14 patients with single-ventricle physiology and 15 patients with two ventricles. Single-ventricle patients had right, left, and apically placed temporary leads. A 15% improvement in cardiac index was seen on average in the entire group, and in two patients CRT facilitated weaning from cardiopulmonary bypass.

Defining Heart Failure in Adult Congenital Heart Disease

There are no current, published guidelines on the use of CRT in patients with CHD of any age. In the most recent iteration of the American College of Cardiology/American Heart Association/Heart Rhythm Society guidelines for device-based therapies there are no comments on CRT in this population.[5] Additionally, in the most recently published 2009 guidelines for management of heart failure there are again no references to the patient with CHD.[6]

Even in the face of a lack of clear guidelines, or a current attempt to develop them, the risk of heart failure in the ACHD population is striking and increases with age. Figure 18-1 shows the probability of heart failure versus age in various CHD types.[7] As these patients gain increasing benefits from technologic advances in both diagnosis and interventional therapies they look toward multiple decades of life, in comparison to the adult postischemic patient with heart failure.

Can the adult classification scheme for heart failure be applied to the ACHD population with any expectation that it will help discern true symptoms and signs? Norozi and associates[8] and Shaddy and Webb[9] examined these issues. Norozi and his group concluded that, based on brain natriuretic peptide values and reduced maximum oxygen consumption as determinants of the presence of heart failure, both the New York Heart Association (NYHA) and Ability index scores were equally valid to judge the presence of heart failure in ACHD patients. However, they emphasized an observed discrepancy between objective and subjective scores that makes their clinical utility to continue to be questioned. Shaddy and Webb[9] reviewed ACHD with respect to the A-D staging system for heart failure: A = at risk for heart failure, B = structural heart disease without signs or symptoms, C = structural heart disease with previous or current symptoms, and D = refractory heart

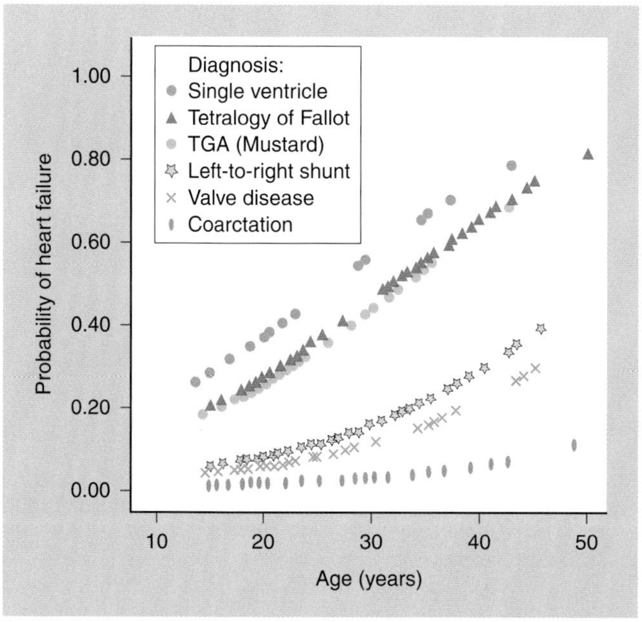

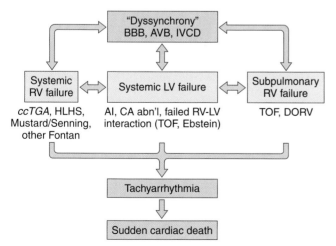

Figure 18-1   The probability of heart failure versus age in various CHD types. *(Redrawn from Norozi K, Wessel A, Alpers V et al. Incidence and risk distribution of heart failure in adolescents and adults with congenital heart disease after cardiac surgery. Am J Cardiol 2006; 97:1238-1243.)*

disease requiring specialized interventions. A detailed review is beyond the scope of this chapter. Briefly, stage A includes all the standard adult risk factors (e.g., hyperlipidemia) plus coronary arterial CHD risks; stage B includes emphasis on "repaired" defects, coarctation, all systemic right ventricular (RV) circulations, and AV valve insufficiency; stage C failure requires anticongestive drug management and consideration of defibrillator and CRT options; and stage D touches on those who may require cardiac transplantation or heart-lung transplantation if refractory pulmonary hypertension is present.

Given the complexity of ACHD anatomy and physiology, an overall examination of risk for heart failure and potential CRT candidate populations may be best approached by means of a diagram of the relationship of myocardial dyssynchrony to systemic RV failure, systemic LV failure, subpulmonary RV failure, and the risk of arrhythmia (Fig. 18-2). Patients with single-ventricle physiology clearly are at risk of heart failure and may realize benefits from CRT as well. Each of these settings will be reviewed individually in this chapter.

Heart Failure: Subpulmonary Right Ventricle

Perhaps one of the more common and potentially fruitful areas of application of CRT techniques is in the large population of postoperative adult CHD patients who have RBBB and diminished subpulmonary RV function. This includes patients with tetralogy of Fallot and many forms of double-outlet right ventricle, those with Ebstein anomaly, and rare patients with decreased function after simple ventricular and AV septal defect repairs. In the conotruncal defect group, the subpulmonary RV often has diminished function in large measure owing to insufficiency (or lack) of the pulmonary valve, leading to chronic RV volume overload, stretch, and poor contractility. Pulmonary regurgitation has been clearly shown to correlate with RV failure,[10] RV size, prolonged QRS complex duration, and ventricular arrhythmia.[11,12] In some patients the poor contractility and other detrimental factors persist well after surgical replacement of the pulmonary valve, especially when valve replacement occurs in a patient with an indexed RV end-diastolic volume of 180 mL/m^2.[13] This naturally leads to the conjecture that an improvement in ventricular synchrony by means of resynchronizing or advancing RV contraction in these patients with RBBB might lead to a clinically beneficial improvement in RV ejection mechanics. There are likely to be similar patients with persistent subpulmonary RV failure following the newer transcatheter approaches to pulmonary valve replacement, currently with the Medtronic Melody valve (Medtronic Inc, Minneapolis, MN, USA).

The target for RV resynchronization in subpulmonary RV failure would appear initially to be the latest areas of RV activation in the presence of RBBB. Pacing at this site, along with intrinsic conduction down the AV node and left fascicles of the conduction system, would result initially in a narrower QRS complex, fusing pacing with intrinsic conduction. Vogel and colleagues[14] and Uebing and associates[15] showed late areas of RV activation in tetralogy of Fallot patients in several disparate areas of the RV free wall, in portions of the interventricular septum, and in the RV outflow tract, so the exact target for RV resynchronization attempts cannot be assumed to be similar from patient to patient. Certainly these recent studies build on the pioneering work of Deanfield and colleagues[16] and Moak and Garson[17] in the mid 1980s and of Horowitz and colleagues[18] in 1979, documenting late activation patterns in animal models of tetralogy and humans. This would appear to advocate for some form of mapping of RV activation as an adjunct to lead placement in RV resynchronization. Thus, Three-dimensional (3D) endocardial mapping techniques can potentially assist in the placement of RV pacing leads in areas of latest RV activation, as shown in Figure 18-3.

A confounding variable in any CRT effort in the setting of subpulmonary RV failure will be the subgroup of patients with RBBB who have LV dysfunction. Tzemos and coworkers showed that a longer QRS complex duration of RBBB correlated with the degree of LV dysfunction in tetralogy patients.[19] This is in good keeping also with many prior studies, including that of van den Berg and associates, who showed increased RV size correlating with later ventricular arrhythmia.[20] The numbers of patients in this category are not insignificant: it is believed that overall 10% to 15% of adult tetralogy of Fallot patients can have systemic LV dysfunction as well, and by some measures of dyssynchrony, as many as 50%. In these cases, isolated attempts to resynchronize the right ventricle, without recognizing the degree of LV dysfunction, will bias early clinical studies, especially when relatively low numbers of patients are typically used for CHD clinical research projects.

RV resynchronization has been the focus of some of the earliest work in CRT for ACHD patients. Dubin and colleagues published their acute study of postoperative tetralogy of Fallot and Ross operation patients who underwent RV resynchronization in the catheterization laboratory.[21] They showed an increase in cardiac output of 17% and increased RV dP/dT of 22%. Six of the seven patients in this early study showed increased cardiac index and also in six of the seven the best output correlated with the shortest QRS duration. This phenomenon can be

Figure 18-2   The interaction of dyssynchrony and risk of tachyarrhythmia and sudden cardiac death in ACHD.

Figure 18-3 Using a 3D electroanatomic mapping technique, areas of late RV activation can be readily identified. Shown is a typical RV map in a patient with tetralogy of Fallot, showing late activation of the far lateral RV free wall in the lower left and right panels. Activation time is early to late, following a spectral red-orange-yellow-green-blue pattern; violet colors are latest activation.

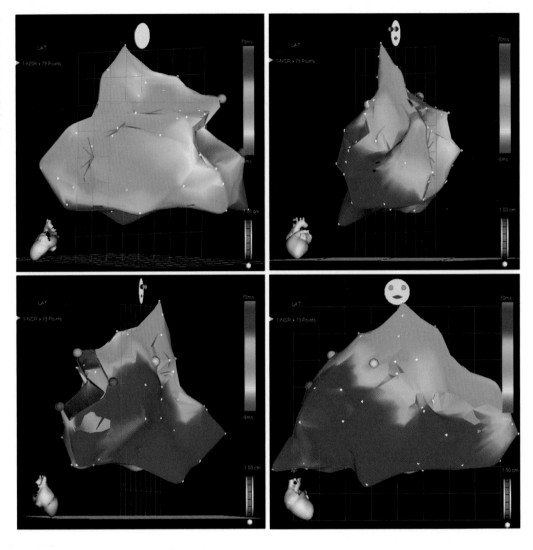

observed frequently in the postoperative care units, especially when temporary pacing wires tend to be placed on the anterior surface of the right ventricle. In patients with diminished cardiac output, RBBB, and elevated central venous pressures, proper programming of the temporary bedside pacing system with a relatively short AV interval can give a beneficial, temporary RV resynchronization and allow more rapid weaning from support. This practice is illustrated in an early postoperative tetralogy patient in an ICU in Figure 18-4. The figure shows clear improvement in blood pressure, a decrease in central venous pressure, and a loss of cannon waveforms. Part of the benefit of RV resynchronization is likely advancing both RV systole and diastole and allowing improved right atrial to RV filling and reduction of tricuspid valve regurgitation.

The ultimate question is whether RV resynchronization (RV-CRT) will reduce the risk of ventricular tachyarrhythmia and sudden cardiac death and, from a functional standpoint, whether RV-CRT can truly improve exercise capacity and/or measures of quality of life on a longer-term basis. In a 2008 study using a single-blinded crossover method of CRT on and off for 3 months each, modest improvements in RV function were found on computed tomography (CT).[22] Quality of life reports were improved, but no clear peak oxygen consumption improvements were noted. Clearly, these are very short-term data and further studies of exercise capacity and long-term arrhythmia burden are needed to examine the potential benefit of RV resynchronization in this setting. It is unknown whether the time course of reverse remodeling of the right ventricle will mimic reports of LV improvements with

standard CRT in adults without CHD. Again, mapping areas of late activation may prove pivotal to predicting measures of RV resynchronization "success," as well as assessment of whether there are benefits to an epicardial pacing approach versus a transvenous approach. Despite the apparent simplicity of these issues, pointing toward a beneficial therapy, the efficacy of RV resynchronization in adult patients with tetralogy is less than clear, with some authors suggesting evidence of no effect.

Finally then, is there a place in this subpopulation for RV-CRT in current ACHD management? Although the patient population is mixed in terms of specific CHD anatomy and details of RV activation patterns and comorbidities, there appears to be solid early data showing benefits, with minor detractors. Consideration of utilizing an RV-CRT intervention could be given at this time to those patients undergoing operative replacement of the pulmonary valve who have very large right ventricles with questionable likelihood for RV recovery. Adjunctive RV-CRT may be of benefit to correct the dyssynchrony of RBBB and restore true improvements in function. Additional candidates may include patients whose right ventricles do not respond to pulmonary valve replacement who are believed to be at risk of sudden cardiac death. These patients could have transvenous approaches with pacing and defibrillation capacity (Fig. 18-5). One may also consider an epicardial approach, especially for patients who have significant tricuspid valve regurgitation or residual tricuspid anatomic abnormalities. A summary of potential CRT settings is presented in Table 18-1.

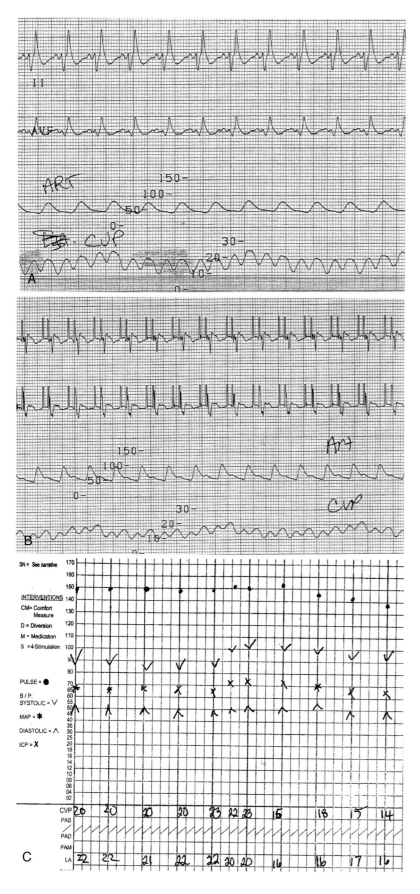

Figure 18-4 RV resynchronization in an early postoperative patient with tetralogy of Fallot using temporary wires. **A,** Sinus rhythm and right bundle-branch block, poor blood pressure, and central venous pressure waveforms. **B,** The heart rate is paced above the intrinsic sinus rate, and the AV delay is programmed to bring about ventricular synchrony with intact left ventricular activation and RV pacing (narrow QRS complex). **C,** This leads to an increased blood pressure and improved central venous pressure, allowing more rapid weaning from support.

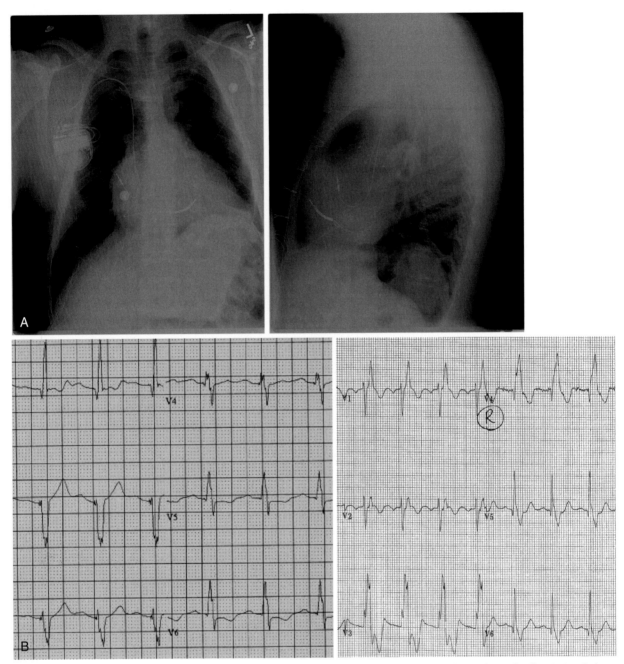

Figure 18-5   Combined implantable cardiac defibrillator (ICD) and CRT therapies in an adult with tetralogy of Fallot. **A,** Lead placement. **B,** Precordial electrocardiogram (ECG) leads before and after CRT.

Heart Failure: Systemic Right Ventricle

When the systemic ventricle in adult CHD patients is a morphologic right ventricle, there are intrinsic factors that lead to a propensity for diminished function and arrhythmia risk despite appropriate early surgical interventions. The most common ACHD settings include the two ventricle physiologies of congenitally corrected transposition of the great arteries (ccTGA) and patients following Mustard or Senning repairs of *d*-TGA along with single ventricle states following a Fontan operation.

CONGENITALLY CORRECTED TRANSPOSITION OF THE GREAT ARTERIES

In the case of ccTGA, the risk factors for RV failure are present even for those who have a systemic right ventricle and no other structural associated cardiac lesion. The structural arrangement of RV coronary arterial supply cannot serve the needs of a systemic ventricular demand. Reports have shown that in nearly all patients with ccTGA, coronary insufficiency is a given, with clear evidence of both fixed and reversible perfusion defects documented on imaging studies.[23] These perfusion deficits were present even in the youngest patients, down to 5 years of age,[24] so the ongoing effects of coronary insufficiency on myocardial performance should not be surprising and must be anticipated. RV ejection fraction in ccTGA is similarly diminished as a rule. The average systemic RV ejection fraction in adults with ccTGA is 41%. In isolated ccTGA without other defects that presents as reduced measures of ejection fraction and heart failure in an adult patient, the true diagnosis may be missed if the systemic ventricular morphology is not recognized in an adult echocardiography suite setting. Clinical symptoms of heart failure in simple ccTGA occur in 34% of patients. For the ccTGA patients with associated defects, such as ventricular septal defect or pulmonary stenosis, the systemic right ventricle reveals systolic dysfunction in as many as 70% and symptoms of heart failure occur in half.[25]

TABLE 18-1	Proposed Applications for Some Cardiac Resynchronization Therapeutic Interventions in Adults with Congenital Heart Disease		
	CHD Types	*Potential Settings*	*Transvenous/Epicardial*
Subpulmonary RV Failure	TOF/DORV Ebstein anomaly Postoperative w/ severe RBBB, poor RV	PVR fails: large RV, poor RVEF With ICD Severe RBBB, min. pulmonary insufficiency Pulmonary insufficiency, CRT to improve exercise Consider if pacing for SND	Transvenous if no shunt Epicardial if TR, venous anomaly or obstruction, surgical procedure, younger age (to avoid lead extractions)
Systemic RV Failure	ccTGA	Pacemaker implant for AVB, prolonged postoperative "transient" block RVEF < 40%, TR	Transvenous depends on coronary sinus "Hybrid" system likely
	d-TGA Mustard/Senning	Pacemaker implant for AVB, prolonged postoperative "transient" block RVEF < 40%, TR With ICD	"Hybrid" system
Systemic LV Failure	Postoperative Ross, Konno Subaortic resections	Standard adult indications Postoperative subaortic surgeries, LBBB, AI Heart failure secondary to chronic RV pacing	Transvenous likely for most, epicardial or hybrid may have long-term benefits
Single Ventricle Failure	All single ventricle physiologies, systemic RV > systemic LV	Systemic EF < 40-45%, poor exercise tolerance, high $\dot{V}_E$ slope With ICD Documented "reservoir" effect on cardiac output (see text)	Epicardial, rare hybrid

AI, aortic insufficiency; AVB, atrioventricular block; ccTGA, congenitally corrected transposition of the great arteries; d-TGA, d-transposition; DORV, double-outlet right ventricle; EF, ejection fraction; ICD, implantable cardiac defibrillator; LBBB, left bundle-branch block; LV, left ventricle; PVR, pulmonary vascular resistance; RBBB, right bundle-branch block; RV, right ventricle; RVEF, right ventricular ejection fraction; SND, sinus node dysfunction; TOF, tetralogy of Fallot; TR, tricuspid valve regurgitation.

When should CRT be considered for the patient with ccTGA? There is a natural, intrinsic risk of acquired complete AV block in these patients as well—6% in those with and 12% in those without associated defects—so dual-chambered pacing systems may be considered or be already in place. One must then attempt to determine how much of the heart failure state is secondary to the inadequate systemic right ventricle and how much could be on the basis of long-term, single-site ventricular pacing. CRT is a reasonable consideration in either case. In most patients, a normal coronary sinus and great vein system (developing with the normal left-sided left atrium) will overly the systemic right ventricle. Although the branching pattern is clearly different from the expected patterns of the LV venous system, access is gained via the coronary sinus to a systemic ventricular venous branch, allowing CRT pacing. Epicardial left-sided systemic RV pacing can be equally efficacious and avoid the long-term risks of thrombosis and subsequent potential lead extraction risks for younger patients. Utilization of an epicardial systemic ventricular lead will also allow placement of the lead in an optimum location and not simply dictated by the branching venous patterns. A "hybrid" of epicardial and transvenous lead systems often results.

There are no firmly established measures of what range of systemic RV ejection fraction constitutes a "failing" ventricle that may be considered for and benefit from CRT. The Diller study used standard adult CRT measures of NYHA class, chamber size, ejection fraction, and arrhythmia but recognized that these variables do not apply directly to the ccTGA patient.[26] For example, if adult ccTGA patients have, on average, a systemic RV ejection fraction of 41%, then many ccTGA patients will have a "reduced" RV ejection fraction (using LV ejection fraction guideline data) and no signs or symptoms of heart failure. The congenital cardiologist needs to ask whether all systemic right ventricles are eventually going to "fail," by what assessment do they fail, and when are these patients therefore deserving of primary preventative measures undertaken by CRT interventions.

d-TRANSPOSITION OF THE GREAT ARTERIES

In patients with d-transposition and intra-atrial repair (Mustard and Senning physiology), systemic RV dysfunction is also to be expected. Systemic RV ejection fraction in adults with atrial baffle repair of d-TGA is reduced in 32% to 48% of these patients with an incidence of clinical signs and symptoms of heart failure in 10% to 22%.[27,28] As is the case for ccTGA, the inherent Erlenmeyer-flask shape of the right ventricle makes precise and reproducible echocardiographic assessments difficult, so measures of RV ejection fraction are done utilizing ejection radionuclide angiography, magnetic resonance, or CT techniques. However, echocardiographic measurements of RV strain by tissue Doppler imaging may prove helpful. Using this method, Chow and associates[29] found that 11% of their d-TGA Mustard/Senning study group had prolonged QRS complex duration and 32% had strain index findings of interventricular dyssynchrony. By most measures there is a high incidence of heart failure and significant ventricular dyssynchrony in the d-TGA Mustard/Senning population that makes for an appealing association and target for therapy.

Many patients with atrial baffle operations develop sinus node dysfunction early and at an increasing prevalence over their lives. The complex anatomy of the intra-atrial baffle poses a problem for some pacing system implanters not adept at CHD and the predilection for stenosis of the baffle conduit both often lead to decisions to place ventricular pacing systems. The resulting loss of AV synchrony may be a contributing factor for subsequent ventricular enlargement, AV valve regurgitation, and the increasing incidence of atrial reentry tachyarrhythmia over many years. All of these factors, including the single-site ventricular pacing alone, contribute to heart failure signs and symptoms.

Cowburn and coworkers[30] reported a similar case in an adult patient after Mustard procedure who had significant improvement in RV ejection fraction, exercise capacity, and renal function and greatly reduced need for diuretic therapy after CRT. The RV ejection fraction improved from 28% to 48% by radionuclide angiography after implantation of an epicardial RV lead, which gave biventricular synchrony along with a transvenous LV (subpulmonary) lead. The patient also received an atrial lead to restore AV synchrony, but the hemodynamic benefit of CRT was first proven. Since then there have been a number of studies, some with a mixed dataset of CHD diagnoses and systemic right ventricles, showing a predominance of benefit of CRT for the failing systemic right ventricle.[9,31-33]

What, then, is the proper place for CRT in the adult population who have had Mustard and Senning procedures? This unusual group of patients is slowly working its way through the ACHD clinic spectrum: the operations are no longer done as a matter of routine with the advent of the arterial switch successes. The youngest patients who received a Mustard or Senning procedure are now nearly 20 years old and the oldest survivors are perhaps in their late 40s. This group of patients has a very significant risk of sudden cardiac death, believed due to the burden of both atrial and ventricular tachyarrhythmia. Rigorous follow-up is required, and electrophysiologic study with risk stratification may be helpful. During placement of primary prevention defibrillator therapies, consideration should be given to an approach that combines the benefits of CRT and implantable cardiac defibrillators.

Heart Failure: Systemic Left Ventricle

In the closest corollary to adult heart failure studies in which CRT has shown benefit there are a relatively small number of scenarios with LBBB and heart failure due to structural disease in ACHD patients. In most of these cases, LBBB in CHD occurs as a postoperative sequela of surgeries to resect myocardium just beneath the aortic valve annulus, where the fascicles of the conduction system emerge from the bundle of His and branch over the LV endocardium in an anterior and posterior generalized fan. Therefore, operations for resection of subaortic stenosis caused by a membrane or hypertrophied myocardium, the Konno operation, and some aortic or mitral valve replacement operations can result in trauma to these conduction tissues and yield LBBB if not complete AV block. In the not uncommon setting in which insufficiency of the semilunar (aortic) valve accompanies a surgically induced postoperative LBBB, both a volume load from insufficiency and abnormal patterns of systemic ventricular myocardial contractility contribute to the development of ventricular remodeling and clinical heart failure. In addition to addressing the hemodynamic abnormality by either open-chest repair or replacement of the aortic valve or, more recently, transcatheter aortic valve replacement, CRT may prove to be of benefit in improving systemic ventricular performance. Again, this can be accomplished either by epicardial or transvenous approach in the majority of these patients.

A less often appreciated setting of systemic LV failure in ACHD patients as noted in sections earlier in this chapter occurs in the patient with tetralogy of Fallot and Ebstein anomaly. In each population, 10% to 15% may develop LV dysfunction in addition to RV dysfunction or as an isolated presentation. A large right ventricle occupies a significant portion of intrapericardial volume, compressing the left ventricle. Additionally, chronic RBBB or at least RV conduction delays and the resulting dyssynchrony may play a role in the development of systemic LV dysfunction in these patients.

An additional important consideration for decreased function of a systemic left ventricle in ACHD patients is the patient who had surgical complete AV block at a young age and required early single-site ventricular pacing or pacing. Also, patients with early pacing systems for congenital AV block have similar if not increased risk of heart failure. Pacing in most of these AV blocks would be either via a transvenous route in an older patient to the right ventricle or from an anterior epicardial approach, especially in the very young patient. The phenomenon of LV dysfunction due to increased duration of RV pacing has been appreciated for several years in adult ischemic patients with heart failure. The DAVID trial[34] revealed increased mortality and hospitalizations in proportion to the amount of ventricular pacing being forced in DDD mode pacing. The MOST trial[35] also showed a relationship of increased pacing in the right ventricle to strong predictors of heart failure and increased risks of atrial fibrillation. It has also been relatively recent that the chronic effect of RV pacing in these patients has been appreciated to contribute in any significant way to the development of systemic LV dysfunction. RV pacing obviously leads to a LBBB pattern of ventricular activation, similar to that seen in the adult postischemic CRT population. In pediatric patients with CHD, the paced QRS duration and site of pacing are believed to be important indicators of the risk of development of heart failure. So-called upgrades of single-chamber pacing systems in pediatric CHD patients from VVI or VVIR pacing to DDD systems resulted in the appearance or worsening of ventricular function, based on percent of ventricular pacing.[36] In a study of chronic RV epicardial pacing in ACHD patients, LV dilation was found to occur in up to 13%.[37]

CRT techniques in the patient with two-ventricle physiology CHD and chronic RV pacing can be quite effective. A picture of dilated cardiomyopathy can present as early as 2 months but on average occurs after about 7 years of pacing. The take-home message for consideration of CRT in ACHD patients with chronic pacing from a young age is one of awareness. There may be a bias toward looking for hemodynamic and structural causes of symptoms in the "repaired" ACHD patient, and the fact may be overlooked that long-term pacing has resulted in either systolic or potentially diastolic forms of heart failure requiring intervention. A final consideration in the patient with congenital complete AV block and what is believed to be pacing-induced heart failure is the possibility of an intrinsic abnormality of the myocardium in some of these patients that may not respond to therapies. Occasional patients with congenital block manifest mutations in *NKX2.5* that cause both loss of conduction system elements and a loss of ventricular trabecular myocytes.[38]

Heart Failure: Single-Ventricle Physiology

The single-ventricle physiology ACHD patient represents perhaps the most complex group of disparate initial CHD diagnoses and, depending on the year of birth, the variability of the surgical interventions that have been performed. Comparisons and global, overarching commentary and guidelines are therefore not only problematic but also likely harmful to development of true CRT indications. The clinician's task is to assess whether there are commonalities in subgroups of this complex population that can be expected to develop heart failure and derive potential benefit from CRT techniques while recognizing that the decision-making process will likely remain a patient-by-patient management exercise. The largest single factor is whether the systemic ventricular mass is of a LV or RV morphology. Those patients with systemic left ventricles and single-ventricle physiology (e.g., tricuspid valve atresia) fare better in the long term than their counterparts with systemic RV morphologies (e.g., forms of hypoplastic left heart syndrome).

Understanding the risk of heart failure in the complex single ventricle population is difficult owing to the variations. Piran and associates[28] provided a solid initial foundation for investigation and plans for therapy by examining a large cohort of 188 ACHD patients with systemic RV and single-ventricle anatomies using radionuclide angiography to measure ejection fraction. The group included 33 Fontan procedure patients with RV or LV morphology, along with 65 ccTGA patients and 90 *d*-TGA (Mustard) patients. Based on classic NYHA staging, 13% of all patients were in class III and 4% in class IV. There were a significant number with symptoms and class II findings. Importantly, 45% of the single-ventricle patients had symptoms, 18% died during 16 years of follow-up, and deaths in one third were secondary to heart failure. Patients with symptoms and heart failure had lower ejection fractions (35% vs. 47%), much higher mortality rates (33% vs. 0%), more potentially life-threatening arrhythmias (58% vs. 24%), and lower exercise capability than asymptomatic patients. Seven of 12 patients with "surgically correctable" lesions had persistent heart failure and/or death after repairs, again indicating a "wait and see" attitude regarding the development of symptoms before intervention is misguided. Also, 82% of those who developed heart failure had an ejection fraction less than 35% before they developed symptoms, leading to the conclusion that greater vigilance for objective measures of heart failure must be obtained on a more routine basis.

Patients with single-ventricle physiology are mixed in with other CHD patients in other reports of CRT in CHD populations,[31,32] but the evidence appears to show that the risk of heart failure in this complex group of patients is high and that attempts to intervene and intervene early are warranted. However, use of quantitative measurements of systemic ejection fraction in Fontan connection patients, as a matter of routine longitudinal follow-up, remains uncommon in the majority of centers. When intervention occurs, CRT strategies remain based on extrapolation and common sense with little ability to predict immediate or long-term outcome. Optimal lead placement at this time is often based on attempts to span as much of the ventricular mass as possible, measurements of tissue Doppler findings, acute blood pressure changes, reduction in AV valve regurgitation, and bringing about a narrower QRS complex. A more robust method of measuring cardiac index quickly and reliably would assist our management.

To complicate matters further, there is what we may call a "reservoir phenomenon" in the group of Fontan connection patients with

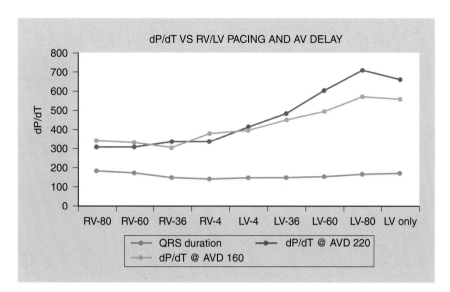

Figure 18-6 Biventricular pacing in a patient with a single ventricle. There is removal of a "reservoir" capacity by activating the passive subaortic outlet chamber first with CRT technique. Measures of dP/dT at two different AV intervals is shown with little change in the QRS complex duration but with marked improvement in dP/dT based on the sequence of activation programmed. See text for further details.

ventricular dyssynchrony and an outflow "pouch" or residual hypoplastic ventricle in continuity with the main ventricular mass. In the presence of asynchronous activation, the force of contractility can be wasted ejecting blood from the main chamber into the "reservoir" chamber or pouch, which when activated later then spills back into a nearly fully contracted ventricle with minimal force to open the semilunar valve and eject into the systemic circulation. Examples could include patients with asynchronous activation and (1) tricuspid atresia and ventricular septal defect, (2) double-inlet LV with remnant hypoplastic ventricle, or (3) all forms with a rudimentary outflow chamber via a bulboventricular foramen. Depending on the pattern of delayed activation, a reservoir capacity could be present and compromise cardiac output. Figure 18-6 shows an example of a patient with complex *l*-TGA and Fontan connection who had improved output by initially pacing the rudimentary LV outlet chamber to prevent its ability to dilate as a reservoir and instead act as a passive conduit for systolic ejection from the main myocardial mass. This finding was seen despite little or no difference in the QRS complex duration. Interestingly, a somewhat similar finding is likely responsible for the beneficial effects reported by Sojak and associates[39] in a case of double-inlet left ventricle, double-outlet right ventricle. AV and VV timing cycles that yielded a sustained 20% increase in cardiac output may have eliminated a reservoir capacitance chamber function in their patient.

An uninvestigated but anecdotal area of concern for CRT in the Fontan population relates to details of device programming. Close attention must be paid not only to the actual programmed AV delay to optimize cardiac output but also to the exact location of the atrial lead and the timing of atrial sensing from that lead. The right-sided atrial epicardium is often buried beneath scar, and in some patients the left atrial surface provides the best location for adequate sensing and capture thresholds. However, sensing of a right-sided atrial rhythm will be quite late, especially owing to obstacles in the atrial conduction route.

The critical factor appears to be whether the atrial lead overlies the AV valve that leads into the main contractile ventricular mass. Timing of atrial filling through that AV valve is what will determine preload and cardiac output, so timing cycles will need to be adjusted accordingly.

For the Fontan patient with a systemic right ventricle, heart failure should be expected relatively early in follow-up. In these patients, diastolic dysfunction in the face of what appears to be a clinically "reasonable" systemic RV systolic contractility may account for a significant incidence of heart failure symptoms as well. Although recent studies point to a potential long-term CRT benefit in adult postischemic heart failure patients as well, the data for such a conclusion in the ACHD patient are a long way away, most likely dependent on assessments of diastolic function and myocardial "twist" in these patients.

CONCLUSION

It is clear that a significant number of ACHD patients will be candidates for CRT systems. Our monitoring protocols during follow-up will require far more rigor and attention to nonechocardiographic measures of cardiac function and ejection fraction if we are to prevent heart failure and sudden cardiac death in patients who seemingly (and quite subjectively) appear to be "doing well." We must think of ACHD as an *electroanatomic defect* rather than remaining focused on the anatomic defects, the electrocardiographic interpretations in isolation, and potentially misleading angiographic images alone.

Care coordination becomes a key component going forward, especially for the ACHD patient with heart failure. These patients need to be included in all adult cardiovascular registries to allow comparison to standard adult heart failure models, and it will be the responsibility of the ACHD cardiologist to generate CHD diagnosis-specific guidelines not only for timing of CRT use but also for the type and frequency of follow-up examinations.

REFERENCES

1. Bradley DJ, Bradley EA, Baughman KL, et al. Cardiac resynchronization and death from progressive heart failure: a meta-analysis of randomized controlled trials. JAMA 2003;289:730–740.
2. Koplan BA, Kaplan AJ, Weiner S, et al. Heart failure decompensation and all-cause mortality in relation to percent biventricular pacing in patients with heart failure: is a goal of 100% pacing necessary? J Am Coll Cardiol 2009;53:355–360.
3. Janousek J, Vojtovic P, Hucin B, et al. Resynchronization pacing is a useful adjunct to the management of acute heart failure after surgery for congenital heart defects. Am J Cardiol 2001;88:145–152.
4. Zimmerman FJ, Starr JP, Koenig PR, et al. Acute hemodynamic benefit of multisite ventricular pacing after congenital heart surgery. Ann Thorac Surg 2003;75:1775–1780.
5. Epstein AE, DiMarco JP, Ellenbogen KA, et al. ACC/AHA/HRS guidelines for device-based therapy of cardiac rhythm abnormalities: executive summary. Heart Rhythm 2008;5:934–955.
6. Jessup M, Abraham WT, Casey DE, et al. Focused update: ACCF/AHA Guidelines for the diagnosis and management of heart failure in adults. A report of the American College of Cardiology Foundation/American Heart Association Task Force on Practice Guidelines. Circulation 2009;119:1977–2016.
7. Norozi K, Wessel A, Alpers V, et al. Incidence and risk distribution of heart failure in adolescents and adults with congenital heart disease after cardiac surgery. Am J Cardiol 2006;97:1238–1243.
8. Norozi K, Wessel A, Buchhorn R, et al. Is the Ability index superior to the NYHA classification for assessing heart failure? Comparison of two classification scales in adolescents and adults with operated congenital heart defects. Clin Res Cardiol 2007;96:542–547.
9. Shaddy RE, Webb G. Applying heart failure guidelines to adult congenital heart patients. Expert Rev Cardiovasc Ther 2008;6:165–174.
10. Frigiola A, Redington AN, Cullen S, Vogel M. Pulmonary regurgitation is an important determinant of right ventricular contractile dysfunction in patients with surgically repaired tetralogy of Fallot. Circulation 2004;110:153–157.
11. Gatzoulis MA, Walters J, McLaughlin PR, et al. Late arrhythmia in adults with the Mustard procedure for transposition of the great arteries: a surrogate marker for right ventricular dysfunction? Heart 2000;84:409–415.
12. Therrien J, Siu SC, Harris L, et al. Impact of pulmonary valve replacement on arrhythmia propensity late after repair of tetralogy of Fallot. Circulation 2002;103:2489–2494.
13. Therrien J, Provost Y, Merchant N, et al. Optimal timing for pulmonary valve replacement in adults after tetralogy of Fallot repair. Am J Cardiol 2005;95:779–782.
14. Vogel M, Sponring J, Cullen S, et al. Regional wall motion and abnormalities of electrical depolarization and repolarization

in patients with repaired tetralogy of Fallot: implications of infundibular disease. Circulation 2007;116:1532–1539.

15. Uebing A, Gibson DG, Babu-Narayan SV, et al. Right ventricular mechanics and QRS duration in patients with repaired tetralogy of Fallot: implications of infundibular disease. Circulation 2007;116:1532–1539.

16. Deanfield J, McKenna W, Rowland E. Local abnormalities of right ventricular depolarization after repair of tetralogy of Fallot: a basis for ventricular arrhythmia. Am J Cardiol 1985;55:522–525.

17. Moak JP, Garson Jr A. Experimental right ventriculotomy: effects on local propagation at a small size scale. Pediatr Res 1988;23:433–438.

18. Horowitz LN, Simson MB, Spear JF, et al. The mechanism of apparent right bundle branch block after transatrial repair of tetralogy of Fallot. Circulation 1979;59:1241–1252.

19. Tzemos N, Harris L, Carasso S, et al. Adverse left ventricular mechanics in adults with repaired tetralogy of Fallot. Am J Cardiol 2009;103:420–542.

20. Van den Berg J, de Bie S, Meijboom FJ, et al. Changes during exercise of ECG intervals related to increased risk for ventricular arrhythmia in repaired tetralogy of Fallot and their relationship to right ventricular size and function. Int J Cardiol 2008;124:332–338.

21. Dubin AM, Feinstein JA, Reddy VM, et al. Electrical resynchronization: a novel therapy for the failing right ventricle. Circulation 2003;107:2287–2289.

22. Dubin AM, Hanisch D, Chin C, et al. A prospective pilot study of right ventricular resynchronization. Heart Rhythm 2008;5:S42.

23. Lubiszewska B, Gosiewska C, Hoffman P, et al. Myocardial perfusion and function of the systemic right ventricle in patients after atrial switch procedure for complete transposition: long-term follow-up. J Am Coll Cardiol 2000;36:1365–1370.

24. Hornung TS, Bernard EJ, Jaeggi E, et al. Myocardial perfusion defects and associated systemic ventricular dysfunction in congenitally corrected transposition of the great arteries. Heart 1998;80:322–326.

25. Graham Jr TP, Bernard YD, Mellen BG, et al. Long-term outcome in congenitally corrected transposition of the great arteries: a multi-institutional study. J Am Coll Cardiol 2000;36:255–261.

26. Diller GP, Okonko D, Uebing A, et al. Cardiac resynchronization therapy for adult congenital heart disease patients with a systemic right ventricle: analysis of feasibility and review of early experience. Europace 2006;8:267–272.

27. Puley G, Siu S, Connelly HM, et al. Arrhythmia and survival in patients > 18 years of age after the Mustard procedure for complete transposition of the great arteries. Am J Cardiol 1999;83:1080–1084.

28. Piran S, Veldtman G, Siu S, et al. Heart failure and ventricular dysfunction in patients with single or systemic right ventricles. Circulation 2002;105:1189–1194.

29. Chow PC, Liang XC, Lam WWM, et al. Mechanical right ventricular dyssynchrony in patients after atrial switch operation for transposition of the great arteries. Am J Cardiol 2008;101:874–881.

30. Cowburn PJ, Parker JD, Cameron DA, Harris L. Cardiac resynchronization therapy: retiming the failing right ventricle. J Cardiovasc Electrophysiol 2005;16:439–443.

31. Dubin AM, Janousek J, Rhee E, et al. Resynchronization therapy in pediatric and congenital heart disease patients: an international multicenter study. J Am Coll Cardiol 2005;46:2277–2283.

32. Cecchin F, Frangini PA, Brown DW, et al. Cardiac resynchronization therapy (and multisite pacing) in pediatrics and congenital heart disease: five years experience in a single institution. J Cardiovasc Electrophysiol 2009;20:58–65.

33. Janousek J, Tomek V, Chaloupecky VA, et al. Cardiac resynchronization therapy: a novel adjunct to the treatment and prevention of systemic right ventricular failure. J Am Coll Cardiol 2004;44:1927–1931.

34. Wilcoff BL, Cook JR, Epstein AE, et al. Dual-chamber pacing or ventricular back-up pacing in patients with an implantable defibrillator: the Dual chamber and VVI Implantable Defibrillator (DAVID) Trial. JAMA 2002;288:3115–3123.

35. Sweeney MO, Hellkamp AS, Ellenbogen KA, et al. Adverse effect of ventricular pacing on heart failure and atrial fibrillation among patients with normal baseline QRS duration in a clinical trial of pacemaker therapy for sinus node dysfunction. Mode Selection Trial Investigators. Circulation 2003;107:2932–2937.

36. Silvetti MS, Drago F. Upgrade of single chamber pacemakers with transvenous leads to dual chamber pacemakers in pediatric and young adult patients. PACE 2004;27:1094–1098.

37. Gebauer RA, Tomek V, Salamah A, et al. Predictors of left ventricular remodeling and failure in right ventricular pacing in the young. Eur Heart J 2009;30:1097–1104.

38. Pashmforoush M, Lu JT, Chen H, et al. Nkx2-5 pathways and congenital heart disease: loss of ventricular myocyte lineage specification leads to progressive cardiomyopathy and complete heart block. Cell 2004;117:373–386.

39. Sojak V, Mazic U, Cesen M, et al. Cardiac resynchronization therapy for the failing Fontan patient. Ann Thorac Surg 2008;85:2136–2138.

Infective Endocarditis

WEI LI | GEORGIOS GIANNAKOULAS

Introduction

Infective endocarditis is a condition characterized by a microbiologic inflammation of the lining of the heart chamber, heart valves, and great vessels. The condition was first described in detail by Osler in 1885, at a time when it was considered universally fatal. Since then great advances have been made in the understanding of the pathophysiologic basis of the disease. There are two major predisposing factors for infective endocarditis: a susceptible cardiac or vascular substrate and a source of bacteremia. The substrate is characterized by lesions associated with high-velocity flow, jet impact, and focal increases in the rate of shear. In the first half of the 20th century, a large proportion of patients with infective endocarditis had previous rheumatic heart disease. Today, with the increasing number of patients with complex congenital heart disease (CHD) surviving to adulthood, and the frequent use of prosthetic devices and indwelling lines in these patients, endocarditis is now observed with increasing frequency in this population.

Incidence and Patients at Risk

The reported incidence of infective endocarditis in CHD is 15 to 140 times higher than that in the general population (the highest estimate originating from a highly specialized unit).[1,2] The reported proportion of CHD in patients with infective endocarditis varies, probably owing to selection bias, between 2% and 18%, with a consistent minor male dominance. In adult CHD patients, the mean age ranges between 28.4 and 32.5 years.[3,4]

Virtually any congenital cardiac defect may predispose to the development of infective endocarditis, and the risk of this actually occurring is not negligible. Both cardiac surgery and catheter-related cardiac interventions constitute risk factors for infective endocarditis, irrespective of the nature of underlying CHD. Shah and associates determined that the lifetime risk of developing infective endocarditis in a patient with an unrepaired, simple ventricular septal defect (VSD) was 12% to 13%.[5] In a large cooperative study on the natural history of aortic stenosis, pulmonary stenosis, and VSD, Gersony and colleagues reported a 9.7% risk of developing infective endocarditis by age 30 years in patients with unoperated VSD.[6] However, in patients who underwent surgical repair the incidence of infective endocarditis was much lower. In contrast, the risk for patients with aortic stenosis (1.4%) was slightly increased after surgical intervention, whereas patients with pulmonary stenosis had only a 0.9% risk of developing infective endocarditis.

A number of pediatric studies have shown that tetralogy of Fallot accounted for the largest percentage of patients with CHD who developed infective endocarditis.[7] VSD was the second most common lesion (16%) in the group, followed by aortic stenosis (8%), patent ductus arteriosus (7%), and transposition of the great arteries (4%). Other studies report VSD and aortic valve disease (bicuspid aortic valve or aortic stenosis) as the most common predisposing lesions.

In a study of infective endocarditis in adults with CHD at the Royal Brompton Hospital, left ventricular outflow tract lesions were the most common cases of infective endocarditis regardless of the presence or absence of previous surgery.[8] Unoperated small VSD was the second most common lesion, followed by cyanotic CHD (25% of the total CHD patients with infective endocarditis); tetralogy of Fallot was the most common cyanotic condition among them. Other lesions included pulmonary atresia with VSD, single ventricular physiology, transposition of the great arteries, atrioventricular septal defect with pulmonary stenosis, truncus arteriosus, and VSD with Eisenmenger physiology.

CHD often consists of multiple cardiac lesions, each contributing to the total risk of infective endocarditis. For example, the incidence of endocarditis is considerably higher in patients with a VSD when there is associated aortic regurgitation.[9] What is noteworthy is that the number of patients with complex types of CHD associated with endocarditis has increased in the past decades. This may be explained by the increased survival of patients with complex type of CHD due to the advances in surgical, interventional, and medical treatment.

Effect of Surgical Repair

Surgical intervention for CHD has had a significant impact on the risk of infective endocarditis. Certain operations (prosthetic valves or conduits) substantially increase the risk, whereas others (division of patent ductus arteriosus, complete closure of VSD) may eliminate it.

In a 25-year postoperative follow-up study the cumulative incidence of infective endocarditis was 1.3% for tetralogy of Fallot, 2.7% for isolated VSD, 3.5% for coarctation of the aorta, 13.3% for valvular aortic stenosis, and 2.8% for primum atrial septal defect.[10] In another group of patients with postoperative follow-up of up to 20 years, the cumulative incidence was 1.1% for complete atrioventricular septal defect, 5.3% for pulmonary atresia with an intact ventricular septum, and 6.4% for pulmonary atresia with VSD. No children with secundum atrial septal defect, patent ductus arteriosus, or pulmonary stenosis have had endocarditis after operation.[10]

Antecedent Events

DENTAL PROCEDURES AND ORAL HYGIENE

Preceding dental procedure is the most frequent precipitating event in patients with infective endocarditis. Cleaning, filling, and extraction of teeth are all accompanied by bacteremia and positive blood cultures in 12% to 85% of dental patients. The most common organisms are streptococci, usually β-hemolytic streptococcus. Bacteremia occurs during extractions performed in children with diseased teeth as well as in children with normal primary or permanent teeth (e.g., wisdom teeth). Elderly edentulous patients, both those who lack dentures and those who have poorly fitting and therefore abrasive dentures, are at risk of *Streptococcus viridans* bacteremia and infective endocarditis. In addition to the different procedures, poor dental hygiene itself predisposes to the growth of similar organisms, which have been cultured from the mouth and blood. As early as 1937, organisms were recovered from blood cultures in patients whose gingival crevices had been painted with *Serratia marcescens* before dental manipulation, indicating the potential for gum disease to introduce microorganisms into the circulation. Patients with cyanotic CHD are at particular risk because of the nature of their fragile, spongy gums. When loose teeth are set into motion by chewing, the incidence of bacteremia is as high as 86%.

OPEN-HEART SURGERY AND NONCARDIAC SURGERY

Open-heart surgery was the most frequently related antecedent event in patients who had undergone surgical repair, especially when it was followed by a long stay in the intensive therapy unit. Intravenous therapy, especially via a central intravenous catheter, and urinary tract instrumentation were most frequent causative events, with a high incidence of *Staphylococcus aureus* infection in these patients. Candidal endocarditis can occur in patients receiving long-term intravenous antibiotics and is difficult to diagnose from cultures; antibody titer may be needed. Noncardiac surgery sets the stage for bacteremia, both from the site itself and the underlying lesion requiring operation.

CARDIAC DIAGNOSTIC AND INTERVENTIONAL PROCEDURES

Diagnostic cardiac catheterization is not frequently associated with infective endocarditis unless complicated by local skin infection or a long procedure. According to the latest recommendations for the prevention of bacterial endocarditis, prophylactic antibiotics are not required in diagnostic catheterization and angiography because with adequate aseptic techniques the occurrence of endocarditis is extremely low. However, in pediatric groups an incidence of cardiac catheter–related infective endocarditis as high as 5% has been reported. The use of cardiovascular devices for treating CHD has become an established therapeutic route, but it carries the risk of device-related infections. Pacemaker systems with intracardiac electrodes account for the majority of cases of intracardiac device–related infective endocarditis. Interventional closure of atrial septal defects or ventricular septal defects, stent implantation, or closure of patent ductus arteriosus may also be followed by infective endocarditis. The number of types of foreign material implanted in the heart or surrounding vessels in permanent contact with the bloodstream are increasing.

OTHER PROCEDURES

The incidence of bacteremia in uncomplicated vaginal delivery is 1% to 5%. The incidence of bacteremia increases with premature rupture of the membranes and with prolonged, difficult labor. Bacteremia occurs in 85% of women undergoing suction abortion as well as in 2.5% of patients during the first year after insertion of a contraceptive device.

Although urologic procedures are much more likely to be accompanied by bacteremia in the presence of urinary tract infection, bacteremia can also occur when the urine is sterile because of the normal urethra flora or because of bacteria that reside in the prostate, commonly enterococci, streptococci, and anaerobic or aerobic gram-negative rods.

Fiberoptic or flexible endoscopy (esophagus, stomach, and duodenum) seldom causes bacteremia. However, transesophageal echocardiography has been reported as a possible cause, although a consensus has emerged that the prevalence of bacteremia in this case is very low, and the incidence of positive blood culture associated with the procedure is indistinguishable from the anticipated contamination rate.

Risk comes from many other sources. In adolescent patients, piercing, tattooing, or intravenous drug abuse must be considered. Unusual occupational and living conditions may lead to infection by unusual organisms: sewer workers have been infected by *Actinobacillus actinomycetem-comitans*, and *Aspergillus* endocarditis has occurred in a patient living in a very damp environment. Nail biting or picking of adjacent soft tissue increases the risk of periungual staphylococcal infection, bacteremia, and infective endocarditis. Acne is a potential source of staphylococcal bacteremia in adolescents and young adults, especially when it is infected.

◼ Clinical Manifestations

The clinical manifestations of infective endocarditis are highly variable and usually nonspecific (Box 19-1; Fig. 19-1). The extent of local involvement of the myocardium or valves, embolization from vegetations, and activation of immunologic mechanisms all play essential roles in the clinical course. Patients with acute infective endocarditis

---

BOX 19-1 SYMPTOMS AND CLINICAL MANIFESTATIONS OF INFECTIVE ENDOCARDITIS

Symptoms

The mean calculated interval between assumed start of bacteremia and first symptoms of infective endocarditis in CHD is approximately 2 weeks. Most common symptoms include the following:
- Fever—manifest as sweating, chills, shivering, or rigors—is the most frequent presenting feature, although it may be absent in up to 10% of cases. Initially continuous, the fever may become intermittent with relatively symptomless intervals. This is particularly so when short nonbactericidal courses of antibiotics have been given.
- Other nonspecific complaints include malaise, anorexia, generalized lethargy, fatigue, and weight loss.
- Arthralgias or arthritis—involvement of the large joints—may occur in up to 20% to 30% of patients.
- Embolic episodes may affect any organ of the body:
  - Renal infarcts due to embolization of relatively large renal arteries may cause frank hematuria.
  - Splenic infarcts usually present as left upper quadrant abdominal pain.
  - Right-sided heart endocarditis may present as hemoptysis or recurrent "chest infections" due to pulmonary emboli.
  - Cerebral infarcts may present in the form of stroke.
  - Blindness in one eye may be caused by emboli of the retinal artery.
  - Chest pain is usually related to myalgia but is sometimes secondary to pulmonary embolism, especially with tricuspid valve involvement.
- Increasing breathlessness and tachycardia may reflect heart failure and anemia. The latter may present as pallor and contributes to the general feeling of malaise. Heart failure may be due to both mechanical and myocardial factors. Diffuse myocarditis may also contribute to heart failure. Involvement of the atrioventricular node may cause atrioventricular block in up to 4% of patients.
- Destruction of valves may cause aortic or mitral incompetence, and coronary emboli may produce myocardial infarction.

- Neurologic manifestations or complications of infective endocarditis are extremely common, being found in 30% to 40% of patients:
  - Acute hemiplegia, ataxia, aphasia, focal neurologic defects, sensory loss, and changing mental status may occur as a presenting feature for years after the disease process has been treated.

Clinical Manifestations
- Patients usually appear ill, pyrexial, and anemic.
- Splenomegaly occurs in about 55% of patients. It is often painless, but there may be tenderness when the spleen is greatly enlarged. Hepatomegaly is also observed in many patients. Infarction of the spleen or abscess formation should be suspected in patients with left upper quadrant pain and tenderness that radiates to the shoulder area. A pleural friction rub or pleural effusion may also be observed.
- Auscultation of the heart reveals signs of the underlying cardiac anomaly, with changes of auscultation findings being particularly characteristic of infective endocarditis (Fig. 19-1).
- Finger clubbing may develop when the course is subacute and clearly must be distinguished from that due to cyanotic heart disease.
- Specific skin lesions associated with infective endocarditis are more common in patients with a "subacute" course. These include splinter hemorrhages, petechiae, Osler nodes, Janeway lesions, and Roth spots. *Splinter hemorrhages* are linear, sublingual and present on the fingers and occasionally the toes. The *petechial lesions* found in infective endocarditis have a characteristically pale center and are seen on the conjunctiva, the backs of the hands, the oral mucous membranes, and occasionally the anterior aspect of the chest or abdomen. *Osler nodes* are small raised red or purple nodules that are tender or painful and found in the pulp of the terminal phalanx of the finger. Rarely, they exist on the back of the toes, on the soles of the feet, or on the thenar or hypothenar eminences. *Janeway lesions* are small, irregular, flat, muscular nontender lesions that blanch with pressure. They are typically also found on the thenar or hypothenar eminence.

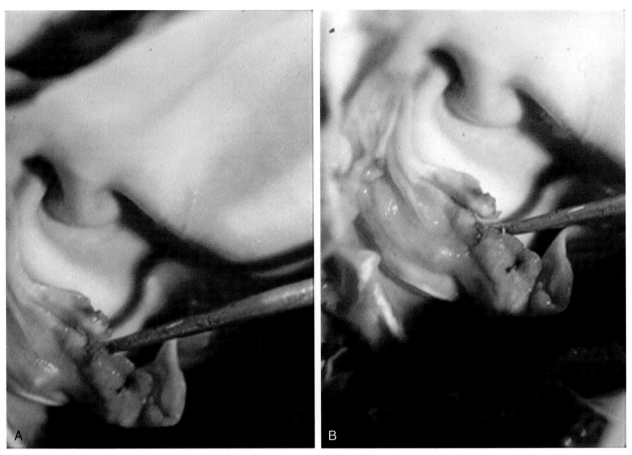

Figure 19-1 **A** and **B,** Autopsy specimen: vegetations on the noncoronary leaflet of the aortic valve with rupture of the valve, which has led to aortic incompetence in a 31-year-old woman with an atrioventricular septal defect palliated with pulmonary artery banding and right Blalock-Taussig shunt. Autopsy also demonstrated a small vegetation on the left atrioventricular valve.

may present in shock and with a clinical picture consistent with over-whelming sepsis, whereas, in some cases, endocarditis may be confirmed only at autopsy. In the subacute form of the disease, the course may be indolent, often blurred by the use of antibiotics, with a diagnosis not established for weeks, months, or even years.

Investigation

BLOOD CULTURE

Blood culture is the most important investigation and should be done as soon as a suspicion of endocarditis is raised. At least three samples from different venepuncture sites are taken over a 24-hour period. Seriously ill patients thought to have endocarditis should be started on antibiotics after two or three samples have been taken. Conversely, it may be best to continue culturing for a few days in less acute cases, particularly when the patient has already had a short course of antibiotic treatment or if initial cultures are negative at 48 hours. Serial sampling can also be a useful way of determining the relevance of an organism such as coagulase-negative *Staphylococcus,* which could be a skin contaminant if found in only one or two samples. Sensitivity of positive blood cultures in CHD-associated endocarditis is 82%.

Negative Blood Culture

The problem of negative blood cultures remains important. Not only is the mortality rate higher in this group, but rational and controlled therapy is impossible to achieve. Some negative results can be explained by poor culture techniques or by previous antibiotic treatment. Blood cultures may remain negative for many days after antibiotic discontinuation, and causative organisms are most often oral streptococci or coagulase-negative staphylococci. Some rare organisms such

as anaerobes, microaerophilic organisms, nutritionally variant streptococci, and fungi need special culture techniques. Some organisms, for example the HACEK (*Haemophilus* spp., *Actinobacillus actinomycetemcomitans, Cardiobacterium hominis, Eikenella corrodens,* and *Kingella* spp.) group, may require several weeks to grow in culture.

HEMATOLOGY

The erythrocyte sedimentation rate (ESR) is raised in 90% of cases, as is the level of C-reactive protein. An artifactually low ESR may be found with renal disease, severe congestive heart failure, or erythrocytosis. The ESR should decrease toward normal if therapy has been successful, and serial measurements may be helpful in monitoring progress of the infection.

Anemia, usually due to a chronic disease state, is seen in approximately 40% of patients. In adult patients with cyanotic CHD who have developed infective endocarditis, the finding of a normal or slightly raised hemoglobin level may represent an anemic state. Although leukocytosis is not uncommon, leukopenia may occur with overwhelming sepsis.

More than 90% of patients will have at least microscopic hematuria. Its absence makes diagnosis unlikely.

Serologic testing for specific organisms may be helpful in culture-negative endocarditis. Antibodies against teichoic acids, which are major components of the cell wall in *S. aureus,* may be present in 85% of adults with infective endocarditis.

ECHOCARDIOGRAPHY

Echocardiography plays an important part in the investigation of patients with endocarditis. It allows accurate scanning of prosthetic valves and may demonstrate vegetations, perforation of valve leaflets, valve-ring abscesses, intracardiac fistulas, and aneurysms when present

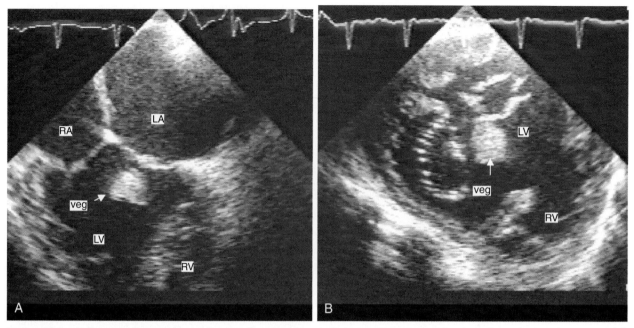

Figure 19-2   **A,** Transesophageal echocardiogram (four-chamber view) shows a large vegetation (*arrow*) attached to the stenotic left atrioventricular valve of a 28-year-old man with a double-inlet left ventricle. **B,** Vegetation on the short-axis view of the atrioventricular valve from the same patient. LA, left atrium; LV, left ventricle; RA, right atrium; RV, right ventricle.

(Fig. 19-2). Two-dimensional (2D) echocardiography can detect vegetations as small as 2 to 3 mm, although it may not always be possible to distinguish these from a thickened, calcified, or surgically repaired valve. Transesophageal echocardiography, on the contrary, gives consistently high-quality pictures and can detect vegetations as small as 1.0 to 1.5 mm with a sensitivity and specificity of more than 90%. If a false aneurysm is suspected, particularly in a patient with coarctation,

transesophageal echocardiography is contraindicated. However, the superiority of transesophageal over transthoracic echocardiography has not been systematically studied in the setting of CHD. Color and pulsed wave and continuous wave Doppler examinations have added significantly to the ability to detect other complications of endocarditis (Fig. 19-3). Full echocardiographic examination should, therefore, always be performed along with the clinical assessment of individual

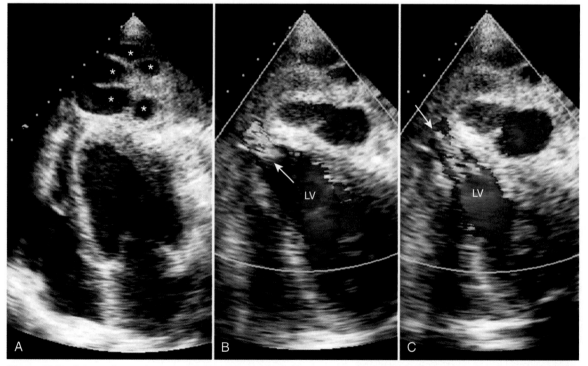

Figure 19-3   Echocardiographic image from a patient who had a previous resection of subaortic membrane. Endocarditis is present at previous left ventricle (LV) apical vent site with rupture, false mycotic aneurysm, and abscess cavity formation. Apical four-chamber view (**A**) showing a multiloculated structure inferior to LV apex (*asterisks*). Color Doppler flow mapping shows laminar flow within cavities as well as turbulent phasic flow (*arrow*) through a defect in the apex of the LV at the onset of systole (**B**) and diastole (**C**).

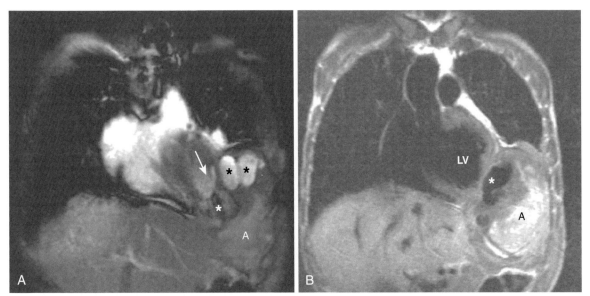

Figure 19-4 Cardiac magnetic resonance (CMR) image from same patient as in Figure 19-3. Steady-state free-procession cine CMR (**A**) and T2-weighted turbo spin-echo (**B**) images in coronal views. A systolic jet (*arrow*) is seen in one of three loculated cavities of the false aneurysm (*asterisks*). The relatively bright signal marked "A" is suggestive of abscess formation below the false aneurysm cavities (LV) left ventricle.

patients and other investigations, including complete microbiologic screening. However, a normal transesophageal echocardiogram does not exclude infective endocarditis. Infection outside the heart, such as that occurring on surgically created shunts, collaterals, or conduits may be very difficult to demonstrate by any method. Magnetic resonance imaging is another useful and reliable technique, particularly for diagnosing false aneurysms and the collection of pus around vessels but not for small vegetations (Fig. 19-4). Finally, multislice computed tomography shows good results in detecting valvular abnormalities in infective endocarditis and could be applied in preoperative planning and exclusion of coronary artery disease before surgery.[11]

Once vegetations are detected, they may show no significant change during therapy. Therefore, a recurrence of disease cannot be supported unless a noticeable increase in vegetation size from baseline has occurred or new vegetations appear. Continued growth of vegetation coexisting with persistent bacteremia or evidence of further endocardial infiltration may indicate a treatment failure and the need for prompt surgical intervention.

▣ Diagnosis

Infective endocarditis should be suspected in all patients with CHD presenting with fever or newly manifesting heart failure. Because the diagnosis of endocarditis is often difficult, attempts have been made to establish criteria that allow for a firm diagnosis to be made. The criteria are based on clinical, microbiologic, echocardiographic, and other investigation results that reflect the four main aspects of endocarditis: a predisposition; a persistent bacteremia with organisms typically causing infective endocarditis; vascular phenomena; and evidence of endocardial involvement, which may be found only by transthoracic or transesophageal echocardiography or direct inspection. The clinical criteria originally proposed by Duke University and subsequent modifications are most commonly used today (Box 19-2).[12,13] It is paramount that patients have some understanding of this potentially devastating complication of CHD. Patients themselves may then request blood cultures to be obtained instead of a prescription of antibiotics for example when pyrexia without an obvious source is present.

BOX 19-2 DIAGNOSIS OF INFECTIVE ENDOCARDITIS (MODIFIED DUKE CRITERIA)

Major Criteria

Blood Cultures Positive for Infective Endocarditis

- Typical microorganisms consistent with infective endocarditis from two separate blood cultures:
  - Viridans streptococci, *Streptococcus bovis*, HACEK group, *Staphylococcus aureus*; or
  - Community-acquired enterococci, in the absence of a primary focus

  or
- Microorganisms consistent with infective endocarditis from persistently positive blood cultures:
  - At least two positive blood cultures of blood samples drawn more than 12 hours apart; *or*
  - All three or a majority of four or more separate cultures of blood (with first and last samples drawn at least 1 hour apart)

  or
- Single positive blood culture for *Coxiella burnetii* or phase I IgG antibody titer greater than 1:800

Evidence of Endocardial Involvement

Echocardiography Positive for Infective Endocarditis

Vegetation—Abscess—New Partial Dehiscence of Prosthetic Valve

New Valvular Regurgitation

Minor Criteria

- Predisposition: predisposing heart condition, intravenous drug use
- Fever: temperature greater than 38° C
- Vascular phenomena: major arterial emboli, septic pulmonary infarcts, mycotic aneurysm, intracranial hemorrhages, conjunctival hemorrhages, Janeway lesions
- Immunologic phenomena: glomerulonephritis, Osler nodes, Roth spots, rheumatoid factor
- Microbiologic evidence: positive blood culture but does not meet a major criterion or show serologic evidence of active infection with organism consistent with infective endocarditis
  Diagnosis of infective endocarditis is definite in the presence of:
- 2 major criteria, *or*
- 1 major or 3 minor criteria, *or*
- 5 minor criteria
  Diagnosis of infective endocarditis is possible in the presence of:
- 1 major and 1 minor criteria, *or*
- 3 minor criteria

Management

The purpose of treatment is to sterilize infected cardiac tissue and, by so doing, to limit the extent of damage and prevent life-threatening complications such as systemic embolism and cardiac failure. In most instances, adequate antibiotic treatment is all that is required, but in selected cases surgery has an important part to play, sometimes early in the course of the disease.

MEDICAL MANAGEMENT

Unless the condition of the patient is deteriorating, initiation of therapy can usually be delayed until the organism has been identified or, more importantly, its antibiotic sensitivities determined.

The principles of antibacterial treatment have been laid down as a result of experimental work in animals and clinical experience in humans. The consensus is that bactericidal drugs should be used in preference to bacteriostatic agents and that bolus intravenous injections are preferable and possibly more effective than intravenous infusions or intramuscular administration. The choice, dose, administration route, and duration of antimicrobial therapy are often complex, so that consulting an infectious disease specialist is desirable. Bacteremia usually resolves within several days after initiation of effective antimicrobial agents, and 75% of the patients become afebrile during the first and 95% during the second week of antibiotic therapy.

Aspirin and other anti-inflammatory agents are not indicated in the management of patients with infective endocarditis.

SURGICAL MANAGEMENT

Operative intervention is sometimes crucial, including surgery during the acute period and surgery followed by antibiotic treatment. The most common indication for surgical intervention is congestive heart failure, together or combined with other conditions (i.e., embolization or persistent infection). Aortic valve involvement by *S. aureus* infection leading to acute aortic regurgitation on a bicuspid aortic valve is a major cause of acute hemodynamic deterioration. Infective endocarditis involving a prosthetic valve is a contentious problem that nearly always requires reoperation, either because of valve dysfunction or because persistent infection leads to dehiscence or a contiguous abscess. Sterilization is difficult if not impossible when infective endocarditis is imposed on the prosthetic valve or prosthetic material. Bioprosthetic valves are not immune from infection, which may prompt the need for their replacement.

Surgery should thus be considered early when (1) medical treatment is failing, particularly when there is hemodynamic deterioration; (2) large mobile vegetations are noted on echocardiographic study; (3) mechanical valve prostheses are involved; (4) there is evidence of an infective abscess (prolongation of the PR interval on the surface electrocardiogram would be suggestive of abscess in patients with aortic valve endocarditis); and (5) when fungal endocarditis is encountered. It is important, and a matter of courtesy, to involve the surgical team early in the management of such patients, and certainly before emergencies occur.

Prognosis

Infective endocarditis is a life-threatening disease with an in-hospital mortality rate of 16% to 20% despite improvement in medical care. Many risk factors for mortality in patients with endocarditis have been reported:
- Age
- Gender
- Presence of heart failure
- Certain causative organisms
- Prosthetic heart valves
- Embolism in the cerebral, pulmonary, renal, and coronary arteries
- Disease severity
- Vegetation size or area
- Hematologic abnormality
- Absence of surgical intervention

Compared with adult endocarditis (especially with those aged older than 60 years), the overall mortality and of the disease in CHD is lower (4% to 10%). This better prognosis of CHD endocarditis compared with other heart disease may reflect the higher proportion of right-sided heart infection in the former, although this is speculative.

Prophylaxis

A clear cause of bacteremia before infective endocarditis is recognized in about two thirds of cases. Apart from intravenous drug users, the mouth, particularly during dental procedures, remains the main portal of entry of organisms. Emphasis should therefore focus on good oral hygiene, including daily brushing and flossing, as well as regular visits to the dentist to decrease the frequency of bacteremia in daily life. However, there is also an educational problem, and efforts to raise awareness in the population of CHD patients of the risk of endocarditis and need for preventive measures should be made. There are no controlled data supporting cardiac surgery or percutaneous interventions (e.g., closure of a patent ductus arteriosus) with the sole purpose of eliminating the risk of endocarditis,[14] although most physicians would consider such interventions after recurrent episodes of endocarditis following antibiotic therapy and complete eradication of sepsis.

Similarly, there are no prospective randomized trials suggesting that prophylactic antibiotic therapy is beneficial. Given the extremely low incidence of endocarditis after procedures such as dental surgery and the medicolegal climate in the United States and Europe, it is unlikely that such a study will ever be undertaken. As a result, over the past years there has been a considerable debate concerning the issue of antibiotic prophylaxis in patients with CHD. Recent recommendations from various professional bodies represent a major departure from the traditional practice of endocarditis prophylaxis and may, sadly, lead to a behavioral change on overall dental and gum hygiene and health promotion.

Risk stratification is determined by the degree of susceptibility of a given substrate to infection. The higher the susceptibility to infective endocarditis, the greater the need for prophylactic regimen. Accordingly, patients are categorized as at low or no risk, moderate risk, or high risk (Box 19-3).[15]

According to the latest guidelines from the European Society of Cardiology,[16] prophylaxis against infective endocarditis is reasonable only for patients at highest risk for adverse outcomes from infective endocarditis who undergo dental procedures that involve manipulation of either gingival tissue or the periapical region of teeth or perforation of the oral mucosa. This is based on the rationale that only an extremely small number of cases of infective endocarditis may be prevented by antibiotic prophylaxis for dental procedures even if such prophylactic therapy were 100% effective. The following patients should be offered prophylaxis:
- Patients with prosthetic cardiac valves or prosthetic material used for cardiac valve repair
- Patients with previous infective endocarditis
- Patients with unrepaired cyanotic CHD, including palliative shunts and conduits or with a congenital heart defect repaired with prosthetic material or device, whether placed by surgery or by catheter intervention, during the first 6 months after the procedure
- Patients with repaired CHD with residual defects at the site or adjacent to the site of a prosthetic patch or prosthetic device (both of which inhibit endothelialization)

Furthermore, infective endocarditis prophylaxis is recommended after surgery or percutaneous intervention in:
- Atrial septal defect: for 6 months after device closure (until endothelialization)
- VSD: for 6 months after device closure and ongoing only when a residual defect is present
- Atrioventricular septal defect: for 6 months if a prosthetic material is used for cardiac valve repair, ongoing only in patients with a prosthetic valve or in patients with previous infective endocarditis

- Patent ductus arteriosus: for 6 months after device closure and ongoing only when a residual defect is present
- Aortic valvular stenosis: only in patients with a prosthetic valve and in patients with previous infective endocarditis
- Aortic coarctation: only with repair using prosthetic material for 6 months after the procedure
- Tetralogy of Fallot: in cyanotic patients with residual defects, palliative shunts, or conduits; in complete repair using prosthetic material for 6 months after procedure (until endothelialization) and ongoing only when a residual defect persists at the site of prosthetic material or in patients with a prosthetic valve or previous endocarditis
- Fontan connection patients: after a recent "redo" Fontan procedure for a duration of 6 months, ongoing only in cyanosis, prosthetic material in the extracardiac conduit, prosthetic valve, residual patch leak, or prior endocarditis
- Univentricular hearts (unoperated and palliated excluding Fontan connection patients): prophylaxis is indicated in all patients.
- Ventricular to pulmonary conduit: recommended in all patients

It is fair to say that among many physicians and experts controversy continues over these recent changes. Many believe that insufficient new evidence exists to justify such a radical change in policy; and because endocarditis may be potentially fatal, prophylaxis should not be restricted to high-risk patients only. Such physicians may extend indications for prophylaxis for infective endocarditis to other patient groups, such as patients with a bicuspid aortic valve, coarctation of the aorta, or severe mitral valve prolapse. The need for both high-level oral hygiene and for reviewing the recent recommendations and their potential impact on epidemiologic trends on endocarditis cannot be overemphasized.

BOX 19-3   RISK STRATIFICATION FOR INFECTIVE ENDOCARDITIS

Low or No Risk
- Surgically repaired atrial septal defect
- Surgically repaired ventricular septal defect
- Surgically repaired patent ductus arteriosus
- Post Fontan or Mustard procedure without residual defect/murmur
- Isolated secundum atrial septal defect
- Mitral valve prolapse without regurgitation
- Pulmonary stenosis

Moderate Risk
- Acquired valvular heart disease (e.g., rheumatic heart disease)
- Aortic stenosis and regurgitation
- Mitral regurgitation
- Bicuspid aortic valve
- Primum atrial septal defect
- Patent ductus arteriosus
- Aortic root replacement
- Coarctation of aorta
- Atrial septal aneurysm/patent foramen ovale
- Ventricular septal defect
- Hypertrophic obstructive cardiomyopathy
- Subaortic membrane

High Risk
- Prosthetic heart valves
- Previous infective endocarditis
- Complex cyanotic congenital heart disease
- Transposition of the great arteries
- Tetralogy of Fallot
- Surgically constructed systemic pulmonary shunts or conduits
- Mitral valve prolapsed with significant mitral regurgitation or thickened leaflets

---

REFERENCES

1. Moller JH, Anderson RC. 1,000 consecutive children with a cardiac malformation with 26- to 37-year follow-up. Am J Cardiol 1992;70:661–667.
2. Niwa K, Nakazawa M, Tateno S, et al. Infective endocarditis in congenital heart disease: Japanese national collaboration study. Heart 2005;91:795–800.
3. Ishiwada N, Niwa K, Tateno S, et al. Causative organism influences clinical profile and outcome of infective endocarditis in pediatric patients and adults with congenital heart disease. Circulation J 2005;69:1266–12670.
4. Niwa K, Nakazawa M, Tateno S, et al. Infective endocarditis in congenital heart disease: Japanese national collaboration study. Heart 2005;91:795–800.
5. Shah P, Singh WSA, Rose V, Keith JD. Incidence of bacterial endocarditis in ventricular septal defects. Circulation 1966;34:127–131.
6. Gersony WM, Hayes CJ, Driscoll DJ, et al. Bacterial endocarditis in patients with aortic stenosis, pulmonary stenosis and ventricular septal defect. Circulation 1993;87(I Suppl. 2):121–126.
7. Di Filippo S, Semiond B, Sassolas F, Bozio A. Influence and usefulness of antibioprophylaxis of infective endocarditis in children and adults with congenital heart disease. Eur Heart J 2001;22(Suppl.):79 (abstract).
8. Li W, Somerville J. Infective endocarditis in the grown-up congenital heart (GUCH) population. Eur Heart J 1998;19:166–173.
9. Gabriel HM, Heger M, Innerhofer P, et al. Long-term outcome of patients with ventricular septal defect considered not to require surgical closure during childhood. J Am Coll Cardiol 2002;39:1066–1071.
10. Morris CD, Reller MD, Menashe VD. Thirty-year incidence of infective endocarditis after surgery for congenital heart defect. JAMA 1998;279:599–603.
11. Feuchtner GM, Stolzmann P, Dichtl W, et al. Multislice computed tomography in infective endocarditis: comparison with transesophageal echocardiography and intraoperative findings. J Am Coll Cardiol 2009;53:436–444.
12. Durack DT, Lukes AS, Bright DK. The DUKE Endocarditis Service. New criteria for diagnosis of infective endocarditis: utilization of specific echocardiographic findings. Am J Med 1994;96:200–209.
13. Li JS, Sexton DJ, Mick N, et al. Proposed modifications to the Duke criteria for the diagnosis of infective endocarditis. Clin Infect Dis 2000;30:633–638.
14. Thilen U, Astrom-Olsson K. Does the risk of infective endarteritis justify routine patent ductus arteriosus closure? Eur Heart J 1997;18:503–506.
15. Bédard E, Shore DF, Gatzoulis MA. Adult congenital heart disease: a 2008 overview. Br Med Bull 2008;85:151–180.
16. Task Force on the Prevention, Diagnosis, and Treatment of Infective Endocarditis of the European Society of Cardiology; European Society of Clinical Microbiology and Infectious Diseases; International Society of Chemotherapy for Infection and Cancer. Guidelines on the prevention, diagnosis, and treatment of infective endocarditis (new version 2009): the Task Force on the Prevention, Diagnosis, and Treatment of Infective Endocarditis of the European Society of Cardiology (ESC). Eur Heart J 2009;30:2369–2413.

20

Transition of the Young Adult with Complex Congenital Heart Disease from Pediatric to Adult Care

MARK D. NORRIS | GARY D. WEBB

Progress in medical and surgical therapy for congenital heart disease (CHD) over the past several decades has greatly increased the number of adults surviving with congenital heart defects, so their number is now greater than the number of children with CHD. The number of adult patients with congenital heart defects continues to grow, and this trend will continue for years to come. Few of these patients or their families have been adequately equipped to understand their conditions and to manage their medical responsibilities in adulthood, and many have been lost to appropriate cardiac follow-up (Box 20-1).[1–3] Many of those who find their way back to cardiac care reappear with new and significant cardiac diagnoses, having missed the opportunities for preventive care, early diagnosis, and intervention.[4] The focus of this chapter is on practices and strategies that can be implemented in childhood and adolescence to improve the understanding and health behaviors of patients and their families so as to improve long-term retention in cardiac care and early recognition of cardiac symptomatology. These interventions can be anticipated to lead to improvements in health status, quality of life, and survival outcomes in patients with simple and complex CHD. Because initiating a comprehensive transition program may appear to be so demanding as to discourage one from approaching the problem at all, some simple, foundational approaches are outlined that individual caregivers and personnel at their care centers may utilize to engage these at-risk patients.

The *transition process* may be defined as an educational and experiential process that prepares patients to take responsibility for their own health care. The process needs to be repetitive and adapted to the patient's individual needs to meet the goal of helping these young people become autonomous patients. The transition process usually culminates with the young adult being transferred to an appropriate adult health care setting, one that is better suited to addressing his or her evolving adult needs. The core messages that young patients with complex congenital heart defects (Box 20-2) need to be taught include:

- They have the potential to live healthy and productive lives, but they are at risk for silent disease progression and have *not been cured.*
- They require lifelong cardiac surveillance.
- They must obtain appropriately skilled care at regular intervals.

The term *transfer of care* refers to an event or series of events through which adolescents and young adults with chronic health conditions move their care from a pediatric to an adult health care environment. For most, care should not be transferred in the absence of appropriate and accessible adult care. If competent adult care is available, transfer is likely to be beneficial to the patient. The pediatric care model focuses on growth and development and directs education toward the parents or guardians. The adult care model can be seen as more of a partnership between the patient and health care professional, with education directed toward the patient while encouraging responsibility and self-reliance.[5]

Health care transition for young people with chronic medical conditions has long been recommended.[6–8] Major American organizations have published a consensus statement on health care transition for young adults with special health care needs.[9,10] In the United Kingdom,

similar guidelines regarding the health care of adolescents have been published.[11] Expert adult CHD task forces in the United States,[12–17] Canada,[18–20] and Europe[21] have recommended patient-appropriate education and structured preparation leading to the transfer of care of young patients with CHD. Despite these efforts, most adolescent patients still do not have the opportunity to participate in such a process. Poor preparation may result in loss to follow-up during or after pediatric care or after an awkward first visit in the adult realm.

Properly equipped health care providers can help these young people navigate the transition and transfer processes, becoming effective and autonomous patients. Therefore, in the following discussion we will:

- Review important aspects of transition
- Outline the key elements of a transition program
- Review the curriculum content appropriate for the young adult with a congenital heart defect
- Discuss the importance of a policy on the timing of transfer from pediatric care
- Outline briefly the types of ongoing care that will need to be available
- Review the steps to an orderly transfer process

Important Aspects of the Transition Process

The transition process has several goals. The main one is to help ensure uninterrupted health care that is patient centered, age and developmentally appropriate, flexible, and comprehensive. Young people are coached to make a smooth transfer from pediatric to adult health care without becoming lost to follow-up. The process involves educating young people about their medical conditions and promoting skills in communication, decision-making, and self-care.

Transition models can be classified as "generic" and "disease based." The generic transition model involves having adolescent health care services operate generic transition programs designed to address general adolescent and transition issues, while relying on subspecialty programs to educate the patient about specific medical issues. In contrast, the disease-based model carries out the transition process within a program that specializes in the medical needs of a patient with a particular diagnosis.

Each practice or institution needs to decide who will be responsible for what elements of the transition process and who will coordinate the overall care plan. Time and space need to be allotted to the transition team for proper implementation of the new processes. In some settings, financial considerations will impact the planning.

Key Elements of an Ideal Transition Program

The transition process is founded on patient and parent preparation and education using a planned curriculum. This progression requires the recognition of the obstacles to transition and transfer that must be addressed, and it depends on the identification of appropriate adult provider services, on a coordinated transfer process with communication between providers, and on a policy regarding the timing of transfer.

Preparation for successful transition should begin early and continue throughout childhood, with the focus shifting from the parent to the child/young person. A major barrier to successful transition for many patients and families is the belief that heart surgery has cured the patient (Case 20-1).[4] Patients with complex CHD and their families must understand that, although in many cases patients will have a normal or near-normal life span, they do not have a normal heart and will require lifelong follow-up. They must also understand that their heart condition is fundamentally different from that of most adult heart patients and that relatively few providers have been trained to knowledgeably monitor their heart condition.

Case 20-1

A 42-year-old father of two children contacted an adult CHD clinic to request an evaluation after prompting from his spouse who works in health care. He had undergone tetralogy of Fallot repair with transannular right ventricular outflow tract patch technique and patch ventricular septal defect closure as a child and understood that he was "fixed." He has remained asymptomatic and has been consistently employed as an electrician, requiring limited physical exertion. Exercise intolerance was denied, but his lifestyle was sedentary. Initial evaluation was consistent with right ventricular dilation, and cardiac MRI confirmed severe pulmonary regurgitation plus substantial right atrial and right ventricular enlargement with diffuse, severe right ventricular dysfunction. After pulmonary valve replacement, his right ventricular size and function improved but did not normalize.

This patient believed he had been cured and had not been taught to remain in lifelong annual surveillance by a CHD expert.

Congenital Heart Disease Curriculum

The transition curriculum should enable young people to understand their diagnosis and medical history. With increasing level of detail with increasing age, they should know how the heart they were born with

differs from the normal and what interventions were undertaken to improve their heart. Having learned that they have not been cured, they need to understand their current residual cardiovascular issues in addition to the potential hemodynamic and arrhythmia complications that they may experience in the future. They should know if medical, surgical, or catheter-based therapies may be considered in the future. Approaching adulthood, these patients need to learn how to navigate the adult health care system: how to find an adult CHD clinic or caregiver; how often they need to be followed up; how to access routine health care; how to access emergency health care; and how to navigate the insurance process (relevant primarily in the United States).

The complete transition curriculum can be quite extensive (Box 20-3), and only one third of surveyed European and United States pediatric cardiology programs reported having a formal transition program.[22] Completion of it would occur over multiple clinic visits with adaptation to individual patients needs. For example, it may be more lengthy and involved for a young person who has learning disabilities, complex cardiac disease, significant physical limitations, and inadequate support systems.

The transition curriculum content can by conveyed using different strategies, with information repeated and presented by different team members, to improve retention and patient buy-in. The information can be conveyed during clinic visits by the pediatric cardiologist or by knowledgeable members of the nursing staff. Additional team members

or oncologist. Some will need cardiac surgery, and some will need diagnostic or therapeutic heart catheterizations. A collection of specialists does not substitute for the care and coordination provided by a "medical home" and a primary care provider. Effective communication between specialists and primary care providers is very important. In addition to the treating physician, additional support personnel including financial aid counselors, social workers, nutritionists, home care providers, and others may favorably impact the health and quality of life for these patients.

Steps to an Orderly Transfer Process

A coordinated transfer process is often the final step in a successful transition process. The last pediatric visit should not be a surprise to the patient or the family. A carefully prepared health summary document is a key element in the successful transfer of care. In addition to the receiving cardiac provider and the primary care provider, the patient should also receive a copy of the summary and understand it. If the patient is under the care of pediatric specialty providers, they should communicate directly with their respective counterparts in the adult health care system. Patients should know to expect a different type of experience in the adult care setting, with the provider focus shifting from the parent to the patient and the style being experienced as more business-like. Transfer provides an opportunity for the patients to see themselves as young adults. The pediatric providers should also reassure the patients that the new adult providers are capable and can be trusted. Some patients describe their attachment to their pediatric cardiology team as a barrier to establishing adult-based care, and the provider is well served by bearing this in mind and even addressing it directly. An independent visit between the cardiac provider and patient in the absence of the parents may facilitate open discussion in preparation for transfer. Direct contact by a pediatric cardiac care team member with the expected adult provider and with the patient after the first scheduled adult visit may prevent loss to follow-up.

How to Design a Transition Process

In our experience, the complexities of the transition process just described may be seen as so daunting that nothing is done to prepare the young patient. It is better that at least some steps be taken and that elements of the transition curriculum become a routine part of the pediatric and adolescent health care experience, rather than simply to be ignored as an unachievable comprehensive process. To begin the transition habit, we recommend starting small and aiming to improve. For a disease-based model, some basic information should be assembled for the patient and conveyed both clearly and repeatedly. Such a minimalist message might resemble the following:

You have had a tetralogy repair involving your heart wall and a valve. As a result, you have a leaky pulmonary valve. You will need to be followed each year by a cardiologist who knows about congenital heart defects. In order to stay healthy, you should see such a person once a year for the rest of your life. Your heart doctor may detect serious heart issues before you can notice any change. If you have any heart problems, you should contact this person. You should become knowledgeable about your health history. You should have a copy of your own health information. You should make sure that you always have good quality health insurance, and know how to get it. You are at risk of infective endocarditis and should be sure your teeth and gums are always healthy to reduce this risk.

This type of information can usually be presented by the pediatric cardiologist as part of a routine visit.

To broaden the agenda beyond the minimalist approach above, the caregiver will need to speak with the patient privately. Indeed, this is standard practice in adolescent care. The acceptability of this practice may be promoted by making a public commitment to the adolescent, such as by posting a sign saying: "When patients become teenagers, it is our standard practice to ensure that they have a chance to speak with their cardiologist on their own."

A pediatric practice can also introduce the topics of transition (education) and transfer (graduation) by posting the following sign in patient waiting areas: "Our pediatric cardiac practice provides education to young patients and their families and prepares them to graduate to adult practice at a goal of age 18."

We have also found it useful to encourage patients to join CHD patient organizations such as the Adult Congenital Heart Association in the United States (www.achaheart.org).

It is the medical and surgical successes of the recent decades that now result in ever-increasing numbers of adults living with CHD. Illusions of single-procedure "fixes" and "cures" have quickly faded, and we must, in honesty, approach our patients as having persistent chronic medical conditions affecting many systems and many aspects of their lives. Although adults must ultimately be responsible for their own medical decisions, it is our responsibility as their providers to partner with them from childhood, to equip them for this transition, and to receive them into adult care so that their longevity and quality of life may be optimized.

REFERENCES

1. Knauth A, Verstappen A, Reiss J, Webb GD. Transition and transfer from pediatric to adult care of the young adult with complex congenital heart disease. Cardiol Clin 2006;24:619–629, vi.
2. Reid GJ, Webb GD, Barzel M, et al. Estimates of life expectancy by adolescents and young adults with congenital heart disease. J Am Coll Cardiol 2006;48:349–355.
3. Verstappen A, Pearson D, Kovacs AH. Adult congenital heart disease: the patient's perspective. Cardiol Clin 2006;24:515–529, v.
4. Yeung E, Kay J, Roosevelt GE, et al. Lapse of care as a predictor for morbidity in adults with congenital heart disease. Int J Cardiol 2008;125:62–65.
5. Bodenheimer T, Wagner EH, Grumbach K. Improving primary care for patients with chronic illness. JAMA 2002;288:1775–1779.
6. Schidlow DV, Fiel SB. Life beyond pediatrics: transition of chronically ill adolescents from pediatric to adult health care systems. Med Clin North Am 1990;74:1113–1120.
7. Blum RW, Garell D, Hodgman CH, et al. Transition from child-centered to adult health-care systems for adolescents with chronic conditions: a position paper of the Society for Adolescent Medicine. J Adolesc Health 1993;14:570–576.
8. Rosen DS. Transition from pediatric to adult-oriented health care for the adolescent with chronic illness or disability. Adolesc Med 1994;5:241–248.
9. A consensus statement on health care transitions for young adults with special health care needs. Pediatrics 2002;110:1304–1306.
10. Rosen DS, Blum RW, Britto M, et al. Transition to adult health care for adolescents and young adults with chronic conditions: position paper of the Society for Adolescent Medicine. J Adolesc Health 2003;33:309–311.
11. Grown-up congenital heart (GUCH) disease: current needs and provision of service for adolescents and adults with congenital heart disease in the UK. Heart 2002;88(Suppl. 1):i1–i14.

12. Warnes CA, Liberthson R, Danielson GK, et al. Task force 1: the changing profile of congenital heart disease in adult life. J Am Coll Cardiol 2001;37:1170–1175.
13. Foster E, Graham TP, Driscoll DJ, et al. Task force 2: special health care needs of adults with congenital heart disease. J Am Coll Cardiol 2001;37:1176–1183.
14. Child JS, Collins-Nakai RL, Alpert JS, et al. Task force 3: workforce description and educational requirements for the care of adults with congenital heart disease. J Am Coll Cardiol 2001;37:1183–1187.
15. Landzberg MJ, Murphy DJ, Davidson WR, et al. Task force 4: organization of delivery systems for adults with congenital heart disease. J Am Coll Cardiol 2001;37:1187–1193.
16. Skorton DJ, Garson A, Allen HD, et al. Task force 5: adults with congenital heart disease: access to care. J Am Coll Cardiol 2001;37:1193–1198.
17. Warnes CA, Williams RG, Bashore TM, et al. ACC/AHA 2008 guidelines for the management of adults with congenital heart disease: executive summary: a report of the American College of Cardiology/American Heart Association Task Force on Practice Guidelines (Writing Committee to Develop Guidelines for the Management of Adults With Congenital Heart Disease) Developed in Collaboration With the American Society of Echocardiography, Heart Rhythm Society, International Society for Adult Congenital Heart Disease, Society for Cardiovascular Angiography and Interventions, and Society of Thoracic Surgeons. J Am Coll Cardiol 2008;52:e1–121.
18. Therrien J, Dore A, Gersony W, et al. Canadian Cardiovascular Society Consensus Conference 2001 update: recommendations for the management of adults with congenital heart disease: I. Can J Cardiol 2001;17:940–959.
19. Therrien J, Gatzoulis M, Graham T, et al. Canadian Cardiovascular Society Consensus Conference 2001 update: recommendations

for the management of adults with congenital heart disease: II. Can J Cardiol 2001;17:1029–1050.
20. Therrien J, Warnes C, Daliento L, et al. Canadian Cardiovascular Society Consensus Conference 2001 update: recommendations for the management of adults with congenital heart disease: III. Can J Cardiol 2001;17:1135–1158.
21. Deanfield J, Thaulow E, Warnes C, et al. Management of grown up congenital heart disease. Eur Heart J 2003;24:1035–1084.
22. Hilderson D, Saidi AS, Van Deyk K, et al. Attitude toward and current practice of transfer and transition of adolescents with congenital heart disease in the United States of America and Europe. Pediatr Cardiol 2009;30:786–793.
23. Thorne S, MacGregor A, Nelson-Piercy C. Risks of contraception and pregnancy in heart disease. Heart 2006;92:1520–1525.
24. Thorne S, Nelson-Piercy C, MacGregor A, et al. Pregnancy and contraception in heart disease and pulmonary arterial hypertension. J Fam Plann Reprod Health Care 2006;32:75–81.
25. Siu SC, Colman JM, Sorensen S, et al. Adverse neonatal and cardiac outcomes are more common in pregnant women with cardiac disease. Circulation 2002;105:2179–2184.
26. Siu SC, Sermer M, Colman JM, et al. Prospective multicenter study of pregnancy outcomes in women with heart disease. Circulation 2001;104:515–521.
27. Reid GJ, Irvine MJ, McCrindle BW, et al. Prevalence and correlates of successful transfer from pediatric to adult health care among a cohort of young adults with complex congenital heart defects. Pediatrics 2004;113:e197–e205.
28. Viner R. Bridging the gaps: transition for young people with cancer. Eur J Cancer 2003;39:2684–2687.

Pregnancy and Contraception

HEIDI M. CONNOLLY | CAROLE A. WARNES

Introduction

Most women with congenital heart disease (CHD) reach childbearing age and are considering pregnancy. As a result, CHD is the predominant form of heart disease encountered during pregnancy in developed countries.[1] Heart disease does not preclude successful pregnancy but increases the risk to both mother and infant and requires special management.

Hemodynamic Changes During Pregnancy, Labor and Delivery, and Postpartum

Substantial hemodynamic changes occur during normal pregnancy. There is a 20% to 30% increase in red blood cell mass and a 30% to 50% increase in plasma volume. These changes result in an increase in total blood volume, with a relative anemia (Fig. 21-1).[2] Heart rate increases by about 10 beats per minute during pregnancy. There is also a reduction in systemic and pulmonary vascular resistance as well as blood pressure during pregnancy. These hemodynamic changes result in a steady increase in cardiac output during pregnancy until the 32nd week of gestation, at which time cardiac output reaches a plateau at 30% to 50% above the pre-pregnancy level. Oxygen consumption increases steadily throughout pregnancy to approximately 30% above the pre-pregnant level by the time of delivery. This increase is due to the metabolic needs of both mother and fetus. During the last half of pregnancy, cardiac output is significantly affected by body position. The enlarging uterus decreases venous return from the lower extremities. The left lateral position minimizes this reduction in venous return. Normally, the hemodynamic changes that occur during pregnancy are well tolerated by the mother. Heart disease may be manifested initially during pregnancy because of increased cardiac output or because minor preexisting symptoms may be exacerbated.

With uterine contractions, an additional 300 to 500 mL of blood enters the circulation. This increase in blood volume in conjunction with increased blood pressure and heart rate during labor increases cardiac output. At the time of delivery, cardiac output increases as much as 80% above the pre-pregnancy level (and may be as great as 9 L/min), owing to the increase in stroke volume and heart rate.

Administration of epidural anesthesia decreases cardiac output to about 8 L/min, and the use of general anesthesia decreases cardiac output further. Approximately 500 mL blood is lost at the time of vaginal delivery, and approximately 1000 mL is lost during a normal cesarean section.

After delivery, venous return increases because of relief from fetal compression on the inferior vena cava. Spontaneous diuresis occurs during the first 24 to 48 hours after delivery; however, it takes 2 to 4 weeks for hemodynamic values to return to baseline after vaginal delivery and longer after cesarean delivery.

Cardiac Examination During Pregnancy

During normal pregnancy, the cardiac examination results may mimic heart disease. There is a brisk and full carotid upstroke, and jugular venous pressure is normal or mildly increased, with prominent a and v waves. The left ventricular impulse is displaced laterally and enlarged. The first heart sound is loud. The pulmonic second sound may be prominent, and there often is persistent splitting of the second heart sound. A third heart sound is audible in more than 80% of normal pregnant women (Fig. 21-2). An early peaking ejection systolic murmur is audible in 90% of normal pregnant women and is caused by a pulmonary outflow murmur. Benign venous hums and mammary continuous murmurs are also common.

Pregnancy Counseling for Patients with Cardiac Disease

Antepartum management of women with heart disease should include an anatomic and hemodynamic assessment of any cardiac abnormality to determine the maternal and fetal risks of pregnancy. Specific cardiovascular conditions pose an unacceptable risk of death to both mother and infant, and in these situations pregnancy should be avoided (Table 21-1).

Pre-pregnancy counseling should include a discussion about the risk of CHD in the infant. The incidence of CHD in the general population is about 1%. Generally, the offspring of women with CHD have a 5% to 6% incidence of CHD.[3] Often the cardiac lesion in the infant is not the same as that in the mother, except for syndromes in which the incidence of recurrence with each pregnancy may be up to 50% (e.g., Marfan syndrome).

Prognosis of Heart Disease in Pregnancy

Maternal prognosis during pregnancy is related to New York Heart Association (NYHA) functional class; the maternal mortality rate for women in NYHA class I or II is less than 1%. However, with NYHA class III or IV symptoms, the maternal mortality rate increases to about 7%. Fetal mortality is also strongly related to maternal functional class; the expected fetal mortality rate is 30% for women in NYHA class IV.

Cardiac Contraindications to Pregnancy

Because of the hemodynamic changes that occur during pregnancy, fixed obstructive cardiac lesions or those associated with pulmonary hypertension generally are poorly tolerated because of the inability to increase cardiac output. In contrast, regurgitant lesions are relatively well tolerated because of the decrease in systemic vascular resistance.

There are certain cardiac conditions in which pregnancy should be avoided and, if pregnancy occurs, termination should be considered (see Table 21-1). These include severe pulmonary hypertension (pulmonary artery pressure ≥ three-fourths systemic pressure), Eisenmenger syndrome,[4] and NYHA class III or IV congestive heart failure due to systemic ventricular dysfunction. Marfan syndrome with an aortic root of 40 mm or more is a contraindication to pregnancy because of the unpredictable risk of aortic dissection and rupture. Severe cyanosis is a relative contraindication to pregnancy, primarily because of adverse fetal outcome. Patients with severe obstructive valve disease should ideally have intervention before proceeding with pregnancy.[5]

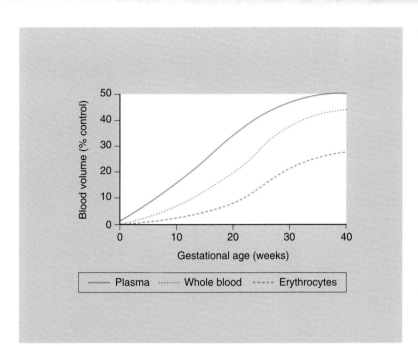

Figure 21-1   Hematologic changes during normal pregnancy.

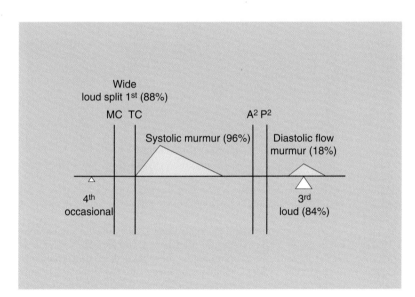

Figure 21-2   Normal auscultatory findings during pregnancy. MC, mitral closure; TC, tricuspid closure.

TABLE 21-1	Contraindications to Pregnancy	
Maternal Lesion	*Death Rate*	
Severe pulmonary hypertension	50%	
Severe obstructive lesions (aortic stenosis, mitral stenosis, pulmonary stenosis, hypertrophic obstructive cardiomyopathy)	17%	
Systemic ventricular dysfunction, class III or IV congestive heart failure	7%	
Marfan syndrome, aortic root > 40 mm		

Management of the Pregnant Patient with Cardiac Disease

The management of pregnant women with cardiovascular disease depends on the NYHA class and underlying cardiac condition. Pregnant patients in NYHA class I or II should limit strenuous exercise, obtain adequate rest, maintain a low-salt diet, avoid anemia (keep hemoglobin concentration above 11 g/dL), have regular prenatal examinations (both obstetric and cardiovascular), and be monitored for arrhythmia. In severely symptomatic women (NYHA class III or IV), pregnancy should be avoided. When pregnancy is established, the option of terminating the pregnancy should be discussed with the patient. If the patient chooses to continue her pregnancy, bed rest is often required during part of the pregnancy and close cardiac and obstetric monitoring is mandatory.

Factors that indicate that a pregnancy may be of high risk include the following:
- Prosthetic valves
- Obstructive cardiac lesions,[6] including unrepaired coarctation of the aorta[7]
- Marfan syndrome
- Cyanotic CHD[8]
- Pulmonary hypertension[9]
- Systemic ventricular dysfunction (ejection fraction ≤ 40%)[10,11]
- Significant unrepaired CHD

During pregnancy, fetal growth and development are monitored with ultrasonography. Fetal cardiac ultrasonography is recommended in women with CHD to identify a congenital cardiac lesion before delivery.

The time and route of delivery should be planned before spontaneous labor to facilitate the delivery and to intervene as appropriate. Elective induction of labor is often preferable in high-risk patients. The optimal anesthesia and analgesia as well as administration of prophylactic treatment for endocarditis should be considered before pregnancy. Cardiac rhythm and, rarely, hemodynamic monitoring should be considered for patients with impaired functional capacity, cardiac dysfunction, pulmonary hypertension, and cyanotic malformations. During delivery, blood and volume loss should be treated promptly. With few exceptions, vaginal delivery, if necessary, with a facilitated second stage (forceps delivery or vacuum extraction), is preferred for women with CHD. Cesarean delivery is indicated primarily for obstetric reasons and when delivery is required in an anticoagulated patient on warfarin (Box 21-1). In addition, cesarean delivery should be considered for patients with fixed cardiac obstructive lesions, pulmonary hypertension, and unstable aortic lesions.

Maternal postpartum care should include early ambulation, attention to neonatal concerns, and consideration of contraception if appropriate.

CARDIOVASCULAR EVALUATION DURING PREGNANCY

A comprehensive history and physical examination is the cornerstone of evaluation of the pregnant patient with CHD. Diagnostic testing may be required, but individual tests should be chosen carefully with consideration of the risk to mother and infant. When evaluating women with cardiovascular disease, the safety of the mother is always the highest priority. Individuals who have knowledge of the hemodynamic changes that occur during pregnancy, and how these changes may affect cardiovascular test results, should interpret studies performed during pregnancy.

Chest radiography and other radiologic procedures requiring radiation are generally avoided during pregnancy. The radiation risk to the fetus is greatest during the first half of pregnancy. Radiation exposure increases the risk of abnormal fetal organogenesis or a subsequent malignancy. If a radiologic procedure is required, it should be delayed as late in the pregnancy as possible, the radiation dose should be kept to a minimum, and shielding of the fetus should be optimal.

Echocardiography is a valuable tool in the assessment of the pregnant patient with suspected structural cardiovascular disease and can be performed safely during pregnancy. Four-chamber dilation is a normal maternal finding during pregnancy and is related to the increase in blood volume and cardiac output. The left ventricular function remains in the normal range. Physiologic tricuspid and pulmonary valve regurgitation is expected, and transient trivial mitral regurgitation may also occur. Transesophageal echocardiography may be performed safely during pregnancy. Sedation may be used with low-dose benzodiazepines such as midazolam and short-acting narcotic analgesic agents such as fentanyl.

Magnetic resonance imaging (MRI) has been used during pregnancy for the assessment of congenital cardiac and aortic disorders (Fig. 21-3). The safety of MRI during pregnancy has not been fully established and should therefore be used only when necessary. The administration of gadolinium has not been demonstrated to cause any serious problems during pregnancy but is not routinely done. Computed tomography results in fetal exposure to high amounts of radiation so is not recommended, especially during early pregnancy.

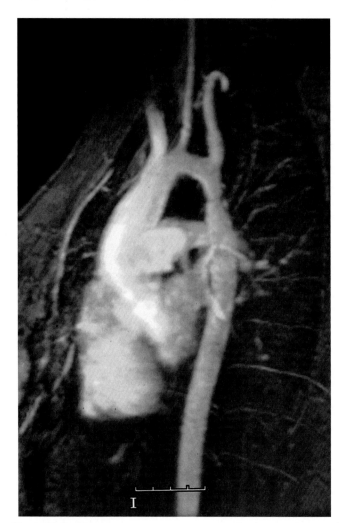

Figure 21-3 MR image in a pregnant patient with a history of repaired coarctation. Recurrent coarctation is demonstrated.

Cardiac catheterization involving fluoroscopy and cine-angiography is associated with a high dose of radiation and should be used only when relevant information cannot be obtained by other methods. Occasionally, patients with serious cardiovascular disorders require cardiac catheterization to secure a diagnosis or intervene with regard to an abnormality. The maternal abdomen should be shielded in an attempt to minimize the degree of fetal radiation. The brachial approach may minimize radiation to the pelvic and abdominal areas and should be used when feasible.

ENDOCARDITIS PROPHYLAXIS

The American Heart Association does not recommend endocarditis prophylaxis for patients expected to have an uncomplicated cesarean section or vaginal delivery. Many institutions are more conservative. We recommend consideration of endocarditis prophylaxis in high-risk cardiac patients (those with prosthetic valves and those with cyanotic heart disease) because of the risk of undiagnosed infections and the significant patient morbidity and mortality should infective endocarditis occur. Antibiotic therapy should be administered 30 to 60 minutes before delivery is expected and repeated 8 hours later.

PERCUTANEOUS PROCEDURES DURING PREGNANCY

Percutaneous balloon valvuloplasty has been reported to be a safe and effective palliative procedure during pregnancy (Fig. 21-4).[12] Percutaneous balloon valvuloplasty during pregnancy should be

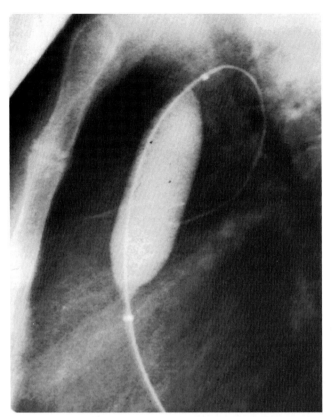

Figure 21-4 Percutaneous pulmonary balloon valvuloplasty performed in a patient with critical pulmonary valve stenosis presenting early in pregnancy. The abdomen and uterus were protected with a lead shield.

attempted only in centers that have extensive experience and surgical backup and is an alternative to surgery in patients with severe symptomatic native aortic or pulmonary stenosis identified during pregnancy.[6] Special considerations for balloon valvuloplasty in the gravid state include radiation exposure and pregnancy outcome. There has been no increase in the incidence of reported congenital malformations or abortions with fetal radiation exposure of less than 5 rads, which can be achieved by shielding the gravid uterus and keeping fluoroscopy time to a minimum. Transesophageal echocardiographic guidance has also been utilized during the procedure to reduce radiation exposure. Valvuloplasty during pregnancy may be complicated by maternal hypotension, which occurs during balloon inflation and may be associated with fetal bradycardia.

CARDIAC SURGERY DURING PREGNANCY

Cardiac surgery should be avoided during pregnancy whenever possible. Cardiopulmonary bypass can adversely affect both the mother and fetus. High-flow, high-pressure, normothermic perfusion appears safest from a fetal standpoint. Fetal heart rate monitoring is mandatory during cardiopulmonary bypass. Fetal bradycardia occurring during cardiopulmonary bypass is often responsive to an increase in flow rates. Even under optimal conditions there is a fetal death rate of approximately 15% associated with cardiac surgery during pregnancy. Therefore, cardiac surgery during pregnancy should be reserved for patients refractory to medical management in whom further delay would prove detrimental to maternal health. When cardiac surgery is necessary during pregnancy, the optimal time is between weeks 24 and 28 of gestation. During this period such surgery is most likely to allow the pregnancy to progress and least likely to cause fetal harm. When cardiac surgery is required during pregnancy it is important to have a short cardiopulmonary bypass time. Cesarean delivery while on cardiac bypass has been reported. This procedure should be

performed only in the setting of extreme risk to mother and fetus. A multidisciplinary team approach is required to optimize maternal and fetal outcomes.

CYANOTIC CONGENITAL HEART DISEASE

Women with complex cyanotic CHD face greater challenges and medical risks than those who have a normal oxygen saturation.[5,8,13–15] The presence of cyanosis means that there is a right-to-left shunt at some level in the circulation, at either the atrial, ventricular, or ductal level. The previously mentioned principles of evaluation for acyanotic patients also apply at the time of pre-pregnancy counseling, with several additional considerations that relate to both maternal and fetal risks.

MATERNAL RISKS

During pregnancy maternal blood becomes more hypercoagulable, and for the cyanotic patient the risk of red cell sludging and thrombus increases. This may manifest as a deep venous thrombosis, pulmonary infarction, or stroke. Deep venous thrombosis poses considerable potential problems because of the likelihood of paradoxical embolus and subsequent stroke. The higher the level of erythrocytosis and hemoglobin, the more likely thrombosis is to occur, although thrombotic complications (both pulmonary and cerebral) have occurred when the hemoglobin concentration is only slightly raised at 17 and 18 g/dL.[5] The role of anticoagulants in this setting is questionable. The erythrocytosis that accompanies cyanosis also carries with it inherent clotting abnormalities with frequent prolongation of the activated partial thromboplastin time (APTT), prothrombin time, reduced platelet count, and abnormal platelet function. This may be exacerbated by heparin or warfarin (Coumadin). More important, probably, is the use of compression stockings or thromboguards, particularly around the time of delivery, along with early ambulation afterward.

The fall in afterload that accompanies pregnancy may augment the right-to-left shunt and exaggerate the hypoxemia. This, in turn, causes symptomatic deterioration. Some patients with cyanosis may have some degree of pulmonary hypertension and pulmonary vascular disease. This increases the risk of pregnancy further and should be evaluated carefully, if necessary with cardiac catheterization before pregnancy. Patients with severe pulmonary hypertension should be counseled strongly against pregnancy because of prohibitive maternal risk (see section on Eisenmenger syndrome).

FETAL RISKS

The fetal risks include those associated with cyanosis itself and relate to the level of maternal hypoxia. With increasing maternal cyanosis, the handicap to fetal growth becomes more pronounced, and infants are likely to have a low birth weight and be premature. With increasing maternal hypoxia, spontaneous abortion is more likely in the first trimester. Presbitero and colleagues[5] retrospectively evaluated the outcomes of 96 pregnancies in 44 women with cyanotic CHD. There were 41 live births (43%), 15 were premature at 26 to 37 weeks' gestation, and only 26 were term deliveries (27% of all pregnancies). There were 49 spontaneous abortions at 6 weeks to 5 months, and six stillbirths at 26 to 38 weeks' gestation. Both maternal hemoglobin level and arterial oxygen saturation displayed a strong relation to the chance of a live birth (Table 21-2). This has also been demonstrated in earlier studies.

The basic maternal cardiac abnormality may also influence fetal outcome, although clearly these variables are highly related. Presbitero and colleagues[5] evaluated four groups of patients: group I had a single ventricle and/or tricuspid atresia; group II had tetralogy of Fallot or pulmonary atresia; group III had Ebstein anomaly and an atrial septal defect; and group IV had corrected transposition of the great arteries, a ventricular septal defect, and pulmonary stenosis. Although the groups were small, it appeared that a higher percentage of live births occurred in groups III and IV, at 86% and 60% respectively, whereas mothers in groups I and II had a 31% and 33% live birth rate, respectively.

After Presbitero P, Somerville J, Stone S et al. Pregnancy in cyanotic congenital heart disease: outcome of mother and fetus. Circulation 1994; 89:2673-2676, with permission of Lippincott Williams & Wilkins.

TABLE 21-2	Live Births and Fetal Outcome Related to Maternal Hemoglobin Level and Oxygen Saturation		
Maternal Factor	No. Pregnancies	No. Live Births	Liveborn (%)
Hemoglobin level (g/dL)			
≤16	28	20	71
17-19	40	18	45
≥20	26	2	8
Arterial oxygen saturation (%)			
≤85	17	2	12
85-89	22	10	45
≥90	13	12	92

EISENMENGER SYNDROME

For women with a right-to-left shunt and pulmonary vascular disease, pregnancy poses a high risk. The fall in peripheral resistance that occurs during pregnancy augments the right-to-left shunt and exaggerates the cyanosis. Any fall in blood pressure, a vasovagal faint, or episode of blood loss can result in sudden death. The maternal mortality rate approaches 50%. The largest series published retrospectively reviewed 44 women with 70 pregnancies, and 52% of women died in connection with a pregnancy.[9] Particularly hazardous were periods of hypovolemia, thromboembolic phenomena, and preeclampsia. Both vaginal delivery and cesarean section are associated with a high maternal death rate. In this series, cesarean section appeared to pose the highest risk but the numbers were small and it may be that the patients having cesarean section were the most hemodynamically tenuous.

More recently a smaller series from a single institution was published.[4] Thirteen pregnancies in 12 women who decided to continue their pregnancy despite medical advice to terminate were reviewed. There were three spontaneous abortions at less than 15 weeks of pregnancy and two stillbirths at 23 weeks' gestation. Eight infants (62%) were born alive, five were premature, and three were term deliveries. Clinical and obstetric examination was carried out every 15 days after the first trimester. Seven patients reached the end of the second trimester. Bed rest, oxygen therapy, and heparin were administered to prolong the APTT to 1.5 times normal. Three (23%) maternal deaths occurred, one at 23 weeks' gestation, one (who had refused hospitalization) in week 27, and the third death on the 30th day of the puerperium. Death in these patients usually occurs because of pulmonary infarction or progressive deterioration of the hemodynamics with a fall in peripheral resistance and worsening cyanosis despite all pharmacologic interventions. Thus the maternal mortality rate remains prohibitively high, and patients should be strongly counseled not to get pregnant. Termination of pregnancy, preferably with cardiac anesthesia, is the better choice.

If patients decide to proceed with pregnancy against advice, the following recommendations may be helpful:

- Coordinated care should be provided with a cardiologist familiar with CHD and high-risk pregnancy along with an obstetrician specializing in high-risk pregnancy.
- Activity should be minimized to reduce cardiac demands and bed rest should be implemented after the second trimester.
- Oxygen therapy may be administered for dyspnea if it appears helpful, although there is no evidence to demonstrate that it improves either maternal or fetal outcome.
- The use of anticoagulants is controversial. Based on the study of Avila and associates,[4] low-dose heparin may be helpful, although there are concerns about the bleeding diathesis that accompanies cyanosis. It may be helpful around the time of delivery, however.
- An early delivery when the fetus is mature should be anticipated. Cesarean section may be the preferable delivery route with cardiac anesthesia and maintenance of blood pressure. Intra-arterial monitoring should be used to monitor both pressure and oxygen saturation so that changes in hemodynamics can be dealt with promptly.

- Ambulation should remain cautious and cardiac monitoring continued for at least 2 weeks after delivery because of the risk of sudden death. Meticulous attention should be paid to the veins of the legs, with compression stockings or compression devices used to minimize the threat of deep venous thrombosis.

MANAGEMENT OF ARRHYTHMIAS DURING PREGNANCY

Cardiac arrhythmias during pregnancy should be investigated similarly to those in nonpregnant patients and the underlying precipitating causes treated. It is preferable to avoid antiarrhythmic drugs during pregnancy, but they may be essential for recurrent arrhythmias or for maternal safety.[16]

Nonmedical treatment of cardiac arrhythmias is occasionally required during pregnancy. Patients who present with hemodynamic compromise related to an arrhythmia should be treated with direct-current cardioversion. Elective and emergent cardioversion has been performed safely for dysrhythmias in all three stages of pregnancy. Energies of up to 300 W/s have been used without affecting the fetus or inducing premature labor, but the fetal heart should be monitored during cardioversion.

Supraventricular Tachycardia

Supraventricular tachycardia may be treated with atrioventricular node blocking agents during pregnancy. This can be achieved with digoxin, β-adrenergic blockers, and calcium channel blockers. Adenosine has also been used successfully to treat acute symptoms related to supraventricular tachycardia during pregnancy. To date, no serious adverse fetal or maternal effects related to adenosine have been reported.

Digoxin is considered to be safe for use during pregnancy. Digoxin crosses the placenta and fetal serum levels approximate to those in the mother. The same digoxin dose will yield lower maternal serum levels during pregnancy than in the nonpregnant state, and the dose may need to be increased. Quinidine is an alternative antiarrhythmic medication, but its use results in gastrointestinal intolerance. Adverse fetal effects have not been reported when quinidine is given at a therapeutic dose. Limited information is available on the use of procainamide and disopyramide during pregnancy, but, to date, no adverse fetal effects have been reported.

Calcium channel blockers have been used to treat hypertension and arrhythmias without adverse effects on the fetus or newborn infant. Relaxation of the uterus can occur with these medications. Verapamil has been used in pregnancy for the management of supraventricular arrhythmias. No adverse effects have been reported. It is recommended that calcium channel blocker therapy be discontinued at the onset of labor to prevent dysfunctional labor or postpartum hemorrhage.

All available β-adrenergic blocking agents cross the placenta, are present in human breast milk, and can reach significant levels in the fetus or the newborn. These agents have been reported to decrease uterine blood flow, initiate premature labor, and result in a small and infarcted placenta with the potential for low-birth-weight infants. Large studies have not confirmed these concerns, and β-adrenergic blocking drugs have been used in a large number of pregnant women without serious adverse effects. They also may be used for the treatment of arrhythmias, hypertrophic cardiomyopathy, hypertension, and hyperthyroidism during pregnancy if clinically indicated. If these agents are used during pregnancy, it is appropriate to monitor fetal heart rates as well as the neonatal heart rate, blood glucose, and respiratory status immediately after delivery. Labetalol with its mixed α- and β-adrenergic blocking effects has been used for the treatment of hypertension without clear detrimental effects during pregnancy.

Ventricular Tachycardia

Ventricular tachycardia may require intravenous drug therapy. Lidocaine is a reasonable first-line therapy. Transient neonatal depression may occur if the neonatal blood level of lidocaine rises excessively, and therefore the dose should be monitored closely during pregnancy.

Fetal levels are 60% of maternal levels. Intravenous procainamide and quinidine may be used during pregnancy but may cause hypotension.

If oral antiarrhythmic therapy is necessary for the management of ventricular tachycardia during pregnancy, it may be appropriate to begin with quinidine because this drug has been used most frequently, without clear adverse fetal affects. There is some information about procainamide, disopyramide, flecainide, and sotalol use during pregnancy, but it is insufficient to recommend routine use unless essential for the mother. Amiodarone used during pregnancy may cause fetal loss or deformity and may result in fetal hypothyroidism.

ANTICOAGULATION DURING PREGNANCY

The management of patients with prosthetic valves or other conditions that require anticoagulation during pregnancy poses a therapeutic dilemma with risks to both mother and fetus.[17] Pre-pregnancy counseling should be done to discuss the risk and benefits to mother and fetus. Data regarding the safety of various anticoagulation regimens are limited, and controversy regarding the best treatment option persists.

Pregnancy results in a hypercoagulable state. This is in part related to an increase in clotting factor concentration and platelet adhesiveness and a reduction in the degree of fibrinolysis and protein S activity. Overall, these coagulation changes result in an increased risk of thrombosis and embolism during pregnancy.

Serious concerns arise regarding the safety of anticoagulation during pregnancy. Concerns include the fact that heparin may not prevent mechanical valve thrombosis and that warfarin can cause embryopathy.

Warfarin
Warfarin crosses the placenta and results in fetal anticoagulation. The effect of warfarin on the fetus is greater than that on the mother, owing to reduced vitamin K–dependent factors present in the fetal liver. Fetal anticoagulation results in an increased risk of spontaneous abortion as well as prematurity, fetal deformity, and stillbirth. Retroplacental hemorrhage and fetal intracranial hemorrhage result in additional risk to the fetus.

Historic reports describe a 30% risk of embryopathy with the administration of warfarin during the first trimester. More recent data suggest the incidence of warfarin embryopathy to be between 4% and 10%[18,19] and apparently related to the maternal dose of warfarin during the first trimester. The risk of warfarin embryopathy appears to be very low with a warfarin dose of less than 5 mg/day.[20] The risk is highest if exposure occurs during weeks 6 to 12 of gestation. Warfarin embryopathy results in bone and cartilaginous abnormalities with chondrodysplasia, nasal hypoplasia, optic atrophy, blindness, intellectual impairment, and seizures. Warfarin does not enter breast milk and, thus, can be administered safely to women who breast-feed their infants.

Heparin
Heparin does not cross the placenta. Its longer-term use subcutaneously may be complicated by sterile abscesses, osteoporosis, alopecia, thrombocytopenia, and bleeding. The greatest concern with heparin is the 12% to 24% incidence of thromboembolic complications, including fatal valve thrombosis, in high-risk pregnant women managed with subcutaneous heparin. Unfortunately, the efficacy of adjusted-dose subcutaneous heparin has not been established. The heparin dose should be adjusted with an APTT two to three times the control level 6 hours after the dose is administered.

Anticoagulation During the First Trimester of Pregnancy
The American Heart Association, American College of Cardiology, and the American College of Chest Physicians have published guidelines regarding anticoagulation during pregnancy.[21–23] They acknowledge that there are insufficient grounds to make definitive recommendations because properly designed studies have not been performed. Patients who elect to discontinue warfarin should receive either continuous intravenous unfractionated heparin with an APTT of at least twice control or dose-adjusted low-molecular-weight heparin administered subcutaneously twice daily to maintain the anti–factor Xa level

between 0.7 and 1.2 U/mL 4 hours after administration. Informed consent should be obtained if warfarin is used during the first trimester of pregnancy.

Anticoagulation During the Second Trimester of Pregnancy
Warfarin is usually utilized during the second trimester of pregnancy after fetal development is accomplished. The dose should be adjusted to a therapeutic international normalized ratio. Use of aspirin is also reasonable at a dose of 75 to 100 mg/day. If unfractionated heparin is continued, the maternal risks of valve thrombosis and thromboembolism are higher.

Anticoagulation During the Third Trimester of Pregnancy
During the third trimester of pregnancy, warfarin should be continued until 36 weeks of pregnancy. In anticipation of delivery, patients should be hospitalized and intravenous heparin should be started. The APTT should be at least twice the control value.

The peripartum period is a particularly high-risk time for the patient who requires anticoagulation during pregnancy. Delivery should be planned, and intravenous heparin should be stopped peripartum and resumed 4 to 6 hours after delivery. Cesarean delivery should be performed if labor occurs during warfarin anticoagulation, because of the risk of fetal intracranial hemorrhage. Heparin should be resumed 4 to 6 hours after delivery in the absence of bleeding.

Additional Anticoagulation Treatment Options in Pregnancy
There is interest and enthusiasm about the use of low-molecular-weight heparin as a form of anticoagulation during pregnancy, and reports of its use are becoming more frequent. There are little data, however, to guide its use during pregnancy. It does not cross the placenta, causes less heparin-induced thrombocytopenia, and has a longer plasma half-life and a more predictable response than unfractionated heparin.[24] Nonetheless, treatment failures have been reported and U.S. Food and Drug Administration (FDA) labeling in 2004 indicated that its use in pregnant women with mechanical prosthetic heart valves had not been studied adequately. If it is utilized it must be recognized that as pregnancy advances the volume distribution for low-molecular-weight heparin changes and meticulous monitoring to maintain optimum anti–factor Xa levels must be undertaken.

Dipyridamole should not be used during pregnancy. There are no data available on the effects of ticlopidine during pregnancy. There is limited information regarding the use of glycoprotein IIB/IIIA inhibitor use during pregnancy.

Thrombolytic therapy has been used in pregnancy. Several cases of emergency use during pregnancy have been reported. Thrombolytic therapy should be considered in the critically ill patient with valve thrombosis or acute coronary syndrome who is not a candidate for cardiac surgery or percutaneous intervention.

In summary, anticoagulation during pregnancy should be avoided if possible. One must weigh the risks and benefits to both mother and fetus and help the patient make an informed decision. Individual assessment and pre-pregnancy planning is mandatory.

CONTRACEPTION

For women with CHD who reach childbearing age, pregnancy must be carefully considered, the risks evaluated, and the timing planned. This is particularly important because it may relate to the prognosis of the woman's condition, the durability of bioprosthetic heart valves, and the need for cardiac operation. Planning involves a detailed discussion with the patient and partner regarding the prognosis. Contraceptive advice should be provided by a physician familiar with the nature of the woman's CHD, the potential benefits, risks, and failures of the contraceptive methods, and an awareness of the desires and potential compliance of the patient. This counseling should be provided early—before the patient presents with an unplanned pregnancy. For patients contemplating sterilization, accurate information must be provided regarding the procedure and any potential risks.

Barrier Methods

The condom and/or diaphragm combined with spermicidal jelly provide safe methods of contraception for the cardiac patient. The condom has the added advantage of preventing the passage of sexually transmitted diseases. Failure rates reportedly are 3 to 5 per 100 woman-years and occur mostly because the method is not used properly or not used during every intercourse.

Hormone Contraceptives
Oral

The "pill" comprises varying doses of estrogen and progestogen, usually ethinylestradiol (20 to 35 μg) combined with progestogen, usually norethindrone. It is recommended that the lowest effective dose of estrogen be used in patients with cardiac disease. When using a 20-μg preparation, the risk of pregnancy increases slightly, particularly if a dose is missed; 30 μg is the dose most commonly prescribed. Nonetheless, oral contraceptives provide the most convenient and reliable method of contraception, provided no doses are missed. The failure rate is approximately 2 per 100 woman-years, and some failures probably relate to missed pills or poor gastrointestinal absorption secondary to diarrhea or interactions with other medications such as antibiotics. The benefits of this reliable method of contraception must be balanced against the risks, which include systemic hypertension, venous thrombosis, myocardial infarction, and pulmonary infarction. This contraceptive method should not be used in any patient with any history of thrombotic complications, pulmonary hypertension, or cyanotic heart disease.

Progestogen-only oral contraceptives (the "mini pill") offer an alternative but are less reliable than the combined pill because they work not by suppressing ovulation but by an effect on the cervical mucus. The mini pill must be taken at the same time every day. If a dose is missed, the effectiveness diminishes considerably. Problems with midcycle bleeding and amenorrhea are common. Few data are available with regard to the safety of progestogen preparations in the setting of cyanosis and pulmonary hypertension, but they probably have less thrombogenic potential, although thromboembolism has been reported with their use and caution should be exercised.

Other Methods

Injectable depot medroxyprogesterone is effective for 3 months and offers an alternative for women in whom compliance is a problem. Its use may be associated with irregular bleeding. Some fluid retention is often associated with its use, so it should be avoided in the setting of significant ventricular dysfunction.

Subcutaneous implants that slowly release progesterone (Implanon) are also available and last for up to 3 years. The fluid retention associated with their use may be less than with injectable preparations. Implantation and removal must be performed with sterile technique.

Intrauterine Devices

These devices are seldom used in cardiac patients and should not be used in any patient with tenuous hemodynamics who cannot tolerate the vagal response that may accompany insertion (e.g., those with pulmonary hypertension such as in Eisenmenger syndrome). Menorrhagia and pelvic inflammatory disease occur about twice as often as in the normal population. The Mirena device releases low-dose progesterone into the uterus and has less risk of infection.

Tubal Ligation

The decision to proceed with a tubal ligation, especially in a patient younger than 30 years old, should be made only after an informed discussion of all the implications. Ligation is performed either laparoscopically or with a laparotomy, usually with general anesthesia. For patients with Eisenmenger syndrome this operation poses a significant risk and should be performed by an experienced surgeon with full monitoring and preferably with cardiac anesthesia. With the laparoscopic approach the abdomen is distended with carbon dioxide, and this may have a deleterious effect on respiration and hemodynamics, so we recommend that, even for this apparently minor surgical procedure, in patients with complex CHD (e.g., postoperative Fontan connection, Eisenmenger syndrome) the operation should be performed in tertiary care centers where expertise in CHD is available.

The Essure is a newer method of sterilization in which stents are inserted hysteroscopically into the fallopian tubes without the need of general anesthesia.[25]

Vasectomy

Vasectomy may be offered as an alternative to tubal ligation, although a careful discussion needs to be undertaken before a final decision is made. A detailed and tactful discussion should occur if the prognosis for the female patient is guarded, and the male partner should not be pressured to undertake this procedure. If the female patient has a limited life span, potentially the male partner may wish to remarry and father children in the future. It may be preferable in this situation for the physician to have the opportunity for discussion with the male partner alone.

CONCLUSION

More women with CHD are considering pregnancy. Despite potential difficulties and complications associated with CHD in pregnancy, careful cardiac and obstetric management in a tertiary referral center results in good maternal and fetal outcomes in the majority of cases.[15] A multidisciplinary approach at a tertiary care center is mandatory for the high-risk pregnant patient with CHD; and for the woman in whom pregnancy is not advisable, appropriate contraceptive advice must be given.

REFERENCES

1. Pitkin R, Peroff J, Koos B, Beall M. Pregnancy and congenital heart disease. Ann Intern Med 1990;112:445–454.
2. Elkayam U, Gleicher N. Hemodynamics and cardiac functioning during normal pregnancy and the puerperium. In: Elkayam U, Gleicher N, editors. Cardiac problems in pregnancy. 3rd ed. New York: Wiley-Liss; 1998. p. 3–19.
3. Romano-Zelekha O, Hirsh R, Blieden L, et al. The risk for congenital heart defects in offspring of individuals with congenital heart defects. Clin Genet 2001;59:325–329.
4. Avila W, Grinberg M, Snitcowsky R, et al. Maternal and fetal outcome in pregnant women with Eisenmenger's syndrome. Eur Heart J 1995;16:460–464.
5. Presbitero P, Somerville J, Stone S, et al. Pregnancy in cyanotic congenital heart disease: outcome of mother and fetus. Circulation 1994;89:2673–2676.
6. Hameed A, Wani O, Karaalp I. Valvular disease in pregnancy. Circulation 1999;100:1–148.
7. Beauchesne L, Connolly H, Ammash N, Warnes C. Outcome of pregnancy in patients with coarctation of the aorta. J Am Coll Cardiol 2001;38:1728–1733.
8. Siu S, Sermer M, Harrison D, et al. Risk and predictors for pregnancy-related complications in women with heart disease. Circulation 1997;96:2789–2794.
9. Gleicher N, Midwall J, Hochberger D, Jaffin H. Eisenmenger's syndrome and pregnancy. Obstet Gynecol Surv 1979;34:721–741.

10. Canobbio MM, Mair DD, van der Velde M, Koos BJ. Pregnancy outcomes after the Fontan repair. J Am Coll Cardiol 1996;28:763–767.
11. Clarkson P, Wilson N, Neutze J, et al. Outcome of pregnancy after the Mustard operation for transposition of the great arteries with intact ventricular septum. J Am Coll Cardiol 1994;24:190–193.
12. Bhargava B, Agarwal R, Yadav R, et al. Percutaneous balloon aortic valvuloplasty during pregnancy: use of the Inoue balloon and the physiologic antegrade approach. Cathet Cardiovasc Diagn 1998;45:422–425.
13. Connolly H, Warnes C. Ebstein's anomaly: outcome of pregnancy. J Am Coll Cardiol 1994;23:1194–1198.
14. Connolly H, Warnes C. Outcome of pregnancy in patients with complex pulmonic valve atresia. Am J Cardiol 1997;79:519–521.
15. Siu S, Sermer M, Colman J, et al. Prospective multicenter study of pregnancy outcomes in women with heart disease. Circulation 2001;104:515–521.
16. Chow T, Galvin J, McGovern B. Antiarrhythmic drug therapy in pregnancy and lactation. Am J Cardiol 1998;82:58I–62I.
17. Salazar E, Zajarias A, Gutierrez N, Iturbe I. The problem of cardiac valve prostheses, anticoagulants, and pregnancy. Circulation 1984;70:I169–I177.
18. Oakley C. Clinical perspective: anticoagulation and pregnancy. Eur Heart J 1995;16:1317–1319.
19. Sbarouni E, Oakley C. Outcome of pregnancy in women with valve prostheses. Br Heart J 1994;71:196–201.

20. Vitale N, DeFeo M, DeSanto LS, et al. Dose-dependent fetal complications of warfarin in pregnant women with mechanical heart valves. J Am Coll Cardiol 1999;33:1637–1641.
21. Bonow RO, Carabello BA, Chatterjee K, et al. 2008 focused update incorporated into the ACC/AHA 2006 guidelines for the management of patients with valvular heart disease: a report of the American College of Cardiology/American Heart Association Task Force on Practice Guidelines (Writing Committee to revise the 1998 guidelines for the management of patients with valvular heart disease). Endorsed by the Society of Cardiovascular Anesthesiologists, Society for Cardiovascular Angiography and Interventions, and Society of Thoracic Surgeons. J Am Coll Cardiol 2008;52:e1–e142.
22. Bates SM, Greer IA, Hirsh J, et al. Use of antithrombotic agents during pregnancy: the Seventh ACCP Conference on Antithrombotic and Thrombolytic Therapy. Chest 2004;126:627S–644S.
23. Salem DN, Stein PD, Al-Ahmad A, et al. Antithrombotic therapy in valvular heart disease—native and prosthetic: the Seventh ACCP Conference on Antithrombotic and Thrombolytic Therapy. Chest 2004;126:457S–482S.
24. Melissari E, Parker C, Wilson N. Use of low molecular weight heparin in pregnancy. Thromb Haemost 1992;68:652–656.
25. Famuyide AO, Hopkins MR, El-Nasher SA, et al. Hysteroscopic sterilization in women with severe cardiac disease: experience at a tertiary center. Mayo Clin Proc 2008;83:431–438.

22

Obstetric Analgesia and Anesthesia

JACQUELINE DURBRIDGE | STEVEN YENTIS

Introduction

Pregnancy in any woman is a physiologic challenge, but in the woman with congenital heart disease (CHD) it may be challenging to the point of considerable risk to the mother and fetus. Superimposing anesthesia on this situation can be like walking a tightrope, balancing the effects on the mother and her fetus against the background of altered cardiovascular physiology, with an unknown net of reserve in the woman with CHD. In this chapter we outline the important physiologic changes in pregnancy that are particularly relevant for anesthesia and analgesia and also discuss some practical aspects of anesthetic techniques that are used.

Physiologic Effects of Pregnancy

Pregnancy is a cardiovascular challenge to all women and may be especially difficult for certain patients with CHD. Pregnancy very early on causes an increase in cardiac output and a reduction in systemic vascular resistance. These changes usually peak at 50% above normal by 20 weeks' gestation and then remain relatively constant after that.[1] Blood pressure initially falls and then during the third trimester starts to climb back to preconception levels. Plasma volume increases by 40% to 45%. Pulmonary blood flow increases, although a reduction in pulmonary vascular resistance normally ensures that pulmonary pressures do not increase. Structural remodeling of the myocardium occurs; this may take up to a year to regress after pregnancy, and some women with CHD may have permanent deterioration in ventricular function.[2] Blood flow to the uterus and kidneys is increased, with uterine blood flow peaking at around term at 500 to 600 mL/min. During labor, cardiac output is further increased by up to 40% with contractions,[3] and immediately after delivery there is an autotransfusion of about 500 mL of blood into the circulation from the contracted uterus. Hematologic changes include a physiologic anemia and a 6-fold increase in risk of thromboembolism during the pregnancy, with a further 11-fold increase during the puerperium.

Superimposing these physiologic changes onto CHD may lead to cardiovascular compromise early in pregnancy, and the importance of pre-pregnancy counseling about the risks and effects of pregnancy cannot be stressed enough. A successful outcome for mother and infant demands early risk assessment, meticulous and frequent antenatal care, and multidisciplinary consultation for planning of delivery and instructions for postnatal care. Anesthetic or analgesic intervention is nowadays often considered essential for all patients with CHD except those with the lowest risk, for whom analgesic and anesthetic considerations can be assumed as routine. Although "traditional" management has included elective cesarean section under general anesthesia for women with CHD, attempted vaginal delivery is now usually preferred for the majority of women, because cesarean section incurs increased risks of hemorrhage, infection, fluid shifts, and thromboembolism. Thus, cesarean section should be undertaken for obstetric indications, although cardiovascular deterioration may prompt early delivery of some women with CHD and this may necessitate cesarean section.

Analgesia for Labor

Effective regional analgesia is the main reason that vaginal delivery has become the preferred option for the majority of women with CHD, because its effects relieve the cardiovascular stress of labor. Unlike alternative methods of pain relief, epidural analgesia can abolish pain and the associated cardiovascular effects, and it allows controlled management of the second stage (delivery of the neonate) without, or with minimal, active pushing from the mother, thus avoiding a major Valsalva-type maneuver. The lower concentrations of local anesthetic and opioid mixtures that are routinely used for modern labor analgesia cause minimal hypotension and other side effects[4]; with careful titration and monitoring they are safe and effective for most patients with CHD.[5] Consideration of adequate cardiovascular monitoring during labor should be made with noninvasive blood pressure measurement, continuous oxygen saturation, and electrocardiographic monitoring used for all patients. Invasive blood pressure monitoring can be usefully added for patients at higher risk with minimal risks aside from maternal discomfort and restriction of movement. Management of the third stage (delivery of the placenta) and control of uterine bleeding need to be planned, because the use of standard oxytocic drugs is relatively contraindicated in cardiac patients owing to the side effects of vasodilation, tachycardia, and hypotension (Syntocinon)[6,7] or intense vasoconstriction and nausea/vomiting (ergometrine). However, postpartum hemorrhage may be poorly tolerated in CHD, so reduction in dosage and slow infusion rather than bolus administration is often preferable to avoidance of the use of these drugs altogether.

Regional analgesia may be contraindicated (e.g., if the patient is receiving anticoagulation therapy), or the mother may choose not to use this option for analgesia. Other alternatives are available but in general are less effective at providing pain relief and therefore may be less suitable. Nitrous oxide in a 50:50 mix with oxygen (Entonox) is commonly offered to women, especially in the early part of labor, and may be at least partially helpful in up to 50% to 70% of women.[8] It commonly causes nausea and vomiting. Opioid drugs have been used for many years to provide analgesia in labor, and intramuscular bolus doses of pethidine (meperidine) or diamorphine are commonly used in U.K. labor wards because midwives are able to prescribe and administer them. More recently the use of short-acting opioids such as fentanyl and remifentanil, given intravenously via a patient-controlled pump, has started to gather favor with women. This affords improved analgesia over pethidine[9] and nitrous oxide.[10] None of these options, however, produces the same quality of analgesia and therefore the cardiovascular benefits as regional analgesia, and they are less suitable for women with significant heart disease.

Anesthesia for Cesarean Section and Other Procedures in Pregnant Patients with Congenital Heart Disease

The majority of cesarean sections in the United Kingdom are performed using regional anesthesia (in our institution, 98% of elective cases and 93% of emergencies) because it is generally accepted that maternal mortality is reduced by avoiding the use of general anesthesia, and in

TABLE 22-1	Comparison of Regional and General Anesthesia for Cesarean Section	
	Regional Anesthesia	*General Anesthesia*
Advantages	Mother awake for delivery of infant Partner may be present Avoids risks of general anesthesia Allows slow titration of drugs against response Better analgesia postoperatively Less nausea/vomiting postoperatively Less blood loss	Avoids maternal intraoperative anxiety Not affected by anticoagulation issues Can give 100% oxygen if required Invasive monitoring easier to site Can apply direct-current cardioversion easily if necessary Avoids risk of inadequate/high block Allows tracheobronchial suction Easy transition to postoperative ventilation if required
Disadvantages	Maternal intraoperative anxiety of mother may have deleterious cardiovascular effects Lying flat may be difficult to tolerate Anticoagulation issues Risk of headache Risk of inadequate block Risk of high block with impaired coughing/breathing and risk of aspiration Marked decrease in systemic vascular resistance; risk of severe hypotension (especially in patients with fixed cardiac output) or worsening hypoxemia (in patients with right-to-left shunts) Inability to give 100% oxygen Discomfort if operative time is long	Failed/difficult tracheal intubation Aspiration of gastric contents Cardiovascular stress from tracheal intubation/extubation Cardiac depressant effect of anesthetic agents Risk of awareness Propensity for nitrous oxide to expand air bubbles (important in patients with right-to-left shunts, who are at risk from systemic air embolism) Volatile anesthetic agents may relax the uterus Fetal and maternal opioid-induced respiratory depression Increased risk of postoperative atelectasis Increased risk of postoperative venous thromboembolism More pain/nausea/vomiting postoperatively Greater blood loss

Reprinted with permission from Richards NA, Yentis SM. Anaesthesia, analgesia and peripartum management in women with pre-existing cardiac and respiratory disease. Fetal Matern Med Rev 2006; 17:327-347. © Cambridge University Press.

particular the risk of a difficult airway, failed intubation, and aspiration of gastric contents.[11] The particular advantages and disadvantages of regional and general anesthesia are summarized in Table 22-1.

The choice of technique will call for proper multidisciplinary assessment of each individual patient and discussion with the woman and her partner about the relevant concerns, advantages, and disadvantages of each technique. Careful, thorough preparation and skillful administration of appropriate drugs, through whichever route is chosen, are thought to be more important than the actual technique selected. Once the decision of regional or general anesthesia has been made, the type of regional technique will need to be considered because there are a variety of methods that offer subtle differences in onset time, character of block, and side effect profile. Choice of method will often depend on the individual anesthetists' preference and experience. Some of the differences in regional techniques are highlighted in Table 22-2. In general, catheter techniques allow for titration of effect and better control, with most techniques affording some postoperative analgesia. All techniques carry a risk of post–dural puncture headache and nerve injury, although the incidence is low and considered acceptable to most women.

During all modes of anesthesia and analgesia, avoidance of aortocaval compression with at least 15° left lateral tilt or the supine wedged position is vital until the neonate is delivered and sometimes after delivery, because the uterus may remain bulky enough to cause cardiovascular effects in high-risk cases. If at all possible, adequate time is required to allow the slow introduction of anesthesia (whether general or regional) after appropriate monitoring has been started, and the avoidance of an emergency situation is clearly of profound benefit in these circumstances. Communication throughout the labor and delivery is essential between anesthetist, obstetrician, midwife, and others, including the cardiologist, to prevent the need for sudden crisis management. Occasionally, an elective procedure will be chosen if the risk from an emergency procedure is believed to be particularly high.

Any complications of delivery must be managed promptly to avoid rapid decompensation in the woman with little or no cardiac reserve. Methods for minimizing blood loss, including appropriate drug therapy and specific surgical techniques (e.g., use of intrauterine balloons and uterine compression sutures) need to be carefully planned. The involvement of senior obstetric and anesthetic staff is crucial, and often the actual presence of a cardiologist can be extremely useful, for example, in advising the team on prevention and/or management of arrhythmias or other complications. Avoidance of excessive fluid therapy in women at risk of cardiac failure, and use of concentrated solutions of drugs, may be indicated.

Continuation of monitoring into the postnatal period must be considered because it is easy to relax when the neonate is safely delivered and the woman has been transferred into recovery or a high-dependency/intensive care area.[12] The physiologic changes of pregnancy take a variable amount of time to revert, and there may be permanent alterations in cardiovascular function in some women. The increased risk of thromboembolism is further increased in the immediate postnatal period and continues for up to 6 weeks.

TABLE 22-2	Differences Between Epidural, Spinal, and Combined Spinal Epidural Techniques			
	Epidural	*Spinal Catheter*	*Spinal*	*Combined Spinal Epidural*
	Injection of LA outside the dura within epidural space, typically with a catheter for repeat dosing	Injection of LA within dura via catheter for repeat dosing	On-off injection of LA within dura	Small dose LA within dura with catheter in epidural space for repeat dosing
	Slow onset	Moderate onset	Fast onset	Moderate onset
	Moderate decrease in SVR/BP	Moderate decrease in SVR/BP	Large decrease in SVR/BP	Moderate decrease in SVR/BP
	Can titrate effect	Can titrate effect	No titration	Can titrate effect
	Large dose LA	Small dose LA	Small dose LA	Moderate dose LA
	Moderate risk failure or technical difficulty	Increased risk technical difficulty	Low risk failure	Moderate risk failure or technical difficulty
	Increased risk pain intraoperatively especially if de novo; more effective if successful analgesia in labor	Minimal risk pain intraoperatively	Minimal risk pain intraoperatively	Minimal risk pain intraoperatively

BP, blood pressure; LA, local anesthetic; SVR, systemic vascular resistance.

Specific Considerations for Certain Conditions

The just described general considerations apply to all women with CHD, but there are specific points to consider for certain conditions.

CONGENITAL SYNDROMES

Patients with some congenital syndromes (e.g., Marfan syndrome or Turner syndrome) may have not only heart disease but also other manifestations such as increased blood vessel fragility and musculoskeletal abnormalities. The latter may impact on the type of anesthesia that can be provided. Regional analgesia and anesthesia may well be preferred, but in women with metal rods in situ to correct scoliosis, for instance, it may not be possible to site an epidural and attempting to do so may carry an increased risk of complications. However, these patients may also be at increased risk of a difficult airway and the risk-benefit ratio must be weighed carefully. If it is not possible to provide effective regional analgesia for labor, then it may be that the safest delivery method is elective cesarean section with general anesthesia.

Patients with aortopathy are particularly at risk of shear stress in the wall of the aorta, which may be induced by a sudden large rise or fall in blood pressure.[13] The proactive management of hypertension and hypotension during any anesthetic intervention is crucial to the successful management of these patients; this may require slow induction of a regional block and careful use of vasopressors or vasodilators.

PULMONARY HYPERTENSION AND RIGHT-TO-LEFT SHUNTS

Patients with pulmonary hypertension are at particular risk of mortality (~30% to 50%) during pregnancy and the puerperium. These patients have an already overburdened right ventricle, and the fluid shifts and cardiovascular stress around the time of delivery inevitably make this a particularly risky time. Patients with the most severe pulmonary hypertension often require preterm delivery owing to failure of the fetus to thrive (through reduced maternal oxygen transport and/or reduced uteroplacental blood flow secondary to erythrocytosis) or worsening cardiac failure or hypoxemia, despite new pulmonary vasodilator therapies. Successful management has been reported with both regional and general anesthesia.[14,15] Careful discussion with the multidisciplinary team and the woman and her family will govern the choice. Those with less severe pulmonary hypertension may reach term, when a managed labor with epidural analgesia and elective instrumental delivery may be preferred. Particular attention should be paid to preventing hemorrhage and monitoring the woman to assess the effect of the fluid shifts on the cardiovascular system and instituting appropriate management. Similarly in those women with a right-to-left shunt, care must be taken to control the shunt with judicious use of vasopressors balanced against the reduction in systemic vascular resistance during anesthesia.

RESTRICTED/FIXED CARDIAC OUTPUT

Patients whose cardiac output is restricted or fixed have traditionally been thought unsuitable for regional anesthesia, owing to the reduction in systemic vascular resistance that this technique produces. However,

this view has changed over the past decade and with carefully instituted regional analgesia or anesthesia these techniques are now helping many women with these conditions deliver safely.[5]

ANTICOAGULATION

Women with CHD may be on prophylactic or therapeutic doses of anticoagulant therapy. Patients taking therapeutic doses, for instance those with prosthetic valves, need careful assessment for anesthesia. Regional anesthesia is contraindicated in the presence of anticoagulation owing to the small but very serious risk of epidural/spinal hematoma. For low-molecular-weight heparin, guidelines suggest a 12-hour treatment-free period for prophylactic doses and 24 hours for treatment doses before attempted neuraxial anesthesia (and also before removal or manipulation of an in-situ epidural/spinal catheter).[16] Therefore, the applicability and timing of specific anesthetic interventions have to be carefully considered, together with the potential increased risk from thrombosis if anticoagulants are withheld. Our anecdotal experience is that achieving adequate control of anticoagulation with intravenous infusions of unfractionated heparin is next to impossible in late pregnancy, presumably owing to altered pharmacokinetics in pregnancy and the heparinase activity of the placenta.

What Anesthetists Want to Know from Cardiologists

At the simplest level, in complex CHD sometimes the most useful question that should be considered is "Where does the blood go?" This may seem elementary to cardiologists, but it is vital that the anesthetist has a picture in his or her head about where the oxygenated and deoxygenated blood travels to understand the potential problems the woman may encounter and the interventions and therapies that may worsen or may help matters. This is particularly relevant to anesthesia because anesthetic drugs tend to have an onset within minutes and the physiology may alter dramatically and, often, very rapidly.

It is helpful also to have an understanding of what the particular risks are in this specific woman (e.g., arrhythmia, ventricular failure, dissection, thrombosis) so that the anesthetist can plan ahead for both the uncomplicated and complicated delivery period.

Guidance on which therapies the cardiologist believes are most likely to be effective for the potential complications for each woman is also helpful, because most obstetric anesthetists will be less familiar with the latest antiarrhythmic therapies and subtleties in their use. The choice of drugs should also include consideration of the safety/advisability of certain drugs in pregnancy and breastfeeding.

CONCLUSION

The safe delivery of anesthesia and analgesia to pregnant women with CHD requires early multidisciplinary planning and experienced, interested obstetric anesthetists available 24 hours a day. The application of any technique or administration of any drugs should be considered and measured with thought to a backup plan for emergencies or complications.

REFERENCES

1. Hunter S, Robson SC. Adaptation of the maternal heart in pregnancy. Br Heart J 1992;68:540–543.
2. Guedes A, Mercier LA, Leduc L, et al. Impact of pregnancy on the systemic right ventricle after a Mustard operation for transposition of the great arteries. J Am Coll Cardiol 2004;44:433–437.
3. Robson SC, Dunlop W, Boys RJ, Hunter S. Cardiac output during labour. Br Med J (Clin Res Ed) 1987;295:1169–1172.
4. Hawthorne L, Slaymaker A, Bamber J, Dresner M. Effect of fluid preload on maternal haemodynamics for low-dose epidural analgesia in labour. Int J Obstet Anesth 2001;10:312–315.
5. Suntharalingum G, Dob D, Yentis SM. Obstetric epidural analgesia in aortic stenosis: a low-dose technique for labour and instrumental delivery. Int J Obstet Anesth 2001;10:129–134.
6. Pinder A, Dresner M, Calow C, et al. Haemodynamic changes caused by oxytocin during caesarean section under spinal anaesthesia. Int J Obstet Anesth 2002;11:156–159.
7. Mukaddam-Daher S, Yin YL, Roy J, et al. Negative inotropic and chronotropic effects of oxytocin. Hypertension 2001;38:292–296.
8. Holdcroft A, Morgan M. Assessment of analgesic effect of pethidine and Entonox. J Obstet Gynaecol Br Common 1974;81:603–607.
9. Blair JM, Dobson GT, Hill DA, et al. Patient controlled analgesia for labour: a comparison of remifentanil with pethidine. Anaesthesia 2005;60:22–27.
10. Volmanen P, Akural E, Raudaskoski T, et al. Comparison of remifentanil and nitrous oxide in labour analgesia. Acta Anaesthesiol Scand 2005;49:453–458.
11. Lewis G, editor. The Confidential Enquiry into Maternal and Child Health (CEMACH). Saving Mothers' Lives: Reviewing Maternal Deaths to Make Motherhood Safer 2003–2005. The Seventh Report on Confidential Enquiries into Maternal Deaths in the United Kingdom. London: CEMACH; 2007.
12. Ramsey M. Management of the puerperium in the women with heart disease. In: Steer PJ, Gatzoulis M, Baker P, editors. Heart disease and pregnancy. London: RCOG Press; 2006. p. 299–311.
13. Immer FF, Bansi AG, Immer-Bansi AS, et al. Aortic dissection in pregnancy: analysis of risk factors and outcome. Ann Thorac Surg 2003;76:309–314.
14. O'Hare R, McLoughlin C, Milligan K, et al. Anaesthesia for caesarean section in the presence of severe primary pulmonary hypertension. Br J Anaesth 1998;81:790–792.
15. Ghai B, Mohan V, Khetarpal M, Malhotra N. Epidural anesthesia for cesarean section in a patient with Eisenmenger's syndrome. Int J Obstet Anesth 2002;11:44–47.
16. Horlocker TT, Wedel DJ, Benzon H, et al. Regional anesthesia in the anticoagulated patient: defining the risks (the Second ASRA Consensus Conference on Neuraxial Anesthesia and Anticoagulation). Reg Anesth Pain Med 2003;28:172–197.

23

Anesthesia in Adult Congenital Heart Disease, Including Anesthesia for Noncardiac Surgery

DAVID ALEXANDER

Introduction

Congenital heart disease is one of the most common birth defects, and with 85% of these children now surviving into adulthood there are an increasing number of patients requiring ongoing care.[1] Many, but not all, will have had some corrective or palliative surgery in infancy or childhood and will require further surgery throughout their life.[2] A comparison of pediatric and adult congenital heart disease (ACHD) defects is shown in Table 23-1 along with the relative frequency of their occurrence.[3,4] With regard to the cardiac lesion, ACHD patients present for cardiac surgery for a number of reasons, among them being late diagnosis, worsening shunting, valvular disease, congenital coronary abnormalities, conduit revision, and pregnancy, which may unmask significant cardiac compromise. Arrhythmias are a common complication in ACHD patients and may necessitate catheter ablation or cardioversion requiring anesthesia. In addition, as their life expectancy increases, many individuals will present with noncardiac disease or traumatic injury requiring surgery.

General Anesthesia for Cardiac Surgery

When general anesthesia is considered for a patient with ACHD, a vital component of patient care is to ensure involvement of all personnel who have experience with the patient's condition. A clear understanding of the functional anatomy is vital. Preoperative assessment of these patients is similar to that for any other surgical patient, with special attention directed toward anticoagulation and assessment of cardiorespiratory function, including the current level of exercise tolerance. Examination should be performed to establish the presence of congestive cardiac failure and cyanosis. In cases in which previous surgery has been undertaken, details of that surgical procedure are important because they will allow a better understanding of the patient's physiologic and anatomic status. Investigations should be tailored to elucidate the cardiac anatomy and actively exclude or diagnose pulmonary hypertension, which is an independent risk factor for perioperative morbidity and mortality. Coronary angiography may be needed. The lateral chest radiograph, useful in assessing the relationship between the sternum and right ventricle, and particularly important in reoperation, has been superseded by magnetic resonance imaging (MRI), which is the radiologic imaging of choice. Special attention should be paid to renal, hepatic, and hematologic tests, particularly the presence of secondary erythrocytosis associated with chronic hypoxia.[5-7]

In many cases this will be "redo" surgery and provision must be made for rapid availability of blood and blood products if these are not readily available on site. Adhesive external defibrillator pads should be used in patients who are undergoing second or subsequent cardiac surgery. The surgical challenges of reoperation in these patients should not be underestimated.

Sedative premedication may be prescribed (with supplemental oxygen), but care must be taken in cases of cyanotic heart disease or pulmonary hypertension in which hypercapnia can have profound deleterious effects on the pulmonary vascular resistance.

Induction of anesthesia should be undertaken with invasive arterial pressure monitoring in situ. All standard induction agents have been used safely in these patients. Some practitioners prefer etomidate for induction because the extent of systemic vasodilation is lessened. Ketamine may confer some hemodynamic advantage but is limited by the frequency of dysphoric reactions. Of greater importance than the choice of agent is the speed and overall dose administered. Many of these patients have slow circulation times, and consequently there is a risk of overdose if the induction drug is injected too rapidly. Some practitioners titrate the induction agent until loss of the lash reflex and then supplement the induction with an opiate (e.g., fentanyl). Paralysis can be achieved with any nondepolarizing muscle relaxant, although many practitioners avoid atracurium because hypotension after histamine release may have a more marked hemodynamic effect in patients reliant on afterload to avoid shunting. Maintenance with an oxygen-air mixture and an inhalational agent is acceptable, as is total intravenous anesthesia.[8] Nitrous oxide should be avoided because it causes myocardial depression. It is seldom necessary or advisable to ventilate with 100% oxygen.

Monitoring should include electrocardiography, saturation, core temperature, and ventilator parameters (e.g., end-tidal carbon dioxide and inspired oxygen concentration). Central venous pressure measurements are essential, but the route of access should be discussed with reference to the surgical approach and care should be taken with univentricular circulations in which thrombotic and embolic events are more common. Pulmonary artery catheters are rarely used because interpretation may be misleading in the presence of significant shunting and the calculation of cardiac output by thermodilution is inaccurate in this setting. In all cases, meticulous attention must be paid during line insertion to prevent air emboli, which can be disastrous in patients with intracardiac defects. Transesophageal echocardiography is an essential additional monitor for the surgical procedure itself and adds useful additional information that may assist the anesthetist. Real-time interpretation allows rapid response to changing hemodynamic conditions.

Every effort should be made in the preoperative period to prevent postoperative hypothermia (shivering increases myocardial work) and hyperglycemia (which may worsen cerebral outcome).[9]

All these patients should receive level 2 or 3 postoperative care (high dependency or intensive care). Detailed handover and discussion between cardiac surgeons, cardiac anesthetists, and intensivists helps to ensure that appropriate care is maintained throughout the perioperative period.[10] The length and complexity of the surgery often necessitates postoperative ventilation, but care must be taken to ensure that the deleterious effects of intermittent positive-pressure ventilation do not worsen cardiac function. Early extubation is preferred and may be associated with an improved outcome.[11]

Fluid management should be carefully guided by hemodynamic response because many of these patients are particularly susceptible to congestive cardiac failure. Current trends in medical management

TABLE 23-1	Comparative Frequencies of Pediatric and Adult Congenital Heart Disease Defects			
Pediatric CHD		**ACHD**		
Defect	%	*Defect*	%	
Ventricular septal defect	35%	Atrial or ventricular septal defects	22%	
Atrial septal defect	9%	Tetralogy of Fallot	14%	
Patent ductus arteriosus	8%	Complex disease (e.g., Fontan)	13%	
Pulmonary stenosis	8%	Obstruction of the left ventricular outflow tract	12%	
Aortic stenosis	6%	Transposition of the great arteries	10%	
Coarctation of the aorta	6%	Obstruction of the right ventricular outflow tract	8%	
Tetralogy of Fallot	5%	Coarctation of the aorta	7%	
Transposition of great vessels	4%	Marfan syndrome	5%	
Atrioventricular septal defect	3%	Corrected transposition of the great vessels	4%	
Other rarer conditions (e.g., tricuspid atresia, bicuspid valves, univentricular heart)	16%	Atrioventricular septal defect	3%	
		Eisenmenger syndrome	2%	

Data from Jordan SC, Scott O. Heart Disease in Paediatrics, 3rd ed. Oxford: Butterworth Heinemann; 1989; and Gatzoulis MA, Hechter S, Siu SC, Webb GD. Outpatient clinics for adults with congenital heart disease: increasing workload and evolving patterns of referral. Heart 1999; 81:57–61.

with regard to fluid resuscitation and oxygen delivery may not apply to this population.

Recent guidelines from the National Institute for Health and Clinical Excellence recommend that routine antibiotic prophylaxis is not beneficial.[12] However, prophylaxis should be considered in accordance with local guidelines, bearing in mind that postoperative sepsis and infective endocarditis carry higher mortalities than in the general population.[13]

Adequate analgesia must be provided. It not only forms part of standard postsurgical care but also reduces the likelihood of pulmonary hypertension in susceptible patients.[14,15]

PULMONARY HYPERTENSION

Pulmonary hypertension may be defined as mean pulmonary artery pressures in excess of 25 mm Hg at rest. The presence of pulmonary hypertension may be a surrogate marker of severity of the associated cardiac disease. Its presence is associated with higher mortality rates. Every effort should be made to avoid iatrogenic rises in pulmonary artery pressure, from, for example, sympathetic stimulation (light anesthesia, pain), acidosis, hypoxia, hypercarbia, hypothermia, increased intrathoracic pressures, and excessive positive end-expiratory pressure. In severe pulmonary hypertension, standard ventilator maneuvers may be of limited value and may worsen the hemodynamics.[16] One useful strategy is moderate hyperventilation, utilizing a shorter inspiratory time, longer expiratory time, and higher peak airway pressures.

It is advisable to employ a specialist physician to assist in the preoperative care of patients with known pulmonary hypertension and to continue that care into the postoperative period when pulmonary hypertensive crises are more common. All the pulmonary hypertension targeted therapies used by the patient preoperatively should continue during the perioperative period.

Hemoptysis is a serious complication in this patient group. Smaller hemorrhages may herald larger, catastrophic events, albeit this is uncommon. Management strategies involve interventional radiology and, again, pulmonary hypertension physicians.

Pulmonary hypertensive crisis is a medical emergency with a very high mortality rate. It is often difficult to diagnose immediately and may present in a variety of ways, largely determined by factors such as ventilation and consciousness. If suspected, rapid treatment must be instituted if there is to be any chance of survival. Correction of any of the precipitants listed earlier should be undertaken, and pharmacologic treatment may include epoprostenol, intravenous nitrates, isoprenaline, phosphodiesterase inhibitors, opiates, sildenafil (which is not widely available in an intravenous form), and inhaled nitric oxide. Mechanical support with intra-aortic balloon counterpulsation or right ventricular assist devices remains a last resort. Despite all these maneuvers, mortality remains high.[17]

UNIVENTRICULAR HEART AND THE FONTAN OPERATION PATIENT

For functionally univentricular hearts, the mainstay of treatment remains the Fontan operation or one of its modifications. The procedure essentially directs venous blood into the pulmonary artery, bypassing the single chamber, which, in turn serves as a pump to the systemic circulation. Pulmonary blood flow, which determines cardiac output, is thus completely passive and highly dependent on preload, pulmonary vascular resistance, and systemic ventricular function. Lateral tunnels or extracardiac conduits are more recent modifications of the Fontan procedure, whereas most older patients had the atriopulmonary type of Fontan operation.

Preoperative anesthetic assessment should aim to identify those patients at higher risk. These include those with ventricular dysfunction, increased pulmonary vascular resistance, abnormal pulmonary anatomy, atrioventricular valve abnormalities, and history of sustained arrhythmia.

Fundamental to the anesthetic management of these patients is the maintenance of low pulmonary artery pressures and adequate venous return, which both dictate eventual cardiac output. Sinus rhythm is clearly desirable.

In addition to standard anesthetic monitoring, central venous pressure may be monitored (and will reflect pulmonary artery pressure after surgical treatment), but great care must be taken to avoid air emboli and protect against the higher than usual risk of intracardiac venous thrombosis.

Positive-pressure ventilation has a profound deleterious effect on these patients, with high intrathoracic pressures severely limiting or abolishing venous return. Early extubation or spontaneous respiration is desirable.

Low cardiac output is usually multifactorial in these patients. Causes include inadequate preload, elevated pulmonary vascular resistance, physical obstruction in the pulmonary or systemic pathway, arrhythmias, and pump failure. These patients are often resistant to standard inotropic support, particularly if the ventricle is hypertrophied and underfilled.

Arrhythmias are common and poorly tolerated. Treatment may include intraoperative pacing, amiodarone, and cardioversion, the latter being the treatment of choice if there are any signs of hemodynamic compromise.

Other common complications include hypoxia (especially in the presence of fenestrated baffles), which may be unresponsive to conventional ventilatory maneuvers; pleural and pericardial effusions; ascites; and thrombosis.

ARRHYTHMIAS

Arrhythmias represent one of the most common reasons for admission among ACHD patients.[18] Any arrhythmia may occur, but commonly they include supraventricular tachycardias (notably in patients who have undergone atrial surgery and in the Fontan circulation), ventricular tachycardias, and, the most common of all, reentrant intra-atrial tachycardias.[19] Most of these arrhythmias are refractory to pharmacologic treatment, and the changes in rhythm can cause serious hemodynamic disturbances in patients with poor cardiac reserve. This means that a common procedure necessitating general anesthesia is urgent/emergency cardioversion, with or without concomitant echocardiography to exclude thrombus. These patients require slow induction and may need intubation if transesophageal echocardiography is to be performed. Remifentanil by infusion is one technique allowing both echocardiography and cardioversion while maintaining cardiac stability. Beware of profound hemodynamic compromise on induction in patients with univentricular hearts. External pacing must be immediately available because there may be no direct venous access to the ventricle in complex disease.

Anesthesia for Noncardiac Surgery

Within this group of patients there may well be the opportunity to use local or regional anesthesia, with substantial benefit in terms of reducing perioperative risks. There is a balance between the risk of avoiding general anesthesia and the effects of central neuraxial blockade on systemic vascular resistance. There is growing evidence that regional techniques are also safe in patients with Eisenmenger syndrome, despite earlier beliefs that general anesthesia was preferable.[14,15]

Whereas those patients undergoing cardiac surgery need to have it and anesthesia performed in specialized cardiac units, the same may not always be true for those patients undergoing the most minor noncardiac surgical procedures.[20] For most, the procedures should be carried out in centers with access to cardiac surgery, cardiac anesthetists, and all the support services these entail. All patients will require level 2 or 3 care postoperatively.[21] Patients with a univentricular heart or Fontan circulations are high-risk cases for noncardiac surgery. Ideally, this surgery should only be undertaken in specialist centers where there is on-site support in the form of cardiac surgery, cardiac anesthesia, and critical care.

The same principles for induction and maintenance in ACHD patients undergoing cardiac surgery apply. Monitoring will be dictated by the extent of the planned surgery and the existing cardiac abnormality. Most patients will have invasive arterial pressure monitoring, but many will not require central venous measurements; and risks associated with insertion must be weighed against any possible advantage.

It is vital to have a complete understanding of the physiologic and anatomic effects of the cardiac disease in these patients and then to classify patients undergoing noncardiac surgery accordingly. A simple physiologic system can be used, such as "too much blood to the lungs" (atrial septal defect, ventricular septal defect, patent ductus arteriosus) in which pulmonary flow and pressure will be raised; "too little blood to the lungs" (tetralogy of Fallot, pulmonary atresia) in which there will be chronic hypoxia and often cyanosis; and "too little blood to the body" (coarctation, Fontan circulation) in which chronic hypoperfusion will exist.

It is also useful to consider the concept of *balanced circulation.* In ACHD patients the blood may mix between left and right sides of the heart and the systemic saturation will depend on what proportion of blood passes through the lungs and the degree of any mixing (e.g., shunt). This is dependent on relative vascular resistances (systemic vs. pulmonary) rather than solely on anatomic connections.

The effect of varying oxygen saturation and arterial carbon dioxide content has marked effects in these patients, and every effort should be made to maintain these levels as close as possible to the preoperative resting values. Supplemental oxygen may do little to improve hypoxia. If further hypoxia occurs, then consider the usual causes (inadequate oxygen supply or hypoventilation) but also the effects of an unbalanced circulation (decreased systemic vascular resistance and increased pulmonary vascular resistance). Induction of anesthesia is associated with myocardial depression and vasodilation, which may lead to hypoxia. Treatment to rebalance the circulation in favor of the pulmonary vasculature includes vasoconstriction, oxygen, and hyperventilation.

Likewise, ACHD patients may have chronic low cardiac outputs and be relatively hypotensive in their everyday lives. Attempts to correct this hemodynamic status quo may be deleterious and unbalance a delicate circulatory state. If patients undergoing surgery become more hypotensive than before, consider the usual causes of hypovolemia, ventricular failure, and reduced systemic vascular resistance. A fall in pulmonary vascular resistance or outflow obstruction may further unbalance the circulation. Apart from treating the usual causes, efforts to rebalance the circulation in favor of the systemic circulation may include reducing the fractional inspired oxygen concentration and allowing the carbon dioxide level to rise.

As noted earlier, postoperative ventilation is not without risk in these patients and should be avoided when possible, but not at the risk of hypoventilation, hypoxia, and hypercarbia. Many of the serious complications (e.g., pulmonary hypertensive crisis, thrombosis) occur in the days after surgery, and these dictate that ongoing careful monitoring is needed. There will be very few, if any, situations in which these patients can be subjected to day surgery type perioperative care.

The reader is referred to Chapters 21 and 22 for a discussion of the complex problem of pregnancy and heart disease.

REFERENCES

1. Wren C, O'Sullivan. Survival with congenital heart disease and the need for follow up in adult life. Heart 2001;85:438–443.
2. Daliento L, Mazzotti E, Mongillo E, et al. Life expectancy and quality of life in adult patients with congenital heart disease. Ital Heart J 2002;3:339–347.
3. Jordan SC, Scott O. Heart Disease in Paediatrics. 3rd ed. Oxford: Butterworth Heinemann; 1989.
4. Gatzoulis MA, Hechter S, Siu SC, Webb GD. Outpatient clinics for adults with congenital heart disease: increasing workload and evolving patterns of referral. Heart 1999;81:57–61.
5. Warner MA, Lunn RJ, O'Leary PW, Schroeder DR. Outcomes of non-cardiac surgical procedures in children and adults with congenital heart disease. Mayo Clin Proc 1998;73:728–734.
6. Flanagan MF, Hourihan M, Keane JF. Incidence of renal dysfunction in adults with cyanotic congenital heart disease. Am J Cardiol 1991;68:403–406.
7. Thorne S. Management of polycythaemia in adults with cyanotic congenital heart disease. Heart 1998;79:315–316.
8. Laird TH, Stayer SA, Rivenes SM, et al. Pulmonary to systemic blood flow ratio effects of sevoflurane, isoflurane, halothane and fentanyl/midazolam with 100% oxygen in congenital heart disease. Anaesth Analg 2002;95:1200–1206.
9. Finney SJ, Zekveld C, Elia A, Evans TW. Glucose control and mortality in critically ill patients. Nutr Clin Pract 2004;19:184–185.
10. Price S, Jaggar SI, Jordan S, et al. Adult congenital heart disease: intensive care management and outcome prediction. Intensive Care Med 2007;33:652–659.
11. Marianeschi SM, Seddio F, McElhinney DB, et al. Fast-track congenital heart operations: a less invasive technique and early extubation. Ann Thorac Surg 2000;69:872–876.
12. National Institute for Health and Clinical Excellence. Antimicrobial prophylaxis against infective endocarditis, clinical guideline (CG64). London: March 2008.
13. Nakatani S, Mitsutake K, Hozumi T, et al. Current characteristics of infective endocarditis in Japan. Circ J 2003;67:901–905.
14. Lovell AT. Anaesthetic implications of grown-up congenital heart disease. Br J Anaesth 2004;93:129–139.
15. Chassot PG, Bettex DA. Anaesthesia and adult congenital heart disease. J Cardiothorac Vasc Anaesth 2006;20:414–437.
16. Cheng DCH, David TE. Perioperative Care in Cardiac Anaesthesia and Surgery. Philadelphia: Lippincott Williams & Wilkins; 2006.
17. Hensley FA, Martin DE, Gravlee GP. A Practical Approach to Cardiac anaesthesia. 3rd ed. Philadelphia: Lippincott Williams & Wilkins; 2003.
18. Kaemmerer H, Fratz S, Bauer U, et al. Emergency hospital admissions and 3 year survival of adults with and without cardiovascular surgery for congenital heart disease. J Thorac Cardiovasc Surg 2003;126:1048–1052.
19. Gatzoulis MA, Freeman M, Siu SC, et al. Atrial arrhythmia after surgical closure of atrial septal defects in adults. N Eng J Med 1999;340:839–846.
20. Ammash NM, Connolly HM, Abel MD, Warnes CD. Non-cardiac surgery in Eisenmenger's syndrome. J Am Coll Cardiol 1999;33:227–229.
21. Bedard E, Shore DF, Gatzoulis MA. Adult congenital heart disease: a 2008 overview. Br Med Bull 2008;85:151–180.

24

Insurability of Adults with Congenital Heart Disease

MICHAEL CUMPER | GORDON CUMMING

Introduction

A 30-year-old woman with tetralogy of Fallot repaired at age 5 years was seen in the adult congenital heart disease (ACHD) clinic. Her physician gave encouraging advice: there was no arrhythmia, the pulmonary regurgitation was only moderate, and right ventricular function was close to normal. With this favorable report the woman asked why an insurer had recently more than doubled her premium for life insurance and declined her individual health and disability insurance applications. Her physician commented that the insurers' actions were possibly unfair, the result of inadequate information.

Insurers have only limited statistics on clients with congenital heart disease (CHD). They rely mostly on the medical literature, combined with "armchair" reasoning and, for some medical directors, clinical experience. At present, clinical follow-up studies contain few patients older than age 50 years and estimation of mortality beyond this is at best an educated guess.

Today, a 30-year-old normal female insurance applicant is expected to survive past age 85, and with a premium increase of 150% is still expected to reach age 77. If medical consensus is that this patient will reach age 85 and not manifest an adverse claims record, why recommend yearly clinic visits to a cardiologist, a yearly electrocardiogram with treadmill testing, and echocardiography or Holter monitoring either yearly or every few years? These recommendations clearly eliminate the possibility of individual health insurance.

Individual health insurance is usually not possible for patients requiring regular cardiac follow-up and will not be discussed further. Income replacement insurance (disability insurance) for CHD patients can be a problem because disability claims are often related to job dissatisfaction, motivation, and mental health status. Subjects with structural heart defects could theoretically use their cardiac problem to support a claim. Nonmedical situations dominate the area of individual disability coverage and will not be discussed further. Subjects with CHD should look to group programs that do not require individual assessment for their health and disability insurance needs and often for life insurance as well. Individual life insurance is individual financial planning, with some applicants requesting coverage for over $10 million. Although it may seem discriminatory to penalize an applicant for health problems not of his or her own making, insurers are legally allowed to categorize subjects according to risk. Without this provision, subjects at the highest risk would load up with insurance, the price would increase, and those at low risk would invest elsewhere. Individual insurance would disappear.

To understand life insurance decisions, it is essential to understand normal and substandard mortality.

Expression of Mortality

Population mortality rates are usually expressed as the number of deaths per 100,000 subjects per year at each age. It is easier for underwriters and medical directors to think in terms of mortality ratio—the observed number of deaths in a population of patients similar to the applicant divided by the expected number of deaths in a normal reference population expressed as a percent. If a patient's group expected mortality is the same as the reference group, the mortality ratio would be 100%; and if there were three times the expected number of deaths, the ratio would be 300%. In subjects younger than age 20 years insurers will often utilize excess death rate as a means of calculating premium rather than mortality ratios.

Longevity (years of life remaining) is strongly related to age and also to gender and smoking status, independent of any medical problems. Life insurers divide the population of applicants into smoker, nonsmoker, male, or female and have four separate tables for expected survival for each age. Table 24-1 shows a partial table for 30-year olds. Using this table, a 30-year-old male nonsmoker with a medical problem predicted to survive 41 instead of 52 years will be assigned a mortality ratio of 300%. Insurance premiums cover agents' commissions and head office administration as well as mortality; the nonmortality costs do not go up with increased mortality. For each 100% increase in mortality, the premium is increased about 90% so that the male projected to reach age 71 would be charged about 280% of standard premium.

Gender Difference in Mortality

Gender differences in mortality are significant. Table 24-2 shows that male mortality at ages 22 and 32 was over twice that for a female, both for an insured normal population and for the 1980 general population of the United States. At ages 52 and 62, male mortality was about 1.5 times the female mortality for the insured population and 1.9 times the mortality for the general population. If the mortality was 3.4 per 1000 per year for both sexes in a population of CHD patients at age 32, the mortality ratio would be 300% for males and 540% for females against an insured standard. Against the general population standard, the mortality ratios would be 200% and 485%. The difference in mortality between insured subjects and the general population is smaller in females compared with males.

Smoking/Nonsmoking Differences

Insurance statistics emphasize the important impact of smoking. Most insurers in North America have separate rates for smokers and nonsmokers. Insurance data (Table 24-3) show that at ages 30 and 40 smoking reduces life expectancy by 7 to 8 years. At age 70 and 80, the difference is 2 years. At age 30, smoking is the equivalent of assigning a mortality ratio of 225% to a nonsmoker. Smoking would lead to a greater increase in premium than many CHD conditions.

Mortality and the Underwriting Process

Insurers have long been aware that mortality in their policyholders is lowest in the first year after clearing the underwriting process, with gradual increases for the next 15 years. The insurance examination that clears the subjects may be nothing other than a medical history or may include a full examination and laboratory tests.

Table 24-4 shows the annual mortality rates for five populations of 32-year-old males: population A with a recent insurance examination, population B having had their examination 5 years previously, population C, 10 years previously, and population D, 15 years previously; population E is a current unexamined general population. The annual mortality in deaths per 1000 is significantly lower in population A than in population D. Fifteen years after policy issue, insurers use the term *ultimate mortality*, and this rate is often used as the reference level for underwriting. From age 20 to 50, this mortality is about two thirds of the mortality

TABLE 24-1	Longevity for Various Mortality Ratios—1993 Insurance Population at 30 Years of Age				
	Life Expectancy in Years				
	Females Aged 30		Males Aged 30		
Mortality Ratio (%)	Nonsmoker	Smoker*	Nonsmoker	Smoker*	
100†	55‡	49	52	44	
150	52	45	48	40	
200	49	42	45	37	
250	47	39	43	35	
300	45	37	41	34	
400	43	34	39	31	
500	40	32	36	29	
700	37	29	34	27	
1000	34	26	31	24	

*Some insurers classify a smoker as a client who answers *yes* to the question: Have you smoked a cigarette within the past 1 year? Other insurers penalize those using any tobacco products. Some are very light smokers; some are 2 pack per day smokers. Applicants who answer *no* but test positive for cotinine and are classified as smokers.

†Subjects accepted as standard mortality after the underwriting process.

‡Many insurers further divide their standard pool of applicants into select and super-select categories based on ideal family history, coronary risk factors, body build, and other positive wellness attributes projecting 1 to 2 years of additional life expectancy.

TABLE 24-2	Male/Female Mortality Comparison: Ultimate Insurance vs. General Population Comparison			
	Mortality—Deaths/1000/Year			
	Insured Ultimate*		General U.S. Population 1986	
Age	Male	Female	Male	Female
22	1.41	0.53	1.9	0.6
32	1.12	0.63	1.7	0.7
42	1.97	1.71	3.2	1.7
52	5.70	3.90	8.5	4.5
62	15.30	9.00	21.2	10.7

*Ultimate = 15 years after policy issue.

TABLE 24-3	Standard (Normal) Insured Males: Comparison of Longevity in Nonsmokers and Smokers			
	Life Expectancy (Years)			
Current Age (Years)	Nonsmoker	Smoker	Difference	Smoker Mortality Ratio vs. Nonsmoker
30	52	44	8	225
40	42	35	7	212
50	33	27	6	200
60	25	20	5	185
70	18	16	2	150
80	12	10	2	130

TABLE 24-4	Effect of Time After Clearing an Insurance Medical Review on Mortality*			
Population	Age at Examination	Current Age	Deaths Per 1000	Description
A	32	32	0.63	Newly issued policies
B	27	32	0.80	Policies underwritten 5 years ago
C	22	32	0.90	Policies underwritten 10 years ago
D	17	32	1.12	Policies underwritten 15 years ago
E	General population	32	1.70	Unexamined general population

*Ultimate mortality.

of the general population. When mortality ratios are calculated in the medical literature, the patient group is compared with a demographically similar general population and insurers would adjust these ratios upward, taking into consideration the lower mortality in insured subjects classified as at normal risk.

Age and Mortality Ratios

Table 24-5 shows the profound effect of age on mortality ratios for a given percent mortality. Medical follow-up studies report percent mortality at specific intervals of follow-up. Because of the marked increase in mortality in the general population with age, any increase in mortality from a congenital heart lesion results in a much less increase in mortality ratio at age 50 compared with age 30. Because most insurers decline to accept clients with mortality ratios of over 500%, subjects with impairments uninsurable at age 30 will find themselves insurable at age 50.

YEAR 2000 LIFE EXPECTANCY: INSURED POPULATION

Table 24-6 provides current life expectancy data from one large insurer for nonsmokers at ages 30 to 70 years. Clients accepted as standard risks have mortality ratios of 100%. A 50-year-old woman is expected to reach age 87, a male, age 83. If a 30-year-old female applicant with a medical problem is assessed at 300% mortality ratio she is still expected to reach age 75 years. This type of table is a useful guideline for the underwriter and the public as to what a given rating means. The 30-year-old subject rated at 300% may be misled into thinking death is near whereas expected survival is to 75 years.

MORTALITY RATIOS FOR ADULTS WITH REPAIRED CONGENITAL HEART LESIONS

Survival results extending up to 40 years are now available for the pioneering survivors of open heart surgery from 1954 to 1964 from many centers and regions, including the Mayo Clinic,[1–5] Minneapolis,[6,7] Oregon,[8] and recently Finland.[9] Few subjects are past age 50, so eventual longevity is uncertain. Mortality results will be presented as mortality ratios, using as a reference population either the control population given by the authors or a 1993 male, nonsmoking insurance population the same mean age.

TABLE 24-5	Mortality Ratios and % Mortality in 10 Years: Male Nonsmokers					
	% Mortality in 10 Years					
Age	1	5	10	15	20	25
30	179	895	1790			
40	89	445	891	1336		
50		64	129	193	258	322
60			59	88	116	147
70						75

TABLE 24-6	Life Expectancy at Various Ages vs. Mortality Ratios: Female and Male Nonsmokers					
Age	Mortality Ratios (%)					
Female	100*	150	200	300	400	500
30	55	52	49	45	43	40
40	46	42	40	36	33	31
50	37	34	31	28	26	24
60	28	25	23	20	19	17
70	21	19	17	15	14	13
Male	100*	150	200	300	400	500
30	52	48	45	41	39	37
40	42	38	36	33	30	29
50	33	30	27	25	22	21
60	25	22	20	18	16	15
70	18	16	14	12	11	10

*100% = Standard or normal expectancy, insured subjects, year 2000.

Atrial Septal Defect Secundum and Sinus Venosum

The Mayo Clinic provided 25-year survival figures for 32 subjects aged 25 to 41 having surgery for atrial septal defect (ASD). The mortality ratio against the reference population was 178%.[1] In the Finnish study[9] there were no deaths 25 to 35 years after repair of ASD in childhood. In other studies of closure in ASD in adults[10] the mortality ratio was about twice the expected whereas the mortality ratio for those who did not have their ASD repaired, for one reason or another, was considerably worse.

Ventricular Septal Defect

The early Minneapolis experience[7] showed 30-year mortality rates of 5% for subjects with pulmonary vascular resistance under 3 units and 44% if over 7 units. Mortality was 78% if there was permanent complete atrioventricular block and 22% if there was transient atrioventricular block. Mortality was 3% with a normal electrocardiogram, 15% with right bundle-branch block, and 22% with right bundle-branch block and left anterior hemiblock. Interval mortality information is available in a report from the Mayo Clinic.[2] Sixteen to 20 years after surgery, mortality was 3.0%, expected ratio was 0.5%, and mortality ratio was 600%; 21 to 25 years after surgery, mortality was 0% and expected ratio was 1.0%; 26 to 30 years after surgery, mortality was 3.0%, expected ratio was 1.5%, and mortality ratio was 200%. The number of cases was small. It appears that high-risk patients died in the first 15 years when the mortality ratios were as high as 1500% and after 20 years, mortality was closer to expected.

Valvular Pulmonary Stenosis

In the Mayo Clinic 25-year follow-up,[3] subjects having surgery between ages 5 and 20 had mortality slightly lower than the reference population. Those having surgery after age 20 had a mortality ratio of about 200%. In this group there were three sudden deaths an average of 17 years after surgery and three other deaths from myocardial infarction and two from cerebral hemorrhage.

In the Minneapolis series[7] and Oregon series,[8] 25-year mortality in all patients having surgery for pulmonary stenosis was similar to that in the reference populations. Catheter intervention patients have not been observed for longer than 20 years.

Valvular Aortic Stenosis

The Second Natural History Study of Congenital Heart Defects (NHS-II) provided 25-year follow-up data.[11] In the group with initial peak gradients of less than 25 mm Hg, 21% eventually had surgery. In those with initial gradients of 26 to 50 mm Hg, many ended up with surgery; and for the whole group, the mortality ratio was about 200%. All subjects with gradients over 80 mm Hg had surgery, and the majority of those with gradients with 50 to 70 mm Hg also ended up with surgery. The 25-year mortality ratio considering all cases with gradients of over 50 mm Hg was over 500%. The data did not allow the assessment of the mortality ratio for subjects who continued to have a good result after age 20 with or without surgery. Subjects with balloon valvuloplasty have not been observed past 20 years.

In the Minneapolis series,[7] the 30-year mortality ratio was 150% for those described with simple cases and 300% for the more complex cases. In the Oregon series,[8] mortality ratio for aortic stenosis for the first 25 years after surgery was 500%.

Coarctation of Aorta

Follow-up for patients having surgery for coarctation of the aorta now extends past 50 years, but the majority of cases operated in the early years were older than 10 years of age and many were adults.

The Mayo Clinic series included subjects aged 1 week to 72 years, and several patients had aortic valve disease. Median age was 16, and mortality between 20 and 30 years after surgery was 12%. The causes of death were coronary disease, 37%; sudden death, 13%; heart failure, 9%; stroke, 7%; aneurysm, 7%; surgical procedures, 7%; and other causes, 7%. The wide range in age and the presence of associated defects make the mean mortality ratio rather unhelpful. Against an insurance population of men ages 36 to 46, the 12% mortality produces a mortality ratio of over 700%.

Insurers select the best cases—those with surgery before age 10, normal blood pressures, arm/leg differences of less than 10 mm Hg, absent or trivial aortic disease, and absence of coronary risk factors—but there are no mortality data to confirm the wisdom of their selection process.

The New Westminster series[12] included 218 survivals of coarctation surgery, but only 27 were observed past 30 years. Fifty-six had surgery from birth to 4 years of age; 76 had surgery from 5 to 14 years of age; and 50 patients had surgery at 15 to 48 years of age. From the Kaplan-Meier survival curves, mortality between 20 to 30 years after surgery was 11%, 11%, and 5% for the three groups, corresponding to mortality ratios of 1200%, 1700%, and 250%. There was surprisingly little difference in the 20- to 30-year survival rate for the three groups, possibly due to the small numbers, comorbidity, and other unknown factors.

In the Turin, Italy, study,[13] 226 patients were followed for up to 30 years after coarctation surgery. For subjects from 4 to 20 years of age at the time of surgery, survival was 97% at 20 years from surgery and 92% at age 30 years. The 5.2% mortality from age 32 to 42 years was said to equal the mortality in the Italian general population; but against a nonsmoking male insurance standard, the mortality ratio would be over 500%. For those aged 20 to 40 years at surgery, survival was 85% after 20 years, down to 68% 10 years later; and the 20% mortality in these 10 years gives a mortality ratio of over 1500%.

Tetralogy of Fallot

The 163 surgical survivors of surgery at the Mayo Clinic from 1955 to 1960 were observed for 30 years.[6] Mortality ratios were 2700% and 670% for the first 10 years but much improved after that. Against a demographically similar general population, mortality ratios were 10 to 20 years, 325%; 21 to 25 years, 275%; and 26 to 30 years, 150%. As for ventricular septal defect (VSD) at the Mayo Clinic, survival was approaching the population average 25 years after surgery in childhood. Very few of these patients were older than age 40 years at the time of the report.

The experience from Munich[14] was the opposite. Four hundred and ninety 1-year survivors of tetralogy surgery were observed for up to 35 years. For the first 25 years, mortality was 0.27% per year. For the next 10 years, mortality was 0.94% per year. The mean age at surgery was 11.8 years. At age 35, a 10-year mortality of 9.4% corresponds to a mortality ratio against male, nonsmoker insured individuals of over 1200%. In this series there were 26 cardiac deaths, 8 noncardiac deaths, and 8 in which the cause was unknown. Over half of the cardiac deaths were sudden and unexpected, with 4 occurring 25 to 30 years after surgery.

The Finnish study[9] revealed mortality ratios of over 2700% for tetralogy of Fallot patients aged about 30 years and observed for 10 years. In the future it is anticipated that the results from tetralogy of Fallot patients having surgery during the first few years of life will be considerably better than the above, and there are several series with up to 20 years follow-up in which survival is as high as 97% after the first year.

Insurers are understandably going to be cautious in their approach to underwriting postoperative tetralogy of Fallot clients until the follow-up of those having surgery in infancy exceeds 30 years.

Transposition of Great Arteries and Atrial Procedures (Mustard and Senning)

The Toronto Adult Congenital Heart Group enrolled 86 transposition of the great arteries post-Mustard procedure patients older than 18 years of age, 54 of who had simple repair.[15] Average follow-up was 8.0 years. Ventricular dysfunction was present in 32%, supraventricular tachycardia in 48%, pacemakers in 22%, and adult admission for heart failure in 10%.

There were eight deaths: two were sudden with no information on their status regarding rhythm or ventricular function, and 1 subject died of a stroke postpartum. Three deaths occurred from the group of 6 subjects with pulmonary hypertension, and 1 death occurred at heart transplantation.

Using the published Kaplan-Meier survival curve, mortality between ages 18 to 28 was 12%, corresponding to mortality ratios of over 1500% for males and 4000% for females using standard insurance populations for reference.

Insurers would automatically exclude the subjects whose conditions presumed higher risks, but there are no data to estimate mortality in the ideal 18-year old with normal rhythm, ventricular function, and exercise response. Even in this large Toronto series there were only 10 survivors past age 32 years who were being followed, so meaningful mortality data will require at least another 30 years of follow-up. Because mortality data after the arterial switch operation do not currently extend past age 20 years, prediction of outcome in the adult years is not currently possible.

Finnish Study

A recent report from Finland[9] provided Kaplan-Meier curves showing survival data for all of the 1-year survivors of congenital heart surgery in that country observed for up to 35 years. The mean age at surgery was 5 years, and all subjects were younger than age 15 years.

Table 24-7 derived from this study provides mortality ratios for the first 25 years using a male insurance population of age 5 years for reference. The mortality ratios ranged from 1.5 times normal for patients with ASD to over 50 times normal for univentricular hearts. This covered the period from a mean age of 5 to age 30 years.

More pertinent to our interest in the adult age group are 10-year mortality ratios for five lesions from 25 to 35 years after surgery. Male and female insurance standards for age 30 were used for reference.

Table 24-8 indicates no mortality for the 259 repaired ASD subjects alive at a mean age of 30 years followed to age 40 years. Subjects with

repaired VSD had relatively low mortality ratios of 175% and 275%, whereas the 153 tetralogy of Fallot survivors at age 30 had mortality ratios in excess of 25 times normal covering the next 10 years. Also high were the mortality ratios for coarctation of the aorta, likely because of the inclusion of complex cases with aortic valve disease.

Oregon Study

Two useful reports[8,16] from Oregon documented the survival of nearly all Oregon residents age 18 and younger having surgery for CHD from 1958 to 1989 (Table 24-9). Data from this follow-up was put into life table format by Singer,[17] and the calculated annual mortality rate from this report was compared with the U.S. general white population 1986. The mortality ratios were high except for VSD repairs against a general U.S. population considering those alive at age 20 observed for 5 years.

LIMITATIONS TO EXISTING LONG-TERM MORTALITY DATA

Published survival information for CHD has several limitations (Table 24-10), but for predicting mortality the main drawbacks are that follow-up information after age 40 is very limited and late survival of subjects having surgery after 1985 may be very different from those who had surgery from 1954 to 1970.

Currently available survival data with surgical survivors from 1954 to 1965 followed for 30 to 40 years reveal calculated mortality ratios in excess of 300% using demographically similar general populations for reference. When an insured population is used for the reference, mortality ratios are in excess of 500%. Insurers may choose to simply decline all cases in a diagnostic category or alternatively eliminate the cases deemed to be at high risk and estimate the expected mortality in the remainder.

The drawback to this is that some of the sudden deaths in adult CHD patients have been unexpected in that a good outcome was expected. There are no detailed longevity studies separating out best result cases, and with follow-up not extending past age 50 years longevity is unknown. This does not prevent insurers from selecting cases believed to be reasonable risks. They are in the risk-taking business and

TABLE 24-7	Finland: 25-Year Mortality After Surgery (Excluding First Year)			
			Mortality Ratios*	
Lesion	% Mortality	No. Alive 25 Years	Female	Male
ASD	2.6	259	350	150
PDA	4.2	1091	650	250
COA	5.3	325	800	325
VSD	10.1	156	1550	625
TOF	15.9	153	2400	1000
TGA	27.2	20	>4000	>3000
UVH	48.5	11	>5000	>4000

*Compared with nonsmoking standard risk, insurance applicants, age 5, 1993. Approximate rounded values.

ASD, atrial septal defect; COA, coarctation of aorta; PDA, patent ductus arteriosus; TGA, transposition of the great arteries; TOF, tetralogy of Fallot; UVH, univentricular heart; VSD, ventricular septal defect.

TABLE 24-8	Finland: 10-Year Mortality: 25 to 35 Years After Surgery		
		Mortality Ratios*	
Lesion	% Mortality	Female	Male
ASD	0	<100	<100
PDA	2.8	650	450
COA	4.4	1200	700
VSD	1.3	275	175
TOF	15.4	4000	2700

*Compared with nonsmoking standard risk insurance applicants age 30 years, 1993. Approximate rounded values.

ASD, atrial septal defect; COA, coarctation of aorta; PDA, patent ductus arteriosus; TOF, tetralogy of Fallot; VSD, ventricular septal defect.

TABLE 24-10	Limitations of Available Survival Studies for Insurers	
No gender breakdown		Unknown smoking status
Wide age range, sometimes 0 to 50+		Limited number of subjects
Few subjects older than age 50 by end of follow-up		Pooling of all subjects with same diagnosis
No survival data separating best result and other cases		Survival may be institution specific
Changes in surgical technique, expertise with time		Improved operative survival with each decade
Myocardial preservation, accurate diagnosis, more complete correction		Surgery at young age before myocardial hypertrophy or fibrosis
Avoidance of palliative surgery creating other problems		More severe cases surviving may increase late mortality.
Data do not permit life-table analysis or require assumptions to do so.		

TABLE 24-9	Oregon Follow-Up Study: Mortality 20 to 25 Years After Surgery						
				Mortality USA 1986 Rate/1000*		**Mortality Ratio (%)**	
Lesion	Median Age After 20 Years	No. Alive After 20 Years	Annual† Mortality 20-25 Years Rate/1000	Male	Female	Male	Female
ASD	29	100	8.4	1.6	0.6	525	1400
VSD	25	81	2.7	1.6	0.5	168	540
COA	28	68	19.0	1.5	0.5	1266	3800
TOF	28	118	7.0	1.6	0.6	438	1166

*U.S. whites: 1986.
†Calculated by Singer.[17]

ASD, atrial septal defect; COA, coarctation of aorta; TOF, tetralogy of Fallot; VSD, ventricular septal defect.

are willing to accept risks based on assumptions. Most insurers decline applications with estimated mortality ratios of over 500%, and a few policies rated at over 300% are actually issued.

CURRENT MORTALITY RATINGS FROM THE MANUALS OF THREE RE-INSURERS

Large insurers have underwriting manuals to guide underwriters, medical directors, and brokers. Only the straightforward cases are given a rating; any variation or complication is covered with the euphemistic "individual consideration (IC)." Insurers do not necessarily price impairments the same. It is not rare for company A to decline a case while company B accepts the case with a modest extra premium. The ratings for congenital disease from three re-insurer manuals are shown in Table 24-11. These ratings are a starting point for the underwriters; the actual ratings given to the client will not always be the published value.

From the three manuals reviewed, subjects with repaired ASD, VSD, pulmonary stenosis, and coarctation of the aorta with near-normal hemodynamics are often allowed standard coverage. Repaired VSD and coarctation of the aorta patients are allowed insurance at ratings better than current statistics support. "Best case" tetralogy of Fallot subjects were rated +100 by company B and +200 up by the others. For tetralogy of Fallot, the ratings listed are more optimistic than the published survival figures would support. Company B gave lighter ratings for mild aortic stenosis in adults. There was no attempt at fine tuning the system, that is, for tetralogy of Fallot considering palliative shunts, outflow patch, degree of pulmonary regurgitation, arrhythmia, age of repair, and so on. One lesion that seems to have been rated more than the evidence would support was small unrepaired VSD. All three companies declined atresias, transposition of the great arteries, corrected transposition, Ebstein anomaly, Eisenmenger complex, truncus arteriosus, and total anomalous pulmonary venous return. Compared with the mortality ratios from published studies, the re-insurers' ratios are significantly less, indicating a level of confidence in selecting out the best risks.

TABLE 24-11	Adult Congenital Heart Disease: Mortality Ratios from Three Re-insurers: A, B, C		
	Mortality Ratios		
Lesion	*A*	*B*	*C*
ASD, small, unoperated	150	150-175	200
ASD repaired	100	100	100
VSD, small			
Age 20-40 unoperated	200	100	100-200
Age 40+ unoperated	150		100-150
Repaired	200	100	100
PDA			
Repaired	100	100	100
Unoperated	200	200	200-300
COA repair			
Age < 20, BP normal	100	100	100-300
Repair 20-40, BP normal	200	100-125	100-300
Bicuspid aortic valve, gradient < 25	150	125	175
Pulmonary stenosis			
Gradient < 25	100	100-150	100-125
Unoperated gradient 25-50	175	125-150	150-200
Unoperated gradient 50-75	200	200 up	300 up
Repaired	100 up	100	100 up
Tetralogy			
Repaired age < 10, good	300	200	300 up
Repaired age < 10, fair	400	300	Decline
Aortic stenosis			
Mild unoperated	300	225	300 up
Moderate	400 up	275	Decline
Subvalvular aortic stenosis—repaired	400 up		300 up

100% = Standard normal expected mortality.

ASD, atrial septal defect; BP, blood pressure; COA, coarctation of aorta; PDA, patent ductus arteriosus; VSD, ventricular septal defect.

ENDOCARDITIS

Endocarditis is more common in adults with structural heart disease than in children. Insured subjects in general are better educated with more sensible health habits and compliance with medical advice than the general population. Assuming a lifetime risk of endocarditis of 3.0% and a fatal outcome of less than 10%, mortality ratio over a life span would be only 110%, well within the range of allowing standard coverage.

How You Can Help Your Patient Obtain Insurance Coverage

EDUCATION OF THE PATIENT

A written diagnosis should be provided to the teenager or young adult including a few specifics concerning severity and interventions and results. Advice should be given concerning education and career choices encouraging education so that manual labor will not be required in later years. The patient who has a potential residual problem should be advised to seek employers with comprehensive employment benefits including life, disability, and health insurance coverage. Patients who graduate from pediatric care or patients who are relocating should be given a summarized record and the names of physicians along with their full records. All too frequently 30-year-old insurance applicants (and unfortunately their attending physician) have no idea as to why they have a chest scar and who put it there.

PROMPT RESPONSE TO INSURERS' REQUEST FOR INFORMATION

Sufficient information should be provided to understand the initial structural defects, the nature of any interventions, and the most recent objective information to include symptomatology, heart sounds and murmurs, reports of electrocardiography, Holter monitoring, echocardiography, stress test, nuclear studies, catheter studies, and so on. There should be the usual general health information and notation of compliance with endocarditis prevention.

Some patients are clearly uninsurable with current knowledge, and detailed responses to the insurer are unnecessary. A simple statement such as univentricular heart or a hypoplastic left heart syndrome suffices.

SHOPPING FOR THE BEST COVERAGE

Some insurers will either decline insurance coverage or suggest higher than expected increases in premiums. The patient can have his or her agent/broker shop for a better deal. Providing the patient with a medical summary will assist this process. CHD is not a high-volume item and is not covered in detail in underwriting manuals.

SIZE OF POLICIES AND NEED FOR MEDICAL INFORMATION

Today, policies under $50,000 or $100,000 are often dealt with by junior underwriters or computer. The profit margins are low, and insurers may wish to avoid paying for medical information and tests, especially if it is doubtful the applicant can be insured. The more information applicants can have on hand from their cardiologists, the better are their chances. Sizable individual insurance policies and large income replacement policies or health policies will be carefully underwritten, and full details would be essential. Most insurers will not go beyond paying for an electrocardiogram, treadmill test, or chest radiograph; and if echocardiograms or other examinations are required, the case will be postponed until the client obtains this procedure through their health insurance or by paying for it.

CONCLUSION

A main concern for our patients with CHD, healthy or otherwise, is to be normal and to be treated by society as normal. Most CHD patients appear normal, feel well, and function normally at school and at work.

Some are surprised, disappointed, and alarmed when they apply for mortgage or bank loan insurance and are declined coverage. This is then their initial exposure to the fact that their longevity may be less than normal.

There are two main types of life insurance—individual life and group life. Group life is when employees of a company or members of an organization are insured for an amount based on their wage while they are working. When a group program is instituted, the insurer requires that at least three fourths of the employees enroll, because this avoids anti-selection, which would occur if mainly those with potential health problems enrolled. New employees are automatically entered if they apply for insurance coverage shortly after employment.

Persons joining a large group are not required to provide any medical information. Coverage is automatic and the group benefits in addition to life insurance include disability insurance (income replacement in case of illness or accident) and health benefits. Persons with health problems that may impact on insurability should consider employment with a firm with a quality group insurance program. Many good programs allow the subject to convert the coverage to individual insurance on termination of employment.

Life insurance continues to be important in the financial planning for families, for estate planning, for business, for loan protection, and so on. Citizens in the United States purchased $2.5 trillion of new life insurance coverage in 1999, 14% more than in 1998; and by the end of 1999, life insurance coverage in force exceeded $15.5 trillion. Fifty-nine percent of that coverage is individual. Total premium income was over $120 billion. The average individual life insurance policy was for $120,000, with some jumbo cases exceeding $50 million.

Life insurance is a highly competitive field, and insurers will often shave any rating to the minimum to acquire the business. Only about 3% of applicants are declined, 90% of these for serious health problems and 10% for hazardous occupations or lifestyle situations. Another 6% of applicants are required to pay extra premiums because of adverse health information. Thus, 90% of those applying for individual life coverage obtain a standard offer.

Creditor life insurance including mortgage insurance is sold at relatively low group rates but requires individual underwriting. Individual pricing is not possible: the client either fits into the mortality range available in the plan or he or she is declined.

Many insurers today subdivide their standard mortality category into super preferred, preferred, and standard. CHD patients would seldom fit into the super preferred and preferred categories, which require complete absence of coronary risk factors, no other potential health problems, and familial longevity. About 65% of applicants receive preferred rates when this is available in the contracts they have applied for.

Life insurers are in the business to assess and insure the risk of premature death. They spend money to acquire a case, which is lost if they decline. In ACHD there does not need to be much concern for subjects with unrepaired mild lesions such as VSD, pulmonary stenosis, and ASD and similarly for subjects with repaired pulmonary stenosis, coarctation of the aorta, VSD, and ASD with excellent results.

At ages 20 to 40 with the low death rates in the general population, especially in a normal insured population, only a few extra deaths from CHD produce high mortality ratios. If insurers were guided only by the mortality ratios available from published follow-up studies, there would be many declines, with others facing a considerable increase in premium. Insurers currently select what they regard as the best risk cases relying on judgment rather than actuarial experience.

It remains to be proven that long-term results achieved from surgical repairs carried out after 1980 or 1990 will be better than in the first 20 years. Insurers tend to be optimistic and, in general, CHD patients can purchase insurance at prices that are very fair considering the existing mortality data.

THE FUTURE …

The problem facing life insurers is illustrated by survivors of the arterial switch operation for transposition of the great arteries. In a report from France,[18] 652 patients with simple repair of transposition of the great arteries survived 3 months and after the first year there were no deaths with over 15 years' follow-up. One hundred eighty-seven subjects were observed to 10 years but only 23 to 15 years. Would you want your pension plan invested in a company that would predict normal survival to age 80 when few of these subjects have yet to see age 20?

Some insurers may accept some atrial switch operation applicants at moderate extra premiums, with the expectation that most of these patients will continue to do well, but any one insurer should not be expected to assume a large volume of unpredictable risks.

Insurers have benefited from the medical advances that prolong life, and as long as their insured population is large, insurers' reserves are sufficient to withstand the unpredictable strains of epidemics such as human immunodeficiency virus infection or of mankind's self-destruction by terrorism.

It is in the public interest that insurers price their financial security products based on fair risk assessments so that sufficient funds are available to cover the billions of dollars paid out every day.

Large CHD centers should keep publishing survival data in a format amenable to life table analysis. To achieve the benefit of a large population, pooled studies such as those of the NHS-II would be of value.

At present, personal financial security through insurance is not possible for the majority of patients with CHD but is more likely for those who are in a group policy or have the simple defects such as an ASD closure. When it comes to vocational choices for the teenager with CHD, this should be taken into account particularly for the patient with moderate to severe CHD who is unlikely to be insurable. Pursuing training and a career in areas that group policies are likely, like health care and larger organizations, would be clearly advantageous.[19]

Life insurance, while very desirable especially if one has dependants, is usually first sought when obtaining a mortgage on a home. This should not prove to be a bar or added expense on home ownership because a repayment mortgage rather than an endowment mortgage can just as easily be obtained.

Another aspect of insurance that would often require an increased premium for patients is travel insurance; however, there are a number of companies with which patients would be able to obtain cover at normal or near-normal premiums. Those who specialize in this market tend to have a set of questions, which are often very reasonable, that as long as one is able to answer adequately would enable cover at normal rates. Matters such as having recently had surgery or awaiting surgery would not result in normal coverage, but as long as travel plans are timed to coincide with periods outside what they regard as greater risk then obtaining coverage should not prove too difficult.

REFERENCES

1. Murphy JG, Gersh BJ, McGoon MD, et al. Long-term outcome after surgical repair of isolated atrial septal defect. N Engl J Med 1990;323:1645–1650.
2. Murphy JG. The late survival after surgical repair of isolated ventricular septal defect (VSD)—Abstract. Circulation 1989;80 (Suppl. II):II490.
3. Hayes CJ, Gersony WM, Driscoll DJ, et al. Results of treatment of patients with pulmonary valvar stenosis. Circulation 1988;78:1150–1156.
4. Cohen M, Forster V, Steele PM, et al. Coarctation of the aorta: long-term follow-up and prediction of outcome after surgical correction. Circulation 1989;80:840–845.
5. Murphy JG, Gersh BJ, Mair RD, et al. Long-term outcome in patients undergoing surgical repair of tetralogy of Fallot. N Engl J Med 1993;3209:53–59.
6. Moller JH, Anderson RC. 1,000 consecutive children with a cardiac malformation with 26- to 37-year follow-up. J Am Coll Cardiol 1991;20:295–300.
7. Moller JH, Patton C, Varco RL, et al. Late results (30–35 years) after operative closure of isolated ventricular septal defect from 1954 to 1960. Am J Cardiol 1991;68:1491–1497.
8. Morris CD, Menashe VD. 25-year mortality after surgical repair of congenital heart defect in childhood: a population-based cohort study. JAMA 1991;226:3447–3472.
9. Nieminen HP, Jokinen EV, Sairanen HI. Late results of pediatric cardiac surgery in Finland: a population-based study with 96% follow-up. Circulation 2001;104:570–575.
10. Konstantinides S, Geibel A, Olschewski M, et al. A comparison of surgical and medical therapy for atrial septal defects in adults. N Engl J Med 1995;333:469–473.
11. Keane JF, Driscoll DJ, Gersony WM, et al. Second Natural History Study of Congenital Heart Defects. Results of treatment of patients with aortic valvar stenosis. Circulation 1993;87(Suppl. I):I16–I27.
12. Bobby JJ, Epami JM, Farmer DT, Newman CGH. Operative survival and 40-year follow-up of surgical repair of aortic coarctation. Br Heart J 1991;65:271–276.

13. Presbitero P, Demarie D, Villani M, et al. Long-term results (15–30 years) of surgical repair of aortic coarctation. Br Heart J 1987;57:462–467.

14. Nollert G, Fischlein T, Bouterwek S, et al. Long-term survival in patients with repair of tetralogy of Fallot: 36 year follow-up of 490 survivors of the first year after surgical repair. J Am Coll Cardiol 1997;30:1374–1383.

15. Puley G, Siu S, Connelly M, et al. Arrhythmia and survival in patients > 18 years after the Mustard procedure for complete transposition of the great arteries. Am J Cardiol 1999;83:1080–1084.

16. Silka MJ, Hardy BG, Menashe VD, Morris CD. A population-based prospective evaluation of risk of sudden cardiac death after operation for common congenital heart defects. J Am Coll Cardiol 1998;32:245–251.

17. Singer RB. Repair of congenital cardiovascular defects: 25-year follow-up. J Insur Med 1993;25:5–10.

18. Losay J, Touchot A, Serraf A, et al. Late outcome after arterial switch operation for transposition of the great arteries. Circulation 2001;104(Suppl. I):1121–1126.

19. Vonder Muhll I, Cumming G, Gatzoulis MA. Risky business: Insuring adults with congenital heart disease. Eur Heart J 2003;24:1595–1600.

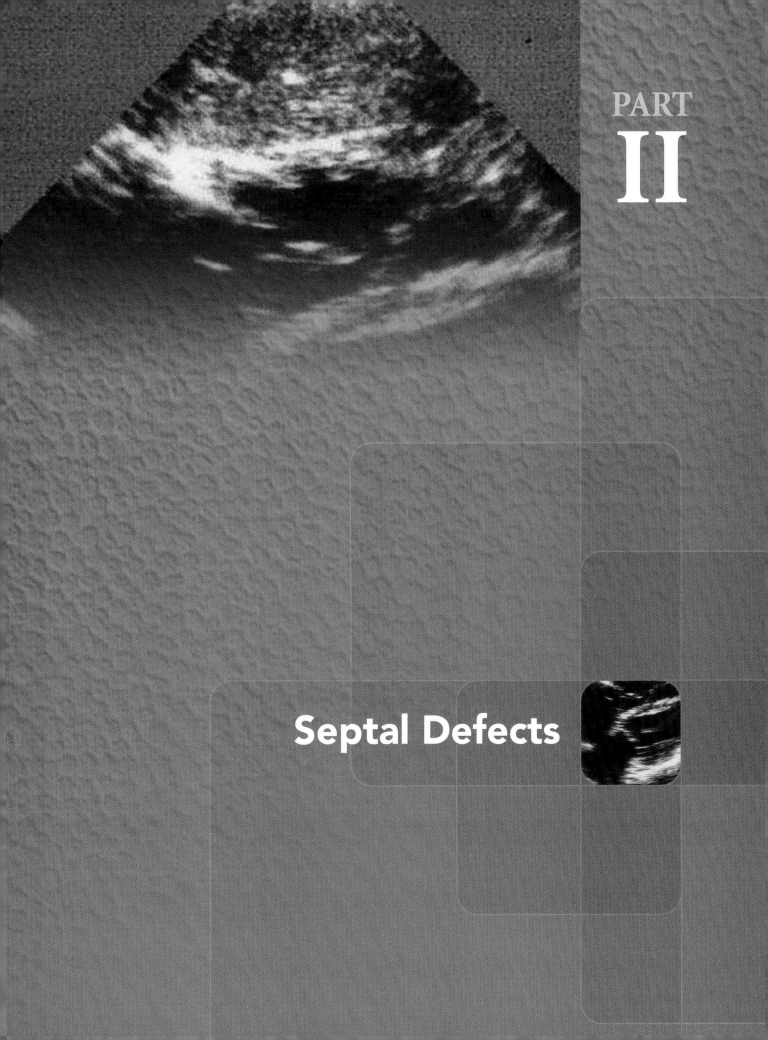

Septal Defects

25

Atrial Septal Defect

JELENA RADOJEVIC | MICHAEL L. RIGBY

Definition and Morphology

An atrial septal defect (ASD) is a direct communication between the cavities of the atrial chambers that permits shunting of blood. In the normal heart the true atrial septum is within the rims of the oval fossa; the majority of the remaining tissue separating the atrial chambers is composed of an infolding of the atrial wall.

The morphology of the various types of interatrial communication has been known since the early description by Rokitansky and forms the basis for that classification (Box 25-1; Fig. 25-1). Defects within the oval fossa are known as secundum defects, in spite of the fact that the oval fossa is the primum septum. They may extend outside the true limits of the oval fossa when there is a deficiency of infolding of the atrial wall. Such extension may occur posteroinferiorly to the mouth of the inferior vena cava (IVC), superiorly to the mouth of the superior vena cava (SVC), inferiorly to the atrioventricular junctions, or posteriorly to the mouth of the coronary sinus. With posterolateral extension to the atrial wall, the defect will encroach toward the entry of the right pulmonary veins into the left atrium. It is not unusual, therefore, for large secundum defects to extend beyond the limits of the oval fossa. In contrast, the most frequent interatrial communication is found when the so-called flap valve of the oval fossa fails to fuse with the rim, sometimes allowing left-to-right shunting but more frequently giving rise to a probe patent foramen ovale, which can permit only right-to-left shunting when the right atrial pressure is higher than that of the left. Although in most instances there is a single defect, it is not unusual to find additional fenestrations; occasionally, multiple small fenestrations occur (Fig. 25-2), often associated with an aneurysm of the oval fossa.

A superior sinus venosus defect occurs when there is a deficiency of infolding of the atrial wall in the environs of the SVC. It is found within the mouth of the SVC, which has a biatrial connection, overriding the rim of the oval fossa so as to produce what is effectively an extracardiac but interatrial communication. Most frequently, the pulmonary veins from part of the right lung are also involved, connecting anomalously to the SVC near its junction with the atria. A defect found similarly in the mouth of the IVC, which has a biatrial connection, is known as an inferior sinus venosus defect. It is much rarer than the superior type, often associated with right-to-left shunting and cyanosis and sometimes difficult to distinguish from an oval fossa defect, which extends posteroinferiorly to the mouth of the IVC. The rarest type is a deficiency of the wall between the coronary sinus and the left atrium, producing an interatrial communication through the mouth of the coronary sinus—a so-called coronary sinus defect. In its most extreme form, a left SVC connects to the roof of the left atrium, the entire wall of the coronary sinus is lacking, and the mouth of the coronary sinus forms a large communication. A primum defect is part of an atrioventricular (AV) septal defect with a common AV junction and is roofed superiorly by the inferior border of the oval fossa and inferiorly by the superior and inferior bridging leaflets, forming two AV valves. Primum defects have a trileaflet left AV valve, which impacts on long-term outcome and is discussed in Chapter 27.

Large interatrial communications may represent a confluence of one type of defect with another. When an ASD is the primary diagnosis, associated malformations occur in about 30% of cases. These include pulmonary valve stenosis, partial anomalous pulmonary venous connection, congenital mitral stenosis, mitral valve prolapse, ventricular septal defect, patent ductus arteriosus, and coarctation of the aorta.

Genetics and Epidemiology

There is a well-recognized association of secundum and primum defects with Down syndrome. Ostium primum ASD may be associated with DiGeorge syndrome and Ellis-van Creveld syndrome. Adults with AV septal defects have an approximate 10% risk of recurrence in their offspring.[1,2] Secundum defects may be associated with skeletal abnormalities of the forearm and hand,[3] which have been shown to result from mutations of *TBX5*, a member of the brachyury family of genes.[4] The familial forms of secundum ASD have been associated with *GATA4* and *NKX2.5* mutations.[5,6] In these forms, prolonged AV conduction times are common. In 250 consecutive patients undergoing closure of a secundum ASD at the Royal Brompton Hospital, London, there was a family history in one or more close relatives in 2%.

Apart from a bicuspid aortic valve, an ASD is the most common congenital heart malformation to be encountered, with a frequency of 10% to 17%. About 60% are found in females. Secundum defects are the most common (60%), with primum defects accounting for 20% and superior sinus venosus defects 15%. The other types are rare.

Although many individuals with an ASD are diagnosed and treated during childhood, a significant number present with symptoms for the first time in adult life. Of all the cases of ASD treated at the Royal Brompton Hospital, London, in the past 3 years, more than 50% presented in adult life.

Early Presentation and Management

Although the occasional infant presents with breathlessness and even heart failure, and a few children have recurrent chest infections or breathlessness on exertion, the majority are symptom free and present with a heart murmur. In the current era, many children are referred to a pediatric cardiologist for spurious reasons and are found to have an ASD on echocardiography. A few children present with cyanosis because of pulmonary stenosis, Ebstein anomaly, or pulmonary vascular disease (uncommon).

Although it has been argued that routine closure is not of proven benefit to every individual, there is a consensus that when a defect gives rise to right ventricular dilation it should be closed. Such holes usually measure 10 mm or more in diameter and occupy at least one third of the length of the atrial septum in echocardiographic four-chamber sections. The hospital mortality rate after operation should be less than 1%, with correspondingly low complication rates. The long-term outcome after surgical repair during childhood is excellent with a reduced incidence of late arrhythmia, heart failure, stroke, pulmonary hypertension, or cardiovascular death.[7]

TRANSCATHETER CLOSURE

The era of transcatheter closure of secundum defects is now well established.[8] It is important to emphasize that defects only within the oval fossa are suitable for transcatheter device closure and there should be a 4- to 5-mm rim between the hole and the atrioventricular valves or the entry of the systemic and pulmonary veins. Three-dimensional (3D) echocardiography can be used to demonstrate the shape and borders of an oval fossa defect. The most reliable imaging modalities for delivery of a device are a combination of fluoroscopy with transesophageal or intravascular ultrasonography.[9]

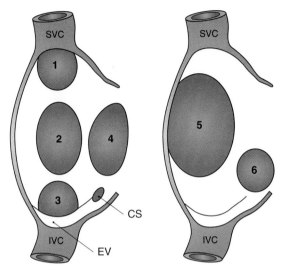

Figure 25-1   Anatomy of atrial septal defects viewed from the right atrium. 1, Superior sinus venosus; 2, secundum; 3, inferior sinus venosus; 4, primum; 5, secundum defect without posterior septal rim; 6, coronary sinus. CS, coronary sinus; EV, eustachian valve; IVC, inferior vena cava; SVC, superior vena cava.

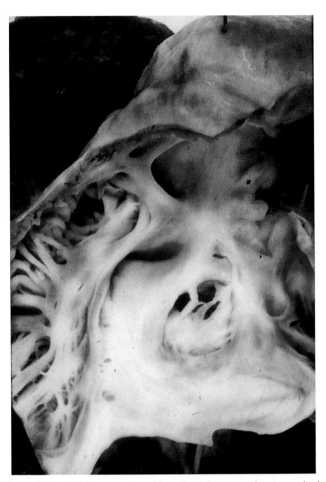

Figure 25-2   Atrial septum viewed from the right atrium, showing multiple fenestrations in the oval fossa.

A variety of devices have been used or are currently available, and modifications to these together with introduction of new systems have resulted in significant changes in practice over the past years. The trend in interventional treatment of septal defects is toward defect-specific systems and new devices minimizing the foreign material in the atria.

Details of the technique for transcatheter closure of suitable interatrial communications are discussed in Chapter 9. In brief, the morphology of the defect is important when selecting which device to use for closure. Oval fossa defects with a stretched diameter of up to 20 mm may be closed with any of the available systems. Larger defects with a stretched diameter of up to 40 mm should be closed with a self-centering device. The best device currently available is the Amplatzer septal occluder (AGA Medical, Golden Valley, MN, USA) (Fig. 25-3), although the STARflex (NMT Medical Inc., Boston, MA, USA) has been used by some. The SolySafe septal occluder (Swissimplant AG, Solothurn, Switzerland) is a self-centering device delivered over a guide wire and can be retrieved after deployment. It has been used for smaller defects up to 25 mm but may be applicable to some patients with a large ASD.[10,11]

Multiple fenestrations in the oval fossa can be closed with a device in which the left and right atrial discs are connected by a thin connecting stem (Cardioseal, Buttoned, or Helex). A septal aneurysm need not be a contraindication to transcatheter closure, but the left atrial disc should cover most of the septum. In general, for all patients, device diameter should never exceed that of the atrial septum.

Other, newer devices currently in use include the BioSTAR septal occluder (NMT Medical, Inc., Boston, MA, USA), which has a bioabsorbable heparin-coated collagen layer matrix. About 24 months after implantation, the collagen matrix is replaced by the host tissue with the theoretical benefit of a reduced risk of thrombus formation.[12,13] The Occlutech device (Occlutech, Jena, Germany) and the Premere occluder (St. Jude Medical, Inc., Maple Grove, MN, USA) are also designed for ASD and patent foramen ovale closure. HeartStitch (Sutura Inc., Fountain Valley, CA, USA) is a new concept in transcatheter patent foramen ovale closure that leaves less material in the atria, with the possible benefit of a reduced risk of thrombus formation, device migration, and eroison.[11]

When an expert neurologist considers that a patient suffers from neurologic symptoms that can be explained on the basis of paradoxic emboli resulting from right-to-left shunting across a patent foramen ovale or small ASD, transcatheter closure can be achieved with conventional devices designed for ASD or those designed specifically for very small defects.

■ Late Outcome

SURVIVAL AND FUNCTIONAL STATUS

The precise natural history of an individual born with an ASD is somewhat unclear, although there is little doubt that in the majority of patients life expectancy is reduced. Campbell, in 1970, reported an early mortality rate during infancy of 1%, increasing to 15% in the third decade of life due to pulmonary hypertension and congestive heart failure, and an actuarial survival rate at 60 years of only 15%.[14] This study clearly exaggerates the poor outcome of isolated ASD. We are now aware that a number of patients with sizeable interatrial communications remain remarkably well and symptom free through early adulthood. They are, however, at risk of premature death due to progressive right ventricular dilation with diminished coronary reserve,[15] right-sided heart failure, recurrent pneumonia and pulmonary hypertension, atrial flutter and fibrillation, and paradoxical embolus and stroke.[16]

Most patients are symptom free during the first and second decades of life. Then an increasing number develop effort intolerance in subsequent decades, although patients are often unaware of any symptoms until

Figure 25-3 Transesophageal echocardiogram from a patient in whom an Amplatzer occluder was used to close an anterior oval fossa defect. AO, aorta; LA, left atrium; RA, right atrium.

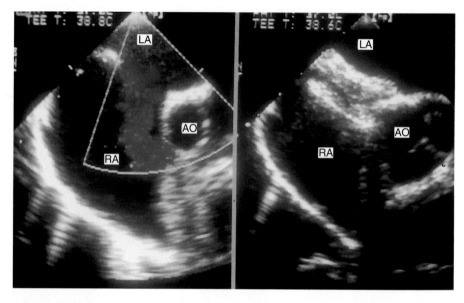

BOX 25-2   COMPLICATIONS OF ATRIAL SEPTAL DEFECTS

- Premature death
- Exercise intolerance
- Right-sided heart failure
- Left ventricular dysfunction
- Tricuspid and mitral valve regurgitation
- Atrial fibrillation or flutter
- Sinus node dysfunction
- Paradoxic thromboembolism
- Endocarditis (rare)
- Pulmonary hypertension or pulmonary vascular disease (uncommon)

closure of the defect results in improved exercise performance.[17,18] Spontaneous closure of a secundum ASD can occur during the first 2 years of life,[19] and our own observations have confirmed that in some patients the defect increases in size in late childhood and early adolescence with somatic growth.[20] The degree of left-to-right shunting may also increase with time, related to decreasing left ventricular compliance and increasing systemic arterial resistance occurring during the fifth to seventh decades. An increasing left-to-right shunt will also tend to give rise to mitral and tricuspid valve regurgitation in later life. As a result of the various later complications, New York Heart Association (NYHA) functional class typically declines from I to II in the first 3 to 5 decades of life to class III to IV in subsequent decades.

Most patients who have undergone early closure of a defect remain well with an excellent outlook and a normal survival (when repair is undertaken before 25 years of age). Older age at repair is a risk factor for premature late death, which becomes progressively more powerful with increasing age at operation.[16,21]

LATE COMPLICATIONS (Box 25-2)

Although pulmonary hypertension is found with increasing frequency with advancing age, a pulmonary vascular resistance greater than 6 units is relatively rare. Advanced pulmonary hypertension is, however, not expected early in the course of an ASD. Right ventricular volume overload and increased end-diastolic dimensions are well tolerated for many years, but eventually diminished right ventricular ejection fraction, hypokinesia, and right ventricular failure tend to occur, usually after the fifth or sixth decade. As outlined earlier, an additional aggravating factor at this time is the increasing left-to-right shunt. There appears to be an interaction between the volume-overloaded right ventricle and the left ventricle. In the latter, diastolic dimensions are reduced and, with increasing age, ejection fraction does not increase with maximal exercise.[22] Important mitral regurgitation is found in a few adult patients, although tricuspid insufficiency is more common, particularly when heart failure begins to develop. By the age of 40 years more than 20% will have developed atrial fibrillation, but by 60 years of age the number will have increased to about 60%. Systemic arterial hypertension is surprisingly common and difficult to explain.[23]

Outpatient Assessment

OPERATED PATIENTS

Patients operated on during the first or second decades for a secundum or superior sinus venosus defect can usually be considered to have a normal heart, so follow-up is not needed. The vast majority are symptom free with no abnormal physical signs and with normal chest radiography, electrocardiography, and echocardiography findings. Such patients are often discharged 1 to 2 years after operation because late problems are extremely rare.

Occasionally, residual ASDs are encountered after either surgical or catheter closure. Unless responsible for a significant left-to-right shunt, they do not require additional intervention.

Progressive pulmonary vascular disease is occasionally encountered after late repair; such patients warrant lifelong follow-up.

A complication specific to superior sinus venosus defects is stenosis of the SVC at its junction with the right atrium. This merits specific attention with echocardiography before the patient is discharged from follow-up.

There is a consensus for periodic, infrequent follow-up of patients operated on after the second decade of life because of the greater risk of chronic right and even left ventricular dysfunction, late atrial arrhythmias, and premature late death.[24] A careful history of lifestyle and symptoms should be an integral part of the review, together with chest radiography, electrocardiography, and cross-sectional echocardiography to assess the atrioventricular valves and ventricular function, with Holter monitoring if appropriate.

There is still no consensus as to the follow-up required for patients undergoing transcatheter device closure of a secundum defect. Most publications about immediate, intermediate-, and long-term follow-up describe the procedure as safe and efficient with low morbidity and mortality.[25,26] When compared with surgical repair in developed countries, hospital stay is shorter and the cost is reduced.[27,28] Immediate and early complications are rare (less than 1%) but can include mitral regurgitation, obstruction of one pulmonary vein, retroperitoneal hematoma, atrial arrhythmias, embolization of the device, cardiac perforation, and even death.[25,29] Cardiac perforation is fortunately very rare (fewer then 30 cases reported in the literature) but is associated with significant morbidity and mortality.[29] It can occur immediately or up to 2 years after the procedure.[29–31] The pathophysiology is not fully understood, but it seems to be related to the forces transmitted by the device to the vulnerable anterosuperior wall of the atria and the aorta.

Another significant mid-term complication is newly developed or deteriorating aortic valve regurgitation. Schoen and associates reported new or worsened aortic regurgitation (usually mild) in up to 10% of patients at 12 months.[32] Although this potential complication should be taken into account when decisions about transcatheter closure are undertaken, the experience of these authors is not universal. Our experience is that this complication is extremely rare even when larger devices are used.

Small residual defects are infrequent but more likely with devices without a self-centering mechanism.

Late complications such as thrombus on the device, thromboembolic events (including stroke and coronary artery embolism), complete heart block, and infective endocarditis have been reported occasionally (up to 8 years after the procedure).[25,33] Because the exact risk of late complications in this group is unknown, our current policy is to review patients annually or every 2 years.

UNOPERATED PATIENTS

The majority of new patients with an ASD seen in the outpatient clinic will have presented with breathlessness on exertion, which in some cases may have been attributed erroneously to asthma. Palpitations due to atrial arrhythmias might also be the presenting symptom, whereas other modes of presentation include cardiac enlargement on a routine chest radiograph, a heart murmur detected during pregnancy or routine physical examination, and, occasionally, cyanosis or symptoms of a paradoxical embolus.

A comprehensive outpatient diagnostic workup should determine:
- The type, number, and size of ASD
- The hemodynamic significance of the defect:
  - The presence and degree of right atrial and ventricular dilation and function
  - Shunt size depicted from $\dot{Q}p/\dot{Q}s$ (in reality this measure is rarely performed)
  - Pulmonary arterial pressure
- The presence of associated anomalies that need to be addressed
- Whether there is a history of sustained arrhythmia that required intervention. The management of the atrial arrhythmia should ideally be performed before the ASD closure, while the antegrade access to the left atrium is still available across the ASD.

History and Clinical Examination
The history and clinical examination includes a search for:
- Right ventricular left parasternal impulse
- Wide and fixed splitting of the second heart sound—cardinal physical sign of an ASD (not always present)
- Pulmonary ejection systolic murmur at the upper left sternal edge
- Tricuspid mid-diastolic murmur at the lower left sternal edge, which might radiate toward the cardiac apex
- An accentuated pulmonary component of the second heart sound, suggesting raised pulmonary arterial pressure
- Cyanosis—this is uncommon and more likely with a large defect or virtually common atrium, an inferior sinus venosus defect, a large coronary sinus defect, pulmonary vascular disease, or associated pulmonary stenosis, right ventricular dysfunction, or Ebstein anomaly.

Pulse Oximetry
On pulse oximetry normal oxygen saturation is expected.

Electrocardiography
Electrocardiography may show the following:
- Right-axis deviation
- Incomplete right bundle-branch block pattern
- Evidence of right ventricular hypertrophy
- Lengthened PR interval
- Abnormal P-wave axis (outside the normal range of 0° to 60°) would suggest a superior sinus venosus ASD
- Extreme right- or left-axis deviation (so-called superior QRS axis) would suggest a primum ASD.

Chest Radiography
Chest radiography in adults with significant ASDs reveals:
- Cardiac enlargement with retrosternal filling in the lateral view
- Right atrial dilation
- Prominent central pulmonary arteries and pulmonary vascular markings
- When severe pulmonary hypertension complicates a large ASD, the heart size is large, in contrast to usually a normal heart size in a patient with a pulmonary hypertensive large VSD.

Echocardiography
The diagnosis is usually confirmed by cross-sectional transthoracic echocardiography, using a combination of subcostal, parasternal, and apical four-chamber sections with color flow Doppler interrogation.

Secundum defects are found within the oval fossa and appear in the middle of the atrial septum. A superior sinus venosus defect, however, is overridden by the SVC and right upper pulmonary vein (Fig. 25-4), an inferior sinus venosus defect is overridden by the IVC, and a coronary sinus defect is seen posterior to the AV valves (Fig. 25-5).

The presence of tricuspid regurgitation will permit a Doppler estimate of pulmonary artery pressure.

In adult patients, however, the reality is that the transthoracic windows may be poor and the only clue to an ASD can be an enlarged right ventricle. For this reason transesophageal studies are often needed to establish the site and size of the defect and the connection of the pulmonary veins. Furthermore, transesophageal echocardiography establishes the morphology and suitability for device closure.

In the current era, live 3D transesophageal echocardiography is a useful complementary tool in assessing the size, site, and shape of an ASD, its borders, and its relations with the neighboring structures (Fig. 25-6). It is also helpful in confirming the good positioning of a device and identifying the site of any residual shunt (Fig. 25-7).[34,35]

Intracardiac echocardiography is expensive and rarely used in routine management.

Cardiac Catheterization
Cardiac catheterization is performed:
- To determine pulmonary artery pressures and resistance, if there are concerns
- To assess pulmonary vascular reactivity if pulmonary arterial hypertension is present
- To delineate anomalous pulmonary venous connection(s)
- For selective coronary angiography, in patients at high risk of coronary artery disease or in patients older than the age of 40 years when surgical repair is contemplated

Magnetic Resonance Imaging
Magnetic resonance imaging (MRI) is an additional means of demonstrating the ASD and its location. It can be used to assess pulmonary venous connections if doubts remain after other imaging modalities have been used, and it can also be used to estimate $\dot{Q}p/\dot{Q}s$.

Computed Tomographic Angiography
Computed tomographic angiography is an additional means of demonstrating the ASD and its location. It can be used to assess pulmonary venous connections, if doubts remain after other imaging modalities have been used. It can also aid in assessing the existence of coronary artery disease in patients older than 40 years of age when surgical repair is contemplated.

Exercise Oxygen Saturation
An exercise oxygen saturation test may be done when more than mild pulmonary hypertension is present.

may include psychiatrists, nutritionists, career counselors, and gynecologists, among others. Seminars for groups of patients and families can be arranged. Group clinic visits have been utilized successfully in noncardiac chronic care models. Patient and family support groups can be organized locally and have been organized on a national level with patient focused meetings. Patients may respond to verbal discussions, pictorial representations, written resources, or online interfaces depending on their personal learning preferences. In many ways, the educational aspects of the transition process should continue indefinitely. If patients are able to independently seek and obtain new knowledge, they can feel a sense of control over their health and medical management.

Specific content should include discussions about the risks and benefits of various forms of contraception and pregnancy should begin before patients reach adolescence. An unplanned pregnancy should not be the stimulus for precipitous transfer to adult care. Both male and female patients should understand the increased chance of congenital abnormalities in their children. Contraceptive options should be discussed with patients before they become sexually active.[23,24] The teratogenicity of warfarin anticoagulation and angiotensin-converting enzyme inhibitors is a critical issue for education and discussion for some patients.

Pregnancy is feasible for many adult patients with CHD, but the potential risks to the mother and unborn child should ideally be discussed before conception (Case 20-2).[25,26] Fetal echocardiography and genetic counseling should be offered to selected patients. Planning regarding the most appropriate number of pregnancies and their timing may be important. Pregnancy, especially in a woman who has a complex congenital heart condition, should be well planned to minimize risks, and a written plan of cardiac care should be developed with the obstetric team.

Case 20-2

A 24-year-old woman, who underwent a Ross procedure for aortic stenosis as a teenager, established care with an adult CHD specialist. Initial review of her medications including a progesterone-only oral contraceptive led to a discussion of contraception and pregnancy. She was previously counseled that women with congenital heart conditions should not take estrogen-containing contraception, and she assumed that in spite of her strong desire it would be very unhealthy to become pregnant. In the absence of residual valvular disease and with normal cardiac function, she was stratified to be low risk for thromboembolism with estrogen-containing contraception. She elected to discontinue contraception completely and successfully carried an infant to full term without cardiovascular sequelae.

This patient had apparently not been educated about family planning options or the feasibility of her having a successful pregnancy.

Patients should learn how to reduce the risk of infective endocarditis through attention to excellent oral health and, in some cases, to the use of antibiotic prophylaxis before dental surgery. They should be able to recognize the symptoms of endocarditis and to access urgent care promptly and appropriately.

If relevant, patients should be educated about arrhythmias that may occur and their presenting symptoms. They should know which arrhythmias should be considered a nuisance, which need nonurgent attention, and which may need emergency care. Arrhythmia management options including medications, catheter ablations, and surgical interventions may be reviewed.

The relevance of their heart condition to noncardiac medical issues and procedures should be reviewed. Many of these patients should have noncardiac surgery performed in a setting where the cardiac staff and the anesthesiologist are familiar with their heart problem and can plan appropriate care.

Many children and young people with congenital heart conditions will be able to have any careers they may choose. The outcome for some complex CHD patients will include physical and/or neurodevelopmental limitations, and they need to be counseled to pursue education and careers that are compatible with such limitations. A patient with a Fontan palliation should know not to become a bricklayer or a commercial trucker. These patients and their parents should have a chance to discuss these matters before the patient reaches high school age and before important decisions are made, such as choosing an inappropriate trade or dropping out of school. Many of these patients will have difficulties obtaining life insurance and should know to expect this and to begin a personal savings program early.[16] In the United States, health insurance may be difficult to obtain and these patients should learn how to position themselves to be able to always have good insurance. This may direct their education and employment choices to improve access to insurance.

Each cardiology visit should include time that the patient spends privately with the provider. Confidentiality should be assured, with the exception of issues risking health or safety. Patients should be made aware that if confidentiality must be broken it will be discussed with them first.

Education around lifestyle issues is important to enable patients to get into the habit of promoting their own good health. Patients should be educated not to smoke cigarettes, to avoid abuse of alcohol and recreational drugs, and to maintain excellent oral hygiene to protect themselves from endocarditis. They should be encouraged to eat a healthy diet and to stay fit. Limitations around physical exercise or hobbies should also be reviewed, including questioning of inappropriate limitations that may be imposed by the patient or family. Much of this preparation should be held privately with the patient. Disclosure of risk taking and substance abuse may be a red flag for a patient at higher risk of loss to follow-up and failure to transfer.[27]

End-of-life decisions and individual preferences for the limits of critical care and resuscitation are often not discussed during adolescence; however it is appropriate for young people with complex congenital heart conditions to explore these topics sooner than their healthy peers. Discussions about such decisions should be part of a comprehensive transition process, and the initiation of this discussion at a time of stable health allows for more educated and less reactionary decision-making. If available and appropriate, the palliative care team may be helpful in addressing these issues.

When possible, skills training in communication, decision-making, and self-care should be available. At least one single independent clinic visit between the patient and pediatric cardiologist should be planned before the transfer of care. This rather simple act serves as a milestone in autonomous medical decision-making and may be associated with improved transfer success.

Policy on the Timing of Transfer from Pediatric Care

There should be a policy on timing of the transfer of care to ensure that transition and transfer actually occur and occur in a predictable way.[28] Transfer most commonly occurs at about age 18 or at the time of completion of high school. Even so, the timing of transfer should be flexible so as to best meet the needs of the patient. It is important that the target age for transfer be explicit and shared among health care providers, patients, and families. Patients should understand that the transfer to adult care is a natural process for all patients, just as each patient can be expected to finish high school. Agreement on the age of transfer also helps ensure that everyone takes full advantage of the opportunity to complete the transition curriculum. As stated earlier, one of the main reasons to delay the transfer process would be the lack of able and available adult cardiac care. For this reason, an inflexible age of discharge from pediatric cardiac care is not in the best interest of the patient.

Types of Services Needed in the Adult Congenital Heart Disease Environment

Although the needs of some patients are straightforward, others have complex needs and may require the involvement of a variety of consultants, including an electrophysiologist, obstetrician, gynecologist, psychiatrist, nephrologist, gastroenterologist, hepatologist, neurologist,

Figure 25-4 Vertical section from a transeso-phageal echocardiogram of a superior sinus venosus defect (*arrow*) in which the superior vena cava (SVC) overrides the atrial septum and therefore connects to both the left atrium (LA) and right atrium (RA). The right upper pulmonary vein (PV) connects to the SVC. The right panel reveals the left-to-right shunt demonstrated by color flow Doppler imaging.

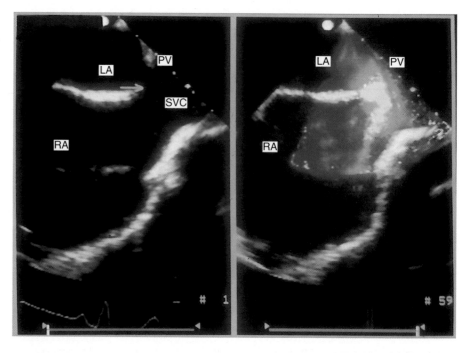

Figure 25-5 Echocardiographic four-chamber section of a confluent coronary sinus atrial septal defect (ASD). Although the defect cannot be visualized in the conventional four-chamber section on the left, sections posterior to this reveal a large defect and unroofing of the coronary sinus. LA, left atrium; LV, left ventricle; RA, right atrium; RV, right ventricle.

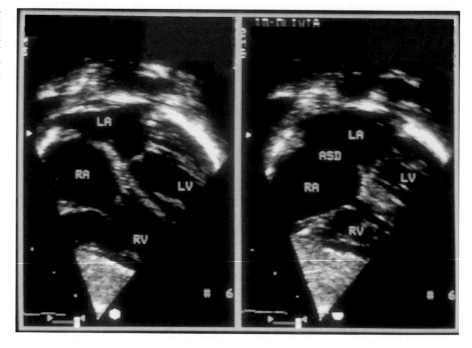

Open-Lung Biopsy

Open-lung biopsy is hardly ever performed in the current era. It may be used when the reversibility of the pulmonary hypertension is uncertain from the hemodynamic data. It is potentially hazardous and should be done only at centers with personnel with substantial relevant experience.

Additional Tests

We consider it important to ascertain what symptoms are present and to establish the degree of exercise intolerance. In our practice we perform exercise treadmill testing (with maximum oxygen uptake), so that any benefits of subsequent closure of an ASD can be documented, and we perform Holter monitoring if there is any suspicion of atrial arrhythmias or atrioventricular block.

Late Management Options

LATE INTERVENTION

The management of ASDs in adults has recently been reviewed by Webb and Gatzoulis (Box 25-3).[36] The decision to close an ASD will be influenced by a number of factors, including symptoms, age, size, and anatomy of the defect; associated lesions; pulmonary artery pressure; and pulmonary vascular resistance.

Many patients would benefit from ASD closure compared with medical therapy in terms of survival,[37] functional class,[16] exercise tolerance,[17,18] reduction of risk of heart failure, and reduction of risk of pulmonary hypertension.[21]

long-term outcome.[27] Roos-Hesselink and coworkers reported a 4% late mortality of patients who survived surgical closure of an isolated VSD during a follow-up period of 22 to 34 years.[28] In the majority of these patients, residual pulmonary hypertension with right ventricular hypertrophy was documented and sudden death in these patients was thought to be related to ventricular arrhythmias resulting from long-standing right ventricular pressure overload. The incidence of pulmonary hypertension after surgical closure of a VSD was in the range of 4%, but the development of pulmonary hypertension from normal pulmonary artery pressures late after surgery was not documented.[28]

Complete heart block was common in the early days of cardiac surgery but now is a rare complication of surgical VSD closure. Transient complete heart block during the early postoperative course, especially when combined with left-axis deviation and complete right bundle-branch block, may well be a precursor of late complete heart block; and this combination is associated with an increased risk of sudden cardiac death.[27]

Sinus node disease can also develop in a small proportion of patients late after VSD closure, possibly resulting from cannulation of the right atrium for cardiopulmonary bypass.[28]

Another common situation after VSD closure is a residual defect. Usually such defects are hemodynamically insignificant, but occasionally they can be large enough to permit considerable left-to-right shunting and need reoperation.

After VSD closure the majority of patients live normal lives and have normal or nearly normal exercise capacity. The clinical condition in the vast majority of the patients is graded as good.[28]

The occurrence of aortic regurgitation may be an issue after VSD closure. Although aortic regurgitation is present in up to 16% of patients, it is usually mild and rarely progresses.[28]

Outpatient Assessment

PHYSICAL EXAMINATION

VSDs can usually be detected by auscultation (Table 26-2). A VSD is characterized by a systolic murmur usually located at the lower left sternal border. The grade of the murmur depends on the velocity of flow across the defect. When the pressure difference between the left and right ventricle is high (restrictive VSD), the systolic murmur is loud and often pansystolic. Smaller defects are loudest and may also have a palpable thrill. The murmur of a small muscular defect can decrease in intensity towards the end of systole because muscular contraction can reduce the size of the defect. With incremental increases in right ventricular pressure, the murmur will get shorter and softer and lower pitched.

TABLE 26-2	Outpatient Assessment of the Adult with a Ventricular Septal Defect
Physical Examination	
Pansystolic murmur ± thrill	Unoperated VSD
	Residual VSD
	Mitral or tricuspid valve regurgitation
Ejection systolic murmur	Right or left ventricular outflow tract obstruction
Diastolic murmur	Significant shunt with increased flow across the mitral valve (low-pitched)
	Aortic regurgitation (high-pitched)
	Pulmonary regurgitation in pulmonary hypertension (high-pitched)
Accentuated pulmonary component of the second heart sound	Pulmonary hypertension
Electrocardiogram	
Broad, notched P wave	Left atrial enlargement
Left ventricular hypertrophy	Left ventricular enlargement
Left-axis deviation	Especially if the defect is in the inlet septum
Right atrial enlargement and right ventricular hypertrophy	Pulmonary vascular disease with right ventricular hypertrophy or right ventricular outflow obstruction
Heart block	Operated VSD, relates to damage to the AV node/conduction system from patch closure
	VSD closed with a device (especially closure of a perimembranous VSD)
Right bundle-branch block ± left-axis deviation (relates to stitches placed to close the VSD or from compression of the right bundle by a closure device [perimembranous VSD])	VSD after closure
	Surgical VSD closure with right ventriculotomy
Chest Radiography	
Dilation of the central pulmonary arteries and increased pulmonary vascularity; increased cardiothoracic ratio	Unoperated VSD or residual VSD with significant left-to-right shunt and low pulmonary vascular resistance leading to pulmonary overcirculation and left-sided heart dilation
Dilation of the central pulmonary arteries, normal heart size, and oligemic lung fields	Large nonrestrictive defects eventually resulting in pulmonary vascular disease
Echocardiography: *interrogate for:*	
Location and size of an unoperated or residual defect	
Direction of any intracardiac shunt flow	
Flow velocity of any intracardiac shunt flow	
Left atrial and left ventricular size	
Left ventricular function	
Aortic regurgitation	
Aortic valve prolapse	
Right ventricular and pulmonary artery pressure (from tricuspid regurgitation jet or from left ventricular to right ventricular pressure gradient)	
Right ventricular size and function	
Right or left ventricular outflow tract obstruction	
Associated left-sided obstructive lesion (e.g., bicuspid aortic valve, coarctation)	
Tricuspid and mitral valve function	
Associated anomalies	

In contrast, device closure of perimembranous defects has been documented to carry a considerable risk of injury to the aortic and tricuspid valves and especially to the conduction system with atrioventricular block potentially progressing to complete heart block in up to 5% of patients.[19] Because surgical VSD closure currently causes complete heart block in less than 1% of patients,[23] transcatheter closure of perimembranous VSDs with the Amplatzer device has been abandoned by some groups.

In young infants with heart failure due to large or multiple muscular VSDs, periventricular device closure (the "hybrid approach") has been proposed as an alternative to primary surgical closure or pulmonary artery banding to avoid an extensive ventriculotomy, cardiopulmonary bypass, or repeated operations in these infants.[24]

Late Outcome and Complications

UNOPERATED PATIENTS

The natural history of patients with a VSD again depends on the size of the defect and the pulmonary vascular resistance.[25] Patients with an isolated VSD that has closed spontaneously and with normal ventricular function have a normal long-term prognosis.

Usually, the outcome of asymptomatic adult patients with an isolated small VSD that has not been closed during childhood is also excellent.[26] Surgical closure does not appear to be required in these patients as long as the left-to-right shunt is small (estimated $\dot{Q}p:\dot{Q}s$ < 1.5:1), and there is no pulmonary hypertension, normal left ventricular size, no VSD-related aortic regurgitation, and no additional heart defects are present.[26] Gabriel and coworkers reported on a mean follow-up period of 7.4 years in 222 consecutive adults with an isolated small VSD and found a spontaneous closure rate of 6%. Infective endocarditis occurred in about 2% of patients of whom all had a perimembranous defect. Aortic regurgitation developed in 5% during the follow-up period and was trivial or mild in all cases. Eighty-seven percent of patients had no arrhythmias on Holter monitoring, with the remainder showing only benign situations such as incomplete or complete right bundle-branch block and complete left bundle-branch block. No heart block was found in any of the patients. Survival free of death, endocarditis, or surgery of 118 patients with a small VSD prospectively observed over 8 years was 95%.[26]

The Second Natural History Study of Congenital Heart Disease (NHS-II) reported a 25-year survival rate of patients with a restrictive VSD of 95.9%.[25] In contrast, patients with moderately sized or large defects who survived into adulthood had a worse prognosis, with a 25-year survival of 86.3 and 61.2%, respectively.[25] Patients with large defects usually developed left ventricular failure and pulmonary vascular disease often progressing to Eisenmenger syndrome.

The incidence of aortic regurgitation and atrial or ventricular arrhythmias and the degree of exercise intolerance are also higher in patients with more than small defects (Table 26-1).[6]

OPERATED PATIENTS

Adult patients with previous VSD closure and no pulmonary hypertension should have a normal life expectancy.

Patients who underwent late repair of a moderately sized or large VSD may have developed a degree of pulmonary vascular disease before surgery that can progress despite surgery and compromise

TABLE 26-1	Complications: Key Issues To Be Monitored in Adults with Ventricular Septal Defects	
	Unoperated Patients	*Patients with Repaired Defects (Surgery of Catheter Closure)*
Infective endocarditis	Especially in perimembranous VSDs	Residual defects at the site of prosthetic patches or near devices
Aortic regurgitation	Secondary to aortic cusp prolapse in perimembranous and outlet VSDs	If any damage to the aortic valve
Tricuspid regurgitation	Rare, potentially resulting from RV enlargement with pulmonary hypertension or from previous endocarditis	If any damage to the tricuspid valve during closure
Left-sided obstructive lesion (subaortic stenosis, bicuspid aortic valve, coarctation)	May be associated with any VSD	Subaortic stenosis due to a VSD patch that obstructs the left ventricular outflow tract, such as after repair of double-outlet right ventricle
Subpulmonary stenosis	Double-chambered right ventricle, especially in patients with a perimembranous VSD	Double-chambered right ventricle, especially in patients with a perimembranous VSD
Left ventricular dysfunction	Left ventricular volume overload from left-to-right shunt	Late VSD closure with long-standing left ventricular volume overload
	Aortic regurgitation	Residual VSD
		Aortic regurgitation
Atrial arrhythmias	Left atrial enlargement, increase in left ventricular end-diastolic volume in the elderly with unoperated VSD	Late repair with the left atrium being exposed to long-standing volume load
		Rare complication after timely closure of a VSD
Conductance disturbance/Complete heart block		Uncommon in contemporary cardiac surgery
		Patients with a transient complete heart block after surgery, left-axis deviation and right bundle-branch block are at risk of developing late complete heart block
Ventricular arrhythmia	Pulmonary hypertension with right ventricular hypertrophy or left ventricular dysfunction	Pulmonary hypertension with right ventricular hypertrophy or left ventricular dysfunction
Exercise intolerance	Left ventricular dysfunction resulting from long-standing left ventricular volume load, or from pulmonary vascular disease	Left ventricular dysfunction after late VSD closure
Sudden cardiac death	Pulmonary vascular disease with right ventricular hypertrophy	Pulmonary vascular disease with right ventricular hypertrophy
		Transient complete heart block + left-axis deviation + right bundle-branch block
Pulmonary vascular disease or Eisenmenger syndrome	Large nonrestrictive defects eventually resulting in shunt reversal	Late repair with persistence or progression of pulmonary vascular disease
		Nonrestrictive residual VSD

If there is significant volume load to the left ventricle in a moderately sized VSD with low pulmonary vascular resistance, the precordial impulse may be displaced laterally and an apical mid-diastolic murmur across the mitral valve and/or a third heart sound may be present.

An increase in pulmonary vascular resistance and pulmonary artery pressure can cause an increase in the pulmonary component of the second heart sound.

Associated tricuspid valve regurgitation may present as a systolic murmur at the right or left lower sternal border, and aortic regurgitation may have a decrescendo diastolic murmur in the aortic area and along the left sternal border.

Patients with shunt reversal from left-to-right to right-to-left (Eisenmenger syndrome) present with cyanosis and clubbing. A right ventricular lift can be felt. The typical systolic murmur disappears. The pulmonary component of the second heart sound is accentuated. There may also be a high-pitched diastolic regurgitant murmur owing to pulmonary regurgitation.

ELECTROCARDIOGRAPHY

The electrocardiogram should be normal in patients with a small and restrictive VSD and no pulmonary hypertension.

With a significant shunt across the defect there may be evidence of left atrial enlargement (broad, notched P wave) and left ventricular dilation (prominent Q wave and tall R wave and upright T wave in the left precordial leads and deep S wave in the right precordial leads) resulting from volume overload of the left side of the heart. The frontal QRS axis can be deviated to the left with left-sided heart enlargement. Even patients with a small or moderately sized VSD can present with left-axis deviation, especially if the defect is perimembranous or in the inlet septum.

In patients with pulmonary hypertension P waves are often peaked and the QRS axis shows variable right-axis deviation and right ventricular hypertrophy.

CHEST RADIOGRAPHY

When a VSD is small and restrictive since birth the radiograph is normal. When the VSD had been larger initially there may be residual signs of previous pulmonary overcirculation with an increase in the size of the pulmonary trunk and its branches.

In patients with a moderately sized VSD and low pulmonary artery resistance, pulmonary vascularity is increased and the pulmonary artery and its branches are dilated. Left atrial and left ventricular dilation may also be evident.

In patients with a large VSD, heart size on radiography decreases as pulmonary resistance increases and left-to-right shunting decreases. The heart size in this situation is normal, but the dilation of the pulmonary trunk and its branches persists or increases and the lung fields are oligemic.

ECHOCARDIOGRAPHY

Two-dimensional (2D) echocardiography with color flow mapping and Doppler echocardiography can establish the presence, location, and physiology of ventricular septal defects.

The anatomy of the defect, its location, and its size can be visualized from multiple planes by 2D echocardiography (Fig. 26-4). However, tiny defects and small multiple defects in the trabecular muscular septum may be difficult to identify and are better visualized by color flow mapping. 2D echocardiography can also identify aneurysm formation that can accompany partial or complete spontaneous closure of a perimembranous VSD or atrioventricular valve straddling that is sometimes present in inlet VSDs. The continuity of the aortic and pulmonary valves in the roof of a doubly committed juxta-arterial VSD located in the outlet septum can be identified as well as any prolapse of the right or noncoronary cusps of the aortic valve potentially leading to aortic regurgitation (see Fig. 26-3).

The direction of shunt flow and the flow pattern (laminar or turbulent) can be determined by color flow mapping.

The velocity of shunt flow across the defect needs to be assessed using Doppler echocardiography. A high-velocity systolic flow signal and a turbulent flow pattern on color flow mapping can typically be obtained in a small restrictive VSD because the left ventricular systolic pressure greatly exceeds the right ventricular systolic pressure. Conversely, a low velocity flow signal and a laminar flow pattern suggest a large, nonrestrictive defect with an elevated right ventricular systolic pressure. An estimation of right ventricular pressure should always be attempted from the systolic peak velocity of any tricuspid regurgitation jet to confirm the accuracy of the transventricular pressure gradient across the VSD.

The hemodynamic significance of a left-to-right shunt across a VSD can be estimated by quantification of the left atrial and left ventricular dimensions because these chambers are subjected to volume overload from increased pulmonary flow returning to the left side of the heart via the pulmonary veins.

Echocardiography also needs to answer whether any associated anomalies such as aortic regurgitation, tricuspid regurgitation, or right ventricular outflow tract obstruction (double-chambered right ventricle or pulmonary valve stenosis) are present.

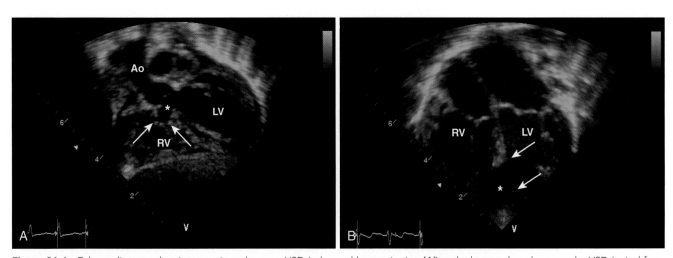

Figure 26-4   Echocardiogram showing a perimembranous VSD (subcostal long-axis view [**A**]) and a large trabecular muscular VSD (apical four-chamber view [**B**]; *arrows* point to the edges of the defect). The defects are marked with an *asterisk*. The perimembranous VSD is partially occluded by tricuspid valve tissue (*arrows* [**A**]). Ao, ascending aorta; LV, left ventricle, RV, right ventricle.

When limitations in the image quality of transthoracic echocardiography hamper the exact evaluation of a VSD and its hemodynamic sequelae, transesophageal echocardiography can be performed.

Three-dimensional (3D) echocardiography may provide additional anatomic information in patients with defects that are difficult to visualize with 2D echocardiography alone.

CARDIAC MAGNETIC RESONANCE IMAGING

Cardiac magnetic resonance imaging is particularly useful in adult patients with a VSD and complex associated lesions or with an inlet or apical VSD that cannot be well seen by echocardiography. It may also be indicated to quantify the severity of aortic insufficiency and to assess left ventricular size and function.

CARDIAC CATHETERIZATION

Cardiac catheterization is indicated in patients in whom pulmonary vascular disease is suspected. Pulmonary vascular pressures and resistances can be calculated and pulmonary vasoreactivity can be tested to guide vasodilator therapy or to decide on surgical treatment.

The amount and direction of intracardiac shunting can be quantified.

Angiocardiography can provide information on the location and number of defects especially when they are located apically in the trabecular muscular septum (Fig. 26-5). Cardiac catheterization also gives information on the severity of aortic insufficiency.

Selective coronary angiography can be performed as part of a catheter study when surgical repair of a VSD is intended and the patient is at risk of coronary artery disease or is older than 40 years of age.

Management

The majority of adult patients with a significant VSD underwent intervention early in life. However, some adult patients have small or moderately sized VSDs that have not been closed. Indications and contraindications for VSD closure in the adult are given in Box 26-1.[11]

Late reoperation for a VSD might also be required for a perimembranous or doubly committed juxta-arterial VSD and more than trivial aortic regurgitation or tricuspid regurgitation or for right ventricular outflow tract obstruction in the form of a double-chambered right ventricle. In the latter, surgery is recommended for patients with a peak midventricular Doppler gradient greater than 60 mm Hg or a mean Doppler gradient greater than 40 mm Hg, regardless of symptoms.

BOX 26-1   LATE TREATMENT: INDICATIONS FOR SURGICAL OR INTERVENTIONAL VENTRICULAR SEPTAL DEFECT CLOSURE IN ADULTS

Surgical VSD Closure
Class I
- Closure of a VSD is indicated when there is a Q̇p:Q̇s of 2.0/1.0 or more and clinical evidence of left ventricular volume overload (*level of evidence*: B)
- Closure of a VSD is indicated when the patient has a history of infective endocarditis (*level of evidence*: C)

Class IIa
- Closure of a VSD is reasonable when net left-to-right shunting is present at a Q̇p:Q̇s greater than 1.5/1.0 with pulmonary artery pressure less than two thirds of systemic pressure and pulmonary vascular resistance less than two thirds of systemic vascular resistance (*level of evidence*: B)
- Closure of a VSD is reasonable when net left-to-right shunting is present at a Q̇p:Q̇s greater than 1.5/1.0 in the presence of left ventricular systolic or diastolic failure (*level of evidence*: B)

Class III
- Closure of a VSD is not recommended in patients with severe irreversible pulmonary arterial hypertension (*level of evidence*: B)

Interventional VSD Closure
Class IIb
- Device closure of a muscular VSD may be considered, especially if the VSD is remote from the tricuspid valve and the aorta, if the VSD is associated with severe left-sided heart chamber enlargement, or if there is pulmonary arterial hypertension (*level of evidence*: C).

Symptomatic patients may be considered for surgical resection if the peak midventricular gradient exceeds 50 mm Hg or the mean Doppler gradient is greater than 30 mm Hg.[11]

Primary closure of an isolated VSD can be performed using prosthetic patches (e.g., Dacron, Gore-Tex) or rarely by direct suture. Early mortality of VSD closure in the adult is approximately 1%, and late survival is excellent when ventricular function is normal. Preoperative pulmonary hypertension may regress, progress, or remain unchanged. Atrial fibrillation may occur especially if chronic volume overload resulted in long-standing left atrial dilation.

Catheter device closure of a VSD can be considered for patients with residual defects after prior surgery or defects with a significant left-to-right shunt. VSD device closure is especially attractive for patients with a

---

Figure 26-5 Left ventriculograms in the left anterior oblique projection demonstrating a perimembranous VSD (**A**) and a VSD located apically in the trabecular muscular septum (**B**). Apical trabecular muscular defects are often difficult to visualize by echocardiography.

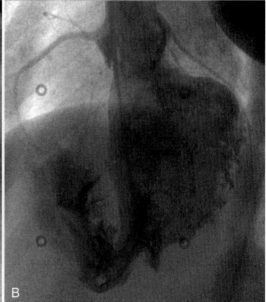

muscular VSD that is sometimes poorly accessible for the surgeon especially when located in the apical part of the trabecular septum. In patients with a perimembranous VSD, suboptimal outcomes have been reported. Even though the closure rates for perimembranous defects are well above 90%, the complications reported include significant conduction abnormalities as well as aortic and tricuspid regurgitation.[19]

Pregnancy

Women with small restrictive VSDs, no pulmonary hypertension, and normal left ventricular function have no increased risk for pregnancy. However, patients with significant pulmonary hypertension should be counseled against pregnancy regardless of whether the defect is closed or not (see Chapter 21).

Patients with a moderate-sized VSD also do well during pregnancy with no maternal mortality and no significant maternal or fetal morbidity. Although the left-to-right shunt may increase during pregnancy as cardiac output increases, this is counterbalanced by a decrease in peripheral vascular resistance.

Women with large left-to-right shunts may experience congestive heart failure, ventricular dysfunction, and atrial or ventricular arrhythmias.

Adults with a VSD should be counseled about the recurrence risk of a congenital heart defect in their offspring. The recurrence risk is about 6% if the mother is affected and about 3% if the father has a VSD.[10]

Level of Follow-Up, Endocarditis Prophylaxis, and Exercise

Adults with no residual VSD, no associated lesion, and no pulmonary hypertension do not require regular follow-up.

In adults with a persistent small VSD and no associated lesions, long-term follow-up is recommended to identify eventual spontaneous closure and to monitor for the appearance of any complications. These patients should be seen at 3- to 5-year intervals.

Adults with a VSD and residual shunt, pulmonary hypertension, aortic regurgitation, or right or left ventricular outflow tract obstruction should be seen at least annually.

Patients who develop bifascicular block or patients with a history of transient complete heart block after surgery are at risk of developing complete heart block later in life and should probably get annual follow-up with electrocardiography, Holter monitoring, and exercise testing.

Patients with a VSD are at an increased risk for infective endocarditis.[6,25] For VSDs, the risk of endocarditis before surgical closure was more than twice that for the surgically closed VSD. In addition, the presence of aortic regurgitation independently increases the risk of infective endocarditis in patients with a VSD. Of those with a surgically repaired VSD who developed endocarditis, at least 22% were known to have a residual VSD leak. The usual sites of vegetations with a restrictive VSD occur where the high-velocity left-to-right jet impacts the right side of the heart (i.e., the tricuspid valve septal leaflet or the mural right ventricular endocardium). Therefore, endocarditis prophylaxis was recommended in all patients with an unoperated or residual VSD until the 2007 American Heart Association guidelines for the prevention of endocarditis were published. The new, simplified recommendations are based on the proposition that most bacteremia occurs during activities of daily living and that infective endocarditis is more likely to result from long-term cumulative exposure to these daily random bacteremias than from procedural bacteremias and that proof is lacking that prophylaxis prevents any or many cases of infective endocarditis. They posit that the risks of antibiotic adverse events in the patient (allergic reactions) and the emergence of resistant organisms exceed any proven benefit of antibiotic prophylaxis against infective endocarditis.

Accordingly, many physicians believe that endocarditis prophylaxis should now only be recommended in patients with residual VSD at the site of a prosthetic VSD patch or closure device and in patients with cyanosis resulting from shunt reversal across a VSD (Eisenmenger syndrome). However, this topic remains controversial.[29]

For patients with small VSDs, no associated lesions, no pulmonary hypertension, and normal ventricular function, no activity restrictions are necessary. If pulmonary vascular disease is present, physical activity is self-restricted and patients should be discouraged from strenuous exercise.

REFERENCES

1. Baker EJ, Leung MP, Anderson RH, et al. The cross sectional anatomy of ventricular septal defects: a reappraisal. Br Heart J 1988;59:339–351.
2. Jacobs JP, Burke RP, Quintessenza JA, et al. Congenital Heart Surgery Nomenclature and Database Project: ventricular septal defect. Ann Thorac Surg 2000;69:S25–S35.
3. Ho S, McCarthy KP, Josen M, et al. Anatomic-echocardiographic correlates: an introduction to normal and congenitally malformed hearts. Heart 2001;86(Suppl. 2):II3–II11.
4. Van Praagh R, Geva T, Kreutzer J. Ventricular septal defects: how shall we describe, name and classify them? J Am Coll Cardiol 1989;14:1298–1299.
5. Anderson RH, Wilcox BR. The surgical anatomy of ventricular septal defect. J Card Surg 1992;7:17–35.
6. Neumayer U, Stone S, Somerville J. Small ventricular septal defects in adults. Eur Heart J 1998;19:1573–1582.
7. Hoffman JI, Kaplan S. The incidence of congenital heart disease. J Am Coll Cardiol 2002;39:1890–1900.
8. Warnes CA, Liberthson R, Danielson GK, et al. Task force 1: the changing profile of congenital heart disease in adult life. J Am Coll Cardiol 2001;37:1170–1175.
9. Garg V, Kathiriya IS, Barnes R, et al. GATA4 mutations cause human congenital heart defects and reveal an interaction with TBX5. Nature 2003;424:443–447.
10. Uebing A, Steer PJ, Yentis SM, et al. Pregnancy and congenital heart disease. BMJ 2006;332:401–406.
11. Warnes CA, Williams RG, Bashore TM, et al. ACC/AHA 2008 Guidelines for the Management of Adults with Congenital Heart Disease: a report of the American College of Cardiology/American Heart Association Task Force on Practice Guidelines (writing committee to develop guidelines on the management of adults with congenital heart disease). Circulation 2008;118:e714–e833.
12. Therrien J, Dore A, Gersony W, et al. CCS Consensus Conference 2001 update: recommendations for the management of adults with congenital heart disease: I. Can J Cardiol 2001;17:940–959.
13. Popelova J, Oechslin E, Kaemmerer H, et al. Congenital Heart Disease in Adults. London: Informa Healthcare Publishers; 2008.
14. Merrick AF, Lal M, Anderson RH, et al. Management of ventricular septal defect: a survey of practice in the United Kingdom. Ann Thorac Surg 1999;68:983–988.
15. Tweddell JS, Pelech AN, Frommelt PC. Ventricular septal defect and aortic valve regurgitation: pathophysiology and indications for surgery. Semin Thorac Cardiovasc Surg Pediatr Card Surg Annu 2006;147–152.
16. Lun K, Li H, Leung MP, et al. Analysis of indications for surgical closure of subarterial ventricular septal defect without associated aortic cusp prolapse and aortic regurgitation. Am J Cardiol 2001;87:1266–1270.
17. Kaplan S, Daoud GI, Benzing 3rd G, et al. Natural history of ventricular septal defect. Am J Dis Child 1963;105:581–587.
18. Lock JE, Block PC, McKay RG, et al. Transcatheter closure of ventricular septal defects. Circulation 1988;78:361–368.
19. Carminati M, Butera G, Chessa M, et al. Transcatheter closure of congenital ventricular septal defects: results of the European Registry. Eur Heart J 2007;28:2361–2368.
20. Butera G, Chessa M, Carminati M. Percutaneous closure of ventricular septal defects. Cardiol Young 2007;17:243–253.
21. Holzer R, Balzer D, Cao QL, et al. Device closure of muscular ventricular septal defects using the Amplatzer muscular ventricular septal defect occluder: immediate and mid-term results of a U.S. registry. J Am Coll Cardiol 2004;43:1257–1263.
22. Arora R, Trehan V, Thakur AK, et al. Transcatheter closure of congenital muscular ventricular septal defect. J Interv Cardiol 2004;17:109–115.
23. Andersen HO, de Leval MR, Tsang VT, et al. Is complete heart block after surgical closure of ventricular septum defects still an issue? Ann Thorac Surg 2006;82:948–956.
24. Crossland DS, Wilkinson JL, Cochrane AD, et al. Initial results of primary device closure of large muscular ventricular septal defects in early infancy using periventricular access. Catheter Cardiovasc Interv 2008;72:386–391.
25. Kidd L, Driscoll DJ, Gersony WM, et al. Second natural history study of congenital heart defects: results of treatment of patients with ventricular septal defect. Circulation 1993;87:I38–I51.
26. Gabriel HM, Heger M, Innerhofer P, et al. Long-term outcome of patients with ventricular septal defect considered not to require surgical closure during childhood. J Am Coll Cardiol 2002;39:1066–1071.
27. Moller JH, Patton C, Varco RL, et al. Late results (30 to 35 years) after operative closure of isolated ventricular septal defect from 1954 to 1960. Am J Cardiol 1991;68:1491–1497.
28. Roos-Hesselink JW, Meijboom FJ, Spitaels SE, et al. Outcome of patients after surgical closure of ventricular septal defect at young age: longitudinal follow-up of 22–34 years. Eur Heart J 2004;25:1057–1062.
29. Child JS, Pagues DA, Perloff JK. Infective endocarditis. In: Perloff JK, Child JS, Aboulhosn J, editors. Congenital Heart Disease in Adults. 3rd ed Philadelphia: Elsevier Saunders; 2008. p. 168–193.

Atrioventricular Septal Defect: Complete and Partial (Ostium Primum Atrial Septal Defect)

ELLIOT A. SHINEBOURNE | SIEW YEN HO

Definition and Morphology

The anatomic hallmark of an atrioventricular septal defect (AVSD, previously called atrioventricular canal defect or endocardial cushion defect) is a common atrioventricular (AV) junction guarded by a common AV valve (Fig. 27-1B).[1]

In a partial AVSD (ostium primum atrial septal defect) the common valve is divided into two orifices (see Fig. 27-1C), whereas in a complete AVSD a common valve guards a common orifice. The terms *partial* and *incomplete* are simply shorthand for the two major patterns of arrangement of the valve leaflets.

In each case the valve consists of five leaflets: superior (anterior) and inferior (posterior) bridging leaflets, each of which overrides the interventricular septum and has chordal attachments to both ventricles, a left mural leaflet, and a right inferior and a right anterosuperior leaflet. In a partial AVSD a tongue of tissue joins the otherwise free margins of the superior and inferior bridging leaflets, dividing the common valve functionally into two valves, although retaining continuity between left and right sides of the bridging leaflets (see Fig. 27-1C). Consequently, in a partial AVSD the left AV valve is trileaflet, made up of the left halves of the superior and inferior bridging leaflets and the left mural leaflet. In an AVSD it is therefore misleading to call the left AV valve a mitral valve, because it is a trileaflet structure, bearing no similarity to a bishop's mitre. More importantly, what is erroneously called a cleft in the mitral valve is not a cleft but the line of apposition of the septal attachments of the superior and inferior bridging leaflets. This may or may not be the site of left AV valve regurgitation. Not only is the arrangement of the valve leaflets different from that in the normal mitral valve, but the left ventricular papillary muscles are also arranged differently. Similarly the right-sided AV valve has four leaflets, unlike the normal tricuspid valve.

In the normal heart the aortic valve is wedged between mitral and tricuspid valves and lies posterior and to the right of the pulmonary valve (see Fig. 27-1A). In an AVSD, because of the common AV junction, the aortic valve is displaced anteriorly and to the right in an unwedged or unsprung position. This contributes to the characteristic "goose neck" deformity of the left ventricle seen on angiography (see later).

In a complete AVSD there is usually:
- An interatrial communication or ostium primum atrial septal defect (ASD) between the inferior margin of the true atrial septum and the superior aspect of the common valve (Fig. 27-2A)
- A large interventricular communication (ventricular septal defect [VSD]) between the crest of the interventricular septum and the inferior aspect of the common valve (see Fig. 27-2B). There is usually, but not always, a VSD beneath the inferior bridging leaflet, which may or may not be attached to the crest of the septum. The defect under the superior bridging leaflet is usually larger.

The attachments of the right ventricular aspect of the superior bridging leaflet form the basis for the Rastelli classification of AVSDs (Fig. 27-3)[2]:
- *Type A:* The superior bridging leaflet is largely contained within the left ventricle with chordal attachments to the crest of the septum, and the right ventricular medial papillary muscle arises in relatively normal fashion from the interventricular septum.

- *Type B:* The superior bridging leaflet extends farther into the right ventricle, being attached to an anomalous right ventricular papillary muscle arising from the trabecula septomarginalis.
- *Type C:* The free-floating superior bridging leaflet extends even farther into the right ventricle and is attached to an anterior papillary muscle.

The Rastelli classification bears some significance in terms of surgical planning and in utilizing the bridging leaflets toward the creation of two separate AV valves, albeit not universally applied today among surgeons.

In a partial AVSD the bridging leaflets are tethered to the crest of the ventricular septum, leaving only an ostium primum ASD (see Fig. 27-2A). Usually there is no VSD, but there may be a small, usually hemodynamically unimportant, interventricular communication between the chordal attachments of the bridging leaflets. We do not endorse use of the term *intermediate AVSD* because its meaning is ambiguous, but we prefer description of the interatrial and interventricular communications, as well as whether or not the common AV valve has divided orifices. Another variant of AVSD that is functionally similar to a large inlet VSD[3] is when the superior and inferior bridging leaflets are fused to the atrial septum, leaving a persistent interventricular communication (see Fig. 27-2C). Finally, for completeness, if the atrial septum is fused to the upper aspect of the AV valves and the crest of the ventricular septum to the inferior aspect, there will be an AVSD with no interatrial and no interventricular communication.[4]

Within the spectrum of AVSD other morphologic features can also have a profound influence on clinical manifestations, outcome, and treatment:
- The common AV valve leaflets may be dysplastic and the valve functionally regurgitant or stenotic.
- Particularly with divided orifices, left AV valve regurgitation or stenosis may affect outcome, as does the presence of a double-orifice left or right AV valve (see later).
- The common AV valve and junction may be dominantly committed to one or other ventricle, resulting in marked ventricular disproportion so that one ventricle is too small to support the circulation. Under these circumstances a biventricular repair is not possible and a total cavopulmonary connection or other variant of the Fontan procedure will be necessary to correct the circulation.
- If more than 75% of the common AV valve is committed to one ventricle, then by definition the category of AV connection becomes a double-inlet ventricle (via a common AV valve).
- Finally, if the commitment of the common AV valve and junction to the right ventricle is extreme, the left ventricle may be so small as to form part of the spectrum of hypoplastic left heart syndrome.

ATRIOVENTRICULAR CONDUCTION TISSUE

In the normal heart, the central fibrous body is where the AV node penetrates from the atrial musculature to become the AV bundle. In an AVSD, because of deficient AV septation and lack of a normal central fibrous body, the atrial septum usually makes contact with the ventricular septum only at the crux of the heart. It is here, therefore, that the AV conduction tissue penetrates and the AV node is displaced

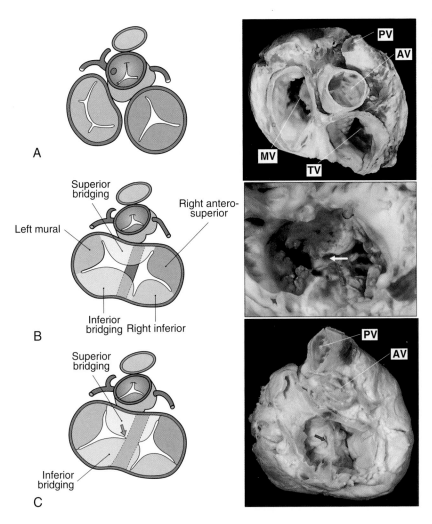

Figure 27-1 The atrioventricular junction viewed from the atrial aspect, depicted diagrammatically and as displayed in corresponding heart specimens to show (**A**) normal, (**B**) atrioventricular septal defect (AVSD) with common valvular orifice or "complete" defect, and (**C**) AVSD with divided valvular orifices or "partial" defect. Note the wedged position of the aortic valve between the mitral and tricuspid valves in the normal heart (not present in patients with AVSD). The common AV junction is oval in both forms of AVSD. The common orifice in **B** is guarded by a valve that has five leaflets. The crest of the ventricular septum (*white arrow*) is visible owing to nonfusion between superior and inferior bridging leaflets. Fusion between the bridging leaflets in **C** produces two valvular orifices and a so-called cleft (*black arrow*) on the left side. AV, aortic valve; MV, mitral valve; PV, pulmonary valve; TV, tricuspid valve.

posteriorly and inferiorly (Fig. 27-4).[5] The area of union of the AV junction that is at the most posterior and inferior extremity of the interventricular septum is the most reliable guide to the position of the conducting tissue. The elongated nonbranching left bundle runs on the crest of the muscular ventricular septum to its left side, being covered by the inferior bridging leaflets. The left ventricular outflow tract, because of its unwedged location, is unrelated to the conduction tissue and, should surgical relief of any associated left ventricular outflow tract obstruction be necessary, heart block is an unlikely complication.

Genetics and Epidemiology

In a population-based study in Liverpool[6] in the 1960s, of 160,480 live births 884 neonates had congenital heart disease, 21 of whom had an AVSD. Of these, 17 had a complete AVSD and all had Down syndrome. Complete AVSDs do occur in chromosomally normal children but are much less common than with trisomy 21. In most surgical series of complete AVSD, 70% to 80% of patients have Down syndrome. In our own hospital series,[7] of 147 children undergoing repair of complete AVSD, 107 (73%) had Down syndrome, compared with 15 (10%) of 152 undergoing repair of a partial AVSD.

In chromosomally normal children with usual atrial situs, a complete AVSD usually occurs as an isolated defect. Autosomal dominant inheritance not linked to chromosome 21 has been described in several large families. AVSDs are also frequently associated with right or left isomerism of the atrial appendages, although AVSD in association with isomerism has not been reported in Down syndrome.

Early Presentation

The most common presentation of an isolated complete AVSD in infancy is with breathlessness when feeding or at rest due to excessive pulmonary blood flow. The magnitude of left-to-right shunting across the interventricular communication (VSD) depends both on the size of the VSD and on the ratio of pulmonary to systemic vascular resistance. The lower the pulmonary vascular resistance (PVR), the greater will be the left-to-right shunt, the stiffer will be the lungs, and the more breathless will be the neonate.

In the normal neonate it takes 7 to 10 days for the PVR to fall from the high level in the fetus to that at which it stays throughout adult life.[8] In the presence of a large VSD, the fall in PVR may be delayed for 3 to 6 weeks, so that the onset of breathlessness is usually delayed for this time. Particularly in children with Down syndrome, the delay in fall of PVR may be longer, or sometimes the PVR does not fall at all and the neonate presents with intermittent cyanosis due to right-to-left shunting.

In Down syndrome, upper airways obstruction with carbon dioxide retention is common, the latter being associated with pulmonary vasoconstriction. Paradoxically the neonate in whom PVR remains high may remain well and be less symptomatic than if the PVR falls, although in the former if untreated the development of progressive pulmonary vascular disease is inevitable.

Another factor influencing presentation is the degree of regurgitation through the common AV valve, this being typically more severe in chromosomally normal children than in those with Down syndrome. Associated anomalies, such as coarctation of the aorta, left ventricular outflow tract obstruction, or right ventricular outflow tract obstruction (i.e., coexistent tetralogy of Fallot), will also profoundly alter the clinical manifestations.

Figure 27-2 **Bottom,** The levels of attachment of the valvular leaflets producing variations in levels of shunting. **Top,** Corresponding heart specimens viewed from the right. **A,** The *double arrows* indicate the deficiency between the free edge of the atrial septum and the atrial surface of the valve, producing interatrial shunting only. **B,** The *double arrow* marks the deficiency between the edge of the atrial septum and the crest of the ventricular septum. Note the bridging leaflets are not completely adherent to the crest, allowing the potential for both interatrial and interventricular shunting. **C,** The bridging leaflets can be seen attached to the edge of the atrial septum, leaving the deficiency at the ventricular level. RA, right atrium; RV, right ventricle.

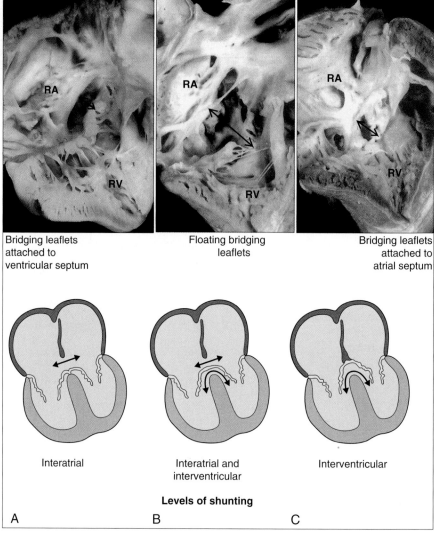

Bridging leaflets attached to ventricular septum

Floating bridging leaflets

Bridging leaflets attached to atrial septum

Interatrial

Interatrial and interventricular

Interventricular

Levels of shunting

A   B   C

Figure 27-3 Rastelli classification. Insertion of the superior bridging leaflet into the right ventricle produces variations in the extent of bridging across the ventricular septum. The atrioventricular valve is viewed from the ventricular aspect. AS, right anterosuperior leaflet; IBL, inferior bridging leaflet; LV, left ventricle; RV, right ventricle; SBL, superior bridging leaflet.

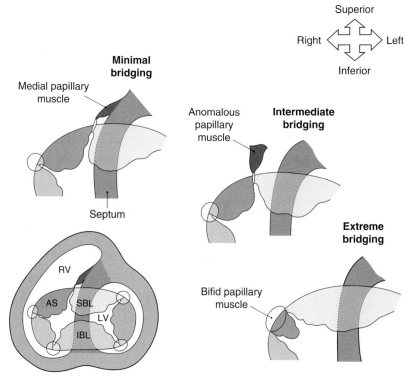

Superior

Right   Left

Inferior

Minimal bridging

Medial papillary muscle

Septum

Anomalous papillary muscle

Intermediate bridging

Extreme bridging

Bifid papillary muscle

RV

AS   SBL

LV

IBL

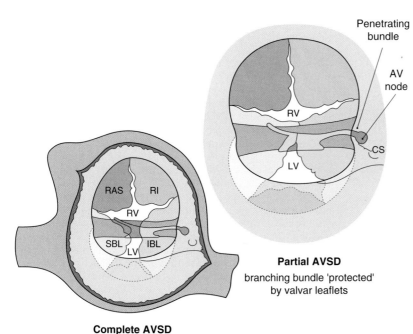

Figure 27-4 Representation of a surgeon's view of hearts with atrioventricular septal defect (AVSD). The atrioventricular (AV) conduction system is shown in the two major forms. Fusion of the bridging leaflets and their adherence to the septal crest provides some protection from risk of surgical trauma to the AV bundle in hearts with divided valvular orifices. The AV penetrating bundle and node are at the site where the ventricular septum meets the AV junction. The distance between this site and the coronary sinus (*marked by brace*) may in some cases be too short to accommodate sutures safely without risk of damage to the atrioventricular node. CS, coronary sinus; IBL, inferior bridging leaflet; LV, left ventricle; RAS, right anterosuperior leaflet; RI, right inferior leaflet; RV, right ventricle; SBL, superior bridging leaflet.

Partial AVSD
branching bundle 'protected'
by valvar leaflets

Complete AVSD
branching bundle exposed on septal crest

Patients with a partial AVSD (ostium primum ASD) are usually asymptomatic as infants or young children, although occasionally a child with a large ASD becomes symptomatic from massive left-to-right shunting with a low systemic output. In this group, left AV valve regurgitation (analogous to mitral regurgitation) may also result in early heart failure.

In summary, clinical features of infants with an AVSD reflect the presence and magnitude of left-to-right shunting—at atrial and/or ventricular level—that is in turn dependent on PVR, modified by left or right ventricular outflow obstruction, if present (see Chapters 4, 25 and 26).

ELECTROCARDIOGRAPHY

First-degree heart block is common in both partial and complete AVSD. A superior mean frontal QRS axis (left-axis deviation) is the most typical finding on an electrocardiogram, with a dominant S wave in aVF.

In a child with Down syndrome such a finding would be virtually diagnostic of an AVSD. The superior QRS axis reflects an abnormal sequence of activation of the ventricles due to deficiency of the intermediate radiation of the left bundle.

CHEST RADIOGRAPHY

When PVR falls there will be cardiomegaly and plethora, but if the resistance remains high the chest radiograph may be normal. Adults with an uncorrected complete AVSD and pulmonary vascular disease will commonly have cardiomegaly (mild, unless advanced ventricular dysfunction ensues) and large proximal, but small peripheral, pulmonary arterial markings (peripheral pruning). Finally, in those who develop increasing common AV valve regurgitation, pulmonary venous markings will increase with upper lobe blood diversion.

CROSS-SECTIONAL ECHOCARDIOGRAPHY

Cross-sectional echocardiography is the imaging method of choice for confirming the diagnosis of AVSD. This applies to the fetus, child, and adult.

Antenatal Diagnosis: Fetal Echocardiography
In the United Kingdom, on a routine 20-week fetal anomaly scan, obstetric ultrasonographers are expected to obtain a four-chamber

view of the heart. This should show two atria and two ventricles of roughly equal size with normal offsetting of the mitral and tricuspid valves. This view shows the crux of the heart and should demonstrate an intact interventricular septum. If there is a complete AVSD, the VSD and common AV valve should be seen on this view. Failure to obtain a normal four-chamber view should prompt referral to a fetal cardiologist.

Echocardiographic Goals and Features
The echocardiographic goals[9] are to establish:
- The diagnosis of AVSD
- The level and direction of shunting (Fig. 27-5)
- Adequacy of ventricular size
- The function of the common or divided AV valve(s): is there valve dysplasia, regurgitation, or stenosis?
- Ventricular function
- The presence of left and/or right ventricular outflow tract obstruction and their severity
- An estimate of pulmonary artery systolic and diastolic pressure (see also Chapter 5)
- Exclusion of other anomalies (e.g., coarctation)

An apical four-chamber view will show the common AV junction with a common AV valve (see Fig. 27-5). An ostium primum ASD and inlet VSD are also seen in this view (see Fig. 27-5A). With both common and divided orifices, the right and left components of the AV valve will be at the same level. Subcostal views typically demonstrate the inferior bridging leaflet, which may or may not be attached to the interventricular septum. Apical four-chamber views with the transducer directed more anteriorly show the superior bridging leaflet and will demonstrate the chordal attachments (see earlier and Fig. 27-3 for the Rastelli classification). An apical four-chamber view also allows comparison of the size of the right and left ventricles. If ventricular disproportion is present, this will be seen on this view. Whether the valve is dysplastic, hypoplastic, or regurgitant can also be demonstrated with a combination of imaging and color flow Doppler evaluation.

From the parasternal short-axis view, the common junction can be demonstrated together with the typical five leaflets of the common AV valve. Most importantly in this view, in both the complete and partial AVSD the left-sided AV valve can be shown to be trileaflet (Fig. 27-6). On cross-sectional echocardiography this is the pathognomonic feature of an AVSD and distinguishes the interventricular component of an AVSD from that of a perimembranous inlet VSD. The arrangement

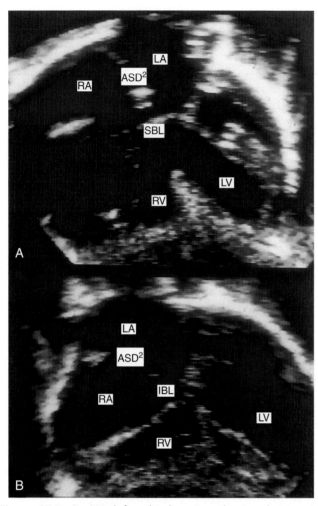

Figure 27-5 **A,** Apical four-chamber view showing the superior bridging leaflet (SBL), immediately above which is an ostium primum atrial septal defect (ASD) and below is a large-inlet ventricular septal defect (VSD). This patient also has an ostium secundum ASD (ASD²). **B,** Subcostal four-chamber view showing inferior bridging leaflet (IBL) with a small VSD beneath. Note marked right ventricular hypertrophy. LA, left atrium; LV, left ventricle; RA, right atrium; RV, right ventricle.

of the left ventricular papillary muscles can also be seen in this view, whereas after angling more superiorly the aorta is seen in its unwedged position. Similarly, should anterior deviation of the outlet septum be present, subvalvular pulmonary stenosis can be identified in this view. This can also be seen on a subcostal right anterior oblique view. The latter also demonstrates the characteristic goose-neck deformity of the left ventricle resulting from the inlet or diaphragmatic surface of the left ventricle being considerably shorter than the outlet portion of the ventricle (Fig. 27-7). This goose-neck deformity was also the pathognomonic feature of the angiographic assessment of AVSD in the days when diagnosis was confirmed by angiography.

CARDIAC CATHETERIZATION AND ANGIOGRAPHY

Cardiac catheterization and angiography are seldom necessary for diagnostic reasons, but a hemodynamic study may be indicated, particularly in older patients, for assessment of PVR.

Early Management of Atrioventricular Septal Defect

Other than in patients with very small atrial or ventricular septal defects and competent AV valves, surgery is the treatment of choice. The aims of surgery are to close the interatrial and interventricular communications and create two competent, nonstenotic AV valves.

Surgery should be performed before pulmonary vascular disease is established and without producing heart block from damage to the conduction system. Left ventricular outflow tract obstruction must also be avoided when placing the VSD patch.

If right ventricular outflow obstruction coexists, this should be relieved at the time of AVSD repair; very occasionally in this setting, a systemic to pulmonary artery shunt may be required in the very small and severely cyanosed infant before repair.

Primary surgical repair within the first 6 months of life is therefore the treatment of choice, although pulmonary artery banding still has a role in those with additional VSDs, very small size, or ventricular disproportion. In the latter group, when one ventricle is too small for a biventricular repair, early pulmonary artery banding is mandatory to reduce pulmonary blood flow and hence distal pulmonary artery pressure so that PVR falls, allowing the possibility of an eventual cavopulmonary connection or univentricular repair. In our own[6] and other[10] series of patients with complete AVSDs undergoing eventual biventricular repair, prior pulmonary artery banding was not an incremental risk factor.

Late Outcome

Overall long-term prognosis after AVSD repair is good. Left AV valve regurgitation is common and can be problematic, hence the need for an individualized surgical approach at the time of AVSD repair (based on valvular anatomy and function) to minimize regurgitation and avoid stenosis.[11–13] Five to 10 percent of patients will require surgical revision for left AV valve repair or replacement during follow-up. Occasionally, previous operation on the left AV valve at the time of primary repair of AVSD results in stenosis. This is more likely when the mural leaflet is short and usually necessitates reoperation. Subaortic stenosis will develop or progress in up to 5% of patients after repair, particularly in patients with primum ASD or those with a complete AVSD who underwent left AV valve replacement. The late complications after AVSD repair[14,15] are summarized in Box 27-1.

Outpatient Assessment of the Adult with Atrioventricular Septal Defect

UNOPERATED PATIENTS

Clinical presentation of the adult with an AVSD depends on the anatomy (presence and size of ASD and/or VSD), competence of the left AV valve, pulmonary artery pressure, and PVR. Presenting features may be:
- Heart murmur; no overt symptoms
- Exercise intolerance and fatigue
- Atrial arrhythmia
- Complete heart block
- Cyanosis with right ventricular outflow obstruction (single second heart sound) or Eisenmenger physiology (accentuated pulmonary component to second sound)
- "Angina" with severe subaortic stenosis
- Heart failure

Adults with an unoperated AVSD would normally fit into one of the following three diagnostic groups:
- Partial AVSD or primum ASD (with or without a small ventricular component)—most would qualify for and benefit from surgery
- Complete AVSD with right ventricular outflow tract obstruction (like tetralogy of Fallot)—should be considered for surgery
- Complete AVSD with irreversible pulmonary vascular disease (Eisenmenger physiology)—diagnosis needs to be confirmed; conventional surgery is not an option but patient should be considered for anti–pulmonary hypertensive therapy such as with an endothelin antagonist, phosphodiesterase-5 inhibitor, and/or prostanoid.

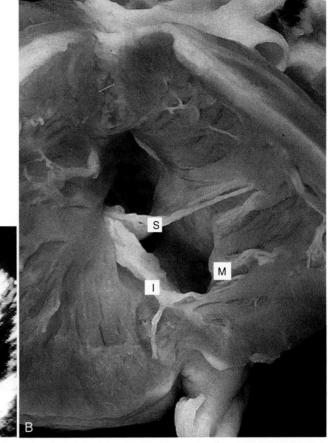

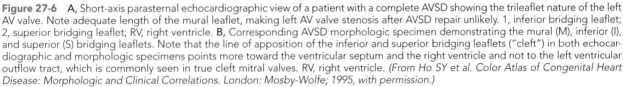

Figure 27-6 **A,** Short-axis parasternal echocardiographic view of a patient with a complete AVSD showing the trileaflet nature of the left AV valve. Note adequate length of the mural leaflet, making left AV valve stenosis after AVSD repair unlikely. 1, inferior bridging leaflet; 2, superior bridging leaflet; RV, right ventricle. **B,** Corresponding AVSD morphologic specimen demonstrating the mural (M), inferior (I), and superior (S) bridging leaflets. Note that the line of apposition of the inferior and superior bridging leaflets ("cleft") in both echocardiographic and morphologic specimens points more toward the ventricular septum and the right ventricle and not to the left ventricular outflow tract, which is commonly seen in true cleft mitral valves. RV, right ventricle. *(From Ho SY et al. Color Atlas of Congenital Heart Disease: Morphologic and Clinical Correlations. London: Mosby-Wolfe; 1995, with permission.)*

Diagnostic workup should include at least:
- A thorough clinical assessment. Particular attention should be paid to left AV valve regurgitation and to the intensity of the pulmonary component of the second heart sound.
- Electrocardiography (as in pediatric patients; see earlier)
- Chest radiography
- Transthoracic echocardiographic/Doppler evaluation (see text and Chapter 5).
  The following tests may also be required:
- Transesophageal echocardiography:
  - If exact anatomy unclear with transthoracic echocardiography
  - To document the presence of intracardiac shunt(s)
  - To define the chordal attachments of the AV valve(s) and severity of left AV valve regurgitation or stenosis
  - To assess further the subaortic stenosis
- Cardiac catheterization is useful to determine:
  - The presence and magnitude of intracardiac shunts
  - PVR
  - Reversibility of any elevation of PVR response to oxygen, nitric oxide, and/or prostaglandins
  - Severity of left AV valve regurgitation (or stenosis, if previous valve repair has been undertaken)
  - The presence and severity of subaortic stenosis
- Coronary angiography in patients at risk of coronary artery disease or in patients older than the age of 40 years if operation is contemplated.

- Open-lung biopsy may be helpful in highly selected cases. It should be considered only when reversibility of pulmonary vascular disease is uncertain from the invasive hemodynamic data. It is potentially hazardous and should be performed only in centers with expertise in pulmonary hypertension and congenital heart disease.
- Holter monitoring to investigate for AV block
- Magnetic resonance imaging to help further define the anatomy.

OPERATED PATIENTS

Operated patients should be asymptomatic. The minimum set of investigations should be performed; if clinical indications are present, additional tests should be considered (see earlier). Late complications, if present (Box 27-2), need to be identified early and addressed in a timely fashion.

Late Management Options

Situations that warrant intervention or re-intervention in adult patients with AVSD are shown in Box 27-2.

Arrhythmia and Sudden Cardiac Death

Complete AV block may occur spontaneously or after repair of AVSD. Sinus node dysfunction may also occur, especially after late repair;

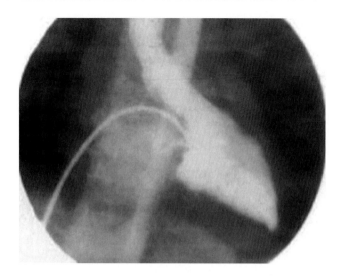

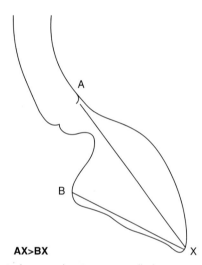

AX>BX

Figure 27-7 Left ventriculogram showing a so-called goose-neck deformity in a patient with a partial AVSD. The appearances are seen to be a consequence of the shorter inlet or diaphragmatic surface of the ventricle (*line BX*) compared with the longer outlet dimension (*line AX*). Note elongated left ventricular outflow tract prone to stenosis and unwedged position of the aorta.

BOX 27-1   COMPLICATIONS AFTER REPAIR OF ATRIOVENTRICULAR SEPTAL DEFECT

- Exercise intolerance and gradual decline in functional status; may relate to residual progressive or new hemodynamic lesions:
  - Left (and right) AV valve regurgitation
  - Subaortic or subpulmonary obstruction (may relate to left AV valve replacement or VSD patch)
  - Residual VSD
- Progressive pulmonary vascular disease (especially in patients who underwent "relatively late" closure of VSD)
- Complete heart block (seen also in patients who did not undergo previous surgery)
- Atrial and ventricular arrhythmia
- Sudden cardiac death
- Endocarditis

---

it may lead to bradycardia and syncope or tachycardia. Atrial flutter and fibrillation in the adult patient with AVSD, usually reflecting long-standing chamber dilation and/or ventricular dysfunction, are not uncommon.

BOX 27-2   LATE TREATMENT INTERVENTION OR RE-INTERVENTION IN ADULTS WITH ATRIOVENTRICULAR SEPTAL DEFECT

- Partial AVSD (primum ASD) with right-sided heart dilation for elective repair irrespective of symptoms (see Chapter 25 for indications); transcatheter closure is not an option, hence operation is required. The left AV valve needs to be assessed and is usually operated on at the time to ensure its competence and avoid stenosis.
- Partial AVSD with an atrial and a restrictive ventricular communication (VSD) with right-sided (and left-sided) heart dilation and without irreversible pulmonary vascular disease, for elective repair
- Complete AVSD with tetralogy of Fallot, for elective repair[16]
- Left AV valve regurgitation (or stenosis from a previous repair) causing symptoms, atrial arrhythmia, or deterioration in ventricular function, for elective repair or replacement
- Subaortic stenosis (catheter peak-to-peak gradient or mean echo gradient greater than 50 mm Hg at rest with evidence of left ventricular hypertrophy), for surgical relief
- Permanent pacing for patients with complete heart block; epicardial pacing should be considered for those who undergo concomitant intracardiac surgery and those with residual intracardiac communications.
- Supportive therapy for patients with Eisenmenger physiology (see Chapter 48). Lung and heart transplantation should be reserved for severely symptomatic patients only, because long-term prospects after lung transplantation remain limited.
- Adults with unbalanced AVSD and protected pulmonary vascular bed (either with a naturally occurring right ventricular outflow tract obstruction or after pulmonary artery banding in infancy), not suitable for biventricular repair, should be considered for palliative surgery in the form of cavopulmonary connection, partial or total (see Chapters 11, 51, and 52).

Sudden death has been reported. Although specific markers for sudden death have not been identified, the potential arrhythmogenic effect of significant residual hemodynamic lesions in this setting should not be underestimated.

Pregnancy

Pregnancy is well tolerated in patients with complete repair and no significant residual lesions. Women in New York Heart Association class I and II with an unoperated partial AVSD usually tolerate pregnancy well but have an increased risk of paradoxical embolization. They should be considered for elective AVSD repair before having a family.

Level of Follow-up, Endocarditis Prophylaxis, and Exercise

Patients with AVSDs warrant lifelong follow-up, ideally by a cardiologist specialized in congenital heart disease. Issues such as left AV valve regurgitation, the development of subaortic stenosis, and late onset of arrhythmia with or without complete AV block need to be addressed appropriately.

Particularly if there are residual hemodynamic lesions such as AV valve regurgitation or a VSD, good oral hygiene and dental care are important in preventing endocarditis but new guidelines from the American Heart Association no longer recommend routine antibiotic prophylaxis for dental procedures. The exception would be if a prosthetic "mitral valve" were required when the adverse consequences of endocarditis are such that antibiotic prophylaxis continues to be recommended.

Exercise restrictions apply only to patients with significant residual or newly developing hemodynamic lesions (particularly subaortic stenosis) or to those with exercise-induced tachyarrhythmia.

REFERENCES

1. Becker AE, Anderson RH. Atrioventricular septal defects: what's in a name? J Thorac Cardiovasc Surg 1982;83:461–469.

2. Rastelli GC, Kirklin JW, Titus JL. Anatomic observations on complete form of persistent atrioventricular canal with special reference to atrioventricular valves. Mayo Clin Proc 1966;41:296–308.

3. Piccoli GP, Ho SY, Wilkinson JL, et al. Morphology and classification of complete atrioventricular septal defects. Br Heart J 1979;42:621–632.

4. Kaski JP, Wolfenden J, Josen M, et al. Can atrioventricular septal defects exist with intact septal structures? Heart 2006;92: 832–835.

5. Feld RH, Du Shane JW, Titus JL. The atrioventricular conduction system in persistent common atrioventricular canal defect: correlations with electrocardiogram. Circulation 1970;42:437–444.

6. Dickinson DF, Arnold R, Wilkinson JL. Congenital heart disease among 160,480 liveborn children in Liverpool 1960 to 1969: implications for surgical treatment. Br Heart J 1981;46:55–62.

7. Al-Hay AA, MacNeill SJ, Yacoub M, et al. Complete atrioventricular septal defect, Down syndrome and surgical outcome: risk factors. Ann Thorac Surg 2003;75:412–421.

8. Rudolph AM. The changes in the circulation after birth: their importance in congenital heart disease. Circulation 1970;41:343–359.

9. Smallhorn JF, Tommasini G, Anderson RH, Macartney FJ. Assessment of atrioventricular septal defects by two dimensional echocardiography. Br Heart J 1982;47:109–121.

10. Gunther T, Mazzitelli D, Hachnel CJ, et al. Long term results after repair of complete atrioventricular septal defects: analysis of risk factors. Ann Thorac Surg 1998;65:754–759.

11. Ebels T, Anderson RH. Atrioventricular septal defects. In: Anderson RH, Baker EJ, Macartney FJ, et al., editors. Paediatric Cardiology. 2nd ed. London: Churchill Livingstone; 2002. p. 939–981.

12. Carpentier A. Surgical anatomy and management of the mitral component of atrioventricular canal defects. In: Anderson RH, Shinebourne EA, editors. Paediatric Cardiology. Churchill Livingstone: Edinburgh; 1977. p. 477–486.

13. Capouya ER, Laks H, Drinkwater DC, et al. Management of the left atrioventricular valve in the repair of complete atrioventricular septal defects. J Thorac Cardiovasc Surg 1992;104:196–201; discussion 201–203.

14. Bergin ML, Washes CA, Tajik AJ, Danielson GK. Partial atrioventricular canal defect: long-term follow-up after initial repair in patients > or = 40 years old. J Am Coll Cardiol 1995;25:1189–1194.

15. Gatzoulis MA, Hechters S, Webb GD, Williams WG. Surgery for partial atrioventricular septal defect in the adult. Ann Thorac Surg 1999;67:504–510.

16. Gatzoulis MA, Shore DF, Yacoub M, Shinebourne EA. Complete atrioventricular septal defect with tetralogy of Fallot: diagnosis and management. Br Heart J 1994;71:579–583.

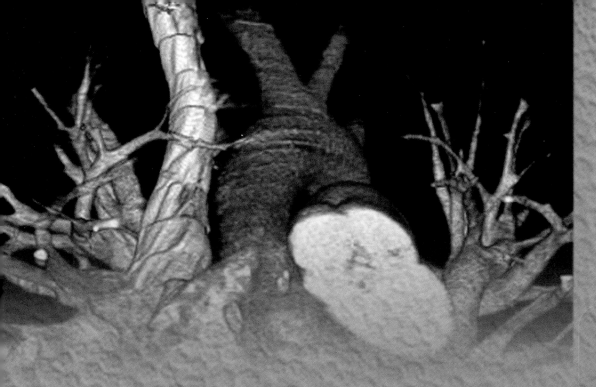

Diseases of the Mitral Valve

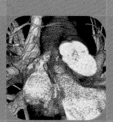

Cor Triatriatum and Mitral Stenosis

DANIEL MURPHY

Introduction

Congenital obstruction to left ventricular inflow has three main causes: congenital mitral stenosis, cor triatriatum, and congenital pulmonary vein stenosis. Congenital pulmonary vein stenosis produces severe symptoms in infancy and is not present in the adult.

COR TRIATRIATUM

Definition and Morphology

Cor triatriatum, sometimes referred to as cor triatriatum sinister, is a rare congenital cardiac anomaly in which the common pulmonary venous chamber is separated from the true left atrium by fibromuscular septum. This anomaly occurs in 0.4% of patients with congenital heart defects, with a slight male predominance.

Cor triatriatum is thought to result from embryologic failure of the common pulmonary vein to become incorporated into the left atrium during the fifth week of embryonic development.[1] The inadequate incorporation of the common pulmonary vein results in an obstructive membrane at the junction of the common pulmonary vein and the left atrium. This creates two separate chambers within the left atrium; the proximal chamber consists of the pulmonary veins and their confluence, whereas the distal chamber includes the true left atrium and left atrial appendage (Fig. 28-1).

Associated Defects

Fifty to 80 percent of cases of cor triatriatum are associated with other cardiac defects (Box 28-1).[1–5] A patent foramen ovale or secundum atrial septal defect may be present. The septal defect establishes a direct communication between the right atrium and the proximal common pulmonary venous chamber or the distal chamber, the true left atrium. Other associated defects include patent ductus arteriosus, persistent left superior vena cava, ventricular septal defect, ostium primum atrial septal defect, and a variety of left-sided cardiac abnormalities including coarctation of the aorta. Other abnormalities of pulmonary venous anatomy can exist in conjunction with cor triatriatum, including total or partial anomalous pulmonary venous connection and sinus venosus atrial septal defect.

Embryology

The embryologic basis of cor triatriatum is controversial. Possibilities include malseptation, malincorporation, and entrapment. The theory of malseptation proposes that the abnormal membrane in the left atrium represents an abnormal growth of the septum primum. The malincorporation hypothesis suggests that cor triatriatum is the result of incomplete incorporation of the embryonic common pulmonary vein into the left atrium. This theory fails to explain the presence of the fossa ovalis in the distal chamber and the presence of atrial muscle fibers in the proximal chamber wall. The final theory—entrapment—proposes that the left horn of the sinus venosus entraps the common pulmonary vein and thereby prevents its incorporation into the left atrium.[1] It has also been proposed that impingement of a persistent left superior vena cava could induce production of an abnormal left atrial membrane. The precise developmental embryology of cor triatriatum is unknown and remains controversial. None of the proposed hypotheses completely explains all anatomic variations and features of this anomaly.

Anatomy

The anatomic feature of cor triatriatum that determines the clinical presentation is the connection between the pulmonary venous confluence and the left atrium. If there is no such connection, complete obstruction of the pulmonary venous drainage occurs, unless there is an alternate site of left atrial decompression. More commonly, there is a small opening or fenestration in the abnormal left atrial membrane that allows decompression of the left atrium, but with some obstruction. Finally, in some cases there is one large opening or several fenestrations in the membrane allowing complete decompression of the pulmonary veins and producing no obstruction to left atrial and left ventricular inflow.

Although the fossa ovalis is usually found between the true left and right atria, the common pulmonary venous chamber may also decompress through a communication with the right atrium. In some cases the decompression will mask signs and symptoms of pulmonary venous congestion and hypertension.

In addition to the most common type of discrete diaphragmatic cor triatriatum, cases have been described in which the proximal left atrial chamber is either hourglass or tubular in shape.

Early Presentation

The age at presentation and clinical symptoms relate directly to the degree of pulmonary venous obstruction. in the most severe forms, clinical presentation occurs during infancy with signs of shock, pulmonary edema, respiratory distress, and pulmonary hypertension.[4,5] The presence of an obstructive membrane in the left atrium associated with clinical symptoms is an indication for surgical resection of the membrane. Most cases of cor triatriatum are identified during childhood. Some 75% of untreated patients with cor triatriatum die in infancy. Symptoms during childhood include dyspnea, tachypnea, cyanosis, exercise intolerance, failure to thrive, and cardiac murmur.[3–5]

Late Presentation

Cor triatriatum can persist unrecognized into adult life (Box 28-2). The adult with cor triatriatum may have no obstruction to left atrial inflow, mild obstruction, or moderately severe obstruction. The anatomic variation is responsible for the varied clinical presentation. The time of onset of symptoms varies, depending on the degree of obstruction at the exit of the accessory chamber. In those with a very large opening, survival without symptoms is possible. Late onset of symptoms is probably caused by increased pulmonary pressure or flow, development of atrial arrhythmias, or mitral valve abnormalities such as mitral regurgitation.[6,7] Adults with moderate obstruction may present with dyspnea on exertion,[8] chest pain,[2] syncope, reactive airway disease, or pulmonary edema.[9] Adult patients usually present

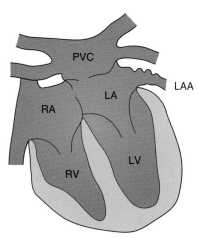

Figure 28-1   Anatomic features of cor triatriatum. A membrane divides the left atrium (LA) into a proximal chamber, containing the pulmonary veins, and a distal "true" left atrium, which contains the left atrial appendage (LAA). LV, left ventricle; PVC, pulmonary venous confluence; RA, right atrium; RV, right ventricle.

BOX 28-1   CARDIAC DEFECTS ASSOCIATED WITH COR TRIATRIATUM

- Atrial septal defect or patent foramen ovale
- Patent ductus arteriosus
- Persistent left superior vena cava
- Partial or total anomalous pulmonary venous connection
- Sinus venosus atrial septal defect
- Ventricular septal defect
- Ostium primum atrial septal defect
- Hypoplastic left ventricle
- Coarctation of the aorta
- Interrupted aortic arch

BOX 28-2   PRESENTING SIGNS AND SYMPTOMS OF COR TRIATRIATUM IN THE ADULT

- Nonobstructive cor triatriatum may be an incidental finding.
- Physical findings are generally nonspecific.
- Symptoms mimic those associated with mitral stenosis, including dyspnea, cough, hemoptysis, and chest pain.
- Atrial fibrillation is the most common arrhythmia and can cause clinical deterioration.
- Left atrial thrombus formation occurs and can cause systemic embolism.

---

with secondary pulmonary hypertension and symptoms that mimic those of mitral stenosis, including cough and hemoptysis.

Late presenting signs and symptoms also include atrial fibrillation[9–11] and left atrial thrombus formation with or without systemic embolization. Cerebral emboli have been reported to be one of the clinical manifestations in cor triatriatum. In most cases, left atrial thrombus developed in the presence of atrial fibrillation. Because of this association, the development of atrial fibrillation in an individual with nonobstructive cor triatriatum may be an indication for surgical resection of the left atrial membrane in order to prevent the formation of thrombus.

There are multiple reports of individuals who have been totally asymptomatic but later develop symptoms during their early adult years or middle age. New or accentuated symptoms can be due to several causes: fibrosis or calcification of the membrane orifice may cause a progressive stenosis, mitral regurgitation may develop as a result of a

degenerative progress that involves the mitral valve, and atrial fibrillation may contribute to clinical decompensation in these cases.

Cor triatriatum can be associated with mitral regurgitation,[2,11] possibly due to abnormal flow through the membrane fenestration damaging or distorting[7] the mitral valve. In some cases there may be contact between the mitral valve leaflets and the left atrial membrane.

Nonobstructive cor triatriatum in adults may be an incidental finding during echocardiography or other imaging procedures. Asymptomatic adult patients have been described who are as old as 93 years of age. Asymptomatic cor triatriatum has also been identified at autopsy in elderly patients who have died from "other causes."

Diagnosis

Before the advent of two-dimensional (2D) echocardiography, the diagnosis of asymptomatic cor triatriatum was rarely made.[3] Physical findings are nonspecific but may include an accentuated pulmonic second heart sound or nonspecific murmur. However, transthoracic and transesophageal echocardiography are key to establishing the diagnosis[2]:

- A nonmobile membrane is seen in the left atrium; the membrane usually originates from the upper portion of the left lateral atrial wall between the pulmonary veins and the left atrial appendage. The location and degree of attachment to the atrial septum vary.
- Echocardiographically, the condition is first suspected by the appearance of a linear structure in the left atrium in the long-axis view (Fig. 28-2).
- The four-chamber view will confirm that this is a definite structure and not an artifact (Fig. 28-3). Adjustment of the scanning plane may show the orifice, and color Doppler imaging will confirm its location.
- The differential diagnosis of cor triatriatum by echocardiography includes a prominent coronary sinus, usually owing to a persistent left superior vena cava (which may coexist with cor triatriatum), a supravalvar mitral ring (which exists between the left atrial appendage and the mitral leaflets), and a prominent fold of the left atrial wall at the junction of the left lower pulmonary vein.
- The most important echocardiographic features of cor triatriatum are the size, number, and location of the membrane openings. The openings can be defined by 2D and three-dimensional (3D) echocardiography,[12,13] and identification of the openings is enhanced through the use of color Doppler imaging.
- It is also crucial to identify the connection of all four pulmonary veins.

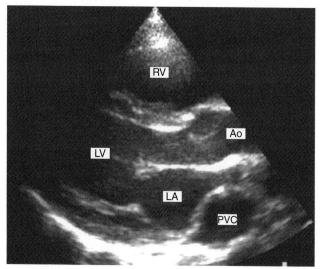

Figure 28-2   Parasternal long-axis echocardiographic image. There is a membrane dividing the left atrium (LA), with the pulmonary venous confluence (PVC) to the right and the "true" left atrium adjacent to the mitral valve. Ao, aorta; LV, left ventricle; RV, right ventricle.

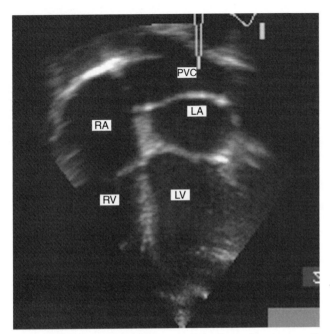

Figure 28-3 Apical four-chamber echocardiographic image. The obstructing membrane in the left atrium (LA) is easily seen. LV, left ventricle; PVC, pulmonary venous confluence; RA, right atrium; RV, right ventricle.

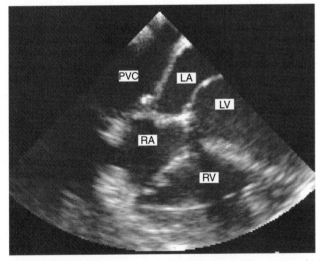

Figure 28-4 Transesophageal echocardiogram. There is a thick membrane in the left atrium (LA), which causes a nearly complete obstruction to left ventricular inflow. LV, left ventricle; PVC, pulmonary venous confluence; RA, right atrium; RV, right ventricle.

- In difficult cases, transesophageal echocardiography (Fig. 28-4) readily shows the membrane and the transmembrane gradient can be measured.[14]
- Echocardiography and other noninvasive modalities are also important in establishing or excluding associated cardiac defects.

  Color, pulsed, and continuous wave Doppler patterns are essential in determining the physiologic significance of the cor triatriatum membrane[15]:
- Low velocity, phasic flow with a peak velocity of less than 1 m/s indicates no obstruction and suggests a large opening between the two atrial chambers.
- Conversely, an accelerating, aliasing narrow Doppler flow signal suggests left atrial obstruction.
- More severe obstruction is associated with higher peak flow velocity and a loss of the phasic character of atrial inflow.

Spectral Doppler imaging also can be used to estimate the pulmonary artery pressure from the tricuspid regurgitation velocity.

Coexisting mitral stenosis can be masked by a moderate obstruction at the level of the atrial membrane. Therefore, it is also important to examine the mitral valve and submitral apparatus for any suggestion of coexisting mitral stenosis.

Although echocardiographic and Doppler measurements are useful in identifying moderate or severe left atrial obstruction, in milder cases there may be no evidence of obstruction at rest. In such patients exercise may produce increased velocity and pressure gradient. Any individual with cor triatriatum and symptoms suggestive of pulmonary venous congestion (exertional dyspnea, wheezing, reactive airway disease, syncope or pulmonary edema) should undergo a provocative test such as exercise echocardiography, volume loading challenge, or exercise cardiac catheterization.[2]

Cor triatriatum is also easily diagnosed by cardiac magnetic resonance imaging[16] and computed tomography.[17] As the resolution of these techniques improves, more precise anatomic detail will be obtained.

2D echocardiography clearly demonstrates the anatomy in most instances and is superior to angiography in the diagnosis of cor triatriatum. Although cardiac catheterization is rarely necessary to establish the diagnosis of cor triatriatum, it may be employed to document the pressure gradient across the membrane and to confirm associated pulmonary hypertension.[2]

For adult patients with previous repair of cor triatriatum, transthoracic echocardiography should demonstrate unobstructed left atrial left ventricular inflow. When tricuspid regurgitation is present, continuous wave Doppler imaging is used to estimate pulmonary artery pressure.

Management

Surgical management is the treatment of choice for symptomatic cor triatriatum and involves excision of the left atrial membrane. Because the degree of obstruction tends to be greater in younger patients[6] and progressive obstruction has rarely been documented, membrane excision may not be necessary in the asymptomatic adult. Although surgical mortality rates may be increased in symptomatic infants,[5] isolated surgical resection of the cor triatriatum membrane in adult patients should be accomplished with very low morbidity and mortality.[10] The right atrial transseptal approach is recommended because it provides excellent exposure with identification of the lesion and complete excision of the diaphragm. In addition, the right atrial approach allows inspection of the pulmonary veins and mitral valve. As is the case with mitral stenosis, in most patients there is regression of pulmonary hypertension and pulmonary arterial pressure may revert to normal levels after cor triatriatum repair.

Dilation of the membrane either intraoperatively or with balloon catheter has been reported but is unlikely to result in permanent relief of symptoms.

Late Outcome

Early surgical resection of cor triatriatum seems to restore normal anatomic and hemodynamic status. There are no reports of recurrence of left atrial membrane after surgical excision for cor triatriatum. There are also few reports of late complications or morbidity after successful surgical repair. Because the operation involves a right atriotomy it is expected that some individuals will be at risk for the development of atrial arrhythmias. Reentrant atrial tachycardia after right atriotomy frequently can be eliminated by means of electrophysiologic mapping and radiofrequency ablation. In the adult who has had long-standing atrial hypertension there may be an increased risk of the late development of atrial fibrillation. However, there are few reports of the late development of atrial arrhythmias in this population.

Pregnancy

After successful repair of cor triatriatum, and provided that there is no residual pulmonary hypertension, there should be no contraindications to pregnancy, which in turn should carry a very low risk.

In the adult with asymptomatic cor triatriatum with no evidence of left atrial obstruction at rest there should be no contraindications to pregnancy. However, pregnancy may produce symptoms in an individual with mild-to-moderate left atrial inflow obstruction at rest. Such cases should be managed in a manner similar to that for cases of mitral stenosis.[18]

Level of Follow-Up, Endocarditis Prophylaxis, and Exercise

After successful surgical excision of the left atrial membrane there should be no need for long-term follow-up of patients with cor triatriatum, provided pulmonary hypertension has resolved. For the individual with asymptomatic unoperated cor triatriatum without evidence of left atrial inflow obstruction, routine cardiac follow-up may not be necessary. There are no reports of progressive constriction or obstruction of left atrial inflow over time. However, for an individual known to have nonobstructive cor triatriatum the development of new symptoms such as atrial fibrillation, dyspnea on exertion, reactive airway disease, or stroke should prompt a reevaluation with reassessment of the need for intervention.

Unless there are associated cardiac defects dictating otherwise, there should be no need for antibiotic prophylaxis for patients with cor triatriatum.

After successful surgical excision of the left atrial membrane there should be no limitations on activities. Specifically, there should be no limitations in occupation or exercise tolerance. Provided that pulmonary hypertension has resolved fully (which is likely), normal activities should be encouraged and there is no contraindication to participation in competitive sports.

MITRAL STENOSIS

Definition and Epidemiology

Congenital mitral stenosis includes a broad spectrum of developmental abnormalities of the mitral valve that result in obstruction of blood flow from the left atrium to the left ventricle. Isolated mitral stenosis is one of the rarest forms of congenital heart disease, occurring in only 0.6% of autopsies. The diagnosis of isolated congenital mitral stenosis is rarely made in the adult. In fact, in an autopsy series from 1972,[19] which included 543 patients older than 14 years of age with severe valve disease, 206 patients had mitral stenosis, all rheumatic in origin. Ruckman and Van Praagh[20] published their autopsy series in 1978. There were 49 cases of mitral stenosis, only 2 of which were in patients older than 18 years of age. There was one 20-year-old patient with a parachute mitral valve and one 28-year-old with coarctation, aortic regurgitation, and mitral stenosis.

Anatomy

A variety of anatomic features may be present and contribute to congenital mitral stenosis. The abnormalities include the following: parachute mitral valve in which a single papillary muscle is present to which all the mitral chordae attach; two closely spaced papillary muscles with an arcade of short chordae limiting leaflet mobility; and a supravalvular mitral ring in which a fibrous membrane is present on the left atrial side of the mitral valve, frequently adherent to the mitral leaflets.

In the Ruckman and Van Praagh[20] series of 49 patients, 24 had short chordae with a mean age at death of 6 months; 20 had hypoplastic left heart syndrome with a mean age at death of 5 days; 6 had a supravalvular mitral ring with a mean age at death of 5.5 years; and 4 had parachute mitral valve with a mean age at death of nearly 10 years.

Double-orifice mitral valve is a rare anomaly that results from excessive leaflet tissue bridging between the anterior and posterior mitral leaflets. The two orifices are typically medial and lateral in position and unequal in size with normal papillary muscles. Double-orifice mitral valves, which are almost always associated with a complex congenital cardiac anomaly,[21] may or may not be obstructed due to restricted excursion of the mitral leaflets.

Patients with atrioventricular septal defects, including ostium primum atrial septal defect, invariably have abnormalities of the "mitral" valve. Most commonly, the anterior "mitral" leaflet is "cleft" with varying degrees of fusion of the superior and inferior bridging leaflets of the anterior "mitral" leaflet. Papillary muscle abnormalities are common in this setting but rarely produce "mitral" stenosis in the unoperated state. However, if a single papillary muscle is present or if the papillary muscles are closely spaced, closure of the anterior "mitral" leaflet cleft can restrict the "mitral" valve orifice and produce "mitral" stenosis.

Associated Defects

Isolated congenital mitral stenosis is uncommon. The most common association is with other left-sided anomalies, particularly obstructive lesions. Minor abnormalities of the mitral valve and the mitral valve support apparatus are common in patients with coarctation of the aorta, bicuspid aortic valve, and subaortic stenosis. Mitral valve abnormalities may also accompany ventricular septal defect or, less commonly, atrial septal defect. Mitral stenosis has also been recognized frequently in patients with tetralogy of Fallot.

A supravalvular mitral membrane or ring can also coexist with other anomalies such as single papillary muscle or short chordae. In 1963, Shone described a constellation of defects including supravalvular mitral membrane, parachute mitral valve, subaortic stenosis, and coarctation of the aorta; the term *Shone syndrome* is applied in patients with some or all of these features. In addition, supravalvular mitral membrane has been described in association with ventricular septal defect, patent ductus arteriosus, atrioventricular septal defects, and double-outlet right ventricle.

Early Presentation

Most cases of congenital mitral stenosis are diagnosed in early childhood. In the past the severity of the mitral valve abnormality and the range of associated defects made surgical repair difficult, with survival to age 18 years only 18%.[22] There are presently few adult survivors of mitral valve operations performed during infancy or childhood, but outcomes for childhood mitral valve repair and replacement are improving.[23–26] Therefore, one should anticipate the emergence of a cohort of young adults born with mitral stenosis.

Although supravalvular mitral ring represents a membrane of fibrous tissue, the natural history suggests that this lesion is not progressive. Occasionally, a child will display progressive symptoms as he or she "outgrows" the effective mitral orifice created by the supravalvular mitral membrane, but this does not appear to be a pattern in adults.

The presence of mild congenital mitral stenosis may exaggerate the effect of an atrial septal defect or left-to-right shunt through a patent foramen ovale. Similar to Lutembacher syndrome, the presence of obstruction to left ventricular inflow raises left atrial pressure and increases the left-to-right shunt. In such cases closure of the atrial septal defect is beneficial to the patient by reducing pulmonary blood flow. The presence of a large unrestrictive atrial septal defect can mask the hemodynamic and echocardiographic signs of mitral stenosis.

Adult Presentation

Severe congenital mitral stenosis is a disease of infancy and early childhood and requires surgical intervention. It is likely that the only adult survivors born with significant congenital mitral stenosis will have undergone mitral valve repair or replacement, single-ventricle repair, or heart transplant by the time they reach adulthood. Therefore, unoperated congenital mitral stenosis in the adult will be limited to mild abnormalities of the mitral valve or support apparatus with or without mild obstruction. The clinical presentation and cardiac symptoms in this group of patients will most likely be dictated by associated findings such as subaortic stenosis, coarctation of the aorta, and aortic valve abnormalities.[27]

A few individuals may survive to adulthood with moderately severe mitral stenosis, particularly if they have not had access to medical care. The presenting symptoms and complications should be identical to those in the adult with rheumatic mitral valve disease. In addition, these individuals may have other associated congenital abnormalities.

Occasionally, an adult patient with double-inlet ventricle and intact atrial septum will present with left atrial hypertension due to mitral stenosis. This situation, which is treated by atrial septectomy, can lead to left atrial thrombus formation, atrial arrhythmias, and pulmonary hypertension.

Investigations

Echocardiography is the definitive diagnostic method for congenital mitral stenosis:
- The valve leaflets and subvalvular apparatus are examined carefully with specific attention to:
  - The placement of the papillary muscles
  - Leaflet tip mobility
  - Presence of a supravalvular fibrous membrane
- A true left ventricular short axis scan is essential:
  - To examine the papillary muscles
  - To detect double-orifice or cleft valves
- Transesophageal echocardiography can be used to improve image quality and resolution if transthoracic images are suboptimal.
- Doppler echocardiography is used to detect mitral regurgitation and to estimate the severity of mitral stenosis, using the same techniques applied to acquired mitral valve disease. Key elements of the Doppler examination are:
  - Peak velocity
  - Mean gradient
  - Estimation of pulmonary artery pressure

In the presence of multiple lesions, hemodynamic assessment by cardiac catheterization can be useful in management planning.

Management

EARLY

In the infant or child with severe congenital mitral stenosis the surgical options include mitral valve repair, mitral valve replacement, or conversion to single-ventricle physiology. The surgical procedure chosen depends on the original mitral valve anatomy, the size of the child and the mitral annulus,[25] and the presence of other intracardiac abnormalities. Mitral valve repair might consist of lengthening chordae, splitting papillary muscles, and removal of a supravalvular mitral membrane.

Mitral valve repair is generally a palliative step designed to allow an infant or child to grow.

Intervention for supravalvular mitral stenosis is usually performed during childhood. In two series of 29 patients who underwent surgery for membranous supravalvular mitral stenosis, none was older than 13 years of age.[28,29]

Balloon valvuloplasty has been attempted with varying success in children with congenital mitral stenosis. Although catheter intervention can reduce transvalvular gradient and symptoms, improvement is frequently temporary.

LATE

Management of the adult with congenital mitral stenosis, as with mitral stenosis of different etiology, includes the initial evaluation, addressing medical management issues and the need for surgical or catheter intervention.

Medical therapy focuses on reduction of atrial pressures, control of atrial arrhythmia, if present, and prevention of embolic events and endocarditis. β-Adrenergic blockers and diuretics have traditionally been used under these circumstances. Anticoagulation with warfarin is indicated in patients with paroxysmal atrial fibrillation or in those with marked left atrial dilation.

The timing of surgical or catheter intervention is based on the clinical status of the patient, the severity of the obstruction, and the risks of continued medical therapy. Because of the frequent involvement of the subvalvular and the occasional involvement of the supravalvular apparatus, surgical intervention in patients failing medical therapy is often in the form of mitral valve replacement. Because hemodynamically significant congenital mitral stenosis is rare in adults, there is little experience with balloon valvuloplasty but the general view is that balloon valvuloplasty is less effective in patients with congenital mitral stenosis than in those with rheumatic heart disease.

Pregnancy

With the exception of the patient with mild mitral stenosis with mild left atrial enlargement and no previous history of atrial fibrillation, pregnancy can be problematic. Cardiac decompensation may occur during the second or third trimester of pregnancy with heart failure. The risk of systemic thromboembolism with atrial fibrillation must not be underestimated. Patients need detailed preconception assessment and counseling, and those who choose to proceed with pregnancy require cardiologic and high-risk obstetric input during pregnancy and the peripartum (see Chapter 21).

Level of Follow-Up, Endocarditis Prophylaxis, and Exercise

All patients with congenital mitral stenosis, operated or not, warrant periodic cardiologic follow-up. All patients with a mechanical mitral prosthesis or a prior history of infective endocarditis require endocarditis prophylaxis. Patients with more than mild mitral stenosis should avoid strenuous exercise.

REFERENCES

1. Van Praagh R, Corsini I. Cor triatriatum: pathologic anatomy and a consideration of morphogenesis based on 13 postmortem cases and a study of normal development of the pulmonary vein and atrial septum in 83 human embryos. Am Heart J 1969;78:379–405.
2. Rorie M, Xie GY, Miles H, Smith MD. Diagnosis and surgical correction of cor triatriatum in an adult: combined use of transesophageal echocardiography and catheterization. Catheter Cardiovasc Interv 2000;51:83–86.
3. Van Son JA, Danielson GK, Schaff HV, et al. Cor triatriatum: diagnosis, operative approach, and late results. Mayo Clin Proc 1993;68:854–859.
4. Gheissari A, Malm JR, Bowman Jr FO, Bierman FZ. Cor triatriatum sinistrum: one institution's 28-year experience. Pediatr Cardiol 1992;13:85–88.
5. Alphonso N, Norgaard MA, Newcom A, et al. Cor triatriatum: presentation, diagnosis and long-term surgical results. Ann Thorac Surg 2005;80:1666–1671.
6. Slight RD, Nzewi OC, Buell R, Mankad PS. Cor-triatriatum sinister presenting in the adult as mitral stenosis: an analysis of factors which may be relevant in late presentation. Heart Lung Circ 2005;14:8–12.
7. Keeble W, Lundmark HJ, Dargie. The paradoxical finding of mitral valve incompetence and cor triatriatum: a mechanism revealed? Heart 2004;90:125.
8. Citro R, Bossone E, Provenza G, et al. Isolated left cor triatriatum: a rare cause of effort dyspnoea in the adult. J Cardiovasc Med 2008;9:926–928.
9. LeClair SJ, Funk KJ, Goff DR. Cor triatriatum presenting as postcesarean section pulmonary edema. J Cardiothorac Vasc Anesth 1996;10:638–639.
10. Chen Q, Guhathakurta S, Vadalapali G, et al. Cor triatriatum in adults: three new cases and a brief review. Tex Heart Inst J 1999;26:206–210.
11. Feld H, Shani J, Rudansky HW, et al. Initial presentation of cor triatriatum in a 55-year-old woman. Am Heart J 1992;124:788–791.
12. Melzer C, Bartel T, Muller S, et al. Dynamic three-dimensional echocardiography in the assessment of cor triatriatum. Clin Cardiol 1997;20:82–83.
13. Mercer-Rosa L, Fedec A, Gruber P, Seliem M. Cor triatriatum sinister with and without left ventricular inflow obstruction: visualization of the entire supravalvular membrane by real-time three-dimensional echocardiography. Impact on clinical management of individual patient. Congenit Heart Dis 2006;1:335–339.
14. Hoffman R, Lambertz H, Flachskampf FA, et al. Transoesophageal echocardiography in the diagnosis of cor triatriatum; incremental value of colour Doppler. Eur Heart J 1992;13:418–420.
15. Vick III GW, Murphy Jr DJ, Ludomirsky A, et al. Pulmonary venous and systemic ventricular inflow obstruction in patients with congenital heart disease: detection by combined two-dimensional and Doppler echocardiography. J Am Coll Cardiol 1987;9:580–587.

On the electrocardiogram LVH is seen in 65% to 85% of all patients and in up to 50% of those with even mild stenosis. Left atrial overload may be present. In postoperative patients, there may be left bundle-branch block.

The chest radiograph is often normal, or there may be prominence of the left ventricle with associated dilation of the ascending aorta.[9,12] Left ventricular dilation may be seen if there is significant aortic regurgitation.

Transthoracic echocardiography will demonstrate a narrow LVOT, seen best in the parasternal long-axis view (PLAX). A "membrane" or ridge is sometimes visualized (owing to limited acoustic window), or a long area of muscular thickening (tunnel type) may be seen. Fluttering or partial early closure of the aortic valve may be seen on two-dimensional (2D) or M-mode echocardiography.

Transesophageal echocardiography usually allows direct imaging of the subaortic "membrane"/ridge, especially if multiplanar imaging is used. The transverse and longitudinal views of the aortic valve and LVOT provide comprehensive definition of discrete membranes (Fig. 32-1) and evaluation of aortic valve competence. The five-chamber transgastric view allows color flow demonstration of the level of obstruction and estimation of pressure gradients by spectral Doppler imaging.

Continuous wave and color flow Doppler imaging quantifies the severity of subaortic obstruction. The severity of discrete stenosis can be estimated using the simplified Bernoulli equation (peak gradient $= 4V^2$), which calculates a peak instantaneous Doppler gradient. This gradient can be higher than the numerical figure of the peak-to-peak gradient recorded at cardiac catheterization and may vary with different loading conditions, heart rate, cardiac output, and circulating catecholamines with beat-to-beat and respiratory variation.[13,14]

The Doppler mean gradient is also useful, taking an average of all instantaneous gradients throughout systole (calculated by tracing the outside border around the continuous wave Doppler velocity profile, using commercially available computer software). Doppler gradient estimation is less accurate with the tunnel form of obstruction, because it neglects the pressure drop caused by viscous friction along its flow path and invalidates some of the physical assumptions in the Doppler gradient calculation. Three-dimensional (3D) echocardiography may also provide accurate definition of these lesions.

Magnetic resonance imaging (MRI) provides an accurate noninvasive assessment of this lesion in both its forms. Spin-echo images define morphology, and gradient reversal images can be utilized to estimate the severity of obstruction. Associated anomalies can also be detected.

Right-sided and left-sided heart catheterization can assess the severity of outflow obstruction by recording pressure withdrawal gradients (peak-to-peak pressure gradients) across the respective outflow tracts. Left and/or right ventriculography can assess ventricular function and delineate the level of obstruction of both discrete and diffuse forms. End-hole or micromanometer-tipped catheters can be used to obtain accurate measurements. Aortography will confirm the presence and severity of aortic regurgitation and associated arch abnormalities.

A combination of investigations may be needed to confirm the diagnosis, define the anatomy, assess severity of the lesion, and detect associated anomalies.

Management

SAS tends to be a progressive lesion with a variable rate of progression. The management of asymptomatic patients is not well defined. The timing of intervention and choice of surgical technique remains controversial. Some advocate early surgery even in the absence of symptoms, to prevent aortic valve damage and recurrence,[15] whereas others adopt a more conservative "watch and wait" approach before performing aggressive myectomy along with membrane excision.[16,17]

In the asymptomatic young adult, a resting peak instantaneous Doppler gradient of more than 50 mm Hg or a mean Doppler gradient of more than 30 mm Hg or, in the setting of smaller gradients, documentation of moderate-to-severe aortic regurgitation and left ventricular dilation are used as criteria for intervention.[18] In patients with lower peak gradients, symptoms can be investigated with exercise Doppler imaging to document how much the gradient increases with exertion.[18]

The controversy regarding timing of surgical intervention reflects conflicting outcome data from mid- and long-term surgical follow-up. A persistent problem is a high postoperative recurrence of SAS (occurring in up to 27% of cases) and the need for late reoperation. The development of progressive aortic regurgitation is also seen (12% to 20% cases) even after successful relief of obstruction. Although recurrence of stenosis is reportedly lower (15%) in those who have early surgical repair,[15] reoperation will be required in some.

For symptomatic patients, who may or may not have had prior surgery, relief of outflow obstruction is needed. Balloon dilation of discrete thin membranes has been described as a safe and effective method of reducing subaortic obstruction, but surgery is traditionally regarded as the preferred treatment option. Surgery is particularly preferred in adults when definitive repair can be performed. The choice of surgical technique remains an area of discussion.

Percutaneous balloon dilation for discrete SAS was first described in 1985.[19,20] Adolescents or young patients with a thin membrane causing a significant gradient (>50 mm Hg), with or without symptoms, may be candidates for this intervention. The membrane should be no more than 1 to 2 mm thick, and transesophageal echocardiography should be used to define the anatomy and guide balloon dilation along with fluoroscopy. A balloon diameter 1 to 2 mm bigger than the aortic valve annulus diameter is used, with a balloon length of 40 to 60 mm. A visible notch in the balloon can be seen during fluoroscopy that should then disappear as the membrane is torn.[21] Early relief of obstruction is described, but there are few long-term follow-up studies, and a recurrence rate of up to 15% has been reported. The technique seems ineffective for membranes with a fibromuscular collar or tunnel-type lesions.[21,22]

The type of surgical treatment of SAS depends on the nature of the obstructive lesion. For discrete obstruction, a membranectomy with or without myomectomy is performed. Myomectomy is favored by several authors who demonstrated better initial and long-term results, with a reduction in recurrence rates of SAS.[16,17] Others, however, have found no difference in recurrence rates whether membranectomy alone, or membranectomy and myectomy is performed.[23] Whichever technique is used, it would appear the main determinant of long-term outcome is the quality of the initial relief of obstruction. The operative mortality is low (0 to 6%).

For tunnel obstruction, the operative mortality is higher in all series. Several types of repair can be performed depending on the size and

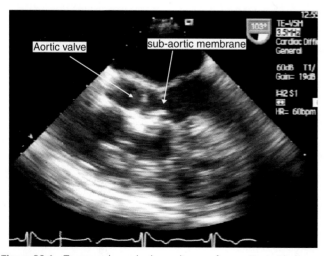

Figure 32-1 Transesophageal echocardiogram from patient with discrete subaortic stenosis.

function of the aortic valve. The valve-sparing (modified Konno) procedure involves patch augmentation of the LVOT to the aortic annulus without aortic valve replacement (aortoventriculoplasty with sparing of the aortic valve). If there is significant aortic regurgitation, then aortic valve replacement is necessary in addition to aortoventriculoplasty (Konno procedure).

More recently, the Ross-Konno procedure has been used in infants with tunnel obstruction and a diminutive aortic annulus. This procedure incorporates the principle of aortic root replacement with a pulmonary autograft and outlet septum enlargement. This provides a new alternative for definitive treatment of this anomaly.[24] Short- and mid-term follow-up data are encouraging with a low operative mortality (1.5%) and good durability. This may well become the technique of choice if long-term follow-up proves satisfactory.

Surgical complications include complete atrioventricular block necessitating permanent pacemaker implantation, perforation of the interventricular septum (acquired ventricular septal defect), damage to the mitral valve apparatus causing mitral regurgitation, delayed pericardial effusions, and diaphragmatic paresis.

Late Outcomes and Complications

Recurrence or persistence of outflow tract obstruction is common in most published series with recurrence rates of between 14% and 27%.[15,23,25,26] An average time to recurrence of 3.6 to 4.7 years has been reported.[15,23] The quality of initial relief of obstruction is the main determinant of recurrence. A peak postoperative systolic LVOT gradient greater than 30 mm Hg, by direct pressure measurement or by Doppler assessment (using the Beekman formula: Peak systolic gradient = 6.02 + 1.49 [mean systolic gradient] - 0.44 [pulse pressure]) has been shown to be an independent risk factor for recurrence of SAS.[15] A resection that reduces immediate postoperative peak LVOT gradient to less than 30 mm Hg is therefore recommended. The preoperative LVOT gradient is also recognized as a risk factor for recurrence with a preoperative catheter or mean Doppler gradient greater than 40 mm Hg associated with a higher rate of recurrence.[15] For patients with discrete SAS, proximity of the lesion to the aortic valve may predict recurrence.[26] Recurrence rates are also higher and more rapidly progressive in those with diffuse tunnel-type obstruction.

Moderate-to-severe late aortic regurgitation is reported in 25% to 40% of cases during long-term follow up. The strongest single predictor of late aortic regurgitation is a significant degree of preoperative aortic regurgitation, even when relief of obstruction has been adequate. A preoperative peak LVOT gradient greater than 40 mm Hg also predicts late progression of aortic regurgitation.[15] Similarly, in children who have not had percutaneous intervention or surgical repair, higher gradients are associated with late moderate-to-severe aortic regurgitation. Thin mobile aortic valve leaflets and an associated ventricular septal defect seem to be protective.[27] Reoperation rates vary between 12% and 20%. Indications for reoperation include relief of recurrent subaortic obstruction, severe aortic regurgitation, and aortic valve endocarditis (Box 32-1).

BOX 32-1 LATE TREATMENT: SUBAORTIC STENOSIS

- SAS is usually progressive.
- Balloon angioplasty may be useful in symptomatic patients with a thin discrete membrane (no long-term data are available).
- Surgery is recommended for symptomatic patients or if there is a peak Doppler instantaneous LVOT gradient greater than 50 mm Hg or mean gradient greater than 30 mm Hg with or without severe aortic regurgitation and left ventricular dilation.
- Recurrence of SAS and moderate-to-severe aortic regurgitation are common postoperative occurrences.
- Long-term follow-up and surveillance of all patients is needed.
- Endocarditis prophylaxis is recommended only in those with prosthetic material used in the surgical repair.

Level of Follow-Up

Long-term observation is needed for all patients whether asymptomatic operated, asymptomatic unoperated, or reoperated. For asymptomatic unoperated patients, regular clinical review and transthoracic echocardiography are needed to assess symptom status, LVOT gradient, left ventricular wall and cavity dimensions, and surveillance/monitoring of aortic regurgitation. Patients who have undergone prior surgical resection of SAS require surveillance for recurrence of obstruction SAS and development of progressive or late aortic regurgitation. At least yearly follow-up is recommended for these groups.[18] Young women should be counseled that the hemodynamic effects of pregnancy will increase any preexisting gradient, possibly making them symptomatic.

Guidelines regarding endocarditis prophylaxis have recently changed such that it is no longer required, apart from those who have had surgical repair employing prosthetic material.[18,28]

Asymptomatic patients with moderate-to-severe gradients should be advised that there may be an increased risk of sudden death with competitive athletic sports and advised to avoid them and strenuous isometric exercise.[29] Reassuring features with regard to exercise would be the presence of a normal exercise tolerance test with no ischemic ST-segment changes, no arrhythmia, a normal blood pressure response, no symptoms, and no or only mild LVH on echocardiography.

SUPRAVALVULAR AORTIC STENOSIS
Definition and Morphology

Congenital SVAS is the least common obstructive lesion of the LVOT. It accounts for 8% of congenital LVOT obstruction, affecting both sexes equally. SVAS tends to be mild if detected in adults and is more commonly encountered in those with Williams syndrome or in patients who previously underwent repair in childhood.

The defining feature of this condition is a fixed aortic narrowing at the level of the sinotubular junction (STJ), which typically produces an hourglass narrowing of the aorta (50% to 75% cases). A wide range of other anatomic variations are seen, including hypoplastic SVAS and membranous SVAS. The obstruction may extend a variable distance along the aorta, and a generalized arteriopathy affecting both systemic and pulmonary arterial systems may be seen.

In 1961, Williams reported a series of four patients with SVAS, mental retardation, and unusual facial features (Williams syndrome).[30] These patients are characterized by elfin facies, stellate iris, short stature, and a "cocktail personality." In addition to SVAS (present in all patients), peripheral pulmonary arterial stenoses are common (70% to 80%), although these tend to regress over time.[31] Arterial hypertension is also common (50% of cases) and, if present, coarctation of the aorta and renal artery stenosis should be excluded as potential causes, in light of the predilection for a generalized arteriopathy of the supra-aortic ostial trunks (e.g., there may be stenosis of the carotids and brachiocephalic arteries).

Approximately 60% of patients with SVAS have Williams syndrome. However, SVAS occurs in the absence of Williams syndrome with recognition of a familial form (~7%) and sporadic cases (~30%). Again, there may be a spectrum of stenoses, from a discrete supravalvular diaphragm to hypoplasia of the ascending aorta.

Associated Lesions

The pathology of SVAS is not simply isolated to the supravalvular region. It tends to involve the aortic valve, the aortic root, and its branches and may be part of a widespread arteriopathy affecting systemic and pulmonary arterial vessels. Multilevel right-sided heart obstruction can also be seen, particularly in Williams syndrome. In a significant proportion of patients, the aortic valve is abnormal (35% to 50% of cases), with abnormal cusp number (bicuspid valve most common), aortic valvular stenosis, and/or incompetence. Subvalvular obstruction (13% to 20% of cases), coarctation of the aorta, and congenital mitral stenosis may also be present (Shone syndrome). Coronary artery anomalies are not uncommon and include diffuse stenosis, ostial stenosis, or isolation of a coronary vessel from the aortic lumen (owing to fusion of an aortic valve cusp to the supravalvular ridge). Because the coronary vessels are proximal to the site of the supravalvular obstruction they are exposed to supranormal pressures, possibly leading to vessel tortuosity and dilation. This may be associated with medial thickening and intimal fibrosis, which in the presence of LVH may result in impaired coronary perfusion.[32] Although the long-term significance of this process has not been confirmed clinically, it is reasonable to suppose that such patients may be at risk of developing premature coronary atherosclerosis.

Genetics and Etiology

Recent genetic linkage and sequencing data have demonstrated alterations in the extracellular matrix protein elastin to be responsible for SVAS and Williams syndrome. SVAS occurs in three settings:

1. In families with an autosomal dominant inheritance pattern, high penetrance, without other major phenotypic anomalies
2. As part of Williams syndrome with its associated phenotypic anomalies
3. As a sporadic form of SVAS with normal phenotype

Williams syndrome is caused by a contiguous hemizygous gene deletion at chromosome 7q11.23.[33,34] Commonly, the deletion involves 1.5- to 1.8-megabase pairs, encompassing 28 genes, with the supravalvular cardiovascular abnormality due to involvement of the elastin gene at this locus. Fluorescent in-situ hybridization allows a definitive diagnosis to be made in young infants who may not have developed the clinical features of Williams syndrome. There is a comparable mouse model, with mutation in just one allele of elastin sufficient to cause SVAS and a general aortopathy.[35] Familial syndromes and sporadic cases of SVAS have also been found to involve mutations in the elastin gene.[36]

Outpatient Assessment

In the absence of Williams syndrome or symptoms, adult patients with SVAS tend to present for evaluation of a murmur. Those with Williams syndrome will usually have been identified in infancy, owing to their characteristic appearance. Patients may complain of exertional chest pain, dyspnea, or syncope.

On examination there may be unequal pulse volume between the carotid arteries and other peripheral pulses and unequal upper limb blood pressures (right arm blood pressure > left arm blood pressure) owing to ostial involvement of the arch vessels or the Coanda effect (whereby the high velocity jet through a stenosis is curved in a particular direction by a curved obstruction). A left ventricular heave may be present if there is LVH with or without a palpable thrill in the suprasternal notch. The S_1 is normal and A_2 may be accentuated with the S_2 sometimes narrowly or paradoxically split. An S_4 may be present over the left ventricular apex. An ejection systolic murmur loudest at the upper right sternal edge, without an ejection click, and radiating to the carotids may be heard. Auscultation over the back and flanks may reveal murmurs of peripheral pulmonary artery or renal artery stenosis.

The 12-lead electrocardiogram may show LVH by voltage criteria in 40% of children with SVAS but LVH rarely seen in adults either because they have had surgical repair or have only mild SVAS. ST-segment/T-wave changes may not regress after surgery despite the elimination of the gradient. The chest radiograph may be normal or show mild to moderate cardiomegaly with left ventricular prominence (~30% cases) in the presence of significant associated aortic regurgitation. On echocardiography, careful color flow or continuous wave Doppler imaging can demonstrate the point of narrowing distal to the aortic valve. Parasternal and suprasternal views will locate the site and extent of obstruction in some adults, but the suprasternal acoustic window is often poor and visualization of the arch can be difficult. Doppler gradients in diffuse SVAS tend to overestimate the gradient due to neglect of the pressure drop caused by viscous friction of fluid along its flow path. Because there is often associated bilateral peripheral pulmonary arterial narrowing, care

must be taken when performing Doppler assessment not to mistake this for ascending aortic flow. MRI and computed tomography (CT) can be used to define the level and severity of the obstructive lesion in addition to its associated vascular anomalies with a high degree of accuracy. The aortic root, proximal coronary arteries, and arch vessels, in addition to the pulmonary arteries and ventricular size and function, can be examined in one thorough investigation, giving useful information to plan future surgery. If the patient has Williams syndrome, imaging of the whole aorta will help assess the presence of arterial stenosis at different levels. Right- and left-sided heart catheterization can determine the severity of arterial stenoses by recording pressure withdrawal gradients across the region or regions of narrowing. Angiography should include images of the ascending aorta and aortic arch (Fig. 32-2) in addition to selective coronary arteriography. Pulmonary arteriography should also be performed to look for peripheral pulmonary artery stenoses.

Late Management

There are little data on the natural history of unoperated SVAS. It may be a progressive lesion or remain stable, but in many cases it may actually regress.[37] Peripheral pulmonary artery stenoses also have a tendency to improve spontaneously with time, with only a small number requiring intervention, usually in the form of balloon angioplasty ± stenting.

In the context of a disease that involves potentially significant secondary changes in the aortic valve, coronary arteries, and left ventricular myocardium, the inability to predict progression poses a management dilemma, especially with regard to the timing of surgical repair. The impact of age and severity of SVAS at the time of repair and their effect on long-term outcome are not clear. The answer must be reached through risk-benefit analysis, taking account of operative risk versus prevention of myocardial hypertrophy and coronary abnormalities. With a low operative mortality and morbidity, it would seem the benefits of repair as early in the course of the disease as possible may be warranted (Box 32-2).[38]

In the asymptomatic young adult, a resting mean Doppler gradient of greater than 50 mm Hg (or peak instantaneous Doppler gradient > 70 mm Hg) has been suggested as an indication for surgery.[18] If there are lesser degrees of obstruction, the presence of left ventricular hypertrophy, left ventricular dysfunction, severe aortic valve dysfunction, and the desire to increase exercise capacity or become pregnant have been used as additional criteria to guide therapy. Symptomatic patients need surgical relief of obstruction. Percutaneous experience is still limited and cannot be recommended routinely, whereas surgical treatment of SVAS is well established, with almost 50 years of experience. Balloon dilation fails to relieve diffuse or tunnel-like SVAS.[39,40] Stenting for SVAS has been described but re-intervention may be required for redevelopment of a significant gradient, and serious complications can occur. The close proximity of the aortic valve leaflets and origin of the coronary ostia are of particular concerns.[41,42]

Surgical repair of discrete SVAS was first performed at the Mayo Clinic.[43] From a surgical perspective there are two forms of SVAS: localized and diffuse. The localized type refers to the discrete supravalvular type of narrowing, whereas the diffuse type refers to a more generalized hypoplasia of the ascending aorta that generally requires more extensive surgery. Past surgical techniques focused purely on relieving outflow obstruction, but it is now appreciated that proper functioning of the aortic valve is dependent on the integrity of the geometry of the aortic root. In SVAS the entire aortic root geometry is disturbed. Current surgical strategies therefore focus on preserving root morphometry and, where possible, salvaging the native aortic valve. There is debate whether a bicuspid valve should be replaced at the time of SVAS repair, even in the absence of valve dysfunction. Delius and associates[44] reported a re-operation rate of 56% in those with a bicuspid valve, compared with 19% with a trileaflet valve. Freedom from reoperation at 5 years was also significantly lower—43% bicuspid versus 86% tricuspid—in their surgical series of 47 patients repaired in the standard way. This has since been supported by McElhinney's series of 36 patients in which 5 of 7 patients with a bicuspid valve required

Figure 32-2 Aortogram showing supravalvular aortic stenosis.

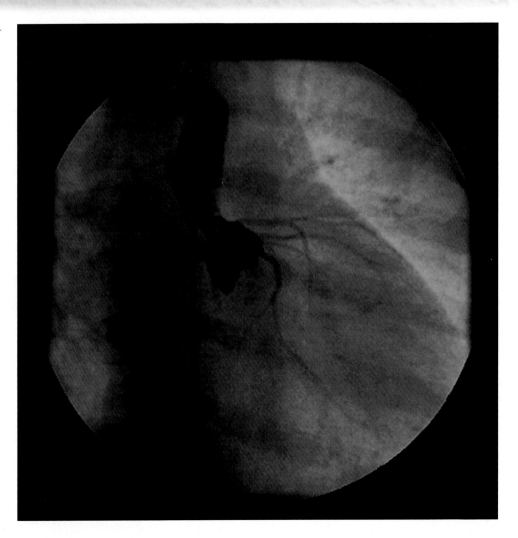

---

reoperation.[38] In light of these findings the Ross procedure has been suggested as the preferred treatment option for such patients.

After the first report of surgical correction of localized SVAS in 1956, various surgical techniques have been tried and developed, with the aim of providing a more symmetrical root augmentation. The initial diamond aortoplasty was modified so that, in addition to excision of the supravalvular ridge, a Y-shaped Dacron vascular graft was extended into both the right and noncoronary sinuses of Valsalva. More recently, techniques that augment all three sinuses have been reported. Where possible, the native aortic valve is salvaged by augmentation, suspension, commissuroplasty, annuloplasty, or thinning. The Ross procedure, using a pulmonary autograft implant, is a newer treatment option for those patients requiring aortic valve replacement. Short- and mid-term results are promising, but as yet its role in this lesion has not been elucidated over long-term follow-up.

The diffuse form of SVAS remains more challenging to treat. Various surgical techniques have been used over the years, including the insertion of a left ventricular apicoaortic conduit. Current strategies involve extensive endarterectomy of the ascending aorta and arch vessels, followed by Dacron patch augmentation, or insertion of an interposition graft if the ascending aorta is severely diseased.

Because this is a heterogeneous surgical population, early surgical mortality has been reported to be between 0 and 11%. Higher mortality figures were reported in earlier surgical series (pre-1970) and for repair of the diffuse form of SVAS. Late mortality (death after the initial operative hospital stay or 30 or more days after surgery) is low, with no significant difference between localized and diffuse repairs. In a study by Stamm and colleagues,[45] Kaplan-Meier estimates of survival, including operative deaths, were 91% at 5 years, 87% at 10 years, and 70% at 20 years. Multivariate analysis revealed that a risk factor for death was the type of operation; it was higher for patients with a diamond-shaped patch, although again this type of operation tended to be performed in the early years of SVAS surgery (pre-1970). The only factor that otherwise seemed to predict reoperation and survival was the presence of diffuse stenosis. In the series reported by van Son, associated aortic valve disease was a predictor of survival and patients with diffuse SVAS did better if they received extended patch repairs.[46] In the most recent surgical series reported by Brown and associates there was a 98% survival at 10 years and 97% survival at 20 years with no clear factor associated with survival, including type of operation, but a key risk factor for reoperation in multivariate analysis was the presence of associated LVOT obstruction at another level.[47]

Late Outcomes

Recurrence of SVAS is uncommon after repair. The most common indication for reoperation is for aortic valve dysfunction. Reoperation has been required in 17% to 40% (nonactuarial) of early operative survivors.[38,45,48] Notably, any abnormality of the aortic valve at the time of original repair has been found to be a significant risk factor for late intervention.[46,47] Isolation of a coronary artery has been reported during follow-up because of fusion of valve cusps to the aortic wall. It is uncommon and develops gradually over time. Collateral recruitment from the contralateral coronary artery tends to prevent myocardial infarction, although ischemic symptoms can occur.

Level of Follow-Up

It is likely that an adult with SVAS either will have undergone surgical repair in childhood or, if unrepaired, will have only mild SVAS. Asymptomatic, unoperated patients should have periodic clinical review and transthoracic echocardiography to assess symptom status, severity of SVAS, and surveillance for aortic valve dysfunction. Patients who have undergone surgical repair require similar assessment and follow-up for progression of aortic valve dysfunction. Endocarditis prophylaxis is required lifelong if prosthetic material has been used in the repair, according to American Heart Association guidelines.[18,28] Guidelines for competitive athletics and strenuous isometric exercise are similar to those suggested for SAS.[29]

PREGNANCY IN SUBVALVULAR AND SUPRAVALVULAR AORTIC STENOSIS

The following issues need to be considered and discussed with regard to pre-pregnancy counseling: prognosis, symptomatic and functional status, severity of LVOT gradient, left ventricular function, the nature of prior surgical correction(s), residua and sequelae of prior surgeries, the need for further surgery, and risk of CHD in the offspring (0.4% to 0.6% in the general population, approximately 5% in those with CHD, and maybe up to 50% in those with Williams syndrome).

The hemodynamic changes of pregnancy have predictable effects on the pathophysiology of LVOT. The stroke volume increases and continues to rise until the 28th week of gestation and peripheral vascular resistance falls. Therefore, the outflow tract gradient will increase late into the second trimester and the intensity of the murmur will increase. The clinical consequences of these hemodynamic changes depend largely on the baseline gradient and in part on the degree of LVH and contractile state of the left ventricle. Experience with pregnancy in patients with either unoperated or repaired SAS or SVAS is limited.

Ideally, those who are symptomatic will undergo surgical repair before conception. For patients who are asymptomatic and unoperated, the experience of pregnancy in valvular aortic stenosis is used to define baseline characteristics associated with a good pregnancy outcome. This includes a normal resting electrocardiogram, mild obstructive Doppler gradient (<30 mm Hg), good exercise tolerance (>7 Mets on exercise tolerance test), and a normal blood pressure response.[49]

In a prospective study of pregnancy outcomes in women with heart disease,[50] one of the four predictors of primary maternal cardiac events or neonatal events was the presence of left-sided heart outflow obstruction (peak LVOT Doppler gradient > 30 mm Hg). Other predictors of maternal cardiac events included prior cardiac event (heart failure, transient ischemic attack, stroke, or arrhythmia), NYHA class II or greater or cyanosis, and left ventricular ejection fraction of less than 40%. In predicting events, one point is assigned to each of these predictors if present. The estimated risk of a cardiac event in pregnancy is 0 points = 5%, 1 point = 27%, more than 1 point = 75%.

Pregnancy should be hemodynamically well tolerated in patients with repaired SAS or SVAS if the degree of residual obstruction is mild (Doppler gradient < 30 mm Hg) and left ventricular function is good. Aortic regurgitation tends to be well tolerated. There remains, however, a potential risk of aortic dissection especially in those with SVAS who have an underlying arteriopathy or who may have undergone prior aortoplasty procedures. This risk has not been quantified but should be discussed.

Epidural anesthesia with adequate volume loading is the technique of choice. In women with substantial gradients, maternal expulsive efforts should be discouraged and assisted delivery advocated.

REFERENCES

1. Oliver JM, Gonzalez A, Gallego P, et al. Discrete subaortic stenosis in adults: increased prevalence and slow rate of progression of the obstruction and aortic regurgitation. J Am Coll Cardiol 2001;38:835–842.
2. Newfeld EA, Muster AJ, Paul MH, et al. Discrete subvalvular aortic stenosis in childhood. Study of 51 patients. Am J Cardiol 1976; 38:53–61.
3. Goodwin JF, Hollman A, Cleland WP, Teare D. Obstructive cardiomyopathy simulating aortic stenosis. Br Heart J 1960; 22:403–414.
4. Hollman A, Goodwin JF, Teare D, Renwick JW. A family with obstructive cardiomyopathy (asymmetrical hypertrophy). Br Heart J 1960;22:449–456.
5. Brock R. Functional obstruction of the left ventricle; acquired aortic subvalvar stenosis. Guys Hosp Rep 1957;106:221–238.
6. Kelly DT, Wulfsberg E, Rowe RD. Discrete subaortic stenosis. Circulation 1972;46:309–322.
7. Abdallah H, Toomey K, O'Riordan AC, et al. Familial occurrence of discrete subaortic membrane. Pediatr Cardiol 1994;15:198–200.
8. Bult CJ, Eppig JT, Kadin JA, et al. Mouse Genome Database (MGD): mouse biology and model systems. Nucleic Acids Res 2009;36(database issue):D724–D728.
9. Somerville J, Stone S, Ross D. Fate of patients with fixed subaortic stenosis after surgical removal. Br Heart J 1980;43:629–647.
10. Cape EG, Vanauker MD, Sigfusson G, et al. Potential role of mechanical stress in the etiology of pediatric heart disease: septal shear stress in subaortic stenosis. J Am Coll Cardiol 1997;30:247–254.
11. Campbell M. The natural history of congenital aortic stenosis. Br Heart J 1968;30:514–526.
12. Katz NM, Buckley MJ, Liberthson RR. Discrete membranous subaortic stenosis: report of 31 patients, review of the literature, and delineation of management. Circulation 1977;56:1034–1038.
13. Currie PJ, Hagler DJ, Seward JB, et al. Instantaneous pressure gradient: a simultaneous Doppler and dual catheter correlative study. J Am Coll Cardiol 1986;7:800–806.
14. Turi ZG. Whom do you trust? Misguided faith in the catheter- or Doppler-derived aortic valve gradient. Catheter Cardiovasc Interv 2005;65:180–182.

15. Brauner R, Laks H, Drinkwater DC, et al. Benefits of early surgical repair in fixed subaortic stenosis. J Am Coll Cardiol 1997;30:1835–1842.
16. Lupinetti FM, Pridjian AK, Callow LB, et al. Optimum treatment of discrete subaortic stenosis. Ann Thorac Surg 1992;54:467–470; discussion 470–471.
17. Rayburn ST, Netherland DE, Heath BJ. Discrete membranous subaortic stenosis: improved results after resection and myectomy. Ann Thorac Surg 1997;64:105–109.
18. Warnes CA, Williams RG, Bashore TM, et al. ACC/AHA 2008 guidelines for the management of adults with congenital heart disease: a report of the American College of Cardiology/American Heart Association Task Force on Practice Guidelines (writing committee to develop guidelines on the management of adults with congenital heart disease). Developed in Collaboration With the American Society of Echocardiography, Heart Rhythm Society, International Society for Adult Congenital Heart Disease, Society for Cardiovascular Angiography and Interventions, and Society of Thoracic Surgeons. J Am Coll Cardiol 2008;52:e1–e121.
19. Suarez de Lezo J, Pan M, Sancho M, et al. Percutaneous transluminal balloon dilatation for discrete subaortic stenosis. Am J Cardiol 1986;58:619–621.
20. Suarez de Lezo J, Pan M, Herrera N, et al. [Left ventricular decompression through a transluminal approach in congenital aortic stenosis]. Rev Esp Cardiol 1985;38:400–407.
21. Suarez de Lezo J, Pan M, Segura J, et al. Discrete Subaortic Stenosis. London: Informa UK Ltd; 2007.
22. Gupta KG, Loya YS, Sharma S. Discrete subaortic stenosis: a study of 20 cases. Indian Heart J 1994;46:157–160.
23. Serraf A, Zoghby J, Lacour-Gayet F, et al. Surgical treatment of subaortic stenosis: a seventeen-year experience. J Thorac Cardiovasc Surg 1999;117:669–678.
24. Starnes VA, Luciani GB, Wells WJ, et al. Aortic root replacement with the pulmonary autograft in children with complex left heart obstruction. Ann Thorac Surg 1996;62:442–448; discussion 448–449.
25. van Son JA, Schaff HV, Danielson GK, et al. Surgical treatment of discrete and tunnel subaortic stenosis: late survival and risk of reoperation. Circulation 1993;88:II159–II169.

26. Geva A, McMahon CJ, Gauvreau K, et al. Risk factors for reoperation after repair of discrete subaortic stenosis in children. J Am Coll Cardiol 2007;50:1498–1504.
27. McMahon CJ, Gauvreau K, Edwards JC, Geva T. Risk factors for aortic valve dysfunction in children with discrete subvalvar aortic stenosis. Am J Cardiol 2004;94:459–464.
28. Nishimura RA, Carabello BA, Faxon DP, et al. ACC/AHA 2008 guideline update on valvular heart disease: focused update on infective endocarditis: a report of the American College of Cardiology/American Heart Association Task Force on Practice Guidelines: endorsed by the Society of Cardiovascular Anesthesiologists, Society for Cardiovascular Angiography and Interventions, and Society of Thoracic Surgeons. Circulation 2008;118:887–896.
29. Graham Jr TP, Driscoll DJ, Gersony WM, et al. Task force 2: congenital heart disease. J Am Coll Cardiol 2005;45:1326–1333.
30. Williams JC, Barratt-Boyes BG, Lowe JB. Supravalvular aortic stenosis. Circulation 1961;24:1311–1318.
31. Giddins NG, Finley JP, Nanton MA, Roy DL. The natural course of supravalvar aortic stenosis and peripheral pulmonary artery stenosis in Williams's syndrome. Br Heart J 1989;62: 315–319.
32. Doty DB, Eastham CL, Hiratzka LF, et al. Determination of coronary reserve in patients with supravalvular aortic stenosis. Circulation 1982;66:I186–I192.
33. Ewart AK, Morris CA, Atkinson D, et al. Hemizygosity at the elastin locus in a developmental disorder, Williams syndrome. Nat Genet 1993;5:11–16.
34. Schubert C. The genomic basis of the Williams-Beuren syndrome. Cell Mol Life Sci 2009;66:1178–1197.
35. Li DY, Brooke B, Davis EC, et al. Elastin is an essential determinant of arterial morphogenesis. Nature 1998;393:276–280.
36. Metcalfe K, Rucka AK, Smoot L, et al. Elastin: mutational spectrum in supravalvular aortic stenosis. Eur J Hum Genet 2000;8: 955–963.
37. Hickey EJ, Jung G, Williams WG, et al. Congenital supravalvular aortic stenosis: defining surgical and nonsurgical outcomes. Ann Thorac Surg 2008;86:1919–1927; discussion 1927.

38. McElhinney DB, Petrossian E, Tworetzky W, et al. Issues and outcomes in the management of supravalvar aortic stenosis. Ann Thorac Surg 2000;69:562–567.

39. Tyagi S, Arora R, Kaul UA, Khalilullah M. Percutaneous transluminal balloon dilatation in supravalvular aortic stenosis. Am Heart J 1989;118:1041–1044.

40. Pinto RJ, Loya Y, Bhagwat A, Sharma S. Balloon dilatation of supravalvular aortic stenosis: a report of two cases. Int J Cardiol 1994;46:179–181.

41. Suarez de Lezo J, Pan M, Romero M, et al. Tailored stent treatment for severe supravalvular aortic stenosis. Am J Cardiol 1996;78:1081–1083.

42. Mullins CE. Not quite ready for prime time!. Catheter Cardiovasc Interv 2004;61:542.

43. McGoon DC, Mankin HT, Vlad P, Kirklin JW. The surgical treatment of supravalvular aortic stenosis. J Thorac Cardiovasc Surg 1961;41:125.

44. Delius RE, Samyn MM, Behrendt DM. Should a bicuspid aortic valve be replaced in the presence of subvalvar or supravalvar aortic stenosis? Ann Thorac Surg 1998;66:1337–1342.

45. Stamm C, Kreutzer C, Zurakowski D, et al. Forty-one years of surgical experience with congenital supravalvular aortic stenosis. J Thorac Cardiovasc Surg 1999;118:874–885.

46. van Son JA, Danielson GK, Puga FJ, et al. Supravalvular aortic stenosis: long-term results of surgical treatment. J Thorac Cardiovasc Surg 1994;107:103–114; discussion 14–15.

47. Brown JW, Ruzmetov M, Vijay P, Turrentine MW. Surgical repair of congenital supravalvular aortic stenosis in children. Eur J Cardiothorac Surg 2002;21:50–56.

48. Sharma BK, Fujiwara H, Hallman GL, et al. Supravalvar aortic stenosis: a 29-year review of surgical experience. Ann Thorac Surg 1991;51:1031–1039.

49. Oakley CM. Pregnancy and congenital heart disease. Heart 1997;78:12–14.

50. Siu SC, Sermer M, Colman JM, et al. Prospective multicenter study of pregnancy outcomes in women with heart disease. Circulation 2001;104:515–521.

33

Aortic Regurgitation

MICHAEL J. MULLEN | NICOLA L. WALKER

Introduction

Aortic regurgitation is rarely present at birth but commonly develops as a consequence of a wide variety of congenital malformations and acquired diseases. Aortic regurgitation may result from direct damage of the valve cusps or alterations of the anatomy and geometry of the supporting structures in the aortic root and/or left ventricular (LV) outflow tract (Table 33-1).

Morphology

The aortic valve is a trileaflet semilunar valve formed within the spherical root of the aorta. The valve leaflets are inserted into the root in a crownlike manner, with the nadir forming the base of the root and the sinotubular junction supporting the superior attachment of the leaflets and delineating the interface with the ascending aorta.[1] The aortic sinuses are the expanded portions of the aortic root delineated below by the attachment of the valve leaflets. They give rise to the coronary arteries but also appear to play an important role in the dynamic function of the aortic valve. Geometric relations between structures within the aortic root are an important factor in maintaining normal valve competency and function.

With the decline in rheumatic heart disease, abnormalities of the aortic root are now the most common cause of aortic regurgitation and are relevant to a number of forms of congenital heart disease (CHD). Aortic regurgitation may be the primary clinical manifestation of the disease process "pure aortic regurgitation" or, as is often the case in congenital cardiac patients, may occur in the context of a range of additional congenital and acquired cardiac abnormalities that are likely to impact on its natural history and management. Mild aortic regurgitation is not associated with significant volume loading of the left ventricle. In contrast, severe aortic regurgitation is often characterized by a marked increase in LV size, LV hypertrophy, and, ultimately, LV failure.

CONGENITAL ABNORMALITIES OF THE AORTIC VALVE

Aortic regurgitation occurs in up to 70% of patients with a functionally abnormal congenitally bicuspid aortic valve.[2] In most cases this is related not only to the abnormal valve structure but also to dilation of the aortic root secondary to intrinsic abnormalities of the aortic wall.[2] In addition, monocuspid or quadricuspid valves are rarely described and these may be intrinsically incompetent. In patients with a bicuspid aortic valve and aortic coarctation, aortic regurgitation might be increased owing to the increased afterload intrinsic to the coarctation itself and to the frequently associated reduced aortic compliance.

AORTIC ROOT PATHOLOGY

Dilation of the aortic root and sinotubular junction may occur spontaneously or in association with a number of forms of congenital and acquired heart disease. These include Marfan syndrome, Loeys-Dietz syndrome, and Ehlers-Danlos syndrome type IV. In this context aortic regurgitation often develops, even in the absence of significant disease of the valve cusps themselves, owing to loss of the normal spherical geometry of the aortic root and displacement of the commissures outward, preventing adequate leaflet coaptation. Aortic regurgitation related to diseases of the aortic root now appears to be more prevalent than that directly related to the valve. In many cases dilation of the aortic root and the risk of spontaneous dissection is the primary clinical concern and may become the main indication for intervention.

VENTRICULAR SEPTAL DEFECT

In the presence of an outlet or doubly committed subarterial ventricular septal defect, the aortic valve cusps are inadequately supported and may prolapse into the right ventricular outflow tract. The subsequent malcoaptation of the valve cusps facilitates aortic regurgitation, which, once present, is usually progressive with time. Histologic studies have demonstrated that an important component of this condition is the loss of continuity between the aortic media and the annulus of the valve. In contrast to other causes of aortic regurgitation, early repair is indicated to prevent further valve damage.[3]

TETRALOGY OF FALLOT, PULMONARY ATRESIA, AND TRUNCUS ARTERIOSUS

Clinically relevant aortic regurgitation occurs in a small proportion of patients with tetralogy of Fallot. It is more common in patients repaired at a later age and also appears to be related to the severity of pulmonary stenosis, underlined by its higher prevalence in patients with Fallot-type pulmonary atresia and ventricular septal defect. The mechanism is unclear, but increased transaortic flow resulting in dilation of the root and ascending aorta have been implicated. Failure to recognize and rectify aortic regurgitation at the time of the initial repair of tetralogy of Fallot appears to be an important factor in later morbidity and mortality.[4] Aortic, strictly speaking truncal valve, regurgitation is also a common finding late after repair of truncus arteriosus. In this context the valve may be congenitally abnormal.

SUBAORTIC STENOSIS

In patients with fibromuscular subaortic stenosis the fibrous ring often impinges on and distorts the aortic valve cusps, and hemodynamically significant aortic regurgitation occurs in about 20% of patients.[5] Even after resection of the fibrous obstruction, aortic regurgitation may be progressive and may become the predominant clinical consideration.

POSTOPERATIVE FINDING

Aortic regurgitation may occur after open valvotomy or as a sequela of balloon dilation of aortic stenosis. Although usually mild, this may occasionally be acute and severe, requiring early surgical intervention. Mild incompetence of the pulmonary autograft is often found after the Ross operation and in the neoaortic valve of patients with transposition of the great arteries after the arterial switch operation. Although rarely progressive, close observation of valve function is required in these patients.

Pathophysiology

The reader is referred to Box 33-1 for an overview of observations regarding the pathophysiology of aortic regurgitation.

BOX 33-1 PATHOPHYSIOLOGY

- Aortic regurgitation may develop in association with, or as a sequela to, a number of congenital cardiac defects.
- Compensatory adaptations mean that most patients remain asymptomatic for many years.
- Understanding the mechanism of aortic regurgitation is important in determining the appropriate management.
- Acute aortic regurgitation may develop as a result of infective endocarditis or xenograft failure and is usually poorly tolerated.
- Thresholds for intervention are poorly defined in patients with aortic regurgitation in the context of a complex congenital defect.

TABLE 33-1 Etiology of Aortic Regurgitation

Disease	Pathologic Process
Bicuspid aortic valve	Deformity of valve cusp and/or dilation of aortic root
Ventricular septal defect	Prolapse of cusp or cusps of aortic valve into the right ventricular outflow tract
Aortic root pathology (Marfan syndrome, bicuspid aortic valve, seronegative arthritides, tetralogy of Fallot)	Dilation of aortic root and change in shape results in failure of coaptation of aortic valve leaflets
Congenital aortic stenosis	Sequela of balloon dilation, open valvotomy, or leaflet degeneration
Subaortic stenosis	Distortion and thickening of aortic cusps caused by jet from subvalvular obstruction
Postoperative	Damaged aortic valve after valvotomy or to autograft after a Ross procedure or arterial switch operation
Infective endocarditis	Valve cusp destruction and deformity; usually with preexisting abnormality such as bicuspid aortic valve
Tetralogy of Fallot/pulmonary atresia	Usually due to dilation of aortic root and subsequent change in shape and coaptation of aortic valve cusps
Rupture of sinus of Valsalva aneurysm	Rupture of localized aneurysm into right ventricle, right atrium, or left ventricle

ACUTE AORTIC REGURGITATION

Acute aortic regurgitation is most commonly seen in the context of infective endocarditis, dissection of the aortic root, or disruption of the valve after balloon dilation. Rarely, acute aortic regurgitation occurs after rupture of a sinus of Valsalva aneurysm. In acute aortic regurgitation, the left ventricle has no time to adapt to the sudden increase in loading and a rapid rise in end-diastolic pressure with reduced ejection fraction and cardiac failure ensues. Without rapid surgical intervention, clinical deterioration can be expected.

CHRONIC AORTIC REGURGITATION

In response to the chronic volume and pressure load induced by aortic regurgitation a number of compensatory physiologic adaptations occur. These include LV dilation and hypertrophy. In contrast to a pure pressure load, hypertrophy results from fiber elongation and replication of sarcomeres in series. As a result, LV compliance increases, the volume load is accommodated without an increase in end-diastolic pressure, and stroke volume is augmented. During this "compensated" phase, which may last for many years, patients are generally asymptomatic and indices of LV function remain normal. However, these adaptations cannot be maintained indefinitely and, as preload reserve becomes exhausted, diastolic filling pressures begin to rise. Simultaneously, systolic failure develops as the degree of LV hypertrophy becomes inadequate in the presence of a continued increase in afterload. Early decompensation is likely to reflect a failure of the left ventricle in the presence of extreme loading conditions, although, ultimately, irreversible myocardial injury develops unless the process is interrupted. The onset of symptoms of LV systolic dysfunction occurs in about 4% of patients per year.[6] Early symptoms are usually exertional dyspnea and fatigue. Patients may complain of angina pectoris related to poor coronary perfusion and increased myocardial oxygen demand. In about 25% of patients LV dysfunction develops before the onset of symptoms, underlying the importance of serial noninvasive measurement of LV function in addition to careful assessment of symptomatic status.

Predictors of progression to symptoms include age, baseline LV end-systolic diameter, baseline ejection fraction, and change in ejection fraction during exercise.[6,7] If the disorder is untreated, the natural history is eventually one of increasing symptoms and death from progressive heart failure or arrhythmia. In the largest natural history study published to date, 246 patients with severe aortic regurgitation were observed for 7 ± 3 years. Within 10 years of diagnosis, 83% of patients had suffered a cardiac event, with 75% dying or requiring aortic valve replacement.[7] The main independent predictor of survival was preoperative functional class. Additional predictors were the presence of comorbidity, baseline LV systolic dimension, and atrial fibrillation. Importantly, in this study, even *very mild symptoms* were associated with an adverse outcome.

Natural History

Most natural history studies have almost exclusively recruited patients with pure aortic regurgitation, and many studies have actively excluded patients with CHD other than isolated bicuspid aortic valve. As a result, the patients in these studies are likely to be older than those who are seen in the context of an adult CHD practice and are predominantly male. Intuitively, when other cardiac abnormalities are present or in patients who have previously undergone cardiac surgery, the progression to symptoms of LV dysfunction and risk associated with chronic severe aortic regurgitation is likely to be greater. Application of risk stratifications derived from studies of pure aortic regurgitation to the management of patients with additional cardiac defects might, therefore, be overly optimistic and inappropriate. The presence of comorbid conditions was a significant risk factor for clinical deterioration in the largest of these studies[7] and the few data published in patients with tetralogy of Fallot[4] and coarctation would support this concept. Furthermore, a number of studies have reported worse survival in women with severe aortic regurgitation compared with men, which does not appear related to differences in baseline risk stratification.[8,9]

Genetics and Epidemiology

Aortic regurgitation has a heterogeneous etiology and, as such, the genetic predisposition will reflect that of the underlying pathologic process. The LV response to aortic regurgitation and progression to surgery might be determined by a number of genetic factors such as angiotensin-converting enzyme (ACE) genotype, although few data have been reported in this area. Aortic regurgitation may occur in association with almost any congenital anomaly and therefore its prevalence is poorly defined. At the Boston Children's Hospital, aortic regurgitation was noted as a factor in approximately 5% of patients.[10] However, the incidence is likely to increase as part of the natural history of many diseases as patients mature.

Early Presentation and Management

Although the majority of patients with chronic aortic regurgitation are asymptomatic, the diagnosis is usually readily made by physical examination and noninvasive testing. A detailed assessment to determine the etiology and exclude additional associated abnormalities should always be performed.

PHYSICAL EXAMINATION

In clinically significant aortic regurgitation, the arterial pulse is typically collapsing in nature. Chronic severe (and sometimes "moderate") aortic regurgitation is characterized by a wide pulse pressure. Systolic blood pressure is increased—secondary to the increased forward stroke volume—and the diastolic blood pressure may be as low as 30 mm Hg. Characteristic signs of severe aortic regurgitation include de Musset sign (head nodding with the pulse), Duroziez sign (audible to-and-fro bruit over a partially compressed femoral artery), "pistol shot" femoral arteries, Quincke sign (visible pulsations in the nail bed), and a pulsatile uvula. The apex beat is displaced laterally with a diffuse forceful impulse. The characteristic blowing early diastolic murmur is usually best heard over the left sternal edge. It is accentuated by factors that increase cardiac afterload, including the Valsalva maneuver and squatting. The murmur may be loudest on the right sternal edge if a dilated aortic root is the primary cause of aortic regurgitation, at which time the aorta closure sound may have a "tambour" quality. In the setting of severe aortic regurgitation with LV decompensation, the diastolic murmur may be short, owing to early equalization of pressures in the aorta and left ventricle. Occasionally a mid-diastolic mitral rumble may be heard due to vibration of the anterior leaflet of the mitral valve (Austin Flint murmur).

A loud ejection systolic murmur may be present with severe aortic regurgitation and does not necessarily imply significant aortic stenosis. The development of a third heart sound after the age of 30 years is an important sign suggesting decompensation.

ROUTINE INVESTIGATIONS

Electrocardiography
The electrocardiogram typically shows sinus rhythm with LV hypertrophy and possibly a "strain" pattern.

Chest Radiography
The cardiac silhouette may be very large. The ascending aorta may be dilated, and the aortic "knuckle" is typically prominent.

Echocardiography
The presence and causes of aortic regurgitation are normally readily detectable by transthoracic echocardiography. LV dimensions and systolic function should be assessed. Important considerations include the morphology and structure of the aortic valve, presence or absence of aortopathy with a typically central jet of aortic regurgitation, subaortic or supra-aortic stenosis, and the presence of a ventricular septal defect with prolapse of (usually) the right coronary cusp into the right ventricular outflow tract. Infective endocarditis is normally suspected by the clinical presentation, and vegetations are often seen on transthoracic echocardiography. Transesophageal echocardiography may be necessary to define the anatomy fully and exclude endocarditis. The severity of aortic regurgitation is reflected by the LV dimension, by the width of the jet on color Doppler imaging, and by the presence of reverse flow in the descending aorta (Fig. 33-1).

NONROUTINE INVESTIGATIONS

Magnetic Resonance Imaging
Magnetic resonance imaging (MRI) may be used to assess the severity of aortic regurgitation and the size and function of the left ventricle. It is ideal for a detailed assessment of the anatomy of the aortic root and ascending aorta and to exclude other significant cardiac abnormalities and coarctation.

Cardiac Catheterization
With the advent of echocardiography, cardiac catheterization is not usually indicated for diagnosis but may be helpful in determining the severity of aortic regurgitation when other tests are equivocal. In older patients, cardiac catheterization should be performed before operation to rule out coronary disease. In patients with complex CHD, a complete hemodynamic assessment is often indicated.

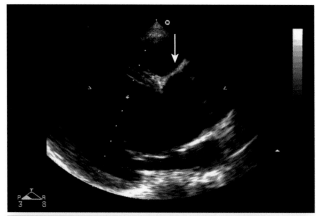
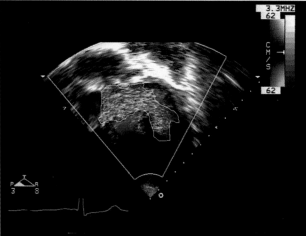

Figure 33-1 Parasternal long-axis (**top**) and four-chamber (**bottom**) echocardiogram with color flow Doppler assessment of patient with repaired tetralogy of Fallot and severe aortic regurgitation. There is a large regurgitant jet (*arrow*) into the left ventricle, resulting in marked dilation.

Exercise Testing
Exercise testing may be useful to assess exercise performance objectively and to document changes with time. Reduced augmentation of LV ejection fraction during exercise may be an early sign of decompensation.

Radionuclide Angiography
This investigation may be used to assess LV function and size when echocardiographic images are inadequate or there are clinical concerns regarding the severity of aortic regurgitation (LV volumes can be estimated) or of LV systolic function both at rest and with exercise.

OUTPATIENT MANAGEMENT

Surgery to replace or repair the aortic valve remains the key therapeutic intervention and should have a good long-term outlook if performed before irreversible LV dysfunction has developed. As a result, serial assessment to identify patients with early symptoms or LV dysfunction is the cornerstone of the management of chronic aortic regurgitation.

All patients other than those with trivial and clinically silent aortic regurgitation should have periodic follow-up. In patients with pure aortic regurgitation, related to valve or aortic root pathology, and no additional cardiac abnormalities, follow-up can be performed adequately in the confines of an adult cardiology clinic. Patients with aortic regurgitation plus additional complex congenital cardiac malformations require follow-up within an adult CHD clinic.

The frequency of follow-up should be determined by the severity of aortic regurgitation and the likelihood of requiring surgical intervention. Patients with mild or moderate aortic regurgitation and minimal LV dilation may be reviewed at 1- to 2-year intervals.

In contrast, patients with severe aortic regurgitation and LV dimensions and function approaching the criteria for surgical intervention require follow-up every 3 to 6 months.

At least annual follow-up is recommended if the aortic root is dilated (Box 33-2).

VASODILATOR THERAPY

Vasodilating agents may reduce cardiac afterload and consequently the regurgitant fraction. This should translate into improved forward stroke volume and reduced cardiac strain. Scognamiglio and colleagues[11] reported the effect of nifedipine, 20 mg, twice daily versus digoxin in patients with chronic severe aortic regurgitation. Over 6 years of follow-up it was shown that nifedipine reduced the need for operation from 34% to 15%, with no apparent deleterious effect on the outcome after surgery. Significant improvement in hemodynamics, with reduction in regurgitant fraction and LV hypertrophy, has also been seen after ACE inhibition.[12] Reduced blood pressure with enalapril and quinapril has been associated with decreases in end-diastolic volume and mass but no change in ejection fraction. Evangelista and associates[13] studied the effect of long-term vasodilator therapy with nifedipine or enalapril, compared with placebo. Neither active agent reduced or delayed the need for aortic valve replacement in patients with asymptomatic severe aortic regurgitation and normal LV systolic function. Results of trials of the impact of ACE inhibition on hard clinical endpoints have been inconsistent to date.

The American College of Cardiology/American Heart Association (ACC/AHA) guidelines[14] suggest that patients with severe aortic regurgitation with LV dilation but preserved systolic function should consider long-term vasodilator therapy. In patients with mild or moderate aortic regurgitation and no significant LV dilation, the long-term outcome is favorable and vasodilator therapy is not currently indicated.

TIMING OF SURGERY

A key objective in the management of chronic aortic regurgitation is the early detection of decompensation, which should trigger a timely surgical intervention.[14] A significant improvement in LV function and good long-term survival can be expected with this approach. Conversely, both longer duration and increased severity of symptoms or LV dysfunction are associated with poor results and ongoing morbidity and mortality.

Most guidelines for the timing of surgical intervention in patients with aortic regurgitation have been developed on the basis of data derived from predominantly adult male populations with pure aortic regurgitation[14] and may not apply to women and patients with additional congenital cardiac defects, who often present at a younger age with a smaller body habitus. Use of a measure of LV function indexed to body size (e.g., end-systolic diameter > 25 mm/m^2)[7] and/or a lower threshold for intervention may be appropriate in these groups. Similarly, in patients with additional defects, surgery may be indicated for reasons other than aortic regurgitation. In this situation consideration should be given to repair or replacement of the aortic valve at the time of operation. Few data are available to guide decision-making, which will need to consider the severity of aortic regurgitation, the presence of LV dysfunction, and surgical risks. Available data suggest that, if untreated, the outcome for aortic regurgitation in the context of additional congenital abnormalities including tetralogy of Fallot and coarctation is poor, and general principles dictate that wherever possible all hemodynamically significant lesions should be dealt with. In patients with Marfan syndrome or other causes of an aortopathy,

dilation of the ascending aorta to more than 50 mm has generally been used as an indication for replacement of the ascending aorta and repair or replacement of the aortic valve to reduce the risk of aortic dissection or rupture.

The algorithm in Figure 33-2 is from the ACC/AHA guidelines.[14] As stated in the text, the majority of evidence for this algorithm is derived from studies of "pure" aortic regurgitation in men. Therefore, there are several points to note in considering a patient with CHD:

- Some 25% of patients with LV dysfunction remain asymptomatic and the decision to refer them for operation remains controversial. However, there is a 20% incidence of symptoms per year. Early intervention may be more important in the context of complex CHD when other factors might increase risk from aortic regurgitation.
- These parameters are derived largely from data obtained in the study of adult males with pure aortic regurgitation. A lower threshold may be appropriate for women and patients with additional defects. Indexing the LV end-systolic diameter to body size may help (e.g., 25 mm/m^2).
- Surgery is usually indicated in patients with an aortic root greater than 50 mm to reduce the risk of spontaneous dissection. In patients with severe aortic regurgitation, aortic valve repair or replacement is indicated even if asymptomatic with normal LV function.
- Mild New York Heart Association (NYHA) functional class II symptoms may be related to other comorbid diseases or physical deconditioning. However, if related to aortic regurgitation, even mild symptoms are likely to progress and are associated with an adverse outcome.
- The change in LV function with time is a risk factor for progression to symptoms.

SURGICAL OPTIONS

The operative mortality rate from elective aortic valve surgery in patients with CHD is low, and long-term survival rates appear to be good (98% and 74% at 5 and 10 years, respectively, in a recent series of aortic valve repair).[15] The choice of surgical approach will depend on the pathologic process underlying the aortic regurgitation and patient factors, including their age, sex, and the wish or need to avoid anticoagulation or further operation (Table 33-2). Patients with CHD are younger than those with acquired aortic valve disease, and, in particular, women of childbearing age may wish to avoid the need for anticoagulation implicit in the implantation of a mechanical prosthetic valve. Aortic valve-sparing surgery is an effective and durable approach in patients with a pathologic process primarily affecting the aortic root or ascending aorta.[16] The Ross operation has been used widely in young patients with aortic valve disease,[17] although recently some doubt has been cast on its long-term durability in younger patients with aortic regurgitation as the primary pathologic process.[18] Concern remains over the durability of bioprosthetic valves in the aortic position, especially in younger patients, although the development of the more hemodynamically efficient stentless porcine valve might offer a better alternative.[19]

The future role of transcatheter aortic valve implantation (TAVI) technology in the management of aortic regurgitation has yet to be examined. There are case reports of the use of TAVI in failed bioprosthetic aortic valves, in failed aortic homografts, and even in native aortic valves. TAVI may offer a therapy that reduces the total number of major cardiac operations required in a patient's lifetime while maintaining a competent valve.

Late Outcome

OUTCOME AFTER SURGERY

The severity and duration of preoperative LV dysfunction appear to be the most important predictors of an adverse course after aortic valve surgery. If surgery is performed before irreversible myocardial dysfunction has occurred, an improvement in symptoms and decrease

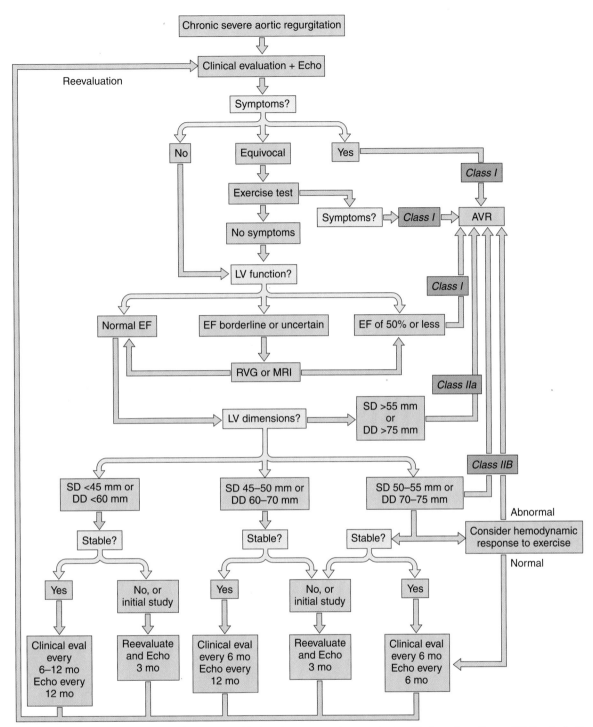

Figure 33-2 Management strategy for patients with chronic severe aortic regurgitation. *(Redrawn from Bonow RO, Carabello B, Chatterjee K et al. 2008 Focused update incorporated into the ACC/AHA 2006 guidelines for the management of patients with valvular heart disease. Circulation 2008; 118:e1-e142).*

in cardiac size usually occurs. LV end-diastolic dimensions usually decline within a few weeks of operation. Failure of this to happen may reflect irreversible LV dysfunction. Somewhat later, LV ejection fraction improves.

Late complications after aortic valve surgery include conduction abnormalities, endocarditis, systemic embolism, and structural deterioration of the valve requiring re-intervention (Box 33-3). As a consequence all patients will continue to require long-term follow-up with a clinical examination, electrocardiography, and echocardiography. This

will normally need to be done on an annual basis, although shorter or longer follow-up intervals may be necessary in individual patients.

ARRHYTHMIA AND SUDDEN DEATH

Clinically important arrhythmias are not common in aortic regurgitation alone. Sudden death is a rare complication of aortic regurgitation and likely to reflect decompensation of LV function and impaired coronary perfusion. The development of syncope, angina, or other symptoms

TABLE 33-2	Surgical Options for Aortic Regurgitation	
	Advantages	*Disadvantages*
Primary Aortic Valve Disease		
Aortic valve repair	May give excellent long-term results with normal hemodynamic profile No need for anticoagulation	May have limited application depending on severity of damage to valve
Bioprosthetic aortic valve repair	Good hemodynamic profile No need for anticoagulation	Valve longevity poor, especially in young people, with near certainty of needing re-do May be better with stentless porcine valves[19]
Ross operation	Excellent hemodynamic profile No need for anticoagulation	Autograft longevity may be significantly lower when aortic regurgitation is main lesion[18] Likely need for re-do pulmonary valve replacement with or without aortic valve repair
Mechanical aortic valve repair	Excellent valve longevity Modern valves have excellent hemodynamic characteristics	Lifelong requirement for anticoagulation use in the young and women of childbearing age
Primary Aortic Root Disease		
Combined aortic valve repair and root replacement (Bentall)	Excellent valve longevity Modern valves have satisfactory hemodynamic characteristics	Lifelong requirement for anticoagulation use in the young and women of childbearing age
Valve-sparing aortic root replacement	Preferred option when aortic root dilation is main problem Aortic competence achieved by reestablishing geometry of aortic root Aortic valve may need repair or modification No need for anticoagulation Good longevity[16]	Late failure of repair may require reoperation and aortic valve replacement

---

BOX 33-3 COMPLICATIONS

- Heart failure
- Myocardial ischemia
- Infective endocarditis

---

should stimulate an early surgical referral. Late risk, after operation, is likely to reflect the presence of irreversible LV disease, with areas of LV fibrosis acting as a substrate for arrhythmia.

Pregnancy

The risk of pregnancy in patients with mild or moderate aortic regurgitation and only minimal or no increase in LV dimensions is low and likely to approach that of the general population. Similarly, in patients with severe chronic aortic regurgitation, pregnancy is likely to be well tolerated provided the patient is asymptomatic and has normal LV systolic function. The decreased afterload seen during pregnancy may compensate for the increase in blood volume and additional cardiac demand, and the murmur of aortic regurgitation may become attenuated. Patients should be counseled by physicians knowledgeable in the assessment and management of pregnant women with heart problems and, wherever possible, should be fully assessed before conception and referred for surgery if criteria are met.

The development of symptoms or heart failure can usually be managed medically during pregnancy, using diuretics and vasodilator therapy. Although nifedipine may be continued during pregnancy, it may not be the ideal vasodilator in the context of heart failure. ACE inhibitors are, however, teratogenic, causing fetal malformations during the second or third trimester. If possible, they should be discontinued before conception or during the first trimester. In patients with heart failure refractory to medical therapy, successful aortic valve repair or replacement has been reported. Antibiotic prophylaxis should be considered at the time of delivery.

Persistent LV dysfunction after aortic valve repair or replacement will also be a factor in the risk of pregnancy. Patients with mechanical prosthetic valves will require careful management of anticoagulation, and this should be a consideration when choosing the surgical approach in women of childbearing age.

Rarely, acute aortic regurgitation may develop during pregnancy. This is most commonly as a result of dissection of the aorta in patients with aortic root disease related to Marfan syndrome but may also occur in the setting of endocarditis. This represents a surgical emergency with increased maternal and fetal mortality.

Level of Follow-Up, Endocarditis Prophylaxis, and Exercise

The level of follow-up will be determined by the underlying pathology of aortic regurgitation, its severity, and LV function. Mild aortic regurgitation is unlikely to progress, and patients may be seen on a 2- to 3-year basis. Patients with severe aortic regurgitation require an annual assessment with a detailed assessment of symptoms and LV size and function. Evidence of increasing LV size—even if not meeting criteria for operation—should stimulate more frequent follow-up. After operation most patients should be observed on an annual basis.

The ACC/AHA guidelines[14] have been rewritten regarding endocarditis prophylaxis. Good oral hygiene should be stressed and appropriate antibiotic prophylaxis administered when dental procedures are performed that involve the manipulation of gingival tissue or the periapical region of the teeth or perforation of oral mucosa. Patients should be counseled on protecting themselves from endocarditis and advised to seek medical attention for unexplained fever.

Aerobic exercise capacity is generally well preserved in patients with aortic regurgitation while LV function is normal. During exercise, peripheral vasodilation and tachycardia serve to decrease the severity of aortic regurgitation. In contrast, the increased afterload associated with isometric exercise may substantially increase the severity of aortic regurgitation and ventricular strain and should be avoided.

REFERENCES

1. Anderson RA. Clinical anatomy of the aortic root. Heart 2000;84:670–673.
2. Keane MG, Wiegers SE, Plappert T, et al. Bicuspid aortic valves are associated with aortic dilation out of proportion to coexistent valvular lesions. Circulation 2000;102(19 Suppl. 3): III35–III39.
3. Yacoub MH, Khan H, Stavri G, et al. Anatomic correction of the syndrome of prolapsing right coronary aortic cusp, dilation of the sinus of Valsalva, and ventricular septal defect. J Thorac Cardiovasc Surg 1997;113:253–260.
4. Capelli H, Ross D, Somerville J. Aortic regurgitation in tetrad of Fallot and pulmonary atresia. Am J Cardiol 1982;49:1979–1983.
5. Oliver JM, Gonzalez A, Gallego P, et al. Discrete subaortic stenosis in adults: increased prevalence and slow rate of progression of the obstruction and aortic regurgitation. J Am Coll Cardiol 2001;38:835–842.
6. Bonow RO, Lakatos E, Maron BJ, Epstein SE. Serial long-term assessment of the natural history of asymptomatic patients with chronic aortic regurgitation and normal left ventricular systolic function. Circulation 1991;84:1625–1635.
7. Dujardin KS, Enriquez-Sarano M, Schaff HV, et al. Mortality and morbidity of aortic regurgitation in clinical practice: a long-term follow-up study. Circulation 1999;99:1851–1857.

8. Klodas E, Enriquez-Sarano M, Tajik AJ, et al. Surgery for aortic regurgitation in women: contrasting indications and outcomes compared with men. Circulation 1996;94:2472–2478.
9. McDonald ML, Smedira NG, Blackstone EH, et al. Reduced survival in women after valve surgery for aortic regurgitation: effect of aortic enlargement and late aortic rupture. J Thorac Cardiovasc Surg 2000;119:1205–1212.
10. Fyler DC. Aortic outflow abnormalities. In: Fyler DC, editor. Nadas' Pediatric Cardiology. Philadelphia: Hanley & Belfus; 1992. p. 493–512.
11. Scognamiglio R, Rahimtoola SH, Fasoli G, et al. Nifedipine in asymptomatic patients with severe aortic regurgitation and normal left ventricular function. N Engl J Med 1994;331:689–694.
12. Schon HR, Dorn R, Barthel P, Schomig A. Effects of 12 months quinapril therapy in asymptomatic patients with chronic aortic regurgitation. J Heart Valve Dis 1994;3:500–509.
13. Evangelista A, Tornos P, Sambola A, et al. Long-term vasodilator therapy in patients with severe aortic regurgitation. N Engl J Med 2005;353:1342–1349.
14. Bonow RO, Carabello B, Chatterjee K, et al. 2008 focused update incorporated into the ACC/AHA 2006 guidelines for the management of patients with valvular heart disease. Circulation 2008;118:e1–e142.
15. Rao V, Van Arsdell GS, David TE, et al. Aortic valve repair for adult congenital heart disease: a 22-year experience. Circulation 2000;102(19 Suppl. 3):III40–III43.
16. David TE, Armstrong S, Ivanov J, et al. Results of aortic valve-sparing operations. J Thorac Cardiovasc Surg 2001;122:39–46.
17. Sievers HH, Hanke T, Stierle U, et al. A critical reappraisal of the Ross operation: renaissance of the subcoronary implantation technique? Circulation 2006;114:I504–I511.
18. Laudito A, Brook MM, Suleman S, et al. The Ross procedure in children and young adults: a word of caution. J Thorac Cardiovasc Surg 2001;122:147–153.
19. David TE, Bos J. Aortic valve replacement with stentless porcine aortic valve: a pioneer series. Semin Thorac Cardiovasc Surg 1999;11(4 Suppl. 1):9–11.

34 Sinus of Valsalva Aneurysms

LORNA SWAN

Introduction

The sinus of Valsalva aneurysm (SV aneurysm), like many other congenital cardiac lesions, has to be defined carefully before there can be meaningful discussion regarding etiology, management, and outcome. Since its first description in 1840 by Thurman, varying terminologies and classifications have been used. In 1962, Sakakibara and Konno[1] documented four types of aneurysm but did not account for a description of the penetration of ruptured aneurysms. The classic congenital SV aneurysm is defined as the dilation or enlargement of one of the aortic sinuses between the aortic valve annulus and the sinotubular ridge. Multiple sinus dilation should be considered as a separate entity, namely, as aneurysmal dilation of the aortic root. By definition, the true SV aneurysm arises from above the aortic annulus, in contrast to the prolapsing aortic cusp which is seen below the annulus (Fig. 34-1). Both of these lesions are known to be associated with the presence of a ventricular septal defect, which may complicate the diagnosis.

The congenital nature of an SV aneurysm was first suggested by Abbott in 1919. Edwards and Burchell[2] later described the histologic features, with separation of the media in the sinus from the media adjacent to the aortic annulus. This congenital absence of the elastic lamellae was thought to give rise to focal weakness in the aortic wall, particularly when subjected to increased aortic pressures. This structural deficiency is the precursor of the clinical sequelae of progressive aneurysmal dilation and, finally, rupture.

An acquired lesion very similar to that seen in primary congenital SV aneurysms can be seen in a variety of conditions such as syphilis, infective endocarditis, trauma, and a group of connective tissue disorders. These acquired lesions are often classified as aneurysms of the aortic root to avoid confusion with the congenital sinus of Valsalva.

A simplified pictorial representation of the lesions affecting the left ventricular outflow tract and aortic root is shown in Figure 34-1.

Recently, a four-level hierarchy of nomenclature has been proposed to encompass sinus of Valsalva aneurysms, aortic root aneurysms, and aortic dissections.[3] This nomenclature has attempted to supersede the classic aneurysmal descriptions of morphology (fusiform or saccular), histology (true, dissected, or false), and anatomy (root, arch, sinuses) (Table 34-1). Hierarchy 1 involves the description of the aortic aneurysm type. If there are multiple areas of dilation, then the aneurysm is referred to as an "aneurysm of the aortic root." Hierarchy level 2 describes the location and anatomy of the lesion, for example, the sinus of origin. Level 3 describes the acuity or current clinical status (ruptured or unruptured), and level 4 describes the pathology and chamber of penetration. This would give a simple descriptive classification, such as sinus of Valsalva defect; right aortic sinus; ruptured; penetrating into right atrium. Other significant modifiers relating to etiology may be added at the end. A similar nomenclature for surgical therapy has also been developed, with the primary aim of standardizing database entry.

Morphology

The morphology of an SV aneurysm can vary from a small isolated enlargement of an aortic sinus (usually the right sinus) to an extended finger-like projection from the body or apex of the sinus. This tubular protrusion may extend into the adjacent structures, causing a myriad of clinical sequelae.

The right coronary sinus is the most common site for aneurysm formation (65% to 85%).[4] The noncoronary sinus and the left sinus account for 10% to 30% and less than 5%, respectively. The rarity of left sinus aneurysms has led several authors to suggest that these may be due to a separate acquired etiology.

Associated Defects

The most frequent associations with SV aneurysm are the presence of a ventricular septal defect (30% to 60%), aortic valve regurgitation (20%), bicuspid aortic valve (10%), pulmonary stenosis, coarctation of the aorta, atrial septal defect, and, occasionally, coronary artery anomalies. There is also a known association with subvalvular aneurysms. Congenital weakness of both the aortic and mitral annuli have been implicated in this subgroup.

Epidemiology

SV aneurysms are rare, accounting for only 0.14% of all open-heart surgical procedures. Because they are often clinically silent for many years, autopsy studies may give a more accurate estimation of prevalence, quoting approximately 0.09% of the general population.[5] SV aneurysms are more common in Asian populations and, in addition, have a marked male preponderance (four times more common in men). The reasons for these racial and sex differences, and the extent of the genetic determination of this lesion, are unclear.[6] A symptomatic SV aneurysm is particularly uncommon in childhood. In these circumstances extra care should be taken to prevent a hereditary connective tissue disorder, such as Ehlers-Danlos or Marfan syndrome, from being overlooked.

Investigations

ELECTROCARDIOGRAPHY AND CHEST RADIOGRAPHY

Electrocardiography and chest radiography are not often helpful in diagnosing SV aneurysm. Evidence of right-sided heart overload, axis deviation, and conduction defects may be present, but the electrocardiogram is often normal. The chest radiograph, in the case of a rupture, often shows cardiomegaly and varying degrees of pulmonary plethora or congestion but again may be normal.

IMAGING

Unruptured and ruptured SV aneurysms are often well visualized on standard transthoracic imaging in echogenic subjects. The classic description of a ruptured aneurysm is that of a "windsock." This is an elongated tubular structure varying from 1 to 5 cm in length.

When SV aneurysms rupture, the discontinuity of the aneurysm wall can be seen. The associated aortic valve cusp can often be seen fluttering. There may also be associated fluttering of the tricuspid leaflets, depending on the direction of the left-to-right shunt lesion. The "windsock" can be seen to collapse and expand with varying stages of the cardiac cycle. The perforating jet is usually well seen on color imag-

assessing the native or residual PDA, later). Occasionally, patients who underwent catheter closure of a PDA during childhood may have a left pulmonary artery stenosis. This is, however, usually mild and unlikely to require further intervention or have any long-term prognostic implications.

PATIENT WITH UNREPAIRED OR RESIDUAL PATENT DUCTUS ARTERIOSUS

At initial diagnostic workup one should:
- Confirm the presence of PDA or residual PDA and identify any associated lesions.
- Assess the magnitude of left-to-right shunting (see later).
- Assess the degree of pulmonary hypertension, if present.
- Identify the presence and size of a ductal aneurysm, if present.
- Determine whether the duct is calcified, if surgical repair is planned.
 The diagnostic workup should include, at a minimum:
- Thorough clinical assessment
- Electrocardiography
- Chest radiography
- Transthoracic echocardiography
- Oximetry (obtained in room air on both fingers and toes)
 The diagnostic workup may require:
- Heart catheterization—to estimate *the degree and direction of shunting when not available by other means* and pulmonary arterial pressure and resistance with reversibility studies, when pulmonary arterial pressure is greater than two thirds of systemic arterial pressure.
- Coronary angiography—in patients with risk factors or patients older than 40 years of age if surgical repair is contemplated.
- Open-lung biopsy—may be helpful in highly selected cases. It should be considered only when reversibility of pulmonary vascular disease is uncertain from the invasive hemodynamic data. It is potentially hazardous and should be rarely performed only in centers where there is particular expertise in management of patients with pulmonary hypertension and congenital heart disease.
- Cardiac magnetic resonance imaging (CMR) or computed tomography (CT) to define the anatomy of the PDA and detect ductal aneurysm or calcification. MRI can also be used to estimate the magnitude of left-to-right shunting.

CLINICAL EXAMINATION

- Full, dynamic pulses (with a wide pulse pressure and low diastolic pressure) suggest a hemodynamically significant PDA.
- A right ventricular lift and palpable second heart sound suggest advanced pulmonary hypertension.
- A continuous murmur in the upper left sternal edge, sometimes radiating to the back, is consistent with a significant PDA; occasionally, a long ejection murmur and not a continuous murmur may be audible. Patients with a large PDA and Eisenmenger complex do not have a continuous murmur but have signs of pulmonary hypertension and lower body cyanosis and toe clubbing.

ELECTROCARDIOGRAPHY

- Broad P waves and tall/deep QRS complexes are suggestive of left atrial and left ventricular overload, respectively.
- Right ventricular hypertrophy, evidenced by tall RV_1 usually with right-axis deviation, suggests significant pulmonary hypertension.

CHEST RADIOGRAPHY

- Dilated central pulmonary arteries with increased pulmonary vascular markings, with left atrial and left ventricular dilation, all suggest a significant left-to-right shunt.
- Calcification may be seen in the posteroanterior and lateral views in the older patient with a PDA; this has clinical implications (see later).

ECHOCARDIOGRAPHY

- Size and maximum diameter of the PDA can be estimated with two-dimensional (2D) echocardiography, but this is usually difficult to ascertain in the adult.
- One should determine whether left atrial and left ventricular dilation is present, which, in turn, suggests a significant left-to-right shunt in the setting of a hemodynamically important PDA.
- Continuous wave Doppler interrogation across the PDA provides indirect information on pulmonary arterial pressures and pulmonary vascular disease. The presence of a systolic pressure gradient greater than 64 mm Hg across the PDA suggests there is no significant pulmonary hypertension. When the systolic pressure gradient between the aorta and the pulmonary artery is less than 64 mm Hg, a significant diastolic pressure gradient may suggest possible reversible pulmonary vascular disease. However, such patients need to be studied formally with cardiac catheterization, including reversibility studies and perhaps test balloon occlusion of the PDA before proceeding to closure.
- Additional assessment of right ventricular and pulmonary arterial systolic pressure should be attempted with continuous wave Doppler imaging, when echocardiographic tricuspid regurgitation is present.

Late Management Options

CLOSURE

PDA closure is recommended (1) for hemodynamic reasons, in patients with substantial left-to-right shunts and left-sided heart dilation; (2) to eliminate the risk of endarteritis (if the risk of endarteritis seems high enough to accept the risks and inconvenience of intervention); and (3) very occasionally in the adult patient to reduce the risk of pulmonary hypertension. The following recommendations apply to both the native and residual PDA in the adult patient.
 PDA closure should be considered in the following situations:
1. The presence of a PDA, with the exception of (a) the silent tiny duct and (b) the presence of severe, irreversible pulmonary vascular disease.
2. The occurrence of an episode of endarteritis, irrespective of the size of the PDA. Closure of the tiny PDA, not audible on auscultation, remains controversial and should not be routinely performed, despite the ease of transcatheter intervention, given the extremely low risk of endarteritis. However, occasional cases of bacterial endocarditis have been documented in adult patients with a clinically silent PDA perhaps suggesting that the risk of endarteritis/endocarditis with a patent duct may not depend entirely on size.[11] It should be also noted that according to the recent American College of Cardiology/American Heart Association guidelines[12] (there is no distinction between tiny and small PDAs) "it is reasonable to close an asymptomatic 'small' PDA by catheter device." Because catheter closure techniques are quite effective and safe in the current era, routine closure of any PDA seems reasonable.

3. If pulmonary hypertension is present (pulmonary arterial pressure more than two thirds of systemic arterial pressure or pulmonary arteriolar resistance exceeding two thirds of systemic arteriolar resistance), there must be a net left-to-right shunt of 1.5:1 or more or evidence of pulmonary artery reactivity with reversibility studies or, in highly selected cases, lung biopsy evidence that pulmonary arterial changes are potentially reversible. These patients may benefit from test balloon occlusion during catheter assessment of hemodynamics prior to permanent PDA closure.

CATHETER INTERVENTION AND SURGICAL CLOSURE

Device closure is the preferred method for the majority of PDAs in most centers today. When possible it should be planned at the same time as the "diagnostic" cardiac catheterization. Pre-intervention aortography can determine the size, configuration, and relationship of the duct to adjacent anatomic structures (particularly to the pulmonary artery, aorta, and tracheal shadow), which have important implications with regard to catheter closure.[4]

The presence of ductal calcification increases surgical risk and favors device closure. If surgical closure is pursued, for whatever reasons, such patients need ductal division, often under cardiopulmonary bypass.

Surgical closure should be reserved for patients with PDAs too large for device closure; when ductal anatomy is so distorted (e.g., ductal aneurysm or after endarteritis) as to make device closure undesirable; and when expert device closure is not available.

Operative repair should probably be undertaken by congenital heart surgeons.

▣ Catheter Intervention and Surgical Outcomes

DEVICE CLOSURE

Successful closure is achieved in the large majority of attempts using a variety of devices. Up to 95% of ducts are closed completely by 1 year after device implantation. Currently, Gianturco coils and Amplatzer duct occluders (standard or modified) are the devices of choice for closure of small (≤2 mm) and moderate to large (>2 mm) PDAs, respectively (Fig. 35-1).[7,8,13] The Amplatzer muscular ventricular septal defect occluder due to its design with two retention discs and large connecting waist seems to be better suited for closure of large PDAs with reversible pulmonary hypertension.[15]

Embolization of the device, usually of coils, can occur but is uncommon. Other important complications are rare and may include stenosis of the left pulmonary artery or descending aorta by a protruding device, hemolysis, and infective endocarditis.

SURGICAL CLOSURE

More than 95% of ducts can be closed by operation. Recanalization is unusual but recognized. Postoperative complications may include recurrent laryngeal or phrenic nerve damage and thoracic duct damage.

▣ Pregnancy

Pregnancy is well tolerated in women with a PDA and left-to-right shunts. Congestive heart failure may occur in patients with moderate shunts and left-sided heart dilation before conception: such patients warrant cardiologic and specialized obstetric input during pregnancy and the peripartum. Patients with a clinically evident PDA should be considered for endocarditis prophylaxis at the time of delivery, recent guidelines notwithstanding.

Pregnancy is contraindicated in patients with a large PDA and Eisenmenger syndrome because of the high maternal and fetal mortality rates.

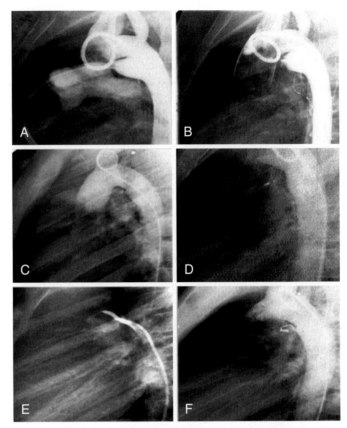

Figure 35-1 Successful closure of type A (**A, B**), B (**C, D**), and E (**E, F**) ("silent") PDAs in three adult patients, using the Amplatzer duct occluder (I and II[14]) and Gianturco coil, respectively.

▣ Level of Follow-Up, Endocarditis Prophylaxis, and Exercise

Patients who have had surgical/device closure of a PDA may benefit from periodic evaluation by a cardiologist familiar with congenital heart disease because recanalization can occur or residual problems (pulmonary hypertension, left ventricular dysfunction, atrial fibrillation) may persist or develop. Patients with devices in situ should also be considered for periodic, infrequent follow-up, because the long-term outcome of device closure remains unknown.

Endocarditis prophylaxis is recommended for 6 months after PDA device or surgical closure or for life if any residual defect persists.

Patients with a silent PDA do not require follow-up or endocarditis prophylaxis.

Patients with a PDA and left-to-right shunt, in general, do not require any exercise restrictions. For those with pulmonary hypertension and Eisenmenger complex, see Chapter 48.

AORTOPULMONARY WINDOW

▣ Definition and Morphology

An aortopulmonary window is a rare lesion that can mimic a PDA and may be difficult to differentiate clinically.[16] It is a direct communication between the ascending aorta and pulmonary artery resulting from an incomplete division of the embryonic common arterial trunk (Figs. 35-2 and 35-3). The defect is usually large; therefore, the likelihood of established pulmonary hypertension in the adult patient is high unless closure took place early in childhood.

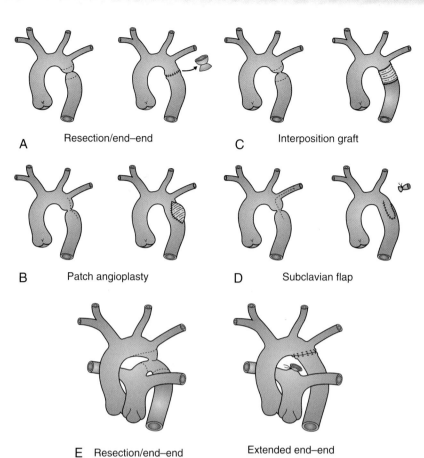

A   Resection/end–end

C   Interposition graft

B   Patch angioplasty

D   Subclavian flap

E   Resection/end–end

Extended end–end

Figure 36-2 **A** to **E**, Major surgical aortic coarctation repair techniques. (*After Rocchini AP. Coarctation of the aorta and interrupted aortic arch. In: Moller JH, Hoffmann JIE, eds. Pediatric Cardiovascular Medicine. New York: Churchill Livingstone; 2000:567–593*).

Late Outcome

SURVIVAL AND FUNCTIONAL STATUS

Unfortunately, satisfactory results are by no means achieved in all patients who undergo operation or angioplasty. Operation improves clinical symptoms and the blood pressure situation, at least in the short term, and also increases survival. Long-term survival after operation, however, continues to be lower than in the general population because of cardiovascular complications and arterial hypertension.

In the largest follow-up study of 646 patients who underwent simple CoA repair at the Mayo Clinic between 1946 and 1981, the postoperative 10-year survival rate was 91%, the 20-year rate was 84%, and the 30-year rate 72%.[10] For patients operated on before the age of 14 years, the 20-year survival rate was 91%, compared with 79% for those operated on after 14 years of age. Among 571 patients with long-term follow-up there were 87 late deaths. The mean age at death of these patients was 38 years.[10] The most common cause of postsurgical death was coronary artery disease, followed by sudden cardiac death, left ventricular failure, stroke, and ruptured aortic aneurysm.

LATE COMPLICATIONS

Long-term problems may occur after all forms of treatment (Table 36-2 and Box 36-1). The most important residua, sequelae, and complications are arterial hypertension, restenosis, or residual stenosis in the region of the previous treatment and aneurysms of the ascending aorta or at the site of intervention. Further problems may develop due to coronary artery disease, bicuspid aortic valves, mitral valve anomalies, infective endocarditis, or cerebral aneurysms.

Arterial Hypertension

Arterial hypertension, either at rest or during exercise, is common, even after successful surgical treatment of aortic coarctation. Patients who underwent surgical correction a long time ago or at an older age are at

TABLE 36-2	Follow-Up Issues and Investigations After Repair of Aortic Coarctation
Problem	*Follow-Up Procedures*
Arterial hypertension	Blood pressure monitoring Exercise testing Ambulatory blood pressure monitoring
Bicuspid aortic valve	Clinical monitoring Echocardiography
Re-coarctation or residual stenosis	Clinical monitoring Blood pressure monitoring Echocardiography Magnetic resonance imaging (MRI) Computed tomography (CT) Cardiac catheterization study
Distention or aneurysm of the ascending aorta	Echocardiography MRI CT
Dilation or aneurysm of the descending aorta	Echocardiography MRI CT Cardiac catheterization
Coronary artery disease	Clinical monitoring Stress scintigraphy (myocardial perfusion imaging) Coronary angiography
New or different quality headache (should raise alarm to possible cerebral aneurysm)	Neurologic evaluation MRI CT

greater risk of abnormal blood pressure responses after operation than those operated on in childhood.

Hypertension associated with CoA is probably related to re-coarctation, structural changes in the wall of peripheral and central vessels, reduced baroreceptor sensitivity, alterations in the renin-angiotensin system, raised plasma concentrations of epinephrine and norepinephrine, or

BOX 36-1   COMPLICATIONS AFTER SURGICAL REPAIR OF AORTIC COARCTATION

- Persistent or new arterial hypertension at rest or during exercise
- Distention and/or aneurysm of the ascending and/or descending aorta
- Re-coarctation or residual stenosis in the region of the aortic isthmus and/or aortic arch
- Coronary artery disease
- Aortic stenosis (in patients with a bicuspid aortic valve)
- Aortic insufficiency (in patients with a bicuspid aortic valve)
- Mitral valve defects (mitral valve prolapse)
- Infective endocarditis or endarteritis
- Rupture of aortic or cerebral aneurysm

the coexistence of essential hypertension. Another significant factor may be a hypoplastic aortic arch that was not corrected. Compared with the general population, arterial hypertension is an important risk factor for increased mortality.

As with other forms of uncontrolled hypertension, affected patients are at risk of premature coronary artery disease, ventricular dysfunction, and rupture of aortic or cerebral aneurysms. Such complications mainly occur in the third and fourth decades of life.

The older the patient at the time of CoA repair, the higher is the incidence of systemic hypertension after operation. The previously mentioned Mayo Clinic study[10] showed a direct correlation between cardiac death and raised blood pressure after surgery. The higher the systolic pressure after operation, the greater the probability of early cardiac death. More recent studies provide evidence that patients operated on in early childhood (between the ages of 2 and 9 years) have a higher rate of normal blood pressure postoperatively. Several studies also suggest an increase in the prevalence of systemic hypertension with increasing length of follow-up after CoA repair: 13% at 8 years, 49% at 17 years, and 68% at 30 years.[9] In a recent rather complete and large cross-sectional study, more than 50% of the patients after CoA repair were hypertensive, and even 30% of those without restenosis and without noncompliant prosthetic material were hypertensive.[11]

I believe that, after CoA repair, systemic hypertension is frequently exacerbated by exercise or occurs only during exercise.[12] The impact of isolated, exercise-induced hypertension is still a matter of debate, but in the follow-up of these patients, regular blood pressure checks, supplemented by selective exercise tests, are necessary.

Re-coarctation or Residual Coarctation

Residual coarctation or restenosis at the site of coarctation is an important cause of morbidity after coarctation treatment, because re-coarctation may induce or aggravate systemic arterial hypertension, left ventricular wall mass, coronary artery disease, or congestive heart failure. After operation, the reported prevalence of re-coarctation was found to be between 3% and 41% in a survey of 11 major studies.[9]

Re-coarctation or residual stenosis may occur with all known surgical techniques: no single technique appears to be superior to the others.

Re-coarctation is associated with smaller patient size, younger age at operation, and the presence of associated transverse arch hypoplasia. The era in which the operation was performed, the surgical technique used, and the duration of follow-up further influence the risk.

Children operated on in infancy or early childhood are at particular risk. After operation in infancy or early childhood, the incidence of residual coarctation and restenosis is very high: 20% to 38%. In patients older than 3 years, it is only about 1.5%.

Not only after operation, but also after angioplasty, re-coarctation is an important issue. In native adult coarctation 8% to 11% of patients develop restenosis. For re-coarctation after previous surgical repair, the results of several large series of angioplasty show an early success rate (pressure gradient < 20 mm Hg) of between 65% and 100%.[9] A multicenter report of 548 patients showed a complication rate of 13%.[13]

In the pediatric balloon angioplasty study of Yetman and associates[14] in 1997, 72% of patients with optimal immediate results did not require re-intervention within a follow-up of 12 years.

Angioplasty of CoA may be unsuccessful because of immediate elastic recoil, long-segment narrowing, or multiple serial obstructions. In such situations balloon-expandable stents were found to be effective and safe, at least in the short term.

Aneurysms of the Ascending Aorta or in the Region of the Aortic Isthmus

Aneurysms of the ascending aorta or in the region of the aortic isthmus are the most dangerous complications because they carry the risk of life-threatening rupture. The cause of an aneurysm in the ascending aorta has not yet been fully explained (Fig. 36-3). Current consensus is that bicuspid aortic valve, independent aortic wall changes, and/or arterial hypertension may together be largely responsible for aneurysm formation in this area.[2]

Several postoperative follow-up studies comprise cases of late death related to dissection of the aorta, particularly in the ascending aorta. As a consequence, supervision with serial assessment of size and morphology of these ascending aortic aneurysms is mandatory.

Practically all surgical techniques carry the risk of postoperative aneurysms (Fig. 36-4). Their occurrence depends to some extent on the era of the operation, the patient's age at the time of surgery, the postoperative interval, and the surgical technique employed.

Recent studies show postoperative aortic aneurysms in only 5% to 9% of patients. The lowest incidence is reported after end-to-end anastomosis or after extra-anatomic tube grafts. In older studies the reported frequency of aneurysm after Dacron patch aortoplasty was up to 33% to 51%.

Whether and when postoperative aneurysms arise cannot be predicted with certainty. Some anastomotic aneurysms have been found after a postoperative interval of more than 30 years. In many patients aneurysms are detected as an incidental finding because their development seldom produces symptoms.

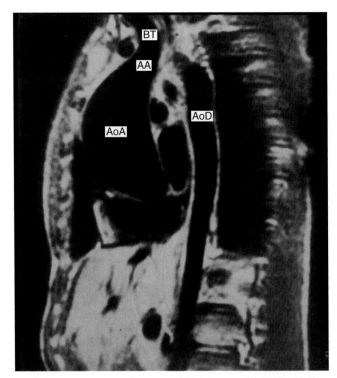

Figure 36-3 MR image of a young adult after coarctation repair showing a massive aneurysm of the ascending aorta. AA, aortic arch; AoA, ascending aorta; AoD, descending aorta; BT, brachiocephalic trunk.

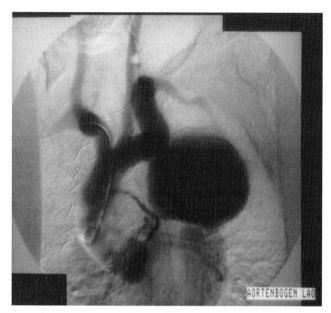

Figure 36-4 Aortic angiogram of a 60-year-old asymptomatic adult after aortic coarctation repair showing a massive aneurysm of the descending aorta as an incidental finding during follow-up.

An aneurysm may also occur after balloon angioplasty of either native coarctation or postoperative obstruction. This may be causally connected to the injury to the endovascular layers and to the presence of histologic medial changes in the pre-coarctation and post-coarctation segments.

The reported frequency of aneurysms after angioplasty in native adult coarctation varies from 4% to 12%. Local aneurysm after previous surgical repair has been described in 5% of patients.[9] This complication has been documented despite the presumption that surgical scar tissue after a previous surgical repair may protect against aneurysm and aortic dissection or rupture. Aneurysms may develop either immediately after angioplasty or after a lag of several months. However, even major tears caused by angioplasty may decrease in size and disappear without aneurysm formation. Because the incidence of aneurysm after surgery or balloon dilation appears to increase with longer follow-up periods, all patients need careful follow-up after angioplasty for CoA.

In addition to the problems just specified, there are certain additional issues that have to be considered during follow-up.

Infective Endocarditis or Endarteritis
Even after treatment, all patients with coarctation continue to be at increased risk for infective endocarditis or endarteritis. Altered arterial wall structure and the effect of abnormal blood flow and pressure associated with aortic and mitral valve anomalies or persistent obstruction at the CoA site predispose to infective endocarditis. Therefore, until recently, lifelong endocarditis prophylaxis was recommended after surgical or interventional treatment of CoA. According to new American Heart Association guidelines, endocarditis prophylaxis is no longer recommended,[15] but this is controversial.[6]

Bicuspid Aortic Valve
Up to 85% of patients with aortic coarctation have a bicuspid aortic valve. The complication rate of bicuspid aortic valves increases with age. Fibrosis, calcification, or myxomatous degeneration may lead to aortic valve stenosis in 59% to 81% and to aortic valve regurgitation in 13% to 22%.[16]

Besides those valvular lesions, 11% to 15% will develop dilation of the ascending aorta, which may progress to aortic aneurysm and even to aortic dissection and rupture. Recently a Mayo Clinic study reported that acute aortic dissection occurred in 2.5% of patients with bicuspid aortic valves.[16]

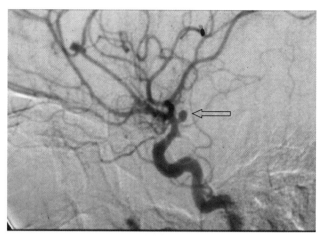

Figure 36-5 Angiogram of a young patient with coarctation and cerebral aneurysm (*arrow*).

Therefore, in addition to valve dysfunction and endocarditis, attention has to be paid to the development of an ascending aortic aneurysm.

Aneurysms of the Circle of Willis
Berry aneurysms of the circle of Willis or other vessels occur in up to 10% of patients with CoA (Fig. 36-5). Aneurysm size, and the likelihood of rupture, increases with age. Uncontrolled hypertension promotes their growth and increases the risk of rupture.

Most patients are asymptomatic until rupture occurs, although some aneurysms may leak prior to rupture, resulting in warning symptoms of headache, photophobia, weakness, or other symptoms.

Because rupture of a cerebral aneurysm is associated with a high mortality rate, this anomaly should be repaired immediately, at least, in symptomatic patients.

The wisdom of screening for cerebrovascular aneurysms is still a matter of debate because of the complex mix of benefits and risks associated with various sized aneurysms and their possible treatment.

Coronary Artery Disease
Premature coronary artery disease may complicate the long-term course of patients with CoA. Probably as a result of the increased blood pressure, the coronary arteries may develop premature narrowing or atherosclerosis. This may lead in early or mid adulthood to typical signs and symptoms of coronary artery disease. In the Mayo Clinic study of 1989, coronary artery disease was the most common cause of late postoperative death.[10]

Elevation of the Left Shoulder
Some degree of elevation of the left shoulder can often be seen in adults after left lateral thoracotomy for aortic coarctation.[17] This alteration may cause noncardiac chest pain, presumably related to functional impairment of peripheral nerves supplying skeletal muscles (latissimus dorsi and serratus anterior muscles).

Outpatient Assessment

Unoperated patients need an initial diagnostic workup, as outlined in Table 36-3. In operated or interventionally treated patients, most of these studies are required to rule out all important residua, sequelae, or complications during periodic follow-up.

PHYSICAL FINDINGS

Cardinal clinical features include upper body hypertension; weak, delayed femoral pulses; a blood pressure decrease between upper and lower extremities; and palpable collateral arteries running over the medial aspects of the scapulae, the lateral chest wall, and between the ribs. The collateral vessels develop from the subclavian, axillary, internal thoracic, scapular, and intercostal arteries.

TABLE 36-3	Diagnostic Workup for Initial Diagnosis and Follow-Up in Patients with Aortic Coarctation	
Investigation	*Details*
Clinical examination	Blood pressure and pulse status of all extremities Palpation/auscultation: associated valvular lesions, collaterals
Electrocardiography	Left ventricular hypertrophy
Chest radiography	"Figure 3" sign Rib notching Descending aortic aneurysm on follow-up Dilated ascending aorta on follow-up
Echocardiographic/Doppler study (transthoracic ± transesophageal)	Site, structure and extent of the stenosis or restenosis Gradient across stenosis or restenosis Left ventricle: diameter, function, hypertrophy, muscle mass Associated valvular lesions Evidence of aneurysm on follow-up
Exercise testing	Arterial hypertension
24-h blood pressure study	Arterial hypertension
MRI or CT (multislice or spiral)	Site, structure and extent of stenosis or restenosis Gradient across stenosis or restenosis (MRI) Collateral circulation Left ventricle: diameter, function, hypertrophy, muscle mass Associated valvular lesions on follow-up
Cardiac catheterization	Anatomy of aorta and supra-aortic vessels Pressure gradient across the coarctation or re-coarctation Associated defects Left ventricular function Coronary status

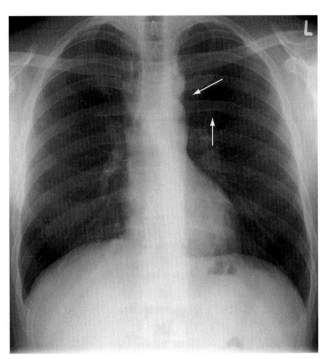

Figure 36-6 Chest radiograph of a 30-year-old man with native aortic coarctation showing the figure-3 sign (*diagonal arrow*), resulting from a prominent aortic knob, the stenotic segment, and the poststenotic aorta, as well as bilateral rib notching of the undersurface of upper ribs (*vertical arrow*).

Other physical findings include a thrill in the suprasternal notch or the neck vessels and a heaving but not displaced apex beat.

Auscultation reveals a loud aortic closure sound and, in patients with a bicuspid aortic valve or an ectatic ascending aorta, an aortic ejection click. An ejection murmur transmitted to the carotids may additionally be found parasternally in the second intercostal space in CoA patients with a bicuspid aortic valve or arterial hypertension. Between the scapulae, a vascular murmur may be heard that is separated from the first heart sound and lasts beyond the second heart sound. Collateral vessels may also be audible as continuous murmurs.

ELECTROCARDIOGRAPHY

Electrocardiography may show varying degrees of left atrial and left ventricular pressure load and signs of left ventricular ischemia or strain.

CHEST RADIOGRAPHY

The chest radiograph (Fig. 36-6) shows a normal heart size and commonly reveals dilation of the ascending aorta, kinking or double contouring in the region of the descending aorta (characteristic "figure 3" sign beneath the aortic knob), and widening of the soft tissue shadow of the left subclavian artery.

Rib notching, at the posteroinferior borders of the third and fourth (to eighth) ribs, is seen in most adults with native CoA. It is caused by the intercostal collateral arteries but is usually not visible until after the fifth year of life.

ECHOCARDIOGRAPHY

The aortic isthmus is not readily detectable in adults. Only the suprasternal view is convincing.

In adults, the proximity of the left bronchus frequently causes artifact superimposition. The site, structure, and extent of the stenosis, as well as left ventricular diameter (hypertrophy) and ventricular function, need to be evaluated.

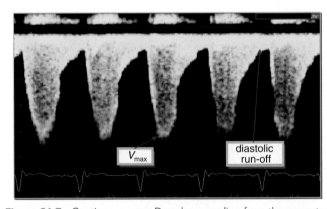

Figure 36-7 Continuous wave Doppler recording from the suprasternal view in an adult with significant re-coarctation, showing a peak systolic velocity greater than 3 m/s and a high-velocity flow continuation persisting during diastole. (*Courtesy of Dr. M. Vogt, German Heart Center, Munich, by permission.*)

Echocardiography may provide additional information on supra-aortic vessels and associated cardiac abnormalities.

Doppler studies (Fig. 36-7) show a turbulent flow pattern with increased flow rates distal to the coarctation and, importantly, a diastolic "runoff" phenomenon.

The Bernoulli equation, estimating the gradient from the peak systolic blood flow velocity, is only validated for valve stenosis and may overestimate CoA, especially in a stiff tubular structure with an enhanced pulse wave velocity.

The flow rates proximal to and within the stenosis should be taken into account to avoid overestimating the pressure gradient. If the proximal flow rate is greater than 1.0 m/s, the expanded Bernoulli equation, $\Delta P = 4 \, (V_2^2 - V_1^2)$, should be used.

Comparison of catheter derived gradients with gradients derived by Doppler echocardiographic maximum and mean velocity is problematic.

However, a resting peak systolic velocity greater than or equal to 3.2 m/s and a diastolic velocity greater than or equal to 1.0 m/s may be suggestive of significant coarctation.

Recent Doppler studies indicate that differentiation between restenosis and enhanced aortic stiffness can be performed by analyzing diastolic flow patterns at the isthmus. In higher-grade stenoses, high flow velocities are maintained during diastole (diastolic runoff).[18] A pandiastolic runoff is the most important echocardiography sign of restenosis.

In the presence of extensive bypassing collateral vessels the systolic and diastolic gradients are not very reliable.

Besides, after surgical coarctation repair a gradient may develop even in the absence of significant narrowing owing to a lack of aortic compliance.

The role of transesophageal echocardiography is a minor one in adults because the quality of aortic isthmus imaging tends to be poor. In experienced hands, intravascular ultrasonography may give important additional information (e.g., restenosis, local aneurysm formation, or intramural hematoma).

MAGNETIC RESONANCE IMAGING AND COMPUTED TOMOGRAPHY

Producing images of the entire aorta in any given plane with no superimpositions, magnetic resonance imaging (MRI) and computed tomography (CT) are the preferred noninvasive techniques to evaluate coarctation before and after operative or interventional treatment in adults. Because CT scans expose patients to a high radiation dose, MR angiography is preferable for repeat imaging. MRI and CT show the site, extent, and degree of the aortic narrowing; the aortic arch, which may be hypoplastic; the prestenotic and poststenotic aorta; and the collateral vessels, if present (Fig. 36-8). State-of-the-art MRI methods provide information on coarctation blood flow, the pressure gradient across the stenosis, and collateral flow.[19]

MRI and CT detect complications related to the natural history or to therapeutic procedures. Of outstanding importance are aneurysms of the ascending aorta or at the operative site, aortic dissections, periaortic hematoma, as well as a residual stenosis or hypoplastic aortic arch. The course and patency of prosthetic bypasses can be depicted with clarity.

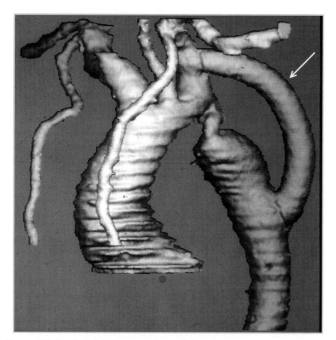

Figure 36-8 Spiral CT image of an adult with severe coarctation after implantation of an extra-anatomic tube graft (*arrow*) between the left subclavian artery and the descending aorta.

CARDIAC CATHETERIZATION

Cardiac catheterization with manometry and angiocardiography is still the "gold standard" for CoA evaluation at many centers before and after operative or interventional treatment. This procedure delineates the anatomy of the aorta and supra-aortic vessels, determines the pressure gradient across the coarctation, detects associated heart defects, and evaluates left ventricular function and coronary status (CoA patients have an increased incidence of coronary artery disease).

At cardiac catheterization a significant coarctation is one with a peak-to-peak gradient greater than 20 mm Hg across the coarctation site in the absence of a well-developed collateral circulation around the coarctation site. In the presence of extensive collateral circulation, there may be a minimal or no pressure gradient, even in high-grade CoA.

Owing to the increased risk of premature coronary artery involvement, coronary angiography may be advisable in patients with coronary risk factors or in those older than 40 years of age.

Late Management Options

The following situations may warrant consideration for intervention or re-intervention (either as operation or as interventional treatment with angioplasty with or without stent implantation[3,20]:

- All *symptomatic* patients with a more than a 20 mm Hg gradient across the CoA
- *Asymptomatic* patients with a greater than 20 mm Hg gradient across the CoA and upper limb hypertension, pathologic blood pressure response during exercise, or significant left ventricular hypertrophy
- Independent from the pressure gradient, *some* patients with 50% or more aortic narrowing (on MRI, CT, or angiography).
- Significant aortic valve stenosis or regurgitation
- Aneurysm of the ascending aorta
- Aneurysm at the previous CoA site
- Symptomatic or large aneurysms of the circle of Willis

MEDICAL INTERVENTION

Patients without a significant residual systolic gradient and with normal blood pressure at rest and exercise do not have to have restrictions on physical activity.

With respect to the risk of early coronary artery disease, cholesterol levels should be controlled and regulated while obesity and smoking are avoided.

Arterial hypertension at rest or during exercise is common, even after successful treatment, and should be treated with β-adrenergic blockers, angiotensin-converting enzyme inhibitors, angiotensin-receptor blockers, and/or diuretics. The impact and treatment of isolated, exercise-induced hypertension is still a matter of debate. However, it has to be kept in mind that blood pressure–lowering medication may have adverse effects in patients with CoA if residual arch obstruction or re-coarctation exists. Medical drug treatment often fails to achieve normotension if a significant restenosis is present. To get these patients "normotensive" may cause an inadequate lower-body perfusion and may produce renal failure.

SURGICAL OR CATHETER INTERVENTIONAL TREATMENT

Intervention for re-coarctation may be either surgical or percutaneous.
- Surgical repair of re-coarctation is technically difficult and associated with high morbidity. Mortality rates of up to 20% and recurrence rates of up to 20% have been described. Even in experienced centers, the mortality rate is 5% to 8%.
- Angioplasty with or without insertion of expandable stents has been found to be an effective and safe management strategy in experienced hands, although long-term follow-up studies are lacking. There is a broad consensus that angioplasty with or without stenting is the preferred approach to re-coarctation or residual stenosis after previous surgery. Recoil after balloon angioplasty can be avoided with endovascular stents. The main indications for balloon-expandable or self-expanding stents are currently recurrent aortic CoA or an aneurysm after prior surgical or balloon therapy (with a covered stent).

- Experience with covered stents in highly selected patients is limited; biodegradable stents are under development.
- Treatment should occur in centers with extensive experience in the treatment of CoA.

The most important residua and sequelae after reoperation or intervention include:
- Re-coarctation
- Aneurysm formation
- Stroke
- Paraplegia due to spinal cord ischemia (tragic, but rare), which may occur during the operation as a result of compromised blood supply to the anterior spinal artery. Paralysis is uncommon in the presence of a well-developed collateral supply. The risk of paralysis is increased with reduced arterial collateral vessels, prolonged aortic crossclamp time, and intraoperative sacrifice of intercostal or collateral vessels. Paraplegia has not been described during ballooning and stenting.
- Early postoperative paradoxical rebound hypertension due to activation of the sympathetic nerve system and renin-angiotensin system
- Phrenic nerve and recurrent laryngeal nerve injury

Pregnancy

Women with CoA need multidisciplinary observation by experienced congenital cardiologists during pregnancy, labor, and delivery and also for a period of time afterward. Hemodynamic and hormonal changes during pregnancy may pose an increased risk to both mother and fetus, especially in the third trimester and in the peripartum period.

Women with unrepaired CoA are at high risk, as are women with arterial hypertension, residual CoA, or aneurysms. Maternal death due to aortic dissection and rupture of a cerebral aneurysm has been reported. After successful treatment of CoA, pregnancy should be tolerated without major problems, although ideally the status of the ascending and descending aorta should be known before conception. However, an excess of miscarriages and the occurrence of pregnancy-related hypertensive disorders (16%) has been reported.[21]

The recurrence risk of CoA increases in the offspring of parents with CoA and with the number of affected relatives. According to Nora and Nora,[22] the recurrence risk of CoA is about 2% if one sibling is affected and approximately 6% if two siblings are affected.

Fetal echocardiography is indicated for pregnancies complicated by maternal congenital heart disease or in women who have previously been delivered of a child with congenital cardiac disease, especially a left-sided heart obstructive lesion.

Level of Follow-Up, Endocarditis Prophylaxis, and Exercise

- CoA is a complex cardiovascular disorder and, as part of a generalized arteriopathy, a lifelong disease.
- Complications may not be evident until many years after initial, apparently successful, treatment.
- Follow-up care after coarctation treatment is required and should include search for late complications including arterial hypertension, recurrent obstruction, aneurysm formation, or other associated anomalies.
- Clinical examination alone is by no means adequate for follow-up in these patients. The use of imaging techniques is essential. Appropriate techniques are echocardiography, angiography, MRI, and CT.
- Treatment, if necessary, should take place in centers with extensive experience in the treatment of CoA.
- Lifelong endocarditis prophylaxis was until recently recommended after surgical or interventional treatment of aortic coarctation. According to the new guidelines it is no longer recommended, but this is controversial.
- Patients without residual obstruction who are normotensive at rest and with exercise should lead normally active lives, without restriction.
- Patients with arterial hypertension, residual obstruction, or other complications should avoid heavy isometric exercises, in proportion to the severity of their problems.

INTERRUPTED AORTIC ARCH

Definition and Morphology

Interrupted aortic arch (IAA) is characterized by a complete discontinuity between two parts of the aortic arch. The first descriptions of IAA came from Steidele in 1777, Siedel in 1818, and Weisman in 1948.[1,23] In 1959, Celoria and Patton classified this anomaly according to the location of interruption into three types (Fig. 36-9)[24]:
- Type A: distal to the left subclavian artery
- Type B: between the left carotid artery and the left subclavian artery
- Type C: between the brachiocephalic trunk and the left carotid artery

IAA type A occurs in approximately one third of cases, type B in two thirds, and type C in less than 1% of cases. The right subclavian artery may arise normally or abnormally in any type.

Moreover, IAA is almost always associated with other important intracardiac and/or extracardiac lesions: ventricular septal defect, patent ductus arteriosus, bicuspid aortic valve, subaortic stenosis, aortopulmonary window, truncus arteriosus, complete transposition of the great arteries, double-outlet right ventricle, single ventricle, or atrioventricular septal defect. Right ventricular outflow tract obstructions are rare. The most common extracardiac anomaly is microdeletion 22q11.

Genetics and Epidemiology

IAA is a rare congenital heart defect. Its overall incidence is 0.2% to 1.4% of all congenital cardiac defects.[25,26] The male-to-female ratio is 1.0:1.0.

The actual cause of IAA is unknown. Altered fetal hemodynamics leading to faulty development of the aortic arch is likely.

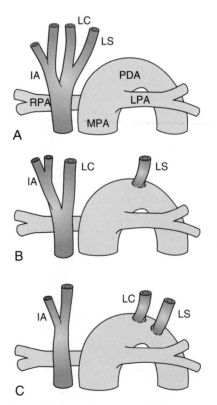

Figure 36-9 **A** to **C,** Anatomic details of an interrupted aortic arch. IA, interrupted aortic arch; LC, left carotid artery; LPA, left pulmonary artery; LS, left subclavian artery; MPA, main pulmonary artery; PDA, patent ductus arteriosus; RPA, right pulmonary artery. *(Redrawn from Schwengel DA, Nichols DG, Cameron DE. Coarctation of the aorta and interrupted aortic arch. In Nichols DG, Cameron DE, Greeley WJ, et al., editors. Critical Heart Disease in Infants and Children. St. Louis: Mosby; 1995.)*

Early Presentation

Almost all patients with IAA have problems in the first days of life. Typical presentation includes respiratory distress, cyanosis, diminished peripheral pulses, congestive heart failure, or shock.

There is some similarity to coarctation, leading to a pressure rise in the left ventricle and the ascending aorta. An associated ventricular septal defect causes a large left-to-right shunt. As the ductus arteriosus closes, perfusion distal to the arch interruption decreases. It is important to mention that severe aortic and subaortic stenosis may be masked by the ventricular septal defect.

Untreated patients usually die within the first days of life, 75% within the first month.[8,27] Only sporadic survival to adulthood has been described.[1] In the rare patient without associated anomalies, the natural history may be similar to that of CoA.

Management

MEDICAL TREATMENT

Prostaglandin E_1 is indicated to maintain patency of the ductus arteriosus until operation is performed.

SURGICAL TREATMENT

Treatment of IAA is achieved by surgical repair of the interruption. A single-stage repair is favored. Continuity of the aorta is established by end-to-end-anastomosis or, in previous years, by interposition of a conduit. If necessary, closure of the ventricular septal defect and resection of subaortic stenosis is performed.

Staged procedures consist of establishing continuity of the aorta, closure of patent ductus arteriosus, and pulmonary artery banding. Subsequently, the ventricular septal defect is closed and the pulmonary artery debanded.

Alternative approaches are the Ross-Konno and Norwood-Rastelli procedures.

Late Outcome

SURVIVAL AND FUNCTIONAL STATUS

Recently Schreiber and associates reported on a 10-year survival of 74%, and the New York Heart Association functional class for long-term survivors was mostly class I or II.[28] Freedom from reoperation at 10 years was 49% in this series.

If surgery is initiated before organ damage has occurred, the long-term prognosis is satisfactory.[28] The morphology of the subaortic outflow tract particularly influences the outcome, and associated complex anomalies carry a high risk.

Reoperation may be needed, for example, for arch obstruction, subaortic stenosis, ventricular septal defect recurrence, or bronchial compression.

LATE COMPLICATIONS

The most important residua, sequelae, and complications are stenosis in the region of the previous anastomosis, conduit obstruction, and left ventricular outflow tract obstruction.

Outpatient Assessment

Operated patients need a diagnostic workup that includes:
- A thorough clinical examination
- Electrocardiography
- Echocardiography/Doppler study (transthoracic ± transesophageal)
- Chest radiography
- MRI or CT (multislice or spiral CT)
- Cardiac catheterization.
- Laboratory studies (regarding microdeletion 22q11, hypoparathyroidism)

Which of these studies may be required depends on the clinical situation.

PHYSICAL FINDINGS

Cardinal clinical features in children include diminished peripheral pulses and cyanosis, symptoms of poor perfusion, or congestive heart failure. Features of microdeletion 22q11 should be sought. Auscultation mainly depends on associated anomalies.

ELECTROCARDIOGRAPHY

Electrocardiography depends widely on associated anomalies. In isolated IAA, electrocardiography in children may include right-axis deviation, right ventricular hypertrophy, and left atrial enlargement due to the left-to-right shunt. Most adults have undergone repair and show left ventricular hypertrophy.

CHEST RADIOGRAPHY

Chest radiography also depends on associated anomalies and is non-specific, because the hemodynamic consequences of IAA vary widely.

ECHOCARDIOGRAPHY

Two-dimensional (2D) echocardiography and Doppler studies are diagnostic for IAA and delineate associated intracardiac and vascular anomalies. The most important information regards the lack of continuity of the aortic arch, the left ventricular outflow obstruction, the aortic valve, and the type and size of ventricular septal defect.[18]

MAGNETIC RESONANCE IMAGING AND COMPUTED TOMOGRAPHY

MRI and CT nicely depict anatomic details of the IAA. Both methods are rarely necessary for the initial diagnosis but may be useful for postoperative follow-up. Both methods reveal complications related to the natural history or to the therapeutic procedures, especially obstruction at the site of anastomosis and patency of prosthetic bypasses.

CARDIAC CATHETERIZATION

Cardiac catheterization and aortography is indicated to delineate anatomy and hemodynamics, particularly if questions remain that cannot be answered by echocardiography alone and when associated cardiac defects are present.

Catheterization may depict the site of arch interruption, the ventricular septal defect, the left ventricular outflow obstruction, and additional vascular abnormalities (e.g., aberrant right subclavian artery).

Late Management Options

The following situations may warrant consideration for intervention or re-intervention:
- Stenosis at the site of aortic arch surgery
- Persistent or developing left ventricular outflow obstruction
- Residual ventricular septal defect
- Microdeletion 22q11

Level of Follow-Up, Endocarditis Prophylaxis, and Exercise

- Follow-up care after IAA treatment is required and should include search for obstruction at the site of anastomosis, left ventricular outflow obstruction, residual ventricular septal defect, and microdeletion 22q11.
- For follow-up, the use of modern imaging techniques is essential: echocardiography, angiography, MRI, and CT.
- Lifelong endocarditis prophylaxis was until recently recommended after surgical treatment. According to new guidelines it is no longer recommended, but this is controversial.[6]
- Patients without residual obstruction at subvalvular, valvular, or aortic levels should lead normally active lives without restriction.

REFERENCES

1. Perloff JK. The Clinical Recognition of Congenital Heart Disease. 4th ed. Philadelphia: WB Saunders; 1994.
2. Niwa K, Perloff JK, Bhuta SM, et al. Structural abnormalities of great arterial walls in congenital heart disease: light and electron microscopic analyses. Circulation 2001;103:393–400.
3. Kaemmerer H, Hager A, Hess J. Coarctation of the aorta in adults. SA Heart 2007;4:4–12.
4. Vriend JW, Zwinderman AH, de Groot E, et al. Predictive value of mild, residual descending aortic narrowing for blood pressure and vascular damage in patients after repair of aortic coarctation. Eur Heart J 2005;26:84–90.
5. Campbell M. Natural history of coarctation of the aorta. Br Heart J 1970;32:633–640.
6. Perloff JK, Child JS, editors. Congenital Heart Disease in Adults. 3rd ed. Philadelphia: WB Saunders; 2008.
7. Connelly MS, Webb GD, Somerville J, et al. Canadian Consensus Conference on Adult Congenital Heart Disease 1996. Can J Cardiol 1998;14:395–452.
8. Kirklin JW, Barrett-Boyes B. Cardiac Surgery. 2nd ed. New York: John Wiley; 1993.
9. Rothman A. Coarctation of the aorta. Curr Probl Pediatr 1998;28:37–60.
10. Cohen M, Foster V, Steele PM, et al. Coarctation of the aorta: long-term follow-up and prediction of outcome after surgical correction. Circulation 1989;80:840–845.
11. Hager A, Kanz S, Kaemmerer H, et al. CoArctation Long-term Assessment (COALA): Significance of arterial hypertension in a cohort of 404 patients up to 27 years after surgical repair of isolated coarctation of the aorta even in the absence of restenosis and prosthetic material. J Thorac Cardiovasc Surg 2007;134:738–745.
12. Kaemmerer H, Oelert F, Bahlmann J, et al. Arterial hypertension in adults after surgical treatment of aortic coarctation. Thorac Cardiovasc Surg 1998;46:121–125.
13. McCrindle BW, Jones TK, Morrow WR, et al. Acute results of acute balloon angioplasty of native coarctation versus recurrent aortic obstruction are equivalent. J Am Coll Cardiol 1996;28:1810–1817.
14. Yetman A, Nykanen D, McCrindle BW, et al. Balloon angioplasty of recurrent aortic arch obstruction: a twelve year review. J Am Coll Cardiol 1997;30:811–816.
15. Wilson W, Taubert KA, Gewitz M, et al. American Heart Association Rheumatic Fever, Endocarditis and Kawasaki Disease Committee, Council on Cardiovascular Disease in the Young; Council on Clinical Cardiology; Council on Cardiovascular Surgery and Anesthesia; Quality of Care and Outcomes Research Interdisciplinary Working Group; American Dental Association. Prevention of infective endocarditis: guidelines from the American Heart Association: a guideline from the American Heart Association Rheumatic Fever, Endocarditis and Kawasaki Disease Committee, Council on Cardiovascular Disease in the Young, and the Council on Clinical Cardiology, Council on Cardiovascular Surgery and Anesthesia, and the Quality of Care and Outcomes Research Interdisciplinary Working Group. J Am Dent Assoc 2007;138:739–745,747–760.
16. Sabet HY, Edwards WD, Tazelaar HD, Daly RC. Congenitally bicuspid aortic valves: a surgical pathology study of 542 cases (1991 through 1996) and a literature review of 2715 additional cases. Mayo Clin Proc 1999;74:14–26.
17. Kaemmerer H, Theissen P, Koenig U, et al. Klinische und magnetresonanztomographische Verlaufskontrollen operative behandelter Aortenisthmusstenosen im Erwachsenenalter. Z Kardiol 1989;78:777–783.
18. Valdez-Cruz LM, Cayre RO. Echocardiographic diagnosis of congenital heart disease. Philadelphia: Lippincott-Raven; 1999.
19. Kaemmerer H, Stern H, Fratz S, et al. Imaging in adults with congenital cardiac disease (ACCD). Thoracic Cardiovasc Surg 2000;48:328–335.
20. Warnes CA, Williams RG, Bashore TM, et al. ACC/AHA 2008 Guidelines for the Management of Adults With Congenital Heart Disease. J Am Coll Cardiol 2008;52:1890–1947.
21. Drenthen W, Pieper PG, Roos-Hesselink JW, et al. ZAHARA Investigators. Outcome of pregnancy in women with congenital heart disease: a literature review. J Am Coll Cardiol 2007;49:2303–2311.
22. Nora JJ, Nora AH. Maternal transmission of congenital heart diseases: new recurrence risk figures and the question of cytoplasmic inheritance and vulnerability to teratogens. Am J Cardiol 1987;59:459–463.
23. Steidele RJ. Sammlung verschiedener in der chirurgischen-praktischen Lehrschule gemachten. Beobachtungen 1777–78;2:114.
24. Celoria GC, Patton RB. Congenital absence of the aortic arch. Am Heart J 1959;58:407–413.
25. Powell CB, Moller JH. Interruption of the aortic arch. In: Moller JH, editor. Perspectives in Pediatric Cardiology. Surgery of Congenital Heart Disease: Pediatric Cardiac Care Consortium 1984–1995. Armonk, NY: Futura; 1998. p. 159–169.
26. Schumacher G, Hess J, Buehlmeyer KH. Diagnostik Angeborener Herzfehler. 3rd ed. Heidelberg: Springer; 2001.
27. Roberts WC, Morrow AG, Braunwald E. Complete interruption of the aortic arch. Circulation 1962;26:39–59.
28. Schreiber C, Eicken A, Vogt M, et al. Repair of interrupted aortic arch: results after more than 20 years. Ann Thorac Surg 2000;70:1896–1899.

37

Truncus Arteriosus

MICHAEL S. CONNELLY

Definition and Morphology

Truncus arteriosus (also known as persistent truncus arteriosus, truncus arteriosus communis, common arterial trunk, or common aorticopulmonary trunk) is an uncommon congenital cardiac malformation that accounts for 1% to 4% of the cardiac malformations found in large autopsy series[1] and 0.6 to 1.4 per 10,000 live births.[2] The natural history without intervention is dismal, and operative repair usually takes place within the neonatal period or infancy. Consequently, the management of adults with this condition involves the care of operative survivors. The original anatomy of truncus arteriosus involves a single arterial vessel arising from the base of the heart that gives rise to the coronary, pulmonary, and systemic arteries. There is a single semilunar valve, the truncal valve. Beneath the truncal valve there is invariably a ventricular septal defect (VSD).

Although usually an isolated defect, truncus arteriosus has been reported in association with other anomalies, particularly the DiGeorge syndrome (in the setting of aortic interruption). It has been reported in monozygotic and dizygotic twins, siblings, and relatives of children with the defect. Embryologically, it is due to abnormal migration of the neural crest tissue and there is a strong association with chromosome 22q11 abnormalities.

The condition was first described in 1798 by Wilson[3] and confirmed in an autopsy report by Buchanan in 1864.[4] Lev and Saphir,[5] in 1942, proposed the basic morphologic criteria defining the anomaly, and Collett and Edwards,[6] in 1949, and, subsequently, Van Praagh and Van Praagh,[1] in 1965, proposed a classification. More recently the Society of Thoracic Surgeons has tried to establish a unified classification for the basis of surgical reporting.[7]

The classification of Collett and Edwards[6] considered four different types of truncus arteriosus based on the origin of the pulmonary arteries, namely:
- *Type I:* A short main pulmonary truncus arising from the truncus arteriosus that gives rise to right and left pulmonary arteries (48% to 68% of cases).
- *Type II:* No main pulmonary truncus but the right and left pulmonary arteries arise close to one another (29% to 48% of cases).
- *Type III:* No main pulmonary truncus and the right and left pulmonary arteries arise distant from one another (6% to 10% of cases).
- *Type IV:* Absence of the pulmonary arteries; the lungs are supplied by large aortopulmonary collateral arteries. This last type is now thought to be a variation of pulmonary atresia with VSD and is no longer considered as part of the spectrum of truncus arteriosus.

The classification of Van Praagh and Van Praagh[1] again recognizes four types, this time based embryologically, rather than anatomically:
- *Type 1:* There is a partially formed aorticopulmonary septum and hence a main pulmonary artery segment is present. This corresponds to Collett and Edwards type I.
- *Type 2:* There is absence of the aorticopulmonary septum, and thus no main pulmonary artery segment is present. The right and left branch pulmonary arteries arise from the truncus arteriosus, but their proximity to one another is not specified. This corresponds to Collett and Edwards types II and III.
- *Type 3:* There is absence of one branch pulmonary artery from the truncus arteriosus (i.e., it arises either from the ductus arteriosus or from the aorta).

- *Type 4:* The aortic arch is either hypoplastic or interrupted, and there is a large patent ductus arteriosus.

The Van Praagh and Van Praagh classification also specifies the presence (type A) or absence (type B) of a VSD.

The Society of Thoracic Surgeons' classification[7] is an attempt to provide a uniform system for reporting that reflects both the anatomy and the features that affect surgical outcome, rather than an attempt to understand the embryology. It is essentially a modification of the Van Praagh and Van Praagh classification (Table 37-1). A comparison between the different classifications is shown in Figure 37-1.

Figure 37-2 demonstrates the typical anatomy of truncus arteriosus, which is discussed further later.

VENTRICULAR SEPTAL DEFECT

The VSD in truncus arteriosus is usually large and nonrestrictive. It results from a deficiency or absence of the infundibular septum. It is subarterial, lying between the two limbs of the septal band (the septomarginal trabeculation), which form the inferior and anterior boundaries. The superior boundary is formed by the truncal valve, and posteriorly it is bounded by the ventriculoinfundibular fold. There is usually a muscle bridge between the tricuspid and truncal valves caused by fusion of the inferior limb and the parietal band. When this is absent (rarely), there is fibrous continuity between the two valves. Under these circumstances, the bundle of His is at risk of damage during surgical repair. Rarely, the VSD is restrictive. This usually occurs when the truncus arteriosus arises exclusively from one ventricle. Very rarely it is absent. This may occur if the truncus arteriosus arises exclusively from the right ventricle.

TRUNCAL VALVE

From various studies, the truncal valve is tricuspid in 69% of cases, quadricuspid in 22%, and bicuspid in 9%. There is fibrous continuity between the posterior leaflets of the truncal valve and the anterior leaflet of the mitral valve (as between the aortic and mitral valves in the normal heart), but only very rarely is there fibrous continuity between the truncal valve and the tricuspid valve. How well the leaflets of the truncal valve are formed impacts on survival: severe myxomatous thickening is found in one third of cases, is associated with significant truncal valve incompetence, and is more common in neonates and young infants who develop severe heart failure or die. Occasionally (18%) the truncal valve may be stenotic.

TRUNCUS ARTERIOSUS

The truncus arteriosus is larger than the normal aorta and is the only vessel exiting the base of the heart. It is often dilated, and histopathologic studies have demonstrated medial wall abnormalities similar to, and sometimes as extreme as, those found in patients with Marfan syndrome. The sinuses of Valsalva are often poorly developed. In the majority of cases (68% to 83%) the truncus arteriosus overrides the ventricular septum and has a biventricular origin. Less commonly (11% to 29%) it arises solely from the right ventricle. Rarely (4% to 6%) it arises from the left ventricle.

TABLE 37-1	Classifications of Truncus Arteriosus Defects		
Society of Thoracic Surgeons[7]		*Van Praagh & Van Praagh*[1]	*Collett & Edwards*[6]
Truncus arteriosus with confluent or nearly confluent pulmonary arteries		Type A1 or A2	Types I, II, II
Truncus arteriosus with absence of one pulmonary artery		Type A3	
Truncus arteriosus with interrupted aortic arch or severe coarctation		Type A4	

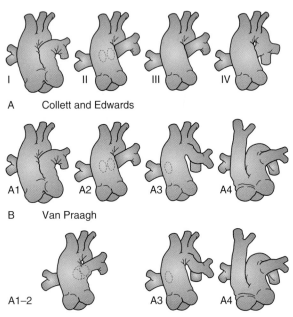

Figure 37-1 **A** to **C**, Comparison of the anatomic classifications of truncus arteriosus. *(Redrawn from Jacobs ML. Congenital heart surgery nomenclature and database project: truncus arteriosus. Ann Thorac Surg 2000; 69:S50-S55.)*

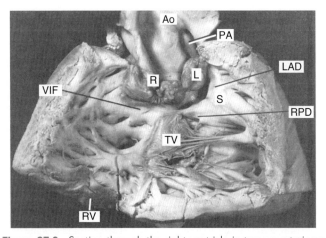

Figure 37-2 Section through the right ventricle in truncus arteriosus type I (Collett and Edwards[6]). The specimen is viewed from the right ventricle. The truncal valve is markedly abnormal. There is a small muscular ridge separating the truncal and tricuspid valves at the posteroinferior margin of the VSD. Ao, aorta; LAD, left anterior division of septal band; L, R, left, right truncal valve leaflets; PA, main pulmonary artery origin; RPD, right posterior division of septal band; RV, right ventricle; S, septal band (septomarginal trabeculation); TV, tricuspid valve; VIF, ventriculoinfundibular fold; VSD, ventricular septal defect. *(From Kirklin JW, Barrett-Boyes BG. Truncus arteriosus. In: Cardiac Surgery, 2nd ed. Edinburgh: Churchill Livingstone; 1993:1140.)*

PULMONARY ARTERIES

The pulmonary arteries usually arise from the left posterolateral aspect of the truncus arteriosus, just above the truncal valve. When there are separate pulmonary artery ostia the left is usually higher than that of the right. Very rarely (in the setting of interrupted aortic arch) the left pulmonary artery ostium may arise to the right of the right ostium, leading to crossing of the pulmonary arteries behind the truncus. Stenoses of the pulmonary artery ostia are uncommon.

CORONARY ARTERIES

The coronary arteries usually arise from the sinuses of Valsalva above the truncal leaflets. In two thirds of cases, the left coronary artery arises from the left posterolateral truncal surface and the right coronary artery arises from the right anterolateral truncal surface, similar to the arrangement found in normal hearts. However, the left anterior descending artery is often relatively small and is displaced to the left and the conus branch of the right is consequently large and supplies branches to the right ventricular outflow tract and septum (which may be important at operation). The coronary circulation is left dominant in about 27% of patients, about three times higher than the prevalence in the normal population. Variations in coronary artery anatomy exist, however.

DUCTUS ARTERIOSUS

The ductus arteriosus is absent in about 50% of cases of truncus arteriosus. When present, however, it tends to remain patent postnatally in approximately two thirds of cases. There is usually an inverse relationship between the diameter of the ductus and that of the ascending aorta and transverse arch: when the ductus is widely patent, the transverse arch is either interrupted or there is severe coarctation, including tubular hypoplasia of the aortic isthmus and arch. Under these circumstances the pulmonary arteries arise separately from the truncus arteriosus (Collett and Edwards type III). When there is neither aortic interruption/coarctation nor discontinuous pulmonary arteries it is exceedingly rare to find a patent ductus arteriosus.

VENTRICLES

The infundibular septum is absent from the right ventricular outflow tract, and the right ventricle is invariably hypertrophied and enlarged. The left ventricular outflow tract is relatively normal.

ASSOCIATED ANOMALIES

The most common cardiovascular anomalies coexisting with truncus arteriosus include interrupted aortic arch or coarctation, occurring in 10% to 20% of cases, in association with a widely patent ductus arteriosus. An interrupted aortic arch is often associated with the DiGeorge syndrome. A right aortic arch with mirror-image brachiocephalic branching occurs in 21% to 36% of patients with truncus arteriosus. Other common associated anomalies include secundum atrial septal defect (9% to 20%), aberrant subclavian artery (4% to 10%), persistent left superior vena cava to coronary sinus (4% to 9%), and mild tricuspid stenosis (6%). In 21% to 30% of patients, extracardiac anomalies are present, particularly skeletal, ureteral, and bowel.

◼ Early Presentation and Management

Truncus arteriosus usually presents in the neonatal period or in early infancy, although intrauterine diagnosis with fetal echocardiography is possible. Presentation is usually with signs of heart failure as the pulmonary vascular resistance falls, namely, tachycardia, tachypnea, excessive sweating, and feeding difficulties, followed by more florid signs of pulmonary and hepatic congestion. Before the fall in pulmonary vascular resistance, mild cyanosis may be detected. The presence of truncal valve insufficiency exacerbates the problem of heart failure and impacts adversely on outcome. Likewise, significant truncal valve stenosis also reduces the likelihood of survival, as does coexisting interrupted aortic arch or coarctation. The presence of truncal valve or aortic anomalies usually results in earlier presentation. Survival is favorably affected by naturally occurring pulmonary stenosis (at the origin of the right, left, or main pulmonary arteries depending on the initial anatomy). Indeed, survival into adult life without surgical intervention has been described but is very uncommon. Nevertheless, the unoperated natural history demonstrates an appalling outlook. Figure 37-3 demonstrates the actuarial survival from a single center[8] and is similar to that in other reports.[1] Death is usually due to heart failure in early infancy and childhood. Beyond early childhood, pulmonary vascular disease is the major cause of death, although endocarditis and cerebral abscess may be responsible.[9]

Surgical History

In view of the poor natural history, surgery is the main form of treatment for truncus arteriosus. Initially, this comprised banding of one or both pulmonary arteries. However, problems are numerous: the

band may be inadequate with subsequent development of pulmonary vascular disease; the band may migrate in type I truncus, leading to obstruction of one pulmonary artery and the development of pulmonary vascular disease in the other; or there may be failure of pulmonary artery growth distal to the band or distortion of the pulmonary arteries. Consequently, primary, complete surgical repair in the neonatal/infant period is preferred. This was successfully accomplished initially in 1967 by McGoon and associates[10] using an aortic homograft and aortic valve. Repair of truncus arteriosus in association with interrupted aortic arch was first successfully accomplished in 1971 by Gomes and McGoon.[11] The basic procedure for repair of truncus arteriosus is demonstrated in Figure 37-4. Numerous iterations of the procedure have taken place subsequently to try to prolong the life of the right ventricle-to-pulmonary artery conduit, including a Dacron conduit with a porcine semilunar valve as well as frozen or fresh homografts. Attempts have been made to repair the truncus arteriosus without the use of an extracardiac conduit, using instead an extracardiac patch with a pericardial monocusp

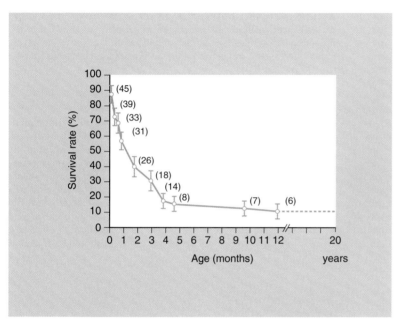

Figure 37-3 Actuarial survival of surgically untreated patients with truncus arteriosus. (After Kirklin JW, Barrett-Boyes BG. Truncus arteriosus. In: Cardiac Surgery, 2nd ed. Edinburgh: Churchill Livingstone; 1993:1140.)

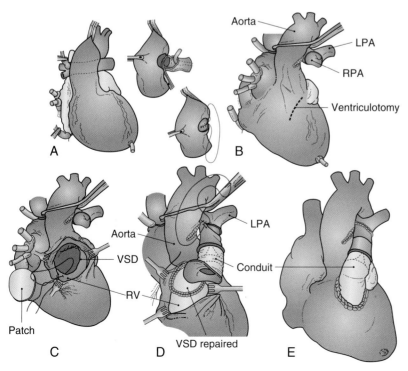

Figure 37-4 Technique for surgical repair of truncus arteriosus. **A,** On cardiopulmonary bypass; origin of pulmonary arteries excised from the truncus arteriosus; defect in truncus arteriosus closed. **B,** Incision made high in right ventricle. **C,** Ventricular septal defect (VSD) closed with prosthetic patch. **D,** Conduit with valve is sutured to pulmonary arteries. **E,** Proximal end of conduit attached to right ventricle. LPA, left pulmonary artery; RPA, right pulmonary artery; RV, right ventricle. (After McGoon DC, Rastelli GC, Ongley PA. An operation for the correction of truncus arteriosus. JAMA 1968; 205:69-73.)

valve.[12] The monocusp valve subsequently shrinks, resulting in free pulmonary incompetence. More recently, a glutaraldehyde-preserved bovine jugular venous valved conduit (Contegra) has been used for the right ventricle-to-pulmonary artery conduit. Although the pulmonary homograft has been considered the most durable, contemporary data suggest that the Contegra conduit is comparable, at least in the short term.[13] Surgical risk is increased if concurrent truncal valve surgery is necessary, and truncal valve repair is preferred over replacement if possible. Concomitant repair of interrupted aortic arch significantly increases the risk of surgery with consequent worse outcomes.[14]

Late Outcome

It follows that initial surgical intervention for truncus arteriosus takes place in infancy and early childhood and only rarely later in life. In a review of a single-center surgical experience spanning 20 years, the median age at repair was 3.5 months and the youngest patient was aged 2 days, with 81% of the patients being operated on within the first year of life.[15] As surgical techniques continue to improve there will be fewer and fewer individuals operated on outside the early childhood period. Factors associated with increased early operative mortality include truncal valve abnormalities, major associated cardiac abnormalities such as interrupted aortic arch, origin of the truncal artery predominantly from the right ventricle, and small size of the right and left pulmonary arteries.[16–18] Not all investigators have found these to be associated with higher risk, however.[19,20] Although the presence of pulmonary vascular disease is associated with adverse outcome, earlier age at operation (<6 months so that pulmonary vascular disease has not developed) should eliminate this problem. More recent results continue to show a trend for improved survival and earlier repair.[21] The best results are obtained at institutions that have the highest case loads and are properly prepared for neonatal and pediatric cardiac surgery.

Long-term survival after initial successful repair of truncus arteriosus is gratifying and continues to improve. Figure 37-5 demonstrates the results of a 20-year follow-up from a single institution of patients who survived to hospital discharge. Similar results have been obtained by others.[19] Of note, the outlook was similar regardless of whether the operation was carried out in infancy.[15] However, survival does not equate to freedom from reoperation. Figure 37-6 demonstrates the actuarial freedom from reoperation in individuals from the same institution. The median time to reoperation was 5.1 years after original repair. The majority of reoperations were for conduit replacement, and initial age at repair was the single most important factor in determining conduit survival; age younger than 3 months at original repair was associated with significantly shorter conduit survival. In this series it did not appear to matter what type of conduit was used at the time of initial operation. The second most common reason for reoperation was surgery to the truncal valve. Truncal valve insufficiency of moderate or greater degree at the time of initial repair was associated with significantly worse outcome. At reoperation, branch pulmonary arterioplasty and closure of residual VSD sometimes had to be performed. Unfortunately, reoperation was the single most important risk factor for late death, with approximately half of the late deaths occurring at the time of reoperation. It is hoped that with the advent of percutaneous valve procedures that reoperation can be delayed and outcomes will improve further. Data on this are lacking, however. Other cardiac causes of late death included arrhythmic, sudden (presumed arrhythmic), and ventricular failure. Of note, however, the great majority of patients surviving initial repair are in New York Heart Association functional class I.

Outpatient Assessment

From the foregoing discussion it is apparent that most individuals encountered in adult life who have a diagnosis of truncus arteriosus will have had previous reparative surgery, sometimes with multiple repeat procedures. Likewise, because the condition is rare and successful surgical repair was first performed in 1967, the number of patients who have successfully reached adulthood is currently small, although with the success of surgery it will continue to increase. Rarely, individuals are encountered who have survived to adult life without surgical intervention, but they will most likely have significant pulmonary vascular disease and Eisenmenger syndrome and should be managed as such.

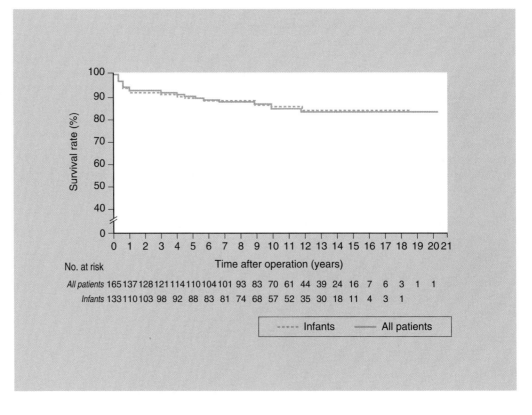

Figure 37-5 Actuarial survival among hospital survivors of complete repair of truncus arteriosus: all patients and infants aged younger than 1 year at time of repair. *(After Rajasinghe HA, McElhinney DB, Reddy VM et al. Long-term follow-up of truncus arteriosus repaired in infancy: a 20-year experience. J Thorac Cardiovasc Surg 1997; 113:869-879.)*

No. at risk

All patients 165 137 128 121 114 110 104 101 93 83 70 61 44 39 24 16 7 6 3 1 1
Infants 133 110 103 98 92 88 83 81 74 68 57 52 35 30 18 11 4 3 1

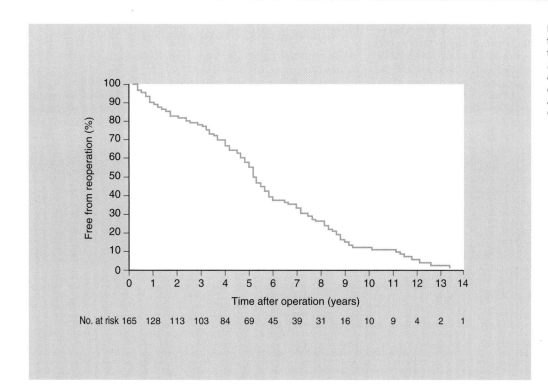

Figure 37-6 Actuarial freedom from reoperation after repair of truncus arteriosus. *(After Rajasinghe HA, McElhinney DB, Reddy VM et al. Long-term follow-up of truncus arteriosus repaired in infancy: a 20-year experience. J Thorac Cardiovasc Surg 1997; 113:869-879.)*

No. at risk 165 128 113 103 84 69 45 39 31 16 10 9 4 2 1

BOX 37-1   COMPLICATIONS

- Conduit stenosis or regurgitation—most likely the former, although use of a pericardial monocusp will increase the likelihood of pulmonary regurgitation
- Truncal (neoaortic) valve regurgitation or stenosis, or prosthetic valve dysfunction if the truncal valve has been replaced
- Myocardial ischemia due to coronary artery abnormalities
- Ventricular dysfunction, which may result from multiple surgical interventions, delayed surgery (with consequent deleterious effects on ventricular function), conduit dysfunction, and myocardial ischemia
- Arrhythmias
- Residual VSD
- Aortic root dilation due to the known medial wall abnormalities found in this condition (although the significance of this is unknown), which may lead to neoaortic valve incompetence
- Branch pulmonary artery stenosis
- Progressive pulmonary vascular disease

Potential complications that need to be considered in the follow-up of adult patients with repaired truncus arteriosus are shown in Box 37-1.

All patients should be observed on a regular basis, at a minimum probably annually, with more frequent follow-up if there are signs of clinical or hemodynamic deterioration. Ideally, patients should be observed at or in conjunction with a center that specializes in the care of adults with congenital heart disease.

Assessment should include:

- Thorough clinical examination, paying particular attention to rhythm status, conduit function, and ventricular function
- Electrocardiography to assess for rhythm abnormalities, signs of developing or worsening right or left ventricular volume, or pressure overload
- Chest radiography (periodically) to assess for conduit or valvar calcification, possible aortic root dilation (although chest radiography is not particularly sensitive for this), or changing ventricular dimensions (cardiothoracic ratio)
- Echocardiographic Doppler examination to assess conduit function, neoaortic valve function, aortic root dimensions, ventricular size

and function, presence of residual VSD, branch pulmonary artery stenosis, and right ventricular pressures

It also may require:

- Myocardial perfusion scan if myocardial ischemia is suspected
- Exercise testing ± assessment of maximal oxygen consumption to assess functional capacity
- Holter monitoring if arrhythmias are suspected
- Magnetic resonance studies (imaging ± hemodynamic studies) or possibly CT angiography if inadequate information is available from echocardiography
- Cardiac catheterization if adequate information cannot be obtained from noninvasive studies

Re-intervention should be considered for:

- Significant right ventricle-to-pulmonary artery conduit stenosis or regurgitation
- Significant neoaortic valve (truncal valve) regurgitation or stenosis or prosthetic valve dysfunction (if the valve has been replaced)
- Significant branch pulmonary artery stenosis
- Significant aortic root dilation, particularly if progressive or associated with neoaortic valvular regurgitation
- Significant residual VSD (although this will usually be dealt with in childhood)
- Important myocardial ischemia

Re-intervention is almost invariably surgical. However, catheter-based techniques may be appropriate as a temporizing measure for conduit and/or branch pulmonary artery stenoses. The role of percutaneous transcatheter valve replacement either to the right ventricle-to-pulmonary artery valved conduit or the neoaortic valve has yet to be determined.

The role of pharmacologic management of ventricular dysfunction is empirical. It seems reasonable to adopt similar strategies to those used in adult patients with heart failure, although there are no data to support such an approach.

Pregnancy

Successful pregnancy and delivery has been reported in postoperative complete repair of truncus arteriosus,[22] although there are few cases in the literature. Worsening neoaortic valve regurgitation has been reported.[23] Because there are few reported cases of pregnancy in such individuals, the prevalence of congenital cardiac disease in their offspring is currently difficult to assess. However, given the association of chromosome 22q11 abnormalities in individuals with truncus arteriosus especially in the setting of interrupted aortic arch, chromosomal analysis using fluorescence in-situ hybridization studies should be offered to all women with the condition contemplating pregnancy. All patients should have pre-pregnancy counseling and careful follow-up during their pregnancy by a specialist cardiologist. Dedicated cardiac fetal ultrasonography should be performed at an appropriate gestational age.

Endocarditis Prophylaxis and Exercise

All individuals with repaired truncus arteriosus should be aware of the need to prevent endocarditis.

Exercise should not be proscribed in individuals who have undergone repair of truncus arteriosus. Advice regarding the intensity of exercise will depend on the outcome of repair, the severity of residual lesions (e.g., conduit stenosis, neoaortic [truncal] valve function) and ventricular function. Formal assessment and involvement in a cardiac rehabilitation program may be useful if available.

REFERENCES

1. Van Praagh R, Van Praagh S. The anatomy of common aorticopulmonary trunk (truncus arteriosus communis) and its embryological implications: a study of 57 necropsy cases. Am J Cardiol 1965;16:406–425.
2. Hoffman JL, Kaplan S. The incidence of congenital heart disease. J Am Coll Cardiol 2002;39:1890–1900.
3. Wilson J. A description of a very unusual malformation of the human heart. Philos Trans R Soc Lond (Biol) 1798;18:346.
4. Buchanan A. Malformation of the heart: undivided truncus arteriosus. Trans Pathol Soc Lond 1864;15:89.
5. Lev M, Saphir O. Truncus arteriosus communis persistens. J Pediatr 1943;20:74.
6. Collett RW, Edwards JE. Persistent truncus arteriosus: a classification according to anatomic types. Surg Clin North Am 1949;29:1245–1270.
7. Jacobs ML. Congenital heart surgery nomenclature and database project: truncus arteriosus. Ann Thorac Surg 2000;69:S50–S55.
8. Kirklin JW, Barratt-Boyes BG. Truncus arteriosus. In: Cardiac Surgery. 2nd ed. Edinburgh: Churchill Livingstone; 1993. p. 1140.
9. Marcelletti C, McGoon DC, Mair DD. The natural history of truncus arteriosus. Circulation 1976;54:108–111.
10. McGoon DC, Rastelli GC, Ongley PA. An operation for the correction of truncus arteriosus. JAMA 1968;205:69–73.
11. Gomes MMR, McGoon DC. Truncus arteriosus with interruption of the aortic arch: report of a case successfully repaired. Mayo Clin Proc 1971;46:40–43.
12. Honjo O, Kotani Y, Agaki T, et al. Right ventricular outflow tract reconstruction in patients with persistent truncus arteriosus—a 15-year experience in a single Japanese center. Circ J 2007;71:1776–1780.
13. Hickey EJ, McCrindle BW, Blackstone EH, et al; CHSS Pulmonary Conduit Working Group. Jugular venous valved conduit (Contegra) matches allograft performance in infant truncus arteriosus repair. Eur J Cardiothorac Surg 2008;33:890–898.
14. Konstantinov IE, Karamlou T, Blackstone EH, et al. Truncus arteriosus associated with interrupted aortic arch in 50 neonates: a Congenital Heart Surgeons Society study. Ann Thorac Surg 2006;81:214–223.
15. Rajasinghe HA, McElhinney DB, Reddy VM, et al. Long-term follow up of truncus arteriosus repaired in infancy: a 20-year experience. J Thorac Cardiovasc Surg 1997;113:869–879.
16. Ebert PA, Turley K, Stanger P, et al. Surgical treatment of truncus arteriosus in the first six months of life. Ann Surg 1984;200:451–456.
17. Thompson LD, McElhinney DB, Reddy M, et al. Neonatal repair of truncus arteriosus: continuing improvement in outcomes. Ann Thorac Surg 2001;72:391–395.
18. De Leval MR, McGoon DC, Wallace RB, et al. Management of truncal valvular regurgitation. Ann Surg 1974;180:427–432.
19. Williams JM, De Leeuw M, Black MD, et al. Factors associated with outcomes of persistent truncus arteriosus. J Am Coll Cardiol 1999;34:545–553.
20. Bove EL, Lupinetti FM, Pridjian AK. Results of a policy of primary repair of truncus arteriosus in the neonate. J Thorac Cardiovasc Surg 1993;105:1057–1066.
21. Kalavrouziotis G, Purohit M, Ciotti C, et al. Truncus arteriosus communis: early and mid-term results of early primary repair. Ann Thorac Surg 2006;82:2200–2206.
22. Perry CP. Childbirth after surgical repair of truncus arteriosus: a case report. J Reprod Med 1990;35:65–67.
23. Hoendermis ES, Drenthem W, Sollie KM, Berger RM. Severe pregnancy-induced deterioration of truncal valve regurgitation in an adolescent patient with repaired truncus arteriosus. Cardiology 2008;109:177–179.

38

Vascular Rings, Pulmonary Slings, and Other Vascular Abnormalities

SHREESHA MAIYA | SIEW YEN HO | PIERS E. F. DAUBENEY

Introduction

Tracheoesophageal compression arises by the close proximity of the heart and great vessels (aortic arch, arterial duct, right and left pulmonary arteries) to the airways and esophagus within the thorax. The true incidence is difficult to estimate, because many cases are asymptomatic, but it has been reported to comprise 1% of all cardiovascular malformations requiring surgical management. Because tracheoesophageal compression can lead to significant morbidity it should always be considered in a patient with unexplained symptoms of dyspnea (difficulty in breathing) or dysphagia (difficulty in swallowing). The vast majority of cases are diagnosed in young children; this is a rare complication in adults either with or without underlying congenital heart disease.

Complications from compression of the airways can be divided into two categories:
- Direct effect of vascular compression on the airway leading to respiratory compromise
- Secondary tracheobronchomalacia and stenoses that result from prolonged compression and degeneration of previously normal cartilage

Normal Embryogenesis

Understanding the normal development of the thoracic vascular system is critical to appreciate the problems that may arise. The aortic arch and pulmonary trunk, together with the main branches, are evolutionally related to the six pairs of arterial arches. These partially encircle the pharynx to connect the ventral aorta to the paired dorsal aortas, which are joined to the future descending aorta. For our purpose this can be simplified to an embryonic double arch system (Fig. 38-1A) as originally proposed by Edwards (see Fig. 38-1B).[1-3] Once the third paired arches have developed, the first and second paired arches disappear. The cephalic extension of the ventral and dorsal aorta beyond the fourth arch becomes the common carotid (portion of ventral aorta between third and fourth arches), internal carotid (cephalic extension of ventral aorta beyond third arch), and external carotid (third arch and cephalic extension of dorsal aorta) arteries respectively on each side. The dorsal aortas between the third and fourth arches regress. The part of the ventral aorta proximal to the fourth arch on the right becomes the brachiocephalic artery (segment D, Fig. 38-1B) and on the left it becomes the future aortic arch between the right brachiocephalic and left common carotid arteries (LCCA) (segment E, Fig. 38-1B). The fourth arch on the left side becomes the future aortic arch between the LCCA and the origin of the future left subclavian artery (LSCA) (segment F, Fig. 38-1B), and on the right it forms the origin of the future right subclavian artery (RSCA) (segment C, Fig. 38-1B). The fifth paired arches usually disappear but may persist.[4,5] The lateral portion of the left sixth arch forms the ductus arteriosus, and the medial portions of both sixth arches form the origins of the pulmonary arteries. The seventh intersegmental arteries migrate cephalad to form the future subclavian arteries (see Fig. 38-1A). Ultimately, the spiral septation of the ventral aorta, or common arterial trunk, provides for separation of the pulmonary trunk from the ascending aorta.

In normal development we observe the disappearance of segment A (see Fig. 38-1B) of the dorsal aorta and distal part of the right sixth arch while the distal part of the left sixth arch persists as the arterial duct (Fig. 38-2), thus giving rise to a left aortic arch.

Classification and Morphology of Individual Lesions (Box 38-1)

NATIVE ANATOMIC ANOMALIES

Congenital malformations of the cardiovascular system are found mainly in neonates and young infants causing either dyspnea or dysphagia, or both, depending on the site of obstruction. These may rarely present de novo in adults.

Vascular Rings
Double Aortic Arch
Double aortic arch (DAA) is the most common cause of tracheoesophageal compression, with an incidence of 46% to 76% in reports of vascular rings.[6,7] Here, persistence of segment A (see Fig. 38-1B) will result in a DAA (Fig. 38-3), completely encircling the trachea and esophagus, sometimes leading to severe obstruction. Each aortic arch gives rise to respective common carotid and subclavian arteries. The arterial duct and the descending aorta are frequently left sided. The right (posterior) arch is usually dominant, although the two arches can be of the same size. The left (anterior) arch is dominant in only approximately 20% of cases. Occasionally, the right or left arch (or a segment) can be atretic. This is more common on the left side, and it is worth remembering that these atretic segments cannot be visualized by any current imaging modalities.[8] Hence, it is sometimes difficult to differentiate the following:
1. Right arch with mirror image branching from a DAA with atresia of the segment beyond the LSCA (segment H, Fig. 38-1B)
2. Right arch with aberrant LSCA from a DAA when the atretic segment is between the LCCA and LSCA (segments F and G, Fig. 38-1B).

DAA is commonly an isolated anomaly but can be seen occasionally in patients with tetralogy of Fallot, transposition of the great arteries, cervical arch, and coarctation of the aorta.

Right Aortic Arch with Aberrant Left Subclavian Artery
Right aortic arch with aberrant left subclavian artery is the next most common cause of vascular ring (30% to 40%) and is due to the absence of the fourth arch on the left side (segments F and G, Fig. 38-1B) with persistence of segments A and H (see Fig. 38-1B). The aberrant LSCA has a retroesophageal course and forms an incomplete vascular ring if the arterial duct is right sided. However, in the presence of a left-sided arterial duct connecting the origin of the aberrant subclavian artery to the left pulmonary artery the vascular ring becomes complete (Fig. 38-4). This is usually loose, but it is tight when coming from a diverticulum of Kommerell, which is an outpouching from the distal remnant of the left aortic arch (see Fig. 38-8). The presence of the diverticulum of Kommerell is indicative of the existence of an arterial ligament (so-called DAA with atretic segment between LCCA and LSCA).[8] It is also worth remembering that the diverticulum of Kommerell can independently cause tracheoesophageal compression; hence, the symptoms might persist in some patients, despite the surgical division of the left-sided ligamentum.[9]

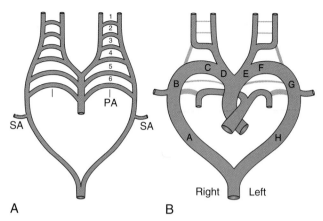

Figure 38-1 **A,** The basic pattern of the six pairs of primitive aortic arches with the position of the primary pulmonary arteries (PA) and subclavian arteries (SA) also indicated. **B,** The embryonic double-arch system is formed by the fourth arches and the dorsal aortas of both sides. The various lettered segments may persist or disappear in different configurations of the great arteries.

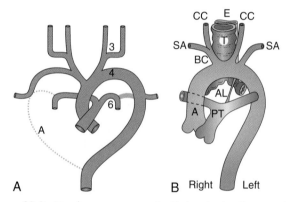

Figure 38-2 Usual arrangement. **A,** Embryologic diagram shows atresia of segment A of the double-arch pattern of Figure 38-1B and the distal portion of the sixth arch on the right side. **B,** The anatomic arrangement shows a left-sided aortic arch and arterial ligament. A, aorta; AL, arterial ligament; BC, brachiocephalic (or innominate) artery; CC, common carotid artery; E, esophagus; PT, pulmonary trunk; SA, subclavian artery; T, trachea.

The right aortic arch with aberrant LSCA and the right-sided arterial duct can occur in patients with tetralogy of Fallot with or without pulmonary atresia or a common arterial trunk.

Right Aortic Arch with Mirror Image Branching
It is worth noting that a right-sided aortic arch with mirror image branching, caused by atresia of segment H (see Fig. 38-1B), is seen in 2% to 3% of the population. The ductus arteriosus is usually left sided, arising from the left subclavian artery. A right-sided arch on its own does not produce a vascular ring, although it may do so in association with other vascular anomalies.[6] Extremely rarely, a duct may originate from a diverticulum of Kommerell and pass retroesophageally to join the left pulmonary artery leading to a tight ring obstructing the left main bronchus (Fig. 38-5).

Left Aortic Arch with Aberrant Right Subclavian Artery
A left aortic arch with aberrant right subclavian artery is found in 0.5% of the normal population and is usually an incidental finding. Usually there is a left duct and no ring. There is persistence of segment A with atresia of segment B and C (see Fig. 38-1B and Fig. 38-6). It is also found commonly in association with tetralogy of Fallot (see Chapter 43).[6] The aberrant RSCA usually takes a retroesophageal course and may cause symptomatic airway compression[10] at the level of the arch and the right subclavian artery (anteroposterior compression). Very rarely it may pass between the esophagus and trachea to cause dysphagia.

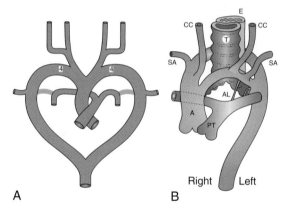

Figure 38-3 Double aortic arch. **A,** Embryologic diagram shows persistence of both fourth arches. **B,** The anatomic arrangement shows persistence of the arterial ligament on the left side only and rotation of the arches, which become anterior and posterior. Abbreviations are as for Figure 38-2.

In the presence of a right-sided arterial duct from the right subclavian artery a complete but loose vascular ring is formed (see Fig. 38-6).

Left Aortic Arch with Retroesophageal Right Descending Aorta
This is an extremely rare anomaly in which the ascending aorta and the descending aorta are on the opposite sides of the spine with the aortic arch looping posterior to the esophagus. With a right duct there can be posterior indentation of the esophagus but it is usually insufficient to cause symptoms (Fig. 38-7A). However, in the presence of an aberrant right subclavian and right duct from a diverticulum of Kommerell there can be a complete ring (see Fig. 38-7B).

Aberrant Left Brachiocephalic (Innominate) Artery
A right aortic arch with an aberrant left brachiocephalic artery (retroesophageal) and left duct can cause a loose vascular ring. Symptoms are variable depending on the extent of compression.

Cervical Arch
Very rarely a third arch component assumes the role of the definitive arch and presents as an abnormal pulsating feature in the neck, the

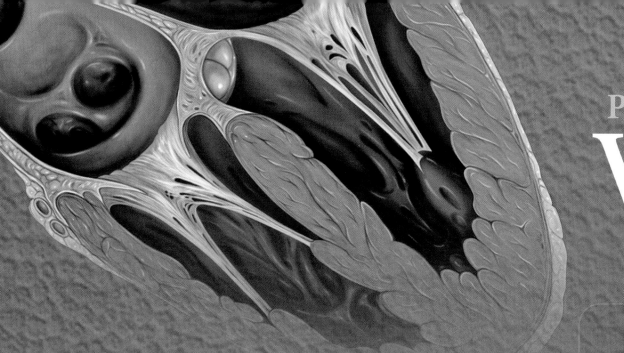

Diseases of the Tricuspid Valve

39

Ebstein Anomaly

MORGAN L. BROWN | JOSEPH A. DEARANI

Definition and Morphology

Ebstein anomaly is a malformation of the tricuspid valve and right ventricle. There is a wide variation of abnormalities that include (1) failure of tricuspid valve delamination (adherence of the leaflets to the underlying myocardium); (2) apical and posterior (downward) displacement of the functional tricuspid annulus (septal > posterior > anterior); (3) dilation of the "atrialized" portion of the right ventricle with variable degrees of hypertrophy and thinning of the wall; (4) fenestrations, redundancy, and tethering of the anterior leaflet; and (5) dilation of the right atrioventricular junction (true tricuspid annulus).

Increased degree of anatomic severity of the malformation results in a posterior and downward displacement of the hinge point of the posterior and septal leaflets in a spiral fashion below the true annulus. The tricuspid leaflets are usually bizarre and dysplastic and are tethered by short chordae and papillary muscles or attached to the underlying myocardium directly by muscular bands. Chordae may be few to absent, and leaflet fenestrations are common. There are varying degrees of delamination of all three leaflets. Although the anterior leaflet is the most delaminated, it may also be severely deformed so that the only mobile leaflet tissue is displaced into the right ventricular outflow tract. The malformed tricuspid valve is usually incompetent, but it may rarely be stenotic.

The atrialized ventricle is characteristically thinned and dilated. In addition, the entire free wall of the right ventricle, including the infundibulum, is dilated. The atrioventricular node is located at the apex of the triangle of Koch, and the conduction system is in its normal position. Atrial septal defect is common, and other associated anomalies may also be present.

Genetics and Epidemiology

The incidence of Ebstein anomaly is approximately 1 per 200,000 live births and accounts for less than 1% of all cases of congenital heart disease.[1] Maternal lithium use may be a risk factor for the development of Ebstein anomaly in the fetus.[2] In rare cases, mutation of transcription factor NKX2.5, 10p13-p14 deletion, and 1p34.3-p36.11 deletion have been described.[3-5]

Early Presentation and Management

Although medical management, including diuretics and antiarrhythmic drugs, may be used to manage some of the symptoms of heart failure and arrhythmias, eventually most patients will require operation. The utility of angiotensin-converting enzyme inhibitors in patients with Ebstein anomaly and right-sided heart failure is unknown. Observation alone may be advised for asymptomatic patients with no right-to-left shunting (acyanotic), mild cardiomegaly, and normal exercise tolerance. Most patients in New York Heart Association (NYHA) classes I and II can be managed medically.

Late Outcome

Ebstein anomaly may remain undetected until late childhood or adulthood. The oldest patient at the Mayo Clinic to undergo primary operation was 79 years of age. However, late survival of *unoperated* adult patients with Ebstein anomaly is less than expected. In a natural history study of 72 unoperated patients with Ebstein anomaly, the mean age at diagnosis was 23.9 ± 10.4 years and arrhythmias were the most common clinical presentation (51%).[6] The estimated cumulative overall survival was 89%, 76%, 53%, and 41% at 1, 10, 15, and 20 years of follow-up, respectively. Univariate predictors of cardiac-related death included cardiothoracic ratio greater than or equal to 0.65, increasing severity of tricuspid valve displacement on echocardiography, NYHA class III or IV, cyanosis, severe tricuspid regurgitation, and younger age at diagnosis. In a multivariate model, younger age at diagnosis, male gender, cardiothoracic ratio greater than or equal to 0.65, and the severity of tricuspid valve leaflet displacement on echocardiography were independent predictors of cardiac mortality.

Late Complications

Late complications in *unoperated* patients with Ebstein anomaly include right and left ventricular failure, atrial and ventricular tachyarrhythmias, and sudden death (Box 39-1). In the same natural history study just mentioned it was found that morbidity was mainly related to arrhythmia and refractory late hemodynamic deterioration.[6] On univariate analysis, the magnitude of tricuspid regurgitation, cyanosis, and NYHA class were risk factors for late deterioration.

Outpatient Assessment

The most common presenting symptom is fatigue in both older children and adults. However, other symptoms may include decreased exercise tolerance, dyspnea on exertion, and cyanosis. Palpitations, often due to paroxysmal atrial arrhythmias or premature ventricular beats, are also common.

Auscultation may demonstrate a systolic murmur of tricuspid regurgitation. Rarely, a low-intensity diastolic and presystolic murmur may be heard that results from anatomic or functional tricuspid stenosis. There is wide splitting of both the first and second heart sounds. Atrial and ventricular filling sounds are relatively common in patients with Ebstein anomaly. Summation of these gallop sounds may result from prolongation of atrioventricular conduction. The arterial and jugular venous pulse forms are usually normal but a large v wave may be seen in the jugular venous pulse. The liver may be palpably enlarged but is rarely pulsatile. Ascites and peripheral edema are rarely present.

The electrocardiogram is not diagnostic but frequently is abnormal. Complete or incomplete right bundle-branch block and right-axis deviation are typically present. On chest radiography the cardiac silhouette can vary from almost normal to the typical Ebstein configuration, which consists of a globular-shaped heart with a narrow waist similar to that seen with pericardial effusion. This appearance is produced by enlargement of the right atrium and displacement of the right ventricular outflow tract outward and upward.

Echocardiography (two-dimensional [2D] and three-dimensional [3D]) allows an accurate evaluation of the tricuspid leaflets and subvalvular apparatus (displacement, tethering, dysplasia, absence), the size of the right atrium, the size and function of the atrialized portion of the right ventricle, and the size and function of the right and left ventricles (Fig. 39-1). The main echocardiographic characteristic that differentiates

Ebstein anomaly from other forms of congenital tricuspid regurgitation is the degree of apical displacement of the septal leaflet at the crux of the heart ($\geq$0.8 cm/m^2).[7] Color flow imaging allows assessment of the site and degree of tricuspid valve regurgitation. Factors that are favorable for tricuspid valve repair include a large, mobile anterior leaflet with a free leading edge, whereas significant leaflet tethering (i.e., adherence of the edge or body of the leaflet to underlying endocardium) and the presence of tricuspid leaflet tissue in the right ventricular outflow tract make successful valve repair more difficult. Any delamination of inferior leaflet tissue is helpful, and the more septal leaflet tissue that is present, the more likely a successful repair can be obtained.

Magnetic resonance imaging (MRI) is being increasingly used in all types of patients with cardiac disease, including those with Ebstein anomaly. Functional assessment can be made including quantitative measurements of left and right ventricular size and function. Currently there is very little information available in the literature to guide therapy on this new imaging modality. We routinely perform MRI examination preoperatively and postoperatively so that we can better understand its role in the evaluation of the patient with Ebstein anomaly. At the present time we prefer echocardiography for evaluation of tricuspid valve anatomy and MRI for longitudinal assessment of right (and left) ventricular size and function.

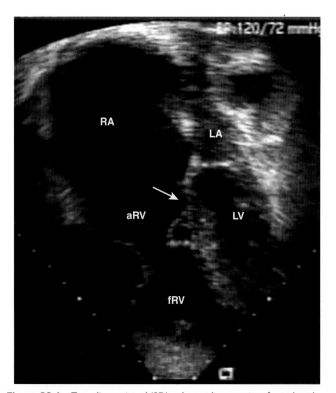

Figure 39-1   Two-dimensional (2D) echocardiogram in a four-chamber view with the apex pointing down. The *arrow* indicates the displaced tricuspid valve septal leaflet. aRV, atrialized right ventricle; fRV, functional right ventricle; LA, left atrium; LV, left ventricle; RA, right atrium.

In general, cardiac catheterization and angiography are usually not necessary after echocardiography and MRI. Hemodynamic catheterization may be required when left ventricular dysfunction is present to measure left- and right-sided pressures, especially if a bidirectional cavopulmonary shunt is being considered (see 1.5-Ventricle Approach).

Twenty-four-hour ambulatory electrocardiographic monitoring is suggested for rhythm assessment in patients with palpitations, tachycardia, or any history of arrhythmia. Invasive electrophysiologic study is performed for all patients with Ebstein anomaly who have evidence of preexcitation on an electrocardiogram or who have a history of recurrent supraventricular tachycardia, undefined wide-complex tachycardia, or syncope as aspects of their clinical presentation.

Late Management

Operation is offered when symptoms are present, when increasing cyanosis becomes evident, or if paradoxical embolism occurs. Operation is also advised if there is objective evidence of deterioration such as decreasing exercise performance by exercise testing, progressive increase in heart size on chest radiography, progressive right ventricular dilation or reduction of systolic function by echocardiography, or appearance of atrial or ventricular arrhythmias. In borderline situations the echocardiographic determination of high probability of tricuspid valve repair makes the decision to proceed earlier with operation easier. Once symptoms develop and patients progress to NYHA class III or IV, medical management has little to offer; operation then becomes the only chance for improvement (Boxes 39-2 and 39-3).

A biventricular repair is possible for the majority of patients. However, in some circumstances a 1.5 ventricle (addition of bidirectional cavopulmonary shunt) is advantageous if there is significant right ventricular dilation or dysfunction or if the resultant tricuspid valve repair has a small effective orifice. The bidirectional cavopulmonary shunt may also reduce hemodynamic stress on a more complex tricuspid valve repair because the volume of the right ventricle is decreased by 35% to 45% with superior vena caval offloading, depending on the patient's age. Cardiac transplantation is rarely indicated and is reserved for patients with severe biventricular dysfunction.

Our operative management of patients with Ebstein anomaly consists of (1) closure of any atrial septal communications; (2) correction of associated anomalies; (3) performance of any indicated antiarrhythmia procedures; (4) consideration of plication of the atrialized portion of the right ventricle; (5) reconstruction of the tricuspid valve or valve replacement (when repair is not possible); and (6) right reduction atrioplasty. Intraoperative transesophageal echocardiography is used routinely.

TRICUSPID VALVE REPAIR

In 1972, Danielson at the Mayo Clinic developed a repair that consisted of longitudinal plication of the free wall of the atrialized right ventricle (i.e., bringing the functional annulus up to true annulus), posterior tricuspid annuloplasty, and excision of redundant right atrial wall (right reduction atrioplasty).[8] The repair is based on the construction of a monocuspid valve by the use of the anterior leaflet of the tricuspid valve, which is usually enlarged in this anomaly; competency is obtained by coaptation of the anterior leaflet with the ventricular septum.[9] Whereas the basic principles of our original repair remain the same, we have frequently incorporated various modifications in the repair as numerous anatomic variants of the anomaly have been encountered. The major change was to repair the valve where it resides in the ventricle. This generally involved bringing the papillary muscle(s) that are attached to the right ventricular free wall down to the ventricular septum to facilitate monocusp coaptation with the ventricular septum and posterior annuloplasty to narrow the tricuspid annulus down to 25 mm in a 70-kg adult. Transverse right ventricular plication (i.e., bringing the acute margin toward the posterior descending coronary artery) was then selectively performed.

Our current surgical experience with Ebstein anomaly now approaches 800 consecutive patients. The early and late (over 25 years' follow-up) outcome for the first 539 patients was recently reported.[10] One hundred and eighty-two patients had initial tricuspid valve repair; however, almost one third of the total patient cohort had already undergone at least one prior cardiac operation elsewhere. Overall early mortality was 5% for the entire cohort; it was 2.3% over the past 5 years of the study (n = 143). In all patients with tricuspid valve repair, survival free from late reoperation (conditional on 30-day survival) on the tricuspid valve was 98%, 93%, 84%, 73%, and 56% at 1, 5, 10, 15, and 20 years. The independent predictors of death or reoperation on the tricuspid valve include male gender, pulmonary valve stenosis, more than moderate postoperative left ventricular dysfunction, prior cardiac procedures, and a maze procedure.

We have more recently applied the "cone reconstruction" as described by da Silva and colleagues[11] because it is a near anatomic repair and can be applied to a wide variety of anatomic abnormalities. The end result of the cone reconstruction is 360 degrees of tricuspid leaflet tissue surrounding the right atrioventricular junction, generally with a neoannulus of 25 mm in a 70-kg adult. In this approach, leaflet tissue coapts with leaflet tissue, similar to what occurs with normal tricuspid valve anatomy. In addition, the reconstructed tricuspid valve is reattached at the true tricuspid valve annulus (atrioventricular junction) so the hinge point of the valve is now in a normal anatomic location. Right ventricular plication also helps reduce the size of the enlarged right ventricle and true annulus, and it decreases tension on the numerous suture lines required for the valve repair. With the exception of some persistent right ventricular dilation and dysfunction in the early postoperative period, the cone reconstruction restores the appearance of normal tricuspid valve anatomy and function more than previously described techniques. Because this technique can be applied to the wider variety of anatomic variations encountered with Ebstein anomaly, we have adopted this repair technique, particularly when there is a septal leaflet to work with. Details of this operation are reported elsewhere (Fig. 39-2).[12]

Relative contraindications to the cone reconstruction include older age (>50 years), moderate pulmonary hypertension, significant left ventricular dysfunction (ejection fraction < 30%), complete failure of delamination of septal and inferior leaflets with poor delamination of the anterior leaflet (i.e., < 50% delamination of the anterior leaflet), severe right ventricular enlargement, and severe dilation of the right atrioventricular junction (true tricuspid annulus). In older patients, porcine bioprosthetic tricuspid valve replacement is a very good alternative.

In 2007, da Silva published his series of 40 patients who underwent the cone reconstruction.[11] In this series the operative mortality was 1 patient (2.5%). After a mean follow-up of 4 years (range, 3 months to 12 years), only 1 patient died and 2 patients required late tricuspid valve re-repair. The cone technique has the potential to cause tricuspid valve stenosis, although no patients in this initial cohort experienced this complication. Additional follow-up is required to determine if this method of repair has long-term durability.

Many others have reported their technique and results of tricuspid repair for Ebstein anomaly in older children and adults, including Carpentier, Hetzer, and Quaegebeur.[13-22] More recently, in the series by Wu and Huang, 34 consecutive patients underwent removal and reattachment of the posterior and septal leaflet with or without pericardial reconstruction of the septal leaflet.[16] There was no operative mortality, and there was only mild or no tricuspid regurgitation in all patients at hospital dismissal. At late follow-up of a mean of 25 months (range, 1 to 55 months) there was no tricuspid regurgitation in 28 patients (82%), mild regurgitation in 3 patients (9%), and moderate regurgitation in 3 patients (9%). Chen and colleagues published their results with vertical plication and valve leaflet reimplantation in 2004.[17] Twenty-five patients with a mean age of 14 years underwent tricuspid valve repair. The majority of patients did well, with good functional outcomes; however, 40% of patients had moderate-severe tricuspid regurgitation perioperatively and 3 patients required reoperation at an average follow-up of 4.1 years. Thus, tricuspid valve repair techniques continue to evolve and there is not one universal repair technique available, owing to the variations in anatomy of patients with Ebstein anomaly.

TRICUSPID VALVE REPLACEMENT

Prosthetic tricuspid valve replacement remains a good alternative for the treatment of Ebstein anomaly when valve repair is not feasible (Fig. 39-3), particularly in older patients. Bioprosthetic (porcine) valve replacement, as opposed to mechanical valve replacement, is generally preferred because of relatively good durability of the porcine bioprosthesis in the tricuspid position and the lack of need for warfarin anticoagulation.

When the tricuspid valve cannot be reconstructed and replacement is necessary, valve leaflet tissue toward the right ventricular outflow tract (which can cause right ventricular outflow tract obstruction) is excised and a prosthetic valve (usually a porcine bioprosthesis) is inserted. Importantly, the suture line is deviated to the atrial side of the atrioventricular node and membranous septum inferiorly to avoid injury to the conduction mechanism (Fig. 39-4) and cephalad to the atrioventricular groove anteriorly (junction of smooth and trabeculated portions of the atrium) to avoid injury to the right coronary artery. The coronary sinus can be left to drain into the right atrium if there is sufficient room between it and the atrioventricular node; if the distance is short, the coronary sinus can be left to drain into the right ventricle so that heart block can be avoided. The struts of the porcine bioprosthesis are oriented so that they straddle the area of the membranous septum and conduction tissue. The valve sutures are tied with the heart beating (after intracardiac communications are closed) to detect any disturbances in atrioventricular conduction.

In our experience with operation for Ebstein anomaly, we make every effort to repair rather than replace the tricuspid valve. However, we believe that bioprostheses in patients with Ebstein anomaly have greater durability in both pediatric and adult populations compared with bioprostheses in other cardiac positions.[23] We speculate that this favorable experience may be related to the relatively larger size of the bioprosthesis that can be implanted relative to patient somatic size and to the normal, low right ventricular systolic pressure after repair in patients with Ebstein anomaly. Both of these factors would tend to reduce turbulence and stress on the bioprosthesis. Short-term warfarin anticoagulation is used for 3 months. For adult patients who are chronically taking warfarin anticoagulation for other reasons and who want to potentially minimize the need for a subsequent reoperation for bioprosthetic deterioration, a mechanical valve can be considered. Importantly, mechanical valves should be avoided when there is significant right ventricular dysfunction because disc motion may not be normal, resulting in a greater propensity for valve thrombosis, even in the presence of therapeutic warfarin anticoagulation. Our algorithm for choice of tricuspid valve prostheses is given in Box 39-4.

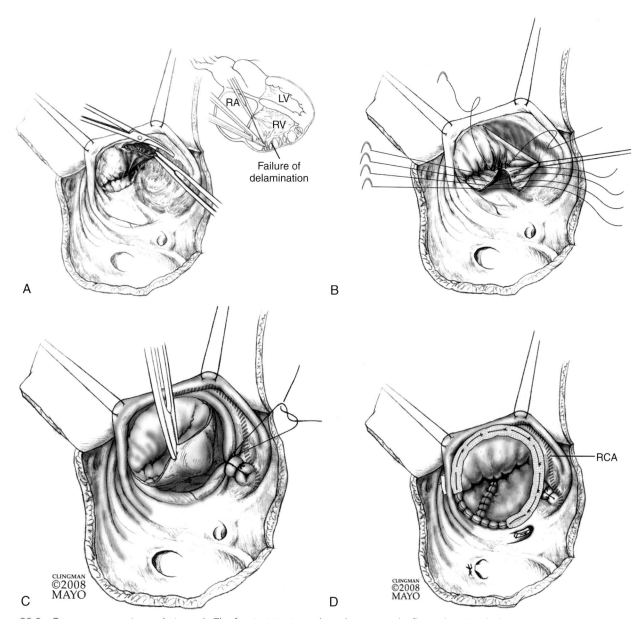

Figure 39-2 Cone reconstruction technique. **A,** The first incision is made in the anterior leaflet at the 12-o'clock position; the incision is a few millimeters away from the true annulus. The incision is extended in a clockwise fashion, and there may be a true space between the anterior leaflet and the right ventricle in this region (i.e., a normally delaminated leaflet). However, when closer to the inferior (posterior) leaflet, it is common for there to be failure of delamination (*inset*), resulting in fibrous and muscular attachments between the leaflet and myocardium. Takedown of these fibrous and muscular attachments is called a "surgical delamination." LV, left ventricle; RA, right atrium; RV, right ventricle. **B,** After all leaflets (anterior, inferior, and septal) are mobilized, the inferior leaflet is cut and rotated clockwise to meet the proximal edge of the septal leaflet. These two leaflets are approximated with interrupted 6-0 monofilament sutures to complete the cone reconstruction. **C,** After the plication or resection of the atrialized right ventricle is completed, the newly constructed tricuspid valve is then reattached at the level of the true tricuspid annulus. A plication of the inferior annulus is necessary to allow the dilated native atrioventricular junction to decrease to meet the size of the neotricuspid valve. **D,** In older children and adults, a flexible annuloplasty band is placed to reinforce the neotricuspid valve annular reconstruction. This is particularly important when there has been a significant reduction in the size of the true annulus during the course of the neotricuspid valve reconstruction. We reinforce each end of the annuloplasty band with a mattress suture backed with felt pledgets; the inferior suture typically incorporates the orifice of the coronary sinus. RCA, right coronary artery. (*Redrawn from Dearani JA, Bacha E, da Silva JP. Cone reconstruction of the tricuspid valve for Ebstein's anomaly: anatomic repair. Oper Tech Thorac Cardiovasc Surg 2008; 13;109-125.*)

1.5-VENTRICLE REPAIR

Although some use the bidirectional cavopulmonary shunt routinely, we use it selectively, and more frequently in the current era. We believe the bidirectional cavopulmonary shunt is helpful in two settings: (1) when the right ventricle is severely dilated and functioning poorly (physiologic abnormality) and (2) when a successful tricuspid valve repair has resulted in an effective valve orifice that has mild to moderate stenosis (mean gradient > 6 mm Hg) (anatomic abnormality). Because concomitant left ventricular dysfunction may be present when there is

significant right ventricular dilation and/or dysfunction, it is important to document by direct pressure measurements that the pulmonary arterial and left atrial pressures are low; otherwise, the bidirectional cavopulmonary shunt will not be feasible. If the left ventricular end-diastolic pressure is less than 15 mm Hg, the transpulmonary gradient is less than 10 mm Hg, and the mean pulmonary arterial pressures are less than 18 to 20 mm Hg, then a bidirectional cavopulmonary shunt is permissible. Even in the presence of moderate left ventricular dysfunction (ejection fraction of 35% to 40%) it is usually feasible to

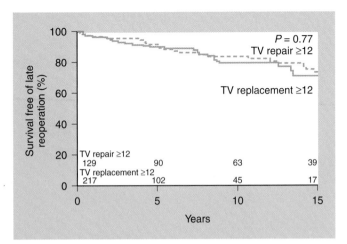

Figure 39-3   Patients 12 years of age or older who had tricuspid valve (TV) repair or replacement. This age was chosen as a cutoff because an adult-sized TV prosthesis can generally be inserted into a 12-year-old patient. In survival free from late reoperation on the TV there was no difference between repair and replacement in adult patients (≥12 years old). *(Used with permission from Brown ML, Dearani JA, Danielson GK, et al. The outcomes of operations for 539 patients with Ebstein anomaly. J Thorac Cardiovasc Surg 2008; 135:1120-1136.)*

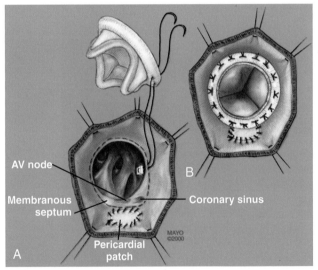

Figure 39-4   Diagrams of technique for tricuspid valve replacement in Ebstein anomaly. **A,** This diagram is a view from the right atrium. The valve suture line is placed on the atrial side of the membranous septum and atrioventricular node to avoid injury to the conduction system. When there is sufficient distance between the coronary sinus and the AV node, the coronary sinus may be left on the atrial side of the suture line. Anteriorly, the suture line is deviated cephalad to the true tricuspid annulus to avoid potential injury to the right coronary artery. Sutures are typically placed at the junction of the smooth and trabeculated portions of the atrium. **B,** The tricuspid valve prosthesis is in place, and the atrial septal defect has been closed. *(Copyrighted and used with permission of Mayo Foundation for Medical Education and Research.)*

perform a bidirectional cavopulmonary shunt in the vast majority of patients with Ebstein anomaly.

Others have suggested that the construction of a bidirectional cavopulmonary shunt may allow for less than perfect tricuspid valve repairs because it will allow for greater amounts of both tricuspid valve regurgitation or tricuspid valve stenosis.[24] In addition, it may allow patients to tolerate longer intervals between repeat tricuspid valve operations for progressive tricuspid regurgitation or failing tricuspid valve prostheses. This is due to a smaller regurgitant volume and therefore a

decreased volume load to the right ventricle. We are in agreement with these principles and rationale.

Chauvaud[18,19] and Quiñonez[25] and their colleagues have proposed that the use of a bidirectional cavopulmonary shunt may decrease operative mortality and facilitate the postoperative management of patients with severe right ventricular dysfunction. The literature suggests that the frequency of bidirectional cavopulmonary shunt application in Ebstein anomaly is increasing; in a series of 150 patients in a European registry, almost 26% underwent a 1.5-ventricle repair.[26] Whereas the early results are clearly improved, late results of a bidirectional cavopulmonary shunt in patients with Ebstein anomaly are unknown. Disadvantages of the bidirectional cavopulmonary shunt may include pulsations of the head and neck veins, facial swelling, and the development of arteriovenous fistulas in the pulmonary vasculature. In addition, the placement of this shunt compromises access to the heart from the internal jugular approach for electrophysiologic studies and for pacemaker lead placement, if needed in the future. The bidirectional cavopulmonary shunt has great appeal in the management of patients with Ebstein anomaly, particularly those with right ventricular dysfunction, but it is our belief that it should be applied selectively until the late outcomes are well described.

PLICATION OF THE ATRIALIZED RIGHT VENTRICLE

There is some controversy as to whether plication (or actual excision) of the atrialized right ventricle is necessary or even desirable. Potential advantages include (1) reduction in the size of the nonfunctional portion of the right ventricle improving the transit of blood flow through the right side of the heart; (2) reduction of compression of the left ventricle (pancake effect of the enlarged right ventricle), thus improving left ventricular function; (3) reduction of tension on the tricuspid valve repair suture lines; and (4) provision of more space for the lungs (more important in neonates). Internal forms of right ventricular plication can interrupt some coronary arterial supply to right ventricular musculature and also have the potential risk of kinking the right coronary artery. This may generate ventricular arrhythmias and compromise right and left ventricular function. The decision to plicate the atrialized right ventricle and how much to plicate are based on the anatomy encountered and the surgeon's personal philosophy. In our practice, we routinely plicate the atrialized right ventricle when (1) the right ventricle is noted to be dilated, thinned, and transparent, (2) a complex tricuspid valve repair has been performed to reduce tension on the suture lines that may be present, (3) there is marked right ventricular dilation, and (4) there is marked tricuspid annular dilation. It is important to emphasize that during the course of any plication technique there should be frequent epicardial inspection of the right coronary artery and its major branches to minimize potential compromise of it. Intraoperative echocardiography can also be helpful in identifying new regional wall motion abnormalities: inferior wall motion abnormalities of the left and right ventricles are a clue that right coronary compromise may have occurred.

HEART TRANSPLANTATION

Transplantation is an option in patients with Ebstein anomaly with severe biventricular dysfunction, that is, a left ventricular ejection fraction less than 25%. In our experience, patients with severe right ventricular dysfunction and normal to moderately depressed left ventricular function can have their defect managed with a conventional operation, which now includes placement of a bidirectional cavopulmonary shunt at the time of tricuspid repair or replacement. Other patients with Ebstein anomaly that should be considered for transplantation are those with significant left ventricular dilation and dysfunction and those with severe mitral regurgitation with significant left ventricular dysfunction. Hemodynamic cardiac catheterization to ascertain left-sided filling pressures and pulmonary arterial pressures may be helpful in this group of patients when trying to determine the feasibility of conventional operation versus transplantation. At the Mayo Clinic, we have been able to achieve successful biventricular or 1.5-ventricular repair in the vast majority of adult patients with Ebstein anomaly, including those with significant left ventricular dysfunction.[27] Transplantation should be considered only in the most severe cases, which is rare in the current era.

Atrial Arrhythmias and Sudden Cardiac Death

Atrial tachyarrhythmias are common and become more likely as time goes on owing to progressive atrial dilation. In addition, 1% to 2% of patients have atrioventricular nodal reentrant tachycardia.[28] Accessory conduction pathways or Wolff-Parkinson-White syndrome is found in approximately 15% of patients. Right ventricular arrhythmias may also be present in patients with end-stage heart failure, and sudden death has been reported in patients with Ebstein anomaly.

A right reduction atrioplasty is performed routinely at the time of atriotomy closure because there is almost always significant right atrial dilation. In all circumstances of right atriotomy closure we avoid placing suture lines in the crista terminalis, which may produce the substrate for atrial tachyarrhythmias.[29]

Atrial fibrillation and atrial flutter are the most frequent atrial tachyarrhythmias that occur in Ebstein anomaly. For most patients, the cut and sew lesions of a Cox maze III right-sided procedure have been successful. With the availability of newer devices (radiofrequency ablation and cryoablation), the time taken to perform the complete biatrial Cox maze III procedure is shortened significantly. Consequently, we perform a biatrial maze procedure more commonly at the present time for all diagnoses associated with atrial arrhythmias. This is particularly important if there is continuous atrial fibrillation, left atrial dilation, or concomitant mitral regurgitation. It is our practice to follow the lesions in both atria that have been previously described.[30,31] In addition, if there is evidence of atrial flutter, we add a line of ablation to the right atrial isthmus, that is, the posterolateral tricuspid annulus to the coronary sinus to the inferior vena cava. We also make an effort to close the left atrial appendage.

For patients with accessory conduction pathway (i.e., Wolff-Parkinson-White syndrome), mapping and ablation is performed preoperatively in all patients in the catheterization laboratory. Rarely is intraoperative mapping and ablation required at the time of repair of Ebstein anomaly in the current era.

Pregnancy

Most patients with Ebstein anomaly will reach childbearing age, and many patients with Ebstein anomaly have successfully carried full-term pregnancies. In our cohort of patients the miscarriage rate for our patients was 24% (32%).[32] This is comparable with the miscarriage rate in the general population of 14% to 26%. Drenthen and associates reported a miscarriage rate for women with Ebstein anomaly of 18% and that 3.9% of 127 pregnancies were complicated by arrhythmias and 3.1% by heart failure.[33] The incidence of congenital heart disease in children of a parent with Ebstein anomaly is estimated at approximately 4%, which is significantly higher than the expected incidence of 0.75% in the general population.[32,33] These estimates of miscarriage and incidence of congenital heart disease are similar to those of children born to parents with aortic stenosis, pulmonary stenosis, or ventricular septal defect.[33]

Level of Follow-Up, Endocarditis Prophylaxis, and Exercise

Patients with Ebstein anomaly need to be observed regularly by a cardiologist who has expertise in congenital heart disease.[34] Prophylaxis for endocarditis is recommended in all cases.

Physical activity recommendations have been summarized by Task Force 1 on Congenital Heart Disease.[35] Patients with mild Ebstein anomaly, nearly normal heart size, and no arrhythmias can participate in all sports. Athletes with severe Ebstein anomaly are precluded from sports unless the anomaly has been optimally repaired, the heart size is nearly normal, the atrial septum is intact, and no history of arrhythmias exists.[35] In general, adults can participate in recreational sports if asymptomatic.[34]

In a recent study of our patients at the Mayo Clinic, the functional outcome after operation for Ebstein anomaly was good and reported exercise tolerance was comparable to patients' peers without heart disease.[32] In a small subset of these patients, formal exercise testing was conducted.[36] There was improvement in the exercise tolerance after operation, but this improvement was believed to be a result of the elimination of the right-to-left shunt at the atrial level rather than due to improvement in ventricular function. Late reoperation, rehospitalization, and atrial tachyarrhythmias continue to be problematic in operated patients with a freedom from rehospitalization for cardiac causes including reoperation of 91%, 79%, 68%, 53%, and 35% at 1, 5, 10, 15, and 20 years, respectively.[32] Thus, improved control of atrial arrhythmias and further improvements in the durability of tricuspid valve repair and replacement may lead to improved quality of life in patients with Ebstein anomaly.

REFERENCES

1. Attenhofer-Jost CH, Connolly HM, Dearani JA, et al. Ebstein's anomaly. Circulation 2007;115:277–285.
2. Cohen LS, Friedman JM, Jefferson JW, et al. A reevaluation of risk of in utero exposure to lithium. JAMA 1994;271:146–150.
3. Benson DW, Silberbach GM, Kavanaugh-McHugh A, et al. Mutations in the cardiac transcription factor NKX2.5 affect diverse cardiac developmental pathways. J Clin Invest 1999;104:1567–1573.
4. Yatsenko SA, Yatsenko AN, Szigeti K, et al. Interstitial deletion of 10p and atrial septal defect in DiGeorge 2 syndrome. Clin Genet 2004;66:128–136.
5. Yang H, Lee CL, Young DC, et al. A rare case of interstitial del(1)(p34.3p36.11) diagnosed prenatally. Fetal Pediatr Pathol 2004;23:251–255.
6. Attie F, Rosas M, Rijlaarsdam M, et al. The adult patient with Ebstein anomaly: outcome in 72 unoperated patients. Medicine (Baltimore) 2000;79:27–36.
7. Seward JB. Ebstein's anomaly: ultrasound imaging and hemodynamic evaluation. Echocardiography 1993;10:641–664.
8. Danielson GK, Maloney JD, Devloo REA. Surgical repair of Ebstein's anomaly. Mayo Clin Proc 1979;54:185–192.
9. Dearani JA, O'Leary PW, Danielson GK. Surgical treatment of Ebstein's malformation: state of the art in 2006. Cardiol Young 2006;16:12–20.
10. Brown ML, Dearani JA, Danielson GK, et al. The outcomes of operations for 539 patients with Ebstein anomaly. J Thorac Cardiovasc Surg 2008;135:1120–1136.
11. da Silva JP, Baumgratz FJ, Fonseca L, et al. The cone reconstruction of the tricuspid valve in Ebstein's anomaly: the operation: early and midterm results. J Thorac Cardiovasc Surg 2007;133:215–223.
12. Dearani JA, Bacha E, da Silva JP. Cone reconstruction of the tricuspid valve for Ebstein's anomaly: anatomic repair. Oper Tech Thorac Cardiovasc Surg 2008;13:109–125.
13. Carpentier A, Chauvaud S, Macé L, et al. A new reconstructive operation for Ebstein's anomaly of the tricuspid valve. J Thorac Cardiovasc Surg 1998;96:92–101.
14. Hetzer R, Nagdyman N, Ewart P, et al. A modified repair technique for tricuspid incompetence in Ebstein's anomaly. J Thorac Cardiovasc Surg 1998;115:857–868.

15. Quaegebeur JM, Sreeram N, Fraser AG, et al. Surgery for Ebstein's anomaly the clinical and echocardiographic evaluation of a new technique. J Am Coll Cardiol 1991;17:722–728.

16. Wu Q, Huang Z. A new procedure for Ebstein's anomaly. Ann Thorac Surg 2004;77:470–776.

17. Chen JM, Mosca RS, Altmann K, et al. Early and medium-term results for repair of Ebstein anomaly. J Thorac Cardiovasc Surg 2004;127:990–999.

18. Chauvaud S, Fuzellier JF, Berrebi A, et al. Bi-directional cavopulmonary shunt associated with ventriculo and valvuloplasty in Ebstein's anomaly: benefits in high risk patients. Eur J Cardiothorac Surg 1998;13:514–519.

19. Chauvaud S. Ebstein's malformation: surgical treatment and results. J Thorac Cardiovasc Surg 2000;48:220–223.

20. Hancock Friesen CL, Chen R, Howlett JG, et al. Posterior annular plication: tricuspid valve repair in Ebstein's anomaly. Ann Thorac Surg 2004;77:2167–2171.

21. van Son JAM, Kinzel P, Mohr FW. Pericardial patch augmentation of anterior tricuspid leaflet in Ebstein's anomaly. Ann Thorac Surg 1998;66:1831–1832.

22. Vargas FJ, Mengo G, Granja MA, et al. Tricuspid annuloplasty and ventricular plication for Ebstein's malformation. Ann Thorac Surg 1998;65:1755–1757.

23. Kiziltan HT, Theodoro DA, Warnes CA, et al. Late results of bioprosthetic tricuspid valve replacement in Ebstein's anomaly. Ann Thorac Surg 1998;66:1539–1545.

24. Marianeschi SM, McElhinney DB, Reddy VM, et al. Alternative approach to the repair of Ebstein's malformation: intracardiac repair with ventricular unloading. Ann Thorac Surg 1998;66:1546–1550.

25. Quiñonez LG, Dearani JA, Puga FJ, et al. Results of the 1.5-ventricle repair for Ebstein anomaly and the failing right ventricle. J Thorac Cardiovasc Surg 2007;133:1303–1310.

26. Sarris GE, Giannopoulos NM, Tsoutsinos AJ, et al. Results of surgery for Ebstein anomaly: a multicenter study from the European Congenital Heart Surgeons Association. J Thorac Cardiovasc Surg 2006;132:50–57.

27. Brown ML, Dearani JA, Danielson GK, et al. Effect of operation for Ebstein anomaly on left ventricular function. Am J Cardiol 2008;102:1724–1727.

28. Khositseth A, Danielson GK, Dearani JA, et al. Supraventricular tachyarrhythmias in Ebstein anomaly: management and outcome. J Thorac Cardiovasc Surg 2004;128:826–833.

29. Durongpisitkul K, Porter CJ, Cetta F, et al. Predictors of early- and late-onset supraventricular tachyarrhythmias after Fontan operation. Circulation 1998;98:1099.

30. Cox JL, Jaquiss RD, Schuessler RB, Boineau JP. Modification of the maze procedure for atrial flutter and atrial fibrillation: II. Surgical technique of the maze III procedure. J Thorac Cardiovasc Surg 1995;110:485–495.

31. Mavroudis C, Deal BJ, Back CL, et al. Arrhythmia surgery in patients with and without congenital heart disease. Ann Thorac Surg 2008;86:857–868.

32. Brown ML, Dearani JA, Danielson GK, et al. Functional status after operation for Ebstein anomaly: the Mayo Clinic experience. J Am Coll Cardiol 2008;52:460–466.

33. Drenthen W, Pieper PG, Roos-Hesselink JW, et al., ZAHARA Investigators. Outcome of pregnancy in women with congenital heart disease: a literature review. J Am Coll Cardiol 2007;49:2303–2311.

34. Deanfield J, Thaulow E, Warnes C, et al. The Task Force on the Management of Grown Up Heart Disease of the European Society of Cardiology: Management of grown up congenital heart disease. Eur Heart J 2003;24:1035–1084.

35. Graham Jr TP, Bricker JT, James FW, Strong WB. 26th Bethesda conference: recommendations for competition in athletes with cardiovascular abnormalities. Task Force 1: congenital heart disease. J Am Coll Cardiol 1994;24:867.

36. MacLellan-Tobert SG, Driscoll DJ, Mottram CD, et al. Exercise tolerance in patients with Ebstein's anomaly. J Am Coll Cardiol 1997;29:1615–1622.

40 Tricuspid Stenosis and Regurgitation

NASER M. AMMASH

Definitions and Morphology

Isolated congenital anomalies of the tricuspid valve (TV) are rare structural malformations that involve one or more components of the TV apparatus and result in tricuspid stenosis (TS) and/or tricuspid regurgitation (TR). The TV components normally include the annulus, three leaflets, and three papillary muscles. When viewed from the ventricular aspect the annulus is shaped like a reversed D and decreases in area by 30% during systole. The septal leaflet lies against the ventricular septum and is apically displaced from the mitral annulus. The posterior, also known as inferior or mural, leaflet makes up the largest portion of the annulus and lies against the inferior wall of the right ventricle. The anterior (anterosuperior) leaflet is the largest and most mobile and extends anteriorly from the right ventricular infundibulum to the inferolateral wall. Each of the papillary muscles has chordal attachments to adjacent leaflets.

TRICUSPID STENOSIS

Isolated congenital malformations of the TV apparatus leading to TS are extremely rare. These include an underdeveloped annulus, shortened chordae, hypoplastic leaflets, underdeveloped fused commissures, parachute deformity (all the chordae arise from a single papillary muscle), and a supravalvular ring at the level of the annulus or midportion of the leaflets. In addition, abnormal persistence of the right venous valve can result in a double-chambered right atrium, also known as cor triatriatum dexter, a condition in which the proximal chamber receives all venous return and the distal chamber contains the TV (Fig. 40-1). This perforated partition within the right atrium mimics the clinical presentation of TS.

TRICUSPID REGURGITATION

Tricuspid regurgitation in adults is usually functional in origin and not due to a congenital deformity of the TV apparatus. Functional TR occurs in the presence of right ventricular dilation and/or dysfunction commonly due to pulmonary hypertension or cardiomyopathy that could be either dilated, ischemic, restrictive, or stress induced. Under those conditions TR is attributed to the dilation of the tricuspid annulus and asymmetrical alterations of the right ventricle geometry that lead to tethering of the TV leaflets and incomplete leaflet coaptation. On the other hand, Ebstein anomaly (see Chapter 39) is the most common cause of congenital TR, followed by TV dysplasia, in which anatomic malformations can include hypoplastic papillary muscles, asymmetrically foreshortened tendinous chordae tethering the leaflets, and underdeveloped, atypical leaflets that prevent the valve from closing completely during systole (Fig. 40-2A, B). Partial or complete agenesis of the valvular tissue is often referred to as an unguarded tricuspid orifice. Both malformations have been associated with pulmonary stenosis and atresia (see Chapters 41 and 44). Other congenital anomalies leading to TR include (1) right-sided congenital partial absence of the pericardium, (2) papillary muscle rupture in the fetus or neonate, (3) the presence of bileaflet TV or cleft of the anterior leaflet (with or without atrial or ventricular septal defects) and (4) Uhl anomaly (best defined as aplasia or hypoplasia of right ventricular myocardium, transforming it into a thin, passive, unexcitable conduit). The latter condition resembles right ventricular dysplasia, in which right ventricular myocardium is progressively replaced by adipose and fibrous tissue; this condition is often associated with ventricular arrhythmia and sudden death. Congenital deformities of the TV leading to TR can be mistaken for acquired diseases of the TV, including TV prolapse, endocarditis, TV involvement by rheumatic or carcinoid heart disease, or collagen vascular diseases.[1] TR has also been reported after chest radiation, penetrating or blunt chest trauma, right ventricular endomyocardial biopsy and pacemaker implantation due to vegetations, leaflet adhesion, deformity, or perforation or secondary to atrioventricular discordance with asynchronous ventricular pacing. In an observational study of 248 patients who had echocardiograms before and after placement of permanent pacemaker and implantable cardioverter defibrillator, TR worsened by at least 1 grade in 24.2%. Patients with an implantable cardioverter defibrillator had a higher rate of TR worsening compared with patients with a pacemaker (32.4% vs. 20.1%; $P < .05$).[2] TR has also been seen in patients with chronic atrial fibrillation due to related atrial remodeling and after repair of ventricular septal defect due to fixation of the septal leaflet to the ventricular septum at the point where it was closed with a pericardial patch.[3] Drugs such as cabergoline (a dopamine receptor-2 agonist used to treat prolactinomas), fenfluramine-phentermine, and ergotamine, which are serotonin-like or can potentiate the effect of circulating serotonin, can lead to valvular injury. In such injury the septal leaflet of the TV becomes thickened and variably fixed to the septum whereas the anterior leaflet exhibits reduced mobility, resulting in loss of coaptation and TR.[4]

Genetics and Epidemiology

Little is known about the genetic predisposition to congenital TS and TR. In 1991 Sharland and associates[5] reported that of 450 cases of structural heart disease diagnosed prenatally 22 (4.9%) were of TV dysplasia and 16 (3.6%) were of Ebstein anomaly.

Review of the surgical pathologic analyses of 363 TVs excised and replaced at the Mayo Clinic between 1963 and 1987 demonstrated that 74% were purely regurgitant, 23% were stenotic and regurgitant, and only 2% were purely stenotic. Rheumatic disease was the most common cause (53%), followed by congenital disease (26%). Female patients accounted for 66% of all TVs excised. Male patients accounted for 61% of the congenital disorders, suggesting a male predominance. This study, however, included both isolated TV anomalies and those associated with other congenital defects and excluded patients who had TV repair. A subgroup analysis of 45 patients with isolated TV defects showed that Ebstein anomaly was by far the most common (39 patients), followed by TV dysplasia (4 patients) and congenital TS (1 patient). Interestingly, the relative frequency of rheumatic disease decreased from 79% during 1963 to 1967 to 24% during 1983 to 1987. However, the frequency of all congenital TV anomalies requiring replacement increased from 7% to 53% during the same time interval.[6]

Early Presentation and Management

Most isolated congenital TV anomalies, especially those leading to TS, present in infancy and childhood and require early intervention. In comparison, congenital TV anomalies resulting in TR can be tolerated for many years and may remain unrecognized until adulthood. Some cases may be severe and require early surgical repair.

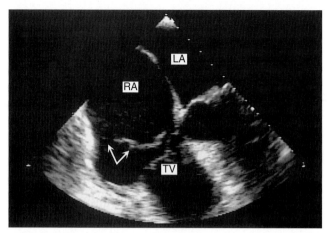

Figure 40-1   Echocardiogram (from the apical four-chamber view) of a 46-year-old man with cor triatriatum dexter. The perforate membrane (*arrows*) within the right atrium (RA) divides it into two chambers, with the distal chamber including the tricuspid valve (TV). LA, left atrium.

Although the initial mortality rates for TV replacement were as high as 30% to 50%, rates have since improved to 7% to 17%.[7] Rizzoli and associates[8] reported a 50% 30-day mortality rate for patients of all age groups with congenital TV diseases. In most cases, death was related to low cardiac output. The interest in repairing the regurgitant TV has increased lately. The three basic reconstructive techniques are the Kay plication, in which the posterior (also known as inferior or mural) leaflet is plicated, converting the TV into a functionally bicuspid valve; the de Vega annuloplasty, which uses purse-string sutures to narrow the annulus along the anterior (anterosuperior) and posterior

(inferior or mural) leaflets; and the Carpentier ring annuloplasty, in which a semiflexible ring is placed along the anterior and posterior aspects of the annulus. McElhinney and associates[9] described the possible application of such a repair in children with TV dysplasia. He described two children with this anomaly, primarily with tethering of the septal leaflet due to abnormally short chordae, who underwent operation at 9 and 11 years of age. The chordae that were tethering the septal leaflet were augmented by interposing appropriate lengths of expanded polytetrafluoroethylene suture and performing commissural annuloplasty. Each patient was reported to be asymptomatic 33 and 42 months after operation. TR resulting from a cleft of the anterior leaflet can be repaired with simple suture and annuloplasty. For patients with Uhl anomaly, various surgical procedures have been performed, including Potts and Glenn anastomoses. None was successful in prolonging life. Cardiac transplantation appears to be the only option for these patients.

Late Outcome

SURVIVAL AND FUNCTIONAL STATUS

When TR is acquired due to pulmonary hypertension, or cardiomyopathy, it may be a marker of worse prognosis as it reflects the severity of the underlying disease.[10] Similarly, TR after heart transplantation has also been associated with increased risk of graft failure.[11] However, because isolated congenital TS and TR (excluding Ebstein anomaly) are extremely rare, their natural history is not well defined. Depending on the severity of the TR, survival into adulthood is not uncommon for patients with conditions such as Uhl anomaly, cleft anterior TV leaflet, or acquired TR. Case reports documenting adults with other congenital deformities of the TV, including TV dysplasia, unguarded tricuspid orifice, and cor triatriatum dexter, have been published.[1] The surgical

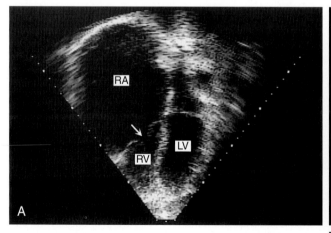

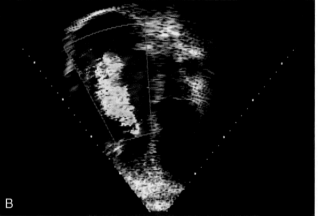

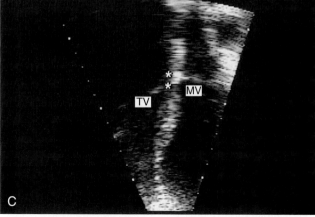

Figure 40-2   Echocardiograms (from the apical four-chamber view) of a 34-year-old man with tricuspid valve dysplasia. **A,** Underdeveloped leaflets tethered to the septum and free wall of the right ventricle (RV), with secondary incomplete coaptation (*arrow*) and tricuspid regurgitation. **B,** As seen on color flow Doppler imaging. **C,** Displacement index of the septal leaflet of the tricuspid valve (TV) of 8 mm or 6 mm/m^2, consistent with non-Ebstein anomaly of the tricuspid valve. LV, left ventricle; MV, mitral valve; RA, right atrium.

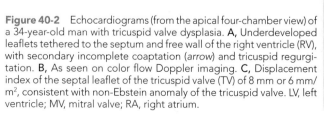

results in these isolated cases are encouraging. However, there are a few reports that focus exclusively on late outcome after medical or surgical treatment of such conditions. Rizzoli and associates[8] reported poorer survival for patients with congenital anomalies (22% survival rate at 5 years) than for the entire group (54% 5-year survival rate). Most survivors report considerable improvement in exercise tolerance after operation, and their New York Heart Association (NYHA) functional classification improves.

Interestingly, although it had been suggested that biologic valves in the TV position have a lower rate of degeneration than valves in the mitral and aortic positions, this study[8] demonstrated that survival did not significantly differ between patients with mechanical prostheses and those with biologic prostheses in the TV position—a reflection, perhaps, of the newer, low-profile mechanical valve with improved hemodynamics, low gradient, reduced turbulence, and a lower thrombosis rate.

Because TV annuloplasty is not commonly performed as an isolated procedure in patients with the rare forms of isolated congenital TV disease (other than Ebstein anomaly), its long-term results are poorly established. When TV annuloplasty is performed for functional TR, the freedom from important TV regurgitation is 94% at 10 years. However, this does not accurately reflect the experience of patients with congenital deformities of the TV. Data presented in Chapter 39 on Ebstein anomaly may be more relevant. Nevertheless, it is believed that intermediate and long-term survival and functional status of any patient having a TV operation are compromised by the preoperative presence of edema, pulmonary hypertension, and right ventricular dysfunction.

LATE COMPLICATIONS AFTER OPERATION

Late complications are summarized in Box 40-1.

BOX 40-1   COMPLICATIONS AFTER OPERATION FOR TRICUSPID STENOSIS OR TRICUSPID REGURGITATION

- Premature death—as high as 19% for isolated TR. Most related to advanced right ventricular dysfunction or arrhythmia. Rarely due to endocarditis or valve thrombosis. Risk factors include earlier date of operation, older age at operation, NYHA functional class, previous valve surgery.
- Complete heart block—as high as 28% after TV replacement in adults. Risk increases with concomitant mitral valve operation. Incidence is reduced by keeping sutures superficial.
- Valve thrombosis—rare in the absence of coagulation abnormalities. Incidence increases with age and is believed to have sharply decreased with the new, low-profile, bileaflet mechanical prosthesis.
- Thromboembolism—systemic (in association with an intra-atrial shunt) and pulmonary embolism rarely have been reported (< 1%)
- Prosthetic valve dysfunction—can be subclinical, identified only on echocardiography
- Anticoagulation-related hemorrhage—incidence increases with age but has declined due to increased awareness.
- Endocarditis—prosthetic valves are at high risk for endocarditis, requiring periodic counseling and strict prophylaxis.
- Right ventricular failure—predominantly related to preoperative right ventricular dysfunction or myocardial preservation at operation. This is a major determinant of prognosis.
- Atrial arrhythmias—related to right atrial hypertension and enlargement or secondary to surgical scars
- Ventricular arrhythmias—caused by right ventricular dysfunction or dysplasia
- Recurrent TR—after TV repair, more than moderate TR is noted in 0% to 12%, necessitating reoperation in 6%.
- Reoperation—predominantly due to operation early in life or to bioprosthetic valve degeneration; rarely due to valve thrombosis; uncommon after repair (< 5%)

Outpatient Assessment

UNOPERATED PATIENTS

Isolated congenital TS is rare and presents exclusively in infancy and childhood. Therefore, whenever TS is suspected clinically or noted on echocardiography in an adult it is almost always the result of acquired heart disease, such as rheumatic or carcinoid heart disease, and less commonly the result of an indwelling central venous catheter or pacemaker wire. In addition, a primary or metastatic right atrial tumor, such as a myxoma (see Chapter 62), renal cell carcinoma and even a right atrial thrombus, can mimic TS by obstructing the TV inflow and possibly precipitating syncope.

Patients with congenital anomalies of the TV or surrounding structures leading to TR can survive well into adulthood with minimal or no symptoms. The typical presentation of adults with TR includes dyspnea, exercise intolerance, palpitation, atrial fibrillation, and, less often, heart failure. The presence of cyanosis should alert one to the possibility of concomitant atrial shunt such as a patent foramen ovale or atrial septal defect with a secondary right-to-left shunt. Furthermore, the presence of hypoalbuminemia should alert one to the possibility of protein-losing enteropathy. Acquired diseases of the TV and right ventricle always should be considered when evaluating patients with TR. These include prolapse, endocarditis, trauma, irradiation, rheumatic or carcinoid heart disease, collagen vascular diseases, use of drugs such as fenfluramine-phentermine and ergotamine preparations, right ventricular dilation, right ventricular dysfunction, or pulmonary hypertension (functional TR).[1,4] Many such conditions present similarly and thus can mimic congenital anomalies of the TV, including Ebstein anomaly (see Chapter 39). An adequate diagnostic evaluation includes the following:
- Careful history and physical examination to assess the severity of TR and to exclude the more common acquired causes of TR (Box 40-2)
- Electrocardiography
- Chest radiography
- Transthoracic echocardiography (see Table 40-1 and Box 40-3)

BOX 40-2   CLINICAL EXAMINATION OF PATIENTS WITH TRICUSPID VALVE REGURGITATION

- Patients are usually acyanotic unless there is a patent foramen ovale or (less commonly) an atrial septal defect. Under these circumstances the raised right atrial pressure related to TR generates a right-to-left shunt at the atrial level.
- Increased venous pressure with large v wave in the neck veins related to severe TR. However, at times the right atrium is so enlarged that it absorbs the regurgitant volume. Other signs of right-sided heart failure (edema, hepatomegaly) are not uncommon.
- Right ventricular heave is common secondary to right ventricular overload. However, the right ventricle is not palpable in patients with a Uhl anomaly.
- Normal first heart sound. Split of the first heart sound is suggestive of Ebstein anomaly. Reduced heart sounds suggest Uhl anomaly.
- Normal or persistent split of the second heart sound. A loud pulmonary closure sound suggests pulmonary hypertension.
- Right ventricle third heart sound due to right ventricular dysfunction
- Early systolic click and ejection murmur suggestive of pulmonary stenosis
- Midsystolic click, mid to late systolic murmur suggestive of TV or mitral valve prolapse
- Systolic murmur of TR is typically diamond shaped if mild and holosystolic if severe in the left lower sternal border. It increases with inspiration. This distinguishes it from mitral regurgitation and ventricular septal defect. If the TR is very severe, the murmur may be brief or absent.
- Diastolic flow rumble if torrential TR or mixed TS and TR
- Pulsating liver in severe TR

	TABLE 40-1 Clinical and Echocardiographic Features of Common Non-Ebstein Anomaly Tricuspid Valve Abnormalities		
TV Abnormalities	*Clinical Findings*		*Echocardiographic Features*
Rheumatic valvular disease	Rheumatic fever, MV involvement		Focal chordal thickening, diffuse fibrous thickening, diffuse marginal or leaflet thickening of the MV or TV, commissural fusions
Tricuspid valve prolapse	Mitral valve prolapse (5%-52% of patients), especially in older women (F:M ratio 3:1); aortic valve prolapse (rare); dilated cardiomyopathy; pulmonary hypertension; hypertensive heart disease; pectus deformity, scoliosis, and straight-back syndrome on chest radiography		Myxomatous degeneration of the TV or MV, with prolapse of one or more leaflets beyond the annular ring (parasternal or apical view); elongated, redundant chordae; large leaflets; TV annular dilation
TV endocarditis	Pneumonia, use of intravenous drugs, habitual alcoholism, immunodeficiency state		TV vegetations, ruptured chordae, valvular indentation
Traumatic TR	Chest trauma, nonpenetrating within 1 month to 37 years; indwelling catheter, wire, etc.		Ruptured TV tensor apparatus (chordae, papillary muscle), leaflet perforation
RV dysplasia, Uhl anomaly	Ventricular tachycardia (in RV dysplasia), family history (in RV dysplasia), reduced intensity of heart sounds, low QRS amplitude on electrocardiography		RV free wall aneurysm, focal RV thinning, RV dysfunction, abnormal septal motion
Tricuspid annular dilation	RV infarction, pulmonary hypertension (any cause), cardiomyopathy, chronic atrial fibrillation (in the elderly)		TV annular dilation, RV or LV enlargement and dysfunction, biatrial enlargement
TV dysplasia, unguarded	Remote history of heart murmur, pulmonary stenosis		Hypoplastic, diminutive or absent leaflets; tricuspid orifice underdeveloped, small papillary muscle; shortened chordae with tethering
Carcinoid heart disease	Gastrointestinal hypermotility; bronchospasm, flushing; pulmonary valve involvement		Thickened margins, chordae; retracted, tethered leaflets; endocardial carcinoid plaques on TV or in RV; pulmonary valve involvement
Other: connective tissue disease, radiation therapy, ergotism or use of diet drugs	History of lupus or rheumatoid arthritis; previous chest irradiation; or history of intake of ergot alkaloid preparations or anorexigens (e.g., fenfluramine-phentermine)		Leaflet contraction, thickening; shortened chordae; or aortic valve or MV involvement

Adapted from Ammash NM, Warnes CA, Connolly HM et al. Mimics of Ebstein's anomaly. Am Heart J 1997; 134:508-513.
LV, left ventricle or ventricular; MV, mitral valve; RV, right ventricle or ventricular; TR, tricuspid regurgitation; TV, tricuspid valve.

BOX 40-3 ROLE OF ECHOCARDIOGRAPHY IN THE EVALUATION OF PATIENTS WITH TRICUSPID REGURGITATION

- Defines the anatomic deformity leading to TR (congenital or acquired)
- Assesses the hemodynamic burden: right atrial size and, more importantly, right ventricular size and function, including visual assessment, dP/dt, or index of myocardial dysfunction.
- Measures the pulmonary artery systolic pressure using the modified Bernoulli equation: Pulmonary artery systolic pressure = $4(TRvelocity)^2$ + estimated right atrial pressure.
- Provides qualitative assessment of the severity of the TR based on three approaches:
  - TR jet size and hepatic veins on color Doppler imaging. Although peripheral intravenous saline injections can enhance the visualization of the TR jet on color Doppler examination, visual assessment of the TR jet size in the right atrium tends to underestimate an eccentric jet and overestimate central ones. It is therefore best used in combination with assessment of hepatic veins and vena cava. Marked dilation of the inferior vena cava (>2 cm) and hepatic veins with systolic flow reversal reflects severe TR.
  - Signal shape of the TR jet on continuous wave Doppler imaging. The presence of a triangular signal with early peak and decline of TR velocity demonstrates a large v-wave notch, which represents equalization of the right atrial and right ventricular pressures with severe TR.
  - Signal intensity of the TR jet on continuous wave Doppler imaging
- TV annulus size of more than 21 mm/m² or 40 mm or tenting area of the TV of more than 8 cm² is indicative of severe TR.
- Direct measurement of the regurgitant volume, fraction, and effective regurgitant orifice by any of the following methods:
  - Continuity equation
  - Proximal isovelocity surface area method with regurgitant volume of more than 45 mL or effective regurgitant orifice > 0.4 cm² indicative of severe TR
  - Vena contracta—the width of the TR jet within the regurgitant orifice is measured from the apical window with standard color scale. Vena contracta greater than 7 mm is suggestive of severe TR.

dP/dt, rate of pressure rise; TR, tricuspid regurgitation.

Role of Echocardiography

A comprehensive echocardiographic examination, especially when supported by clinical findings, is the procedure of choice for the diagnosis of congenital and acquired TV anomalies (see Table 40-1). The two-dimensional (2D) echocardiographic features of the TV are best seen on the parasternal long-axis view with medial angulation and on the parasternal short-axis view. Both views allow visualization of the right ventricular inflow, including the anterior (anterosuperior) and septal leaflets of the TV (especially the leading edges) and their attachment to the free wall and septum. In addition, both views often help in the assessment of right atrial size and right ventricular size and function. The posterior (inferior or mural) leaflet of the TV, however, is best visualized by the subcostal sagittal view with lateral angulation. To exclude the diagnosis of Ebstein anomaly, an apical four-chamber view is needed to evaluate the internal cardiac crux and measure the degree of apical displacement of the septal leaflet of the TV. We have previously demonstrated that an apical displacement index of less than 8 mm/m² is suggestive of other congenital and acquired diseases of the TV (see Fig. 40-2C).[1]

Transesophageal echocardiography or three dimensional (3D) transthoracic echocardiography should be considered if optimal anatomic and hemodynamic data are not provided by the precordial 2D echocardiographic examination. 2D transthoracic echocardiography typically shows the TV in its long axis. However, short-axis views of the TV leaflets could be difficult to obtain. Real-time 3D echocardiography overcomes this limitation and facilitates obtaining a short-axis view (en face view) of the TV. This new technique could be very helpful in assessing the precise TV pathology leading to TR thus giving it an incremental value over the 2D technique.[12,13]

The crucial role of echocardiography in the assessment of anatomic and hemodynamic disturbances in congenital and acquired TR has limited the role of invasive cardiac catheterization and other imaging techniques except in patients with suspected Uhl anomaly or right ventricular dysplasia. In these patients, ultrafast computed tomography of the heart and magnetic resonance imaging are more often superior to echocardiography. In addition, early opacification of the inferior vena cava or hepatic veins on first-pass contrast-study using either technique could be used to assess the severity of TR.

OPERATED PATIENTS

Most adult patients with a previously repaired or replaced congenital deformity of the TV lead unrestricted lives with excellent functional capacity, often requiring no additional operation. However, late complications (see Box 40-1) do occur and account for up to 11% of late deaths. Periodic evaluation is therefore recommended. A history of new-onset dyspnea, palpitation, or fatigue should prompt further evaluation for residual or recurrent TR, prosthetic valve stenosis or thrombosis, right ventricular dysfunction, and dysrhythmias. Occasionally, an exercise stress test or Holter monitoring is performed to assess functional capacity and exercise tolerance and to exclude exercise-induced arrhythmias in patients with unexplained dyspnea and weakness. A normal cardiac response to exercise as measured by functional aerobic capacity and oxygen consumption can be suggestive of a noncardiac cause.

On examination, operated patients may have a residual right ventricular heave if they have persistent right ventricular dysfunction or enlargement. No murmurs (systolic or diastolic) should be noted in the absence of residual TR or prosthetic valve dysfunction. Leg edema and hepatomegaly can be a sign of right ventricular or prosthetic valve dysfunction. Periodic chest radiography permits detection of an increasing cardiothoracic ratio and should prompt further evaluation to exclude prosthetic valve dysfunction, residual TR, or right ventricular dysfunction and enlargement. At times, cardiomegaly can be secondary to atrial enlargement due to chronic atrial arrhythmias such as atrial fibrillation.

Periodic echocardiographic assessment after TV repair or replacement is recommended even in asymptomatic patients because subclinical prosthetic valve dysfunction is not uncommon.[14] This examination should include assessment of atrial size and right ventricular size and function, including the myocardial performance index, the rate of pressure rise, and assessment of the repaired or replaced TV. Assessment of the TV should include direct visualization of the valve as well as Doppler imaging to assess the gradient and pressure half-time across the valve, which allows calculation of the valve area.

A repaired TV typically causes a mean diastolic gradient of 1 to 3 mm Hg and often demonstrates mild to moderate residual regurgitation. The normal ranges for Doppler hemodynamics of various TV prostheses have been established by Connolly and coworkers.[15] In a normally functioning TV prosthesis, the mean gradient is 3 ± 1 mm Hg regardless of the valve used. However, the pressure half-time varies according to the model. For example, the pressure half-time is markedly lower for a St. Jude prosthesis than for a heterograft prosthesis (108 ± 32 vs. 146 ± 39 ms).[15] If the findings on transthoracic echocardiography are suggestive of prosthetic valve dysfunction, then 3D transthoracic/transesophageal echocardiography and/or a fluoroscopic examination should be considered.

In a recent study performed to identify echocardiographic parameters related to postoperative clinical outcome in patients who had surgery for severe TR after mitral valve surgery, echocardiographic examinations were performed before and 15 ± 7 months after surgery. Only systolic tricuspid annulus velocity was found to be associated with postoperative clinical outcome (favorable vs. unfavorable postoperative clinical outcome 12.9 ± 2.1 vs. 9.7 ± 1.7 cm/s, $P < .05$). For systolic tricuspid annulus velocity of less than 9.5 cm/s, the sensitivity, specificity, and positive and negative predictive values for predicting an unfavorable postoperative clinical outcome were 67%, 100%, 100%, and 75%, respectively.[16]

▨ Late Management Options

LATE INTERVENTION

There are no standard guidelines on the timing of operation for patients with congenital TV anomalies. Unoperated patients with severe isolated congenital TR should be considered for TV repair or replacement if they have one of the following indications:
- Symptoms of dyspnea, palpitation, or fatigue thought to be due to TR
- A patent foramen ovale causing resting or exercise-induced oxygen desaturation

- Progressive cardiomegaly on chest radiography or right ventricular enlargement on echocardiography
- Echocardiographic signs of early right ventricular dysfunction
- Poorly tolerated, uncontrolled atrial arrhythmias
- Deteriorating functional capacity
- Bacteriologically proven TV endocarditis not responding to antibiotics or complicated by pulmonary embolism

Congenital anomalies and acquired diseases of the TV can be repaired with good results depending on the etiology and severity of TV deformity with TV annuloplasty with or without chordal extension being the most favorable approach.[1,17,18] Earlier reports from the Cleveland Clinic suggest worse outcome after TV replacement compared with TV repair.[19] The 8-year survival rate was 50% in 401 adults who had undergone TV repair or replacement, with an increased risk of death or adverse clinical events for patients with TV replacement (relative risk 3.3) or concomitant coronary artery bypass grafting (relative risk 1.5). Other studies demonstrated similar unfavorable outcome after TV replacement. The in-hospital mortality rate of patients with either congenital or acquired TV disease undergoing TV replacement was reported at 16% to 19%.[20,21] The predictors of postoperative death include anemia, right ventricular dysfunction, and anasarca but not the type of prosthesis implanted.[20-22] A study by Van Nooten and colleagues[20] demonstrated an in-hospital mortality rate of 16% in 146 adults who had TV replacement. The 5-year survival rate was 74%, with no difference between patients with bioprosthetic and those with bileaflet mechanical valves. Nakano and coworkers[14] reported a 10-year experience with the Carpentier-Edwards pericardial prosthesis implanted in the TV position in 66 patients whose average age was 53 years, with aortic or mitral valve replacement in 46; the actuarial survival rate was $75 \pm 6\%$ at 9 years. Echocardiography demonstrated subclinical prosthetic valve dysfunction in 35%, with a mean gradient of more than 5 mm Hg, or more than moderate TR. Kawano and associates[23] reported on 23 patients who had 25 St. Jude TV replacements at a mean age of 40 years. The overall survival rate, including in-hospital death, was 83% at 10 and 15 years. The clinical and echocardiographic factors associated with poorer long-term prognosis include coronary disease, congestive heart failure, primary pulmonary disease, NYHA functional class, and evidence of left or right ventricular dysfunction on the preoperative echocardiogram. Therefore recent data suggest better outcome which still appears to be largely dependent on the cause of the TV dysfunction.

When TV replacement was performed in 20 patients with isolated acquired TR caused by endocarditis, trauma, endomyocardial fibrosis, constrictive pericarditis, or prior heart transplantation, Maleszka reported one perioperative mortality (5%). Two patients underwent a "re-do" operation during follow-up, one due to prosthetic endocarditis and one after thrombosis of a mechanical prosthesis. There was no structural deterioration of biological prostheses and no bleeding due to anticoagulation with mechanical prostheses. Among the surviving patients, 13 were in NYHA class I and one was in class II/III at the time of follow up.[24] Cardarelli more recently suggested the use of a stentless aortic root placed inverted in the tricuspid annulus with a reported hospital survival of 100% in 8 patients and no TV stenosis or insufficiency by echocardiography after a mean follow-up of 17.2 months (1 to 38 months). The potential advantages of this stentless prosthesis over other prostheses include minimization of blood contact with nonbiologic surfaces, preservation of annular motion, freedom from anticoagulation, and a theoretical lower rate of calcification.[25]

Although TV repair can be accomplished with excellent results in patients with flail leaflets, the durability of TV repair, in absence of flail segments, may be limited.[26] Recurrent or residual TR after annuloplasty has been associated with the degree of preoperative TV leaflet tethering as well as postoperative left ventricular function and right ventricular function and pressure. These factors could identify patients at risk for repair failure, and therefore such individuals may require development of additional surgical strategies to improve results of TV repair.[27] More recently, De Bonis and colleagues described a new surgical approach for TV repair, which consists of stitching together the central part of the free edges of the leaflets producing a "clover-shaped" valve. This novel technique in combination with annuloplasty was performed in 14 patients (mean age 57 ± 17 years) with severe tricuspid regurgitation. The hospital mortality was 7.1% (1/14). At follow-up extending to 22 months (mean 12 ± 6.3), all survivors were asymptomatic. At the last echocardiogram TR was absent or mild in 13 patients and moderate in 1. Mean tricuspid valve area and gradient were 4.2 ± 0.4 cm^2 and 2.7 ± 1.4 mm Hg, respectively.[28] When TV annuloplasty is performed with concomitant disease of the mitral or aortic valve due to functional, rheumatic or degenerative disease, the hospital and late mortality rates were noted to be 8.1% and 23.3%, respectively, in a study by Bernal and colleagues.[29] The predictors of hospital mortality were biologic prosthesis, renal insufficiency, time of cardiopulmonary bypass, and use of inotropic drugs. Predictors of late mortality were age older than 60 years, left ventricular ejection fraction less than 0.50, and NYHA functional class IV. At 12 years, the actuarial survival rate was 50.5% ± 6.1%, and the actuarial curve free from reoperation was 75.7% ± 7.3%. The actuarial curve for freedom from valve-related complication was 39.0% ± 6.3% at 11 years.

In patients with TR due to blunt chest trauma, a simple and effective method of choice is the de Vega tricuspid annuloplasty with excellent surgical results.[30] However, if the structural integrity of the TV is very distorted as seen after orthotopic cardiac transplantation due to accumulated injury from repeated endomyocardial biopsies, the durability of repair in this setting was shown to be suboptimal. Replacement with a bioprosthesis was found to be durable and relieved symptoms of heart failure associated with TR in the majority of patients.[31] When TV replacement is contemplated, the decision of mechanical versus bioprosthetic valve must be discussed thoroughly with the patient, cardiologist, and surgeon. The issue of chronic anticoagulation is important in women of childbearing age because of the concern about warfarin embryopathy.

In patients undergoing TV replacement it would be reasonable to place prophylactic epicardial pacing leads given the possibility of postoperative heart block and the need to avoid placement of an endocardial lead across the TV prosthesis. Alternatively, the TV prosthesis can be placed below the coronary sinus ostium, allowing the future use of a coronary sinus lead to provide ventricular pacing if heart block develops. Finally, in patients who already have a pacemaker at the time of their TV replacement, or needing a pacemaker at the time of surgical repair, moving that lead to the exterior of the TV prosthesis and allowing it to pass between two pledgeted sutures is recommended.

There is less experience with surgical repair of TS because organic involvement of the TV is uncommon. Pande and associates reported their experience with TV valvuloplasty (commissurotomy with or without deVega annuloplasty) in 37 patients. There were significant reductions in peak and mean tricuspid gradients and right ventricular systolic pressure in both groups. There was no postoperative death but less residual TR in patients who underwent commissurotomy and annuloplasty, and therefore they recommended supporting the tricuspid annulus with annuloplasty in patients with organic tricuspid valve disease and no dilation of the annulus if annular shortening is less than 30%.[32]

LATE RE-INTERVENTION

Although most patients undergoing TV operation show improvement in their functional capacity and exercise tolerance, re-intervention (see Box 40-1) after any kind of TV operation is not uncommon. The probability of remaining free of reoperation was 90%, 66%, and 52% at 5, 10, and 15 years, respectively, in the experience of Rizzoli and coworkers.[8] The rate of mechanical valve dysfunction was 2.2% per patient-year, compared with 4.7% per patient-year for biologic valves.

Valve thrombosis occurs even with the newer, low-profile, bileaflet mechanical valve. The incidence of such an event in the TV position has been reported to be as high as 20% for the St. Jude prosthesis and 11% for the Starr-Edwards prosthesis[33]; and although this could be treated successfully with thrombolytic agents such as streptokinase, reoperation for valve thrombosis has been reported to be 2.8% per patient-year, with reoperation occurring at a mean interval of 9.5 years.[23]

The reoperation rate for bioprosthetic valve dysfunction is very low in the first few years after implantation. Rizzoli and coworkers[8] demonstrated that the cumulative failure rate increased after the seventh postoperative year. Late re-intervention for prosthetic valve regurgitation is uncommon in the absence of endocarditis or an iatrogenic cause such as pacemaker-induced TV regurgitation. The rate of biologic valve re-replacement was approximately 5% or less per patient year.[14]

Arrhythmia and Sudden Cardiac Death

Atrial arrhythmia, especially atrial fibrillation and flutter, in association with congenital TV anomalies can reduce the quality of life and be the source of considerable morbidity and mortality, even after surgical intervention. In our experience, the incidence of arrhythmia decreases by approximately 30% after surgical repair. The surgical scars and residual atrial enlargement continue to provide the nidus for such electrical instability. Asymptomatic atrial arrhythmias have been noted in our experience, suggesting the need for periodic Holter monitoring because of the associated increased risk of stroke, heart failure, and death. Treatment includes anticoagulation as well as rate or rhythm control using pharmacologic agents or catheter-based treatments. Although rhythm control improves exercise tolerance and may preserve ventricular function, its beneficial effect on mortality is not yet proven.

A concomitant right-sided maze procedure has been suggested as a way to eliminate or reduce the incidence of atrial arrhythmia after surgical repair. Initial experience at the Mayo Clinic in 18 congenital patients, including 15 with Ebstein anomaly, 2 with congenital TR, and 1 with an atrial septal defect, with atrial fibrillation demonstrated no operative deaths.[34] At 8-month follow-up, all patients were in NYHA functional class I or II. One patient had a permanent pacemaker placed for chronotropic incompetence, and recurrent atrial flutter or fibrillation occurred in only 3 patients.

Ventricular arrhythmia and sudden cardiac death associated with congenital TV disease are almost always secondary to underlying right ventricular dysplasia or right ventricular dysfunction, resulting from chronic volume overload or intraventricular conduction delay manifested by prolonged QRS complex on electrocardiography. Therefore, every effort should be made to preserve right ventricular function, including early operation, especially when early signs of dysfunction are noted on noninvasive testing or ventricular arrhythmias are detected. Treatment of these arrhythmias should be considered even in asymptomatic patients if ventricular dysfunction is documented. The use of antiarrhythmic medications or devices is guided by the severity of the symptoms and right ventricular dysfunction.

Pregnancy, Exercise, and Endocarditis Prophylaxis

Isolated cases of successful pregnancy in patients with congenital TS or TR, and even Uhl anomaly, have been reported.[35] When pregnancy is being considered by such patients, information gathered from a comprehensive history, physical examination, echocardiogram, and exercise stress testing should be used to evaluate the risk of pregnancy or exercise. The major concerns are that the hemodynamic changes associated with pregnancy, including increased heart rate and blood volume, lead to a decreased diastolic filling time, an increase in right atrial pressure, and, as a result, worsening of the gradient in patients with TS and lowering of the cardiac output. Similarly, the increase in blood volume leads to worsening TR without increasing the stroke volume, and thus could precipitate heart failure.

Common sense leads one to believe that patients who have any of the previously mentioned indications for surgical repair should be counseled against pregnancy because of the risk of heart failure and arrhythmia. Patients with mild or moderate TS should be considered for an exercise stress echocardiogram to evaluate the gradient across the TV with exercise and to assess functional capacity. If uncontrolled heart failure develops in a pregnant patient with TS, open-heart operation or percutaneous balloon valvuloplasty should be considered.

The latter has been performed successfully in pregnant patients with TS predominantly of rheumatic origin.

In the presence of TR, pregnancy may be contemplated in well-compensated patients with less than severe regurgitation, no marked right ventricular enlargement, normal right ventricular function, and preserved functional capacity (>80% of predicted) on exercise stress testing, with no exercise-induced serious arrhythmia. Similar guidelines can be followed for patients seeking advice about exercise activity. All pregnant patients should be offered fetal echocardiography.

In the absence of any history of endocarditis, or prior heart transplantation, patients with isolated TR and/or TS due to congenital or acquired heart disease do not need prophylaxis against endocarditis for dental or surgical procedures. Endocarditis prophylaxis is recommended for dental procedures in patients with prior history of endocarditis or after prosthetic TV replacement and in patients who had undergone TV repair using an annuloplasty ring in the presence residual regurgitation that is in the vicinity of the prosthetic ring.

REFERENCES

1. Ammash NM, Warnes CA, Connolly HM, et al. Mimics of Ebstein's anomaly. Am Heart J 1997;134:508–513.
2. Kim JB, Spevack DM, Tunick PA, et al. The effect of transvenous pacemaker and implantable cardioverter defibrillator lead placement on tricuspid valve function: an observational study. J Am Soc Echocardiogr 2008;21:284–287.
3. Totsugawa T, Kuinose M, Tsushima Y, et al. Sliding tricuspid valvuloplasty for severe tricuspid regurgitation after corrective surgery of a ventricular septal defect. Gen Thorac Cardiovasc Surg 2007;55:222–224.
4. Connolly HM, Crary JL, McGoon MD, et al. Valvular heart disease associated with fenfluramine-phentermine. N Engl J Med 1997;337:581–588.
5. Sharland GK, Chita SK, Allan LD. Tricuspid valve dysplasia or displacement in intrauterine life. J Am Coll Cardiol 1991;17:944–949.
6. Hauck AJ, Freeman DP, Ackermann DM, et al. Surgical pathology of the tricuspid valve: a study of 363 cases spanning 25 years. Mayo Clin Proc 1988;63:851–863.
7. Ratnatunga CP, Edwards MB, Dore CJ, Taylor KM. Tricuspid valve replacement: UK Heart Valve Registry mid-term results comparing mechanical and biological prostheses. Ann Thorac Surg 1998;66:1940–1947.
8. Rizzoli G, De Perini L, Bottio T, et al. Prosthetic replacement of the tricuspid valve: biological or mechanical? Ann Thorac Surg 1998;66(Suppl. 6):S62–S67.
9. McElhinney DB, Silverman NH, Brook MM, et al. Asymmetrically short tendinous cords causing congenital tricuspid regurgitation: improved understanding of tricuspid valvar dysplasia in the era of color flow echocardiography. Cardiol Young 1999;9:300–304.
10. Behm CZ, Nath J, Foster E. Clinical correlates and mortality of hemodynamically significant tricuspid regurgitation. J Heart Valve Dis 2004;13:784–789.
11. Ben Sivarajan V, Chrisant MR, Ittenbach RF, et al. Prevalence and risk factors for tricuspid valve regurgitation after pediatric heart transplantation. J Heart Lung Transplant 2008;27:494–500.
12. Pothineni KR, Duncan K, Yelamanchili P, et al. Live/real time three-dimensional transthoracic echocardiographic assessment of tricuspid valve pathology: incremental value over the two-dimensional technique. Echocardiography 2007;24:541–552.
13. Sugeng L, Weinert L, Lang RM. Real-time 3-dimensional color Doppler flow of mitral and tricuspid regurgitation: feasibility and initial quantitative comparison with 2-dimensional methods. J Am Soc Echocardiogr 2007;20:1050–1057.
14. Nakano K, Eishi K, Kosakai Y, et al. Ten-year experience with the Carpentier-Edwards pericardial xenograft in the tricuspid position. J Thorac Cardiovasc Surg 1996;111:605–612.
15. Connolly HM, Miller FA, Taylor CL, et al. Doppler hemodynamic profiles of 82 clinically and echocardiographically normal tricuspid valve prostheses. Circulation 1993;88:2722–2727.
16. Kwon DA, Park JS, Chang HJ, et al. Prediction of outcome in patients undergoing surgery for severe tricuspid regurgitation following mitral valve surgery and role of tricuspid annular systolic velocity. Am J Cardiol 2006;98:659–661.
17. Katogi T, Aeba R, Ito T, et al. Surgical management of isolated congenital tricuspid regurgitation. Ann Thorac Surg 1998;66:1571–1574.
18. van Son JA, Danielson GK, Schaff HV, Miller FA. Traumatic tricuspid valve insufficiency: experience in thirteen patients. J Thorac Cardiovasc Surg 1994;108:893–898.
19. Bajzer CT, Stewart WJ, Cosgrove DM, et al. Tricuspid valve surgery and intraoperative echocardiography: factors affecting survival, clinical outcome, and echocardiographic success. J Am Coll Cardiol 1998;32:1023–1031.
20. Van Nooten GJ, Caes F, Taeymans Y, et al. Tricuspid valve replacement: postoperative and long-term results. J Thorac Cardiovasc Surg 1995;110:672–679.
21. Scully HE, Armstrong CS. Tricuspid valve replacement: fifteen years of experience with mechanical prostheses and bioprostheses. J Thorac Cardiovasc Surg 1995;109:1035–1041.
22. Nagel E, Stuber M, Hess OM. Importance of the right ventricle in valvular heart disease. Eur Heart J 1996;17:829–836.
23. Kawano H, Oda T, Fukunaga S, et al. Tricuspid valve replacement with the St. Jude Medical valve: 19 years of experience. Eur J Cardiothorac Surg 2000;18:565–569.
24. Maleszka A, Kleikamp G, Koerfer R. Tricuspid valve replacement: clinical long-term results for acquired isolated tricuspid valve regurgitation. J Heart Valve Dis 2004;13:957–961.
25. Cardarelli MG, Gammie JS, Brown JM, et al. A novel approach to tricuspid valve replacement: the upside down stentless aortic bioprosthesis. Ann Thorac Surg 2005;80:507–510.
26. Messika-Zeitoun D, Thomson H, Bellamy M, et al. Medical and surgical outcome of tricuspid regurgitation caused by flail leaflets. J Thorac Cardiovasc Surg 2004;128:296–302.
27. Fukuda S, Gillinov AM, McCarthy PM, et al. Determinants of recurrent or residual functional tricuspid regurgitation after tricuspid annuloplasty. Circulation 2006;114(Suppl. 1): I582–I587.
28. De Bonis M, Lapenna E, La Canna G, et al. A novel technique for correction of severe tricuspid valve regurgitation due to complex lesions. Eur J Cardiothorac Surg 2004;25:760–765.
29. Bernal JM, Gutierrez-Morlote J, Llorca J, et al. Tricuspid valve repair: an old disease, a modern experience. Ann Thorac Surg 2004;78:2069–74; discussion 2074–2075.
30. Bara C, Zhang R, Haverich A. De Vega annuloplasty for tricuspid valve repair in posttraumatic tricuspid insufficiency—16 years experience. Int J Cardiol 2008;126:e61–e62.
31. Badiwala MV, Rao V. Tricuspid valve replacement after cardiac transplantation. Curr Opin Cardiol 2007;22:123–127.
32. Pande S, Agarwal SK, Majumdar G, et al. Valvuloplasty in the treatment of rheumatic tricuspid disease. Asian Cardiovasc Thorac Ann 2008;16:107–111.
33. Vander Veer Jr JB, Rhyneer GS, Hodam RP, Kloster FE. Obstruction of tricuspid ball-valve prostheses. Circulation 1971;43(Suppl. 5): I62–I67.
34. Theodoro DA, Danielson GK, Porter CJ, Warnes CA. Right-sided maze procedure for right atrial arrhythmias in congenital heart disease. Ann Thorac Surg 1998;65:149–153 discussion 153–154.
35. Chuah SY, Hughes-Nurse J, Rowlands DB. A successful pregnancy in a patient with congenital tricuspid stenosis and a patent oval foramen. Int J Cardiol 1992;34:112–114.

Diseases of the Right Ventricular Outflow Tract

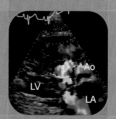

41

Pulmonary Stenosis

ANNIE DORE

Definition and Morphology

Pulmonary valvular stenosis is usually an isolated congenital anomaly and occurs in 7% to 10% of patients with congenital heart disease. It can sometimes be associated with other congenital heart defects such as atrial septal defect or peripheral pulmonary artery stenosis. It is the most common form of right-sided obstruction and results from fusion of the valve leaflets. The pulmonary valve appears conical or dome shaped with a narrow opening at its apex; the leaflets are fused, and in adults calcifications may be present. The valve is sometimes called dysplastic when the leaflets are very thick, but there is no fusion of the cusps. Rarely, pulmonary valve stenosis is due to rheumatic inflammation or carcinoid involvement. Pulmonary stenosis may be associated with various genetic or chromosomal disorders, the most common being Noonan, Williams, and Alagille syndromes. The functional consequence of pulmonary stenosis is obstruction to the ejection of blood from the right ventricle leading to an increase in right ventricular pressure. Right ventricular output is maintained by the development of right ventricular hypertrophy, which may sustain a large pressure gradient across the pulmonary valve for many years without symptoms, the development of right ventricular dilation, or a reduction in cardiac output.

Early Presentation and Management

Severe pulmonary stenosis in neonates is frequently associated with a hypoplastic right ventricular cavity and may be fatal without rapid intervention. The main clinical symptom is cyanosis due to right-to-left shunting through a patent foramen ovale caused by increased right-sided pressures. The diagnosis of severe pulmonary valvular stenosis can be made by echocardiography in the neonatal unit. Balloon dilation of the pulmonary valve is the procedure of choice to relieve the obstruction. Pulmonary valvotomy or systemic to pulmonary arterial shunt may be necessary if there is underdevelopment of the right ventricle, the pulmonary valve annulus, or the pulmonary artery branches.

Clinical presentation in childhood depends on the severity of the obstruction and the degree of hypoplasia of the right ventricle. Most children are asymptomatic, and pulmonary stenosis is often discovered during routine examination. When symptoms are present, children experience exertional symptoms: dyspnea, fatigue, mild cyanosis, chest pain, or syncope. Mild pulmonary stenosis has a favorable course. Relief of the obstruction is indicated for children with moderate to severe stenosis, even in the absence of symptoms. The severity of the obstruction on echocardiography is classified by the level of the maximal Doppler-derived systolic pressure gradient across the pulmonary valve (Table 41-1).

Late Outcome

SURVIVAL AND FUNCTIONAL STATUS

Pulmonary valve stenosis is generally better tolerated than aortic stenosis and is associated with a more benign course. Today, survival into adolescence and adulthood is the rule. Hayes and associates,[1] in the Second Natural History Study of Congenital Heart Defects, reported a probability of survival similar to that of the general population among 592 patients with different degrees of obstruction who were managed either medically or surgically and observed for more than 15 years. In that series, unoperated adults with trivial stenosis were asymptomatic and had no significant progression of the obstruction with time. For those with a peak systolic gradient between 25 and 49 mm Hg at initial heart catheterization there was an approximately 20% chance of eventually needing an intervention, whereas most patients with a peak systolic gradient greater than 50 mm Hg ultimately required an intervention. Children with severe pulmonary stenosis will usually have had a valvotomy (surgical or balloon). Kopecky and colleagues[2] reported a normal life expectancy over a 20- to 30-year period for 191 hospital survivors who underwent repair at age 21 years or younger between 1956 and 1967. Most patients, operated on or not, are thus asymptomatic and in New York Heart Association (NYHA) functional class I to II when they reach adulthood.

Late Complications

Obstruction to the ejection of blood from the right ventricle leads to an increase in right-sided pressures and to secondary right ventricular hypertrophy. The right ventricular hypertrophy may be particularly noticeable in the infundibular region, producing dynamic narrowing of the outflow tract and contributing to an increase in the degree of obstruction. With time, such patients may present with decreased exercise tolerance, dyspnea, and signs of right ventricular failure. Right ventricular failure is the most common mode of death in unoperated patients with moderate to severe obstruction and generally occurs after the fourth decade. Supraventricular arrhythmias (atrial fibrillation or flutter) may precipitate symptoms of right ventricular failure. Bacterial endocarditis is a rare complication. Complications after pulmonary valvotomy (surgical or balloon) include pulmonary regurgitation with right ventricular dilation, residual valvular or infundibular obstruction, supraventricular or ventricular arrhythmias, and sudden death (Box 41-1).

Outpatient Assessment (Box 41-2)

THE UNOPERATED ADULT

Pulmonary stenosis may be found during a routine examination because adults with mild to moderate obstruction are asymptomatic. Some patients are referred because of enlarged pulmonary arteries detected on chest radiography or because a murmur was heard. Moderate to severe obstruction can be associated with:

- The development of right ventricular hypertrophy
- Symptoms such as decreased exercise tolerance, dyspnea, fatigue, syncope, chest pain, and palpitations
- Mild cyanosis and clubbing in patients with severe obstruction, due to right-to-left shunting through a foramen ovale or an atrial septal defect

Physical Examination

Physical examination includes assessment of:

- A prominent jugular a wave due to a forceful right atrial contraction, which is essential to fill the hypertrophied, noncompliant right ventricle.
- A right ventricular lift
- A systolic thrill along the left sternal border

TABLE 41-1	Pulmonary Stenosis: Severity of the Obstruction	
Maximal Doppler-Derived Systolic Pressure	*Right Ventricular Systolic Pressure (mm Hg)*	*Transvalvular Pressure Gradient (mm Hg)*
Trivial	<25	<50
Mild	25-49	50-74
Moderate	50-79	75-100
Severe or critical	>80	>100

BOX 41-1   COMPLICATIONS

Not Operated
- Subvalvular dynamic obstruction
- Right ventricular heart failure
- Arrhythmias
- Sudden death

Operated
- Pulmonary regurgitation
- Right ventricular dilation
- Right ventricular heart failure
- Arrhythmias
- Sudden death

- A normal first heart sound
- A soft and delayed pulmonary component of the second heart sound due to prolonged ejection time
- Further delayed splitting of the second heart sound (when the pulmonary component is audible) with increasing obstruction
- A fourth heart sound that may be present
- A systolic ejection click at the upper left sternal edge (produced by sudden opening of the valve) that is louder during expiration (may not be present in severe obstruction, when the cusps remain immobile)
- A harsh, crescendo-decrescendo systolic ejection murmur heard best at the upper left sternal border, which radiates to the back and may be augmented by inspiration. With increasing obstruction, the murmur lengthens and peaks later in systole.

Physical signs suggestive of severe obstruction are summarized in Box 41-3.

Electrocardiography

There may be right-axis deviation, right ventricular hypertrophy, and right atrial enlargement with moderate to severe pulmonary stenosis. The electrocardiogram is usually normal in the presence of mild obstruction.

BOX 41-2   ASSESSMENT

- Clinical assessment
- Oximetry
- Electrocardiography
- Chest radiography
- Echocardiography
- Magnetic resonance imaging
- Cardiac catheterization

BOX 41-3   PHYSICAL SIGNS SUGGESTIVE OF SEVERE OBSTRUCTION IN PULMONARY STENOSIS

- Cyanosis and clubbing
- Widely split S_2
- Reduced or absent P_2
- Short S_1-ejection click interval
- Long systolic ejection murmur
- Peak of murmur late in systole

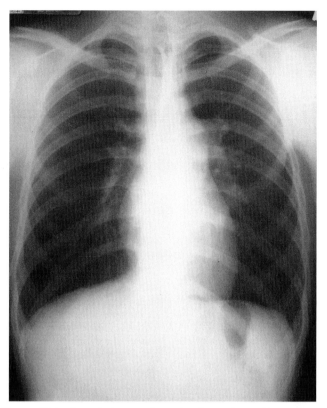

Figure 41-1 Frontal chest radiograph of a patient with moderate stenosis showing dilation of the left pulmonary artery. Heart size and lung vascularity are normal.

Chest Radiography

The most striking feature is a prominent main pulmonary artery due to dilation of the pulmonary trunk and left pulmonary artery (Fig. 41-1). The physics and the direction of the jet dispersion may be the reason for the asymmetric dilation of the left and right pulmonary arteries, although such dilation may occur in patients with mild or even trivial pulmonary stenosis.

Heart size and pulmonary vascular markings are normal in patients with mild to moderate obstruction. In patients with severe stenosis, right atrial and ventricular enlargement and decreased pulmonary vascular markings may be seen. Pulmonary valve calcification may occasionally be present.

Echocardiography

Echocardiography is the diagnostic method of choice. It allows for visualization of the valve anatomy and evaluation of the hemodynamic repercussions of the stenosis.

The valve is more difficult to visualize in adults than in children but may appear thickened with a dome-shaped deformity in systole. Nishimura and associates[3] studied the morphology of the pulmonary valve by echocardiography in 325 patients with various degrees of stenosis and detected doming in 31%, leaflet thickening in 24%, and calcifications in 1% to 2%.

Continuous wave Doppler imaging allows estimation of the transvalvular gradient and must be performed in the parasternal, apical, and subcostal views to ensure the recording of the maximal jet velocity (Fig. 41-2). The modified Bernoulli equation is used to derive the maximal instantaneous Doppler pulmonary valve gradient (gradient in mm Hg = 4 × squared peak Doppler velocity across the pulmonary valve in meters/second). Contrary to aortic valvular stenosis there is a fairly good correlation between the maximal Doppler-derived systolic pulmonary gradient and the catheter-derived peak-to-peak gradient because the pressures are lower in amplitude in the pulmonary artery than in the aorta and the dP/dt is slightly different on the right side.[4] For this reason, most centers employ the maximal Doppler-derived gradient for

Figure 41-2 Continuous wave Doppler assessment across the pulmonary valve, showing a maximal velocity of 3.6 m/s, corresponding to a maximal systolic gradient of 52 mm Hg.

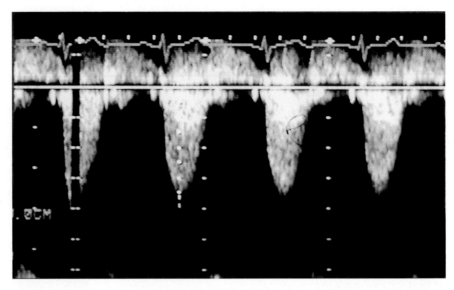

the evaluation of pulmonary valve stenosis. However, in a recent study of 132 patients with complex pulmonary stenosis, Silvilairat and associates[5] suggest that the mean Doppler-derived gradient showed superior correlation with the peak-to-peak gradient at heart catheterization and should be included in the echocardiographic evaluation.

The modified Bernoulli equation can be used when the obstruction is discrete and confined to one level, but the equation is less reliable in the presence of long stenoses or multiple stenoses in series. With infundibular hypertrophy causing dynamic narrowing of the outflow tract and creating a long stenosis, evaluation of the transvalvular gradient by continuous wave Doppler imaging is difficult and cardiac catheterization may be needed to accurately determine the levels and the degree of obstruction.

Tricuspid jet velocity, when tricuspid regurgitation is present, provides an estimate of right ventricular systolic pressure.

Forward late diastolic pulmonary blood flow, coinciding with atrial systole ("restrictive" right ventricular physiology), is more pronounced during inspiration. Increased venous return translates into increased pressure in the right atrium and in the presence of a hypertrophic and noncompliant right ventricle may result in partial presystolic opening of the pulmonary valve.

Size and function of the right ventricle, as well as integrity of the atrial septum, should be assessed carefully. The right ventricle is usually of normal size and function, with variable degrees of hypertrophy in unoperated patients.[2]

Magnetic Resonance Imaging

Magnetic resonance imaging (MRI) may add to the assessment of:
- The level of obstruction (infundibular, valvular, supravalvular)
- The size and function of the right ventricle
- The size of the pulmonary arteries

It also may detect other associated lesions such as pulmonary artery stenosis, coexisting pulmonary regurgitation and its severity, and the presence of atrial and ventricular septal defects.

Cardiac Catheterization

Catheterization (including angiocardiography) is occasionally indicated to determine:
- The severity and level(s) of obstruction
- Tricuspid valve and pulmonary artery abnormalities
- The presence of intracardiac shunts when noninvasive imaging cannot provide complete information
- Coronary artery anatomy in high-risk subjects or if a patient scheduled for intervention is older than 40 years of age.

THE OPERATED ADULT

Patients who needed an intervention to relieve the obstruction had either a surgical pulmonary valvulotomy or a balloon pulmonary valvuloplasty. The surgical techniques include a closed valvotomy, as pioneered by Lord Brock in 1948, or an open pulmonary valvotomy performed under cardiopulmonary bypass, allowing the possibility of incising the valve, excising redundant cusp tissue, dealing with subvalvular stenosis, and closing the atrial septum. Balloon pulmonary valvuloplasty has, however, become the procedure of choice for the past 15 to 20 years. After successful intervention, patients are usually asymptomatic and findings on physical examination may be unimpressive. Some patients may have secondary pulmonary regurgitation, which may eventually lead to exertional dyspnea or palpitations. Progression of a residual stenosis can also occur. McCrindle[6] reported the intermediate follow-up of an early cohort of 533 patients who required balloon valvuloplasty between 1981 and 1986. Moderate to severe pulmonary regurgitation was present in 7% of the patients after intervention, and 6.5% of the patients who had an immediate reduction of the gradient to less than 36 mm Hg progressed to require further therapy for recurrent stenosis.

On physical examination patients usually have no cyanosis or clubbing after a successful intervention. The jugular pulse is normal; there is no ventricular lift unless the right ventricle is dilated secondary to significant residual pulmonary regurgitation. The second heart sound is usually normal. A soft systolic ejection murmur may be heard at the second intercostal space; and, if regurgitation is present, a short decrescendo diastolic murmur may also be heard. After relief of the obstruction, cardiac performance as assessed by exercise testing improves in children and young adults but preoperative cardiac dysfunction and myocardial fibrosis may explain a lack of improvement in older adults.[7]

On the electrocardiogram the criteria for right ventricular hypertrophy usually regress. A right bundle-branch block may be present after a surgical valvotomy. On chest radiography the main and left pulmonary arteries remain dilated even after successful relief of the obstruction but the heart size returns to normal. The echocardiographic examination will determine the degree of residual stenosis and the presence/degree of pulmonary regurgitation as well as the size and function of the right ventricle. In patients with severe residual pulmonary regurgitation, stress testing will help to determine the functional capacity.

Late Management Options (Box 41-4)

INDICATIONS FOR INTERVENTION

Asymptomatic patients with moderate to severe pulmonary stenosis, defined as a peak Doppler transvalvular gradient greater than 60 mm Hg or a mean Doppler gradient over 40 mm Hg (in association with less than moderate pulmonary valve regurgitation), should have relief of the obstruction.[8] Relief of the obstruction could also be

BOX 41-4   LATE TREATMENT

Indications for Intervention
- Moderate to severe stenosis
- Symptomatic or not

Indications for Re-intervention
- Moderate to severe obstruction
- Severe pulmonary regurgitation with:
  - Reduced exercise tolerance *or*
  - Severe right ventricular dilation *or*
  - Sustained atrial or ventricular arrhythmias

considered in symptomatic patients with a peak Doppler transvalvular gradient greater than 50 mm Hg or a mean Doppler gradient over 30 mm Hg. Percutaneous balloon valvuloplasty has been accepted as the treatment of choice, but it might be unsuccessful, especially if the valve is calcified or in the presence of a dysplastic valve (valve with thick leaflets but limited or no cusp fusion), in which case surgical valvotomy or pulmonary valve replacement is usually necessary. Furthermore, patients with supravalvular stenosis, such as those with Noonan syndrome, tend to be resistant to balloon dilation. Balloon valvuloplasty works by causing commissural splitting of the pulmonary valve. It is an effective and safe procedure. Stanger and coworkers[9] published, in 1990, the first large-scale study on the efficacy and safety of pulmonary balloon valvuloplasty in 822 cases performed between 1981 and 1986 mainly in children (and only 35 adults). They reported a significant decrease in systolic pressure gradient across the pulmonary valve (from a mean of 71 ± 33 to 28 ± 21 mm Hg), although an infundibular gradient was sometimes present at the end of the procedure. This infundibular gradient did not correlate with the initial severity of the lesion and can regress after 3 to 12 months. In Stanger's series, the rate of major complications (death, tamponade, tricuspid regurgitation) was less than 1%, a result that is comparable to surgery. Chen and associates[10] reported the results of balloon valvuloplasty in 53 adults and also found a significant decrease in systolic pressure gradient (from a mean of 91 ± 46 to 38 ± 32 mm Hg), with a significant increase in the diameter of the pulmonic valve orifice (from a mean of 8.9 ± 3.6 to 17.4 ± 4.6 mm), without causing severe valve incompetence.

INDICATIONS FOR RE-INTERVENTION

Residual right ventricular outflow tract obstruction, either infundibular because of a hypertrophied ventricle or valvular with a peak Doppler systolic gradient greater than 60 mm Hg, should be readdressed. Patients who have severe pulmonary regurgitation with severe right ventricular dilation and/or reduced exercise capacity should have pulmonary valve replacement. Pulmonary valve replacement should also be considered in patients with severe pulmonary regurgitation and sustained atrial and/or ventricular tachycardia.

Arrhythmia and Sudden Cardiac Death

The unoperated adult with pulmonary stenosis may present with supraventricular arrhythmias, mainly atrial flutter, resulting from right ventricular pressure overload and tricuspid regurgitation. The onset of supraventricular arrhythmias may precipitate signs of right ventricular failure. The adult who underwent valvotomy may also present with supraventricular and ventricular arrhythmias, especially if significant residual hemodynamic lesions are present. Rare cases of sudden death have been reported.

Pregnancy

Asymptomatic women are sometimes first seen by a cardiologist during pregnancy because of a loud systolic murmur. Pregnancy is well tolerated in women with mild to moderate pulmonary stenosis and in women who have undergone valvuloplasty or surgery. In women with severe stenosis, however, the increased hemodynamic load of pregnancy may precipitate right-sided heart failure and atrial arrhythmias, regardless of the functional class before pregnancy. These women should undergo relief of the obstruction before conception. Percutaneous valvuloplasty may be done during pregnancy if symptoms of heart failure develop.

Level of Follow-Up, Endocarditis Prophylaxis, and Exercise

Adults with a peak systolic gradient of less than 25 mm Hg do not need regular cardiology follow-up and should live normal lives. Patients with systolic gradients above 25 mm Hg, and those with other hemodynamic issues after valvotomy (either surgical or balloon), require lifelong follow-up because intervention or re-intervention may be needed. Attention should be paid to progressive stenosis, right ventricular size and function in the context of pulmonary regurgitation, the severity of tricuspid regurgitation (often reflecting right ventricular dilation and dysfunction), and evidence of intracardiac shunting.

The risk of endocarditis is low and antibiotic prophylaxis is not indicated except in patients who have had a pulmonary valve replacement.

Patients with mild pulmonary stenosis and those with a good hemodynamic result after previous intervention and preserved biventricular function need no exercise restrictions. They can participate in endurance sports, athletic competitions, and contact sports. Patients with mild to moderate pulmonary stenosis and normal biventricular function should be encouraged to participate in moderate levels of exercise. Patients with moderate to severe pulmonary stenosis (right ventricular outflow tract Doppler maximal gradient greater than 50 mm Hg) should under normal circumstances undergo elective intervention or re-intervention before resuming unrestricted physical activity. Similarly, patients with severe pulmonary regurgitation with or without residual stenosis, after previous intervention, and with progressive right ventricular dilation should be considered for elective pulmonary valve implantation and then return to increased physical activity, after staged rehabilitation.

REFERENCES

1. Hayes CJ, Gersony WM, Driscoll DJ, et al. Second Natural History Study of Congenital Heart Defects: results of treatment of patients with pulmonary valvar stenosis. Circulation 1993;87(Suppl. I):I28–I37.
2. Kopecky SL, Gersh BJ, McGoon MD, et al. Long-term outcome of patients undergoing surgical repair of isolated pulmonary valve stenosis: follow-up at 20-30 years. Circulation 1988;78:1150–1156.
3. Nishimura RA, Pieroni DR, Bierman FZ, et al. Second Natural History Study of Congenital Heart Defects. Pulmonary stenosis: echocardiography. Circulation 1993;87(Suppl. I):I73–I79.
4. Currie PJ, Hagler DJ, Seward JB, et al. Instantaneous pressure gradient: a simultaneous Doppler and dual catheter correlative study. J Am Coll Cardiol 1986;7:800–806.
5. Silvilairat S, Cabalka AK, Cetta F, et al. Outpatient echocardiographic assessment of complex pulmonary outflow stenosis: Doppler mean gradient is superior to the maximum instantaneous gradient. J Am Soc Echocardiogr 2005;18:1143–1148.
6. McCrindle BW. Independent predictors of long-term results after balloon pulmonary valvuloplasty. Circulation 1994;89:1751–1759.
7. Krabill KA, Wang Y, Einzig S, et al. Rest and exercise hemodynamics in pulmonary stenosis: comparison of children and adults. Am J Cardiol 1985;56:360–365.
8. Warnes CA, Williams RG, Bashore TM, et al. ACC/AHA 2008 guidelines for the management of adults with congenital heart disease: executive summary. A report of the American College of Cardiology/American Heart Association Task Force on Practice Guidelines (Writing Committee to Develop Guidelines for the Management of Adults With Congenital Heart Disease) developed in collaboration with the American Society of Echocardiography, Heart Rhythm Society, International Society for Adult Congenital Heart Disease, Society for Cardiovascular Angiography and Interventions, and Society of Thoracic Surgeons. J Am Coll Cardiol 2008;52:1890–1947.
9. Stanger P, Cassidy SC, Girod DA, et al. Balloon pulmonary valvuloplasty: results of the Valvuloplasty and Angioplasty of Congenital Anomalies Registry. Am J Cardiol 1990;65:775–783.
10. Chen CR, Cheng TO, Huang T, et al. Percutaneous balloon valvuloplasty for pulmonic stenosis in adolescents and adults. N Engl J Med 1996;335:21–25.

Double-Chambered Right Ventricle

MICHAEL N. SINGH | DOFF B. MCELHINNEY

Definition and Morphology

Double-chambered right ventricle (DCRV) is characterized by anomalous or hypertrophied muscle bundles that cause a form of subvalvular right ventricular outflow tract (RVOT) obstruction, dividing the right ventricle into a high-pressure proximal chamber and a low-pressure distal chamber. Anatomic descriptions of what was thought to be DCRV date to at least the 1860s, but it was not until 100 years later, in the 1960s, that the hemodynamic abnormalities and surgical concerns were described.[1] Terms such as *anomalous muscle bundle of the right ventricle, cor triventriculare* (with the right ventricular [RV] infundibular area depicted as the third ventricle), and *aberrant muscle bundle of the right ventricle,* among others, were used to describe what is currently known as DCRV.

The nature of the single or multiple muscle bundles causing the obstruction varies, with descriptions including (1) an anomalous hypertrophied moderator band with its origin at a high point on the RV septal surface; (2) hypertrophied accessory septoparietal bands; (3) anomalous muscle bundles originating from the body of the septal band (septomarginal trabeculation) in the area of the supraventricular crest and attaching to the RV anterior wall near the base of the anterior tricuspid valve papillary muscle; and (4) RV apical trabeculation. Two basic morphologic patterns based on angiographic findings have been identified: a high-position abnormal muscle bundle with a horizontal orientation and a low-position muscle bundle with an oblique orientation across the apical component of the right ventricle.[2-4] The two patterns appear to occur with similar frequency and have no significant clinical differences. DCRV is morphologically distinct from tetralogy of Fallot (TOF) (see Chapter 43). In TOF the RV infundibulum is hypoplastic due to anterior and superior displacement of the crista supraventricularis, but in DCRV the infundibular septum is not involved.

The obstructing muscle bundles likely have an underlying congenital anatomic substrate, which through an ongoing hemodynamic process may enlarge and cause progressive obstruction over time ranging from trivial to severe.[5] One explanation is that these individuals have a genetic susceptibility for cellular proliferation and given certain hemodynamic factors may have progressive anomalous RV muscle bundle hypertrophy causing insignificant RVOT obstruction earlier in life and severe obstruction in adulthood requiring surgical intervention.[6] A retrospective study of adolescents and adults with unrepaired DCRV showed the rate of progression of midventricular obstruction by Doppler assessment ranged from 3.3 to 11.1 mm Hg per year, with a mean of 6.2 mm Hg per year.[6] Histologic evaluation of the anomalous muscle bundles postoperatively has shown subendocardial thickening, disarrayed myocardial tissue, heterogeneous staining of myofilaments, vacuolization, nuclei of irregular size, and partial replacement of myocardium with fibrous tissue.[7]

The majority of patients with DCRV have coexisting cardiac lesions: (1) ventricular septal defect (VSD; 60% to 90%), with the majority being perimembranous, followed by muscular and subarterial; (2) pulmonary valve stenosis (~40%); (3) atrial septal defect (~17%); (4) double-outlet right ventricle (~8%); and (5) TOF.[8,9] Adult individuals presenting with isolated DCRV may have had a VSD present at a younger age that spontaneously closed from mechanisms such as adherence of tricuspid valve tissue, fibromuscular proliferation adjacent to the anomalous muscle bundles, or hypertrophy of the anomalous muscle bundles and/or

ventricular septum. In a subset of patients, the combination of DCRV and discrete subaortic stenosis may occur with an incidence of approximately 0.5% (nine times the expected rate) and is likely caused by the hemodynamic disturbances from the commonly associated VSD.[10] It is believed that progression of the obstruction over time, in patients with DCRV and VSD or DCRV and discrete subaortic stenosis, is brought on by altered hemodynamic flow that triggers a genetic predisposition to cellular proliferation from increased muscular shear stress.[6] The location of the VSD relative to the obstructing muscle bundles plays a role in the flow profile and clinical features. If the obstructing anomalous muscle bundles are located distal to the VSD (~60% of cases), pulmonary blood flow will be decreased and may lead to right-to-left shunting across the VSD, causing cyanosis in the setting of severe obstruction.[11] Echocardiographic data have shown that a shorter distance between the pulmonary valve and moderator band in infants with a VSD may predict development of DCRV later in life.[11]

The natural history of DCRV is not well defined because it was not recognized as a clinical entity until the early 1960s, but it is likely related to the presence of other cardiac lesions. Prior to that time patients were often diagnosed with TOF even though they may have undergone surgery for DCRV. One series showed that 11% of patients who underwent surgical repair for what was thought to be TOF actually met diagnostic criteria (based on operative reports, cardiac catheterization, and angiograms) for DCRV and not TOF.[12] In patients with associated congenital heart defects, DCRV may develop either before or after the primary anomaly has been repaired and is similarly progressive in either event. Patients who are diagnosed at an older age or undergo evaluation or repair of unrepaired DCRV at an older age are less likely to have coexisting congenital cardiac anomalies than younger patients.

Genetics and Epidemiology

DCRV is an uncommon cardiac anomaly with an incidence of 0.5% to 2% of all congenital heart disease. It has not been associated with any particular genetic abnormality, although sporadic cases have been associated with Noonan's syndrome and Down syndrome.[13,14] There is no known pattern of inheritance, association with teratogen exposure, epidemiologic pattern of occurrence, gender predilection (45% to 75% males[3,6,8]), ethnic/racial background, or geographic origin. Series have shown an association of DCRV with VSD and TOF. The development of DCRV occurs in 3% to 10% of patients with VSD[5] and in approximately 3% of patients with TOF.[15] Although data have shown that a shorter distance between the pulmonary valve and moderator band in patients with a VSD may predict development of DCRV later in life,[11] the epidemiologic value of this observation is limited because of the lack of prospective evaluations.

Early Presentation and Management

The majority of DCRV cases with significant RVOT obstruction are identified and treated during childhood or adolescence. The initial clinical presentation varies, with most patients having an asymptomatic systolic murmur. The diagnosis of DCVR may be missed if the loud systolic murmur at the left sternal border is attributed to a restrictive VSD. Symptoms may include cyanosis, dyspnea, failure to thrive, excessive sweating, and congestive heart failure. Symptoms are also

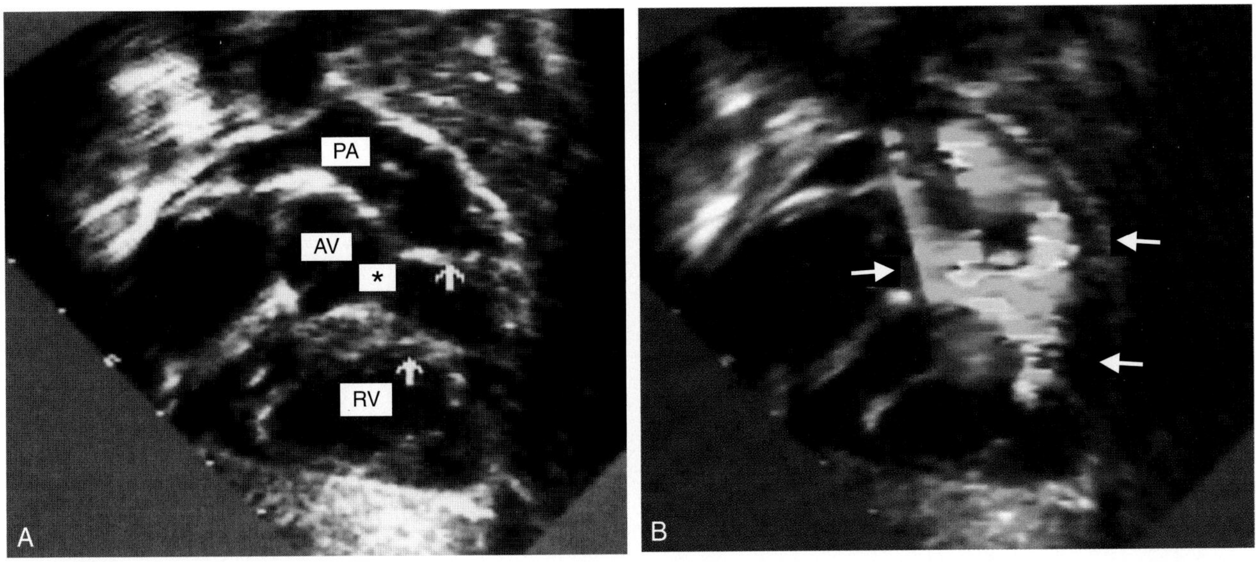

Figure 42-1 Echocardiographic images in a patient with double-chambered right ventricle and a permembranous ventricular septal defect (VSD). Cross-sectional (**A**) and corresponding Doppler color flow (**B**) images from an oblique subcostal view, showing the RVOT. **A**, The *arrows* indicate obstructing RV muscle bundles. The pulmonary valve is just proximal to the pulmonary artery label (PA). A VSD is indicated by the *asterisk,* just to the right of the aortic valve (AV). **B**, Acceleration of flow through the RVOT (*left facing arrows*) is seen at the locations of the obstructing RV muscle bundles and through the VSD (*right-facing arrow*).

dependent on any associated VSD (presence, location, and size), degree of RVOT obstruction, and other associated cardiac anomalies.[16] Adult patients with DCRV have limited clinical findings unless there is significant RVOT obstruction. The primary murmur heard is a grade 2-3/6 harsh systolic murmur at the left sternal border in the second intercostal space. Approximately 25% of patients have an associated thrill. Almost all patients with significant obstruction have an RV heave. The first heart sound is single. The second heart sound is physiologically split and usually has normal intensity of the pulmonary component. Other physical findings in the right side of the heart such as a tricuspid regurgitant murmur, increased jugular venous v wave, right-sided gallop, and hepatomegaly depend on the severity and duration of the RVOT obstruction. Lower extremity edema secondary to severe RV failure is uncommon. Other physical findings depend on the presence of associated cardiac abnormalities.

Electrocardiographic (ECG) findings include RV hypertrophy in the majority of patients, incomplete right bundle-branch block in approximately 25% of patients, and right-axis deviation in a few patients. There is typically a prominent R wave in lead V_4R with no significant S wave and normal voltage in the precordial leads including V_1. It is suggested that the ECG findings are related to the absence of distal RV chamber hypertrophy.[17] A small proportion of patients have normal ECG results. In 40% of patients in one series, the only ECG finding suggestive of RV hypertrophy was an upright T wave in V_3R.[17] This is typically not seen in patients with an isolated VSD or TOF and may be a valuable distinguishing feature if present.

Even though there may be clinical, physical, and ECG findings in patients with DCRV, the only reliable methods for confirming the diagnosis are noninvasive imaging, cardiac catheterization with hemodynamic assessment and angiography, and direct inspection during surgery or autopsy. In younger patients with adequate echocardiographic windows, transthoracic echocardiography is the primary method of diagnosing DCRV (Fig. 42-1). Cross-sectional and Doppler echocardiographic evaluation using a subxiphoid window can delineate the anatomy of DCRV in very young patients, but adequate imaging may be difficult to obtain in older patients. Transesophageal echocardiography is diagnostic in most cases, if transthoracic echocardiographic windows are suboptimal. Cardiac magnetic resonance imaging (CMR) provides excellent images to define the RV anatomy as well as the functional characteristics of DCRV (Fig. 42-2). Its use is becoming

more common, especially in patients with suboptimal echocardiographic windows. Cardiac catheterization with hemodynamic assessment and angiography (Fig. 42-3) may be necessary if the diagnosis remains in question or other information is needed before proceeding to surgical repair, such as coronary anatomy.

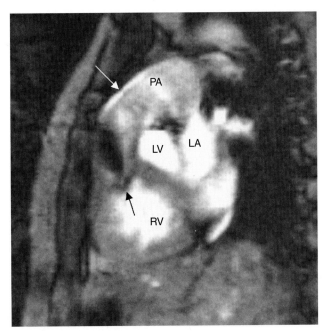

Figure 42-2 This gradient-echo cine MR image (TE = 14 ms) in an oblique parasagittal plane aligned with the RVOT is from an adult with double-chambered right ventricle. Taken during systole, it demonstrates the obstructing muscle bundles (*black arrow*) dividing the hypertrophied proximal right ventricle (RV) and the thin-walled infundibular region. High-velocity flow distal to the obstructing muscle bundles is represented by the dark jet. The *white arrow* indicates the level of the pulmonary valve. LA, left atrium; LV, left ventricular outflow tract; PA, main pulmonary artery. (*Courtesy Philip Kilner, Royal Brompton Hospital, London, UK.*)

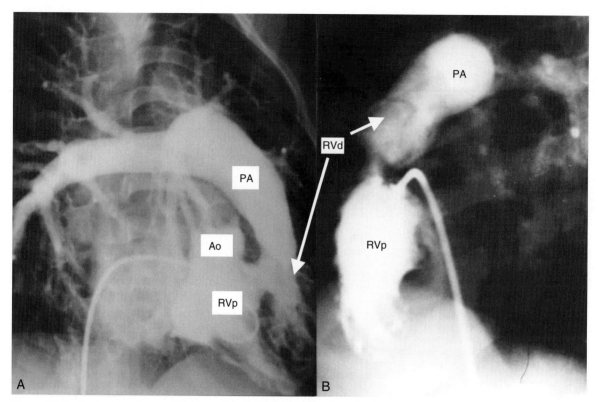

Figure 42-3 Angiograms in two different patients with double-chambered right ventricle and a permembranous ventricular septal defect (VSD). Right (**A**) and left (**B**) anterior oblique views of a right ventriculogram, demonstrating the division of the right ventricle into proximal (RVp) and distal (RVd) chambers. The anomalous muscle bundles are located more distally in **B** than in **A**. In A the pulmonary valve is at the level of the pulmonary artery (PA). Flow through the VSD, which is located in the proximal chamber of the RV, can be seen passing into the left ventricle posterior to the infundibular septum. AO, aorta. *(Courtesy Shi-Joon Yoo, The Hospital for Sick Children, Toronto, Canada.)*

Surgical intervention is generally recommended in patients with DCRV and significant RVOT obstruction, regardless of the age at diagnosis. The associated cardiac defects that are often present will usually require repair as well. There is no routine, effective transcatheter therapy for DCRV. Medical management with β-adrenergic blockers in atypical cases of DCRV with dynamic intraventricular obstruction[18] or with diuretics in patients with congestive heart failure is only palliative; definitive surgical repair is required given the obstruction is a fixed anatomic structure. Delaying surgical repair is not indicated from a cardiovascular standpoint, unless the degree of RVOT obstruction is mild, because DCRV is frequently a progressive condition resulting in more prominent hypertrophy of the anomalous muscle bundles and proximal RV chamber, which leads to progression of the obstruction. Repair becomes more complicated as symptoms, hypertrophy, and fibrosis progress.

Surgical repair consists of resection of the obstructing anomalous RV muscle bundles, partial resection of the septal and parietal bands, and resection of any hypertrophied trabecular muscle that may impede RV outflow.[8,15,19–21] When a VSD is present, it is closed with a patch or direct suture and any other associated defects are repaired. Depending on the presence and type of associated defects, DCRV repair is generally straightforward. It is usually approached through a median sternotomy incision with cardiopulmonary bypass and cardioplegic arrest. The right ventricle is accessed through a right atriotomy or a combination of pulmonary arteriotomy and right atriotomy. A longitudinal right ventriculotomy was used in the past but is generally avoided to decrease the risk of early and late complications.[8,15,19–21] Intraoperative transesophageal echocardiography with Doppler interrogation is used after repair and discontinuation of cardiopulmonary bypass to assess the hemodynamic result. In most cases, the RVOT gradient can be decreased to less than 10 mm Hg.[8,15,19–21]

In the current era, early postoperative complications are uncommon, as are in-hospital and late deaths. The most important postoperative consideration after repair of DCRV is low cardiac output, which is likely related to RV trauma from extensive muscle bundle resection[8,15,19–21] and can usually be managed with inotropic support until the right ventricle recovers.

Late Outcomes

SURVIVAL AND FUNCTIONAL STATUS

Mid- and long-term survival is very favorable in patients with repaired DCRV, and most patients remain asymptomatic. The few long-term follow-up studies available showed no in-hospital or late deaths.[12,16,19] Residual associated cardiac defects such as hemodynamically significant VSD or subvalvular aortic stenosis are more likely to require reoperation than residual RVOT obstruction from DCRV, which is usually trivial to mild after repair.[12,16,19] Patients infrequently have significant ventricular arrhythmias or myocardial dysfunction postoperatively.

Outpatient Assessment

PATIENTS WITH REPAIRED DOUBLE-CHAMBERED RIGHT VENTRICLE

Most patients with repaired DCRV are relatively asymptomatic and have few physical limitations because they usually have only trivial to mild residual RVOT obstruction. There is rarely recurrence or progression of RVOT obstruction due to anomalous muscle bands in patients with adequate surgical repair. Patients with an increased murmur intensity and progression of RV hypertrophy on ECG evaluation should undergo routine follow-up evaluation.

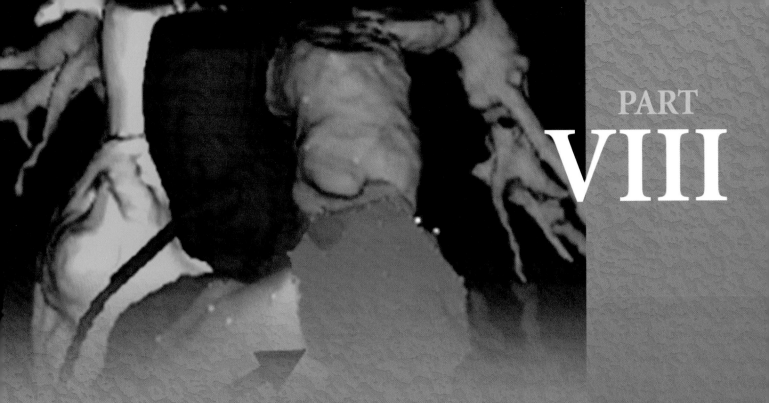

PART

VIII

Cyanotic Conditions

Tetralogy of Fallot

SONYA V. BABU-NARAYAN | MICHAEL A. GATZOULIS

Definition and Morphology

It was Etienne-Louis Arthur Fallot who, in a series of papers in 1888, separated the malformation we now describe with his name from other anatomic lesions responsible for the "maladie bleue." Although autopsy cases had been recognized previously, he was the first to correlate clinical features with pathologic findings. In anatomic terms, the malformation is composed of four constant features, namely, subpulmonary infundibular stenosis, ventricular septal defect (VSD), rightward deviation of the aortic valve with biventricular origin of its leaflets, and right ventricular (RV) hypertrophy (Fig. 43-1).

Nonetheless, the malformation represents a morphologic spectrum. At one end it can be difficult to distinguish hearts with tetralogy of Fallot (TOF) from those with VSD and overriding aorta with minimal pulmonary stenosis. At the other extreme, the pulmonary obstruction is so severe as to represent the most common variant of pulmonary atresia with VSD (see Chapter 44). One morphologic marker, however, usually unifies the overall entity. This is anterocephalad deviation of the outlet septum (the muscular structure that separates the subaortic from the subpulmonary outlets) in relationship to the rest of the muscular septum. However, something over and above septal deviation is needed to produce TOF. This is hypertrophy of the septoparietal trabeculations, a series of normally small trabeculations, extending from the anterior margin of the septomarginal trabeculations and encircling the parietal margin of the subpulmonary infundibulum. Together with the deviated outlet septum this complex forms the narrowed path to the pulmonary valve (which itself is often small and bicuspid).

VENTRICULAR SEPTAL DEFECT

The VSD in TOF is usually single and almost always large and nonrestrictive, except in very rare cases where its right ventricular margin is shielded by accessory tricuspid valve tissue or where marked septal hypertrophy narrows the defect. In about 80% of cases the defect is perimembranous, the remainder having a muscular posteroinferior rim. Much less commonly the defect can be doubly committed juxta-arterial, with its cephalad border being formed by the conjoined aortic and pulmonary valves. It is questionable if such a heart defect should be called TOF because the outlet "septum is absent. But the anatomy otherwise is exactly that of TOF. Furthermore, the free wall of the subpulmonary infundibulum is present and can possess hypertrophied trabeculations that may be obstructive after closure of the defect.

PULMONARY STENOSIS

There is infundibular stenosis in almost all cases, which commonly coexists with obstruction(s) at other sites. The crucial importance of anterocephalad deviation of the outlet septum and the hypertrophied septoparietal trabeculations has been described. Hypertrophy of the anterior limb of the septomarginal trabeculation may contribute to this, but a second level of "subinfundibular pulmonary" obstruction may be seen in which there is hypertrophy of the moderator band and apical trabeculations, which produces more proximal stenosis and gives the appearance of a two-chambered right ventricle. The pulmonary valve is abnormal in most cases, although rarely the major cause of obstruction. In young infants, however, valvular stenosis has been found at surgery to be the major obstructive lesion. Acquired atresia of the infundibulum or the

valve can also occur. Stenoses within the pulmonary arteries themselves are of major surgical significance, usually occurring at branch points from the bifurcation onward. Hypoplasia of the pulmonary arteries has been reported to be as frequent as 50%. Lack of origin of one pulmonary artery (typically the left) from the pulmonary trunk is not infrequent. The nonconnected pulmonary artery is almost always present, usually being connected by the arterial duct to some part of the aortic arch. Rarely, it may arise directly from the ascending aorta, but then it is more often the right pulmonary artery that is anomalously connected.

AORTIC OVERRIDING

The degree of aortic override can vary from 5% to 95% of the valve being connected to the right ventricle. TOF, therefore, coexists with double-outlet RV, when more than half of the aorta connects to the right ventricle. This feature has surgical significance in that a much larger patch is required to connect the left ventricle to the aorta when it originates predominantly from the right ventricle.

ASSOCIATED LESIONS

Patency of the oval fossa, atrial septal defect (ASD), a second muscular inlet VSD, or an atrioventricular septal defect, usually in the setting of Down syndrome, can coexist with TOF. A right aortic arch is common. Coronary arterial abnormalities, the most common being a left anterior descending artery from the right coronary artery crossing the right ventricular outflow tract (RVOT), occur in about 3% and may be of surgical importance, sometimes necessitating the use of a right ventricular-to-pulmonary arterial (RV-PA) conduit.

CONDUCTION SYSTEM

The atrioventricular node is normally located in patients with TOF. When the VSD is perimembranous, the bundle of His penetrates at the posteroinferior rim of the defect in the area of tricuspid and mitral valve continuity. In most cases the bundle and its left branch proceed on the left side of the defect, although occasionally they run directly on the crest of the septum. Nevertheless, most surgeons place their sutures along the RV aspect of the defect, thus avoiding heart block. When the defect is muscular, that is, there is muscular interruption between the tricuspid and aortic valve fibrous continuity, the bundle runs along the anterosuperior aspect of the defect and sutures can be placed safely on the lower rim of the VSD.

Furthermore, the conduction tissue never runs along the outlet septum, the muscular structure separating the aortic from the pulmonary valve, which can be safely resected without risk of producing heart block.

Genetics and Epidemiology

TOF is the most common form of cyanotic congenital heart defect, accounting for approximately 10% of all congenital heart disease. There is a slight male-to-female predominance. Approximately 15% of patients with TOF have a deletion of chromosome 22q11. This is tested with fluorescence in-situ hybridization (FISH) test. The incidence of 22q11 deletion is especially high in patients with right aortic arch, pulmonary atresia, and aortic-to-pulmonary collateral vessels. The 22q11 deletion

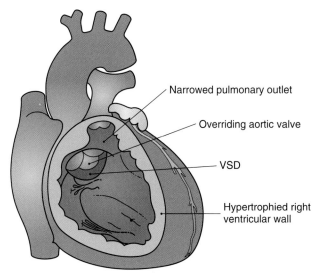

Figure 43-1 Anatomic features of tetralogy of Fallot. Tetralogy (Gk. *tetralogia* meaning "four parts") of Fallot is composed of four constant features: subpulmonary infundibular stenosis, ventricular septal defect (VSD), aortic overriding, and right ventricular hypertrophy. *(After Ho SY, Baker EJ, Rigby ML, Anderson RH. Color Atlas of Congenital Heart Disease: Morphologic and Clinical Correlation. St. Louis: Mosby; 1995 with permission.)*

is also referred to as the DiGeorge syndrome and historically was summarized in the so-called CATCH 22 acronym (Cardiac defect, Abnormal facies, Thymic hypoplasia, Cleft palate, Hypocalcemia [neonatal], and 22q11 deletion). Given that 22q11 deletion results in a spectrum of disease, it is therefore not always associated with cardiac abnormality; however, affected subjects have a 50% risk of transmission, hence the indication for family screening and genetic counseling. Deletion of 22q11 is usually sporadic. Patients with 22q11 deletion may be small for dates with respect to birth weight, have nasal speech, cleft palate, learning difficulties, and a propensity to early psychiatric disorder, most commonly depression or schizophrenia in adolescence or young adulthood. Other mutations such as *NKX2.5* have also been described but are not yet recommended for clinical screening. In those without 22q11 deletion there is a 3% risk of vertical transmission of congenital heart disease that is greater for mothers with TOF than for fathers.

Early Presentation and Management

Patients with TOF invariably present with cyanosis. This is due to right-to-left shunting at the ventricular level through the large, nonrestrictive VSD. RV pressure is at systemic levels from birth. RV hypertrophy is rarely extreme and does not lead to cavity obliteration in the way seen in patients with critical pulmonary stenosis or atresia with an intact ventricular septum. Patients with TOF, therefore, always have a right ventricle of adequate size, and from this perspective they are always suitable for biventricular repair. In contrast, extreme pulmonary artery hypoplasia, which is more common in patients with pulmonary atresia, may deem the occasional patient unsuitable for repair. The timing of presentation, with cyanosis, depends on the degree of RVOT obstruction. The latter can be labile, owing to its infundibular component, leading to variable degrees of cyanosis for the individual patient. Although the severity of RVOT obstruction varies considerably, there always seems to be sufficient obstruction to protect the patient from developing pulmonary vascular disease. Patients with pulmonary atresia and multiple aortopulmonary collateral vessels represent an exemption to this, however, because parts of the lungs supplied by nonrestrictive collateral vessels may become hypertensive.

The vast majority of patients with TOF present in infancy. However, when the RVOT obstruction is mild, patients often have minimal cyanosis (so-called pink tetralogy or acyanotic Fallot) and may occasionally present in adulthood.

Most adults will have had surgery, either palliative or, more commonly, reparative, by the time they present to the adult congenital heart disease cardiologist. Rarely, adults present without previous operations. For these patients, surgical repair is still recommended because the results are gratifying and the operative risk is comparable to that in pediatric series (provided there is no significant coexisting morbidity). However, late morbidity and mortality in patients undergoing late repair is higher compared with those who underwent repair in early childhood.[1] This, in turn, is due to higher incidence of ventricular dysfunction, right-sided heart failure, and sudden cardiac death.

Reparative surgery involves closing the VSD and relieving the RVOT obstruction. The latter may involve the following:
- Pulmonary valvotomy (because in most instances the pulmonary valve is involved, being "bicuspid" and dysplastic)
- Resection of infundibular muscle (which represents the major site of RVOT obstruction)
- RVOT patch (a patch across the RVOT that does not disrupt the integrity of the pulmonary valve annulus), which may be combined with infundibular resection
- Transannular patch (a patch across the pulmonary valve annulus that disrupts the integrity of the pulmonary valve annulus and creates the potential for free pulmonary regurgitation). A transannular patch is used when the pulmonary valve annulus is restrictive.
- Pulmonary valve implantation (human homograft valve or porcine bioprosthesis). This is "routinely" performed in adolescents and adults undergoing late repair, because these patients usually do not tolerate pulmonary regurgitation well, hence the need for a competent RVOT and bioprosthetic valve implantation.
- An extracardiac RV-PA conduit (in patients with pulmonary atresia, either congenital or acquired)
- Angioplasty/patch augmentation of central pulmonary arteries, in patients with hypoplastic main pulmonary trunk and/or stenoses of the central pulmonary arteries
- Closure of a patent foramen ovale or secundum ASD, if present
- Additional treatable lesions such as aortic regurgitation or muscular VSDs may also need to be addressed.

The nature of the surgical approach to repair of TOF has evolved over the years. Early cohorts underwent repair through a right ventriculotomy. Furthermore, complete relief of RVOT obstruction often necessitated the use of a transannular patch, which creates the potential for free pulmonary regurgitation. Recent data, however, have shown detrimental long-term effects of right ventriculotomy and chronic pulmonary regurgitation on RV function and the propensity to clinical arrhythmia and sudden cardiac death. This has led to a modified approach of repairing the lesion with a combined transatrial/transpulmonary approach involving closure of the VSD and relief of the RVOT obstruction through the right atrium and the pulmonary artery. A limited RV incision is often required for patch augmentation of the RVOT and/or the pulmonary valve annulus. Routine and generous transannular patching has been abandoned. In summary, every effort is now made to maintain the integrity and competence of the pulmonary valve even when this implies insertion of a bioprosthetic valve. It is of note that residual RVOT pressure gradients present in the immediate postoperative period, previously thought to carry a poor long-term prognosis, often regress within days. Furthermore, mild to moderate residual RVOT obstruction in isolation is well tolerated in the long term. Avoidance of free pulmonary regurgitation, at the expense of residual mild to moderate pulmonary stenosis, is well within the current therapeutic goal of reparative surgery.

The timing of surgical repair has also changed. Contemporary patients often undergo primary repair at presentation or when they become symptomatic. This approach may convey long-term benefits because it abolishes cyanosis early and, by normalizing pulmonary blood flow, promotes pulmonary artery growth. Many contemporary adult patients with repaired TOF, however, had one or more palliative procedures before undergoing repair.

There are occasional patients who reach adulthood with a palliative procedure only. The types of different palliative procedures that augment pulmonary blood flow in the setting of TOF are shown in Table 43-1.

TABLE 43-1	Palliative Procedures Augmenting Pulmonary Blood Flow
Procedure	**Description**
❑ Blalock-Taussig shunt (classic)	Subclavian artery-to-pulmonary artery anastomosis (end-to-side). Infrequently, this may lead to pulmonary hypertension.
❑ Blalock-Taussig shunt (modified)	Interposition graft between subclavian artery and ipsilateral pulmonary artery. Controlled augmentation of pulmonary blood flow. Usually a 4-mm Gore-Tex shunt is required early in infancy. Larger shunts would be required for older patients, although the possibility of repair should always be explored first.
❑ Waterston shunt	Ascending aorta-to-main or right pulmonary artery (side-by-side). No artificial material used; shunt grows with the patient. May lead to pulmonary hypertension. Problems have also been encountered with pulmonary artery disruption, requiring extensive arterioplasty.
❑ Potts shunt	Descending aorta-to-left pulmonary artery (side-by-side). Frequent complication with narrowing and kinking of the left pulmonary artery at the site of the anastomosis. The latter necessitates reconstructive surgery during repair, occasionally through an additional thoracotomy, which made this shunt unpopular.
❑ Central interposition tube graft	A Gore-Tex graft is often used for patients not suitable for early repair.
❑ Infundibular resection (Brock procedure) or closed pulmonary valvotomy	Often effective palliative procedure from an earlier surgical era
❑ Relief of RVOT obstruction without VSD closure or with fenestrated VSD closure	Used in patients with multiple pulmonary artery stenoses or hypoplasia

Late Outcomes

SURVIVAL AND FUNCTIONAL STATUS

Patients with Repaired Tetralogy of Fallot

The overall survival of patients who have had operative repair is excellent, provided the VSD has been closed, the RVOT obstruction relieved satisfactorily, and there is no severe pulmonary regurgitation that may lead to RV dilation and RV dysfunction. Findings of 32- and 36-year survival of 86% and 85%, respectively, have been reported.[1,2] Older age at repair is consistently associated with decreased late survival. Death occurs usually suddenly or is due to congestive heart failure. The reported incidence of sudden death, presumably arrhythmic, in late follow-up series varies between 0.5% and 6%, accounting approximately for one third to one half of late deaths. In a recent study the risk of sudden death increased incrementally after the first 20 years from repair of TOF (1.2% and 2.2% at 10 and 20 years, respectively, increased to 4% and 6% at 25 and 35 years).[2] With increasing age, acquired heart disease may be contributory to late mortality for these patients and should not be overlooked.

Palliated Patients

Palliation with arterial shunts and relief of severe cyanosis has dramatically improved the early and mid-term outcome for patients with TOF. Recognized complications after palliative procedures for TOF comprise pulmonary arterial distortion and pulmonary hypertension. Pulmonary arterial distortion has been described with any type of previous arterial shunts, although more commonly seen after a Potts or Waterston shunt. Pulmonary hypertension due to a large left-to-right shunt with volume and pressure pulmonary artery overload is more common after a Waterston anastomosis. Despite early dramatic relief of symptoms, very long-term outcome for patients who underwent only palliative procedures for TOF is limited, compared with those who ultimately underwent repair. This is because in patients with palliative procedures only, residual cyanosis, volume overload of the left ventricle, and pressure overload of the right ventricle (with RV pressures at systemic pressures due to the large VSD) persist. With time, biventricular dysfunction ensues and ultimately patients die prematurely usually from heart failure or sudden cardiac death.

Unoperated Patients

Twenty-five percent of patients die in the first year of life if their defect is not surgically treated. Forty percent die before 3 years of age, 70% before 10 years, and 95% before 40 years of age. Morbidity in adult survivors of TOF without surgery is high and relates to progressive cyanosis, exercise intolerance, arrhythmia, tendency to thrombosis, and cerebral abscess. In those few naturally surviving into the fourth and fifth decades of life, death usually occurs due to chronic congestive heart failure, secondary to long-standing RV hypertension, or suddenly, presumably from an arrhythmia.

Outpatient Assessment

PATIENTS WITH REPAIRED TETRALOGY OF FALLOT

Most adults with previous repair of TOF lead lives without restrictions.[1-4] Late symptoms can comprise exertional dyspnea, palpitations, syncope, or sudden cardiac death. The latter can indeed be the first presentation in patients previously free of overt symptoms. Investigations are directed toward late complications (Box 43-1) and preservation of biventricular function. Investigations may vary according to the type of operation performed, the locally available facilities, and the status of the patient.

All patients should have, periodically, a minimum of:
- A thorough clinical examination (Box 43-2)
- A 12-lead electrocardiogram to assess for sinus rhythm, PR interval, QRS duration (Fig. 43-2),[5] QRS prolongation over time, and, finally, QT dispersion (for high-risk patients).[6] The last three variables have been shown to relate to propensity to sustained ventricular tachycardia and risk of sudden death (see Arrhythmia and Sudden Cardiac Death, later).[4]
- Chest radiography. The cardiothoracic ratio on the posteroanterior view, presence of a left or right aortic arch, dilation or not of the ascending aorta and central pulmonary arteries, presence of retrosternal filling on the lateral view suggestive of RV dilation, and features of a calcified RV-PA conduit should be noted.

BOX 43-1 COMPLICATIONS AFTER REPAIR

- Endocarditis
- Aortic regurgitation with or without aortic root dilation: due to damage to the aortic valve during VSD closure or secondary to intrinsic aortic root abnormality (common in patients with pulmonary atresia and systemic to pulmonary artery collateral vessels)[3]
- Left ventricular (LV) dysfunction: secondary to inadequate myocardial protection during previous repair, chronic LV volume overload due to long-standing palliative arterial shunts and/or residual VSD, injury to anomalous coronary artery (uncommon)
- Residual RVOT obstruction: infundibular, at the level of the pulmonary valve and main pulmonary trunk and, distally, beyond the bifurcation and occasionally into the branches of the left and right pulmonary arteries
- Residual pulmonary regurgitation: usually well tolerated if mild to moderate. Severe chronic pulmonary regurgitation, however, may lead to symptomatic RV dysfunction. Severity of pulmonary regurgitation and its deleterious long-term effects are exacerbated by coexisting proximal or distal pulmonary artery stenosis
- RV dysfunction: usually due to residual RVOT lesions and can also be due to inadequate myocardial protection during initial repair
- Exercise intolerance: often due to pulmonary regurgitation and RV dysfunction
- Heart block, late postoperative (uncommon)
- Atrial tachyarrhythmia: atrial flutter and or atrial fibrillation
- Sustained ventricular tachycardia
- Sudden cardiac death

BOX 43-2 ASSESSMENT

- Patients with repaired TOF should have normal oxygen saturation.
- A right ventricular heave is common.
- Signs of right-sided heart failure (edema, elevated jugular veins, and hepatomegaly) are uncommon. The presence of any of these signs may suggest neglected underlying right-sided hemodynamic lesions. Patients need to be investigated thoroughly and the option of re-intervention explored.
- A single S_2 sound is common because only the aortic component can be heard.
- A to-and-fro murmur in the pulmonary area is very common. The degree of pulmonary regurgitation can be difficult to ascertain on clinical grounds only.
- Diastolic murmurs may be due to either pulmonary regurgitation (common) or aortic regurgitation (less common, but with increasing frequency observed with longer follow-up).
- A new pansystolic heart murmur in the left lower sternal edge, varying with respiration, would often indicate new-onset tricuspid regurgitation. This, in turn, may be the result of further RV dilation secondary to pulmonary regurgitation and may necessitate pulmonary valve implantation with or without tricuspid valve annuloplasty.

- Echocardiography[7] (Fig 43-3, Box 43-3)
- Exercise testing to document functional capacity. Change with time of exercise capacity may be useful in defining optimal timing for intervention.
- Holter monitoring (when clinically indicated)

Assessments that also may be required include:
- Cardiovascular magnetic resonance (CMR) for assessing (1) RV and left ventricular (LV) volumes and function, (2) assessing the presence of RV outflow tract aneurysms or akinetic regions (Fig. 43-4),[8] (3) assessing conduits that may be difficult to evaluate with transthoracic echocardiography alone due to a retrosternal anterior location, (4) quantifying pulmonary regurgitation (Fig. 43-5),[9,10] and (5) demonstrating pulmonary artery and aortic anomalies, either proximal or distal. In selected cases three-dimensional (3D) MR angiography or 3D steady-state free precession imaging can be used for further anatomic delineation, including, for example, determining the presence and extent of major aortopulmonary collateral arteries or for further assessment of suitability for percutaneous pulmonary valve insertion.[11] Late gadolinium enhanced CMR (Fig. 43-6) for detection of myocardial fibrosis may also be considered in selected cases although longitudinal correlation with outcomes is still pending.[12]
- Gated CT should also be considered in selected cases when CMR is not readily available, or contraindicated, and echocardiographic windows are poor. In addition to anatomy including branch pulmonary arteries, this can be used when relevant to assess the coronary arteries. In patients being considered for percutaneous pulmonary valve implantation the extent of calcification, dimensions of the RVOT and pulmonary artery, and proximal coronary course with respect to the RVOT can be assessed. RV and LV function can also be quantified.
- Quantitative lung perfusion scintigraphy in patients with suspected pulmonary artery branch stenosis, when this cannot be ascertained by nonionizing radiation CMR.

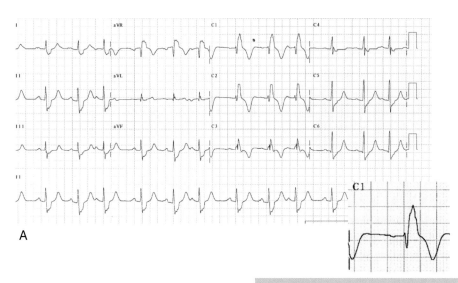

A

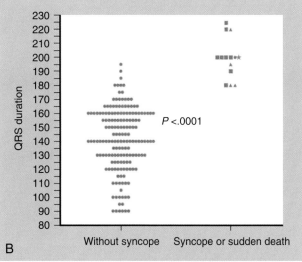

B

Figure 43-2 QRS duration predicts sustained ventricular tachycardia and sudden cardiac death. **A,** Standard 12-lead surface electrocardiogram from a patient presenting with sustained monomorphic ventricular tachycardia 20 years after TOF repair. Maximum QRS duration in V_1 (*inset*) occupies a large square (200 ms). **B,** Plot of maximum QRS duration in eight patients with repaired TOF. Those with syncope due to sustained monomorphic ventricular tachycardia (nine patients, *squares*), atrial flutter (one patient, *asterisk*) and sudden cardiac death (four patients, *triangles*) are plotted separately on the right column. *P* < .0001 signifies statistical difference in mean QRS duration between patients without syncope and those with syncope or sudden death. (*After Gatzoulis MA, Till JA, Somerville J et al. Mechanoelectrical interaction in tetralogy of Fallot: QRS prolongation relates to right ventricular size and predicts malignant ventricular arrhythmias and sudden death. Circulation 1995; 92:231-237, with permission.*)

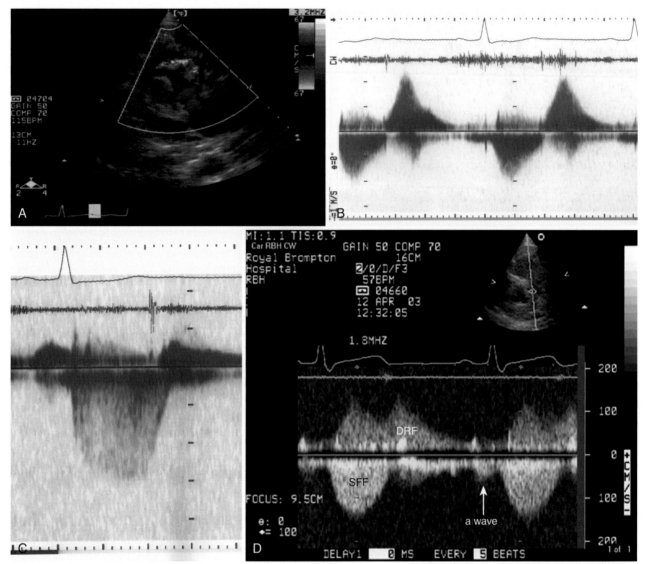

Figure 43-3 Echocardiographic assessment after repair of TOF. **A,** Color Doppler interrogation of the right ventricular outflow tract (RVOT) in the parasternal short-axis view: patient with free pulmonary regurgitation after previous TOF repair with a transannular patch. Laminar (broad jet) retrograde flow in red from the pulmonary artery in the RV outflow. Note RVOT aneurysm. **B,** Pulsed-wave Doppler image from the same patient. Note early termination of pulmonary regurgitation (flow above the curve returning to equilibrium by mid-diastole) indicative of severe pulmonary regurgitation. Forward blood velocity is not increased, suggesting the absence of pulmonary stenosis. **C,** Continuous wave Doppler interrogation of the tricuspid valve from the same patient. Maximum pressure drop across the tricuspid valve is 36 mm Hg, excluding severe proximal or distal pulmonary stenosis. **D,** Pulsed wave Doppler interrogation of the RVOT in the parasternal short-axis view in a patient with free PR after repair of TOF. As in **B,** the systolic forward flow (SFF) trace does not demonstrate evidence of pulmonary stenosis and early termination of the diastolic reverse flow (DRF) suggests severe pulmonary regurgitation. There is the additional finding of antegrade flow in late diastole (a wave, *arrow*) present throughout the respiratory cycle and suggesting so-called RV restrictive physiology. *(Courtesy Dr. Wei Li.)*

BOX 43-3   ECHOCARDIOGRAPHY

- Measure RV size and assess RV function; changes with time may guide optimal timing for re-intervention.
- Assess septal motion (indirect sign of RV dilation) and RV hypertrophy
- Interrogate the RVOT with two-dimensional (2D), Doppler, and color flow mapping for residual pulmonary stenosis and regurgitation (see Fig. 43-3A-C).
  Measure maximum continuous wave Doppler velocities. Assess for features of RV restrictive physiology including searching for anterograde flow in the pulmonary artery in late diastole throughout the respiratory cycle (see Fig. 43-3D).[7]

- Detect and quantify tricuspid regurgitation.
- Estimate RV systolic pressure (from tricuspid regurgitation). This may disclose proximal and or peripheral pulmonary artery stenosis; the latter can be difficult to image.
- Exclude residual VSD. If it is present, assess Doppler gradient across the VSD.
- Assess LV size and function.
- Exclude intra-atrial communications.
- Document left and right atrial size.
- Measure aortic root size and interrogate for aortic regurgitation.

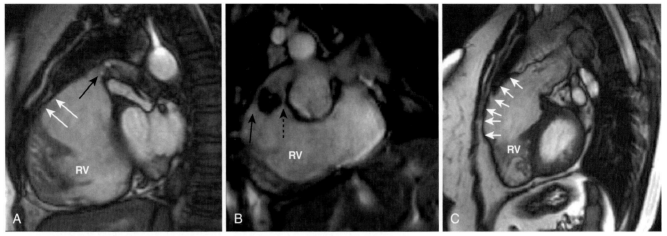

Figure 43-4 CMR for assessment of conduits and RVOT akinetic or aneurysmal areas after repair of TOF. Still frames from CMR steady-state free precession cine imaging are shown. **A,** There is a large akinetic area of thin RV myocardium (*white arrows*) in the RVOT in this 16-year old lost to follow-up after a repair involving an RV-PA conduit in childhood. The jet of pulmonary stenosis and narrow pulmonary trunk is shown by the *black arrow.* **B,** The native RVOT (*dotted arrow*) and more anterior stenosed RV-PA conduit (*solid arrow*) are both seen in this adult after repair of TOF in infancy and attempted percutaneous pulmonary valve insertion into the conduit (a small metallic artifact is visible). The proximal coronary arteries were also assessed at CMR and an anomalous left anterior descending artery passed in front of the RVOT and behind the conduit. **C,** The akinetic area below the pulmonary valve in the RVOT is particularly large (*arrows*) in this example of a patient with repaired TOF with pulmonary regurgitation.

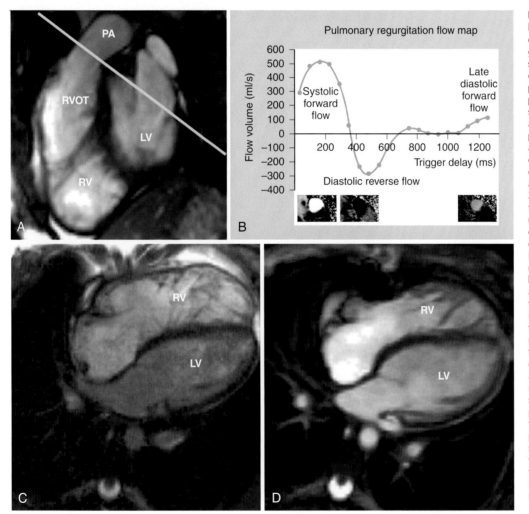

Figure 43-5 CMR for biventricular volumes, mass, function, and quantification of pulmonary regurgitation after repair of TOF. **A,** CMR still frame from steady-state free precession cine imaging in diastole in a plane located through the RVOT and pulmonary artery. The *yellow line* shows the through-plane in which a phase-encoded velocity mapping sequence was subsequently acquired. **B,** A flow curve was produced and through integrating areas containing forward and reverse flow a pulmonary regurgitant fraction of 36% was quantified. The regurgitant volume, net forward pulmonary flow, anatomic appearances of the outflow tract, appearances of jet widths, and flow on in-plane RVOT-PA phase-encoded velocity mapping, size and pulsatility[9] of the branch pulmonary arteries, as well as the consequent size[10] and function of the right ventricle are also important in determining precisely the severity and relevance of pulmonary regurgitation.[9] **C,** CMR still frame from steady-state free precession cine imaging in diastole in a four-chamber plane before pulmonary valve replacement. **D,** CMR still frame from steady-state free precession cine imaging in diastole in a four-chamber plane after pulmonary valve replacement in the same patient shown in **C.** The right ventricle is no longer dilated, and the left ventricular volumes have increased. There was no pulmonary regurgitation at follow-up.

Figure 43-6 **A,** Rows i, ii, and iii are selected late gadolinium enhancement (LGE) images from three different individuals that are examples of extensive RV LGE (*arrows*) seen in repaired TOF. *From left to right:* **i,** RVOT, short axis (SA) and LV outflow tract (LVOT) views. The large enhanced area of the RVOT and RV anterior wall corresponded to akinesia on cine imaging. LGE extends to the trabeculated myocardium including the moderator band. **ii,** RV long-axis view, SA, and four-chamber views. LGE corresponded to akinesia of the anterior wall on cine imaging, extending more inferiorly than is commonly seen. LGE of the trabeculated RV myocardium is present (*asterisk*). **iii,** The left and middle panels show the same mid-SA slice imaged twice showing extensive subendocardial LGE. The phase encode direction has been swapped between the two to exclude artifact as a cause. On the right, the LVOT plane shows RVOT LGE (*arrows*). **B,** RV LGE and markers of clinical outcome. Differences in clinical, neurohormonal, and CMR variables between patients classified according to lower quartile, middle quartiles, and upper quartile. Variables are illustrated in the bar chart with different bars representing RV LGE score. RV LGE extent is related to adverse markers of clinical outcome as shown. (*After Babu-Narayan SV, Kilner PJ, Li W, et al. Ventricular fibrosis suggested by cardiovascular magnetic resonance in adults with repaired tetralogy of Fallot and its relationship to adverse markers of clinical outcome. Circulation 2006; 113:405–413, with permission.*)

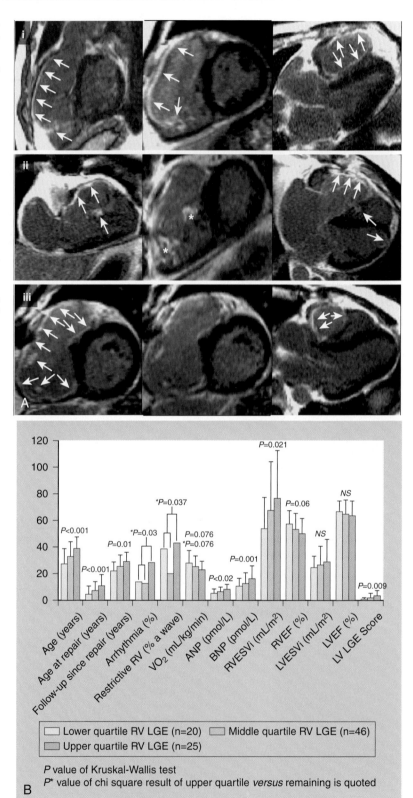

- Cardiac catheterization if adequate assessment of hemodynamics cannot be obtained by noninvasive means, for catheter intervention, and usually when surgical re-intervention is planned. Selective coronary angiography, when clinically indicated or as part of the preoperative assessment, can be done.
- Electrophysiologic studies for patients being evaluated for clinical or suspected arrhythmia

PALLIATED-ONLY OR UNOPERATED PATIENTS

Late repair should be considered because it improves long-term outcome. For those patients who have had previous palliation(s), assessment of pulmonary arterial pressure and anatomy is mandatory at some point, because these shunts have inherent complications (distortion of the pulmonary arteries, development of pulmonary hypertension [rare], and LV dysfunction secondary to volume overload). Peripheral pulmonary artery stenosis, when present, may exacerbate pulmonary regurgitation, with its deleterious long-term effects on the right ventricle.

Patients presenting as adults who have not undergone repair may have elevated pulmonary arterial pressures despite severe RVOT obstruction. This can be due to either chronic cyanosis or LV dysfunction.

However, this does not preclude repair, because the RV functions at systemic pressure levels from birth and, therefore, is "prepared" for postoperative hypertension. Lung "reperfusion injury" immediately after late repair presenting as pulmonary edema (bilateral or unilateral) is a recognized complication in adult patients with marked cyanosis and severely restricted pulmonary blood flow. It may require positive-pressure ventilation and usually resolves after several days.

Late Management Options

PATIENTS WITH REPAIRED TETRALOGY OF FALLOF

Indications for Re-intervention

Re-intervention is necessary in approximately 10% of patients after reparative surgery over a 20-year follow-up.[13] It is anticipated that with increasing lengths of follow-up from repair the incidence of re-intervention, particularly on the RVOT, will increase (Box 43-4).

The following situations after repair warrant consideration for re-intervention:

- Residual VSD with a shunt greater than 1.5:1
- Residual patent arterial shunts (leading to LV volume overload)
- Residual pulmonary stenosis with RV pressure greater than or equal to two thirds of systemic pressure (native RVOT or valved conduit)
- Aneurysmal dilation of the RVOT usually associated with regional RV hypokinesis. This is common and can be extensive especially in patients with previous RVOT or transannular patch repair and significant pulmonary regurgitation. Furthermore, this area can be the focus of subsequent sustained ventricular tachycardia.
- Branch pulmonary artery stenosis, particularly when combined with significant pulmonary regurgitation
- Free pulmonary regurgitation associated with progressive RV enlargement, new-onset tricuspid regurgitation, arrhythmia, or symptoms such as deteriorating exercise tolerance[14]
- Significant aortic regurgitation associated with symptoms and/or progressive LV dilation or deterioration of LV function
- Progressive aortic root enlargement (patients with aortic root ≥ 55 mm in diameter) and aortic regurgitation
- The development of clinical arrhythmia, most commonly atrial flutter or fibrillation, or sustained ventricular tachycardia with underlying hemodynamic substrate (often RV dilation with or without hypertrophy) amenable to intervention
- The combination of residual ASD or VSD, residual pulmonary stenosis, and pulmonary regurgitation, all mild to moderate but leading to progressive RV enlargement, reduced RV function, or symptoms

---

BOX 43-4 LATE TREATMENT

- Repair of suitable patients: with previous palliative procedures or the occasional adult survivor without previous surgery
- Preservation of RV function by RV volume offloading (restoration of RVOT competence, when severe pulmonary regurgitation with progressive RV dilation is present) and relief of RV hypertension (due to native RVOT, conduit, and or distal pulmonary artery stenoses)
- Preservation of LV function: by volume offloading (closure of significant residual VSDs, residual palliative shunts and, very occasionally—in the setting of TOF with pulmonary atresia—occlusion of systemic-to-pulmonary artery collateral vessels)
- Risk modification for sustained arrhythmia and sudden cardiac death

---

Surgical/Catheter Interventional Options

Patients requiring intervention should be treated at a tertiary referral center with appropriate cardiology and cardiac surgical expertise. The following are possible interventional options:

- Surgery may be necessary for residual pulmonary stenosis and may involve resection of residual infundibular stenosis or placement of an RVOT or transannular patch. A valved conduit may be necessary.
- Pulmonary valve implantation (either homograft or porcine bioprosthesis) may be necessary for severe pulmonary regurgitation or a grossly calcified pulmonary valve. It carries a low operative risk and leads to symptomatic improvement and improved RV function.[14] Timing of pulmonary valve implantation for asymptomatic pulmonary regurgitation is still the focus of much research and debate. Pulmonary regurgitation after repair of TOF, hitherto considered relatively benign, is in fact associated with arrhythmia, late heart failure, and sudden cardiac death. If there were such a thing as a perfect pulmonary valve prosthesis, the decision regarding timing of pulmonary valve replacement would be easier. All currently available bioprostheses, however, have a finite life span, and the longevity of a second homograft may be shorter than the first. Balancing the risk of late RV dysfunction, arrhythmia, and sudden cardiac death in these patients against the finite life span of a bioprosthetic valve leads to debate over the optimal timing of pulmonary valve replacement. There is an increasingly held view that pulmonary valve replacement is happening too late for optimal benefit and that delayed intervention may risk avoidable irreversible RV damage. Our current indications are summarized in Box 43-5. Recently, transcatheter pulmonary valve implantation using a stent-mounted bovine jugular venous valve in patients with pulmonary regurgitation and a degree of residual stenosis after previous surgical implantation of a valved conduit has been introduced. This pioneering technique is currently best suited to conduits with a degree of residual stenosis and calcium on which to anchor the device. Work is in development to make it applicable to wider substrates that will extend the group of patients for whom this technique

---

BOX 43-5 CURRENT INDICATIONS FOR PULMONARY VALVE IMPLANTATION LATE AFTER TETRALOGY OF FALLOT REPAIR IN THE PRESENCE OF SIGNIFICANT PULMONARY REGURGITATION

Consider pulmonary valve implantation if at least one of the following criteria is present:

- Symptoms, particularly subjective decrease in exercise tolerance, also fatigue
- Arrhythmia—atrial or ventricular or syncope
- Documented decrease in exercise tolerance
- Serial RV dilation and/or evidence of impaired RV ejection fraction or decrease in RV ejection fraction
- New-onset tricuspid regurgitation reflecting serial RV dilation
- QRS duration greater than or equal to 180 ms and evidence of serial increase in QRS duration[9]

Or at least two of the following criteria are present:

- RV:LV volume ratio greater than or equal to 2:1[16]
- RVEDVi[15] of 150 mL/m² or RVEDVi[16] of 140 mL/m²*
- Severe pulmonary regurgitation with any degree of residual stenosis
- Combined lesions that may not have been indications for intervention in isolation
- Contemplating pregnancy[17]

Additional points to consider:

- Large akinetic area may alter the decision in either direction
- Degree of ventricular fibrosis/scarring[12]
- Availability and suitability for percutaneous pulmonary valve implantation
- RV end-systolic volume index RV:LV systolic volume ratios
- Autonomic nervous system dysfunction[18]
- Neurohormonal activation[19]

*These indexed volume cutoffs for RV end-diastolic volume indexed to body surface area (RVEDVi) are quoted from the referenced published literature. Each unit should establish its own reproducible CMR protocol for such measurements and may need to interpret volumes reported from other centers in this context.

could be used and potentially change the face of further interventions after surgical pulmonary valve implantation. Tricuspid valve annuloplasty may also be necessary when at least moderate tricuspid regurgitation is present. Metallic prostheses in the pulmonary position have been complicated with a relatively high incidence of valve thromboses and early valve failure and are hence not widely used.

- RVOT aneurysm resection is usually performed at the time of surgical pulmonary valve implantation but may be an independent consideration.
- Balloon dilation and stenting or surgery for branch pulmonary artery stenosis may be considered to relieve distal peripheral pulmonary stenosis and reduce severity of pulmonary regurgitation.[9] However, such patients may ultimately require pulmonary valve implantation. Joint management strategy between cardiologists and cardiac surgeons is, therefore, essential. Patients with free pulmonary regurgitation and evidence of RV dysfunction should undergo pulmonary valve implantation with concomitant relief of proximal pulmonary artery stenosis with pulmonary angioplasty. More distal peripheral pulmonary artery stenoses can be dealt by balloon dilation and stenting.
- Suture or patch closure of a residual VSD (if the shunt is ≥ 1.5:1) is indicated or if the patient is undergoing reoperation for other reasons.
- Catheter or surgical closure of residual arterial shunts can be done to reduce LV volume overload.
- Aortic valve and/or root replacement may be necessary for those with aortic valve regurgitation and/or root dilation.
- Ablative therapy for arrhythmia, either atrial or ventricular, can be performed either percutaneously or intraoperatively during reoperations to restore residual hemodynamic lesions and include the modified maze procedure for patients with documented atrial flutter undergoing reoperation for residual hemodynamic problems.
- Biventricular pacing may be useful in patients with symptomatic heart failure on medical therapy. About a third of repaired TOF patients have evidence of asynchrony. However, although there is interventricular delay, a large contribution to delay is intraventricular between the right ventricle and RVOT and within the RVOT itself,[20] meaning resynchronization therapy would need to address the RV infundibulum successfully.
- Insertion of an automatic implantable cardioverter-defibrillator (AICD) can be done for secondary prevention of sudden cardiac death if sustained ventricular tachycardia recurs after restoration of hemodynamics. In the absence of a residual hemodynamic substrate amenable to catheter or surgical re-intervention, an AICD should be part of secondary prevention of sudden cardiac death for patients presenting with sustained monomorphic ventricular tachycardia. An AICD should also be considered for primary prevention of patients at risk of sudden cardiac death without target hemodynamic lesions, although prospective data for these patients are clearly required (see later).
- Closure of ASD or persistent foramen ovale is necessary if there is persistent cyanosis, history of transient ischemic attacks, or evidence of significant left-to-right shunt leading to RV dilation.

PALLIATED-ONLY OR UNOPERATED PATIENTS

Late repair of TOF should be considered in unoperated adult patients or those with previous palliative shunts only because most of them are suitable for repair. Their workup should include:
- Assessment of biventricular size and function
- Assessment of pulmonary arterial size and pressure
- Demonstration of additional VSDs, if present
- Exclusion of systemic-to-pulmonary artery collateral vessels (amenable to catheter occlusion prior to repair)
- Exclusion of coronary artery disease (which can be addressed at the time of repair)

Arrhythmia and Sudden Cardiac Death

CONDUCTION ABNORMALITIES

A right bundle-branch block (RBBB) pattern is almost universal in patients who underwent repair of TOF via a right ventriculotomy. Characteristically, the RBBB involves a short and narrow first part with

a taller and broader second part of the QRS complex (see Fig. 43-2). RBBB with left anterior hemiblock, so-called bifascicular block, is also common (occurring in approximately 15% of postoperative patients). Bifascicular block, when isolated, seldom leads to complete heart block (unless there has been transient atrioventricular block in the immediate postoperative period) nor does it relate to increased risk of sudden death. Bifascicular block combined with late PR prolongation, however, occasionally heralds high-degree atrioventricular block. Such patients warrant further investigation and may require pacing. Pacemaker implantation is mandatory in all cases of postoperative complete heart block and in true trifascicular block, confirmed by electrophysiologic study. For the majority of patients with previous TOF repair, late onset of complete heart block is rare.

SUPRAVENTRICULAR ARRHYTHMIA

Atrial flutter and atrial fibrillation are relatively common in the adult with previous TOF repair. Atrial tachyarrhythmia occurred in one third of adult patients in a single-institutional report and was contributory to late morbidity and even mortality.[21] Atrial flutter and fibrillation were more common in patients who had long-lasting systemic-to-pulmonary artery shunts, and therefore persisting volume overload, and those who required early reoperations for residual hemodynamic lesions, that is, patients with suboptimal result from reparative surgery. Older age at repair and moderate-to-severe tricuspid regurgitation were found to be additional predictors of late sustained atrial flutter and/or fibrillation in a multicenter study.[4] It is of note that previously documented atrial flutter or fibrillation does not preclude sustained ventricular tachycardia or propensity to it in these patients. Such an overlap between sustained atrial and ventricular tachyarrhythmia is more likely in patients with residual right-sided hemodynamic lesions, most often in the setting of pulmonary regurgitation and progressive RV dilation. Atrial tachyarrhythmia usually presents as palpitations. Occasionally, however, patients can present with presyncope or syncope, and atrial flutter has been postulated as a possible cause of sudden cardiac death, because these relatively young adult patients have the ability for one-to-one atrioventricular conduction. Patients presenting with sustained atrial flutter and/or atrial fibrillation should undergo thorough assessment of their hemodynamics and should have target residual hemodynamic lesions restored. Radiofrequency ablation after mapping for atrial reentry is now yielding better results for classic atrial flutter and/or incisional reentry tachycardia and has to be considered. Antiarrhythmic medication and the new-generation atrial antitachycardia pacemakers are further therapeutic tools that are available.

VENTRICULAR ARRHYTHMIA

Nonsustained Ventricular Arrhythmia
Nonsustained ventricular arrhythmia on Holter monitoring is very common (up to 60%) after repair of TOF. Ventricular ectopy of greater than grade II according to the modified Lown criteria (>30 uniform ventricular extrasystoles in any hour) appeared to be associated with increased risk of sudden cardiac death. However, more recent studies failed to show such a relationship.[4,22] Sudden cardiac death after repair of TOF is relatively uncommon.[1,2,4] There is no justification, therefore, for prophylactic antiarrhythmic therapy to suppress Holter ventricular arrhythmia in this relatively low-risk population.

Sustained Monomorphic Ventricular Tachycardia
Sustained monomorphic ventricular tachycardia, in contrast, is relatively uncommon.[4] Reentry is the most common pathophysiologic mechanism, and multiple factors have been implicated for its pathogenesis. The usual arrhythmic focus is in the RVOT, in the area of previous infundibulectomy or VSD closure. In approximately 20% of cases the reentry foci can be multiple, involving the body of the right ventricle. RV dilation and stretch with slowed ventricular activation[5] are also contributory to the creation of reentry circuits within the right ventricle,

whereas impaired hemodynamics are responsible for sustaining ventricular tachycardia, once initiated. QRS duration from the standard surface electrocardiogram has been shown to correlate well with RV size in these patients.[5] A maximum QRS duration of 180 ms or more is a highly sensitive, and relatively specific, marker for sustained ventricular tachycardia and sudden cardiac death in adult patients with previous repair of TOF (see Fig. 43-2B).[5] QRS prolongation in these patients reflects (1) initial damage to the bundle during TOF repair (right ventriculotomy, relief of muscular subpulmonary stenosis, and suture placement for VSD closure) and (2) late progressive QRS prolongation, secondary to RV dilation, almost invariably the result of chronic pulmonary regurgitation. In a multicenter study[4] it was shown that QRS change with time may be a more sensitive and specific predictor of patients at risk. New, absolute QRS predictive values for sustained ventricular tachycardia will be required for patients undergoing TOF repair in the current era, because most of them undergo repair via the right atrium and pulmonary artery and not through a right ventriculotomy, which used to be the norm until the late 1980s. Initial QRS prolongation immediately after repair is, therefore, significantly shorter in contemporary cohorts. QT dispersion (the difference between the shortest and longest QT interval in any of the 12 leads of the standard surface electrocardiogram), a marker of inhomogeneous repolarization, has also been shown to be predictive of sustained monomorphic ventricular tachycardia late after repair of TOF.[6] A QT dispersion greater than 60 ms combined with a QRS duration of 180 ms or more refines further risk stratification for sustained ventricular tachycardia for adult patients. Recent reports demonstrating depressed heart rate variability and baroreflex sensitivity suggest that the autonomic nervous system may also be involved in arrhythmogenesis.[18] Abnormal right-sided hemodynamics, predominantly RV dilation due to pulmonary regurgitation with or without pulmonary stenosis, are very common in patients presenting with sustained ventricular tachycardia (Fig. 43-7).[4]

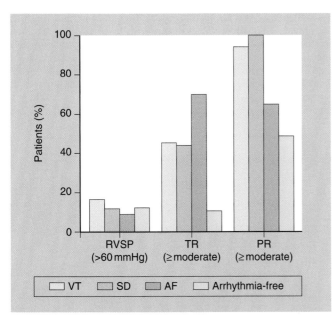

Figure 43-7 Hemodynamic substrate in patients with sustained ventricular tachycardia and sudden cardiac death late after repair of TOF. Echocardiographic data from 456 patients obtained during the preceding 12 months from the occurrence of sustained ventricular tachycardia (VT), sudden cardiac death (SD), or atrial flutter or fibrillation (AF) and, at the end of the study, for arrhythmia-free patients. Pulmonary regurgitation (PR) was the main underlying hemodynamic lesion for patients with sustained VT and SD. RVSP, right ventricular systolic pressure; TR, tricuspid regurgitation. (*After Gatzoulis MA, Balaji S, Webber SA et al. Risk factors for arrhythmia and sudden cardiac death late after repair of tetralogy of Fallot: a multicentre study. Lancet 2000; 356:975–981, with permission.*)

Detailed hemodynamic assessment is, therefore, of paramount importance. Furthermore, interventions to restore underlying residual lesions, usually right sided, should be an essential part of risk modification and arrhythmia management in these patients.[23] Other invasive therapeutic tools are transcatheter or intraoperative ablative procedures and AICD implantation. AICD implantation is usually an adjuvant therapy for secondary prevention of sustained ventricular tachycardia and sudden cardiac death after restoration of residual hemodynamic problems. Antiarrhythmic therapy clearly has a role for the symptomatic patient, but one cannot overemphasize the need for addressing underlying hemodynamic lesions. Prophylactic antiarrhythmic therapy, in contrast, has no role for the asymptomatic patient with ventricular ectopy on Holter monitoring. Patients with repaired TOF are at low risk for sustained ventricular tachycardia and sudden cardiac death, and the potential proarrhythmic side effects of antiarrhythmic therapy can be more hazardous.

SUDDEN CARDIAC DEATH AND RISK STRATIFICATION

Sudden cardiac death has been reported in all large series with an incidence varying between 0.5% and 6%.[1,2,4] Older age at repair and relative postoperative RV hypertension (compared with LV pressure) have been previously shown to be risk factors for late sudden death.[1] Transannular patching, predisposing to free pulmonary regurgitation, and accelerated rate of QRS prolongation were additional predictors of sudden death in a multicenter study (see Fig. 43-2B).[4] RV hypertension (RV systolic pressure > 60 mm Hg) in isolation was not predictive of sudden cardiac death or sustained ventricular tachycardia in this study. Patients with sustained monomorphic ventricular tachycardia and those dying suddenly shared a common electrophysiologic and hemodynamic substrate, which suggests a common pathogenic and pathophysiologic mechanism. Patients who died suddenly, however, had a much later repair compared with patients presenting with sustained ventricular tachycardia. This, in turn, suggests that LV dysfunction, secondary to long-lasting cyanosis and volume overload (from palliative arterial shunts) may also be contributory to sudden death. It is of note that none of the 16 patients who died suddenly from this multicenter study had undergone reoperations or catheter intervention to address existing important residual hemodynamic problems.[4] LV dysfunction is an additional risk factor for impaired clinical status[8,24] and moderate or severe LV dysfunction combined with QRS duration greater than or equal to 180 ms appears to have high positive and negative predictive value for sudden death.[25] Despite obvious limitations with available retrospective data,[25] it is becoming clear that preservation or restoration of RV and pulmonary valve function may reduce the risk of sudden cardiac death in these patients. As with sustained ventricular tachycardia, addressing residual hemodynamic lesions should be part of the risk modification approach for sudden cardiac death. Furthermore, this approach is shown to preserve ventricular function,[14,26] which, in turn, is a major determinant of the very long-term outcome for these patients.

Selected patients presenting with symptomatic ventricular tachycardia, biventricular dysfunction, or inducible ventricular tachycardia on a ventricular stimulation study may warrant internal insertion of an AICD. Insertion of an AICD may also be considered for primary prevention for patients at risk. This is particularly the case when advanced ventricular dysfunction is present and no target hemodynamic lesions for catheter and/or surgical intervention are to be found, but inappropriate shocks are common, as well as appropriate ones, with reported complication rates up to 30%.[27,28] It may be that late gadolinium enhanced CMR to detect the burden of myocardial fibrosis is relevant to risk stratification for defibrillator insertion, but this still needs to be investigated (see Fig. 43-5).[12] Invasive electrophysiologic studies may help in selection of appropriate patients (Box 43-6). Programmed ventricular stimulation appears to be more specific and less sensitive for suspected sustained ventricular tachycardia in the adult patients compared with pediatric patients. Failure to induce sustained monomorphic ventricular tachycardia in the catheter laboratory does not exclude clinical ventricular tachycardia. Invasive electrophysiologic investigation can also have a therapeutic goal—to guide drug therapy or attempt ablation of reentry circuits. Inappropriate AICD shock may relate to supraventricular tachycardia and may be avoided if atrial ablation procedures are performed. VT ablation may reduce the need for appropriate device therapy (Box 43-7, Fig. 43-8).

BOX 43-6 USE OF VENTRICULAR STIMULATION STUDIES IN RISK STRATIFICATION OF REPAIRED TETRALOGY OF FALLOT

Ventricular stimulation study is useful if at least one of the following criteria is present:
- Clinically documented sustained ventricular tachycardia or ventricular fibrillation
- History of cardiac syncope
- At atrial ablation procedures*

Ventricular stimulation study is potentially useful if at least two of the following criteria are present:
- QRS duration greater than 180 ms[4]
- Rapid QRS prolongation during follow-up[4]
- LV dysfunction in addition to significant pulmonary regurgitation
- Nonapical vent LV fibrosis suggested by late gadolinium CMR[†]
- Extensive RV fibrosis suggested by late gadolinium CMR
- Severe RV dysfunction
- Patient considered at risk of perioperative ventricular tachycardia
- Arrhythmia evident on Holter monitoring in patients assessed/ investigated for ventricular tachycardia/sudden cardiac death

*Atrial arrhythmia is considered a marker of ventricular dysfunction.
[†]Apical vent LV fibrosis was described as small areas of late gadolinium enhancement at the LV apex in keeping with the insertion of an apical vent perioperatively, as documented in the operation notes of many patients studied, that was found to be clinically significant in the cited paper. Nonapical vent LV fibrosis was LV fibrosis not corresponding to, or in addition to, a potential previous apical vent.

BOX 43-7 INDICATIONS FOR ABLATION OF VENTRICULAR TACHYCARDIA

- Clinically documented sustained ventricular tachycardia or ventricular fibrillation
- Appropriate shock from AICD
- Preceding AICD insertion
- A positive ventricular stimulation study

Pregnancy

Pregnancy in unoperated patients constitutes a considerable risk of maternal and fetal complications and death. This risk is greater when resting oxygen saturations in air are less than 85%. The fall in peripheral vascular resistance during pregnancy and hypotension during labor and delivery may increase the right-to-left shunt and aggravate preexisting cyanosis. Fetal loss may be as high as 30% and maternal mortality is reported at 4% to 15%, with risk increasing proportional to hematocrit.

The risk of pregnancy in patients who have undergone repair depends on the hemodynamic status. The risk is low, approaching that of the general population, in patients with good underlying hemodynamics. In patients with significant residual RVOT obstruction, severe pulmonary regurgitation with or without tricuspid regurgitation, and RV dysfunction, the increased volume load of pregnancy may lead to heart failure and arrhythmia. Recent data suggest there is concern with regard to incomplete reverse cardiac remodeling after pregnancy in patients with pulmonary regurgitation and RV dysfunction.[17] Furthermore, LV dysfunction, usually due to previous volume overload, may be present. This, in turn, increases the likelihood of complications during pregnancy and requires independent consideration.

All patients with TOF should have specialist cardiologic counseling before conception, fetal echocardiography during the second trimester, and cardiologic as well as antenatal follow-up during pregnancy. The FISH test to exclude 22q11 deletion (i.e., DiGeorge syndrome [see earlier]) should also be offered.

Level of Follow-Up

All patients should have periodic review at an adult congenital heart disease center. A minimum of history taking, physical examination, electrocardiography, and echocardiography is required per visit. Further assessment of RV size and function, preferably by CMR, is advisable because it provides robust data on biventricular size and function; interval change in these parameters provides reliable guidance on the need for, and optimal timing of, re-intervention. CMR should be considered as a baseline assessment for all patients and can be repeated with variable frequency depending on the severity of residual hemodynamic lesions.

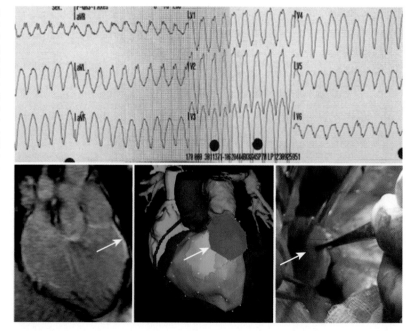

Figure 43-8 This patient with pulmonary regurgitation late after TOF re-presented to follow-up with sustained ventricular tachycardia with a left bundle-branch block pattern (**top**). Late gadolinium imaging showed evidence of scarring in her RVOT (**bottom left**, *arrow*). A 3D CMR dataset was made to provide a roadmap of the heart (**bottom middle**) and an image of the RVOT scar (*arrow*). The scar on noninvasive CMR corresponded to a low-voltage area in the RVOT at electrophysiology study performed by Dr. Sabine Ernst. Ventricular tachycardia replicating the clinical tachycardia was induced at electrophysiologic study and successfully ablated before pulmonary valve implantation and RVOT scar resection (**bottom right**). There were no perioperative events, and there has been no ventricular tachycardia during follow-up.

Endocarditis Prophylaxis

New guidelines are still refining current practice. Currently our view remains that it is reasonable that not only palliated or unoperated patients with TOF but also patients with repair of their defect have life-long antibiotic endocarditis prophylaxis together with high level dental and gum hygiene. This may, however, change.

Exercise

Recommendations for exercise include the following:
- Patients with a good hemodynamic result after repair of TOF, preserved biventricular function, and mild residual lesions need no exercise restriction. They can participate in endurance sports, athletic competition and contact sports.
- Patients with moderate residual lesions (defined as RV systolic pressure less than half systemic pressure, or moderate pulmonary regurgitation or residual VSD) and normal biventricular function should be encouraged to participate in moderate levels of exercise, including running, tennis, football, and aerobics.
- Patients with moderate to severe residual lesions (RV systolic pressure between one half and two thirds of systemic pressure and severe pulmonary regurgitation) with preserved biventricular function, not suitable for or not considered for re-intervention, can participate in light exercise, including recreational swimming, cycling, and golf.
- Patients with moderate to severe lesions with progressive RV dilation and evidence of early dysfunction requiring re-intervention may return to increased physical activity after staged rehabilitation.

- Patients with advanced biventricular dysfunction and patients with marked ascending aortopathy should limit themselves to low intensity activity/sports and avoid isometric exercise.

Future Therapies

The true potential for targeting abnormalities recently demonstrated in this population group using medical therapy is not yet known. Such targets include neurohormonal activation,[19] autonomic dysfunction,[18] cystic medial necrosis in the aorta,[3,29] and myocardial fibrosis.[12] Currently, therapy is generally symptom directed or empirical based on current or emerging available evidence, be it for management of arrhythmia or ventricular dysfunction. There is one randomized controlled trial of pharmacologic therapies in the setting of pulmonary regurgitation after repair of TOF.[30] In this trial of angiotensin-converting enzyme inhibitors, 6 months of ramipril led to improvement in measures of biventricular long-axis function in the treated cohort, but the clinical relevance of these effects with regard to outcomes needs to be precisely determined with longer and larger studies. Patients with repaired TOF and restrictive RV physiology had improved left-sided heart function with ramipril and may merit treatment. This is particularly so if they are unsuitable for pulmonary valve implantation due to comorbidity and if there are other indications for angiotensin-converting enzyme inhibition such as diabetes or hypertension. Pulmonary valve implantation, whether surgical or transcatheter, is likely to remain the mainstay of treatment. The spectrum of patients suitable for less invasive transcatheter pulmonary valve implantation may increase with advances in device design, and this may supersede "re-do" surgical pulmonary valve implantation more frequently. Strategies preserving pulmonary competence may become more aggressive, and it is not inconceivable that in the future no patient will be allowed to have long-term pulmonary incompetence.

REFERENCES

1. Murphy JG, Gersh BJ, Mair DD, et al. Long-term outcome in patients undergoing surgical repair of tetralogy of Fallot. N Engl J Med 1993;329:593–599.
2. Nollert G, Fischlein T, Bouterwek S, et al. Long-term survival in patients with repair of tetralogy of Fallot: 36-year follow-up of 490 survivors of the first year after surgical repair. J Am Coll Cardiol 1997;30:1374–1383.
3. Niwa K, Siu SC, Webb GD, et al. Progressive aortic root dilation in adults late after repair of tetralogy of Fallot. Circulation 2002;106:1374–1378.
4. Gatzoulis MA, Balaji S, Webber SA, et al. Risk factors for arrhythmia and sudden cardiac death late after repair of tetralogy of Fallot: a multicentre study. Lancet 2000;356:975–981.
5. Gatzoulis MA, Till JA, Somerville J, et al. Mechanoelectrical interaction in tetralogy of Fallot: QRS prolongation relates to right ventricular size and predicts malignant ventricular arrhythmias and sudden death. Circulation 1995;92:231–237.
6. Gatzoulis MA, Till JA, Redington AN. Depolarization-repolarization inhomogeneity after repair of tetralogy of Fallot: The substrate for malignant ventricular tachycardia? Circulation 1997;95:401–404.
7. Gatzoulis MA, Clark AL, Cullen S, et al. Right ventricular diastolic function 15 to 35 years after repair of tetralogy of Fallot: Restrictive physiology predicts superior exercise performance. Circulation 1995;91:1775–1781.
8. Davlouros PA, Kilner PJ, Hornung TS, et al. Right ventricular function in adults with repaired tetralogy of Fallot assessed with cardiovascular magnetic resonance imaging: detrimental role of right ventricular outflow aneurysms or akinesia and adverse right-to-left ventricular interaction. J Am Coll Cardiol 2002;40:2044–2052.
9. Kilner PJ, Balossino R, Dubini G, et al. Pulmonary regurgitation: the effects of varying pulmonary artery compliance and of increased resistance proximal or distal to the compliance. Int J Cardiol 2009;133:157–166.
10. Chaturvedi RR, Kilner PJ, White PA, et al. Increased airway pressure and simulated branch pulmonary artery stenosis increase pulmonary regurgitation after repair of tetralogy of Fallot: real-time

analysis with a conductance catheter technique. Circulation 1997;95:643–649.
11. Khambadkone S, Coats L, Taylor A, et al. Percutaneous pulmonary valve implantation in humans: results in 59 consecutive patients. Circulation 2005;112:1189–1197.
12. Babu-Narayan SV, Kilner PJ, Li W, et al. Ventricular fibrosis suggested by cardiovascular magnetic resonance in adults with repaired tetralogy of Fallot and its relationship to adverse markers of clinical outcome. Circulation 2006;113:405–413.
13. Oechslin EN, Harrison DA, Harris L, et al. Reoperation in adults with repair of tetralogy of Fallot: indications and outcomes. J Thorac Cardiovasc Surg 1999;118:245–251.
14. Vliegen HW, van Straten A, de Roos A, et al. Magnetic resonance imaging to assess the hemodynamic effects of pulmonary valve replacement in adults late after repair of tetralogy of Fallot. Circulation 2002;106:1703–1707.
15. Dave HH, Buechel ER, Dodge-Khatami A, et al. Early insertion of a pulmonary valve for chronic regurgitation helps restoration of ventricular dimensions. Ann Thorac Surg 2005;80:1615–1620 discussion 1620–1621.
16. Frigiola A, Tsang V, Bull C, et al. Biventricular response after pulmonary valve replacement for right ventricular outflow tract dysfunction: is age a predictor of outcome? Circulation 2008;118(Suppl. 14):S182–S190.
17. Uebing A, Arvanitis P, Li W, et al. Effect of pregnancy on clinical status and ventricular function in women with heart disease. Int J Cardiol 2010;139:50–59.
18. Davos CH, Davlouros PA, Wensel R, et al. Global impairment of cardiac autonomic nervous activity late after repair of tetralogy of Fallot. Circulation 2002;106(12 Suppl. 1):I69–I75.
19. Bolger AP, Sharma R, Li W, et al. Neurohormonal activation and the chronic heart failure syndrome in adults with congenital heart disease. Circulation 2002;106:92–99.
20. Uebing A, Gibson DG, Babu-Narayan SV, et al. Right ventricular mechanics and QRS duration in patients with repaired tetralogy of Fallot: implications of infundibular disease. Circulation 2007;116:1532–1539.

21. Roos-Hesselink J, Perlroth MG, McGhie J, et al. Atrial arrhythmias in adults after repair of tetralogy of Fallot: correlations with clinical, exercise, and echocardiographic findings. Circulation 1995;91:2214–2219.
22. Cullen S, Celermajer DS, Franklin RC, et al. Prognostic significance of ventricular arrhythmia after repair of tetralogy of Fallot: a 12-year prospective study. J Am Coll Cardiol 1994;23:1151–1155.
23. Therrien J, Siu SC, Harris L, et al. Impact of pulmonary valve replacement on arrhythmia propensity late after repair of tetralogy of Fallot. Circulation 2001;103:2489–2494.
24. Geva T, Sandweiss BM, Gauvreau K, et al. Factors associated with impaired clinical status in long-term survivors of tetralogy of Fallot repair evaluated by magnetic resonance imaging. J Am Coll Cardiol 2004;43:1068–1074.
25. Ghai A, Silversides C, Harris L, et al. Left ventricular dysfunction is a risk factor for sudden cardiac death in adults late after repair of tetralogy of Fallot. J Am Coll Cardiol 2002;40:1675–1680.
26. Bove EL, Byrum CJ, Thomas FD, et al. The influence of pulmonary insufficiency on ventricular function following repair of tetralogy of Fallot: evaluation using radionuclide ventriculography. J Thorac Cardiovasc Surg 1983;85:691–696.
27. Khairy P, Harris L, Landzberg MJ, et al. Implantable cardioverter-defibrillators in tetralogy of Fallot. Circulation 2008;117:363–370.
28. Witte KK, Pepper CB, Cowan JC, et al. Implantable cardioverter-defibrillator therapy in adult patients with tetralogy of Fallot. Europace 2008;10:926–930.
29. Tan JL, Davlouros PA, McCarthy KP, et al. Intrinsic histological abnormalities of aortic root and ascending aorta in tetralogy of Fallot: evidence of causative mechanism for aortic dilation and aortopathy. Circulation 2005;112:961–968.
30. Babu-Narayan SV, Uebing A, Davlouros PA, et al. ACE inhibitors for potential prevention of the deleterious effects of pulmonary regurgitation in adults with tetralogy of fallot repair—the appropriate Study—a randomised, double-blinded, placebo-controlled trial in adults with congenital heart disease. Circulation 2006;114:II409.

Pulmonary Atresia with Ventricular Septal Defect

CRAIG S. BROBERG | GEORGE A. PANTELY

Introduction

Pulmonary atresia, or absence of a communication between the right ventricle and the main pulmonary artery, exists in two forms based on the presence or absence of a ventricular septal defect (VSD). Despite similar nomenclature they are very different entities, each with a distinct management strategy and expected outcome. Pulmonary atresia with a VSD (PA+VSD), discussed here, is similar to tetralogy of Fallot. Patients usually have two functional ventricles, a VSD below the aortic valve (i.e., "subaortic"), and, unlike tetralogy, collateral arteries to the lungs. In contrast, pulmonary atresia with an intact ventricular septum (PA+IVS) is characterized by a hypoplastic right ventricle, a patent ductus arteriosus supplying blood to the lungs, and coronary fistulas, most often treated with a single ventricle palliation. PA+IVS is discussed in Chapter 46.

PA+VSD varies from simple to complex. In its simplest form the lesion is merely an extreme variant of tetralogy of Fallot with an imperforate pulmonary valve. Accordingly, the clinical management of tetralogy of Fallot (see Chapter 43) also largely applies to PA+VSD. In its more complex form there is atresia of the main pulmonary artery or its major branches and some or all of the lung parenchyma is instead supplied by collateral arteries arising from the aorta or its major branches. This is similar to type 4 truncus arteriosus.[1,2] In either case, blood leaving the right ventricle exits through the overriding aortic valve, mixes with left ventricular output, and contributes to both the pulmonic and systemic circulations.

The challenge in the management of PA+VSD is optimizing pulmonary blood flow and pressure, that is, having neither too little nor too much. Heterogeneity of pulmonary blood flow is the rule and complicates treatment considerably. The amount of native pulmonary vasculature present and the extent of collateral blood flow to the lungs determine the treatment approach for each individual.[3,4] These collateral vessels, known as major aortopulmonary collateral arteries (MAPCAs), are crucial for gas exchange and for the development of lung tissue but can also present difficulty in the long term.

Anatomy

PULMONARY VASCULATURE

In simple cases the main pulmonary artery may be present but small with only pulmonary valve atresia. In more severe cases the pulmonary artery itself may be severely atretic or nonexistent, with the exception of a small fibrous band connected to the infundibulum. Absent flow through the pulmonary arteries in utero contributes to further atresia of the distal vessels, such that the lesion can essentially propagate itself downstream. The extent of distal arborization may not be sufficient for blood to reach all portions of lung parenchyma. Lung segments not in communication with the branch pulmonary arteries are usually perfused via MAPCAs. Either lung may be smaller than usual as a result of inadequate perfusion.

Confluence between the right pulmonary artery (RPA) and the left pulmonary artery (LPA) is an important variable that aids in differentiating individuals along the spectrum of lesion severity. Confluence occurs in the majority (85%) and simplifies the initial management,[4] because the pulmonary arteries are in communication and

the pulmonary blood flow arises predominantly from either a patent ductus arteriosus (Fig. 44-1A) or from MAPCAs, especially if the RPA and LPA are hypoplastic (see Fig. 44-1B). When the RPA and LPA are not confluent, different parts of the lung are perfused strictly via MAPCAs (see Fig. 44-1C).

MAPCAs can be vessels of substantial diameter (>10 mm at times) with a muscular layer. They typically arise from the descending thoracic aorta (Fig. 44-2) or any of its branches, including the subclavian, intercostal, bronchial, or celiac arteries. Rarely, coronary arteries can be the origin of collateral arteries to the pulmonary circulation,[5] usually without significant coronary steal.[6] MAPCAs most often anastomose with the pulmonary artery branches fairly proximally, and with somatic growth these anastomoses can become stenotic over time. These differ from acquired collateral blood vessels to the lungs associated with cyanosis, which usually join the pulmonary blood supply more distally at or near the precapillary level.

Intracardiac Anatomy

The VSD is typically a large, perimembranous subaortic defect, as seen in tetralogy of Fallot (Fig. 44-3A). Less commonly, the defect may be subpulmonic, when the aorta is malposed anteriorly (such as a Taussig-Bing anomaly with transposition of the great arteries). The terminology may become inconsistent because there is only one semilunar valve. Hence the terms *double-outlet right ventricle* or *transposition of the great arteries,* although convenient, may be misnomers in the setting of coexistent pulmonary atresia.

PA+VSD can also be associated with other congenital defects, including a right-sided aortic arch (25% of cases), dextrocardia, L-type malrotation, atrioventricular septal defects, or heterotaxy syndromes,[7] especially when 22q11 deletion is present.[8] Management is more complex with these additional anatomic variants.

Genetics and Epidemiology

PA+VSD comprises 1% to 2% of all congenital heart defects or 7/100,000 live births.[9] Roughly 10% of individuals with tetralogy of Fallot have the PA+VSD variant.[10] Importantly, 22q11 deletions are more commonly found in patients with PA+VSD (40%) than in those with tetralogy of Fallot.[11] Those with the deletion typically have a more complex pattern, with small pulmonary arteries and MAPCA dependence.[8]

Early Presentation

Patients with PA+VSD present with varying severity of cyanosis determined by the extent of their native pulmonary arterial supply and the presence of MAPCAs. These are critical to sustain life if or when the ductus arteriosus closes (often later than usual).[12] If MAPCAs are insufficient, a child will be given prostaglandins until a surgical shunt is created to provide adequate pulmonary blood flow. If MAPCAs are too abundant or unrestricted (less common), pulmonary blood flow increases as the pulmonary vascular resistance falls and pulmonary congestion with heart failure symptoms may result. Without surgery to either increase or limit pulmonary blood flow prolonged survival is unlikely.[13,14] Those with adequate but not excessive pulmonary blood flow can survive into adulthood without surgery, although such a well-balanced circulation occurs infrequently.

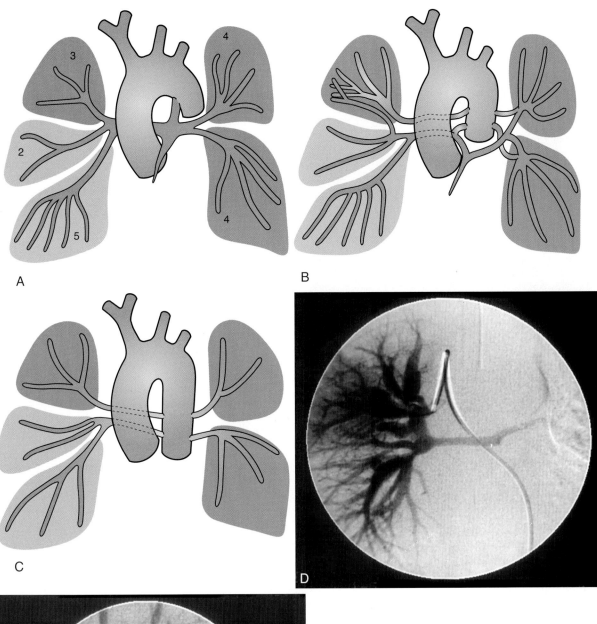

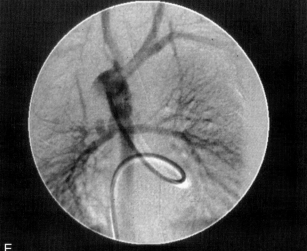

Figure 44-1 Three patterns of pulmonary arterial anatomy in PA+VSD. **A,** Well-formed central pulmonary arteries with normal arborization are present. Pulmonary blood supply is via a patent ductus. **B,** Central but hypoplastic pulmonary arteries are present and coexist with MAPCAs. **C,** Central pulmonary arteries are absent and pulmonary blood supply is entirely via MAPCAs. **D,** Angiogram demonstrating the pattern in **B**: selective injection into a MAPCA retrogradely fills small pulmonary arteries that taper toward the atretic main pulmonary artery, producing a "sea gull" sign. **E,** Angiogram demonstrating the pattern in **C**: an aortogram with injection into the descending aorta reveals large bilateral MAPCAs. (*A to C, After Baker EJ. Tetralogy of Fallot with pulmonary atresia. In: Anderson RH, Baker EJ, Macartney FJ, et al, eds. Paediatric Cardiology. London: Churchill Livingstone; 2002:1251–1280, with permission.*)

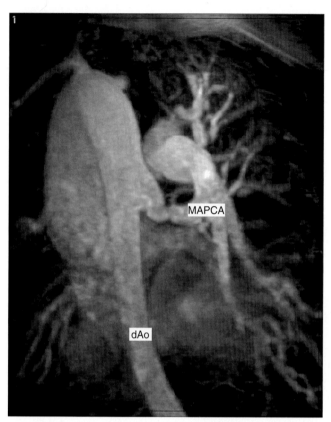

Figure 44-2 Cardiac magnetic resonance (CMR) angiography with gadolinium contrast enhancement for visualization of pulmonary blood supply. Variations in major aortopulmonary collateral artery (MAPCA) anatomy can be well demonstrated with this modality. This is a posterior view of a patient with a very large MAPCA arising from the descending aorta (dAo) to supply most of the vasculature of the right lung.

Management

Providers for adults are obliged to understand the early interventions made on an individual patient. The major goals of initial management are to ensure adequate pulmonary blood flow without overcirculation, specifically to (1) establish a confluent, functional pulmonary vasculature if possible, (2) achieve a right ventricular-to-pulmonary arterial (RV-PA) connection, and (3) close the VSD with a patch (see Fig. 44-3B). The means of achieving this have evolved over the past several decades. In most adult patients, this likely involved a multistage approach with several operations in childhood (Fig. 44-4). Surgeons are now more frequently able to meet these goals with a single surgery.[15]

The vast majority of adults will have undergone a palliative systemic to pulmonary arterial shunt procedure early in life to improve pulmonary blood flow. Several types of shunts have been used over the years and are well described elsewhere (see Chapter 43). These shunts increase pulmonary blood flow and promote growth of the pulmonary vasculature. A Blalock-Taussig shunt, first performed in 1944, marked the beginning of the era of surgical intervention in cyanotic congenital heart disease. The shunt connected the subclavian artery with the ipsilateral pulmonary artery. It was usually placed on the side opposite the aortic arch to avoid kinking. The modern Blalock-Taussig shunt uses a Gore-Tex conduit between the subclavian and pulmonary artery to better control the shunt volume (see Fig. 44-4B) and is presently the most common systemic to pulmonary arterial shunt.

Other options include a Waterston-Cooley shunt (an interposition graft between the ascending aorta and the RPA), Potts shunt (anastomosis between the descending aorta and LPA), or central shunt (ascending aorta to the main pulmonary artery via a synthetic conduit). These are rarely used by surgeons presently, because complications such as severe distortion of the pulmonary arteries or pulmonary arterial hypertension were more common. However, they all may be seen in surviving adult patients today. A Melbourne shunt, introduced more recently, uses an end-to-side anastomosis of the ascending aorta to the pulmonary artery.[16]

For patients with severely atretic native pulmonary arteries, unifocalization is required to reconstruct the pulmonary vascular bed from available vascular tissue, including MAPCAs.[4,17] Unifocalization involves painstaking dissection and reunion of vessels, with synthetic material placed to bring the "RPA" and "LPA" into communication. This process is often staged through several surgeries (see Fig. 44-4). When successful, unifocalization allows for placement of a valved RV-PA conduit and VSD closure. Treatment with a single-stage surgical procedure is becoming more common,[15] as is a hybrid catheter/surgical approach.[18] An assessment of the adequacy of arborization, sometimes using schemes for objectively measuring pulmonary vasculature such as the McGoon ratio,[19] or Nakata index,[20] can guide decision-making early on. Decisions are sometimes based on intraoperative assessment of pulmonary blood flow.[21]

Single-ventricle palliation may be necessary if the right ventricle is too small to sustain a biventricular circulation.[4] However, creation of a Fontan pathway may not be an option if the pulmonary vasculature is not favorable.

Figure 44-3 **A,** Oblique coronal MR image showing a large VSD with the aorta overriding both the right and left ventricles. The patient had not undergone repair, and hence there is persistent RV hypertrophy from systemic level pressures. **B,** MR image in a similar plane from a different patient with a patch (*arrow*) over the VSD. LV, left ventricle; RV, right ventricle.

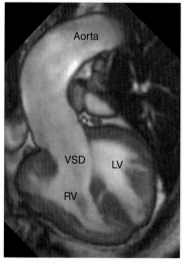

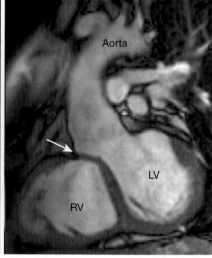

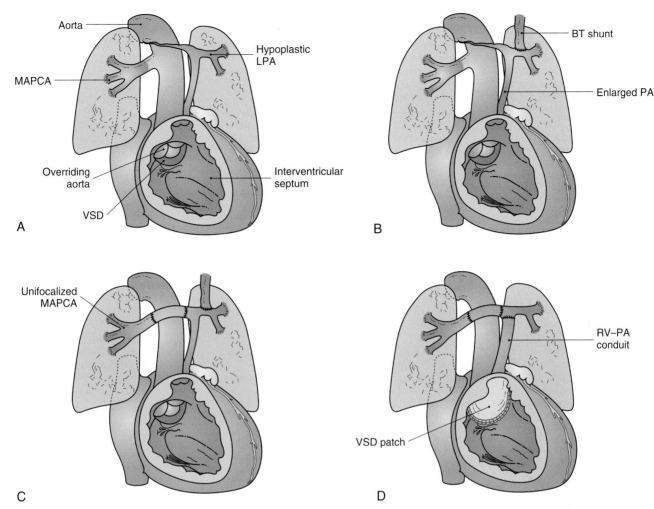

Figure 44-4 Multistage surgical repair of PA+VSD. **A,** Before repair, the left main pulmonary artery (LPA) is hypoplastic. Large major aortopulmonary collateral arteries (MAPCAs) supply the right and left lung. Intracardiac anatomy is consistent with tetralogy of Fallot. **B,** A left Blalock-Taussig (BT) shunt is created to increase pulmonary blood flow to left lung, resulting in growth of the main pulmonary artery (PA). **C,** The MAPCA to the right lung is now unifocalized with the left using a prosthetic interposition graft. **D,** Once an independent pulmonary circulation has been created, a conduit connects the right ventricular mass to the pulmonary artery and the VSD is closed.

▥ Long-Term Outcome

Complications are the rule rather than the exception in PA+VSD, and all patients deserve close, informed follow-up. The provider must review the past records to understand details of the patient's original anatomy and the interventions subsequently performed (Box 44-1).

Unoperated adult patients are uncommon. They either have protected pulmonary blood flow from adequate resistance in the MAPCAs or unprotected pulmonary blood flow and Eisenmenger syndrome physiology. Intervention on such a patient is rarely justified but is determined based on thorough review of clinical status, existing pulmonary blood flow and pressure, and biventricular function.

BOX 44-1   COMPLICATIONS

Patients with Repaired Pulmonary Atresia and Ventricular Septal Defect
- RV-PA conduit stenosis and regurgitation—due to calcification and degeneration of the conduit over time
- Right ventricular pressure overload—due to conduit stenosis, branch pulmonary artery stenosis, stenoses in unifocalized MAPCAs or hypoplastic pulmonary arteries, or arborization defects of pulmonary vasculature
- Right-sided heart failure—due to right ventricular pressure or volume overload
- Tricuspid regurgitation—due to right ventricular dysfunction
- Left-sided heart failure—due to long-standing volume overload (excess circulation from MAPCAs or aortic insufficiency) or coexistent right ventricular failure
- Aortic root dilation and regurgitation—may be progressive
- Endocarditis—in a conduit or on other residual lesions
- Arrhythmias—supraventricular (atrial fibrillation, atrial flutter, or

atrial tachycardia), usually related to right-sided heart failure. Ventricular arrhythmias may be related to ventriculotomy, intrinsic myocardial abnormalities, or progressive ventricular dilation and dysfunction.

Palliated and Unoperated Patients
- Cyanosis—due to inadequate pulmonary blood flow
- Pulmonary hypertension—may be segmental, due to chronically excessive blood flow in lung segments supplied by large, unrestrictive MAPCAs or shunts
- Left ventricular dysfunction—due to long-standing volume overload from MAPCAs or aortic regurgitation, myocardial ischemia from cyanosis, or right ventricular failure.
- Aortic root dilation and regurgitation—may be progressive
- Arrhythmias—as above
- Stroke—due to paradoxical emboli from intracardiac communications or in-situ thrombosis related to erythropoiesis

Palliated patients will usually have undergone a shunt or unifocalization, but VSD closure and RV-PA connection may not have been possible. These patients remain cyanotic. If their condition is stable and they have few or no symptoms, then long-term survival is reasonable. Thus, further complex, risky surgical procedures may not be warranted. Palliated patients or those who have not undergone repair and who are without an RPA-LPA confluence may have a different response in the two lungs: low pulmonary vascular resistance in one and high pulmonary vascular resistance in the other (Fig. 44-5).

The vast majority of adults will have undergone repair, meaning VSD closure and RV-PA flow, but are not free from complications or further intervention. Although patients with repaired tetralogy of Fallot commonly have pulmonary regurgitation, PA+VSD patients are more likely to develop pulmonary stenosis (Fig. 44-6B). Common locations include the RV-PA conduit valve, conduit anastomoses, or major branch pulmonary arteries. Approximately one half of patients will have required reoperation within 10 years of initial repair, and two thirds of patients will do so within 20 years.[22]

Patients may be at risk for problems related to overcirculation of the lungs from MAPCAs. Although these arteries are critical in early life, after repair they can become disadvantageous by causing overperfusion, heart failure, or increased pulmonary vascular resistance. Catheterization for coil occlusion of these vessels may be required.

Both chronic pulmonary stenosis and regurgitation have implications for the long-term function of the right ventricle. Ventricular fibrosis, restriction, dilation, and dysfunction are all encountered and can be manifest by arrhythmia (atrial or ventricular) or heart failure symptoms such as fatigue, dyspnea with exertion, edema, or ascites. Earlier intervention aims at improving the hemodynamic burden for the right ventricle. When right ventricular dysfunction is severe, further surgical intervention may be too risky and sometimes should not be undertaken without the option of mechanical support as a bridge to transplantation if the right ventricle fails to recover postoperatively.

The left ventricle may also become dysfunctional. This may be due to coexisting right ventricular failure, prior repeated cardiopulmonary bypass, or volume overload from aortic insufficiency. The latter usually relates to enlargement of the ascending aorta, which is more common in PA+VSD patients than in those with tetralogy of Fallot.[23] Reasons for ascending aortic dilation are not entirely known but may relate to the increased circulation through the aorta after a shunt procedure since it is then carrying both systemic and pulmonary flow, and possibly increased after a shunt procedure.

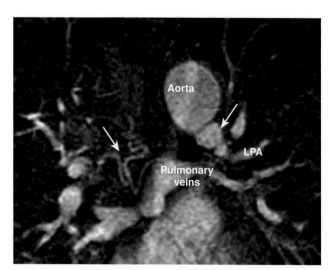

Figure 44-5 Patient with a Potts shunt from descending aorta to LPA (*right arrow*), eventually leading to pulmonary hypertension in the left lung only. There was no confluence between the right and left pulmonary arteries. The right lung was supplied via collateral arteries (a small one is shown [*left arrow*]) and had low circulating pressure. LPA, left pulmonary artery.

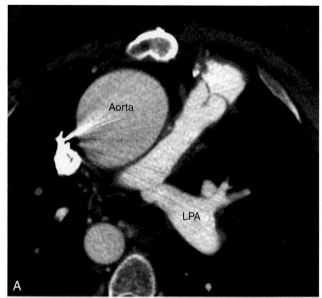

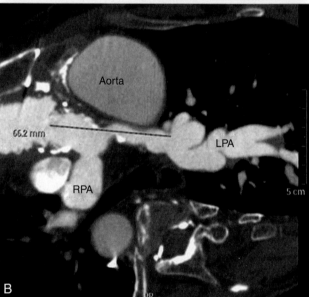

Figure 44-6 **A,** A valved RV-PA conduit arising from the anterior free wall of the RV, left of the ascending aorta. The left pulmonary artery (LPA) takes off at a 90° angle, with slight stenosis at this anastomosis. Note the enlarged ascending aorta. **B,** An RV-PA conduit from a patient with dextrocardia. The conduit arises from the right ventricle, right of the ascending aorta. It is severely calcified and stenosed along most of its course. The proximal right pulmonary artery (RPA) is also mildly stenosed. The LPA appears tortuous where several large collateral arteries join the artery.

Outpatient Assessment

Guidelines for the management of adults with congenital heart disease have been recently published.[24] Patients with PA+VSD (considered under the tetralogy of Fallot section of the guidelines) should be seen at least yearly by informed providers familiar with this lesion and its complications, together with appropriate imaging (see later; Box 44-2).

Patients should be questioned about exertional capacity, oral hygiene, contraception/pregnancy issues, unexplained fevers, hemoptysis, or chest pain. Any history of syncope, near-syncope, or arrhythmia should be investigated. The presence of significant arrhythmia should prompt a thorough assessment of the hemodynamics.

On physical examination a systolic ejection murmur in the pulmonic position is commonly heard, usually from the conduit. It may radiate

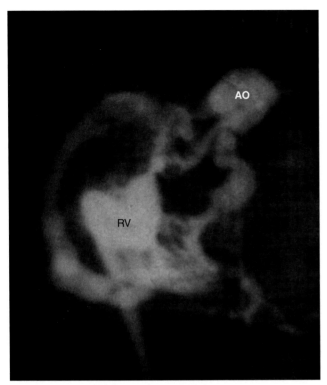

Figure 46-5 RV angiogram showing RV to coronary artery fistula and retrograde filling of the aorta. Ao, aorta; RV, right ventricle.

TABLE 46-1	Morphologic Variables in Pulmonary Atresia with Intact Ventricular Septum
Tricuspid valve diameter (Z score)	
Tricuspid valve function: stenosis and/or regurgitation	
Tripartite/bipartite/unipartite right ventricle	
RV cavity size	
RV outflow obstruction: membranous/muscular	
Presence of RV to coronary artery fistulas	
RV-dependent coronary circulation: coronary ectasia, stenoses, and interruptions	

RV, right ventricular.
Modified from Shinebourne EA, Rigby ML, Carvalho JS. Pulmonary atresia with intact ventricular septum: from fetus to adult: congenital heart disease. Heart 2008; 94:1350–1357.

repair. When this is not clear-cut, the strategy is usually to aim toward a biventricular repair, establish RV to pulmonary artery continuity, and maximize RV growth, because an arterial shunt alone may preclude this in the future. Management options are listed in Table 46-2.

BIVENTRICULAR STRATEGY

The long-term aim of biventricular strategy is to achieve separated pulmonary and systemic circulations with *two* pumping chambers. This requires a reasonable-sized RV, without significant coronary artery abnormalities (i.e., RV to coronary artery fistulas are permissible, coronary stenosis/interruptions/ectasia is not permissible) and with adequate TV size and function (see Fig. 46-1). Traditionally this involved surgical intervention to reconstruct the RV outflow tract (see Table 46-2). When there is concern as to whether the RV can generate sufficient pulmonary blood flow, then a systemic-to-pulmonary shunt is created in addition (modified Blalock-Taussig shunt). Since the 1990s it has become feasible to achieve transcatheter radiofrequency perforation of the atretic pulmonary membrane when there is membranous rather than muscular atresia (Fig. 46-6).[20] A total of 40% to 60% of patients subsequently require a surgical arterial shunt because of continuing cyanosis, leading some groups to stent the arterial duct routinely. Some also ultimately need a surgical RV outflow tract procedure.[20] However, a biventricular circulation is usually achieved, with transcatheter closure of the shunt performed 2 to 4 years later.[14,20]

1.5-VENTRICLE REPAIR

In some cases in which the RV is of borderline size it becomes apparent that the RV will not be capable of totally supporting the pulmonary circulation alone. In such cases, after an initial RV outflow tract procedure, a superior bidirectional cavopulmonary anastomosis can be fashioned to provide an additional source of pulmonary blood flow. Once any arterial shunts and/or atrial septal defects (ASDs) are closed this is known as a 1.5-ventricle repair.

UNIVENTRICULAR STRATEGY

The long-term aim of a univentricular strategy is to achieve separated pulmonary and systemic circulations with only *one* contributory pumping chamber (the left ventricle). It tends to be performed in those with small RVs (see Fig. 46-3) or an RV-dependent coronary circulation (see Figs. 46-4 and 46-5). A balloon atrial septostomy is initially performed to enable the obligatory right-to-left shunt and prevent obstruction, followed by an arterial shunt, a superior cavopulmonary anastomosis (bidirectional Glenn procedure), and then finally a total cavopulmonary connection (TCPC).

TABLE 46-2	Management Options in Childhood for Each Initial Strategy			
Initial Strategy		*Procedure Sequence*		
Biventricular repair	**Catheter procedure** Wire/laser/radiofrequency perforation of pulmonary valve + Balloon valvuloplasty +/– **Surgery** Surgical systemic to pulmonary shunt (modified Blalock-Taussig shunt)	**Catheter procedure** Device occlusion of systemic to pulmonary shunt Device occlusion of residual ASD		
	Surgery Pulmonary valvotomy/valvectomy +/–Transannular patch +/– Monocusp homograft +/– Surgical systemic to pulmonary shunt (modified Blalock-Taussig shunt) +/– **Hybrid procedure** Stenting of patent ductus arteriosus			
Univentricular repair	Balloon atrial septostomy	**Surgery** Systemic to pulmonary shunt (modified Blalock-Taussig shunt)	**Surgery** Superior cavopulmonary anastomosis (bidirectional Glenn)	**Surgery** Total cavopulmonary connection (TCPC)

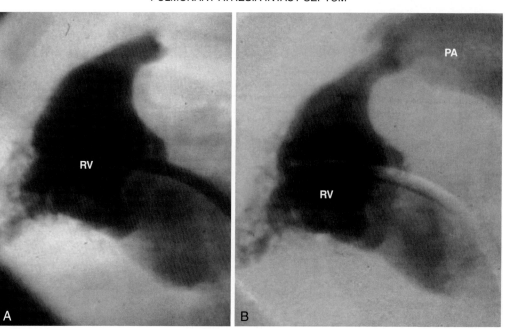

Figure 46-6 Lateral angiograms showing **(A)** contrast medium injected into the right ventricle (RV) filling the infundibulum but ending at the level of the imperforate pulmonary valve and **(B)** contrast medium passing into the pulmonary artery (PA) after radiofrequency perforation of the imperforate pulmonary valve.

PULMONARY ATRESIA INTACT SEPTUM

SEVERELY DILATED RIGHT VENTRICLES

When there is gross dilation of the RV at presentation, often due to severe tricuspid regurgitation, the mortality is high with little improvement despite advances in fetal diagnosis and surgical management.[4,12,16] The operative strategy must include TV repair or, in many cases, occlusion of the TV with construction of a systemic to pulmonary arterial shunt (Starnes procedure) followed by a univentricular route.

There is substantial debate as to which initial strategy should be adopted. Most groups utilize single or multiple morphologic features on presentation as a guide to the initial management. These include (selected from many others):

- Tricuspid size (often expressed as a Z score[4,6,23]
- Partite classification of the RV (tripartite, bipartite, or unipartite)[23]
- Infundibular size[24]
- Indices of right ventricular size[9,10]
- Presence of coronary artery stenoses[25]

Late Outcome

SURVIVAL AND FUNCTIONAL STATUS

Survivors are now reaching adulthood. Their numbers are few (but increasing), and this relates to the rarity of the disease and high early mortality. Correspondingly, there are scant data about survival and functional status in adulthood. The Toronto Hospital for Sick Children reported 10-year survival of 43%, the Congenital Heart Surgeons study reported 15-year survival at 58%, the Swedish Collaborative study noted 10-year survival of 68%, but more reassuringly a recent series from the University of California, Los Angeles (UCLA), reported a 10-year survival of 86%.[6–9] In the future an increasing number of patients will be expected to reach adulthood.

Biventricular Repair

Mortality with biventricular repair tends to occur in the first 6 months of life, and the survival curves then flatten.[4,12,26] A Japanese study documented 14-year survival after biventricular repair at 86%.[26] Twenty percent of patients had late arrhythmias, and right atrial dilation was found in all patients.

Although intuitive there is limited actual evidence that biventricular repair is better than univentricular repair. Sanghavi and associates[27] found no statistical difference in exercise capacity between those with biventricular versus

univentricular repair using programmed bicycle ergonometry. Most patients in both groups had subnormal peak oxygen consumption and a trend toward impaired performance with increasing age. Similarly, Ekman-Joelsson and colleagues, in the Swedish Collaborative Study,[28] found no difference in exercise capacity in patients after biventricular versus univentricular repair, although the group with RV to coronary artery fistulas and a biventricular repair did worse. Decreased lung function was noted in all groups.

There are several possible explanations for these findings. It is known that after biventricular repair patients have evidence of RV diastolic dysfunction with restrictive RV physiology. With atrial contraction there is retrograde flow in the superior vena cava and antegrade flow in the pulmonary artery. In addition, widespread perfusion defects have been found using myocardial perfusion scintigraphy, particularly in the ventricular septum.[29] Mi and Cheung have documented abnormalities of both RV and left ventricular (LV) long-axis function in patients late after biventricular repair.[30]

Until more specific data are available, prediction of longer-term outcome can be made only by drawing parallels with other diseases. After a biventricular repair for PAIVS, patients show many similarities with patients who have undergone definitive repair of pulmonary stenosis and tetralogy of Fallot (see Chapters 41 and 43). When there is minimal residual hemodynamic disturbance, long-term outlook is probably excellent with good quality of life. Mild residual pulmonary stenosis should be well tolerated; if it is more severe it may lead to arrhythmia from atrial dilation. Long-standing pulmonary regurgitation has been shown to be detrimental to RV function in tetralogy of Fallot (see Chapter 43) and may be expected to cause similar problems in PAIVS. Little is known about the risks of sudden death and ventricular tachycardia in patients with PAIVS in adult life, but they may be expected in patients with residual pulmonary regurgitation. Long-term complications are shown in Table 46-3.

1.5-Ventricle Repair

Numata and coworkers explored whether there was any functional benefit in having a 1.5-ventricle repair compared with a univentricular repair. At 5 and 10 years there was no difference in exercise capacity. Atrial arrhythmias were common in the 1.5-ventricle repair group.[31]

Univentricular Repair

In those embarking down the route toward a Fontan circulation, mortality tends to occur early in childhood, often within a few months of

TABLE 46-3	Late Complications After Repair of Pulmonary Atresia with Intact Ventricular Septum		
	Type of Circulation	*Residual Lesion*	*Complication*
Separate pulmonary and systemic circulations	Biventricular	Pulmonary stenosis	Atrial arrhythmias Angina Syncope
		Pulmonary regurgitation	Atrial and ventricular arrhythmias Sudden death Exercise intolerance
		Tricuspid regurgitation	Atrial and ventricular arrhythmias Exercise intolerance Fatigability
	1.5-Ventricle repair	As above	As above
	Univentricular	Right atrial dilation	Atrial arrhythmia Thromboembolism Right pulmonary vein occlusion
		Coronary stenoses	Sudden death Angina Ventricular arrhythmias Left ventricular dysfunction
		High systemic venous pressure	Protein-losing enteropathy Hepatic dysfunction
		Systemic to pulmonary venous collateralization	Cyanosis
Incomplete separation of pulmonary and systemic circulations	Mixed circulation	Common mixing of systemic and pulmonary circulations	Cyanosis Erythrocytosis Thromboembolism Fatigability Arrhythmias

the initial procedure.[4,12,32] There is an ongoing mortality hazard, but the data available indicate that the influence of coronary abnormalities may be less than predicted.

A study from the Mayo Clinic of 40 patients who underwent the Fontan procedure for PAIVS found three operative deaths and also three later deaths at 2.5, 8, and 8 years postoperatively.[32] Cause of death was presumed dysrhythmia in 2 patients and protein-losing enteropathy in the third. The median age of survivors was 13 years (range: 4 to 30 years); all but 1 were in New York Heart Association (NYHA) functional class I or II. This was a highly preselected group with a low incidence of coronary fistulas (10%) and RV-dependent coronary blood flow (2.5%).

A study from Toronto reported survival after the Fontan procedure of 80% at 10 years with only one late death 1 year after procedure.[33] This was in spite of a relatively high occurrence of coronary fistulas (68%) and RV-dependent coronary blood flow (22%). It is known that persisting RV hypertension and RV to coronary connections can lead to progression of coronary abnormalities such as stenoses, ectasia, and interruptions that can in themselves lead to sudden death. It is pertinent in the Toronto study that patients with fistulas underwent thromboexclusion (patch closure) of the TV, a technique that is believed indicated in this group to prevent ongoing coronary artery damage. Further follow-up will be required to ascertain whether this strategy leads to improved late outcome. Late complications are shown in Table 46-3.

More recently a study from Boston examined the outcome of 32 patients with RV-dependent coronary circulation and following the univentricular route.[34] There was a surprisingly good outcome with actuarial survival of 81% at 5, 10, and 15 years. All mortality occurred within 3 months of the initial systemic-to-pulmonary shunt. All patients with aortocoronary atresia died. The researchers' conclusion was that "single ventricle palliation yields excellent long-term survival and should be the preferred management strategy for these patients."[34]

Outpatient Assessment

PAIVS is a complex lesion with great morphologic heterogeneity.[1,2] After operation the complexity increases. In the outpatient setting, assessment is required for each of the residual morphologic lesions (Table 46-4). A careful history needs to be taken, in particular documenting each intervention.

TABLE 46-4	Assessment
History	Documentation of surgical and interventional procedures Symptoms
Clinical examination	Degree of cyanosis with erythrocytosis and clubbing Scars: thoracotomy and sternotomy Presence of right-sided heart failure including hepatic congestion Single second heart sound Pansystolic murmur (tricuspid regurgitation) To and fro murmur (pulmonary stenosis and regurgitation) Continuous murmurs (residual systemic shunt)
Electrocardiography	Rhythm abnormalities, right atrial hypertrophy (P pulmonale), atrial arrhythmias, ischemic changes
Chest radiography	Dilated right atrium and ventricle, pulmonary oligemia
Echocardiography	Documentation of systemic venous return Atrial baffle obstruction Right atrial size ± thrombus Presence of ASD and direction of interatrial shunt TV size, Z score and function
Angiography	RV size and function including restriction Pulmonary valve stenosis and/or regurgitation Pulmonary artery size and distortion Presence of systemic shunts Coronary artery origins LV function and mitral regurgitation RV size and function Distortion of pulmonary arteries Documentation of RV to coronary artery fistulas Presence of coronary stenoses, interruptions and ectasia Baffle leaks in Fontan circuit
MRI	Documentation of cardiac anatomy and function Degree of pulmonary stenosis and regurgitation Myocardial scarring Perfusion defects
CT Angiography	Coronary artery abnormalities
Scintigraphy	Coronary perfusion and areas of myocardial ischemia

Clinical findings will depend on which type of surgery the patient has received. After a *biventricular repair*:

- The patient should be pink, with normal volume pulses.
- The jugular venous pulse may be elevated and the RV impulse increased.
- There will usually be a normal first heart sound with a single second sound (which may be split if a homograft is inserted).
- Murmurs of residual pulmonary stenosis, regurgitation, and tricuspid regurgitation may be present.
- Hepatomegaly may be present (if tricuspid regurgitation is severe, the liver may be pulsatile).
- Patients are prone to atrial arrhythmia.

After a *Fontan procedure*:

- The patient should be pink, with saturations in the 90s.
- Brachial pulses may be absent after previous arterial shunt procedures.
- The jugular venous pulse will be greatly elevated and may only be visible on sitting up.
- There will be a single heart second.
- There may be a murmur from tricuspid regurgitation or a systolic murmur caused by blood flow from a high-pressure RV into a coronary fistula.
- Hepatic congestion may be evident.

For patients with a *mixed circulation*, the patient will be cyanosed with clubbing, erythrocytosis, and possible continuous murmurs due to patent systemic shunts and may have features of either circulation described previously.

Chest radiography will often show an increased cardiothoracic ratio with, in particular, a dilated right atrial contour. In patients with severe tricuspid regurgitation the RV may also be dilated. In a mixed circulation there may be pulmonary oligemia.

The electrocardiogram may show the presence of arrhythmias, either atrial or ventricular. There is often P pulmonale due to right atrial dilation. The QRS axis usually shows LV dominance.

Echocardiography should be used to:

- Document systematically and sequentially all the morphologic features discussed at the beginning of this chapter
- Seek residual lesions such as ASDs and patent systemic shunts
- For those with a *biventricular circulation*, document the presence and degree of tricuspid regurgitation, pulmonary regurgitation, and stenosis. The size and Z-score of the TV should be documented.
- For those with a *Fontan circulation*, assess the anastomoses as well as LV function, mitral regurgitation, and the presence of right atrial thrombus.
- Imaging of the coronary artery origins and their size to check for significant RV to coronary fistulas.

Cardiac catheterization may be required to assess the hemodynamics of the Fontan circuit. Coronary arteriography is essential because stenoses and interruptions may play a significant part in the prognosis. Assessment of the pulmonary artery anatomy is important because the patient may have had a systemic-to-pulmonary shunt in the past with pulmonary artery distortion. In contrast to pulmonary atresia with tetralogy of Fallot, native pulmonary artery stenoses or hypoplasia is relatively uncommon in patients with PAIVS. Baffle leaks should be sought in a Fontan circulation.

Magnetic resonance imaging (MRI) may supplant catheterization as a means of noninvasive assessment of the range of morphologic lesions found in this condition. It gives excellent anatomic and functional information. Evidence of myocardial scarring and abnormalities of myocardial perfusion should also be sought.

Computed tomographic angiography has excellent resolution and may be helpful in determining abnormal coronary anatomy.

Nuclear imaging conveys important information about myocardial perfusion and ischemia, particularly for those patients with significant coronary artery lesions, although abnormal anatomy imposes technical challenges.

Late Management Options

Patients with PAIVS surviving to adulthood would always have had previous operations. Until there are good adult data, management must be guided by reference to other similar anatomic lesions. Late interventions can be conveniently divided into those who have achieved separation of the pulmonary and systemic blood flow and those who have not (Table 46-5). The former may have ongoing hemodynamic lesions that need addressing; the latter may have been stable but should be considered for separation of their circulations, particularly if progression of symptoms occurs.

SEPARATED PULMONARY AND SYSTEMIC CIRCULATIONS ACHIEVED

Biventricular Repair

Many of these patients may be well with minimal residual lesions. However, after an outflow tract procedure there may be hemodynamic sequelae. Residual pulmonary stenosis should be managed as for native pulmonary stenosis. Balloon valvuloplasty is the treatment of choice for re-intervention and should be performed in cases of severe pulmonary stenosis (gradient at catheter > 50 mm Hg), where symptoms are present (exertional dyspnea, angina, presyncope, syncope), or where important atrial arrhythmias are present. Residual pulmonary regurgitation should be managed as it is after repair of pulmonary stenosis or tetralogy of Fallot (see Chapters 41 and 43). Re-intervention should be performed if there is reduced exercise capacity of cardiovascular origin, deteriorating RV function, progressive tricuspid regurgitation, atrial arrhythmias, or sustained ventricular tachycardia. This could be with surgical pulmonary valve replacement using a bioprosthesis or via transcatheter insertion of a stent-mounted valve. Substantial tricuspid regurgitation may be related to intrinsic dysplasia of this valve and if very severe may need TV repair.

1.5-Ventricle Repair

Many of the residual lesions in this group relate to the function of the TV/RV/pulmonary valve complex and are covered in the previous section.

Univentricular Repair

Many of the problems in patients with a Fontan-type circulation are more germane to the Fontan physiology rather than to PAIVS (see Chapters 11, 12, and 52). The presence of atrial arrhythmias may be due to dilation of all or part of the right atrium. This may require revision of the Fontan circuit with the possibility of creation of an external conduit. This may be combined with arrhythmia surgery. The presence of severe hepatic dysfunction, protein-losing enteropathy, or arrhythmias should promote a search for a hemodynamic cause such as pulmonary artery distortion, baffle obstruction, residual systemic to pulmonary shunt, or significant tricuspid regurgitation (into either systemic or pulmonary pathways). These may be amenable to a transcatheter approach (balloon angioplasty, stenting, coil occlusion) or alternatively to a surgical revision, including TV closure. When there is no obvious anatomic cause for high venous pressure then it may be necessary to create a fenestration in the baffle allowing a right-to-left shunt. Cyanosis may be due to right-to-left shunts arising from baffle leaks or systemic to pulmonary venous collateralization. These may be sought and embolized, preferably by a transcatheter approach.

The management of cardiac ischemia is controversial. It should prompt a thorough search to determine the cause and, in particular, the presence of coronary artery fistulas or stenoses. When it is deemed to be due to the coronary sinus draining into the high-pressure systemic venous pathway, then a Fontan revision may be necessary.

TABLE 46-5	Late Interventions		
	Type of Circulation	*Residual Lesion*	*Procedure*
Separation of pulmonary and systemic circulations	Biventricular	Pulmonary stenosis	Balloon dilation
		Pulmonary regurgitation	Surgical pulmonary valve replacement homograft
			Catheter implantable pulmonary valve
		Tricuspid regurgitation	Tricuspid valve repair or replacement
	1.5-Ventricle (RV outflow procedure and superior cavopulmonary anastomosis)	As above	As above
	Univentricular	Restrictive atrial septum/cardiac output (prior to TCPC)	Enlargement of ASD
		Arrhythmias secondary to dilated right atrium	Fontan revision surgery e.g., external conduit
			Catheter or surgical arrhythmia surgery ± Fontan revision
		Coronary ischemia	Baffle revision if coronary sinus drains to higher pressure systemic venous pathway
			Coil occlusion considered for gross ectasia
			Angioplasty of coronary stenoses
			RV to aorta shunt considered for stenoses
			Transplantation
		Tricuspid regurgitation	Tricuspid valve patch occlusion
Incomplete separation of pulmonary and systemic circulations	Good-sized RV		*Strategy toward a biventricular repair*
		ASD	Catheter or surgical closure
		Systemic to pulmonary shunt	Catheter closure
		Heavily trabeculated RV	Surgical removal of excessive muscular overgrowth "RV overhaul"[35]
	Medium-sized RV		*Strategy toward 1.5 ventricle repair*
		Volume-loaded LV with cyanosis (low PA pressures)	Cavopulmonary anastomosis alone
			As above with RV outflow procedure
			As above with closure ASD and any systemic shunts (1.5 ventricle repair)
	Small RV		Status quo or univentricular repair (provided PA pressures are low)
		Cyanosis	Total cavopulmonary anastomosis
			Repeat systemic to pulmonary shunt

ASD, atrial septal defect; LV, left ventricle; PA, pulmonary artery; RV, right ventricle; TCPC, total cavopulmonary connection.

When coronary fistulas alone are present, then thromboexclusion of the TV has been advocated.[33] Patients with coronary artery ectasia may benefit from coil occlusion; and those with stenoses may benefit from catheter intervention. When ischemia is due to severe and multiple coronary artery stenoses, then consideration should be given to cardiac transplantation, because sudden death may be an ongoing risk.

INCOMPLETE SEPARATION OF PULMONARY AND SYSTEMIC CIRCULATIONS

A significant proportion of adults with PAIVS will have a "mixed" circulation. This means there is incomplete separation of the pulmonary and systemic circuits owing to the presence of patent arterial shunts or an ASD. Many of these patients will be stable, and so intervention will be guided by symptomatology, the arterial hemoglobin oxygen saturation, the hematocrit, the size of the RV and TV, and the functional status of the LV.

Good-Sized Right Ventricle
The aim here would be to achieve separated pulmonary and systemic circulations with a biventricular repair. This may require closure of an ASD (by device preferably) and occlusion of systemic-to-pulmonary shunts (by coil preferably). If the RV is heavily trabeculated, this may require removal of muscle bundles from the body of the RV (RV overhaul).[35]

Medium-Sized Right Ventricle
The aim here would be to separate circulations with a 1.5-ventricle repair. This is the combination of a superior bidirectional cavopulmonary anastomosis and an RV outflow tract procedure. Either may have been performed previously. The advantage is considered to be that the

RV will contribute some additional pulmonary blood flow in addition to the cavopulmonary anastomosis. When the RV proves capable of this task it may be possible to close subsequently the ASD (with a device) and any arterial shunts that remain by catheter intervention.

Small-Sized Right Ventricle
The aim here would be to achieve separated circulations via a Fontan type circulation or, if not possible, optimization of the pulmonary blood flow. For a Fontan procedure the heart would have to satisfy the currently accepted criteria, which may be more stringent in adults than in children because of the chronic pressure and volumes that these ventricle have been exposed to. If these criteria are not achievable, then enhancement of pulmonary blood flow may be achieved with a systemic to pulmonary artery shunt with or without pulmonary artery repair, although this will lead to further ventricular volume overload (see Late Management Options in Chapter 51). An unrestrictive atrial septum would be essential in this case.

Arrhythmia and Sudden Cardiac Death

Limited data exist about arrhythmia and sudden cardiac death in adults with PAIVS; again, a parallel must be drawn from other congenital heart conditions. Even after a biventricular repair, many patients with PAIVS have a chronically dilated RA that may predispose to atrial arrhythmias.[26] When patients have long-standing pulmonary regurgitation and/or tricuspid regurgitation with RV dilation, the parallel with tetralogy of Fallot (see Chapter 43) suggests there may be a risk of arrhythmias, particularly ventricular tachycardia and sudden death. Long-standing atrial dilation after the Fontan procedure also predisposes to atrial arrhythmias (see Chapter 12).

Antiarrhythmic medication is required in the majority, but in each case hemodynamic abnormalities should be sought and addressed. This may involve pulmonary valve replacement or conversion of an atriopulmonary to a total cavopulmonary connection in patients with a Fontan circulation. Concomitant arrhythmia surgery forms an integral part of management.

Patients with coronary artery stenoses, interruptions, and ectasia and hence the substrate for coronary artery steal may have an additional risk of arrhythmia and sudden cardiac death (or may be already dead). Thorough documentation of the coronary abnormalities by angiography and use of nuclear or MRI perfusion scintigraphy to identify areas of ischemia are mandated in these circumstances. Treatment, however, is more problematic (see Late Management Options).

Pregnancy

Successful pregnancies have been reported in women with PAIVS after biventricular repair. There was no increased prevalence of infertility or menstrual disorders.[36]

BIVENTRICULAR REPAIR WITH RESIDUAL PULMONARY STENOSIS OR REGURGITATION

The increased hemodynamic load of pregnancy may precipitate right-sided heart failure, atrial arrhythmias, or tricuspid regurgitation. Balloon dilation can be performed during pregnancy (preferably after organogenesis), although it is better to treat the defect before conception.

UNIVENTRICULAR CIRCULATION

There are increased risks of systemic venous congestion, deterioration in ventricular function, atrial arrhythmias, thromboemboli, and paradoxical emboli if there is a fenestration in the atrial baffle. Successful pregnancy is possible, however, with meticulous cardiac and obstetric planning and supervision. If anticoagulation is required, additional risks to the fetus are involved (see Chapter 21).

MIXED CIRCULATIONS WITH CYANOSIS

There is an increased risk of maternal cardiovascular complications, prematurity, and fetal death, particularly when baseline maternal resting saturations are less than 85%.

All patients with PAIVS should have pre-pregnancy cardiology counseling and follow-up by a cardiologist specializing in adult congenital heart disease and by an obstetrician with experience in high-risk pregnancy during pregnancy and the peripartum. Fetal echocardiography is recommended.

Follow-Up, Endocarditis Prophylaxis, and Exercise

Follow-up should be life-long. For those with a biventricular repair and minimal residual hemodynamic lesion this should be every 1 to 3 years by a cardiologist. When there are significant residual lesions, follow-up should be yearly by a cardiologist specializing in adult congenital heart disease. Similarly, patients with mixed or univentricular circulations warrant tertiary care follow-up. For patients with venous shunts or the Fontan procedure, strong consideration should be given to full anticoagulation, particularly if there is suspicion of coronary artery abnormalities.

All patients should be advised of the importance of good oral hygiene in reducing the risk of endocarditis. Antibiotic prophylaxis has become controversial: it is no longer recommended routinely in the United Kingdom and the United States.

Exercise limitations need to be reviewed on an individual basis depending on the type of surgical route followed, the underlying hemodynamics, and the overall status of the patient. Generally, limitation is not necessary.

REFERENCES

1. Daubeney PE, Delany DJ, Anderson RH, et al. Pulmonary atresia with intact ventricular septum: range of morphology in a population-based study. J Am Coll Cardiol 2002;39:1670–1679.
2. Freedom RM, Mawson JB, Yoo S-J, Benson LN. Pulmonary atresia and intact ventricular septum. In: Freedom RM, Mawson JB, Yoo S-J, , Benson LN, editors. Congenital Heart Disease. Textbook of Angiocardiography. Armonk, NY: Futura Publishing; 1997. p. 617–622.
3. Bull C, Kostelka M, Sorensen K, de Leval M. Outcome measures for the neonatal management of pulmonary atresia with intact ventricular septum. J Thorac Cardiovasc Surg 1994;107:359–366.
4. Hanley FL, Sade RM, Blackstone EH, et al. Outcomes in neonatal pulmonary atresia with intact ventricular septum. J Thorac Cardiovasc Surg 1993;105:406–427.
5. Jahangiri M, Zurakowski D, Bichell D, et al. Improved results with selective management in pulmonary atresia with intact ventricular septum. J Thorac Cardiovasc Surg 1999;118:1046–1055.
6. Ashburn DA, Blackstone EH, Wells WJ, et al. Determinants of mortality and type of repair in neonates with pulmonary atresia and intact ventricular septum. J Thorac Cardiovasc Surg 2004;127:1000–1007; discussion 1007–1008.
7. Dyamenahalli U, McCrindle BW, McDonald C, et al. Pulmonary atresia with intact ventricular septum: management of, and outcomes for, a cohort of 210 consecutive patients. Cardiol Young 2004;14:299–308.
8. Ekman Joelsson BM, Sunnegardh J, Hanseus K, et al. The outcome of children born with pulmonary atresia and intact ventricular septum in Sweden from 1980 to 1999. Scand Cardiovasc J 2001;35:192–198.
9. Odim J, Laks H, Plunkett MD, Tung TC. Successful management of patients with pulmonary atresia with intact ventricular septum using a three tier grading system for right ventricular hypoplasia. Ann Thorac Surg 2006;81:678–684.
10. Yoshimura N, Yamaguchi M, Ohashi H, et al. Pulmonary atresia with intact ventricular septum: strategy based on right ventricular morphology. J Thorac Cardiovasc Surg 2003;126:1417–1426.
11. Rychik J, Levy H, Gaynor JW, et al. Outcome after operations for pulmonary atresia with intact ventricular septum. J Thorac Cardiovasc Surg 1998;116:924–931.
12. Daubeney PE, Wang D, Delany DJ, et al. Pulmonary atresia with intact ventricular septum: predictors of early and medium-term outcome in a population-based study. J Thorac Cardiovasc Surg 2005;130:1071.

13. Daubeney PE, Delany DJ, Anderson RH, et al. Pulmonary atresia with intact ventricular septum: range of morphology in a population-based study. J Am Coll Cardiol 2002;39:1670–1679.
14. Shinebourne EA, Rigby ML, Carvalho JS. Pulmonary atresia with intact ventricular septum: from fetus to adult: congenital heart disease. Heart 2008;94:1350–1357.
15. Bull C, De Leval M, Mercanti C, et al. Pulmonary atresia and intact ventricular septum: a revised classification. Circulation 1982;66:266–272.
16. Freedom RM, Jaeggi E, Perrin D, et al. The "wall-to-wall" heart in the patient with pulmonary atresia and intact ventricular septum. Cardiol Young 2006;16:18–29.
17. Freedom RM, Anderson RH, Perrin D. The significance of ventriculo-coronary arterial connections in the setting of pulmonary atresia with an intact ventricular septum. Cardiol Young 2005;15:447–468.
18. Daubeney PE, Sharland GK, Cook AC, et al. Pulmonary atresia with intact ventricular septum: impact of fetal echocardiography on incidence at birth and postnatal outcome. UK and Eire Collaborative Study of Pulmonary Atresia with Intact Ventricular Septum. Circulation 1998;98:562–566.
19. Allan LD, Cook A. Pulmonary atresia with intact ventricular septum in the fetus. Cardiol Young 1992;2:367–376.
20. Daubeney PEF. Pulmonary atresia with intact ventricular septum: United Kingdom And Ireland Collaborative study, thesis. Oxford, UK: University of Oxford; 2007.
21. Kleinman CS. The echocardiographic assessment of pulmonary atresia with intact ventricular septum. Catheter Cardiovasc Interv 2006;68:131–135.
22. Tworetzky W, McElhinney DB, Marx GR, et al. In utero valvuloplasty for pulmonary atresia with hypoplastic right ventricle: techniques and outcomes. Pediatrics 2009; Aug 24 [Epub ahead of print].
23. Bull C, Kostelka M, Sorensen K, de Leval M. Outcome measures for the neonatal management of pulmonary atresia with intact ventricular septum. J Thorac Cardiovasc Surg 1994;107:359–366.
24. Pawade A, Capuani A, Penny DJ, et al. Pulmonary atresia with intact ventricular septum: surgical management based on right ventricular infundibulum. J Card Surg 1993;8:371–383.
25. Giglia TM, Jenkins KJ, Matitiau A, et al. Influence of right heart size on outcome in pulmonary atresia with intact ventricular septum. Circulation 1993;88:2248–2256.

26. Mishima A, Asano M, Sasaki S, et al. Long-term outcome for right heart function after biventricular repair of pulmonary atresia and intact ventricular septum. Jpn J Thorac Cardiovasc Surg 2000;48:145–152.
27. Sanghavi DM, Flanagan M, Powell AJ, et al. Determinants of exercise function following univentricular versus biventricular repair for pulmonary atresia/intact ventricular septum. Am J Cardiol 2006;97:1638–1643.
28. Ekman-Joelsson BM, Gustafsson PM, Sunnegardh J. Exercise performance after surgery for pulmonary atresia and intact ventricular septum. Pediatr Cardiol 2009;30:752–762.
29. Ekman-Joelsson BM, Berggren H, Boll AB, et al. Abnormalities in myocardial perfusion after surgical correction of pulmonary atresia with intact ventricular septum. Cardiol Young 2008;18:89–95.
30. Mi YP, Cheung YF. Assessment of right and left ventricular function by tissue Doppler echocardiography in patients after biventricular repair of pulmonary atresia with intact ventricular septum. Int J Cardiol 2006;109:329–334.
31. Numata S, Uemura H, Yagihara T, et al. Long-term functional results of the one and one half ventricular repair for the spectrum of patients with pulmonary atresia/stenosis with intact ventricular septum. Eur J Cardiothorac Surg 2003;24:516–520.
32. Mair DD, Julsrud PR, Puga FJ, Danielson GK. The Fontan procedure for pulmonary atresia with intact ventricular septum: operative and late results. J Am Coll Cardiol 1997;29:1359–1364.
33. Najm HK, Williams WG, Coles JG, et al. Pulmonary atresia with intact ventricular septum: results of the Fontan procedure. Ann Thorac Surg 1997;63:669–675.
34. Guleserian KJ, Armsby LB, Thiagarajan RR, et al. Natural history of pulmonary atresia with intact ventricular septum and right-ventricle-dependent coronary circulation managed by the single-ventricle approach. Ann Thorac Surg 2006;81:2250–2257 discussion 2258.
35. Pawade A, Mee RBB, Karl T. Right ventricular "overhaul"—as an intermediate step in the biventricular repair of pulmonary atresia with intact ventricular septum. Cardiol Young 2003;24:516–520.
36. Drenthen W, Pieper PG, Roos-Hesselink JW, et al. Fertility, pregnancy, and delivery after biventricular repair for pulmonary atresia with an intact ventricular septum. Am J Cardiol 2006;98:259–261.

47

Transposition of the Great Arteries

TIM HORNUNG

Definition and Morphology

The term *transposition of the great arteries* (TGA) describes the anatomic arrangement in which the aorta arises from the right ventricle and the pulmonary artery from the left ventricle. This malformation was first described in 1797 by Baillie and later in 1814 by Farre. Associated abnormalities are relatively common, occurring in approximately 50% of patients. The most frequently associated lesions are ventricular septal defect (VSD), left ventricular outflow tract (LVOT) obstruction, and coarctation of the aorta. Although patients with more complex intracardiac anatomy, for example, tricuspid atresia or double-inlet left ventricle, may be described as having transposition of the great arteries, this terminology may be confusing and should be avoided. In these complex hearts the anatomy is most reliably described using the sequential analysis concept in which the term *ventriculoarterial discordance* would be used to describe the arrangement of the great arteries. The discussion in this chapter will therefore be restricted to that of TGA as just described.

GREAT ARTERY ORIGINS

In the great majority of patients with TGA the aorta arises from the right ventricle via a subaortic infundibulum, in a fashion analogous to the pulmonary artery in the normal heart. Conversely, the transposed pulmonary artery arises directly from the left ventricle without a subpulmonary infundibulum; there is, therefore, fibrous continuity between the mitral and pulmonary valves but no continuity between aortic and tricuspid valves.

The abnormal origins of the great arteries result in an altered relationship between the ascending aorta and main pulmonary artery. Instead of the normal crossover or spiral relationship, in TGA hearts the two vessels run parallel to each other, which is an echocardiographic feature that helps to make the diagnosis of TGA in the cyanosed neonate.

There is some morphologic variation in terms of the relative positions of the great arteries. The most common relationship of the great arteries is an anterior and rightward position of the aorta relative to the pulmonary artery. This occurs in approximately 95% of all patients. Many other arrangements have been recognized, the most common being an anterior but leftward position of the aorta. In rare cases of TGA, the aorta is the posterior vessel.

CORONARY ARTERIES

The anatomy of the coronary arteries is quite variable in patients with TGA. As shown in Figure 47-1, the coronary ostia arise from the aortic sinuses closest to the pulmonary artery, the so-called facing sinuses. The figure shows the most common arrangement of the coronary arteries, with the left main arising from the left facing sinus and bifurcating to give rise to the left anterior descending and circumflex arteries while the right coronary artery arises from the right facing sinus. This arrangement is present in 67% of all patients with TGA. There are many possible variations on this theme, including the circumflex artery arising from the right coronary artery, a single left or right coronary artery giving rise to all three branches, or an inverted coronary pattern.[1] Perhaps the most important variation from a management perspective occurs when one or another coronary artery takes an intramural course between the aorta and pulmonary artery.

This variation occurs in approximately 3% of all cases and, although outcome has improved for patients with this arrangement, it continues to be associated with an increased surgical mortality from the arterial switch procedure in many centers.[2]

Associated Defects

VENTRICULAR SEPTAL DEFECT

A VSD is the most common abnormality to coexist with TGA, occurring in 40% to 45% of cases. The position and size of such defects within the ventricular septum is variable, but the most common types are perimembranous defects and muscular defects, occurring with approximately equal frequency. Associated malalignment of the outlet septum is common in these types of defect, with some degree of malalignment in up to 75% of cases. Less common types of defect are atrioventricular septal defects and doubly committed subarterial defects, each making up approximately 5% of the total. Small defects, especially in the muscular septum, are likely to close spontaneously, but larger defects will generally need surgical management.

LEFT VENTRICULAR OUTFLOW TRACT OBSTRUCTION

This abnormality is second in frequency to VSDs, occurring to some degree in up to 25% of patients. It is more likely to occur in patients who also have a VSD. The anatomy of the obstruction is somewhat variable but most commonly involves either a subvalvular fibrous membrane or a combination of valvular and muscular subvalvular stenosis. Less common types of obstruction are due to abnormal chordal attachments of the mitral valve into the ventricular septum below the pulmonary valve or aneurysm formation of the membranous septum.

In patients who have undergone atrial baffle repair of TGA there is commonly a gradient across the LVOT due either to bulging of the ventricular septum into the LVOT or to systolic anterior motion of the mitral valve. In most cases the gradient is relatively mild, although in a minority it may be more severe, leading to the development of systemic pressures within the left ventricle. Such pressure loading of the left ventricle may be potentially beneficial in that it may render the patient suitable for a late arterial switch conversion (see later).

COARCTATION OF THE AORTA

Aortic coarctation is seen in approximately 5% of patients with TGA. It may be a discrete shelflike lesion or may be associated with hypoplasia of the distal aortic arch. Coarctation is more common in patients with malalignment-type VSDs and may be associated with some degree of subaortic narrowing in this situation.

Genetics and Epidemiology

TGA is the most common form of cyanotic congenital heart disease (CHD) presenting in the neonatal period. Of all forms of cyanotic CHD, only tetralogy of Fallot is more common. TGA represents 5% to 7% of all CHD and has a birth incidence of 20 to 30/100,000 live births, with a male preponderance of approximately 2:1.

There have been a small number of reports of possible genetic associations in individual cases of TGA, involving deletions at chromo-

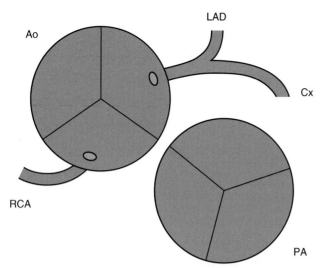

Figure 47-1 Coronary artery pattern in transposition of the great arteries (TGA). The aortic sinuses in TGA are described in terms of their relationship to the pulmonary artery (PA). Therefore, the left- and right-facing sinuses face the PA and the nonfacing sinus does not. The figure shows the most frequent coronary pattern seen in TGA. The left main coronary artery arises from the left-facing sinus and gives rise to the left anterior descending (LAD) and circumflex (Cx) arteries. The right coronary artery (RCA) arises from the right-facing sinus. Ao, aorta.

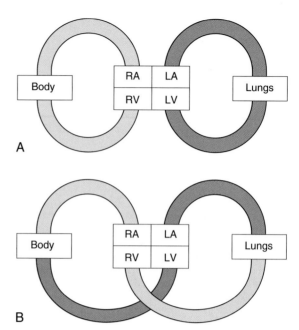

Figure 47-2 Blood flow in transposition of the great arteries (TGA). The anatomic arrangement of the TGA heart causes blood to circulate in (A) two separate parallel circuits rather than (B) the normal single series circuit. In patients with TGA, oxygenated blood (dark) circulates continuously around the pulmonary circuit, whereas deoxygenated blood (light) circulates around the right side of the heart without picking up oxygen from the lungs. LA, left atrium; LV, left ventricle; RA, right atrium; RV, right ventricle.

some 22q11 and, in one family, the *ZIC3* gene on the X-chromosome. Nevertheless, in the great majority of cases, TGA is not currently known to be associated with any specific single gene defects. In mice, great arterial septation abnormalities have been induced by the administration of retinoic acid to the developing embryo and a very high incidence of TGA has also been observed in the perlecan-null mouse. There has been some suggestion that TGA in human fetuses may be related to maternal intrauterine hormonal imbalance, and there is also a higher than expected incidence of TGA in infants of diabetic mothers.

In one large study of patients with TGA the incidence of congenital heart defects in both siblings and parents of affected children was less than 1%. An accurate recurrence rate in offspring of parents with TGA is not available, but this would appear to be 1% to 2%.

■ Early Presentation and Management

Antenatal diagnosis of TGA is becoming more frequent; however, most commonly the infant with complete transposition will be diagnosed after being recognized as a "blue baby," often within the first day of life. Examination of these infants reveals a varying degree of cyanosis; the remainder of the cardiac examination reveals a murmurless heart in the absence of associated lesions. The second heart sound is single and loud because of the relationship of the great arteries, with the aortic valve being anterior.

The anatomic arrangement of the TGA heart causes blood to circulate in two separate parallel circuits rather than the normal single series circuit (Fig. 47-2). The systemic arteries receive blood that has not passed through the pulmonary circulation and therefore remains deoxygenated. Mixing of blood between the two parallel circuits is essential for small amounts of oxygenated blood to enter the systemic circuit and supply vital organs. Mixing can take place at the level of the atrial septum via a patent oval foramen and at the level of the great arteries via a patent arterial duct. From the time that a diagnosis of TGA is suspected, patients are managed with intravenous prostaglandin E$_1$ to restore and/or maintain patency of the arterial duct and allow mixing between the circuits.

BALLOON ATRIAL SEPTOSTOMY

To maintain acceptable systemic arterial oxygen saturations before definitive surgery, the early management of these patients at most centers includes balloon atrial septostomy. This procedure disrupts

the foramen flap, thus creating a larger communication between the atria and allowing better atrial-level mixing between the two parallel circuits.[3]

The procedure is performed using an angulated balloon-tipped Fogarty or Miller-Edwards catheter, with the reinforced latex balloons having a volume of 1.8 or 3 mL. The catheter is introduced via a femoral venous or umbilical venous approach and passed into the right atrium, across the oval foramen, and into the left atrium under echocardiographic or angiographic control. The balloon is then inflated and drawn back sharply across the oval foramen to the junction of the right atrium and inferior caval vein, producing a tear of the foramen flap. After successful balloon atrial septostomy, most infants can be weaned off intravenous prostaglandin therapy and will maintain a systemic arterial oxygen saturation of between 50% and 80%. In the era of atrial baffle repairs this procedure allowed adequate oxygenation for growth until such time as the atrial switch operation was performed—often beyond 6 months of age. In the current era most infants undergo definitive repair with the arterial switch operation within the first 2 weeks of life.

ATRIAL BAFFLE REPAIR

Mustard and Senning Operations

The first definitive operations for TGA were described by Senning[4] in 1959 and Mustard[5] in 1964. Both of these procedures "correct" the physiologic abnormality of the transposed great arteries by forming a baffle within the atria to "switch" the flow of blood at inflow level. This results in a reversion to the normal flow of blood with the heart and lungs being in series; however, the left ventricle remains the pulmonary ventricle and the right ventricle remains the systemic ventricle.

The main difference between the two procedures is that in the Senning operation the baffle is created from right atrial wall and atrial septal tissue without the use of extrinsic materials; the Mustard operation, however, involves resection of the atrial septum and the creation

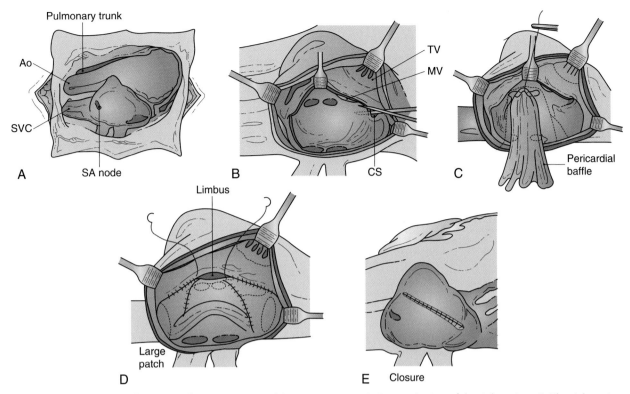

Figure 47-3 The Mustard operation for transposition of the great arteries. **A,** Surgeon's view of the right atrium. **B,** The right atrium is opened and the atrial septum is excised. **C,** The pericardial baffle is initially sutured around the left pulmonary veins. **D,** The baffle is completed. **E,** The right atrium is closed. Ao, aorta; CS, coronary sinus; MV, mitral valve; SA, sinoatrial; SVC, superior vena cava; TV, tricuspid valve. *(After Kirklin JW, Barrett-Boyes BG. Complete transposition of the great arteries. In: Cardiac Surgery, 2nd ed. White Plains, NY: Churchill Livingstone; 1993:1383–1467.)*

of a baffle from pericardium or synthetic material (Fig. 47-3). These operations were performed at varying stages of life but usually between 1 month and 1 year of age.[6] In experienced hands, the early mortality rate associated with these procedures is low, with a surgical mortality rate generally between 1% and 10% (Box 47-1).

BOX 47-1 COMPLICATIONS AFTER REPAIR

Mustard and Senning Operations
- Endocarditis
- Sinus node dysfunction
- Interatrial reentry tachycardia
- Sudden cardiac death
- Baffle leaks
- Baffle obstruction
- Tricuspid valve regurgitation
- Right ventricular systolic and diastolic dysfunction
- Residual hemodynamic lesions
- Pulmonary hypertension

Rastelli Operation
- Endocarditis
- Atrial and ventricular tachycardias
- Sudden death
- Complete heart block
- Left and right ventricular dysfunction
- Conduit stenosis
- Residual hemodynamic lesions

Arterial Switch Operation
- Endocarditis
- Pulmonary outflow obstruction
- Neoaortic regurgitation
- Coronary artery stenosis

Rastelli Operation

The most frequently used surgical option for patients with the combination of TGA, pulmonary outflow tract obstruction, and VSD is the Rastelli operation (Fig. 47-4), which was originally described in 1969.[7] This operation utilizes the VSD as part of the LVOT and involves placement of a baffle within the right ventricle, directing blood from the VSD to the aorta. The pulmonary valve or subpulmonary region is oversewn, and a conduit is inserted between the right ventricle and the pulmonary artery. Suitability for the Rastelli operation is dependent on appropriate VSD anatomy: the defect should be large and subaortic. Surgical enlargement of the VSD may be undertaken but carries with it a risk of inducing complete heart block.

The main advantage of this operation is that the left ventricle becomes the systemic ventricle. The most important limitation is that the patient is committed to further operations, because the conduit is likely to need replacing several times during the patient's life.

There is continuing debate regarding the most appropriate timing of the Rastelli operation. Some believe that the procedure should be performed during early infancy, citing the advantages of early physiologic correction, less time spent with systemic hypoxemia, and avoidance of a left-to-right shunt from palliative procedures. Others believe that a palliative procedure is the most appropriate first intervention, usually a modified Blalock-Taussig shunt. The reasons cited would be the higher risks associated with early repair and the fact that a smaller conduit will require earlier reoperation.

ARTERIAL SWITCH OPERATION

The successful anatomic correction of TGA was first described in 1975 by Jatene and associates.[8] This procedure involves the transection of the aorta and pulmonary artery at a level above the valve sinuses. The coronary arteries are detached from the aorta with a surrounding "button" of aortic wall and sutured into place in the neoaorta. Finally,

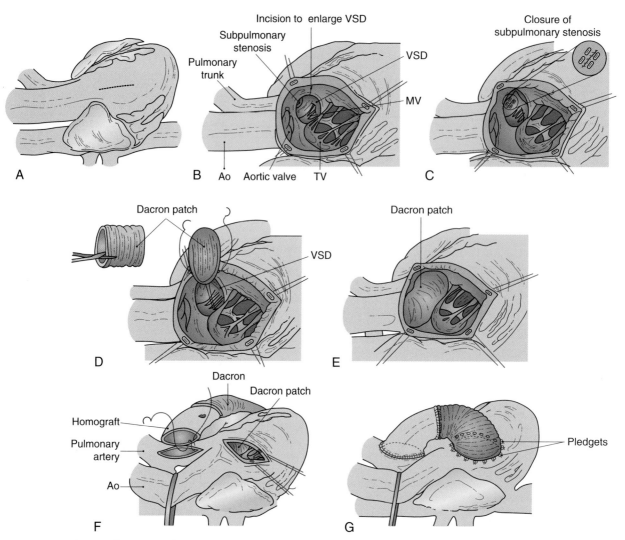

Figure 47-4 The Rastelli operation for transposition of the great arteries with ventricular septal defect (VSD) and pulmonary outflow obstruction. **A,** Surgeon's view of the right ventricle. **B,** The right ventricle is opened and the VSD enlarged if necessary. **C,** The entrance to the pulmonary artery is closed. **D** and **E,** A patch is sewn into place to create a tunnel from the left ventricle across the VSD to the aortic valve. **F,** A valved conduit is prepared and sutured to the pulmonary artery. **G,** The proximal end of the conduit is sutured to the right ventriculotomy. Ao, aorta; MV, mitral valve; TV, tricuspid valve. *(After Kirklin JW, Barrett-Boyes BG. Complete transposition of the great arteries. In: Cardiac Surgery, 2nd ed. White Plains, NY: Churchill Livingstone; 1993:1383-1467.)*

the pulmonary trunk is moved forward into its new position anterior to the aorta and the switched great arteries are sutured into place (Fig. 47-5). The arterial switch is a technically challenging operation but has the great advantage over the Mustard or Senning procedure in that the left ventricle becomes the systemic ventricle.

The procedure is usually performed within the first 2 weeks of life and should be undertaken at the latest by 4 to 6 weeks of life. After this time, the patient with TGA and intact ventricular septum will have suffered significant regression of left ventricular muscle mass due to its functioning at low pressure in the pulmonary circuit. This thinning of the left ventricular myocardium increases the potential for left ventricular failure after the arterial switch procedure and increases surgical risk.

Late Outcome

NATURAL HISTORY

Without surgical intervention, the survival rates of patients with TGA are poor. Most patients will die in the first few months of life, with about 90% of patients dying in infancy.[9] Patients with isolated TGA and no associated lesions (approximately 50% of the total) have

the worst outcome—only 30% survive beyond the first month of life (Fig. 47-6). Patients with a large VSD have a somewhat better outcome, but less than 50% will survive the first year of life. The subset of patients with coexistent LVOT obstruction and VSD has the best outcome, with approximately 50% surviving to 3 years of age. These patients may occasionally be seen as cyanosed adults with "balanced" circulation despite no previous surgical intervention.

ATRIAL BAFFLE REPAIRS

Survival and Functional Status

Surgical mortality rates after the Mustard and Senning operations were low in most centers that performed large numbers of these operations. A review of the literature concerning operations performed between 1971 and 1979 showed a mean hospital mortality rate of 4.8%.[10] A large single-center review showed that the surgical mortality rate fell significantly in the second half of the series, with a mortality rate of 10.4% for 1963 to 1973 and 0.9% for 1974 to 1985.[11] Early mortality after repair of patients with associated lesions is significantly higher. In the literature review just cited, the average mortality for patients with TGA and VSD was 23%,[10] and, although more recent results show improved outcome for this population, the surgical risk is clearly higher.

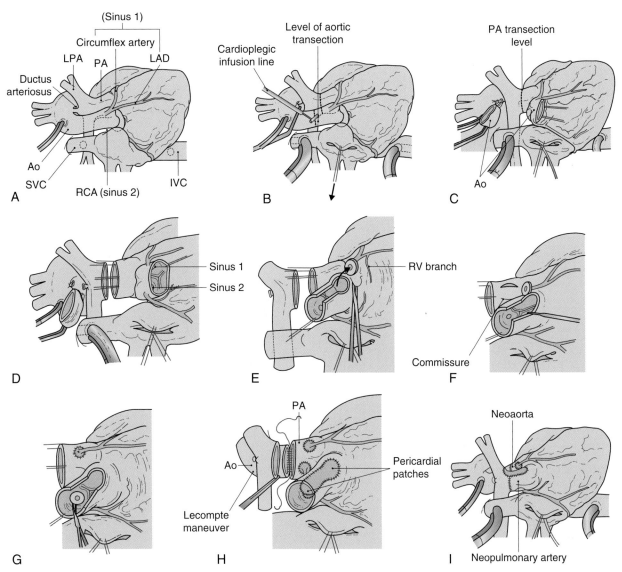

Figure 47-5 The arterial switch operation for transposition of the great arteries. **A,** Surgeon's view of the heart. Sinus 1, left-facing sinus; sinus 2, right-facing sinus. **B,** *Dashed lines* indicate the sites of transection of the aorta and main pulmonary artery. **C,** The aorta is transected. **D,** The pulmonary trunk is transected. **E,** A button of aorta is excised around the ostium of the left main coronary artery. **F,** An incision is made in the left-facing sinus of the neoaorta, into which the left coronary button will be sutured. **G,** The right coronary artery button is excised and sutured onto the neoaorta in similar fashion. **H,** The distal ascending aorta is brought under the pulmonary bifurcation (the Lecompte maneuver) and is anastomosed to the proximal portion. Pericardial patches are sewn into the neopulmonary trunk to fill the defects left by the coronary buttons. **I,** The proximal and distal portions of the neopulmonary trunk are anastomosed. Ao, aorta; IVC, inferior vena cava; LAD, left anterior descending artery; LPA, left pulmonary artery; PA, pulmonary artery; RCA, right coronary artery; RV, right ventricle; SVC, superior vena cava. (*After Kirklin JW, Barrett-Boyes BG. Complete transposition of the great arteries. In: Cardiac Surgery, 2nd ed. White Plains, NY: Churchill Livingstone; 1993:1383-1467.*)

The Mustard and Senning procedures were superseded by the arterial switch operation in the mid to late 1980s in most surgical centers, and the population of patients who have undergone these procedures is therefore essentially complete. Unfortunately, these patients have several issues leading to late morbidity and mortality, especially as the population ages.

Late survival data after atrial baffle repair show a small but ongoing attrition rate, with the most frequent causes of death being sudden death and systemic right ventricular failure. In one large single-center series, the 5-year survival rate was 89% and the 20-year survival rate was 76%.[12] Another large series showed a 90% 10-year survival rate and an 80% 20-year survival rate.[13] Some studies have suggested somewhat better long-term survival in Senning procedure patients compared with Mustard procedure patients.

Survival rates after repair of TGA and VSD are again less good, with 5-year survival rates of 60% to 70%. Risk of late death after atrial baffle repairs is 2.7 times greater in patients with a VSD, relative to those with an intact ventricular septum.

Functional status is reasonably good in this population, with 60% to 80% of patients in many series being in New York Heart Association (NYHA) functional class I and the majority of the remainder being in class II.[11,13] Nevertheless, overall functional class does appear to be declining with increasing length of follow-up.[14] Formal testing demonstrates that the exercise capacity of the atrial switch population as a whole is reduced relative to the normal population, with the most significant cause of limitation appearing to be chronotropic incompetence.[15] The stroke volume response to exercise is also reduced secondary to a failure to augment ventricular filling rates during tachycardia, presumably due to the abnormal characteristics of the atrial baffles.[16]

Figure 47-6 Actuarial survival curves of various subsets of patients with transposition of the great arteries. ASD, atrial septal defect; IPBF, increased pulmonary blood flow; PDA, patent ductus arteriosus; PFO, patent foramen ovale; PS, pulmonary stenosis; PVD, pulmonary vascular disease; VSD, ventricular septal defect greater than or equal to 3 mm.

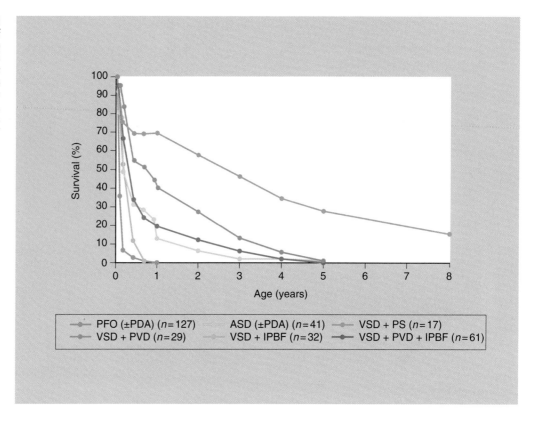

Arrhythmias and Sudden Cardiac Death

Patients who have undergone the Mustard or Senning procedure are at risk of both bradyarrhythmias and tachyarrhythmias. The most common tachyarrhythmia is an incisional atrial reentry tachycardia, sometimes described as atypical atrial flutter. The most common bradyarrhythmia is sinus node dysfunction leading to sinus bradycardia with a junctional escape rhythm.

Bradyarrhythmias

Resting bradycardia is frequently seen in atrial switch patients, representing a resting sinus bradycardia often with a slow junctional escape rhythm, typically 40 to 60 beats per minute. This is usually asymptomatic. Sinus node dysfunction in this group appears to be more likely with increasing time from operation. One series demonstrated a probability of being in sinus rhythm of 72% at 1 year, 56% at 5 years, 50% at 10 years, and 43% at 13 years.[10] There appears to be an incidence of late loss of sinus rhythm of approximately 2.4% per year. Histologic examination of the sinus node region demonstrates abnormalities of the sinus node and sinus node artery, and electrophysiologic studies show that abnormal function of the sinus node is present in at least 50% of patients.[17]

The chronotropic response to exercise is variable in this situation: a minority of patients have a very poor response with maximal rates of 70 to 80 beats per minute, whereas many will achieve a maximal rate between 100 and 150 beats per minute. A normal exercise chronotropic response is relatively unusual in this population, and indeed the maximal exercise heart rate is the most important predictor of exercise capacity for these patients. For those with a poor chronotropic response to exercise, rate-responsive atrial pacing may result in a symptomatic improvement in terms of exercise capacity.

Tachyarrhythmias

Intra-atrial reentry tachycardia occurs in up to 50% of patients after atrial baffle repair of TGA. A study with a mean follow-up of 23 years after the Mustard procedure demonstrated that 48% of patients had had at least one episode of supraventricular tachycardia.[18] Of these patients, 73% had "atrial flutter." Catheter radiofrequency ablation of these arrhythmias has produced procedural success in many cases, although there is a risk of high-grade atrioventricular block as a result of this procedure.[19,20]

Sudden Death

Sudden death is a well-documented occurrence after atrial baffle repair, occurring in 7% to 15% of patients.[13] A multicenter Dutch paper exploring predictors of sudden death found that symptoms of arrhythmia or heart failure, as well as previous documented atrial flutter or fibrillation, increased the risk of sudden death.[21] Other data have suggested that loss of sinus rhythm may also be a predictor. Sudden death is likely to be arrhythmic in most cases, and in the Dutch study ventricular fibrillation and ventricular tachycardia were the most frequent arrhythmias in documented cases.

Ventricular Function

The main concern regarding the long-term outlook for patients with atrial baffle repairs of TGA has been the function of the systemic right ventricle. Although it is clear that the right ventricle can tolerate functioning at systemic pressures in the short to medium term without difficulty, it may potentially fail when required to do this in the long term. A study from the Netherlands reviewing 91 patients after the Mustard operation showed that all patients had good function or mild dysfunction 14 years after repair. When the group was restudied at a median follow-up of 25 years, however, 61% had moderate or severe dysfunction.[14] Our concern therefore is that patients with mild right ventricular dysfunction in the third decade of life may progress to more severe dysfunction over the decades to come. We have observed several patients in our own clinic who have had quite rapid progression of right ventricular systolic dysfunction to the stage where this becomes severe. As yet there are no clear risk factors that predict the development of severe right ventricular dysfunction in this population, although early research in our group suggests that there may be a relationship with the degree of right ventricular hypertrophy, with those with the most severe hypertrophy having less good ventricular function. This research potentially fits in with the finding that the great majority of atrial baffle repair patients have right ventricular myocardial perfusion abnormalities.[22] It is possible that the greatly increased coronary demand of the systemic right ventricle outstrips the available coronary supply from a morphologic right coronary artery system. Further research will be required to determine whether pharmacologic measures to reduce hypertrophy and/or improve myocardial perfusion will be beneficial for this population; however, at this stage limited research has not demonstrated any significant benefit from drugs such as angiotensin-converting enzyme inhibitors or β-adrenergic blockers.

Tricuspid Valve Function

Mild to moderate tricuspid regurgitation is relatively common in patients after atrial baffle repair of TGA. The reversal of the right and left ventricular pressure relationship results in altered geometry of the ventricular septum. The tricuspid valve therefore takes on a more rounded shape, which in combination with the displaced septal chordal attachments of the valve results in an increased tendency to tricuspid regurgitation. Severe tricuspid regurgitation in patients without associated lesions is unusual in most series and when present may reflect severe ventricular dysfunction and dilation. In patients with associated VSD the incidence of important tricuspid regurgitation is higher— about 5% to 10%—due to damage to the valve and its support apparatus during operation. In this case, repair or replacement of the valve may be justified to reduce volume loading and prevent progressive deterioration of right ventricular function. However, tricuspid valve repair in the context of moderate or severe right ventricular dysfunction is unlikely to be beneficial.

Baffle Obstruction and Baffle Leaks

Baffle obstruction is an infrequent but important late complication after the Mustard and Senning operations. Superior limb systemic venous baffle obstruction occurs with a frequency of 5% to 10% in Mustard patients, whereas inferior limb obstruction occurs infrequently, with an incidence of only 1% to 2%. Mild obstruction can be managed expectantly, although more severe stenosis may require surgical or catheter intervention. Pulmonary venous baffle obstruction is also infrequent, occurring with a frequency of about 2%. Severe obstruction of the pulmonary venous channel will lead to the development of pulmonary hypertension and therefore pressure loading of the morphologic left ventricle, which, in turn, may render the patient suitable for consideration of late arterial switch conversion.

Baffle leaks are more common than obstruction, with the most common site being at the suture line of the superior limb of the systemic venous baffle. Baffle leaks have been shown to be present in up to 25% of patients,[23] although most are not hemodynamically significant. Shunting may be either left to right or right to left. In patients with a large left-to-right shunt, the consequent volume loading of the systemic right ventricle may necessitate re-intervention to close the defect. In patients with important right-to-left shunts, systemic arterial desaturation will develop, likewise necessitating closure. These large shunts are rare, however, and only 1% to 2% of atrial baffle patients will require re-intervention for baffle leaks.

Pulmonary Hypertension

The late development of pulmonary vascular disease is a recognized complication after atrial switch procedures, occurring with a frequency of about 7%. This complication is more common after late repair and in patients with an associated VSD.

RASTELLI OPERATION

Survival and Functional Status

Operative survival after the Rastelli operation was poor early in the surgical experience, with mortality rates of up to 30%; however, this has improved substantially such that more recent series report an operative mortality rate of 5% or less.[10,23] There is a significant incidence of late mortality after Rastelli repair, with a recent large series reporting a survival rate of 82% at 5 years, 80% at 10 years, 68% at 15 years, and 52% at 20 years.[24] The most common causes of late death or transplantation were left ventricular failure and sudden death.

Functional status is often good in these patients, although the presence of conduit stenosis or important ventricular dysfunction may be limiting factors. Exercise capacity in the Rastelli population overall is reduced compared with that in the normal population.

Arrhythmias and Sudden Cardiac Death

There is a significant incidence of sudden death after the Rastelli operation, which is considered likely to be arrhythmic in nature. In one large series there was a high incidence of documented late arrhythmias, with approximately equal rates of ventricular and supraventricular tachycardia.[24] There is also a risk of early or late development of heart block in these patients. The occurrence of ventricular tachycardia in particular may be associated with conduit obstruction and right ventricular hypertension and should direct the physician toward a detailed hemodynamic assessment of the patient.

Ventricular Function

Left ventricular dysfunction is present in about 25% of Rastelli patients at late follow-up and is a cause of late death in a significant minority. Right ventricular dysfunction is also common, often secondary to the abnormal pressure and/or volume load related to conduit dysfunction.

Conduit Stenosis and Outflow Tract Obstruction

Development of stenosis of the right ventricle/pulmonary artery conduit after childhood Rastelli procedure is inevitable. Most patients who undergo the Rastelli procedure will require multiple conduit replacements during a normal lifespan, because the longevity of currently used bioprosthetic conduits is between 10 and 20 years. The role of percutaneous implantable valves in these situations is developing rapidly and is likely to be the method of choice in the future. Vigilance for the development of conduit stenosis or regurgitation is important throughout life in this population. LVOT obstruction is less common but equally important and should be detected by careful clinical and echocardiographic evaluation.

ARTERIAL SWITCH OPERATION

Survival and Functional Status

Operative survival after the arterial switch in the current era is very good, with a surgical mortality rate of between 2% and 5% for patients without associated lesions.[6,25] The operative mortality rate is higher in patients with an associated VSD but is still less than 5% in many series.[26] Functional status is normal in the great majority of patients, and aerobic exercise capacity has been shown to be normal or low-normal relative to age- and sex-predicted values.[27]

Mid- to long-term follow-up studies for the arterial switch operation are reassuring at this relatively early stage in the history of this procedure. A review of over 1000 survivors showed an overall survival rate of 88% at both 10 and 15 years with no deaths later than 5 years after operation.[28] The results are somewhat less good in patients with associated lesions, with a survival rate of 80% at both 10 and 15 years, although the difference largely represents differing operative risk.

Although these results are encouraging, it must be remembered that the follow-up for this operation remains relatively short at this stage with the oldest patients at most centers being younger than 25 years of age.

Arrhythmias and Sudden Cardiac Death

Sinus rhythm with normal conduction is maintained at medium- to long-term follow-up in 95% to 98% of arterial switch patients. There is a low incidence, less than 2%, of complete heart block, usually in patients who had an associated VSD. In one study, the incidence of supraventricular tachycardia at medium-term follow-up was 4%, the majority occurring more than 1 year after the surgery. The incidence of late sustained ventricular arrhythmias was less than 0.5%.[29] Sudden death is unusual in most series and is related to myocardial infarction secondary to coronary artery obstruction.

Ventricular Function

Good left ventricular function is the norm after the arterial switch operation, with more than 95% of patients having normal left ventricular systolic function at medium- to long-term follow-up. Severe ventricular dysfunction is an occasional complication in a small proportion of patients and is often associated with coronary artery abnormalities. Left ventricular dysfunction is a recognized cause of death in less than 1% of patients.

Pulmonary Artery Stenosis

Re-intervention is required in at least 10% of patients after the arterial switch operation and in many cases is due to supravalvular main pulmonary artery stenosis or branch pulmonary artery stenosis. This occurs in at least 5%—and in as many as 25% of patients in some series—although recent results appear better. One large multicenter study showed freedom from pulmonary artery stenosis of 95%, 90%, and 86% at 1, 5, and 10 years, respectively. Surgical or catheter intervention to address pulmonary arterial stenosis is required in a significant minority of arterial switch operation patients.

Neoaortic Valve Regurgitation

There appears to be an ongoing risk of the development of important aortic regurgitation, although only a small proportion has needed intervention at current stages of follow-up. In one large study the incidence of all grades of aortic regurgitation was 16% at a median follow-up of 4.9 years; however, only 3.8% had regurgitation of grade 2 or more.[28] Freedom from reoperation for aortic regurgitation was 99.1%, 97.6%, and 96.2% at 5, 10, and 15 years, respectively. Some degree of aortic root dilation is almost universal in this population, and several studies have shown serial increases in aortic root Z scores with serial follow-up. Early data suggest that aortic dilation may stabilize in adult life, but follow-up is too short at this stage to be certain of the natural history of this complication in adulthood. To date we have not seen complications such as aortic dissection or rupture, but patients with severe aortic dilation clearly need careful follow-up.

Coronary Arteries

In a large study of 1198 hospital survivors of the arterial switch procedure 7.2% had coronary events, defined as death from myocardial ischemia/infarction, sudden death, nonfatal infarction, or reoperation for coronary stenosis. The great majority of these events occurred in the first 3 months after the surgery. In a subset of 324 who underwent coronary angiography, 6.8% had significant lesions, 13 with coronary occlusions and 9 with stenoses. A further 4% had minor coronary stenoses.[30] Several other series have also reported coronary abnormalities and late deaths due to coronary events.

Because of the denervation of the heart at the time of the arterial switch operation, the symptoms of myocardial ischemia may be atypical, without classic angina; and it is therefore important to remain vigilant for the possibility of this complication.

Outpatient Assessment

ATRIAL BAFFLE REPAIR AND RASTELLI OPERATION PATIENTS

These patients require the following (Box 47-2):
- *Regular clinical examination:* This should focus on signs of atrioventricular valve regurgitation and congestive cardiac failure. In atrial baffle repair patients, audible splitting of the second heart sound may indicate development of pulmonary hypertension. In Rastelli operation patients the character of the pulmonary ejection murmur should be noted to exclude conduit stenosis.
- *Electrocardiography:* Cardiac rhythm should be noted: there is a significant incidence of loss of sinus rhythm in the Mustard and Senning procedure populations, with junctional rhythm being a common baseline rhythm. Right-axis deviation and right ventricular hypertrophy are present owing to the systemic pressure in the right ventricle in this population. Patients after the Rastelli operation will have a surgical right bundle-branch block pattern and are also at risk of late development of complete heart block.
- *Chest radiography:* Patients with TGA have a narrow mediastinal shadow owing to the parallel relationship of the great arteries. Cardiothoracic ratio is normal in the patient without ventricular dilation, and pulmonary vascular markings should be normal in the absence of pulmonary hypertension.
- *Echocardiography:* Echocardiography in the atrial switch population allows assessment of the degree of tricuspid regurgitation as well as interrogation for baffle stenosis and baffle leaks (although more

detailed analysis may require transesophageal echocardiography). Two-dimensional (2D) echocardiography also allows an approximate estimation of systemic right ventricular function, and early experience suggests that transthoracic three-dimensional (3D) echocardiography will allow volumetric measurement of right ventricular ejection fraction in those with good transthoracic echocardiographic windows. In Rastelli operation patients, echocardiography will exclude residual VSDs, allow assessment of left ventricular function and exclude LVOT obstruction, as well as estimate right ventricular systolic pressure and degree of conduit stenosis.
- *Magnetic resonance imaging (MRI):* MRI is the most valuable imaging modality in these patients (see Box 47-2 and Figs. 47-7 to 47-9).

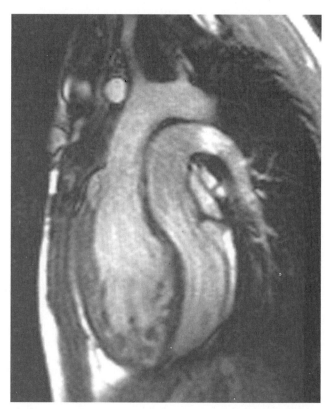

Figure 47-7 Long-axis MR image of a patient after the Mustard operation showing the parallel relationship of the great vessels. The deviation of the ventricular septum to the left shows the high-pressure right ventricle and low-pressure left ventricle. There is significant right ventricular hypertrophy.

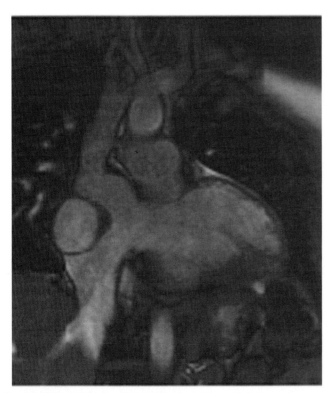

Figure 47-8 MR image showing the superior and inferior venae cavae draining into the systemic venous baffle in a Mustard patient. In this case both limbs of the baffle are widely patent.

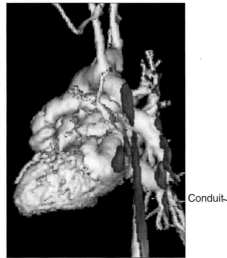
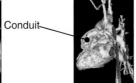

Conduit

Figure 47-9 Three-dimensional MRI reconstruction of the heart after a Rastelli repair. The conduit is seen arising from the anterior surface of the right ventricle and is mildly stenosed at its insertion into the pulmonary artery.

It allows detailed quantitative assessment of right and left ventricular systolic function as well as assessment of baffle anatomy in the atrial switch population and conduit flow imaging in the Rastelli procedure population.
- *Radionuclear ventriculography:* This is a useful imaging modality for analysis of systemic right ventricular function in patients who are unable to undergo MRI.
- *Cardiopulmonary exercise testing:* Regular exercise testing is useful in terms of recognizing change of clinical status in the individual patient. In Mustard and Senning procedure patients the chronotropic response to exercise is frequently impaired, and these patients may occasionally benefit from pacemaker implantation.
- *24-Hour Holter monitoring:* This can detect heart block or severe sinus node dysfunction resulting in prolonged pauses, as well as episodes of atrial or ventricular tachyarrhythmia, and should be performed on a regular basis.

ARTERIAL SWITCH OPERATION PATIENTS

Arterial switch operation patients need assessment with the following:
- *Regular clinical examination:* Focus should be placed on signs of pulmonary artery stenosis and neoaortic valve regurgitation.
- *Electrocardiography:* Care should be taken to exclude signs of myocardial ischemia and right ventricular hypertrophy suggesting pulmonary outflow obstruction.
- *Echocardiography:* Regular echocardiography should be done to exclude supravalvular and branch pulmonary artery stenosis, neoaortic regurgitation, and left ventricular dysfunction. Note, however, that the branch pulmonary arteries may be difficult to image with this modality in this population, necessitating MRI or computed tomography (CT) in some patients.
- *Exercise stress testing:* We would perform routine exercise testing in the early teenage years, or earlier if there are concerns of possible myocardial ischemia.
- *Selective coronary angiography (or coronary CT):* In patients in whom there is a suspicion of coronary artery stenosis these investigations should be performed. There is currently no consensus as to the utility of routine aortography or coronary angiography after the arterial switch operation.
- *MRI:* This is useful for assessing the anatomy of the branch pulmonary arteries to exclude stenosis. With improvements in technology, MRI is also becoming a valuable tool for assessment of the coronary arteries and myocardial perfusion in this population.

Late Management Options

MEDICAL THERAPY

For patients with dysfunction of the systemic right ventricle after the Mustard and Senning operations, standard drug treatment has been widely used as for a failing systemic left ventricle. Studies have not yet demonstrated statistically significant benefit from drugs such as angiotensin-converting enzyme inhibitors or β-adrenergic blockers and have been limited by small patient numbers at individual centers. In most cases these drugs will be well tolerated, but β-blockers in particular need to be initiated carefully in the context of the sinus bradycardia that is frequently seen in this population.

SURGICAL AND CATHETER INTERVENTIONS

Atrial Baffle Repair Patients

Atrial Baffle Revision
Patients with important baffle stenosis may require surgical or catheter intervention. The procedure of choice is a transcatheter intervention using either balloon dilation or primary implantation of self-expanding or balloon expandable stents. These procedures have been widely used in patients with systemic venous baffle obstruction.[31] Transcatheter dilation of pulmonary venous baffle obstruction has been performed successfully but is more technically challenging, and these patients, as well as those with complete obstruction of a systemic venous baffle limb, may require surgical revision.

Baffle leaks are also amenable to transcatheter therapy in many cases. Most reports have documented the successful use of septal occluder devices, although covered stents have also been used for this purpose.

Arterial Switch Conversion
The arterial switch operation is likely to have medium- and long-term benefits over atrial baffle repairs, the most important of which is that the left ventricle is returned to the systemic circulation.

In atrial baffle repair patients with systemic right ventricular failure, the ideal option would be to convert the patient to an arterial switch operation with takedown of the atrial baffle and closure of the atrial septum. Although this procedure has had quite good success rates in some pediatric patients, its success in adult patients is less encouraging. In most atrial baffle repair patients, the left ventricular pressure is low and the left ventricle therefore requires "retraining" to function at systemic pressures. Retraining of the left ventricle is accomplished by the application of a pulmonary artery band to increase left ventricular pressure and induce myocardial hypertrophy, a procedure that may need to be staged. The left ventricular response to this procedure is variable, and in adult patients in particular it has had limited success owing to the frequent development of left ventricular failure.[32] There is a small subgroup of atrial baffle patients with systemic left ventricular pressure due to either LVOT obstruction or pulmonary venous baffle obstruction: these patients are likely to be have a more favorable outcome from late switch conversion.

Pulmonary Artery Banding

Some observers have advocated the use of pulmonary artery banding as a therapeutic measure in its own right for patients with important tricuspid regurgitation. The rise in left ventricular pressure results in a resetting of ventricular septal geometry, with the ventricular septum moving toward the right ventricle and thus closer to its position in the normal heart. The tricuspid valve therefore assumes a geometry closer to normal and has been shown to result in a reduction of tricuspid regurgitation in the short term. Despite this, there are risks associated with pulmonary artery banding in this population. This strategy has not been widely adopted at this stage, and its long-term benefits remain unclear.

Radiofrequency Ablation of Arrhythmias

Intra-atrial reentry tachycardias and other supraventricular tachycardias in atrial switch patients have been addressed by both surgical and, more recently, catheter radiofrequency ablative techniques.[19,20] Procedural success rates up to 80% to 90% have been reported and have improved with the application of newer 3D mapping in combination with entrainment mapping techniques.

Some series have reported an important risk of high-degree atrioventricular block complicating radiofrequency ablation in this population. The widespread scarring present in the atria of these patients makes assessment and treatment of reentry tachycardia a complex procedure requiring detailed knowledge of the surgical anatomy; these procedures should be performed only by electrophysiologists familiar with this patient population.

Resynchronization Therapy

Data regarding cardiac resynchronization therapy for the failing systemic right ventricle are limited to case reports and small case series. Nevertheless, these suggest that in some patients improvement may be gained by this technique either as definitive therapy or as a bridge to transplantation.

Rastelli Operation Patients
Conduit Replacement and Dilation

All patients with a right ventricle to pulmonary artery conduit will eventually require conduit replacement. Although gaining initial surgical access to the heart in this situation may be technically challenging, surgical mortality from conduit replacement is low. The recent development of a stent-mounted bovine jugular valve for transcatheter pulmonary valve replacement has shown good medium-term results and may substantially reduce the number of operative interventions required for these patients.

Repair of Residual Lesions

There is a risk of both LVOT obstruction and residual VSDs after the Rastelli operation. In some cases residual VSDs may be amenable to transcatheter device closure but many patients with hemodynamically important residual lesions will need surgical revision.

Arterial Switch Operation Patients
Pulmonary Artery Dilation or Surgery

Balloon angioplasty of pulmonary artery stenosis after the arterial switch operation has a relatively high failure rate, with most series quoting success rates of about 50%. The best results appear to be in patients with branch pulmonary artery stenosis.[33] Primary stent implantation appears to have higher initial success rates, although most operators would reserve the use of stents for older children and adolescents. Proximal pulmonary artery stents will press onto the ascending aorta and may potentially compromise the coronary arteries and therefore may not be suitable in all cases. Surgical relief of pulmonary stenosis, often requiring the use of a patch, may be required in those who do not respond to interventional catheter techniques.

Coronary Artery Interventions

Coronary artery lesions after the arterial switch have been treated successfully using surgical bypass grafting as well as percutaneous catheter procedures.[30]

Repair of Residual Lesions

Severe neoaortic regurgitation may require surgical attention. There have been reports of valve replacement, valve repair, and autograft replacement using the neopulmonary valve. Other hemodynamically significant residual lesions will also require repair, with examples being residual VSDs, LVOT obstruction, and mitral valve regurgitation.

Palliative Atrial Baffle Procedure

Rarely, adult patients are encountered with unoperated TGA and a large VSD. These patients have pulmonary vascular disease that precludes closure of the VSD. If these patients are found to have a pulmonary arterial oxygen saturation significantly higher than their aortic saturation, a palliative Mustard or Senning operation without closure of the VSD is likely to be beneficial by improving their systemic oxygenation. The operative mortality rate from this procedure in one series was 7%, with a survival rate of 92% at 7 years.

Transplantation

For many atrial baffle repair patients with a failing systemic right ventricle or Rastelli procedure patients with a failing left ventricle, heart transplantation will be the only available surgical option. Assessment of pulmonary arterial pressures is particularly important in the patient with an atrial baffle with evidence of pulmonary venous baffle obstruction.

Pregnancy
MATERNAL RISK

Mustard and Senning Operation Patients

There is a significant risk of maternal pregnancy complications in this population, although the majority will have uncomplicated pregnancies. A recent U.S. multicenter review of 70 pregnancies in 40 women reported 10 miscarriages and 6 therapeutic abortions, with live births in the remaining 54. Cardiac complications occurred in 36% of pregnancies, including arrhythmia, heart failure, and hemoptysis, with these complications largely developing in the third trimester but some developing in the first 2 weeks after delivery. One patient who developed heart failure died, and one required transplantation during the postpartum period.[34] The Toronto Congenital Cardiac Centre for Adults reported 25 pregnancies in women with atrial baffle repairs of TGA with cardiac complications in 6, including congestive cardiac failure, arrhythmia, and death from postpartum heart failure in 1 patient.[35]

In patients with good or mildly impaired ventricular function and no previous arrhythmias, the maternal risk from pregnancy is likely to be relatively low; however, there is a risk of deterioration of systemic right ventricular function during pregnancy in patients with atrial baffle repairs, which may not recover after the pregnancy. In patients with symptomatic congestive heart failure or those with previous arrhythmia, the risk from pregnancy is clearly higher. We would actively discourage pregnancy in patients with moderate or severe ventricular dysfunction or symptomatic heart failure.

Obstetric care should be in a unit experienced in the management of pregnancy in women with CHD. Ideal management is in a program run jointly between a high-risk obstetric service and a congenital cardiology service, with regular follow-up during the pregnancy. Potential mothers should be counseled before becoming pregnant, and detailed up-to-date imaging including MRI assessment of right ventricular function should be available to aid the counseling process. This process should include discussion of the uncertain maternal longevity in this population. If residual hemodynamic lesions are present, consideration should be given to addressing these lesions before conception. Patients can have normal vaginal deliveries; and other than trying to minimize pain and keep the second stage short, labor and delivery usually do not need to be modified for cardiac reasons.

FETAL RISK

There is an increased risk of prematurity and small-for-gestational-age birth weight. In the multicenter U.S. study just described, prematurity was frequent (39%) and the average birth weight was 2.7 kg, with 31% of infants weighing less than 2.5 kg. The risk of CHD in children of parents with TGA is thought to be 1% to 2%, although accurate rates are not available. All mothers should be offered detailed fetal echocardiography at 16 to 18 weeks' gestation.

Level of Follow-Up, Endocarditis Prophylaxis, and Exercise

All patients who have had repair of TGA in addition to the rare unoperated survivors should be observed at a center specializing in adult CHD. Most Mustard, Senning, and Rastelli procedure patients can be seen annually, although those with complicating factors such as severe systemic right ventricular dysfunction will require more frequent visits. Arterial switch operation patients may be able to be seen less frequently unless there are specific reasons for concern, such as severe aortic root dilation. Patients should have a clinical history taken and examination performed, as well as electrocardiography and echocardiography at each visit. The "gold standard" imaging modality for atrial baffle repair patients is cardiac MRI; and as this modality becomes more widely available it should be performed at least every 3 years for these patients. In patients who are unable to undergo MRI, radionuclide ventriculography is a suitable alternative for the assessment of right ventricular function.

The most recent revisions of the various international guidelines for endocarditis prophylaxis would not support the use of prophylaxis in most patients who have had repair of their transposition, although many would continue to recommend prophylaxis for Rastelli procedure patients because of the bioprosthetic pulmonary valve.

For atrial baffle repair patients with good or mildly impaired systemic ventricular function, few exercise limitations need to be imposed. We would advocate avoidance of isometric exercise to protect the systemic right ventricle, although there is no evidence that any form of exercise is detrimental. It is worth noting that in the Dutch multicenter study of sudden death in this population, 81% of deaths occurred during exercise. Patients with moderate or severe right ventricular dysfunction should be advised to avoid more strenuous and competitive exercise but encouraged to pursue regular light to moderate social exercise.

Rastelli operation patients without residual hemodynamic lesions and with good ventricular function should receive similar advice to the atrial baffle repair group. Patients with moderate or severe ventricular dysfunction or outflow obstruction should likewise avoid more strenuous exercise.

Patients who have had an arterial switch operation and who are without residual hemodynamic lesions and with good ventricular function should not be restricted in terms of exercise. In patients with significant aortic root dilation isometric and competitive exercise should probably be avoided. Exercise testing should be undertaken in all arterial switch operation patients in their early teenage years to exclude ischemia resulting from coronary arterial complications.

In all groups of TGA patients, as for all patients with CHD, aerobic exercises such as walking, cycling, and swimming should be encouraged.

REFERENCES

1. Wernovsky G, Sanders SP. Coronary artery anatomy and transposition of the great arteries. Coron Artery Dis 1993;4:148–157.
2. Pasquali SK, Hasselblad V, Li JS, et al. Coronary artery pattern and outcome of arterial switch operation for transposition of the great arteries: a meta-analysis. Circulation 2002;106:2575–2580.
3. Rashkind WJ, Miller WW. Creation of an atrial septal defect without thoracotomy: a palliative approach to complete transposition of the great arteries. JAMA 1966;196:991–992.
4. Senning A. Surgical correction of transposition of the great vessels. Surgery 1959;45:966–980.
5. Mustard WT. Successful two-stage correction of transposition of the great vessels. Surgery 1964;55:469–472.
6. Castañeda AR, Trusler GA, Paul MH, et al. The early results of treatment of simple transposition in the current era. J Thorac Cardiovasc Surg 1988;95:14–27.
7. Rastelli GC, McGoon DC, Wallace RB. Anatomic correction of transposition of the great arteries with ventricular septal defect and sub-pulmonary stenosis. J Thorac Cardiovasc Surg 1969;58:545–552.
8. Jatene AD, Fontes VF, Paulista PP, et al. Anatomic correction of transposition of the great arteries. J Thorac Cardiovasc Surg 1976;72:364–370.
9. Liebman J, Cullum L, Belloc NB. Natural history of transposition of the great arteries: anatomy and birth and death characteristics. Circulation 1969;40:237–262.
10. Kirklin JW, Barratt-Boyes BG. Complete transposition of the great arteries. In: Cardiac Surgery. 2nd ed. White Plains, NY: Churchill Livingstone; 1993. p. 1383–1467.
11. Trusler GA, Williams WG, Duncan KF, et al. Results with the Mustard operation in simple transposition of the great arteries 1963–1985. Ann Surg 1987;206:251–260.
12. Gelatt M, Hamilton RM, McCrindle BW, et al. Arrhythmia and mortality after the Mustard procedure: a 30-year single-center experience. J Am Coll Cardiol 1997;29:194–201.
13. Wilson NJ, Clarkson PM, Barratt-Boyes BG, et al. Long-term outcome after the Mustard repair for simple transposition of the great arteries. 28-year follow-up. J Am Coll Cardiol 1998; 32:758–765.
14. Roos-Hesselink JW, Meijboom FJ, Spitaels SEC, et al. Decline in ventricular function and clinical condition after Mustard repair for transposition of the great arteries (a prospective study of 22–29 years). Eur Heart J 2004;25:1264–1270.
15. Paul MH, Wessel HU. Exercise studies in patients with transposition of the great arteries after atrial repair operations (Mustard/Senning): a review. Pediatr Cardiol 1999;20:49–55.
16. Derrick GP, Narang I, White PA, et al. Failure of stroke volume augmentation during exercise and dobutamine stress is unrelated to load-independent indexes of right ventricular performance after the Mustard operation. Circulation 2000;102(Suppl. III):154–159.
17. Gillette PC, Kugler JD, Garson Jr A, et al. Mechanisms of cardiac arrhythmias after the Mustard operation for transposition of the great arteries. Am J Cardiol 1980;45:1225–1230.
18. Puley G, Siu S, Connelly M, et al. Arrhythmia and survival in patients > 18 years of age after the Mustard procedure for complete transposition of the great arteries. Am J Cardiol 1999;83:1080–1084.
19. Kanter RJ, Papagiannis J, Carboni MP, et al. Radiofrequency catheter ablation of supraventricular tachycardia substrates after Mustard and Senning operations for d-transposition of the great arteries. J Am Coll Cardiol 2000;35:428–441.
20. Zrenner B, Dong J, Schreieck J, et al. Delineation of intra-atrial reentrant tachycardia circuits after Mustard operation for transposition of the great arteries using biatrial electroanatomic mapping and entrainment mapping. J Cardiovasc Electrophysiol 2003;14:1302–1310.
21. Kammeraad JA, van Deurzen CH, Sreeram N, et al. J Am Coll Cardiol 2004;44:1095–1102.
22. Millane T, Bernard EJ, Jaeggi E, et al. Role of ischemia and infarction in late right ventricular dysfunction after atrial repair of transposition of the great arteries. J Am Coll Cardiol 2000;35:1661–1668.
23. Park SC, Neches WH, Mathews RA, et al. Haemodynamic function after the Mustard operation for transposition of the great arteries. Am J Cardiol 1985;55:1238–1239.
24. Kreutzer C, De Vive J, Oppido G, et al. Twenty-five-year experience with Rastelli repair for transposition of the great arteries. J Thorac Cardiovasc Surg 2000;120:211–223.
25. Sarris GE, Chatzis AC, Giannopoulos NM, et al. The arterial switch operation in Europe for transposition of the great arteries: a multi-institutional study from the European congenital heart surgeons association. J Thorac Cardiovasc Surg 2006; 132:633–639.
26. Wetter J, Belli E, Sinzobahamvya N, et al. Transposition of the great arteries associated with ventricular septal defect: surgical results and long-term outcome. Eur J Cardiothorac Surg 2001;20: 816–823.
27. Reybrouck T, Eyskens B, Mertens L, et al. Cardiorespiratory exercise function after the arterial switch operation for transposition of the great arteries. Eur Heart J 2001;22:1052–1059.
28. Losay J, Touchot A, Serraf A, et al. Late outcome after arterial switch operation for transposition of the great arteries. Circulation 2001;104(Suppl. I):121–126.
29. Hayashi G, Kurosaki K, Echigo S, et al. Prevalence of arrhythmias and their risk factors mid- and long-term after the arterial switch operation. Pediatr Cardiol 2006;27:689–694.
30. Legendre A, Losay J, Touchot-Koné A, et al. Coronary events after arterial switch operation for transposition of the great arteries. Circulation 2003;108(Suppl. II):186–190.
31. Bu'Lock FA, Tometzki AJ, Kitchiner DJ, et al. Balloon expandable stents for systemic venous pathway stenosis late after Mustard's operation. Heart 1998;79:225–229.
32. Poirier NC, Mee RB. Left ventricular reconditioning and anatomical correction for systemic right ventricular dysfunction. Semin Thorac Cardiovasc Surg Pediatr Card Surg Annu 2000; 3:198–215.
33. Nakanishi T, Matsumoto Y, Seguchi M, et al. Balloon angioplasty for postoperative pulmonary artery stenosis in transposition of the great arteries. J Am Coll Cardiol 1993;22:859–866.
34. Canobbio MM, Morris CD, Graham TP, Landzberg MJ. Pregnancy outcomes after atrial repair for transposition of the great arteries. Am J Cardiol 2006;98:668–672.
35. Siu SC, Sermer M, Colman JM, et al. Prospective multicenter study of pregnancy outcomes in women with heart disease. Circulation 2001;104:515–521.

48

Eisenmenger Syndrome

ERWIN OECHSLIN

Definition and Morphology

In 1897, Victor Eisenmenger, a German physician, first described both the clinical and pathologic features of irreversible pulmonary vascular disease in a 32-year-old man with a nonrestrictive ventricular septal defect, cyanosis, and dyspnea since infancy. The patient had led a reasonably active life until 3 years before his death as an adult when he developed progressive congestive heart failure and died of hemoptysis.[1] Eisenmenger described in detail the cardiac and pulmonary pathology, including a large, perimembranous ventricular septal defect, right and left ventricular hypertrophy, right ventricular dilation, pulmonary atherosclerosis, pulmonary emboli, and subsequent pulmonary infarction.

Sixty years later, Paul Wood elucidated the distinctive clinical and physiologic characteristics in 127 individuals with Eisenmenger physiology in his classic and thoughtful work on the Eisenmenger syndrome.[2] He coined the term *Eisenmenger complex* to describe the presence of "pulmonary hypertension at systemic level, due to a high pulmonary vascular resistance (over 800 dyn.s.cm^{-5}), with reversed or bidirectional shunt through a large ventricular septal defect," as originally described by Victor Eisenmenger.[2] Because any large communication between the systemic and pulmonary circulation may result in a similar physiologic condition, when a markedly increased pulmonary vascular resistance occurs, and the localization of the defect is difficult at the bedside, Wood suggested using the term *Eisenmenger syndrome,* which was defined as pulmonary hypertension with reversed or bidirectional shunting at any level to embrace all conditions that behave physiologically like Eisenmenger complex: "it matters very little where the shunt happens to be. The distinguishing feature is not anatomy but the physiologic behavior of the pulmonary circulation".[2] A large communication was common in Wood's population and exceeded 0.7 cm in diameter at necropsy when it was aortopulmonary, 1.5 cm when interventricular, and 3.0 cm when interatrial.

Etiology

The presence of a nonrestrictive communication at any level with consequent increased pulmonary blood flow and transmission of (near) systemic pressures to the pulmonary arteries are the driving forces for the development of irreversible pulmonary vascular disease. This pulmonary obstructive arteriopathy causes an increase in pulmonary vascular resistance and reversal of the shunt. Eisenmenger syndrome is the most advanced form and extreme manifestation of pulmonary arterial hypertension associated with congenital heart disease (CHD) and may occur in natural and surgically created communications between the systemic and pulmonary circulations.

SEPTAL DEFECTS WITHOUT PULMONARY OUTFLOW TRACT OBSTRUCTION

- Defect at the atrial level (sinus venosus defect, secundum and primum atrial septal defects)
- Ventricular septal defect (Fig. 48-1)
- Atrioventricular septal defect

COMPLEX LESIONS WITHOUT PULMONARY OUTFLOW TRACT OBSTRUCTION

- Discordant ventriculoarterial connection (*d*-transposition of the great arteries) or discordant atrioventricular and ventriculoarterial connections (*l*-transposition of the great arteries in cardiac situs solitus or dextro-position in cardiac situs inversus) with a nonrestrictive ventricular septal defect
- Various forms of common arterial trunk
- Various forms of univentricular hearts

LARGE AORTOPULMONARY CONNECTIONS

- Patent ductus arteriosus
- Aortopulmonary window
- Aortopulmonary collateral vessels in patients with pulmonary atresia
- Surgically created aortopulmonary connections (e.g., Potts and Waterston anastomoses)

PULMONARY VASCULAR PATHOLOGY

The structural reactions of the pulmonary vascular bed start in early childhood and are progressive. They are the deleterious response and the key to the pathophysiology of Eisenmenger syndrome.[2] The exact process initiating the pathologic changes is still unknown. The underlying pathobiology is multifactorial and involves various biochemical pathways and cell types. Increased pulmonary blood flow and pulmonary arterial pressure cause increased shear stress on the endothelium and increased circumferential stretch on the pulmonary arteries, especially the pulmonary artery smooth muscle cells. These hemodynamic forces are translated into biochemical signals through messengers at the cellular level with an impressive array of molecular abnormalities.[3] Only three pathways have been translated into clinical practice: the prostacyclin pathway, the nitric oxide pathway, and the endothelin pathway.

Obliterative remodeling of the pulmonary vessels includes vasoconstriction and occlusion of the lumen in medium-sized and small pulmonary arteries due to excessive cellular proliferation in the vascular wall, inflammation, and thrombosis.[4] New concepts in the molecular biology and development of pulmonary arterial hypertension are emerging: recent evidence suggests that the proliferative and anti-apoptotic environment in the vascular wall of medium and small pulmonary arteries share common features with *neoplasia;* the loss of endothelial cells and microvessels has features of *degenerative disease;* and circulating and vascular inflammatory cells and mediators appear to play an important role in *inflammation.*[4] Clinical translation of therapies addressing apoptosis/proliferation, regeneration, and inflammation may be attractive in the future.

Increased activity of an endogenous vascular elastase is one of the key enzymes in the pathobiology of irreversible pulmonary vascular disease. Elastase production and release or activation induce mediators (e.g., growth factors, the glycoprotein tenascin) and result in smooth muscle cell differentiation from precursor cells, smooth muscle hypertrophy, and migration in the context of neointimal formation and stimulation of elastin and collagen synthesis.[5] A number of experimental

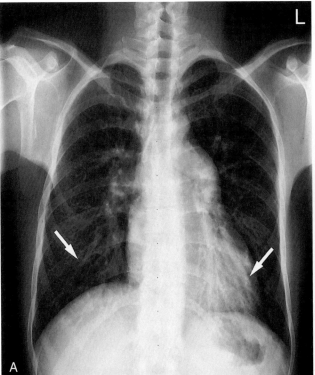

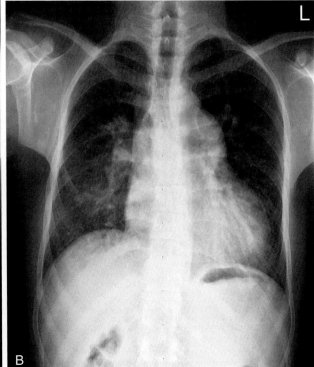

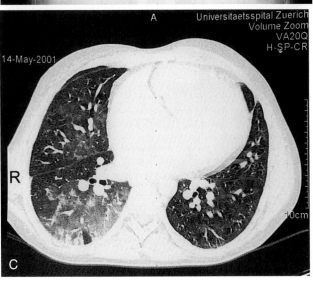

Figure 48-2 Intrapulmonary hemorrhage in a 29-year-old man with atrioventricular concordance and ventriculoarterial discordance (*d*-transposition of the great arteries), nonrestrictive subaortic ventricular septal defect, previous Blalock-Hanlon atrial septectomy, patent ductus arteriosus, and Eisenmenger syndrome. **A,** Chest radiograph at age of 26 years shows dilation of the main pulmonary trunk and the smaller division branches uniformly throughout the lungs (*arrows*). The aortic arch is small. The lungs are clear. **B,** The patient presented 3 years later with mild hemoptysis. Acinar consolidation is present in the right lower lung and represents intrapulmonary hemorrhage. Cardiothoracic ratio has increased from 0.52 to 0.60. **C,** Computed tomogram obtained on the same day shows extensive acinar consolidation (intrapulmonary hemorrhage) in the right lower lobe and in the middle lobe. (*Courtesy of B. Marincek, Institute of Diagnostic Radiology, University Hospital, Zurich, Switzerland.*)

these patients have.[31-33] A multidisciplinary approach is advisable in case of special problems or needs (e.g., respirology, hematology, infectious diseases, anesthesia, psychology or psychiatry, gynecology, social work, nursing).

All patients should periodically have a minimum of:
- A thorough medical history and clinical assessment (see Box 48-2)
- Electrocardiography: to assess cardiac rhythm, atrial and ventricular pressure overload
- Chest radiography: to assess the cardiothoracic ratio on the posteroanterior view; right or left aortic arch; dilation, aneurysm or calcification of the central pulmonary arteries; narrowing of the peripheral pulmonary vessels throughout the lungs; retrosternal filling on the lateral view (right ventricular dilation or transposition of the great arteries); pulmonary infiltrates; and calcified ductus arteriosus on the lateral view

- Doppler echocardiography (Box 48-3)
- Exercise testing: 6-minute walk test (cardiopulmonary study is optional)
- Holter monitoring: only if there is an indication (not a routine test)
- Hematologic studies:
  - Blood cell count including mean corpuscular volume (MCV) to recognize iron deficiency; MCV, however, is not a good indicator for iron deficiency in cyanotic patients[34]
  - Serum ferritin and transferrin saturation to define iron stores and stage of iron deficiency (Box 48-4).
  - Serum uric acid, serum creatinine levels
  - Clotting profile (INR, aPTT, thrombin time, fibrinogen)
  - Bleeding time is not useful to assess impaired homeostasis in patients with Eisenmenger syndrome (see Hemostatic Abnormalities).

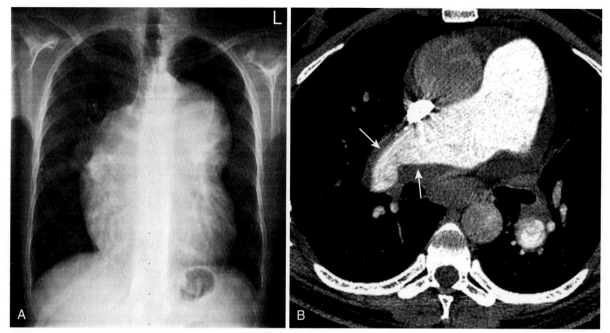

Figure 48-3 **A,** Giant pulmonary artery aneurysm in an 18-year-old man with nonrestrictive, perimembranous and multiple muscular ventricular septal defects and Eisenmenger syndrome. Chest radiograph shows an aneurysm of the pulmonary trunk, dilation of the central right and left pulmonary arteries, and pulmonary artery branch narrowing toward the periphery of the lungs. The heart is grossly enlarged (cardiothoracic ratio 0.67). **B,** Laminated thrombus in the proximal right pulmonary artery in a 40-year-old man with nonrestrictive patent ductus arteriosus. (*A, Courtesy of B. Marincek, Institute of Diagnostic Radiology, University Hospital, Zurich, Switzerland.*)

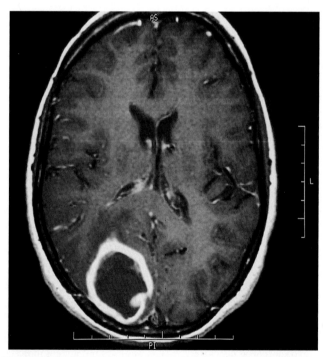

Figure 48-4 Cerebral abscess in a 33-year-old woman with cyanotic and pulmonary hypertensive congenital heart disease. Axial T1-weighted post-contrast magnetic resonance image shows an abscess (*Streptococcus intermedius,* 5 × 3.6 × 3.6 cm in diameter) in the right occipital lobe. Typical contrast enhancement of the abscess wall and perilesional edema are present. (*Courtesy of A. Valavanis, Institute of Diagnostic Neuroradiology, University Hospital, Zurich, Switzerland.*)

BOX 48-3 DOPPLER ECHOCARDIOGRAPHY

- Define cardiac anatomy (sequential analysis) and communication between systemic and pulmonary circulation; is the communication restrictive or nonrestrictive?
- Assess or exclude aortopulmonary collateral vessels.
- Assess the pressure gradient across the communication if possible.
- Assess ventricular size and function (right and left or univentricular; calculate ejection fraction and/or fractional area change and/or tricuspid/mitral annular motion).
- Determine right ventricular systolic pressure from tricuspid regurgitation.
- Assess atrioventricular valve regurgitation.
- Exclude or determine pulmonary and/or systemic outflow tract obstruction.

BOX 48-4 CONCEPT OF NEGATIVE IRON BALANCE AND IRON-DEFICIENT ERYTHROPOIESIS

Stages of Iron Deficiency
- Iron store depletion: the result of an imbalance between normal physiologic demands and the level of dietary intake
- Iron-deficient erythropoiesis: reduced red blood cell production
- Iron-deficiency anemia: the result of a prolonged period of negative iron imbalance. Phlebotomy is the main cause of microcytic, hypochromic red blood cell morphology in patients with Eisenmenger syndrome.

Laboratory Assessment of Iron Deficiency
- Measurement of hemoglobin, mean corpuscular volume, serum ferritin, and transferrin saturation concentration is essential; determination of the other parameters is optional. Findings are shown in Table 48-1.

TABLE 48-1	Stage of Iron Deficiency and Laboratory Findings		
	Early Iron Store Depletion	Iron-Deficient Erythropoiesis	Iron-Deficiency Anemia
Hemoglobin	Normal	Normal to ↓	↓↓
Mean corpuscular volume	Normal	Normal	↓↓
Erythrocyte protoporphyrin	Normal	↑	↑↑
Serum iron	Normal	↓↓	↓↓↓
Total iron-binding capacity	Normal	↑	↑
Serum ferritin	↓	↓↓	↓↓
Transferrin saturation	↓	↓↓	↓↓

LABORATORY PRECAUTIONS

Coagulation Parameters
Caution is required for accurate measurement of the coagulation parameters because secondary erythrocytosis increases hematocrit and decreases plasma volume. Adjustment of the amount of liquid anticoagulants is essential for accurate measurement of the coagulation parameters.[17] Two useful formulas are:
- The Toronto formula: anticoagulant (3.8% citrate) in mL = 1.6 [(100 − hematocrit)/100] + 0.02 for a draw of 10 mL whole blood
- Dr. Perloff's formula[23]: anticoagulant (3.8% citrate) in mL whole blood = (100 − hematocrit)/595 − hematocrit)

Hematocrit
Determination of the hematocrit level must be based on automated electronic particle counts because microhematocrit centrifugation results in plasma trapping and falsely raised hematocrit.[23]

Blood Glucose
There is increased in-vitro glycolysis resulting from the greater than normal number of red blood cells. Reduced blood glucose levels are not uncommon (artificial "hypoglycemia"). Sodium fluoride must be added to the tube to prevent red cell glycolysis and to determine an accurate blood glucose level.[23]

OPTIONAL DIAGNOSTIC WORKUP

Transesophageal Echocardiography
Transesophageal echocardiography is used to define cardiac and cardiovascular anatomy and the communication between the two circuits if they were not adequately obtained by transthoracic echocardiography. Sedation may decrease systemic vascular resistance and cause hypotension with a subsequent increase in right-to-left shunting. Transesophageal echocardiography should be performed only by very experienced and skilled ultrasonographers.

Spiral or High-Resolution Computed Tomography or Cardiac Magnetic Resonance Imaging
These techniques are especially useful in patients with poor echocardiographic windows and in those with previous cardiac surgery. They are used:
- To visualize better the defects between the systemic and pulmonary circuits and to evaluate their size(s) and location(s)
- To describe pulmonary artery dilation or aneurysm formation and to visualize mural or obstructive thrombi
- To define the severity of intrapulmonary hemorrhage or infarction if the chest radiograph is showing pulmonary infiltrates or consolidation (see Fig. 48-2)
- To visualize in-situ thromboses in the aneurysmal proximal pulmonary arteries

Cardiac Catheterization
Cardiac catheterization is used to evaluate the hemodynamics in the setting of inadequate assessment by noninvasive means and to determine the potential reversibility of pulmonary arterial pressure and vascular resistance with pulmonary vasodilators (100% oxygen, nitric oxide, prostacyclin) if not adequately assessed by other means.

Open-Lung Biopsy
Open-lung biopsy is useful to define reversibility of pulmonary vascular disease if hemodynamic data are not conclusive. This procedure may be hazardous because of the multisystemic disorder in patients with Eisenmenger syndrome and should be performed only at centers with personnel with substantial experience in management of CHD and supported by a pathologist skilled in the assessment of pulmonary hypertension. Open-lung biopsies are very rarely performed.

Late Management Options

Advances in medicine and the introduction of new technologies have had little influence on the care and management of patients with Eisenmenger syndrome. Once the syndrome has become established, efforts must be directed toward avoiding complications and mismanagement associated with increased morbidity and mortality (Box 48-5). The basic principle and mainstay of the care and medical therapy are to avoid medications that have not been proven to be beneficial, to alleviate symptoms without increasing or adding risks, to counsel against special risks, to intervene only when needed and, finally, not to destabilize the balanced physiology. Although specific, pulmonary vascular disease targeting therapies have emerged and are considered in selected patients, supportive and preventive care remains the cornerstone.

THERAPEUTIC INTERVENTIONS

Phlebotomy
Prophylactic phlebotomy to maintain the hematocrit within an arbitrary predetermined level (hematocrit < 65%) and to prevent cerebrovascular events is never justified and is one of the major misconceptions in the management of patients with cyanotic CHD.[22] An increased hematocrit level, in and of itself, is no indication for phlebotomy. Inappropriate and repeated phlebotomies do not offer

---

BOX 48-5   LATE TREATMENT

- The mainstay of care is not to destabilize the balanced physiology.
- Phlebotomy must be restricted to patients with moderate to severe hyperviscosity symptoms in the absence of dehydration and iron deficiency.
- Iron supplements: iron deficiency is hazardous and must be prevented or treated.
- Avoidance and treatment of "anemia" (*caveat*: Eisenmenger syndrome patients require a higher hemoglobin level than healthy adults).
- Rehydration: if dehydration present.
- Anticoagulation: the risk-benefit ratio has to be evaluated carefully. Oral anticoagulation is justified by strong indications (atrial flutter, atrial fibrillation, pulmonary emboli, mechanical heart valves) but at an increased risk of major bleeding. Meticulous surveillance of anticoagulation is mandatory. Prophylactic anticoagulation reinforces hemostatic abnormalities.
- Bleeding complications: care should be provided by a multidisciplinary team. Discontinuation of aspirin or any oral anticoagulant is essential. Bronchoscopy seldom has any diagnostic impact on the management of patients with hemoptysis and should be avoided. Chest radiography should be performed and computed tomography considered.
- Arterial hypertension must be evaluated and treated. β-Adrenergic blockers are usually well tolerated.
- End-stage heart and lung disease: consider transplantation and refer to a transplant team sooner rather than later.
- Specific, pulmonary vascular disease targeting therapy. Endothelin receptor antagonists should be considered in NYHA functional class III patients; there are anecdotal experiences regarding other specific therapies or combination therapies.

any clinical benefit to the patient and pose the potential hazard of iron deficiency. Iron-deficient microspherocytosis mimics or worsens hyperviscosity symptoms and is a recognized risk factor for cerebrovascular events.[14,23,25,29,30] Relative iron-deficiency anemia is frequently ignored or not recognized in these patients, because the hemoglobin may be less than 15 g/dL but should be greater than 18 g/dL.

There are two indications for phlebotomy: (1) moderate to severe hyperviscosity symptoms (see Boxes 48-1 and 48-2) and (2) preoperative phlebotomy to improve hemostasis if hematocrit is greater than 65%.

The primary goal of phlebotomy is temporary relief of moderate to severe hyperviscosity symptoms, which should be achieved by the withdrawal of only enough blood to alleviate symptoms. The strongest indication for phlebotomy is moderate to severe hyperviscosity symptoms in the absence of both iron deficiency and dehydration (see Boxes 48-2 and 48-5). Patients with compensated secondary erythrocytosis do not usually complain of intrusive hyperviscosity symptoms interfering with their daily activities; they do not need phlebotomies, although the hematocrit level may exceed 70%.

The hyperviscosity symptoms(s) should disappear after adequate phlebotomy. The patient will develop the same symptom(s) should hyperviscosity recur. Symptomatic improvement from phlebotomy results from increased cardiac output and systemic blood flow due to decreased whole blood viscosity and systemic vascular resistance. Oxygen delivery to tissue is improved, which leads to an increase in exercise performance. This therapeutic effect is evident within 24 hours after phlebotomy.[23]

METHOD OF PHLEBOTOMY

Phlebotomy is a safe outpatient procedure in the adult setting utilizing the withdrawal of 250 to 500 mL whole blood preceded by or concurrent with volume replacement (e.g., 750 to 1000 mL isotonic saline). If moderate to severe hyperviscosity symptoms persist in the absence of dehydration and iron deficiency, phlebotomy may be repeated after 24 to 48 hours.

Administration of salt-free albumin or fresh frozen plasma is not necessary. From the experience in Toronto, oral fluid replacement may be effective in selected, well hydrated, and stable patients.

Blood pressure is recorded before phlebotomy and every 15 minutes after the procedure for the next 60 minutes. Further fluid replacement may be necessary until the patient's blood pressure stabilizes.

No more than four phlebotomies should be performed per year. If hyperviscosity symptoms persist despite repeat phlebotomy, iron deficiency must be strongly considered.

Iron Replacement
Iron deficiency is hazardous for patients with cyanotic CHD and must be avoided by all means and corrected without delay if there is biochemical evidence of iron deficiency (low ferritin, low transferrin saturation, and usually microcytosis). A low dose of ferrous sulfate (325 mg once daily, 65 mg elemental iron once daily) is orally administered to avoid an excessive erythrocytotic response.[23]

Parenteral iron therapy can be considered in patients who are intolerant of iron preparations or in those with severe iron deficiency. Iron dextran has been intravenously administered for many years. It is usually well tolerated, safe, and effective but can cause an anaphylactic reaction. Iron saccharose is a new preparation that is much better tolerated and does not appear to have allergic side effects.

Anemia
Anemia is frequently ignored or easily missed in the setting of Eisenmenger syndrome. The hemoglobin level and hematocrit must be increased in accordance with the severity of hypoxia. A hemoglobin level of 15 g/dL is normal for healthy adults, but it is too low for patients with Eisenmenger syndrome. Inappropriate, repeated phlebotomies or menorrhagia are the main causes of a relative iron-deficiency anemia. Of course, other causes of anemia have to be considered. Blood transfusion must be considered in the presence of iron-repleted anemia with a hemoglobin inadequate to compensate for marked oxygen desaturation.

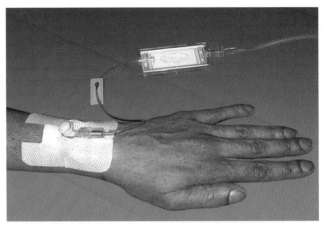

Figure 48-5 Posidyne ELD Filter (Pall Corporation, Port Washington, NY). An air-eliminating filter with a 0.2-μm Posidyne membrane may be used for up to 96 hours in an Eisenmenger syndrome patient with an intravenous line.

Rehydration
Dehydration may be multifactorial (i.e., diarrhea, vomiting, fever, heat, air travel), may destabilize the patient's delicate pathophysiology, and can be fatal. Adequate fluid intake or replacement is crucial. An air filter must be used to avoid air embolism if an intravenous line is in place (Fig. 48-5).

Ischemic Complications
There is a therapeutic dilemma in the management of patients with Eisenmenger syndrome facing both bleeding and thromboembolic complications. Because hemostatic abnormalities are an integral part of the multisystem disorder in patients with cyanotic CHD, indications for anticoagulation must be strong, and both indications and contraindications must be evaluated carefully. Anticoagulation has a favorable effect on survival and morbidity, based on retrospective, nonrandomized studies, and is widely used in patients with idiopathic pulmonary hypertension.[10,35] Thus, it is tempting to draw similar conclusions for adults with Eisenmenger syndrome. However, the routine use of anticoagulants is very controversial and no data exist to support this approach in these patients. All available data are empirical and retrospective, and there are legitimate arguments against routine anticoagulation.[10,27,36,37] Thus, prophylactic, routine administration of aspirin or oral anticoagulants cannot be recommended because such interventions reinforce hemostatic abnormalities and bleeding tendency with the risk of intrapulmonary hemorrhage.[31–33]

Strong indications for anticoagulation in the setting of cyanosis and pulmonary hypertension may include:
- Atrial flutter or fibrillation
- Recurrent thromboembolic events in the absence of iron deficiency or dehydration
- Pulmonary artery thrombosis with pulmonary emboli and absent or only mild hemoptysis
- Mechanical heart valves or other high-risk anatomy

Warfarin (Coumadin), unfractionated heparin, or low-molecular-weight heparin (LMWH) may be used. Subcutaneous LMWH administration may be convenient but may cause hematomas, which can be painful and become infected.

Meticulous surveillance of anticoagulation is required and includes withdrawal of whole blood into tubes containing anticoagulants, which are adjusted to the hematocrit. The optimal range of the INR or aPTT has not been evaluated. Recommendations for therapeutic anticoagulation in Eisenmenger syndrome patients are empirical:
- Therapeutic aPTT: 1.5 times the control value
- Target INR: 2.0 to 2.5
- Target INR for mechanical valves presumably higher: 2.5 to 3.0

Risk reduction strategies for ischemic events also include:

- Avoidance and treatment of dehydration and iron deficiency
- Special care to avoid systemic air embolism, including the use of an air filter in all intravenous lines (see Fig. 48-5)
- Iron supplementation in patients subjected to recurrent phlebotomy

The incidence and extent of large in-situ thromboses within the dilated pulmonary arteries is frightening.[18,27,28,37] This may be thought to be an indication for oral anticoagulation, but the significance of such thrombi and the results of treatment are unknown. No therapeutic modality satisfactorily addresses these in-situ laminated thromboses. Thrombolytic agents are ineffective and the risk-benefit ratio does not justify the use of oral anticoagulants.[18] Short-term administration of low-dose warfarin is indicated to stabilize the proximal thromboses if proximal thrombotic material embolizes into distal pulmonary arteries and causes pulmonary infarction with subsequent intrapulmonary hemorrhage and hemoptysis.[10,11,27,36]

Bleeding Complications

A multidisciplinary team including coagulation experts and other specialists can best manage major hemorrhage and the risk of serious morbidity and mortality.

Hemoptysis is external and may not reflect the extent of intrapulmonary hemorrhage (see Fig. 48-2). It should be regarded as potentially life threatening and requires meticulous evaluation, including both general and specific aspects.[23,31-33]

General diagnostic and therapeutic aspects include:
- Hospital admission
- Reduction of physical activity (typically bed rest)
- Suppression of nonproductive cough
- Avoidance of bronchoscopy, which incurs risk while seldom providing useful information
- Chest radiography
- Thoracic computed tomography if there are infiltrates or acinar consolidation on the chest radiograph to assess the severity of intrapulmonary hemorrhage or to visualize in-situ thromboses in the proximal dilated pulmonary arteries
- Immediate discontinuation of aspirin, nonsteroidal anti-inflammatory drugs, and oral anticoagulants
- Bleeding diathesis:
  - Consider administration of platelets, especially if platelet count is less than 100 000/μL
  - Consider administration of fresh frozen plasma (FFP), factor VIII, vitamin K, cryoprecipitate, desmopressin, etc.
- Treatment of hypovolemia and anemia

Specific diagnostic and/or therapeutic aspects include treatable causes of hemoptysis that must be excluded and/or treated:
- Infectious disease: take sputum culture and treat infectious disease (e.g., bronchitis, pneumonia). Consider tuberculosis as a cause of hemoptysis.
- Aortography with selective embolization of the artery supplying the source of blood loss may be considered in the setting of severe and/or incessant bleeding.
- Pulmonary emboli or pulmonary infarction: anticoagulate and consider implantation of an inferior vena caval filter in case of deep vein thrombosis and recurrent pulmonary emboli. Anticoagulate in the presence of embolizing thrombus material from the dilated proximal pulmonary arteries. Be aware of the risk of pulmonary hemorrhage in the setting of pulmonary infarction.
- Rupture of aortopulmonary collateral vessels or pulmonary artery aneurysms is usually fatal—interventional closure of aortopulmonary collateral vessels may be considered (high-risk procedures with uncertain benefit).

Arterial Hypertension

Systemic arterial hypertension, which is transmitted to the pulmonary circulation, must be evaluated as in patients without Eisenmenger syndrome. Arterial hypertension is frequently ignored and may have a serious impact on morbidity and mortality in these patients. As systemic artery pressures rise, pulmonary arterial pressure increases and may facilitate intrapulmonary bleeding or rupture of a dilated or aneurysmal pulmonary artery. Meticulous therapy is warranted. Administration of a β-adrenergic blocker started at a low dose is safe. Other antihypertensive agents may decrease systemic vascular resistance and may result in an increase in right-to-left shunting and cyanosis but can be used if required to control systemic hypertension.

Noncardiac Surgery

Adults with Eisenmenger syndrome, who are very vulnerable to any hemodynamic alterations, may require noncardiac surgery and should undergo the procedures only in centers with expertise in the care of such patients.[31-33] Eisenmenger physiology precludes rapid adaptive mechanisms to any change in hemodynamics caused by anesthetics, fluid shifts, and/or surgery.[23,38] Thus, every surgical procedure carries a high risk of morbidity and substantial risk of mortality.[38] There is no prospective study that has evaluated the risks of noncardiac surgery in Eisenmenger syndrome patients.

Perioperative risks include:
- Decrease in systemic vascular resistance, which may result in an increase in right-to-left shunting, increased cyanosis, and possibly collapse and death
- Sudden increase in systemic vascular resistance, which may depress ventricular function
- Supraventricular and ventricular arrhythmias
- Increased blood loss because of a bleeding diathesis
- Risk of thrombotic and/or embolic complications due to the thrombotic diathesis.

Key points in the perioperative management of adults with Eisenmenger syndrome who undergo noncardiac surgery include the following[31-33,38]:
- The patient's care should be managed by a team including a cardiac anesthetist experienced in the management of patients with pulmonary arterial hypertension.
- Meticulous preoperative evaluation is essential (i.e., medical history, physical examination, electrocardiography, chest radiography, complete blood cell count, blood chemistry, clotting studies, Doppler echocardiography).
- Local anesthesia is preferred whenever possible.
- The choice of general versus epidural-spinal anesthesia is controversial. General anesthesia is preferred. Epidural anesthesia resulting in sympathetic blockade and decrease in both preload and afterload may be hazardous, although it has been employed successfully for minor operations; a bleeding diathesis may be a contraindication to epidural anesthesia.
- Preoperative phlebotomy with at least isovolumic fluid replacement can be considered if the hematocrit exceeds 65%. This strategy may increase platelet count and reduce the risk of intraoperative bleeding. The blood so withdrawn should be reserved for autologous blood donation if required.[23,38]
- Careful intraoperative monitoring (arterial line ± central venous line) to detect sudden pressure and volume changes should be done, with pulse oximetry to assess oxygen saturation.
- Surgery must be performed by an experienced surgeon (every surgical procedure in these patients can be major and demanding).
- Endocarditis prophylaxis is required as is use of an air filter (see Fig. 48-5).

Transplantation

Transplantation is a widely accepted surgical option in patients with end-stage diseases to improve survival and quality of life. It must be addressed and discussed as soon as possible after the recognition of a high mortality risk. Early referral to a transplant team and assessment are crucial for the complex and long process of being listed. This topic is addressed in detail in Chapter 13.

Oxygen Therapy

Oxygen therapy does not substantially improve arterial oxygen saturation. There is a drying effect of the nonhumidified oxygen predisposing to epistaxis. Oxygen therapy may have a psychologic (placebo) benefit.[39]

PROPHYLACTIC INTERVENTIONS AND RISK REDUCTION STRATEGIES

A prophylactic approach is the key point in the management of adults with Eisenmenger syndrome to avoid infectious, thromboembolic, hemorrhagic, and other serious complications:

- Administration of a flu shot annually and of Pneumovax 23, a multivalent pneumococcal polysaccharide vaccine, every 5 years
- Avoidance of iron deficiency
- Avoidance of dehydration
- Avoidance of cigarette smoking and recreational drug use
- Avoidance of drugs that impair renal function (e.g., aspirin, nonsteroidal anti-inflammatory drugs)
- Consultation with an adult CHD cardiologist before administering any drugs
- Use of an air filter to avoid systemic air embolism if intravenous access is needed (see Fig. 48-5)
- Avoidance of strenuous exercise
- Avoidance of exposure to excessive heat (sauna, hot tube/shower)
- Avoidance of pregnancy
- Use of a toothbrush with soft bristles (brushing should be gentle)

SPECIFIC DISEASE-TARGETING THERAPIES

New pulmonary vascular disease targeting therapies have evolved and many randomized controlled studies demonstrated safety and efficacy in patients with idiopathic pulmonary arterial hypertension and other forms associated with it. Despite many described molecular abnormalities, only three of them have been translated into clinical practice: prostacyclin pathway (prostacyclin analogues), nitric oxide pathway (phosphodiesterase type-5 inhibitors), and endothelin pathway (endothelin receptor antagonists). Only a few studies included patients with Eisenmenger syndrome, and conclusions cannot be extrapolated to this population. Treatment strategies and algorithms have been updated recently (Fig. 48-6).[10,11,35,36,40]

Endothelin receptor antagonists are attractive substances targeting the intimately involved endothelin-1 system in the pathobiology

and pathophysiology. The BREATHE-5 trial, the first multicenter, double-blind randomized study in patients with Eisenmenger syndrome, confirmed the safety and efficacy of bosentan, a dual endothelin-receptor receptor antagonist.[41] There was no negative effect on oxygen saturation, and bosentan significantly improved the 6-minute walk distance and decreased pulmonary vascular resistance after 16 weeks of therapy in NYHA functional class III patients. Sustained improvement was demonstrated in the extension study (40 weeks' follow-up).[42] Bosentan is approved in many countries for NYHA functional class III Eisenmenger syndrome patients. No studies similar to BREATHE-5 are available for other endothelin antagonists.

Prostanoids have been used in patients with Eisenmenger syndrome with favorable effects on hemodynamics and exercise capacity, but the need for a central line to administer intravenous epoprostenol and the exposure of the patients to paradoxical emboli and infection are major issues. Insufficient data exist with the use of other prostanoids.

Phosphodiesterase-5 inhibitors (sildenafil, tadalafil) have shown favorable results, but there are only anecdotal experiences with their use in patients with Eisenmenger syndrome.

Combination therapy is used in selected patients, but there are only anecdotal experiences in Eisenmenger syndrome patients.

Any disease-targeting therapy must be initiated in a specialized center with expertise in both CHD and pulmonary hypertension.

Management strategies for idiopathic pulmonary hypertension are discussed in Chapter 64.

Arrhythmia and Sudden Cardiac Death

Arrhythmias such as atrial flutter or fibrillation may be a result of a failing heart, are usually poorly tolerated, and thus often cause important morbidity and mortality.

SUPRAVENTRICULAR ARRHYTHMIAS

Supraventricular tachyarrhythmias (atrial flutter, atrial fibrillation, ectopic atrial tachycardia) are common. They occurred in 13%, 36%, and 25% of patients with ventricular septal defect, truncus arteriosus, and univentricular heart, respectively, and were recorded in 35.5% of a heterogeneous population of Eisenmenger syndrome patients during 24-hour Holter monitoring.[14,18] These arrhythmias usually heralded clinical deterioration with heart failure, peripheral embolism, collapse, and death.[14] A history of arrhythmia requiring cardioversion or antiarrhythmic therapy was documented in a minority of patients (13%).[16] A history of supraventricular arrhythmias requiring treatment was identified to be an independent predictor for mortality (hazard ratio 3.44).[17] This was confirmed by another retrospective study (odds ratio of 9.0).[16]

Restoration of sinus rhythm is a high priority and is best achieved by cardioversion. A trial of amiodarone may be an option in a hemodynamically stable patient. There has been no clinical trial to evaluate the proarrhythmic impact of antiarrhythmic drugs on the hypertrophic ventricles exposed to chronic hypoxemia. Thus, individualized antiarrhythmic therapy is recommended with special attention to the proarrhythmic effect of these drugs.

The presence of subacute or chronic atrial flutter or fibrillation increases the risk of intracardiac thrombi and thromboembolic complications. Transesophageal echocardiography performed by a skilled ultrasonographer with special expertise may be required to exclude intracardiac thrombi before electrical cardioversion if the arrhythmia has lasted for more than 48 hours. As explained earlier, anticoagulation must be initiated with caution.

VENTRICULAR ARRHYTHMIAS

Ventricular arrhythmias are less common than supraventricular ones. Nonsustained monomorphic ventricular tachycardia was observed in 13% of patients with a ventricular septal defect and in 6% of those with a univentricular heart but no sustained ventricular tachycardia

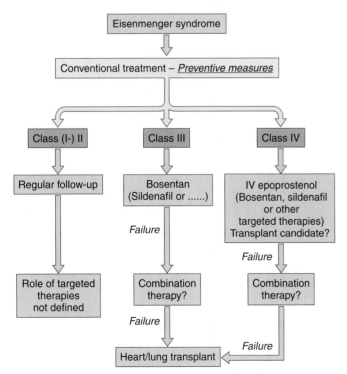

Figure 48-6 Treatment strategy and algorithm for Eisenmenger syndrome.

was recorded.[18] Although 22% of patients (n = 10) in one study had at least one recorded episode of either nonsustained (n = 5) or sustained (n = 5) ventricular tachycardia there was no correlation between arrhythmias and sudden death.[14]

There is no reported experience with respect to used of an automatic implantable cardioverter-defibrillator in the presence of syncope and malignant ventricular arrhythmias in this population.

SYMPTOMATIC BRADYCARDIA

Pacemaker implantation is required in patients with complete heart block and may be an option in those with nodal bradycardia to prevent sudden cardiac death and/or to offer functional improvement. Transvenous leads incur a significant risk of systemic thromboemboli in patients with intracardiac shunts.[43] Thus, cyanotic patients must have epicardial pacing electrodes to reduce the thromboembolic risk. Implantation may be complicated by the bleeding tendency.

SUDDEN DEATH

Sudden death was reported in 21% to 63% of all deaths in Eisenmenger syndrome patients and is due to a variety of causes.[14,16–18,44] Arrhythmias, massive hemoptysis, and intrapulmonary hemorrhage caused by rupture of aneurysmal pulmonary arteries or of a bronchial artery, dissection of the ascending aorta, thromboemboli in large pulmonary arteries, vasospastic cerebral infarction, severe dehydration, and intracranial hemorrhage in patients on anticoagulants have all been implicated. Tachyarrhythmias as a cause of sudden death were probably overestimated in the past but may still have a role.

Sudden death was frequently related to lifestyle—during holidays, dancing, or undue physical activity.[14] Lifestyle counseling is very important in Eisenmenger syndrome patients to avoid such hazards.

Pregnancy

Pregnancy in a patient with Eisenmenger syndrome incurs a high risk for both maternal and fetal complications. This subject is dealt with in Chapter 21.

Level of Follow-Up and Endocarditis Prophylaxis

All patients with Eisenmenger syndrome need a careful and periodic follow-up at an adult CHD center by a cardiologist with expertise in the management of such a complex defect.[31–33] Involvement of other specialists (e.g., pulmonary hypertension specialist) is advisable and beneficial because these patients have a multisystemic disorder. Every patient should be seen once or twice a year, or even more, depending on the clinical condition (see Outpatient Assessment).

Patients with Eisenmenger syndrome carry a high risk of endocarditis and require meticulous endocarditis prophylaxis.

Exercise, Air Travel, and Exposure to High Altitude

The cardiovascular and pulmonary response to exercise of patients with Eisenmenger syndrome is complex and includes some special aspects[23]:

- Increased cyanosis during exercise caused by an increase in right-to-left shunting and limited pulmonary blood flow
- A smaller increase in oxygen uptake immediately after the onset of exercise and a delayed and slower increase with continued activity
- A high ventilatory cost to eliminate even a small amount of carbon dioxide and to maintain acid-base homeostasis.

Delayed recovery from acidosis and phosphocreatinine depletion compared with that in controls reflects abnormal muscle metabolism.

Adults with Eisenmenger syndrome are at risk of sudden death during strenuous exercise. Participation in competitive sports activities, endurance sports, and contact sports is prohibited. Individual advice is important. Low-intensity sports activities (billiards, cricket, bowling, golfing) are safe. Patients must respect their limitations and restrict their level of activity to their symptoms.

Commercial air travel is usually well tolerated without supplemental oxygen.[45,46] Actual decrease in oxygen saturation during ascent follows a similar pattern in patients and in healthy controls.[45] Travel- and non–travel-related stress must be avoided (trip organization well in advance, easy transportation). Intake of an adequate amount of fluid (no alcoholic drinks) is important because of the low humidity in commercial aircraft. Prevention of deep vein thrombosis with the potential of paradoxical emboli is critical (e.g., aisle seat, extension of the legs, periodic walks, fluid intake).

Because commercial air travel (cabin pressure altitude maintained between 1800 and 2400 m above sea level) is well tolerated, exposure to high altitude (>1500 m above sea level) may be safe. Acute exposure to high altitude (>2500 m) on land should be avoided. A gradual or stepwise ascent is important and a time for acclimatization may be wise. A transport medium must be available for immediate descent if health problems occur. Eisenmenger syndrome patients have traveled to the Grand Canyon and to the Alps in Switzerland (>3000 m above sea level) without health problems! Exercise at high altitude must be very limited and strongly restricted by symptoms.

REFERENCES

1. Eisenmenger V. Die angeborenen Defecte der Kammerscheidewand des Herzens. Z Klin Med 1897;32(Suppl.):1–28.
2. Wood P. The Eisenmenger syndrome or pulmonary hypertension with reversed central shunt. BMJ 1958;ii:701–709, 755–762.
3. Morrell NW, Adnot S, Archer SL, et al. Cellular and molecular basis of pulmonary arterial hypertension. J Am Coll Cardiol 2009;54(Suppl. 1):S20–S31.
4. Michelakis ED, Wilkins MR, Rabinovitch M. Emerging concepts and translational priorities in pulmonary arterial hypertension. Circulation 2008;118:1486–1495.
5. Rabinovitch M. Elastase and the pathobiology of unexplained pulmonary hypertension. Chest 1998;114(Suppl. 3):213S–224S.
6. Heath D, Edwards JE. The pathology of hypertensive pulmonary vascular disease; a description of six grades of structural changes in the pulmonary arteries with special reference to congenital cardiac septal defects. Circulation 1958;18:533–547.
7. Rabinovitch M, Haworth SG, Castaneda AR, et al. Lung biopsy in congenital heart disease: a morphometric approach to pulmonary vascular disease. Circulation 1978;58:1107–1122.
8. Rabinovitch M, Keane JF, Norwood WI, et al. Vascular structure in lung tissue obtained at biopsy correlated with pulmonary hemodynamic findings after repair of congenital heart defects. Circulation 1984;69:655–667.
9. Simonneau G, Robbins IM, Beghetti M, et al. Updated clinical classification of pulmonary hypertension. J Am Coll Cardiol 2009;54(Suppl. 1):S43–S54.
10. Galie N, Hoeper MM, Humbert M, et al. Guidelines for the diagnosis and treatment of pulmonary hypertension: The Task Force for the Diagnosis and Treatment of Pulmonary Hypertension of the European Society of Cardiology (ESC) and the European Respiratory Society (ERS), endorsed by the International Society of Heart and Lung Transplantation (ISHLT). Eur Heart J 2009;30:2493–2537.
11. Dimopoulos K, Giannakoulas G, Wort SJ, Gatzoulis MA. Pulmonary arterial hypertension in adults with congenital heart disease: distinct differences from other causes of pulmonary arterial hypertension and management implications. Curr Opin Cardiol 2008;23:545–554.
12. Engelfriet P, Boersma E, Oechslin E, et al. The spectrum of adult congenital heart disease in Europe: morbidity and mortality in a 5 year follow-up period. The Euro Heart Survey on adult congenital heart disease. Eur Heart J 2005;26:2325–2333.
13. Duffels MG, Engelfriet PM, Berger RM, et al. Pulmonary arterial hypertension in congenital heart disease: an epidemiologic perspective from a Dutch registry. Int J Cardiol 2007;120:198–204.
14. Daliento L, Somerville J, Presbitero P, et al. Eisenmenger syndrome: factors relating to deterioration and death. Eur Heart J 1998;19:1845–1855.
15. Hopkins WE, Ochoa LL, Richardson GW, Trulock EP. Comparison of the hemodynamics and survival of adults with severe primary pulmonary hypertension or Eisenmenger syndrome. J Heart Lung Transplant 1996;15:100–105.
16. Diller GP, Dimopoulos K, Broberg CS, et al. Presentation, survival prospects, and predictors of death in Eisenmenger syndrome: a combined retrospective and case-control study. Eur Heart J 2006;27:1737–1742.
17. Cantor WJ, Harrison DA, Moussadji JS, et al. Determinants of survival and length of survival in adults with Eisenmenger syndrome. Am J Cardiol 1999;84:677–681.
18. Niwa K, Perloff JK, Kaplan S, et al. Eisenmenger syndrome in adults: ventricular septal defect, truncus arteriosus, univentricular heart. J Am Coll Cardiol 1999;34:223–232.
19. Oya H, Nagaya N, Satoh T, et al. Haemodynamic correlates and prognostic significance of serum uric acid in adult patients with Eisenmenger syndrome. Heart 2000;84:53–58.
20. Oya H, Nagaya N, Uematsu M, et al. Poor prognosis and related factors in adults with Eisenmenger syndrome. Am Heart J 2002;143:739–744.
21. Diller GP, Dimopoulos K, Okonko D, et al. Exercise intolerance in adult congenital heart disease: comparative severity, correlates, and prognostic implication. Circulation 2005;112:828–835.
22. Oechslin E. Hematological management of the cyanotic adult with congenital heart disease. Int J Cardiol 2004;97(Suppl. 1): 109–115.
23. Perloff JK. Cyanotic congenital heart disease: a multisystem disorder. In: Perloff JK, Child JS, Aboulhosn J, editors. Congenital Heart Disease in Adults. 3rd ed. Philadelphia: Elsevier; 2008. p. 265–289.

24. Broberg CS, Bax BE, Okonko DO, et al. Blood viscosity and its relationship to iron deficiency, symptoms, and exercise capacity in adults with cyanotic congenital heart disease. J Am Coll Cardiol 2006;48:356–365.

25. Perloff JK, Rosove MH, Child JS, Wright GB. Adults with cyanotic congenital heart disease: hematologic management. Ann Intern Med 1988;109:406–413.

26. Oechslin E, Kiowski W, Schindler R, et al. Systemic endothelial dysfunction in adults with cyanotic congenital heart disease. Circulation 2005;112:1106–1112.

27. Broberg CS, Ujita M, Prasad S, et al. Pulmonary arterial thrombosis in Eisenmenger syndrome is associated with biventricular dysfunction and decreased pulmonary flow velocity. J Am Coll Cardiol 2007;50:634–642.

28. Silversides CK, Granton JT, Konen E, et al. Pulmonary thrombosis in adults with Eisenmenger syndrome. J Am Coll Cardiol 2003;42:1982–1987.

29. Perloff JK, Marelli AJ, Miner PD. Risk of stroke in adults with cyanotic congenital heart disease. Circulation 1993;87:1954–1959.

30. Ammash N, Warnes CA. Cerebrovascular events in adult patients with cyanotic congenital heart disease. J Am Coll Cardiol 1996;28:768–772.

31. Silversides CK, Salehian O, Oechslin E, et al. Canadian Cardiovascular Society 2009 Consensus Conference on the management of adults with congenital heart disease: complex congenital heart lesions. Can J Cardiol 2010;26:e98–e117.

32. Deanfield J, Thaulow E, Warnes C, et al. Management of grown up congenital heart disease. Eur Heart J 2003;24:1035–1084.

33. Warnes CA, Williams RG, Bashore TM, et al. ACC/AHA 2008 Guidelines for the Management of Adults with Congenital Heart Disease: Executive Summary: a report of the American College of Cardiology/American Heart Association Task Force on Practice Guidelines (writing committee to develop guidelines for the management of adults with congenital heart disease). Circulation 2008;118:2395–2451.

34. Kaemmerer H, Fratz S, Braun SL, et al. Erythrocyte indexes, iron metabolism, and hyperhomocysteinemia in adults with cyanotic congenital cardiac disease. Am J Cardiol 2004;94:825–828.

35. Barst RJ, Gibbs JS, Ghofrani HA, et al. Updated evidence-based treatment algorithm in pulmonary arterial hypertension. J Am Coll Cardiol 2009;54(Suppl. 1):S78–S84.

36. Beghetti M, Galie N. Eisenmenger syndrome a clinical perspective in a new therapeutic era of pulmonary arterial hypertension. J Am Coll Cardiol 2009;53:733–740.

37. Perloff JK, Hart EM, Greaves SM, et al. Proximal pulmonary arterial and intrapulmonary radiologic features of Eisenmenger syndrome and primary pulmonary hypertension. Am J Cardiol 2003;92:182–187.

38. Ammash NM, Connolly HM, Abel MD, Warnes CA. Noncardiac surgery in Eisenmenger syndrome. J Am Coll Cardiol 1999;33:222–227.

39. Sandoval J, Aguirre JS, Pulido T, et al. Nocturnal oxygen therapy in patients with the Eisenmenger syndrome. Am J Respir Crit Care Med 2001;164:1682–1687.

40. Galie N, Manes A, Palazzini M, et al. Management of pulmonary arterial hypertension associated with congenital systemic-to-pulmonary shunts and Eisenmenger syndrome. Drugs 2008;68:1049–1066.

41. Galie N, Beghetti M, Gatzoulis MA, et al. Bosentan therapy in patients with Eisenmenger syndrome: a multicenter, double-blind, randomized, placebo-controlled study. Circulation 2006;114:48–54.

42. Gatzoulis MA, Beghetti M, Galie N, et al. Longer-term bosentan therapy improves functional capacity in Eisenmenger syndrome: results of the BREATHE-5 open-label extension study. Int J Cardiol 2008;127:27–32.

43. Khairy P, Landzberg MJ, Gatzoulis MA, et al. Transvenous pacing leads and systemic thromboemboli in patients with intracardiac shunts: a multicenter study. Circulation 2006;113:2391–2397.

44. Oechslin EN, Harrison DA, Connelly MS, et al. Mode of death in adults with congenital heart disease. Am J Cardiol 2000;86:1111–1116.

45. Harinck E, Hutter PA, Hoorntje TM, et al. Air travel and adults with cyanotic congenital heart disease. Circulation 1996;93:272–276.

46. Broberg CS, Uebing A, Cuomo L, et al. Adult patients with Eisenmenger syndrome report flying safely on commercial airlines. Heart 2007;93:1599–1603.

49

Congenitally Corrected Transposition of the Great Arteries

THOMAS P. GRAHAM, JR. | **LARRY W. MARKHAM**

Definition and Morphology

Congenitally corrected transposition of the great arteries (CCTGA) is defined as that condition in which the atria are connected to the opposite ventricle (right atrium to left ventricle, left atrium to right ventricle) and the ventricles are connected to the "wrong" great artery (left ventricle to pulmonary artery, right ventricle to aorta). The aorta lies in a leftward (or levo versus the normal dextro or rightward) position relative to the pulmonary artery. These multiple anatomic abnormalities have led to a number of different synonyms for CCTGA. These include *double discordance* or *discordant atrioventricular and ventricular arterial connections,* as just described, *l-TGA* because of the position of the aorta, and simply *corrected transposition.*

We prefer to use *CCTGA* because this term defines the condition and indicates a physiologic or hemodynamic congenital "correction" such that, in the absence of associated anomalies, systemic venous return is appropriately pumped to the lungs by the anatomic left ventricle with pulmonary venous return to the aorta by the anatomic right ventricle. *l-TGA* is a incomplete term and is misleading, because many complex conditions, including univentricular hearts, have an "L"-positioned aorta. Simply *corrected transposition* also is incomplete because complete transposition of the great arteries (TGA) with an atrial, arterial, or intraventricular switch operation is also "corrected," but not on a congenital basis.

CCTGA was first described by Von Rokitansky[1] in 1875. He described hearts from two patients in which the great arteries were transposed but the arrangement of the ventricles and ventricular septum resulted in physiologic correction of blood flow.

For the purposes of this review, univentricular hearts, hearts with crisscross atrioventricular connections, and hearts with aortic atresia will not be discussed. A small proportion of patients (probably 1% to 9%) with CCTGA have no associated lesions[2-6]; this percentage is a best estimate because patients without symptoms easily can go undiagnosed for many years.

The heart position in the chest is usually normal (levocardia) or midline (mesocardia) but is right sided (dextrocardia) in approximately 20% of these patients. Atrial situs is normal (solitus) in 95% and inversus in 5%. The ventricles are usually in a side-to-side configuration with the systemic anatomic right ventricle slightly anterior to the left ventricle and the septum in a midline position.

ASSOCIATED LESIONS

The most common associated defects are ventricular septal defect (VSD), pulmonary stenosis or atresia, and tricuspid valve abnormalities (Box 49-1).[2-6] Patients with VSD and pulmonary stenosis represent the largest group. The VSD is usually large, but all types and sizes can be seen, including multiple VSDs.

Pulmonary stenosis (more appropriately left ventricular outflow obstruction) comes in a variety of forms, including valvular and subvalvular pulmonary stenosis, "aneurysm" of the ventricular septum with aneurysmal tricuspid valve tissue prolapsing through a VSD, and various tissue tags or abnormal mitral or tricuspid valve attachments, which can obstruct outflow.

Tricuspid valve abnormalities are common, with an Ebstein-like malformation frequently occurring. In this condition there is lack of normal delamination of the valve from the right ventricular endocardium and/or tethering of the valve by short chordae, which can prevent normal closure. In addition, the valve is on the systemic side of the circulation and subjected to higher systolic pressure than normal, a factor that may also contribute to the high incidence of progressive tricuspid regurgitation with increasing age.

Other conditions are listed in Box 49-1 and should be considered in any full anatomicophysiologic patient assessment. Aortic regurgitation is not commented on by many authors but was reported recently in 25% to 36% of adult patients assessed by clinical and echocardiographic/Doppler studies.[6] Symptomatic aortic regurgitation as an isolated lesion with the need for operation has not been reported.

CORONARY ARTERIES

The coronary arteries[2,7] have been described as being inverted. Normally they arise from the posterior-facing sinuses of the aortic valve, with the right-sided coronary artery having the epicardial distribution of a normal left coronary artery. It bifurcates into an anterior descending coronary artery running along the midline interventricular groove and a circumflex branch that runs in the right atrioventricular (AV) sulcus to the posterior surface of the heart. The left-sided coronary artery arises from the left posterior sinus and continues its course into the left AV groove, reaching the crux.

CONDUCTION SYSTEM

Although the sinus node is normal, the AV node and bundle of His have an unusual location and course.[8,9] There appear to be dual AV nodes in many, if not most, patients. In patients with the usual perimembranous, subpulmonary VSD, the bundle of His passes along the anterior and superior rim of the defect in a markedly different location from that in hearts with normally related great arteries. This conduction system is a fragile one, with an increasing incidence of AV block with increasing age and a particularly high incidence with VSD or tricuspid valve surgery.

Genetics and Epidemiology

The incidence of CCTGA in patients with congenital heart disease (CHD) is approximately 0.5%, and there is a slight male preponderance. The recurrence risk of CHD for siblings in families with CCTGA has been estimated at 5.2%, which is higher than expected. A specific genetic etiology of this condition has not been reported. Extracardiac anomalies are uncommon.[2,3,10]

Early Presentation and Management

CONGESTIVE HEART FAILURE

Infants and children can present with congestive heart failure (CHF), usually secondary to a large VSD or severe tricuspid regurgitation. Initial medical management includes diuretics, afterload reduction with an angiotensin-converting enzyme (ACE) inhibitor, and usually digoxin. Patients with a large VSD, excessive pulmonary blood flow, and pulmonary hypertension require an early operation for VSD closure, a double-switch operation, or pulmonary artery banding in certain patients.

BOX 49-1 ASSOCIATED CARDIAC DEFECTS IN PATIENTS WITH CCTGA

Most Common Defects
- Ventricular septal defect (60% to 80%):
  - Usually perimembranous and subpulmonary
  - Muscular and inlet defects also possible
- Pulmonary stenosis (30% to 50%):
  - Usually present with an associated VSD
  - Frequently fibromuscular
  - Valvular stenosis also occurs
  - Less common—aneurysm of the ventricular septum, tissue tags from mitral or tricuspid valve
- Tricuspid valve abnormalities (14% to 56%)
  - Ebstein-like malformation (15% to 45%)
  - Dysplasia and abnormal ventricular attachments also possible

Less Common Conditions (1% to 10%)
- Atrial septal defect, patent ductus arteriosus
- Pulmonary atresia
- Double-outlet right ventricle
- Aortic regurgitation
- Mitral valve abnormalities—usually without significant stenosis or regurgitation
- Supravalvular stenosis in the left atrium
- Subaortic stenosis

Surgical VSD closure is performed, with the attempt made to put sutures on the morphologic right ventricular side of the septum to avoid heart block if possible.[11] Relatively common complications include the onset or worsening of tricuspid regurgitation and heart block, despite attempts to prevent it.

Tricuspid valve repair for severe tricuspid regurgitation is rarely successful; most patients require tricuspid valve replacement. A mechanical valve is preferred because of the difficulties with bioprosthetic valves in young children. Tricuspid valve replacement is a difficult option in young children because of the relatively large prosthesis needed to allow for growth and the need for long-term warfarin therapy.

In considering tricuspid valve replacement, systemic ventricular function must be evaluated rigorously. If it is significantly depressed despite afterload reduction therapy, other options such as the double-switch operation (see later) or transplantation should be considered.

One of the intriguing features of tricuspid regurgitation in patients with CCTGA is the tendency for it to worsen after VSD closure and to improve after pulmonary artery banding. The most likely explanation for this phenomenon is a shift in the position of the ventricular septum; VSD closure lowers the subpulmonary left ventricular pressure causing failure of tricuspid leaflet co-optation; pulmonary artery banding raises the subpulmonary left ventricular pressure, improving tricuspid leaflet co-optation.

Young patients with a large VSD or severe tricuspid regurgitation are also candidates for a double switch of the arterial plus atrial type[12,13] because of the long-term progressive nature of right ventricular dysfunction and tricuspid regurgitation.[6] This is a difficult and complex operation, with the potential disadvantages of an atrial switch procedure including atrial arrhythmia, sinus node dysfunction, and baffle obstruction. It avoids the problems of the anatomic right ventricle being subjected to systemic afterload and has been associated with a good early outcome in selected patients.[12,13] Patients with a low left ventricular pressure (<60% to 70% of systemic pressure) usually need preoperative pulmonary artery banding to prepare the left ventricle to generate adequate systemic pressure. It is difficult to determine how tight to make the pulmonary band; left ventricular failure can ensue quickly or within a few days or weeks of the procedure if the band is too restrictive. Infants and young children handle the banding best, and it is rare for banding to be successful in an adolescent or adult. Multiple reoperations to tighten or loosen the band may be necessary to achieve the appropriate degree of hypertrophy without ventricular damage. Late left ventricular dysfunction has been reported after banding and then a successful double-switch procedure.[14]

CYANOSIS

Approximately 50% of patients with CCTGA have significant left ventricular outflow tract obstruction (LVOTO) associated with VSD. If the cyanosis is moderately severe, a modified Blalock-Taussig shunt is needed in infancy. For older patients without the need for an early shunt, or those who have outgrown the shunt, VSD closure plus relief of LVOTO is required—usually with the use of a valved or nonvalved conduit.[15] In selected patients, relief of valvular pulmonary stenosis, resection of tissue tags, resection of an "aneurysm" of the ventricular septum, or resection of subvalvular fibrous tissue or muscle may relieve the obstruction. Conduits, however, are needed for the majority of patients and must be placed to avoid the papillary muscles and conduction tissue. The conduit should be placed to avoid sternal compression and sufficiently to the side of the sternum to avoid direct entry into the conduit with reoperation.[15] The major problem with conduits of all types is the deterioration with time and the need for their replacement in the majority of older patients within 10 years. In children, growth alone can lead to the need for early reoperation at less than 10 years after the initial conduit placement.

Again because of problems with late ventricular dysfunction and tricuspid regurgitation, a double-switch including arterial switch plus intraventricular (Rastelli) type procedure has been advocated for patients with VSD plus left ventricular outflow obstruction.[16] This procedure combines a Mustard or Senning atrial baffle with an intraventricular (Rastelli) baffle and an anatomic right ventricle to pulmonary artery conduit. This is a long and complex surgical procedure but one with reasonably good early results.[12,13,16] It will still be subject to the problems of repeated conduit replacement, baffle obstruction, and rhythm abnormalities, such as are seen after conventional atrial repairs of TGA.

Late Outcome

SURVIVAL

Classic Repairs (Table 49-1)

Yeh and associates[17] published data on 127 patients undergoing biventricular repair for CCTGA between 1959 and 1997. Repair was performed at a median age of 8 years but varied by diagnosis: VSD, 3.5 years; VSD and tricuspid valve repair or replacement, 5 years; VSD and pulmonary stenosis, 9 years; and tricuspid valve replacement alone, 16.6 years.

The operative mortality rate for the initial repair was 6%, but Kaplan-Meier survival 20 years after initial repair was only 48%. The small number of patients (n = 5) observed for a total of 20 years, however, makes this survival rate of 48% questionable: it is probably significantly higher with present surgical and medical therapy.

Late death after initial operation occurred in 28 patients; causes included reoperation, 36%; sudden or unexplained death, 29%; progressive myocardial failure, 21%; documented arrhythmia, 11%; and infection, 1 patient (3%).

TABLE 49-1	Results of Biventricular Repair of CCTGA
Age at initial operation	Median 8 years. Earlier with ventricular septal defect only
Operative mortality rate	6%
Late mortality	28 of 120 (23%). *Causes:* reoperation, sudden unexplained, myocardial failure, arrhythmia, infection
Reoperation rate	35% by 10 years
	80% of reoperations were for tricuspid valve replacement or pulmonary conduit stenosis
	50% of conduits replaced by 10 years
Atrioventricular block	12% before operation
	38% immediately after operation

Data from Ilbawi MN, Deleon SY, Backer CL et al. An alternative approach to the surgical management of physiologically corrected transposition with ventricular septal defect and pulmonary stenosis or atresia. J Thorac Cardiovasc Surg 1990; 100:410–415.

The overall survival rate after open repair in three recent studies[18–20] with smaller numbers of patients ranged from 55% to 85% at 10 years.

In the study by Yeh and associates, reoperation was required in 35% of all patients by 10 years and in approximately 50% of patients with VSD/pulmonary stenosis or tricuspid valve repair or replacement. Notably, 80% of all reoperations were for tricuspid valve replacement or pulmonary conduit stenosis.

Complete AV block was present in 12% of patients before operation and in 38% after surgery. Twenty years after the initial operation 40% of patients were free of pacemaker placement. Serious arrhythmias were relatively uncommon; supraventricular tachycardia or atrial fibrillation occurred in 3% immediately before operation and in 4% immediately afterward.

Double-Switch Repairs

Yeh and associates[17] have recently reviewed the mortality and actuarial survival data of patients with CCTGA after conventional versus double-switch repairs (Table 49-2). The operative mortality rate for double-switch procedures (80% of which involve a conduit) averaged 8% (range 0% to 11%).

Alghamdi and colleagues[21] recently reported a meta-analysis of 11 nonrandomized studies involving 124 patients comparing "physiologic" (the circulation is altered without changing the ventriculoarterial discordance) versus "anatomic" (the circulation is altered and the ventriculoarterial discordance corrected) repairs; 69 patients had anatomic/Rastelli repair, 25 had anatomic/arterial switch repair, and 30 had physiologic repair. Age at repair ranged from 3 months to 55 years. Anatomic/Rastelli repair had a lower hospital mortality, and operation before 1995 had an increased risk. In addition, this report showed an increased use of the anatomic repairs after 1995 in these centers.

The double-switch procedure remains a long and complex operation, with only a few centers having significant experience and no long-term follow-up data available. Most patients will have a conduit, and all have the potential for atrial arrhythmias and baffle obstruc-tion as seen in Mustard and Senning repairs. Nevertheless, results look promising, with a reasonably low operative mortality rate and a normal or near-normal left ventricular ejection fraction in most of patients studied early after repair.[13,14]

UNOPERATED PATIENTS

There are a relatively small number of patients with CCTGA with no associated defects or minimal defects such as small VSD, mild pulmonary stenosis, and/or mild tricuspid regurgitation.

In Table 49-3, data from three studies[6,21,22] are shown, with the complications of heart block, significant tricuspid regurgitation, and clinical CHF. Although there have been occasional reports of patients with isolated TGA having normal or near-normal right ventricular function in their 60s and 70s, such a course is exceedingly rare. Figure 49-1 shows

TABLE 49-2	Comparison of Operative Mortality and Actuarial Survival for Conventional Versus Double-Switch Repair of CCTGA	
Parameter	*Conventional Repair (8 Reports)*	*Double-Switch Repair (7 Reports)*
Total no. of patients	480	48 (arterial switch 10)
Operative death	61 (13%) (range 4%–27%)	4 (8%) (range 0%–11%)
Overall mortality rate (cohort to date)	32% (range 4%–80%)	7% (range 0%–30%)
Perioperative heart block requiring pacemaker	116 (24%)	7 (15%)
Actuarial survival rate		
10 years	70% (range 54%–83%)	NA
20 years	48% (only one study)	NA

NA, not available.
Data from Ilbawi MN, Deleon SY, Backer CL et al. An alternative approach to the surgical management of physiologically corrected transposition with ventricular septal defect and pulmonary stenosis or atresia. J Thorac Cardiovasc Surg 1990; 100:410–415.

TABLE 49-3	Long-Term Follow-Up of "Isolated" CCTGA*				
Reference	*No. of Patients*	*Age Range (years)*	*Heart Block*	*Tricuspid Regurgitation*	*Congestive Heart Failure*
Masden and Franch[21]	42	1–73	24%	NA	17% (all over 30 years)
Presbitero et al[22]	18	16–61	39%	44%	22% (all over 40 years)
Graham et al[6]	50	18–75	27%	40%	34%

*Minimal or no associated lesions (includes mild pulmonary stenosis, small ventricular septal defect).
NA, not available.

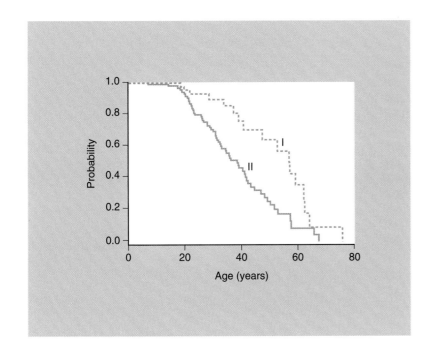

Figure 49-1 Freedom from congestive heart failure in group I (associated lesions, n = 125) and group II (no significant associated lesions, n = 50) as a function of increasing age. *P* = .0013. (*After Graham TP Jr, Bernard YD, Mellen BG et al. Long-term outcome in congenitally corrected transposition of the great arteries: a multi-institutional study. J Am Coll Cardiol 2000; 36:255–261.*)

data on freedom from clinical CHF in 50 patients with CCTGA without significant associated lesions; there is a progressive increase with advancing age, with 25% of patients having developed CHF by 45 years of age.[6]

FUNCTIONAL STATUS

Despite the problems of CHF, right ventricular dysfunction, heart block, and associated lesions, many patients report a reasonably good functional status. Of patients with associated lesions, 60% report no symptoms and 25% describe only mild symptoms; of patients with no associated lesions, 73% report no symptoms and 22% only mild symptoms.[6] This method of patient reporting of symptoms usually underestimates cardiovascular symptoms. Exercise performance in 26 patients with CCTGA was reported by Connelly and coworkers[23]: workload was only 38% of the normal value, and the exercise right ventricular ejection fraction was 43% compared with a normal value of 71%.

LATE COMPLICATIONS

CCTGA is a complex condition with a number of associated late complications, some of which have been discussed previously (Box 49-2). Right ventricular dysfunction and clinical CHF are the most common complications; increasing age, tricuspid regurgitation, associated defects, and open-heart surgery are definite risk factors for these problems.[6] The question of whether tricuspid regurgitation is a cause or effect of systemic right ventricular dilation and CHF remains unanswered. The progressive nature of tricuspid regurgitation and its worsening with open-heart surgery have been well documented.[24,25]

Myocardial perfusion defects,[26] impaired coronary flow reserve,[27] and abnormal areas of myocardium (presumably fibrosis)[28] of the right ventricle have been reported in patients with CCTGA associated with abnormalities of wall motion and impaired function. One interpretation of these findings is that intermittent silent myocardial ischemia occurs at times of high myocardial oxygen consumption (stress, exercise, hypertension). Inadequate coronary flow to a markedly hypertrophied right ventricle supplied by a coronary artery system with limited ability to provide adequate perfusion during the extremes of high metabolic demand could lead to microinfarction and fibrosis. Patients whose ventricular function is well preserved may have more favorable coronary arterial systems and microcirculation.

Heart block increases with time at a rate of approximately 2% per year; it is also a common complication of VSD or tricuspid valve surgery. Arrhythmias are another complication that increases with time. The onset of atrial flutter or fibrillation may precipitate symptoms of CHF. Ventricular arrhythmias may be associated with hemodynamic abnormalities and/or ventricular dysfunction. Although sudden death is relatively uncommon, probable risk factors include ventricular dysfunction, CHF, hemodynamic abnormalities, and a history of arrhythmia.

Because so many of the operative procedures in patients with CCTGA (conventional or double switch) require a conduit, stenosis of the conduit is a common late complication, with reoperation or reintervention in the catheterization laboratory every 10 to 20 years a likely scenario in virtually all such patients.

◼ Outpatient Assessment

OPERATED AND UNOPERATED PATIENTS

Most young adults with successful repair lead relatively normal lives. The increasing incidence of right ventricular dysfunction, worsening tricuspid regurgitation, CHF, heart block, and arrhythmias with age makes for an important checklist for outpatient assessment (Box 49-3). Late symptoms can include easy fatigability, exertional dyspnea, palpitations, and syncope.

All patients should periodically have a minimum of the following (Box 49-4):
- A thorough clinical examination
- Electrocardiogram—observe for heart block. Superior QRS axis is relatively common. Wolff-Parkinson-White syndrome is present in 2% to 4% of patients. There is frequently a QR pattern in V_4R and/or V_1 and rS in V_6 (reversal of ventricular septal depolarization).
- Chest radiography—dextrocardia occurs in 20%, usually with normal situs. Mesocardia is also relatively common. The cardiothoracic ratio on the posteroanterior view gives a fair estimate of overall systemic ventricular dilation. There is a straight upper left cardiac border bulge due to presence of left-positioned ascending aorta. Pulmonary venous congestion and pulmonary edema should be sought. In patients with a conduit, one must check for calcification.
- Echocardiographic/Doppler examination[2,3,5]

ECHOCARDIOGRAPHY

Echocardiography in CCTGA is usually not straightforward, and initial scans can be confusing if the diagnosis is unexpected. Because 25% of patients will have dextrocardia or mesocardia, knowledge of cardiac position should be known from chest radiography before echocardiography is performed. Initially, multiple subcostal planes should be used to verify atrial and ventricular connections and atrial

---

BOX 49-2 COMPLICATIONS

- Right ventricular dysfunction or congestive heart failure—progressive dysfunction with advancing age. Risk factors include tricuspid regurgitation, associated lesions, open-heart surgery and possibly also heart block and arrhythmia.
- Tricuspid regurgitation—progressive worsening with age. Cause and/or effect of right ventricular dysfunction. Increases after VSD repair.
- Heart block—progressive increased incidence of pacemaker requirements with age, open-heart surgery (VSD, tricuspid valve replacement). Develops at rate of approximately 2% per year in the absence of open-heart surgery.
- Arrhythmia—progressive increase with age: atrial greater than ventricular. Effect of right ventricular dysfunction.
- Sudden death—relatively rare. Usually associated with ventricular dysfunction, hemodynamic abnormalities, and arrhythmia.
- Conduit stenosis—appears inevitable with time. Approximately 50% of patients will need conduit replacement within 10 years
- Mitral regurgitation, aortic regurgitation—less common.
- Endocarditis—more common with residual VSD, tricuspid valve abnormalities, Blalock-Taussig shunt.

BOX 49-3 FINDINGS ON ASSESSMENT

- Normal oxygen saturation (unless unrepaired with VSD and pulmonary stenosis or pulmonary atresia, or with VSD and pulmonary vascular disease)
- Dextrocardia—20%
- Right ventricular parasternal lift—common
- Loud aortic component of S_2. S_2 is frequently single, and the pulmonary component is soft or inaudible (pulmonary valve more posterior/dorsal than normal).
- Murmur of tricuspid regurgitation—common at the apex or left sternal border
- If a conduit is present, systolic ejection murmur at upper left sternal border or upper right sternal border is invariable. Intensity correlates fairly well with severity of obstruction. Residual pulmonary stenosis is also possible in patients without conduit.
- VSD or mitral regurgitation murmur at left sternal border is less common.
- Diastolic murmur common—pulmonary (conduit) regurgitation most likely. Aortic regurgitation is also possible in older patients.
- Signs of CHF—S_3 or S_4, fluid accumulation, jugular venous distention, hepatomegaly—will be more common with increasing age, after open-heart surgery, and with progressive tricuspid regurgitation.
- Observe for signs of heart block—slow heart rate, variable cannon waves, variable S_1 intensity.

and ventricular morphology. Atrial situs is usually normal and atrial morphology determined by the systemic and pulmonary venous return and the atrial appendages. Multiple, nonconventional planes from subcostal, parasternal short-axis, and suprasternal notch coronal views may be needed. Ventricular morphology is usually best defined from the subcostal and apical four-chamber views and the parasternal short-axis views. The ventricular septum is usually oriented in a straight anteroposterior direction. The systemic right ventricle is on the patient's left; it is heavily trabeculated and has a prominent moderator band with tricuspid valve attachments to the interventricular septum. The tricuspid valve mural leaflet is often significantly displaced toward the right ventricular apex (Fig. 49-2). Mitral-pulmonary valve fibrous continuity usually can be determined from a four-chamber view. The ventriculoarterial connections and spatial relationships of the great arteries are best defined using multiple subcostal, apical, and parasternal views. There can be multiple levels of outflow obstruction in the left (pulmonary) ventricle. Transesophageal echocardiography can be a useful adjunct to transthoracic echocardiography because adults frequently do not have the multiple echocardiographic windows needed for mapping the anatomy and valvular function in CCTGA.[29] Both main and branch pulmonary arteries are usually difficult to visualize with either echocardiographic modality.

Assessment of biventricular systolic function is quite important, and attempts should be made to quantify right ventricular ejection fraction as well as assess the severity of tricuspid regurgitation. Unfortunately, both of these determinations in adults with CCTGA remain relatively qualitative by echocardiographic/Doppler studies.

CARDIAC MAGNETIC RESONANCE

Cardiac magnetic resonance imaging (CMR) is a useful modality for anatomic and functional assessment in patients with CCTGA (Fig. 49-3). Intracardiac and great vessel anatomy are well demonstrated, and cine data can be used to quantify volume, mass, and ejection fraction.[30] Advances continue, with more rapid image acquisition and three-dimensional (3D) reconstruction being two of the more useful innovations for cardiovascular imaging. In addition, myocardial perfusion studies and scanning for myocardial ischemia or scarring with late gadolinium enhancement are important additions to this diagnostic modality.

BOX 49-4   LATE TREATMENT

- Afterload reduction—therapy with an angiotensin-converting enzyme inhibitor or angiotensin receptor blocker to treat or prevent right ventricular dysfunction is being used with increasing frequency. Data on efficacy are not available.
- Tricuspid valve replacement—should be considered earlier rather than later, before severe right ventricular volume overload and deterioration of right ventricular function.[36]
- Double switch (Mustard and Rastelli type)—for patients with normal left ventricular function, markedly depressed right ventricular function, VSD, and left ventricular outflow obstruction.
- Double switch (Mustard and arterial switch)—rarely, if ever, possible in adults. For patients with normal left ventricular function, markedly depressed right ventricular function, intact ventricular septum, and no left ventricular outflow obstruction. These patients usually have low left ventricular pressure and are not candidates for an arterial switch procedure. Pulmonary artery banding may decrease tricuspid regurgitation but does not usually successfully prepare an adult left ventricle for a double-switch operation.
- Conduit revision replacement—needed every 5 to 15 years in children with a conduit-type repair because conduit becomes obstructed; long-term outcomes in adults are better, and there is an emerging role for percutaneous valves and stents.
- Catheter interventions—some patients may have pulmonary artery stenosis or conduit stenosis, which can be dilated or stented, or conduit regurgitation, possibly amenable to percutaneous valve placement.
- Pacemaker implant or replacement—high incidence of heart block. Atrioventricular pacing is preferred to preserve atrial transport function, because many patients have ventricular dysfunction.
- Radiofrequency ablation—may be needed in the occasional patient with atrial or ventricular tachycardia
- Exercise rehabilitation—may be useful in sedentary patients to determine true cardiovascular symptoms, degree of disability, and need for surgery
- Cardiac transplant—final option for patients with severe CHF unresponsive to medical treatment and who are not good candidates for double-switch repair

---

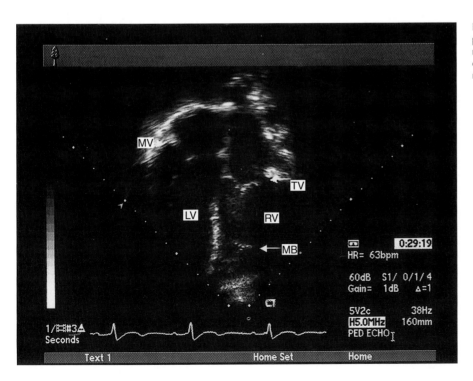

Figure 49-2 Four-chamber view showing prominent moderator band (MB) in left-sided right ventricle (RV) and tricuspid valve (TV) displaced farther toward the apex than the mitral valve (MV). LV, left ventricle.

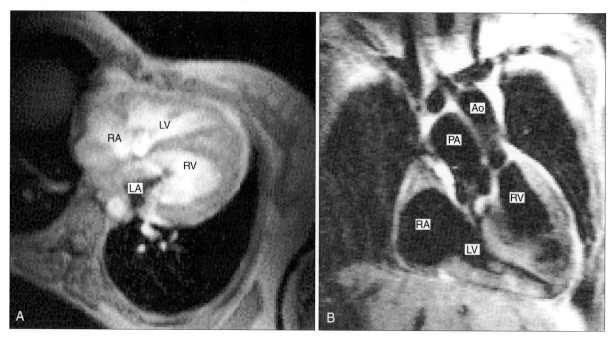

Figure 49-3   MR images of the heart of a woman with unoperated congenitally corrected transposition of the great arteries. **A,** The systolic cine image shows relations between the four heart chambers, viewed from below. There is tricuspid regurgitation, with a dark jet directed back from the left-sided right ventricle (RV) to the left atrium (LA). **B,** The coronal spin-echo image shows the aorta (Ao) arising from the left-sided RV and the pulmonary artery (PA) arising from the right-sided left ventricle (LV). There is a ridge of tissue causing subpulmonary stenosis in this patient. RA, right atrium. *(Courtesy Philip Kilner.)*

In patients with pacemakers or other contraindications for CMR, or to avoid images that are distorted because of sternal wires, ultrafast computed tomography can be used to obtain many of the same data as CMR.

EXERCISE TESTING

The use of exercise testing (usually treadmill) with measurement of oxygen consumption is an important adjunct for patient management.[31] Exercise duration, maximal oxygen consumption, and anaerobic threshold should all be measured and compared with normal values. Sequential testing can be useful as an aid to the assessment of overall cardiopulmonary function and response to medical, rehabilitative, or surgical therapy.

ELECTROCARDIOGRAPHIC MONITORING

Ambulatory electrocardiographic monitoring with a 24- to 48-hour device, a transtelephonic system, or implanted rhythm detector is potentially useful when serious arrhythmias are suggested by the history. In addition, this monitoring may reveal progression of heart block and the need for a pacemaker.

Transesophageal or invasive electrophysiologic study may be indicated if serious atrial or ventricular arrhythmias are suspected or detected from data obtained noninvasively.

CARDIAC CATHETERIZATION

Cardiac catheterization and angiography are indicated when interventional procedures such as pulmonary artery or conduit dilation or stenting are possible. In addition, assessment of left- and right-sided heart pressures, systolic function, and valvular regurgitation is usually needed before surgical procedures.

Arrhythmia and Sudden Death

As described earlier, both supraventricular and ventricular arrhythmias are known complications for patients with CCTGA. Wolff-Parkinson-White syndrome is present in 2% to 4% of patients and should be treated by radiofrequency ablation in patients with symptomatic AV reentry tachycardia. Supraventricular tachycardia, atrial flutter, and atrial fibrillation occur with increasing frequency with age, atrial enlargement, and atrial surgery or suture lines from surgical cannulation. These arrhythmias should be treated aggressively with medical and/or radiofrequency ablation therapy. Referral to a specialist in adult CHD and arrhythmia treatment for evaluation and management is an important aspect of overall patient care.

Ventricular arrhythmia is less common than atrial arrhythmia and is frequently associated with hemodynamic abnormalities such as tricuspid regurgitation and left ventricular outflow obstruction and/or ventricular dysfunction. Sudden death is not common and is usually associated with ventricular arrhythmia, ventricular dysfunction, and/or hemodynamic abnormalities, as described previously. Cardiac resynchronization therapy should be considered in patients with a pacemaker, wide QRS complex, and impaired systemic right ventricular function. An implantable cardiac defibrillator should be considered in patients at high risk for ventricular arrhythmia.[32,33]

Pregnancy

Pregnancy outcome in 22 women with CCTGA has been reported by a group at the Mayo Clinic.[34] There were 60 pregnancies with 50 live births (83%). One patient developed CHF late during pregnancy because of progressive tricuspid regurgitation and required tricuspid valve replacement 2 months post partum. One patient had 12 pregnancies with a history of toxemia, CHF, and endocarditis but is alive at age 80 years. There were no perinatal deaths, and CHD was not reported in the offspring. Therrien and colleagues[35] reported on 45 pregnancies in 19 patients with CCTGA. Cardiovascular complications included 3 patients with CHF, one with increased cyanosis, and one with a stroke. There were no maternal deaths and 27 live births (60%). These authors recommended (and we concur) a comprehensive cardiovascular evaluation before pregnancy be undertaken, including examination, electrocardiography, chest radiography, exercise study, and echocardiography and/or CMR for evaluation of any hemodynamic abnormalities and ventricular function.

Catheterization may be indicated for patients with conditions potentially requiring operation. Patients with more than mild cardiovascular symptoms, significant systemic ventricular dysfunction, or significant tricuspid regurgitation should be advised against pregnancy.

Level of Follow-Up, Endocarditis Prophylaxis, and Exercise

All adult patients with CCTGA should have regular evaluations by a specialist in adult CHD. In those with minimal or no symptoms, evaluation yearly or every other year should suffice. More frequent evaluations are needed for patients with symptoms, ventricular dysfunction, and significant tricuspid regurgitation. Periodic evaluations of ventricular dysfunction and tricuspid regurgitation are vital; echocardiography and cine CMR are valuable aids to clinical evaluation.

As a result of changes in endocarditis prophylaxis recommendations, only patients with prosthetic valves and those with ongoing cyanosis and those with a prior history of endocarditis are advised to take antibiotics before dental surgery.

Moderate to strenuous aerobic exercise, as tolerated, should be encouraged. Exercise rehabilitation with electrocardiography and blood pressure monitoring can be useful to improve fitness, quality of life, and the patient's knowledge of his or her own physical abilities. Excessive (power) weight-lifting should be actively discouraged because of the theoretic potential for excessive afterload increase with resultant increase in the degree of tricuspid regurgitation.

REFERENCES

1. Von Rokitansky C. Die defecte der scheidewande des Herzens. Vienna: Wilhelm Braumiller; 1875.
2. Freedom RM, Dyck JD. Congenitally corrected transposition of the great arteries. In: Emmanouilides GC, Riemenschneider TA, Allen HD, Gutgesell HD, editors. Moss and Adams Heart Disease in Infants, Children and Adolescents, 5th ed., Vol. II. Baltimore: Williams & Wilkins; 1995. p. 1225–1245.
3. Webb CL. Congenitally corrected transposition of the great arteries: clinical features, diagnosis, and progresses. Prog Pediatr Cardiol 1999;10:17–30.
4. Lundstrom U, Bull C, Wyse RKH, Somerville J. The natural and "unnatural" history of congenitally corrected transposition. Am J Cardiol 1990;65:1222–1229.
5. Silverman NH, Gerlis LM, Horowitz ES, et al. Pathologic elucidation of the echocardiographic features of Ebstein's malformation of the morphologically tricuspid valve in discordant atrioventricular connections. Am J Cardiol 1995;76:1277–1283.
6. Graham Jr TP, Bernard YD, Mellen BG, et al. Long-term outcome in congenitally corrected transposition of the great arteries: a multi-institutional study. J Am Coll Cardiol 2000;36:255–261.
7. Dabizzi RP, Barletta GA, Caprioli G, et al. Coronary artery anatomy in corrected transposition of the great arteries. J Am Coll Cardiol 1988;12:486–491.
8. Fischbach PS, Law JH, Serwer GS. Congenitally corrected transposition of the great arteries: abnormalities of atrioventricular conduction. Prog Pediatr Cardiol 1999;10:37–43.
9. Anderson R, Becker A, Arnold R, Wilkinson J. The conducting tissues in congenitally corrected transposition. Circulation 1974;50:811–823.
10. Piacentini G, Digilio M, Capolino R, et al. Familial recurrence of heart defects in subjects with congenitally corrected transposition of the great arteries. Am J Med Genet 2005;137A:176–180.
11. deLeval M, Bastos P, Stark J, et al. Surgical technique to reduce risk of heart block following closure of ventricular septal defect in atrioventricular discordance. J Thorac Cardiovasc Surg 1979;78:515–526.
12. Yagihara T, Kishimoto H, Isobe F, et al. Double switch operation in cardiac anomalies with atrioventricular and ventriculoarterial discordance. J Thorac Cardiovasc Surg 1994;107:351–358.
13. Imai Y, Sawatari K, Hoshino S, et al. Ventricular function after anatomic repair in patients with atrioventricular discordance. J Thorac Cardiovasc Surg 1994;107:1272–1283.
14. Quinn DW, McGuirk SP, Mehta C, et al. The morphologic left ventricle that requires training by means of pulmonary artery banding before the double-switch procedure for congenitally corrected transposition of the great arteries is at risk of late dysfunction. J Thorac Cardiovasc Surg 2008;135:1137–1142.
15. Bove E. Congenitally corrected transposition of the great arteries: surgical options for biventricular repair. Prog Pediatr Cardiol 1999;10:45–49.
16. Ilbawi MN, Deleon SY, Backer CL, et al. An alternative approach to the surgical management of physiologically corrected transposition with ventricular septal defect and pulmonary stenosis or atresia. J Thorac Cardiovasc Surg 1990;100:410–415.
17. Yeh T, Connelly MS, Coles JG, et al. Atrioventricular discordance: results of repair in 127 patients. J Thorac Cardiovasc Surg 1999;117:1190–203.
18. Sano T, Riesenfeld T, Karl TR, Wilkinson JL. Intermediate-term outcome after intracardiac repair of associated defects with atrioventricular and ventriculoarterial discordance. Circulation 1995;92(Suppl. II):II272–II278.
19. Termignon JL, Leca F, Vouhe PR, et al. "Classic" repair of congenitally corrected transposition and ventricular septal defect. Ann Thorac Surg 1996;62:199–206.
20. Voskuil M, Hazekamp MG, Kroft LJM, et al. Postsurgical course of patients with congenitally corrected transposition of the great arteries. Am J Cardiol 1999;83:558–562.
21. Alghamdi AA, McCrindle BW, Van Arsdell GS. Physiologic versus anatomic repair of congenitally corrected transposition of the great arteries: meta-analysis of individual patient data. Ann Thorac Surg 2006;81:1529–1535.
22. Presbitero P, Somerville J, Rabajoli F, et al. Corrected transposition of the great arteries without associated defects in adult patients: clinical profile and follow-up. Br Heart J 1995;74:57–59.
23. Connelly MS, Liu PP, Williams WG, et al. Congenitally corrected transposition of the great arteries in the adult: functional status and complications. J Am Coll Cardiol 1996;27:1238–1243.
24. Prieto L, Hordof AJ, Secic M, et al. Progressive tricuspid valve disease in patients with congenitally corrected transposition of the great arteries. Circulation 1998;98:997–1005.
25. Acar P, Sidi D, Bonnet D, et al. Maintaining tricuspid valve competence in double discordance: a challenge for the pediatric cardiologist. Heart 1998;80:479–483.
26. Hornung TS, Bernard EJ, Celermajer DS, et al. Right ventricular dysfunction in congenitally corrected transposition of the great arteries. Am J Cardiol 1999;84:1116–1119.
27. Hauser M, Bengel FM, Hager A, et al. Impaired myocardial blood flow and coronary flow reserve of the anatomical right systemic ventricle in patients with congenitally corrected transposition of the great arteries. Heart 2003;89:1231–1235.
28. Giardini A, Lovato L, Donti A, et al. Relation between right ventricular structural alterations and markers of adverse clinical outcome in adults with systemic rigth ventricle and either congenital complete (after Senning operation) or congenitally corrected transposition of the great arteries. Am J Cardiol 2006;98:1277–1282.
29. Caso P, Ascione L, Lange A, et al. Diagnostic value of transesophageal echocardiography in the assessment of congenitally corrected transposition of the great arteries in adult patients. Am Heart J 1998;135:43–50.
30. Lorenz CH, Walker EJ, Morgan VL, et al. Normal right and left ventricular mass systolic function and gender differences by cine magnetic resonance imaging. J Cardiovasc Magn Reson 1999;1:7–21.
31. Diller GP, et al. Exercise intolerance in adult congenital heart disease: comparative severity, correlates, and prognostic implication. Circulation 2005;112(6):828–835.
32. Walsh EP. Practical aspects of implantable defibrillator therapy in patients with congenital heart disease. Pacing Clin Electrophysiol 2008;31(Suppl. 1):S38–S40.
33. Khairy P. Defibrillators and cardiac resynchronization therapy in congenital heart disease: evolving indications. Expert Rev Med Devices 2008;5:267–271.
34. Connolly HM, Grogan M, Warnes CA. Pregnancy among women with congenitally corrected transposition of the great arteries. J Am Coll Cardiol 1999;33:1692–1695.
35. Therrien J, Barnes I, Somerville J. Outcome of pregnancy with congenitally corrected transposition of the great arteries. Am J Cardiol 1999;84:820–824.
36. van Son JA, Danielson GK, Huhta JC, et al. Late results of systemic atrioventricular valve replacement in corrected transposition. J Thorac Cardiovasc Surg 1995;109:642–652 discussion 652–653.

50

Double-Outlet Right Ventricle

ABDULLAH A. ALGHAMDI | GLEN S. VAN ARSDELL

Introduction

Double-outlet right ventricle (DORV) is a "disease" that includes a family of anatomically related complex congenital heart lesions involving the right ventricular outflow tract. There are a number of variations within the diagnostic category of DORV that give rise to a wide spectrum of physiology ranging from that of tetralogy of Fallot to transposition of the great arteries (TGA) to true single ventricle physiology. It therefore encompasses virtually the entire spectrum of cardiac physiology.

Determining treatment requires an understanding of the specific relationship of the ventricular septal defect (VSD) to the great vessels, the size of the VSD, the size of the great vessels, the ventricular size, and the status of the atrioventricular (AV) valves. Understanding these components and their relationship allows one to predict the physiology and therefore consider appropriate treatment algorithms. Repair may consist of one-stage biventricular repair, biventricular repair with a conduit, or staged palliative single-ventricle surgery (Table 50-1).

Definition

A consensus definition derived from the Congenital Heart Surgery Nomenclature and Database Project states that "DORV is a type of ventriculoarterial connection in which both great vessels arise either entirely or predominantly from the right ventricle."[1] This definition implies that more than 50% of each of the great vessels arises from the morphologic right ventricle (RV), which is known as "the 50% rule."[2] This definition may not be sufficient in cases of tetralogy of Fallot with extreme aortic override or transposition with extreme pulmonary override. An additional morphologic criterion that could differentiate between these conditions and DORV is the aortic-mitral fibrous continuity (in patients with tetralogy of Fallot) and pulmonary-mitral continuity (in patients with transposition). Some suggest that the absence of the fibrous continuity between the arterial and AV valves is a feature of DORV.[3–8] Hearts with DORV, remote VSD, and both great vessels arising entirely from the RV constitute a complete DORV known as the "200% DORV."[9]

History

The earliest description of DORV probably dates to 1703 in a report by Mery.[10] In 1793 Abernathy described a heart with the origin of both great arteries from the RV.[11] In 1893 a subsequent similar description was reported by Birmingham.[11] The designation of "double-outlet ventricle" was probably first reported by Braun and associates in 1952. The specimen had both great vessels arising from the RV.[12] Another "double-outlet right ventricle" designation is also found in a report by Witham in 1957.[13] A form of DORV, in which the VSD was associated with the pulmonary artery (PA), was described by Taussig and Bing in 1949 but was initially classified as transposition of the great arteries.[14] Lev and coworkers subsequently clarified what became known as the Taussig-Bing heart to be part of the spectrum of DORV.[4] DORV was first repaired at the Mayo Clinic in 1957 by John Kirklin.[4]

Embryology

Embryologic development of the heart includes a phase in which a common arterial trunk arises from the RV. As the common trunk separates into the two great vessels, they both arise from the RV for a period of time. Regression of muscle between the aorta and the mitral valve results in the aorta arising from the left ventricle in fibrous continuity with the mitral valve.[15] In some situations the muscle between the mitral and aortic valve does not regress, resulting in what is known as a *persistent left ventriculoinfundibular fold (VIF)*. An alternative term is *persistent left-sided conus*. A persistent left VIF can be, but is not necessarily, associated with DORV.

Epidemiology

DORV may exist as an isolated condition or in association with cardiac or extracardiac anomalies. The reported incidence ranges from 0.03 to 0.14 per 1000 live births.[16–22] It occurs in about 1% of all congenital heart disease.[23] There may be associated aortic coarctation, aortic arch hypoplasia, or interrupted aortic arch—particularly at the transposition end of the spectrum.[24] Additionally, in hearts with right atrial isomerism, DORV is a frequent finding.[25,26] Several chromosomal abnormalities have been associated with DORV, including trisomy 13, trisomy 18, and chromosome 22q11 deletion.[10]

Classification

The traditional classification of DORV is based on the position of the VSD relative to the great vessels. Lev and associates classified the VSD associated with DORV to subaortic, subpulmonary, doubly committed, and noncommitted (remote).[4] This classification system has the advantage of relative simplicity and providing a means by which DORV outcomes can be examined. However, this classification system alone is not adequate to determine the management algorithm. In addition, in rare cases of the DORV the ventricular septum may be intact.[27] From a practical standpoint it is the specific location of the VSD in combination with associated lesions and the resultant pathophysiology that allows one to determine management strategy.

DORV can also be classified based on "clinical" presentation: a VSD type (with subaortic or doubly committed VSD), a tetralogy of Fallot type (VSD with infundibular deviation), a TGA type (Taussig-Bing with subpulmonary VSD), and a single ventricle type (noncommitted VSD).[1,28] This clinical classification system has the advantage of predicting the natural and modified history of DORV. Specifically, a VSD-type DORV will have similar presentation, surgical options, and outcomes to VSD and Fallot-type DORV will have similar presentation, surgical options, and outcomes to tetralogy of Fallot.

The VSD of DORV is typically large and unrestrictive. Occasionally it can be shallow and restrictive or potentially restrictive. In DORV with a subaortic or subpulmonary VSD, the VSD sits between the two limbs of the trabeculae septomarginalis (TSM) (Fig. 50-1A, B). The TSM is a Y-shaped muscle bar in which the two limbs of the Y are the muscular rim of the VSD. The respective limbs of the Y are known as the anterior and posterior limbs of the TSM. The attachment of the infundibular septum to either the anterior or posterior limb predicts which great vessel is related to the VSD. Attachment of the infundibular

TABLE 50-1	Double-Outlet Right Ventricle: Morphologic Spectrum, Associated Physiology, and Interventions		
Location of VSD	*Associated Lesions*	*Physiology (like)*	*Intervention*
Subaortic		VSD	Tunnel repair
	Subpulmonary stenosis	Tetralogy of Fallot	Tetralogy of Fallot–type repair
Subpulmonary		Transposition	Arterial switch procedure
	Coarctation of aorta (CoA)	Transposition and CoA	Tunnel repair with repair of aortic arch
Doubly committed		VSD	Tunnel repair
			Arterial switch (see text)
Remote		VSD	Fontan route or occasionally biventricular repair

septum to the anterior limb of the TSM leaves the VSD in the subaortic position (see Fig. 50-1A). Attachment of the septum to the posterior limb of the TSM leaves the VSD in the subpulmonary position (see Fig. 50-1B). Absence of the infundibular septum leaves a doubly committed VSD (committed to both great arteries) (see Fig. 50-1C).

Pathophysiology and Presentation

SUBAORTIC VENTRICULAR SEPTAL DEFECT

DORV with subaortic VSD (see Fig. 50-1A) is the most common type of DORV occurring in about 50% of the cases.[1] The resultant pathophysiology depends on the degree of anterior deviation of the infundibular septum toward the PA. In the presence of anterior deviation there is associated right ventricular outflow tract (RVOT) obstruction with stenosis in the subvalvular or valvular region. Pulmonary blood flow is decreased. The degree of cyanosis is variable as is seen with tetralogy of Fallot. In the absence of anterior deviation of the infundibular septum (i.e., no RVOT obstruction), the pulmonary blood flow is increased and heart failure is usually the presenting symptom. In the latter situation the pathophysiology is similar to that of a very large VSD.

SUBPULMONARY VENTRICULAR SEPTAL DEFECT

The subpulmonary position VSD with DORV (see Fig. 50-1B) occurs in about 30% of the cases.[1] In this anatomic configuration there is unfavorable streaming of cyanotic blood to the aorta and saturated blood to the PA (transposition-type physiology). This occurs because the VSD is closely associated with the PA. The PA preferentially receives left ventricular oxygenated blood, whereas the desaturated blood from the RV streams to the aorta. The Taussig-Bing anomaly is the classic example for this morphology. Associated coarctation or arch hypoplasia may occur in up to 50% of neonates presenting with DORV and subpulmonary VSD. There is usually a small outlet to the RV with a substantial size mismatch between the aortic and pulmonary trunks. Clinical presentation is similar to that of transposition with associated severe cyanosis and increased pulmonary blood flow.

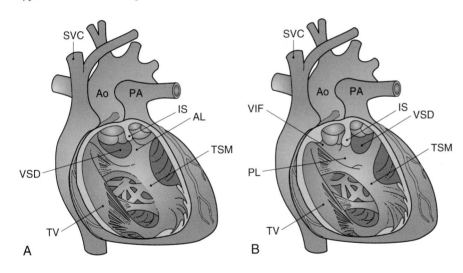

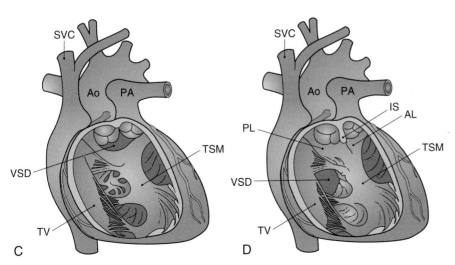

Figure 50-1 **A,** Double-outlet right ventricle (DORV) with subaortic ventricular septal defect (VSD). Infundibular septum (IS) is attached to the anterior limb of the trabeculae septomarginalis (TSM). **B,** DORV with subpulmonary VSD. IS is attached to the posterior limb (PL) of the TSM. **C,** DORV with doubly committed VSD. Absent or virtually absent IS. **D,** DORV with remote VSD. Here the VSD is in the inlet portion of the septum; remote VSDs also occur as muscular VSDs unrelated to either great vessel. AL, anterior limb of TSM; Ao, aorta; PA, pulmonary artery; SVC, superior vena cava; TV, tricuspid valve; VIF, ventricular infundibular fold (same as conus).

DOUBLY COMMITTED VENTRICULAR SEPTAL DEFECT

In a doubly committed type DORV (see Fig. 50-1C) both semilunar valves (aortic and pulmonary) are related to the VSD. There is no infundibular septum separating the aortic and pulmonary valves. The lesion is an uncommon variant (perhaps 5%). It may have streaming, which can be favorable or unfavorable. Pulmonary stenosis may be an association. Therefore, the clinical picture is similar to that of VSD with or without pulmonary stenosis.

REMOTE (NONCOMMITTED) VENTRICULAR SEPTAL DEFECT

A remote VSD may be an inlet VSD (see Fig. 50-1D) or trabecular muscular VSD. Either could be unrelated to either great vessel. Saturations typically would be that of complete mixing. These children behave physiologically as patients with a single ventricle. There may be too much, too little, or appropriate pulmonary blood flow for a single ventricle.

◼ Other Considerations

POSITION OF THE AORTA

The position of the aorta in DORV is variable. In most cases the relationship to the PA is posterior and slightly rightward (usual spiraling pattern). Completely normal relationships may occur. In the absence of spiraling (i.e., parallel configuration), the aorta could be side by side and to the right of the PA (d-malposition—most common) or side by side and to the left of the PA (l-malposition—rare). Occasionally, the aorta is parallel and anterior to the PA.

CONDUCTION TISSUE

AV node and bundle of His pathways follow the normal pathways for specific AV connections. The VSD in DORV is frequently in the perimembranous position and thereby is in jeopardy at the time of surgical repair at the margin of the tricuspid annulus and VSD closest to the crux of the heart. DORV associated with AV discordance has conduction pathways that match the AV discordance, that is, anterior to the typical VSD where it is associated with the PA.

OTHER ANATOMIC CHARACTERISTICS

Other intracardiac components may be abnormal, impacting on both physiology and management options. AV valve tissue may be attached to the infundibular septum. AV valve apparatus from either AV valve may straddle the VSD. DORV can occur with a hypoplastic ventricle, thereby acting as a functional single ventricle. Unusual relationships can be superoinferior ventricles with twisted (or crisscross) AV connections.

DORV may also occur with AV discordance, in which both great arteries arise from the left-sided systemic morphologic RV (Fig. 50-2). It may also occur with pulmonary atresia or other complex lesions such as right atrial isomerism and total anomalous pulmonary venous return. Most cases of right atrial isomerism and DORV are palliated with staged single-ventricle surgery. Occasionally, DORV presents as an isolated associated anomaly of an AV septal defect. A biventricular repair in this circumstance is possible, but challenging.

◼ Indications for Repair and Preoperative Evaluation

The spectrum of the pathophysiology of DORV is wide, thus making the natural history variable. Generalization can be applied based on natural history studies obtained from pathophysiologies that are similar. A DORV with subaortic VSD and no pulmonary stenosis will have a natural history similar to that of a large VSD. There is congestive heart failure and risk of development of pulmonary vascular obstructive disease. Similarly, at the tetralogy of Fallot or transposition ends of the spectrum, the natural history may resemble those conditions.

Spontaneous closure of the VSD is rare, and when it occurs it is fatal.[29] The diagnosis of DORV is sufficient indication for surgical repair. Preoperative evaluation includes performing a thorough

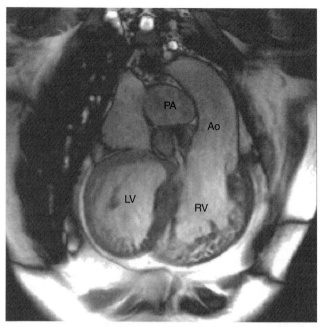

Figure 50-2 Magnetic resonance image of DORV in an adult with atrioventricular discordance in whom satisfactory imaging for three-dimensional (3D) relationships could not be fully achieved with other modalities. Note the left-sided systemic right ventricle (RV; coarse trabeculations) giving rise to both the aorta (Ao) and more than 50% of the pulmonary artery (PA), and thus the DORV relationship. Also note subvalvular and valvular pulmonary stenosis. LV, left ventricle.

echocardiographic examination that provides information regarding the AV valves, ventricular size and function, location and size of the VSD, relationship of the great vessels, status of the semilunar valves, associated lesions (e.g., coarctation), and coronary anatomy. Cardiac catheterization may be necessary for therapeutic reasons (at the transposition end of the spectrum to perform balloon atrial septostomy) or for diagnostic reasons (in late presentation when pulmonary vascular disease is in question or if the anatomy is unclear by echocardiography or magnetic resonance imaging [MRI]). Three-dimensional (3D) echocardiography and cardiac MRI (CMR) are now approaching the level of functionality that their utilization may assist with decision-making with regard to repair strategy. 3D printing is also emerging as a potentially interesting tool for preoperative preparation (Box 50-1).

BOX 50-1   IMAGING ASSESSMENT

- Transthoracic echocardiography is invaluable in the assessment of DORV. It will detail most of the anatomic and physiologic variables shown in Table 50-1.
- Transesophageal echocardiography can provide clearer information of complex AV arrangements such as straddle or override.
- When cyanosis is present, further imaging may be needed to ascertain whether it is due to:
  - Decreased pulmonary blood flow
  - Eisenmenger complex (see Chapter 48)
  - Impaired ventricular function
- Magnetic resonance imaging provides complementary and important information on:
  - Intracardiac anatomy
  - Aortic arch
  - Morphology of the pulmonary arteries
  - 3D relationship of the chambers and great vessels
  - Right and left ventricular function
- Cardiac catheterization may be performed to:
  - Determine the hemodynamics
  - Exclude pulmonary vascular disease
  - Assess the course of the coronary arteries

Surgical Repair

SUBAORTIC VENTRICULAR SEPTAL DEFECT

In patients with no anterior deviation of the infundibular septum and, therefore, no RVOT obstruction, the physiology of the lesion is typically that of a large VSD. These children often present with overt heart failure early in life. Because of the left VIF the outlet to the aorta is completely muscular with the potential to cause subaortic obstruction. Repair consists of intraventricular tunnel repair (VSD to aorta), usually within the first 6 months of life. Occasionally this may leave a residual VSD from trabeculations in the tubular muscular outlet. Some resection of the infundibular septum may be required during repair, with or without enlargement of the VSD. Occasionally an infant may have a PA band as initial therapy followed by an intraventricular tunnel and debanding in early childhood.

With anterior deviation of the infundibular septum, repair is much like repair for tetralogy of Fallot and therefore is frequently referred to as tetralogy-type DORV (Fig. 50-3). Greater override than in tetralogy of Fallot necessitates a patch in the shape of an opened tube. Resection and release of obstructing muscle must be performed. A pulmonary valvotomy or transannular patch also needs to be performed. In some instances the VSD may be shallow, thereby being a source of obstruction for left ventricular outflow once the intraventricular tunnel has been created. Obstruction is avoided by enlarging the VSD. Occasionally there is a need to insert a valved conduit between the RV and the PA for reasons of coronary anatomy or ventricular function.

Surgical timing for repair varies, depending on the era. One or two decades ago, repair was commonly performed in childhood. Significant cyanosis in infancy would have been treated with a Blalock-Taussig shunt. Presently, most large centers perform repair in the first year of life, although some would still palliate first with an arterial shunt should surgical treatment be necessary within the first 2 to 3 months of life. After repair, the physiology is similar to that in patients who have had repair of tetralogy of Fallot.

SUBPULMONARY VENTRICULAR SEPTAL DEFECT

The most common current treatment for DORV and subpulmonary VSD is an arterial switch procedure (Fig. 50-4). Flow from the left ventricle can easily be directed to the pulmonary valve by simply closing the VSD. An arterial switch converts the pulmonary valve to a neoaortic valve.

Intraventricular tunneling may also be performed for DORV with a subpulmonary VSD (known as a Kawashima repair).[30] This operation is best accomplished with side-by-side great vessels and when the distance between the pulmonary valve and tricuspid annulus is at least the width of the aortic valve. VSD enlargement along with resection of the infundibular septum is usually necessary. Increasing expertise in the arterial switch procedure has made the Kawashima repair for the Taussig-Bing anomaly less appealing.

If arch obstruction is present, most surgeons would perform a single-stage complete repair, although in the past there have been advocates of initial arch reconstruction followed by later intracardiac repair.

DOUBLY COMMITTED VENTRICULAR SEPTAL DEFECT

This unusual lesion is repaired as a large VSD. Repair is typically performed in the first 6 months of life. The lack of an infundibular septum may complicate closure of that portion of the VSD. Enlargement of the VSD may be required to prevent outlet obstruction.

If the VSD is slightly more related to the PA and thus the left ventricle is closer to the pulmonary valve, the best treatment option may be to perform an arterial switch with routing of the VSD to the original

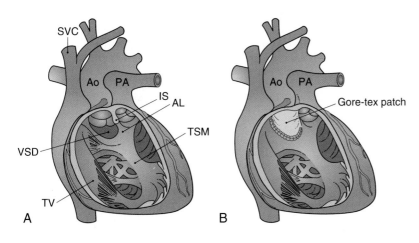

A

B

Figure 50-3 **A** and **B,** Intraventricular tunnel repair of subaortic DORV. Tunnels may be longer than illustrated here. Enlargement of the VSD may be necessary to prevent early subaortic stenosis. AL, anterior limb of the trabeculae septomarginalis; Ao, aorta; IS, infundibular septum; PA, pulmonary artery; SVC, superior vena cava; TSM, trabeculae septomarginalis; TV, tricuspid valve; VSD, ventricular septal defect.

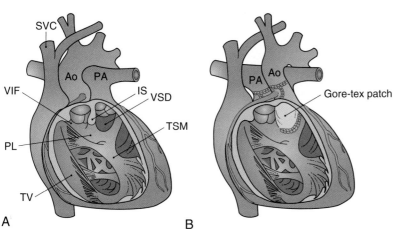

A

B

Figure 50-4 **A** and **B,** Arterial switch repair and VSD closure for DORV with subpulmonary VSD. By moving the aorta (Ao) over the VSD, the intraventricular tunnel is shortened, thereby lessening the risk for subaortic stenosis. IS, infundibular septum; PA, pulmonary artery; PL, posterior limb of the trabeculae septomarginalis; RCA, right coronary artery; SVC, superior vena cava; TSM, trabeculae septomarginalis; TV, tricuspid valve; VIF, ventricular infundibular fold (same as conus).

PA. One may thus preclude the potential for either RVOT obstruction or left ventricular outflow tract obstruction from a complex intraventricular tunnel.

REMOTE VENTRICULAR SEPTAL DEFECT

Decision-making in patients with this lesion is complex. Because two good-sized and completely functional ventricles and two normal AV valves are frequently present there is a natural desire to achieve a biventricular repair. In some cases, long tunnel repairs can be performed. These are usually performed with VSD enlargement and resection of some infundibular muscle. Late subaortic obstruction is a possibility. An arterial switch may bring the aorta closer to the remote VSD, thereby making an intraventricular tunnel repair less problematic. In most cases, however, the best course of action appears to be a single-ventricle palliation. Although technically feasible, routing of a remote VSD to the aorta can be associated with high initial mortality related to the complexities of creating a nonobstructed tunnel to the left ventricular outlet, the right ventricular outlet (around the tunnel), and the tricuspid inlet (again, around the tunnel). Reoperation for conduits or other residual lesions may be more frequent than desired.[31]

Single-ventricle palliation for children with remote VSDs typically involve a PA band as a neonate followed by a bidirectional cavopulmonary connection at around 6 months of age. A Fontan procedure is typically performed between 18 months and 4 years of age.

▣ Special Situations

DOUBLE-OUTLET RIGHT VENTRICLE WITH TRANSPOSITION-LIKE PHYSIOLOGY AND PULMONARY STENOSIS

In DORV with pathophysiology closer to the transposition end of the spectrum and pulmonary stenosis there are three described surgical options:
- Rastelli repair
- REV procedure
- Nikaidoh repair

In the Rastelli-type repair, an intraventricular tunnel repair between the VSD and aorta is constructed followed by placing a conduit between the RV and PA.[32] The REV procedure (réparation à l'étage ventriculaire) entails division of the main PA with extensive mobilization, translocation of the PA anterior to aorta (Lecompte maneuver), and direct connection of the PA to the RV, thus eliminating the use of prosthetic materials.[33,34] The Nikaidoh procedure is an aortic root translocation procedure into the enlarged pulmonary root position. A right ventricle-to-pulmonary artery (RV-PA) conduit is then placed.[35]

RIGHT ATRIOVENTRICULAR VALVE OVERRIDING AND STRADDLING

DORV may be associated with overriding and/or straddling of the AV valve apparatus. Straddling of the right AV valve chordae may sometimes still allow biventricular repair. Typically chordae are detached and then reimplanted on the right ventricular side.[8] Valve repair is performed (Fig. 50-5).

Substantial overriding of the right AV valve can be problematic because subsequent to septation of the VSD the inlet size of the RV may be small. Unloading of the volume flow across the right AV valve may be necessary. A concomitant bidirectional cavopulmonary shunt (so-called 1.5-ventricle repair) unloads the volume going to the right side of the heart by about 25% in fully grown patients.[36]

▣ Surgical Outcomes

Results of surgical repair for congenital cardiac lesions have improved significantly over time, and the surgical repair of DORV is no exception. In most recent large series, 15-year overall survival ranges from 56% to 90%.[37-39] In the simple forms of DORV (e.g., VSD type and tetralogy type), early survival, late survival, and freedom from reoperation are

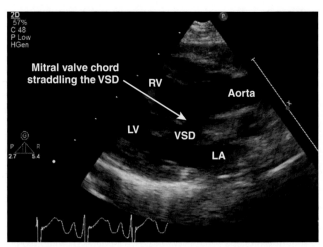

Figure 50-5 Echocardiogram in the parasternal long-axis view in DORV. The *arrow* demonstrates a chord from the anterior leaflet of the mitral valve that straddles the VSD and is attached to the crest of the ventricular septum on the right ventricular aspect. Note the anteriorly placed aorta. LA, left atrium; LV, left ventricle; RV, right ventricle.

excellent and comparable to the outcomes of those patients with VSD and tetralogy of Fallot.[38] Patients requiring repair with an RV-PA conduit (Rastelli-type repair) will inevitably need conduit replacement.[36] Although the REV procedure seems to lessen the need for reoperation, this, however, may occur at the expense of right ventricular dilation and risk of late right ventricular failure.[40]

Those with complex intraventricular tunnels are at substantial risk of developing subaortic stenosis.[41] Depending on the individual anatomy, risk of reoperation varies from approximately 5% to 50%; this risk is particularly high after intraventricular tunnel repair of DORV with subpulmonary VSD.[37]

In contrast, subaortic stenosis, after the arterial switch for DORV and subpulmonary stenosis, seems to be minimal despite the need for VSD enlargement at the original repair approaching 50%.

Those with transposition physiology treated with an arterial switch have excellent late survival.[42] However, neoaortic valve incompetence in these patients is more common than in standard transposition, suggesting that there may be a need for future aortic valve repair or replacement.[43]

These results underline what is becoming a clear understanding in congenital heart disease: complex intracardiac biventricular repairs are associated with a high risk of reoperation but not necessarily death. At least in the intermediate term, Fontan procedures for complex hearts are associated with less early mortality and lower reoperation rates. However, the functional benefits of complex biventricular repairs in comparison with single-ventricle palliation are not well defined.

For patients considered for biventricular repair, the complicating risk factors include[11]:
- Restrictive VSD
- Multiple VSDs
- Straddling AV valve
- Ventricular hypoplasia
- Obstructive anatomy of the aortic arch
- Complex coronary anatomy

▣ Outpatient Assessment of the Adult with Double-Outlet Right Ventricle

OPERATED PATIENTS

Thorough outpatient assessment for postrepair patients with DORV is necessary to screen for and manage the potential complications. Exercise intolerance and gradual decline in functional status is particularly important and may relate to residual progressive hemodynamic lesions shown in Box 50-2. Evaluation of the heart rhythm is essential.

UNOPERATED PATIENTS

Most adult survivors with DORV would have received a childhood operation. For the occasional primary adult presentation of DORV there will be natural selection factors determining physiologic status. Adults with subpulmonary or subaortic VSDs without restriction to pulmonary flow will almost certainly have high pulmonary vascular resistance and irreversible pulmonary vascular disease. Those with pulmonary stenosis may be candidates for biventricular repair provided both ventricles are of good size and the PA pressures and pulmonary vascular resistance are low. One has to be cautious about ventricular size in adult presentation of tetralogy-like DORV. It is not uncommon that left ventricular size is borderline and associated with poor ventricular compliance. The risk of cardiac failure is thereby increased after repair.

There may be occasional patients, presenting late, with appropriately balanced DORV and single-ventricle physiology, who may be good candidates for a primary Fontan procedure. CMR followed by a hemodynamic assessment with cardiac catheterization will be required to determine suitability for a Fontan operation.

When cyanosis is present in the unrepaired patient with DORV, one needs to establish whether this is due to decreased pulmonary blood flow from anatomic causes or due to Eisenmenger complex (see Chapter 48). Echocardiographic windows may be inadequate even with transesophageal imaging. CMR provides complementary and important information on intracardiac anatomy, status of the aortic arch, size of the pulmonary arteries, 3D relationship of chambers and great vessels, and right and left ventricular function. Cardiac catheterization is invariably performed to determine whether the hemodynamics are suitable for repair, to exclude pulmonary vascular disease and to assess the course of coronary arteries (Box 50-3).

Arrhythmias and Sudden Cardiac Death

Adult patients with DORV, whether operated on or not, are at risk of both atrial and ventricular tachycardia. Onset of arrhythmia in these patients may reflect progressive abnormal underlying hemodynamics with chamber dilation and hypertrophy and/or ventricular dysfunction.

Previous intracardiac surgery, particularly in the form of complex tunnel repair, and severely stenosed conduits are additional risk factors for both arrhythmia and sudden cardiac death.

Right bundle-branch block on the surface electrocardiogram is common after VSD closure (30% to 80%).[44] QRS prolongation may occur in patients with tetralogy-like physiology or repair and may suggest an increased risk of sustained ventricular tachycardia and sudden cardiac death. Patients with compromised AV valve function that may be related to complex intracardiac repair, and those with small "noncompliant" ventricles, are susceptible to atrial arrhythmia, secondary to long-standing atrial dilation. Patients who have had a previous Fontan operation are predominantly at risk of atrial arrhythmia, whereas those with complex intracardiac repair are at risk of ventricular tachycardia. Both are at risk of sudden cardiac death.

Pregnancy

After biventricular repair of DORV, successful pregnancy and delivery have been reported.[45] However, because large studies are lacking it is reasonable to assume that pregnancy physiology and outcomes would follow that of tetralogy of Fallot in which there is tetralogy of Fallot-type DORV. These cases are low risk provided no significant residual hemodynamic lesions are present.[46–48] In general, patients with a biventricular repair of DORV should have a low pregnancy risk, assuming good biventricular function, normal oxygen saturations, and absence of significant hemodynamic lesions. For patients with a Fontan-type repair, pregnancy outcomes should be comparable to those of Fontan patients with other single-ventricle anatomic substrates. Successful pregnancy and delivery after a Fontan procedure for DORV have been reported.[49] All patients with DORV who are contemplating starting a family should undergo a thorough evaluation by a congenital cardiologist and a high-risk obstetrician so that appropriate risk counseling may be given.

Follow-Up and Endocarditis Prophylaxis

Patients with DORV, whether they have undergone repair or not, benefit from periodic follow-up at a specialized adult congenital heart disease center. Patients with a subaortic VSD, who underwent early repair, may see their local general cardiologist instead. Patients with DORV no longer require routine endocarditis prophylaxis except if there is:
- Prosthetic cardiac valve
- Previous endocarditis
- Unrepaired cyanotic congenital heart disease (including patients with palliative shunts and conduits)
- Completely repaired congenital heart disease with prosthetic material or device, whether placed by surgery or catheter intervention, during the first 6 months after the procedure
- Repaired congenital heart disease with residual defects at the site or adjacent to the site of a prosthetic patch or prosthetic device (which inhibit endothelialization)

Regular physical activity is advisable for all patients. The level of intensity should be based on individual anatomic substrates, single versus biventricular type of repair, and the type and severity of residual hemodynamic lesions, particularly outflow tract stenosis and the presence of residual coarctation of the aorta.

Conclusion

DORV is a complex form of congenital heart disease that is best understood by knowledge of the intraventricular anatomy. Awareness of the location of the VSD and associated lesions helps one determine the physiology. The physiology of DORV varies with subtypes having similarities to a simple VSD, tetralogy of Fallot, transposition, or single-ventricle type physiology. Knowledge of the physiology allows appropriate surgical treatment to be planned. The long-term outlook today is quite favorable for the majority of patients with DORV, although the need for reoperation may be present.

REFERENCES

1. Walters III HL, Mavroudis C, Tchervenkov CI, et al. Congenital Heart Surgery Nomenclature and Database Project: double outlet right ventricle. Ann Thorac Surg 2000;69(Suppl. 4):63.
2. Becker AE, Anderson RH. Double outlet ventricles. In: Becker AE, Anderson RH, editors. Pathology of Congenital Heart Disease. London: Butterworths; 1981. p. 297–307.
3. Howell CE, Ho SY, Anderson RH, Elliott MJ. Variations within the fibrous skeleton and ventricular outflow tracts in tetralogy of Fallot. Ann Thorac Surg 1990;50:450–457.
4. Lev M, Bharati S, Meng CC, et al. A concept of double-outlet right ventricle. J Thorac Cardiovasc Surg 1972;64:271–281.
5. Van Praagh R. What is the Taussig-Bing malformation? Circulation 1968;38:445–449.
6. Bacha EA. Ventricular septal defect and double-outlet right ventricle. In: Sellke FW, del Nido PJ, Swanton SJ, editors. Sabiston & Spencer Surgery of the Chest. 7th ed. Philadelphia: Elsevier Saunders; 2005. p. 1981–1997.
7. Jonas RA. Double outlet right ventricle. In: Jonas RA, DiNardo J, Laussen PC, et al., editors. Comprehensive Surgical Management of Congenital Heart Disease. London: Arnold; 2004. p. 413–428.
8. Anderson RH, McCarthy K, Cook AC. Continuing medical education: double outlet right ventricle. Cardiol Young 2001;11:329–344.
9. Lacour-Gayet F. Intracardiac repair of double outlet right ventricle. Semin Thorac Cardiovasc Surg Pediatr Card Surg Annu 2008;39–43.
10. Obler D, Juraszek AL, Smoot LB, Natowicz MR. Double outlet right ventricle: aetiologies and associations. J Med Genet 2008;45:481–497.
11. Freedom RM, Yoo S-J, Williams WG. Double-outlet ventricle. In: Freedom RM, Yoo S.-J., Mikailian H, et al., editors. The Natural and Modified History of Congenital Heart Disease. New York: Blackwell; 2004. p. 370–380.
12. Braun K, De Vries A, Feingold DS, et al. Complete dextroposition of the aorta, pulmonary stenosis, interventricular septal defect, and patent foramen ovale. Am Heart J 1952;43:773–780.
13. Witham AC. Double outlet right ventricle: a partial transposition complex. Am Heart J 1957;53:928–939.
14. Taussig HB, Bing RJ. Complete transposition of the aorta and a levoposition of the pulmonary artery: clinical, physiological, and pathological findings. Am Heart J 1949;37:551–559.
15. Anderson RH, Wilkinson JL, Arnold R, Lubkiewicz K. Morphogenesis of bulboventricular malformations: I. Consideration of embryogenesis in the normal heart. Br Heart J 1974;36:242–255.
16. Botto LD, Correa A. Decreasing the burden of congenital heart anomalies: an epidemiologic evaluation of risk factors and survival. Prog Pediatr Cardiol 2003;18:111–121.
17. Loffredo CA. Epidemiology of cardiovascular malformations: prevalence and risk factors. Am J Med Genet 2000;97:319–325.
18. Pradat P, Francannet C, Harris JA, Robert E. The epidemiology of cardiovascular defects: I. A study based on data from three large registries of congenital malformations. Pediatr Cardiol 2003;24:195–221.
19. Samanek M, Voriskova M. Congenital heart disease among 815,569 children born between 1980 and 1990 and their 15-year survival: a prospective Bohemia survival study. Pediatr Cardiol 1999;20:411–417.
20. Grabitz RG, Joffres MR, Collins-Nakai RL. Congenital heart disease: incidence in the first year of life. The Alberta Heritage Pediatric Cardiology Program. Am J Epidemiol 1988;128:381–388.
21. Ferencz C, Rubin JD, McCarter RJ, et al. Congenital heart disease: prevalence at livebirth. The Baltimore-Washington Infant Study. Am J Epidemiol 1985;121:31–36.
22. Davachi F, Moller JH. The electrocardiogram and vector-cardiogram in single ventricle: anatomic correlations. Am J Cardiol 1969;23:19–31.
23. Park MK. Cyanotic congenital heart defects. In: Park MK, editor. Pediatric Cardiology for Practitioners. 5th ed. St. Louis: Mosby Elsevier; 2008. p. 215–302.
24. Sondheimer HM, Freedom RM, Olley PM. Double outlet right ventricle: clinical spectrum and prognosis. Am J Cardiol 1977;39:709–714.
25. Hashmi A, Abu-Sulaiman R, McCrindle BW, et al. Management and outcomes of right atrial isomerism: a 26-year experience. J Am Coll Cardiol 1998;31:1120–1126.
26. De TS, Daliento L, Ho SY, et al. Analysis of atrioventricular junction, ventricular mass, and ventriculoarterial junction in 43 specimens with atrial isomerism. Br Heart J 1981;45:236–247.
27. Kouchoukos NT, Blackstone EH, Doty DB, et al. Double outlet right ventricle. In: Kouchoukos NT, Blackstone EH, Doty DB, et al., editors. Kirklin/Barratt-Boyes Cardiac Surgery. 3rd ed. Edinburgh: Churchill Livingstone; 2003. p. 1509–1539.
28. Franklin RC, Anderson RH, Daniels O, et al. Coding Committee of the Association for European Paediatric Cardiology. Report of the Coding Committee of the Association for European Paediatric Cardiology. Cardiol Young 2002;12:611–618.
29. Marino B, Loperfido F, Sardi CS. Spontaneous closure of ventricular septal defect in a case of double outlet right ventricle. Br Heart J 1983;49:608–611.
30. Kawashima Y, Fujita T, Miyamoto T, Manabe H. Intraventricular rerouting of blood for the correction of Taussig-Bing malformation. J Thorac Cardiovasc Surg 1971;62:825–829.
31. Delius RE, Rademecker MA, de Leval MR, et al. Is a high-risk biventricular repair always preferable to conversion to a single ventricle repair? J Thorac Cardiovasc Surg 1996;112:1561–1568.
32. Rastelli GC. A new approach to "anatomic" repair of transposition of the great arteries. Mayo Clin Proc 1969;44:1–12.
33. Borromee L, Lecompte Y, Batisse A, et al. Anatomic repair of anomalies of ventriculoarterial connection associated with ventricular septal defect. J Thorac Cardiovasc Surg 1988;95:96–102.
34. Lecompte Y, Neveux JY, Leca F, et al. Reconstruction of the pulmonary outflow tract without prosthetic conduit. J Thorac Cardiovasc Surg 1982;84:727–733.
35. Nikaidoh H. Aortic translocation and biventricular outflow tract reconstruction: a new surgical repair for transposition of the great arteries associated with ventricular septal defect and pulmonary stenosis. J Thorac Cardiovasc Surg 1984;88:365–372.
36. Kreutzer C, De Vive J, Oppido G, et al. Twenty-five-year experience with rastelli repair for transposition of the great arteries. J Thorac Cardiovasc Surg 2000;120:211–223.
37. Bradley TJ, Karamlou T, Kulik A, et al. Determinants of repair type, reintervention, and mortality in 393 children with double-outlet right ventricle. J Thorac Cardiovasc Surg 2007;134:967–973.
38. Brown JW, Ruzmetov M, Okada Y, et al. Surgical results in patients with double outlet right ventricle: a 20-year experience. Ann Thorac Surg 2001;72:1630–1635.
39. Vogt PR, Carrel T, Pasic M, et al. Early and late results after correction for double-outlet right ventricle: uni- and multivariate analysis of risk factors. Eur J Cardiothorac Surg 1994;8:301–307.
40. Rubay J, Lecompte Y, Batisse A, et al. Anatomic repair of anomalies of ventriculo-arterial connection (REV): results of a new technique in cases associated with pulmonary outflow tract obstruction. Eur J Cardiothorac Surg 1988;2:305–311.
41. Belli E, Serraf A, Lacour-Gayet F, et al. Surgical treatment of subaortic stenosis after biventricular repair of double-outlet right ventricle. J Thorac Cardiovasc Surg 1999;112:1570–1578.
42. Alsoufi B, Cai S, Williams WG, et al. Improved results with single-stage total correction of Taussig-Bing anomaly. Eur J Cardiothorac Surg 2008;33:244–250.
43. Haas F, Wottke M, Poppert H, Meisner H. Long-term survival and functional follow-up in patients after the arterial switch operation. Ann Thorac Surg 1999;68:1692–1697.
44. Houyel L, Vaksmann G, Fournier A, Davignon A. Ventricular arrhythmias after correction of ventricular septal defects: importance of surgical approach. J Am Coll Cardiol 1990;16:1224–1228.
45. Drenthen W, Pieper PG, van der Tuuk K, et al. Fertility, pregnancy and delivery in women after biventricular repair for double outlet right ventricle. Cardiology 2008;109:105–109.
46. Bashore TM. Adult congenital heart disease: right ventricular outflow tract lesions. Circulation 2007;115:1933–1947.
47. Meijer JM, Pieper PG, Drenthen W, et al. Pregnancy, fertility, and recurrence risk in corrected tetralogy of Fallot. Heart 2005;91:801–805.
48. Veldtman GR, Connolly HM, Grogan M, et al. Outcomes of pregnancy in women with tetralogy of Fallot. J Am Coll Cardiol 2004;44:174–180.
49. Ito M, Takagi N, Sugimoto S, et al. Pregnancy after undergoing the Fontan procedure for a double outlet right ventricle: report of a case. Surg Today 2002;32:63–65.

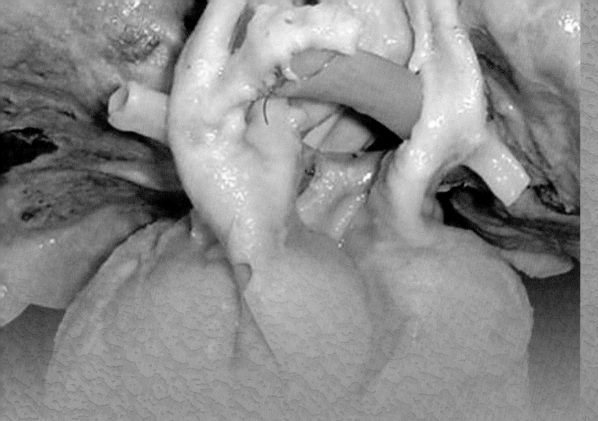

Univentricular Hearts

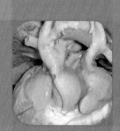

51 Double-Inlet Ventricle

NANCY C. POIRIER | MICHAEL A. GATZOULIS

Definition and Morphology

Double-inlet ventricle is defined as the morphologic arrangement in which more than 50% of both atria are connected to one dominant ventricular chamber. The connection can be either through two separate atrioventricular (AV) valves (one of them may be imperforate) or through a common AV valve (Box 51-1). The term *single ventricle* is often used in patients with a double-inlet ventricle, although in most instances a rudimentary second ventricle is present. The rudimentary ventricle may receive direct drainage from the atrium. However, by definition, more than 50% of the corresponding AV valve must override the ventricular septum and drain into the main ventricular chamber.[1]

Full appreciation of the morphology helps in understanding of the different presentation patterns, the natural history, and the surgical options available, including surgical septation, and the potential long-term complications.

The most common clinical scenario is of a double-inlet left ventricle in the setting of situs solitus with transposed great vessels or double-outlet right ventricular connection, as recently confirmed by Uemura and colleagues (Fig. 51-1).[2] The right nondominant ventricle is usually small, precluding a biventricular repair. There is one or occasionally multiple ventricular septal defects (VSDs) that may or may not be restrictive, leading to subaortic stenosis. Pulmonary stenosis (valvular and subvalvular) and, occasionally, pulmonary atresia are often associated.

CONDUCTION SYSTEM

The anatomy of the specialized conduction tissue in double-inlet ventricles is a preoccupation for surgeons, particularly when septation or muscular resection is considered. The atrial situs determines the position of the sinoatrial node. Dual nodes are seen in right atrial isomerism, and hypoplastic nodes occur in left atrial isomerism. The AV conduction is determined by the AV connection and ventricular morphology. A ring of conduction tissue associated with the AV valve annulus forms the AV node(s) and bundles. In the usual situation of a dominant left ventricle (also called l-loop configuration), the AV node and bundle are anterior and to the right, with the bundle across the anterior aspect of the outflow tract then onto the right margin of the VSD. If the VSD in this situation needs enlargement (to relieve subaortic stenosis), septal resection must be done posteriorly.

ASSOCIATED LESIONS

Associated cardiac lesions are common. AV valve anomalies in the form of valvular hypoplasia, straddling, leaflet dysplasia, and clefting are prevalent, potentially leading to valvular stenosis or insufficiency. Valvular pulmonary stenosis or atresia occurs secondary to leaflet dysplasia or to a hypoplastic annulus. Subvalvular pulmonary stenosis occurs due to muscle hypertrophy, infundibular hypoplasia, septal displacement, or a restrictive VSD. Subaortic stenosis is usually due to a restrictive VSD. Aortic arch abnormalities (coarctation or interruption) are also common.

Genetics and Epidemiology

Double-inlet ventricle is an uncommon defect; it has been found in 1.5% of patients with congenital heart disease at the Hospital for Sick Children in Toronto. Recurrence of congenital heart disease was 2.8% among siblings of children with double-inlet ventricles, although this was much higher among patients with left atrial isomerism (28%). As in the majority of patients with single-ventricle physiology, no chromosomal abnormalities have been associated with double-inlet ventricles.

Early Presentation and Management

The clinical presentation of patients with double-inlet ventricle is determined by the degree of pulmonary blood flow and associated lesions (Box 51-2).

Management

The majority of patients with double-inlet ventricle are not suitable for biventricular repair and are considered for staged palliative procedures with a view to an ultimate Fontan operation.

Early interventions usually address one or more of the following:
- Pulmonary blood flow:
  - Augmentation of flow (for patients with pulmonary stenosis) with a systemic to pulmonary arterial shunt or a bidirectional cavopulmonary anastomosis; the former is preferred when pulmonary vascular resistance is raised
  - Reduction of flow with pulmonary artery banding for patients without pulmonary stenosis who are at risk of pulmonary hypertension
- Relief of outflow tract obstruction with:
  - VSD enlargement in patients with discordant ventriculoarterial connections and a restrictive VSD leading to subaortic stenosis; the latter may not be evident from the outset and may develop after pulmonary artery banding. It is also common in patients who underwent aortic arch repair for coarctation or interruption. Infants with these anatomic substrates, therefore, need early reassessment of the subaortic outflow tract (with cardiac catheterization and angiography, if necessary), after pulmonary artery banding and/or aortic arch surgery. VSD enlargement may leave residual stenosis and cause postoperative complete heart block. However, with VSD enlargement by means of resection at the inferior part of the septum, the latter complication is less common; and this approach has become the treatment of choice in a number of centers.
  - A Damus-Kaye-Stansel (D-K-S) operation is the alternative approach for relieving subaortic stenosis in this setting. It consists of an aortopulmonary window with distal ligation of the main pulmonary artery, thus using both left and right ventricular outflow tracts to supply the aorta and effectively relieving subaortic stenosis. If a D-K-S operation needs to be considered and pulmonary artery banding is required, the latter should be placed closer to the bifurcation of the pulmonary arteries (i.e., distal to the pulmonary valve). This maneuver provides adequate space for anastomosing the proximal pulmonary artery with the ascending aorta when the D-K-S procedure is performed subsequently.
- Atrial septectomy, occasionally—particularly if there is stenosis or atresia of one of the AV valves with a restrictive atrial septum

These palliative procedures are followed by cavopulmonary anastomosis and finally a Fontan completion or, in a minority of patients, ventricular septation.

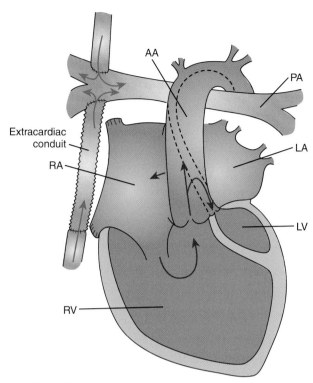

Figure 52-4 Stage 3 Fontan completion for hypoplastic left heart syndrome. The shunt or right ventricle to pulmonary artery conduit is taken down. The Fontan circuit is usually completed by means of an extracardiac total cavopulmonary connection. *Red* indicates oxygenated blood—pulmonary venous return. *Blue* indicates deoxygenated blood—systemic venous return. AA, ascending aorta; LA, left atrium; LV, left ventricle; PA, pulmonary artery; RA, right atrium; RV, right ventricle.

may occur, leading to ischemia and sudden death. Furthermore, great care must be taken with stent placement to avoid encroachment over the ascending aorta. In addition, the second-stage operation is more extensive than after a conventional surgical approach, involving reconstruction of the aorta and pulmonary arteries, removal of the stent, and creation of the cavopulmonary anastomosis. Nonetheless, a hybrid approach is likely to be useful in high-risk cases such as those with intact interatrial septum, low birth weight (<2 kg), and those with additional noncardiac problems. It is not suitable for those in whom the aorta is diminutive.

Neonatal cardiac transplantation is not widely available and is a realistic option in only a few centers worldwide. Dedicated centers performing neonatal transplantation for hypoplastic left heart syndrome have achieved mid-term results comparable to those of the staged Fontan approach. However, multicenter studies show a 25% mortality for neonates awaiting transplantation.[12] Transplantation is a more widespread option for children who have embarked on the staged Fontan approach but who have developed cardiac failure. Those who do receive a transplant have the advantage of a biventricular circulation, albeit at the expense of requiring lifelong immunosuppression.

Late Outcome

Long-term survival in tricuspid atresia is expected after aortopulmonary shunt or Fontan-type surgery. Although a Fontan circulation is the goal for most patients with tricuspid atresia, it carries long-term complications, which have been appreciated increasingly over the past decade and are discussed later and in Chapter 12.

Whether palliated by aortopulmonary or cavopulmonary shunt, or by a Fontan operation, all patients remain at risk from a panoply

of serious long-term complications (Boxes 52-1 to 52-5). Nonetheless, quality-of-life scores are comparable to those of the general population, the only difference being poorer perceptions of physical health among those with persistent cyanosis.[13]

Survivors of staged Fontan surgery for hypoplastic left heart syndrome are only just beginning to be seen at adult congenital heart disease clinics, so their long-term future is unknown. However, they can be expected to have all the complications of tricuspid atresia palliated with a Fontan procedure with additional possible complications, which

BOX 52-1   COMPLICATIONS OF PALLIATIVE SHUNT SURGERY FOR TRICUSPID ATRESIA

- After aortopulmonary shunt:
  - Ventricular volume overload
  - Risk of ventricular dysfunction and atrial arrhythmia
- After cavopulmonary shunt (superior vena cava to pulmonary artery) (bidirectional Glenn shunt):
  - Inadequate sole source of pulmonary blood supply in an adult
  - Increasing cyanosis—pulmonary arteriovenous fistulas may develop if pulmonary circulation is deprived of hepatic venous blood.
- Endocarditis
- Atrial and ventricular arrhythmias
- Complications of cyanosis:
  - Hypoxia-induced erythrocytosis and hyperviscosity
  - Paradoxic embolism because of persistent right-to-left shunt
  - Cerebral abscess because of persistent right-to-left shunt and previous hypoxic brain injury
  - Hemoptysis
  - Renal impairment
  - Pigment gallstones secondary to high hemoglobin turnover
  - Gingival hypertrophy if poor oral hygiene
  - High plasma uric acid level and gout
  - Acne
  - Clubbing and hypertrophic osteoarthropathy

BOX 52-2   COMPLICATIONS AFTER FONTAN-TYPE OPERATION FOR TRICUSPID ATRESIA

- Chronic low cardiac output state dependent on high systemic venous filling pressures
- Atrial arrhythmia
- Atrioventricular valve regurgitation
- Thromboembolism—the Fontan circulation is prethrombotic.
- Fontan pathway obstruction
- Protein-losing enteropathy
- Recurrent effusions, ascites, peripheral edema
- Development of subaortic stenosis (if ventriculoarterial discordance)
- Right lower pulmonary vein compression by dilated right atrium
- Cyanosis (due to development of collateral veins to the left atrium or pulmonary arteriovenous fistulas)
- Endocarditis

BOX 52-3   ADDITIONAL POTENTIAL COMPLICATIONS AFTER THE FONTAN PROCEDURE FOR PATIENTS WITH HYPOPLASTIC LEFT HEART SYNDROME

- Re-coarctation and residual arch hypoplasia
- Pulmonary artery stenosis
- Restrictive atrial septal defect
- Systemic right ventricular failure
- Systemic tricuspid valve regurgitation
- Myocardial ischemia secondary to poor perfusion of the coronary arteries as they arise from a diminutive aorta

BOX 52-4 CLINICAL EXAMINATION AFTER A FONTAN PROCEDURE

- Most post–Fontan operation patients are acyanotic. New or deepening cyanosis is a cause for concern.
- Jugular venous pressure is normally marginally raised. A high venous pressure may be a cause for concern. Note any visible flutter waves.
- There is a palpable A_2 in patients with ventriculoarterial discordance.
- The second heart sound is usually single.
- There should be no loud systolic murmur. A pansystolic murmur of mitral regurgitation may be audible. A loud ejection systolic murmur may indicate subaortic stenosis in patients with ventriculoarterial discordance.
- A liver edge is commonly palpable, but new or increasing hepatomegaly is a cause for concern.
- Ascites often precedes peripheral edema in young patients with complications after this procedure.
- Clinical thyroid status should be noted in patients taking amiodarone.

BOX 52-5 LATE TREATMENT INDICATIONS FOR CONSIDERATION OF LATE RE-INTERVENTION AND THEIR MANAGEMENT OPTIONS POST FONTAN

- Obstruction within cavopulmonary connection: transcatheter balloon dilation ± stent placement, reoperation
- Atrial arrhythmia: if drug therapy fails, consider conversion to cavopulmonary connection: (TCPC) + maze procedure.
- Atrial thrombus: begin or intensify anticoagulation; consider conversion to TCPC
- Increasing cyanosis due to:
  - Shunt across fenestrated Fontan: consider device closure of fenestration if pulmonary arterial pressure is low.
  - Collateral veins to left atrium: consider coil occlusion (often recur)
  - Pulmonary arteriovenous fistulas: see earlier; consider inclusion of hepatic veins to pulmonary circulation.
- Protein-losing enteropathy: nutritional therapy: high protein, low fat, high medium-chain triglyceride; drug therapy: unfractionated heparin, corticosteroids, somatostatin analogues, sildenafil. Consider loperamide if diarrhea is present.
- Intervention: atrial pacing, fenestration, possible conversion of Fontan procedure to TCPC, transplant
- Right upper pulmonary vein compression by dilated right atrium: consider conversion to TCPC.
- AVV regurgitation: valve repair or replacement if ventricular function is adequate

may include re-coarctation and residual arch hypoplasia, pulmonary artery stenosis, restrictive atrial septal defect, systemic right ventricular failure, systemic tricuspid valve regurgitation, and myocardial ischemia secondary to poor perfusion of the coronary arteries because they arise from a diminutive aorta.

Outpatient Assessment

The purpose of follow-up is to detect, and if possible treat, long-term complications. An important additional role of the cardiologist caring for patients with complex anatomy and physiology is to advise other health care professionals with whom the patient comes into contact.

Because failure to recognize and treat arrhythmia (usually interatrial reentry tachycardia, atypical atrial flutter) is common and life threatening, all patients should carry a copy of their electrocardiogram in sinus rhythm (and flutter) with management instructions and contact details of their specialist center for advice.

UNOPERATED OR POST-SHUNT PATIENTS WITH TRICUSPID ATRESIA

History should seek evidence of complications of cyanosis and exercise capacity. Examination findings, including oxygen saturation, should be compared with values obtained at previous visits.

All patients should have periodic assessment with:
- Electrocardiography—to check for sinus rhythm, atrial arrhythmia
- Chest radiography—to evaluate cardiothoracic ratio, pulmonary vasculature
- Echocardiography—to assess ventricular cavity size and function, atrioventricular and aortic valve regurgitation, and patency of shunts
- Exercise testing—to assess functional capacity and degree of desaturation on exercise
- Ambulatory electrocardiographic monitoring—if the patient describes palpitations or faintness
- Thyroid function—for patients on amiodarone. The incidence of amiodarone-associated thyroid dysfunction is high in cyanotic patients; thyrotoxicosis can cause worsening atrial arrhythmia and heart failure.[14]

All unoperated or shunted patients are cyanosed and have restricted physical activity. It is not usually necessary to impose additional limitations on physical activities because most patients will have adapted their lifestyle so that they live within their limits.

Post-Fontan or Post–Total Cavopulmonary Connection Patients with Tricuspid Atresia or Hypoplastic Left Heart Syndrome

The history should seek evidence of changes in exercise capacity, new-onset arrhythmia or syncope, and protein-losing enteropathy (weight loss and ascites or edema). Examination should include oxygen saturation, because cyanosis can develop late after a Fontan procedure.

All patients should have periodic assessment with:
- Electrocardiography—to check for sinus rhythm, atypical atrial flutter
- Chest radiography—to evaluate cardiothoracic ratio, pulmonary vasculature
- Echocardiography—to assess ventricular cavity size and function, AVV valve regurgitation, right atrial dilation and spontaneous contrast or thrombus, restrictive atrial septal defect, restrictive ventricular septal defect, and subaortic stenosis in patients with ventriculoarterial discordance
- Magnetic resonance imaging—to assess Fontan connections, quantify ventricular function, aortic arch, and coarctation repair sites, search for pulmonary artery stenoses
- Magnetic resonance imaging or echocardiographic stress imaging—to identify myocardial ischemia
- Exercise testing—to assess functional capacity, blood pressure response, and any desaturation on exercise
- Ambulatory electrocardiographic monitoring—if the patient describes palpitations or faintness
- Thyroid function—for patients on amiodarone. The incidence of amiodarone-associated thyroid dysfunction is high after a Fontan procedure; thyrotoxicosis can cause worsening atrial arrhythmia and heart failure.
- Fecal α_1-antitrypsin and serum albumin levels—if protein-losing enteropathy is suspected.

Most patients have restricted physical activity, and it is not usually necessary to impose additional limitations. However, many patients find that emotional stress, fatigue, and alcohol and drug misuse precipitate atrial flutter; counseling to avoid precipitating factors is often helpful. Young adults leaving home for the first time are at particular risk; some patients develop their first episode of arrhythmia once freed from parental constraints.

Late Management Options

No late operative intervention should be undertaken lightly in adults with AVV atresia, whatever their previous surgical history. The risk of surgery is high both in patients with long-standing cyanosis and in Fontan operation patients with low cardiac output. There is a risk of bleeding from collateral vessels or because of abnormal hemostasis. Both cyanotic patients and Fontan operation patients with chronic low cardiac output state are at risk of perioperative renal failure.

LATE INTERVENTION IN UNOPERATED OR SHUNT-PALLIATED PATIENTS WITH TRICUSPID ATRESIA

Patients with tricuspid atresia who have survived to adulthood, either unoperated or shunt-palliated, are a highly select group who are likely to have a "well-balanced" circulation and either (1) have always had low pulmonary blood flow and therefore low pulmonary vascular resistance or (2) have now, or in the past, had pulmonary blood flow at high pressure and therefore have high pulmonary vascular resistance.

The group with raised pulmonary vascular resistance is unsuitable for conversion to a Fontan-type circulation, and these patients are usually best managed conservatively. Late ventricular dysfunction and atrial arrhythmia are common, and there is a continuing attrition, with death occurring early in the fourth decade.[15] Heart or heart-lung transplantation is an option for these patients.

Patients with low pulmonary vascular resistance may be suitable for conversion to a Fontan-type circulation; with careful patient selection an 80% 1-year survival rate can be achieved.[16] Nonetheless, despite offloading the ventricle there is a continuing late attrition with declining ventricular function and atrial arrhythmia.

The shunt-palliated adult who is being considered for conversion to a Fontan-type circulation needs full and frank discussion with both cardiologist and surgeon. The aims and risks of surgery must be carefully considered; although a Fontan operation or TCPC may be possible technically, surgery should be performed only if there is a good chance of improved quality of life. The patient will be exchanging a complex cyanotic condition with the long-term complications of volume overload for a complex acyanotic (it is hoped) condition with the long-term complications of a Fontan circulation.

Increasing cyanosis may be due to:

- A reduction in pulmonary blood flow secondary to progression of pulmonary or subpulmonary stenosis or to narrowing of an aortopulmonary shunt. The options here are to improve pulmonary blood flow with a controlled pulmonary valvotomy or a further aortopulmonary shunt or to consider conversion to a Fontan circulation.
- Development of pulmonary arteriovenous fistulas if the pulmonary vascular bed is deprived of hepatic venous blood (e.g., in patients with tricuspid atresia in whom a classic Glenn anastomosis was performed such that the right lung receives only superior vena caval blood). It may also occur after Fontan-type surgery in patients with anomalous systemic venous connections where hepatic venous return is directly to the heart and not the pulmonary circuit. The fistulas are often too small and numerous to be successfully coil occluded. Operative intervention to direct hepatic venous blood to the pulmonary circulation may reduce the fistulas and improve cyanosis.
- Progression of pulmonary vascular disease in patients with unrestrictive pulmonary blood flow, unsuitable for a Fontan operation (for management see Chapter 48).

LATE RE-INTERVENTION IN PATIENTS AFTER A FONTAN PROCEDURE

Conversion from an atriopulmonary (Fontan) connection to a TCPC is an option for selected patients with post-Fontan complications and adequate ventricular function (see Chapter 11).[17] In practice, this approach is usually possible only for young adults.

Protein-losing enteropathy is a debilitating and grave complication of Fontan-type surgery that carries a 5-year survival rate of less than 50% and may occur in up to 13% of long-term survivors.[18] Its pathogenesis is not fully understood but probably relates to the detrimental effects of the Fontan circulation on lower-body systemic venous, and therefore lymphatic, pressure. High lymphatic pressures result in gastrointestinal protein loss and hypoproteinemia, causing malnutrition, edema, effusions, and ascites, as well as infections secondary to hypogammaglobulinemia. A low serum albumin level and increased fecal α_1-antitrypsin concentration confirm the diagnosis.

Treatment is difficult; the extensive and diverse list given in the Box 52-5 points to a generally limited response and poor outcome. Specialist diets may be helpful but are restrictive and unpalatable. Treatment with unfractionated heparin, corticosteroids, or somatostatin analogues may be helpful,[19] and transcatheter fenestration of the atrial septum may reduce systemic venous pressure and improve symptoms. Atrial pacing may be beneficial for patients with sinus node dysfunction.[20] Surgical relief of any Fontan obstruction may be successful but carries a high mortality rate, and cardiac transplantation may be the only option, although protein-losing enteropathy may recur. There are anecdotal reports of sildenafil producing beneficial effects in protein-losing enteropathy,[21] most likely by an improvement in pulmonary blood flow. If the diarrhea associated with protein-losing enteropathy is debilitating, simple antidiarrheal measures such as loperamide may improve symptoms and improve the serum albumin concentration.

Arrhythmia

Intra-atrial reentry tachycardia (atypical atrial flutter) is common in long-term follow-up after Fontan surgery. Risk factors for the development of arrhythmia are right atrial distention, high atrial pressures, systemic AVV regurgitation, atrial suture lines, and obstruction to the Fontan circuit.

Atrial flutter impairs left atrial filling and is poorly tolerated, so cardioversion should be undertaken without delay. Atrial arrhythmias may be difficult to control, and amiodarone may be the most effective and well-tolerated therapy. However, post–Fontan operation patients appear to be particularly vulnerable to amiodarone-induced thyrotoxicosis, so thyroid function should be monitored closely. Catheter ablation of atrial arrhythmias in patients who have had the Fontan procedure is challenging because these patients often have multiple pathways and a distended right atrium (see Chapters 16 and 17). Advances in electrophysiologic mapping techniques may improve arrhythmia ablation success rates in patients with complex atrial anatomy. It is hoped that more recent modifications of the Fontan operation, including lateral and extracardiac tunnels, may be associated with fewer long-term atrial tachyarrhythmias. However, these modifications leave no catheter access to the atrial mass, so, if arrhythmias occur, catheter ablation is unlikely to be possible.

Operative conversion from a Fontan procedure to TCPC in combination with cryoablation has shown promising early results in reducing arrhythmia in selected patients.[22]

Pregnancy and Contraception

CONTRACEPTION

The risks of pregnancy are considerable for all patients with AVV atresia, so safe and effective contraception is vital. The combined oral contraceptive pill is contraindicated because of the risk of thromboembolism. Barrier methods and progestogen-only hormonal contraception are safe in terms of cardiovascular effects. The progestogen only "mini-pill" is not advised, because it has poor contraceptive efficacy. Cerazette is a newer progestogen-only pill that has an efficacy similar to that of the combined oral contraceptive pill and is therefore a good option for women who wish to use oral contraception. Long-acting progestogen-only preparations are highly effective; Depo-Provera (3-monthly intramuscular injection) and Implanon (3-yearly subdermal implant) have no cardiac contraindications.

The progestogen-eluting intrauterine device (Mirena IUS) is similarly effective, but there is a risk of vasovagal syncope at insertion, especially in nulliparous women; in those who remain cyanosed and those with a Fontan circulation, such a reaction may cause cardiovascular collapse.[23]

For the first few months of use all progestogen-only preparations may cause irregular prolonged menstrual bleeding and menorrhagia in those who are cyanosed or anticoagulated. For some women, however, especially those using the Mirena IUS, amenorrhea may subsequently develop.

UNOPERATED OR SHUNT-PALLIATED PATIENTS

The risk of pregnancy depends on ventricular function and the degree of cyanosis. Maternal risk is increased if ventricular function is impaired or there is significant aortic valve regurgitation. Cyanosis *per se* does not pose a significant risk of death (unless associated with pulmonary hypertension), but the right-to-left shunt may result in paradoxical embolism, and the hematologic changes associated with cyanotic heart disease put the mother at risk of both thrombosis and peripartum hemorrhage. Cyanosis is a major risk factor for the fetus; a live birth results from only 12% of pregnancies in which the mother's resting oxygen saturation is less than 85%. The risk of recurrence is about 5%.

POST–FONTAN OPERATION PATIENTS

Advice on contraception is the same as for unoperated or shunt-palliated patients. The maternal risk of pregnancy depends on ventricular function, patency of the Fontan circuit, and AVV regurgitation. Arrhythmias may become more troublesome during pregnancy. Maternal risk appears to be low in women with good pre-pregnancy exercise capacity. However, spontaneous abortion may occur in nearly one third of pregnancies. The effects of drugs on the fetus should be considered at pre-pregnancy counseling. Low-molecular-weight heparin should be substituted for warfarin once pregnancy is confirmed, and therapy with angiotensin-converting enzyme inhibitors should be stopped. Amiodarone poses a difficult problem; because of its long half-life it needs to be stopped several months before conception to ensure no or minimal fetal exposure. However, most patients take amiodarone only if other antiarrhythmic agents have failed to control serious arrhythmias; and, given the increased incidence of any arrhythmia during pregnancy, it may be safer for the mother to continue to take it. The potential risk to the fetus of thyroid abnormality needs to be weighed against the risk to the mother—and therefore to the fetus—of hemodynamically significant arrhythmia.[24,25]

Level of Follow-Up, Endocarditis Prophylaxis, and Exercise

All patients should have periodic review in an adult congenital heart disease center. It is particularly important to maintain good lines of communication with the adult cardiology team at the patient's local hospital, because this is where the patient is most likely to go in an emergency. The local team should have access to immediate advice from the specialist center, for example in case of atrial arrhythmia, or the need for emergency noncardiac surgery.

All patients should be advised of the importance of good oral hygiene in reducing the risk of endocarditis. Antibiotic prophylaxis has become controversial: it is no longer recommended routinely in the United Kingdom and United States.

All patients have restricted physical capability, but most limit themselves and do not need restraint. They should be discouraged from extremes of exercise, especially when there is a risk of dehydration, and patients on warfarin should avoid contact sports in which there is a risk of significant injury.

REFERENCES

1. Ho SY, Baker EJ, Rigby ML, Anderson RL. Hearts with a univentricular atrioventricular connexion. In: Ho SY, Baker EJ, Rigby ML, Anderson RL, editors. Color Atlas of Congenital Heart Disease. Morphologic and Clinical Correlations. London: Mosby-Wolfe Times Mirror International; 1995. p. 77–90.
2. Norwood WI, Lang P, Hansen DD. Physiologic repair of aortic atresia–hypoplastic left heart syndrome. N Engl J Med 1983;308:23–6.
3. Marino B, Diglio MC, Novelli G, et al. Tricuspid atresia and 22q11 deletion. Am J Med Genet 1997;72:40–42.
4. Svensson EC, Huggins GS, Lin H, et al. A syndrome of tricuspid atresia in mice with targeted mutation of the gene encoding Fog-2. Nat Genet 2000;25:353–356.
5. Tchervenkov CI, Jacobs JP, Weinberg PM, et al. The nomenclature, definition and classification of hypoplastic left heart syndrome. Cardiol Young 2006;16:339–368.
6. Report of the New England Regional Infant Cardiac Program. Pediatrics 1980;65:375–461.
7. Hinton RB, Martin LJ, Tabangin ME, et al. J Am Coll Cardiol 2007;50:1590–1595.
8. McGuirk SP, Griselli M, Stumper OF, et al. Staged surgical management of hypoplastic left heart syndrome: a single institution 12 year experience. Heart 2006;92:364–370.
9. Mahle WT, Spray TL, Wernovsky G, et al. Survival after reconstructive surgery for hypoplastic left heart syndrome: a 15-year experience from a single institution. Circulation 2000;102(19 Suppl. 3):III136–III141.
10. Pizarro C, Malec E, Maher KO, et al. Right ventricle to pulmonary artery conduit improves outcome after stage I Norwood for hypoplastic left heart syndrome. Circulation 2003;108(Suppl. 1): II155–II160.
11. Akintürk H, Michel-Behnke I, Valeske K, et al. Hybrid transcatheter-surgical palliation: basis for univentricular or biventricular repair: the Giessen experience. Pediatr Cardiol 2007;28:79–87.
12. Chrisant MR, Naftel DC, Drummond-Webb J, et al., Pediatric Heart Transplant Study Group. Fate of infants with hypoplastic left heart syndrome listed for cardiac transplantation: a multicenter study. J Heart Lung Transplant 2005;24:576–582.
13. Salba Z, Butera G, Bonnet D, et al. Quality of life and perceived health status in surviving adults with univentricular heart. Heart 2001;86:69–73.
14. Thorne SA, Barnes I, Cullinan P, Somerville J. Amiodarone-associated thyroid dysfunction in adults with congenital heart disease. Circulation 1999;100:149–154.
15. Gatzoulis MA, Munk MD, Williams WG, Webb GD. Definitive palliation with cavopulmonary or aortopulmonary shunts for adults with single ventricle physiology. Heart 2000;83:51–57.
16. Veldtman GR, Nishimoto A, Siu S, et al. The Fontan procedure in adults. Heart 2001;86:330–335.
17. Marcelletti CF, Hanley FL, Mavroudis C, et al. Revision of previous Fontan connections to a total extracardiac cavopulmonary anastomosis: a multicentre experience. J Thorac Cardiovasc Surg 2000;119:240–246.
18. Feldt RH, Driscoll DJ, Offord KP, et al. Protein-losing enteropathy after the Fontan operation. J Thorac Cardiovasc Surg 1996;112:672–680.
19. Pratap U, Slavil Z, Ofoe V, et al. Octreotide to treat postoperative chylothorax after cardiac operations in children. Ann Thorac Surg 2001;72:1740–1742.
20. Cohen MI, Rhodes LA, Wernovsky G, et al. Atrial pacing: an alternative treatment for protein losing enteropathy after the Fontan operation. J Thorac Cardiovasc Surg 2001;121:582–583.
21. Uzun O, Wong JK, Bhole V, Stumper O. Resolution of protein-losing enteropathy and normalization of mesenteric Doppler flow with sildenafil after Fontan. Ann Thorac Surg 2006;82: e39–e40.
22. Deal BJ, Mavroudis C, Backer CL, et al. Impact of arrhythmia circuit cryoablation during Fontan conversion for refractory atrial arrhythmia. Am J Cardiol 1999;83:563–568.
23. Thorne SA, MacGregor AE, Nelson-Piercy C. Risk of contraception and pregnancy in heart disease. Ed Heart 2006;92:1520–1525.
24. Canobbio MM, Mair DD, van de Velde M, Koos BJ. Pregnancy outcomes after the Fontan repair. J Am Cardiol 1996;28:763–767.
25. Walker F. Pregnancy and the various forms of the Fontan operation. Heart 2007;93:152–154.

53

Heterotaxy and Isomerism of the Atrial Appendages

ELISABETH BÉDARD | JOSEP RODÉS-CABAU | HIDEKI UEMURA

Definitions

The term *heterotaxy* comes from the Greek *heteros,* meaning "other" and *taxis,* meaning arrangement. The nomenclature and definition of heterotaxy have been a matter of debate for years and remain controversial. The complex combinations of cardiac malformations found in this syndrome make its description challenging. Heterotaxy can be defined as an abnormal arrangement of the internal thoracoabdominal organs across the left-right axis of the body.[1] Heterotaxy syndrome does not include "situs inversus," in which patients have complete mirror-imaged arrangement of their internal organs along the left-right axis.

Isomerism (from the Greek *isos,* meaning "equal," and *meros,* meaning "part") can be defined as "a situation where some paired structures on opposite sides of the left-right axis of the body are, in morphologic terms, symmetrical mirror images of each other."[1] The concept of "atrial isomerism" is not universally accepted[2] because atrial chambers as a whole are not entirely isomeric. However, true isomerism of the atrial appendages (considered in isolation) has been demonstrated previously[3]; the concepts of isomerism of the right and left atrial appendages (IRAA and ILAA) are therefore more accurate. These two entities represent, in fact, two different subgroups of the heterotaxy syndrome itself. IRAA is most often associated with asplenia (asplenia syndrome), and ILAA is usually found with polysplenia (polysplenia syndrome). As described later (Tables 53-1 and 53-2), IRAA and ILAA are typically, but not always, associated with a variety of cardiac and other thoracoabdominal abnormalities. The spleen is most commonly affected. Although certain associations of cardiac and noncardiac abnormalities are frequent, it is important to keep in mind that almost any combination can be found.

The complex anatomy of patients with heterotaxy syndrome should therefore be described by using a sequential segmental approach, which allows for a complete description of the cardiac structures' relations and connections to each other (see Table 53-1 and Chapters 2 and 5).[1] However, in a minority of patients, the exact diagnosis will remain uncertain despite the most thorough assessment. The sequential segmental approach includes separate documentation of the following:

1. The position of the heart in the chest and the orientation of the cardiac apex
   - Significant variations can occur in heterotaxy syndrome and can have major impact on surgical interventions
2. Cardiac segmental anatomy
   - Arrangement of the atrial appendages (atrial situs)
   - Ventricular topology (ventricular loop)
   - Morphology of the venoatrial, the atrioventricular (AV), and ventriculoarterial junctions
   - Relationships of the arterial trunks in space
3. Other malformations within the heart such as septal structures and coronary arterial distribution
4. Description of the remaining thoracoabdominal organs, including:
   - The spleen
   - The lungs
   - The intestines

Presented here is a comprehensive and contemporary overview of heterotaxy syndrome, one of the most complex congenital heart diseases.

Morphology

THE ATRIUM

Morphologically right and morphologically left atria can be differentiated by studying the anatomy of their atrial appendages and the morphology of the atrial septum[1]:
- Anatomy of the atrial appendages (Fig. 53-1)
  - The morphologically right atrial appendage is a broad structure, and the pectinate muscles extend around the muscular AV vestibules.[3]
  - The morphologically left atrial appendage is a narrow finger-shaped structure to which the pectinate muscles are confined; there is continuity between the vestibule of the AV junction and the smooth-walled venous component of the atrium, uninterrupted by the presence of pectinate muscles.[3]
- Morphology of the atrial septum
  - The morphologically right side of the atrial septum contains the rim of the oval fossa, whereas its flap is on the left side.

BRONCHOPULMONARY ANATOMY

In heterotaxy syndrome, bronchopulmonary anatomy is often (but not always) consistent with the morphology of the atrial appendages.
- In ILAA, patients typically have bilateral bilobed lungs, with two morphologically left-sided bronchi that follow a long course before the first branching and branch inferior to the first lobar division of the pulmonary artery (hyparterial).
- In IRAA the following features are usually found: bilateral trilobed lungs with two morphologically right-sided bronchi that follow a short course before the first branching and a branch superior to the first lobar division of the pulmonary artery (eparterial).

THE SPLEEN

Most patients with heterotaxy have splenic abnormalities. As mentioned earlier, the spleen is absent in most patients with IRAA whereas ILAA is associated with multiple spleens. However, the correlation between the morphology of the atrial appendages and the anatomy of the spleen is poorer than with the bronchopulmonary anatomy.[4] The cardiac anatomy or subgroup of heterotaxy syndrome should therefore never be deduced from the splenic morphology; rather, each should be assessed and described separately.

ATRIOVENTRICULAR JUNCTIONS

In hearts of patients with univentricular physiology three types of AV connections can be found: absent right, absent left, or double inlet. In patients with ILAA or IRAA who have biventricular arrangement there is a concordant AV connection in half of the heart (with two mitral or two tricuspid valves) and a discordant connection in the other half (mixed or nonconcordant/nondiscordant AV connections). A common AV junction with a common valve is frequent in both subgroups of heterotaxy syndrome, but particularly in IRAA.

TABLE 53-1	Sequential Segmental Approach, Echocardiographic Views, and Cardiac Findings in Heterotaxy Syndrome		
Steps	*Echocardiographic Views*	**Cardiac Findings in Heterotaxy Syndrome**	
		IRAA	*ILAA*
1. Localization of the heart in the chest + orientation of apex	Subcostal and apical	The heart is right sided in up to half of all patients and in the middle in up to one tenth	
2. Assessment of situs	Subcostal short axis	Aorta and IVC on the same side of the spine, with IVC anterior to aorta	Azygos vein posterior and to the left of aorta (azygos continuation of IVC)
3. Atrial morphology	RAA: high parasternal long axis (angulation toward RVOT), subcostal short axis, right subclavicular LAA: parasternal short axis at the level of the aortic valve	Bilateral RAA Frequent anomalies of the interatrial septum[15]	Bilateral LAA
4. Atrioventricular junction	Modified subcostal, apical four-chamber view	A common AV junction is frequent	
5. Ventricular morphology	All views, including modified subcostal, apical four-chamber	Left ventricular hypoplasia in up to 40%	
6. Ventriculoarterial connections	Parasternal long and short axis, apical four-chamber with anterior angulations	Frequent DORV or TGA, and RVOTO	RVOTO in ~ 40%, aortic obstruction in one fourth, occasional DORV
7. Venoatrial connections			
a. Inferior vena cava and azygos vein	Abdominal and subcostal (long and short axis)	Usually intact	Interrupted with azygos continuation
b. Superior vena cava	RSVC: Subcostal (long and short axis), suprasternal, and right subclavicular LSVC: Parasternal and suprasternal short axis with transducer directed leftward; most easily seen in the so-called ductal view	Bilateral superior venae cavae in up to 70%	
c. Coronary sinus	Parasternal (long and short axis), suprasternal short axis	Usually absent	Can be absent up to 70%[16]
d. Hepatic drainage	Subcostal (long and short axis) and apical	Hepatic veins usually drain to IVC	Anomalous hepatic venous drainage directly to the atrium in up to 30%
e. Pulmonary veins	Apical four-chamber, suprasternal short axis, subcostal four-chamber	TAPVC is the rule, frequently to an extracardiac site	Bilateral return (right pulmonary veins draining into the right sided atrium and left veins to the left-sided atrium) common (approximately 60%)

AV, atrioventricular; DORV, double-outlet right ventricle; ILAA, isomeric left atrial appendages; IRAA, isomeric right atrial appendages; IVC, inferior vena cava; RVOTO, right ventricular outflow tract obstruction; SVC, superior vena cava; TAPVC, Total anomalous pulmonary venous connection; TGA, transposition of great arteries.

TABLE 53-2	Most Common Extracardiac Anomalies in Heterotaxy Syndrome	
*Extracardiac Anomalies**	*Isomerism of Right Atrial Appendage*	*Isomerism of Left Atrial Appendage*
Pulmonary morphology	Bilaterally short and eparterial bronchi Three lobes found bilaterally (73%)	Bilaterally long and hyparterial bronchi Two lobes on both sides (74%)
Spleen anomalies	Functional asplenia with immunodeficiency	Polysplenia
Gastrointestinal anomalies	Malrotation of the gut Dextroposition of the stomach	Biliary atresia Malrotation of the gut Dextroposition of the stomach

*Genitourinary, musculoskeletal, craniofacial abnormalities as well as anomalies of the central nervous system are also found in less than or equal to 15% of patients with heterotaxy syndrome (IRAA or ILAA).

Data from references 3, 6, 7, and 17.

VENTRICULOARTERIAL JUNCTIONS

In patients with heterotaxy syndrome, any type of ventriculoarterial connection may exist, regardless of the subgroup. However, discordant or double-outlet ventriculoarterial connections (often with pulmonary atresia) are more likely to occur in patients with IRAA whereas concordant ventriculoarterial connections are more frequent in those with ILAA.[1,5]

VENOATRIAL CONNECTIONS

Venoatrial connection abnormalities are almost universal in patients with heterotaxy syndrome and, depending on their nature, have a profound impact on clinical presentation.

- In IRAA, total anomalous pulmonary venous connection (TAPVC) of the extracardiac type is common. Even when the pulmonary veins are directly connected to the atrial cavity, the pattern of connection of the pulmonary veins to the atrial wall is almost always abnormal. The coronary sinus is not formed according to the standard definition and is usually considered absent.
- In ILAA, interruption of the inferior caval vein with azygos continuation is frequent and the hepatic veins often connect directly to one or both atria.

■ Epidemiology and Genetics

IRAA or ILAA is diagnosed in 0.4% to 2% of all infants with congenital heart disease but accounts for at least 6% of the cardiac defects detected in utero.[6–8] The embryonic development of the left-right axis is a complex process and has not been fully elucidated. Over the past decades, outstanding improvements in molecular embryology and genetics have been made, leading to new insights into the etiology of heterotaxy. Animal models have helped to improve our understanding of the mechanisms underlying the defects of laterality. In mice, mutations in an axonemal dynein heavy-chain gene (*lrd*; iv/iv mice) led to randomization of the process of lateralization; half of iv/iv mice exhibit situs inversus, and half have normal situs.[9,10] Abnormalities in nodal cilia are found in these mutants.[11] Embryonic nodal cilia seem to play a key role in organogenesis and lateralization.[12] The fact that heterotaxy syndrome has recently been identified in 6.3% of patients with primary ciliary dyskinesia, a recessive genetic disorder characterized by recurrent sinopulmonary disease, supports this hypothesis.[12] In this study, an increased prevalence of mutations in *DNAI1* and *DNAH5* genes that code for respiratory and ciliary outer dynein arm proteins was observed in patients with heterotaxy.[12]

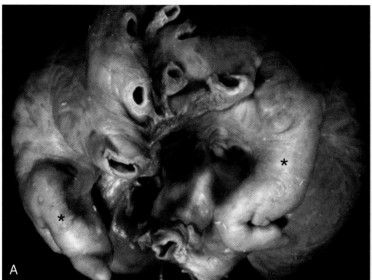 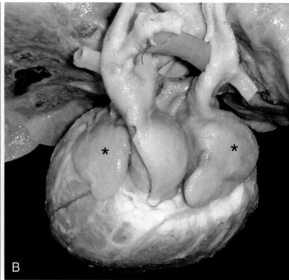

Figure 53-1 Heart specimens with ILAA and IRAA. **A,** This heart specimen viewed from above, with the great arteries retracted forward, shows bilateral narrow and finger-like left atrial appendages (*asterisks*) indicative of left isomerism. **B,** Both atrial appendages (*asterisks*) in this heart with right isomerism are triangular with broad bases.

Despite these major advances, additional studies are needed to clarify further the genetic and molecular determinants of laterality and the causes of heterotaxy.[11]

Associated Cardiac Lesions in Heterotaxy Syndrome

Associated cardiac findings in heterotaxy syndrome are presented in Table 53-1.[3,4,6,7,11,13–16] Intracardiac involvement is found in 83% of ILAA and 100% of IRAA diagnosed in utero.[14] It is usually more complex and severe in IRAA, leading to poorer prognosis.[6] Anomalies of the conduction system are also frequent in heterotaxy syndrome and are described later (see Conduction System Abnormalities and Arrhythmias).

NONCARDIAC MALFORMATIONS

Extracardiac anomalies observed in heterotaxy syndrome are presented in Table 53-2.[3,6,7,17] The spleen is most often affected, and malrotation of the gut is also common in both IRAA and ILAA. Up to 10% of infants with ILAA may have biliary atresia. Complete multisystem assessment is mandatory in infants with heterotaxy syndrome.

Early Presentation and Initial Management

Despite major advances in pediatric surgery over the past decades, the prognosis of patients with heterotaxy syndrome and complex cardiovascular anomalies remains poor, especially for IRAA: 5-year survival in patients with ILAA and IRAA is reported to be only 64% and 29%, respectively.[6] Only half of the patients with IRAA survive the first year of life.[18] In these patients, TAPVC with obstructed pulmonary veins and pulmonary arterial obstruction further increase the risk of death.[19,20] Although cardiac anomalies in ILAA tend to be less severe than in IRAA and prognosis slightly better, one fifth of these patients die shortly after birth or are not suitable candidates for surgery.[7]

The early clinical presentation depends on the nature and severity of cardiac involvement. Because right ventricular outflow tract obstruction is common in IRAA, infants will often present with symptoms related to the severity of obstruction, such as cyanosis,[6,18] acidosis, and even cardiovascular collapse. The pulmonary circulation is often arterial duct dependent. In infants with ILAA, left-to-right shunts often dominate the clinical picture, leading to heart failure.[7] Congenital heart

block is another significant lesion related to mortality and morbidity in infants with ILAA. However, patients with ILAA may also initially present with gastrointestinal symptoms or other noncardiac features.[7]

INITIAL MANAGEMENT

Initial management of infants with heterotaxy syndrome varies, depending on the cardiovascular malformations. Patients with inadequate pulmonary blood supply will first require construction of a systemic-to-pulmonary shunt. When patients are able to survive early infancy without such palliation, the first surgical procedure can be superior cavopulmonary anastomosis using the bidirectional Glenn procedure. Many patients with IRAA have a functionally single ventricle; some of them will be candidates for establishment of the Fontan circulation. Only a few selected cases of IRAA are suitable for biventricular repair,[21] compared with more than half of the patients with ILAA.[6,7]

As mentioned earlier, heterotaxy syndrome was found in 6.3% of patients with primary ciliary dyskinesia.[12] Assessment of ciliary function is therefore suggested in patients with heterotaxy syndrome for subsequent aggressive pulmonary management in affected cases.[12,22]

Patients with asplenia should receive antibiotic prophylaxis. Polysaccharide encapsulated bacteria are the most common causative organisms of sepsis in such patients. In infants younger than 3 months of age, coliform bacilli are the most common pathogens, whereas older children and adults require prophylaxis against *Streptococcus pneumoniae* and *Haemophilus influenzae*.[23] Vaccination for pneumococcus, *Haemophilus influenzae* type b, varicella, and influenza is recommended.

Late Presentation and Outcomes

Owing to the dramatic progress of pediatric cardiology and surgery, an increasing number of patients with heterotaxy syndrome now survive into adulthood. Most of them will have undergone palliative and/or reparative surgery (biventricular repair or the Fontan-type procedure), depending on the underlying cardiovascular malformations. These adults may present with symptoms associated with complications such as arrhythmias (see later), heart failure, thrombotic events, cyanosis, exercise intolerance, endocarditis, and sepsis (particularly in patients with asplenia).

The 10-year survival rate after biventricular repair in patients with ILAA is reported to be 66%.[7] Heterotaxy syndrome was previously considered to be an independent risk factor for early and late death after the Fontan operation. Recent data have shown improved results; early and midterm mortality has decreased in heterotaxy syndrome and are now similar to that of nonheterotaxy patients.[13,24,25] Ten-year survival in heterotaxy syndrome after completion of the Fontan circuit now reaches 90%.[24,25] However, complications such as arrhythmias, AV valve regurgitation, and prolonged pleural effusions remain significantly high.[24,25] Moreover, as mentioned earlier, a significant proportion of patients with IRAA are not good candidates for the Fontan operation and will die before 5 years of age.[6]

Complications and Late Management Options

Complications and their management after previous interventions in adults with heterotaxy syndrome are presented in Table 53-3. Patients with a Fontan circuit are subject to the residua and sequelae described in this population (see Chapter 12). There seem to be no differences in exercise tolerance between patients with heterotaxy syndrome and other survivors with a Fontan circulation.[26] Arrhythmias, as described later, are particularly frequent and contribute considerably to the high late morbidity of patients with heterotaxy syndrome.[24] Surgical correction for anomalous pulmonary venous connection has often been performed initially; residual pulmonary venous stenosis should be considered when a patient presents with decreased exercise tolerance. AV valve regurgitation after repair for complete AV septal defect is another well-recognized complication.[24] Severe progressive cyanosis, for which there may be several possible causes, may also occur (see Table 53-3).

Outpatient Assessment

Most adults with heterotaxy syndrome have a complex cardiovascular anatomy and are at high risk of developing the just-discussed complications. Therefore, regular outpatient assessment is mandatory

TABLE 53-3	Complications and Late Management Options
Complications	*Late Management Options*
Arrhythmias ILAA: Sinus bradycardia, AV block, SVT IRAA: SVT	Pacemaker implantation for symptomatic sinus bradycardia and AV block Electrophysiologic study and ablation should be considered for SVT and failure of medical treatment or prior to the Fontan type procedure

Cyanosis, secondary to:
    Pulmonary arteriovenous malformations
    Systemic venous collaterals to the pulmonary venous atrium or pulmonary veins
    Residual interatrial communication
    Connection of hepatic veins to the pulmonary venous atrium
    Developing communication between the portal vein and the systemic veins
	Iron deficiency should be assessed and treated
	Avoid and treat anemia and dehydration
	In selected cases:
	    Coil embolization of aortopulmonary and systemic venous collaterals
	    Percutaneous closure of residual interatrial communication

Pulmonary or systemic venous stenosis	Angioplasty and stenting in selected cases
AV valve regurgitation or stenosis	Consider AV valve repair/replacement
Systemic ventricular dysfunction	Diuretics with avoidance of fluid overload No proven effect of angiotensin-converting enzyme inhibitors or β-adrenergic blockers
Endocarditis and sepsis (particularly in patients with asplenia)	Endocarditis prophylaxis Antibiotic prophylaxis and immunization for patients with asplenia
Thromboembolic events	Anticoagulation with warfarin should be considered in most patients (particularly in those with a Fontan circulation)

AV, atrioventricular; SVT, supraventricular tachycardia.

and should include a detailed physical examination, electrocardiography, chest radiography, hematologic studies (for renal and liver function and iron status in patients with cyanosis), and echocardiography. Exercise testing with monitoring of oxygen saturation and 24-hour Holter monitoring should also be performed periodically.

ELECTROCARDIOGRAPHY

In ILAA, the P-wave axis is superior in nearly half of the patients.[27] Junctional rhythm, sinus bradycardia, or AV block can also be found (see Conduction System Abnormalities and Arrhythmias). Junctional ectopic tachycardia may occur after completion of the Fontan-type operation.[28] Multiple P-wave morphologies are found in one sixth of patients with IRAA, and supraventricular tachycardia is not uncommon (see later).[29] Left-axis deviation may suggest the presence of AV septal defect.

CHEST RADIOGRAPHY

The chest radiograph may show discordance between the direction of the cardiac apex and the stomach gas bubble (Fig. 53-2). Scoliosis may also be present. In ILAA, bilateral morphologic left (long) bronchi are usually present (see Fig. 53-2) and absence of the inferior vena caval contour on the lateral view may also be noted. In IRAA, bilateral short bronchi may be observed. Pulmonary venous congestion in these patients may suggest pulmonary venous obstruction.

ECHOCARDIOGRAPHY

Fetal echocardiography for the diagnosis of heterotaxy syndrome is challenging; accurate description of congenital heart disease requires a segmental approach. Fetal echocardiography is highly specific and sensitive for all findings but has low sensitivity for anomalous pulmonary veins.[11,30] Although fetal diagnosis may have a beneficial impact on outcome in some congenital heart diseases such as hypoplastic left heart syndrome,[31] it does not improve outcome in heterotaxy syndrome.[6,30] However, prenatal diagnosis allows for counseling of affected families regarding prognosis and potential treatments.[11]

Postnatal and adult echocardiography in patients with heterotaxy syndrome should be performed using a step-by-step protocol,

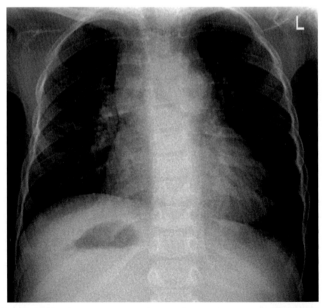

Figure 53-2   Anteroposterior chest radiograph in a patient with ILAA shows left-sided cardiac apex but the stomach bubble is on the right. Moreover, the main bronchi appear symmetrical with both having left-sided morphology (widening of the mediastinum due to right Blalock shunt).

as described in Table 53-1. The position of the heart within the chest, apex orientation, and situs should first be assessed. A sequential segmental approach then allows detailed description of the AV junction, ventricular morphology, ventriculoarterial connections, and venoatrial connections. Careful examination of the latter is mandatory, because they are typically abnormal in heterotaxy syndrome (see Table 53-1).

MAGNETIC RESONANCE IMAGING AND COMPUTED TOMOGRAPHY

The contemporary refinement of imaging technologies allows for complete assessment of these complex congenital malformations using multiple noninvasive modalities.[32]

In patients with heterotaxy syndrome, magnetic resonance imaging (MRI; Fig. 53-3) provides an excellent anatomic and functional description of:
- The complexity of the cardiovascular system, including hemodynamic information such as ventricular size and function, cardiac output, and pulmonary and systemic blood flow
- Tracheobronchial anatomy and bronchial-arterial relationships
- Abdominal abnormalities (status of the spleen, stomach, and liver)

MRI is therefore extremely useful for the follow-up of patients with heterotaxy syndrome and for preoperative evaluation, such as before the Fontan-type procedure. Moreover, MRI is known to be superior to echocardiography and often to catheterization in delineating systemic and pulmonary venous anatomy and its relation to mediastinal structures.[33] Computed tomographic angiography may offer adjunctive information, especially on vascular anomalies or abdominal and thoracic malformations.[32]

CARDIAC CATHETERIZATION

Although noninvasive modalities often provide most of the information required, angiography remains helpful for hemodynamic assessment and delineation of venous and pulmonary arterial anatomy, especially before surgical interventions.[11] Moreover, angiography allows identification and coil embolization of aortopulmonary and systemic collateral veins,[34] angioplasty and stenting of pulmonary or systemic venous obstructions,[35] and percutaneous closure of residual interatrial shunt in selected cases.

▨ Conduction System Abnormalities and Arrhythmias

In ILAA the sinus node is present in less than 50% of cases and is usually hypoplastic and abnormally positioned.[36,37] As a result, patients with ILAA may present with junctional rhythm or sinus bradycardia due to sinus nodal dysfunction. Hearts with IRAA, however, have bilateral sinus nodes; about one sixth of them show multiple P-wave morphologies on the ECG.[11,29]

Discontinuity between the AV node and the ventricular conduction tissues is found in 83% of hearts with ILAA[38]; complete AV block occurs in up to one third of patients with ILAA and is a predictive factor of poor outcome.[39] In hearts with IRAA, a sling of conduction tissue between two AV nodes is present.[37,38] Supraventricular tachycardia is reported in a fourth of these patients and is presumed to be a reentry tachycardia between the paired AV nodes via the conduction sling.[40] When medical management with nodal blocking agents fails and/or when total cavopulmonary connection is contemplated, electrophysiologic study and radiofrequency ablation should be considered.[40,41] Atrial and junctional tachycardia are also common in ILAA and may be caused by abnormal hemodynamics with atrial dilation or be due to previous surgeries.[27,28,42]

▨ Pregnancy

Pregnancy outcomes in women with heterotaxy syndrome have not been reported. Maternal and fetal risks are highly variable, depending on the nature of the cardiac defect and the patient's hemodynamic status and functional class. As described in Chapter 21, counseling of these patients should include information about contraception, life expectancy, maternal and fetal risks, and peripartum management. Women with cyanosis, ventricular dysfunction, functional class greater than New York Heart Association class II, and anticoagulation are at higher risk for complications.[43,44] In patients with a previous Fontan operation, patency of the circuit should be assessed before pregnancy. Arrhythmias are particularly frequent in patients with heterotaxy syndrome and may worsen during pregnancy, complicating its course.

In most cases, pregnant women with heterotaxy syndrome are at moderate if not high risk of adverse events; follow-up in a tertiary center with a multidisciplinary team is therefore highly recommended.

▨ Level of Follow-Up and Endocarditis Prophylaxis

Most adults with heterotaxy syndrome have a complex cardiac anatomy, have had multiple previous surgical interventions, and are at significant risk of developing complications. Regular follow-up should take place in a tertiary care center with expertise in adult congenital heart disease. Endocarditis prophylaxis should be considered in nearly all patients with heterotaxy syndrome, particularly because many of them will have residual shunt and cyanosis, which increase the risk of endocarditis.

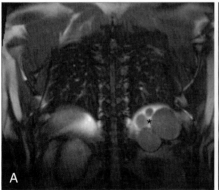 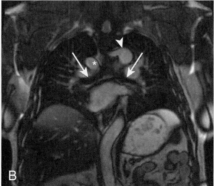 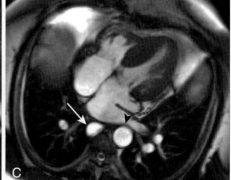

Figure 53-3 MRI in a patient with ILAA. **A,** Coronal view revealing polysplenia (*asterisk*). **B,** Note bilateral left bronchi (*white arrows*), large azygos arch on right (*asterisk*), and anomalous origin of right subclavian artery from descending aorta (*white arrowhead*). **C,** Four-chamber view during systole showing repaired partial AVSD, azygos vein on right (*white arrow*), and descending aorta on left (*black arrowhead*).

REFERENCES

1. Jacobs JP, Anderson RH, Weinberg PM, et al. The nomenclature, definition and classification of cardiac structures in the setting of heterotaxy. Cardiol Young 2007;17(Suppl. 2):1–28.
2. Van Praagh R, Van Praagh S. Atrial isomerism in the heterotaxy syndromes with asplenia, or polysplenia, or normally formed spleen: an erroneous concept. Am J Cardiol 1990;66:1504–1506.
3. Uemura H, Ho SY, Devine WA, et al. Atrial appendages and venoatrial connections in hearts from patients with visceral heterotaxy. Ann Thorac Surg 1995;60:561–569.
4. Uemura H, Ho SY, Devine WA, Anderson RH. Analysis of visceral heterotaxy according to splenic status, appendage morphology, or both. Am J Cardiol 1995;76:846–849.
5. Uemura H, Ho SY, Anderson RH, Yagihara T. Ventricular morphology and coronary arterial anatomy in hearts with isomeric atrial appendages. Ann Thorac Surg 1999;67:1403–1411.
6. Lim JS, McCrindle BW, Smallhorn JF, et al. Clinical features, management, and outcome of children with fetal and postnatal diagnoses of isomerism syndromes. Circulation 2005;112:2454–2461.
7. Gilljam T, McCrindle BW, Smallhorn JF, et al. Outcomes of left atrial isomerism over a 28-year period at a single institution. J Am Coll Cardiol 2000;36:908–916.
8. Ferencz C, Rubin JD, McCarter RJ, et al. Congenital heart disease: prevalence at livebirth. The Baltimore-Washington Infant Study. Am J Epidemiol 1985;121:31–36.
9. Brueckner M, D'Eustachio P, Horwich AL. Linkage mapping of a mouse gene, iv, that controls left-right asymmetry of the heart and viscera. Proc Natl Acad Sci U S A 1989;86:5035–5038.
10. Supp DM, Witte DP, Potter SS, Brueckner M. Mutation of an axonemal dynein affects left-right asymmetry in inversum viscerum mice. Nature 1997;389:963–966.
11. Cohen MS, Anderson RH, Cohen MI, et al. Controversies, genetics, diagnostic assessment, and outcomes relating to the heterotaxy syndrome. Cardiol Young 2007;17(Suppl. 2):29–43.
12. Kennedy MP, Omran H, Leigh MW, et al. Congenital heart disease and other heterotaxic defects in a large cohort of patients with primary ciliary dyskinesia. Circulation 2007;115:2814–2821.
13. Bartz PJ, Driscoll DJ, Dearani JA, et al. Early and late results of the modified Fontan operation for heterotaxy syndrome 30 years of experience in 142 patients. J Am Coll Cardiol 2006;48:2301–2305.
14. Taketazu M, Lougheed J, Yoo SJ, et al. Spectrum of cardiovascular disease, accuracy of diagnosis, and outcome in fetal heterotaxy syndrome. Am J Cardiol 2006;97:720–724.
15. Van Praagh S, Carrera ME, Sanders S, et al. Partial or total direct pulmonary venous drainage to right atrium due to malposition of septum primum: anatomic and echocardiographic findings

16. Uemura H, Ho SY, Anderson RH, et al. The surgical anatomy of coronary venous return in hearts with isomeric atrial appendages. J Thorac Cardiovasc Surg 1995;110:436–444.
17. Ticho BS, Goldstein AM, Van Praagh R. Extracardiac anomalies in the heterotaxy syndromes with focus on anomalies of midline-associated structures. Am J Cardiol 2000;85:729–734.
18. Hashmi A, Abu-Sulaiman R, McCrindle BW, et al. Management and outcomes of right atrial isomerism: a 26-year experience. J Am Coll Cardiol 1998;31:1120–1126.
19. Yildirim SV, Tokel K, Varan B, Aslamaci S, Ekici E. Clinical investigations over 13 years to establish the nature of the cardiac defects in patients having abnormalities of lateralization. Cardiol Young 2007;17:275–282.
20. Foerster SR, Gauvreau K, McElhinney DB, Geva T. Importance of totally anomalous pulmonary venous connection and postoperative pulmonary vein stenosis in outcomes of heterotaxy syndrome. Pediatr Cardiol 2008;29:536–544.
21. Koh M, Yagihara T, Uemura H, et al. Biventricular repair for right atrial isomerism. Ann Thorac Surg 2006;81:1808–1816; discussion 1816.
22. Brueckner M. Heterotaxia, congenital heart disease, and primary ciliary dyskinesia. Circulation 2007;115:2793–2795.
23. Price VE, Blanchette VS, Ford-Jones EL. The prevention and management of infections in children with asplenia or hyposplenia. Infect Dis Clin North Am 2007;21:697–710, viii–viix.
24. Kim SJ, Kim WH, Lim HG, et al. Improving results of the Fontan procedure in patients with heterotaxy syndrome. Ann Thorac Surg 2006;82:1245–1251.
25. Stamm C, Friehs I, Duebener LF, et al. Improving results of the modified Fontan operation in patients with heterotaxy syndrome. Ann Thorac Surg 2002;74:1967–1977; discussion 1978.
26. Atz AM, Cohen MS, Sleeper LA, et al. Functional state of patients with heterotaxy syndrome following the Fontan operation. Cardiol Young 2007;17(Suppl. 2):44–53.
27. Wren C, Macartney FJ, Deanfield JE. Cardiac rhythm in atrial isomerism. Am J Cardiol 1987;59:1156–1158.
28. Wu MH, Wang JK, Lin JL, et al. Cardiac rhythm disturbances in patients with left atrial isomerism. Pacing Clin Electrophysiol 2001;24:1631–1638.
29. Cheung YF, Cheng VY, Yung TC, Chau AK. Cardiac rhythm and symptomatic arrhythmia in right atrial isomerism. Am Heart J 2002;144:159–164.
30. Cohen MS, Schultz AH, Tian ZY, et al. Heterotaxy syndrome with functional single ventricle: does prenatal diagnosis improve survival? Ann Thorac Surg 2006;82:1629–1636.

31. Tworetzky W, McElhinney DB, Reddy VM, et al. Improved surgical outcome after fetal diagnosis of hypoplastic left heart syndrome. Circulation 2001;103:1269–1773.
32. Alharthi M, Mookadam F, Collins J, et al. Images in cardiovascular medicine: extracardiac venous heterotaxy syndrome: complete noninvasive diagnosis by multimodality imaging. Circulation 2008;117:e498–e503.
33. Geva T, Vick 3rd GW, Wendt RE, Rokey R. Role of spin echo and cine magnetic resonance imaging in presurgical planning of heterotaxy syndrome: comparison with echocardiography and catheterization. Circulation 1994;90:348–356.
34. Kaulitz R, Ziemer G, Paul T, et al. Fontan-type procedures: residual lesions and late interventions. Ann Thorac Surg 2002;74:778–785.
35. Miura T, Sano T, Matsuda H. Intravascular stenting of systemic venous baffle stenosis after corrective surgery for double outlet right ventricle with left isomerism. Heart 1999;81:218–220.
36. Smith A, Ho SY, Anderson RH, et al. The diverse cardiac morphology seen in hearts with isomerism of the atrial appendages with reference to the disposition of the specialised conduction system. Cardiol Young 2006;16:437–454.
37. Dickinson DF, Wilkinson JL, Anderson KR, et al. The cardiac conduction system in situs ambiguus. Circulation 1979;59:879–885.
38. Ho SY, Fagg N, Anderson RH, et al. Disposition of the atrioventricular conduction tissues in the heart with isomerism of the atrial appendages: its relation to congenital complete heart block. J Am Coll Cardiol 1992;20:904–910.
39. Lopes LM, Tavares GM, Damiano AP, et al. Perinatal outcome of fetal atrioventricular block: one-hundred-sixteen cases from a single institution. Circulation 2008;118:1268–1275.
40. Wu MH, Wang JK, Lin JL, et al. Supraventricular tachycardia in patients with right atrial isomerism. J Am Coll Cardiol 1998;32:773–779.
41. Epstein MR, Saul JP, Weindling SN, et al. Atrioventricular reciprocating tachycardia involving twin atrioventricular nodes in patients with complex congenital heart disease. J Cardiovasc Electrophysiol 2001;12:671–679.
42. Frogoudaki A, Sutton R, Gatzoulis MA. Pacing for adult patients with left atrial isomerism: efficacy and technical considerations. Europace 2003;5:189–193.
43. Siu SC, Sermer M, Colman JM, et al. Prospective multicenter study of pregnancy outcomes in women with heart disease. Circulation 2001;104:515–521.
44. Siu SC, Colman JM, Sorensen S, et al. Adverse neonatal and cardiac outcomes are more common in pregnant women with cardiac disease. Circulation 2002;105:2179–2184.

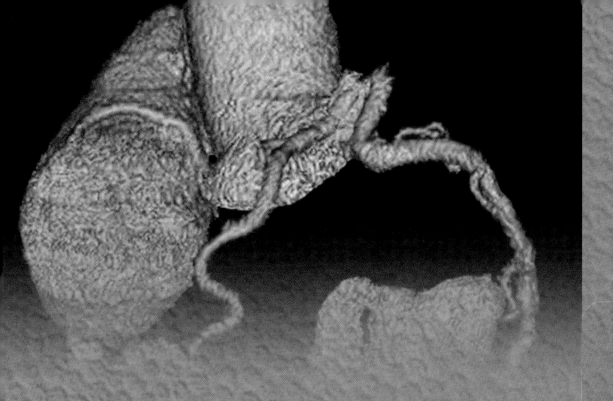

PART
X

Coronary Artery Abnormalities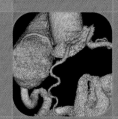

Congenital Anomalies of the Coronary Arteries

HUBERT W. VLIEGEN | ALBERT V. G. BRUSCHKE

Anomalous coronary arteries are frequently seen in conjunction with certain other congenital cardiac defects and may even be considered inherent in some anomalies, such as in transposition of the great vessels. These abnormalities, which may be called secondary coronary artery anomalies, will be discussed in brief at the end of this chapter.

Abnormalities of the origin or the course of coronary arteries in the absence of other congenital cardiac defects, the so-called primary or isolated congenital coronary anomalies, constitute a separate category of congenital cardiac defects.

Primary Congenital Coronary Anomalies

In view of the great "normal" variability of the coronary anatomy the division between normal and abnormal anatomy is subject to a certain degree of subjectivity. Furthermore, some relatively common anomalies are generally believed to have no pathologic significance and have therefore been classified as "normal variations." This has been the basis of a classification system of a working group of the World Health Organization[1] that divides coronary anomalies primarily into two categories (Box 54-1):

1. *Normal variations* or anomalies (benign anomalies)
2. *Abnormal variations*, that is, anomalies generally considered to have clinical relevance

As will be discussed later, the clinical significance of many anomalies is still unclear and therefore the second category may be divided into anomalies that unequivocally have pathologic significance (also called malignant or serious anomalies) and those that may have pathologic significance under certain circumstances (also called potentially malignant or serious anomalies).

Several proposals have been made to classify coronary artery anomalies on an anatomic basis.[2] Undoubtedly a gross anatomic classification, as in part already given above, is useful. However, these anomalies are very rare and therefore proposals for detailed anatomic classification systems comprising many categories may be more confusing than helpful. Most importantly, proper interpretation and evaluation of coronary anomalies is of great clinical importance, irrespective of the merits and limitations of various classification schemes.

PREVALENCE

Most large studies on the occurrence of congenital coronary anomalies are based on reviews of data obtained at coronary angiography. There is considerable variation in reported prevalence that may in part be explained by differences in the definition of abnormal anatomy; however, in all angiographic databases coronary anomalies appear to be rare (Table 54-1).[3–6]

It should also be noted that in the numbers of cases listed in Table 54-1 many minor, or at least benign, variations are included, which constitute the majority of cases. If, for example, in the Cleveland Clinic series, reported by Yamanaka and Hobbs,[5] anomalies such as abnormal origin of the circumflex artery and separate origin of the left anterior descending and left circumflex arteries in the left sinus are excluded, then the prevalence of anomalies drops from 1.33% to 0.56%. Likewise, in the large series reported by Göl and associates[6] if

similar abnormalities are disregarded the prevalence of the remaining anomalies is in the order of 0.2%.

These figures are based on findings in patients who were candidates for coronary arteriography, and it is conceivable that the prevalence in the population at large is different. On the other hand, most patients underwent coronary arteriography for evaluation of coronary atherosclerosis and the presence or suspicion of a congenital coronary anomaly was practically never a selection criterion. It is therefore unlikely that the prevalence of congenital coronary anomalies in this "angiographic population" is much different from the prevalence in the general population. It is hoped that data will become available from screening by noninvasive methods of large asymptomatic populations that will allow a more accurate estimate of the true prevalence.

There may still be some uncertainty about the real prevalence of coronary artery anomalies, but there can be no doubt that these anomalies are rare, which is even more true for (potentially) serious anomalies.

The anomalies that have the greatest practical significance are discussed in the most detail. Because most anomalies are detected at coronary arteriography, focus is placed on angiographic findings but other imaging modalities such as magnetic resonance imaging (MRI)[7] and multislice computed tomographic angiography (CTA) may provide valuable diagnostic information.[8]

ORIGIN OF CORONARY ARTERIES FROM OPPOSITE SINUS

In various respects the most important group of anomalies concerns coronary arteries or coronary artery branches with ectopic origin, that is, arteries or branches arising from the opposite sinus. This is also the group of anomalies that causes most diagnostic problems, particularly with regard to the course of the anomalously originating artery. To facilitate analysis of angiographic recordings of anomalous coronary arteries, Serota and colleagues[9] called attention to a diagnostic characteristic they called "dot and eye." An artery that makes a gradual bend or loop may be seen as an ellipse or "eye" if looked on slightly from above or below, whereas an artery that is seen "on end" will appear as a "dot." A "dot" is often best recognized if the involved coronary artery is not very densely filled with contrast medium, which is usually the case in an aortogram or left ventricular angiogram. Some examples given in the figures illustrate the usefulness of this diagnostic tool.

Anatomy and Physiologic Consequence
Left Coronary Artery Arising from Right Sinus of Valsalva
If the left main coronary artery originates in the right sinus of Valsalva it may, before it divides into the left anterior descending and left circumflex arteries, follow one of the following courses: (1) anterior to the pulmonary artery, the anterior course; (2) between the aorta and pulmonary artery, the interarterial course; (3) posterior to the aorta, the posterior course; or (4) in the interventricular septum, the intraseptal (or intramyocardial) course (Fig. 54-1). The intraseptal course is the most common variant; in this case the left main coronary artery crosses the superior aspect of the crista supraventricularis, then passes a variable distance through the interventricular septum where it gives off one or more septal branches, and finally reaches an epicardial position where

BOX 54-1 NORMAL AND ABNORMAL VARIATIONS OF THE CORONARY ANATOMY

Normal variations include:
- Separate origin of left anterior descending and left circumflex arteries from left sinus of Valsalva
- Large conus branch with separate origin in right sinus
- Abnormal origin of first septal branch (e.g., from first diagonal branch or right coronary artery)
- Dual left anterior descending arteries
- Circumflex originating from right sinus or from proximal right coronary artery and coursing behind aorta
- Most variations in the course of normally originating coronary arteries

Abnormal variations include:
- Origin of coronary artery or main branch from the opposite sinus or from the opposite coronary artery
- Single coronary artery
- Origin of left or right coronary artery from pulmonary artery
- Tunneling or extensive myocardial bridging of a coronary artery

TABLE 54-1	Prevalence of Congenital Coronary Anomalies in Large Series of Coronary Angiographies			
First Author	*Year of Publication*	*No. of Patients*	*Prevalence*	
			No.	%
Wilkins[3]	1988	10,661	83	0.78
Click[4]	1989	24,959	73	0. 30
Yamanaka[5]	1990	126,595	1,686	1.33
Göl[6]	2002	58,023	257	0.44
Total		220,238	2,099	0.95

it divides into the left anterior descending and left circumflex arteries. The most malignant variant is the type in which the left main coronary artery courses between the aorta and pulmonary artery. This variant may be the cause of sudden death, especially after strenuous exercise. Formerly the mechanism underlying sudden death was thought to be compression of the left main coronary artery between the aorta and pulmonary artery. Currently most investigators assume that the sharp angle between the aorta and ectopic left coronary artery with interarterial course, which is associated with a slitlike orifice and easily collapsible proximal portion of the left coronary artery, is responsible. Collapse of the left main coronary artery in a valvelike manner, for example by stretch of the aortic wall during vigorous exercise and concomitant rise of blood pressure, may cause occlusion of the left main coronary artery and eventually death. This is most likely to occur if a relatively long portion of the left main coronary artery is embedded in the aortic wall (Fig. 54-2). In addition, in this situation the origin or proximal portion of the left main coronary artery is often hypoplastic.

An intraseptal, posterior, or anterior course of an ectopic left coronary artery usually has no pathologic significance, but it is uncertain if this is always the case.

In a substantial number of cases the course of the left anterior descending and the left circumflex arteries is different: there may be an intraseptal course of the left anterior descending artery in combination with a posterior course of the left circumflex artery.

Right Coronary Artery Arising from the Left Sinus of Valsalva

If the right coronary artery arises in the left sinus it courses toward the right atrioventricular groove. To reach the atrioventricular groove it may, similar to an ectopic left coronary artery, pass, respectively, anterior to the pulmonary artery (anterior course), between aorta and pulmonary artery (interarterial course), and posterior to the aorta (posterior course). The most frequent and also most malignant variant is the interarterial course. The latter is associated with a sharp angle with the aorta and a slitlike orifice that produce an easily collapsible proximal portion, similar to an ectopic left coronary artery with interarterial course.

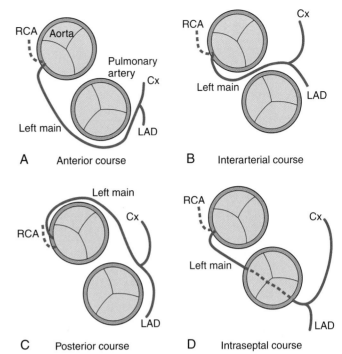

Figure 54-1 Schematic representation of anatomic variations in cases with origin of the left coronary artery from the right sinus of Valsalva. The ectopic artery may course: (**A**) anterior to aorta and pulmonary artery, (**B**) between aorta and pulmonary artery, and (**C**) posterior to the aorta. In addition, an ectopic left coronary artery may follow an intraseptal course in the crista supraventricularis and interventricular septum (**D**). Cx, circumflex artery; LAD, left anterior descending artery, RCA, right coronary artery. *(Adapted with permission from Vliegen HW et al: Congenital Coronary Artery Anomalies. Almere, The Netherlands: PCC; 2006.)*

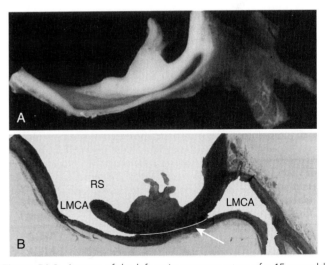

Figure 54-2 Images of the left main coronary artery of a 15-year-old male soccer player who died suddenly during a game. **A,** Transverse section of the aortic root at the commissural level. The anomalous left main coronary artery (LMCA) originates in the right sinus (RS) and shows an intramural aortic course. **B,** The intramural part of the LMCA (*white line and arrow*) is collapsed. *(Adapted with permission from Basso C, Maron BJ, Corrado D, Thiene G. Clinical profile of congenital coronary artery anomalies with origin from the wrong aortic sinus leading to sudden death in young competitive athletes. J Am Coll Cardiol 2000; 35:1493–1501.)*

Clinical Manifestations of Ectopic Coronary Arteries

Often patients with an ectopic coronary artery are asymptomatic and the anomaly remains unrecognized or is found by coincidence if the patient is examined by coronary arteriography for coronary atherosclerosis or valvular disease.

Sudden death may be the only symptom of an ectopic coronary artery. This occurs mainly during episodes of vigorous exercise and is nearly always related to an interarterial course. Basso and associates[10] reviewed 27 cases of sudden death in young athletes with a congenital coronary artery anomaly and found that all patients had an ectopic origin of either the right (n = 4) or left main (n = 23) coronary artery and that each case was characterized by both an acute angled takeoff of the anomalous coronary artery with a slitlike lumen at its point of origin from the wrong sinus and a proximal course between the aorta and pulmonary trunk. Taylor and coworkers[11] reviewed the clinicopathologic records of 242 patients with isolated coronary artery anomalies. Cardiac death had occurred in 142 cases (59%). The anomaly most frequently leading to sudden death was a left main coronary artery originating from the right sinus, and it was noted that in these cases acute angle takeoff of the left main coronary artery and an interarterial course were frequently present. Eckart and associates,[12] who investigated the causes of sudden nontraumatic death in military recruits, found that an ectopic left coronary artery with interarterial course accounted for one third (21 of 64) of the cardiac causes. These figures indicate that this is a serious congenital anomaly, but the absolute incidence of sudden death fortunately is low. The total prevalence of athletic field deaths in high school-age athletes is estimated to be in the range of 1:100,000 to 1:300,000, and in military recruits sudden death due to an anomalous coronary artery was calculated to be 2.2 per 100,000 recruit-years.[13]

There is no consensus about the incidence of premonitory symptoms in patients who eventually are subject to sudden death. Most reports indicate that premonitory symptoms are rare. However, Basso and associates[10] noted that in 10 of the 27 cases they studied premonitory symptoms, such as syncope, palpitations, or chest pain, had been reported. The occurrence of such symptoms in young athletes warrants a cardiac examination with special attention for ectopic coronary arteries.

The electrocardiogram is usually normal. Exercise testing may reveal evidence of ischemia if the proximal left main coronary artery is hypoplastic, but a normal exercise test has little predictive value with regard to the occurrence of future events, which is not surprising in view of the possibility of a suddenly collapsing proximal portion of the ectopic artery.

Diagnosis of an Ectopic Coronary Artery

If an ectopic coronary artery is found unexpectedly at coronary arteriography its course in relation to aorta, pulmonary artery, and interventricular septum should be determined. This is practically always possible solely on the basis of the coronary arteriogram, if adequate recordings in left and right anterior oblique projections, preferably without caudal or cranial angulation, are available. Unfortunately the quality of the angiographic recordings is sometimes less than optimal because the angiographer may not be familiar with the abnormal anatomic situation or may be unable to engage and adequately opacify the ectopic artery.

Angiographic characteristics listed in Box 54-2 are helpful to determine the course of an ectopic left coronary artery (Fig. 54-3).

Management

Most patients with ectopic origin of a coronary artery require no therapy and should not be restricted in their physical activities. However, ectopic origin of a coronary artery with interarterial course is considered the most malignant congenital coronary anomaly and usually requires surgical intervention. Surgical intervention is mandatory if the patient has symptoms that might be interpreted as premonitory symptoms of sudden death. The most threatening symptom is syncope during vigorous exercise but angina-like chest pain and ventricular arrhythmias may also be warnings. There is no consensus about the

---

BOX 54-2 ANGIOGRAPHIC CHARACTERISTICS OF AN ECTOPIC LEFT CORONARY ARTERY

- An *anterior course* produces in the right anterior oblique projection an anterior and cranial loop of the left main coronary artery, similar to a large conus branch. The left main coronary artery then divides into the left anterior descending and the left circumflex arteries. This configuration produces an "eye" between the left main artery and left circumflex artery.
- An *interarterial course* is characterized by a left main coronary artery that in the right anterior oblique projection appears to be short and is seen on end where it passes between the aorta and pulmonary artery. This produces a "dot" on the left ventricular angiogram.
- The *posterior course* resembles the angiographic configuration of a circumflex artery originating in the right sinus. In a right anterior oblique projection the left main coronary artery courses posterior and caudal to turn around the aortic root. Where the left main courses around the posterior aspect of the aorta it is seen in RAO projection on end, which produces a "dot" on the left ventricular angiogram or aortogram. Careful motion study may reveal that from the left main coronary artery first the left circumflex artery and then the left anterior descending artery is opacified.
- The *intraseptal* variant shows in right anterior oblique projection a typical "hammock" configuration in which the left main coronary artery passes through the septum. Usually a first septal branch, which originates in the left main coronary artery close to the origin and proximal from the division into the left anterior descending and left circumflex arteries, is visible (see Fig. 54-3).

Multislice CTA and MRI may show clearly the three-dimensional (3D) aspects but are rarely necessary to determine the course of an ectopic left coronary artery detected at coronary arteriography.

---

indications for intervention in asymptomatic patients. If a large left coronary artery is involved there may be an indication for intervention irrespective of the presence of symptoms, especially if the patient regularly performs vigorous exercise. Exercise testing may be helpful in asymptomatic patients, but the absence of inducible ischemia does not necessarily mean that there is no indication for surgery.

When the aberrant artery is embedded in the aortic wall (Fig. 54-4), which appears to be usually the case, the preferred surgical procedure is "unroofing" (Fig. 54-5). This technique may be used for both an abnormal right or left coronary artery and creates a large neo-orifice in the appropriate sinus. After the procedure the ectopic artery arises in a normal fashion perpendicularly from the aortic root. If unroofing is not feasible, then coronary bypass grafting may be the best option.

When a high profile athlete has suddenly died, the question has been raised whether all athletes engaged in top level sports should be screened for coronary artery abnormalities (e.g., by transthoracic echocardiography). Because of the low prevalence of ectopic coronary arteries with interarterial course this may not be necessary. However, Brothers and coworkers[14] found evidence for a genetic link for this anomaly; therefore, screening of first-degree relatives may be advisable, especially of relatives who regularly perform competitive sports activities.

ANOMALOUS ORIGIN OF A CORONARY ARTERY FROM THE PULMONARY ARTERY

One or more coronary arteries may originate from the pulmonary artery. An anomalous origin of the left coronary artery from the pulmonary artery (ALCAPA, Fig. 54-6) is seen in approximately 1 in 300,000 live births. An anomalous origin of the right coronary artery, left anterior descending artery, or left circumflex artery from the pulmonary artery is extremely rare. The names of Bland, White, and Garland are associated with ALCAPA because these authors were the first to describe the symptoms of this anomaly in a case report published in 1933. In ALCAPA, the left coronary artery is a small vessel with a thin wall whereas the right coronary artery is large, dilated, and

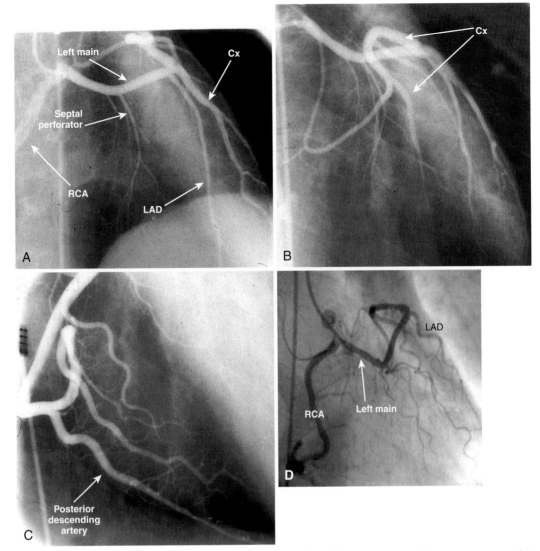

Figure 54-3 Two cases of ectopic left coronary artery with intraseptal course. **A** to **C,** A typical ectopic left coronary artery with intraseptal course, viewed in a right anterior oblique projection. In **A** some craniocaudal tilt was applied that demonstrates the position of the septal perforators nicely, whereas the circumflex artery (Cx) is better depicted in **B**. The distal right coronary artery (RCA) in a right anterior oblique projection is shown in **C**; the large posterior descending artery explains why the left anterior descending artery (LAD) is relatively small. This patient underwent coronary arteriography in the course of evaluation for ventricular tachycardias. **D,** An ectopic left coronary artery with intraseptal course (in the right anterior oblique projection) in another patient who underwent evaluation for ventricular arrhythmias. *(Adapted with permission from Vliegen HW et al. Congenital Coronary Artery Anomalies. Almere, The Netherlands, PCC; 2006.)*

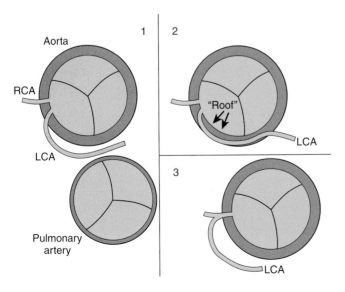

Figure 54-4 Schematic drawing of potential consequences of origin of left main coronary artery from the right sinus with interarterial course of the left coronary artery. In panel 1 the left main coronary artery runs almost entirely outside of the aortic wall. In panel 2 the left main, as is usually the case, follows over a certain distance an intramural course that creates an easily collapsible "roof," which may cause sudden occlusion and death. In panel 3 the left main coronary artery arises from the proximal RCA, which appears to be a less hazardous situation. *(Adapted with permission from Vliegen HW et al. Congenital Coronary Artery Anomalies. Almere, The Netherlands, PCC; 2006.)*

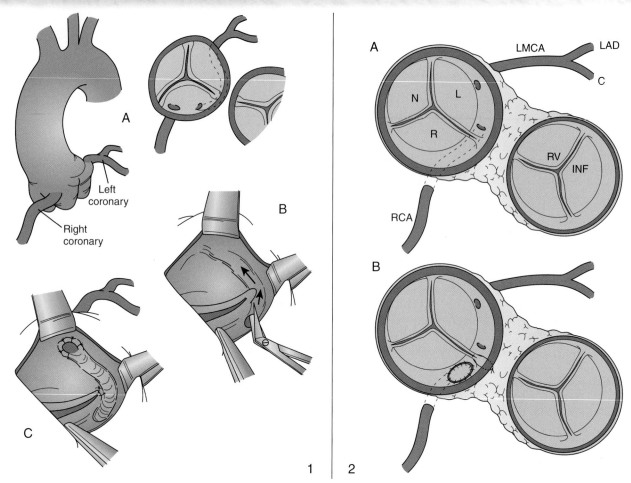

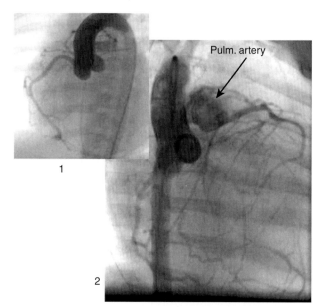

Figure 54-5 "Unroofing" of, respectively, ectopic left coronary artery (**1**) and ectopic right coronary artery (**2**). The intramural portion of the aberrant artery is unroofed, and a neo-orifice is created in the appropriate sinus. Because of the unroofing procedure sometimes re-suspension of the commissure between left and right aortic cusps is required. (*1 redrawn from Frommelt PC et al. Prospective echocardiographic diagnosis and surgical repair of anomalous origin of a coronary artery from the opposite sinus with an interarterial course. J Am Coll Cardiol 2003; 42:148–154; 2 from Nelson-Piercy C, et al: Aberrant origin of the right coronary artery as a potential cause of sudden death: successful anatomical correction. Br Heart J 1990; 644:208–210.*)

Figure 54-6 Anomalous left coronary artery arising from the pulmonary artery (ALCAPA) in a 5-month-old boy. An aortogram first shows opacification of the right coronary artery but no opacification of the left coronary artery (panel 1). Later (panel 2) the left coronary artery fills by collateral arteries from the right coronary artery and drains into the pulmonary artery. (*Adapted with permission from Vliegen HW et al. Congenital Coronary Artery Anomalies. Almere, The Netherlands, PCC; 2006.*)

tortuous. The hypoperfused but viable part of the myocardium shows hypertrophy. The endocardium often shows fibroelastosis.

In the neonate the initial high pulmonary pressure maintains adequate perfusion via the anomalous artery. The low saturation of the pulmonary blood is usually well tolerated. The decline in pulmonary pressure leads to a reduction of the flow in the anomalous coronary artery. Subsequently, myocardial perfusion is provided solely by the right coronary artery and eventually the direction of flow in the left coronary artery reverses, that is, the direction of flow is now toward the pulmonary artery; in other words the left coronary artery drains into the pulmonary artery. This results in ischemia unless adequate collateral circulation has developed. In principle, collateral arteries have a beneficial effect on myocardial perfusion, but in these cases the drawback is that increasing collateral flow entails increasing shunting toward the pulmonary artery, resulting in increasing coronary steal.

Diagnosis

Most instances of this defect have been found in neonates who had died in the first year of life. However, survival into adult life without treatment is possible, and this appears to occur in approximately 15% of cases. Infants with this anomaly appear normal at birth and during the first month of life. Usually signs or symptoms are present for several weeks preceding a terminal event. Symptoms are heart failure, failure to thrive, and respiratory infections, almost invariably occurring in the first year of life.

Occasionally the anomaly is first detected in adult patients who present with dyspnea, angina pectoris, or life-threatening rhythm disturbances. Sudden death without warning symptoms has also been reported. The chest radiograph usually shows cardiomegaly and frequently pulmonary congestion. The electrocardiogram may show anterior or anterolateral myocardial infarction or evidence of ischemia.

The diagnosis may be confirmed by CT, but coronary arteriography is required to demonstrate more clearly the development of collateral arteries. Frequently there is evidence of (severe) mitral regurgitation due to papillary muscle dysfunction.

Management

Surgery for ALCAPA was already performed in the early days of heart surgery and initially consisted of ligation of the anomalous left coronary artery or closure of its orifice in the pulmonary artery. This was meant to abolish coronary steal and thus raise coronary perfusion pressure. A similar but percutaneous technique, that is, transcatheter occlusion of the orifice in the pulmonary artery using a vascular plug, has recently been reported and may be an option if there is a well-developed collateral network and surgery is contraindicated.[15]

At present, surgical repair tries to restore a dual coronary artery system. This may be accomplished by several techniques: (1) a connection of the left coronary artery with the aorta is established by re-implantation in the sinus of Valsalva; (2) bypass grafting and ligation of the orifice in the pulmonary artery; (3) subclavian artery interposition and ligation of the orifice; and (4) creation of an intrapulmonary tunnel from the aortopulmonary window to the aortic sinus (Takeuchi procedure). Mitral valve repair may be needed if mitral regurgitation is severe. Surgical repair may improve left ventricular function and myocardial perfusion considerably, but both generally remain impaired, even if the anatomic result of surgery is good. The earlier the patient is operated on, the better is the recovery of left ventricular function.[16]

CORONARY ARTERIOVENOUS SHUNTS

Anatomy and Physiology

Arteriovenous shunts are abnormal connections between coronary arteries and a compartment of the venous side of the heart. The abnormal connection may originate in the right or left coronary artery, or, more rarely, multiple shunts originating in both arteries may be present. The shunt may drain into the right atrium, the coronary sinus, the right ventricle, or the pulmonary artery. Often the shunt volume is small and hemodynamically insignificant, but occasionally the shunt volume is large enough to cause right-sided heart volume overload. The shunt may cause coronary "steal" because it provides a low resistance pathway that may divert blood from the coronary circulation. However, usually the flow capacity of the proximal coronary arteries is large enough to adapt to the extra flow and therefore the steal phenomenon is only significant in the presence of a large shunt or of an already compromised coronary circulation (Fig. 54-7). Large shunts are often accompanied by marked, sometimes aneurysmal, dilation of the coronary artery in which the shunt originates.

Diagnosis

Often these shunts are asymptomatic and found by chance in patients undergoing coronary arteriography for other reasons. Symptoms of sizable shunts include angina pectoris (often atypical), dyspnea, palpitations, and peripheral edema.

Coronary arteriovenous shunts, like other arteriovenous shunts, may produce continuous murmurs. These murmurs may lead to a presumptive diagnosis of patent ductus arteriosus but, depending on the location of the shunt, the location of the maximum intensity of the murmurs is often different. The chest radiograph is usually unremarkable but may show cardiomegaly and occasionally a local bulge indicative of a dilated coronary artery.

The electrocardiogram shows no specific changes.

Management

Small coronary arteriovenous shunts require no therapy, but prophylaxis against subacute bacterial endocarditis is advisable if the shunt volume is more than minimal.

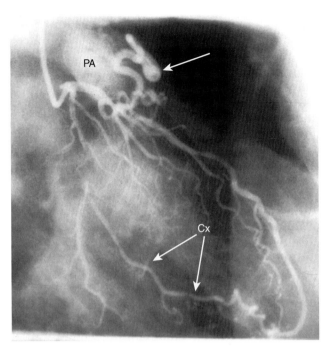

Figure 54-7 Arteriovenous shunt to pulmonary artery. Small arteriovenous shunts or fistulas are frequently detected unexpectedly. This figure shows a left coronary artery in a right anterior oblique projection. The patient underwent coronary angiography for angina pectoris, and the main obstructive lesion was an occlusion of the circumflex artery (Cx), which is filled in retrograde fashion by collateral vessels arising from a moderately narrowed left anterior descending artery. In addition, an abnormal artery (*arrow*) arises from the proximal left anterior descending artery and terminates as a small shunt to the pulmonary artery (PA). Probably this shunt has no hemodynamic significance, although a "steal" effect to the left anterior descending arterial territory, which in this case includes myocardium normally supplied by the circumflex artery, cannot be ruled out. (*Adapted with permission from Vliegen HW et al. Congenital Coronary Artery Anomalies. Almere, The Netherlands, PCC; 2006.*)

Large arteriovenous shunts that have significant hemodynamic consequences or which, under special circumstances, cause coronary steal require closure. In general, shunts with a pulmonary-to-systemic flow ($\dot{Q}p:\dot{Q}s$) less than 1.5 require no closure and shunts with a $\dot{Q}p:\dot{Q}s$ greater than 2.0 should be treated. Traditionally, closure has been achieved surgically, but, more recently, good results have been reported from transcatheter occlusion using embolic coil devices or covered stents.

Secondary Congenital Coronary Anomalies

Secondary congenital coronary artery anomalies are anomalies in patients with congenital heart disease. The course of the coronary arteries is especially important in patients with congenital heart disease who require surgery.[8,17] The presence of an anomaly may require modification of the surgical procedure. We will discuss the major congenital defects that are associated with coronary anomalies. Currently the coronary anatomy can be accurately evaluated with multislice CT.

TETRALOGY OF FALLOT

Several variants of tetralogy of Fallot are possible. Of major importance is an anomalous vessel that courses over the right ventricular outflow tract. Such a vessel may be damaged during surgery to relieve right ventricular outflow tract obstruction.

Frequently observed anomalies are:
- A large conus branch from the right coronary artery or right sinus
- A left anterior descending artery from the right coronary artery or right sinus
- A single coronary artery from the right sinus with a left anterior descending artery running over the right ventricular outflow tract

TRANSPOSITION OF THE GREAT ARTERIES

The anatomy of the coronary arteries is highly variable in patients with TGA. In complete TGA the most common pattern is a right coronary artery from the posterior sinus and the left coronary artery from the left coronary sinus. The anatomic patterns that are associated with increased operative risks during surgery are an inverted pattern, a single coronary artery, and an intramural coronary artery.

BICUSPID AORTIC VALVE

The coronary artery pattern follows the location of the cusps. In anteroposterior cusps, both coronary arteries originate in the anterior cusp. In right-to-left cusps, the right coronary artery origins in the right cusp and the left coronary artery comes from the left cusp.

TRUNCUS ARTERIOSUS

Truncus arteriosus is frequently associated with coronary artery anomalies. The most important is a high and posterior origin of the left coronary artery just below the pulmonary artery origin. This anatomy complicates surgical repair and may result in postoperative stenosis or occlusion.

PULMONARY ATRESIA WITH INTACT VENTRICULAR SEPTUM

Persistent sinusoidal–coronary artery connections in the right ventricle may be observed. Coronary arteries involved show characteristic histopathologic changes of myointimal hyperplasia, which is thought to be a consequence of repeated injury from the high-pressure turbulent right ventricular systolic flow.

REFERENCES

1. James TN, Bruschke AVG, Böthig S, et al. Report of WHO/ISFC Task Force on nomenclature of coronary arteriograms. Circulation 1986;74:451A–455A.
2. Angelini P, Velasco JA, Flamm S. Coronary anomalies: incidence, pathophysiology, and clinical relevance. Circulation 2002;105:2449–2454.
3. Wilkins CE, Betancourt B, Mathur VS, et al. Coronary artery anomalies: a review of more than 10,000 patients from the Clayton Cardiovascular Laboratories. Tex Heart Inst J 1988;15:166–173.
4. Click RL, Holmes DR, Vlietstra RE, et al., the participants of the Coronary Artery Surgery Study (CASS). Anomalous coronary arteries: location, degree of atherosclerosis and effect on survival—a report from the Coronary Artery Surgery Study. J Am Coll Cardiol 1989;13:531–537.
5. Yamanaka O, Hobbs RE. Coronary artery anomalies in 126,595 patients undergoing coronary arteriography. Cathet Cardiovasc Diagn 1990;21:28–40.
6. Göl MK, Ozatik MA, Kunt A, et al. Coronary anomalies in adult patients. Med Sci Monit 2002;8:CR636–CR641.
7. Vliegen HW, Doornbos J, de Roos A, et al. Value of fast gradient echo magnetic resonance angiography as an adjunct coronary arteriography in detecting and confirming the course of clinical significant coronary artery anomalies. Am J Cardiol 1997;79:773–776.
8. Goo HW, Seo DM, Yun TJ, et al. Coronary artery anomalies and clinically important anatomy in patients with congenital heart disease: multislice CT findings. Pediatr Radiol 2009;39:265–273.
9. Serota H, Barth CW, Seuc CA, et al. Rapid identification of the course of anomalous coronary arteries in adults: the "Dot and Eye" method. Am J Cardiol 1990;65:891–898.
10. Basso C, Maron BJ, Corrado D, Thiene G. Clinical profile of congenital coronary artery anomalies with origin from the wrong aortic sinus leading to sudden death in young competitive athletes. J Am Coll Cardiol 2000;35:1493–1501.
11. Taylor AJ, Rogan KM, Virmani R. Sudden cardiac death associated with isolated congenital coronary artery anomalies. J Am Coll Cardiol 1992;20:640–647.
12. Eckart RE, Scoville SL, Campbell CL, et al. Sudden death in young adults: a 25-year review of autopsies in military recruits. Ann Intern Med 2004;141:829–834.
13. Maron BJ, Thompson PD, Puffer JC, et al. Cardiovascular preparticipation screening of competitive athletes: a statement for health professionals from the Sudden Death Committee (Clinical Cardiology) and Congenital Cardiac Defects Committee (Cardiovascular Disease in the Young), American Heart Association. Circulation 1996;94:850–856.
14. Brothers JA, Stephens P, Gaynor JW, et al. Anomalous aortic origin of a coronary artery with an interarterial course: should family screening be routine? J Am Coll Cardiol 2008;51:2062–2064.
15. Collins N, Colman J, Benson L, et al. Successful percutaneous treatment of anomalous left coronary artery from pulmonary artery. Int J Cardiol 2007;122:e29–e31.
16. Michielon G, Di Carlo D, Brancaccio G, et al. Anomalous coronary artery origin from the pulmonary artery: correlation between surgical timing and left ventricular function recovery. Ann Thorac Surg 2003;76:581–588.
17. Mawson JB. Congenital heart defects and coronary anatomy. Tex Heart Inst J 2002;29:279–289.

55

Kawasaki Disease

KOICHIRO NIWA | SHIGERU TATENO

Definition and Morphology

Tomisaku Kawasaki first reported Kawasaki disease (KD) in 1967.[1] At first, KD was thought to be an acute and self-limiting febrile disorder; however, the first nationwide survey in Japan revealed that 1.7% of patients had died of acute cardiac failure, with necropsy showing coronary arteritis accompanied by aneurysms and thrombotic occlusion.[2] KD is an acute febrile multisystem vasculitic syndrome of unknown etiology occurring predominantly in infants and young children and involving small and medium-sized arteries, particularly the coronary arteries.[1,2] Although based entirely on clinical features, the diagnosis is easy when characteristic cutaneous and mucosal manifestations are expressed.[1–3]

Genetics, Epidemiology, and Etiology

A fascinating constellation of signs designated as KD was noted initially in Japan and later in many other countries. More than 200,000 cases have been recognized in Japanese children. Now more than 10,000 new patients per year in Japan develop KD and, therefore, 181.1 per 100,000 children develop KD.[4] It affects children primarily in the first 5 years of life, although cases can also occur in older children and, rarely, in adults. The preponderance of males is notable (male-to-female ratio of 1.5:1). Furthermore, complications and serious and fatal cases of KD are much more common in males than females.[5] With longer follow-up, eventual recurrence rates reach 3% or more. It is documented that secondary sibling cases occur in about 1% of all cases. In Japan, the nationwide epidemics of KD have been recognized in several different years.

The etiology of KD remains unknown. Many investigators believe that KD has an infectious cause or is the result of an immune response to an infectious agent. A wide variety of microorganisms have been proposed as causative agents with little or no evidence of an etiologic relationship. It has been suggested that KD may be caused by bacterial superantigens.[6] The agent responsible for KD and the mechanism by which such agents lead to coronary vasculitis in a minority of affected patients remains to be elucidated.[7,8] Investigations have demonstrated immunologic derangement in the serum of KD patients, including abnormalities in T-cell population and increase in circulating cytokine levels.[9] The expanding body of descriptive immunologic data is of interest but does not point to any specific mechanism of immunopathogenesis. The factors leading to coronary vasculitis are still unknown, but there is certainly involvement of activated endothelial cells, monocytes/macrophages, cytotoxic lymphocytes, and IgA plasma cells.[10,11]

Early Presentation and Management

Acute systematic vasculitis usually subsides within several weeks or months after onset. KD is normally acute and self-limiting; however, cardiac damage sustained when KD is active and severe may be progressive. The diagnosis rests entirely on clinical grounds, even in adults: there is a characteristic combination of prolonged high fever, multiform rash, stomatitis, conjunctivitis, erythema of the hands and feet with characteristic late peeling of the digits, and lymphadenopathy (Box 55-1).[1,3] There are no specific laboratory tests diagnostic of the disease, but supportive evidence includes marked thrombocytosis. However, thrombocytopenia is one of the risk factors for future development of coronary artery aneurysm (CAA) and acute myocardial infarction (AMI).[12] Two-dimensional (2D) echocardiography can accurately demonstrate dilation and aneurysms of the proximal coronary arteries as well as specific signs of cardiac inflammation, including abnormal ventricular wall motion, pericardial effusion, mitral regurgitation (MR), and diminished cardiac function. From multiple studies, it is clear that 15% to 30% of patients who do not receive intravenous gammaglobulin (IVIG) develop CAA detectable by angiography, 2D echocardiography, magnetic resonance imaging (MRI),[13,14] or multislice computed tomography (CT).[15] These abnormalities may appear between 7 days and as late as 4 weeks after onset. After the clinical diagnosis in the acute stage of illness, the treatment of choice is IVIG. Efficacy has been demonstrated in several studies.[16] The risk of CAA now has been lowered to less than about 5% when IVIG is given during the first 10 days of illness. However, for infants, even with IVIG treatment, the risk of coronary abnormalities at 8 weeks is still 15%. Pericarditis and pericardial effusion are observed in approximately 15% of cases, and myocarditis occurs in about 40%. However, these complications are usually mild and subside after the acute phase of illness. Most valvular abnormalities during the acute phase are due to valvulitis leading to regurgitation and involve especially the mitral and rarely the aortic valve. These abnormalities usually disappear several months after onset. However, MR due to papillary muscle dysfunction is progressive and will become an important late complication.[17]

Salicylates (aspirin, acetylsalicylic acid) are used as adjunctive therapy during the early acute phase because coagulation activation has been shown to occur in the first 3 weeks of the illness. Corticosteroids can be used and are effective in some cases[18]; however, currently corticosteroids are not established as the initial treatment. Once symptoms of acute inflammation have subsided, single doses of aspirin, 3 to 5 mg/kg/day, are used until 2D echocardiography and/or coronary angiography have confirmed the absence of dilated or aneurysmal coronary arteries approximately 4 to 8 weeks after the onset of illness. In the presence of persistent coronary abnormalities, low-dose aspirin is continued indefinitely. Giant aneurysms, defined as lesions exceeding 8 mm in diameter, are associated more frequently with myocardial ischemia, infarction, and/or death. Although more aggressive therapy would seem indicated (e.g., warfarin, dipyridamole), no single approach has been universally accepted.

Adult-Onset Kawasaki Disease

KD is seen almost exclusively in children. Reports of adult cases are viewed with skepticism, although nearly 60 adult cases have been reported in the English literature using the accepted diagnostic criteria. In adults with KD, the incidence of specific diagnostic criteria is similar to that in children.[19,20] Sterile pyuria is more common in children than adults, whereas arthralgia, gastrointestinal complications, and liver function abnormalities are more common among adults.[19] Electrocardiographic abnormalities occur in about the same percentage of adults as children, as does the reported incidence of heart failure. The incidence of CAA in adults is reported to be lower than in children (5 in 57 reported adult cases).[20] The other reason for a lower incidence of CAA in adults may reflect the difficulty in visualizing the adult coronary arteries with transthoracic echocardiography; this may underestimate the true incidence. There are no published guidelines from consensus panels on the treatment of KD in the adult. The majority of adults have been treated with aspirin therapy in the manner recommended for children. There are more than five reported cases in adults of treatment with IVIG; these patients demonstrated a clinical response and shortened recovery time without coronary involvement, similar to the experience in many children. Although case reports described the benefit of IVIG therapy in adults with acute KD, there are no controlled studies regarding the optimal dose, timing, and clinical benefit of IVIG therapy in adults. Internists treating adults with infectious conditions must be aware of this disease.

Late Outcome and Long-Term Management

The important late cardiovascular complications in KD are shown in Box 55-2. Although a mortality rate for KD of approximately 2% was reported in the mid 1970s, this has dropped to approximately 0.1% recently.[21] This improvement coincides with the widespread use of aspirin, increased recognition of KD, and greater awareness of cardiac complications, leading to more intensive follow-up and better supportive care. Ten- to 20-year follow-up studies of KD are now being conducted.[21] These demonstrate that large and medium aneurysms may progress to stenosis, leading to the risk of AMI, sudden death, and myocardial ischemia.

It is reasonable to divide late outcomes into three different groups depending on coronary abnormalities observed in the acute phase: (1) patients with no evidence of coronary artery abnormalities, (2) patients with transient or small (<5 mm diameter) or medium (5 to 8 mm) CAA, and (3) patients with large and giant (>8 mm) CAA.

Because there are no criteria for the size of CAA in adults with KD, the definitions of small, medium, and large are taken from the pediatric guidelines.[11]

PATIENTS WITH NO EVIDENCE OF CORONARY ARTERY ABNORMALITIES

For patients without CAA, there is no need for aspirin or other antiplatelet medication 6 to 8 weeks after onset or for restriction of physical activities beyond the first 6 to 8 weeks. Cardiovascular risk assessment and counseling should be performed at 5-year intervals.

To date, there is no evidence of significant cardiovascular sequelae in patients without any evidence of coronary artery abnormalities in the first month after onset. A limited number of postmortem studies of adults with a history of KD or compatible clinical illness have been performed.[22] Fatty deposits and advanced changes similar to

atherosclerotic disease have been found,[22–24] raising the important issue of whether patients with KD are at an increased risk of earlier or more severe atherosclerosis. There may be long-lasting changes in endothelial function in the vessels, even in those with no evidence of coronary artery abnormalities in the acute and subacute phase. Newer imaging methods such as tissue Doppler imaging, intravascular ultrasonography, and MRI have demonstrated coronary intimal changes in patients with no history of abnormalities in the acute phase.[23–25] It is unclear what is the long-term significance of these persistent, pervasive, vascular abnormalities in those thought to have escaped coronary abnormalities in the acute phase. The prevalence of the disease and its uncertain long-term effects suggest that ongoing follow-up may be necessary. The question of whether childhood KD increases the long-term risk for coronary atherosclerosis will only be answered by long-term prospective cohort studies.[22,26,27]

PATIENTS WITH TRANSIENT OR SMALL OR MEDIUM CORONARY ARTERY ANEURYSMS

Patients with CAAs that do not include large or giant aneurysms should be started on long-term therapy with aspirin, 3 to 5 mg/kg/day, at least until resolution of abnormalities and preferably indefinitely. Regression of small aneurysms appears to be common.[21] Such patients should be observed at yearly cardiac evaluations. There is no need for restriction of physical activities beyond the first 6 to 8 weeks in patients younger than age 11 years, and exercise restrictions should be guided by the results of stress testing in patients 11 to 20 years of age and, if necessary, older. Angiography is recommended if noninvasive tests suggest ischemia.

PATIENTS WITH LARGE AND GIANT CORONARY ARTERY ANEURYSMS OR AFTER CORONARY ARTERY OCCLUSION

The risk of giant aneurysms, estimated at affecting 3% to 7% untreated patients, has been lowered dramatically by the administration of IVIG. For those with acute coronary artery abnormalities, the greatest risk is in children with large aneurysms, who are at risk of myocardial ischemia, infarction, and sudden death, particularly in the first year after onset. In the first 2 years after onset, regression of aneurysms with restoration of a normal lumen size occurs in one third to one half of such cases. Regression of the internal lumen of the aneurysm to normal diameter may occur by intimal proliferation or by thrombus organization and recanalization. These patients have persistent functional and structural abnormalities but appear to have a good short- to mid-term prognosis without evidence of ischemia. Previously aneurysmal segments are known to have an abnormal functional response with decreased ability to dilate in response to exercise or pharmacologic agents.[23] Most patients with regressed aneurysms do not progress to stenosis, but tortuosity and coronary thrombosis may still occur.[21] Intravascular ultrasonography shows thickened arteries and coronary calcification present in the areas of regressed aneurysm. These changes resemble those of atherosclerosis.[23] There is no need for restriction of physical activities in patients without stress test abnormalities. Angiography is indicated if electrocardiographic or stress test abnormalities develop.

Those with persistent large or giant CAA are known to be at risk ultimately of the development of hemodynamically significant stenoses with resultant myocardial ischemia and the need for medical and catheter/surgical intervention.[21,28] The risk of developing significant stenosis in the area of a large CAA shows a steady rise over 15 to 20 years of observation.[21] These markedly abnormal vessels are subject to calcification and thrombosis and may cause myocardial ischemia or infarction. Therapy with aspirin, 3 to 5 mg/kg/day, with or without dipyridamole, 2 to 6 mg/kg day, is indicated and should be continued indefinitely. All such patients should be under the care of a cardiologist with extensive experience in managing patients with KD. Anticoagulant therapy with warfarin can be added, especially during the first 2 years after disease onset. Follow-up at 6 months should include an electrocardiogram and echocardiogram, with annual stress test and myocardial perfusion scan. Angiography should be performed initially to define the extent

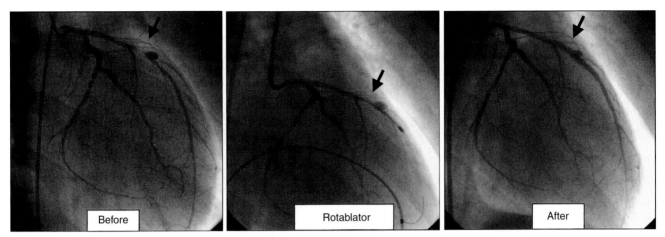

Figure 55-1 Coronary arteriography in an 18-year-old man who had left anterior coronary artery (LAD) aneurysm with severe LAD stenosis and calcification. Catheter intervention (rotablator) was performed. **Left,** Appearance before intervention. Note severe LAD stenosis (*arrow*). **Middle,** Appearance during rotablator procedure. **Right,** Appearance after intervention. The LAD was dilated with a stent after intervention. *(Courtesy Masatake Shirai, MD.)*

of disease and whenever symptoms or stress tests indicate myocardial ischemia. Physical activity should be regulated on the basis of stress test results and the severity of the coronary artery stenosis by angiography.

Patients with obstructive lesions or signs of ischemia may need to be evaluated for possible catheter/surgical intervention.[28,29] Balloon angioplasty, rotablator angioplasty, stent implantation (Fig. 55-1),[23,28] coronary artery bypass grafting (CABG),[29] and cardiac transplantation have all been used for patients with serious coronary artery pathology. MR due to coronary ischemia and papillary muscle dysfunction may persist and occasionally requires mitral valve replacement.[18] In adults with KD after MI, angiotensin-converting enzyme inhibitors and/or beta-adrenergic receptor blockers can be useful to prevent further progression of myocardial damage or MR, but there is no evidence of efficacy of these medications at present.

MYOCARDIAL INFARCTION

The most common cause of death in KD is AMI. A collaborative study in Japan involving 195 patients found that the first infarction was fatal in 22% and asymptomatic in 37%.[30] It was most common in the first year after onset of illness but not rare in adult patients with a history of childhood KD. Fatal infarctions tended to involve the left main trunk and left anterior descending artery. Survivors were most likely to have right coronary artery involvement. Around half of survivors after an AMI had one or more complications, such as ventricular dysfunction, MR, or arrhythmia. In some patients with an occluded coronary artery with ischemia, heparin and exercise therapy can be effective in increasing collateralization and alleviating myocardial ischemia in the collateral-dependent region (Fig. 55-2).[31]

CORONARY ARTERY SEQUELAE

Because the cardiac complications of KD were not familiar among pediatricians in the 1960s and 1970s, most patients were not observed by cardiologists. Recently there have been several reports of patients with childhood KD who presented with AMI, ischemic heart disease, significant arrhythmia, or congestive heart failure in their 20s or 30s. These symptoms may be sequelae from KD. The possible contribution of antecedent KD to the genesis of cardiovascular disease in adults was investigated by Kato and colleagues.[32] A survey of adult cardiologists throughout Japan identified 130 adult patients with CAA, 21 of whom (mean age 34 years) had a history compatible with KD in childhood. These patients had severe clinical coronary artery disease with an AMI, angina, MR, arrhythmias, or congestive heart failure or needed CABG. The investigators suspected that many of the remaining 109 patients might have had antecedent KD, but information regarding childhood

illness was unclear or absent. This study indicated that the coronary artery sequelae of KD might be an important cause of ischemic heart disease in adults.

A study by Burns and associates[33] documented coronary artery involvement in adolescent and young adults attributable to antecedent KD in childhood by respective review of cases reported in the literature on adult coronary artery disease. Of 74 patients with presumed late sequelae of KD (mean age of presentation 27 years), chest pain or AMI was present in 61%, arrhythmia in 11%, and sudden death in 16%, with symptoms precipitated by exercise in 82%. CAA was identified in 93% of patients, with coronary occlusion in 66%. Necropsy findings included CAA in 100% and coronary artery occlusion in 72%. The authors concluded that KD in childhood could cause permanent coronary artery damage that may remain clinically silent until adulthood. From these reports, a history of KD should be sought in adult patients with CAA in the absence of atherosclerotic risk and/or generalized atherosclerotic disease.

OUTPATIENT ASSESSMENT OF THE ADULT WITH KAWASAKI DISEASE

Assessment of the Adult with KD includes the following:
- Electrocardiography: to evaluate ischemia or infarction
- Exercise stress testing for documented or suspected coronary artery disease
- Radioisotope myocardial perfusion scintigraphy *or*
- Echocardiography: for regional wall assessment; when this is combined with stress testing or dobutamine there appears to be a higher sensitivity for detecting ischemia.
- MRI: for detection of AMI, wall motion abnormalities, and wall thinning in previous infarction[14,34]
- Serial stress tests and myocardial imaging: mandatory in the management of patients with KD and coronary artery stenosis to determine the need for coronary angiography and for surgical or transcatheter intervention
- Serial angiography: in patients with CAA without stenosis for detection of progression of coronary artery stenosis
- Transthoracic echocardiography: with inclusion of dobutamine stress echocardiography may be sufficiently sensitive or specific in detecting adult coronary artery abnormalities[24,25]
- Transesophageal echocardiography: may be useful but would also probably not be adequate as a screening test for coronary lesions
- MRI or multislice CT: can be useful to visualize CAA and evaluate coronary flow reserve[24,35]
- Coronary angiography: still the gold standard for assessing the level of risk in an individual patient

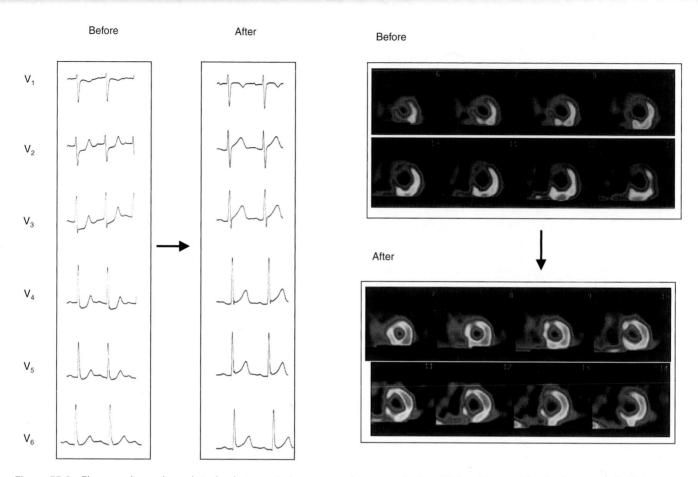

Before   After   Before

After

Figure 55-2 Electrocardiography and single photon emission computed tomography (SPECT) in a 13-year-old girl with an occluded left anterior descending artery (LAD) who underwent heparin and exercise therapy. **Left,** Ischemic ST-segment depression (V$_1$-V$_4$) present before therapy (*left*) disappeared after therapy (*right*). **Right,** Stress SPECT imaging before (*top*) and after (*bottom*) therapy revealed improved myocardial perfusion in the anteroseptal wall after therapy.

Late Management Options

The surgical experience involving CABG for symptomatic patients or for critically narrowed vessels, in the absence of symptoms, has improved greatly (see Fig. 55-1 and Box 55-3).[29] The results over the first decade after CABG are good, and graft patency in adult life after CABG in childhood is encouraging.[36] In long-term KD because the stenotic region of the coronary artery is stiff and often associated with severe calcification, simple balloon angioplasty usually is ineffectual. Instead, rotablator therapy with or without stent implantation appears promising especially for severe calcified lesions (see Fig. 55-2).[22,23,28,37] Cardiac transplantation has been performed in a small number of patients with severe ischemic heart disease resulting from KD.[38] This procedure should be considered only for individuals with severe, irreversible myocardial dysfunction and coronary lesions for which intervention is not feasible.

Pregnancy

Many female patients with a history of KD are now reaching childbearing age. However, experience of pregnancy and delivery in patients with KD, especially those with CAA and/or coronary stenosis, is still limited. Based on the English literature regarding pregnancy and delivery in patients with KD and CAA, including a recent multicenter report from Japan, there are at least 60 recorded pregnancies and deliveries. This includes 7 patients after CABG, 2 of whom who had an AMI during pregnancy.[39,40] All patients with normal left ventricular ejection fraction and without coronary stenosis tolerated pregnancy without complication. Nearly half of the patients had

---

BOX 55-3   LATE TREATMENT

Patients with Small (5 mm) to Medium (5 to 8 mm) Coronary Artery Aneurysms
- Aspirin, 3 to 5 mg/kg/day

Patients with Giant (>8 mm) or Multiple Small-to-Moderate Coronary Artery Aneurysms
- Aspirin, 3 to 5 mg/kg/day, and warfarin (target INR 2.0 to 2.5)

Patients with Coronary Artery Occlusion
- Aspirin, 3 to 5 mg/kg/day, and warfarin (target INR 2.0 to 2.5)
- Consideration of β-adrenergic blocker to reduce myocardial oxygen consumption, calcium-channel blockers, angiotensin-converting enzyme inhibitors, and nitrates
- Coronary artery bypass grafting
- Percutaneous coronary intervention
- Stent implantation
- Rotablator angioplasty
- Mitral valve replacement
- Heparin and exercise therapy
- Cardiac transplantation

INR, international normalized ratio.

---

vaginal or assisted vaginal delivery, and the others had cesarean section—all with successful outcomes. There were no maternal deaths. Three neonates were born small for gestational age and one was born with a ventricular septal defect. All other neonates were healthy. Low-dose aspirin, nitroglycerin, heparin, or dipyridamole was administered to all these reported patients. The use of low-dose aspirin during pregnancy is thought to be useful, with no unfavorable effects on the fetus. For patients with CAA and stenosis as a result of KD, intervention is recommended before getting pregnant. Choice of anesthesia and method of delivery in patients with KD and CAA remain unclear. From available data, pregnancy and delivery in such patients can be recommended with appropriate thorough care and management. Guidelines need to be developed to improve the management of pregnancy and delivery, to avoid unnecessary poor outcomes such as a miscarriage, and to provide more opportunities for childbearing in these patients with KD and CAA.

Level of Follow-Up

The level of follow-up for patients with KD depends on the degree of coronary artery involvement and is set out by the American Heart Association (Box 55-4).[11]

BOX 55-4 ASSESSMENT

No Coronary Artery Changes at Any Stage of Illness
- Cardiovascular risk assessment and counseling at 5-year intervals. Noninvasive testing is recommended.

Transient Coronary Artery Ectasia Disappearing Within First 6 to 8 Weeks
- Cardiovascular risk assessment and counseling at 3- to 5-year intervals. Noninvasive testing is recommended.

Small-to-Medium Coronary Artery Aneurysm/Major Coronary Artery (<5 mm or 5 to 8 mm in internal diameter)
- Yearly cardiac evaluation
- No need for restriction of physical activities beyond first 6 to 8 weeks in patients younger than age 11 years and as guided by stress testing in patients 11 to 20 years of age and possibly older

- When echocardiography or stress testing suggests stenosis/ischemia, coronary angiography should be performed.

Large or Giant Coronary Artery Aneurysm (>8 mm in internal diameter) or Multiple or Complex Aneurysm in Same Coronary Artery With or Without Obstruction
- Six-month follow-up should include electrocardiography and echocardiography.
- Annual stress test/evaluation by myocardial perfusion scintigraphy is recommended.
- Angiography should be performed 6 to 12 months after initial illness to define the extent of disease and thereafter whenever symptoms or stress tests indicate myocardial ischemia.
- Physical activity should be regulated on the basis of stress test results and the severity of the coronary artery stenosis by angiography.

From Newburger JW, Takahashi M, Gerber MA et al. Diagnosis, treatment, and long-term management of Kawasaki disease: a statement for health professionals from the Committee on Rheumatic Fever, Endocarditis and Kawasaki Disease, Council on Cardiovascular Disease in the Young, American Heart Association. Circulation 2004; 110:2747–2771. Available at http://www.circulationaha.org.

REFERENCES

1. Kawasaki T. Acute febrile mucocutaneous syndrome with lymphoid involvement with specific desquamation of the fingers and toes in children. Jpn J Allergy 1967;116:178–222.
2. Kato H. Cardiovascular involvement in Kawasaki disease: evaluation and natural history. Prog Clin Biol Res 1987;250:277–286.
3. Ayusawa M, Sonobe T, Uemura S, et al. Kawasaki Disease Research Committee: Revision of diagnostic guidelines for Kawasaki disease (the 5th revised edition). Pediatr Int 2005;47:232–234.
4. Nakamura Y, Yanagawa Y. The worldwide epidemiology of Kawasaki disease. Prog Pediatr Cardiol 2004;19:99–108.
5. Nakamura Y, Aso E, Yashiro M, et al. Mortality among persons with a history of Kawasaki disease in Japan—mortality among males with cardiac sequelae is significantly higher than that of the general population. Circ J 2008;72:134–138.
6. Leung DY, Meissner HC, Shulman ST, et al. Prevalence of superantigen s-secreting bacteria in patients with Kawasaki disease. J Pediatr 2002;140:742–746.
7. Abe J, Jibiki T, Noma S, et al. Gene expression profiling of the effect of high-dose intravenous Ig in patients with Kawasaki disease. J Immunol 2005;174:5837–58345.
8. Onouchi Y, Tamari M, Takahashi A, et al. A genomewide linkage analysis of Kawasaki disease: evidence for linkage to chromosome 12. J Hum Genet 2007;52:179–190.
9. Rowley AH, Shulman ST. New developments in the search for the etiologic agent of Kawasaki disease. Curr Opin Pediatr 2007;19:71–74.
10. Ogawa S, Akagi T, Ishi M, et al. [Guidelines for diagnosis and management of cardiovascular sequelae in Kawasaki disease]. Available at: http://www.j-circ.or.jp/guideline/index.htm.
11. Newburger JW, Takahashi M, Gerber MA, et al. Diagnosis, treatment, and long-term management of Kawasaki disease: a statement for health professionals from the Committee on Rheumatic Fever, Endocarditis and Kawasaki Disease, Council on Cardiovascular Disease in the Young, American Heart Association. Circulation 2004;110:2747–2771. Available at: http://www.circulationaha.org.
12. Niwa K, Aotsuka M, Hamada H, et al. Thrombocytopenia: a risk factor for acute myocardial infarction during the acute phase of Kawasaki disease. Coron Artery Dis 1995;6:857–864.
13. Greil GF, Stuber M, Botnar RM, et al. Coronary magnetic resonance angiography in adolescents and young adults with Kawasaki disease. Circulation 2002;105:908–911.
14. Fujiwara M, Yamada TN, Ono Y, et al. Magnetic resonance imaging of old myocardial infarction in young patients with a history of Kawasaki disease. Clin Cardiol 2001;24:247–252.
15. Arnold R, Lev S, Lev-Zaporozhan J, et al. Visualization of coronary arteries in a patients after childhood Kawasaki syndrome: value of by multidetector CT and MRI image in comparison to conventional coronary catheterization. Pediatr Radiol 2007;37:998–1006.
16. Newburger JW, Takahashi M, Burns JC, et al. The treatment of Kawasaki syndrome with intravenous gammaglobulin. N Engl J Med 1986;315:341–347.
17. Takao A, Niwa K, Kondo C, et al. Mitral regurgitation in Kawasaki disease. Prog Clin Biol Res 1987;250:311–323.
18. Okada Y, Shinohara M, Kobayashi T, et al. Gunma Kawasaki disease Study Group. Effect of corticosteroids in addition to intravenous gamma globulin therapy on serum cytokine levels in the acute phase of Kawasaki disease in children. J Pediatr 2003;143:363–367.
19. Wolff AE, Hansen KE, Zakawski L. Acute Kawasaki disease: not just for kids. J Gen Intern Med 2007;22:681–684.
20. Seve P, Stankovic K, Smail A, et al. Adult Kawasaki disease: report of two cases and literature review. Semin Arthritis Rheum 2005;34:785–792.
21. Kato H, Sugimura T, Akagi T, et al. Long-term consequences of Kawasaki disease: a 10–21 year follow-up study of 594 patients. Circulation 1996;94:1379–1385.
22. Takahashi K, Oharaseki T, Naoe S. Pathological study of post arteritis in adolescents and young adults: with reference to the relationship between sequelae of Kawasaki disease and atherosclerosis. Pediatr Cardiol 2001;22:138–142.
23. Ishii M, Ueno T, Ikeda H, et al. Sequential follow-up results of catheter intervention for coronary artery lesions after Kawasaki disease: quantitative coronary artery angiography and intravascular ultrasound imaging study. Circulation 2002;105:3004–3010.
24. Hiraishi S, Hirota H, Horiguchi Y, et al. Transthoracic Doppler assessment of coronary flow velocity reserve in children with Kawasaki disease: comparison with coronary angiography and thallium-201 imaging. J Am Coll Cardiol 2002;40:1816–1824.
25. Karasawa K, Miyashita M, Taniguchi K, et al. Detection of myocardial contractile reserve by low-dose dobutamine quantitative gated single-photon emission computed tomography in patients with Kawasaki disease and severe coronary artery lesions. Am J Cardiol 2003;92:865–868.
26. Noto N, Okada T, Karasawa K, et al. Age-related acceleration of endothelial dysfunction and subclinical atherosclerosis in subjects with coronary artery lesions after Kawasaki disease. Pediatr Cardiol 2009;30:262–268.
27. Niboshi A, Hamaoka K, Sakata K, et al. Endothelial dysfunction in adult patients with a history of Kawasaki disease. Eur J Pediatr 2008;167:189–196.
28. Akagi T. Interventions in Kawasaki disease. Pediatr Cardiol 2005;26:206–212.
29. Kitamura S, Kameda Y, Seki T, et al. Long-term outcome of myocardial revascularization in patients with Kawasaki coronary artery disease: a multicenter cooperative study. J Thorac Cardiovasc Surg 1994;107:663–673.
30. Kato H, Ichinose E, Kawasaki T. Myocardial infarction in Kawasaki disease. J Pediatr 1986;108:923–928.
31. Tateno S, Terai M, Niwa K, et al. Alleviation of myocardial ischemia after Kawasaki disease by heparin and exercise therapy. Circulation 2001;103:2591–2597.
32. Kato H, Inoue O, Kawasaki T, et al. Adult coronary artery disease probably due to childhood Kawasaki disease. Lancet 1992;340:1127–1129.
33. Burns JC, Shike H, Gordon JB, et al. Sequelae of Kawasaki disease in adolescents and young adults. J Am Coll Cardiol 1996;28:253–257.
34. Niwa K, Tashima K, Kawasoe Y, et al. Magnetic resonance imaging of myocardial infarction in Kawasaki disease. Am Heart J 1990;119:1293–1302.
35. Hauser M, Bengel F, Kuehn A, et al. Myocardial blood flow and coronary flow reserve in children with "normal" epicardial coronary arteries after the onset of Kawasaki disease assessed by positron emission tomography. Pediatr Cardiol 2004;25:108–112.
36. Tsuda E, et al. National survey of coronary artery bypass grafting for coronary stenosis caused by Kawasaki disease in Japan. Circulation 2004;110:II61–II66.
37. Sugimura T, Yokoi H, Sato N, et al. Interventional treatment for children with severe coronary artery stenosis with calcification after long-term Kawasaki disease. Circulation 1997;96:3928–3933.
38. Checchia PA, Pahl E, Shaddy RE, et al. Cardiac transplantation for Kawasaki disease. Pediatrics 1997;100:695–699.
39. Nolan TE, Savage RW. Peripartum myocardial infarction from presumed Kawasaki's disease. South Med J 1990;83:1360–1361.
40. Tsuda E, Kawamata K, Neki R, et al. Nationwide survey of pregnancy and delivery in patients with coronary arterial lesions caused by Kawasaki disease in Japan. Cardiol Young 2006;16:173–178.

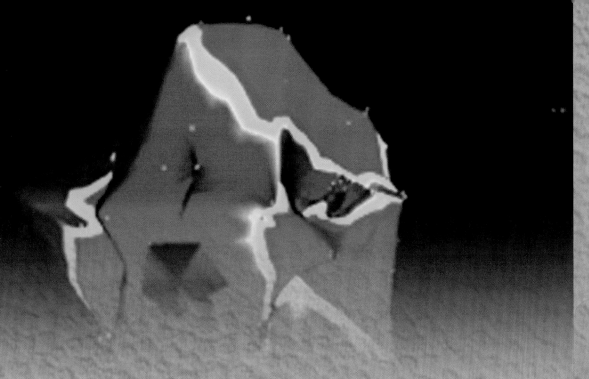

PART
XI

Other Lesions

56

Myocarditis and Dilated Cardiomyopathy

RAVI ASSOMULL | ANKUR GULATI | SANJAY K. PRASAD

Introduction

The cardiomyopathies represent an important group of heart muscle disorders that are all associated with significant morbidity and mortality. The most prevalent of these conditions is dilated cardiomyopathy (DCM), which accounts for over half of all cases. A proportion of cases of DCM result from the progression of an initial inflammatory insult to the myocardium during an episode of acute myocarditis. During the past decade, significant efforts have been made to further our understanding of the underlying disease pathophysiology, which in turn have led to refinements in diagnosis and management. In particular, novel imaging techniques have provided a new insight into risk stratification of DCM patients, who may consequently benefit from more aggressive therapy earlier on in the disease course. In this chapter the diagnostic cascade, current management, and prognosis of DCM and myocarditis are reviewed.

Definition

DCM is characterized by enlargement and impaired contractility of the left ventricle in the absence of an ischemic etiology. The World Health Organization suggests echocardiographic criteria of a left ventricular end-diastolic value greater than 117% of predicted value (corrected for age and body surface area), associated with a fractional shortening of less than 25%.[1] In a proportion of cases the right ventricle may also be involved, resulting in biventricular systolic dysfunction.

The condition should not be considered a single disease entity but is more accurately regarded as the final common pathway for multiple heterogenous disease processes. DCM has a familial etiology in approximately 20% of cases, and many different genes have been implicated in its pathogenesis (Table 56-1).[2] In addition, a wide range of environmental factors and systemic disorders are also known to trigger the DCM phenotype (Table 56-2). However, in over half of DCM patients an underlying cause is never identified and these cases are often labeled as "idiopathic."[3] Idiopathic DCM may partially reflect undiagnosed factors such as infectious, genetic, or toxic causes. The number of patients labeled as having idiopathic DCM is likely to diminish in the future as our understanding of the pathophysiologic mechanisms, specifically genetic-environmental interactions, is enhanced.

Myocarditis is defined histologically by myocardial inflammation and subsequent myocyte necrosis. The condition typically presents acutely and may be associated with transient ventricular impairment, followed by complete or partial ventricular recovery. A proportion of patients who fail to recover ventricular function develop progressive systolic impairment. In these patients acute myocarditis may therefore be the precursor for chronic DCM.

Epidemiology and Etiology

DCM has an annual incidence of 4.8/100,000 in infancy, 0.7 in early childhood (birth to age 10 years),[4] and 5 to 8/100,000 in adulthood, and is associated with an annual mortality in adults of between 10% and 50%.[5] Whereas most cases of clinically apparent myocarditis have an infectious etiology, a vast array of differing causes are recognized in DCM. Identification of the precise underlying etiology in DCM is critical in targeting appropriate therapy. One fifth of cases are genetically linked, which emphasizes the importance of familial screening.

Common underlying causes are presented in Table 56-2, but in 50% of cases no underlying cause is found. When alcohol, drugs, or toxins are implicated, cessation of exposure to the responsible agent may yield dramatic improvement in ventricular function. Peripartum cardiomyopathy has an incidence of 1 in 3000 live births.[6] In this condition, cardiomyopathy typically develops in the last month of pregnancy or in the first 5 months postpartum. Chemotherapeutic agents such as anthracyclines are also a common cause of DCM. Despite steps to monitor cardiac function during anthracycline treatment, cardiac dysfunction can develop as early as 2 months after initiation of chemotherapy and the risk of cardiotoxicity rises markedly after an exposure of 400 mg/m^2.[7]

A significant proportion of idiopathic cases are likely to be the result of an initial viral myocarditis that may have been clinically silent in its acute phase.[8] Symptoms may develop insidiously, by which point a DCM phenotype has fully evolved. In autopsy series of previously asymptomatic individuals, the incidence of myocarditis is quoted at approximately 5%, consistent with the assertion that patients with an acute viremia may have a significant subclinical period before either recovery or progression to a DCM phenotype.[9]

Cardiotropic viruses such as the enteroviruses (e.g., coxsackievirus group B serotypes) have traditionally been thought to be the most commonly implicated serotypes in the pathogenesis of DCM. However, more recent studies have revealed a changing picture with differences also noted depending on location. In Germany, Kuhl and colleagues have demonstrated a high prevalence of parvovirus B19 along with human herpesvirus-6, whereas in the United States, adenovirus appears to be more common.[10,11] In Japan, hepatitis C virus is reported more frequently as the causative agent.[12]

The prevalence of myocarditis and DCM associated with human immunodeficiency virus (HIV) is also increasing. In HIV-infected patients diagnosed with heart failure, autopsy series have revealed histopathologic findings consistent with myocarditis in over half of cases.[13] This situation is clouded by the fact that the antiretroviral drugs used to treat these patients may themselves cause myocarditis in addition to the infection with the virus.

Pathogenesis

Current understanding of the pathophysiologic processes underpinning myocarditis is predominantly derived from a mouse-based enteroviral model. Both humoral and cellular immune responses are thought to play important roles.[14] The process is initially triggered by myocyte invasion by a cardiotropic virus that itself may cause direct cytotoxicity in the acute phase. This invasion triggers a secondary immunologic cascade with CD8-positive T-lymphocyte–mediated eradication of virus-infected cells. Inadequate negative modulation results in an excessive inflammatory response with release of cytokines (e.g., tumor necrosis factor-α) and activation of enzymes (e.g., nitrous oxide synthase) that cause further myocardial damage.

The virus itself utilizes elaborate systems to escape immunologic detection, and its persistence in myocytes stimulates a chronic immune response. The resulting expansion of CD4-positive activated cells results in autoimmune myocytolysis by cardiac-specific autoantibodies. The ensuing vicious cycle of myocardial injury and repair may lead to adverse cardiac remodeling and fibrosis, eventually culminating in significant ventricular dysfunction.

TABLE 56-1	Genes Implicated in the Pathogenesis of Dilated Cardiomyopathy		
	Gene	*Protein*	*Function*
Autosomal Dominant Familial Dilated Cardiomyopathy Phenotype	*ACTC*	Cardiac actin	Sarcomeric protein; muscle contraction
	DES	Desmin	Dystrophin-associated glycoprotein complex; transduces contractile forces
	SGCD	δ-Sarcoglycan	Dystrophin-associated glycoprotein complex; transduces contractile forces
	MYH7	β-Myosin heavy chain	Sarcomeric protein; muscle contraction
	TNNT2	Cardiac troponin T	Sarcomeric protein; muscle contraction
	TPM1	α-Tropomyosin	Sarcomeric protein; muscle contraction
	TTN	Titin	Sarcomere structure/extensible scaffold for other proteins
	VCL	Metavinculin	Sarcomere structure; intercalated discs
	MYBPC	Myosin-binding protein C	Sarcomeric protein; muscle contraction
	MLP/CSRP3	Muscle LIM protein	Sacromere stretch; sensor/Z discs
	ACTN2	α-Actinin-2	Sarcomere structure; anchor for myofibrillar actin
	PLN	Phospholamban	Sarcoplasmic reticulum Ca^{2+} regulator; inhibits SERCA2 pump
	ZASP/LBD3	Cypher/LIM binding domain 3	Cytoskeletal assembly; involved in targeting and clustering of membrane proteins
	MYH6	α-Myosin heavy chain	Sarcomeric protein; muscle contraction
	ABCC	SUR2A	Regulatory subunit of Kir6.2, an inwardly rectifying cardiac K_{ATP} channel
	LMNA	Lamin A/C	Inner leaflet, nuclear membrane protein; confers stability to nuclear membrane; gene expression
X-linked Familial Dilated Cardiomyopathy	*DMD*	Dystrophin	Primary component of dystrophin-associated glycoprotein complex; transduces contractile force
	TAZ/G4.5	Tafazzin	Unknown
Recessive Familial Dilated Cardiomyopathy	*TNN13*	Cardiac troponin I	Sarcomeric protein, muscle contraction

From Burkett EL, Hershberger RE. Clinical and genetic issues in familial dilated cardiomyopathy. J Am Coll Cardiol 2005; 45:969.

The pathogenesis of DCM remains unresolved, largely hindered by the fact that most patients present at a stage when the pathogenesis is complete. Histologic findings are nonspecific and not suggestive of any particular pathogenesis. The typical microscopic appearance is consistent with a healed myocarditis, with patchy perimyocyte and interstitial fibrosis, myocyte death and hypertrophy, and occasional scattered inflammatory cells. The potential for viral involvement or an autoimmune basis is supported by the murine models of myocarditis discussed earlier. Current opinion therefore favors an autoimmune pathogenesis, possibly with a viral trigger, in genetically susceptible individuals.

TABLE 56-2	Etiology of Dilated Cardiomyopathy
Cause	*Comment*
Drugs and toxins	Ethanol*, cocaine*, doxorubicin, clozapine, cyclophosphamide, phenothiazines*, zidovudine, didanosine, cobalt*, mercury*
Infectious	Viruses (coxsackie, HIV, adenovirus, cytomegalovirus) Parasites (*Trypanosoma cruzi*, toxoplasmosis*, trichinosis) Bacteria (diphtheria)
Genetic	Muscular dystrophy (Duchenne, Becker, fascioscapulohumeral, myotonic) Friedreich ataxia Familial cardiomyopathy (see Table 56-1) Mitochondrial myopathies
Immunologic	Systemic lupus erythematosus, scleroderma, dermatomyositis Kawasaki disease Sarcoidosis* Hypersensitivity myocarditis*
Arrhythmias	Tachycardias*, congenital complete heart block
Metabolic	Iron overload (hemochromatosis, multiple blood transfusions*) Endocrine* (hypothyroidism, hyperthyroidism, acromegaly, pheochromocytoma, Cushing syndrome) Electrolyte disorder* (hypocalcemia, hypophosphatemia) Nutritional deficiency (thiamine, selenium) Congenital metabolic defects (carnitine)
Peripartum	

*Potentially reversible.

Clinical Presentation and Management

Clinical presentation can vary from the asymptomatic individual with electrocardiographic abnormalities through to heart failure (the most common presentation), arrhythmia, chest pain mimicking an acute coronary syndrome, embolic stroke, and sudden cardiac death. A careful history to ascertain the aforementioned symptoms and any features of a viral prodrome, coupled with findings observed on abnormal electrocardiographic recordings and a chest radiograph, may alert the physician to the possibility of DCM and/or myocarditis. The history should also focus on uncovering the etiology of the ventricular dysfunction, including careful questioning regarding drug and alcohol use. In patients in whom chest pain is associated with electrocardiographic changes consistent with acute ischemia, prompt coronary angiography is advisable to exclude clinically significant coronary artery disease.[15]

Serum biomarkers are often elevated in myocarditis, and serum troponin T levels of more than 0.1 ng/mL have been shown to increase sensitivity to approximately 53% with a specificity of 93%.[16] Further investigations include viral serology (e.g., coxsackievirus, hepatitis C virus, HIV), serum iron studies, appropriate endocrine testing, and screening for causative drugs/toxins. Brain-natriuretic peptide is useful for screening in the initial presentation phase and may have value in monitoring disease progress. Echocardiography provides readily available imaging to quantify the extent of ventricular dilation and cardiac dysfunction. Careful screening for arrhythmia should be considered, especially in patients presenting with palpitations, presyncope, or syncope, because the prevalence of supraventricular and ventricular arrhythmias may be as high as 50%.[17]

Management depends on the nature of presentation (Boxes 56-1 to 56-4). In patients presenting with acute heart failure with severe hemodynamic compromise, inotropes, intra-aortic balloon pumps, or even a ventricular-assist device may be required very early in their treatment. Early transfer of these patients to a specialist center is advised. For patients whose condition is hemodynamically stable, treatment should mirror that of someone with heart failure with the administration of oxygen, diuretics, and nitrates for symptomatic relief as well as the gradual introduction and upward titration of angiotensin-converting enzyme inhibitors, β-adrenergic blockers, and aldosterone antagonists for clinical and prognostic benefit. The value of corticosteroids and other immunosuppressants in myocarditis remains unproven. The best studied cohort is described in The Myocarditis Treatment Trial in which 111 patients identified from 2233 initially recruited patients were randomized to receive conventional heart failure therapy with or without immunosuppression.[18] The mortality in this group was 20% at 1 year and 56% at just over 4 years. The addition of prednisolone and cyclosporine did not improve left ventricular parameters or survival. Other studies looking at immunoglobulins have similarly shown no survival benefits.[19]

Outpatient Assessment, Level of Follow-Up, and Exercise

The mainstay of outpatient assessment is to assess the response to treatment both in terms of symptoms and ventricular function. A careful history coupled with serial electrocardiography and echocardiography is essential to make a judgment on the extent of recovery. Patients should have their drug therapy reviewed and stringent efforts made to upwardly titrate doses of angiotensin-converting enzyme inhibitors and β-blockers. An assessment of fluid overload should also be made with diuretic regimens being modified appropriately. Judicious monitoring of serum electrolyte levels, especially in the context of increasing doses of potentially nephrotoxic drug therapy, is also mandatory. For stable patients, follow-up at 6-month intervals would be reasonable. More frequent follow-up is recommended in those who remain severely symptomatic or have a history of recent decompensation requiring hospital admission.

Patients with DCM are limited by the nature of their disease. However, exercise should be encouraged and specially formulated exercise training programs offered. These programs should avoid isometric exercises such as weight lifting. Like all therapies for this condition, exercise programs must be tailored specifically to each individual.

Arrhythmia and Sudden Cardiac Death

Device implantation is increasingly being used in DCM patients. The benefits of implantable cardioverter-defibrillators or cardiac resynchronization therapy in this population are reasonably well established. The use of such devices should therefore be considered in all DCM patients who meet the relevant clinical criteria as per published guidelines.[20] Serial assessment should continue after discharge from the hospital. A history of unexplained syncope should trigger investigations seeking out evidence of malignant arrhythmia. In patients with severe left ventricular systolic impairment who remain symptomatic, current guidelines would also suggest use of an implantable cardioverter-defibrillator as a reasonable therapeutic maneuver.

In patients with heart failure due to DCM who are failing to respond to therapy, cardiac transplantation can be considered in severe cases.

Evidence of Myocardial Inflammation and Infection

Endomyocardial biopsy has widely been regarded as the "gold standard" for confirming the diagnosis of myocarditis. Samples obtained from the right ventricular surface of the interventricular septum at right-sided heart catheterization can be examined histologically, with further analysis by immunohistologic staining and viral polymerase chain reaction.

The rates of biopsy-proven myocarditis in new-onset heart failure vary greatly in published studies from 3% to 63%.[21] The Dallas criteria are the standardized histopathologic classification system used to define myocarditis.[22] These criteria are based on the finding of an inflammatory infiltrate with necrosis and/or degeneration of myocytes that are not typical of ischemic injury. Samples are classified into three categories:

1. Active (all features present)
2. Borderline (typically no myocyte degeneration)
3. Absent (no features present)

The patchy nature of inflammation explains why the diagnostic yield of biopsies in true cases of myocarditis is heavily dependent on the number of samples taken. Previous studies indicate that endomyocardial biopsy has a sensitivity of only 50% with the standard 5 samples, but this figure rises to over 80% when 17 or more samples are obtained.[23] Moreover, the timing of biopsy also affects the sensitivity, because samples taken within a week of symptom onset often have a higher yield than those taken when symptoms have been of long standing.

Further challenges with endomyocardial biopsy relate to the interpretation of the obtained samples. In the patients recruited for the National Institutes of Health Myocarditis Treatment Trial, only 64% of the cases obtained were confirmed as truly showing features of myocarditis by an expert consensus panel.[18] This observation was made despite the fact that the initial biopsy had been graded as positive for the condition by a pathologist at enrollment.

Finally, complications from myocardial biopsy occur in about 1% of cases and can be life threatening. For these reasons, endomyocardial biopsy is not routinely recommended unless it is likely to impact on management significantly. Indications may include unexplained, rapidly progressive cardiomyopathies that are refractory to conventional therapies or associated with life-threatening arrhythmias.

Emerging Role of Cardiovascular Magnetic Resonance

Cardiovascular magnetic resonance (CMR) imaging is an important new technique that yields high-resolution and high-contrast images of the heart by radiofrequency excitation of hydrogen nuclei in a powerful magnetic field. CMR is widely considered to be the "gold standard" investigation in the assessment of cardiac function, volumes, and mass.

An additional strength of CMR lies in its unique ability to facilitate myocardial tissue characterization. Increases in both T1- and T2-weighted signals can be used to demonstrate global myocardial inflammation. Short tau inversion recovery (STIR) T2-weighted images can specifically define focal areas of edema, which are particularly evident in the first 3 weeks from symptom onset in myocarditis. This technique may therefore assist with the diagnosis of myocarditis in the acute phase.[24]

Late gadolinium-enhanced (LGE) CMR can also be used to directly visualize focal areas of myocardial fibrosis that are seen in both myocarditis and DCM. In approximately one third of patients with myocarditis, healing by organization occurs, resulting in myocardial scarring. The resulting scar is identifiable as areas of bright signal or enhancement on LGE images. These changes in signal characteristics have been validated in biopsy-proven studies in which CMR was proven to be both useful in establishing the diagnosis in myocarditis and in guiding biopsy.[25] The use of CMR-guided biopsy increased the diagnostic yield of this invasive procedure to 90% (Fig. 56-1) and may be considered a noninvasive alternative in establishing a diagnosis. In patients presenting with suspected acute coronary syndromes but unobstructed coronary arteries, CMR has been found to show changes consistent with myocarditis in 30% of cases.[26]

In approximately one third of DCM patients, LGE CMR reveals patchy or linear striae of enhancement confined to the mid wall.[27]

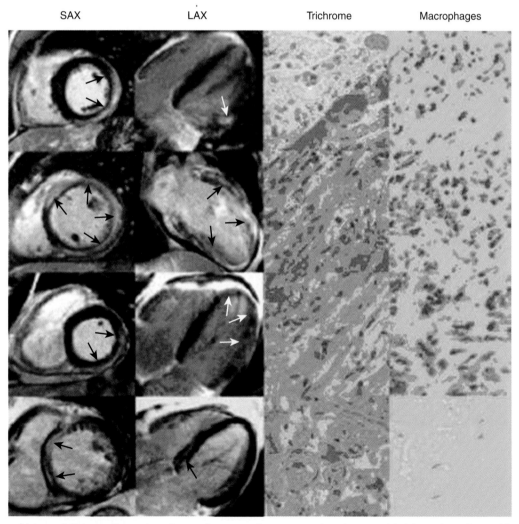

SAX   LAX   Trichrome   Macrophages

Figure 56-1 Use of late gadolinium-enhanced cardiovascular magnetic resonance imaging to guide biopsy in patients with myocarditis. LAX, long axis view; SAX, short axis view. *(From Mahrholdt H, Goedecke C, Wagner A et al. Cardiovascular magnetic resonance assessment of human myocarditis: a comparison to histology and molecular pathology. Circulation 2004; 109:1250–1258.)*

The histologic basis for this is focal replacement fibrosis, which is seen at autopsy in up to half of DCM patients. The absence of subendocardial late enhancement has been shown to have a high sensitivity in excluding significant coronary artery disease.[28] Differentiation between DCM and ischemic cardiomyopathy is important for prognostic and therapeutic reasons. Although historically coronary angiography is routinely performed for this task, several studies have since proposed a role for LGE CMR to distinguish between these two causes noninvasively based on their different patterns of late enhancement.

Prognosis

The factors governing eventual outcome, including the likelihood of transplantation or death, are poorly understood. In DCM, the underlying etiology will often portend an expected range of outcomes. Mortality is generally high, being quoted at 20% at 5 years. In a study by Felker and associates of 1230 patients with DCM, multivariate modeling identified etiology, sex, age, pulse pressure, and raised pulmonary pressures as independent risks for death or transplantation.[3] Patients with peripartum cardiomyopathy seem to have the best survival rates, with almost all patients showing some improvement in left ventricular function on conventional therapy. Conversely, patients with anthracycline-associated, infiltrative, and HIV-associated cardiomyopathy have the worst prognosis (Fig. 56-2).

In patients with myocarditis the mode of presentation may subsequently govern eventual outcome. In the classification adopted by Lieberman, patients are categorized as having fulminant myocarditis when they present with severe acute ventricular failure after a short viral prodrome. Patients with this mode of presentation surprisingly fare better than patients presenting with acute nonfulminant myocarditis, with survival quoted at 93% at 11 years' follow-up (Fig. 56-3).[29] Other series have demonstrated that a diagnosis of giant cell myocarditis is associated with a median survival of only 6 months after the onset of symptoms. Patients with a persistent viremia resulting in chronic active myocarditis also have a poor outcome, with 4-year mortality rates in excess of 50%. In general, however, the majority of myocarditis patients initially have only a mild degree of ventricular impairment and subsequently make a full recovery.

Giant cell myocarditis is a poorly understood but clinically devastating variant of uncertain cause. It is characterized by the presence of multinucleated giant cells on biopsy, most likely the result of an autoimmune process, which results in an acute and often lethal presentation of heart failure.[18]

Finally, risk stratification in DCM is a challenging and complex area. Recent prospective studies using LGE CMR have demonstrated that the presence of mid-wall fibrosis predicts a worse outcome in terms of death, hospitalization, or cardiac arrhythmia (Fig. 56-4).[30] In these patients, early and aggressive institution of maximal medical and device therapy may therefore be required.

Pregnancy

Women with a history of DCM should be carefully counseled on the risk of pregnancy. As well as the potential to exacerbate left ventricular dysfunction due to the physiologic stresses that pregnancy presents, these women will have to stop prognostically important medication such as angiotensin-converting enzyme inhibitors to prevent teratogenic complications in the early stages of pregnancy.

Even in women who have responded to therapy with normalized left ventricular function, the stress of pregnancy has a high risk of unmasking a very limited cardiac reserve. In women with DCM who do get pregnant, serial echocardiography with extremely close monitoring by a perinatal center with experience in management of high-risk pregnancy should be sought.

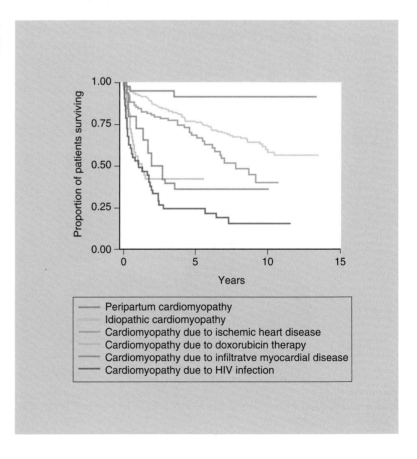

Figure 56-2 The etiology of DCM affects survival. *(After Felker GM, Thompson RE, Hare JM et al. Underlying causes and long-term survival in patients with initially unexplained cardiomyopathy. N Engl J Med 2000; 342:1077–1084.)*

diagnosis.[11] Although most patients have asymmetrical septal hypertrophy (Fig. 57-2), any pattern of LV hypertrophy is consistent with the diagnosis of HCM, including concentric, eccentric, distal, and apical patterns.[12]

LVOT obstruction is present at rest in approximately 25% of patients, although as many as 70% may have latent or provokable outflow tract obstruction,[4] caused by systolic anterior motion of the mitral valve (Fig. 57-3). Echocardiographically, dynamic obstruction in the LVOT is associated with midsystolic closure of the aortic valve, often associated with coarse fluttering of the aortic valve on M-mode echocardiography. Continuous wave Doppler assessment is used to quantify the severity of LVOT obstruction, with a characteristic high-velocity, late-systolic peak seen (Fig. 57-4). Most patients with systolic anterior motion of the mitral valve and LVOT obstruction have a posteriorly directed jet of mitral regurgitation; the presence of anteriorly directed or central regurgitant jets should prompt a search for primary mitral valve abnormalities. In some patients there may complete obliteration

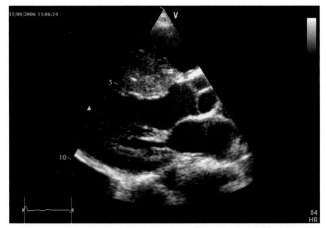

Figure 57-2 Two-dimensional (2D) echocardiogram of a patient with asymmetrical septal hypertrophy.

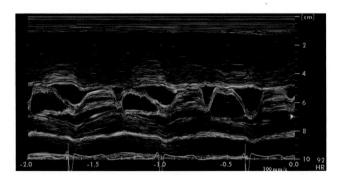

Figure 57-3 M-mode echocardiogram showing systolic anterior motion of the mitral valve in a patient with obstructive hypertrophic cardiomyopathy.

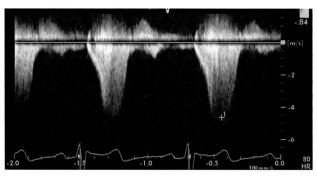

Figure 57-4 Continuous wave Doppler image of the left ventricular outflow tract in a patient with obstructive hypertrophic cardiomyopathy. Note the characteristic "dagger shape" with a late systolic peak.

of the ventricular cavity in systole, which may be associated with a high-velocity gradient in the mid ventricle.

LV global systolic function is typically increased in HCM. However, regional and long-axis function is often reduced.[13] A proportion of adults (5% to 15%) with HCM develop progressive myocardial thinning, global LV systolic impairment, and cavity dilation.[3,14] LV diastolic function is often impaired in patients with HCM and can be assessed using Doppler echocardiography, including tissue Doppler imaging.

AMBULATORY ELECTROCARDIOGRAPHY

Ambulatory electrocardiographic monitoring reveals supraventricular arrhythmias in 30% to 50% (most commonly atrial fibrillation) and nonsustained ventricular tachycardia in 25% of individuals. Sustained ventricular tachycardia is uncommon, except in patients with apical aneurysms.

CARDIOPULMONARY EXERCISE TESTING

Individuals with HCM usually have a reduced peak oxygen consumption. In addition, 25% of adults with HCM have a flat or hypotensive blood pressure response to exercise, resulting from abnormal vasodilation of the nonexercising vascular beds and impaired cardiac output responses; such abnormal blood pressure responses to exercise are associated with an increased risk of sudden death in young adults.[15]

CARDIAC MAGNETIC RESONANCE IMAGING

Like echocardiography, cardiac magnetic resonance imaging can be used to evaluate the distribution and severity of LV hypertrophy and provide functional measurements of systolic and diastolic function. Many patients with HCM have areas of patchy gadolinium hyperenhancement in the ventricular myocardium, the extent of which may correlate with increased risk of sudden death and progressive LV remodeling.[16]

Late Outcomes

The natural history of HCM is heterogeneous. Many patients follow a stable and benign course, but a large number may experience progressive symptoms, caused by gradual deterioration in LV systolic and diastolic function and atrial arrhythmias. Sudden death is the most common mode of HCM-related death. Recent studies report annual sudden death rates of 1% or less in adults[17] and 1.0% to 1.5% per year in children and adolescents.[18] In the United States, HCM accounts for 36% of cases of sudden death in competitive athletes younger than 35 years of age.[19] A proportion of individuals die of progressive heart failure, whereas others may die of thromboembolism (often associated with atrial fibrillation) and, rarely, infective endocarditis.

BOX 57-2 AIMS OF MANAGEMENT

- Alleviation of symptoms caused by left ventricular outflow tract obstruction
- Alleviation of symptoms associated with left ventricular diastolic dysfunction and ischemia
- Identification of patients at high risk of ventricular arrhythmia and sudden cardiac death
- Screening of first-degree relatives of individuals with HCM

Management

The management of patients with HCM is focused on three main areas: the screening and counseling of other family members, the management of symptoms, and the prevention of disease-related complications (Box 57-2).

FAMILY SCREENING

Careful pedigree analysis can identify relatives who may be at risk of inheriting the disease and for whom clinical screening with electrocardiography and echocardiography may be appropriate after counseling. Current guidelines recommend screening at intervals of 12 to 18 months throughout adolescence until full growth and maturation is achieved (usually by the age of 18 to 21 years). After this, if there are no signs of phenotypic expression, screening approximately every 5 years is advised, because the onset of LV hypertrophy may be delayed until well into adulthood in some families.[11] For individuals with unequivocal disease it may be possible to offer relatively rapid genetic testing. If a disease-causing mutation is identified, relatives can be offered predictive testing after appropriate genetic counseling and consideration of issues relating to patient autonomy, confidentiality, and psychosocial harm.

MANAGEMENT OF SYMPTOMS RELATED TO LEFT VENTRICULAR OUTFLOW TRACT OBSTRUCTION

The first-line treatment for symptomatic patients with obstructive HCM is medical therapy with β-adrenergic receptor blockers. At standard doses, β-blockers can reduce symptoms of chest pain, dyspnea, and pre-syncope on exertion, although they probably do not reduce LVOT obstruction at rest. The addition of disopyramide to a β-blocker can reduce obstruction and improve symptoms via its negative inotropic action. Although disopyramide is usually well tolerated, some patients (particularly the elderly) may experience marked anticholinergic side effects. Disopyramide should ideally be administered in combination with drugs that slow atrioventricular conduction because it causes accelerated atrioventricular node conduction and may increase the ventricular rate during atrial fibrillation. The calcium antagonist verapamil is also used to treat symptoms caused by LVOT obstruction. It is thought to act by reducing myocardial contractility and relieving myocardial ischemia. Verapamil must be used with caution in patients with severe symptoms caused by large gradients (>100 mm Hg) and pulmonary hypertension because it can cause rapid hemodynamic deterioration.

For patients with obstructive HCM who do not tolerate drugs or whose symptoms are refractory to medical therapy, the gold standard procedure is surgical septal myotomy-myectomy, in which a trough of muscle is removed from the interventricular septum through an aortic incision. In experienced surgical centers, the mortality is less than 1% and the success rate is high, with complete and permanent abolition of the outflow gradient and a marked improvement in symptoms and functional class in over 90% of patients. Complications are rare and include complete heart block requiring permanent pacemaker insertion in less than 5% of patients and small ventricular septal defects.

Initial studies of dual-chamber atrioventricular pacing appeared to show a reduction in LV outflow gradients. However, subsequent randomized trials showed no objective improvement in exercise capacity and a significant placebo effect.[20,21]

Nevertheless, there is a subgroup of elderly patients with relatively mild hypertrophy who may benefit from pacing.

Percutaneous transcoronary alcohol septal myocardial ablation is an alternative to surgery for patients with obstructive HCM. The procedure involves injecting 95% alcohol into a septal perforator coronary artery branch to produce an area of localized myocardial necrosis within the basal septum.[22] The area supplied by the perforator branch is first visualized using echocardiographic contrast injection, thus minimizing myocardial damage. Although short-term results are promising, the long-term effects are unknown and there is the potential for the resulting myocardial scar to act as a substrate for ventricular arrhythmia and sudden death.

MANAGEMENT OF SYMPTOMS WITHOUT LEFT VENTRICULAR OUTFLOW TRACT OBSTRUCTION

Symptoms in patients without LVOT obstruction are usually caused by LV diastolic dysfunction and myocardial ischemia. Although β-blockers and calcium antagonists can reduce symptoms by improving LV relaxation and filling, reducing LV contractility and relieving myocardial ischemia, treatment in this group of patients is often suboptimal. Other drugs such as nitrates and angiotensin-converting enzyme inhibitors may be of use in some patients but should be avoided in patients with provokable LVOT obstruction. Individuals who progress to the burnt-out phase of the disease receive conventional heart failure treatment, including angiotensin-converting enzyme inhibitors, angiotensin-II receptor antagonists, spironolactone, β-blockers such as carvedilol or bisoprolol, digoxin, and, if necessary, cardiac transplantation. Biventricular pacing improves heart failure symptoms and results in reverse atrial and ventricular remodeling in up to 40% of patients with end-stage HCM.[23]

SUDDEN CARDIAC DEATH

Although the overall risk of sudden death in patients with HCM is only approximately 1% per year, a minority of individuals are at much greater risk of ventricular arrhythmia and sudden death (Boxes 57-3 and 57-4). In the majority of patients, the mechanism of sudden death is thought to be ventricular arrhythmia, which can sometimes be triggered by atrial arrhythmia, myocardial ischemia, and exercise. The most reliable predictor of sudden cardiac death in HCM is a history of previous cardiac arrest.[24] However, identifying those patients without such a history who nevertheless have a high risk of dying suddenly is an important aspect of the management of individuals with HCM.

BOX 57-3 RISK FACTORS FOR SUDDEN CARDIAC DEATH

- Resuscitated cardiac arrest
- Family history of sudden death due to HCM
- Nonsustained ventricular tachycardia
- Flat or hypotensive blood pressure response to upright exercise
- Severe left ventricular hypertrophy (>30 mm)
- Unexplained syncope

BOX 57-4 COMPLICATIONS

- Ventricular arrhythmia and sudden cardiac death
- Progression to "end-stage" disease characterized by left ventricular wall thinning, dilation, and systolic impairment (occurs in 5% to 15% of individuals)
- Atrial arrhythmia and thromboembolic disease
- Patients with obstructive HCM are at increased risk of infective endocarditis
- Serious complications during pregnancy in women with HCM are rare.

The most clinically useful markers of risk are a family history of sudden cardiac death, unexplained syncope (unrelated to neurocardiogenic mechanisms), an abnormal blood pressure response to upright exercise, nonsustained ventricular tachycardia on ambulatory electrocardiographic monitoring or during exercise, and severe LV hypertrophy on echocardiography (defined as a maximal LV wall thickness of ≥ 30 mm).[25] Patients with two or more risk factors are at substantially higher risk of dying suddenly, with estimated annual mortality rates of 3% for those with two risk factors rising to 6% in those with three or more risk factors.[25] Patients with a single risk factor represent a more difficult group to risk stratify because the annual mortality rate in this group is low (1.2%) but the confidence intervals are wide (0.2% to 2.2%).[25] Therefore, some individuals with a single risk factor may be twice as more likely to die suddenly than patients without risk factors. In these patients, patient-specific variables such as age and the significance of the individual risk factor have to be taken into account. Additional factors, such as LVOT obstruction[26,27] or the presence of late gadolinium enhancement on magnetic resonance imaging,[16] may represent an incremental risk factor in combination with other conventional markers.

THERAPY

In patients considered to be at high risk of sudden death, the treatment of choice is insertion of an implantable cardioverter-defibrillator (ICD). Registry data show that ICDs prevent sudden death in patients with HCM, with annual appropriate discharge rates of 11% in patients with a history of cardiac arrest or sustained ventricular arrhythmia and 35% in the primary prevention group.[28] Amiodarone was used in high-risk HCM patients before the advent of ICDs[29] but does not prevent sudden cardiac death in this high-risk group. Amiodarone is, however, useful for the treatment of atrial fibrillation in patients with HCM.

Pregnancy

Serious complications during pregnancy in women with HCM are rare, occurring in less than 2% of pregnancies. Women with higher-risk profiles may have an increased risk of maternal mortality.[30] During delivery, the vasodilation associated with standard epidural analgesia may worsen LVOT obstruction, and care must be taken when administering cardioactive drugs. In general, however, most pregnant women with HCM undergo normal vaginal delivery without the need for cesarean section. Women considered to be at high risk should be offered specialized obstetric antenatal and perinatal care.

Endocarditis Prophylaxis and Exercise

Patients with obstructive HCM have an increased risk of developing infective endocarditis.[31] Therefore, patients with HCM and LVOT obstruction should receive antibiotic prophylaxis at times of potential bacteremia, according to current American College of Cardiology/American Heart Association guidelines.[32]

Because a substantial proportion of sudden deaths in HCM occur during or just after exercise, abstention from strenuous or competitive sporting activities is recommended. In addition, patients with LVOT obstruction should avoid dehydration and circumstances where vasodilation may occur, such as hot baths or saunas.

REFERENCES

1. Elliott P, Andersson B, Arbustini E, et al. Classification of the cardiomyopathies: a position statement from the European Society of Cardiology Working Group on Myocardial and Pericardial Diseases. Eur Heart J 2008;29:270–276.
2. Hughes SE. The pathology of hypertrophic cardiomyopathy. Histopathology 2004;44:412–427.
3. Thaman R, Gimeno JR, Murphy RT, et al. Prevalence and clinical significance of systolic impairment in hypertrophic cardiomyopathy. Heart 2005;91:920–925.
4. Maron MS, Olivotto I, Zenovich AG, et al. Hypertrophic cardiomyopathy is predominantly a disease of left ventricular outflow tract obstruction. Circulation 2006;114:2232–2239.
5. Monserrat L, Elliott PM, Gimeno JR, et al. Non-sustained ventricular tachycardia in hypertrophic cardiomyopathy: an independent marker of sudden death risk in young patients. J Am Coll Cardiol 2003;42:873–879.
6. Maron BJ, Gardin JM, Flack JM, et al. Prevalence of hypertrophic cardiomyopathy in a general population of young adults: echocardiographic analysis of 4111 subjects in the CARDIA Study. Coronary Artery Risk Development in (Young) Adults. Circulation 1995;92:785–789.
7. Lipshultz SE, Sleeper LA, Towbin JA, et al. The incidence of pediatric cardiomyopathy in two regions of the United States. N Engl J Med 2003;348:1647–1655.
8. Nugent AW, Daubeney PE, Chondros P, et al. The epidemiology of childhood cardiomyopathy in Australia. N Engl J Med 2003; 348:1639–1646.
9. Richard P, Charron P, Carrier L, et al. Hypertrophic cardiomyopathy: distribution of disease genes, spectrum of mutations, and implications for a molecular diagnosis strategy. Circulation 2003;107:2227–2232.
10. Seidman JG, Seidman C. The genetic basis for cardiomyopathy: from mutation identification to mechanistic paradigms. Cell 2001;104:557–567.
11. Maron BJ, McKenna WJ, Danielson GK, et al., American College of Cardiology/European Society of Cardiology Clinical Expert Consensus Document on Hypertrophic Cardiomyopathy. A report of the American College of Cardiology Foundation Task Force on Clinical Expert Consensus Documents and the European Society of Cardiology Committee for Practice Guidelines. Eur Heart J 2003;24:1965–1991.

12. Maron BJ, Gottdiener JS, Epstein SE. Patterns and significance of distribution of left ventricular hypertrophy in hypertrophic cardiomyopathy: a wide angle, two dimensional echocardiographic study of 125 patients. Am J Cardiol 1981;48:418–428.
13. Ganame J, Mertens L, Eidem BW, et al. Regional myocardial deformation in children with hypertrophic cardiomyopathy: morphological and clinical correlations. Eur Heart J 2007; 28:2886–2894.
14. Harris KM, Spirito P, Maron MS, et al. Prevalence, clinical profile, and significance of left ventricular remodeling in the end-stage phase of hypertrophic cardiomyopathy. Circulation 2006;114:216–225.
15. Frenneaux MP, Counihan PJ, Caforio AL, et al. Abnormal blood pressure response during exercise in hypertrophic cardiomyopathy. Circulation 1990;82:1995–2002.
16. Moon JC, McKenna WJ, McCrohon JA, et al. Toward clinical risk assessment in hypertrophic cardiomyopathy with gadolinium cardiovascular magnetic resonance. J Am Coll Cardiol 2003; 41:1561–1567.
17. Maron BJ, Casey SA, Poliac LC, et al. Clinical course of hypertrophic cardiomyopathy in a regional United States cohort. JAMA 1999;281:650–665.
18. Nugent AW, Daubeney PE, Chondros P, et al. Clinical features and outcomes of childhood hypertrophic cardiomyopathy: results from a national population-based study. Circulation 2005; 112:1332–1338.
19. Maron BJ, Carney KP, Lever HM, et al. Relationship of race to sudden cardiac death in competitive athletes with hypertrophic cardiomyopathy. J Am Coll Cardiol 2003;41:974–980.
20. Maron BJ, Nishimura RA, McKenna WJ, et al. Assessment of permanent dual-chamber pacing as a treatment for drug-refractory symptomatic patients with obstructive hypertrophic cardiomyopathy: a randomized, double-blind, crossover study (M-PATHY). Circulation 1999;99:2927–2933.
21. Nishimura RA, Trusty JM, Hayes DL, et al. Dual-chamber pacing for hypertrophic cardiomyopathy: a randomized, double-blind, crossover trial. J Am Coll Cardiol 1997;29:435–441.
22. Knight C, Kurbaan AS, Seggewiss H, et al. Nonsurgical septal reduction for hypertrophic obstructive cardiomyopathy: outcome in the first series of patients. Circulation 1997;95:2075–2081.

23. Rogers DP, Marazia S, Chow AW, et al. Effect of biventricular pacing on symptoms and cardiac remodeling in patients with end-stage hypertrophic cardiomyopathy. Eur J Heart Fail 2008;10:507–513.
24. Elliott PM, Sharma S, Varnava A, et al. Survival after cardiac arrest or sustained ventricular tachycardia in patients with hypertrophic cardiomyopathy. J Am Coll Cardiol 1999;33:1596–1601.
25. Elliott PM, Poloniecki J, Dickie S, et al. Sudden death in hypertrophic cardiomyopathy: identification of high-risk patients. J Am Coll Cardiol 2000;36:2212–2218.
26. Elliott PM, Gimeno JR, Tome MT, et al. Left ventricular outflow tract obstruction and sudden death risk in patients with hypertrophic cardiomyopathy. Eur Heart J 2006;27:1933–1941.
27. Maron MS, Olivotto I, Betocchi S, et al. Effect of left ventricular outflow tract obstruction on clinical outcome in hypertrophic cardiomyopathy. N Engl J Med 2003;348:295–303.
28. Maron BJ, Shen WK, Link MS, et al. Efficacy of implantable cardioverter-defibrillators for the prevention of sudden death in patients with hypertrophic cardiomyopathy. N Engl J Med 2000;342:365–373.
29. McKenna WJ, Oakley CM, Krikler DM, Goodwin JF. Improved survival with amiodarone in patients with hypertrophic cardiomyopathy and ventricular tachycardia. Br Heart J 1985;53:412–416.
30. Thaman R, Varnava A, Hamid MS, et al. Pregnancy related complications in women with hypertrophic cardiomyopathy. Heart 2003;89:752–756.
31. Spirito P, Rapezzi C, Bellone P, et al. Infective endocarditis in hypertrophic cardiomyopathy: prevalence, incidence, and indications for antibiotic prophylaxis. Circulation 1999; 99:2132–2137.
32. Nishimura RA, Carabello BA, Faxon DP, et al. ACC/AHA 2008 guideline update on valvular heart disease: focused update on infective endocarditis: a report of the American College of Cardiology/American Heart Association Task Force on Practice Guidelines: endorsed by the Society of Cardiovascular Anesthesiologists, Society for Cardiovascular Angiography and Interventions, and Society of Thoracic Surgeons. Circulation 2008;118:887–896.

58

Constrictive Pericarditis and Restrictive Cardiomyopathy

PEDRO T. TRINDADE | FOLKERT J. MEIJBOOM

Introduction

The clinical presentation of constrictive pericarditis is identical to that of restrictive cardiomyopathy: predominantly signs of systemic venous congestion and, less pronounced, signs of a low cardiac output. The differentiation between these two diagnoses is difficult but very important because constrictive pericarditis is treatable and restrictive cardiomyopathy is likely not. In this chapter the emphasis will be on the hemodynamic differences and on the diagnostic techniques that can be used to differentiate between these two diseases.

Definition and Morphology

Restrictive cardiomyopathy is a disease of the myocardium. The key element is a decreased ventricular compliance, whereas ventricular volumes are normal or reduced and ventricular wall thickness is normal. Systolic function is often considered to be normal, but contractility is seldom truly normal.[1,2] The restriction is to flow into the ventricles; there is no problem with filling of the atria. The increased filling pressures, necessary for ventricular filling against an increased resistance, will lead to gross enlargement of both atria and marked dilation of the systemic veins.

Constrictive pericarditis is the end stage of an inflammatory process, most often infectious, following operation or irradiation, involving the pericardium. The visceral and parietal pericardium, originally two smooth separate layers, becomes a thickened, fibrosed, often calcified, rigid case around the entire heart. The causative inflammatory process may have affected the myocardium as well, leading to decreased ventricular function, but in "pure" constrictive pericarditis the ventricular (myocardial) function is normal—both systolic and diastolic. Because the pericardium encases the whole heart there is restriction to filling of the entire heart, not only of the ventricles. Characteristic findings include normal-sized ventricles, atria that are slightly enlarged, all surrounded by a thickened pericardium and marked dilation of the systemic veins. However, although the entire heart, including the atria, is encapsulated in the pericardium, ventricular filling is the predominant problem and atrial dilation can become impressive.

Epidemiology and Genetics

Constrictive pericarditis is a rare, acquired disease. There is no known genetic predisposition and there are no reliable data regarding the occurrence in the general population. Tuberculosis was by the far the most common cause of constrictive pericarditis, and since its incidence has decreased substantially the incidence of constrictive pericarditis has dropped. Nowadays most patients present without a clear history of one of the known predisposing factors: cardiac surgery, chest irradiation, pericarditis, and autoimmune disorders.[3] Chest irradiation, mainly for Hodgkin disease, is associated with constrictive pericarditis in up to 4% of cases.[4] Constrictive pericarditis as a complication of cardiac surgery is even more rare: among 5207 adults who underwent cardiac surgery, postoperative constrictive pericarditis was recognized in 11 patients (0.2%).[5] Others also report a very low incidence after cardiac surgery. However, it is a diagnosis that is often missed. Therefore, the reported incidence probably underestimates the real incidence.

Restrictive cardiomyopathy is less rare. In the western world, amyloidosis is by far the most common cause of restrictive cardiomyopathy, accounting for approximately 10% of all nonischemic cardiomyopathies. It is often secondary, but a familial, autosomal-dominant form exists and accounts for 10% to 20% of clinically manifest cases. Idiopathic restrictive cardiomyopathy is a very rare disease, probably autosomal-dominantly inherited, with variable penetration. However, sporadic cases have been reported. Its pathogenesis is unclear; it is diagnosed mainly in young adults or children. Endomyocardial fibrosis is rare in areas in the world with moderate temperatures, but in the tropics it is a serious health problem. In equatorial Africa it accounts for approximately 20% of all cases of heart failure and up to 15% of cardiac deaths.[6] Environmental and nutritional factors (cassava roots) possibly play an important role in this tropical form of endomyocardial fibrosis. Hypereosinophilic endomyocardial fibrosis, better known as Loeffler endomyocardial fibrosis, is more common in moderate climates but is still considered very rare.

Early Presentation and Management

In terms of the history and physical examination, constrictive pericarditis is virtually indistinguishable from restrictive cardiomyopathy: congestive heart failure is often the first presentation of both entities. The symptoms are usually dyspnea on mild exertion and fatigue. Chest pain is rare. At physical examination the signs of right-sided heart failure are prominent: jugular vein distention, hepatomegaly, and edema of the legs. In advanced cases ascites will be present.

DIAGNOSIS

There is no single diagnostic test that has sufficient specificity and sensitivity to differentiate between constrictive pericarditis and restrictive cardiomyopathy. The information that is acquired by all diagnostic modalities, together with a thorough understanding of the pathophysiologic differences between these two diseases, should be used to come to the diagnosis (Box 58-1). Table 58-1 gives an overview of features that are helpful in the differential diagnosis.[7,8]

Pathophysiology
Ventricular filling is restricted in both constrictive pericarditis and restrictive cardiomyopathy, leading to raised atrial pressures in both. High atrial pressures in the case of restrictive cardiomyopathy will lead to (often gross) atrial enlargement. Atrial dilation is limited in constrictive pericarditis because of the rigid pericardium, which also encapsulates the atria.

At the onset of diastole, at the time of atrioventricular valve opening, the high atrial pressures will lead to a rapid early ventricular filling. Ventricular compliance is normal in constrictive pericarditis, but ventricular filling is soon halted by the pericardial constraint. In restrictive cardiomyopathy it is the stiff myocardium with its decreased compliance that causes the restriction to ventricular filling. The mechanisms differ, but the effect is the same: ventricular diastolic pressures will increase sharply after the small increase in volume that occurs during early filling. This is represented by the typical "square root" or "dip and plateau" appearance of ventricular pressure curves that constrictive pericarditis and restrictive cardiomyopathy have in common

(Fig. 58-1).[9] At the moment when ventricular pressure equals atrial pressure, atrioventricular flow will stop. This happens at the end of the early filling period.

In a normal heart, differences in diastolic pressures can exist between left- and right-sided chambers, because of differences in their individual compliance. In patients with constrictive pericarditis this individual compliance is overruled by a common restrictive force: the rigid pericardium. The entire heart now functions as a single cylinder, allowing only marginal differences in intracardiac diastolic pressure between the individual chambers. This equalization of pressures is, together with the "square root" sign, the hallmark of a restrictive physiology in constrictive pericarditis. However, it is often also seen in restrictive cardiomyopathy.

It was the breakthrough work of Hatle and associates[10] in 1989 that illuminated the hemodynamic changes with respiration that occurred in constrictive pericarditis but not in restrictive cardiomyopathy: (1) dissociation between intrathoracic and intracardiac pressure and (2) enhanced ventricular interaction. In the heart with a normal pericardium, inspiration causes a decrease in pressure of all intrathoracic structures, including the heart. Because the pulmonary veins, left atrium, and left ventricle are all equally affected by these changes in intrathoracic pressure there will be no change in driving force from pulmonary veins to left atrium and left ventricle. This is true also for patients with restrictive cardiomyopathy. In contrast, in case of constrictive pericarditis, the rigid pericardium shields the intracardiac chambers from these respiration-related changes in intrathoracic pressure. During inspiration, the pressure in the pulmonary veins will decrease, while pressure in the left atrium and left ventricle remains unaltered. The diminished driving force during inspiration results in underfilling of the left side of the heart. During expiration, the opposite occurs.

Enhanced ventricular interaction is the second effect of pericardial restraint but closely related to the first. At inspiration, the driving force for left ventricular filling is decreased while the driving forces for filling of the right ventricle increases: the lowering of the intrathoracic pressure will lead to increased systemic venous return. The combination of left ventricular underfilling and increased systemic venous return will allow increased right ventricular filling at inspiration. This is called enhanced ventricular interaction.

Past Medical History

In the population of adults with congenital heart disease many will have had cardiac surgery in the past. Scarring of the pericardium is always reported as a possible cause of constrictive pericarditis. However, on the basis of the (sparse) data regarding the incidence of constrictive pericarditis after cardiac surgery, there is little chance of ever diagnosing one. Chest irradiation can cause both diseases. A history of connective tissue disease is compatible with constrictive pericarditis. A (family) history of amyloidosis is suggestive of restrictive cardiomyopathy.

TABLE 58-1	Features Useful in Differentiating Constrictive Pericarditis from Restrictive Cardiomyopathy	
Feature	**Constrictive Pericarditis**	**Restrictive Cardiomyopathy**
Past medical history	Previous pericarditis, cardiac surgery, trauma, radiotherapy, connective tissue disease	Items in previous column rare
Jugular venous waveform	Dips in x and y troughs brief and "flicking"; not conspicuous positive waves	Dips in x and y troughs less brief; may have conspicuous a wave or v wave
Extra sounds in diastole	Early S_3, high-pitched "pericardial knock," no S_4	Later S_3, low-pitched "triple rhythm," S_4 in some cases
Mitral or tricuspid regurgitation	Usually absent	Often present
Electrocardiogram	P waves reflect intra-atrial conduction delay. Atrioventricular or intraventricular conduction defects are rare.	P waves reflect right or left atrial hypertrophy or overload. Atrioventricular or intraventricular conduction defects are not unusual.
Plain chest radiography	Pericardial calcification in 20% to 30%	Pericardial calcification rare
Ventricular septal movement in diastole	Abrupt septal movement ("notch") in early diastole in most cases	Abrupt septal movement in early diastole seen only occasionally
Ventricular septal movement with respiration	Notable movement toward left ventricle in inspiration usually seen	Relatively little movement toward left ventricle in most cases
Atrial enlargement	Slight or moderate in most cases	Pronounced in most cases
Respiratory variation in mitral and tricuspid flow velocity	>25% in most cases	<15% in most cases
Equilibration of diastolic pressures in all cardiac chambers	Within 5 mm Hg in nearly all cases; often essentially the same	Within 5 mm Hg in a small proportion of cases
Dip-plateau waveform in the right ventricular pressure waveform	End-diastolic pressure more than one third of systolic pressure in many cases	End-diastolic pressure often less than one third of systolic pressure
Peak right ventricular systolic pressure	Nearly always < 60 mm Hg, often < 40 mm Hg	Frequently > 40 mm Hg and occasionally > 60 mm Hg
Discordant respiratory variation of ventricular peak systolic pressures	Right and left ventricular peak systolic pressure variations are out of phase	Right and left ventricular peak systolic pressure variations are in phase
Paradoxical pulse	Often present to a moderate degree	Rarely present
MRI or CT	Shows thick pericardium in most cases	Shows thick pericardium only rarely
Endomyocardial biopsy	Normal or nonspecific abnormalities	Shows amyloid in some cases; rarely other specific infiltrative disease

From Hancock EW. Differential diagnosis of restrictive cardiomyopathy and constrictive pericarditis. Heart 2001; 86:343–349, with permission.

Figure 58-1 **A,** Simultaneous left ventricular (LV) and right ventricular (RV) pressure recording in a patient with constrictive pericarditis showing the typical "square root" sign as well as equalization of diastolic pressures. **B,** Equalization of pressures on simultaneous right atrial (RA) and left ventricular (LV) diastolic pressure tracing. *(After Vaitkus PT, Cooper KA, Shuman WP, Hardin NJ. Images in cardiovascular medicine: constrictive pericarditis. Circulation 1996; 93:834–835, with permission.)*

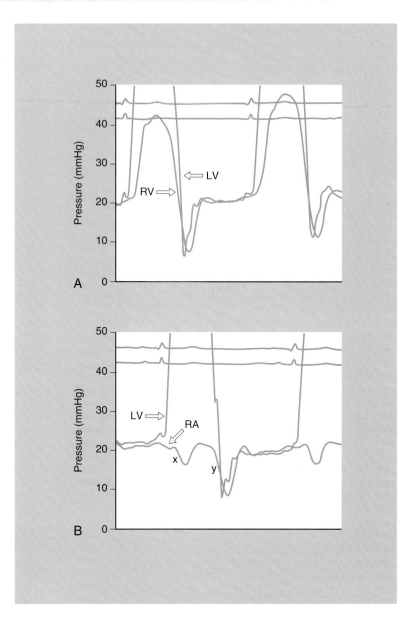

Physical Examination

The central venous pressure is raised. In the distended jugular veins the two dips—the x and y troughs, respectively, in systole and early diastole—are more prominent than normal in both constrictive pericarditis and restrictive cardiomyopathy. The atrial contraction is often more forceful in restrictive cardiomyopathy than in constrictive pericarditis, reflected by a large—and clearly visible—a wave in the jugular vein, not seen in constrictive pericarditis. At auscultation, a third heart sound can be heard in both diseases. Audible mitral regurgitation is often present in restrictive cardiomyopathy but rarely in constrictive pericarditis.

Electrocardiography

There are no specific differences in the electrocardiographic findings.

Chest Radiography

Pericardial calcification on a chest radiograph in patients with heart failure suggests constrictive pericarditis. In the past it was often observed with tuberculous pericarditis. However, since the incidence of tuberculosis has decreased in western countries, pericardial calcification is often associated with idiopathic pericardial disease. Pericardial calcifications are not a feature of restrictive cardiomyopathy.

Two-Dimensional and Doppler Echocardiography

Two-dimensional (2D) echocardiography is particularly helpful in the exclusion of other causes of right-sided heart failure, which include left ventricular systolic dysfunction, mitral valve abnormalities, right ventricular infarction, pulmonary hypertension, and pulmonary stenosis. Hepatic vein and inferior vena caval distention will be present in right-sided heart failure, irrespective of the causative mechanism. 2D echocardiography may provide some clues for the differentiation between constrictive pericarditis and restrictive cardiomyopathy. However, the findings are often not sufficiently specific and not very sensitive.

Flow Doppler and tissue Doppler ultrasonographic studies have an important place in the differential diagnosis of the two diseases.

Constrictive pericarditis and restrictive cardiomyopathy have in common that the atrial pressures are high and ventricular relaxation is normal. There is no increased resistance to atrioventricular filling in early diastole. The result is a high E wave of the transmitral and transtricuspid flow velocity contour. The restriction to further ventricular filling is represented by a short deceleration time of the E wave, frequently less than 150 ms. Atrial contraction will not result in much antegrade flow because the end-diastolic pressure of the ventricle is high; the a wave will show a low velocity.

The difference in mitral flow pattern between constrictive pericarditis and restrictive cardiomyopathy lies in the different response to respiration. At inspiration, the intrathoracic pressure drops. The left ventricle is shielded from this lowering of pressure by the rigid pericardium. This results in a decreased pressure difference between the pulmonary veins and the left atrium and ventricle, leading to a decrease of left ventricular filling. A marked decrease—often more than 25%—of the E-wave velocity over the mitral valve is seen in the first beat after beginning of the inspiration. At expiration there is a pronounced increase of mitral flow velocity in comparison with previous inspiratory beats. In hearts with a normal pericardium, including hearts with restrictive cardiomyopathy, there is only minimal variation of mitral flow during the cardiac cycle. A pitfall in using variation of mitral flow with respiration is the condition of very high left atrial pressures, which sometimes exist in patients with constrictive pericarditis. This very high atrial pressure may overrule the respiratory variation and be responsible for absence of respiratory variation of the mitral flow. This phenomenon can be unmasked by giving diuretics.[11]

In constrictive pericarditis, the combination of a decreased left ventricular filling and an increased systemic venous return results in a substantially increased tricuspid flow velocity at inspiration. At expiration the opposite occurs. Respiratory changes of tricuspid flow per se are difficult to interpret as signs of constrictive pericarditis because there is also a marked variation of tricuspid flow with respiration in normal hearts and in hearts with restrictive cardiomyopathy. The effects of respiration can also be seen in the pulmonary veins and in the hepatic and caval veins.

The combination of mitral and tricuspid flow velocities, together with flows in the hepatic, caval, and pulmonary veins at inspiration and expiration, is considered a sensitive method (88% in the report of Oh and colleagues)[12] to distinguish between constrictive pericarditis and restrictive cardiomyopathy (Fig. 58-2). Characteristic flow Doppler changes occurring in restrictive cardiomyopathy are more difficult to assess and therefore a less sensitive tool for discrimination between the two diseases. Both patients with constrictive pericarditis and those with restrictive cardiomyopathy have a borderline or shortened deceleration time of the mitral and tricuspid E wave, but only patients with restrictive cardiomyopathy show an additional shortening of the deceleration time with inspiration. Mitral and tricuspid regurgitation, both systolic and late diastolic, are often seen in restrictive cardiomyopathy but rarely in constrictive pericarditis.

Echocardiographic/Doppler evaluation, although helpful in most cases, does not always lead to the right diagnosis. Atrial fibrillation, which is not uncommon, especially in restrictive cardiomyopathy with its dilated atria, will make the interpretation of mitral valve flow velocities hazardous: changes in the RR interval will lead to changes in mitral E-wave velocity, resembling constrictive pericarditis. Larger than normal variations in intrathoracic pressure, as seen in patients with chronic obstructive pulmonary disease or asthma, may also lead to substantial variation in E-wave velocity.

The limitations of flow Doppler imaging in the distinction between these two entities and the advent of tissue Doppler imaging have led to several studies with this more recent technique. Initially it could be shown that the peak early velocity of longitudinal axis expansion (Ea) was markedly reduced in patients with restrictive cardiomyopathy while it was preserved, or even exaggerated, in constrictive pericarditis.[13] This longitudinal axis expansion is blunted in restrictive cardiomyopathy because this is a disease of the myocardium, whereas in constrictive pericarditis the longitudinal motion of the mitral annulus is exaggerated because lateral expansion is limited. This observation was extended subsequently, and it was found that a peak value of Ea greater than 8 cm/s differentiates patients with constriction from restriction with a sensitivity of 95% and sensitivity of 96%.[14,15] However, the sensitivity of this cutoff value might be lower in patients with constrictive pericarditis and underlying myocardial disease. To address this issue, investigators evaluated the incremental value of the systolic mitral annular velocity (S′), an index of left ventricular longitudinal contraction. In their report, when compared with Ea alone, the sensitivity for differentiation of the two entities, when combined with S′, could be increased from 70% to 88%.[16] In summary, tissue Doppler imaging plays an important role in the discrimination between restrictive cardiomyopathy and constrictive pericarditis and should be at present an integral component of diagnostic ultrasound examination.

Computed Tomography and Magnetic Resonance Imaging

The value of both computed tomography (CT) and cardiac magnetic resonance imaging (CMR) in the differential diagnosis between restrictive cardiomyopathy and constrictive pericarditis is that they can directly visualize the pericardium. Because both techniques can measure its thickness, they can provide evidence for pericardial disease. The normal pericardium has a thickness of approximately 1 mm; if it is thicker than 2 to 3 mm, constrictive pericarditis should be considered (Fig. 58-3). However, a thickened pericardium does not necessarily imply it is constrictive and constrictive pericarditis also may be present with a pericardium of normal thickness. CT is also well suited to detect pericardial calcifications and to evaluate their distribution, which can be very helpful in surgical planning before pericardiectomy (Fig. 58-4).

The imaging features of restrictive cardiomyopathy are nonspecific, but tissue characterization can be accomplished by CMR. Hence, a variety of pathologic processes, known to lead to this entity, including amyloidosis, sarcoidosis, and iron overload, can be detected.[17]

A thickened ventricular myocardium in combination with a thickened interatrial septum and right atrial wall hypertrophy suggests amyloid heart disease. Furthermore, a typical late gadolinium enhancement pattern, with widespread enhancement preferentially

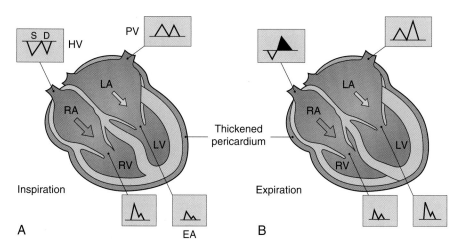

Figure 58-2 Schematic drawing of respiratory variation in transvalvular and central venous flow velocities in constrictive pericarditis. **A,** During inspiration the decrease in left ventricular filling results in a leftward shift of the interventricular septum, allowing increased right ventricular filling. **B,** The opposite occurs at expiration. A, ventricular filling due to atrial contraction; D, diastolic venous flow; E, early ventricular filling; HV, hepatic vein; LA, left atrium; LV, left ventricle; PV, pulmonary vein; RA, right atrium; RV, right ventricle; S, systolic venous flow. *(After Oh JK, Hatle LK, Seward JB et al. Diagnostic role of Doppler echocardiography in constrictive pericarditis. J Am Coll Cardiol 1994; 23:154–162, with permission.)*

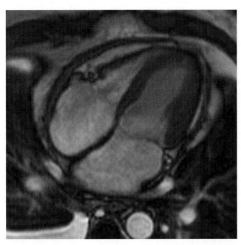

Figure 58-3   CMR image showing a thickened pericardium in a patient with constrictive pericarditis. *(Courtesy D. Didier, MD, University Hospital Geneva, Switzerland.)*

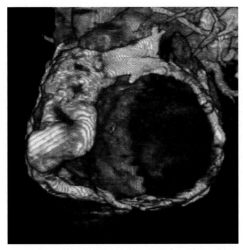

Figure 58-4   CT image showing extensive pericardial calcifications in a patient with constrictive pericarditis. *(Courtesy D. Didier, MD, University Hospital Geneva, Switzerland.)*

affecting the subendocardium and sparing the mid myocardium, is seen. These imaging features have been referred to the "zebra" pattern of enhancement. The wash-in and wash-out kinetics of gadolinium are also abnormal. These characteristics help in diagnosing amyloid heart disease (Fig. 58-5).[18]

Cardiac sarcoidosis can be seen on CMR as areas of abnormal high myocardial signal intensity, which is more prominent on T2-weighted images compared with T1-weighted images. Gadolinium enhances the signal intensity of the inflamed myocardium on T1-weighted images. Typical findings are patchy mid-wall and epicardial enhancement affecting the basal lateral walls. These features are not diagnostic of cardiac sarcoidosis, because they indicate myocardial inflammation, but are suggestive in the appropriate clinical setting (Fig. 58-6). Recently it has been shown that delayed enhancement CMR is more sensitive in detecting cardiac involvement in patients with sarcoidosis as current consensus criteria and that myocardial damage by this method seems to be associated with future cardiac adverse events.[19] Furthermore, CMR is likely to be of value in monitoring treatment in these patients.

CMR is an excellent imaging technique to diagnose iron-overload cardiomyopathy. T2* is a relaxation parameter due to local magnetic field inhomogeneities that are increased with particulate storage iron deposition. This parameter correlates with myocardial iron stores, which can now be quantified, The median value of T2* in the normal population is about 40 ms. A threshold of T2* less than 10 ms indicates severe iron loading. This method is highly useful not only for diagnosis but also for monitoring treatment with chelation therapies and has led to a reduction in mortality rates in this condition in the United Kingdom.[20]

Cardiac Catheterization

A thorough, invasive hemodynamic evaluation should be done by simultaneous right- and left-sided heart catheterization. Constrictive pericarditis and restrictive cardiomyopathy share the restrictive physiology, of which the characteristic "square root" or "dip and plateau" pattern is the hallmark (see Fig. 58-1). In the classic presentation of a constrictive pericarditis, the diastolic pressures are increased and almost equal, with less than a 5 mm Hg difference in all four cardiac chambers. However, the same phenomenon is not infrequently seen in restrictive cardiomyopathy.

The atrial pressure curves show a rapid descent of both x and y troughs in both constrictive pericarditis and restrictive cardiomyopathy. The end-diastolic pressure is often more than one third of the peak systolic pressure in constrictive pericarditis. It is often lower than that in restrictive cardiomyopathy, but exceptions, in both conditions, are seen frequently. This indicates that, although the differences between groups of patients with the two diseases are reported to be significant in many aspects, the overlap is such that discrimination in the individual patient is often difficult. The most important clue for the differentiation between constrictive pericarditis and restrictive cardiomyopathy is the simultaneous measurement of left and right ventricular peak systolic pressures at inspiration and expiration. In patients with constrictive pericarditis, with an enhanced ventricular interaction, the peak systolic left ventricular pressure drops while the peak systolic pressure of the right ventricle rises with inspiration. With expiration the opposite occurs. In other words, there is discordance in the direction of change of left and right peak systolic ventricular

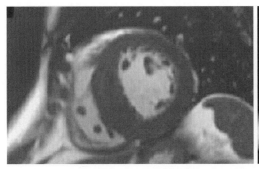
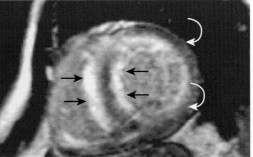

Figure 58-5   Cardiac amyloidosis. CMR with late gadolinium enhancement showing diffuse subendocardial enhancement in both left and right ventricles *(straight arrows)* with sparing of the epicardium and mid wall *(curved arrows)*. *(From O'Hanlon R, Pennell DJ. Cardiovascular magnetic resonance in the evaluation of hypertrophic and infiltrative cardiomyopathies. Heart Failure Clin 2009; 5:369–387, with permission.)*

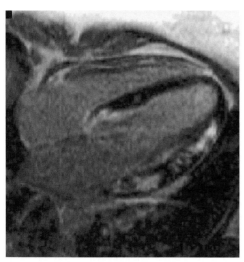

Figure 58-6   Cardiac sarcoidosis. CMR with late gadolinium enhancement showing patchy mid-wall patterns affecting the lateral wall at the base and apex in the four-chamber view. *(From O'Hanlon R, Pennell DJ. Cardiovascular magnetic resonance in the evaluation of hypertrophic and infiltrative cardiomyopathies. Heart Failure Clin 2009; 5:369–387, with permission.)*

pressures with respiration (Fig. 58-7). In restrictive cardiomyopathy, as in normal hearts, both right and left peak systolic ventricular pressure drop with inspiration and increase with expiration, parallel with the changes in the intrathoracic pressures. There is concordance in the direction of change of left and right ventricular pressures with respiration (see Fig. 58-7).

More recently the ratio between the right ventricular to left ventricular systolic pressure-time area during inspiration versus expiration (systolic area index) was used as a measurement of enhanced ventricular interaction. The systolic area index had a sensitivity of 97% in identifying patients with surgically proven constrictive pericarditis.[21]

Endomyocardial Biopsy

A positive biopsy for amyloidosis—by far the most common cause of restrictive cardiomyopathy—is 100% diagnostic. Other specific infiltrative diseases can be detected this way, but, because of a sometimes patchy distribution of the disease throughout the myocardium, a negative biopsy does not completely rule out the disease. However, the advent of tissue characterization by CMR will likely increase the diagnostic yield of endomyocardial biopsy in providing guidance for the procedure. The idiopathic form of restrictive cardiomyopathy has a nonspecific microscopic presentation. Similar nonspecific abnormalities are also reported in myocardial biopsies in patients who are proved to have constrictive pericarditis.

Figure 58-7   **A,** Simultaneous pressure tracing from the left ventricle (LV) and right ventricle (RV) of a patient with restrictive cardiomyopathy. At inspiration both RV and LV peak systolic pressures decrease. **B,** In a patient with constrictive pericarditis, RV pressure rises at inspiration whereas LV pressure decreases. *(After Hatle LK, Appleton CP, Popp RL. Differentiation of constrictive pericarditis and restrictive cardiomyopathy by Doppler echocardiography. Circulation 1989; 79:357–370, with permission.)*

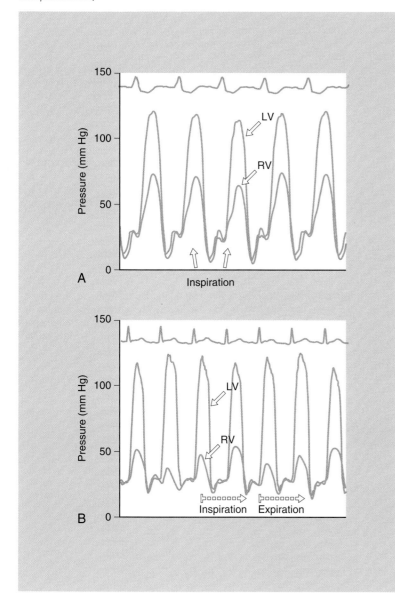

Exploratory Thoracotomy

If all else fails to distinguish between constrictive pericarditis and restrictive cardiomyopathy, an exploratory thoracotomy can be considered.

TREATMENT

Because patients present with signs of predominantly right-sided heart failure, symptomatic relief is achieved by diuretic treatment and salt restriction, irrespective of the diagnosis. If, after the diagnostic workup, constrictive pericarditis is the likely diagnosis, surgical pericardiectomy will have to be considered. Although the natural history of constrictive pericarditis remains unknown, case reports indicate a poor outcome without surgical intervention. However, there is a substantial perioperative mortality rate, ranging from about 6% in more recent reports[22] to nearly 15% in older series. The perioperative mortality relates to the etiologic subgroup: hence, patients with idiopathic constrictive pericarditis have a better prognosis than patients with postsurgical or postradiation constriction. In some reports, pericardial calcification is an independent predictor of increased perioperative mortality rates. Symptomatic improvement is reported in over 90% of the patients.

The treatment of idiopathic restrictive cardiomyopathy consists of general measures to reduce venous congestion, such as diuretics and fluid and salt restriction. Because the ventricles need high filling pressures in restrictive cardiomyopathy, the reduction in filling pressures by these general measurements will lead to a diminished stroke volume and cardiac output. Therefore, diuretic treatment should be implemented with the utmost care. Often patients will present with atrial fibrillation, in which case they will need oral anticoagulation.

▩ Late Outcome

In a recent study[22] examining the late outcome after pericardiectomy for constrictive pericarditis, the authors were able to show that long-term survival was related to the underlying etiology, left ventricular systolic function, renal function, and pulmonary artery pressure. Patients in the subgroup of idiopathic constrictive pericarditis had the best prognosis with a 7-year survival rate of 88%. However, patients with a history of chest irradiation had a 7-year survival rate of only 27% and had the poorest outcome.

There are concerns that long-term ventricular function is affected negatively by the absence of the pericardial support and that ventricular failure might occur at a relatively early age. However, there are no data to support this concern and, in the absence of a short-term alternative to pericardiectomy, it remains the treatment of choice.

The clinical course of restrictive cardiomyopathy is that of progressive heart failure. Although the clinical presentation might be variable, the condition is often fatal within 5 years of the diagnosis. In a study[23] analyzing patients with idiopathic restrictive cardiomyopathy the 5-year survival rate was 64% compared with an expected survival rate of 85%. By multivariate analysis the risk of death increased with male sex, older age, New York Heart Association functional class, and large left atrial dimensions.

If untreated, constrictive pericarditis follows the same clinical course. There are no late complications specific to either of the two diseases in comparison to other forms of heart failure, even though the occurrence of ascites might be more pronounced (Box 58-2).

BOX 58-2   COMPLICATIONS

- Refractory heart failure with end organ dysfunction
- Arrhythmias and sudden death
- Thromboembolism
- Cachexia
- Depression

▩ Outpatient Assessment

Once the diagnosis has been made, follow-up can be done by a general physician because clinical decision-making is based mainly on the patient's history and physical examination. Changes in body weight, liver enlargement, central venous pressure, peripheral edema, ascites, heart rate, and blood pressure will guide the dosage of diuretics and the strictness of salt and fluid restriction. Regular laboratory tests are necessary to monitor electrolyte levels and kidney function, especially during diuretic treatment.

▩ Late Management Options

Cardiac transplantation remains the only option in the end stage of restrictive cardiomyopathy and for patients with constrictive pericarditis in whom pericardectomy did not allow clinical improvement. Cardiac transplantation should be considered only when medical treatment fails and chronic right-sided heart failure has developed and not at the time when the diagnosis of restrictive cardiomyopathy or constrictive pericarditis is made, since the clinical course cannot be anticipated (Box 58-3).

▩ Arrhythmia and Sudden Cardiac Death

Supraventricular arrhythmias may be the initial presentation in both restrictive cardiomyopathy and constrictive pericarditis. In both entities there is severe dilation of the right and left atria, providing a substrate for atrial fibrillation or intra-atrial reentry tachycardia. Loss of sinus rhythm and consequently atrial contraction, which is an important contributor to ventricular filling in these compromised hemodynamic states, may lead to rapid clinical deterioration. The clinical presentation is of progressive heart failure and not of sudden cardiac death. In the case of restrictive cardiomyopathy due to amyloidosis, or of any other type of storage disease affecting the myocardium, there is an increased risk of ventricular arrhythmia, including ventricular fibrillation leading to sudden death.

▩ Pregnancy

Symptomatic patients with either restrictive cardiomyopathy or constrictive pericarditis carry a high additional risk in pregnancy. Cardiac output can only slightly increase by means of a higher heart rate and not by an increase in stroke volume. Hence, the raised metabolic needs required during pregnancy may not be matched. There is a high risk of fetal loss, and even of maternal death.

▩ Level of Follow-Up, Endocarditis Prophylaxis, and Exercise

Once the diagnosis has been made, follow-up should be provided by a physician familiar with the medical treatment of heart failure; this can be either a general physician or a cardiologist. The frequency of follow-up visits depends on the clinical status of the individual patient. Good access to, and good communication with, a center for cardiac

---

BOX 58-3   LATE TREATMENT

- Outpatient management of restrictive cardiomyopathy should aim to deliver a patient in the best possible medical condition for cardiac transplantation. This includes maintaining nutrition, treating anemia and hypertension, and trying to preserve renal function.
- Drug therapy is limited for restrictive cardiomyopathy. Judicious use of diuretics may help symptoms of congestion, but excessive reduction of preload may be counterproductive or even dangerous. Salt restriction is recommended. Angiotensin-converting enzyme inhibitors may occasionally have a role.
- Surgical pericardectomy is the treatment of choice for constrictive pericarditis.

transplantation is essential for optimal timing of cardiac transplantation in the end-stage phase of these diseases.

As a rule, endocarditis prophylaxis is not indicated for patients with restrictive cardiomyopathy or constrictive pericarditis without concomitant intracardiac abnormalities.

Patients will be limited in their exercise capacity, because cardiac output can only be increased to a modest degree. Within these limitations, patients should be encouraged to exercise to maintain an optimal level of physical fitness. The risk of sudden death during exercise is estimated to be very small.

REFERENCES

1. Elliott P, Andersson B, Arbustini E, et al. Classification of the cardiomyopathies: a position statement from the European Society of Cardiology Working Group on Myocardial and Pericardial Diseases. Eur Heart J 2008;29:270–276.
2. Maron BJ, Towbin JA, Thiene G, et al. Contemporary definitions and classification of the cardiomyopathies: an American Heart Association scientific statement from the Council on Clinical Cardiology, Heart Failure and Transplantation Committee. Circulation 2006;113:1807–1816.
3. Ling LH, Oh JK, Schaff HV, et al. Constrictive pericarditis in the modern era: evolving clinical spectrum and impact on outcome after pericardiectomy. Circulation 1999;100:1380–1416.
4. Piovaccari G, Ferretti RM, Prati F, et al. Cardiac disease after chest irradiation for Hodgkin's disease: incidence in 108 patients with long follow-up. Int J Cardiol 1995;49:39–43.
5. Kutcher MA, King III SB, Alimurung BN, et al. Constrictive pericarditis as a complication of cardiac surgery: recognition of an entity. Am J Cardiol 1982;50:742–748.
6. Kabbani SS, LeWinter M. Pericardial disease. In: Crawford MH, DiMarco JP, editors. Cardiology. London: Mosby; 2001. p. 5.15.1–5.15.14.
7. Nishimura RA. Constrictive pericarditis in the modern era: a diagnostic dilemma. Heart 2001;86:619–623.
8. Hancock EW. Differential diagnosis of restrictive cardiomyopathy and constrictive pericarditis. Heart 2001;86:343–349.
9. Vaitkus PT, Cooper KA, Shuman WP, Hardin NJ. Images in cardiovascular medicine. Constrictive pericarditis. Circulation 1996;93:834–835.
10. Hatle LK, Appleton CP, Popp RL. Differentiation of constrictive pericarditis and restrictive cardiomyopathy by Doppler echocardiography. Circulation 1989;79:357–370.
11. Oh JK, Tajik AJ, Appleton CP, et al. Preload reduction to unmask the characteristic Doppler features of constrictive pericarditis: a new observation. Circulation 1997;95:796–799.
12. Oh JK, Hatle LK, Seward JB, et al. Diagnostic role of Doppler echocardiography in constrictive pericarditis. J Am Coll Cardiol 1994;23:154–162.
13. Garcia MJ, Rodriguez L, Ares M, et al. Differentiation of constrictive pericarditis from restrictive cardiomyopathy: assessment of left ventricular diastolic velocities in longitudinal axis by Doppler tissue imaging. J Am Coll Cardiol 1996;27:108–114.
14. Ragajoplan N, Garcia MJ, Rodriguez L, et al. Comparison of new Doppler echocardiographic methods to differentiate pericardial heart disease and restrictive cardiomyopathy. Am J Cardiol 2001;87:86–94.
15. Ha JW, Ommen SR, Tajik AJ, et al. Differentiation of constrictive pericarditis from restrictive cardiomyopathy using mitral annular velocity by tissue Doppler echocardiography. Am J Cardiol 2004;94:316–319.
16. Choi EY, Ha JW, Kim JM, et al. Incremental value of combining systolic mitral annular velocity and time difference between mitral inflow and diastolic mitral annular velocity to early diastolic annular velocity for differentiating constrictive pericarditis from restrictive cardiomyopathy. J Am Soc Echocardiogr 2007; 20:738–743.
17. O'Hanlon R, Pennell DJ. Cardiovascular magnetic resonance in the evaluation of hypertrophic and infiltrative cardiomyopathies. Heart Failure Clin 2009;5:369–387.
18. Maceira AM, Joshi J, Prasad SK, et al. Cardiovascular magnetic resonance in cardiac amyloidosis. Circulation 2005;111:186–193.
19. Patel MR, Cawley PJ, Heitner JF, et al. Detection of myocardial damage in patients with sarcoidosis. Circulation 2009;120: 1969–1977.
20. Anderson LJ, Holden S, Davis B, et al. Cardiovascular T2-star (T2*) magnetic resonance for the early diagnosis of myocardial iron overload. Eur Heart J 2001;22:2171–2179.
21. Talreja DR, Nishimura RA, Oh JK, et al. Constrictive pericarditis in the modern era: novel criteria for diagnosis in the cardiac catheterization laboratory. J Am Coll Cardiol 2008;51:315–319.
22. Bertog SC, Thambidorai SK, Parakh K, et al. Constrictive pericarditis: etiology and cause-specific survival after pericardiectomy. J Am Coll Cardiol 2004;43:1445–1452.
23. Ammash NM, Seward JB, Bailey KR, et al. Clinical profile and outcome of idiopathic restrictive cardiomyopathy. Circulation 2000;101:2490–2496.

59 Arrhythmogenic Right Ventricular Cardiomyopathy

KALLIOPI PILICHOU | GAETANO THIENE | DOMENICO CORRADO | CRISTINA BASSO

Introduction

Arrhythmogenic right ventricular cardiomyopathy/dysplasia (ARVC/D) is a unique heart muscle disease clinically characterized by nonischemic right ventricular (RV) arrhythmias that can cause sudden death in the young and in athletes.[1-4] The pathology consists of progressive dystrophy of the RV myocardium with fibrofatty replacement.[3,5] In the general population the estimated prevalence of the disease varies from 1:2000 to 1:5000.[2]

Clinical Features and Natural History

Traditionally, the following clinical phases of the disease have been observed:

1. Subclinical phase with concealed structural abnormalities, during which the affected patient presents no symptoms and cardiac arrest may be the first and last manifestation of the disease. ARVC/D has been reported as the second most cause of sudden death in the young (Fig. 59-1).[3]
2. Overt electrical disorder, with palpitations and syncope. The most typical clinical presentation is symptomatic ventricular arrhythmias of RV origin, usually triggered by effort. Arrhythmias range from isolated premature ventricular beat to sustained ventricular tachycardia (VT) with left bundle-branch block (LBBB) morphology (Figs. 59-1 and 59-2) and ventricular fibrillation.
3. RV failure due to progressive loss of the RV myocardium, which may impair the mechanical function with severe pump failure.
4. Biventricular failure, when the disease involves the ventricular septum and the left ventricle mimicking dilated cardiomyopathy. Endocavitary mural thrombosis may occur, within aneurysms or in the atrial appendages, when heart failure is complicated by atrial fibrillation and may account for thromboembolism. In such conditions, contractile dysfunction may be so severe as to require cardiac transplantation.

Pathology and Pathogenesis

The disease consists of a progressive replacement of the RV myocardium by fibrofatty tissue,[3,5] which starts from the epicardium and extends down to reach the endocardium to become transmural. This implies thinning of the free wall, resulting in RV dilation and aneurysm formation, typically located at the inferior, apical, and infundibular walls (the so-called triangle of dysplasia).[6] The myocardial atrophy is not present at birth and is progressive with time. The disease should not be confused with Uhl disease, which is a congenital heart defect in which the RV myocardium failed to develop during embryonic life.[7] Apoptotic myocyte death has been observed both post mortem[8] and in vivo in endomyocardial biopsy specimens.[9]

Transvenous endomyocardial biopsy may be of great help for an in-vivo morphologic demonstration of fibrofatty myocardial replacement.[10] Samples should be retrieved from the RV free wall, where the fibrofatty replacement is usually transmural and thus detectable through the endocardial approach, whereas the ventricular septum is usually spared. A residual amount of myocardium less than 60%, due to fibrous or fibrofatty replacement, has been proven to have a high diagnostic accuracy.[11]

Clinical and Differential Diagnosis

In-vivo diagnosis may be achieved by demonstrating alterations of the RV function and structure, typical electrocardiographic depolarization and repolarization abnormalities, arrhythmias of LBBB morphology, fibrofatty replacement of the myocardium, and positive family history. Diagnostic criteria have been proposed[12] and divided into major and minor (Box 59-1). The diagnosis of ARVC/D will be fulfilled by the presence of two major or one major plus two minor or four minor criteria.

Morphologic changes accounting for global and/or regional dysfunction are detectable by echocardiography, angiography, cardiac magnetic resonance imaging (CMR), or radionuclide scintigraphy. Major criteria consist of severe dilation and reduction in systolic function of the right ventricle with no (or only mild) impairment of left ventricular (LV) function; localized RV aneurysms (akinesia or dyskinetic areas with diastolic bulging); and severe segmental dilation of the right ventricle. Minor criteria are mild global RV dilation and/or reduction in ejection fraction with normal LV size and function, mild segmental dilation of the RV free wall, and regional RV hypokinesia.

RV angiography is usually reported as the gold standard for the diagnosis of ARVC/D. Angiographic evidence of akinetic/dyskinetic bulging localized in the infundibular, apical, and subtricuspid region has high diagnostic specificity (>90%).[13] Echocardiography represents the first-line diagnostic imaging approach for suspected ARVC/D or for screening of family members. Echocardiography also allows serial examinations aimed to assess the disease onset and progression during the follow-up of affected patients, family members, or asymptomatic genetic carriers. CMR is an attractive imaging tool because it is noninvasive and has the ability to characterize tissue by distinguishing fat from muscle. However, recent studies have shown a high degree of interobserver variability in assessing fatty deposition, which may be observed even in normal hearts. Cine-CMR may be of value in estimating RV volume and wall motion abnormalities with akinesia, dyskinesia, and aneurysms. Tissue characterization of the RV free wall by histopathology with fibrofatty replacement of the myocardium, as demonstrated on endomyocardial biopsy or surgical resection, is considered a major criterion.

Repolarization abnormalities consisting of inverted T waves in right precordial leads (V_2 and V_3) in the absence of right bundle-branch block (RBBB) in individuals older than 12 years of age are considered a minor criterion (see Fig. 59-1). As far as depolarization/conduction abnormalities, epsilon wave or localized prolongation of the QRS complex greater than 110 ms in V_1 to V_3 is a major criterion, whereas the presence of late potentials on signal-averaged electrocardiography is considered minor. Arrhythmias such as sustained or nonsustained VT with LBBB morphology and premature ventricular beats of more than 1000 over 24-hour Holter monitoring are considered minor (see Fig. 59-2). Finally, family history is a major criterion when familial disease is confirmed at necropsy or surgery, whereas it is minor in patients with a family history of premature sudden death (<35 years) with diagnosis based on the present criteria.

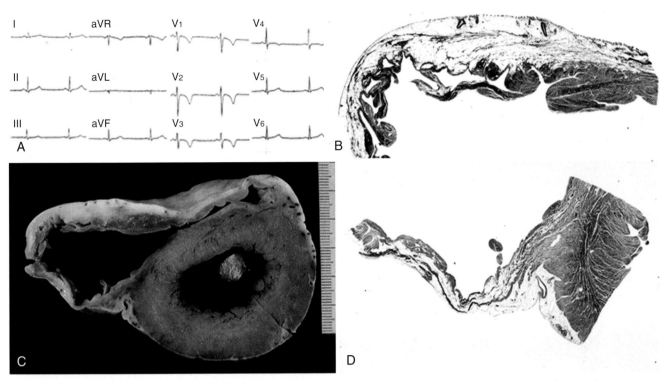

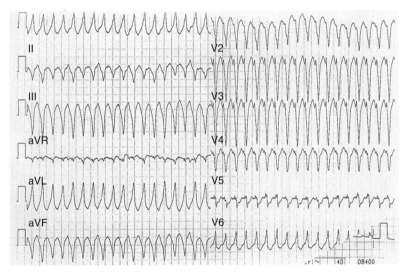

Figure 59-1   A 17-year-old asymptomatic male athlete died suddenly during a soccer game. **A,** Twelve-lead electrocardiogram showing inverted T waves up to V$_4$. **B,** Cross section of the heart shows RV dilation with anterior and posterior aneurysms and spotty left ventricular (LV) involvement. **C** and **D,** Histology of the anterior and posterior RV free walls with transmural fibrofatty replacement. (*Modified from Basso C, Thiene G, Corrado D et al. Arrhythmogenic right ventricular cardiomyopathy: dysplasia, dystrophy or myocarditis? Circulation 1996; 94:983–991.*)

Figure 59-2   Twelve-lead electrocardiographic recording of ventricular tachycardia with left bundle-branch block morphology.

A modification by a joint European-American task force of the criteria for the diagnosis of ARVC/D has been proposed for early detection of the disease in family members.[14] In first-degree relatives of a patient confirmed to be affected by ARVC/D, the presence of right precordial T-wave inversion (V$_2$ and V$_3$) or late potentials on signal-averaged electrocardiogram (ECG), or VT with LBBB morphology, or mild functional or morphologic RV changes on imaging should be considered diagnostic for members of familial ARVC/D. In addition, the threshold of premature ventricular beats has been reduced from 1000 to 200 over 24-hour Holter monitoring to suggest familial disease expression (Table 59-1).

New tools for improving diagnostic accuracy have been introduced in recent years. Among noninvasive investigations, CMR with gadolinium late enhancement has been demonstrated to be able to detect fibrosis both in the RV and LV myocardium.[15] Among invasive procedures, three-dimensional (3D) electroanatomic mapping shows low-voltage areas in ARVC/D that correspond to fibrofatty myocardial replacement (Fig. 59-3).[16] This technique is able to differentiate ARVC/D from active myocarditis with tachyarrhythmias, which shows a preserved electrogram voltage and has a better arrhythmic outcome. Moreover, this procedure is useful to distinguish early minor forms

BOX 59-1   1996 CRITERIA FOR DIAGNOSIS OF ARRHYTHMOGENIC RIGHT VENTRICULAR CARDIOMYOPATHY/DYSPLASIA

Family History

Major
- Familial disease confirmed at necropsy or surgery

Minor
- Family history of premature sudden death (<35 years of age) due to suspected ARVC/D
- Family history (clinical diagnosis based on present criteria)

Electrocardiographic Depolarization/Conduction Abnormalities

Major
- Epsilon waves or localized prolongation (>110 ms) of QRS complex in right precordial leads (V$_1$ to V$_3$)

Minor
- Late potentials on signal-averaged electrocardiography

Electrocardiographic Repolarization Abnormalities

Minor
- Inverted T waves in right precordial leads (V$_2$ and V$_3$) in individuals older than 12 years of age and in the absence of right bundle-branch block

Arrhythmias

Minor
- Sustained or nonsustained left bundle-branch block–type ventricular tachycardia documented on electrocardiographic or Holter monitoring or during exercise testing

- Frequent ventricular extrasystoles (>1000/24 hr on Holter monitoring)

Global or Regional Dysfunction and Structural Alterations*

Major
- Severe dilation and reduction of RV ejection fraction with no or mild LV involvement
- Localized RV aneurysms (akinetic or dyskinetic areas with diastolic bulging)
- Severe segmental dilation of the right ventricle

Minor
- Mild global RV dilation or ejection fraction reduction with normal left ventricle
- Mild segmental dilation of the right ventricle
- Regional RV hypokinesia

Tissue Characteristics of Walls

Major
- Fibrofatty replacement of myocardium on endomyocardial biopsy

*Detected by echocardiography, angiography, magnetic resonance imaging, or radionuclide scintigraphy.
Modified from McKenna WJ, Thiene G, Nava A et al. Diagnosis of arrhythmogenic right ventricular dysplasia/cardiomyopathy. Task Force of the Working Group Myocardial and Pericardial Disease of the European Society of Cardiology and of the Scientific Council on Cardiomyopathies of the International Society and Federation of Cardiology. Br Heart J 1994; 71:215–218.

TABLE 59-1	Proposed Modification of Task Force Criteria for the Diagnosis of Familial Arrhythmogenic Right Ventricular Cardiomyopathy/Dysplasia	
ARVC/D in First-Degree Relative Plus One of the Following:	
Electrocardiography	T-wave inversion in right precordial leads (V$_2$ and V$_3$)
Signal-averaged electrocardiography	Late potentials evident
Arrhythmia	Left bundle-branch block–type ventricular tachycardia on electrocardiography, on Holter monitoring, or during exercise testing
	Extrasystoles > 200 over a 24-hr period*
Structural or functional abnormality of the right ventricle	Mild global RV dilation and/or ejection fraction reduction with normal left ventricle
	Mild segmental dilation of the right ventricle
	Regional RV hypokinesia

*Greater than 1000/24-hr period in previous task force criteria.
Modified from Hamid MS, Norman M, Quraishi A et al. Prospective evaluation of relatives for familial arrhythmogenic right ventricular cardiomyopathy/dysplasia reveals a need to broaden diagnostic criteria. J Am Coll Cardiol 2002; 40:1445–1450.

of ARVC/D from idiopathic RV outflow tract tachycardia, which is a nonfamilial benign arrhythmic disorder without substrate and normal electrocardiographic mapping.[17] More recently, a joint European-American task force modified the diagnostic criteria by incorporating new knowledge and technology to improve diagnostic sensitivity but maintaining diagnostic specificity. Box 59-2 contains updated criteria. Quantitative criteria have been proposed and abnormalities were defined based on comparison with normal subject data.[18]

◼ Genetics

ARVC/D is heredofamilial in nearly 50% of cases, and the classic form is an autosomal dominant disease with variable penetrance.[19,20] The key to the discovery of gene defects came from a recessive form of ARVC/D, the so-called Naxos disease, a cardiocutaneous syndrome

characterized by palmoplantar keratosis, woolly hair, and heart muscle disease.[21] Importantly, epidermal cells and myocytes share a similar mechanical junctional apparatus, that is, desmosomes and fascia adherens, which provides cell-to-cell connections. This explains why genes coding proteins of the intercellular junction became candidate genes for ARVC/D. Desmosomes, together with adherens junctions, provide mechanical attachment between cells. In contrast to adherens junctions, desmosomes are not linked to the actin network but to intermediate filaments, namely, desmin in the heart and keratin in the skin. Proteins from three separate families assemble to form desmosomes: the desmosomal cadherins, armadillo proteins, and plakins (Fig. 59-4). In addition to the first deletion in plakoglobin found in Naxos disease in 2000,[21] other mutations have been described for dominant forms of ARVC/D to desmoplakin in 2002,[22] plakophilin-2 in 2004,[23] desmoglein-2 in 2006,[24] desmocollin-2 in 2006,[25] and the plakoglobin gene in 2007 (Table 59-2).[26] Thus, ARVC/D was also found to be a cell junction disease in its dominant form, with plakophilin-2 as the most frequently associated gene. Genotype-phenotype correlations revealed that the desmoplakin mutations are associated with a high occurrence of sudden death and frequent LV involvement.[27] Ultrastructural studies of endomyocardial biopsies of patients with ARVC/D and cell junction gene mutations revealed intercalated disc remodeling with a reduced number and length of desmosomes and intercellular gap widening.[28]

A recessive mutation in desmoplakin has been associated to Carvajal syndrome, another cardiocutaneous disorder characterized by keratoderma, woolly hair, and a biventricular form of ARVC/D, with distinct ultrastructural abnormalities of intercalated discs and decreased immunoreactive signals for desmoplakin, plakoglobin, and connexin 43.[29,30] Recently, routine immunohistochemical analysis of plakoglobin on conventional endomyocardial biopsy samples has been shown to be a highly sensitive and specific diagnostic test for ARVC/D.[31] With gene mutations available, transgenic mice are now being developed to gain an insight into the pathogenetic mechanisms of the disease, with possible therapeutic implications.[32–34]

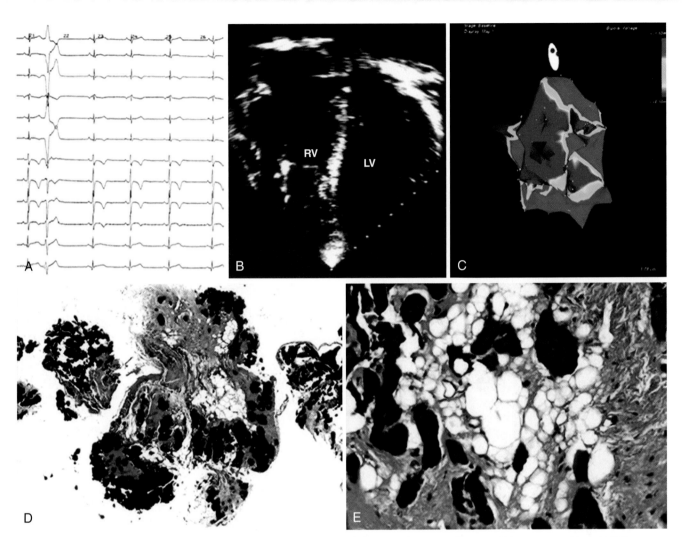

Figure 59-3   Invasive electroanatomic mapping by CARTO. **A,** Twelve-lead electrocardiogram with inverted T waves up to V$_4$ and LBBB premature ventricular beat. **B,** Four-chamber two-dimensional (2D) echocardiogram showing right ventricular (RV) dilation and apical aneurysm. LV, left ventricle. **C,** Low-voltage RV areas (*red*) shown by CARTO mapping. **D** and **E,** Extensive fibrofatty replacement of the RV myocardium at endomyocardial biopsy. *(Modified from Corrado D, Basso C, Leoni L et al. Three-dimensional electroanatomic voltage mapping increases accuracy of diagnosing arrhythmogenic right ventricular cardiomyopathy/dysplasia. Circulation 2005;111:3042–3050.)*

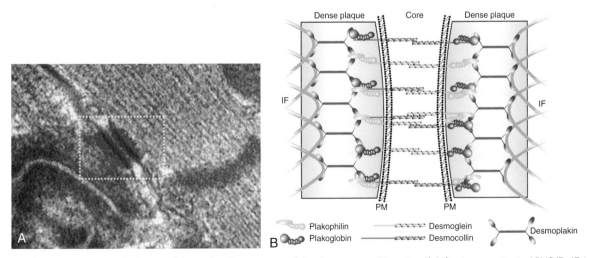

Figure 59-4   Ultrastructure (**A**) and scheme of the molecular structure of the desmosome (**B**) at site of defective proteins in ARVC/D. IF, intermediate filaments; PM, plasma membrane. *(From Basso C, Corrado D, Marcus FI, et al. Arrhythmogenic right ventricular cardiomyopathy. Lancet 2009; 373:1289-1300.)*

TABLE 59-2	Desmosomal Genes Involved in Arrhythmogenic Right Ventricular Cardiomyopathy/Dysplasia and Cardiocutaneous Syndromes		
Abbreviation	Disease Gene	Transmission Trait	Study
JUP	Plakoglobin	AR	McKoy et al, 2000[21]
DSP	Desmoplakin	AR	Norgett et al, 2000[29]
DSP	Desmoplakin	AD	Rampazzo et al, 2002[22]
PKP2	Plakophilin-2	AD	Gerull et al, 2004[23]
DSG2	Desmoglein-2	AD	Pilichou et al, 2006[24]
DSC2	Desmocollin-2	AD	Syrris et al, 2006[22]
JUP	Plakoglobin	AD	Asimaki et al, 2007[23]

In particular, our group recently demonstrated that myocyte necrosis underlies progressive myocardial dystrophy in mouse *dsg2*-related ARVC/D.[34]

■ Risk Stratification and Therapy

Young age, "malignant" family history, QRS dispersion greater than or equal to 40 ms, T-wave inversion beyond V_1, LV involvement, ventricular tachycardia, syncope, or previous cardiac arrest are considered the major determinants for adverse prognosis and impending sudden death.[35] Different antiarrhythmic drugs have been employed, including sodium blockers, β-adrenergic blockers, sotalol, amiodarone, and verapamil alone or in combinations.

BOX 59-2   2010 REVISED TASK FORCE CRITERIA FOR ARVC/D

Global or Regional Dysfunction and Structural Alterations*
Major
By 2D echo:
- Regional RV akinesia, dyskinesia, or aneurysm
- *and* 1 of the following (end diastole):
  - PLAX RVOT ≥32 mm (corrected for body size [PLAX/BSA] ≥19 mm/m²)
  - PSAX RVOT ≥36 mm (corrected for body size [PSAX/BSA] ≥21 mm/m²)
  - *or* fractional area change ≤33%
By MRI:
- Regional RV akinesia or dyskinesia or dyssynchronous RV contraction
- *and* 1 of the following:
  - Ratio of RV end-diastolic volume to BSA ≥110 mL/m² (male) or ≥100 mL/m² (female)
  - *or* RV ejection fraction ≤40%
By RV angiography:
- Regional RV akinesia, dyskinesia, or aneurysm

Minor
By 2D echo:
- Regional RV akinesia or dyskinesia
- *and* 1 of the following (end diastole):
  - PLAX RVOT ≥29 to <32 mm (corrected for body size [PLAX/BSA] ≥16 to <19 m/m²)
  - PSAX RVOT ≥32 to <36 mm (corrected for body size [PSAX/BSA] ≥18 to <21 mm/m²)
  - *or* fractional area change >33% to ≤40%
By MRI:
- Regional RV akinesia or dyskinesia or dyssynchronous RV contraction
- *and* 1 of the following:
  - Ratio of RV end-diastolic volume to BSA ≥100 to <110 mL/m² (male) or ≥90 to <100 mL/m² (female)
  - *or* RV ejection fraction >40% to ≤45%

Tissue Characterization of Wall
Major
- Residual myocytes <60% by morphometric analysis (or <50% if estimated), with fibrous replacement of the RV free wall myocardium in ≥1 sample, with or without fatty replacement of tissue on endomyocardial biopsy
Minor
- Residual myocytes 60% to 75% by morphometric analysis (or 50% to 65% if estimated), with fibrous replacement of the RV free wall myocardium in ≥1 sample, with or without fatty replacement of tissue on endomyocardial biopsy

Repolarization Abnormalities
Major
- Inverted T waves in right precordial leads (V_1, V_2, and V_3) or beyond in individuals >14 years of age (in the absence of complete right bundle-branch block QRS ≥120 ms)

Minor
- Inverted T waves in leads V_1 and V_2 in individuals >14 years of age (in the absence of complete right bundle-branch block) or in V_4, V_5, or V_6
- Inverted T waves in leads V_1, V_2, V_3, and V_4 in individuals 14 years of age in the presence of complete right bundle-branch block

Depolarization/Conduction Abnormalities
Major
- Epsilon wave (reproducible low-amplitude signals between end of QRS complex to onset of the T wave) in the right precordial leads (V_1 to V_3)

Minor
- Late potentials by SAECG in ≥1 of 3 parameters in the absence of a QRS duration of 110 ms on the standard ECG
- Filtered QRS duration (fQRS) ≥114 ms
- Duration of terminal QRS <40 μV (low-amplitude signal duration) ≥38 ms
- Root-mean-square voltage of terminal 40 ms ≤20 μV
- Terminal activation duration of QRS ≥55 ms measured from the nadir of the S wave to the end of the QRS, including R', in V_1, V_2, or V_3, in the absence of complete right bundle-branch block

Arrhythmias
Major
- Nonsustained or sustained ventricular tachycardia of left bundle-branch morphology with superior axis (negative or indeterminate QRS in leads II, III, and aVF and positive in lead aVL)

Minor
- Nonsustained or sustained ventricular tachycardia of RV outflow configuration, left bundle-branch block morphology with inferior axis (positive QRS in leads II, III, and aVF and negative in lead aVL) or of unknown axis
- >500 ventricular extrasystoles per 24 hours (Holter)

Family History
Major
- ARVC confirmed in a first-degree relative who meets current Task Force criteria
- ARVC confirmed pathologically at autopsy or surgery in a first-degree relative
- Identification of a pathogenic mutation† categorized as associated or probably associated with ARVC in the patient under evaluation

Minor
- History of ARVC/D in a first-degree relative in whom it is not possible or practical to determine whether the family member meets current Task Force criteria
  - †Premature sudden death (35 years of age) due to suspected ARVC/D in a first-degree relative
  - †ARVC/D confirmed pathologically or by current Task Force Criteria in second-degree relative

---

*Hypokinesis is not included in this or subsequent definitions of RV regional wall motion abnormalities for the proposed modified criteria.
†A pathogenic mutation is a DNA alteration associated with ARVC that alters or is expected to alter the encoded protein, is unobserved or rare in a large non–ARVC control population, and either alters or is predicted to alter the structure or function of the protein or has demonstrated linkage to the disease phenotype in a conclusive pedigree.
ARVC/D, arrhythmogenic right ventricular cardiomyopathy/dysplasia; BSA, body surface area; 2D, two-dimensional; ECG, electrocardiogram; echo, echocardiogram; MRI, magnetic resonance imaging; PLAX, parasternal long-axis view; PSAX, parasternal short-axis view; RVOT, RV outflow tract; SAECG, signal-averaged electrocardiogram.

Wichter and associates reported the various efficacy rates by demonstrating that sotalol is superior with complete or partial efficacy in 68% of patients versus 26% for amiodarone.[36] Catheter ablation has been accomplished in VT refractory to drug treatment. Although the treatment may be effective in the short term, the procedure is associated with high rate of recurrence, clearly indicating its palliative nature.[36] Nonetheless, in terms of survival, the outcome is satisfactory.

Use of an implantable cardioverter-defibrillator has been proven to be lifesaving. Corrado and colleagues[35] found a 76% freedom from electric shock, delivered in case of ventricular flutter/fibrillation, at 48 months after implantation, with a survival of 96%. Considering that each episode followed by electric shock would have been fatal, 20% of patients were saved by this device. Finally, in refractory congestive heart failure or electric storms, cardiac transplantation remains the only therapeutic option.

▪ Prevention of Sudden Death

Cardiac arrest in ARVC/D is the consequence of a combination of various factors (substrate, trigger, arrhythmias), and measures for prevention should focus on these various steps.

Effort, by volume overload and stretching of the RV myocardium, is considered a major trigger. Sport activity increases fivefold the risk of sudden death in the young.[37] Thus, identification of asymptomatic ARVC/D carriers is crucial to inform them about the risk during intense physical effort. Pre-participation screening and sport disqualification, with a choice of lifestyle without strenuous effort, has been shown to be lifesaving.[4] In the Veneto region in Italy, after implementation of obligatory pre-participation screening there was a sharp decline in sudden death in athletes from 1:28,000 per year in the pre-screening period to 1/250,000 per year in the late screening period, mostly due to identification and disqualification of patients affected by ARVC/D.[4]

REFERENCES

1. Marcus FI, Nava A, Thiene G, editors. Arrhythmogenic RV Cardiomyopathy/Dysplasia: Recent Advances. Milan: Springer Verlag; 2007.
2. Basso C, Corrado D, Marcus FI, et al. Arrhythmogenic right ventricular cardiomyopathy. Lancet 2009;373:1289–1300.
3. Thiene G, Nava A, Corrado D, et al. Right ventricular cardiomyopathy and sudden death in young people. N Engl J Med 1988;318:129–133.
4. Corrado D, Basso C, Pavei A, et al. Trends in sudden cardiovascular death in young competitive athletes after implementation of a preparticipation screening program. JAMA 2006;296:1593–1601.
5. Basso C, Thiene G, Corrado D, et al. Arrhythmogenic right ventricular cardiomyopathy: dysplasia, dystrophy or myocarditis? Circulation 1996;94:983–991.
6. Marcus F, Fontaine G, Guiraudon G, et al. Right ventricular dysplasia: a report of 24 adult cases. Circulation 1982; 65:384–398.
7. Uhl HS. A previously undescribed congenital malformation of the heart: almost total absence of the myocardium of the right ventricle. Bull Johns Hopkins Hosp 1952;91:197–209.
8. Mallat Z, Tedgui A, Fontaliran F, et al. Evidence of apoptosis in arrhythmogenic right ventricular dysplasia. N Engl J Med 1996;335:1190–1196.
9. Valente M, Calabrese F, Thiene G, et al. In vivo evidence of apoptosis in arrhythmogenic right ventricular cardiomyopathy. Am J Pathol 1998;152:479–484.
10. Angelini A, Basso C, Nava A, Thiene G. Endomyocardial biopsy in arrhythmogenic right ventricular cardiomyopathy. Am Heart J 1996;132:203–206.
11. Marcus F, Ronco F, Marcus F, et al. Quantitative assessment of endomyocardial biopsy in arrhythmogenic right ventricular cardiomyopathy/dysplasia: an in vitro validation of diagnostic criteria. Eur Heart J 2008;29:2760–2771.
12. McKenna WJ, Thiene G, Nava A, et al. Diagnosis of arrhythmogenic right ventricular dysplasia/cardiomyopathy. Task Force of the Working Group Myocardial and Pericardial Disease of the European Society of Cardiology and of the Scientific Council on Cardiomyopathies of the International Society and Federation of Cardiology. Br Heart J 1994;71:215–218.
13. Daliento L, Rizzoli G, Thiene G, et al. Diagnostic accuracy of right ventriculography in arrhythmogenic right ventricular cardiomyopathy. Am J Cardiol 1990;66:741–745.
14. Hamid MS, Norman M, Quraishi A, et al. Prospective evaluation of relatives for familial arrhythmogenic right ventricular cardiomyopathy/dysplasia reveals a need to broaden diagnostic criteria. J Am Coll Cardiol 2002;40:1445–1450.
15. Tandri H, Saranathan M, Rodriguez ER, et al. Noninvasive detection of myocardial fibrosis in arrhythmogenic right ventricular cardiomyopathy using delayed-enhancement magnetic resonance imaging. J Am Coll Cardiol 2005;45:98–103.
16. Corrado D, Basso C, Leoni L, et al. Three-dimensional electroanatomic voltage mapping increases accuracy of diagnosing arrhythmogenic right ventricular cardiomyopathy/dysplasia. Circulation 2005;111:3042–3050.
17. Corrado D, Basso C, Leoni L, et al. Three-dimensional electroanatomic voltage mapping and histological evaluation of myocardial substrate in right ventricular outflow tract tachycardia. J Am Coll Cardiol 2008;51:731–739.
18. Marcus FI, McKenna WJ, Sherrill D, et al. Diagnosis of arrhythmogenic right ventricular cardiomyopathy/dysplasia (ARVC/D); Proposed Modification of the Task Force Criteria. Circulation 2010;121:1533–1541.
19. Thiene G, Corrado D, Basso C. Arrhythmogenic right ventricular cardiomyopathy/dysplasia. Orphanet J Rare Dis 2007;2:45.
20. Nava A, Thiene G, Canciani B, et al. Familial occurrence of right ventricular dysplasia: a study involving nine families. J Am Coll Cardiol 1988;12:1222–1228.
21. McKoy G, Protonotarios N, Crosby A, et al. Identification of a deletion in plakoglobin in arrhythmogenic right ventricular cardiomyopathy with palmoplantar keratoderma and woolly hair (Naxos disease). Lancet 2000;355:2119–2124.
22. Rampazzo A, Nava A, Malacrida S, et al. Mutation in human desmoplakin domain binding to plakoglobin causes a dominant form of arrhythmogenic right ventricular cardiomyopathy. Am J Hum Genet 2002;71:1200–1206.
23. Gerull B, Heuser A, Wichter T, et al. Mutations in the desmosomal protein plakophilin-2 are common in arrhythmogenic right ventricular cardiomyopathy. Nat Genet 2004;36:1162–1164.
24. Pilichou K, Nava A, Basso C, et al. Mutations in desmoglein-2 gene are associated with arrhythmogenic right ventricular cardiomyopathy. Circulation 2006;113:1171–1179.
25. Syrris P, Ward D, Evans A, et al. Arrhythmogenic right ventricular dysplasia/cardiomyopathy associated with mutations in the desmosomal gene desmocollin-2. Am J Hum Genet 2006;79:978–984.
26. Asimaki A, Syrris P, Wichter T, et al. A novel dominant mutation in plakoglobin causes arrhythmogenic right ventricular cardiomyopathy. Am J Hum Genet 2007;81:964–973.
27. Bauce B, Basso C, Rampazzo A, et al. Clinical profile of four families with arrhythmogenic right ventricular cardiomyopathy caused by dominant desmoplakin mutations. Eur Heart J 2005; 26:1666–1675.
28. Basso C, Czarnowska E, Della Barbera M, et al. Ultrastructural evidence of intercalated disc remodelling in arrhythmogenic right ventricular cardiomyopathy: an electron microscopy investigation on endomyocardial biopsies. Eur Heart J 2006;27:1847–1854.
29. Norgett EE, Hatsell SJ, Carvajal-Huerta L, et al. Recessive mutation in desmoplakin disrupts desmoplakin-intermediate filament interactions and causes dilated cardiomyopathy, woolly hair and keratoderma. Hum Mol Genet 2000;9:2761–2766.
30. Kaplan SR, Gard JJ, Carvajal-Huerta L, et al. Structural and molecular pathology of the heart in Carvajal syndrome. Cardiovasc Pathol 2004;13:26–32.
31. Asimaki A, Tandri H, Huang H, et al. A new diagnostic test for arrhythmogenic right ventricular cardiomyopathy. N Engl J Med 2009;360:1075–1084.
32. Garcia-Gras E, Lombardi R, Giocondo MJ, et al. Suppression of canonical Wnt/beta-catenin signaling by nuclear plakoglobin recapitulates phenotype of arrhythmogenic right ventricular cardiomyopathy. J Clin Invest 2006;116:2012–2021.
33. Yang Z, Bowles NE, Scherer SE, et al. Desmosomal dysfunction due to mutations in desmoplakin causes arrhythmogenic right ventricular dysplasia/cardiomyopathy. Circ Res 2006;99:646–655.
34. Pilichou L, Remme CA, Basso C, et al. Myocyte necrosis underlies progressive myocardial dystrophy in mouse dsg2-related arrhythmogenic right ventricular cardiomyopathy. J Exp Med 2009;206:1787–1802.
35. Corrado D, Leoni L, Link MS, et al. Implantable cardioverter-defibrillator therapy for prevention of sudden death in patients with arrhythmogenic right ventricular cardiomyopathy/dysplasia. Circulation 2003;108:3084–3091.
36. Wichter T, Paul M, Eckardt L, et al. Arrhythmogenic right ventricular cardiomyopathy. Antiarrhythmic drugs, catheter ablation, or ICD? Herz 2005;30:91–101.
37. Corrado D, Basso C, Rizzoli G, et al. Does sports activity enhance the risk of sudden death in adolescents and young adults? J Am Coll Cardiol 2003;42:1959–1963.

Noncompacted Myocardium

ALIDA L. P. CAFORIO | GAETANO THIENE | ANNALISA ANGELINI

Introduction and Definitions

Noncompacted myocardium is an anatomic condition of the myocardial wall characterized by prominent left ventricular trabeculae and deep intertrabecular recesses (Fig. 60-1).[1] Noncompaction of the left ventricle (LVNC) can occur as an isolated cardiac feature or in association with idiopathic dilated cardiomyopathy (DCM) or with hypertrophic cardiomyopathy (HCM) as well as with metabolic and neuromuscular disorders and genetic syndromes (e.g., Barth syndrome) or with congenital heart defects (nonisolated LVNC). The definition of isolated LVNC was first used by Chin and colleagues[2] in 1990 to describe eight pediatric cases with the cardiac phenotype in the absence of congenital heart defects. There is no consensus about etiology, pathogenesis, diagnosis, and management of LVNC. In the 1995 World Health Organization/International Society and Federation of Cardiology classification of cardiomyopathies LVNC was regarded as unclassified.[3] It has been included in the North American revision,[4] but not all experts agree that it represents a cardiomyopathy or a disease of its own.[5,6] The clinical presentation is that of a sporadic or familial heart muscle disorder with presumed persistence of the embryonic pattern of trabeculation of the left ventricle. The apparent failure to undergo the normal "compaction process," which occurs between days 30 and 70 of embryogenesis, is thought to predispose to systolic and diastolic dysfunction, cavity dilation, hypertrophy, and arrhythmia.

Pathology and Pathogenesis

Noncompacted myocardium is characterized by involvement of the apical and mid segments of the left ventricular trabeculated component, with a thick noncompacted subendothelial layer and a thin compacted subepicardial layer in the transmural wall (see Fig. 60-1).[1,7,8] The ratio between noncompacted and compacted layers is of importance for the clinical and pathologic diagnoses. Suggested diagnostic criteria are a ratio more than 2 between the noncompacted and compacted layers or the presence of intertrabecular recesses extending to half the thickness of the myocardium.[7] The subendocardium contains deep intertrabecular recesses communicating with the ventricular cavity and prominent trabeculations (see Fig. 60-1), resulting, according to the most popular pathogenetic hypothesis, from an arrest of compaction of myocardial fibers during embryogenesis. This arrest usually occurs at 5 to 8 weeks of gestation when the myocardium is gradually compacted and the intertrabecular spaces are transformed into capillaries and the coronary circulation develops. The process occurs from the epicardium toward the endocardium and from the base toward the apex.[9] The right ventricle is affected in less than 50% of patients, even though the evaluation of the right ventricle could be somewhat more difficult. The absence of well-formed papillary muscle is considered an important aspect in the diagnosis.[7]

Histologic examination confirms that the spongy appearance is due to the deep intertrabecular recesses, lined by endothelium, which spread close to the epicardial surface (see Fig. 60-1). This feature strongly resembles the spongy myocardium pattern of nonmammalian vertebrates such as fish, amphibians, and reptiles. Increased subendocardial fibrosis is a common feature. In a series of 14 cases, predominantly consisting of autopsied hearts, endocardial fibroelastosis was also another characteristic histologic finding.[7] Subendocardial scar suggesting ischemic damage is often observed.

No differences in gross or histologic patterns of the noncompacted regions between the isolated and nonisolated LVNC have been reported.[7,10] A wide range of heterogeneity in patterns of trabeculation and recesses have been described: broad anastomosing trabeculae, coarse trabeculae resembling multiple papillary muscles, and interlacing smaller papillary muscles or relatively smooth endocardial surface with compressed recesses. Even though the noncompaction hypothesis is recognized as the most likely pathogenetic hypothesis, other hypotheses have been put forward. The compensatory hypothesis acknowledges a genetic defect, which should in turn produce an adaptive reaction in a poorly contracting myocardium. A hemodynamic hypothesis suggests that ischemia and/or microinfarcts may result in myocardial hypoxia and LVNC-like changes. Finally an inflammatory process (e.g., myocarditis) might produce a similar result. Diversity of mutated genes and frequent familial occurrence suggest a complex interplay among structural, contractile, and metabolic factors producing either arrest of compaction or induction of noncompaction.[11]

Diagnostic Criteria

The diagnosis of LVNC is difficult. Current diagnostic criteria that rely on standard transthoracic echocardiography are debated (Box 60-1) and may change in the future to include contrast echocardiography and cardiovascular magnetic resonance imaging. One of the defining features is a two-layered myocardium, a thin and compacted layer adjacent to the epicardium and a thick noncompacted layer near the endocardium, with prominent trabeculations separated by recesses. The first proposed criteria by Chin and colleagues[2] required an x/y ratio of less than or equal to 0.5 at end diastole. Because the differentiation of the two layers in diastole is difficult to determine, a subsequent set of criteria, suggested by Jenni and associates,[12] focused on a noncompacted (N) to compacted (C) ratio measured at end systole and requires an N/C ratio greater than 2 in adults and greater than 1.4 in children. In addition, Jenni and associates[12] proposed additional diagnostic requirements: the absence of coexisting cardiac structural abnormalities; the demonstration of numerous, excessively prominent trabeculations and deep intertrabecular recesses supplied by intraventricular blood on color flow Doppler imaging; and the prevalent localization of noncompacted regions to the lateral, inferior, or apical left ventricular segments. It is relevant to mention that the distribution of prominent trabeculations and interventricular recesses is segmental in LVNC whereas it is often diffuse in non-LVNC hearts. The most recently proposed criteria by Stollberger and coworkers[13] focus on more than three trabeculations protruding from the left ventricular wall, apically to the papillary muscles, visible in a single image plane and on the finding of intertrabecular spaces perfused from the ventricular cavity on color Doppler imaging. These authors justified their approach as a way to overcome the technical difficulties in the differentiation between papillary muscles, aberrant bands, false tendons, and trabeculations in the short-axis views used by Jenni and associates.[12] It should be noted that, most recently, Finsterer and Stollberger have proposed that if both the criteria of Stollberger and Jenni and their associates are satisfied then the diagnosis should be considered as "definite" LVNC whereas if only one set is satisfied the diagnosis should be of "probable" LVNC.[14] Patients with fewer than four trabeculations or an N/C ratio less than 2 would be considered

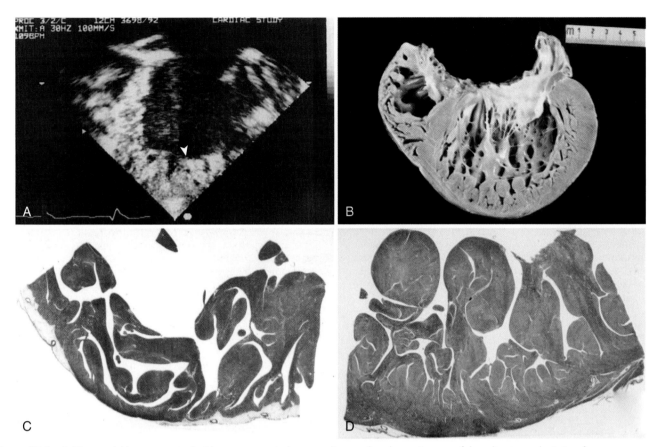

Figure 60-1 A 15-year-old boy presented with noncompacted myocardium and underwent successful cardiac transplantation for severe congestive heart failure. **A,** Two-dimensional (2D) echocardiography disclosed biventricular dilation and endocardial hyperechogenic coarse trabeculation. **B,** The heart removed at transplantation revealed the gross morphologic features of noncompaction with biventricular involvement. Histologic examination of the right (**C**) and left (**D**) ventricular wall confirmed that the spongy appearance was due to the deep intertrabecular recesses, lined by endothelium, which spread close to the epicardial surface both in the right and the left ventricle (Azan-Mallory stain, modified Heidenheim). *(Modified from Angelini A, Melacini P, Barbero F, Thiene G. Evolutionary persistence of spongy myocardium in humans. Circulation 1999; 99:2475.)*

as "possible" LVNC.[14] The current limitations in the diagnostic criteria have been recently highlighted by Kohli and coworkers,[15] who compared the three sets of LVNC criteria in an adult population referred to a heart failure clinic and found limited concordance and lack of specificity, especially in Afro-Caribbeans. These authors found an unexpectedly high proportion of heart failure patients (23.6%) and controls (8%) fulfilling one or more of the echocardiographic definitions and suggested that current criteria may be too sensitive, particularly in black subjects. Further work is needed to define the range of normal and LVNC morphology in different racial groups.

Clinical Presentation (Cardiac and Noncardiac Findings)

Clinical features of LVNC in major published series are summarized in Table 60-1. Noncardiac features in isolated LVNC include dysmorphic facial appearance, prominent forehead, bilateral strabismus, low-set ears, micrognathia, high-arched palate, and contractures of the left elbow.[2] Facial dysmorphism and motor delays are more common in children than in adults. In its extreme pediatric form LVNC may have severe presentation as fetal hydrops, neonatal heart failure, or ventricular fibrillation, which, if occurring in the absence of prodromes, may manifest as sudden infant death syndrome.[2,16–18] However, most pediatric cases are asymptomatic and the diagnosis

BOX 60-1 ECHOCARDIOGRAPHIC DIAGNOSTIC CRITERIA FOR LEFT VENTRICULAR NONCOMPACTION

Chin and colleagues[2]
- LVNC is defined by a ratio of x/y less than or equal to 0.5.
  - x = Distance from the epicardial surface to the trough of the trabecular recess
  - y = Distance from the epicardial surface to peak of trabeculation
- These criteria focus on trabeculae at the left ventricular apex on the parasternal short-axis and apical views and on left ventricular free wall thickness at end diastole.

Jenni and colleagues[12]
- A two-layer structure, with a thin compacted layer and a thick noncompacted layer measured in end systole on parasternal short-axis views
- LVNC is defined by a ratio of N/C greater than 2 in adults and greater than 1.4 in children, where N = noncompacted layer of myocardium and C = compacted layer of myocardium.
- Absence of coexisting cardiac structural abnormalities
- Numerous, excessively prominent trabeculations and deep intertrabecular recesses
- Recesses supplied by intraventricular blood on color Doppler imaging

Stollberger and colleagues[13]
- More than three trabeculations protruding from the left ventricular wall, apically to the papillary muscles, in a single-image plane, with same echogenicity as the myocardium, moving synchronously with it, not connected to the papillary muscles
- Intertrabecular spaces perfused from the ventricular cavity on color Doppler imaging

TABLE 60-1	Clinical Features in Patients with Isolated and Nonisolated Left Ventricular Noncompaction								
	Pediatric Patients				**Adult Patients**				
Study	Chin et al, 1990[2]	Ichida et al, 1999[16]	Pignatelli et al, 2003[17]	Lilje et al, 2006[18]	Oechslin et al, 2000[23]	Sengupta et al, 2004[24]	Murphy et al, 2005[19]	Stöllberger et al, 2002[13]	Lofiego et al, 2007[20]
No. of Patients	8	27	36	66	34	32	45	62	65
Age at Diagnosis (yr)	7	5	0.3	4	40	49	37 (mean)	50 (mean)	42
% Male	63%	56%	55%		74%	53%	62%	79%	
Ratio of Isolated to Nonisolated LVNC (Patients)	8:0	27:0	31:5	25:41	34:0	29:3	45:0	62:0	65:0
% Familial	50%	44%			18%				31%
Follow-Up (yr)	Up to 5	Up to 17	Up to 12	Up to 4	Up to 11				Up to 16
Bundle-Branch Block	25%	15%	0%		56%		29%	23%	32%
Wolff-Parkinson-White Syndrome	13%	15%	17%		0%			3%	1.5%
Ventricular Tachycardia	38%	0%	2.7%		41%		20%	18%	6%
Heart Failure	63%	30%	89%	68%	68%	62.5%	62%	73%	34%
Systemic Emboli	38%	0%	0%		21%		4%		5%
Pulmonary Emboli	0%	7%	0%		9%				
Ventricular Thrombi	25%	0%	2.7%		9%	6%			
Facial Dysmorphism	38%	33%	2.7%		0%				1.5%
Neuromuscular Disorders			14%					82%	9%
Deaths	38%	7%	14%	7.5%	35%		2%		11%
Heart Transplantation	0%	4%	11%	0%	12%				14%

is made at family screening or after an abnormal electrocardiogram or chest radiograph. LVNC seems to be more common in children than in adults and may account for up to 10% of the pediatric cardiomyopathies in children aged younger than 10 years.[2,16-18] In symptomatic pediatric cases tachypnea is the most common presentation, whereas arrhythmia and sudden death seem to be less common. Wolff-Parkinson-White syndrome is found in up to 17% of pediatric cases but is rare in adults. Heart failure in the pediatric forms has been reported with a frequency ranging from 30% to 89% (see Table 60-1). Death in children with LVNC ranged from 7% to 38%.[2,16-18] Heart failure symptoms with left ventricular dilation and reduced systolic function by echocardiography are also common in adults. Thromboembolic events and tachyarrhythmia, with or without an associated Wolff-Parkinson-White syndrome are known features (see Table 60-1). Electrocardiographic abnormalities in LVNC, described in up to 91% of cases, may include paroxysmal supraventricular tachycardia, atrial fibrillation, Wolff-Parkinson-White syndrome, complete heart block, abnormal Q waves, ST-segment abnormalities, T-wave changes, left ventricular hypertrophy, bigeminal ventricular ectopic beats, left bundle-branch block, ventricular tachycardia, and fibrillation.

Heart transplantation has been performed in up to 11% of pediatric LVNC cases.[2,16-18] Recent studies have however reported more favorable outcomes, particularly in adult patients (see Table 60-1). Among 45 adult patients with LVNC from a series from the United Kingdom, the mean survival free from death or transplantation was 97% at 46 months.[19] It is uncertain whether this difference of outcome in pediatric versus adult LVNC is related to selection bias or etiologic and/or genetic heterogeneity. In addition the frequency of detection has increased with improvements in cardiac imaging. It is not yet clear whether noncompaction detected incidentally in healthy subjects undergoing routine cardiac imaging relates to early disease or overdiagnosis. It has been speculated that the extent of noncompaction may be a continuous trait within the population, with only the extreme of the distribution representing a disease state.[6] In keeping with this hypothesis, a recent study in an adult cohort identified by echocardiographic laboratories showed that symptom-free patients, with incidental or familial discovery of LVNC at diagnosis, had no major cardiovascular events at 46-month follow-up whereas 31% of those who had symptoms of heart failure (New York Heart Association class III to IV), sustained ventricular arrhythmias, or an enlarged left atrium at diagnosis experienced cardiovascular death or heart transplantation.[20]

ASSOCIATION WITH NEUROMUSCULAR DISORDERS, METABOLIC AND GENETIC SYNDROMES, AND CONGENITAL HEART DEFECTS

The association of LVNC with various genetically determined neuro-muscular disorders (including dystrophinopathies, α-dystrobre-vinopathy, laminopathies, zaspopathy, miotonic dystrophy type 1, Friedreich ataxia, and Charcot-Marie-Tooth disease) as well as rare metabolic or genetic syndromes[21,22] suggests a genetic cause (Table 60-2). In addition, familial aggregation is described in 30% to 50% of pediatric and adult cases.[2,16-18,23,24] In familial disease there is an overlap of LVNC with the DCM phenotype.[19]

In nonisolated LVNC cases, several congenital heart defects may coexist: hypoplastic right ventricle, right ventricular muscle bands with pulmonary stenosis, pulmonary hypertension, anomalous pulmonary venous return, atrial isomerism, atrial septal defects, Ebstein anomaly, mitral valve cleft, double orifice mitral valve, congenital mitral valve stenosis, polyvalvular dysplasia, ventricular septal defects, hypoplastic left heart syndrome, tetralogy of Fallot, aortic stenosis, bicuspid aortic valve, transposition of the great arteries, coarctation of the aorta, and patent ductus arteriosus.[21]

Genetics

LVNC in adults is typically transmitted as an autosomal dominant trait with incomplete penetrance,[22,25] but autosomal recessive and X-linked forms are also recognized.[17,22-27] A proportion of the sporadic cases may represent de novo mutations.[27] Initial genetic insights in LVNC came from the discovery of the *G4.5* gene in the distal portion of Xq28, encoding a family of proteins named tafazzins; these

TABLE 60-2	Left Ventricular Noncompaction: Metabolic and Genetic Syndromes	
Syndrome	*Loci (Genes)*	*Clinical Phenotype*
Barth syndrome	Xq28 (*TAZ*)	Dilated cardiomyopathy, growth retardation, neutropenia, *3-methylglutaconic* aciduria
Charcot-Marie-Tooth disease 1	17p11.2 (*PMP22*)	Muscle atrophy and weakness, reduced *nerve conduction velocity*, hollow feet
Cobalamin C deficiency	1p34.1 (*MMACHC*)	Failure to thrive, neurologic deficits and mental retardation, retinopathy, hematologic abnormalities
Congenital contractural arachnodactyly	5q23.2 (*FBN2*)	Marfanoid habitus, flexion contractures, "crumpled" outer helices
Duchenne/Becker muscular dystrophy	Xp21.2 (*DMD*)	Muscle degeneration
Leber hereditary optic neuropathy	Mitochondrial DNA	Retinal degeneration, cardiac dysrhythmia
Limb-girdle muscular dystrophy	Several	Limb musculature weakness
Mitochondrial myopathy, encephalopathy, lactic acidosis, and stroke (MELAS)	Mitochondrial DNA	Mitochondrial myopathy, encephalopathy, lactic acidosis, stroke-like episodes
Melnick-Needles syndrome	Xq28 (*FLNA*)	Short stature, osteodysplasty, craniofacial abnormalities
Microphthalmia with linear skin defects	Xp22 (*HCCS*)	Microphthalmia, linear skin defects, sclerocornea, microcephaly and mental retardation, cardiac anomalies
Myoadenylate-deaminase deficiency	1p13.2 (*AMPD1*)	Exercise-related myopathy
Myotonic dystrophy 1	19q13.32 (*DMPK*)	Myotonia, distal muscle wasting, cataract, hypogonadism, cardiac arrhythmias
Nail-patella syndrome	9q33.3 (*LMX1B*)	Dysplasia of the nails, absent/hypoplastic patellae, nephropathy
Noonan syndrome	12q24.13-primary locus (*PTPN11*)	Short stature, facial dysmorphism, cardiac anomalies, bleeding diathesis
Roifman syndrome	X (unknown)	Antibody deficiency, spondyloepiphyseal dysplasia, growth retardation, retinal dystrophy
Succinate dehydrogenase deficiency	5p15.33 (SHDA), 1p36.13 (SDHB), 1q23.3 (SDHC), 11q23 (SDHD)	Mitochondrial encephalomyopathy, leukodystrophy, late-onset optic atrophy, myopathy

Adapted from Zaragoza MV, Arbustini E, Narula J. Noncompaction of the left ventricle: primary cardiomyopathy with an elusive genetic etiology. Curr Opin Pediatr 2007; 19:619–627.

proteins are expressed in heart and muscle cells and may function as acyltransferases within mitochondria[27] and are the cause of Barth syndrome (see Table 60-2).[28] It was lately discovered that severe X-linked LVNC with neonatal onset was allelic with Barth syndrome.[29] Ichida and coworkers[30] subsequently showed that mutations in the *G4.5* gene might be associated with various cardiac phenotypes, including infantile DCM, classic Barth syndrome, endocardial fibroelastosis, isolated LVNC, and a DCM-HCM overlapping phenotype. Cardiac phenotype may change among different family members and over time, possibly in response to therapy.[30] In addition, the same group of researchers identified mutations in α-dystrobrevin, a component of the dystrophin-associated glycoprotein complex, which connects the cytoskeleton of cardiac myocytes to the extracellular matrix, as genetic causes of nonisolated LVNC.[29] Further evidence for wide genetic heterogeneity in LVNC came from the demonstration of mutations in genes encoding for sarcomeric (β-myosin heavy chain and α-cardiac actin),[31,32] cytoskeletal (α-dystrobrevin, Lamin A/C),[22,30] Z-line (Cypher/ZASP),[33] and mitochondrial proteins,[22] as well as in LVNC families where various other cardiac phenotypes were observed in distinct family members, including DCM, HCM, restrictive cardiomyopathy, arrhythmogenic cardiomyopathy,[6] and even congenital heart defects.[34] Currently, the various mutations described in LVNC are rare among probands; thus the yield of genetic testing is low, implying a genetic heterogeneity similar to what is observed in familial DCM.[35]

Management

Management of LVNC is symptomatic and should be conducted according to general heart failure and arrhythmia guidelines (Box 60-2). Incidental or symptom-guided discovery of LVNC in children or adults should prompt noninvasive cardiac screening of first-degree relatives to detect early disease similar to familial DCM.[35] Genotype/phenotype correlation studies are needed to clarify whether LVNC is a distinct cardiomyopathy or a morphologic trait associated with other cardiomyopathy phenotypes.[36]

BOX 60-2 LATE TREATMENT

- Mechanical assist devices as bridge to heart transplantation
- Automatic implantable cardioverter-defibrillator
- Heart transplantation

REFERENCES

1. Angelini A, Melacini P, Barbero F, Thiene G. Evolutionary persistence of spongy myocardium in humans. Circulation 1999;99:2475.
2. Chin TK, Perloff JK, Williams RG, et al. Isolated noncompaction of left ventricular myocardium: a study of eight cases. Circulation 1990;82:507–513.
3. Richardson P, McKenna WJ, Bristow M, et al. Report of the 1995 World Health Organization/International Society and Federation of Cardiology Task Force on the definition and classification of cardiomyopathies. Circulation 1996;93:841–842.
4. Maron BJ, Towbin JA, Thiene G, et al. Contemporary definitions and classification of cardiomyopathies: an American Heart Association scientific statement from the Council on Clinical Cardiology, Heart Failure and Transplantation Committee; Quality of Care and Outcome Research and Functional Genomics and Translational Biology Interdisciplinary Working Groups; and Council on Epidemiology and Prevention. Circulation 2006;113: 1807–1816.
5. Elliott P, Andersson B, Arbustini E, et al. Classification of the cardiomyopathies: a position statement from the European Society of Cardiology Working Group on Myocardial and Pericardial Disease. Eur Heart J 2007;29:270–276.
6. Sen-Chowdhry S, McKenna WJ. Left ventricular noncompaction and cardiomyopathy: cause, contributor, or epiphenomenon? Curr Opin Cardiol 2008;23:171–175.
7. Burke A, Mont E, Kutys R, Virmani R. Left ventricular noncompaction: a pathological study of 14 cases. Hum Pathol 2005;36:403–411.
8. Freedom RM, Yoo SJ, Perrin D, et al. The morphological spectrum of ventricular noncompaction. Cardiol Young 2005;15: 345–364.
9. Sedmera D, Pexieder T, Vuillemin M, et al. Developmental pattering of the myocardium. Anat Rec 2000;258:319–337.
10. Ritter M, Oechslin E, Sutsch G, et al. Isolated noncompaction of the myocardium in adults. Mayo Clin Proc 1997;72:26–31.
11. Finsterer J. Cardiogenetics, neurogenetics, and pathogenetics of left ventricular hypertrabeculation/noncompaction. Pediatr Cardiol 2009;30:659–681.
12. Jenni R, Oechslin E, Schneider J, et al. Echocardiographic and pathoanatomical characteristics of isolated left ventricular noncompaction: a step towards classification as a distinct cardiomyopathy. Heart 2001;86:666–671.
13. Stöllberger C, Finsterer J, Blazek G. Left ventricular hypertrabeculation, noncompaction and association with additional cardiac abnormalities and neuromuscular disorders. Am J Cardiol 2002;90:899–902.
14. Finsterer J, Stöllberger C. Definite, probable, or possible left ventricular hypertrabeculation/noncompaction. Int J Cardiol 2008;123:175–176.
15. Kohli SK, Pantazis AA, Shah JS, et al. Diagnosis of left-ventricular noncompaction in patients with left-ventricular systolic

dysfunction: time to reappraisal of diagnostic criteria? Eur Heart J 2008;29:89–95.

16. Ichida F, Hamamichi Y, Miyawaki T, et al. Clinical features of isolated noncompaction of the ventricular myocardium: long-term clinical course, hemodynamic properties, and genetic background. J Am Coll Cardiol 1999;34:233–240.

17. Pignatelli RH, McMahon CJ, Dreyer WJ, et al. Clinical characterization of left ventricular noncompaction in children: a relatively common form of cardiomyopathy. Circulation 2003;108:2672–2678.

18. Lilje C, Razek V, Joyce JJ, et al. Complications of noncompaction of the left ventricular myocardium in a paediatric population: a prospective study. Eur Heart J 2006;27:1855–1860.

19. Murphy RT, Thaman R, Blanes JG, et al. Natural history and familial characteristics of isolated left ventricular noncompaction. Eur Heart J 2005;26:187–192.

20. Lofiego C, Biagini E, Pasquale F, et al. Wide spectrum of presentation and variable outcomes of isolated left ventricular noncompaction. Heart 2007;93:65–71.

21. Finsterer J, Stöllberger C, Blazek G. Neuromuscular implications in left ventricular hypertrabeculation/noncompaction. Int J Cardiol 2006;110:288–300.

22. Zaragoza MV, Arbustini E, Narula J. Noncompaction of the left ventricle: primary cardiomyopathy with an elusive genetic etiology. Curr Opin Pediatr 2007;19:619–627.

23. Oechslin EN, Attenhofer Jost CH, Rojas JR, et al. Long-term follow-up of 34 adults with isolated left ventricular noncompaction: a distinct cardiomyopathy with poor prognosis. J Am Coll Cardiol 2000;36:493–500.

24. Sengupta PP, Mohan JC, Mehta V, et al. Comparison of echocardiographic features of noncompaction of the left ventricle in adults versus idiopathic dilated cardiomyopathy in adults. Am J Cardiol 2004;94:389–391.

25. Sasse-Klaassen S, Gerull B, Oechslin E, et al. Isolated noncompaction of the left ventricular myocardium in the adult is an autosomal dominant disorder in the majority of patients. Am J Med Genet A 2003;119:162–267.

26. Bleyl SB, Mumfrod BR, Brown-Harrison MC, et al. Xq28-linked noncompaction of the ventricular myocardium: prenatal diagnosis and pathologic analysis of affected individuals. Am J Med Genet 1997;72:257–265.

27. Xing Y, Ichida F, Matsuoka T, et al. Genetic analysis in patients with left ventricular noncompaction and evidence for genetic heterogeneity. Mol Genet Metab 2006;88:71–77.

28. Bione S, D'Adamo P, Maestrini E, et al. A novel X-linked gene, G4.5 is responsible for Barth syndrome. Nat Genet 1996;12:385–389.

29. Bleyl SB, Mumford BR, Thompson V, et al. Neonatal, lethal noncompaction of the left ventricular myocardium is allelic with Barth syndrome. Am J Hum Genet 1997;61:868–872.

30. Ichida F, Tsubata S, Bowles KR, et al. Novel gene mutations in patients with left ventricular noncompaction or Barth syndrome. Circulation 2001;103:1256–1263.

31. Klaassen S, Probst S, Oechslin E, et al. Mutations in sarcomere protein genes in left ventricular noncompaction. Circulation 2008;117:2893–2901.

32. McNally E, Dellefave L. Sarcomere mutations in cardiogenesis and ventricular noncompaction. Trends Cardiovasc Med 2009;19:17–21.

33. Vatta M, Mohapatra B, Jimenez S, et al. Mutations in Cypher/ZASP in patients with dilated cardiomyopathy and left ventricular noncompaction. J Am Coll Cardiol 2003;42:2014–2027.

34. Monserrat L, Hermida-Prieto M, Fernandez X, et al. Mutation in the alpha-cardiac actin gene associated with apical hypertrophic cardiomyopathy, left ventricular noncompaction, and septal defects. Eur Heart J 2007;28:1953–1961.

35. Hershberger H, Lindenfeld J, Mestroni L, et al. Genetic evaluation of cardiomyopathy—A Heart Failure Society of America practice guideline. J Card Fail 2009;15:83–97.

36. Thiene G, Corrado D, Basso C. Cardiomyopathies: is it time for a molecular classification? Eur Heart J 2004;25:1772–1775.

61

Rheumatic Fever

DENNIS V. COKKINOS

Introduction

Rheumatic fever is an inflammatory disease that affects the skin, brain, cardiovascular system, and many mucosal membranes, including the pericardium, pleura, and peritoneum. The joints are involved to a great extent. However, although the peripheral joints produce the most obvious symptoms, it is the cardiovascular system that suffers the most long-lasting influences. It remains the most common pathogenic cause of acquired heart disease in children and young adults, because, although in developed countries its incidence has decreased very sharply, it remains a major problem in the developing world.[1,2]

Pathogenesis

The etiologic agent is the group A streptococcus, which causes untreated tonsillopharyngitis. Skin infections (impetigo) are not believed to cause rheumatic fever. However, Carapetis and colleagues point out that skin infections may represent an important reservoir of all strains of group A streptococcus in areas with high rates of acute rheumatic fever.[3]

As already stressed, not all group A streptococcal strains cause rheumatic fever. The common strains M2, 4, and 12 are not causative. Homology has been shown to exist between the M protein of the surface of the streptococcus and the human heart myosin and tropomyosin. This M protein is characterized by an epitope that differs between those causing or not causing rheumatic fever. Guilherme and colleagues[4] found that T lymphocytes from the cardiac tissue of patients with rheumatic heart disease recognized streptococcal M protein and peptides as well as the cardiac proteins.

The human leukocyte antigen (HLA) system may be responsible for the propensity of certain individuals to develop rheumatic fever; susceptibility has been linked to HLA-DR[1,3] haplotypes.[5]

The propensity to develop rheumatic fever after streptococcal involvement depends on characteristics of both the infecting organism and the host:

- The infecting organism: The strains belonging to types M1, 3, 5, 6, and 18 have been more frequently involved in the appearance of rheumatic fever. All these strains have a long terminal antigenic domain. Moreover, they share epitopes with human cardiac tissue.
- The incidence of rheumatic fever is much higher in patients with a previous episode of the disease (50% vs. 3%).
- The specific B-cell alloantigen is present in 99% of patients with rheumatic fever versus only 14% of those without.
- Susceptibility to rheumatic fever is associated with HLA-DR1, HLA-DR2, HLA-DR3, and HLA-DR4 haplotypes.

Epidemiology

The incidence of acute rheumatic fever varies from 2/100,000 in the United States up to 100/100,000 in developing countries. In New Zealand the incidence is 2.5/100,000 population; it is much higher in Maori and Pacific Islander children at between 50 and 70/100,000.[6] Tibazarwa and associates have provided an excellent review.[7] Briefly, they state that the incidence is less than 10/10,000 per year in the Americas and Western Europe; however, in areas with higher rates (20 to 30/100,000) rates are steadily falling. Similarly, mortality due to

rheumatic heart disease declined 42% between 1994 and 2004 in the United States.[1,2]

The incidence of rheumatic heart disease in school-aged children varies from 0.6/1000 in the United States to 15 to 19/1000 in South Africa and South America.[8] Interesting data have emerged from the global use of echocardiography in areas where the prevalence of rheumatic fever is still high. In Cambodia, rheumatic heart disease was detected clinically in 8 of 3677 children but in 79 with echocardiographic screening.[9] The corresponding rates in Mozambique were 5 and 66 of 2170 children, respectively. Similar results were seen in schoolchildren in Tonga.[10] However, cases of rheumatic fever are still being underreported.[3] Also, unfortunately, register-based programs are waning, mostly owing to underfunding.

In Greece, in one of the two main pediatric hospitals in Athens, between 1980 and 1997 the diagnosis of rheumatic fever was made in 66 children: carditis and arthritis were the major manifestations in 70% and 68% of the cases, respectively.[11]

Clinical Presentation

Specific clinical manifestations exist that establish the diagnosis as described later. The Jones criteria have been employed for many years.[3] It should be stressed that they concern the first attack of rheumatic fever and not recurrence.

DIAGNOSTIC CRITERIA

If evidence of an antecedent group A streptococcal infection exists, the presence of two major or one major and two minor criteria render the diagnosis of rheumatic fever highly likely.

Major criteria are:
- Carditis
- Polyarthritis
- Erythema marginatum
- Subcutaneous nodules

Minor criteria are:
- Arthralgia
- Fever
- Raised erythrocyte sedimentation rate
- PR-interval prolongation

The supporting evidence of antecedent A streptococcal infection is a positive throat culture, rapid streptococcal antigen test, or elevated streptococcal antibody titers (e.g., anti–streptolysin O).

The World Health Organization (WHO) proposed criteria in 2002–2003. Carapetis and colleagues,[3] in a seminal review in 2005, point out criteria may have somewhat different functions according to their epidemiologic setting. In regions of high prevalence, sensitivity may be more important. They believe that the 1992 Jones criteria may not be sensitive enough in this milieu and that the 2002–2003 WHO criteria are more appropriate.

The erythrocyte sedimentation rate and C-reactive protein are invariably increased during the acute stage of rheumatic fever. However, their levels may have returned to normal when chorea develops. The C-reactive protein measurement is more specific because it is not affected by anemia or heart failure.

The PR-interval prolongation is a nonspecific finding. It is not associated with carditis or long-term valvular lesions.

As regards evidence of antecedent group A streptococcal infection, it must be remembered that because rheumatic fever develops approximately 3 weeks after the streptococcal infection, throat cultures are rarely positive at this time for streptococci. The rapid streptococcal antigen detection tests have high specificity but low sensitivity. The antibody tests are used more widely: anti–streptolysin O and anti–deoxyribonuclease B (anti–DNase B). The former is performed first and only if it is negative is the latter performed. However, elevated anti–streptolysin O or anti-DNase B titers may persist for months after a previous streptococcal infection. A rapid antigen detection test has been found to have high sensibility and specificity.[12]

SPECIFIC CLINICAL MANIFESTATIONS

Carditis
Carditis has been described as a pancarditis (endocarditis, myocarditis, and pericarditis). Its incidence is approximately 50% cases. In a study by Voss and coworkers the incidence was 39 of 59 cases (66%).[13]

Symptoms may range from severe, leading to death, to mild. In the latter case the murmur of valvulitis signifying endocardial involvement can be missed by auscultation.

The mitral and aortic valves are those predominantly affected, in order of frequency. Myocarditis or pericarditis in the absence of valvulitis is unlikely.

Essentially, the carditis is diagnosed clinically by valvular regurgitation. Some authors have described diffuse and focal thickening by echocardiographic examination. The impact of the use of echocardiographic criteria by the American Heart Association has already been discussed.[9,10] The 1995 guidelines require valvular involvement either by clinical or echocardiographic criteria.[14]

Echocardiographic criteria are useful for the confirmation of subclinical rheumatic carditis.[3,15]

Mitral regurgitation jet characteristics include:
- Extension 1 cm back into the left atrium
- Appearance in two planes
- Mosaic pattern indicative of chaotic flow
- Holosystolic flow as confirmed by Doppler imaging
  Aortic regurgitation jet characteristics include:
- Extension 1 cm into left ventricle
- Appearance in two planes
- Holodiastolic flow

Veasy[16] points out that these criteria should also be used for the follow-up management of patients with rheumatic fever. In this context, Ozkutlu and associates[17] observed 26 consecutive patients with silent valvulitis without clinical sign of carditis for 4.5 months. They concluded that rheumatic fever with silent carditis is not a benign entity.

Arthritis
The incidence of arthritis is approximately 55%. It is characterized by asymmetric and migratory involvement of the large joints (knees, elbows, ankles, wrists). Involvement is always transient with permanent residua. Its duration is limited (up to 2 to 3 weeks). It responds very readily to salicylates.

Chorea
Chorea occurs in about 20% of cases. It is ascribed to an autoimmune inflammatory response involving primarily the basal ganglia and caudate nuclei. The latent period of appearance is about 3 months. Accordingly, in its presence the diagnosis of rheumatic fever can be made even if the other Jones criteria are lacking. It resolves in 1 to 2 weeks. The first line of treatment is valproic acid; risperidone and haloperidol may also prove useful.[18]

Erythema Marginatum
Erythema marginatum is rare (<5%) and present only in severe cases. It involves mostly the trunk and proximal extremities with highly variable size.

Subcutaneous Nodules
Subcutaneous nodules are also seen infrequently (3%), mostly in severe cases, especially in the extensor joint surfaces and the scalp.

However, one should be aware that just as the incidence has changed so have the clinical manifestations of rheumatic fever. Thus, Carapetis and Currie[19] found monarthritis in only 17% of confirmed non-chorea cases and fever greater than 39° C (102.2° F) in only 25%.

The diagnosis of streptococcal pharyngeal tonsillitis is essential. The main symptoms are sore throat, fever above 38° C (100.4° F), headache, abdominal pain, nausea, and vomiting.

The tonsils are reddened with or without exudates, and lymphadenitis is common. The differential diagnosis from viral involvement is not always easy. Findings not common in streptococcal infection are conjunctivitis, stomatitis, and ulcerative pharyngeal lesions. Other organisms causing pharyngitis include adenoviruses, enteroviruses, herpes simplex, *Neisseria gonorrhoeae*, *Mycoplasma pneumoniae*, *Chlamydia pneumoniae*, and *Arcanobacterium haemolyticum*. The best diagnostic modality is a swab culture of both tonsils and posterior pharynges. However, culture cannot always differentiate true streptococcal pharyngeal tonsillitis from viral infection because many individuals chronically harbor streptococci. A negative culture allows the physician to avoid the institution of antibiotic therapy. Bisno[20] gave a very thorough description of streptococcal pharyngitis. He stressed the importance of the tonsillopharyngeal exudate and anterior cervical lymphadenitis. The absence of fever and pharyngeal erythema diminish the likelihood. He also stated that a correctly performed and interpreted throat culture has a sensitivity greater than 90%. Definitive results are obtained within 24 to 48 hours. Bisno also believed that a positive rapid test could be considered equivalent to a positive throat culture; however its sensitivity, in comparison with the throat culture, was only 80% to 90%.

Pathology

Rheumatic fever represents a generalized vasculitis affecting small blood vessels. The collagen appearance is that of fibrinoid degeneration with disintegration of the collagen fibers. Aschoff cells are large, modified fibrohistiocytic cells. The Aschoff nodule of rheumatic carditis is pathognomonic. It is characterized by central areas of necrotic myocardium surrounded by large lymphocytes and plasmacytes.[21] Fraser and associates,[22] after studying 16 fresh valve specimens from patients with acute rheumatic fever, classified the nodules into three stages:
- Stage 1 with macrophages only, secreting tumor necrosis factor-α and interleukin-1, which activate lymphocytes
- Stage 2 with a few T lymphocytes
- Stage 3 with many B and T lymphocytes

The vasculitis may persist for many years after an initial attack. The initial inflammation of valvular tissue persists and causes valvular insufficiency whereas fibrosis and calcification cause long-term stenosis.

Natural History

A clear-cut picture of the natural history exists because of many careful longitudinal studies.[3,21] Typically, the first attacks are seen in children aged 5 to 15. They are rarer beyond the age of 30 years. Increased frequency of rheumatic fever occurs during military service. Death may occur at an early stage because of acute heart failure, although this is uncommon. Individuals who develop heart failure during the acute phase have a poorer prognosis, however. In contrast, patients with Sydenham chorea have a benign prognosis. Cardiac involvement increases with each recurrence of rheumatic fever. Typically it is seen in 20% during the first 5 years after the first attack, 10% during the next 5 years, 5% during the third 5-year period, and only 1.5% after 15 to 20 years. During recurrences of rheumatic fever, if the initial attack involved the heart there is always new cardiac involvement. If prevention of recurrences is effective, 70% of patients who develop a murmur of mitral insufficiency will be free of valvular regurgitation during the next 5 years.

Restating these facts in a different way, 27% of patients with initial carditis had no valvular sequelae within a year and 41% of regurgitant aortic or mitral valves were no longer regurgitant after 6 months.[3] Chronic rheumatic heart disease has recently been considered to increase with the *MBL2* polymorphism.[23]

In recent years, many older individuals with previous rheumatic fever have had only mild rheumatic valve lesions, probably as a result of antibiotic therapy early during the initial or subsequent attacks (Box 61-1). Atrial fibrillation is a major complication in patients with rheumatic heart disease,[24] perhaps secondary to atrial remodeling.[25]

Treatment

ACUTE PHARYNGITIS

Penicillin V is the drug of choice. Up to now resistant streptococci have not been found. Even if started after 9 days, penicillin can effectively prevent the occurrence of rheumatic fever; and even if started later than this period, morbidity is decreased. The patient cannot transmit the infection after 24 hours from the start of treatment. Dosages are shown in Table 61-1. Treatment must continue for 10 days even after symptoms subside. Ampicillin and amoxicillin are being used as alternatives, but they do not seem to be more effective than common penicillin V. However, amoxicillin has the advantage that it can be given in one single daily dose of 750 mg for 10 days whereas penicillin needs to be given three times daily. Intramuscular benzathine penicillin G is given in a dose of 600,000 units to individuals weighing less than below 28 kg (62 lb), and 1.2 million units is used in individuals weighing more than this weight. Its use is preferred when compliance with oral treatment is a problem.

Intramuscular injections can be painful. The pain may diminish when the solution is heated before use. Allergic reactions are more frequent in adults and after intramuscular injections. Their main manifestations are urticaria and angioneurotic edema. Anaphylactic reactions are rare but can be fatal. The best way to avoid them is careful history taking. In patients allergic to penicillin, erythromycin can be considered. This also is given for 10 days. Azithromycin is another alternative; it can be given in a dose of 500 mg on the first day and continued for 4 more days with a daily dose of 250 mg. It is better tolerated than erythromycin. However, it is much more expensive than penicillin and resistant streptococci may develop rapidly. Cephalosporins are probably preferable to azithromycin: those with a narrow range of effectiveness are a better choice. Some authors believe that 5 days of cephalosporin treatment are equivalent to 9 days' treatment with penicillin. In one study cephalosporins achieved a bacteriologic cure,

TABLE 61-1	Drug Dosages in Acute Rheumatic Fever— Streptococcal Pharyngitis		
Drug	*Route*	*Dose*	*Duration*
Penicillin V	Oral	Children: 250 mg bid to tid Adolescents: 250 mg qid Adults: 500 mg bid	10 days
Penicillin G benzathine	IM	Weight < 27 kg: 600,000 U Weight > 27 kg: 1.2 million U	1 dose
For Patients Allergic to Penicillin			
Erythromycin estolate	Oral	20–40 mg/kg/day in two to four divided doses	10 days
Erythromycin ethylsuccinate	Oral	40 mg/kg/day in two to four divided doses	10 days
Erythromycin stearate	Oral	1 g/day in two to four divided doses	10 days

as documented by throat swab cultures, of 92%, compared with 84% for penicillin.[26] They may eradicate carriage better than penicillin. It should not be forgotten that a rate of treatment failure of 38% has been reported with penicillin. However, 20% of individuals allergic to penicillin are also allergic to cephalosporins; hence, cephalosporins should be avoided in patients with a history of anaphylactic reactions to penicillin. Tetracyclines, sulfonamides, and trimethoprim-sulfamethoxazole are not indicated because they are not bactericidal.

A new throat swab taken 2 to 7 days after the completion of therapy is indicated in individuals who remain symptomatic or develop recurrences or who have in the past developed rheumatic fever. Only in the latter group can a second full penicillin course be recommended. Some clinicians advise that the second treatment course be different from the first. Thus, if penicillin were used during the first course, cephalosporins or clindamycin would be recommended subsequently. Asymptomatic patients should not be treated with penicillin.

PREVENTION OF RECURRENCES

The recommended drugs are shown in Table 61-2. As already stressed, the danger of rheumatic carditis increases with the number of recurrences. Thus, the duration of chemoprophylaxis should be longer in patients with previous rheumatic fever and carditis, with or without valvular involvement.

Dajani[27] recommends treatment for 5 years or until age 21 for patients without carditis for 10 years *or* until adulthood in patients with carditis but without residual valvular heart disease, *and* for at least 10 years after the last episode or at least until 40 years of age in patients with residual valvular disease.

INFLAMMATORY MANIFESTATIONS

The mainstay of treatment for inflammation is still acetylsalicylic acid in a dose of 50 to 100 mg/kg/day in children and 6 to 8 g/day in adults, in four divided doses. Some clinicians currently recommend lower doses, up to 25 mg/kg. Desirable salicylate blood levels are 15 to 25 mg/dL. With this treatment symptoms subside within 12 to 24 hours. Toxic findings are not rare. Nausea and tinnitus are not uncommon. However, they can subside with continuation of the drug. After 2 weeks of therapy the dose is decreased to 70% of the initial dose for a further 6 weeks. The previously given dosage is recommended for 6 to 10 weeks with gradual tapering for 2 more weeks. In patients who do not tolerate aspirin or are allergic to it nonsteroidal anti-inflammatory agents may be given, although there is no appreciable experience with these drugs.

Corticosteroids are indicated in patients with significant cardiac involvement, especially pericarditis or heart failure because patients seem to respond more favorably or when the clinical symptoms do not subside readily with aspirin. The initial corticosteroid dose is prednisone, 1 to 2 mg/kg/day, tapered after 2 to 3 weeks for 3 further weeks. Usual side effects of corticosteroids should be heeded, such as gastric bleeding, sodium retention, and glucose intolerance. Stolerman,[28] in a thorough review, does not recommend corticosteroids as routine therapy. Neither salicylates nor corticosteroids seem to prevent the occurrence of rheumatic carditis or the occurrence of significant valvular disease.[1] After discontinuation of either corticosteroids or aspirin, a rebound manifestation may be seen usually within 2 weeks. If these

TABLE 61-2	Drug Therapy for Secondary Prevention	
Drug	*Route*	*Dose*
Penicillin V	Oral	250 mg bid
Penicillin G benzathine	IM	1.2 million U q 20 days
Sulfadiazine	Oral	Weight < 27 kg: 0.5 g/day Weight > 27 kg: 1.0 g/day
For Patients Allergic to Penicillin and Sulfadiazine		
Erythromycin	Oral	250 mg bid

symptoms are mild, no treatment is needed. If they are more severe, treatment may be restarted. Some clinicians use salicylates during corticosteroid tapering. Lowering of erythrocyte sedimentation rate and C-reactive protein levels are reliable indices of anti-inflammatory success.

The indications for ambulation are becoming more difficult to formulate with the decreased incidence of the disease and the current propensity of individuals for increased activity. Ambulation can be permitted once apyrexia is achieved and the erythrocyte sedimentation rate or C-reactive protein level reverts to normal. However, if carditis is present, restriction of activity should be advised. Strenuous exercise is not recommended if carditis has been diagnosed.

In many immune-mediated cardiac disorders such as Kawasaki disease, myocarditis, and postpartum cardiomyopathy, intravenous immunoglobulin therapy is considered to be beneficial. However, Voss and associates[13] could not demonstrate any influence on the natural history or clinical, laboratory, and echocardiographic indices in patients with rheumatic fever.

If severe mitral regurgitation occurs during the acute phase, valve repair or replacement may be lifesaving (Box 61-2). Reddy and coworkers[29] reported excellent results in 9 children aged 2 to 13 years with mitral valve repair. Kalangos and colleagues[30] also reported excellent results with a biodegradable mitral ring in 220 children (mean age 12 ± 3 years) between 1994 and 2006, without hospital deaths. Survival without recurrent mitral valve insufficiency or stenosis was 27% at 10 years. Even mitral valve replacement has excellent results when the chordae can be preserved. In the longer term, tricuspid regurgitation can become a problem.

BOX 61-2 LATE TREATMENT

- For mitral stenosis, open-heart surgery remains an option.
- For pliable, not heavily calcified or regurgitant valves, percutaneous mitral valvotomy is an option.
- For mitral regurgitation, reconstruction is possible, although valve replacement is often necessary—as is usually the case for aortic lesions.

It is becoming apparent that infective endocarditis is a major sequelae of rheumatic heart disease. Carapetis[31] estimates that in most Asian countries at least half of cases of infective endocarditis are due to underlying rheumatic heart disease. It also causes a considerable number of strokes from valvular lesions.

▣ Conclusion

In summary it should be stressed that the incidence of rheumatic fever can be gradually reduced, even in developing countries, with appropriate public health and medical awareness. Encouraging results have been reported recently from Cuba, where recurrent attacks decreased from 6.4/100,000 in 1986 to 0.4/100,000 in 1996.[32] The eradication of rheumatic fever should be the aim of all countries where the population is significantly affected. It is extremely encouraging that many countries where the prevalence of rheumatic fever is still high have developed working groups to formulate consensus guidelines on an integrated approach to this still important entity.[33]

REFERENCES

1. World Health Organization. Rheumatic Fever and Rheumatic Heart Disease: Report of a WHO Expert Consultation, Geneva, 29 October–1 November 2001. Geneva: World Health Organization; 2004.
2. Rosamond W, Flegal K, Furie K, et al. Heart disease and stroke statistics 2008 update: a report from the American Heart Association Statistics subcommittee. Circulation 2008; 117:e25–e146.
3. Carapetis JR, McDonald M, Wilson N. Acute rheumatic fever. Lancet 2005;366:155–168.
4. Guilherme L, Cunha-Neto E, Coelho V, et al. Human heart infiltrating T-cell clones from rheumatic heart disease patients recognize both streptococcal and cardiac proteins. Circulation 1995;92:415–420.
5. Ayoub EM, Barrett DJ, Maclaren NK, et al. Association of class II human histocompatibility leukocyte antigens with rheumatic fever. J Clin Invest 1986;77:2019–2028.
6. Baker M, Chakraborty M. Rheumatic fever in New Zealand in the 1990s: still cause for concern. N Z Public Health Rep 1996;3:17–19.
7. Tibazarwa KB, Volmink JA, Mayosi BM. Incidence of acute rheumatic fever in the world: a systematic review of population-based studies. Heart 2008;94:1534–1540.
8. McLaren MJ, Hawkins DM, Koornhof HJ, et al. Epidemiology of rheumatic heart disease in black schoolchildren in Soweto, Johannesburg. BMJ 1975;3:474–478.
9. Marijon E, Ou P, Celermajer DS, et al. Prevalence of rheumatic heart disease detected by echocardiographic screening. N Engl J Med 2007;357:470–476.
10. Carapetis JR, Hardy M, Fakakovikaetau T, et al. Evaluation of a screening protocol using auscultation and portable echocardiography to detect asymptomatic rheumatic heart disease in Tongan schoolchildren. Nat Clin Pract Cardiovasc Med 2008;4:411–417.
11. Giannoulia-Karantana A, Anagnostopoulos G, Kostaridou S, et al. Childhood acute rheumatic fever in Greece: experience of the past 18 years. Acta Paediatr 2001;90:809–812.
12. Camurdan AD, Camurdan OM, Ok I, et al. Diagnostic value of rapid antigen detection test for streptococcal pharyngitis in a pediatric population. Int J Pediatr Otorhinolaryngol 2008; 72:1203–1206.
13. Voss LM, Wilson NJ, Neutze JM, et al. Intravenous immunoglobulin in acute rheumatic fever. Circulation 2001;103:401–406.
14. American Heart Association. Treatment of acute streptococcal pharyngitis and prevention of rheumatic acute streptococcal pharyngitis and prevention of rheumatic fever: a statement for health professionals. Pediatrics 1995;96:758–764.
15. Abernathy M, Bass M, Sharpe N, et al. Doppler echocardiography and the early diagnosis of carditis in acute rheumatic fever. Aust N Z J Med 1994;24:530–533.
16. Veasy LG. Time to take soundings in acute rheumatic fever. Lancet 2001;357:1994–1995.
17. Ozkutlu S, Ayabakan C, Saraclar M. Can subclinical valvitis detected by echocardiography be accepted as evidence of carditis in the diagnosis of acute rheumatic fever? Cardiol Young 2001;11:255–260.
18. Cardoso F. Sydenham's chorea. Curr Treat Options Neurol 2008;10:230–235.
19. Carapetis JR, Currie BJ. Rheumatic fever in a high incidence population: the importance of monoarthritis and low grade fever. Arch Dis Child 2001;85:223–227.
20. Bisno AL. Acute pharyngitis. N Engl J Med 2001;344:205–211.
21. Leachman RD, Leachman DR. Acute rheumatic fever. In: Willerson JT, Cohn JN, editors. Cardiovascular Medicine. New York: Churchill Livingstone; 1995. p. 227–238.
22. Fraser WJ, Haffeje Z, Jankelow D, et al. Rheumatic Aschoff nodules revisited: II. Cytokine expression corroborates recently proposed sequential stages. Histopathology 1997;31:460–464.
23. Schafranski MD, Pereira Ferrari L, Scherner D, et al. High-producing MBL2 genotypes increase the risk of acute and chronic carditis in patients with history of rheumatic fever. Mol Immunol 2008;45:3827–3831.
24. Mohan N, Shah P, Batra R, et al. Chronic atrial fibrillation in patients with rheumatic heart disease. Circulation 2001;104:802.
25. John B, Stiles MK, Kuklik P, et al. Electrical remodeling of the left and right atria due to rheumatic mitral stenosis. Eur Heart J 2008;29:2234–2243.
26. Pichichero ME, Margolis PA. A comparison of cephalosporins and penicillins in the treatment of group A beta-hemolytic streptococcal pharyngitis: a meta-analysis supporting the concept of microbial copathogenicity. Pediatr Infect Dis 1991;10:275–281.
27. Dajani AS. Rheumatic fever. In: Braunwald E, Zipes DP, Libby P, editors. Heart Disease. 6th ed. Philadelphia: WB Saunders; 2001. p. 2192–2298.
28. Stolerman GH. Rheumatic fever. Lancet 1997;349:935–942.
29. Reddy PK, Dharmapuram AK, Swain SK, et al. Valve repair in rheumatic heart disease in pediatric age group. Asian Cardiovasc Thorac Ann 2008;16:129–133.
30. Kalangos A, Christenson JT, Beghetti M, et al. Mitral valve repair for rheumatic valve disease in children: midterm results and impact of the use of a biodegradable mitral ring. Ann Thorac Surg 2008;86:161–169.
31. Carapetis JR. Rheumatic heart disease in Asia. Circulation 2008;118:2748–2753.
32. Nordet P, Lopez R, Duenas A, et al. Prevention and control of rheumatic fever and rheumatic heart disease: the Cuban experience (1986-1996-2002). Cardiovasc J Afr 2008;19:135–140.
33. Working group on Pediatric Acute Rheumatic Fever and Cardiology Chapter of Indian Academy of Pediatrics', Saxena A, Kumar RK, Gera RP, et al. Consensus guidelines of pediatric acute rheumatic fever and rheumatic heart disease. Indian Pediatr 2008;45:565–573.

62 Cardiac Tumors

STELLA D. BRILI | CHRISTODOULOS STEFANADIS

Introduction

Cardiac tumors in infants and children are rare. Their atypical clinical presentation prevented timely diagnosis in the past, when cardiac tumors were often a postmortem finding. The widespread use of echocardiography and other noninvasive diagnostic methods in recent years, however, has resulted in a marked increase in the detection of cardiac tumors during childhood, when the patients are often asymptomatic, and also in fetal life. In turn, early recognition of cardiac tumors has resulted in better understanding of their natural history and, combined with advances in surgical techniques, an improved overall outcome.

Definition and Morphology

Primary cardiac tumors are benign in 75% cases[1] and considered malignant in 25% from evidence of tumor cellular mitosis and metastases.[2]

BENIGN TUMORS

Myxomas

Myxomas are cardiac tumors with a size ranging from 1 to 15 cm (Box 62-1). They have a semitransparent and round appearance with a gelatinous glistening surface and may have a distinct stalk.[1] They are usually solitary (90%) and are most commonly located in the left atrium (75% to 90%) principally in the fossa ovalis (Fig. 62-1).[1–5] Location on the posterior left atrial wall suggests malignancy.[1] Right atrial myxomas comprise 15% to 20% of cases, and ventricular myxomas comprise 3% to 4% of cases.[1,4,5] Myxomas appear to grow rather quickly.[1,4] They stem from subendocardial primitive mesenchymal cells that persist as embryonal residues during septation of the heart.[1,6] This may explain the predilection of the tumor for the atrial septum.[2] These cells can potentially differentiate into endothelial cells, smooth muscle cells, angioblasts, fibroblasts, cartilage cells, and myoblasts.[1,6] The typical myxoma cells, called "lipidic," resemble endothelial cells and are embedded in a myxoid stroma rich in glycosaminoglycans and also line the surface of the tumor.[1,7] Stromal cells originate from multipotent mesenchyme capable of neural and endothelial differentiation. They are polygonal and eosinophilic and arranged as small groups or irregular cell nests adjacent to the endothelial cells.[6] Inflammatory cells are common, and calcification is often present (10% to 20%).[1] Some cells express features of glandular epithelium and disclose an immunoreactivity that overlaps with endocrine cells from normal human gut epithelium, supporting the hypothesis that they may represent nests of entrapped embryonic foregut.[6] Interleukin-6 overproduction by myxomas seems to be responsible for some constitutional symptoms or immunologic abnormalities. When the tumor is removed the systemic signs disappear. The pluripotent differentiation potential of the cells in myxomas may explain many of the noncardiac manifestations such as fever, diarrhea, and spotty skin pigmentation.[6] Some myxomas show increased mitotic activity and pleomorphism, which are histologic signs considered to designate malignancy.[6] Local invasion has also been considered as evidence of malignant potential. However, the existence of truly malignant myxomas is controversial[6]

and most previously reported cases represented embolic phenomena, local recurrence after excision, multiple myxomas, or sarcomas with myxoid degeneration.[1,6,8]

Rhabdomyomas

They are almost always multiple and ventricular (most frequently on the interventricular septum), and 50% have an intracavitary component (Fig. 62-2).[2–4,7] Calcification or necrosis is rare, and there is a high rate of spontaneous regression.[9]

Fibromas

Fibromas are low-grade neoplasms, most frequently solitary, arising from the connective tissue of the left ventricle and interventricular septum.[3] Rarely they are multiple and/or arise from the right ventricle or the atria. They do not regress and, on the contrary, continue to enlarge and may develop central calcification, necrosis, and cystic degeneration.[2,3,7]

Papillary Fibroelastomas

Papillary fibroelastomas are small pedunculated tumors located on the cardiac valves.[2,10] The frondlike appearance is typical with a short attaching pedicle, resembling a "sea anemone."[10] Approximately 50% have a stalk; and when they do, they are always mobile (Fig. 62-3). They are more frequently located on the aortic and mitral valves. They appear to be very infrequent on the right side, but this may be due to a paucity of symptoms from embolization. Microscopically, each frond is formed of a central fibroelastic core, an overlying myxomatous layer, and an endothelial covering. Their histologic origin, however, remains elusive.[2]

Lipomas

Lipomas are usually subepicardial encapsulated tumors discovered incidentally during cardiac imaging or at autopsy.[2,4]

Angiomas

Angiomas localize principally to the interventricular septum and are visualized as subendocardial nodules that are usually 2 to 4 cm in diameter.[2,8]

MALIGNANT TUMORS

Ninety-five percent of malignant tumors are sarcomas, and 5% are lymphomas.[2] Sarcomas derive from mesenchyme and may potentially differentiate to angiosarcomas, rhabdomyosarcomas, osteosarcomas, fibrosarcomas, and liposarcomas, among others. Angiosarcomas and rhabdomyosarcomas are the most common histologic types (Box 62-2). The right atrium is most frequently affected, followed by the left atrium, right ventricle, left ventricle, and interventricular septum.[2,8] Angiosarcomas usually originate from the right atrium and tend to metastasize to the pericardium and lungs. Kaposi sarcoma belongs to this category.[2,4] Rhabdomyosarcomas have elements of striated muscle and frequently infiltrate the myocardium diffusely. In contrast to angiosarcomas there is no predilection for one cardiac chamber and the tumors rarely infiltrate beyond the parietal pericardium.[4] Fibrosarcomas stem from fibroblasts and widely infiltrate the heart muscle. Thrombus formation in the pulmonary veins, inferior vena cava, or over the tumor surface occurs frequently. Lymphomas present as nodular or diffuse infiltrates with appearances similar to hypertrophic cardiomyopathy when extensive.[4]

BOX 62-1 MYXOMAS

- Myxomas are the most frequent cardiac tumors (50% of primary tumors).
- Ninety percent are left atrial (usually on the interatrial septum), and 90% are solitary; hence, differentiation from thrombus is important.
- Mobile pedunculated tumors are more prone to embolize than laminar calcified nonmobile masses.
- Facial freckling is suggestive of Carney syndrome; screening is needed for detection of possible multiple foci and affected family members.
- Clinical features may mimic infective endocarditis, vasculitis, or other inflammatory disorders.
- Surgical resection is advisable immediately after diagnosis, because the risk of embolization is high.
- Recurrence is possible; long-term echocardiographic follow-up is recommended for detection of secondary growth. Interleukin-6 levels may prove to be a useful marker of disease recurrence.

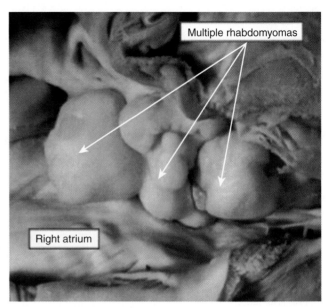

Figure 62-2 These multiple rhabdomyomas, occupying an intracavitary position, are growing from the wall of the right ventricle and the adjacent right atrium. (From Bédard E, Becker AE, Gatzoulis MA. Cardiac tumours. In Anderson RH, Baker EJ, Redington A, et al, eds. Pediatric Cardiology, 3rd ed. Philadelphia: Elsevier Churchill Livingstone; 2010.)

Cardiac metastases find their way to the heart either directly (lung, breast, and rarely renal cell carcinomas) or via hematogenous spread (leukemia, reticuloendothelial tumors, melanomas).[2,4] Renal cell carcinomas, hypernephromas, or lung cancer metastasizing to the adrenal glands may infiltrate the inferior vena cava.[2,4] Heart involvement in the case of melanoma takes the form of diffuse metastatic foci. Leukemia and lymphoma commonly metastasize in the heart (25% of lymphomas). Leukemia produces widespread intramyocardial infiltrates, whereas lymphomatous deposits are usually grossly discernible.[4]

Genetics and Epidemiology

Primary cardiac tumors have an incidence of 0.02% to 0.1% in adults and 0.027% in children, percentages that are increasing with advancement in noninvasive imaging.[1-3,5,8,11,12] Secondary metastases are more frequent than primary cardiac tumors, occurring in up to 1% at postmortem examination and usually in the context of widely disseminated malignancy.[2] Myxomas are the most frequent primary cardiac tumors, accounting for 30% to 50% of all benign tumors.[1,4,6,8] They present at between 30 and 70 years of age and more often in women (70%).[1,2,5,8,13]

The majority of the rest of the benign tumors are lipomas, papillary fibroelastomas, and rhabdomyomas. Fibromas, hemangiomas, teratomas, and mesotheliomas of the atrioventricular node are found less frequently, whereas granular cell tumors, neurofibromas, and lymphangiomas are very rare.[2,4] Angiomas are extremely rare tumors, accounting for 5% to 10% of benign tumors in surgical series.[2,8]

Malignant tumors almost always affect adults (mean age 41 years)[1] and more frequently men.[1,8] Sarcomas comprise the second most common cardiac tumor after myxoma in surgical series (10%).[1] Angiosarcomas represent 30% of sarcomas and occur more frequently in men.[1] Because Kaposi sarcoma belongs to this category

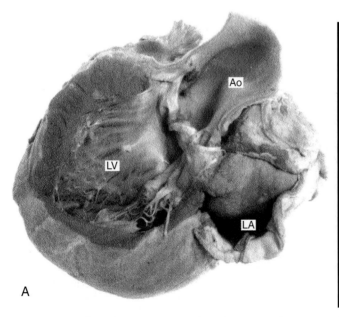

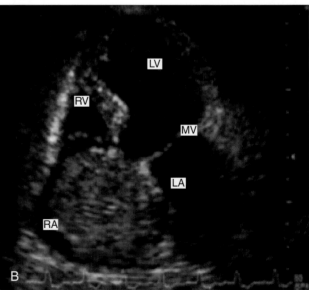

Figure 62-1 **A,** Left atrial myxoma arising from the interatrial septum and extending toward the mitral valve. **B,** Transthoracic echocardiogram: four-chamber view depicting a large right atrial myxoma. Ao, aorta; LA, left atrium; LV, left ventricle; MV, mitral valve; RA, right atrium; RV, right ventricle.

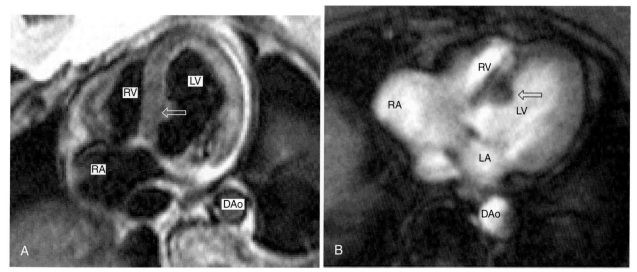

Figure 62-3 **A,** Spin-echo CMR image (black blood) showing a pedunculated papillary fibroelastoma (15 mm × 4 mm) extending from the basal ventricular septum (*arrow*). The tumor has similar signal intensity to myocardium. **B,** Gradient-echo CMR image (white blood) of the same papillary fibroelastomas (*arrow*). The tumor has low signal intensity. Cine images demonstrate the lesion's movement in the left ventricular outflow tract. DAo, descending aorta; LA, left atrium; LV, left ventricle; RA, right atrium; RV, right ventricle.

there has been a rise in the incidence of angiosarcomas in the past 20 years as part of the acquired immunodeficiency syndrome (AIDS). Rhabdomyosarcomas constitute the second most common primary sarcoma of the heart. Lymphomas are very uncommon primary heart tumors; however, their incidence is increasing in the context of AIDS.[4] Sarcomas of other cell types are infrequent. The most frequent cardiac metastases are due to lung neoplasia and then, in decreasing frequency, breast cancer, lymphoma, and leukemia. However, the most frequently metastasizing tumor to the heart is melanoma, followed by malignant germ cell tumors, leukemia, lymphoma, lung cancer, and noncardiac sarcomas.[2,4]

Myxomas are familial (<10% cases) with autosomal dominant transmission and variable phenotype.[1] Carney syndrome comprises myxomas in noncardiac locations (breast, skin), spotty pigmentation (lentigines, pigmented nevi), and endocrine tumors (pituitary adenoma, primary pigmented nodular adrenocortical disease, testicular

---

BOX 62-2 MALIGNANT TUMORS AND CARDIAC METASTASES

- Majority of malignant primary cardiac tumors are sarcomas, usually angiosarcomas or rhabdomyosarcomas.
- They are mostly located in the right atrium, although their presence on the posterior left atrial wall is suggestive of malignancy.
- Incidence of primary intracardiac lymphomas is increasing as part of the acquired immunodeficiency syndrome.
- Combination of surgery, radiation therapy, chemotherapy, or palliative surgery may prolong survival or improve quality of life. Mean survival reported is 1 to 3 years.
- Secondary cardiac tumors are usually epicardial and asymptomatic.
- Metastasis is rarely limited solely to the heart. Pericardial effusion is common.
- Screening for cardiac involvement should be done in patients with malignancies known to have a high predilection for the heart such as hypernephroma, metastatic melanoma, leukemia, lymphoma, and primary intrathoracic tumors.
- Mesothelial (monocytic) incidental cardiac excrescences (MICE) are incidental small peculiar masses found during surgery attached to valves or on cardiac masses. They are not neoplastic and are believed to be transported via catheters or cardiotomy suction tips.

Sertoli cell tumors).[14] It has been mapped to chromosomes 2p16 and 17q2.[2–4] Patients are young (mean age 20 years), are usually male, and may have bilateral tumors; recurrences are frequent after resection.[1,4] The syndrome resembles von Recklinghausen neurofibromatosis. NAME (nevi, atrial myxoma, myxoid neurofibromas and ephelides) and LAMB (lentigines, atrial myxoma, mucocutaneous myxoma and blue nevi) syndromes are other terms describing myxoma syndromes, but recent nomenclature suggests that they should be brought together under Carney syndrome.[2]

Tuberous sclerosis is a rare (birth prevalence 0.017%) autosomal dominant neuroectodermal disease with variable penetrance and expression characterized by hamartomas in several organs, epilepsy, mental deficiency, and adenoma sebaceum. It affects the brain, retina, pancreas, kidneys, and skin.[3,4,7] Two tuberous sclerosis genes have been identified on chromosomes 9q34 and 16p13.[7,12] At least 80% of patients with cardiac rhabdomyomas have tuberous sclerosis, and 40% to 86% of patients with this disease have cardiac rhabdomyomas.[7,12] The diagnosis of multiple rhabdomyomas during fetal or early neonatal life is considered the earliest detectable marker of tuberous sclerosis. The most common cause of death is renal disease.[7]

▣ Early Presentation and Management

Cardiac tumors may be found incidentally at autopsy or during cardiac imaging. Symptoms of primary tumors may be local, owing to invasion of the heart and neighboring organs, or systemic as a result of a variety of cytokines produced by the tumor, embolization, or metastasis (Table 62-1). Metastatic heart disease is associated with extracardiac symptoms arising from the primary focus, although cardiac symptoms may be the first manifestation. Less frequently noncardiac symptoms may be well-recognized manifestations of a syndrome with an accompanying primary cardiac tumor. Pericardial involvement may be the result of a primary tumor or metastatic disease.

Myxomas may present as fever, fatigue, arthralgia, myalgia, weight loss, anemia, increased erythrocyte sedimentation rate, elevated C-reactive protein, and globulins. These findings may be confused with infective endocarditis, rheumatic fever, connective tissue diseases, or malignancy.[1,2] Damage to the atrioventricular valve apparatus may lead to valvular regurgitation, the "wrecking ball effect" (see Table 62-1).[1,4,5] Obstruction to the tricuspid valve leads to constrictive physiology, and central cyanosis may result from the opening of the foramen ovale owing to increased right atrial pressure with subsequent right-to-left

TABLE 62-1	Clinical Signs and Symptoms at Presentation
	Comments
Systemic Findings	
Fever General malaise Weight loss Fatigue	May mimic endocarditis or malignant disease
Digital clubbing Raynaud phenomenon Myalgia and arthralgia	May mimic collagen, rheumatic, or malignant disease
Embolic Findings	
Systemic embolism	May affect almost any organ Caused by embolization of left-sided tumor fragments or thrombi aggregated at its surface
Pulmonary embolism	Caused by embolization of right-sided tumors
Cardiac Findings	
Arrhythmias	Almost any arrhythmias can occur. Complete atrioventricular block and sudden death are seen as the extreme.
Cardiac failure	May mimic dilated, restrictive, or hypertrophic obstructive cardiomyopathy. May present as cardiomegaly, respiratory distress, hydrops, pulmonary edema, or cyanosis.
Pericardial effusion and tamponade	Mainly seen in teratoma, malignant tumors, and secondary lesions
Obstruction	May cause outflow tract or atrioventricular valve obstruction and mimic valvular disease May present as new murmur, syncope, sudden death, or acute pulmonary edema Symptoms and murmur may relate to the patient's position.
Tumor plop	Is almost the only specific sign (with the postural variation of a murmur) Results from sudden tension on the stalk of the tumor as it prolapses during diastole into the left ventricular cavity with the possible impact of the mass on the ventricular wall.

Modified from Bédard E, Becker AE, Gatzoulis MA. Cardiac tumours. In Anderson RH, Baker EJ, Redington A, et al, eds. Pediatric Cardiology, 3rd ed. Philadelphia: Elsevier Churchill Livingstone; 2010.

shunting.[1,4] Embolization is most frequent in the cerebral, retinal, or other systemic arteries, but pulmonary embolism with chronic pulmonary hypertension has been reported.[1,2,4]

Rhabdomyomas are strongly associated with tuberous sclerosis.[2] Presenting symptoms may be due to obstruction, arrhythmias, pericardial effusion, or even sudden death.[4] Right ventricular tumors may produce cyanosis and symptoms mimicking severe pulmonary stenosis or pulmonary atresia. Hypoxic spells indistinguishable from those in tetralogy of Fallot have been reported.[4]

Fibromas may produce subaortic obstruction with evidence of left ventricular hypertrophy on the electrocardiogram and can be confused with hypertrophic cardiomyopathy. Sudden death has been reported in a third of patients.[2–4,7]

Papillary fibroelastomas do not appear to be the cause of valve dysfunction; however, they are frequently associated with valvular heart disease.[10] These tumors were considered to be benign and insignificant, but despite their firm consistency they can fragment and embolize or lead to endocardial thrombus deposition.[8,10] The presence of a stalk and associated mobility is a significant predictor of embolic risk.[10]

Lipomas are usually asymptomatic but rarely cause arrhythmias. When they are in the pericardium they may be quite large and can be mistaken for pericardial cysts and they can lead to pericardial effusion. They have also been discovered on cardiac valves simulating vegetations or myxomas.[2,4] Lipomatous hypertrophy of the interatrial septum is a separate, non-neoplastic condition usually found in obese patients older than 50 years of age in which the atrial septum is heavily infiltrated with adipose tissue. This is seen by ultrasound as a very thickened atrial septum (up to 7 cm cephalad and 4 cm caudad to the fossa

ovalis) with low echocardiographic density.[4] This disorder is usually asymptomatic but may be associated with atrial tachyarrhythmias.[2,4]

Malignant tumors have symptoms resembling those of benign tumors but are rapidly progressive. Signs of right-sided heart failure result from obstruction of the right atrium or right ventricle. In addition, obstruction of the superior vena cava may result in swelling of the face and upper extremities whereas obstruction of the inferior vena cava may result in visceral congestion. Pericardial involvement is frequent, usually with hemorrhagic pericardial fluid resulting in tamponade. Primary malignant tumors of the heart have a grave prognosis and metastasize widely; 75% of the patients have metastases at the time of death. They metastasize directly to neighboring organs or spread via the bloodstream to the liver, kidneys, adrenals, pancreas, bone, spleen, and bowel. A continuous precordial murmur may be produced by blood flowing in the highly vascularized angiosarcoma.[4] Echocardiography usually shows a broad-based right atrial mass near the inferior vena cava.[2] With rhabdomyosarcomas, nonspecific symptoms of malignancy are the rule, although arrhythmias, obstructive symptoms, pleuropericardial symptoms, and distal embolization may occur.[2] Extensive infiltration by lymphoma may mimic hypertrophic cardiomyopathy.[4] Sarcomas of other cell types produce the same nonspecific or cardiac symptoms as the more common sarcomas.[4] Only 10% of patients with cardiac metastases develop signs and/or symptoms of cardiac dysfunction.[2,4] Ninety percent of them result from pericardial involvement and only 10% from direct intramyocardial or intracavity involvement.[4] The development of cardiac enlargement, pericarditis, tachycardia, heart failure, or arrhythmias in a patient with cancer is suggestive of cardiac metastases and widespread organ involvement by the primary tumor.[2,4]

Neoplastic pericarditis manifests as the clinical syndrome of dyspnea, chest pain, and pericardial friction rub. Cardiac tamponade may be the initial manifestation of cancer, leukemia, or primary pericardial tumors. Rarely, constrictive pericarditis may result from neoplastic pericardial infiltration from lung or breast cancer, Hodgkin disease, and lymphoma. Electrocardiographic and radiographic signs of pericarditis or effusion-tamponade aid in the diagnosis of pericardial involvement but are not helpful in unraveling the specific neoplastic etiology.[15] The diagnostic yield of the cytologic examination of the pericardial fluid in patients with suspected neoplastic pericarditis is increased with measurement of carcinoembryonic antigen. However, if the cytologic examination is negative, open pericardial biopsy may be required.[15]

Treatment of cardiac tumors depends on the specific histologic type (Box 62-3). Metastases, local invasion, location on the right side of the heart or on the atrial free wall, rapid growth, hemorrhagic pericardial effusion, evidence of combined intramural and intracavitary location, and extension into the pulmonary veins are considered signs of malignancy. However, embolization of benign tumors in the lungs or systemic circulation may mimic malignant metastases.[1] Biopsy of embolization material may aid in the preoperative differential diagnosis.[1] Light microscopy and, recently, immunohistochemistry using antibodies against various antigens (factor VIII-related, desmin, myoglobin, muscle-specific actin, smooth muscle-specific actin, vimentin, cytokeratins, neurofilaments, and S-100 protein) offer the most valuable tools for differential diagnosis between primary and secondary tumors, malignant and benign forms, and non-neoplastic masses.[6,8]

Since the first successful excision of a left atrial myxoma by Craaford in 1954, surgical resection has become the treatment of choice.[1,2,5] Benign cardiac tumors can be life threatening, owing to local pressure-obstructive characteristics or distal embolization. Therefore, surgical resection is considered mandatory once the diagnosis has been made and this is usually curative.[2,5] Resection is done under cardiopulmonary bypass, and care is taken to excise the tumor in its entirety and with as little manipulation as possible because this may result in intracavitary seeding with further metastatic implantation or emboli. Most surgeons usually induce ventricular standstill with cardioplegic solution before any manipulation of the heart.[1,4,5] Operative mortality is about 3% for atrial myxomas. Resection is more difficult for ventricular tumors and sometimes necessitates valve replacement or pacemaker implantation.[1]

BOX 62-3   TREATMENT

- Benign cardiac tumors can be life threatening, owing to local pressure/obstruction or distal embolization. Surgical resection is mandatory and usually curative.
- Resection is done using cardiopulmonary bypass with care taken to excise the tumor en bloc with as little manipulation as possible.
- Atrial myxoma resection has an operative mortality about 3%. Resection is more difficult for ventricular tumors, sometimes necessitating valve replacement or pacemaker implantation.
- Fibromas should be surgically excised, whereas rhabdomyomas are resected only when they cause severe symptoms because they may regress.
- Large papillary fibroelastomas should be excised owing to the relatively high incidence of embolization. Survival is excellent after surgical excision without tumor recurrence.
- Lipomas do not warrant surgical excision because they reduce in size with weight loss.
- Angiomas are difficult to excise surgically because of the highly vascular nature of the tumor.
- Malignant tumors have a grave prognosis and are very difficult to resect.
- When primary benign or malignant heart tumors are not respectable, orthotopic heart transplantation is an alternative.

Surgical excision is recommended for fibromas. Because of the high rate of spontaneous regression (up to 54%),[9] the management is more conservative, unless the patients are symptomatic.[2–4,7]

Asymptomatic patients with small, left-sided, nonmobile papillary fibroelastomas can usually be observed. However, owing to the relatively high incidence of embolization of these tumors to cerebral and coronary arteries, especially when they are larger (≥1 cm) and mobile, they should be considered for excision.[10] Survival is excellent after surgical excision without tumor recurrence.[10] Lipomas usually do not warrant surgical excision.[2,4] For teratomas in children, surgery is necessary only to rule out more serious tumors. Angiomas are difficult to excise surgically because of the highly vascular nature of the tumor. However, regression, spontaneously or after corticosteroid therapy, has been reported.[4] Malignant tumors are very difficult to resect and have a grave prognosis. The combination of surgery, radiation therapy, chemotherapy, or palliative surgery may prolong survival or improve quality of life.[5]

When primary benign or malignant heart tumors are not resectable, orthotopic heart transplantation is an alternative.[8] Palliative surgery such as bidirectional cavopulmonary anastomosis to offload the right ventricle and augment pulmonary blood flow has been reported in cases of unresectable right ventricular fibromas. Palliative procedures such as Blalock-Taussig shunts have also been implemented with the hope that an obstructive right ventricular rhabdomyoma will eventually regress.[3,7]

Late Outcome

The probability of recurrence is low for benign tumors. Sporadic myxomas recur in 1% to 3% of cases usually due to incomplete resection, preexisting second tumor focus, or seeding during the operation.[1–3,5,7] This usually happens within 4 years after resection.[1,4] In patients with familial myxomas, or with multiple primary myxomas at presentation, the probability of a second tumor appearing in the future is quite high, sometimes reaching even 20% to 22%.[1] Therefore, in such cases careful preoperative screening is needed for detection of possible multiple foci and close follow-up for detection of secondary growth is mandatory for all types of myxomas. Interleukin-6 might be a useful marker of disease recurrence.

For malignant tumors mean survival is reported to be 1 to 3 years. Survival after surgical treatment of sarcomas (mean 11 months, median 6 months) correlates with clinical and histologic parameters.[8]

For angiosarcomas survival beyond 6 months after diagnosis is rare.[2,4] Response to chemotherapy has been reported for rhabdomyosarcomas, and tumor bulk may be followed sequentially with magnetic resonance imaging, but survival remains poor.[2] When cardiectomy results in surgical margins free of tumor, orthotopic heart transplantation may provide long-term survival (range 14 to 78 months) without tumor recurrence despite therapeutic immunosuppression.[8]

ASSESSMENT OF PATIENT WITH SUSPECTED CARDIAC TUMOR (Table 62-2)

Because of the versatile symptoms and signs of cardiac tumors, primarily myxoma, any known cardiac or systemic disease can be mimicked. The differential diagnosis of an intracardiac mass encompasses heart tumors, thrombi, and, rarely, vegetations.[1] An intracardiac tumor should be suspected in patients with hemodynamic or auscultatory findings suggesting intermittent obstruction of intracardiac flow.[1,2] A delayed or widely split first heart sound, positional change of a heart murmur, and a tumor plop (mimicking a third heart sound) are signs suggestive of a mobile atrial mass.[1,2] Tumor plop, murmurs that increase on inspiration, or a paradoxically split second heart sound (early pulmonary valve closure) are suggestive of right atrial tumors.[1]

Atrial or ventricular arrhythmias are nonspecific signs, and the electrocardiogram is usually inconclusive.[1] The chest radiograph is also nonspecific and may disclose various findings of organic heart disease (e.g., signs of mitral stenosis with a left atrial myxoma).[1] Pericardial effusion and mediastinal widening or pericardial masses should raise the suspicion of primary malignant or metastatic tumors. Cardiac calcification may suggest a tumor, although it may also be present in coronary artery disease, pericardial disease, thrombus, valvular heart disease, or parasitic infestations.

Echocardiography is the gold standard for diagnosis.[16] It is easy, quick, and reliable for identifying masses within the cardiac chambers and useful for risk stratification (see Fig. 62-1B).[1,5] Gated blood pool scanning can identify filling defects in the ventricles, but it is not the preferred method of diagnosis.[1] Computed tomography (CT) helps in identification of the degree of intramural tumor extension and in evaluation of extracardiac structures. Ultrafast CT with electrocardiographic gating provides a short scanning acquisition time and better accuracy than conventional CT. Tumors at least 0.5 to 1.0 cm in diameter can be visualized by electron beam CT and cardiovascular magnetic resonance imaging (CMR).[1] These techniques provide addi-

TABLE 62-2	Potential Investigations and Their Merits in Patients with Suspected Cardiac Tumors
Investigations	**Comments**
Blood	Nonspecific; may include elevated erythrocytic sedimentation rate and serum C-reactive protein, hypergammaglobulinemia, thrombocytosis or thrombocytopenia, polycythemia, leukocytosis, and anemia.
Electrocardiogram	Nonspecific; all kinds of rhythm and conduction disturbances or voltage and ST-segment/T-wave abnormalities may be seen.
Chest radiograph	Nonspecific; may show abnormal contours of the heart. Signs of pulmonary venous obstruction may occur with obstructive left-sided tumors. It may be possible to show calcification of the tumor.
Echocardiogram	Main diagnostic modality; allows accurate determination of the size, shape, "texture," location, attachment, mobility, and hemodynamic consequences of the tumor
Magnetic resonance imaging	Allows for better soft tissue contrast and offers a larger field of view, demonstrating the extension to the adjacent structures Requires sedation in children to suppress deep respiration and movements

Modified from Bédard E, Becker AE, Gatzoulis MA. Cardiac tumours. In: Anderson RH, Baker EJ, Redington A, et al, eds. Pediatric Cardiology, 3rd ed. Philadelphia: Elsevier Churchill Livingstone; 2010.

tional information about tissue composition and characteristics, aiding in the differentiation of solid, liquid, hemorrhagic, and fatty tumors or in the differentiation of thrombus from tumor masses.[1–4,7] Multislice cine CMR gives an excellent evaluation of size, shape, and surface characteristics of the tumor and also provides dynamic information such as tumor prolapse and valve obstruction (see Fig. 62-3). The use of angiocardiography has declined because of the superior imaging quality of the aforementioned techniques and the concomitant risk of tissue embolization from catheter manipulation.[1] Transseptal puncture should be avoided when suspecting a myxoma. Angiocardiography is particularly helpful in the diagnosis of hemangiomas (characteristic "tumor blush") and in the preoperative delineation of the tumor's blood supply.[1,12] Coronary angiography is mandatory for all patients older than age 40 years scheduled for operation and for the rare patient with coronary artery complications (e.g., embolization, compression).[1,5]

Arrhythmia and Sudden Cardiac Death

Arrhythmias are a common manifestation of cardiac tumors, especially those infiltrating the cardiac muscle. Sudden cardiac death (SCD) is a rare but devastating complication resulting from electrical or mechanical causes. Myxomas very rarely lead to SCD as a result of mechanical obstruction. Preexcitation is common with rhabdomyomas (9% to 13%) probably owing to abnormally conducting tumor tissue, and SCD has been reported.[4] SCD has been reported in a third of patients with fibromas and is related to ventricular tachycardia, conduction defects, or obstruction of ventricular outflow.[2–4,7] Lipomas can rarely become large and cause arrhythmias, including atrioventricular block.[2,4] Atrial tachyarrhythmias may be a manifestation of lipomatous hypertrophy of the interatrial septum and are the only kind of arrhythmia curable with starvation.[2,4] Rarely, ventricular tachycardia and cardiac tamponade may result from angiomas.[1]

REFERENCES

1. Reynen K. Cardiac myxomas. N Engl J Med 1995;333:1610–1617.
2. Shapiro LM. Cardiac tumours: diagnosis and management. Heart 2001;85:218–222.
3. Holley DG, Martin GR, Brenner JI, et al. Diagnosis and management of fetal cardiac tumors: a multicenter experience and review of published reports. J Am Coll Cardiol 1995;26:516–520.
4. Roberts WC. Primary and secondary neoplasms of the heart. Am J Cardiol 1997;80:671–682.
5. Centofanti P, Di Rosa E, Deorsola L, et al. Primary cardiac tumors: early and late results of surgical treatment in 91 patients. Ann Thorac Surg 1999;68:1236–1241.
6. Pucci A, Gagliardotto P, Zanini C, et al. Histopathologic and clinical characterization of cardiac myxoma: review of 53 cases from a single institution. Am Heart J 2000;140:134–138.
7. Freedom RM, Lee KJ, MacDonald C, Taylor G. Selected aspects of cardiac tumors in infancy and childhood. Pediatr Cardiol 2000;21:299–316.
8. Basso C, Valente M, Poletti A, et al. Surgical pathology of primary cardiac and pericardial tumors. Eur J Cardiothorac Surg 1997;12:730–737 discussion 737–738.
9. Smythe JF, Dyck JD, Smallhorn JF, Freedom RM. Natural history of cardiac rhabdomyoma in infancy and childhood. Am J Cardiol 1990;66:1247–1249.
10. Sun JP, Asher CR, Yang XS, et al. Clinical and echocardiographic characteristics of papillary fibroelastomas: a retrospective and prospective study in 162 patients. Circulation 2001;103:2687–2693.
11. Butany J, Nair V, Naseemuddin A, et al. Cardiac tumours: diagnosis and management. Lancet Oncol 2005;6:219–228.
12. Sallee D, Spector ML, van Heeckeren DW, Patel CR. Primary pediatric cardiac tumors: a 17-year experience. Cardiol Young 1999;9:155–162.
13. Heath D. Pathology of cardiac tumors. Am J Cardiol 1968;21:315–327.
14. Carney JA, Hruska LS, Beauchamp GD, Gordon H. Dominant inheritance of the complex of myxomas, spotty pigmentation, and endocrine overactivity. Mayo Clin Proc 1986;61:165–172.
15. Lorell BH. Pericardial diseases. In: Brawnwald E, editor. Heart Disease: A Textbook of Cardiovascular Medicine. Philadelphia: WB Saunders; 1997. p. 1478–1534.
16. Mehmood F, Nanda NC, Vengala S, et al. Live three-dimensional transthoracic echocardiographic assessment of left atrial tumors. Echocardiography 2005;22:137–143.

Marfan Syndrome: A Cardiovascular Perspective

BARBARA J. M. MULDER | GARY D. WEBB

Introduction

The Marfan syndrome is an autosomal dominant disorder of connective tissue in which cardiovascular, skeletal, and ocular abnormalities may be present to a highly variable degree. Prevalence has been estimated at 2 to 3/10,000, and 25% to 30% of cases represent new mutations. Prognosis is mainly determined by progressive dilation of the aorta, potentially leading to aortic dissection and death at a young age (Fig. 63-1).[1] Prophylactic surgery can prevent aortic dissection, and early identification of patients with Marfan syndrome is therefore of considerable importance.

Genetics

The Marfan syndrome is caused by mutations in the *FBN1* gene on chromosome 15q21 encoding a large glycoprotein called fibrillin-1, a glycoprotein in the extracellular matrix.[1] A deficiency of fibrillin may lead to weakening of the supporting tissues. Additionally, fibrillin-1 has a regulating role of transforming growth factor-β (TGF-β). In a mouse model of Marfan syndrome, increased TGF-β signaling appeared to play a causal role in progressive aortic root dilation.[2] Furthermore, increased TGF-β signaling provides an explanation for changes in architecture of the aortic wall, such as aberrant thickening of the aortic media with increased collagen deposition that cannot be explained only by structural weakness of the wall.[3]

More than 1000 mutations in the *FBN1* gene have been identified, and almost all are unique to an affected individual or family. In approximately 10% of the patients with a definite diagnosis of Marfan syndrome it is still not possible to find an *FBN1* mutation.

Genotype-phenotype correlations in Marfan syndrome have been complicated by the large number of unique mutations reported, as well as by clinical heterogeneity among individuals with the same mutation. Moreover, mutations in the *FBN1* gene have also been found in patients with other fibrillinopathies.

Clinical Presentation and Natural History

DIAGNOSIS

Early identification and establishment of the diagnosis in patients with Marfan syndrome is of considerable importance because prophylactic surgery can prevent aortic dissection and rupture. Elucidation of the molecular mechanisms behind Marfan syndrome will allow improvement in diagnostic testing, but so far the diagnosis Marfan syndrome has to be made on clinical grounds, following the Ghent criteria (Table 63-1).[4] Because of the variability in clinical expression, a multidisciplinary approach in a center for Marfan screening is required for complete evaluation and screening of a patient and his or her relatives. A definite diagnosis requires the occurrence of a major manifestation in two different organ systems and involvement of a third organ system.

CLINICAL FINDINGS

Prognosis of patients with Marfan syndrome is mainly determined by progressive dilation of the aorta, potentially leading to aortic dissection and aortic rupture, which are the major causes of death. Mean survival of untreated patients is 40 years, but the variance is large. Dilation of the sinus of Valsalva is found in 60% to 80% of adults with Marfan syndrome (Figs. 63-2 and 63-3). The rate of dilation is heterogeneous and unpredictable. The risk of type A dissection clearly increases with increasing aortic root diameter, but dissection may occasionally occur in patients with no or only mild aortic dilation. Not only the aortic root, but also other parts of the aorta may be dilated.[5] As an additional potential predictor for aortic dissection, noninvasive aortic elasticity has been investigated in patients with Marfan syndrome.[6-8] Decreased aortic elasticity determined by measurement of local distensibility and flow wave velocity with magnetic resonance imaging (MRI) has been demonstrated in many but not all unoperated patients with Marfan syndrome. Aortic elasticity of the descending thoracic aorta has been shown to be an independent predictor of progressive descending aortic dilation.[9]

Although not included in the diagnostic criteria for Marfan syndrome, it has been speculated that a fibrillin defect in the myocardium may predispose patients with Marfan syndrome to left ventricular dilation and reduced left ventricular function. In an echocardiographic study of 234 patients with Marfan syndrome without significant valvular regurgitation, left ventricular dimensions and systolic function were found to be normal in most patients and none of the patients fulfilled the criteria for dilated cardiomyopathy.[10]

Patients with a dilated aorta are usually asymptomatic. The presence of significant aortic, tricuspid, or mitral regurgitation may lead to symptoms of ventricular volume overload. Patients with Marfan syndrome tend to feel fatigued, which may, at least partly, be explained by orthostatic hypotension. The combination of increased height and a structural abnormality of the blood vessels may cause impaired orthostatic tolerance. In Marfan patients, fatigue and low orthostatic tolerance have been correlated.[11] Patients can be educated in physical counterpressure maneuvers, such as leg crossing and muscle tensing, to counteract orthostatic drops in blood pressure. Adequate muscle mass is, however, a prerequisite for these maneuvers.

Marfan syndrome can be confused with other heritable connective tissue disorders that closely mimic some Marfan syndrome manifestations, such as Loeys-Dietz syndrome, familial aortic aneurysm, bicuspid aortic valve with aortic dilation, familial ectopia lentis, MASS phenotype, and Ehlers-Danlos syndrome, because of the considerable clinical overlap between the various syndromes.

Treatment

MEDICAL TREATMENT

Both medical and surgical therapies have improved life expectancy substantially up to a median survival of 60 to 70 years.[12] β-Adrenergic blockers may reduce the rate of aortic dilation and improve survival in patients with Marfan syndrome.[13,14] Rigorous antihypertensive medical treatment, aiming at a systolic blood pressure less than 120 mm Hg, and 110 mm Hg in patients with aortic dissection, is important. β-Blocker therapy may be protective, independent of its effects on blood pressure, by reducing the force of left ventricular ejection. The angiotensin II receptor 1 blocker (AT1) losartan is potentially useful

Figure 63-1 Magnetic resonance (MR) image of a type B dissection. *(From Mulder BJM. The distal aorta in the Marfan syndrome. Neth Heart J 2008; 16:382–386.)*

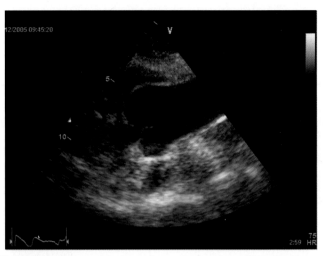

Figure 63-2 Long-axis echocardiography showing a dilated aortic root in a patient with Marfan syndrome. *(From Mulder BJM. The distal aorta in the Marfan syndrome. Neth Heart J 2008; 16:382–386.)*

TABLE 63-1	Diagnostic Criteria for Marfan Syndrome*	
Category	*Major Criteria*	*Minor Criteria*
Family history	Independent diagnosis in parent, child, sibling	None
Genetics	Mutation of *FBN1*	None
Cardiovascular	Aortic root dilation Dissection of ascending aorta	Mitral valve prolapse Calcification of the mitral valve (<40 yr) Dilation of the pulmonary artery Dilation/dissection of descending aorta
Ocular	Ectopia lentis	*Two needed:* flat cornea, myopia, elongated globe
Skeletal	*Four needed:* Pectus excavatum needing surgery Pectus carinatum Pes planus Wrist and thumb sign Scoliosis >20° or spondylolisthesis Arm span–height ratio > 1.05 Protrusio acetabuli (radiographic, MRI) Diminished extension elbows (<170°)	*Two to three major, or one major and two minor signs:* Moderate pectus excavatum High narrowly arched palate Typical face Joint hypermobility
Pulmonary		Spontaneous pneumothorax, apical bulla
Skin		Unexplained stretch marks (striae) Recurrent or incisional hernias
Central nervous system	Lumbosacral dural ectasia (CT or MRI)	

*The diagnosis requires major criteria in at least two different organ systems and involvement of a third organ system.

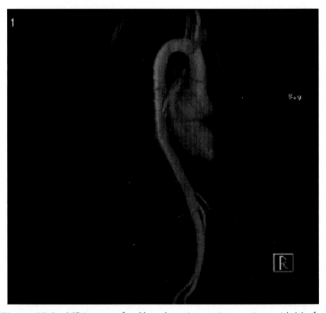

Figure 63-3 MR image of a dilated aortic root in a patient with Marfan syndrome. *(From Mulder BJM. The distal aorta in the Marfan syndrome. Neth Heart J 2008; 16:382–386.)*

in Marfan syndrome because it leads to TGF-β antagonism. A recent study with losartan in a mouse model of Marfan syndrome has shown a reduction in the rate and even elimination of aortic dilation and progressive degeneration of the aortic wall.[15] Clinical trials are presently being conducted to evaluate the beneficial effect of losartan in human patients with Marfan syndrome.

SURGICAL TREATMENT

Indications for aortic surgery are shown in Box 63-1.[16] Until recently, composite replacement of the aortic valve and ascending aorta was the standard operation for aortic root aneurysm in patients with Marfan syndrome. Over the past 30 years, the composite valve graft or Bentall procedure has become a low risk operation and a very durable one for these patients. In a large series of aortic root surgery in 675 patients with Marfan syndrome, the operative mortality was 1.5% for elective

Figure 63-4 **A,** Aortic root replacement with remodeling of the aortic root. Re-implantation of the aortic valve—the three commissures are resuspended inside a Dacron graft, and the remnants of the aortic sinuses are sutured to the Dacron. The coronary arteries are re-implanted into their respective neoaortic sinuses. **B,** Aortic root replacement with re-implantation of the aortic valve. Remodeling of the aortic root—the coronary arteries are re-implanted into their respective neoaortic sinuses.

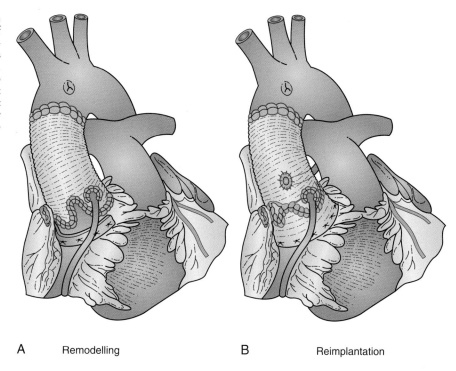

A   Remodelling   B   Reimplantation

BOX 63-1 INDICATIONS FOR (PREFERABLY VALVE-SPARING) AORTIC SURGERY IN PATIENTS WITH MARFAN SYNDROME

Aortic Root:
- 50 mm
- 45 to 50 mm with family history of dissection
  - or progressive dilation > 2 mm/yr, as confirmed by repeated measurement
  - or severe aortic or mitral valve regurgitation
  - or if pregnancy is desired

Other Parts of the Aorta:
- 50 mm or progressive dilation

is usually recommended already before reaching 50 mm, which is the threshold for intervention in aortic diseases of any etiology.

Surgery is also indicated when rapidly progressive aortic dilation is observed. Surgery should be performed in a center with substantial experience with great vessel surgery.

Although there are few reports of short-term success after endovascular stent grafting of the descending thoracic aorta, stent grafting in patients with Marfan syndrome is not recommended unless

operations and 11.7% for emergency operations.[17] In patients with initially normal aortic valves, in whom aortic insufficiency is due to the dilated annulus or dissection, valve-sparing operations with root replacement by a Dacron prosthesis and with reimplantation of the coronary arteries into the prosthesis (the David procedure) or remodeling of the aortic root (the Yacoub procedure) have now become the preferred choice of surgery (Fig. 63-4). Either type of valve-sparing aortic root replacement appears to be safe, reproducible, and associated with excellent 5- to 10-year results for selected patients, at least in institutions with cardiac surgeons who have considerable personal experience and success with this procedure. Late aortic regurgitation requires reoperation in 20% of patients after 10 years.[18] A homograft or bioprosthetic valve may also be considered to avoid anticoagulant therapy, yet at the cost of a considerable reoperation rate in young patients.

Women have on average a smaller aorta (by 5 mm), which is only partly explained by a smaller body surface area (BSA).[19] In small individuals the use of an indexed aortic diameter adjusted for a BSA of 2.75 cm/m^2 should perhaps be used for operative decision-making.[20] Using this approach, surgery would be indicated at an aortic diameter of 4.5 cm in patients with a BSA of 1.65 m^2, 5.0 cm at a BSA of 1.8 m^2, and 5.5 cm at a BSA of 2 m^2.

If necessary, all parts of the aorta can be replaced by prostheses (Fig. 63-5). In Marfan syndrome, replacement of the distal parts of the aorta

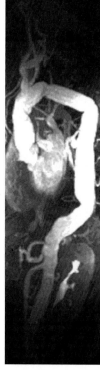

Figure 63-5 MR angiogram of a patient with entire aortic replacement. *(From Mulder BJM. The distal aorta in the Marfan syndrome. Neth Heart J 2008; 16:382–386.)*

intervention is clearly indicated and the risk of conventional open surgical repair is deemed to be prohibitive.[21]

Outpatient Assessment

Regular imaging of the aortic root and all other parts of the aorta is crucial in the follow-up of patients with Marfan syndrome (Box 63-2).

Echocardiography in the parasternal long-axis view is mostly used for measurement of the aortic root. By means of Doppler echocardiography the presence and hemodynamic consequences of aortic regurgitation, mitral valve prolapse, mitral regurgitation, and occasionally tricuspid valve prolapse can be assessed. MRI is particularly useful for imaging of the entire aorta, for patients with deformation of the chest wall and asymmetrical aortic roots.[22] Imaging of the entire aorta should be performed in every patient. When parts of the aorta are dilated, regular follow-up should be performed at least once every year. Even when the aorta shows no abnormalities, imaging should be repeated within 5 years. Computed tomography (CT) may be used when MRI cannot be performed because of contraindications or unavailability. With MRI, aortic elasticity can be measured and is often reduced. Aortic elasticity of the thoracic descending aorta appeared to be an independent predictor for progressive descending aortic dilation.[9] Coronary angiography should be performed in patients 50 years and older in whom cardiac surgery is planned. Transesophageal echocardiography may be useful if aortic dissection is suspected. Holter monitoring should be performed in symptomatic patients, because ventricular arrhythmias, conduction disturbances, and sudden cardiac death may occasionally occur.

LATE OUTCOME

Because of the advances in medical and surgical therapy, the life expectancy of patients with Marfan syndrome has improved substantially. Five- and 10-year survival after aortic root replacement has been

reported to be 84% and 75%, respectively.[17] After aortic root replacement, both electively operated patients with Marfan syndrome and especially patients presenting with dissection at the time of the operation deserve intensive surveillance because aneurysms and dissection of the aorta may develop distal to the site of the graft (Fig. 63-6 and Box 63-3).[23,24] Aortic root replacement in Marfan syndrome has been associated with a considerably higher risk of re-dissection and

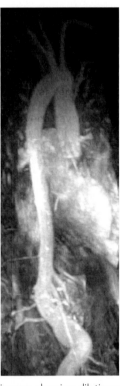

Figure 63-6 MR angiogram showing dilation of the abdominal aorta after previous aortic root replacement in a patient with Marfan syndrome. (*From Mulder BJM. The distal aorta in the Marfan syndrome. Neth Heart J 2008; 16:382–386.*)

BOX 63-2   ASSESSMENT

Transthoracic Echocardiography
This imaging method may show the following:
• Aortic root dilation
• Presence and severity of aortic regurgitation
• Presence and severity of mitral regurgitation
• Dilation of the pulmonary trunk
• Evidence of endocarditis
• Presence of ascending aortic dissection with or without pericardial and pleural effusion

Transesophageal Echocardiography
This is used to assess:
• Aortic dissection
• Severity of mitral regurgitation
• Reparability of mitral and aortic valves
• Intraoperative evaluation of aortic valve-sparing and mitral repair surgery

Magnetic Resonance Imaging or Computed Tomography
These methods are used to evaluate:
• The entire aorta and its major branches (especially after dissection)
• Dimensions of any artery and its false lumen after dissection
• Source and threats to perfusion of viscera after dissection and repair
• Sequelae of surgical repair.
• Presence of lumbosacral dural ectasia

Cardiac Catheterization
This may be useful to assess:
• The coronary arteries in patients older than 50 years of age when contemplating elective surgery

---

BOX 63-3   COMPLICATIONS

Aortic Dilation or Dissection
• Aortic root dilation, requiring β-blockers. Elective—preferably valve-sparing—surgery is indicated when the aortic root diameter is between 45 and 50 mm, depending on risk factors and available surgical resources.
• Dilation of other parts of the aorta. Surgery is usually performed before the aortic diameter reaches 50 mm.
• Type A dissection, requiring emergency operation
• Type B dissection, usually conservative treatment and rigorous antihypertensive medical treatment. Surgery is indicated when complications (progressive dilation, progressive dissection, branch occlusion, organ malperfusion) occur.

Valve Regurgitation
• Aortic valve regurgitation, requiring surgery when hemodynamically important (refer to American College of Cardiology/American Heart Association/European Society of Cardiology valve guidelines) or when aortic surgery is performed
• Mitral valve regurgitation, requiring surgery, preferably repair, when hemodynamically important (refer to ACC/AHA/ESC valve guidelines)
• Tricuspid valve regurgitation, requiring surgery, preferably repair, when hemodynamically important

recurrent aneurysm than in patients with other causes of aortic disease. The presence of dissection, either acute or chronic, at the time of the first operation is a significant predictor of subsequent repeat aortic procedures. Other risk factors for reoperation are hypertension and smoking. Long-term results of valve-sparing aortic root replacement in Marfan syndrome are still becoming known.

In a European survey of Marfan patients, of all aortic events observed during follow-up, almost one in three occurred in the distal aorta.[25] In 18% of these patients the distal aorta was the site of first complications. In a study by Finkbohner and colleagues, the first aortic event occurred in the distal aorta in 16% of patients.[26] Elective replacement of the aortic root removes the most important site for aneurysms, but the distal aorta remains at risk. In the European survey, the rate of events involving the distal aorta increased after elective aortic root surgery. Diameters of the distal aorta were greater in patients who had undergone aortic root surgery than in those who had not.[25] One possible explanation of this finding is that patients who undergo elective surgery have more advanced disease. Another explanation is that intervention at the level of the root has an impact on the more distal aorta, as a result of hemodynamic factors or altered wall mechanics or because of clamping of the aorta during the operation.

A little recognized postoperative complication, both after aortic valve-sparing operations and after composite aortic valve replacement, is coronary ostial aneurysm.[27] In a series of 40 patients with Marfan syndrome who underwent MRI 3 months to 19 years after elective aortic root surgery 27 (43%) patients had coronary ostial aneurysms. Time after operation did not influence the prevalence of coronary ostial aneurysms. Therefore, it seems likely that coronary ostial aneurysms are not progressive and develop due to perioperative stretch of the weakened wall of the coronary ostium. Follow-up studies, however, are needed to confirm that these aneurysms are not clinically relevant.

Pregnancy

For women with Marfan syndrome, pregnancy presents a twofold problem: a 50% chance that the child will be affected and an increased risk of aortic dissection during or (especially) shortly after pregnancy. Women with an aortic diameter above 45 mm are strongly discouraged from becoming pregnant before surgical repair. An aortic diameter below 40 mm rarely presents a problem, although a completely safe diameter does not exist. With an aorta between 40 and 45 mm, recent aortic growth and a family history of aortic events are important for advising pregnancy with or without preconception aortic repair.[28] In addition to cardiovascular complications, pregnancy in women with Marfan syndrome is associated with a high rate of premature deliveries, preterm premature rupture of membranes, and increased mortality in the offspring.[29]

Level of Follow-Up

Optimal long-term outcome demands lifelong follow-up with imaging of the aortic root by means of echocardiography and the entire aorta by means of MRI at regular intervals. This is particularly true if a dissection has occurred and its stability is being monitored. Patients with mitral valve prolapse and moderate or severe mitral regurgitation should also be followed with yearly echocardiography.

Antihypertensive medical treatment, aiming at a systolic blood pressure less than 120 mm Hg, is important in all patients with Marfan syndrome. After aortic dissection, systolic blood pressure should not exceed 110 mm Hg. Clinical trials presently are being conducted to evaluate the possible beneficial effect of losartan in human patients with Marfan syndrome.

Lifelong and regular follow-up of these patients requires involvement of trained specialists with ample expertise in a tertiary referral center.

Endocarditis Prophylaxis

Endocarditis prophylaxis is recommended only in patients with a prosthetic valve and in patients with previous endocarditis; in patients with complete repair using prosthetic material (surgical or percutaneous) for up to 6 months after the procedure (until endothelialization); and ongoing only when a residual defect persists at the site of prosthetic material.[30]

Exercise

Patients should be advised to avoid both physical and emotional situations that increase blood pressure and heart rate dramatically. Furthermore, patients should be advised to avoid exertion at maximal capacity, competitive sports, contact sports, and isometric sports.

REFERENCES

1. McKusick VA. The cardiovascular aspects of Marfan's syndrome: a heritable disorder of connective tissue. Circulation 1955; 11:321–342.
2. Neptune ER, Frischmeyer PA, Arking DE, et al. Dysregulation of TGF-beta activation contributes to pathogenesis in Marfan syndrome. Nat Genet 2003;33:407–411.
3. Yetman AT, Graham T. The dilated aorta in patients with congenital cardiac defects. J Am Coll Cardiol 2009;53:461–467.
4. DePaepe A, Devereux RB, Dietz HC, et al. Revised diagnostic criteria for the Marfan syndrome. Am J Med Genet 1996;62:417–426.
5. Mulder BJM. The distal aorta in the Marfan syndrome. Neth Heart J 2008;16:382–386.
6. Adams JN, Brooks M, Redpath TW, et al. Aortic distensibility and stiffness index measured by magnetic resonance imaging in patients with Marfan's syndrome. Br Heart J 1995;73:265–269.
7. Groenink M, De Roos A, Mulder BJ, et al. Biophysical properties of the normal-sized aorta in patients with Marfan syndrome: evaluation with MR flow mapping. Radiology 2001;219:535–540.
8. Hirata K, Triposkiadis F, Sparks E, et al. The Marfan syndrome: abnormal aortic elastic properties. J Am Coll Cardiol 1991;18:57.
9. Nollen GJ, Groenink M, Tijssen JGP, et al. Aortic stiffness and diameter predict progressive aortic dilation in patients with Marfan syndrome. Eur Heart J 2004;25:1146–1152.
10. Meijboom LJ, Timmermans J, Van Tintelen JP, et al. Evaluation of left ventricular dimensions and function in Marfan's syndrome without significant valvular regurgitation. Am J Cardiol 2005;95:795–797.
11. Van Dijk N, Boer MC, Mulder BJM, et al. Is fatigue in Marfan syndrome related to orthostatic intolerance? Clin Auton Res 2008; 18:187–193.
12. Silverman DI, Gray JG, Roman MJ, et al. Family history of severe cardiovascular disease in Marfan syndrome is associated with increased aortic diameter and decreased survival. J Am Coll Cardiol 1995;26:1062–1067.
13. Shores J, Berger KR, Murphy EA, Pyeritz RE. Progression of aortic dilation and the benefit of long-term beta-adrenergic blockade in Marfan's syndrome. N Engl J Med 1994;330:1335–1341.
14. Engelfriet P, Mulder BJM. Is there benefit of beta-blocking agents in the treatment of patients with the Marfan syndrome? Int J Cardiol 2007;114:300–302.
15. Habashi JP, Judge DP, Holm TM, et al. Losartan, an AT1 antagonist, prevents aortic aneurysm in a mouse model of Marfan syndrome. Science 2006;312:117–121.
16. Groenink M, Lohuis TAJ, Tijssen JPG, et al. Survival and complication free survival in Marfan's syndrome: implications of current guidelines. Heart 1999;82:499–504.
17. Gott VL, Greene PS, Alejo DE, et al. Replacement of the aortic root in patients with Marfan's syndrome. N Engl J Med 1990;340:1307–1313.
18. Kallenbach K, Baraki H, Khaladj N, et al. Aortic valve-sparing operation in Marfan syndrome, what do we know after a decade? Ann Thorac Surg 2007;83:S764–S768.
19. Meijboom LJ, Timmermans J, Zwinderman AH, et al. Aortic root growth in men and women with the Marfan's syndrome. Am J Cardiol 2005;96:1441–1444.
20. Davies RR, Gallo A, Coady MA, et al. Novel measurement of relative aortic size predicts rupture of thoracic aortic aneurysms. Ann Thorac Surg 2006;81:169–177.
21. Svensson LG, Kouchoukos NT, Miller DC, et al. Wheatley III expert consensus document on the treatment of descending thoracic aortic disease using endovascular stent-grafts. Ann Thorac Surg 2008;85(Suppl.):S1–S41.
22. Meijboom LJ, Groenink M, Van der Wall EE, et al. Aortic root asymmetry in Marfan patients; evaluation by magnetic resonance imaging and comparison with standard echocardiography. Int J Card Imaging 2000;16:161–168.
23. Engelfriet P, Boersma E, Oechslin E, et al. The spectrum of adult congenital heart disease in Europe: morbidity and mortality in a 5 year follow-up period. The Euro Heart Survey on adult congenital heart disease. Eur Heart J 2005;26:2325–2333.
24. Kawamoto S, Bluemke DA, Traill TA, Zerhouni EA. Thoracoabdominal aorta in Marfan syndrome: MR imaging findings of progression of vasculopathy after surgical repair. Radiology 1997;203:727–732.
25. Engelfriet PM, Boersma E, Tijssen JGP, et al. Beyond the root: dilation of the distal aorta in the Marfan's syndrome. Heart 2006;92:1238–1243.
26. Finkbohner R, Johnston D, Crawford ES, et al. Marfan syndrome: Long term survival and complications after aortic aneurysm repair. Circulation 1995;91:728–733.
27. Meijboom LJ, Nollen GJ, Merchant N, et al. Frequency of coronary ostial aneurysms after aortic root surgery in patients with the Marfan syndrome. Circulation 2002;89:1135–1138.
28. Meijboom LJ, Vos FE, Timmermans J, et al. Pregnancy and aortic root growth in the Marfan syndrome: a prospective study. Eur Heart J 2005;26:914–920.
29. Meijboom LJ, Drenthen W, Pieper PG, et al. Obstetric complications in Marfan syndrome. Int J Cardiol 2006;110:53–59.
30. Nishimura RA, Carabello BA, Faxon DP, et al., American College of Cardiology/American Heart Association Task Force. ACC/AHA 2008 guideline update on valvular heart disease: focused update on infective endocarditis: a report of the American College of Cardiology/American Heart Association Task Force on Practice Guidelines: endorsed by the Society of Cardiovascular Anesthesiologists, Society for Cardiovascular Angiography and Interventions, and Society of Thoracic Surgeons. Circulation 2008;118:887–896.

64

Idiopathic Pulmonary Arterial Hypertension

GERHARD-PAUL DILLER | MICHAEL J. LANDZBERG

Introduction

Idiopathic pulmonary arterial hypertension (IPAH) is a rare progressive disease that eventually, if left untreated, leads to right-sided heart failure and death. The first pathologic description of the condition dates to 1891,[1] but, until about a decade ago, no adequate treatment existed and the disorder received relatively little clinical attention. With the advent of disease-targeting therapies the prognosis has improved greatly; and this has stimulated research into the condition, providing novel insights into pathophysiology and therapy. The etiology, epidemiology, pathophysiology, clinical aspects, and treatment options for IPAH are reviewed here.

Epidemiology

The incidence of IPAH in the general population has been estimated to 1 to 2 cases/million/ year.[2] Estimations on the prevalence of the disease traditionally have been based on autopsy data and data from patients with cardiopulmonary disease.[3,4] A recent study based on the Scottish Morbidity Record scheme compiling data from all adults aged 16 to 65 years estimated an IPAH incidence of approximately 3.3 cases/million/year and a prevalence of approximately 25 cases/million inhabitants.[5] This is roughly consistent with data from a French registry suggesting a prevalence of approximately 65 cases/million. Most published studies suggest that there is a female predominance with a female-to-male ratio of approximately 1.7:1 to 3.5:1.[6]

Definition and Clinical Classification

Pulmonary arterial hypertension (PAH) is defined as an elevated mean pulmonary arterial pressure of more than 25 mm Hg at rest.[7] Traditionally it had been classified according to the presence or absence of an identifiable underlying cause into primary or secondary PAH. Improved pathophysiologic insight as well as a more accurate detection of underlying causes have led to the introduction of a new clinical classification at the 3rd World Symposium on Pulmonary Arterial Hypertension, in Venice in 2003, which has replaced the previous Evian classification.[2] PAH is classified as idiopathic (IPAH), familial, or PAH related to other risk factors (oPAH) and associated conditions. Recently the 4th World Symposium on Pulmonary Hypertension generated new "consensus, recommendations, and directions." (Box 64-1) Owing to a large variability of pulmonary arterial pressures during exercise in healthy individuals the previous definition of PAH as an elevated mean pulmonary arterial pressure of more than 30 mm Hg during exercise has now been abandoned. Acknowledging that mean pulmonary arterial pressures in normal individuals are 13.9 ± 3.3 mm Hg at rest, resulting in an upper 95% confidence interval (mean + 2 standard deviations) of 20.5 mm Hg, mean pulmonary arterial pressures between 20 and 25 mm Hg at rest have been defined as borderline PAH.[8] For clinical purposes we suggest stratifying severity of PAH according to mean pulmonary arterial pressures into mild (25 to 45 mm Hg), moderate (46 to 65 mm Hg), and severe (>65 mm Hg) forms.[9]

Pulmonary Vascular Pathophysiology and Genetic Factors

PAH represents a dynamic and multifactorial process linked to vasoconstriction and remodeling of the pulmonary vascular bed that may be aggravated by thrombosis.[10] Histologically, PAH is characterized by smooth muscle cell hypertrophy, formation of plexiform lesions, and migration of smooth muscle cells distally into normally nonmuscular arterioles. Based on these characteristics histologic classifications of PAH have been developed that show some correlations to the clinical severity of the disease.[11,12]

Several pathophysiologic mechanisms responsible for the development of the disease have been proposed that probably act synergistically in leading to overt PAH. It has been suggested that IPAH requires a permissive genotype, a vulnerable cell phenotype (either endothelial, smooth muscle cell, or both), and potentially an additional exogenous trigger.[13] Pulmonary endothelial damage (e.g., toxic, immunologic, or due to shear stress as a consequence of high pulmonary blood flow and pressure) may induce adverse pulmonary vascular remodeling. This is associated with degeneration and degradation of extracellular matrix as well as release of growth factors (e.g., transforming growth factor-β or fibroblast growth factor). These and other unknown factors also induce smooth muscle cell hypertrophy, proliferation, and failure to sustain normal apoptosis pathways, resulting in the known histopathologic changes in PAH. Endothelial dysfunction also favors platelet adherence and activation, immune inflammation, and activation of coagulation pathways. Furthermore, endothelial dysfunction also affects the production of vasoconstrictors (e.g., endothelin-1 and thromboxane) and vasodilators (e.g., nitric oxide), shifting the balance in favor of vasoconstrictors and, ultimately, pulmonary vascular remodeling (Fig. 64-1). In addition, numerous humoral factors influencing pulmonary vascular tone have been identified. This area of research has received considerable clinical interest because some of these factors are now amenable to pharmacologic therapy.

Pulmonary hypertension is characterized by reduced nitric oxide bioavailability. Nitric oxide (formerly known as endothelium-derived relaxing factor) is a potent vasodilator. Nitric oxide leads to increased intracellular levels of cyclic guanylate monophosphate (cGMP) in vascular smooth muscle cells, which induce vasodilation and inhibit cell proliferation. cGMP in turn is degraded by phosphodiesterases. Pharmacologic inhibition of phosphodiesterases, therefore, provides a way to augment intracellular cGMP levels. Sildenafil represents such a phosphodiesterase-5 inhibitor currently employed in the treatment of PAH. In addition, PAH is characterized by activation of the endothelin system with increased endothelin levels in tissue and plasma.[14,15] Endothelin-1 is a potent vasoconstrictor with mitogenic, profibrotic, and proinflammatory properties.[16] Reduced production of prostacyclin is an additional hallmark of PAH. Prostacyclin, a metabolite of arachidonic acid, is a potent pulmonary and systemic vasodilator. Excretion of prostacyclin metabolites has been reported to be reduced in patients with PAH.[17] Similar to endothelin, it has important antiproliferative properties. Additional abnormalities involved in the pathophysiology of PAH include increased serotonin (a vasoconstrictor) turnover, increased intrapulmonary expression of transforming growth factor-β (a profibrotic factor),[18] immune inflammation with intrapulmonary inflammatory infiltration,[19] impaired endothelial cell apoptosis and progenitor cell homing to the site of pulmonary vascular changes,[20] as well as altered expression of pulmonary potassium channels associated with an accentuated response to hypoxia. These mechanisms have been reviewed in detail elsewhere and provide the basis for investigation of novel agents to treat PAH, including activation of endothelial cell progenitor cells; inhibition of NFAT, elastase, or an endothelial growth factor receptor; or the use of imatinib, dichloroacetate, cyclosporine, or simvastatin.[21] Recently, important insights into the genetic components involved in the pathobiology of PAH have also been gained. Mutations in receptors of the transforming growth factor-β family (bone morphogenetic protein type II [*BMPR2*] and activin-like kinase type-1) have been identified as causes of familial PAH. In a recent study, 26% of patients with IPAH were found to have *BMPR2* mutations.[22] This suggests that *BMPR2* mutations are important cofactors for the development of the disease. However, it appears that a *BMPR2* mutation in itself is not sufficient to develop PAH and additional environmental factors are required for the phenotype to develop.

Cardiac Pathophysiology

"…as the right ventricle goes, so goes the patient"[23]

Whereas PAH primarily involves the pulmonary vasculature, symptoms and survival prospects are mainly determined by the long-term ability of the right ventricle to cope with increased afterload, which is typically described as pulmonary vascular resistance but perhaps best characterized in terms of impedance changes.[24] The individual

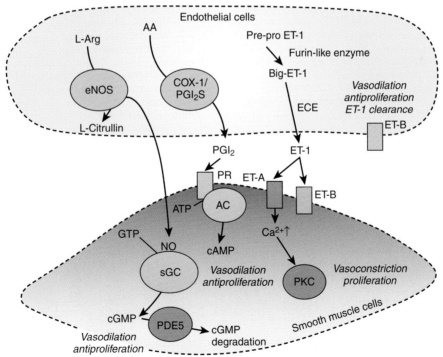

Figure 64-1   Components of the nitric oxide (NO), prostacyclin (PGI_2), and endothelin pathway regulating pulmonary vascular tone and pulmonary vascular remodeling. Nitric oxide is synthesized by endothelial NO-synthase (eNOS) from l-arginine. NO stimulates soluble guanylate cyclase (sGC) in smooth muscle cells, resulting in increased production of cyclic guanosine monophosphate (cGMP), inducing vasodilation and antiproliferatory effects. cGMP, in turn, is degraded by phosphodiesterase-5 (PDE5). Prostacyclin (PGI_2) is produced by cyclooxygenase-1 (COX-1) and PGI_2 synthase (PGI_2S) from arachidonic acid (AA). Activation of prostacyclin receptors (PR) on smooth muscle cells induces stimulation of adenylate cyclase, thus increasing intracellular cyclic adenosine monophosphate (cAMP) levels and leading to vasodilation and antiproliferative effects. Pre-pro-endothelin (pre-pro ET-1) is formed after translation from mRNA and is subsequently processed by furin-like enzymes to big-ET-1. Big-ET-1 is cleaved by endothelin-converting enzymes (ECEs) to ET-1. ET-1 induces vasoconstriction and leads to smooth muscle cell proliferation via activation of ET-A and ET-B receptors with subsequent calcium release and activation of protein kinase C (PKC). Factors inducing vasodilation/antiproliferation are in *green,* and those leading to vasoconstriction/proliferation are in *red.*

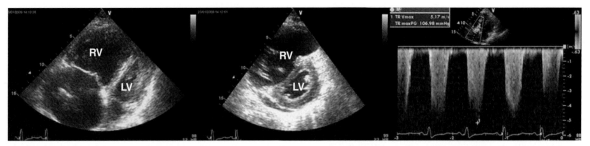

Figure 64-2   Echocardiographic images from a patient with severe PAH. The right ventricle (RV) is dilated, and the septum curves leftward, compressing the left ventricle (LV) in diastole. At right a transtricuspid gradient of more than 100 mm Hg indicates severe PAH.

response of the right ventricle to PAH varies significantly. However, right ventricular dilation and deterioration are thought to be major contributing factors to the adverse prognosis in this setting.[25]

As established by previous physiologic and animal studies, an acute increase in afterload is not well tolerated by the right ventricle.[26] In contrast, a chronic increase in afterload is much better tolerated but increased contractility occurs at the price of right ventricular diastolic dysfunction and compensatory augmented right atrial contraction.[27] Furthermore, it has been demonstrated in young lambs that after 8 weeks of adjustable pulmonary artery banding the right ventricle has a reduced response to dobutamine, indicating a diminished inotropic reserve.[28] With time, right ventricular pressure overload leads to ventricular dilation, thus reducing right ventricular mass to volume ratio and increasing wall tension, according to Laplace law. This, in turn, augments wall stress and induces right ventricular systolic dysfunction. With time, remodeling and compensatory mechanisms of the right ventricle fail, leading to overt right ventricular failure. In addition to the direct effect on the right ventricle, right ventricular dilation and interventricular septal shift impact left ventricular shape and function, thus aggravating biventricular function (Fig. 64-2).[29] Interventricular interdependence is paramount in defining systemic cardiac output in patients with IPAH and acts in various ways. Left ventricular filling and, consequently, systemic cardiac output can be affected by reduced pulmonary venous return. Increased right ventricular pressure results in deviation of the ventricular septum toward the left ventricle (the characteristic D-shaped left ventricle) and a reduction of the left ventricular capacitance.

Clinical Presentation and Assessment

Clinical signs and symptoms in IPAH are variable, and the onset of symptoms is usually subtle, with several years elapsing before the diagnosis is actually made (Box 64-2). Common symptoms are breathlessness, chest pain, and syncope. The physical signs in IPAH patients include peripheral cyanosis of hypoperfusion and signs of right ventricular failure, such as a raised jugular venous pressure, a right ventricular heave, and a pronounced pulmonary second heart sound. In addition, a pansystolic murmur of tricuspid regurgitation or a loud diastolic murmur of high pressure pulmonary regurgitation may be audible. There may be pulsatile hepatomegaly, ascites, and peripheral pitting edema.

Patients with a suspected diagnosis of IPAH benefit from referral to a specialized center where the diagnosis can be confirmed and therapy initiated early, when it is most likely to be of benefit.

Evaluation of IPAH patients should include a chest radiograph, electrocardiogram, measurement of arterial oxygen saturations, laboratory investigations of blood and serum, pulmonary function testing, assessment of portal venous flow and pressures, objective measure of exercise tolerance, and echocardiography. In addition, high-resolution chest computed tomography (CT) or magnetic resonance imaging (MRI) provides additional information concerning the pulmonary vascular bed and the right ventricle in selected patients.

CHEST RADIOGRAPHY

Typical abnormal radiologic findings in patients with IPAH include enlargement or calcification of the main pulmonary artery and the hilar pulmonary vessels. In addition, attenuation of peripheral vascular markings (pruning) may be present (Fig. 64-3). Furthermore, signs of right atrial and right ventricular enlargement may be noticed (the cardiothoracic ratio should be recorded). Radiographic findings, however, are variable and the chest radiograph may be remarkably normal in some patients.

BOX 64-2   CLINICAL EXAMINATION

- Signs and symptoms are variable and nonspecific.
- Symptom onset is usually subtle.
- Common symptoms include:
  - Shortness of breath
  - Chest pain
  - Syncope
- Physical signs are:
  - Peripheral cyanosis
  - Signs of right-sided heart failure
  - Pronounced second heart sound
  - Occasionally pansystolic murmur of tricuspid regurgitation
  - Occasionally loud diastolic murmur of high pressure pulmonary regurgitation
  - Hepatomegaly, ascites, and peripheral pitting edema in patients with right-sided heart failure

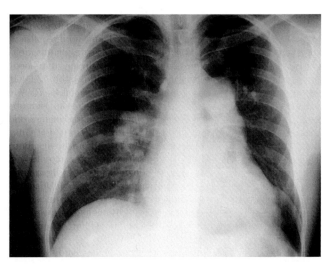

Figure 64-3   Chest radiograph of a patient with IPAH. There is significant enlargement of the main pulmonary artery and of the hilar pulmonary vessels bilaterally. The peripheral parenchymal vascularity appears diminished.

ELECTROCARDIOGRAPHY

The electrocardiogram will show the heart rhythm and may indicate atrial dilation or right ventricular strain. In addition, voltage criteria for right ventricular hypertrophy, derived as the sum of the R-wave amplitude in V_1 and the maximum amplitude of the S wave in V_5 or V_6, may be present.

FORMAL EXERCISE TESTING

Exercise capacity in patients with IPAH reflects disease severity and is of prognostic significance.[30,31] Exercise capacity can be formally assessed either by measurement of the 6-minute walk test distance or cardiopulmonary exercise testing with measurement of peak oxygen consumption. Both measurements have been successfully employed to evaluate objective exercise limitation in patients with IPAH. The 6-minute walk test is relatively robust and the only exercise test modality recommended by the U. S. Food and Drug Administration as an endpoint for prospective clinical trials in the setting of PAH.[32] It should be considered for the periodic assessment of IPAH patients.

TRANSTHORACIC ECHOCARDIOGRAPHY

Echocardiography is the preferred imaging modality for the initial screening of all patients and should be used to exclude underlying cardiac defects (Box 64-3). It enables the estimation of subpulmonary ventricular pressure (from Doppler pressure gradients across the tricuspid valve) (see Fig. 64-2) and provides information on biventricular dimensions and function.

CARDIAC CATHETERIZATION

Cardiac catheterization is the gold standard for establishing the diagnosis of PAH and is useful for assessing the presence of more occult additional contributors to pulmonary hypertension, as well as defining the severity of pulmonary vascular disease. The potential vasoreactivity of the pulmonary vascular bed (using 100% oxygen via a rebreathing mask, inhaled nitric oxide, intravenous adenosine, or prostacyclin) should be assessed as part of the invasive evaluation because this carries important prognostic information. However, an absent pulmonary vasoreactivity study should not preclude initiation of disease-targeting therapy.

CARDIAC MAGNETIC RESONANCE IMAGING OR HIGH-RESOLUTION COMPUTED TOMOGRAPHY

Cardiac MRI can be employed in selected patients to provide information on right ventricular function and the pulmonary vascular bed. High-resolution CT is useful to assess pulmonary arterial thrombi and to exclude intrapulmonary hemorrhage or infarction in patients with IPAH. It is also the imaging modality of choice for assessing the lung parenchyma.

ROUTINE LABORATORY TESTING

In addition to routine investigations including complete blood cell count and biochemistry (electrolytes, urea and creatinine, liver function tests, and uric acid), additional tests should be performed to exclude connective tissue disease (antinuclear antibodies, antineutrophil cytoplasmic antibody, and rheumatoid factor).

Additional tests, including liver ultrasonography with Doppler assessment of portal flow, pulmonary function testing, and ventilation-perfusion lung scintigraphy may be particularly useful to exclude additional causes of PAH. In addition, human immunodeficiency virus testing should be considered in selected patients.

Management Options

EXERCISE TRAINING

When added in randomized, controlled fashion to stable medical therapy for PAH (see later), highly structured and comprehensive low-dose exercise and respiratory training was found to significantly improve exercise capacity, 6-minute walking test, quality of life, World Health Organization functional class, and peak oxygen consumption.[33] Although most PAH centers do not offer such intensive exercise training, the guided use of formal cardiopulmonary fitness and conditioning programs in particular patients with IPAH at appropriate points in therapy may offer substantive benefit in functional outcomes.

MEDICAL TREATMENT

In patients with IPAH or familial PAH without contraindications, oral anticoagulation is recommended (Fig. 64-4).[34,35] In addition, patients with signs and symptoms of right-sided heart failure will generally benefit from diuretics. Digoxin should be considered in selected patients, especially those presenting with atrial fibrillation or flutter.

Calcium-channel blockers are only recommended for patients who have responded to acute vasodilator challenge. *Responsiveness* is commonly defined as a reduction in mean pulmonary arterial pressure of at least 10 mm Hg, resulting in a mean pulmonary arterial pressure below 40 mm Hg. This definition is based on the results of a large study using nitric oxide for vasoreactivity testing.[36] Other criteria may apply for patients undergoing vasoreactivity testing with epoprostenol or adenosine.[2] Although less than 10% of IPAH patients are long-term responders to calcium-channel blockers,[36] high doses of these agents (nifedipine, up to 240 mg/day, and diltiazem, up to 700 mg/day, although variability exists) improve hemodynamics and exercise capacity and thus these drugs are recommended for first-line treatment in current guidelines. Calcium-channel blockers should be started with close monitoring in a hospital and titrated carefully to avoid systemic vasodilation and right-sided heart failure. Sustained response to calcium-channel blocking treatment needs to be reevaluated regularly and patients started on targeted therapies if they fail to exhibit a sustained response to high-dose treatment with these drugs.

Targeted therapies should be begun in patients not responding to vasodilator challenge or failing to exhibit a sustained response to treatment with calcium channel blockers. These therapies include endothelin antagonists (e.g., bosentan or sitaxsentan), phosphodiesterase-5 inhibitors (e.g., sildenafil), or prostaglandins.

In less impaired patients, oral or inhaled therapies are generally preferred, although continuous intravenous prostacyclin (epoprostenol) may be used. In contrast, intravenous prostacyclin is generally regarded as first-line treatment in patients presenting unstable or in New York Heart Association (NYHA) class IV.[37] Prostacyclin administration is technically challenging, and prolonged intravenous therapy is associated with frequent complications such as sepsis and line dislocation. Therefore, continuous intravenous prostacyclin administration requires special expertise and extensive patient training and should be reserved for specialist centers for PAH. Treprostinil has been demonstrated to improve functional capacity and pulmonary hemodynamics and can be delivered subcutaneously. However, pain at the infusion site (in up to 85% of patients) prompting discontinuation of therapy in 8% of patients limits its use.[38] Inhaled iloprost has been demonstrated to improve 6-minute walk test distance and NYHA class in patients with

---

BOX 64-3 ECHOCARDIOGRAPHY

- Echocardiography is the preferred imaging modality for initial screening and follow-up.
- It allows estimation of right ventricular pressure from Doppler pressure gradients across the tricuspid valve.
- The following parameters should be assessed:
  - Biventricular dimensions and systolic function
  - Degree of tricuspid and pulmonary regurgitation
  - Presence of pericardial effusion
  - Dimensions of the main and branch pulmonary artery

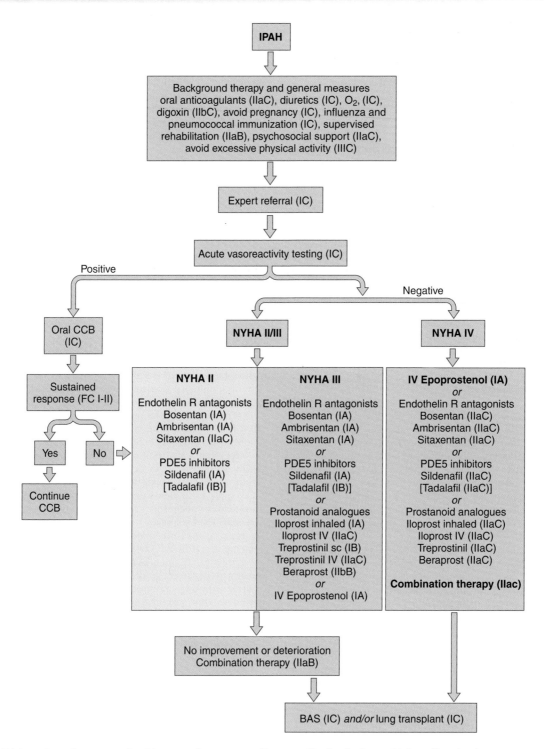

Figure 64-4 Evidence-based treatment algorithm according to current European Cardiac Society guidelines. Sustained response to calcium-channel blockers is defined as patients being in NYHA functional class I or II with near-normal hemodynamics. BAS, balloon atrioseptostomy; CCB, calcium-channel blockers; IV, continuous intravenous; PDE, phosphodiesterase; R, receptor. *(From Galiè N, Hoeper MM, Humbert M, et al. Guidelines for the diagnosis and treatment of pulmonary arterial hypertension: The Task Force for the Diagnosis and Treatment of Pulmonary Hypertension of the European Society of Cardiology [ESC] and the European Respiratory Society [ERS], endorsed by the International Society of Heart and Lung Transplantation [ISHLT]. Eur Heart J 2009;30:2493–2537, with permission. Tadalafil is under regulatory review in the European Union.)*

IPAH, PAH associated with connective tissue disease, and thromboembolic PAH and may represent an alternative to intravenous or subcutaneous prostacyclin analogues in selected patients.[39]

Endothelin receptor antagonists have been demonstrated to improve pulmonary hemodynamics and attenuate pulmonary fibrosis and inflammation.[40] Their efficacy in improving 6-minute walk test distance as well as time to clinical worsening has been confirmed by several randomised controlled trials.[41–47] Preliminary results also suggest that bosentan may prolong survival in IPAH patients with advanced pulmonary hypertension.[48] As a consequence, endothelin receptor antagonists have become the mainstay of PAH therapy. Their role as first-line treatment of PAH has been recently challenged by phosphodiesterase-5 inhibitors (mainly due to cost considerations) despite superior data and longer experience with endothelin receptor antagonists.

Recently, the SUPER-1 trial showed a significant improvement in 6-minute walk test distance, NYHA class, and pulmonary hemodynamics after 3 months of sildenafil therapy. The study included IPAH and PAH associated with connective tissue disease patients in NYHA class II or III.[49]

Response to therapy is typically gauged by clinical improvement in symptoms in concert with measured testing that has been correlated with outcomes benefits (low right atrial pressure or improved cardiac index at hemodynamic catheterization; 6-minute walking distance > 380 m). Likewise, poor functional outcome has been correlated with presence of pericardial effusion or otherwise unexplained left ventricular dysfunction on echocardiography and inability to walk more than 150 m on the 6-minute walk test, failure to achieve a peak oxygen consumption of more than 10.4 mL/kg/min at cardiopulmonary exercise testing, and inability to raise the systolic blood pressure more than 120 mm Hg with more routine treadmill testing.[50] The presence of such poor outcomes measures emphasizes that, in particular patients, pulmonary hypertension may remain a progressive disease and that escalation of medical therapy may be required. Different studies have demonstrated the benefit of combination therapy,[51-53] and the number of IPAH patients treated with two or more disease-targeting drugs is expected to increase, eventually probably becoming the standard form of treatment.

OXYGEN THERAPY

Oxygen therapy is recommended in PAH patients with oxygen-responsive hypoxemia. However, the majority of IPAH patients do not exhibit pronounced hypoxemia and these patients do not usually benefit from long-term oxygen therapy. Current guidelines, however, highlight the importance of maintaining oxygen saturation above 90% at all times. Thus, supplemental oxygen should be considered in patients who acutely improve oxygen saturation with supplementation and who have baseline oxygen saturations below this threshold.[37]

SURGICAL TREATMENT

Atrial septostomy has been shown to be beneficial in selected patients with advanced PAH, especially those with recurrent syncope. By creating a right-to-left shunt at the atrial level it is possible to decompress the right ventricle and improve left ventricular filling pressure, thus maintaining cardiac output. There is, however, a risk of severe systemic desaturation with this procedure. Atrial septostomy can thus be considered in patients with severe pulmonary hypertension despite

---

> **BOX 64-4   COMPLICATIONS**
>
> - Right-sided heart failure
> - Sudden cardiac death
>   - Malignant arrhythmias
>   - Pulmonary hypertensive crises
> - Thrombosis

maximum medical therapy and that which is associated with recurrent syncope. Atrial septostomy should be carried out only by experienced interventionalists and is contraindicated in patients with severe right ventricular failure on maximum cardiorespiratory support.[54-56]

In some patients with PAH there is a progressive deterioration despite medical therapy. In this situation transplantation may provide the optimal potential for survival. With the continuing improvements in surgical technique and advances in immunosuppressive therapy the survival for heart and lung transplantation in this group of patients has reached 65% to 70% at 1 year. Obliterative bronchiolitis, however, remains the major complication of long-term survival in lung transplant recipients (Box 64-4).

Additional management strategies include avoidance of strenuous exercise and competitive sports, annual immunization against influenza, careful planning, and intraoperative monitoring during noncardiac surgery, which carries significant mortality risks in this population.

Pregnancy

Even in the current era, pregnancy carries a very high risk of maternal death (up to 20% to 50%) and should be discouraged.[57]

Level of Follow-Up, Endocarditis Prophylaxis, and Exercise

Patients require regular follow-up at a center specializing in the treatment of IPAH. Regular 6-minute walk tests and echocardiographic assessment is recommended.

Antibiotic prophylaxis is not recommended for IPAH, unless independent risk factors (e.g., prosthetic valves, previous endocarditis) exist.

Competitive sports and strenuous exercise, in general, is not recommended, nor is isometric exercise. Low-intensity aerobic exercise is safe and may improve symptoms, objective exercise capacity, and quality of life,[33] although some controversy exists about the level of medical supervision required during exercise training.

REFERENCES

1. Romberg E. Ueber die Sklerose der Lungenarterie. Dtsch Arch Klin Med 1891;48:197–206.
2. Simonneau G, Galie N, Rubin LJ, et al. Clinical classification of pulmonary hypertension. J Am Coll Cardiol 2004;43:5S–12S.
3. Goodale Jr F, Thomas WA. Primary pulmonary arterial disease; observations with special reference to medial thickening of small arteries and arterioles. AMA Arch Pathol 1954;58:568–575.
4. Wood P. Pulmonary hypertension. In: Wood P, editor. Diseases of the Heart and Circulation. 3rd ed. London: Eyre & Spottiswoode; 1968.
5. Peacock AJ, Murphy NF, McMurray JJ, et al. An epidemiological study of pulmonary arterial hypertension. Eur Respir J 2007; 30:104–109.
6. Moride Y, Abenhaim L, Xu J. Epidemiology of primary pulmonary hypertension. In: Rubin LJ, Rich S, editors. Primary Pulmonary Hypertension. New York: Marcel Dekker; 1997.
7. Barst RJ, McGoon M, Torbicki A, et al. Diagnosis and differential assessment of pulmonary arterial hypertension. J Am Coll Cardiol 2004;43:40S–47S.
8. Olschewski H. [Dana Point: what is new in the diagnosis of pulmonary hypertension?] Dtsch Med Wochenschr 2008; 133(Suppl 6):S180–S182.
9. Stewart S. Pulmonary Arterial Hypertension: A Pocketbook Guide. London: Taylor & Francis; 2005.
10. Diller GP, Gatzoulis MA. Pulmonary vascular disease in adults with congenital heart disease. Circulation 2007;115:1039–1050.
11. Heath D, Edwards JE. The pathology of hypertensive pulmonary vascular disease; a description of six grades of structural changes

in the pulmonary arteries with special reference to congenital cardiac septal defects. Circulation 1958;18:533–547.
12. Rabinovitch M, Haworth SG, Castaneda AR, et al. Lung biopsy in congenital heart disease: a morphometric approach to pulmonary vascular disease. Circulation 1978;58:1107–1122.
13. Haworth SG. Role of the endothelium in pulmonary arterial hypertension. Vasc Pharmacol 2006;45:317–325.
14. Giaid A, Yanagisawa M, Langleben D, et al. Expression of endothelin-1 in the lungs of patients with pulmonary hypertension. N Engl J Med 1993;328:1732–1739.
15. Stewart DJ, Levy RD, Cernacek P, Langleben D. Increased plasma endothelin-1 in pulmonary hypertension: marker or mediator of disease? Ann Intern Med 1991;114:464–469.
16. Zamora MR, Stelzner TJ, Webb S, et al. Overexpression of endothelin-1 and enhanced growth of pulmonary artery smooth muscle cells from fawn-hooded rats. Am J Physiol 1996;270:L101–L109.
17. Christman BW, McPherson CD, Newman JH, et al. An imbalance between the excretion of thromboxane and prostacyclin metabolites in pulmonary hypertension. N Engl J Med 1992; 327:70–75.
18. Mata-Greenwood E, Meyrick B, Steinhorn RH, et al. Alterations in TGF-beta1 expression in lambs with increased pulmonary blood flow and pulmonary hypertension. Am J Physiol Lung Cell Mol Physiol 2003;285:L209–L221.
19. Dorfmuller P, Humbert M, Perros F, et al. Fibrous remodeling of the pulmonary venous system in pulmonary arterial hypertension associated with connective tissue diseases. Hum Pathol 2007; 38:893–902.

20. Levy M, Maurey C, Celermajer DS, et al. Impaired apoptosis of pulmonary endothelial cells is associated with intimal proliferation and irreversibility of pulmonary hypertension in congenital heart disease. J Am Coll Cardiol 2007;49:803–810.
21. Rabinovitch M. Molecular pathogenesis of pulmonary arterial hypertension. J Clin Invest 2008;118:2372–2379.
22. Thomson JR, Machado RD, Pauciulo MW, et al. Sporadic primary pulmonary hypertension is associated with germline mutations of the gene encoding BMPR-II, a receptor member of the TGF-beta family. J Med Genet 2000;37:741–745.
23. Shapiro S. Management of pulmonary hypertension resulting from interstitial lung disease. Curr Opin Pulm Med 2003;9:426–430.
24. Hunter KS, Lee PF, Lanning CJ, et al. Pulmonary vascular input impedance is a combined measure of pulmonary vascular resistance and stiffness and predicts clinical outcomes better than pulmonary vascular resistance alone in pediatric patients with pulmonary hypertension. Am Heart J 2008;155:166–174.
25. Raymond RJ, Hinderliter AL, Willis PW, et al. Echocardiographic predictors of adverse outcomes in primary pulmonary hypertension. J Am Coll Cardiol 2002;39:1214–1219.
26. Guyton AC, Lindsey AW, Gilluly JJ. The limits of right ventricular compensation following acute increase in pulmonary circulatory resistance. Circ Res 1954;2:326–332.
27. Gaynor SL, Maniar HS, Bloch JB, et al. Right atrial and ventricular adaptation to chronic right ventricular pressure overload. Circulation 2005;112:1212–1218.
28. Leeuwenburgh BP, Helbing WA, Steendijk P, et al. Biventricular systolic function in young lambs subject to chronic systemic right

ventricular pressure overload. Am J Physiol Heart Circ Physiol 2001;281:H2697–H2704.

29. Haddad F, Doyle R, Murphy DJ, Hunt SA. Right ventricular function in cardiovascular disease: II. Pathophysiology, clinical importance, and management of right ventricular failure. Circulation 2008;117:1717–1731.

30. Miyamoto S, Nagaya N, Satoh T, et al. Clinical correlates and prognostic significance of six-minute walk test in patients with primary pulmonary hypertension: comparison with cardiopulmonary exercise testing. Am J Respir Crit Care Med 2000;161:487–492.

31. Wensel R, Opitz CF, Anker SD, et al. Assessment of survival in patients with primary pulmonary hypertension: importance of cardiopulmonary exercise testing. Circulation 2002; 106:319–324.

32. ATS statement: guidelines for the six-minute walk test. Am J Respir Crit Care Med 2002;166:111–117.

33. Mereles D, Ehlken N, Kreuscher S, et al. Exercise and respiratory training improve exercise capacity and quality of life in patients with severe chronic pulmonary hypertension. Circulation 2006; 114:1482–1489.

34. Fuster V, Steele PM, Edwards WD, et al. Primary pulmonary hypertension: natural history and the importance of thrombosis. Circulation 1984;70:580–587.

35. Rich S, Kaufmann E, Levy PS. The effect of high doses of calcium-channel blockers on survival in primary pulmonary hypertension. N Engl J Med 1992;327:76–81.

36. Sitbon O, Humbert M, Jais X, et al. Long-term response to calcium channel blockers in idiopathic pulmonary arterial hypertension. Circulation 2005;111:3105–3111.

37. Galie N, Torbicki A, Barst R, et al. Guidelines on diagnosis and treatment of pulmonary arterial hypertension. The Task Force on Diagnosis and Treatment of Pulmonary Arterial Hypertension of the European Society of Cardiology. Eur Heart J 2004;25:2243–2278.

38. Simonneau G, Barst RJ, Galie N, et al. Continuous subcutaneous infusion of treprostinil, a prostacyclin analogue, in patients with pulmonary arterial hypertension: a double-blind, randomized, placebo-controlled trial. Am J Respir Crit Care Med 2002;165:800–804.

39. Olschewski H, Simonneau G, Galie N, et al. Inhaled iloprost for severe pulmonary hypertension. N Engl J Med 2002;347:322–329.

40. Farber HW, Loscalzo J. Pulmonary arterial hypertension. N Engl J Med 2004;351:1655–1665.

41. Channick RN, Simonneau G, Sitbon O, et al. Effects of the dual endothelin-receptor antagonist bosentan in patients with pulmonary hypertension: a randomised placebo-controlled study. Lancet 2001;358:1119–1123.

42. Rubin LJ, Badesch DB, Barst RJ, et al. Bosentan therapy for pulmonary arterial hypertension. N Engl J Med 2002; 346:896–903.

43. Barst RJ, Langleben D, Badesch D, et al. Treatment of pulmonary arterial hypertension with the selective endothelin-A receptor antagonist sitaxsentan. J Am Coll Cardiol 2006;47:2049–2056.

44. Barst RJ, Langleben D, Frost A, et al. Sitaxsentan therapy for pulmonary arterial hypertension. Am J Respir Crit Care Med 2004;169:441–447.

45. Galie N, Badesch D, Oudiz R, et al. Ambrisentan therapy for pulmonary arterial hypertension. J Am Coll Cardiol 2005; 46:529–535.

46. Galie N, Olschewski H, Oudiz RJ, et al. Ambrisentan for the treatment of pulmonary arterial hypertension: results of the ambrisentan in pulmonary arterial hypertension, randomized, double-blind, placebo-controlled, multicenter, efficacy (ARIES) study 1 and 2. Circulation 2008;117:3010–3019.

47. Galie N, Rubin L, Hoeper M, et al. Treatment of patients with mildly symptomatic pulmonary arterial hypertension with bosentan (EARLY study): a double-blind, randomised controlled trial. Lancet 2008;371:2093–2100.

48. McLaughlin VV, Sitbon O, Badesch DB, et al. Survival with first-line bosentan in patients with primary pulmonary hypertension. Eur Respir J 2005;25:244–249.

49. Galie N, Ghofrani HA, Torbicki A, et al. Sildenafil citrate therapy for pulmonary arterial hypertension. N Engl J Med 2005;353:2148–2157.

50. McLaughlin VV, McGoon MD. Pulmonary arterial hypertension. Circulation 2006;114:1417–1431.

51. Humbert M, Barst RJ, Robbins IM, et al. Combination of bosentan with epoprostenol in pulmonary arterial hypertension: BREATHE-2. Eur Respir J 2004;24:353–359.

52. McLaughlin VV, Oudiz RJ, Frost A, et al. Randomized study of adding inhaled iloprost to existing bosentan in pulmonary arterial hypertension. Am J Respir Crit Care Med 2006; 174:1257–1263.

53. Simonneau G, Rubin LJ, Galie N, et al. Addition of sildenafil to long-term intravenous epoprostenol therapy in patients with pulmonary arterial hypertension: a randomized trial. Ann Intern Med 2008;149:521–530.

54. Kerstein D, Levy PS, Hsu DT, et al. Blade balloon atrial septostomy in patients with severe primary pulmonary hypertension. Circulation 1995;91:2028–2035.

55. Law MA, Grifka RG, Mullins CE, Nihill MR. Atrial septostomy improves survival in select patients with pulmonary hypertension. Am Heart J 2007;153:779–84.

56. Reichenberger F, Pepke-Zaba J, McNeil K, et al. Atrial septostomy in the treatment of severe pulmonary arterial hypertension. Thorax 2003;58:797–800.

57. Bedard E, Dimopoulos K, Gatzoulis MA. Has there been any progress made on pregnancy outcomes among women with pulmonary arterial hypertension? Eur Heart J 2009;30:256–265.

Selected Terms Used in Adult Congenital Heart Disease

JACK M. COLMAN | ERWIN OECHSLIN | DYLAN A. TAYLOR

aberrant innominate artery   A rare abnormality associated with right aortic arch comprising a sequence of arteries arising from the aortic arch—right carotid artery, right subclavian artery, and then (left) innominate artery— with the last one passing behind the esophagus. This is in contrast to the general rule that the first arch artery gives rise to the carotid artery contralateral to the side of the aortic arch (i.e., right carotid artery in left aortic arch and left carotid artery in right aortic arch). *Syn:* retroesophageal innominate artery.

aberrant subclavian artery   Right subclavian artery arising from the aorta distal to the left subclavian artery. Left aortic arch with (retroesophageal) aberrant right subclavian artery is the most common aortic arch anomaly. It was first described in 1735 by Hunauld and occurs in 0.5% of the general population. *See also* vascular ring.

absent pulmonary valve syndrome   Absent pulmonary valvular tissue, resulting in pulmonary regurgitation. This rare anomaly uncommonly may be isolated, or it may be associated with ventricular septal defect, obstructed pulmonary valve annulus, and massive dilation and distortion of the pulmonary arteries. Absent pulmonary valve may occur in association with other simple or complex congenital heart lesions, for instance as a variant of tetralogy of Fallot.

ACHD   Adult congenital heart disease.

Alagille syndrome   *See* arteriohepatic dysplasia.

ALCAPA   Anomalous left coronary artery arising from the pulmonary artery. *See* Bland-White-Garland syndrome.

ambiguus   With reference to cardiac situs, neither right nor left sided (indeterminate). Latin spelling is generally used for situs ambiguus. *Syn:* ambiguous sidedness. *See also* situs.

Amplatzer device   A group of self-centering devices delivered percutaneously by catheter for closure of abnormal intracardiac and vascular connections such as secundum atrial septal defect, patent foramen ovale, or patent ductus arteriosus.

aneurysm of sinus of Valsalva   *See* sinus of Valsalva/aneurysm.

anomalous pulmonary venous connection   Pulmonary venous return to the right side of the heart, which may be total or partial.

- **partial anomalous pulmonary venous connection (PAPVC):** One or more, but not all, of the pulmonary veins connect to the right atrium directly or via a vena cava. This anomaly is frequently associated with sinus venosus defect.
  See also scimitar syndrome and sinus venosus defect.
- **total anomalous pulmonary venous connection (TAPVC):** All pulmonary veins connect to the right side of the heart, either directly or via venous tributaries. The connection may be supradiaphragmatic, usually via a vertical vein to the innominate vein or the superior vena cava. The connection may also be infradiaphragmatic via a descending vein to the portal vein, the inferior vena cava, or one of its tributaries. Pulmonary venous obstruction is common in supradiaphragmatic connection and almost universal in infradiaphragmatic connection.

aortic arch anomalies   Abnormalities of the aortic arch and its branching. Left or right aortic arch is defined by the main-stem bronchus that is crossed by the descending thoracic aorta and does not refer to the side of the midline on which the aorta descends. In left aortic arch (normal anatomic arrangement) the descending thoracic aorta crosses over the left main-stem bronchus; the innominate artery branching into the right carotid and right subclavian artery arises first, the left carotid artery second, and the left subclavian artery third. Usually, the first aortic arch vessel gives rise to the carotid artery that is opposite to the side of the aortic arch (i.e., the right carotid artery in left aortic arch and the left carotid artery in right aortic arch). The most important anomalies are described below.

- **abnormal left aortic arch:**   Left aortic arch with minor branching anomalies; left aortic arch with aberrant right subclavian artery.
- **cervical aortic arch:** The arch extends above the level of the clavicle.
- **double aortic arch:** Both right and left aortic arches are present; that is, the ascending aorta splits into two limbs encircling the trachea and esophagus, and the two limbs join to form a single descending aorta. There are several forms, such as widely open right and left arches or hypoplasia/atresia of one arch (usually the left). This anomaly is commonly associated with patent ductus arteriosus. Double aortic arch creates a vascular ring around the trachea and the esophagus. *See also* vascular ring.
- **interrupted aortic arch:** Complete discontinuation between the ascending and descending thoracic aorta.
  - type A: Interruption distal to the subclavian artery that is ipsilateral to the second carotid artery.
  - type B: Interruption between the second carotid artery and the ipsilateral subclavian artery.
  - type C: Interruption between carotid arteries.
- **isolation of contralateral arch vessels:** an aortic arch vessel arises from the pulmonary artery via the ductus arteriosus without connection to the aorta; this anomaly is very uncommon. Isolation of the left subclavian artery is the most common form.
- **persistent fifth aortic arch:** Double-lumen aortic arch with both lumina on the same side of the trachea. Degree of luminal patency varies from full patency of both lumina to complete atresia of one of them.
- **right aortic arch:**   The descending thoracic aorta crosses the right main-stem bronchus. Right aortic arch is often associated with tetralogy of Fallot, pulmonary atresia, truncus arteriosus, and other conotruncal anomalies. Types of right aortic arch branching include:
  - mirror image branching (left innominate artery, right carotid artery, right subclavian artery).
  - aberrant left subclavian artery with a normal caliber; sequence of branching: left carotid artery, right carotid artery, right subclavian artery, left subclavian artery.
  - retroesophageal diverticulum of Kommerell; *see* diverticulum of Kommerell.
  - right aortic arch with left descending aorta (i.e., retroesophageal segment of right aortic arch); the descending aortic arch crosses the midline toward the left by a retroesophageal route.

aortic–left ventricular defect (tunnel)   Vascular connection between the aorta and the left ventricle resulting in left ventricular volume overload due to regurgitation from the aorta via the tunnel to the left ventricle.

aortic override   *See* tetralogy of Fallot.

aortic valve-sparing aortic root replacement   *See* David operation; Yacoub procedure.

aortopulmonary collateral   Abnormal arterial vessel arising from the aorta, providing blood supply to the lungs. This vessel may be single or multiple and small or large (*see also* MAPCA) and may be associated with tetralogy of Fallot, pulmonary atresia, or other complex cyanotic congenital heart disease.

aortopulmonary septal defect   *See* aortopulmonary window.

aortopulmonary window   A congenital connection between the ascending aorta and the main pulmonary artery, which may be contiguous with the semilunar valves or, less often, separated from them. It simulates the physiology of a large patent ductus arteriosus but requires a more demanding repair. *Syn:* aortopulmonary septal defect.

APSACHD   Asia-Pacific Society for Adult Congenital Heart Disease (http://www.apsachd.org)

arterial switch operation (ASO)   *See* Jatene procedure.

arteriohepatic dysplasia   An autosomal dominant multisystem syndrome consisting of intrahepatic cholestasis, characteristic facies, butterfly-like vertebral anomalies, and varying degrees of peripheral pulmonary artery stenosis or diffuse hypoplasia of the pulmonary artery and its branches. It is associated with microdeletion in chromosome 20p. *Syn:* Alagille syndrome.

ASO   arterial switch operation. *See* Jatene procedure.

asplenia syndrome   *See* isomerism/right isomerism.

atresia, atretic   Imperforate; used with reference to an orifice, valve, or vessel.

atrial maze procedure   An intervention for atrial fibrillation directed toward restoring normal rhythm by interrupting conduction of the abnormal atrial impulses. It was originally (and is still) performed by creating surgical incisions in the atrium that are then re-sewn, thus creating electrical barriers that disrupt reentrant circuits. Similar electrical barriers often can be created in the electrophysiology laboratory without the need for thoracotomy. The originally described procedure, involving incisions in both atria, is called the Cox maze procedure (Cox J, et al. The surgical treatment of atrial fibrillation: III. Development of a definitive surgical procedure. J Thorac Cardiovasc Surg 1991; 101:569-583).

atrial septal defect (ASD)   An interatrial communication, classified according to its location relative to the oval fossa (fossa ovalis).

- **coronary sinus "ASD":**   (properly termed *coronary sinus defect*): Inferior and anterior to the oval fossa at the anticipated site of the orifice of the coronary sinus. May be part of a complex anomaly including absence of the coronary sinus and a persistent left superior vena cava.
- **ostium primum ASD:**   Part of the spectrum of atrioventricular septal defect (AVSD). Located anterior and inferior to the oval fossa such that there is no atrial septal tissue between the lower edge of the defect and the atrioventricular valves. The atrioventricular valves are located on the same plane. An ostium primum ASD is almost always associated with a "cleft" in the "anterior mitral leaflet." This cleft is actually the separation between the left-sided portions of the primitive anterosuperior and posteroinferior bridging leaflets. *See also* atrioventricular septal defect (AVSD).
- **ostium secundum ASD:**   Located within the true interatrial septum at the level of the oval fossa. The defect is actually a defect in the embryologic septum primum that otherwise constitutes the floor of the fossa ovale.
- **sinus venosus "ASD":**   *see* sinus venosus defect.

atrial switch procedure   A procedure to redirect venous return to the contralateral ventricle. When used in complete transposition of the great arteries (Mustard or Senning procedure), this accomplishes physiologic correction of the circulation while leaving the right ventricle to support the systemic circulation. It is also used in congenitally corrected transposition of the great arteries in combination with an arterial switch operation (Jatene procedure). *See also* double-switch procedure.

atrioventricular concordance   *See* concordant atrioventricular connections.

atrioventricular discordance   *See* discordant atrioventricular connections.

atrioventricular septal defect (AVSD)   A group of anomalies resulting from a deficiency of the atrioventricular (AV) septum that have in common (1) a common AV junction with a common fibrous ring and a unique, five-leaflet, AV valve; (2) unwedging of the aorta from its usual position deeply wedged between the mitral and tricuspid valves; (3) a narrowed subaortic outflow tract; (4) disproportion between the inlet and outlet portions of the ventricular septum. Echocardiographic recognition is aided by the observation that left and right AV valves are located in the same anatomic plane. Included in this group of conditions are anomalies previously known as (and often still described as) ostium primum ASD (partial AVSD), "cleft" anterior mitral and/or septal tricuspid valve leaflet, inlet VSD, and complete AVSD ("complete AV canal defect"). An older, obsolete term describing such a defect is *endocardial cushion defect. See also* endocardial cushion defect.

atrioventricular septum   The atrioventricular septum separates the left ventricular inlet from the right atrium. It has two parts: a muscular portion that exists because the attachment of the septal leaflet of the tricuspid valve is more toward the apex of the ventricle than the corresponding attachment of the mitral valve and a fibrous portion superior to the attachment of the septal leaflet of the tricuspid valve. This latter portion separates the right atrium from the subaortic left ventricular outflow tract. *See also* Gerbode defect.

atrioventricular valve (AV valve)   A valve guarding the inlet to a ventricle. AV valves correspond with their respective ventricles: the tricuspid valve is always associated with the right ventricle, and the mitral valve is associated with the left ventricle. However, in the setting of an atrioventricular septal defect there is neither a true mitral nor a true tricuspid valve. Rather, in severe forms there is a single atrioventricular orifice, guarded by a five-leaflet AV valve. The left AV valve comprises the left lateral leaflet and the left portions of the superior (anterior) and inferior (posterior) bridging leaflets, while the right AV valve comprises the right inferior leaflet, the right anterosuperior leaflet, and the right portions of the superior and inferior bridging leaflets.

- **cleft AV valve:**   A defect due to incomplete fusion of the superior and inferior bridging leaflets that conjoin to form the left AV valve in AVSD. A cleft may also be seen in the septal tricuspid leaflet. A similar-appearing, but morphogenetically distinct, entity may involve the anterior or rarely the posterior leaflet of the mitral valve in otherwise normal hearts.
- **common AV valve:**   Describes a five-leaflet AV valve in complete AVSD that is related to both ventricles.
- **overriding AV valve:**   Describes an AV valve that empties into both ventricles. It overrides the interventricular septum above a ventricular septal defect.
- **straddling AV valve:**   Describes an AV valve with anomalous insertion of tendinous cords or papillary muscles into the contralateral ventricle (an associated ventricular septal defect is obligatory).

autograft   Tissue or organ transplanted to a new site within the same individual.

AV septal defect (AVSD)   *See* atrioventricular septal defect (AVSD).

AV valve   *See* atrioventricular valve.

azygos continuation of the inferior vena cava   An anomaly of systemic venous connections in which the inferior vena cava (IVC) is interrupted distal to its passage through the liver. IVC flow reaches the right atrium through an enlarged azygos vein connecting the IVC to the superior vena cava. Usually, only hepatic venous flow reaches the right atrium from below. *See also* isomerism.

Baffes operation   Anastomosis of the right pulmonary veins to the right atrium and the inferior vena cava (IVC) to the left atrium by using an allograft aortic tube to connect the IVC and the left atrium (Baffes TG. A new method for surgical correction of transposition of the aorta and pulmonary artery. Surg Gynecol Obstet 1956; 102:227-233). This operation provided partial physiologic correction in patients with complete transposition of the great arteries and was originally described by Lillehei and Varco in 1953 (Lillehei CW, Varco RL. Certain physiologic, pathologic, and surgical features of complete transposition of great vessels. Surgery 1953; 34:376-400).

baffle   A structure created surgically to divert blood flow. For instance, in atrial switch operations for complete transposition of the great arteries an intra-atrial baffle is constructed to divert systemic venous return across the mitral valve thence to left ventricle and pulmonary artery and to divert pulmonary venous return across the tricuspid valve thence to right ventricle and aorta. *See also* Mustard procedure and Senning procedure.

balanced   As in "balanced circulation," for example, in the setting of ventricular septal defect and pulmonary stenosis. The pulmonary stenosis is such that there is neither excessive pulmonary blood flow (which might lead to pulmonary hypertension) nor inadequate pulmonary blood flow (which might lead to marked cyanosis). *See also* ventricular imbalance.

balloon atrial septostomy   *See* Rashkind procedure.

Bentall procedure   Replacement of the ascending aorta and aortic valve with a composite graft/valve device and re-implantation of the coronary ostia into the sides of the conduit (Bentall H, DeBono A. A technique for complete replacement of the ascending aorta. Thorax 1968; 23:338-339).
- **exclusion technique:** The native aorta is resected and replaced by the prosthetic graft.
- **inclusion technique:** The walls of the native aorta are wrapped around the graft so that the prosthetic material is "included."

bicuspid aortic valve   An anomaly in which the aortic valve is composed of only two cusps instead of the usual three. There is often a raphe or aborted commissure dividing the larger cusp anatomically but not functionally. This anomaly is seen in approximately 2% of the general population and in approximately 75% of patients with aortic coarctation.

bidirectional cavopulmonary anastomosis   *See* Glenn anastomosis/bidirectional Glenn.

Björk modification   *See* Fontan procedure/RA-RV Fontan.

Blalock-Hanlon atrial septectomy   A palliative procedure to improve arterial oxygen saturation in patients with complete transposition of the great arteries. A surgical atrial septectomy is accomplished through a right lateral thoracotomy, excising the posterior aspect of the interatrial septum to provide mixing of systemic and pulmonary venous return at the atrial level (Blalock A, Hanlon CR. Surgical treatment of complete transposition of aorta and pulmonary artery. Surg Gynecol Obstet 1950; 90:1-15).

Blalock-Taussig anastomosis   A palliative operation (sometimes called Blalock-Taussig shunt) for the purpose of increasing pulmonary blood flow and hence systemic oxygen saturation. It involves creating an anastomosis between a subclavian artery and the ipsilateral pulmonary artery either directly with an end-to-side anastomosis (classic) or using an interposition tube graft (modified) (Blalock A, Taussig HB. The surgical treatment of malformations of the heart in which there is pulmonary stenosis or pulmonary atresia. JAMA 1945; 128:189-202).

Bland-White-Garland syndrome   The left main coronary artery arises from the main pulmonary artery (Bland EF, White PD, Garland J. Congenital anomalies of the coronary arteries: report of

an unusual case associated with cardiac hypertrophy. Am Heart J 1933; 8:787-801). *Syn:* ALCAPA.

bridging leaflets   The superior and the inferior bridging leaflets of the AV valve are two leaflets uniquely found in association with AVSD. They "bridge," or pass across, the interventricular septum. When the central part of the bridging leaflet tissue runs within the interventricular septum, the AV valve is functionally separated into left and right components; when the bridging leaflets do not run within the interventricular septum, but pass over its crest, a common AV valve guarding a common AV orifice (with an obligatory ventricular septal defect) is the result.

Brock procedure   A palliative operation to increase pulmonary blood flow and reduce right-to-left shunting in tetralogy of Fallot. It involved resection of part of the right ventricular infundibulum using a punch or biopsy-like instrument introduced through the right ventricle so as to reduce right ventricular outflow tract obstruction without closure of the ventricular septal defect. The operation was performed without cardiopulmonary bypass (Brock RC. Pulmonary valvotomy for the relief of congenital pulmonary stenosis: report of three cases. BMJ 1948; 1:1121-1126).

bulboventricular foramen   An embryologic term describing the connection between the left-sided inflow segments (primitive atrium and presumptive left ventricle) and the right-sided outflow segments (presumptive right ventricle and conotruncus) in the primitive heart tube. *Syn:* primary foramen, primary ventricular foramen, primary interventricular foramen.

Canadian Adult Congenital Heart (CACH) Network   A cooperative nationwide association of Canadian cardiologists, cardiac surgeons, and others, many of whom are situated in regional referral centers for adult congenital heart disease, dedicated to improving the care of patients with ACHD (http://cachnet.ca).

cardiac position   Position of the heart in the chest with regard to its location and the orientation of its apex.
- **cardiac location:** Location of the heart in the chest. Cardiac location is affected by many factors, including underlying cardiac malformation, abnormalities of mediastinal and thoracic structures, tumors, kyphoscoliosis, and abnormalities of the diaphragm:
  - levoposition: to the left
  - mesoposition: central
  - dextroposition: to the right
- **cardiac orientation:** The orientation of the apex of the heart relative to the base. The base to apex axis of the heart is defined by the alignment of the ventricles and is independent of cardiac situs (sidedness). This axis is best described by echocardiography using the subcostal four-chamber views:
  - levocardia: apex directed to the left
  - mesocardia: apex oriented inferiorly
  - dextrocardia: apex directed to the right

cardiac sidedness   *See* situs.

cardiopulmonary study   A rest and stress study of cardiopulmonary physiology, including at least the following elements: resting pulmonary function, stress study to assess maximum workload, maximum oxygen uptake (Vo_2max), anaerobic threshold (AT), ventilatory efficiency ($\dot{V}_E/\dot{V}_{CO_2}$), and oxygen saturation with effort.

Cardio-Seal device   A device delivered percutaneously by catheter for closure of a secundum atrial septal defect or patent foramen ovale.

CATCH-22   *See* microdeletion 22q11.2 syndrome.

cat's eye syndrome   A syndrome due to a tandem duplication of chromosome 22q or an isodicentric chromosome 22 such that the critical region 22pter-22q11 is duplicated. Phenotypic features include mental deficiency, anal and renal malformations, hypertelorism, and others. Total anomalous pulmonary venous return is the most common congenital cardiac lesion, occurring in up to 40% of patients.

cavopulmonary connection   Surgically created connection between a vena cava and the pulmonary artery intended to deliver systemic venous blood to the pulmonary circulation. *See also* Glenn anastomosis.

- **bidirectional cavopulmonary connection:**   A cavopulmonary connection between the superior vena cava and the pulmonary arteries in which the pulmonary arteries are confluent, allowing caval blood to be delivered to both lungs.
- **total cavopulmonary connection (TCPC):**   *see* Fontan procedure/total cavopulmonary connection.

CHARGE association   Anomaly characterized by the presence of coloboma or choanal atresia and three of the following defects: congenital heart disease, nervous system anomaly or intellectual impairment, genital abnormalities, and ear abnormality or deafness. If coloboma and choanal atresia are both present, only two of the additional (minor) abnormalities are needed for diagnosis. Congenital heart defects seen in the CHARGE association are tetralogy of Fallot with or without other cardiac defects, atrioventricular septal defect, double-outlet right ventricle, double-inlet left ventricle, transposition of the great arteries, interrupted aortic arch, and others.

Chiari network   Fenestrated remnant of the right valve of the sinus venosus resulting from incomplete regression of this structure during embryogenesis. It was first described in 1897 (Chiari H. Ueber Netzbildungen im rechten Vorhof. Beitr Pathol Anat 1897; 22:1-10). The prevalence is 2% in autopsy and echocardiographic studies. It presents as coarse right atrial reticula connected to the eustachian and thebesian valves and attached to the crista terminalis. It may be associated with a patent foramen ovale and interatrial septal aneurysm. *See also* sinus venosus.

cleft AV valve   *See* atrioventricular valve; *see also* atrial septal defect/ostium primum ASD.

coarctation of the aorta   A stenosis of the proximal descending aorta varying in anatomy, physiology, and clinical presentation. It may present as discrete or long-segment stenosis, is frequently associated with hypoplasia of the aortic arch and bicuspid aortic valve, and may be part of a Shone complex.

common (as in AV valve, atrium, ventricle, etc.)   Implies bilateral structures with absent septation. Contrasts to "single," which implies absence of corresponding contralateral structure. *See also* single.

common arterial trunk   *See* truncus arteriosus.

common atrium   Large atrium characterized by a nonrestrictive communication between the bilateral atria due to absence of most of the atrial septum. Frequently associated with complex congenital heart disease (e.g., isomerism, AVSD). *See also* single (atrium).

complete transposition of the great arteries (TGA)   An anomaly in which the aorta arises from the right ventricle and the pulmonary artery arises from the left ventricle. The right ventricle supports the systemic circulation. *Syn:* classic transposition; atrioventricular concordance with ventriculoarterial discordance; the terms *d*-transposition and *d*-TGA, although not true synonyms, are often used to refer to complete transposition of the great arteries.

concordant atrioventricular connections   Appropriate connection of morphologic right atrium to morphologic right ventricle and of morphologic left atrium to morphologic left ventricle. *Syn:* atrioventricular concordance.

concordant ventriculoarterial connections   Appropriate origin of pulmonary trunk from morphologic right ventricle and of aorta from morphologic left ventricle. *Syn:* ventriculoarterial concordance.

conduit   A structure that connects nonadjacent parts of the cardiovascular system, allowing blood to flow between them. It is often fashioned from prosthetic material and may include a valve.

cone reconstruction   A technique for tricuspid valve repair in Ebstein anomaly involving mobilization of the anterior and posterior tricuspid valve leaflets from their anomalous attachments in the right ventricle, rotating the complex clockwise to be sutured to the septal border of the anterior leaflet, thus creating a cone the vertex of which remains fixed at the right ventricular apex and the base of which is sutured to the true tricuspid valve annulus. The septal leaflet is incorporated into the cone wall if possible and the atrial septal defect is closed (da Silva JP, et al. The cone reconstruction of the tricuspid valve in Ebstein anomaly: the operation: early and midterm results. J Thorac Cardiovasc Surg 2007; 133:215-223).

congenital coronary arteriovenous fistula (CCAVF)   A direct communication between a coronary artery and cardiac chamber, great artery, or vena cava, bypassing the coronary capillary network.

congenital heart disease   Anomalies of the heart originating in fetal life. Their expression may, however, be delayed beyond the neonatal period and may change with time as further postnatal physiologic and anatomic changes occur.

congenital pericardial defect   A defect in the pericardium due to defective formation of the pleuropericardial membrane of the septum transversum. The spectrum of pericardial deficiency is wide. It may be partial or total. Its clinical diagnosis is difficult. Left-sided defects are more common. Total absence of the pericardium may be associated with other defects such as bronchogenic cyst, pulmonary sequestration, hypoplastic lung, and other congenital heart diseases.

congenitally corrected transposition of the great arteries   An anomaly in which the atrioventricular connection is discordant such that the right atrium connects to the left ventricle and the left atrium connects to the right ventricle and the ventriculoarterial connection is discordant such that the aorta arises from the right ventricle and the pulmonary artery from the left ventricle. There are usually associated anomalies, the most common being ventricular septal defect, pulmonic stenosis, and/or hypoplastic ventricle. The right ventricle supports the systemic circulation. *Syn:* CCTGA, atrioventricular discordance with ventriculoarterial discordance, double discordance. The terms *l*-transposition and *l*-TGA, although not true synonyms, are often used to refer to congenitally corrected transposition of the great arteries.

connection   Anatomic link between two structures (e.g., venoatrial, atrioventricular, ventriculoarterial). An abnormal connection implies abnormal anatomic attachment of the structures. *Connection* and *drainage* are not interchangeable terms. *See also* drainage.

conotruncal abnormality   Neural crest cell migration is crucial for conotruncal septation and the development of both the pulmonary and aortic outflow tracts. If neural crest cell migration fails, conotruncal abnormalities occur. Conotruncal anomalies include tetralogy of Fallot, truncus arteriosus, interrupted aortic arch, pulmonary atresia with ventricular septal defect, absent pulmonary valve, and *d*-malposition of the great arteries with double-outlet right ventricle, single ventricle, or tricuspid atresia. Abnormal neural crest migration may also be associated with complex clinical entities, such as CATCH-22.

conus   *See* infundibulum.

cor triatriatum dexter   Abnormal septation of the right atrium due to failure of regression of the right valve of the sinus venosus. This yields a smooth-walled posteromedial "sinus" chamber (arising embryologically from the sinus venosus) that receives the venae cavae and (usually) the coronary sinus and a trabeculated anterolateral "atrial" chamber (arising embryologically from the primitive right atrium) that includes the right atrial appendage and is related to the tricuspid valve. Usually there is free communication between these two compartments, but variable obstruction to systemic venous flow from the "sinus" chamber to the "atrial" chamber may occur and may be associated with underdevelopment of downstream right-sided heart structures (e.g., hypoplastic tricuspid valve, tricuspid atresia, pulmonary stenosis, or pulmonary atresia). A patent foramen ovale or an atrial septal defect is often present in relation to the posteromedial sinus chamber. *See also* sinus venosus.

cor triatriatum sinister   A membrane divides the left atrium into an accessory pulmonary venous chamber and a left atrial chamber contiguous with the mitral valve. The pulmonary veins enter the accessory chamber, and the left atrial appendage is associated with the true left atrium. The connection between the accessory chamber and the true left atrium varies in size and may produce pulmonary venous obstruction. *Cor triatriatum* otherwise unmodified implies cor triatriatum sinister.

coronary sinus defect   *See* atrial septal defect(ASD)/coronary sinus "ASD."

Cox maze procedure   *See* atrial maze procedure.

crisscross heart   A rotational abnormality of the ventricular mass around its long axis resulting in relationships of the ventricular chambers not anticipated from the given atrioventricular connections. If the rotated ventricles are in a markedly superoinferior relationship, the heart may also be described as a superoinferior or upstairs-downstairs heart. There may be ventriculoarterial concordance or discordance. *Syn:* crisscross atrioventricular connection.

crista supraventricularis   A saddle-shaped muscular crest in the right ventricular outflow tract intervening between the tricuspid valve and the pulmonary valve, consisting of septal and parietal components, which demarcates the junction between the outlet septum and the pulmonary infundibulum. Occasionally, but less accurately, this is termed *crista ventricularis.*

crista terminalis   A vestigial remnant of the right valve of the sinus venosus located at the junction of the trabeculated right atrial appendage and the smooth-walled "sinus" component of the right atrium that receives the inferior vena cava, the superior vena cava, and the coronary sinus. This is a feature of normal right atrial internal anatomy. *Syn:* terminal crest.

crista ventricularis   *See* crista supraventricularis.

cyanosis   A bluish discoloration due to the presence of an increased quantity of desaturated hemoglobin in tissues. In congenital heart disease cyanosis is generally due to right-to-left shunting through congenital cardiac defects, bypassing the pulmonary alveoli, or due to acquired intrapulmonary shunts (central cyanosis). Cyanosis can also occur as a result of increased peripheral extraction due, for instance, to critically reduced cutaneous flow (peripheral cyanosis).

Dacron   A synthetic material often used to fashion conduits and other prosthetic devices for the surgical palliation or repair of congenital heart disease.

Damus-Kaye-Stansel operation   A procedure reserved for patients with abnormal ventriculoarterial connections who are not suitable for an arterial switch operation (e.g., transposition of the great arteries and nonsuitable coronary patterns, double-outlet right ventricle with severe subaortic stenosis). The operation involves anastomosis of the proximal end of the transected main pulmonary artery in an end-to-side fashion to the ascending aorta to provide blood flow from the systemic ventricle to the aorta; coronary arteries are not translocated and are perfused in a retrograde fashion. The aortic orifice and a ventricular septal defect (if present) are closed with a patch. A conduit between the right ventricle and the distal pulmonary artery provides venous blood to the lungs. The procedure was described in 1975 (Damus PS. Correspondence. Ann Thorac Surg 1975; 20:724-725; Kaye MP. Anatomic correction of transposition of the great arteries. Mayo Clin Proc 1975; 50:638-640; and Stansel HC Jr. A new operation for *d*-loop transposition of the great vessels. Ann Thorac Surg 1975; 19:565–567).

David operation   A form of valve-sparing aortic root replacement for the management of aortic root and ascending aortic aneurysm. In the David I procedure, described as the "re-implantation" procedure, a tailored synthetic tube graft is fixed to the left ventricular outflow tract at the subannular level and the native aortic valve is re-implanted inside the fabric graft, thus stabilizing the size of the aortic annulus (David TE, Feindel CM. An aortic valve sparing operation for patients with aortic incompetence and aneurysm of the ascending aorta. J Thorac Cardiovasc Surg 1992; 103:617-621). *See also* Yacoub procedure.

DCRV   *See* double-chambered right ventricle.

De Vega annuloplasty   A surgical method for management of tricuspid regurgitation that involves decreasing the size of the tricuspid valve annulus by placing a circumferential suture around the tricuspid valve, with due care to avoid the atrioventricular node.

dextrocardia   Cardiac apex directed to the right relative to the cardiac base. *See* cardiac position.

dextroposition   Rightward shift of the heart. *See* cardiac position.

dextroversion   An older term for dextrocardia. *See* cardiac position.

differential hypoxemia, differential cyanosis   A difference in the degree of hypoxemia or cyanosis in different extremities as a result of the site of a right-to-left shunt. The most common situation involves greater hypoxemia and cyanosis in the feet, and sometimes the left hand, compared with the right hand and head, in a patient with an Eisenmenger patent ductus arteriosus.

DiGeorge syndrome   An autosomal dominant syndrome now known to be part of microdeletion 22q11.2 or CATCH-22 syndrome. As originally described, it consisted of infantile hypocalcemia, immunodeficiency due to thymic hypoplasia, and a conotruncal cardiac abnormality. *See also* microdeletion 22q11.2 syndrome.

discordant atrioventricular connections   Anomalous connection of atria and ventricles such that the morphologic right atrium connects via a mitral valve to a morphologic left ventricle while the morphologic left atrium connects via a tricuspid valve to a morphologic right ventricle.

discordant ventriculoarterial connections   Anomalous connection of the great arteries and ventricles such that the pulmonary trunk arises from the left ventricle and the aorta arises from the right ventricle.

diverticulum of Kommerell   Enlarged origin of an aberrant subclavian artery associated with right aortic arch. Its diameter may be equal to that of the descending aorta and tapers to the left subclavian diameter. It is found at the origin of the aberrant left subclavian artery, the fourth branch off the right aortic arch.

double aortic arch   *See* aortic arch anomalies.

double-chambered right ventricle   Separation of the right ventricle into a higher-pressure inflow chamber and a lower-pressure infundibular chamber, the separation usually being produced by hypertrophy of the septomarginal trabeculation. When a ventricular septal defect is present it usually communicates with the higher pressure right ventricular inflow chamber.

double discordance   *See* congenitally corrected transposition of the great arteries.

double-inlet left/right ventricle (DILV/DIRV)   *See* univentricular connection.

double-orifice mitral valve   The mitral valve orifice is partially or completely divided into two parts by a fibrous bridge of tissue. Both orifices enter the left ventricle. Mitral regurgitation and/or mitral stenosis may be present. Aortic coarctation and atrioventricular septal defect may be associated.

double-outlet left ventricle (DOLV)   Both the pulmonary artery and the aorta arise predominantly from the morphologic left ventricle. DOLV is rare and much less frequent than double-outlet right ventricle (DORV).

double-outlet right ventricle (DORV)   Both great arteries arise predominantly from the morphologic right ventricle; there is usually no fibrous continuity between the semilunar and the AV valves; a ventricular septal defect (VSD) is present. When the VSD is in the subaortic position without right ventricular (RV) outflow tract obstruction the physiology simulates a simple VSD. With RV outflow tract obstruction the physiology simulates tetralogy of Fallot. When the VSD is in the subpulmonary position (Taussig-Bing anomaly) the physiology simulates complete transposition of the great arteries with VSD. *See also* Taussig-Bing anomaly.

double-switch procedure   An operation used in patients with congenitally corrected transposition of the great arteries (*l*-transposition of the great arteries, *l*-TGA CCTGA) and also in patients who have had a previous Mustard or Senning atrial switch operation for complete transposition of the great arteries (*d*-TGA). It leads to anatomic correction of the ventricle to great artery relationships such that the left ventricle supports the systemic circulation. It includes an arterial switch procedure (*see* Jatene procedure) in all cases, as well as an atrial switch procedure (Mustard or Senning) in the case of CCTGA, or reversal of the previous Mustard or Senning procedure in the case of complete transposition of the great arteries. When used to refer to revision of a prior Mustard or Senning operation it is more accurately termed a *switch-reversal* or *switch-conversion.*

doubly committed VSD   *See* ventricular septal defect.

Down syndrome   The most common malformation caused by trisomy 21. Most patients (95%) have complete trisomy of chromosome 21; some have translocation or mosaic forms. The phenotype is diagnostic (short stature, characteristic facial appearance, intellectual impairment, brachydactyly, atlantoaxial instability, thyroid and white blood cell disorders). Congenital heart defects are frequent, with atrioventricular septal defect and ventricular septal defect being the most common. Mitral valve prolapse and aortic regurgitation may be present. Patients with Down syndrome are prone to earlier and more severe pulmonary vascular disease than might otherwise be expected as a consequence of the lesions identified.

drainage   A physiologic term describing the direction of blood flow. Anomalous drainage can occur in the absence of anomalous connection (e.g., common atrium with normal connection of the pulmonary veins). *See also* connection.

dural ectasia   Expansion of the dural sac in the lumbosacral area, seen on computed tomography or magnetic resonance imaging. It is one of the criteria used to confirm the diagnosis of Marfan syndrome (Pyeritz RE, et al. Dural ectasia is a common feature of the Marfan syndrome. Am J Hum Genet 1988; 43:726-732; Fattori R, et al. Importance of dural ectasia in phenotypic assessment of Marfan's syndrome. Lancet 1999; 354:910-913).

Ebstein anomaly   An anomaly of the tricuspid valve in which the basal attachments of both the septal and the posterior valve leaflets are displaced apically within the right ventricle. Apical displacement of the septal tricuspid leaflet of more than 8 mm/m² is diagnostic (the extent of apical displacement should be indexed to body surface area). Abnormal structure of all three leaflets is seen, with the anterior leaflet typically large with abnormal attachments to the right ventricular wall. The pathologic and clinical spectrum is broad and includes not only valve abnormalities but also myocardial structural changes in both ventricles. Tricuspid regurgitation is common, tricuspid stenosis occurs occasionally, and right-to-left shunting through a patent foramen ovale or atrial septal defect is a regular but not invariable concomitant. Other congenital lesions are often associated, such as ventricular septal defect, pulmonary stenosis, and/or accessory conduction pathways.

Ehlers-Danlos syndrome (EDS)   A group of heritable disorders of connective tissue (specifically, abnormalities of collagen). Hyperextensibility of the joints and hyperelasticity and fragility of the skin are common to all forms; patients bruise easily.

- **EDS types I, II and III:**   demonstrate autosomal dominant inheritance and are the most common forms, each representing about 30% of cases. The cardiovascular abnormalities are generally mild, consisting of mitral and tricuspid valve prolapse. Dilation of major arteries, including the aorta, may occur. Aortic rupture is seen rarely in type I, but not in types II and III.
- **EDS type IV:**   also autosomal dominant but frequently appears de novo. This is the "arterial" form, presenting with aortic dilation and rupture of medium and large arteries spontaneously or after trauma. It is due to an abnormality of type III procollagen and comprises about 10% of cases of EDS.
- There are six other rare types of EDS.

Eisenmenger syndrome   An extreme form of pulmonary vascular obstructive disease arising as a consequence of preexisting systemic to pulmonary shunting in which pulmonary vascular resistance increases such that pulmonary pressures are at or near systemic levels and there is reversed (right to left) or bidirectional shunting at great artery, ventricular, and/or atrial levels. *See also* Heath-Edwards classification.

Ellis–van Creveld syndrome   An autosomal recessive syndrome in which common atrium and partial atrioventricular septal defect (including primum atrial septal defect) are the most common cardiac lesions.

endocardial cushion defect   *See* atrioventricular septal defect. The term *endocardial cushion defect* has fallen into disuse because it infers an outdated concept of the morphogenesis of the atrioventricular septum.

erythrocytosis   Increased red blood cell concentration secondary to chronic tissue hypoxia, as seen in cyanotic congenital heart disease and in chronic pulmonary disease. It results from a hypoxia-induced physiologic response resulting in increased erythropoietin levels and affects only the red cell line. It is also called secondary erythrocytosis. The term *polycythemia* is inaccurate in this context because other blood cell lines are not affected. *See also* polycythemia vera. Erythrocytosis may cause hyperviscosity symptoms. *See also* hyperviscosity.

eustachian valve   A remnant of the right valve of the sinus venosus guarding the entrance to the right atrium from the inferior vena cava.

extracardiac Fontan   *See* Fontan procedure.

fenestration   An opening or "window" (usually small) between two structures, which may be spontaneous, traumatic, or created interventionally or surgically.

fibrillin   A large glycoprotein closely involved with collagen in the structure of connective tissue. Mutations in the fibrillin gene on chromosome 15 are responsible for all manifestations of Marfan syndrome. *See also* Marfan syndrome.

fluorescence in-situ hybridization (FISH)   A cytogenetic technique to detect and to localize the presence or absence of specific nucleic acids sequences (DNA sequences) on a chromosome by the use of fluorescent probes that bind to those parts of the chromosome with a high degree of sequence similarity (e.g., in diagnosis of microdeletion 22q11.2).

Fontan procedure (operation)   A palliative operation for patients with a univentricular circulation involving diversion of the systemic venous return to the pulmonary artery usually without the interposition of a subpulmonary ventricle. There are many variations, all directed toward normalization of systemic oxygen saturation and elimination of volume overload of the functioning ventricle.

- **atriopulmonary Fontan:**   An early modification of the original Fontan operation in which a non-valved connection is created between the right atrium and the pulmonary artery by a variety of techniques. *See also* Kreutzer procedure.
- **classic Fontan:**   Originally a valved conduit between the right atrium and the pulmonary artery (Fontan F, Baudet E. Surgical repair of tricuspid atresia. Thorax 1971; 26:240-248). Subsequently modified to a direct anastomosis between the right atrium and the pulmonary artery.
- **extracardiac Fontan:**   *See* Fontan procedure/total cavopulmonary connection (TCPC).
- **fenestrated Fontan:**   Surgical creation of a defect in the atrial patch or baffle to provide a pressure-relief valve, allowing some right-to-left shunting and thus reducing pressure in the systemic venous circuit and increasing systemic blood flow at the expense of some systemic hypoxemia.

- **lateral tunnel Fontan:** Inferior vena caval flow is directed by a baffle within the right atrium into the lower portion of the divided superior vena cava or the right atrial appendage, which is connected to the pulmonary artery. The upper part of the superior vena cava is connected to the superior aspect of the pulmonary artery as in the bidirectional Glenn anastomosis. The majority of the right atrium is excluded from the systemic venous circuit.
- **RA-RV Fontan:** Conduit (often valved) between the right atrium and the right ventricle. Also known as the Björk modification (Björk VO, et al. Right atrial-right ventricular anastomosis for correction of tricuspid atresia. J Thorac Cardiovasc Surg 1979; 77:452-458).
- **total cavopulmonary connection (TCPC):** Inferior vena caval blood is directed to the pulmonary artery via an extracardiac conduit. The superior vena cava is anastomosed to the pulmonary artery as in the bidirectional Glenn anastomosis.

fossa ovalis An oval depression in the lower part of the right atrial surface of the interatrial septum. It is a vestige of the foramen ovale and its floor corresponds to the septum primum of the fetal heart. *Syn: oval fossa.*

Gerbode defect An unusual variant of atrioventricular septal defect in which the defect is in the superior portion of the atrioventricular septum above the insertion of the septal leaflet of the tricuspid valve, resulting in a direct connection and shunt between the left ventricle and the right atrium. *See also* atrioventricular septum.

Ghent criteria A set of criteria for the diagnosis of Marfan syndrome requiring the involvement of three organ systems (two systems must have "major" involvement) or of two organ systems (one major) and a positive family history (DePaepe A, et al. Revised diagnostic criteria for the Marfan syndrome. Am J Med Genet 1996; 62:417-426).

Glenn anastomosis *Syn: Glenn operation* (often called "Glenn shunt"). A palliative operation for the purpose of increasing pulmonary blood flow, and hence systemic oxygen saturation, in which a direct anastomosis is created between the superior vena cava (SVC) and a pulmonary artery. This procedure does not cause subaortic (systemic) ventricular volume overload.
- **bidirectional Glenn:** End-to-side anastomosis of the divided SVC to the undivided pulmonary artery (Haller JA Jr, et al. Experimental studies in permanent bypass of the right heart. Surgery 1966; 59:1128-1132; Azzolina G, et al. Tricuspid atresia: experience in surgical management with a modified cavo-pulmonary anastomosis. Thorax 1972; 27:111-115; Hopkins RA, et al. Physiologic rationale for a bi-directional cavo-pulmonary shunt: a versatile complement to the Fontan principle. J Thorac Cardiovasc Surg 1985; 90:391-398). *Syn: bi-directional cavo-pulmonary anastomosis.*
- **classic Glenn:** Anastomosis of the SVC to the distal end of the divided right pulmonary artery with division/ligation of the SVC below the anastomosis. Acquired pulmonary arteriovenous malformations with associated systemic arterial desaturation are a common long-term complication (Glenn WW. Circulatory bypass of the right side of the heart. IV. Shunt between superior vena cava and distal right pulmonary artery: report of clinical application. N Engl J Med 1958; 259:117-120).

goose-neck deformity Describes the angiographic appearance of the distorted, elongated and narrowed left ventricular outflow tract and ascending aorta during diastole in patients with AV septal defect.

Gore-Tex A synthetic material often used to fashion conduits and other prosthetic devices for the surgical palliation or repair of congenital heart disease.

GUCH Grown-up congenital heart disease. A term originated by Dr. Jane Somerville, a famous cardiologist, one of the founders of the discipline of ACHD/GUCH. *Syn:* adult congenital heart disease (ACHD).

GUCH Working Group 22 Working Group for Grown-Up Congenital Heart Disease of the European Society of Cardiology (Working Group 22) (http://www.escardio.org/communities/Working-Groups/guch/Pages/welcome.aspx)

Heath-Edwards classification A histopathologic classification useful in assessing the potential for reversibility of pulmonary vascular disease (Heath D, Edwards JE. The pathology of hypertensive pulmonary vascular disease: a description of six grades of structural changes in the pulmonary arteries with special reference to congenital cardiac septal defects. Circulation 1958; 18:533-547).
- **Grade I:** Hypertrophy of the media of small muscular arteries and arterioles
- **Grade II:** Intimal cellular proliferation in addition to medial hypertrophy
- **Grade III:** Advanced medial thickening with hypertrophy and hyperplasia including progressive intimal proliferation and concentric fibrosis. This results in obliteration of arterioles and small arteries.
- **Grade IV:** "Plexiform lesions" of the muscular pulmonary arteries and arterioles with a plexiform network of capillary-like channels within a dilated segment
- **Grade V:** Complex plexiform, angiomatous and cavernous lesions, and hyalinization of intimal fibrosis
- **Grade VI:** Necrotizing arteritis

hemi-Fontan A modification of the bidirectional cavopulmonary anastomosis utilizing the right atrium, believed to improve the flow dynamics from the superior vena cava into the pulmonary arteries and also to simplify the additional surgery required to complete a Fontan procedure that may be "completed" at a later time. *See also* Glenn anastomosis/bidirectional Glenn.

hemi-truncus An older term describing an anomalous pulmonary artery branch to one lung arising from the ascending aorta in the presence of a main pulmonary artery arising normally from the right ventricle and supplying the other lung. It is better described as an aberrant pulmonary artery arising from the aorta, because it is morphogenetically distinct from "truncus." Individual aortic and pulmonary valves arise from the ventricle, and there is no truncal valve. *See also* truncus arteriosus.

heterograft Transplanted tissue or organ from a different species.

heterotaxy Abnormal arrangement (Gk. *taxo*) of viscera that differs from the arrangement seen in either situs solitus or situs inversus. It is often described as "visceral heterotaxy."

heterotopic Located in an anatomically abnormal site, often in reference to transplantation of an organ.

Holt-Oram syndrome Autosomal dominant syndrome consisting of radial abnormalities of the forearm and hand associated with secundum atrial septal defect (most common), ventricular septal defect, or, rarely, other cardiac malformations (Holt M, Oram S. Familial heart disease with skeletal manifestations. Br Heart J 1960; 22:236-242). The gene for this syndrome is on chromosome 12q2 (Basson CT, Bachinsky DR, Lin RC, et al. Mutations in human TBX5 cause limb and cardiac malformation in Holt-Oram syndrome. Nat Genet 1997; 15:30-35).

homograft Transplanted tissue or organ from another individual of the same species.

Hunter syndrome A genetic syndrome due to a deficiency of the enzyme iduronate sulfate (mucopolysaccharidase) with X-linked recessive inheritance. Clinical spectrum is wide. Patients present with skeletal changes, intellectual impairment, arterial hypertension, and involvement of atrioventricular and semilunar valves resulting in valve regurgitation.

Hurler syndrome A genetic syndrome due to a deficiency of the enzyme α-l-iduronidase (mucopolysaccharidase) with autosomal recessive inheritance. Phenotype presents with a wide spectrum including severe skeletal abnormalities, corneal clouding, hepatosplenomegaly, intellectual impairment, and mitral valve stenosis.

hyperviscosity   An excessive increase in viscosity of blood as may occur secondary to erythrocytosis in patients with cyanotic congenital heart disease. Hyperviscosity symptoms include headache; impaired alertness, depressed mentation, or a sense of distance; visual disturbances (blurred vision, double vision, amaurosis fugax); paresthesias of fingers, toes, or lips; tinnitus; fatigue, lassitude; myalgias (including chest, abdominal muscles) and muscle weakness (Perloff JK, et al. Adults with cyanotic congenital heart disease: hematologic management. Ann Intern Med 1988; 109:406-413). Restless legs or a sensation of cold legs may reflect hyperviscosity (observation of Dr. E. Oechslin). Because the symptoms are nonspecific, their relation to hyperviscosity is supported if they are alleviated by phlebotomy. Iron deficiency and dehydration worsen hyperviscosity and must be avoided—or treated if present.

hypoplastic left heart syndrome   A heterogeneous syndrome with a wide variety and severity of manifestations involving hypoplasia, stenosis, or atresia at different levels of the left heart including the aorta, aortic valve, left ventricular outflow tract, left ventricular body, mitral valve, and left atrium.

Ilbawi procedure (operation)   An operation for congenitally corrected transposition of the great arteries with ventricular septal defect (VSD) and pulmonary stenosis in which a communication is established between the left ventricle and the aorta via the VSD using a baffle within the right ventricle. The right ventricle is connected to the pulmonary artery using a valved conduit. An atrial switch procedure is done. The left ventricle then supports the systemic circulation (Ilbawi MN, et al. An alternative approach to the surgical management of physiologically corrected transposition with ventricular septal defect and pulmonary stenosis or atresia. J Thorac Cardiovasc Surg 1990; 100:410-415).

infracristal   Located below the crista supraventricularis in the right ventricular outflow tract. *See also* crista supraventricularis.

infundibular, infundibulum   (Pertaining to) a ventricular–great arterial connecting segment that normally is subpulmonary but can be subaortic and may be bilateral or absent. Bilateral infundibulum may be seen in patients with transposition of the great arteries with ventricular septal defect (VSD) and pulmonary stenosis (PS), double-outlet right ventricle with VSD and PS, and anatomically corrected malposition. *Syn:* conus.

inlet VSD   *See* ventricular septal defect.

interrupted aortic arch   *See* aortic arch anomaly.

interrupted inferior vena cava   The inferior vena cava is interrupted below the hepatic veins with subsequent systemic venous drainage via the azygos vein to the superior vena cava. The hepatic veins enter the right atrium directly. This anomaly is frequently associated with complex congenital heart disease, particularly left isomerism.

ISACHD   International Society for Adult Congenital Heart Disease (formerly called ISACCD, International Society for Adult Congenital Cardiac Disease) (http://www.isachd.org)

isolation of arch vessels   *See* aortic arch anomalies.

isomerism   Paired, mirror-image sets of normally single or nonidentical organ systems (atria, lungs, and viscera), often associated with other abnormalities
- **left isomerism:** *Syn:* polysplenia syndrome. A congenital syndrome consisting of paired, morphologically left structures: multiple bilateral spleens, bilateral left bronchi, bilateral bilobed (left) lungs, midline liver, two morphologic left atria, multiple anomalies of systemic venous connections, and other complex cardiac and noncardiac malformations.
- **right isomerism:** *Syn:* asplenia syndrome. Congenital syndrome consisting of paired morphologically right structures: absence of spleen, bilateral right bronchi, bilateral trilobed (right) lungs, two morphologic right atria, multiple anomalies of pulmonary venous connections, and other complex cardiac and noncardiac anomalies.

Jatene procedure (operation)   An operation used in complete transposition of the great arteries, involving removal of the aorta from its attachment to the right ventricle, removal of the pulmonary artery from the left ventricle, and the reattachment of the great arteries to the contralateral ventricles, with re-implantation of the coronary arteries into the neoaorta. As a consequence, the left ventricle supports the systemic circulation (Jatene AD, et al. Anatomic correction of transposition of the great vessels. J Thorac Cardiovasc Surg 1976; 72:364-370). *Syn:* arterial switch operation (ASO). *See also* LeCompte maneuver.

juxtaposition of atrial appendages   A rare anomaly seen in patients with transposition of the great arteries and other complex congenital heart defects in which the atrial appendages are situated side by side. The right atrial appendage passes immediately behind the transposed main pulmonary artery in patients with leftward juxtaposition of atrial appendages.

Kartagener syndrome   Autosomal recessive syndrome consisting of situs inversus totalis, dextrocardia, and defect of ciliary motility leading to sinusitis, bronchiectasis, and sperm immobility (Kartagener M. Zur Pathogenese der Bronchiektasien: Bronchiektasien bei Situs viscerum inversus. Beitr Klink Tuberkul 1933; 28:231-234; Kartagener M, et al. Bronchiectasis with situs inversus. Arch Pediatr 1962; 79:193-196; Miller RD, et al. Kartagener's syndrome. Chest 1972; 62:130-136).

Kawashima repair   An operation for repair of double-outlet right ventricle with subpulmonary ventricular septal defect (Taussig-Bing anomaly) consisting of an intraventricular diversion using a pericardial patch to direct left ventricular output through the ventricular septal defect to the aorta. This procedure is to be distinguished from a different Kawashima procedure, which is a modified bidirectional cavopulmonary anastomosis performed in patients with interrupted inferior vena cava and azygos continuation.

Konno procedure (operation)   Repair of tunnel-like subvalvular left ventricular outflow tract obstruction (LVOTO) by aortoventriculoplasty. The operation involves enlargement of the left ventricular outflow tract by inserting a patch in the ventricular septum, as well as aortic valve replacement and enlargement of the aortic annulus and ascending aorta (Konno S, et al. A new method for prosthetic valve replacement in congenital aortic stenosis associated with hypoplasia of the aortic valve ring. J Thorac Cardiovasc Surg 1975; 70:909-917). Modification of the original technique with preservation of the aortic valve is described as the "modified Konno procedure." In severe forms of LVOTO, a prosthetic valve-containing conduit may be inserted between the left ventricular apex and descending aorta (DiDonato RM, et al. Left ventricular–aortic conduits in paediatric patients. J Thorac Cardiovasc Surg 1984; 88:82-91; Frommelt PC, et al. Natural history of apical left ventricular to aortic conduits in paediatric patients. Circulation 1991; 84[Suppl III]:213-218).

Kreutzer procedure   An operation performed for the management of tricuspid atresia, in which, in contrast to the classic Fontan procedure, an atriopulmonary anastomosis was performed without interposition of a valve between the right atrial appendage and the main pulmonary artery. Kreutzer used a homograft in his first patient; in subsequent patients he performed a direct atriopulmonary anastomosis with the patient's own pulmonary valve removed from the outflow tract of the right ventricle (Kreutzer G, et al. An operation for the correction of tricuspid atresia. J Thorac Cardiovasc Surg 1973; 66:613-621).
- **Fontan-Kreutzer procedure:** direct atriopulmonary connection in patients with a Fontan circulation.

LeCompte maneuver   The pulmonary artery is brought anterior to the aorta during an arterial switch procedure in patients with *d*-transposition of the great arteries. *See also* Jatene procedure.

LEOPARD syndrome   This autosomal dominant condition includes **l**entigines, **e**lectrocardiographic abnormalities, **o**cular hypertelorism, **p**ulmonary stenosis, **a**bnormal genitalia, **r**etardation of growth, and **d**eafness. Rarely, cardiomyopathy or complex congenital heart disease may be present.

levocardia Leftward-oriented cardiac apex (normal). *See* cardiac position.

levoposition Leftward shift of the heart. *See* cardiac position.

ligamentum arteriosum A normal fibrous structure that is the residuum of the ductus arteriosus after its spontaneous closure.

Loeys-Dietz syndrome An autosomal dominant aneurysm syndrome characterized by the triad of arterial tortuosity and aneurysms, hypertelorism, and bifid uvula or cleft palate (Loeys BL, et al. A syndrome of altered cardiovascular, craniofacial, neurocognitive and skeletal development caused by mutations in *TGFBR1*. Nat Genet 2005; 37:275-281). It is caused by mutations in the transforming growth factor-β receptor gene (Loeys BL, et al. Aneurysm syndromes caused by mutations in the TGF-beta receptor. N Engl J Med 2006; 355:788-798).

long QT syndrome Abnormal prolongation of QT duration with subsequent risk of torsades de pointes, syncope, and sudden cardiac death. It may be congenital or acquired (from medications such as antiarrhythmics, antihistamines, some antibiotics; electrolyte disturbances such as hypocalcemia, hypomagnesemia, hypokalemia; hypothyroidism; and other factors). QT interval must be adjusted to heart rate.

looping Bending of the primitive heart tube (normally to the right, dextro, d-) which determines the atrioventricular relationship.
- *d*-loop: Morphologic right ventricle lies to the right of the morphologic left ventricle (normal rightward bend).
- *l*-loop: Morphologic right ventricle lies to the left of the morphologic left ventricle (leftward bend).

Lutembacher syndrome Atrial septal defect associated with mitral valve stenosis. The mitral valve stenosis is usually acquired (rheumatic).

LVOTO Left ventricular outflow tract obstruction.

maladie de Roger Eponymous designation for a small restrictive ventricular septal defect (VSD) that is not associated with significant left ventricular volume overload or raised pulmonary artery pressure. There is a loud VSD murmur due to the high-velocity turbulent left-to-right shunt across the defect.

malposition An abnormality of cardiac position. *See* cardiac position.

MAPCA Major aortopulmonary collateral artery. A large abnormal arterial vessel arising from the aorta connects to a pulmonary artery (usually in the pulmonary hilum) and provides blood supply to the lungs. It is found in complex pulmonary atresia and other complex congenital heart disorders associated with a severe reduction or absence of antegrade pulmonary blood flow from the ventricle(s).

Marfan syndrome A connective tissue disorder with autosomal dominant inheritance caused by a defect in the fibrillin gene on chromosome 15. The phenotypic expression varies. Patients may have tall stature, abnormal body proportions, ocular abnormalities, dural ectasia, and protrusio acetabulae and present with skeletal and cardiovascular abnormalities. Mitral valve prolapse with mitral regurgitation, ascending aortic dilation or aneurysm with subsequent aortic regurgitation, and aortic dissection are the most common cardiovascular abnormalities. *See also* Ghent criteria.

McGoon ratio Angiographic index to determine if the branch pulmonary arteries are large enough to permit surgical repair in patients with tetralogy of Fallot/pulmonary atresia. The McGoon ratio is the ratio of the combined diameter of the right and left pulmonary artery at the prebranching point divided by the diameter of the aorta at the level of the diaphragm. A ratio greater than 2 is normal. A ratio greater than 1.2 is associated with an acceptable postoperative right ventricular pressure; a ratio less than 0.8 is deemed inadequate for surgical repair. This ratio tends to overestimate the adequacy of the size of pulmonary arteries because the diameter of descending thoracic aorta at the level of diaphragm is frequently smaller in patients with pulmonary atresia/tetralogy of Fallot. *See also* Nakata index.

Melbourne shunt An operation involving the creation of an end-to-side anastomosis between the hypoplastic pulmonary artery and the aorta to increase pulmonary blood flow and promote growth of the central pulmonary artery (e.g., in a patient with pulmonary atresia, ventricular septal defect, and major systemic-to-pulmonary collateral arteries who has a diminutive central pulmonary artery). It was developed by Dr. Roger Mee's group from Melbourne, Australia (Watterson KG, et al. Very small pulmonary arteries: central end-to-side shunt. Ann Thorac Surg 1991; 52:1132-1137).

mesocardia Cardiac apex directed to mid-chest. *See* cardiac position.

mesoposition Shift of the heart toward the midline. *See* cardiac position.

microdeletion 22q11.2 syndrome Syndrome due to a microdeletion at chromosome 22q11.2 resulting in a wide clinical spectrum, commonly called CATCH-22 syndrome. CATCH stands for **c**ardiac defect, **a**bnormal facies, **t**hymic hypoplasia, **c**left palate and **h**ypocalcemia. Cardiac defects include conotruncal defects such as interrupted aortic arch, tetralogy of Fallot, truncus arteriosus, and double-outlet right ventricle. *See also* DiGeorge syndrome, velocardiofacial syndrome.

mitral arcade Chordae of the mitral valve are shortened or absent, and the thickened mitral valve leaflets insert directly into the papillary muscle ("hammock valve"). Mitral valve excursion is limited and results in mitral stenosis.

mitral valve prolapse Systolic billowing of one or both mitral valve leaflets into the left atrium superior to the annular plane with or without associated mitral regurgitation. Echocardiographic definition: dislocation greater than 2 mm into the left atrium of at least one of the mitral valve leaflets during systole and a thickening of 5 mm or more of the prolapsing valve leaflet during diastole.

moderator band A prominent muscular structure traversing the right ventricle from the base of the anterior papillary muscle to the septum near the apex.

muscular VSD *See* ventricular septal defect.

Mustard procedure (operation) An operation for complete transposition of the great arteries in which venous return is directed to the contralateral ventricle by means of an atrial baffle made from autologous pericardial tissue or (rarely) synthetic material, after resection of most of the atrial septum. As a consequence the right ventricle supports the systemic circulation. This is a type of "atrial switch" operation (*see also* Senning procedure, atrial switch procedure; double-switch procedure) (Mustard WT. Successful two-stage correction of transposition of the great vessels. Surgery 1964; 55:469-472).

Nakata index Angiographic index to determine if the branch pulmonary arteries are large enough to permit surgical repair in patients with tetralogy of Fallot. The Nakata index is the sum of the combined cross-sectional area of the branch pulmonary arteries indexed to body surface area (normal value: 330 ± 30 mm²/m²; a Nakata index less than 150 mm²/m² is considered diminutive [Nakata S, et al. A new method for the quantitative standardization of cross-sectional areas of the pulmonary arteries in congenital heart diseases with decreased pulmonary blood flow. J Thorac Cardiovasc Surg 1984; 88:610-619]). *See also* McGoon ratio.

national referral center *See* supraregional referral center (SRRC).

neoaortic valve/neo-pulmonary valve In patients undergoing an arterial switch operation (Jatene procedure), the pulmonary root and aortic root are detached from their native sites and reattached to the opposite valve; thus, the pulmonary valve becomes the neoaortic valve and the aortic valve becomes the neo-pulmonary valve. *See* Jatene procedure.

Nikaidoh procedure Surgical repair of double-outlet right ventricle or transposition with pulmonary stenosis consisting of aortic translocation with reconstruction of the right ventricular outflow tract. The aortic root, with valve and coronary arteries attached, is removed from the right ventricular outflow tract and translocated posteriorly to lie primarily over the left ventricle. The ventricular septal defect is repaired with a patch that is attached to the aortic root at its superior margin. The pulmonary artery is attached to the right ventriculotomy with another pericardial patch.

nonrestrictive VSD *See* ventricular septal defect.

Noonan syndrome An autosomal dominant syndrome phenotypically somewhat similar to Turner syndrome, with a normal chromosomal complement, due to an abnormality in chromosome 12q. It is associated with congenital cardiac anomalies, especially dysplastic pulmonic valve stenosis, pulmonary artery stenosis, atrial septal defect, tetralogy of Fallot, and hypertrophic cardiomyopathy. Congenital lymphedema is a common associated anomaly that may be unrecognized (Noonan JA, Ehmke DA. Associated non-cardiac malformations in children with congenital heart disease. Midwest Soc Pediatr Res 1963; 63:468.)

Norwood procedure The first operation in a multistage strategy for management of hypoplastic left heart syndrome. In stage 1 (Norwood), a systemic to pulmonary arterial shunt (generally a modified Blalock-Taussig anastomosis) is created to maintain pulmonary blood flow and the main pulmonary artery is disconnected from the lungs and anastomosed to a reconstructed aorta to provide systemic blood flow. By this strategy, the right ventricle becomes the subaortic ventricle supporting the systemic circulation. This procedure is followed by a second stage some months later when a bidirectional cavopulmonary anastomosis is created to increase pulmonary blood flow and decrease volume loading of the subaortic right ventricle. The third stage is the completion of a Fontan-type operation, resulting in single-ventricle physiology.

Norwood-Rastelli procedure An operation for transposed great arteries associated with a ventricular septal defect (VSD), left ventricular outflow tract obstruction, and hypoplastic ascending aorta and arch, in which the proximal main pulmonary artery is anastomosed to and augments the ascending aorta and arch (Norwood) while the left ventricle is baffled to the pulmonary, now neoaortic, valve via the VSD and a right ventricle (RV) to distal pulmonary artery (PA) conduit is construction to restore RV-PA continuity (Rastelli).

orthotopic Located in an anatomically normal recipient site, often in reference to transplantation of an organ.

ostium primum ASD *See* atrial septal defect.

outlet VSD *See* ventricular septal defect.

oval fossa *See* fossa ovalis.

over-and-under ventricles *See* superoinferior heart.

overriding valve An atrioventricular valve that empties into both ventricles, or a semilunar valve that originates from both ventricles.

palliation, palliative operation A procedure carried out for the purpose of relieving symptoms or ameliorating some of the adverse effects of an anomaly that does not address the fundamental anatomic or physiologic disturbance. Contrasts to "repair" or "reparative operation."

PAPVC Partial anomalous pulmonary venous connection. *See* anomalous pulmonary venous connection.

parachute mitral valve A mitral valve abnormality in which all chordae tendineae of the mitral valve, which may be shortened and thickened, insert in a single, abnormal, papillary muscle, usually causing mitral stenosis. The parachute mitral valve may be part of the Shone complex. *See also* Shone complex.

partial AV septal defect *See* atrioventricular septal defect.

patent ductus arteriosus (PDA) An arterial duct that fails to undergo normal closure in the early postnatal period. *Syn:* persistently patent ductus arteriosus, persistent arterial duct.

patent foramen ovale Failure of anatomic fusion of the valve of the foramen ovale with the limbus of the fossa ovalis that normally occurs when left atrial pressure exceeds right atrial pressure after birth. There is no structural deficiency of tissue of the atrial septum. The foramen is functionally closed as long as left atrial pressure exceeds right atrial pressure but can reopen if right atrial pressure rises. Patent foramen ovale is found in up to 35% of the adult population in pathologic studies. The lower and variable prevalence reported in clinical series depends on the techniques used to find it. Patent foramen ovale is not classified as atrial septal defect or as a heart condition; it is a frequently found normal variant. *Syn:* probe-patent foramen ovale, PFO.

pentalogy of Fallot Tetralogy of Fallot with an atrial septal defect or patent foramen ovale. *See* tetralogy of Fallot.

perimembranous ventricular septal defect *See* ventricular septal defect.

persistent left superior vena cava (LSVC) Persistence of the left anterior cardinal vein (which normally obliterates during embryogenesis) results in persistent LSVC. LSVC connects via the coronary sinus to the right atrium in more than 90% of patients; rarely, it may directly connect to the left atrium in association with other congenital heart defects (e.g., isomerism). Its prevalence is up to 0.5% in the general population and higher in patients with congenital heart disease.

PFO *See* patent foramen ovale.

phlebotomy A palliative procedure involving withdrawal of whole blood (usually in up to 500-mL increments) that may be offered to patients with cyanotic congenital heart disease and secondary erythrocytosis who are experiencing hyperviscosity symptoms. Concomitant volume replacement is usually indicated.

pink tetralogy of Fallot *See* tetralogy of Fallot.

polycythemia vera A neoplastic transformation of all blood cell lines (erythrocyte, leukocyte, and platelet) associated with increased numbers of cells in the peripheral blood. Contrast to secondary erythrocytosis as seen in cyanotic heart disease. *See also* erythrocytosis.

polysplenia syndrome *See* isomerism/left isomerism.

Potts anastomosis A palliative operation for the purpose of increasing pulmonary blood flow, and hence systemic oxygen saturation. The procedure involves creating a small communication between a pulmonary artery and the ipsilateral descending thoracic aorta. It is often complicated by the development of pulmonary vascular obstructive disease if too large or by acquired stenosis or atresia of the pulmonary artery if distortion occurs. It is sometimes called "Potts shunt" (Potts WJ, et al. Anastomosis of aorta to pulmonary artery: certain types of congenital heart disease. JAMA 1946; 132:627-631).

PPH Primary pulmonary hypertension, an obsolete term, now reclassified as idiopathic pulmonary arterial hypertension. *See* pulmonary arterial hypertension.

probe-patent foramen ovale *See* patent foramen ovale.

protein-losing enteropathy (PLE) A complication that may be seen after the Fontan operation (as well as in other conditions) in which protein is lost via the gut resulting in ascites, peripheral edema, and pleural and pericardial effusions. It is of unknown cause although exacerbated by high systemic venous pressure. If serum protein and albumin levels are low, increased α1-antitrypsin in the stool supports the diagnosis.

protrusio acetabulae Abnormal medial displacement of the head of the femur within the acetabulum. This is a radiologic finding useful in the diagnosis of Marfan syndrome.

pseudotruncus arteriosus An old term used to describe pulmonary atresia with a ventricular septal defect, biventricular aorta, and pulmonary blood flow provided by systemic to pulmonary collaterals (MAPCAs). This anatomic arrangement had previously been called "truncus arteriosus type IV" but is morphogenetically a separate lesion from truncus arteriosus. In pseudotruncus the single vessel arising from the ventricles is an aorta with an aortic valve, not a truncus with a truncal valve, and pulmonary blood flow derives from aortopulmonary collateral arteries, not from anomalously connected true pulmonary arteries. *Syn:* Tetralogy of Fallot with pulmonary atresia and MAPCAs.

pulmonary arterial hypertension (PAH)　Raised pulmonary arterial pressure. A common method to define the severity of PAH is the pulmonary-aortic systolic pressure ratio: mild: ≥ 0.3, < 0.6; moderate: ≥ 0.6, < 0.9; severe: ≥ 0.9. In adults mean PAH may be used: borderline PAH: 20-24 mm Hg; mild PAH: 25-45 mm Hg; moderate PAH: 46-65 mm Hg; severe PAH: > 65 mm Hg.

pulmonary arteriovenous malformation (PAVM)　Defect of the pulmonary circulation consisting of direct connection between arterioles and venules without intervening capillaries. These defects are believed to arise during fetal development or very soon after birth and may enlarge under certain circumstances (e.g., in a lung supplied by a classic Glenn anastomosis). When large enough they may cause central cyanosis.

pulmonary artery band　Surgically created stenosis of the main pulmonary artery performed as a palliative procedure to protect the lungs against high blood flow and pressure when definitive correction of an underlying anomaly is not immediately advisable (e.g., in the setting of a nonrestrictive ventricular septal defect).

pulmonary artery sling　Anomalous origin of the left pulmonary artery from the right pulmonary artery such that it loops around the trachea. It may be associated with complete cartilaginous rings in the distal trachea and tracheal stenosis. It may occur as an isolated entity or in association with other congenital heart defects.

pulmonary atresia　An imperforate pulmonary valve. When associated with a ventricular septal defect (VSD) (variant of tetralogy of Fallot), pulmonary blood flow arises from aortopulmonary collateral vessels and systemic venous return exits the right side of the heart via the VSD. When associated with intact interventricular septum, pulmonary artery blood supply is via a patent ductus arteriosus and the systemic venous return exits the right side of the heart via an obligatory atrial septal defect.

Rashkind procedure　A balloon atrial septostomy performed as a palliative procedure to allow increased mixing of pulmonary and systemic venous return in infants born with complete transposition of the great arteries (*d*-TGA) (Rashkind WJ, Miller WW. Creation of an atrial septal defect without thoracotomy: a palliative approach to complete transposition of the great arteries. JAMA 1966; 196:991-992).

Rastelli procedure (operation)　An operation for repair of complete transposition of the great arteries in association with a large ventricular septal defect (VSD) and pulmonary stenosis in which a communication is established between the left ventricle (LV) and the aorta via the VSD using a baffle within the right ventricle (RV). The RV is connected to the pulmonary artery using a valved conduit, and the LV–pulmonary artery (PA) connection is obliterated. As a consequence, the LV supports the systemic circulation (Rastelli GC, et al. Anatomic correction of transposition of the great arteries with ventricular septal defect and subpulmonary stenosis. J Thorac Cardiovasc Surg 1969; 58: 545-552).

regional referral center (RRC)　A center for the care of adult patients with congenital heart disease incorporating, at a minimum, cardiology staff with special skills, training, and experience in the management of such patients and highly skilled echocardiographers.

restrictive right ventricular physiology　Physiologic behavior of the ventricles of some patients (e.g., after repair of tetralogy of Fallot). It may be defined by echocardiography as antegrade pulmonary artery flow in late diastole (a wave) through all phases of respiration. The pulsed recordings are obtained with the sample volume at the midpoint between the pulmonary valve cusps or remnants and the pulmonary artery bifurcation (Redington AN, et al. Antegrade diastolic pulmonary artery flow as a marker of right ventricular restriction after complete repair of pulmonary atresia with intact ventricular septum and critical pulmonary valve stenosis. Cardiol Young 1992; 2:382-386).

restrictive VSD　*See* ventricular septal defect.

REV procedure (réparation à l'étage ventriculaire)　A surgical technique used to treat transposition of the great arteries with ventricular septal defect (VSD) and pulmonary stenosis and malpositions similar to transposition of the great arteries (TGA) such as double-outlet right ventricle. Resection of a posteriorly deviated conal septum enlarges the VSD and facilitates the construction of a wide and straight left ventricular to aorta tunnel. Transection of the great arteries and the LeCompte maneuver permit direct implantation of the pulmonary artery on the right ventriculotomy.

right aortic arch　*See* aortic arch anomalies.

right ventricular dysplasia　*See* Uhl anomaly.

Ross procedure; Ross operation　A method of aortic valve replacement involving autograft transplantation of the pulmonary valve, annulus, and trunk into the aortic position, with re-implantation of the coronary ostia into the neoaorta. The right ventricular outflow tract is reconstructed with a homograft conduit (or a bioprosthetic valve and conduit) (Ross DN. Replacement of aortic valve with a pulmonary autograft. Lancet 1967; 2:956-958; Ross D. Pulmonary valve autotransplantation (the Ross operation). J Cardiac Surg 1988; 3:313-319).

rubella syndrome　A wide spectrum of malformations caused by rubella infection early in pregnancy, including cataracts, retinopathy, deafness, congenital heart disease, bone lesions, intellectual impairment, etc. The spectrum of congenital heart lesions is wide and includes pulmonary artery stenosis, patent ductus arteriosus, tetralogy of Fallot, and ventricular septal defect.

RV infundibulum　A normal connecting segment between the body of the right ventricle and the pulmonary artery. *Syn:* RV conus. *See also* infundibulum.

RVOTO　Right ventricular outflow tract obstruction.

sail sound　An auscultatory finding in some patients with Ebstein anomaly. The first heart sound includes mitral valve closure as its first component with a delayed tricuspid component. The abnormally large tricuspid anterior leaflet snapping like a sail catching the wind causes this delayed closure sound. The sail sound is not an ejection click, although it may simulate one.

Sano modification　A modification of the Norwood procedure for hypoplastic left heart syndrome in which a right ventricular–pulmonary artery (RV-PA) conduit is constructed to maintain pulmonary blood flow instead of a modified Blalock-Taussig anastomosis. *See* Norwood procedure.

scimitar syndrome　A constellation of anomalies including infradiaphragmatic total or partial anomalous pulmonary venous connection of the right lung to the inferior vena cava, often associated with hypoplasia of the right lung and right pulmonary artery. The lower portion of the right lung tends to receive its arterial supply from the abdominal aorta. The name of the syndrome derives from the appearance on the posteroanterior chest radiograph of the shadow formed by the anomalous pulmonary venous connection that resembles a Turkish sword, or scimitar.

secondary erythrocytosis　*See* erythrocytosis; *see also* polycythemia vera.

Senning procedure (operation)　An operation for complete transposition of the great arteries in which venous return is directed to the contralateral ventricle by means of an atrial baffle fashioned in situ by using the right atrial wall and interatrial septum. As a consequence, the right ventricle supports the systemic circulation. This is a type of "atrial switch" operation. (Senning A. Surgical correction of transposition of the great vessels. Surgery 1959; 45:966-980.) *See also* Mustard procedure, atrial switch procedure, double-switch procedure, and Ilbawi procedure.

septomarginal trabeculation   Prominent muscular structure on the septal surface of the right ventricle consisting of a body and two limbs. The body extends distally towards the apex of the right ventricle. Proximally, the septomarginal trabeculation splits into two limbs at the base of the right ventricle: the posteroinferior or posterocaudal limb, which gives rise to the papillary muscle; and the anterosuperior or anterocephalad limb, which extends to the pulmonary valve. The supraventricular crest inserts between the two limbs of the septomarginal trabeculation. The ventricular septal defect in tetralogy of Fallot is between the limbs of the septomarginal trabeculation. *Syn:* septal band.

septoparietal trabeculation   Prominent muscular structure that extends from the anterior surface of the septomarginal trabeculation to the lateral (parietal) wall of the right ventricle.

Shone complex (syndrome)   An association of multiple levels of left ventricular inflow and outflow obstruction: subvalvular and valvular left ventricular outflow tract obstruction, coarctation of the aorta, and mitral stenosis (parachute mitral valve and supramitral ring) (Shone JD, et al. The developmental complex of "parachute mitral valve," supravalvular ring of left atrium, subaortic stenosis and coarctation of aorta. Am J Cardiol 1963; 11:714-725).

Shprintzen syndrome   *See* velocardiofacial syndrome, CATCH 22.

shunt   Movement of blood through a congenitally abnormal or surgically created connection between two circuits, at the level of the atria, ventricles, or great arteries. *Shunt* is a physiologic term, in contrast to *connection*, which is an anatomic term.

single (as in atrium, ventricle, etc.)   Implies absence of the corresponding contralateral structure. Contrasts to "common," which implies bilateral structures with absent septation. *See also* common.

sinus of Valsalva   An anatomic dilation of the ascending aorta that occurs just above the aortic valve (also known as aortic sinus, sinus of Morgagni, or Petit sinus). There are generally three aortic sinuses: the left, which gives rise to the left coronary artery; the right, which gives rise to the right coronary artery; and the posterior, or noncoronary sinus.

- **aneurysm of sinus of Valsalva:**   Localized dilation of a sinus of Valsalva due to a separation between the aortic media and the annulus fibrosus, associated with a deficiency of elastic tissue and abnormal development of the bulbus cordis. Congenital sinus of Valsalva aneurysm typically involves only one sinus, whereas acquired sinus of Valsalva aneurysms (e.g., atherosclerosis, trauma, syphilis) usually involve multiple sinuses.

sinus venosus   An embryologic structure, the anatomic precursor of the inferior vena cava, superior vena cava, coronary sinus, and part of the definitive right atrium, which is located external to the primitive right atrium in the early embryologic period (3 to 4 weeks' gestation). The sinus portion of the right atrium receives the inferior vena cava, superior vena cava, and coronary sinus. The right and left valves of the sinus venosus separate the sinus venosus from the primitive right atrium, the embryologic precursor of the trabeculated or muscular portion of the right atrium, which includes the right atrial appendage, which in turn communicates with the tricuspid valve. The left valve of the sinus venosus joins the interatrial septum, retrogresses, and is absorbed. The right valve of the sinus venosus enlarges and functions to deflect the oxygenated fetal blood coming from the placenta and via the inferior vena cava across the foramen ovale. Through partial resorption of the right valve of the sinus venosus, remnants form the eustachian valve related to the inferior vena cava, the thebesian valve related to the coronary sinus, and the crista terminalis. *Chiari network* describes right atrial reticula that are an extensively fenestrated remnant of the right valve of the sinus venosus. *See also* cor triatriatum dexter and sinus venosus defect.

sinus venosus defect   A communication located posterosuperior to the oval fossa (called superior sinus venosus defect) or, rarely, posteroinferior to the oval fossa (called inferior sinus venosus defect). It is commonly associated with partial anomalous pulmonary venous connection (most often right pulmonary veins, especially the right upper pulmonary vein in association with a superior sinus venosus defect), which is functionally identical to an atrial septal defect but properly named a sinus venosus defect because it occurs due to abnormal development of the sinus venosus in relation to the systemic and pulmonary veins and is not a defect in the interatrial septum. *See also* atrial septal defect.

situs   Sidedness. The position of the morphologic right atrium determines the sidedness and is independent of the direction of the cardiac apex or the position of the ventricles or the great arteries.

- **situs ambiguus:**   Indeterminate sidedness (in the setting of atrial isomerism)
- **situs inversus:**   Mirror-image sidedness (i.e., opposite of normal); left-sided morphologic right atrium
- **situs inversus totalis:**   Total mirror-image sidedness; the position of all lateralized organs is inverted.
- **situs solitus:**   Normal sidedness; right-sided morphologic right atrium

stent   Intravascular (intraluminal) prosthesis to scaffold a vessel for the purpose of maintaining patency.

Sterling-Edwards procedure   A palliative operation for transposition of the great arteries in which the atrial septum was resected, repositioned, and sutured to the left of the right pulmonary veins to produce drainage into the right atrium. The procedure produced left-to-right shunt of oxygenated blood directly into the systemic atrium and ventricle and offloaded the pulmonary circulation in patients with complete transposition of the great arteries and high pulmonary flow (Edwards WS, et al. Reposition of right pulmonary veins in transposition of the great vessels. JAMA 1964; 188:522-523; Edwards WS, Bargeron LM. More effective palliation of the transposition of the great vessels. J Thorac Cardiovasc Surg 1965; 19:790-795).

straddling atrioventricular valve   *See* atrioventricular valve.

subaortic ventricle   The ventricle that relates most directly to the aorta.

subpulmonary ventricle   The ventricle that relates most directly to the pulmonary artery.

superoinferior heart   A term applied to a heart in which the ventricles are in a markedly superoinferior relationship due to abnormal displacement of the ventricular mass along the horizontal plane of its long axis. This anomaly often coexists with crisscross atrioventricular relationships. *See also* crisscross heart. *Syn:* over-and-under ventricles; upstairs-downstairs heart.

supracristal   Located above the crista supraventricularis in the right ventricular outflow tract; hence contiguous with the origin of the great arteries. *See* crista supraventricularis.

supraregional referral center (SRRC)   A "full service" center for providing optimal care of adult patients with congenital heart disease comprising specialized resources, the availability of cardiology specialists with specific training and experience in ACHD, the availability of other cardiology subspecialists, and other medical and paramedical personnel with special training or experience in the problems of congenital heart disease and offering opportunities for training, research, and education in the field. *Syn:* national referral center.

supravalvular mitral ring   An anomaly found in the left atrium that may produce congenital mitral stenosis. *See also* Shone complex. This should be differentiated from cor triatriatum.

switch conversion of transposition   An operation performed in patients who had previously had a Mustard or Senning procedure for complete transposition of the great arteries to allow the left ventricle to assume the function of the systemic ventricle. The first stage may involve pulmonary artery banding to induce subpulmonary left ventricular hypertrophy. The second stage involves an arterial switch operation, removal of the Mustard/Senning atrial baffle, and reconstruction of an atrial septum. *See also* double-switch operation.

systemic AV valve   The atrioventricular valve guarding the inlet to the subaortic (systemic) ventricle.

Takeuchi procedure   A surgical procedure for the management of anomalous left coronary artery arising from the pulmonary artery (ALCAPA) that involves creating an aortopulmonary window and an intrapulmonary-artery tunnel to connect the ostium of the anomalous left coronary artery to the ascending aorta.

TAPVC   Total anomalous pulmonary venous connection. *See* anomalous pulmonary venous connection.

TAPVD   Total anomalous pulmonary venous drainage. This term is sometimes used to refer to the entity properly called total anomalous pulmonary venous connection. *See* anomalous pulmonary venous connection. *See also* connection, drainage.

Taussig-Bing anomaly   A form of double-outlet right ventricle in which the great arteries arise side by side with the aorta to the right of the pulmonary artery and the ventricular septal defect (VSD) in a subpulmonary position. Because the left ventricle empties across the VSD preferentially into the pulmonary artery, the physiology simulates complete transposition of the great arteries with a VSD.

TCPC   *See* Fontan procedure/total cavopulmonary connection.

tetralogy of Fallot   A congenital anomaly, the primary pathophysiologic components of which are obstruction to right ventricular outflow at the infundibular level and a large nonrestrictive ventricular septal defect (VSD). The other two components of the "tetralogy" are an overriding aorta and concentric right ventricular hypertrophy. Valvular right ventricular outflow tract obstruction (RVOTO; pulmonic stenosis) and distal pulmonary artery stenosis are often present. The essential morphogenetic anomaly is malalignment of the infundibular (outlet) septum such that it fails to unite with the trabecular septum (hence the VSD) owing to anterior deviation (hence the RVOTO). Lillehei and coworkers first described the repair in 1955 (Lillehei CW, et al. Direct vision intracardiac surgical correction of the tetralogy of Fallot, pentalogy of Fallot, and pulmonary atresia defects; reports of first ten cases. Ann Surg 1955; 142:418-445).

- **pentalogy of Fallot:**   Tetralogy of Fallot with an associated atrial septal defect or patent foramen ovale.
- **pink tetralogy of Fallot:**   Tetralogy of Fallot presenting with increased pulmonary blood flow and minimal cyanosis because of a lesser degree of RVOTO. *Syn:* acyanotic Fallot.

thebesian valve   A remnant of the right valve of the sinus venosus guarding the opening of the coronary sinus.

total anomalous pulmonary venous connection (drainage, return)   *See* anomalous pulmonary venous connection/total anomalous pulmonary venous connection.

total cavopulmonary connection (TCPC)   *See* Fontan procedure/total cavopulmonary connection.

trabecular VSD   *See* ventricular septal defect.

transannular   Crossing the annulus. In connection with the right ventricular outflow tract in tetralogy of Fallot, the term refers to the pulmonary valve annulus, which often must be enlarged by a transannular patch, with consequent obligatory pulmonary insufficiency. Transannular patching was first described in 1959 (Kirklin JW, et al. Surgical treatment for tetralogy of Fallot by open intracardiac repair. J Thorac Surg 1959; 37:22-51).

transfer   The physical relocation of patients and their health records from one institution or practitioner to another. Transfer refers to an event and is to be differentiated from "transition," which describes a process. *See also* transition.

transition   The purposeful, planned movement of adolescents and young adults with chronic physical and medical conditions from child-centered to adult-oriented health care systems. Transition is a process and is to be differentiated from the event of "transfer" (Rosen DS, et al. Transition to adult health care for adolescents and young adults with chronic conditions: a position paper of the Society for Adolescent Medicine. J Adolesc Health 2003; 33: 309-311). *See also* transfer.

transposition of the great arteries (TGA)   *Syn:* complete transposition of the great arteries. *See* discordant ventriculoarterial connections; *see also* congenitally corrected transposition of the great arteries.

- **complex transposition of the great arteries:**   Discordant connection of the great arteries and ventricles such that the pulmonary trunk arises from the left ventricle and the aorta arises from the right ventricle, with associated abnormalities, most commonly a ventricular septal defect.
- **simple transposition of the great arteries:**   Discordant connection of the great arteries and ventricles such that the pulmonary trunk arises from the left ventricle and the aorta arises from the right ventricle, without any additional associated abnormality.

tricuspid atresia   A congenital anomaly in which there is no physiologic or gross morphologic connection between the right atrium and right ventricle. An internal connection allows mixing of systemic and pulmonary venous return at the atrial level. There is a variable degree of hypoplasia of the right ventricle. The left ventricle and mitral valve are normal.

truncus arteriosus   A single artery (truncus, trunk) arises from the base of the heart because of failure of proximal septation into the aorta and the pulmonary artery. Both pulmonary and systemic arteries, as well as the coronary arteries, arise from the common trunk. Truncus arteriosus is divided into two types depending on whether there is a ventricular septal defect or an intact ventricular septum. *Syn:* common arterial trunk.

Turner syndrome   A clinical syndrome due to the 45 XO karyotype in about 50% of cases, with 45XO/45XX mosaicism and other X-chromosome abnormalities comprising the remainder. There is a characteristic but variable phenotype, and association with congenital cardiac anomalies, especially postductal coarctation of the aorta and other left-sided obstructive lesions, as well as partial anomalous pulmonary venous drainage without atrial septal defect. The female phenotype varies and is somewhat similar to that of Noonan syndrome.

Uhl anomaly   Congenital malformation consisting of nearly total absence of the right ventricular myocardium, presenting with marked enlargement of both the right ventricle and right atrium and consequent tricuspid regurgitation. Arrhythmogenic right ventricular dysplasia may be one end of a spectrum and Uhl anomaly the other.

unbalanced atrioventricular canal   *See* ventricular imbalance.

unifocalization   A surgical technique that creates a common trunk for major aortopulmonary collateral arteries (MAPCAs), often utilizing a Blalock-Taussig shunt or conduit, as part of the surgical management of complex pulmonary atresia.

univentricular connection   Both atria are connected to only one ventricle. The connection is univentricular, but the heart is usually biventricular. *Syn:* double-inlet ventricle.

unroofed coronary sinus   An anomaly in which there is a deficiency in the normal separation of the coronary sinus from the left atrium as the coronary sinus passes behind the left atrium in the atrioventricular groove, such that the coronary sinus drains into the left atrium. This is a form of absence of the coronary sinus.

upstairs-downstairs heart   *See* superoinferior heart.

VACTERL association   Describes a spectrum of defects including vertebral abnormalities, anal atresia, tracheoesophageal fistula, radial dysplasia, renal abnormalities, and congenital heart defects (atrial and ventricular septal defect, tetralogy of Fallot, truncus arteriosus, aortic coarctation, patent ductus arteriosus, etc.).

Valsalva, sinus of   *See* sinus of Valsalva.

valve-sparing aortic root replacement   *See* David operation; Yacoub procedure.

vascular ring   A wide spectrum of aortic arch anomalies including double aortic arch and other vascular structures that surround the trachea and the esophagus resulting in their compression. The vascular structures may or may not be patent. Vascular rings may be isolated (in 1% to 2% of patients with congenital heart disease) or associated with other congenital heart malformations, such as tetralogy of Fallot. *See* aortic arch anomalies.

velocardiofacial syndrome   Syndrome of cleft palate, abnormal facies (square nasal root, long nose with narrow alar base, long face with malar hypoplasia, long philtrum, thickened helix, low-set ears), velopharyngeal incompetence, and congenital cardiac defects (conotruncal anomalies, isolated ventricular septal defect, tetralogy of Fallot). It is due to microdeletion at chromosome 22q11.2. *Syn:* Shprintzen syndrome. *See also* CATCH-22.

venous (or subpulmonary) AV valve   The atrioventricular valve guarding the inlet to the subpulmonary or "venous" ventricle.

ventricle repair

- **1-ventricle repair:**   *See* Fontan procedure.
- **1.5-ventricle repair:**   A term used to describe operations for cyanotic congenital heart disease performed when the subpulmonary ventricle is insufficiently developed to accept the entire systemic venous return. A bidirectional cavopulmonary connection is constructed to divert superior vena cava flow directly to the lungs, while inferior vena cava flow is directed to the lungs via the functioning but small subpulmonary ventricle.
- **2-ventricle repair:**   A term used to describe operations for cyanotic congenital heart disease with a common ventricle in which functioning systemic and pulmonary ventricles are created by means of surgical septation of the common ventricle.

ventricular imbalance   In the setting of atrioventricular septal defect, ventricular imbalance refers to relative hypoplasia of one or the other of the ventricles in association with small size of the ipsilateral component of the atrioventricular annulus.

ventricular septal defect (VSD)   A defect in the ventricular septum, such that there is direct communication between the two ventricles. The anatomic classification system for VSDs proposed by the Society for Thoracic Surgery—Congenital Heart Surgery Database Committee in association with the European Association for Cardiothoracic Surgery is presented, followed by additional definitions for specific types of VSD:

- **doubly committed (juxta-arterial) VSD:**   A defect in the outlet septum such that there is fibrous continuity between the aortic and pulmonary valves, with the VSD situated directly beneath both semilunar valves. *See* type 1 VSD.
- **inlet VSD:**   A defect in the lightly trabeculated inlet portion of the muscular interventricular septum, typically seen as part of an atrioventricular septal defect. *See* type 3 VSD.
- **muscular VSD:**   A defect entirely surrounded by muscular interventricular septum. *See* type 4 VSD.
- **nonrestrictive VSD:**   A ventricular septal defect of such a size that there is no significant pressure gradient between the ventricles. Hence the pulmonary artery is exposed to systemic pressure unless there is right ventricular outflow tract obstruction.
- **outlet VSD:**   A defect in the nontrabeculated outlet portion of the muscular interventricular septum, hence above the crista supraventricularis. *Syn:* supracristal VSD. Sometimes also described as subpulmonary, subarterial, or doubly committed subarterial VSD. *See* type 1 VSD.
- **perimembranous VSD:**   A VSD located in the membranous portion of the interventricular septum with variable extension into the contiguous portions of the inlet, trabecular, or outlet portions of the muscular septum but not involving the atrioventricular septum. *Syn:* membranous VSD; infracristal VSD, type 2 VSD.
- **restrictive VSD:**   A VSD of sufficiently small size that there is a pressure gradient between the ventricles, such that the pulmonary ventricle (hence pulmonary vasculature) is protected from the systemic pressure of the contralateral ventricle.
- **Swiss cheese VSD:**   multiple muscular VSDs. *See* type 4 VSD.
- **trabecular VSD:**   A defect in the heavily trabeculated central or trabecular portion of the muscular interventricular septum. May be multiple. *See* type 4 VSD.

- **type 1 VSD:**   Located in the outlet portion of the muscular septum. It is also termed a conal, subpulmonary, infundibular, or supracristal defect and also in this category is the doubly committed juxta-arterial VSD.
- **type 2 VSD:**   Confluent with the membranous septum. These defects usually extend into one of the three components of the muscular septum. *Syn:* perimembranous or membranous VSD.
- **type 3 VSD:**   Located in the inlet portion of the muscular septum inferior to the atrioventricular valves. *Syn:* inlet VSD or atrioventricular canal type VSD.
- **type 4 VSD:**   Located in the trabecular portion of the muscular septum completely surrounded by muscle. *Syn:* trabecular VSD, muscular VSD. Location may be midmuscular, apical, posterior, or anterior.

ventriculoarterial concordance   *See* concordant ventriculoarterial connections.

ventriculoarterial discordance   *See* discordant ventriculoarterial connections.

ventriculoinfundibular fold   Muscle interposed between the leaflets of an atrioventricular and of a subarterial valve, thus separating the inlet and outlet portions of a ventricle.

Waterston anastomosis   Sometimes called a Waterston shunt, a palliative operation for the purpose of increasing pulmonary blood flow, and hence systemic oxygen saturation, which involves creating a small communication between the main pulmonary artery and the ascending aorta. It is often complicated by the development of pulmonary vascular obstructive disease, if too large. Not uncommonly it causes distortion of the pulmonary artery (Waterston DJ. Treatment of Fallot's tetralogy in children under one year of age. Rozhl Chir 1962; 41:181-183).

Williams syndrome   An autosomal dominant syndrome, often arising de novo, associated with an abnormality of elastin, infantile hypercalcemia, mild cognitive impairment, and the so-called cocktail personality and congenital heart disease, especially supravalvular aortic stenosis and multiple peripheral pulmonary stenoses (Williams JC, et al. Supravalvular aortic stenosis. Circulation 1961; 24:1311-1318; Beuren A, et al. Supravalvular aortic stenosis in association with mental retardation and certain facial features. Circulation 1962; 26:1235-1240).

Wolff-Parkinson-White (WPW) syndrome   Accessory lateral atrioventricular conduction pathway causing characteristic electrocardiographic changes and atrial (and sometimes ventricular) arrhythmias. WPW syndrome may be isolated or associated with congenital heart defects. It is found in up to 25% of patients with Ebstein anomaly, who typically have more than one accessory pathway.

Wood unit   A nonstandard unit for expressing pulmonary vascular resistance (mm Hg/L), named after Paul Wood, the famous British cardiologist. One Wood unit is equivalent to 80 dyn•cm•s^{-5}.

xenograft   Tissue or organ used for transplant derived from another species. *Syn:* heterograft.

Yacoub procedure   A form of valve-sparing aortic root replacement described as the "remodeling" procedure, in which an aortic tube graft is sutured onto the aortic annulus above the insertion line of the aortic cusps, thus leaving the annulus mobile (but unsupported) and allowing billowing of the graft. This contrasts to the David I valve-sparing aortic root replacement, described as the "re-implantation" procedure, in which the graft is fixed to the left ventricular outflow tract at the subannular level and the valve is re-implanted inside the fabric graft, thus fixing the size of the aortic annulus permanently. The Yacoub procedure has also been called the David II procedure. *See also* David operation.

Z score, Z value   The number of standard deviations a measurement departs from mean normal. It is a way of expressing a physiologic variable in a form corrected for age and body size that is important in pediatrics (Rimoldi HJA, et al. A note on the concept of normality and abnormality in quantitation of pathologic findings in congenital heart disease. Pediatr Clin North Am 1963; 10:589-591; Daubeney PEF, et al. Relationship of the dimension of cardiac structures to body size: an echocardiographic study in infants and children. Cardiol Young 1999; 9:402-410).

Acknowledgments

The first iteration of this glossary was published in 1998 as an appendix to the Canadian Cardiovascular Society's first Canadian Consensus Conference on Adult Congenital Heart Disease (Colman JM, Oechslin E, Taylor D. Glossary of Terms. In: Connelly M, Webb GD, Somerville J, et al. Canadian Consensus Conference on Adult Congenital Heart Disease, 1996. Can J Cardiol 1998; 14:395-452).

The glossary has been reproduced in several formats since and was included in the first edition of this textbook. It is available online (at www.isachd.org/proglossary/ and also at www.cachnet.org/achd_index.htm). The authors thank colleagues and friends who have made suggestions for its improvement over the years. In particular we thank Drs. Luke Burchill, May Ling Mah, Lucy Roche, Nakul Sharma, Daniel Tobler, Jonathan Windram, and Sergey Yalonetsky, all of whom assisted in a major update of the glossary for the second edition of the textbook *Diagnosis and Management of Adult Congenital Heart Disease*.

Index

Pages followed by *f* indicate figures; *t*, tables, *b*, boxes.